LAROUSSE

Dictionary of
WORLD
HISTORY

LAROUSSE

Dictionary of

WORLD HISTORY

Consultant Editor
Bruce P Lenman

LAROUSSE

LAROUSSE

Larousse plc
43–45 Annandale Street, Edinburgh EH7 4AZ
Larousse Kingfisher Chambers Inc.,
95 Madison Avenue, New York, New York 10016

First published by Chambers Harrap Publishers Ltd 1993
Copyright © Chambers Harrap Publishers Ltd 1993

First issued under the Larousse imprint 1994
First published in paperback by Larousse plc 1995
Copyright © Larousse plc 1995

10 9 8 7 6 5 4 3 2 1

British Library Cataloguing in Publication Data
for this book is available from the British Library

Library of Congress Catalog Card Number: 94-73378

ISBN 0 7523 5008 0

Cover illustration: Henry VIII in Parliament
(from the Wriothesley manuscript)
The Royal Collection © Her Majesty Queen Elizabeth II

Typeset by Pillans & Wilson Ltd, Edinburgh
Printed in England by Clays Ltd, St Ives plc

Consultants and Contributors

Consultant Editor
Bruce P Lenman

Managing Editor
Katharine Boyd

Dr Peter Ashdown, Head of History, Slindon College, Nr Arundel, West Sussex

Dr P Bailey, Senior Lecturer in History, University of Edinburgh

Dr Crispin Bates, Lecturer in Modern South Asian History, University of Edinburgh

Dr John L Brockington, Reader in Sanskrit, University of Edinburgh

Dr Ian Brown, Senior Lecturer in the Economic History of South East Asia, School of Oriental and African Studies, University of London

Dr Jonathan G Campbell, Lecturer in Jewish Studies, St David's University College, University of Wales

Dr F Colson, Lecturer in History, University of Southampton

Professor Eric J Evans, Professor of Social History, Lancaster University

Dr Conan Fischer, Senior Lecturer in History, University of Strathclyde

Dr Mary Fischer, Lecturer in German, Napier University

Professor R Hodder-Williams, Head of Department of Politics, University of Bristol

Dr D E P Jackson, Senior Lecturer in Arabic Studies, University of St Andrews

Dr Henry Kamen, Professor, Higher Council for Scientific Research, Spain

Dr David S Laven, Lecturer, Department of History, University of Keele

Dr Richard Mackenney, Senior Lecturer in History, University of Edinburgh

Professor John M MacKenzie, Professor of Imperial History, Lancaster University

Dr R Muhs, former Lecturer, School of Slavonic and East European Studies, University of London

Dr William G Naphy, Tutor and Honorary Lecturer, Department of Modern History, University of St Andrews

Dr Stewart P Oakley, Senior Lecturer in History, University of East Anglia

Mr S Ravi Rajan, Junior Research Fellow, Wolfson College, Oxford

Dr Jane L Rowlandson, Lecturer in Ancient History, King's College, London

Dr Patrick Salmon, Senior Lecturer in History, University of Newcastle

Dr Catherine Simpson, Research Fellow, Robinson College, Cambridge

Dr S G F Spackman, Lecturer in Modern History, University of St Andrews

Dr Jonathan Spencer, Lecturer, Department of Social Anthropology, University of Edinburgh

Mr Alan Sykes, Lecturer in Modern History, University of St Andrews

Mr Bjarne Thorup Thomsen, Lecturer in Danish, University of Edinburgh

Mr James K Thomson, Curator, Ancient Civilizations, Glasgow Museums

Mr D Townson, Historian and former Head of History, Sevenoaks School, Kent

Dr Nigel Townson, Historian and journalist

Professor Bill Wallace, Honorary Senior Research Fellow, University of Glasgow

Mrs Susan Walton, University of St Andrews

Dr David R Watson, Senior Lecturer in History, University of Dundee

Dr Margaret H Williams, Tutor, Open University

Dr Michael Wintle, Senior Lecturer in European Studies, University of Hull

Introduction

Larousse, distinguished in the tradition of biographical and encyclopedic information, has built upon its reputation in the creation of this single-volume comprehensive survey of political, military and diplomatic history. Although there are many multi-volume works of historical reference, there seemed a need for a single substantial (7500-entry) work providing a world overview from earliest times to the present. Obviously, even with 1000 pages, selectivity was a difficult question, and we have had to concentrate on the three main categories given above. Thus, a cultural figure will only feature if he or she is of importance in one of the other three categories.

Every effort has been made to produce a balanced international selection covering all major cultures and we have relied heavily on a team of over 40 specialist contributors, based in universities throughout the UK. Larousse's extensive computerized databases have been exploited in the making of this dictionary; however, all existing entries have been revised by the team of contributors or have been specially commissioned for the work.

It has been our aim to provide in a single volume of substantial size an adequate global survey which will be useful for most quick reference purposes for professional and educational users. The cross-referencing of entries should facilitate browsing and enable the reader to explore connections between personalities and topics. It is an important feature of the dictionary that it draws on Larousse's extensive biographical expertise, supplementing this information with wide-ranging topic entries. Every effort has been made to avoid a purely Eurocentric balance of entries. We have endeavoured to be even-handed between continents and cultures, giving as much or more coverage in matters American as, for example, British. In European entries we have consciously striven to provide a more extensive coverage of Eastern Europe than has hitherto been usual in general works, not least in the light of recent events.

Of course, there are always problems in treading on the skirts of very recent history. Although our decision to increase Eastern European coverage has been more than justified by these events, those events, especially in the Balkans, move at such a pace that we had to accept that our entries could only be updated to the latter part of 1992. In fact, it has proved possible to update some material a little beyond that point. However, in the last analysis, we simply have to keep databanks up-to-date and we hope that future editions will benefit from this.

Although phrases like 'the end of history' were current long before the end of the Cold War, events since the disintegration of the Soviet Union have underlined yet again the endless surprises which historical events generate for even the best-informed observer, and we hope that this volume will serve to meet the historical needs of constantly changing and increasingly globalized societies.

Bruce P Lenman

Using the Dictionary

The *Larousse Dictionary of World History* aims to be both comprehensive (within the scope defined in the Introduction) and as accessible and easy to use as possible.

It is arranged in a straightforward A–Z format and each entry is placed according to what has been judged to be the most familiar form. Where we felt that there was any potential for confusion, either in the order of the elements in a headword (eg **Alliance, Holy** ▷ **Holy Alliance**) or in terminology (eg **US War of Independence** ▷ **American Revolution**), we have provided a cross-reference.

Some foreign words and names pose special difficulties insofar as they may be transliterated in a variety of ways. Here, as elsewhere, we have relied heavily upon the expertise of our team of specialist contributors. We have taken their advice regarding the most commonly-used forms, and have added cross-references from other less widely-found or up-to-date forms of words and names. As far as Chinese names are concerned, most entries are found listed alphabetically under the Pinyin transliteration, with a cross-reference given from the corresponding Wade-Giles transliteration; exceptions to this rule are specific Chinese names which are traditionally expressed in the Wade-Giles system and which would therefore be unfamiliar to most readers if given in the Pinyin form (eg Chiang Kai-shek, Sun Yat-sen) and Taiwanese names (since the Wade-Giles system is always used to transliterate these). Each of these entries is listed under its Wade-Giles transliteration (although, in the case of People's Republic of China names, a cross-reference is still provided from the Pinyin form).

We have highlighted in bold type, either in the body of an entry or following the open arrow symbol (▷) at the end of an entry, other biographical or topic entries found in the dictionary which provide additional information.

Acknowledgements

We would like to thank the following specialists for their help in the compilation of headword lists:

Dr Jeremy M Black, Reader in History, University of Durham

Dr R M Burrell, Lecturer, Department of History, School of Oriental and African Studies, University of London

Dr A C Duke, Reader in History, Department of History, University of Southampton

Dr Ruth J Macrides, Teaching and Research Fellow, Department of Medieval History, University of St Andrews

Dr T Munck, Senior Lecturer in Modern History, University of Glasgow

Dr F Rexroth, Institut für Geschichtswissenschaften, Humboldt-Universität, Berlin

Professor J S Richardson, Professor of Classics, University of Edinburgh

Dr Peter Robb, Senior Lecturer in Modern South Asian History, School of Oriental and African Studies, University of London

Dr M Wheeler, Lecturer, School of Slavonic and East European Studies, University of London

Dr D Wood, Reader Emeritus in History, University of Sussex

A

Abahai (1592–1643) Manchu (Jurchen) leader. He was the eighth son of **Nurhaci**, whom he succeeded as dominant leader of the Manchu tribes in 1626. He enhanced his power by gradually reducing the influence of other senior princes, or banner chiefs, thereby transforming a collective leadership into unitary rule. Under Abahai, the Manchus extended their control over Korea and Mongolia and conducted raids into north China. With the assistance of captured Chinese officials and scholars, Abahai created the structures of a bureaucratic state modelled on that of China. In 1636, at his capital in Mukden, Abahai proclaimed himself Emperor of the **Qing Dynasty**, and by the time of his death the Manchus were poised to launch a full-scale invasion of China. ▷ **Banner System**

Abalkin, Leonid Ivanovich (1930–) Soviet economist. He was for a time Director of the Institute of Economics of the USSR Academy of Sciences and a member of the Supreme Soviet of the USSR, with special responsibility for economic affairs. His published works centre on the theoretical problems of political economy under socialism. Under Mikhail **Gorbachev** he was one of the major advocates of rapid economic reform.

'Abbas (566–652) The uncle of the Prophet **Muhammad**. 'Abbas was at first hostile to him, but ultimately became the chief promoter of Islam. It was from 'Abbas that the **'Abbasid Dynasty** of rulers took their name.

'Abbas I, 'the Great' (1571–1629) Safavid Shah of Persia (1588/1629). After his accession, he set about establishing a counterweight to the Turkmen tribal chiefs who under his father, Muhammad Khudabanda, had constituted the principal political and military powers in the state, and whose propensity for feuding was a major cause of instability. This was achieved by the creation of a standing army drawn especially from Caucasian prisoners and immigrants and financed by an increase in the extent of the crown lands. From 1598 he was able to recover Azerbaijan and parts of Armenia from the Ottomans, and Khurasan from the Uzbeks. He transferred his capital from Qazvin to Isfahan, which he developed with a major programme of public works, and established diplomatic and economic relations with Western Europe.

'Abbas I (1813–54) Khedive of Egypt (1848/54). A grandson of the great **Muhammad 'Ali**, he took an active part in his grandfather's Syrian war, but later did much to undo the progress made under him, for example by blocking the construction of the Suez Canal.

'Abbas II (1874–1943) Khedive of Egypt (1892/1914). He succeeded his father, Tewfik Pasha, and attempted to rule independently of British influence. At the outbreak of **World War I** in 1914 he sided with Turkey and was deposed when the British made Egypt a protectorate.

Abbas, Ferhat (1899–1955) Algerian nationalist leader. He founded a Muslim Students' Association in 1924, before becoming a chemist. He served as a volunteer in the French army in 1939, but after France's defeat he produced in 1942 a 'Manifesto of the Algerian People'. In 1955 he joined the *Front de Libération Nationale* (**FLN**), the main Algerian resistance organization, and worked with **Ben Bella** in Cairo, before founding in 1958 a 'Provisional Government of the Algerian Republic' in Tunis. After independence in 1962, he was appointed President of the National Constituent Assembly but he fell out favour and was exiled. He was rehabilitated shortly before his death. ▷ **Algerian War of Independence**

Abbas Hilmi Pasha ▷ **'Abbas II**

'Abbasid Dynasty A dynasty of caliphs, which replaced that of the Umayyads in 749, establishing itself in Baghdad until its sack by the **Mongols** in 1258. Early 'Abbasid power reached its peak under **Harun al-Rashid** (786/809). The 'Abbasids traced their descent from the family of the Prophet **Muhammad**'s uncle, **'Abbas**, and were thus able to claim legitimacy in the eyes of the pious. See panel p2.

'Abbas Pasha ▷ **'Abbas I**

'ABBASID DYNASTY

Regnal Dates	Name	Regnal Dates	Name	Regnal Dates	Name
Caliphs in Iraq		944/6	al-Mustakfi	1352/62	al-Mu'tadid I
and Baghdad		946/74	al-Muti'	1362/77	al-Mutawakkil I
749/54	al-Saffah	974/91	al-Ta'i'		(1st reign)
754/75	al-Mansur	991/1031	al-Qadir	1377	al-Mu'tasim (1st reign)
775/85	al-Mahdi	1031/75	al-Qa'im	1377/83	al-Mutawakkil I
785/6	al-Hadi	1075/94	al-Muqtadi		(2nd reign)
786/809	Harun al-Rashid	1094/1118	al-Mustazhir	1383/5	al-Wathiq II
809/13	al-Amin	1118/35	al-Mustarshid	1385/9	al-Mu'tasim (2nd reign)
813/33	al-Ma'mun	1135/6	al-Rashid	1389/1406	al-Mutawakkil I
833/42	al-Mu'tasim	1136/60	al-Muqtafi		(3rd reign)
842/7	al-Wathiq	1160/70	al-Mustanjid	1406/14	al-Musta'in
847/61	al-Mutawakkil	1170/80	al-Mustadi'	1414/41	al-Mu'tadid II
861/2	al-Muntasir	1180/1225	al-Nasir	1441/51	al-Mustakfi II
862/6	al-Musta'in	1225/6	al-Zahir	1451/5	al-Qa'im
866/9	al-Mu'tazz	1226/42	al-Mustansir	1455/79	al-Mustanjid
869/70	al-Muhtadi	1242/58	al-Musta'sim	1479/97	al-Mutawakkil II
870/92	al-Mu'tamid			1497/1508	al-Mustamsik
892/902	al-Mu'tadid	**Caliphs in Cairo**			(1st reign)
902/8	al-Muktafi	1261	al-Mustansir	1508/16	al-Mutawakkil III
908/32	al-Muqtadir	1261/1302	al-Hakim I		(1st reign)
932/4	al-Qahir	1302/40	al-Mustakfi I	1516/17	al-Mustamsik (2nd reign)
934/40	al-Radi	1340/1	al-Wathiq I	1517	al-Mutawakkil III
940/4	al-Muttaqi	1341/52	al-Hakim II		(2nd reign)

Abboud, Ibrahim (1900–83) Sudanese soldier. Commander-in-Chief of the Sudanese army from the time of attainment of independence (1956), he was the leader of the military regime in the Sudan which obtained power when Abdullah Khalil surrendered the reins of government to the army in 1958. Abboud's regime was unable either politically or economically to maintain effective rule over the country, and was overthrown in 1964. Abboud himself resigned and retired into private life.

Abd al-Hadi, Awni (1889–1970) Palestinian politician. He was involved in Arab nationalist activity directed against the Turks prior to **World War I**, and helped to organize the 1st Arab Congress in Paris in 1913. A member of King Abdullah of Transjordan's staff after the so-called 'liberation' of Palestine in the latter years of the war, Abd al-Hadi subsequently became involved in the pan-Arab movement, was a member of the Arab Higher Committee in 1936 and was also behind the Arab 'Rebellion' of the same year. Exiled by the British from 1937 until 1941, he was subsequently involved in the formation of the Arab League in 1944. He was Jordanian Ambassador to Britain (1951–5) and, despite holding government posts in Jordan, spent the later years of his life in Egypt. ▷ **Alexandria Protocol**

Abd al-Krim, Muhammad (1882–1963) Berber chief. Born at Ajdir, Morocco, he led revolts in 1921 and 1924 against Spain and France, but surrendered before their combined forces in 1926. He was exiled to the Island of Réunion, and later amnestied (1947). He then went to Egypt, where he formed the North African Liberation Committee. He died in Cairo.

Abd ul-Hamid II (1842–1918) Ottoman Sultan (1876/1909). Known as the 'Great Assassin', he was the second son of Sultan **Abd ul-Majid I** and successor to his brother, Murad V. He promulgated the first Ottoman constitution in 1876, but his reign was notable for his cruel suppression of revolts in the Balkans, which led to wars with Russia (1877–8), and especially for the appalling Armenian massacres of 1894–6. He suspended the constitution in 1878 and ruled autocratically. Revolts in Crete in 1896–7 led to war with Greece. Later a reform movement by the revolutionary **Young Turks** forced him to restore the constitution and summon a parliament in 1908, but he was deposed and exiled in 1909.

'Abd al-Malik (646/7–705) Umayyad Caliph (685/705). Regarded, with his sons, al-Walid and Hisham, as one of the greatest of the Umayyad caliphs, he succeeded his father,

Marwan, and went on to defeat the forces of the so-called anti-caliph, al-Zubayr, in 691, thus establishing the **Umayyad Dynasty** on a firm footing. Credited with building the Dome of the Rock in Jerusalem, 'Abd al-Malik was known for his accessibility to his subjects. He minted his own coinage, established Arabic as the language of the Damascus administration (instead of Byzantine Greek) and, once he had rid himself of rival claimants to his position, prosecuted the conflict with Byzantium with renewed vigour. He was succeeded by his son, al-Walid I. ▷ **Camel, Battle of the**

Abd al-Qadir (1807–83) Algerian military and religious leader. After the French conquest of Algiers, the Arab tribes of Oran elected him as their Amir. He waged a long struggle against the French (1832–47), defeating them at Makta (1835). Eventually crushed by overpowering force, he took refuge in Morocco and began a crusade against the enemies of Islam. He finally surrendered in 1847 and was sent to France. He later lived in Bursa and in Damascus, where he died.

Abd al-Rahman The name of five amirs of Cordoba, Muslim Spain; most notably, Abd al-Rahman III (891–961), who ruled from 912. Under him, the caliphate reached the peak of its power, extending its boundaries in successful campaigns against the Fatimids and the Kings of Leon and **Navarre**. A patron of the arts, he made a cultural centre of Cordoba, where he died. ▷ **Fatimid Dynasty**

Abd al-Rahman (c.1840–1901) Amir of Afghanistan. The grandson of Dost Muhammad Khan, he was driven into exile in Russia in 1869. He was brought back and proclaimed emir with British support in 1880. Abd al-Rahman consolidated his power and arranged for the withdrawal of British troops, leaving Britain in control of foreign affairs, and in 1893 subscribed to the Durand Line as the India–Afghanistan border.

Abd el Kader ▷ **Abd al-Qadir**

Abduh, Muhammad (1849–1905) Egyptian reformer. A prime mover behind the reform movement in late 19c Egypt, after graduating from the Azhar, he became convinced of the need for educational reorganization and a reappraisal of Islam's position in the modern world. Exiled after the suppression of the **'Urabi Revolt**, he went eventually to Paris, where he renewed his acquaintanceship with

Jamal al-Din al-**Afghani**. Permitted to return to Cairo, by 1889 he had been appointed to the highest (clerical) post, that of state Mufti, which he held until his death. His activities were dominated by a strong Egyptian patriotism and he was thus opposed to control of Egypt being vested in despots, whether European or Oriental. He was, however, first and foremost a theologian and the maintenance of the true religion of Islam, shorn of falsifying abuses was his prime motivation.

Abd ul-Aziz (1830–76) Ottoman Sultan (1861/76). He succeeded his brother, **Abd ul-Majid I**, and continued his brother's liberal and Westernizing reforms. He promulgated the first Ottoman civil code, and visited Western Europe (1871). Thereafter, he became more autocratic and, after revolts in Bosnia, Herzegovina and Bulgaria, was forced to abdicate. He was found dead five days later.

Abdullah, Sheikh Muhammad (1905–82) Kashmiri politician. Known as the 'Lion of Kashmir', he was a leading figure in the struggle for India's independence and the fight for the rights of Kashmir. He participated actively in the Muslim struggle to overthrow the Hindu maharajah and substitute constitutional government, for which he was imprisoned several times. He was the founder of the Kashmir Muslim (later, National) Conference, and then the Quit Kashmir movement in 1946, when he was again detained. A year later, he was released by the emergency administration and in 1948 he was appointed Prime Minister of Kashmir. However, for his championing of the cause of an independent Kashmir, and his subsequent treasonable refusal to pledge his loyalty to India, he was again imprisoned for most of the period 1953–68. He contested the 1972 elections at the head of his Plebiscite Front, but lost to the Congress Party. As Chief Minister of Jammu and Kashmir from 1975 until his death, he was instrumental in persuading the Indian Prime Minister, Indira **Gandhi**, to grant Kashmir a degree of autonomy, making him a central figure in the fight for Kashmiri national rights.

Abdullah ibn Husayn (1882–1951) King of Jordan (1946/51). Born in Mecca, he was the second son of **Husayn ibn 'Ali**, and the grandfather of King Husayn. He was made the ruler of the British-mandated territory of Transjordan in 1921, and became the first King of Jordan when the mandate ended in 1946. He was assassinated in Jerusalem.

3

Abd ul-Majid I (1823–61) Ottoman Sultan (1839/61). He succeeded his father, **Mahmud II**, and continued the reforms of the previous reign, reorganizing the court system and education, and granting various rights to citizens, including Christians. In 1850 he chivalrously refused to give up the Hungarian political refugee Lajos **Kossuth** to the Habsburgs. In 1854 he secured an alliance with Britain and France to resist Russian demands, thus precipitating the **Crimean War** (1854–6). Thereafter, however, the **Ottoman Empire** was increasingly weakened by financial difficulties and internal nationalist problems. ▷ **Habsburg Dynasty**

Abdul Rahman, Tunka Putra (1903–90) Malaysian politician. The son of the Sultan of Kedah, he trained as a lawyer and joined the Civil Service in Kedah in 1931, becoming a public prosecutor in 1949. In 1952 he was nominated to the Executive and Legislative Councils of the Federation of Malaya, becoming Chief Minister in 1955 and Prime Minister, on independence, in 1957. He negotiated the formation of the Federation of Malaysia, to embrace Sabah, Sarawak and Singapore (1961–2) and remained Prime Minister of that enlarged entity when it came into being in 1963. After the outbreak of violent Malay–Chinese riots in Kuala Lumpur (May 1969), he withdrew from active politics. In his later years, he became an outspoken newspaper columnist.

Abercromby, Sir Ralph (1734–1801) British general. He studied law at Edinburgh and Leipzig, then joined the Dragoons in 1756 and fought in the **Seven Years War**. He became an MP in 1774, later serving in Holland and the West Indies, capturing Trinidad (1797). In 1801 he commanded the expedition to the Mediterranean, and effected a successful landing at **Aboukir Bay**, but was mortally wounded in the ensuing battle. ▷ **Napoleonic Wars**

Aberdeen, George Hamilton Gordon, 4th Earl (1784–1860) British politician. He succeeded to his earldom in 1801, and became a Scottish representative peer (1806), Ambassador to Vienna (1813–14), and Foreign Secretary (1828–30 and 1841–6). From 1852 to 1855, he headed a coalition ministry, which for some time was extremely popular. However, vacillating policy and mismanagement during the **Crimean War** led to his resignation.

Abernathy, Ralph (1926–90) US civil rights leader. A Baptist minister, he became chief aide to Martin Luther **King**, Jr, and helped organize the boycott of buses by the black community in Montgomery in 1955. He assumed the presidency of the **SCLC** (Southern Christian Leadership Conference) after King was assassinated in 1968 and continued in that post until his resignation in 1977. ▷ **civil rights movement; Parks, Rosa Lee**

Abgrenzung A German term meaning 'delimitation'. Following the success of Federal (West) Germany's **Ostpolitik** in the early 1970s, the East German authorities feared that increased personal contact between East and West Germans might undermine the GDR's legitimacy. They therefore stressed the differences between 'socialist' and 'capitalist' Germany, which were deemed more significant than a common German nationhood. ▷ **Germany, East; Germany, West**

abolitionism A 19c movement to end slavery in the US South, it was distinguished from earlier anti-slavery movements by its uncompromising attitude. It crystallized around the American Anti-Slavery Society, founded in 1833, and made slavery an issue that could not be ignored. Blacks as well as whites, and women as well as men, actively participated in the movement. ▷ **Douglass, Frederick; Garrison, William Lloyd; Howe, Julia Ward**

Aboriginals The native inhabitants of Australia, who reached the country some 40 000 years ago. By 1788, there were c.600 territorially defined groups, with a population of 300 000–1 million. Numbers fell dramatically thereafter, partly through conflict with Europeans, but mainly through epidemics of European diseases such as smallpox, and by 1933 the population was only c.66 000. As white settlement progressed, the Aboriginals lost control of the land and their daily lives. Government actions and those of Christian missionaries, whilst well-intentioned, attempted to civilize the Aboriginals in the European image. The alternative to assimilation was segregation: in the 1830s the government of Van Diemen's Land (Tasmania) attempted to clear the island, removing the Aboriginals to Flinders Island. Elsewhere, most Aboriginals were confined to government or mission reserves, which offered little protection against the demands for land from pastoral and, later, mining interests, or from the government's own policies such as **closer settlement**. Social Darwinist theories that the Aboriginals, as an inferior race, were doomed to extinction, made the Aboriginal question appear temporary. Defying European theory, the Aboriginal population rose from the nadir of the 1930s to reach 145 000 in 1981. Aboriginal confidence also grew: a day of mourning was planned to mark the 150th anniversary of the European invasion in 1838 and Aboriginal stockmen went on strike for better wages, with the Arbitration Commission awarding them equal pay in 1965. In 1967 a referendum gave the federal government powers to legislate for Aboriginals, making aid available. Aboriginal Land Trusts, to which remaining reserves were transferred, were set up in most states from the mid-1960s, but the European doctrine of *terra nullius*, reaffirmed by the courts, left the Aboriginals with little or no claim to the land in law. Aboriginal activism, however, kept the issue alive. The **Whitlam** government set up the Aboriginal Land Fund and the Aboriginal Land Rights (Northern Territory) Act (1976) to enable land transfers. In 1981, land for Aboriginal use amounted to some nine per cent of the total land area, but much of this was in the desert centre. Since then, the momentum has slowed, with growing opposition from commercial interests and economic difficulties reducing the scope for positive government action. Although Aboriginals have gradually been appointed in the Department of Aboriginal Affairs, they remain the most deprived section of the population.

Aboukir Bay, Battle of (Aug 1798) A naval battle during the War of the Second Coalition, in which the British Admiral **Nelson** destroyed the French fleet under Brueys off the coast of Egypt; the engagement is also known as the Battle of the Nile. This victory forced **Napoleon I** to abandon his Egyptian campaign, aimed at threatening British territory in India, and return to France.

Aboukir Bay, Battle of (July 1799) The last French victory of the Egyptian campaign, in which **Napoleon I**'s Army of Egypt captured Aboukir citadel, north-east of Alexandria, defeating an Ottoman Turkish force over twice the size, led by Mustafa Pasha.

Abraham, Plains/Heights of, Battle of (1759) The site of a battle in Quebec City, Canada, in which British forces under James **Wolfe** defeated a French/Canadian force under **Montcalm** and **Vaudreuil**, and gained control over Quebec. Wolfe and Montcalm were both killed in the battle.

Absalon (Axel) (1128–1201) Danish prelate and statesman. The foster-brother of

Valdemar I, 'the Great' whom he helped to the throne in 1157, he was appointed Bishop of Roskilde in 1158 and elected Archbishop of Lund in 1177. As Chief Minister to Valdemar, he led an army against the Wends in 1169 and extended Danish territories in the Baltic by capturing Rügen. In 1169 he built a fortress at Havn which became the nucleus of Copenhagen. As Chief Minister to Knud VI he led an expedition in 1184 that captured Mecklenburg and Pomerania. As Archbishop of Lund, he was largely responsible for the systematization of Danish ecclesiastical law.

absolutism The prevalent type of government in 17–18c continental Europe, characterized by the concentration of all state power in the hands of the ruler and best exemplified by France under **Louis XIV**. The establishment of absolute rule involved the suspension of the estates' tax-voting rights and the streamlining of all intermediate authorities between subject and state. This required, and thus caused, the creation of a standing army and an efficient bureaucracy. State and monarch were conceived of as one and regarded as above the law. The notion of the divine right of kings provided the justification for this claim to undivided sovereignty, which found its visible expression in a magnificent court. In many countries the arbitrariness of monarchical power was later tempered by concepts of responsibility to God and the common good, and used to implement a variety of reforms. ▷ **enlightened despots**

Abu Bakr (573–634) First of the Rashidun (or 'Rightly-Guided'), Caliphs (632/4). One of the earliest converts to Islam, he became chief adviser to **Muhammad**, who married his daughter, **'Aisha**. On Muhammad's death (632), Abu Bakr was elected leader of the Muslim community, with the title *khalifat Rasul Allah* ('Successor of the Messenger of God'). In his short reign he put down the Wars of the **Apostasy**, a religious and political revolt directed against the government at Medina, and set in motion the great wave of Arab conquests over Persia, Iraq and the Middle East. It was Abu Bakr who began the compilation of the Quran.

Abu Nidal (Sabri Khalil al-Banna) (1937–) Palestinian terrorist. Having joined Yasser **Arafat**'s Fatah guerrilla group in the late 1950s, he grew impatient with its relatively 'moderate' stance and established his own group, the 'Revolutionary Council of

5

Fatah' (often simply called the 'Abu Nidal Group'), in 1973. Sentenced to death for his extremism by the 'mainstream' **PLO** the following year, Abu Nidal went on to head a group which gained notoriety for its brutal activities. The group has targeted Arabs viewed as traitors to the Palestinian cause, and its attacks have included the killing of 'moderate' PLO member Issam Sartawi in 1983 and that of the Israeli-appointed Mayor of Nablus in 1986. It also killed passengers at Rome and Vienna airports. Bowing to pressure from Arab states and the PLO, in 1988 Abu Nidal reportedly agreed to abide by the latter's ban on terrorism.

Abyssinia, Conquest of (1935) The bellicose venture by **Mussolini** aimed at winning popular support at home, an increase in Italian prestige and strategic gains to pressurize the British in the Eastern Mediterranean. The invasion began in Oct 1935, against the advice of **Victor Emmanuel III** and most of his generals. Victory was achieved by General **Badoglio** in May 1936 and the King was declared Emperor. However, the campaign was not a success: Italy had to commit over 650 000 men to subduing an ill-equipped and badly organized army and won the profound enmity of the British government. Limited economic sanctions were also imposed by the **League of Nations**. ▷ **autarchia; De Bono, Emilio**

Acadia Part of France's American empire; what is today Prince Edward Island, Nova Scotia, New Brunswick, and the mainland coast from the Gulf of St Lawrence to Maine. The first settlement was established at Port Royal in 1605 by the sieur de Monts, and the area was exchanged between France and England until the Treaty of **Utrecht** (1713) handed most of Acadia to Britain. In 1755 10 000 Acadians were evicted from the territory for resolving to pursue a policy of neutrality in the conflicts between France and Britain. The last French stronghold, Louisbourg, fell in 1758. ▷ **New France**

Aceh A major state at the northern extremity of the island of Sumatra, renowned for the fierceness of its Islamic tradition and for its trading prowess. As Dutch rule advanced from Java though the outer islands of the Indonesian archipelago in the second half of the 19c, the Acehnese put up the most stubborn resistance. The Dutch occupied the capital of the sultanate in the early 1870s but then found themselves drawn into a protracted resistance struggle. The colonial power launched ceaseless attacks from 1896 and subdued the sultanate by 1902.

Achaean League In ancient Greece, the association of the 12 cities of Achaea in the north-west Peloponnese. Its membership expanded considerably from 251BC, under the leadership of **Aratus of Sicyon**, to include by 228BC much of the north Peloponnese, **Corinth** and Aegina. Weakened by warfare against Cleomenes III of **Sparta** (c.222BC), its support for Rome in the early 2c BC was rewarded with dominance in the Peloponnese. It was dissolved when Rome created the province of Achaea in 146BC.

Achaemenids The first royal house of Persia, founded by the early 7c ruler, Achaemenes. Its capitals included Parsagadae and Persepolis. ▷ **Cyrus II; Darius I, 'the Great'; Persian Empire; Xerxes I**

Acheampong, Ignatius Katu (1931–79) Ghanaian soldier and politician. He taught in commercial colleges before joining the army in 1953. Trained in the UK and USA, he served with the **UN** in the Congo (Zaire) and, following the 1966 military overthrow of **Nkrumah**, was Chairman of the Western Region's administration for the National Liberation Council. Acting head of the 1st Brigade when he led the coup overthrowing Kofi **Busia** (13 Jan 1972), he became Chairman of the National Redemption Council and then Chairman of the Supreme Military Council and head of state (1972–8), until he was deposed and later executed.

Acheson, Dean Gooderham (1893–1971) US lawyer and politician. Educated at Yale and Harvard, he was Under-Secretary (1945–7) and then Secretary of State (1949–53) in the Truman administration. He developed US policy for the containment of **communism**, helped to formulate the **Marshall Plan** (1947–8) and participated in the establishment of **NATO** (1949).

Achille Lauro Hijacking (7–9 Oct 1985) The Italian cruise liner hijacked, when sailing between Alexandria and Port Said, by four members of the Tunis-based faction of the Palestine Liberation Front (PLF), part of the **PLO** (Palestine Liberation Organization). The hijackers demanded the release of 50 Palestinians being held in Israel and threatened to kill the ship's 180 passengers if their demands were not met. However, after negotiations with Egyptian and Italian intermediaries and PLO officials, the terrorists surrendered. Despite the hijackers' claims that no-one had been harmed, after their surrender it transpired that a US Jewish passenger, Leon Klinghoffer, had been shot dead and thrown overboard. The hijackers and an alleged Syrian accomplice were tried on charges of illegal possession of arms and explosives in Genoa the following month; all were convicted and sentenced to between four and nine years' imprisonment.

Achimota College A college founded in the Gold Coast by the Governor Sir Gordon Guggisberg in 1924 with the intention of developing an educated African elite capable of taking over a large proportion of the administrative tasks in the colony. By 1938 it was offering degree courses to a small number of students.

Achin War ▷ **Atjeh War**

Acker, Achille Henry van (1898–1975) Belgian politician. A socialist, he began his career in trade unions after **World War I** and was MP for his home town of Bruges (1927–74). He was appointed Cabinet Minister for Labour and Social Affairs in 1944, and thereafter became Prime Minister on four occasions. He is remembered for his role in the education debate, in the controversy leading to the King's abdication, and in social legislation. After 1958 he took less controversial political roles, first as a minister of state, and then as chairman of the House of Representatives until 1974. ▷ **Belgian Socialist Party**

ACLU ▷ **American Civil Liberties Union**

Actium, Battle of (31BC) The victory of Octavian (later the Emperor **Augustus**) over the forces of Mark **Antony** and **Cleopatra VII** off the coast of north-west Greece. It traditionally marks the end of the **Roman Republic** and the beginning of the **Roman Empire**.

Adalbert (c.1000–72) German prelate. Born of a noble Saxon family in 1043 he was appointed Archbishop of Bremen and Hamburg. As papal legate to the north (1053), he extended his spiritual sway over Scandinavia, and carried Christianity to the Slavonic Wends. In 1063 he became tutor to the young **Henry IV** (of the Germans) and ruled over the whole kingdom for three years until he was deposed by enemy princes in 1066. He never regained his earlier authority and even lost Bremen, from which he was banished for three years.

Adams, Charles Francis (1807–86) US diplomat. The son of John Quincy **Adams**, he studied at Harvard, was admitted to the Bar (1828), and became a representative from Massachusetts (1858–61). As Minister to Britain (1861–8), he strove to maintain British neutrality during the **American Civil War**.

Adams, Sir Grantley Herbert (1898–1971) Barbadian politician. After studying classics at Oxford, he was called to the English Bar in 1924 and returned to the West Indies to practise. He was a prominent figure in Caribbean politics and became Premier of Barbados (1954–8) before being elected the first Prime Minister of the short-lived Federation of the **West Indies** (1958–62), which would have united seven former British colonies into a single state.

Adams, John (1735–1826) US politician and 2nd President. Educated at Harvard, and admitted to the Bar in 1758, he emerged as a leader of US resistance to Britain's imposition of the **Stamp Act** (1765), and led the debate that resulted in the **Declaration of Independence**. He served in Congress until 1777, after which he had an extensive diplomatic career in Europe. He took part in negotiating a peace treaty with Great Britain, and then served as Minister to Great Britain (1785–8). He became the first US Vice-President, under George **Washington** (1789) an office he found frustrating. Both were re-elected in 1792, and in 1796 Adams was elected President with Thomas **Jefferson** as Vice-President. Adams's presidency was marked by factionalism within his cabinet and his party, especially over the issue of war with France. Adams opposed a war, which made him an unpopular president, and he was defeated by Jefferson on seeking re-election in 1800. He retired to his home at Quincy, where he died. ▷ **Federalist Party**

Adams, John Quincy (1767–1848) US politician and 6th President. The son of John **Adams**, he studied at Harvard, and was admitted to the Bar in 1790. He had an extensive and brilliant diplomatic career between 1794 and 1817, except when he served in the US Senate (1803–8). As Secretary of State under James **Monroe**, he negotiated with Spain the treaty for the acquisition of Florida, and played an important part in the formulation of the **Monroe Doctrine**. As President (1825–9), he failed to establish a strong base of public and political support and was therefore frustrated by executive and congressional factionalism. After his defeat by Andrew **Jackson** in 1828, he was elected to House of Representatives, where through the 1830s and 1840s he became a strong opponent of the extension of slavery.

Adams, Samuel (1722–1803) American revolutionary political leader. Educated at Harvard, he became Lieùtenant-Governor (1789–94) and Governor (1794–7) of Massachusetts. He was a strong supporter of revolution against Britain, and helped to plan the **Boston Tea Party**. Adams was a member of the **Continental Congress** (1774–81) and one of the signatories of the **Declaration of Independence**. ▷ **American Revolution**

Adams, Will(iam) (1564–1620) English sailor. He was pilot of a Dutch ship stranded off Japan in 1600, and was kept by **Tokugawa Ieyasu**, the first **Shogun**, as an adviser on such areas as shipbuilding, navigation, gunnery, foreign relations, and trade. He built the first European type of ocean-going vessel in Japan. The first Englishman to enter the service of a Japanese ruler, he lived at **Edo** (now Tokyo), where he was given an estate by Ieyasu. He is buried at Pilot Hill, Yokosuka, and is commemorated by monuments at Ito and Tokyo. ▷ **Tokugawa Shogunate**

Addams, Jane (1860–1935) US social reformer. She founded the first US settlement house, Hull House in Chicago, dedicated to settlement work among the immigrant poor, where she made her home. Addams worked to secure social justice by sponsoring legislation relating to housing, factory inspection, female suffrage, and the cause of pacifism. She also campaigned for the abolition of child labour and the recognition of labour unions. Many of these reforms were adopted by the Progressive Party as part of its platform in 1912; Addams seconded Theodore **Roosevelt**'s nomination for President and was an active campaigner on his behalf. In 1931 she shared the Nobel Peace Prize, awarded in recognition of her efforts to end hostilities in **World War I**.

Addington, **Henry** ▷ **Sidmouth, Henry Addington, 1st Viscount**

Addison, **Joseph** (1672–1719) English essayist and poet. In 1708–11 he was Secretary to the Lord-Lieutenant of Ireland, where he formed a warm friendship with Alexander Swift. He became an MP, and contributed largely to the *Tatler*. In 1711 the *Spectator*, 274 numbers of which were his work, was founded. He was satirized by Pope in the famous character of Atticus. Addison was made a commissioner for trade and the colonies, and in 1717 was appointed Secretary of State, but a year later resigned his post on health grounds.

Addled Parliament In Britain, the name given to the brief parliament of Apr–June 1614 which saw disputes over money between **James VI and I** and the House of Commons. The Commons attempted to coerce the King into giving up prerogative revenue from 'impositions' on goods entering and leaving the country. The King dismissed the parliament, which passed no legislation.

Adelfi Secret society inspired and organized by the Tuscan revolutionary Filippo **Buonarroti** which pursued radical and patriotic goals from the 1790s until the Restoration era. ▷ **Carbonari**

Adenauer, Konrad (1876–1967) German politician. He studied at Freiburg, Munich, and Bonn, before practising law in Cologne, where he became Lord Mayor (1917). He was President of the Prussian State Council (1920–33). In 1933 the Nazis dismissed him from all his offices, and imprisoned him in 1934, and again in 1944. In 1945, under Allied occupation, he helped to found the Christian Democratic Union (**CDU**) and served briefly again as Lord Mayor of Cologne. As the first Chancellor of the Federal Republic of Germany (1949–63), he established closer links with the French, and aimed to rebuild West **Germany** on a basis of partnership with other West European nations through **NATO** and the **EEC**. Although relations were restored with the USSR, relations with other countries in Eastern Europe remained frigid.

ADGB (*Allgemeiner Deutscher Gewerkschaftsbund*, 'General German Trade Union Federation') The predominant, socialist-inclined German trade-union organization in the **Weimar Republic**. Founded in 1919, the ADGB strove to unite all employees in a single federation and to gain recognition from the employers as the legitimate representative of German labour. Initial successes were undermined by a vigorous employers' counter-offensive, but the ADGB remained a significant organization with a membership of around 4 to 5 million. On 2 May 1933 it was banned by the National Socialist government. ▷ **Nazi Party**

Adolf Frederick (1710–71) King of Sweden (1751/71). The first king of the House of Holstein–Gottorp, he was the son of Christian Augustus, Prince-Bishop of Lübeck, and was descended on his mother's side from King **Charles XI** of Sweden. A favourite of Empress **Elizabeth Petrovna** of Russia, he was imposed by her on the Swedes as successor-designate to the childless King **Frederick I** in 1743 as a condition for ending a war in which Sweden had been humiliatingly defeated. The following year he married **Lovisa Ulrika**, the sister of King **Frederick II, 'the Great'** of Prussia, by whom he was dominated. His powers as king were severely limited by the constitution of the '**Age of Liberty**', but in 1768 his brief abdication forced the calling of an election to the Diet, which returned the Hat Party to power.

Adolf of Nassau (1250–98) King of Germany (1292/8). Relatively powerless himself, Adolf was unanimously elected King in 1292 as a means of refuting Habsburg claims to a hereditary right to the monarchy, represented by Albert of Austria. Adolf attempted to build up a power base in Meissen and Thuringia and had military successes there in 1294–5, but his ambitions alarmed the **Electors** and he was deposed in 1298 by a coalition of Bohemia, Austria and Mainz. He fell in battle against Albert of Austria and was buried in the cathedral in Speyer in 1309. ▷ **Göllheim, Battle of; Habsburg Dynasty**

Adowa, Battle of (1 Mar 1896) A battle between Ethiopian forces, under Emperor **Menelik**, and Italian forces, in which the latter were decisively defeated. In the 1880s Italy had become involved in the Scramble for Africa, taking Eritrea (1884) and the Indian Ocean coast of Somalia (1890). The Italian defeat at Adowa was the worst reverse suffered by Europeans in the Partition of Africa, and ensured Ethiopian independence for another 40 years. It was also probably the biggest factor in bringing down the second **Crispi** ministry. **Mussolini**'s invasion of 1935 was a conscious act of revenge. ▷ **Africa, Partition of**

Adrian IV (Nicholas Breakspear) (c.1100–59) English Pope (1154/9). The only Englishman to hold the office, he became first a lay brother in the monastery of St Rufus, near Avignon, and in 1137 was elected its Abbot. His zeal for strict discipline led to an attempt to defame his character, and he had to appear before **Eugenius III** at Rome. Here he not only cleared himself, but also acquired the esteem of the Pope, who appointed him Cardinal Bishop of Albano in 1146. As Pope, he is said to have granted Ireland to **Henry II** of England.

Adrian VI (Adrian Dedel) (1459–1523) Dutch Pope (1522/3). After studying with the Brethren of the Common Life and in Leuven (Louvain), he was made Professor of Theology (1491) and was appointed tutor in 1507 to the 7-year-old Charles (later Charles I of Spain and Emperor **Charles V**), who in 1516, commencing rule in Spain, made Adrian Inquisitor-General of Aragon and effective co-regent with Ximenes, the choice of the dying **Ferdinand II, 'the Catholic'**. On Ximenes's death, Charles worked closely with Adrian and made him regent in his absence from 1520, but in 1522 on the death of Leo X, Adrian was almost unanimously elected Pope. He tried to attack the sale of indulgences which had prompted **Luther**'s first revolt, but was blocked by interested officials. He called openly for widespread reform of the curia at the Diet of Nuremberg, but also demanded Luther's punishment for heresy. He allied with the Emperor, England and Venice against France, thus failing to unite Christendom against the Turks, who captured Rhodes. He died before his attempted reforms could be effective, and was the last non-Italian Pope before **John Paul II** in 1978.

Adrianople, Battle of (378) A battle between the Romans and the **Visigoths** at present-day Edirne in European Turkey. This was one of the crucial battles of the ancient world, as the crushing Visigoth victory, under Fritigern, opened up Roman territory to Germanic invasion. Two-thirds of the Roman army, including Emperor **Valens**, were killed. ▷

Adrianople, Treaty of (1829) The treaty ending the Russo-Turkish War of 1828–9 which began when, partly as a diversion from domestic unrest, **Nicholas I** of Russia renewed his predecessors' policy of southwards expansion by moving his forces across the River Danube in 1828. It marked an important stage in the advance of both Serbia and Greece towards independent statehood. Russian troops also crossed the Balkan mountains for the first time; and, although under the treaty Russia gave up all its conquests, it gave notice that it was now a military power to be reckoned with in the Near East and the Mediterranean. ▷ **Russo-Turkish Wars**

Adullamites A nickname coined by the radical British Liberal MP John **Bright** to describe those in his party who opposed **Gladstone**'s parliamentary reform bill in 1866. Bright's reference was to the 'Cave Adullam' in the First Book of Samuel which housed 'everyone that was in distress ... and everyone that was discontented'. The Adullamite leaders, Robert Lowe and Lord Elcho, succeeded in bringing down the Liberal government (1866). ▷ **radicalism**

Aegospotami (Aigospotamoi), Battle of (405BC) The naval victory near Sestos on the Hellespont when the Peloponnesian fleet under **Lysander** destroyed the last fleet the Athenians could equip in the **Peloponnesian War**. It thus allowed Lysander to cut off Athens's corn supply and to besiege Athens itself, soon bringing the war to an end.

Aeolians A sub-group of Hellenic peoples who colonized the north-west coast of Asia Minor and the islands of the northern Aegean (eg Lesbos) towards the end of the second millennium BC.

Aerssen, Cornelis van (1546–1627) Founder of an important Dutch political family of the 16–17c. He became Pensionary of Brussels in 1580, and then Secretary to the States General in 1584, a post he held until 1623. He was closely involved in the negotiations leading to the **Twelve Years' Truce**. His son François (1572–1641) became Lord of Sommelsdijk in 1612 and was a diplomat and adviser to Oldenbarnevelt, but later transferred his allegiance to Prince **Maurice**, and exerted a major influence on the foreign policy of the Dutch Republic. François' son Cornelis (1600–62), a military leader, was thought to be the richest man in Holland of his day. Several other members of the family achieved prominence in the public life of the republic.

Aeschines (c.390–c.315BC) Athenian orator, second only to **Demosthenes**. Prominent in Athenian politics between 348 and 330BC, his advocacy of peace with **Macedonia** brought him frequently into bitter conflict with Demosthenes, his chief opponent. Defeated in his attempt to undermine Demosthenes in 330BC, he went into voluntary exile in Rhodes, where he taught rhetoric, and later died. Of his speeches, only three survive. ▷ **Philip II** of Macedon

Aethelstan ▷ **Athelstan**

Aethelred ▷ **Ethelred**

Aëtius (d.454) Roman general. He effectively ruled the western Roman Empire for **Valentinian III**. His main achievements were the destruction of the Burgundian Kingdom in eastern **Gaul**, and the defeat of **Attila** the Hun in 451. ▷ **Catalaunian Plains, Battle of the**

Aetolia In antiquity, a district of north-western Greece on the north of the Corinthian Gulf. Its principal cities included Thermon, Calydon and Pleuron. An area of minor importance in the Archaic and Classical periods of Greek history, the Aetolian League, formed by its main cities in the later 4c BC, became increasingly powerful, dominating all central Greece by 245BC, and later extending its influence into the Peloponnese and the Aegean. An ally of Rome against **Philip V** of Macedonia at Cynoscephalae (197BC), the League soon found its own power restricted by Rome after it had brought about war between Rome and Antiochus III.

Aetolian League ▷ **Aetolia**

affirmative action The name given to US policies requiring businesses and other institutions to enact employment practices concerning minorities ranging from the employment and promotion of ethnic minorities and women, to the setting of employment quotas. Such policies were established in the early 1970s to counteract discrimination in the past, but have been challenged in recent times as 'reverse discrimination'.

Afghani, Jamal al-Din al- (1838/9–97) Muslim reformer and political agitator. Born at Asadabad near Kabul, his life's work was directed towards fomenting agitation for his country's liberation from European exploitation, the independent internal development of Muslim countries along liberal lines, and towards his overriding vision of a union of all Islamic states under a single caliph ('pan-Islam'). He visited India, Egypt and Turkey, where he fell foul of the authorities and returned to Cairo. In what was to become a familiar pattern, after an initially good reception, he annoyed both the British and the Azharis by his inflammatory behaviour and was deported to India. Noted particularly for his later opposition to the Persian tobacco concession, which became a cause célèbre, he became a thoroughly embarrassing figure to the authorities in the countries he had visited. In 1892 he was, however, invited to retire to Turkey, where he spent the last five years of his life. His activities were primarily directed towards the goal of universal Pan-Islam. He sought to achieve this by means of inflammatory articles, appearing notably in two major publications, *Al-Urwa al-Wuthqa* (in collaboration with Muhammad **Abduh**), and the bilingual Arabic-English monthly, *Diya' al-Khafiqin*, which contained many attacks on the Shah of Persia and his government.

Afghan Wars (1838–42, 1878–80 and 1919) A series of wars between Britain and Afghanistan, prompted by the British desire to extend control in the region to prevent the advance of Russian influence towards India. The treaties which followed the third Afghan War (1919) reinforced the country's independent political status.

Aflaq, Michel (1912–89) Syrian politician. A schoolteacher and then journalist in Damascus, he was, with Salah al-Din **Bitar**, the founder of the Ba'ath Party. The ideology behind the party was essentially socialist, with an emphasis on Arab unity. It was also anti-Zionist and instrumental in the foundation with Gamal Abd al-**Nasser** of the **United Arab Republic** (1958–61). Ousted from Syria in 1966, his own political influence declined, but even today (hostile) Arab presses are inclined to refer to the Ba'ath Party as being Aflaqi.

AFL–CIO (American Federation of Labor and Congress of Industrial Organizations) A federation of labour unions in the US, Canada, Mexico, Panama and US dependencies, formed in 1955 from the merger of the AFL (mainly craft unions, founded in 1886) with the CIO (mainly industrial workers' unions, founded in 1935). Its aims include educational campaigns on behalf of the labour movement, the settlement of disputes among affiliates, and political support for beneficial legislation. ▷ **Lewis, John L; United Automobile Workers**

afrancesados The term applied to those 'Frenchified' Spanish politicians and intellectuals who during the War of Independence (1793–1814) supported Joseph **Bonaparte** and the programme of reforms introduced by the French administration. They were opposed by the 'patriot' reformers who supported Ferdinand VII. When the French troops withdrew from Spain, some 10 000 *afrancesados* were driven into exile by a decree of 1814.

Africa, Partition of The division of the continent of Africa into colonial territories, which occurred in the last three decades of the 19c. Europeans had traded with Africa for several centuries, using a series of coastal settlements. Portuguese efforts to penetrate the interior in the 16–17c had largely failed, and only the Dutch at the Cape had been able to establish a dynamic permanent settlement. In the course of the 19c, efforts to abolish the **slave trade**, missionary endeavours, and optimistic views of African riches helped to encourage colonial ambitions. The countries involved in the Partition included Britain, France, Germany, Portugal, and Italy, as well as the Boers in the south, and (in his private capacity) King **Leopold II** of the Belgians. When the French and the Italians completed the Partition of North Africa in the years before **World War I**, only Liberia and Ethiopia remained independent. At the end of the two World Wars, a repartitioning occurred with the confiscation of German and Italian territories. Most of the countries created by the Partition achieved independence in or after the 1960s, and the **Organization of African Unity** pledged itself to the maintenance of the existing boundaries. See maps p12 and p13.

African Development Bank Established in 1963 in the same year as the **Organization of African Unity** and based in Abidjan, it began operations in 1966. Its funds come from both individual countries and multilateral sources and loans are made, on preferential rates, for development schemes.

African Lakes Company A company founded in 1878, originally called the Livingstonia Central Africa Company, to assist the Scottish Presbyterian missionaries in Nyasaland, now Malawi. Its founders, the two brothers Fred and John Moir, placed steamers on Lake Nyasa and became embroiled in campaigns against Muslim rivals. The under-capitalized company was poorly managed and it was bought out by Cecil Rhodes who, in 1893, turned it into the African Lakes Trading Corporation. It remained a leading trading and retailing company throughout the period of colonial rule in central Africa.

African National Congress ▷ **ANC**

African National Council A Zimbabwean political organization founded in 1972 on the roots of the **Zimbabwe African People's Union** to express to the Pierce Commission black opposition to a proposed constitutional

Africa, 1895

arrangement agreed between Ian **Smith** and British Prime Minister Sir Alec Douglas-Home. Its leader was Bishop Abel **Muzorewa** who developed it into a political party. Its success in the late 1970s depended upon the continued banning of its forerunners and its strength rapidly reduced after independence in 1980. ▷ **Home of the Hirsel, Baron**

Afrifa, Akwasi A (1936–79) Ghanaian soldier and politician. Educated at Adisadel College, he joined the colonial army in 1956, trained at Sandhurst and twice served with the **UN** in the Congo (Zaire). He was one of the group which overthrew **Nkrumah** in 1966 and became a member, later chairman, of the National Liberation Council. He handed power over to civilians in 1969, but, when the military intervened again in 1972, he was for a while detained. When civilian rule returned,

he was tried and executed for corrupt practices.

Afrika Corps A German expeditionary force of two divisions under the command of **Rommel**, sent to North Africa (Mar 1941) to reinforce Italian troops there. It had been given special desert training in Germany, and proved highly effective in desert warfare between 1941 and 1943. ▷ **North African Campaign; World War II**

Afrikaner Bond A society founded in 1880 as part of the political and cultural revival of the Boers or **Afrikaners** in South Africa. It coined the slogan 'Afrika voor de Afrikaners' and promoted the Dutch language and strict Calvinism. There were branches in the Cape, Orange Free State and Transvaal. At the Cape the Bond was prepared to form a

Decolonization of Africa

political alliance with English-speaking South Africans, particularly supporting Cecil Rhodes, but elsewhere it became virulently anti-British. In 1918 a new body, the Afrikaner **Broederbond**, emerged. It was much more secretive and became the driving force of more radical Afrikaner nationalism in the 20c.

Afrikaners An early 18c term to describe those Europeans who had been born in the Dutch colony at the Cape and were therefore 'Africans', also known as **Boers** (in Dutch, 'farmers'). They emerged as a separate people derived from an admixture of Dutch, German, French, and non-White. During the 18c they penetrated the interior of the Cape as pastoral farmers. After 1835, groups left Cape Colony and established independent republics in the interior, which later coale-

sced into the Orange Free State and the South African Republic. After the Boer War (1899–1902) the British hoped to encourage emigration to South Africa, transforming the Afrikaners into a minority. Such large-scale emigration failed to materialize, and after the Union of South Africa in 1910 the Afrikaners became the dominant force in White South African politics. Never a monolithic force, they have produced repeated political fission in the search for security against the African majority. ▷ **apartheid; Boer Wars; Great Trek; Smuts, Jan**

Agadir A port on the Atlantic coast of Morocco which was visited in July 1911 by the German gunboat *Panther*, supposedly to protect German interests in Morocco threatened by the French, whom Kiderlen-Wächter had accused of acting contrary to the agree-

13

ments reached at the 1906 Conference of **Algeciras**. It was the British government, however, who were the more alarmed by the presence of the *Panther* in a port relatively close to Gibraltar. They suspected the Germans of seeking to establish a naval presence in Agadir, thereby posing a threat to British trade routes. The 'Second Moroccan Crisis' came close to precipitating hostilities. These were, however, averted.

Aga Khan The title of the hereditary head of the Nizari Ismailian sect of Muslims, notably Aga Khan III (1877–1957), in full Aga Sultan Sir Mohammed Shah, born at Karachi, who succeeded to the title in 1885. He worked for the British cause in both World Wars, and in 1937 was president of the **League of Nations**. He owned several Derby winners. He died at Versoix, Switzerland, and was succeeded as 49th Imam by his grandson, Aga Khan IV (1936–), Karim, the son of Aly Khan. ▷ **Word War I; World War II**

Aganbegyan, Abel Gazevich (1932–) Soviet economist. Part-Armenian, part-Hungarian, he was born in Tbilisi in Georgia, studied economics in Moscow and made his name in the Institute of Industrial Production in Novosibirsk, eventually as Director (1967–85). He met Mikhail **Gorbachev** through **Zaslavskaya** and was initially one of the main contributors to his reform programme. An early influence on Gorbachev's **perestroika**, although he transferred to Moscow, he fell into the background in the late 1980s.

Age of Greatness (Sweden) The period in the 17c when Sweden acquired and maintained the status of a great European power. It is usually taken to begin with the accession of **Gustav II Adolf** in 1611 and to end with the Peace of Nystadt in 1721 at the end of the **Great Northern War**. During this time Sweden won Livonia in the south-eastern Baltic, western Pomerania, the city of Wismar and the bishoprics of Bremen and Verden in northern Germany, as well as the provinces of Halland, Scania and Blekinge from Denmark, and Bohuslän, Jämtland and Härjedalen from Norway. Under a series of capable kings and ministers, Sweden's government and military machine became among the most efficient in Europe.

Age of Liberty (Sweden) The period between the death of **Charles XII** in 1718 and the coup d'état of **Gustav III** in 1772, when Sweden was governed under a constitution

(finalized in 1720) which granted political power to the Diet dominated by the Estate of Nobles. It saw the rise of political parties, divided on foreign, economic and social policy, beginning with the pro-French Hat Party in the later 1730s, who dominated the scene until ousted in 1765 by the Cap Party, who then developed a social policy which aimed at the reduction of noble privileges. The intensity of the struggle between these two groups was ended by Gustav III, who restored a degree of monarchical power.

Agesilaus (444–360BC) King of **Sparta** (399/ 360BC). Initially an active and successful defender of Spartan interests, both in Asia Minor (396–395BC) and mainland Greece, he ultimately brought about her total eclipse by precipitating the Battle of **Leuctra** against **Thebes** (371BC). He died fighting overseas, trying to raise money for the state he had helped to impoverish. ▷ **Epaminondas; Peloponnesian War**

Agincourt, Battle of (1415) A battle between France and England during the **Hundred Years War**. **Henry V** of England was forced to fight near Hesdin (Pas-de-Calais) by the French who, ignoring the lessons of the Battles of **Crécy** and Poitiers (1356), pitched cavalry against dismounted men-at-arms and archers. Though heavily outnumbered, the English won another overwhelming victory, and returned in 1417 to begin the systematic conquest of **Normandy**.

Agitprop An abbreviation for the Department of Agitation and Propaganda, established in 1920 as a section of the Central Committee Secretariat of the Soviet Communist Party. Its role was to ensure the compatibility of activities within society with Communist Party ideology. The term later came to be widely used in an artistic or literary context for works which adopted an ideological stance. ▷ **communism**

Agnadello, Battle of ▷ **Italian Wars**

Agnew, Spiro Theodore (1918–) US politician. The son of a Greek immigrant, after service in **World War II** he studied law at the University of Maryland. In 1966 he was elected Governor of Maryland on a liberal platform, supporting anti-discrimination and anti-poverty legislation, but by 1968, he had become considerably more conservative. As a compromise figure acceptable to many in the Republican party, he became Richard **Nixon**'s running mate in the 1968 election, and took office as Vice-President in 1969. He resigned in 1973 after charges of corruption during his years in Maryland politics were brought against him. ▷ **Republican Party**

Agrarian Party (Sweden) ▷ **Centre Party**

Agrarian Reform Law (1950) One of the first measures implemented by the Chinese People's Republic established in 1949. It aimed to complete the process, begun in the late 1940s in areas under communist control, to redistribute land amongst landless and poor peasants. In contrast to previous measures, however, agrarian reform in 1950 was to be relatively moderate, in line with the prevailing view that there was to be a gradual transition towards socialism and collectivization. Although the land and property of landlords (who made up about four per cent of the population and owned 30 per cent of the cultivated land) were to be confiscated and redistributed, dispossessed landlords could still be given a share. Moreover, land worked by rich peasants was protected and they could even rent land to tenant farmers, providing it did not exceed the amount of land they cultivated themselves. Nevertheless, agrarian reform, completed in 1952, produced a large class of individual peasant owner-cultivators. Socially and politically, the influence of the landlord class was eliminated; many landlords were subject to denunciation and even execution by communist-organized peasant associations.

agregado A term used in Brazil (literally, 'a dependant') with various connotations, all of which denote the dependence of the *agregado* on the patronage of a powerful proprietor. The agregado was a rural labourer, dependent on the favour of a landowner for access to subsistence plot and hut, in exchange for labour services specified by customary law. Such agreements were always verbal, and could generally be revoked by the landowner. Agregados were often tied by fictitious rental agreements, which obliged them to vote for the candidate chosen by the landowner: they were seen variously, as the property of the landowner or as his personal militia.

Agricola, Gnaeus Julius (AD40–93) Roman general. Rome's longest-serving and most successful governor in Britain (78–84), he skilfully implemented a two-pronged policy, of conquest in the north and Romanization in the south. He subdued northern England and Lowland Scotland, and actively encouraged the development of Roman-style towns in the south. Though his plans to conquer the extreme north of Scotland and Ireland came to nothing, the circumnavigation of Britain by his fleet greatly impressed contemporaries. Recalled c.84 by Emperor **Domitian**, probably out of jealousy, he lived quietly in retirement in Rome until his death.

Agricultural Revolution The name popularly given to a series of changes in farming practice occurring first in England and later throughout Western Europe. Some historians date these as far back as the end of the 16c, but the term usually covers the period 1700–1850. The main changes included: greater intensity of productive land use; the reduction of fallow land and waste lands; the introduction of crop rotation; the development of artificial grasses; and scientific animal breeding. Many such changes were facilitated by the replacement of open fields by enclosures. They also depended upon tenant farming and market production replacing subsistence and peasant agriculture. The widespread use of mechanized farming techniques, such as threshing machines and mechanical ploughs, mostly post-dated the changes of this agricultural revolution. ▷ **Industrial Revolution**

Agrippa, Marcus Vipsanius (c.63–12BC) Roman general. The administrator and right-hand man of Octavian (Emperor **Augustus**), he was the architect of the latter's victory at **Actium** (31BC). Agrippa subsequently used his great wealth to popularize the new regime by vastly improving the public amenities of Rome. Through his marriage to Augustus's daughter, Julia, he gave Rome the emperors **Caligula** and **Nero**.

Agrippina the Elder (c.14BC–AD33) The daughter of Agrippina, granddaughter of the Roman emperor Augustus and mother of the emperor Caligula. She became the focal point of opposition to the emperor Tiberius, and hence the chief target of his henchman, Sejanus, after the suspicious death of her husband, Germanicus, in 19. She was banished to the barren island of Pandeteria in 29, where she died of voluntary starvation.

Agrippina the Younger (AD15–59) The eldest daughter of Agrippina (the Elder) and **Germanicus**, and mother of Emperor **Nero** by her first husband Cnaeus Domitius Ahenobarbus. In AD54 she ruthlessly engineered Nero's succession to the throne by supplanting the true heir Britannicus, and poisoning the reigning Emperor **Claudius**, her husband at the time. Initially she ruled as virtual co-regent with Nero, but he tired of her influence and had her murdered.

Aguinaldo, Emilio (1870–1964) Filipino revolutionary. He was a central figure in the rising against Spain (1896–8), and against the USA (1899–1901). After capture by the Americans in 1901, he took the oath of allegiance to the USA, the new colonial power.

Aguirre, José Antonio (1904–60) Basque politician. Born into a middle-class, Carlist family, he became leader of the conservative Basque Nationalist Party (**PNV**), the main Basque party of the 1930s. He was elected as the first President (or *Lendakari*) of the Basque country (or *Euzkadi*) after the Republic passed the Autonomy Statute in Oct 1936. After the fall of Bilbao in June 1937, Aguirre took the government into exile in France. Following the outbreak of **World War II**, he was denied passage to England, and so undertook an extraordinary journey via Nazi Germany (complete with artificial moustache and glasses), Sweden, and Brazil to Uruguay. After the war, he headed the government in exile in France. ▷ **Basque Autonomy Statutes**

Aguiyi-Ironsi, Johnson (1925–66) Nigerian soldier and politician. He joined the colonial army in 1942 and was trained in the UK before commanding the Nigerian contingent in the **UN** involvement in the Congo (Zaire). Appointed Commander-in-Chief in 1965, he assumed power following the officers' coup of Jan 1966, but was killed in the counter-coup, led by **Gowon** (July 1966).

Ahidjo, Ahmadou (1924–89) Cameroonian politician. Educated at the Ecole Supérieure d'Administration, Yaounde, he was a radio operator in the post office before entering politics in 1947, being elected to the Territorial Assembly. He represented Cameroon in the Assembly of French Union 1953–7. From 1957 to 1960 he held senior positions in the Territorial Assembly of Cameroon. In 1960, when most of the British Cameroons was amalgamated with the French Cameroons, he became President and was re-elected to that post in 1972, 1975 and 1980. He resigned in 1982 and went into voluntary exile in France. His one-party state, although severe on the rival, but outlawed, *Union des Populations Camerounaises* (UPC), was relatively successful economically and less repressive than many West African states.

Ahmad al-Mansur (1549–1603) Sultan of Maghrib (Morocco) (1578/1603). He brought peace and prosperity to the country, instituting administrative reforms and developing trade, especially in sugar and saltpetre.

Ahmad Gran (c.1506–43) Sultan of Adal in Somalia. He declared a **jihad** or holy war against Christian Ethiopia in the 1530s and, with assistance from the Ottomans, he was able to maintain control of the empire until his defeat in battle by Emperor **Galawdewos** in 1543.

Ahmad Khan, Sir Sayyid (1817–98) Indian lawyer and educator. One of the most important and influential Indian Muslims of the 19c, he was an employee of the British **East India Company** and later a judge, who embraced European civilization and many aspects of British rule and worked to further the Muslim cause in India within the British system. An opponent of Muslim participation in the **Indian National Congress**, following the **Indian Uprising** of 1857–8, Khan wrote a widely read book and a pamphlet demonstrating that Muslims were neither primarily responsible nor generally involved in the rebellion. He held progressive views on the issue of the social position of women, which brought him into conflict with orthodox Islamic leaders, but his greatest legacy was his establishment of the Mohammedan Anglo-Oriental College (now Aligarh Muslim University) in 1875 and the development of the Muslim Educational Conference, which eventually spread across India.

Ahmad of Rai Bareilly, Sayyid (1786–1831) Muslim Indian leader hostile to British rule. Sayyid Ahmad of Rai Bareilly came from the circle of Islamic thinkers whose spiritual forebears had tried to convince the Afghan Shah Ahmad to wage a **jihad** against all non-Muslim powers in India. Sayyid Ahmad led an Islamic revival in the early 19c, seeking to rid Indian Islam of all Hindu practices, to end popular belief in the intercessionary power of Sufi saints, and to establish an exemplary Muslim society in India. In order to wage jihad upon the Sikhs, Sayyid Ahmad and his followers eventually moved into the North West Frontier, where he was killed in 1831.

Ahmad Shah Durrani (1722–73) Central Asian warlord. He was the founder of the short-lived Durrani empire in Afghanistan and northern India. A commander of the Afghan ruler Nadir Shah's bodyguard,

Ahmad Shah founded his own regime in Kandahar after Nadir's death in 1747. By 1761, through decisive victory at the Battle of **Panipat**, he had established supremacy over the Marathas and much of north-western India. After severely weakening the Mughal power base, however, Ahmad Shah and his successors were unable to exploit fully his opportunity and it was left to European powers, most notably Britain, to fill the vacuum.

Ahmadu ibn Hammadu (c.1775–1844) West African Islamic leader. Influenced by the example of **Usman dan Fodio** in northern Nigeria, he led a **jihad** or holy war in the western Sudan. It started about 1818 and made Ahmadu master of a state of some 50000 square miles, including within its borders the important centres of Jenne and Timbuktu. In 1862 it was conquered by another leader of a jihad, al-Hajj **Umar ibn Tal**.

Ahmad 'Urabi ▷ **'Urabi Pasha**

Ahmadzai Najibullah (1947–) Afghan communist leader. A Pusthtun (Pathan), he was educated at Kabul University and trained as a doctor. He joined the Communist People's Democratic Party of Afghanistan (PDPA) in 1965, allying with its gradualist Parcham (banner) faction, and was twice imprisoned for anti-government political activities during the 1960s and 1970s. After the Soviet invasion of Dec 1979 he was appointed head of KHAD, the State Information Service (secret police), and, inducted into the PDPA's Politburo (1981). In May 1986 he replaced Babrak Karmal as Party, and thus national, leader and was formally elected State President in Oct 1987. He sought to broaden support for the PDPA regime, encouraging non-communist politicians to join the government and promulgating a non-Marxist constitution which enshrined a multi-party system, mixed economy and dominant position for Islam. However, his hold over power became imperilled following the withdrawal of Soviet military forces in Feb 1989.

Ahmed I (1590–1617) Ottoman Sultan (1603/17). He was the son of **Mehmed III**, whom he succeeded. The was most notable feature of his reign was the losing war he waged against Persia (1602–12).

Ahmed II (1642–95) Ottoman Sultan (1691/5). He was the son of Ibrahim, whom he succeeded. The disastrous Ottoman defeat at **Slankamen** (1691) at the hands of the Habsburgs lost him Hungary. ▷ **Habsburg Dynasty**

Ahmed III (1673–1736) Ottoman Sultan (1703/30). He was the son of Mehmed IV, whom he succeeded. He sheltered **Charles XII** of Sweden after the Battle of **Poltava** (1709), thus falling foul of **Peter I, 'the Great'**, with whom he waged a successful war which was terminated by the Peace of the Pruth (1711). He successfully fought the Venetians (1715), but soon after was defeated by the Austrians, losing territories around the Danube. He was deposed by the **Janissaries** (1730) and died in prison.

Ahmose I (Nebpehtire) (c.1570/1546BC) King of Egypt. He was the dynast of Thebes, who drove the **Hyksos** from Egypt, became the first pharaoh of the 18th Dynasty and established the **New Kingdom**, the period of the Egyptian Empire.

Ahmose II (Khnumibre) (570/526BC) King of Egypt. He acceded to the throne following the defeat of his predecessor, Apries. Ahmose II relied on Greek support during his long, peaceful reign. It was during this time that a Greek trading emporium was founded at Naukratis, in the Nile Delta; by such a balancing of native Egyptian and Greek aspirations, the prosperity of Egypt was promoted. ▷ **Polycrates**

Ain Jalut, Battle of ▷ **Ayn Jalut, Battle of**

'Aisha (c.613–78) Third and favourite of the nine wives of the Prophet **Muhammad**. The daughter of **Abu Bakr**, the first caliph, she married at the age of nine, but had no children. When Muhammad died in 632 she resisted the claims to the caliphate of **'Ali**, Muhammad's son-in-law (who had accused her of infidelity), in favour of her father. When 'Ali became the fourth caliph in 656, she led a revolt against him, but was defeated and captured at the Battle of the **Camel** at Basra, and was exiled to Medina. She is known as 'the mother of believers'.

Aiskhines ▷ **Aeschines**

Akali Movement (and Akali Dal) Primary Sikh political organization in Punjab. The original Akalis were 17c Sikh zealots who became censors for the community. During the Independence movement, the Akalis cooperated with Congress but tended to promote Sikh communal concerns. They were especially concerned with the control of Sikh shrines. Following Muslim agitation for the creation of Pakistan, the Akalis agitated for an independent Sikh state within the Punjab, but settled for a greater language-based autonomy in 1966. In recent years the Akali Dal has once again become active in the Sikh independence cause.

Akbar the Great (Jalal ud-Din Muhammad Akbar) (1542–1605) Mughal Emperor of India (1556/1605). He succeeded his father, **Humayun**, in 1556, and took over the administration from his regent in 1560. Within a few years, he had gained control of the whole of India north of the Vindhya Mountains. He constructed roads, established a uniform system of weights and measures, and adjusted taxation. He was unusually tolerant towards non-Muslims, and greatly encouraged literature and the arts. ▷ **Mughal Empire**

Akhenaten ▷ **Amenhotpe IV**

Akhromeyev, Sergei Fedorovich (1923–91) Soviet commander in **World War II**. He joined the **Red Army** in 1940 and was in command of a tank battalion by 1945. He then rose steadily to be first Deputy-Chief of the General Staff by 1979 and Marshal by 1981. Opposed to escalating military expenditure, he was called in to replace **Ogarkov** as Chief of the General Staff in 1984 and aided Mikhail **Gorbachev** in his post-1985 arms control talks. He tried, but failed, to accommodate fully to the Gorbachev era, and resigned in 1988 in disgust at Gorbachev's unilateral troop cuts. He committed suicide in the aftermath of the attempted coup in 1991, in apparent dismay at **perestroika**'s results. ▷ **August Coup**

Akihito (1933–) Emperor of Japan (1989/). The eldest son of Emperor **Hirohito**, he was born and educated in Tokyo, where he studied politics and economics. Invested as Crown Prince in 1952, he became the first Crown Prince to marry a commoner, Michiko Shoda, in 1959.

Akkerman, Convention of (1826) The Russians imposed terms upon the Ottoman Sultan **Mahmud II** whereby Russia was acknowledged as the protector of **Serbia** and the **Danubian Principalities**. The internal organization of the Principalities was also to be modified: new statutes were to be drawn up for the administration of each province

and the **hospodars** (governors) were to be elected by the boyar divans for seven years subject to Russian and Ottoman approval. The terms of the Convention, which met in the course of the **Greek War of Independence**, built upon the Treaty of **Bucharest** (1813) and confirmed Russian influence over the emergent Balkan nations. ▷ **Organic Statutes**

Akritas, Digenis ▷ **Grivas, Georgeios**

Aksakov, Ivan Sergeievich (1823–86) Russian lyric poet and publicist. Born in Nadeshdino, he was the son of Sergei Aksakov. He was the founder and editor of various Slavophil and Panslavic periodicals, and a supporter of the liberation of Slavs in the Balkans.

Akwamu A state founded about 1600 by the Abrade people, an Akan group in the Gold Coast in the immediate hinterland of Accra. It commanded trade routes and eventually built up its power along almost the entire length of the Gold Coast to Dahomey. It collapsed in 1730 when conquered by Akim, its neighbour to the West.

Ala al-Din Khalji (Ala-ud-Din Khilji) (1296/1316) Second ruler of the Khalji Dynasty in Delhi. After murdering his uncle and seizing power in 1296, Ala al-Din embarked on a programme of Southern expansion made possible by the recession of the Mongol threat to the north. In a series of brutal military expeditions he subdued the Gujarat and the Rajput princes, spreading his rule and Islam deep into south India. During his reign, Delhi enjoyed a prosperity sustained by the spoils of war, and was transformed by the Sultan's grandiose building campaign.

Alabama Claims (1869–72) A diplomatic dispute in which the USA held Britain accountable for damage inflicted to the Union during the **American Civil War** by Confederate naval vessels (the *Alabama*, *Florida* and *Shenandoah*) built in Britain. The dispute was resolved in 1872 when an international tribunal (Italy, Switzerland and Brazil), ruled that Britain should pay an indemnity to the USA of US$15 500 000. ▷ **Washington, Treaty of**

Alamán, Lucas (1792–1853) Mexican politician and historian. The intellectual father of Mexican conservatism, his views were shaped by the wrecking of Guanajuato (his birthplace) in **Hidalgo (y Costilla)**'s revolt in 1810, and his training as a mining engineer. Repelled by the aftermath of the Riego Revolt in Spain (1820), he argued that monarchical rule would provide stability for an independent Mexico. After independence (1821), he negotiated with the Vatican and France to set up a Mexican royal house. Minister of State under **Iturbide**, and Foreign Minister and Minister of State for Anastasio Bustamante and **Santa Anna**, he was a friend of the Church and writer of the monumental, and still readable, *Historia de México*.

Alamo, The A fortified mission in San Antonio, Texas, held in 1836 during the Texas War of independence against Mexico. In a heroic act of resistance, some 180 Texans defended the Alamo for 12 days against several thousand Mexicans, until the last survivors were overwhelmed. ▷ **Mexican War**

Alanbrooke (of Brookeborough), Alan Francis Brooke, 1st Viscount (1883–1963) British field marshal and leading strategist of **World War II**. He joined the Royal Field Artillery in 1902, and fought in **World War I**. He commanded the 2nd Corps of the **British Expeditionary Force** in France (1940), and later was Commander-in-Chief Home Forces. Chief of the Imperial General Staff 1941–6, he was Winston **Churchill**'s principal strategic adviser at the conferences with **Roosevelt** and **Stalin**. He was created baron (1945) and viscount (1946).

Alaric I (c.370–410) Chief of the **Visigoths** (395/410) and the first Germanic conqueror of Rome. The sack of Rome by his troops in 410, the first capture of the city by foreigners in 800 years, marks the beginning of the end of the western Roman Empire.

Alaska, Sale of (1867) Tsarist Russian interests in Alaska were sold to the USA for $7 million, a price which seemed so high at the time that the Tsarist government had to spend a large sum of money influencing both members of Congress and influential newspapers. Russian efforts to establish a position on both sides of the North Pacific had begun more than a century before. However, defeat in the **Crimean War** and the acquisition of the Amur Basin from China by the Treaty of **Beijing** (1860) made **Alexander II** decide to concentrate on the north-west Pacific. Once the **American Civil War** was over, Secretary of State William Seward was quick to realize the long-term strategic and economic value of Alaska both for the continental USA and for its expansion into the Pacific.

Alaunghpaya (1714–60) Founder of the Konbaung Dynasty in Burma (the country's last royal line). He came to prominence during the final collapse of the restored Toungoo Dynasty at the beginning of the 1750s. A local official, he rapidly brought under his authority, by skilful organization, the great force of his personality and also by military might, the many competing elements jostling for power in the vacuum left by the disintegration of the old state. With the fall of Pegu to Alaunghpaya's forces in May 1757, internal consolidation was complete. He then turned his attention to the Tai states to the east, but in an unsuccessful attack on the Thai capital of Ayudhya (May 1760), he was fatally wounded, dying on the retreat.

Alava, Don Miguel Ricardo de (1771–1843) Spanish soldier and politician. He served under **Wellington** in the **Peninsular War** (from 1811) and was Ambassador to the Netherlands for King **Ferdinand VII**. However, as President of the **Cortes** in 1822, he aided in the deposition of the monarch. He fled when the French reinstated Ferdinand in 1823, but later served Queen **María Cristina** as Ambassador to London and Paris. Having refused to take the oath to the Constitution of 1837, he went into exile in France, where he died.

Alawi An alternative name for Nusayri Shiites, who currently hold power in Syria. The Syrian leader Hafez al-**Asad** is an Alawi (Alawite). ▷ **Shiites**

Alba, Fernando Álvarez de Toledo, 3rd Duke of (1507–82) Spanish general and political figure. He served with distinction in Germany under Emperor **Charles V** against the Protestant princes, notably at the siege of Metz (1552). Under **Philip II** of Spain his three most important commands were in the **Italian Wars** against the forces of Pope **Paul IV**, in the army of Flanders, and in the conquest of Portugal (1580). He also served in several diplomatic roles. He is most associated with the Flanders campaigns, when he was sent (1567) to deal with the **Dutch Revolt** and, as Regent, adopted a hardline policy through the Council of **Blood**, the body he set up to try rebels and heretics. His harsh policies, including his prosecution of ferocious military campaigns against the rebels and the introduction of new centralized taxes, aggravated rather than calmed the revolt, which he was unable to subdue militarily; his actions signalled the start of the **Eighty Years War** in 1568. Recalled in 1573, he was pulled out of retirement to lead the successful occupation of Portugal in 1580.

Albanian League ▷ **Prizren, League of**

Albanians Their name first appears in 2c AD, Ptolemy referring to a tribe, the Albanoi, in the region of modern Albania. The Albanian Ghegs and Tosks speak two forms of an Indo-European language now considered a dialect of Illyrian, the Albanians being recognized as descendants of the ancient Illyrians but with Slav, Greek, Vlah and Turkish blood. In the Middle Ages they were included within the empires of Byzantium, **Samuel** (of Macedonia) and **Stephen Nemanja** of **Serbia**, but from the 12c an independent Albanian enclave developed around Krujë. Their decentralized tribal way of life was little changed under Ottoman rule (1503–1913) and was only destroyed with the establishment of the communist regime (1945). After local uprisings against Ottoman officials, the Albanian national movement formerly began with the League of **Prizren** (1878–81). The first general uprising was in 1912 and in 1913 the first independent Albanian state was established with boundaries which excluded many Albanians; in 1989 c.3.2 million lived in Albania and at least 1.7 million in Yugoslavia with many million more immigrants in the USA, Canada, Greece and Australia. ▷ **Balli Kombëtar; London, Treaties of; LNC**

Albany Congress (1754) A meeting in Albany, New York, of representatives from seven British colonies in North America at which Benjamin Franklin proposed his 'plan of union' to unite the separate American British colonies. The Albany Plan of Union was rejected by the Colonial governments and the Crown. However, the plan served as a model for the joint action of the mainland colonies in the **American Revolution**.

Albany Regency A group of Democrats organized (c.1817) by Martin **Van Buren** to run New York while he served in the US Senate in Washington. Situated in Albany, New York, which he had established as his power base, the Regency was one of the first effective political machines using the '**spoils system**' to fill public office, and influenced the future development of US political parties.

Alberdi, Juan Bautista (1810–84) Argentine political thinker. A creole of Basque inheritance, he studied law in Buenos Aires.

Persecuted by Juan Manuel de **Rosas**, he was exiled to Montevideo in 1839, travelled in Europe and returned to Valparaíso in Chile for 10 years. Author of a treatise which profoundly influenced the Constituent Congress of Santa Fé, which drew up the constitution of 1853, he is regarded as its intellectual godfather. He argued that a democratic future for Argentina could only be guaranteed by the attainment of economic and educational equality: to achieve this, European immigration should be encouraged and the economy opened up to foreign investment by a strong federal government. He coined the phrase 'To govern is to populate' which had an enduring, if equivocal, impact on modern Argentina. Appointed Minister to France and England in 1854 by General Justo José de Urquiza, Alberdi spent most of the remainder of his life in Europe.

Albero (c.1080–1152) Archbishop of Trier. The son of a noble family, he held many high offices in the Church, culminating in his election as Archbishop of Trier in 1131. A supporter of the papacy against Emperor **Henry V**, he was made papal legate in Germany in 1137. The following year he was instrumental in having the papal candidate, **Conrad III**, elected to the German throne, bypassing **Lothair III**'s designated successor, Henry the Proud, and strengthening his own political and territorial position. As a church reformer he had close links with Pope **Eugenius III** and **Bernard of Clairvaux**.

Alberoni, Giulio (1664–1752) Spanish-Italian cardinal and statesman. After a diplomatic career in France and Spain, he gained the favour of **Philip V** of Spain, and arranged his marriage to Elizabeth Farnese (1714), daughter of the Duke of Parma. He used his influence to develop the resources of Spain, remodel the army and fleet, increase foreign trade, and extend Spanish power in Italy. His aggressive European foreign policy finally lost him Philip's support. He was banished, fled to Rome (1721), and through papal influence resumed his career in the Church. ▷ **Farnese Family**

Albert (1819–61) Prince Consort of Queen **Victoria** of Great Britain. The youngest son of the Duke of **Saxe-Coburg-Gotha**, he married his cousin, an infatuated Queen Victoria, in 1840. He became her chief adviser, first as Consort (1842), then as Prince Consort (1857). Ministerial distrust and public misgivings combined to obstruct his interference in politics, but he developed a congenial sphere of self-expression by encouraging the arts and social and industrial reforms. It was largely on his initiative that the Great Exhibition of 1851 took place.

Albert I (c.1255–1308) King of Germany (1298/1308). The son of **Rudolf I** of Habsburg, he was elected King of Germany in opposition to the deposed **Adolf of Nassau**, whom he then defeated and killed in battle at **Göllheim** (1298). He proceeded energetically to restore the power of the monarchy and reduce that of the electoral princes, but was murdered while crossing the River Reuss by his disaffected nephew, John. ▷ **Habsburg Dynasty**

Albert I (1875–1934) King of the Belgians (1909/34). The younger son of Philip, Count of Flanders, he succeeded his uncle, **Leopold II**. At the outbreak of **World War I** he refused a German demand for the free passage of their troops, and after a heroic resistance led the Belgian Army in retreat to Flanders. He commanded the Belgian and French Army in the final offensive on the Belgian coast in 1918, and re-entered Brussels in triumph on 22 Nov. After the war he took an active part in the industrial reconstruction of the country; the Albert Canal, linking Liège with Antwerp, is named after him. He was killed in a climbing accident in the Ardennes, and was succeeded by his son, **Leopold III**.

Albert V (1528–79) Duke of Bavaria. Educated at the Jesuit College at Ingolstadt, he was a strong Catholic, and established the pattern of Wittelsbach absolutism in Bavaria based upon the suppression of Protestantism and the centralization of ducal authority.

Albert of Hohenzollern (1490–1568) Last Grand Master of the **Teutonic Knights** (1510/23). The younger son of the Margrave of Ansbach, he failed to shake off Polish overlordship but, embracing the Reformation, was able to convert the Order's lands into a hereditary duchy. In 1525, he became the first secular Duke of Prussia, a title which subsequently passed to the Brandenburg line of the House of Hohenzollern. ▷ **Holhenzollern Dynasty**

Albert the Bear (1100–70) First Count of Brandenburg. The only son of Otto of Ballenstädt, he succeeded his father in 1123. Thwarted in his ambitions to become Duke of Saxony, by King **Lothair III** in 1127 and then,

after becoming Duke in 1138, by the **Welfs**, to whom he lost the title irrevocably in 1142, he expanded his territory instead to the east. He gained control of the North Mark, Pomerania and Brandenburg, and settled and christianized the area with the help of settlers from the Rhineland and Saxony. He is regarded as the founder of the state of Brandenburg and the first to begin German colonization east of the River Elbe.

Albigenses (Albigensians) Followers of a form of Christianity which in the 11c and 12c especially had its main strength in the town of Albi, south-western France. It was derived from 3c followers of the Persian religious teacher, Mani, whose ideas gradually spread along trade routes to Europe, especially Italy and France. Also known as Cathars or Bogomils, they believed life on Earth to be a struggle between good (spirit) and evil (matter). In extreme cases, they were rigidly ascetic, with marriage, food, and procreation all condemned. They believed in the transmigration of souls. Condemned by Rome and the **Inquisition**, they were devastated in the early 13c crusade against them, which also broke down the distinctive civilization of Provence, France.

Alboin (d.574) King of the **Lombards** in Pannonia (561/74). He fought against the Ostrogoths, and slew Kunimond, King of the Gepids (566), marrying his daughter, Rosamond. In 568 he invaded Italy, subdued the north, and made his capital at Pavia before he was murdered by his wife's lover.

Albuquerque, Affonso d', 'the Great' (1453–1515) Portuguese Viceroy of the Indies. He landed on the Malabar coast of India in 1502, and conquered Goa, Ceylon, the Sundra Islands, Malacca, and (in 1515) the island of Hormuz in the Persian Gulf. He gained a reputation for wisdom and justice, but through his enemies at court he was replaced in office, and died soon afterwards at sea near Goa.

alcabala A traditional Spanish sales tax, also imposed in Spanish America (in Mexico from 1575 and in Peru from 1591). Generally 10 per cent in Castile and six per cent in Spanish America, its collection was often farmed out to local traders and continued to be the major source of revenue for local governments in the first decades after independence. Its abolition, in the late 19c, marked the emergence of effective national governments under rulers such as Mexico's Porfirio **Díaz** and the development of the railroads. Equivalent taxes (*registros*) continued to be levied in Brazil until the **Vargas** governments of the 1930s.

Alcalá Zamora, Niceto (1877–1949) Spanish politician. A lawyer and landowner from Andalucia, he was Liberal Minister of Development in 1917 and Minister of War in 1922. In opposing the dictatorship of **Primo de Rivera**, he joined the Republican cause and, with the establishment of the Republic, headed both the provisional government and the Constituent Cortes's first administration. He resigned in Oct 1931 over the new constitution's anticlerical clauses, but accepted the presidency in Dec of the same year. A florid orator, he proved a highly conscientious if conservative and interventionist president, finally being removed in Apr 1936 after a decisive vote of the Cortes (238–5) against him. He died in exile in Buenos Aires.

Alcantara, Order of One of the military orders founded in **Castile** during the **Reconquest** of Spain. It was founded in 1156, with a green cross as its symbol, and came to possess extensive estates (*encomiendas*), numbering 38 in 1616. Members were in theory subject to semi-monastic discipline. From 1523, the crown of Spain became, with papal permission, head of the orders. ▷ **encomienda**

Alcazarquivir, Battle of (4 Aug 1578) The battle fought by the young King **Sebastian** of Portugal at the head of the flower of Portuguese nobility and troops, whom he led out into a disastrous adventure in Morocco, where they were annihilated by superior Muslim forces. Some 7000 of the Portuguese troops were killed, and 8000 were taken prisoner. King Sebastian's body was never clearly identified, leading to later claims by impostors; the throne was left without an heir, as a consequence of which **Philip II** of Spain was able to claim the succession in 1580.

Alcibiades (c.450–404BC) Athenian politician and general. A member of the aristocratic Alcmaeonid family, he was a ward of **Pericles** and a pupil of Socrates. He was a leader against **Sparta** in the **Peloponnesian War**, and a commander of the Sicilian expedition (415BC). Recalled from there to stand trial for sacrilege, he fled to Sparta and gave advice which contributed substantially to Athens's defeat in Sicily (413BC) and her economic discomfiture at home. Having

fallen out with the Spartans in 412BC, he began to direct Athenian operations in the eastern Aegean, and won several notable victories. Unjustly blamed for the Athenian defeat off Notium (406BC), he went into voluntary exile, where he actively intrigued with the Persians until his assassination in 404BC. ▷ **Alcmaeonids**

Alcmaeonids An aristocratic Athenian family to which many prominent Athenian politicians belonged. It was particularly influential in the period 632–415BC. The actions of the Alcmaeonid Megacles in putting down the attempted tyranny of Cylon in 632BC placed the family under a curse for sacrilege, a charge used to good effect by later political opponents of the family. ▷ **Alcibiades; Cleisthenes; Pericles**

Alcock Convention (1869) A proposed treaty agreed upon by the British ambassador to China, Sir Rutherford Alcock, and Chinese officials in Beijing. Reflecting the British government's view that undue pressure to extract greater trade concessions should not be exerted on the Chinese government, the proposed treaty allowed the Chinese government to increase import duties on opium and export duties on silk, as well as to open a consulate in the British colony of Hong Kong. However, due to protests from British merchant interests eager for a considerable expansion of commercial opportunities in China, the treaty was not ratified by the British government.

Alesia, Siege of (52BC) Julius **Caesar**'s military operation at the hill-fort of that name in central France, which brought the revolt of **Vercingetorix** to an end and, with it, all serious resistance to the Roman conquest of Gaul. By penning the Gallic leader and his army inside the hill-fort by means of a double ring of earthworks, Caesar forced his surrender since he could neither break out nor be relieved. ▷ **Gallic Wars**

Alessandri (Palma), Arturo (1868–1950) Chilean politician. He became a member of the Chamber of Deputies (1897–1915), Senator (1915–18 and 1944–50) and Minister of the Interior (1918–20). Elected President on a reform platform in 1920, he was ousted, but was soon recalled by the armed forces (1924–5). In 1932–8 he served a second, more conservative, term.

Alexander (1893–1920) King of Greece (1917/20). The second son of **Constantine I**

and Queen Sophia, he became King in June 1917 after his father, under pressure from Eleuthérios **Venizélos** and the Allies to enter **World War I**, was obliged to abdicate. Greece then entered the war on the side of the Allies and Venizélos returned as Prime Minister. Alexander's death in Oct 1920, after being bitten by a pet monkey, precipitated a constitutional crisis which led to the election defeat of Venizélos and the triumphant return of his father as king.

Alexander I (c.1077–1124) King of Scots (1107/24). He ruled north of the Forth–Clyde line while his younger brother David (later **David I**) controlled southern Scotland in his name. The second of the three sons of **Malcolm III, 'Canmore'** and Queen (later St) Margaret to become king, he succeeded his brother, Edgar. He founded an Augustinian monastery at Scone, and maintained friendly relations with England by marrying Sybilla, an illegitimate daughter of **Henry I**, and fighting alongside Henry in Wales (1114). ▷ **Margaret, St**

Alexander I (1777–1825) Emperor of Russia (1801/25). The grandson of **Catherine II, 'the Great'**, the early years of his reign were marked by the promise of liberal constitutional reforms and the pursuit of a vigorous foreign policy. In 1805 Russia joined the coalition against Napoleon, but after a series of military defeats was forced to conclude the Treaty of **Tilsit** (1807) with France. When Napoleon broke the Treaty by invading Russia in 1812, Alexander pursued the French back to Paris. At the Congress of **Vienna** (1814–15) he laid claim to Poland. During the last years of his reign his increased political reactionism and religious mysticism resulted in the founding of the Holy Alliance. His mysterious death at Taganrog caused a succession crisis which led to the attempted revolutionary coup of the **Decembrists**. ▷ **Congress Kingdom of Poland; Napoleon I; Romanov Dynasty**

Alexander II (Anselm of Lucca) Italian Pope (1061/73). Bishop of Lucca from 1057, he undertook reforms and campaigned against immorality and corruption in the Church. He was a founder of the Patarine Party, which opposed the marriage of priests. On his election in 1061 as the choice of Hildebrand (the future Pope **Gregory VII**), the German court elected Honorius (II) as anti-pope (1061/72).

Alexander II (1198–1249) King of Scots (1214/49). The son and successor of

William I, 'the Lion', he supported the English barons against King **John**, later concluding a peace treaty with **Henry III** (1217), and marrying Henry's eldest sister, Joan (1221). In 1239 he married Marie, the daughter of Enguerrand de Coucy. His reign represents an important landmark in the making of the Scottish kingdom. He renounced his hereditary claims to Northumberland, Cumberland, and Westmorland by the Treaty of York (1237), and concentrated on the vigorous assertion of royal authority in the north and west. He died of a fever on Kerrera, near Oban, while leading an expedition to wrest the Western Isles from Norwegian control. ▷ **Barons Wars**

Alexander II (1818–81) Emperor of Russia (1855/81). The son of **Nicholas I**, the main achievement of his reign was the emancipation of the serfs (1861), followed by local government judicial and military reforms. During his reign, the Russian Empire was widely extended in central Asia and the Far East. He defeated Turkey in the war of 1877–8. The latter part of his reign was marked by the struggle with populist terrorists. One of their organizations, the People's Will, finally succeeded in assassinating him by bombing his coach in St Petersburg. ▷ **Romanov Dynasty; Russian Serfs, Emancipation of the;**

Alexander III (Rolando Bandinelli) (c.1105–81) Italian Pope (1159–81). He taught law at Bologna, and became adviser to Pope **Adrian IV**. As pope, he was engaged in a struggle with the Emperor **Frederick I, 'Barbarossa'** who supported anti-popes against him. The Emperor was finally defeated at the Battle of **Legnano** (1176) and peace was concluded by the Treaty of Venice (1177). The other notable conflict of church and state in which he was involved was that between **Henry II** of England and Thomas à **Becket**. He also called the third Lateran Council (1179). ▷ **Lateran Councils**

Alexander III (1241–86) King of Scots (1249/86). The son of **Alexander II** of Scotland, in 1251 he married Princess Margaret, eldest daughter of Henry III of England. Soon after he had come of age, he defended the kingdom against the Norwegians, who were routed at Largs (1263). By the Treaty of Perth (1266), Scotland gained the Hebrides and the Isle of Man. In the later part of his reign, the kingdom enjoyed a period of peace and prosperity. He was killed in a riding accident.

Alexander III (1845–94) Emperor of Russia (1881/94). The son of **Alexander II**, his reign was marked by policies of extreme political reactionism, Great Russian chauvinism, religious bigotry, and attempts to reverse some of his father's liberal reforms. On the other hand, the Russian economy made some progress and the foundations were laid for the industrial boom of the late 1890s. ▷ **Romanov Dynasty**

Alexander III, 'the Great' (356–323BC) King of **Macedonia** (336/323BC). The son of **Philip II** of Macedon and Olympias, he was tutored by Aristotle, and ascended the throne when less than 20 years old. After crushing all opposition at home, he set out to conquer Greece's hereditary enemy, Achaemenid Persia. This he achieved with great rapidity in a series of famous battles: Granicus (334BC), Issus (333BC), and Gaugamela (331BC). He had taken over Egypt from the **Achaemenids** in winter 332–331BC, founding the city of Alexandria and consulting the oracle of Ammon at Siwah Oasis (which apparently fostered his belief in his divine descent). By 330BC, **Darius III, 'Codommanus'** had fled, and the capitals of Babylon, Susa, Persepolis, and Ecbatana had been taken. In the next three years, the eastern half of the empire followed, and Alexander set out for India. He reached the Punjab, and had set his sights on the Ganges, when his troops mutinied and forced his return. He died shortly after at Babylon. Attempts to introduce Persian customs at court had provoked dissent among his Macedonian entourage; his desire for divine honours also met with a mixed response in the Greek cities. ▷ **Hellenistic Age; Hellenization**

Alexander VI (Rodrigo Borgia) (1431–1503) Spanish Pope (1492/1503). He was made a cardinal (1455) by his uncle, Calixtus III, and became Pope on the death of Innocent VIII as a result of flagrant bribery. Father to Cesare and Lucrezia **Borgia**, and two other illegitimate children, he endeavoured to break the power of the Italian princes, and to gain their possessions for his own family. Under his pontificate, he apportioned the New World between Spain and Portugal, and despite introducing the censorship of books, he was a generous patron of the arts. ▷ **Borgia**

Alexander VII (Fabio Chigi) (1599–1667) Italian Pope (1655/67). As nuncio, he had protested against the Treaty of **Westphalia**

(1648), which ended the **Thirty Years War**. His election was said to have been clinched by belief in his opposition to nepotism, to which he later succumbed. He supported the Jesuits against the Jansenists and forbade the translation of the Roman Missal into French. He was also responsible for the construction of the colonnade in the piazza at St Peter's.

Alexander VIII (Pietro Vito Ottoboni) (1610–91) Italian Pope (1689/91). On his deathbed he issued the Bull *Inter multiplices*, based on ideas already developed by **Innocent XI**, which reaffirmed the Papal condemnation of the Gallican Articles published by the French Synod summoned by **Louis XIV** in 1682. Despite this, it was during Alexander's pontificate that the bases were established for the reconciliation which took place between France and the papacy under **Innocent XII**.

Alexander I Karageorgević (1888–1934) King of the Kingdom of Serbs, Croats and Slovenes (1921/9) and King of Yugoslavia (1929/34). The second son of **Peter I Karageorgević** of **Serbia**), he was Commander-in-Chief of the Serbian Army during **World War I** while acting as Prince-Regent of Serbia (1914/21). A Serbian nationalist, he aimed to create a centralized state governed from Belgrade and roused the resistance of other non-Serb national groups in the kingdom. In 1929, after the collapse of the constitutional system hastened by the murder of the Croatian leader Stjepan **Radić**, he imposed a royal dictatorship, dissolving the assembly, abolishing the political parties and imprisoning many of their leaders. Supported by the **Little Entente** and France, in 1934 he was assassinated while on a state visit to Marseilles by a Macedonian terrorist linked to the Italian-backed Croatian **Ustaša**. ▷ **Korošec, Anton; Maček, Vladko; Pavelić, Ante; Pribićević, Svetozar; Trumbić, Ante; VMRO**

Alexander Karageorgević (1806–85) Prince of Serbia (1842/58). The son of George **Karageorge**, he lived in exile until he was chosen as the new Prince of Serbia after the regency of Michael **Obrenović** collapsed (1842). The Constitutionalist Party hoped to control the new prince through a constitution and to establish a civil code and a centralized, bureaucratic state system. In 1844 Ilija **Garašanin** presented the weak and inexperienced Alexander with a programme for government, the **Nacertanije**, but relations between the prince and the Constitutionalists swiftly deteriorated. He further lost support through his conciliatory policy towards Austria which led him to remain neutral during the Serbian revolt in Hungary (1848) and during the **Crimean War** (1854–6). On St Andrew's Day 1858, the assembly deposed Alexander and called for the return of the old absolutist prince, Miloš **Obrenović**.

Alexander Nevsky (c.1220–63) Russian Grand Prince, hero and saint. He received his surname from his victory over the Swedes on the River **Neva** (1240). He later defeated the **Teutonic Knights** (1242) and the Lithuanians (1245), and also helped maintain Novgorod's de facto independence from the Mongol Empire. He died at Gorodets, and was canonized by the Russian Church in 1547. ▷ **Golden Horde**

Alexander Severus (c.208–235) Roman Emperor (222/35). Last ruler of the **Severan Dynasty**, Alexander Severus came to power after the murder of his eccentric cousin, Emperor **Elagabalus**. Only fourteen on accession to the throne, he left the running of affairs in the capable hands of his grandmother, Julia Maesa (d.226) and his formidable mother, Julia Mamaea. Lack of success in foreign affairs proved their undoing. A lacklustre campaign against the Sassanids in the East, followed by fumbled dealings with the German tribes in the West, cost Severus the support of the troops and both he and his mother were butchered in an army mutiny at Mainz.

Alexander (of Tunis), Harold Rupert Leofric George, 1st Earl (1891–1969) British field marshal. In **World War I** he commanded a brigade on the Western Front, and in 1940 was the last officer out of Dunkirk. He served in Burma, and in 1942–3 was Commander-in-Chief, Middle East, his **North African Campaign** being one of the most complete victories in military history. Appointed field marshal on the capture of Rome in June 1944, he became Supreme Allied Commander, Mediterranean Theatre, for the rest of the war. He later became Governor-General of Canada (1946–52) and Minister of Defence (1952–4), and was created Viscount (1946) and Earl (1952). ▷ **World War II**

Alexander, Sir William ▷ **Stirling, William Alexander, 1st Earl of**

Alexandra Feodorovna (1872–1918) Empress of Russia. A princess of Hesse-Darmstadt, and granddaughter of Queen **Victoria**, she became Empress upon her marriage to **Nicholas II** in 1894. Alexandra came under the influence of **Rasputin**, and meddled disastrously in politics, eventually being imprisoned and shot by Bolshevik revolutionaries, along with her husband and children, at Ekaterinburg. ▷ **Bolsheviks; February Revolution** (Russia)

Alexandria Protocol (1944) This agreement was the outcome of a conference of Arab states convened in Alexandria by the Egyptian Prime Minister Mustafa al-**Nahhas**. His aim was to determine the form that future Arab unity should take. Al-Nahhas, backed on this issue by King Farouk, wished to obtain agreement to the formation of a 'League of Arab States' consisting of the sovereign states in the Arab world, and this was embodied in the Alexandria Protocol.

Alexei (Sergei Vladimirovich Simansky) (1877–1970) Russian Orthodox ecclesiastic. He accommodated to the Soviet regime to save Orthodoxy. First elected to a bishopric in 1913, he was made Metropolitan of Leningrad in 1933 and, despite one spell of exile, he was able to survive to earn a reputation for his courage during the Siege of **Leningrad**. He was then elected Patriarch of Moscow and All Russia in 1944, in succession to Patriarch **Sergei**, and generally supported Soviet attitudes to the world at large in order to protect his Christian flock at home, in which he was certainly not unsuccessful.

Alexeiev, Mikhail Vasilevich (1857–1918) Russian soldier. He fought in the **Russo-Japanese War** (1904–5) and was promoted general. In **World War I** he was appointed Chief of the Imperial General Staff in 1915, and directed the retreat from Warsaw after the crushing German victory. After the **Russian Revolution** in 1917 he organized the volunteer army against the **Bolsheviks**.

Alexei Mikhailovich (1629–76) Romanov Tsar of Russia (1645/76). He succeeded his father, **Michael Romanov** and, although personally pious and abstemious, presided over a court notorious for its splendour and excess. Abroad, he waged war against Poland (1654–67), regaining Smolensk and Kiev, while at home his attempts to place the Orthodox Church under secular authority brought him into conflict with Patriarch **Nikon**. In 1670–1 he suppressed a great peasant revolt; and his new code of laws (1649) legitimized peasant serfdom in Russia.

By his second wife he was the father of **Peter I, 'the Great'**. ▷ **Romanov Dynasty**

Alexei Petrovich (1690–1718) Heir to the Russian throne. Having opposed the reforms and wars of his father, **Peter I, 'the Great'**, he was excluded from the succession when Peter's second wife, Catherine, provided him with another male heir. Alexei fled to Vienna, where he was sheltered by the Holy Roman Emperor, **Charles VI**, and Naples. Having been induced to return to Russia by Peter, who was fearful of the possibility of foreign support for his son, Alexei found himself condemned to death on a charge of treason. He was later pardoned, only to die in prison under torture a few days later. Alexei's son subsequently became Tsar as **Peter II**. ▷ **Catherine I**

Alexius I Comnenus (1048–1118) Byzantine Emperor (1081/1118). The founder of the Comnenian Dynasty, he strengthened the weakened Byzantine state, and defeated the attacking Turks and Normans. He was able to use the warriors of the First Crusade to Palestine (1096) to recover lands in Asia Minor, but relations with them were complicated by the setting up of the Latin States in Antioch, Edessa, Jerusalem and Tripoli. ▷ **Crusade, First**

Alfonsín (Foulkes), Raúl (1927–) Argentine politician. Educated at military and law schools, he joined the Radical Union Party (UCR) in 1945. He later served in local government (1951–62), but was imprisoned by the **Perón** government for his political activities in 1953. During two brief periods of civilian rule, between 1963 and 1976, he was a member of the Chamber of Deputies, at other times practising as a lawyer. When constitutional government returned in 1983, he was elected President. He ensured that several leading military figures were brought to trial for human rights abuses and in 1986 was joint winner of the Council of Europe's human rights prize. His conduct of economic policy remained equivocal: an initial success, the *Plao Austral*, failed to dampen inflation, and he proved unable to open up the economy to international investment. The failure of economic policy under the UCR resulted in the election in 1989 of Carlos **Menem**, of the Peronist Party, as President.

Alfonso I, 'Henriques' (c.1110–85) King of Portugal (1139/85). He was only two years old at the death of his father, Henry of Burgundy, first Count of Portugal. Wresting

power from his mother in 1128, he fought the **Moors**, defeating them at Ourique (1139), and proclaimed himself King. He took Lisbon (1147), and later all Galicia, Estremadura, and Elvas.

Alfonso III, 'the Great' (d.910) King of Leon, Asturias and Galicia (866/910). He fought over 30 campaigns and gained numerous victories over the **Moors**, occupied Coimbra, and extended his territory as far as Portugal and Old Castile. His three sons conspired against him and eventually dethroned him.

Alfonso V, 'the Magnanimous' (1394–1458) King of **Aragon** (1416/58). He took the Catalan–Aragonese empire to its peak of expansion. After his succession, Alfonso largely neglected his peninsular dominions and devoted himself to campaigns against the Mediterranean islands of Corsica and Sardinia. He was concerned, above all, with the capture of the Kingdom of Naples, which he secured in 1442.

Alfonso X, 'the Astronomer' or **'the Wise'** (1221–84) King of Leon and Castile (1252/84). He succeeded his father, **Ferdinand III**, in 1252. His victories over the **Moors** enabled him to unite Murcia with Castile, but an insurrection headed by one of his sons in 1282 seriously undermined his power. He was the founder of a Castilian national literature, and fostered work on Spanish history and the Bible, as well as compiling a code of laws and a planetary table.

Alfonso XII (1857–85) King of Spain (1874/85). After a period of Republican rule following the overthrow of his mother, **Isabella II**, by the army in 1868, he was formally proclaimed King in 1874. In 1876 he suppressed the last opposition of the Carlists (supporters of the Spanish pretender, Don Carlos (1788–1855), and his successors). Alfonso summoned the **Cortes** to provide a new constitution and, under the influence of his Prime Minister, **Cánovas del Castillo**, a parliamentary system based on rigged elections was introduced to protect the interests of the predominantly landed oligarchy. The last years of his reign were beset by difficulties, including several military revolts, a devastating cholera epidemic, and continuing unrest in Cuba. In 1879 he married **María Cristina**, daughter of Archduke Charles Ferdinand of Austria, and was succeeded by his posthumously-born son, **Alfonso XIII**.

Alfonso XII's reign was distinguished more by hope than accomplishment, its major achievement being the stabilization of the dynasty.

Alfonso XIII (1886–1941) King of Spain (1886/1931). A member of the Spanish House of Bourbon, he was the posthumous son of **Alfonso XII**. Until 1902, his mother, **María Cristina** of Austria, acted as regent on his behalf. At 16 he assumed his majority, thereafter frequently attempting to influence politics, and showing marked sympathy for the Spanish army. In 1923 he allowed General Miguel **Primo de Rivera** to destroy the parliamentary system and establish a dictatorship: the dictator's fall in 1930 left Alfonso discredited and, in 1931, after sweeping Republican gains in local elections, he left Spain, never to return. In 1941, shortly before his death in Rome, he 'abdicated' in favour of his third son, Don Juan.

Alfred, 'the Great' (849–99) King of **Wessex** (871/99). He was the fifth son of King Ethelwulf. When Alfred came to the throne, the Danes had already conquered Northumbria, East **Mercia**, and East Anglia, and threatened to subdue Wessex itself. He inflicted on them their first major reverse at the Battle of **Edington** in Wiltshire (878), and began to win back Danish-occupied territory by capturing the former Mercian town of London (886). He stole the military initiative from the Danes by reorganizing his forces into a standing army, building a navy, and establishing a network of burhs (fortified centres). These developments were complemented by his revival of religion and learning, a programme designed to win God's support for victory over the pagan Danes and to consolidate loyalty to himself as a Christian king. He forged close ties with other English peoples not under Danish rule, and provided his successors with the means to reconquer the **Danelaw** and secure the unity of England. The famous story of his being scolded by a peasant woman for letting her cakes burn has no contemporary authority, and is first recorded in the 11c. ▷ **Anglo-Saxons; Athelstan; Edward the Elder; Vikings**

Algeciras, Conference of (1906) This conference was called to defuse the differences between France and Germany which derived from the First Moroccan Crisis. The conference resulted in the acceptance by Germany, outmanoeuvred diplomatically by the French and particularly by the British, of the Act of Algeciras. The Germans had hoped both to curb the growth of French influence in Morocco and to harm the developing cordiality in relations between France and Britain. They were, however, constrained under the Act to accept provisions whereby, with due respect to the authority of the Sultan of Morocco, France and Spain were authorized to 'police' Morocco under the supervision of a Swiss Inspector-General.

Algerian War of Independence (1954–62) Growing resentment against French colonial rule in Algeria, fuelled by Arab nationalism (which had been gathering strength since **World War II**) and ignited by the **FLN** (*Front de Libération Nationale*), first expressed itself on the night of 1 Nov 1954, when Algerian nationalists attacked French military and civilian targets. By 1956, guerrilla warfare was widespread in rural areas; by the late 1950s, between 60 000 and 100 000 nationalists, with Tunisian support, were actively involved in the fight for independence. The 400 000–500 000-strong French army under General Jacques Massu, responded, but its harsh methods led to widespread criticism, and public opinion in France began to turn. In May 1958 there was a revolt in Algiers by French officers under Massu, who suspected that the **Mendès-France** government might enter negotiations with the FLN. This came close to triggering civil war in France, and brought about the fall of the government. This led to the inauguration of the Fifth Republic of General de **Gaulle** (1 June 1958) who, later that year, promised self-determination to Algeria. Despite subsequent attempts by right-wing French colonists, the army general, Raoul **Salan**, and the **OAS** (*Organisation Armée Secrète*), to prevent the attainment of Algerian independence, peace talks began at Evian-les-Bains in France (Mar 1962), and a cease-fire was agreed. Algeria was declared independent on 3 July 1962, with Ahmed **Ben Bella** as Premier of the new Algerian government. ▷ **Evian Agreements; Republic, Fifth** (France)

Algiers Agreement (1975) This agreement, negotiated between the government of the Shah of Iran and Saddam **Hussein** of Iraq, granted a considerable area of border territory north of the Shatt al-Arab waterway to Iran, coupled with the recognition of the waterway itself as constituting the border between the two states (as opposed to the low-water mark on the Iranian side), in return for a cessation of military assistance by

Iran to the Kurds in the north of Iraq. The abrogation of this agreement by Saddam Hussein may be regarded as effectively provoking the 1980–8 Iran–Iraq War.

Algonquin A small group of Native North Americans speaking Algonquian languages and living along the Ottawa River in Canada. They were allied with the French during the French and Indian War, and most were killed by the Iroquois. The few remaining Algonquin live near Quebec and Ontario.

'Ali (d.661) Fourth and last of the Rashidun, or 'Rightly-guided', Caliphs (656/61). The cousin and son-in-law of **Muhammad**, he converted to Islam while still a boy, and later married the prophet's daughter, **Fatima**. He withdrew, or was excluded from government during the caliphates of **Abu Bakr** and **'Umar**, and disagreed with **'Uthman** in the interpretation of the Quran and application of the law. Although not involved in 'Uthman's death, he was elected Caliph soon after, but encountered considerable opposition, led by **Mu'awiya**, Governor of Syria, the beginning of a major division within Islam which has persisted to the present day. The issue was still undecided when he was murdered in the mosque at Kufa, his capital, by a member of a third Muslim party, the **Kharijites**.

Ali, (Chaudri) Muhammad (1905–80) Pakistani politician. He was educated at Punjab University and, in 1947, on the partition of India, became the first Secretary-General of the Pakistani government. In 1951 he became Finance Minister, and in 1955 Prime Minister. He resigned a year later because of lack of support from members of his own party, the **Muslim League**.

Ali, Maulana Muhammad (1878–1931) and **Ali, Maulana Shaukat** (1873–1938) Muslim Indian political activists and leaders of the **Khilafat Movement**. Muhammad 'Ali was closely associated with the states of Rampur and Baroda, and in the internal politics of Aligarh College prior to **World War I**. In 1911 he founded *Comrade*, an English-language weekly paper espousing pan-Islamic views. Shortly thereafter he moved the paper to the new seat of government, Delhi, and also bought an Urdu paper, *Hamdard*, which he used to set forth his political views. Shaukat Ali was also prominent in Aligarh College politics and in 1913 organized *Anjuman-i-Khuddam-i-Kaaba* to provide Indian support of Muslim causes in the Middle East. The continued

activities of this movement after the outbreak of World War I resulted in the detention of both brothers between 1915 and 1919. On their release, they joined the Khilafat Conference, of which Muhammad soon became the leader. Because of M K **Gandhi**'s support of the Khilafat Movement, the brothers allied with the **Indian National Congress** and Muhammad convinced the Khilafat Conference to adopt M K Gandhi's **Satyagraha** strategy. As a result of a Khilafat Conference resolution calling upon Muslims to refuse to serve in the Indian army, the brothers were again arrested in 1921. In 1923, Muhammad Ali was elected President of the Congress. Mustafa **Kemal**'s 1924 abolition of the Caliphate undermined the Khilafat movement, which continued on with dwindling support and influence. During the late 1920s both brothers broke with Congress over the issue of safeguards for Muslims in an autonomous India. Following this, they concentrated on affairs solely concerning the Muslim community, although they remained highly influential national political leaders.

Alia, Ramiz (1925–) Albanian communist leader. Born of poor Muslim peasants, during **World War II** he fought in the Army of National Liberation, attaining in 1945 the rank of Lieutenant Colonel and receiving a Yugoslav military decoration. In 1949 he became a member of the Central Committee of the Albanian Workers Party, was Minister for Education and Culture (1955–8) and member of the Agitation and Propaganda Department (1958). He was made an alternate member of the Politburo in 1966, becoming a full member and Secretary of the People's Assembly in 1982. As Chairman of the Presidium of the People's Assembly in 1982 he became nominal head of state. On the death of Enver **Hoxha** (1985), he took over as First Secretary of the Albanian Workers Party Central Committee, thus becoming the national leader.

'Ali Bey (1728–73) Caucasian slave. In 1763 he rose to be chief of the **Mamluks** in Egypt. After being proclaimed Sultan (1768), he made himself independent of Turkey, and conquered Syria and part of Arabia. He died soon after being defeated by an army raised by one of his sons-in-law.

Alien and Sedition Acts (1798) Four US laws passed by a Federalist-controlled Congress intended to restrain the political opposition, at a time of crisis in US relations with the warring powers of Europe. The Alien

Acts delayed citizenship and gave the President great power over foreigners, while the Sedition Act authorized fining and imprisonment for public criticism of the government.
▷ **Kentucky and Virginia Resolutions**

Aliev, Geidar Alievich (1923–) Azerbaijani secret police officer. He moved to politics and survived from Leonid **Brezhnev**'s to Mikhail **Gorbachev**'s time. His move to the Central Committee came in 1971 and to the Supreme Soviet in 1974. Yuri **Andropov** made him a full member of the **Politburo** in 1982 as someone from a non-Russian republic, and in this respect he was useful to Gorbachev, too. The latter, however, pushed him out in 1987 for his lack of enthusiasm for reform, and on account of allegations of corruption. ▷ **perestroika**

Alinagar, Treaty of (7 Feb 1757) The treaty concluded by **Clive of Plassey** following his recapture of Calcutta from the Nawab of Bengal, **Siraj ud-Daula**. Under its terms, Calcutta was returned to the British **East India Company**, its privileges were renewed and the rights to fortify the town and mint money were secured. This absolutely secured a bridgehead from which to increase the Company's power in Bengal.

Ali Pasha (1744–1822) Rumeliot notable (ayan). A semi-independent feudal lord in south Albania, he became Pasha of Trikala in 1787 and was known as 'the Lion of Janina' after the region of Greece which he took in 1788. In 1803 he became *beglerbeg* (governor) of **Rumelia**. He received at his court Lord Byron and other European travellers and developed contacts with Britain and with revolutionary France and the **Philiki Etairia**, which worked for independence from the Ottoman Porte. Anticipating Russian support, in 1819 he declared his independence from the Porte but after the long siege of Janina he surrendered to the Sultan **Mahmud II**, and was put to death in 1822. ▷ **Greek War of Independence; Ottoman Empire; Porte, The Sublime**

Ali Salim Rubay (1934–78) Yemeni politician. He was the president of the People's Democratic Republic of Yemen during the period of left-wing socialist rule there and was overthrown and executed in 1978.

Alivardi Khan (1678–1756) Ruler of Bengal, Bihar and Orissa. He was an officer in the Mughal bureaucracy who rose steadily to become Deputy Governor of Bihar under the Nawab of Bengal, Shuja-ad-Din. Following Shuja's death, his successor was overthrown by Alivardi. His reign was largely spent suppressing rebellions and unsuccessfully defending Bengal against the Maratha invasion. A strong ruler, Alivardi was independent of Delhi, but never secure in his position due to the method of its attainment.

Aliyah The name given to the Jewish migrations from Europe to Palestine, which started in 1882, and laid the foundations of the modern state of Israel. The ideals of the second Aliyah (1904–14) were redemption of the soil, and personal labour as a means of salvation. It pioneered the cooperative settlement which was to develop into the modern kibbutz. The third Aliyah was associated with a search for a National Home, while the fourth (1925) reflected Jewish persecution in Eastern Europe, mainly Poland. The fifth Aliyah (1932) represented flight from early Nazi Persecution. ▷ **Zionism**

Al-Kasr al al-Kabir, Battle of ▷ **Alcazarquivir, Battle of**

Allan, Sir Hugh (1810–82) Canadian entrepreneur. He emigrated to Montreal in 1826, became partner in an ocean-going shipping line and by 1859 was one of the wealthiest men in the province. His relationship with Conservative politicians enabled him to win back the contract to deepen the St Lawrence in 1854. In 1862 the British Secretary for War accused him of charging excessive fares, and causing the death of many immigrants. He was also charged with bribery in the Pacific Scandal of 1873 which brought down the Conservative government. In return for donating campaign funds to the party, he had hoped to receive the charter for building the Canadian Pacific Railway.

Allen, Ethan (1738–89) American soldier, revolutionary leader, and writer. Allen distinguished himself early in the Revolutionary War when he led Vermont's **Green Mountain Boys** in the capture of Fort Ticonderoga from the British (10 May 1775). He then assisted in an effort to capture Montreal, but was himself captured. He returned to Vermont and continued to campaign for its independence. ▷ **American Revolution**

Allenby, Edmund Henry Hynman, 1st Viscount (1861–1936) British field marshal. As Commander of the 3rd Army during the Battle of Arras (1917), he came close to breaching the German line. He then took

29

command of the Egyptian Expeditionary Force, and conducted a masterly campaign against the Turks in Palestine and Syria, capturing Jerusalem (1917), Damascus and Aleppo (1918), and securing an armistice. He was made a viscount in 1919. ▷ **World War I**

Allende (Gossens), Salvador (1908–73) Chilean politician. A medical doctor who helped found the Chilean Socialist Party (1933), he was a member of the Chamber of Deputies (1937–9), Minister of Health (1939–41), and Senator (1945–70). Unsuccessfully standing for the presidency in 1952, 1958 and 1964, he was finally elected in 1970 as leader of the left-wing **Unidad Popular** ('Popular Unity') coalition, which promised a 'transition to socialism'. Undermined by US policy under Richard **Nixon** and Henry **Kissinger**, he was overthrown in 1973 by the army under General Augusto **Pinochet** and gunned down in the Casa Rosada, the presidential palace.

Alliance, Holy ▷ **Holy Alliance**

Alliance, Tripe ▷ **Triple Alliance**

Alliance for Progress A 10-year programme (1961–71) of modernization and reform for 22 countries in Latin America, sponsored by the US government in reaction to the advent of Fidel **Castro**'s Cuba and **Kubitschek (de Oliveira)**'s abortive 'Operation Pan American' initiative. However, it fell foul of the Kennedy administration's **Cold War** impulse and its partiality for orthodox economic policies, and few of its aims were achieved. ▷ **Kennedy, John F**

Alliance of Free Democrats (1989) The most immediately successful of the new non-communist parties in Hungary after the Democratic Forum. Events in 1989 intensified public interest in reform and many new groupings emerged. The Alliance showed greater concern for marketization and, in coalition with the Democratic Forum following the 1990 elections, it moved policy in this direction. However, there was already a Federation of Young Democrats in position to press for more radical restructuring still.

Allied Intervention in Russia (1918–22) The term refers to the intervention of foreign troops in Russian affairs following the Bolshevik **October Revolution** (1917). France, Britain, Japan and the USA were initially concerned to stiffen resistance to Germany by landing contingents in the north

and the south of Russia and in eastern Siberia. Before these could become effective, **Lenin** had concluded the separate Treaty of **Brest-Litovsk** (Mar 1918), and they got drawn instead into the **Russian Civil War** on the side of his opponents. This did nothing to help defeat Germany and soured Western–Soviet relations for years to come. Most of the troops had been withdrawn by 1920, but it was Oct 1922 before the Japanese left Vladivostok. ▷ **Bolsheviks**

All-India Muslim League ▷ **Muslim League**

Allon, Yigal (1918–) Israeli military commander and politician. After Israeli independence in 1948, he attended university in Jerusalem and Oxford. Under the British Mandate, Allon was prominent in the **Haganah** and Palmach, involved both in the allied occupation of Syria and Lebanon and in military activities against the British administration in Palestine. Having played a vital role in the War of Independence, Allon turned to academia and politics during the 1950s and 1960s. He became Deputy Prime Minister in 1968, having helped to shape Israeli strategy in the **Six-Day War**, and became Foreign Minister in 1974. ▷ **Israel, State of**

Almagro, Diego de (c.1475–1538) Spanish conquistador and collaborator of **Pizarro**. He briefly invaded Chile in 1536. Bitter rivalry then developed between Almagro and Pizarro, who defeated him in a desperate engagement near Cuzco. Shortly thereafter, Almagro was executed.

Almansa, Battle of (25 Apr 1707) A crucial episode in the War of the **Spanish Succession** in the Iberian Peninsula. The Franco-Spanish army of some 25 000 men under the Duke of **Berwick** was faced by the Allied forces, mainly Portuguese and English, numbering some 15 000 and commanded by the Earl of Galway and the Portuguese general, Das Minas, near the town of Almansa (Valencia). Berwick won a decisive victory which, despite subsequent minor reverses, permanently assured the Bourbon cause in Spain.

Almanzor ▷ **Mansur**

Almeida-Garrett, João Baptista da Silva Leitão (1799–1854) Portuguese writer and politician. Brought up in the Azores, he graduated in law from the University of Coimbra in 1820. He was exiled after the 1820 revolt because of his liberalism, but returned to support **Pedro I**, becoming Minister of the Interior. He was also a pioneer of the romantic movement and of modern Portuguese drama.

Almohads The Muslim dynasty which dominated North Africa and Andalusia for a century from c.1100 to c.1200, after the preceding dynasty of **Almoravids**. In 1160 they invaded Spain and established their control over the Muslim kingdoms there.

Almoravids The Muslim dynasty which dominated North Africa from c.1055 to c.1147. They invaded Spain during the same period and controlled the Muslim kingdoms there from 1091 to 1146. They were noted for their severe religious principles. ▷ **Almohads**

Alp Arslan (1029–72) Seljuk Sultan (1062/72). He succeeded his uncle, Tughrul Beg. A skilful and courageous commander, he devoted his energies to extending the frontiers of the Seljuk empire, entrusting the central administration to his capable vizier, Nizam al-Mulk. He restored good relations with the 'Abbasid Caliph and, in his role as protector of the caliphate, was about to launch a major offensive against its rivals, the Fatimids, when he was recalled to meet a Byzantine offensive in Armenia; at Manzikert (1071) he defeated a numerically superior army and captured the Emperor, Romanus IV, opening up the interior of Anatolia to penetration by the nomadic Turkmen tribes. Killed in a struggle with a prisoner while on campaign in Persia, he was succeeded by his son, Malik Shah. ▷ **'Abbasid Dynasty; Fatimid Dynasty**

Alpujarras, Revolts of (1499–1501 and 1568–70) The Alpujarra Mountains in the formerly Muslim kingdom of Granada were the setting for several revolts after the kingdom was captured by Christian Spain in 1492. The Islamic faith had been guaranteed in the terms of surrender, but social exploitation and religious persecution fuelled rebellions in 1499 and 1500. These led to the government of Queen **Isabella I**, 'the Catholic' decreeing (12 Feb 1502) that all **Mudejars** of **Castile** must choose between conversion or exile. Continued pressures provoked another great revolt in 1568–70, which was put down in 1570 by Don **John of Austria**. Thousands of **Moriscos** were slaughtered, and some 80000 were forcibly expelled to other parts of Spain; the population of Granada was reduced by a third.

Alsace Region of north-east France, comprising the departments of Bas-Rhin and Haut-Rhin, occupying part of the Upper Rhine Plain on the frontier with Germany. A traditional scene of Franco-German conflict, it was historically part of Lorraine before becoming part of the German Empire. The Peace of **Westphalia** (1648) and Treaty of **Rijswijk** (1697) ceded most of Alsace to France, but it was reannexed by Germany in 1871. Alsace was subsequently returned to France in 1919 and temporarily regained by Germany in **World War II**. Predominantly Germanic in language and culture, various autonomist movements have, since 1871, sought a special cultural or political status in Germany/France respectively.

Altan Khan (1507–82) Leader of the Tumet Mongols (a branch of the **Khalkas** who inhabited eastern Mongolia). He asserted control over the Western Mongols, or Oirat, and captured the former imperial Mongol capital at Karakorum. Altan Khan was responsible for the revival of Tibetan Buddhism (or Lamaism), whose influence in Mongolia had waned from the 14c onwards. In particular he patronized the Yellow Sect of Lamaism, personally conferring on the sect's leader, Sonam Gyatso, the title of **Dalai Lama**. Altan Khan's settlement at Köke Qota became the first permanent Mongol city of modern times. After his death, the influence of the Tumet Mongols waned and all the Khalka Mongols came under the sway of the **Qing Dynasty** in the 17c. ▷ **Mongols**

Alternate Attendance System (*Sankin-kotai*) An arrangement in 17–19c Japan whereby the **Tokugawa Shogunate** was able to ensure its control over the feudal lords, or **daimyo**. Each *daimyo* was required to spend six months of the year in the Tokugawa capital of **Edo** (present-day Tokyo). Such a prolonged stay, along with the need to maintain a large household, was a continual drain on the daimyo's financial resources. When the daimyo returned to his own domain, his family had to remain in Edo as virtual hostages. With the weakening of the shogunate from the 1850s, such controls lapsed in 1862.

Althing The Icelandic parliament. The original *Althing* was established in 930 at Thingvellir, near the modern capital of Reykjavik. It met for two weeks in the summer of each year and was attended by the leaders of Icelandic society and their followers. Its legislative assembly of 48 chieftains, presided over by a 'lawspeaker' elected every three years, considered changes in the law code. It survived the loss of Iceland's independence in 1262/4, but by the end of the 18c had become purely a court of law, and in 1800 was abolished. It was, however, revived as a consultative body by the Danish crown in 1843, and in 1874 was granted legislative powers. From 1983 it has had 63 members, divided after election into an upper and (smaller) lower chamber.

Alumbrados (Illuminists) The name applied to groups of religious mystics active in **Castile** in the 16c. The first groups appeared between 1510 and 1520 in the area between Toledo and Valladolid and were patronized by elements of the higher aristocracy. Their members were mostly of Jewish descent (**Conversos**), with women (*beatas*) playing a prominent role. From 1525 they were persecuted by the **Inquisition**, but without any of them suffering grave penalties. A later group, also subsequently persecuted by the Inquisition, appeared in Llerena in 1570. Illuminism was regarded with suspicion largely because it appeared at a period when Protestant heresy was spreading outside Spain.

Alva, Fernando Álvarez de Toledo, 3rd Duke of ▷ **Alba, Fernando Álvarez de Toldeo, 3rd Duke of**

Alvarado, Pedro de (c.1485–1541) Spanish conquistador. The companion of Hernando **Cortés** during the conquest of Mexico (1519–21), he became Governor of Tenochtitlán, where the harshness of his rule incited an Aztec revolt which drove the Spaniards out. In the following year Tenochtitlán was recaptured and razed, and Mexico City built in its place. From 1523 to 1527 he was sent by Cortés on an expedition to Guatemala, which also conquered parts of El Salvador. He returned to Spain, and in 1529 was appointed Governor of Guatemala. He embarked on an expedition to conquer Quito (Ecuador) in 1534, but was bought off by Francisco **Pizarro**.

Álvarez Mendizábal, Juan (1790–1853) Spanish politician. He was Liberal Minister of Finance in 1835 and Prime Minister in 1835–6. Álvarez initiated one of the most important programmes of **disentailment** in Spanish history in an endeavour to reduce the government's debts and create an independent peasantry.

Amadeus VIII, 'the Peaceful' (1383–1451) Anti-Pope, as Felix V (1439/49). Count and Duke (from 1416) of Savoy, he became ruler of Piedmont in 1419. In 1434 he retired to the monastery of Ripaille beside Lake Geneva, but in 1439 was elected Pope as Felix V (an anti-pope, in opposition to **Eugenius IV**). He resigned in 1449.

Amal A Lebanese Shiite movement established by the Imam Musa Sadr in the early 1970s. After Sadr's disappearance in 1978 during a trip to Libya, Nabih Berri assumed the leadership of the organization. Amal has a fighting force of over 4000 men. ▷ **Shiites**

Amanullah Khan (1892–1960) Amir and King of Afghanistan (1919/29). He established Afghan independence (1922) after a war with Britain. His push for internal reforms provoked opposition, and led to his abdication. He spent the rest of his life in exile, and died in Zurich, Switzerland.

Amasis ▷ **Ahmose II**

Amban Civil officials (usually Manchu or Chinese) appointed by the authorities of the **Qing Dynasty** from the 18c onwards to supervise administration in Tibet and Mongolia, with the support of armed garrisons. With the abolition of the Tibetan monarchy in 1750, the *amban* ('imperial resident') assumed a more extensive supervision of the Tibetan government, while in Mongolia the amban was also responsible for regulating the increasing numbers of Chinese traders and merchants entering the region.

Ambedkar, Bhimrao Ranji (1893–1956) Indian politician. A champion of the depressed castes, he was born in a Ratnagiri village, Bombay. Educated in Bombay, New York and London, he became a London barrister, later a member of the Bombay Legislative Assembly and leader of 60000000 Untouchables. Appointed Minister of Law in 1947, he took a leading part in framing the Indian Constitution. With thousands of his followers, he publicly embraced the Buddhist faith not long before his death, in New Delhi. ▷ **India, Partition of**

Amboise, Georges d' (1460–1510) French prelate and statesman. A cardinal, he became Prime Minister under **Louis XII** in 1498. In an attempt to secure his election as pope, he encouraged a schism between the French Church and Rome. An able minister, in 1505 he effected the Treaty of Blois which brought about an alliance between France and Spain.

Amboyna (Ambon), Massacre of (1623) The execution by the Dutch authorities of 10 Englishmen, 10 Japanese and a Portuguese on the island of Ambon in the Dutch East Indies; it has been used ever since as a propaganda tool to whip up anti-Dutch feeling among the English. The Governor of Ambon, Herman van Speult, ordered the arrests after learning of an alleged plot by the English (who were permitted to reside in the Dutch fort at Victoria on Ambon) to overthrow the Dutch authorities with the help of some Japanese soldiers in Dutch service. The prisoners were tortured, confessed, and were executed; this was subsequently used as a symbol for Dutch brutality and barbarism, especially during the **Anglo-Dutch Wars** of the 17c.

Amelioration The term used to denote the various improvements in slave conditions urged on the British West Indies between 1807 and 1831. The abolition of the slave trade led to the abolitionists seeking to attack **slavery** itself, and in 1815 parliament secured the compulsory registration of slaves in Crown Colonies. Pressure from abolitionists and the self-interest of some sections of the West India lobby produced the Amelioration Proposals of Lord Bathurst (1823). The instructions of the Colonial Secretary included the abolition of the flogging of women, punishment record books, religious instruction for slaves and the acceptance of slave testimony in law. They were widely resisted by the plantocracy and only produced unfulfilled slave expectations which led to revolts in Demerara (1823) and Jamaica (1831–2).

Amendola, Giovanni (1882–1926) Italian journalist, politician and philosopher. He was elected to parliament in 1919 and was made Under-Secretary for Finances in the **Nitti** government (1920) and Minister for Colonies under **Facta** (1922). He vehemently opposed the fascist seizure of power and led the **Aventine Secession**. Attacked several times by fascist thugs, he fled to France after a particularly savage beating, dying shortly afterwards of his injuries. ▷ **fascism**

Amenemhat I (Shetepibre) (c.1991/ 1962BC) King of Egypt. He was the founder of the 12th Dynasty, one of the most successful line of kings to rule Egypt. Amenemhat checked incursions of Libyans and Asiatic

nomads and extended Egyptian control into Nubia. He also regulated the activities of the provincial governors for the benefit of the country as a whole. A sound government was established, with a smooth transition of power ensured through his appointment of his son, **Senusret I**, as co-regent, the two kings ruling jointly for a decade. Although he was by birth a Theban, he moved the capital from Thebes to It-tawy ('Seizer-of-the-Two-Lands'), 18 miles south of Memphis, and built his pyramid nearby, at modern-day Lisht.

Amenemhat III (Nemaatre) (1842/1797BC) King of Egypt. As the sixth king of the 12th Dynasty, he enjoyed a long and successful reign in which he continued and enlarged his grandfather **Senusret II**'s agricultural scheme in the Fayum. By land reclamation and flood water control, the area became the most fertile part of Egypt. He constructed two pyramids: one at Dahshur south of Sakkara, and the second at Hawara at the entrance to the Fayum. It was apparently at Hawara that Amenemhat III was buried. The funerary temple of this pyramid, now reduced to a huge expanse of debris, was described by classical writers as the 'Labyrinth'.

Amenhotpe I (Amenophis) (Djeserkare) (c.1546/1526BC) King of Egypt. The second king of the 18th Dynasty, he consolidated the emerging **New Kingdom**. Through records of his contemporaries, we learn of campaigns in Nubia, the building of temples in that region and hints of hostile action in western Asia. Most of Amenhotpe's constructions in Egypt were dismantled by his successors, but one structure, an alabaster shrine, was recovered from the 3rd pylon at Karnak. For his tomb, Amenhotpe changed the old system of tomb and mortuary temple adjoining each other and separated the two elements. This concept was continued throughout the New Kingdom. Amenhotpe and his mother, Ahmose-Nefertiry, were later deified and their cult as patrons of the necropolis workers was long maintained.

Amenhotpe II (Aakheperure) (c.1436/ 1411BC) King of Egypt. A member of the 18th Dynasty, he was the son of **Thutmose III** and his chief wife, Hatshepsut-meryetre. He was a celebrated archer, horseman and oarsman, who campaigned in Syria and Palestine.

Amenhotpe III (Nebmaatre) (c.1397/ 1360BC) King of Egypt. The son of Thutmose IV, it was in his reign that Egypt reached her peak in cultural, political and artistic achievements. The country enjoyed diplomatic relations with neighbouring powers, Babylonia and Mitanni, and the immense wealth and prosperity of Egypt was reflected in magnificent buildings at Thebes, such as the Luxor temple, the third pylon of the temple of Amun at Karnak and the famous 'Colossi of Memnon' (two statues of Amenhotpe which stood in front of his now vanished mortuary temple).

Amenhotpe IV (Akhenaten) (Neferkheperure) (c.1370/1353BC) King of Egypt. Known as the 'Heretic Pharoah', he was a ruler in the 18th Dynasty, and was possibly associated on the throne with his father, **Amenhotpe III**, in the last years of the latter's reign. In his sixth year as King, he adopted formally the cult of the sun-disc (Aten), changing his name to Akhenaten, and moved the capital to El-Amarna (Akhetaten). Here he devoted himself to the practice of the new religion; the cult of the Aten was personal to the King and his family, and had no appeal to the population as a whole. Meanwhile, the Asiatic empire, left to its own devices, began to disintegrate. By his Queen, **Nefertiti**, Amenhotpe had six daughters, one of whom married **Tutankhamun**.

Amenophis ▷ **Amenhotpe I**

Amer, Abd al-Hakim (d.1967) Egyptian politician. He was one of the nine officers who, meeting in the aftermath of the disastrous 1948 war, formed the original constituent committee of the **Free Officers** movement in 1949. In 1950 Gamal Abd al-**Nasser** was elected Chairman of this committee and, when he became Prime Minister in 1954, it was Amer (by this time a general) who took over the War Ministry. In 1967, following the **Six-Day War**, Amer (now field marshal), disillusioned by what he saw as Nasser's betrayal of the army, allegedly took part in a conspiracy against him. Arrested for his supposed part in this plot, Amer was arrested and subjected to a campaign of vilification by the press. He committed suicide while in custody.

America First Committee Political organization (1940–1) opposing US involvement on behalf of the Allies in **World War II**. The committee attracted support from many conservatives fearing costly military commitment as well as pro-Nazi sympathizers, and the renowned aviator Charles **Lindbergh** was a chief spokesman. It campaigned unsuccess-

fully against the **Lend-Lease Agreement** and the repeal of the **Neutrality Acts**, but its propaganda was undoubtedly effective in the early years of the war. After the Japanese attack on **Pearl Harbor** (7 Dec 1941), however, the committee ended its activities, urging its members to support the war effort.

America, Hispanic This term, used to define the region of the Western Hemisphere from the Rio Grande 7000 miles to Cape Horn, emerged as late 19c scholars attempted to coin a word which would encapsulate the Iberian heritage of the region. It was convenient in that it emphasized European and non-Anglo-Saxon roots, in contrast to those of the rapidly emerging 'Colossus of the North', the USA. It reiterated the importance of Roman Law and Catholicism, tracing its roots back to the Roman Empire. Inherently elitist, the term implicitly excludes those many and varied peoples of the region whose heritage is either Indian or African. Nevertheless, its prevalence indicates the extent of the difficulties embraced when the history of this vast region is summarized.

American Civil Liberties Union (ACLU) US legal defence association founded to protect the constitutional rights of free speech, privacy, and equal protection under the law. The ACLU board selects areas where **civil rights** and liberties are under threat and provides legal assistance and expenses for litigants in its test cases. In its early days the ACLU provided the defence counsel in the **Sacco and Vanzetti Affair** and the Scopes **Monkey Trial**. During **World War II** it protested against the internment of the **Nisei** and in the post-war years acted on behalf of many harassed by McCarthyism and subjected to blacklisting. Throughout its existence it has been associated with unpopular political causes and has won cases concerning academic freedom, labour/ business relations and civil rights. ▷ **McCarthy, Joseph**

American Civil War (1861–5) A conflict between Northern states (the Union) and Southern states that had seceded (the Confederacy). The causes of the war included disagreement over slavery (which by then existed only in the South) and conflict over how much control the federal government should exert over the states (states' rights). The election in 1860 of Abraham **Lincoln**, who was hostile to slavery and opposed its extension to new territories (although he did not believe at first that he could interfere with

it where it already existed) precipitated the conflict. South Carolina seceded almost at once from the Union, followed within a short time by 10 other states. These 11 states formed the **Confederacy** early in 1861. War broke out on 12 Apr 1861, when Southern forces opened fire on **Fort Sumter**, South Carolina, and took possession of the fort. Most of the Civil War battles were fought in the South, and the Confederacy won some early victories, particularly at **Bull Run** and **Fredericksburg** and in the **Peninsula Campaign**. But **Antietam** (1862) was a victory for the North. Shortly after Antietam, President Lincoln signed the **Emancipation Proclamation** freeing all slaves in the Confederacy. This further reduced the available manpower in the South and as the war continued, the Union, with its far greater manpower and industrial resources, gradually began to prevail. The Battle of **Vicksburg** in 1863 was a major victory, and the Battle of Gettysburg, followed by Lincoln's **Gettysburg Address**, marked a turning point in the war. By 1864, Union forces captured Atlanta and completed a march of destruction through Georgia to the sea. The war ended on 9 Apr 1865, when Confederate General Robert E **Lee** surrendered to Ulysses S **Grant** at **Appomattox Court House**. At enormous cost of life, the war had succeeded in keeping the Union together and in bringing an end to slavery in the USA. See maps p35.

American Colonization Society A US group founded in 1816 whose goal was to resettle freed slaves in Africa. By 1860, 11 000 former slaves had been transported to Liberia. The society was attacked by abolitionists but supported by some slaveholders anxious to keep freed blacks separate from slaves. It was dissolved in 1912. ▷ **abolitionism**

American Federation of Labor ▷ **AFL–CIO**

American Indians ▷ **Native Americans**

American Legion In the USA, an association for former members of the armed forces (veterans) of **World War I** and **World War II**, the **Korean War** and the **Vietnam War**. It is the largest such organization in the world. Incorporated in 1919, its aims are to rehabilitate veterans, promote child welfare, ensure a strong national defence, and encourage patriotism.

American Revolution (1775–83) The war that established the 13 American colonies as

independent from Britain, often called the American War of Independence. In the years 1763 to 1775 relations between the North American colonies and Britain became increasingly strained as Britain began taking measures to tighten control over the colonies. Colonial resistance was especially high over the issue of whether the British parliament had the right to tax the colonies without their representation. Anti-British sentiment was more organized in the major port towns, with considerable support coming from the elected assemblies. The tension during this period was reflected in the **Stamp Act** crisis (1765–6), resistance to the **Townshend Acts** (1767–70), the **Boston Massacre** (1770), the burning of the customs cruiser *Gaspée* (1772), and the **Boston Tea Party** (1773). The British Parliament's passage of the **Intolerable Acts** (1774) to punish Massachusetts for the Tea Party led to the calling of the First **Continental Congress** (1774). In Apr 1775 fighting broke out between British troops and the colonial militia known as the **Minutemen** at the Battles of **Lexington and Concord** in Massachusetts. Other military engagements followed, including the colonial capture of Fort Ticonderoga (May 1775), the Battle of

American Revolution

Bunker Hill, and the unsuccessful colonial expedition in Quebec, Canada. In June 1775 the Second Continental Congress elected George Washington to command the Continental Army and in July adopted the Declaration of Independence. Following the British evacuation of Boston in May 1776, the main theatre shifted to New York, New Jersey, and Pennsylvania. Washington's troops suffered a number of defeats in the New York area, including the Battle of Long Island (Aug 1776), but his surprise attacks at Trenton (25 Dec 1776) and Princeton (Jan 1777), New Jersey, though small victories, did much to reinvigorate the colonial cause. In the Battle of Brandywine (Sep 1777) in Pennsylvania, however, Washington's troops were once again defeated. In June 1777 British troops had begun to move down from Canada and at first seemed assured of victory, but shrewd American manoeuvring resulted in defeat of the British and the surrender of Burgoyne following the Battle of Saratoga in upstate New York. This American triumph convinced the French to enter the war officially, bringing to the colonists badly needed material support, troops, monetary credit, and a fleet. During the winter of 1778 Washington's troops suffered great hardship while wintering in Valley Forge. By the spring the colonial forces had regathered their strength and Washington's men made a good showing at the Battle of Monmouth (June). Later that year fighting shifted southward, when Sir Henry Clinton commanded an invasion of South Carolina. Clinton's successor, Lord Cornwallis, led the army gradually north until Washington and the French Admiral de Grasse trapped him on the Yorktown Peninsula in Virginia, where he surrendered in 1781. The defeat resulted in the fall of the British Prime Minister, Lord North, who had prosecuted the war, and ended British will for further fighting. After almost two years of negotiating, the Treaty of Paris was signed in Sep 1783, recognizing the independence of the USA. The revolution had an impact felt far beyond the battlefield. Although support had not been universal — many loyalists fled at the war's end and became the core of English-speaking Canada — the various coalitions uniting entrepreneurs, professionals, planters, farmers, and urban working people had given form to the most advanced political hopes of their time. The newly created republic was an institution that political thinkers of the day had doubted was capable of governing a large area or of even surviving at all. The new country, founded by a democratic movement and based on an ideology of 'equal rights' opened the way for the long-term decline of monarchy in the rest of the world. See map p36. ▷ **Camden, Battle of; Charleston, Battles of; Committees of Correspondence; Camden, Battle of; Charleston, Battles of; Constitutional Convention; Cowpens, Battle of; Gaspée; Green Mountain Boys; Sons of Liberty; Sugar Act; Yorktown Campaign**

American War of Independence ▷ **American Revolution**

Amhara A Semitic-speaking people of the Ethiopian central highlands who, with the Tigray, dominate the country. They are descended from the original Semitic conquerors from southern Arabia. The Christian empire of Ethiopia was ruled by Amhara dynasties (1260–1974) which, by intermarriage and cultural assimilation, incorporated people from almost every ethnic group of the empire. Amharic is the official language of Ethiopia.

Amherst, Jeffrey, 1st Baron Amherst (1717–97) British general. He successfully commanded an expedition against the French fortress at Louisbourg (Nova Scotia) in 1758. After the fall of **Quebec** the following year, he completed the conquest of Canada by taking Montreal in 1760. He became a peer in 1776, and served as Commander-in-Chief of the British army.

Amiens, Treaty of (1802) A treaty between Britain and France, marking the end of the first stage of the wars with revolutionary France. Most of the conquests made by either power since 1793 were agreed to be returned. The peace held for only a brief period; war broke out afresh in 1803, and continued until 1815. ▷ **Napoleonic Wars**

Amin (Dada), Idi (c.1925–) Ugandan soldier and President. He joined the King's African Rifles in 1946, fought with the British army in the Kenyan **Mau Mau** uprising and was heavyweight boxing champion of Uganda. He benefited from the rapid Africanization of the army after Uganda's independence in 1961 and was promoted to major-general in 1968. He seized power from President **Obote** in Jan 1971, dissolved parliament and was proclaimed President. During his presidency, there was widespread violence in Uganda, a mass expulsion of British Asians and the massacre of opponents, especially from the Langi and Acholi peoples. Deposed by exiled Ugandans with the help of the Tanzanian army in 1979, he fled to Libya and thence he went to Saudi Arabia (1980–8). After a brief sojourn in Zaire, he returned to the Arab world.

Amitabha A Buddhist deity, or bodhisattva, worshipped by the Pure Land Sect, a branch of Mahayana Buddhism that teaches salvation through faith rather than good deeds. The worship of Amitabha originated in India during the 2c and was introduced to China from the 5c and to Japan from the 7c, where he was known as Amida. The worship of Amitabha became a feature of popular Buddhist sects in imperial China, which at times of economic crisis and government suppression often resorted to open rebellion against the state.

Amnesty International A British-based pressure group, founded in London in 1961, that campaigns for the release of any person detained for their political or religious beliefs or who has been unjustly imprisoned for any other reason.

Amorites The name borne by various Semitic peoples who lived in Mesopotamia, Syria, and Palestine in Old Testament times.

Amr Ibn al-As (d.664) Arab soldier. A convert to Islam, he joined **Muhammad** in 629, and took part in the conquest of Palestine in 638. In 639 he undertook the conquest of Egypt; in 642 he captured Alexandria after a 14-month siege, and accepted the capitulation of Egypt and became the first Muslim Governor of Egypt (642–4), where he founded the first city on the site of Cairo. He helped **Mu'awiya**, founder of the **Umayyad Dynasty**, to seize the caliphate from **'Ali** by capturing Alexandria again in 658, and was Governor of Egypt again from 661 to 663.

Amritsar Massacre (13 Apr 1919) On 10 Apr 1919 riots broke out in Amritsar in the Punjab in the course of an agitation for Indian self-rule. A gathering assembled three days later at Jallianwalla Bagh, a public park, on the festive occasion of Baisakhi. While they were being addressed, General Dyer, the local British commander, marched in. With barely a warning to the assembly and leaving no adequate means for the crowd to disperse, he ordered his troops to fire on the unarmed crowd, which included women and children, killing 379 Indians and wounding nearly 1 200. A government commission of inquiry severely censured Dyer and he had to resign his commission. Back in England, however, the House of Lords passed a motion approving of his actions and Dyer was widely acclaimed as 'the man who saved India' (the *Morning Post* launched a fund for him, raising £26 000 towards his retirement). The long-term effect of the massacre was the reverse of what Dyer had intended: many Indians were driven into supporting the **Indian National Congress**, and M K **Gandhi** himself became convinced of the impossibility of just rule under the British and the necessity for Indian independence.

Amselfeld, Battle of ▷ **Kosovo, Battle of**

Anabaptists (Rebaptizers) The collective name given to various groups of believers on the radical wing of the 16c Reformation committed to the baptism of believing adults only. They emphasized adherence to the word of scripture and strict Church discipline as ranking higher than the law of the state, which made them liable to much harassment and persecution. Infant baptism was first challenged by the 'Zwickau Prophets' who visited Wittenberg in 1521, and their protests were carried further by Thomas **Müntzer**, whose religious reforming zeal soon escalated into advocacy of social revolution. After his execution in 1525 Switzerland, Moravia and Holland emerged as the main centres of Anabaptist activity and, most spectacularly, Münster, where a short-lived 'Kingdom of the Saints' was established (1533–5), the antics of which did much to discredit the movement. Redoubled persecution by both Roman Catholics and Protestants followed, and Anabaptism was all but stamped out. Some of its more pacifically-minded followers were able to regroup under the name of Mennonites, while modern-day Baptists can be considered a more distant offshoot.

anarchism A generic term for political ideas and movements that reject the state and other forms of authority and coercion, in favour of a society based exclusively upon voluntary cooperation between individuals. To anarchists the state, whether democratic or not, is always seen as a means of supporting a ruling class or elite, and as an encumbrance to social relations. However, they differ in their view of the nature of their future society, their proposals ranging from a communist society based on mutual aid to one based on essentially self-interested voluntary exchange. They reject involvement in political institutions, and support civil disobedience action against the state, and on occasions political violence. Anarchist movements were most prevalent in Europe in the second half of the 19c and early 20c, but virtually died out apart from fringe groups after the **Spanish Civil War**.

Anastasia (Grand Duchess Anastasia Nikolaievna Romanova) (1901–19) Daughter of Tsar **Nicholas II**. She is thought to have died when the Romanov family were executed by the **Bolsheviks** in Ekaterinburg (19 July 1918). Several women claimed to be Anastasia, notably Anna Anderson, from the Black Forest (d.1984). Conflicting opinions by members of the Romanov family and others failed to establish the truth, and her claim was finally rejected by a Hamburg court in May 1961. The mystery has been the theme of books, plays, and films and has not been resolved by further evidence produced following the collapse of the USSR. ▷ **Romanov Dynasty; Russian Revolution**

ANC (African National Congress) The most important of the South African nationalist organizations opposed to white minority rule. It began life in 1912 as the South African Native National Congress and, under the influence of M K **Gandhi**, organized passive resistance to white power. Led by members of a growing black middle class, it steadily extended its support both into the urban black community and also into some liberal white quarters. Its central policy document, the **Freedom Charter**, was issued in 1956 and is social democratic, believing in non-racialism rather than the racial exclusivity of its rival **Pan-Africanist Congress**. When the party was declared an unlawful organization (Apr 1960), it began a campaign of industrial and economic sabotage through its military wing (**Umkhonto we Sizwe**), but essentially followed a two-track policy of direct action within South Africa and diplomacy abroad. It was generally recognized as the dominant voice of Black protest, by the **National Party** inside South Africa as well as the international community, and was unbanned in Feb 1990. It suspended its armed struggle in Aug 1990 and its leaders, notably Nelson **Mandela**, Walter **Sisulu** and Cyril **Ramaphosa** were involved in talks about a transition to a democratic South Africa.

ancien régime The social and political system of France existing from the late 16c to the outbreak of the **French Revolution** (1789). The term denotes a hierarchical,

corporative society, bound closely to the dynastic state, and is associated particularly with mechanisms upholding traditional orders and privileges. ▷ **Parlement**

Anckarström, Johan Jakob (1762–92) Swedish army officer and assassin of King **Gustav III** of Sweden. He served as the instrument of a ring of nobles opposed to the King's autocracy and, in 1792, mortally wounded Gustav during a masked ball in the Royal Opera House in Stockholm. He was soon seized and executed.

Ancus Marcius (7c BC) Fourth of the legendary Kings of Rome. His dates, though unknown, are conventionally given as 642/617BC. Many achievements were later accredited him (for example, the conquest of the lands at the mouth of the River Tiber, the building of the first bridge across it and the enlargement and embellishment of the city of Rome), but their historicity is altogether difficult to establish.

Andalus, al- The name given by the Arabs to the southern part of Spain (modern Andalusia) under Muslim rule from the 8c, when it was controlled by the Umayyad caliphs of Cordoba, who fashioned it into the most powerful and civilized state of Western Europe. The great cultural achievements of the era can still be seen in the mosques of Cordoba and Granada, and the Palace of Seville. ▷ **Umayyad Dynasty**

Anders, Władysław (1892–1970) Polish general. He was Commander-in-Chief of the Polish forces in the Middle East and Italy in **World War II**. After the war, deprived of his nationality by the Polish communist government (1946), he became Inspector-General of the Polish forces in exile, and a leading figure in the 140 000-strong Free Polish community in Britain. He died in London.

Andhra Dynasty ▷ **Satavahana Dynasty**

Andrada e Silva, José Bonifácio de (1763–1838) Brazilian politician and geologist. After holding academic posts in Portugal, he returned to Brazil in 1819 to take part in the independence movement that overturned the Portuguese regency of Prince Pedro in 1820–2. He was adviser and First Minister to Pedro in 1822, forming his first administration under the new empire of Brazil. Authoritarian by instinct, he closed newspapers and advocated a strong executive, but argued for the gradual end of the African slave trade as a means of eradicating slavery from the empire. Deported once **Pedro I** had dissolved the constituent assembly, he returned in 1829. After Pedro's abdication in Apr 1831, he served as tutor to the young **Pedro II**.

Andrada Family Arguably one of the most impressive political dynasties of Latin America, founded by three brothers, José Bonifácio de **Andrada e Silva**, Antônio Carlos de Andrada e Silva and Martim Francisco Ribeiro de Andrada. All educated at Coimbra University, Portugal, they played major roles in the making of the Brazilian empire between 1815 and 1826, either as First Minister to **Pedro I**, or as protagonists of constitutional reform. All headed powerful regional factions, and were known for taking fearless, if highly controversial, stances on constitutional issues, as well as slavery and the abolition of the slave trade. Their descendants often achieved powerful positions as councillors to **Pedro II**, and as senators or deputies, generally for São Paulo and Minas Gerais; they were often lawyers and drawn from families holding landed property in the most prosperous regions of those provinces. The more conservative, Minas, branch of the family played a leading role in support of Getúlio **Vargas**'s 1930 'revolution' as Governor of Minas and during his subsequent vice-presidency. José Bonifácio de Andrada e Silva served as President of the Chamber under the Costa e Silva government in 1967–9.

Andrássy, Gyula, Count (1823–90) Hungarian politician. A supporter of Lajos **Kossuth**, he was prominent in the struggle for independence (1848–9), after which he remained in exile until 1858. When the Dual Monarchy came into being, he was made Prime Minister of Hungary (1867–71). ▷ **Austria-Hungary, Dual Monarchy of**

Andrássy, Gyula, Count (1860–1929) Hungarian politician. The son of Count Gyula **Andrássy** (1823–90), he became Minister of the Interior in 1900, and Foreign Minister in 1918. In 1921 he attempted to restore the monarchy, and was imprisoned, but after his release became leader of the royalist opposition.

Andreev, Andrei Andreevich (1895–) Russian government minister and long-serving apparatchik. He joined the Communist Party in 1914 and was active in the Petrograd

metal workers union in the period 1917–19. He was a member of the Central Committee by 1935 and a secretary by 1938. In 1946 he moved on to be Deputy Chairman of the Ministerial Council and, as such, had special responsibility for improving agriculture. Pressure did little to increase yields, though, and in the early 1950s Nikita **Khrushchev** took on the job and began enlarging collectives instead. However, this did very little good either, and agriculture became institutionalized as the major economic problem.

Andropov, Yuri (1914–84) Soviet politician. The son of a railwayman, he became head of the **KGB** (1967–82), and in 1973 was made a member of the **Politburo**. On the death of Leonid **Brezhnev** (1982), he became General-Secretary of the Soviet Communist Party, consolidating his power (June 1983) with the presidency. He fell ill later that year, and died soon after, in Moscow. ▷ **communism; Hungarian Uprising**

Andrusovo, Treaty of (1667) The treaty ending the Russo–Polish war which began when Tsar **Alexei Mikhailovich** agreed (1654) to give military assistance to the Ukrainian Cossack rebel, Bohdan Khmelnitsky. The River Dnieper became the new frontier, except that Kiev on the right bank went to Russia. While the Ukrainians were fortunate to escape from the Poles, they were subsequently to consider that they had gone from the frying pan into the fire.

Angevins The name conventionally given to the English monarchs from 1154 to 1216: **Henry II** and his sons, **Richard I** and **John**. It derives from the lordship of the medieval county (and later, duchy) of Anjou in western France via Henry, son of Geoffrey Plantagenet, Count of Anjou. Henry created a wider 'Angevin Empire' comprising also Normandy, Maine and Aquitaine. The Angevin line continued as Plantagenets after the death of John, although John is usually considered the last Angevin king because it was during his reign that Anjou was lost to the French. ▷ **Plantagenet Dynasty**

Angkor Thom The ancient capital of the Khmer Empire, 150 miles (240 km) northwest of Phnom Penh, Cambodia. The moated and walled city was built on a square plan, extending over 40 square miles (100 sq km), and completed in the 12c. Abandoned in the 15c, it was rediscovered in 1861. Angkor Wat is the largest of the temples surrounding the site—linked, richly sculpted sanctuaries on a massive platform, the work of Suryavarman III (1112–52).

Angles A Germanic people from the southern Danish peninsula and neighbourhood. With the **Saxons**, they formed the bulk of the invaders who, in the two centuries following the Roman withdrawal from Britain (409), conquered and colonized most of what became England. Anglian rulers were apparently dominant by the 8c, and the Angles ultimately gave their name to England, its language and people. ▷ **Anglo-Saxons**

Anglesey, Henry William Paget, 1st Marquis of (1768–1854) British field marshal, who commanded the British cavalry at the Battle of **Waterloo** (1815), where he lost a leg. He sat in parliament at various times between 1790 and 1810, succeeding his father as Earl of Uxbridge in 1812. He served in the army with distinction in Flanders (1794), Holland (1799), and the **Peninsular War** (1808–14), and was made Marquis of Anglesey for his services at Waterloo. He was Lord Lieutenant of Ireland (1828–9 and 1830–3), where he supported Catholic emancipation, and Master-General of the Ordnance (1846–52).

Anglo-Burmese Wars (1824–6, 1852–3 and 1885) Three wars which secured British control of Burma: the first (1824–6) brought control of Arakan and Tehnasserim; the second (1852–3) led to the occupation of Pegu; the third (1885) saw the occupation of Upper Burma, and in 1886 all Burma was proclaimed a province of British India.

Anglo-Dutch Wars (1652–4, 1665–7, 1672–4 and 1780–4) Four naval wars fought between the Dutch Republic and England caused mainly by commercial and colonial rivalry between the two great sea powers. The first three, in the second half of the 17c, did not result in the supremacy of either nation; the fourth (1780–4), shortly before the French revolutionary period, was heavily lost by the Dutch, and signalled the end of their claims to commercial domination. The wars were the occasion of great naval heroics on both sides, for instance in the persons of Robert **Blake**, Maarten and Cornelis **Tromp**, and Michiel de **Ruyter**. ▷ **French Revolution**

Anglo-Egyptian Treaty (1936) In 1922 the British government had issued a declaration which recognized Egypt as an 'independent sovereign state', but retained for Britain control of the Suez Canal, the right to keep troops in the Canal Zone and the condominium in the Sudan. The 1936 treaty gave more of the substance of independence to Egypt. British residents in Egypt lost their legal and financial privileges, the British occupation was formally ended and Egypt gained control of her armed forces for the first time since 1882. In wartime, the British had the right to reoccupy the country, a right they exercised in 1939.

Anglo-Iraqi Treaty (1930) This treaty prepared the way for ending Britain's mandate in Iraq. The two countries formed a 25-year alliance in which they agreed to consult each other where they had common interests in foreign policy. Britain would retain the use of some air bases in Iraq and would train the Iraqi army. In 1932 Iraq became independent and joined the **League of Nations**.

Anglo-Irish Agreement (1985) A joint agreement allowing the Irish Republic to contribute to policy in Northern Ireland for the first time since 1922, signed (15 Nov 1985) by the British and Irish Prime Ministers, Margaret **Thatcher** and Garrett **Fitzgerald**. It established an intergovernmental conference to discuss political, security, and legal matters affecting Northern Ireland; early meetings focused on border cooperation. Both governments pledged not to change the status of Northern Ireland without the consent of the majority. The agreement was opposed by the Irish Republic's opposition party, **Fianna Fáil**; in Northern Ireland, Unionist leaders withdrew cooperation with ministers and boycotted official bodies.

Anglo-Japanese Alliance (1902) The first modern alliance between a Western and Asian power, which lasted until 1921. It reflected the anxiety both countries felt at increasing Russian encroachment in **Manchuria**. The alliance took account of each country's interests in China, as well as Japan's interests in Korea, and provided for joint action in the event that either of the signatories was involved in war with more than one power in East Asia. Each signatory would remain neutral if the other fought only one power. The alliance was renewed twice (1905 and 1911), extending its scope to the protection of Britain's interests in India and recognizing Japan's annexation of Korea in 1910. Although the alliance brought benefits to both countries, the irrelevance of Russia as a threat in East Asia after 1918 and persistent US hostility led to its replacement in 1921 at the Washington Conference by a much looser consultative Four-Power Pact (USA, Britain, France and Japan).

Anglo-Russian Entente (1907) A crucial settling of differences between Russia and Britain which in the event almost amounted to an alliance. The Russian and British empires had been rivals in the Near, Middle and Far East for at least a century. However, they were gradually brought together by mutual distrust of an aggressive Germany and mutual interest in friendship with a worried France, with which Russia had had an alliance since 1894 and Britain an entente since 1904. Neither was prepared to sink their differences so far as to conclude a treaty. However, agreeing their respective spheres of influence, particularly in Persia, enabled them to operate as a diplomatic bloc that went to war in 1914.

Anglo-Saxons A term probably first used to distinguish the **Saxons** of England from those of the Continent; occasionally adopted by the 10c English kings for all their subjects, though 'English' was preferred; now commonly employed for the entire Old English people from the incoming of **Angles**, Saxons, and **Jutes** in the 5c to the **Norman Conquest**. Among the main themes in Anglo-Saxon history are the emergence of the early kingdoms, their conversion to Christianity, their response to attacks by the **Vikings**, and their eventual unification in the 10c into a single realm, England, literally 'land of the Angles'. The Anglo-Saxons left an enduring legacy, including a developed system of government and a rich economy. ▷ **Alfred, 'the Great'; Athelstan; Edgar; Edward the Elder; Offa; Wessex**

Anglo-Tibetan Agreement (1904) The agreement reached in Lhasa between Tibetan officials and a British expeditionary force (under Sir Francis Younghusband) fearful of potential Russian influence. Tibet recognized British overlordship of Sikkim and agreed to open relations with India. Trade marts were also to be opened in Gyantse and Gartok (western Tibet), where British officials and troops could be stationed. This agreement was virtually repudiated by the British government when it signed a convention with China in 1906 reaffirming China's position in Tibet and promising not to interfere in Tibetan affairs, in return for China's guarantee to keep Tibet free from encroachment by a third power.

Angry Brigade A left-wing group with anarchist sympathies, active in Britain in the 1960s and early 1970s, which took sporadic violent action against representatives of the establishment in the name of the working class. Its leaders were tried and imprisoned for a bomb attack on the home of Robert Carr, Secretary of State for Employment, in 1971. ▷ **anarchism**

Anhalt A principality of the **Holy Roman Empire**, originally a part of the Duchy of Saxony, then ruled by Brandenburg. Prince George III introduced Lutheranism in 1526. Anhalt was devastated in the **Thirty Years War** as a result of the activities of the Prince, Christian I, in siding against the Empire. The principality straddles the River Elbe between Magdeburg and Wittenberg.

Ankara, Battle of (21 July 1402) This represented a devastating defeat for the Ottomans at the hands of **Timur**. Throughout the 14c, the Ottomans had gradually increased their hold over Anatolia and in the second half of the century they had established a European capital at Edirne (Adrianople). Their defeat by Timur lost them Anatolia at a stroke. It was as well for the Ottomans that they had invaded Europe as their sultanate was able to hold on in the Balkans with its capital at Edirne until, after Timur's departure, they were able in the 15c to re-establish themselves in their former territories. ▷ **Edirne, Capture of; Ottoman Empire**

An Lu-shan, Rebellion of (755–63) A large-scale rebellion in China initiated by a frontier general from the north-east, An Lu-shan (705–57), during the reign of Emperor **Tang Xuanzong**. An Lu-shan, of Turkish and Sogdian origins, was one of many non-Chinese militarists who amassed considerable power at the periphery of the Tang Empire. Feeling his ambitions blocked by hostile advisers at court, he invaded Hebei in 755. Tang Xuanzong was forced to flee the capital, Chang'an, and in 756 An Lu-shan declared himself the Emperor of a new dynasty. Although An Lu-shan was assassinated by his own son in 757, the rebellion continued until 763, fatally undermining the **Tang Dynasty**.

Anna Comnena (1083–1148) Byzantine Princess. The daughter of Emperor **Alexius I Comnenus**, she tried in vain to secure the imperial crown, and failed in her attempt to overthrow or poison her brother (1118).

Disappointed and ashamed, she withdrew from the court, and sought solace in literature. On the death of her husband (1137), she wrote a life of her father, the *Alexiad*, which contains an account of the First Crusade. ▷ **Comnenus Family; Crusade, First**

Anna Ivanovna (1693–1740) Empress of Russia (1730/40). She was the younger daughter of Ivan V and the niece of **Peter I, 'the Great'**. In 1710 she married the Duke of Courland, who died the following year. After the early death of **Peter II**, she was elected to the throne by the Supreme Council in 1730, with conditions that severely limited her authority. She trumped the council by abolishing it and ruled as an autocrat with her German favourite, Ernst Johann **Biron**, who assumed the title of Duke of Courland and became the real power behind the throne. Together they established a reign of terror, in which 20 000 people are said to have been banished to Siberia.

Annam A French protectorate, occupying the central part of Vietnam. The name was originally a T'ang Chinese term for Vietnam (literally, 'the pacified south'), but was then revived by the French. The French protectorate was established in 1883, following the final French assault on the Vietnamese court. In 1887, Annam was brought together with the French colony of **Cochin-China** and the Cambodia and Tonkin protectorates to form the *Union Indochinoise*. Economic conditions in parts of Annam were notably harsh. This was an important element in the fierceness of the local opposition to French rule, as demonstrated in the uprisings in Nghe-An and Ha-Tinh at the beginning of the 1930s. The imperial capital of Vietnam, Hue, was situated in Annam.

Anna Pavlovna (1795–1865) Queen of the Netherlands. She was Tsar **Alexander I**'s sister, and married the Dutch Crown Prince, the future King **William II**, in 1816. They ascended the throne in 1840, on the abdication of Wiliam's father, William I. William himself died in 1849 and was succeeded by their son, **William III**. An indefatigable charity organizer, she is remembered as a stickler for ceremony, and brought international sophistication to the Dutch court.

Anne (1665–1714) Queen of Great Britain and Ireland (1702/14). The second daughter of **James VII and II**, she was the last Stuart sovereign. In 1672 her father became a Catholic, but she was brought up in the Church of England. In 1683 she married Prince George of Denmark (1653–1708); and Sarah Jennings (1660–1744), the wife of Lord Churchill (afterwards 1st Duke of **Marlborough**), was appointed a lady of her bedchamber. Lady Churchill speedily acquired supreme influence over her, which she exerted in favour of her husband. During her father's reign, Anne lived in retirement, taking no part in politics, but later was drawn into intrigues for his restoration, or to secure the succession for his son. She was herself childless when she succeeded to the throne in 1702. She bore 17 children, but only William, Duke of Gloucester, survived infancy. The influence of Marlborough and his wife was powerfully felt in all public affairs during the greater part of her reign, which was marked by pronounced party political conflict between **Whigs** and **Tories**, the Union of England and Scotland (1707), and the long struggle against **Louis XIV** of France known as the War of the **Spanish Succession**. Towards the end of her reign she quarrelled with the Marlboroughs and **Godolphin**, her Lord Treasurer. Anne found a new favourite in Abigail Masham, and under her influence appointed a Tory government (1710); but quarrels between the new ministers prevented her securing the succession for her brother. ▷ **Stuart, House of; Union, Acts of; Whigs**

Anne of Austria (1601–66) Queen of France. The eldest daughter of **Philip III** of Spain, she married **Louis XIII** of France in 1615. Their first son was born in 1638; he succeeded to the throne on his father's death in 1643, as **Louis XIV**, with Anne as regent. She wielded power with her lover, Cardinal Jules **Mazarin**, as Prime Minister. They steered France through the difficult period of the **Fronde** and, although Louis came of age in 1651, they continued to rule the country jointly until Mazarin's death (1661), when Anne retired to the convent of Val de Grâce, and Louis XIV became absolute monarch.

Anne of Brittany (1477–1514) Duchess of Brittany (1488/1514). She married **Charles VIII** (1491), then **Louis XII** of France (1499), and devoted herself to preserving the autonomy of Brittany, her hereditary dominion.

Anne of Cleves (1515–57) Lutheran princess. She became the fourth queen of **Henry VIII** of England in Jan 1540, as part of Thomas **Cromwell**'s strategy of developing an alliance with German Protestant rulers. The marriage was declared null and void, on grounds of non-consummation six months afterwards. On agreeing to the divorce, Anne was given a large income, and she remained in England until her death.

Anne of Denmark (1574–1619) Wife (from 1589) of **James VI** of Scotland, later James I of England. Much of her time was spent in planning extravagant court entertainments, and she became a patron of the masque and other art forms.

Annexation Manifesto (1849) A Canadian proposal (produced chiefly by Montreal **Tories**, A T **Galt** among them, and some **Rouges**), which argued that annexation to the USA was preferable to the proposed union of the colonies. Since the ending of colonial preference, Canadian trading problems had become very severe, and with the repeal of the **Navigation Acts** it looked as if the colonies were being abandoned. Annexation would raise farm prices, lower import costs, and make US capital available for industrial development. The reaction to the proposal was disappointing for the signatories: not only were the French thoroughly opposed, but the USA showed little interest.

Anno (c.1010–75) Archbishop of Cologne. Elected Archbishop of Cologne in 1056, after Emperor **Henry III**'s death he led the opposition to the Regent, the Empress Agnes; he seized the young King, Henry IV, and took control of the Empire (1062). From 1063 onwards he was forced to share government with **Adalbert** of Bremen and increasingly lost the favour of Henry IV, although he continued to support him, even when the King sided with the people of Cologne in their revolt against the Archbishop in 1074. Anno contributed greatly to the power of the Church and created a centre for reform in the Rhineland. He was canonized in 1183.

Ansbach-Bayreuth A principality of the **Holy Roman Empire** in Franconia which became Lutheran under Margrave George (d.1543). Margrave Christian Ernst (d.1712) settled Huguenots in Erlangen, where a university was founded in 1743. It was annexed to Bavaria in 1810.

Anschluss The concept of union between **Austria** and Germany, expressly forbidden by the Treaties of **Versailles** and **St Germain** (1919), but with widespread support, especially in Austria, after the collapse of the Habsburg Empire. A proposed customs union (1931) was vetoed by France and Czechoslovakia. **Hitler** pursued the idea once in power, and in 1938, after the forced resignation of the Austrian Chancellor von **Schuschnigg**, the Germans occupied Austria. The union of Austria and Germany was formally proclaimed on 13 Mar 1938. ▷ **Habsburg Dynasty**

Antall, Jozsef (1932–93) Hungarian historian and reforming politician. After working as an academic in Budapest, he came to politics in 1956 when he led one of the revolutionary committees. Active in the Smallholders Party, he was arrested in 1957 and banned from practising his profession until 1963. He did not enter politics again until the late 1980s, when he became President of the Democratic Forum in 1989. He entered parliament in 1990 and was chosen Prime Minister later the same year, with the difficult task of presiding over a coalition government.

Anthony, Susan Brownell (1820–1906) US reformer and champion of women's rights. After teaching and pursuing temperance work, she was instrumental in the passage of the Women's Property Rights Act (1860). From 1869 she was a leader of the National Woman Suffrage Association, becoming President of the US branch in 1892. ▷ **National American Woman Suffrage Association**

Anti-Comintern Pact An agreement between Germany and Japan, concluded in 1936, which outlined both countries' hostility to international **communism**. The pact was also signed by Italy in 1937. In addition to being specifically aimed against Soviet Russia, it also recognized Japanese rule in Manchuria. ▷ **Comintern**

Anti-Confucian Campaign (1973–4) An ideological campaign launched by the Chinese Communist Party on the eve of its Tenth Congress (Aug 1973). It was apparently the inspiration of **Mao Zedong**'s radical supporters who used the campaign, ostensibly to condemn the persistence of traditional ideas, as a veiled attack on the policies of Premier **Zhou Enlai**. Just as **Confucius** and his followers attempted to restore feudal society and practices, so Zhou was seen as trying to roll back **Cultural Revolution** innovations (in such areas as education) and rehabilitate purged party officials. After the Congress, however, the campaign was specifically linked to a denunciation of **Lin Biao**, Mao's former deputy, who was identified with the excesses of the Cultural Revolution, suggesting that the campaign had been taken over by Zhou and his more moderate allies.

Anti-Corn Law League (Sep 1838) An association formed in Manchester, largely under the patronage of businessmen and industrialists, to repeal the British **Corn Laws**, which imposed protective tariffs on the import of foreign corn. League propaganda aided the growing movement for free trade in early 19c Britain, and the league was an influential political pressure group with many supporters in parliament. The Corn Laws were repealed by Robert **Peel** (1846). ▷ **Bright, John**

Antietam, Battle of (16–17 Sep 1862) A battle of the **American Civil War** (also known as the Battle of Sharpsburg), fought in Maryland. In military terms the North won a technical victory, but both McClellan's and Robert E **Lee**'s troops suffered huge casualties. The Union cause gained enough credibility to allow President **Lincoln** to issue his preliminary **Emancipation Proclamation**. ▷ **Confederate States of America**

Antigonus Gonatas (c.320–239BC) King of **Macedonia**. He did not mount his throne until 276BC, seven years after the death of his father, **Demetrius Poliorcetes**. **Pyrrhus** of **Epirus** overran Macedonia in 274BC, but Antigonus soon recovered his kingdom, and consolidated it despite incessant wars.

Antigonus Monophthalmos ('the One-Eyed') (c.382–301BC) Macedonian soldier. He was one of the generals of **Alexander III, 'the Great'**, and after Alexander's death received the provinces of Phrygia Major, Lycia, and Pamphylia. However, he aspired to reunite Alexander's empire under his rule, and waged war against the other generals, making himself master of all Asia Minor and Syria. In 306BC he assumed the title of King together with his son **Demetrius Poliorcetes**, but was defeated and slain by his rivals at Ipsus in Phrygia. ▷ **Cassander; Hellenistic Age**

Anti-Masonic Party (1830–6) US political party. Dedicated to driving Freemasons out of public life, it arose from the highly publicized disappearance (1826) of the author of a book revealing Masonic secrets. It was the first 'third party' in the USA, nominating a presidential candidate in 1832 at the first national party convention.

Antioch, Capture of (June 1098) After the successes of the First Crusade over the Turks at Dorylaeum and Heraclea, the main body of the Crusader army split up and moved on Antioch (which had been lost to the Turks in 1085). The city was taken after a seven-month siege, Bohemond having achieved this success by obtaining a betrayal from one of its citizens. Despite an attempt to recapture the city by the the the Seljuk Atabeg of Mosul, Kitbugha, the Crusaders repelled his force and the gateway to northern Syria was in Crusader hands. ▷ **Crusade, First**

Anti-Party Plot (1957) The name given by Nikita **Khrushchev** to the attempt made by senior opponents to oust him from his position as First Secretary of the Communist Party. Ever since **Stalin**'s death he had been strengthening his position and, in the process, introducing changes to existing policies. He had therefore incurred the hostility of hardliners and opponents of reform such as **Malenkov, Molotov, Kaganovich** and **Shepilov**, who succeeded in defeating his decentralization proposals at a meeting of the Party Presidium. However, Khrushchev managed with great skill to convene a meeting of the Central Committee, where he commanded a majority, and had the Presidium vote overturned and the plotters expelled. In a similar situation in 1964, he was unable to repeat his success since many of his reforms had proved useless.

Antipater (398–319BC) Macedonian general and loyal servant of the royal family. He was **Philip II** of Macedon's closest aide, Governor of **Macedonia** during the wars of conquest of **Alexander III, 'the Great'** (334–323BC), and Regent of Alexander's former empire after the death of Perdiccas (320–319BC). ▷ **Cassander**

anti-pope In the Roman Catholic Church, a claimant to the office of **pope** in opposition to one regularly and canonically appointed. Anti-popes featured prominently in the period of **Great Schism** in the Western Church (1378–1417). They included **Clement VII** and Benedict XIII (in Avignon, France) and Alexander V and **John XXIII** (in Pisa, Italy).

Anti-Revolutionary Party (*Anti-Revolutionaire Partij*, ARP) Dutch political party founded in 1878 by Abraham **Kuyper** on principles of Calvinist opposition to the Enlightenment and the **French Revolution** (hence 'anti-revolutionary'). Since the

1840s there had been a loose grouping of Dutch MPs calling themselves 'Anti-Revolutionaries', led by **Groen van Prinsterer**, but in 1878 under Kuyper it became the first true political party in the Netherlands, with a published manifesto and a quasi-democratic structure. Its programme was for limited social and political reform, together with a Calvinist approach to all things including politics: thus it was an early Christian–Democrat party. Since 1888 the ARP has regularly taken part in Dutch government coalitions, usually with the Catholics. Kuyper's successor, **Colijn**, led the country during the 1930s, and in 1973 the ARP joined the other Dutch confessional political parties in the **Christian Democratic Appeal**. As a result of this merger, the ARP ceased to exist in Sep 1980.

Anti-Saloon League US organization. Established in 1893, its aim was to end the use of alcohol by state and local anti-alcohol laws and by amending the **US Constitution**. The League remained in existence during and after the **Prohibition** period, and became part of the National Temperance League in 1950.

Anti-Spiritual Pollution Campaign (1983) Ideological campaign promoted by the Chinese Communist Party and initially encouraged by **Deng Xiaoping**. At a time of economic reform, which aimed to dismantle state controls, and increasing contacts with the West, 'spiritual pollution' referred to pernicious Western influences in the realm of political thought and culture that were seen to encourage excessive individualism and hedonism. Intellectuals were criticized for their espousal of humanism and the notion that alienation could exist in a socialist society, while Western trends in dress and music were condemned as decadent.

Anti-Trust Acts US legislation passed to control the development of monopoly capitalism. The Sherman Act (1890) forbade all combinations 'in restraint of trade'. Ambiguities in wording led to its use against labour unions instead of corporations, or *trusts*. The Clayton Act (1914) was intended to clear up the ambiguities and make enforcement easier.

Antonescu, Ion (1882–1946) Romanian general and politician. He was military attaché in Rome and London and served as Minister of War from 1934 to 1938. Rightwing and nationalistic, while out of office he maintained links with the **Iron Guard**. In 1940 he established a dictatorship with the trappings of fascism, taking the title *conducător* (leader) and assuring **Hitler** of his support. In Jan 1941, to maintain the internal stability essential for German interests, he crushed an uprising of the Iron Guard with the Romanian army backed by German forces. He was executed as a war criminal. ▷ **Codreanu, Corneliu Zelea; Michael** of Romania

Antonine Emperors (AD138–192) The dynasty which ruled over the Roman Empire after the death of **Hadrian**, consisting of Hadrian's adopted son, **Antoninus Pius** (138/161), Pius's adopted sons, **Marcus Aurelius** (161/80) and Lucius Verus (161/9) and Marcus Aurelius's natural son, **Commodus** (177/92). The experiment with collegiate rule, seen for the first time in the joint reign of Marcus Aurelius and Lucius Verus (161/9), though abandoned on Aurelius's death, was repeated frequently in the 3c when the task of governing the empire became recognized once more as simply too much for one man.

Antonine Wall A defensive frontier barrier commissioned by the Roman Emperor Antoninus Pius in AD142, which extended the northern limit of Roman Britain into Scotland. Constructed of turf upon a foundation of cobbles, guarded by 19 forts, and with a ditch in front and a military road behind it, the 'wall' extended from the Forth estuary to the Clyde. ▷ **Britain, Roman**

Antoninus Pius (86–161) Roman Emperor (138/161). His title *Pius* ('dutiful') was probably conferred because of his exemplary behaviour towards his adoptive father, **Hadrian**. His reign, though depicted by establishment writers as peaceful and happy, saw much unrest. In Britain, defensive measures (the Antonine Wall) against the northern barbarians had to be taken, and there was also trouble in Germany, Africa, Palestine and Dacia.

Antony, Mark (Marcus Antonius) (c.83–30BC) Roman politician and soldier. Related to Julius **Caesar** on his mother's side, he assisted Caesar in **Gaul**, and supported him in Rome. He was a commander in Caesar's war against **Pompey the Great**, and governed Italy while Caesar was in Africa. In 44BC, as consul, he tried in vain to have Caesar made emperor. After Caesar's assassination, his speeches caused the flight of the conspirators from Rome, and left him with almost absolute power. After his defeat at Mutina (43BC) by Octavian (**Augustus**), he fled to Gaul, but returned in triumph with a large army. A triumvirate was formed with Octavian and **Lepidus** to share the Roman world among themselves. The 'triumvirs' secured Italy, then defeated **Brutus** and **Cassius** at Philippi. While reorganizing the Eastern provinces, Antony met and was captivated by Queen **Cleopatra VII**, whom he followed to Egypt (41BC), and with whom he lived in idleness and luxury. On his return to Italy in 40BC to patch up a quarrel with Octavian, a new division of the Roman world was made at Brundisium, with Antony taking the East, but the agreement failed to heal the breach between them. Antony's renewed liaison with Cleopatra, and his donation to his children by her of large parts of the Roman Empire, provided Octavian with reasons to arouse the Roman people against him. War was declared. Defeat at Actium (31BC) followed, and Antony and Cleopatra both committed suicide.

Antraigues, Emanuel Delaunay, Count of (1755–1812) French politician. His *Mémoires sur les Etats-généraux* (1788) was one of the first sparks of the **French Revolution**; but in 1789, when he was chosen a Deputy, he defended the hereditary privileges and the kingly veto, and ranked himself against the union of the three estates. After 1790 he was employed in diplomacy at St Petersburg, Vienna, and Dresden. In England he acquired great influence with George **Canning**; he was murdered, with his wife, near London, by an Italian servant.

Antwerp, Sack of (Nov 1576) Also known as the Spanish Fury, the Sack occurred during the **Eighty Years War** when the prosperous trading port was plundered by mutinous Spanish troops who had not been paid in campaigns against the northern Dutch provinces. The sack lasted several days, and cost 7000 citizens their lives, together with huge amounts of booty.

Anuradhapura A city in northern Sri Lanka, which was the centre of the island's Buddhist kingdoms from 4c BC to AD 12c. The centre of government then shifted to Polonnaruwa, partly as a result of hostile invasions from South Indian kingdoms. In the late 19c the city became the focus of archaeological attention and in the 20c many of its monuments have been restored by Buddhist revivalists.

ANZAC (Australia and New Zealand Army Corps) A unit in which troops from both countries fought during **World War I** in the Middle East and on the Western Front. Anzac Day (25 Apr) commemorates the Gallipoli landing in 1915; the fighting lasted until Jan 1916, during which time 7600 were killed and 19500 wounded. ▷ **Gallipoli Campaign**

Anzio Landing (22–3 Jan 1944) Landing by 50000 US and British troops during **World War II** at a small port 60 miles behind the German defences of the so-called Gustav Line. Although the Germans were taken by surprise, they were able to confine the Allied troops and prevent them from using Anzio as a bridgehead. In late May the forces at Anzio eventually made contact with the advancing troops of General Alexander who had over-run the Gustav Line.

ANZUS (1951) An acronym for the treaty concluded between Australia, **New Zealand**, and the United States for mutual security in the Pacific against armed attack. The treaty encompasses not only the metropolitan territories of the three, but also island territories under their jurisdiction, their armed forces, and their aircraft and shipping. New Zealand participation lapsed in 1985, following that country's refusal to admit US nuclear-powered warships to its waters.

Apache Native North Americans; members of the Athapascan linguistic group, who originally migrated from Canada, settling in the south-western USA. During the 19c their fierce warriors dominated the region, leading raids against both Native American and white settlements. They proved formidable opponents of the US army when from 1861, led by **Cochise** and **Geronimo**, they fought against federal troops in the Apache Wars. Following their defeat in 1886, they were assigned to reservations in Arizona and New Mexico. ▷ **Indian Wars; Native Americans**

apartheid (Afrikaans 'apartness') The policy of separate racial development in the Republic of South Africa, supported traditionally by the Nationalist Party, and more recently by other right-wing parties. The ideology has several roots: Boer concepts of racial, cultural, and religious separation arising out of their sense of national uniqueness; British liberal notions of indirect rule; the need to preserve African traditional life while promoting gradualism in their Christianization and westernization; and the concern for job protection, promoted by White workers to maintain their status in the face of a large and cheaper Black proletariat. Under the policy, different races are given different rights. In practice, the system was one of White supremacy, Blacks having no representation in the central state parliament. Many of the provisions of apartheid regarding labour, land segregation (reserves, Homelands, Bantustans), municipal segregation, social and educational separation, and a virtually exclusive White franchise, were in place before the Nationalist victory of 1948, but after that date it was erected into a complete political, social, and economic system, down to the provisions of 'petty apartheid' relating to transport, beaches, lavatories, park benches, etc. Its principal architect, Hendrik **Verwoerd**, was assassinated in 1966. At the end of the 1980s F W **De Klerk** began the liberalization movement which resulted in the election of Nelson **Mandela** as president in 1994. ▷ **Afrikaners; Black Consciousness Movement; indirect rule; Sharpeville Massacre**

Apartheid Laws A body of legislation in South Africa passed by the Nationalist government after its victory in 1948. **Apartheid** was based on a combination of ideas derived both from the Boers' sense of separateness and from the British colonial practice of indirect rule (ruling through chiefs on reserves). Earlier laws such as the Natives Land Act of 1913 and the Natives (Urban Areas) Act of 1923 created a foundation for the more extreme form of separation promoted by the Nationalists. The laws included the Prohibition of Mixed Marriages Act and the Population Registration Act (both 1949), the Immorality Act and the Group Areas Act of 1950, the Prevention of Illegal Squatting Act (1951), the Bantu Authorities Act and the Bantu Education Act (1953). The intention of these Acts was to separate white and black living areas, educational provision and social intercourse. Jobs were also reserved according to race, but the apartheid system was ultimately destroyed because it failed to match economic realities. Most of these laws were repealed after F W **De Klerk** became President of South Africa in 1989 and announced the abandonment of the apartheid programme.

Apis ▷ **Dimitrijević, Dragutin**

APO (*Ausser parlamentarische Opposition*, 'Extra-parliamentary Opposition') After the formation of an **SPD–CDU** coalition in Federal Germany in 1966, there was no effective opposition in the **Bundestag**. Radi-

cal, student-dominated, groups therefore took their opposition to the political system into the streets, declaring the Federal Republic to be a parliamentary dictatorship. The formation of an SPD–**FDP** coalition in 1969 (leaving the CDU/**CSU** as a credible opposition) defused much of the criticism, but the **Baader–Meinhof Group** had roots in the APO.

Apollo-Soyuz Project A landmark joint space mission conducted by the USA and USSR in July 1975, following an agreement signed by President Richard **Nixon** and Premier Alexei **Kosygin** in May 1972. A project of the period of US–Soviet **détente**, Apollo-Soyuz also demonstrated the capability for joint operations between the major space powers and, as such, the potential for on-orbit emergency rescue missions. The rendezvous (17 July 1975) lasted nearly two days. The crews (T Stafford, V Brand, D Slayton and A Leonov, V Kubasov) conducted a series of joint experiments. A special adaptor docking module was constructed for the mission.

Apostasy, Wars of the The so-called Apostasy of the tribes of the Arabian Peninsula after the death of the Prophet **Muhammad** (632) depends for its name on the acceptance of the conversion of the Peninsula prior to the Prophet's death. Whatever view is taken of this, the Muslims during the caliphate of **Abu Bakr** (632/4) undertook a series of campaigns in the Peninsula which brought the tribes (back) into the fold of Islam. The Muslim victories over the 'Apostates' led to complete control of the Peninsula and hence directly to the subsequent Muslim conquests in the Fertile Crescent, Egypt and Persia.

apparat The aggregate of full-time officials of the **Communist Party of the Soviet Union** (*apparatchiki*). Originally drawn from professional revolutionaries, and based on **Lenin**'s doctrine of democratic centralism, the role of the *apparat* is to execute the decisions of the party leadership in a disciplined, bureaucratic manner with little scope for discussion or discretion. The term *apparatchik* is used to refer to a functionary.

appeasement A foreign policy based on conciliation of the grievances of rival states by negotiation and concession to avoid war. The term is most often applied to the unsuccessful British and French attempts before **World War II** to satisfy **Hitler**'s demands over German grievances arising out of the Treaty of **Versailles**. As a result, Hitler remilitarized the **Rhineland**, secured **Anschluss** with **Austria**, and gained the **Sudetenland** from Czechoslovakia. ▷ **Chamberlain, Neville**

Appius Claudius (5c BC) Roman jurist. He was the leader of the 10-man commission (*decemviri*) which was appointed in 451BC to produce Rome's first written code of laws. Although he died in the violent backlash that the commission's activities provoked, the decemviral code itself survived. Known as the **Twelve Tables**, it was still taught in Roman schools as late as Cicero's day.

Appius Claudius Caecus (4c–3cBC) Aristocratic Roman politician and general. His fame rests primarily on his great reforming censorship (312 BC), during which he opened up the political process to the lower orders, made the Senate less exclusive and launched a number of projects to improve the quality of life at Rome (like the building of the city's first aqueduct, the Aqua Appia). A fervent expansionist, he actively participated in Rome's wars against the **Etruscans**, **Sabines** and **Samnites** and began Rome's first major trunk road in Italy, the Appian Way (Via Appia). Despite blindness in old age (whence the nickname 'caecus'), he continued to be active in politics, especially during the war against Pyrrhus of Epirus (280–79 BC). A skilled orator, as well as a writer, he was regarded by the Romans as the father of Latin oratory and prose-writing.

Appomattox Court House The site in Virginia, USA, of the surrender (9 Apr 1865) of the Confederate Army under Robert E **Lee** to Union forces under Ulysses S **Grant**. Although a few Confederates remained under arms, the surrender marked the effective end of the **American Civil War**.

Apponyi, Albert Georg, Count (1846–1933) Hungarian politician. He entered the Hungarian Diet in 1872, and showing himself to be a brilliant orator, soon became leader of the moderate opposition which became the National Party in 1891. In 1899 he and his supporters went over to the Liberal Government party, and from 1901 to 1903 he was president of the Diet. From 1906 to 1910 he was Minister of Culture and, a devout Catholic, gave asylum to the expelled French Jesuits. He introduced free public education. In 1920 he led the Hungarian peace delegation, protested bitterly against the terms

imposed under the Treaty of **Trianon** and resigned. He frequently represented his country at the **League of Nations**.

Apprenticeship System (1834–8) The technique introduced into the British West Indies after emancipation in order to preserve the labour force of the plantation economy. Fearful of the expected social upheaval and economic consequences of the immediate freedom of some 750000 slaves, the British government totally freed only children under six years in 1834. Field slaves remained apprenticed to their masters for another six years and domestic slaves for four years, and were bound to give 40 hours of unpaid work each week. Stipendiary magistrates were appointed to oversee apprenticeship, which worked well only in colonies without large tracts of crown-land. Antigua ignored apprenticeship, while slaves in Guyana and Jamaica left to found 'free villages'. In all the British West Indies the system was ended in 1838.

Apraxin, Fyodor Matveevich, Count (1671–1728) Russian naval commander, known as the 'Father of the Russian Navy'. In the service of **Peter I, 'the Great'** from 1682, he was appointed admiral in 1707 and built up the navy into a powerful fighting force. In the Great Northern War (1700–21) he fought off the Swedes at St Petersburg (1708), captured Viborg, Åbo and Helsinki, and routed the Swedish fleet in 1713, thus taking control of the Baltic. Later he commanded successful engagements against Turkey and Persia.

Apraxin, Stephen Fyodorovich, Count (1702–58) Russian soldier. The nephew of Count Fyodor **Apraxin**, he served in the war against the Turks (1736–9), and at the outbreak of the **Seven Years War** (1756–63) was appointed marshal. He commanded the Russian forces invading East Prussia in 1757, and defeated the Prussians at the Battle of Gross-Jägersdorf, but fell from favour and died in prison. ▷ **Russo-Turkish Wars**

April Movement (1853) Popular Protestant protest in the Netherlands against the re-establishment of the Roman Catholic episcopal hierarchy. On 4 Mar 1853 Pope Pius IX set up five new bishoprics (Breda, Haarlem, Roermond, 's-Hertogenbosch, and the Archbishopric of Utrecht) in the Netherlands, which had not had a proper hierarchy since the Reformation (the country had been a 'mission area', under the *Propaganda Fide* in Rome). Petitions were raised, demonstrations took place, Catholic employees were dismissed, Catholics were molested on the streets, and the liberal government of the day was forced to resign. Thereafter the row subsided, and the new bishops took over their sees.

April Theses A programme of revolutionary action announced by **Lenin** in Apr 1917 shortly after the **February Revolution** and his return to Russia. In it he advocated the transformation of the Russian 'bourgeois-democratic' revolution into a 'proletarian-socialist' revolution under the slogan of 'All power to the Soviets'. ▷ **Bolsheviks; July Days; October Revolution; Russian Revolution**

Aquino, Benigno ('Ninoy') (1932–83) Filipino politician. Born into a political family, he rose rapidly through provincial politics to become a senator at the age of 35. He was the principal opposition leader during the period of martial law, declared by President Ferdinand **Marcos** in 1972; it is generally accepted that if martial law had not been declared then, and the 1973 presidential election thereby abandoned, Aquino would have succeeded Marcos as President. However, Aquino was arrested and sentenced to death on charges of murder and subversion (Nov 1977). In 1980, suffering from a heart condition, he was allowed to leave for the USA for surgery (and exile). On his return to the Philippines (21 Aug 1983), he was assassinated at Manila airport; this, it was widely believed, on the orders of the established regime. His death unleashed mass demonstrations against the Marcos order, which were to lead, in Feb 1986, to the collapse of the Marcos presidency and the succession of Benigno's widow, Corazon **Aquino**.

Aquino, Corazón ('Cory') (1933–) Filipino politician. In 1956 she married Benigno **Aquino**, and after his imprisonment in 1972 by President **Marcos** kept him in touch with the outside world. She lived in exile with Benigno in the USA until 1983, when he returned to the Philippines and was assassinated at Manila airport. She took up her husband's cause, and with widespread support claimed victory in the 1986 presidential elections, accusing President Marcos of ballot-rigging. The nonviolent 'people's power' movement which followed brought the overthrow of Marcos and Aquino's installation as President. Her presidency was, however, much troubled by internal oppo-

sition; in 1989 the sixth, and most serious, attempted coup against her was resisted with assistance from the USA.

Arab Cooperation Council (ACC) The ACC was founded by Egypt in 1989 in cooperation with Iraq, Jordan and Yemen when Saddam **Hussein** appeared to have been excluded from the Gulf Cooperation Council (GCC). Its establishment had as its formal aim, economic cooperation between the member states, but the underlying objective was to establish a consultative assembly whereby the more extravagant policies of Iraq might be subjected to at least some form of control. The ACC ceased to function as an effective body when Saddam Hussein annexed Kuwait (Aug 1990).

Arabi Revolt ▷ **'Urabi Revolt**

Arab-Israeli Wars Four wars (1948, 1956, 1967 and 1973) fought between Israel and the Arab states over the existence of the state of Israel and the rights of the Palestinians. The June 1967 war is known by supporters of Israel as the '**Six-Day War**' and by others as 'The June War.' The 1973 war is called the '**Yom Kippur War**' by Israelis, the 'Ramadan War' by Arabs, and the '**October War**' by others. See map p51. ▷ **Zionism**

Arab League A League of Arab States, founded (Mar 1945) with the aim of encouraging Arab unity. The League's headquarters was established in Egypt, but moved to Tunis after the signing of Egypt's peace treaty with Israel in 1979. Today the Arab League has 22 member states including Palestine, which is represented by the **PLO** (Palestine Liberation Organization).

Arab Legion (1921) Established in the state of Transjordan in 1921, initially as a police force, command of the force passed in 1939 to Major John Bagot Glubb (later known as Glubb Pasha), under whose training it developed into a military force of the highest discipline and quality. Making a considerable contribution to the **World War II** effort in the Middle East, the legion was also instrumental in the 1948 struggle with Israel in retaining East Jerusalem and the West Bank for the Arabs. This provided the basis of additional territory, which enabled King Abdullah to proclaim his Hashimite Kingdom of Jordan which consisted of the former Transjordan and the territories won by the legion. Glubb Pasha (now Colonel Sir John Glubb), resigned in 1956, at which time the legion became part of the regular Jordanian army.

State of Israel after armistices of 1949

Cease-fire lines:
—— June 1967 —— 1974

Territory occupied by Israel since 1967

Territory annexed by Israel in July 1967 (East Jerusalem) and Dec 1981 (Golan Heights)

Territory occupied by Israel in 1967, handed back to Egypt in 1982

Territory occupied by Israel 1982-5 (South Lebanon)

Israel and her neighbours since 1949

Arab Revolt (1916) The result of British negotiations with Sharif **Husayn ibn 'Ali** of Mecca, in part at least encouraged by the **Husayn–McMahon Correspondence**, the revolt was led by the Sharif's son, Faysal. Attached to the Arab forces during the revolt was T E **Lawrence** ('Lawrence of Arabia'). Amongst the achievements of the revolt was the destruction of the **Hijaz Railway** between Ma'an and Medina, and the capture of Aqaba. Essentially a revolt against Turkish occupation, the Arabs were also under the impression that a greater Arab nation had been promised them by the British. The revolt cleared the way for British troops under **Allenby** to advance northwards into Syria, where the capture of Damascus

effectively brought Turkish hegemony to a close. Unsurprisingly, the Arabs felt aggrieved, if not betrayed, by the provisions of the subsequent **Balfour Declaration** (providing for a national home for the Jews in Palestine) and by the provisions for British and French 'spheres of influence', initially negotiated by Sykes and Picot and confirmed after **World War I** by the **League of Nations**. ▷ **Faysal I; Sykes–Picot Agreement**

Arabs A diverse group of people, united by their use of Arabic as a first language, who live primarily in south-west Iran, Iraq, Syria, the Arabian Peninsula, the Maghrib region of North Africa, Egypt, and Mauritania. They are mostly Caucasoid, but with Negroid and Mongoloid admixture in certain areas. A great unifying force is Islam, the religion of 95 per cent of all Arabs. The majority live in cities and towns; five per cent are pastoral nomads living in deserts.

Arab Socialism This was the ideology of President Gamal Abd al-**Nasser** of Egypt. He denounced Western parliamentary democracy as 'a shameful farce' because the masses were still exploited. 'Democracy,' he wrote, 'means that the government should not be the monopoly of feudalism and exploiting capitalism but should be for the welfare of the whole nation.' Nasser put his ideas into practice by nationalizing nearly all large-scale businesses and landholdings in 1961 and by forming the Arab Socialist Union, with 'basic units' in villages, factories and workshops. There were elected councils at local levels, rising to the National Executive, headed by Nasser himself. In all elected bodies, half the seats were reserved for farmers and workers, so that for the first time all Egyptians could participate in running the country.

Arafat, Yasser or **Yasir**, originally **Mohammed Abed Ar'ouf Arafat** (1929–) Palestinian resistance leader, born in Cairo of Palestinian parents. He led the Palestinian Students' Union at Cairo University, and co-founded the Fatah resistance group in 1956, which gained control of the Palestinian Liberation Organization (**PLO**) in 1964. Acknowledged (though not universally popular) as the PLO leader, he skilfully managed the uneasy juxtaposition of militancy and diplomacy, and gradually gained world acceptance of the PLO. In 1983 however, his policies lost majority PLO support, and he was forced to leave Lebanon with his remaining followers. Since then he has been based at the PLO headquarters in

Tunis, though he spends much of his time in Baghdad. The *intifada* (uprising) in the West Bank in 1988 paved the way for his dramatic recognition of Israel and renunciation of terrorism in Dec 1988. In Sep 1993 he and the Prime Minister of Israel, Itzhak **Rabin**, negotiated a peace agreement at the White House (signed in Cairo in 1994), by which Israel agreed to withdraw from Jericho and the **Gaza Strip.**

Arago, Dominique François Jean (1786–1853) French scientist and politician. At 17 he entered the Polytechnic, in 1804 became Secretary to the Observatory, and in 1830 its Chief Director. He took a prominent part in the **July Revolution** (1830), and as member of the Chamber of Deputies voted with the extreme left. In 1848 he was a member of the provisional government, but refused to take the oath of allegiance to **Napoleon III** after the events of 1851–2. His achievements were mainly in the fields of astronomy, magnetism, and optics.

Aragon, House of The ruling house of one of Spain's component kingdoms, founded in 1035 by Ramiro I, the illegitimate son of Sancho the Great of Navarre. It was united by marriage with the ruling house of Barcelona in 1131. Fernando II of Aragon (**Ferdinand II, 'the Catholic'**) married Isabella of Castile in 1469, and the crowns of Aragon and **Castile** were finally united in 1479. ▷ **Isabella I, 'the Catholic'**

Aragon, Kingdom of The kingdom, with its capital in Saragossa, began to emerge in the 11c. It came to form part of the confederation of the 'Crown of Aragon', which took shape from the 12c, when Aragon and Catalonia came under one ruler. Subsequent territorial extensions took in Valencia and much of the western Mediterranean. The Aragonese empire reached its height in the 13c.

Arai Hakuseki (1657–1725) Japanese Confucian scholar and official. He came from a **samurai** family and in 1694 was appointed personal tutor to the future sixth Tokugawa Shogun, later becoming his adviser. Arai vainly attempted to transform the shogunate from a military-style government to a Confucian monarchy replete with the appropriate rituals and ceremony. He also wrote extensively on early Japanese myths and history, military affairs, and geography. ▷ **Tokugawa Shogunate**

Arakcheev, Alexei Andreevich, Count (1769–1834) Russian landowner, officer and

imperial minister. Commandant of St Petersburg for a time under **Paul I**, he became Minister of War under **Alexander I** in 1807 and then a state councillor in 1810. He did much to improve the efficiency of the army, but he also acted as a conservative counterweight to the reformist Count **Speransky**. Then, and also for a time under **Nicholas I**, he was responsible for the notorious military colonies which organized ex-soldiers and their families in agricultural settlements run along military lines. Typical of the best and the worst of Tsarist rule, he acquired a reputation for brutality excessive even for the administration of his time.

Araki Sadao (1877–1966) Japanese soldier and politician. An ultra-nationalist, he was a leader of the right-wing **Imperial Way Faction** (*Kodo-ha*) of the army. He was Minister for War (1931–3) and for Education (1938–40). After **World War II** he was convicted as a war criminal and sentenced to life imprisonment, but was released in 1965.

Arana Goiri, Sabino de (1865–1903) Basque nationalist. From a well-to-do Carlist family, he created much of the language and symbolism of Basque nationalism. Not only did he revive the Basque language, by publishing grammars, textbooks, histories, newspapers and magazines, but he also created the word *Euzkadi* for the Basque ethnic nation, designed the first Basque flag (the *ikurrina*), founded the first Basque cultural club, and coined many of its key political slogans. He founded the Basque Nationalist Party (**PNV**) in 1895. He was also the first Basque nationalist to win public office. ▷ **Carlism**

Aranda, Pedro Pablo Abarca y Bolea, Count of (1718–99) Spanish statesman and general. He was made Ambassador to Poland in 1760, but in 1766 was recalled to Madrid and made Prime Minister in the wake of the Esquilache riots of that year. He engineered, in 1767, the expulsion from Spain of the Jesuits, who were blamed for the risings, but in 1773 fell from power and was sent to France as ambassador. Returning in 1787, he became Prime Minister again in 1792, but antagonized Manuel de **Godoy**, and died in Aragon in enforced retirement.

Aratus of Sicyon (c.271–213BC) One of the leading politicians of 3c BC Greece. He joined Sicyon to the hitherto small **Achaean League** in 251BC, which he then gradually built up as a major power, seizing the Acrocorinth from

Macedonian control in 243BC, and bringing new Peloponnesian cities into membership of the League. However, the revival of Spartan power under Cleomenes III caused him to turn for support to Antigonus Doson of **Macedonia**.

Arawaks The original inhabitants of the Bahamas (Lucayos) and the Greater Antilles (Tainos) who practised a subsistence agriculture based on seafood, game, maize and cassava using neolithic technology. They lived mainly in coastal settlements of large villages with *caneyes* (family houses) and *bohios* (chiefs' houses) and had a hierarchical politico-religious structure based on a hereditary ruler, the *cacique*, who possessed a ceremonial stool (*duho*). A priestly caste controlled worship of gods of place and nature (*zemis*) and ceremonies which led to *coyaba* (heaven). Notable Arawak caciques included Hautey (Cuba) and Guarionex and Anacaona (Hispaniola). They were exterminated as a people by the Spanish after 1519. The words maize, tobacco, potato, hammock, canoe and hurricane all derive from the Arawak language.

Arbatov, Georgi Arkadevich (1923–) Soviet journalist, academic, party official and adviser to Mikhail **Gorbachev**. A Russian born in the Ukraine, he graduated in international relations, was a contributor to serious periodicals and got his first academic posting in 1962. His first Communist Party appointment came in 1964 and his major breakthrough was in 1967, becoming Director of the Institute for American Studies. This made him chief Soviet interpreter of US policies, a role that acquired a new importance with Gorbachev's rise to power. He clearly influenced the **Gorbachev–Reagan** link that ended the **Cold War**. In the late 1980s, however, the need for his talents declined.

arbitristas The name given to the writers who put forward proposals (*arbitrios*) to solve the problems of **Castile** in the late 16c and early 17c. The majority of them were concerned with questions of economy, inflation, taxation and population decline; but some were also concerned with questions of imperial power. Among the best known of them were Martín González de Cellorigo, Sancho de Moncada and Pedro Fernández de Navarrete.

Arbroath, Declaration of (6 Apr 1320) A response by Scottish barons, with the support of the Church, to a demand from Pope **John** **XXII** that the Scots make peace with England. The Pope did not recognize Robert **Bruce** as King of Scotland. Almost certainly written by Bruce's Chancellor, Bernard de Linton, also Abbot of Arbroath, the declaration asserted the separate nationhood of Scotland and the integrity of its 'uninterrupted succession of 113 Kings, all of our own native and royal stock'. The declaration, a skilful and effective piece of anti-English propaganda, declared that the signatories would never 'consent to subject our selves to the dominion of the English' and urged the Pope to take note of the wrong and calamities to the Church and state which had been wrought by the English incursions. Unsurprisingly, it has since become a key document for supporters of a separate Scottish nation.

Arcadius (377–408) Roman emperor(395/408). He was born in Spain, and after the death of his father, Emperor **Theodosius**, in 395, received the Eastern half of the Roman Empire, the Western falling to his brother, **Honorius**. Arcadius lived in oriental state and splendour, and his dominion extended from the Adriatic to the Tigris, and from Scythia to Ethiopia; but the real rulers over this vast empire were the Gaul Rufinus, the eunuch Eutropius, and the Empress Eudoxia, who persecuted and banished St John Chrysostom in 404.

Archaic Period ▷ **Early Dynastic Period**

Archelaus (c.413/399BC) King of **Macedonia**. He developed Macedonian military power and economic strength. He encouraged Greek culture at his court, which he moved from Aegae to Pella for easier access to the sea.

archon In ancient Athens, a public official whose duties were mainly legal and religious. Each year nine were chosen, of whom the chief was the 'eponymous archon': the Athenian system for dating years was based on the list of eponymous archons. The political importance of archons declined from 487BC, when election to the office was replaced by selection by lot.

Arcot Small town and principality in India near Madras, capital of the Carnatic under the **Mughal Empire**. Arcot is principally known for the daring diversionary tactic of **Clive of Plassey**, embarking on his first command in 1751. By capturing the town and defending it against a much larger force of French and Carnatic troops, Clive forced the

Nawab and the French to move troops from Trichinopoly, ending the stalemate which had pervaded the war. Ultimately, Clive's victory at Arcot resulted in British control of the Madras region.

Arditi Volunteer commandos set up in Italy by General **Diaz** towards the end of **World War I**. Many joined the **Fascist Party** after the war, feeling betrayed by the Peace Settlements. It was in imitation of their uniform that the fascists adopted black shirts.
▷ **mutilated victory**

Aref, Abd al-Salam (1921–66) Iraqi politician. He took over as Ba'ath socialist President of Iraq from Abd al-Krim **Qassim** in 1963. Amongst his achievements were improved relations with Gamal Abd al-**Nasser**'s Egypt and the nationalization of the oil industry. Under Ba'athist ideological influences, he moved further towards the establishment of Iraq as a secular state, but his rule ended suddenly with his death in a helicopter crash. He was succeeded by his brother, Abd al-Rahman Aref, until he was toppled in the Ba'ath coup of July 1968 and replaced as President by Hasan al-**Bakr**, who ruled in concert with the Ba'ath leader, Saddam **Hussein**.

Arens, Moshe (1925–) Israeli politician, born in Lithuania. Educated at Massachusetts and California Institutes of Technology, he lectured in aeronautical engineering at the Israel Institute of Technology, Haifa, and was Deputy Director of Israel Aircraft Industries before entering the Knesset in 1973. He served as Ambassador to the USA (1982–3), and was then a Minister without portfolio until 1987, when he was appointed Foreign Minister. ▷ **Likud**

Areopagus In ancient Athens, the name of the oldest Council, and also of the hill on which it met. Composed of ex-archons, the Areopagus had jurisdiction in cases of homicide; its political power was reduced by **Ephialtes** in 462–461BC, but revived in the later 4c BC. The name literally means 'the hill of Ares' (the god of war). ▷ **archon**

Argenson, René Louis, Marquis of (1694–1757) French politician, the son of the Marquis of Argenson (1652–1721) who created the secret police and established the **lettres de cachet**. He became councillor to the **Parlement** of Paris in 1716, and Foreign Minister (1744–7). He fell a victim in 1747 to the machinations of Madame de **Pompadour**,

as 10 years later did his brother, Marc Pierre, Count of Argenson (1696–1764), who became War Minister in 1743.

Argentine-Brazilian War (1825–8) A war fought to decide the possession of the Banda Oriental, territory to the east of the River Uruguay, whose separate status was confirmed by the adoption of a constitution in 1830. The vicissitudes of the war provoked profound political change in both major combatants, contributing to the fall of both Bernardino Rividavia and the *unitarios* in Buenos Aires and **Pedro I** in Rio de Janeiro. ▷ **Artigas, José Gervasio; Rosas, Juan Manuel de**

Argos Ancient Greek city-state, situated in the north-east Peloponnese. It was repeatedly involved in wars, punctuated by periods of truce, with its traditional enemy, **Sparta**. Because of this enmity, it did not help the Greeks to repel the Persian invasion of **Xerxes** (480–479BC). Its alliance with Athens in the 5c BC was also motivated by their common hostility to Sparta. ▷ **Cleomenes I; Persian Wars**

Arianism Arius of Alexandria (AD 3–4c) maintained a doctrine holding that Jesus Christ was not of one substance with God but had been created by God as father and, although therefore not God by nature, was called the 'Son of God' because of his perfect goodness. After its founder, the doctrine came to be known as Arianism and Arian views were subsequently condemned at the Council of Nicaea in the early 4c.

Arias Navarro, Carlos (1908–) Spanish politician. Notorious as the 'Butcher of Malaga' for being state prosecutor there during the Nationalists' savage repression during the **Spanish Civil War**, between 1957 and 1965 he was the Director-General of Security and from 1965 to 1973 the Mayor of Madrid. Named Minister of the Interior (June 1973), he became Prime Minister after the assassination of **Carrero Blanco** in Dec 1973. Following **Franco**'s death, he was confirmed as the first Prime Minister of the monarchy. He resigned in July 1976, having proven too hardline to effect the transition to democracy.

Arias Sanchez, Oscar (1940–) Costa Rican politician. He was educated in the UK, then returned to Costa Rica, where he started a law practice. He entered politics, joining the left-wing National Liberation Party

(PLN) and eventually becoming its Secretary-General. Elected President of Costa Rica in 1986, on a neutralist platform, Arias Sanchez was the major author of a Central American Peace Agreement aimed at securing peace in the region, and particularly in Nicaragua.

Aristides (c.550–c.467BC) Athenian politician and general, whose reputation for fair dealing earned him the title 'the Just'. A respected general in the Graeco-**Persian Wars**, he held command at the Battles of **Marathon** (490BC), **Salamis** (480BC), and Plataea (479BC). His greatest achievement was the organization of the **Delian League** after the defeat of the Persians.

Aris Veloukhiotis ▷ **Klaras Athanasios**

Arius (c.250–336) Founder of **Arianism**. Born in Libya, he trained in Antioch, and became a presbyter in Alexandria. He claimed (c.319) that, in the doctrine of the Trinity, the Son was not co-equal or co-eternal with the Father, but only the first and highest of all finite beings, created out of nothing by an act of God's free will. He won some support, but was deposed and excommunicated in 321 by a synod of bishops at Alexandria. The subsequent controversy was fierce, so the Council of Nicaea was called in 325 to settle the issue. Out of this came the definition of the absolute unity of the divine essence, and the equality of the three persons of the Trinity. Arius was banished, but recalled in 334, and died in Constantinople. After his death the strife spread more widely abroad: the West was mainly orthodox, the East largely Arian or semi-Arian; but despite later revivals the doctrine was largely suppressed by the end of the 4c. ▷

Arlington, Henry Bennet, 1st Earl of (1618–85) English statesman. A member of the **Cabal** ministry under **Charles II**, and Secretary of State (1662–74), he was created Earl of Arlington in 1672. In 1674 he was impeached for embezzlement, and although cleared, resigned and became Lord Chamberlain. He negotiated the Triple Alliance against France (1668), and helped to develop the English party system.

Armada, Spanish A fleet of 130 Spanish ships, commanded by Medina Sidonia, carrying 20 000 soldiers and 8 500 sailors, sent by **Philip II** of Spain to invade England in 1588. The invasion was in retaliation for English support of Protestant rebels in the Netherlands, the execution of **Mary, Queen of Scots** (1587), and raids on Spanish shipping, such as **Drake**'s at Cadiz (1587); Philip's aim was to gain control of the English Channel. The fleet, hampered by orders to rendezvous with Spanish forces in the Netherlands, was routed by English attacks off Gravelines (28–9 July 1588); 44 ships were lost in battles and during the flight home around Scotland and Ireland. Although a victory for the English, counter-armadas were unsuccessful, and the war lasted until 1604. ▷ **Elizabeth I**

Armand, Inessa (1875–1920) Russian politician. One of the most active women **Bolsheviks**, she was a champion of Soviet women's causes. Born in Paris where her French father lived, she was brought up in Russia by a rich family after her parents died. Her intellectual interests and travels brought her into contact with **Lenin** and she joined his party in 1905. She was twice exiled, but she returned to Russia in 1917, and in 1919 became the founding head of *zhenotdel*, the women's section of the Communist Party. She set to, organizing branches everywhere, but died shortly thereafter of overwork and cholera. Zhenotdel, however, continued at least until 1930.

Armenia, Independence of (1991) One of the 14 non-Russian Republics that gained their independence with the disintegration of the USSR. The Armenians had a history going back to the Roman period and including years of relative independence. Those who were not retained under Turkish control were taken over by the Russians in 1828. Christians, galvanized by earlier Turkish massacres and encouraged by **Lenin**, they declared their independence in 1918; however, they lost it again on his orders in 1920 for allegedly consorting with Soviet enemies. In 1991 they emerged not only with a distaste for Russia, but in an armed dispute with **Azerbaijan** over the Armenian enclave trapped across the border in the autonomous region that **Stalin** had set up in Nagorno-Karabakh.

Armenian Massacres (19–20c) These killings resulted from the persecution of Armenians in the **Ottoman Empire** by Sultan **Abd ul-Hamid II** in 1894–6 and by the Young Turk government in 1915. By the late 1880s there were, in the Ottoman Empire, two and a half million Armenians who, encouraged by Russia, sought autonomy. When they refused to pay vastly increased taxes in 1894, Turkish troops killed thousands and burnt their villages. Two years later, Armenians seized the Ottoman Bank in Istanbul to draw European attention to their plight: this sparked off riots in which over 50 000 Armenians were killed. In **World War I** the secret recruitment of Turkish Armenians to fight on the side of Russia led the Turkish government to deport the Armenian population to Syria and Palestine, during which a million died of starvation or were killed.

Armenians A people who came from Armenia, now north-east Turkey and the Armenian Soviet Socialist Republic. Of Indo-European origin, they speak a language of that family with some Caucasian features, and are Christians, affiliated to the Armenian Catholic branch of the Roman Catholic Church, or the Monophysite Armenian Apostolic (Orthodox) Church. Their highly developed ancient culture, particularly in fine art, architecture, and sculpture, reached its zenith in the 14c. Highly nationalistic, their resentment of foreign domination during the 19c provoked their Russian and Turkish rulers. During **World War I**, the Turks deported two-thirds of Armenians (1.75 million) to Syria and Palestine; 600 000 were either killed or died of starvation during the journey; later, many settled in Europe, the USA and the USSR.

Armfelt, Gustaf Mauritz (1757–1814) Swedish soldier and politician. Born in Finland, he was a favourite of King **Gustav III** towards the end of his reign. He fought in Gustav's war against Russia (1788–90) and helped to negotiate the Peace of Värälä. Armfelt was a member of the regency council during the minority of **Gustav IV Adolf** and was Swedish ambassador in Vienna in 1802–4. He commanded the Swedish army against **Napoleon I** in Pomerania. After the deposition of Gustav IV Adolf in 1809, Armfelt was exiled by his successor, **Charles XIII**, and entered Russian service. He became Governor-General of Finland, now a grand duchy under the Russian tsar.

Arminius (c.18BC–AD19) Chief of the German Cherusci. He ambushed three Roman legions in the **Teutoburg Forest**, probably near Detmold, in AD9, and thus inflicted on the Romans one of their worst defeats. It was called the 'Varian' disaster, after the defeated Roman commander, Publius Quinctilius **Varus**.

Army, (British) Indian (1748–1947) British-controlled and officered military

force in India in which the rank and file were recruited from the native populace, although some purely European regiments existed until 1860. The Indian Army served abroad as well as in India, and was a mainstay of the Pax Britannica. It was originally formed from guards used to protect properties of the British **East India Company** and Indian soldiers known as sepoys. In 1748 the growing French presence in Madras and continuing bad relations between France and Britain caused the Company to organize a permanent military force in India. Until 1759, when the size and organization of units were standardized, the armies of the Bengal, Bombay and Madras presidencies developed entirely independently, and expanded at different rates. By 1796, when two-battalion native infantry regiments were instituted, Bengal had 12, Madras 11, and Bombay 6. Bengal and Madras also had cavalry regiments, although these were less strictly regulated and sometimes amounted to elite private units raised and commanded by enthusiastic Company officials. The growth of the military reflecting the Company's increased territorial acquisitions and responsibility for what had been Mughal administration. For all its size, the Indian Army in the first half of the 19c was inefficient and amateur; defects became apparent especially amongst the exclusively European officer cadre. Following the mutiny of the Bengal army and the **Indian Uprising** of 1857–8, the East India Company was dissolved and the Indian Army became the property of the Crown; by 1861 European regiments had been transferred to the British Army. The main functions of the Army between 1858 and 1914 were guarding the North-West Frontier and maintenance of order, although it was designed to be used in emergencies between Suez and Hong Kong. In 1895, the armies of the three Presidencies were amalgamated into one British Indian Army. In 1903 Lord Kitchener administratively combined the Staff and Troops, and renamed the force the Indian Army. Because of their performance during **World War I** and the changing political climate, Indians became eligible for the King's Commission in 1917. In 1922 the army was again reorganized and 'Indianization' of the officer corps was accelerated. By 1924 there were 8 wholly Indian units and in 1934 an Indian Military Academy for the training of officers was opened at Dehra Dun. In **World War II** units of the Indian Army were employed throughout the world in the Allied cause, although the bulk of the force fought in

Burma and remained in India to maintain order. With Indian independence in 1947, the British Indian Army ceased to exist, its resources having been divided equally between India and Pakistan. ▷ **British India**

Arnarson, Ingólfur (late 9c) Norwegian Viking. From Hördaland in south-western Norway, he is honoured as the first settler of Iceland in AD874. According to early historical traditions in *Landnámabók*, the Icelandic 'Book of Settlements', he left Norway after some local disputes and settled with his family and friends on a farm he named Reykjavík ('Steamy Bay') because of its hotsprings, and which later became the country's capital. His descendants held the hereditary and honorary post of supreme chieftain (*alsherjargoði*) of the Icelandic parliament (**Althing**) after its foundation in 930.

Arnhem, Battle of (Sep 1944) Major confict in occupied Dutch territory towards the end of **World War II**, in which the German forces thwarted Allied attempts to break through. Operation 'Market Garden' was designed by Field Marshal **Montgomery**, and involved the largest airlift operation of the war, parachuting 10 000 troops on 17 Sep 1944 into the Dutch rivers area, to take key bridges over the Rhine, Maas and Waal. Allied forces advanced to Nijmegen, but at Arnhem met the 9th and 10th German Panzer divisions, which successfully resisted attack and eventually forced an Allied withdrawal on 25 Sep to behind the Rhine River.

Arnim, Hans Georg von (1581–1641) German soldier and diplomat. Born in Brandenburg, he joined the Swedish army and served in the war with Russia (1613–17). However, after falling out with **Gustav II Adolf**, he transferred to Poland to fight Sweden in 1621. Although a Protestant, he next entered the service of the emperor in 1626 and soon rose to be the right hand of **Wallenstein**. However when, in 1629, the edict of restitution was passed, Arnim resigned; he devoted himself to the formation of a third force in the raging conflict, decidedly Protestant but ready for compromise and with a view to maintaining the unity of the Reich against all foreign interventions. He took command of the Saxon army and advocated an alliance with Sweden (1631), but stayed in close contact with Wallenstein all the same. The latter's fall destroyed what slim chances of success there were for his scheme. Lacking full support from his master, the Elector of Saxony, and

distrusted by both the Emperor and Sweden, Arnim retired in 1635.

Arnold of Brescia (c.1100–55) Italian churchman and politician. Born at Brescia, he was possibly educated in France under Abelard. He adopted the monastic life, but his preaching against the wealth and power of the Church led to his banishment from Italy (1139). He returned to Rome in 1145 and became involved in an insurrection against the papal government, which continued for some 10 years. When this movement failed, he fled, but was captured by the forces of Emperor **Frederick I, 'Barbarossa'**, brought to Rome, condemned for heresy, and hanged.

Arnold, Benedict (1741–1801) US general and turncoat. In the **American Revolution** he joined the colonial forces, and for his gallantry at the siege of Quebec (1775) was made a brigadier-general. He also fought with distinction at the Battles of Ridgefield and **Saratoga**, and in 1778 was placed in command of Philadelphia. His resentment at being passed over for promotion, followed by his marriage to a woman of loyalist sympathies, led him to conspire with John André to deliver West Point to the British. When the plan was detected and André was captured, Arnold fled behind British lines, and was given a command in the royal army. After the war he lived in obscurity in London, where he died.

Arnulf (d.937) Duke of Bavaria. Son of Count Liutpold, Arnulf succeeded his father to the Dukedom of Bavaria in 907, defended it successfully against the Hungarians and secured his domestic position by ruthlessly seizing church land, in spite of the opposition of **Conrad I** of Germany and the Bavarian bishops. In 919 he was chosen as a candidate for the kingship but was defeated by Conrad's candidate, **Henry I, 'the Fowler'**. He submitted to Henry and was granted a free hand in his own territories. After his death, Bavaria once more came under the control of the crown.

Árpád (d.c.907) National hero of Hungary. A Magyar chieftain in the Caucusus, he led the Magyars from the Black Sea into the Valley of the Danube after defeat by the Pechenigs (c.896) and occupied modern Hungary. He founded the Árpád Dynasty of Hungary, from St Stephen (997) to 1301 under whom the Magyars first gained a footing in that country about 884.

Arras, Union of (6 Jan 1579) During the **Eighty Years War** the southern Netherlands principalities of Artois, Hainaut and Douai formed the union with the intention of returning to the Catholic rule of **Philip II** of Spain. Later the same month, on 23 Jan, the other Netherlands provinces formed the Union of **Utrecht** in opposition. Together with other French-speaking southern provinces in the Netherlands, the members of the Union of Arras signed a treaty (17 May 1579) which contributed to the final separation of the southern from the northern Netherlands, and therefore to the eventual independence of the Dutch Republic.

Arriaga, Manoel José de (1840–1917) Portuguese politician. He took part in the revolution of 1910 which overthrew King **Manuel II**, and was the first elected President of the Republic (1911–15).

Arrow Cross (1938–45) Hungarian right-wing fascist-type party. Like similar parties in other East European countries, it emerged from a combination of nationalist dissatisfaction, anti-**communism** and anti-Semitism that was rooted in the failure of successive Hungarian governments to reverse the defeat marked by the Treaty of **Trianon** in 1920 or to overcome the 1929 depression. These feelings were strengthened by the successes of **Mussolini** and **Hitler**, and leaders were found in malcontents such as **Szalasi**, a former officer who became Prime Minister in 1944.

Arrow War (Second Opium War) (1856–60) A conflict between Britain and China, which began when the Hong Kong-registered ship *Arrow*, flying the British flag, was boarded at Canton (Guangzhou) by the Chinese, who arrested most of the crew for piracy. British warships and troops then attacked Canton and were initially repulsed, but a combined British and French force took it the following year, and proceeded north, threatening Beijing. The Treaty of **Tianjin** (Tientsin) that concluded hostilities opened additional **treaty ports** to foreign trade, legalized the opium traffic, and facilitated Christian missionary activity. ▷ **Opium Wars**

Arsacids A dynasty of Parthian kings, so called from the founder, Arsaces, who wrested a kingdom for himself from the grasp of the Seleucid Antiochus II, c.250BC. This ultimately extended from Bactria to the Euphrates, and included Persia. Its greatest kings were Mithridates, Phraates, Mithridates 'the Great', and Artabanus, who fell

at Hormizdján in AD226 attempting to stem the conquering career of **Artaxerxes I** (Ardashir), founder of the Sassanian Dynasty of Persia.

Arsenije III Črnojević (Arsen III) (1633–1706) Serbian Patriarch of Peć. During the Vienna War (1684–99) he met General Piccolomini at Prizren in southern **Kosovo** and arranged for c.20 000 Serbs and Albanians from Ottoman territory to enter the service of Emperor Leopold I. In 1690 he led 70 000–80 000 Serbs into southern Hungary and established a religious and cultural centre for the Serbs at Sremski Karlovci in the **Vojvodina**. During the 19c the descendants of these migrants, known as the *prečani* ('across-the-river') Serbs, were to play an important role in the Serbian national revival.

Artaxerxes I (Ardashir) (c.211–42) King of Persia (224/42). He was the destroyer of the Arsacid Dynasty of Parthia, and founder of the new Persian **Sassanid Dynasty**. A vigorous ruler, his expansionist policies brought him twice into conflict with Rome (230–2 and 238). ▷ **Parthians**

Artaxerxes I, Longimanus ('the Long-handed') (5c BC) King of Persia (464/425BC). The second son of **Xerxes I**, in a long and peaceful reign, he sanctioned Jewish religion in Jerusalem, and appointed Nehemiah Governor of Judea (445BC).

Artaxerxes II, Mnemon ('the Mindful') (4c BC) King of Persia (404/358BC). He lost control of Egypt, but rebuilt the royal palace at Susa.

Artaxerxes III, Ochus King of Persia (358/338BC). The son of **Artaxerxes II, Mnemon**, he found the empire disintegrating on his accession, but did much to build it up again. He was poisoned in 338BC by his favourite eunuch, Bagoas.

Artevelde, Jacob van (c.1290–1345) Flemish statesman. A burgess of Ghent, he led his town in a revolt against the pro-French policies of Count **Louis of Nevers**. Thus he sided with England at the beginning of the **Hundred Years War**. He concluded a treaty with **Edward III** (1340), and was effectively Governor of Flanders, but when he proposed that the Black Prince should be elected Count of Flanders, he was killed in a popular insurrection.

Artevelde, Philip van (1340–82) Flemish leader. He was taken to England when his father, Jacob van **Artevelde**, was murdered in 1345. He returned in 1360, and in 1382 led the people of Ghent in their uprising against Count Louis II of Flanders. Against all odds Van Artevelde won the Battle of Beverhoutsveld (May 1382), but lost to Count Louis and his French allies at the Battle of Westrozebeke (Nov 1382), where he perished.

Arthashastra Ancient Indian text on statecraft in Sanskrit ascribed to Kautilya and reaching its present form around 2c AD The majority of the text is devoted to explaining how a king, desirous of increasing his power and expanding his domain, should rule his kingdom. There are also sections dealing with society, politics, management of agriculture and natural resources and technology as well as other related topics.

Arthur (?6c) A probably legendary king of the Britons. He is represented as the unifier of the British tribes against the pagan invaders (5–6c AD), and as the champion of Christianity. It is very doubtful that he actually lived: he is claimed alike as a prince in Brittany, Cornwall, Wales, Cumberland, and the Lowlands of Scotland. His story passed into literature and many legends became interwoven with it, including those of the Round Table and the Holy Grail (both from the 12c–13c). The stories were developed by French writers (notably Chrétien de Troyes), and Lancelot, Percival, and the Grail were added. Malory's English version, *Morte d'Arthur*, was the final medieval compilation from which most later retellings are derived.

Arthur (1187–1203) Claimant to the English throne. He was the posthumous son of Geoffrey (**Henry II**'s fourth son) by Constance, Duchess of Brittany. On the death of **Richard I** (1199), Arthur claimed the English crown; and the French King, **Philip II**, for a while supported his bid for the throne. However, King **John** had him captured and murdered.

Arthur, Chester Alan (1830–86) US politician and 21st President. He qualified in law, and then became leader of the **Republican Party** in New York State. He was Vice-President when James A **Garfield** became President (1881), and succeeded him on his death, holding the presidency from 1881 until 1885. During his administration he supported civil service and vetoed a Chinese exclusion bill.

Articles of Confederation The constitution of the USA from 1781 to 1788. Prepared by the **Continental Congress**, it established a single-house Congress, with one vote for each state and with no executive, courts, or independent revenue. Its weaknesses led to its replacement by the present **US Constitution** in 1788.

Artigas, José Gervasio (1774–1850) Spanish American soldier and revolutionary hero of Uruguay. A **gaucho** in his youth, and then army officer in Spanish service, he sided with Buenos Aires against Spain in 1811, and fought Buenos Aires in 1813–14, and the Portuguese between 1817 and 1820. Unable to hold the littoral, Artigas fled to **Francia**'s Paraguay (1920), where he lived in exile until his death. Uruguay finally became independent on 27 Aug 1828. ▷ **Spanish–American Wars of Independence**

Artyukhina, Alexandra Vasilevna (1889–1969) Soviet politician. An early champion of Soviet women's rights, she failed in the face of traditional male chauvinism. A textile worker, she was active in the union movement in the pre-revolutionary period and was arrested several times. She held various government jobs after the **Russian Revolution**, but in 1927 she was appointed head of *zhenotdel*, the women's section of the **Communist Party of the Soviet Union**. In this she did much good work until it was shut down in 1930. Thereafter, her jobs were more honorific than real, but at least she survived **Stalin**.

Arunchalam, Ponnambalam (1853–1924) Ceylonese civil servant and politician. He was the first Tamil to gain a place in the Ceylonese Civil Service through open competition, eventually rising to be Registrar-General of Ceylon. He later entered politics and ardently championed the cause of the Ceylon National Congress. He eventually left the Ceylonese National Congress owing to his disillusionment at the lack of Tamil representation in the Legislative Council provided for by the 1924 constitution.

Arundel, Thomas (1353–1414) English prelate and statesman, third son of Robert Fitzalan, Earl of Arundel. He became Archdeacon of Taunton and Bishop of Ely (1373), then Archbishop of York (1388), and finally of Canterbury (1396). He supported the nobles opposed to **Richard II**, who banished him (1397), but he returned to help seat Henry of Lancaster on the throne (1399). He was a vigorous opponent of the **Lollards**.

Arusha Declaration (29 Jan 1967) Although strictly only Part IV, the Arusha Declaration usually refers to all of an important document, written under President Julius **Nyerere**'s direction and accepted by **Tanganyika African National Union** (TANU)'s National Executive Committee in Arusha on 29 Jan 1967. It set out the assumptions underlying Tanzania's version of African Socialism, emphasizing the dignity and equality of people, the primacy of rural production, self-reliance, the importance of hard work and the role of the party. Later documents ('Education for Self-Reliance', 'Socialism and Rural Development' and 'After the Arusha Declaration') developed Nyerere's ideas of creating a uniquely African and egalitarian socialism in Africa, but it proved economically disastrous although, for the most part, politically popular.

Aryabhata (c.6c) Indian astronomer and mathematician. He made numerous corrections to the earlier basic astronomical text, the *Suryasiddhanta*. Aryabhata demonstrated a clear understanding of the Earth's rotation centuries before Copernicus or Galileo. In his 121-verse *Aryabhatiya* he expostulated on astronomy, arithmetic, geometry, algebra, trigonometry, methods to determine the positions of the planets and descriptions of their movement, and a method to calculate the movements of the sun and moon and predict their eclipses. In his honour, India's first geosynchronous satellite was named Aryabhata.

Aryan A prehistoric people and their language, an extinct member of the Indo-European language family. Aryans reputedly colonized Iran and northern India, and gave rise to the Indian subcontinent's Indo-Aryan languages. Nazi Germany embraced unscientific notions of Germanic peoples as the purest members of an Aryan race of Indo-European-speaking peoples responsible for human progress. ▷ **Nazi Party**

Arya Samaj A dogmatic and militant Hindu sect (literally, 'Society of Nobles') founded c.1875 by Dyananda Sarasawati (1824–83). The latter demanded a return to the purity of the *Rig Veda* and its principles, as opposed to the accretions and corruptions that subsequently entered Hinduism. Many militant nationalists in the north-west of India, such as Lala **Lajpat Rai**, belonged to this sect.

Asad, Hafez al- (1928–) Syrian general and politician. He was Minister of Defence and Commander of the Air Force (1966–70), instigated a coup in 1970 and became Prime Minister and then President (1971–). He belongs to the minority **Alawi** sect of Islam. After the 1973 Arab–Israeli War, he negotiated a partial withdrawal of Israeli troops from Syria. In 1976 he sent Syrian troops into Lebanon, and did so again in early 1987. By 1989 he had imposed Syrian control over the greater part of Lebanon. He has long enjoyed Soviet support, and was one of the few Arab leaders to support Iran in its war with Iraq. He also supports the Palestinian radicals against **Arafat**'s mainstream **PLO** (Palestine Liberation Organization). ▷ **Iran–Iraq War**

Asaf ud-Daula (1775/97) Nawab of Awadh (Oudh) during the governor-generalship of Warren **Hastings**. During his reign, Awadh was a Mughal buffer against the rising power of the British in Bengal. While Hastings was Governor of Bengal, his administrative council imposed the Treaty of Faizabad, also known as the Second Treaty of Benares (1775), on Asaf, increasing the subsidy he paid for the British military presence in Awadh, and ceding the sovereignty of Benares, Jaunpur and Ghazipur to the British **East India Company**. With the Treaty of Chunar (1781), Hastings attempted to interfere with the administration of Awadh. Hastings' part in the resumption of jagirs and removal of the treasures of Awadh formed a large part of the charges brought against him at his subsequent impeachment.

Asanuma Inejiro (1898–1960) Japanese politician. Initially he was a member of the **Japan Communist Party** and in 1924 was imprisoned for participating in anti-government demonstrations. In 1936 he was elected to the Diet as a member of the Social Masses Party (*Shakai Taishuto*), one of many pre-**World War II** socialist parties. After 1945 he helped found the **Japan Socialist Party**, becoming its Secretary-General. He acquired notoriety in 1959 on a visit to Beijing when he declared that US imperialism was the common enemy of China and Japan. In 1960 he was assassinated by a right-wing fanatic while attending a televised political rally.

Asen Dynasty The dynasty which ruled Bulgaria from 1187 to 1257. John (Ivan) Asen I (1187/96), with his brother Peter led the rebellion which freed Bulgaria from Byzantine suzerainty (c.1185). John then founded the second Bulgarian Empire and established his throne at Trnovo. John II (1190–1241) ruled from 1218 until his death. He renewed the Bulgarian patriarchate (1235), thereby securing the independence of the Bulgarian Church. ▷ **Bulgarian Exarchate**

Ashanti (Asante) A Kwa-speaking Akan people of southern Ghana and adjacent areas of Togo and Ivory Coast. They form a confederacy of chiefdoms, founded by the ruler Osei Tutu in the late 17c; the paramount chief was established at Kumasi, and the Golden Stool was the symbol of Ashanti unity. The independent Ashanti state was at the height of its powers in the early 19c, and became a major threat to British trade on the coast, until defeated (1873) by a force under Sir Garnet **Wolseley**. The state was annexed by the British in 1902 after a further campaign in which the Golden Stool was seized and removed to London. Traditional culture and religion still flourish, with rich ceremonial and internationally famous art.

Ashdown, Jeremy John Durham (Paddy) (1941–) British politician. After a career in the Royal Marines (1959–71) and the diplomatic service (1971–6) he entered politics, becoming Liberal MP for Yeovil (1983). He was Liberal spokesman on trade and industry (1983–6) and succeeded David **Steel** as leader of the Social and Liberal Democrats (1988). ▷ **Liberal Party** (UK)

Ashida Hitoshi (1887–1959) Japanese politician. Formerly a Finance Ministry bureaucrat, he was first elected to the Diet in 1932. In the first post-**World War II** cabinet (Oct 1945) he was Minister of Health and Welfare. In 1947 he helped to organize the Democratic Party (*Nihon Minshuto*), one of the two principal conservative parties at the time. In June 1947 he joined a coalition cabinet headed by the socialist **Katayama** Tetsu and became Prime Minister when the coalition collapsed (Mar 1948). Ashida was a vigorous advocate of Japanese rearmament. In Oct 1948 he was forced to resign following alleged involvement in the Showa Denko Scandal.

Ashikaga Shogunate (1338–1573) In Japan, the second shogunal government, located in the vicinity of the imperial capital of Kyoto. The Ashikaga family, from central Honshu, was an offshoot of the **Minamoto Family**, founders of the first shogunate. There were altogether 15 Ashikaga shoguns. Under the third shogun, Yoshimitsu (1369/95), the imperial schism, originally caused by **Daigo II**'s exile and establishment of a rival imperial

ASHIKAGA SHOGUNATE

Regnal Dates	Name
1338/58	Ashikaga Takauji
1358/67	Ashikaga Yoshiakira
1368/94	Ashikaga Yoshimitsu
1394/1423	Ashikaga Yoshimochi
1423/5	Ashikaga Yoshikazu
1429/41	Ashikaga Yoshinori
1442/3	Ashikaga Yoshikatsu
1449/73	Ashikaga Yoshimasa
1473/89	Ashikaga Yoshihisa
1490/3	Ashikaga Yoshitane (1st reign)
1494/1508	Ashikaga Yoshizumi
1508/21	Ashikaga Yoshitane (2nd reign)
1521/46	Ashikaga Yoshiharu
1546/65	Ashikaga Yoshiteru
1568	Ashikaga Yoshihide
1568/73	Ashikaga Yoshiaki

court south of Kyoto, was ended when the two rival branches of the imperial family were united in 1392. During the 15c, however, increasingly powerful military governments undermined its control, leading to a series of bloody wars, with the result that the last Ashikaga shoguns became virtual puppets of their leading vassals.

Ashikaga Takauji (1305–58) Japanese warrior leader. He was the founder of the second shogunal government, the **Ashikaga** (or Muromachi) **Shogunate**. Originally sent by the previous **Kamakura Shogunate** to quell forces loyal to Emperor **Daigo II**, who had been exiled (1324) for attempting to assert direct imperial rule, Takauji turned against his former masters and allowed Daigo II to return. Yet in 1336 he himself forced the exile of Daigo II and installed a rival claimant on the throne, who conferred on Takauji the title of **shogun** in 1338. For his betrayal of the Emperor, Takauji is condemned in Japanese historiography.

Ashoka (3c BC) Third ruler of the Mauryan Dynasty in north India (c.269/232 BC). The conqueror of **Kalinga**, he is noted for the many edicts he had engraved on rocks and pillars detailing his policies of rule by *dharma* (broadly, moral responsibility), in which he was influenced by his personal conversion to Buddhism around the time of the Kalinga War.

Ashurbanipal ▷ **Assurbanipal**

asiento de negros Literally 'negro (slave) contract', this was the means whereby the

61

Spanish Crown farmed out the slave trade between Spain, Africa, and the Spanish American empire. The contractors were usually non-Spaniards: originally Genoese, from 1595 to 1640 they were Portuguese; from 1702 to 1713, French; and, from the Treaties of **Utrecht** in 1713 until 1750, British. ▷ **slavery**

Askiya The dynastic title of the rulers of **Songhai**, founded by *Sunni* Ali (1464/92) out of the disintegrating empire of Mali in Western Africa. The first *askiya*, Muhammad Toure (d.1528), deposed Sunni Ali's successor c.1500 and extended the empire into Easter Mali and the upper Volta basin. He also re-established Timbuktu as a centre of Islamic faith and learning. He was deposed by his son in 1528 and Songhai went into decline. The empire dissolved altogether in 1591, when it was invaded by a Moroccan army, but descendants of the Songhai askiyas continued to fight on against their Moroccan rulers well into the 17c.

Aspromonte, Battle of (Sep 1862) Frustrated by the reluctance of the Italian government to seize Rome, **Garibaldi** sought to take the city with a group of volunteers he had mustered in Sicily. **Rattazzi**, who hitherto had not opposed Garibaldi's plans openly, feared **Red Shirts** would clash with the French garrison in Rome and sent regular troops to prevent their northward advance. The two forces met at Aspromonte, where a skirmish took place in which Garibaldi was wounded and captured. He was briefly held under arrest at La Spezia before receiving a royal amnesty.

Asquith, H(erbert) H(enry), 1st Earl of Oxford and Asquith (1852–1928) British Liberal politician and Prime Minister. He was called to the Bar (1876), and became a QC (1890) and MP (1886), Home Secretary (1892–5), Chancellor of the Exchequer (1905–8), and Premier (1908–16). His regime was notable for the upholding of free trade, the introduction of old-age pensions, payment for MPs, the Parliament Act of 1911, Welsh disestablishment, suffragette troubles, the declaration of war (1914), the coalition ministry (1915), and the **Sinn Féin** rebellion (1916). His replacement as Premier by Lloyd George provoked lasting bitterness; in 1918 he led the Independent Liberals who rejected Lloyd George's continuing coalition with the Conservatives. He was created an earl in 1925. ▷ **Liberal Party** (UK); **suffragettes**

Assassins An Ismaili Shiite grouping. An offshoot of the **Fatimid Dynasty** of Cairo, the sect was founded by an Isma'ili *da'i* (missionary) called Hasan-i Sabbah in the late 11c in northern Persia. The name 'Assassins' is thought to have derived from their use of hashish, designed to give them the courage to carry out the attacks they believed their faith demanded as a duty. The sect's headquarters was at the virtually impregnable castle of Alamut in the Elburz Mountains in Iran, from where they achieved their ends by using murder (or assassination) as a political weapon. The sect spread also to Syria, where it was based in the Ansariyya Mountains and caused considerable problems for the Crusaders and for **Saladin**. As a sect, it was finally dissolved by the **Mongols** in the mid-13c. The Nizaris, with whom the sect was linked, still exist as a sevener Shiite sect to this day, with the Aga Khan as their leader.

Assemblies A unique feature of the 'Old Representative System' which existed in the pre-19c British West Indies colonies. When the previous proprietary system of government was abolished in 1663, real legislative and financial power quickly devolved on to a forum of the unrepresentative, rich plantocracy, whose wealth made London's responsibility for the administration somewhat illusory. Aping the powers and prerogatives of the House of Commons in England, the Assemblies resisted progressive legislation and imperial edict and countered all attempts to abolish them. So obstructive, oligarchic, self-interested and obscurantist had the Assemblies become, that when Britain took over Trinidad, Berbice-Essequibo and St Lucia after the **Napoleonic Wars**, they were incorporated into the empire under **Crown Colony Government**. Jamaica gave up its assembly after the **Morant Bay Rebellion** (1866), but Barbados maintained an assembly until 1966.

Assietta, Battle of (19 July 1747) Famous Piedmontese victory in the War of **Austrian Succession** in which the troops of **Charles Emmanuel III** halted the advance on Turin of a Franco-Spanish army.

assignats Originally, paper bonds issued by the Constituent Assembly in France (1789). They were later (1790) accepted as currency notes, in view of the shortage of coin, until the abolition of paper currency in 1797. ▷ **French Revolution**

Assize Court A legal system in England and Wales, dating from the time of **Henry II** of

England, which was abolished by the Courts Act, 1971. Assize courts were presided over by High Court judges, who travelled on circuit to hear criminal and civil cases. The functions of Assize courts continue to be exercised by High Court judges sitting in Crown Courts throughout England and Wales.

Association of German Princes An association of 17 important German states organized by **Frederick II, 'the Great'** of Prussia. They agreed to uphold Imperial law and to defend one another's territory. It was designed to thwart the centralizing plans of Emperor **Joseph II** for the **Holy Roman Empire**. The association collapsed after Frederick's death (1786).

Association of South-East Asian Nations (ASEAN) An association formed in 1967 to promote economic cooperation between Indonesia, Malaysia, the Philippines, Singapore, and Thailand; Brunei joined in 1984. It has become an important political force, particularly with respect to the Vietnamese incursion into Cambodia in 1978.

Assurbanipal (Ashurbanipal) (7c BC) King of Assyria (668/627BC). The last of the great Assyrian kings, he was the son of Esarhaddon and grandson of Sennacherib. A patron of the arts, he founded the first systematically gathered and organized library in the ancient Middle East.

Assyria The name given first to the small area around the town of Assur on the Tigris in Upper Mesopotamia, and then much later to the vast empire that the rulers of Assur acquired through conquering their neighbours on all sides. At its height in the 9c and 8c BC, the Assyrian Empire stretched from the eastern Mediterranean to Iran, and from the Persian Gulf as far north as the mountains of eastern Turkey. The Empire was destroyed in an uprising of Medes and Babylonians in 612BC.

Astor, John Jacob (1763–1848) German-born US millionaire. The son of a butcher, he emigrated to the USA in 1783 and eventually became the wealthiest man in America, worth more than US$20m at his death. His first fortune was made through the Western fur trade, the second in New York real estate. Astor used his friendship with **Jefferson** to advantage, in one instance gaining permission for one of his ships to sail to Canton during the 1807 embargo. Astor helped the government finance the **War of 1812** by taking over and selling to the public the unsubscribed portion of a government loan. He also used his influence to ease through **Congress** the Act establishing the Second Bank of United States. His major philanthropy was the endowment of the Astor Library, now the New York Public Library.

Astor, Nancy Witcher Langhorne, Viscountess (1879–1964) British politician. The first woman MP to sit in the House of Commons (1919–45), she succeeded her husband as MP for Plymouth in 1919, and became known for her interest in women's rights and social problems, especially temperance.

Astrid (1905–35) Queen of the Belgians (1934/5). The daughter of Prince Charles of Sweden and Princess Ingeborg of Denmark, on 4 Nov 1926 she married **Leopold III**, Crown Prince of Belgium, who succeeded to the throne on 23 Feb 1934, with Astrid as Queen. The mother of three children, Josephine-Charlotte, **Baudouin I** (later king), and Albert, she was killed in a car accident near Küssnacht in Switzerland.

Asturias, Principality of A former principality of northern Spain, co-extensive with the modern province of Oviedo. It was the centre of Christian resistance to Muslim invasion during the 8–9c and became part of the Kingdom of Leon in 911. In the 20c it was the scene of an unsuccessful left-wing revolution in 1934.

Atahualpa (d.1533) Last King of the Incas (1527/33). On his father's death (1527), he received the Kingdom of Quito, and in 1532, overwhelming his elder brother Huascar, seized Peru. At times overconfident of his strength, at others apprehensive of the Spaniards, his vacillations encouraged initial Spanish penetration and subsequent control. He was captured by the Spaniards, accused of plotting against **Pizarro**, and executed.

Atatürk, Kemal (Mustafa Kemal) (1881–1938) Turkish army officer and politician. During **World War I** he fought against the British in the Dardanelles and earned the title *pasha*. He drove the **Greeks** from Anatolia (1919–22), raising a nationalist rebellion in protest against the post-war division of Turkey. In 1921 he established a provisional government in Ankara. The following year the Ottoman Sultanate was formally abolished, and Turkey was declared a secular republic, with Kemal as President (1923–38). The focus of a strong personality cult, he launched a programme of revolutionary social and political reform intended to transform Turkey from a feudal absolute monarchy into a modern republic. His reforms included the political emancipation of women (1934) and the introduction of the Latin alphabet to replace Arabic script, as well as increased educational opportunities and the suppression of traditional Islamic loyalties in favour of a secular Turkish nationalism. In 1934, upon the introduction of surnames into Turkey, he took the name Atatürk ('Father of the Turks'). ▷ **Graeco-Turkish War; Lausanne, Treaty of**

Athelstan (c.895–939) King of England (927/39). The son of **Edward the Elder**, and the grandson of **Alfred, 'the Great'**, he was elected King of **Wessex** and Mercia on his father's death in 924. He built upon his predecessors' achievements by invading **Northumbria**, securing his direct rule over it, and thus establishing himself as effectively the first King of all England (927). He stabilized his position by defeating a powerful coalition of enemies at Brunanburh (location unknown) in 937. ▷ **Anglo-Saxons**

Athenian Empire The name used for the 5c BC Athenian naval hegemony in the Aegean after the **Delian League** treasury was moved from Delos to Athens (c.454BC), and warfare against Persia, the original purpose of the League, ceased. By 431BC all cities contributed tribute in coin to fund the Athenian fleet, except the islands of Lesbos and Chios, which still retained their own ships. Although the cities in the hegemony were internally self-governing, they were subjected to increasing interference by Athenian officials. Some cities, particularly after attempted revolts, had political constitutions imposed, garrisons installed, or Athenians settled on their land in 'cleruchies'. Revolts were unsuccessful unless backed by **Sparta**; encouraging revolt became a primary Spartan strategy towards the end of the **Peloponnesian War**. The empire was dissolved on Athens's defeat in 404BC. ▷ **Thucydides**

Athos, Mount The site of a complex of 20 Orthodox monasteries on the easternmost peninsula of Chalcidice in Greece. The first monastic community was established c.963 and it reached the peak of its influence in the 15c and later maintained good relations with the Ottoman **Porte, Selim I, 'the Grim'**, making a state visit. During the **Greek War of Independence** it joined the Greek insurgents but was defeated. Russian influence dominated in the period after the Treaty of **Adrianople** (1829). During the first of the **Balkan Wars** it was occupied by Greek troops and was declared independent and neutral by the Treaties of **London** (1913). In 1926 it became a theocratic republic under the suzerainty of Greece. As well as the Greek, the Russian, Bulgarian, Serbian and Romanian Orthodox Churches have communities on the mountain. ▷ **Constantinople, Patriarchate of; Sava, St**

Atjeh War (1873–1914) Dutch colonial war fought between the Dutch East Indies (now Indonesia) and the inhabitants of Atjeh, the northernmost part of the island of Sumatra. In order to limit the activities of the pirates, the Dutch sent a series of military expeditions against Atjeh which until 1900 proved unsuccessful and sometimes disastrous. The campaigns intensified as the imperialist movement meant that investment opportunities were sought in oil, mines and plantations; under Governor-General J B van Heutsz (1851–1924) resistance was finally broken by 1912, not without reports of extreme atrocities. The Dutch then installed a full-scale civil administration in Atjeh. The war is estimated to have cost more than 100 000 lives, nearly all Indonesian.

Atlantic, Battle of the (1940–3) The conflict arising out of German attacks on shipping in the Atlantic during **World War II**. The German strategy was to cut off Britain's supplies of food and munitions by submarine action. Only at the end of 1943 were the attacks countered, and the threat brought under control.

Atlantic Charter (Aug 1941) A declaration of principles to govern the national policies issued by US President Franklin D **Roosevelt** and British Prime Minister Winston **Churchill** after a secret meeting off the Newfoundland coast. Echoing Woodrow **Wilson**'s **Fourteen Points**, and the **Four Freedoms** of Roosevelt's Jan 1941 State of the Union Address, the charter called for the rights of self-determination, self-government and free speech for all peoples, promised a more equitable international economic system, and called for the abandonment of the use of force, pending the establishment of a system of general security. After the entry of the USA into the war, the charter was endorsed internationally by the inclusion of its provisions in the Declaration of the United

Nations signed by the USA, Great Britain, the USSR and China, on 1 Jan 1942, and by 22 other states on the following day. It served as an ideological basis for Allied cooperation during the war. ▷ **World War II**

Attalids The Hellenistic dynasty that ruled over large parts of western Asia Minor from the 3c to the 1c BC. Keen patrons of the arts, they made their beautiful capital, Pergamum, one of the main cultural centres of the Graeco-Roman world.

Attila (c.406–53) Hunnish King (434/53). Called the 'Scourge of God', his dominion extended from the Rhine to the Caspian Sea. In 447 he devastated all the countries between the Black Sea and the Mediterranean, and defeated the Emperor **Theodosius I**. In 451 he invaded **Gaul**, but was defeated at the Battle of the **Catalaunian Plains** by a joint army of Romans and **Visigoths**. He then invaded Italy (452), sacking several cities, Rome itself being saved only by the personal mediation of Pope **Leo I**, who bought off Attila with large sums. The Hunnish Empire decayed after Attila's death. ▷ **Aëtius; Huns**

Attlee (of Walthamstow), Clement (Richard), 1st Earl (1883–1967) British politician. Early converted to **socialism**, he became the first Labour Mayor of Stepney (1919–20), an MP (1922), Deputy Leader of the Opposition (1931–5), and then Leader (1935). He was Dominions Secretary (1942–3) and Deputy Prime Minister (1942–5) in Winston **Churchill**'s war cabinet. As Prime Minister (1945–51), he carried through a vigorous programme of nationalization and social welfare, including the introduction of the National Health Service (1948). His government granted independence to India (1947) and Burma (1948). He was Leader of the Opposition again (1951–5) until he resigned and accepted an earldom.

Auchinleck, Sir Claude (John Eyre) (1884–1981) British field marshal. He joined the 62nd Punjabis in 1904, and served in Egypt and Mesopotamia. In **World War II**, he commanded in northern Norway and India, and then moved to the Middle East (1941). He made a successful advance into Cyrenaica, but was later thrown back by **Rommel**. His regrouping of the 8th Army on **El Alamein** is now recognized as a successful defensive operation, but at the time he was made a scapegoat for the retreat, and replaced (1942). In 1943 he returned to India,

serving subsequently as Supreme Commander India and Pakistan (1947). ▷ **North African Campaign**

audiencia A high court in each of the Spanish realms. First established in Santo Domingo (1511), Mexico (1535) and Lima (1544), additional *audiencias* were subsequently created in Guatemala, Guadalajara, Charcas, Quito and Panama. These courts were far more than judicial entities: they served in the Viceroy's stead, and the judges (*oidores*) stood at the apex of colonial society. Personally linked to the Council of the Indies in Madrid, the oidores brought family retinues plus lawyers and credit arrangements, which tied to them to both local and metropolitan society. Although some Spanish-born individuals (*peninsulares*) were always appointed to them, by the mid-18c the audiencias were dominated by members of Criollo (American-born) families; **Charles III** of Spain's reforms barely altered this trend. Additional audiencias were created in Bogota (1739) and Buenos Aires (1776) for military and economic reasons. Their Portuguese equivalent was the *Relação*, or High Court, established in Bahia (1751) and subsequently Rio de Janeiro; judges (*desembargadores*) were recruited from among both Brazilian and Portuguese-born magistrates.

Augsburg, League of (1686) The alliance against French territorial expansionism (the *réunion* policy of **Louis XIV**), formed by Emperor Leopold I, Spain, Bavaria and various circles of the empire. The accession to it of England, the Netherlands and Savoy during the subsequent War of the League of Augsburg (1688–97, also known as the War of the Palatinate Succession) created the so-called Grand Alliance. Following the devastation of the Palatinate (1689) and a joint English–Dutch naval victory at the Battle of La Hogue (1692), the eventual peace treaty (Treaty of **Rijswijk**, 1697) restored the independence of Lorraine but confirmed France's possession of Alsace.

Augsburg, Peace of (25 Sep 1555) The treaty signed by Catholics and Lutherans in Germany, recognizing the legitimacy of the **Augsburg Confession** (1530) and the Catholic faith. It marked the failure of Emperor **Charles V**'s attempt to destroy Protestantism in the Empire. The treaty was negotiated by his brother, Ferdinand. It confirmed the appropriation of ecclesiastical properties by the Protestant princes and declared that the religion of a ruler became the religion of his state (hence the phrase: *cuius regio, eius religio*).

Augsburg Confession A statement of faith composed by Luther, Melanchthon, and others for the Diet of Augsburg (1530), the official text being written by Melanchthon in 1531. The earliest of Protestant Confessions, it became authoritative for the Lutheran Church.

Augsburg Interim (1548) A formula designed at the Diet of Augsburg (30 June 1548) by **Charles V** to solve the Empire's religious divisions by devising a loosely defined Catholicism acceptable to the Protestant princes. It allowed the laity to receive the Communion cup and for Protestant ministers to keep their wives. The Catholic princes signed without enthusiasm while most of the Protestant princes rejected it outright. Pope Paul refused to endorse it until Aug 1549. Most Catholic priests refused to give the wine to the laity, which they considered a Protestant innovation. The Protestant ministers considered it an attempt to reintroduce Catholicism. ▷ **Holy Roman Empire**

August Coup (1991) The conservative attempt to reverse the process of reform in the USSR, which ended in failure. Communist opponents of Mikhail **Gorbachev**'s policies had been able to slow down, but not to stop, the reforms. The coup's leaders included **Yanaev**, the Vice-President, and **Yazov**, Defence Minister. The military in particular were split, and the planning left Boris **Yeltsin** free to act in full view of the world. The plotters achieved the very opposite of what they wanted: Yeltsin took over from Gorbachev and accelerated the reforms. Those behind the coup succeeded, however, in undermining the USSR; the Commonwealth of Independent States (CIS), its emasculated successor, may yet give them another opportunity.

Augustine, St (d.604) The first Archbishop of Canterbury. He was prior of a Benedictine monastery at Rome, when in 596 Pope **Gregory** I sent him with 40 other monks to convert the **Anglo-Saxons** to Christianity. He was kindly received by **Ethelbert**, King of Kent, whose wife was a Christian, and the conversion and baptism of the King contributed greatly to his success. Augustine was made Bishop of the English in 597, and established his church at Canterbury. His efforts to extend his authority over the native

Celtic Christianity were less successful. He died at Canterbury, and in 612 his body was transferred to the abbey of Saints Peter and Paul, now the site of St Augustine's Missionary College (1848).

Augustus (Gaius Julius Caesar Octavianus) (63BC–AD14) Founder of the **Roman Empire**. He was the son of Gaius Octavius, senator and praetor, and great-nephew, through his mother Atia, of Julius **Caesar**. On Caesar's assassination (44BC), he abandoned his studies in Illyricum and returned to Italy, where, using Caesar's money and name (he had acquired both under his will), he raised an army, defeated Mark **Antony**, and extorted a wholly unconstitutional consulship from the Senate (43BC). When Antony returned from **Gaul** in force later that year with **Lepidus**, Octavian made a deal with his former enemies, joining the so-called Second Triumvirate with them, and taking Africa, Sardinia, and Sicily as his province. A later redivision of power gave him the entire Western half of the Roman world, and Antony the Eastern. While Antony was distracted there by his military schemes against Parthia, and his liaison with **Cleopatra VII**, Octavian consistently undermined him at home. Matters came to a head in 31BC, and the Battle of Actium followed, Octavian emerging victorious as the sole ruler of the Roman world. Though taking the inoffensive title *princeps* ('first citizen'), he was in all but name an absolute monarch. His new name, Augustus ('sacred'), had historical and religious overtones, and was deliberately chosen to enhance his prestige. His long reign (27BC–AD14) was a time of peace and reconstruction at home, sound administration and steady conquest abroad. In gratitude, the Romans awarded him the title *Pater Patriae* ('Father of his Country') in 2BC, and on his death made him a god (*Divus Augustus*). ▷ **Herod the Great; Agrippa, Marcus Vipsanius; Livia; Maecenas, Gaius (Cilnius)**

Augustus I (1526–86) Elector of Saxony (1553/86). The younger son of Henry, Duke of Saxony, he was raised a Lutheran and educated at Leipzig University. He became Elector upon the death of his brother, Maurice. Married (Oct 1548) to Anna, daughter of Christian III, King of Denmark, he worked hard to avoid religious disputes in the Empire and, although a Lutheran, supported the Habsburgs. He was actively involved in bringing about the Peace of **Augsburg**. He strove to unite the Lutherans and the Calvinists but after 1574 and the expulsion of the Crypto-Calvinists from Saxony he adopted a strict form of Lutheranism. He continued to hope that the Calvinists could be persuaded to accept the **Augsburg Confession**. ▷ **Habsburg Dynasty**

Augustus II, 'the Strong' (1670–1733) King of Poland (1697/1706 and 1710/33). After being elected King, he tried to recover the provinces lost to Sweden, but was defeated, and then deposed. In 1709 he returned to Poland, formed a fresh alliance with the Tsar, and recommenced a war with Sweden, which raged until the death of **Charles XII** of Sweden (1718). The Saxon court became known as the most dissolute in Europe, and poor government hastened Poland's decline. Augustus is said to have had around 300 illegitimate children; his one legitimate child became **Augustus III** of Poland. He died in Warsaw.

Augustus III (1696–1763) Elector of Saxony and King of Poland (1733/63). Unlike his father, **Augustus II, 'the Strong'**, he had no ambition to make his combined dominions a great power in Europe. He ruled from Dresden, not Warsaw, and made no attempt to control the Polish magnates and gentry, famed for their unpatriotic selfishness. He permitted foreign interference in Poland's internal affairs, thus preparing the ground for the partitions of Poland which followed his reign. He squandered much of the considerable wealth of the country, helped in this activity by the nobility. ▷ **Poland, Partitions of**

Auletes ▷ **Ptolemy XII Neos Dionysos**

Aung San (1915–47) Burmese nationalist. He was the dominant figure in the nationalist movement during and after the Pacific War. At the beginning of the 1940s, Aung San, working with Japanese agents, formed the anti-British Burma Independence Army, which entered Burma with the invading Japanese in Jan 1942. He rapidly became disillusioned with the Japanese, however, and, as a leading figure in the Anti-Fascist People's Freedom League (AFPFL), turned his troops against them (Mar 1945). In the immediate post-war period he became President of the AFPFL and, in 1946, was effectively Prime Minister in the Governor's Executive Council. In Jan 1947 he travelled to London to negotiate, with success, Burma's independence. On 19 July, however, he was assassinated by a political rival. His death removed the one figure who might have held together Burma's warring political interests as the country achieved independence (4 Jan 1948).

Aurangzeb (1618–1707) Mughal Emperor (1658/1707). The last, and most magnificent, of the Mughal Emperors of India, he took the kingly title Alamgir. The youngest son of Shah Jahan, he struggled for power with his brothers, finally putting them to death. He was a fervent Muslim, which alienated the Hindus and led to war with the Marathas and the extension of the boundaries of the Empire into the Deccan in the south. His long reign was distinguished by prosperity. However, in the long term, most of his enterprises failed, and after his death the empire began rapidly to decline. ▷ **Mughal Empire**

Aurelian (215–75) Roman Emperor (270/75). A man of humble provincial origin, but outstanding military talents, he ended the chaos of 40 years in a brief but brilliant reign. Army discipline and domestic order were restored, and action successfully taken against the **Goths** and Carpi on the Danube, **Zenobia** of Palmyra in the East, and the breakaway Gallic Empire in the West. For his efforts, he was awarded the title 'Restorer of the Roman World'.

Auriol, Vincent (1884–1966) French politician. A socialist, he studied law, and was a Deputy (1914–40 and 1945–7), Minister of Finance in the **Popular Front** government (1936–7) and Minister of Justice (1937–8). He opposed the granting of power to **Pétain** in 1940, and joined the French Resistance, escaping to Algeria in 1943, where he became President of the Foreign Affairs Committee of the Consultative Assembly. He represented France at the first meeting of the **UN**, was elected President of the Constituent Assembly in 1946, and was first President of the Fourth Republic (1947–53). ▷ **Republic, Fourth** (France); **Resistance Movement** (France)

Aurora (1917) The Russian warship that went over to the **Bolsheviks** in Oct 1917, and thus tipped the balance in their favour. Although ordered by the **Russian Provisional Government** to put to sea, it stayed in the River Neva across from the **Winter Palace**, fired a blank shell that frightened away many of the government's supporters and eventually fired some live shells to help overcome its defenders. Its action was, however, essentially symbolic, indicating that the authorities had lost a major source of power.

Auschwitz The largest Nazi **concentration camp**, founded in 1941, on the outskirts of Oświecim, south-west Poland, where 3–4 million people, mainly Jews and Poles, were murdered between 1940 and 1945. Gas chambers, watch towers, and prison huts are preserved at the camp, part of which is now a museum. ▷ **Holocaust**

Ausgleich The arrangement (literally, 'compromise') made in 1867 between the Imperial government of **Austria** and representatives of Hungary, following the Austrian defeat by **Prussia** (1866), which created the Dual Monarchy of **Austria-Hungary**.

Austerlitz, Battle of (2 Dec 1805) The victory of **Napoleon I** over a combined Austrian-Russian army in Moravia. The Treaty of **Pressburg** (Bratislava) followed on 26 Dec, by which Austria renounced all interests in Italy, lost most of her western Alpine lands, and saw French hegemony established in western Germany.

Australia An independent country and the smallest continent in the world, entirely in the southern hemisphere. The **Aboriginals** are thought to have arrived in Australia from south-east Asia c.40000 years ago. The first

European visitors were the Dutch, who explored the Gulf of Carpentaria in 1606 and landed in 1642. Captain James Cook arrived in **Botany Bay** in 1770, and claimed the east coast for Britain. New South Wales was established as a penal colony in 1788. In 1829, all the territory now known as Australia was constituted a dependency of Britain. Increasing numbers of settlers were attracted to Australia, especially after the introduction of Spanish Merino sheep. Gold was discovered in New South Wales and Victoria (1851) and in Western Australia (1892). **Transportation** of convicts to eastern Australia ended in 1840, but continued until 1853 in Tasmania and 1868 in Western Australia. During this period, the colonies drafted their own constitutions and set up governments: New South Wales (1855), Tasmania and Victoria (1856), South Australia (1857), Queensland (1860), and Western Australia (1890). In 1901 the Commonwealth of Australia was established with Canberra chosen as the site for its capital. A policy of preventing immigration by non-Whites stayed in force from the end of the 19c until 1974. The growing movement for independence in recent years culminated with the pledge of Paul Keating in 1993 to make Australia a republic by 2001, subject to a referendum.

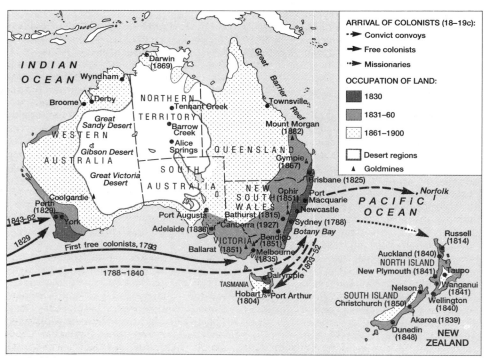

British penetration of Australia and New Zealand, 18–19c

Australian Council of Trade Unions (ACTU) Australia's national trade-union organization, formed in 1927. Its prestige has come from representing the unions' case before the Australian Conciliation and Arbitration Commission, and in helping to settle industrial disputes. By 1986 162 unions were affiliated, with a claimed total membership of 2.6 million. In 1983 the ACTU and the **Australian Labor Party** (ALP) signed an accord on economic policy, which was put into effect when the ALP came to power. ▷ **Australian Workers' Union (AWU)**

Australian Gold Rush Traces of gold were first found in Australia in 1823, but the first significant find was in 1851, when Edward Hargraves publicized his find and attracted 2000 to the site at Ophir, New South Wales. In the same year, large gold finds were made in Victoria, which accounted for 35 per cent of world gold production (1851–60). Gold was also found in Queensland (1867) and Western Australia (1893). The discovery transformed Australia: it drew thousands of immigrants (342000 arrived from overseas, 1852–61), created a mass movement for democracy, and gave a tremendous boost to the economy. Cities, in particular Melbourne (which grew from 29000 to 473000 in 1851–91), symbolized the new-found prosperity. Although some miners struck it rich, most did not, and this led to pressure to open pastoral land for farming. Gold also attracted thousands of Chinese miners, who were greatly resented by the Europeans; this led to anti-Chinese laws and the beginning of the **White Australia Policy.** ▷ **Eureka; Lambing Flat Riots**

Australian Labor Party (ALP) Australia's oldest political party, founded in 1891 in New South Wales following the defeat of the trade unions in the 1890 maritime strike. The party spread to all states by the mid-1900s and formed the world's first labour government in Queensland in 1899 for one week. It has always been a social democratic party, committed to evolutionary not revolutionary change. Despite a commitment to **'socialism'**, it has generally been moderate and pragmatic when in government. Three major splits in the ALP occurred: in 1916–17 over conscription, in 1931 over economic policy to combat the Depression and in 1955 over attitudes to **communism.** ALP has had only some success in winning federal government (1908–9, 1910–13, 1914–15, 1929–32, 1941–9, 1972–5 and 1983–), but has done better at state level. Its most important national figures

have been Prime Ministers W M **Hughes** (1915–16), James Scullin (1929–32), John **Curtin** (1941–5), Ben **Chifley** (1945–9), Gough **Whitlam** (1972–5), and R J L ('Bob') **Hawke** (1983–). In 1988, the party had about 60000 members; it has always had fewer members than its main rival, the **Liberal Party of Australia.** ▷ **Democratic Labor Party; Petrov Affair**

Australian Workers' Union (AWU) The largest Australian trade union from the early 1900s to 1970, and still one of the largest, with over 120000 members in 1985. It was formed in 1894 by the merging of the Amalgamated Shearers' Union (formed 1886) and the General Labourers' Union (formed 1890), and has traditionally recruited lesser paid workers. It has always been a conservative force in trade union and labour politics. ▷ **Australian Council of Trade Unions**

Austrasia The eastern Frankish kingdom in the Merovingian period (6–8c). It covered present north-eastern France and parts of western and central Germany. The ambitions of the Austrasian nobles led to the area having its own king from 623. In 687 the Austrasian mayor of the palace, **Pepin II, 'of Heristal'**, defeated the Neustrians at Tertry and secured Austrasian ascendancy. ▷ **Dagobert I; Neustria**

Austria, Republic of Following the collapse of Austria-Hungary at the end of **World War I**, those German-speaking lands of the Habsburg Empire not annexed by other successor states constituted themselves on 12 Nov 1918 as 'German Austria', renamed Austria on the insistence of the victor powers. Between the wars the republic led an uneasy existence, with most of public opinion and most politicians seeking union with Germany. Union with **Hitler**'s Germany, which occurred in Mar 1938 (**Anschluss**), was more controversial. After **World War II**, Austria was reconstituted as a distinct territory by the Allies and in 1955 became an independent, neutral state. ▷ **Austrian State Treaty; Habsburg Dynasty**

Austria-Hungary, Dual Monarchy of A constitutional arrangement created by the **Ausgleich**, or 'compromise', of 1867. In Austria-Hungary the **Habsburg** Emperors **Francis Joseph** (until 1916), and **Charles** (1916/18), ruled over the twin kingdoms of **Austria** (incorporating German-, Czech-, Polish-, Slovenian-, and Ruthenian-speaking regions of their empire) as well as Dalmatia and Hungary (incorporating Magyar, Romanian, Slovak, and most Croatian and Serb regions). The separate kingdoms possessed considerable autonomy over internal policy, with overall foreign and financial policy remaining in the hands of the Imperial government. The Dual Monarchy provided a temporary solution to the internal problems of the Habsburg Empire, but was ultimately destroyed by defeat in **World War I**.

Austrian State Treaty (May 1955) The agreement between **Austria** and the four Allied victor powers under which Austria regained its independence as a federal republic in return for restrictions on armaments and curbs on close relations with Germany. In Oct 1955 this was supplemented by an Austrian declaration of permanent neutrality.

Austrian Succession, War of the (1740–8) The European conflict over the succession to the hereditary Habsburg lands of **Maria Theresa**. On the death of Emperor **Charles VI**, Bavaria, Saxony and Spain, backed by France, refused to recognize the **Pragmatic Sanction** and invaded Bohemia and Upper Austria. At this juncture, Prussia claimed and, on being rebuffed, conquered Silesia in two campaigns. 1745, the year when the second Silesian War ended, also saw the withdrawal of Bavaria from the struggle, when the son and successor of Charles Albert, holder of the Bohemian and imperial crowns, renounced all claims to them. The subsequent intervention on Austria's side of Russia led to peace negotiations and, by 1748, to the Treaty of Aachen, under the terms of which the Habsburg monarchy retained almost all her dominions with the exception of Silesia. ▷ **Habsburg Dynasty**

Austro-Prussian Dualism The period which spanned the reign of **Frederick II, 'the Great'** of Prussia. For the first time, power within the Empire was evenly divided between Prussia and Austria and they were both substantially stronger than any other Imperial state. Neither seemed inclined to strive for absolute mastery over the Empire.

Austro-Prussian War (1866) A war between **Austria** and **Prussia** occasioned by a dispute over the Duchies of Schleswig and Holstein. It was declared on 14 June, decided by the Prussian victory at the Battle of **Königgrätz-Sadowa** on 3 July, and ended by the Treaty of Prague on 23 Aug. Austria's defeat hastened German unification (since

she had been the main advocate and defender of particularism in the **German Confederation**, now dissolved by Prussia); allowed Italy, Prussia's ally, to acquire Venetia; and precipitated the creation of Austria-Hungary.

Austro-Slavism A federalist movement among the Slavs within the Habsburg Empire. It developed after 1848 as a reaction to German nationalism and Pan-Germanism which, in its extreme forms, denied the existence of Slav nationhood. Representatives of the Habsburg Slavs, under the leadership of the Czech František **Palacký**, demanded the reorganization of the monarchy on a federal basis which would give full weight to the Slav nations. Having ably exploited Austro-Magyar antagonisms, the advocates of Austro-Slavism had their hopes crushed with the establishment of the Dual Monarchy. Their ideas were later taken up by the Czench national leader, T G Masaryk. ▷ **Austria-Hungary, Dual Monarchy of**

autarchia The Italian word ('autarchy' or 'self-sufficiency') used to describe the policy of economic self-sufficiency pursued by the fascist regime in Italy. Originally it was largely limited to a drive for greater grain production, the so-called 'battle for wheat'. However, when limited economic sanctions were imposed in response to Italy's invasion of Abyssinia in 1935, an increased effort was made to replace imports with ersatz goods. ▷ **Abyssinia, Conquest of; fascism**

authoritarianism A form of government, or a theory advocating such government, which is the opposite of democracy, in that the consent of society to rulers and their decisions is not necessary. Voting and discussion are not usually employed, except to give the appearance of democratic legitimacy to the government, and such arrangements remain firmly under the control of the rulers. Authoritarian rulers draw their authority from what are claimed to be special qualities of a religious, nationalistic or ideological nature, which are used to justify their dispensing with constitutional restrictions. Their rule, however, relies heavily upon coercion. ▷ **totalitarianism**

auto-de-fe (Portuguese, *auto da fé*) Literally an 'act of faith', practised originally by the Spanish and later by the Portuguese **Inquisition**, it was a public ceremony, including a procession and mass, at which prisoners were made to express repentance for sins.

Very frequent in the late 15c and 16c, the ceremony was rarely held in later epochs. Burning of heretics at the stake never formed part of the *auto-de-fe*, and was carried out in a separate act afterwards.

Autumn Harvest Uprisings (1927) A series of attempted peasant insurrections launched by the Chinese Communist Party in the provinces of Hunan and Hubei following the collapse of the United Front (June 1927). An emergency party conference in Aug 1927 called for communist-led attacks on major cities in the hope of igniting urban revolution. **Mao Zedong** led one such uprising, but following its defeat he led the remnants of his ragtag force to the mountains of **Jinggangshan** where he began to create a rural base area. By the end of 1927, all other insurrections had collapsed.

Aventine Secession (June 1924) In protest at fascist vote-rigging and the murder of **Matteotti**, the deputies of the main Italian opposition parties staged a walk-out from parliament. Designed to register protest and deny legitimacy to **Mussolini**'s regime, the actual consequence was to hand the fascists dominance of the Italian Chamber. The measure was further undermined by the reluctance of **Giolitti** and other leading liberals to support what they felt to be a useless boycott. Those deputies who joined the walk-out were said to have 'gone to the Aventine hill'.

Avis Dynasty The dynasty which ruled Portugal from 1385 to 1580 and took its name from the medieval military order of Avis, founded in 1147. The first of the line was King João (John) I (1385–1433), and the last was **Sebastian**, who died at the Battle of **Alcazarquivir** in 1578.

AVNOJ (*Antifašističko Veče Narodnog Oslobodjenja Jugoslavije*, 'Anti-Fascist Council for the National Liberation of Yugoslavia') Organized by the partisan leader, **Tito**, the council first met at Bihać in Bosnia to establish a central government for Yugoslavia (Nov 1942). Communist-dominated, it challenged the authority of the royalist government-in-exile in London. In Nov 1943 it met at Jajce and declared itself the true representative government of Yugoslavia. Its political programme included the reorganization of the country on a federal basis and the establishment of a republic. At the end of **World War II**, it had created an effective administrative structure throughout the country and became the national provisional assembly until the Nov 1945 elections. That Yugoslavia alone of the Balkan countries was under communist control at the end of the war was due to the successful organization of AVNOJ. ▷ **Djilas, Milovan; Kardelj, Edvard; Stojadinović, Milan**

Awadh, Annexation of A semi-independent northern Indian province within the **Mughal Empire**, Awadh (Oudh) was annexed in 1856 by the British **East India Company**. Loss of rights by hereditary land revenue receivers caused resentment, and contributed towards the 1857–8 **Indian Uprising**.

Awami League East Pakistani (later Bangladeshi) political party founded initially to promote East Pakistani autonomy, and later Bangladeshi independence. The Awami League rose to political prominence in the late 1960s when, under the leadership of Sheikh Mujibur Rahman, it protested against the fact that profits from jute, produced in highly populated East Pakistan, were being kept in relatively sparsely populated West Pakistan. The Awami League's second cause was for parliamentary representation by population. As the government of General **Ayub Khan** became increasingly unstable in 1968, Sheikh Mujib and the Awami League publicized a six-point programme to limit the powers of the central government in East Pakistan. The central government responded by imprisoning all opposition leaders. The following year Ayub Khan resigned and was replaced by General Yahya Khan who proceeded with a policy of political militarization while preparing to return parliamentary democracy. Although representation by population was part of Yahya Khan's plan, dissatisfaction in East Pakistan grew and popular feeling began to call for independence. In the election of 7 Dec 1970, the Awami League won 160 of 162 seats in East Pakistan. In Mar 1971 Sheikh Mujib set forth full internal autonomy as his condition for the Awami League's participation in the National Assembly. He was arrested shortly thereafter and the Awami League was outlawed. These actions on the part of the central government led directly to the bloody 1971 Pakistani civil war, which saw the emergence of the new state of Bangladesh following India's military invasion in support of the Awami League. While the League managed to retain democratic control of Bangladesh through the nation's first independent election in 1973, it was overthrown by a coup in 1975. Since then, the Awami League has remained a major political party in Bangladesh.

AWB (*Afrikaanse Weestand Beweging*, 'Afrikaner Resistance Movement') A paramilitary group founded in 1973, and led by Eugene Terr'Blanche, it is prepared to support its aim of preserving white control of South Africa by force.

Awolowo, Chief Obafemi (1909–87) Nigerian politician. Educated in Protestant schools, he was a teacher, trader, trade union organizer and journalist, before being an external student of law at London University and becoming a solicitor and advocate of the Nigerian Supreme Court. He helped found and then led the Action Group, a party based on the Yoruba of Western Nigeria, 1951–66 (when the party was banned). He was Premier of the Western Region (1954–9) and then leader of the opposition in the federal parliament from 1960 to 1962, when he was imprisoned. Released after the 1966 coup, he was Federal Commissioner for Finance and Vice-President, Federal Executive Council of Nigeria (1967–71), when he returned to private practice. But he returned to politics in 1979 as the unsuccessful presidential candidate for the Unity Party of Nigeria.

Axis Powers The name given to the co-operation of Nazi Germany and Fascist Italy (1936–45), first used by **Mussolini**. In May 1939 the two countries signed a formal treaty, the 'Pact of Steel'. In Sep 1940, Germany, Italy and Japan signed a tripartite agreement, after which all three were referred to as Axis Powers. ▷ **Nazi Party; World War II**

Axum A Greek-influenced Semitic trading state on the Eritrean coast, founded about the beginning of the Christian era and trading with Meroe. From its port at Adulis it dominated the trade of the Red Sea, and in the 3c extended its power to Yemen. At the height of its influence under King Ezana (c.320–50), who accepted Christianity, it later became the basis of the Christian kingdom of Ethiopia.

Ayacucho, Battle of (9 Dec 1824) The final major battle of the **Spanish–American Wars of Independence**, fought in the Peruvian Andes by **Bolívar** and **Sucre** against Field Marshal José de la Serna, the last Viceroy of Peru. The revolutionary forces (comprising Venezuelans, Colombians, Argentines, Chileans and Peruvians) defeated the royalist army, and the Spanish Viceroy and his generals were taken prisoner. All Spanish forces were then withdrawn from Peru and Charcas (Bolivia), ensuring the independence of the newly-emerged South American republics from Spanish rule.

Ayans Muslim notables who, as landowners, enjoyed considerable political influence at local level in the **Ottoman Empire**. Often rebellious, during the 18c their independence increased as Ottoman central authority weakened.

Ayn Jalut, Battle of (3 Sep 1260) A major battle between the **Mongols** and the **Mamluks** which effectively stopped the Mongol westward advance. The armies met at Ayn Jalut near Nazareth in Palestine, where the Mongols, under Kitbugha, were trapped and suffered a crushing defeat at the hands of the Mamluks, led by Baybars. This was the Mongols' first defeat in pitched battle.

Ayub Khan, Mohammed (1907–74) Pakistani soldier and politician. Educated at Aligarh Moslem University and Sandhurst, he served in **World War II**, became first commander-in-chief of Pakistan's army in 1951 and field marshal in 1959. He became President of Pakistan in 1958 after a bloodless army coup, and established a stable economy and political autocracy. In Mar 1969, after widespread civil disorder and violent opposition from both right and left wings, Ayub Khan relinquished power and martial law was re-established.

Ayudhya Classical Thai kingdom (1351–1767) situated in the heart of the great plain of the Chaophraya River, and the name of that kingdom's capital. Ayudhya was established (1351) by Prince U Thong, as the power of the Cambodian empire of Angkor in the region began to wane. In the mid-15c, Ayudhya, securing the final collapse of Angkor and the elimination of the rival Tai state of Sukhothai, emerged as an expansive regional power. Sacked by the Burmese in 1569 and reconstructed towards the end of the 16c, Ayudhya became a major trading centre and host to many nationalities (including Europeans) in the 17c. However, in 1688, following French intrigues at the court, an internal revolt ended the Western presence, although intra-Asian trade continued to flourish. Burmese attacks were revived from the late 1750s and in 1767 the capital was sacked by Burmese forces. A new royal line and a new state, was established at Thonburi-Bangkok in 1782.

Ayyubid Dynasty The Kurdish dynasty of the 12c and 13c established by **Saladin**. His empire, based essentially on Egypt, included Yemen, Syria and enough of the Fertile Crescent to cause him at one time to be a matter of concern to the 'Abbasid caliph, al-Nasir (1180/1225). Saladin's greatest achievements were the defeat of the field army of the Latin Kingdom of Jerusalem at **Hittin** (1187) and his subsequent capture of Jerusalem, enabled him to negotiate a settlement with the Crusaders. By this, the latter retained control of much of the Levantine littoral, while Saladin (and his descendants) had control of the Syrian and Palestinian hinterland as well as Egypt. The failure of the Ayyubids to survive as a dynasty more than 60 years after Saladin's death was largely due to squabbling between those who considered themselves his heirs. The cession by negotiation of Jerusalem to Frederick II by the Ayyubid al-Kamil in the early 13c (which 'did not count' because Frederick was excommunicated at the time) served in some degree to emphasize the futility of the Holy Wars of the 12c and 13c. Internal disagreements in the Ayyubid House opened the way for Mamluk control of Egypt and then Palestine in the mid-13c. ▷ **'Abbasid Dynasty; Mamluks**

Azad, Abu'l-Kalam (1888–1958) Muslim Indian politician and leader of the **Indian National Congress**. His pan-Islamic articles in his newspaper, *Al-Hilal*, resulted in detention in 1915, after release from which he became active in the **Khilafat Movement**. In 1923 Azad presided over a special session of the Indian National Congress, and in 1940 he was elected President — a position which he held until 1946. While President of Congress he conducted important negotiations with Sir Stafford Cripps and Field Marshal Lord **Wavell**. He was interned throughout most of the war. Following Indian independence, Azad became India's Education Minister, a post he held until his death.

Azaña (y Díaz), Manuel (1880–1940) Spanish politician and intellectual. He qualified as a lawyer, served as a bureaucrat, but became eminent in the literary and political world. In 1925 he founded a political party, *Acción Republicana*. With the advent of the Second Republic (1931), he became Minister of War and then Prime Minister (1931–3) of a reforming government. An outstanding orator and thinker, he himself was closely identified with army reform and anticlericalism. In opposition from Sep 1933 to Feb 1936, he was the chief architect of the Popular Front coalition which triumphed in the general election of Feb 1936. He resumed the premiership then, and was elevated to the presidency in May 1936. He remained President during the **Spanish Civil War** until Feb 1939, then went into exile in France, where he died. Azaña was the leading politician of the Second Republic and the greatest embodiment of its liberal, reformist vision. ▷ **Republic, Second** (Spain)

Azania (Zanj) The names given by ancient and medieval Greek and Arab geographers to the northern part of the East African coast. 'Azanians' were the early, pre-Bantu-speaking inhabitants of the coast. In modern times, the name Azania has been used by some nationalist groups, especially the **Pan-Africanist Congress**, to denote a post-**apartheid** South Africa.

Azcona del Hoyo, José Simon (1927–) Honduran politician. He trained as a civil engineer in Honduras and Mexico and developed a particular interest in urban development and low-cost housing. As a student he became interested in politics and fought the 1963 general election as a candidate for the Liberal Party of Honduras (PLH) but his career was interrupted by a series of military coups. He served in the governments of Roberto Suazo and Walter Lopez (1982–6), which were ostensibly civilian administrations but, in reality, controlled by the army commander-in-chief, General Gustavo Alvarez. The latter was removed by junior officers in 1984 and in 1986 Azcona narrowly won the presidential election.

Azerbaijan, Independence of (1991) One of the non-Russian Republics that gained their independence with the disintegration of the USSR. The Azeris had a long history, mainly of subjection to the neighbouring empires. A Turkish people converted to Islam, they came under Tsarist Russian rule in 1813. The development of the oil industry in and around Baku produced leaders who, encouraged by **Lenin**, declared for independence in 1918. However, in 1920 they were reconquered on his instructions for allegedly siding with Soviet enemies. Before re-emerging in 1991, Azerbaijan became locked in a struggle with **Armenia** over the autonomous region that **Stalin** had set up for the latter's co-nationals in Nagorno-Karabakh.

Azhari, Ismail al- (1900–69) Sudanese politician. He was the leader of the Sudanese

Unionist Party which, to the surprise and indeed disappointment of the British, was the victor of the first Sudanese parliamentary elections in 1953. Al-Azhari formed the first government in 1954. Opposed by the Mahdists, he was nonetheless able to guide the Sudan towards independence, which was achieved on 1 Jan 1956. After the deposition of Ibrahim **Abboud** in 1964, al-Azhari became President of the Supreme Council of the Sudan. However, a military coup in 1969 resulted in his being placed under house arrest and he died during this confinement.

Azikiwe, Nnamdi (1904–   ) Nigerian journalist and politician. He spent four years as a government clerk before going to the USA, where he studied at Storer College, Lincoln University and Howard University. He then taught at Lincoln, where he obtained two further degrees. He returned to Africa in 1934 and edited the *African Morning Post* in Accra before going back to Nigeria to take up the editorship of the *West African Pilot* in 1937. He was a member of the executive of the Nigerian Youth Movement (1934–41) and helped found the National Council of Nigeria and the Cameroons (NCNC) of which he was Secretary (1944–6) and President (1946–60). A member of the Nigerian Legco in 1947–51, he became Premier of the Eastern Region in 1954 after two years as Leader of the Opposition. He was appointed the first black Governor-General of Nigeria in 1960 and was President of the first Nigerian Republic in 1963–6. He was in Britain at the time of the 1966 military coup, but returned as a private citizen to Nigeria soon afterwards. He returned to politics in 1979 as leader of, and successful candidate for, the Nigerian People's Party. He was a member of the Council of State 1979–83.

Aztecs The most powerful people of Mesoamerica during the 15–16c. Their main city, Tenochtitlán (present-day Mexico City), near Lake Texcoco, became the most densely populated city of the region. They built up a great and powerful despotic state, with a strong military force, subjugating nearly all the people of central Mexico, and eventually ruling 400–500 small tribute-paying states (probably 5–6 million people), which provided them with raw materials and produce. People captured in wars were offered for human sacrifice to the Aztec gods. The Aztecs were famous for their agriculture, cultivating all available land, introducing irrigation, draining swamps, and creating artificial islands in the lakes. Their best-known ruler was **Montezuma II**. They developed a form of hieroglyphic writing, a complex calendar system, and built famous pyramids and temples. The Aztec empire was finally destroyed by the Spanish under **Cortés** in 1521.

B

Baader–Meinhof Group The popular name for *Rote Armee Fraktion* (RAF), after its leaders, Andreas Baader (1943–77) and Ulrike Meinhof (1934–76). A left-wing German revolutionary, terrorist group, which recruited largely from the middle-class, younger generation, it carried out political bombings in Germany in the early 1970s. Baader, Meinhof, and 18 other members were arrested in 1972. On a much smaller scale RAF continued into the 1980s.

Ba'ath Socialist Party The political manifestation of Ba'athism, an Islamic ideology of the 1930s. Founded by Michel **Aflaq** and Salah al-Din **Bitar**, the party's ideology faced problems in coping with combining a Marxist social analysis with an Islamic religious basis, but eventually became the ruling party in both Syria and Iraq. However, rather than closening relations between the two countries, the term became divorced from its ideological bases and has in no way served to reduce the rancour which has existed between the two countries over the ages.

Bab al-Mandab The straits lying between Yemen on the east and Djibouti and Ethiopia on the west. Strategically important, they lie at the southern entrance to the Red Sea and thus control access to Jordan's only seaport, Aqaba. The straits were of considerable importance, for example, during the Iran–Iraq War. Since Iraq had no significant freedom of navigation in the Persian Gulf, all seaborne material destined for Iraq had to pass through Aqaba at the head of the Red Sea, with entry to there being controlled at the Bab al-Mandab.

Babangida, Ibrahim (1941–) Nigerian soldier and politician. Educated at military schools in Nigeria and later in India, UK and USA, he was commissioned in 1963 and became an instructor at the Nigerian Defence Academy. During the Nigerian Civil War, he commanded an infantry battalion, then became an instructor at the Nigerian Defence Academy (1970–2) and later commander of the Armoured Corps (1975–81). Involved in the military overthrow of President **Shagari** in 1983, he became a member of the Supreme Military Council and Chief of Staff in 1985

and was himself the leader of the coup which overthrew **Buhari** in 1985. He was mainly responsible for the cautious and controlled way Nigeria returned to civilian rule, imposing a two-party system and staged elections on the country.

Bab-ed-Din (1819–50) Persian religious leader. This title, meaning 'Gate of the Faith', was assumed by a merchant of Shiraz, Mirza Ali Mohammed. In 1844 he declared himself the Bab (Gateway) to the prophesied 12th Imam; later he claimed to be the Imam himself. He was imprisoned in 1847 and later executed at Tabriz. The religion he founded (Babism) was the forerunner of the Baha'i faith. ▷ **Baha-Allah**

Babeuf, François-Noël (1760–97) French politician. During the **French Revolution** (as 'Gracchus Babeuf'), he advocated a rigorous system of **communism** (Babouvism). His conspiracy to destroy the **Directory** (1796) and establish an extreme democratic and communistic system (a 'Republic of Equals') was discovered, and he was guillotined.

Babington, Antony (1561–86) English Roman Catholic conspirator. He served as a page to **Mary, Queen of Scots**, when she was a prisoner at Sheffield. In 1586, he was induced by John Ballard and others to lead a conspiracy towards **Elizabeth I**'s murder and Mary's release (the Babington Plot). Cipher messages were intercepted by **Walsingham** in which Mary warmly approved the plot, and these were later used against her. Babington fled, but was captured and executed with the others.

Babi Yar A huge ravine near Kiev in the Ukraine into which over 30 000 Jews were herded and massacred by Nazi German troops in 1941. It is also the title of a poem by Yevegeny Yevtushenko (1961) and a novel by Anatoly Kuznetsov (1966) dedicated to the victims. ▷ **Holocaust; Nazi Party**

Babur (Zahiruddin Muhammad) (1483–1530) First Mughal Emperor of India (1526/30). Born in Fergana, Central Asia, a small principality ruled by his father, he was a descendant of **Genghis Khan** and of **Timur**.

The nephew of Sultan Mahmud Mirza of Samarkand, he attempted unsuccessfully as a young man to establish himself as ruler there, but in 1504 turned his attention with greater success towards Afghanistan, entering Kabul in that year. A further attempt to win Samarkand in 1511 was again unsuccessful. The death of Sikander Lodi in 1517 brought civil war to the Afghan Lodi Empire in India and Babur took advantage of this to invade India, defeating Ibrahim Lodi decisively at the Battle of **Panipat** in 1526 and laying the foundation for the Mughal Empire. The following year he defeated the Hindu Rajput Confederacy and, despite continuing resistance from the Hindus and from the Afghans, the military strength of the Mughlas enabled him to consolidate his gains. A soldier of genius, he was also a cultured man with interests in architecture, music and literature. Himself a Muslim, he initiated a policy of toleration towards his non-Muslim subjects that was continued by his successors and became a hallmark of the Mughal Empire at its zenith.

Babylonia The region in Lower Mesopotamia around the ancient city of Babylon, which formed the core twice in antiquity of extensive but short-lived empires. The first, covering the whole of Mesopotamia, was created by the great Amorite King Hammurabi (c.1795–1750BC) but destroyed by the Hittites c.1595BC. The second came into being with the Babylonian overthrow of Assyria in 612BC and lasted until the Persian conquest in 539–538BC. Under its greatest monarch, Nebuchadnezzar (605/562BC), it stretched as far east as the Mediterranean. Although the Persians ended Babylonian political power for good, culturally Babylonian influence lasted for centuries, particularly in the fields of astrology, astronomy and mathematics.

Babylonian Exile The mass deportation of the Jews from Palestine to Babylonia in 587–586BC, after the failure of their revolt against **Nebuchadnezzar**.

Bach, Alexander, Baron von (1813–93) Austrian politician. A prominent supporter of the Mar 1848 revolution in Vienna, Bach became Minister of Justice in the revolutionary government of Wessenberg-Doblhof. After he resigned from office in Oct 1848 his rapid personal conversion from liberalism to neo-absolutism brought him high office in the counter-revolutionary government led by **Schwarzenberg**. Here he served as Interior Minister and achieved reforms in the system of provincial government which influence **Austria** to this day. ▷ **Revolution of 1848**

Bacon, Francis, Viscount St Albans (1561–1626) English p hilosopher and statesman. He became an MP in 1584, and was knighted by **James VI and I** in 1603. He was successively Solicitor-General (1607), Attorney-General (1613), Privy Counsellor (1616), Lord Keeper (1617), and Lord Chancellor (1618). He became Lord Verulam in 1618, and was made viscount in 1621. However, complaints were made that he accepted bribes from suitors in his court, and he was publicly accused before his fellow peers, fined, imprisoned, and banished from parliament and the court. Although soon released, and later pardoned, he never returned to public office, and died deeply in debt.

Bacon's Rebellion (1675–6) A rising against the royal governor in the American colony of Virginia, rooted in a conflict between small frontier farmers and the indigenous peoples. The rebellion reflected the rift between the western farmers and the eastern aristocracy represented by the colonian government. When Governor Berkeley, perhaps protecting trading interests with the Native Americans, failed to respond to a Native American attack against western settlers, Nathaniel Bacon led a misguided reprisal against innocent Native Americans. In 1676 Berkeley sought to bring the farmers to trial, but the opposition escalated, resulting in the burning of **Jamestown**. After Bacon's death, the rebellion collapsed.

Bactria The name given in antiquity to the area roughly corresponding to northern Afghanistan and the adjacent parts of southern Russia. It was ruled for centuries by foreign conquerors, notably the Achaemenids and the Seleucids. In the second half of the 3c BC Bactria at last became an independent state, and under a series of able Indo-Greek rulers went on to establish an empire that at its height covered not only all Afghanistan but large parts of Soviet Central Asia and Pakistan. ▷ **Persian Empire**

Baden, Treaty of (1714) The treaty which ended the War of the **Spanish Succession** between France and the **Holy Roman Empire**. It completed the peace process which began with the Peace of Utrecht (1713). Emperor **Charles VI** renounced his claim to the Spanish throne though he refused to recognize the French-backed claimant, **Philip V** of Spain (a Bourbon), until 1720.

Baden-Powell, Robert (Stephenson Smyth), 1st Baron (1857–1941) British general. Educated at Charterhouse, he joined the army, served in India and Afghanistan, was on the staff in Ashanti and Matabeleland, and won fame as the defender of Mafeking in the second Boer War. He founded the Boy Scout movement (1908) and, with his sister Agnes (1858–1945), the Girl Guides (1910). ▷ **Boer Wars; Mafeking, Siege of**

Badoglio, Pietro (1871–1956) Italian general. Governor of Libya (1929–34), by 1932 he had achieved the pacification of the Sanusi tribesmen. In 1935 he replaced **De Bono** at the head of the Conquest of **Abyssinia** where he conducted a campaign of extreme brutality; he became Viceroy of the new colony in May 1936. At the outbreak of **World War II** he initially favoured neutrality but rapidly dropped his opposition to intervention and in June 1940 was made Commander-in-Chief. Humiliating defeats suffered by the Italian Army in Greece and Albania prompted Badoglio's resignation (Dec 1940). In 1943 he was asked by **Victor Emmanuel III** to form an anti-fascist government after the arrest of **Mussolini**. On 25 Sep Badoglio signed an armistice with the Allies at Malta and in mid-Oct declared war on Germany. Apr 1944 saw the formation of a broad coalition government under Badoglio's leadership (including **Togliatti**, **Croce** and Carlo **Sforza**), but after the liberation of Rome in June he was obliged to stand down under pressure from the Americans and politicians with better anti-fascist credentials. He was replaced by Ivanoe **Bonomi**.

Bagaza, Jean-Baptiste (1946–) Burundian politician and soldier. After attending military schools in Belgium he returned to Burundi and became assistant to the head of the armed forces, with the rank of lieutenant-colonel. In 1976 he led a coup to overthrow President Micombero and was appointed President by a Supreme Revolutionary Council. In 1984 the post of prime minister was abolished and Bagaza was elected Head of State and Government. In 1987 he was himself ousted in a coup led by Major Pierre Buyoya.

Bagehot, Walter (1826–77) British economist, journalist, and political theorist. He studied mathematics at London, and spent some time as a banker in his father's firm, then became editor of the *Economist* in 1860. His *English Constitution* (1867) is still considered a standard work. His *Physics and Politics* (1872) applied the theory of evolution to politics. He advocated many constitutional reforms, including the introduction of life peers.

Baghdad, Sack of (1258) The sack of Baghdad carried out by the Mongol armies of Hulagu Khan, grandson of Genghis Khan. The initial wrath of Genghis had been kindled by the murder of three of his diplomatic envoys by the Khwarazm-Shah, an action which made the invasion of the Khwarazm-Shah's territories inevitable. By extension, the incident also led to the eventual devastation of the Muslim territories by the Mongols, the sack of Baghdad and the death of the last 'Abbasid Caliph of Baghdad, al-Mustasim. The latter surrendered on 10 Feb 1258 and the sack of Baghdad, beginning on 13 Feb with the concomitant pillaging, lasted for some seven days.

Baghdad, Siege of (812) This siege represented the culmination of the civil war between al-Amin and al-**Ma'mun**, two of the sons of **Harun al-Rashid**. Harun's dispositions for the succession, giving al-Amin control of Baghdad and Iraq, and al-Ma'mun control of the eastern empire (Khurasan and Transoxiana), were so arranged as to make civil war more likely than not. The siege itself was prosecuted by al-Ma'mun's generals, Tahir ibn al-Husayn and Harthama ibn A'yan. Al-Amin's armies were completely defeated, and, despite assurances of safe conduct from Harthama, al-Amin was killed by Tahir's forces.

Baghdad Pact Originally a treaty between Turkey and Iraq (1955) aimed at mutual cooperation against militants of the left. Britain, Pakistan and Iran joined later in 1955 but there was general opposition in Jordan when King Hussein proposed becoming a signatory. The Suez Crisis compromised Britain's position in 1956 and after the withdrawal of Iraq in 1958 (after the murder of the royal family) the pact ceased to exist as such and was supplanted by the Central Treaty Organization (CENTO).

Baghdad Railway A railway planned in 1899 by a German company to link Berlin via the Bosphorus to Baghdad and possibly to the Shatt-el-Arab, thereby providing a link between Central Europe and the Persian Gulf. The British feared that this would threaten their interests in the Gulf, southern Persia, and above all India, while the Russians sought to develop Persian railways themselves. The British kept a careful watch on the progress of the line, but it was incomplete before the outbreak of **World War I**, and by 1919 the British controlled Mesopotamia (Iraq).

Bagot, Sir Charles (1781–1843) British diplomat and Governor General of Canada. On taking office in 1842, he was advised by the British Colonial Secretary to depend on the **Family Compact**. However he discovered that 'you cannot rule Canada without the French', and that the **Durham**–Sydenham programme of anglicization was causing great resentment amongst the French Canadians. He therefore appointed as advisers Louis H **Lafontaine** as well as Robert **Baldwin**, and invariably listened to their advice. Since these two men held a majority in the Assembly, this almost amounted to ministerial government or collective responsibility, but Bagot still retained the ultimate decision-making power. In 1843 a fatal illness forced him to resign.

Bagration, Peer Ivanovich, Prince (1765–1812) Russian soldier. Descended from the royal Bagratidae of Georgia, he entered the Russian army in 1783, and, after much active service, distinguished himself by holding up **Murat** in a rearguard action at Schongraben (1805). He fought, too, at **Austerlitz** (1805), Eylau, **Friedland** (1807), and the siege of Silistria (1809). He was mortally wounded at the Battle of **Borodino**.

Baha-Ullah (1817–92) Persian religious leader. This was the name, meaning 'Glory of God', given to Mirza Huseyn Ali, founder of the Islamic Baha'i sect. He became a follower of the Shiraz merchant Mirza Ali Mohammed (**Bab-ed-din**), founder of the Persian Babi sect. Persecuted and imprisoned in 1852, he was exiled to Baghdad, Constantinople and Acre. In 1863 he proclaimed himself as the prophet that Bab-ed-din had foretold, and became the leader of the new Baha'i faith.

Bahmani Sultanate (1347–1518) A Muslim sultanate in the Deccan, India, founded by Alauddin Bahman Shah, an official of the Tughluq Dynasty of the **Delhi Sultanate**, who declared his independence in that year. The early Bahmani period is mostly recalled for

wars and uneasy truces with the Hindu empire of Vijayanagar and for the brutality and intolerance of the early sultans. In sharp contrast, the later Bahmani period, beginning in the 15c, is remembered for the open-mindedness of its rulers, who practised religious tolerance towards the local majority Hindu population and promoted an air of Persian intellectual diversity similar to that of the Mughal Empire at its height. The sultanate's capital was Gulbarga (Ahsanabad) until c.1425, when it was transferred to Bidar (Muhammadabad). At the peak of its power, during the period 1466–81, it ruled everything between the Penganga River in the north to Vijayanagar in the south.

Bailly, Jean Sylvain (1736–93) French astronomer and politician. From art he turned to literature, and then to astronomy, writing his great *Histoire de l'astronomie* (1775–87). As President of the National Assembly and Mayor of Paris during the **French Revolution** in 1789, he conducted himself with great integrity; but lost his popularity by allowing the **National Guard** to fire on anti-royalist crowds. He withdrew from public affairs but was arrested and taken to Paris, where he was guillotined.

Bairakdar, Mustafa (1755–1808) Turkish Grand Vizier and Pasha of Rustchuk. After the revolt of the **Janissaries** in 1807 by which **Selim III** was deposed in favour of Mustafa IV, he marched his troops to Constantinople in 1808, but found Selim already dead. Bairakdar executed the murderers, deposed Mustafa, and then proclaimed his brother, **Mahmud II**, sultan. As Grand Vizier, he endeavoured to carry out Selim's reforms and to annihilate the Janissaries who, however, rebelled and, backed by the fleet, demanded the restoration of Mustafa. Bairakdar defended himself bravely until, having strangled Mustafa, he threw the latter's head to the besiegers, and then blew himself up.

Bakatin, Vadim Viktorovich (1937–) Russian politician. Educated as an engineer in Novosibirsk, he worked in the construction industry before being selected for political work in the Communist Party of the USSR. With further training in social sciences he worked his way up from First Secretary in Kirov (1985–7) and in Kemerovo (1987–8) to the Central Secretariat in Moscow. In search of new blood, Mikhail **Gorbachev** appointed him Minister of the Interior in 1988 but dismissed him under right-wing pressure (Dec 1990) as too liberal, particularly on the nationalities question. In June 1991 he ran against Boris **Yeltsin** and others for election as President of the Russian Federation, allegedly as Gorbachev's candidate, but he came bottom of the poll. After the failure of the **August Coup** of the same year, Gorbachev appointed him head of the **KGB** with instructions to convert it to a normal police force as he struggled to retain Soviet power.

Baker, James Addison (1930–) US public official. He was educated at Princeton and the University of Texas. Baker served President Ford as Under-Secretary of Commerce, and President **Reagan** as White House Chief of Staff (1981–5) and Secretary of the Treasury (1985–8) before resigning to manage George **Bush**'s campaign for the presidency. After winning the election, Bush made him Secretary of State.

Baker v Carr (1962) The US Supreme Court decision that state electoral districts must contain approximately the same voting population, bringing to an end the long-standing rural domination of state legislatures.

Bakhtiyaris A nomad tribe from the south of what is now Iran. In early 20c Persia they supported the nationalist cause which had been given impetus by gaining the agreement, albeit reluctant, of the Qajar Shah Muzaffar al-Din to the formation of a national assembly. Muzaffar al-Din was succeeded by his son Muhammad Ali who was just as reluctant to have his powers circumscribed as his father had been and, after a bomb attack in an attempt to assassinate him, he called upon Russian-officered Cossack brigades to crush the nationalists in Tehran and Tabriz. Against this background, the Bakhtiyaris, under their leader Sirdari Asad, moved first against Isfahan where they put an end to the autocratic rule of the local governor, and then led a combined nationalist combat force against Tehran. The nationalists succeeded in seizing the capital and deposing the Shah. The Bakhtiyaris were thus instrumental in assisting the Persian nationalists to a triumph albeit short lived as a result of Great Power (in this case Russia and Britain) involvement in the politics of the country.

Bakr, Hasan al- (1914–82) President of Iraq. He succeeded Abd al-Rahman Aref as President in 1968, following the Ba'ath coup of July 1968. A leader of the socialist Ba'ath Renaissance Party, he held power with Saddam **Hussein**, the Ba'ath leader. Because of his border claims against Iran, al-Bakr was involved in conflict with the Kurds in the north of Iraq, a problem he eventually resolved through an agreement reached in 1975. On the economic front, he developed the modernization of both agriculture and industry, the former particularly as a result of irrigation financed by oil revenues. Politically, he made an alliance with the USSR, supported the **PLO** (Palestine Liberation Organization) and was an ally of Syria and Egypt in the 1973 Yom Kippur War. He was succeeded by Saddam Hussein in 1979.

Bakunin, Mikhail Alexeevich (1814–76) Russian anarchist. He took part in the German revolutionary movement (1848–9) and was condemned to death. Sent to Siberia in 1855, he escaped to Japan, and arrived in England in 1861. In the First International (1868), he was the opponent of Karl **Marx**; but at the Hague Congress in 1872 he was outvoted and expelled.

Balaclava, Battle of (25 Oct 1854) A battle fought between British and Russian forces during the early stages of the **Crimean War**. The Russian attack on the British base at Balaclava was unsuccessful, but the British sustained the heavier losses. ▷ **Charge of the Light Brigade**

Balaguer, Joaquim (1907–) Dominican Republic politician. He was Professor of Law at Santo Domingo University from 1938 and Ambassador to Colombia and Mexico in the 1940s before entering politics. He served in the dictatorial regime of Rafael **Trujillo**, after whose assassination in 1961 he fled to the USA in 1962, returning in 1965 to win the presidency in 1966 as leader of the Christian Social Reform Party (PRSC). He was re-elected in 1970 and 1974. The failure of the economic policies of the Dominican Revolutionary Party (PRD) brought the PRSC and Balaguer back to power in 1986, at the age of 79.

Balaguer (i Cirera), Victor (1824–1901) Catalan poet, politician and historian. A leading figure of the Catalan renaissance, he wrote a *History of Catalonia*, a *Political and Literary History of the Troubadours*, and poems in both Catalan and Spanish.

Balbo, Cesare (1789–1853) Piedmontese politician and political writer. He wrote widely on political problems and Italian history, his most important work, *Delle Speranze d'Italia* (Of the Hopes of Italy), appearing in 1844. Echoing **Gioberti**, to whom it was dedicated, *Delle Speranze* called for the creation of an Italian Confederation. It also demanded the end of Austrian rule in **Lombardy-Venetia** and that the Habsburgs seek compensation by expansion into the Balkans. In 1847, in a growing climate of reform, Balbo accepted the invitation of **Charles Albert** to enter a moderate government and the following year fleetingly held office as Piedmont's first constitutional Prime Minister. In his final years he supported the policies of **D'Azeglio** and **Cavour** despite reservations about their anticlericalism. ▷ **Habsburg Dynasty**

Balbo, Italo (1896–1940) Italian politician. An early supporter of Italian intervention in **World War I**, Balbo served from 1915 as an officer in the Alpini. From 1920 he played a key part in the fascist movement: he was one of the most energetic **ras** and a Quadrumvir in the **March on Rome**. During 1923–4 he was commander of the **MVSN** and in 1926 became Secretary of State for Aviation. In Jan 1934 he was made Governor of Libya, but he was killed when his plane was accidentally brought down by Italian anti-aircraft fire in 1940. He was one of several fascist leaders who disliked **Mussolini**'s move towards **Hitler** and who spoke out in defence of the Jews.

Balczerowicz, Leszek (1947–) Polish economist and politician. A talented economic researcher at the Central School of Planning in Warsaw, he was also a strong supporter and adviser of **Solidarity**. In 1989 he was appointed Finance Minister after the **Wałesa** revolution and achieved something of an economic miracle in stabilizing the currency and introducing the first stage of marketization. Following the 1991 elections, Wałesa judged his economic stringency too unpopular and engineered his dismissal in 1992. His achievement, nonetheless, won wide international praise.

Baldwin I (1172–c.1205) Count of Flanders, as Baldwin IX (1194/1205), and Hainaut, as Baldwin VI (1195/1205), and Latin Emperor of Constantinople (1204/5). The youngest brother of Godfrey of Bouillon, in 1202 he joined the Fourth Crusade, and in 1204 was crowned Baldwin I of the Latin Empire in Constantinople. The **Greeks**, invoking the aid of the Bulgarians, rose and took Adrianople. Baldwin laid siege to the town, but was defeated in 1205 and died in captivity. ▷ **Crusades**

Baldwin II (1217–73) Latin Emperor of Constantinople (1228/61). The nephew of **Baldwin I**, he succeeded his brother, Robert, as fourth and last Emperor of Constantinople, the Greeks taking the city in 1261 and extinguishing the Latin Empire. Thereafter, Baldwin lived as a fugitive, having sold his rights to **Charles of Anjou**.

Baldwin II, 'of Bourcq' (d.1131) King of Jerusalem (1118/31). He was a son of Count Hugh of Rethel and succeeded his cousin, Baldwin I, as Count of Edessa (1100) and King of Jerusalem (1118).

Baldwin III (1129–62) King of Jerusalem (1143/62). The grandson of **Baldwin II, 'of Bourcq'**, he succeeded his father, Fulk of Anjou, in 1143, but enjoyed sole authority only after long disputes and even civil war with his mother, Melisend. Baldwin's main achievement was the capture of Ascalon, the last Fatimid stronghold in Palestine (1153). ▷ **Fatimid Dynasty**

Baldwin, Robert (1804–58) Canadian lawyer and politician. He was the leader of the **Canada West** reforming clique who formed a coalition with Louis H **Lafontaine** to establish a reform party, which became a precursor of the **Liberal Party**. With his father, William Baldwin, he devised the theory of **Responsible Government**. This was rejected initially by the British government and governors such as Sir Francis Bond Head and Sir Charles **Metcalfe**, although Sir Charles **Bagot** accepted a level of participation by the Executive Council in government. Metcalfe's autocratic government led both Baldwin and Lafontaine to resign. In 1848 Baldwin came into power again as a partner with Lafontaine in the 'Great Ministry', during the period of transition from colonial rule to self-government.

Baldwin (of Bewdley), Stanley, 1st Earl (1867–1947) British politician. He worked in his family business before becoming a Conservative MP in 1908. He was President of the Board of Trade (1921–2) and Chancellor of the Exchequer (1922–3), and then unexpectedly succeeded Bonar **Law** as Prime Minister. His periods of office (1923–4, 1924–9 and 1935–7) included the **General Strike** (1926) and were interrupted by the two minority Labour governments of 1924 and 1929–31. During the **MacDonald** coalition (1931–5), he served as Lord President of the Council. He played a leading role in arranging the abdication of **Edward VIII** in 1936. He resigned from politics in 1937, when he was made an earl. ▷ **Conservative Party** (UK)

Balewa, Sir Abubakar Tafawa (1912–66) Nigerian politician. After a career as a teacher and education officer, he entered the Nigerian Legco and was a founder member of the Northern People's Congress. He entered the Federal Assembly in 1947 and was appointed consecutively Federal Minister of Works (1952–4), Minister of Trade (1954–7), Chief Minister (1957–9) and Prime Minister (1959–66). Essentially sympathetic to Western priorities, he was seen within Nigeria as a supporter of northern interests in the first years of independence. He was overthrown and assassinated in the 1966 coup.

Balfour, Arthur James, 1st Earl (1848–1930) British politician. He entered parliament in 1874, becoming Secretary for Scotland (1886) and Chief Secretary for Ireland (1887–91), where his policy of suppression earned him the name of 'Bloody Balfour'. A Conservative, he became Prime Minister (1902–5) and First Lord of the Admiralty (1915–16). As Foreign Secretary (1916–19), he was responsible for the **Balfour Declaration** (1917), which promised Zionists a national home in Palestine. He resigned in 1922, was created an earl, but served again as Lord President (1925–9). ▷ **Zionism**

Balfour Declaration (2 Nov 1917) A short communication from the British Foreign Secretary, A J Balfour, to Lord Rothschild, expressing the British government's disposition towards a Jewish national home in Palestine. The central portion reads: 'His Majesty's Government view with favour the establishment in Palestine of a national home for the Jewish people … it being clearly understood that nothing shall be done which may prejudice the civil and religious rights of existing non-Jewish communities'. Britain having received the Mandate for Palestine in 1920, the vagueness of the Balfour Declaration was clarified in 1923: Jewish immigration was to be encouraged; an appropriate Jewish body formed to that end; the rights of non-Jews were to be protected; and English, Hebrew and Arabic were to be given equal status. However, the ensuing two decades showed Britain to be either unwilling or unable to deliver its promise to the Jews, especially in view of increasing Arab hostility to Jewish immigration. ▷ **Haganah; Irgun; Jewish National Fund; Zionism**

Balilla The umbrella term for the youth movement founded by the **Fascist Party** in 1926. Its official name, the *Opera nazionale Balilla*, was altered to *Gioventù Italiana del Littorio* in 1937. The organization had many branches for boys and girls of different age groups and aimed at fascist indoctrination and the cultivation of patriotic fervour; it also provided youth clubs, sports facilities and rudimentary military training. Its success in attracting members can be largely attributed to the fascist abolition of the Catholic Boy Scouts Movement in 1928.

Balkan Entente (1930) A cultural and political alliance formed between Greece, Yugoslavia, Romania and Turkey after the first Balkan Conference held in Athens. It became in effect a defensive alliance against revisionist Bulgaria, which sought to regain territory lost to Greece and Yugoslavia by the Treaty of **Neuilly** (1919). In 1934 the member states signed a pact of mutual security and consultation, but cooperation was limited and the Entente could not counteract great power interference in the Balkans. During the 1930s, with the establishment of authoritarian regimes in all the Balkan states, the whole region moved closer to the German and Italian camp.

Balkan Wars (1912–13) A series of military campaigns fought in the Balkans. In 1912 Bulgaria, Serbia, Greece and Montenegro attacked Turkey, securing swift victories. A preliminary peace was drawn up by the Great Powers in May 1913, in which Turkey surrendered most of her European territories and the new state of Albania was created. Disputes between the Balkan allies over the spoils of war led to a second war, in which Bulgaria attacked her former allies, and was defeated. As a result of the two wars, Turkish territory in Europe was reduced to an area around Adrianople and Constantinople, Albania was established, Macedonia was partitioned, Serbia and Montenegro almost doubled in size, and tension among the Great Powers in Europe was considerably increased.

Balli Kombëtar The National Front Albanian resistance movement during **World War II**. Formed in Oct 1942 under Ali Klissura and Midhat Frashëri, it was nationalistic and liberal, favouring the establishment of a republic and an extensive programme of domestic reform. Relations with the communist-led resistance were vexed by the issue of **Kosovo**, which since 1941 had been included within Albania by the Italians: while Balli Kombëtar wanted to retain Kosovo, the Albanian communists, under pressure from their Yugoslav masters, did not. In 1943, under Allied pressure, the two resistance groups joined to form the Committee for the Salvation of Albania, but at the end of the war many members of Balli Kombëtar fell victim to Enver **Hoxha**'s drive to destroy all internal opposition to communist rule. ▷ **Albanians**

Balliol, Edward (c.1283–1364) King of Scots (1332/56). He was the elder son of John **Balliol**. In 1332, accompanied by the 'disinherited barons' bent on recovering their forfeited Scottish estates, he landed with 3400 followers at Kinghorn, Fife; and at Dupplin Moor, Perthshire, on 12 Aug, surprised and routed the Scottish Army under the new Regent, the Earl of Mar. On 24 Sep he was crowned King of Scotland at Scone. Less than three months later, he was himself surprised at Annan and fled across the Border on an unsaddled horse. Two further incursions into Scotland, in 1334–35, were unsuccessful and he resigned his claims to the Scottish throne to **Edward III** in 1356. He died without heirs.

Balliol, John (c.1250–1313) King of Scots (1292/96). On the death of Margaret, the 'Maid of Norway' in 1290, he became a claimant to the crown of Scotland; and was supported by **Edward I** of England against Robert **Bruce**, Lord of Annandale. Balliol swore fealty to Edward before and after his investiture at Scone (1292) and was forced to repudiate the Treaty of Bingham of 1290 with its guarantees of Scottish liberties. By 1295 a council of 12 of the magnates had taken control of government out of his hands and concluded an alliance with France, then at war with England; Edward invaded Scotland, took Balliol prisoner, and forced him to surrender his crown (10 July 1296). Balliol was confined for three years at Hertford and in the Tower; in 1302 he was permitted to retire to his estates in **Normandy**.

Balmaceda, José Manuel (1840–91) Chilean politician. A Liberal, he was elected to Congress in 1870, and served in the cabinet of President Santa María (1881–6). His strong presidency (1886–91) provoked resistance from Congress; this led to civil war, in which the President was defeated (1891). His suicide mythologized his rule as a struggle against the dominion of foreign, principally British, interests.

Baltimore and Ohio Railroad The first US passenger-carrying railroad. Its foundation stone was laid on 4 July 1828 by the last surviving signatory of the **Declaration of Independence**. In 1830 its first section was opened, running horse-powered vehicles over the 13 miles from Baltimore to Ellicott's Mills. Later that year the railroad turned to steam after Peter Cooper's Tom Thumb covered the distance in one hour. By the Civil War the system had become a major element in the transportation links between the mid-west and the east coast.

Baltimore Incident (1891) A brief but serious dispute between the USA and Chile, stemming from the death of two US sailors from the cruiser *Baltimore* in a brawl in Valparaiso. A war between the two countries was averted by a Chilean apology.

Bambuk A region in the valley of the middle and upper Senegal and its tributary the Faleme famous for its goldfields, exploited from medieval until modern times and important in trade and the rise and fall of West African kingdoms.

Banat of Temesvár ▷ **Temesvár, Banat of**

Ban Chao (Pan Ch'ao) (AD32–102) Chinese military commander. The brother of **Ban Gu**, he helped re-establish Han control of Central Asia between AD73 and 94, after it had been lost during the interregnum of Wang Mang (AD9/23). In AD97 Ban Chao led a Chinese army as far as the Caspian Sea, with the aim of protecting the oases along the **Silk Road**. ▷ **Han Dynasties**

Banda, Hastings Kamuzu (Officially 1905, probably 1898–) Doctor and politician. He left Malawi by foot for South Africa, from where he travelled to the USA and Britain to obtain medical qualifications. He set up practice first in Liverpool and then on Tyneside before moving to London, where he became deeply involved in opposition to the Central African Federation, but, after a scandal involving his liaison with a white woman, he went to Ghana, from where he was persuaded to return to Malawi to lead the Nyasaland African National Congress there. He was jailed in 1959 but was soon released and was appointed Minister of National Resources and Local Government (1961–3), Prime Minister of Nyasaland (1963–4) and then of independent Malawi (1964–6). When the country became a republic, he was its first President and Life President from 1971. He retained many portfolios, notably Defence, throughout his period as President. He made himself Life President of the only political party, the **Malawi Congress Party**. Depending on a unique mix of populism, a functioning political party and ruthless use of his security apparatus, he has survived as the dominant figure in Malawi for over 30 years.

Bandaranaike, Sirimavo (1916–) Sri Lankan politician. The widow of S W R D **Bandaranaike**, who was assassinated in 1959, she became the first woman prime minister in the world when she was elected in 1960. She held office from 1960 to 1965, and again from 1970 to 1977. Her second term was especially turbulent, with the 1971 **JVP** (People's Liberation Front) insurrection followed by the introduction of a new republican constitution in 1972 and a period of severe economic shortages. The **UNP** (United National Party) government of J R **Jayawardene** stripped her of her civil rights in 1980, forcing her to relinquish temporarily the leadership of the **SLFP** (Sri Lanka Freedom Party) to her son, Anura.

Bandaranaike, S(olomon) W(est) R(idgeway) D(ias) (1899–1959) Ceylonese (Sri Lankan) politician. Educated in Colombo and Oxford, he was called to the Bar in 1925. He became President of the Ceylon National Congress, and helped to found the **UNP** (United National Party). He was Leader of the House in Ceylon's first parliament, and Minister of Health. In 1951 he resigned from the government and organized the **SLFP** (Sri Lanka Freedom Party). In 1956 he was the main partner in a populist coalition which defeated the UNP in an election dominated by the issue of national language and the spirit of Buddhist revivalism. Bandaranaike's Sinhala-only proposals were opposed by representatives of the Tamil minority and swiftly followed by outbreaks of Sinhala–Tamil violence. In 1959 he was assassinated by a Buddhist monk. ▷ **Bandaranaike, Sirimavo**

Bandiera, Attilio (c.1810–44) and **Emilio** (1819–44) Italian revolutionaries. Sons of a Venetian admiral and lieutenants in the Habsburg navy, in 1840 they founded a nationalist secret society and planned to seize an Austrian frigate and launch a mutiny. Their plans discovered, they deserted ship in Corfu and travelled to the Kingdom of the **Two Sicilies** with the intention of launching an insurrection; captured by Neapolitan troops, they were tried and executed along with seven of their co-conspirators.

bandeirante A 17c Brazilian slave-raider and explorer. Parties of *bandeirantes* (literally, followers of the *bandeira* standard) sought Indian slaves from the interior from among the sedentary Jesuit-led Guarani peoples of the Platine Basin and peoples of the Amazon to labour on the coastal plantations. Initially permitted by the colonial government, their expeditions into the interior became a means by which the Portuguese could extend their rule well beyond the formal limits established by the Treaty of Tordesillas. Their conflicts with Indian peoples took them into the gold- and diamond-bearing districts of Minas Gerais and Bahia, which had been discovered by the late 17c. Their legendary feats in securing the interior of Brazil against Spanish, French or Dutch penetration secured them the mythical role of 'pioneers' (equivalent to the Canadian Voyageurs or South African **Voortrekkers**) in Brazil's history.

Bandung Conference (Apr 1955) A meeting in Bandung, Indonesia, of 29 newly-independent Afro-Asian countries, anxious to distance themselves from the superpower rivalry between the USA and the USSR. Representatives included **Zhou Enlai** (China), **Nehru** (India), **Sihanouk** (Cambodia), U **Nu** (Burma) and Gamal Abd al-**Nasser** (Egypt). Communist China's participation, which signalled its emergence as an actor on the world stage, indicated Beijing's determination to pursue a foreign policy independent of that of Moscow and a desire to deal amicably with those governments (such as that of India) hitherto deemed 'lackeys' of US imperialism. Zhou Enlai expressed this new conciliatory policy with his Five Principles of Peaceful Co-Existence (first enunciated in 1954), which looked forward to peaceful relations with all countries (including the USA) on the basis of mutual respect for each other's territorial integrity, non-interference in each other's affairs, and non-aggression. Thus, the conference sought to establish the non-aligned, newly-emerging nations as a major force in world politics, free from the shabby self-interest and manipulative interventions practised by the established blocs. It was a major triumph, domestically and internationally, for the Indonesian president, **Sukarno**.

Banerjea, Sir Surendranath (1848–1925) Indian politician and journalist. A fervent nationalist, he founded the Calcutta Indian Association in 1876 and was editor of *The Bengali* newspaper from 1879 to 1921.

Initially regarded as 'extremist' by the British, but later as a moderate, he was important in the **Indian National Congress** (of which he was President in 1902), a member of the Calcutta Corporation and twice returned to the Central Legislature. He welcomed the Montagu–Chelmsford reforms for the government of India, and subsequently broke with Congress over the non-cooperation question. ▷ **Non-Cooperation Movement**

Bánffy, Dezsö, Baron (1843–1911) Hungarian politician. He was born into an aristocratic family in Transylvania, where the population was ethnically mixed. In 1876 he became Lord Lieutenant of the county of Szolnok-Doboka, acquiring a reputation for denying the rights of nationalities other than his fellow Magyars. In 1892 he became Speaker of the Hungarian parliament, and from 1895 to 1899 he was Prime Minister. In these capacities he was much concerned with developing the ruthless policy of enforced Magyarization as an antidote to the emerging nationalism of the subject peoples of the Hungarian half of the Austro-Hungarian Empire.

Bangladesh War (1971) The suspension of democracy following a sweeping electoral victory by the **Awami League** in East Pakistan (1970), the devastation of this province of Pakistan by a cyclone in the same year, and the Dacca government's ineffectual response to the disaster—which claimed 220 000 lives and countless homes and crops—triggered fighting, which developed into a full-scale border war in 1971. Pakistan surrendered the territory only months later, following a popular uprising and military intervention by India, which had accepted huge numbers of Bangladeshi refugees, and the independent republic of Bangladesh was created. It joined the Commonwealth a year later.

Ban Gu (Pan Ku) (AD32–92) Chinese historian. He initiated a tradition of dynastic histories under imperial patronage unparalleled in other civilizations. In AD82 he completed a history of the Western Han Dynasty (202BC–AD9). The tradition pioneered by Ban Gu served a crucial political and moral role in imperial China. The history of a preceding dynasty highlighted its shortcomings in providing wise and benevolent government, thus serving as lessons for the future and enhancing the legitimacy of the current ruling dynasty. ▷ **Han Dynasties**

Bani-Sadr, Abolhassan (1935–) Iranian politician. He studied economics and sociology at the Sorbonne in Paris, having fled there in 1963 after being imprisoned in Iran for involvement in riots against the Shah's regime. He was an important figure in the Iranian Revolution of 1978–9, a member of the Revolutionary Council, and was elected first President of the Islamic Republic of Iran in 1980. From the start, however, he was threatened by a deepening conflict with the fundamentalist Muslim clergy; he was eventually criticised by Ayatollah **Khomeini**, and dismissed (mid-1981). He fled to France, where he was granted political asylum.

Banjaras An aboriginal tribe of Rajputhanis, known for centuries as itinerant artisans and traders.

Bank War (1832) An anti-national bank policy adopted by US President Andrew **Jackson**, when he vetoed the re-charter of the Second Bank of the United States which had been passed through Congress under the patronage of the **National Republican Party**. Like many Americans, especially in the West, Jackson believed that the bank had been responsible for the depression of the 1820s. He accused the bank of being a monopoly and representing big business, of allowing foreigners too much influence, of showing favour to congressmen, and of having too much power over state banks. Jackson refused, against the advice of two Secretaries of the Treasury, to allow any more federal revenues to be deposited with the bank, placing them instead with favoured state banks. Flush with new deposits and without the restraints which the national Bank had placed on their activities, the state banks encouraged another speculative boom which collapsed in the Panic of 1837, after Jackson had been succeeded by Martin **Van Buren**.

Banna, Hasan al- (1906–49) Islamic fundamentalist. Born at Mahmudiya, near Cairo, he was the founder in Egypt in 1928 of the Society of Muslim Brothers (better known as the **Muslim Brotherhood** or Brethren), which preached a return to the purity of early Islam. In 1948 the Egyptian Prime Minister, Nuqrashi Pasha, was killed by a Brotherhood member, and the following year al-Banna was himself murdered, although he had condemned the assassination. His movement has had considerable influence on contemporary Islamic fundamentalism.

Banna, Sabri Khalil al- ▷ **Abu Nidal**

Banner System A system of military organization in China, created by **Nurhaci** and used by the Manchu tribes. By the early 17c, the Manchus were organized into companies of 300 troops under at first four and then eight banners. By 1644, eight Chinese and eight Mongol banners had been formed, comprising an army of 170 000 men. The system survived throughout the **Qing Dynasty**.

Bannockburn, Battle of (21 June 1314) A battle fought near Stirling between English forces under **Edward II** and the Scots under Robert **Bruce**. It resulted in a decisive victory for the Scots. The English Army was largely destroyed, and many English nobles were killed or captured. The battle made Bruce a national hero, and inspired Scottish counter-attacks against northern England.

Bantustans ▷ **apartheid**

Ban Zhao (Pan Chao) (AD45–c.114) Chinese historian and moralist. The sister of **Ban Chao** and **Ban Gu**, she helped complete Ban Gu's history of the former Han Dynasty and became a tutor to empresses and court ladies. Ban Zhao compiled a book for moral admonitions for women, emphasizing the virtues of deference and modesty, which exerted a lasting influence on attitudes towards women in China. A crucial assumption underpinning these moral admonitions was that women should not play any public role. ▷ **Han Dynasties**

Bao Dai (1913–) Indo-Chinese ruler. He succeeded his father in 1925, ascending the throne in 1932. He collaborated with the Japanese during **World War II** and, after the Japanese surrender, found very brief favour with **Ho Chi Minh**. He abdicated in 1945, but returned to Saigon in 1949 (having renounced his hereditary title), as Chief of the State of Vietnam within the French Union. In 1955 he was deposed by **Ngo Dinh Diem** and South Vietnam became a republic.

Baojia (Pao-chia) System An administrative arrangement of household control and surveillance in China dating from the **Song Dynasty** (960–1279). Village families were grouped into units of 100 (*jia*) and 1 000 (*bao*), presided over by local elders. Originally responsible for providing and provisioning militia conscripts, by the time of the **Qing Dynasty** (1644–1911) the baojia system simply fulfilled a police function of mutual surveillance. All households were registered and were made responsible for the actions of their members.

Bar, Confederation of (1768) A military alliance of Polish gentry established at Bar, Podolia, directed against the Russian-backed king, Stanisław Poniatowski. The Confederation advocated the preservation of the privileges of the Polish aristocracy and the Catholic Church. Its suppression in 1772 led to the first partition of Poland. ▷ **Poland, Partitions of**

Barbary Coast The coast of North Africa from Morocco to Tripolitania (Libya), famous for piracy between the 16c and 18c. This coast and the Barbary States of Morocco, Algeria, Tunisia, and Tripolitania take their name from Barbarossa, who led the Turkish conquest of the region in the 1530s, preventing Spanish invasion. ▷ **Frederick I, 'Barbarossa'**

Barberini A Tuscan family which acquired wealth by trade in the 16c, and rose to the front rank of the Roman nobility on the elevation of Maffeo to the papacy as **Urban VIII** in 1623. Francesco (1597–1679), brother of Cardinal Taddeo, founded the Barberini Library. Antonio (1608–71) was cardinal and high chamberlain under Urban VIII. Their power and ambition aroused the jealousy of neighbouring princes and led to war (1641–4) and the defeat of papal troops by the Duke of Parma. The Barberini fled to France, but returned in 1652.

Barbosa, Ruí (1849–1923) Brazilian politician and lawyer. After studying law, he practised in Salvador and then in Rio de Janeiro. A Liberal, he was elected a deputy in 1878, and became prominent in 1884–5 at the peak of the anti-slavery campaign. A radical, he campaigned against the last Cabinet of the Monarchy, siding with the Republicans in Nov 1889. He was Finance Minister and also briefly Vice-Chief of the Provisional Government of the Republic. His controversial 14 months of power saw the introduction of financial measures which stimulated hyperinflation and massive government deficits, a legacy which meant that he never succeeded in regaining high office. As Senator for Bahia from 1891 until his death, he campaigned in favour of a more liberal regime, being exiled in 1893–4, and defeated on an 'anti-military' ticket in the presidential election of 1910. Special Ambassador to the

Hague Conference in 1907, he defended the idea that all states were equal in international law.

Barcelona, Siege of (1713–14) The final drama of the War of the **Spanish Succession**, when the Catalans were abandoned by their allies, the Germans and the English, and forced to defend themselves or accept unconditional surrender. After a bloody siege, the Duke of **Berwick** at the head of the Franco-Spanish army entered the city and abolished its privileges (*fueros*) and those of all Catalonia. The date of the surrender (11 Sep) is now commemorated as the national day of Catalonia. Barcelona was the seat of a principality from the 9c, and the centre of resistance to Castilian rule during the revolution of 1640. It was besieged several times, notably by the French in 1697.

Barclay de Tolly, Mikhail Bogdanovich, Prince (1761–1818) Russian field marshal. He joined the Russian army in 1786, and served in Turkey, Sweden, and Poland, losing an arm at the Battle of Eylau (1807). He was appointed Minister of War in 1810. Defeated by Napoleon at Smolensk (1812), and replaced, he later served again as Commander-in-Chief, and took part in the invasion of France. He was made a prince in 1815, and died at Insterburg, eastern Prussia. ▷ **Alexander I; Napoleon I**

Bardi and **Peruzzi** These Florentine families gave their names to two great banking companies of the 14c, commanding assets far greater than those of the later and more famous Medici bank. They advanced loans to European monarchs, most notably **Edward I**, who used the money to finance his campaigns in the **Hundred Years War**. He reneged on his debts in 1345, which led to bankruptcy for the Bardi and Peruzzi firms and sent shock waves through the European economy.

Bardoli A town in Surat district, near Bombay, it was the scene of a very successful tax reduction campaign lasting from 12 Feb to 4 Aug 1928. Led by Sardar **Patel**, using M K **Gandhi**'s **Satyagraha** technique, the protest called for an impartial review of an apparently arbitrary increase in local land revenue forecast used for tax assessments. In Mar 1929 an appointed committee reported that the increase was excessive by 15.75 per cent, and the rate was lowered.

Barebone's Parliament (4 July–12 Dec 1653) The English 'Parliament of Saints', nominated by the Council of Officers of the Army to succeed the **Rump Parliament**; named after radical member Praise-God Barebone. It instituted civil marriage and sought legal reforms; but collapsed after disagreements over the abolition of tithes and lay patronage in church.

Barère (de Vieuzac), Bertrand (1755–1841) French revolutionary and regicide, noted for his achievement of survival. Originally a monarchist, he went over to **Robespierre**'s camp, becoming a member of the Committee of Public Safety. He was later imprisoned (1794), but escaped into exile, not returning to Paris until 1830. ▷ **French Revolution; Public Safety, Committee of**

Bar Kokhba, Simon (d.135) The leader of the Jews in their great but fruitless insurrection against the Emperor Hadrian (130–5). He was killed at Bethar. In 1960 some of his letters were found in caves near the Dead Sea.

Bar–Lev Line The chain of fortifications established after the **Six-Day War** on the east of the Suez Canal by Chaim Bar Lev, Israeli Chief of Staff. This was in response to continued Egyptian attacks under Gamal Abd al-**Nasser**, despite cease-fire agreements. In the **Yom Kippur War** of 1973, however, the Bar–Lev Line was not able to withstand the initial onslaught of Egyptian forces. ▷ **Arab-Israeli Wars**

Barmakids A Persian family descended from a Buddhist priest (parmak) at Balkh (now Afghanistan). In the mid-8c Khalid ibn Barmak and his brothers came to Iraq, converted to Islam, and rose in the bureaucracy of the 'Abbasid caliphate. The height of their power was a 17-year period during the reign of **Harun al-Rashid**, when the vizier, Yahya ibn Khalid, and his sons, al-Fadl and Jafar effectively controlled the central administration. The family patronized poets and theologians and built sumptuous palaces in Baghdad, but lacked military power, and in 803 Harun had its members imprisoned or executed and their property seized.

Barnave, Antoine (Pierre Joseph Marie) (1761–93) French revolutionary. He studied law, and became a member of the new National Assembly (1799), where he established a reputation as an orator, and helped to carry through the **Civil Constitution of the Clergy**. He brought back the royal family from Varennes, but, after advocating more moderate courses, was guillotined. ▷ **French Revolution**

Barneveldt, Jan van Olden (1547–1619) Dutch politician and lawyer. As adviser to Prince **Maurice**, he opposed his warlike schemes and in 1609 concluded a truce with Spain. This caused a political rift which eventually resulted in his being represented as a secret friend of Spain. He was illegally arrested, condemned as a traitor, and executed. Of his two sons, the elder escaped to Antwerp, the younger was executed.

Barons Wars (1215–17) and 1263–7) Two wars in England during the reigns of **John** and **Henry III**. The first came about after the sealing of **Magna Carta**: many barons still defied John, and offered the crown to Prince Louis (later **Louis VIII**) of France. After John's death, the French and baronial army was routed at Lincoln (May 1217), and the war was effectively ended by the Treaty of Kingston-on-Thames (Sep 1217). The second war broke out after the Provisions of Oxford failed to achieve a settlement, and some barons led by Simon de **Montfort**, captured Henry III at Lewes (1264). Earl Simon was killed at Evesham (1265), and the King was restored to power by the Dictum of Kenilworth (1266). ▷ **Oxford, Provisions of**

Barras, Paul François Jean Nicolas, Count of (1755–1829) French revolutionary. An original member of the Jacobin Club, and a regicide, he played the chief part in the overthrow of **Robespierre**, and was given dictatorial powers by the National Convention. In 1795, acting against a royalist uprising, he was aided by his friend Bonaparte, who fired on the rebels (the historical 'whiff of grape-shot'). Barras became one of the five members of the **Directory** (1795). Once more dictator in 1797, he guided the state almost alone, until his hedonism and corruption made him so unpopular that Bonaparte overthrew him easily (1799). After travelling abroad, he died at Paris-Chaillot. ▷ **Convention, National; French Revolution; Jacobins; Napoleon I**

Barre, Mohamed Siad (1919–) Somali soldier and politician. Educated locally and at an Italian military academy, he was a police officer in Somaliland, under both Italian and British Trusteeship, before joining the Somali army in 1960. He led a successful coup in 1969. Using a **KGB**-trained secret service and manipulating the clan

divisions of the Somalis, he was backed first by the USSR and then by the USA. When uprisings took place in 1989, his use of the air force and army to stamp out the opposition proved unavailing and he was forced to leave Mogadishu (Jan 1991), leaving behind an impoverished country divided into competing warring factions.

Barre, Raymond (1924–) French conservative politician. He made his reputation as an influential neo-liberal economist at the Sorbonne and as Vice-President of the European Commission (1967–72). He was Minister of Foreign Trade under President **Giscard d'Estaing** and was appointed Prime Minister (1976–81) after the resignation of Jacques **Chirac** in 1976. Holding concurrently the Finance Ministry portfolio, he concentrated on economic affairs, gaining a reputation as a determined budget-cutter. With unemployment mounting between 1976 and 1981, he became deeply unpopular, but his term as Prime Minister was later favourably reassessed after the failure of the 1981–3 socialist administration's reflationary experiment. During the 1980s he built up a firm political base in the Lyons region, representing the centre-right Union for French Democracy (UDF). He contested the 1988 presidential election but was eliminated in the first ballot.

Barrès, Maurice (1862–1923) French novelist and politician. A member of the Chamber of Deputies (1889–93), he was an apostle of nationalism, individualism, provincial patriotism and national energy. He wrote a trilogy on his own self-analysis (*Le Culte du moi*, 1888–91), and a nationalistic trilogy that included *L'Appel au soldat* (1906), and many other works, including *Colette Baudoche* (1909).

Barreto, Francisco de (1520–73) Portuguese military commander. He attempted an ambitious conquest of the Zambezi Valley, the Mashonaland plateau and the kingdom of Mwene Mutapa in 1572. In 1575 a treaty was concluded between the Portuguese and the Mwene Mutapa ruler whereby Muslims would be expelled and the Portuguese be allowed to trade, to seek gold and conduct missionary work. The Portuguese maintained trading footholds in the interior of what is now Zimbabwe until expelled in the 1690s.

Barrier Treaties (1697, 1709 and 1715) A series of agreements giving the Dutch

Republic the right to garrison certain towns in the southern Netherlands as a protection against potential French encroachments. The first was signed between the Dutch and Spain in 1697, the second between the Dutch and the English in 1709, and the third between the Dutch, the English, and the Austrians in 1715. In the War of the Austrian Succession (1740–8) the towns were overrun by the French; in 1781 Emperor Joseph II declared the treaties void and returned the garrisons to the Netherlands.

Barrow, Errol Walton (1920–87) Barbadian politician. Born in Barbados, he flew with the Royal Air Force (1940–7) and then studied at London University and Lincoln's Inn. Returning to Barbados, he became active in the Barbados Labour Party (BLP) and was elected to the House of Assembly in 1951. In 1955 he left the BLP and co-founded the **Democratic Labour Party (DLP)**, becoming its Chairman in 1958. In the elections following independence in 1961 the DLP was victorious and Barrow became the first Prime Minister. His unbroken tenure was ended in 1976 by the BLP, led by 'Tom' Adams. In 1986, a year after Adams's death, Barrow returned to power with a decisive majority but he died in the following year and was succeeded by Erskine Lloyd Sandiford.

Barry, Marie-Jeanne Gomard de Vaubernier, Countess du (c.1743–93) French noblewoman. The favourite mistress of **Louis XV**, her influence reigned supreme until his death (1774), when she was dismissed from court. She was tried before the Revolutionary Tribunal, and guillotined. ▷ **French Revolution**

Bart (Barth), Jean (1650–1702) French privateer. He served first in the Dutch Navy, turning to French service on the outbreak of the war with Holland (1672). In 1691 he commanded a small squadron in the North Sea, where he destroyed many English vessels. In the War of the **Grand Alliance** (1689–97), he was taken prisoner, but escaped from Plymouth to France, where **Louis XIV** received him, rewarding him with command of a squadron, and later giving him noble status.

Barthou, Jean Louis (1862–1934) French politician. He practised law, and was a member of parliament from 1889 until his death. From 1894 onwards he frequently held ministerial office, becoming Prime Minister in 1913, when he introduced three-year

conscription. He was briefly Foreign Minister in 1917 and criticized the Treaty of **Versailles** (1919) for not providing enough security for France. After **World War I** he was again almost continually in office, as Minister of War (1921–2, 1930–1), Minister of Justice (1922–4, 1926–9) and Foreign Minister (1934). He presided over the French delegation at the Genoa Conference (1922), and was President of the Reparations Committee. As part of his attempt to strengthen French links with the states of Eastern Europe against the threat from Germany (an 'Eastern Locarno Treaty'), he invited King Alexander I of Yugoslavia to France; he was assassinated with him by Croatian terrorists in Marseilles.

Barton, Clara (Clarissa Harlowe) (1821–1912) US humanitarian and founder of the American Red Cross. A schoolteacher (1836–54) and clerk in the Patent Office in Washington DC (1854–7), during the **American Civil War**, she organized the distribution of hospital supplies and nursed the wounded, becoming known as the 'Angel of the battlefield'. She worked for the International Red Cross in Europe during the **Franco-Prussian War** (1870–1). After returning to the USA she established the US branch of the Red Cross in 1881 and became its first President (1881–1904). As a result of her campaigning, in 1882 the USA signed the Geneva Convention for the humane treatment of the wounded and prisoners of war.

Barton, Sir Edmund (1849–1920) Australian jurist and politician, the first Prime Minister of the Australian Commonwealth (1901–3). He was elected to the New South Wales legislature in 1879, becoming speaker (1883–7) and Attorney-General (1889 and 1891–3). He was leader of the **federation** movement from 1891, headed the committee that drafted the Commonwealth Constitution Bill and led the delegation that presented it to the British parliament in 1900. From 1903 until his death he served as a High Court judge.

Baruch, Bernard Mannes (1870–1965) US financier. In 1918 he was appointed by President Woodrow **Wilson** to head the War Industries Board, with sweeping powers to establish priorities and increase production. His appointment symbolized a new alliance between a Democratic administration which had previously acted against the excesses of big business, and industry which now wished to combine patriotism with its own interests. A conservative Democrat and supporter of Al **Smith**, Baruch was one of the few speculators who anticipated the **Wall Street Crash** and so preserved his fortune. Often critical of the more radical aspects of the **New Deal**, he nevertheless frequently advised President Franklin D **Roosevelt**. In 1946 he presented the US plan for atomic energy control to the UN.

Barzani, Mustafa al- (1904–79) Kurdish military leader and mullah. He commanded the peshmerga guerrillas and negotiated a promise of autonomy for the Kurds in northern Iraq in 1970. However, President **Bakr**'s failure to honour his pledge led to further Iraqi-Kurdish conflict, resulting in the defeat of the peshmerga by Saddam **Hussein**, who took over the presidency in 1979.

Basic Law (*Grundgesetz*) The Basic Law forms a major component within the Federal German constitutional order. In the period 1949–90, the Basic Law accepted the western Allied provision that Federal Germany have a market-oriented economy (although it did not exclude alternative options in the future) and that in political matters ultimate sovereignty lay with the (non-functioning) Allied Control Commission. With German reunification these limitations on sovereignty have lapsed. In its content the Basic Law represents a summation of previous German constitutional experience which learns from previous successes and failures. It establishes the principle of constitutional democracy with ultimate sovereignty lying with the people and it defines the rights of the **Bund** and *Länder*. The Basic Law has been amended dozens of times by act of parliament and although previously regarded as a provisional creation, pending eventual reunification, it has survived in slightly amended form in a reunited Germany. ▷ **Land**

Basic Treaty (*Grundvertrag*) (8 Nov 1972) The treaty signed between Federal (West) and East **Germany** under which each promised to respect the other's independence and sovereignty. East **Germany** claimed that the agreement finalized Germany's division, the West maintained in a note delivered to East **Berlin** that it did not preclude the possibility of unification in a future, more peaceful Europe. The treaty marked a key success in Willy **Brandt**'s policy of **Ostpolitik**, not least because it allowed the resumption of personal contacts between East and West Germans.

Basil, St (c.329–79) One of the greatest of the Greek Fathers. He was born and died at Caesarea, Cappadocia. After living a monastic life, in 370 he succeeded Eusebius as Bishop of Caesarea. Along with his brother, St Gregory of Nyssa, and St Gregory of Nazianzus, he defended Christian philosophy against Arianism.

Basil I, 'the Macedonian' (d.886) Byzantine Emperor (867/86). Born in Thrace, he founded the Macedonian Dynasty. He was at first joint ruler with Michael III, but assassinated him in 868. He began the work of reissuing the Justinianic legal corpus.

Basil II Bulgaroctonus (c.958–1025) Byzantine Emperor (963(976)/1025). The son of Romanus II, he came to the throne as sole ruler in 976. A revolt by the nobleman Bardas Sclerus was quashed with the help of the general Bardas Phocas, but a decade later both men revolted in turn with much of the army and aristocracy. Basil was saved by his alliance with **Vladimir I, 'the Great'**, Prince of Kiev, who married his sister Anna and converted to Christianity. In return, Vladimir sent 6000 Russian troops who defeated the uprising (989) and became the core of the future Varangian Guard, the elite unit of the Byzantine army. Thereafter Basil supported the peasantry at the expense of the great landowners. His 15-year war against the Bulgarians culminated in the victory in the Belasica mountains which earned him his surname of 'Bulgar-slayer': thousands of prisoners were blinded and in groups of a hundred, each led by a one-eyed man, sent back to their Tsar Samuel, who died of shock (1015). Bulgaria was annexed to the empire by 1018, while the eastern frontier was extended to Lake Van in Armenia.

Basle, Council of (1431–49) A controversial Council of the Church. It was intended to continue the work of the Council of Constance, against heresy and initiating reform, but fell into dispute with Pope **Eugenius IV** for asserting the authority of the Council over that of the Pope. When the Pope attempted to dissolve it, the Council appointed Felix V (**Amadeus VIII, 'the Peaceful'**), the last of the anti-popes.

Basle, Treaties of (7 Sep 1795) Two separate treaties were signed during the wars associated with the **French Revolution**. The first was between France and Prussia (5 Apr) and accepted the French occupation of German lands west of the Rhine. In the second (22 July) Spain ceded the Dominican Republic to France. The treaty is connected with the Treaty of Rastatt.

Basle, **Treaty of** (22 Sep 1499) The treaty which put an end to the so-called Swiss or Swabian War between **Maximilian I** and the Swiss Confederation. In it the Swiss obtained stewardship of the Thurgau but had to accept Austrian overlordship in Graubünden. More significantly, the treaty declared that Switzerland was not subject to the imperial court of taxes, thus hastening its separation from the Holy Roman Empire.

Basque Autonomy Statutes (1936 and 1979) One of the oldest peoples in Europe, the Basques first formed a political entity with their unification under the Kingdom of Navarre in the 10c and 11c. With the decline of Navarre, the Basque provinces became integrated into the Kingdom of Castile by the 16c. The Basques retained their feudal laws and privileges until these were steadily abolished during the 19c. The Second Republic (1931–6) created an autonomous regime through the Statute of Oct 1936, but this was rescinded at the end of the **Spanish Civil War** by General **Franco**. Franco's dictatorship (1939–75) tried to suppress all aspects of Basque independence and culture. In 1979 a new Basque Autonomy Statute was passed, although it did not include Navarre, which obtained its own autonomous arrangement in 1982. The 1979 Autonomy Statute provided for the Basque country's own parliament, police force, tax authority, and control of the means vital to the survival of Basque culture, such as Basque schools and television in Euskera (the Basque language). The fight for outright independence is maintained by **ETA**. ▷ **Republic, Second** Spain

Basque Nationalist Party ▷ **PNV**

Basques A people of uncertain origin living in north-west Spain and neighbouring areas in France. They are physically similar to their neighbours, and are Roman Catholics, but their language, Basque, spoken by c.500 000, does not relate to any other European language, and is thought to be a remnant of the languages spoken in Western Europe before the advent of the Indo-European family. Despite extensive cultural and linguistic assimilation, urbanized Basques retain strong ethnic identity, and their main city, Bilbao, is a centre of Basque nationalism. Most Basques supported the Spanish Republic, which granted an autonomy

statute in Oct 1936, during the **Spanish Civil War**. After the fall of Bilbao (June 1937), many went into exile. Since the death of **Franco** (1975), the new liberal Spanish monarchy has granted Basques some local autonomy (1978–9), but the more militant continue to agitate for a separate Basque state through the terrorist organization, **ETA**.

Bastille A medieval fortress and prison in east Paris, the symbol of Bourbon despotism, stormed by a Parisian mob on 14 July 1789. Its destruction came to have a unique place in French revolutionary ideology as marking the end of the **ancien régime**. The anniversary of the day is a French national holiday. ▷ **Bourbon, House of**; **French Revolution**

Batavian Republic The name given to the Dutch Republic 1795–1806, after that country had been conquered by revolutionary French forces in 1794–5. Much influence was exerted from Paris, but the Dutch retained a degree of independence, and fought out their own battles between radicals and conservatives during the revolutionary era. Between 1806 and 1810 the Kingdom of Holland was ruled by **Napoleon I**'s brother, **Louis Napoleon**; in 1810 the Netherlands was incorporated into France until the collapse of French rule in 1813. ▷ **French Revolutionary Wars**; **Napoleonic Wars**

Batavians A Germanic tribe inhabiting part of the Low Countries during the Roman occupation. Traditionally they were allies of the Romans, and provided valued soldiers for their legions. In 1c BC, at the request of the Romans, they colonized the present-day Dutch region of the Betuwe, in order to defend it from attack by other Germanic tribes across the Rhine. In AD 69–70 the Batavian Revolt took place, a temporary alliance of a number of Germanic tribes under the Batavian Julius **Civilis** (his Romanized name). His forces laid siege to Roman positions on the Rhine, and the rebellion was brought to a conclusion by a peace-with-honour agreement with the Roman general Cerialis. Thereafter the Batavians disappeared as a distinct group, but lived on in the history of the Dutch people, who have always admired their heroic independence against foreign domination.

Batista (y Zaldívar), Fulgencio (1901–73) Cuban dictator. In 1933 he organized a military coup (the 'Sergeants' Revolt'), consolidated his power, and became President (1940–4). In 1952 he overthrew President Prio Socorras, and ruled as dictator until his overthrow by Fidel **Castro** (Jan 1959), when he found refuge in the Dominican Republic.

Batlle y Ordóñez, José (1856–1929) Uruguayan politician. Educated in Montevideo and Europe, he founded the newspaper *El día* in 1886, rallying suport of the articulate middle sectors of Montevideo. He was elected Senator (1896), President (1903–7 and 1911–15). Nominally a Colorado (or liberal constitutionalist), he crushed the conservative Blancos (*estancieros* who had dominated the interior of the country). Supported by foreign immigrants and workers, he designed a political system where power was shared between the President and a nine-member National Council. He was a notable social reformer and exponent of democratic ideals.

Batman, John (1801–39) Australian colonizer, the 'Founder of Victoria'. He became a grazier in Tasmania (1821) and found fame by capturing the bushranger, Matthew Brady. In May 1835 he colonized the shores of Port Phillip from Tasmania. He was the main founder of Melbourne, seeing the potential of its site.

Battenberg, Prince Alexander of (1857–93) First Prince of Bulgaria (1879/86). The uncle of Earl **Mountbatten**, he was the second son of Prince Alexander of Hesse and, through his mother, a nephew of Tsar **Alexander II** of Russia. In 1879 he was named as a suitable candidate as Prince of Bulgaria by the Great Powers which, while accepting that Russia would be Bulgaria's protector, did not want the new principality to fall to a major ruling dynasty. A German aristocrat with miltary training, Prince Alexander had no sympathy with the ideas of the predominant Bulgarian Liberal Party. After the accession of his reactionary cousin, **Alexander III**, as Tsar of Russia, he suspended the highly liberal Bulgarian constitution. Bulgarian-Russian relations deteriorated as the new tsar treated Bulgaria as tantamount to a Russian province. In 1886 Prince Alexander was overpowered by pro-Russian army conspirators at Sofia and was forced to abdicate. Unable to overcome the hostility of Alexander III, he retired to Darmstadt in Austria as Count Hartenau.

Batthyányi, Louis, Count (1806–49) Hungarian politician. A member of the Hungarian assembly, and a leader of the independence movement, he was executed by the Austrians for his part in the Hungarian insurrection of 1849. His estates were confiscated, but were restored to his family in 1867. In 1870 his body was removed and interred anew with great solemnity.

Baudouin I (1930–93) King of the Belgians (1951/93). The elder son of **Leopold III** and his first wife, Queen **Astrid**, he succeeded to the throne on the abdication of his father over the controversy of the latter's conduct during **World War II**. In 1960 he married the Spanish Fabiola de Mora y Aragon.

Baudouin IX of Flanders ▷ **Baldwin I**

Bauer, Gustav (1870–1944) German politician. A senior trade unionist before **World War I**, Bauer became an **SPD** member of the **Reichstag** in 1912. In Oct 1918 he was appointed a Junior Minister of Labour and became Minister of Labour in Feb 1919. He succeeded **Scheidemann** as Chancellor and on 26 June 1919 headed the government which signed the Treaty of **Versailles** under protest. He resigned as Chancellor during the **Kapp Putsch** (Mar 1920) and, after holding various further ministerial posts, eventually resigned from parliament in 1928 on becoming involved in a corruption trial.

Bava Beccaris, Fiorenzo (1831–1924) Italian general. His brutality in suppressing the Milan bread riots in 1898 was pivotal in both the fall of the **di Rudini** government and the decline in popularity of **Umberto I**.

Bavaria A south-east German region and, although much changed in size and structure in the course of time, one of the oldest existing political entities in Europe. First documented as a duchy under Frankish overlordship in the 6c, Bavaria included most of present-day Austria until 1156 and was ruled by a succession of dynasties, including the **Guelfs**, before the House of Wittelsbach took over in 1180. Presiding over the country until 1918, members of this family won the German crown on two occasions (Louis IV, 1314/47 and Charles VII, 1742/5), and for centuries held the dignity of Electors of the **Holy Roman Empire**. Bavaria fought in the vanguard of the counter-reformation and was among the pioneers of monarchical absolutism in Germany. During the revolutionary wars, she deserted the cause of the Reich by signing the Treaty of Lunéville (1803) for which Napoleon subsequently rewarded her with considerable territorial enlargement and, in 1806, elevation to the status of kingdom. One of the first German states to introduce constitutional government (1818), Bavaria tried to pursue an independent policy between Austria and Prussia during the period of the German Confederation. Having sided with Austria against Prussia in 1866 she did, however, join the newly created German Empire in 1871, and is now one of the component federal states of Germany.

Bavarian Succession, War of the (1778–9) A brief campaign waged by Frederick II of Prussia against Austria when, on the dying out of the Bavarian branch of the Wittelsbach family, Joseph II sought to gain parts of Bavaria and thereby strengthen the Habsburg position in Germany. Military manoeuvring soon gave way to stalemate, and the Treaty of Teschen by and large reaffirmed the status quo. Austria was forced to recognize the succession of the Palatinate line of the Wittelsbachs to the Bavarian throne, but succeeded in winning the Innviertel, including the town of Braunau which was destined to become the birthplace of Hitler. The 'Potato War' as the whole affair is often referred to, because of the absence of any conclusive battles, further tarnished Frederick the Great's prestige in the last years of his reign.

Bayard, Pierre du Terrail, Lord of (c.1473–1524) French soldier. Known as 'the good knight without fear and without reproach', he fought for **Charles VIII** of France in Italy (1494–5), and for **Louis XII** of France in Italy and Spain. At Marignano (1515), he gained a victory for **Francis I** (of France). When **Charles V** invaded Champagne with a large army, Bayard successfully defended Mézières. He was mortally wounded by a shot from an arquebus while defending the passage of the Sesia.

Bayazid ▷ **Bayezid**

Bayezid I (c.1360–1403) Ottoman Sultan (1389/1402). He succeeded his father, Murad I, who was slain in the Battle of **Kosovo**. Within three years he had conquered Bulgaria, with parts of Serbia, Macedonia, and Thessaly, and most of Asia Minor. His rapid conquests earned him the name of *Yildirim* — 'Lightning'. For 10 years he blockaded Constantinople, to rescue which King Sigismund of Hungary (later Emperor) assembled a large army, including 2 000 French nobles, and laid siege to Nicopolis, on the Danube.

Bayezid hastened to meet him, and gained a decisive victory (1396). Bayezid would have entirely destroyed the Greek empire if he had not, in 1402, been completely defeated by **Timur** near Ankara. Bayezid himself fell into the hands of the conqueror, who treated him with great generosity (his incarceration in an iron cage being a myth), and in whose camp he died. He was succeeded by his son, **Suleyman I, 'the Magnificent'**. ▷ **Ankara, Battle of**

Bayezid II (1448–1512) Ottoman Sultan (1481/1512). He succeeded his father, **Mehmed II**, the conqueror of Constantinople, in 1481. His long reign was a succession of wars against Hungary, Poland, Venice, Egypt, and Persia, which served on the whole to establish the Ottoman power.

Bay of Pigs (Apr 1961) The failed invasion of Cuba by anti-**Castro** Cuban exiles sponsored by the USA. The invasion force of 1 500 men landed at Bahía de Cochinos ('Bay of Pigs') on the southern coast, but failed to win local support and was rapidly overwhelmed and defeated by Cuban troops. The episode was an embarrassment to John F **Kennedy**'s administration.

Bazaine, Achille (François) (1811–88) Marshal of France. He joined the army in 1831, serving in Algeria, Spain, the Crimea, the Italian campaign of 1859, and notably the French expedition to Mexico (1862–7). For his surrender at Metz (1870), during the **Franco-Prussian War**, he was court-martialled and imprisoned, but he later escaped and fled to Spain, where he died. ▷ **Mexican War**

Beaton (Bethune), David (1494–1546) Scottish statesman and Roman Catholic prelate. He resided at the French court (1519) and was appointed Bishop of Mirepoix by **Francis I** (1537). In 1525 he took his seat in the Scots parliament as Abbot of Arbroath and became Privy Seal. Elevated to cardinal (1538), and made Archbishop of St Andrews (1539), he championed French interests at the expense of English influence. A persecutor of the Scottish Protestants, he had the reformer George Wishart burnt at St Andrews (1546), but was murdered in revenge three months later by a group of Protestant conspirators. ▷ **Reformation** (Scotland)

Beatrix (Wilhelmina Armgard) (1938–) Queen of the Netherlands (1980/). The eldest daughter of Queen **Juliana** and Prince Bernhard zur Lippe-Biesterfeld, she acceded to the throne on the abdication of her mother. In 1966 she married West German diplomat Claus-Georg Wilhelm Otto Friedrich Gerd von Amsberg, causing much controversy in the Netherlands; there were hostile demonstrations at her wedding and her coronation. Their son, Prince Willem-Alexander Claus George Ferdinand, is the first male heir to the Dutch throne in over a century. There are two other sons: Johan Friso Bernhard Christiaan David and Constantijn Christof Frederik Aschwin.

Beatty, David Beatty, 1st Earl (1871–1936) British admiral. He served in the Sudan (1896–8), and as battleship commander took part in the China War (1900). At the outbreak of **World War I** he steamed into Heligoland Bight, and destroyed three German cruisers. He later sank the *Blücher* (Jan 1915), and took part in the Battle of **Jutland** (May 1916). He became Commander-in-Chief of the Grand Fleet in 1916 and First Sea Lord in 1919, when he was created an earl.

Beaufort, Henry (1377–1447) English cardinal and political figure. He studied at Oxford and Aix-la-Chapelle, was consecrated Bishop of Lincoln (1398) and Winchester (1405), and became a cardinal in 1426. He was Lord Chancellor on three occasions (1403–5, 1413–17, 1424–6). In 1427 the Pope sent him as legate into Germany, to organize a crusade against the **Hussites**; this undertaking failed, and he fell from papal pleasure. During the 1430s he controlled the government of the young King **Henry VI** of England. He retired from politics in 1443. ▷ **Hussite Wars**

Beaufort, Margaret (1443–1509) Daughter of John, 1st Duke of Somerset, and great-granddaughter of **John of Gaunt**, Duke of Lancaster. She married Edmund Tudor, Earl of Richmond (1455), and became the mother of **Henry VII**, to whom she conveyed the Lancastrian claim to the English crown. She was twice widowed before her third husband, Thomas, Lord Stanley, was instrumental in helping Henry VII assume the crown. She was a benefactress of William Caxton, and of Oxford and Cambridge.

Beauharnais, Alexandre, Viscount of (1760–94) French army officer. He served in the American War of Independence, and in 1789 eagerly embraced the **French Revolution**. He was made Secretary of the National Assembly, but was guillotined (1794) for his failure to relieve Metz. In 1779 he had married **Josephine**, afterwards wife of **Napoleon I**, and his daughter **Hortense** in 1802 married Napoleon's brother Louis. Beauharnais was thus the grandfather of **Napoleon III**. ▷ **American Revolution**

Beauharnais, Eugène Rose de (1781–1824) French soldier. After the marriage of his mother, **Josephine**, to **Napoleon I**, he served with his stepfather in Italy and Egypt, and rapidly rose to the highest military rank. In 1805 he was made a prince of France, and from 1805 to 1814 was Viceroy of Italy. As Viceroy he established his court at Milan but was allowed little rein by his stepfather in running the affairs of the kingdom. In 1806 he married Augusta, daughter of Maximilian of Bavaria. In 1813–14 Beauharnais tried to resist the Austrian invasion of Italy but eventually fled to Munich where he was offered protection by his father-in-law.

Beauregard, Pierre Gustave Toutant (1818–93) US Confederate general. He graduated from the US Military Academy at West Point (1838), served with distinction in the **Mexican War**, and was appointed by the Confederate government to the command at Charleston, where he commenced the war by the bombardment of **Fort Sumter** (12 Apr 1861). He fought at **Bull Run** (1861), then took command at **Shiloh** (1862), and later defended Charleston and Richmond. ▷ **American Civil War**

Bebel, Ferdinand August (1840–1913) German socialist. By 1871 he had become leader of the German Social Democratic movement and its chief spokesman in the **Reichstag**. He wrote much on **socialism**, on the Peasants' War, and on the status of women, as well as several philosophical works and an autobiography. ▷ **SPD**

Becket, St Thomas (à) (1118–70) English saint and martyr, Archbishop of Canterbury. The son of a wealthy Norman merchant, he studied canon law at Bologna and Auxerre. In 1155, he became Chancellor, the first Englishman since the **Norman Conquest** to hold high office. A skilled diplomat and brilliant courtly figure, he changed dramatically when created Archbishop of Canterbury (1162), resigning the chancellorship, and becoming a zealous ascetic, serving the Church as vigorously as he had **Henry II**. He thus came into conflict with the King's aims to keep the clergy in subordination to the state. He unwillingly consented to the Constitutions of Clarendon (1164) defining the powers of Church and state, but remained in disfavour. He fled the country after having his goods confiscated and the revenues of his sees sequestered. After two years in France, he pleaded personally to the Pope, and was reinstated in his see. In 1170 he was reconciled with Henry, and returned to Canterbury, amid great public rejoicing. New quarrels soon broke out, however, and Henry's rashly-voiced wish to be rid of 'this turbulent priest' led to Becket's murder in Canterbury cathedral (29 Dec 1170) by four of the King's knights. He was canonized in 1173, and Henry did public penance at his tomb in 1174.

Beck, Jozef (1894–1944) Polish colonel. He helped Marshal **Piłsudski** to seize control in his 1926 coup, became Deputy Foreign Minister in 1930 and was finally Foreign Minister from 1932 to 1939. Following **Hitler**'s rise to power, he tried to maintain first an equilibrium between Nazi Germany and the USSR and then a policy of partial cooperation with Hitler to expand and defend his country. He assisted in the dismemberment of Czechoslovakia (Sep 1938) and defeated the Anglo-French bid to form an alliance with the USSR (May 1939). In Aug of the same year, he had to face the consequences when Hitler invaded a Poland that was virtually defenceless. Beck escaped abroad.

Bedchamber Crisis A British political crisis which occurred in May 1839, after **Melbourne**, Prime Minister in the Whig government, offered to resign, and advised the young Queen **Victoria** to appoint **Peel** and the **Tories**. The Queen refused to dismiss certain ladies of the Bedchamber with Whig sympathies, whereupon Peel refused office and the Whig government continued. ▷ **Whigs**

Bedford, John of Lancaster, Duke of (1389–1435) English general and statesman. He was the third son of **Henry IV**. In 1414 his brother, **Henry V**, created him Duke of Bedford, and during the King's campaigns against France he was appointed Lieutenant of the Kingdom. After Henry's death (1422), he became Guardian of England and Regent of France. When **Charles VI** died, he had his nephew proclaimed King of France and England as **Henry VI**. In the **Hundred Years War**, he defeated the French in several battles, notably at Verneuil (1424), but an army under **Joan of Arc** forced him onto the defensive (1429).

Bedmar, Alfonso de Cueva, Marquis of (1572–1655) Spanish conspirator. He was sent in 1607 as ambassador to Venice, and in 1618 plotted the overthrow of the republic. One of the conspirators betrayed the plot, which forms the theme of Otway's *Venice Preserved*. Bedmar was dismissed, and went to Flanders, where he became president of the council. In 1622 he was made a cardinal, and finally Bishop of Oviedo.

Bedouin Arabic-speaking nomads of Arabia, Syria, Jordan, Iraq, and other desert areas in the Middle East. They mainly herd animals in the desert during winter months and cultivate land in summer; camel herders have the highest prestige. Many have been forced to settle in one locality, because of political or economic moves, such as restrictions on their grazing land, or nationalization of their land. They are divided into largely independent, endogamous patrilineal tribal groups, each controlled by its sheikh and council of male elders. There are also several vassal tribes, whose members work for others as artisans, blacksmiths, entertainers, etc. ▷

Beecroft, John (1790–1854) British trader, explorer and consul. He was influential in promoting the conquest of Lagos in 1851. Beecroft arrived in West Africa in 1828 as a trader on the island of Fernando Po, which the British occupied as a naval base and settlement for freed slaves during the period 1827–34. He administered the island under the Spanish flag, but later he explored the Niger Delta and in 1849 was appointed Consul for the Bights of Benin and Biafra. He promoted legitimate commerce and the suppression of the slave trade.

Beernaert, Auguste (1829–1912) Belgian politician. He trained as a lawyer, entered politics and was appointed Minister for Public Works in 1873. He became a member of the Belgian parliament in 1874, opposing the ruling liberal governments of the day. He was appointed Minister of Agriculture, Trade, and Industry in 1884, and took over the leadership of the government in Oct of the same year. He was responsible for introducing multiple-vote universal suffrage to Belgium in 1893, and for important reforms in labour law; he was also a supporter of King **Leopold II**'s colonial policies in the Congo. He left the government in 1894, and became Chairman of the Belgian Senate for five years until 1899. His work on weapons reduction and international law earned him the Nobel Peace Prize in 1909.

Beggars (*Gueux*; *Geuzen*) The name given to the resistance in the Netherlands to the rule of **Philip II** of Spain in the earlier part of the **Eighty Years War**. The name was apparently taken as a matter of inverted pride from a remark made by Count C Berlaymont (1510–78) in 1565 about the lesser nobles of the Low Countries: *Ce ne sont que les gueux* ('They're only beggars'). As well as land-based guerrilla forces (*bosgeuzen*), the Beggars took to the sea as privateers (*watergeuzen*), allied with adventurers and refugees from the Spanish campaigns in the Low Countries. The Sea-Beggars harassed the shipping and coastal positions of Spain and her allies, and on 1 Apr 1572 they took the Dutch port of Brill with the surrounding countryside, which led directly to the spread of the revolt to the northern provinces.

Begin, Menachem (1913–92) Israeli politician. Born and educated in Brest-Litovsk, Poland (now Russia), he studied law at Warsaw University. An active Zionist, he became head of the Polish Zionist movement in 1931. He fled to Russia in 1939, enlisted in the Free Polish Army (1941), and was sent to British-mandated Palestine. In 1943 he commanded the **Irgun** Zvai Leumi resistance group in Israel, and in 1948 founded the Herut Freedom Movement, becoming Chairman of the Herut Party. In 1973 three parties combined to form the nationalist **Likud** Front with Begin as its leader, and in the 1977 elections he became Prime Minister at the head of a coalition government. In the late 1970s he attended peace conferences in Jerusalem (Dec 1977) and at Camp David (Sep 1978) at the invitation of President **Carter**. In 1978 he and President Anwar **Sadat** of Egypt were jointly awarded the Nobel Peace Prize. He resigned the premiership in 1983.

Beijing, Treaty of (1860) The treaty which gave Tsarist Russia all the territory it wanted between the Ussuri River and the Pacific coast in order to establish a strong presence in the Far East. Russia had been expanding towards the Pacific at China's expense since the 17c. **Alexander II** took advantage of China's weakness in face of British and French military attacks and US diplomatic pressure to secure without war, but through the negotiating skill of Count Nikolai Pavlo-

vich **Ignatiev**, the territory on which he then built the port and naval base of Vladivostok (literally, 'Ruler of the East').

Beiyang (Pei-yang) Army China's first modern army dating from 1899. Under the command of **Yuan Shikai**, the Beiyang army grew in size during the last decade of the **Qing Dynasty**. Many of its officers were either trained in Japan or in new military academies in China. After 1911 the army was the basis of Yuan Shikai's power in his struggle with the **Guomindang**. Many of Yuan's generals later went on to become influential militarists (warlords) in their own right.

Belaúnde, Terry Fernando (1913–) Peruvian politician. He was an architect before entering politics, leading the Popular Action Party (AP) in 1956. He campaigned for the presidency in 1956 and 1962, eventually winning it in 1963, but was deposed by the army in a bloodless coup in 1968. He fled to the USA where he lectured at Harvard. He returned to Peru two years later but was deported and did not re-establish himself until 1976. He won the presidency again in 1980, and was the first civilian to hand over to another constitutionally elected civilian (1985).

Belgian Revolution (1830) The revolt of the southern Netherlands provinces against the government of King **William I** of the Netherlands, ending the union of the northern (Dutch) and southern (Belgian) provinces which existed between 1815 and 1830, and leading to the creation of the independent state of Belgium. The southern provinces were unhappy with the union because of William's religious, linguistic and economic policies. There were republican riots in Brussels on the evening of 25 Aug 1830 after a performance of the opera *La muette de Portici*, which celebrated the rebellion of Naples against the Spanish in 1648. The riots were put down by the local militia, which then took control of the city. During negotiations William ordered an attack on Brussels (23 Sep), which was beaten off after four days, but which spelt the end of any negotiated settlement. A provisional government, called a National Convention, declared the independence of Belgium and drafted a new constitution (7 Feb 1831), which made Belgium a constitutional monarchy with **Leopold I** as its first king. The Great Powers, notably England, no longer felt the need to contain France's northern borders as they had done in 1815, and recognized Belgian independence, drawing up a set of conditions of separation at the Conference of London (20 Jan 1831). William I refused to cooperate, and indeed ordered the **Ten Days Campaign** of 2–12 Aug 1831 against the Belgians, in which the Dutch were successful; as a result an armed standoff accompanied by bitter negotiations dragged on for most of the 1830s. Finally in Apr 1839 the Dutch government capitulated and signed a treaty which completed the independence of Belgium.

Belgian Socialist Party (*Parti Socialiste Belge*; *Belgische Socialistische Partij*) The principal left-wing political party in Belgium, formed in 1940 after the German invasion had caused the abolition of its predecessor, the Belgian Workers' Party (founded in 1885). The party first gained important political influence after the constitutional revision of 1893 had introduced universal suffrage, and gave the socialists 27 MPs. After **World War I** the party dropped its Marxist and revolutionary attitude, and became a regular coalition partner in Belgian governments, often leading them in the 1950s and 1960s. After years of dispute between the French-speaking and Flemish-speaking sections of the party, they formally broke apart in 1978, with their own leaders, programmes and policies. Since the mid-1950s, when the socialists had 37 per cent of the vote, their popularity has declined, but they remain a major force in Belgian politics. Principal leaders have been E **Vandervelde**, H de **Man**, P H **Spaak**, A van **Acker**, and C **Huysmans**.

Belisarius (505–65) Byzantine general. Under Emperor **Justinian I, 'the Great'**, he defeated the Persians (530), suppressed an insurrection in Constantinople (532), and defeated the **Vandals** in Africa (533–4) and the Ostrogoths in Italy (535–40). He later again drove back the Persians (542), and repelled an assault of the **Huns** on Constantinople (559). Falsely accused of conspiracy against the Emperor, he was imprisoned (562), but was soon restored to favour. ▷ **Narses**

Bello, Sir Ahmadu (1910–66) Nigerian politician. Educated at Katsina College, he started his career as a teacher but became a major political figure following his appointment as Saudana of Sokoto (1938). He led the Northern People's Congress from 1951, reaching the post of Prime Minister in 1954. He was a major figure in national politics, exercising his power through the NPC from

his base in the Hause-dominated north of the country and was assassinated in the coup of Jan 1966.

Belorussia, Independence of (1991) One of the 14 non-Russian Republics that gained their independence with the disintegration of the USSR. The Belorussians were one of the original Slav tribes, like the Russians themselves. They remained slightly distinct because they lived in the exposed western border area and were subject to long periods of foreign, particularly Polish rule. Under Tsarist control from 1795, they eventually developed a national movement which declared independence in 1917. However, a feeble Belorussia had a troubled existence and was incorporated into the USSR in 1921. In 1945 its territory was expanded at the expense of Poland and, for Soviet political reasons, it was given separate membership of the **UN**. Yet its sense of national identity remained comparatively undeveloped until its chance came in 1991.

Bem, Joseph (1794–1850) Polish soldier. He fought against the Russians in Napoleon's army and then in the Polish insurrection of 1830–1. He commanded Hungarian forces in the unsuccessful Hungarian insurrection of 1848–9, after which he escaped into Turkey. There he became a Muslim and was appointed Governor of Aleppo, where he died of fever 10 months later.

Bemis Heights, Battle of (7 Oct 1777) A preliminary conflict during the Saratoga campaign, in the US War of Independence. ▷ **Saratoga, Battle of**

Ben Ali, Zine el Abidine (1936–) Tunisian politician. After studying electronics at military schools in France and the USA, he began a career in military security, rising to the position of Director-General of National Security. He became Minister of the Interior and then Prime Minister under 'President-for-life' Habib **Bourguiba**, who had been in power since 1956. In 1987 he forced Bourguiba to retire and assumed the presidency and immediately embarked on constitutional reforms, promising a greater degree of democracy.

Ben Bella, Ahmed (1918–) Algerian politician. A key figure in the **Algerian War of Independence** against France, he fought with the Free French in **World War II**, and in 1949 became head of the *Organisation Spéciale* ('Special Organization'), the paramilitary wing of the Algerian nationalist *Parti du Peuple Algérien* (Party of the Algerian People'). In 1952 he escaped from a French-Algerian prison to Cairo, where he became a key member of the **FLN** (*Front de Libération Nationale*). Captured by the French in 1956, he spent the remainder of the war in a French prison. Following independence in 1962, he became Algeria's first Prime Minister (1962–3), and President (1963–5). His deposition in 1965 was followed by 15 years of imprisonment, from which he was released in 1980.

Benbow, John (1653–1702) British admiral. His main engagements were in the Nine Years War (1690, 1693 and 1694) and the War of the **Spanish Succession**, when he came upon a superior French force in the West Indies (1702). For four days he kept up a running fight from Santa Marta, almost deserted by the rest of his squadron, until he was wounded. He was forced to return to Jamaica, where he died.

Benckendorff, Alexander, Count (1849–1917) Russian diplomat. As ambassador in London (from 1903), he greatly promoted Anglo-Russian friendship and played a part in forming the Triple Entente (1907).

Benedict VIII (d.1024) First of the Tusculan Popes, members of the Tusculani family, (1012/24). He was temporarily driven from Rome by the anti-pope Gregory VI, of the Crescenti family, but was restored to the papal chair by Emperor **Henry II**, whom he crowned in 1014. Later he defeated the **Saracens** and the **Greeks** in northern Italy, and introduced clerical and monastic reforms.

Benedict IX (d.c.1065) Last of the Tusculan Popes (1032/44. 1045 and 1047/8). The nephew of **Benedict VIII**, he succeeded another uncle, John XIX, in 1032, obtaining the papal throne by simony while still a youth. However, in 1036 the Romans banished him on account of his licentiousness. He was reinstalled and deposed on at least three occasions. He died in the convent of Grotta Ferrata, probably before 1065.

Benedict XIV (1675–1758) Pope (1740/58). Perhaps the greatest of 18c pontiffs, he was a fine scholar who won praise for his moderation and reforming tendencies. In the domestic affairs of the **Papal States** he sought energetically to stimulate the economy through liberal commercial policies, the reduction of taxes and agricultural improvement. He was similarly far-sighted and realistic in the conciliatory approach he adopted towards the many monarchs of his day, who were increasingly eager to extend the realm of secular jurisdiction and to bring Church patronage under their personal control. In the face of growing interest across Europe in Enlightenment ideas, he urged that restraint be exercised by those responsible for compiling the *Index* of prohibited literature. He was also anxious to avoid too open a breach with Jansenism and, in 1756, condemned those who refused last rites to clergy who opposed the Bull *Unigenitus*. However, he was not merely a doctrinal pragmatist: in the *Ex quo singulari* (1742) and the *Omnium sollicitudinum* (1744) he forcefully denounced as incompatible with the Catholic faith, and prohibited, the various traditional practices which Jesuits had tolerated among converts in India and China. While these measures undoubtedly set back the progress of Jesuit missionary work, they were important in maintaining the theological integrity of the Church in Asia.

Benelux An economic union between Belgium, the Netherlands and Luxembourg. It began as a customs union which came into existence in 1948 as the result of a convention concluded in London in 1944. Despite the difficulties of achieving economic integration and the exclusion of agriculture from the union, mutual trade between the three countries expanded. A treaty established a more ambitious economic union between the three in 1958.

Beneš, Edvard (1884–1948) Czechoslovak politician. He was Professor of Sociology at Prague, then as an émigré during **World War I** worked in Paris with Masaryk for Czech independence, becoming Foreign Minister of the new state (1918–35), and for a while Premier (1921–2). In 1935 he succeeded Masaryk as President, but resigned in 1938 following the Munich Agreement. He then left the country, setting up a government in exile, first in France, then in Britain. Beneš returned to Czechoslovakia in 1945 and was re-elected President the following year, but resigned after the Communist takeover in 1948.

Benevento, Battle of (1266) Victory of the **Guelfs** over the Ghibellines in the papal-imperial struggle in Italy. The Pope had brought **Charles of Anjou** into Italy to counterbalance the imperial power in the south. **Manfred**, the illegitimate son of **Frederick II**, was killed in the battle, and the Angevin position was further consolidated by victory at the Battle of **Tagliacozzo** (1268), before the expulsion of the French in the **Sicilian Vespers** of 1282. ▷ **Angevins**

Bengal, Partition of (1905) The division of Bengal for administrative purposes, conceived and carried out by Lord Curzon while he was Viceroy. Because of Bengal's combination with Orissa and Bihar for administrative purposes, the provincial population was become unwieldy, and administration had become unwieldy. Largely because of this and poor communications to the east of Calcutta, East Bengal had been neglected in favour of West Bengal, Orissa and Bihar. Curzon decided to combine East Bengal with Assam, making Dacca the capital, and to leave Calcutta as the capital of West Bengal and India. Because the partition created an East Bengal with a large Muslim majority, Hindus felt that they would be marginalized in that region. Many Bengalis believed that the partition was an attempt to destroy nationalism, which was more highly developed in Bengal than elsewhere. The public outcry was manifested in rural agitation, mass meetings, boycott of foreign goods and even terrorism. Although the partition took place, East and West Bengal were reunited in 1911, with Assam and Orissa-Bihar becoming two new administrative districts. The outrage of nationalists and Bengali Hindus over the partition was largely responsible for both Curzon's early removal from the Viceroyalty, and the transformation of the **Indian National Congress** from a middle-class pressure group to a popular nationwide political party.

Bengal Presidency The original British **East India Company** designation for lands around Calcutta under its direct administrative control. The Bengal Presidency bordered Bihar and Orissa to the west, Sikkim and Bhutan to the north and Assam and Burma to the east. It was from the Bengal Presidency that the Company's greatest expansion of influence and control took place in the 18c and 19c, and it was also from there that most of the old Mughal Empire was informally controlled until 1858. The Bengal Presidency was the senior administrative area, and the Governor of Bengal was in fact the Governor-General of British India. The term and administrative area of the Bengal Presidency remained current even after the dissolution of the Company.

Ben-Gurion, David (1886–1973) Israeli politician. Born in Poland, he emigrated to Palestine in 1906. Expelled by the Turks during **World War I**, he recruited Jews in the British Army in North America. In Palestine in 1919 he founded a socialist party and became Secretary to the **Histadrut** in 1921. He led the **Mapai Party** from its formation in 1930 and headed the **Jewish Agency** in 1935. Ben-Gurion moulded the Mapai into the main party of the **Yishuv** during British rule and became Prime Minister after independence (1948–53), when he was responsible for Israel absorbing large numbers of refugees from Europe and Arab countries. He was Prime Minister again from 1955 to 1963. ▷ **Jewish Labour Movement in Palestine**

Benin, Kingdom of A powerful kingdom in the south Nigerian rainforest, founded in the 13c, which survived until the 19c. The dynastic title of the rulers was Oba, and Benin reached its imperial apogee under Ewuare the Great (1440/73). The Portuguese turned to Benin as a source of cloth, beads, and slaves in the 15–16c, and it was later involved in the **slave trade**. It became one of the most prosperous towns in Africa. Benin was conquered by the British in 1897, and in 1975 the name was adopted by the former French colony of Dahomey.

Benn, Tony (Anthony (Neil) Wedgwood Benn) (1925–) British politician. The son of Viscount Stansgate, he became a Labour MP in 1950 but was debarred from the Commons on succeeding to his father's title. He renounced his title, and was re-elected in a by-election in 1963. He held various government posts under Harold **Wilson** and James **Callaghan**, notably Minister of Technology (1966–70), Secretary for Industry (1974–5) and Secretary for Energy (1975–9). He was the main focus for the left-wing challenge to the Labour leadership in the late 1970s and 1980s which ultimately failed but which persuaded some on the right to leave the party and form the **Social Democratic Party**. ▷ **Foot, Michael; Kinnock, Neil; Labour Party** (UK)

Bennett, Richard Bedford, 1st Viscount (1870–1947) Canadian politician. Educated in Nova Scotia, he trained as a lawyer, and entered politics in 1897. He was Conservative leader from 1927, and while Prime Minister (1930–5) convened the Imperial Economic Conference in Ottawa (1932), from which emerged a system of empire trade preference. He retired to England in 1938 and was made a peer in 1941. ▷ **New Deal** (Canada); **Price Spreads Commission**

Bentham, Jeremy (1748–1832) British writer on jurisprudence and utilitarian ethics. He was called to the Bar in 1767, though he never practised, being more interested in the theory of the law. His publications include *A Fragment on Government* (1776), and *Introduction to the Principles of Morals and Legislation* (1789), which present his theory of hedonistic utilitarianism. He held that laws should be socially useful and not merely reflect the *status quo*, and that all actions are right when they promote 'the happiness of the greatest number' (a phrase which he popularized). He travelled widely on the Continent. Supporters of his utilitarian ideas (the Benthamites) attempted to apply them to public policy (1830s and 1840s). He was also a founder of University College, London, where his skeleton, dressed in his clothes, is preserved.

Bentinck, Hans Willem, Baron (1649–1709) Friend, confidant and agent of **Stadholder** William III (later King **William III** of England). Bentinck was a page to William III, and in time took on vital missions for his master, such as the marriage negotiations between William and Princess Mary, daughter of **Charles I** of England, and the role and input of Amsterdam in the invasion of England by William's forces in 1688. When William had succeeded to the English throne, he made Bentinck the first Duke of Portland in 1689; Bentinck remained a key figure at William's court, in war, peace and diplomacy. ▷ **Glorious Revolution**

Bentinck, William (Henry Cavendish), Lord (1774–1839) British soldier and Governor-General of India. The second son of the 3rd Duke of **Portland**, in 1791 he became an army officer. Appointed Governor of Madras in 1803, he was recalled from India following a mutiny of native soldiers, and commanded troops in Spain and Sicily during the **Napoleonic Wars**. A liberal Whig in his political sympathies, in 1811 he was entrusted with reorganizing Sicily where he forced a constitution on the reactionary Bourbon King, Ferdinand I. In 1814–15 he championed the cause of Italian independence and constitutional government but was unable to persuade the authorities in Britain to share his vision. On his return to Britain he was elected to parliament. He later became Governor-General of India (1828–35), where

he introduced important administrative reforms.

Benton, Thomas Hart (1782–1858) US politician. He was a Missouri Senator for 30 years, and a leader of the **Democratic Party**, becoming known as 'Old Bullion' from his opposition to paper currency. In his later years, he adopted an anti-slavery position which finally lost him his seat in the Senate.

Ben-Zvi, Itzhak (1884–1963) Israeli politician. Born in Poltava in the USSR, he emigrated to Palestine in 1907. He became a prominent Zionist and was a founder of the Jewish Labour Party. Ben-Zvi was elected President of Israel on the death of Chaim **Weizmann** in 1952. A prominent scholar and archaeologist, he wrote on the history of the Middle East. ▷ **Aliyah; Zionism**

Beran, Josef (1888–1969) Czech Catholic priest and archbishop. Imprisoned in **Dachau** concentration camp in **World War II**, he became Archbishop of Prague in 1946. Although the Catholic Church was anxious to avoid too close an involvement in politics, he spoke out in favour of democracy during the communist seizure of power in Feb 1948. Within a year the Church was persecuted, and Beran and most churchmen were cut off from contact with Rome. It was 1965 before the situation eased sufficiently for him to leave for Rome, where he was appointed cardinal.

Beran, Rudolf (1887–1954) Czechoslovak politician. He became Secretary-General of the powerful right-wing Agrarian Party in 1918 and its President in 1935. Torn between dislike of **Hitler** and hatred for **Stalin**, he quickly opted for a policy of appeasing Germany in the hope of securing local concessions. His behaviour in 1938 was close to treasonable as he negotiated behind President **Beneš**'s back. His reward was to become Prime Minister for a time after the **Munich Agreement**, but in 1946 he was imprisoned as a Nazi collaborator. He undoubtedly undermined the Czechoslovak position in the face of Hitler.

Berber Hamito-Semitic-speaking peoples of Egypt, Algeria, Libya, Tunisia, and Morocco. They were originally settled in one area, but the Bedouin Arabs who invaded N Africa in the 12c turned many of them into nomads. Most Berber tribes ultimately accepted Islam, and in the 11c formed themselves into a military federation known as the **Almoravids**, who conquered the medieval state of Ghana, Morocco, Algeria, and S Spain. In the 12c their power began to wane, and the **Almohads**, a new group influenced by Sufism, by 1169 came to command the entire Maghrib to Tripoli, as well as Muslim Spain. The Almohad Empire declined in the 13c. Today, some Berbers are sedentary farmers, while others are nomadic or transhumant pastoralists. Many work as migrant labourers in southern Europe. The best-known groups include the Kabyle, Shluh, and Tuareg.

Berdyaev, Nikolai (1874–1948) Russian religious philosopher. Born into an aristocratic family in Kiev, he developed strong revolutionary sympathies as a student and supported the **Russian Revolution** of 1917. He secured a professorship at Moscow but his unorthodox spiritual and libertarian ideals led to his dismissal in 1922. He moved to found in Berlin an Academy of the Philosophy of Religion which he later transferred to Clamart, near Paris, where he died. He described himself as a 'believing freethinker' and his fierce commitment to freedom and individualism brought him into conflict with both ecclesiastical and political powers.

Berengar I (d.924) King of Italy (888 /924) and Holy Roman Emperor (915/24). He succeeded his father, Eberhard, a count of Frankish origin, as Margrave of Friuli. He died at the hands of his own men.

Berezina River, Crossing of (1812) A typical example of **Napoleon** I's mixture of skill and luck in extricating himself from complete disaster. During the retreat from Moscow, his depleted army faced crossing the Berezina River, its supplies and morale low, the bridges destroyed, and two Russian armies closing in in a pincer movement. But he deceived the enemy, found a crossing-place, built pontoons, and escaped with two-thirds of his numbers. That his losses were not greater, however, was due to Russian mistakes, and shortly afterwards he recognized defeat and hastened off to Paris.

Berg A duchy of the **Holy Roman Empire**, it became a possession of John III, Duke of Cleves in 1511. A centre for iron and textile manufacturing in the 17c and 18c, Berg passed into Prussian hands, as the Rhine Province, after the Congress of **Vienna** (1814–15).

Berggrav, Eivind (1884–1959) Norwegian Lutheran bishop. After some years as a teacher, pastor and prison chaplain, he became Bishop of Troms and then Bishop of Oslo and Primate of the Norwegian Church (1937–50). Following the Nazi occupation of 1940, he led the Church's opposition to the **Quisling** government, refusing to endorse the war against Russia as a fight against atheism, and opposing Nazi attempts to monopolize the education of young people. For this he was imprisoned (1941–5). He wrote some 30 books and was a strong supporter of the ecumenical movement, becoming a president of the World Council of Churches (1950–4).

Beria, Lavrenti Pavlovich (1899–1953) Soviet secret police chief. After holding local positions in his native Georgia, he became Soviet Commissar for Internal Affairs in 1938. During **World War II** he was Vice-President of the State Committee for Defence, and was active in purging **Stalin**'s opponents. After **Stalin**'s death (1953), he belonged briefly with Giorgiy **Malenkov** and Molotov to the collective leadership. Accused by his colleagues of conspiracy, he was shot after a mock 'treason' trial.

Berlin, Battle of (Apr–May 1945) On 25 Apr 1945 advancing Soviet troops surrounded **Berlin**. **Hitler** had ordered the 9th and 11th Armies to relieve Berlin on 24 Apr, but they were unable to break through the Soviet lines. There followed a Soviet offensive on the city which resulted in days of bitter street fighting. On 30 Apr, Hitler committed suicide and on 2 May the German Commander in Berlin, General Weidling, surrendered to the Soviet commander, Marshall **Zhukov**.

Berlin, Congress of (Nov 1884–Feb 1885) A conference summoned by the German Chancellor, **Bismarck**, to consider rival claims to Africa and the internationalization of the Congo region under the aegis of the African Association of King **Leopold II** of the Belgians. All the major European powers attended, together with the USA and the **Ottoman Empire**, but there were no representatives from Africa. The General Act of the conference, signed in Feb 1885, established freedom of navigation on African rivers and free trade areas. It also effectively laid down the ground rules for the Scramble for Africa, which was speeding up even as the conference was meeting. Bismarck achieved his objective of maintaining tension between Britain and France and won electoral support in Germany by securing colonies in West, East and South-West Africa.

Berlin, Congress of (1878) An international congress following the Russian defeat of Turkey and the one-sided Treaty of **San Stefano**. The chief results were: Serbia, Romania, and Bulgaria had their independence from Turkey recognized but gained less territory than they were entitled to; Austria-Hungary occupied Bosnia-Herzegovina; Russia retained gains in southern Bessarabia and the Caucasus, but conceded a reduction in the size of its protégé, Bulgaria, and generally suffered a diplomatic defeat; and Britain occupied Cyprus. ▷ **Ottoman Empire**

Berlin, Partition of Founded in the 13c, Berlin became the residence of the **Hohenzollern Dynasty** and the capital of Brandenburg. Later it was the capital of **Prussia**, becoming an industrial and commercial centre in the 18c. As the capital of Germany, it was partitioned during the late 1940s into East Berlin and West Berlin. In 1949, West Berlin became associated with the Federal Republic of Germany (although under Four Power control) and East Berlin became, *de facto*, a county of the German Democratic Republic. The two halves of the city were separated by a wall built around West Berlin in 1961 to prevent the movement of citizens from East to West. Contact between the two halves of the city was restored in Nov 1989, following the **Revolution of 1989** in East Germany, and it was made the capital of unified Germany in 1990. ▷ **Berlin Wall; Germany, East**

Berlin, Treaty of (1728) The treaty by which Frederick William of Prussia accepted the **Pragmatic Sanction** of **Charles VI** confirming the rights of Charles's daughter, **Maria Theresa**, to succeed to the Imperial throne. Charles's machinations made him unable to deliver his part of the treaty relating to Prussia's claims to parts of Jülich and Berg. As a result, Prussia disputed Maria's right to the throne after Charles's death.

Berlin Airlift (1948–9) A massive airlift of essential supplies flown in to **Cold War** Berlin by British and US aircraft in round-the-clock missions. It was carried out in response to the action of the Soviet military authorities in Berlin, who had attempted to isolate the city from the West by severing all overland communication routes (June 1948). **Stalin** lifted the blockade in May 1949.

Berlin–Baghdad Railway ▷ **Baghdad Railway**

Berlin Blockade (1948–9) An attempt by **Stalin** to weaken US preparedness to remain in Europe indefinitely following **World War II**, and also to secure his control over Eastern Europe by strengthening his hold on the east of Germany. Specifically, the idea was to prevent supplies getting through to the western zones of Berlin, in the hope that the Allies would withdraw. In the event, the Allies flew in food and fuel for almost 11 months until Stalin had to back down. It was after this that the **Cold War** intensified, with the establishment of **NATO** and **Comecon** in 1949.

Berlinguer, Enrico (1922–84) Italian politician. Son of a wealthy Sardinian landowning family, from 1943 he was a member of the Italian Communist Party (PCI) and played an active role in the resistance. Secretary-General of the Federation of Young Communists (1949–56), he was elected to parliament in 1968 and became Vice-Secretary of the party in 1969; in 1972 he was made Secretary-General. In Sep 1973 he proposed the 'historic compromise' with the **Christian Democrat Party**: in return for social reforms and an increased say on policy formation, the PCI agreed to respect the Church and constitutional institutions and discourage labour militancy. Shortly afterwards, he also endorsed **NATO** and, in Dec 1977, PCI deputies voted in favour of Italy's foreign and defence policies. Under Berlinguer's influence, Italian communism flourished in the 1970s: in the 1976 elections, the PCI received 34.4 per cent of votes, rivalling the 38.7 per cent polled by the DC, and by Mar 1978 the PCI had entered the government's parliamentary majority. However, traditional DC suspicion of the left, the openly anti-communist stance of Pope **John Paul II** (elected Oct 1978), and the anti-Soviet feeling generated by the invasion of Afghanistan undermined the coalition. So too did the more militant wing of the PCI which never welcomed cooperation with the DC. Berlinguer was consequently forced to jettison his conciliatory position and by 1979 was once again in opposition. During the remaining years of his life, he continued to pursue his vision of 'Eurocommunism" which rejected the rigid Stalinist doctrines of the USSR. However, support for the PCI never again reached its peak of the late 1970s.

Berlin Wall A concrete wall built by the East German government in 1961 to seal off East **Berlin** from the part of the city occupied by the three main Western powers. Built largely to prevent mass illegal emigration to the West, which was threatening the East German economy, the wall was the scene of the shooting of many East Germans who tried to escape from the eastern sector. The wall, seen by many as a major symbol of the denial of human rights in Eastern Europe, was unexpectedly opened in Nov 1989, following revolutionary upheaval in East **Germany**. Following reunification, most of the wall has now been taken down. ▷ **Revolution of 1989**

Bernadotte, House of The royal dynasty of Sweden since 1818. The House was founded by Jean Baptiste Jules Bernadotte, one of **Napoleon**'s marshals, who became King **Charles XIV John**. On his death he was succeeded by his son, **Oscar I**, only child of his marriage to Désirée Clary, sister-in-law of Napoleon's brother, Joseph **Bonaparte**. The reigning monarchs of Denmark, Norway, Sweden and Belgium are direct descendants of the couple. Count Folke Bernadotte, nephew of King **Gustav V**, acted as mediator in both world wars. ▷ **Bernadotte, Count Folke**

Bernadotte, Count Folke (1895–1948) Swedish diplomat. He was the nephew of King **Gustav V** of Sweden. He acted as a mediator in **World War I** and, as the Vice-President of the Swedish Red Cross, negotiated with **Himmler** in spring of 1945 for the liberation of Scandinavian prisoners from German concentration camps. Appointed by the **UN** to try to reach a settlement of the Palestine question, he produced a plan of partition but was assassinated by the **Stern Gang** in Jerusalem.

Bernadotte, Jean Baptiste Jules ▷ **Charles XIV John**

Bernard of Clairvaux, St (1090–1153) French theologian and reformer. Born of a noble family, in 1113 he entered the Cister-

cian monastery of Cîteaux, and in 1115 became the first Abbot of Clairvaux. His studious, ascetic life and stirring eloquence made him the oracle of Christendom; he founded more than 70 monasteries; and his preaching kindled the enthusiasm of France for the Second Crusade (1146). His writings include hundreds of epistles and sermons, and several theological treatises. He died at Clairvaux, and was canonized in 1174. The monks of his reformed branch of the Cistercians are often called Bernardines. ▷ **Crusades**

Bernhard Leopold (1911–) Prince of the Netherlands. The son of Prince Bernhard Casimir of Lippe and Armgard von Cramm, in 1937 he married **Juliana**, the only daughter of **Wilhelmina**, Queen of the Netherlands. During **World War II** he commanded the Netherlands Forces of the Interior (1944–5). In 1976 he was involved in a bribery scandal, in which he was found to have received money for promoting the Dutch purchase of aircraft from the Lockheed Aircraft Corporation.

Bernstein, Eduard (1850–1932) German socialist leader. An associate of **Engels**, he played a major part in unifying the German socialist movement in 1875. As a leading intellectual in the Social Democratic Party (**SPD**), he was prominent in establishing its Marxist ideology. Later he was an advocate of revisionism, an evolutionary form of **Marxism**, and a member of the **Reichstag** periodically (1902–28). He was exiled for his beliefs (1888–1901), during which time he lived in London, where he influenced, and was in turn influenced by, the British Fabians and other socialists. ▷ **Fabian Society**

Bernstorff, Andreas Peter (1735–97) Danish politician. A Count of Hanoverian descent, he was Minister of Foreign Affairs (1773–80 and 1784–97) and, after the summer of 1788, he was Denmark's de facto Prime Minister. He was in charge of the pragmatic and cautious policy of neutrality that kept Denmark clear of the wars between the great powers and achieved continued Danish prosperity, while at the same time not unduly provoking British shipping and naval interests. In domestic matters, he played the role of mediator between those who demanded agricultural reforms, such as the abolition of serfdom and the introduction of freehold, and the influential landowners who saw their feudal interests threatened. On Bernstorff's death, Crown Prince Frederick (later King

HOUSE OF BERNADOTTE

Regnal Dates	Name
1818/44	Charles XIV John
1844/59	Oscar I
1859/72	Charles XV
1872/1907	Oscar II
1907/50	Gustav V
1950/73	Gustav VI Adolf
1973/	Carl XVI Gustaf

Frederick VI), took over the leading political role, resulting in a more confrontational Danish foreign policy which (Apr 1801) led to the first of two naval Battles of Copenhagen between Denmark and the UK.

Bernstorff, Johan Heinrich, Count (1862–1939) German diplomat. After a varied diplomatic career, Bernstorff became German ambassador to the USA in 1908. During **World War I** he sought unsuccessfully to dissuade his government from waging submarine warfare, the latter bringing the USA into the war. He then became German Ambassador to the **Ottoman Empire** before serving as a member of the **Reichstag** for the liberal **DDP** during the Weimar era and as German delegate on the League of Nations Disarmament Commission. In 1933 he sought exile in Switzerland where he pursued his publishing interests. ▷ **Weimar Republic**

Bernward (d.1022) Bishop of Hildesheim. After an extensive education in theology, administration and art, Bernward became tutor to **Otto III** in 987. In 993 he was appointed Bishop of Hildesheim and with his brother Tammo, a Saxon count and the King's steward, he was at the centre of a Saxon faction at court. He took a less prominent role in the administration of Otto's successor, **Henry II, the Holy**, and died as a monk in the monastery he had founded in Hildesheim. He was responsible for a period of great vitality in the arts under Otto and was canonized in 1192. ▷ **Ottonians**

Berri, Nabih (1939–) Lebanese politician and soldier. Born in Freetown, Sierra Leone, he was the son of an expatriate Lebanese merchant. He studied law at Beirut University and practised as a lawyer for a time. In 1978 he became leader of Amal ('Hope'), a branch of the Shiite nationalist movement founded by Iman Musa Sadr. Backed by Syria, he became the main Shiite military force in West Beirut and Southern Lebanon during the country's civil wars, but in 1988 its Beirut branch was heavily defeated by the Iranian-backed Hezbollah ('Party of God') and was then disbanded. Berri joined the Lebanese government in 1984 as Minister of Justice.

Bersaglieri Piedmontese light infantry (in Italian literally 'sharpshooters') established in 1836 by General Alessandro Ferrero La Marmora (1799–1856), brother of Alfonso **La Marmora**. They fought in the **Crimean War** and the campaigns of 1859–60, and were subsequently incorporated into the Italian Army.

Berthier, Alexandre (1753–1815) Prince of Neuchâtel and Wagram, Marshal of the First French Empire. Entering the army in 1770, he fought with **Lafayette** in the American War of Independence. In the **French Revolution** he soon rose to be Chief of Staff in the Army of Italy (1795), and in 1798 proclaimed the republic in Rome. He became Chief of Staff to **Napoleon I**, on whose fall he had to surrender the principality of Neuchâtel, but was allowed to keep his rank as peer and marshal. Napoleon made overtures to him from Elba; but he retired to Bamberg. On 1 July 1815, at the sight of a Russian division marching towards the French frontier, he threw himself from a window. ▷ **American Revolution**

Berwick, James Fitzjames, 1st Duke of (1670–1734) French and Jacobite general. He was the illegitimate son of James VII of Scotland and II of England. Educated in France as a Catholic, he was created Duke of Berwick (1687), but fled from England at the Glorious Revolution. He fought in his father's Irish campaign (1689–91), and then in Flanders and against the **Camisards**. In 1706 he was created a Marshal of France, and in Spain established the throne of **Philip V** by the decisive victory of **Almansa** (1707) in the War of the **Spanish Succession**. Appointed Commander-in-Chief of the French forces in 1733, he was killed while besieging Phillippsburg. ▷ **James VII and II; Jacobites**

Besant, Annie (1847–1933) British theosophist and social reformer. Brought up in Harrow, she married the Rev Frank Besant, but was separated from him in 1873. From secularism and **Bradlaugh** she passed in 1889 to Madame Blavatsky and theosophy, becoming its high priestess from 1891. In her later years she went to India, where she championed the causes of nationalism and education.

Bessarabia The region between the Prut and Dniester Rivers, the Black Sea and Danube delta. Settled by the Slavs (6c), then the Mongols (13c), at the end of the 14c it became part of Wallachia and was named after the ruling Wallachian Dynasty. In the 15c it passed to Moldavia and from the 16c was subject to the Ottomans until 1812 when, by the Treaty of **Bucharest**, together with half of Moldavia, it passed to Russia. In 1918 it declared itself independent, voted to join

Romania and under the Treaty of **Paris** (1920) was awarded to Romania. In the **German–Soviet Pact** (1939) the USSR was promised Bessarabia with northern **Bukovina** and in 1940, with part of the Ukraine, it became part of the Soviet Socialist Republic of Moldavia. Although occupied by the Romanian Army during **World War II**, it was returned to the USSR in 1947, since when it has been an irredentist issue between the Soviet and Romanian governments. ▷ **Moldavia and Wallachia; Romanians**

Bestuzhev-Ryumin, Alexei Petrovich, Count (1693–1766) Russian politician and diplomat. After foreign service in Hanover and England (1713–17), he became Russian Resident (1720) and later Ambassador (1730–40) in Denmark. In 1741 he was sentenced to death (later commuted to exile) for participation in a plot to seize the throne by the royal favourite, Ernst Biron. On the accession of Empress Elizabeth the same year, he was pardoned, and made Chancellor in charge of foreign affairs (1744–58). At first he strengthened the alliance with England, Holland, and Austria against France, Prussia, and Turkey, but on the outbreak of the Seven Years War (1756–63) was forced to ally with France. In 1758 he was banished again for complicity in the political intrigues of the future Empress **Catherine II, 'the Great'**, but when Catherine came to the throne (1762) he was restored to favour and granted the title of General Field Marshal. He then took no further part in political life.

Betancourt, Rómulo (1908–81) Venezuelan politician and reformer. One of the founders of the *Partido Democrático Nacional* (National Democratic Party) in 1936, he held power from 1945 to 1947. On the fall of the Pérez Jiménez dictatorship (1950–8), he was elected President (1959–64) of the new Venezuelan democracy. He chose a moderate course, adopting an agrarian law in Mar 1960, and ambitious economic development plans which provided for a transition from the dictatorship.

Bethlen, Gabriel (Bethlen Gábor) (1580–1629) Protestant Prince of Transylvania (1613/29). A brilliant soldier and diplomat, he opposed Emperor Ferdinand II in the Thirty Years War. In 1619 he invaded Hungary, and the following year was chosen its King; however, in 1621 he concluded peace with Ferdinand, and resigned his claims, obtaining large accessions of territory. He later renewed hostilities with the

Emperor (1624 and 1626), before finally withdrawing (1629).

Bethlen, István (Stephen), Count (1874–1947) Hungarian politician. He was a leader of the counter-revolutionary movement after **World War I**, and as Prime Minister from 1921 to 1931 promoted Hungary's economic reconstruction.

Bethmann-Hollweg, Theobald von (1856–1921) German politician. Having qualified in law, he rose in the service of **Prussia** and the German Empire, becoming Imperial Chancellor in 1909. Although not identified with the German élite's most bellicose elements, and fearing the effects of war upon German society, he nevertheless played an important part in the events which brought about general war in 1914. Anxious for a negotiated peace in 1917, he was forced from office. ▷ **World War I**

Bethune, Mary McLeod (1875–1955) US educator and administrator. She was founder and President of the National Council of Negro Women and of Bethune-Cookman College. Serving as adviser to President Franklin D **Roosevelt**'s **New Deal** administration, she worked to expand awareness of minority issues within government agencies. She was director of the division of Negro Affairs within the National Youth Administration at a time when 40 per cent of black youths were suffering unemployment. As such she was quietly insistent that the number of blacks enrolled in the programme be increased despite the reluctance of state administrators. Black college students also benefited from the Special Negro Fund which she administered. In 1945 she was accredited by the State Department to attend the San Francisco Conference to establish the UN.

Beust, Friedrich Ferdinand, Count von (1809–86) Saxon and Austrian politician. He was appointed Foreign Secretary (1866–71) and Imperial Chancellor (1867–71), then Ambassador in London (1871–8) and Paris (1878–82). His chief achievement was the reconciliation of Hungary to **Austria** (the **Ausgleich**, 1867).

Bevan, Aneurin (1897–1960) British politician. One of 13 children, he worked in the pits on leaving school at 13, and led the Welsh miners in the 1926 **General Strike**. He entered parliament for the **Independent Labour Party** in 1929, joining the **Labour Party** in 1931. He established a reputation as a brilliant, irreverent, and often tempestuous orator. As Minister of Health (1945–51), he introduced the National Health Service (1948). He became Minister of Labour in 1951, but resigned in the same year over the National Health charges proposed in the Budget. From this period dated 'Bevanism', a left-wing movement to make the Labour Party more socialist and less 'reformist'. He married Jennie **Lee** in 1934, and died while still an MP. ▷ **socialism**

Beveridge, William Henry Beveridge, 1st Baron (1879–1963) British economist, administrator, and social reformer. He entered the Board of Trade (1908) and became Director of Labour Exchanges (1909–16). He was Director of the London School of Economics (1919–37) and Master of University College, Oxford (1937–45). He is best known as the author of the *Report on Social Insurance and Allied Services* (The Beveridge Report, 1942), which provided a blueprint for the creation of the welfare state. He was knighted in 1919, became a Liberal MP (1944–6), and was made a baron in 1946. ▷ **Liberal Party** (UK)

Bevin, Ernest (1881–1951) British politician. Orphaned by the age of seven, and self-taught, he early came under the influence of trade unionism and the Baptists, and was for a time a lay preacher. A paid official of the dockers' union, he gained a national reputation in 1920 when he won most of his union's claims against an eminent barrister, earning the title of 'the dockers' KC'. He built up the National Transport and General Workers' Union, and became its General-Secretary (1921–40). In 1940 he became a Labour MP, Minister of Labour and National Service in Winston **Churchill**'s coalition government, and was Foreign Secretary in the Labour governments (1945–51). ▷ **Labour Party** (UK)

Bhadralok A highly-educated elite class distinguished by its westernizing tendencies, which flourished in late 19c and early 20c Bengal. Well-represented in the **Brahmo Samaj**, it played a leading role in Indian nationalist activity.

Bhattari, Krishna Prasad (1925–) Nepalese politician. As an opponent of absolute monarchy, he was in hiding for 12 years until 1990, when, as Leader of the centrist Nepali Congress Party, he became Prime Minister in the wake of the revolution that year, which ended the uncontested rule

of King **Birendra**. However, in May 1991, in Nepal's first multi-party elections in three decades, he offered his resignation to the King after losing his own seat in the 205-member House of Representatives to the Marxist leader of the United Communist Party, Madan Bhandari.

Bhave, Vinoba (1895–1982) Indian social and land reformer. M K **Gandhi** took him under his care as a young scholar, an event which changed his life. Distressed in 1951 by the land hunger riots in Telengana, Hyderabad, Bhave began a walking mission throughout India to persuade landlords to give land to the peasants and thus founded the **Bhoodan** movement. A barefoot, ascetic saint, his silent revolution led to 4 000 000 acres of land being redistributed in four years. He was claimed to be the most notable spiritual figure in India after the death of Gandhi, whose ardent disciple he was.

Bhindranwale, Sant Jarnail Singh (1947–84) Indian politician and former Sikh extremist leader. Born into a poor Punjabi Jat farming family, he trained at the orthodox Damdani Taksal Sikh missionary school, becoming its head priest in 1971 and assuming the name Bhindranwale. Initially encouraged by Sanjay Gandhi (1946–80), the son and political adviser of Indira **Gandhi**, who sought to divide the Sikh Akali Dal movement, he campaigned violently against the heretical activities of Nirankari Sikhs during the later 1970s. His campaign broadened into a demand for a separate state of 'Khalistan' during the early 1980s, precipitating a bloody Hindu-Sikh conflict in Punjab. After taking refuge in the Golden Temple complex at Amritsar and building up an arms cache for terrorist activities, with about 500 devoted followers, he died at the hands of the Indian Security Forces who stormed the temple in 'Operation Blue Star'. ▷ **Akali Movement**

Bhoodan (Bhudan) Literally 'land-giving' in Hindi, Bhoodan is a late 20c agrarian Indian social movement, which encouraged the donation of land to the landless peasantry. Bhoodan was conceived and led by Vinoba **Bhave**.

Bhumibol Adulyadej (1927–) King of Thailand (1946/). The second son of Prince Mahidol of Songkhola and grandson of King **Chulalongkorn**, he was educated in Bangkok and Switzerland and became monarch, as King Rama IX, after the death, in controversial circumstances, of his elder brother, King Ananda Mahidol. He married Queen Sirikit in 1950 and has one son and three daughters. As king, he has been a stabilizing influence in a country noted for its political turbulence, and was active, with popular support, in helping to overthrow the military government of Field Marshal Thanom Kittikachorn in 1973. He is a highly respected figure, viewed in some quarters as semi-divine, and wields considerable political influence behind the scenes.

Bhutto, Benazir (1953–) Pakistani politician. After an education at Oxford University, she returned to Pakistan and was placed under house arrest between 1977 and 1984 by General **Zia ul-Haq**, who had executed her father Zulfikar Ali **Bhutto**, following the 1977 coup against him. During her subsequent exile in England with her mother, she formed the Pakistan People's Party, returning to Pakistan with the lifting of martial law in 1986 and beginning her campaign for open elections. She married in 1987, and, following General Zia's death the same year, she was elected Prime Minister in 1988, taking Pakistan back into the Commonwealth in 1989. Increasing friction between her Administration and the conservative presidency resulted in her Government being dismissed in Aug 1990, and soon after corruption charges were made against her; her husband was placed in custody on related alleged criminal offences. At the start of 1991, she began a lecture tour of America and Europe, but she dismissed speculation that she was choosing self-exile in return for her husband's release.

Bhutto, Zulfikar Ali (1928–79) Pakistani politician. A graduate of the Universities of California and Oxford, he began a career in law. He joined the Pakistani Cabinet in 1958 as Minister of Commerce, and became Foreign Minister in 1963. Dropped from the Cabinet, he founded the Pakistan People's Party (PPP) in 1967. After the secession of East Pakistan (now Bangladesh) in 1971, he became President (1971–3) and Prime Minister (1973–7). He introduced social and economic reforms, but opposition to his policies, especially from right-wing Islamic parties, led to the army under General **Zia ul-Haq** seizing control after the 1977 elections. Tried for corruption and murder, he was sentenced to death in 1978. In spite of worldwide appeals for clemency, the sentence was carried out in 1979.

Biafra The south-eastern province of Nigeria, inhabited by the **Igbo** people. Under the leadership of Colonel Ojukwu, it attempted to break away from the federation, thus precipitating the civil war of 1967–70. After the war, Nigeria was reorganized into a new provincial structure in an attempt to avert continuing instability.

Biafran War (1967–70) Two military coups in 1966 left Nigeria racked by ethnic divisions and on 26 May 1967 Lt-Col Chukuvemoka **Ojukwu** was mandated by the Ibo consultative assembly to declare the Eastern Region of Nigeria independent as the state of Biafra. Civil war then broke out as the Federal government, led by **Gowon**, sought to keep Nigeria one. It was not until Jan 1970 that the federal forces prevailed and, with Ojukwu's exile, peace was restored.

Bibó, István (1911–) Hungarian political writer and, briefly, revolutionary politician. A supporter of the so-called Smallholders Party, he held middle-of-the-road views and had a difficult time practising as a writer in the early 1950s. However, in 1956, between the two Soviet interventions, he was chosen to be a member of Imre **Nagy**'s cabinet and tried to exert a calming influence. He was subsequently condemned to death by the **Kádár** government and was only saved by protests from the West. It was not until 1963 that he was released from prison as a sign that reform was on the way.

Bicocca, Battle of ▷ **Italian Wars**

Bidault, Georges (1899–1982) French politician. He became a professor of history, served in both world wars, and was a member of the French Resistance. He became leader of the MRP (*Mouvement républicain populaire*), and apart from his periods as Premier (1946 and 1949–50), was Deputy Prime Minister (1950 and 1951), and Foreign Minister (1944, 1947 and 1953–4). After 1958 he opposed de **Gaulle** over the **Algerian War of Independence**, was charged with plotting against the security of the state, and went into exile (1962–8). ▷ **Resistance Movement** (France)

Bierut, Bolesław (1892–1956) Polish Communist Party functionary. In the interwar period he was in and out of prison and of Poland; then and later he spent formative periods in Moscow. In 1946 he was appointed Interim President, and the following year he was elected President. In 1948 he took over from **Gomułka** as Secretary of the party, and then from 1952 to 1954 he was Prime

Minister. His main claim to fame was following the Stalinist line and doing much damage to his country and colleagues in the process.

Big-Character Poster (*Dazibao/Ta-tzu pao*) A form of wall-poster in China that has served as a unique means of public expression free of government or party control. Often anonymous, and handwritten, these posters have appeared on walls or billboards erected in public places. The first wallposter to gain notoriety was the one displayed by the Philosophy Department of Beijing University on 25 May 1966, criticizing university authorities for stifling political debate. In Aug 1966 **Mao Zedong** himself wrote a wallposter which denounced revisionism. Although the right to erect wallposters expressing one's opinions was guaranteed in the 1975 and 1978 Constitutions, such a privilege was withdrawn in 1980 following a protest movement the previous year calling for greater democracy.

Big Sword Society (*Dadao hui*) A Chinese sect active in the south-western region of the province of Shandong during the 1890s. In an area of endemic economic poverty and banditry, the Big Swords were formed and led by wealthy landlords to provide protection. Like the Boxers in north-west Shandong, they practised martial arts and invulnerability rituals, as well as coming into conflict with native Christian congregations. At first tolerated by local officials, the Big Swords were finally suppressed in 1896. ▷ **Boxer Rising**

Biko, Steve (Stephen) (1947–77) South African black activist. He studied medicine at Natal University from where he became President of the all-black South African Students Organization (1969) and Honorary President of the Black People's Convention (1972). He was the major figure in the **Black Consciousness Movement** and his challenge to **apartheid**, expressed in his organization of the Black Community Programme, led to his being banned and then detained. He died in police custody as a result of the beatings he received.

Bil'ak, Vasil (1917–) Czechoslovak politician. He had a fairly undistinguished career in the Communist Party until 1968 when, as a Slovak, he succeeded Alexander **Dubček** as Secretary of the Central Committee of the Slovak Section. It was at this point that Dubček moved up to the secretaryship of the whole party and initiated the **Prague Spring**. Bil'ak was a reluctant reformer and in July and Aug of 1968 turned against Dubček, eventually welcoming the Soviet invasion. He was subsequently too unpopular to achieve high office but he remained a member of the party presidium, resisting any change, for two decades.

Bilingualism and Biculturalism, Royal Commission on (1963–71) Canadian governmental inquiry. Instituted by the Pearson administration, it was a response to the increasing separatist pressure in Quebec. Its aims were to research the origins of the crisis and to propose measures which would lead to a more equitable relationship between francophones and anglophones. Joint presidents of the commission were André Laurendeau, editor of the newspaper *Le Devoir*, and A Davidson Dunton, President of Ottawa's Carleton University. The final report revealed the extent to which French-Canadians were disadvantaged, both economically and culturally by their origins. It recommended the adoption of both French and English as official languages throughout the federal bureaucracy and in business. Whilst the report refused to advocate separate nationhood for Quebec, it did propose the concept of a two-nation federation, and the establishment of a ministry for multiculturalism, which was enacted in 1972.

Billaud-Varenne, Jean Nicolas (1756–1819) French revolutionary and supporter of the Reign of **Terror**. He became Secretary, then Vice-President, of the Jacobin Club (1792) and was one of those responsible for the September Massacres (1792) in which the mob, urged on by demagogic extremists, seized and murdered innocent victims from Paris prisons. He attacked the **Girondins**, was elected to the Convention and became a member of the Committee of Public Safety (1793). He supported **Robespierre** at first, but deserted him at the time of **Thermidor**. He was nevertheless transported to Cayenne (Guiana), where he lived until 1815. He then fled to Haiti, where he died. ▷ **Convention, National; Jacobins; Public Safety, Committee of**

Bill of Rights (1689) A Bill to enact the **Declaration of Rights** (1689), it asserted that **James II** (of England) had abdicated, established **William III** and Mary II as monarchs, forbade Roman Catholics from succeeding to the throne, and declared illegal exercise of royal power, such as the maintenance of an army in peacetime, without the consent of parliament.

bill of rights A list of citizens' rights set out in constitutional documents. Usually accompanying the document is an elaboration of the institutional means and powers by which such rights may be enforced. The best-known example is the one adopted in 1791 as the first 10 amendments to the **US Constitution**. The American Bill of Rights protects the liberties of private citizens in relation to the federal and state governments in such matters as freedom of speech, religion, the press and assembly, and legal procedure. It was adopted because of popular pressure during the campaign to ratify the constitution (1787–8), and its meaning has been expounded in many cases decided by the Supreme Court.

Billy the Kid ▷ **Bonney, William H**

Bird, Vere Cornwall (1910–) Antiguan politician. In 1939 he was a founder-member of the Antigua Trades and Labour Union and then leader of the Antigua Labour Party (ALP). In the pre-independence period he was elected to the Legislative Council and became Chief Minister (1960–7) and Premier (1967–71 and 1976–81). When total independence, as Antigua and Barbuda, was achieved in 1981 he became Prime Minister; he and his party were re-elected in 1984, and again in 1989.

Birdwood, William Riddell, 1st Baron Birdwood of Anjac and Totnes (1865–1951) Australian military leader, he served in the Indian Army, became Secretary of the Indian Army Department and a member of the Viceroy's legislative council (1912). In 1914 he was put in command of the Australian and New Zealand Army contingents, and planned the landing at Gallipoli, on Anzac Cove as it was subsequently known. Upon evacuation from the Peninsula, he took his troops to the Western Front, through the Battles of the Somme and Ypres in 1916 and 1917. After **World War I** he returned to India to command the Northern Army, becoming Commander-in-Chief in 1925, and retiring in 1930. ▷ **Gallipoli Campaign; Somme, Battle of the**

Birendra, Bir Bikram Shah Dev (1945–) King of Nepal (1972/). Educated at St Joseph's College, Darjeeling, Eton, and Tokyo and Harvard Universities, he married Queen Aishwarya Rajya Laxmi Devi Rana in 1970, and has two sons and one daughter. Appointed Grand Master and Colonel-in-Chief of the Royal Nepalese Army in 1964, he became King on the death of his father, King Mahendra. During his reign, there has been gradual progress towards political reform, but Nepal remained essentially an absolute monarchy, with political activity banned, until 1990, when Birendra was forced to concede much of his power.

Birkenhead, Frederick Edwin Smith, 1st Earl of (1872–1930) British politician and lawyer. A Conservative, he entered parliament in 1906, where he became known as a brilliant orator. In the Irish crisis (1914) he supported resistance to **Home Rule**, but later helped to negotiate the Irish settlement of 1921. He became Attorney-General (1915–19) and Lord Chancellor (1919–22) and was made an earl in 1922. His conduct as Secretary of State for India (1924–8) caused much criticism, and he resigned to devote himself to a commercial career. ▷ **Conservative Party** (UK)

Birla, G D (1894–1983) Indian industrialist. Until recently, he was India's biggest paper magnate, in charge of the huge Oriental Paper empire. He was also a large-scale philanthropist, contributing to the causes of scientific and medical research. Most famous for his close friendship with M K **Gandhi** and his strong support for the **Indian National Congress** in the 1920s, 1930s and 1940s. He was himself elected to the Indian Central Legislative Assembly in 1926. In 1944 he compiled the so-called Bombay Plan, along with two other businessmen, Thakurdas and J R D Tata, which set the pattern of state and private investment that was characteristic of India's five-year plans after Independence.

Biron, Ernst Johann (1690–1772) Baltic German nobleman. He assumed the name and arms of the French dukes of Biron, when, as favourite of **Anna Ivanovna**, he became the real ruler of Russia on her ascent to the Russian throne in 1730. He was blamed for most of the ills which befell Russia at this time, but greatly improved the country's administration. In 1737 Anna made him Duke of Courland. On the Empress's death (1740), he assumed the regency and acted with great moderation, but was arrested and banished for a time to Siberia. **Peter III** allowed him to return in 1762 and his titles were eventually restored to him.

Biryukova, Alexandra Pavlovna (1929–) Soviet politician. She was trained as a textile engineer and continued until as late as 1968 with her professional job in a factory. However, she had earlier taken official jobs, and in 1968 she became Secretary of the Trade Union Presidium and in 1985 Deputy Chairman. In 1986 Mikhail **Gorbachev** selected her for the Secretariat of the Central Committee of the Communist Party and in 1988 appointed her Deputy Prime Minister responsible for Social Development. She was also made a candidate member of the **Politburo**, the first woman since **Furtseva** to achieve this distinction. One of the few Soviet women to reach positions of political importance, in the turmoil of 1990–1, she was, however, pushed aside.

Bishop, Maurice (1946–83) Grenadian politician. He was the leader of the New Jewel Movement which overthrew the government of Eric **Gairy** in 1979 and set up a Marxist People's Revolutionary Government. Disagreements over policy resulted in Bishop's overthrow and murder by his deputy, Bernard Coard, and the Commander of the Armed Forces, General Austin (Oct 1983), and the creation of a Revolutionary Military Council (RMC). The USA and moderate Caribbean governments, shocked by the bloody coup and fearful of imagined Cuban influence, instigated military intervention to depose the RMC and arrest the coup leaders. Coard, Austin and 12 others were sentenced to death, but these sentences were commuted to life imprisonment in 1991.

Bishops Wars (1639–40) Two wars between **Charles I** of England and the Scottish **Covenanters**, caused by his unpopular policies towards the Scottish Kirk. They resulted in English defeats, and bankruptcy for Charles, who was then forced to call the Short and Long Parliaments (1640), bringing to an end his 'personal rule' (1629–40). ▷ **Long Parliament; Short Parliament**

Bismarck, Otto Edward Leopold von (1815–98) Prusso-German politician. He studied law and agriculture at Göttingen, Berlin, and Greifswald. In the new Prussian parliament (1847) he became known as an ultra-royalist, resenting Austria's predominance and demanding equal rights for **Prussia**. He was Ambassador to Russia (1859–62), and was appointed Prime Minister in 1862, with an explicit remit to thwart liberal pressure for a constitutional monarchy. During the Schleswig-Holstein question and the Seven Weeks War between **Prussia** and **Austria**, he was a guiding figure, becoming a national hero and reconciling the liberals to Prussian monarchism. Uniting German feeling, he deliberately provoked the **Franco-Prussian War** (1870–1) and acted as Germany's spokesman. He was made a count in 1866, and created a prince and was the first Chancellor of the new German Empire (1871–90). After the Peace of Frankfurt (1871), his policies aimed at consolidating and protecting the young empire. His domestic policy included universal suffrage, reformed coinage, welfare legislation and the codification of the law, although he ensured that ultimate political power resided with the Emperor and aristocracy. He engaged in a lengthy conflict with the Vatican (known as the **Kulturkampf**), which proved to be a failure, and from 1878 pursued a vigorous anti-socialist policy. In 1879, to counteract Russia and France, he formed the Austro-German Treaty of Alliance, which was later joined by Italy. Called the 'Iron Chancellor', he resigned the chancellorship in 1890, out of disapproval of Emperor **William II**'s initially liberal policy. In the same year he was made Duke of Lauenburg, and was finally reconciled to his sovereign (1894).

Bitar, Salah al-Din Syrian politician. Co-founder in 1943 with Michel **Aflaq** of the **Ba'ath Socialist Party**, he played a considerable part in the founding of the short-lived **United Arab Republic** (UAR), a union of Egypt and Syria established in 1958, from which Syria seceded in 1961. Despite a broad influence through its essentially socialist and pan-Arab ideology, the failure of the UAR dealt a considerable blow to the Ba'ath as originally conceived by Bitar and Aflaq, and paved the way for the separate development of one-party Ba'athist rule in Syria and Iraq.

Bithynia The name in antiquity for the area to the south-west of the Black Sea. Inhabited mainly by warlike Thracians, it eluded Achaemenid and Seleucid control, becoming an independent kingdom under a Hellenizing dynasty of Thracian stock c.300BC. In 75–74BC, under the will of its last king, Nicomedes IV, it passed to Rome. Bithynia's strategic importance grew during the imperial period: in the late 3cAD, its leading city, Nicomedia, became a while the capital of the entire eastern half of the Empire. ▷ **Hellenization; Persian Empire**

Bixio, Gerolamo ('Nino') (1821–73) Italian soldier. One of **Garibaldi**'s most able lieutenants and one of the few *garibaldini* to be fully accepted by the regular army, he was elected a deputy in the Italian parliament in 1861 and became a senator in 1870.

Biya, Paul (1933–) Cameroonian politician. He graduated with a law degree from Paris University and entered politics under the aegis of **Ahidjo**. He was a junior minister in 1962, a minister of state in 1968 and Prime Minister in 1975. When Ahidjo unexpectedly retired in 1982, he became President and reconstituted the government with his own supporters. He survived a coup attempt in Apr 1984 (almost certainly instigated by Ahidjo) and was re-elected President in 1988 with more than 98 per cent of the vote.

Bjelke-Petersen, Sir Jo(hannes) (1911–) New Zealand-born Australian politician, of Danish parents. In 1913 the family moved to Kingaroy, Queensland. He entered state politics in 1947 as a Country Party (later National Party) member of the Legislative Assembly, becoming a minister in 1963. In 1968, as a result of his firm stand on law and order, he was made Police Minister, then Deputy Leader and, following the sudden death of Jack Pizzey, became Premier of Queensland. A vocal supporter of states' rights against federal intervention, he controlled a strongly right-wing government, first in coalition with the **Liberal Party of Australia** and after 1983 in his own right. He was knighted in 1982 and retired from the premiership in 1987. ▷ **National Party of Australia**

Björnsson, Sveinn (1881–1952) Icelandic diplomat and politician. Born in Copenhagen, he was the son of an Icelandic newspaper editor. He studied law in Copenhagen and was elected a member of the Icelandic parliament in 1914–16 and 1920. During **World War I** he was envoy to the USA and Britain, and was ambassador to Denmark in 1920–4 and 1926–41. During the German occupation of Denmark he was elected regent of Iceland and, when Iceland declared its independence of Denmark in 1944, he was elected the new republic's first President. Re-elected in 1948, he died in office.

Black, Hugo Lafayette (1886–1971) US jurist. He practised law in his home state of Alabama and became a police court judge. In 1927 he entered the US Senate and as a liberal leader promoted the Tennessee Valley Authority as well as legislation that would set minimum wages and impose limits on working hours. In 1937 he was appointed to the US Supreme Court, where he served until his death. Black, a libertarian, opposed undue economic regulation by the states or the federal government. Central to his philosophy was the conviction that the Fourteenth Amendment made the Bill of Rights generally applicable to the states and that the First Amendment's guarantees of freedoms were absolute. Late in his career he supported civil rights legislation.

Black and Tans Additional members of the Royal Irish Constabulary, recruited by the British government to cope with Irish nationalist unrest in 1920. The shortage of regulation uniforms led to the recruits being issued with khaki tunics and trousers and very dark green caps, hence their name. Terrorist activities provoked severe and brutal reprisals by the Black and Tans, which caused an outcry in Britain and the USA.

Black Codes Laws enacted in 1865–6 by Southern state legislatures following the **American Civil War** which severely restricted many rights of the newly freed slaves. Varying significantly from state to state, these laws were interpreted by the North as Southern unwillingness to change its racial attitudes. The Freedman's Bureau prevented their implementation and they were later repealed.

Black Consciousness Movement (South Africa) A loose movement formed by Steve **Biko** in 1969, when he led African students out of the multi-racial National Union of South African Students and founded the South African Students Organization. From this emerged the Black People's Convention in 1972 which sought to create cooperation in social and cultural fields among all non-white peoples. Banned in 1976, most of its leaders were imprisoned in 1977 and Biko himself died in police custody soon afterwards.

Black Dragon Society (*Kokuryukai*) A Japanese ultra-nationalist conspiratorial organization founded in 1901 by Uchida Ryohei and Toyama Mitsuru. Strongly influenced by the concept of Pan-Asianism, the society sought to enhance Japan's influence on the Asian mainland, initially in Manchuria (and thereby eliminate Russian influence) and then throughout China. It maintained ties with a number of government officials,

Diet politicians and military officers, continually pressing for an assertive foreign policy to combat Western influence in Asia, an aim that was often linked with domestic renovation. The society also carried out espionage work on the Asian mainland. As with other ultra-nationalist organizations, the Black Dragon Society was disbanded in 1945 following Japan's defeat in **World War II**.

Black Friday The name given to 24 Sep 1869, the day of a US financial crisis, when the price of gold dropped severely as a result of an attempt by such financiers as Jay Gould (1836–92) and James Fisk (1834–72) to corner the gold market. Many speculators lost their fortunes in the ensuing panic.

Black Hand The common name for the secret organization 'Unification or Death' (*Ujedinjenje ili Smrt*) formed by Serbian nationalist army officers in 1911. Led by Colonel Dragutin **Dimitrijević**, alias Apis, its objective was the political unification of all the Serbs. It lay behind the assassination by the Bosnian Serb Gavrilo **Princip** of **Francis Ferdinand**, Archduke of Austria, in Sarajevo (June 1914), an event which led directly to the outbreak of **World War I**. ▷ **Mlada Bosna**

Black Hawk War (1832) A military conflict between the USA and Sauk and Fox peoples, which led to the completion of the policy of removing Native Americans from 'the Old North-West' to beyond the Mississippi River. ▷ **Indian Wars**

Black Hole of Calcutta A small, badly-ventilated room in which surviving British defenders were imprisoned following Calcutta's capture (June 1756) by **Siraj ud-Daula**, Nawab of Bengal. It was claimed that only 23 out of 146 prisoners survived. Following possibly self-serving publicity by J Z Holwell, the incident became famous in the history of British imperialism, but the circumstances are controversial, and the total number of prisoners was probably much smaller.

Black Hundreds (post-1905) The name given to the right-wing terrorists opposed to the reforms conceded by **Nicholas II** during the Russian **Revolution of 1905**. Operating under fine-sounding names such as Union of the Russian People, Union of the Russian Land, or Russian Orthodox Committee, they were well-to-do and well connected. Often with official connivance, they resorted to violence against individuals or groups supporting democratic reform and helped to discredit such representative institutions as were tolerated.

Black Muslims A black religious movement in the USA, also known as the Nation of Islam, founded in 1930 by Wali Farad (Wallace D Fard), who proclaimed that black Americans are descended from an ancient Muslim tribe. Followers adopted Muslim names and believed Farad to be an incarnation of God. Following Farad's mysterious disappearance in 1934, Elijah **Muhammad** became leader of the movement until his death in 1975. Muhammad urged his followers to avoid contact with whites and demanded a separate state for blacks as well as reparation for past injustices. **Malcolm X** was one of the movement's most inspiring preachers, while the boxer Muhammad Ali was one of its most famous members. After Elijah Muhammad's son, Warith Dean (Wallace D), assumed leadership, the organization adopted orthodox Muslim beliefs. There were some, however, who continued to hold to the original tenets of the movement, including its separatist stance. Louis Farrakhan emerged as that faction's spokesman and has continued in that role.

Black Panthers US militant black political party, founded by Huey P Newton and Bobby Seale in 1966, promoting the use of physical force and armed confrontation for black liberation. The party was active in the 1960s, but was split by rival groups in the 1970s and diminished in importance.

Black Power The slogan used by black activists in the USA from the mid-1960s to reflect the aspiration of increased black political power. It formed part of the more radical wing of the **civil rights** movement, was against integrationist policies, and rejected non-violence. Some political results were achieved in terms of registering black voters, together with much wider attitudinal change. ▷ **Black Panthers; Congress of Racial Equality (CORE)**

Black Saturday (26 Jan 1952) After guerrilla attacks on their bases in Egypt, the British acted against suspects, including the Egyptian police. British forces surrounded police headquarters at Ismailia and called on the police to surrender; they refused and 50 were killed in the attack on their headquarters. The next day — Black Saturday — Egyptian crowds, led by the Muslim Brotherhood, burnt down British and foreign shops and restaurants in the centre of Cairo. Egyptian troops did not intervene to bring the situation under control until evening. King Farouk and the government blamed each other for the delay and there began a period of ministerial instability, while governments followed one another rapidly. This led the Free Officers to bring forward the coup they were planning for 1954 or 1955 to July 1952, when army units seized key points in the capital and Farouk was forced into exile.

Black September (Sep 1970) This refers to the month when Fedayeen and the **PLO** (Palestine Liberation Organization) resisted an attempt by the Jordanian government to establish control over them and their guerrillas who were carrying out operations against Israel. A civil war resulted and King Hussein was saved by the loyalty of his Bedouin regiments.

blackshirts The colloquial name for members of Oswald **Mosley**'s British Union of Fascists (BUF), formed in Oct 1932. It derived from the colour of the uniforms worn at mass rallies and demonstrations organized by the BUF on the model of European fascist parties. After clashes and disturbances in Jewish areas of London (1936), the Public Order Act prohibited the wearing of uniforms by political groups. ▷ **Union Movement**

Black Thursday (24 Oct 1929) The date of the crash of the New York stockmarket that marked the onset of the **Great Depression**.

Blackwell, Elizabeth (1821–1910) US physician and feminist. Born in Bristol, UK, she received a degree in medicine, from Geneva College in New York State. Blackwell, who faced hostility throughout her education and career, was responsible for opening the field of medicine to women. She also established an infirmary for the poor of New York City. In later life she returned to England, where she died at Hastings, Sussex.

Blaize, Herbert Augustus (1918–89) Grenadian politician. After qualifying and practising as a solicitor, he entered politics and helped to found the centrist Grenada National Party (GNP), being elected to parliament in 1957. He held ministerial posts before becoming Premier in 1967. After full independence, in 1974, he led the official opposition and then went into hiding (1979–83) following the left-wing coup by

Maurice **Bishop**. After the US invasion of 1983, when normal political activity resumed, he returned to lead a reconstituted New National Party (NNP) and win the 1984 general election.

Blake, Edward (1833–1912) Canadian lawyer and politician. A Liberal, he became Premier of Ontario in 1871 and minister without portfolio in the **Mackenzie** federal administration in 1873. Uncomfortable with Mackenzie's policies, he resigned in 1874 and with a fervent speech assumed the leadership of the **Canada First** movement. He returned to government as the Minister of Justice in 1875 and succeeded in gaining the British government's acceptance of the Supreme Court Act and a reduction in the powers of the Governor General. Leader of the Liberals (1880–87), he resigned from the party in 1891 because he could not accept its **reciprocity** proposals. Long interested in the Irish question, he left Canada in 1892 and became an Irish nationalist MP in the British parliament, but eventually returned to Canada in 1906. ▷ **Liberal Party** (Canada)

Blake, Robert (1599–1657) English admiral. He lived in Oxford as a quiet country gentleman until he was 40. In 1640 he was returned for Bridgwater to the **Short Parliament**, and later served in the **Long Parliament** (1645–53) and the **Barebone's Parliament** (1653). In 1649 he blockaded Lisbon, destroying the squadron of Prince **Rupert**, and in 1652–3 routed the Dutch in several battles. His greatest victory was his last, at Santa Cruz, when he destroyed a Spanish treasure fleet off Tenerife; but he died on the return journey to England. ▷ **Anglo-Dutch Wars; English Civil Wars**

Blamey, Sir Thomas (1884–1951) Australian soldier. He joined the regular army in 1906 and attended Staff College at Quetta. He saw service on the north-west frontier of India, and in **World War I** played an important part in the evacuation of Gallipoli. He became Chief of Staff of the Australian Corps in 1918 and between 1925 and 1936 was Chief Commissioner of Police in Victoria. At the outbreak of **World War II** he was given command of the Australian Imperial Forces in the Middle East. He had command of Commonwealth operations in Greece (1941) and served as Deputy Commander-in-Chief to Wavell. On the establishment of the south-west Pacific command he became Commander-in-Chief of Allied land forces (1942) and received the Japanese surrender

in 1945. In 1950 he was made a field marshal, the first Australian soldier to hold this rank.
▷ **Gallipoli Campaign**

Blanc, (Jean Joseph) Louis (1811–82) French politician and historian. A socialist, he studied in Paris, where in 1839 he founded the *Revue du Progrès* and wrote his chief work on socialism, the *L'Organisation du travail* (1839), proposing the establishment of cooperative workshops subsidized by the state. After the **February Revolution** (1848) he became a member of the provisional government, without portfolio, acting as President of the Luxembourg Committee set up to discuss ways of improving labour conditions; it had no power and achieved nothing. Charged, unjustly, with fomenting the **June Days** rising of Parisian workers, he fled in Aug 1848 to Belgium, moving to London in 1851. On the fall of the Second Empire, he returned to France, and was elected to the National Assembly in 1871, being re-elected 1878–7. He opposed the **Paris Commune** (1871), but led the extreme left in the first parliaments of the Third Republic. ▷ **Empire, Second** (France); **Republic, Third** (France)

Blanqui, (Louis) Auguste (1805–81) French revolutionary leader. A socialist, he studied law and medicine, demonstrated against the Bourbon regime, and organized an abortive insurrection in 1839, which led to his imprisonment until 1848. He founded the Central Republican Society, and was again imprisoned after the demonstrations of May 1848. He remained politically active during the Second Empire, and was arrested on the eve of the **Paris Commune**, of which he was nevertheless elected President (1871). A passionate extremist, whose supporters were known as Blanquists, he spent 37 years of his life in prison. ▷ **Bourbon, House of; Empire, Second** (France)

Blasco Ibáñez, Vicente (1867–1928) Spanish politician and writer. A federalist Republican leader of revolutionary leanings, he was first elected to parliament in 1898. His populist appeal laid the foundations for the PURA (Party of Republican Autonomist Union), otherwise known as the 'Blasquist' movement, which became the dominant political force in Valencia until the **Spanish Civil War**. At the same time as the Barcelona leader Alejandro **Lerroux** (an ally), Blasco Ibáñez formed the first modern political party in Spain. Although Blasco abandoned politics for writing in 1907, his political

pronouncements made a greater impact than ever. During **World War I** he backed the Allies, most notably through his novel *The Four Horsemen of the Apocalypse*. His broadsides against the monarchy and **Primo de Rivera**'s dictatorship (1923–30) were highly effective. During the early part of the 20c he was probably the most famous living Spanish writer in the world. He died in exile in France.

Blenheim, Battle of (1704) The greatest military triumph of **Marlborough** and his Imperial ally, Prince Eugene of Savoy, in the War of the **Spanish Succession**. Fought on the Danube to prevent a combined Franco-Bavarian thrust on Vienna, it marked the first major defeat of **Louis XIV** of France's armies, and the first major English victory on the European mainland since the Battle of **Agincourt**.

Bleus French-Canadian moderate reform followers of Louis Hippolyte. **Lafontaine** (the term dating from 1850 in contradistinction to the radical **Rouges**). From 1854 they became the French-Canadian wing of the new Conservative Party. In 1862, with the introduction of the **Militia Bill, the bloc split into two wings, the** *Ultra-bleus*, led by Sir Hector **Langevin**, who were on the extreme right, and the moderate *Bleus*, led by Adolphe **Chapleau**. The party had problems when **Canada West** and **Canada East** were united in 1864 because the French Canadians suffered a numerical disadvantage in the legislature. However, under the leadership of George Étienne **Cartier**, the Bleus sought to protect the cultural rights of the French Canadians. The support of the party was essential to the Conservative domination of federal politics during the late 19c, but with D'Alton **McCarthy**'s Equal Rights Association and the **Manitoba Schools Act** controversy, Quebec swung its vote behind the Liberals who then won the 1896 federal election.

Bligh, William (c.1753–c.1817) British sailor. He sailed under Captain James **Cook** in his second world voyage (1772–4), and in 1787 was sent as commander of the *Bounty* to Tahiti. On the return voyage, the men mutinied under his harsh treatment. In Apr 1789, Bligh and 18 men were cast adrift in an open boat without charts. In June, after great hardship, he arrived at Timor, near Java, having sailed his frail craft for 3 618 miles. In 1805 he was appointed Governor of New South Wales, where his conduct led to his imprisonment for two years. He was promoted admiral in 1811.

blitz The colloquial name for the series of air raids on British cities by the German Air Force (Sep 1940–May 1941). The purpose of the raids was to weaken British resistance to projected invasion. The cities of London and Coventry were particularly badly affected. ▷ **Blitzkrieg; Luftwaffe; World War II**

Blitzkrieg A term (literally, 'lightning war') coined, in Sep 1939, to describe the German armed forces' use of fast-moving tanks and deep-ranging aircraft in techniques which involve bypassing resistance and aiming the focus of effort at the enemy's rear areas rather than making frontal attacks. *Blitzkrieg* tactics were used with great success by the Germans in 1939–41 to achieve rapid and conclusive victories. ▷ **World War II**

Bloc national (1919) A French electoral coalition which won the 1919 elections, producing a Chamber of Deputies with a conservative majority, called the 'blue horizon' Chamber, so named after the colour of French Army uniforms. It was defeated by the **Cartel des gauches** ('Left-wing Cartel') in 1924. The term 'bloc' in this context had been coined by **Clemenceau** in 1891, in a famous phrase describing the **French Revolution**, and first applied to the *Bloc de Défense républicaine* ('Republican Defence') at the time of the **Dreyfus** Affair (1899–1902).

Bloc Populaire Quebecois nationalist political party. It was formed in 1942 by liberals who opposed Canadian participation in **World War II** and the introduction of conscription, and by Catholic radicals like André Laurendeau who wished to base industrial relations on papal encyclicals and to forbid the entry of foreign capital. After winning four seats in the provincial elections of 1944, the party fragmented, with the **Union Nationale** having benefited considerably from its extremism.

Blood, Council of (1567–76) A court established by the Duke of **Alva**, the Spanish Habsburg military commander in the Low Countries, on **Philip II**'s orders, to suppress heresy and opposition during the Revolt of the Netherlands. Also known as the Council of Troubles, it comprised seven members (three of them Spaniards). The council's proceedings were rigorous and strict, especially against Protestants, and took no account of rank or privilege. Its deliberations were widely resented, and helped intensify the **Eighty Years War**. ▷ **Habsburg Dynasty**

Blood, Thomas (c.1618–80) Irish adventurer. Celebrated for his activities during the **English Civil Wars** and **Restoration**, his most famous exploit was the attempt, disguised as a clergyman, to steal the crown jewels from the Tower of London (May 1671). After nearly murdering the keeper of the jewels, he succeeded in taking the crown, while one of his associates bore away the orb. He was pursued, captured, and imprisoned, but later pardoned by King **Charles II** of England.

Blood River, Battle of (Dec 1838) A battle in which the Boers of the trekker republic of Natalia defeated the Zulu. Andries Pretorius with a commando of some 500 men avenged the killing of Piet **Retief** and attacks on Boer settlements ordered by Dingane, the Zulu king, in Feb of that year. As a result, the Boers re-established themselves in Natal, although many left when the British annexed the colony in 1843. The battle has remained a central aspect of Boer mythology in relation to Africans ever since and is the subject of annual commemorations.

Bloody Assizes The name given to the western circuit assizes in England in the summer of 1685, presided over by Lord Chief Justice George **Jeffreys** after the defeat of the Duke of **Monmouth** at the Battle of **Sedgemoor**. About 150 of Monmouth's followers, mostly poorer farmers and clothworkers, were executed, and 800 transported to the West Indies.

Bloody Sunday (13 Nov 1887) The name conventionally given to clashes between police and demonstrators in Trafalgar Square, London, at a meeting called to protest against a ban on open-air meetings and to call for the release of an Irish MP who had been supporting a rent strike. Two demonstrators were killed. The meeting took place against a background of economic depression, widespread unemployment and Irish nationalist unrest.

Bloody Sunday (9 Jan 1905) Political opposition to Tsarist autocracy had intensified in 1904 as Russia suffered defeats in its war with Japan. In the new year, on this day, Father **Gapon** led a group of workers to the **Winter Palace** in St Petersburg to present a petition to **Nicholas II**. They were joined by a large but peaceful crowd. Troops opened fire, killing over 100 people and wounding several hundred more. This marked the beginning of the Russian **Revolution of 1905** and, symbolically, made something like the **February Revolution** (1917) more or less inevitable.

Bloody Sunday (30 Jan 1972) The name given, especially by Republicans in Northern Ireland, to events occurring during a Catholic civil rights protest march in Londonderry. The British Army opened fire, killing 14, mainly young, demonstrators. This action led to increased support for the **IRA** and also to many more deaths from political violence. Indirectly, it led to the ending of the **Stormont** parliament and the reimposition of direct rule by the British government over Northern Ireland.

Blücher, Gebbard Leberecht von, Prince von Wahlstadt (1742–1819) Prussian field marshal. He fought against the French in 1793 and 1806, and in 1813 took chief command in **Silesia**, defeating **Napoleon I** at the Battle of **Leipzig**, and entering Paris (1814). In 1815 he assumed the general command, suffered a severe defeat at Ligny, but completed **Wellington**'s victory at the Battle of **Waterloo** by his timely appearance on the field. He was known as 'Marshal Forward', his victories being due mainly to dash and energy. ▷ **Prussia**

Blueshirts The pejorative term coined by the Japanese to refer to a Chinese elite revolutionary corps set up within the **Guomindang** (Nationalist Party). Founded in 1932 by close associates of **Chiang Kai-shek**, it sought to root out corruption within the Guomindang, promote state-sponsored industrial development, and create a militarized and disciplined society. Admirers of European fascism, the Blueshirts also wished to see Chiang Kai-shek elevated to the position of supreme leader, around whom national unity would be forged. They made little headway amongst the entrenched interests and factions within the Guomindang, however, and were disbanded in 1938.

bluestockings A nickname, usually with derogatory connotations, for educated women. The term was widely used when opportunities expanded for the education of middle-class women in the late 19c, but it originated in the Blue Stocking Club at Montagu House, London, c.1750.

Blum, Léon (1872–1950) French politician. He trained in the law and was elected a Deputy in 1919, becoming the leader of the Parliamentary Group of Socialists, and an influential writer in the party newspaper. He was Prime Minister of the **Popular Front** governments (1936–7 and 1938). He opposed the **Vichy** regime, and was arrested and put

on trial at Riom as one of those responsible for the defeat of 1940. The trial was abandoned, but he remained in prison, and was deported to Germany. He returned to France in 1944 and resumed his position as leader of the **Socialist Party**, becoming Prime Minister of a brief caretaker government (1946–7), before retiring from active politics. ▷ **Riom Trial**

Blundell, Sir Michael (1907–93) Kenyan farmer and politician, born in London. He emigrated to Kenya in 1925 to farm, and served throughout **World War II**. He then involved himself in settler politics, being a member of Legco 1948–63 and leader of the European members in 1952–4 and then Minister of Agriculture (1955–9 and 1961–3). He broke with the dominant white group to espouse political change involving black Kenyans in national politics and was much vilified for this. However, he was an essential bridge between the white-dominated colonial years and the black majority rule of independent Kenya.

Blunt, Anthony (Frederick) (1907–83) British double agent. An art historian, he became a Fellow at Trinity College, Cambridge (1932), where he shared in the left-wing communist-respecting tendencies of the time, and first met **Burgess**, **Philby** and **Maclean**. Influenced by Burgess, he acted as a 'talent-spotter', supplying to him the names of likely recruits to the Soviet communist cause, and during his war-service in British Intelligence, was in a position to pass on information to the Soviet government. Although his spying activities appear to have ceased after the war, he was still able to assist the defection of Burgess and Maclean in 1951, although suspected by British Intelligence. In 1964, after the defection of Philby, a confession was obtained from Blunt in return for his immunity, and he continued as Surveyor of the Queen's Pictures until 1972. His full involvement in espionage was made public only in 1979, and his knighthood (awarded 1956) was annulled.

Blyden, Edward Wilmot (1832–1912) West Indian writer and educational philosopher. He spent most of his life in West Africa and is generally regarded as one of the founders of the concept of negritude and the precursor of the intellectual and political nationalism of the 20c. Blyden believed in the establishment of a vast colony under British rule in West Africa as the means whereby the Continent could modernize itself. Such a colony would aspire to Dominion status and be ruled by its own elite fully educated in western ways but also re-discovering its own essential African characteristics. At one stage he favoured Christian missionary endeavour as a means of reaching this goal, but later turned increasingly to traditional beliefs and Islam. He wrote many works on these issues and worked for the foundation of a West African University.

Blyukher, Vasili Konstantinovich (1890–1938) Russian soldier. A **Red Army** hero in the **Russian Civil War**, he ended up commanding the forces that expelled the Japanese from the Soviet Far East. In 1924–7 he was military adviser to **Chiang Kai-shek's Guomindang**. In 1929 he was put in command of Soviet troops in the Far East and fought successfully with the Chinese that year and with the Japanese in 1938. However, he proved too successful for **Stalin** who had him arrested, tried and executed; this, among other things, left the USSR particularly powerless against Japan.

Boabdil (Abu Abdallah Muhammad) (d.c.1493) Last Moorish King of Granada (1482/92). He dethroned his father, Abu al-Hasan (1482) and, while he continued to struggle for power against his father and uncle, the Christians gradually conquered the kingdom. Malaga fell in 1487, and after a two-year siege Granada itself capitulated to **Ferdinand II, 'the Catholic'** and **Isabella I, 'the Catholic'** (2 Jan 1492). Boabdil was granted a small lordship in the Alpujarras, but in 1493 sold his rights to the Spanish crown and retired to Morocco, where he died. ▷ **Granada, Conquest of**

Boadicea ▷ **Boudicca**

boat people Vietnamese who fled Vietnam by boat after the communist victory in 1975, travelling to Australia, Hong Kong, Japan, and several other parts of South-East Asia. Many died on the long voyages, or were killed by pirates. Voluntary repatriation schemes gained momentum in 1989, and the first involuntary repatriation operation from Hong Kong was carried out in Dec 1989.

Boccanegra, Simone (c.1301–63) Doge of Genoa. Born of an illustrious Genoese family, Boccanegra rose to power when the factional strife of Guelf and Ghibelline had plunged the city into anarchy. In the interests of order he was given the title of perpetual doge in 1339. The burden of taxation which he imposed provoked discontent, and he went into exile in Pisa (1344). He returned to his native city to stiffen a revolt against the **Visconti** and was again appointed perpetual Doge in 1356. His career is the subject of Verdi's famous opera. ▷ **Guelfs; Ghibellines**

Bocskai, István (1557–1606) Prince of Transylvania (1604/6). A landowner in the region around the River Tisza, he was elected Prince of Transylvania. He made his reputation first in the long wars against the Ottoman Turks, and then in the struggle of the Hungarian nobles against Austrian Habsburg domination, culminating in the insurrection of 1604. With the Peace of Vienna in 1606, he won self-government for the Hungarian nobility and religious freedom for Protestant Transylvania; this was the foundation on which **Bethlen Gábor** later built the remarkably powerful independent principality of Transylvania that made its mark on the **Thirty Years War**.

Boeotia (Boiotia) In antiquity, the area in central Greece bordering on Attica. Its chief city-state was **Thebes**. Its inhabitants were largely of Aeolian stock, and proverbial for their stupidity. ▷ **Aeolians**

Boers ▷ **Afrikaners**

Boer Wars (1880–1 and 1899–1902) Two wars fought by the British and the Boers for the mastery of southern Africa. The British had made several attempts to re-incorporate the Boers, who had left the Cape Colony in the **Great Trek**, within a South African confederation. The first Boer War ended with the defeat of the British at **Majuba Hill**, and the signing of the Pretoria and London Conventions of 1881 and 1884. In 1896 the **Jameson Raid** was a clumsy private effort to achieve the same objective. The second Boer War can be divided into three phases: (1) (Oct 1899–Jan 1900) a series of Boer successes, including the sieges of **Ladysmith**, **Kimberley**, and **Mafeking**, as well as victories at Stormberg, Modder River, Magersfontein, Colenso, and Modderspruit; (2) (Feb–Aug 1900) counter-offensives by Lord **Roberts**, including the raising of the sieges, the victory at Paardeberg, and the capture of Pretoria; (3) (Sep 1900–May 1902) a period of guerrilla warfare when **Kitchener** attempted to prevent Boer commando raids on isolated British units and lines of communication. The Boers effectively won the peace. They maintained control of 'native affairs', won back representative government in 1907, and federated South Africa on their terms in 1910. On the other hand, British interests in South Africa were protected and, despite internal strains, the Union of South Africa entered both **World War I** and **World War II** on the British side. ▷ **Vereeniging, Peace of**

Bogomils The name, meaning 'pleasing to God', given to Balkan followers of the Manichean heresy which thrived in the 10–15c, especially in Bosnia, where espousal of Bogomilism was closely tied to a desire for a national Bosnian church free from Rome and Constantinople. The dualistic heresy — that God had two sons, Christ and Satan — first took root in Macedonia towards the end of the reign of the Bulgarian Emperor, **Simeon** (d.927), then spread throughout the Balkans in the mid-11c, dominating intellectual life in Bulgaria and Bosnia until the 15c. It spread into Italy and thence to Lombardy and the Pyrenees, where its followers were known as the Cathars.

Bogomolov, Alexei Yefremovich (1900–) Soviet soldier, diplomat and lecturer. He served in the **Red Army** from 1919 to 1930 and spent the period 1930–8 teaching. His career changed again in 1939 when he became a deputy, and in 1941 when he became an ambassador. He served two years in the UK, helping to get the British government accustomed to the idea of a **Czechoslovak–Soviet Alliance**. Later, he spent the years 1954–7 in Prague, as Czechoslovakia escaped from some of the less happy consequences of the 1943 treaty.

Bogomolov, Oleg Timofeevich (1927–) Soviet economist and official. He was educated at the Moscow Institute of Foreign Trade and moved, after a short spell at the Soviet Ministry of Foreign Trade, to a long spell at **Comecon**. He then served on the State Planning Commission and the Communist Party Central Committee, before becoming Director of the Institute of the Economics of the World Socialist System in 1969. There he was involved in attempts to improve Comecon output in Leonid **Brezhnev**'s time, and he became a reformist adviser to both Yuri **Andropov** and Mikhail **Gorbachev**. In 1990 he was elected to the Soviet Congress of Deputies, but his influence appeared to decline as more radical ideas came to the fore.

bogotazo (9 Apr 1948) A serious urban riot in Bogota, Colombia, fired by the assassination of the popular liberal and nationalist politician, Jorge Eliécer Gaitán. A turning-point in the history of modern Colombia, it resulted in hundreds of deaths and much material damage. The mob violence was inspired by both the ultra-right followers of Laureano Gómez and Gaitáns's leftists; this in turn sparked off sporadic revolts in the countryside and the spread of martial law under moderate conservative Mariano Ospina Pérez. Gómez, an admirer of **Hitler** and **Franco**, was elected President in 1950.

Bohemia Historic province of western Czechoslovakia, bounded to the east by Moravia, west and south by Germany and Austria and north by Poland. Part of the Moravian Empire in the 9c, it was at its peak in the early Middle Ages, especially in the 14c under Charles I. Bohemia came under Habsburg rule in the early 16c and became a province of Czechoslovakia in 1918. It became part of the Czech Socialist Republic of western Czechoslovakia in 1968.

Bohemian Museum, Foundation of the (1818) The second most important development, after the Royal **Bohemian Society**, in the Czech cultural revival. It was established under the patronage of German-speaking nobles to house important local scientific objects. However, it became a centre for Czech-speaking intellectuals and, when its German-language journal failed in 1831, the Czech-language version rapidly increased its circulation. The most famous of the Czechs who frequented it was the great historian, and subsequently politician, František **Palacký**, who used the journal effectively to spread nationalist thinking.

Bohemian Protectorate (1939–45) The form of government **Hitler** used to control Bohemia and Moravia following the destruction of Czechoslovakia in Mar 1939. Officially, there was a Czech president, **Hácha**, and a ruling cabinet, but they were instruments of the German protector, particularly after the murder of **Heydrich** in 1942. However, while terror was used, Hitler was careful not to push the Czechs too far since their agricultural and industrial production was essential for his war effort. In the end, though, he faced resistance there as well as elsewhere in Europe.

Bohemian Revolt (1618) A major uprising against the Habsburgs. The revolt was led by Protestants who were unwilling to tolerate Imperial attempts to reintroduce Catholicism. The revolt, one of many, can be traced to tensions which arose out of the earlier Hussite religious reforms as well as later Protestantism. By 1621 the Bohemians had been crushed and the country was subjected to strong, centralized rule by the Habsburgs. The defeat of the revolt was used as a pretext to crush Protestantism but only in those areas which rebelled. Protestants continued to enjoy their traditional rights and freedoms in other Austrian areas. ▷ **Habsburg Dynasty**

Bohemian Society of Sciences, Foundation of the Royal (1790) An important development in the revival of Czech culture, it was in part a product of the Enlightenment. However, the nobles who founded it in Prague, German-speaking though they were, intended it as a means of resisting the centralizing pressures of the Habsburg Emperors by stressing and developing their local links. The long-term effect was to contribute to the emergence of Czech nationalism.

Boissy d'Anglas, François Antoine de (1756–1826) French politician. A member of the **Estates General** (1789), he joined the successful conspiracy against **Robespierre**. He was elected Secretary of the Convention, and a member of the Committee of Public Safety, in which capacity he displayed remarkable talent. He was later called to the Senate by **Napoleon I** and made a peer by **Louis XVIII**. ▷ **Convention, National; Public Safety, Committee of**

Bokassa, Jean Bedel (1921–) Central African soldier and politician. He was educated in mission schools before joining the French army in 1929. He rose through the ranks and, after independence, was made Army Commander-in-Chief, with the rank of colonel. On 1 Jan 1966 he led the coup which overthrew President **Dacko** and steadily entrenched his own power, first making himself Life President; then in 1976, modelling himself on **Napoleon**, he crowned himself Emperor of the renamed Central African Empire. His rule was noted for its gratuitous violence and in Sep 1979 he was driven from the country and went into exile, first in the Ivory Coast and then France, being sentenced to death in absentia. However, in 1986 he was returned for trial and found guilty of murder and other crimes, being sentenced to life imprisonment.

Bokelson, Jan (Jan van Leyden) (d.1536) Leader (styled King) of the radical Ana-baptists. He seized power in Münster in 1534, but was executed in 1536 with two other Anabaptist leaders, after the city was captured by a combined Catholic-Protestant force in 1535. Jan introduced many changes into his 'New Jerusalem' (Münster) including polygamy. His views were militant and millennial.

Boleyn, Anne (c.1504–36) Queen of England. She was the second wife of **Henry VIII** and the daughter of Sir Thomas Boleyn by Elizabeth Howard. Secretly married to Henry (Jan 1533), she was soon declared his legal wife (May); but within three months his passion for her had cooled. It was not revived by the birth (Sep 1533) of a daughter (later **Elizabeth I**), still less by that of a stillborn son (Jan 1536). She was arrested and brought to the Tower, convicted of treason on fragile evidence, and beheaded (19 May). Henry married Jane **Seymour** 11 days later.

Bolgikh, Vladimir Ivanovich (1924–) Soviet politician and engineer. Born in the Krasnoyarsk region and educated in Irkutsk, he worked in engineering for 20 years before being drawn into the party machine in 1969. He climbed the political ladder quickly in **Brezhnev**'s command economy and in 1972 became a secretary in the Central Committee, and in 1982 a candidate member of the **Politburo**. He appeared to be in line for further promotion, but in 1988 Mikhail **Gorbachev** dismissed him and closed down the heavy industry section of the party secretariat as no longer relevant to a marketizing economy.

Bolingbroke, Henry St John, 1st Viscount (1678–1751) English politician. After travelling in Europe, he entered parliament (1701), becoming Secretary for War (1704), Foreign Secretary (1710), and joint leader of the Tory Party. He was made a peer in 1712. On the death of Queen **Anne** (1714), his Jacobite sympathies forced him to flee to France, where he wrote *Reflections on Exile*. He returned for a while to England (1725–35), but unable to attain political office he went back to France (1735–42). His last years were spent in London, where his works included the influential *Idea of a Patriot King* (1749). ▷ **Tories**

Bolívar, Simón ('the Liberator') (1783–1830) A founding father of Venezuela, Colombia, Ecuador, Peru, and Bolivia. Born and educated in Caracas, Venezuela, after travelling in Europe he played the most prominent part in the **Spanish–American Wars of Independence** in northern South America. In 1819, he proclaimed and became President of the vast Republic of Colombia (modern Colombia, Venezuela, and Ecuador), which was finally liberated in 1822. He then took charge of the last campaigns of independence in Peru (1824). In 1826 he returned north to face growing political dissension. He resigned office (1830), and died on his way into exile, near Santa Marta, Colombia.

Bollandists A Roman Catholic religious order of Belgian Jesuits formed to carry on the work of the hagiographer Jean Bolland (1596–1665). Since the 17c the Bollandists have worked on and published the *Acta Sanctorum*, a set of detailed and critical biographies of the saints of the Roman Church, which has now reached well over 60 volumes but is not yet finished. Until 1778 the work was carried out in Antwerp, and after an interlude caused by the suppression of the Jesuits in 1773, was resumed in Brussels in 1837.

Bolsheviks From the Russian meaning 'majority-ites', the term describes members of the hard-line faction of the Marxist Russian Social Democratic Labour Party, formed by **Lenin** when he split the party at its second congress in London in 1903 and won a spurious majority; the forerunner of the modern **Communist Party of the Soviet Union**. In Oct 1917 the Bolsheviks led the revolution in Petrograd which established the first Soviet government. ▷ **April Theses; Cheka; July Days; Mensheviks; October Revolution; Russian Revolution**

Bombay Presidency The original British **East India Company** designation for lands around Bombay under its direct administrative control. The Bombay Presidency bordered Baroda and the Rajput States to the north, the Central Provinces, the Principality of Hyderabad to the east and Mysore to the south. The term and administrative area of the Bombay Presidency remained current even after the dissolution of the Company. ▷ **British India**

Bonaparte, Jérôme (1784–1860) Youngest brother of **Napoleon I**. He served in the war against Prussia, was made King and ruled Westphalia (1807–14), and fought at the Battle of **Waterloo**. He lived for many years in exile in Florence, but in 1848 was appointed Governor of the Invalides, and in 1850 was made a French marshal by **Napoleon III**. His first marriage to an American, Elizabeth Patterson (1785–1879), resulted in a son, Jérôme (1805–70), who went to live in the USA.

Bonaparte, Joseph (1768–1844) King of Naples (1806/8) and Spain (1808/13). The eldest brother of **Napoleon I**, he carried out various diplomatic duties for his brother, and was made ruler of the Two Sicilies (1805) and King of Naples (1806). In 1808 he was summarily transferred to the throne of Spain, but after the defeat of the French at Vitoria (1813) he abdicated and returned to France. After the Battle of **Waterloo** he escaped to the USA, and lived in New Jersey as a farmer, but in 1832 returned to Europe, where he died.

Bonaparte, Napoleon ▷ **Napoleon I; Napoleon III**

Bonapartism The cult of Napoleon Bonaparte, inspired by the traditions of **Napoleon I**, the Emperor of the French (1804/14), and sustained by his heirs, notably by his nephew, Louis-Napoleon, later Emperor **Napoleon III** (1852/70).

Bongo, El Hadj Omar (Albert-Bernard) (1935–) Gabonese politician. Educated in Brazzaville, he joined the French civil service in 1957, becoming Head of the Ministry of Information and Tourism (1963), and then Minister of National Defence (1964–5). He was made Vice-President in 1967. When President **M'ba** died in 1967, he took over the interlocking posts of President, Prime Minister and Secretary-General of the *Parti Democratique Gabonais*, establishing a one-party state in 1968. Converting to Islam in 1973, he has presided over the exploitation of Gabon's rich mineral resources (it has the highest per capita income of any African country) without notably diminishing inequalities. In 1986 he was re-elected for the third time.

Boniface, St (originally, **Wynfrith**) (c.672–754) English Benedictine missionary, known as the 'Apostle of Germany'. He became a monk in Exeter, and in 718 was commissioned to preach the Gospel to all the tribes of Germany. He met with great success, and was made Bishop, Primate of Germany (732), and Archbishop of Mainz (746). His work in christianizing Bavaria paved the way for its being incorporated into the Carolingian Empire. He enjoyed the whole-hearted support of **Charles Martel, Carloman** and **Pepin III, 'the Short'**, who used the discipline of the Church as a means of subduing rebellious magnates. The opposition this aroused forced Boniface into a less prominent role after 747 and he was killed by the heathen in Frisia in 754.

Boniface VIII (Benedetto Gaetani) (c.1235–1303) Italian Pope (1294/1303). His reign was marked by the strong assertion of papal authority, claiming supreme power in temporal affairs in the Bull *Unam Sanctam* (1302). His authority was challenged, most notably by **Philip IV, 'the Fair'** of France, who had Boniface taken prisoner at Anagni in 1303. He died soon after and the papacy took up residence at Avignon.

Boniface IX (Pietro Tomacelli) (d.1404) Italian Pope (1389/1404). He was chosen Pope in 1389 to succeed Urban VI in opposition to **Clement VII**, who was pope in Avignon. Boniface was notoriously inexperienced in papal administration but he acquired despotic power in Rome.

Bonifacio, Andres (1863–97) Filipino revolutionary leader. Born in Manila in humble circumstances, he received little formal education. Bonifacio was strongly influenced by the writings of José **Rizal** and, when the latter was sent in to exile in 1892, he founded the *Katipunan*, a secret revolutionary organization. In Aug 1896 the organization was betrayed, forcing it prematurely into open rebellion. Even so, the uprising, and particularly those revolutionary forces under Emilio **Aguinaldo**, achieved considerable success against the Spanish colonial regime. In 1897, however, serious divisions appeared between Bonifacio and Aguinaldo. The former's limited educational background was held against him as the revolutionary leaders set to the task of forming an administration. These divisions threatened the revolution and in May 1897, following a farcical trial, Bonifacio was executed, with the assent of Aguinaldo.

Bonn Former capital city of West **Germany** (1949–90) and current seat of the administration and government of Germany, in North Rhine-Westphalia. The site of an early Roman fort on the Rhine, Bonn was the seat of the Electors of Cologne from the 13c to the 16c. In 1815, it became part of **Prussia**. The city was badly bombed in **World War II**.

Bonner, Yelena (1923–) Soviet civil rights campaigner. After the arrest of her parents in

Stalin's 'great purge' of 1937, and the subsequent execution of her father and imprisonment of her mother, Bonner was brought up in Leningrad by her grandmother. In **World War II** she served in the army, becoming a lieutenant, but suffered serious eye injuries. After the war she married and worked as a doctor. On separating from her husband (1965), she joined the CPSU, but became disillusioned after the Soviet invasion of Czechoslovakia (1968) and drifted into 'dissident' activities. She married Andrei **Sakharov** in 1971 and resigned from the CPSU a year later. During the next 14 years she and her husband led the Soviet dissident movement. Following a **KGB** crackdown, Sakharov was banished to internal exile in Gorky in 1980 and Bonner suffered a similar fate in 1984. After hunger strikes, she was given permission to travel to Italy for specialist eye treatment in 1981 and 1984. The couple were finally released from Gorky in 1986, as part of a new 'liberalization' policy under Mikhail **Gorbachev**'s administration, and remained prominent campaigners for greater democratization.

Bonney, William H ('Billy the Kid') (1859–81) US outlaw. He achieved legendary notoriety for his robberies and murders in the south-west, supposedly from the age of 12. He was captured by Sheriff Patrick F Garrett in 1880, and sentenced to hang. He escaped, but was finally tracked down by Garrett and shot.

Bonomi, Ivanoe (1873–1952) Italian politician. A graduate in natural sciences and law, Bonomi took up journalism in 1898, writing for *Avanti!* and *Critica socialista*. In 1909 he was elected to parliament. Expelled from the Italian Socialist Party in 1912, he founded a reformist socialist movement. In 1916–21 he was a minister on a number of occasions, serving under **Orlando, Nitti** and **Giolitti**, and was briefly Premier himself (1921–2). He opposed **Mussolini**'s seizure of power but left politics in 1924. From 1942, he was a leading figure in the anti-fascist struggle, replacing **Badoglio** as Prime Minister (June 1944) and establishing a broad, anti-fascist coalition government. In 1945 he was forced to resign in favour of the more radical **Parri**; he became President of the Senate in 1948.

Bonus Army (June 1932) A US protest march of some 20000 unemployed ex-servicemen on Washington DC, demanding Congressional passage of a bill authorizing the immediate payment of a bonus due to

World War I veterans. When the bill was defeated in the Senate, some veterans refused to return home. At the end of July, on the orders of President Herbert **Hoover**, General **MacArthur** evicted the marchers but incurred great odium by doing so with violence and cruelty.

Boone, Daniel (1735–1820) US frontiersman. He made a trail, the 'wilderness road', through the Cumberland Gap (1767) and became one of the first to explore Kentucky (1769–73). Twice captured by Native Americans, he repeatedly repelled (1775–8) native attacks on his stockade fort, now Boonesboro. Boone was a successful surveyor, trapper, and landowner, ushering new settlers into Kentucky. After losing his large landholdings to debt and legal mismanagement, he moved further west into Missouri, where he died.

Booth, John Wilkes (1839–65) US assassin. An actor, he was the brother of Edwin Booth. In 1865 he entered into a conspiracy to avenge the defeat of the Confederates and shot President Abraham **Lincoln** at Ford's Theatre, Washington (14 Apr). He broke his leg while escaping, but managed to flee to Virginia. He was tracked down and was either shot by his pursuers or shot himself.

Borah, William Edgar (1865–1940) US politician. He was elected as a Republican senator for Idaho in 1907. An advocate of disarmament and a leading isolationist, Borah was instrumental in blocking the USA's entry into the **League of Nations** in 1919.

Borden, Sir Robert Laird (1854–1937) Canadian politician. He practised as a barrister, and became leader of the Conservative Party in 1901. As Conservative Prime Minister (1911–20), he led Canada through **World War I**, the Conscription crisis, and the introduction of income tax. At the Imperial War Conference of 1917, he called for greater recognition of the dominions' autonomy, a step towards the building of a Commonwealth. ▷ **Compulsory Service Act; Lapointe, Ernest; War Measures Act**

Borgå, Diet of (1809) ▷ **Porvoo, Diet of** (1809)

Borghese A great 13c family of ambassadors and jurists of Siena, afterwards (16c) at Rome. Their members include Camillo Borghese, who ascended the papal throne in 1605

as **Paul V**, and Prince Camillo Filippo Ludovico Borghese (1775–1832), who joined the French Army, married **Napoleon I**'s sister Marie Pauline (1803), and was Governor-General of Piedmont. The Borghese Palace still contains one of the finest collections of paintings in Rome.

Borgia (Borja) An ancient family from Valencia in Spain. Alfonso (1378–1458) accompanied Alfonso of Aragon to Rome, and became Pope Calixtus III (1455/8). His nephew, Rodrigo, became pope as **Alexander VI** (1492/1503) and sought to further the interests of his notorious children Cesare and Lucrezia Borgia. By contrast, a descendant of another of Alexander's sons, Francisco (1510–72), was to become General of the Jesuits. ▷ **Borgia, Cesare; Borgia, Lucrezia**

Borgia, Cesare (1476–1507) Italian soldier. He was the illegitimate son of Pope **Alexander VI** and brother of Lucrezia **Borgia**. A brilliant soldier and administrator, he succeeded his elder brother (whom he is rumoured to have murdered) as Captain-General of the armies of the Church. In two campaigns he became the master of the Romagna, Perugia, Siena, Piombino and Urbino, and planned a kingdom of Central Italy. After the death of his father (1503), his enemies rallied. He surrendered at Naples, was imprisoned and escaped (1506) only to die fighting in the service of the King of Navarre soon afterwards. His campaigns greatly impressed Machiavelli, who discussed Cesare's career at length in the notorious seventh chapter of *The Prince*. ▷ **Borgia**

Borgia, Lucrezia (1480–1519) Illegitimate daughter of Pope **Alexander VI**. She was three times married to further her father's political interests: first, in 1493, at the age of 12 to Giovanni Sforza, Lord of Pesaro, but this marriage was annulled by her father in 1497; second, in 1498, to Alfonso of Aragon, nephew of the King of Naples, but this marriage was ended in 1500 when Alfonso was murdered by her brother, Cesare **Borgia**; and third, in 1501, to Alfonso d'Este (1486–1534), son of the Duke of Este. Alfonso d'Este inherited the duchy of Ferrara, where Lucrezia established a brilliant court of artists and men of letters. ▷ **Borgia**

Boris I (d.907) Emperor of Bulgaria (852/89). He adopted Christianity in 865 and at the Fourth Council of Constantinople (869–70), he gained the sanction for the establishment of an independent Bulgarian archbishopric. He abdicated and became a monk in 889, and was canonized by the Orthodox Church.

Boris III (1894–1943) King of Bulgaria (1918/43). He was the son of **Ferdinand I** and Maria Luisa Bourbon-Parma. After his father's abdication, he became king, the numeral III implying his succession to the great medieval Bulgarian emperors. After a series of military coups, in 1935 he established an authoritarian regime, securing the removal of Colonel Kimon Georgiev, abolishing the **Zveno**-backed Military League and returning the country to civilian control. Married to the daughter of the King of Italy and an admirer of German culture, he maintained good terms with Benito **Mussolini** and **Hitler**. Although formally neutral at the outbreak of **World War II**, Bulgaria through Boris's diplomacy was firmly in the Axis camp. He died suddenly, shortly after a stormy visit to Hitler, and recent research has lent credence to the rumour that he was poisoned. He was succeeded by his son, **Simeon II**.

Boris Godunov (c.1552–1605) Tsar of Russia (1598/1605). Of Tatar stock, he became an intimate friend of **Ivan IV, 'the Terrible'**, who entrusted to Boris the care of his feeble son, Fyodor. During the reign of Tsar Fyodor (1584/98), Boris Godunov was virtual ruler of the country with the title of 'the Great Sovereign's brother-in-law', becoming Tsar himself on Fyodor's death (1598). He continued Ivan's expansionist policies, going to war against both Poland and Sweden. At home, he disposed finally of the Tatar threat but was embroiled in the last years of his reign in a civil war against a pretender, claiming to be Dmitri, younger son of Ivan IV. The pretender was murdered the year after Boris's death. Boris's reign is regarded as the beginning of the **Time of Troubles**.

Borja ▷ **Borgia**

Bormann, Martin (1900–45) German Nazi politician. One of **Hitler**'s closest advisers, he became *Reichs-minister* (1941) after **Hess**'s flight to Scotland, and was with Hitler to the last. His own fate was uncertain, but he is now known to have committed suicide by a poison capsule during the breakout by Hitler's staff from the Chancellory (1 May 1945). He was sentenced to death in his absence by the Nuremberg Court (1946). ▷ **Nuremberg Trials; World War II**

Bornu A state in northern Nigeria and southern Niger lying to the west of Lake Chad. In the 15c Bornu replaced **Kanem** as a great trading empire linking the forest and the desert, and reached its apogee in the 16c. Its people, the Kanuri, had been Muslim since the 11c and developed a highly stratified social organization.

Borodin, Mikhail (1884–1951) Russian adviser in China from 1923 to 1927. Born Mikhail Markovich Grusenberg, Borodin participated in the Jewish worker movement in his native Russia and met **Lenin** in 1904. After 1905 he lived in exile in Britain and the USA. When the United Front was formed between the **Guomindang** and the Chinese Communist Party in 1923 Borodin, as the representative of both the **Comintern** and the Soviet Communist Party, became a personal adviser to **Sun Yat-sen**. He helped transform the Guomindang into a disciplined and centrally-controlled revolutionary party, as well as convincing Sun of the necessity of creating mass-based organizations. When the United Front broke down in 1927 Borodin was compelled to leave China. Made the scapegoat for the failure of **Stalin**'s policy in China, Borodin was henceforth given only minor posts. He died in a Siberian prison camp.

Borodino, Battle of (7 Sep 1812) A costly victory for **Napoleon I**'s army. He inflicted 40 000 casualties on **Alexander I**'s forces, but lost 30 000 dead and wounded, a quarter of his own men. One of the Russian commanders, General Bagration, subsequently died of his wounds. A second, General Barclay, showed immense courage and greatly raised his men's morale. Napoleon, although tempted to advance on Moscow, which was abandoned to him, was left with no alternative but to retreat through the snow, harried all the way by more numerous and better-spirited Russian forces.

Bosch, Johannes van den (1780–1844) Dutch reformer and politician. Van den Bosch took a career in the Dutch East Indian Army, rapidly reaching the rank of Colonel. Returning to the Netherlands in 1815 he was put in charge of East Indies military affairs. He produced two important political essays which shaped his further career and to some extent the Dutch state as well. One was on poor-relief, resulting in 1818 in the foundation of the Society for Charity, which tried to take urban paupers and compel them to be agricultural labourers in a number of 'colonies' in the east of the country. The other was his plan to make the Dutch colonies earn money for the mother country: known as the '**Culture System**', it was launched in 1834, and was in time highly successful in financial terms, if not in human ones. Van den Bosch had the ear of King **William I**; he served as Governor-General of the Dutch East Indies (1828–33), and as Minister of Colonies (1834–9).

Bosch, Juan (1909–   ) Dominican Republic politician and writer. The founder of the Dominican Revolutionary Party, Bosch lived in exile in Cuba and Costa Rica during the **Trujillo** dictatorship. He became President in 1963 but his reformist government lasted only six months before it was overthrown by the army (Sep 1963) and he was again exiled. He has been the losing candidate in every presidential election since 1966 and, although by 1990 he had moderated his **Marxism**, his Dominican Liberation Party again lost the election of that year, despite having appeared to be the front runner.

Bose, Subhas Chandra (1897–1945) Indian nationalist leader. A successful candidate for the **Indian Civil Service** in 1920, he did not take up his appointment, returning instead to Calcutta to work in the **Non-Cooperation Movement** and the **Swaraj** Party. He also managed the Calcutta newspaper, *Forward*, and became Chief Executive Officer of the Calcutta Corporation when Congress won its control in 1924. He spent the years 1925–7 under detention in Mandalay. In 1928 Bose formed an Independence League with Jawaharlal **Nehru** in opposition to Congress's objective of dominion status. Throughout the 1930s Bose took part in the **civil disobedience** movement, but became increasingly dissatisfied with the non-violent methods of M K **Gandhi** and increasingly radical in his beliefs. Bose felt that a disciplined mass revolutionary movement, espousing a combination of Fascism and communism was the fastest and best path toward Indian statehood. He was twice in succession President of the **Indian National Congress** (1938). Having resigned from the organization (1939), he formed Forward Bloc, a militant nationalist party. With the outbreak of **World War II**, he supported the Axis Powers. Escaping from detention, he fled to Nazi Germany, then (1943) sailed to Singapore to take command of the Indian National Army (INA), a force formed of prisoners of war of the Japanese army. This force fought against the British in Burma and participated in the disastrous Japanese attempt to invade India from Burma. In Oct 1943 he announced the formation of the Provisional Government of Free India. He was reported killed in an aircrash in Taiwan. For many years, however, his most devoted followers still refused to believe that he was dead, and many still cherish his ideas, attitudes and beliefs.

Bosnia and Herzegovina, Province of
After a series of peasant revolts culminating between 1875 and 1878 in mass uprisings against the Ottomans (the medieval state of Bosnia had fallen to the Turks in 1463, the Duchy of Herzegovina in 1482), Bosnia and Herzegovina became an Austrian protectorate (1879) and were then annexed by Austria in 1908; in 1914 it was at Sarajevo, the capital of Bosnia, that a Bosnian Serb nationalist assassinated the Austrian Archduke Francis Ferdinand, prompting Austria to declare war on Serbia and thus precipitating **World War I**. In 1918 Bosnia and Herzegovina became part of the Kingdom of Serbs, Croats and Slovenes (later Yugoslavia). In **World War II** it was the scene of some of the heaviest fighting between the occupying forces and **Tito**'s partisans who held the first and second meetings of **AVNOJ** at Bihać and Jajce. In 1945 Bosnia-Herzegovina was established as one of the six republics within the Socialist Federal People's Republic of Yugoslavia. ▷ **Mlada Bosna**

Bosnia and Herzegovina, Republic of
Formerly one of the six republics established in 1945 within the Socialist Federal People's Republic of Yugoslavia, in Mar 1992 under its elected president, Alia Izetbegović, it followed the Republics of Slovenia and Croatia in declaring its independence from Yugoslavia. Civil war broke out among die-hard communist and nationalist elements from the Yugoslav National Army and extreme nationalist paramilitary groups and has gradually and brutally engulfed the civilian population until all civil order has dissolved.

Boston Massacre (5 Mar 1770) The first bloodshed of the **American Revolution**. In an atmosphere of intense resentment against British troops and regulations, on 5 Mar 1770 British guards opened fire on an unruly crowd, killing five. Of the nine British soldiers tried for murder, seven, including the commander, were acquitted and two were found guilty of manslaughter.

Boston Tea Party (1773) During the **American Revolution**, the climactic event of resistance to British attempts at direct taxation, resulting in the destruction of 342 chests of dutied tea by working men disguised as Native Americans. Other ports had refused to let the tea ships enter. ▷ **Intolerable Acts**

Boström, Erik Gustaf (1842–1907) Swedish politician. Elected to the Second Chamber of Parliament in 1876, he became leader of the protectionist wing of the Ruralist (Conservative) Party in 1888 and Prime Minister in 1891. He admired **Bismarck** and proposed similar welfare legislation as had been introduced in Germany. He resigned in 1900, but returned to office in 1902 for three years.

Bosworth Field, Battle of (22 Aug 1485) The battle which put **Henry VII** on the English throne after victory over **Richard III**, who died in the conflict. Henry Tudor's forces were possibly inferior in number, but proved more loyal; they received crucial support from the Stanley family, who had feet in both camps. ▷ **Tudor, House of**

Botany Bay The shallow inlet five miles south of Sydney, New South Wales, Australia (now a residential part of Sydney) where Captain James **Cook** made his first landing in 1770, naming the bay after the number of new plants discovered there. It was chosen as a penal settlement in 1787 but, on his arrival, Arthur Phillip (1738–1814), the commander of the **First Fleet**, found it to be unsuitable, and chose Sydney Cove instead; the name Botany Bay, however, was for many years synonymous with Australian convict settlements. ▷ **transportation**

Botev, Khristo (1848–76) Bulgarian journalist, poet and revolutionary leader. A schoolteacher's son, in 1863 he went to study in Odessa, where he met members of the Russian revolutionary circle. Having returned to Bulgaria to teach, he was one of the leaders of the ill-fated Bulgarian uprising of Apr 1876 and was killed after leading a band of rebels across the Danube.

Botha, Louis (1862–1919) South African politician and soldier. Born in Greytown, Natal, he was a member of the Transvaal Volksraad, and commanded the Boer forces during the war. In 1907 he became Prime Minister of the Transvaal colony, and subsequently became the first Prime Minister of the new Union of South Africa (1910–19). He

suppressed De Wet's rebellion (1914), and then conquered German south-west Africa (1914–15). He died at Pretoria. ▷ **Boer Wars**

Botha, P(ieter) W(illem) (1916–) South African politician. The son of an internee in the Anglo-Boer War, he was steeped in politics. His early life lacked success (he dropped out of university), but he found his metier as a party organizer. With his confidence and courage, he was a formidable operator. An advocate of **apartheid** before the **National Party** gained power, he entered Parliament in 1948 and became Deputy Minister of the Interior (1958–61), Minister of Community Development, Public Works and Coloured Affairs (1961–6), Minister of Defence (1966–78) and Prime Minister (1978–89). Leader of the Cape section of the National Party, in 1966 he was chosen as leader of the Party on **Vorster**'s resignation on the second ballot only because the Transvaal Nationalists were divided. He thus became Prime Minister. Having built up the defence forces and supported the invasion of Angola in 1975, he now sought constitutional changes, but his ideas, although too progressive for some of his Party (some members defected in 1982 to form the **Conservative Party**), were too cautious to appeal to the Black opposition. He suffered a stroke in 1989 and resigned later that year.

Bothwell, James Hepburn, 4th Earl of (c.1535–78) Scottish nobleman and third husband of **Mary, Queen of Scots**. One of the greatest nobles in Scotland, he was held responsible for the abduction and murder of Mary's second husband, Lord **Darnley** (1567). He was made Duke of Orkney, then married Mary, but faced opposition from the nobles. He fled to Denmark after Mary's surrender to rebel forces at Carberry Hill, and was imprisoned in Dragsholm, where he died insane.

Bottai, Giuseppe (1895–1959) Italian politician. One of the founders of the **Fascist Party**, Bottai took an active part in the **March on Rome**. He was one of the **Fascist Grand Council** members who demanded **Mussolini**'s resignation in July 1943. Sentenced to death by the Republic of **Salò** and to life imprisonment by the Italian authorities after **World War II**, he escaped and joined the French Foreign Legion. He returned to Italy on being amnestied.

Botzaris, Marcos (1788–1823) Greek patriot. In 1803 he was forced to retreat to the

Ionian Islands by **Ali Pasha**. In 1820, at the head of 800 expatriated Suliotes, he gained several victories for Ali against the Sultan; in 1822 he skilfully defended Missolonghi, but was killed in an attack on the Turkish-Albanian Army at Karpenisi.

Boudicca (1c AD) British warrior-queen. She was the wife of Prasutagus, King of the **Iceni**, a tribe inhabiting what is now Norfolk and Suffolk. On her husband's death (AD60), the Romans seized her territory, and treated the inhabitants brutally. She gathered a large army, destroyed the Roman colony of Camulodunum, took Londinium and Verulamium, and put to death as many as 70000 Romans. Defeated in battle by Suetonius Paulinus, she took poison.

Boulanger, Georges Ernest Jean Marie (1837–91) French soldier and politician. Educated at Saint-Cyr, he served in Italy, China, the Franco-German War (1870–1), and helped suppress the **Paris Commune** (1871). In 1886, as the protégé of **Clemenceau**, he was appointed Minister of War. He introduced many reforms in soldiers' pay and living conditions and became a popular national figure amongst the Parisians, often appearing amongst them on horseback. When he lost office in 1887, 'Boulanger fever' only increased. He was 'exiled' by the army to a command at Clermont-Ferrand, and although deprived of his command in 1888, was immediately elected Deputy for Dordogne and Nord, and demanded a revision of the constitution. He was wounded in a duel with **Floquet**, the Minister-President, in the same year. 'Boulangism' became really formidable in 1889, and was supported with large sums of money by leading royalists for their own ends. Fearing a coup d'état, the government prosecuted Boulanger, who lost courage and fled the country in 1889. He was condemned in absentia; his schemes wholly collapsed, and he eventually shot himself on his mistress's grave in Brussels.

Boumédienne, Houari (Mohammed Bou Kharrouba) (1925–78) Algerian soldier and statesman. Educated at Constantine and El Azhar University in Cairo, he became a teacher. In 1954 he joined the **FLN** for whom for eight years he conducted guerrilla operations against the French, serving as chief of staff (1960–62) with the rank of colonel. When Algeria gained independence in 1962, he became minister of national defence. In 1965 he led a military coup against President **Ben Bella** and established an Islamic socialist government, presiding over the Council of Revolution as effective head of state until he formally accepted election as president in 1976. In home affairs, he directed a four-year plan which increased industrial output and revolutionized agricultural production. Not long before his death, he was seeking to establish a North African socialist federation.

Bourassa, Henri (Joseph-Napoléon-Henri) (1868–1952) Canadian politician and journalist (as a founder and editor of *Le Devoir*). A grandson of Louis Joseph **Papineau**, he was a French-Canadian nationalist who consistently opposed French Canada's forced participation in British wars. He resigned his independent Liberal seat in the federal House of Commons when **Laurier** sent Canadian troops to the Boer War, but, since most French-Canadians felt the same way, he was returned by acclamation. Bourassa was also the focal point for French-Canadian outrage at the Naval Act of 1910, using *Le Devoir* to advocate his views and making an important contribution to the **Liberal Party** defeat in the election of 1911. He was also a vigorous opponent of Canadian involvement in **World War I**. An advocate of European liberal Catholic thinking, he was opposed to industrial capitalism and emerged as a social reformer in the 1920s and 1930s. ▷ **Boer Wars**

Bourassa, Robert (1933–) Canadian politician. Leader of the Quebec Liberal Party when it won an emphatic election victory in 1970, despite the nationalist unrest of the period. By refusing to give prominence to the constitutional and language controversies and promising to help the unemployment crisis by generating 100000 jobs, his party won 41.8 per cent of the vote and 72 seats. During the **October Crisis** Bourassa was accused of being too ready to hand over power to Ottawa by those who suspected that he hoped to undermine his nationaliste and left-wing opponents. Bourassa responded by reinforcing his demands for a special status for Quebec within the Confederation. He resigned as party leader when the Liberals lost the 1976 provincial elections to the **Péquistes**, but he was re-elected in 1983 and led the party to victory in 1986, this time with a huge hydro-electric project as the electoral promise.

Bourbon, Charles (1490–1527) French soldier. Known as 'Constable de Bourbon', he was the son of Gilbert de Bourbon, Count of Montpensier, and the only daughter of the

Duke of Bourbon. For his bravery at the Battle of Marignano (1515) he was made Constable of France; but losing the favour of **Francis I** of France he concluded a private alliance with Emperor **Charles V** and **Henry VIII** of England. He invaded France in 1524, and was chief imperial commander at Pavia, in which Francis I was taken prisoner. He was made Duke of Milan, and commanded in northern Italy, but was killed while attacking Rome in 1527. ▷ **Bourbon, House of**

Bourbon, House of The French royal house descended from the Capetian St **Louis IX**, associated with absolutist traditions at home and the extension of French influence abroad. Succeeding the last member of the **Valois Dynasty**, **Henry III** (1589) and Henry of Navarre (**Henry IV**) firmly established the dynasty. Under the latter's son (**Louis XIII**) and grandson (**Louis XIV**), the long-standing rivalry between France and the Spanish Habsburgs came to a climax; it was concluded when a descendant, Philip of Anjou, ascended to the Spanish throne (**Philip V**), thereby founding the Spanish House of Bourbon. Under **Louis XV** and **Louis XVI**, the prestige of the French Bourbons gradually declined; with the latter's execution (1793) the line was interrupted, to be briefly restored (1814–30). ▷ **Capetian Dynasty; Charles X** of France; **Condé, House of; Habsburg Dynasty; Orléans, House of**

Bourgeois, Léon (Victor Auguste) (1851–1925) French politician. A socialist, he studied law and later served as Minister of Public Instruction (1890–2 and 1898), Prime

HOUSE OF BOURBON

Regnal Dates	Name
FRANCE	
1589/1610	Henry IV
1610/43	Louis XIII
1643/1715	Louis XIV
1715/74	Louis XV
1774/93	Louis XVI
1793/1814	Interregnum
1814/24	Louis XVIII
1824/30	Charles X
SPAIN	
1700/24	Philip V
1724/5	Louis I
1725/46	Philip V
1746/59	Ferdinand VI
1759/88	Charles III
1788/1808	Charles IV
1814/33	Ferdinand VII

Minister (1895–6) and Minister of Labour (1912–13 and 1917). A delegate to the Hague Conference (1907), he was one of the founders of the **League of Nations**, and in 1920 was awarded the Nobel Peace Prize. He advocated a form of socialism called *solidarisme*, which stressed the obligations of individuals as members of society.

Bourguiba, Habib ibn Ali (1903–) Tunisian politician. He studied law in Paris and became a radical Tunisian nationalist in 1934. Over the next 20 years he served three prison sentences imposed by the French authorities. In 1956, however, the French government of **Mendès-France** in Paris recognized that, in contrast to other Arab leaders, Bourguiba was moderate in his demands and he was accepted as Tunisia's first prime minister, becoming president in 1957. By 1962 he had secured the withdrawal of the French from their Tunisian military bases; thereafter he was able to improve trading contacts with the former imperial power. In 1975 he was declared president for life. His authority, however, was threatened by riots instigated by Islamic fundamentalists in 1983 and 1984, and subsequently he exercised little influence on policy. In 1987 he was deposed by his prime minister, General **Ben Ali**, on the grounds of senility.

Bourj al-Barajneh Palestinian refugee camp on the outskirts of Beirut, Lebanon. It was created following the evacuation of Palestinians from the city after Israeli attacks on Palestinians and Syrians (June 1982). The camp was the scene of a prolonged siege in 1987.

Bouvines, Battle of (27 July 1214) The battle near Valenciennes in northern France, at which King Philip Augustus of France defeated the armies of the Holy Roman Emperor **Otto IV**, the Count of Flanders, and King **John** (Lackland) of England. This victory consolidated the power of the French monarchy over its vassals, led to Otto's deposition as Emperor, to the loss of **Normandy** by King John, and probably contributed to his acceptance of **Magna Carta** (1215).

Bowell, Sir Mackenzie (1823–1917) Canadian politician. In 1878, as Grand Master of the **Orange Order** (a position he filled with a certain tact towards the sensibilities of Catholics), he was included in the cabinet of Sir John **Macdonald** in order to balance the leadership of the **Bleus**. In 1895 Bowell became Prime Minister, faced not only with the Depression but also with the crisis caused by the **Manitoba Schools Act**. When the province refused to restore the rights of the Catholic minority, he introduced a Remedial Bill and seven ministers resigned. They were concerned not so much with the actual issue but to remove Bowell, whose stand had alienated the Orange Order from the party, and they returned to office when he had yielded to Sir Charles **Tupper**. Nevertheless, the Conservatives were defeated in the election of 1896, after which Bowell led their opposition in the Senate.

Bowie, Colonel James ('Jim') (1790–1836) US adventurer. He is mainly remembered for his role in defending the **Alamo** (1836) during the Texas revolution. He was the inventor of the curved sheath knife named after him.

Boxer Rising (1898–1900) An anti-foreign uprising in China (in Chinese, *Ye He Tuan*). Its popular name derives from the secret society to which the rebels belonged, the 'Righteous Harmonious Fists', whose members adopted boxing and ritual forms of combat, in the belief that foreign weapons would thus not harm them. The movement originated in Shandong, where it destroyed churches and expelled missionaries. It also defeated the Qing forces dispatched to suppress it. It spread across north China, invading Beijing and Tianjin. The foreign powers sent a combined force to rescue their envoys in Beijing, occupying the capital, and the rising was suppressed. By the International Protocol of 1901, the Qing court agreed to pay a massive indemnity, and a foreign garrison was established in the Legation Quarter of Beijing. ▷ **Qing Dynasty**

Boyacá, Battle of (7 Aug 1819) A decisive victory for the patriot forces under Simón **Bolívar** in the **Spanish–American Wars of Independence**. It resulted in the liberation of New Granada (now Colombia) from Spanish rule and marked the beginning of the last great military campaign to destroy Spanish rule. The victory enabled Bolívar to announce the creation of Gran Colombia (Venezuela, New Granada and Ecuador), establish the rule of **Santander**, and led to the expulsion of General Morillo's forces from the Venezuelan coastal region by 1823.

boyars Members of the highest stratum of the Russian feudal aristocracy from the 10c to the early 18c. The *Boyarskaya Duma* ('Boyars' Council') was a major legislative and deliberative assembly under the early tsars. During the reign of **Ivan IV, 'the Terrible'**, the boyars' authority was drastically curtailed, and the *Boyarskaya Duma* was finally abolished by **Peter I, 'the Great'** in 1711. ▷ **Duma; feudalism**

boycott A general refusal to have dealings — usually in relation to trade — with a person, company, or country. A trade union may boycott talks with a company as a negotiating ploy. Individuals may refuse to buy a country's goods as a gesture of political protest — for example, goods from South Africa, in protest against **apartheid**. Boycotts have also been used in international sporting events, such as by the USA and UK at the 1980 Moscow Olympic Games. They are often only effective if legally enforced; for example, the ban on the import of Cuban cigars into the USA.

Boycott, Charles Cunningham (1832–97) British soldier. As land agent for Lord Erne in County Mayo, he was one of the first victims in 1880 of **Parnell**'s system of social excommunication. His name is the source of the word 'boycott' in English.

Boyer, Jean Pierre (1776–1850) Haitian mulatto politician. Sent to France at an early age, in 1792 he entered the army. He distinguished himself against the British on their invasion of Haiti, and established an independent republic in the western part of the island. President Pétion, on his deathbed, recommended him as his successor (1818). After the death of Henri **Christophe**, he united the Negro district with the mulatto in 1820. The following year he also added the eastern district, hitherto Spanish, and in 1825, for 150 million francs, obtained recognition of independence from France. He governed Haiti well for 15 years, but his partiality to the mulattos made the pure Negroes rise in 1843. Boyer fled, and died in Paris.

Boyne, Battle of the (12 July 1690) A battle fought near Drogheda, County Louth, Ireland, between Protestant forces under **William III** of Great Britain and smaller Catholic forces led by **James VII and II**. William's decisive victory enabled him to capture Dublin, and marked a critical stage in the English reconquest of Ireland. It ended James's campaign to regain the English throne. The anniversary is celebrated annually by Protestant marches in Northern Ireland.

Brabant, Duchy of Brabant is now the name of a province in the northern part of Belgium, and also of a province in the Netherlands (Noord-Brabant), but in the Middle Ages it was a powerful duchy covering both those areas and also the present Belgian province of Antwerp. Its nucleus was originally the County of Leuven (Louvain), whose Count Gottfried was made the first Duke in 1106. The early dukes set about increasing their power at the expense of other local magnates, and then of the towns, which were rising commercial and industrial centres. The expansion of the Duchy continued throughout the 12–13c, and in 1406 the Burgundian Anton (son of **Philip the Bold**) succeeded to Brabant. The Burgundian connection was confirmed in 1430 when **Philip the Good** inherited the Brabant Duchy; as an integral part of the Burgundian state in the Low Countries it eventually passed into Habsburg control, and at the Peace of Utrecht in 1648 the northern half was split off and went to the newly recognized Dutch Republic. The southern Duchy was dismantled under the rule of the French (1795–1813) and now the title of Duke of Brabant is given to the eldest son of the Belgian monarch. ▷ **Habsburg Dynasty**

Brabant Revolution (1789) The name given to the revolt in the Austrian southern Netherlands (now Belgium) against the rule of the enlightened despot Emperor **Joseph II** of Austria, who planned a major modernization and rationalization of church, state and legal system. The revolutionaries fell into two groups: one inspired by the ideals of the **French Revolution** and led by J F Vonck (**Vonckists**), and the other more conservative and looking to restore the pre-Josephan *status quo*, led by H van der Noot (**Statists**). They had early successes, and proclaimed the independence of the 'United States of Belgium', but the Austrians regained control within a year.

Braccio da Montone, otherwise **Brancaccio,** or **Fortebraccio** (1368–1424) Italian mercenary captain or **condottiere**. He commanded the troops of Queen Giovanna of Naples, and coveted the throne of Naples, but he died of his wounds in a battle before Aquila.

bracero The term used to describe seasonal labour from Central and Southern Mexico, working on large-scale agroindustrial enterprises in California and Texas. Often 'wetbacks', who had illegally entered the USA by crossing the Rio Grande, they did not benefit from minimum wage and employee-protection legislation in either California, Texas or New Mexico. They had often been used as 'scab' or strike-breaking labour in both states, so were not easily accepted into US trade unions. Drives to unionize them began in the mid-1960s, thanks to the activities of leaders such as Cesar Chavez; against heavy opposition from both the **AFL–CIO** and local employers, they were supported by the Republican Governor, Ronald **Reagan**. The influx of *braceros* increased during the 1980s, in the wake of the Mexican debt crisis and the endemic civil wars of Central America.

Bradford, William (1590–1656) American colonist and religious leader. One of the Pilgrim Fathers, he was born near Doncaster, England. A nonconformist from boyhood, he joined a separatist group in 1606 and went with them to Holland in 1609, seeking freedom of worship. In Leiden he became a tradesman and read widely. One of the moving spirits in the Pilgrim Fathers' expedition to the New World in 1620, he sailed on the *Mayflower* and signed the Mayflower Compact. In 1621 he was elected as the second governor of Plymouth colony, taking over from John Carver. Re-elected governor 30 times between 1622 and 1656 (elections were held yearly), he guided the fledgling colony with exemplary fairness and firmness.

Bradlaugh, Charles (1833–91) British freethinking social reformer. He became a busy secularist lecturer, and a pamphleteer under the name of 'Iconoclast'. In 1880 he became an MP, and claimed the right as an unbeliever to make affirmation of allegiance instead of taking the parliamentary oath; but the House refused to allow him to do either. He was re-elected on three occasions, and finally was admitted (1886). ▷ **Besant, Annie**

Bradshaw, Robert (1916–78) St Kitts-Nevis politician. Bradshaw took St Kitts-Nevis to associated statehood in 1967. The founder and leader of the St Kitts-Nevis Labour Party (1940) and Federal Minister of Finance (1958–62), he briefly made the world press in 1969, when his dispute with Anguilla forced that island to declare its independence of St Kitts; this action resulted in a farcical British military intervention.

Braganza, House of The Portuguese royal house which originated in 1442 but succeeded to the throne only in 1640, when the rebellion

HOUSE OF BRAGANZA

Regnal Dates	Name
1640/56	John (João) IV
1656/67	Alfonso VI
1667/1706	Pedro II
1706/50	John (João) V
1750/77	José
1777/1816	Maria I and (until 1786) Pedro III
1816/26	John (João) VI
1826	Pedro IV (Emperor of Brazil, as Pedro I, 1822/31)
1826/8	Maria II da Gloria
1828/34	Miguel
1834/53	Maria II da Gloria
1853/61	Pedro V (Emperor of Brazil, as Pedro II, 1831/89)
1861/89	Luis I
1889/1908	Carlos I
1908/10	Manuel II

against Spain put the 8th Duke, John (João), on the throne as John (João) IV. The family ruled continuously until 1910.

Brahmins The highest of the four Hindu social classes. A priestly class, the Brahmins dominated Indian society for many centuries. Owing to modern economic and social changes, many of their descendants took up secular occupations. Chitpavan Brahmins figured largely amongst nationalist politicians in Western India in the late colonial period. Recently they have come under critical attack by some lower-caste movements. ▷ **caste**

Brahmo Samaj Literally 'Divine Society', the theistic movement founded by Ram Mohan Roy in 1828 which argued that reason should form the true basis of Hinduism. Influenced by Islam, Christianity, and modern science, it sought a return to the purity of Hindu worship through an emphasis on monotheism, the rejection of idol-worship and the reform of Hindu social practices. This, and other movements of social and religious reform, has had a profound influence on many social and political thinkers in modern India.

Brand, Sir Jan Hendrik (1823–88) South African politician. President of the Orange Free State from 1864 till his death, he defeated the Basutos (1865–9), and favoured friendship with Britain.

Brandeis, Louis Dembitz (1856–1941) US judge. He was educated in the USA and in Europe and, after graduating from Harvard Law School, he practised law in Boston. He conducted many labour arbitrations, and was frequently involved in cases challenging the power of monopolies and cartels, as well as others that dealt with the constitutionality of maximum hours and minimum wages legislation. He formulated the economic doctrine of the New Freedom adopted by Woodrow **Wilson** for his 1912 presidential campaign. Appointed to the US Supreme Court in 1916, he favoured governmental intervention to control the economy where public interest required it, but was also a strong defender of the principle of private property. Brandeis, who supported most of **Roosevelt**'s New Deal legislation, is remembered as one of the most perceptive and thoughtful Supreme Court judges.

Brandenburg, Duchy of The original core of the Kingdom of **Prussia**. Effective German control was gained in 1106 by Lothair, Duke of Saxony (later German Emperor). It came under Hohenzollern control with the appointment of Frederick II as Elector by Emperor **Sigismund** in 1415. The Electors Joachim and John introduced Lutheranism. Brandenburg was invaded and occupied by the Swedes in the **Thirty Years War**. Independence and order were restored by **Frederick William** (the 'Great Elector'). In 1701, Elector Frederick III (1688–1713) proclaimed himself King of Prussia, which became the new title of the region. ▷ **Lothair III, 'of Supplinburg'**

Brandt, Willy (1913–92) West German politician. Born Karl Herbert Frahm, he was an anti-Nazi who fled in 1933 to Norway. There he changed his name, adopted Norwegian nationality and worked as a journalist, until the occupation of Norway (1940) forced him to move to Sweden. In 1945 he returned to Germany, and was a member of the **Bundestag** (1949–57). A pro-Western leader, he was Mayor of West Berlin (1957–66), and chairman of the Social Democratic Party (1964). In 1966 he led his party into a coalition government with the **Christian Democrats**, and in 1969 was elected Chancellor in a coalition government with the Free Democrats. Dedicated to restoring relations with Eastern Europe and especially East Germany, his success brought him the 1971 Nobel Peace Prize. He resigned as Chancellor in 1974, and later chaired a commission on the world economy (the Brandt Commission Report, 1980). ▷ **Ostpolitik**

Brant, Joseph (1742–1807) Mohawk chief. He fought for the British in the French and Indian Wars and the American Revolution. In later years an earnest Christian, he translated St Mark's Gospel and the Book of Common Prayer into Mohawk, and in 1786 visited England, where he was received at court.

Branting, Karl Hjalmar (1860–1925) Swedish politician. He was co-founder of the **Social Democratic Party** of Sweden in 1889 and was its first parliamentary representative in 1896. He became Chairman of the party in 1907 and helped to lead it away from revolutionary Marxism towards a more moderate 'revisionist' programme. He was Prime Minister in 1920, 1921–3 and 1924–5. In 1921 he shared the Nobel Peace Prize and was Sweden's first representative at the **League of Nations** in 1922–5.

Brătianu, Constantine (1866–?1948) Romanian politician. He became the leader of the Liberal Party after the assassination of the Liberal Prime Minister, Ion Duca (Dec 1933). Opposed to the dictatorship of **Charles II**, he operated part of the 'tolerated opposition' under Ion **Antonescu**. He advocated Romania's withdrawal from the war after the winning back of **Bessarabia** and **Bukovina**. In 1944 he was involved in the anti-fascist coup against Antonescu and became a minister without portfolio in the new government. He refused to hold office in the communist regime of Petru **Groza** and was arrested and imprisoned without trial. The year of his death, in prison, is not known, but is generally held to be between 1948 and 1952.

Brătianu, Ion (1821–91) Romanian politician. With his brother, Demeter (1818–92), he founded the Romanian Liberal Party. He was Premier from 1876 to 1888, while Demeter held the office for a short time in 1881. He was the father of Ion C **Brătianu**.

Brătianu, Ion Constantine (1864–1927) Romanian politician. A Liberal, he was the son of the great 19c minister Ion **Brătianu**, in 1916 he brought Romania into **World War I** against the **Central Powers**. At the **Paris Peace Conference** he secured maximum territorial gains for Romania. His brother, Vintila (1867–1930), was Premier from 1927 to 1928.

Braun, Otto (1872–1955) German politician. After an early career in political journalism and in municipal and Prussian state politics as a member of the **SPD**, Braun

became a member of the German National (Constituent) Assembly in 1919 and a member of the **Reichstag** in 1920. His main role, however, was as SPD Minister-President of **Prussia** from 1920 to 1932, where he carried out some important welfare and Civil Service reforms which earned his government the hostility of the political right. The unsuccessful SPD candidate for the German presidency in 1925, he sought exile in Switzerland in 1933.

Brazzaville, Conference (30 Jan 1944) French colonial governors and delegates of the French Consultative Assembly met at Brazzaville, the capital of French Equatorial Africa, in the presence of de **Gaulle** to lay down the principles which were to govern relations between France and her colonies in the **French Union**, created by the constitution of 1946. They envisaged assimilation and integration, rather than independence or even autonomy.

Breda, Peace of (31 July 1667) The treaty which brought an end to the second of the **Anglo-Dutch Wars**, following hard on the heels of Michiel de **Ruyter**'s raid on Chatham Docks (June 1667). This improved the terms of the peace for the Dutch Republic: they lost their North American colonies to England (New Amsterdam became New York, after James Duke of York, the King's brother and future monarch himself), but the Dutch retained Surinam in South America and the English gave up their claims to the Moluccan islands in the East Indies. The English Navigation Acts were also relaxed to allow more Dutch trade into England. ▷ **Chatham, Dutch Descent on**

brehon laws A corpus of ancient Irish customary law written down by the 8c; the name derives from Irish *breitheamh* 'judge'. Following the Anglo-Norman invasion of Ireland in the late 12c, Irish law gave much ground to English common law. It was finally abolished by statute in the early 17c.

Breitenfeld, Battle of (1631) The crushing defeat inflicted upon **Tilly**, commander of the forces of the Habsburg Empire and the **Catholic League**. Tilly was overcome by the Swedes in the only major defeat he suffered in the **Thirty Years War**.

Brennan, William Joseph Jr (1906–) US jurist. He was educated at the University of Pennsylvania and Harvard, and after practising law he rose in the New Jersey court system to the state Supreme Court. Named to the US Supreme Court in 1956, he took an active role in the liberal decisions handed down under Chief Justice Earl **Warren**. He retired from the Court in 1990.

Breshko-Breshkovskaya, Ekaterina Konstantinova (1844–1934) Russian revolutionary. The colourful and independent-minded daughter of a Polish landowner and a Russian aristocrat, she associated with various liberal and revolutionary groups in the more open society of St Petersburg under **Alexander II**. In the 1870s she worked with the **Narodniki** and was arrested and sent to Siberia in 1874; she was not allowed back into European Russia until 1896. In 1901 she helped to found the **Socialist Revolutionary Party** but in 1908 she was again exiled to Siberia, from which she was able to return only in 1917. Dubbed the 'Grandmother of the Revolution', she fell out with the **Bolsheviks** after their victory in Oct 1917, and died in Prague a firm anti-communist.

Brest-Litovsk, Treaty of (Mar 1918) A bilateral treaty signed at Brest-Litovsk between the new Soviet state and the **Central Powers**. Under its terms, Russia withdrew from **World War I**, hostilities ceased on Germany's Eastern front, and the new Soviet state ceded vast areas of territory and economic resources to Germany and her newly-created protectorates. **Lenin** argued against his opponents that Russia must 'sacrifice space in order to gain time'.

Bretton Woods Conference An international conference held at Bretton Woods, New Hampshire, USA, in 1944, which led to the establishment of the International Monetary System, including the International Monetary Fund (IMF) and the World Bank (International Bank for Reconstruction and Development). The agreement, signed by the USA, UK and 43 other nations, aimed at controlling exchange rates, which were fixed for members in terms of gold and the dollar. The system was used until 1973, when floating exchange rates were introduced.

Brezhnev, Leonid Ilich (1906–82) Russian politician. Born in the Ukraine, he trained as a metallurgist and became a political commissar in the **Red Army** in **World War II**. After the war, he was a party official in the Ukraine and Moldavia, becoming a member (1952–7) and then Chairman (1960–4) of the Presidium of the Supreme Soviet. He succeeded Nikita **Khrushchev** as General-Secretary of the **Communist Party of the Soviet Union** (1964–82), and gradually emerged as the most powerful figure in the USSR, the first to hold simultaneously the position of General-Secretary and President of the Supreme Soviet (1977–82). He was largely responsible for the enormous military machine and ailing economy that Mikhail **Gorbachev** inherited. ▷ **Brezhnev Doctrine**

Brezhnev Doctrine The term applied to the policies of Leonid **Brezhnev**, General-Secretary of the Soviet Communist Party (1964–82), which, while combining strict political control internally with peaceful co-existence and détente abroad, specifically justified intervention (including military) in the internal affairs of other socialist states, as in Czechoslovakia (1968).

Brian (c.926–1014) King of Ireland (1002/14). The Brian Boroimhe or Boru ('Brian of the tribute') of the annalists, in 976 he became chief of Dál Cais, and after much fighting he made himself King of Leinster (984). After further campaigns in all parts of the country, his rule was acknowledged over the whole of Ireland. He was killed after defeating the **Vikings** at Clontarf.

Briand, Aristide (1862–1932) French politician. He began his political career on the extreme left, advocating a revolutionary general strike, but soon moved to the centre as a 'republican socialist', refusing to join the United Socialist Party (SFIO), which did not allow its members to join 'bourgeois' governments. He held ministerial office almost continuously from 1906, being a cabinet minister 25 times, and Prime Minister 11 times. Apart from his periods as Prime Minister (1909–11, 1913, 1915–17, 1921–2, 1925–6 and 1929), his most important offices were as Minister of Public Instruction and of Religion (1906–8), during which he implemented the **Separation of Church and State** (voted 1905), and as Foreign Minister (1925–32), when he became known as the 'apostle of peace'. He was a fervent advocate of the **League of Nations**, and of Franco-German reconciliation. He shared the Nobel Peace Prize in 1926, concluded the **Kellogg–Briand Pact** outlawing war (1928), and launched the idea of a United States of Europe (1929). ▷ **Socialist Party** (France)

Bright, John (1811–89) British politician and orator. A quaker, he worked in his father's cotton mill, and took an interest in public questions. He became a leading member of the **Anti-Corn Law League** (1839), and engaged in free-trade agitation. A radical-Liberal, he was MP for Durham (1843), Manchester (1847), and Birmingham (1857), and was closely associated with the Reform Act of 1867. He later held several government posts, until his retirement in 1882. ▷ **Reform Acts**

Brissot (de Warville), Jacques Pierre (1754–93) French revolutionary politician. He trained as a lawyer, but then became an author, writing on criminal law. In 1789 he was elected to the National Assembly, where he influenced all the early movements of the Revolution. He established *Le Patriote français*, the organ of the earliest republicans, and became leader of the **Girondins** (or Brissotins). In the National **Convention** his moderation made him suspect to **Robespierre** and the **Jacobins**, and, with other Girondins, he was guillotined. ▷ **French Revolution**

Britain, Battle of (1940) The name given to the air war campaign of late summer 1940 in which the German **Luftwaffe** attempted to destroy the Royal Air Force (RAF) as a prelude to the invasion of Great Britain. The aerial offensive began in Aug, the German bomber aircraft and fighter escorts concentrating on wiping out the RAF both by combat in the air and by bombing their vital airfields in the south of the country. British resistance proved stubborn, with the Spitfires and Hurricanes of RAF Fighter Command being directed by radar onto the incoming bomber streams. Badly mauled, the *Luftwaffe* switched their offensive from attacks on airfields to attacks on British cities (the '**blitz**'), losing their opportunity to gain true air superiority. Between 1 July and 31 Oct the *Luftwaffe* lost 2 848 aircraft to the RAF's 1 446. ▷ **World War II**

Britain, Roman Known to the Graeco-Roman world from the late 4c BC, Britain escaped invasion until the time of Julius **Caesar** (55–54BC) and conquest until the time of Emperor **Claudius** (AD43); Roman military occupation then followed, the main garrison towns being Lincoln, York, Caerleon on the Usk, and Chester. Conquest of the whole island was initially intended, but the fierce resistance of the tribes in the north (Caledonia) ruled this out. Instead, defensive barriers were erected in northern England and southern Scotland: Hadrian's Wall (AD122–9) and the Antonine Wall (AD c.150). To the south, control was exerted through the army and the policy of Romanizing the natives. Military occupation lasted until c.400, when troubles elsewhere in the Empire forced the withdrawal of the garrison troops. ▷ **Iceni; Picts**

British Empire There were in fact several British Empires: the empire of commerce and settlement in the Caribbean and North America, founded in the 17c and partly lost when the 13 colonies declared their independence in 1776; the empire in the East, founded in the 17c but developed through the extensive conquest of India (1757–1857) and the acquisition of islands, trading posts, and strategic positions from Aden to Hong Kong; the empire of white settlement in Canada, Australia, New Zealand and the Cape in South Africa, each of which had been federated as 'dominions' by 1910; and the 'dependent territories' in Africa and elsewhere acquired during the 'New Imperialism' of the last few decades of the 19c. To this must be added the British 'informal empire': territories which the Empire did not rule directly, but which fell under its influence because of its industrial and commercial power. These included parts of South America, the Middle East, the Persian Gulf and China. In 1919 the Empire reached its fullest extent through the acquisition of mandates over German and Ottoman territories in Africa and the Middle East. It was this diversity which gave rise to such famous phrases as 'the empire on which the sun never sets'. By the late 19c the empire was bonded together not only by industrial strength, but by Britain's vast merchant marine and powerful navy. After **World War I** it was apparent that Britain could not control such an extensive empire: the dominions secured effective independence in 1931; the Middle Eastern mandates were virtually lost by **World War II**; India gained her independence in 1947, and the other Asian colonies soon followed; while most of the rest of the Empire was decolonized in the 1960s. Many of the countries of the Empire remained in the British **Commonwealth of Nations**.

British Expeditionary Force (BEF) An army, first established in 1906, sent to France (Aug 1914 and Sep 1939) to support the left wing of the French armies against German attack. In **World War II** its total strength was 394 000, of whom 224 000 were safely evacuated, mainly from Dunkirk, in May–June 1940. ▷ **French, John; Haig, Douglas; Marne, Battle of the; World War I**

British India The term commonly used to designate the whole of India during the

Independent Princely States

British India:
- in 1805, on Wellesley's departure
- 1805–58
- post-1858
- Empire of India, proclaimed in 1877

◆ French settlements

◻▼ Portuguese possessions

India, 1753–1890

period of British hegemony, more properly it refers to those districts of India under direct British rule. This area may be said to have varied from the first granting of Zamindari rights over 24 parganas near Calcutta to the British **East India Company** in 1701. By 1766 the Company directly ruled the area around Madras, the Northern Circars and a sizable area of Bengal and Bihar, while the Crown had control of the city of Bombay. More properly, British India came into being in 1858 when the Company was dissolved and its lands taken over by the crown. At its height, just before independence in 1947, British India included North-West Frontier province and the provinces of Baluchistan, Sind, Punjab, Ajmer, Merwara, Delhi, United Provinces, Bombay, Coorg, Madras, Ceylon, Central Provinces, Bihar, Orissa, Bengal and Assam; Sikkim and Bhutan were protectorates. Although not officially part of British

India, there were in addition many princely states which are often viewed as part of British India. Though nominally independent vassal states of the Crown, the princely states were watched over by British Residents and advisers. All control over foreign affairs and policy, and a wide variety of continent-wide matters, were ceded by the princely states to British India's government, under informal terms of paramountcy by which Britain had filled the vacuum left by the Mughal Empire. Although India moved gradually toward representative government between 1858 and 1947, British India was effectively governed by a viceroy or governor-general and some sort of advisory council throughout the period. Along with a small elected assembly, this was the government of India. The viceroy was responsible only to the Crown and the government of England. Below the government of India was the small

133

but effective bureaucracy of the **Indian Civil Service (ICS)**, which was focused on provincial centres, with district commissioners in rural areas. The **ICS** was supported by the local police forces under its control. The entire government was supported by the British Indian Army which was an integral part of both government and society, especially after the **Indian Uprising** (1857–8).

British–Iraqi Treaty (1930) This treaty carried, amongst others, clauses providing for mutual assistance between Iraq and Britain in time of war and special rights for Britain in respect of 'essential communications' through Iraq and was, in effect, the treaty which brought to a close the British mandate in Iraq. It also granted Britain two air bases on the condition that these were not in any way to be regarded as constituting an occupation; nor were they to be seen as interfering with the principle of Iraqi sovereignty. The treaty, therefore, although ending the mandate and securing full independence for Iraq, bound Iraq to Britain in what was *de facto* a military alliance, due under the treaty to last for 25 years.

British North America Act (1867) An act passed by the British parliament which sanctioned the confederation of Nova Scotia, New Brunswick, Quebec and Ontario, thus giving rise to the dominion of **Canada**. In 1982 it was renamed the Constitution Act (1867).

British South Africa Company A company, formed by Cecil **Rhodes**, which used a series of concessions from King Lobengula and other Central African chiefs to secure a Royal Charter from the British government in 1889. Mashonaland was invaded in 1890 and by 1900 the Company ruled much of Central Africa despite considerable African resistance. In 1923–4 its territories were divided into Northern Rhodesia (Zambia after 1964) and Southern Rhodesia (Zimbabwe after 1980). It retained extensive mineral rights.

British Union of Fascists ▷ **Blackshirts**

Brizola, Leonel de Moura (1922–) Brazilian politician. He became a state deputy in 1947 on a **Vargas** ticket, and went on to become leader of the *Partido Trabalhista Brasileiro* (PTB, 'Brazilian Workers' Party') a decade later. As Governor of Rio Grande do Sul, his support for his brother-in-law, João **Goulart**, Getúlio Vargas's heir, was crucial in Aug 1961, when he enabled Goulart to assume office as President and in Mar 1964 when, as Popular Deputy for Guanabara, he urged the Left to take to the streets in defence of the President. Exiled in 1964, he advocated armed opposition to the new regime, and by the 1970s had become the standard-bearer of the exiled Social Democrats. Amnestied in 1979, he founded the *Partido Democratico Trabalhista* ('Democratic Workers' Party'), a grouping based on his personal appeal, but limited to his personal following in Rio and Rio Grande do Sul. He became Governor of Rio de Janeiro in the first direct elections in 1982 and led the successful campaign in 1985 which ended the military government. Narrowly defeated by **Lula** in 1989 for the left-wing candidacy for the presidency, he was elected Governor of Rio de Janeiro in 1990; he is viewed as the éminence grise of the nationalists.

Broederbond A secret Afrikaner organization founded in 1918. Membership, limited to male Afrikaners, is by invitation only and was intended to integrate potential leaders across the country first to promote Afrikaner political ambitions and then to protect them. Since the early 1980s, it has become somewhat more open as it split between its reformist (or verligte) and its reactionary (*verkrampte*) wings.

Broglie, Achille Charles Léonce Victor, 3rd Duke of (1785–1870) French politician. The grandson of Victor Broglie, and son of Prince Claude Victor (1757–94), he distinguished himself as a liberal politician and advocate of the abolition of slavery. He became Foreign Secretary and Prime Minister (1835–6) under **Louis-Philippe** (1757–94).

Brooke, Sir James (1803–68) British soldier, and Rajah of Sarawak. He sailed in 1838 in a schooner-yacht from London for Sarawak, on the north-west coast of Borneo, with the object of putting down piracy. Made Rajah of Sarawak (1841) for assisting the local sultan against Dayak rebel tribes, he instituted free trade, framed a new code of laws, declared the Dayak custom of head-hunting a capital crime, and vigorously set about suppressing piracy. In 1857 Brooke repelled, with native forces, a series of attacks by a large body of Chinese, who had been irritated by his efforts to prevent opium-smuggling. He was succeeded as rajah in 1868 by his nephew, Sir Charles Johnson, who changed his name to Brooke. He was succeeded in turn in 1917 by his son, Sir Charles Vyner, who in 1946 ceded Sarawak to the British crown.

Brookeborough, Basil Stanlake Brooke, 1st Viscount (1888–1973) Irish politician. He was elected to the Northern Ireland parliament in 1929, became Minister of Agriculture (1933), Commerce (1941–5), and then Prime Minister (1943–63). A staunch supporter of union with Great Britain, he was created viscount in 1952, and retired from politics in 1968.

Brown, George (1818–80) Canadian politician and journalist. A supporter of **Responsible Government** in 1848, he became a member of the Canadian legislative assembly in 1851. As editor of the *Toronto Globe* he used his considerable influence to speak for the **Clear Grits**, pressing the case for representation-by-population ('rep by pop'), to give **Canada West** a majority of seats in the legislature. After the Liberal-Conservatives took over government in 1854, Brown reorganized the party, and won the 1857 elections by advocating the acquisition of the North West from the **Hudson's Bay Company**. In 1858, in alliance with A A Dorion, the leader of the Liberals of **Canada East**, he formed a government which survived only a few days. It was perhaps this experience which helped him to realize the inherent instability of provincial government under the system established by the Act of Union. He therefore played a major role with Alexander **Galt**, J A **Macdonald**, and George Étienne **Cartier**, in a coalition government established to devise the constitutional reforms required for confederation. This he continued to support even after resigning in Dec 1865. Brown was also an anti-slavery activist, involved in the settlement of fugitive slaves during the 1850s. He was shot and killed by an employee sacked from the *Globe*. ▷ **Liberal Party** (Canada)

Brown, John (1800–59) US militant abolitionist. He supported himself with many different jobs while wandering through the country advocating anti-slavery. He was twice married and had 20 children. In 1859, he led a raid on the US armory at Harpers Ferry in Virginia (now West Virginia), intending to launch a slave insurrection. The raid failed, and after being convicted of treason against Virginia, he was hanged at Charles Town. The song 'John Brown's Body' commemorates the **Harpers Ferry Raid**. ▷ **abolitionism**

Brown v Board of Education of Topeka, Kansas (1954) US Supreme Court case in which Chief Justice Earl **Warren**, speaking for a unanimous bench declared that separate educational facilities were inherently unequal and inhumane. With this decision the court overturned **Plessy v Ferguson** (1896), which had supported 'separate but equal' facilities, and undermined the major principle upon which **Jim Crow Laws** depended. Critics contended that it encroached on **states' rights**, and that it represented judicial legislation rather than interpretation. In 'Brown II' (1955) the Supreme Court acknowledged the problems faced by school boards in implementing the earlier decision; they ordered district courts therefore to integrate schools 'with all deliberate speed'. ▷ **segregation**

Broz, Josip ▷ **Tito**

Bruce, Blanche Kelso (1848–98) US politician. Born in Farmville, Virginia, he was a former slave who became a planter. He went on to become the first black American to serve a full term in the US Senate.

Bruce, Robert (1274–1329) King of Scots (1306/29) and hero of the Scottish War of Independence. As Earl of Carrick, in 1296 he swore fealty to **Edward I** of England, but soon joined the Scottish revolt under **Wallace**. In 1306 he quarrelled with John Comyn, his political rival, stabbing him to death; then assembled his vassals and was crowned king at Scone. He was forced to flee to Ireland, but returned in 1307 and defeated the English at Loudoun Hill. After Edward's death (1307), the English were forced from the country and all the great castles recovered except Berwick and Stirling. This led to the Battle of **Bannockburn** (1314), when the English were routed. Sporadic war with England continued until the Treaty of Northampton (1328), which recognized the independence of Scotland and Bruce's right to the throne. He was succeeded by **David II**, the son of his second wife. ▷ **Scottish War of Indpendence**

Bruce, Stanley Melbourne, 1st Viscount Bruce of Melbourne (1883–1967) Australian politician. Bruce attended Trinity Hall, Cambridge (1902–5), and spent much time in England because of business interests. After service in **World War I** with a British regiment, he entered Australian federal politics in 1918, representing Australia at the **League of Nations** in 1921 (and again 1932–9).

He became treasurer in 1921 and Prime Minister and Minister for External Affairs (1923–9) in a coalition with **Page**'s Country Party. Bruce's primary concern was Australian economic development within the framework of the British Empire, to which end he encouraged immigration, overseas investment and imperial preference. Attacks on the arbitration system and the trade-union movement led to the fall of his government in 1929. He led the Australian delegation at the **Ottawa Conference** in 1932 and was High Commissioner in London (1933–45). He became Viscount Bruce in 1947 and was the first Chancellor of the Australian National University (1951–61). ▷ **National Party of Australia**

Bruges, Matins of (18 May 1302) The overpowering of the French garrison in the Flemish town of Bruges. The raid was carried out mainly by members of the lower classes of Bruges, who rejected the pro-French policies of the town's leaders. Thus the incident had a democratic character; it led to a general rising of Flanders against French domination, and culminated in the Battle of the **Golden Spurs** later the same year.

Bruges, Treaty of (15 Aug 1521) The agreement between King **Henry VIII** of England and the Emperor **Charles V** against France, despite the Anglo-French friendliness of the **Field of the Cloth of Gold** the year before. The treaty meant that England was involved in long campaigns in northern Europe in support of the Emperor.

Brühl, Heinrich, Count von (1700–63) Saxon courtier and diplomat. He helped his master, Elector **Augustus III**, gain the Polish crown in 1733 and was appointed Prime Minister in 1746. His aim of securing a territorial connection between Saxony and Poland at Prussia's expense aroused the unremitting hostility of **Frederick II, 'the Great'** and was ultimately frustrated by the outcome of the **Seven Years War**. Brühl's ambitious political schemes, his generous sponsorship of baroque culture and his lavish private lifestyle drained the state's coffers and burdened the country with debt.

Brumaire Coup (9–10 Nov 1799) Named after its date in the **French Republican Calendar**, this was a plot, organized by **Sieyès**, one of the five Directors, together with **Talleyrand** and Cambacérès, with Napoleon Bonaparte as its military leader. Napoleon, however, bungled his part in it

136

and had to be rescued by his brother, Lucien Bonaparte. It was intended by its organizers to produce limited constitutional changes, but ended with the overthrow of the **Directory** and the establishment of absolute power in the hands of **Napoleon I** as First Consul.

Brun (c.925–65) Archbishop of Cologne. The son of **Henry I, 'the Fowler'**, he became Chancellor at the court of his brother, **Otto I, 'the Great'** (940). Appointed Archbishop of Cologne and Duke of Lotharingia in 953, he played an important role in securing border territories for the empire. Brun attempted to mediate in rivalries within the royal family, as in 953 when the King's son, Liudolf, Duke of Swabia, rebelled against his father; he himself remained a supporter of the King. During his episcopacy Cologne became a centre for the training of clerics and this led to a great strengthening of the links between the crown and the German Church. ▷ **Ottonians**

Brundtland, Gro Harlem (1939–) Norwegian politician. She studied medicine at Oslo and Harvard, qualifying as a physician. She married (1960) a leader of the opposition Conservative Party, Arne Olav, and worked in public medicine services in Oslo until, in 1969, she joined the Labour Party and entered politics. She was appointed Environment Minister (1974–9) and then, as leader of the Labour Party group, became (1981) Prime Minister of Norway, the first woman to hold the post. She was Prime Minister again in 1986, and in 1987 chaired the World Commission on Environment and Development which produced the report *Our Common Future*. In 1988 she was awarded the Third World Foundation prize for leadership in environmental issues.

Brunhilde (567–613) Frankish queen. She was the daughter of the Visigothic king, Athanagild. She married King Sigbert of **Austrasia**, and afterwards, as regent for her two grandsons, Theodobert II, King of Austrasia, and Theodoric II, King of Burgundy, divided the government of the whole Frankish world with her rival, **Fredegond**, who governed **Neustria** for the youthful Clotaire II. On Fredegond's death in 598 she seized Neustria, and for a time united under her rule the whole Merovingian dominions, but was overthrown by the Austrasian nobels under Clotaire, and put to death by being dragged at the heels of a wild horse.

Brüning, Heinrich (1885–1970) German politician. He studied in **Bonn** and at the

London School of Economics, and during the **Weimar Republic** became (1929) leader of the predominantly Catholic *Zentrum* (**Centre Party**) and then Chancellor (1930–2). Faced with the problems of economic depression, he attempted to rule by decree, but was eventually forced out of office, to make way for the more conservative Franz von **Papen**. In 1934 he left Germany, spending most of the rest of his life in US universities.

Bruno, Giordano (1548–1600) Italian hermetic thinker. At first a Dominican, his opinions caused him to flee to Geneva (1578). He then went to Paris (1581), where he lectured, then (1583) to London. He travelled throughout Europe until 1591, when he was arrested by the **Inquisition** and, after an eight-year trial, burnt in Rome. His philosophy was pantheist and sympathetic to Copernicus's theory of the universe. His most famous works are *De l'infinito universo et mondi* (1584, On the Infinite Universe and Worlds) and *Spaccio de la bestia trionfante* (1584, The Expulsion of the Triumphant Beast).

Brunswick Manifesto (12 July 1792) The manifesto issued by Charles William Ferdinand, Duke of Brunswick, warning the Jacobins in Revolutionary France that Paris would face heavy reprisals if any harm were to befall the French King or Queen. It marked the commencement of the Wars of the Coalition. ▷ **French Revolution**

Brusilov, Alexei (1856–1926) Russian soldier. He served in the war against Turkey (1877). In **World War I** he led the invasion of Galicia (1914) and the Carpathians. From 1916 he distinguished himself on the eastern front, notably in command of the South Western Army Group in the only partly successful 'Brusilov Offensive' against the Austrians in 1916. He became Chief of Staff in 1917, but the second 'Brusilov Offensive' was frustrated, many of his troops mutinied and added to the unrest that produced the Bolshevik Revolution. ▷ **Brusilov Offensives**

Brusilov Offensives (1916 and 1917) Two crucial Russian actions during **World War I**. In June 1916 General **Brusilov** launched a massive offensive against Austria at the request of the Western powers. He advanced into Galicia, relieved the Italians and encouraged the Romanians to enter the war. This helped eventually to destroy the Austrian Empire, but the cost in men and materials damaged Russian morale and weakened the

Russian economy. The second offensive in July 1917, intended to strengthen the **Russian Provisional Government** that followed the **February Revolution**, was an abysmal failure and contributed to the worsening social and political unrest that the **Bolsheviks** then exploited in Oct of the same year.

Brussels Conference, Declaration of (1874) An early statement of regulations covering many aspects of warfare. All the European powers were signatories, and much of the declaration was incorporated into that of the Hague Conference of 1899.

Brutus, Lucius Junius (6c BC) Legendary Roman hero. He was revered for his overthrow of the tyrannical king **Tarquinius Superbus** after the rape of **Lucretia** and his foundation of the **Roman Republic** (509BC). He was appointed (also in 509BC) as one of Rome's first two consuls, his partner being Publius **Valerius Poplicola**.

Brutus, Marcus Junius (c.85–42BC) A leader of the group who assassinated Julius **Caesar**. He sided with **Pompey** when the civil war broke out, but after the Battle of **Pharsalus** (48BC) submitted to Caesar, and was appointed Governor of Cisalpine **Gaul**. **Cassius** prevailed on him to join the conspiracy against Caesar (44BC). Defeated by Mark **Antony** and Octavian at Philippi, he killed himself. ▷ **Augustus**

Bryan, William Jennings (1860–1925) US politician. Educated at Illinois College, he entered the House of Representatives as a Democrat in 1890 and won his party's presidential nomination in 1896 on a Populist platform. He was Democratic nominee three times, and became Secretary of State under Woodrow **Wilson**. His last public act was assisting the anti-evolutionist prosecutor in the Scopes Monkey Trial in Dayton, Tennessee. ▷ **Darrow, Clarence; Democratic Party; free silver; Populist Party**

Bryce, James, 1st Viscount (1838–1922) British politician. He entered parliament in 1880, and was made Irish Secretary (1905) and Ambassador to the USA (1907–13). As chairman of the Bryce Commission (1894–5), he recommended the establishment of a Ministry of Education. His best-known work is *The American Commonwealth* (1888).

Bubnov, Andrei Sergeevich (1883–1940) Russian politician. He was a typical middle-ranking Bolshevik who suffered for the cause and was then consumed by it. Expelled from the Agricultural Institute in Moscow for political activity, he was quickly drawn into organizing and making propaganda for **Lenin** and his colleagues. He was arrested many times before 1917 and became a **Politburo** member in that year. Between 1918 and 1924 he was associated with **Trotsky**, but he broke clear and was entrusted with political education in the Russian Republic in 1929. That, however, did not save him from **Stalin**'s vengeance in 1937 and he died in prison three years later.

buccaneers The term used to denote legalized pirates operating in the Caribbean in the period 1650–98. The name derives from the French *boucanier* ('buyer of smoked beef'). The initial buccaneer stronghold was the island of Tortuga off Hispaniola, but this transferred itself to Port Royal after the English capture of Jamaica in 1655. As with the **privateers** a century earlier, the home governments often used the buccaneers as instruments of policy, issuing them with Commissions of Reprisal entitling them to attack Spanish shipping and settlements. The most infamous buccaneers were the Frenchmen L'Ollonais, Du Casse and De Maintenon and the Welshman Henry **Morgan**. English buccaneering was ended by the Treaty of Madrid (1670) and French by the Treaty of **Rijswijk** (1697).

Buchan, John, 1st Baron Tweedsmuir (1875–1940) British author and politician. During **World War I** he served on HQ staff (1916–17), when he became Director of Information. He was MP for the Scottish Universities (1927–35), when he was made a baron, and became Governor-General of Canada until 1940. In 1937 he was made a Privy Councillor and chancellor of Edinburgh University. Despite his busy public life, Buchan wrote more than 50 books, especially fast-moving adventure stories, such as *Prester John* (1910) and *The Thirty-Nine Steps* (1915).

Buchanan, George (1506–82) Scottish humanist and reformer. He was imprisoned for a satirical poem on the **Franciscans**. He escaped to France (1539), and taught at Bordeaux, Paris, and Coimbra, Portugal (1549), where he was arrested as a suspected heretic. Released in 1552, he returned to Scotland in 1561, and was tutor to **Mary, Queen of Scots**. Abandoning Mary after the death of **Darnley**, he became tutor to James I of England, and Keeper of the Privy Seal

138

(1570–8). His European reputation rested mainly on his skill in Latin poetry; his Latin paraphrase of the Psalms was used as a textbook until the 19c. ▷ **James VI and I**

Buchanan, James (1791–1868) US politician and 15th President. Educated at Dickinson College, he was admitted to the Bar in 1812. Elected to the US Senate in 1834, he became Secretary of State under President James K **Polk** (1845), an office he held during the **Mexican War**. He served as Minister to Great Britain under President Pierce (1853–6), and was elected president as a Democrat in 1856. During his administration the slavery question came to a head and he tried to maintain a balance between pro-slavery and anti-slavery forces. He supported the establishment of Kansas as a slave state, which alienated many in the North, but his moderate position also displeased radicals in the South. Defeated in the presidential election by Abraham **Lincoln**, but before Lincoln's inauguration, Buchanan was faced with the secession of the Southern states. Determined to avert a civil war, he rejected a military response and instead pursued a policy of compromise.

Bucharest, Treaties of (1812 and 1913) Two treaties, marking important stages in the achievement of Balkan nationhood. The 1812 Russo-Turkish treaty, concluding the Serbian revolt which had begun in 1804, granted **Serbia** autonomy within the **Ottoman Empire** and launched her on the path to outright independence in 1878. The treaty of Aug 1913 ended the second Balkan War between Bulgaria and Greece, Serbia and Romania, her recent allies against Turkey in the first of the **Balkan Wars** (1912–13). Its terms, involving Bulgaria's surrender of north **Macedonia** to Serbia, south Macedonia to Greece, and the south Dobrudja to Romania, finally extinguished any prospect of a 'Greater Bulgaria'.

Buchenwald German concentration camp. Established near Weimar in Aug 1937, it became a major part of the **SS**'s economic empire during **World War II**. Among its 239 000 internees (of whom 56 000 died) were many Soviet and Polish prisoners of war as well as German political detainees. Many major firms, as well as the SS's own Earth and Stone Co Ltd, exploited its inmates as forced labour. Liberated by the US Army in Apr 1945, Buchenwald subsequently passed under Soviet control and served as an internment camp until 1950. ▷ **Holocaust**

Buck, Edward Charles (1838-1916) British Indian administrator. Buck, a graduate of Clare College Cambridge, joined the **Indian Civil Service** in 1886, being immediately posted to Bengal. Having proved a great asset to the Bengal Civil Service, Buck moved through the ranks and eventually became Secretary of the government of India in 1882, a post he held until his retirement in 1897. In 1886 he represented the government of India at the Great Colonial Exhibition. In 1897, marking both his retirement and Queen **Victoria**'s diamond jubilee, Buck was made a Knight Commander of the Star of India.

Buckingham, George Villiers, 1st Duke of (1592–1628) English statesman and court favourite. He was knighted by **James I** (of England), and raised to the peerage as Viscount Villiers (1616), Earl of Buckingham (1617), Marquis (1618), and Duke (1623). In 1623 he failed to negotiate the marriage of Prince Charles to the daughter of the Spanish King, but later arranged the marriage to Henrietta Maria of France. The abortive expedition against Cadiz (1625) exposed him to impeachment by the Commons, and only a dissolution rescued him. An expedition against France failed (1627), and while planning a second attack, he was assassinated at Portsmouth by John Felton, a discontented subaltern.

Buckingham, George Villiers, 2nd Duke of (1628–87) English statesman. After his father's assassination, he was brought up with **Charles I**'s children, and went into exile after the royalist defeat in the **English Civil Wars**. His estates were recovered at the **Restoration** and he became a member of the **Cabal** of **Charles II**. He was instrumental in **Clarendon**'s downfall (1667), but lost power to **Arlington** and was dismissed in 1674 for alleged Catholic sympathies.

Budenny, Simeon Mikhailovich (1883–1973) Russian soldier. The son of a Cossack farmer, he fought as a Cossack private in the **Russo-Japanese War** (1904–5) and as an NCO in **World War I**. After the revolution he became a Bolshevik and raised a Cossack unit to fight the White forces on the Don, and defeated the Whites in the battles of Tsaritsyn (1918–19). He served in the war against Poland (1920), and was made a marshal in 1935. In 1941 he commanded the south-west sector against the German invasion, but was relieved by **Timoshenko** after a disaster at Kiev. ▷ **Bolsheviks; Russian Revolution**

Budi Utomo The first and most important of the ethnic-based organizations formed in the **Dutch East Indies** just before **World War I**. Founded in 1908, it drew in younger members of the Dutch-educated Javanese aristocracy who, in seeking to create a modernized Javanese culture, wished to establish for themselves a greater influence in the colonial world. Moderate in tone and unable to decide whether to pursue a purely cultural programme or whether to take up political ambitions, it was soon overshadowed by overtly political indigenous movements, although it remained in existence until the mid-1930s.

Buffalo Bill ▷ **Cody, William Frederick**

Buganda One of the states of Uganda, occupying territory on the north-west shore of Lake Victoria. It began to expand in the 17c, and was very powerful by the 19c. It was involved in trade in ivory and other commodities with the **Nyamwezi** in the 18c, and later became a focus of the struggle among Muslim, Catholic, and Protestant parties. The British ruled Uganda through the **indirect rule** system, and the continuing existence of the kingdom caused serious strains for independent Uganda. ▷ **Bunyoro, Kingdom of**

Buhari, Muhammadu (1942–) Nigerian soldier and politician. Educated locally and then at military academies in Nigeria, England and India, he was military governor of North-Eastern State (1975–6), of Bornu State (1976), and then Federal Commissioner for Petroleum Resources (1976–8) and Chairman of the Nigerian National Petroleum Corporation (1976–9). He returned to army duties (July 1976) but led the military coup which ousted Shehu **Shagari** (31 Dec 1983), when he became President. He was himself removed in a coup led by Ibrahim **Babangida** on 27 Aug 1985.

Bukharin, Nikolai Ivanovich (1888–1938) Russian Marxist revolutionary and political theorist. Dubbed by **Lenin** 'the darling of the Party', he was active in the Bolshevik underground (1905–17), and after the **February Revolution** returned to Russia, playing a leading role in the organization of the **October Revolution** in Moscow. He was a considerable theorist. As a member of the **Politburo** he came round to supporting Lenin's **New Economic Policy**, but had an ambivalent attitude to **Stalin**'s collectivization campaign. In 1937 he was arrested in

139

Stalin's Great Purge, expelled from the Party, tried on trumped-up charges, and shot. In 1987 he was officially rehabilitated by a board of judicial inquiry, and posthumously readmitted to the Party in 1988. ▷ **Bolsheviks; Brest-Litovsk, Treaty of**

Bukovina The region lying in the north-east of the Carpathian Mountains, which was settled by Ruthenians and Moldavians, and became part of Moldavia in the 14c. It was ceded to Austria by the Turks (1775) and governed by a mainly Polish administration as part of Galicia, first as a duchy and then as a crown land (1786–1849). During 1848, demands were made for separation and in 1853 it received its own diet and a separate administration. Romania, after gaining full independence (1879), sought Bukovina, occupied it during **World War I** and received it by the Treaty of **Trianon** (1920). The Romanian government then began to impose a Romanian cultural identity in the region. In **World War II** Soviet troops seized northern Bukovina and in 1947 incorporated it into the Ukrainian Soviet Socialist Republic, while the southern part around Suceava remained within Romania. Populated by Ukrainians, Romanians, Germans, Jews, Poles and Hungarians, under **Ceauşescu** it became an irredentist issue with the USSR. ▷ **Moldavia and Wallachia**

Bulganin, Nikolai Alexandrovich (1895–1975) Soviet politician. An early member of the Communist Party, he was Mayor of Moscow (1931–7), a member of the Military Council in **World War II**, and held various defence appointments after the war. Following **Stalin**'s death he became Vice-Premier in Malenkov's government, and was Premier after Giorgiy **Malenkov** resigned (1955–8), with Nikita **Khrushchev** wielding real power. 'B and K' travelled extensively abroad for propaganda purposes. Bulganin was dismissed in 1958, and retired into obscurity.

Bulgarian Exarchate During the 19c, Bulgarian national sentiment first focused on founding a Bulgarian exarchate, an autonomous ecclesiastical province which would free the Bulgarians from Greek domination, although they would still be ultimately subject to the ecumenical patriarch at Constantinople. In 1849 Sultan **Abd ul-Majid I** allowed the Bulgarians to open a church in Constantinople, an act which for the first time recognized their existence as a separate nation. The Bulgarian Church was finally declared independent in 1872, when Antim I was appointed exarch.

Bulgars Originally a Turkic-speaking people inhabiting the steppes north of the Black Sea, renowned as fierce warriors and horsemen. In the 5c AD they split into two groups, one of which later migrated west into the Danube region, where they became assimilated with the Balkan Slavs, and established the Kingdom of Bulgaria.

Bulge, Battle of the (1944) The last desperate German armoured counter-offensive through the Ardennes in **World War II** (beginning 16 Dec), to prevent the Allied invasion of Germany. It achieved early success, but ground to a halt, and the Germans were then pushed to retreat by the Allies by the end of Jan 1945.

Bull Run, Battles of (21 July 1861 and 29–30 Aug 1862) Major victories by Confederate forces in the **American Civil War**; also known as the Battles of Manassas. The first battle, which was the first major clash of the Civil War, pitted untrained Northern troops attempting to capture Richmond, Virginia (the Southern capital), against well-commanded Southerners. 'Stonewall' **Jackson**'s stand caused the Northern troops to retreat and the retreat became a rout. In the second battle, a large Northern force under John Pope was trapped by combined Confederate forces under 'Stonewall' Jackson and James Longstreet.

Bülow, Bernhard (Heinrich Martin Karl), Prince von (1849–1929) German politician. He was Foreign Secretary (1897) before becoming Chancellor, and was made a count (1899) and a prince (1905). Identified with an aggressive foreign policy in the years before **World War I**, Bülow, as Chancellor (1900–9), was the first to govern through a parliamentary coalition, which provoked conflict with the Emperor, **William II**, and precipitated his dismissal.

Bummei-kaika ('Civilization and Enlightenment') A slogan much used by Japanese government leaders and intellectuals following the **Meiji Restoration** of 1868. It was used with reference to government promotion of Western-style reforms in politics, society, and the economy, with the aim of making Japan a strong and wealthy power: for a period in the 1870s and 1880s, everything Western — from constitutions to dress and eating habits — was regarded worthy of emulation. A nativist reaction set in by the end of the 1880s, when traditional values were once again championed.

Bunau-Varilla, Philippe Jean (1859–1940) French engineer. The chief organizer of the Panama Canal project, he was instrumental in getting the waterway routed through Panama instead of Nicaragua. He incited the Panama revolution (1903), was made Panamanian minister to the USA and negotiated the Hay-Bunau-Varilla Treaty (1903) giving the USA control of the Canal Zone.

Bunche, Ralph (Johnson) (1904–71) US diplomat. He studied at Harvard and the University of California, then taught political science at Howard University, Washington (1928–50). In 1944 he assisted the Swedish Nobel prize winner Gunnar Myrdal in the creation of *An American Dilemma*, a study on American blacks. He directed the **UN** Trusteeship department (1946–54), and became UN mediator in Palestine, where he arranged for a ceasefire. Awarded the Nobel Peace Prize (1950), he became a UN under-secretary for Special Political Affairs from 1957 to his death.

Bund Literally 'federation', this is the name given to the German federal level of government and its competences, as against those of the states (*Länder*) and of local government. The *Bund* shares sovereignty with the Länder. ▷ **Basic Law; Germany, West; Land**

Bund, The (1897) The short name for the General Union of Jewish Workers in Russia and Poland. In the wave of official and popular anti-Semitism that afflicted Russia following the assassination of **Alexander II** (1881), Jewish intellectuals and workers inevitably found themselves drawn into opposition activities, including Marxist groups. The Bund had its own *raison d'être*. However, in 1898 at a secret congress in Minsk, it was one of the founder members of the Russian Social Democratic Labour Party.

Bundesrat (1867–1918) The upper and more powerful house of the North German (1867–70) and then German (1871–1918) parliament. Its members were appointed by the member states/princes of the German federation (**Reich**) and had extensive legislative powers as well as the power to resolve disputes between member states of the federation. Its influence declined with time as the elected, lower house of parliament (**Reichstag**) played a more prominent role in public affairs.

Bundesrat (1949–) The upper house of the current German parliament. Its members are appointed by the state (**Land**) governments and scrutinize all federal legislation. A two-thirds majority can block legislation proposed by the lower, elected house (**Bundestag**). The *Bundesrat* also serves to represent state interests at federal level. ▷ **Basic Law**

Bundestag The lower house of parliament of the Federal Republic of Germany, elections for which are held every four years in the autumn. It is possible for the *Bundestag* to be dissolved and elections held before the end of the fixed term, as in 1972 and 1983 when the government actually lost, or contrived to lose, its majority. In addition to legislating, the Bundestag selects the Chancellor and supports his government.

Bundeswehr (Federal German Armed Forces) Following Federal German entry into **NATO** on 9 May 1955, the *Bundeswehr* accepted 101 volunteers on 12 Nov. This ended the period of disarmament following capitulation in May 1945. In contrast to earlier German armed forces, the Bundeswehr was unequivocally subordinated to parliament and its conscripts perceived as 'citizens in uniform'. Virtually entirely within the NATO command structure, the Bundeswehr became the largest element in NATO with 340 000 soldiers and 8 600 tanks, 104 000 airmen and 400 front-line aircraft and 37 500 sailors. Following reunification, the Bundeswehr absorbed the surviving elements of the East German armed forces.

Bunge, Nikolai Khristyanovich (1823–95) Russian politician. Formerly Professor of Economics at Kiev University, he was Minister of Finance (1881–6). He was responsible for introducing a series of enlightened tax reforms that continued the policy of **Alexander II** after the latter's assassination in 1881. Bunge also introduced labour laws, and both of these measures benefited peasants and manual workers. In 1884 he established the **Peasants Land Bank** which for a period helped peasants buy land. In addition, he began the purchasing of private railways and the building of state-owned lines as a means of promoting industrial development. He resigned rather than raise new taxes to pay for fresh foreign wars. However, despite the atmosphere of political repression, he initiated two decades of economic modernization.

Bunker Hill, Battle of (1775) The first pitched battle of the **American Revolution**, technically a US defeat. The British garrison dislodged New England troops from their position overlooking occupied Boston, but very high British casualties demonstrated American fighting capacity, and forbade attempts on other American emplacements. The battle was actually fought on Breed's Hill, above Charlestown, not on nearby Bunker Hill.

Bunyoro, Kingdom of One of the kingdoms of Uganda occupying territory north of Buganda. It was formerly the most powerful of these states, originally known as Kitara, before it was colonized by the Nilotic Bito. It declined in influence when **Buganda** rose in the 17c.

Buonarroti, Filippo (1761–1837) Italian revolutionary. One of the most colourful and radical of Italian revolutionary leaders, in the 1790s he frequented Jacobin circles in Paris and went on a number of missions to Italy, Corsica and Lyons for the revolutionary regime. After the **Thermidor** coup he was imprisoned twice, the second time for his involvement in **Babeuf**'s 'Conspiracy of Equals". Freed by **Napoleon I**, he returned once more to conspiracy both in France and Italy where he joined the **Carbonari** and founded the **Adelfi**. Forced to leave Italy, he settled in Paris, mixing in revolutionary circles until the very end. ▷ **Jacobins**

Buraimi Dispute (1952) Buraimi, a group of oases on the borders of Abu Dhabi (now one of the United Arab Emirates) and Oman, was the subject of a territorial claim voiced by Saudi Arabia in 1949. A small armed force from Saudi Arabia occupied Buraimi in 1952, but was expelled on behalf of the rulers of Abu Dhabi and Oman by the Trucial Oman Scouts, a local force with British officers. There seems little doubt that the motivation behind the original claims and the occupation of Buraimi was the oil-bearing potential of the area recognized by the American oil concerns operating in Saudi Arabia; also that the **CIA** was involved in the organization of the attempted military seizure of the oasis.

burakumin An outcaste group in Japanese society, concentrated in about 6 000 ghetto communities and numbering 1–3 million; the target of extreme discrimination with regard to employment, marriage and residential segregation. Their origins go back to the Edo feudal period of the 17c, when impoverished Japanese in lowly occupations were segregated. The class was officially abolished in

1871, but to no great effect: some militancy within the group since the 1920s has also had little impact.

Bureau of Indian Affairs (BIA) A US government agency established in 1824 as part of the War Department and transferred in 1849 to the Department of the Interior. The BIA is in charge of the administration of Native American affairs, acting on behalf of the USA, which is the trustee of tribal lands and property.

Burgenland The easternmost state of the Austrian federation. Settled by Germans in the 9c, this territory was part of Hungary until 1922 when, with the exception of its capital, Odenburg (Sopron), it passed to **Austria** under the terms of the Treaty of **St Germain** (1919).

Burger, Warren Earl (1907–   ) US jurist. Educated at the University of Minnesota, he taught and practised law in St Paul from 1931 before he became Assistant Attorney-General of the USA (1953) and US Court of Appeals judge for the District of Columbia in 1955. Richard **Nixon** appointed him Chief Justice of the US Supreme Court in 1969. Burger, whose philosophy inclined toward judicial restraint and caution toward change, reined in the liberal tendencies the Court had shown in previous years. He resigned from the Court in 1986.

Burgess, Guy (Francis de Moncy) (1910–63) British double agent. Recruited as a Soviet agent in the 1930s, he worked with the BBC (1936–9), wrote war propaganda (1939–41), and again joined the BBC (1941–4) while working for MI5. Thereafter, he was a member of the Foreign Office, and second secretary under **Philby** in Washington in 1950. Recalled in 1951 for 'serious misconduct', he and **Maclean** disappeared, reemerging in the USSR in 1956. He died in Moscow. ▷ **Blunt, Anthony**

Burgh, Hubert de (d.1243) Justiciar of England under King **John** and **Henry III** (1215–32). He is chiefly remembered as the jailer of Prince **Arthur**. He was created Earl of Kent in 1227, but was imprisoned after falling from favour (1232–4), then pardoned.

Burghers A term related to 'burgess', which referred to citizens of a chartered community (a burgh or borough). A burgher possessed certain civic rights and responsibilities associated with citizenship, whether by birth or through purchase of burgher status.

Burgos, Carmen (1879–1932) Spanish feminist. Born in the remote province of Almeria, she married young but moved to Madrid after being abandoned by her husband. Having become a teacher, Burgos was elected to the presidency of the International League of Iberian and Hispanoamerican Women. She was an outstanding advocate of women's rights, above all through her writing. Not only did she publish a vast quantity of journalism both in Spain and Latin America (being the first Spanish female war correspondent in 1909), but also many books on women's issues under the pseudonym 'Colombine'.

Burgos, Javier de (1778–1849) Spanish politician and administrative reformer. An adherent of enlightened despotism (rejecting liberalism as a political system), he was a founder of the conservative **Moderate Party** in the 1830s. As a minister 1833–4, he replaced the powerful Council of Castile with a Ministry of the Interior and a Supreme Court. He also redrew the political geography of Spain into provinces.

Burgoyne, John (1723–92) British general. He entered the army in 1740, and gave distinguished service in the **Seven Years War** (1756–63). He then sat in parliament as a Tory, and in 1777 was sent to America, where he led an expedition from Canada, taking Ticonderoga, but being forced to surrender at Saratoga. He later joined the **Whigs**, and commanded in Ireland (1782–3). ▷ **American Revolution; Tories**

Burgundians An eastern Germanic people who migrated c.100BC from Scandinavia into the area between the Oder and the Weichsel. By the 4c, under pressure from the **Goths** and the Rugians, they had reached the Rhine. They were defeated by the **Huns** in 436 and settled in the area around the rivers Rhone and Saone, making Lyons their capital in 461. In 534 they were defeated by the **Franks** and Burgundy was assimilated into the Frankish empire. ▷ **Germanic Invasions**

Burgundy, House of A dynasty of French nobles, originating from the French royal family of Capet when **Philip the Bold**, the fourth son of King John the Good of France, was made the first Duke in 1363. The family's possessions in French Burgundy were hardly more important than their holdings in the Low Countries, where the dukes began an expansion policy which continued apace throughout the 15c and early 16c. After the

male line died out with the death of **Charles the Bold** in 1477, Burgundian possessions passed by marriage to the Austrian imperial house, which brought them into Habsburg control. The new leaders continued the consolidation of the Burgundian State in the Low Countries in the early 16c, which covered present-day Belgium, the Netherlands, and parts of northern France. In the 15c the court of the House of Burgundy was one of the major cultural centres of Europe, vying with France and England as the home of chivalry and art. ▷ **Capetian Dynasty; Habsburg Dynasty**

Burgundy, Kingdom of and Duchy of The first Kingdom of Burgundy was a successor state of the Roman Empire in the 5c. Incorporated in the Carolingian Empire, it was divided by the Treaty of **Verdun** (843), and was then united with the Kingdom of Provence in 10c. The dukes of **Burgundy** were some of the greatest vassals of the French monarchy, and frequently endeavoured to obtain independence at least *de facto*. They came closest to achieving this during 15c as allies of the English during the **Hundred Years War**, and under **Charles** 'the Bold', Duke of Burgundy (1467–77). The basis of Burgundian strength at this time was the dynastic marriages that had united Burgundy with Flanders, bringing the great wealth of the cities of the Netherlands to the dukes. However, the French monarchy retained its hold on Champagne, separating the two parts of the ducal territory. The death of Charles 'the Bold' in battle (1477) brought Burgundy back within the French kingdom. ▷ **Carolingians**

Burke, Edmund (1729–97) British politician and political philosopher. He began in 1750 to study law, but then took up literary work. His early writing includes his *Philosophical Inquiry into the Origin of our Ideas of the Sublime and Beautiful* (1756). He became Secretary for Ireland, and entered parliament in 1765. His main speeches and writings belong to the period when his party was opposed to Lord **North**'s American policy (1770–82). His *Reflections on the French Revolution* (1790) was read all over Europe. ▷ **American Revolution; Hastings, Warren**

Burlatsky, Fedor Mikhailovich (1927–) Soviet intellectual. Born in Kiev, he studied law and philosophy in Tashkent and Moscow and went on to be an academic, journalist and political consultant in the 1950s and 1960s.

Under a slight cloud in the 1970s, he transferred first to the Institute of State and Law and then to the Institute of Social Sciences, where his work in political science and sociology prepared some of the ground for the 1980s. As a journalist and politician in Mikhail **Gorbachev**'s time, he did much to propagate constitutional practices and to increase concern for Soviet human rights. He played a critical ideological role within the establishment from Nikita **Khrushchev** to Gorbachev.

Burlingame Mission (1868) A Chinese official mission to the West led by the former US Minister to China, Anson Burlingame. With revision of the 1858 Treaty of Tianjin due in 1868 the Chinese government was anxious to dissuade Western governments from forcing the pace of westernization in China, and invited Burlingame to mediate on China's behalf. The mission first visited the USA, where Burlingame actually signed a treaty on his own authority with the US Secretary of State. The treaty committed the USA to a policy of non-interference in China and provided for reciprocal rights of residence, religion and travel. In London and Berlin, likewise, Burlingame extracted vague promises of restraint and moderation. While in St Petersburg, in Feb 1869, Burlingame died of pneumonia.

Burma Road A road linking the Burmese railhead at Lashio with Kunming, 700 miles distant in Yunnan province, China. Completed by the Chinese in 1938, it was of great strategic importance to the Allies during **World War II**.

Burnham, Forbes (1923–85) Guyanese politician. British-educated, Burnham represented the African element in the Guyanese population and was co-leader with **Jagan** of the multiracial People's Progressive Party until 1955. In that year he split with Jagan over the latter's support for international **communism** and set up a rival African-based party, the **People's National Congress** (PNC). The PNC slowly gained adherents in Jagan's troubled years after 1961 and in 1964 Burnham became Prime Minister. He negotiated an independence constitution in 1966 and in 1970 established Guyana as a 'cooperative socialist republic', remaining its President until his death.

Burr, Aaron (1756–1836) US politician. Educated at Princeton and called to the Bar in 1782, he became state Attorney-General

(1789–91), then US Senator (1791–7), and Republican Vice-President (1801–5). His political career ended in 1804 when he killed his political rival, Alexander **Hamilton**, in a duel. Thought to be conspiring to take Louisiana and establish it as an independent republic, he was tried for treason (1807) and acquitted. In 1812 he resumed his law practice in New York City, where he died.

Bursa, Capture of (1326) The capture of the city by **Orhan** for the Ottoman Turks, who were expanding their power in Anatolia not only at the expense of the Byzantines, but also that of other Turkish groups. Orhan's capture of Bursa took place shortly before the death of his father, **Osman I**, eponymous leader of the Osmanli (or Ottoman) Turks, whose holy city Bursa became. Bursa also became the capital of a sanjaq placed initially under the control of 'Crown Prince' Murad, his father, Orhan, having succeeded to the leadership after the death of his own father.

Bush, George (Herbert Walker) (1924–) Politician and 41st US President. He served in the US Navy (1942–5) and after the war received a degree in economics from Yale and established an oil-drilling business in Texas. In 1966 he devoted himself to politics, and was elected to the House of Representatives. Unsuccessful in his bid for the Senate in 1970, he became US ambassador to the **UN**. During the **Watergate** scandal he was chairman of the Republican National Committee. Under President **Ford** he served as US envoy to China, and then became Director of the **CIA**. In 1980 he sought the Republican presidential nomination, but lost to Ronald **Reagan**, later becoming his Vice-President. He became President in 1988, defeating the Democratic candidate, Governor Michael Dukakis of Massachusetts. As President, he focused on US foreign policy, which was changed most dramatically by the dissolution of the USSR, and he presided over the USA-led UN coalition to defeat Iraq in the **Gulf War**. In 1992 he failed to be re-elected, perhaps because of the perception that he had ignored US domestic issues. ▷ **Republican Party**

bushido The Japanese notion of 'way of the warrior'. The samurai code until 1868, which taught personal loyalty to a master, death rather than capture/surrender, and stoic indifference to material goods. Like European knights, **samurai** rode into battle in armour. The bushido tradition is still seen in modern times, eg Japanese officers carried swords in **World War II**.

bushrangers Australian rural outlaws who operated from 1790 to 1900. Concentrated in New South Wales, Victoria, and Van Dieman's Land (Tasmania), the first bushrangers were ex-convicts (Donahoe in New South Wales, and Howe, Brady and Cash in Van Dieman's Land). The opportunities of the gold rushes led to a revival in the 1860s and 1870s. Products of a lawless frontier society, the gangs which included Frank Gardiner, Ben **Hall** and Ned **Kelly**, relied heavily on the sympathy of the local poor settlers for whom they were symbols of resistance to a heavy-handed government. Immortalized in ballads, they became a central part of the mythology of the Australian past.

Busia, Kofi (1913–78) Ghanaian academic and politician. Educated in Kumasi and at Achimota College, he then obtained an external BA degree from London and a DPhil from Oxford. He was one of the first Africans to be appointed an administrative officer in the Gold Coast (Ghana). He resigned that position to become a lecturer, and later Professor of Sociology, at the University College of Ghana. Elected to Legco (1951), he became a leader of the National Liberation Movement (1954–9) in opposition to **Nkrumah** and went into exile (1959–66), taking up the chair of sociology at Leiden University. After the 1966 coup, he returned as adviser to the National Liberation Council and then founded, and led, the Progress Party which won the 1969 election. He was Prime Minister (1969–72) before being overthrown in another coup, going into exile again in 1972. He held various academic posts and died in Oxford.

Buss, Frances Mary (1827–94) British pioneer of higher education of women. She founded the North London Collegiate School for Ladies, which became a model for the High Schools of the Girls' Public Day Schools Company. She also campaigned for women to be admitted to university.

Bustamante, (William) Alexander, originally **William Alexander Clarke** (1884–1977) Jamaican politician. The son of an Irish planter, he was adopted at the age of 15 by a Spanish seaman called Bustamante and spent an adventurous youth abroad before returning in 1932 to become a trade-union leader. In 1943 he founded the **Jamaica Labour Party** (**JLP**) as the political wing of his union and in 1962, the year Jamaica achieved independence, became its first Prime Minister. He was knighted in 1955.

Bute, John Stuart, 3rd Earl of (1713–92) British politician. After early court appointments, he became a favourite of **George III**, who made him one of the principal Secretaries of State (1761). As Prime Minister (1762–3), his government was decidedly unpopular. Its principal objective was the supremacy of the royal prerogative, and he was soon forced to resign. From 1768 he lived chiefly in the country, where he engaged in scientific study.

Buthelezi, Chief Mangosuthu Gatsha (1928–) South African politician and Zulu leader. Expelled from Fort Hare University College in 1950, where he was a member of the **ANC** (African National Congress), he was a government interpreter in the Native Affairs Department (1951–7). Officially appointed as Chief of the Buthelezi tribe in 1957, he was also assistant to the Zulu King, Cyprian (1953/68), before being elected leader of the Zulu Territorial Authority in 1970 and Chief Minister of KwaZulu in 1976, with the ANC's approval. He was sympathetic to the ANC's opposition to **apartheid** and he rejected the South African plan to turn Zululand into a 'bantustan' or 'homeland', but increasingly his readiness to work within the system and his Zulu nationalism distanced him from the radical forces of South Africa's opposition. He founded, and remains President of, the **Inkatha Freedom Party**.

Butler, Benjamin F(ranklin) (1818–93) US politician, lawyer and general. He graduated from Waterville College, Maine, and was admitted to the Bar in 1840, becoming a criminal lawyer. In the **American Civil War**, he and his troops took possession of New Orleans (1862), where they crushed all opposition. Elected to Congress in 1866, he was prominent in the Republican efforts for the reconstruction of the Southern states and in the impeachment of President **Johnson**. He was Governor of Massachusetts (1882–4), and unsuccessfully ran (as the candidate for the Greenback Party) for President in 1884.
▷ **greenback; Reconstruction**

Butler, R(ichard) A(usten), Baron (1902–82) British politician. He became Conservative MP for Saffron Walden in 1929. After a series of junior ministerial appointments, he became Minister of Education (1941–5), introducing the forward-looking Education Act of 1944, and then Minister of Labour (1945). He became Chancellor of the Exchequer (1951), Lord Privy Seal (1955),

Leader of the House of Commons (1955), Home Secretary (1957), First Secretary of State and Deputy Prime Minister (1962). He narrowly lost the premiership to Douglas-Home in 1963, and became Foreign Secretary (1963–4). He was appointed Master of Trinity College, Cambridge (1965–78), and was made a life peer. ▷ **Butskellism; Conservative Party** (UK)**; Home of the Hirsel, Baron**

Butler, Uriah 'Buzz' (1897–1977) Gre-nadian-born politician and labour leader. In 1921 he emigrated to Trinidad to work in the oilfields. An industrial accident in 1929 led him towards the Moravian Baptist Church and organized labour and in 1935 he broke with **Cipriani**'s Trinidad Labour Party (TLP) and set up the British Empire and Citizens' Home Rule and Workers' Party. In 1937 his fiery oratory whipped up agitation in the oilfields, and an attempt to arrest him at Fyzabad led to rioting and several deaths at

BYZANTINE EMPERORS

Regnal Dates	Name	Regnal Dates	Name
474/91	Zeno	1055/6	Theodora
475/6	Basiliscus	1056/7	Michael VI
491/518	Anastasius I	1057/9	Isaac I Comnenus
518/27	Justin I	1059/67	Constantine X
527 (518)/565	Justinian I, 'the Great'	1068/71	Romanus IV
565/78	Justin II	1071/8	Michael VII
578 (574)/582	Tiberius II	1078/81	Nicephorus III
582/602	Maurice V	1081/1118	Alexius I Comnenus
602/10	Phocas I	1118/43	John II Comnenus
610/41	Heraclius	1143/80	Manuel I Comnenus
641	Constantine III	1180/3	Alexius II Comnenus
641	Heracleon	1183/5	Andronicus I Comnenus
641/68	Constans II	1185/95	Isaac II
668/85	Constantine IV	1195/1203	Alexius III
685/95	Justinian II	1203/4	Isaac II (restored)
695/8	Leontius	1203/4	Alexius IV
698/705	Tiberius II	1204	Alexius V
705/11	Justinian II (restored)		
711/13	Philippicus	**Latin Emperors**	
713/15	Anastasius II	1204/5	Baldwin I
715/17	Theodosius III	1205/16	Henry
717/41	Leo III	1216/17	Peter of Courtenay
720/75	Constantine V Copronymus	1217/19	Yolande
775/80	Leo IV	1219/28	Robert of Courtenay
780/97	Constantine VI Porphyrogenitus	1228/61	Baldwin II
797/802	Irene	1231/7	John of Brienne (Co-Emperor)
802/11	Nicephorus I		
811	Stauracius	**Nicaean Emperors**	
811/13	Michael I	1204/22	Theodore I Lascaris
813/20	Leo V	1222/54	John III
820/9	Michael II	1254/8	Theodore II Lascaris
829 (820)/42	Theophilus I	1258/61	John IV Lascaris
842/67	Michael III	1259/61	Michael VIII Palaeologus
867/886	Basil I, 'the Macedonian'		
886/911	Leo VI	**Palaeologi**	
912/13	Alexander II	1261(1259)/82	Michael VIII Palaeologus
911/59	Constantine VII Porphyrogenitus	1282/1328	Andronicus II
920/44	Romanus I Lecapenus	1295/1320	Michael IX (Co-Emperor)
959/63	Romanus II	1328/41	Andronicus III
963(976)/1025	Basil II Bulgaroctonus	1341/7	John V Palaeologus
963/9	Nicephorus II Phocas	1347(1341)/54	John VI
969/76	John I Tzimisces	1355/76	John V (restored)
1025(976)/1028	Constantine VIII	1376/9	Andronicus IV
1028/50	Zoë	1379/91	John V (restored)
1028/34	Romanus III	1390	John VII
1034/41	Michael IV	1391/1425	Manuel II Palaeologus
1041//2	Michael V	1425/48	John VIII
1042/55	Constantine IX	1448/53	Constantine XI Palaeologus

Byzantine Empire (at the death of Justinian I, 'the Great')

Port Fortin. Interned for sedition in **World War II**, he returned to politics in 1945, but by then was a spent force.

Butskellism A compound of the names of British Conservative politician R A **Butler** and the Labour leader Hugh **Gaitskell**, used in the 1950s and early 1960s to imply a high degree of similarity between the policies of the two main parties. 'Mr Butskell' was first referred to in *The Economist* (Feb 1954).

Buyids (Buwayhids) A twelver or *imami* Shiite grouping from Daylam, which lies just south of the Caspian Sea in what is now Iran. Obtaining control of much of the central Islamic lands, they achieved control of Baghdad in 945 while allowing the Sunni 'Abbasid caliph to retain his position. This gave rise to the anomalous situation of an 'Abbasid caliph's being forced to surrender secular control to twelver Shiites while himself having to be content with what was not much more under the circumstances than the relatively empty prestige of his position. Eventually declining into a group of squabbling princelings, the Buyids were ousted in the mid-11c by the Sunni Great Seljuks (Turks who had migrated from Central Asia) who restored Sunni secular control in Baghdad. For all their differences and difficulties, however, Buyid rule saw great advances in learning and scholarship, and private patronage of scholars was encouraged.

Byng, George, 1st Viscount Torrington (1663–1733) English sailor. He joined the navy at 15, and gained rapid promotion as a supporter of William of Orange. Made rear-admiral in 1703, he captured Gibraltar, and was knighted for his gallant conduct at Málaga. In 1708 he defeated the French fleet of James **Stuart**, the Pretender, and in 1718 destroyed the Spanish fleet off Messina. He was created viscount in 1721. ▷ **William III**

Byng, John (1704–57) English sailor. He was the fourth son of George **Byng**, 1st Viscount Torrington. He joined the navy at 14, and was rapidly promoted, becoming admiral in 1756. For his failure to relieve Minorca, blockaded by a French fleet, and for retreating to Gibraltar, he was found guilty of neglect of duty, and shot at Portsmouth.

Byng (of Vimy), Julian Hedworth George, 1st Viscount (1862–1935) British general. He commanded the 9th Army Corps in the **Gallipoli Campaign** (1915), the Canadian Army Corps (1916–17), and the 3rd Army (1917–18). After **World War I** he became Governor-General of Canada (1921–6) and Commissioner of the Metropolitan Police (1928–31), and was made a viscount in 1928 and a field marshal in 1932.

Byzantine Empire The eastern half of the Roman Empire, with its capital at Constantinople (founded AD330), formerly Byzantium. The Eastern Roman Empire survived the collapse of the Western Empire by nearly a thousand years, only falling to the Ottoman Turks in 1453, when Constantinople was taken. One of its greatest rulers was **Justinian I, 'the Great'** (527/65). See panel on p146 and map on p147.

C

Cabal An acronym taken from the initials of the five leading advisers of **Charles II** of England between 1667 and 1673: Clifford, Arlington, Buckingham, Ashley Cooper (Shaftesbury), and Lauderdale. The name is misleading, since these five were by no means Charles's only advisers; nor did they agree on a common policy. Arlington and Buckingham were bitter rivals. ▷ **Arlington, Henry Bennet, 1st Earl of; Buckingham, George Villiers, 2nd Duke of; Lauderdale, John; Shaftesbury, Anthony Ashley Cooper, 1st Earl of**

cabildo A Spanish (specifically Castilian) municipal council, transplanted to colonial Spanish America during the 16c. Its members were usually appointed by the colonial authorities, but membership was often bought and sold. It declined in power during the 17c, but during the later 18c re-emerged as a focus for creole assertiveness against Spanish centralizing designs.

Cabral, Amilcar (1924–73) Guinean nationalist leader. Educated at Lisbon University, he worked as an agronomist and agricultural engineer for the colonial authorities. He founded the PAIGC in 1956 and, after abortive constitutional discussions with the Portuguese government, initiated a revolutionary war in 1963. Noted for his commitment to politicizing the peasantry and establishing alternative institutions in liberated territories, he presided over a successful war which forced the Portuguese to concede independence. He was murdered in 1973 just as his aim was being achieved.

Cabral, Luiz (1931–) Guinean nationalist leader. The brother of Amilcar **Cabral**, he was educated in Portuguese Guinea and became a clerk and a trade union organizer. As a member of the PAIGC, he went into exile in 1960 and took part in the guerrilla struggle to win independence for Guinea Bissau. Success made him President of the new Republic (1974–80), but he was then overthrown in a coup.

Cabrera, Ramón (1810–77) Spanish Carlist general and political figure. He was the leader of the Carlists in 1833–40 and 1848–9.

In 1839 Don **Carlos** created him Count of Morella in recognition of his resounding victory there the previous year against forces loyal to **Isabella II**. Cabrera died at Wentworth near Staines, having married a wealthy English lady.

cacique Originally a Caribbean Indian word meaning 'chief', the term was adapted and applied in 19c Spain to the local power-holders or bosses whose influence generally derived from their economic power, which was invariably rooted in their ownership of land. After the Restoration of 1875, the *caciques'* role as intermediaries of the state became institutionalized. They controlled political life by fixing elections so that Liberal and Conservative parties rotated in power in a pre-arranged manner, otherwise known as the *turno pacífico* ('peaceful rotation'). The caciques thereby became the cornerstone of the **Restoration System**. This fraudulent parliamentary system survived until the establishment of the dictatorship of General **Primo de Rivera** in 1923. Although the monarchist parties were disbanded by the dictatorship, the socio-economic power of the caciques often remained intact. Consequently, under the Second Republic of 1931–6 they proved a redoubtable obstacle to the implementation of the democratic and progressive reforms envisaged by the new regime. ▷ **Republic, Second Spain**

Cade, Jack (d.1450) Irish leader of the insurrection of 1450 against **Henry VI** of England. After an unsettled early career he lived in Sussex, possibly as a physician. Assuming the name of Mortimer, and the title of Captain of Kent, he marched on London with a great number of followers, and entered the city. A promise of pardon sowed dissension among the insurgents; they dispersed, and a price was set upon Cade's head. He attempted to reach the coast, but was killed near Heathfield, Sussex.

Cadorna, Luigi (1850–1928) Italian general. Commander-in-Chief of the Italian Army from 1914, he held the Austrian forces successfully from the outbreak of war in Mar 1915 until the the disastrous defeat of the Battle of **Caporetto**, after which he was replaced by the more flexible **Diaz**.

1	Collo	6	Carpi	11	Thysdrus
2	Rusicade	7	Clupea	12	Cirta
3	Thabraca	8	Curubis	13	Milev
4	Hippo Diarrhytus	9	Neapolis	14	Arles
5	Carthage	10	Hadrumetum	15	Buthrotum

Julius Caesar's campaigns

Cadoudal, Georges (1771–1804) French insurgent. A miller's son from Auray, Lower Brittany, from 1793 to 1800 he led the royalist **Chouans** against the republicans. He was guillotined for conspiring, with **Pichegru**, against **Napoleon I**.

Caesar, Julius (c.100–44BC) Roman politician. A man of patrician origins but slender means, his military genius, as displayed in the **Gallic Wars** (58–51BC), enabled Rome to extend her empire permanently to the Atlantic seaboard, but his ruthless ambition led to the breakdown of the republican system of government at home. Never one to allow himself to be blocked by constitutional niceties, in 60BC he joined with **Pompey the Great** and **Crassus** (the so-called First Triumvirate) to protect his interests in the state, and in 49BC, to avoid being humbled by his enemies at Rome, he led his army across the River Rubicon into Italy and plunged the state into civil war. Victory over the Pompeian forces at the Battle of **Pharsalus** (48BC), Zela (47BC), **Thapsus** (46BC), and Munda (45BC) left him in sole control at Rome. He did not disguise his absolute power, taking the title 'Dictator for Life' in 44BC, and allowing himself to be paid extravagant

honours which suggested he was aiming at regal and even divine status. This was too much for many republican-minded Romans, and under the leadership of **Brutus** and **Cassius** they conspired to murder him. His brief period of power left him with little time to carry through the many reforms, social, economic, and administrative, that he had intended. It was left to his great-nephew and heir, Octavian (Emperor **Augustus**) to reap where he had sown, and also to learn from his mistakes.

Caesars, Twelve The modern collective name for the Republican dictator, Julius **Caesar**, and the first eleven emperors of Rome. The idea for bracketing them together goes back to the second century writer Suetonius whose work 'Lives of the Caesars' consists of short biographical sketches of precisely these twelve rulers. By his time the word 'Caesar', which in Julius' day been a personal name meaning hairy, had come to be a virtual title for the Emperor of Rome.

Caetano, Marcelo (1906–80) Portuguese politician and academic. The son of a schoolteacher, Caetano had a meteoric rise during the counter-revolution following the

150

First Republic. He played a key judicial role in the establishment of the **Estado Novo**. From 1944 to 1947 he was Minister of the Colonies, and from 1955 until 1958 Deputy Prime Minister. Extrovert, ambitious and less submissive than other ministers, in 1951 Caetano had attempted to replace **Salazar** as Prime Minister. Yet in 1968 he was chosen as Salazar's successor as one of the most notable figures in Estado Novo politics. From 1969 to 1971 he liberalized the country in certain respects, but there was no promise of a liberal democracy; he was simply too closely identified with the authoritarian regime to execute authentic liberalization. Enormous discontent within the army over the costly and militarily unsuccessful 13-year war waged in Portuguese Africa against independence movements led to the bloodless coup of 25 Apr 1974 which, in its turn, resulted in the revolution of 1974–5. He died in exile in Brazil. ▷ **Republic, First** (Portugal)

Cai Chang (Ts'ai Ch'ang) (1900–90) Chinese revolutionary and women's leader. The younger sister of Cai Hesen (1890–1931), friend and colleague of **Mao Zedong**, she went to France in 1919 on a work-study scheme. She returned to China in 1924 after further study in Moscow. During 1924–6 she helped organize women textile workers in Shanghai and was Head of the Women's Department in Mao Zedong's **Jiangxi Soviet** from 1931 to 1934. At the Seventh National Congress of the Chinese Communist Party in 1945, Cai Chang was the sole woman elected to full membership of the Central Committee. With the establishment of the People's Republic in 1949 Cai Chang founded and led the All-China Federation of Democratic Women.

Caillaux, Joseph (1863–1944) French radical politician. He was several times Finance Minister (1899–1902, 1906–9, 1911, 1913–14 and 1925), unsuccessfully advocating a progressive income tax. As Prime Minister (1911–12), he negotiated the treaty with Germany, following the Agadir Incident, by which France was given a free hand to subjugate Morocco, and to turn it into a protectorate. He was attacked for being too ready to conciliate Germany, and was arrested in 1918 on a charge of contacting the enemy. Tried by the Senate, acting as a special High Court, he was sentenced in 1920 to three years' imprisonment, and to loss of political rights. Amnestied in 1925, he resumed his political career in the influential post of President of the Finance Committee

of the Senate, and as one of the leading elder statesmen of the **Radical Party**. In 1914 his second wife shot and killed Gaston Calmette, editor of *Le Figaro*, who had published letters written to her by Caillaux while he was married to his first wife; she was acquitted after a sensational trial.

Cairo Conference (1921) Convened by Winston **Churchill**, this conference had as its objective the consideration of the many problems afflicting the Middle East, particularly those thrown up by **World War I**. Discussions covered such questions as defence in the area and the treatment of the Iraqi Kurds (on which no decision was reached), but perhaps the most important result (if not actual decision) of the conference was the emergence of two Hashimite rulers: the King of Iraq and the Amir of Transjordan. The latter subsequently became King of Jordan after the creation of the state of Israel and the addition to the former Transjordan of the West Bank and the Old City of Jerusalem.

Cairo Conference (1943) A meeting held between Winston **Churchill** and **Roosevelt** which was attended by **Chiang Kai-shek**. Chiang was anxious that the allies continue to support the war effort in China at a time when they were considering inviting **Stalin** to bring the USSR into the Pacific War and whether to concentrate on capturing the Pacific Islands (from where Japan might be bombed rather than from Chinese airfields). Both developments would render the China Theatre marginal. Chiang was handicapped by both Anglo-American differences over strategy and by Roosevelt's increasing hostility to Chiang's regime, which was seen as hopelessly corrupt. The Cairo Conference was a significant turning-point in Washington's policy towards Chiang Kai-shek, hitherto considered a crucial actor in the war against Japan. Chiang did not receive the assurances he desired, while later in the same year Stalin pledged to enter the war in return for privileges in Manchuria.

Cai Yuanpei (Ts'ai Yuan-p'ei) (1868–1940) Chinese educator, scholar and politician. One of the youngest candidates ever to obtain the highest degree in the classical **Civil Service Examination System**, Cai taught in various schools and colleges in his home province of Zhejiang and in Shanghai. He joined **Sun Yat-sen**'s anti-Manchu republican movement and in 1911 became the first Minister of Education of the new Chinese

Republic, presiding over the creation of a new school system. Although he resigned in 1912, Cai continued to be active in educational affairs, helping to promote a work-study programme for Chinese students in France and assuming the chancellorship of Beijing University in 1916. He encouraged free debate and scholarship at the university, transforming it into one of the country's foremost intellectual centres. He later became a member of the **Guomindang**, but became increasingly critical of the party's suppression of free speech. He died in Hong Kong.

Calas Affair (1762) A famous miscarriage of justice in Toulouse, publicized by Voltaire. A Protestant merchant, Jean Calas, whose son had committed suicide, was accused of having killed him because he wished to convert to Catholicism. He was executed in 1762, but posthumously rehabilitated in 1765 after Voltaire's campaign; the affair did much to discredit the **ancien régime** in France.

Calatrava, Order of One of the military orders founded in **Castile** during the **Reconquest**. It was founded in 1155, with a red cross as its symbol, and came to possess extensive estates (*encomiendas*), numbering 51 in 1616. Members were in theory subject to semi-monastic discipline. From 1523 the crown of Spain became, with papal permission, head of the orders. ▷ **encomienda**

Calhoun, John Caldwell (1782–1850) US politician. He graduated from Yale (1804), studied law, then entered politics, becoming (1817) Secretary of War, Vice-President under John Quincy **Adams** and **Jackson** (1825–32), and Secretary of State under **Tyler**. He is best known for his 'nullification' theory (1828), in which he argued that states have the right to nullify laws they considered unconstitutional. He later entered the Senate, where he championed the interests of the slave-holding states.

Caligula (Gaius Caesar) (AD12–41) Roman Emperor (AD37/41). The youngest son of **Germanicus** and Agrippina the Elder, he was brought up in an army camp and nicknamed Caligula from his little soldier's boots (*caligae*). His official name, once Emperor, was Gaius. Extravagant, autocratic, vicious, and mentally unstable, he wreaked havoc with the finances of the state, and terrorized those around him, until he was assassinated. Under him, Hellenistic court practices, such as ritual obeisance, made

their first (though not last) appearance in Rome.

Caliphate The term caliph (*khalifa*), literally meaning 'successor', came to be applied to successive rulers of the Islamic state after the death of **Muhammad**. As an institution, it evolved slowly through the periods of the so-called Orthodox caliphs (632–61), the **Umayyad Dynasty** (661–750) and the **'Abbasid Dynasty** (750–1258). Succession was always a problem in Islam as, according to the Sunnis, Muhammad had made no explicit provision for a successor. The first definitive attempt to lay down qualifications for being caliph were made by al-Mawardi in his al-Ahkam al-Sultaniyya, significantly during a period of Shiite (Buyid) control of the central Islamic lands and are effectively a back-projection designed to bolster the position of the Sunni caliph then forced to accept Shiite secular rule, the main qualification being that any caliph should be (however remote) a member of the Meccan tribe of Quraysh.

Calixtus II (Guy de Bourgogne) (d.1124) Pope (1119/24). Formerly Count of Burgundy and Archbishop of Vienne. In 1121 he overcame the anti-pope Burdinus (Gregory VIII), who was supported by the German Emperor **Henry V**, and in 1122 concluded with Henry the Concordat of **Worms**, which settled the **Investiture Controversy**.

Callaghan, (Leonard) James ('Jim') (1912–) British politician. After a secondary education, he joined the Civil Service (1929), and in 1945 was elected Labour MP for South Cardiff. As Chancellor of the Exchequer under **Wilson** (1964–7), he introduced the controversial corporation and selective employment taxes. He was Home Secretary (1967–70) and Foreign Secretary (1974–6), and became Prime Minister (1976–9) on Wilson's resignation. He resigned as Leader of the Opposition in 1980. ▷ **Labour Party** (UK)

Calles, Plutarco Elías (1877–1945) Mexican politician. A former schoolmaster, he became Governor of Sonora (1917), and President of Mexico (1924–8). Anticlerical, he challenged the pretensions of the Church, implementing the 1917 constitution and provoking the **Cristero Revolt**; he dominated the presidency until 1934, enhancing the power of the state, creating the PNR but limiting agrarian reform. Defeated by his protégé, **Cárdenas**, he was exiled to the USA, but was allowed to return in 1941.

Calonne, Charles Alexandre de (1734–1802) French politician; in 1783 was made Controller-General of Finance. In 1786 he advised King **Louis XVI** to convoke the Assembly of Notables, and distribute the burden of taxation more equally. In opening the Assembly (1787), he described the general prosperity of France, but confessed that the annual deficit of the treasury had risen to 115 million francs, and that during 1776–86 the government had borrowed 1 250 millions. The Notables demanded a statement of accounts; failing to satisfy them, he was banished to Lorraine. After this, he resided chiefly in England, until in 1802 **Napoleon I** permitted him to return. ▷ **Notables, Assemblies of the**

Calvin, John (1509–64) French Protestant reformer. He studied Latin at Paris, then law at Orléans, where he developed his interest in theology. In Bourges and other centres, he began to preach the reformed doctrines, but he was forced to flee from France to escape persecution. At Basle he issued his influential *Christianae Religionis Institutio* (1536), and at Geneva was persuaded by Guillaume **Farel** to help with the **Reformation**. The reformers proclaimed a Protestant Confession of Faith, under which moral severity took the place of licence. When a rebellious party, the Libertines, rose against this, Calvin and Farel were expelled from the city (1538). Calvin withdrew to Strasbourg, where he worked on New Testament criticism, and married. In 1541 the Genevans recalled him, and he founded a theocracy which controlled almost all the city's affairs. By 1555 his authority was confirmed into an absolute supremacy. The father figure of Reformed theology, he left a double legacy to Protestantism by systematizing its doctrine and organizing its ecclesiastical discipline. His commentaries, which embrace most of the Old and New Testaments, were collected and published in 1617. ▷ **Basle, Council of**

Calvo Sotelo, José (1893–1936) Spanish politician. Under the dictator **Primo de Rivera**, he was made the Director-General of Local Government, introducing the stillborn Municipal Statute in 1924. He was also a controversial Minister of Finance, attempting to overhaul the tax system (only to be thwarted by the banks) and creating state monopolies, in particular the petroleum company, CAMPSA. His much-criticized monetary policies contributed to the regime's fall. He went into exile on the advent of the Second Republic in 1931, returning with the amnesty of 1934. Having founded the totalitarian National Bloc, he soon became the most powerful civilian figure on the extreme Right. His assassination on 13 July 1936 triggered off the military rising that led to the **Spanish Civil War**. ▷ **Republic, Second** (Spain)

Camacho, Marcelino (1918–) Spanish trade union leader. He joined the Communist Party in 1934 and fought for the Republicans in the **Spanish Civil War**. Jailed by the Nationalists, he escaped to French Morocco and then Algeria, where he earned his living as a millwright (1944–57). An amnesty in 1957 allowed him to return to Spain and during the 1960s he rose within the clandestine Workers' Commissions (**CCOO**) to become the leading trade union leader in Spain by the early 1970s. For most of the period 1967–75 he was in jail. He was a Communist Party Deputy (1977–82) as well as being a member of the Party's Central Committee. Following the Communists' dismal showing in 1982, he was one of those who pressed **Carrillo** to resign. In 1987 he retired as Secretary-General of the CCOO, but remained its Honorary President.

Cambacérès, Jean Jacques Régis de (1753–1824) French lawyer. A member of the National **Convention**, he voted for the pursuit of the **Girondins**, but then effaced himself during the Reign of **Terror**, resuming a prominent role under the **Directory** and the **Consulate**. He became Archchancellor of the First French Empire (1804) and Duke of Parma (1808). As **Napoleon I**'s chief legal adviser, his civil code formed the basis of the **Code Napoléon**. ▷ **Empire, First** (France)

Cambaluc The westernized term, popularized by Marco Polo, for *Khanbalikh* (Turkish, 'City of the Khan'), the capital **Kublai Khan** built on the site of present-day Beijing. Also known as *Ta-tu* (in Chinese) and *Dadu* (in Mongol), the city was constructed between 1266 and 1272 and served as the capital of the Mongol empire. By transferring his capital from Kharakorum (Qaraqorum) in the Mongol heartland to north China, Kublai Khan demonstrated his commitment to China, hoping thereby to gain the acceptance of Chinese elites. In order to ensure grain supplies from the south, Kublai Khan extended the Grand Canal to his new capital.

Cambó, Francesc (1876–1947) Catalan politician. The leader of conservative Catalan nationalists, he was a businessman and banker, who founded with Enric **Prat de la Riba** the *Lliga Regionalista* in 1901. As a middleman for foreign companies, he became the most prominent self-made businessman of that period. His overriding political objective was to establish the Catalan bourgeoisie as the ruling class in Spain. To this end, he attempted to organize a nationwide movement for political reform, but the general strike of 1917 led him to change course. From this time on, he was closely allied to the central ruling oligarchy, joining the 'National Government' of Antonio **Maura** in 1918 as Minister of Economic Development and remaining in government until Mar 1922. During the Second Republic he relaunched the **Lliga** (as the *Lliga Catalana*), but his oligarchical nationalism was overshadowed throughout by the Catalan Left. He spent the **Spanish Civil War** in Italy, thereafter living in Argentina until his death. ▷ **Republic, Second** (Spain)

Cambrai, League of An alliance, formed in 1508, as a result of Pope Julius II's schemes to reduce the power of the Venetians and acquire their possessions in Romagna, the league included Emperor Maximilian, Louis XII and Ferdinand II, 'the Catholic'. It succeeded in the destruction of the Venetian army at the Battle of Agnadello (14 May 1509), although the Venetians subsequently recovered their territories as the victors quarrelled amongst themselves. In 1510 Julius abandoned the league to side with Venice; Ferdinand declared his neutrality, but the next year also went over to Venice. After the French victory at Ravenna (1512), even the Emperor and Swiss cantons became part of the coalition against them, and the French were driven out of Milan (May 1512). The French won a victory at Ravenna then lost at Novara in 1513 to the Swiss mercenaries who were now operating as an independent force. This was revenged by the French at Marignano amid terrible slaughter in 1515. By now it was clear that Italy was merely the theatre for the conflicts of other powers and was no longer in control of its own affairs. Pope **Clement VII**, fearful of imperial dominance, dispensed Francis from his vow to keep the peace and formed the League of Cognac between the papacy, Venice, Florence and France. This was swept aside by the imperial advance and the full wrath of the unpaid imperial mercenaries was unleashed in the Sack of Rome in 1527, an event so shattering that in many ways it can be said to have brought the Italian **Renaissance** to an end. ▷ **Italian Wars**

Cambrai, Treaty of (5 Aug 1529) A treaty concluded between **Francis I** of France and Emperor **Charles V** in 1529, following the latter's victory at Landriano in the **Italian Wars**. Francis renounced his claims in Italy and Flanders and Charles his claim to **Burgundy**. Although peace was short-lived, these terms were reflected in the final settlement at **Cateau-Cambrésis** a generation later (1559).

Cambyses II (d.522BC) Second Achaemenid King of Persia (530/522BC). The son of Cyrus the Great, his one solid achievement was the conquest of Egypt (525BC). He died in Syria while trying to put down a rival for the throne. ▷ **Achaemenids; Cyrus II**

Camden, Battle of (1780) A battle of the **American Revolution**, fought in South Carolina. After the British capture of **Charleston**, Camden was the first major battle of the Southern campaign. Americans under Horatio Gates were defeated by British troops under Lord **Cornwallis**.

Camel, Battle of the (656) This battle, following the murder of the Caliph '**Uthman** (644/56), is significant as being the first Muslim civil war, thus posing serious problems for religious theorists. The death of 'Uthman, resulting as it did in the acclamation as Caliph of '**Ali**, provoked considerable hostility amongst two completely separate groups of Muslims. First, and most obviously, the Umayyad kinsmen of 'Uthman, including the powerful Governor of Syria, **Mu'awiya**. More dangerous perhaps for Islam was the reaction of a second group, led by Talha and al-Zubayr, companions of **Muhammad**, and the prophet's favourite wife, '**Aisha**. These three and their adherents, regarding 'Ali's caliphate as fatally flawed insofar as much of his support came from the groups involved in the murder of 'Uthman, set out for Basra. 'Ali's forces, by now based in Kufa, defeated them at this battle (so called because of the camel on which 'Aisha sat throughout it), but the damage to Islam was done. The way was then open for Mu'awiya and his Syrians to demand vengeance for 'Uthman, a demand which, in view of 'Ali's inability to meet it, led to the disastrous Battle of **Siffin** (657).

Camillus, Marcus Furius (5c–4c BC) Aristocratic Roman general and politician, famous primarily for the capture and destruction in 396 BC, of Rome's greatest rival of the day, the Etruscan city of **Veii**, and for his repulse of the Gallic attack on Rome under Brennus in 387/6 BC. For this he came to be regarded as the saviour and second founder of Rome. Many other military achievements were later attributed to him, as well as numerous civic offices, but most of these (eg at least three of his five dictatorships) are no longer considered to be historical.

Camisards The last major Protestant rebellion in early modern Europe, centred on the Cévennes Mountains in northern Languedoc (1700–4). It was provoked by the Revocation of the Edict of **Nantes** (1685), which had guaranteed limited toleration, and the failure of the Treaty of **Rijswijk** (1697) to safeguard French Protestants. The uprising was put down with difficulty by royal troops under Marshal Villars.

campanilismo The Italian word, derived from *campanile* ('bell-tower'), which is commonly used to describe the intense particularism which has always been a characteristic of Italian culture and politics.

Campbell, Sir Colin (Baron Clyde) (1792–1863) British field marshal. He fought in the **Peninsular War** against **Napoleon I**, where he was twice badly wounded, and after 30 years of duty in various garrisons, fought in China (1842) and in the second of the **Sikh Wars** (1848–9). In the **Crimean War** he commanded the Highland Brigade in a campaign which included the renowned repulse of the Russians by the 'thin red line' at the Battle of **Balaclava** (1854). During the 1857–8 **Indian Uprising** he commanded the forces in India, and effected the final relief of Lucknow. He was created baron in 1858.

Campbell-Bannerman, Sir Henry (1836–1908) British politician. He became a Liberal MP in 1868, was Chief Secretary for Ireland (1884), War Secretary (1886 and 1892–5), Liberal leader (1899), and Prime Minister (1905–8). A 'pro-Boer', he granted the ex-republics responsible government, and his popularity helped to reunite a divided **Liberal Party**. He supported the Lib–Lab pact of 1903, which played a part in the Liberal landslide of 1906. ▷ **Boer Wars**

Camp David Accords (1978) Documents signed by Anwar **Sadat**, President of Egypt, and Menachem **Begin**, Prime Minister of Israel, and witnessed by US President Jimmy **Carter** at Camp David, Maryland, USA, in Sep 1978. Regarded by many as a triumph of US diplomacy, they were preliminary to the

signing of the formal peace treaty (1979) between the two countries, which gave Egypt back the Sinai Desert, captured in the 1967 War. ▷ **Arab-Israeli Wars; PLO**

Camperdown, Battle of (1797) A naval battle fought between British and Dutch fleets off Texel Island, Holland. Admiral Adam Duncan (1731–1804) virtually destroyed the Dutch fleet, frustrating the attempt to disable the British North Sea squadron and thus facilitate the invasion of Britain.

Campoamor, Clara (1888–1972) Spanish politician and feminist. Of working-class origin, she graduated in law in 1924, and from then onwards agitated widely on behalf of women's issues. In 1931 she was elected to the Constituent Cortes of the Second Republic as a deputy for the **Radical Republican Party**. She was responsible more than anyone else for the inclusion of women's suffrage in the Constitution of 1931. During the legislature of 1931–3 she was Vice-President of the Labour Commission and participated in the reform of the Civil Code. In addition, she represented Spain at the **League of Nations** and founded the Republican Feminine Union. In 1933–4 she was also the Director-General of Charity. During the 1930s she wrote extensively on women's rights and aspirations. In 1938 she chose exile in Buenos Aires, moving in 1955 to Lausanne, where she died. She was one of the principal figures of the 20c in the struggle for women's rights in Spain. ▷ **Republic, Second** (Spain)

Campo Formio (Campoformido), Treaty of (18 Oct 1797) A treaty between France and Austria. Negotiated and signed by **Napoleon I** and ratified by the **Directory**, the treaty marked the end of the first of the Wars of the Coalition and it represented the climax of the young French general's successful campaigns of 1796–7. By its terms, Francis II of Austria recognized French possession of the Austrian Netherlands and French claims to territory on the left bank of the Rhine. The Austrian Emperor also ceded Lombardy and Mantua to the newly established **Cisalpine Republic**, receiving in compensation Venetia, Istria, Dalmatia and Friuli.

Campomanes, Pedro Rodríguez, Count of (1723–1803) In 1762 he became *fiscal* (chief legal officer) of the Council of **Castile** under **Charles III**, King of Spain since 1759. His programme was expressed in *The Right of*

Mortmain (1765), designed to limit acquisition of property by the Church, and he became identified with a liberal policy of free trade with America. Plans were interrupted by the outbreak of riots in Madrid (1766) and popular risings throughout Spain which forced the King to sack his minister, **Esquilache**. Under the new Chief Minister, **Aranda**, Campomanes prepared a prosecution of the Jesuits, considered instigators of the riots; they were expelled by decree in 1767 from both Spain and America. In 1774 he encouraged the spread of Economic Societies of Friends of the Country, a group which played a key role in bringing the elite into the reform programme. In 1783 he was appointed head of the Council of Castile but was relieved of the post in 1791. An accomplished scholar, historian and practical intellectual, his writings represent the most advanced thinking of the Enlightenment in Spain.

Campos, Roberto de Oliveira (1926–) Brazilian political economist and diplomat. A Jesuit-trained economist, he served as a diplomat on the US-Brazil Economic Commission in the 1950s, and was later Director of the National Economic Development Bank (BNDE) under **Kubitschek (de Oliveira)**. Associated with attempts to achieve an 'orthodox' economic policy by the nationalist press, he was the natural choice for Planning Minister under **Castelo Branco**. He co-authored the 'Government Economic Action Programme, 1964–6' (PAEG), with Otávio Gouveia de Bulhões: this introduced modern fiscal and monetary policy instruments, as well as indexation and the centralization of expenditure, while encouraging 'corporate' management of the economy, drawing on the heritage of the **Vargas** era. He espoused the trickle-down theory of economic growth and the encouragement of foreign investment.

Campos Salles, Manuel Ferraz de (1841–1913) Brazilian politician. The 'Political Architect of the Republic', he was a slave-owner, **fazendeiro** and lawyer in Campinas, then the centre of the coffee-growing region of Brazil. He became a Republican in the 1870s and was Minister of Justice in the Provisional Government of the Republic (1889–91), when he was responsible for the separation of Church and State and the introduction of civil marriage. He was Governor of São Paulo in 1896–8, and then became President (1898–1902). Charged with radical financial reform, designed to protect the country from foreign intervention, and

pledged to a 'privatization' programme, he emasculated a nationalist Congress by agreeing a pact with incumbent governors: the President would protect them from federal intervention if they, in their turn, pledged their support for him in Congress. This system, known as the 'Politics of the Governors', led to one-party state administrations and provided the basis for political management until 1930; vestiges of it remain to this day.

Canaan The land of the ancient Semitic-speaking peoples, living in the coastal areas of modern Israel and Syria, but perhaps also extending inland to the Jordan River and the Dead Sea. It was divided into various city-states during the early 2nd millennium BC, but mostly fell under the control of Israelites and other powers from the late 13c BC.

Canada, Lower (1791–1841) The name given to Quebec by the Constitutional Act of 1791. The decision to divide Canada in two was reached with the realization that it would not be possible to establish a form of government which would satisfy both English-speaking Protestant Canadians and French-speaking Catholics. Lower Canada was dominated by French-Canadians, the Catholic Church was established and the Custom of Paris accepted as its legal system. With its borders drawn up on the old seigniorial property boundaries, Montreal, despite being dominated by English merchants was also included. In Lower Canada the problems associated with colonial rule existed along with the friction caused by the fractious relationship between the two communities. This friction increased with the influx of English-speaking immigrants so that the French-Canadians were afraid for their ascendancy and the English-speaking immigrants suffered from the domination of French custom and language. In 1822 the Montreal Chateau Clique originated a bill which united both provinces. They aimed to bar most Frenchmen from the vote through a high property franchise and to limit the power of the Catholic Church. The bill was dropped after **Papineau** went to London to appeal. Although by 1831 control of the revenue had been given to the Assembly, the majority in the House was not given any official ministerial recognition. By 1834 the French only held a quarter of the public posts although they formed three-quarters of the population. The situation was aggravated by the depression of 1837, and rebellion broke out, but was put down fairly quickly. With the Act of Union (1840) Lower Canada became **Canada East** (in 1841), and was given equal representation within a united province, so the French were yet again at a disadvantage. ▷ **Canada, Upper; Craig, Sir James Henry; Durham Report; Ninety-Two Resolutions**

Canada, Upper (1791–1841) The name given to the western region of the province of Quebec when it was made, like Lower Canada, a separate province by the Constitutional Act of 1791. At that time it had a population of 14000, but by 1812, with an influx of settlers mostly from the USA, it had grown to 90000. The first governor was Sir John Graves **Simcoe** who initiated a system of distributing free land grants in return for a loyalty oath. However, the distribution of land according to social rank created an elite known as the **Family Compact**. Similarly the Anglican Church's semi-established status gave it advantages at the expense of the Methodist Church, although the latter's members outnumbered the Anglicans. These dissatisfactions led William Lyon **Mackenzie**, after the failure of rebellion in Lower Canada, to call settlers to action, but his inability to organize a military uprising matched the inability of the governor, Sir Francis Bond Head to govern. Nevertheless it did bring the problems out into the open, and after the **Durham Report**, Upper Canada was made **Canada West** in the united Province of Canada.

Canada East (1841–67) The name given to Lower Canada (Quebec) when it became a district of the united Province of Canada established by the Act of Union in 1840 as a result of the **Durham Report**. After confederation in 1867, Canada East became the Province of Quebec within the **Dominion of Canada**. ▷ **Confederation Movement; Papineau, Louis Joseph**

Canada First (1867–76) Canadian patriotic movement. It was founded by a number of young intellectuals who were later joined by business and professional men of Toronto disenchanted by the Treaty of **Washington**. Its journal, *The Nation* (edited by Goldwin **Smith**) was noted for its political commentary and in 1874 Edward **Blake** became the chief spokesman for the movement during his temporary defection from the **Liberal Party**. The **Clear Grits** and many Liberals disliked the movement because its demand that Canada be given the authority to negotiate its own treaties seemed to imply the dissolution

of the **British Empire**. Some of its members believed in the racial supremacy of the Anglo-Saxon inheritance, thinking French-Canada corrupt and priest-ridden and therefore likely to retard Canada's progress. Many however, like Blake, believed Canada's potential for greatness would only be realized if French Canada's cultural inheritance was recognized, so that her leaders would be free to cooperate in federal politics.

Canada West (1841–67) The name given to Upper Canada when it became a district of the united Province of Canada established by the Act of Union in 1840 as a result of the **Durham Report**. After confederation in 1867, Canada West became the Province of Ontario within the **Dominion of Canada**. ▷ **Confederation Movement**

Canaris, Wilhelm (1887–1945) German naval commander. He entered the Imperial German Navy in 1905, and served in the *Dresden* at the Battles of Coronel and the Falklands in **World War I**. He escaped from internment in Chile and made his way back to Germany, and served in U-boats in the Mediterranean. He retired with the rank of rear-admiral in 1934. Though disapproving of aspects of the Nazi regime, he rose under **Hitler** to become admiral of the German Navy and chief of the *Abwehr*, the military intelligence service of the High Command of the armed forces. Involved in the anti-Nazi resistance and associated with the 1944 bomb plot against Hitler, he was arrested, imprisoned and hanged in Apr 1945, just before the entry of the Soviet Army into **Berlin**. ▷ **Nazi Party**

Candia, War of The war fought between the Republic of Venice and the Turks for control of Crete. The conflict hinged on the defence of Candia which was besieged for over 20 years before surrendering in Sep 1669. Even after the fall of Candia, the Venetians did retain a presence on the island at Grabusa, Spinalonga and Suda, but these fell to the Turks between 1691 and 1715.

cangaço The golden age of the *cangaço*, the rural banditry in north-eastern Brazil, occurred between 1860 and 1930. The great droughts of 1877–9 and 1888–90, and the demise of slavery coincided with the decline of the region's importance in national politics and a long boom in cotton production. The result was to intensify feuding between powerful local landowners, whose ancient prerogative of *homísio* (personal protection to any individual seeking it) protected bandits. *Cangaceiros* were recruited from, and formed part of, the irregular forces which *coroneis* retained in order to preserve their local hegemonies, and their forces were enlisted by both federal and state authorities during the 1920s. Bandit leaders such as Antônio Silvino and **Lampião**, who led large and well-equipped bands in the sertão capitalized on the notion of the 'good thief', but were liquidated by the centralized federal government after the 1930 revolution. Their defiance of authority has made them popular heroes to this day.

Canisius, Petrus, SJ (1521–97) Dutch-born Jesuit reformer who was the leader of the Counter-Reformation in Germany. His Dutch name was Pieter Kanis, and in his function as the first Provincial of the German Jesuits he became known as the 'Second Apostle of Germany'.

Cannae, Battle of (216BC) The crushing defeat in southern Italy in the second of the **Punic Wars** of the Romans at the hands of **Hannibal**, the great Carthaginian general.

Canning, Charles John, 1st Earl (1812–62) British politician. He entered parliament in 1836 as Conservative MP for Warwick, but next year was raised to the Upper House as Viscount Canning by his mother's death, both his elder brothers having predeceased her. In 1841 he became Under-Secretary in the Foreign Office, and in 1856 he succeeded Lord **Dalhousie** as Governor-General of India. The war with Persia was brought to a successful close in 1857. In the same year (10 May), the **Indian Uprising** began with the outbreak at Meerut. Canning's conduct was described at the time as weak — he was nicknamed 'Clemency Canning' — but the general opinion later was that he acted with courage, moderation and judiciousness. In 1858 he became the first Viceroy of India, and in 1859 was raised to an earldom.

Canning, George (1770–1827) British politician. He entered parliament for Newport, Isle of Wight (1794) as a supporter of **Pitt**, 'the Younger'. He became Under-Secretary of State (1796), Treasurer of the Navy (1804–6), and Minister for Foreign Affairs (1807). His disapproval of the Walcheren expedition led to a misunderstanding with **Castlereagh**, which resulted in a duel. He became MP for Liverpool (1812), Ambassador to Lisbon (1814), President of

the Board of Control (1816), and MP for Harwich (1822). Nominated Governor-General of India (1822), he was on the eve of departure when Castlereagh's suicide saw him installed as Foreign Secretary. In this post he gave a new impetus to commerce by advocating tariff reductions. He was the first to recognize the free states of Spanish America; promoted the union of Britain, France, and Russia in the cause of Greece (1827); protected Portugal from Spanish invasion; contended earnestly for **Catholic Emancipation** (1829); and prepared the way for a repeal of the **Corn Laws**. In 1827 he formed an administration with the aid of the **Whigs**, but died the same year.

Canossa (1077) During the conflict between the empire and the papacy known as the **Investiture Controversy**, **Henry IV** (of Germans) had been excommunicated and his subjects thus released from their oath of allegiance to him. Henry offered unconditional submission to Pope **Gregory VII** at Canossa, spending three days barefoot in the snow in the dress of a penitent and was freed from the ban of excommunication. This allowed him to regain the support of the majority of the German nobles. It is debatable whether his move represented a genuine change of heart or shrewd political tactics, but Canossa marks the turning point in the empire's relationship with the papacy and the end of the tradition of imperial protection and domination of the Church in Germany. ▷ **Tribur, Princes' Meeting at**

Cánovas del Castillo, Antonio (1828–97) Spanish politician and historian. A Conservative, he became a member of the **Cortes** in 1854, and was Premier in 1875–81, 1884–5, 1890–2 and 1895–7, when he was shot by an anarchist. Cánovas was the architect of the oligarchical **Restoration System**, which survived until the dictatorship of General **Primo de Rivera** (1923–30).

Cantonalist Risings (1873) The failure of the Spanish First Republic to establish a unitary regime led to the emergence by July 1873 of scores of independent city-states, or cantons. Inspired by the ideas of the Catalan federalist **Pi i Margall**, the movement swept through eastern and southern Spain, embracing Barcelona, Cartagena, Granada, Malaga, Seville and Valencia. The cantonalists pursued a form of primitive communism, dividing up the large estates or common lands and adopting anticlerical measures. Under the presidency of **Castelar** the cantonalists were crushed by the army under General Pavía, Cartagena holding out until Jan 1874. ▷ **Republic, First** Spain

Canton System This term refers to the trading arrangements imposed by the Qing authorities on China's south-east coast during the latter half of the 18c and early decades of the 19c. Portuguese, Spanish, Dutch and British traders had begun arriving off China's coast from the 17c onwards but by the mid-1750s the **Qing Dynasty**, with the aim of regulating and supervising maritime trade, had limited contact to the port of Canton (Guangzhou). Foreigners (mostly British) had to deal with a licensed group of merchants (**Cohong**) and could only trade at certain times of the year. While at Canton they had to reside outside the city walls and their movements were restricted. Until the British East India Company's monopoly of the China trade was abolished, the system worked reasonably well; thereafter, with the increasing hostility of private British traders towards the restrictions and duties on commercial transactions and with the Chinese government's attempts to halt the increase of illegal opium sales, the system broke down. After the **Opium War** (1839–42) it was dismantled and China was compelled to open five treaty ports in which foreigners could reside and trade freely.

Canudos Campaign (1896–7) One of the bloodiest conflicts in Brazilian history, pitting one third of the federal army and police forces from several southern states against the local populace, led by Antônio Vicente Mendes Maciel, or the 'Councillor'. An educated messianic figure, who had long preached in the drought-stricken north-eastern interior, the Councillor founded Canudos as a centre of pilgrimage, but his practice of lay preaching brought him into conflict with the Church, and the economic independence of the settlement led to violent clashes with powerful politicians. The military capabilities of the Councillor's following were such that Canudos was seen as a 'monarchist redoubt': total destruction of his forces was necessary for the consolidation of the Republic under **Campos Salles**. This was widely viewed as a titanic clash between tradition and modernity: one which precipitated the demise of Jacobin nationalism in political life.

Canute (c.995–1035) King of England (1016/35), Denmark (1019/35) and Norway (1028/35). The younger son of **Svein I** Haraldsson, 'Fork Beard', he first campaigned in England in 1013, and after his father's death (1014) successively challenged **Ethelred the Unready** and **Edmund II, 'Ironside'** for the English throne. He defeated Edmund in 1016 at the Battle of Assandun, secured Mercia and Northumbria, and became King of all England after Edmund's death. In 1017 he married Emma of Normandy, the widow of Ethelred. He ruled England, according to the accepted traditions of English kingship, and maintained the peace throughout his reign. He died at Shaftesbury, Dorset. The story of his failure to make the tide recede was invented by the 12c historian, Henry of Huntingdon, to demonstrate the frailty of earthly power compared to the might of God. ▷ **Anglo-Saxons**

Cao Cao (Ts'ao Ts'ao) (150–220) Chinese military commander and poet. During the latter years of the Han Dynasty he was the predominant influence at court and became the virtual protector of the emperor. His military power was enhanced when he helped suppress the Yellow Turban Rebellion (184–215). The dynasty was fatally weakened, however, and imperial rivals established autonomous regimes in the south. Although Cao Cao consolidated his hold over north China, he was never able to extend his control to the south. On his death, Cao Cao's son, Cao Pei (Ts'ao P'ei), established a new dynasty in the north, the Wei. Although Chinese historiography has condemned Cao Cao as an unprincipled hegemon, he is credited with the promotion of efficiency in administration, devising a rating system for officials, and with the creation of state agricultural colonies in which dispossessed peasants were settled. ▷ **Han Dynasties**

Cao Dai/Hoa Hao Two major religious movements, established in **Cochin-China** (southern Vietnam) from the final decades of French rule. The Cao Dai religion, officially founded in 1926, claimed to be heir to all the religions of the world. It preached the virtues of spiritualism, Confucian piety and vegetarianism. Hoa Hao Buddhism, founded in 1939 by a charismatic faith-healer, Huynh Phu So, was extremely puritanical. It sought to eliminate idol worship and elaborate ritual. In the late 1940s the attractiveness of Cao Dai and Hoa Hao were a major obstacle to the advance of the **Viet Minh** in the rural south. The Hoa Hao was strongly hostile to the communists, to the extent that it was allied with the French against them. In 1947 the communists seized, tried and executed Huynh Phu So. The power of the sects in the politics of post-war southern Vietnam, reinforced over a number of years by French subventions, was sharply curbed by **Ngo Dinh Diem** in 1955.

Cape Coloured or **Coloured** A term used by the South African government to refer to a group of people of mixed descent, arising from the unions of Europeans with slaves (from Madagascar, Mozambique, or the East) or Khoikhoi (Hottentots). They number about 2.5 million people (c.nine per cent of the total population), mainly living in the towns and rural areas of the western Cape province. Culturally akin to White South Africans, most Coloureds speak Afrikaans and are Christian, with a small Muslim minority (Cape Malays). In South Africa's racial hierarchy, they are ranked between Europeans and Black Africans. They live in separate areas on city outskirts, with their own schools and other facilities, and have limited rights within the country's political system. They are mostly farm labourers, factory workers, and artisans, with a small middle class. Coloureds reject the classification Cape Coloured, and refer to themselves as 'so-called Cape Coloureds'. ▷ **apartheid**

Capellen tot den Poll, Joan Derk van der (1741–84) Dutch politician. He studied in Utrecht, and joined the States (Provincial Assembly) of Overijssel in 1772, where he vigorously opposed the policies of the aristocracy and urban patricians. In 1781 he published anonymously the pamphlet *To the People of the Netherlands*, which attacked the **Stadholder**'s government and proposed a democratic state based on popular sovereignty. This work had a profound effect on the Dutch **Patriot Movement**, which spread the ideals of the **French Revolution** to the Netherlands.

Cape St Vincent, Battle of (1797) A naval battle fought between British and Spanish fleets. Admiral Sir John Jervis (1735–1823) defeated a numerically superior Spanish force, thus preventing French plans for the assembly of a combined invasion fleet to conquer Britain. ▷ **French Revolutionary Wars**

Capet, Hugh (c.938–96) King of France (987/96). He was the founder of the third Frankish royal dynasty (the **Capetian Dynasty**), which ruled France until 1328. Son of

Hugh the Great, whom he succeeded as Duke of the **Franks** in 956, he was elected King and crowned at Noyon (987). His 40 years in power were marked by constant political intrigue and struggle, both among the feudal aristocracy and with his Carolingian rivals, but his position was invariably saved by the disunity of his enemies. ▷ **Carolingians**

Capetian Dynasty A French ruling dynasty for over 300 years (987–1328), founded by Hugh **Capet** in succession to the Carolingians. Two dynamic royal descendants were **Philip II** of France and St **Louis IX**. By increasing territorial control, enforcing the right to inherit of an eldest son, and devoting themselves to administration and justice, the Capetians laid the foundations of the French nation-state. ▷ **Bourbon, House of**

CAPETIAN DYNASTY

Regnal Dates	Name
987/96	Hugh Capet
996/1031	Robert II
1031/60	Henry I
1060/1108	Philip I
1108/37	Louis VI, 'the Fat'
1137/80	Louis VII
1180/1223	Philip II
1223/6	Louis VIII, 'the Lion'
1226/70	Louis IX (St Louis)
1270/85	Philip III, 'the Bold'
1285/1314	Philip IV, 'the Fair'
1314/16	Louis X, 'the Quarrelsome'
1316	John I
1316/22	Philip V, 'the Tall'
1322/8	Charles IV, 'the Fair'

Capitalist Encirclement (1928–53) An excuse used by **Stalin** to justify his dictatorship. In his attitude to the outside world, Stalin moved from advocating World Revolution to accepting peaceful co-existence. However, in order to maintain his control over the Communist Party and the people, he exaggerated the hostility of surrounding states, especially Britain, Germany, Japan and the USA, by raising the spectre of a terrible capitalist encirclement.

capitulary A document, normally divided into articles or chapters (Lat. *capitula*), recording individual verbal pronouncements made by a Carolingian king after consultation with his advisers. Some capitularies address a specific area of concern, such as legal or ecclesiastical matters; others are general in scope and mixed in content. ▷ **Carolingians**

Capitulations Originally these were commercial concessions dating back as far as Crusader and Mamluk times, such as freedom from customs duties and other forms of taxation, coupled with a civil form of diplomatic immunity so that foreign nationals were effectively under the jurisdiction of their consuls. These, as far as modern Egypt was concerned, were effectively a number of humiliating discriminatory privileges and concessions granted to certain foreign powers in Egypt, the end of which was finally negotiated in the Montreux Convention of 1937.

Capo d'Istrias, Ionnes Antonios ▷ **Kapodistrias, Ioannis**

Capone, Al(phonse) (1899–1947) US gangster. He achieved worldwide notoriety as a racketeer during the prohibition era in Chicago. Such was his power that no evidence sufficient to support a charge against him was forthcoming until 1931, when he was sentenced to 10 years' imprisonment for tax evasion. Released on health grounds in 1939, he retired to his estate in Florida, where he died.

Caporetto, Battle of (24 Oct–4 Nov 1917) The disastrous defeat for the Italian Army under **Cadorna** by the Austro-German forces of General Belov. The battle broke the stalemate which had characterized the first two years of the war in Italy. The Italians lost 300000 men and were forced back to the River Piave, where, with the assistance of French and British divisions, they managed to establish a defensive line. The defeat led to Cadorna's replacement by **Diaz**.

Cappadocia The ancient name for the mountainous region of central Turkey, between the Black Sea and the Taurus Mountains; a poor area without good natural defences, it tended to be ruled by whatever power was dominant in Asia Minor; a province of the Roman Empire from AD17.

Cap Party (Sweden) ▷ **Age of Liberty**

Caprivi, Georg Leo, Count von (1831–99) German soldier and politician. Entering the Prussian Army in 1849, he fought in the campaigns of 1864 and 1866, and in the **Franco-Prussian War** (1870–1) was Chief of Staff to the 10th Army Corps. As head of the Admiralty (1883–8), he reorganized the navy and then was made commander of his old army corps in Hanover. On **Bismarck**'s fall in 1890, he became Imperial Chancellor and Prussian Prime Minister. His principal measures were the army bills of 1892–3 and the commercial treaty with Russia in 1894. He was dismissed by the Emperor in 1894 for pursuing too liberal a policy. ▷ **Prussia**

Carabobo, Battle of (24 June 1821) A decisive victory by Simón **Bolívar** in the **Spanish–American Wars of Independence**, fought near Valencia, Venezuela. Bolívar and **Páez**'s forces of 6500 men defeated a smaller Spanish army, securing independence from Spanish forces demoralized by the return of General Morillo to Spain in the aftermath of the Riego revolt. However, the last royalist garrisons were not dislodged from Venezuelan soil until 1823.

Caracalla (188–217) Roman Emperor (211/17). The son of **Septimius Severus**, he is chiefly remembered for his enactment, the *constitutio Antoniniana* (212), which made all the free inhabitants of the empire Roman citizens, and for his sumptuous baths, whose impressive remains can still be seen in Rome. ▷ **Severan Dynasty**

Caracciolo, Prince Francesco (1752–99) Neapolitan naval commander. He served with the British in the American War of Independence, then entered the service of Ferdinand of Naples and became supreme commander of the Neapolitan navy. In Dec 1798 he fled with the King before the French from Naples to Palermo, but returned to Naples in 1798 and entered the service of the 'Parthenopean Republic'. For two months he ably directed the operations of the revolutionists, but was captured trying to escape in peasant disguise, and was hanged. ▷ **American Revolution**

Caractacus (Caratacus or **Caradoc)** (1c AD) Chief of the Catuvellauni. The son of Cunobelinus, he mounted a gallant but unsuccessful guerrilla operation in Wales against the Romans in the years following the Claudian conquest (AD43). Betrayed by the Brigantian queen, Cartimandua, he was taken to Rome (AD51), where he was exhibited in triumph, pardoned by **Claudius**, and later died. ▷ **Britain, Roman**

Carausius (Marcus Aurelius Mausaeus Carausius) (3c AD) Roman commander of the English Channel under **Diocletian** and Maximian. He rebelled and established an independent empire in Britain and north-east **Gaul** (c.287), which he ruled capably until his assassination (c.293).

Carbonari The members (literally, 'charcoal burners') of a liberal and patriotic secret society (the *Carboneria*) that emerged in southern Italy during the **Napoleonic Wars** and which spread to other areas of Italy, particularly after the Vienna Settlement. Usually anticlerical, the society borrowed many rituals and symbols from freemasonry, with which its origins are certainly connected. Although *Carbonari* were involved in a number of conspiracies and insurrections in different Italian states during the period 1817–31, they never possessed a clear programme or achieved any lasting victories. It is often hard to distinguish between the Carboneria and other similar but smaller groups such as the **Adelfi**, Guelfi and Federati. By the 1830s, however, most of these so-called sects had been superseded by better organized groups with more clearly defined (although by no means more realistic) liberal aims, usually seeking some degree of Italian unity and an end to Austrian hegemony in the peninsula. The Italian Carboneria was copied elsewhere in Europe, notably in Spain and France.

Cárdenas (del Río), Lázaro (1895–1970) Mexican general and politician. His presidency (1934–40) shaped modern Mexico. He promoted the return of the **ejido** in the south and the extension of the rancho (small property) principally in the north. His presidency also witnessed the creation of **PEMEX** from nationalized foreign (mainly British) companies, and the PRM (*Partido de la Revolución Mexicana*, Mexican Revolutionary Party), precursor of the **PRI**. Left-wing in his sympathies, he introduced many social reforms and reorganized the ruling party.

Cardigan, James Thomas Brudenell, 7th Earl of (1797–1868) British general. He entered the army in 1824, and purchased his promotion, commanding the 15th Hussars (until 1833), and then the 11th Hussars (1836–47). He commanded a cavalry brigade in the Crimea, and led the fatal charge of the Six Hundred (the **Charge of the Light Brigade**) against the Russians at the Battle of **Balaclava** (25 Oct 1854) in the **Crimean War**. He then became Inspector-General of Cavalry (1855–60). The woollen jacket known as a cardigan is named after him.

Cardozo, Benjamin (1870–1938) US jurist. He sat on the bench of the New York Court of Appeals from 1913 to 1932, during which time the court became internationally famous. Appointed to the US Supreme Court by President Herbert Hoover, he succeeded Oliver Wendell Holmes, serving for six years, 1932–8. Although he served for such a relatively brief time, and although many of his opinions dissented from the majority, he was remarkably influential because of his eloquence and learnedness. He was generally liberal and believed that the courts could effect social change.

Cardwell, Edward, 1st Viscount (1813–86) British politician. He became a lawyer (1838) and an MP (1842). First a Peelite, then a Liberal, he served as President of the Board of Trade (1852–55), Chief Secretary for Ireland (1859–61), Chancellor of the Duchy of Lancaster (1861–4), and Colonial Secretary (1864–6). As Secretary for War (1868–74), he carried out a major reorganization of the British Army. He was made a peer in 1874.

Carib American-Indian groups of the Lesser Antilles and neighbouring South America (the Guianas and Venezuela). The island Caribs were maritime people and warriors, who slowly drove the **Arawaks** from the islands. Most were slaughtered by Spaniards or wiped out by diseases brought in by Europeans in the 16c, and the survivors mixed with Spanish conquerors and later Negro slaves. The mainland Caribs led a more peaceful existence in small autonomous settlements in the tropical forests.

Caribbean Community (CARICOM) An association of former British colonies in the Caribbean, some of which (Barbados, Jamaica, and the Leeward Islands) existed as the Caribbean Federation, with the aim of full self-government, until the establishment of the Federation of the **West Indies** (1958–63). When Jamaica became independent in 1962, the Federation was dissolved. In 1969 certain of the remaining islands in the Windward and Leeward Islands were offered associated status within the **Commonwealth of Nations**, and in 1969 the West Indies Associated States was formed. In 1968 many of the islands agreed to the establishment of the Caribbean Free Trade Area (CARIFTA).

Carinthia (Kärnten) A federal state in southern Austria bordered by Styria, Italy and Slovenia. Part of Roman Noricum, it was settled by the Teutons, Avars and Slavs, and in the 8c became a part of Bavaria. Briefly subject to Bohemia, it passed to **Rudolf I** of Habsburg (1276) and then to the Count of

Tyrol (1286), finally becoming a Habsburg crown land in 1335. Remaining a distinct district with its capital at Klagenfurt, together with Styria and **Carniola** it formed Inner Austria. At the end of **World War I**, though it remained within Austria, parts were ceded to Italy and the Kingdom of Serbs, Croats and Slovenes (later Yugoslavia). During the **Anschluss** it became part of the Reichsgau Kärnten (1938–45) and since 1945 has been a federal state within Austria. It is populated mainly by Germans but has a large Slovene minority.

Carl XVI Gustav ▷ **Charles XVI Gustav**

Carleton, Sir Guy (Lord Dorchester) (1724–1808) Acting Governor (1767–70) and Governor (1786–91) of Quebec and Governor-in-Chief of British North America until 1798. General James **Wolfe**'s quartermaster at the capture of **Quebec** in 1759, he realized during his first tour of duty as Governor that the 13 North American colonies were close to rebellion and that British imperial authority would require a base which he set out to establish in Quebec. His belief that the maintenance of the seigniorial system would ensure French-Canadian loyalty was embodied in the **Quebec Act** of 1774 which, despite protests from the increased English-speaking population, was pushed through the House of Commons against bitter opposition. Carleton refused to consider the English speaking settlers' demands for *habeas corpus* and other aspects of English law, but in spite of resentment against this, it was they who took up arms against the US rebels when they invaded in 1775–6. Carleton's successful defence, however, was criticized for the slowness with which he pursued the rebels and he resigned. Sent out as Governor of Quebec again in 1786, he became Governor-General after the Constitutional Act of 1791. He disliked the division of Quebec into Upper and Lower **Canada**, and the introduction of elected assemblies, but his advice that Montreal be retained within Lower Canada was accepted. His continued concern for the military defence of Canada was illustrated by the inflammatory speech he made to Native Americans just before **Jay's Treaty** was signed in 1794, when he was sure that war with the USA was imminent. He resigned in 1794 and left the province in 1796.

Carlism A Spanish dynastic cause and political movement, officially born in 1833, but with its origins in the 1820s. Against the claim to the Spanish throne by **Isabella II**, daughter of Ferdinand VII, Carlists supported the claim of the latter's brother, Don **Carlos**. In the 19c, Carlism attracted widespread popular support chiefly in conservative, Catholic districts of rural northern Spain. In 1833–40, 1846–9 and 1872–6, Carlists fought unsuccessful civil wars against Spanish liberalism. After 1876, Carlism ceased to be a vehicle for widespread anti-capitalist protest and became a narrower movement espousing ultra-rightist, 'traditionalist' principles. It took the Nationalist side in the **Spanish Civil War**, providing c.100 000 volunteers. Since 1939, both during and after the **Franco** regime, the cause has suffered division and serious decline, although small Carlist groups persist.

Carloman (d.754) Frankish Mayor of the Palace. After the death of **Charles Martel**, his sons Carloman and **Pepin III, 'the Short'** shared the government of the Frankish kingdom under the Merovingian puppet king, Childeric III. Carloman ruled **Austrasia**, Thuringia and Alemannia and together the brothers subjected Aquitaine (745) and defeated Duke Gottfried of Alemannia. In 747 Carloman relinquished his rights in the government and withdrew to a monastery. ▷ **Franks; Merovingians**

Carloman (751–71) Frankish prince. The younger son of **Pepin III, 'the Short'** and brother of **Charlemagne**, he ruled the eastern **Franks** from 768. At his death Charlemagne took over his lands.

Carloman (c.829–80) King of the Eastern **Franks** and of Italy. The eldest son of **Louis the German**, on the death of his father in 876 he inherited Bavaria, Carinthia and Pannonia as well as a shaky claim to Bohemia and Moravia. He became King of Italy in 877. A serious illness forced him to abandon plans to be crowned Emperor and in 879 he relinquished his claims to Italy in favour of his brother **Charles III, the Fat**. His successor in Bavaria was his older brother, Louis III.

Carlos, Don (1545–68) Heir to the Spanish throne. The son of **Philip II** of Spain by his first wife, Maria of Portugal, he was recognized as heir to the Spanish throne by the Cortes of **Castile** (1560). A sickly child, who later showed signs of instability, he was alienated from his father while young, and was sent to study at Alcala de Henares. Twice (1565 and 1567) he attempted to escape from Spain, to Flanders and Germany. His hatred for his father led to his being tried for

163

conspiracy with rebel nobles from the Spanish Netherlands. He was found guilty (although sentence of death was not formally recorded) and died shortly afterwards in prison in unclear circumstances.

Carlos, Don (1788–1855) Spanish pretender. He was the second son of Charles IV of Spain. On the accession of his niece, **Isabella II**, in 1833, he asserted his claim to the throne. This claim was reasserted by his son, Don Carlos, the Count de Montemolin (1818–61), and by *his* nephew, Don Carlos (1848–1909). Carlist risings, whose principal strength lay in the Basque provinces and Navarre, occurred in 1833–40, 1846–9 and 1872–6. ▷ **Carlism**

Carlsson, Ingvar Costa (1934–) Swedish politician. Educated at Lund (Sweden) and North Western (USA) universities, he was secretary in the prime minister's office (1958–60) before entering active party politics. He became president of the youth league of the Social Democratic Labour party (SAP) in 1961, and in 1964 was elected to the Riksdag (parliament). After holding a number of junior posts (1967–76), he became deputy to Olof **Palme** in 1982 and succeeded him as prime minister and SAP leader after Palme's assassination in 1986.

Carmona, António (1869–1951) Portuguese politician and soldier. Having entered the army in 1888, he was made a general in 1922 and briefly served under the First Republic as Minister of War (1923). Following the coup d'état of 28 May 1926 against the Republic, Carmona emerged as de facto Prime Minister (from July 1926) and as President (from Nov 1926). Although he lacked a political programme, he was able to consolidate his position by balancing the various factions within the armed forces. As military dictator for six years (1926–32), he adopted a low profile, partly because he was an uncharismatic bureaucratic officer and partly because the regime was headed by a coalition of officers. Carmona oversaw the rise of **Salazar** and the **Estado Novo**, protecting him against opposition, especially during the major cabinet crises of 1929 and 1930. On the other hand, Salazar's success ensured Carmona's own future. Once Salazar was established as dictator, Carmona was content to act as a figurehead president. Although by 1945 he had become disillusioned with Salazar, his control over national affairs was by now negligible. He died as President, bitter at his political impotence. ▷ **Republic, First** (Portugal)

Carneiro Leão, Honorio Hermeto (Marquis de Paraná) (1801–56) Brazilian politician. Born into a powerful mercantile-landowning family, he became a lawyer and then Deputy for his native Minas Gerais (1833–41). A senator and councillor of state from 1842 to 1856, he was a moderate Conservative, who led a group responsible for the charting of policies which would enable the more powerful provinces, such as Minas Gerais, to accept the centralist rule of **Pedro II**. A shrewd political manager of the Chamber, he articulated the structure of the Empire, whereby central power was offset by the limited autonomy of local interests, tempered by the distribution of patronage. Master of the **conciliação**, he was Prime Minister in 1853–6 at the head of a cabinet of 'All the Talents', drawn from the ranks of moderate Liberals and Conservatives alike, committed to a broad programme of administrative reform and railroad building.

Carniola (Krain) A part of Roman Pannonia, it was settled by the Slavs (6c), emerging as a distinct district in the 10c. Subject to various princes and bishops, it became a Habsburg crown land (1335) and, remaining a distinct district with its capital at Laibach (Ljubljana), with **Carinthia** and Styria formed Inner Austria. Conquered by **Napoleon I**, Carniola was included within the **Illyrian Provinces** from 1809 to 1813. During the 19c it was the centre of the Slovene national awakening; in 1848, nationalists tried to form an autonomous Slovene kingdom within the Habsburg Monarchy but in 1849 Carniola was again organized as a crown land. In 1918 it became part of the Kingdom of Serbs, Croats and Slovenes (later Yugoslavia) and after 1947 it was absorbed, in its entirety, within Slovenia.

Carnot, Lazare (Nicolas Marguerite) (1753–1823) French politician. Known as the 'organizer of victory' during the **French Revolutionary Wars**, he entered the army as an engineer, and in 1791 became a member of the **Legislative Assembly** (1791–2). He survived the Reign of **Terror**, and became one of the Directors (1795), but in 1797, suspected of royalist sympathies, he escaped to Germany. Back in Paris, he became Minister of War (1800), and helped to organize the Italian and Rhenish campaigns. He commanded at Antwerp in 1814, and during the **Hundred Days** was Minister of the Interior. ▷ **French Revolution**

Carnot, Marie François Sadi (1837–94) President of the French Third Republic, grandson of Lazare **Carnot**. He studied at the Ecole Polytechnique, and became a civil engineer. In 1887 he was elected President and proceeded to stand firm against the Boulangist movement. Carnot was stabbed to death at Lyons by an Italian anarchist. ▷ **Boulanger, Georges; Republic, Third** (France)

Carol I, **Carol II** ▷ **Charles I, Charles II** of Romania

Caroline (of Brunswick), Amelia Elizabeth (1768–1821) Wife of **George IV** of the UK, the daughter of **George III**'s sister, Augusta. She married the Prince of Wales in 1795; but the marriage was disagreeable to him, and although she bore him a daughter, the Princess Charlotte, they lived apart. When George became King (1820), she was offered an annuity to renounce the title of Queen and live abroad; when she refused, the King persuaded the government to introduce a Divorce Bill. Although this failed, she was not allowed into Westminster Abbey at the coronation (July 1821).

Carolingians A Frankish ruling dynasty which rose to power as mayors of the palace, and ultimately replaced the **Merovingians** when **Pepin III, 'the Short'** became King of the **Franks** in 751. The Carolingian Empire created by **Charlemagne** embraced most of the former territory of the Roman Empire in the West. However, the Frankish custom of dividing land among all male heirs meant that the empire rapidly declined after Charlemagne's death. In 843, at the Treaty of **Verdun**, his three grandsons divided it into Eastern Francia, Western Francia, and the 'Middle Kingdom' stretching from the North Sea to Italy, and these soon dissolved into smaller states. ▷ **Charles Martel**

Carpetbaggers A derogatory term for US Northerners who went to the defeated South after the **American Civil War** to aid freed blacks and take advantage of the economic opportunities offered by Reconstruction. The term derived from Southerners' characterization of them as opportunistic transients who carried all their worldly goods in luggage made of carpet fabric. Though many were well-intentioned, others earned their reputation of corruption and rise to political power through exploitation of the black vote.

Carranza, Bartholomé de (1503–76) Spanish theologian. A Dominican, he became Professor of Theology at Valladolid, and in 1554 accompanied **Philip II** of Spain to England, where he was confessor to Queen **Mary I**, and where his zealous efforts to re-establish Catholicism gained him the confidence of Philip and the Archbishopric of Toledo. Here, however, he was accused of heresy, and imprisoned by the **Inquisition** in 1559. In 1567 he was removed to Rome, and confined in the castle of St Angelo. He died a few days after his release.

Carranza, Venustiano (1859–1920) Mexican politician. A senator under Porfirio **Díaz** and a supporter of **Madero**, he emerged as the leader of Constitutionalist forces against the dictator, Victoriano Huerta, in 1914. A fervent protagonist of Liberal aims, he was forced to accept the radical constitution of 1917, but limited agrarian reform to military measures, destroying **Zapata** and **Villa** in the process. He was assassinated when attempting to retain the presidency.

Carrero Blanco, Luis (1903–73) Spanish politician and naval officer. Director of Naval Operations in 1939, he later rose to the rank of admiral (1966). In 1941 he became an under-secretary to the presidency, and for the next 32 years he was effectively **Franco**'s right-hand man. He became a minister in 1951, Vice-Premier in 1967 and, in 1973, the first prime minister other than Franco since 1939. He was the political alter ego of Franco, not only because of his absolute loyalty, but also because he shared the same ultra-reactionary outlook, hating 'communists', 'freemasons', and 'liberals', although his visceral anti-Semitism set him apart. The key figure of the regime after Franco and the embodiment of continuity, his assassination by **ETA** (Dec 1973) was a grave blow to the regime.

Carrier, Jean Baptiste (1756–94) French revolutionary. In the National **Convention** he voted for the death of King **Louis XVI**, demanded the arrest of Louis Philippe Joseph, the Duke of **Orléans** (known as Philippe Egalité after renouncing his title), and assisted in the overthrow of the **Girondins**. At Nantes in 1793 he massacred 16 000 prisoners, chiefly by drowning them in the Loire (the *noyades*), but also by shooting them, as in a battue. After the fall of **Robespierre** he was tried, and perished by the guillotine.

Carrillo, Santiago (1915–) Spanish political leader. He became Secretary-General of the Socialist Youth at only 19. Jailed for participation in the Asturian rising of Oct 1934, he was a key figure in the merger of the Socialist Youth with the Communists before the **Spanish Civil War**. He has been widely held responsible for the massacre of Nationalist prisoners at Paracuellos de Jarama in Nov 1936. He became General-Secretary of the exiled **PCE** in 1960 and took the party from its neo-Stalinism to, in the 1970s, Eurocommunism. He returned to Spain in 1976. Although the PCE won 23 seats in the 1979 general election, it plummeted to a mere four in 1982. He resigned to found his own communist party, finally entering the **PSOE** in 1991. ▷ **Stalinism**

Carrington, Peter (Alexander Rupert), 6th Baron (1919–) British politician. A Conservative, he held several junior posts in government (1951–6), before becoming High Commissioner to Australia (1956–9). He then served as First Lord of the Admiralty (1959–63) and Leader of the House of Lords (1963–4). He was Secretary of State for Defence (1970–4) and briefly for Energy (1974), and also Chairman of the Conservative Party organization (1972–4). Upon the Conservative return to office he was Foreign Secretary (1979–82), until he and his ministerial team resigned over the Argentinian invasion of the Falkland Islands. He later became Secretary-General of **NATO** (1984–8), and **EC** mediator during the crisis in Yugoslavia (1991–2). ▷ **Conservative Party** (UK)

Carson, Edward Henry, Baron (1854–1935) Irish politician and barrister. He became a Conservative MP (1892–1921), a QC of the Irish Bar (1880) and English Bar (1894), and in 1895 became known for his successful prosecution of Oscar Wilde. He was Solicitor-General for Ireland (1892) and for England (1900–6), Attorney-General (1915), First Lord of the Admiralty (1916–17), and Lord of Appeal (1921–9). Strongly opposed to **Home Rule**, he organized the Ulster Volunteers. ▷ **Conservative Party** (UK)

Carson, Kit (Christopher) (1809–68) US frontiersman. A trapper and hunter, his knowledge of Native American habits and languages led to his becoming a guide in 1841 for John Frémont's explorations. He fought in the Mexican War (1846), was Indian agent in New Mexico (1853), and served the Union in the **American Civil War**.

Cartel des gauches (1924) Literally 'left-wing cartel', this term describes an electoral coalition in France of the radical, socialist and other left-wing parties which defeated the **Bloc national**.

Carter, Jimmy (James Earl) (1924–) US politician and 39th President. Educated at the US Naval Academy, he served in the US Navy until 1953, when he took over the family peanut business and other enterprises. As Governor of Georgia (1971–5), he showed sensitivity towards the rights of blacks and women. In the aftermath of the **Watergate** crisis he won the Democratic presidential nomination in 1976, and went on to win a narrow victory over Gerald **Ford**. As president (1977–81), he arranged the peace treaty between Egypt and Israel (1979), known as the **Camp David Accords**, and was concerned with human rights both at home and abroad. His administration ended in difficulties over the **Iran Hostage Crisis**, and the Soviet invasion of Afghanistan, and he was defeated by Ronald **Reagan** in the 1980 election.

Carteret, John, 1st Earl Granville (1690–1763) English politician. He entered the House of Lords in 1711, and became Ambassador to Sweden (1719), Secretary of State (1721), and Lord-Lieutenant of Ireland (1724–9). Chief Minister from 1742 to 1744, he was driven from power by the Pelhams (1744) because of his pro-Hanoverian policies, though from 1751 he was President of the Council under Henry **Pelham**, and twice refused the premiership. ▷ **Pelham, Thomas Pelham-Holles, 1st Duke of Newcastle; Walpole, Robert**

Carthage Ancient town in Tunisia, North Africa, now a suburb of Tunis; a world heritage site. Reputedly founded by the Phoenicians in 814BC, it was destroyed by Rome following the **Punic Wars** (146BC), but was refounded by **Caesar** and Octavian (29BC). Carthage was restored as a capital by the **Vandals** (AD439–533), but was again destroyed, by the Arabs, in 698.

Cartier, Sir George Étienne (1814–73) Canadian politician. Leader of the *Bleu* bloc of **Canada East**, he served with John **Macdonald** in 1854 to form a Conservative ministry. Cartier believed that the French Canadian nation would only survive if French Canadians worked together with English-speaking Canadians. He also recognized that his people not only needed legislation to maintain their cultural identity but that their economic betterment required the development of transportation and commercial schemes. As Attorney-General for the province and solicitor for the Grand Trunk Railway he was able to advance his people's interests as well as his own. In 1858 the Macdonald–Cartier administration was defeated, but reformed as the Cartier–Macdonald ministry in a mutual exchange of posts (the so-called 'double-shuffle'). This lasted until 1862, and Cartier returned to government in the great coalition of 1864 which negotiated confederation. Perhaps his greatest contribution to Canadian history was to impress the need for Union upon French-Canadians, although many modern French-Canadians think of him as the first *vendu*. Because of his involvement with the Canadian Pacific Railway and Sir Hugh **Allan**, he was defeated in 1872, became ill and died. ▷ **Bleus; Confederation Movement**

Carton de Wiart, Count Henri (1869–1951) Belgian politician, writer and historian. A Catholic, he founded the Christian-Democratic newspaper *L'Avenir Social* in 1891, and represented Brussels in the Belgian parliament. From 1911 to 1950 he was frequently a cabinet minister, holding at various times the portfolios of Justice, Home Affairs, Social Services and Public Health; in 1920–1 he was also Prime Minister.

Cartright, Sir Richard John (1835–1912) Canadian banker and politician. Having broken with the conservatives over the railway scandal of 1873, he became Finance Minister in Alexander **Mackenzie**'s Liberal administration of 1873–8, when he was the most prominent advocate of free trade and alienated many transport and industrial interests by his opposition to tariffs. After the liberals' victory in 1896 he was made minister for trade and commerce in **Laurier**'s cabinet. ▷ **Liberal Party** (Canada)

Casablanca Conference (Jan 1943) A meeting in North Africa between Franklin D **Roosevelt** and Winston **Churchill** during **World War II**, at which it was decided to insist on the eventual 'unconditional surrender' of Germany and Japan. Attempts to overcome friction between Roosevelt and the Free French under de **Gaulle** had only limited success. The combined Chiefs of Staff settled strategic differences over the projected invasion of Sicily and Italy.

casa del pueblo Spanish grass-roots political institution. Literally 'House of the People', the term describes a meeting-place and

educational, social and welfare centre for political activists. Based on a Belgian socialist model, the *casa del pueblo* was introduced into Spain in 1906 by the Republican populist Alejandro **Lerroux**. The first casa del pueblo opened in Barcelona with a clinic, theatre and a consumer cooperative, which provided insurance and pension schemes as well as legal aid. It was designed to replace the traditional and more exclusive Republican casinos, thereby helping to create a truly mass party by forging a new basis for collaboration between workers and the Republicans. The casas compensated for some of the glaring deficencies of the state's welfare provisions and became best-known as an important focus of support for the Socialist Party and its trade union movement, the **UGT**.

Casas, Bartolomé de las (1474–1566) Spanish priest and 'Protector of the Indians'. He sailed in the third voyage of Columbus (1502) to Hispaniola, where he settled as an *encomendero*. Convinced of the evil of the **encomienda**, in 1514 he gave up his Indians and began a campaign to achieve liberty for the natives with the help of the crown. In 1517 he was appointed 'Protector of the Indians' and began a series of unsuccessful experiments to set up colonies of Indian farmers. Disappointed by his failure, he entered the Dominican Order (c.1521) and went into retirement for about 10 years, during which time he began his major writings. Thereafter he dedicated his career to the liberation of the Indians. He undertook at least one more scheme for peaceful colonization of the natives, in Guatemala (1537–50), and was the first to suggest that black slaves be imported to substitute for Indian labour. He was influential in the Spanish court, from which in 1542 he obtained the New Laws, which decreed the end of **slavery** in America. Appointed Bishop of Chiapa in Guatemala (1544), he had to resign in the face of settler protests. In Spain in 1550 he took part in a famous debate in Valladolid on the morality of conquest in America.

Casement, Roger (David) (1864–1916) British consular official. He acted as Consul in various parts of Africa (1895–1904) and Brazil (1906–11), where he denounced the Congo and Putumayo rubber atrocities. Knighted in 1911, ill health caused him to retire to Ireland in 1912. An ardent Irish nationalist, he tried to obtain German help for the cause. In 1916 he was arrested on landing in Ireland from a German submarine to head the **Sinn Féin** rebellion, and hanged for high treason in London. His controversial 'Black Diaries', revealing, among other things, homosexual practices, were long suppressed by the government but ultimately published in 1959.

Casey, Richard Gardiner, Baron Casey (1890–1976) Australian politician. He was elected to the House of Representatives in 1931. He became first Australian Minister to the USA in 1940, Minister of State in the Middle East (a war-cabinet rank) in 1942, and Minister for External Affairs in 1951. A life peerage was conferred on him in 1960.

Casimir-Périer, Pierre (1777–1832) French politician and banker. He belonged to the liberal opposition under **Louis XVIII** and **Charles X**, joining the first government of **Louis-Philippe** after the **July Revolution** (1830), and was Prime Minister and Minister of the Interior (1831–2). He repressed insurrections in Paris and Lyons (1832).

Cassander (c.358–297BC) King of Macedonia (306/297 BC). He assumed power over Macedonia after the death of his father, **Antipater**, in 319BC, and became its king some thirteen years later. An active figure in the power struggle after the death of **Alexander III, 'the Great'** (323BC), he murdered Alexander's mother, widow and son, and contributed to the defeat of **Antigonus Monophthalmos** at Ipsus in 301BC.

Cassin, René (1887–1976) French jurist and politician. During **World War II** he joined General de **Gaulle** in London. He was principal legal adviser in negotiations with the British government and, in the later years of the war, held important posts in the French government in exile in London and Algiers, and subsequently in the Council of State (of which he was President, 1944–60) in liberated France. He was the principal author of the Universal Declaration of the Rights of Man (1948) and played a leading part in the establishment of UNESCO. He was a member of the European Court of Human Rights from 1959, and its President (1965–8). In 1968 he was awarded the Nobel Prize for Peace.

Cassius (Gaius Cassius Longinus) (d.42BC) Roman soldier, politician, and tyrannicide. An opponent of Julius **Caesar** during the civil war with **Pompey the Great**, he was pardoned by Caesar after their defeat at the Battle of **Pharsalus** (48BC). Despite

168

gaining political advancement through Caesar, he later turned against him again, and played a leading part in the conspiracy to murder him (44BC). Defeated by Caesar's avengers at Philippi (42BC), he committed suicide. ▷ **Brutus, Marcus Junius**

Cassivellaunus (1c BC) King of the Catuvellauni, a British tribe living in the area of modern Hertfordshire. He led the Catuvellauni in resistance to Julius **Caesar** on his second invasion (54BC). ▷ **Britain, Roman**

Castanos, Francisco Xavier de, Duke of Bailen (1756–1852) Spanish soldier. During the **Peninsular War** (1808–14) he compelled 18000 French to surrender at the Battle of Bailén (1808), but was defeated by Lannes at Tudela. Under **Wellington** he took part in the Battles of Albuera, Salamanca, and Vitoria (1813). In 1843 he was appointed guardian of Queen **Isabella II** of Spain.

caste A system of inequality, most prevalent in Hindu Indian society, in which status is determined by the membership of a particular lineage and associated occupational group into which a person is born. The groups are ordered according to a notion of religious purity or spirituality thus, the Brahmin or priest caste, as the most spiritual of occupations, claims highest status. Contact between castes is held to be polluting, and must be avoided. Caste was officially abolished in the Constitution of Independent India in 1951. However, controversy has erupted in the 1980s and 1990s over the extension of 'reservations' — a policy of positive discrimination in the allocation of government posts and student places in universities — intended to remove the disadvantages of, and prejudices against, the lower castes created by the caste system. ▷ **Mandal Commissions**

Castelar Y Ripoll, Emilio (1832–99) Spanish politician and writer. He studied at Madrid, where he was Professor of History and Philosophy (1856–65). A leader of the Republicans, he fled to Paris in 1866 but returned at the 1868 revolution, and in 1873 helped to bring about the downfall of King Amadeus I. He was made head of government in Sep 1873, crushing the **Cantonalist Risings** in the provinces. He resigned in Jan 1874, and fled on **Alfonso XII**'s accession. He returned to Spain in 1876, becoming leader of the Possibilist Republican Party, which merged with the monarchist Liberal Party upon his withdrawal from political life in 1893.

Castelo Branco, Humberto de Alencar (1900–67) Brazilian politician. He was educated at the Pôrto Alegre Military Academy in Rio Grande do Sul and at France's École Supérieure de Guerre, as well as the General Command course at Fort Leavenworth, USA. He went on to fight with the Brazilian army in Italy, and coordinated the anti-**Goulart** military conspiracy of 1964. Linked to other veteran officers in the Escola Superior da Guerra, founded in the 1940s in Rio de Janeiro, his foreign policy was anti-communist, and he believed that short-term arbitary technocratic measures should be taken to create the conditions for democracy. As President from 1964 to 1967, although the economy had been stabilized, the financial system reorganized and foreign debt renegotiated, his government failed to alter traditional patterns of authority and prevent the emergence of hard-line factions amongst the military, which established the 'tutelary regime' which survived until 1985.

Castiglione, Baldassare, Count (1478–1529) Italian author and diplomat. Educated at Milan, he began a career at court, and in 1505 was sent by the Duke of Urbino as envoy to **Henry VII** of England, who made him a knight. His chief work, *Il Cortegiano* (1528, The Courtier), is a manual for courtiers. He also wrote Italian and Latin poems, and many letters illustrating political and literary history.

Castiglione, Battle of (5 Aug 1796) An important victory for **Napoleon I** over the Austrian forces commanded by General Wurmser sent from the South Tyrol to relieve the blockade of Mantua.

Castile, Kingdom of The central region and component kingdom of Spain. The United County of Spain was formed in 970, and during the 11c and most of the 12c was subject to the suzerainty of Leon of Navarre. Hegemony over Leon was established in 1188, and the union of the Castilian and Leonese crowns took place in 1230. The union of crowns with the Kingdom of Aragon (1469–79), the Conquest of Granada (1492), and the annexation of Navarre (1512) created the basis of the modern Spanish state. ▷ **Granada, Conquest of**

Castle, Barbara Anne (1911–) British politician. She became Labour MP for Blackburn (1945–87) and was Chairman of the Labour Party (1958–9), Minister of Overseas Development (1964–5), and a controversial Minister of Transport (1965–8), introducing a 70 mph speed limit and the 'breathalyser' test for drunken drivers. She became Secretary of State for Employment and Productivity (1968–70) and Minister of Health and Social Security (1974–8). She then returned to the backbenches, but became Vice-Chairman of the Socialist Group in the European Parliament in 1979, when she became an elected member of that body, a post she held until 1985. ▷ **Labour Party** (UK); **socialism**

Castlereagh, Robert Stewart, Viscount (1769–1822) British politician. The son of an Ulster proprietor, he became Whig MP for County Down in 1790, turning Tory in 1795. He was created Viscount Castlereagh in 1796, and became Irish Secretary (1797), President of the Board of Control (1802), and Minister of War (1805–6 and 1807–9). His major achievements date from 1812, when, as Foreign Secretary under Lord **Liverpool**, he was at the heart of the coalition against **Napoleon I** (1813–14). He represented England at Chaumont and the Congress of **Vienna** (1814–15), Paris (1815), and Aix-la-Chapelle (1818). He advocated 'Congress diplomacy' among the great powers, to avoid further warfare. Believing that he was being blackmailed for homosexuality, he committed suicide at Foots Cray, his home in Kent. ▷ **Tories; Whigs**

Castors Canadian political epithet. *Castor* (meaning 'beaver') was the signature on a pamphlet of 1882, entitled *Le Pays, le parti et le grand homme*, which attacked Joseph Adolphe **Chapleau** and J A Mousseau for becoming members of **Macdonald**'s cabinet. The name was given to right-wing conservatives in Quebec in the following year when their newspaper adopted the beaver as its emblem. *Castors* were ultramontane Catholics and racialists, the counterparts of extremist British Protestants.

Castro (Ruz), Fidel (1927–) Cuban revolutionary. He studied law in Havana and in 1953 was imprisoned after an unsuccessful rising against **Batista**, but released under an amnesty. He fled to the USA and Mexico, then in 1956 landed in Cuba with a small band of insurgents. In 1958 he mounted a full-scale attack and Batista was forced to flee. He became Prime Minister (1959–), later proclaimed a 'Marxist-Leninist programme', and set about far-reaching reforms. His overthrow of US economic dominance, and the routing of the US-connived émigré invasion at the **Bay of Pigs** (1961) was balanced by his dependence on Soviet aid. Castro became President in 1976. Although Cubans gained substantially in terms of general social provision, by the late 1980s the economic experiment had failed, and the collapse of the USSR isolated his regime.

Catalan Autonomy Statutes (1932 and 1979) Catalonia (the 'land of castles') has always been distinguished from the rest of Spain by its culture, language and geography. The dynastic union of Ferdinand of Aragon (which included Catalonia) and Isabella of Castile in 1469 allowed Catalonia to retain its laws and privileges until the end of the War of the **Spanish Succession** in 1714. **Philip V** of Spain thereupon abolished the *fueros* (medieval laws and customs) and the **Generalitat**, a parliament of medieval origin. During the late 19c a Catalan nationalist movement developed which eventually led to the establishment of a limited form of self-government in the shape of the Mancomunitat in 1913, only to be abolished by the dictatorship of General **Primo de Rivera** in 1923. However, the Second Republic (1931–6) provided Catalonia with an autonomy statute in Sep 1932. This restored the Generalitat, proclaimed Catalan as the official language, and gave the Catalans control over most regional issues, although the period of self-government was cut short by **Franco**'s victory in the **Spanish Civil War**. In 1977 the Generalitat was revived and in 1979 Catalonia regained its autonomy with a substantial measure of home rule. ▷ **Republic, Second** (Spain)

Catalaunian Plains, Battle of the (451) The decisive defeat in eastern France suffered by **Attila** the Hun at the hands of the Romans and **Visigoths**. Deflected from France, he turned south to Italy, which he ravaged the following year.

Catalonia An autonomous region of northeast Spain, comprising the provinces of Barcelona, Gerona, Lérida, and Tarragona, and formerly including Roussillon and Cerdana. Catalonia united with Aragon in 1137, and a medieval trading empire developed in the 13c and 14c. It became part of Spain following the union of the Castilian and Aragonese crowns (1469–79). There has been a strong Catalan separatist movement since the 17c, and a Catalan autonomy statute was eventually granted in Sep 1932. This was, however, abolished by **Franco** during the **Spanish Civil War**. A new government was established in 1979. ▷ **Catalan Autonomy Statutes**

Catalonia, Revolt of (1640–52) The rising which took place after decades of political tension between the Catalan authorities and the central government of **Castile**. It was provoked directly by the Count-Duke of **Olivares**, whose imperial ambitions spawned a plan for a Union of Arms, which the Catalans rejected. In 1635, when Spain went to war against France, Olivares deliberately centred the conflict on the Catalan frontier, in order to stir the Catalans to defend themselves. The billeting of Castilian troops in the province provoked uprisings, and the murder of the Castilian viceroy in Barcelona during the 'Corpus of Blood' in 1640. The Catalan leadership used the crisis to declare the separation of the province from Spain and its adherence to France. The experience of French rule was, if anything, worse and, after a long siege, the city of Barcelona capitulated to the Castilian army under Don **Juan José of Austria** in 1652.

Cataví Massacre (21 Dec 1941) An attack on striking Bolivian tin-miners and their families by Bolivian soldiers at the Cataví mining camp, in which several hundred people were killed. The incident brought about the emergence of the powerful silver miners' union, culminating in the upheaval of Dec 1943, which brought the MNR (*Movimiento Nacionalista Revolucionario*) to power, with Víctor **Paz Estenssoro** as mentor. Cataví was chosen as the ceremonial site for the nationalization of Bolivia's tin mines in Oct 1952, under Estenssoro's presidency.

Cateau-Cambrésis, Treaty of (2–3 Apr 1559) The treaty agreed between the French and Spanish crowns which brought an end to the wars of **Charles V** in Europe. It recognized Italy as an area of Spanish influence and Franche-Comté as part of the Spanish monarchy, and confirmed France in possession of Metz, Toul and Verdun. A dynastic marriage was also agreed between **Philip II** of Spain and Elizabeth Valois, daughter of **Henry II** of France.

Cathay A name for China made famous by Marco Polo in the 13c. It derived from the Mongol *Khitai*, another name for the **Khitan**, a semi-nomadic tribe that founded the Liao Dynasty (916–1125) and controlled northern China (to which this term originally referred) from its southern capital in what is now Beijing.

Catherine I (1684–1727) Empress of Russia (1725/7). Of lowly birth (probably Lithuanian peasant stock), she was baptized a Roman Catholic with the name of Martha. Married as a young girl to a Swedish army officer who deserted her, she subsequently became mistress to a Russian general, Boris Sheremetev, and to the Tsar's principal minister, Prince Alexander **Menshikov**. In 1705 she became mistress to Tsar **Peter I, 'the Great'**, changing her name to Catherine and converting to Orthodoxy in 1708. The Tsar married her (his second wife) in 1712, following her distinguished conduct while on campaign with her husband during the wars against Sweden. In 1722 Peter passed a law allowing the tsar to nominate a successor and in 1724 chose Catherine, having her crowned Empress in that year. After his death in 1725, Prince Menshikov ensured her succession to the throne. Although she continued her husband's reforms, she had neither Peter's strong will nor his sense of purpose. She was, however, concerned to alleviate conditions for the peasantry, lowering taxation and reducing the power of local bureaucracies. She was succeeded by his grandson, **Peter II**.

Catherine II, 'the Great' (1729–96)

Empress of Russia (1762/96). Originally Princess Sophia Augusta of Anhalt-Zerbst, she was born at Stettin and in 1745 was married to the heir to the Russian throne (later **Peter III**). Their marriage was an unhappy one, and Catherine (now baptized into the Russian Orthodox Church under that name) spent much of her time in political intriguing and extra-marital affairs. In 1762 a palace coup overthrew her unpopular husband, and she was proclaimed Empress. She carried out an energetic foreign policy and extended the Russian Empire south to the Black Sea as a result of the **Russo-Turkish Wars** (1774 and 1792) while in the west she brought about the three partitions of Poland. Despite pretensions to enlightened ideas, her domestic policies achieved little for the mass of the Russian people, though great cultural advances were made among the nobility. In 1774 she suppressed the popular rebellion led by Pugachev, and later actively persecuted members of the progressive-minded nobility. Her private life was dominated by a long series of lovers, most notably Potemkin. ▷ **Poland, Partitions of; Pugachev, Emelyan; Romanov Dynasty**

Catherine de' Medici (1519–89) Queen of

France. The daughter of Lorenzo de' Medici, she became the wife of **Henry II** of France, and was Regent from 1560 to 1574. During the minority of her sons, **Francis II** (1559–60)

and **Charles IX** (1560–3), she assumed political influence which she retained as Queen Mother until 1588. She tried to pursue moderation and toleration, to give unity to a state increasingly torn by religious division and aristocratic faction, but she nursed dynastic ambitions, and was drawn into political and religious intrigues, conniving in the **St Bartholomew's Day Massacre** (1572). ▷ **Huguenots**

Catherine of Aragon (1485–1536) Queen of

England. The fourth daughter of **Ferdinand II, 'the Catholic'** and **Isabella I, 'the Catholic'** of Spain, she became the first wife of **Henry VIII**. She was first married in 1501 to Arthur (1486–1502), the son of **Henry VII**, and following his early death was betrothed to her brother-in-law, Henry, then a boy of 11. She married him in 1509, and bore him five children, of whom only the Princess Mary (later **Mary I**) survived. In 1527 Henry began a procedure for divorce, which he obtained in 1533, thereby breaking with the Pope, and starting the English Reformation. Catherine then retired to lead an austere religious life until her death. ▷ **Reformation** (England)

Catherine of Braganza (1638–1705) Wife

of **Charles II** of England. The daughter of King **John IV** of Portugal, she was married to Charles in 1662 as part of an alliance between England and Portugal, but failed to produce an heir. She helped to convert him to Catholicism just before his death, after which she returned to Portugal (1692), where she died.

Catholic Emancipation (1829) A reluctant

religious concession granted by the British Tory government, headed by the Duke of **Wellington**, following mounting agitation in Ireland led by Daniel **O'Connell** and the Catholic Association. Roman Catholics were permitted to become MPs; and all offices of state in Ireland, except Viceroy and Chancellor, were also opened to Catholics. ▷ **Tories**

Catholic League The league formed during

the **Jülich–Cleves Succession Conflict** (1609–14) by the German Catholic princes, led by **Maximilian I** of Bavaria. It sided with the Emperor in the **Thirty Years War** and was instrumental in his victory at the Battle of the **White Mountain** (1620). The league withdrew its support from Emperor Ferdinand and **Wallenstein** because of the radical changes proposed by Ferdinand. The league's terms, imposed on Ferdinand with French support at Regensburg (1630), weakened the Emperor and encouraged the invasion of Pomerania by **Gustav II Adolf** of Sweden. The league dissolved after the Swedes defeated the Imperial army under **Tilly** at Magdeburg (1631).

Catholic People's Party (*Katholieke Volkspartij*, KVP) Dutch political party, founded in 1945 as a continuation of the Roman Catholic National Party (RKSP, founded 1922). Traditionally the Catholic Party in the Netherlands polled about a third of the votes; in the 1960s that percentage began to drop radically, due to general secularization and the departure of various Catholic splinter groups. As a result the KVP decided in 1973 to join the Dutch Protestant parties in an interconfessional grouping, the **Christian Democratic Appeal** (CDA), and in 1980 the KVP ceased to exist as a separate party. As a centre party the KVP was regularly in government, and it (or the CDA) has taken part in all Dutch cabinets since **World War II**.

Catiline (Lucius Sergius Catalina) (d.62BC) An impoverished Roman politician of patrician extraction who tried to exploit the economic unrest of Rome and Italy in the 60s BC for his own political ends. His conspiracy against the state was foiled by **Cicero** late in 63BC, and he fell in battle early in 62BC.

Cato, Marcus Porcius, 'the Elder' (234–149BC) Roman politician, orator and man of letters. Deeply conservative, and strongly opposed to the contemporary fashion of all things Greek, when made censor (184BC) he conducted such a vigorous campaign that he was thereafter known as 'Censor'. Sent on a mission to Carthage (175BC), he was so impressed by the power of the Carthaginians that afterwards he ended every speech in the Senate with the words: *Carthago delenda est* ('Carthage must be destroyed'). ▷ **Punic Wars**

Cato, Marcus Porcius, 'the Younger' (95–46BC) Roman politician. He was the great-grandson of **Cato, 'the Elder'**. A man of uncompromising principles and deep conservatism, his career was marked by an unswerving opposition to Julius **Caesar**. A supporter of **Pompey the Great** in the civil war, after the Battle of **Pharsalus** (48BC) he escaped to Africa. On hearing of Caesar's overwhelming victory at **Thapsus** (46BC), he killed himself.

Cato Street Conspiracy (Feb 1820) A plot formulated by Arthur Thistlewood (1770–1820) and fellow radical conspirators, to blow up the British Tory cabinet as it attended a dinner at the house of the Earl of Harrowby. The plot was infiltrated by a government agent, and the leaders were arrested and hanged. ▷ **radicalism; Tories**

Cats, Jacob (1577–1660) Dutch statesman and poet. After studying law at Leiden and Orléans, he settled at Middelburg. He rose to a position of authority in the state, and was twice ambassador in England (1627 and 1652). From then till his death, 'Father Cats' lived at his villa near the Hague, writing the autobiography printed in the 1700 edition of his Poems.

Catt, Carrie Clinton Chapman (1859–1947) US suffragist. In 1887 she joined the Iowa Woman Suffrage Association and quickly climbed the ranks of the national movement. Succeeding Susan B **Anthony** as president of the **National American Woman Suffrage Association** in 1900, her strategy of working on both state and national levels and through both political parties led to the ratification of the 19th Amendment in 1920 and secured the suffrage for women. She organized the Women's Peace Party during **World War I**.

Cattaneo, Carlo (1801–69) Italian politician and political economist. He wrote extensively during the pre-1848 period on agriculture, communications, education, finance, charity and public works. In 1835 he married an English noblewoman and was consulted during the 1830s by the British government on reform and agriculture in India and Ireland. Essentially a gradualist reformer who never preached open rebellion against Austrian rule, he nevertheless became head of the Milanese council of war during the anti-Austrian **Cinque Giornate** (Mar 1848). He was, however, suspicious of the pro-Piedmontese, aristocratic faction which soon came to dominate Milan and left for Paris. After the collapse of the **Revolutions of 1848–9**, he spent many years in exile in Switzerland; he returned to Milan in 1859 after its annexation by the Kingdom of **Sardinia**. He was elected Deputy in 1860 and 1867 but never attended parliament. He did, however, continue to write on politics and in 1860 was summoned to Naples by **Garibaldi** to serve as *prodittatore*.

caudillo The term (literally 'chief') often used in Spanish-speaking countries to refer to a dictator, especially (but not exclusively) in the 19c. It was much used of General **Franco** of Spain.

Cavaco Silva, Anibal (1939–) Portuguese politician. After studying economics in Britain and the USA, he became a university teacher and then a research director in the Bank of Portugal. With the gradual re-establishment of constitutional government after 1976, he was persuaded by colleagues to enter politics and was Minister of Finance (1980–1). In 1985 he became leader of the Social Democratic Party (PSD) and Prime Minister. Under his cautious, conservative leadership, Portugal joined the European Community (EC) in 1985 and the Western European Union (WEU) in 1988.

Cavaignac, Louis Eugène (1802–57) French soldier. Having commanded the French Army in Algeria, he became Governor-General there in 1848, but was soon recalled to Paris and became Minister of War. He quelled the formidable insurrection of the **June Days** (1848), and ruled France thereafter as Prime Minister, until the election of Louis Napoleon (**Napoleon III**) as President in Dec 1848. In the coup d'état of Dec 1851 he was arrested but soon released; and though he refused to adhere to the Second Empire, he was permitted to reside in France.

Cavalier Parliament The name given to the British parliament of 1661–79. Until the crisis over the **Popish Plot** it usually supported the King, its name deriving from royalist support during the **English Civil Wars**. It passed legislation in the 1660s and early 1670s to strengthen the Church of England and to discriminate against Puritans and Nonconformists who had been dominant during the English revolution. ▷ **Charles II** (of England)**; Puritanism**

Cavaliers Those who fought for **Charles I** in the **English Civil Wars**. The name was used derogatorily in 1642 by supporters of parliament to describe swaggering courtiers with long hair and swords, who reportedly welcomed the prospect of war. Similarly, the parliamentarians were labelled 'Roundheads' by Cavaliers, dating from the riotous assemblies in Westminster during **Strafford's** trial in 1641, when short-haired apprentices mobbed Charles I's supporters outside the House of Lords.

Cavendish, Spencer Compton, 8th Duke of Devonshire (1833–1908) British politician, known as the Marquis of Hartington. A Liberal, he entered parliament in 1857, and between 1863 and 1874 was a Lord of the Admiralty, Under-Secretary for War, War Secretary, Postmaster-General, and Chief Secretary for Ireland. In 1875 he became leader of the Liberal Opposition during **Gladstone's** temporary abdication, later serving under him as Secretary of State for India (1880–2) and as War Secretary (1882–5). He disapproved of Irish **Home Rule**, and, having lead the breakaway from the **Liberal Party**, became head of the Liberal Unionists from 1886, serving in the Unionist government as Lord President of the Council (1895–1903).

Cavendish, William, Duke of Newcastle (1592–1676) English soldier and patron of the arts. He was created Knight of the Bath in 1610, Viscount Mansfield in 1620, and Earl (1628), Marquess (1643), and Duke (1665) of Newcastle. He gave strong support to **Charles I** in the **English Civil Wars**, and was general of all forces north of the Trent. After the Battle of **Marston Moor** (1644) he lived on the Continent, at times in great poverty, until the Restoration. A noted patron of poets and dramatists, he was himself the author of several plays, and of two works on horsemanship.

Cavour, Camillo Benso di, Count (1810–61) Italian politician. Abandoning his early military career, he spent most of the 1830s and 1840s concentrating on the scientific farming of his estates or travelling. His visits to England left him a deep admirer of the British liberal institutions, railways, industry and banking. In 1847 he founded a progressive journal, *Il Risorgimento*, but he played no part in the events of 1848. He entered politics in 1849, and held various ministerial posts under **D'Azeglio** before replacing him as Prime Minister (Nov 1852); he was to remain Premier until his death, except for a few months in 1859. Cavour's early policy was based on the economic development and modernization of the Kingdom of Sardinia-Piedmont, fostering commerce, ending restrictions on banking and improving communications. From 1855, however, he concentrated increasingly on foreign affairs, perhaps achieving his greatest success with the **Plombières Agreement** which laid the basis for the Piedmontese acquisition of Lombardy. In 1860 the Expedition of the **Thousand** to Sicily and **Garibaldi's** subsequent victories in the **Mezzogiorno** caused Cavour considerable anxiety: he feared that the former Mazzinian might establish a republican government in the south or attempt to capture Rome, which would jeopardize good relations with France. He consequently tried to place the south under more moderate leadership. Having failed to achieve this end, he sent Piedmontese troops through the **Papal States** (annexing Umbria and the Marche en route) to block Garibaldi's northward advance. Much to his relief, Garibaldi happily surrendered his conquests to **Victor Emmanuel II**. In the last months of his life, Cavour made an abortive attempt to secure Rome through purchase and diplomacy.

CCF (Cooperative Commonwealth Federation) Canadian socialist political party. Founded in Calgary in 1932, and first meeting held at Regina in 1933 by representatives of intellectual groups, organized labour, socialists and farmers, it was led by J S **Woodsworth**. The 'Regina Manifesto' included economic planning, central financial control and price stabilization, the extension of public ownership in communications and natural resources, the creation of a welfare state and an emergency relief programme. By 1934 the party had become the official opposition in Saskatchewan and in British Columbia, and hundreds of CCF clubs had sprung up throughout the country (except in the Maritimes Provinces and Quebec). The party avoided the fate of the US **Socialist Party** because of its strong adherence to parliamentary principles and the support it was given by both trade unionists and intellectuals, although it was damaged severely by **Duplessis**'s **Padlock Act**. In Ontario the CCF became the official opposition in 1943, while in the following year it was elected into government in Saskatchewan. Its challenge forced the Liberals into a far stronger emphasis on social reforms, and such federal legislation as the 1944 Families Allowances Act led to a decrease in support for CCF during the election of 1945. The continuation of this trend in **Liberal Party** policies eventually led the CCF to drop the most doctrinaire elements from its manifesto in 1956. In 1961 the party evolved into the **New Democratic Party** with 'Tommy' **Douglas**, the CCF Premier of Saskatchewan, as its leader.

CCM ▷ **Chama Cha Mapinduzi**

CCOO (Comisiones Obreras) Spanish trade union organization (literally, 'Workers' Commissions'). Its origins lay in the spontaneous rank and file committees set up in the late 1950s in the Asturian coalfields and the Basque country to organize strike action. By the mid-1960s, it had established a parallel organization to the official syndicate; thereby it became the first democratic broadly-based union organization in Spain since the **Spanish Civil War**. By the late 1960s it was firmly under Communist control, being severely repressed after the major demonstration of 1967 until **Franco**'s death in 1975. It is now one of the two main trade union forces in Spain.

CDU (*Christlich Demokratische* Union, 'Christian Democratic Union') German political party. An ideologically heterogeneous collection of regional organizations gradually coalesced between 1947 and 1950 to form the main party of government in post-war Federal Germany. The CDU has roots in the pre-1933 **Centre Party**, but it functions as a multi-denominational, 'people's' party committed to social progress within a **social market economy**. Its membership is socially diverse, but with a definite middle-class flavour; initially more within the independent middle classes, now among salaried and professional groups. It dominated government under the leadership of Konrad **Adenauer** (1949–63) and presided over Germany's great economic miracle (**Wirtschaftswunder**), but in 1966 was forced into coalition with the **SPD** and in 1969 went into opposition. Under Helmut **Kohl** the CDU regained power in 1982 with its customary ally, the **CSU**, and with the **FDP**. This coalition oversaw the reunification of Germany during 1989 and 1990.

Ceauşescu, Nicolae (1918–89) Romanian politician. Born into a peasant family, he joined the Communist Party in 1936 and was imprisoned for anti-government activities (1936–8). He became a member of the Central Committee of the Romanian Communist Party (RCP) in 1952 and of the Politburo in 1955. In 1965 he succeeded **Gheorgiu-Dej** as *de facto* party leader, becoming General-Secretary of the RCP in 1965 and its first President in 1967. Under his leadership, Romania became increasingly independent of the USSR and pursued its own foreign policy, for which Ceauşescu was decorated by many Western governments. In internal affairs he extended the rigid programme of his Stalinist predecessor, instituting a strong personality cult and filling offices with his family. He manipulated Romanian nationalism and ruthlessly forced national minorities to adopt Romanian culture. His policy of 'systematization' in the countryside, uprooting traditional villages, roused an international outcry in the late 1980s. In 1989 he was deposed when elements in the army joined a popular revolt. Following a trial by military tribunal, he and his wife, Elena, who had been second only to him in political influence, were shot.

Cecil, Robert, 1st Earl of Salisbury (c.1563–1612) English minister, son of William **Cecil**, 1st Baron Burghley. He entered parliament in 1584. He became a Privy Councillor (1591) and was appointed **Elizabeth I**'s Secretary of State (1596). His years of control in the last years of the reign helped to smooth the succession of James VI of Scotland to the English throne. James maintained him in office and he negotiated peace terms ending the long war with Spain (1604). He was an efficient administrator and financial manager who fought a losing battle against mounting royal debts. ▷ **James VI and I**

Cecil, Robert (Arthur Talbot Gascoyne), 3rd Marquis of Salisbury (1830–1903) British politician. He became a Conservative MP in 1853. In 1865 he was made Viscount Cranborne, and in 1868 Marquis of Salisbury. He was twice Indian Secretary (1866 and 1874), became Foreign Secretary (1878) and, on **Disraeli**'s death (1881), Leader of the Opposition. He was Prime Minister on three occasions (1885–6, 1886–92 and 1895–1902), also serving much of the time as his own Foreign Secretary. He resigned as Foreign Secretary in 1900, but remained as head of government during the **Boer Wars** (1899–1902). He retired in 1902.

Cecil, William, 1st Baron Burghley (Burghleigh) (1520–98) English statesman. He served under Somerset and Northumberland, was made Secretary of State (1550) and knighted (1551). During **Mary I**'s reign he conformed to Catholicism. In 1558 **Elizabeth I** appointed him chief Secretary of State, and for the next 40 years he was the chief architect of the Elizabethan regime, controlling the administration, influencing her pro-Protestant foreign policy, securing the execution of **Mary, Queen of Scots**, and preparing for the Spanish **Armada**. In 1571 he was created Baron Burghley, and in 1572 became Lord High Treasurer (an office he held until his death).

CEDA (*Confederación Española de Derechas Autónomas*, 'Spanish Confederation of Autonomous Rightist Groups') Spanish political party. The CEDA, founded in Feb 1933, was the principal non-Republican conservative force under the Second Republic. Ultimately, the proto-fascist CEDA aimed to replace the Republic by an authoritarian, corporatist state: many of its goals were assumed by **Franco**. The CEDA dominated the governments of 1933–5 through an alliance with the **Radical Republican Party**, demolishing the reforms of 1931–3 and preparing the army for a rising. Its legalistic strategy for power was thwarted by the collapse of the Radicals, the President's refusal to allow the CEDA to head an administration and, finally, its failure to win the general election of Feb 1936. The party not only provided funds for the rising of July 1936, but the vast majority of its members joined the Nationalists. However, there was no place for the CEDA in Nationalist Spain, so it was dissolved in Apr 1937. ▷ **Republic, Second** (Spain)

Ceka The gang of hired thugs, often recruited from the criminal classes, employed by **Mussolini** to intimidate his political opponents. Their attacks were responsible for the death of **Matteotti** and for the flight from Italy of, among others, **Nitti** and **Amendola**. They were also used to harass **fuorusciti**.

Celtiberia The territory in north-central Spain inhabited by the Celtiberians, a warlike people of mixed Celtic and Iberian ancestry. Staunch opponents of the Romans, they were pacified in 133BC after decades of intermittent but fierce resistance.

Celts Different groups of prehistoric peoples who all spoke Celtic languages and lived in most parts of Europe from the Balkan regions to Ireland. Most powerful during the 4c BC, they probably originated in present-day France, southern Germany, and adjacent territories during the Bronze Age. Celtic-speaking societies developed in the later first millennium BC, expanding through armed raids into the Iberian Peninsula, British Islands, Central Europe, Italy, Greece, Anatolia, Egypt, Bulgaria, Romania, Thrace, and **Macedonia**. They were finally repulsed by the Romans and Germanic tribes, and in Europe withdrew into Gaul in the 1c BC. Celtic tradition survived most, and for longest in Ireland and Britain. They were famous for their burial sites and hill forts, and their bronze and iron art and jewellery.

Censorate A Chinese government institution during imperial times with its origins in the 3c BC, which was responsible for the investigation of official conduct in central and local administration. Censors could report directly to the emperor and impeach officials for violating administrative regulations or moral standards. As the upholders of proper moral conduct in government, censors occasionally criticized emperors, although they might be treated harshly for such action. By the time of the **Ming Dynasty** and **Qing Dynasty**, the censorate had virtually become merely the emperor's tool for controlling the bureaucracy.

CENTO (Central Treaty Organization)
A political-military alliance signed in 1955 between Iran (which withdrew after the fall of the Shah), Turkey, Pakistan, Iraq (which withdrew in 1958), and the UK, as a defence against the USSR.

Central African Federation (1953–63) A
federal territory established by the British Government to bring together the administrations of Northern and Southern Rhodesia and Nyasaland (now Zambia, Zimbabwe and Malawi). It was designed to act as a counterweight to South Africa, which had been dominated by the Afrikaans Nationalists since the election of 1948, and to encourage investment in the region. Theoretically its society and government were to be developed on the basis of racial partnership, but in reality it became a means for the extension of white settler power. It stimulated African nationalist resistance and an emergency was declared after disturbances broke out in Nyasaland in 1959, together with strikes and political activism in Northern Rhodesia. After the Devlin and Monckton Commission reports the Federation was wound up, leading to the independence of Zambia and Malawi and the unilateral declaration of independence in Rhodesia.

Central American Common Market (CACM) An economic association initiated
in 1960 between Guatemala, Honduras, El Salvador, Nicaragua, and (from 1963) Costa Rica. Its early apparent success was offset by growing political crisis in the late 1970s. ▷ EEC

Central American Federation (CAF) A
federation formed in 1823, following independence from Spain, by Costa Rica, Nicaragua, Honduras, El Salvador, and Guatemala. Despite vigorous leadership by Francisco Morazán (1792–1842) of Honduras, internal tensions brought about the collapse of the federation by 1838.

Central Committee of the Communist Party of the Soviet Union Under Soviet
party rules, this was the highest decision-making authority in the USSR, apart from the Party Congress, which elected it. Except in rare circumstances (twice in Nikita **Khrushchev**'s time), however, it exercised little influence, partly because of its unwieldy size and partly because of the concentration of power in the **Politburo**.

Central Intelligence Agency ▷ CIA

Central Powers Initially, the members of
the **Triple Alliance** (Germany, Austria-Hungary, Italy) created by **Bismarck** in 1882. As Italy remained neutral in 1914, the term was later used to describe Germany, Austria-Hungary, their ally Turkey, and later Bulgaria in **World War I**.

Centre Party (Germany; *Zentrum*) Ger-
man political party. This interest-group party was founded in 1870–1 after the creation of the German **Reich**, to defend the rights and identity of the Catholic Church and the Catholic minority (33 per cent of the population) within the country. By the turn of the century, the Centre Party had long escaped the **Kulturkampf**, or political persecution it initially suffered under **Bismarck** and from 1918 onward played a key role in the creation and governance of the **Weimar Republic**. It contained politicians and supporters right across the social spectrum, whose politics were only accommodated with difficulty during the 20c. A staunch opponent of **Hitler** at the end of Weimar, the Centre Party then supported his enabling legislation in Mar 1933 in return for guarantees on the rights of Catholics. The Centre dissolved itself in July 1933.

Centre Party (Sweden) The name adopted
in 1958 by the Agrarian Party, which had been formed in 1921 by the union of a number of farmers' groups. It supported the Social Democrats between 1932 and the later 1950s and indeed joined them in coalition governments in 1936–45 and 1951–7. After this, the party moved away from its former allies. It took up the environmentalist and anti-nuclear cause and succeeded in broadening its electoral base. In 1976–82 the leader of the party, Torbjörn Fälldin, headed non-socialist coalition governments.

Centurioni The members of the militia established in the **Papal States** by Cardinal Tommaso Bernetti after the liberal uprisings of the early 1830s. They were stigmatized by liberal writers as little better than bandits.

Ceresole, Battle of ▷ **Italian Wars**

Cerezo Arevalo, Mario Vinicio (1942–) Guatemalan politician. Educated at San Carlos University, Guatemala, he joined the Christian Democratic Party (PDCG), founded in 1968. From 1974 there was widespread political violence and democratic government was virtually suspended. With the adoption of a new constitution in 1985, the PDCG won the congressional elections and Cerezo became the first civilian president for 20 years.

Cerignola, Battle of ▷ **Italian Wars**

Černík, Oldřich (1921–) Czechoslovak politician. A man of reasonable ability, he worked his way up through the official hierarchy to become Chairman of the State Planning Commission in 1963. As such, he favoured moderate change to make the economy more efficient. However, in Jan 1968, when Alexander **Dubček** became General-Secretary, Černík became Prime Minister and followed a more far-reaching reform policy. In July and Aug of the same year he tried to restrain the more radical supporters of the **Prague Spring**, and after the Soviet invasion he struggled to try to retain something of its achievements. But within two years, like Dubček, he was removed from the party and the government.

Černý, Jan (1874–1959) Czechoslovak official and politician. Partly as a result of its proportional representation system, interwar Czechoslovakia had, on occasions, difficulty in finding a coalition government. In two such periods (1920–1 and 1926), President **Masaryk** employed the device of appointing a cabinet of officials. In both of these, Černý acted as Prime Minister and did an efficient job. His experience as an official in the Ministry of the Interior stood him in good stead, although it added to his unpopularity among the social democrats in particular. He subsequently served brief periods as Minister of the Interior, including just before and after the **Munich Agreement**.

Céspedes, Carlos Manuel de (1819–73) Cuban nationalist. 'The Father of the Country' came from a wealthy plantation family and studied law in Spain before returning to Cuba. There he raised a revolt against the Spanish colonial government instigating the **Ten Years War** in Oriente. With 200 poorly-armed men, he took Santiago and freed the slaves and in 1869 devised a constitution and was elected provisional President of the incipient republic. However, in 1873 he was deposed by the revolutionary council; he went into hiding, but was captured by the Spanish and shot.

Cetewayo (c.1826–84) King of the Zulu (1872/9). In Jan 1879 he defeated an entire British regiment at Isandhlwana, but was himself overcome by British forces under Sir Garnet **Wolseley** at Ulundi in July of the same year. However, so eloquently did Cetewayo present his case in London, that in Jan 1883 he was restored by the British as ruler of central Zululand. Shortly thereafter, though, he was driven out by his subjects, and died at Ekowe.

CGT (*Confédération générale du travail*, 'General Confederation of Labour') French trade-union organization, formed in 1895, which today claims a membership of about 2 million, mainly production and blue-collar workers. It is now closely linked to the **Communist Party**, but originally adopted by the Charter of Amiens (1906) a policy of avoiding all links with political parties and espousing the doctrines of revolutionary syndicalism (according to which the trade union movement should destroy capitalist society through strike action, and create a new society run by the workers' unions, as opposed to State socialism). By 1921 it had evolved to a moderate position, which led to a schism, and the founding of the CGTU (*Confédération générale du travail unitaire*), which soon came to be controlled by the Communist Party. The CGT and CGTU were reunited in 1936, under the CGT banner; after being banned during **World War II**, the CGT emerged under communist control, which led to a new schism in 1948, with the formation of the CGT *Force ouvrière*, ('Workers' Force'), close at that time to the **Socialist Party** and consisting mainly of civil servants and clerical workers. There are several other trade-union federations, of which the most important are the *Confédération française démocratique du travail* (CFDT, 'French Democratic Confederation of Labour') formed in 1964, out of the *Confédération française des travailleurs chrétiens* (CFTC, 'French Confederation of Christian Workers'), a Catholic federation originally established in 1920, which however also continued to exist. There is also the *Confédération générale des cadres* (CGC) founded in 1944, consisting mainly of white-collar workers. One of the largest unionized workforces, the schoolteachers, have their own *Fédération de l'éducation nationale* (FEN) independent of all the general federations. The main characteristics of French trade-unionism are its fragmentation and weakness; a much smaller proportion of workers are members of any trade union than in comparable economies.

Chaadayev, Pyotr A (1794–1856) Russian writer and political critic. Particularly in periods of repression, it became the function of Russian authors overtly or covertly to discuss political issues. In 1836, during **Nicholas I**'s autocratic reign, Chaadayev published his *Philosophical Letters*, critical of Russia's political and cultural achievements and specifically of the link between the state and the Orthodox Church. For a time, Nicholas declared him mad and ordered him to be examined regularly by doctors. However, his ideas were much discussed and opened what became a prolonged and heated debate between the old 'easterners' and new 'westerners'.

Chaco War (1932–5) A territorial struggle between Bolivia and Paraguay in the disputed Northern Chaco area. Owing to the brilliant tactics of Colonel José Félix **Estigarribia**, Paraguay won most of the area, and a peace treaty was signed in 1938. Around 50 000 Bolivians and 35 000 Paraguayans died in the war. The outcome of the war decisively shaped the history of the decades which followed, defeat ultimately contributing to the formation of the MNR (*Movimiento Nacionalista Revolucionario*) in Bolivia, and victory to a succession of dictatorships in Paraguay, culminating in that of Alfredo **Stroessner** in 1954.

Chadli, Benjadid (1929–) Algerian politician and soldier. In 1955 he joined the guerrillas (*maquisards*) who were fighting for independence as part of the **FLN**. Under Houari **Boumédienne**, Defence Minister in **Ben Bella**'s government, he was military commander of Algiers, and then when Boumédienne overthrew Ben Bella in 1965 he joined the Revolutionary Council. He succeeded Boumédienne as Secretary-General of the FLN and President of Algeria in 1979.

Chaeronea (Khaironeia), Battle of (338BC) The decisive defeat in **Boeotia** of the Greeks at the hands of **Philip II** of Macedon which effectively ended the political independence of the Greek city-states.

Chahamanas ▷ **Chauhans**

Chak(k)ri Dynasty A Siamese dynasty founded in 1782 by General P'raya Chakri, who as Rama I (1782/1809) established his capital at Bangkok, and instituted a period of stability and prosperity in Siam; also known as the 'Bangkok Dynasty'. His successors, especially Rama III (1824/51), Rama IV (1851/68), and Rama V (1868/1910), opened the country to foreign trade and championed modernization. The dynasty still reigns under the constitutional monarchy established after a bloodless revolution in 1932. ▷ **Chulalongkorn**

Chalcedon, Council of (AD451) The fourth ecumenical council, called by Emperor Marcian. This council formulated the doctrine of two natures of Christ, perfect, indivisible yet separate. It thus, by standing midway between the two, condemned both monophysites and Nestorians. It maintained that the source of salvation was a saviour, at the same time perfect God and perfect man. In condemning both monophysites and Nestorians it naturally led to contentiousness between the 'new' Byzantine orthodoxy and the monophysitism of Syria and Egypt and the Nestorians, who (Nestorius having been condemned by the (third) Council of Ephesus) were beginning to flourish in the East.

Chaldaeans Originally the name of a Semitic people (Kaldu) from Arabia who settled in the region of Ur in Lower Mesopotamia, in the 7c and 6c BC, it became a generic term for Babylonians.

Chalukyas An Indian ruling dynasty which flourished in two main branches. The Western Chalukyas controlled Deccan (543–757 and c.975–c.1189), with capitals at Vatapi and Kalyani. The Eastern Chalukyas ruled what is present-day Andhra Pradesh from Vengi (c.624–c.1070).

Chama Cha Mapinduzi (CCM) Sometimes referred to as the Revolutionary Party of Tanzania, this party was formed in 1977 by the merger of **Tanganyika African National Union** (TANU) and the Afro-Shirazi Party. It is the only legal party in Tanzania, but is relatively pluralist with active women's, youth, and local branches.

Chamberlain, Sir (Joseph) Austen (1863–1937) British politician. The eldest son of Joseph **Chamberlain**, he was elected a Liberal Unionist MP in 1892, and sat as a Conservative MP until his death in 1937. He was Chancellor of the Exchequer (1903–6 and 1919–21), Secretary for India (1915–17), Unionist leader (1921–2), Foreign Secretary (1924–9), and First Lord of the Admiralty (1931). He received the 1925 Nobel Peace Prize for negotiating the **Locarno Pact**. ▷ **Conservative Party** (UK)

Chamberlain, Joseph (1836–1914) British politician. He entered the family business at 16, and became Mayor of Birmingham (1873–5), and a Liberal MP (1876). In 1880 he became President of the Board of Trade, but in 1886 resigned over **Gladstone**'s **Home Rule** Bill, which split the **Liberal Party**. From 1889 he was leader of the Liberal Unionists, and in the coalition government of 1895 took office as Secretary for the Colonies. In 1903 he resigned office to be free to advocate his ideas on tariff reform, which split the Conservative and Unionist Party. In 1906 he withdrew from public life after a stroke. ▷ **Chamberlain, Austen; Chamberlain, Neville; Conservative Party** (UK); **radicalism**

Chamberlain, (Arthur) Neville (1869–1940) British politician. He was the son of Joseph **Chamberlain** by his second marriage. He was Mayor of Birmingham (1915–16), a Conservative MP from 1918, Chancellor of the Exchequer (1923–4 and 1931–7), and three times Minister for Health (1923, 1924–9 and 1931), where he effected notable social reforms. He played a leading part in the formation of the National Government (1931). As Prime Minister (1937–40), he advocated '**appeasement**' of Italy and Germany, returning from Munich with his claim to have found 'peace in our time' (1938). Criticism of his war leadership and initial military reverses led to his resignation as Prime Minister (1940), and his appointment as Lord President of the Council. ▷ **Conservative Party** (UK); **Munich Agreement; World War II**

Chambord, Henri Charles Dieudonné, Count of (1820–83) French **Bourbon** pretender as 'Henri V', grandson of King **Charles X** of France. Born in Paris after the assassination of his father, the Duke of Berry, he was taken into exile after the abdication of Charles in 1830. The National Assembly elected in 1871 had a royalist majority and his restoration to the throne seemed possible,

but his refusal to accept the tricolour flag rendered this abortive.

Chamoun, Camille (1900–87) Lebanese politician. The curious constitutional provisions of Lebanon after its independence provided for a Muslim Prime Minister and a (Maronite) Christian President. Camille Chamoun held the presidency from 1952 until 1958. A pro-USA Maronite, his reluctance to surrender the presidency to Fuad Chehab, a Maronite more acceptable to Lebanese Muslims, led to the outbreak of civil war. His policy aimed at peaceful coexistence between Christians and Muslims, but his support for France and Britain during the Suez Crisis seriously undermined the credibility of his regime. His position was only saved during the civil war by the intervention, in 1958, of US Marines (who caused a stir by coming ashore on the bathing beaches of the Lebanese coast). Although he did not seek re-election, he continued in politics and in 1980 his National Liberal Party split from the Phalangists. He survived an assassination attempt in 1987, but died later the same year.

Champa A state founded on the east coast of Vietnam in the 2c AD that developed along the Indian pattern of state organization and was a serious rival to Khmer and Vietnamese power in the peninsula up to the 16c. Less than 100 000 Chams survive today.

Champlain, Samuel de (c.1570–1635) French navigator and Governor of **New France**. In a series of voyages he travelled to North America (1603), exploring the east coast (1604–7), and founding Quebec (1608). He was appointed commandant of New France (1612), and established alliances with several Indian nations. When Quebec fell briefly to the British, he was taken prisoner (1629–32). From 1633 he was Governor of Quebec. Lake Champlain is named after him. ▷ **fur trade**

Chandellas A North Indian dynasty prominent in the 10–12c as one of the successor states to their former overlords, the **Pratiharas**. The first major reigns of Harsha (c.900/ c.925) and Yashovarman (c.925/c.950) saw their rise at the expense of the Pratiharas, as well as the start of their notable temple building at their early capital, Khajuraho (later to become a purely religious centre), in a distinctive and highly ornate style. Their main rivals were the neighbouring dynasty, the Kalachuris of Tripuri. The last significant ruler was Paramardi (1165/1202), the latter half of whose reign saw prolonged conflicts with the Chahamanas of Shakambhari (**Chauhans**) and the plundering of their later capital, Mahoba, in 1182. The dynasty was overthrown in the Muslim conquest of North India with the capture of their stronghold, Kalanjara, in 1202 by **Qutb-ud-Din Aibak**.

Chandragupta (Sandracottus) (c.350–c.250BC) Hindu Emperor of **Pataliputra** (Palibothra), to whom Megasthenes was sent by Seleucus I Nicator (c.300BC).

Chandragupta II (Vikramaditya) (c.380/c.415) Indian Emperor. The third of the imperial Guptas of northern India, he extended control over his neighbours by both military and peaceful means. A devout Hindu, he tolerated Buddhism and Jainism, and patronized learning. During his reign, art, architecture and sculpture flourished, and the cultural development of ancient India reached its climax.

Changamire The dynastic title of the rulers of southern Zimbabwe from 1480 until the mid-17c. In 1480 a vassal-ruler of the Changa people took advantage of the weakness of the empire of Monomotapa to declare himself an independent amir (Changa Amir). During the 17c the Changamire also conquered most of northern Zimbabwe (Mutapa) and formed a powerful barrier to the incursions of Portuguese traders, eager to obtain access to the substantial gold-mining industry there.

Chang'an (Ch'ang-an) Chinese imperial capital on the site of present-day Xi'an (Sian) in Shaanxi (Shensi) province. Known as Xianyang during the **Qin Dynasty** (221–207BC), Chang'an became the capital of the Former Han Dynasty (202BC–9AD). During this time it became an important metropolis surrounded by a wall 33 feet high and 16 miles in circumference. Sacked by northern nomadic tribes in AD316, the city became an imperial capital again during the **Sui Dynasty** (581–618). It reached its apogee during the **Tang Dynasty** (618–907), when it became a cosmopolitan centre embracing cultural and religious influences from central Asia and beyond. After the fall of the Tang the city declined in importance and was never again used as the imperial capital. ▷ **Han Dynasties**

Chang Kuo-t'ao ▷ **Zhang Guotao**

Chao Tzu-yang ▷ **Zhao Ziyang**

Chapleau, Sir Joseph Adolphe (1840–98) Canadian politician. As leader of the

180

moderate **Bleus**, John **Macdonald** invited him into the cabinet in 1882 to balance the inclusion of the extremist Sir Hector **Langevin**. The Rouge leader, Honoré **Mercier**, asked him to lead the movement of protest at the execution of **Riel** but since he believed the sentence was just, he refused. However, he did resign in 1892 to become Lieutenant-Governor of Quebec. ▷ **Rouges**

Chaptal, Jean Antoine (Count of Chantaloupe) (1756–1832) French politician and chemist. He took a leading part in the introduction of the metric system of weights and measures. He was equally successful as a chemical manufacturer and a writer on industrial chemistry. He was Minister of the Interior from 1800 to 1804. Ennobled by **Napoleon I**, he served as a minister in his **Hundred Days** (1815).

Chapultepec, Act of (1945) Signed in Mexico, this act established that American states should aid each other in the event of aggression from any source whatsoever. It also met the need to coordinate, by a single instrument, the various measures calling for the peaceful settlement of disputes in the Inter-American system. It was designed as a regional counterpoise to the UN. Its corollary was the Inter-American Treaty of Mutual Assistance (TIAR), subsequently signed in Rio de Janeiro, and the Organization of American States (OAS), drawn up in Bogotá in 1948, as well as the Inter-American Treaty on Pacific Settlement (Pact of Bogotá) outlining procedures for the peaceful settlement of Inter-American disputes. Subsequent amendments have strengthened the economic and social functions of the OAS.

Charge of the Light Brigade An incident during the Battle of **Balaclava** (1854), when the Light Brigade, under the command of the Earl of **Cardigan**, charged the main Russian artillery. The charge involved massive loss of life. It resulted from the misunderstanding of an order given by the commanding officer, Lord **Raglan**, to stop guns captured by the Russians being carried away during their retreat.

Charlemagne (742–814) King of the **Franks** (771/814) and Emperor of the West (800/14). He was the eldest son of **Pepin III, 'the Short'**. He defeated the **Saxons** (772–804), as well as the **Lombards** (773–4), fought the Arabs in Spain, and took control of most of Christian Western Europe. In 800 he was crowned Emperor by Pope **Leo III**. In his later years he consolidated his vast empire, building palaces and churches, and promoting Christianity, education, agriculture, the arts, manufacture and commerce, so much so that the period has become known as the Carolingian Renaissance. ▷ **Carolingians**

Charles I of Spain ▷ **Charles V** (Holy Roman Emperor)

Charles I (1600–49) King of England and Ireland (1625/49). He failed in his attempt to marry the Infanta Maria of Spain (1623), marrying instead the French princess, Henrietta Maria (1609–69). This disturbed the nation, since the marriage articles permitted her the free exercise of the Catholic religion. Three parliaments were summoned and dissolved in the first four years of his reign; then for 11 years (1629–40) he ruled without one, making much use of prerogative courts. He warred with France (1627–9), and in 1630 made peace with Spain, but his growing need for money led to unpopular economic policies. His attempt to anglicize the Scottish Church brought active resistance in the **Bishops Wars** (1639–40), and he then called a parliament (1640). Having alienated much of the realm, Charles entered into the First of the **English Civil Wars** (1642–6), which saw the defeat of his cause at the Battle of **Naseby**, and he surrendered to the Scots at Newark (1646). After many negotiations, during which his duplicity exasperated opponents, and a second Civil War (1646–8), he came to trial at Westminster, where his dignified refusal to plead was interpreted as a confession of guilt. He was beheaded at Whitehall (30 Jan 1649). ▷ **Long Parliament**

Charles I (1839–1914) King of Romania (1881/1914). He was the second son of Prince Karl Anton, head of the Catholic southern branch of the Prussian ruling dynasty. Designated as a suitable candidate by the liberal Ion **Brătianu**, he was made Prince of Romania in 1866 and became Romania's first king after the country received full independence from the **Ottoman Empire**. A patriotic Prussian yet loyal to Romanian interests, active in government as a constitutional monarch and a clever politician, he became a strong and popular leader. On account of his concern for economic development, Romania was in this respect the most advanced of the Balkan states on the eve of **World War I**.

Charles I (1887–1922) Last ruler of the Austro-Hungarian monarchy (1916/18). He succeeded his grand-uncle, Francis Joseph, in 1916, having become heir presumptive on the assassination at Sarajevo (1914) of his uncle, Archduke Francis Ferdinand. In Nov 1918 he was compelled to abdicate upon the collapse of Austria-Hungary. Two attempts at restoration in Hungary (1921) failed, and he died in exile in Madeira.

Charles II (1630–85) King of England and Ireland (1660/85). He was the son of King **Charles I**. As Prince of Wales, he sided with his father in the **English Civil Wars**, and was then forced into exile. On his father's execution (1649), he assumed the title of King, and was crowned at Scone (1651). Leading poorly organized forces into England, he met disastrous defeat at the Battle of **Worcester** (1651). The next nine years were spent in exile until an impoverished England, in dread of a revival of military despotism, invited him back as King (1660). In 1662 he married the Portuguese Princess **Catherine of Braganza**. It was a childless marriage, though Charles was the father of many illegitimate children. His wars against the Dutch (1665–7 and 1672–4) were unpopular, and the first of these led to the dismissal of his adviser, Lord **Clarendon** (1667), who was replaced by a group of ministers (the **Cabal**). He negotiated subsidies from France in the Secret Treaty of Dover (1670), by which he also promised **Louis XIV** to make England Catholic once more. He negotiated skilfully and sometimes unscrupulously between conflicting political and religious pressures, and, during the **Exclusion Crisis** (1678–81) refused to deny the succession of his Catholic brother, James. For the last four years of his life, he ruled without parliament. ▷ **Anglo-Dutch Wars; Popish Plot**

Charles II (1661–1700) King of Spain (1665/1700). The son of **Philip IV** of Spain, he was the last ruler of the Habsburg Dynasty in Spain. Congenital ill health made him unfit to rule, and government was conducted first by a regency under his mother, then by his half-brother, Don **Juan José of Austria**, and finally by various noble factions. The reign was one of positive advances in many areas of economy, demography and culture, but the dominant reality was the collapse of Spanish power in Europe as a result of the aggressions of **Louis XIV** of France. Peace treaties of 1684 and 1697 resulted in substantial territorial gains for France. The King's inability to produce an heir precipitated disputes over the succession, and his nomination of the

French Duke of Anjou (later **Philip V** of Spain) as next king led directly to the War of the **Spanish Succession**.

Charles II (1893–1953) King of Romania (1930/40). Involved in a scandalous affair with Magda Lupescu, he renounced his right of succession (1925) and went to live in Paris. In 1930 he returned to Romania as King and succeeded in concentrating political power in his own hands during the subsequent rapid changes of ministry. In 1938 he established a royal dictatorship, gaining full powers through a new constitution, organizing his own political party, the Front of National Rebirth, and adopting many of the themes of the fascist-style **Iron Guard**. In 1940, after agreeing to the Vienna Award, which gave part of Transylvania to Hungary, he became so unpopular that he was obliged to abdicate in favour of his son, **Michael**.

Charles II, 'the Bald' (823–77) King of the West Franks (843/77). He became king as a result of the Treaty of **Verdun**, following a series of civil wars with his brothers. He was Emperor of the West (875/7) and ruler of the Kingdom of Italy from 876. The Pope called on him to fight the Saracens, but he died at Brides-les-Bain, fleeing from his brother, **Carloman** who disputed his right to the Imperial and Italian crowns. Charles was responsible for a revival of the Carolingian Renaissance. ▷ **Carolingians**

Charles III (1716–88) King of Spain (1759/88) and, as Charles IV, King of Naples and Sicily (1734/59). The younger son of **Philip V** of Spain, he conquered Naples and Sicily during the War of the **Polish Succession** and, on his accession to the Spanish throne, handed them over to his son, Ferdinand I. Charles subordinated the Church to the crown, did much to revive the economic and cultural standing of Spain in Europe, and reformed Spanish links with her colonies. He sided with France in the **Seven Years War**, when Florida was lost to Britain. France ceded Louisiana to Spain in compensation, and Spain recovered Florida (1783) after the **American Revolution**.

Charles III, 'the Fat' (839–88) King of Swabia (876/87) and Italy (879/87), and Emperor of the West (881/7). He reunited under his rule the whole Empire of **Charlemagne**, save for Burgundy. His failure to defeat the **Vikings** in 881 and 886 led to his deposition in 887, when the Carolingian Empire finally disintegrated. ▷ **Carolingians**

Charles III, 'the Simple' (879–929) King of the **Franks** (893/922). He was the son of **Louis II, 'the Stammerer'**. He made peace with the **Vikings**, ceding Normandy to Rollo, and was deposed in 922.

Charles IV (1316–78) Holy Roman Emperor (1346/78). He became Margrave of Moravia in 1334 and gradually assumed an increasing role in the government of the Czech lands during the frequent absences of his father, King John. On the latter's death, he became both Holy Roman Emperor and King of Bohemia. Unlike his predecessors, he tried to avoid being drawn into Italian conflicts. Instead, through shrewd diplomacy, he built up a dynastic empire based round his domains of Bohemia and Moravia, with his capital at Prague, where he founded the first university within the Empire (1348). His *Golden Bull* of 1356 became the new constitutional framework for the empire; it laid down procedure for the election of the monarch, excluded papal pretensions, and defined the rights of the seven Electors, whose domains were declared indivisible. He was the first emperor since **Frederick I** to be succeeded by his son (**Wenceslas IV**).

Charles IV (1783–1819) King of Spain (1788/1808). The son of **Charles III**, his government was largely in the hands of his wife, Maria Luisa (1751–1819), and her favourite, Manuel de **Godoy**. **Nelson** destroyed his fleet at the Battle of **Trafalgar**, and in 1808 he abdicated under pressure from **Napoleon I**. He spent the rest of his life in exile, and died in Rome.

Charles IV, 'the Fair' (1294–1328) King of France (1322/8) and (as Charles I) of Navarre. He renewed war with England by his invasion of Aquitaine.

Charles V (1500–58) Holy Roman Emperor (1519/56). The son of **Philip I, 'the Handsome'** and **Juana the Mad**, he inherited the Habsburg lands in 1506, Spain in 1516 and was elected Holy Roman Emperor in 1519. His rivalry with Francis I of France led to four wars but left him in control of the disputed territories in Italy and the Netherlands. During the **Reformation** Charles sought to defend and restore the unity of faith, and although he was forced to make concessions to the Protestants in 1532, these were revoked at the height of his power in 1546. The internally divided **Schmalkaldic League** of Protestant princes was subsequently defeated at **Mühlberg** (1547) but the attempted reunification of the religious parties by the compromise formula of the Augsburg Interim (1548) proved unacceptable and had to be abandoned in 1555. Exhausted and frustrated, Charles abdicated in 1556, dividing the empire between his son, **Philip II** of Spain, and his brother, Ferdinand I of Austria. He retired to the monastery of San Yuste in Spain, where he died.

Charles V, 'the Wise' (1337–80) King of France (1364/80). As **Dauphin** he acted as regent during the long captivity of his father **John II**, after the Battle of Poitiers, finally succeeding him in 1364. In a series of victories, he regained most of the territory lost to the English in the **Hundred Years War**.

Charles VI (1685–1740) Holy Roman Emperor (1711/40). As Charles III he was also a claimant to the Spanish throne. His goal was to re-establish the global empire of **Charles V**. He devised the **Pragmatic Sanction** to ensure the succession of his daughter, **Maria Theresa**, after the failure of the direct male Habsburg line. A son of **Leopold I**, he attempted to seize Spain after the death of **Charles II** (1700). He was initially recognized by the Netherlands, Britain, and Portugal who abandoned him when he came to the Austrian throne. He gained lands from France in the Treaty of **Rastatt** (1714) and from the Turks in Hungary and Serbia (1716–18). He failed to secure Maria Theresa's succession, lost the War of the **Polish Succession** (1733–8) and returned land to the Turks as a result of defeats (1736–9).

Charles VI, 'the Foolish' (1368–1422) King of France (1380/1422). He was defeated by **Henry V** of England at the Battle of **Agincourt** (1415). From 1392, he suffered from fits of madness.

Charles VII (Albert of Wittelsbach) (1697–1745) Elector of Bavaria (1726/45) and Holy Roman Emperor (1742/5). He opposed the Imperial claims of **Francis I**, Duke of Tuscany, husband of **Maria Theresa**, although he had originally accepted the **Pragmatic Sanction** and Maria's claim to the throne. He was defeated and ousted by the Austrians but restored to his Bavarian lands by Prussia and France shortly before his death.

Charles VII, 'the Victorious' (1403–61) King of France (1422/61). At his accession, the north of the country was in English hands, with **Henry VI** of England proclaimed King of France. However, after **Joan of Arc** roused the fervour of both nobles and people, the Siege of **Orléans** was raised (1429), and the English gradually lost nearly all they had gained in France. Under his rule France recovered in some measure from her terrible calamities. ▷ **Hundred Years War**

Charles VIII (1470–98) King of France (1483/98). The son of **Louis XI**, his marriage to **Anne of Brittany** (1491) enabled him to free himself from the political domination of his sister and brother-in-law, the Beaujeus, and secure his kingdom. His Italian campaign (1494–5) initiated 60 years of French military involvement in Italy. The Kingdom of Naples was temporarily secured, but Charles was driven from Italy by the League of Venice (1495).

Charles VIII of Sweden ▷ **Karl Knutsson**

Charles IX (1550–74) King of France (1560/74). The second son of **Henry II** and **Catherine de' Medici**, he succeeded his brother, **Francis II**. His reign coincided with the Wars of **Religion**. He was completely subject to his mother, whose counsels drove him to authorize the slaughter of **Huguenots** known as the **St Bartholomew's Day Massacre** (1572).

Charles IX (1550–1611) King of Sweden (1604/11). He was the son of **Gustav I Vasa** by his second wife, Margareta Leijohuvfud. On the accession in 1592 of his Catholic nephew, Sigismund, Charles led the Protestant nobility against him and secured the firm adherence of the Swedish church to Lutheran doctrine. After Sigismund had been driven from Sweden (1598), Charles was appointed regent. He crushed Sigismund's leading supporters in Sweden in the Linköping Bloodbath in 1600 and finally accepted the crown in 1604. His action against Sigismund involved Sweden in war with Poland, to which wars with Russia and Denmark were added before the end of his reign. He alienated many nobles by his use of non-noble servants and by leaving vacant a number of the great offices of state so that his son, **Gustav II Adolf**, had on his accession to promise to rule in association with the nobility.

Charles X (1757–1836) Last Bourbon King of France (1824/30). The grandson of **Louis XV**, he received the title of Count of Artois. He lived in England during the **French Revolution**, returning to France in 1814 as Lieutenant-General of the kingdom. He succeeded his brother **Louis XVIII**, but his repressive rule led to the **July Revolution** (1830), and his eventual abdication and exile. ▷ **Bourbon, House of**

Charles X Gustav (1622–60) King of Sweden (1654/60). He was the son of John Pfalz-Zweibrücken by **Gustav II Adolf's** sister, Katarina. He served with the Swedish army in the **Thirty Years War**. Plans for his marriage to Queen **Christina** came to naught, but she named him her heir and on her abdication in 1654, Charles ascended the throne. In 1655 he invaded Poland and in 1657 became embroiled also in war with Denmark, which he forced to make a humiliating peace at Roskilde (1658) after a dramatic march over the frozen waters between the Danish islands. He attacked Denmark again, but died in Gothenburg before he could secure a decisive victory. In many ways his style of ruling anticipated the absolutism introduced by his son and successor, **Charles XI**.

Charles XI (1655–97) King of Sweden (1660/97). He was the son and successor of **Charles X Gustav**. After a 12-year regency dominated by the nobility, he assumed power in 1672. Two years later he helped to staunch a Danish invasion through his leadership at the Battle of Lund, and won favourable terms at the ensuing peace treaty in 1679. In the aftermath of the war he severely punished the regents and members of the council held to be responsible for it and resumed much of the royal lands and tax revenues which had been alienated under previous monarchs (the *reduktion*). With the additional revenue this provided he reorganized the administration and armed forces, which were both placed on a much firmer financial basis. He was also no longer reliant on the Diet, and established absolute monarchy. He was married to the Danish princess Ulrika Eleonora and was succeeded by his son, **Charles XII**.

Charles XII (1682–1718) King of Sweden (1697/1718). He was the son of **Charles XI** of Sweden. Three years after coming to the throne, he was attacked by an alliance of Denmark, Saxony and Russia, which was attempting to deprive Sweden of its gains during the 17c. After forcing Denmark to make peace, Charles defeated the Russians at Narva (1700) and forced Augustus of Saxony to abandon the throne of Poland, on which he placed his ally, Stanislas Leszczyński. In 1707 he turned against Russia, but was defeated by the Tsar's forces at **Poltava** in the Ukraine in 1709 and fled to Turkey. After a conflict with the local Turkish authorities (the *kalabalik*) in 1713, he was taken to Constantinople as a virtual prisoner, but managed to leave Turkey the following year and reached Stralsund, Sweden's almost last remaining foothold on the southern coast of the Baltic, after a dramatic ride across central Europe. Once back in Sweden, he mobilized the country to continue the struggle against a formidable coalition. He attacked Denmark twice on Norwegian soil, but on the second of these campaigns (1718) was shot dead in the trenches before the Norwegian fortress of Frederikshald, whether by the enemy or from his own side has never been satisfactorily determined. He never married and was succeeded by his younger sister, **Ulrika Eleonora**.

Charles XIII (1748–1818) King of Sweden (1809/18) and of Norway (1814/18). The younger brother of **Gustav III**, he was the uncle and successor to **Gustav IV Adolf**. As Duke of Södermanland, he commanded the Swedish fleet against Russia in the war of 1788–90 and, after his brother's assassination in 1792, was regent until his nephew's coming-of-age in 1796. When Gustav was deposed in 1809, Charles was elected King and agreed to a new constitution which limited the monarch's powers. He had no children and in 1810 the Diet chose the French marshal, Jean Baptiste Jules Bernadotte (later **Charles XIV John**), as heir to the throne. Bernadotte in effect ruled the country until Charles's death. Charles was married to Charlotte of Oldenburg, whose diary is an important source for the history of her time. ▷ **Bernadotte, House of**

Charles XIV John (1763–1844) King of Sweden (1818/44). Born Jean Baptiste Jules Bernadotte, the son of a lawyer, at Pau, France, he joined the French army in 1780, and fought his way up to become marshal in 1804. In 1799 he was Minister of War, and for his conduct at the Battle of **Austerlitz** (1805) was named Prince of Pontecorvo. He fought in several Napoleonic campaigns and in 1810 was made heir to the Swedish throne by a group of Swedes who had been impressed by his conduct and wished to please Napoleon, then at the height of his power. On coming to Sweden, Bernadotte was received into the Lutheran faith and adopted the name Charles John (Karl Johan). He took control of his adopted country's foreign policy and steered it away from France. He concluded an alliance with Russia and took command of the allied forces in northern Germany in the final campaigns, forcing France's ally, Denmark, to surrender Norway to Sweden at the Treaty of Kiel (1814). His autocratic rule after his accession and his alliance with Russia caused opposition to him in the 1830s. He died in Stockholm and was succeeded by his son, **Oscar I**. ▷ **Bernadotte, House of; Napoleon I**

Charles XV (1826–72) King of Norway and Sweden (1859/72). He was the son and successor of **Oscar I**. As Crown Prince he had been an enthusiastic supporter of the idea of the political union of the Scandinavian monarchies, but after his accession this idea died. Without consulting his ministers, he promised support to Denmark in the event of war with Germany over Schleswig-Holstein. However, when war broke out in 1864, he was unable to fulfil his promise. During his reign the old four-Estate Diet was replaced (1865–6) by a bicameral parliament, elected on a narrow franchise. A cheerful and flamboyant character, Charles was also a poet and artist. Married to Lovisa of the Netherlands, who predeceased him, he left no surviving male heir and was succeeded by his younger brother, **Oscar II**.

Charles XVI Gustav (1946–) King of Sweden (1973/). As his father had died in an air accident in 1947, he became Crown Prince from the time of the accession of his grandfather, King **Gustav VI Adolf**, in 1950. A new constitution, which reduced the king to a purely ceremonial head of state, was approved by the Swedish Parliament just before his accession. In 1976 he married Silvia Sommerlath, the daughter of a West German businessman. They had two daughters, Victoria and Madeleine, and a son, Charles Philip.

Charles Albert (1789–1849) King of Sardinia-Piedmont (1831/49). Born into a junior branch of the House of **Savoy**, Charles Albert was schooled in Paris and Geneva and made a Count of the Empire by **Napoleon I**. In 1821 he was made regent following the **Santarosa** mutiny and the abdication of the elderly **Victor Emmanuel I**. Responding to popular demands he granted a liberal constitution which was promptly revoked by the new King, **Charles Felix**. With the latter's accession and the collapse of the insurrection, he was exiled from the court in disgrace but was saved from disinheritance by the intervention of **Metternich**, who demanded in return

guarantees that he would not alter the status quo. However, on ascending the throne Charles Albert embarked on a foreign policy which showed increasing readiness to resist Austrian hegemony in the Italian peninsula. Despite subsequent attempts to portray him as an Italian patriot, he was essentially reactionary and adopted very repressive measures against Mazzinian agitation in 1833–4. The surge of liberal feeling that greeted the election of **Pius IX** and the growing strength of the moderate movement of Cesare **Balbo**, **D'Azeglio** and **Gioberti** encouraged him to appoint a more progressive ministry in Oct 1847. In Mar 1848, in the midst of a growing climate of revolution, he granted a new constitution, the **Statuto,** and launched a somewhat half-hearted military campaign to assist the Lombard insurgents against Austrian rule. Following defeat by **Radetzky** at **Custozza** (25 July 1848), he signed the **Salasco Armistice**. War was renewed the following year but he was once again defeated by the Austrians at the Battle of **Novara** (23 Mar 1849). He abdicated in favour of his son, **Victor Emmanuel II**.

Charles Emmanuel II (1634–75) Duke of Savoy (1638/75). He was the son of Victor Amadeus I of Savoy and Christine de Bourbon (sister of **Louis XIII** of France). Under the regency of his mother, Savoy remained firmly within the French orbit, a policy which Charles Emmanuel did not alter when he began to govern in his own right in 1663. **Louis XIV** of France tended to treat him as little more than a vassal, virtually requiring him to furnish troops for his campaigns.

Charles Emmanuel III (1701–73) Duke of Savoy and King of Sardinia (1730/73). The second son of **Victor Amadeus II**, he became heir to the throne when his brother died in 1715 and became King himself on his father's abdication. When, shortly afterwards, his father tried to return to power, Victor Emmanuel had him imprisoned in the fortress of Rivoli. Like his father, he was prepared to back either France or Austria as his interests dictated, supporting the former in the War of the **Polish Succession** (1733–8) and the latter in the War of the **Austrian Succession** (1740–2). This policy brought territorial gains in Lombardy. He avoided involvement in the **Seven Years War**, preferring instead to concentrate on domestic reform, introducing a new legal code, the *Corpus Carolinum*, in 1770.

Charles Emmanuel IV (1751–1819) King of Sardinia (1796/1802). The elder son of **Victor Amadeus III**, he had the misfortune to come to the throne as the French armies of the **Directory** began their first great successes. He flirted with the idea of saving his dynasty through an alliance with France against Austria, but was unable to realize this scheme because of the agreement reached between **Francis II** and **Napoleon I** at the Treaty of **Campo Formio**. In 1798 he fled to Sardinia where he abdicated in favour of his brother, **Victor Emmanuel I**, in 1802. He died having entered the Church in a Monastery in Rome.

Charles Felix (1765–1831) King of Sardinia-Piedmont (1821/31). He was the fifth son of **Victor Amadeus III** and younger brother of **Victor Emmanuel I**. When the latter abdicated in 1821, Charles Felix was in Modena and was horrified to discover, on his return to Turin, that the young regent, **Charles Albert**, had granted a constitution. He immediately revoked the constitution and embarked on a policy of repression which characterized the remainder of his otherwise undistinguished reign.

Charles Frederick of Baden (1728–1811) Duke of Baden-Durlach (1746–1811). He was an enlightened ruler who made substantial changes in Baden (eg emancipation of the peasants). Although he opposed Revolutionary France, he signed a separate truce with France and later (1806) became a Grand-Duke under Napoleon.

Charles Martel (c.688–741) Mayor of the Palace for the last Merovingian kings of the **Franks**. He was the illegitimate son of **Pepin II, 'of Heristal'**, and the undisputed head of the Carolingian family by 723. He conducted many campaigns against the Frisians and **Saxons**, and in Aquitaine, Bavaria, and **Burgundy**. He halted Muslim expansion in Western Europe at the Battle of **Poitiers** (732). Established as effective ruler of much of **Gaul**, but never crowned king, he left the kingdom to his sons, **Carloman** and **Pepin III, 'the Short'**, who in 751 was anointed as the first Carolingian King of the Franks. ▷ **Carolingians**

Charles Robert (1288–1342) First King of Hungary of the Angevin Dynasty (304/42). He claimed the throne (through his mother) on the death of the last male member of the House of Árpád, Andrew III (1301), and after the defeat of rival claimants was crowned in 1308. He restored the royal authority in a struggle against the rebellious great magnates, whose lands he redistributed to the minor nobility, thus creating a new aristocracy loyal to him. The reforms which followed included the reorganization of military service and the introduction of a royal monopoly on gold and silver production. He married Elizabeth, daughter of Casimir III of Poland, and in 1337 obtained recognition of his son Louis, the future **Louis I, 'the Great'**, as heir also to the Polish throne.

Charles the Bold (1433–77) Duke of Burgundy (1467/77). Though a French vassal, he was continually at war with **Louis XI** of France, aiming to restore the old Kingdom of **Burgundy**, by conquering Lorraine, Provence, Dauphiné, and Switzerland. He gained Lorraine (1475) and invaded Switzerland, but was defeated at Granson and Morat. He laid siege to Nancy, but was killed in the battle.

Charles Theodore of Bavaria (1724–99) Elector of the Palatinate (1743/77) and later (1777/99) of the Palatinate and Bavaria. His control of Bavaria was recognized by his rival Charles Zweibrücken after the War of the Bavarian Succession (1778–9).

Charles William Ferdinand, Duke of Brunswick (1735–1806) A renowned military leader of the **Seven Years War**, he began his military career as an officer to the Duke of Cumberland in 1757. A nephew of **Frederick II, 'the Great'**, he was made a Prussian field marshal. He was acclaimed as an enlightened ruler when he succeeded his father, Charles I, in 1780. He accepted command of the allied Austro-German army sent to defeat Revolutionary France, having refused command of the French army shortly before.

Charles (Philip Arthur George), Prince of Wales (1948–) Eldest son of HM Queen **Elizabeth II** and HRH Prince Philip, Duke of **Edinburgh**, and heir apparent to the throne of Great Britain. Duke of Cornwall as the eldest son of the monarch, he was given the title of Prince of Wales in 1958, and invested at Caernarvon (1969). He served in the RAF and the Royal Navy (1971–6), and in 1981 married Lady Diana Frances, younger daughter of the 8th Earl Spencer, from whom he separated in 1992. They have two sons, Prince William Arthur Philip Louis and Prince Henry Charles Albert David. In the 1980s he made a number of controversial statements about public issues, including architecture and educational standards.

Charles (Karl Ludwig Johann) (1771–1847) Archduke of Austria and soldier. The third son of the Emperor **Leopold II** and brother of the Emperor **Francis II**, he entered the Austrian Army in 1792 and became Governor-General of the Netherlands (1793). As commander of the Austrian Army on the Rhine in 1796, he defeated Moreau and Jourdan in several battles, drove the French over the Rhine, and took Kehl. He was forced back from the Tagliamento by **Napoleon I** as he invaded Austria in 1797, but defeated Jourdan again at Stockach in 1799, only to be worsted by Masséna. In 1799 he was again victorious over Jourdan. Next year ill health compelled him to accept the governor-generalship of Bohemia. Recalled after the Austrian defeat at Hohenlinden (1800) to the chief command, he checked the progress of Moreau. In 1805 he commanded against Masséna in Italy; then, after news of the crushing defeat at the Battle of **Austerlitz** (1805), he made a masterly retreat to Croatia. In 1809 he won the great Battle of Aspern, but had to give best at the ferocious Battle of **Wagram**, leading to the Treaty of **Vienna**. He retired thereafter and became Governor of Mainz in 1815.

Charles of Anjou (1227–85) Angevin King of Naples and Sicily. The posthumous son of **Louis VIII** of France, he was invested with the crown of Naples and Sicily by Pope Urban IV (1265). After defeating his Hohenstaufen rivals **Manfred** (1266) and **Conradin of Swabia** (1268), he and his French supporters had established control of the kingdom. He conquered Corfu and much of mainland Greece, and planned to capture Constantinople and re-establish the Latin Empire, but his schemes were wrecked by the revolt known as the **Sicilian Vespers** (1282), which allowed Manfred's son-in-law, Peter III of Aragon, to seize the entire island of Sicily. ▷ **Angevins; Hohenstaufen Dynasty**

Charles of Valois (1270–1325) Second son of **Philip III** of France and Isabelle of Aragon. He was put forward as French claimant to the Kingdom of Aragon which he was unable to conquer (1283–9). He was an unsuccessful candidate for the thrones of Constantinople (1301–7) and the **Holy Roman Empire** (1308) but achieved great influence during the short reigns of Philip's three sons, **Louis X, Philip V** and **Charles IV**. His only son, **Philip VI**, founded the **Valois Dynasty**.

Charles, (Mary) Eugenia (1919–) Dominican politician. After qualifying in London as a barrister, she returned to the West Indies to practise in the Windward and Leeward Islands. She entered politics in 1968 and two years later became co-founder and first leader of the centrist Dominica Freedom Party (DFP). She became an MP in 1975. Two years after independence, the DFP won the 1980 general election and she became the Caribbean's first female Prime Minister. She was re-elected Prime Minister in 1985 and again in 1990.

Charleston, Battles of (11 Feb–12 May 1780) During the **American Revolution**, the victorious British siege of Charleston, South Carolina, which marked the beginning of the Southern phase of British strategy. At a small cost, the troops of Sir Henry Clinton (c.1738–95) captured a 5 400-strong American garrison and a squadron of four ships.

Charter 77 (post-1977) An informal association of individuals devoted to the assertion of lost human rights in Czechoslovakia. The 'normalization' following the Soviet invasion of Czechoslovakia in 1968 suppressed many civil rights, including that to free expression of views. However, in 1976 the Czechoslovak government signed the international convention on human rights confirmed in the Helsinki Final Act. This gave the opposition the opportunity to protest and publish its 'charter' on 1 Jan 1977. The founders included the Foreign Minister from 1968, Jiří **Hajek**, and the President since Dec 1989, Václav **Havel**. Charter 77 suffered much harassment, but it attracted international condemnation of the communists and eventually contributed to their downfall in 1989. ▷ **Helsinki Conference**

Chartered companies A series of companies chartered to rule colonies in late Victorian times, designed to produce imperialism on the cheap. The idea for these companies was based upon the monopolistic ventures of the mercantilist period, like the East India Company of 1599 and the Hudson's Bay Company of 1670, whose charters had been abrogated in the 19c. The British North Borneo Company was chartered in 1882 and survived until the Japanese invasion of 1941. The Royal Niger Company ruled in Nigeria between 1886 and 1898; the Imperial British East Africa Company was chartered to run British East Africa (Kenya and Uganda) from 1888 to 1893; and the British South Africa Company received a charter to rule in Southern and Northern Rhodesia between 1889 and 1923.

Charter Oath (6 Apr 1868) A broad policy statement issued in the name of the Japanese **Meiji** Emperor after the overthrow of the **Tokugawa Shogunate**. By calling for deliberative assemblies and public discussion of national affairs, the oath was initially designed to attract **samurai** support for the new regime, although it was later cited as justification for parliamentary government. The charter oath also declared that status distinctions and other backward feudal practices of the past would be eliminated, and sanctioned a policy of westernization to enhance national strength by promising to 'seek knowledge throughout the world'. The oath thus came to be seen as a manifesto anticipating the modernization programme of the new government after 1868.

Charter of the Nobility (1785) The entrenchment of the privileges of the Russian nobility, intended by **Catherine II, 'the Great'** to ensure their loyalty for the future. She had already divided her empire into 50 provinces, each with approximately 10 districts. The nobles were now given the right to elect provincial and district marshals, to convene assemblies and to petition the Tsar. Their existing rights freed them from taxation and service, and they were now given fresh property rights. They had immense privileges but no obligations other than to keep down the serfs and not to question the Tsar's authority. At the same time, Catherine extended the system of serfdom and worsened the condition of the serfs. They became chattels with no privileges and few rights, forced to slave to support the Tsar and the nobles, and to fight to win the Tsar's wars: it was a political recipe for ultimate revolution.

Chartism ▷ **Chartists**

Chartists In the UK, supporters of democratic political reform, most active between 1838 and 1849. Their name derives from the 'People's Charter' presented twice to parliament (1839 and 1842) which called for universal manhood suffrage, voting by secret ballot, the abolition of property qualifications for MPs, payment for MPs, equally-sized constituencies and annually elected parliaments. All but the last of these were obtained but this movement, largely of working people, threatened and occasionally alarmed the authorities, who arrested and imprisoned its leaders during the main phase of the agitation. Chartism was an important cultural and educational force in working-class development. ▷ **O'Connor, Feargus**

Chassé, David Hendrik, Baron (1765–1849) Dutch soldier. Nicknamed 'General Baïonette' by **Napoleon I**, he joined the French army in 1789 and fought with great distinction in Germany and Spain. As Lieutenant-General of the Dutch forces in 1815 he fought at **Waterloo** against his old comrades, the French. In the struggle for Belgian independence, he held the citadel at Antwerp (1830–2), but finally surrendered to superior French and Belgian forces, with some Pontish naval assistance.

Chateaubriand, François Auguste René, Viscount of (1768–1848) French writer and politician. His *Atala* (1801) established his literary reputation; and *Le Génie du christianisme* (1802, The Genius of Christianity) made him prominent among men of letters. He held various political and diplomatic posts after the Restoration, but was disappointed in his hope of becoming Prime Minister. In his later years, he wrote his celebrated autobiography, *Mémoires d'outre-tombe*, not published as a whole until 1902.

Chatham, Dutch Descent on (17–24 June 1667) A Dutch naval expedition at the end of the second of the **Anglo-Dutch Wars**, which had the effect of forcing the hand of the English at the negotiations for the Peace of **Breda**. The Dutch Pensionary Johan de **Witt** sent the expedition under his brother, Cornelius, and Admiral Michiel de **Ruyter**; they sailed up the Thames and captured the fort at Sheerness. They proceeded up the Medway to the Royal Docks at Chatham, destroyed a number of ships, and carried off the English flagship the *Royal Charles*, causing panic in London. Traditionally, this event is underreported in English history books. ▷ **Chatham, Dutch Descent on**

Chatila Palestinian refugee camp on the outskirts of Beirut in Lebanon. It was created following the evacuation of Palestinians from the city after Israeli attacks on Palestinians and Syrians (June 1982). The camp was the scene of a massacre by Christian Phalangists (Sep 1983).

Chattanooga Campaign (Aug–Nov 1863) A series of battles in Tennessee, during the **American Civil War**, leading to Southern victory at Chickamauga, and Northern victories at Lookout Mountain and Missionary Ridge. It was of military importance, because it placed Northern troops in a position to bisect the Confederacy on an east–west axis.

Chatterjee, Bankim Chandra (1838–94) Indian author and social critic. While his primary career was as a district magistrate in Bengal, his greatest skill was as an author and philosopher. A contemporary of Rabindranath Tagore, he founded (1872) *Bangadarshan*, a Bengali newspaper which soon became a vehicle for expounding on Hindu philosophy and culture. An influential philosophical writer, Chatterjee was also a poet and a master of the historical novel, as he demonstrated in *Ananda Math*, which is set against the Sannyasi revolt in the Bengal of Warren **Hastings**. He was also a social activist, publishing *Kamalakanter Daptar* in 1885. In this novel he pleaded for a degree of social equality which was not to be found in India. Chatterjee's French rationalist bent allowed him to forge a sense of Indian nationality in his novels, and at the same time point out the inequities institutionalized in Hindu society.

Chauhans (Chahamanas) of Shakambhari A prominent Rajput dynasty of North India, originating from the 8c feudatory to the **Pratiharas**, but emerging as independent rulers in the 11–12c. Several related branches of the family ruled other small states in Rajasthan. Vigraharaja IV (known dates, 1150/63) captured Delhi from the Tomaras and from then on the dynasty was involved in conflict with the Muslims by now established in the Punjab. Prithviraja III (1177/92) is famous for his conflicts both with the Gahadavalas (Gahrwals) of **Kanauj** and with **Muhammad Ghuri**, whom he defeated in the first Battle of Tarain in 1191; the second Battle of Tarain (1192) was a decisive victory for the Muslims and spelt the end of this branch of the Chauhans. These events are celebrated in the bardic chronicle, the *Prithvirajaraso of Chand Bardai*, one of the earliest works of Rajasthani literature.

Chaumette, Pierre Gaspard (1763–94) French revolutionary, a shoemaker's son. At the Revolution he joined with Camille **Desmoulins**, and soon gained such popularity by his extremism that he was appointed procurator of the Paris commune, the elected municipal government of the city of Paris, which played an important part in the developing extremism of the Revolution, 1792–3. His extravagances disgusted **Robespierre**, and he died on the scaffold. ▷ **French Revolution**

Chautauqua Movement A late 19c and early 20c US adult education movement, organized at Lake Chautauqua, New York, under Methodist auspices by Lewis Miller (1829–99) and Bishop John H Vincent (1832–1920), with home reading programmes and lectures in the arts, sciences, and humanities. At its peak it attracted up to 60 000 participants annually to regional centres in the USA and elsewhere.

Chebrikov, Viktor Mikhailovich (1923–) Soviet **KGB** operative. A Russian, he served in the army in **World War II** and afterwards qualified in metallurgy in Dnepropetrovsk in the Ukraine. Having transferred to party work, he came into contact with Leonid **Brezhnev** who, in 1967, appointed him to the KGB to keep an eye on Yuri **Andropov**. He eventually switched his loyalty, and in 1982 Andropov made him chairman of the KGB. In 1985 he cast his vital note for Mikhail **Gorbachev**, who made him a full member of the **Politburo**. As he began to take fright at the implications of Gorbachev's reforms and veered towards Yegor **Ligachev**; he was carefully but firmly removed from all his posts in 1988–9.

Chefoo Convention (1876) An agreement signed by the British Minister to China, Thomas Wade, and **Li Hongzhang**, representing the Chinese government. The previous year a British consular official, Margary, was killed in south-west China en route to meet a British expedition from Burma. The agreement both provided for Chinese government compensation and an official mission of apology to Britain, as well as stipulating that four more **treaty ports** were to be opened. In return, however, the Chinese government was allowed to increase taxes on opium imports and could impose the *likin* (internal transit tax) on foreign goods outside the treaty ports. These two concessions outraged British mercantile opinion, and the convention was not ratified until 1885.

Chehab, Fuad (1902–73) Lebanese politician and soldier. From a Maronite Christian family who had settled initially in the Chouf Mountains of Lebanon in Ottoman times, he came to prominence when he was appointed to command the new Lebanese army in 1945. He rose to become Minister of Defence in Camille **Chamoun**'s government, formed in the aftermath of the Suez affair in 1956. During the insurrection and disturbances following the declaration of the **United Arab Republic** of Egypt and Syria in 1958, Chehab refused to use the Lebanese army to crush the rebellion. This, coupled with the call by the rebels for the resignation of Chamoun, won Chehab the respect of the Muslim section of the community; and in July 1958 Chehab, who had by this time resigned command of the army, was elected President, to succeed Chamoun when the latter demitted office. Despite initial problems, he succeeded in restoring stability to Lebanon. His six-year term of office saw an attempt to establish a social policy aimed at improving the lot of the common people. That this was unsuccessful may be seen, to some extent, as a contributing factor to the disastrous currents which were to overwhelm Lebanon a decade later.

Cheka An acronym from Russian letters **che+ka**, for the All-Russian Extraordinary Commission for Combating Counter-Revolution and Sabotage, established in 1917. It was in effect a political police force whose duties were to investigate and punish anti-Bolshevik activities. During the **Russian Civil War** it was responsible for executing thousands of political opponents in what came to be called the 'Red Terror'. ▷ **Bolsheviks; communism**

Chelčický, Petr (c.1390–1460) Czech reformer and theologian. A radical follower of the Hussites, he abjured towns, commerce and violence, and founded the sect which eventually became the Moravian Brothers. The Christian doctrine of his *The Net of True Faith* (1450) was later promulgated by **Tolstoy.**

Chen, Eugene (Ch'en Yu-jen) (1878–1944) Chinese lawyer and politician. Born in Trinidad he had a Catholic education and trained to be a lawyer. After the creation of the Chinese republic in 1912, Chen was appointed legal adviser to the Ministry of Communications. He became particularly close to **Sun Yat-sen** and served as his foreign affairs adviser. Chen was identified with the left wing of the **Guomindang**, which established its own government in Wuhan in early 1927 in opposition to **Chiang Kai-shek**. As Foreign Minister in the Wuhan government he pursued a vigorous anti-imperialist policy, negotiating the return of the British concessions of Hankou and Jiujiang. After 1927, when the Wuhan government was dissolved, Chen was briefly associated with anti-Chiang Kai-shek separatist movements.

Chen Boda (Ch'en Po-ta) (1905–) Chinese political propagandist and interpreter of **Mao Zedong**'s thought. He joined the Chinese Communist Party (CCP) in 1927 and studied in Moscow until 1930. After teaching in Beijing, Chen went to the communist base at Yan'an (Yenan) in 1937. He became Mao Zedong's personal secretary and helped popularize Mao's concept of the 'Sinification of Marxism' (adapting Marxism to Chinese conditions). After 1949 he continued to be influential in the party's propaganda department, becoming chief editor of the party organ, *Hongqi* (Red Flag), in 1958. During the **Cultural Revolution** Chen became associated with the radicals and in 1969 reached the apogee of his influence when he was appointed to the Politbureau. In the campaign against leftist excesses the following year, however, Chen was arrested and expelled from the CCP. In 1980–1 he was put on public trial along with the **Gang of Four** and sentenced to 18 years in prison. ▷ **Communist Party, Chinese**

Chen Duxiu (Ch'en Tu-hsiu) (1879–1942) Chinese revolutionary and publicist. In 1915 Chen founded the journal 'New Youth' (*Xin Qingnian*), which heralded the beginnings of a new cultural movement calling for a rejection of the Confucian tradition and the promotion of democracy and science. In 1917 he became Dean of the College of Letters at Beijing University, where he attracted a large student following. By 1920, disillusioned with the prospects of cultural change, he had become attracted to Marxism and established a communist cell in Shanghai. Although Chen was in Canton when the Chinese Communist Party (CCP) was formally created in Shanghai (July 1921), he was a founder member and was elected its first Secretary-General. With **Comintern** prodding, he led the CCP into the first United Front with the **Guomindang** in 1923 and oversaw a considerable expansion of the party's membership. When the Guomindang turned on its erstwhile communist allies in 1927, which resulted in the near total annihilation of the party, Chen was made a scapegoat for the disaster and replaced as Secretary-General.

Ch'en Po-ta ▷ **Chen Boda**

Chen Tu-hsiu ▷ **Chen Duxiu**

Chen Yi (1901–72) Chinese communist leader. He studied in France, and joined the Chinese Communist Party on his return. He supported **Mao Zedong** in the struggle with the **Guomindang**, and the Japanese (1934). Chen Yi formed the 4th Route Army in Jiangxi (1940), commanded the East China

Liberation Army (1946) and restyled the 3rd (East China) Army (1948). He prepared an amphibious operation against Taiwan, but failed to capture Quemoy Island in 1949. Created Marshal of the People's Republic in 1955, he became Foreign Minister in 1958, but was dropped from the Politburo during the **Cultural Revolution** in 1969.

Chen Yong'gui (Ch'en Yung-kuei) (1915–86) Chinese 'model' peasant and politician. During the **Cultural Revolution** Chen, an illiterate peasant, was hailed as a model worker in the Dazhai Production Brigade in the north-western province of Shanxi. As leader of the brigade and supporter of Maoist policies, Chen was elected to the Central Committee in 1969 and elevated to the Politbureau in 1973. After **Mao Zedong**'s death in 1976, amidst a general reversal of Maoist policies, doubts were raised about Dazhai's claim as the successful embodiment of self-reliance and egalitarianism. Chen increasingly lost influence and he was dropped from the Politbureau in 1981. ▷ **Maoism**

Chen Yün (Ch'en Yun) (1905–) Chinese communist leader and economic planner. Chen joined the Chinese Communist Party in 1924 and became a labour organizer in Shanghai. By 1940 he was a member of the Politbureau. As Minister of Heavy Industry (1949–50) and a member of the State Planning Commission (1952–4), Chen was an important economic planner in the new communist government, helping to formulate the first Five-Year Plan. As an advocate of central planning and the need to maintain production, he clashed with **Mao Zedong** over the **Great Leap Forward** campaign in 1958, which led to his official eclipse until after Mao's death. In 1978 he was reinstated as party Vice-Chairman and appointed a vice-premier in 1979, overseeing economic policies. He has been a consistent critic of the post-Mao leadership's attempt to introduce elements of a market economy, arguing for the need to maintain the dominant role of the state sector. Chen retired from party posts in 1987.

Ch'en Yung-kuei ▷ **Chen Yong'gui**

Cheops ▷ **Khufu**

Chephren ▷ **Khafre**

Cherasco, Peace of (1631) The death of the last **Gonzaga** duke in 1627 meant that the

French Prince of Nevers would inherit Mantua. The Habsburgs, fearing a French presence in northern Italy, diverted troops from the north to Mantua, and **Richelieu** countered with a French force. The Peace of Cherasco ended the war; it gave Pinerolo to France and invested Nevers with Mantua. ▷ **Habsburg Dynasty**

Cherikov, V (1900–) Soviet marshal and typical post-**Russian Revolution** commander. A Russian peasant, he joined the **Red Army** in 1918 and the Communist Party in 1919. He became a regimental commander in the **Russian Civil War** and graduated from the Frunze Military Academy in 1925. During **World War II** his activities included serving as adviser to **Chiang Kai-shek** and then participating in the Battle of **Stalingrad** (1943) and the final assault on Berlin in 1945. He was Deputy Commander (1946–53), then Commander-in-Chief of Soviet forces in Germany, and Deputy Minister of Defence (1960–5).

Chernenko, Konstantin Ustinovich (1911–85) Soviet politician. He joined the Communist Party in 1931, and held several local posts. An associate of Leonid **Brezhnev** for many years, he became a member of the **Politburo** in 1978, and the Party's chief ideologist after the death of Mikhail **Suslov** (1982). Regarded as a conservative, Chernenko was a rival of Yuri **Andropov** in the Party leadership contest of 1982, and became Party General-Secretary and Head of State after Andropov's death in 1984. He suffered from ill health, and died soon after in Moscow, to be succeeded by Mikhail **Gorbachev**.

Chernov, Viktor Mikhailovich (1876–1952) Russian peasant politician. Although the peasants were not fully emancipated until 1905, individuals and groups participated increasingly in the opposition to **Nicholas II**. Chernov was originally a populist but, influenced by Marxism, he helped to found the **Socialist Revolutionary Party** in 1901, a party oscillating between terrorism and peaceful advocacy of far-reaching land reform. Halfway through the Provisional Government's life in 1917, he joined it as Minister of Agriculture and supported the peasants' seizure of all available land. This divided it in the face of the Bolshevik threat. His party gained a majority in the **Russian Constituent Assembly** elected in Nov 1917 and convened in Jan 1918 under his chairmanship. But power lay not with the peasants and their representatives, but with the **Bolsheviks** and their soldiers. Within two days, **Lenin** dissolved the assembly and consigned it and Chernov to history.

Chernyshevsky, Nikolai Gavrilovich (1828–89) Russian writer and political activist. The well-educated son of a Saratov priest, a graduate in history from the University of St Petersburg, and a brilliant journalist, he was contributor to and editor of the critical magazine *Sovremennik* ('Contemporary') from 1855 to 1862. He abandoned the liberalism of his predecessors and developed a primitive revolutionary socialist philosophy based on his faith in the Russian peasantry. He was disappointed with **Alexander II**'s rather tentative reforms and, on somewhat doubtful evidence of political subversion, he was imprisoned in 1862 and sent to Siberia in 1864. He was not allowed to return to Saratov until 1889 when he was already dying. Through his writings and his suffering he inspired a whole generation of emerging revolutionaries. ▷ **nihilism**

Cherokee Native North Americans formerly living in southeastern USA, now living in Oklahoma and North Carolina. They sided with the British in the **American Revolution**, and later, in 1827, established the Cherokee Nation with its own constitution and elected government. After gold was discovered on their land, they were removed by US troops and forced to move west to unsettled **Indian Territory** in Oklahoma. Thousands died from cold, disease and starvation during their 800-mile mid-winter march that became known as the Trail of Tears. The survivors settled in Oklahoma with other displaced SE tribes. Over 250 000 Cherokee live in the USA today; most live in Oklahoma, but some who refused to leave the SE still live in North Carolina. ▷ **Five Civilized Tribes**

Cherry Blossom Society (*Sakurakai*) The secret society formed by young Japanese army officers in 1930 under the leadership of Lieutenant-Colonel Hashimoto Kingoro of the Army General Staff. Violating the ban on army involvement in politics, the society met to discuss the renovation of the state, reflecting increasing army dissatisfaction with civilian government run by political parties. It was involved in two abortive coups in 1931, in alliance with ultra-nationalist civilians, to set up a military cabinet. The society was dissolved shortly afterwards.

Chervenkov, Vulko (1900–80) Bulgarian politician. He joined the Bulgarian Communist Party (BCP) in 1919 and went to the USSR where he studied at the Moscow Military Academy and Lenin International School and acted as secretary to Georgi **Dimitrov**. Returning to Bulgaria in 1944, he held a series of appointments within the BCP: Secretary for AgitProp (1949–50), Deputy Prime Minister (1949–50), General-Secretary (1950–61), Prime Minister (1950–6) and Deputy Prime Minister (1956–61). Known as Bulgaria's 'Little **Stalin**', he fell victim to Nikita **Khrushchev**'s anti-Stalinist campaign in the early 1960s. In 1962 he was expelled from the party and replaced by Todor **Zhivkov** who had denounced him at the 1961 and 1962 party conferences. Later he was rehabilitated (1969) and awarded a state pension.

Chesterfield, Philip Dormer Stanhope, 4th Earl of (1694–1773) English politician, orator, and man of letters. He studied at Cambridge, made the Grand Tour, became an MP (1715), and in 1726 succeeded his father as Earl. A bitter antagonist of **Walpole**, he joined the **Pelham** ministry (1744), became Irish Lord-Lieutenant (1745), and one of the principal Secretaries of State (1746–8).

Chetniks (*Četnici*) Bands of royalist Serbian guerrilla fighters active in Yugoslavia during **World War II**. Organized by Colonel Draža **Mihailović** and a small group of Serbian officers after the collapse of the Yugoslav Army (1941), anti-communist and anti-Croat, they fought **Tito**'s communist partisans rather than the Axis occupiers and so forfeited Allied support in 1944.

Cheyenne Native North Americans, members of the Algonquian linguistic group, who originally lived east of the Missouri River and migrated to the Great Plains in the 17c, becoming skilled horsemen and buffalo hunters. A northern group settled along the North Platte River, while a southern contingent lived along the upper Arkansas River. Following the incursion of white prospectors and settlers on their land and attack by US troops, including a massacre at Sand Creek, Colorado, they joined the Arapaho and Sioux to fight the army, taking part in the Battle of the **Little Bighorn**. Eventually defeated, their few remaining members were assigned to reservations in Oklahoma and Montana. ▷ **Indian Wars**

Chiang Ch'ing ▷ **Jiang Qing**

Chiang Ching-kuo (1910–88) Taiwanese politician. The son of **Chiang Kai-shek**, he studied in the USSR during the early 1930s, returning to China with a Russian wife in 1937 at the time of the Japanese invasion. After the defeat of Japan in 1945 he held a number of government posts before fleeing with his father and the defeated **Guomindang** forces to Taiwan in 1949. He became Defence Minister (1965–72), and was Prime Minister from 1972 to 1978. He succeeded to the post of Guomindang leader on his father's death (1975) and became state President in 1978. Under his stewardship, Taiwan's post-war 'economic miracle' continued, but in the political sphere there was repression. During the closing years of his life, with his health failing, he instituted a progressive pro-gramme of political liberalization and demo-cratization, which was continued by his successor, **Lee Teng-hui**.

Chiang Kai-shek (Jiang Jieshi) (1887–1975) Chinese revolutionary leader. He was the effective head of the Nationalist Republic (1928–49), and head thereafter of the émigré Nationalist Party regime in Taiwan. Born into a merchant family in Zhejiang, he interrupted his military education in Japan to return to China and join the Nationalist revolution. In 1918 he joined the separatist revolutionary government of **Sun Yat-sen** in Canton, where he was appointed Commandant of the new Whampoa Military Academy. After Sun's death (1925), he launched an expedition against the **warlords** and the Beijing government, entering Beijing in 1928, but fixed the Nationalist capital at Nanjing (Nanking). During the ensuing decade the Nationalist Party steadily lost support to the Communists. When Japan launched a cam-paign to conquer China (1937), Nationalist resistance was weak. Defeated by the Com-munist forces, he was forced to retreat to Taiwan (1949), where he presided over the beginnings of Taiwan's 'economic miracle'. His son, **Jiang Jing'guo**, became Prime Minister in 1971 and President in 1978.

Chibcha (Miusca) An Indian people of South America who lived in the central highlands of Colombia from about 1200. They developed the largest and most highly centralized political system in the area, made up of smaller units under hereditary chiefs. They were defeated by the Spanish in the 16c, and were later assimilated.

Chicherin, Grigoriy Vasilevich (1872–1936) Russian revolutionary, politician, and diplomat. He joined the Russian Social Democratic Labour Party in 1905 and engaged in party work in Germany, France and England. At first he sided with the **Mensheviks**, but after the **October Revolution** he supported the **Bolsheviks** and was arrested for subversive activities in Britain. He was later exchanged for the ex-British ambas-sador in Russia. In 1918 he helped negotiate the Treaty of **Brest-Litovsk**, and became People's Commissar for Foreign Affairs. During the 1920s he represented the USSR at many international conferences. In 1930, ill health and differences with **Stalin** over his conduct of foreign affairs led to his being relieved of his post, and he lived in retirement until his death.

Chidzero, Bernard Thomas G (1927–) Zimbabwean politician and **UN** admini-strator. Educated in Southern Rhodesia and Marianhill in South Africa, he went to Pius XII Catholic College Lesotho, Ottawa Uni-versity and then Nuffield Colege, Oxford, from where he graduated with a DPhil in 1960. He was successively assistant research officer Economic Commission for Africa in Addis Ababa (1961–3), representative of UN Technical Assistance Board in Kenya (1963–6), Resident Representative UNDP, Kenya (1966–8), Director Commodities Division UNCTAD (1968–77) and Deputy President General (1977–80). Elected to the Zimbabwe Senate (1980), he has been Minister of Economic Planning and Develop-ment since then. Although not a member of the Politburo, he has been the chief architect of Zimbabwe's economic policy and the leading figure among reformists who pre-vailed over the radicals' wish for a more socialist and Leninist state.

Ch'ien-lung ▷ **Qianlong**

Chifley, Joseph Benedict (1885–1951) Australian politician and Labor Prime Minister (1945–9). In early life an engine driver, he entered parliament in 1928, and became Defence Minister in 1931. Defeated in the 1931 election, he returned to parlia-ment in 1940, becoming Treasurer in 1941, a post he combined with that of Minister for Post-War Reconstruction (1942–5), and Prime Minister on **Curtin**'s death in 1945. As Prime Minister, he expanded social services and reformed the banking system, although his attempt to nationalize the banks failed. He continued as leader of the **Australian Labor Party** until his death.

DYNASTIES OF CHINA

Dates	Name	Dates	Name
1766–1122BC	Shang Dynasty	420–589	Southern Dynasties
1122–256BC	Zhou (Chou) Dynasty	581–618	Sui Dynasty
403–222BC	Warring States Period	618–907	Tang Dynasty
221–206BC	Qin (Ch'in) Dynasty	907–60	Five Dynasties and Ten Kingdoms Period
206BC–AD24	Western ('Former') Han Dynasty	960–1279	Song (Sung) Dynasty
AD8–23	Interregnum (Wang Mang)	1122–1234	Jin (Jurchen) Dynasty
25–220	Eastern Han Dynasty	1279–1368	Yuan Dynasty
220–80	Three Kingdoms Period	1368–1644	Ming Dynasty
266–317	Western Jin (Chin) Dynasty	1644–1911	Qing Dynasty
318–420	Eastern Jin (Chin) Dynasty		

Childers, (Robert) Erskine (1870–1922) Irish nationalist and writer. He fought in the **Boer Wars** and **World War I**, and wrote a popular spy story, *The Riddle of the Sands* (1903), and several works of nonfiction. After the establishment of the **Irish Free State**, he joined the IRA, and was active in the civil war. He was captured and executed at Dublin. His son, Erskine Childers (1905–74) was President of Ireland in 1973–4.

Children's Crusade, The (1212) The crusade began in the Rhineland and Lower Lorraine and was led by a boy called Nicholas. The children, unarmed and ranging in age from about 10 to 18, intended to travel to Jerusalem and recapture the Holy Sepulchre. When they reach Genoa they numbered around 7000, but the Lombards refused to supply them with ships, hoped-for miracles did not happen, and they gradually dispersed. The crusade had its origins in the fanaticism of contemporary preaching against the **Albigenses** and in the ideal of poverty, which suggested that the pure and innocent were the most effective servants of God.

Chilembwe, John (c.1871–1915) Nyasaland religious and military leader. After receiving his education in the USA, he returned to Nyasaland (Malawi) where he established his Providence Industrial Mission, an independent African church and mission in 1906. He became increasingly discontented with white rule and petitioned for black rights in various limited areas. When his appeals were ignored, in 1915 he led a rising against the British, through which he hoped to replace white rule by divine assistance. Two Europeans were killed, but the revolt was suppressed and Chilembwe died while trying to escape. It was the first major act of black resistance in Malawi, and an inspiration to subsequent African nationalism.

Chiltern Hundreds In the UK, a legally fictitious office of profit under the crown: Steward or Bailiff of Her Majesty's Chiltern Hundreds of Stoke, Desborough, and Burnham. To accept this office disqualifies an MP from the House of Commons. As an MP cannot resign, application to the Chiltern Hundreds is the conventional manner of leaving the Commons.

Chin ▷ **Jin**

China A socialist state in central and eastern Asia, which also claims the island of Taiwan. Chinese civilization is believed to date from the Xia Dynasty of 2200–1700BC; the western **Zhou Dynasty** ruled over a prosperous feudal agricultural society c.1066–771BC; the eastern Zhou Dynasty (770BC–256BC) was the era of **Confucius** and **Lao Zi** (Lao-tzu); the **Qin Dynasty** (221BC–206BC) unified the warring states and provided a system of centralized control; there was expansion west during the Western and Eastern **Han Dynasties** (206BC–AD265. From the 4c, a series of northern dynasties was set up by invaders, with several dynasties in the south; these were gradually reunited during the **Sui** (581–618) and **Tang** (618–907) dynasties. After a period of partition into Five Dynasties (907–60) there emerged the **Song Dynasty** (960–1279), remembered for literature, philosophy, and inventions (eg movable type, gunpowder); **Genghis Khan** established the Mongol Yuan dynasty (1279–1368). There followed visits by Europeans, such as Marco Polo, in the 13c–14c, and the **Ming Dynasty** (1368–1644) increased contacts with the West. It was overthrown by Manchus, who ruled until 1911, and enlarged the empire to include **Manchuria**, **Mongolia**, Tibet, Taiwan, and parts of Turkestan. Opposition to foreign imports led to the **Opium Wars** (1839–42, 1858–60), which opened ports to foreign

trade. The **Sino-Japanese War** (1895) gave control of Taiwan and Korea to Japan. The **Boxer Rising** (1898–1900) was the last attempt to oppose foreign influence; the Republic of China was founded by **Sun Yat-sen** (1912), and unification came under Jiang Jieshi (**Chiang Kai-shek**), who made Nanjing the capital in 1928. Conflict between nationalists and communists led to the **Long March** (1934–5), with communists moving to north-west China under **Mao Zedong** (Mao Tse-tung). The nationalists were defeated in 1950 and withdrew to Taiwan. The People's Republic of China was proclaimed in 1949, with its capital at Beijing (Peking). The first Five-Year Plan (1953–7) was a period of nationalization and collectivization; the **Great Leap Forward** (1958–9) emphasized local authority and establishment of rural communes; the **Cultural Revolution** was initiated by Mao Zedong in 1966; many policies were reversed after Mao's death in 1976, and there was a drive towards rapid industrialization and wider trade relations with the West. The killing of student-led pro-democracy protesters in **Tiananmen Square**, Beijing, in 1989 provoked international outrage and the introduction of economic sanctions, relaxed after 1990. Tough economic controls were imposed in 1993. China has a population of 1.2 billion (1990), and is governed by an elected National People's Congress of 2 978 deputies and a State Council of over 45 ministers, led by a prime minister. See panel p194.
▷ **Five Dynasties and Ten Kingdoms, Period of; Mongols; Manchu**

China Democratic League A political group formed in 1944 in response to **Chiang Kai-shek**'s attempt to ease controls on minority party activity and thereby enhance the credibility of the **Guomindang** government. Calling for constitutional guarantees as well as the creation of a coalition government, the league's criticism of Chiang's intransigence towards the Chinese Communist Party (CCP) and its condemnation of the renewed civil war in 1946 aroused the hostility of the authorities. Outlawed in 1947, the league was resuscitated after 1949 by the new communist regime and its leaders allowed to participate in government. In 1957, following general criticism of the CCP during the **Hundred Flowers Campaign**, the leaders of the league were accused of being rightists and were purged from official life.

Ch'in Dynasty ▷ **Qin Dynasty**

Chinese Civil War (1946–9) After Japan's **World War II** defeat (Aug 1945), civil war broke out again in China between the communists and the **Guomindang** (Nationalist) forces under **Chiang Kai-shek**. A truce (14 Jan 1946), mediated by US envoy General George Marshall, broke down and US supplies to the Guomindang were stopped (July 1946). Nonetheless, the better-equipped Guomindang took the communist capital, Yan'an, on 19 Mar 1947. The communists, meanwhile, stepped up their campaign from rural-based guerrilla warfare to full-scale battles, recapturing the city a year later. The communists' strategy of focusing on rural rather than urban areas had succeeded in isolating the Guomindang and severely taxing their resources. They followed up their advantage in late 1948 and in early 1949 with the so-called Battle of **Huai-Hai**, the series of decisive engagements in the civil war, in which the Guomindang lost more than half a million men. The communists went on, in 1949, to capture Beijing and Tianjin (Jan), Nanjing (Apr) and Shanghai (May) and Canton (Oct). The People's Republic of China was formally proclaimed by **Mao Zedong** on 1 Oct 1949; the Nationalists withdrew to Taiwan (Formosa) on 7 Dec of the same year.

Chinese Eastern Railway (CER) The railroad in north Manchuria, covering a distance of 1 073 miles. In 1896 China granted Tsarist Russia the concession of building the railway as an extension of the Trans-Siberian railroad begun in 1891; Russia also obtained the right of policing the line. The 1896 agreement stipulated that the line would either be redeemed by China after 36 years for 700 million roubles or would pass to Chinese control without compensation after 80 years. Although the new Bolshevik government in 1920 promised to abolish all Tsarist Russia's privileges in China, the CER remained under Soviet control until 1935, when it was sold to Japan. In 1945 the CER came under joint Sino-Russian control as part of the price paid for Soviet entry into the war against Japan. The CER was not restored to full Chinese control until 1954.

Chinese Labour (Canada) The reputation of the Chinese for hard work meant they were in great demand, especially by the railway interests for the building of the British Columbian sections of the Canadian Pacific Railway. Their rate of immigration into British Columbia was such that the province attempted to restrict their entry with the introduction of a 'head tax'. This rose from $50 in 1885 to $100 in 1900; by 1903 it had risen to $500, but still did not put off those seeking fortune in the 'Land of the Golden Mountains'. Anti-Chinese sentiment was pronounced among the trade unions who feared that the labour movement would be undermined, while throughout the province there were fears that society would be destabilized. In 1902 the **Laurier** government set up a royal commission and as a result Chinese immigration was severely restricted. In response companies, led by the Canadian Pacific, began to bring in East Indians and Japanese in their stead. The unions became even more alarmed by the arrival of the Japanese, for they were considered more competitive and were supported by a government whom neither the Canadian nor the British governments wished to displease. With the formation of the Asiatic Exclusion League and after the violent riots of 1907, the Laurier government introduced severe restrictions on the entry of all Oriental immigrants.

Chinese Revolution (1911) The events relating to the overthrow of the Manchu **Qing Dynasty** and the subsequent creation of a republic in China. It broke out in Wuchang, Hubei province (central China) on 10 Oct 1911 with a mutiny in one of the new army units created by the Qing as part of its reform programme designed to strengthen the dynasty. Officers in these army units, while studying in Japan, had been influenced by the republicanism of **Sun Yat-sen** and his followers, who attributed China's weakness to the corruption of the Qing monarchy and its subservience to the foreign powers. The anti-Qing uprising quickly spread to other central and southern provinces, where mutinous army units were joined by provincial gentry elites disillusioned with the Qing government's half-hearted attempts at constitutional reform and its failure to prevent foreign encroachment in China, particularly with regard to railway concessions. By 1 Jan 1912 delegates from 16 provinces had elected Sun Yat-sen provisional president of a Chinese republic. Aware of the weakness of his own military forces and fearful that the foreign powers might intervene to protect their economic interests, Sun offered the presidency to **Yuan Shikai**, commander of the Qing forces, on the condition he abide by a republican constitution. On 12 Feb 1912 the court announced the abdication of the boy-emperor, **Puyi**, and Yuan Shikai became President of a unified republic. The 1911

Revolution can be viewed as a nationalist revolution, but in other respects it was an ambivalent one. Spearheaded by traditional elites, who were its principal beneficiaries (rather than Sun Yat-sen's republican revolutionaries), the revolution brought no significant social change in its wake, while the new president had been an important official of the *ancien régime* who, as events were to show, had scant respect for constitutional government.

Ch'ing Dynasty ▷ **Qing Dynasty**

Ch'in Shih Huang-ti ▷ **Qin Shi Huangdi**

Chioggia, War of (1378–81) This was the climax of the struggle between Venice and Genoa for commercial supremacy in the Mediterranean. The fact that the Genoese had reached the lagoon is commemorated in the name of the war, and, with the bell tower of St Mark's in sight, it seemed that victory would be theirs. From an apparently impossible position, the Venetians contrived an astonishing naval victory.

Chirac, Jacques (René) (1932–) French politician. A Gaullist, he was first elected to the National Assembly in 1967, and gained extensive governmental experience before being appointed Prime Minister by **Giscard d'Estaing**. In office from 1974 to 1976, he resigned over differences with Giscard and broke away to lead the Gaullist Party. Mayor of Paris since 1977, he was an unsuccessful candidate in the 1981 and 1988 presidential elections. ▷ **Gaulle, Charles de; Gaullists**

Ch'i-shan ▷ **Qishan**

Chisholm, Caroline (1808–77) British-born Australian philanthropist. In 1830 she married an East India Company officer, Archibald Chisholm, and they moved from Madras, where she founded a school for the daughters of European soldiers, to Sydney in 1838. Concerned at the moral and physical dangers faced by poor women immigrants dumped in Sydney without resettlement facilities, she began her campaign to publicize their plight when Captain Chisholm returned to duty in 1840. She met the ships, established an employment register and a temporary Female Immigrants' Home, and sought work for the immigrants in rural areas, often accompanying groups herself. In the 1840s over 11000 women and children passed through the network she established. Returning to England in 1846, convinced of the positive effect women and families would have on Australian frontier society, she secured free passages for the families of emancipated convicts, and in 1849 established the Family Colonization Loan Society in London, with branches in Australia. The New South Wales government voted £10 000 to assist her work in 1852; the *Caroline Chisholm* was built for the society by a London shipbuilder. In 1854 she returned to Australia and toured the gold-rush settlements, publicizing the poor conditions, but personal financial difficulties and ill health ended her philanthropic work.

Chisholm, Shirley (1924–) US politician. She was elected to the New York State Assembly in 1964, and was the first black woman to become a member of the House of Representatives when elected as a Democrat in 1968. In the 1972 Democratic Convention she won a 10 per cent vote for the presidential nomination. ▷ **Democratic Party**

Chissano, Joaquim (1939–) Mozambique politician. He graduated from high school in Maputo and went to Portugal to study medicine, where he became involved in political activity. He was a founder member of **Frelimo** and was in charge of its Department of Security and Defence. A close confidant of Samora **Machel**, he became Foreign Minister after independence in 1975, being responsible for negotiating the **Nkomati Accord** with South Africa. He succeded Machel in 1986 and began the process of change inside Mozambique.

Ch'i-tan ▷ **Khitan**

Ch'iu Chin ▷ **Qiu Jin**

Ch'i-ying ▷ **Qiying**

Chłopicki, Józef (1771–1854) Polish soldier and patriot. He served under **Napoleon I**, was made a general by the Emperor Alexander, and took part for a time in the Polish insurrection of 1830–1. However, although declared dictator, his rather conservative attitude compelled him to give up this role and he died in exile in Kraków.

Chlotar I (498–561) King of all the **Franks** (558/61). The son of the Frankish king **Clovis I**, he inherited the kingdom jointly with his three brothers in 511, but gradually added to his holdings until with the death of his brother Childebert I in 558 he became ruler of all the Franks. His realm extended from the Pyrenees to Carinthia, but was split up once more at his death.

Chlotar II (584–629) King of the **Franks** (613/29). The grandson of **Chlotar I**, he assumed rule in 613 after a period of regency, recovered lost territories by defeating **Brunhilde** (613) and extended rule over all the Franks. However, he was forced to appease the Austrasian nobles who had supported him by setting up his son **Dagobert** as King of **Austrasia** in 623.

Choibalsan (d.1952) Mongolian revolutionary leader. Originally trained as a lamaist monk, he went to Siberia, where he made contact with Russian revolutionaries. He founded his first revolutionary organization in 1919 and joined up with Sukhe Bator in 1921 to establish the Mongolian People's Revolutionary Party. When Soviet **Red Army** units entered Urga, the capital of Outer Mongolia (which had broken free of Chinese control in 1912) in 1921 and sponsored the creation of a pro-Soviet government, Choibalsan became a deputy War Minister. In succeeding years he became the dominant leader of the Mongolian People's Republic (formally established in 1924) and had eliminated all his rivals by 1940. His policies were modelled on those of **Stalin**, including the cultivation of a personality cult and harsh treatment of landowners. He was also responsible for the execution of thousands of lamaist monks.

Choiseul-Amboise, Etienne François, Duke of (1719–85) French politician. A minister of **Louis XV**, he became Duke of Choiseul and Foreign Minister in 1758. He arranged in 1756 the alliance between France and Austria against **Frederick II, 'the Great'**, and obtained good terms for France at the end of the **Seven Years War** (1763). He improved the army and navy, and developed trade and industry. However, he was alienated from Louis by Madame du **Barry** and he retired in 1770.

Chola Dynasty An ancient Tamil dynasty, which ruled much of southern India between the 8c and 13c. The height of power was under Rajaraja (985/1014) and Rajendra (1014/44), who extended the kingdom to include Ceylon. It introduced highly developed revenue administration, village self-organization, and irrigation systems. Tamil architecture and literature flourished.

Choshu A Japanese feudal domain (*han*) situated in south-west Honshu and founded during the **Ashikaga Shogunate** (1338–1573). After 1603 Choshu, as one of the domains that had resisted the establishment of the **Tokugawa Shogunate** (1603–1868), was classified as an 'outside fief' (*tozama*) *and stripped of land*. *Middle-ranking* **samurai** from Choshu played an important part in the overthrow of the Tokugawa and restoration of imperial rule in 1868. In subsequent decades they occupied key posts in the national government and army.

Choson The semi-sinicized Korean state occupying north Korea and south Manchuria, established in 190BC. In the centuries preceding the creation of Choson, the neolithic tribal culture of north Korea had been influenced by incoming waves of people from Manchuria, who brought with them knowledge of Chinese agriculture as well as iron and bronze technology. Although Choson began to extend its political control over the Korean Peninsula, it was conquered by the Chinese Han Dynasty in 108BC and divided into commanderies. ▷ **Han Dynasties**

Chosroes I, 'Anushirvan' (d.579) Sasanid King of Persia (531/79). After a long succession struggle, during the course of which he had his brothers put to death, he eventually succeeded his father, Kavadh. The empire he inherited was in disorder, rocked by the upheaval caused by revolution fomented by a religious sect, the Mazdakites. Once Chosroes had restored order, he set about implementing a series of reforms designed to strengthen his ailing empire. Most importantly, he created a new and fairer taxation system, based on a fixed, rather than variable, annual payment. He reorganized the army and the bureaucracy, developing a system of ministries or divans under a prime minister, and invested greater power in the hands of the aristocracy, rather than the previously powerful feudal lords. He also promoted agriculture, commerce and science. Chosroes waged war against Emperor **Justinian I, 'the Great'** for 20 years.

Chosroes II, 'Parviz' (d.628) Sasanid King of Persia (588/627). The grandson of **Chosroes I, 'Anushirvan'**, he conquered Syria, Palestine, Egypt and parts of Asia Minor (613–19), almost bringing the **Byzantine Empire** to its knees. However, Emperor **Heraclius** led a brillliant recovery and penetrated Persia, defeating Chosroes at

Nineveh (627), after which he was deposed and executed by his son, Kavadh II.

Chouans Peasant guerrilla bands from the western provinces of France, who rose against the republican government in Paris (1793), opposing attempts to enforce conscription and subdue the clergy. Their name comes from the Breton word for 'screech-owl', allegedly the nickname of their leader, Jean Cottereau. ▷ **French Revolution**

Chou Dynasty ▷ **Zhou Dynasty**

Chrétien, Joseph-Jacques-Jean (1934–) Canadian politician. As Chancellor in Pierre **Trudeau**'s administration he introduced two budgets in 1978 in an attempt to encourage industrial growth and fight inflation, but he failed in the latter since he also introduced tax cuts. In 1980 as Minister of Justice he fought against the concept of an independent Quebec, organizing the campaign leading up to the referendum. After Trudeau's resignation in 1984, the **Liberal Party**'s tradition of alternating francophone and anglophone leaders meant that it was John Turner who took over the leadership of the party rather than Chrétien.

Christelijk Historische Unie ▷ **Christian Historical Union**

Christen-Democratisch Appèl ▷ **Christian Democratic Appeal**

Christian I (1426–81) King of Denmark (1448/81), Norway (1450/81), and Sweden (1457/64). The founder of the Oldenburg royal line, he was the son of Dietrich, Count of Oldenburg, and Hedvig, heiress of Schleswig and Holstein. He was elected King of Denmark in succession to Christopher III (Christopher of Bavaria). In 1450 he was accepted as King of Norway, ousting **Karl Knutsson** of Sweden, and in 1457 he ousted Karl from the throne of Sweden as well (although he lost the crown to Karl again in 1464). In 1460 he was elected sovereign ruler of Schleswig and Holstein. Improvident and spendthrift, he maintained a splendid court in Copenhagen, but was always chronically short of money; to provide a dowry of 60 000 guilders for the marriage of his daughter, Margaret, to **James III** of Scotland, he mortgaged the Orkneys and Shetland for 8 000 guilders to make up the balance — a pledge that was never redeemed. In Denmark, however, he founded the University of Copenhagen in 1478. He was succeeded by his son, Hans I.

Christian II (1481–1559) King of Denmark and Norway (1513/23) and Sweden (1520/3). He mounted the throne of Denmark and Norway in 1513 and, in 1515, married Elisabeth of Habsburg, sister of Emperor **Charles V**. In 1520 he overthrew Sten **Sture, 'the Younger'**, the regent of Sweden, and thereafter was crowned king. But his treacherous massacre in the **Stockholm Bloodbath** of the foremost men in Sweden (8–10 Nov 1520) roused such opposition that he was driven out by **Gustav I Vasa** in 1523, marking the end of the **Kalmar Union** between the three kingdoms. In Denmark a popular revolt drove him for refuge to the Netherlands, and placed his uncle, **Frederick I**, on the throne. Assisted, however, by Charles V, Christian landed in Norway in 1531, but at Akershus next year was totally defeated, and spent his remaining years in imprisonment.

Christian III (1503–59) King of Denmark and Norway (1534/59). The elder son and successor of **Frederick I**, he was an ardent Lutheran, imposing the Reformation on Denmark, Norway and Iceland, and establishing the Lutheran state church. He acceded to the throne in the midst of a civil war, the so-called 'Count's War' (1533–6) between Catholic supporters of the ex-king **Christian II** and the Protestant son of Frederick. It ended only with the capitulation of Copenhagen (Aug 1536). Six days later, Christian arrested all the Catholic bishops who had opposed him, and confiscated church lands. He then encouraged agriculture and trade, brought out a Danish translation of the German Bible (1550), and hugely strengthened the monarchy. He was succeeded by his son, **Frederick II**.

Christian IV (1577–1648) King of Denmark and Norway (1588/1648). One of the best-remembered monarchs of Scandinavia, he was the son of **Frederick II**, whom he succeeded, ruling under regents until 1596. A man of action and heroic stature, he made the Danish navy and army stronger, and enhanced the city of Copenhagen with magnificent new buildings. He also founded the city of Kristiania (Christiania) on the site of medieval Oslo after it was burnt down in 1624. He invaded the Sweden of the young **Gustav II Adolf** in 1611, but failed to capture Stockholm and made peace in 1613 with the Treaty of Knærød (Knäred). In the **Thirty Years War** (1618–48) he joined the Protestant Union in 1625 to help his niece, Elizabeth of Bohemia, but retired from the fray after a catastrophic defeat at Lutter am Barenberge, near Hamelin, by Count von Tilley and **Wallenstein** in 1626. Denmark's power and prestige were now shattered, and the rest of Christian's reign was a story of steady decline. In 1628 he formed a defensive Baltic alliance with Gustav II Adolf against Wallenstein; but in a second war with the Sweden of Queen **Christina** in 1643–5, he lost the dominion of the Baltic he had previously gained. He was succeeded by his son, **Frederick III**.

Christian VII (1749–1808) King of Denmark and Norway (1766/1808). The son and successor of Frederick V, from an early age he suffered from dementia praecox, aggravated by the harshness of his tutor. He married in 1766 his English cousin, Caroline Matilda, sister of King **George III** of Britain, and in 1768 made a glittering tour of Europe, accompanied by his court physician, Count Johann Friedrich **Struensee**, whom he soon appointed a privy councillor. Struensee became the Queen's lover and seized effective power, but in 1772 was charged with treason and executed, while the Queen was divorced and exiled to Hanover. In 1784 the king was adjudged insane, and relinquished control to his son, Crown Prince Frederick, who eventually succeeded to the throne as **Frederick VI**.

Christian VIII (1786–1848) King of Denmark (1839/48). The son and successor of **Frederick VI**, as Crown Prince of Denmark he was elected King of Norway in 1814 to go with a new constitution (17 May). However, he was promptly ousted when Norway was taken by **Charles XIV John** of Sweden. As King of Denmark he revived the ancient **Althing** (parliament) of Iceland as a consultative assembly (1843), and allowed freedom of trade with Iceland. Early in 1848 he signed an order abolishing monarchical absolutism, which was implemented by his son and successor, **Frederick VII**, the following year.

Christian IX (1818–1906) King of Denmark (1863/1906). A prince of Glücksburg, he succeeded the childless **Frederick VII**. He was confirmed as Crown Prince of Denmark by the Protocol of London, signed by all the great powers in 1852 when it became clear that the old Oldenburg line would become extinct. On succeeding to the throne in 1863, he was immediately obliged to sign the 'November Constitution' of that year incorporating Schleswig into the Danish kingdom; this led to war with Prussia and Austria and the loss of both Schleswig and Holstein. In 1874, on the 1000th anniversary of the settlement of Iceland, he paid the first royal visit by a reigning monarch, and granted Iceland's first constitution, of limited autonomy under a governor. He was succeeded in 1906 by his elder son as **Frederick VIII**, while his younger son became King **George I** of Greece. His elder daughter, **Alexandra**, married the future King **Edward VII** of Britain, and his younger daughter, Mari Dagmar, married the future Tsar **Alexander III** of Russia.

Christian X (1870–1947) King of Denmark (1912/47) and of Iceland (1888/1944). The son of **Frederick VIII**, he was revered as a symbol of resistance during the German occupation in **World War II**. In 1915 he signed a new constitution granting the vote to women, and in 1918 signed the Act of Union with Iceland which granted Iceland full independence in personal union with the Danish sovereign (this ended in 1944). During World War II he elected to stay on in Denmark; he would ride on horseback through the streets as a defiant reminder of his presence, until he was put under house arrest by the Germans (1943–5). He married Alexandrine, Duchess of Mecklenburg-Schwerin, and was succeeded by their son, **Frederick IX**.

Christian of Brunswick (1599–1626) He was a son of the Duke of Brunswick and a Protestant commander and mercenary during the first part of the **Thirty Years War**. He fought against the Spanish in the Netherlands (1521) and raised an army to support the Elector Palatine, Frederick V. He was twice defeated by **Tilly** in five years of campaigning. He was called 'mad Christian'.

Christian, Fletcher (fl.18c) British seaman. He was the ringleader in the mutiny on the *Bounty*, which sailed to Tahiti 1787–8. In 1808 his descendants were found on Pitcairn Islands. ▷ **Bligh, William**

Christian Democrats Members of Christian Democratic political parties, most of which were formed in Western Europe after 1945, and which have since become a major political force. The Christian Democratic philosophy is based upon strong links with the Catholic Church and its notions of social and economic justice. It emphasizes the traditional conservative values of the family and church, but also more progressive, liberal values such as state intervention in the

economy and significant social welfare provision. Christian Democrat parties emerged to fill the vacuum created by the general disillusionment with parties of the right and left after **World War II**, a major exception being the UK, which has no such party. Electorally, the most successful example is the West German Christian Democratic Union (**CDU**) which, in alliance with its Bavarian sister party, the **CSU**, polled nearly 50 per cent of the votes in 1983. ▷ **Bundestag**

Christian Democrat Party (*Democrazia Cristiana*, DC) The most powerful of Italian parties in the post-fascist era and invariably the chief component in the coalition governments which form the basis of modern Italian politics. Emerging in 1942 as a clandestine anti-fascist group that was Catholic, but formally secular and non-confessional, it was the ideological heir of the **Popolari** from which its early leaders (eg **Gronchi** and **De Gasperi**) were drawn. Although embracing quite a wide range of views, the Christian Democrat Party is essentially made up of moderate conservatives of clerical sympathies.

Christian Democratic Appeal (*Christen-Democratisch Appèl*, CDA) Dutch political party, founded in 1973 as an amalgamation of the three main confessional parties: the **Catholic People's Party**, the **Anti-Revolutionary Party**, and the **Christian Historical Union**. The CDA was formed as a common defence against falling electoral support for the three member parties in the 1960s and 1970s, which was a result of general secularization. At first the CDA was a loose federation, but in 1976 it campaigned on a single electoral list, and in 1980 the member parties dissolved themselves as separate entities. The CDA is the party of Ruud **Lubbers**, the Dutch Prime Minister since 1982.

Christian Democratic Union (Germany) ▷ **CDU**

Christian Historical Union (*Christelijk Historische Unie*, CHU) Dutch Calvinist political party founded in 1908 as an extension of the Free **Anti-Revolutionary Party** (ARP, founded 1895). At the end of the 19c some Dutch Calvinist politicians, members of the Anti-Revolutionary Party (ARP), expressed their doubts about the democratic and religiously schismatic tendencies of the ARP leader, Abraham **Kuyper**. These more conservative and perhaps more patrician Christian Democrats eventually gathered in the CHU, led by A F de **Savornin Lohman**. The CHU has been a regular party of government, combining with other Christian Democrat parties. In the late 1960s increasing secularization began to reduce the CHU's support, to less than five per cent in 1972. In 1976 it joined the **Christian Democratic Appeal**, and in 1980 the CHU ceased to exist as a separate party.

Christian People's Party (*Parti Social Chrétien*, PSC; *Christelijke Volkspartij*, CVP) Belgian Roman Catholic political party founded in 1945 as a renewal of the previous Catholic Block (founded 1936). The first modern Catholic Party in Belgium was formed in 1884, which then dominated politics until 1914. Between the world wars it underwent changes of structure and name (1921, Belgian Catholic Union), and as the largest party in the country, the CVP/PSC has participated in all Belgian coalitions since 1950, with the exception of 1954–8. In 1968 the French and Dutch-speaking wings of the party split apart over the Leuven University language affair, although they still vote together except on language-related issues. As a broad party, it has seen some friction between the representatives of employers and Catholic trade unions.

Christina (1626–89) Queen of Sweden (1632/54). The daughter and successor of King **Gustav II Adolf**, she was educated like a boy during her minority, when the affairs of the kingdom were ably managed by her father's chancellor, Count Axel **Oxenstierna**. After she came of age in 1644, she adopted an independent line in both domestic and foreign policy and worked to bring an end to the costly **Thirty Years War** in which Sweden was engaged. She patronized the arts and attracted to her court some of the best minds in Europe, including Hugo Grotius, Salamatius and Descartes, who died there in 1650. She was strongly averse to marriage and found child-bearing repugnant. She refused to marry her cousin (later **Charles X Gustav**), but instead had him proclaimed Crown Prince. Then, having secretly embraced Catholicism and impatient of the personal restraints imposed on her as a ruler, she abdicated in 1654. She left Sweden for Italy, was openly received into the Catholic Church in Innsbruck and rode into Rome on horseback. She spent the remainder of her life in Rome as a pensioner of the pope and a generous patron of the arts.

Christophe, Henri (1767–1829) Haitian revolutionary. Born a slave on the island of Grenada, he joined the black insurgents on Haiti against the French (1790), and became one of their leaders, under **Toussaint L'Ouverture**. He was appointed President in 1807, and despite civil war was proclaimed King, as Henri I, in the northern part of the island in 1811. He ruled with vigour, but his avarice and cruelty led to an insurrection, and his subsequent suicide.

Christophersen, Henning (1939–) Danish politician. A member of the Danish parliament (**Folketinget**) from 1971 to 1984, he led the Danish Liberal Party (*Venstre*) from 1978 to 1984. In 1978–9 he was Minister of Foreign Affairs and in 1982–4 was Minister of Finance and Deputy Prime Minister. He has been a member of the EC Commission since 1984 and is a vice-president, in charge of economic and monetary cooperation.

Chulalongkorn (Rama V) (1853–1910) King of Siam (1868/1910). The son of King Maha Mong Kut, he was educated largely by English teachers, acquiring Western linguistic and cultural skills, after which he went, as traditionally prescribed, to a Buddhist monastery. He succeeded his father, as a minor, in 1868 and became king in his full right in 1873. He toured India and the **Dutch East Indies**, abolished slavery, freed his subjects from approaching him on hands and knees, built schools, hospitals, roads, railways and modernized the armed forces. He standardized the coinage, introduced posts and telegraphs, and policed, sanitized and electrified Bangkok. He sent his Crown Prince to study in Britain and visited Queen **Victoria** in 1897. He was forced to accept treaties with France (removing Siam's claims over Cambodia and Laos) and with Britain (removing Siamese sovereignty over the northern Malay states) as the imperial pressures bore down on his kingdom towards the end of the 19c.

Ch'u Min-i ▷ Chu Minyi

Chu Minyi (Ch'u Min-i) (1884–1946) Chinese politician and educator. He studied medicine at the University of Strasbourg (1915–21) and subsequently became Vice-President of the Institut Franco-Chinois attached to Lyons University. In 1925 he joined the **Guomindang** and was closely associated with **Wang Jingwei**, leader of the party's left wing. Following their invasion of China in 1937, the Japanese sponsored a separate Chinese nationalist regime under

Wang Jingwei in 1940 and Chu accepted the position of Foreign Minister in the new government. The regime gained little international support and crumbled with Japan's defeat in **World War II**. Chu was executed in 1946 for collaborating with the Japanese.

Chun Doo-hwan (1931–) South Korean soldier and politician. He trained at the Korean Military Academy and was commissioned as a second lieutenant in the South Korean army in 1955. After further training at the US Army Infantry School, in 1960 he worked with the Special Airborne Forces group and in military intelligence. After President **Park**'s assassination (Oct 1979), he took charge of the Korean Central Intelligence Agency (KCIA) and led the investigation into Park's murder. He assumed control of the army and the government after a coup in 1979. In 1981 he was appointed President and retired from the army to head the newly formed Democratic Justice Party (DJP). Under his rule, the country's 'economic miracle' continued, but popular opposition to the authoritarian nature of the regime mounted, which eventually forced his retirement in 1988.

Churchill, Lord Randolph (Henry Spencer) (1849–95) British politician. He was the third son of the 7th Duke of Marlborough, and the father of Winston **Churchill**. He entered parliament in 1874, and became conspicuous in 1880 as the leader of a ginger group of Conservatives known as the 'Fourth Party'. He was Secretary for India (1885–6), and for a short while Chancellor of the Exchequer and Leader of the House of Commons. His powers rapidly diminished by syphilis, he resigned after his first budget proved unacceptable, and thereafter devoted little time to politics. ▷ **Conservative Party** (UK)

Churchill, Sir Winston (Leonard Spencer) (1874–1965) British politician and author. The eldest son of Randolph **Churchill**, he was gazetted to the 4th Hussars in 1895, and his army career included fighting at Omdurman during the 1898 Nile Expeditionary Force. During the second Boer War he acted as a London newspaper correspondent. Initially a Conservative MP (1900), he joined the Liberals in 1904, and was Colonial Under-Secretary (1905), President of the Board of Trade (1908), Home Secretary (1910), and First Lord of the Admiralty (1911). In 1915 he was made the scapegoat for the Dardanelles disaster, but in 1917

became Minister of Munitions. After **World War I** he was Secretary of State for War and Air (1919–21), and (as a 'Constitutionalist' supporter of the Conservatives) Chancellor of the Exchequer (1924–9). In 1929 he returned to the Conservative fold, but remained out of step with the leadership until **World War II**, when he returned to the Admiralty; then, on Neville **Chamberlain**'s defeat (May 1940) formed a coalition government, and, holding both the premiership (1940–5) and the defence portfolio, led Britain through the war against Germany and Italy with steely resolution. Defeated in the July 1945 election, he became a pugnacious Leader of the Opposition. In 1951 he became Prime Minister again, though he was less effective after a stroke (1953) which was concealed from the public. From 1955 until his resignation in 1964, he remained a venerated backbencher. He achieved a world reputation not only as a great strategist and inspiring war leader, but as a classic orator with a supreme command of English, a talented painter and a writer with a great breadth of mind and a profound sense of history. He was knighted in 1953, and won the Nobel Prize for Literature the same year. ▷ **Boer Wars; Conservative Party** (UK); **Liberal Party** (UK)

Chvalkovský, František (1885–1944) Czechoslovak politician. He was Foreign Minister in the unhappy post-Munich period. A career diplomat, he served as Ambassador to Rome, endeavouring to win strong Italian support for Czechoslovakia against Germany. As this became impossible, he veered towards cooperation with the Axis powers, which made him a natural choice for his post-Munich post. However, in 1939 he was bullied into accepting **Hitler**'s demands and, with President **Hácha**, acceding to the division and domination of Czechoslovakia in Mar. He had the dubious privilege of proving that **appeasement** backfires.

CIA (Central Intelligence Agency) The official US intelligence gathering organization responsible for external security, established under the National Security Act (1947) and reporting directly to the President. The CIA was conceived as the coordinator of foreign intelligence and counterintelligence, but it has also engaged in domestic operations. As a result of abuses of power in both the domestic (notably in the **Watergate** affair) and foreign arenas, the CIA must now coordinate domestic activities with the FBI and report on covert activities to Congress.

Cialdini, Enrico, Duke of Gaeta (1811–92) Italian general and politician. He left Italy after his part in the abortive risings of Parma and Modena (1831) and took refuge in Paris, where he studied medicine. In 1833 he joined the liberal forces in Spain but returned to serve in the Piedmontese army in 1848–9. He remained in the service of **Victor Emmanuel II** after the Battle of **Novara**, fighting in the Crimea, and at Palestro (1859) and Gaeta (1860). After failing as a commander in the war of 1866, he retired from the army. He subsequently pursued a successful diplomatic career: he was Ambassador to Madrid (1870–3), and to Paris (1876–81).

Ciano, Galeazzo, di Galeazzo, Count (1903–44) Italian politician and diplomat. Son of an admiral, he took part in the **March on Rome** and had a successful diplomatic career from 1925 to 1930, when, after marrying **Mussolini**'s daughter, he was rapidly promoted to Under-Secretary for Press and Propaganda and a seat on the **Fascist Grand Council**. In June 1936 he became Foreign Minister. He negotiated the Axis Agreement with Germany and supported the Italian invasion of Albania (1939) and the Balkans (1940–1), but was unenthusiastic about the invasion of France, especially after **Hitler**'s unilateral and early declaration of war. Dismissed as Foreign Minister (Feb 1943), Ciano was one of those who called for the **Duce**'s resignation in July 1943. He fled to Germany after his father-in-law's arrest but was blamed by Hitler and **Ribbentrop** for Mussolini's defeat and was executed.

Cicero, Marcus Tullius (106–43BC) Roman orator, politician and man of letters. At Rome he studied law, oratory, philosophy and literature, and embarked upon a political career, attaining the consulship in 63BC. Though he foiled **Catiline**'s revolutionary plot, he broke the law by executing Roman citizens without a trial, and when charges were pressed, went into exile at Thessalonica (58BC). In 57BC he was recalled by the people, but lost the esteem of both **Caesar**'s and **Pompey the Great**'s factions by vacillating between the two. Living in retirement (46–44BC), he wrote most of his chief works on rhetoric and philosophy. In 43BC he delivered his famous speeches against Mark Antony, the so-called 'Philippics'. He was murdered near Caieta by Antony's soldiers as he tried to escape. ▷ **Augustus**

Cid, El (c.1043–99) Spanish hero. His real name was Rodrigo (Ruy) Díaz de Vivar, but he soon became known as the *Cid* (from the Moorish *Sidi*, 'lord'); *Campeador* ('warrior') is often added. A soldier of fortune and great patriot, he was constantly fighting from 1065; his great achievement was the capture of Valencia (1094), where later he died.

científicos The pejorative term (literally, 'scientists') used to describe the intellectual supporters of Mexico's President Porfirio **Díaz** from 1876 to 1911. *Científicos* were generally Positivists, who championed the application of practical scientific (especially social sciences') methods to the solution of national problems such as industrialization and education, arguing that 'individual absolute right is worth as much as absolute monarchy'. They were pre-eminent in the period 1876 to 1906, arguing that the government's duty was to assure landowners of their rights. They also believed that 'scientific-technical progress' decreed the demise of the Indian, the end to customary law which protected him, and the integration of Mexico into the international economy and European society.

Çiflik In the **Ottoman Empire**, a type of estate acquired by lease or as a tax farm and which, unlike a **timar**, was treated by its owner as private property. Like a feudal landowner in Europe, the owner of a *çiflik* could claim labour service and between a third and a half of his tenants' produce. The çiflik system developed from the 17c in some of the best agricultural areas of the Balkans (but not in **Moldavia and Wallachia**) and resulted in a shift in the balance of power between the provinces and the Ottoman Porte.

Cimbri A Germanic people from the area around Jutland who migrated south with the neighbouring Teutons towards the end of the 2c BC in search of new lands. Their raids into **Gaul**, initially successful, spread panic on all sides — the 'Terror Cimbricus'. They were defeated and destroyed by the Roman General Marius (101BC) on the Raudian Fields in the plain of Vercellae, in the region of the upper Po River. ▷ **Germanic Invasions**

Cimon (c.507–c.450BC) Athenian soldier and politician, the son of **Miltiades**, the conqueror at **Marathon**. He fought at the Battle of **Salamis** (480BC), and from 476BC he was the most notable commander of the forces of the **Delian League** in the patriotic struggle against the Persians. His greatest exploit was his destruction of a Persian fleet and army at the River Eurymedon (c.467BC). He led an unsuccessful expedition to support the Spartans during the helot uprising in 462BC, and was dismissed and ostracized (461BC). He was recalled in 454BC, and may have been instrumental in obtaining a five-years armistice with **Sparta**. He died at the siege of a town in Cyprus. ▷ **Athenian Empire; helots; ostracism**

Cincinnatus, Lucius Quinctius (5c BC)
Roman politician, farmer and folk hero. Called from the plough and given absolute power to rescue the Roman Army of the consul Minucius, which had been trapped by the Aequi (458BC), he voluntarily gave up this power and returned to his farm, as soon as the crisis was over.

Cinna, Lucius Cornelius (d.84BC)
Prominent Roman politician of the turbulent 80s BC. Driven from Rome and illegally deposed while consul in 87BC, he recaptured the city with the help of Gaius **Marius** amid much bloodshed, and was all-powerful there until his murder in 84BC. ▷ **Sulla**

Cinque Giornate (Mar 1848)
The Italian term (literally, 'the five days') used to describe ferocious street fighting in Milan that heralded the outbreak of the anti-Austrian revolution in Lombardy. Having heard the news of the overthrow of **Metternich**, insurgents drove **Radetzky** from the city, establishing a provisional government under Carlo **Cattaneo**.

Cinque Ports
Originally, the five southern English coast ports of Dover, Hastings, Hythe, Romney, and Sandwich, associated by royal authority (under **Edward the Confessor**) to provide ships for naval defence; Rye and Winchelsea were added later. They received royal privileges, including (from 1265) the right to send barons to parliament, and charters, the first dating from 1278; they were governed by a Lord Warden who was also Constable of Dover Castle. Their role declined with the growth of the navy under the Tudors and Stuarts, and the status was abolished in 1835. ▷ **Stuart, House of; Tudor, House of**

Ciompi, Revolt of the (1378)
A popular rebellion in Florence during the painful adjustments which the city's economy had to make in the aftermath of the Black Death. It was led by workers who were not allowed guild membership and who were therefore disenfranchised. The merchant oligarchy was briefly overthrown in favour of popular government but returned to power in a counter-coup.

Cipriani, Arthur 'Tattoo' (1875–1945)
Trinidadian white labour leader. Cipriani represented the working man in the Trinidad legislature in the 1920s and 1930s. Of French-Corsican origin, he served as an officer in **World War I** and on his return set up the Trinidad Workingmen's Association (1922). Once elected to the Legislative Council, he championed the cause of the 'barefoot man' and, in 1932, founded the moderate Trinidad Labour Party which campaigned for a strong trade-union movement, racial harmony and constitutional change. His failure to effect substantial socio-political progress in part led to the **Disturbances** (1935–7), and the conversion of labour to the more militant policies of Uriah **Butler**.

Circles of the Empire (*Reichskreise*)
Administrative districts established (1500) by Maximilian I in the Empire. The original six (Bavaria, Swabia, Franconia, Rhineland, Westphalia, Saxony) were later (1512) joined by four more (Upper Saxony, Austria, Burgundy, Palatinate). These areas had various responsibilities associated with the Imperial administration (eg collecting tolls, taxes, customs).

CIS (Commonwealth of Independent States)
A grouping (1991) of 11 independent states out of the 15 republics which formerly made up the Soviet Union. They are Armenia, Azerbaijan, Belorussia, Kazakhstan, Kirghizia, Moldavia, Russia, Tajikistan, Turkmenistan, Ukraine and Uzbekistan. ▷ **USSR**

Cisalpine Republic
The satellite republic established by Bonaparte in Lombardy in Apr 1797. Later the same year, the territories of the smaller Cispadane Republic (Reggio, Modena, Massa and Carrara, and Ferrara and Bologna) were added, followed by the western regions of the old Venetian Republic, Mantua, the Romagna and the Valtellina. Although the republic was briefly suppressed in 1799–1800, after being overrun by Austrian and Russian forces, it was re-established after the Battle of **Marengo** (1800). In 1801 it was renamed the Republic of Italy. ▷ **Napoleon I**

Cisar, Cestmir (1920–)
Czechoslovak communist and reformer. He worked his way up through the party apparatus to become a

secretary to the Central Committee and also the Minister of Education in 1963. But, having studied in France, he proved too liberal a minister for the establishment and was appointed Ambassador to Bucharest in 1965. In 1968 he was brought back by Alexander **Dubček** to be Chairman of the Czech National Council and proved very popular with young people in particular. Inevitably, he was dismissed from office and from the Communist Party following the Soviet invasion: the young had to wait 20 years for their peaceful revolution.

Cisneros, Francisco Jiménez de (1436–1517) Castilian statesman. He entered the Franciscan Order and was appointed confessor to Queen **Isabella I, 'the Catholic'** in 1492 and then (1495) Archbishop of Toledo, and cardinal and Inquisitor-General (1507). He was a zealous reformer of his own Franciscan order in **Castile** and promoter of spiritual literature and influenced the Queen's decision to prohibit the Muslim faith in Castile (1502). After her death he was active in military expeditions into North Africa (1507–9), resulting notably in the capture of Orán (1509). Twice regent, the second time on the death of King **Ferdinand II, 'the Catholic'**, he died on his way to greet Charles of Burgundy as the new King of Spain. His achievements for Castilian culture include the foundation of the new university at Alcalá de Henares (1508), and the publication of the famous Complutensian Polyglot Bible (1522).

Civic Forum (1989) The broad-based alliance of anti-communist groups in Czechoslovakia that came together to force the resignation of the communist government in Nov. This was subsequently christened the **Velvet Revolution**, since the toppling of the government had been achieved without serious bloodshed. The moving force had for long been **Charter 77** led by Václav **Havel** who subsequently became President. Civic Forum won 51 per cent of the votes in the June 1990 election but split into two rival groups in Jan 1991.

Civil Constitution of the Clergy (1790) A decree of the National Assembly confiscating the property of the Catholic Church, and reorganizing it on the model of the new administrative system of France. Bishops and priests were to be elected by all voters in their areas. The Pope, who had not been consulted, condemned the measure in Mar 1791. The Assembly had already imposed an oath of loyalty on existing clergy. Nearly all the bishops, and about half of the parish priests, refused to take the oath, thus dividing the clergy into the constitutional clergy, those who agreed, and the refractory clergy, those who refused. This was an important factor in producing resistance to the **French Revolution**. At the most extreme period of the Revolution (1793–4), attempts were made to replace Christianity by the 'Worship of Reason'; although this remained a brief aberration, the Catholic Church took a long time to recover from its persecution during the Revolution. It was restored to the position of an established Church by the **Concordat** (1801).

civil disobedience A political strategy adopted by M K **Gandhi** and his followers in India in 1930, in opposition to Britain's imperial rule: launched by a march to the coast in order to break the law symbolically by making salt (on which tax was payable), it was a non-violent, mass, illegal protest, intended to discredit the authority of the state. The movement was banned, and many were arrested, including Gandhi; but a pact was reached in 1931, and Gandhi then participated in the second of the **Round Table Conferences**. The strategy was later used by Martin Luther King Jr to good effect, and is a path sometimes advocated by opponents of nuclear weapons.

Civil Guard Founded in Spain as a militarized police force in 1844 to keep down banditry, the Civil Guard was organized like an army, led by a general and officers with military rank. Its brutal vigilance of the countryside in defence of the status quo led the ruling classes to regard it as the *Benemérita* (the 'well-deserving'), while for the lower classes its distinctive three-cornered hat, green uniforms, and great cloaks made it one of the most hated symbols of the *ancien régime*. Most of the Civil Guard sided with the Nationalists in the **Spanish Civil War**, though it played a leading role in holding places such as Madrid and Barcelona for the Republic. Under **Franco** the Civil Guard's dominance of the countryside was consolidated. In 1986 the first civilian appointee was made its Director General. Today it numbers 60000, with its energies divided between controlling the traffic on the highways, patrolling the countryside, guarding foreign embassies, and combating terrorism.

Civilis, Claudius (Julius) (fl.69–70AD) Dutch folk-hero, from Roman times. He was one of the favoured Batavian tribe who in opposition to Roman conscription and gubernatorial exactions took advantage of the imperial crisis after **Nero**'s fall to lead his people into revolt in alliance with the Germans (especially the Frisians) and then also the Gauls. Civilis seems to have been sufficiently Romanized to win over troops and captains. But **Vespasian**, once master of Rome, despatched Petillius Cerialis to end the revolt. Civilis refused terms of surrender, but Gauls and Roman mutineers were overawed and Civilis was defeated by the Romans at Trier in AD70, and after further fighting fell back on sea-protected Batavia. Nothing more is known of him.

civil rights The rights guaranteed by certain states to its citizens. Fundamental to the concept of civil rights is the premise that a government should not arbitrarily act to infringe upon these rights, and that individuals and groups, through political action, have a legitimate role in determining and influencing what constitutes them. Historically, civil rights in England have been protected by the **Magna Carta** and in the USA by the **Constitution** and **Bill of Rights**. In common usage, the term often refers to the rights of groups, particularly ethnic and racial minorities, as well as to the rights of the individual.

Civil Rights Acts US legislation which prohibits the states from discriminating against any citizen on the grounds of race or colour. The act of 1866 included blacks within its definition of US citizenship. President Andrew **Johnson**'s veto so angered Republican moderates in Congress that radicals were able to override the veto, and incorporated its provisions in the **Fourteenth Amendment**. However the act was undermined by the Supreme Court in the Slaughterhouse Cases (1873) and US v Cruikshank (1875). The act of 1875, passed as a memorial to Charles Sumner, upheld the equal rights of blacks in the use of inns, theatres and public transport (though education was specifically excluded), but was declared unconstitutional in the civil rights cases of 1883. By the 1950s only about a quarter of those Southern blacks who were qualified to vote could actually do so because state officials were adept at preventing them from registration. The Act of 1957 therefore established the Civil Rights Commission to examine such cases. It was backed up by a new Civil Rights Division in the Justice Department which could seek injunctions to prevent denial of the right to

vote. Even when bolstered in 1960 the Act did not prove very effective. By the act of 1964 the Attorney General was authorized to institute proceedings directly when voting rights were abused, and empowered to accelerate the desegregation of schools. Agencies which practised racial discrimination were liable to lose federal funding, and an Equal Opportunities Commission was set up to end job discrimination on the grounds of race, religion or sex. Discrimination was also prohibited in hotels and public transport. This legislation, together with the establishment of the Community Relations Service, indicated the federal government's awareness of the difficulties in dismantling the structures of white supremacy and was more effective than any previous **civil rights** legislation.

civil rights movement A movement in the USA, especially 1954-68, aimed at securing through legal means the enforcement of the guarantees of racial equality contained in the Civil War Amendments to the US **Constitution**, namely, the Thirteenth, Fourteenth, and Fifteenth Amendments, and by civil rights acts of the 1860s and 1870s. These guarantees were severely curtailed by later legislation. In particular, the Supreme Court rulings of 1883, which declared the Civil Rights Act of 1875 unconstitutional because Congress had no right to trespass on the states' internal powers of economic regulation, opened the way to racial segregation. The civil rights movement began as an attack on specific forms of segregation in the South, then broadened into a massive challenge to all forms of racial discrimination. It made considerable gains, especially at the level of legal and juridical reform, culminating in the Supreme Court case of **Brown v Board of Education of Topeka, Kansas** (1954), in which Thurgood **Marshall** successfully argued against school segregation. The first major challenge was the Montgomery bus boycott of 1955, which was sparked by an incident in which a black woman, Rosa **Parks**, refused to give up her seat to a white man. As a result of the boycott, the buses were desegregated and Martin Luther **King**, Jr, emerged as the movement's leader. King was a major force in establishing the **SCLC** (Southern Christian Leadership Conference). Forming a coalition with the **NAACP** and other organizations such as the **National Urban League**, the **Congress of Racial Equality** (**CORE**) and the Student Non-Violent Coordinating Committee (SNCC), he led a campaign aimed at desegregating all public facilities, including schools, restaurants, stores, and transportation, by nonviolent means, and at winning for blacks the unrestricted right to vote and to hold public office. Major actions included the first big clash over school desegregation (1957), which took place in Little Rock, Arkansas; the efforts of the 'freedom riders', groups of blacks and whites who challenged segregation in interstate transport (1961); the national March on Washington (1963), in which over 200 000 blacks and whites participated; and the voter registration drive in Alabama, which culminated in the march from Selma to Montgomery (1965). As white resistance grew, many participants in the marches and demonstrations were arrested, many were beaten, and some lost their lives. But by the late 1960s most of the original goals had been achieved as a result of Court decisions, major legislation and the actions of Presidents **Eisenhower**, **Kennedy** and especially Lyndon **Johnson** in enforcing the law. The Civil Rights Act of 1964 barred discrimination in public accommodations and in employment; the Voting Rights Act (1965) ensured blacks' right to vote in places where it had hitherto been denied; and the Civil Rights Act of 1968 prohibited discrimination in the sale or rental of housing. One result of the 60s legislation was the increased participation of blacks in political life, even in Southern communities that were once bastions of segregation. But by the mid-60s, different problems were arising in the black ghettos of the Northern cities when blacks began rioting to protest their poverty, high unemployment and poor living conditions. Both King, who turned his attention northward in the last three years of his life, and more militant black leaders such as **Malcolm X**, recognized that the struggle for equality was moving into the economic sphere. So did Jesse **Jackson**, an associate of King's, who focused on the importance of creating jobs by investment in black businesses. But, unlike King, Malcolm X and his followers were advocating black separatism rather than integration, and the use of force to reach their goals. Significantly, widespread rioting followed King's assassination in 1968. In the decades since his death, although the economic condition of US blacks improved, the large gap between blacks and whites remained, and has led to racial tensions that have yet to be resolved.

Civil Service Examination System

A system in China for recruiting government officials based on merit rather than birth, dating from the 8c. As early as the 2c BC local officials had been called upon to 'recommend' talented candidates for official posts, but until the 8c officialdom continued to be monopolized by powerful aristocratic families. The examination system aimed to break down the hereditary principle and draw upon a larger pool from which to recruit the bureaucracy. Begun during the **Tang Dynasty** and systematized during the **Song Dynasty**, examinations were held triennally at prefectural, provincial and metropolitan levels, each one conferring a civil service degree. Initially the curriculum on which the examinations were based was a wide-ranging one, but by the 14c was limited to knowledge of the **Confucian Classics**. While success at even the lowest level conferred on the candidate membership of the gentry-literati class, important official posts went to those who had passed the provincial and metropolitan level examinations. The system became increasingly rigid and corrupt during the 19c and was abolished in 1905, to be replaced by a network of modern schools offering a wider curriculum.

Cixi (Tz'u Hsi) (1835–1908) Chinese consort of the Xianfeng Emperor (1851/62). She rose to dominate China by manipulating the succession to the throne and bore the Xianfeng Emperor his only son, who succeeded at the age of five as the Tongzhi Emperor. Cixi (whose personal name was Yehenala), however, kept control even after his majority in 1873. After his death (1875), she flouted the succession laws of the Imperial clan to ensure the succession of **Zai Tian**, another minor, as the **Guangxu** (Kuang-hsu) Emperor, and continued to assert control even when the new Emperor reached maturity. In 1900 she took China into war against the combined treaty powers in support of the Boxer movement. Only after her death in Beijing was it possible to begin reforms. ▷ **Boxer Rising; Hundred Days of Reform; Qing Dynasty**

Clam-Martinic, Jindrich, Count (1826–87) Bohemian landowner and provincial politician. From the turn of the 18c and 19c, the landed nobility of the Czech lands, none of Czech nationality, began to associate with the emerging Czech intelligentsia and politicians as a means of asserting their provincial rights against centralist rule from Habsburg Vienna. In the 1860s and 1870s Clam-Martinic played a leading role in pursuing this policy in conjunction with František **Palacký** and **Rieger**, the leaders of the so-called Young Czech Party. But their combined tactics achieved nothing, and by the mid-1870s a purely Czech party emerged, the so-called Young Czechs, aiming for at least national autonomy with little regard for Germans, ennobled or otherwise.

Clarendon, Edward Hyde, 1st Earl of (1609–74) English statesman and historian. He trained as a lawyer, and in 1640 became a member of the **Short Parliament**. At first he supported parliamentary claims, but in 1641 became a close adviser of **Charles I**, and headed the royalist opposition in the Commons until 1642. He was knighted in 1643, and made Chancellor of the Exchequer, became High Chancellor in 1658, and at the **Restoration** (1660) was created Baron Hyde and (1661) Earl of Clarendon. In 1660 his daughter Anne (1638–71) secretly married the King's brother, James (later **James VII and II**). Unpopular as a statesman, Clarendon irritated Cavaliers and Puritans alike, and in 1667 he fell victim to a conspiracy at court. Impeached for high treason, he left the country for France, where he died. ▷ **English Civil Wars**

Clarendon Code A series of Acts passed by the **Cavalier Parliament** (1661–79) between 1661 and 1665 which reasserted the supremacy of the Church of England over Protestant nonconformity after the collapse of the 'Puritan Revolution' in 1660. The most important were the Corporation Act (1661) and the Act of Uniformity (1662). Nonconformity was recognized as lawful, but severe restrictions were placed on the activities of Nonconformists. ▷ **Puritanism; Uniformity, Acts of**

Clarendon, Constitutions of (1164) A written declaration of rights claimed by **Henry II** of England in ecclesiastical affairs, with the purpose of restoring royal control over the English Church. Promulgated at Clarendon, near Salisbury, the Constitutions (especially Clause 3, which jeopardized benefit of clergy and threatened clerical criminals with secular penalties) brought Thomas Becket and Henry II into open conflict. ▷ **Becket, St Thomas (à)**

Clark, Joe (Charles Joseph) (1939–) Canadian politician. At first a journalist and then Professor of Political Science, he was elected to the Federal Parliament in 1972, becoming leader of the Progressive Conservative Party (1976) and of the Opposition (1980–83). In 1979 he became Canada's

youngest-ever Prime Minister. His minority government lost the general election the following year, and he was deposed as party leader in 1983. In 1984 he became Canada's Secretary of State for External Affairs.

Clark, Mark Wayne (1896–1984) US army officer. Chosen by Dwight D **Eisenhower** to plan the 1943 Allied invasion of North Africa, he became commander of the Allied armies in Italy in 1944. In 1945, after **World War II**, he headed the US forces occupation in Austria. During the **Korean War** he served as commander of the **UN** forces, participated in the lengthy peace talks of 1952–3, and signed the armistice.

Claudius (10BC–AD54) Roman Emperor (AD41/54). He was the grandson of the Empress **Livia**, brother of **Germanicus**, and nephew of the Emperor **Tiberius**. Kept in the background because of his physical disabilities, he devoted himself to historical studies, and thus survived the vicious in-fighting of the imperial house. Becoming Emperor largely by accident in the chaos after **Caligula**'s murder, he proved to be an able and progressive ruler, despite his gross and sometimes ridiculous indulgence of his wives and freedmen. Through his lavish public works and administrative reforms, he made a lasting contribution to the government of Rome and the empire, and through the annexation of Britain, Mauretania, and Thrace, a significant extension of its size. He died in AD54, poisoned, it was widely believed, by his fourth wife, **Agrippina the Younger**.

Claudius II Gothicus (d.AD270) Roman Emperor (268/70). He was the officer of, and successor to, Emperor **Gallienus**. His short reign was notable chiefly for his decisive defeat of the **Goths** and his ending of their threat to the Balkan provinces — whence his title, 'Gothicus'. He died of the plague.

Clausewitz, Karl (Philip Gottlieb) von (1780–1831) Prussian general. He served with distinction in the Prussian and Russian Armies, and ultimately became Director of the Prussian army school, and **Gneisenau**'s Chief of Staff. His posthumously published *Vom Kriege* ('On War'), in which war was regarded as a continuation of diplomacy by other means, revolutionized military theory, and was extremely influential in Germany and beyond. ▷ **Prussia**

Clay, Henry (1777–1852) US politician. The son of a Baptist preacher, he became a lawyer

(1797), entered the House of Representatives in 1811, and was chosen its speaker, a post he held for many years. He was one of the Congressional 'war hawks' active in bringing on the **War of 1812**–15 with Britain, and was one of the commissioners who arranged the Treaty of **Ghent** which ended it. His attempts to hold the Union together in the face of the issue of slavery, earned him the title of 'the great pacificator'. In 1824, 1832 and 1844 he was an unsuccessful National Republican and Whig candidate for the presidency.

Clayton–Bulwer Treaty (19 Apr 1850) A US–British agreement on the terms for building a canal across Central America. It remained in effect until 1901, when it was superseded by the Hay–Pauncefote Treaty. Its major provision was to forbid either party to exercise exclusive control or to build fortifications. The parties involved were the US Secretary of State, John M Clayton, and the British Minister to Washington, Sir Henry Lytton Bulwer. The Panama Canal was not completed until 1914.

CLC (Canadian Labour Congress) Canadian labour organization. It was established in 1956 with the merger of the Trades and Labor Congress (associated with the US AFL) and the Canadian Congress of Labour (similarly associated with the US CIO). Unlike the US labour movement, the CLC was ready to take direct political action and in 1961 it united with the **CCF** (Cooperative Commonwealth Federation) to form the **New Democratic Party.** ▷ **AFL–CIO Clear Grits** Canadian political party. The name given to a radical reform group in Upper **Canada (Canada West**/Ontario) in the 1850s. The term derived from the group's attitude of uncompromising determination. It promoted major constitutional reform, including representation by population, direct election to executive posts, and secularization of **Clergy Reserves**. It played an important part in Confederation and after 1867 it formed the core of the Canadian **Liberal Party.** ▷ **Brown, George**

Cleisthenes (6c BC) Athenian politician. A member of the Alcmaeonid family, he was the founder of Athenian democracy. His constitutional reforms (c.507BC) undermined traditional local loyalties by dividing the citizen body of Athens into 10 tribes (*phylai*), each comprising citizens from all regions of Attica: the city, coast and inland areas. Each tribe contributed 50 members annually to the democratic council of 500, and in all respects the Cleisthenic tribes provided the organizational basis for the democracy as it developed in the 5c–4c BC. ▷ **Alcmaeonids**

Clemenceau, Georges Eugène Benjamin (1841–1929) French politician. He studied medicine and visited the USA (1865–9), where he married an American. Elected to the National Assembly (1871), he resigned his seat in protest at the actions of the government that provoked the uprising in Paris known as the **Paris Commune**. Re-elected in 1876, he became the leader of the radicals (on the extreme Left). Implication in the Panama scandal led to his defeat in the 1893 elections. He was a leader of the campaign for the rehabilitation of **Dreyfus**, which allowed his return to parliament as a Senator in 1903. Clemenceau was Prime Minister in 1906–9 and 1917–20, when his determination spurred France to make the effort to pursue victory in **World War I**. He presided at the **Paris Peace Conference** (1919), where he sought unsuccessfully to obtain in the Treaty of **Versailles** a settlement that would preserve France from another German attack. Nicknamed 'the Tiger' for the ferocity of his oratorical attacks on his political opponents, he was equally renowned for his journalism, in *L'Aurore*, at the time of the Dreyfus Affair, and in his own newspaper, *L'Homme libre* (renamed *L'Homme enchaîné* after a quarrel with the censor) during the war.

Clement V (Bertrand de Got) (c.1260–1314) French Pope (1305/14). He became Archbishop of Bordeaux in 1299. As Pope, he suppressed the **Templars**, and removed the seat of the papacy to Avignon (1309), a movement disastrous to Italy.

Clement VII (Giulio de' Medici) (1478–1534) Italian Pope (1523/34). He allied himself with **Francis I** of France against the Holy Roman Emperor **Charles V**, whose troops sacked Rome in 1527, and for a while became his prisoner. His indecisiveness, along with his refusal to sanction **Henry VIII**'s divorce from **Catherine of Aragon**, hastened the **Reformation.** ▷ **Rome, Sack of**

Clement IX (Giulio Rospigliosi) (1600–69) Italian Pope (1667/9). He was papal ambassador to Spain (1644/53) and Secretary of State to Alexander VII, and sought, through the so-called Clementine Peace (Jan 1669), to prevent **Louis XIV** of France from persecuting the Jansenists. The issue of Jansenism, however, took on a lesser significance than Louis's increasing insistence on Gallican rights to limit the authority of the papacy within France. Louis's refusal to respond to Clement's pleas that he assist the Venetians in their struggle against the Turks during the War of **Candia** further strained relations. The slight assistance the Pope was able to offer was insufficient to avert Turkish victory and Clement died while mourning the Christians killed by the infidel in the final stages of the conflict.

Clement X (1590–1676) Pope (1670/6). Made a Cardinal in 1669, he had previously held a number of important Church offices, including that of papal ambassador to Naples. As Pope, he sought vainly to rouse Europe against the Turkish threat in the Mediterranean and in Eastern Europe. Absence of support from **Louis XIV** (generated in part by Clement's refusal to allow the French king to collect revenues from vacant sees), coupled with a general uninterest among other European princes, stymied any chance of a general crusade. However, Clement did manage to strengthen papal finances sufficiently to provide subsidies for the Poles in their struggle against the Turks.

Clement XI (1649–1721) Pope (1700/21). He was elected Pope at a difficult time for the papacy, with its political role in sharp decline and its control of national Churches increasingly threatened. Although from the outset Clement hoped to avoid conflict with either of the great ruling houses of Europe, he succeeded in antagonizing first the Austrian Habsburgs, by supporting the recognition of **Louis XIV**'s grandson, Philip of Anjou, as King of Spain, and then the Bourbons, when he gave in to the demands of Joseph I of Austria to recognize his brother, Charles, as the rightful pretender to the Spanish throne. By the Treaties of **Utrecht** (1713) and **Rastatt** (1714), Clement was forced to concede suzerainty over Naples, Sicily, Parma and Piacenza, while papal influence in France was increasingly marginalized by the growth of Gallicanism and the rise of Jansenism. It was against this latter that, in Sep 1713, he issued the Bull *Unigenitus* which prompted widespread opposition among the many French clergy who supported the now outlawed heresy. ▷ **Habsburg Dynasty**

Clement XIII (1693–1769) Pope (1758/69). He held several important ecclesiastical positions before he became Cardinal in 1737. As Pope, he faced considerable hostility from most of Europe's more powerful Catholic princes who, at the time, were seeking to exert greater control over their own national Churches. This was especially true of the Portuguese and the Bourbon rulers of Spain, Naples and France, who were all engaged in anti-Jesuit campaigns, but it was also evident within the Habsburg Empire, which witnessed the development of Febronianism, the German equivalent of Gallicanism. Despite Clement's attempts to defend the Jesuits, they were expelled from Portugal (1759), France and its dominions (1764), the Spanish Empire (1767) and the Kingdom of Naples and Sicily (1768). Finally in 1769 the ambassadors of the three Bourbon powers demanded that the Society of Jesus be suppressed totally; Clement refused, but within a month had a stroke and died.

Clement XIV (1705–74) Pope (1769/74). Educated by the Jesuits, he was made a Cardinal by **Clement XIII**, who hoped he would prove a useful ally in his struggle against the rulers of Portugal, Spain, France and Naples. The latter had proved themselves determined to destroy the Society of Jesus, not least because it was seen as a symbol of papal interference in their domestic affairs. However, when elected Pope on Clement XIII's death, he feared that open schism might emerge unless he placated the great Bourbon powers. In July 1773 he, therefore, issued the *Dominus ac Redemptor* dissolving the Society; the suppression lasted until 1814.

Clementis, Vladimír (1902–52) Slovak politician. He became a Czechoslovak communist MP in 1935 but criticized the Nazi–Soviet Pact in 1939 and spent **World War II** in London. In 1945 he became Vice-Minister of Foreign Affairs in the first postwar government. One of the organizers of the 1948 coup, he succeeded Jan **Masaryk** as Foreign Minister, but was forced to resign in 1950 as a 'deviationist'. During the Stalinist purges, he was hanged along with Rudolf **Slánský**. ▷ **German–Soviet Pact**

Cleomenes I (d.490BC) King of **Sparta** (c.520/490BC) in the Agiad royal family. He sought to extend Sparta's power in mainland Greece: he intervened repeatedly in Athens (expelling the **tyrant** Hippias, son of **Pisistratus**, in 510BC), defeated Sparta's main Peloponnesian enemy, **Argos** (c.494BC), and engineered the deposition of his fellow king at Sparta, Demaratus, in order to intervene in Aegina. However, he avoided more distant commitments, refusing to intervene in Samos c.517BC, or to support the **Ionian Revolt** against Persia (499BC). The historian Herodotus recounts his eventual madness and suicide.

Cleopatra VII (69–30BC) Queen of Egypt (51/48BC and 47/30BC). She was the daughter of **Ptolemy XII Neos Dionysos (Auletes)**. A woman of great intelligence, she made the most of her undoubted physical charms to strengthen her own position within Egypt, and to save the country from annexation by Rome. Thus, Julius **Caesar**, whom she bore a son, Caesarion, supported her claim to the throne against her brother (47BC), while Mark **Antony**, by whom she had three children, restored to her several portions of the old Ptolemaic Empire, and even gave to their joint offspring substantial areas of the Roman East (34BC). Defeated along with Antony at **Actium** (31BC), she preferred suicide to being captured and exhibited at Rome in Octavian's victory parade. The asp, which she used to cause her death, was an Egyptian symbol of royalty.

Clergy Reserves A seventh of the public land in Upper and Lower **Canada** (Ontario and Quebec), set aside for the future use of Protestant clergy; established under the Constitutional Act (1791). In practice, the reserves became bastions of wealth and power for the predominantly Anglican elite (the **Family Compact**) in Upper Canada, drawing fierce criticism from Methodists and disestablishmentarians. They were secularized in 1854.

Cleveland, (Stephen) Grover (1837–1908) US politician and 22nd and 24th President. The son of a Presbyterian minister, he became a lawyer, Mayor of Buffalo, and in 1883 Governor of New York. An honest and independent politician who abhorred **machine** politics, he was nominated for president by the Democrats in 1884 and won the election. In his first term he strongly advised a reduction in the high tariff. He was not re-elected in 1888, but regained the presidency in 1892. His second term began with an industrial depression that led to labour unrest and a split in the Democratic Party. In foreign affairs, he took a firm stand in the boundary dispute between Great Britain and Venezuela, asserting the US right, under the Monroe Doctrine, to determine that boundary.

Clinton, De Witt (1769–1828) US politician. He was admitted to the bar in 1790, sat in the New York state legislature (1798–1802) and US Senate (1798–1802), was three times Mayor of New York (1803–07, 1808–10, 1811–15). He was, however, defeated by James **Madison** in the presidential election of 1812. He led the way in the fight to build the Erie Canal, known as 'Clinton's Ditch', which opened in 1825.

Clinton, William ('Bill') (1946–   ) US politician and 42nd President. Educated at Georgetown University and Yale Law School, and a Rhodes scholar at Oxford, he taught law at the University of Arkansas (1973–6) before being elected state attorney general in 1976. In 1978, at the age of 32, he was elected Governor of Arkansas, the youngest person ever to hold that office, and served for five terms (1979–81 and 1983–92). In 1992 he was elected President, campaigning on a platform of hope and change in a climate of economic recession and voter disillusionment and finishing a 12-year Republican hold on the office.

Clive of Plassey, Robert (1725–74) British soldier and administrator. In 1743 he joined the British **East India Company** in Madras, and took part in the campaigns against the French. In 1755 he was called to avenge the so-called **Black Hole of Calcutta**, and at the Battle of **Plassey** (1757) defeated a large Indian force — much of which defected to the British side following the offer of inducements to the commanding general, Mir Jaffar, and the payment of bribes by Indian merchants to the soldiers of the Mughal Nawab (Governor), **Siraj ud-Daula**. For three years, Clive was sole ruler in all but name of Bengal. In 1760, he returned to England, entered parliament, and was made a baron (1762). In 1765 he returned to Calcutta, effectively reformed the civil service, and reestablished military discipline. His measures were seen as drastic, and he became the subject of a select committee inquiry upon his return to England in 1767. He committed suicide in London.

Cloots, Jean Baptiste du Val-de-Grâce, Baron de (1755–94) French revolutionary. Born a subject of Prussia, he established himself in France in 1776. There he adopted the name Anacharsis, became one of the **Philosophes** and lavished his money to promote the union of all nations in one family. In the **French Revolution** he saw the fulfilment of his dreams. He was both hated and feared by **Robespierre**, who involved him in **Hébert**'s downfall, and he was guillotined.

closer settlement The name given to Australian colonial and state government laws (1894–1906) designed to settle individuals or groups of unemployed persons on small farm blocks. Based on New Zealand's example (1892), the laws provided for the repurchase of land by the government, either by arrangement or compulsorily at a fair price, and its sale in small blocks to settlers on easy terms. The principles of closer settlement and government assistance for land settlement were also applied to soldier settlement schemes after both world wars. ▷ **selectors; Squatters**

Clotaire I, II ▷ **Chlotar I, II**

Clovis I (c.465–511) Merovingian King. He succeeded his father, Childeric, in 481, as King of the **Franks**. He overthrew the Gallo-Romans, and took possession of the whole country between the Somme and the Loire by 496. In 493 he married the Burgundian princess (St) Clotilda, and was converted by her to Christianity along with several thousand warriors after routing the Alemanni. In 507 he defeated the Visigoth, Alaric II, captured Bordeaux and Toulouse, but was checked at Arles by the Ostrogoth, Theodoric. He then took up residence in Paris, where he died. ▷ **Gaul; Ostrogoths; Visigoths**

CMEA–EEC Agreement (1988) The mutual recognition and trade agreement between **Comecon**, based in Moscow, and the Brussels-based **EEC**. Their hostility was linked with the continuance of the **Cold War** and with a specific disagreement concerning how trade should be conducted. Mikhail **Gorbachev**'s emergence helped calm tension and a compromise was found according to which individual CMEA members made comprehensive deals with the EEC as a whole. This further reduced tension and contributed to the dissolution of CMEA in 1990.

CNCA (*Confederación Nacional Católico-Agraria*, 'National Catholic-Agrarian Confederation') (1917–42) Spanish agrarian organization. Organized and funded by large landowners, the CNCA built up a large following among smallholders of north and central Spain through its propaganda and services. It claimed 500 000 members by 1919. Conservative and religious in outlook, its aim was to combat the rising power of the urban and rural working class by mobilizing middle-class support for the ruling classes. In

this respect it was similar to the ACNP (National Catholic Association of Propagandists). It was an important source of support for the Right during the Second Republic, especially for the **CEDA**. In 1942 it was transformed into the National Union of Rural Cooperatives (UNCC), more recently the UNACO. ▷ **Republic, Second** (Spain)

CND (Campaign for Nuclear Disarmament) An organization formed in 1958 to oppose Britain's development of a nuclear weapons programme. It organized annual Aldermaston marches and briefly persuaded the Labour Party to declare a policy of unilateral disarmament in 1960, only to see it effectively reverse that decision a year later. An effective pressure group in the 1960s, its popularity and influence had already begun to decline before the signing of nuclear non-proliferation pacts in the 1980s, although supporters agreed that as part of a European movement it played a part in halting the arms race.

CNI ▷ **Independents** (France)

CNT (*Confederación Nacional de Trabajo*, 'National Confederation of Labour') Spanish anarcho-syndicalist movement. The emergence of the CNT in 1911 provided Spanish anarcho-syndicalism with its first national framework. It was based on already existing trade unions, most of them in Catalonia, which were sympathetic to anarchism. Centred on Barcelona, Saragossa, and rural Andalucia, the CNT became the largest trade union movement in Spain during the social crisis sparked by **World War I**. The CNT's influence in Catalonia was at its greatest from 1918 to 1923, but it met with the brutal resistance of the employers. The CNT was severely repressed under the **Primo de Rivera** dictatorship of 1923–30. Under the Second Republic, against a background of continuing if lesser repression, it spurned electoral politics (though many CNT members voted for the Left in 1931 and 1936), split over the issue of revolutionary confrontation with the Republic, and pursued a series of largely fruitless strikes and risings, most notably those of Jan and Dec 1933. However, it also extended its influence in Madrid and other areas as the voice of the marginalized sections of the working class. While the anarchist rural and industrial collectives during the **Spanish Civil War** often proved both a social and an economic success, the failure of the anarchist militia undoubtedly undermined the Republican war effort. The

CNT's revolutionary conception of the war clashed with that of most other Republican forces. Nonetheless in Nov 1936 four anarchists joined the government — the only occasion in the history of anarchism. The Communist assault on the CNT in May 1937 lost it the political initiative, and it declined thereafter. Anarchist opposition to **Franco** was ineffectual, its revival after his death being unimpressive. ▷ **Republic, Second** (Spain)

Coastal Command A separate functional Command within the British Royal Air Force (1936–69). Moves to transfer it to the Royal Navy caused a political storm in 1958–9. During **World War II**, the Command destroyed 184 German U-boats and 470 000 tonnes of enemy shipping, and played a decisive role in winning the Battle of the **Atlantic**.

Cobbett, William (1763–1835) British journalist and reformer. The son of a farmer, he moved on impulse to London (1783), spent a year reading widely, and joined the army, serving in New Brunswick (1785–91). In 1792 he married and went to the USA, where he wrote fierce pieces against the native Democrats under the name 'Peter Porcupine'. Returning to England in 1800, he was welcomed by the **Tories**, and started his famous *Weekly Political Register* (1802), which continued until his death, changing in 1804 from its original Toryism to an uncompromising radicalism. In 1810 he was imprisoned for two years for criticizing the flogging of militiamen by German mercenaries, and in 1817 he went again to the USA, fearing a second imprisonment. Returning in 1819 he travelled widely in Britain, and finally became an MP (1832). ▷ **Democratic Party**

Cobden, Richard (1804–65) British economist and politician. He worked as a clerk and commercial traveller in London, then went into the calico business, settling in Manchester. In 1835 he visited the USA, and in 1836–7 the Levant, after which he published two pamphlets preaching free trade (thus earning the nickname 'the Apostle of Free Trade'), non-intervention, and speaking against 'Russophobia'. A radical-Liberal, in 1838 he helped to found the **Anti-Corn Law League**, becoming its most prominent member. He became an MP in 1841. His lectures and parliamentary speeches focused opinion on the **Corn Laws**, which were repealed in 1846.

Cocceji, Samuel von (1679-1755) A famous jurist under Frederick II of Prussia. In 1749–51 he wrote the Project des Corporis Juris Fredericiani. The Project formed the basis for the later Prussian Law Code of Count J H C von Carmer (1721–1801) which became (1794) Germany's first legal code.

Cochin-China A French colony, occupying the southern part of Vietnam. The colony was established in 1862 when, following hostilities with the Vietnamese court, the court was forced to cede three eastern provinces to the French. Three western provinces were added in 1867. In 1887, Cochin-China was brought together with the French protectorates of **Annam**, Tonkin and Cambodia to form the *Union Indochinoise*. During the period of French administration, Cochin-China emerged as a major rice-exporting region. In the 1930s it became an important focus of rural unrest. In 1949 as the French sought to establish a Vietnamese alternative to **Ho Chi Minh** in the north, Cochin-China became part of the Associated State of Vietnam within the French Union.

Cochise (c.1812–74) Chief of the Chiricahua Apache. He lived in the American Southwest and was known for his bravery and military prowess. In 1861 he was wrongfully accused of stealing and abducting a rancher's child, and was arrested by the US Army. He escaped, and after hostages were taken on both sides, and eventually killed, he began a protracted guerrilla-type war against the Army, together with other tribes, that lasted for 10 years. In 1872, General Oliver Howard finally reached a peace settlement with Cochise by promising the Chiricahua a reservation on their native land.

Code Napoléon The French civil code, introduced (though not devised) by Napoleon Bonaparte as First Consul in 1804, to fill the void left by the abolition of the legal and social customs of pre-revolutionary France. It established the principles of equality between people, liberty of person and contract, and the inviolability of private property. From 1804 the code was introduced into those areas of Europe under direct French control. The civil code of the newly-united Italian state (1865) bore close affinity to it, and it was widely emulated in South America. It is still substantially extant in France, Belgium, Luxembourg, and Monaco today. ▷ **Napoleon I**

Codreanu, Corneliu Zelea (1899–1938) Romanian political leader. From a peasant family of Ukrainian or Polish ancestry, in 1927 he organized the Legion of the Archangel Michael, the quasi-religious and nationalist organization of which the **Iron Guard** formed the military wing. In 1938 he was tried for treason and sentenced to 10 years in prison; later that year, he and a group of followers were shot, apparently while trying to escape. ▷ **Antonescu, Ion; Charles II of Romania**

Cody, William Frederick ('Buffalo Bill') (1846–1917) US showman. He earned his nickname after killing nearly 5000 buffalo in 18 months for a contract to supply workers on the Kansas Pacific Railway with meat. He served as a scout in the **Sioux** wars, but from 1883 toured with his Wild West Show. The town of Cody in Wyoming stands on part of his former ranch.

Coehoorn, Menno van (1641–1704) Dutch soldier and engineer. Coehoorn specialized in the building of fortifications. He achieved great fame through his treatises and by his practical demonstrations of his theories in the wars against France. Built the fortifications of eg Breda, Nijmegen, Zwolle and Bergen op Zoom.

Coen, Jan Pieterzoon (1587–1629) Dutch colonial administrator. One of the founders of the Dutch East Indies, Coen joined the Dutch **East India Company** at the age of 20 as a junior merchant. In 1618 he was made Governor-General and the next year he conquered the Javanese town of Jacatra and founded in its place Batavia (now Jakarta), the capital of the Dutch East Indies. He resigned in 1623 and returned to the Netherlands, but was reappointed in 1624. He died (probably of cholera) in the capital he had founded, during its siege by a Mataram army. His achievement was crucial in setting up the colony in its early days, and in excluding English and Spanish competition in the Indonesian archipelago. He is probably best remembered for his brutal handling of the Bantanese people, which brought the Dutch a global monopoly in nutmeg and mace.

Cognac, League of ▷ **Italian Wars**

Cohong The westernized form of the Chinese *gonghang* ('official firms'), which referred to a monopolistic guild of Chinese merchants licensed by the government to trade with Westerners at the port of Canton in the years 1760–1839. Each member of the Cohong was made responsible for the behaviour of Western traders, and served as intermediaries between them and local Chinese officials. Although some Cohong merchants made huge fortunes in their transactions with Westerners, the guild as a whole was always subject to arbitrary impositions by the Chinese government. The Cohong was abolished in the wake of China's defeat in the first of the **Opium Wars** in 1842.

Coke, Sir Edward (1552–1634) English jurist. He became Speaker of the House of Commons (1593), Attorney-General (1594), Chief Justice of the Common Pleas (1606), Chief Justice of the King's Bench (1613), and Privy Councillor. He vigorously prosecuted **Essex**, **Raleigh**, and the **Gunpowder Plot** conspirators, but after 1606 increasingly supported the idea of national liberties vested in parliament, against the royal prerogative. He was dismissed in 1617, and from 1620 led the popular party in parliament, serving nine months in prison. The petition of right (1628) was largely his doing. Most of his epoch-making Law Reports were published during the period 1600–15.

Colbert, Jean Baptiste (1619–83) French administrator and politician. He reorganized the colonies, provided a strong fleet and introduced a code of marine law. His attempts to develop the economy through state intervention, and in the interests of State power, had some success at first, but his endeavours were undermined by court extravagance and continual warfare. His policies have been systematized by historians under the name of 'Colbertism', a term which is used in a French context as the equivalent of 'Mercantilism'. ▷ **Le Tellier, Michel**

Cold Harbor, Battles of (1–3 June 1864) A battle of the **American Civil War**, fought in Virginia, with General Ulysses S **Grant's** forces suffering heavy losses (12000 men in one day's fighting) in an ill-advised attack on General Robert E **Lee's** secure Confederate position. The battle, however, did serve to further Grant's strategy of keeping unrelenting pressure on the South.

Cold War A state of tension or hostility between states that stops short of military action or a 'hot' war. The term is most frequently used to describe the relationship between the USSR and the major Western powers — especially the USA — following **World War II**. Tension was particularly high in the 1960s when the nuclear 'arms race' intensified. The process of detente, begun in the late 1960s, led through two decades of arms reduction and control negotiations to the 'end' of the Cold War in 1990, mainly as a result of a dramatic change in the Soviet attitude under Mikhail **Gorbachev**.

Colenso, Battle of (1899) A reverse suffered by the British in the Boer War. General Sir Redvers Buller (1838–1908), fearing that his forces might be cut off in his efforts to relieve Ladysmith, changed his plans and attempted to take Colenso, an important crossing-point on the Tugela River. He was defeated by Boer force under Louis **Botha**. ▷ **Boer Wars**

Coligny, Gaspard II de, Lord of Châtillon (1519–72) French Huguenot leader. He fought in the wars of **Francis I** and **Henry II** of France, and in 1552 was made Admiral of France. In 1557 he became a Protestant, and commanded the **Huguenots** during the second and third Wars of **Religion**. **Catherine de' Medici** made him one of the first victims in the **St Bartholomew's Day Massacre** in Paris (1572).

Colijn, Hendrikus (1869–1944) Dutch politician. His first career was in the Dutch colonial army (1892–1909); then he became a member of the Dutch parliament for the Calvinist **Anti-Revolutionary Party**, of which he was the leader from 1920 on. He also had business interests (as Director of the Batavian Oil Company) and was chief editor of the Calvinist daily newspaper *The Standard* from 1922. He first took cabinet office as Minister of War (1911–13) and then as Minister of Finance (1923–5). From 1925 to 1939 he was Prime Minister of no less than six cabinets, and was the figurehead of the tough deflationary Dutch government policies of the 1930s. When the Germans invaded his country in 1940 he toyed with accepting the New Order; he soon rejected this, and was interned in 1941. He died in Ilmenau in Germany.

collaboration (France) (1940–4) The act of collaborating with the Germans during their occupation of France in **World War II**. It could take various forms: economic, literary, journalistic and political. The latter applies especially to political figures who remained in Paris, rather than following the French government to **Vichy**, although the distinction became blurred in 1943–4. The most extreme collaborators fought on the Eastern Front: LGF (*Légion des volontaires français*

contre le bolchévisme, 'French Legion of Volunteers against Bolshevism') or in the auxiliary police force (*Milice*) within France, which committed appalling atrocities. ▷ **French State**

collective security The concept of maintaining security and territorial integrity by the collective actions of nation states, especially through international organizations such as the League of Nations, where the principle is embodied in its Covenant, and the UN, in its Charter. Individual member states must be prepared to accept collective decisions and implement them, if necessary, through military action. Because of the difficulty of obtaining such agreements, collective security has never been fully established.

Collective Leadership (post-1956) In the USSR, the term used, with occasional justification, to differentiate between the leadership methods of **Stalin**, who was accused of the **Cult of Personality**, and those of his successors. But as general-secretaries of the Communist Party both Nikita **Khrushchev** and Leonid **Brezhnev** reverted to virtual single-handed rule in the later years of their tenure. Mikhail **Gorbachev** amended the party's rules in 1986 to include collective leadership but had himself appointed President as well as General-Secretary in 1990.

Collectivization (post-1929) The process, initiated by **Stalin** in the USSR, of forcing peasants into large communal farms where in theory they worked for one another and not for themselves or their own families. Stalin's aims were to solve the food crisis through large-scale farming, by the same means to accumulate capital and secure spare labour for industrial development, and to create a revolutionary peasantry to maintain and intensify the spirit of revolution. Despite fierce resistance and pauses to gather breath, the main aims were achieved; casualties were, however, very high. Productivity also remained remarkably low, and agriculture became one of the weak points of the economy, leading to the collapse of Soviet socialism in recent years. The extension of collectivization to much of Eastern Europe after **World War II** led to very similar results.

Colleoni, Bartolomeo (1400–75) Italian soldier and **condottiere**. He fought on both sides in the strife between Milan and Venice, where he finally settled in 1454, becoming *generalissimo* for life. He is the subject of a famous Venetian equestrian statue by Verrochio.

Collier, Jeremy (1650–1726) English bishop. He became a priest in 1677, and refused to take the oath of allegiance to **William III** and Mary II (1689). Arrested in 1692 on suspicion of being involved in a Jacobite plot, in 1696 he was outlawed for giving absolution to two would-be assassins on the scaffold. Returning to London, he continued to preach to a congregation of those who had not taken the oath (non-jurors), and was consecrated bishop in 1713. He was also the author of a celebrated attack on the immorality of the English stage (1698). ▷ **Jacobites**

Collingwood, Cuthbert, Baron (1750–1810) British admiral. He joined the navy at 11, and from 1778 his career was closely connected with that of **Nelson**. He fought at the Battles of Brest (1794), **Cape St Vincent** (1797), and **Trafalgar** (1805), where he succeeded Nelson as commander. He was created baron after Trafalgar, died at sea, and is buried beside Nelson in St Paul's Cathedral, London.

Collins, Michael (1890–1922) Irish politician and **Sinn Féin** leader. He was an MP (1918–22), and organized the nationalist intelligence system against the British. With Arthur **Griffith**, he was largely responsible for the negotiation of the treaty with Great Britain in 1921. Commander-General of the government forces in the civil war, he was killed in an ambush between Bandon and Macroom.

Collor de Mello, Fernando (1950–) Brazilian politician. Born into a family in the north-eastern state of Alagoas, he grew up in Rio de Janeiro. He made use of his family's extensive media holdings to lever himself into the Prefecture of Maceió (1979–82) and then become Governor of Alagoas (1986). A political conservative, he leapt to prominence as a critic of 'corruption', achieving a leading position, at the head of his National Renovation Party, in the race for the presidency in Nov 1989. His ability to project the image of a young and dynamic 'messias', professing a modern social democratic approach, caught the traditional PMDB and radical PT off guard. Once in office (Mar 1990), he embarked on a bold programme of economic reform, before he built up a significant base within Congress. Control over Congress lay in the hands of groups which had benefited from the 1988 Constitution, which protected special interests directly affected by the presidential pro-

gramme. He resigned in Dec 1992 as his impeachment, on charges of corruption, began in the Senate.

Collot d'Herbois, Jean Marie (1751–96) French revolutionary. Originally a provincial actor, he joined the Jacobin Club in 1791. His self-confidence, his loud voice and his *Almanach du Père Gérard* (1791) secured his election to the National **Convention**. In 1793 he became President of the Convention and a member of the Committee of **Public Safety**. Sent to Lyons, he took bloody revenge by guillotine and grapeshot on the inhabitants for having once hissed him off the stage. He played a major part in the successful plot against **Robespierre** (1794), but himself was expelled from the Convention, and banished to Cayenne (1795), where he died. ▷ **French Revolution; Jacobins**

Colonial and Imperial Conferences A series of conferences at which representatives of the British colonies and dominions discussed matters of common imperial concern; usually held in London. The first Colonial Conference was held in 1887, and this was followed by others in 1894, 1897, 1902 and 1907. They were particularly concerned with defence, although they also dealt with issues of trade and communications. The first Imperial Conference was held in 1911, the change of name implying a new status for the colonies, and was followed by others in 1921, 1923, 1926, 1930 and 1937, mainly concerned with constitutional changes and economic matters. After **World War II** they were replaced by the Conferences of Commonwealth Prime Ministers, now by the Commonwealth Heads of Government meetings. ▷ **British Empire; Commonwealth of Nations**

Colonial Development and Welfare Acts (1929, 1940, 1945, 1949 and 1950) A series of acts designed to offer funds for the development of British colonies. They represented a departure from the notion that colonies should be self-supporting and a recognition that development might serve to combine colonial idealism with British economic self-interest. The 1929 act made available £1 million; the 1940 act was partly a response to riots in the West Indies and partly designed to encourage sympathy and loyalty during **World War II**. £20 million was set aside, but only £3 million was spent in the first four years. The principle was extended in the post-war climate of trusteeship when £120 million was invested under the three acts introduced by Clement **Attlee**'s Labour government.

colonialism A form of imperial domination of one country (the colonial power) over others (its colonies) for political, economic, or strategic purposes. The main period of colonial rule was 1870–1960, when Western European powers 'scrambled' to gain control over territories in Africa, Asia and the Far East. The French and British had the largest colonial empires. Colonialism is said by some to have established a system of 'dependency' in the colony, whose economy and political administration served primarily not its own needs but those of the colonial power. This has made it difficult for the colony to develop on its own terms and in its own direction. This situation is said to prevail even after the granting of 'independence', and these dependent countries make up the 'underdeveloped' Third World.

Colonna Roman family, whose members included a pope (**Martin V**), several cardinals, generals, statesman and scholars, as well as the poet Vittoria (1492–1547), who was a close friend of Michelangelo.

colônos Colonist labourers, they were introduced from Europe to Brazilian coffee plantations in the mid-19c, in order to supplant slave labourers, then declining in numbers. *Colônos* were initially allotted housing and a given area of coffee groves, and received a cash income from sales of coffee to the **fazendeiro**. By the 1880s, planters were prepared to concede fresh lands to families of Italian- and Spanish-born immigrants, many of whom cultivated and sold foodstuff crops, while tending young coffee trees. Colôno settlements became crucial to the opening up of the west and south of Brazil, with distinctive patterns of landholding: they have only recently been displaced by agro-businesses. The term is generally used to describe official settlements in the western and Amazon regions.

Comanche Shoshonean-speaking Native North American Plains people. Among the first to acquire horses from the Spanish, they migrated south into Colorado, Kansas, Oklahoma, Texas, and New Mexico. They dominated the Plains and warred against both Apache and white settlers. By the 1870s the Comanche were settled on reservations in Oklahoma, where today they number about 3 500.

Combes, Emile (1835–1921) French politician. Originally intended for the Church, after education in a seminary, he studied medicine and practised as a doctor. He was elected to the Senate (1885), and became Prime Minister (1902–4). He used the law on Associations (1901), first presented as little more than a tidying-up of administrative regulations, but turned by strained interpretation into a measure to dissolve nearly all religious orders and confiscate their property. This opened a conflict with the papacy that led, perhaps against his own intentions, to the **Separation of Church and State** (1905).

Combination Acts (1799 and 1800) British legislation which prohibited the coming together ('combination') of workers in trade unions. The Acts were part of anti-reformist legislation passed by the Pitt government during the French wars, though combinations in many trades were already illegal. The Acts were repealed in 1824–5, and trade unions, though under severe restrictions, legalized. ▷ **Pitt, William, 'the Younger'**

Combined Operations Command A British force established in 1940 when Winston **Churchill** appointed Admiral of the Fleet Lord Keyes to coordinate British commando raids against German-occupied Europe. Keyes's successor Lord **Mountbatten** (1941–3) directed larger operations involving all three Services, and prepared for the eventual Allied invasion of France, in which Combined Operations techniques were to play a crucial role. ▷ **D-Day; World War II**

COMECON (Council for Mutual Economic Assistance) A body founded in 1949 by **Stalin**, dominated by the USSR, but frequently thwarted by other member states. Its purpose was ostensibly the economic integration of the Eastern bloc as a means of counteracting the economic power and political influence of the West. The 10 member states were eventually the USSR, Bulgaria, Cuba, Czechoslovakia, Hungary, Poland, Romania, East Germany, Mongolia, and Vietnam. With the overthrow of **communism** in Eastern Europe in 1989–90 and the weakening of the USSR, COMECON was disbanded in 1991.

Comenius, John Amos (1592–1670) Czech educational reformer. He studied at Herborn and Heidelberg, and became Rector of the Moravian School in Přerov (1614–16) and minister at Fulnek, but fled to Poland in 1628 at the height of Ferdinand II's oppression of Czech Protestants following his victory at the White Mountain in 1620. Settling at Leszno, he worked out a new theory of education and was chosen Bishop of the Unity of Brethren (later known as the **Moravian Brethren**) in 1632. He visited England, the Netherlands and Sweden, and wrote and published extensively. He then settled in Holland, where he died. He tried, without success, to interest other countries in freeing the Czechs from Austrian rule, but his main contribution to history was as an influential educational innovator.

Comines, Philippe de (c.1445–1511) French politician and historian. In 1463 he entered the court of Burgundy, but in 1472 began to serve **Louis XI** of France. After Louis's death, he was imprisoned, but in 1493 was restored to favour, and accompanied **Charles VIII** on his Italian expedition (1494). His *Mémoires* (written 1489–98, published 1524) provide an important record of his times.

Cominform (Communist Information Bureau) An organization founded by **Stalin** in 1947 as a successor to the **Comintern**, which had been established in 1943. Its purpose was the coordination of the propoganda and politics of the communist parties of Bulgaria, Czechoslovakia, France, Hungary, Italy, Poland, Romania, the USSR, and Yugoslavia. Its headquarters were moved from Belgrade to Bucharest following the break between Stalin and **Tito** which culminated in Yugoslavia's expulsion in 1948. Cominform became an instrument in the **Cold War**, expressing hostility towards capitalism, and was also used by Stalin as an additional means of dominating Eastern Europe. After the rapprochement between the USSR and Yugoslavia in 1956, the Cominform was dissolved.

Comintern An abbreviation for the Third or Communist International, founded in Moscow in Mar 1919 at the behest of the Soviet Communist Party, its purpose being to promote the expected international proletarian revolution by rallying communists and left-wing socialists. It adopted Leninist principles in its policies, rejecting reformism in favour of revolutionary action, which it encouraged against capitalist governments. It gradually became an instrument of **Stalin**'s foreign policy and was ultimately little used. It was disbanded in May 1943 when Stalin was

anxious to strengthen his **World War II** friendship with **Roosevelt** and Winston **Churchill**. ▷ **Cominform; Marxism–Leninism**

Commando Civilian militia in the Cape, originally called out by the Dutch East India Company in the early 18c, but later organized by the Boers themselves and regarded as a prime symbol of their self-sufficiency in the interior of the Continent. The commando was used to defend Boer settlements, but increasingly went on to the offensive attacking Khoisan and Bantu-speaking peoples as a means of expanding Boer power, landholding and herds of cattle. The word has come to mean any forces specializing in irregular actions.

'Commercial Union' A Canadian movement for economic union with the USA which became a major political issue in 1887. Confederation had failed to generate growth, probably because the number of outlets for Canadian staples had not increased, while John A **Macdonald**'s policy of protection resulted in retaliatory tariffs in the USA. Britain, an advocate of free trade, already took half of Canada's export trade, whilst there seemed little chance that trade with other European countries or South America would expand. Canadian manufacturers, anxious to maintain their protected position argued that 'Commercial Union' was akin to Annexation, and would lead to Washington dictating fiscal policy to Ottawa. The **Liberal Party** itself was initially split, with **Laurier** for **reciprocity** rather than 'Commercial Union' and Richard **Cartright** for free trade, and in 1888 it committed itself not to 'Commercial Union' but to 'unrestricted reciprocity'.

Committee for the Liberation of Upper Italy (*Comitato di Liberazione nazionale Alta Italia*, CLNAI) The organization established (Jan 1944) to coordinate the activities of anti-German and anti-fascist partisans, often already grouped within local **Committees of National Liberation** (CLNs). Originally the CLNAI asserted its claims to power not only against the Germans and fascists but also against the Allies and the anti-fascist government in Rome. In Dec 1944, CLNAI delegates agreed to the so-called 'Protocols of Rome' by which, in exchange for a subsidy from the Allies, they promised to hand over all authority after liberation to the Allied Military Government. During the last months of **World War II** the CLNAI burgeoned, assisted by a remarkable degree of political collaboration among the leaders of all the main anti-fascist parties. By late Apr 1945 most of the north had fallen to the CLNAI, which established its own *de facto* administration before the arrival of the Allies. Although the CLNAI laid down its weapons, it retained a strong bargaining position which its leaders used to win much greater representation in Rome, forcing the resignation of **Bonomi** and the appointment of **Parri** as Prime Minister. The new CLNAI-dominated government carried out widespread purges against anyone associated with the former fascist regime, alienating a good deal of public opinion in the process. Blamed for the prevailing dire economic conditions and high unemployment, as well as for the anti-fascist witch-hunts, the Parri government fell from office (Dec 1945); it was replaced by the **De Gasperi** government.

Committee of National Liberation (Algeria) The committee set up by Charles de **Gaulle** on 3 June 1943, through which the Algerians were promised a full voice in the running of their country. The failure to fulfil this promise was, more than any other single factor, responsible for the hardening of native Algerian resistance to the presumptions of the French in Algeria, which eventually resulted in the **Algerian War of Independence**.

Committees of Correspondence In the **American Revolution**, an informal network linking towns for the purpose of sharing political information. Committees, which held town meetings, began to appear in 1772. During the crisis over independence (1775–6) they assumed active power in many places.

Committees of National Liberation (*Comitati di Liberazione nazionale*, CLNs) The first CLN emerged in the autumn of 1943 from the 'United Freedom Front' set up by Ivanoe **Bonomi** in Apr of that year. Bonomi's organization was aimed at coordinating the efforts of the main anti-fascists, whether Catholic, communist or socialist. However, as the Allies advanced through Italy, autonomous CLNs were established throughout Italy to organize partisan activity; these usually had no affiliation to Bonomi's central organization. In German-occupied northern Italy especially, the CLNs often became a *de facto* government in areas where the anti-fascist resistance was victorious, and in Jan 1944 the **Committee for the Liberation of Upper Italy** was established to

coordinate their efforts. ▷ **Parri, Ferruccio; Party of Action**

Commodus (161–92) Roman Emperor (180/92). The son of **Marcus Aurelius**, he was carefully educated, but ruled with extraordinary savagery, especially after the discovery of his sister Lucilla's plot against his life in 183. He became increasingly unbalanced, imagining that he was the god Hercules. At length his mistress, Marcia, had him strangled by Narcissus, a champion athlete. ▷ **Antonine Emperors**

Commons, House of The lower, and effectively the ruling, chamber of the bicameral legislature of the UK. It contains 650 members, elected by universal adult suffrage, each representing a single constituency. The Commons is elected for a maximum period of five years, though the prime minister may call an election at any time within that period, and the government is drawn from the party that wins the majority of seats. The ascendancy of the House of Commons over the House of Lords began during the 16c, and was completed with the passage of the Parliament Acts of 1911 and 1949. The Commons is dominated by a disciplined party system, which means that governments are generally assured of a majority in the passage of legislation. In this sense the Commons serves a legitimizing rather than a legislating function. ▷ **Lords, House of**

Commonwealth English republican regime created by Oliver **Cromwell**, based on the **Rump Parliament** established in 1649, which lasted until the Instrument of Government created a **Protectorate** in 1653. It failed to achieve political settlement at home, but its armies pacified Scotland and Ireland. The Navigation Acts (1650 and 1651) and the **Anglo-Dutch Wars** (1652–4) fostered overseas trade and colonies. ▷ **English Civil Wars**

Commonwealth of Independent States ▷ **CIS**

Commonwealth of Nations A voluntary organization of autonomous states which had been imperial possessions of Britain. Its head is the reigning British monarch. It was formally established by the Statute of Westminster (1931) and meets frequently to discuss matters of mutual interest and concern. While most states, on independence, chose to become members of the Commonwealth, four have left (Irish Republic, 1949;

South Africa, 1961; Pakistan, 1972; Fiji, 1987). ▷ **Westminster, Statutes of**

communalism The term used in India to characterize the use of religion for political ends, particularly by Muslims and Hindus. Early expressions of communalism arose within the Cow Protection Societies formed by Hindus, to whom the cow is sacred; these often came into conflict with Muslims, to whom the slaughter of animals is required during some religious festivals. Conflict also arose over holy sites used by both Hindus and Muslims for worship. British intervention in such disputes often only exacerbated them: nationalists have argued that this was a conscious policy, part of the colonial tactic of 'divide and rule'. Certainly, from an early stage the British colonial government treated Hindus and Muslims (as well as tribals) as entirely separate communities, making co-operation between them very difficult to achieve. Despite this, there was a considerable degree of cooperation between Hindu and Muslim politicians in the Indian independence movement, particularly in 1915–22 when both Mohammed Ali **Jinnah** (the leader of the **Muslim League**) and M K **Gandhi** (by 1917 the leader of the **Indian National Congress**) strove to forge a united front against the British during the Khilafat, Rowlatt and Non-Cooperation campaigns. This unity collapsed, however, in 1922 after the suspension of the **Non-Cooperation Movement** by Gandhi. Conflict between the two communities increased markedly during the Great Depression, in the late 1930s when Congress provincial governments were formed, and during **World War II**, when the League supported the British and the Congress was banned in the wake of the **Quit India** Campaign of 1942. Jinnah's demands for Muslims to have their own separate nation led ultimately to the partition of India into separate Hindu and Muslim nations (India and Pakistan) in 1947. Three wars between India and Pakistan have fuelled the conflict since, and within India itself the 110 million-strong Muslim population remains the focus of fierce political dispute. A secular constitution and a secular majority amongst Indian politicians has tended to curb serious conflict, but at times of social and economic crisis the threat of 'communalism' has always reemerged.

Commune A sworn association of equals which developed as the distinctive political organization of European towns in the Middle Ages, first and most notably from the

later 11c in northern Italy. They revived the traditions of republican Rome in the office of consul but added a corporatist dimension to civic life which reflected the new economic strength of the medieval town. The **Lombard League** of Italian communes won a notable success against the feudal host of the German emperor **Frederick I, 'Barbarossa'** at the Battle of **Legnano** in 1176. In the later Middle Ages in Italy and elsewhere, communal political structures proved vulnerable to family factionalism, and many succumbed to tyranny for the sake of stability and were absorbed into larger territorial states.

Communes, People's The basic unit of government in the Chinese countryside, first created in 1958 as part of the **Great Leap Forward** campaign. Originating in 1957 with the large-scale mobilization of rural labour for irrigation and water conservancy projects, the communes amalgamated previously-existing collectives and combined administrative, economic and social functions. **Mao Zedong** hailed the communes as a symbol of China's transition to **communism** that would boost rural productivity and enhance collective life. By the end of 1958 740 000 collectives had been amalgamated into 26 000 communes; private plots were abolished, communal mess-halls and nurseries created, and rural industrialization promoted. Disastrous economic results and widespread peasant opposition forced the leadership after 1959 to modify the extreme forms of collectivism and devolve some of the communes' functions to the production brigade (the former collective). During the 1980s the communes were virtually dismantled as the individual peasant household became the unit of agricultural production.

communism A political ideology which has as its central principle the communal ownership of all property, and thereby the abolition of private property. Although examples of early social and religious groupings based upon communal sharing of property have been cited, modern communism is specifically associated with the theories of Karl **Marx**. Marx saw the emergence of a communist society as being the final stage in a historical process that was rooted in human material needs, preceded by feudalism, capitalism, and (a transitional stage) socialism. Communism, according to Marx, would abolish class distinctions and end the exploitation of the masses inherent in the capitalist system. The working class, or proletariat, would be the instrument of a revolution that would overthrow the capitalist system and liberate human potential. A fully developed communist system would operate according to the principle of 'from each according to his ability, to each according to his need', and as there would be no cause for the state to regulate society, it would 'wither away'. Marx's writings provided a powerful ideological basis for communist and many socialist parties and governments, which legitimized the implementation of their policies by reference to them. The **Communist Party of the Soviet Union** (CPSU), first of all under **Lenin**'s leadership and then under **Stalin**'s, reinterpreted Marxist ideology as Marxism–Leninism–Stalinism, a major feature of which came to be democratic centralism. Unlike the spontaneous, decentralized organization envisaged by Marx, the CPSU was a highly centralized, monolithic, and secretive organization. Under Stalin's leadership it became an instrument in the development of a totalitarian dictatorship. The CPSU provided the ideological lead for European communist parties; indeed, at the creation of the Third **International** or **Comintern** in 1919, it was clear that only those socialist parties which accepted the discipline, leadership, and organizational structure of the Soviet Communist Party would be allowed to join. Much the same was true of the **Cominform** established in 1947. Increasingly from the 1960s onwards, however, the compulsory leadership of the CPSU was questioned and challenged, partly because of the economic difficulties resulting from the rigidities of democratic centralism in industrial states, where decentralization and flexibility were required. Nonetheless, Yugoslavia had been the only country to challenge Soviet dominance successfully (it was expelled from the Cominform in 1948); other countries such as Hungary (1956), Czechoslovakia (1968), and Poland (1980–1) were prevented by military force from breaking away from the Soviet model. But in 1989–90, the establishment of a non-communist government in Poland and popular uprisings elsewhere in Eastern Europe, followed by reasonably free elections, saw the almost total eclipse of communism there. The uprisings were political and economic, and one reason for their success was the changing nature of Soviet communism under Mikhail **Gorbachev**'s reforming leadership and the growing demand in the USSR for the same kind of changes as Eastern Europe wanted. Within a year of the failed coup against Gorbachev in Aug 1991, the Soviet Communist Party was declared illegal and much of the mechanism of communist rule was dismantled. There remains the possibility of some kind of communist recovery in the USSR as well as in Eastern Europe. But faith in communism worldwide has been seriously weakened, at least in its manifestations hitherto. And even Chinese communism, which was never slavishly Soviet in its ideology and practices, is changing quite noticeably.

Communist Party, Chinese (CCP) Formally created in July 1921 by 14 delegates (including **Mao Zedong**), the party represented six communist cells established the previous year. **Comintern** representatives from Moscow persuaded **Chen Duxiu**, the party's first Secretary-General, to join with the more powerful **Guomindang** (Nationalist Party) in a United Front to combat imperialism and restore national unity, the long term aim being to take over leadership 'from within'. During this period of cooperation (1923–7) the CCP increased its membership to 6000 and gained significant influence over mass organizations. The party's urban base was destroyed after 1927 when the Guomindang turned on its erstwhile communist allies. Henceforth, Mao Zedong's strategy of protracted rural revolution, emphasizing the creation of base areas and reliance on a peasant Red Army, came to be accepted by the CCP leadership. Membership of the party again increased substantially during the war with Japan (1937–45) and totalled 1.2 million by 1945. With Mao confirmed as Leader at the Party's Seventh Congress (1945), the CCP emerged victorious from the civil war with the nationalists (1946–9) and established the People's Republic in 1949. By the time of the party's Eighth Congress (1956), membership totalled 10.5 million. Party authority was undermined during the **Cultural Revolution** (1966–9) but at the party's Ninth Congress (1969) the policy of rebuilding and reasserting party control was confirmed. Since Mao's death in 1976, **Deng Xiaoping** has sought to rejuvenate and reform the party, but this has not prevented it gradually losing credibility amongst the population during the 1980s. ▷ **communism**

Communist Party (Cuba) The only political party in existence in Cuba since 1959. Originally named the Popular Socialist Party and then the United Party of the Socialist Revolution (when **Castro** was not yet a hard-line Marxist), it became the Communist Party of Cuba in 1965. Castro has always sought to maintain the ideological purity of the party, enunciating policy in the party newspaper, *Granma*, resisting Mikhail **Gorbachev**'s call for **perestroika** and purging the state of undesirables (no matter how high), such as General Ochao (a member of the Central Committee of the Party and a Hero of the Revolution, who was executed in 1989 for drug offences). ▷ **communism**

Communist Party (Finland) Founded in Moscow (Aug 1918) by members of the Finnish Red Army and **Social Democratic Party** who had been defeated by the Finnish Whites and their German allies in the civil war earlier in the year, its most prominent leader was Otto **Kuusinen**. In 1919 it joined the **Comintern** and was declared illegal in Finland the same year. Suppressed by the Finnish authorities, it worked underground and, although it failed to win the allegiance of the majority of the working class, who were loyal to the Social Democrats, it nevertheless gained significant footholds in working-class organizations through a front organization, the Socialist Workers' Party. However, its organizations in Finland were effectively smashed by anti-communist legislation introduced in 1930 under pressure from the **Lapua Movement**. The party remained largely inactive until it was legalized in 1944, following Finland's defeat in the **Continuation War** of 1941–4. Despite its widespread perception as a tool of Moscow, the party was able to draw on solid support among both industrial workers in the south and the small farmers of northern and eastern Finland. Through its front organization, the Finnish People's Democratic League (SKDL), the party did well in the immediate post-war period. Following electoral success in 1945, they were represented in government from 1945 to 1948, and in 1958 gained their best ever result, with 25 per cent of the vote, becoming the largest party in parliament. They were, however, kept from office for many years by the other parties' refusal to cooperate with them. From 1966 onwards the Communist Party was weakened by conflicts between Moscow loyalists and those advocating a reformist, Eurocommunist line, but it was a regular participant in government. Ultimately, the party split, with the reformist minority breaking away to form the Democratic Alternative. At the same time, the party's electoral support declined, falling to 13 per cent in 1983. ▷ **communism**

Communist Party (France) Founded in 1920 when a majority of members of the **Socialist Party** (SFIO) voted to join the Third International and to become the Communist Party, officially known until 1943 as SFIC (*Section française de l'Internationale communiste*, 'French Section of the Communist International'). The 1924 elections showed that few voters were prepared to support the new party, and by 1932 it had only 11 Deputies. It was saved by the **Popular Front**, and emerged after **World War II** as a major political force with over a quarter of the vote and representation in a coalition cabinet (1945–7). In spite of retaining substantial electoral support (usually around 20 per cent of the vote), it never again held office until the victory of the left in the election of 1981, when it joined in a coalition with the socialists until 1984. This apparent success coincided with a rapid decline in voting support, to under 10 per cent in 1986. ▷ **communism**

Community Party (Germany) ▷ **KPD**

Communist Party of Great Britain Formed in 1920 through the merger of various leftist groups, it acknowledged from its inception the authority of Moscow. Its fortunes improved with Soviet intervention in **World War II,** but it never won more than four seats in parliament, and the 1956 **Hungarian Uprising** saw many defections. Unlike many European parties, its influence was minimal long before the collapse of the USSR (1990–1). ▷ **communism**

Communist Party (Greece) ▷ **KKE**

Communist Party of India (CPI) Founded in Dec 1926, it was an expatriate Bengali, M N Roy, who recruited and trained the first party members in the USSR. Early attempts to link up with radicals in India were frustrated by the Kanpur and Meerut conspiracy trials (1923 and 1929), but the communists, although persecuted and effectively illegal, were able to establish a network of members and supporters, infiltrating not only the **Indian National Congress** and trade union movements, but also setting up workers' and peasants' societies, with a view to mobilizing the masses in the struggle against colonialism. Relations with the Gandhian Congress were not always easy, although members of the Congress Socialist Party and Congress leaders such as Jawaharlal **Nehru** were sympathetic. This was due not only to disagreements over tactics, particularly the use of violence, but also because the **Comintern** policy between 1929 and 1935 was to reject cooperation with bourgeois–democratic movements. Before and after these dates, however, CPI members occupied prominent positions in the Indian National Congress. Increasingly active in the late 1930s, after the collapse of Gandhi's **civil disobedience** movement, and despite the fact that officially the CPI supported the British government in the struggle against fascism during **World War II**, local level members of the Workers' and Peasants' Parties played a prominent part in the violent Quit India agitation of 1942. In 1946 the CPI contested elections held by the British to the provincial and central assemblies and won a considerable number of votes, though a limited number of seats, as the runner-up to the Congress in most constituencies. Despite this, the CPI was not consulted by the British in the negotiations over Independence, and party members organized strikes and agitations, particularly in the independent princely states, which threatened to break away from the Indian Union and set up their own autocratic regimes. Of greatest importance was the **Telengana Disturbances** in Hyderabad. After Independence, CPI members continued to contest elections and gained a number of seats in parliament. However, they were closely allied with the Congress Party (at least until 1974) and therefore generally supported the government. ▷ **Bengal, Partition of; Communalism; Ghadr Party and Movement; India, Partition of; Indian National Congress; Quit India Movement**

Communist Party of India (Marxist) The split between the USSR and China caused a split within the ranks of the Communist Party of India, the splinter group becoming the CPI (M) or CPM (where 'M' stands for 'Marxist') in 1964, a party which has since opposed the dominant political party, the Indian National Congress, in national and state elections. Its greatest success has been in Bengal, where it has been the party in power for much of the time since first forming a coalition government in 1967. The first government though lasted only briefly after another faction split from the party, calling itself the CPM–L (where 'M–L' stands for 'Marxist–Leninist'), and attempted to raise a general revolt by undertaking direct action against class enemies, beginning in the district of Naxalbari, from which they derived the name 'Naxalites'. Having committed themselves, like the CPI, to the parliamentary route to socialism, violent confrontations between the CPM supporters and the CPM–L resulted, leading to intervention by the central government. After a period of Congress rule and Indira Gandhi's Emergency in 1975–7,

the CPM again returned to office with a huge majority in 1977, with Jyoti Basu as Chief Minister, and it has remained there ever since, as the leading party in a Left coalition, its popularity based on its successful land reform and rural development programmes and its pragmatic, secular, social policies, which have made Bengal, despite its poverty, the only Indian state with a considerable Muslim population in recent years to have largely escaped the threat of communal violence. ▷ **communism; Communist Party of India; Indian National Congress**

Community Party (Italy) ▷ **PCI**

Communist Party of the Soviet Union (CPSU) The party which controlled political, economic, and social life in the USSR from the Bolshevik Revolution in 1917 until its abolition in 1991. It was the only party with the right to put forward candidates in elections, and most of the country's important jobs were filled by selected party members. Membership comprised only c.10 per cent of the population, and the party itself was highly undemocratic, being run by the small **Politburo** or the slightly larger Central Committee. ▷ **communism**

Communist Party (Spain) ▷ **PCE**

Commynes, Philippe de ▷ **Comines, Philippe de**

Comnenus Family (1057–1461) A family, with estates in Asia Minor, of which many members occupied the Byzantine throne from 1057 to 1185 and that of Trebizond from 1204 to 1461. David Comnenus, the last in Trebizond, was executed at Adrianople in 1462, with all his family, by **Mehmed II**. ▷ **Alexius I Comnenus; Anna Comnena; Isaac I, Comnenus**

Compact Theory of Confederation Canadian constitutional theory. An interpretation of the **British North America Act** which argued that confederation meant the entrusting of certain powers to Ottawa while the provinces still retained their autonomy. As a compact, the agreement could not be altered without the acceptance of the signatories and could even be nullified if they so wished. The theory was supported in the 1880s by Quebeckers such as Honoré **Mercier** and by English-speaking provincial leaders like Mowat in Ontario and Norquay in Manitoba. The federal power which provincial governments most wanted to remove was that of disallowing provincial legislation, because, along with a policy of economic centralization, it would result in the severe limitation of provincial rights. At the 1927 Dominion-Provincial Conference the compact theory was proclaimed the true interpretation of confederation by both the Liberal Premier of Quebec and the Tory Premier of Ontario and during the 1930s it was used to place the Prime Minister, Richard **Bennett**, under political pressure. The theory actually disintegrates under examination because the original signatories comprised only three provinces.

Compaore, Blaise (1940–) Burkino Faso soldier and politician. Educated locally and in military academies in Senegal and France, including St Cyr, he joined the army in 1958 rising to command the Artillery Group (1975–6). In 1980 he was appointed Minister of Rural Development and was second in command to Thomas **Sankara** (1983–7), when he overthrew his colleague on 15 Oct 1987 and became Chairman of the Popular Front of Burkino Faso and Head of Government. Originally a very close friend and confrere of Sankara's, he came to reject what he felt was the overly egalitarian thrust of Sankara's policies.

Compradors The Chinese managers of foreign enterprises in China's **treaty ports** during the 19c and early 20c. Condemned by Chinese nationalists as the tools of Western imperialism, many compradors in fact invested in modern Chinese-owned enterprises that successfully competed with Western-owned firms. In the late 19c some compradors were also keen advocates of political and educational reform.

Compromise of 1850 A major but ultimately unsuccessful attempt by the Congress of the United States to resolve by legislation the conflict between the North and the South over slavery. Specifically involved was the expansion of slavery into new territories such as California and the South-West. Its major terms were the admission of California as a free (nonslave) state, and the passage of a strong fugitive slave law to placate the South. ▷ **American Civil War**

Compromise of Nobility (1565) A league of the lesser nobility of the Low Countries formed in resistance to Spanish rule at the beginning of the **Eighty Years War**. In Brussels in Nov 1565 a number of the lesser aristocracy or gentry joined the compromise against the introduction of the Spanish **Inquisition** and other forms of religious persecution; both Catholics and Calvinists were affiliated. Membership grew fast, and it provided the leadership of the revolt until there was an accord reached in late 1566 with the Spanish Regent, **Margaret of Parma**, after which the compromise was dissolved.

Compton, John George Melvin (1926–) St Lucian politician. He graduated at the London School of Economics and was called to the English Bar. In 1951 he established a law practice in St Lucia and three years later joined the St Lucia Labour Party (SLP), becoming its Deputy Leader. He left in 1961 to form the United Workers' Party (UWP) and, on independence in 1979, was St Lucia's first Prime Minister. He was defeated in the same year by the Labour Party but returned in 1982, and was narrowly re-elected in 1987.

Compton, Spencer, Earl of Wilmington (1673–1743) British politician. He was Paymaster-General from 1722 to 1730 and **George II** attempted to make him his First Minister on succeeding to the throne (1727), but was outmanoeuvred by **Walpole**. Compton remained a strong supporter of the King as Walpole's popularity waned after the outbreak of war with Spain (1739). As First Lord of the Treasury (1742–3), he was leader of the administration in name only, being overshadowed by Thomas **Pelham**-Holles, 1st Duke of Newcastle, and **Carteret**. ▷ **Whigs**

Compulsory Service Act (1917) Canadian conscription legislation. It was introduced because Canada's voluntary militia had been unable to fulfil the commitment to provide four full divisions on the Western Front. **Borden**'s Minister for Militia, Sir Sam Hughes, had deterred many French-Canadians from volunteering by his Ulster Protestant prejudices. The Act was particularly unpopular in Quebec, where many believed they were being asked to fight for the empire, while being denied equal rights at home. With **World War II** the government tried to maintain a policy of 'no conscription' to ensure national unity, despite continuous pressure coming from the English-speaking provinces, especially after the fall of France. In response **King** held a referendum which showed that although 80 per cent of the English-speaking population wished to free the government from its pledge, 72 per cent of French-Canadians were against doing so. King therefore retained the policy and sacked his Defence Minister when he was advised that there were not enough volunteers to maintain the Canadian commitment after the Normandy landings in 1944. But with the failure of the policy to enlist home defence draftees, King was forced to reintroduce conscription. Protest from the French-Canadians, both among civilians and in the forces, was fierce, while one French-Canadian minister resigned from the government and 34 Quebec Liberals voted against it in a vote of confidence. Even so, King managed to survive the election of 1945, albeit with a reduced majority.

Comuneros, Revolt of the (1520–1) The name given to those who participated in the rebellion (the *Comunidades*) of the chief cities of **Castile** against Emperor **Charles V** (Charles I of Spain) in 1520–1. On Charles's arrival in Spain in 1516, the privileges awarded to his foreign entourage aggravated other complaints that the cities had against the crown. The uprising began in Toledo, under Juan de **Padilla**, and rapidly took in the major cities of central Castile, which banded themselves into a junta and sought the help of Queen **Juana the Mad** at Tordesillas. The nobility, however, rallied to help the royal cause, and defeated the *Comunero* forces at the Battle of **Villalar** (1521). Padilla and the other leading rebels were executed the following day. The popular appeal of the *Comuneros* persisted through time, and rebel movements in Spanish South America also adopted the name in the 18c.

Comuneros, Revolt of the (1781) One of the largest rebellions in 18c Latin America, it occurred in the Spanish viceroyalty of New Granada (now Colombia) as a protest by lower classes against new fiscal levies on tobacco and aguardiente production by the new administration under the Visitor-General, who had been appointed by Carlos III to supersede previous administrations. Unlike many popular revolts, the scale of this one was substantial, involving over 20 000 armed men, and its local creole leadership coalesced around a programme of 'capitulations' which included demands against arbitrary imprisonment, preference for local men (not Spaniards) in the distribution of patronage and the freedom of Indians to retain their reserves as individual proprietors. Initially successful in halting the imposition of new legislation, the scale of revolt shook the viceregal administration, and the four principal leaders of the revolt were caught and executed the following year.

concentration camp A detention centre for political prisoners; known primarily from the camps established in Germany soon after the Nazi seizure of power, which soon came under **SS** control and were administered with extreme cruelty. The coming of war swelled the camp population with millions of Jews, Gypsies, slave workers, Soviet prisoners of war, and other 'enemies of the state' whom the SS regarded as an economic unit of resource. Following the Wannsee Conference (Jan 1942), which plotted the destruction of European Jewry, the concentration camps established in Poland, such as **Auschwitz** and Treblinka, became purpose-made extermination centres in which over 6 million Jews died. ▷ **Holocaust; Nazi Party**

Concessions, Scramble for (1897–8) The term used to describe competition amongst the foreign powers in China to secure leasehold territories from an increasingly enfeebled **Qing Dynasty**. It began in 1897 with Germany obtaining a 99-year lease on the port of Qingdao (Tsingtao) in Shandong province as 'compensation' for the murder of two German missionaries there. Russia then demanded from the Chinese government a similar lease agreement for Port Arthur, in south Manchuria. Britain obtained a lease on Weihaiwei (Shandong province) and Hong Kong's New Territories, while France acquired a lease on Guangzhou Bay in south China. At the same time, the Chinese government had to accept informal spheres of economic influence carved out by the foreign powers. Such concessions stimulated the development of Chinese nationalism.

conciliação The Brazilian tradition of reaching a consensus among the powerful propertied groups, rather than risk civil war. Invoked by Antônio Carlos Ribeiro de Andrada Machado é Silva in 1840, at the close of a decade of civil war, *conciliação* implied that incoming administrations would respect minor appointments made by their predecessors. This was seen as a recipe for peace in the interior and implied that the central government would mediate in local disputes, rather than allow them to threaten the political or social integrity of the empire. 'Compromise' or conciliação ministries governed the empire through the mid-19c. ▷ **Andrada Family**

Concordat (1516) The agreement between King **Francis I** (of France) and Pope Leo X which governed relations between Church and state in France until 1789. It gave the king the right to nominate bishops and abbots, and thus granted him a high degre of control over the Church.

Concordat (1801) The **Concordat** (1516) having been broken by the **French Revolution**, this new agreement between **Napoleon I** and Pope Pius VII established a system that lasted until 1905. The government regained the right to nominate bishops, who in turn appointed parish priests; the Church did not regain its property, but the clergy were to be paid salaries by the state. The Concordat said nothing about the monastic clergy, but they came to be tolerated in practice. ▷ **Separation of Church and State**

Condé, House of The junior branch of the French royal line, the House of **Bourbon**, which played a prominent role in French dynastic politics, particularly in the 16–17c. Ten generations bore the title of 'Prince of Condé', the most eminent being Louis II of Bourbon, Prince of Condé, better known as 'the Great Condé'. ▷ **Condé, Louis I; Condé, Louis II of Bourbon**

Condé, Louis I of Bourbon, Prince of (1530–69) French Huguenot leader. The younger brother of Antony of Bourbon, King of Navarre, he led the **Huguenots** during the French Wars of **Religion**. He fought in the wars between **Henry II** of France and Spain (1551–7), and joined the Huguenots on the accession of **Francis II** (1559). He was defeated at Dreux during the first civil war (1562); and in the second war (1567–9) was defeated at Jarnac, taken prisoner, and shot. ▷ **Condé, House of**

Condé, Louis II of Bourbon, Prince of ('the Great Condé') (1621–86) French military leader. During the **Thirty Years War** he defeated the Spaniards (1643 and 1648) and Bavarians (1645–6). The court party came to terms with the **Fronde** by his help; but his arrogance led to his imprisonment, and when he was released he joined the rebels. Defeated at the Battle of the Dunes, near Dunkirk (1658), he was then pardoned, and became one of **Louis XIV**'s greatest generals, defeating the Spanish in Franche-Comté (1668) and **William III**, of Orange, at Seneffe (1674). ▷ **Condé, House of**

Condominium (Anglo/Egyptian Sudan) After the defeat of the Mahdist forces by **Kitchener**, the area of the Upper Nile was linked with Egypt, named the Anglo/Egyptian Sudan and controlled nominally by

Britain and Egypt as a 'condominium'. In practice, though, real power lay in British hands as Britain was, at the time, in effective control of Egypt. The period of the condominium, initially both economically and socially advantageous to the Sudan, led (through the development of an educated class) to a desire for independence. Some progress was made and in 1948 Britain recognized the validity of these aspirations. However, the movement of the Sudanese towards independence received a setback when, in 1951, King Farouk of Egypt proclaimed himself also King of the Sudan. Farouk's subsequent fall led to Egypt's recognition, in principle, of the Sudanese right to independence, and full independence was declared in 1955.

Condorcet, Marie Jean Antoine Nicolas de Caritat, Marquis of (1743–94) French politician, philosopher, and mathematician. He studied at Paris, and his work in mathematics became highly regarded in the 1760s. He was elected to the **Legislative Assembly** (1791–2), and became its President, siding usually with the **Girondins**. Accused and condemned by the **Jacobins**, he was captured, and found dead in prison, at Bourg-la-Reine. In his philosophy, he proclaimed the ideal of progress, and the indefinite perfectibility of the human race. ▷ **French Revolution**

condottiere A leader of mercenary soldiers in 14–15c Italy; from Italian *condotta* 'contract'. Hired by city-states and the papacy, they were often of foreign origin (eg the Englishman Sir John Hawkwood or Giovanni Acuto), but they also included Italian noblemen (eg the d'Este dukes of Ferrara, Gonzaga marquises of Mantua, and Sforza dukes of Milan).

Confederacy ▷ **Confederate States of America**

Confederacy, Second Athenian The name for the revived Athenian naval hegemony created in 378/7BC. Its constitution was designed to avoid provoking the unpopularity which had characterized the 5c BC **Athenian Empire**. However, in 357BC Chios, Cos, **Rhodes** and Byzantium revolted from the alliance, and by 354BC all the important members had seceded. ▷ **Mausolus**

Confederate States of America The official name of the states that seceded in 1860–1, precipitating the **American Civil War**:

Virginia, North Carolina, South Carolina, Georgia, Florida, Tennessee, Alabama, Mississippi, Louisiana, Texas and Arkansas. The Confederacy's constitution was modelled on the **US Constitution**. Its only President was Jefferson **Davis** of Mississippi. It never won foreign recognition, and collapsed after military defeat by the North in 1865. The other four slave states (Delaware, Maryland, Kentucky, and Missouri) did not secede, and neither did the north-west counties of Virginia, which became West Virginia.

Confederation, Articles of ▷ **Articles of Confederation**

Confederation Movement Canadian political movement for unification within the British North American provinces. Prefigured at various times from the **American Revolution** onwards, consideration of the project by Earl **Grey**, the British Colonial Secretary (1846–52), set in train discussions within the maritime provinces. At the same time a growing paralysis of government was becoming evident within the Province of Canada. A T **Galt**'s entry into the **Cartier–Macdonald** government in 1858 was only secured on condition that it sought confederation, which was rapidly being seen as a necessity. The English-speaking business community believed it to be essential for economic growth and expansion to the west against American competition, while the threat to reciprocity demanded closer trading links between Canada and the Maritimes. The British government's commitment to Canadian defence had been called into question since the Oregon dispute, and with the onset of the **American Civil War**, the provinces became aware that they were very vulnerable to retaliation from the Northern states because of British policies and because Confederates were ready to use Canada as a base for raids. In 1864 the 'great coalition' of Canadian reformers and conservatives under the leadership of Sir Étienne-Paschal Tache broached the idea of a general union at the Charlottetown Conference called by the Maritimes. Discussions continued at the Quebec Conference, where agreement was quickly reached. Acceptance by the provincial legislatures was much more difficult to obtain, and was achieved in Canada (where it needed all George Étienne Cartier's political acumen to persuade the French-Canadians) only after lengthy debate. In the Maritimes, Newfoundland and Prince Edward Island rejected confederation, but Samuel **Tilley** and Charles **Tupper** eventually secured its

adoption in New Brunswick and Nova Scotia. The final resolutions were agreed at the London Conference of 1866 and embodied in the **British North America Act** of 1867. ▷ **Dominion of Canada**

Confederation of the Rhine (1806–14) A union of all the German states except **Prussia** and **Austria**, established by **Napoleon I** on the dissolution of the **Holy Roman Empire** in 1806. The 18 states were placed under French control to assist the French war effort, although the long-term effect was to stimulate the movement for German unification. ▷ **Napoleonic Wars**

Confessing Church A Church formed in Germany by Evangelical Christians opposed to Nazism and the Nazi-supported 'German Christian Church Movement'. Its Synod of Barmen published the *Barmen Declaration* (1934), which became influential in Germany and beyond as a basis for resistance to oppressive civil authorities, It was succeeded in 1948 by the 'Evangelical Church in Germany'. ▷ **Nazi Party**

confino The practice of internal exile or banishment to remote provinces and islands; it was used extensively against critics of **Mussolini**'s government after Nov 1926.

Confucian Classics A collection of texts thought to embody the ideas of the Chinese philosopher **Confucius** (551–479BC) on ethics, government and ritual. Composed principally during the **Zhou Dynasty** and Western ('Former') Han Dynasty, these works comprised the Five Classics (Classic of Changes, Book of History, Classic of Odes, Classic of Rites, and the Spring and Autumn Annals) and the Four Books (Analects of Confucius, Mencius, Book of Great Learning, and Doctrine of the Mean). The former were officially canonized during the Han Dynasty, while the latter were similarly exalted during the **Song Dynasty**. As the official canon, these works constituted the entire curriculum of the civil service examinations from the 14c onwards. ▷ **Han Dynasties**

Confucius (K'ung Fu-tse) (551–479BC) Chinese philosopher. Largely self-educated, he married at 19, became a local administrator, and in 531BC began his career as a teacher. In 501BC he was appointed Governor of Chengdu, then Minister of Works, and later Minister of Justice. His ideas for social reform made him the idol of the people; but his enemies caused him to leave his home state of Lu, and he travelled widely, followed by many disciples. He later edited the ancient writings, and the *Confucian Analects*, memorabilia compiled soon after his death, are a collection of his sayings and doings. His moral teaching stressed the importance of the traditional relations of filial piety and brotherly respect.

Congress (USA) The national, or federal, legislature of the USA, consisting of two elected chambers: the Senate and the House of Representatives. The Senate contains two members from each state (irrespective of size), serving six-year terms, with a third of the terms expiring every two years. Representation in the House is for a two-year term, and is calculated on the basis of population. Congress initiates legislation, and significantly amends or rejects presidential legislative proposals. The **US Constitution** endows it with the 'power of the purse', and all revenue bills must originate in the House. For a bill to become law it must be passed in identical form by both chambers and signed by the President. A presidential veto may be overturned by a two-thirds majority in each chamber. Legislation receives detailed consideration in the powerful Congressional committees. Although the chambers are organized along party lines, party discipline is weak. The majority party leader of the House occupies the influential position of Speaker.

Congress Kingdom of Poland The name of that part of Poland given to Russia at the Congress of **Vienna** in 1815. Tsar **Alexander I** granted it a constitution which established it theoretically as a constitutional monarchy united to the Russian Empire. After the Polish uprising of 1830 the constitution was suspended, and after that of 1863 the kingdom was fully absorbed and subjected to a campaign of Russification. ▷ **Poland, Partitions of**

Congress of Racial Equality (CORE) US **civil rights** organization founded in 1942. In the 1960s CORE sponsored sit-in demonstrations, the freedom riders' challenge to segregation in interstate public buses, and registration of black voters in the South.

Congress Party (India) ▷ **Indian National Congress**

Connubio The Italian word (literally 'marriage') used to describe the parliamentary alliance established by **Cavour** with **Rattazzi**

in 1852, ushering in a period of anticlerical legislation and paving the way for Cavour to become Prime Minister of Sardinia-Piedmont. The alliance lasted until the sweeping electoral gains of the clericals in 1857, when Cavour promptly adopted a more conservative stance.

conquistador Literally 'conqueror', this is the standard term for the leaders of the Spanish expeditions of the early 16c which undertook the invasion and conquest of America. The ethos of conquest pervaded Castilian society and was inherited from the long successful struggle against the Moors, permanent settlement, formal rule, a change of religion, and the division of lands among successful conquistadores. The expectation that conquistadores would receive labouring peoples in encomienda preceded the discovery of the Americas and led to friction between the crown, conquistadores, and the Church during the early 16c. ▷ **Cortés**

Conrad I (d.918) King of Germany (911/18). He was the son of the Count of Franconia, and nephew of the Emperor Arnulf. Elected king on the extinction of the direct Carolingian line in 911, he gradually re-established the imperial authority over most of the German princes, carried on an unsuccessful war with France, and at last fell mortally wounded at Quedlinburg in a battle with the Hungarians. ▷ **Carolingians**

Conrad II (c.990–1039) German King (1024/39). The son of the Count of Speyer, he was crowned King in Mainz in 1024 and, after overcoming Lotharingian opposition, was crowned Emperor of the West in 1027. He restored German ascendancy over the Poles and Bohemians, and succeeded in 1032 to the Kingdom of Burgundy, but was unable to subdue rebellion in Italy in 1036–8. In 1035 he regulated the conditions of his unfree palace officials, laying the basis for the important role these **Ministeriales** were to play in his successors' administrations. ▷ **Lotharingia**

Conrad III (1093–1152) The first Hohenstaufen King of the Germans (1138/52). The son of Frederick of Swabia, he unsuccessfully contested the crown of Italy with Lothair of Saxony, and became King on his death. He was immediately involved in a quarrel with Henry the Proud, head of the Guelfs in Germany, the struggle being continued under Henry's son. When St **Bernard of Clairvaux** preached a new crusade, Conrad

set out for Palestine with a large army (1147).
▷ **Crusade, Second; Hohenstaufen Dynasty**

Conrad IV (1228–54) King of Germany and Jerusalem. The son of Emperor **Frederick II** and the heiress of the Kingdom of Jerusalem, Isabella of Brienne, he became Duke of Swabia in 1235 and was elected King in 1237. He ruled under the tutelage of Siegfried of Mainz (until 1241) and **Henry Raspe** of Thuringia (until 1246). His rule in Germany was secured on the support of Swabian **Ministeriales** and towns. In 1251 he began the fight for his Sicilian inheritance. He landed in Apulia in 1252 and took over the government of the Norman Kingdom from his half brother, Manfred, but Pope **Innocent III** refused to recognize his claim and excommunicated him. He died of malaria in Apulia and was succeeded by his infant son, **Conradin**.

Conradin of Swabia (1252–68) King of Jerusalem and Sicily and the last Hohenstaufen. The son of **Conrad IV**, he was formally recognized as Duke of Swabia in 1254. His uncle, **Manfred**, had assumed the crown of Sicily on a rumour of Conradin's death, and Pope Urban IV's hatred of the **Hohenstaufen Dynasty** led him to offer the crown of the Two Sicilies to **Charles of Anjou**, who invaded Italy and slew Manfred at Benevento (1266). Conradin, invited by the Neapolitans to assert his rights, appeared in Italy with 10 000 men, but was defeated near Tagliacozzo, taken prisoner, and executed.

Conrad of Montferrat (d.1192) Italian Crusader. He distinguished himself during the defence of Tyre against **Saladin** (1187) and in 1192 he was elected King of Jerusalem as consort of the heiress Isabella, daughter of Amalric I. He was, however, murdered by the **Assassins** before he could be crowned.

Conrad the Red (d.955) Duke of Lotharingia. A loyal follower of **Otto I, 'the Great'**, he was rewarded with Lotharingia in 944. He married Otto's daughter Liudgard (947) and successfully fulfilled commissions from Otto to settle disputes between his vassals (948–52) and bring Count Berengar of Ivrea to heel (952). However, the terms of his settlement with Berengar led to a breach with Otto and, embittered, Conrad joined Otto's son Liudolf's rebellion (953–4). He was forced to submit to Otto's authority in 954 and was deprived of all his lands in Franconia. Later reconciled with the king, he was killed in the Battle of **Lechfeld** against the Hungarians.

Consalvi, Ercole, Cardinal (1757–1824) Italian statesman and prelate. Made a cardinal and Secretary of State by **Pius VII** (1800), he was an extremely able diplomat and administrator. In 1801 he concluded the Papal Concordat with **Napoleon I**, and, at the Congress of **Vienna** (1814–15), managed to block **Metternich**'s schemes to establish an Italian Confederation under Austrian presidency along the same lines as that of Germany. In domestic affairs, he was a reformer but found his policies constantly opposed by reactionary cardinals (who were known as **Zelanti**).

conscription The practice of compelling young men of eligible age and fitness to serve by statute in the armed forces of a nation. To meet the huge manpower needs of **World War I**, conscription was introduced in Great Britain in early 1916. Conscription was again enforced in Britain from 1939 to 1945, continuing in peacetime as National Service, which was finally abolished in 1962.

Consejo Real First created as an advisory body in 1385, as the royal council of **Castile** its powers and functions were specified clearly in a law of 1406 and its structure reformed in 1459, when it was laid down that eight of its 12 members must be university-trained lawyers (*letrados*). The council was further reformed in 1480, and by 1493 all its members were required to be *letrados*. The body, the supreme court of the realm, was later also known as the Council of Castile.

Conservative Party of South Africa A South African party formed in 1982 by reactionary (*verkrampte*) members of the **National Party** who had been expelled from Parliament. It was led by Andries **Treurnicht** and, after the 1987 general election, became the chief opposition party in the white parliament and opposed the liberalization measures of President **De Klerk**.

Conservative Party (Sweden) ▷ **Moderate Unity Party**

Conservative Party (UK) One of the two major political parties in the UK, its full name being the Conservative and Unionist Party. It developed from the Tory Party during the 19c and pursued policies, first under **Peel** and then **Disraeli**, designed to broaden its appeal beyond the English landowners and supporters of the Church of England. It has largely succeeded in this, having been in power either solely or as the dominant element in coalitions for approximately two-thirds of the period since Disraeli's election victory of 1874. Its main support, however, has remained English rather than British and the party is stronger in rural than in urban areas. ▷ **Tories; Whigs**

Constans (c.323–50) Roman Emperor (337/50). The youngest son of **Constantine I, 'the Great'**, Constans received only Italy, Africa and Illyricum in the division of the empire after his father's death (337), his older, more aggressive, brother Constantine II, taking the lion's share of the West—Gaul, Britain and Spain. After defeating him at Aquileia in north Italy (340), Constans became sole Emperor of the West, a position he held until his death in an army mutiny. His visit to Britain (343) was the last ever to be made by a legitimate Roman Emperor.

Constans II (Flavius Heraclius) (630–68) Byzantine Emperor (641/68). He succeeded his father, Constantine III, and his reign was marked by the loss of Egypt and much of the Middle East to the Arabs. His despotism and church policies aroused antagonism, and he was murdered in his bath by a chamberlain five years after transferring his capital to Syracuse.

Constant (de Rebeque), (Henri) Benjamin (1767–1830) French novelist and politician. Educated at Oxford, Erlangen, and Edinburgh, he settled in Paris (1795). As a journalist, he supported the Revolution, but was banished in 1802 for his opposition to **Napoleon I**. He returned in 1814, and became leader of the liberal opposition. His best-known work is the novel *Adolphe* (1816), based on his relationship with Madame de Staël. ▷ **French Revolution**

Constantine I, 'the Great' (c.285–337) Roman Emperor (306/37). Though proclaimed Emperor by the army at York on the death of his father, **Constantius I, 'Chlorus'** in 306, it was not until his defeat of **Maxentius** at the Milvian Bridge in Rome (312) that he became Emperor of the West; and only with his victory over **Licinius**, the Emperor of the East, that he became sole Emperor (324). Believing that his victory in 312 was the work of the Christian God, he became the first emperor to promote Christianity, whence his title 'Great'. His Edict of Milan (313), issued jointly with Licinius, brought toleration to Christians throughout the empire, and his new capital at Constantinople, founded on the strategically important site of Byzantium

(324), was from the outset a Christian city. On his death, the empire was once more partitioned, with his sons, **Constantine II** and **Constans**, dividing the western provinces between them and Constantius II taking over the entire East. ▷ **Byzantine Empire; Milan, Edict of**

Constantine I (1868–1923) King of Greece (1913/17 and 1920/2). He was the son and successor of **George I**. As a military commander he was unsuccessful in the Turkish War of 1897, but led the Greeks to victory in the **Balkan Wars** (1912–13). As the brother-in-law of Kaiser **William II** of Germany, he insisted on Greek neutrality in **World War I**, but was forced to retire in favour of his son, Alexander, by the rival government of Eleuthérios **Venizélos** and the Allies in 1917. In 1920 he was restored to the throne by plebiscite, but after a military revolt in 1922, abdicated again in favour of his son, **George II**.

Constantine II (317–40) Roman Emperor (337/40). He was the second son of **Constantine I, 'the Great'**, on whose death he became the ruler of Britain, Gaul and Spain. His attempt to suppress his younger brother, **Constans,** the ruler of Italy, Africa and Illyricum, resulted in his own death in battle at Aquileia in north Italy.

Constantine II (1940–   ) King of Greece (1964/73). The son and successor of **Paul I** of Greece, soon after his accession he married Princess Anne-Marie, younger daughter of **Frederick IX** of Denmark and sister of Queen **Margrethe** of Denmark. In Apr 1967 the 'Colonels' seized power in a military coup; Constantine made an abortive attempt to regain power, then fled into exile in Rome (Dec 1967). He was formally deposed in June 1973, and the monarchy was abolished by national referendum in 1974. His heir is Crown Prince Paul (1967–   ).

Constantine V Copronymus (718–75) Byzantine Emperor (720/75). The son of **Leo III**, he was crowned Co-Emperor at the age of two. On the death of his father (741), he defeated a revolt by his brother-in-law, Artabasdus, and thereafter intensified Leo's iconoclastic policies. A well-managed Council of the church (754) promulgated the destruction of icons, inaugurating an era of persecution of the orthodox party. A talented leader of soldiers, Constantine directed numerous expeditions against the Bulgarians, whom he defeated in battle in 763 and 773, and died while on campaign.

Constantine VII Porphyrogenitus (905–59) Byzantine Emperor (911/59). He was the son of Leo VI. Although crowned Emperor in 911, for over 30 years he was overshadowed by his father-in-law, the regent Romanus Lecapenus, who created his own sons Co-Emperors. However, in 945 a struggle within this family allowed Constantine to seize sole power. A scholar rather than a ruler by nature, he wrote or compiled numerous works of history and geography, including the life of his grandfather, **Basil I**.

Constantine XI Palaeologus Dragases (1404–53) The last Byzantine Emperor (1448/53). He was the fourth son of Manuel II and the Serbian princess, Helen Dragaš. During the reign of his elder brother, John VIII, he and his other brothers jointly ruled the despotate of Morea, a Byzantine apanage in the Peloponnese; on John's death (1448), Constantine succeeded to an empire consisting of little more than Constantinople and its environs, threatened by the vast **Ottoman Empire** which surrounded it. His proclamation of the union of the Greek Church with Rome (1452) secured only limited military assistance from the West and was repudiated by his indignant subjects. Powerless to prevent the inevitable Ottoman siege, Constantine died fighting in the final Turkish assault.

Constantine Nikolaevich (1827–92) Russian naval commander. A grand duke, he was the second son of Tsar **Nicholas I**. In the **Crimean War** he commanded the Russian fleet, and held the British and French in check before Kronstadt. He played an important role in preparing and implementing the social and political reforms of Tsar **Alexander II** after the war.

Constantinople, Capture of (29 May 1453) Constantinople eventually fell to the Ottoman Turks under **Mehmed II, 'the Conqueror'**. Mehmed had been provoked by the Byzantine Emperor, Constantine IX, who had proposed setting up a pretender against Mehmed if the latter refused to double the financial contribution he made to Constantine for his (Constantine's) custodianship of the very prince Constantine was proposing as would-be pretender. Mehmed responded by building Rumeli Hisar, a fortress on the Constantinople side of the Bosporus, and when envoys were sent in protest by Constantine, Mehmed had them beheaded. This was the signal for open hostilities to begin. The siege took some two months, with the Byzantines, aided only by a

Genoese colony on Chios, hopelessly inadequately provided with manpower for the defence of their city. After a two-month siege, Constantinople was taken by a general frontal assault and the Emperor was killed in the mêlée.

Constantinople, Council of (869–70) Originally held to establish the status of Photius, Patriarch of Constantinople, whose efforts were directed to the establishment of independence for the Byzantine Church. The Council, before the legates of Hadrian II, declared Photius excommunicated; this, regarded by the Roman Church as the eighth ecumenical council, resulted in a lack of agreement between Basil I and the papal legates over the rights of the Roman See. An unexpected development, at least from the Roman viewpoint, was the arrival of a Bulgarian delegation, forcing a reassembly of the Council to decide whether the Bulgarian Church came under Rome or Byzantium. Boris, the Bulgar, had hoped for an independent Bulgarian Church, and with this in view had turned to Rome. Unsuccessful, he turned again to Byzantium, where he was able, as a result of the Council's decision, to have an archbishop and several bishops consecrated by the then Patriarch, Ignatius.

Constantinople, Latin Empire of A 13c empire based at Constantinople (ancient Byzantium, modern Istanbul), the capital of the medieval (Eastern) Roman or Byzantine Empire. The army of the Fourth Crusade took Constantinople (1204) and created a Latin Empire, with **Baldwin I**, Count of Flanders as the first emperor. It succumbed in 1261 to the army of **Michael VIII Palaeologus**, after a precarious existence.

Constantinople, Latin Occupation of (1204–61) The Fourth Crusade, originally destined for Egypt, with the Venetians supplying the ships, was tragically diverted at Venetian behest to Constantinople, because, as a result of failure to meet the cost of the ships, the Crusaders found themselves beholden to Venice virtually to the extent of being in Venetian service. It was this diversion which led to the Latins' taking Constantinople in 1204 and to the subsequent Latin occupation. Control of events appears to have been securely in the hands of Enrico Dandolo, the aging Doge of Venice, and it was he who contrived the election of Count Baldwin of Flanders as the first Latin Emperor. The division of imperial territory which followed was complex, but it was certainly the Venetians who gained the most. The Latin Occupation was heartily detested by the Byzantines themselves who, quite apart from their religious differences with the papacy, found the overweening arrogance of the Latins hard to stomach. It was eventually the statesmanship of Michael VIII which led to what might be seen, given the antipathy of the Byzantines towards the Latins and the constant factional differences among the Latins themselves, as the not wholly unexpected demise of the Latin 'Empire' and the restoration of the Byzantine Empire as such.

Constantinople, Patriarchate of The highest ecclesiastical office in the Orthodox Church. Under the **Ottoman Empire**, the ecumenical patriarch had jurisdiction over the members of the Orthodox **millet** and represented its interests to the Ottoman Porte. Control of the patriarchate long lay in the hands of the **Greeks** who used it to dominate the cultural and religious life of the Balkans, securing the abolition of the Serb patriarchate at Peć (1766) and the Bulgarian patriarchate at Ohrid (1767). In the 19c, Bulgarian, Serb and Romanian nationalists sought to free themselves from the Greeks no less than the Turks. ▷ **Bulgarian Exarchate**

Constantinople, Siege of (674–8) The Umayyad Caliph **Mu'awiya** (661/80), effectively the founder of the **Umayyad Dynasty**, maintained a policy of hostile relations with the Byzantines consisting largely of raids into Byzantine territory with the object of acquiring booty. He did, however, prosecute hostilities against Constantinople itself, the major attack being this siege. The Arabs acquired a base on an island in the Sea of Marmora from which they were able to conduct operations. There was a continuous series of naval engagements before the city, although not in the winter which the Arab forces spent at their base. Accounts of the actions themselves are confused but there appears to be general agreement that it was the Byzantine's eventual successful use of Greek fire which finally caused the Arab withdrawal.

Constantinople, Siege of (717–18) This siege, conducted by Maslama ibn Abd al-Malik, began during the caliphate of his brother, Sulayman (715/17). During the siege the Arabs were well supplied with reinforcements both by sea and land, but again Greek fire was used to good effect and also a chain was drawn across the Golden Horn, entry to Arab vessels thus being barred. The

operation came to an end on the accession of the new caliph, 'Umar ibn Abd al-Aziz, who ordered the fleet (which suffered devastation at the hands of the elements on its return voyage) to withdraw.

Constantinople, Siege of (1391–8) In 1391 the Ottomans had conquered most of the Balkans, and from 1391 until 1398, Constantinople was in an almost continuous state of siege from the land and blockade from the sea. The only reason for its survival was the strength of its defences which depended largely on the sea- and land-walls of the city. At this time Imperial City and Empire were almost coterminous (the principality in the Morea still held out) and, in some ways, this siege was not so much an attempt by the Ottomans to take the city, as the surrounding of Constantinople by Turks on all sides. There was little or no prospect of relief, as the Turks had reduced the surrounding area and there was nowhere whence that relief could come. This left **Manuel II Palaeologus** (1391/1425) able to do little more than appeal for aid to Russia and the West.

Constantinople, Siege of (1422) A degree of relief having been afforded the beleaguered Byzantines by the devastating activities of **Timur**, it was not long before the Ottomans (who had lost Asia Minor after the Battle of **Ankara** in 1402) re-established their ascendancy, having survived as a result of their foothold in the Balkans. Sultan **Murad II** (1421/51) presided over a renewal of Ottoman aggression, and initiated (22 June) a purposeful siege of Constantinople. The strength of the Byzantine defences was again too much for the besieging Ottomans, but Murad was only deflected from his intent by his having to deal with the threat to his throne posed by his younger brother, Mustafa.

Constantinople, Treaty of (1700) The treaty ending the Russo-Turkish War that included Austria on the anti-Turkish side when it broke out in 1697. Austria made peace at **Karlowitz** in 1699, but **Peter I, 'the Great'** struggled on to strengthen his hold on the Black Sea. He acquired the fortress of Azov, was excused the tribute hitherto paid to the Crimean Tatars, and won the right to diplomatic representation at Constantinople. Russia now had a springboard for further encroachment on the **Ottoman Empire**.

Constantinople Agreements (Mar–Apr 1915) Britain and France feared that Russia would make a separate peace with Germany unless she was offered significant territorial gains. They secretly agreed, therefore, that after **World War I** Russia should receive Constantinople (Istanbul) and land along the Straits. This was a remarkable change in British policy particularly, as throughout the 19c Britain had opposed Russia gaining control of the Straits. After the **October Revolution**, however, the **Bolsheviks** rejected all agreements made by the Tsarist government.

Constantius I, 'Chlorus' (c.250–306) Deputy Roman Emperor of the West (293/305) and Emperor of the West (305/6). Appointed by **Diocletian** as deputy to **Maximian** in 293, he turned out to be an outstanding general and enlightened ruler. Chiefly remembered now as the father of **Constantine I, 'the Great'** by his concubine, Helena, it was above all as a military man, the conqueror of the rebel emperor in Britain, **Carausius** (293–6), that contemporaries valued him. He died in York, after defeating the Picts in battle.

Constitution Act of 1982 The statute which 'patriated' the constitution of Canada, adding a Charter of Rights and Freedoms, and a general amendment procedure. It was the result of 18 months of hectic negotiation following the 1980 Quebec referendum on independence during which the federal government had promised a national settlement of constitutional issues. Through the summer of 1980 a series of very public discussions explored the items of a prepared agenda for a First Ministers' conference in Sep. After this broke down in acrimony, the federal government announced a unilateral approach to the British parliament, a resolution whose validity was finally accepted by the Supreme Court in Sep 1981 as allowable though objectionable. 'Constitutional convention plus constitutional law equal the total constitution of the country,' it said in a judgement that was used to support the arguments of both sides. At a final conference in Nov 1981, the so-called Kitchen Meeting paved the way for compromise, which, however was rejected by Quebec. ▷ **Meech Lake Accord**

Constitutional Convention (1787) A gathering at Philadelphia that drafted the **US Constitution**; 12 of the original 13 states were represented (Rhode Island did not send a delegate). The term, by extension, is also used for any political meeting empowered to write a state or national constitution.

consulado The Spanish term used to describe the merchant guild (to which most traders belonged) established in the viceregal capitals of Mexico City (1592) and Lima (1613). Each *consulado* had the right to regulate its own custom and practice and adjudicate disputes among its members. The administrative reorganization under Charles III saw the establishment of consulados in Caracas, Guatemala, Buenos Aires, Havana, Cartagena, Santiago, Guadalajara and Veracruz. By the 1780s, dynasties of merchants stood at the apex of colonial society, passing the export-import business from generation to generation through the marriage of daughters to Spanish-born nephews (often from the same small towns of the peninsula), and of sons to the families of local worthies. By loans to local government and the Church, they sustained the privileges of the consulado. ▷ **cabildo**

Consulate (France) (1799–1804) The system of government established by the constitution of the year VIII (1799). Power was placed theoretically in the hands of three consuls, but in reality was from the first monopolized by **Napoleon I**, who abolished the Consulate in 1804, to proclaim himself Emperor.

Conte, Lansana (c.1945–) Guinean soldier and politician. As military commander of the Boke Region, he led a bloodless coup on the death of Sekou **Toure** (Mar 1984) and set up the Military Committee for National Recovery with himself as President. He relaxed the centralizing policies of Toure and successfully encouraged many exiles to return. An attempted coup was thwarted by loyal troups in 1985 and the process of reintegrating into the Western world was continued.

Continental Congress (1774–8) In North America, the federal legislature consisting of delegates from each of the 13 colonies (the United States after 1776). The First Continental Congress met from 5 Sep to 26 Oct 1774, in response to Britain's passing the **Intolerable Acts**, and its delegates petitioned the King. When no appropriate response was received, the Second Continental Congress convened in May 1775, shortly after the Battles of **Lexington and Concord**, and created an army. Agreeing to seek independence in the summer of 1776, the Congress formally adopted the **Declaration of Independence** on July 4. The Congress remained the political voice of the young country under the

Articles of Confederation until the US **Constitution** took effect in 1789. ▷ **American Revolution; Ordinance of 1787**

Continuation War (1941–4) Known also as the Soviet–Finnish War, Finland's attack on the USSR (June 1941) in partnership with Nazi Germany was intended to reverse the verdict of the **Russo-Finnish War** of 1939–40. After initial success, the Finnish front was stabilized until the great Russian offensive of June 1944. However, the Finnish government had decided as early as Feb 1943 that it must seek peace. With the assistance of Swedish mediation, an armistice was signed (Sep 1944) and the war was formally ended by the Treaty of Paris (Feb 1947). ▷ **Tanner, Väinö; World War II**

Contra-Remonstrants ▷ **Counter-Remonstrants**

Contreras, Battle of (1847) An engagement in the **Mexican War** (1846–8) in which the Mexican army under **Santa Anna** was badly defeated by a smaller US force under Winfield Scott (1786–1866), opening the way to Mexico City and leading to the collapse of Mexican resistance.

Convention, National (France) (1792–5) The assembly which ruled France from 1792 to 1795. It originated with the insurrection of 10 Aug 1792, which overthrew the **Legislative Assembly** elected in 1791 and called for new elections on a completely democratic franchise. In practice, however, very few dared to vote. The Convention proclaimed the First Republic, tried and executed King **Louis XVI** and allowed itself to be terrorized into authorizing the most extreme measures of the **French Revolution** (1793–4), under **Robespierre** and the Committee of **Public Safety**. With the downfall of Robespierre at **Thermidor** (July 1794), the Convention recovered its own authority, recalled the surviving **Girondins**, established a new constitution, the **Directory** (1795), and dissolved itself. ▷ **Republic, First** (France)

Convention People's Party (CPP) Formed in 1949 by Nkwame **Nkrumah** as a breakaway from the **United Gold Coast Convention** (UGCC), the CPP appealed to a mass, especially urban, following and was instrumental in propelling Ghana to independence in 1957 and Nkrumah to the premiership. It became the only legal party in 1964 (with the slogan 'the CPP is Ghana and Ghana the CPP') and lost popular support quickly,

putting up no defence for Nkrumah when he was ousted in a coup in 1966. Nevertheless, later parties were built upon CPP foundations.

Conversos In medieval Spain, the name given to those who had converted to Christianity from the Jewish faith; the term also applied to their descendants. Known also as New Christians to distinguish them from Old or non-Semitic Christians, they were in popular parlance vilified as **Marranos** (or 'pigs'). They made a major impact on public life from 1392, when anti-Jewish riots in the major Spanish towns forced most Jews to convert to Christianity. As Christians, they had right of access to public office: by the late 15c they were an influential force in many towns and could be found in the episcopate and in the royal councils. Many were suspected of still following Jewish religious practices, which helped to bring about the establishment of the Spanish **Inquisition** in 1478 and the Expulsion of the Jews in 1492. From 1480, when it commenced operations, to the 1520s, the Inquisition in Spain executed thousands of *Conversos* accused of secret judaizing. By the early 16c, judaizers were becoming a rarity and Conversos were more readily absorbed into Spanish life. Conversos made a notable contribution to cultural life through such figures as St Teresa of Avila and the poet Luis de León. ▷ **Jews, Expulsion of the**

Cook, Sir Joseph (1860–1947) British-born Australian politician. A miner, he emigrated to Australia in 1885 and was elected to the New South Wales Assembly in 1891 as a Labor member. He left the **Australian Labor Party** (1894) and joined G H **Reid**'s Liberal ministry. He entered federal politics in 1901, supporting Reid's opposition free-trade group of which he became Deputy Leader in 1905 and leader in 1908. By now anti-socialist, he formed a coalition government with **Deakin** in 1909, serving as Minister of Defence. He was Prime Minister (1913–14), Deputy Prime Minister in **Hughes**'s Nationalist government (1917), Treasurer (1920–1) and Australian High Commissioner in London (1921–7).

Coolidge, (John) Calvin (1872–1933) US politician and 30th President. He became a lawyer, and was Governor of Massachusetts (1919–20) when he gained national attention for his firm handling of the Boston police strike. Elected Vice-President (1921–3), on Warren G Harding's death, he became

President (1923). A strong supporter of US business interests, he was triumphantly re-elected in 1924, but refused renomination in 1928. Coolidge's policies were successful while he was in office, but were partly responsible for the **Great Depression** that followed.

Cooperative Party (UK) A British political party which grew out of the ideas of voluntary mutual economic assistance developed in the 19c by Robert Owen (1771–1858). Established in 1917, one candidate, who joined with the parliamentary **Labour Party**, was elected to the House of Commons in 1918. Thereafter it became closely integrated with the Labour Party.

Coornhert, Dirck Volkertzoon (1522–90) Dutch politician, theologian, writer, poet and philosopher. One of the most important thinkers of the 16c, he was outspoken in his criticism of others and so spent most of his mature life being pursued around the Low Countries by his enemies. He became Town Clerk of Haarlem in 1562: after imprisonment in 1567 he fled to Germany where he worked for **William** of Orange against Spanish rule. In 1572 he returned to Haarlem and became Secretary to the States of Holland, but regularly was obliged to flee to escape persecution. His 145 surviving publications show he was a champion of toleration and a sworn enemy of prejudice: these views brought him into conflict with both Calvinists and Catholics.

Copenhagen, Battles of (1801 and 1807) British naval operations aimed at preventing Danish neutrality from benefiting France during the **Napoleonic Wars**. The first engagement (Apr 1801), led by Admirals Hyde Parker (1739–1807) and **Nelson**, resulted in Denmark's withdrawal from the Armed Neutrality. After the bombardment of Copenhagen (Sep 1807) by Admiral James Gambier (1756–1833) and Arthur Wellesley (later Duke of **Wellington**), the Danes surrendered their fleet and stores.

Corday (d'Armont), (Marie) Charlotte (1768–93) French noblewoman. She sympathized with the aims of the **French Revolution**, but was horrified by the acts of the **Jacobins**. Having managed to obtain an audience with the revolutionary leader, Jean Paul **Marat**, she stabbed him to death while he was in his bath. She was guillotined four days later.

Cordeliers' Club An extreme revolutionary club founded in Paris (1790) by **Danton** and **Marat**; also called the Society of the Friends of the Rights of Man and Citizen. Under **Hébert**'s leadership its programme became increasingly radical (1792–4), contributing to the downfall of the **Girondins** (1793). ▷ **French Revolution**

Cordobazo (May 1969) The name given to a period of major unrest in Córdoba, Argentina, during which trade unionists and students briefly took control of the city in protest against the military dictatorship of Juan Carlos Onganía. The event indicated the potential for an alliance between left-wing **Peronism** and student activists inspired by more traditional (ie European) left-wing ideologies. It also revealed the structural weaknesses of the military regime.

Corfu, Declaration of (20 July 1917) During **World War I**, in anticipation of the break-up of the Austro-Hungarian monarchy, the government of Serbia (then in exile on the island of Corfu), together with the **Yugoslav Committee**, agreed to work together to create a South Slav or Yugoslav state. This was to be a 'constitutional, democratic and parliamentary monarchy' under the Serbian Karageorgević Dynasty. The declaration, although it had no legal force, marked an important stage in the creation of the Kingdom of Serbs, Croats and Slovenes (later Yugoslavia).

Corfu Incident (Aug 1923) When an Italian general and four members of his staff were shot while on a mission determining the Greek–Albanian frontier, **Mussolini** saw it as an insult to national pride and an opportunity to test Italian strength. The Greek island of Corfu was bombarded and occupied. A Greek appeal to the **League of Nations** was successful in getting the Italians to evacuate the island, but the Greeks were also ordered to pay Italy a large indemnity. After the Corfu incident, Mussolini adopted a more conciliatory position in international relations for a number of years.

Corinth Located on the isthmus between northern Greece and the Peloponnese, with easy access to both the Corinthian and Saronic Gulfs, by the 8c BC it had developed into a prosperous trading and colonizing city: its colonies included **Syracuse** and Corcyra (Corfu). In the late 6c BC, it joined the **Peloponnesian League** under **Sparta**, and after c.460BC actively encouraged Sparta to go to war against Athens. However, Corinth's prosperity suffered greatly in the resulting **Peloponnesian War** (431–404BC). After his victory at the Battle of **Chaeronea** (338BC), **Philip II** of Macedon convened a congress at Corinth to set up a league of Greek states under his hegemony (the 'Corinthian League'); a Macedonian garrison was also strategically placed in Corinth's citadel. The city was sacked and destroyed in 146BC, but rebuilt by Julius **Caesar**.

Corinthian War (395–386BC) The war which resulted from **Sparta**'s imperialistic policy and consequent unpopularity in the years after the end of the **Peloponnesian War** (404BC), so-called because much of the fighting took place around the isthmus of **Corinth**. By 386BC, Sparta had secured the support of the Persian King Artaxerxes for imposing peace: Persian control of the Greek cities of Asia Minor, and of Cyprus, was recognized; all other Greek cities (with three minor exceptions) were declared autonomous (the 'King's Peace', or 'Peace of Antalcidas').

Coriolanus, Gaius or **Gnaeus Marcius** (5c BC) Roman folk hero, so named from his capture of the Volscian town of Corioli. Banished by the Romans for tyrannical behaviour (491BC), he took refuge with the Volscians, and proceeded to lead them against his native city. After entreaties from his mother and wife, he spared Rome, and was executed by the Volscians.

Corn Laws British legislation regulating the trade in corn. This was common in the 18c, but the most famous Corn Law was that enacted by Lord **Liverpool**'s government in 1815. Passed at a time when market prices were dropping rapidly, it imposed prohibitively high duties on the import of foreign corn when the domestic price was lower than 80 shillings (£4) a quarter. Widely criticized by radical politicians as legislation designed to protect the landed interest at the expense of the ordinary consumer, the Corn Law was amended in 1828, with the introduction of a sliding scale, and duties were further reduced by **Peel** in 1842. The Laws were repealed in 1846. ▷ **Anti-Corn Law League**

Cornwallis, Charles, 1st Marquis (1738–1805) British general and politician. He served in the **Seven Years War**, although he was personally opposed to taxing the American colonists, accepting a command in the war. He defeated Gates at Camden (1780),

but was forced to surrender at Yorktown (1781). In 1786 he became Governor-General of India, where he defeated **Tippoo Sahib** of Mysore, and introduced the series of reforms known as the Cornwallis Code. He returned in 1793, to be made marquis. He was Lord-Lieutenant of Ireland (1798–1801), and negotiated the Peace of Amiens (1802). Reappointed Governor-General of India (1804), he died at Ghazipur.

coronelismo The Spanish term denoting the unfettered rule of a proprietor (frequently a trader) over a community, which was a natural result of the settlement of the vast interior of Brazil. Such men were often heads of extended families (*parentelas*) and were frequently nominated to public office, especially the National Guard, in recognition of their rule. Their position was vastly strengthened under **Campos Salles**, who encouraged the creation of one-party government in the states. Though many never held formal office in the Guard, the title *coronel* implied the ability to muster a substantial vote from local tenants and clients, and to produce *agregados* as personal militia in support of a state governor. The golden age of *coronelismo* ended with the Estado Novo in 1937. ▷ **agregado; parentela**

Corporation Act (1661) A British Act passed by the **Cavalier Parliament** (1661–79), soon after the **Restoration** of **Charles II**. Office in municipal corporations was restricted to those who took the sacrament according to the usage of the Church of England. Part of the reassertion of Anglican supremacy represented by the **Clarendon Code**, the Act remained on the statute book until 1828.

Corporations Fascist labour organizations in **Mussolini**'s Italy. They were first established in 1926 to replace the old socialist-dominated unions and were to include both employers and employees. They were supposed to minimize industrial conflict and maximize efficiency. In practice, while not a disaster, the bargaining power of workers was greatly decreased, while grateful industrialists continued to do much as they pleased. In 1930 the National Council of Corporations was set up to act as a consultative body on the economy; in reality, its views were rarely canvassed and it was most important as a means of providing jobs for loyal party members.

corregidor The Spanish term (literally, 'corrector') originally denoting Spanish government officials, first appointed by Alfonso XI of Castile in the 14c; the word was then applied to the short-term lieutenant-governors, nominated by viceroys, who headed the **cabildos** in all Spanish settlements, hearing appeal cases from the *alcaldes* (local magistrates). Often of creole (American-born) origin, and sometimes known as *alcalde mayor*, in major cities such as Puebla in Mexico or Cuzco in Peru they were rarely strong enough to serve as a counterpoise to the *cabildo*. The *corregidor de Indios* acted as the Viceroy's representative in Indian settlements or *corregimientos*, and was also known as alcalde mayor. He was responsible for the collection of taxes, organization of labour services and *repartimientos*; often closely linked to the consulado traders, to whom he was generally indebted, the corregidor was supplanted by the *subdelegado* during the reign of Carlos III.

Corsica, Rebellions of In the 18c, Corsica was characterized by regular uprisings, first against Genoese rule (1729–68) and, after its acquisition by France, against its new French overlords. The main rebellions of the latter period were led by Pasquale de **Paoli** who ably resisted the French for over a year in 1768–9 and sought to turn the island into a British protectorate in 1793–5. Separatism was eventually crushed in the 1790s by the island's most famous son, Napoleon Bonaparte himself. ▷ **Napoleon I**

Cortes The Spanish parliament. The late 12c Cortes of Leon is thought by many to have been the earliest of all medieval parliaments, antedating the **Magna Carta**. The Cortes exercised full democratic rights for the first time under the Second Republic of 1931–6. It continued to exist under the **Franco** regime of 1939–75, but only in a consultative capacity. In 1977 it was established as the lower chamber of a two-chamber parliament based on universal suffrage. With the Constitution of 1978 the Cortes's powers were extended. ▷ **Republic, Second** (Spain)

Cortés, Hernán (1485–1547) Spanish conqueror of Mexico. He studied at Salamanca, then accompanied Velázquez in his expedition to Cuba (1511). In 1519 he commanded an expedition against Mexico, fighting his first battle at Tabasco. He founded Vera Cruz, marched to Tlascala, and made allies of the natives. He then marched on the Aztec capital, capturing King **Montezuma**, but the Mexicans rose and Cortés was forced to flee. He then launched a successful siege of the capital, which fell in 1521. He was formally appointed Governor and Captain-General of New Spain in 1522, but his authority was later superseded. He spent the years 1530–40 in Mexico, then returned to Spain. ▷ **Aztecs**

Cortes of Cadiz (1810–13) The first Spanish constituent legislature. During the War of Independence the Cortes of Cadiz, initially called by the regency, staged an internal revolution by drawing up a liberal constitution. The Constitution of 1812 established a constitutional monarchy, embracing popular sovereignty, the division of powers, a unicameral Cortes, and the centralization of government. Although principally a liberal document, the Constitution did maintain Catholicism as the state religion. The Cortes of Cadiz and the Constitution of 1812 became potent symbols of liberalism throughout southern Europe and Latin America. In Spain, the constitution was resurrected in 1820, 1837, 1854 and 1869.

Cosgrave, William Thomas (1880–1965) Irish politician. He joined the **Sinn Féin** movement at an early age, and took part in the **Easter Rising** (1916). He was elected a Sinn Féin MP (1918–22) and, after holding office as first President of the **Irish Free State** (1922–32), became Leader of the Opposition (1932–44). His son, Liam, was Leader of the **Fine Gael** Party (1965–7) and Prime Minister (1973–7).

Cossacks Originally, members of semi-independent communities of fugitive peasants and military adventurers who inhabited the steppelands of South Russia and the Ukraine. Attempts to limit Cossack freedom led to several large-scale rebellions against the Russian government in the 17–18c. In the 18–19c Cossack horsemen were formed into military organizations (*hosts*), and earned a reputation for ferocious fighting.

Costa, Afonso (1871–1937) Portuguese politician. Born in the clerical Beira Baixa province, as Minister of Justice under the First Republic he led a vigorous anticlerical campaign culminating in the separation of church and state in 1911. Between Jan 1913 and Feb 1914 Costa, a capable and energetic administrator, headed the most popular Portuguese Republican Party (PRP) government of the Republican era, being the only government to balance the budget. Costa's PRP was the vehicle of the urban lower middle classes, disenfranchising much of the working class by reducing the electorate by more than half to 400 000. The Costa government fell in 1914 partly through the internal divisions of the PRP and partly because it had alienated various interests, above all the army. Premier again (1916–17), Costa took Portugal into **World War I** on the side of the Allies out of fear for its colonies in the post-war settlement. But the economic impact of the war and bad military losses paved the way for a coup (Dec 1917). Disenchantment with the Republic led Costa to go into exile in Paris in 1919. ▷ **Republic, First** (Portugal)

Costa, Joaquín (1846–1911) Spanish reformer and historian. A prolific writer and campaigner, he was the most prominent member of the radical 'regenerationists'. This was a diffuse reform movement which emerged in late 19c Spain in reaction to the country's decline, a process which culminated in the loss of the final remnants of the Spanish empire in the 'Disaster of 1898'. A critic of the oligarchical **Restoration System**, Costa constantly publicized the need for a development policy, drawing up detailed education, irrigation and agricultural plans for the modernization of Spain, while drawing on certain collective traditions. He co-founded the National League of Producers (1899), the National Union (1900), and in 1903 was elected as a deputy for the Republican Union. In his exasperation with the Restoration System, he advocated a 'revolution from above', endorsing the use of an 'iron surgeon' to carry out the necessary reforms. He failed, however, to articulate a coherent political doctrine. A unique publicist and reformer, Costa left a legacy of radical populism and corporatism, and all later regenerationists were to be in his debt.

Costa, Manuel Pinto da (1937–) Sao Tome politician. In 1972 he founded the Movement for the Liberation of Sao Tome and Principe (MLSTP) in Gabon and in 1974, taking advantage of a military coup in Portugal, returned and persuaded the new government in Lisbon to recognize the MLSTP as the sole representative of the people and to grant independence a year later. He became president in 1975 and set his country on a politically non-aligned course.

Coty, René (1882–1962) French politician. A barrister, he was elected a Deputy in 1923, entered the Senate in 1935 and was Minister of Reconstruction in 1947. The last President of the French Fourth Republic (1953–9), after the constitutional crisis precipitated by

the generals in Algeria (May 1958), he assisted the return to power of General de **Gaulle** and the consequent birth of the Fifth Republic (Jan 1959), with de Gaulle as his successor. ▷ **Republic, Fifth** (France); **Republic, Fourth** (France)

Counter-Reformation A general movement of reform and missionary activity in the Roman Catholic Church starting in the mid-16c, stimulated in part by the Protestant Reformation. It included the revival of the monastic movement (eg Capuchins, 1528; Oratorians, 1575), especially the creation of the Jesuit Order. It provided for the enforcement of disciplinary measures by the Roman Inquisition; its doctrinal formulations were made by the Council of Trent; and liturgical and moral reforms were also introduced throughout the Church. There was a strong influence from mystics (eg John of the Cross, Teresa of Avila) and devotional teachers (eg Francis of Sales). In a secular sense, the term also refers to the success of Roman Catholic powers in Europe in the late 16c and early 17c.

Counter-Remonstrants The name given to a party of orthodox Calvinist activists in the Dutch Republic in the early 17c. They opposed the **Remonstrants** who had petitioned in 1610 for a more liberal Calvinist theology. The beliefs of the Counter-Remonstrants were enshrined in the canons of the Synod of **Dordrecht**; they were also known as Gomarists, after their leader, Francis Gomarus.

Coureurs du bois The French-Canadian term for fur-traders who 'went Indian'. Indians began to realize that their identity was threatened through contact with settlements and trading posts. They also grew to understand that they were in a strong position to play off the French against English fur-traders from Albany. French-Canadian fur-traders therefore made annual trips into the hinterland or *pays d'en haut* to deal directly with the Indians, and frequently decided not to return to the settlements.

Court, Pieter de la (1618–85) Dutch economist and publicist. Although trained as a lawyer, he worked as cloth manufacturer in Leiden before moving to Amsterdam in 1673. He published several important works, especially *Holland's Welfare* (1662), which were characterized by their support for political, religious, and especially economic liberty. He was a forerunner of Adam Smith, and was closely linked with the party of Johan de **Witt**, leader of the merchant interest in the Dutch Republic, whose policies he articulated.

Couthon, Georges (1756–94) French revolutionary. A lawyer at the outbreak of the **French Revolution**, he was elected to the National **Convention**, where he demonstrated his hatred of the priesthood and the monarchy. In July 1793 he became a member of the Committee of **Public Safety**. At Lyons he crushed the insurrection with merciless severity (1793), and helped to usher in the Reign of **Terror**. **Robespierre**'s fall brought down Couthon also; he was thrown into prison, freed by the mob with whom he was popular, recaptured by the soldiers of the Convention, and executed, with **Saint-Just** and Robespierre.

Covenanters Originally, signatories (and their successors) of the National Covenant (1638) and the **Solemn League and Covenant** (1643) in Scotland, who resisted the theory of 'Divine Right of Kings' and the imposition of an episcopal system on the Presbyterian Church of Scotland. When declared rebels, they resorted to open-air preaching. Until Presbyterianism was restored in 1690, they were savagely persecuted, with imprisonment, execution without trial, and banishment (eg to Holland or the USA).

cowboys Cattle herders in 19c USA who flourished on the trans-Mississippi plains during the 'open range' period of the cattle industry (c.1865–85). They were particularly important in the 'long drive' from Texas to the railheads in Missouri and Kansas. Cowboys included many Confederate veterans, as well as former slaves and Mexicans. Contrary to popular imagery, the cowboy's life was one of hard work and privation. In the popular mind the cowboy remains the embodiment of the American hero who stands for rugged self-sufficiency and frontier justice.

Cowpens, Battle of (1781) During the **American Revolution**, an engagement in South Carolina in which a small American army under Daniel Morgan (1736–1802) defeated a British force under Banastre Tarleton (1754–1833).

Cox, Percy (1864–1937) British diplomat. After receiving his military training, he served in India. During his time there, he left the army to work in the Indian political service in the Persian Gulf area; he was

subsequently made Foreign Secretary in India but his major work was in Iraq, where he moved in 1914. He attended the Cairo Conference of 1921 which resulted, on his returning to Iraq, in his supervision of the emergence by resolution of the Council of Ministers of the Amir Faysal, second son of Sharif **Husayn ibn** 'Ali of Mecca, as King of Iraq (as **Faysal I**), a resolution which was ratified by a referendum upon which Cox insisted. Given his military background, he was also tasked with supervising the creation of an army for the country, and with looking after its constitutional arrangements. His last act in Iraq was his signature on behalf of British of a Protocol to the 1922 Anglo-Iraqi Treaty which, amongst other things, reduced the effective period of the Treaty to four years, a provision which was welcomed by the King and a majority of the politicians.

CPP ▷ **Convention People's Party**

Craig, James, 1st Viscount Craigavon (1871–1940) Ulster politician. His early career was as a stockbroker. He was MP in the UK parliament (1906–21) where he vigorously campaigned to preserve the Act of Union against the Irish Nationalists. After Northern Ireland refused to join the South in 1921, he worked as its first Prime Minister (1921–40) to maintain order in the Province and then to develop social and educational services under powers devolved to **Stormont**. His Unionist beliefs ensured that the interests of the Protestant majority in Northern Ireland would be paramount. While still in office, he died suddenly. ▷ **Carson, Edward**

Craig, Sir James Henry (1748–1812) British soldier and colonial administrator. He fought in the **American Revolution**, being wounded at the Battle of Bunker Hill (1775) and serving with distinction in the invasion of the Hudson River Valley. After playing a prominent part in the capture of the Dutch colony of the Cape of Good Hope, he was made the colony's temporary governor from 1795 to 1797. After further commands in India, England and in the **Napoleonic Wars**, he became Governor-General of Canada (1807–11). There, with the backing of London and the English-speaking Montreal merchants, he sought to anglicize the province. To that end he dissolved the assembly, and cashiered many French officers from the militia. In 1810 the printers and proprietor of the critical newspaper, *Le Canadien*, were arrested for treason and, when war broke out with the USA, he introduced a special Act which enabled him to suppress the newspaper altogether. This provoked both riots and the election of an increased number of radical French-Canadian deputies. The British government drew back from its policy and Craig was recalled. His name is still hated in the province, and the period of his governorship is known as the 'Reign of Terror'.

Cranmer, Thomas (1489–1556) Archbishop of Canterbury. His suggestion that **Henry VIII** appeal for his divorce to the universities of Christendom won him the King's favour, and he was appointed a royal chaplain. He was made Archbishop of Canterbury in 1533, making allegiance to the Pope 'for form's sake'. He later annulled Henry's marriages to **Catherine of Aragon** (1533) and to Anne **Boleyn** (1536), and divorced him from **Anne of Cleves** (1540). He was largely responsible for the Book of Common Prayer (1549 and 1552). On Henry's death, Cranmer rushed Protestant changes through. He had little to do with affairs of state, but agreed to the plan to divert the succession from Mary to Lady Jane **Grey** (1553), for which he was later arraigned for treason. Sentenced to death, he retracted the seven recantations he had been forced to sign, before being burnt alive. ▷ **Reformation** (England)

Crassus, Marcus Licinius, **'Dives'** (c.115–53BC) Roman politician. As praetor he defeated **Spartacus** at the Battle of Lucania (71BC), and in 70BC was made consul with **Pompey the Great**. One of the richest Roman citizens (hence his byname 'Dives', 'wealthy'), he became a friend of **Caesar**, and formed the first triumvirate with him and Pompey (60BC). In 53BC, as Governor of Syria, he attacked the Parthians, but was routed and killed at the Battle of Carrhae.

Craxi, Bettino (1934–) Italian politician. After being active in the Socialist Youth Movement, he became a member of the Central Committee of the Italian Socialist Party (PSI) in 1957, a member of the National Executive (1965) and a Deputy Secretary (1970–6). In 1976 he became General-Secretary, and after the July 1983 election he became Italy's first socialist Prime Minister, successfully leading a broad-based coalition until 1987.

Crazy Horse (Ta-Sunko-Witko) (c.1849–77) Oglala **Sioux** Chief, regarded as the foremost Sioux military leader. He defeated

General **Custer** at the Battle of **Little Bighorn** (1876), leading a combined force of Sioux and **Cheyenne**. He and his followers surrendered the following year, and he died in custody at Fort Robinson, Nebraska, stabbed in the back, according to a well-known Native American pictograph.

Crécy, Battle of (1346) A battle between France and England in the **Hundred Years War**. Using tactics perfected against the Scots, **Edward III** routed a larger French Army, mainly cavalry, near Abbeville (Somme). It was a classic demonstration of the superiority over mounted knights of a coordinated force of dismounted men-at-arms, and archers providing offensive firepower.

Créditistes French-Canadian partner of the **Social Credit Party**. After a revival in their fortunes the party gained 26 seats in the 1962 federal elections but declined to 24 seats in 1963 when the Quebec representatives set up their own organization. Since then the party's popularity declined with the size of the rural population and by 1980 it was eliminated.

Creek Native North Americans originally organized in a confederacy living in Georgia and Alabama. Members of the Muskhogean linguistic group, they were an agricultural people with a highly developed social system. During the colonial period they gave assistance to both the French and the British. They rose up in the Creek War of 1813–14 to stop white invasion of their territory, but were defeated and forced to cede much of their land. In the 1830s they were part of the 'removal' of the **Five Civilized Tribes** to Oklahoma, where most of the remaining Creeks continue to live today.

Crerar, Thomas Alexander (1876–1975) Canadian politician. Founder of the **Progressive Party** when he bolted from the Liberals in protest against their high tariff budget of 1920, he led the party to second place in the 1921 elections with 65 seats. Preferring to hold the balance of power, he left official opposition to the Conservatives. Within a year he resigned as leader, at least in part because he insisted on conventional principles of party organization and representation in conflict with those of his Alberta and Ontario membership. He re-entered politics, becoming Minister of Railways and Canals in Mackenzie **King**'s administration in 1929. Although he lost his seat in 1930, he won again with the Liberals in 1933, and served in the government as Minister of Mines and Resources. In 1945 he became a Senator and resigned in 1966.

Crespy, Peace of (1544) An agreement between **Francis I** of France and Emperor **Charles V**, under the terms of which France agreed to help Charles in his struggle against the Protestants, and Charles agreed to give up territory in either northern Italy or the Netherlands. By the next year, circumstances had changed, and Charles saw no reason to maintain his offer of territory.

Crete An island in the south Aegean, in antiquity the centre of the **Minoan Civilization** (3400–1100BC). Part of Byzantium (5–9c), then occupied by the **Saracens** (c.823–961), it was purchased by the Venetian Republic in 1210. Having enjoyed an artistic renaissance, after falling to the Ottomans (1669) it went into a long decline. During the **Greek War of Independence**, the Cretans joined the insurgents but were quickly crushed and made subject to the Egyptian Viceroy, **Ali Pasha**. Once again under Ottoman control from 1840, Cretan demands for **enosis** grew apace with revolts (1858, 1866–9 and 1895), but these were handled cautiously by the Greek government lest it antagonize the Porte. After a brief military campaign, Crete was declared independent under a High Commissioner appointed by the Great Powers (1898). The Cretan assembly declared its enosis in 1908, but not until the Treaties of **London** (1913) was it joined to the Kingdom of Greece. It was a stronghold of support for its native son, Eleuthérios **Venizélos**, and rebelled against **Metaxas** (1938). During **World War II**, it was occupied by the Germans (May 1941) and several thousand Allied troops were forced to evacuate.

Crimean War (1854–6) A war fought in the Crimean Peninsula by Britain and France against Russia. Its origins lay in Russian successes in the Black Sea area and the British and French desire to prevent further expansion into the **Ottoman Empire** by the Russians, since this would threaten the Mediterranean and overland routes to India. Major battles were fought in 1854 at the River Alma (20 Sep), **Balaclava** (25 Oct), and Inkerman (5 Nov). The war was notable both for the nursing exploits of Florence Nightingale at Scutari and the pioneer war reports of W H Russell in *The Times*. The fall of the Russian fortress at **Sevastopol** (Sep 1855) led to peace negotiations. Under the treaty finally agreed at Paris (Mar 1856),

Russia returned southern Bessarabia to neighbouring Moldavia and had to accept the neutralization of the Black Sea; Moldavia and Wallachia were soon to unite as an independent Romania. Shattered by its defeat in the war, Russia turned to overdue internal reform.

Cripps, (Richard) Stafford (1889–1952) British politician. He made a fortune in patent and compensation cases. In 1930 he was appointed Solicitor-General in the second Labour government, and became an MP in 1931. During the 1930s he was associated with several extreme left-wing movements, and was expelled from the **Labour Party** in 1939 for his 'popular front' opposing Neville **Chamberlain**'s policy of **appeasement**. He sat as an independent MP during **World War II**, was Ambassador to the USSR (1940–2), and in 1942 became Lord Privy Seal, and later Minister of Aircraft Production. In the 1945 Labour government, he was readmitted to the party and appointed President of the Board of Trade (1942–5). In 1947 he became Minister of Economic Affairs and then was Chancellor of the Exchequer, introducing a successful austerity policy. He resigned due to illness in 1950.

Crispi, Francesco (1819–1901) Italian politician. A member of the provisional government established in Palermo after the insurrection of Jan 1848, he was exiled from the Kingdom of the **Two Sicilies** in 1849 and settled in Turin; in 1853 he was expelled from Piedmont for supporting a Mazzinian conspiracy in Milan. He helped to organize the Expedition of the **Thousand** to his native Sicily in 1860 and, as a member of the interim government established there by **Garibaldi**, sought to prevent its annexation by Piedmont. After unification, he initially led the extreme left in the Italian parliament but by 1865 had been converted to monarchism. In the 1870s he achieved fame by campaigning against parliamentary corruption and in 1877–8 served as Interior Minister under **Depretis**. He was Prime Minister twice (1887–91 and 1893–6), leaving politics between these two terms of office because of allegations of bigamy. As Prime Minister, his foreign policy was characterized by a loathing for the French and by a strengthening of ties with Germany and Austria. This forced him to neglect **irredentism** and to concentrate on colonial expansion, culminating in the disaster of the Battle of **Adowa** (1896), which brought his second government to an ignominious end. On the domestic front, his period of office was notable for violent anti-clericalism (a response in large part to Leo XIII's refusal to recognize the annexation of Rome) and the energetic and brutal suppression of peasant and worker unrest.

Cristero Revolt (1927–9) Rural guerrilla warfare against the Mexican government. Confined to the states of Guadalajara, Morelos, Colima, Jalisco, and Michoacán, the rebels fought under the banner 'Viva Christo Rey!'. Unlike their predecessors, they did not merely seek to restore the traditional pre-eminence of the Church in Mexico, but also to carry through social reforms; they thus presented a fundamental challenge to the revolutionary governments led by **Calles** and Obregón. By the end of 1927, Church and State were at stalemate: the Church suspended public worship and the State persecuted the clergy. In June 1929 the Vatican and the US Ambassador Dwight Morrow achieved a compromise by which Church property was returned to the clergy and religious instruction was permitted in the Churches.

Critchlow, Hubert (1884–1958) Guyanese trade unionist. In 1906, as an employee of Booker Brothers, he led an unofficial dockers' strike and became the mouthpiece of Guyanese labour. In Jan 1917 another 13-day strike resulted in a nine-hour day and increased wages for waterfront workers, and two years later Critchlow founded the British Guiana Labour Union, the first registered trade union in the British West Indies (1921) when unions were legalized. Although Critchlow and the BGLU lost some of their dynamism in the 1930s (when the sugar workers Manpower Citizens' Association became the dominant force in Guyanese labour), as 'father' of Guyanese unionism, he was honoured with the Secretaryship of the British Guiana Trades Union Congress in 1941.

Critias (Kritias) (c.460–403 BC) Athenian orator and politician. A pupil of Socrates, he was implicated with **Alcibiades** in the mutilation of the Hermae on the eve of the Sicilian expedition (415 BC), but nonetheless escaped punishment. In 411 BC he took part in the oligarchical revolution that set up the government of Four Hundred. Exiled from 406 BC to 404 BC, as a strong supporter of **Sparta**, he became one of the **Thirty Tyrants** set up by the Spartans after their defeat of Athens at the end of the **Peloponnesian War** (431–404 BC). In the same year he fell at

Munychia, resisting Thrasybulus and the exiles. He had a high reputation as an orator, and wrote poetry and tragedies.

Croatia, Independent State of (1941–5) During **World War II**, after the disintegration of Yugoslavia, part of Croatia and Bosnia Herzegovina formed the Independent State of Croatia, a satellite state of the Axis powers. Benito **Mussolini** chose Prince Aimone of Saxony, the Duke of Spoleto, to be King, but the Prince never took over his kingdom. The state was, instead, subject to the brutal regime of Ante Pavelić, the leader of the **Ustaša** fascist movement. In 1945 Croatia became one of the constituent republics of the Socialist Federal Republic of Yugoslavia. The Croatian President Franjo **Tudjman** declared Croatia's independence from the Yugoslav federation in 1991.

Croatia, Kingdom of An independent kingdom of Croatia existed from 910 until 1102, when the Croatian crown was inherited by the Hungarian Árpád Dynasty. The Croatian and Hungarian crowns continued to be joined under the **Habsburg Dynasty** from 1526 until 1918 when, with the end of the Habsburg monarchy, the Croatian royal title became truly obsolete and Croatia became part of the Kingdom of Serbs, Croats and Slovenes (later Yugoslavia).

Croats Slav settlers in the Balkans, the Croats migrated (6–7c) from White Croatia in the Ukraine to the old Roman provinces of Pannonia and **Dalmatia**. The Croats established their own kingdom and were ruled by Croatian kings until 1102, when the Croatian crown passed to the Árpád house of Hungary. In the 15–16c the Croats became divided between three empires: the Croats in Dalmatia were subject to Venice; those in Croatia and Slavonia to the Habsburgs; and those in Bosnia and Herzegovina to the Ottomans. Following the fall of the Venetian Republic (1797) and the disbandment of the **Illyrian Provinces** (1809–13), the Dalmatian Croats were subject to direct rule from Vienna. The **Ausgleich** (1867) divided the Croats of the Habsburg Empire between the governments at Budapest and Vienna, while those in Bosnia-Herzegovina, having revolted against Ottoman rule, found themselves within an Austrian protectorate (1879). Not until 1918 and the creation of the Kingdom of Serbs, Croats and Slovenes (later Yugoslavia) were the Croats all subject to one government. The Croatian national revival began in the 1830s under the leadership of

Ljudevit **Gaj**. ▷ **Dubrovnik; Nagodba; South Slavs; trialism; Ustaša; Yugoslav Committee; Yugoslavism; Yugoslavs**

Croce, Benedetto (1866–1952) Italian philosopher, historian, literary critic and politician. Although best remembered as a scholar, Croce had an active political life. Under the last **Giolitti** ministry he was Education Minister (1920–1) while, as a Senator following the fascist seizure of power, he profited from the virtual immunity afforded by his enormous reputation to criticize the fascist regime constantly. In 1943 he played a prominent part in organizing the anti-fascists, and was a minister in both the **Badoglio** and **Bonomi** governments of 1944. He became President of the Italian Liberal Party in 1947 and a member of the Constituent Assembly; he became a Senator again in 1948.

Crockett, Davy (David) (1786–1836) US frontiersman. He distinguished himself against the **Creek** in Jackson's campaign of 1814, and was elected to the US House of Representatives from Tennessee (1827–31 and 1833–5). He died fighting for Texas at the Battle of the **Alamo**. Highly embellished stories of his exploits have assumed mythological proportions.

Croesus (c.560/546BC) Last King of Lydia. After succeeding his father, Alyattes, he made the Greeks of Asia Minor his tributaries, and extended his kingdom eastward from the Aegean to the Halys. His conquests and mines made his wealth proverbial. **Cyrus II** defeated and imprisoned him (546 BC), but his death is a mystery. ▷ **Lydia**

Croix de Feu, Ligue des A French political movement (1927–36), which was originally an organization of veteran soldiers of **World War I**, under the leadership of Colonel de **La Rocque**. It developed into a mass movement with a membership of about 250 000, campaigning for political change in a fashion which suggested that it could be a French version of **fascism**. That this was not really the case was shown when, uniformed **leagues** having been prohibited in 1936, it transformed itself into a legal political party, the PSF (*Parti social français*, 'French Social Party').

Cromer, Evelyn Baring, Earl (1841–1917) British colonial administrator. He was private secretary to his cousin, Lord **Northbrook**, when Viceroy of India (1872–6),

British Controller-General of Egyptian Finance (1879–80), Finance Minister of India (1880-83), and Agent and Consul-General in Egypt (1883–1907). Effectively the ruler of Egypt, he reformed its administration and agricultural policies, and put its finances on a good footing.

Cromwell, Oliver (1599–1658) English soldier and statesman. A convinced Puritan, after studying law in London, he sat in both the **Short Parliament** and the **Long Parliament** (1640), and when war broke out (1642) fought on the parliamentary side at Edgehill (1642). He formed his unconquerable Ironsides, combining rigid discipline with strict morality, and it was his cavalry that secured the victory at the Battle of **Marston Moor** (1644), while under **Fairfax** he led the **New Model Army** to decisive success at **Naseby** (1645). He quelled insurrection in Wales in support of **Charles I**, and defeated the invading army of Hamilton. He then brought the King to trial, and was one of the signatories of his death warrant (1649). Having established the **Commonwealth**, Cromwell suppressed the **Levellers**, the Irish (1649–50), and the Scots (under **Charles II**) at **Dunbar** (1650) and Worcester (1651). Using the power of the army, he dissolved the Rump of the Long Parliament (1653), and after the failure of a nominated **Barebone's Parliament**, then established a **Protectorate** (1653). As Protector (1653–8), he refused the offer of the crown (1657). At home he extended religious toleration, and gave Scotland and Ireland parliamentary representation. Under him the Commonwealth became the head and champion of Protestant Europe. ▷ **English Civil Wars**

Cromwell, Thomas, Earl of Essex (c.1485–1540) English statesman, known as *malleus monachorum* ('the Hammer of the Monks'). He served as a soldier on the Continent (1504–12), then entered **Wolsey**'s service in 1514, and became his agent and secretary. He arranged **Henry VIII**'s divorce with **Catherine of Aragon**, and put into effect the Act of Supremacy (1534) and the dissolution of the monasteries (1536–9). He became Privy Councillor (1531), Chancellor of the Exchequer (1533), Secretary of State and Master of the Rolls (1534), Vicar-General (1535), Lord Privy Seal and Baron Cromwell of Oakham (1536), Knight of the Garter and Dean of Wells (1537), Lord Great Chamberlain (1539), and finally Earl of Essex (1540). In each of his offices, he proved himself a highly efficient administrator and adviser to the King; but Henry's aversion to **Anne of Cleves**, consort of Cromwell's choosing, led to his ruin. He was accused of treason, sent to the Tower and beheaded. ▷ **Reformation** (England)

Cronje, Piet (1835–1911) Boer general. Born at Colesberg, South Africa, he was a leader in the **Boer Wars** (1881 and 1899–1900), defeated Methuen at Magersfontein, but surrendered to Lord Roberts at **Paardeberg** (1900). He died at Potchefstroom, Transvaal.

Crosland, Tony (Charles Anthony Raven) (1918–77) British politician. He taught in Oxford after serving in **World War II**. Elected as a Labour MP in 1950, he became Secretary for Education and Science (1965–7), President of the Board of Trade (1967–9), Secretary for Local Government and Regional Planning (1969–70), Environment Secretary (1974–6), and Foreign Secretary (1976–7). A strong supporter of Hugh **Gaitskell**, he was a key member of the revisionist wing of the **Labour Party** aiming to modernize socialist ideology, and wrote one of its seminal texts, *The Future of Socialism* (1956). ▷ **socialism**

Crossman, Richard (Howard Stafford) (1907–74) British politician. He became a philosophy tutor at Oxford, and leader of the Labour group on Oxford City Council (1934–40). In 1938 he joined the staff of the *New Statesman*. In 1945 he became a Labour MP, and under **Wilson** was Minister of Housing and Local Government (1964–6), then Secretary of State for Social Services and head of the Department of Health (1968–70). He was editor of the *New Statesman* (1970–2). His best-known work is his series of political diaries, begun in 1952, keeping a detailed, and frequently indiscreet, record of the day-to-day workings of government and political life. They were published in four volumes (1975–81), despite attempts to suppress them. ▷ **Labour Party** (UK)

Crown Colony Government British imperial system of trusteeship government in which full executive power was vested in the Governor. Introduced into Trinidad and St Lucia in 1797 and 1803 respectively, 'the direct protection of the Crown of the unrepresented classes, which takes the place of representation' was meant to be a panacea to cure the evils of the **Assemblies**. The elective principle was absent from the constitution,

the Governor's Executive Council being composed of his chief officials and the Legislative Council which, while it had nominated unofficial members, possessed an unofficial majority. The system was in place in most of the British West Indies by 1898 and, although reformist and impartial, it excluded the rising coloured middle-class from the decision-making process and was viewed as imposed, alien and paternalistic.

Crusade, First (1095–9) Proclaimed by Pope **Urban II** in 1095, this crusade was ostensibly in response to a request by the Byzantine Emperor **Alexius I Comnenus** for assistance against the Seljuk Turks whose encroachments in Anatolia had become ever more threatening since the catastrophic defeat some years previously of the Byzantine forces at **Manzikert** in 1071. Urban's preaching, insisting as it did on the liberation of Jerusalem from Muslim control, aroused such fervour that an ill-fated 'People's Crusade' under Peter the Hermit and Walter Sansavoir set out prior to the main body of the Crusade. This disorganized and motley crew were ferried across the Bosporus, having created much mayhem on their passage through Europe; once in Anatolia, they were wiped out by the Seljuks of Rum. The Crusade proper, however, inflicted a major defeat on the Turks at Dorylaeum (July 1097) and went on to establish a foothold in northern Syria at Antioch (1098). The capture of Jerusalem, accompanied by looting and massacre, was accomplished in 1099, crusading counties having been established in Edessa, Antioch and Tripoli. **Godfrey of Bouillon**, one of the leaders of the Crusade, became ruler of the new Latin Kingdom of Jerusalem and the crusade itself was distinguished from its successors by the presence of Adhemar of Le Puy as Papal Legate. The successful prosecution of the First Crusade was aided not a little by the disarray into which the petty Turkish princedoms of the Levant had fallen at this time. See map p245.

Crusade, Second (1147–9) Proclaimed by Pope **Eugenius III**, this crusade was led by **Louis VII** of France and **Conrad III** of Germany, and was launched in response to the capture (1144) of Edessa and the consequent discomfiture of the Franks at the hands of the Turkish Atabeg, 'Imad al-Din Zangi. After disastrous campaigns in Anatolia and in Syria, Damascus was unsuccessfully besieged. This achieved nothing apart from damage to the Crusaders' name as a power to be reckoned with in Palestine and Syria and

The First, Second and Third Crusades (11–12c)

was a great disappointment to St Bernard who had expended much effort in its promotion. See map p245. ▷ **Zangid Dynasty**

Crusade, Third (1189–92) This was proclaimed by Pope Gregory VIII following the defeat by **Saladin** of the field army of the Latin Kingdom of Jerusalem at the Battle of **Hittin** (July 1187), and his subsequent capture of the Holy City itself (Oct 1187). Led by the three great rulers of Western Christendom, **Frederick I, 'Barbarossa'**, **Philip II** of France and **Richard I, 'the Lionheart'**, the Crusade promised much. It did not, in the event, live up to this promise. Barbarossa perished by drowning in the River Cydnus in Anatolia before even arriving in the Holy Land, with the consequent disintegration of the German effort; the leisurely outward progress of Philip and Richard, the pillaging and capture of Cyprus from their thoroughly disillusioned Byzantine co-religionists, and the scarcely-veiled hostility between the French and English (which led to Philip's early return to France and Richard's subsequent preoccupation with affairs at home and his own departure (1192)) meant that the Crusade failed in its objective of regaining Jerusalem. It did, however, bring **Guy of Lusignan**'s siege of Acre to a successful close in 1191 and gained, if not an overwhelming, at least morale-lifting victory over Saladin's forces at Arsuf in the same year. Richard managed to achieve a compromise settlement whereby pilgrimage to the Holy Places was safeguarded and the Crusaders maintained their position on the Levantine littoral with the Muslims (in this case the **Ayyubid Dynasty**) controlling the hinterland. See map p245.

Crusade, Fourth (1202–4) Proclaimed by **Innocent IV**, with the aim of recovering the Holy Places in Palestine, the Crusade faced financial difficulties over the provision of ships and finished up by being beholden to the Venetians, who diverted it to their own ends. First of all, Zara (the modern Zadar) in Dalmatia was taken then, under Venetian pressure, attention was redirected to Constantinople. The latter was sacked and pillaged under the pretext of restoring Isaac II Angelus and his son, Alexius, to their positions of power in Byzantium. The aging Doge, Enrico Dandolo, played a leading part in the operation and in the subsequent establishment of a Latin Empire (which lasted until 1261) and particularly in the election of Baldwin of Flanders to be the first Latin Emperor of Constantinople as **Baldwin**

I. The **Byzantine Empire**, although surviving for a further 200 years or so, was unable fully to recover from the blow. In consequence, such credibility as the Crusading enterprise had in the eyes of the Eastern Christians (which was precious little if we are to take the reactions of **Anna Comnena** as at all typical) evaporated. The original objectives of Innocent IV were not addressed at all.

Crusades, Later These were mostly directed towards Egypt and North Africa, it having been supposed that the route to the control of Palestine was through the defeat of the Ayyubids (and subsequently the **Mamluks**) in Egypt. Failure in the Nile Delta by the Fifth and Seventh Crusades, despite initial success in the capture of Damietta by the former in 1219 and by the latter in 1249, prevented these crusades having a significant impact on the Holy Land. The Eighth Crusade (1270–2) had a limited success in the negotiation of a truce with the Mamluks by the future King **Edward I** of England and the treaty between **Charles of Anjou**, King of Naples and Sicily, with Tunis (although this last does seem to relate more to the interest of his twin realms than to any intention of assisting the Latins in Palestine). Of these later crusades only the so-called Sixth Crusade of the Emperor **Frederick II** (*Stupor Mundi*) made any considerable impact on the Holy Land itself. Frederick's negotiation of the peaceful cession to his rule of Jerusalem by the Ayyubid al-Kamil, while still under excommunication by Gregory IX because of his delays in setting out on the Crusade (which meant that, in the eyes of the papacy, his gaining control of Jerusalem 'did not count'), serves to underline how futile much of the Crusading effort had been and was still to be. As a result of Frederick's negotiations, Jerusalem was again in the hands of the Latins from 1229 (when Frederick was crowned King of Jerusalem) until 1244, when the Latin forces were defeated by a joint Egyptian and Khwarizmian army. The Latins were finally driven from the Holy Land by Al-Ashraf Khalil, son of the Mamluk Sultan, Qalawun (1291). ▷ **Ayyubid Dynasty**

CSU (*Christlich-Soziale Union*, 'Christian Social Union') Bavarian political party. As the successor to the pre-1933 Bavarian People's Party, the CSU functions as the Christian Democratic Party of Bavaria (within which the **CDU** does not organize). Founded in Jan 1946 it dominates Bavarian state politics by virtue of its absolute majority in the **Landtag** obtained in 1962 and operates in coalition with the CDU in the **Bundestag**. Somewhat to the right of the CDU, it is a staunch exponent both of Bavarian particularist, and all-German interests (with a European democratic federation as a long-term aim). Its membership is socially diverse, but is dominated by independent and salaried members of the middle classes. While leader of the CSU, the late Franz-Josef **Strauss** was a prominent advocate of right-wing Christian Democracy within Bavaria and Germany as a whole.

cuartelazo A Spanish pejorative term meaning 'barrack room coup': one which puts first the interests of the military, narrowly defined as the motivation for the coup. Such coups have often occurred when the incumbent government was judged to have accorded a high priority to health and education, rather than military expenditure. Rulers in the 20c who owed their pre-eminence to *cuartelazos* include Chaves (Paraguay), Onganía and Videla (Argentina), Torrijos and Robles (Panama), Tinoco (Costa Rica) and Perez Jimenez (Venezuela).

Cuauhtémoc (c.1495–1525) Last Aztec ruler. He was the successor to **Montezuma**, who resisted the Spaniards under **Cortés** at the siege of Tenochtitlán (now Mexico City) in 1521. He was later executed while on an expedition with Cortés to Honduras. ▷ **Aztecs**

Cuban Missile Crisis (Oct 1962) A period of acute international tension and potential military confrontation between the USA and USSR, following the USA's discovery of Soviet nuclear missile sites in Cuba. President John F **Kennedy** demanded the dismantling of the base and the return of the missiles, and threw a naval blockade around the island. The crisis ended on 28 Oct, when Soviet leader **Khrushchev** agreed to Kennedy's demands, in return for the withdrawal of US missiles from Turkey.

Cuban Revolution (1895–8) Sometimes known as the War of Independence, the nationalist revolt against Spanish imperialism started in Apr 1895 when a force landed by **Marti** and Gomez in Oriente province joined that of Maceo near Santiago. A provisional government was proclaimed and, although Marti was killed soon afterwards, Gomez and Maceo triumphed everywhere until 'Butcher' Weyler, the Spanish Commander-in-Chief, resorted to a policy of terror. Weyler's atrocities, however, provoked popular sym-

pathy for the rebel cause in the USA and when the USS *Maine* blew up in Havana harbour (Feb 1898), the Americans blamed the Spanish authorities and instituted a military intervention, the **Spanish–American War** (1898).

Culdees Originally, monks in the Irish church in the 8c and the Scottish Church in the 9c, who later became secular clergy. In Scotland, they were respected for their high ideals and spirituality, and survived in St Andrews until the 14c.

Culloden, Battle of (16 Apr 1746) A battle fought near Inverness, the last major battle on British soil, which marked the end of the Jacobite **Forty-Five Rebellion** led by Charles Edward **Stuart**. His force, mainly of Scottish Highlanders, was crushed by a superior force of English and lowland Scots under the Duke of **Cumberland**. ▷ **Jacobites**

Cultivation System An economic system introduced into Java in 1830 by Governor-General Johannes van den Bosch. Using the traditional structures of deference and obligation within Javanese society, the Cultivation System coerced the rural population of Java into a remarkable expansion of the cultivation of tropical crops for export, notably sugar, coffee and indigo. The Dutch colonial state and many Dutch officials made huge profits from the system. Its impact on the Javanese themselves has long been a matter of great controversy, between those who have argued that the system brought impoverishment and economic stagnation and those who have argued that, for many Javanese, it secured an important advance in their material condition. Under fierce attack from liberal elements in Holland from the mid-19c, the Cultivation System began to be dismantled in the 1870s, although it did not finally disappear until 1918–19.

Cult of Personality (1956) The formula used to condemn Joseph **Stalin** and his dictatorship at the Twentieth Congress of the Communist Party of the USSR. It took some time after Stalin's death in 1953 for Nikita **Khrushchev** to establish himself and to build a suable case against him. Many of Stalin's crimes were made known, but they were attributed to his being led astray, and not to the system that allowed him to act dictatorially. Khrushchev and his successors could, therefore, still be communists and run their country autocratically, so long as they steered clear of Stalin's excesses.

Cultural Revolution (1966–76) An abbreviation for the Great Proletarian Cultural Revolution, a radical Maoist mass movement in China initiated as a rectification campaign in 1966, which ended only with the death of **Mao Zedong** and the arrest of the **Gang of Four** in the autumn of 1976. To prevent the Chinese revolution from stagnating and to avoid 'revisionism', Mao aimed at replacing the old guard, including Liu Shaoqi (died in prison in 1969), Peng Zhen, and **Deng Xiaoping** (both disgraced in 1966), with a new generation of fervent revolutionaries. He appealed directly to the masses, in particular to young students, the **Red Guards**, who with the support of the **People's Liberation Army** overthrew not only party leaders but all so-called 'bourgeois reactionaries' and 'capitalist-roaders' in authority in schools, universities, factories, and the administration. The 10 years of social and political turmoil saw the closure of schools and universities, factories at a standstill, and millions of people sent to undertake manual labour in the countryside as re-education. ▷ **Maoism**

Culture System A system of taxation in the Dutch East Indies, in general use 1830–70. Governor-General J van den **Bosch** first conceived the idea of making the colony more lucrative by imposing a tax in kind of about 20 per cent on the land and labour of the natives. These resources were used to cultivate crops such as coffee, tea, indigo, and tobacco, which then became the property of the colonial regime. The profits of the system were transferred annually to the Dutch treasury, and were of considerable help to the home economy. After 1865, under pressure from economic and humanitarian liberalism, the system was gradually dismantled; it was much admired by other colonial powers, like Britain and Belgium.

Cumberland, William Augustus, Duke of (1721–65) British general. The second son of King **George II**, he adopted a military career, and in the War of the **Austrian Succession** (1740–8) was wounded at Dettingen (1743) and defeated at Fontenoy (1745). He crushed Charles Edward **Stuart**'s rebellion at the Battle of **Culloden** (1746), and by his harsh policies against the Highland clans thereafter earned the lasting title of 'Butcher'. In the **Seven Years War**, he surrendered to the French (1757), and thereafter retired.

Cunaxa, Battle of (401BC) The occasion of the defeat of **Cyrus the Younger** at the hands of his brother **Artaxerxes II**, north of Babylon. ▷ **Achaemenids**

Cuno, Wilhelm (1876–1933) German politician. After an early career in the senior civil service and commerce (from 1918 Director-General of the Hamburg–America Shipping Line, Hapag), Cuno served as an economic adviser to the German government at the Treaty of **Versailles** negotiations and at the subsequent **reparations** talks. In Nov 1922 he became Chancellor of Germany, despite belonging to no party, at the head of a pro-business government. His foreign and economic policies collapsed as a result of the crisis precipitated by the French occupation of the Ruhr in 1923, leading to his resignation on 12 Aug, after which he returned to the business world.

Curtin, John (Joseph) (1885–1945) Australian politician. He was active in trade-union work, and edited a Perth newspaper. In 1928 he entered parliament, and became leader of the **Australian Labor Party** in 1935. As Prime Minister (1941–5), he appealed for support from the US and organized national mobilization during the war against Japan. He died in office.

Curzon (of Kedleston), George Nathaniel, Marquis (1859–1925) British politician. He became an MP in 1886, and then travelled widely in the East. He became Under-Secretary for India (1891–2), and for Foreign Affairs (1895), and in 1898 was made Viceroy of India and given an Irish barony. He introduced many social and political changes, establishing in the interests of imperial security a new North-West Frontier province (1901) under a Chief Commissioner responsible to the government of India alone. He also partitioned Bengal (1905). He resigned after a disagreement with Lord **Kitchener** (1905), returning to politics in 1915 as Lord Privy Seal. He became Foreign Secretary (1919–24), and was created a marquis in 1921. ▷ **Curzon Line**

Curzon Line A line of territorial demarcation between Russia and Poland proposed in 1920 by the British Foreign Secretary, Lord Curzon. Poland rejected the proposal, subsequently gaining larger territories. In Sep 1939 a boundary similar to the Curzon Line became the border between German- and Soviet-occupied Poland, and in 1945 was recognized as the frontier between Poland and the USSR. ▷ **Yalta Conference**

Cush ▷ **Kush**

Custer, George Armstrong (1839–76) US army officer. He graduated from the US Military Academy at West Point (1861), and after a brilliant career as a cavalry commander in the **American Civil War** served in the campaigns against the tribes of the Great Plains. His actions were controversial, but his gift for self-publicity made him a symbol of the cavalry. He and over 200 of his men were killed at the Battle of **Little Bighorn**, Montana (25 June 1876), by a combined force of Sioux and Cheyenne. ▷ **Indian Wars**

Custozza (Custoza), Battles of (25 July 1848 and 24 June 1866) Two of the most important battles of the **Risorgimento**. In the former, the Piedmontese Army of **Charles Albert** was routed by the Austrian army of **Radetzky**. The second battle was part of the Italian campaign to seize Venetia. Once again, it resulted in Austrian victory, Archduke Albrecht defeating the Italian Army commanded by **La Marmora** and **Victor Emmanuel II**. ▷ **Lissa, Battle of; Salasco Armistice**

Cuza, Alexander Ioan (1820–73) Hospodar (governor) of Moldavia and Wallachia. Born into a boyar family, he studied in Paris and Bologna. In 1848 he led the meeting of liberal landowners at Jassy, where he put forward a programme of limited social and political reform and in 1857 he emerged as a leading member of the Moldavian *divan ad hoc*. His election as hospodar by Moldavia (Jan 1859) and Wallachia (Feb 1859) effected the unification of the two **Danubian Principalities**. As hospodar, he worked for the administrative union of the two provinces, a goal which was achieved in 1862. With **Kogălniceanu** as Prime Minister, he introduced a programme of social and economic change, issuing a civil code based on the Code Napoléon, sequestering the lands of the Dedicated Monasteries, giving land to peasants, abolishing payments and dues to landowners and encouraging foreign investment. He roused opposition from the conservatives led by Ion **Brătianu** and the liberals led by C A **Rosetti**, and in 1866 was forced by a group of army officers to abdicate. ▷ **Romanians**

Cvetković, Dragiša (1893–1969) Serbian politician. After studying law at Subotica, he entered politics as a member of the Serbian Radical Party and held a series of minor government posts until 1939 when he succeeded **Stojadinović** as Prime Minister. Supported by Prince Paul Karageorgević, he negotiated the **Sporazum** with Vladko **Maček** which led to a measure of cooperation between the **Croats** and the Yugoslav government. In Mar 1941 he and Cincar-Marković signed an agreement with the Axis powers in which they pledged Yugoslavia's neutrality. A few days later, his government was overthrown in a coup led by General Dušan Simović. He went abroad in 1943, and eventually settled in France.

Cymbeline (d.c.43) Pro-Roman King of the Catuvellauni. From his capital at Camulodunum (Colchester), he ruled most of southeast Britain. Shakespeare's character was based on Holinshed's half-historical Cunobelinus. ▷ **Britain, Roman; Caractacus; Cassivellaunus**

Cyprus, Kingdom of The conquest of Cyprus by **Richard I, 'the Lionheart'**, on his way to Palestine in prosecution of the Third Crusade, marked the end of Byzantine control of the island (at that time, it was under the nominal suzerainty of Isaac Comnenus). Richard established **Guy of Lusignan** as King of Cyprus in compensation for his loss of the Kingdom of Jerusalem (his right having lapsed with the death of his queen in 1190). This marked the beginning of a long period in which aspiring Crusaders could look on Cyprus as a relatively safe haven. St Louis's Crusaders, for instance, wintered in Cyprus in 1248–9 and as late as 1365 Peter I of Lusignan, titular King of Jerusalem, was King of Cyprus. However, the presence of a Christian state in Cyprus did nothing to reassure Muslim shipowners and the piracy out of the island remained a constant threat to Muslim seaborne trade in the eastern Mediterranean. The Circassian Mamluk Sultan al-Ashraf Barsbay recognized the problem and in 1426 reduced Cyprus, capturing the King and establishing Mamluk influence in the island. A Christian vassal king was then established in the island, with tribute paid to the Mamluk sultanate. The island was then for a time effectively a Venetian protectorate because of marriage alliances, although it still paid tribute to the Mamluk Sultan. The last vestige of Frankish influence in the eastern Mediterranean, Cyprus fell to the Ottoman Sultan, **Selim II**, in 1571. ▷ **Crusade, Third; Mamluks**

Cyrankiewicz, Jozef (1911–89) Polish politician. He became Secretary of the Socialist Party in Kraków in 1935. Taken prisoner by the Germans (1939), he escaped and organized resistance, but was sent to

Auschwitz in 1941. In 1945 he became Secretary-General of the Socialist Party, and after two periods as Premier (1947–52 and 1954–70) became Chairman of the Council of State (1970–2) and of the All-Poland Peace Committee (1973).

Cyrus II, 'the Great' (d.529BC) Founder of the Achaemenid Persian Empire. The son of Cambyses I, he defeated the Medes (549BC), became King of Persia (548BC), and took Lydia (c.546BC) and Babylon (539BC). His empire eventually ran from the Mediterranean to the Hindu Kush. He had a policy of religious conciliation: the nations who had been carried into captivity in Babylon along with the Jews were restored to their native countries, and allowed to take their gods with them. ▷ **Achaemenids; Croesus**

Cyrus the Younger (424–401BC) Second son of the Achaemenid King, **Darius II Ochus**. Cyrus was accused of conspiring against his brother, Artaxerxes II, and sentenced to death (404BC), but was afterwards pardoned and restored as Satrap of Asia Minor. In 401BC he led an army of Greek mercenaries against his brother, but was killed at Cunaxa. ▷ **Achaemenids; Xenophon**

Czartoryski, Adam Jerzy (1770–1861) Polish politician. The outstanding member of a famous family, he fought against Russia in the Polish insurrection of 1792. Sent, in 1795, to St Petersburg to serve in the imperial civil service, he gained the friendship of the imperial Grand Duke Alexander and the confidence of Emperor **Paul**, who made him ambassador to Sardinia. When **Alexander** ascended the throne, he appointed him assistant to the Minister of Foreign Affairs. As curator of the University of Wilno (1803) he strove to keep alive a spirit of nationality, and when some of the students were sent to Siberia, resigned his office. Disappointed with the treatment Poland received at the Congress of **Vienna** (1814–15), he threw himself wholeheartedly into the Revolution of 1830. He was elected President of the provisional government and summoned a national diet; this declared (Jan 1831) the Polish throne vacant and elected him head of the national government. He immediately devoted half of his large estates to the public service; although he resigned his post (Aug), he continued to fight as a common soldier. After the suppression of the rising, excluded from the amnesty and with his Polish estates confiscated, he escaped to Paris, where he lived thereafter. During the 1848 revolutions

he freed all his serfs in Galicia, and during the **Crimean War** he endeavoured to induce the allies to identify the cause of Poland with that of Turkey. He refused the amnesty offered to him by **Alexander II**, and died near Paris.

Czech Baroque (17c and 18c) One of the two most outstanding periods in Czech architecture and art, associated with important historical developments. The centre of Prague was particularly well endowed, with the ornate designs of many churches such as St Francis and St Nicholas, the Clementinium with its rich libraries, the Loretto and Strahov monasteries, and the town palaces of great noble families. The Czechs had finally lost their independence at the Battle of the **White Mountain** and were subjected to the rigours of the Habsburg Counter-Reformation. But compensation came in financial and cultural investment that even Mozart could tolerate and benefit from. However, later nationalists tended to denigrate what appeared to them a 'period of darkness'.

Czech Gothic (14–15c) One of the two most outstanding periods in Czech architecture and art, associated with important historical developments. The centre of Prague was particularly well endowed, with the clean lines of the Cathedral and the Castle, the Charles Bridge, the Carolinum which was the seat of the University set up in 1348, the Old and the New Town Halls and many churches. The Czech Lands were rich in agriculture and silver-mining and formed a crossing-point for European trade. **Charles IV** made them the centre of the **Holy Roman Empire** for half a century, and Jan Hus gave them the leading place in reform of the Church for all of a century. It was to this period that Czech nationalists in the 19c looked back for inspiration.

Czech National Movement (late 18c–early 20c) One of the last national movements that between them destroyed the Europe of the empires. The Czech revolt against Habsburg rule began slowly through a cultural revival fuelled by a German provincial nobility. It gained strength following the emancipation of the peasantry in 1849, which allowed Czechs from the countryside to swamp German towns and build up grievances, part social, part national. Imperial resistance to change, wider education and a growing literature, and Czech politicians harking back to the comparative prosperity and relative independence of the Czech Lands in the period of Jan **Hus** and before the Battle of the

White Mountain did the rest. The heroic figures were František **Palacký** and **Masaryk**. In 1918 the Czech and Slovak national movements came together to produce united Czechoslovakia. ▷ **Habsburg Dynasty**

Czechoslovak Independence, Declaration of (1918) The moment when the Czechs and Slovaks declared themselves free of Austria-Hungary and came together in a united state. Significantly, the declaration came out simultaneously in Geneva and Prague on 28 Oct, and on 30 Oct in Slovakia. Exiled politicians such as Tomáš **Masaryk** and Edvard **Beneš** played at least as great a role as those at home; and the Slovaks trailed behind the Czechs in their nationalist activities as in their economic development. Indeed it was the Czechs abroad who pressed the case for union, with support from the Allied Powers. And this has caused the union to be questioned at least twice, once following the **Munich Agreement**, and the second time after the so-called **Velvet Revolution**.

Czechoslovak Legion A corps of 30 000–40 000 Czech and Slovak volunteers and ex-prisoners of war in Russia, who fought briefly on the Eastern front and became embroiled with the **Bolsheviks** (May 1918) while being transported home along the Trans-Siberian railway. They seized many towns along the railway and for a time controlled much of Siberia. Their activities intensified the **Russian Civil War**, but also helped Tomáš **Masaryk** to gain recognition from the Allied powers for a provisional Czechoslovak government abroad.

Czechoslovak–Soviet Alliance (1935) The treaty linking the two countries against the growing threat from Germany. Relations had been strained since 1917 and the involvement of the **Czechoslovak Legion** in the **Russian Civil War**. It was 1934 before Czechoslovakia recognized the USSR *de jure*. However, things changed in 1935 when **Hitler** announced the reintroduction of conscription and the Franco-Soviet alliance was signed. But **Beneš** only agreed to the new treaty on condition that its operation would depend on the previous functioning of the Franco-Soviet alliance. This was to ensure that he would not be left to fight Hitler with **Stalin** as his sole ally. During the Munich crisis France reneged on its international obligations and Beneš did not attempt to activate his Soviet pact.

Czechoslovak–Soviet Alliance (1943) Treaty linking the two countries against the proven threat from Germany. Relations had been strained since the **Munich Agreement** and the **German–Soviet Pact** but improved following the German invasion of the USSR in 1941. **Beneš** was anxious to liberate his country and prevent another Munich. **Stalin** wanted all possible allies to win the war and negotiate a satisfactory peace. So in 1943 a new treaty replaced that of 1935. This time it was a direct alliance, not dependent upon a third party. In return, the USSR promised non-interference in Czechoslovakia's internal affairs. Unfortunately, similar treaties signed with Poland and other states were abused along with this one. The Soviet government did not interfere; but the Communist Party did. However, in 1989 all that was reversed with the collapse of Soviet power in Eastern Europe.

Czech Reformation (15c) One of the more important attempts to reform the medieval Christian Church before the 16c Protestant **Reformation**. It arose from the intellectual and social ferment aroused in Bohemia and Moravia when **Charles IV** made his imperial seal in Prague and in 1348 founded a university there. It drew strength from the preachings and in 1415 the martyrdom of Jan **Hus** and a strong streak of anti-German feeling. It produced the Czech Brethren and other more extreme groups. But it declined as the Czech Lands faded in prosperity and independence, and gave way first to Lutheranism and Calvinism and finally, after 1620, to the Counter-Reformation. But its spirit remained as an inspiration to Czech nationalists in the 19c.

D

Dabrowski, Jan Henryk (1755–1818) Polish soldier. He fought against Russia with Tadeusz **Kościuszko** (1794), then formed a Polish legion in the French army and played a distinguished part throughout the Napoleonic campaigns. On **Napoleon**'s fall he returned to Poland, and was appointed by Emperor **Alexander I** a general of cavalry and Polish senator. ▷ **Napoleonic Wars**

Dachau German concentration camp. Founded on **Himmler**'s orders on 20 Mar 1933 to accommodate political detainees under brutal conditions, Dachau was expanded during **World War II** to hold detainees from throughout Europe. By the time it was liberated by US troops in Apr 1945 about 30 000 people had died there. ▷ **Holocaust**

Dacia In antiquity, the name given to the area north of the River Danube, roughly corresponding to modern Romania, inhabited by the Dacians, a Thracian people. The Romans, under Emperor **Trajan**, conquered Dacia in the early 2c AD, and long lines of Dacian captives are depicted in the reliefs on the Column of Trajan in Rome. Colonists from all over the **Roman Empire** settled in Dacia to work the rich gold, silver and salt mines. In 271 the Romans withdrew from Dacia, abandoning the province to the **Goths**, but leaving a cultural legacy evident still in the modern name of the region's inhabitants, the Romanians.

Dacko, David (1930–) Central African politician. Educated at a teachers' training college in Mouyoundzi, he was a teacher and trade unionist before being elected to the territorial assembly in 1957, becoming successively Minister of Agriculture (1957–8), Minister of Administrative Affairs (1958), Minister of the Interior (1958–9) and Prime Minister (1959–60). He became the first President of the Central African Republic (1960) but was deposed in a coup, led by **Bokassa**, in 1966 and was imprisoned until 1976, when he was appointed one of Bokassa's advisers. With the help of the French, he was responsible for removing Bokassa in 1979, becoming President, a post to which he was re-elected in 1981, but was

then removed from office by a military coup led by Andre-Dieudonné Kolingba.

Daendels, Herman Willem (1762–1818) Dutch soldier and colonialist. He joined the French revolutionary army as a general in 1793, and in 1796 entered Dutch service under a succession of governments. He was appointed Governor-General of the Dutch East Indies (1807–10). In 1815 he was made Governor of the Dutch colonies on the coast of Africa, where he died.

Dagobert I (605–39) Last Frankish King of the Merovingian Dynasty (629/39). The son of **Chlotar II**, he was installed as King of **Austrasia** in 623 at the insistence of local nobles, and succeeded his father as King of a combined Frankish Kingdom from 629. His vigorous foreign and domestic policy restored the Merovingian Kingdom to a position of authority, but his policy of unifying the kingdom alienated the Austrasian nobles, who withdrew their support in 633–4 and forced him to set up his son, Sigibert III, as King there. ▷ **Merovingians**

Dahomey, Kingdom of A West African kingdom based on its capital at Abomey, which in the late 17c and early 18c extended its authority from the coast to the interior, to the west of the Yoruba states. In the 1720s the cavalry of the Oyo kingdom of the Yoruba devastated Dahomey, but when the Oyo Empire collapsed in the early 19c, Dahomey regained its power. It became famous for its trade in palm oil and slaves and was influenced by the neighbouring Yoruba. The state was annexed by the French in 1883, and regained its independence (later renaming itself Benin) in 1960.

Daigo II (Go-Daigo) (1288–1339) Japanese Emperor (1318/39). He attempted to restore direct imperial rule after it had been eclipsed by the **Kamakura Shogunate**. An abortive attempt to overthrow the shogunate in 1324 resulted in his banishment to the south-west. He escaped in 1333 and returned to the imperial capital, Kyoto, in triumph after the leader of the shogun's army, **Ashikaga** Takauji, changed sides. Daigo then exercised personal rule, but his attempts to intervene directly in administration aroused the enmity of his erstwhile supporter, Ashikaga, who rose in revolt. Daigo fled to Nara prefecture, south of Kyoto, where he continued to maintain his claim to the throne in opposition to the new emperor (from another line of the imperial family) installed in Kyoto by Ashikaga. The two rival imperial families (known as the Northern and Southern Courts) were not to be reunited until 1392. No emperor after Daigo ever attempted to rule directly.

Dáil Eireann The lower house of the parliament of the Irish Republic. Unlike the upper house, the Senate (*Seanad Eireann*), which is appointed, the Dáil is elected by universal suffrage by proportional representation for a period of five years. It nominates the Prime Minister for appointment by the President. There are 144 members, who are called *Teatcha Dala*.

daimyo A Japanese feudal lord, equivalent to a medieval baron in Europe. Powerful under the **Tokugawa Shogunate**, *daimyo* lost power at the **Meiji Restoration**. They had responsibility for keeping the peace, and the amount of rice their domains produced showed their prestige. ▷ **samurai**

Daladier, Edouard (1884–1970) French politician. In 1927 he became a leader of the **Radical Party**, and in 1933 Minister of War and Prime Minister of a short-lived government, a pattern which was repeated in 1934. In 1936 he was Minister of War in the **Popular Front** cabinet, and as Premier (1938–40) supported appeasement policies and signed the **Munich Agreement**. On 20 Mar 1940 he resigned as Prime Minister, becoming successively War and Foreign Minister in **Reynaud**'s cabinet, and on the fall of France was arrested and interned until 1945. He was one of the defendants in the **Riom Trial** (1942) of Third Republic leaders. After the war he continued in politics until 1958. ▷ **Republic, Third** (France)

Dalai Lama The traditional religious and temporal head of Tibet, whose name literally means 'ocean-like guru', regarded as an incarnation of the Bodhisattva Avalokiteshavara. Tensin Gyamtsho (1935–), held to be the 14th incarnation, ruled in Tibet from 1940 to 1959. After temporarily fleeing Tibet (1950–1) during the Chinese invasion of the country, he escaped to India during a local uprising in 1959. Tibetans still regard him as their spiritual leader. He won the Nobel Peace Prize in 1989.

Dalberg, Karl Theodore von (1744–1817) Son of an important noble family, he studied canon law at Göttingen and Heidelberg before being made administrator of the Erfurt bishopric (1772). He supported the League of Princes and Frederick of Prussia in 1785 to promote German unity. In 1802 he became archbishop of Mainz and Arch Chancellor of the Empire. After the reorganization of the Empire in 1803 he was primate of Germany controlling Mainz, Cologne, and Trier. He supported Napoleon to foster German unity and was made prince primate of the Rhine Confederation. As a result of Napoleon's changes to German territories in 1810 he became Grand Duke of Frankfurt. After Napoleon's defeat and the Congress of **Vienna** (1814–15) he was left with only the Archbishopric of Regensburg.

Daley, Richard J (1902–76) US politician. As Democratic mayor of Chicago (1955–76) and city boss, his political machine was so powerful that Democratic candidates at both the state and national level sought his backing. He became notorious during the 1968 Democratic Convention in Chicago, when the city's police force clubbed and gassed demonstrators protesting against the **Vietnam War**. By 1972 his influence had waned as a result of reforms which increased the representation of women, blacks and other minorities in the Democratic Party.

Dalhousie, James Andrew Broun Ramsay, 1st Marquis of (1812–60) British politician and colonial administrator. He became an MP in 1837, was made Earl of Dalhousie in 1838, and President of the Board of Trade in 1845. As Governor-General of India (1847–56), he encouraged the development of railways and irrigation works. He annexed Satara (1847) and Punjab (1849), but the annexation of Awadh (Oudh) (1856) caused resentment which fuelled the 1857–8 **Indian Uprising**. He was made a marquis in 1849, and retired through ill health in 1856.

Dalmatia The name given since antiquity to the narrow strip of land and over 1 000 islands along the eastern Adriatic coast from the south end of Pag to Cavtat, south of **Dubrovnik**. A Roman province inhabited by Illyrians, then settled by Slavs (7c), in the Middle Ages Dalmatia was governed by the kings of **Croatia** and later those of Hungary. From the 14c, most of Dalmatia was ruled by the Republic of Venice and the towns, notably Zadar, Šibenik, Split and Dubrovnik, still show the influence of Venetian culture. Occupied by **Napoleon I**'s army and included in the **Illyrian Provinces** (1809–13), following the Congress of **Vienna** (1814–15), Dalmatia was governed by Austria until 1918 when it became part of the Kingdom of Serbs, Croats and Slovenes, later Yugoslavia. Annexed by **Mussolini**'s Italy in **World War II**, in 1943 it was handed over to the **Ustaša** regime of Ante **Pavelić**. Since 1945 Dalmatia has been part of the Republic of Croatia within the Socialist Federal Republic of Yugoslavia.

Dalton, (Edward) Hugh (John Neale), Baron (1887–1962) British politician. First elected as a Labour MP in 1924, he held the posts of Minister of Economic Warfare (1940–2) and then President of the Board of Trade (1942–5). In the post-war Labour government he was Chancellor of the Exchequer (1945–7), Chancellor of the Duchy of Lancaster (1948–50), Minister of Town and Country Planning (1950–1), and, briefly, Minister of Local Government (1951). He was elevated to the peerage in 1960. ▷ **Labour Party (UK)**

Damascus, Capture of (1154) In the early 12c Damascus had been held largely through the astute capacities of the Seljuk princeling Tughtegin against both Muslim and Crusaders alike, and towards the middle of the century became an objective of the Atabeg Imad al-Din Zangi. Zangi's death (1146), followed by his son Nur al-Din's accession to control over Aleppo, in no way diminished the threat to Damascus which, although possessed of astute statesmen, was by this time ruled by the enfeebled Burid Dynasty. The effect of the Second Crusade's attack on Damascus (1148) led to the Burid statesman Unur's appealing to Nur al-Din for assistance. The Second Crusade's abandoning of the siege of Damascus was in some respects a result of the threat posed by Nur al-Din, but it was now clear that Damascus was essential to the control of Syria. The death of Unur (1149) followed by a recognition by the citizenry of Damascus of the need for strong rule led to Nur al-Din's army besieging Damascus (1154), being admitted to the town by the Damascenes themselves and the fall of the last Burid. ▷ **Crusade, Second; Zangid Dynasty**

Damaskinos, Demetrios Papandreou (1891–1949) Greek archbishop and regent of Greece. After serving in the army during the **Balkan Wars**, he was ordained priest (1917)

and elected Bishop of Corinth (1922) and Archbishop of Athens (1938), but was exiled because of his opposition to **Metaxas**. Returning to Greece in 1941, he was able to give secret assistance to the British during the German occupation. After the withdrawal from Greece of German troops, Winston **Churchill**, eager to establish peace between the warring factions and to settle the constitutional crisis, agreed to Damaskinos' appointment as regent until a plebiscite could be held over the issue of the monarchy (Dec 1944). When the **Greeks** voted for the return of their king, Damaskinos resigned as regent (Sep 1946) and continued his work as archbishop. ▷ **Plastiras, Nikolaos**

Danby, Thomas Osborne, 1st Earl of ▷ **Leeds, Thomas Osborne, 1st Duke of**

Dandolo, Enrico (c.1110–1205) Doge of Venice (1192–1205). He sailed at the head of the Fourth Crusade in 1202. The Crusaders could not raise the sum which they had negotiated for the ships which the Venetians had supplied. Dandolo proposed that the debt be paid in military service to Venice. This resulted in the subjugation of Trieste and Zara, the coasts of Albania and the Ionian Islands. Most notoriously, it led to the Sack of Constantinople in 1204, from which much of the plunder was carried off to Venice.

Danegeld In a narrow sense, the royal tax (Old English *geld*) levied in England between 991 and 1012 according to hidage, but distinct from the ordinary geld, in order to buy peace from Danish invaders. After 1066, the term was used for the general geld, which was effectively abandoned in 1162. ▷ **Danelaw; Ethelred the Unready; Vikings**

Danelaw That part of England where Danish conquest and colonization in the late 9c left an imprint on not only legal and administrative practices, but on placenames, language, and culture. Danish-derived customs survived even the **Norman Conquest**, and in the 12c all eastern England from the Thames to the Tees was so designated. ▷ **Vikings; Wessex**

Danish-German War (1863–4) The origins of this war lay in a dispute between Denmark and the **German Confederation** over the status of the Duchies of Schleswig, Holstein and Lauenburg. These predominantly German-speaking areas enjoyed autonomy under the Danish crown, but in 1863 King

Christian IX sought to integrate Schleswig (which had a large Danish minority) fully into Denmark. Austrian and Prussian forces invaded the duchies on behalf of the Confederation and soon defeated the Danish armies. After an unsuccessful attempt at international mediation (London Conference), further military action forced the Danes to terms at the Peace of Vienna (30 Oct 1864). After a brief period of joint Austrian-Prussian rule, the duchies passed to **Prussia**.

Danish West Indies, Sale of (1917) The result of an agreement reached in Jan 1916 between the governments of Denmark and the USA concerning the Danish West Indian colonies, the main islands being St Croix, St Jan and St Thomas, acquired in the 18c. The agreement stipulated that the US government would pay the Danish government the sum of $25 million for the islands, which the US considered part of its sphere of influence and of strategic importance after the opening of the Panama Canal. To the agreement was annexed a declaration in which the US government recognized the sovereignty of Denmark over the whole of Greenland. On 14 Dec 1916 a referendum about the agreement was held in Denmark with 64.3 per cent of the votes in favour of the sale and 35.7 per cent, a surprisingly high proportion, against. On 1 Apr 1917 — five days before the US declared war on Germany — the islands were handed over by the Danish government to the USA and renamed the 'Virgin Islands of the US'.

D'Annunzio, Gabriele (1863–1938) Italian writer. One of Italy's most important literary figures of the late 19c and early 20c. He was a fervent supporter of the **Tripolitanian War** and an active advocate of Italian intervention in **World War I**, during which he saw action as an airman. In Sep 1919 he occupied the disputed port of **Fiume** with a force of volunteer 'legionaries', where he introduced a constitution drafted by his syndicalist friend, Alceste **De Ambris**. Expelled from Fiume by the Italian navy in Jan 1921, D'Annunzio then flirted with the fascist movement and in Aug 1921 was actually invited by Dino **Grandi** and Italo **Balbo** to take over its leadership. Although D'Annunzio refused to usurp **Mussolini**'s position, the latter both admired him and considered him a threat to his dominance of the **Fascist Party** especially in the aftermath of the **Matteotti** crisis. Such fears were unfounded, as D'Annunzio never sought to challenge Mussolini for power.

Danquah, Joseph Boakye (1895–1965) Ghanaian nationalist and politician. After pursuing his studies in London, where he qualified as a lawyer, he returned to Ghana and founded the Times of West Africa in 1931. He was a leader of the **United Gold Coast Convention** (UGCC), which campaigned for independence, but he fell out with its successor, the **CPP**, and became leader of the opposition. He was imprisoned in 1961–2 and 1964–5 and died in prison.

Danton, Georges (Jacques) (1759–94) French revolutionary politician. He became a lawyer, and was practising in Paris at the outbreak of the **French Revolution**. In 1790 he formed the **Cordeliers' Club**, a rallying point for revolutionary extremists, and in 1792 became Minister of Justice. He voted for the death of **Louis XVI** (1793), and was one of the original members of the Committee of **Public Safety**. He tried to abate the pitiless severity of his own Revolutionary Tribunal, but lost the leadership to **Robespierre**. He was arrested and brought before the Tribunal, charged with conspiracy. Despite a heroic and eloquent defence, he was guillotined.

Danubian Principalities (Moldavia and Wallachia) The two principalities of Moldavia and Wallachia which merged in 1862 to form the Principality of Romania.

Dardanelles or **Hellespont** Narrow strait in north-west Turkey, connecting the Aegean Sea and the Sea of Marmara, part of the important waterway linking the Mediterranean and the Black Sea. It was the scene of an unsuccessful Allied campaign in **World War I**. Intending to overcome the Turks and come to the aid of Russia, the British War Council approved a naval expedition to capture Constantinople by forcing a route up the Dardanelles. Many of the Anglo-French battleships were destroyed during the attempted passage, and efforts were subsequently concentrated on the land attack at **Gallipoli**.

Darius I, 'the Great' (548–486BC) Achaemenid King of Persia (521/486BC). One of the greatest of the Achaemenids, he is noteworthy for his administrative reforms, military conquests, and religious toleration. His division of the empire into provinces called *satrapies* outlasted the Achaemenids. His conquests, especially in the East and Europe (Thrace and Macedonia) consolidated the frontiers of the empire. Patriotic

Greek writers made much of the failure of his two punitive expeditions against Athens, the first miscarrying through the wreck of his fleet off Mount Athos (492BC), the second coming to grief at Marathon (490BC); but in Persian eyes they were probably not very important. Although a worshipper himself of Ahura Mazda, who turned Zoroastrianism into a state religion, he showed an unusual respect for the religions of his subjects. ▷ **Persian Wars**

Darius II, 'Ochus' (d.404BC) Achaemenid King of Persia (423/404BC). He was an illegitimate son of **Artaxerxes I**, hence his being dubbed by the Greeks *Nothos*, 'bastard'. He seized power in the dynastic struggle which followed his father's death, but was the tool of his cruel half-sister and spouse, Parysatis, and his reign was a long series of struggles and revolts ruthlessly suppressed. After the failure of the Sicilian expedition of the Athenians in 413BC, Darius resumed active Persian intervention in Greek affairs. He died at Babylon, and was succeeded by his eldest son, **Artaxerxes II**.

Darius III, 'Codommanus' (d.330BC) Achaemenid King of Persia (336/330BC). The son of a daughter of **Artaxerxes II**, he was defeated by **Alexander III, 'the Great'** at the Granicus (334BC), at Issus (333BC) and at Gaugamela or Arbela (331BC), and, during flight, treacherously slain by a Bactrian satrap, Bessus.

Darlan, Jean (Louis Xavier) François (1881–1942) French admiral. He passed through the Ecole Navale in 1899, became captain in 1918, and navy Commander-in-Chief in 1939. He served in the **Vichy** government as Minister of the Navy and Mercantile Marine, Vice-President of the Council of Ministers, and Secretary of State for Foreign Affairs and the Navy. He then commanded French forces in North Africa (1942), where he concluded an armistice with the Allies. He was killed by an anti-Vichy assassin in Algiers. ▷ **World War II**

Darnand, Joseph (1897–1945) French politician. A militant in extreme-right movements, he was involved in the 1938 *Cagoule* ('hooded men') conspiracy, all financed by **Mussolini**, to murder left-wing Italian exiles in France. He collaborated with the Germans in **World War II**, organizing the *Milice*, an auxiliary police force responsible for many atrocities. He fled to Germany, was captured, tried and executed. ▷ **Vichy**

Darnley, Henry Stewart, Lord (1545–67) English nobleman. He was the second husband of **Mary, Queen of Scots** and father of James VI of Scotland and I of England. He married Mary (his cousin) in 1565, and was made Earl of Ross and Duke of Albany. In Scotland, this debauchery and arrogance made him unpopular, and his part in the murder (1566) of the Queen's secretary, David Rizzio, caused his downfall. He became estranged from the Queen, and during an illness was killed at Edinburgh, when Kirk O'Field, the house in which he was sleeping, was destroyed by gunpowder (the result of a plot probably organized by the Earl of **Bothwell**, perhaps with Mary's knowledge). ▷ **James VI and I**

Darrow, Clarence Seward (1857–1938) US civil liberties lawyer. In 1907 he successfully defended 'Big Bill' **Haywood** and Charles Moyer of the Western Federation of Miners implicated in the murder of Frank Steunenberg, ex-governor of Idaho. In 1924, his defence of Richard Loeb and Nathan Leopold in the most sensational murder trial of the age saved them from the death penalty; and in the Monkey Trial of 1925, at Dayton, Tennessee, he defended the high school biology teacher John Scopes who was charged under the Tennessee state law forbidding the teaching of Darwin's Theory of Evolution. Although Scopes was found guilty and fined US$100, Darrow demolished the views which lay behind the law and the arguments of the the prosecution, led by William Jennings Bryan, the elderly champion of Protestant fundamentalism. In 1934 Darrow was appointed to investigate Senator Gerald Nye's charge that the codes introduced by the National Recovery Board were favouring monopolies. His scathing report led eventually to the demise of price control.

Das, Chittaranjan (1870–1925) Bengali patriot and politician. Called to the Bar in 1894, he soon acquired a reputation for skilfully representing nationalists, such as Aurobindo Ghose (1908), accused of terrorism by the British colonial government in India. He participated in the campaign against the partition of Bengal, chaired Bengal Provincial Congress (1917) and the **Indian National Congress** (1918), and in 1920 renounced his legal practice and all his property to join M K **Gandhi**'s **Non-Cooperation Movement**. Imprisoned in 1921, he emerged (1922) to help form the **Swaraj** Party to contest district and provincial council elections (then boycotted by the Indian

National Congress). Opposed to Hindu **communalism**, he was popular with both Muslim and Hindu communities in Bengal and with Congressmen in Bengal, the Swarajists winning a majority of seats in the Bengal Council elections of 1923–4, and Das being elected Mayor of Calcutta City Corporation in 1924. Soon after, he came to an agreement with Gandhi which allowed both Swarajists and Gandhians to campaign from the Congress platform. Although he himself rejected violence, many of his followers were either involved in terrorism or openly advocated the use of violence in opposition to colonial rule. A strong supporter of the trade union movement, Das campaigned on behalf of railway workers and labourers on the Assam tea plantations; he and his followers were thus a powerful force for radicalism within the Indian Nationalist movement, a radicalism that grew in the years following his death. Sadly, his achievements in forging unity between Hindus and Muslims in Bengal survived his death by only a few years: factionalism and violence led ultimately to the partition of the province on independence in 1947. ▷ **Bengal, Partition of; Bose, Subhas Chandra**

Dashkova, Ekaterina Romanovna (1743–1810) Russian princess and author. In 1759 she married Prince Dashkov. She was an intimate friend and leading supporter of the Empress **Catherine II, 'the Great'** in the conspiracy that deposed her husband, **Peter III**, in 1762. She travelled widely in Europe, and was director of the Academy of Arts and Sciences in St Petersburg (1783-96). She wrote several plays, and was the first president of the Russian Academy (1783). On Catherine's death in 1796 she was ordered by the new emperor, her son **Paul**, to retire to her estates at Novgorod.

Daudet, Léon (1867–1942) French writer and political activist, son of Alphonse Daudet. He studied medicine but turned to journalism, and in 1904 began to associate with the right-wing royalist *Ligue de l'action française* ('League of French Action'), whose newspaper, *Action française*, he edited from 1908 (jointly with Charles Maurras after 1917). He sat in the Chamber of Deputies as a leader of the extreme right from 1919 to 1924. He wrote several novels, but is best remembered for his numerous memoirs and critical works, especially *Le Stupide XIXe Siècle* (1922).

Daughters of the American Revolution (DAR) A patriotic society organized in the USA in 1890; members must be directly descended from soldiers or patriots of the revolutionary period. It has three divisions: historical, educational and patriotic. ▷ **American Revolution**

Dauphin The title of the eldest son of the reigning French monarch in the period 1350–1830, acquired in 1349 when the future King **Charles V** purchased the lands known as Dauphin.

David (d.c.962BC) Second King of Israel. He was the first king of the dynasty that governed Judah and Israel until the exile, and the youngest son of Jesse of Bethlehem. According to Jewish tradition, he was the author of several of the Psalms, and according to some Christian traditions the ancestor of Jesus. David was a warrior under King Saul, but his successes against the Philistines (including the killing of Goliath) caused the King's jealousy, and he was forced to become an outlaw. After Saul's death, he became King over Judah in Hebron, and later was chosen King of all Israel. He made Jerusalem the political and religious centre of his kingdom, building a palace for himself on its highest hill, Zion (the 'city of David'), and placing the Ark of the Covenant there under a tent. He united the many tribes of Israel, and extended his territory from Egypt to the Euphrates. The later part of his reign was troubled by the revolts by his sons, Absalom and Adonijah. He was succeeded by Solomon, his son by Bathsheba.

David I (c.1085–1153) King of Scots (1124/53). He was the youngest son of **Malcolm III** and Queen (later St) **Margaret**. Educated at the court of **Henry I** of England, he became Earl of Huntingdon through his marriage to Maud de Senlis (c.1113). Once King, he emphasized his independence, systematically strengthened royal power, and firmly secured the foundations of the medieval Kingdom of Scotland. In 1136, as a nominal supporter of the claims of his niece, Empress Matilda, to the English crown, he embarked on wars of territorial conquest against Stephen. He was defeated in 1138 at the Battle of the Standard, near Northallerton, but from 1141 occupied the whole of northern England to the Ribble and the Tees.

David II (1324–71) King of Scots (1329/71). The only surviving son of Robert **Bruce**, he became King at the age of 5. In 1334, after the victory of **Edward III** of England at the Battle of **Halidon Hill** (1333), he fled to France. He returned in 1341, and later invaded England, but was defeated and captured at Neville's Cross, near Dunbar (1346), and was kept prisoner for 11 years. After his death at Edinburgh he was succeeded by his sister's son, **Robert II**.

Davies, Clement (Edward) (1884–1962) British politician. Elected MP for Montgomeryshire in 1929, he held his seat until his death. Although offered a post as Education Secretary in Winston **Churchill**'s 1951–5 government, he declined, and thus helped to preserve the independent existence of the **Liberal Party**, which he led from 1945 to 1956.

Davis, Jefferson (1808–89) US politician. After studying at the US Military Academy at West Point, he served in several frontier campaigns. He entered US House of Representatives for Mississippi (1845), fought in the **Mexican War** (1846–7), and became Secretary of War (1853–7). In the Senate (1847–51) he led the extreme State Rights Party, and supported slavery. President of the Confederate States of Americas at the close of the **American Civil War** (1865), he was imprisoned for two years, then released on bail. Though indicted for treason, he was never brought to trial, and he was included in the amnesty of 1872.

Davitt, Michael (1846–1906) Founder of the Irish Land League. Before becoming a journalist, he worked in a cotton mill, where he lost an arm in an accident. In 1866 he joined the Fenian Movement, was arrested in 1870 for sending guns to Ireland, and sentenced to 15 years' penal servitude. Released in 1877, he began an anti-landlord crusade which culminated in the Land League (1879). During a further period of imprisonment, he was elected an MP (1882), but disqualified from taking his seat. A strong Home Ruler but opponent of **Parnell**, he was twice more an MP (1892–3 and 1895–9). ▷ **Fenians; Home Rule**

Davout, Louis Nicolas (1770–1823) French general. He was educated with **Napoleon I** at the military school of Brienne. As general he accompanied Napoleon to the East, and mainly secured the victory at the Battle of **Aboukir Bay** (1799). A Marshal of the Empire (1804), he acted a brilliant part at **Austerlitz** (1805) and Auerstädt (1806), and was made Duke of Auerstädt (1808). As governor of Poland he ruled that country with the harshest despotism; after the retreat from

Moscow he became Governor-General of the Hanse towns. On Napoleon's return from Elba in 1815, Davout was appointed War Minister; and after the Battle of **Waterloo** he received the command of the remnant of the French Army under the walls of Paris. In 1819 he was made a peer of France. ▷ **Jena and Auerstädt, Battles of**

Dawes Plan A report on Germany's economic problems issued in 1924 by a committee presided over by US banker Charles G Dawes. The plan laid down a schedule of annual German payments of **reparations**, outlined the reorganization of the German Reichsbank, and recommended a large foreign loan for Germany. A further report was drawn up in 1929 by an international commission chaired by US Corporation official Owen Young (1874–1962).

Dayan, Moshe (1915–81) Israeli general and politician. During the 1930s he joined the illegal Jewish defence organization, the **Haganah**, and was imprisoned by the British (1939–41), then released to fight with the Allies in **World War II** (when he lost his left eye, thereafter wearing his distinctive black eye-patch). He became Chief-of-Staff (1953–8), joined the Knesset as a Labour member in 1959, but left the Labour Party in 1966 to set up the Rafi Party with David **Ben-Gurion**. He won international acclaim as Defence Minister in 1967 when his heavily-outnumbered forces triumphed over Egypt, Jordan and Syria in the **Six-Day War**, and he himself became a symbol of Israeli dash and courage. As Foreign Minister, he helped to secure the historic peace treaty with Egypt (1977). He resigned from the **Begin** government in 1979, and launched a new centre party in 1981, but died the same year.

D'Azeglio, Massimo Tarpelli (1798–1866) Piedmontese politician, painter and novelist. Influenced by his friend Cesare **Balbo** and the exiled Vincenzo **Gioberti**, D'Azeglio published his famous *Degli ultimi casi di Romagna* in 1846, in which he developed a moderate, patriotic programme. As well as developing the ideas of Balbo and Gioberti, he succeeded them as Piedmontese Prime Minister, replacing the latter in May 1849 and retaining the post until 1852. During his period of office, extensive anticlerical legislation was initiated which was to continue under his successor, **Cavour**. In 1860 D'Azeglio was made Governor of Milan after its acquisition from the Austrians, but he remained unenthusiastic about annexation of the south of Italy, judging the time not yet right.

Dazhai A production brigade in the Chinese province of Shanxi that was personally hailed by **Mao Zedong** in 1964 as a national model for agricultural development, embodying the ideals of self-help, egalitarianism and ideological correctness. Peasants in Dazhai were said to have transformed the barren hillsides into fertile terraced fields. After Mao's death in 1976, the achievements of Dazhai were increasingly called into question and its production figures were said to have been falsified.

D-Day (6 June 1944) The day when the Allies launched the greatest amphibious operation in history (codenamed 'Overlord'), and invaded German-occupied Europe. By the end of D-Day, 130000 troops had been landed on five beach-heads along an 80km/50ml stretch of the coast of **Normandy**, at a cost of 10000 casualties. ▷ **Normandy Campaign; World War II**

DDP (*Deutsche Demokratische Partei*, 'German Democratic Party') German political party. The DDP was founded on 20 Nov 1918 from left-liberal elements who supported the transformation of post-**World War I** Germany from a semi-absolutist monarchy to a parliamentary democracy. Until its dissolution in 1930, the DDP participated actively in Weimar coalition governments, particularly with the **SPD** and the **Centre Party**. Its middle-class supporters, however, became increasingly disenchanted with the republic and abandoned the DDP in large numbers. On 9 Nov 1930 the party was wound up and its remnants integrated in the small DSP (German State Party). ▷ **Weimar Republic**

Deák, Ferenc (1803–76) Hungarian politician. Born into the gentry class, he practised as an advocate, and entered the national Diet in 1832, playing a moderate liberal role. In 1848 he became Minister of Justice, dissociating himself from Lajos **Kossuth**'s more extreme Magyar nationalism. In the restored Diet of 1860–1, he emerged as leader of moderate liberalism; his efforts helped Hungary to recover her constitution (1867), and on her behalf he negotiated the **Ausgleich** of 1867, establishing the Dual Monarchy of Austria-Hungary.

Deakin, Alfred (1856–1919) Australian politician. He entered the Victorian Legisla-tive Assembly in 1879 and held various offices, including that of Chief Secretary (1886–90). Out of office after 1890, his political interests increasingly centred on **federation**. He was a member of the committees which drew up draft constitutions at both the National Australasian Convention in 1891 and the Federal Convention of 1897–8, and went to Britain with **Barton**'s delegation to present the draft constitution to the British parliament in 1900. He became Attorney-General in Barton's first federal government and was largely responsible for the immigration legislation that created the **White Australia Policy** and the Judiciary Act which established the High Court. He became Prime Minister after Barton's retirement (1903), and held the office again in 1905–8 with the support of Labor. His second ministry created much of the distinctive structure of Australian government, including 'New Protection' which attempted to link wage rates to the new protective tariff. Although a lifelong social reformer, Deakin was wary of trade union power and the strict party discipline of Labor, and his third ministry (1909–10) was in coalition with Sir Joseph **Cook**'s anti-socialists, marking a fundamental realignment in Australian politics. A nationalist, Deakin sought greater Australian influence in imperial affairs, criticizing the naval subsidy to Britain and promoting an Australian navy and compulsory military service. Yet he was also an imperialist, so effective as an advocate of imperial preference and closer union at the 1907 Imperial Conference that some British imperialists considered inviting him to lead an imperial party in Britain. Failing health forced his political retirement in 1913.

De Ambris, Alceste (1874–1934) Italian politician and trade unionist. After leading a long strike in the Parma region in 1908, he was forced into political exile, but in 1913 was elected to the Italian parliament. He campaigned for intervention in **World War I** in the hope that it would trigger a revolution and in 1919 he joined Gabriele **D'Annunzio** in **Fiume** where he was responsible for drafting a bizarre, guild-based constitution which was later to inspire the fascist **Corporations**. He left Italy in 1922 after **Mussolini**'s seizure of power.

Déat, Marcel (1894–1955) French socialist politician. He left the SFIO in 1933 as co-founder of the 'neo-socialist' *Parti social-iste de France* ('Socialist Party of France') which did not long survive. A visceral hatred of war led him from appeasement to **colla-boration**. In 1941 he created the RNP (*Rassemblement national populaire*, 'National Popular Assembly') in the zone of German occupation. In Mar 1944 German pressure forced **Laval** to accept him as Minister of Labour in the **Vichy** government; he fled to Germany, was sentenced to death *in absentia*, but evaded arrest until his death in Italy. ▷ **Socialist Party**

De Beers Consolidated Mines The diamond mining company formed by Cecil Rhodes in 1887 from the amalgamation of several companies operating at Kimberley, Cape Province. The De Beers mine was one of the original diamond concessions named after the Boer farmer on whose land the diamonds were found. Rhodes and his associate, Rudd, formed the De Beers Mining Company in 1880 and set about the gradual acquisition of other mines. Kimberley became virtually a company town and by 1900 De Beers was contributing 50 per cent of all the exports of the Cape Colony. Rhodes used both his personal wealth derived from the Company and the Company's own finances to help to advance his interests on the Rand and to form the British South Africa Company to pursue his dreams in Central Africa. De Beers developed the closed compound system for migrant black labourers which became a major feature of South African urban life and remained one of the most powerful companies in 20c South Africa.

De Bono, Emilio (1866–1944) Italian soldier and politician. Present at the humiliating defeat of the Battle of **Adowa** in 1896, De Bono commanded a corps in **World War I**. After the war, he rallied to **fascism** and took part in the **March on Rome**. He was Director of Police and then Governor of Tripolitania from 1925. In 1935 he was placed in charge of the forces to invade Ethiopia but was quickly replaced by **Badoglio**. As early as 1940 De Bono began to have doubts over **Mussolini**'s fitness to lead Italy in a war, worried by the latter's desire to control all policy personally. He was present at the meeting of the **Fascist Grand Council** of 25 July 1943 which toppled Mussolini and was later put on trial and executed by the Republic of **Salò**.

Debray, Regis (1941–) French Marxist theorist. Educated at the Ecole Normale Supérieure, he gained international fame through his association with the Marxist revolutionary Ernesto Che **Guevara** in

Latin America during the 1960s. His most influential writings have been *Strategy for Revolution* (1970) and *The Power of the Intellectual in France* (1979), the latter a broadside against the growing influence of 'mediacrats'.

Debré, Michel (1912–) French politician. After taking part in the **Resistance Movement**, he helped to set up of the *Ecole Nationale d'Administration* (ENA, 'National School of Administration') in 1945, the training ground for France's governing élites in politics, industry and the Civil Service in subsequent years. He was elected to parliament as a member of the Gaullist Party (RPF) in 1948, and violently attacked the constitution of the Fourth Republic. In 1958 de **Gaulle** charged him with the task of producing the new constitution of the Fifth Republic, and made him its first Prime Minister (1959–62). ▷ **Gaullists; Republic, Fifth** (France)**; Republic, Fourth** (France)

Debs, Eugene Victor (1855–1926) US politician. He worked as a locomotive fireman, and in 1893 was founder and first President of the American Railway Union, in 1894 leading the **Pullman Strike** for higher wages. He helped to establish the Socialist Party of America, was imprisoned for labour agitation, and between 1900 and 1920 stood five times as socialist candidate for President. His indictment for violation of Espionage Act brought him imprisonment (1918–21).

Decatur, Stephen (1779–1820) US naval commander of French descent. He served against the French, and gained great distinction in the war with Tripoli (1801–5), burning the captured Philadelphia, and escaping under the fire of 141 guns. Promoted captain in 1804 and commodore in 1810, in the **War of 1812** with England he captured the frigate *Macedonian*, but in 1814 surrendered to the British. He was killed in a duel at Bladensburg, Maryland.

Deccani Sultanates Successors in the Deccan to the Bahmani Sultanate, comprising the Imad Shahi Dynasty of Berar (1484–1575), Barid Shahi Dynasty of Bidar (1492–1619), Qutb Shahi Dynasty of Golconda (1518–1687), Nizam Shahi Dynasty of Ahmadnagar (1490–1637) and Adil Shahi Dynasty of Bijapur (1489–1686). Usually disunited, the four sultans of Ahmadnagar, Bidar, Bijapur and Golconda united in 1565 to inflict a decisive defeat on Ramaraja, the Vijayanaraga ruler. Shia by persuasion, they were the target of Aurangzeb's Sunni ortho-doxy and finally eliminated him.

December Ninth Movement (1935) A massive student demonstration in the Chinese capital of Beijing to protest against Japanese military incursions in north China and to call upon the Chinese government of **Chiang Kai-shek** to lead a campaign of national resistance. Although the demon-stration was brutally suppressed, the movement provided many supporters for the Chinese Communist Party, increasingly per-ceived as the genuine representative of Chinese nationalism because of its call for an anti-Japanese war. ▷ **Communist Party, Chinese**

Decembrists A group of Russian progress-ive-minded army officers who had long been discussing constitutional reform and who attempted a coup against the autocratic government of the new tsar, **Nicholas I** (12 Dec 1825). The rebellion was quickly sup-pressed, five of its leaders hanged, and over 200 conspirators exiled to Siberia. They were later regarded as martyrs and founders of the 19c Russian revolutionary movement. ▷ **Romanov Dynasty**

Decius, Gaius Messius Quintus Trajanus (d.251) Roman Emperor (249/51). Roman army commander in the Danubian province of Moesia who was proclaimed Emperor by his troops in 249. His brief reign is notable for two things: the first systematic attempt to stamp out Christianity throughout the Roman Empire and the emergence of the **Goths** as a major threat to the security of the Roman Empire. It was in battle against them that Decius and his son, Herennius, whom he had made his co-emperor, were killed.

Declaration of Independence (1776) The document adopted by the US **Continental Congress** to proclaim the separation of the 13 colonies from Britain. Drawn up by a committee of John **Adams**, Benjamin **Frank-lin**, Thomas **Jefferson**, Robert R Livingston, and Roger Sherman, it announced the right of revolution, detailing the Americans' reasons for the break, and asserted that American government should be based on a theory of natural law, and should respect the fundamental rights of individuals.

Declaration of Rights (1689) An English statute which ended the brief interregnum after **James VII and II** quit the throne in Dec 1688, establishing **William III** and Mary II as joint monarchs. The Bill effectively ensured that monarchs must operate with the consent of parliament, and must not suspend or dispense with laws passed by that body. ▷ **bill of rights**

Declaration of the Rights of Man and Citizen (27 Aug 1789) A declaration made by the French National Assembly, proclaim-ing liberty of conscience, of property, and of the press, and freedom from arbitrary imprisonment. It finally ended the privileged system of the **ancien régime**. ▷ **French Revolution**

Declaratory Act (1766) A British Act passed by the **Rockingham** government. After much opposition in the US colonies to the introduction of taxes by the preceding George **Grenville** administration, Rock-ingham repealed the **Stamp Act** (1765); but this legislation reasserted the British parlia-ment's general right to legislate for the colonies 'in all cases whatsoever'.

Decumates Agri This term, which comes from Tacitus (*Germania* 29,5), describes the lands between the rivers Rhine, Danube and Main, originally settled by Celts and then by **Suebi**. Its meaning is controversial but it possibly derives from a Celtic term meaning 'tithe land' or 'very fertile land'. It was settled by the Romans in the first half of the 1c AD and was lost to the Alemanni c.260.

Defence of the Realm Act ('DORA') (Nov 1914) A British Act introduced to give the government greater controls over the activi-ties of its citizens. The most important control related to restrictions on press reporting and other forms of censorship. The restrictions were increased as **World War I** progressed.

Defenestration of Prague (1618) The dramatic gesture with which the Czech Protestants challenged the authority and religion of the Habsburg Emperors within the Czech Lands. On an issue of church-building a crowd of nobles and knights marched on Prague Castle and, after a dispute, threw two imperial councillors, the Counts Martinic and Slavata, and their secretary out of a high window. Falling on rubbish, the victims survived. But in due course the Czech estates proceeded to depose Ferdinand II from the thrones of Bohemia and Moravia and to replace him with Frederick V of the Palati-nate. The course was set for the Battle of the **White Mountain** and the end of Czech independence. ▷ **Habsburg Dynasty**

De Gasperi, Alcide (1881–1954) Italian politician. An Austrian subject until the end of **World War I**, he was elected to the Austrian parliament in 1911 as a deputy for the Trentino and became known as an ardent defender of the interests of the Italian minority. In 1919 after Italian annexation of his native region, he attended the first congress of the **Popolari** at Bologna and in 1921 was elected to the Italian parliament. Although he originally backed **Mussolini**'s government, he soon withdrew his support and was arrested while trying to flee the country with false papers; he was sentenced to four years in prison but served only six months. On his release, he became Vatican Librarian, a post he held until the liberation of Rome. Made Secretary-General of the **Christian Democrat Party (DC)**, he was Minister without Portfolio in the first **Bonomi** ministry, while **Parri** made him Foreign Minister. In June 1946 he became Prime Minister, successfully supporting Italy's transition from monarchy to republic and signing the peace treaty with the Allies (Feb 1947). In Jan 1947 he formed a government with the support of both socialists and communists but he soon jettisoned this alliance, excluding them from his government in May 1947. Foremost among his reasons for ending a policy of cooperation with the left was the heightening tension between the USA (on which Italy was heavily dependent for investment and aid) and the USSR and increasing pressure from Pope Pius XII, who had made it clear as early as June 1946 that he saw it as his 'main aim to fight communism'. Despite a narrower basis for his government, De Gasperi remained Prime Minister until July 1953, providing continuity even though he presided over eight separate governments. He remained Secretary-General of the DC until his death.

De Geer, Louis G (1818–96) Swedish politician. In 1858 he was appointed Minister of Justice, a post which made him in effect Prime Minister, and which he held until 1870. He was largely responsible for the replacement of the Diet of four estates (nobles, clergy, burghers and peasants) with a parliament of two houses (1866), one indirectly elected through county councils and one directly elected on a narrow franchise. He was appointed Prime Minister (the title being then accepted) in 1876, but resigned four years later after defeat in parliament.

Degrelle, Léon (1906–94) Belgian politician. From French-speaking Belgium, he founded the fascist **Rexism** movement in the 1930s, and achieved considerable support in the elections of 1936. During **World War II** he collaborated with the German forces, commanding the Walloon (French-speaking Belgian) regiment on the Russian front, and was briefly put in charge of German-occupied Belgium towards the end of the war. He escaped in 1945 to Spain, and was condemned to death in his absence. In 1974 he was declared an undesirable alien in Belgium.

Dekker, Eduard Douwes (Multatuli) (1820–87) Dutch radical publicist and novelist. He served for many years in the Dutch civil service in Java, and in his novel *Max Havelaar* (1860), and in many bitter satires, he protested in particular against the abuses of the Dutch colonial **Culture System**.

De Klerk, F(rederik) W(illem) (1936–) South African politician. Born into a prominent Nationalist family (his father was a cabinet minister and President of the Senate, his uncle the Prime Minister Johannes **Strijdom**), he graduated from Potchestroom University and established a legal practice in Vereeniging, which he represented as a **National Party** member in the South African parliament from 1972. He served in the cabinets of both B J **Vorster** and P W **Botha**, but never in major positions. Elected National Party leader for the Transvaal in 1982, when **Treurnicht** left to form the Conservative Party, he used that position as the political base from which to replace Botha on his retirement in 1989. He has been chiefly responsible for the public policy of ending **apartheid**, successfully winning elections in Sep 1989 (but with a reduced majority), and a referendum supporting negotiations with the **ANC**, which he had unbanned in Feb 1990. Although attacked from the right for betraying Afrikaner and white interests, and from the left for sanctioning state and Inkatha violence, his leadership of the white population towards an accord with the Blacks in South Africa has been essential for the peaceful transition towards majority rule in South Africa.

Delaney, Martin Robinson (1812–85) US anti-slavery activist. The grandson of slaves, he became a doctor and a journalist, his major work being *The Condition, Elevation, Emigration and Destiny of the Colored Peoples of the United States* (1852). By 1854, despairing of ever achieving black **civil rights** in the North, he began to advocate emigration of blacks to Africa. This he abandoned after travelling in West Africa on the eve of the **American Civil War**, resuming the struggle for racial equality within the USA, and becoming active in the Freedmen's Bureau.

Delcassé, Théophile (1852–1923) French politician. He was twice Foreign Minister (1898–1905 and 1914–15), during which time he promoted the **Entente Cordiale** with Britain (1904), and worked towards the **Triple Entente** with Britain and Russia.

Delescluze, (Louis) Charles (1809–71) French radical republican and journalist. His revolutionary politics drove him from France to journalism in Belgium (1835), but the **February Revolution** (1848) brought him back to Paris. His writing made him popular, but brought him imprisonment (1849–53), and he was transported until 1859. He played a prominent part in the **Paris Commune**, and died on its last barricade.

Delfim Neto, Antônio (1929–) Brazilian economist and politician. The son of Italian immigrants, he is widely viewed as the typical technocrat, an econometrician who believed in rapid GDP growth and centralization as an antidote to the social problems of Brazil. He was Economic Secretary to São Paulo State (1966) and Planning Minister under Costa e Silva, becoming 'economic Tsar' under his successor, Emílio **Médici**. Heavily reliant upon repression to curb the labour unions, he became the darling of the propertied class as the author of the 'Economic Miracle' of 1968–73 and was recalled to office (Aug 1979–Mar 1985). He attempted to sustain GDP and export growth as antidotes to soaring international oil prices, interest rates and a deteriorating balance of payments.

Delgado, Humberto (1906–65) Portuguese general and politician. Born into a modest military family, in the 1920s he keenly supported the counter-revolution as a junior officer. His vertiginous rise through the military ranks led him to become, at 46, the youngest general in the Portuguese armed forces. However, **Salazar** never entirely trusted Delgado, considering him too independent. Delgado's democratic experience abroad, especially in the USA (1953–7), caused him to reject the Salazar regime and in Apr 1958 Delgado scandalized the dictatorship by standing against the official presidential candidate. His charismatic appeal led to huge demonstrations of support in Lisbon and Oporto, but a heavily-rigged vote ensured his defeat. The humiliated Salazar

soon got rid of direct presidential elections, restrictive as they had been. Delgado tried to stage three coup attempts in 1958, but failed on each occasion for lack of support. He left Portugal in 1959 and attempted unsuccessfully to win over the armed forces from abroad. He was murdered in Spain, near the Portuguese border, by the **PIDE** in mysterious circumstances.

Delhi Sultanate (1200–1526) The principal northern Indian Muslim kingdom between the 13c and 16c, in which Sultan **Iltutmish** (1211/36) made his permanent capital at Delhi. It became an imperial power under the Khalji Dynasty (1290–1320), but its power was much reduced under the Saiyid and Lodi Dynasties, and the sultanate was destroyed by **Babur** at the Battle of **Panipat** in 1526. ▷ **Mughal Empire**

Delian League The association of Greek city-states under Athenian leadership that was formed (478–477BC) after the **Persian Wars** for the continuing defence of the Aegean area against the Persians. It was so called because the treasury of the League was initially on the island of Delos. ▷ **Aristides; Athenian Empire; Cimon**

Deligiannis (Deliyannes), Theodoros (1824–1905) Greek politician. From a prominent family of landowners, he entered politics as a Conservative, first serving as Foreign Minister (1878) and later as Prime Minister (1885, 1890 and 1895). An advocate of the **Megale Idea**, he conducted an extravagant foreign policy intended to bring about the creation of Greater Greece. In Mar 1905 he was assassinated on the steps of the National Assembly.

Delors, Jacques (1925–) French politician. He served as social affairs adviser to Prime Minister Jacques Chaban-Delmas (1969–72). He joined the **Socialist Party** in 1973 and served as Minister of Economy and Finance in the administration of President **Mitterrand** (1981–4), overseeing a programme of austerity (*rigueur*). He became President of the European Commission in 1985 and was elected to a second four-year term as President in 1988. As Commission President he oversaw significant budgetary reforms and the move towards the removal of all internal barriers in the EC in 1992, with increased powers residing in Brussels.

Delphi, Oracle of The oracular shrine of Apollo at Delphi in central Greece. It was the most prestigious oracle in the Graeco-Roman world, for centuries (from the 8c BC onwards) being consulted by states about public policy and by individuals about private matters. On the payment of a fee, enquirers put their questions to Apollo's medium, a priestess called the Pythia. Her ecstatic responses (oracles) were notorious for their ambiguity.

Delta Works Series of public works in the Netherlands to protect the coastline against storms, designed after the disastrous floods of Feb 1953. The Delta Plan (5 Nov 1957) laid down projects to strengthen the water defences by building new or improved dams, bridges and surge barriers in the south-west of the country, effectively closing off the sea-arms between Rotterdam and Antwerp. The project, costing enormous sums of public money, has opened up the Dutch province of Zeeland to economic development, has been generally successful in achieving its aims, and was officially completed in 1986.

Dembiński, Henryk (1791–1864) Polish soldier. He entered the Polish army in 1809 and fought under **Napoleon** against Russia and at **Leipzig** (1813). In the Polish revolution of 1830 he eventually became Commander-in-Chief; in 1833 he entered the service of **Muhammad Ali**. On the outbreak of the Hungarian insurrection in 1848, Lajos **Kossuth** appointed him Commander-in-Chief. He was hampered by the jealousy of **Görgey**, and after the defeat of Kapolna (1849) was forced to resign. On Kossuth's resignation he fled to Turkey, but in 1850 returned to Paris.

Demetrius Poliorcetes (d.283BC) King of Macedonia (294/288BC). The son of Alexander the Great's general, **Antigonus Monophthalmos**, he assumed the royal title together with his father in 306BC, and was king in **Macedonia** from 294BC until his expulsion in 288BC. Named 'the Besieger of Cities' after his famous, although unsuccessful, siege of **Rhodes** (305BC), he died the prisoner of Seleucus I.

Demirel, Süleyman (1924–) Turkish politician. He qualified as an engineer at Istanbul Technical University and worked on hydro-electric schemes in the USA and Turkey before making the transition from public service to politics. In 1964 he became President of the centrist Justice Party (JP), now subsumed in the True Path Party (TPP). He served three terms as Prime Minister from 1965, until a military coup in 1980 resulted in

a three-year ban on political activity. He was placed in detention but released in 1983.

Democracy Wall Movement (1978–9) A protest movement in China against the excesses of the **Cultural Revolution**, the corruption of the Chinese Communist Party, and infringement of human rights. Ironically, the movement initially may well have been unofficially encouraged by **Deng Xiaoping**, who was at the time intent on reducing the influence of his Maoist opponents. At the Third Party Plenum (Dec 1978) Deng succeeded in gaining approval for his economic reforms. Wall-posters started to appear in the centre of the city during the Third Plenum, which not only criticized **Mao Zedong** and the Cultural Revolution, but also called into question the socialist system itself. Magazines were also published advocating greater democratic and artistic freedom. Many of the people involved were young urbanites, including workers, students, and former **Red Guards** disillusioned with the party. In Mar 1979 Deng Xiaoping, fearing that the protests had gone too far, ordered a clampdown and a number of dissidents were arrested. By the end of 1979 the movement had virtually come to an end; a limited number of wall-posters were allowed only to be displayed in a park far from the city centre. ▷ **Maoism**

Democratic Centralism (post-1906) The term used by **Lenin** in 1906 to describe the operating principles that would govern the Communist Party and the Soviet state. Elections and accountability were mandatory, but it was also ordained that lower bodies must implement the decisions of higher bodies. This was used to eliminate whatever democracy the revolutionaries of 1917 might have envisaged and to institute dictatorship. It was implicit in the 1936 constitution, explicit in that of 1977. It continued as a party rule to the end and helps to explain why **communism** was doomed as soon as open debate was allowed after 1985.

Democratic Labor Party (DLP) Australian political party, formed in 1957 from anti-communist groups which had formerly been part of the **Australian Labor Party** (ALP). The DLP was largely centred in Victoria, and drew most of its support from parts of the Catholic section of Australian society. At its height, in the late 1950s and through the 1960s, its importance lay in its ability to prevent the ALP from winning national government. Its policies were strongly anti-communist and pro-defence, and incorporated elements of Catholic teaching on social matters. No DLP representative has been elected to the national parliament since 1974.

Democratic Labour Party (DLP) One of the two political parties which has shared power in Barbados since 1938. From that date, Grantley **Adams**'s Barbados Labour Party dominated politics until 1961 when the DLP, led by Errol **Barrow**, took a majority of seats in the legislature. The DLP was ousted in the 1976 election by the BLP, led by 'Tom' Adams but with Adams's death in 1985, the DLP returned to power (under Barrow) later in 1986. Barrow's death that year saw the leadership of the party pass into the hands of Erskine Sandiford, and Sandiford and the DLP were again victorious in the 1991 election.

Democratic Party US political party. It was originally composed in the late 18c of those opposed to the economic policies of Alexander Hamilton and in sympathy with France rather than Britain (during the Anglo-French Wars of the 1790s). Its first successful presidential candidate was Thomas Jefferson, and in the early 1800s dominated its opponent, the **Federalist Party**. During the 1830s, under Presidents Andrew **Jackson** and Martin **Van Buren**, the party gained mass appeal among the electorate through shrewd political management, and was identified as representative of the 'common man'. The party was split over slavery and secession during the **American Civil War**, and its position of national dominance was taken over by the **Republican Party**. After the war the party became conservative, based in the South and West, achieving only intermittent success. It returned to a majority position in 1932, with Franklin D **Roosevelt**'s 'New Deal', and added large urban areas and ethnic, racial, and religious support to its conservative Southern base. It also became associated with a more liberal stance on social reform and minority rights, especially in the 1960s. It retains the preference of the majority of Americans, reflected in the Democrat-dominated House and Senate, but since the early 1960s it has had great difficulty winning the presidency, with the exception of Jimmy **Carter** (1977–81) and Bill **Clinton** (1993–). ▷ **Whig Party**

Democratic Unionist Party The political party formed in Northern Ireland in 1971 under the leadership of Rev Ian **Paisley** after a split in the Unionist Party over Protestant reaction to demands both by Catholics in the Province and from Westminster for greater social and political equality. It has had strong appeal to many working-class Protestants and during the 1980s attracted about one-third of the Unionist vote. Frequently suspicious in the 1970s and early 1980s that the official Unionists were less zealous in their support for Protestantism, the two Unionist parties agreed on concerted opposition to the **Anglo-Irish Agreement** (1985) and agreed in the 1987 general election not to nominate candidates against one another, thus avoiding a split in the Unionist vote.

Democrats 66 (*Democraten 66*, **'D66'**) Dutch political party formed in 1966 on a programme of radical constitutional reform. It wished to break the mould of 'compromise politics' and **Verzuiling** in the Netherlands by introducing a directly elected President, and by changing pure proportional representation to a more district-based system. In other matters D66 is generally left-of-centre.

Demosthenes (384–322BC) Athenian orator. He entered politics c.354BC, but did not gain prominence until 351BC, with the first of a long series of passionate speeches (the 'First Philippic') advocating all-out resistance to **Philip II** of Macedon. Swayed by his oratory, the Athenians did eventually go to war (340BC), only to be thoroughly defeated at the Battle of **Chaeronea** (338BC). Put on trial by the peace party of **Aeschines**, he vindicated himself in his oratorical masterpiece, *On the Crown*. It was the high point of his career. Exile for embezzlement followed in 325BC, and enforced suicide in 322BC, after the failure of the Athenian revolt from **Macedonia** after the death of **Alexander III, 'the Great'**.

Deng Xiaoping (Teng Hsiao-p'ing) (1902–) Chinese politician. Leader of the Chinese Communist Party, since 1978 he has been the dominant figure in Chinese politics. Educated in France, where he joined the Communist Party, and in the USSR, he became associated with **Mao Zedong** during the period of the **Jiangxi Soviet** (1928–34). In 1954 he became Secretary-General of the Chinese Communist Party, but reacted strongly against the excesses of the **Great Leap Forward** (1958–9). When Mao launched the **Cultural Revolution** (1966), Deng was criticized and purged along with **Liu Shaoqi**, but retained the confidence of Premier **Zhou Enlai** and was restored to power in 1974. Again dismissed in 1976, after

265

the death of Mao he was restored once more to power, and since 1978 has taken China through a rapid course of pragmatic reforms.

Denikin, Anton Ivanovich (1872–1947) Russian soldier. He entered the army at the age of 15, and rose to lieutenant general in **World War I**. After the **Russian Revolution** of 1917 he led the White Army in the south against the **Bolsheviks** (1918–20). He won the Ukraine, but was defeated by the **Red Army** at Orel (1919), and in 1920 resigned his command and escaped to Constantinople. Thereafter he lived in exile in France (1926–45) and the USA (1945–7), and wrote books on his military experiences.

Denkyira A state developed in the mid-17c by one of the princelings of the Akan people in the western Gold Coast. Its power was based on gold and trade with Europeans on the coast. However, its ruler never developed an effective imperial administration and it was weakened and eventually destroyed by competition and conflict with its eastern neighbour, the **Akwamu** state, in the early 18c. Akwamu in its turn was defeated by Akin and then by the **Ashanti** in the 1730s and 1740s.

Denmark, German Invasion of (8–9 Apr 1940) An adjunct to the German invasion of Norway which met with little or no resistance on the part of the Danish armed forces and government. The latter continued in office until dismissed by the German occupying authorities in 1943. ▷ **Norway, German Invasion of; World War II**

Deoband The 'House of Learning'. This leading Muslim theological centre of India was founded in 1867 by Muhammad Abid Husain in Saharanpur district in the state of Uttar Pradesh. Deoband has a puritanical and orthodox outlook, and prepares students mainly for religious leadership of the Muslim community. Students study jurisprudence, Quranic exegesis, Islamic traditions, scholastic theology and philosophy. Deoband enrols students from all parts of the Muslim world. It has a library which contains Arabic, Persian and Urdu manuscripts. It also has a mosque, lecture halls and student residences.

Deodoro da Fonseca, Manuel (1827–92) Brazilian general and politician. A **tarimbeiro**, he served in the front-line in the War of the **Triple Alliance** and was promoted for valour. A traditional Conservative follower of the Marshal Duke of Caxias, he was eventually alienated by Liberal and Conservative politicians' insensitive treatment of the army during the 1880s; idolized by junior officers, he agreed to lead them against the Ouro Preto cabinet on 15 Nov 1889, and was manoeuvered by republicans into declaring against **Pedro II**. A sick man, his presidency (1889–91) rested on the support of the armed forces. He was outmanoeuvred by Congress, but assumed dictatorial powers in early Nov 1891. A few weeks later he was toppled by a constitutionalist revolt under Floriano **Peixoto**.

Department of Regional Economic Expansion (DREE) Canadian Federal Department. In 1969 it became responsible for the administration of the Agricultural Rehabilitation and Development Act (ARDA) and the Fund for Rural Economic Development (FRED). Parliament gave the department extraordinary powers under the Regional Development Incentives Act. The choice of regions or firms which qualified for capital assistance grants was made by the minister appointed by Pierre **Trudeau**, Pierre Marchand. Up to $12 million could be allotted to the projects of his choice and soon the department was involved in many different federal/provincial development schemes, so that by 1979 the department's expenditure had grown to half a billion dollars per year.

Depretis, Agostino (1813–87) Italian politician. A friend of both **Garibaldi** and **Mazzini**, he broke with the latter after the abortive Milanese insurrection of 1853. Depretis played a key part in the Expedition of the **Thousand** to Sicily in 1860, serving for a while as the island's 'prodictator'. Although he began his parliamentary career on the political left, he abandoned his earlier radicalism and achieved ministerial office in 1862 and 1866. He was to be Prime Minister for all but two years in the period 1876–87 and became the arch-exponent of **trasformismo**. Depretis played a key part in orientating Italy towards the **Triple Alliance** with Germany and Austria-Hungary.

De Priest, Oscar Stanton (1871–1951) US politician. Born in Alabama, he ran away from home to Chicago where he was the first black to be elected to the City Council (as a Republican in 1915). He became an alderman in 1927, and the first black congressman from the North in 1928. Holding office until 1934, when he was defeated by a black Democrat, he secured passage for a bill to reduce discrimination in the Civilian Conservation Corps.

Derby, Edward Geoffrey Smith Stanley, 14th Earl (1799–1869) British politician. He entered parliament as a Whig in 1828, and became Chief-Secretary for Ireland (1830) and Colonial Secretary (1833), when he carried the Act for the emancipation of West Indian slaves. In 1834 he withdrew from the party and soon after joined the Conservatives, subsequently becoming party leader, 1846–68. In 1844 he entered the House of Lords as a baronet. He retired from the cabinet in 1845, when **Peel** decided to repeal the **Corn Laws**, and in 1846 headed the Protectionists in the Lords. In 1851 he succeeded his father as Earl of Derby. Leader of minority governments on three occasions (1852, 1858–9 and 1866–8), his third administration nevertheless passed the second Reform Act (1867). ▷ **Conservative Party (UK); Reform Acts; Tories; Whigs**

Dergue The name, meaning 'committee', given to the Provisional Administrative Council in Ethiopia after the military's overthrow of Emperor **Haile Selassie** in 1974 and chaired by Haile Mariam **Mengistu**. Operating like a politburo, its members increasingly also came to fill governmental positions and it was responsible for organizing the creation of the Worker's Revolutionary Party to advance its radical socialist policies.

Déroulède, Paul (1846–1914) French politician and poet. A fervent nationalist, founder of the *Ligue des patriotes* ('League of Patriots') in 1882, and the author of patriotic verses, his writings called for revenge on Germany, and he was active in the campaign against **Dreyfus**. In 1900 he was exiled for 10 years for sedition, but returned in 1905.

Desai, Morarji (Ranchhodji) (1896–) Indian politician. Educated at Bombay University, he became a civil servant, entering politics in 1930. After various ministerial posts, he became a candidate for the premiership in 1964 and 1966, but was defeated by Indira **Gandhi**. He became Deputy Prime Minister but led a breakaway faction of Congress, the Congress (S), following the party's split in 1969. Detained during the state of emergency (1975–7), he was then appointed leader of the newly-formed Janata Party, and elected Premier (1977–9). The Janata government was, however, characterized by internal strife and he was forced to resign in 1979.

desamortización ▷ **disentailment**

Desert Rats Members of the 7th British Armoured Division, which in 1940 took as its badge the jerboa or desert rat, noted for remarkable leaps. The media applied the name generally to all British servicemen in the **North African Campaign**, and it was readily adopted by those not entitled to wear the jerboa shoulder flash. ▷ **World War II**

Deshima A small island in Nagasaki Bay, south-west Japan, the site of a Dutch trading factory between the 17c and 19c. The first Europeans to arrive in Japan were Portuguese and Spanish missionaries in the 16c, followed in the early 17c by Dutch and English traders. Suspicion of Christianity by the Japanese authorities, who perceived it as a political threat, led to the expulsion of the Spanish and Portuguese by the 1630s. The new **Tokugawa Shogunate** officially proclaimed a policy of isolation (*Sakoku*) after 1636, curtailing all foreign trade and contact. The one exception was the permission granted the Dutch to reside and trade at Deshima. It was through Japanese contact with the Dutch that Western learning was introduced into Japan in the 18c and early 19c. A small number of dedicated Japanese scholars translated Dutch texts on anatomy, medicine, shipbuilding, astronomy and gunnery, providing the foundation for early modernization. The significance of Deshima faded once Japan was opened up to Western trade after 1854.

Desmoulins, (Lucie Simplice) Camille (Benoist) (1760–94) French revolutionary and journalist. He studied law in Paris. He played a dramatic part in the storming of the **Bastille**. He was also an influential pamphleteer. A member of the **Cordeliers' Club** from its foundation, he was elected to the National **Convention**, and voted for the death of King **Louis XVI**. He actively attacked the **Girondins**, but by the end of 1793 argued for moderation, thus incurring the hostility of **Robespierre**. He was arrested and guillotined. ▷ **French Revolution**

Dessalines, Jean Jacques (c.1758–1806) Guinea-born Emperor of Haiti. Imported into Haiti as a slave, he was bought by a French planter, whose name he assumed. In the slave insurrection of 1791 he was second only to **Toussaint L'Ouverture**. After compelling the French to leave Haiti (1803), he was created Governor and crowned Emperor as Jacques I. But his cruelty and debauchery alienated his adherents, and he was assassinated near Port-au-Prince.

détente An attempt to lower the tension between states as a means of reducing the possibility of war and of achieving peaceful coexistence between different social and political systems. A prominent feature of relations between the USA and USSR in the 1970s, it led to several agreements over arms (SALT) and security and cooperation (Helsinki). In the early 1980s, there was a cooling towards detente on the part of the USA, on the grounds that too many concessions had been made and that the USSR did not adhere to the spirit of such agreements; but there was a considerable improvement in relations in the later part of the decade. ▷ **Cold War; Helsinki Conference**

Dettingen, Battle of (27 June 1743) Fought during the War of the **Austrian Succession** on the banks of the River Main between British, Hanoverian and Austrian forces, under the nominal command of **George II**, and a French army under Marshal Noailles. The resulting French defeat was not followed up, reducing the battle's strategic importance. This was the last occasion on which a ruling British sovereign took command of troops in battle.

De Valera, Eamon (1882–1975) Irish politician. Brought up on a farm in County Limerick, he became a teacher in Dublin, and was active in various republican movements. A commandant of the Irish Volunteers in the **Easter Rising** (1916), he was arrested and narrowly escaped the firing squad. He became an MP in 1917 and was Leader of **Sinn Féin** from 1917 to 1926. He was elected President of **Dáil Eireann**, and in 1926 became Leader of **Fianna Fáil**, his newly-formed republican opposition party, which won the 1932 elections. As Prime Minister (1932–48, 1951–4 and 1957–9), he instituted social, industrial and agricultural reforms and was instrumental in framing the constitution of 1937, which established the **Irish Free State** as **Eire**. He was President of Ireland from 1959 to 1973.

Devolution, War of (1667–8) A Franco-Spanish conflict prompted by **Louis XIV** of France in pursuit of his wife's legal claims to the Spanish Netherlands. According to the laws of devolution of the provinces of **Brabant** and Hainaut, females of a first marriage took precedence over males of a second with regard to property inheritance. To uphold the claims of Queen **Maria Theresa**, the elder daughter of **Philip IV** of Spain, Louis's armies overran Flanders, prompting the Dutch Republic, England,

and Sweden to negotiate the Triple Alliance (1668); to this, France responded with the invasion of Franche-Comté. When a secret treaty of compromise between Louis and the Emperor **Leopold I** was signed in early 1668, France agreed to peace at the Treaty of Aix-la-Chapelle (2 May 1668).

Devonshire, William Cavendish, 4th Duke of (1720–64) British politician. His family connections enabled him to embark early upon a political career: he became a Whig MP in 1741 and Privy Councillor in 1751. He was appointed Lord Lieutenant and Governor-General of Ireland (1754), succeeding to the dukedom in 1755. He was appointed First Lord of the Treasury by **George II** in 1756 at the beginning of the **Seven Years War**, largely because William **Pitt** 'the Elder', whose inclusion in a war ministry was considered vital, refused to serve under the Duke of Newcastle. He was ineffectual in the post, resigning after six months. He was Lord Chamberlain of the Household from 1757 to 1762.

devşirme In the **Ottoman Empire**, the levy made every five years of one out of every four Christian boys aged between 10 and 20. The youths chosen were then educated and converted to Islam. Many became **Janissaries** but some, like Sokolović, attained high office at court, rising to the office of Grand Vizir. Skanderbeg was also recruited into Ottoman service by this system. The practice of *devşirme* ended in the 17c.

de Wet, Christian (Rudolf) (1854–1922) Afrikaner politician and general. He became conspicuous in the Transvaal war of 1880–1; and in the war of 1899–1902 was the most audacious of all the Boer commanders. In 1907 he became Minister of Agriculture of the Orange River Colony, and in 1914 joined the South African insurrection, but was captured. Sentenced to six years' imprisonment, he was released in 1915. He died in Dewetsdorp district, South Africa. ▷ **Boer Wars**

Dewey, George (1837–1917) US admiral. He served with the Union naval forces in the Civil War (1861–5), and as Commodore in the **Spanish–American War** (1898) defeated the Spanish fleet at Manila Bay without losing a man.

DGB (*Deutscher Gewerkschaftsbund*, 'German Trade Union Federation') Founded in the western zones of Germany in

1949, the DGB was the successor to **Weimar Republic**'s **ADGB** as well as its liberal and Christian trade unions. It embraces 16 individual unions, each representing a major sector of the economy, and by the 1970s had organized over 7 million employees. It is closely involved in most areas of economic and social policymaking and formulates its pay policy (*Tarifpolitik*) in the light of official assessments of Germany's economic health. Consensus rather than confrontation characterizes its actions.

Dhaka (Dacca) Capital of present-day Bangladesh. The town was adorned, as the prosperous capital of Bengal, with fine buildings by Shayista Khan, the Mughal Governor of Bengal (1664–77 and 1680–8). In 1668, the British **East India Company** started a factory in Dhaka, a centre for the purchase of fine cotton and muslin goods. Dhaka was ceded by the Dutch to the British in 1824. Subsequently, it became a hotbed of nationalist political activists such as the Bengali revolutionaries during the Indian Freedom Struggle. Following the partition of India in 1947, Dhaka became the capital of East Pakistan, and later following the formation of Bangladesh in 1971, its capital. ▷ **India, Partition of**

Dharmapala, Anagarika (1864–1930) Sri Lankan nationalist and religious reformer. He was born Don David Hewavitarana and took the name Anagarika Dharmapala as a result of his activities with the Buddhist Theosophical Society. He wrote and spoke as the champion of Buddhist reformism and the interests of the **Sinhala** people, but never formed or led any significant political grouping. Instead he devoted his attention in his later years to campaigning for the return into Buddhist hands of Buddhist sacred sites in North India.

Dharmashastra The 'Law Books', translated in 1776 from the original Sanskrit first into Persian and only then into English at the orders of Warren **Hastings**, then Governor-General of Bengal under the British **East India Company**. These ancient codes of law are generally assigned to various ancient worthies, among whom Manu, who is the author of the law-book of Manu (*Manava Dharmashastra*), is generally regarded as the most important. The *Dharmashastras*, unlike the *Dharmasutras*, deal usually with formal law, and not so much with religious and ethical domestic duties. Amalgamated with English (and some Muslim) law, the *Dharmashastra* helped to frame the colonial legal system, which is still largely used in India today.

Diane de Poitiers (1499–1566) Mistress of **Henry II** of France. She was married at 13 and left a widow at 32; she then won the affections of the boy **Dauphin**, already wedded to **Catherine de' Medici**. On his accession (1547), Diane enjoyed great influence, and was made Duchess of Valentinois. After his death (1559), she retired to her Château d'Anet.

diarchy A system where political authority is divided; associated with constitutional reforms introduced by the British into India in 1919. Under the reforms, some departments of provincial government were under Indian control, while others including finance and security remained under British control. The reforms did not extend to central government, and the system is seen by some as a concession to 'moderate' opinion in an attempt to seduce the Indians into cooperation with the British Raj.

Diaspora The term (literally, 'scattering') used to describe the Jews scattered in the world outside the land of Israel, from either voluntary or compulsory resettlements, such as the Assyrian and Babylonian deportations in the 8c and 6c BC, or later dispersions in the Graeco-Roman period; also known as the Dispersion. The Babylonian Talmud and the Septuagint were important literary products of those Jews that had settled 'abroad'.

Díaz, Armando, Duke (1861–1928) Italian soldier. Wounded in Tripoli in 1913, he was promoted major-general in 1914. He he replaced **Cadorna** after the disaster of **Caporetto** (Nov 1917) and led the Italian Army to victory at **Vittorio Veneto**. He served as War Minister in **Mussolini**'s first cabinet (1922–4) and was made a marshal in 1927.

Díaz, (José de la Cruz) Porfirio (1830–1915) Mexican politician. A follower of Benito **Juárez**, he fought against the conservatives and Emperor **Maximilian**'s French-imposed rule in 1864–7. He seized power in 1876 and was President until 1880, returning in 1884 to remain in office until 1911, when he was ousted by Francisco **Madero**. His long period of office saw the impact of the changes brought about by the laws of La **Reforma**, including the emergence of a wage-earning rural populace, the rise of a powerful northern economy, export-led economic growth stimulated by the railroad and extensive foreign investment. Though a master manipulator, his regime became a gerentocracy, and his patronage of the **científicos'** attempt to 'whiten the nation' meant that he was open to the accusation of having betrayed Mexico to foreign, mainly Anglo-American, interests. Nonetheless, his regime (known as the Porfiriato) did much to stimulate material progress in Mexico. He died in Paris, in the midst of a revolution whose outcome was influenced by the changes he had fomented.

Dictation Test A method used by Australian governments (1902–58) to exclude certain classes of intending immigrants. Based on the example of Natal (1897), under the Immigration Act of 1901, immigrants received a test in a European language. Non-Europeans were the main target, but it was also used with those considered politically undesirable; the most celebrated case was the anti-fascist, Egon Kisch (1885–1948), who was tested in Scottish Gaelic (1934). Kisch was eventually admitted when the High Court decided that this was not a European language. ▷ **White Australia Policy**

dictatorship of the proletariat A term used by Marx to describe the period of transition from capitalism to socialism, when the working class has seized political power either through revolution or through the use of democratic political institutions. Under the influence of **Lenin**, the term was transformed from its original use to that of a dictatorship imposed on behalf of, and ultimately on, the revolutionaries. ▷ **Marxism–Leninism**

Diebitsch, Hans Karl Friedrich, Count (1785–1831) German-born Russian soldier. He joined the Russian army in 1801, and was a major-general in the campaigns of 1805 and 1812–14. In the Russo-Turkish War of 1828–9 he won the surname of Zabalkanski ('Crosser of the Balkans'), and was promoted field marshal. He died of cholera while suppressing the Polish insurrection of 1830–1. ▷ **Russo-Turkish Wars**

Diefenbaker, John George (1895–1979) Canadian politician. In 1940 he entered the Canadian Federal House of Commons, becoming leader of the Progressive Conservatives (1956) and Prime Minister (1957–63) after 22 years of **Liberal Party** rule. His government introduced important agricultural reforms, and extended the federal franchise to Canada's Amerindian peoples. He

remained active in national politics until his death in Ottawa.

Dien Bien Phu A district capital in northwest Vietnam, some 10 miles from the border with Laos, and the site of the major battle which brought an end to the French colonial presence in Vietnam. Dien Bien Phu is situated in a wide valley, surrounded by steep hills. In late 1953, it was reoccupied by French military forces, who intended to use it as a major base to disrupt **Viet Minh** operations. The Vietnam People's Army, under Vo Nguyen Giap, surrounded the base with heavy artillery, dragged up into the hills by human and animal carriers — an extraordinary feat of endurance. The Vietnamese assault began on 13 Mar 1954 and on 7 May the French base was overrun, with over 10 000 prisoners being taken. It was a humiliating defeat for the French.

Diggers A radical group in England formed during the **Commonwealth**, led by Gerrard Winstanley (1609–72), preaching and practising agrarian **communism** on common and waste land. From Apr 1649 they established the Digger community at St George's Hill, Surrey, followed by colonies in nine other southern and Midland counties. The movement was suppressed and its communities dispersed by local landowners. ▷ **Fifth Monarchists**

Diktat The name given to the Treaty of **Versailles** (1919) by its critics in Germany. Adolf **Hitler** and the **Nazi Party** in particular lambasted the republican parties for signing the *Diktat* which had, undoubtedly, triggered resentment and outrage across the political spectrum. The republicans, however, felt they had had no realistic choice but to sign under protest.

Dimitrijević, Dragutin (alias **Apis**) (1876–1917) Serbian army officer. The son of a craftsman, he rose swiftly through the army to become a member of the Serbian General Staff (1901), Head of Intelligence (1913) and a colonel (1916). His reputation rests on his near prodigious enthusiasm for conspiracy: he took part in the assassination of King Alexander **Obrenović** (1903); he founded the secret society the **Black Hand** (1911); he plotted at various times against the kings of Bulgaria and of Greece and Emperor **Francis Joseph**; and he seems to have had a part in the fateful assassination of **Francis Ferdinand**, Archduke of Austria, at Sarajevo (1914). Finally he was executed on a charge, probably trumped up by Nikola **Pašić**, of conspiracy against the Regent, **Alexander I Karageorgević** (1917).

Dimitrov, Gemeto (1903–72) Bulgarian politician. After studying medicine in Belgrade and Sofia, he began to take an active part in left-wing politics as a member of the Pladne Group of the Agrarian Union. Like many others during the dictatorship of **Boris III**, he was arrested and tortured (1935). After the outbreak of **World War II**, he organized opposition to the Tripartite Pact and had to flee to Turkey. He returned to Bulgaria in 1944 and began to reorganize the Agrarian Party. Placed under house arrest, with US assistance he escaped to the USA, where he founded the Bulgarian National Committee and the newspaper, *Free and Independent Bulgaria*.

Dimitrov, Georgi Mikhailovich (1882–1949) Bulgarian politician. A leading figure in the Bulgarian Socialist Party before **World War I**, he helped to found the Bulgarian Communist Party in 1919. After visiting Moscow, he returned to Bulgaria and led an uprising which earned him a death sentence (1923). He fled to Yugoslavia, then lived in Vienna and Berlin and worked for **Comintern**. One of the communist leaders accused of setting fire to the **Reichstag**, he conducted a brilliant defence against the charges engineered by the Nazi prosecution and was acquitted. He then went to Moscow and served as Secretary-General of the Executive Committee of Comintern (1935–43). Returning to Bulgaria in 1945, he was elected President of the Central Committee of the **Fatherland Front** and became Prime Minister after the elections in Oct 1946 which established communist rule. ▷ **Kostov, Traicho; Velchev, Damian**

Ding The name (in Old English, literally 'thing') for the legislative assembly of the early Germanic tribes, consisting of all the freemen of the tribe. It elected the King or Duke, who had unlimited powers in the time of war but who had to give up office in peace time. The Ding also functioned as a court of justice.

Dingane (d.1843) King of the Zulu (1828/40). The successor to Shaka, he ruled at a time of increasing white penetration of Natal. He had good relations with the traders at Port Natal, but became alarmed at land concessions to whites in northern Natal. In Feb 1838 Piet Retief, one of the leaders of the Boer Voortrekkers, secured a grant of land, but he and his party were murdered on Dingane's orders on the same day. Retief was avenged at the Battle of **Blood River**, when Andries Pretorius defeated Dingane. The latter was subsequently overthrown by his brother, Mpande (1840/72), and fled to Swaziland, where he was killed.

Dingiswayo (d.1818) Chief of the Mthethwa, one of the northern Zulu **Nguni** tribe peoples. He is credited with laying the foundations of the Zulu state developed by **Shaka** in the 1820s. Dingiswayo succeeded some time in the 1790s and set about a more centralized system among the northern Nguni, perhaps as a result of developing trade with Delagoa Bay or ecological problems in the region caused by a combination of rising population and severe drought. Dingiswayo began the military revolution taken up by the Zulu, particularly the development of age regiments, and abolished traditional ceremonies like circumcision, but was killed in 1818 following conflict with the rival Ndwandwe group. He was succeeded by **Shaka**.

Ding Ling (Ting Ling) (1902–86) Chinese feminist writer and Communist Party activist. From a landowning family, she went to Shanghai University in 1923–4 and published her first short story in 1927. She became increasingly politicized and joined the Chinese Communist Party in 1932, becoming active in the League of Left-Wing Writers. Arrested and placed under house arrest by the **Guomindang** authorities (1933–6), she succeeded in escaping to the communist stronghold in the north-west. In 1942 Ding Ling was censured in a rectification campaign for a series of stories and essays expressing disillusion with the failure of communist ideals to be put into practice. One essay, in particular, criticized male party attitudes towards women. After 1949 she once again became a member of the literary establishment but in the 1957 anti-rightist campaign she again fell foul of party authorities. She was expelled from the Party and Writers' Union, sent to prison and then to a labour reform camp. She was finally rehabilitated in 1979.

Dinka Eastern Sudanic-speaking transhumant cattle herders of the Upper Nile in the Sudan Republic, occupying a vast area of low-lying and often swampy country. Lacking centralized political authority, they comprise many subgroups recognizing only the authority of religious chiefs.

Diocletian (Gaius Aurelius Valerius Diocletianus) (245–316) Roman Emperor (284/305). A Dalmatian of humble birth, he rose through the ranks of the army to become the greatest of the soldier emperors of the 3c. Diocletian saw the answer to the empire's problems in a division of power at the top and reorganization of the provincial structure below. In 286 the empire was split in two, with Diocletian retaining the East, and **Maximian**, a loyal friend, taking the West. Further refinement followed in 293 when, under the famous tetrarchy, the empire was divided into four. Diocletian abdicated in 305. ▷ **Galerius**

Dionysius the Elder (c.430–367BC) Tyrant of Syracuse (405/367BC) and ruler of half of Sicily. His influence extended over most of southern Italy and his reign was dominated by intermittent warfare with the Carthaginians, his chief rivals for power in Sicily. A patron of the arts, he invited Plato to his court, and even won a prize himself for tragedy at one of the great Athenian dramatic festivals.

Diori, Hamani (1916–87) Niger politician. He was educated in Dahomey and then at the William Ponty School in Dakar. A teacher and then instructor in the language school for colonial administrators (1938–46), he helped form the **Rassemblement Democratique Africain** in 1946 and represented Niger in the French National Assembly (1946–51 and 1956–7). In 1956 he became Prime Minister of Niger and in 1960, at independence, its first President. Building on close relations with France, he ran one of the most stable countries in West Africa, being re-elected in 1965 and 1970, but opposition within his party (the Niger Progressive Party) led to his overthrow in Apr 1974 through a military coup. He was placed under house arrest for 13 years, before he left for Morocco, where he died.

Diouf, Abdu (1935–) Senegalese politician. He studied at Dakar and Paris Universities before graduating with a law degree and returning to Senegal to work as a civil servant. After holding a number of posts, including that of Secretary-General to President **Senghor**, he became Prime Minister in 1970 and succeeded Senghor on the latter's retirement (1 Jan 1981). He was re-elected President of Senegal in 1983 and 1988.

Dipanagara (1785–1855) Javanese prince and the central figure in a major revolt against Dutch colonial rule on Java in the early 19c. The eldest son of Sultan Hamengkubuwana III, but raised by his grandmother away from the court at Yogyakarta, Dipanagara strongly disliked the intrigue, decadence and corrupt European influence found at court. In his early twenties he underwent a profound religious experience which convinced him that he was to be, in the millenarian tradition, the divinely appointed saviour King of Java. Harsh economic conditions and violent conflict within the court in the early 1820s led Dipanagara into open rebellion. The Java War (1825–30) cost some 200000 Javanese lives. In 1830, with the rebellion broken, Dipanagara was exiled from Java, eventually to Makasar, to live out his days.

Directory The government of the First Republic of France (1795–9), established in the Thermidorian reaction to the Reign of **Terror**, with five executive Directors. Its limited franchise and narrow social base added to the difficulties of rampant inflation. After political conspiracies from left and right, it was overthrown by the coup of 18 Brumaire (9–10 Nov), bringing **Napoleon I** to power. ▷ **Brumaire coup; French Revolution; Republic, First** (France); **Thermidor**

di Rudini, Antonio Starabba, Marquis (1839–1908) Italian politician. Having taken part in the revolutionary uprising in his native Sicily before the arrival of **Garibaldi**, di Rudini became Mayor (1864) and then Prefect (1866) of Palermo. He was made Prefect of Naples in 1868. Elected to parliament, he became Minister of the Interior (1869) and Prime Minister (1891–2 and 1896–8). He owed his second term of office to **Crispi**'s fall after the Battle of **Adowa** (1896). He had to resign in 1898 after his extremely tough repression of strikers and left-wing protesters. ▷ **Bava Beccaris, Fiorenzo**

disarmament Arms control which seeks to promote international security by a reduction in armed forces and/or weapons. The levels are set by agreement, and then opened up for inspection and enforcement by the other side or an independent inspectorate. General (ie applies to all countries) and comprehensive (ie applies to all categories of forces and weapons) disarmament was first attempted in 1927 and 1934 by the **League of Nations**, and by the United Nations in the 1950s, but such moves have not been successful. Disarmament is therefore limited to agreements between two or a few countries, and restricted to particular classes of weapons and troop levels. Problems arise in determining equivalences between different types of weapons held by different countries, and in verifying arms reduction treaties, especially in respect of nuclear weapons, largely because weapons can be re-assembled. There is also the possibility of nuclear disarmament involving no agreement with other countries, used as a means of encouraging others to follow. Such *unilateral* action may also be taken for moral reasons and as a means of diminishing the chances of being attacked, particularly as regards nuclear and chemical weapons.

disentailment The modern process of disentailment (*desamortización*) in Spain, which aimed to bolster the royal finances and implement agrarian reform, began under Charles IV in 1798; by 1808, about one sixth of all church property had been disentailed. Major ecclesiastical disentailment in 1833–43 took place. The last and most important period was after the revolution of 1854, when roughly a third of all land changed hands. The beneficiaries were not the urban bourgeoisie, but those whose wealth derived from the state, church and the land; later, bourgeois purchasers joined, rather than replaced, the old class. Although the process accelerated the commercialization of agriculture, it also produced appalling social hardship.

Disraeli, Benjamin, 1st Earl of Beaconsfield (1804–81) British politician. He made his early reputation as a novelist, publishing his first novel, *Vivian Grey*, in 1826. He is better known for his two political novels, *Coningsby* (1844) and *Sybil* (1845), which date from his period as a Romantic Tory, critical of industrial developments. He became leader of the 'Young England' movement which espoused these values, and came to prominence as a critic of **Peel**'s free-trade policies, especially the repeal of the **Corn Laws** (1845–6). He became leader in the Commons of the Conservatives, after the Peelites left the party, and was Chancellor of the Exchequer in Derby's minority governments of 1852 and 1858–9. While Chancellor in the government of 1866–8, he piloted the 1867 Reform Bill through the Commons. He became Prime Minister on **Derby**'s resignation in 1868, but was defeated the same year in the general election. His second administration (1874–80) was notable both for diplomacy and social reform, though much of the latter only consolidated legislation begun under **Gladstone**. During his administration, Britain became half-owner of

the Suez Canal (1875), and the Queen assumed the title Empress of India (1876). His skilful diplomacy at the Congress of **Berlin** (1878) contributed to the preservation of European peace after conflict between the Russians and the Turks in the Balkans. Defeated in 1880 by Gladstone and the Liberals, he then effectively retired, dying the following year. ▷ **Reform Acts; Tories; Victoria**

Disturbances (1935–8) A series of strikes and riots which took place in the British West Indies, sometimes known as 'The Troubles'. These had their roots in post-1918 socio-economic deprivation and this was exacerbated by the **Great Depression** after 1929 and the lack of political representation in the Crown Colonies. Discontent surfaced first in Belize and Jamaica (1934), spread to the sugar workers in St Kitts and Guyana (1935) and culminated in serious disorder in Trinidad, Jamaica and Barbados (1937–8). In Trinidad **Butler**'s oratory provoked the oilfield workers, in Barbados Clement Payne's deportation led to the deaths of 14 people and in Jamaica the Jamaica Worker's Union of **Bustamante** brought rioting to the sugar estates and docks and the arrest of 700 people. Stung into action by the degree of unrest, the imperial government set up the **Moyne Commission**.

Ditch, Battle of the (627) The name given to the siege of Medina by the hostile Meccans. The Prophet **Muhammad**'s defence of Medina at this time, the success of which was in large measure due to the defensive ditch dug around the city, led to a strengthening of the Muslim position physically and, more importantly, morally. After this battle, Muhammad was able finally to eliminate Jewish influence in Medina and the Muslim success against the combined efforts of the Meccans and their allies can be seen as marking the beginning of that final rise in the Muslims' position which was to culminate in the reduction of Mecca in 630, the conversion of the Meccans to Islam, and the pre-eminent standing of the Prophet among the tribes of the Arabian Peninsula as a whole (if not necessarily in their conversion).

divine kingship The notion that rulers are descended from the gods and are therefore themselves deities first propounded in Ancient Egypt. Diffusionists believed that this legitimating idea passed through the kingdom of Kush on the upper Nile to West, East and Central Africa, where there are many instances of states whose rulers underpin their power with this concept. More modern views see divine kingship as being a spontaneous and independent development in many different parts of the world.

Divine Right of Kings The concept of the divinely-ordained authority of monarchs, widely held in the medieval and early modern periods, and often associated with the absolutism of **Louis XIV** of France and the assertions of the House of **Stuart**.

Djilas, Milovan (1911–) Yugoslav politician and writer. Born in Montenegro, he was active in the outlawed Yugoslav Communist Party in the 1930s and was subsequently imprisoned (1933–6). He was, with **Tito**, a remarkable partisan leader during **World War II**. In the post-war government, he was Vice-President of Yugoslavia but concern for doctrine led him to criticize the communist system practised in Yugoslavia. Expelled from the party in 1954 and imprisoned (1956–61 and 1962–6), he was released under amnesty. He was formally rehabilitated by the Yugoslav authorities in 1989.

Djoser (Neterikhet) (c.2700BC) King of Egypt. He was the first king of the 3rd Dynasty at the beginning of the Egyptian **Old Kingdom**. The outstanding monument of his reign was the Step Pyramid at Sakkara, the earliest free-standing stone structure to be built, rising in six stages to a height of 204 feet. It formed part of a complex of buildings such as imitation shrines connected to the magical celebrations of the Sed-festival or jubilee of the dead king. The architect responsible for the monument was Imhotep, later deified and identified with Asclepios by the Greeks. The reliefs and architectural features, together with a masterly seated statue of Djoser, demonstrate the technical skill reached at this early stage of the Old Kingdom.

Dmitri (1583–91) Russian prince. The youngest son of Tsar **Ivan IV, 'the Terrible'**, he appears to have been murdered. It was popularly believed at the time that his murderer was the regent, **Boris Godunov**. In about 1603 Dmitri was impersonated by a runaway Moscow monk, Grigori Otrepiev. The latter, dubbed the 'false Dmitri', was crowned Tsar by the army in 1605 but killed in a rebellion the following year. Other subsequent pretenders suffered a similar fate.

DNVP (*Deutsch nationale Volks partei*, 'German National People's Party')

German political party. Founded in late Nov 1918 by a coalition of conservative politicians, the DNVP came to represent much of the old, German imperial élite. It never accepted the legitimacy of the new **Weimar Republic**, cooperated sporadically and unwillingly in coalition governments, and pursued particularly virulent campaigns against any compromise agreements between Germany and her erstwhile enemies. In Jan 1933 the DNVP entered a coalition with the **Nazi Party** which paved the way for **Hitler**'s overthrow of the republic, before dissolving itself in the middle of that year.

Dobi, Istvan (1898–1968) Hungarian politician. He spent the earlier part of his life as a day labourer on various characteristically large estates. He had a brief experience as a soldier in the Hungarian Red Army in 1919, but it was not until 1935 that he joined the Independent Smallholders Party. During and after **World War II** he rose within its ranks and, as leader of its left wing, became Prime Minister within the predominantly communist government of 1949. He remained in office until 1952 during the worst of the Stalinist purges, and was president of the state council through to 1967, including during the **Hungarian Uprising** of 1956.

Dobrudja The region lying between the Black Sea and the Danube, now divided between Bulgaria and Romania. Settled by the **Greeks**, Romans, Byzantines, **Goths**, Alani and **Huns**, and conquered by the Ottoman Turks, in the 18–19c it was the object first of Russian, then of Romanian and Bulgarian ambitions. ▷ **Romanians**

Dobrynin, Anatoly Fedorovich (1919–) Soviet diplomat and politician. He worked as an engineer at an aircraft plant during **World War II**, then joined the diplomatic service in 1946. He served as Counsellor at the Soviet Embassy in Washington (1952–5), assistant to the Minister for Foreign Affairs (1955–7), Under-Secretary at the **UN** (1957–9) and head of the USSR's American Department (1960–1), before being appointed the Soviet ambassador to Washington (1962–86). Dobrynin played an important part in resolving the **Cuban Missile Crisis** in 1962 and was influential in promoting Soviet–US entente. A member of the Communist Party (CPSU) from 1945, he became a full member of its Central Committee in 1971. In 1986, the new Soviet leader, Mikhail **Gorbachev**, appointed him Secretary for Foreign Affairs and head of the International Department. He retired in 1988.

Doctors' Plot (1952–3) Alleged plot by nine doctors, seven of them Jewish and all paid by the USA, to get rid of several Soviet politicians. It was a fabrication by the secret police and was intended to prepare the ground for a public trial that would herald a new round of **Stalin**'s purges. Anti-Semitism and anti-Americanism were judged to be good bases on which to win support for removing Stalin's opponents. Fortunately Stalin died, and Nikita **Khrushchev** subsequently used this and other evidence to condemn his entire behaviour.

Doe, Samuel Kenyon (1951–90) Liberian soldier and politician. He joined the army as a private in 1969, reaching the rank of sergeant in 1975. In Apr 1980 he led a coup of junior officers in which President **Tolbert** was killed. In 1981 he made himself general and army Commander-in-Chief and established a party (the National Democratic Party of Liberia) in 1984 under whose aegis he narrowly won the 1985 presidential election. Widespread dissatisfaction with his rule generated several opposition groups and a virtual civil war erupted in 1989, which the **ECOWAS** attempted to mediate. Doe was killed in the ensuing internal struggle for power.

Dogali Ambush (1887) A dramatic defeat for the Italian Army in which 500 troops were massacred by Abyssinians resisting Italy's policy of forcing trade through the port of Massawa on the Red Sea (acquired by Italy in 1885). Public outcry led to an Italian blockade of Abyssinia until Emperor John IV agreed to pay compensation and to use Massawa as a trading post. Nonetheless, Dogali was seen as a major blow to national pride, which was to find an echo in the defeat at **Adowa** nine years later.

Doihara Kenji (1883–1948) Japanese army general. He served in China (1913–20) and in 1931 became Director of Military Intelligence at Mukden in Manchuria. Doihara was a key participant in the Japanese military's plans to overrun Manchuria, which culminated in the creation of the Japanese puppet-state of **Manzhuguo** in 1933. He then became involved in a relentless campaign to expand Japan's influence in north China, a campaign that was ultimately to lead to full-scale war with China in 1937. In 1948 Doihara was executed as a Class A war criminal.

Doi Takako (1929–) Japanese politician. After lecturing on the Japanese constitution at Doshisha University, she entered the Diet in 1969 and since 1986 has been the leader of the Japanese Socialist Party, the first woman party leader in Japan. In 1989, she became the Leader of the Upper House.

Dolgorukova, Katarina, Princess Yurevskaya (1847–1922) Russian noblewoman. She was the mistress of Emperor **Alexander II**, who married her in 1880 after his first wife's death. Under the pseudonym of Victor Laferté, she published *Alexandre II, Détails inédits sur sa vie intime et sa mort* (1882). Her *Mémoires* (1890) were suppressed by the Russian government.

Dolle Mina Dutch feminist movement, named after *Dolle* ('Wild') Wilhel*mina* Drucker (1847–1925), an early Dutch activist for the emancipation of women. Growing out of the political upheaval in the late 1960s, the name *Dolle Mina* was first used in 1970, when for a few years the world saw a number of demonstrations designed to promote awareness of women's issues and rights, such as equal pay, child care, divorce, and abortion. After 1972 membership declined.

Dollfuss, Engelbert (1892–1934) Austrian politician. He studied in Vienna and **Berlin**, and became leader of the Christian Socialist Party. As Chancellor (1932–4), he suspended parliamentary government, drove the socialists into revolt and militarily crushed them (Feb 1934). In July 1934 an attempted Nazi putsch in Vienna culminated in his assassination. ▷ **Nazi Party**

Domela Nieuwenhuis, Ferdinand (1846–1919) Dutch socialist and anarchist leader. He began his career as a Lutheran minister, but left the Church in 1879 when he became a socialist, founding the newspaper 'Rights for All' (*Recht voor Allen*). He was Secretary of the Social-Democratic League, the first Dutch socialist party (1882–7), and was imprisoned in 1886–7 for treasonous newspaper articles, and elected to parliament in 1888–91. Thereafter he rejected the parliamentary way, and became an anarchist, co-founding the National Labour Secretariat in 1893 as a socialist trade-union federation. Often ridiculed for his extreme views, he was nonetheless one of the founders of the modern Dutch socialist labour movement. He had numerous international socialist contacts, and the widespread emotional support he enjoyed amongst working people was shown at his funeral when tens of thousands poured into Amsterdam for the occasion.

Domesday Book The great survey of England south of the Ribble and Tees Rivers (London and Winchester excepted), compiled in 1086 on the orders of **William I**; sometimes spelled Doomsday Book. Information is arranged by county and, within each county, according to tenure by major landholders; each manor is described according to value and resources. Domesday is one of the greatest administrative achievements of the **Middle Ages**, yet its central purpose remains unclear. Most probably, it was to assist the royal exploitation of crown lands and feudal rights, and to provide the new nobility with a formal record and confirmation of their lands, thus putting a final seal on the Norman occupation. ▷ **Norman Conquest**

Dominic, St (c.1170–1221) Spanish founder of the Order of Friars Preachers. He studied at Palencia, where he acquired such a name for piety and learning that he was made a canon in 1193. He led a life of rigorous asceticism, and was especially devoted to missionary work, notably among the **Albigenses** of southern France. His preaching order was approved by Pope Honorius III in 1216. By the time of his death, at Bologna, his order occupied 60 houses, and had spread as far as England, where from their dress the monks were called Black Friars. He was canonized in 1234 by **Gregory IX**. ▷ **Honorius**

Dominion of Canada Established on 1 July 1867, by the **British North America Act** of 29 Mar, the Dominion consisted of three provinces, Canada (now divided into Quebec and Ontario), Nova Scotia and New Brunswick, all united by the **Confederation Movement**. Desire for unification had intensified because of the need for improvements in transport and because of the proximity of the USA, which instilled emulation as well as fear. The ending of **reciprocity** in 1866 and the failure of the USA to curb the **Fenians** perhaps accentuated the provinces' link with the British crown, which was a distinguishing feature of the confederation (although the term 'Dominion' was chosen rather than 'Kingdom' in deference to US republican sentiment). Manitoba joined the Dominion in 1870, British Columbia in 1871, Prince Edward Island in 1873, Alberta and Saskatchewan in 1905, and Newfoundland in

1949. ▷ **Brown, George; Cartier, George Étienne; Compact Theory of Confederation; Macdonald, John Alexander**

domino theory A strategic theory first used by President **Eisenhower** in 1954, reflecting the view that, as neighbouring states are so interdependent, the collapse of one will spread to the others. Originally referring to the belief that if one country became Communist, others would follow, the theory relates to military collapse, as well as insurgence, and has been used to justify intervention in a country not immediately threatened, but whose neighbour is. It was an important element in the US policy of intervention in South-East Asia in the 1960s and 1970s, and in Central America in the 1980s. ▷ **Vietnam War**

Domitian (Titus Flavius Domitianus) (AD51–96) Roman Emperor (AD81/96). He was the younger son of **Vespasian**, and the last of the Flavian emperors. An able but autocratic ruler, he thoroughly alienated the ruling class by his rapacity and tyrannical ways. Becoming paranoid about opposition after the armed revolt of Saturninus, the Governor of Upper Germany (AD89), he unleashed a reign of terror in Rome which lasted until his own assassination. ▷ **Agricola, Gnaeus Julius; Flavian Dynasty**

DOM-TOM (*Départements d'outre-mer* and *Territoires d'outre-mer*, 'Overseas Departments and Territories') French colonial possessions which are now treated as being an integral part of French metropolitan territory, electing representatives to the French National Assembly, etc. They were part of the **French Union** (*Union française*), established in 1946, renamed the *Communauté* ('Community') in 1958, and are all that remained when the other colonies and associated states (protectorates) became independent.

Donald III ('Donald Bane') (c.1033–c.1100) King of Scots (1093/4 and 1094/7). He was the younger son of **Duncan I**, who seized the throne on **Malcolm III**'s death and killed Malcolm's eldest son, **Duncan II**. Donald's reign was brief and turbulent. He was briefly supplanted by Duncan II and finally overthrown in 1097 by an English army in support of the claim of Edgar, Malcolm's eldest surviving son by his marriage to Margaret, 'Maid of Norway'. Edgar had him blinded and he was buried on Iona.

Donglin (Tunglin) Movement A movement of political and moral reform led by scholars and officials in China during the 1620s. Associated with the Donglin Academy, established in 1604 in the city of Wuxi near Shanghai, the movement advocated a return to classical Confucianism and condemned corruption at court. During the reign of Ming Tianqi (1620/7) Donglin followers gained official positions and became deeply involved in factional politics. Their criticism of misgovernment brought them into conflict with the powerful eunuch Wei Zhongxian (1568–1627), who launched a terror campaign against them. Most were dismissed from office and some were executed.

Dong Zhongshu (Tung Chung-shu) (c.179–104BC) Chinese philosopher of the Han Dynasty. His eclectic Confucianism, incorporating contemporary cosmological notions, became the basis of the official state orthodoxy during the reign of **Han Wudi**. Dong exalted the position of the ruler, whose function was to ensure the preservation of a harmonious and hierarchical order reflecting that of the cosmos. As the intermediary between Heaven and Earth, the ruler's position was paramount; any disorder or natural calamity, however, could be interpreted as the ruler's failure to govern in accordance with the correct moral precepts. ▷ **Han Dynasties**

Dönitz, Karl (1891–1980) German Nazi politician and naval commander. He entered the submarine service of the German Navy in 1916, and became a staunch advocate of **U-boat** warfare. He planned **Hitler**'s U-boat fleet, was made its commander in 1936, and in 1943 became Commander-in-Chief of the German Navy. Becoming *Führer* on the death of Hitler, he was responsible for the final surrender to the Allies, and in 1946 was sentenced to 10 years' imprisonment for war crimes. ▷ **World War II**

Donoughmore Commission A committee sent by the British government to Ceylon in 1927 to examine the Ceylonese constitution and recommend reforms. These recommendations were reluctantly accepted by Ceylonese political leaders and served as the basis for the new constitution of 1931. The reforms replaced communal electorates by territorial constituencies and extended the franchise to all resident adults. An assembly or state council with legislative and executive powers was also established under the recommendations of the Donoughmore Commis-

sion. The new constitution was in effect until 1946.

Dopolavoro (*Opera Nazionale Dopolavoro*) In Italy, the national network of clubs and other recreational and welfare centres established by the fascists in 1925. The membership of the *Dopolavoro* (literally, 'after work') expanded massively to include 4 million by 1939. The Dopolavoro provided bars, sports facilities, libraries, dances and concerts as well as organizing holidays and was undoubtedly one of the most successful and popular innovations of the fascist state. ▷ **Balilla; fascism; Fascist Party**

Dordrecht (Dordt), Synod of (13 Nov 1618–9 May 1619) An important church council held in the Dutch Republic to resolve the disputes between the **Remonstrants** and the **Counter-Remonstrants**. The Dutch Calvinists had been squabbling for some time over theology, and the Synod was a resounding victory for the orthodox Counter-Remonstrants, who silenced or banished their enemies. The Synod promulgated many of the documents which have been the foundation of Dutch Calvinism, and commissioned the great States Bible translation, comparable to the English Authorized Version. The Synod had a political impact: the Orangist party had supported the Counter-Remonstrants, and with their victory they were able to dispose of many enemies, and to relaunch the war with Spain, ending the **Twelve Years' Truce**.

Dorgon (1612–50) Manchu prince. The 14th son of **Nurhaci**, he commanded the Manchu armies that invaded China in 1644. As regent for the first Manchu Emperor of China, Shunzhi (1644/61), Dorgon oversaw the completion of the Manchu conquest of China. He amassed much personal power, alienating the other Manchu princes in the process. Although he was responsible for the forced imposition of the queue (or pigtail) amongst the Chinese as a sign of subservience to the Manchus, he also made use of Chinese officials in government and continued to rely on Chinese institutions. He died while on a hunting trip and was posthumously denounced for usurping power.

Doria, Andrea (c.1466–1560) Genoese mercenary and admiral. After serving under various Italian princes, he was given command of the Genoese fleet, defeating the Turks in 1519. When the imperial faction

277

came to power (1522), he transferred his allegiance to **Francis I** of France, and commanded the French fleet, defeating Emperor **Charles V** in Italy and Provence. After a period of papal service, he rejoined the French, but in 1529, fearing Francis's power, he went over to Charles V, entered Genoa, and established an oligarchy under his domination. He continued to fight the Turks with many successes, but was defeated at Algiers (1541) and Djerba (1560). His family continued to rule at Genoa until the end of the 18c.

Dorians A sub-group of Hellenic peoples, thought to have migrated into southern Greece around 1100BC. Dorian settlements there included **Argos**, **Corinth** and **Sparta**; later Dorian foundations include Halicarnassus and **Syracuse**.

Doriot, Jacques (1898–1945) French politician. A metalworker, communist Deputy (1924) and Mayor of St Denis, a working-class suburb of Paris, he was excluded from the **Communist Party** in 1934 for advocating a **Popular Front** before it was adopted as party policy. He then co-founded the *Parti populaire français* ('French People's Party'), regarded as the only fascist-type party in France to have much popular support. However, it had already entered a period of crisis in 1938. During **World War II** he collaborated with the Germans, organizing the LVF (*Légion des volontaires français contre le bolchévisme*, 'League of French Volunteers against Bolshevism') to fight on the Eastern Front. At the liberation he fled to Germany, where he was killed in an Allied air raid. ▷ **collaboration** (France)

Dos Santos, Jose Eduardo (1942–) Angolan nationalist and politician. He joined the **MPLA** in 1961 and was forced into exile in Zaire, where he founded the MPLA Youth League. In 1963 he went to the USSR to study petroleum engineering and telecommunications and then to Lisbon to study medicine. He returned to Angola in 1970 to participate in the war of liberation, being responsible for the MPLA's medical services. A close confidant of Agostinho **Neto**, he became Foreign Minister on independence and First Deputy Prime Minister, Planning Minister and head of the National Planning Commission. When Neto died in 1979, he succeeded to the presidency and, conscious that the cost of fighting **UNITA** with its South African backers was destroying Angola, negotiated the withdrawal of Cuban and

South African forces in 1989 and then a ceasefire between MPLA and UNITA.

Dost Muhammad (1783–1863) Ruler of Afghanistan (1826/38 and 1843/63). He lost Peshawar from the Afghan state in 1834, and subsequently made claims to the British on Peshawar. Dost Muhammad was ousted in 1839 by Shah Shuja, a descendant of Afghan kings, and the British. Following his defeat by British forces in 1840, Dost Muhammad surrendered. Upon Lord Ellenborough's proclamation, Dost Muhammad returned to the throne of Afghanistan in 1843, later becoming a British ally as a result of a treaty signed in 1855. He was assisted by the British in some subsequent battles against the Persians, and died at the age of 80 after recapturing Herat from the Persians.

Douglas A Scottish family which includes William the Hardy, Crusader, who harried the monks of Melrose and joined **Wallace** in the rising against the English in 1297. His son, Sir James Douglas (c.1286–1330), called also 'the Black Douglas' from his swarthy complexion, effectively shared command with Robert **Bruce** of Scottish forces victorious at the Battle of **Bannockburn** (1314). The hero of 70 fights, he was slain in Andalusia. His son, William, died at the Battle of **Halidon Hill**; and the next Lord of Douglas, Hugh, brother of James, made over the now great domains of the family in 1342 to his nephew, Sir William. ▷ **Scottish War of Independence**

Douglas, Stephen Arnold (1813–61) US political leader. Appointed to the Illinois Supreme Court in 1841, he was elected to the House of Representatives, where he served from 1843–47, and then to the US Senate, serving from 1847 to 1861. In 1858 he ran against Abraham **Lincoln** in the senatorial race, participating in a number of debates that gained national attention for Lincoln. Douglas's position on slavery in the territories was that each territory should decide for itself. In 1860 he was nominated for the presidency, but was defeated by Lincoln.

Douglas, William Orville (1898–1980) US judge. Educated at Whitman College and Columbia University, he was a law professor at Yale, then a member (1936) and chairman (1937–39) of the Securities and Exchange Commission. A strong supporter of the New Deal legislation, he was appointed to the Supreme Court in 1939 to replace Louis **Brandeis**. As a justice he strongly supported civil rights and liberties, and guarantees of freedom of speech. He wrote *We the Judges* (1956), *A Living Bill of Rights* (1961) and autobiographical works and many books on his travels.

Douglas-Home, Sir Alec ▷ Home of the Hirsel, Baron

Douglass, Frederick (c.1817–95) US abolitionist. Born into slavery, he escaped in 1838, and in 1841 emerged as a major anti-slavery force. He founded the abolitionist paper *North Star* in Rochester in 1847 and edited it for 17 years. During the Civil War he encouraged Negroes to join Union forces. He also supported the cause of women's rights, and became US Minister to Haiti. ▷ **abolitionism**

Doumer, Paul (1857–1932) French politician. He was a working jeweller, journalist, Deputy (1888), and then Governor-General of French **Indochina** from 1897 to 1902 (where he is credited with the creation of the modern French colonial state). Doumer was President of the Chamber (1905–6), of the Senate (1927–31), and of the Third Republic (1931–2). He was shot by a Russian émigré, Gorgalov. ▷ **Republic, Third** (France)

Doumergue, Gaston (1863–1937) French politician and first Protestant President of the French Republic (1924–31). He was Prime Minister in 1913–14 and 1934 (when he failed to carry constitutional changes); and President of the Senate 1923–4. ▷ **Republic, Third** (France)

Dover, Treaty of (1670) A treaty, some of whose terms were kept secret from the British parliament and some of the King's ministers, between **Charles II** of Great Britain and **Louis XIV** of France. Under its terms, Charles received French subsidies and agreed to maintain amity with France and, at an appropriate time, declare himself a convert to Roman Catholicism. Charles received almost £750 000 during the 1670s, a crucial supplement to inadequate income. Though the secret terms were not revealed until 1682, they were guessed by many in parliament in the later 1670s, doing much to sour relations with the King. ▷ **Exclusion Crisis; Popish Plot**

Dowding, Hugh (Caswell Tremenheere), 1st Baron (1882–1970) British air chief marshal. He served in the Royal Artillery and the Royal Flying Corps in **World War I**. As Commander-in-Chief of Fighter Command

(1936–40), he organized the air defence of Britain during **World War II**, which resulted in the victorious Battle of **Britain** (1940). He retired in 1942 and was created a peer in 1943.

Dozsa, Gyorgy (d.1514) Hungarian soldier. He was ennobled for his exploits in fighting the Turks as a member of the Belgrade garrison. In 1514 Archbishop Tamas Bakocz appointed him to command a crusade. However, fired by the grievances of the peasants who joined his army, and frustrated by the delaying tactics of the majority of the Hungarian nobles, he turned away from the Turks and marched against them instead. Despite his initial success and his heroism, he was defeated at Temesvár and put cruelly to death.

Draco (fl.7c BC) Athenian legislator. His harsh codification of the law in 621 BC has given us the word 'draconian'. With death the penalty for almost every offence, the code was so unpopular that it was largely abolished by **Solon** (594 BC); only Draco's ruling on homicide remained.

Draft US conscription. It was introduced first in 1777 when the number of volunteers failed to meet the quotas demanded by the **Continental Congress**. During the **American Civil War** it was enacted first by the South in 1862, followed by the North in 1863. Both acts caused great opposition, with a major riot taking place in New York, because the draft flouted the US tradition of voluntary service, while in the South it was believed to be an abuse of states' rights. On both sides, provisions for substitution and exemption gave rise to the slogan 'a rich man's war and a poor man's fight'. The draft was introduced for **World War I** with the passage of the Selective Service Act of 1917, and again in 1940 in anticipation of the United States' entry into **World War II**, and again in various crises such as the invasion of Korea, the **Berlin Airlift**, and the **Cuban Missile Crisis**. Much of the opposition to the **Vietnam War**, especially the student protest, centred on the draft. Eventually offenders numbered 570 000, so that under President Richard **Nixon** a fairer lottery system was introduced in 1969, with the draft itself being ended in 1973.

dragonnades In France, a system of billeting troops on Protestant households in order to 'persuade' them to convert to Catholicism. It was instituted in 1681 and continued for the rest of the reign of **Louis XIV**.

Drake, Sir Francis (c.1540–96) English seaman and explorer. In 1567 he commanded the *Judith* in his kinsman John Hawkins's ill-fated expedition to the West Indies, and returned there several times to recover the losses sustained from the Spaniards, his exploits gaining him great popularity in England. In 1577 he set out with five ships for the Pacific, through the Straits of Magellan, but after his fleet was battered by storm and fire, he alone continued in the *Golden Hind*. He then struck out across the Pacific, reached Pelew Island, and returned to England via the Cape of Good Hope in 1580 having circumnavigated the globe. The following year, Queen **Elizabeth I** visited his ship and knighted him. In 1585 he sailed with 25 ships against the Spanish Indies, bringing home tobacco, potatoes, and the dispirited Virginian colonists. In the battle against the Spanish **Armada** (1588), which raged for a week in the Channel, his seamanship and courage brought him further distinction. In 1595 he sailed again to the West Indies, but died of dysentery off Porto Bello.

Drakon ▷ **Draco**

Drapeau, Jean (1916–) Canadian politician. He became Mayor of Montreal in 1954, backed both by those wanting improved municipal services and those who demanded the elimination of gambling and prostitution. Drapeau sought more autonomy for the city and when he was thwarted by **Duplessis** he became a strong critic of the provincial Premier. When the **October Crisis** occurred in 1970 Drapeau, along with the Montreal chief of police and Robert **Bourassa**, asked the federal government to implement the **War Measures Act**. When Pierre Laporte's body was found, Montreal public opinion was so hardened that Drapeau was given 92 per cent of the votes in the following city elections. His administration backed Expo 67 (when General de **Gaulle** delivered his notorious 'Vive le Québec libre' speech), and Montreal's successful bid to hold the 1976 Olympic Games, and although the financial entanglements were still being unravelled in 1980, the increase in jobs certainly benefited the working population.

Dravida Munnetra Kazhagam (DMK) A Tamil regional nationalist party and now one of the two main political parties in the southern Indian state of Tamil Nadu. The DMK traces its origins to the Dravidian movement of the 19c, as well as to the Non-Brahmin movement of the 20c. It stands

primarily for the promotion of Tamil regional cultural identity. After the death of its leader C N Annadurai in 1969, the DMK split into its two present offshoots, the DMK and the AIADMK. The AIADMK ruled Tamil Nadu from 1977 to 1987. The DMK was then briefly returned to power with Karunanidhi as Chief Minister, but lost heavily in the 1991 elections.

Dred Scott v Sandford (1857) US Supreme Court case in which the slave Dred Scott sued for his freedom on the grounds of residence in a free state (Illinois) and territory (Wisconsin) to which a former owner had taken him. The US Supreme Court Chief Justice Roger B Taney ruled that slaves were not US citizens and therefore lacked standing in the court. Going beyond the case, the court also ruled that the **Missouri Compromise**, which excluded slavery from the northern territories, was unconstitutional. This decision and other remarks by Taney, such as his comment that blacks had no rights which a white man was bound to respect, increased sectional tension and helped to bring on the **American Civil War**.

Drees, Willem (1886–1988) Dutch politician. After a short period working in a bank, he moved to the Hague as a government stenographer and then entered politics, joining the Socialist Democratic Workers' Party and becoming its chairman in 1911. He sat in the Second Chamber from 1933 until the German invasion of 1940, after which he played an important part in the resistance movement. In 1947, as Minister of Social Affairs, he introduced the state pension and then became Prime Minister (1948–58). A modest, puritanical man, he became one of the most durable figures in Dutch politics.

Drees, Willem (1922–) Dutch economist and politician. The son of Willem **Drees** (1886–1988), after graduating at the Netherlands School of Economics, Rotterdam, he joined the International Monetary Fund (IMF) in Washington (1947–50), and then worked in the Dutch embassy in Jakarta (1950–5). He returned to the Netherlands as Director of the Budget in the Ministry of Finance, as well as being Professor of Public Finance at Rotterdam.

Dresden, Battle of (1813) **Napoleon I**'s last victory in Germany, fought outside the Saxon capital, Dresden, then a major French depot, against an allied force of Austrian, Prussian, and Russian troops under Prince Schwarzenberg (1771–1820). The French, however, were denied complete success, being twice defeated by the Allies in the following ten days. ▷ **Napoleonic Wars**

Dresden, Treaty of (1745) This treaty ended the second of the **Silesian Wars** in which **Frederick II, 'the Great'** of Prussia retained Silesia but had to recognize **Francis I** as Holy Roman Emperor.

Dreyfus, Alfred (1859–1935) French Jewish army officer. An artillery captain on the General Staff, in 1893–4 he was falsely charged with delivering defence secrets to the Germans. He was court-martialled and transported to Devil's Island, French Guiana. The efforts of his wife and friends to prove him innocent provoked a vigorous response from militarists and anti-Semites, and deeply divided the French intellectual and political world. After the case was tried again (1899), he was found guilty but pardoned, and in 1906 the verdict was reversed. Proof of his innocence came when German military documents were uncovered in 1930.

Druze A religious faith which originated during the closing years of the Fatimid caliph al-Hakim (996–1021), who some extremist Ismailis regarded as a manifestation of the Divinity. The Druze, who survive in parts of Jordan, Lebanon, and Syria, deviate considerably in belief and practice from the main Muslim body. They await the return from divine concealment of both al-Hakim and his disciple, Hamza ibn Ali. They assemble on Thursdays, instead of the usual Fridays, reject many of the prescriptions of the Shari'a, affirm monogamous marriage, and believe in the transmigration of souls. Today they number c.500 000.

Dual Alliance (1879) A defensive alliance between the German and Austro-Hungarian Empires, assuring 'reciprocal protection' from direct Russian attack, and at least benevolent neutrality in case of an attack from any other power. It expanded to the **Triple Alliance** in 1882, by the inclusion of Italy, and remained the focus of German and Austro-Hungarian foreign policy until 1918. ▷ **Austria-Hungary, Dual Monarchy of**

Duan Qirui (Tuan Ch'i-jui) (1865–1926) Chinese politician. He took up a military career, rising to prominence as a protégé of **Yuan Shikai**, becoming his Prime Minister and remaining in office after his death (1916). His aim was to reunite the country, but his resort to force and his increasing dependence on Japan proved highly unpopular in China, and the Northern generals facing the Southern Nationalist regime refused to fight. His decision to force them to obey plunged China into the successive civil wars of its 'period of warlordism' (1916–25), in which four groups fought for control. Defeated, he retired from politics in 1920, except for a brief return in 1924. ▷ **warlords**

Duarte, José Napoléon (1925–90) El Salvador politician. Trained as a civil engineer in the USA, he founded the Christian Democratic Party (PDC) in 1960. After serving as Mayor of El Salvador (1964–70), he was elected President in 1972 but was soon impeached and exiled for seven years in Venezuela. He returned and in 1980 regained the presidency with US backing. He lost the 1982 election and for two years witnessed a fierce struggle between right- and left-wing elements. He returned as President in 1984 but in 1988, stricken by terminal cancer, was forced to resign.

Dubček, Alexander (1921–92) Czechoslovak politician. After living with his parents in the USSR from 1925 to 1938, he returned home and joined the Communist Party in 1939, worked underground during **World War II** and took part in the Slovak uprising in 1944. He rose through various Party and parliamentary offices to become a full member of the Presidium in 1963 and, on the forced resignation of Antonín Novotný, First Secretary in Jan 1968. He began to introduce a series of far-reaching reforms, including the abolition of censorship and increased freedom of speech. His political liberalization policy during the **Prague Spring** provoked Soviet hostility to what he called **Socialism with a Human Face** and led to the occupation of Czechoslovakia by **Warsaw Pact** forces (Aug 1968). In 1969 he was replaced as First Secretary by Gustav Husák. He became President of the Federal Assembly for a few months in 1969, but was then expelled from the Presidium and deprived of Party membership in 1970. In 1989, following the popular uprising and the resignation of the communist government, he became Chairman of the new Federal Assembly. Not quite as radical as the post-1989 reformers, he did not play a prominent political role and, before he could develop one, he died as the result of a car accident.

Dubois, Guillaume (1656–1723) French prelate. The son of a poor apothecary, he was first tutor and then secretary to the Duke of Chartres; when the latter (Philippe, Duke of **Orléans**) became Regent in 1715, Dubois was virtually all powerful. He was appointed Foreign Minister and Archbishop of Cambrai (1720), a cardinal (1721), and Prime Minister of France (1722).

Du Bois, William Edward Burghardt

(1868–1963) US civil rights activist, historian and sociologist. He studied at Fisk, Harvard, and Berlin, and in his writings explored the history and lives of black Americans. In politics he campaigned for full equality, opposing the tactics of Booker T **Washington**. He helped found the National Association for the Advancement of Colored People (**NAACP**), and in his later years lived in Ghana, where he died.

Dubrovnik, Republic of A wealthy independent city state after 1358, when it ceased to acknowledge Venetian suzerainty, Dubrovnik was governed by an oligarchy of noble families. A flourishing centre of trade, literature and art, in 1667 it was almost totally destroyed in an earthquake. Occupied by **Napoleon I**'s army in 1806, it lost its status as an independent republic in 1808, after which it became part of the **Illyrian Provinces** (1809–13). The Congress of **Vienna** (1814–15) granted the republic to Austria and, as part of the province of Dalmatia, it remained subject to Vienna until 1918, when it became part of the Kingdom of Serbs, Croats and Slovenes (later Yugoslavia).

Duce The Italian word (lit. 'leader') commonly applied to **Mussolini**; it corresponds with **Hitler**'s title, *Führer*.

Dulles, John Foster (1888–1959) US politician. Educated at Princeton and the Sorbonne, he became a lawyer. During **World War II** he advocated a world governmental organization, and in 1945 advised at the Charter Conference of the **UN**, thereafter becoming US delegate to the General Assembly. In 1953 he became US Secretary of State, and was known chiefly for his aggressive anti-communist rhetoric and his policy of brinkmanship.

Duma The name given to various forms of political assembly in pre-revolutionary Russia, such as the medieval 'Boyars' Council'. Municipal *dumas* (town councils) similar to the rural *zemstvos* were introduced as part of local government reforms in 1870. After the Russian **Revolution of 1905**, the State

Duma, a quasi-parliamentary body, was established with progressively limited constitutional powers. Four State Dumas were elected between 1906 and the 1917 revolution, when the institution was abolished. ▷ **Russian Revolution; zemstvo**

Dumouriez, Charles François (du Périer) (1739–1823) French general. In 1792 he defeated the Prussians at Valmy and the Austrians at Jemappes, but in 1793 lost to the Austrians at Neerwinden. His leanings towards the monarchy caused him to be denounced by the revolutionaries, and to save his head he went over to the Austrians. He later settled in England. ▷ **French Revolutionary Wars**

Dunant, (Jean) Henri (1828–1910) Swiss philanthropist. He inspired the foundation of the international **Red Cross** after seeing the plight of the wounded on the battlefield of **Solferino**. His efforts brought about the conference at Geneva (1863) from which came the **Geneva Convention** (1864), and in 1901 he shared the first Nobel Peace Prize.

Dunbar, Battle of (27 Apr 1296) The battle fought between English and Scottish forces after Scottish magnates had deprived King John (**Balliol**) of independent authority and had negotiated alliances with France and Norway. **Edward I** marched north and his victory resulted in Balliol's resignation of the throne. He was taken to England as prisoner. Scotland remained without a King until Robert **Bruce** was crowned in 1306. ▷ **Scottish War of Independence**

Dunbar, Battle of (3 Sep 1650) Fought between an English army under Oliver **Cromwell** and Scots forces supporting the recognition of **Charles II** after **Charles I**'s execution. Hemmed in by Scottish forces under the Earl of **Leven**, Cromwell launched a surprise counter-attack which was entirely successful. ▷ **English Civil Wars**

Duncan I (c.1010–40) King of Scots (1034/40). He was the grandson of Malcolm II (1005–34) and the son of Bethoc and Crinan, Abbot of Dunkeld. He succeeded to Strathclyde and probably ruled over most of Scotland except the islands and the far north. He attempted southwards expansion and a long and unsuccessful siege of Durham weakened his position. He was killed by **Macbeth** at Pitgaveney, near Elgin.

Duncan II (c.1060–94) King of Scots (1094). The son of **Malcolm III** and Ingibjorg, he was held hostage by **William I** of England from 1072 but was released and knighted by **William II**. Aided by an English army, he overthrew **Donald III**. Attempting to appease anti-English feeling, he tried to rule without English support but only weakened his position and was killed on 12 Nov 1094 by the mormaer of the Mearns, probably at the instigation of Donald. ▷ **Duncan I**

Dundee, John Graham of Claverhouse, 1st Viscount (c.1649–89) Scottish soldier, known as 'Bonnie Dundee' or 'Bloody Claverhouse'. In 1672 he entered the Prince of Orange's horseguards, and at the Battle of Seneff saved the future **William III**'s life. He returned to Scotland in 1677, and defeated the **Covenanters** at Bothwell Brig (1679). He was made a Privy Councillor in 1683, and became Viscount Dundee (1688). Joined by the Jacobite clans, he raised the standard for **James VII and II** against William and Mary, but died from a musket wound after his successful battle against Mackay at the Pass of Killiecrankie. ▷ **Jacobites**

Dunois, Jean d'Orléans, Count ('The Bastard of Orléans') (1403–68) French soldier. The illegitimate son of Louis, Duke of Orléans, he was a general in the **Hundred Years War**. He defeated the English at Montargis (1427), defended Orléans with a small force until its relief by **Joan of Arc** (1429), then inflicted further defeats on the English, forcing them out of Paris, and by 1453 from Normandy and Guyenne.

Dupleix, Joseph François (1697–1763) French colonial administrator. In 1741 he became Governor-General of all the French Indies; and his skilful diplomacy among the native princes almost made the Carnatic a French province. His power alarmed the British **East India Company**. When war broke out in Europe between France and England, several engagements took place between the French and the Nawab of the Carnatic, who endeavoured in vain to seize Madras. Dupleix's science and courage were displayed in the defence of Pondicherry, which Admiral Boscawen attacked in vain for five weeks. However, Dupleix's ambitious project of founding a French empire in India on the ruins of the Mughal monarchy was frustrated by **Clive of Plassey**; though the struggle continued until Dupleix's recall in 1754. The French Company refused to reimburse him for the vast sums he had spent out of his (alleged) private fortune, and he

died in poverty and neglect in 1763. ▷ **East India Company, French**

Duplessis, Maurice le Noblet (1890–1959) Canadian politician. He led the **Union Nationale** to power in Quebec in 1936, gaining power through a methodical exploitation of *nationalisme* and fear of anglicization, and yet he encouraged further encroachments by US corporations on Quebec's economic life. His campaign against radical reformers gained him the support of the Catholic Church, which he retained almost throughout his political career. His attitude towards labour was expressed in the notorious **Padlock Act** (1937) which crippled the **CCF**, but it was his antagonistic attitude towards federal government (which he claimed was invading provincial rights through the **War Measures Act**) which contributed most to his defeat in 1939, when Ernest **Lapointe** and other French-Canadian ministers threatened to resign if he was returned to office. He did regain power in 1944, defeating both the incumbent Liberals under Adélard **Godbout** and the extremist **Bloc Populaire**, and maintained his pre-war policies. An alliance between labour, professionals, academics and even some churchmen, eventually succeeded in demonstrating the scale of corruption in his government and although Duplessis himself died suddenly in 1959, the *Union Nationale* was defeated by the Liberals in 1960.

Duquesne, Abraham, Marquis of (1610–88) French naval officer. He distinguished himself from 1637 to 1643 in the war with Spain. After serving Sweden (1644–7), he returned to France, capturing Bordeaux, which had declared for the **Fronde** (1650). He defeated the Dutch and the Spanish fleets (1672–6). On the revocation of the Edict of **Nantes**, Duquesne was the only Protestant excepted.

Durando, Giacomo (1807–94) Italian soldier and politician. The brother of Giovanni **Durando**, he was implicated in a plot in 1831; forced to flee Sardinia-Piedmont, he lived in exile in Belgium, Portugal and Spain until 1848. He commanded a corps in the war against the Austrians and was the aide-de-camp of **Charles Albert** at the Battle of Novara (1849). In 1855 he became Piedmontese Minister for War and from 1856 to 1861 was the Italian ambassador in Istanbul. In 1862 he entered the government again, this time as Foreign Minister. He presided over the Italian Senate from 1884 to 1887.

Durando, Giovanni (1804–69) Italian soldier. Cashiered by **Charles Felix** in 1821, he served in Portugal and Spain before returning to Italy in 1848. He became Commander-in-Chief of the Papal Army that was sent to assist the Venetian rising against the Austrians, before the **Papal Allocution** of Apr 1848 forbade him to continue his advance against fellow Catholics. Disregarding **Pius IX**'s instructions, he retreated to Vicenza, where he was forced to surrender. He then entered Piedmontese service, fighting at the Battle of **Novara**, in the Crimean campaign and at **Solferino** (1859).

Durbar The audience-chamber or body of officials at the Indian royal court. In British India the term was applied to formal assemblies marking important state occasions to which leading Indians were invited, eg the Delhi Durbar of 1911 celebrating the visit of King **George V** and Queen Mary.

Durcansky, Ferdinand (1906–74) Slovak Populist Party politician. Upset by the union of Czechs and Slovaks in a single state in 1918, he was active in the 1930s in trying to negotiate Slovak independence. After the **Munich Agreement** he visited **Goering** and others in Berlin and he was encouraged to make trouble for the rump Czechoslovak government in Prague. Eventually **Hitler** virtually ordered him and his superior, **Tiso**, to declare independence: this was the signal for the Nazis to sweep into Prague in Mar 1939 and establish the **Bohemian Protectorate**. Durcansky was immediately made Slovak Foreign Minister, although about a year later he was dismissed as insufficiently compliant. He was condemned to death *in absentia* in 1947, and spent the remainder of his life abroad.

Durham, John George Lambton, 1st Earl of (1792–1840) British politician. He served in the dragoons, and in 1813 became a Whig MP. In 1828 he was created Baron Durham. He became Lord Privy Seal (1830), and was one of those who drew up the Reform Bill. He was made an earl in 1833, and became Ambassador to St Petersburg (1835). As Governor-General of Canada (1838), his measures were statesman-like, but the House of Lords voted disapproval of his amnesty to several of the French-Canadian rebels, and he resigned. His report on Canada (1839) advocated the union of Upper and Lower Canada, which was accepted in 1841. ▷ **Reform Acts; Whigs**

Durham Report A British government report of 1839 recommending the union of Upper and Lower **Canada** into a single political structure; produced by Lord Durham, the governor general of Canada, it called for the assimilation of French-Canadian into English-Canadian economic and linguistic culture. It also recommended responsible government.

Dürnkrut, Battle of (1278) Refusing to accept defeat after his battle with **Rudolf I** of Habsburg in 1276, Ottokar II of Bohemia began to prepare for battle again in 1278. In a pre-emptive strike, Rudolf attacked him with an army of 2 000 horsemen and the support of Ladislav of Hungary. Ottokar's army was put to flight and he himself was killed. The battle paved the way for the rise of the **Habsburg Dynasty**.

Durruti, Buenaventura (1896–1936) Spanish revolutionary anarchist. He was the most prominent violent activist to emerge from the ferocious urban guerrilla warfare of 1919–23 in Barcelona between the employers (backed by the state) and the **CNT**. Exiled in Europe and South America during the period 1923–31, Durruti was the principal leader of the revolutionary **FAI**. During the Second Republic, he agitated for an immediate revolution from below, and was frequently jailed. He led the anarchist militia in the **Spanish Civil War** until he was shot dead in Nov 1936 in mysterious circumstances, probably by a Nationalist sniper. His funeral procession in Barcelona was the last great demonstration of strength by the anarchist movement. ▷ **Republic, Second** (Spain)

Dushan, Stephen ▷ Stephen Dushan

Dutch East Indies A name applied to Indonesia until 1945, when **Sukarno** declared independence: the area included the islands of Java, Sumatra, the Celebes, most of Borneo, the Moluccas, and Bali. The Dutch recognized Indonesia's independence in 1949.

Dutch Revolt ▷ **Eighty Years War**

Dutch West India Company The organization of Dutch merchants responsible for the settlement of New Netherland, now New York. The Company was established in 1621, and was dissolved in 1674. It was later reorganized as a trading venture.

Duvalier, François ('Papa Doc') (1907–71) Haitian politician. He held power from 1957 until his death, ruling in an increasingly arbitrary fashion. His regime saw the creation of the civilian militia known as the Tonton Macoute, and the exile of many people. He became President for life in 1964, and was succeeded in this post by his son, Jean-Claude ('Baby Doc') **Duvalier**, whose regime lasted until 1986.

Duvalier, Jean-Claude ('Baby Doc') (1951–) Haitian politician, son of François ('Papa Doc') **Duvalier**. After studying law at the University of Haiti, he followed his father into politics. At the age of 20 he became President for life, ruling, as had his father, through a private army. In 1986 he was deposed in a military coup led by General Henri Namphrey and went into exile in Grasse, in the south of France.

DVP (*Deutsche Volks partei*, 'German People's Party') German political party. Founded in Dec 1918, the DVP represented the interests of right-wing liberalism and heavy industry in the **Weimar Republic**. Although its attitude to Weimar was equivocal, its leader, **Stresemann**, served continuously as German Foreign Minister from 1923 until his death in Oct 1929 in which post he did much to revise the more onerous provisions of the Treaty of **Versailles**. During the early 1930s, the DVP lost most of its electoral support and on 4 July 1933 the party was wound up.

Dzerzhinsky, Felix Edmundovich (1877–1926) Russian revolutionary, of Polish descent. In 1897 he was exiled to Siberia for political agitation, fought in the Russian **Revolution of 1905**, and in 1917, as one of the organizers of the coup d'état, became chairman of the secret police and a member of the Bolshevik Central Committee until his death. After 1921 he also reorganized the railway system, and was chairman of the Supreme Economic Council (1924–6), trying to combine industrialization with good relations with the peasantry.

Dzungars Western Mongols (also known as Eleuthes or Kalmuks) who resisted the Manchu expansion into Central Asia during the 18c. A series of campaigns by the Manchu Emperor **Qianlong** during the 1750s resulted in their destruction and the incorporation of their territory in Turkestan (henceforth known as Xinjiang) into the Qing Empire in 1759. ▷ **Qing Dynasty**

E

EAM (*Ethnikón Apeleftherotikón Métopon*, 'National Liberation Front') A coalition of left-wing parties in Greece during **World War II**, it was founded and dominated by the **KKE** (Communist Party of Greece) which hoped to take power upon liberation. EAM organized a military wing, **ELAS**, established a system of government, education, health care and justice in the areas it liberated, and in Mar 1944 created the Political Committee of National Liberation (PEEA) which challenged the Greek government-in-exile. By the end of the war, the EAM enjoyed support throughout Greece and, bitterly opposed to the return of **George II**, it continued to demand a plebiscite to decide the future constitution of Greece. By 1945, dissension among its various left-wing members weakened EAM and its role was superseded by the KKE, which remained the strongest party on the Left. With armed bands at their command, the communists, royalists and republicans embarked on civil war, which lasted until 1949. ▷ **Aris Veloukhiotis; EDES; EKKA; Greek Civil War; Plastiras, Nikolaos; Vafiadis, Markos; Zachariadis, Nikos; Zervas, Napoleon**

Eanes, António Ramalho dos Santos (1935–) Portuguese general and politician. For his role in quashing the Far Left at the end of the Revolution of Apr 1974–Nov 1975, he was promoted from an unknown colonel to Chief of Staff. With his remote, austere and humourless manner, and his dark glasses, he often appeared to be a hangover from the **Salazar** regime. In 1976 he was elected President as the principal non-communist candidate. During his 10-year presidency, the laconic and enigmatic Eanes did much to uphold the new democratic regime amidst the debilitating squabbles of the political parties, and his essential honesty won him wide popular support. Politically, he proved to be left-of-centre (though he drifted rightwards), and was distrusted by the Right. From 1986 to 1987 he was leader of the Portuguese Democratic Renewal Party.

Early Dynastic Period (Archaic Period) (c.3100/2780BC) This period, which consists of the 1st and 2nd Dynasties, was the formative era of Egyptian culture. A central-ized administration was based on the newly founded capital of Memphis at the apex of the Delta. At the same time, a system of writing — hieroglyphic script — was devised in order to convey information on vital matters such as flood control and agricultural production. At this time, artistic conventions, craft methods and the lifestyle of the Egyptians quickly assumed the forms which were to become characteristic and remain little altered for centuries. The skill and resources of the people is shown by their rapid mastery in the working of stone initially for various vessels but soon applied to architectural elements. Little is known of the internal activities of the country, but the prime concern was to counteract, by means of a strong central authority, the tendency for the newly created union of north and south to dissolve into scattered units.

East Bank The region in Jordan, east of the River Jordan, which comprises the governorates of Amman, Al Balqa, Irbid, Al Karak, and Maan. It corresponds roughly to the former Emirate of Transjordan.

Eastern Question A complex set of diplomatic problems affecting 18c, 19c and early 20c Europe. It was created by the slowly declining power of the **Ottoman Empire**, the emergence of the Balkan nations and nationalism, and the ambitions in south-east Europe of the Great Powers, especially Russia and Austria (later Austria-Hungary).

Eastern Rumelia The region lying between the Balkan and Rhodope mountains which was created by the Treaty of Berlin (1878) from the Bulgarian lands remaining after the establishment of the autonomous principality of Bulgaria and the return of Thrace and Macedonia to the Ottoman Porte. Eastern Rumelia was ruled by a governor appointed by the Ottomans and subject to the approval of the Great Powers. The separation of Eastern Rumelia from Bulgaria was temporary: in 1885 the two regions were united after a bloodless revolution.

Easter Rising (24–9 Apr 1916) A rebellion of Irish nationalists in Dublin, organized by two revolutionary groups, the Irish Republican Brotherhood led by Patrick **Pearse** (1879–1916), and **Sinn Féin** under James Connolly (1870–1916). The focal point of the rebellion was the seizing of the General Post Office. The rising was put down and several leaders were executed. The extent of the reprisals increased support for the nationalist cause in Ireland.

East India Company, British A British trading monopoly, established in India in 1600, which later became involved in politics. Its first 'factory' (trading station) was at Surat (1612), and others were at Madras (1639), Bombay (1688) and Calcutta (1690). A rival company was chartered in 1698, but the two companies merged in 1708. During the 18c it received competition from other European countries, in particular France. The company benefited territorially from local Indian disputes and Mughal weakness, gaining control of Bengal (1757), and after the Battle of Baksar receiving the right to collect revenue from the Mughal emperor (1765). Financial indiscipline among company servants led to the 1773 Regulating Act and Pitt's 1784 India Act, which established a Board of Control responsible to Parliament. Thereafter it gradually lost independence. Its monopoly was broken in 1813, and its powers handed over to the British Crown in 1858. It ceased to exist as a legal entity in 1873.

East India Company, Dutch (*Vereenigde Oostindische Compagnie*) A trading company founded in 1602 to protect trade in the Indian Ocean and assist in the war against Spain. It established 'factories' (trading stations) on the Indian subcontinent, but made little political/cultural contact there; it founded long-term colonies in South Africa, Ceylon, and especially the Indonesian archipelago. It was at the height of its prosperity during the 17c and was dissolved in 1799.

East India Company, French (*Compagnie des Indes Orientales*) A commercial/political organization, founded in 1664, which directed French colonial activities in India. It established major trading stations at Chandernagore, Pondicherry, and Mahé, and competed for power with the British during the 18c. Its governer, **Dupleix**, captured Madras (1746), but was defeated during the **Seven Years War** (1756–63). The Company lost government support and ceased to exist during the **French Revolution**. ▷ **East India Company, British**

Eban, Abba (1915–) Israeli diplomat and politician. Born in South Africa, he was educated in England and taught oriental languages at Cambridge before serving as a liaison officer at Allied HQ during **World War II**. In 1944 he worked in the Middle East Arab Centre in Jerusalem and in 1948 was Israeli **UN** representative in New York and then ambassador in Washington (1950–9). He returned to Israel where he won a seat in the Knesset and joined David **Ben-Gurion**'s government. Between 1959 and 1974 he held several posts, under various prime ministers, and was Foreign Minister from 1966 to 1974. In the 1989 general election he was unexpectedly defeated by the opposition leader, George Price. ▷ **Mapai Party**

Ebert, Friedrich (1871–1925) German politician. He started life as a saddler, then became a journalist on a Social Democratic newspaper and **Reichstag** member (1912). Chairman of his party (1913), he was a leader in the **Revolution of 1918**–19; his firm line against groups on the far left and deals with the old order to achieve this have provoked much controversy. He was the first President of the German Republic (1919–25).

Eboli, Ruy Gómez de Silva, Prince of (1516–73) Portuguese nobleman. He became the adviser and confidant of **Philip II** of Spain from 1559 until his own death. Even more famous was his wife, Ana Mendoza de la Cerda (1540–91), who married Ruy Gómez in 1552 and is featured in portraits with an eye-patch over one eye. She became involved in the intrigues of the King's secretary, Antonio Pérez, and was kept in confinement from 1579.

Ebroin (d.681) Neustrian Mayor of the Palace (c.656/81). After the death of the Merovingian puppet king, Chlotar III, Ebroin elected Theodoric III as his successor. This was opposed by the Neustrian magnates, who elected the Austrasian king Childeric II in his place and imprisoned Ebroin. After Childeric's death, Ebroin was restored to power. His campaigns against the Austrasians led to his assassination and to the end of Neustrian predominance in Frankish affairs. ▷ **Austrasia; Franks; Merovingians; Neustria**

EC (European Community) A community of 12 states in Western Europe created for the purpose of achieving economic and political integration. It comprises three communities. The first of these was the *European Steel and Coal Community*, established in 1952 under the Treaty of Paris by France, West Germany, Italy, Belgium, the Netherlands, and Luxembourg. It created common institutions for regulating the coal and steel industries under a common framework of law and institutions, thereby producing the first breach in the principle of national sovereignty. In the early 1950s, unsuccessful attempts were made to establish a European Defence Community and a European Political Community. In 1958, under the Treaty of Rome, the six states established the *European Economic Community* and the *European Atomic Energy Community*, which provided for collaboration in the civilian sector of nuclear power. Six members have been added to the original six: Denmark, Ireland, and the UK (1973); Greece (1981); and Portugal and Spain (1986). Turkey is seeking to become a member. To develop and oversee the policies of economic and political integration there are a number of supranational community institutions: the Commission, the Council, the European Parliament, and the European Court of Justice. While the Community has grown in the 1970s and 1980s and continues to progress towards economic integration, a political union seems still a distant possibility. ▷ **EEC**

Ecclesiastical Principalities The states in the **Holy Roman Empire** ruled directly by church officials. The rulers were elected by the cathedral chapters. Although unable to establish strong dynasties, the church princes functioned in every other way as secular princes. Three were Electors: the Archbishops of Mainz, Cologne, and Trier. Other prominent states were the bishoprics of Speyer, Worms, Würzburg, and Bamberg and the territories of the the Abbots of Fulda and Lorsch.

Ecevit, Bülent (1925–) Turkish politician. After working as a government official and a journalist, he became an MP for the centre-left Republican People's Party in 1957. He was Minister of Labour, then in 1966 became Secretary-General of his party and subsequently (1972) Chairman. He headed a coalition government in 1974 and during office ordered the invasion of Cyprus. He was Prime Minister again in 1977 and in 1978–9, when he imposed martial law on Turkey. After the military coup of 1980, he was imprisoned twice for criticizing the military regime.

Echegaray y Eizaguirre, José (1833–1916) Spanish dramatist, scientist, and politician. Born of Basque descent in Madrid, he taught

mathematics, held portfolios in various ministries (1868–74), then won literary fame by many plays in prose and verse, notably *The Great Galeoto* (1881). He shared the Nobel Prize for Literature in 1904. In 1905 he returned to politics as Minister of Finance (1905), and to science as Professor of Physics at Madrid.

Economic Community of West African States (ECOWAS) An organization formed (May 1975) by 15 West African states through the Treaty of Lagos: Benin, the Gambia, Ghana, Guinea, Guinea-Bissau, Ivory Coast (Cote d'Ivoire), Liberia, Mali, Mauritania, Niger, Nigeria, Senegal, Sierra Leone, Togo, and Upper Volta (now Burkina Faso). Cape Verde joined in 1977. It is based in Abuja, Nigeria. Its principle objectives are the ending of restrictions on trade between the signatories, the establishment of a common customs tariff, the harmonization of economic and industrial policies, and equalization of the levels of development of member states. In 1990 it set up a Standing Mediation Committee to mediate disputes between member states. It has also supported the free movement of peoples and has overseen a collaborative military involvement in Liberia.

Economic Societies of Friends of the Country The most active expression of the Enlightenment in 18c Spain, they originated in the Basque country in a group formed in 1748 by the Count of Peñaflorida and others, which in 1765 took the name the Basque Society of Friends of the Country, receiving royal approval the following year. The societies functioned mainly as discussion groups, and published various proposals for economic and technical reform. The minister **Campomanes** encouraged them, and in the 1770s some 60 were founded under royal patronage in the main cities of Spain. The society in Madrid commissioned Jovellanos to draw up his famous *Report on the Agrarian Law*. ▷ **Basques**

Eda Saburo (1907–77) Japanese politician. Active in the pre-war Farmers' Movement, Eda joined the Japan Socialist Party (JSP) in 1946 and was elected to the House of Councillors (upper house) in 1950. During the 1960s he served as Secretary-General of the JSP, when he incurred the wrath of the party's dominant left wing for suggesting a shift in the party's approach of confrontation with the existing capitalist system to one of promoting gradual change within the system.

Edde, Emile (1886–1949) Lebanese nationalist and lawyer. A Maronite, he spent **World War I** in France, having been sentenced to death *in absentia* by the Turks. After the war he was adviser to Picot's deputy, Robert Coulondre, thereby acquiring considerable prestige in the eyes of the Lebanese. Disagreement between the two meant, however, that this arrangement did not last long. Edde, though, was destined to play a leading part in Lebanese politics. In 1924 he was elected President of the Representative Council of Greater Lebanon, which was dissolved by the French High-Commissioner early the following year. By 1927 a rival to Edde's position had emerged in Bishara al-Khouri: where Edde was more at home with the French language and culture, al-Khouri, although a French-speaker, had excellent Arabic; where Edde was outspoken, al-Khouri tended to be reserved. The two politicians, however, regarded Lebanon as more a part of the Mediterranean culture than of a greater Arab world. Elected to the presidency again in 1936, Edde managed to survive, relying heavily on French support, until 1941; at this point, however, wartime shortages became too much for his already weak regime, and he was forced to resign. Edde was again active in public life from 1942, establishing his Francophile following as the National Bloc. However, despite some sympathy amongst the Christian element of the population, Edde's stance made him out of touch with the country as a whole.

Eden (of Avon), Sir (Robert) Anthony, 1st Earl (1897–1977) British politician. He became a Conservative MP in 1923, and was Foreign Under-Secretary (1931), Lord Privy Seal (1933), and Foreign Secretary (1935), resigning in 1938 over differences with Neville **Chamberlain**. In **World War II** he was first Dominions Secretary, then Secretary of State for War, and Foreign Secretary (1940–5). Again Foreign Secretary (1951–5), he was involved with the negotiations in Korea and Indo-China, and the 1954 Geneva Summit Conference. He succeeded Winston **Churchill** as Prime Minister (1955–7), and in 1956 ordered British forces (in collaboration with the French and Israelis) to occupy the Suez Canal Zone. His action was condemned by the **UN** and caused a bitter controversy in Britain which did not subside when he ordered a withdrawal. In failing health, he resigned abruptly in 1957. He was created an earl in 1961. ▷ **Conservative Party** (UK)

EDES (*Ellinikos Dimokratikos Ethnikos Stratos*, 'National Republican Greek League') One of the three major Greek resistance groups operating after the German invasion of Greece (6 Apr 1941). Formed during the winter 1941–2, its leader in Greece was the republican Napoleon **Zervas**. It rivalled **EAM/ELAS** in power and influence, and was favoured by the British government as a counterweight to the communists. It cooperated with Special Operations Executive and EAM/ELAS in Sep 1942, cutting German supply lines over the Gorgopotamos viaduct and, following the National Bands Agreement (summer 1943), it took part in Operation Animals. With the withdrawal of the Axis forces, conflict between the rival resistance groups grew and EDES was forced from the field by EAM/ELAS. ▷ **EKKA; Greeks; Plastiras, Nikolaos; Vafiadis, Markos; Zachariadis, Nikos**

Edgar (943–75) King of Mercia and Northumbria (957/75) and the King of all England (959/75). He was the younger son of **Edmund I**. He encouraged the reform of the English Church as a means of enhancing his prestige and power, though his lavish support for the monasteries, caused bitterness among an important section of the nobility. He introduced a uniform currency based on new silver pennies c.973. ▷ **Anglo-Saxons**

Edgar the Atheling (c.1050–1125) Anglo-Saxon prince, the grandson of **Edmund II, 'Ironside'**. Though chosen as king by some influential Englishmen after the Battle of **Hastings**, he was never crowned. He submitted to **William I, 'the Conqueror'** (by Dec 1066), but then rebelled and fled to Scotland (1068), where his sister Margaret married **Malcolm III, 'Canmore'**. He was finally reconciled with King William in 1074. He was taken prisoner at the Battle of Tinchebrai (1106), fighting for Duke Robert of Normandy against **Henry I** of England, and lived in obscurity after his release.

Edinburgh, Duke of, Prince Philip The husband of Queen Elizabeth II, the son of Prince Andrew of Greece and Princess Alice of Battenberg, born at Corfu. He became a naturalized British subject in 1947, when he was married to the Princess Elizabeth (20 Nov). In 1956 he began the Duke of Edinburgh Award Scheme to foster the leisure activities of young people. ▷ **Elizabeth II**

Edington, Battle of (878) Decisive victory in Wiltshire for **Alfred, 'the Great'**, King of

Wessex against an invading Danish army. The Danes sought peace, left Wessex and their king, **Guthrum**, was baptized a Christian. The peace settled the frontier between Wessex and the Danes, greatly enlarged Alfred's territory and established the West Saxons as the leading English power.

Edirne, Capture of (1362) Edirne (Adrianople), which was to be the Ottoman capital from 1366 to 1453 (the year in which Constantinople fell), was lost to the Byzantines in 1362. This Turkish success formed a part of what was a systematic reduction of the Balkans. Achieved either right at the end of **Orhan**'s reign or at the beginning of the reign of **Murad I**, it paved the way for the Turkish control of the Balkans which stood them in such good stead when Asia Minor was overrun by **Timur**.

Edmund I (921–46) King of the English (939/46). He was the half-brother of **Athelstan**. On Edmund's accession, Scandinavian forces from Northumbria, reinforced by levies from Ireland, quickly overran the East Midlands. He re-established his control over the southern **Danelaw** (942) and **Northumbria** (944), and for the remainder of his life ruled a reunited England. He was killed by an outlaw. ▷ **Anglo-Saxons**

Edmund II, 'Ironside' (c.980–1016) King of the English (1016). The son of **Ethelred the Unready**, he was chosen King by the Londoners on his father's death (Apr 1016), while **Canute** was elected at Southampton by the **witan**. Edmund hastily levied an army, defeated Canute, and attempted to raise the siege of London, but was routed at Ashingdon or possibly Ashdon, Essex (Oct 1016). He agreed to a partition of the country, but died a few weeks later, leaving Canute as sole ruler.

Edo The former name for Tokyo, capital of Japan. Edo became a castle town at the end of the 16c and the capital of the **Tokugawa Shogunate** after 1601. Due to its administrative and economic importance, Edo became one of the most populous cities in the world during the 18c, with an estimated population of 1 million. With the overthrow of the Tokugawa in 1868 and the restoration of imperial rule (the **Meiji Restoration**), the city was renamed Tokyo (Eastern Capital) and became the capital of the new Meiji state.

Edomites According to the Bible, the descendants of Esau who settled in the mountainous area south of the Dead Sea to the Gulf of Aqaba; in Greek, *Idumeans*. They often appear as enemies of Israel, having been conquered by **David**, but retaking parts of Judah and becoming a kingdom in the 8c BC. They participated in the overthrow of Judah in 587 BC by the Babylonians, but were eventually conquered by John **Hyrcanus** in the late 2c BC, forcing their integration into the Jewish people. Herod I (the Great) was of Edomite descent.

Edward I (1239–1307) King of England (1272/1307). The elder son of **Henry III** and Eleanor of Provence, he married **Eleanor of Castile** (1254) and later Margaret of France, the sister of **Philip IV** (1299). In the **Barons Wars**, he at first supported Simon de **Montfort**, but rejoined his father, and defeated de Montfort at Evesham (1265). He then won renown as a crusader to the Holy Land, and did not return to England until 1274, two years after his father's death. In two devastating campaigns (1276–7 and 1282–3), he annexed north-west Wales, and ensured the permanence of his conquests by building magnificent castles. He reasserted English claims to the overlordship of Scotland when the line of succession failed, and decided in favour of John **Balliol** as King (1292). However Edward's insistence on full rights of suzerainty provoked the Scottish magnates to force Balliol to repudiate Edward and ally with France (1295), thus beginning the Scottish Wars of Independence. Despite prolonged campaigning and victories such as Falkirk (1298), he could not subdue Scotland as he had done Wales. He died while leading his army against Robert **Bruce**. ▷ **Crusades; Scottish War of Independence; Wallace, William; Westminster, Statutes of**

Edward II (1284–1327) King of England (1307/27). He was the fourth son of **Edward I** and **Eleanor of Castile**. In 1301 he was created Prince of Wales, the first English heir-apparent to bear the title, and in 1308 married **Isabella of France**, the daughter of **Philip IV**. Throughout his reign, Edward mismanaged the barons, who sought to rid the country of royal favourites and restore their rightful place in government. The Ordinances of 1311 restricted the royal prerogative in matters such as appointments to the King's household, and demanded the banishment of Edward's favourite, Piers Gaveston, who was ultimately captured and executed (1312). Edward was humiliated by reverses in Scotland, where he was decisively defeated by Robert **Bruce** at the Battle of

Bannockburn (1314). The Ordinances were formally annulled (1322), but the King's new favourites, the Despensers, were acquisitive and unpopular, and earned the particular enmity of Queen Isabella. With her lover Roger Mortimer, she toppled the Despensers (1326) and imprisoned Edward in Kenilworth Castle. He renounced the throne in 1327 in favour of his eldest son, **Edward III**, and was then murdered in Berkeley Castle, near Gloucester.

Edward III (1312–77) King of England (1327/77). The elder son of **Edward II** and **Isabella of France**, he married Philippa of Hainault in 1328, and their eldest child, Edward (later called **Edward, the Black Prince**), was born in 1330. By banishing Queen Isabella from court and executing her lover, Roger Mortimer, he assumed full control of the government (1330), and began to restore the monarchy's authority and prestige. He supported Edward **Balliol**'s attempts to wrest the Scots throne from **David II**, and his victory at the Battle of **Halidon Hill** (1333) forced David to seek refuge in France until 1341. In 1337, after **Philip VI** had declared **Guyenne** forfeit, he revived his hereditary claim to the French crown through Isabella, the daughter of **Philip IV**, thus beginning the **Hundred Years War**. He destroyed the French navy at the Battle of Sluys (1340), and won another major victory at the Battle of **Crécy** (1346). David II was captured two months later at the Battle of Neville's Cross, near Durham, and remained a prisoner until 1357. Edward was renowned for his valour and military skill. ▷
William of Wykeham

Edward IV (1442–83) King of England (1461/70 and 1471/83). He was the eldest son of Richard, Duke of York. His father claimed the throne as the lineal descendant of **Edward III**'s third and fifth sons (respectively Lionel, Duke of Clarence, and Edmund, Duke of York), against the Lancastrian King **Henry VI** (the lineal descendant of Edward III's fourth son, **John of Gaunt**). Richard was killed at the Battle of Wakefield (1460), but Edward entered London in 1461, was recognized as King on Henry VI's deposition, and with the support of his cousin Richard Neville, Earl of **Warwick**, decisively defeated the Lancastrians at Towton. He threw off his dependence on Warwick, and secretly married Elizabeth Woodville (1464). Warwick forced him into exile in Holland (Oct 1470), and Henry VI regained the throne. Edward returned to England (Mar 1471), was restored to kingship (11 Apr), then defeated and killed Warwick at the Battle of Barnet (14 Apr), and destroyed the remaining Lancastrian forces at the Battle of **Tewkesbury** (4 May). Henry VI was murdered soon afterwards, and Edward remained secure for the rest of his reign. ▷ **Lancaster, House of; Roses, Wars of the**

Edward V (1470–83) King of England (Apr/June 1483). He was the son of King **Edward IV** and Elizabeth Woodville. Shortly after his accession, he and his younger brother, Richard, Duke of York, were imprisoned in the Tower by their uncle, Richard, Duke of Gloucester, who usurped the throne as **Richard III**. The two princes were never heard of again, and were most likely murdered (Aug 1483) on their uncle's orders. In 1674 a wooden chest containing the bones of two children was discovered in the Tower, and these were interred in Westminster Abbey as their presumed remains. ▷ **Roses, Wars of the**

Edward VI (1537–53) King of England (1547/53). He was the son of **Henry VIII** by his third queen, Jane **Seymour**. During Edward's reign, power was first in the hands of his uncle, the Duke of Somerset, and after his execution in 1552, of John Dudley, Duke of Northumberland. Edward became a devout Protestant, and under the Protectors the English Reformation flourished. He died of tuberculosis, having agreed to the succession of Lady Jane **Grey** (overthrown after nine days by **Mary I**). ▷ **Reformation** (England)

Edward VII (1841–1910) King of the UK (1901/10). The eldest son of Queen **Victoria**, in 1863 he married Alexandra, the eldest daughter of **Christian IX** of Denmark. They had three sons and three daughters: Albert Victor, Duke of Clarence; George; Louise, Princess Royal; Victoria; Maud, who married **Haakon VII** of Norway; and Alexander. As Prince of Wales, his behaviour led him into several social scandals, and the Queen excluded him from affairs of state. As King, he carried out several visits to Continental capitals which strove to allay international animosities. ▷ **George V**

Edward VIII (1894–1972) King of the UK (Jan/Dec 1936). He was the eldest son of King **George V**. He joined the navy and, during **World War I**, the army, travelled much, and achieved considerable popularity. He succeeded his father in Jan 1936, but abdicated (11 Dec) in the face of opposition to his proposed marriage to Mrs Ernest Simpson, a commoner who had been twice divorced. He was then given the title of Duke of Windsor, and the marriage took place in France in 1937. The Duke and Duchess of Windsor lived in Paris, apart from a period in the Bahamas (1940–5), where Edward was Governor.

Edward, 'the Black Prince' (1330–76) Eldest son of **Edward III**. He was created Earl of Chester (1333), Duke of Cornwall (1337), and Prince of Wales (1343). In 1346, though still a boy, he fought at the Battle of **Crécy**, and is said to have won his popular title (first cited in a 16c work) from his black armour. He won several victories in the **Hundred Years War**, including the Battle of **Poitiers** (1356). He had two sons, Edward (1365–70) and the future **Richard II**. In 1362 he was created Prince of Aquitaine and lived there until 1371, when a revolt forced him to return to England. A great soldier, he was a failure as an administrator.

Edward the Confessor (c.1003–66) King of England (1042/66). He was the elder son of **Ethelred the Unready** and Emma of Normandy, and the last king of the Old English royal line. After living in exile in Normandy, he joined the household of his half-brother **Hardaknut** in 1041, and then succeeded him on the throne. Until 1052 he maintained his position against the ambitious Godwin family by building up Norman favourites, and in 1051 he very probably recognized Duke William of Normandy (later **William I**) as his heir. However, the Godwins regained their ascendancy, and on his deathbed in London, Edward, who remained childless, nominated Harold Godwin (**Harold II**) to succeed, the **Norman Conquest** following soon after. Edward's reputation for holiness began in his lifetime, and he rebuilt Westminster Abbey, where he was buried, in the Romanesque style. His cult grew in popularity, and he was canonized in 1161.

Edward the Elder (c.870–924) King of **Wessex** (899/924). The elder son of **Alfred, 'the Great'**, he built on his father's successes and established himself as the strongest ruler in Britain. By one of the most decisive military campaigns of the whole Anglo-Saxon period, he conquered and annexed to **Wessex** the southern **Danelaw** (910–18). He also assumed control of **Mercia** (918), and although he exercised no direct power in the north, all the chief rulers beyond the

Humber, including the King of Scots, formally recognized his overlordship in 920. ▷ **Anglo-Saxons**

Edward the Martyr (c.962–78) King of England (975/8). During his reign there was a reaction against the policies in support of monasticism espoused by his father, **Edgar**. He was murdered at Corfe, Dorset, by supporters of his stepmother, Elfrida, and canonized in 1001.

EEC (European Economic Community) An association within the European Community, established in 1958 after the Treaties of Rome (1957), often referred to as the Common Market. It is essentially a customs union, with a common external tariff and a common market with the removal of barriers to trade among the members. In addition it has a number of common policies, the most important of which is the Common Agricultural Policy, providing for external tariffs to protect domestic agriculture and mechanisms for price support. The cost of support to agriculture takes up about 70 per cent of the European Community's budget and has shown an alarming propensity to grow. Reform of agricultural policy has been on the agenda for a number of years, but many member governments are reluctant to entertain the wrath of the farming vote which remains sizable in their countries. There are common policies for fisheries, regional development, industrial intervention, and economic and social affairs. There is also a European Monetary System, which regulates exchange rate movements among the member states' currencies in an attempt to achieve monetary stability. In 1986 the Single European Act was passed, allowing for the completion of the process of creating a common market within the community by the beginning of 1993. ▷ **EC (European Community)**

Eelam The name of the proposed independent state in north and east Sri Lanka, demanded by some Tamil groups including the militant **LTTE**.

EFTA (European Free Trade Association) An association originally of seven Western European states who were not members of the European Economic Community (**EEC**), intended as a counter to the EEC; it was established in 1959 under the Stockholm Convention. The members (Austria, Denmark, Norway, Portugal, Sweden, Switzerland, and the UK) agreed to eliminate over a period of time trade restrictions between them, without having to bring into line individual tariffs and trade policies with other countries. Agriculture was excluded from the agreement, although individual arrangements were permitted. Both the UK (1973) and Portugal (1986) left to join the EEC, but there has been a free trade agreement between the remaining EFTA countries and the European Community, and considerable trade between the two groupings. Finland joined in 1985. ▷ **EC (European Community)**

Egbert (d.839) King of **Wessex** (802/39). After his victory in 825 over the Mercians at Ellendun (now Wroughton) in Wiltshire, Essex, Kent, Surrey, and Sussex submitted to him; but his conquest of **Mercia** itself (829) was soon reversed. He extended his control over Cornwall, defeating an alliance between the **Vikings** and Britons at Hingston Down (838). These successes gave him mastery over southern England from Kent to Land's End, and established Wessex as the strongest Anglo-Saxon kingdom. ▷ **Anglo-Saxons**

Eger, Golden Bull of (1213) An agreement between the Holy Roman Emperor **Frederick II** and Pope **Innocent III** that repeated and formalized the terms of an agreement made by **Otto IV** at Speyer. It recognized the territorial aspirations of the papacy in full and emancipated the German Church from imperial control.

Egidian Constitution (1357) This political settlement takes its name from the warrior cardinal and constitutional lawyer, Egidio Albornoz. He imposed it on the **Papal States** after his skilful reconquest (with slender miltary means) of the petty tyrannies which had developed there, and it was to remain valid for virtually the entire history of these territories.

Egmond, Lamoral, Count of, Prince of Gavre (1522–68) Dutch soldier and political figure. As one of the foremost nobles of the Netherlands, he accompanied the Emperor **Charles V** to Algiers in 1541 and in all his later campaigns, distinguishing himself at St Quentin (1557) and Gravelines (1558), for which he was made **Stadholder** of Flanders and Artois in 1559. He now sided with the party in the Netherlands that opposed **Philip II** of Spain's policies in the Low Countries, and left the Council of State. He went on a special mission to Spain in 1565 to tell the King of conditions in the Netherlands, and after the **Image-breaking Riots** (1566), he distanced himself from the Prince of Orange and the 'Beggars'. He seemed to have restored order and to have gained the

ANCIENT EGYPT: DYNASTIES

Date BC	Dynasty	Period	Date BC	Dynasty	Period
c.3100–2890	I	**Early Dynastic Period (Archaic Period)**	c.1684–1567	XVI	
			c.1660–1567	XVII	
c.2890–2686	II	First use of stone in building	1567–1320	XVIII	**New Kingdom**
c.2686–2613	III	**Old Kingdom**	1320–1200	XIX	Began with colonial expansion, ended in divided rule
c.2613–2494	IV	The age of the great pyramid builders			
c.2494–2345	V	Longest reign in history: Pepi II, 90 years	1200–1085	XX	
c.2345–2181	VI		1085–945	XXI	**Third Intermediate Period**
c.2181–2173	VII	**First Intermediate Period**	945–730	XXII	Revival of prosperity and restoration of cults
c.2173–2160	VIII	Social order upset; few monuments built	817–730	XXIII	
			720–715	XXIV	
c.2160–2130	IX		751–668	XXV	
c.2130–2040	X				
c.2133–1991	XI		664–525	XXVI	**Late Period**
1991–1786	XII	**Middle Kingdom**	525–404	XXVII	Completion of Nile–Red Sea canal
1786–1633	XIII	Golden age of art and craftsmanship	404–399	XXVIII	
			399–380	XXIX	
1786–c.1603	XIV	**Second Intermediate Period**	380–343	XXX	
1674–1567	XV	Country divided into principalities	343–332	XXXI	Alexander III, 'the Great' reaches Alexandria, 332BC

confidence of the Duke of **Alva**, now (1567) Lieutenant-General to the Netherlands; but suddenly he was seized, condemned to death, and beheaded in Brussels.

Egypt A republic in north-east Africa. The history of Egypt can be traced as far back as c.6000BC, to Neolithic cultures on the River Nile. A unified kingdom embracing lower and upper Egypt was first created in c.3100BC, ruled by Pharaoh dynasties; the pyramids at El Giza were constructed during the Fourth Dynasty. Egyptian power was greatest during the New Empire period (1567–1085BC). It became a Persian province during the 6c BC and was conquered by Alexander the Great in the 4c BC. Ptolemaic Pharaohs ruled Egypt until 30BC. It was conquered by Arabs in AD672. From 1798 until 1801, it was occupied by France under Napoleon. The Suez Canal was constructed in 1869. A revolt in 1879 was put down by the British in 1882. Egypt became a British protectorate in 1914, and declared its independence in 1922. It was used as a base for Allied forces during **World War II**. King Farouk was deposed by **Nasser** in 1952, and Egypt was declared a republic the following year. An attack on Israel, followed by Israeli invasion in 1967, resulted in the loss of the Sinai Peninsula and control of part of the Suez Canal (regained following negotiations in the 1970s). In 1981, President **Sadat** was assassinated, and relations with Arab nations were strained, but improved throughout the 1980s. In the early 1990s there were violent attacks and clashes between Muslim and Coptic Christians. See panel p293.

Ehrenburg, Ilya Grigorevich (1891–1967) Soviet novelist and journalist. Born in Kiev, he was in exile in Paris before 1917 and returned to fight against the communists. Yet he was allowed back again in 1923 and wrote novels in praise of the system that were accepted abroad. In the **Khrushchev** period he wrote in favour of an East–West thaw and managed to open the eyes of the Soviet public to some genuine truths about the West.

Eichmann, Karl Adolf (1906–62) Austrian SS officer. A fanatical Nazi and anti-Semite, he became a member of the SS in 1932 and organized anti-Jewish activities, particularly their deportation to concentration camps. Captured by US forces in 1945, he escaped from prison some months later, having kept his identity hidden, and in 1950 reached Argentina. He was traced by Israeli agents and in 1960, seized, taken to Israel, condem-

ned for 'crimes against humanity' and executed.

Eighth Route Army The Chinese 'Red Army', formed by the communists in 1927. It was given this name in 1937 when it entered into an uneasy alliance with the Nationalist Army of **Chiang Kai-shek** against the Japanese invaders of China.

'Eight-Legged Essay' (*baguwen*) The standard form of essay written in the Chinese **Civil Service Examination System** during the **Ming Dynasty** and **Qing Dynasty**. The introduction of this form, the composition of balanced prose in a rigid eight-part structure, coincided with a reduction in the scope of the examinations themselves; only approved classical interpretations of Confucian texts could be used and preparation increasingly came to rely on rote memorization. By the 18c, form and calligraphy assumed more importance than the presentation of original ideas. Handbooks on the writing of eight-legged essays were produced for potential examination candidates. The eight-legged essay was finally abolished in 1902 and replaced with a more topical dissertation. Three years later, the civil service examinations themselves were abolished.

Eighty Years War (1568–1648) Uprisings and wars against Spanish Habsburg rule by 17 provinces in the Low Countries, also called the War of Independence, the Revolt of the Netherlands, and the Dutch Revolt. The provinces, previously separate principalities in the Burgundian sphere of influence, were finally united by **Charles V**, who was also King of Spain. His son, **Philip II**, pursued through his regents policies of centralization, increased taxation, and persecution of non-Catholics; resistance to centralization and religious persecution began in the 1550s. The wars devastated the 10 southern provinces retained by the Spanish. The rebels, led by William of Orange and his Protestant naval and land force of **'Beggars'**, took refuge in the seven northern provinces, chiefly Holland, and which were declared a republic in 1588, with the Orange family as stadholders. Independence was finally recognized by Spain in 1648. ▷ **Blood, Council of; Habsburg Dynasty; Stadholder; William I** of the Netherlands

Einaudi, Luigi (1874–1961) Italian politician. Professor of Public Finance in Turin (1902–49), he was a Senator (1915–45) and President of Italy (1948–55). His most important role was as Budget Minister (a post specially created for him in 1947 by **De Gasperi**): he devised a rigorous deflationary policy of tight monetary control and high interest rates which was not abandoned until 1950. While this arguably slowed Italy's post-war industrial recovery and certainly contributed to high unemployment, it also helped to revive confidence in the lira and to lay the foundation for growth in the post-1950 era.

Eire Name superseding '**Irish Free State**' under the Irish constitution of 1937 which declared the country a sovereign, independent and democratic state with a directly elected President, a restored but weakened Senate and a **Dáil Eireann** elected by proportional representation. ▷ **de Valera, Eamon; Irish Republic**

Eisenhower, Dwight David ('Ike') (1890–1969) US general and 34th President. He graduated from the US Military Academy at West Point, and by 1939 had become chief military assistant to General Douglas **MacArthur** in the Philippines. In 1942 he commanded Allied forces for the amphibious descent on French North Africa. His ability to coordinate the Allied forces and staff led to his selection as Supreme Commander of the Allied Expeditionary Force which spearheaded the 1944 invasion of Europe. In 1950 he was made Supreme Commander of the NATO forces in Europe. In 1952 the popularity that he had gained as a war hero swept him to victory in the US presidential election, in which he ran as a Republican; he was re-elected in 1956. During his administration (1953–61) he negotiated a truce in the **Korean War** (1953) and continued US efforts to contain **communism**. During his second term the administration became more active in civil rights issues, sending troops to Little Rock, Arkansas to enforce a school desegregation order. ▷ **Republican Party; World War II**

Eisenhower Doctrine (1957) The US declaration to protect the Middle East against communist aggression, intended to reassure the Western allies after the Suez Crisis. Addressing Congress, President **Eisenhower** stated that the USA regarded the Middle East as vital to its security and that it should give economic and military aid to any country in the region that requested it.

ejido A traditional form of communal land-holding in Mexico: *ejido* lands existed in the Valley of Mexico at the time of the conquest and were areas claimed as common or **cabildo** properties outside the settlement or village, which were to be protected from alienation to private holders. The idea of the ejido as a communal property was revived by the followers of Emiliano **Zapata**, who believed that title to lands should be vested in the village. Communal ejidos were created under Lázaro **Cárdenas**, who expropriated large integrated haciendas created under Porfirio **Díaz**, as a means of forming loyal peasant communities immune to pressure from the Cristeros and supporting the PRM (*Partido de la Revolución Mexicana*). Some 16.8 million hectares were distributed.

EKKA (*Ethnike Kai Koinonike Apeleutherosis*, 'National and Social Liberation') The smallest of the three major resistance groups in Greece during **World War II**. Led by Colonel Dimitrios Psarros, its politics were liberal and republican. It took an active part in the resistance from summer 1943 onwards, but was forced from the field when its leader was murdered by ELAS (Apr 1944). ▷ **EAM; EDES; Greeks**

Elagabalus (204–22) Roman Emperor (218/22). Born Varius Avitus Bassianus but called Elagabalus after the Syro-Phoenician Sun God Elagabal, whose hereditary priest he was, he became Emperor of Rome after an army coup in Syria engineered by his grandmother, Julia Maesa, the sister-in-law of the late Roman emperor **Septimius Severus**. Interested in little but the cult of the god whose priest he was and which he had introduced to Rome, Elagabalus left the running of affairs largely in the hands of his formidable grandmother. He died in a palace coup, murdered by the **Praetorian Guard**. ▷ **Severan Dynasty**

El Alamein, Battle of (23 Oct–4 Nov 1943) A battle in **World War II**, named after a village on Egypt's Mediterranean coast, which ended in the victory of the British Eighth Army commanded by **Montgomery** over **Rommel**'s Afrika Corps. It proved to be a turning point in the war in the war in Africa. ▷ **North African Campaign**

Elam The name given in antiquity to what is now south-west Iran. Its main city was Susa, and at its zenith in the 13c BC it ruled an empire stretching from Babylonia in the west to Persepolis in the east. ▷ **Babylonia; Persepolis; Susa**

ELAS (*Ethnikós Laïkós Apeleftherotikós Strátos*, 'National Popular Liberation Army') The Greek resistance army founded in Dec 1941 as the military wing of the communist-dominated **EAM**. In the field from summer 1942, while fighting to liberate Greece from the Axis forces, its ultimate goal was the establishment of communist rule at the end of the war. It worked to eliminate rival resistance bands, cooperating with **EDES** only under the auspices of the British **Special Operations Executive (SOE)**. At the end of the war, with c.70 000 men, it controlled most of Greece and refused to cooperate with the British-backed government of George **Papandreou**. Although it agreed to disarm in Feb 1945, the fighting between communists, republicans and royalists continued, erupting into the **Greek Civil War** of 1946–9.

El Dorado Literally 'the gilded one', the term refers to a powerful early colonial Spanish-American legend of a ruler coated in gold, believed to exist in New Granada (now Colombia). By extension, it came to mean a land of fabulous wealth. Sir Walter **Raleigh** organized two expeditions (1595 and 1617) from England in search of El Dorado. ▷ **Incas**

Eleanor of Aquitaine (c.1122–1204) Queen consort of **Louis VII** of France (1137–52) and, after the annulment of this marriage, of the future **Henry II** of England (1154–89). She was imprisoned (1174–89) for supporting the rebellion of her sons, two of whom became kings of England (**Richard I** in 1189, and **John** in 1199).

Eleanor of Castile (c.1245–1290) Queen consort of **Edward I** of England (1254/90). The daughter of **Ferdinand III**, she accompanied Edward to the Crusades, and is said to have saved his life by sucking the poison from a wound he had. She died at Harby, Nottinghamshire, and the 'Eleanor Crosses' at Northampton, Geddington, and Waltham Cross are survivors of the 12 erected by Edward at the halting places of her cortège. The last stopping place was Charing Cross, where a replica now stands.

Electors Members of the electoral college that chose Holy Roman Emperors. By the 13c, membership was limited to seven: the Duke of Saxony, King of Bohemia, Count Palatine of the Rhine, Margrave of Brandenburg, and Archbishops of Cologne, Mainz, and Trier. The *Golden Bull* (1356) of Emperor **Charles IV** permanently granted the right of election to the seven. ▷ **Holy Roman Empire**

ELF ▷ **Eritrea Liberation Front**

Eliot, Sir John (1592–1632) English statesman. He entered parliament in 1614, and was knighted in 1618. He became a supporter of **Charles I**'s favourite, the 1st Duke of **Buckingham**, but in 1625 turned against him, and moved his impeachment. His policy of antagonism to the King led to his imprisonment on three occasions. He died in the Tower, thus becoming a martyr to the parliamentary cause.

Elizabeth, St (1207–31) Hungarian princess. The daughter of Andreas II of Hungary, at the age of four she was betrothed to Louis IV, Landgrave of Thuringia. She was educated at his father's court, the Wartburg, near Eisenach, and at 14 she was married; a boy and two girls were the fruit of their union. Louis, who admired her for her piety and ceaseless alms-giving, died as a crusader at Otranto in 1227, whereupon Elizabeth was deprived of her regency by her husband's brother, and exiled on the plea that she wasted state treasures by her charities. After severe privations, she was received into the monastery of Kitzingen by the abbess, her aunt. Later she retired to a cottage near the castle of Marburg and lived in cloistered simplicity for the remainder of her days. She was canonized by Pope **Gregory IX** in 1235.

Elizabeth I (1533–1603) Queen of England (1558/1603). She was the daughter of **Henry VIII** by his second wife, Anne **Boleyn**. On the death of **Edward VI** (1553), she sided with her Catholic half-sister, Mary, against Lady Jane **Grey** and the Duke of Northumberland, but her identification with Protestantism made Mary suspicious, and so she was imprisoned for her alleged part in the rebellion led by Sir Thomas Wyatt (1554). Ascending the throne on **Mary I**'s death, she reduced animosities and promoted stability by engineering a moderate Protestant Church settlement, and it is from this time that a distinctive Anglican Church was effectively established. She made peace with France and Scotland, and strengthened her position by secretly helping Protestants in these countries. **Mary, Queen of Scots**, was thrown into her power (1568) and imprisoned, causing numerous conspiracies among English Catholics. After the most sinister plot was discovered (1586), Elizabeth was reluctantly persuaded to execute Mary (1587); many other Catholics were persecuted in the 1580s and 1590s. Infuriated by this, and by Elizabeth's part in inciting the Netherlands against him, Philip of Spain attacked England with his 'invincible **Armada**' (1588), but England managed to repel the attack, though war continued until 1604. Of all Elizabeth's personal relationships, only one touched her deeply, that with Robert Dudley, Earl of **Leicester**, whom she would probably have married had it not been for her adviser **Cecil**'s remonstrations. A strong and astute, but sometimes cruel and capricious, woman, the 'Virgin Queen' was nevertheless popular with her subjects, becoming later known as 'Good Queen Bess', and her reign is seen as a period of generally effective government and increased international status.

Elizabeth II (1926–), Queen of the UK (1952/   ) and Head of the **Commonwealth of Nations**. The elder daughter of King **George VI**, she was proclaimed Queen on 6 Feb 1952, and crowned on 2 June 1953. Her husband was created Duke of Edinburgh on the eve of their wedding (20 Nov 1947), and styled Prince Philip in 1957. They have three sons, Prince **Charles**, Prince Andrew, and Prince Edward, and a daughter, Princess Anne.

Elizabeth Petrovna (1709–62) Empress of Russia (1741/62). The daughter of **Peter I, 'the Great'** and **Catherine I**, she was passed over for the succession in 1727, 1730 and 1740, finally becoming empress on the deposition of Ivan VI. She was guided by favourites throughout her reign, some better than others. A war with Sweden was brought to a successful conclusion, but her animosity towards **Frederick II, 'the Great'** led her to take part in the War of the **Austrian Succession** and in the **Seven Years War**, which helped to establish Russia as a European power. At home, she contributed considerably to the extension and entrenchment of serfdom.

Ellenborough, Edward Law, 1st Earl of (1790–1871) British politician. He became a Tory MP in 1813, held office under several administrations, and was Governor-General of India (1841). Parliament approved his Afghan policy in 1843, but his subsequent policy led to his early recall (1844). He was then created Viscount Southam and Earl of Ellenborough. He became First Lord of the Admiralty in 1846,

and in 1858 was made Minister for India, but the publication of a dispatch in which he rebuked Viscount **Canning** forced him to resign and he held no further office.

Elphinstone, Mountstuart, 11th Lord Elphinstone (1779–1859) British colonial administrator and historian. He entered the Bengal civil service in 1795, served with distinction on **Wellesley**'s staff (1803) at the Battle of Assaye, and was appointed Resident at Nagpur. In 1808 he was sent as the first British Envoy to Kabul; and as Resident from 1810 at Pune ended the Maratha War of 1817 and organized the newly-acquired territory. He was Governor-General of Bombay (1819–27), where he founded the system of administration, and did much to advance state education in India. He returned to Britain in 1829, and, declining the governor-generalship of India, lived in comparative retirement until his death.

Emancipation Acts Statutes of imperial legislatures which freed colonial slaves. The bill to emancipate slaves in the **British Empire** was introduced by Buxton and was passed in Aug 1833. It granted financial compensation to the slave owners and freed the slaves under a system of **Apprenticeship** on 1 Aug 1834. On that date 750 000 slaves became free in the British West Indies and it was reported that the expected trouble had not materialized and that the ex-slaves had spent the weekend in chapels and churches in thanksgiving. France freed its slaves in 1848, the Netherlands in 1863, the USA in 1865 and Spain in 1885.

Emancipation Proclamation (1 Jan 1863) A document issued by President Abraham **Lincoln** during the **American Civil War**, that declared the freedom of all slaves in areas then in rebellion against the US government. Originally set forth in a preliminary statement on 22 Sep 1862, it was intended as a war measure to reduce the reserves of manpower in the South. It freed the slaves in the Confederacy but did not free the slaves in areas that supported the US government (the Union).

Emanuel (Manuel) I, 'the Great' (1469–1521) King of Portugal (1495/1521). He consolidated royal power, and his reign, marred only by persecution of the Jews, was the golden age of Portugal. He prepared the code of laws which bears his name, and made his court a centre of chivalry, art, and science. He sponsored the voyages of Vasco da

Gama, Cabral, and others, which helped to make Portugal the first naval power of Europe and a world centre of commerce.

Emma (Adelheid Emma Wilhelmina Theresia) (1858–1934) Queen and Regent of the Netherlands (1879/98). The daughter of Prince George Victor of Waldeck-Pyrmont and Helena of Nassau-Weilburg, she became the second wife of the Dutch King **William III** on 7 Jan 1879. In 1880 her daughter, the future Queen **Wilhelmina**, was born; Emma became Regent shortly before the death of her husband in Dec 1890 until her daughter came of age in 1898. After William III's unpopularity, Emma succeeded in restoring the esteem of the Dutch for their monarchy.

Emmet, Robert (1778–1803) Irish patriot. He left Trinity College to join the United Irishmen, and travelled on the Continent for the Irish cause, at one point meeting **Napoleon I**. In 1803, he plotted an insurrection against the English, but it proved a failure. He was captured and hanged in Dublin.

Empecinado, El (Juan Martín Díaz) (1775–1825) Spanish soldier and patriot. El Empecinado (literally, 'the Stubborn One') acquired great distinction as a guerrilla leader against the French in the **Peninsular War** (1808–14). He became a general in 1814, but for petitioning Ferdinand III to re-establish the **Cortes** was banished to Valladolid (1818). On the outbreak of the insurrection in 1820, he joined the Constitutionalists; and on the Absolutists' triumph in 1823 he was exhibited in an iron cage, and fatally stabbed by a soldier.

Empire, First (France) The system of government established by **Napoleon I** in 1804, which continued until his fall in 1814, restored for the **Hundred Days** in 1815, then abolished after his defeat at the Battle of **Waterloo**.

Empire, Second (France) The system of government established by Louis Napoleon (**Napoleon III**) in 1852, which continued until he fell from power in Sep 1870.

encomienda A feudal-type tenure or grant, applied especially to the tenure of landed property, and known in Spain since the Middle Ages. The best-known *encomiendas* were those of the Military Orders, such as those of the Orders of **Alcantara** and **Santiago**, their holders being known as *encomen-*

deros. In America, from the 16c the word *encomienda* was applied to the tenure or grant of the labour of native Indians, and was known also as a *repartimiento*.

Encyclopedists A collective term for the distinguished editors (Diderot and d'Alembert) and contributors (notably Voltaire, **Montesquieu, Condorcet,** Helvetius, and **Rousseau**) to the *Encyclopédie*, a major work of social and political reference published in France (1751–72), associated with the French Enlightenment. ▷ **Philosophes**

Engelbrekt Engelbrektsson (c.1390–1436) Swedish rebel and military commander. He was born in Bergslagen of an iron-mining family of German ancestry. When the war between King **Erik of Pomerania** and the Hanseatic League disrupted iron exports, he led a series of rebellions against the King, and in 1434 forced the Council of the Realm to retract its oath of loyalty to Erik. In the following year, at a meeting of the Estates at Arboga (often described as the first Swedish Parliament), he was appointed commander-in-chief of the realm. Within a few months the Council reversed its decision, but a year later Erik was again deposed, and Engelbrekt was appointed joint commander-in-chief with the noble, **Karl Knutsson**. Shortly after this Engelbrekt was murdered, as the result of a personal quarrel, while travelling from his castle at Örebro to Stockholm. His reputation as a hero of national liberation has ensured him a place in literature, not least in the 'Song of Liberty' by Bishop Thomas of Strangnas, the greatest Swedish poem of the Middle Ages.

Engels, Friedrich (1820–95) German socialist philosopher, collaborator with Karl **Marx**, and founder of 'scientific socialism'. From 1842 he lived mostly in England. He first met Marx in Brussels in 1844 and collaborated with him on the *Communist Manifesto* (1848). He died in London, after spending his later years editing and translating Marx's writings. ▷ **communism; Marxism; Marxism–Leninism; socialism**

Enghien, Louis Antoine Henri de Bourbon, Duke of (1772–1804) French soldier, the only son of Louis Henri Joseph, Prince of Condé. He commanded the emigré vanguard from 1796 to 1799. At the peace of Lunéville (1801) he went to reside in Baden. Bonaparte, claiming that Enghien was involved in a conspiracy against him, violated the neutral territory of Baden, captured the duke and took him to Vincennes. In Mar 1804, he was shot in the castle moat. Boulay de la Meurthe said of this act that it was worse than a crime — it was a blunder, a saying often wrongly attributed to **Fouché** or to **Talleyrand**. ▷ **Napoleon I**

Englandspiel (1942–4) The codename given to a highly successful German counter-espionage operation in the Netherlands in **World War II**. The occupying German forces obtained the codes used by the Dutch resistance in radio contact with Britain, and by impersonating the resistance the Germans were able to capture 57 agents sent in from England, and to arrest hundreds of resistance personnel. Several English bombers were also brought down by them. ▷ **Resistance Movement** (Netherlands)

English Civil Wars (1642–8) The country's greatest internal conflict, between supporters of parliament and supporters of **Charles I**, caused by parliamentary opposition to what it considered growing royal power. Although the King left London in Mar 1642, open hostilities between royalists and parliamentarians did not immediately break out. The prospect of compromise was bleak, but both sides, fearing the consequences of civil strife, moved slowly towards the use of armed force. Charles finally issued commissions of array (June 1642), and raised his standard two months later at Nottingham. The first major engagement took place at Edgehill in Oct. It was inconclusive, but royalist forces then threatened London, the key parliamentary stronghold. Royalist strategy in 1643 centred upon taking the capital by a three-pronged attack from armies in the north, the south-west and the Thames valley. By autumn the north and the west (apart from a garrison in Gloucester) were in their hands, although parliament held back the tide in the (drawn) first Battle of Newbury. The crucial event of 1643 was parliament's alliance with the Scots in the **Solemn League and Covenant**, which strengthened its hand militarily and threatened the King's forces on a new front. In 1644 parliament, assisted by the Scots, became a formidable foe. This was clear in July when its forces, aided by Scottish invaders, inflicted a serious defeat upon the royalists at the Battle of **Marston Moor**. However, the King's forces were swamped in the west. In 1643 they were victorious over the Earl of Essex in the Battle of Lostwithiel, and in the second Battle of Newbury they were successful against the combined forces of Essex, the Earl of Manchester, and Sir William Waller.

In 1645, strengthened by the creation of the **New Model Army**, parliament's cause advanced in the Midlands and the west, with important victories at the Battles of **Naseby** and Langport. The First Civil War ended in 1646 when Charles surrendered to the Scots at Newark in May, and his stronghold of Oxford fell in June. He was taken into parliamentary custody (Jan 1647) when the Scots left for home, and in June was seized by the army. From June 1646 to Apr 1648 there was an uneasy peace and attempts at compromise. Negotiations between the King and parliament had begun as early as 1645, but they achieved little. The main sticking points were religion, particularly parliament's disestablishment of the Church, and the King's prerogative rights, many of which had been abolished by parliament. The climax came (Aug 1647) when the army presented the King with the Heads of Proposals, calling for religious toleration, and parliamentary control of the armed forces. Charles made a secret alliance with the Scots, promising to establish Presbyterianism in England which parliament had failed to do; they invaded England (Apr 1648), and were repulsed only after the Battle of Preston (Aug). Bitterly fought, the second war earned Charles the epithet 'that man of blood' and, ultimately, his execution (30 Jan 1649). Possibly 100 000 died in the two wars: 1 in 10 of adult males. ▷ **Cavaliers; Commonwealth; Covenanters; Cromwell, Oliver; Independents** (England); **Ireton, Henry**

Enlightened Despots The misnomer for a number of European absolute monarchs who, under the influence of the ideas of the Enlightenment, used their power to pursue comprehensive legal, social and educational reforms. However, while they acknowledged responsibility for the common good, political consultation and popular participation remained firmly ruled out. Best-known examples are **Frederick II, 'the Great'** of Prussia, **Joseph II** of Austria, Leopold II (as Duke of Tuscany), **Catherine II, 'the Great'** of Russia and **Charles Frederick of Baden**.

enosis The Greek term for the policy of seeking union with Greece, first applied in the 1840s to the Cretans' agitation for union with the Kingdom of Greece. In Cyprus in the 1950s, demands for independence from Britain and enosis became insistent, giving rise to the underground movement **EOKA**. There followed a serious and long-running conflict amounting to civil war between the island's Greek and Turkish inhabitants, with the latter bitterly opposed to enosis. ▷ **Makarios III; Grivas, Georgeios; Karamanlis, Constantine**

enragés Literally 'madmen', the term refers to a group of French revolutionary extremists, led by Jacques Roux. Enjoying popular support (1793), and dedicated to radical social and economic measures (eg controls on food), they were supplanted by the Hébertists (Sep 1793). Roux was executed by the Jacobin government. ▷ **French Revolution; Hébert, Jacques René; Jacobins**

Entente Cordiale A term first used in the 1840s to describe a close relationship between the UK and France; then given to a series of agreements in 1904 between the two countries, dealing with a range of issues, in particular establishing the predominant role of the UK in Egypt, and France's interests in Morocco.

Enver Pasha (1881–1922) Turkish soldier and politician. A leader in the 1908 revolution of **Young Turks**, in Aug 1914 as the pro-German Minister of War he steered the Turkish government into a secret alliance with Germany directed against Russia. After the Turkish surrender in 1918 at the end of **World War I**, he fled to Russia and was killed in an insurrection in Turkestan.

EOKA (*Ethniki Organosis Kipriakou Agono*, 'National Organization of Cypriot Struggle') A Greek-Cypriot underground movement which sought both to end British rule and achieve **enosis** (union with Greece). Founded in 1955 by a Greek army officer, Colonel Georgeios **Grivas**, and supported by Archbishop **Makarios III**, it pursued a campaign of anti-British violence which came to a climax in 1956–7. EOKA declined and was disbanded after Makarios's acceptance in 1958 of independence for Cyprus rather than enosis. The organization was resurrected unsuccessfully as EOKA B during the period 1971–4. ▷ **Karamanlis, Constantine**

Eötvös, József, Baron (1813–71) Hungarian author and politician. He became an advocate in 1833, but soon devoting himself to literature, published a work on prison reform, and the novels, *The Carthusian* (1838–41), *The Village Notary* (1846) and others. In 1848 he was Minister of Religion and Public Instruction, and held the post again under **Andrássy** in 1867–71. He was responsible for some liberal legislation.

Epaminondas (c.420–362BC) Theban general and politician. His victory at the Battle of **Leuctra** (371BC) broke the military power of **Sparta** and made **Thebes** the most powerful state in Greece. His death at the Battle of Mantinea, however, brought this supremacy to an abrupt end.

Ephialtes (d.461BC) Athenian politician. He enacted the constitutional reforms (462–461BC) which broke the power of the **Areopagus** and ushered in radical democracy at Athens. He was murdered shortly afterwards by his political opponents. ▷ **Cleisthenes**

Ephors 'Overseers'; in ancient **Sparta**, the name for the chief magistrates. Five were elected annually, of whom one was 'eponymous' (ie gave his name to the year).

Epirus The region divided between Albania and Greece lying between the Pindos Mountains and the Ionian Sea. A kingdom in antiquity, the ruling family of the dominant Molossian tribe included Olympias, wife of **Philip II** of Macedon and mother of **Alexander III, 'the Great'**; her brother Alexander became the first King of Epirus. Its most notable king was **Pyrrhus** (c.319–272BC). In 168BC it became part of the Roman province of Macedonia and was repeatedly invaded during the Middle Ages. Under Byzantine rule, it was divided with centres at Dyrrachium (Durrës in modern Albania) and Acarnania. After 1204 it was established as a despotate but it returned to Byzantine rule (1335) until it was taken by the Serbs (1348–86). During the 15c the Turks and Venetians occupied much of Epirus. The part under Turkish rule was freed in 1881 and, although the Greek Army occupied north Epirus during the **Balkan Wars**, in 1913 most of Epirus went to form the newly independent Albanian state. ▷ **Greeks**

Equal-Field System (*juntian*) A system of land distribution carried out by the state in imperial China. It had its origins in the attempts by the sinicized Northern Wei Dynasty (386–534) of the Toba Turks to reduce the influence of a powerful landed aristocracy by limiting landholdings and controlling acquisition of landed property and reached its apogee in the **Tang Dynasty**. During the first half of the Tang Dynasty, the state claimed ownership of all agricultural land and assumed the duty of allocating landholdings equitably on the basis of labour power. In theory, land was to revert to the state on the owner's death and be reallocated. The system was, however, gradually undermined by population growth and the granting of large inheritable tracts to officials and favourites. After the mid-8c, inequalities in land ownership were accepted and the principle that the state had the duty to intervene and correct inequalities in land distribution was abandoned.

Equal Rights Amendment Proposed amendment to the US Constitution stating that equal rights shall not be denied on account of sex. First introduced in 1923, it was not approved by Congress until 1972. Although the adoption deadline was extended from 1979 to 1982, the amendment fell just short of ratification by the required 38 states.

Erfurt, Congress of (27 Sep–14 Oct 1808) This settlement of European affairs between **Napoleon I** and the Russian Tsar **Alexander I** was also attended by the 34 princes of the Confederation of the Rhine. They were treated dismissively by Napoleon, but Alexander was able to achieve a reduction in Prussian **reparations** due to France from 140 to 120 million francs. In return for territorial gains in Eastern Europe (Finland, Moldavia, Wallachia), Russia agreed not to hinder the French war effort in Spain and to join France if the latter were attacked by **Austria**.

Erfurt Programme (Oct 1891) A programme formulated by the **SPD** in a conference which lent German social democracy an explicitly Marxist flavour. The SPD still subscribed to the principles of political liberty, but adopted a Marxist view of economics and future economic development which coexisted uneasily with the social reformist character of many of its day-to-day policies. ▷ **Gotha, Congress of; Marxism**

Erhard, Ludwig (1897–1977) German economist and politician. Professor of Economics at Munich, he was appointed by the Americans as Economic Director of the Bizone in 1948. In the following year he was elected to the Federal Parliament in **Bonn** and made Economics Minister in the **Adenauer** administration. He was a leading architect of the **social market economy**, a key element of the West German 'economic miracle' of recovery from wartime devastation. He succeeded **Adenauer** as Chancellor (1963–6), but economic difficulties forced his resignation. ▷ **Christian Democrats**

Eridu The oldest of the Sumerian city-states, lying south-west of Ur. Excavations of the site have revealed a continuous series of temples starting in the sixth millennium BC and ending in the third with the great ziggurat. ▷ **Sumer; Ur**

Erie Railroad US railroad linking the Great Lakes with New York City. Its construction became a by-word for fraud, financial manipulation and political corruption by speculators Jim Fisk and Jay Gould, who also issued millions of dollars of watered stock in order to beat off a takeover bid from Cornelius Vanderbilt in 1868. The railroad collapsed under this burden of debt in the depression of 1893, but underwent several subsequent reorganizations and bankruptcies.

Erik XIII of Sweden ▷ **Erik of Pomerania**

Erik XIV (1533–77) King of Sweden (1560/9). He was the eldest son and successor of **Gustav I Vasa**. Tutored by a German Lutheran nobleman, his outlook was that of a Renaissance prince. His temperament was, however, highly unstable. Suspicious of others to the point of paranoia, in 1563 he imprisoned his half-brother, John (III), who had been conducting an independent foreign policy as Duke of Finland. In the same year Erik became involved in a seven-year war with the Denmark of **Frederick II**, Lübeck and Poland, which ended inconclusively with the Peace of Stettin (1570). Before it ended he had several members of the Sture family butchered on unjustified suspicion of having designs on the Swedish throne, and in 1568 married privately a lowly soldier's daughter, Karin Månsdotter. This provided a pretext for a rebellion amongst the nobles led by his half-brothers, John and Charles (IX), who in 1569 dethroned him in favour of John. Erik spent the rest of his days in captivity and probably died of arsenic poisoning, administered on John's orders. In his early years he was a suitor for the hand of both **Elizabeth I** of England and **Mary, Queen of Scots**.

Erik Bloodaxe (d.954) King of Norway (942/7) and later of the Viking kingdom of York (948/54). The eldest son of **Harald Fairhair**, he succeeded to the throne of Norway on his 80-year-old father's abdication. His wife was Gunnlaug, the imperious and ruthless sister of King **Harald Bluetooth** of Denmark. His reign in Norway was marked by much violence, and Erik killed several of his half-brothers who had rebelled against him. He was deposed by his youngest brother, **Haakon the Good**, in 947 and sought refuge in England, where he was accepted as king in York of the Norse realm in Northumbria. He was eventually expelled in 954 and killed in battle at Stainmore in Yorkshire.

Erik Jedvarsson, Saint (d.c.1160) King of Sweden (c.1158/60). The patron saint of Sweden, he is said to have led a Christian crusade for the conversion of the Finns and to have been murdered at mass in Uppsala by a Danish pretender to his throne. He was married to Kristina, who was descended from a royal line of Swedish kings, and was the father of King Knut Eriksson (c.1173/96).

Erik of Pomerania (1382–1459) King of Sweden (1397/1438), Denmark (1397/1439) and Norway (1397/1442). The son of Duke Wratislaw VII of Pomerania and Maria, the niece of Queen **Margrethe I**, he was adopted as heir to the triple monarchy by his great-aunt, in 1389, and crowned at Kalmar in Sweden in 1397, when the treaty of union between the three countries was formally sealed. In 1405 he married Philippa, the daughter of King **Henry IV** of England. It was not until 1412, however, on Queen Margrethe's death, that he gained actual power. Aggressive commercial and military policies against the **Hanseatic League** that ultimately failed, led to economic disasters that fomented rebellion, and he was deposed by all three countries one by one: Sweden in 1438, Denmark in 1439 and Norway in 1442. He was succeeded by his nephew, Christopher of Bavaria. ▷ **Kalmar Union**

Eritrea Liberation Front (ELF) A movement seeking independence from Ethiopia, founded in 1958. Eritrea, an Italian colony from 1884, was federated with Ethiopia at the request of the **UN** in 1952 and then incorporated as a province in 1962. This galvanized the Front into action and, despite some divisions, it managed, through support from the Eastern bloc and some Arab countries, to prevent its destruction both while **Haile Selassie** was Emperor and when **Mengistu** was President. The collapse of the **Dergue** in 1991 advanced its position.

Erlander, Tage Fritiof (1901–85) Swedish politician. He became active in the Social Democratic Party while he was studying at the University of Lund and was elected to parliament in 1933. He was minister without portfolio in the wartime coalition government from 1944, and was Minister for Ecclesiastical Affairs when chosen to succeed

Per Albin **Hansson** as party leader and Prime Minister in 1946. He made way for the younger Sven Olof **Palme** in 1969. A moderate, his brand of consensual government was dubbed 'Harpsund democracy' after his country estate, where he consulted with leaders in all walks of society.

Ershad, Hussain Muhammad (1929–   ) Bangladesh soldier and chief martial law administrator. Appointed army Chief-of-Staff by President **Ziaur Rahman** in 1978, he repeatedly demanded that the armed forces should be involved in the country's administration. In 1982 he led a bloodless military coup, becoming President the following year.

Erskine, Thomas, 1st Baron (1750–1823) British jurist. He sought a career in the navy and army before studying law. Called to the Bar in 1778, his success was immediate and unprecedented, and he became a KC and MP (1783). His sympathy with the **French Revolution** led him to join the 'Friends of the People', and to undertake the defence in many political prosecutions of 1793–4, notably of Thomas **Paine**. He became a peer in 1806 and for a while acted as Lord Chancellor (1806–7), after which he retired into private life.

Erzberger, Matthias (1875–1921) German politician. He became controversial when, as a leading member of the Centre Party, he began to advocate peace without annexations as early as 1917 and again (1918–19) when, as a member of the armistice delegation, he advocated acceptance, despite some fierce German opposition, of the terms of the Treaty of **Versailles**. Finance Minister and Vice-Premier in 1919, he drastically reformed the tax system and nationalized the German railways. Unsuccessful in a libel action against an unscrupulous political opponent, he resigned in Feb 1921 and was assassinated in Aug of the same year by members of an extremist group (*Organisation Consul*) in the Black Forest.

Erzerum, Treaty of (1823, confirmed 1847) More usually regarded as two treaties, the Treaty of Erzerum in its first manifestation was signed on 18 July 1823 and was expressly aimed at defining the frontier in lower Iraq between the territories of the Ottoman Sultan and those of the Qajar Shah of Persia. However, the disputes which had arisen over the frontier, centring on the foundation (1812) of the town of Muhammara at the mouth of the Karun River, were not effectively solved by the 1823 treaty. Both Sultan and Shah continued to claim the town, and the dispute led to the signing of the so-called 'Second' Treaty of Erzerum in 1847, by which Muhammara was granted to the Persians.

Esarhaddon (d.669BC) King of Assyria (680/669BC). The son of Sennacherib and father of Assurbanipal, he is best-known for his conquest of Egypt (671BC).

Eshkol, Levi (1895–1969) Israeli politician. Born in the Ukraine to parents of traditional Jewish piety, he settled in Palestine as an agricultural worker in 1914. After Israeli independence in 1948, he supervised the founding of several hundred new villages to absorb immigrants. A member of the **Mapai Party**, Eshkol served as Minister of Finance (1952–63) and as Prime Minister and Defence Minister (1963–9), transferring the latter post to Moshe **Dayan** during the **Six-Day War** of 1967. Eshkol established diplomatic relations with West Germany and was also the first Israeli leader to visit the USA. Despite internal political difficulties in 1964–5, he remained Prime Minister until his death. ▷ **Restitution Agreement**

Espartero, Baldomero (1793–1879) Spanish general and politician. He spent the period 1815–25 in South America, fighting the independence movements. After the accession of **Isabella II** in 1833, he played a leading role in defeating the Carlist supporters of her uncle, Don **Carlos**, driving Don Carlos from Spain (1884) and being made Duke of Vitoria. In 1841 he was instrumental in forcing Isabella's mother, **María Cristina**, to leave Spain, becoming sole regent (1841/3). He was, therefore, Spain's first modern **caudillo**. Driven out by Ramón **Narváez** in 1843, he lived abroad in England and in retirement in Spain, but in 1854, with Leopold **O'Donnell**, led a successful revolution. In 1856 he resigned as head of the revolutionary government in favour of O'Donnell. In 1870 his name was put forward for the throne, which he refused; and in 1875 he tendered his allegiance to **Alfonso XII** after his accession.

Esquilache (Squillace), Leopoldo de Gregorio, Marquis of (d.1785) Spanish politician. Secretary of War and Finance under **Charles III** of Spain, he held the post of Minister of Finance in Naples before he came with the new monarch from Italy in 1759. He attempted a number of reforms in the Spanish fiscal system, but was frustrated by opposition and by a series of bad harvests (1760–6) which precipitated agitation in several cities. He was sacked (Mar 1766) after major riots in Madrid ('the Esquilache Riots'), apparently provoked by a new decree regulating dress. The Jesuits were blamed for the events and expelled. Esquilache returned to Naples the following month and was then appointed Spanish ambassador in Venice.

Essex, Robert Devereux, 2nd Earl of (1566–1601) English soldier and courtier. He served in the Netherlands (1585–6), and distinguished himself at Zutphen. At court, he quickly rose in the favour of **Elizabeth I**, despite his clandestine marriage in 1590 with Sir Philip Sidney's widow. In 1591 he commanded the forces sent to help **Henry IV** of France, and took part in the sacking of Cadiz (1595). He became a Privy Councillor (1593) and Earl Marshal (1597). He alienated the Queen's advisers, and there were constant quarrels with Elizabeth (notably the occasion when he turned his back on her, and she boxed his ears). His six months' lord-lieutenancy of Ireland (1599) proved a failure; he was imprisoned and deprived of his dignities. He attempted to raise the City of London, was found guilty of high treason, and beheaded in the Tower.

Estado Novo (Brazil) Literally 'New State', this was the name given by President Getúlio **Vargas** to his authoritarian regime in Brazil (1937–45). The term was copied from the Estado Novo established in **Salazar**'s Portugal. The Estado Novo had a profound influence on the party political structure of Brazil until 1965. The political leadership of the various states imposed by Vargas in 1937 formed the backbone of the **PSD**, while the labour unions formed the 'nationalist' PTB (*Partido Trabalhista Brasileiro*). Francisco Campos and Carlos Medeiros Silva, architects of the Estado Novo, were brought back to reshape the constitution of 1946 in an authoritarian mould. ▷ **Estado Novo** (Portugal)

Estado Novo (Portugal) The authoritarian political system (literally, 'New State') under **Salazar** which ruled Portugal from the early 1930s to 1969. This entailed the abolition of political parties and trade unions, total censorship, the vesting of power in an all-powerful executive, and the glorification of the values of 'God, Country, and Family'. Despite its fascist trappings and corporatist aspirations, the aim of the Estado Novo was mass depoliticization rather than mobilization within a single party totally identified with the state. The heavily centralized and authoritarian Estado Novo effectively allowed the old elite to retain political and social control.

estancia A standard term used in Spanish America to denote a ranch. By the early 16c, *estancia* denoted a private landholding held by a Spaniard or creole, supplying cattle to the towns and *encomenderos*. By the mid-17c, they had absorbed Indian lands and were combined as haciendas. Estancias emerged in late 18c Rio de la Plata as large tracts of open land owned by merchants of Buenos Aires, such as Juan Manuel de **Rosas**, on which cattle were bred and driven for slaughter in coastal *saladeros* (salting plants). Enclosed by barbed wire a century later, their vast wealth supported the Argentine economy. The same development can also be charted for the rise of analogous groups in Uruguay and Rio Grande do Sul, Brazil. ▷ **encomienda; hacienda**

Estates The divisions in medieval society recognized by law. Most European societies were divided into clergy, nobles and commoners. However, within each group there were often strict delineations. Thus, for example, the clergy were divided into bishops, parish priests and monks, the nobles had various gradations of aristocracy and the commoners would have been separated into urban dwellers with civic rights, those without, and peasants bound to the land. All of these distinctions were of some legal and social importance though the distinctions varied according to place and time.

Estates General (*Etats-Généraux*) (France) An assembly representing the different provinces of the French monarchy, called by the King primarily to grant taxes, roughly equivalent to the English parliament, beginning in 14c (the normally accepted date for its first meeting is 1347). Although it never met on such a regular basis as the English parliament, it appeared by 16c to be on the way to becoming a regular institution, but after the meeting of 1614 no more were called until 1789. In the intervening period the king ruled as an absolute monarch, although some provincial Estates continued to meet intermittently. Both the Estates General and the provincial Estates met and voted in three separate houses: the First Estate (the clergy), the Second Estate (the nobility) and the

Third Estate (the commoners). Hence the Third Estate was the whole non-noble population, except for the clergy.

Este (1000–1875) Italian family who became rulers of Ferrara towards the end of the 12c and maintained their hegemony over the city until 1598, when it was incorporated into the **Papal States**. Azzo D'Este (1205–64), the first marquess, had established his authority over the area by the time of his death, and the office of *signore* of Ferrara was made hereditary in the family during the time of his son, Obizzo (d.1293), and the territories of Modena and Reggio were annexed to it. Niccolo III (1383–1441) brought peace and security to the state during his long reign while his sons and successors Leonello (1407–50), Borso (1413–71) and Ercole (1431–1505) were notable patrons of the arts and of humanist scholarship, a tradition continued by Isabella (1474–1539) and Beatrice (1475–97), daughters of Ercole, who married respectively Francesco **Gonzaga** of Mantua and Lodovico **Sforza** of Milan. Alfonso I (d.1534) quarrelled with Popes **Julius II** and **Leo X** and lost the family's papal fiefs in 1527 while his son Ippolito (d.1572) erected the magnificent Villa d'Este at Tivoli. Although Ferrara was lost in 1598, the family retained the duchy of Modena until 1859 when Francis V (1819–75) resigned his territories to **Victor Emmanuel II**.

Esterházy A powerful Hungarian aristocratic family, which flourished in several branches between the 16c and 19c. Among its many members were Count Pál Esterházy of Fraknó (1635–1713), the Habsburg field marshal, who was made a Prince of the Empire in 1687 for promoting the dynasty's cause and for his successes against the Turks. Prince Miklós IV (1765–1833) fought against Napoleon, but by extravagance brought his vast estates into sequestration. Prince Pál Antal (1786–1866), represented Austria in London until 1842, and in 1848 was Minister of Foreign Affairs.

Estigarribia, José Félix (1888–1940) Paraguayan general and war hero. He won fame as a brilliant commander in the **Chaco War** (1932–5), on the strength of which he became President (1939–40). He died in a plane crash near Asunción.

Estrada Palma, Tomás (1835–1908) Cuban nationalist and politician. A commander in the **Ten Years War**, he was captured by the

Spanish in 1877 and on his release moved to New York where he became Principal of the Central High School for Boys and leader of the Cuban exiles in the USA. For his work for the struggle for Cuban independence in the USA, he was elected President of the new republic (1901 and 1905) but, after having to call in US troops in 1906 to put down a rebellion against his government, was forced into retirement.

ETA (*Euskadi Ta Askatasuna*, 'Basque Homeland and Freedom') The extremist Basque nationalist organization set up in 1959 to secure the independence of the Basque country. It was later influenced by Third World nationalism, Marxism, and the use of violence, all of which led to much inner feuding and divisions. ETA initiated a campaign of armed struggle in 1968, which has led to over 400 assassinations. Its killing of Admiral **Carrero Blanco** in 1973 undoubtedly altered the course of the post-Francoist transition. The organization's political front, *Herri Batasuna* ('Popular Unity'), generally wins about 12 per cent of the vote in the Basque country, and elected seven deputies to the Cortes in the 1986 election.

Ethelbert (c.552–616) King of Kent (560/616). In his reign Kent achieved (c.590) control over England south of the Humber, and Christianity was introduced by St **Augustine** (597). To him we owe the first written English laws. ▷ **Anglo-Saxons**

Ethelred I (c.830–71) King of Wessex (865/71). He was the elder brother of **Alfred, 'the Great'**. It was during Ethelred's reign that the Danes launched their main invasion of England. He died soon after his victory over the invaders. ▷ **Wessex**

Ethelred the Unready (c.968–1016) King of England (978/1016). The son of **Edgar**, he was aged about 10 when the murder of his half-brother, **Edward the Martyr**, placed him on the throne. In 1002 he confirmed an alliance with **Normandy** by marrying, as his second wife, Duke Richard's daughter Emma — the first dynastic link between the two countries. Renewed attacks by the **Vikings** on England began as raids in the 980s, and in 1013 Sweyn Forkbeard secured mastery over the whole country, and forced Ethelred into exile in Normandy. After Sweyn's death (1014), he returned to oppose **Canute**, but the unity of English resistance was broken when his son, **Edmund II, 'Ironside'**, rebelled. 'Unready' is a mistranslation of *Unraed*, not recorded as his nickname until after the **Norman Conquest**, which means 'ill-advised' and is a pun on his given name, Ethelred (literally, 'good counsel').

Ethiopia formerly **Abyssinia** A state in north-east Africa. It is the oldest independent country in sub-Saharan Africa, and the first African country to be Christianized. Abyssinian independence was recognized by the League of Nations in 1923, but after the invasion of Italy in 1935 the country was annexed as Italian East Africa from 1936 to 1941, when Emperor **Haile Seslassie** returned from exile. A military coup led to the establishment of the Provisional Military Administrative Council (PMAC) in 1974, and left-wing opposition was met by mass arrests and executions in 1977–8. In addition to conflict with Somalia over the Ogaden district during the 1970s and 1980s, there was internal division with separatist Eritrean and Tigrean forces, who secured victories over government troops in the early 1980s, while the country suffered severe famine. PMAC dissolved in 1987, with the transfer of power to the People's Democratic Republic, but an attempted coup in 1989 was followed by the collapse of the government in 1991 and renewed famine in 1992. Eritrea secured independence in 1993.

ethnic cleansing The removal from an area by the militarily superior ethnic group, either by extermination or forced migration, of members of the other ethnic groups; the term was used originally in the former Yugoslavia.

Eto Shimpei (1834–74) Japanese politician. From a lower-ranking **samurai** family, he was a participant in the overthrow of the **Tokugawa Shogunate** and was awarded a minor government post. In 1872, as Minister of Justice, he helped draft a new penal code. He resigned the following year in protest against the government's refusal to sanction a military expedition to Korea and began to champion the disgruntled samurai in his home prefecture of Saga, most of whom had fallen on hard times following the political and social reforms of the new government. By 1874 Eto was calling for a national representative assembly, condemning the monopoly of power held by those from the former feudal domains of **Satsuma** and **Choshu**. Following his attempted armed uprising in Saga in 1874, he was tried and executed.

Etruria The heartland of the Etruscan people, roughly corresponding to modern Tuscany. In antiquity, it was defined as the area between the Arno, Tiber, Apennines, and Tyrrhenian Sea. ▷ **Etruscans**

Etruscans A people of obscure origin who sprang to prominence in western central Italy in the 8c BC. At the height of their power their influence extended from the Po valley to Campania, taking in Rome itself. Although they succumbed to the Romans politically in the 3c, culturally their influence remained strong. In religion, civil engineering, and urban planning the Romans owed much to them. Their lavishly equipped tombs show that they were particularly skilled in metalwork, and heavily engaged in trade with the Greek world. ▷ **Camillus, Marcus Furius; Etruria; Veii**

Euboea (Euboia) A large island off the north-east coast of Greece; excavations at Lefkandi show its prosperity until the late 8c BC, when a war between its chief cities, Chalcis and Eretria, over control of the Lelantine plain, involved (according to **Thucydides**) all the major states of Greece. In the 5c BC, it became part of the **Athenian Empire**; after an unsuccessful revolt in 446BC, it successfully seceded in 411BC. It also belonged to the Second Athenian **Confederacy**.

Eugene of Savoy, Prince (François Eugène de Savoie Carignan) (1663–1736) Austrian general. Born in Paris and brought up at the court of **Louis XIV** of France, he left when refused a commission and, at the age of 19, entered the service of Emperor Leopold I. Having distinguished himself in the war against the Turks, he was appointed field marshal in 1694. On the outbreak of the War of the **Spanish Succession** (1701), he was made commander of the imperial army in Italy, joined forces with Marlborough at the Danube in 1704, leading up to the decisive victory at Blenheim. Their cooperation was renewed in 1708 in the Netherlands, resulting in the victories of **Oudenarde** (11 July 1708) and **Malplaquet** (1709). After Marlborough's recall, he succeeded to the allied supreme command but, abandoned by England, had to accept the terms of the Peace of **Rastatt** (1714). By 1716 he was again in the field against the Turks, putting an end to their power in Hungary and capturing Belgrade (1718). Distrusted by Emperor **Charles VI** and plotted against at court, he retired from active service to devote himself to the arts

and literature and to the building of his palace of Belvedere in Vienna, where he died.

Eugenius III (Bernardo Paganelli) Italian Pope (1145/53). He was a Cistercian monk. His predecessor (Lucius II) having died during a rebellion against the papacy in Rome, he was obliged to flee to Viterbo immediately upon his election. Soon after his return he was again driven out by a revolt initiated by **Arnold of Brescia** and turned his attention to promoting a second crusade in France.

Eugenius IV (Gabriele Condulmer) (1383–1447) Italian Pope (1431/47). By birth a Venetian nobleman, he quarrelled with the Council of Basle which it sought to limit papal power. In 1434 he was driven from Rome by the **Colonna** and opened a new council which met at Ferrara, then Florence, where it achieved a fleeting reunion of the Greek and Latin Churches. He excommunicated the bishops at Basel, but the council there deposed him in 1439 and elected **Amadeus VIII, 'the Peaceful'** of Savoy as Felix V.

eunuchs Castrated male attendants employed at the Chinese imperial court from the time of the **Qin Dynasty** (221–207BC). Initially introduced to wait upon the female members of the imperial family, eunuchs often became the personal confidants of the emperor, wielding enormous influence. During the later Han Dynasty (25–220) they were able to manipulate the dynastic succession, and by the time of the **Tang Dynasty** (618–907) had infiltrated every level of government. Most eunuchs were castrated before the age of 10 and were either younger sons of poor families or children from non-Chinese frontier peoples. Their influence reached its height during the latter decades of the **Ming Dynasty** (1368–1644), when they controlled appointments and tax-collection. Eunuch influence was greatly reduced during the succeeding **Qing Dynasty** (1644–1911). ▷ **Han Dynasties**

Eureka In Australian history, an armed clash between goldminers and a combined police and military force at the Eureka Stockade, Ballarat, Victoria (1854), which cost the lives of 30 miners and 5 soldiers, with many others wounded. The miners had objected to the expensive mining licence imposed by the government. Public opinion swung behind the miners, juries refused to convict, and reforms to the goldfields were put into effect. The miners' rejection of government authority and use of a southern cross flag gave the incident symbolic significance for Australian democracy and national identity. ▷ **Australian Gold Rush**

Euric (c.420–80) King of the Visigoths. He is best known for the law code to which he gave his name, the Code of Euric. He came to the throne after assassinating his brother, Theodoric II, and ruled as a federate of the Roman Empire until 475, when he became an independent king. He continued to extend his realm into the Iberian Peninsula and **Gaul**, defying Roman authority. ▷ **Germanic Invasions**

European Community ▷ EC

Eusebius of Nicomedia (d.342) Syrian prelate. He was bishop first of Beryta in Syria, and then of Nicomedia. Eusebius defended **Arius** at the Council of Nicaea (325) and afterwards became the head of the Arian party. Exiled to Gaul for his views, he came back in 328 and influenced Emperor **Constantine** to move towards Arianism, baptizing him in 337, just before his death. He was also responsible for the deposition of Athanasius in 335. In 339 he was appointed Patriach of Constantinople, and enjoyed the favour of Emperor Constantius.

Evangelical Union Suspicious of the intentions of Maximilian, Duke of Bavaria, the Protestant German princes formed this Union in 1608. The Catholics, under Maximilian, reacted by forming the **Catholic League**. The Union was headed by the Elector Palatine, Frederick IV, a Calvinist, and was viewed with suspicion by many Lutherans. Initially allied with France and prepared for war in the **Jülich–Cleves Succession Conflict**, the Union down after the assassination of **Henry IV** of France (May 1610). The Union took the field in the **Thirty Years War** and was destroyed at the Battle of the **White Mountain** (1620).

Evatt, Herbert Vere (1894–1965) Australian jurist and politician. He served in the state Assembly (1925–30), and was justice of the High Court of Australia (1930–40), when he entered federal politics. As Minister of External Affairs (1941–9), he was a prominent figure in the United Nations Organization and President of the General Assembly (1948–9). He was leader of the **Australian Labor Party** in opposition (1951–60) to Britain and delegate at interna-

tional conferences. He represented Australia in Winston **Churchill's** war cabinet, and was Leader of the Opposition in the federal parliament (1951–60), when he became Chief Justice of New South Wales until his retirement in 1962.

Ever-Normal Granaries A system of state regulation of grain supplies of imperial China dating from the reign of **Han Wudi** (141/87BC). With its aim of stabilizing grain supplies and prices, the system was underpinned by the assumption that the state had the duty to prevent private speculation and provide for the people's well-being. Surplus grain was purchased and stored by government agencies and sold whenever supplies were inadequate. Grain supplies might also be transported to other regions experiencing shortages. The system remained virtually intact until the 19c when increasing government weakness and corruption led to its breakdown.

Evers, Medgar (1925–63) US **civil rights** activist. Field Secretary of the **NAACP** with responsibility for registering black voters and organizing boycotts of establishments which practised racial discrimination, he was shot dead outside his home in Jackson, Mississippi. His murder illustrated the dangers faced by black civil rights activists working in the South. A white man, Byron de la Beckwith, boasted of and was indicted for his murder, but was freed after two trials ended in hung juries.

'Ever-Victorious Army' A foreign-led Chinese army which assisted the Qing imperial forces in the suppression of the **Taiping Rebellion** (1850–64) in its closing stages. It was first commanded by an American, Frederick Townsend Ward, and then, following his death, by Charles Gordon, a British artillery officer. The army made use of steam-driven gunboats and modern weapons. Although it played only a minor role in the suppression of the Taipings, its fighting efficiency prompted some Chinese provincial officials to advocate the introduction of Western technology (especially military) into China on a larger scale. ▷ **Qing Dynasty**

Evian Agreements (1962) These agreements were the result of secret talks held at Evian, on the French shore of Lake Geneva, to end the war in Algeria. The government of General de **Gaulle** and representatives of the provisional government of Algeria, led by

Ben Bella, agreed to a cease-fire and to the establishment of an independent Algeria after a referendum. The agreements were given massive support in referenda in both France and Algeria, in spite of the attempts of the **OAS** (*Organisation Armée Secrète*) to undermine them. ▷ **Algerian War of Independence**

Exclusion Crisis (1678–81) The name given to events, beginning with the **Popish Plot**, during a campaign in parliament to exclude **Charles II**'s brother, James, Duke of York (later **James II**), from succession to the throne on grounds of his Catholicism. Showing considerable political skill, the King outmanoeuvred his Whig opponents and undermined their power base. Many were arrested or fled abroad. ▷ **Whigs**

Extensive Development (post-1928) The term used by Soviet-style economists to describe the massive, planned build-up of basic industries in backward societies like the early USSR. The emphasis was on production, not on producers or on consumers. The twin objectives were the creation of a national capital and the expansion of the working class. The technique was imposed on the states of Eastern Europe after **World War II**, irrespective of their levèl of development. By the 1960s, the cry went up for intensive development, the establishment of consumer industries and the employment of new technologies. The fact that too little came too late seriously undermined Soviet-style **communism** in the 1980s.

Eyadema, (Etienne) Gnassingbe (1937–) Togolese soldier and politician. He joined the French army in 1953, serving outside Africa for many years, and became Army Chief of Staff in 1965. He led a bloodless military coup in 1967, deposing President Grunitsky. He banned all political parties until 1969, when he founded a new organization, the Rassemblement du Peuple Togolais, as a vehicle for the organization of support for the government. Despite opposition, he has survived and responded by a degree of democratization.

Eylan, Battle of (1807) The indecisive battle between Russian and French armies as

Alexander I tried to halt **Napoleon I**'s drive from Prussia through Poland. Casualties were high on both sides but Alexander stuck to his anti-French alliance. His reaction was quite different a few months later after his army's defeat at **Friedland**.

Eyre, Edward John (1815–1901) British explorer and colonial governor. He emigrated to Australia in 1833, where he drove stock from Sydney to Melbourne and Adelaide. From Adelaide in 1839–40 he made exploratory forays to the north, reaching Lake Eyre, and west across the Eyre Peninsula, but without finding a route out of South Australia. In 1841, with just his overseer, Baxter, and three **Aboriginals**, he set out to reach Albany in the west. On the way Baxter died and two Aboriginals deserted, but fresh supplies provided by a French whaler enabled Eyre to complete the first crossing from South to Western Australia. In 1841 he was appointed protector of Aboriginals at Moorundie, South Australia, returning to England in 1844. He became Lieutenant-Governor of New Zealand (1846), Lieutenant-Governor of St Vincent (1854), acting Governor (1861) and then Governor of Jamaica (1864). There, his severe repression of a Negro rebellion (1865) created a political storm in England and led to his recall and retirement.

Eyskens, Gaston (1905–) Belgian economist and politician. After studying in Leuven and the USA, he became Professor of Economics at Leuven (1934–75). In 1939 he was elected MP for the **Christian People's Party (Belgium)**, and in 1965 became a Senator in the Upper House. He was Minister of Finance in 1945 and in 1947–9, and from 1949 to 1950 was Prime Minister for the first time. In the mid-1950s he was Minister for Economic Affairs, and led the government again in 1958–61. Appointed Minister for Finance (1965–6), he became Prime Minister twice more (1968–72 and 1972–3). He led coalitions with both left and right, and was one of the pivotal figures of post-war Belgian politics, playing a central role in the negotiations surrounding the abdication of King **Leopold III**, the debate on education funding, and the decolonization of the Congo.

F

Fabian Society A socialist group established in 1884 which took its name from the Roman general, **Fabius Maximus** *Cunctator* ('the Delayer'), noted for his cautious military tactics. It adopts a gradualist approach to social reform, and sometimes 'Fabian' is applied to people who are not members of the society but who believe in reformist **socialism**. The society has remained a small select group, but has a close association with the British **Labour Party**, and has been a source of socialist ideas and arguments.

Fabius, Laurent (1946–) French socialist politician. He had a brilliant academic career and became economic adviser to the **Socialist Party** (PS) leader, François **Mitterrand**, in 1976. Elected to the National Assembly in 1978, he was appointed Budget Minister when the PS gained power in 1981, and Minister for Research and Industry in 1983. In 1984 he was appointed Prime Minister and introduced a more free-market economic programme, which had some success, but resigned following his party's electoral defeat in Mar 1986. A popular and moderate social democrat, he heads an influential faction within the PS.

Fabius Maximus, Quintus (c.260–203BC) Roman general and statesman. He was the hero of the second of the **Punic Wars**, whose refusal to engage **Hannibal** in set battle earned him his nickname, *Cunctator* ('the Delayer'). Originally a term of abuse, it became an honorific title after 216BC, when Rome's massive and unnecessary defeat at the Battle of **Cannae** proved that his cautious tactics had been right.

Facta, Luigi (1861–1930) Italian politician. As Prime Minister in Mar 1922, after the collapse of the **Bonomi** ministry, he made no real effort to resist the fascist seizure of power, even given the refusal of **Victor Emmanuel III** to declare a state of emergency. His government collapsed (28 Oct 1922) and was replaced by that of **Mussolini**. ▷ **March on Rome**

Factory Acts Legislation passed in Britain from 1802 onwards to regulate employment in factories. The early Acts were generally concerned to limit the hours of work of women and children in textile factories only. The 1833 Factory Act prohibited children under nine from working in textile mills, and was the first to appoint factory inspectors. A maximum 10-hour working day for women and older children was enacted in 1847.

Fagel, Gaspar (1634–88) Dutch politician. A member of a prominent family in the Dutch Republic, he trained as a lawyer and set up practice in The Hague. In 1663 he became Pensionary of the town of Haarlem, through the influence of Johan de **Witt**. Fagel followed De Witt's anti-Orange policies, and in 1670 he became Secretary to the States General; in 1672 he changed sides to support the Stadholder **William III**, and became his **Grand Pensionary**.

Fahd (ibn Abd al-Aziz al-Saud) (1923–) King of Saudi Arabia (1982/). As effective ruler since the assassination of his older half-brother, Faysal, in 1975, he became King on the death of his other half-brother, Khalid. A great promoter of the modernization of his country, he was also a central figure in the shaping of Saudi Arabia's foreign policy in the 1970s and 1980s, countering Soviet influence through financial assistance to moderate Arab states such as Egypt. He opposed the **Camp David Accords** and demanded a **jihad** against Israel after its annexation in 1980 of East Jerusalem. Despite this, in 1981 he produced a plan for a Middle Eastern peace settlement, apparently recognizing Israel's right to secure boundaries. This plan, however, was never endorsed.

Fa-hsien ▷ **Fa Xian**

FAI (*Federación Anarquista Ibérica*, 'Iberian Anarchist Federation') A semi-secret group of activists established in Spain in 1927 to preserve the purist and revolutionary anarchist tradition in reaction against the increasing syndicalism of the **CNT**. Though loosely organized, the FAI came to exercise great influence within the CNT during the Second Republic, being the major force in its split of 1932. The FAI also promoted the disastrous revolutionary risings of Jan and Dec 1933.

During the **Spanish Civil War**, the FAI became a bureaucracy within the CNT, playing an important role not only in the successful agrarian and industrial collectives, but also in the often ineffective anarchist militia. ▷ **Republic, Second** (Spain)

Faidherbe, Louis (Léon César) (1818–89) French general and colonial administrator. When Governor of Senegal (1854–61 and 1863–5), he greatly extended the frontiers of his province, laying the foundation of France's empire in Africa. In the **Franco-Prussian War**, he commanded the army of the North, but was defeated near St Quentin (1871). He was twice elected as a Deputy (1871 and 1879).

Fair Deal The name adopted by US President Harry S **Truman** for his post-**World War II** liberal and pro-labour domestic policies. ▷ **New Deal**

Fair Employment Practices Committee (FEPC) Established (1941) by President Franklin D **Roosevelt**, the FEPC was created to eliminate racial discrimination in the war production industries and in government employment. President Harry S **Truman**'s efforts to establish permanent status for the committee were met with rejection by the Senate in 1946. In 1964 the Fair Employment Opportunity Commission was established to prevent discrimination in employment. ▷ **Randolph, A Philip**

Fairfax (of Cameron), Thomas, 3rd Baron (1612–71) English parliamentary general. In the **English Civil Wars**, he distinguished himself at the Battle of **Marston Moor** (1644), and in 1645 was given command of the **New Model Army**, defeating **Charles I** at the Battle of **Naseby**. He was replaced by **Cromwell** in 1650 for refusing to march against the Scots, who had proclaimed **Charles II** king, and withdrew into private life. In 1660 he was head of the commission sent to The Hague to arrange for the King's return.

Fakhr al-Din (1572–1635) Member of the Druze sect which, at the time in question, was not even regarded as properly Muslim by the orthodox. The Druzes, since the foundation of their sect in the early 11c by al-Darazi, an adherent of the Fatimid caliph al-Hakim bi-Amrillah, have wielded considerable influence in areas of Syria but more particularly Lebanon up to the present day. Fakhr al-Din was able then to make himself master

(1591–1613) of Lebanon and parts of northern Palestine, then part of the **Ottoman Empire**. He treated independently with the European powers, having a certain amount of success particularly as regards commerce. The Ottomans procured his exile to Tuscany, but not to be so easily restrained, Fakhr al-Din organized his return to Lebanon in 1618 and his reinstatement as master of the territories in which he had previously held sway. Despite his considerable influence, particularly between 1623 and 1631, the replacement in Istanbul of a weak Ottoman regime by a strong one led by Sultan Murad IV saw a speedy reduction in the power and influence of Fakhr al-Din who was defeated by Ottoman forces and captured. He was taken to Istanbul and there executed.

Falange Española Principal fascist movement (literally, 'Spanish Falange') active in 20c Spain. Founded (Oct 1933) by José Antonio **Primo de Rivera**, the son of the military dictator of the 1920s, the Falange remained a small if vocal and violent movement during its first two years. In the general election of Feb 1936 it won a mere 0.7 per cent of the vote. Following the triumph of the Popular Front, the Falange grew rapidly as disillusioned middle-class youth deserted the mainstream right-wing parties. Party activists played a key role in the street-fighting that helped polarize the political climate in the spring and summer of 1936. The Falange also assisted in the military rebellion of July 1936 against the Republic. During the **Spanish Civil War** the Falange became the dominant political movement in the Nationalist zone and controlled the press and propaganda. But the mass influx into the Falange and the loss of its leadership (especially José Antonio, executed in Alicante jail in Nov 1936) diluted its radical spirit. The political fate of the Falange was sealed in Apr 1937 when General **Franco**, as the Nationalists' head of state and military leader, forcibly united it with the Carlists to become the *Falange Española Tradicionalista y de las JONS*. Under the Franco dictatorship of 1939–75 the Falange adopted a subordinate role, serving as the regime's dependent and clientelist administrative arm. It organized the labour force through the 'vertical syndicates', helped control the middle classes, and acted as the political cheerleader of the dictator.

Faliero, Marino (c.1274–1355) Doge of Venice (1354/5). He is notorious for conspiring to replace the republic with a principate.

His swift execution (before the public at large was aware of the crisis) enhanced the reputation of the Venetian constitution for stability and justice, though Faliero's fate inspired plays by Byron and Swinburne and a painting by Delacroix.

Falin, Valentin Mikhailovich (1926–) Soviet specialist in international relations. Born in Leningrad and educated in Moscow, he held a range of Communist Party and Foreign Ministry postings from 1950 onwards. In 1968–71 he was head of the German department of the Foreign Ministry and in 1971–8 Ambassador to West Germany, the period when relations were 'normalized'. In the 1980s he was for a time influential in journalism, and in 1988 he succeeded **Dobrynin** as head of the international department of the party, but its days were numbered.

Falkenhayn, Erich von (1861–1922) German military commander. Following a varied military career, Falkenhayn succeeded **Moltke** as Chief of the German General Staff in the autumn of 1914. He decided against a German retreat in the West, despite the French success at the first Battle of the **Marne** and during 1915 pursued limited objectives in the East. In 1916 he launched the offensive at the Battle of **Verdun** which sought to destroy the French Army through a process of massive and rapid attrition. His failure here, and other setbacks, led to his replacement by **Hindenburg** and **Ludendorff** in 1917. He brilliantly commanded the German forces in the occupation of Romania when it entered the war, and continued to serve successfully as a field commander. ▷ **World War I**

Falklands War (Apr–June 1982) A war between Britain and Argentina, precipitated by the Argentine invasion of the Falkland Islands (known to Argentinians as the Malvinas). Britain had ruled these islands continuously since 1833, but Argentina claimed them by inheritance from the Spanish Empire and through proximity to her shores. The British had been conducting talks with Argentina on sovereignty over the Falklands, involving either a leaseback arrangement or a joint administration. When these talks broke down, the government of General **Galtieri** issued a warning to the British. The British government announced the withdrawal of HMS *Endurance* from the South Atlantic, and on 19 Mar scrap merchants landed on South Georgia, ostensibly to demolish a whaling station, but they also raised the Argentine flag. On the night of 1–2 Apr the full-scale invasion of the Falklands began. The 70 Royal Marines on the islands were overwhelmed, and the Governor was deported to Uruguay. The British immediately fitted out a task force to retake the islands, and the Foreign Office team, including Lord Carrington, resigned. The task force consisted of almost 70 ships, including some 40 requisitioned merchantmen and some well-known passenger vessels such as the *Queen Elizabeth 2*. A 200-mile maritime exclusion zone was declared around the Falklands, and on 2 May the Argentine cruiser, *General Belgrano*, was sunk by the nuclear submarine, *HMS Conqueror*. This brought to an end peace initiatives conducted by the US Secretary of State, Alexander Haig, and the Peruvian government. South Georgia was retaken (25 Apr); the destroyer HMS *Sheffield* was sunk by an Exocet missile (4 May); 5 000 British troops were landed at Port San Carlos (21 May); and more troops were landed at Bluff Cove (6–8 June), an operation attended by much loss of life when the Argentine air force attacked the *Sir Tristram* and *Sir Galahad*. The British forces took Darwin and Goose Green on 28 May, and after the recapture of the capital, Port Stanley, the Argentinians surrendered (14 June). The war cost the British £700 million; 254 British and 750 Argentine lives were lost; and some political commentators claim that it did much to save the declining fortunes of the government of Margaret **Thatcher**.

Fallières, Armand (1841–1931) French politician. He became an advocate and was a Deputy from 1876 to 1890. After a series of minor posts in **Ferry**'s Cabinet, he was Minister of the Interior under Charles Duclerc (1882–3) and then Prime Minister for a matter of weeks in 1883. A Senator from 1890 to 1906, he became its President (1899–1906), before becoming President of the Third Republic (1906–13). ▷ **Republic, Third** (France)

Family Compact The high Tory political and social elite of Upper **Canada**. The phrase was coined in 1828 by Marshall Spring Bidwell, speaker of the House of Assembly, but it described a situation that been developing from the first years of the 19c. The regulations which governed land grants were not only complicated but designed to serve the 'well-affected and respectable classes' already established. The Family Compact also controlled the seats in the two councils and most of those in the elective assembly. Its members monopolized patronage and obtained canal and bank charters as well as land. This political control also ensured that only the Anglican Church benefited from the **Clergy Reserves**, and denied financial support for the fledgling public education system. Reform agitation resulted in the expulsion of the leaders from the province, while London refused even to acknowledge petitions of protest. The resulting social tensions fuelled the radical leadership of William Lyon **Mackenzie** and were a major cause of the rebellions of 1837. ▷ **Bagot, Charles; Durham Report**

Fan Chung-yen ▷ **Fan Zhongyan**

Fanfani, Amintore (1908–) Italian politician. A professor of political economy, he was elected as a Christian Democrat deputy in 1946 and held a number of ministerial posts until 1954 when he was elected General-Secretary of the DC. He has been Foreign Minister three times (1958–9, 1960–3 and 1965–8), a post which he has twice combined with his five periods as Prime Minister (1954, 1958–9, twice in 1960–3, and 1982–3). Nominated a life Senator in 1972, he was President of the Italian Senate in 1968–73 and 1976–82. ▷ **Christian Democrat Party**

Fang Li-chih ▷ **Fang Lizhi**

Fang Lizhi (Fang Li-chih) (1936–) Chinese astrophysicist and dissident. During the 1957 anti-rightist campaign he was dismissed from the Chinese Communist Party, but was rehabilitated during the late 1970s at a time of relative cultural freedom. As Vice-President of the University of Science and Technology in Hefei (Anhui province), he called for greater democracy and condemned party corruption. He supported student demonstrations in Dec 1986 and was once again expelled from the party for his advocacy of 'bourgeois liberalism'. In the wake of the brutal suppression of the democracy movement in 1989, Fang Lizhi was accused of being one of the ringleaders. He sought refuge in the US Embassy and was eventually allowed to leave for the West.

Fanon, Frantz (1925–61) Martinique-born doctor and revolutionary. His study of the Algerian revolution, *The Wretched of the Earth* (1961), became the inspiration and manifesto for liberation struggles throughout the Third World. Educated as a psychiatrist in France and sent to Algeria, Fanon changed

sides and joined the rebels, but died of leukaemia before seeing the achievement of independence for Algeria.

Fanti States Separate traditional states, each under the authority of a royal chief in southern Ghana. The Fanti are Kwa-speaking farmers and fishermen, but formerly they traded with the Europeans in coastal towns such as Elmina and Cape Coast.

Fan Zhongyan (Fan Chung-yen) (989–1052) Chinese reforming scholar-official of the **Song Dynasty**. He championed a Confucian activism in government in reaction against the otherworldly concerns of Buddhism, stressing the importance of Confucian scholars participating in public life and the need for social welfare projects. Fan is especially known for his promotion of the clan (a corporate organization bringing together related families in a particular region) as the ideal basis of society, providing for a stable and harmonious political order. He helped to devise clan rules that laid down standards for personal conduct and management of clan institutions such as schools and orphanages.

Fara'izi Movements A religious sect founded in eastern Bengal in 1802 by Haji Shariatullah upon his return after 20 years from Mecca. Shariatullah asked the rural Muslims of Bengal to purge themselves of non-Muslim accretions, both Hindu and animist. He held that Muslims under the British lived in a land of war where the Id and Friday prayers could not be held properly. His son, Dhadu Miyan, organized the sect on community lines and also started an agrarian movement against Hindu landlords, which was suppressed by the British.

Farel, Guillaume (1489–1565) French reformer. He studied in Paris, and became a convert to Protestantism in 1521. He fled to Basle, and moved to Geneva in 1532. The severity of the ecclesiastical discipline imposed by **Calvin** produced a reaction, so that in 1538 the two reformers were expelled from the city. He became a pastor in Neuchâtel in 1538, and worked there for the rest of his life.

Farinacci, Roberto (1892–1945) Italian politician. One of the founding members of Italian **fascism** and perhaps the most intransigent **ras**. He was a deputy (1921–2), Secretary-General of the **Fascist Party** (1925–6), a member of the **Fascist Grand**

Council (from 1935) and a Minister of State (1938). An ardent anti-Semite, he was ideologically much closer to Nazism than most other **gerarchi**. In the famous meeting of the Fascist Grand Council (25 July 1943), he was one of the minority who voted for total loyalty to the alliance with Germany. At the end of the war he was captured and executed on the same day and by the same partisans as **Mussolini**.

Farini, Luigi Carlo (1812–66) Italian revolutionary and politician. Involved in the Bologna uprising against papal rule in 1831 and expelled from the **Papal States** in 1843, Farini was summoned back to Rome by **Pius IX** who appointed him Under-Secretary of State. When Pius fled to Gaeta after the murder of Pellegrino **Rossi**, Farini followed but he was subsequently dismissed and exiled because of his liberal sympathies. He settled in Turin and collaborated with **Cavour** on *Il Risorgimento*, the latter's liberal and progressive journal. He became a minister in the **D'Azeglio** government and supported Cavour during the 1850s. In June 1859 he was appointed as Commissioner Extraordinary in Modena and the following year was recognized as 'dictator' in Parma and the Papal Legations as well; in Mar 1860 he orchestrated their transfer by plebiscite to the new united Italy. After the annexation of the Kingdom of the **Two Sicilies**, he was made Lieutenant-General of Naples. He became Prime Minister on the resignation of **Rattazzi** (Dec 1862), but resigned himself because of ill health in Mar 1863. His admiration and close cooperation with Cavour earned him the nickname 'Cavour's shadow'.

Farnese, Alessandro (1545–92) Italian general. He fought in the service of **Philip II** of Spain, who was his uncle, and distinguished himself against the Turks at the Battle of **Lepanto** (1571). As Governor-General of the Spanish Netherlands (1578–92), he captured Antwerp (1585), and compelled **Henry IV** of France to raise the siege of Paris (1590).

Farnese Family The ruling family of the Principality of Parma, with important Spanish links. Alessandro **Farnese** was one of the greatest generals of his day, serving with distinction in the Netherlands against the rebels. Elizabeth Farnese (1692–1766) was the Queen (1714/46) of **Philip V** of Spain, and played an active role in Spanish foreign policy. ▷ **Farnese, Alessandro**

Faroe Islands, Possession of the The group of islands lying between the Shetland Islands and Iceland and subject to the Danish crown. The islands were settled from Norway and the Norse settlements in Scotland from the beginning of the 9c. They were converted to Christianity c.1000 and made tributary to the Norwegian crown c.1035. A bishopric was established at Kirkjuböur at the beginning of the 12c, but abolished in 1557, after the introduction of the Reformation. The islands were governed as a Danish province, but in the 17c were granted for long periods as a fief of the Danish crown. With the abolition of absolute monarchy in Denmark in 1848, the islands were granted a seat in both the Upper and Lower House of the Danish parliament in Copenhagen, and a provincial assembly (*Lagting*) was set up in 1852. During **World War II** the Faroes were occupied by British troops. A referendum held in 1946 voted for independence, but this was disallowed and home rule was introduced in 1948. When Denmark joined the **EEC** in 1973, the islands were excluded because of their special fishing interests.

Farouk I (1920–65) Last King of Egypt (1936–52), born in Cairo. He was educated in England, and studied at the Royal Military Academy, Woolwich. After **World War II** he turned increasingly to a life of pleasure. The defeat of Egypt by Israel (1948) and continuing British occupation led to increasing unrest, and General **Neguib**'s coup (1952) forced his abdication and exile. In 1959 he became a citizen of Monaco, and he died in Rome.

Farragut, David Glasgow (1801–70) US naval commander. He entered the navy in 1810 and saw service against the British in the War of 1812, and against pirates in 1820. In the **American Civil War** he served with the Federal forces and commanded the armament fitted out for the capture of New Orleans (1862). He took part in the siege and capture of **Vicksburg** (1863), and destroyed the enemy's gunboats in Mobile Bay, leading to the town's surrender. He was made Vice Admiral, the rank being created for him by special Act of Congress, as was also that of Admiral (1866).

Farroupilha Revolt A separatist rebellion in the southern provinces of Brazil, especially Rio Grande do Sul. The rebels, known as *farropos* ('ragamuffins'), proclaimed an independent republic in 1836, but the south was restored to Brazil by 1845. The revolt was eventually brought to an end under the strong government of Luís Alves de Lima e Silva (who was later created Duke of Caxias) by a combination of his tactics and the conciliation of *estanciero* interests in an amnesty. The last major civil war under the Brazilian Empire, the divisions it left remained an integral part of **gaucho** politics to the 1970s.

Fasci Siciliani The first *fasci* (literally, 'bundles') were established in Sicilian towns in the late 19c as mutual aid societies for workers and peasants, which could also operate as primitive trade unions. The leadership of the Fasci was very varied, often being run by anarchists but also by local gentry, academics, professionals and even *mafiosi*. In 1893 they began to gain widespread support among the Sicilian peasantry and were instrumental in coordinating a number of agricultural strikes. The traditional rural violence which accompanied some strike action was used as a pretext by the recently formed government of Francesco **Crispi** to take repressive action. In Jan 1894 the Fasci were officially dissolved and martial law was declared in Sicily. Many members of the Fasci were arrested and sentenced to imprisonment; others were deported to nearby islands without trial.

Crispi also used the disorder as an excuse to strike off the names of thousands of potential socialist or anarchist supporters from the electoral rolls.

fascism A term applied generically, and often inaccurately, to a variety of extremely nationalistic and authoritarian, populist movements that reached their pinnacle in the inter-war years. The movement originated in Italy, centred on **Mussolini**. It is hard to define the central tenets of fascism even in Italy, where it began as a republican, anti-capitalist, anticlerical movement with a strong syndicalist influence and yet quickly switched to supporting the free market, the monarchy and the Church. However, all fascist movements (Oswald **Mosley**'s **Black-shirts** in Britain, the **Iron Guard** in Romania, the **Croix de Feu** in France or any other of its legion manifestations across Europe) shared common features: an aggressive and unquestioning nationalism; a disrespect for democratic and liberal institutions which did not, however, preclude using them to attain power; a profound hatred for socialism; an emphasis on a single charismatic leader; a strong association with militarism. There are

European dictatorships, 1920–39

many similarities between fascism and Nazism, the latter often being described as simply an extreme manifestation of the former. However, it should be stressed that, although xenophobic, there was nothing intrinsically anti-Semitic about Italian fascism, at least in its early stages. After the end of **World War II**, fascism was largely discredited, although groups such as the **Italian Social Movement** and the British and French National Fronts show many similarities. See map p314.

Fascist Grand Council (*Gran Consiglio di Fascismo*) Established in 1923 as a parallel fascist cabinet alongside the constitutional one, the *Gran Consiglio* did relatively little. Instead, **Mussolini** created it primarily to provide apparently prestigious posts to occupy potentially dangerous *ras*. By 1928, it had become in theory the most powerful organ of both party and state, composed almost entirely of ministers. In practice, its powers were extremely limited: it was purely advisory and could only convene on the orders of Mussolini: he did not summon it at all between 1939 and July 1943. Despite his attempts to keep the Council as no more than a forum for careerists, nonentities and sycophants, it did eventually assert itself in the famous meeting of 25 July 1943 when it voted by a majority of 17 to 7 in favour of Dino **Grandi**'s motion to remove the **Duce** from office: Mussolini was dismissed by King **Umberto II** and arrested the following day.

Fascist Party (*Partito Nazionale Fascista*, PNF) The fascist movement was founded by **Mussolini** at a meeting in Milan in Mar 1919, anticlerical, anti-capitalist and republican in philosophy. It contested elections in 1919 disastrously and was not put on a formal party footing until Oct 1921, when the PNF was established. Its remarkable growth, both in membership and electoral support, has much to do with the chaotic political climate of the post-war years, the weakness of liberal institutions and widespread fear of **communism**, but the PNF's ideology also changed, Mussolini realizing that if it were to appeal broadly it could not continue to be anticlerical, against the free market or hostile to the monarchy. By Oct 1922 it was already the most significant political force in Italy and by 1929 had effectively become the sole Italian political party, dominating an essentially totalitarian regime. However, the nature of the party also altered: largely as a result of purges undertaken by the **Duce** it lost its revolutionary edge and became increasingly bureaucratic. By the 1930s membership was seen more as a prerequisite for advancement than a sign of genuine commitment to the ideals of **fascism**.

Fashoda Incident (1898) The settlement of Fashoda (now Kodok) on the upper White Nile, was the scene of a major Anglo-French crisis in this year. French forces under Captain Jean Baptiste Marchand had reached the Nile after an 18-month journey from Brazzaville. The British, who were in the process of retaking the Sudan, issued an ultimatum; France was not prepared to go to war, and Marchand was ordered to withdraw. The incident destroyed French ambitions for a trans-continental African empire, and confirmed British mastery of the Nile region. ▷ **Africa, Partition of; Kitchener, 1st Earl**

Fatah, al- The popular name (in Arabic, 'Victory') for the Palestine National Liberation Movement (PNLM), created in 1957 and headed by Yasser **Arafat**. It is the single biggest Palestinian movement, and operates under the umbrella of the **PLO** (Palestine Liberation Organization).

Fateh Singh, Sant (1911–72) Sikh religious leader. A campaigner for Sikh rights, he was involved in religious and educational activity in Rajasthan, founding many schools and colleges there. In 1942 he joined the **Quit India Movement**, and was imprisoned for his political activities. During the 1950s he agitated for a Punjabi-speaking state, which was achieved once Haryana was created as a separate state in 1966.

Fatherland Front The popular front organized by the communists in Bulgaria during **World War II**. Formed (June 1942) from a combination of Social Democrats, **Zveno** and the left-wing Pladne Agrarians, it was from the first dominated by its communist members. In Sep 1944 it organized strikes and prepared to take over the government. Through the Front, the communists held key positions in the pro-Western government of the right-wing Agrarian Kosta Muraviev. It attacked its opponents, organized a 'people's militia', and tried and executed members of the past governments and the regents. In Mar 1945 Georgi **Dimitrov** was elected President of the Central Committee and in Nov of the same year the Front won a majority in the elections through fraud. Its activities ensured that Bulgaria was completely under communist control by Nov 1947.

Fatima (c.605–33) The youngest daughter of **Muhammad**, and wife of the fourth Muslim caliph, **'Ali**. From this couple descended the **Fatimid Dynasty**, which ruled over Egypt and North Africa (909–1171), and later over Syria and Palestine. ▷ **Shiites**

Fatimid Dynasty An Arab dynasty tracing its descent from **Fatima**, daughter of the Prophet **Muhammad**, and her husband, **'Ali**. The dynasty came to prominence through its leadership of the Ismaili movement, a branch of Shia Islam which believed that the government of the Muslim community should reside in a series of divinely-guided *imams* drawn from the family of the Prophet. The first Fatimid publicly to proclaim himself was Ubayd Allah who, in 910, established himself as Caliph in North Africa with the support of the Berber Kutama people, taking the title al-Mahdi ('Rightly-Guided One'). Al-Mu'izz (952/75) conquered Egypt and built a new capital at Cairo; he and his successors extended their rule to Palestine, Syria and the holy places of Mecca and Medina. The principal aim of the Fatimids was the establishment of a universal caliphate, to be attained both by military means and by the maintenance of a vast missionary network intended to subvert the rule of their 'Abbasid rivals and to propagate the Isma'ili faith throughout the Middle East. However, the Sunni Muslims and Coptic Christians who constituted the majority of the Egyptian population were left in relative peace, except during the turbulent reign of al-**Hakim** (996/1021). That of al-Mustansir (1036/94) marked a turning point in Fatimid fortunes, with the independence of the Zirid emirs in North Africa, and the loss of much of Syria to the Seljuks, while from 1099 Palestine was conquered by the Frankish Crusaders. By this time the caliphs, who were frequently minors, had fallen under the domination of viziers and generals, and in the course of the 12c, Egypt came under increasing pressure from the Franks of Jerusalem and **Nur al-Din**, the ruler of Muslim Syria, who recognized the religious authority of the 'Abbasids. In 1168 Egypt was occupied by a Syrian army and, on the death of al-'Adid (1171), the caliphate was abolished by Nur al-Din's general, **Saladin**. ▷ **'Abbasid Dynasty**

Faure, Edgar (Jean) (1908–88) French politician. He entered politics as a radical, before becoming a Gaullist. He was Minister of Finance and Economic Affairs several times in the 1950s, becoming Premier for two short periods (1952 and 1955–6). He was later Minister of Agriculture (1966), Education (1968), and Social Affairs (1969), and President of the National Assembly (1973–8). He became a Member of the European Parliament in 1979.

Faure, (François) Félix (1841–99) French politician. A merchant and shipowner in Le Havre, he became a deputy for that town in 1881 and, after holding posts in several administrations, in Jan 1895 he succeeded **Casimir-Périer** as President of the French Third Republic. He was a moderate republican, whose period in office was notable for the strengthening of links with Russia, and rocky diplomatic relations with the UK following the **Fashoda Incident**. It was during his presidency that Madagascar was declared a French colony. ▷ **Republic, Third** (France)

favela The original *favela* was erected on the Morro de Castelo in Rio de Janeiro by the families of soldiers returning from the **Canudos Campaign** of 1897, to beg for their salaries. Currently, the word is a generic term for shanty towns around Rio and the southern cities of Brazil. Favelas have their own distinctive political organizations and provide housing for the low paid and support for populist politicians and popular religious sects alike.

Favre, Jules Claude Gabriel (1809–80) French lawyer and politician. He took part in the **July Revolution** of 1830, defended Orsini (the Italian revolutionary executed for his abortive attempt to assassinate Emperor **Napoleon III**), became a republican leader, and after the fall of Napoleon III became Foreign Minister in the Government of **National Defence**, and in **Thiers'** first government, in which capacity he negotiated the treaty of Frankfurt in 1871.

Fawcett, Dame Millicent (1847–1929) British women's rights campaigner. Keenly interested in the higher education of women and the extension of the franchise to her sex, she was made President of the National Union of Women's Suffrage Societies (1897–1919).

Fawkes, Guy (1570–1606) English conspirator. Born of Protestant parentage, he became a Catholic at an early age, and served in the Spanish Army in the Netherlands (1593–1604). He crossed to England at Robert Catesby's invitation, and became a member of the **Gunpowder Plot** to blow up parliament. Caught red-handed, he was tried and hanged.

Fa Xian (Fa-hsien) (fl.400) Chinese Buddhist monk and traveller. At the beginning of the 5c AD, he made a pilgrimage to India across the Takla Makan desert and Pamirs, following the Upper Indus River south to Sri Lanka in search of holy texts. He returned by sea through South-East Asia.

Faysal I (1885–1933) King of Iraq (1921/33). He was the son of **Husayn ibn 'Ali**, King of the Hijaz. He played a major role in the **Arab Revolt** of 1916, and was for a short while King of Syria after **World War I**. Installed as King of Iraq by the British, he became a leader of Arab nationalism. He died in Berne, Switzerland.

Faysal II (1935–58) King of Iraq (1939/58). He was the great-grandson of **Husayn ibn 'Ali**, King of the Hijaz. He succeeded his father, King **Ghazi**, who was killed in an accident, and after an education at Harrow was installed as king. In Feb 1958 he concluded with his cousin, King **Hussein** of Jordan, a federation of the two countries in opposition to the **United Arab Republic** of Egypt and Syria. In July 1958, he and his entire household were assassinated during a military coup, and Iraq became a republic.

Faysal ibn 'Abd al-'Aziz (1904–75) King of Saudi Arabia (1964/75). Appointed Viceroy of the Hijaz in 1926, he became Minister for Foreign Affairs in 1930, Crown Prince in 1953, and succeeded his half-brother, Sa'ud, as King. He was assassinated in the royal palace in Riyadh by his nephew, Faysal ibn Musayd.

fazenda The term used to describe a large plantation in Brazil. In colonial times (16–18c), the term was identified with cattle ranching and the production of cotton or subsistence crops, especially in the north-east and Minas Gerais, often with the use of *caboclo* (part-Indian) and free black labour using huge tracts of land. Similar to ranches in other parts of Latin America, north-eastern fazendas employed very few slaves; only in Minas were slaves introduced to supply food for the mining camps. By the 1840s, the word had become synonymous with the *fazenda do café* (coffee-estate), especially in the Valley of the Paraíba, using large-scale slave labour and **agregados**, displacing local *sitiantes*. Such fazendas became ever more mechanized and specialized: by 1900, they employed immigrant **colônos** and freedmen and grew millions of coffee trees. Land-hungry, they surged across the high-quality western plateau of São Paulo into Paraná. By the 1980s, the term applied to any large-scale extensive farming enterprise producing cash crops (such as the **hacienda**). The diminutive form of the word, *fazendola*, implies small-scale landholding, not producing significant cash crops. ▷ **sitiante**

fazendeiro The owner of a **fazenda**; the head of the patriarchal family, exercising quasi-regal powers within its lands. These lands were often obtained by a combination of force — the dispossession of *posseiros* (squatters) or *sitiantes* (smallholders) — and possession of royal land grants (*sesmarías*). Generally, the term is synonymous with 'slaveowner', since slaves performed many functions in both pastoral, cotton and coffee culture. Currently, *fazendeiros* exercise control over labour forces (*bois-frias*) in surrounding and tributary areas. This has generally been achieved by influence over *vendas*, or general stores, which offered credit to **colônos**, posseiros and sitiantes.

Fazl al-Haq (1873–1962) Bengali Muslim leader. Formerly a lawyer, teacher and journalist in Calcutta, the reunification of Bengal in 1912 saw Haq become a political leader of the Muslims. He became Secretary and then President of the **Muslim League** and was chiefly concerned with the political organization of rural interest groups. Haq was Chief Minister of Bengal from 1937 to 1943. After breaking with the Muslim League in 1941, Haq reconstructed his ministry with the help of Hindus. In Pakistan, Haq was first Advocate-General of East Pakistan and then its Chief Minister, before being appointed Governor (1956–8).

Fazl-i Husain (1877–1936) Punjabi Muslim political leader. He participated in both Congress and **Muslim League** activities in Punjab. Husain saw the 1919 reforms as advantageous to the Punjabi Muslims, for these would give the Muslims a Legislative Council majority. Thus, he opposed the non-cooperation boycott of the legislatures and was elected to the Punjab council. He served afterwards in various high offices in the Punjab government and in the government of India, handling education and revenue. Husain was a strong supporter of separate Muslim electorates and intervened successfully to prevent his fellow-Muslims from surrendering these during negotiations in 1930–1. ▷ **Non-Cooperation Movement**

FBI (Federal Bureau of Investigation) The US organization primarily concerned with internal security or counter-intelligence operations, although it also has responsibility for investigating violations of federal law not remitted by the federal government to any other organization. The FBI is a branch of the Department of Justice. ▷ **Hoover, J Edgar**

FDP (*Freie Demokratische Partei*, 'Free Democratic Party') German political party. Founded in the Federal Republic in Dec 1948, the FDP was the successor to previous German liberal parties. Initially a centre-right party with close links to business, the FDP adopted a centre-left slant in its Freiburg Theses (1971) which included support for economic democracy (**Mitbestimmung**), equal opportunity in education and the fostering of individual political responsibility. The FDP has always been a minority party, typically gaining 10 per cent of the vote (and therefore 10 per cent of seats in the **Bundestag**). However, this has enabled it to hold the balance of power for most of the period since 1949, thereby modifying the programmes and policies of both **CDU/CSU** and **SPD** governments. FDP politicians such as Hans-Dietrich **Genscher** have played a major role in German government.

FEB (*Fôrça Expedicionária Brasileira*) The only Latin American troops to serve in the European theatre in **World War II**, the 25 000-strong FEB ('Brazilian Expeditionary Force') fought alongside the US Fifth Army in Italy in 1944–5 under the command of General Mascarenhas de Moraes. Trained in US bases, combat in Italy forged a group of officers who were strongly anti-communist and committed to democracy; they were also convinced that, in the short run, arbitrary government might be necessary. Veteran FEB officers formed key groups within both the high command and the Escola Superior da Guerra. They became a diehard opposition to Getúlio **Vargas** in 1945 and **Goulart** in 1961–4, and formed the backbone of the 1964–7 **Castelo Branco** government.

February Revolution (Czechoslovakia; 1948) The name given by the communists to their assumption of power in Czechoslovakia. The National Front government was divided down the middle in the approach to fresh elections due in Apr or May 1948, with communists and non-communists exchanging accusations of impropriety. East–West tension was also growing. The communists resorted to extra-parliamentary tactics, whereupon the non-communists resigned to try to force an earlier election; however, it

was a minority resignation. The communists called out their militia, leaving President **Beneš** with little alternative but to ask Klement **Gottwald** to take power. However, it was hardly a revolution, and the communists soon changed their monopoly position.

February Revolution (France; 22–4 Feb 1848) The revolution in France which resulted in the abdication of King **Louis-Philippe**, the proclamation of a republic, and the establishment of a provisional government. Although not the first of the European revolutions of 1848, it inspired subsequent revolutionary activity in Germany and Austria. ▷ **Republic, Second** (France); **Revolutions of 1848–9**

February Revolution (Russia; Feb–Mar 1917) Popular demonstrations, strikes and military mutinies in Petrograd, Russia, resulting from pre-war misgovernment and wartime privation, which led to the abdication of Tsar **Nicholas II** and the collapse of the tsarist government. The old regime was succeeded by a series of provisional governments composed of ostensibly liberal and moderate socialist ministers, and simultaneously by the establishment of the Soviet ('Council') of Workers' and Soldiers' Deputies. This 'dual power' prevented the emergence of decisive government and provided the opportunity for the **Bolsheviks** to prepare for their revolution, which materialized in Oct/Nov of the same year. ▷ **April Theses; July Days; Mensheviks; October Revolution**

Fedayeen Derived from the Arabic *fidai*, 'one who sacrifices oneself' (for a cause or country), the term is now generally translated as 'commando' or 'guerrilla fighter'. A number of organizations, including the **PLO** (Palestine Liberation Organization), have trained military or paramilitary groups who are termed 'fedayeen'. The word first appeared in general use in the late 11c or early 12c, when the operatives of the **Assassins** of Alamut and in Syria were known thus because of their willingness to sacrifice their own lives in pursuit of their murderous objectives.

Federal Bureau of Investigation ▷ **FBI**

Federal Constitutional Convention ▷ **Constitutional Convention**

Federalist Papers A series of 85 essays defending the **US Constitution**, most of which were published in New York newspapers between Oct 1787 and Aug 1788, and subsequently collected in book form. Under the pen name of 'Publius', Alexander **Hamilton** and James **Madison** were the major contributors, with John **Jay** writing five of the articles. The papers provide important insights into the objectives sought by the framers of the US Constitution. They discuss the importance of establishing a strong centralized government while preserving state and individual freedoms. Although written in an effort to win over the citizens of New York to the constitution, the Federalist essays have become one of the most important US contributions to democratic political philosophy. ▷ **Federalist Party**

Federalist Party US political party that favoured a strong centralized government. It was formed in support of the domestic policies of Secretary of the Treasury, Alexander **Hamilton**, who represented the interests of merchants and men of property, and President **Washington**'s foreign policy. **Washington** (in office 1789–97) and John **Adams** were Federalist Presidents, but after Thomas **Jefferson**'s victory in the 1800 election the Federalists never again held the presidency, and the party's opposition to the War of 1812 led to its demise. ▷ **Hartford Convention**

Federal Reserve System (FRS) The US central banking system, set up in 1913. Under the system, the USA is divided into 12 districts, each with its own Federal Reserve Bank. The system is supervised by a central board of governors called the Federal Reserve Board. Its responsibilities include maintaining credit and monetary conditions as well as monitoring member banks. Less than half of the 14 000 banks in the USA are members of the 'Fed'.

federation (Australia) In Australian history, the events leading up to the political union of the colonies (1 Jan 1901). The eastern states of Australia gained self-government in the 1850s, and Western Australia in 1890. By the 1880s, colonial development raised the issue of intercolonial trade and internal tariff barriers, while the extension of European imperialism into the Pacific raised that of defence. A Federal Council was established in 1883 which New South Wales refused to join. The rivalry between free-trade New South Wales and protectionist Victoria was the greatest of the problems federationists had to overcome. Negotiations began in earnest after Sir Henry **Parkes**'s speech

at Tenterfield (1889), arguing that federation was essential to Australian defence, led to the Australasian Federation Conference (1890) and the National Australasian Convention (1891). Agreement was reached on the US model of federation which protected state rights, with a lower house based on population, a senate representing the states, and a high court to adjudicate on constitutional disputes. Discussions continued through the 1890s, culminating in the Federal Convention of 1897–8 which amended the constitution drafted in 1891. Anti-federalist interests remained powerful, and it required two referendums and further amendments before the constitution was accepted by all states.

Federation, Festival of (14 July 1790) A grandiose celebration of the first anniversary of the fall of the **Bastille**, attended by delegates from all over France. It epitomized the decentralizing and libertarian aspirations of the first period of the **French Revolution**.

Federation Riots (1876) An outburst of violence in Barbados provoked by the Governor's attempt to force the Assembly to join a federation of the Windward Islands. Hennessy, a maverick Irishman, angered by the reactionary nature of the Barbadian plantocracy's attitudes towards his reforms, threatened to 'raise up the blacks, if he could not bend the whites' and gave the black estate workers to understand that it was their masters' intransigence towards the proposed federation which was holding up land reform and wage increases. In Mar 1876 disorder broke out, eight people died and troops had to be brought in from Jamaica and Guyana. The planters blamed Hennessy, claiming he was attempting to deprive Barbados of its age-old 'representative' government; he was recalled, Barbados never submitted to **Crown Colony Government** and successfully resisted incorporation into the Windwards federation.

Fehrbellin, Battle of (1675) A battle in which **Frederick William**, Elector of Brandenburg, defeated a Swedish army allied with **Louis XIV** of France. He was unable to pursue this victory with a conquest of all of Swedish Pomerania because of additional French pressure.

Fehrenbach, Konstantin (1852–1926) German politician. After an early legal career, Fehrenbach was elected to the Baden state parliament in 1885 and to the **Reichstag**

in 1903. On the right of the **Centre Party**, Fehrenbach served as President of the National (constituent) Assembly in 1919 and as German Chancellor from June 1920 to May 1921. He played a leading role in **reparations** negotiations with the Allies, but his willingness to make concessions was undermined by the hostility of one of his partners in the ruling coalition, the **DNVP**.

Feijoo, Benito Jerónimo (1676–1764) Spanish theologian. His career as a Benedictine monk and Professor of Theology at the University of Oviedo (**Asturias**) spanned four reigns, and he is commonly regarded as the 'father' of the Spanish Enlightenment. Not until the age of 50 did he begin to produce his seminal writings. Through the nine volumes of his *Teatro Crítico* (1726–39) and the five of his *Erudite Letters* (1742–60), he reached a Spanish public to whom he introduced Newtonian science and a spirit of criticism of superstition. His work provoked considerable attacks and controversy, but in 1750 **Ferdinand VI** prohibited any further attacks on his works, which were declared to enjoy royal favour. He continued writing until 1759. His work as an early diffuser of the Enlightenment in Spain was complemented by other writers, notably Mayans i Ciscar, but he enjoyed unrivalled popularity among the elite, and numerous editions of his works were issued in the generation after his death.

Felix V ▷ Amadeus VIII, 'the Peaceful'

Feng Guifen (Feng Kuei-fen) (1809–74) Chinese scholar-official. He helped defend his native district during the **Taiping Rebellion** and became an administrative adviser to the powerful provincial official **Li Hongzhang** in 1864. He is credited with being one of the first Chinese scholars to advocate administrative reform and the introduction of Western technology in what became known as the **Self-Strengthening Movement** of the 1860s and 1870s.

Feng Guozhang (Feng Kuo-chang) (1859–1919) Chinese militarist. He trained at the Beiyang Military Academy, one of the military schools established during the last decades of the **Qing Dynasty**. On graduating, he entered the service of **Yuan Shikai**, Commander of the Beiyang Army, China's first modern army. After the creation of a republic in 1912 he became one of a number of influential militarists known as the 'Beiyang Clique'. He served as a provincial military governor before becoming Acting

President of the Chinese Republic (1917–18). During his one year in office China declared war on Germany.

Feng Kuei-fen ▷ Feng Guifen

Feng Kuo-chang ▷ Feng Guozhang

Feng Yu-hsiang ▷ Feng Yuxiang

Feng Yuxiang (Feng Yu-hsiang) (1882–1948) Chinese warlord. Known as the 'Christian General', he rose through the ranks to command an independent force. In 1924 he took Beijing, and set up a government which included members of the Nationalist Party. He supported the Nationalist government in 1927, but became apprehensive of the growing personal power of **Chiang Kai-shek**, and joined in two successive revolts, both of which failed. He left China in 1947 to visit the USA, and died in a ship fire on his return journey. ▷ **Guomindang; warlords**

Fenian Raids A series of attacks on Canada from 1866 to 1870 led by the Fenian Brotherhood. The Fenians (mostly New York Irish immigrants) hoped to take advantage of the anti-British sentiment felt by many Northerners in the aftermath of the **American Civil War**, and to invade Britain's North American possessions. Once established in Canada, the Fenians hoped to force Britain to negotiate the independence of Ireland. Although they did capture Fort Erie before withdrawing, the Canadian militia's resistance, divisions within the Fenian organization and the US authorities' hostility left no real prospect of success. However, their threat did encourage support for the **Confederation Movement**, especially in the Maritime Provinces.

Fenians The short title of the Irish Republican Brotherhood, a nationalist organization founded in New York in 1857. The movement quickly espoused violence as a means of achieving its objective, and is best known for attacks in Manchester and London in 1867 to rescue imprisoned supporters. The fatalities which occurred caused these to be called 'The Fenian Outrages'. ▷ **Sinn Féin**

Ferdinand (1865–1927) King of Romania (1914/27). The nephew of King **Charles I** of Romania, he was named as heir to the throne in 1880. He married Princess Marie of Edinburgh, granddaughter of Queen **Victoria** and Tsar **Alexander II**. He succeeded his uncle in Oct 1914 and led Romania into

World War I on the side of the Allies. Romania almost doubled in size at the end of the war and in 1922 he was crowned King of Greater Romania at Alba Iulia. Distrusting his son, the future **Charles II** of Romania, he named his grandson, **Michael**, as his successor.

Ferdinand I (1503–64) Holy Roman Emperor (1556/64). The son of Philip I of Spain, he was the brother and successor of Emperor **Charles V** who, as early as 1521, made over to him the Habsburg possessions in Germany. Married to the sister of Lewis II of Hungary and Bohemia, he claimed these kingdoms on his brother-in-law's fall against the Turks in 1526. However, while he succeeded without difficulty in Bohemia, there ensued a 12-year struggle over Hungary with a Magyar rival, John Zapolya (1487–1540), before the permanent union between Austria, Bohemia and Hungary was secured. Ferdinand advocated compromise with the Protestants and negotiated the religious Peace of **Augsburg** (1555). The creator of a unified administration in the Austrian lands, he died in Vienna, and was succeeded by his son, Maximilian II.

Ferdinand I (1751–1825) King of Naples, as Ferdinand IV (1759/99, 1799/1806 and 1815/16), King of Sicily, as Ferdinand III (1759/1816) and King of the **Two Sicilies** (1816/25). Until 1777, he was guided in most aspects of his rule by his able adviser, Tanucci. With the latter's fall from favour, Ferdinand came almost solely under the influence of his wife, **Maria Carolina**, and her half-English, half-French lover, John Acton. It was they who persuaded him to join the anti-French coalition of 1793 and to march on French-occupied Rome in 1796. In 1798–9 a French army led by Championnet counter-attacked and seized Naples: Ferdinand was forced to flee to Sicily and the **Parthenopean Republic** was established. The French satellite was, however, short-lived, overthrown by the **Sanfedisti**. In 1801 Ferdinand signed the Armistice of Foligno with the French, but two years later he again declared war; defeated by **Napoleon I**'s armies, he was replaced on the throne of Naples by Napoleon's brother, Joseph (1806). Ferdinand again fled to Sicily, placing himself under British protection until 1815. In return for providing him with continued safe haven, the British forced Ferdinand to send away his wife (1811) and to grant a constitution (1812). In 1815 he returned to Naples, surviving an attempted insurrection by **Murat**. After his restoration, Ferdinand avoided the worst excesses of reaction, guided by the shrewd counsel of his able minister, Prince Luigi de' Medici. Medici, however, was no liberal; nor could he prevent ultra-reactionaries, such as Prince Antonio Canosa, Chief of Police. From his appointment in 1816, the latter waged an energetic campaign against the **Carbonari** and other sects. Canosa's measures were probably counter-productive in the long run since the Carbonari were heavily involved in the July 1820 revolution in Naples. Led by Florestano **Pepe**, this bloodless coup brought about the concession of a liberal constitution. However, Pepe, faced with both a separatist rising in Sicily and an army sent by **Metternich** to restore the old order, was defeated by the Austrians at the Battle of Rieti. After the collapse of the revolution, the Kingdom of the **Two Sicilies** was brought much more firmly within the Austrian sphere of influence.

Ferdinand I (1861–1948) Prince and first King of modern Bulgaria (1887/1918). On the abdication of Prince Alexander of Battenberg, he accepted the crown, as Prince, in 1887. Dominated at first by the Premier Stephan **Stambolov**, he later took increasing control of the government. After proclaiming Bulgaria independent of the Ottoman Porte in 1908, he took the title Tsar. In 1912 he joined the Balkan League against Turkey. Allying himself with the **Central Powers**, he invaded **Serbia** in 1915. His armies routed, he abdicated in 1918, to be succeeded by his son, **Boris III**. ▷ **Balkan Wars**

Ferdinand II (1578–1637) Holy Roman Emperor (1619/37). The grandson of **Ferdinand I**, in 1596 he assumed the government in his paternal duchies of Styria, Carniola and Carinthia, where he pursued a policy of recatholicization with great severity and success. Nominated head of the **Habsburg Dynasty**, he became King of Bohemia in 1617, of Hungary in 1618 and was elected Emperor in 1619. His rigorous Catholicism and absolutist tendencies sparked off a rebellion against him in Bohemia which developed into the **Thirty Years War**. After a series of spectacular successes (thanks largely to his general, **Wallenstein**), he issued the Edict of Restitution (1629) which made even many Catholic princes suspicious of his aims. The subsequent intervention of Sweden and France, as well as Wallenstein's dismissal (1630) and murder (1634), turned the war against the Habsburg forces. The compromise Peace of Prague, two years before his death in Vienna, clearly marked the failure of Ferdinand's bid to restore uniform Catholicism and imperial supremacy in Germany.

Ferdinand II (1810–59) King of the Two Sicilies (1830/59). Despite granting a political amnesty early in his reign, Ferdinand II was even more reactionary than his predecessor, **Francis I**: when his first Minister of Police, Francesco Intoni, suggested moderate liberal reforms, he was promptly exiled. Together with Intoni's replacement, Francesco Delcarretto, Ferdinand managed to make his kingdom one of the most reactionary states in Europe. Yet despite, perhaps because of, his terror of conspiracy and insurrection, his reign was characterized by frequent uprisings, most significantly in 1848–9. In Jan 1848 insurrection in Palermo, the capital of Sicily, heralded the beginning of revolutions throughout his territories. On the mainland he managed to check the revolutionary upheavals rather more rapidly, and soon re-established his authority in Naples. His ruthless bombardment of the Sicilian city of Messina (Sep 1848) earned him the sobriquet of 'Bomba'; he was finally able to restore complete order on the island in the summer of 1849. The 1850s witnessed renewed persecution by Ferdinand of any of those who advocated reform.

Ferdinand II, 'the Catholic' (1452–1516) King of Aragon and King of **Castile**, as Ferdinand V (1479/1516), of Sicily as Ferdinand II and of Naples as Ferdinand III (1503/16). In 1469 he married Isabella of Castile, sister of Henry IV of Castile, and ruled jointly with her until her death. He introduced the **Inquisition** (1478–80), and in 1492, after the defeat of the **Moors**, the Expulsion of the **Jews**. Under him, Spain gained supremacy following the discovery of America, and in 1503 he took Naples from the French, with the help of the **Holy League**. To him and Isabella, Spain owed her unity and greatness as a nation and the foundation of her imperial influence. ▷ **Isabella I, 'the Catholic'**

Ferdinand III (1200–52) King of **Castile** (1217/52) and of Leon (1230/52). From 1224 he devoted himself to a series of offensives against the weakened Almohad caliphate in Andalusia. After achieving a major breakthrough with the capture of Cordoba (1236), he went on to take Jaen, Seville, Cadiz and the surrounding territories, settling his conquests with Christian inhabitants. By the time

of his death, he had annexed more Muslim territory than any other Spanish king, and reduced the remaining Muslim states to vassal kingdoms of Castile.

Ferdinand III (1608–57) Holy Roman Emperor (1637/57). The son of Emperor **Ferdinand II**, he became King of Hungary in 1625 and of Bohemia in 1627. A more moderate representative of the counter-reformation than his father, he succeeded **Wallenstein** as commander of the imperial armies in 1634 and headed a peace party at the imperial court. On his succession to the imperial crown, he sought to halt the fighting, but the struggle continued for another decade, ending only with the Peace of **Westphalia** (1648). Interested in philosophy and the natural sciences, he was also an accomplished musician and a notable patron of the arts.

Ferdinand VI (1711–59) King of Spain (1746/59). Having succeeded his father, **Philip V**, he played no active role in the government of his country, which was occupied throughout the reign in resisting English aggression in both Europe and the colonies. He had the good fortune to be served by able ministers, notably Zenón de Somodevilla, Marquis de Ensenada, who from service in the military administration rose to become Chief Secretary of State (1743–54). Ensenada's term in office was, however, balanced by the appointment in 1746 as minister of José de Carvajal. Carvajal believed in a rapprochement with England which he carried through in 1750; after his death in 1754, his policies were continued by the Irishman, Ricardo Wall. Ensenada, whose lasting historical monument is the great survey (*catastro*) of **Castile** carried out in 1749, was removed from power in 1754, shortly after Carvajal's death, as a result of English intrigues. In 1758 Ferdinand's wife, Bárbara of Braganza, died; the King was deeply affected, and died mad the following year. ▷ **Braganza, House of**

Ferdinand VII (1784–1833) King of Spain (1808/33). The eldest son of Charles IV and Queen Luisa, he intrigued against his parents and was banished from Madrid in 1807. When **Napoleon** invaded Spain in 1808, Charles abdicated in favour of his son, but Ferdinand was brushed aside by the French emperor and replaced as king by Napoleon's brother Joseph **Bonaparte**. For six years Ferdinand lived in exile on the estate of the French foreign minister, **Talleyrand**, at

Valençay, where the treaty was signed with Napoleon in 1813 that restored him to the throne. He refused to accept Napoleon's liberal Constitution of Cadiz (1812) and inaugurated a period of counter-revolutionary terror. A revolution in 1820 obliged Ferdinand briefly to recognize the 1812 constitution but repressive absolutism was reinstated three years later with the aid of French troops. The second terror lasted until his death in 1833, which signalled the outbreak of the first Carlist War (1833–9).

Fernández de Córdoba, Gonzalo (1453–1515) Spanish soldier, known as 'the Great Captain'. He served with distinction against the **Moors** of Granada, and afterwards in Portugal. Sent to assist **Ferdinand II 'the Catholic'** in his Holy League against the French (1495), he conquered the greater part of the Kingdom of Naples, and expelled the French. When the partition of Naples was determined upon in 1500, Gonzalo again set out for Italy, but first took Zante and Cephalonia from the Turks, and restored them to the Venetians. He then landed in Sicily, occupied Naples and Calabria, and ultimately won a great battle (1503) at the Garigliano River, which by careful planning and tactics he crossed five miles above Minturno, at a spot where in 1943 the 56th British Division found a crossing. His victory secured Naples for Spain. Recalled in 1506, and treated by the King with neglect, Gonzalo withdrew to his estates in Granada.

Ferraro, Geraldine Anne (1935–) US Democrat politician. The daughter of Italian Roman Catholic immigrants, she was educated at Marymount College, Fordham University and New York Law School and, after marrying wealthy businessman John Zaccaro in 1960, established a successful law practice (1961–74). She served as assistant district attorney for the Queens district of New York between 1974 and 1978 and worked at the Supreme Court from 1978, heading a special bureau for victims of violent crime, before being elected to the House of Representatives in 1981. In Congress, she gained a reputation as an effective, liberal-minded politician and was selected in 1984 by Walter Mondale to be the first female vice-presidential candidate of a major party, in an effort to add sparkle to the Democrat ticket. After the Democrats' convincing defeat, she returned to private law practice and in 1992 unsuccessfully sought the New York Democratic nomination for US Senator.

Ferrer, Francisco (1849–1909) Spanish anarchist and educationist. A follower of the Republican **Ruiz Zorrilla**, Ferrer participated in the abortive Villacampa rising of 1886, the last Republican rising for over 40 years. In 1901 he established the Escuela Moderna (Modern School) in Barcelona, an influential secular and experimental school following libertarian principles. He was made a scapegoat for the popular rising of the **Tragic Week** in July 1909. His execution in Oct 1909 caused an international outcry which contributed to the fall from power of the conservative Prime Minister, Antonio **Maura**.

Ferry, Jules François Camille (1832–93) French politician. Secretary of the Government of National Defence, he was Mayor of Paris during the siege (1870–1) and incurred popular hostility. He became Minister of Public Instruction in 1879 and Prime Minister (1880–1). **Gambetta**'s death made him the undisputed leader of the moderate republicans, and his second period as Prime Minister (1883–5) saw major reforms. A modern education system was created (state primary education became free, compulsory and secular), constitutional reforms were voted, and a vast colonial empire acquired, in Madagascar and Indo-China. A trivial incident there (the Lang-son Incident, in which it was wrongly reported that the French Army had suffered a major defeat at the hands of the Chinese) led to the fall of his government (Mar 1885); he never again held office, although he had just been elected President of the Senate when he died. ▷ **National Defence, Government of; Paris, Siege of**

Fersen, Fredrik Axel von (1719–94) Swedish soldier and politician. A descendant of the Scottish Macphersons, he served successively in the French and Swedish armies and was made a field marshal in 1770. He was leader of the Hat Party in the 1750s and 1760s and, after the victory of the rival Caps in 1765, cooperated with the Court Party to work for an increase in royal power. This was achieved after the coup d'état of King **Gustav III** in 1771, but Fersen became disillusioned with the new monarch and joined the opposition to him.

Fersen, Hans Axel von (1755–1810) Swedish soldier and politician. The son of Count Frederik Axel von **Fersen**, he fought as a volunteer with the French army in America during the War of Independence.

On his return, he served at the French court, where he became closely attached to Queen Marie Antoinette. In 1791, disguised as a coachman, he drove the royal family on their flight to Varennes. He returned to Sweden in 1799 and in 1801 was appointed Earl Marshal. It was in this capacity that, in 1810, he rode in the funeral procession of Christian August of Augustenburg, the recently-elected heir to the Swedish throne, and was murdered by a mob who suspected him of having poisoned the prince.

feudalism A modern construct from the Latin word *feudum* ('fief'), originally coined in 1839, referring to phenomena associated more or less closely with the **Middle Ages**. In a narrow sense, the word is used to describe the medieval military and political order based on reciprocal ties between lords and vassals, in which the main elements were the giving of homage and the tenure of fiefs. Though normally associated with political fragmentation, feudalism as here defined could serve as the ally of royal power. Polemicists apply it to whatever appears backward or reactionary in the modern world.

Feuillants, Club of the An association of moderate Deputies and former members of the Jacobin Club, led by the Marquis of **Lafayette**, Antoine **Barnave**, and Jean **Bailly**, who aimed at establishing a constitutional monarchy in France during the first stage of the Revolution (1791). ▷ **French Revolution; Jacobins**

FFI (*Forces français de l'intérieur*, 'French Interior Forces') The armed forces of the French Resistance within France, as distinct from the **Free French** fighting overseas; they played an important part in the battle for the liberation of France, and were incorporated into the regular army in Nov 1944. ▷ **Resistance Movement** (France); **World War II**

Fianna Fáil Irish political party founded in 1926 by those opposed to the 1921 Anglo-Irish Treaty. It first came to power under **De Valera** in 1932, and has been the governing party for most of the period since. In the 1930s it emphasized separation from the British, and has consistently supported the unification of Ireland. In domestic issues its approach is more pragmatic than ideological.

Fielding, William Stevens (1848–1929) Canadian journalist and politician. Liberal Premier of Nova Scotia, he threatened to

secede in 1886 if the federal government refused to lower tariffs and redress other provincial complaints. In 1896 he became the finance minister in **Laurier**'s administration and introduced a two-tier tariff system which answered the needs of farmers for a low tariff, while still maintaining some high rates to protect manufacturers. In 1910 he negotiated a trade agreement with the USA which, like his earlier system, took into account the needs of both agriculture and industry. While the US Congress ratified it in the summer, the Conservatives under Robert Laird **Borden** filibustered the bill in the House of Commons. In response Laurier called an election, the government was defeated, and Fielding lost his seat. ▷ **Liberal Party** (Canada)

Field of the Cloth of Gold (June 1520) The ceremonial meeting in Picardy between **Henry VIII** of England and **Francis I** of France. Francis was trying (in vain) to woo England away from its alliance with the Emperor **Charles V**. The lavish finery of the occasion gave the meeting its name, and enhanced the standing of the English monarchy.

Fierlinger, Zdenek (1891–1976) Czechoslovak diplomat and politician. He was appointed Ambassador in Moscow in 1937 and therefore played an important role in maintaining a liaison between Edvard **Beneš** and **Stalin** before, during and after the **Munich Agreement** and again following the Soviet entry into **World War II**. A social democrat by persuasion, he inclined increasingly to the communist point of view, was Prime Minister in the interim post-war government 1945–6, and then Minister of Industry in Klement **Gottwald**'s coalition government between 1946 and 1948. In Feb 1948 he played a crucial role in persuading most of the social democrats to join the communists in taking over power and putting an end to traditional Czechoslovak democracy for more than 40 years. His influence declined particularly after Gottwald's death in 1953, but he remained useful for propaganda purposes.

Fieschi, Count Giovanni Luigi de (c.1523–1547) Italian nobleman. He belonged to a Genoese noble line which by tradition feuded with the Doria, who had restored republican government in Genoa. In 1547 Fieschi and his brothers organized an unsuccessful plot to establish an oligarchy. However, Fieschi, stepping from one galley to another at night, fell overboard, and was drowned in the harbour. The scheme ended there, and Doria returned to wreak merciless vengeance on the other plotters.

Fifteen Rebellion The name given to the first of the Jacobite rebellions against Hanoverian monarchy to restore the Catholic Stuart Kings to the British throne. The rising began at Braemar (Sep 1715) by the Earl of Mar proclaiming James Edward **Stuart** (the 'Old Pretender') as King. Jacobite forces were defeated at Preston in Nov, and the rebellion collapsed early in 1716. ▷ **Jacobites; Stuart, House of**

Fifth Amendment (1791) Amendment to the **US Constitution** which protects against self-incrimination. This gained notoriety during the **Cold War** anti-communist investigations, when 'taking the Fifth' became synonomous with an admission of guilt. More important constitutionally, however, has been the amendment's clause prohibiting the deprivation of 'life, liberty, or property without due process of law'. Before the **American Civil War** it was used to defend **slavery** (**Dred Scott v Sanford**), and afterwards, when this clause was incorporated into the **Fourteenth Amendment**, it was used as an argument (known as 'substantive due process') against economic regulation.

fifth column A popular expression from the early days of **World War II** to describe enemy sympathizers who might provide active help to an invader. The name originally described the rebel sympathizers in Madrid in 1936 during the **Spanish Civil War**, when four rebel columns were advancing on the city.

Fifth Monarchists A millenarian religio-political grouping in England in the 1650s which believed that the second coming of Christ was imminent. The name derived from the Bible (Daniel 2.44), adherents seeking a 'fifth monarchy' to succeed the empires of Assyria, Persia, Greece and Rome. Though radical Puritans, Fifth Monarchists did not form a coherent sect. They opposed the new establishment represented by the **Protectorate** of Oliver **Cromwell** supported by the army after the dissolution of **Barebone's Parliament** (1653). Under Thomas Venner, they mounted uprisings against both Cromwell (1657) and the restored monarchy of **Charles II** (1661) after the second of which Venner was executed. ▷ **Restoration**

'Fifty-Four Forty or Fight' US political slogan used by the **Democratic Party** in the 1844 presidential election. It referred to the US claim to the Oregon country lying between the northern border of California (latitude 42°N) and the southern border of what is now Alaska (54° 40′N). The UK also claimed the region for similar reasons of discovery and settlement. In spite of the expansionist arguments of Stephen Douglas and Lewis Cass in Congress, and those of President **Polk** in his inaugural speech and his first annual message to Congress, a compromise was reached with Britain in 1846 drawing the frontier along the 49th parallel.

Figueras, Estanislao (1819–82) Spanish politician. For taking part in Republican plots in 1866 he was imprisoned but, after the expulsion of **Isabella II**, he became a member of the Republican government. On the abdication of King Amadeus I in 1873, he became President of the Spanish Republic, but soon resigned.

Figueres (Ferrer), José (Don Pepe) (1906–90) Costa Rican politician. In May 1948 he led a civilian rising against an attempt to annul the legal election of Otilio Ulate. Figueres headed a junta for 18 months, during which he carried through fundamental reforms of a social democratic nature: abolishing the armed forces; nationalizing the banking system; creating an electoral law and another law promoting rural cooperatives; and the modernization of the educational and social security systems. The constitution of 1949 embodied these reforms. He was President twice (1953–8 and 1970–4), and is commonly known as the person who created a regime which was strong enough to survive the buffeting of civil war in neighbouring Nicaragua and El Salvador.

Filiki Etairia (Philike Hetairia) Literally 'the Society of Friends', this Greek revolutionary organization was founded in Odessa in 1814 and drew its support from Greek merchants and professionals. Modelling themselves on the Freemasons, secretive and conspiratorial, its members aimed to liberate the Greeks from Ottoman rule. Hoping for Russian support, the society organized the revolt in the **Danubian Principalities** which marked the beginning of the **Greek War of Independence** (1821).

Fillmore, Millard (1800–74) US politician and 13th President. He educated himself, and became a lawyer. A member of the US House of Representatives from New York for eight years (1833–5 and 1837–43), he was elected

Vice-President when Zachary **Taylor** won the 1848 election, becoming President (1850) on Taylor's death. A moderate on the **slavery** issue, he signed the **Compromise of 1850** and tried to enforce the Fugitive Slave Act.

finca This term is used to describe a substantial property in Colombia (the Chilean equivalent is *fundo*). The property, which is smaller than a **hacienda**, is often managed by an administrator (*mayordomo*) and produces cash crops for sale in the cities; it utilizes various forms of labour, including tenant farmers (*arrendatarios*) and day-labourers.

Fine Gael Irish political party created out of the pro-Anglo-Irish Treaty (1921) wing of **Sinn Féin**. It was known as *Cumann na nGaedheal* from 1923 until it changed its name in 1933. The first government of the **Irish Free State**, it has largely been in opposition since the 1930s, and has never held power on its own. It supports an Irish confederation, and is largely pragmatic in domestic matters.

Finkenstein, Treaty of (4 May 1807) An agreement negotiated between France and Persia, which provided for French cooperation with Persia by way of the supply of material and aid by military advisers, in an attempt to force the Russians to leave Georgia. The Persian side of the agreement was the provision of assistance to France should she decide to invade India.

Finlandization Supposedly the policy of influencing the internal politics and foreign policy of a small neighbouring country by bringing pressure to bear on it. The notion refers specifically to the Soviet trade and diplomatic sanctions applied to Finland in 1958, because the Finnish government formed after the elections did not contain any communist members, although they had won a quarter of the seats. The sanctions were effective; a number of ministers resigned and a government more acceptable to the USSR was formed. But, in general, Finland retained a great freedom of action in return for unimportant concessions.

Finnbogadóttir, Vígdis (1930–) Icelandic politician. Born in Reykjavík, she studied French language and literature in France and returned to Iceland to teach French in secondary school and French drama at the University of Iceland in Reykjavík. The first woman to be elected head of any state, she

was first elected President against three male candidates (1980), was returned unopposed in 1984 and re-elected in 1988.

Finnish–Soviet War ▷ **Russo-Finnish War**

Finn MacCool Legendary Irish hero. The son of Cumhall and father of Ossian (Oisin), he became leader of the **Fenians**, and was famous for his generosity.

Firmian, Carlo (Karl Gotthard), Count of (1718–82) Austrian nobleman, administrator and diplomat. Born in Trento, Firmian became an Aulic Councillor at the remarkably young age of 22. As a young man, he travelled extensively in Europe and most especially in Italy. In 1752, he benefited from the patronage of Kaunitz and was sent on a diplomatic mission to Naples; then, in 1759, he was made Governor of the important Austrian province of Lombardy where he proved an able and reforming administrator: under his administration the tax system was made more equitable and rationalized, economic restrictions were removed and many Church privileges abolished. Firmian's mild and tolerant rule created fertile ground for the lively academic debate epitomized in the publication of Cesare Beccaria's masterpiece, *Dei delitti e delle penne*.

First Fleet In Australian history, the name given to the 11 ships which left Portsmouth, England, carrying the first European settlers to eastern Australia (1787). The fleet carried officials, 212 marines and their families, and 759 convicts plus provisions. The fleet's captain, Arthur Phillip, decided that **Botany Bay** was unsuitable and proceeded north to Sydney Cove, Port Jackson, where he hoisted the British flag (26 Jan 1788).

Firuz Shah (1305–88) Tughlaq ruler of the Kingdom of Delhi (1351/88). As the third Tughlaq ruler of the kingdom, Firuz Shah restored peace and order to his realm, encouraged agriculture, and implemented irrigation schemes (traces of his canals still remain). He indulged a passion for building and founded a new capital, Firuzabad, which is part of present-day Delhi. Firuz Shah embarked on various military missions, with mixed results. During his reign there was a disastrous attempt to transfer the capital from Delhi to Daulatabad.

Fisher, Andrew (1862–1928) British-born Australian politician. A coalminer from the age of 12, he emigrated to Queensland in

1885. From mining, he gradually moved into trade-union activity and politics, entering the Queensland state assembly in 1893 and the first federal parliament in 1901. He became **Australian Labor Party** (ALP) leader in 1907 and then Prime Minister (1908–09, 1910–13 and 1914–15). At the start of **World War I** he made the dramatic promise to support the war effort 'to the last man and the last shilling'. He was Australian High Commissioner in London (1916–21).

Fisher (of Kilverstone), John Arbuthnot, 1st Baron (1841–1920) British admiral. He joined the navy as a boy in 1854, and rose to be First Sea Lord (1904–10 and 1914–15). His major reforms of the Royal Navy prepared the country for **World War I**, including the introduction of the 'Dreadnought' battleship and 'Invincible' cruiser. He was made a peer in 1909.

fitna Literally 'trial' or 'test', in Islamic usage the term refers to a heretical uprising, especially the internal struggle (656–61) within Islam which resulted in civil war and a religious schism between the orthodox **Sunnis** and the heterodox **Shiites**. The third Caliph, '**Uthman** (644/56), favoured Meccans over Medinese. He was murdered and when the fourth caliph, '**Ali**, failed to comply with Meccan demands for revenge, he was opposed by the Meccans under **Mu'awiya**. There was at this time an irrevocable split in Islam by the formation of the *Shiat* 'Ali ('Party of 'Ali'). The war ended in 661, when 'Ali was assassinated and Mu'awiya became caliph, but Sunnis and Shiites remained divided. The term 'fitna' has subsequently been applied to a variety of rebellious social, religious and political movements within Islam.

Fitzgerald, Garrett (Michael) (1926–) Irish politician. He became a barrister and a lecturer in political economy (1959–73) and in 1969 he was elected **Fine Gael** member of the Irish parliament for Dublin South-East. He became Minister for Foreign Affairs (1973–7), Prime Minister (1981–2 and 1982–7) and Leader of the Fine Gael Party (1977–87).

Fiume (Rijeka) Port in Croatia of mixed Slav and Italian population. Although not included in the areas promised to Italy by the Treaty of **London** (1915), Fiume was claimed by the Italian delegation at the Paris Peace Conference. Italian claims were rejected and the port was afforded free city status, but in Sep 1919 it was seized by the Italian poet Gabriele **D'Annunzio** and a band of nationalist 'legionaries' who ran it as an independent 'Italian producers' republic'. By the Treaty of **Rapallo** (12 Nov 1920), Yugoslavia and Italy agreed that Fiume should regain free city status and in Jan 1921 D'Annunzio was ejected by the Italian navy. Free city status was, however, never restored, the terms of Rapallo being abandoned on **Mussolini**'s seizure of power. In Jan 1924 Yugoslavia recognized Fiume as Italian, although the adjoining harbour of Susak remained under Yugoslavian control. At the end of **World War II**, it became part of the Republic of Croatia within the Socialist Federal Republic of Yugoslavia.

Five Civilized Tribes The native tribes (Chickasaws, Creeks, Choctaws, Cherokees, Seminoles) who originally inhabited the present south-east USA, so called because they adapted relatively easily to the European way of life. Nevertheless, they were forced to leave the area under the Removal Act of 1830, and were relocated west of the Mississippi River. Large numbers of **Native Americans** died as a result of exposure, disease and the hardships suffered en route and in the new **Indian Territory**. The name given to the Cherokee ordeal, the 'trail of tears', sums up the fate of these tribes.

Five Dynasties and Ten Kingdoms, Period of (907–60) The period following the collapse of the **Tang Dynasty**, when north China was ruled by a succession of dynasties: Later Liang (907–23); Later Tang (923–34); Later Jin (936–47); Later Han (947–51); and Later Zhou (951–60). These were founded for the most part by Turkic mercenaries, and southern China came under the sway of regional warlords who established their own independent kingdoms. A period of political and social turmoil, it witnessed the further decline of aristocratic families, particularly in the north, and the emergence of new merchant and military elites. After the mid-10c, much of the area around Beijing was ceded to the **Khitan** nomads from the north. A general of the Later Zhou, Zhao Guangyin, succeeded in establishing his own dynasty, the **Song Dynasty**, in 960 and began the process of reuniting China. ▷ **Han Dynasties**

Five Emperors, The The term which refers to the mythical rulers of Chinese antiquity who were exalted in Confucian philosophy as the builders of Chinese civilization and the embodiment of virtuous government. They included Fuxi (Fu-hsi), who taught his subjects how to domesticate animals, Shen'ong (Shen-nung), who invented the plough and taught men how to grow millet, Huangdi (Huang-ti) or the Yellow Emperor, who was credited with the establishment of the first empire and is associated with the development of medicine, Yao (supposedly 2357/2256BC) and Shun (supposedly 2255/2205BC). The last two were particularly esteemed as model rulers who provided moral guidance and benevolent administration.

Five Pecks of Rice Band, Revolt of the (AD184) A revolt which broke out towards the end of the Later Han Dynasty, when large-scale natural disasters and increasing taxes led to widespread poverty and discontent. The Five Pecks of Rice Band was a congregation of believers (each of whom had to pay 'five pecks of rice' in contributions) belonging to a popular Daoist church that practised mystical faith-healing and provided social welfare. It resorted to open rebellion when the authorities attempted to suppress the movement. Although the rebellion was put down, it helped to undermine fatally the dynasty. ▷ **Han Dynasties**

Five-Year Plans Independent India adapted this model (initiated in the USSR under **Stalin** in 1928) for organizing the economy during the 1950s. The Indian Planning Commission was set up in 1950 to enable the government to supervise economic development. The commission was asked to assess development resources, formulate a national five-year plan, and assess progress, and the first plan was implemented during the period 1951–6. The plans covered the activities of both central and state governments, although states controlled their own plans.

Flandin, Pierre Etienne (1889–1958) French politician. From 1914 to 1940 he was President of the *Alliance démocratique* ('Democratic Alliance') a moderate republican group. He frequently held cabinet office, notably as Finance Minister (1931–2); as Prime Minister (1934–5) he vainly tried to solve the economic crisis by deflation, and to counter-balance the German threat by joining with Italy in the Stresa front. He supported appeasement, and voted for **Pétain** in 1940. He was briefly in office under **Vichy** (14 Dec 1941) which ended his active political career.

Flavian Dynasty (AD70–96) The second dynasty to rule the **Roman Empire**; it consis-

ted of Vespasian (Titus Flavius Vespasianus) and his two sons, Titus and Domitian. Domitian's assassination in 96 brought the dynasty to an end, since his own children had died in infancy.

Flemish Movement A cultural and political emancipation movement in Belgium, aimed at the recognition of the rights of the Dutch-speaking inhabitants of the northern part of the country (Flanders) as opposed to the interests of the French-speaking inhabitants of southern Belgium (Wallonia) and increasingly of the capital Brussels. Born of the **Belgian Revolution**, it was originally a cultural movement concerned principally with the recognition of Flemish (the Belgian form of Dutch) as a language in literature, education and politics. Many petitions and pressure-groups resulted in a number of language laws in the 1870s and 1880s which recognized the existence of Flemish; as the suffrage was widened in 1893 beyond the Francophone bourgeoisie, the movement gained political power and achieved an 'Equality Law' in 1898, giving the two languages equal status. There followed a long dispute over the University in Ghent, which the movement wanted as a Dutch-language institution: this was finally agreed in 1930. During both world wars elements of the Flemish Movement chose to work with the German authorities in the hope of achieving their aims: this brought the movement into some temporary disrepute. Since the war the Flemish Movement has ridden on the rising economic power of coastal Flanders, and has contributed to the political federalization of Belgium, which is now almost complete.

Fleury, André-Hercule de (1653–1743) French prelate and politician. Replacing the Duke de Bourbon as Chief Minister (1726), he was made cardinal, and effectively controlled the government of **Louis XV** until 1743. Through skilful diplomacy he limited French involvement in the War of the Polish Succession (1733–8), restoring the country's prestige as a mediator.

FLN (*Front de Libération Nationale*) An organization founded in the early 1950s, which campaigned and fought for Algerian independence from France, under the leadership of Mohammed **Ben Bella**. The war with the FLN led to the collapse of the French Fourth Republic in 1958, and the return to power of de **Gaulle**. France's inability to defeat the FLN led to the Evian conference in 1962, and complete Algerian independence. ▷ **OAS; Republic, Fourth** (France)

Flodden, Battle of (9 Sep 1513) A victory of the English over the Scots, fought in Northumberland. **James IV** of Scotland, allied with France, invaded England in Aug, but was defeated by English forces under Thomas Howard, Earl of Surrey. The Scottish dead included James, 13 earls, and three bishops; the battle ended the Scottish threat for a generation.

Flood, Henry (1723–91) Irish politician. He became leader of the popular party in the Irish parliament after his election in 1759. In 1775 he became Vice-Treasurer of Ireland, but was removed in 1781 as a strong nationalist. In 1783 he was returned for Winchester, and in 1785 for Seaford, but he failed to make a great mark at Westminster.

Floquet, Charles Thomas (1828–96) French lawyer and radical politician. He opposed the Second Empire, and was elected to the National Assembly in 1871 as a republican. Having resigned in Apr 1871, he sought to mediate between the government and the **Paris Commune**. He was elected to the Chamber of Deputies in 1876, was President of the Chamber (1885–8, 1889–93) and Prime Minister (1888–9). Floquet opposed 'Boulangism' and wounded the movement's leader, Georges **Boulanger**, in a duel in 1888. His political influence waned after his implication in the Panama scandal of 1893, although he was later a Senator (1894–6). ▷ **Empire, Second** (France)

Flores, Juan José (1801–64) Ecuadorean politician. One of **Bolívar**'s principal aides, he fought with distinction in the **Spanish–American Wars of Independence** and became the first President of Ecuador (1830–5 and 1839–43) after the collapse of Gran Colombia. Illiterate and capricious, he imposed an autocratic constitution in 1830. As the representative for conservative Quito, he alternated in government with his Liberal opponent, Vicente Rocafuerte (1835–9), returning in 1839 and retaining power until 1845. He eventually sided with Gabriel **García Moreno** against the Liberals of Guayaquil under Guillermo Franco to create a conservative state in 1860.

Floridablanca, Count of (1728–1808) Spanish administrator and minister. A leading member of the group of civil servants and ministers under **Charles III** that aimed to modernize the monarchy. A cautious and conservative civil servant, he planned the road system radiating from Madrid. He was

also the architect of the French alliance, the cornerstone of Spain's foreign policy until the war with France in 1793. Chief Minister (1777–92) during the last years of Charles III's reign, his hostility to revolutionary France hastened the end of his ministerial career because he was unable to resolve Franco-Spanish relations.

Floris V (1254–96) Count of Holland (1256/96). He was the son of Count William II (1227–56), who was murdered when Floris was a baby. A regency ensued, first by his uncle, Floris the Guardian (c.1228–58), and then by his aunt, Aleidis of Holland (d.1284), who was replaced in 1263 by Otto II of Gelre (c.1200–71). In 1266, at the age of 12, he was declared of age, and succeeded to his title, in order to escape the Gelre influence. In c.1270 he married Beatrix, daughter of the Count of Flanders. Floris was responsible for an expansion of the Count's power within his own territory, and also for territorial gain, mainly at the expense of the Bishop of Utrecht and the West Frisians, whom he finally defeated in 1289. As King **Edward I** of England's principal ally on the Continent against the French, he won the English wool staple for the Holland town of Dordrecht in 1295, but then changed sides to support the French. This resulted in his kidnap by some of his nobles, who intended to send him to England; he was, however, murdered when others tried to effect his release.

Flourens, Gustave (1838–71) French republican politician. He distinguished himself by his book, *La Science de l'homme* (1865); as an ardent republican, he took part in the Cretan insurrection against the Turks (1866), and fell fighting for the **Paris Commune** (1871).

FNLA (*Frente Nacional de Libertação de Angola*) Formed in 1962, the FNLA established a government in exile under Holden Roberto in Zaire and, with US assistance, was active in northern Angola, especially after the Portuguese left the country. Poor leadership and reduced US support weakened its effectiveness and it ceased operations in the early 1980s.

Foch, Ferdinand (1851–1929) French marshal. He taught at the Ecole de Guerre, proved himself a great strategist at the Battle of the **Marne** (1914), Ypres, and other **World War I** battles, and became Allied Commander-in-Chief in Mar 1918. He quarelled with the Prime Minister, **Clemenceau**, about the peace settlement, regarding it as not providing adequately for French security.

Foix, Gaston (1489–1512) French nobleman and soldier, nephew of **Louis XII** of France. He became Duke of Nemours in 1505. He twice overthrew the Swiss, at Como and Milan (1511); chased the papal troops from Bologna; seized Brescia from the Venetians (1512); and defeated the Spaniards at Ravenna, where he was killed.

Folketinget Literally 'the People's Thing', the parliament of Denmark located at Christiansborg Palace in Copenhagen. It has 179 members of whom two are elected in the Faroe Islands and two in Greenland, both self-governing regions of the Kingdom of Denmark. The members of the *Folketinget* are elected for periods of four years by universal adult suffrage. The system of voting is proportional representation. Folketinget was established by the Danish constitution of 5 June 1849 as a result of popular pressure for democratic reforms following the February Revolution in France and the death of the absolute monarch, King **Christian VIII** in 1848. The 1849 Danish parliament, *Rigsdagen*, consisted of two chambers: a lower chamber, Folketinget, and an upper chamber, *Landstinget*. In 1901, a Danish political consensus was reached to the effect that a government could not continue if a majority of the members of the Folketinget was against it, thus giving priority to the more democratically elected of the parliament's two chambers. In 1915, female suffrage was introduced in Denmark. On 5 June 1953, as part of a revision of the Danish constitution, the upper chamber of the Rigsdagen was abolished and the name Folketinget was carried on as the name of the Danish parliament as such.

Fontenoy, Battle of (1745) A battle in which French forces under **Louis XIV** of France and Maurice, Marshal of Saxony, decisively defeated an Anglo-Dutch-Austrian army commanded by William Augustus, Duke of Cumberland. Fought in Hainaut in the Austrian Netherlands, the battle ensured the French conquest of Flanders in the War of the **Austrian Succession**, and was the last major military victory for a French army until the French Revolution.

Foot, Michael (Mackintosh) (1913–) British Labour politician. He joined the staff of the *Tribune* in 1937, becoming editor (1948–52 and 1955–60). He was also acting

330

editor of the *Evening Standard* (1942–4) and a political columnist on the *Daily Herald* (1944–64). He became an MP in 1945, serving until 1992, and was Secretary of State for Employment (1974–6), Deputy Leader (1976–80) then Leader (1980–3) of the **Labour Party**, resigning after his party's heavy defeat in the general election. A prominent figure on the party's left and a pacifist, he has long been a supporter of the Campaign for Nuclear Disarmament (**CND**). A prolific writer, his best-known work is his biography of Aneurin **Bevan**.

Football War (July 1969) A lightning war fought over several days between Honduras and El Salvador, which was rapidly halted by international pressure. It was provoked by the wave of migration from overpopulated Salvador to the unoccupied territories of Western Honduras, and was so named because recriminations between the two Central American states came to a head during the qualifying matches for the 1970 World Cup.

forced labour camp A prison camp where those regarded as politically undesirable or of an unwanted nationality are deported to carry out forced labour on behalf of the state. In the modern world they date back to 1918 in Soviet Russia, where millions of citizens regarded with suspicion by the authorities were sent for 'correction' in the 1920s, 30s and 50s. The camps were used more as a means of punishment and social control than of political correction, and most inmates died in the camps. It is estimated that at its peak there were between 12 and 15 million people in Soviet camps. **Hitler** also established forced labour camps. The camps in what was the USSR have largely disappeared since Mikhail **Gorbachev**'s time.

Ford, Gerald Rudolph (1913–) US politician and 38th President. Educated at the Universities of Michigan and Yale, he served in the US Navy during **World War II**. He became a Republican member of the House of Representatives (1949–73), and on the resignation of Spiro **Agnew** in 1973 became the first appointed Vice-President. He became President (1974–6) when Richard **Nixon** resigned because of the **Watergate** scandal. The full pardon he granted to Nixon the same year, combined with an economic recession and inflation, made him unpopular, and he was defeated in the 1976 presidential election by Jimmy **Carter**. ▷ **Republican Party**

Foreign Legion The elite formation of the French Army, recruited from non-French nationals. '*La Légion étrangère*' was first raised in 1831, and has seen action almost wherever French arms have been engaged. Always the subject of romance and adventure, the legion retains its reputation for toughness.

Formigny, Battle of (1450) The decisive defeat near Bayeux (Calvados) during the **Hundred Years War** of an army sent by the English government, then bankrupt and bereft of allies, to stem French advances in Normandy. Having lost their previous tactical superiority, the English were bombarded out of their positions by artillery, and routed by infantry. The French reconquest of Normandy was swiftly completed.

Fornovo, Battle of ▷ **Italian Wars**

Forrest, John, 1st Baron Forrest of Bunbury (1847–1918) Australian explorer and politician. From 1865 he was a colonial surveyor. In 1869 he explored inland from Perth; in 1870 he reached South Australia from the west along the south coast and in 1874 made the eastward journey across the centre. Surveyor-General for the colony from 1883, he was the first Premier of Western Australia (1890–1901), exploiting the rise in wealth and population from the gold-rush boom of the decade to develop the port of Freemantle and provide basic services throughout the colony. An active but cautious federalist, he moved to federal politics in 1901 and was, in turn, Minister for Defence, Home Affairs and five times Treasurer in various governments (1901–18). He died at sea off Sierra Leone.

Fortescue, Sir John (c.1385–c.1479) English jurist. He was called to the Bar, and became Lord Chief-Justice of the King's Bench (1442). He sided with the Lancastrians, fled with **Margaret of Anjou** and her son to Scotland, and in 1463 embarked with them for Holland. During exile he wrote his *De Laudibus Legum Angliae* (In Praise of the Laws of England, printed 1537) for the instruction of Prince Edward, a work which came to be of great value to later jurists. After the defeat of the Lancastrians at the Battle of **Tewkesbury**, he submitted to **Edward IV**. ▷ **Lancaster, House of**

Fort Sumter (12–13 Apr 1861) The US federal installation in Charleston (South Carolina) harbour, bombarded in the first military engagement of the **American Civil War**. Shortly after President Abraham **Lincoln**'s inauguration, the fort's commanding officer, Captain Robert Anderson, informed the Union government that he had only enough supplies to last until early Apr. On 6 Apr 1861 Lincoln informed the Governor of the seceded state of South Carolina that he intended to provision the garrison. Confederate General Pierre **Beauregard** issued an ultimatum to surrender, which Anderson refused. On 12 Apr the fort came under fire, and Union troops departed two days later for lack of ammunition. The Confederate states thus having opened hostilities, Lincoln issued a call to the states for troops and began to blockade Southern ports.

Forty-Five Rebellion (1745–6) The Jacobite rebellion which aimed to restore the Catholic Stuart kings to the British throne and displace the Hanoverians. It began in July 1745 when Charles Edward **Stuart** (the 'Young Pretender') arrived in Scotland and proclaimed his father King James III. Support came mainly from the Scottish Highland Clans, and there were some early successes. The Jacobite forces reached as far south as Derby, but the rebellion lost support, and was crushingly defeated at the Battle of **Culloden** in 1746. After the '45, the Hanoverian regime brutally suppressed the clan system. ▷ **Jacobites; Stuart, House of**

forty-niners Adventurers who swarmed to California in 1849, after the discovery of gold there the previous year. Their number may have been as high as 100000. ▷ **gold rush**

Forty-Seven Ronin, Incident of the (1701–3) An incident that took place in Japan which provided a potent symbol of self-sacrificing loyalty for later generations. Following a quarrel, a minor feudal lord wounded a powerful official at the **Shogun**'s court in **Edo**. He was ordered to commit suicide and his domain was confiscated for this breach of etiquette. The lord's **samurai** retainers then became *ronin* (masterless samurai) with their status much diminished. Forty-seven of these ronin vowed to take vengeance for their former lord and after biding their time for two years they succeeded in killing the shogunal official in 1703, knowing full well they would have to die themselves for such an act. For their unflinching loyalty to their lord, the 47 ronin became heroes.

Foscari, Francesco (c.1370–1457) Doge of Venice (1423/57). His warlike policies on the

Italian mainland were vital to the creation of a territorial state under Venetian rule. However, his princely style of government and his promotion of the interests of his family resulted in his deposition, and to his death from rage and grief soon afterwards. His career is the subject of a play by Byron.

Fouché, Joseph, Duke of Otranto (1763–1829) French revolutionary politician. A member of a Catholic teaching order before 1789, he was elected to the National **Convention** (1792), and became an extreme revolutionary, being noted for his zealous support of attacks on the Christian religion, and for his part in the bloody suppression of opposition at Lyons. He then turned against **Robespierre**, being one of the main organizers of the **Thermidor** coup. Appointed Chief of Police in 1799, he helped to bring **Napoleon I** to power, and retained the post until 1815, surviving all the rapid changes of 1814–15. The First Empire gave him his titles of nobility, and great wealth. He was banished in 1816. ▷ **Empire, First** (France); **French Revolution; Jacobins**

Fould, Achille (1800–67) French financier and politician. Elected in 1842 to parliament, after the revolution of 1848 he served the Provisional Government. During the presidency of Louis Napoleon (**Napoleon III**), he was four times Minister of Finance during which time he stabilized the country's finances. He resigned (1852) on the confiscation of the property of the Orléans family, but again served as Minister of Finance from 1861 to 1867. ▷ **Orléans, House of**

Foulques ▷ **Fulk**

Fouquet, Nicolas (1615–80) French politician. Cardinal **Mazarin** made him *Procureur-Général* to the parliament of Paris (1650) and Superintendent of Finance (1653). He became extremely rich, and was ambitious to succeed Mazarin, but **Louis XIV** himself took up the reins of power on Mazarin's death, and Fouquet was arrested for embezzlement (1661). He was sentenced to life imprisonment in the fortress of Pignerol, where he died.

Fouquier-Tinville, Antoine Quentin (1747–95) French revolutionary politician. He was Public Prosecutor to the Revolutionary Tribunal from 1793. He superintended all the political executions during the Reign of **Terror** until July 1794, sending his friends, among them **Robespierre**, **Danton**

and **Hébert**, to execution as cheerfully as he sent their enemies; at last he himself was guillotined. ▷ **French Revolution**

Fourah Bay College A college in Sierra Leone founded as a missionary establishment as early as 1814, the first institution of Western education in West Africa. In 1827 it became a training college for teachers and missionaries and in 1876 became affiliated to the University of Durham for the award of degrees. Many of the members of the elite of West Africa were educated there and the first nationalist movements were founded by its former students.

Four Emperors, Year of the (AD69) Popular name for the year of civil war following **Nero**'s overthrow and the termination of Julio-Claudian rule at Rome, during which no less than four provincial governors, **Galba**, **Otho**, **Vitellius** and **Vespasian**, backed by their troops, were declared emperor in turn. Only with Vespasian's defeat of Vitellius and his establishment of the Flavian dynasty did peace and stability return to Rome. ▷ **Julio-Claudian Dynasty**

Four Freedoms (1941) Four basic human rights proclaimed in an annual message to Congress by President Franklin D **Roosevelt** as basic human rights. They included freedom of speech and worship, and freedom from want and fear.

Four Modernizations, The This refers to the long-term policy aim of the Chinese Communist Party to achieve advanced development in the fields of agriculture, industry, science and technology, and national defence. Coined by Premier **Zhou Enlai** at the Third National People's Congress (1964), the phrase was downplayed during the **Cultural Revolution** when ideological correctness took precedence over strictly economic development. After **Mao Zedong**'s death in 1976 the term was revived by **Deng Xiaoping**, and at the Third Plenum of the Party's Eleventh Central Committee (Dec 1978) priority was given to the implementation of the Four Modernizations. Although ambitious targets set in 1978 had to be modified subsequently, the policy has led to free market reforms in the countryside, more autonomy being granted to urban enterprises, increasing professionalization of the army, and encouragement of foreign investment and more extensive trade with the West.

Fourteen Points A peace programme outlined by US President Woodrow **Wilson** in a message to Congress in 1918, at the end of **World War I**. The programme offered the possibility of an acceptable peace to the Central Powers, and as a result Wilson came to be perceived as a moral leader. It was largely instrumental in bringing about the surrender of Germany and the beginning of peace talks. Several of the points, however, were compromised or defeated in the actual treaty.

Fourteenth Amendment (1868) US constitutional amendment adopted during **Reconstruction** after the **American Civil War** to guarantee equality before the law to blacks and whites alike. Its first section defined federal and state citizenship for all American-born or naturalized persons specifically to include the ex-slaves, and it prohibited the states from abridging their 'privileges and immunities' and denying them the 'equal protection of the laws'. Judicial interpretation of the amendment soon turned it to purposes for which it was never intended. Since corporations were legal 'persons', the amendment became used as a shield against state regulation, particularly of railroads and working conditions. Its negative wording was also taken to allow individual discrimination, while the 'separate but equal' argument even gave the amendment's sanction to formal legislative segregation. This flagrant abuse was reversed during the 1950s and 1960s, but in the last two decades it has also been used with success against policies of affirmative action and positive discrimination. ▷ **Brown v Board of Education of Topeka, Kansas; Civil Rights Cases; Plessy v Ferguson**

Fox, Charles James (1749–1806) British politician. He became an MP at 19, and two years later was a junior Lord of the Admiralty. He supported Lord **North**, but in 1772 resigned over American policy. Foreign Secretary in 1782 and 1783, he became Secretary of State after North's downfall, and formed a coalition with him, which held office for a short period in 1783. He supported the **French Revolution**, and strongly opposed the war with France. After **Pitt**, the Younger's death (1806) he was recalled to office as Foreign Secretary, but died soon afterwards.

Fraga Iribarne, Manuel (1922–) Spanish politician and academic. As Minister of Information and Tourism under **Franco** (1962–9) he liberalized the regime, above all

through the Press Law of 1966. By contrast, he was a hardline Minister of the Interior in 1975–6. In Sep 1976 he founded *Alianza Popular*, which became the main opposition party to the **PSOE** in 1982 and was renamed the **PP** in 1988. A conservative of authoritarian temperament, he was a dynamic, if abrasive, leader of *Alianza* in 1979–86 and was elected again in 1989. In 1990 Fraga was elected President of the regional government of Galicia, his home region.

Francesco IV d'Este (1779–1846) Duke of Modena (1815/46). He was an extremely reactionary ruler of the restoration period who served as the model for Stendhal's Enrico IV in *La Chartreuse de Parme*. He harboured ambitions for the Piedmontese throne in 1821 and seems to have briefly flirted with the idea of cooperating with liberal revolutionaries, who hoped to persuade him to lead a nationalist insurrection (1829–30). He was responsible for the summary execution of Ciro **Menotti**. ▷ **Misley, Enrico**

Franchet d'Esperey, Louis Félix Marie François (1856–1942) French soldier. He was made commanding general of the French 5th Army in 1914, gaining success at the Battle of the **Marne**. In 1918 he was appointed Commander-in-Chief of Allied armies in **Macedonia**, where from Salonica he overthrew Bulgaria and advanced as far as Budapest; only the end of the war prevented his dash for Berlin. He was made Marshal of France in 1922. He had some links to the French extreme right but refused to support **Pétain** in 1940. ▷ **World War I; World War II**

Francia, José Gaspar Rodríguez de (1766–1840) Paraguayan dictator. Educated in Paraguay and Argentina in theology and law, he assumed a prominent role in Paraguay's movement for independence. Francia ('El Supremo') held absolute power from 1814 until his death, adopting a policy of isolating Paraguay from the outside world.

Francis I (1494–1547) King of France (1515/47). He was Count of Angoulême and Duke of Valois before succeeding **Louis XII** as King and marrying his daughter, Claude. He combined many of the attributes of medieval chivalry and a Renaissance prince, the dominant feature of his reign being his rivalry with Emperor **Charles V**, which led to a series of wars (1521–6, 1528–9, 1536–8 and 1542–4). After establishing his military reputation against the Swiss at Marignano (1515) in his first Italian campaign, he later suffered a number of reverses, including his capture at Pavia (1525) and imprisonment in Madrid. Though he avoided religious fanaticism, he became increasingly hostile to Protestantism after 1534. ▷ **Italian Wars; Valois Dynasty**

Francis I (1708–65) Holy Roman Emperor (1745/65). He was the eldest son of Leopold, Duke of Lorraine, whom he succeeded in 1729. However, he resigned his dominions in return for French recognition of his claim to the German imperial throne upon his marriage to the Habsburg heiress, **Maria Theresa**, in 1736. Awarded the Grand Duchy of Tuscany in compensation, he was finally elected Holy Roman Emperor in 1745. This office gave him little political influence, though, and in spite of being made co-regent of Austria, affairs of state remained firmly in the hands of his wife.

Francis II (1544–60) King of France (1559/60). He was the eldest son of **Henry II** and **Catherine de' Medici**. In 1558 he married **Mary, Queen of Scots**. His short reign was dominated by the Guise family, in their struggle against the Protestants. ▷ **Guise, House of; Religion, Wars of**

Francis II (of Austria) (1768–1835) Holy Roman Emperor (1792/1806). He was also, as Francis I, first Emperor of Austria (1804/35), and King of Hungary (1792/30) and Bohemia (1792/1836). Defeated on several occasions by **Napoleon I** (1797, 1801, 1805 and 1809), he made a short-lived alliance with him, sealed by the marriage of his daughter, **Marie Louise**, to the French Emperor. Later he joined with Russia and **Prussia** to win the Battle of **Leipzig** (1813). By the Congress of **Vienna** (1814–15), thanks to **Metternich**, he recovered several territories (including Lombardy-Venetia and **Dalmatia**). ▷ **Napoleonic Wars**

Francis II (1836–94) King of the Two Sicilies (1860/1). A weak and cowardly monarch, who was often referred to by his nickname, 'Bombino' (the diminutive form of 'Bomba', the sobriquet of **Ferdinand II**). In July 1860 he restored the 1848 constitution in a vain attempt to win over public support in the face of the threat posed by **Garibaldi**, who had seized Sicily and crossed to the mainland of the Kingdom of the **Two Sicilies**. He fled in the face of Garibaldi's advance and capitulated at Gaeta (13 Feb 1861). He played a small part in trying to stimulate unrest in his former territories during the **Grande Brigantaggio**.

Franciscans Religious orders founded by St Francis of Assisi in the early 13c. The first order, of Friars Minor, is now divided into three groups: the Observants (OFM), the Conventuals (OFMConv), and the Capuchins (OFMCap). These lead active lives preaching to the poor and needy. The second order is made up of nuns, known as the Poor Clares (PC). The third order is a lay fraternity. Together, they constitute the largest religious order in the Roman Catholic Church, notable for missionary and social work.

Francis Ferdinand (1863–1914) Archduke of Austria, nephew and heir-apparent (from 1896) to the Emperor **Francis Joseph**. On a visit to Sarajevo, Bosnia (in former Yugoslavia) in June 1914 he and his wife, Sophie, were assassinated by the **Black Hand**, a group of young Serbian nationalists, among whom was the perpetrator, Gavrilo **Princip**. Austria, encouraged by Germany, used the incident as a pretext for attacking **Serbia**, which precipitated **World War I**.

Francis Joseph (1830–1916) Emperor of Austria (1848/1916) and King of Hungary (1867/1916). He was the grandson of Emperor **Francis I**. During his reign the aspirations of the various nationalities of the empire were rigorously suppressed. He was defeated by the Prussians in 1866, and established the Dual Monarchy of **Austria-Hungary** in 1867. His annexation of Bosnia-Herzegovina in 1908 agitated Europe and especially Russia, and his government's attack on **Serbia** in 1914 precipitated **World War I**.

Franco (Bahamonde), Francisco (1892–1975) Spanish general and dictator. He graduated from Toledo military academy in 1910, rising rapidly through the ranks in Spanish Morocco, to become Europe's youngest general in 1926. He oversaw the repression of the Asturias miners' revolt (1934), and during 1935 served as Chief of Staff. In 1936 he joined, at the last moment, the conspiracy against the Popular Front government (elected Feb 1936) which was launched on 17–18 July; the rebellion led to the **Spanish Civil War**. Franco's leadership of the vital Army of Africa, and his close relations with the rebels' Italian and German allies, led to his becoming (Sep 1936) *generalísimo* of the rebel forces and chief of the Nationalist state. Between Oct 1936 and Apr 1939, he led the Nationalists to victory, and presided over the construction of an authoritarian regime that endured until his death. During **World War II**, he wanted to join Germany and Italy, but **Hitler** was not prepared to pay his price of France's north African territories, at Hendaye (Oct 1940). Franco therefore kept Spain out of the war, but sent the Blue Division to fight in the USSR, and provided the Germans with logistical and intelligence support. During the 1950s, his anti-communism made possible a rapprochement with the Western powers, the Bases Agreement of 1953 with the USA providing Franco with his breakthrough. The greatest paradox of Franco was that he oversaw the modernization of the Spanish economy in the 1950s and 60s which undermined the political foundations of his police state and prepared it for the transition to democracy. In 1969 he announced that upon his death the monarchy would return in the person of **Juan Carlos**, grandson of Spain's last ruling king. Franco died in Madrid, and within two years almost every vestige of his dictatorship had disappeared.

Franco-German Treaty of Cooperation (Jan 1963) The treaty signed by President de **Gaulle** and Chancellor **Adenauer** signalling a rapprochement and the ending of centuries of conflict. It made provisions for regular summit meetings, and cooperation and consultation in foreign, economic, and cultural affairs. A symbol of the new, post-war order in Europe, the treaty also underpinned the **EEC**.

Franconia One of the tribal duchies of early medieval central Europe, with its core around the valley of the River Main, and part of the realm of the Franks. When their lands were divided upon the Treaty of **Verdun** (843), Franconia passed to the eastern kingdom and became one of the constituent parts of Germany, the first elected king of which, Conrad I (911/18), hailed from the ducal family of Franconia. Remaining closely associated with the German crown until the 13c, the duchy later disintegrated into a mass of principalities. Some of these, notably the bishoprics of Würzburg and Bamberg, were grouped into a Franconian circle on the administrative reorganization of the empire after 1500 and since the territorial revolution have been part of Bavaria.

Franco-Prussian War (1870–1) The conflict occasioned by the Hohenzollern candidature for the Spanish throne and the Ems telegram, and caused by the changing balance of power in Europe. It resulted in crushing defeats for France at the Battles of **Sedan** and Metz by **Moltke**'s reformed Prussian Army, the Siege of **Paris**, and the humiliating Treaty of Frankfurt. ▷ **Hohenzollern Dynasty**

Franco-Russian Alliance (1894) The treaty under which Russia guaranteed France against Germany or Italy, France guaranteed Russia against Germany or Austria, and both agreed to mobilize if all three of Germany, Austria and Italy did so. It was largely the result of a change in German policy towards Russia from friendly reassurance to careless disregard. Already smarting from Germany's triumph in 1870, France was ready to provide loans when opportunity offered from 1887 onwards and to make military and naval overtures soon after **William II** dismissed **Bismarck** in 1890. The treaty overcame a tradition of hostility stretching back to Napoleon Bonaparte's invasion of Russia and retreat from Moscow and helped prepare the setting for **World War I**.

Frangipani A noble Roman family which figured in the Guelf and Ghibelline quarrels of the 12c and 13c causing a schism in the Church and the election of an anti-pope, Gregory VIII. ▷ **Guelfs; Ghibellines**

Franjiyeh, Suleyman (1910–92) Lebanese politician. President of Lebanon (and thus a Maronite) from 1970 to 1976, he presided over Lebanon at a particularly tense time in that Palestinian guerrillas ejected from Jordan in 1970–1 began conducting their operations from Palestinian refugee camps in Lebanon. He was President when the civil war broke out in 1975 and demitted office in 1976, the year of the Syrian invasion. He was, however, still active in Maronite politics in 1978 when, as a result of his pro-Syrian stance (which lasted until 1984), a split occurred in Maronite ranks and Phalangist militiamen murdered his son, Tony Franjieh, and other members of his family.

Frank, Anne (1929–45) Dutch Jewish girl. Her family went into hiding in Amsterdam to evade capture by the occupying German forces during **World War II**. The diary she kept of her life during this period (1942–4) was published in 1947 and is probably the most moving single testament against oppression and persecution. The family was betrayed, and Anne died in a German **concentration camp** in 1945. ▷ **Holocaust**

Frankfurter, Felix (1882–1965) Austrian-born US law teacher and judge. Educated at

335

the College of the City of New York and at Harvard, he taught at the Harvard Law School (1914–39) and served as an associate justice of the US Supreme Court (1939–62). He was a noted supporter of civil liberties and helped found the American Civil Liberties Union, although in court he advocated judicial restraint in opposing legislative and executive policy. In constitutional cases he claimed that judges should consider whether legislators could reasonably have enacted such a law.

Frankfurt Ghetto The Jewish quarter of Frankfurt. It was destroyed in 24 hours on 14 June 1711 by one of the largest fires in German history prior to the present century.

Frankfurt Parliament An elected assembly convened following the German revolutions of Mar 1848 to draft a liberal constitution for all of Germany. It represented every state in the **German Confederation**, but proved to be disunited and powerless. After its offer of the imperial crown to the King of **Prussia** was repudiated by **Austria** and rejected by the King himself, the parliament disintegrated. ▷ **Revolutions of 1848–9**

Franklin, Benjamin (1706–90) US politician, author and scientist. He set up a printing house in Philadelphia, bought the *Pennsylvania Gazette* (1730), and built a reputation as a journalist. In 1736 he became Clerk of the Pennsylvania legislature, in 1737 Deputy Postmaster of Philadelphia, and in 1753 Deputy Postmaster-General for the colonies, and was sent on various diplomatic missions to England. In 1748 he began his research into electricity, proving that lightning and electricity are identical, and suggesting that buildings be protected by lightning-conductors. In 1776 he was actively involved in framing the **Declaration of Independence**. A skilled negotiator, he successfully won Britain's recognition of US independence (1783). He was US Minister in Paris until 1785, three times President of the State of Pennsylvania, and a member of the **Constitutional Convention**. In 1788 he retired from public life. ▷ **Albany Congress**

Franks Germanic peoples, originally from the lower Rhine region. **Clovis I** led the Salian and Ripuarian Franks and founded a kingdom embracing much of **Gaul**; **Charlemagne**, their greatest ruler, attempted to revive the **Roman Empire** in the West. They gave their name to Francia and to Franconia, which by the 13c stood for what is now

France, but earlier had diverse territorial connotations, reflecting the vicissitudes of Frankish royal power. ▷ **Carolingians; Merovingians; Salic Law**

Franz Josef ▷ **Francis Joseph**

Fraser, (John) Malcolm (1930–) Australian politician. In 1955 he became the youngest MP in the House of Representatives. He was Minister for the Army (1966–8), Defence (1969–71), and Education and Science (1968–9, 1971–2). He became leader of the **Liberal Party of Australia** in 1975, and was Prime Minister in a Liberal–National Country coalition from the same year, retiring from politics after his government's defeat in 1983.

Fraser, Peter (1884–1950) British-born New Zealand politician. In 1910 he emigrated to New Zealand, and became involved in trade union organization. A founder member of the New Zealand Labour Party (1916), he was imprisoned during **World War I** for opposing conscription. He entered parliament in 1918, became Deputy Party Leader in 1933, and Leader and Prime Minister in 1940, holding office until 1949, when his government was defeated.

Fraser, Simon (1776–1862) Canadian fur-trader and explorer. In 1792 Fraser joined the North-West Company as a clerk, becoming a partner in 1801. In 1805 he was given responsibility for the company's operations beyond the Rockies, and established the first settlements in New Caledonia, now central British Columbia. Hoping to discover a water route which would cut the company's transport costs, in 1808 he braved the dangerous reach now known as the Fraser River Canyon. In 1815 he was arrested with other company officers at Fort William in retaliation for the Seven Oaks Incident (a North West Company attack on the **Hudson's Bay Company**'s Red River Settlement). The charges could not be sustained and Fraser had retired to Upper Canada by the time his trial took place.

Fratricide, Law of This law was promulgated by the Ottoman Sultan **Mehmed II, 'the Conqueror'**. 'To whichever of my sons the Sultanate may be granted, it is proper for him to put his brothers to death, to preserve the order of the world'. The law was designed to provide a stable regime and prevent dynastic conflicts for the succession to the throne. For a century and a half, each new sultan had his brothers strangled by a silken bowstring. The last such killings were in 1595, when Sultan Mehmed III ordered the execution of his 19 brothers. After this, the succession went to the eldest male member of the Ottoman house. The system of sending Ottoman princes to govern provinces of the Empire and so learn how to rule, now came to an end. Instead, they spent their lives in the *kafe* or cage, a group of buildings in the royal palace. There, surrounded by concubines, they lived lives of luxurious imprisonment, from which they emerged only to rule or when they were dead. The result was a marked decline in the quality of the sultans, who were often feeble in mind or body, a serious deficiency in a state where all power was in the hands of the Sultan.

Fredegond (d.597) Frankish Queen. She was first mistress, then wife, of Chilperic, King of **Neustria**. Fredegond waged a relentless feud with **Brunhilde**, wife of Sigbert, King of **Austrasia**, and sister of Chilperic of Neustria's first wife, a feud intensified by the rivalry between the two kingdoms.

Frederick I (1249–68) Duke of Austria. The son of Count Hermann of Baden and Gertrude, widow of Leopold of Austria, after the death of his father (1250) he was forced to relinquish Austria to Ottokar of Bohemia and fled to Bohemia. There he became friendly with **Conradin** and went with him to Italy in 1267 to reconquer the Hohenstaufen lands. He was captured at the Battle of Tagliacozzo and was beheaded in Naples along with Conradin, at the insistence of King Ottokar. ▷ **Hohenstaufen Dynasty**

Frederick I (1371–1440) Elector of Brandenburg. As Frederick VI, Count of Nuremberg, he was the founder of the Brandenburg line of the **Hohenzollern Dynasty**. In 1410 he was instrumental in having **Sigismund** elected German King and as a reward was made Governor of Brandenburg (1411) and confirmed as Elector and Margrave in 1417. He led the imperial army against the Hussites (1422 and 1427–31) but his lack of success led him to support the peace negotiated in the pacts of Prague (1433) and Iglau (1436). ▷ **Electors; Hussite Wars**

Frederick I (1471–1533) King of Denmark (1523/33) and Norway (1524/33). He was the son of **Christian I** and uncle of **Christian II** and, as Duke of Holstein, was chosen king when Christian II, who had just lost Sweden to **Gustav I Vasa**, was dethroned in 1523 by a rebellion in Denmark. In 1531–2 he fended off an invasion of Norway by the ex-king; he then tricked him into accepting safe-conduct for a parley in Copenhagen, and imprisoned him for life instead. Frederick died soon afterwards, on the verge of accepting Lutheranism, and was succeeded by his son, **Christian III**.

Frederick I (1657–1713) Elector of Brandenburg (1688/1713) and King in Prussia (1701/13). He was the son of **Frederick William**, the 'Great Elector', whom he succeeded in 1688 (as Frederick III of Brandenburg). In 1701 he assumed the title of King in Prussia, the only part of the Hohenzollern dominions outside the **Holy Roman Empire**. His foreign policy was generally supportive of the Habsburgs, and during the War of the **Spanish Succession** he took part in the Grand Alliance against France. Unlike his predecessors and most of his successors, his main interests were not military. Instead, he maintained a splendid court life and was a great patron of the arts and of learning. ▷ **Habsburg Dynasty; Hohenzollern Dynasty**

Frederick I, 'Barbarossa' (c.1123–90) German King and Holy Roman Emperor (1152/90). Born of the **Hohenstaufen Dynasty**, he succeeded his uncle, **Conrad III**, in 1152. His reign was a continuous struggle against unruly vassals at home, the city-republics of Lombardy, and the papacy. He went on several campaigns in Italy, and though severely defeated at **Legnano** (1176), he quelled **Henry the Lion** of Bavaria, and asserted his feudal superiority over Poland, Hungary, Denmark, and Burgundy. He led the Third Crusade against **Saladin** (1189), and was victorious at Philomelium and Iconium. ▷ **Crusade, Third; Lombard League**

Frederick II (1194–1250) German King (1212/50) and Holy Roman Emperor (1215/50). The grandson of **Frederick I, 'Barbarossa'**, he was the last Emperor of the Hohenstaufen line. He was also King of Sicily (1198) and of Germany (1212). He keenly desired to consolidate imperial power in Italy at the expense of the papacy, and devoted himself to organizing his Italian territories, but his plans were frustrated by the Lombard cities and by the popes. Embarking on the Fifth Crusade in 1228, he took possession of Jerusalem, and crowned himself King there (1229). Returning to Italy, he continued his struggles with the papacy until his death, at

Fiorentino. ▷ **Crusades, Later; Hohenstaufen Dynasty; Lombard League**

Frederick II (1534–88) King of Denmark and Norway (1559/88). He was the son and successor of **Christian III**. In the early years of his reign he was engaged in a seven-year war against the Sweden of the deranged **Erik XIV**, which was brought to an inconclusive ending with the Treaty of Stettin (1370). The remainder of his reign was a period of peace and prosperity. A pleasure-loving monarch, he built the magnificent Renaissance castle of Kronborg at Elsinore, to which he brought English musicians to provide entertainment, and was a patron of the astronomer Tycho Brahe and other scientists. He was succeeded by his young son, **Christian IV**. His daughter, **Anne of Denmark**, married King James VI of Scotland and I of England. ▷ **James VI and I**

Frederick II, 'the Great' (1712–86) King of Prussia (1740/86). He was the son of **Frederick William I** and Sophia Dorothea, daughter of **George I** of England. He developed an early devotion to French culture and his desire for independence resulted in bitter conflict with, and permanent alienation from, his despotic father. Almost immediately on his accession to the throne, he invaded the Austrian province of Silesia which he managed to hold on to through three wars, although Prussia was brought to the brink of annihilation more than once. In domestic affairs, he continued his father's policy of centralization and personal absolutism, but redefined the king's role as that of the first servant of the state. However, his promotion of agriculture, commerce and industry proved meddlesome in many respects. Committed to religious tolerance he had, on the other hand, little regard for civil and national self-determination and in 1772 became involved in the first partition of Poland. A misanthropist and recluse in his last years, Frederick left Prussia a great power when he died at Potsdam. ▷ **Austrian Succession, War of the; Austro-Prussian Dualism; Poland, Partitions of; Seven Years War; Silesian Wars**

Frederick III (1415–93) King of Germany, as Frederick IV (1440/93), and Emperor (1452/93). His reign was turbulent, and he lost his hold on many territories. He surrendered the Empire to the Pope by the Vienna Concordat of 1448, and failed to oppose the Turkish invasions of 1469 and 1475. Nevertheless, by the marriage (1477) of his son, Maximilian I, to Mary, daughter of **Charles the Bold**, Duke of Burgundy, he laid the foundation of the subsequent greatness of the **Habsburg Dynasty**.

Frederick III (1609–70) King of Denmark and Norway (1648/70). He was the son and successor of **Christian IV**. The first half of his reign was taken up with costly wars against Sweden, but after the peace settlement of 1660 he established absolute hereditary monarchy over Denmark, Norway and Iceland, embodied in the Royal Law (*Kongelov*) of 1665. He was an enlightened patron of scientific and antiquarian studies, and founded the Royal Library in Copenhagen.

Frederick III (1831–88) German Emperor and eighth King of **Prussia**. The only son of **William I**, in 1858 he married Victoria, Princess Royal of England. As Crown Prince of Prussia (from 1861) he protested against **Bismarck**'s reactionary policy in relation to constitutional questions and the press. In the **Franco-Prussian** War he commanded the 3rd Army and was made field marshal (1870). In 1871 he became Crown Prince of the German Empire. In 1878, when the Emperor was wounded by an assassin, the Crown Prince was appointed provisional Regent. When, in 1888, Emperor William I died, Frederick was already ill, with cancer of the throat. He was proclaimed emperor as Frederick III, but he died at Potsdam. His son, **William II**, succeeded him. Frederick had a great horror of war, intensely disliked autocratic ideas, and sought to liberalize German institutions.

Frederick V (1596–1632) Elector of the Palatinate (1610/23) and King of Bohemia (as Frederick I, 1619/20). Born at Amberg in the Upper Palatinate, he was the leading calvinist prince of Germany and was married to Elizabeth, the daughter of James VI of Scotland and I of England. As head of the Evangelical Union he was offered, and accepted, the Bohemian crown when the estates rose in rebellion against **Ferdinand II**. Swiftly defeated by the imperial forces at the Battle of the **White Mountain** outside Prague (1620), the 'Winter King' went into exile in Holland, eventually losing the Palatinate as well as Bohemia. ▷ **James VI and I**

Frederick VI (1768–1839) King of Denmark (1808/39) and Norway (1808/14). He was the son of **Christian VII**. During his reign, Frederick supported liberal measures: feudal serfdom was abolished, the criminal code amended, and the slave trade prohibited in the Danish colonies. However, he refused to join Britain against Napoleon, and after the war lost Norway to Sweden (1814). The state became bankrupt in 1813, and did not recover for many years. In 1831 he granted a more liberal constitution to his subjects. ▷ **Napoleonic Wars**

Frederick VII (1808–63) King of Denmark (1848/63). He was the son and successor of **Christian VIII**, and the last of the Oldenburg line. In 1849 he promulgated a new and liberal constitution abolishing monarchical absolutism. He died childless, and was succeeded by **Christian IX**.

Frederick VIII (1843–1912) King of Denmark (1906/12). He was the son and successor of **Christian IX**, and brother of Queen Alexandra of Britain. In 1907 he made a state visit to Iceland to celebrate the granting of home rule there (1904). He married Princess Louise of Sweden, and was well-liked for his simple lifestyle. His second son, Prince Carl, became King **Haakon VII** of Norway. He was succeeded by his eldest son, **Christian X**.

Frederick IX (1899–1972) King of Denmark (1947/72). The son and successor of **Christian X**, he trained as a naval officer (rising to rear-admiral in 1946), and was Crown Prince from 1912. During **World War II** he assisted his father in resistance to the German occupation, and was held under house arrest (1943–5). He granted home rule to the Faroes in 1948, and in 1953 a new constitution provided for female succession to the throne. In 1935 he had married Ingrid, daughter of King **Gustav VI Adolf** of Sweden; their eldest daughter now became crown princess and succeeded him as Queen **Margrethe II** in 1972. Their youngest daughter, Anne-Marie, married King **Constantine II** of Greece, who was later dethroned.

Frederick (Augustus) (1763–1827) Duke of York. He was the second son of King **George III** of Great Britain. A soldier by profession, he was unsuccessful both in the field in the Netherlands (1793–9) and as British commander-in-chief (1798–1809), and earned the nickname of the 'grand old Duke of York' in the nursery rhyme. However, his painstaking reform of the army proved of lasting benefit, especially to **Wellington**. In 1809 he resigned because of the traffic in appointments conducted by his mistress, Mary Anne Clarke, but he was exonerated and reinstated in 1811.

Frederick Augustus I (1750–1827) Elector, as Frederick Augustus III (1763/27), and

First King of Saxony (1806/87). Under his rule Saxony recovered rapidly from the **Seven Years War**, but fared less well during the Napoleonic era. Defeated alongside **Prussia** at the Battles of **Jena and Auerstädt** by France in Oct 1806, Frederick Augustus subsequently allied with **Napoleon I** and remained loyal to him almost to the end. Although confirmed on his throne by the Congress of **Vienna** (1814–15), Saxony lost much territory to Prussia as a result of his alliance with France.

Frederick Henry (1584–1647) Stadholder of the United Provinces (1625/47). The son of **William I, 'the Silent'** and Louise de Coligny, he led the Dutch Republic after 1625, when he became **Stadholder** of the provinces Holland, Zeeland, Utrecht, Gelderland and Overijssel. In 1640 Groningen and Drente also elected him. As military leader of the northern Dutch territories in their revolt against Spain (the **Eighty Years War**), he had considerable success, especially in **Brabant** and Limburg. Although not a hereditary monarch, he set up a court and, after 1640, applied a dynastic foreign policy, marrying off his children (by Amalia of Solms-Braunfels) to the royal families of England and Germany.

Fredericksburg, Battle of (13 Dec 1862) In the **American Civil War**, a fruitless attempt by a Northern army of well over 100 000 to capture the town of Fredericksburg, Virginia, from a Southern army that was heavily outnumbered.

Frederick William ('The Great Elector') (1620–88) Elector of Brandenburg (1640/88). On his accession, Brandenburg was at its weakest, but ruthless manoeuvring during the last stages of the **Thirty Years War** enabled him to make considerable territorial gains in the Peace of **Westphalia** (1648), and in 1660 he acquired full sovereignty in Prussia. His designs on Swedish Pomerania were frustrated, though, when French intervention invalidated Brandenburg's victory at Fehrbellin (1675). This prompted the diplomatic orientation towards Austria which was to dominate Hohenzollern foreign policy until 1740. Keeping a small standing army to serve foreign policy as well as domestic purposes, he established the rule of princely absolutism by breaking the traditional tax voting rights of the estates. The Junker nobility were compensated for their loss of political influence with social privileges over the peasantry. With a view to the economic development of his dominions, he offered asylum to large numbers of Huguenot refugees. ▷ **Hohenzollern Dynasty**

Frederick William I (1688–1740) King of Prussia (1713/40). He was the son of **Frederick I**, whom he succeeded. Known as the 'Soldier King', his reign saw everything and everybody being subordinated to the push for a massive increase of the army. The enforcement of strict discipline gave even the civil service a decidedly military character. His suppression of the estates' influence and the creation of a centralized administrative directory (1723) transformed the scattered dominions of the **Hohenzollern Dynasty** into a unified state, albeit one resembling a large barracks. In many ways he can be regarded as the real creator of Prussia, and although his foreign policy was peaceful throughout, it was he who laid the foundation for his country's subsequent expansion.

Frederick William II (1744–97) King of Prussia (1786/97). He was the nephew and successor of **Frederick II, 'the Great'**. Although some of the latter's more unpopular measures were revoked, no comprehensive reforms were undertaken and Prussia became increasingly ossified. A weak character, he relied on the suggestions of mistresses and favourites, and under the influence of a mystic sect ordered a reactionary clampdown in religious and educational matters. Under him, Prussia became involved in the wars of the European coalition against revolutionary France, and in the second and third partitions of Poland (1792 and 1795). ▷ **Poland, Partitions of**

Frederick William III (1770–1840) King of Prussia (1797/1849). He was the son of Frederick William II. At first cautiously neutral towards **Napoleon I**'s conquests, he eventually declared war (1806) and was severely defeated at the Battles of **Jena and Auerstädt**, with the loss of all territory west of the Elbe. To further Prussia's recovery, he sanctioned the liberalizing reforms of **Hardenberg** and **Stein** and the military reorganization of **Scharnhorst** and **Gneisenau**, sharing in the decisive victory at the Battle of **Leipzig** with Tsar Alexander I (1813). By the Congress of **Vienna** (1814–15) he recovered many of his possessions, gained vital new territories on the Rhine and Ruhr, and thereafter tended to support the forces of conservatism. ▷ **Napoleonic Wars**

Frederick William IV (1795–1861) King of Prussia (1840/61). The son of **Frederick**

William III, he began his reign by granting minor reforms and promising radical changes, which were never implemented. He opposed the popular movement of 1848, but was forced to grant a representative parliament (1850). In 1857, afflicted with insanity, he resigned the administration to his brother.

Frederikshamn, Peace of (1809) The treaty ending the Russo-Swedish War of 1808–9 and transferring the Grand Duchy of Finland from Swedish to Russian rule. This completed the expansion of Russia towards the Baltic, giving it control of strategic Finnish fortresses. It also began the gradual process of undermining the supremacy of the Swedish elite within Finland by cutting it off from its mother country and by recognizing the privileges of the Finnish estates which were at that time a Swedish preserve but eventually became a target for Finnish nationalists. A century later the same nationalists were to turn against Russia.

Free Coloured The intermediate class which resulted from unsanctified unions between members of the white plantocracy and its slaves and which became an economic force in the British West Indies c.1800. Varying from Mustifino (15/16 white) to Sambo (1/4 white), these illegitimate offspring were often emancipated by their fathers and had property settled upon them. While the group grew in economic importance after 1750, its members becoming craftsmen, merchants, professionals and even planters and slave owners, it was excluded by law from any role in the legal and political process. Its disabilities were removed by 1830 and after that date prominent coloured men, such as George William Gordon and Edward Jordan in Jamaica and Samuel Prescod Jackson and Conrad Reeves in Barbados, were to be found as legislative councillors and magistrates. Known as *affranchis* in the French colonies, the group played a key role in the outbreak of the **Haitian Revolution**.

Freedom and People's Rights Movement (*Jiyu minken undo*) A political movement in early Meiji Japan during the 1870s and 1880s calling for a national representative assembly along Western lines. The movement originated in 1873 with a split in the new Meiji government over whether to send a punitive expedition to Korea. Some members, like **Itagaki Taisuke**, resigned when the decision was taken not to send an expedition. He founded political societies in his own domain of Tosa, denouncing the monopoly of power

by leaders from **Choshu** and **Satsuma** and calling for a nationally-elected assembly. At first comprising dissident **samurai**, the movement spread nationwide and obtained the support of landowners and wealthy farmers; these political societies formed the *Jiyuto* (Liberal Party) in 1881. The ideology of the movement was influenced by Anglo-Saxon liberalism, although more radical members were influenced by Rousseau's concept of popular sovereignty. Government suppression and the internal rift between moderates and radicals severely hampered the movement and, after a series of violent incidents (1882–4), the government dissolved the Jiyuto. The movement, however, hastened the government's own plans for a constitution, which was promulgated in 1889.
▷ **Meiji Constitution**

Freedom Charter The policy document adopted by the Congress Alliance (June 1955), when 3 000 opposition delegates from all regions of South Africa met to coordinate policies, and which was issued by the **ANC** (African National Congress) itself in 1956, setting out its non-racial policy for South Africa, emphasizing its Fabian principles as well as its commitment to racial equality.

Free French Frenchmen who answered General de **Gaulle**'s appeal, broadcast from London (18 June 1940), to reject the impending armistice between France and Germany, and join him in fighting on. He became leader of the Free French forces, and the 2nd French Armoured Division helped to liberate Paris (25 Aug 1944). ▷ **Resistance Movement** (France); **World War II**

Free Officers In Egypt, a small group of army officers formed after the fiasco of the 1948 war, who were bent on the expulsion of the British from Egypt and the removal of the politicians in power at the time. In the aftermath of the riots of **Black Saturday** (Jan 1952), the Free Officers, fearing that King Farouk might be about to have them arrested, rose and forced Farouk into abdication (July 1952). The Free Officers (with Neguib nominally at their head, but actually led by Gamal Abd al-**Nasser**) took control of the country; Nasser went on to run the country until his death in 1969. The Free Officers played a leading role in Egypt throughout the period until the June War of 1967 when, with the growing rift between Abd al-Hakim **Amer** and Nasser and the former's subsequent suicide, the solidarity of the Free Officers was broken.

Free Officers' Movement (Libya) Libya became an independent country in 1951 with the Sanusi leader, Amir Idris, as King. His regime was, however, soon condemned by students and young army officers as corrupt and for being dependent on foreign support. Inspired by the pan-Arab and socialist doctrines of Gamal Abd al-**Nasser** and the Ba'ath Party, the Free Officers' Movement, consisting of middle-ranking officers and NCOs and led by Muammar al-**Gaddafi**, seized power. They set up a Revolutionary Command Council and established a military dictatorship. Foreign banks and businesses were nationalized and politcal parties and trade unions were outlawed.

free silver A demand made within the US **Democratic Party** in 1895 for the unlimited coinage of silver at a ratio of 16:1 with gold. Intended as a reflationary solution for agrarian economic problems, in the 1896 presidential election, free silver became a major plank of the Democratic Party platform. But after Democrat William Jennings **Bryan** lost to Republican William **McKinley**, interest in the issue faded.

Free-Soil Party (1848) A US political party whose slogan was 'free soil, free speech, free labor, and free men.' Opposed to the expansion of slavery into territories annexed after the **Mexican War**, it ran former President Martin **Van Buren** as its presidential candidate in 1848. Van Buren lost, but the slavery issue was later taken up by the **Republican Party**.

Frei (Montalva), Eduardo (1911–82) Chilean politician. He became one of the leaders of the Social-Christian Falange Party in the late 1930s, and of the new Christian Democratic Party after 1957. His presidency (1964–70) saw an ambitious programme of social reform, which brought Chile substantial international support. His initial scepticism of the **Pinochet** regime turned into outright opposition. By the time of his death, he was widely seen as the father of opposition to the dictatorship.

Freikorps German paramilitary organizations. Formed in late 1918 and 1919 by military officers who recruited demobilized soldiers, sailors, students and members of the unemployed, the *Freikorps* (literally, 'volunteer corps') played an equivocal and often violent role in the early history of the **Weimar Republic**. Sanctioned by the Social Democratic Army Minister, Noske, their initial purpose was to suppress extreme left-wing insurgency and subsequently to defend Germany's eastern frontier, particularly in Upper Silesia, against Polish irregular forces. However, they were strongly anti-republican in spirit and engaged in a campaign of terror and assassination against prominent republican figures as well as attempting to topple the republic in the **Kapp Putsch** of 1920. Despite their official dissolution in 1920, the Freikorps maintained a clandestine existence and were involved in **Hitler**'s failed 1923 putsch. Subsequently quiescent, many Freikorps officers later resurfaced as leaders of the **SA** of the **Nazi Party**.

Frelimo (*Frente de Libertação de Moçambique*, 'Mozambique Liberation Front') Founded in 1962, it was led by Eduardo **Mondlane** and was based in Dar es Salaam. When Mondlane was assassinated, the leadership passed to Samora **Machel** and Frelimo waged a successful guerrilla war against the Portuguese, establishing liberated zones in which rudimentary governmental structures were established. At independence in 1975, it became the only legal party in Mozambique.

Frémont, John Charles (1813–90) US explorer and politician. In 1843 he crossed the Rocky Mountains (where a peak is named after him), and found an overland route across the continent. He explored the Great Salt Lake (1843), fought in the **Mexican War** (1846), then went to California, where he made a fortune in the **gold rush**, and became a Senator. In 1856 he was the first presidential candidate of the new **Republican Party**, losing to James Buchanan, but receiving 1 million votes and making the party a major force in national politics. He later became Governor of Arizona (1878–83). ▷ **Republican Party**

French, John (Denton Pinkstone), Earl of Ypres (1852–1925) British field marshal. He joined the navy (1866), then the army (1874), and distinguished himself in the Sudan (1884–5) and South Africa (1899–1901). Chief of Imperial General Staff (1911–14), he held supreme command of the British Expeditionary Force in France (1914–15), but was criticized for indecision, and resigned. He was made a viscount (1915) and earl (1921), and was Lord-Lieutenant of Ireland (1918–21). ▷ **World War I**

French and Indian War (1756–63) The last of the 18c wars between France and Britain for the control of North America. France

accepted final defeat at the Treaty of Paris (1763). ▷ **Seven Years War**

French Community A grouping of some former French colonies which under the constitution of the Fifth Republic (1958) opted to stay closely associated with France. The member states had full internal autonomy, but many matters, including currency, defence, and foreign affairs remained the responsibility of the Community, which in effect meant France. Some 12 overseas territories opted to join. Pressures for full independence continued to build up, and in 1960 it became possible to be fully independent within the Community, thus rendering it of no practical relevance. ▷ **French Union; Republic, Fifth** (France)

French Republican Calendar A calendar introduced during the **French Revolution** by the National Convention to herald the beginning of a new epoch for France and for humanity in general, and to further the anti-clerical campaign for de-christianization. The structure and nomenclature were devised by a committee under the Deputy, Fabre d'Eglantine, Year 1 dating from the abolition of the monarchy and the declaration of the First Republic (22 Sep 1792). Twelve 30-day months were introduced and divided into three 10-day weeks of *decadi*, eliminating Sundays. They were given names derived from nature, notably from the seasons: Vendémiaire, Brumaire, Frimaire, Nivôse, Pluviôse, Ventôse, Germinal, Floréal, Prairial, Messidor, **Thermidor**, and Fructidor. The system was abolished under **Napoleon I** (1805). ▷ **Brumaire coup; Vendémiaire, 12th and 13th**

French Revolution (1789) A complex upheaval, profoundly affecting every aspect of government and society, and therefore considered a significant turning-point in French history. Although its causes have been subject to conflicting interpretation, conventionally the start was the summoning of the **Estates General** (spring 1789), which became the National Assembly when its three houses combined; it is also known as the Constituent Assembly. It responded to public pressure, such as the storming of the **Bastille** (14 July 1789), with wide-ranging political, social and economic measures (1789–91). These included the abolition of feudal, aristocratic and clerical privileges, a **Declaration of the Rights of Man and Citizen** (1789), the establishment of a constitutional government, the confiscation of Church property, and a reorganization of Church–state relations in the **Civil Constitution of the Clergy** (1790). Thus the **ancien régime** was effectively dismantled in the name of 'Liberty, Equality, Fraternity'. Meanwhile, the royal family had been removed from Versailles to Paris (Oct 1789), but after their flight to Varennes (June 1791) their fate was sealed. A **Legislative Assembly** was elected; however, after an insurrection on 10 Aug 1792, France was declared a republic (1792), and a new assembly (the National Convention) was effected in Sep 1792. At the same time, the September Massacres occurred. The Paris crowd, in panic at the advance of invading armies, and incited by demagogues, entered the prisons and massacred thousands of innocent victims. **Louis XVI** and his queen, **Marie Antoinette**, were executed (1793). The Revolution then entered more dramatic phases, marked by political extremism and bitter rivalry between **Girondins** and **Jacobins** (the latter led by **Robespierre**). Although the Jacobins seized control of the Committee of Public Safety (July 1793) and instituted the dictatorship of the Reign of **Terror**, Robespierre's short-lived triumph ended with his execution (1794). The Convention suppressed opponents from both sides, Jacobins and royalists, with military force before establishing the government of the **Directory** (1795), which was in turn overthrown by Napoleon Bonaparte (**Napoleon I**) in the **Brumaire coup** (1799). Under the **Consulate** (1799–1804) and the First Empire (1804–15), many of the ideas of the Revolution, such as popular sovereignty and civil equality, were disseminated in those areas of Europe subjected to French rule. ▷ **Chouans; Convention, National; Empire, First** (France); **French Republican Calendar; French Revolutionary Wars; Mountain, The; Plain, The; Public Safety, Committee of; Terror, Reign of; sans-culottes**

French Revolutionary Wars (1792–9) A series of campaigns between France and neighbouring European states hostile to the Revolution and to French hegemony, merging ultimately into the **Napoleonic Wars** (1799–1815). Starting with France's declaration of war on Emperor **Francis II**, Prussia, and Sardinia, which precipitated the War of the First Coalition (1792–7), French forces attacked the Rhine, the Netherlands, and Savoy, after checking an initial Austro-Prussian advance at Valmy (1792). France later extended hostilities to Britain, Holland, and Spain (1793); after successfully invading the Netherlands (1794), the French broke the Coalition (1795–6), isolating Britain (1797). A Second Coalition (1798) expelled French forces from Italy and the Rhinelands, before suffering defeat by **Napoleon I** (1799–1800). ▷ **Dumouriez, Charles François (du Périer); French Revolution; Murat, Joachim**

French State (*Etat français*) (1940–4) The name given to the regime established after the French defeat in 1940, in which all power was placed in the hands of **Pétain**, to emphasize the break made with the Third Republic; Pétain was given power to promulgate a new constitution, but one was never drawn up. The French State is also known unofficially as the **Vichy** regime, from its capital in the zone not originally occupied by the German Army; it was abolished upon the liberation of occupied France, by an ordinance of Aug 1944. ▷ **collaboration,** (France); **Republic, Third** (France); **World War II**

French Union (*Union française*) A term for the French Empire introduced by the constitution of the Fourth Republic in 1946. Former colonies were reclassified as departments of France or overseas territories; trust territories became overseas territories; and former protectorates became associated states. The latter had all become independent when the Union was renamed the *Communauté* ('community') in 1958; the former colonies rapidly gained their independence also, leaving only a few small overseas departments and territories (**DOM-TOM**). ▷ **Republic, Fourth** (France)

Frère-Orban, Hubert Joseph Walthère (1812–96) Belgian politician. He trained as a lawyer, and was one of the most prominent Francophone liberal leaders in Belgium of the 19c. He took part in most liberal cabinets from 1847 onwards, and was Prime Minister (1867–70 and 1878–84). His liberalism was primarily economic, and aimed against restrictions on entrepreneurial freedom; in political matters his liberalism was moderate or 'doctrinaire', not extending to universal suffrage or social reforms.

Frescobaldi One of several banking families in 14–15c Florence with European-wide interests. Their clients included **Edward II** of England, whose wars with Scotland they financed in exchange for customs revenues. The royal default on debts led to a crisis for the Frescobaldi bank in 1311. ▷ **Bardi and Peruzzi**

Freycinet, Charles Louis de Saulces de (1818–1923) French politician. An engineer, in 1870 he was called by **Gambetta** to the War Department where he rendered great services. He was a Senator from 1876 to 1920, and his ministerial career spanned the years 1877 to 1916, during which he was four times Prime Minister (1879–80, 1882, 1886 and 1890–2). He was Prime Minister and Foreign Minister at a crucial moment, in 1882, when French withdrawal from a proposed joint expedition led to British control of Egypt: his major contribution was at the Ministry of War (1888–93).

Friedland, Battle of (June 1807) A battle fought in northern Prussia between French and Russian forces. It resulted in a complete, if costly, victory for **Napoleon I**, forcing the Russians to sue for peace, which was signed the next month under the terms of the Treaty of **Tilsit**. It was one of the crucial encounters in the collapse of the Fourth Coalition (Britain, Russia and Prussia) against France. Prussia suffered most; Russia, although defeated, strengthened its position as a major European power since Tsar **Alexander I** reached a number of ruler-to-ruler agreements with Napoleon.

Friends, Society of A Christian sect founded by George Fox and others in mid-17c England, and formally organized in 1667; members are popularly known as Quakers, possibly because of Fox's injunction 'to quake at the word of the Lord'. Persecution led William Penn to establish a Quaker colony (Pennsylvania) in 1682. Belief in the 'inner light', a living contact with the divine Spirit, is the basis of its meetings for worship, where Friends gather in silence until moved by the Spirit to speak. They emphasize simplicity in all things, and are active reformers promoting tolerance, justice, and peace. Today most meetings have programmed orders of worship, though meetings based on silence (unprogrammed) still prevail in the UK and parts of the USA.

Frihedsråd Literally 'Freedom Council', a coordinating body established in Denmark (Sep 1943) in order to regulate and escalate the country's resistance against the Nazi occupation (1940–5). The formation of the *Frihedsråd* came in response to the dismissal of the Danish government by the German occupation force (29 Aug 1943), following extensive strike action and several acts of sabotage in Danish towns and cities. The Frihedsråd gathered all factions of the Danish resistance movement, from Communists to Conservatives. By definition, the organization carried no official authority, but it played a vital role in organizing the growing sabotage campaign and in the formation and command of a Danish underground army numbering 43000 men at the time of the German capitulation. The Frihedsråd was supported by the Allied nations, particularly the UK, and its activities contributed greatly to the recognition of Demnark as an Allied nation after **World War II**. During the war, the Frihedsråd was also involved in formulating the broadly democratic political direction that peacetime Denmark was to follow. Several of its members took office in the first Danish post-war government, formed in May 1945 immediately after the liberation of Denmark by Allied forces. ▷ **Denmark, German Invasion of**

Frolov, Ivan Timofeevich (1929–) Soviet philosopher, ideologist and journalist. He had a long education in Moscow before turning to journalism in the 1960s and 1970s when he had two spells on the *World Marxist Review* in Prague divided by a turn as editor of *Problems of Philosophy* in Moscow. In the latter case he had some disagreements with orthodox views that made him a target for Mikhail **Gorbachev**'s recruiting policy. In 1986 he was appointed editor of *Communist*, in 1989 editor-in-chief of *Pravda*, and in 1990 a member of the **Politburo**. However, Gorbachev's role was all but past.

Fronde, The (1648–53) A series of civil revolts in France during the regency of **Anne of Austria**, caused by economic grievances and opposition to Cardinal **Mazarin** and the central government. The disturbances, named after a contemporary street urchins' game, developed into two phases: the *Fronde Parlementaire* (1648–9), and that of the Princes (1650–3). After the declaration of **Louis XIV**'s majority (1651), the Princes' opposition was slowly undermined; royal forces under **Turenne** recovered Paris (1652) and the provinces (1652–3), ending the most serious threat to the central government during the **ancien régime**.

Front de Libération de Québec (FLQ) Canadian terrorist organization. On the extreme left wing and anti-capitalist, it targeted the prosperous English-speaking sector of Quebec society. The FLQ had little formal organization, although arrangements were made for its members to train with the **PLO**. It gave the impression of being a much larger conspiracy than it actually was, for its name was simply appropriated by small independent groups to indicate responsibility for terrorist attacks. The arrest of Pierre Vallière and Charles Gagnon, two of the movement's theorists, set off its most active period which culminated in the **October Crisis** of 1970.

Frontenac, Louis de Buade, Count of (1622–98) French-Canadian politician. He served in the army, and in 1672 was appointed Governor of the French possessions in North America. He was recalled for misgovernment in 1682, but was sent out again in 1689. He extended the boundaries of **New France** down the Mississippi, launched attacks on New England villages, repulsed the British siege of Quebec (1690), and broke the power of the Iroquois (1696).

Frundsberg, Georg von (1473–1528) German soldier. He was the founder and leader of German *Landsknechte* during the Italian Wars of **Maximilian I** and **Charles V**. He fought in 20 pitched battles, and the victory at **Pavia** (1525) was largely due to him.

Frunze, Mikhail Vasilevich (1885–1925) Russian revolutionary and professional soldier. Frunze exercised profound influence upon Soviet military doctrine. A Bolshevik from 1904, active in both the 1905 and 1917 events, he rose to prominence in the **Russian Civil War** with successful commands on the eastern and southern fronts. But he was soon engaged in debate with **Trotsky**, commissar for War, about creating a **Red Army** fit for the future. In 1925 he displaced him but died during an operation, often claimed to have been a medical murder. But his concept of unified command and policy won through. ▷ **Bolsheviks**

Fuad I (1868–1936) King of Egypt (1922/36). The son of Khedive **Ismail Pasha**, he was Sultan of Egypt from 1917, and became King when the British protectorate was ended. His position in Egypt was not helped by the fact that his father had been responsible for the sale (at a farcically low price) of Egyptian Suez Canal shares to Britain, and his brother Tawfiq's incapacity as a ruler, which had led to the British occupation of 1883. The Egyptian nationalists of the Wafd Party despised his dispensation, and his acquisition and flaunting of conspicuous wealth, coupled with his corrupt entourage of hangers-on, provoked adverse comment. In an attempt to control the party, he suspended the constitution in 1931, but was forced to restore it in 1935. He was succeeded by his son, Farouk I, who was to be the last King of Egypt.

Fuad Pasha, Mehmed (1814–69) Turkish politician and littérateur. He was the son of the poet, Izzet-Mollah, became an Admiralty physician, but in 1835 took up history and politics. After diplomatic service in London and Madrid, he became Grand Interpreter to the Porte, Minister of Foreign Affairs (1852 and 1855), and Grand Vizier (1861–66). To him Turkey owed the hatti-sherif of 1856.

fuero A traditional Spanish (and Spanish-American) term for a set of legal privileges and immunities attaching to a specific group, such as the clergy or the army, or to a region, most notably the Basque country.

Fugger A south German family of merchants and bankers who reached their greatest importance during the late 15c and early 16c. Weavers by origin and settled at Augsburg since 1367, they rose to prominence through a series of judicious marriages and success in the spice and cloth trade. Their business interests spread over much of central, southern and eastern Europe, culminating in the financing of the imperial election of **Charles V**, who subsequently elevated one of their number, Jakob II 'the Rich' (1459–1525), to the rank of imperial count. The latter was also responsible for setting up the still extant Fuggerei, a charitable foundation providing houses for the poor of Augsburg. From the late 16c, the family's influence declined.

Fugitive Slave Laws (1793 and 1850) US federal legislation requiring the return of runaway slaves who fled to states where slavery had been abolished. Enforcement was hindered by the 'personal liberty laws' of several Northern states, which allowed runaway slaves the benefit of a trial by jury, and sometimes by popular 'rescues' of captured runaways. The laws were repealed in 1864. ▷ **Compromise of 1850**

Fujiwara Family An influential Japanese courtier family during the **Heian Era** (794–1185). The Fujiwara achieved prominence through inter-marriage with the imperial family: as the fathers of empresses, Fujiwara family heads were able to exercise de facto authority. In the 9c they often assumed the post of regent (*sessho*) for child emperors, controlling finances and appointments. One of the most influential of Fujiwara family heads was Fujiwara no Michinaga (966–1028), the father of four empresses and grandfather of three emperors, who dominated the court for 30 years. The family's influence gradually waned as increasingly ambitious military families in the provinces began to encroach on its vast landholdings, the basis of Fujiwara economic power.

Fukoku-Kyohei ('Wealthy Country and Strong Army') A slogan used in Japan by government leaders after the **Meiji Restoration** in 1868 to describe national policy. Priority was given to a programme of industrial and military modernization to strengthen the country against the perceived threat of Western imperialism. Such a programme, it was hoped, would also convince the Western powers to treat Japan on an equal basis and revise the unequal treaties signed under the **Tokugawa Shogunate** in the 1850s and 1860s.

Fukuda Takeo (1905–) Japanese politician and financier. He worked at the Ministry of Finance (1929–50) and was Deputy Vice-Minister (1945–6), Director of the Banking Bureau (1946–7), and Director of the Budget Bureau (1947–50). A member of the House of Representatives since 1952, he served as Minister of Finance (1965–6, 1968–71 and 1973–4). In 1974 he became deputy Prime Minister and Director of the Economic Planning Agency, until his appointment as Prime Minister (1976–8). He was President of the **Liberal Democratic Party** in 1966–8 and 1976–8.

Fukuzawa Yukichi (1835–1901) Japanese political thinker and educator. From a lower-ranking **samurai** family, he was an avid student of the West and was a member of the first official Japanese missions to the USA (1860) and Europe (1862). After the **Meiji Restoration** (1868) Fukuzawa championed the virtues of individualism, cosmopolitanism and a scientific spirit, arguing that only a reformed people would achieve national wealth and strength. He also played a crucial role in the development of higher education and a modern press.

Fulani Emirates Muslim states formed by the Fulbe or Peul Fula-speaking peoples of the Sahel zone of West Africa. The pastoral Fulani established their authority over the agricultural Hausa in a series of holy wars in the early 19c. The kingdoms were subsequently conquered by the British and in the early 20c they became one of the prototypes of the **indirect rule** system.

Fulbright, James William (1905–) US politician. Educated at the University of Arkansas, and George Washington University Law School, he was a Rhodes scholar at Oxford, and taught law in Washington and Arkansas. He was elected to the US House of Representatives as a Democrat in 1942 and to the Senate in 1944. He sponsored the Fulbright Act (1946), which established an exchange scholarship system for students and teachers between the USA and other countries. As Chairman of the Senate Foreign Relations Committee, he became a major critic of the escalation of the **Vietnam War**. He lost his Senate seat in 1974. ▷ **Democratic Party**

Fulk V (1095–1143) Count of Anjou (1109/31) and King of Jerusalem (1131/43). He was proposed by **Louis VI, 'the Fat'** of France, to be King of Jerusalem at the request of King **Baldwin II, 'of Bourcq'**, who had no male heirs. Fulk arrived in the Holy Land in May 1129 and moved to Jerusalem where he married Melisend, one of Baldwin's four daughters. On Baldwin's death (1131), Fulk and Melisend were crowned King and Queen of Jerusalem. Fulk's accession was the occasion for an outburst of the internal rivalries which so bedevilled the Latin Kingdom. More serious problems, however, were in store as, after a period of damaging internecine strife amongst the Muslim princelings in the Levant, the Turkish Atabeg, Imad al-Din Zangi, was setting in train the harnessing of Muslim effort against the Franks in the north and in 1136 the Damascenes also went on the offensive. Fulk was, however, capable of handling the Muslims both in the military and diplomatic spheres and when, later, Damascus itself was threatened by Zangi, it was an alliance with Fulk which saved the city. Thus, despite problems internally with his fellow Franks and externally with the Muslims, by 1140 King Fulk was securely established in his own kingdom.

Fuller, (Sarah) Margaret (1810–50) US feminist and journalist. She became part of the Transcendentalist circle that centred around Ralph Waldo Emerson, and despite a lack of higher education was known as one of its brightest stars. Her *Woman in the Nineteenth Century* (1845) is the earliest major piece of US feminist writing. She died in a shipwreck while returning to the USA after taking part in the abortive Italian revolution of 1848.

Funan The earliest known state in South-East Asia. Located in the delta of the Mekong River, Funan was founded, according to Chinese sources, in the 1c AD. It evolved a pattern of statecraft from the Indian model, although it is not accepted by all scholars that Indian Brahmans were actually resident, in large numbers, in Funan. Some have argued that Funan's rulers constructed complex irrigation systems to sustain large-scale, wet-rice agriculture, but again not all scholars agree. It is accepted, however, that Funan was a major international trading centre, from which the state, at the height of its power, derived great prosperity. Funan went into decline in the 6c.

Fundamental Orders of Connecticut (1639) US colonial charter. An agreement for self-government adopted by the Connecticut towns of Hartford, Windsor, and Wethersfield, and extended to other towns. It was replaced by a royal charter in 1662.

Funding Loan This term refers to the loan of £10 million contracted (June 1898) between **Campos Salles** and the Rothschilds to enable Brazil to meet its external obligations for 12 years, and thus prevent a formal declaration of state bankruptcy. Guaranteed by the Rio Customs receipts, it enabled the government to stabilize the exchange rate and control expenditure, introduce sales taxes in Rio, raise excise taxes, dramatically reduce the money supply, and lease railroads to international firms. The measure consolidated financial institutions, stimulated the cartelization of coffee exports, and the growth of industry; opposition to it was met by the imposition of one-party rule in the states. At the outset of **World War I**, another loan (of £15 million) was negotiated; this operation terminated in 1927.

fuorusciti The Italian word (literally, 'exile', 'outlaw', 'émigré') often applied to political opponents of the fascist regime who fled, or were forced to leave, Italy during the 1920s and 1930s. Many served in the republican armies in the **Spanish Civil War** and consequently fought against Italian troops sent by **Mussolini** to assist **Franco**. They achieved a famous victory over Italian fascist 'volunteers' at the Battle of Guadalajara (Mar 1937). ▷ **fascism**

fur trade The history of the fur trade in North America is inextricably linked with the exploration of the continent and the struggle between France and Britain for its control. The trade was first centred along the St Lawrence River and the Atlantic coast around Newfoundland and **Acadia** during the late 16c and early 17c. The furs were brought to the fishing stations by **Native Americans** attracted by the exchange for relatively cheap

trinkets and other manufactured goods. In 1608 Samuel **Champlain** established a base at Quebec and contacts with the **Algonquin** and **Huron** tribes, whom he assisted against their traditional enemies the Iroquois. With the advance of settlement and the opening up of trading routes into the interior, it became clear by the late 17c that the French were caught between the British colonies to the south and the **Hudson's Bay Company** (set up in 1670 as the result of information from two disaffected French traders) to the north and west. While the Iroquois acted as middlemen bringing the trade into British hands at Albany, the French re-established a forward position with the chain of forts and trading posts which controlled the Great Lakes region and the upper Mississippi and Ohio valleys until the cession of **New France** to Britain in 1763. In the late 18c and early 19c the north-western fur trade was bitterly contested between the independents who organized themselves as the **North West Company** (opening up new routes to the Pacific seaboard, where they found John Jacob **Astor**'s Pacific Fur Company already established) and the Hudson's Bay Company. After the amalgamation of the two Canadian companies in 1821, the HBC organized the trade on a continental basis, ceding its lands to the Dominion in 1869 but continuing as the most important economic force in the north. ▷ **Iroquois Confederacy**

Furtseva, Yekaterina Alexeevna (1910–74) The first woman member of the Soviet Communist Party's **Politburo**. Following a technical education, she became a party worker and rose to be district secretary in Moscow in 1942 and a member of the Central Committee in 1956. A supporter of Nikita **Khrushchev**, she was brought into the Politburo in 1957 in the aftermath of the **Anti-Party Plot**. Hardly a major political figure, she was pushed out in 1961. However, from 1960 until her death she was Minister of Culture and apparently had no difficulty in insisting on ever greater conformity.

Futa Jalon and **Futa Toro** Regions in West Africa, respectively the highlands near the source of the River Senegal and the valley of the lower Senegal, where a sequence of jihads or holy wars broke out among the Fulani herdsmen in the 17–18c. These wars produced Islamic states which were the forerunners of their more significant 19c successors. West African history became essentially a conflict of two imperialisms, African Islamic and European.

G

Gaddafi, Muammar (1942–) Libyan political and military leader. He abandoned his university studies in favour of military training in 1963, and went on to form the **Free Officers' Movement** which overthrew King Idris in 1969. He became Chairman of the Revolutionary Command Council, promoted himself to colonel (the highest rank in the revolutionary army) and became Commander-in-Chief of the Libyan Armed Forces. As de facto head of state, he set about eradicating colonialism by expelling foreigners and closing down British and US bases. He also encouraged a religious revival and return to the fundamental principles of Islam. A somewhat unpredictable figure, Gaddafi has openly supported violent revolutionaries in other parts of the world while ruthlessly pursuing Libyan dissidents both at home and abroad. He has waged a war in Chad, threatened other neighbours, and in the 1980s saw his territory bombed and aircraft shot down by the Americans.

Gadsden Purchase (1853) A strip of land in south Arizona and New Mexico bought by the US from Mexico for US$10 000 000. The purchase was negotiated by the minister to Mexico, James Gadsden, as a feasible route for a southern railroad to the Pacific.

Gage, Thomas (1721–87) British general. In 1760 he became Military Governor of Montreal, in 1763 Commander-in-Chief of the British forces in America, and in 1774 Governor of Massachusetts. In 1775 (18 Apr) he sent a force to seize a quantity of arms at Concord; and next day the skirmish of Lexington took place which began the **American Revolution**. After the Battle of Bunker Hill (June 1775) he resigned, and returned to England, where he died.

Gairy, Eric Matthew (1922–) Grenadian politician. In 1950 he founded the country's first political party, the left-of-centre Grenada United Labour Party (GULP) and was soon a dominant figure in Caribbean politics. He held the posts of Chief Minister in the Federation of the **West Indies** (1957–62), Premier of Grenada (1967–74) and, on independence in 1974, Prime Minister. He was ousted by the left-wing leader, Maurice

Bishop, in 1979 and GULP was defeated in the 1990 election by the National Democratic Congress of Nicholas Braithwaite. ▷ **West Indies, Federation of the**

Gaiseric (c.390–477) King of the Vandals and Alans (428/77), who led the Vandals in their invasion of Gaul. He crossed from Spain to Numidia (429), captured and sacked Hippo (430), seized Carthage (439), and made it the capital of his new dominions. He built up a large maritime power, and his fleets carried the terror of his name as far as the Peloponnese. He sacked Rome in 455, and defeated fleets sent against him. The greatest of the Vandal kings, he was succeeded by his son, Huneric.

Gaitskell, Hugh (Todd Naylor) (1906–63) British politician. He became a socialist during the 1926 **General Strike**. He became an MP in 1945, he was Minister of Fuel and Power (1947) and of Economic Affairs (1950), and Chancellor of the Exchequer (1950–1). In 1955 he was elected Leader of the Opposition by a large majority over **Bevan**. He bitterly opposed **Eden**'s Suez action (1956), and refused to accept a narrow conference vote for unilateral disarmament (1960). This caused a crisis of leadership in which he was challenged by Harold **Wilson** (1960) and Arthur Greenwood (1961), but he retained the loyalty of most Labour MPs. ▷ **Butskellism; Labour Party** (UK); **Suez Crisis**

Gaj, Ljudevit (1809–72) Croatian nationalist. Inspired in his youth by the romantic nationalism of Kollár, Šafařík and Herder, his belief in the common nationality of the South Slavs (whom he referred to as Illyrians) led him to formulate a standard South Slav literary language and found a Croatian newspaper. Through his literary activities, he became increasingly involved in opposition to Hungarian and German political and cultural influence in Croatia. To counter the pro-Hungarian party in Croatia, in 1841 he founded the Illyrian National Party, which espoused the ideas of the **Illyrian Movement** and championed Croatian state-right. Ever-hopeful for the support of Vienna against the Hungarian nationalists, he concluded a pact with the Hungarian conservatives in a move designed to gain the confidence of the Austrian minister, **Metternich** (1845). Under the government of Ban Josip **Jelačić**, in Mar 1848 Gaj led a delegation to Vienna and presented the Emperor with the Croats' requests for the reorganization of the Habsburg Monarchy as a federation. Later that year, he was elected to the Croatian *sabor* (parliament) but shortly afterwards was obliged to leave political life, following his apparent involvement in a financial scandal with the Serbian prince, Miloš **Obrenović**. ▷ **Strossmayer, Josip Juraj; Yugoslavism**

Galawdewos (d.1559) Emperor of Ethiopia (1540/59). With Portuguese aid he defeated the Muslims who, under Ahmad Gran, (Ahmad Ibn Ibrahim Al-Ghazi) had dominated Ethiopia in the early years of the 16c. He strengthened the authority of the monarchy and reformed the cultural and religious institutions of the empire. Towards the end of his reign he was preoccupied with the migration of Galla tribesmen but, despite various successes in battle (1554–5), was unable permanently to check their advance.

Galba, Servius Sulpicius (c.3BC–AD69) Roman Emperor (69). Despite an outstanding track-record as governor in Gaul, Germany, Africa and Spain under the **Julio-Claudian Dynasty**, as an emperor (the first of four to rule at Rome in the year after **Nero**'s downfall) he proved to be a disaster. Mean and inconsistent, he rapidly offended even his closest backers and after only a few months in power was overthrown by them, being murdered in a palace coup led by his one-time supporter and fellow governor in Spain, **Otho**.

Galdan (c.1632–97) Chief of the western Mongols, or Dzungars. He resisted the encroachment of the Manchu **Qing Dynasty** and, following the Qing subjugation of the eastern Mongols in 1675, took the offensive. By the late 1670s, Galdan had taken control of several central Asian oases such as Kashgar and Turfan. The Qing Emperor **Kangxi** had to undertake three campaigns in the 1690s before defeating Galdan at the Battle of Jao Modo (Outer Mongolia) and forcing him to commit suicide.

Galerius (Gaius Galerius Valerius Maximianus) (c.250–311) Roman Emperor (305/11). A Roman soldier of humble extraction, he rose from the ranks to become deputy ruler of the eastern half of the empire

under **Diocletian** (293), and its chief ruler after Diocletian's abdication in 305. He was a notorious persecutor of the Christians (303–11) until near the end of his reign, when after an illness he granted them some toleration.

Galileo (Galileo Galilei) (1564–1642) Italian astronomer and mathematician. He entered the university at Pisa as a medical student in 1581. He became Professor of Mathematics at Padua (1592–1610), where he improved the refracting telescope (1610), and was the first to use it for astronomy. His realization that the ancient Aristotelian teachings were unacceptable brought severe ecclesiastical censure, and he was forced to retract before the **Inquisition**.

Gallicanism A French religious doctrine, emphasizing royal or episcopal authority over matters pertaining to the French Church at the expense of papal sovereignty. It emerged during **Philip IV**'s struggle with **Boniface VIII** (1297–1303), and remained a traditional, though controversial force in France, invoked to defend established liberties against **Ultramontanism** and papal interference.

Gallic Wars The name traditionally given to Julius **Caesar**'s brutal campaigns (58–51BC) against the Celtic tribes of **Gaul** (ancient France). They were also the occasion of his two unsuccessful invasions of Britain. ▷ **Alesia, Siege of; Britain, Roman; Vercingetorix**

Galliéni, Joseph Simon (1849–1916) French soldier. He served in the war of 1870–1, also in West Africa and Tonkin, was Governor of Upper Senegal from 1886, and Governor-General of Madagascar 1897–1905. As Minister for War, and Military Governor of Paris from 1914, he saw to its fortifications and contributed to the victory of the Marne (1914) by his foresight and planning. He was posthumously created Marshal of France in 1921.

Gallienus, Publius Licinius Egnatius (d.268) Roman Emperor (AD253/68). Proclaimed Emperor jointly with his father, **Valerian**, by the Roman army in Raetia (Switzerland), Gallienus operated in the western half of the empire while his father was alive. From 260, when he ruled alone, he was assailed on all sides by revolts (eg **Postumus** in Gaul) and raids (eg the **Goths** into Greece) but somehow he managed to keep the Empire more or less intact. More tolerant than Valerian was towards the Christians, he abandoned his policy of persecution. He died at Milan, cut down by his soldiers.

Gallipoli Campaign (1915–16) A major campaign of **World War I**. With stalemate on the Western Front, the British War Council advocated operations against the Turks to secure the **Dardanelles** and aid Russia. The land campaign began with amphibious assaults on the Gallipoli Peninsula (Apr 1915). Australian and New Zealand forces were heavily involved: the beach where they landed is still known as Anzac Cove. Allied casualties were 250 000 out of 480 000 engaged. The operation was abandoned as a costly failure, with successful evacuations of all remaining troops in Jan 1916.

Galt, Sir Alexander Tilloch (1817–93) Canadian politician. In 1844–55 he was High Commissioner of the British American Land Company which made huge profits from lands obtained through its influence with the **Château Clique** and in London. As a business leader of the English-speaking community in **Canada East** his signature on the **Annexation Manifesto** in 1849 reflected fears for its future in markets no longer protected by the British **Navigation Acts**. However he recognized that **reciprocity** would only be of benefit with a more integrated Canadian economy and in 1858 he was persuaded by **Macdonald** and George Étienne **Cartier** (with whom he was involved in the Grand Trunk Railway) to enter politics on the understanding that they would work towards confederation. As Finance Minister in the Macdonald–Cartier administration he introduced the high tariffs of 1859, and he served in the 'great coalition' of 1864 that negotiated the terms of confederation. In 1880 he became the first Canadian High Commissioner in London. ▷ **Confederation Movement**

Galtieri, Leopoldo Fortunato (1926–) Argentine soldier and politician. After training at the National Military College, he was commissioned in 1945 and progressed steadily to the rank of lieutenant-general in 1979, when he joined the junta which had been in power since the military coup which ousted Isabelita **Perón** in 1976. In 1981 the leader of the junta, General Viola, died and Galtieri succeeded him as President. The state of the Argentine economy worsened and, to counter mounting domestic criticism, in Apr

1982 Galtieri ordered the invasion of the long-disputed Malvinas (Falkland) Islands. Their recovery by Britain, after a brief and humiliating war, brought about his downfall. He was court-martialled in 1983 and sentenced to 12 years' imprisonment for negligence in starting and losing the **Falklands War**.

Gambetta, Léon (Michel) (1838–82) French politician. A republican, he was one of the opposition deputies in 1869. After the surrender of **Napoleon III**, he helped to proclaim the Third Republic (1870), became Minister of the Interior in the Government of **National Defence**, made a spectacular escape from the Siege of Paris in a balloon, and for five months ruled France as leader of the Tours Delegation until the armistice of 28 Jan 1871. Re-emerging as leader of the republicans, his role was important in the voting of the constitutional laws of 1875, and in the defeat of **MacMahon**'s abortive coup in 1877. The jealousy of other republican politicians, and fear of the role that could be played by such a popular and strong leader, meant that he was subsequently virtually excluded from office, only forming a weak and brief ministry in 1882, before his early accidental death. ▷ **Paris, Siege of; Republic, Third** (France)

Gamelin, Maurice Gustave (1872–1958) French soldier. He attained lieutenant-colonel's rank in 1914, but no divisional command until 1925. In 1935 seniority brought him the post of Chief of Staff of the army and membership of the *Conseil supérieur de la guerre* ('Supreme War Council') (1930); but his unfitness for overall command was exposed in his pronouncement that 'To attack is to lose'. In 1940 he refused to rethink his outmoded defensive strategy of 'solid fronts', which crumbled under the German **Blitzkrieg**. He was hurriedly replaced by General **Weygand**, tried, and imprisoned (1943–5). ▷ **Riom Trial**

Gandhara The area in antiquity corresponding roughly to north-west Pakistan. An Achaemenid satrapy, it was conquered by Alexander III, 'the Great', and ended up being ruled in the 2c BC by the Indo-Greeks of neighbouring **Bactria**. Through their influence, Gandhara evolved a distinctive art style in which Greek and Indian elements were fused. ▷ **Achaemenids**

Gandhi, Indira (Priyadarshini) (1917–84) Indian politician. The daughter of Jawaharlal Nehru, she was educated at Visva-Bharati

University (Bengal) and Oxford, and in 1942 married Feroze Gandhi (d.1960). She became President of the Indian Congress Party (1959–60), Minister of Information (1964) and Prime Minister (1966–77) after the death of Shastri. After her conviction for election malpractices, she declared a state of emergency (1975–7), was defeated in elections by the Janata Party, and was Premier again (1980–4). She achieved a considerable reputation through her work as a leader of the developing nations, but was unable to stem sectarian violence at home. She was assassinated in New Delhi by Sikh extremists who were members of her bodyguard, and succeeded by her elder son, Rajiv **Gandhi.** ▷ **Indian National Congress**

Gandhi, M(ohandas) K(aramchand) (1869–1948) Indian nationalist leader. He studied law in London, but in 1893 went to South Africa, where he spent 21 years opposing discriminatory legislation against Indians. In 1914 he returned to India, where he supported the Home Rule movement, and became leader of the **Indian National Congress**, advocating a policy of non-violent non-cooperation to achieve independence. Following his first major non-cooperation and **civil disobedience** campaign (1919–22), he was jailed for conspiracy (1922–4). In 1930 he led a 200-mile march to the sea to collect salt in symbolic defiance of the government monopoly; this marked the beginning of the second major campaign of civil disobedience. On his release from prison (1931), he attended the London Round Table Conference on Indian constitutional reform. In 1946 he negotiated with the Cabinet Mission which recommended the new constitutional structure. After independence (1947), he tried to stop the Hindu/Muslim conflict in Bengal, a policy which led to his assassination in Delhi by Nathuram Godse, a Hindu fanatic. ▷ **Non-Cooperation Movement; Round Table Conferences; Swaraj**

Gandhi, Rajiv (1944–91) Indian politician. As the eldest son of Indira **Gandhi** and the grandson of **Nehru**, he was born into a Kashmiri-Brahmin family which had governed India for all but four years since 1947. He was educated at Doon School (Dehra Dun) and Cambridge University, where he failed his engineering degree. In contrast to his younger brother, Sanjay (1946–80), he exhibited little interest in politics and became a pilot with Indian Airlines. Following Sanjay's death in an air crash, he assumed the family's political

mantle, being elected to his brother's Amethi parliamentary seat (1981) and appointed a General-Secretary of the Congress (I) Party (1983). After his mother's assassination in 1984, he became Prime Minister and secured a record majority in the parliamentary elections later that year. He attempted to cleanse and rejuvenate the Congress (I), inducting new technocrats, and introducing a freer market economic programme. Congress (I), however, suffered heavy losses under his leadership in the 1989 general election, and he was forced to resign as Premier after his party was defeated in the general election of Nov 1989. He was assassinated by Tamil terrorists during a subsequent election campaign in May 1991.

Gang of Four A description given by **Mao Zedong** to the Shanghai-based hard-core radicals of the Chinese **Cultural Revolution**: Zhang Chunqiao, Yao Wenyuan, Wang Hongwen, and Jiang Qing. Zhang and Yao were veterans of the Shanghai party machine. Wang emerged as a workers' leader in the Shanghai 'January Revolution' of 1967. Jiang, Mao's wife, enjoyed his trust and was the acknowledged leader of the Gang. All were members of the politburo when they were arrested and disgraced in 1976.

Gao A medieval state in West Africa, with its capital at Gao, east of Timbuktu. It emerged in the 9–10c with an economy based on fishing, salt, and irrigation water from the Niger, and controlled the Saharan trade to eastern Algeria. Its rulers embraced Islam, but did not force the religion on their peoples.

Gao Gang (Kao Kang) (c.1902–55) Chinese political leader. In the mid-1930s he was in charge of a small independent communist area at Baoan, Shaanxi, where the **Long March** led by **Mao Zedong** ended. Mao and Gao Gang became close political allies, and he later became Chief Party Secretary of Manchuria (1949). He set the national pace in economic development, but in 1955 was accused of attempting to set up a 'separate kingdom'. He apparently committed suicide. ▷ **Communist Party, Chinese**

Gapon, Georgei Apollonovich (1870–1906) Ukrainian priest and reformer. In 1902 he became leader of the so-called Union of Russian Factory Workers. Without his knowledge, this seems to have been financed by the Tsarist police as a means of penetrating and controlling the working-class movement. However, with deteriorating economic conditions, its numbers grew; and in Jan 1905 Gapon was quite happy to lead them in a procession to the Winter Palace in the sincere belief that the Tsar **Nicholas II** would accede to their demands. The result was **Bloody Sunday**. Thereafter, idealists like Gapon could exercise less and less influence on Russian developments.

Garang, Colonel John (1943–) Sudanese soldier. After studying agricultural economics in the USA, he returned to Sudan, where he joined the army. Another period in the USA, for military training, was followed by a post at the Military Research Centre in Khartoum. In 1983 he formed the Sudanese People's Liberation Movement in the southern Sudan. Backed by Marxists in Ethiopia, the movement grew out of Garang's belief that the resources of southern Sudan were being exploited by the country's northerners. Waging a relentless guerrilla campaign, the organization has posed a considerable threat to the stability of the Sudan. Involving conflict with the regular Sudanese army, the movement's activities have done much to increase the sufferings of the people in a country already racked by famine.

Garašanin, Ilija (1812–74) Serb politician. Having supported the constitutionalists during the 1830s, in 1842 he took part in the deposition of Prince Michael **Obrenović**. He became prominent in the pro-constitution government under Alexander Karageorgević and was Minister for Internal Affairs (1843–52), organizing the police and bureaucracy. Very conservative, in 1844 he wrote the **Nacertanije** for the guidance of the Prince, believing that Serbia would be the core around which the other **South Slavs** would unite. He remained a prominent minister after the return of Michael Obrenović (1861–7), but lost his pre-eminence when the prince changed direction in foreign affairs. After the succession of Milan **Obrenović**, he retired into private life.

García, Perez Alan (1949–) Peruvian politician. After studying law in Lima, he continued his education in Guatemala, Spain and France. He returned to Peru in 1978 and was elected to the National Congress, for the moderate, left-wing APRA Party, which he had joined as a youth. Four years later he became Secretary-General of the party and in 1985 succeeded Fernando **Belaúnde** as President, becoming the first civilian to do so in

democratic elections. He inherited an ailing economy which forced him to trim his socialist programme. By 1991 the economy was in tatters, and García was a prisoner of the deepening struggle between the **Sendero Luminoso** and the armed forces in the Andes and a conservative Congress in Lima. He was succeeded by the conservative Alberto Fujimori.

García Moreno, Gabriel (1821–75) Ecuadorean dictator. Born in Guayaquil in Ecuador, he studied theology and witnessed the **Revolutions of 1848–9** in Europe. Elected Mayor of Quito, he seized power in 1860 with the support of Juan José **Flores**, and was President from 1861 to 1865 and from 1869 to 1875. He was assassinated on the eve of re-election. García Moreno proclaimed two constitutions, both of which were theocratic structures: citizenship was limited to Catholics and all others were stripped of civil rights. These survived his death, enduring until 1895.

Garfield, James A(bram) (1831–81) US politician and 20th President. He was a farmworker, teacher, lay preacher and lawyer before being elected to the Ohio State Senate in 1859. He fought in the **American Civil War** until 1863, when he entered the US House of Representatives, eventually becoming a leader of the **Republican Party**. After his election as President (a post he held only from Mar to Sep 1881), he alienated the 'Stalwarts', a major faction of the Republican Party, by passing them over for federal appointments. On 2 July 1881, he was shot in the Washington railroad station by a disappointed office-seeker, Charles Guiteau, and died two months later.

Garibaldi, Giuseppe (1807–82) Italian revolutionary, soldier and politician. The greatest hero of the **Risorgimento**, he was a member of **Young Italy** and took part in an abortive Mazzinian insurrection in Genoa in 1834. He subsequently fled to South America, where he fought in defence of the Rio Grande do Sul republic against the Brazilian Empire and in Uruguay against the Argentine dictator, de Rosas. He returned to Italy (1848) and offered his services to **Charles Albert** against the Austrians but was rejected. He instead took part in the government and defence of the Roman Republic, before attempting to relieve the Venetian republic of Daniele **Manin**. After the **Revolutions of 1848–9** he visited America before settling on the island of Caprera. In 1856 he backed the

Italian National Society and played a minor but brilliant part in the 1859 campaign against the Austrians. In 1860 he set sail from Genoa with his **Thousand** volunteers to assist the anti-Bourbon rebellion which had broken out in Sicily. Having seized control of the island, he crossed to the mainland of the Kingdom of the **Two Sicilies** and overran much of the **Mezzogiorno** before handing it over to **Victor Emmanuel II**. In 1862 he attempted to march on Rome but was stopped by Piedmontese troops at **Aspromonte**; a similar attempt to seize the Papal capital was blocked by French forces at **Mentana** in 1867. He fought with limited success against the Austrians in 1866 and in 1870 he offered his services to the French after the Battle of Sedan. In 1870 he was elected a deputy at the Bordeaux Assembly. He passed his last years as a farmer on Caprera.

Garneau, Francis Xavier (1809–66) Canadian historian. His *Histoire du Canada* (1845–8) was written to rebut Lord **Durham**'s assertions that French Canadians had neither a history or a culture of any significance. His work provided Quebec nationalism with an intellectual basis and a body of material on which later writers drew freely.

Garnet, Henry Highland (1815–82) US abolitionist. A former slave, who with Frederick **Douglass** helped promote racial pride and dispel popular stereotypes of blacks. A persuasive and witty speaker, he argued at the National Convention of Coloured Citizens in 1843 that a slave was justified in using violence to gain his freedom. By the 1850s, like another anti-slavery activist Martin **Delaney**, he despaired of achieving racial justice and advocated the emigration of blacks to Africa. ▷ **abolitionism**

Garnier-Pagès, Louis Antoine (1803–78) French politician. A member of the Chamber of Deputies (1842–48), he led the extreme left. Mayor of Paris (1848) and Finance Minister of the Provisional Government, he was a member of the *Corps Législatif* in 1864, and of the Provisional Government in 1871. He wrote *Histoire de la Révolution de 1848* (1861–62) and *L'Opposition et l'Empire* (1872).

Garrison, William Lloyd (1805–79) US abolitionist. Educated informally, he emerged in 1830 as one of the foremost anti-slavery voices in the USA. His newspaper *The Liberator* argued the case for immediate abolition, and his American Anti-Slavery Society drew thousands of people to the cause. ▷ **abolitionism**

Garvey, Marcus (1887–1940) Advocate of black nationalism. Born and brought up in poverty in Jamaica, he promoted self-help for blacks and black pride and in 1914 founded the Universal Negro Improvement Association. Two years later, he left Jamaica for New York, his arrival in New York coinciding with the wave of black migration into Harlem. Despite little formal education, he proved to be a gifted writer and speaker. It was in the ghettos of the northern cities that he found his greatest following, reaching blacks through his weekly *Negro World* and greatly expanding his Association, a forerunner of the black nationalist movement. However, his call for a return to Africa attracted little interest. He founded such enterprises as the Black Factories Corporation and the Black Star Line, a steamship line owned and operated by blacks, which, however, collapsed in 1921 due to mismanagement. In 1923 he was convicted of mail fraud, imprisoned, and later deported. After he left the country, his black nationalist movement went into decline. He died in obscurity in London.

Gaspée A British customs schooner set afire and destroyed by colonists after it went aground near Providence, Rhode Island (9 June 1772). The schooner had been stationed off the coast to counter the profitable smuggling trade of the region. A subsequent investigation by the British into the incident ended in failure.

Gastarbeiter A German term for the foreign, usually Mediterranean, workers who have been employed in large numbers in the Federal German economy since the 1960s. The term (literally 'guest workers') belies the fact that many of these migrants have settled in Germany with their families and that their presence is indispensable to the German economy. However, only a few have become German citizens and many return to their country of origin after completing a predetermined period of employment.

Gates, Horatio (1728–1806) British-born US general. He joined the British Army, served in America in the **Seven Years War** (1756–63), and then settled in Virginia. In the **American Revolution** he sided with his adoptive country and fought for its cause. In 1777 he took command of the Northern department, and forced the British Army to surrender at the Battle of **Saratoga**. In 1780 he commanded the Southern department, but his army was routed by **Cornwallis** at the Battle of **Camden**, and he was superseded. He returned to Virginia, but in 1790 emancipated his slaves and then settled near New York City.

Gau A National Socialist administrative district created initially to organize the **Nazi Party** during the **Weimar Republic** and coordinate electoral and other work. The *Gau* became a form of administration parallel to the traditional one in Nazi Germany. The *Gaue* were retained after **Hitler**'s takeover, each headed by a *Gauleiter* who was a party official answerable to Hitler, not the civil authorities. In this way, the Nazis created a regional administrative structure which operated parallel to the traditional one and allowed the party to bypass the civil service when it so desired. Needless to say, conflict developed between the party and civil authorities over their precise areas of competence.

gaucho A nomadic, fiercely independent mestizo horseman of the Argentine pampa, first appearing in the 17c. With the advent of ranches, railways, and settled government in the 19c, the gaucho vanished, though gaucho skills live on among the rural population of Argentina and Uruguay. The gaucho myth tradition suffuses Argentine political and social life: enshrined in the tango, echoed in **Peronism**, it is both elemental and conservative. The inhabitants of Rio Grande do Sul in Brazil are known as gauchos: their distinctive politics — their support of a series of charismatic political leaders and resort to war — have given 'gaucho politics' a specific tenor.

Gaul In Roman times, the term *Gallia* was normally used for Transalpine Gaul, bounded by the Alps, the Rhine, and the Pyrenees. Julius **Caesar** completed the Roman conquest in 58–51BC, the impact of Romanization being felt most in the south, where Roman law remained in use until 1789. With the gradual Roman withdrawal in the 5c, Germanic colonies became independent kingdoms. Unity was superficially achieved under **Clovis I** and **Charlemagne**; later, after many vicissitudes, Gaul (its easternmost territories excluded) developed into the medieval Kingdom of France. Cisalpine Gaul lay south of the Alps and north of the Apennines. Conquered by the Romans in 201–191BC, it was incorporated into Italy in 42BC. ▷ **Franks; Visigoths**

Gaulle, Charles (André Joseph Marie) de (1898–1970) French general and politician. Born into a devout Catholic and conservative family, he was educated by the Jesuits and at Saint-Cyr military college, and fought with distinction in **World War I**. Only a colonel in 1940, he was known as the author of several books on military and historical topics, especially one advocating mechanized warfare. He was promoted temporary General of Brigade (1 June 1940), and four days later entered the government as Under-Secretary at the Ministry of National Defence. Refusing to accept the armistice, he fled to England, where (18 June 1940) he appealed to the French people to continue the struggle. As the leader of the **Free French**, he fought many diplomatic battles against President **Roosevelt** to ensure that France was treated as a co-belligerent, thus emerging in 1944 as head of the Provisional Government. He organized the election of an assembly to draw up a new constitution, but resigned in protest at the trend of its deliberations (Jan 1946), thus consigning himself to the political sidelines until 1958 when the Algerian crisis led to his recall to power as the last Prime Minister of the Fourth Republic. He used this position to draw up a new constitution for the Fifth Republic, which embodied the presidential system he had wanted in 1946. It was approved by a referendum (Sep 1958) and he became its first President (1959–69). He defeated two attempted coups, launched by supporters of a French Algeria, and negotiated Algerian independence (1962). France's colonies were also granted independence, while he concentrated on winning France a leading place in Europe by excluding Britain from the **EC** (European Community) and by signing an historic reconciliation treaty with Germany (both 1963). He developed a French nuclear deterrent, and removed France from its military obligations under **NATO** (1965). His supporters won by a big majority in the elections following the 'events' of 1968, but he lost a referendum on constitutional reform in 1969, and resigned. ▷ **National Defence, Government of; Republic, Fifth** (France); **Republic, Fourth** (France)

Gaullist Party ▷ **Gaullists**

Gaullists Supporters of General de **Gaulle**, more specifically members of political parties which followed him in his lifetime, and claimed to embody his legacy after his death. Their names have changed frequently. The principal ones are RPF (*Rassemblement du* *peuple français*, 'Assembly of the French People') (1947–54), UNR, later UNR-UDT (*Union pour la nouvelle république*, 'Union for the New Republic') (1958–67), UDR (*Union des démocrates pour la Ve République*, 'Union of Democrats for the Fifth Republic') (1967–76); and RPR (*Rassemblement pour la République*, 'Assembly for the Republic') since 1976. Gaullists emphasize the need for a strong foreign policy, and have become one of the two main constituents of the right wing. ▷ **Independent Republican Party**

Gaylani, Rashid Ali al- (1892–1965) Iraqi politician. He was Prime Minister of Iraq in 1933, 1936–8 and 1940–1. An opponent of Nuri al-**Said** and a fervent nationalist, he eventually fell in with the prevailing Iraqi opinion, which resented the British presence in the country; after initially permitting British reinforcement in Iraq, he was later implicated in supporting Iraqi armed resistance to the British and was expelled after the surrender of the Iraqi army. He returned to Iraq but, accused of plotting against Abd al-Krim **Qassim**, fled and died in exile.

Gaza Kingdom One of the kingdoms established by the northern **Nguni** people (of whom the Zulu are the most famous) after their dispersal in southern Africa known as the *Mfecane*. After the defeat of Zwide by Shaka in 1819, Shoshangane (d.1858), one of Zwide's military leaders, led his followers across the Limpopo and established his sovereignty over the Tsonga people in Mozambique. The state became a thorn in the side of the Portuguese and was not fully subdued until the 19c. The 'Shangaans' of the Gaza state became celebrated as labour migrants on the gold mines of the Witwatersrand.

Gaza Strip An Israeli-occupied Mediterranean coastal area under military administration from 1967 to 1994. It was formerly part of Egyptian Sinai, after the Arab–Israeli War in 1948–9. A Palestinian uprising (*intifada*) began in 1988. In 1993 and 1994 peace agreements between Israel and the PLO (Palestine Liberation Organization) were signed, by which Israel agreed to withdraw from Jericho and the Gaza Strip. ▷ **West Bank**

Gdańsk (formerly **Danzig**) Industrial port and capital of Gdańsk voivodship, north Poland. A German city, it passed to Poland in 1466, on the Peace of Thorn, but was regained by **Prussia** (1793–1919). It became a free city within the Polish tariff area in 1919 and its annexation by Germany in 1939 precipitated **World War II**. Its German population fled, or were expelled, at the end of the war in 1945. In the 1980s, the city's Lenin shipyard was the scene of much labour unrest, in support of **Solidarity**.

Gdlyan, Telman Khorenovich (1940–) Soviet lawyer. Of Armenian extraction, he, along with **Ivanov**, exposed misdemeanours in Uzbekistan involving the late Leonid **Brezhnev**'s son-in-law, he then proceeded to attack other figures such as Yegor **Ligachev** but encountered hostility even among Mikhail **Gorbachev**'s supporters. Both Gdlyan and Ivanov were very popular with the general public, and they certainly undermined communist credibility.

Geisel, Ernesto (1908–) Brazilian general and dictator. Prominent in both the **Quadros** and **Castelo Branco** administrations, his ascendancy in 1973–4, largely a result of his brother Orlando's control of the military, marked the re-emergence of Golberi de Couto e Silva, nemesis of the hardliners, such as Air Force Minister Sousa e Melo and Navy Minister Rademakr, who believed in an uncompromising dictatorship. During Geisel's presidency (1974–9), he and Golberi successfully masterminded a return to a regime in which the military acted in their traditional role as a moderating power. Geisel's imperial style allowed him subsequently to play a discrete role in politics. His support for Tancredo **Neves** in early 1985 was decisive in persuading the army to acquiesce in a return to civilian rule.

Gelasius II (John of Gaeta) (1058–1119) Italian Pope (1118/19). He was formerly cardinal and chancellor under **Urban II** and Paschal II. On the death of the latter in 1118 he was chosen pope by the party hostile to the Emperor **Henry V**. Gelasius fled to Gaeta to escape the advancing imperialists, and excommunicated Henry and Gregory VIII, the anti-pope he had set up. Shortly after he was able to return to Rome, but in the same autumn had to flee to France, where he died in the monastery at Cluny.

Gemayel, Amin (1942–) Lebanese politician. The son of Pierre **Gemayel**, he trained as a lawyer and supported his brother, Bashir **Gemayel**, in the 1975–6 civil war, becoming President (1982–) after the latter's assassination. Politically more moderate, his policies initially proved no more successful in determining a peaceful settlement of the problems of Lebanese government.

Gemayel, Bashir (1947–82) Lebanese army officer and politician. The youngest son of Pierre **Gemayel**, he joined the militia of his father's Phalangist Party and came to be the party's Political Director in the Ashrefieh sector of East Beirut, where he was an active leader of the Christian militia in the civil war of 1975–6. By the systematic elimination of rivals, he came to command the military forces of East Beirut. He distanced his party from Israeli support, and aimed to expel all foreign influence from Lebanese affairs. Having twice escaped assassination, he was killed in a bomb explosion while president-elect, ten days before he was due to take office. His brother, Amin **Gemayel**, was elected President in his stead, one week later.

Gemayel, Pierre (1905–   ) Lebanese politician. A member of the Maronite Christian community of Lebanon, he was educated in Beirut and Paris and trained as a pharmacist. In 1936 he founded the Kataeb or Phalangist Party, modelled on the Spanish and German fascist organizations, and in 1937 became its leader. He was twice imprisoned (1937 and 1943), held various ministerial posts (1960–7), and led the Phalangist Militia in the 1975–6 civil war. ▷ **Gemayel, Amin; Gemayel, Bashir**

Generalitat The Catalan autonomous government; an institution of medieval origin restored under the Second Republic of 1931–6 by the Catalan Autonomy Statute of Sep 1932. Dominated by the Catalan Left, it clashed repeatedly with the right-wing administration in Madrid. In Oct 1934 it joined the left-wing rising against the central government by declaring a Catalan Republic within a Federal Republic of Spain. Following its defeat, the Generalitat was suspended until the victory of the Popular Front in Feb 1936. At the beginning of the **Spanish Civil War**, it shared power with the **CNT**-dominated Anti-Fascist Militia Committee, but lost a great deal of power to the central government after the CNT and **POUM** had been crushed in the May Days of 1937. Dissolved under **Franco**, the Generalitat was re-established after his death. ▷ **Catalan Autonomy Statutes; Republic, Second (Spain)**

Generality Lands The name given to buffer-territories between the northern Dutch

Republic and the southern (Spanish/Austrian) Netherlands during and after the **Eighty Years War**. In 1648 they included northern **Brabant**, Dutch Limburg and Zeeland Flanders, which had been conquered by the Dutch in the wars against Spain; in 1713 part of Gelderland was added. The districts were governed by the Dutch States General, in which they had no voice; they were also punitively taxed. They now form part of the modern Dutch state, and remain distinct by being Catholic, whereas the rest of the country is either Protestant or of mixed religion.

General Strike (4–12 May 1926) A national strike in Britain, organized by the Trades Union Congress (TUC) in support of an existing miners' strike to resist wage cuts. The government organized special constables and volunteers to counter the most serious effects of the strike, and issued an anti-strike propaganda journal, *The British Gazette*. The TUC called off the strike, though the miners' strike continued fruitlessly for three more months.

Geneva Convention An international agreement on the conduct of warfare first framed in 1864 and ratified in 1906. It is chiefly concerned with the protection of wounded and the sanctity of the Red Cross, while prohibiting methods of war (such as the use of 'dumdum' bullets, which expand on impact) that might cause unnecessary suffering. The terms were extended in 1950 and again in 1978 to confirm the prohibition of attacks on non-defended civilians, reprisals against civilians, and the prisoner-of-war rights of guerrilla fighters.

Geneva Peace Conference (1973) The conference, arranged by Henry Kissinger under the auspices of the **UN**, to discuss the disengagement of Israeli and Arab forces and to achieve a peace settlement after the **October War**. Despite its failure to achieve substantial results, the conference (convened 21 Dec 1973), was remarkable for its efforts towards getting Egypt, Jordan and Israel together. The USA and USSR attended in what was really an observational capacity, but the actual ceasefire arrangements were achieved by Kissinger in his so-called 'shuttle' diplomacy.

Genghis Khan (c.1162–1227) Mongol conqueror. He succeeded his father, a Mongol chief, at the age of 13 and had to struggle hard for years against hostile tribes. His ambition awakening with his continued success, he spent six years in subjugating the Naimans and in conquering Tangut. From the Turkish Uighurs, who voluntarily submitted, the Mongols derived their civilization, alphabet and laws. In 1206 he dropped his name Temujin for that of Genghis (Jingis or Chingis) Khan ('Universal Ruler'). He overran the empire of northern China (Khitai) in 1217, and the following year he attacked the powerful empire of Khwarazm, took Bokhara, Samarkand, Khwarazm and other chief cities, returning home in 1225. Two of Genghis' lieutenants penetrated northwards from the southern shore of the Caspian through Georgia into southern Russian and the Crimea, everywhere routing and slaying, and returned by way of the Volga. Meanwhile, in the Far East, another of his generals had completed the conquest of all northern China (1217–23) except Hunan. After a few months' rest, Genghis set out once again; he died after thoroughly subduing the kingdom of the Tanguts. Genghis was not only a warrior and conqueror, but a skilful administrator and ruler; having conquered empires stretching from the Black Sea to the Pacific, he organized them into khanates, some of which lasted until the 17c.

Genoa, Economic Conference (Apr–May 1922) Conference of 34 states hosted by Italy to promote European economic reconstruction and to discuss the restoration of economic and diplomatic relations with the USSR. Presided over by Luigi **Facta**, the conference achieved little on either front. Instead, it served to bring together Soviet and German delegates who took the opportunity to arrange closer military collaboration, signing the Treaty of **Rapallo** (16 Apr 1922).

genocide The deliberate mass extermination of a population, usually an ethnic group, on cultural or biological grounds. The most nefarious historical example was the slaughter, in specially constructed extermination camps, of almost six million Jews by the Nazis during **World War II**. Combining anti-Semitism and racial science theories of Social Darwinism, the Nazis justified such extermination according to an extreme hierarchical view of mankind. Genocide was one of the principal charges brought against the defendants at the **Nuremberg Trials**, and in 1948 in its approval of the Convention on the Punishment of the Crime of Genocide, the **UN** classified genocide as a crime under International Law. ▷ **Nazi Party**

genro The unofficial term (literally, 'senior statesman') for influential Japanese leaders who had spearheaded the **Meiji Restoration** (1868) and continued to serve the Emperor as chief advisers. Originally seven in number (with two added in 1912), they were mostly middle- or lower-ranking **samurai** from the two former domains of **Choshu** and **Satsuma**. The three most significant *genro* were **Ito Hirobumi**, **Yamagata** Aritomo and **Matsukata** Masayoshi. They oversaw political, military and economic reforms in the 1870s and 1880s and, after the adoption of the **Meiji Constitution** in 1889, either served as Prime Minister or collectively chose one. The genro were a force for stability and continuity, and with their passing the political system became more unstable as competing institutions (the Diet, military, Imperial Household Ministry) jostled for pre-eminence.

Genscher, Hans-Dietrich (1927–) German politician. He trained as a lawyer, studying at Leipzig before he moved to West **Germany** in 1952. He became Secretary-General of the Free Democratic Party (**FDP**) in 1959, and was Minister of the Interior for five years before becoming, in 1974, Vice-Chancellor and Foreign Minister in **Schmidt**'s coalition government. In the same year, he became Chairman of the FDP, a post to which he was re-elected in 1982. He retained his cabinet post after 1982 in the coalition between the FDP and the **Christian Democrats**. He played a crucial role in the maintenance and furtherance of the **Ostpolitik** after the fall of the Social Democratic Party (**SPD**).

Genseric ▷ **Gaiseric**

Gentile, Giovanni (1875–1944) Italian philosopher and politician. Unlike his friend Benedetto **Croce**, Gentile became a firm supporter of **fascism**, being chosen by **Mussolini** to serve as Education Minister in 1922. He twice served as a member of the **Fascist Grand Council** (1923–4 and 1925–9) and rallied to the **Duce** in the autumn of 1943 when he established the fascist Republic of **Salò**. He was killed in Florence by anti-fascist partisans.

Gentiloni, Vincenzo Ottorino, Count (1865–1916) Italian politician. President of the 'Catholic Electoral Union', he urged that good Catholics reject their traditional hostility to the Italian state and that they participate actively in Italian political life. In 1913 he made the so-called 'Gentiloni Pact' with

Giolitti, in which Catholic votes were promised to liberal candidates on condition that they would not pursue anticlerical policies.

Gentlemen's Agreement (1907) An informal pact between the USA and Japan under which Japan agreed to limit Japanese migration to the USA in return for a promise by President Theodore **Roosevelt** not to discriminate against the Japanese.

Genyosha A Japanese ultra-nationalist organization (literally, 'Black Ocean Society') created by ex-**samurai** from Fukuoka prefecture in 1881. Dissatisfied with their lot and critical of the new Meiji state, these ex-samurai promoted conservative values at home and vigorous expansion abroad. The *Genyosha* was responsible in the 1880s for several terrorist attacks on government ministers thought to be 'soft' in their dealings with the West, and engaged in conspiratorial activity in Korea and Manchuria. While some members of the Genyosha sought genuine cooperation with Asian revolutionaries, most supported the aggressive actions of the Japanese military during the 1930s. The Genyosha was forcibly disbanded in 1945.

George I (1660–1727) King of Great Britain and Ireland (1714/27). Born in Hanover, he was the great-grandson of James I of England, and was proclaimed King on the death of Queen **Anne**. Elector of Hanover since 1698, he had commanded the Imperial forces in the **Marlborough** wars. He divorced his wife and cousin, the Princess Dorothea of Zell, imprisoning her in the castle of Ahlde, where she died (1726). He took relatively little part in the government of the country. His affections remained with Hanover, and he lived there as much as possible. ▷ **Jacobites; James VI and I; Walpole, Robert**

George I (1845–1913) King of Greece (1863/1913). The second son of King **Christian IX** of Denmark, he served in the Danish navy. On the deposition of King **Othon** of Greece, he was elected king by the Greek National Assembly. In 1867 he married the Grand Duchess Olga, the niece of Tsar **Alexander II** of Russia. His reign saw the consolidation of Greek territory in **Thessaly** and **Epirus**, and the suppression of a Cretan insurrection in 1896–7. Involved in the **Balkan Wars** (1912–13), he was assassinated at Salonica, and was succeeded by his son, **Constantine I**.

George II (1683–1760) King of Great Britain and Ireland (1727/60) and Elector of Hanover. Born in Hanover, he was the son of **George I**. In 1705 he married Caroline of Anspach (1683–1737). Though he involved himself more in the government of the country than his father had, the policy pursued during the first half of the reign was that of Robert **Walpole**. In the War of the **Austrian Succession**, he was present at the Battle of **Dettingen** (1743), the last occasion on which a British sovereign commanded an army in the field. His reign also saw the crushing of Jacobite hopes at the Battle of **Culloden** (1746), the foundation of British India after the Battle of Plassey (1757), the beginning of the **Seven Years War**, and the capture of **Quebec** (1759). ▷ **Stuart, Charles**

George II (1890–1947) King of Greece (1922/3 and 1935/47). The son of **Constantine I** and grandson of **George I** of Greece, he succeeded to the throne on his father's second abdication in 1922, but was deposed the following year by a military junta. Restored to the throne by plebiscite in 1935, he worked closely with his dictatorial Prime Minister, Ioannis **Metaxas**. When Greece was overrun by the Germans, after the country had successfully resisted the Italian invasion of 1940–1, he withdrew to Crete and then England. In 1946 he was restored to the throne, again by plebiscite. He was succeeded by his brother, **Paul I**.

George III (1738–1820) King of Great Britain and Ireland (1760/1820), and Elector (1760/1815) and King (1815/20) of Hanover. The eldest son of Frederick Louis, Prince of Wales (1707/51), his father predeceased him, and he thus succeeded his grandfather, **George II**. Eager to govern as well as reign, he did not lack ability but was not politically adept and caused considerable friction. With Lord **North** he shared in the blame for the loss of the American colonies, and popular feeling ran high against him for a time in the 1770s. In 1783 he called **Pitt, 'the Younger'** to office, an important stage in reducing the political influence of a small group of established Whig families. In 1810 he suffered a recurrence of a mental derangement, and the Prince of Wales was made Regent. He died, insane and blind. ▷ **American Revolution**

George IV (1762–1830) King of the United Kingdom and of Hanover (1820/30). The eldest son of **George III**, he became Prince Regent in 1810, because of his father's insanity. Rebelling against a strict upbringing, he went through a marriage ceremony with Mrs Fitzherbert, a Roman Catholic, in 1785, thus forfeiting his title to the crown. The marriage was later declared invalid, and in 1795 he married Princess Caroline of Brunswick, whom he tried to divorce when he was King. Her death in 1821 ended a scandal in which the people sympathized with the Queen. A frequently vilified and always extravagant monarch, he was responsible for the building of the pavilion at Brighton.

George V (1865–1936) King of the United Kingdom (1910/36). He was the second son of **Edward VII**. He served in the navy, travelled in many parts of the Empire, and was created Prince of Wales in 1901. His reign saw the creation of the Union of South Africa (1910), **World War I**, the **Irish Free State** settlement (1922), and the **General Strike** (1926). His consort, Mary (1867–1953), married him in 1893; she organized women's war work (1914–18), and continued with many public and philanthropic activities after the death of her husband. They had five sons and one daughter.

George VI (1895–1952) King of the United Kingdom (1936/52). The second son of **George V**, he served in the Grand Fleet at the Battle of Jutland (1916). In 1920 he was created Duke of York, and married in 1923. He played at Wimbledon in the All-England tennis championships in 1926. He ascended the throne on the abdication of his elder brother, **Edward VIII**. During **World War II** he continued to reside in bomb-damaged Buckingham Palace, visited all theatres of war, and delivered many broadcasts, for which task he mastered a speech impediment. He and his wife, Elizabeth, (née Elizabeth Bowes-Lyon), had two children, Princess Elizabeth (later Queen **Elizabeth II**) and Princess Margaret.

George of Podiebrad (1420–71) King of Bohemia (1458/71). Born into the Czech nobility in Podiebrad, he became an adherent of the moderate reformist followers of Jan **Hus**, the so-called Utraquists. In the interregnum and civil strife following the death of Albert II in 1439, Podiebrad gradually emerged as leader of the Utraquists, seized Prague in 1448, and finally and officially had himself made regent for the new young king, Ladislav Posthumus in 1453. Following Ladislav's death in 1457, Podiebrad was crowned his successor (1458). He succeeded for a while in allaying the bitternesses of religious controversy. But in 1462 he inevitably

refused to abolish the *compactata* of Prague (1433) which legitimized the Utraquists; this angered Pope **Pius II**, but the Emperor restrained him from excommunicating Podiebrad. The next pope (Paul II), however, excommunicated him in 1466. King **Matthias I, 'Corvinus'** of Hungary took the field to enforce the ban and to make a bid for the Czech crown, but Podiebrad captured him and forced him into a truce at Vilémov (1469). When Matthias was nevertheless invited to be King of Bohemia by the Catholic nobles, Podiebrad persuaded the Czech estates to offer the succession instead to the Polish prince, Władysław Jagiełło. This was typical of his diplomatic moves intended to help preserve Czech independence. So was the proposal he made, unsuccessfully, in the years 1462–4 for a league of European princes to keep the peace.

gerarchi The Italian word (literally, 'hierarch') applied by **Mussolini** to the leading figures of the **Fascist Party**; hence the name of the party periodical, *Gerarchia*.

Gerhardsen, Einar (1897–) Norwegian politician. Of working-class origin, he rose to prominence in the Norwegian Labour Party between the wars but was not a member of the Labour government which was in power when the German invasion of Norway took place in 1940. This, together with his active participation in the Resistance, made him well qualified to lead the first post-war government in Norway. He was Prime Minister (1945–51 and 1955–65), leading Norway into membership of **NATO** in 1949 and presiding over a long period of economic growth and social welfare legislation. ▷ **Norway, German Invasion of**

German Confederation A Central European state system created at the Congress of **Vienna** (1814–15) to fill the void left by **Napoleon I's** destruction (1801–6) of the **Holy Roman Empire**. Dominated until after 1848 by **Austria**, it was rendered unstable by the subsequent rising power of **Prussia**, and was dissolved in 1866 following the **Austro-Prussian War**. ▷ **North German Confederation**

German–Danish War (1864) The Schleswig-Holstein question was reopened in Nov 1863 by the death of King **Frederick VII** of Denmark, followed by the promulgation of a new constitution by his successor, **Christian IX**, which altered the status of the duchy of Schleswig in contravention of the

London Protocol of 1852. German nationalist outrage against Denmark was exploited by Otto von **Bismarck**, Minister President of Prussia. Prussia, Austria and other German states carried out a 'federal execution' against Denmark on behalf of the **German Confederation**. In Dec 1863 German troops entered the duchy of Holstein and the Danes withdrew their forces into Schleswig. Following a Danish refusal to withdraw from Schleswig, German forces entered the duchy and hostilities began (1 Feb 1864). The Danes retreated to the fortified position of Dybböl, which guarded the approach to the island of Als and thus the route to the Danish capital, Copenhagen. Dybböl was under intense bombardment (2–18 Apr 1864) before being stormed by Austrian and Prussian troops, who outnumbered the defenders six to one. An armistice came into force and an attempt was made to reach a negotiated settlement at the London Conference (May–June 1864) but, in the vain hope of obtaining active British support, the Danes rejected a compromise agreement (22 June). When the war was resumed, German forces captured Als and occupied most of the Jutland Peninsula. A new armistice was signed (20 July) and in the Treaty of Vienna (30 Oct 1864) Denmark surrendered Schleswig-Holstein to Prussia and Austria. The duchies came under Prussian control following the **Austro-Prussian War** of 1866.

German–Danish Wars (1848–50) Wars which resulted from the clash of German and Danish nationalisms in the duchies of Schleswig and Holstein during the **Revolutions of 1848–9**. Both duchies had mixed German and Danish populations; both were ruled by the Danish crown, but Holstein was also part of the **German Confederation**. Following a declaration (Mar 1848) that Schleswig was to be brought into a closer relationship with the Kingdom of Denmark, a provisional government for Schleswig-Holstein was formed at Kiel and appealed to Prussia for assistance. Prussian troops crossed the border of Holstein (4 Apr 1848) and the Danish army was obliged to retreat but managed to hold a line on the Jutland Peninsula, while Danish naval forces blockaded Prussian ports. A seven-month armistice concluded at Malmö (26 Aug 1848) was regarded as a betrayal of the German national cause by the delegates assembled at the **Frankfurt Parliament**. War between Denmark and the government of Schleswig-Holstein, again backed by Prussian and other German forces, was resumed in the spring of

1849 and led to further Danish setbacks which were ended by the defensive victory at Fredericia (6 July 1849). The third and final round was fought in July 1850 between Denmark and Schleswig-Holstein, this time without official support from the German states, and ended with a Danish victory at Isted (25 July 1850). The Schleswig-Holstein question was formally settled by the London Protocol of 8 May 1852. ▷ **German-Danish War** (1864)

German East Africa Company The company established by the Germans to exploit its newly acquired territory of Tanganyika. It acquired a charter on the British model in 1885 after Karl Peters and his associates in the Society for German Colonization had collected treaties from East African chiefs. However the charter was lost by 1892 because Peters's company proved unable to cope with Swahili and African resistance to its rule.

Germania Magna/Barbara Between 12 and 9BC the Roman Empire pushed as far east as the River Elbe and proposed to create a new province, to be known as *Germania Magna*, but the success was short-lived and by 9BC the Romans were pushed back to the Rhine. *Germania Barbara* was the name given by the Romans to the land occupied by Germanic tribes east of the Rhine and north of the Danube and the Limes.

Germanías Revolutionary movements (literally, 'brotherhoods') which were active between 1519 and 1523 in Valencia and Mallorca, at the same time as the **Comuneros** in **Castile**. Led in Valencia by Juan Llorens, an artisan, and then after his death in battle by Vicent Peris, a more radical figure, the *Germanías* represented the interests of the guilds and middle sectors against the upper aristocracy. They were also hostile to the **Mudejars** of the province and forced them to baptize. Peris was executed (Mar 1522) and a harsh repression took place. In Mallorca a violent Germanía was led eventually by Juan Colom, and not crushed until Mar 1523.

Germanic Invasions This mass movement of the Germanic peoples, caused by the shortage of arable land in their homeland and by increases in population, contributed to the downfall of the Roman Empire and was the last phase of the Indo-European migration. The tribes originally expanded southwards, at the expense of the Celts, from the area around the southern part of Sweden, but from the beginning of the 2c BC began to encroach on the Mediterranean world. A major impetus was given to the invasions by the arrival of the **Huns** in 375, which drove the Germanic peoples south and west into the Roman Empire. The defeat of the Romans by the **Visigoths** at **Adrianople** (378) marked the beginning of the end of the Western Empire. The Germanic kingdoms which originated during the period of migration were generally short-lived, with the exception of those of the **Franks** and the **Anglo-Saxons**. The synthesis of Roman and Germanic values which emerged after the migrations formed the basis of medieval Europe. ▷ **Burgundians; Cimbri; Herules; Marcomanni; Ostrogoths; Suebi; Teutons; Teutoburg Forest, Battle of**

Germanicus (Gaius Germanicus Caesar)

(15BC–AD19) Roman general. He was the son, father, and brother of the Roman emperors **Tiberius**, **Caligula**, and **Claudius** respectively, and heir-apparent himself from AD14. A man of great charm but mediocre ability, his sudden and suspicious death in Antioch marked a turning point in Tiberius' reign. It crystallized the growing disenchantment with the Emperor, and sent his reign on its downward spiral. ▷ **Agrippina the Elder**

German South-West Africa Company

A company formed to exploit the German colony in South-West Africa proclaimed by **Bismarck** in 1884 out of the trading positions of Adolf Luderitz. The company was never chartered and was always under-capitalized. In the 1890s it faced competition from a more financially secure British company, the South-West Africa Company.

German–Soviet Pact (Hitler–Stalin Pact)

(23 Aug 1939) Following Germany's failure to gain British support for, or even toleration of, her expansionist plans after 1938 and following difficulties surrounding the conclusion of a British–French–Soviet pact of mutual assistance directed against Germany, the German and Soviet governments moved swiftly to settle their differences. The respective Foreign Ministers, **Ribbentrop** and **Molotov**, signed an agreement (including a Secret Protocol) which defined territorial interests in Eastern Europe (effectively partitioning the region between them) renounced the use of force against one another, guaranteed friendly relations and allowed extensive economic relations to develop. The fate of Poland was thereby sealed, but **Hitler**'s attack on the USSR in June 1941 ended what was always an opportunistic and cynical agreement.

Germany, East (Deutsche Demokratische Republik, 'German Democratic Republic')

Former socialist republic of north central Europe, divided into 14 counties, with East **Berlin** as its capital. Administered by the USSR after the 1945 partition of Germany, a Soviet model of government was established, with the Socialist Unity Party (**SED**) guaranteed a pre-eminent role, in 1949. Anti-Soviet demonstrations were put down in 1953, and East Germany was recognized by the USSR as an independent republic the following year. The flow of refugees to West Germany continued until 1961, but was largely stopped by the building of the **Berlin Wall**. East Germany was governed by the People's Chamber, a single-chamber parliament (*Volkskammer*) of 500 Deputies, which elected a 29-member Council of State (*Staatsrat*), a Council of Ministers (*Ministerrat*), and a National Defence Council. The movement for democratic reform, as well as mounting economic crisis, culminated (Nov 1989) in the opening of the **Berlin Wall** and other border crossings to the West, and a more open government policy. Free elections (Mar 1990) paved the way for a currency union with West Germany (July) and full political unification (Oct). ▷ **Germany, West.** See map p362.

Germany, West (Deutschland or Deutsches Reich; Bundesrepublik Deutschland, 'Federal Republic of Germany')

Former Central European state, divided into 15 states (*Länder*), with **Berlin** as federal capital and **Bonn** as seat of government. Location of the union of the ancient Germanic tribes within the Frankish Empire of **Charlemagne** in the 8c and of an elective monarchy after 918 under **Otto I**, with the **Holy Roman Empire** divided into several hundred states. Many reforms and territorial changes took place during the Napoleonic era, and after the Congress of **Vienna** (1814–15) a **German Confederation** of 39 states under **Austria** was formed. Under **Bismarck**, **Prussia** succeeded Austria as the leading German power and excluded her from the **North German Confederation**. The union of Germany and foundation of the Second **Reich** (1871), with the King of Prussia as hereditary German Emperor, gave rise, from around 1900, to an aggressive foreign policy which eventually led to **World War I**. After the German defeat, the Second *Reich* was replaced by the democratic **Weimar Republic** and, in 1933,

Germany following World War II

political power passed to the **Nazi Party**. **Hitler**'s acts of aggression as Chancellor and Leader (*Führer*) of the totalitarian Third *Reich*, eventually led to **World War II** and a second defeat for Germany, with the collapse of the German political regime. The area of Germany was subsequently reduced, and occupied by the UK, USA, France, USSR and Poland whose zone is now recognized as sovereign Polish territory. This Western occupation softened with the creation of the Federal Republic of Germany (1949) out of the three western zones. Its federal system of government, built around 10 states (*Länder*) with considerable powers, has since absorbed East Germany (Oct 1990) as five additional states. A leading industrial and trading nation, following major reconstruction after World War II, Germany is now a dominant force in the European Monetary System. ▷ **Land**

Geronimo (Goyathlay) (1829–1909) Mexican-born Chiricahua **Apache** chief. The best known and most fearsome of all Apaches, he led numerous raiding parties in Mexico and Arizona following the massacre of his family by Mexican soldiers. He forcibly resisted the internment of his people on a reservation, escaping from white control on several

362

occasions, but made a final surrender in 1886. In his old age he became a Christian and a figure in public spectacles, including President Theodore **Roosevelt**'s inauguration parade. ▷ **Indian Wars**

gerrymander A term describing the redrawing of electoral districts so as to benefit the party in power in forthcoming elections. It was first coined in the USA in 1812 by combining the last name of Elbridge Gerry, then Governor of Massachusetts, with salamander, the shape of which animal the newly created electoral district was said to resemble.

Gestapo An abbreviation of *Geheime Staatspolizei*, the political police of the German Third **Reich**, founded in 1933 by **Goering** on the basis of the Prussian political police. It soon extended throughout Germany, and from 1936 came under the control of **Himmler**, as head of the **SS**. ▷ **Nazi Party**

Gettysburg, Battle of (1–3 July 1863) Marking the turning point in the **American Civil War**, the Gettysburg campaign began in June 1863. It consisted of a major series of engagements in Pennsylvania between the army of north Virginia (Confederate) and the army of the Potomac (Union), after Robert E **Lee**, the Southern commander, decided to take the war into the North. The Battle of Gettysburg ended with a Union victory, but with heavy losses on both sides (Union 23 000; Confederate 25 000). On 4 July, Lee's severely reduced troops retreated, with the defeat ending any prospect of foreign recognition for the Confederacy.

Gettysburg Address (19 Nov 1863) A speech given by President **Lincoln** during the **American Civil War**, at the dedication of a war cemetery in Pennsylvania on the site of the Battle of **Gettysburg**. Ill-regarded at the time, it is now thought of as one of the masterpieces of US oratory, from its often-quoted opening, 'Fourscore and seven years ago our fathers brought forth on this continent a new nation', to its memorable conclusion, 'that government of the people, by the people, for the people, shall not perish from the earth'.

Geyl, Pieter (1887–1966) Dutch historian and patriot. He was educated in The Hague, at Leiden and in Italy. After serving as London correspondent of the *Nieuwe Rotterdamsche Courant* (1913–19), he was appointed the first Professor of Dutch Studies at London University (1919–36) and Professor of Modern History at Utrecht (1936–58). During **World War II**, he was imprisoned in **Buchenwald** and other Nazi concentration camps. He was a believer in a 'greater Netherlands', always mourning the loss of Dutch-speaking Flanders and **Brabant** during the Eighty Years War in the late 16c. As a historian, however, he was a climatologist and environmentalist, arguing that the outcome of the Dutch revolt against Habsburg Spain was dictated by movements of rivers and water-currents rather than religion or economics. His multi-volume history of the Eighty Years War and its sequels were published in the 1930s, translated into English as *The Revolt of the Netherlands* and *The Netherlands Divided*, while his struggle against Hitlerian domination of Europe is reflected in his *Napoleon, For and Against* (1944). He was also a poet and essayist, debating with numerous living and dead historians, and was the leading interpreter of the Dutch past to his country and the world.

Ghadr Party and Movement Originally an organization of Indian migrants, especially Punjabis, settled in British Columbia and on the West Coast of the USA, it derived its name from the title of its journal, *Ghadr* (Urdu, 'revolution'). Influenced by the activities of Irish radicals and Russian revolutionaries, a highly-organized conspiracy was hatched at the start of **World War I**, the Indian–Berlin Committee of the 'Hindustan Ghadr Party' offering money and arms to help raise a revolt against the British in India. Accordingly, large numbers of Ghadrites returned to the subcontinent. Many were arrested, but by late 1914 a substantial body of party members and suppporters was established in the Punjab. Led by men such as Rashbehari Bose and Sachin Sayal, attempts were made to foster mutiny in the Indian army; bombs were manufactured, robberies committed and arsenals raided in order to raise arms and supplies for a general uprising. However, the British pre-empted this plan, arresting large numbers of Ghadrites in Punjab, Bengal, Singapore and elsewhere. A series of trials, including the 1915 Lahore Conspiracy Case, resulted, in which Ghadrites and others accused of revolutionary activities were prosecuted under the Defence of India Act; 46 people were hanged and 194 were imprisoned. A total of 145 revolutionaries were hanged or killed by the police, and some 306 sentenced to transportation. Later, further trials of Ghadrites were held in the USA, whilst in India those revolutionary cells still active were riven by factionalism. Attempts to revive the Ghadr Movement in India after 1919 failed due to the growing popularity and success of the Gandhian Congress, although in the 1930s and 1940s returning Ghadrites, having served out their term in prison, often became activists once again in the Indian Communist movement.

Ghaffar Khan, Abd al- (1891–1988) Muslim Indian politician. He was from North-West Frontier Province, where in 1921 he formed *Khudai Khidmatgar* ('Servants of God') to act as an agent of social welfare and peaceful political change in the mostly Muslim province. Because of his close links with the **Indian National Congress** and his strict adherence to M K **Gandhi**'s technique of **Satyagraha** he became popularly known as the 'Frontier Gandhi'. Due to the close cooperation of Khudai Khidmatgar and the Congress, North-West Frontier province became the only one with a Muslim majority to be controlled by the Congress after the 1937 national election. Abd al-Ghaffar boycotted the July 1947 referendum on the issue of North-West Frontier province's accession to Pakistan, and this led to his political decline and that of his party. His later demands for an independent Pathan state resulted in repeated imprisonment in Pakistan and eventual exile in Afghanistan.

Ghana, Kingdom of An African kingdom in the western Sudan which may have its origins as early as the 5–6c, but which certainly flourished in the 8–11c. It probably derived its name from the title of its king, and bears no geographical relationship to the modern state, which lies further to the south and east. It was one of a series of states on the margin between the savanna and the desert, controlling the trade of the Sahara. Its capital was sacked by the **Almoravids** c.1076 and its power broken, though it lingered on until the 13c. ▷ **Berber**

Ghazi (1912–39) King of Iraq (1933/9). The son of King **Faysal I**, he proved not to be of his father's calibre and was seen as inadequate when faced with the duties required of the King of Iraq. Despite, or possibly because of, his popularity with Iraqi army officers (educated, as he himself had been, in the UK), his reign saw a general increase in anti-British sentiment throughout his country.

Ghaznevids The dynasty founded by Sebuktegin, son of Alptegin, a Turkish slave of the Samanids who had attained to a position of great influence in Samanid government circles. The most famous member of the dynasty was Sebuktegin's son, Mahmud (999/1030). Ghazna, situated as it is high in Afghanistan overlooking the plain of what is now Pakistan, to which access could be gained through the valley of Kabul, enabled Mahmud in the early 11c to annex the Punjab, Multan and part of Sind. Mahmud's westward expansion extended to capturing most of Persia from the Buyids. He thus established control over a wide empire, and, with the riches therefrom accruing, he was able to beautify his capital and play patron to men of science, learning and the arts, notable among whom was the poet Firdawsi, author of the *Shahnama*, the Persian national epic, to name but one. After the death of Mahmud, the dynasty soon began to show signs of decay. Various powers in east and west gradually gained control of elements of the Ghaznevid Empire and the last Ghaznevid finally fell in 1186 in Lahore at the hands of the Ghurids.

Ghegs The northern **Albanians** who, until **World War II**, retained their strong tribal

organization and lived in isolated communities in the mountains. Under Ottoman rule, they were Sunni Muslims. They speak Gheg, one of the Albanian dialects.

Ghent, Pacification of (8 Nov 1576) The peace treaty signed by almost all the provinces of the northern and southern Netherlands in the early stages of the **Eighty Years War** against Spain. It agreed to stop all religious persecution (except against the Catholics in Holland and Zeeland) and to leave the religious question to be decided by the States General; confiscated property was to be returned and political prisoners released. **William I** of Orange was recognized as **Stadholder** of Holland and Zeeland. This was a highpoint of the revolt: all the Netherlands provinces united against Spain, with freedom of religion. Two years later, however, the Union of **Arras** broke ranks, and the southern Netherlands drifted back to Spain.

Ghent, Treaty of (1814) The treaty between the USA and Britain which ended the **War of 1812**, without any resolution of the major issues from which the conflict had grown. These had included maritime rights and military control of the Great Lakes.

Gheorgiu-Dej, Gheorghe (1901–65) Romanian politician. As a railway worker, he joined the Romanian Communist Party (RCP) in 1930 and was imprisoned in 1933 for his role in the Griviţa railway strike. On his release in 1944, he became Secretary-General of the RCP and Minister of Communications (1944–6) and in 1945 was instrumental in the ousting of the coalition government of Nicolae Radescu (1874–1953) and the establishment of a communist regime. He then served in a variety of economic posts (1946–52) and as Prime Minister (1952–5), before becoming state President in 1961. A Stalinist, he nonetheless retained the support of Nikita **Khrushchev's** Moscow, while developing increasingly independent policies during the 1950s and 1960s. ▷ **Ceauşescu, Nicolae**

Ghibellines The pro-imperial party in Italian cities of the 13–14c, favouring the involvement of the Holy Roman Emperor in Italian politics, even after the decline of the Hohenstaufen state from 1266. They supported the invasion of the Holy Roman Emperor **Henry VII** in 1308, although the power and status of the Empire had much diminished by that date. ▷ **Guelfs; Hohenstaufen Dynasty**

Ghosh (Ghose), Aurobindo (1872–1950) Bengali nationalist and poet. He started the philosophy of cosmic salvation through spiritual evolution. Educated in Christian convents in India and at Cambridge, he took administrative and professorial posts in India, and then turned to the study of Indian culture. A teacher in Baroda, Ghosh showed only a passing interest in nationalist politics through the writing of a few articles prior to 1905. Coincident with the partition of Bengal, however, he returned to Calcutta to become Principal of the National College, and became prominent in the **Swadeshi** movement. Taking editorial control of the newspaper, *Bande Mataram*, he wrote and published articles which greatly increased Hindu nationalist fervour in the Bengali contingent of Congress. Acquitted of a charge of sedition in 1908, he became an acknowledged leader of the so-called 'extremist' group within the Bengal Congress. He started a new journal, *Karmayogin*, in 1910 but fled Bengal soon afterward to escape government surveillance. He went to the French colony of Pondicherry near Madras, where he founded Auroville, an international centre for spiritual development. ▷ **Bengal, Partition of**

Gia Long (Nguyen Phuoc Anh) (1762–1820) Vietnamese emperor, the founder of the Nguyen Dynasty. In a series of military campaigns in the 1790s, he extended and consolidated the authority of the Nguyen clan, taking advantage of the disintegration of the existing, Tay Son, order. Final victory was achieved in 1802 and, for the first time in Vietnam's history, a single court (at Hue) could claim authority over the whole territory: from the border with China in the north to the Mekong delta in the south. Emperor Gia Long's reign sought to secure Nguyen power within a highly centralized administration. His Law Code, promulgated in 1815 and drawing heavily on Chinese models, greatly strengthened the position of the ruling elite.

Giap, Vo Nguyen (1912–) Vietnamese military leader. He studied law at Hanoi University, joined the Vietnamese Communist Party, and trained in China. He led the **Viet Minh** against the French after 1945, and planned and executed the decisive defeat of their garrison at **Dien Bien Phu** in 1954. As Vice-Premier and Defence Minister of North Vietnam, he masterminded the military strategy that forced US forces to leave South Vietnam (1973) and led to the reunification of Vietnam in 1975. He was a member of the politburo from 1976 to 1982. He wrote *People's War, People's Army* (1961), which became a textbook for revolutionaries. ▷ **Vietnam War**

Gibraltar The narrow peninsula rising steeply from the low-lying coast of south-west Spain at the eastern end of the Strait of Gibraltar, which is an important strategic point of control for the western Mediterranean. Settled by the Moors in 711, Gibraltar was taken by Spain in 1462, and ceded to Britain in 1713, becoming a British Crown Colony in 1830. As a Crown Colony, it played a key role in Allied naval operations during both World Wars. A proposal to end British rule was defeated by a referendum in 1967. The frontier with Spain was closed from 1969 until 1985, and Spain continues to claim sovereignty.

Gierek, Edward (1913–) Polish politician. He lived in France (1923–34) during the **Piłsudski** dictatorship, and joined the French Communist party in 1931. He was deported to Poland in 1934, but moved to Belgium (1937–48), becoming a member of the Belgian resistance. On his return to Poland in 1948, he joined the ruling Polish United Workers' Party (PUWP), being inducted into its Politburo in 1956 and appointed party boss of Silesia. He became First Secretary and leader of the PUWP in 1970 when **Gomułka** resigned after strikes and riots in Gdansk, Gdynia and Szczecin. Head of the party's 'technocrat faction', he embarked on an ambitious industrialization programme which, with foreign loans, also involved high consumer spending. This plunged the country heavily into debt and, following a wave of strikes in Warsaw and Gdansk, spearheaded by the **Solidarity** free trade union movement, he was forced to resign in 1980.

Giers, Nikolai Karlovich (1820–95) Russian diplomat and politician. He gained wide experience serving in various diplomatic posts in the Balkans and the Middle East before becoming Deputy Foreign Minister in 1875 and Foreign Minister in 1882. Concerned to protect his country against its traditional rivals, France and Britain, he was inclined to lean towards Germany. He struggled hard to retain the special German connection both before and after **Bismarck**'s dismissal in 1890. Initially he resisted the **Franco-Russian Alliance** signed in 1894, but he was forced to recognize changing circumstances.

Gilded Age A derogatory term for a period in the latter part of the 19c in the USA. Taken from the title of a novel by Mark Twain and Charles Dudley Warner (1829–1900) it referred to the widespread political corruption and scandals of the time.

Gil Robles, José María (1898–1980) Spanish politician and academic. As a young and pugnacious leader of the **CEDA**, he was the principal figure of the Right during the Second Republic. Effectively dominating the governments of Nov 1933–Dec 1935, as Minister of War he prepared the army for the rising of July 1936. Exiled as a member of the monarchist opposition to the **Franco** regime (1936–53 and 1962–5), he was the founder and first President of the Popular Democratic Federation, and also created the Christian Social Democratic Party. However, in the 1977 general election his party was annihilated. ▷ **Republic, Second** (Spain)

Ginkel, Godert de (1630–1703) Dutch general. He accompanied **William III** to England in 1688, and fought at the Battle of the **Boyne** (1690). As Commander-in-Chief in Ireland, he defeated the remaining rebels, and was created Earl of Athlone (1692). He later led the Dutch troops under the Duke of Marlborough.

Gioberti, Vincenzo (1801–52) Piedmontese writer and politician. Ordained in 1825 and expelled from Piedmont in 1833 because of his outspoken defence of the Polish cause, he wrote extensively on Italian history and politics. His most important work, *Del primato morale e civile degli italiani* (On the Moral and Civil Primacy of the Italians), written in exile in Brussels and published in 1843, called for an Italian Confederation under papal presidency. His dreams seemed to have been realized with the election of the apparently liberal **Pius IX** in 1846 and the outbreak of revolution in 1848. Briefly Prime Minister of Piedmont (Dec 1848–Mar 1849), he became disillusioned with, and retired from, politics and was condemned by an increasingly reactionary Pius. ▷ **Balbo, Cesare; Charles Albert; D'Azeglio, Massimo**

Giolitti, Giovanni (1842–1928) Italian politician. An astute and unprincipled parliamentary manager, Giolitti entered parliament in 1882 as a liberal. He became **Crispi**'s Minister of Finance in 1889. Prime Minister from 1892 to 1893, he was brought down by a banking scandal. He returned to politics as Interior Minister under **Zanardelli** in 1901, becoming Prime Minister again from 1903 to 1909, except for a brief spell out of office in 1905–6. As Prime Minister, he sought to

combat leftist strikes and disorders through economic policy rather than confrontation; in foreign policy he strengthened Italy's ties with Austria and Germany. During his fourth spell as Prime Minister (1911–14), he brought Italy into the **Tripolitanian War**, gaining Libya, Rhodes and the Dodecanese. However, the war resulted in unpopular tax increases. A general strike forced him from office in 1914. In opposition, he urged neutrality in 1915. His fifth ministry (1920–1) failed to cope with post-war disorder or the violence of the **squadristi**, and he was unable to block **Mussolini**'s ascent to power.

Giraud, Henri Honoré (1879–1949) French soldier. Commander of the 7th and 9th Armies in 1940, he was captured by the Germans, but escaped. Reaching North Africa in 1942, he joined the Allied cause, and was imposed by the USA as joint chairman with de **Gaulle** of the committee of National Liberation. Rapidly outmanoeuvred by the latter, he resigned and played no further political role of any consequence. ▷ **World War II**

Girondins (Girondists) A group of deputies in the **Legislative Assembly** (1791–2) and French Convention (1792–5), led by Jean Roland, Charles **Dumouriez**, and Jacques **Brissot**. Their name derived from the Gironde region of south-western France. They aroused the hostility of **Robespierre** and the 'Mountain' in the Convention, many being executed during the Terror (1793). ▷ **Convention, National; French Revolution; Plain, the; Terror, Reign of**

Giscard d'Estaing, Valéry (1926–) French politician. He entered the Ministry of Finance as a civil servant and was appointed Finance Minister in 1962. He led that faction of the **Independents** who remained loyal to de **Gaulle** after Algerian independence, and turned them into a new political party, the **Independent Republican Party**. He returned to the Finance Ministry in 1969, defeated **Mitterrand** and the Gaullist candidate to become President in 1974, and was then beaten by Mitterrand in 1981. ▷ **Gaullists**

Giulio de' Medici ▷ **Clement VII**

Gladstone, W(illiam) E(wart) (1809–98) British politician. He entered parliament in 1832 as a Conservative, working closely with **Peel**. From 1834 he held various junior posts, becoming President of the Board of Trade (1843–5). He was Chancellor of the Exchequer in **Aberdeen**'s coalition (1852–5) and then again under **Palmerston** and **Russell** (1859–66). In 1867 he became leader of the **Liberal Party**, and soon after served his first term as Premier (1868–74). In a ministry notable for administrative reform, he disestablished and disendowed the Irish Church, reformed the Civil Service and established a system of national elementary education (1870). Frequently in office (1880–5, 1886 and 1892–4) until his resignation in 1894, he succeeded in carrying out a scheme of parliamentary reform (1884) which went a long way towards universal male suffrage. In his last two ministries he introduced bills for Irish **Home Rule**, but both were defeated. ▷ **Conservative Party** (UK)

Glanvill, Ranulf de (d.1190) Chief Justiciary of England (1180–9). He was adviser to **Henry II** and reputed author of the earliest treatise on the laws of England. In 1174 he raised a body of knights and captured **William I**, 'the Lion', of Scotland. He joined the third crusade and died during the siege of Acre. ▷ **Crusades**

glasnost A Russian term, usually translated as 'openness', describing the changes in attitude on the part of leaders of the former USSR following Mikhail **Gorbachev**'s rise to power in 1985, which brought about a wider and franker dissemination of information and the opportunity for genuine debate both within Soviet society and in Soviet relations with foreign powers. ▷ **perestroika**

Glemp, Jozef (1929–) Polish ecclesiastic. He became Bishop of Warmia in 1979 and succeeded Cardinal Stefan Wyszinski as Archbishop of Gniezno and Warsaw and Primate of Poland after the latter's death in 1981. A specialist in civil and canonical law, Glemp was a prominent figure during Poland's internal political unrest, attempting with some success to moderate hardline communist attitudes. He was made a cardinal in 1983.

Glendower, Owen (c.1354–1416) Welsh chief. He studied law at Westminster, and became esquire to the Earl of Arundel. In 1401 he rebelled against **Henry IV**, proclaimed himself Prince of Wales, established an independent Welsh parliament, and joined the coalition with Harry Percy (Hotspur), who was defeated at the Battle of Shrewsbury (1403). He continued to fight for Welsh independence until his death. ▷ **Percy**

Gleneagles Agreement (1977) An undertaking entered into by Commonwealth Heads of Government, meeting at Gleneagles in Scotland, to discourage sporting links with South Africa as a symbol of disapproval of **apartheid**.

Glistrup, Mogens (1926–) Danish politician. From 1956 to 1963 he was a member of the Faculty of Law at Copenhagen University. In 1972 he founded the anti-tax Progress Party (*Fremskridtspartiet*), which after the general election in 1973 became a right-wing force in Danish politics. Since 1973 he has been a member of the Danish parliament (**Folketinget**).

Glorious First of June, Battle of the (1794) A naval battle fought off the Isle d'Ouessant (near Brest) between British and French navies. The victory for Admiral Richard **Howe** resulted in the capture of a third of the French ships, and confirmation of British naval supremacy. ▷ **French Revolutionary Wars**

Glorious Revolution (Dec 1688–Feb 1689) The name given to the events during which **James VII and II** fled from England, effectively abdicating the throne, and **William III** and Mary II were established by parliament as joint monarchs. The title, coined by **Whigs** who in the long term benefited most from it, celebrates the bloodlessness of the event, and the assertion of the constitutional importance of parliament.

Gloucester, Humphrey, Duke of (1391–1447) Youngest son of **Henry IV**, and protector during the minority of **Henry VI** (1422–9). He greatly increased the difficulties of his brother, Bedford, by his greed, irresponsibility, and factious quarrels with their uncle, Cardinal Henry **Beaufort**. In 1447 he was arrested for high treason at Bury St Edmunds and five days later was found dead in bed (apparently from natural causes). His patronage of literature led to his nickname 'the Good Duke Humphrey'

Glubb, John Bagot (Glubb Pasha) (1897–1986) British soldier. Educated in Cheltenham and the Royal Military Academy, Woolwich, he served in **World War I**, and became the first organizer of the native police force in the new state of Iraq (1920). In 1930 he was transferred to British-mandated Transjordan, organizing the Arab Legion's Desert Patrol, and becoming Legion Commandant (1939). He had immense prestige among the Bedouin, but was dismissed from his post in 1956 following Arab criticism. Knighted in 1956, he then became a writer and lecturer.

Glyndwr, Owain ▷ **Glendower, Owen**

Gneisenau, August (Wilhelm Anton), Count Neithardt von (1760–1831) Prussian general. In 1786 he joined the Prussian Army, fought at Saalfeld and **Jena and Auerstädt** (1806), helped to reorganize the army after its defeat by **Napoleon I** (1807), and in the war of liberation gave distinguished service at the Battle of **Leipzig** (1813). In the **Waterloo** campaign as chief of **Blücher**'s staff he directed the strategy of the Prussian Army. ▷ **Napoleonic Wars; Prussia**

Gobind Singh (1666–1708) Last of the 10 Sikh Gurus (1675/1708). He completed the process by which the Sikhs developed from the quietist faith propagated by Guru Nanak to a militant creed. Coming to the leadership on the execution by the Mughals of his father, Guru Tegh Bahadur (1664/75), he was implacably hostile to them, and in the final years of the 17c established a small Sikh state in the Punjab foothills by military means. At the Baisakhi festival in 1699 he instituted the Khalsa, the new Sikh brotherhood marked by a new code of discipline, the 'Five Ks' (visible symbols, including the uncut hair and beard), and common adoption of the name Singh for males and Kaur for females. Following Aurangzeb's death in 1707, there were moves towards an accommodation between Sikhs and Mughals, ended by Gobind Singh's death the following year at the hands of Pathan assassins. Traditionally, Gobind Singh declared on his deathbed that guruship would henceforth reside in the Sikh scripture (*Guru Granth*) and the Sikh community (*Guru Panth*), his sons having already died in battle or been executed by the Mughals.

Godbout, Adélard (1892–1956) Canadian politician. He became Liberal Premier of Quebec in 1939, defeating Maurice **Duplessis** and the **Union Nationale**. In 1944 his administration placed the Montreal Light, Heat and Power Company in public ownership, the first move in breaking free from the English-speaking community's hold on the economy of Quebec. ▷ **Liberal Party** (Canada)

Goderich, Viscount, Robinson, Frederick John (1st Earl of Ripon) (1782–1859) British politician. He entered parliament as a Tory MP in 1806, later becoming

President of the Board of Trade (1918–23 and 1841–3) and Chancellor of the Exchequer (1823–7). He was associated with financial reforms to reduce government debt and promote greater freedom of trade. His success earned him the sobriquet 'Prosperity Robinson'. He was Secretary of State for War and the Colonies (1827) under **Canning**, whom he succeeded. His weak leadership was soon exposed and he resigned willingly before meeting parliament as Prime Minister (1827–8), the only Premier to do so. Briefly changing parties, he served in **Grey**'s Whig governments as Secretary for War and the Colonies (1830–3) and Lord Privy Seal (1834–5). His last government office was under **Peel** as President of the Board of Control (1843–6) and he introduced the Bill to repeal the **Corn Laws** (1846). His extensive governmental career testifies to administrative competence but not to leadership. ▷ **Tories; Whigs**

Godfrey of Bouillon (c.1061–1100) French Crusader. Duke of Lower Lorraine from 1089 to 1095, he was elected one of the principal commanders of the First Crusade. After the capture of Jerusalem (1099) he was proclaimed King, but he refused the crown, accepting only the title Defender of the Holy Sepulchre. He died at Jerusalem. ▷ **Crusade, First**

Godolphin, Sidney Godolphin, 1st Earl of (1645–1712) English statesman. He entered parliament (1668), visited Holland (1678), and was made head of the Treasury and a baron (1684). He stood by **James VII and II** when William of Orange landed (1688), and voted for a regency; yet in 1689 William reinstated him as First Commissioner of the Treasury. He was ousted in 1696, but made Lord High Treasurer by Queen **Anne** (1702) and created earl (1706). His able management of the finances helped **Marlborough** in the War of the **Spanish Succession** (1700–13); but court intrigues led to his dismissal in 1710. ▷ **William III**

Godoy, Manuel de (1767–1851) Spanish court favourite and Chief Minister (1792–1808) under Charles IV. An obscure guards officer, he achieved dictatorial power at the age of 25 through the favour of the Queen, Maria Luisa, whose lover he was. In 1795 he assumed the title 'Prince of the Peace', following Spain's defeat by Revolutionary France; in 1796 he allied with France against England — a disastrous move which turned Spain into a virtual French satellite, and contributed massively to her losing her American Empire. In 1808 he was overthrown, spending the rest of his life exiled in Rome and in Paris, where he died.

Godwin (d.1053) Earl of Wessex. He was probably the son of the South Saxon, Wulfnoth. Godwin became powerful under King **Canute**, and in 1042 helped to raise **Edward the Confessor** to the throne, marrying him to his daughter, Edith. He led the struggle against the King's foreign favourites, which Edward revenged by confining Edith in a monastery, and banishing Godwin and his sons (1051). In 1052 Godwin landed in England, received the support of the people, and was reinstated. His son, **Harold II**, was, for a few months, Edward's successor. ▷ **Anglo-Saxons**

Goebbels, (Paul) Joseph (1897–1945) German Nazi politician. A deformed foot absolved him from military service, and he attended several universities, obtaining his doctorate at Heidelberg. He became **Hitler**'s enthusiastic supporter, led the **Nazi Party** in **Berlin** from 1926 and was appointed head of the Ministry of Public Enlightenment and Propaganda in 1933. A political radical and bitter anti-Semite, his gift of mob oratory made him a powerful exponent of Nazi philosophy. Wartime conditions greatly expanded his role as a propagandist, and from 1943 Goebbels did much to squeeze every last effort from the population and economy. He retained Hitler's confidence to the last, being appointed Plenipotentiary for the Pursuit of Total War in July 1944. In the Berlin bunker, he and his wife committed suicide, after taking the lives of their six children. His diaries now constitute a major historical source. ▷ **World War II**

Goerdeler, Carl (1884–1945) German politician. He served under **Hitler** as Commissar for Price Control (1934), but resigned from his mayoralty of Leipzig in 1937 and became one of the leaders who opposed Hitler. This opposition culminated in **Stauffenberg**'s unsuccessful bomb plot of 20 July 1944, for which Goerdeler was executed together with a number of generals.

Goering, Hermann (Wilhelm) (1893–1946) German Nazi politician. In **World War I** he fought on the Western Front, then transferred to the Air Force, and commanded the famous 'von Richthofen Squadron'. In 1922 he joined the **Nazi Party** and was given command of **Hitler**'s stormtroopers

(SA) until the unsuccessful 1923 putsch. In exile until 1927, he became President of the **Reichstag** in 1932, and joined the Nazi government in 1933 with responsibility for **Prussia** and air travel. He founded the **Gestapo**, and set up the concentration camps for political, racial, and religious suspects. In 1935 he took charge of the reconstituted **Luftwaffe** and in 1936 became director of the Four Year Plan, renewed in 1940, to prepare the economy for war. He played a major part in the **Anschluss** with **Austria** (1938) and in the annexation of the **Sudetenland** (1938). In 1940 he was made Marshal of the **Reich**, the first and only holder of the rank, but his political influence and personal drive declined as his wish for aggressive diplomacy was superseded by open warfare. As **World War II** went against Germany and the *Luftwaffe* failed to meet expectations, his prestige waned further. In 1945 he attempted a palace revolution, was condemned to death, but escaped, to be captured by US troops. In 1946 he was sentenced to death at the **Nuremberg Trials**, but before his execution could take place he committed suicide.

Gökalp, Ziya (Mehmet Ziya) (c.1875–1924) Turkish thinker. He owed his education, in the major Islamic languages (Arabic and Persian in addition to his native Turkish) and in the sciences both religious and secular, to his uncle. His career was spent in an intellectual attempt to contain the contrasting and not infrequently conflicting influences of orthodox religion, mysticism and modern science with which he had come into contact. Initially a thorn in the flesh of the authorities in Istanbul with his liberal and revolutionary views, he was arraigned in 1897 and in due course exiled to his native Diyarbakir. By 1908, he was recognized as a prominent liberal writer and lecturer in his home province and in course of time returned to Istanbul where he lived from 1912 to 1919. During this period he emerged as the propounder of a nationalist ideology for the Turks, which involved a reorientation of Turkish leanings emphasizing a Western approach. Exiled to Malta by the British after **World War I**, he occasioned no surprise when, after his release in 1921, he associated himself with Mustafa Kemal (**Atatürk**) and his national movement. Gökalp died with a reputation throughout his country as a thinker who had prepared the ground for the emergence of modern Turkey.

Gokhale, Gopal Krishna (1866–1915) Indian social reformer and nationalist. He founded the Servants of India Society (1905) to work for the relief of the underprivileged, and in the same year, was elected President of the **Indian National Congress**. He advocated moderate and constitutional methods of agitation and gradual reform, and died in Pune.

Golden Bull Any document whose importance was stressed by authentication with a golden seal (Latin, *bulla*). Specifically, the term is used for the edict promulgated by Emperor **Charles IV** in 1356 to define the German constitution. It formally affirmed that election of an emperor was by a college of seven princes, and recognized them as virtually independent rulers.

Golden Fleece, Order of the The exclusive chivalric order founded in 1430 by **Philip the Good**, Duke of Burgundy, in order to increase the dependence of his highest nobles on his leadership; in this sense it was comparable to the English Order of the Garter. Later, the order passed from the House of **Burgundy** to the **Habsburg Dynasty**, and so to the royal houses of Spain and Austria. The knights could only be tried by their sovereign and fellow knights, and were members of the Council of State; it was thus an order of great political significance and prestige. The derivation of the order's name is uncertain: it might refer to the object of the quest of Jason and the Argonauts, or to Gideon's fleece.

Golden Horde A feudal state, constituting at its height from the mid-13c to the end of the 14c the western part of the Mongol Empire, and occupying most of central and southern Russia and western Siberia. Its capital was first at Sarai Batu and then at Sarai Berbe on the River Volga. The Russian princes were vassals of the Khan of the Golden Horde, and paid regular tribute. The state was weakened by the Black Death (1346–7) and then soon overthrown by the Grand Princes of Moscow. ▷ **Mongols**

Golden Spurs, Battle of the (11 July 1302) A great victory by Flemish foot-soldiers over a French army of knights; about 1 000 French nobles perished, and their golden spurs gave the battle its name. After the Matins of **Bruges**, the whole of Flanders rose up against France, and pinned down the French forces near Kortrijk. A great French army came to relieve the town and punish the Flemings, but was heavily defeated by the citizens' army from the Flemish industrial towns. The

victory granted temporary independence to Flanders from France, and increased the democratic factor in Flemish urban politics.

Goldie, Sir George Taubman (1846-1925) British soldier and trader. After service as an army officer, became a trader in West Africa. He foresaw the developing Partition of Africa and believed that British interests must be secured against the French in the Oil Rivers region and along the Niger as a great commercial highway to the interior. By 1884 he had amalgamated all the British companies as the National Africa Company and set out to secure treaties from chiefs throughout the Niger Delta and in northern Nigeria. In 1886 he secured a charter for his renamed Royal Niger Company and effectively ruled the Niger regions until 1898. Frederick Lugard joined his employ and conquered the emirates of Northern Nigeria. ▷ **Africa, Partition of**

Goldman, Emma (1869–1940) US anarchist, feminist and birth-control advocate. Her Jewish family left Russia for Germany to avoid persecution and, in 1885, she migrated to the USA, where she began her anarchist career. Imprisoned during **World War I** for opposing government policy, she was deported to the USSR and eventually settled in France.

gold rush A burst of enthusiasm for mining, following the discovery of gold deposits in Sutter's Mill, California, in 1848. Major rushes of prospectors included California (1849), Colorado (1858–60), Idaho (1861–4), Montana (1862–4), South Dakota (1876–8), and Yukon territory (1896). ▷ **Klondike Gold Rush**

Goldwater, Barry Morris (1909–) US politician. Educated at the University of Arizona, he became a US Senator for that state in 1952. In 1964 he gave up his Senate seat to become Republican nominee for the presidency, but was overwhelmingly defeated by Lyndon B **Johnson**. He returned to the Senate in 1968, serving until 1987, and was one of the architects of the conservative revival within the **Republican Party**.

Göllheim, Battle of (1298) The decisive encounter between King **Adolf of Nassau** and the anti-king **Albert I** of Habsburg, in which Adolf was defeated and killed.

Gombos, Gyula (1886–1936) Hungarian politician. An army officer during **World**

War I, he found himself fighting Béla **Kun**'s Soviet Republic alongside Admiral **Horthy** in 1919. Following Hungary's reduction in size and status in the post-war settlement, he drifted further to the right. He became Minister of Defence (1929) and was Prime Minister (1932–6). He strengthened the totalitarian tendencies in Hungarian politics; and in foreign policy he flirted with Italy and Germany. In 1933 he was one of the first foreign statesmen to visit **Hitler** and congratulate him on his coming to power.

Gomes, Albert (1911–78) Trinidadian politician, trade unionist and novelist. He edited an anti-establishment periodical, *The Beacon*, and founded (1937) the Federated Workers Union. As a member of the Port of Spain city council, he attacked the colonial government and maintained this criticism when elected to the Legislative Council in 1946. However, on becoming Minister of Labour (1950), with a policy of 'industrialization by invitation', he lost his earlier radicalism and quickly became less influential after the nationalist upsurge of 1956. Gomes was Deputy Leader of the Democratic Labour Party in the federation elections of 1958.

Gómez, Juan Vicente (1857–1935) Venezuelan dictator. A rancher with no formal education, he became Vice-President under Cipriano Castro in 1899. He deposed Castro in 1908 and his dictatorial rule (1908–35) witnessed the dramatic expansion of the oil industry, mainly Standard Oil and Anglo-Dutch Shell, in the Maracaibo region. He played off the major multinationals and the army benefited accordingly.

Gompers, Samuel (1850–1924) British-born US labour leader. After migrating to the USA in 1863, he followed his father's trade as a cigar maker, joining a union the following year. Self-educated, he studied and rejected Marxism and socialism, developing instead the US practice of nonpolitical trade unionism. He helped found (1886), and was long-time president of, the American Federation of Labor (AFL), and with the AFL's triumph as the main force in organized labour he became a major public figure.

Gomułka, Władysław (1905–82) Polish political leader. A professional trade unionist, in 1943 he became Secretary of the outlawed Communist Party. He was Vice-President of the first postwar Polish government (1945–8), but his criticism of the

USSR led to his expulsion from the party in 1949 and his imprisonment from 1951 to 1954. He returned to power as Party First Secretary in 1956. In 1970, following a political crisis, he resigned office, and spent his remaining years largely in retirement.

Gondomar, Diego Sarmiento de Acuña, Count of (1567–1626) Spanish diplomat. As Ambassador in England (1613–18 and 1620–22), he worked to arrange the marriage of Prince Charles (later **Charles I**) with the Infanta. He had great influence over **James VI and I**, but caused public hostility in England. He was recalled to Spain in 1622, and lost influence after the Anglo-Dutch alliance of 1624.

Gong (Kung) (1833–98) Manchu Prince. The sixth son of the Manchu Qing Emperor Daoguang (1821/51), he was given the task of signing the Convention of Beijing (1860) with invading British and French forces. The convention, which ratified the 1858 Treaty of **Tianjin**, guaranteed as a treaty port, and gave Britain a lease on Kowloon. Originally anti-foreign, Prince Gong after 1860 advocated conciliation and the use of diplomacy. In 1861 he became Head of the *Zongli Yamen* (*Tsungli Yamen*), a government institution created to deal with the foreign powers. Following the death of Emperor Xianfeng (1851/62) and the accession of a boy-emperor, Tongzhi (1862/74), Prince Gong assisted the two Empress-Dowagers in regency government. His authority was increasingly diminished after 1875 with the growing influence of Empress-Dowager **Cixi** and in 1884 he was stripped of his official positions.

Gonzaga A princely northern Italian family who ruled Mantua for three centuries, from 1432 as marquises, from 1530 as dukes. They championed imperial interests and were often at war with the **Visconti** of Milan. In the 15c, and to a lesser extent in the 16c, the Gonzaga presided over one of the most splendid of **Renaissance** courts. The last Gonzaga duke died in 1627 opening the so-called Mantuan phase of the **Thirty Years War**. The duchy itself survived until 1708, when the 10th and last duke was deprived of his estates and sent into exile by the Emperor Joseph I. A branch of the family became Dukes of Montferrat.

González, Felipe (1942–) Spanish politician. He practised as a lawyer, and in 1962 joined the Spanish Socialist Workers' Party

371

(**PSOE**), then an illegal organization. The Party regained legal status in 1977, three years after he became Secretary-General. He persuaded the PSOE to adopt a more moderate policy, and in the 1982 elections they won a substantial majority. González then became Prime Minister in the first left-wing administration since 1939.

Gorbachev, Mikhail Sergeevich

(1931–) Soviet politician. Educated at the Law Faculty of Moscow State University and Stavropol Agricultural Institute, he began work as a machine operator (1946), and joined the Communist Party in 1952. He held a variety of senior posts in the Stavropol city and district Komsomol and Party organizations (1956–70), and was elected a deputy to the USSR Supreme Soviet (1970) and a member of the Party Central Committee (1971). He became Central Committee Secretary for Agriculture (1979–85); candidate member of the **Politburo** (1979–80) and full member (1980–91) of the Central Committee (1979–80); and, on the death of **Chernenko**, General-Secretary of the Party (1985–91). In 1988 he also became Chairman of the Presidium of the Supreme Soviet, ie head of state, and in 1990, the first executive President of the USSR. On becoming General-Secretary he launched a radical programme of reform and restructuring (**perestroika**) of the Soviet economic and political system. A greater degree of political participation, civil liberty, public debate, and journalistic and cultural freedom were allowed under the policy of **glasnost** (openness). In defence and foreign affairs he reduced military expenditure and pursued a policy of detente, disarmament and arms control with the West. He ended the Soviet military occupation of Afghanistan (1989) and accepted the break-up of Comecon and the **Warsaw Pact**, the withdrawal of Soviet troops from Eastern Europe and the reunification of Germany. But he failed to fulfil his promise to reform the economy and improve the living standards of the Soviet people, and proved unable to cope with the rising tide of nationalism. Following the unsuccessful coup against him in Aug 1991, he lost power to Boris **Yeltsin** despite accepting the demise of the Communist Party. In Dec 1991 he felt obliged to resign from the presidency as the USSR itself collapsed into 15 separate republics.

Gorbacheva, Raisa Maximova (1932–)

Wife of Mikhail **Gorbachev**, and the first ever wife of a Soviet leader to play a public role.

Born of a railway family in the Altai region, she graduated from Moscow University and pursued a career in sociological research and lecturing. A woman of considerable intelligence and obvious charm, she had standing in her own right before 1985 when, as the General-Secretary's wife, she began to appear with him on important occasions, including overseas tours. In an unsettled society she attracted criticism, but abroad she added to her husband's political and popular prestige and did a great deal to make a success of East–West arms talks.

Gorchakov, Prince Alexander Mikhailovich

(1798–1883) Russian politician. A cousin of Prince Mikhail **Gorchakov**, he was ambassador at Vienna (1854–6), then succeeded **Nesselrode** as Foreign Minister was, until **Bismarck**'s rise, the most powerful minister in Europe. He secured Austrian neutrality in the Franco-German War of 1870, and in 1871 the freeing of Russia from the Black Sea neutralization clauses of the Treaty of Paris (1856). After the conclusion of the Russo-Turkish War (1878), the repudiation of the Treaty of **San Stefano**, and the signing of the Treaty of Berlin, his influence began to wane, and he retired in 1882. ▷ **Russo-Turkish Wars**

Gorchakov, Prince Mikhail (1793–1861)

Russian soldier. A cousin of Prince Alexander **Gorchakov**, he served against the French in the Napoleonic campaign of 1812–14, and in the Russo-Turkish War of 1828–9. He helped to suppress the Polish revolution of 1831 and took part in the capture of Warsaw, and he assisted in the suppression of the Hungarian insurrection in 1849. On the outbreak of the **Crimean War** (1854–6), he commanded in the Danubian Principalities, but as Commander-in-Chief in the Crimea (1855) he was defeated on the Chernaya, although he recovered his laurels by his gallant defence of **Sevastopol**. He was military governor of Poland from 1856 to 1861. ▷ **Russo-Turkish Wars**

Gordon, Charles George (1833–85)

British general. He joined the Royal Engineers in 1852, and in 1855–6 fought in the **Crimean War**. In 1860 he went to China, where he crushed the **Taiping Rebellion**, for which he became known as 'Chinese Gordon'. In 1877 he was appointed Governor of the Sudan. He resigned in poor health in 1880, but returned in 1884 to relieve Egyptian garrisons which lay in rebel territory. He was besieged at Khartoum for 10 months by the Mahdi's troops, and was killed there two days before a relief force arrived.

Gordon Riots Anti-Catholic riots in London which caused a breakdown of law and order in parts of the capital for several days in early June 1780. They occurred after Lord George Gordon (1751–93), leader of the Protestant Association, had failed in his attempt to have clauses in the 1778 Catholic Relief Act (removing restrictions on the activities of priests) repealed. ▷ **Catholic Emancipation**

Gore, 'Al' (Albert) Jr (1948–) US politician. He was educated at Harvard, and at Vanderbilt University, where he studied law and divinity. He worked as an investigative reporter for *The Tennessean* (1971–6) and in 1976 was elected as a Democrat from Tennessee to the US House of Representatives, a position he held for eight years. He became a US Senator in 1984. Four years later he mounted an unsuccessful campaign for President but in 1992 made a successful bid for vice-president on the Democratic ticket with Bill **Clinton**. An ardent environmentalist, he is the author of *Earth in the Balance* (1992).

Gorée Island A small island off the Cape Verde Peninsula, Senegal. Throughout the 18c and early 19c, when Gorée was first a French, and then a British colony, it was a major centre of slave storage before shipping to the Americas. ▷ **slave trade**

Görgey, Artúr (1818–1916) Hungarian rebel soldier. During the revolt of 1848 he compelled Jelačić and his 10 000 Croats to capitulate at Ozora. As Hungarian Commander-in-Chief, although often in dispute with Lajos **Kossuth**, he relieved Komorn by inflicting a series of severe reverses on the Austrians, practically driving them out of the country. In 1849 he was repeatedly defeated and in Aug surrendered to the Russians with his army of 24 000 men, at Világos near Arad. Görgey was imprisoned at Klagenfurt, but was eventually set free in 1867 and returned to Hungary in 1868.

Göring, Hermann ▷ **Goering, Hermann**

Gorky, Maxim (1868–1936) Russian and Soviet writer and revolutionary. Born in Nizhni Novgorod, subsequently rechristened after him, he had little formal education and learned most from his frequent wanderings. From the turn of the century his inclinations were revolutionary and in 1905 he officially joined the **Bolsheviks**. However, he was in and out of friendship with **Lenin** and disapproved of what the Bolsheviks did in the years 1917–18, but he was on good and influential terms in years 1918–21 before going abroad for his health. But he returned in 1931 to preside over the new Writers' Union and sing the praises of much of what **Stalin** was doing. This was in the spirit of the socialist realist philosophy he helped create. He died less happy in 1936; and in 1991 his birthplace took back its old name.

Gorshkov, Sergei Georgievich (1910–88) Soviet admiral. He joined the navy in 1927 and, after graduating from the Frunze Naval Academy in 1931, he served in the Black Sea and in the Far East. From 1940 to 1955 he served mostly in the Black Sea fleet. His wartime exploits won him great fame and by 1951 he commanded the fleet. He was appointed commander-in-chief of the entire Soviet navy by Nikita **Khrushchev** in 1956, with the brief to cut back expenditure. However, after the **Cuban Missile Crisis** in 1962 and Khrushchev's ousting in 1964, the new Soviet leader, Leonid **Brezhnev**, pressed for naval expansion to enable the USSR to project itself globally. Gorshkov supported this view and oversaw a massive naval build-up, both surface and underwater, creating a force capable of challenging the West's by the 1970s. He remained in command of the navy until his death, although his influence declined rapidly after Mikhail **Gorbachev** came to power in 1985.

Gorton, Sir John Grey (1911–) Australian politician. He was a Liberal Senator for Victoria (1949–68) and a member of the House of Representatives (1968–75). He served in the governments of Sir Robert **Menzies** and Harold **Holt** and succeeded Holt as Prime Minister in 1967. In 1971 he was defeated on a vote of confidence and resigned in favour of William McMahon. ▷ **Liberal Party of Australia**

Goshi ('Rural Samurai') A lower-ranking status group in feudal Japan, which before the late 16c included all retainers expected to support themselves from income of the land granted to them as fiefs. The *goshi* became a distinct group after the 1590s when most **samurai** were separated from the land and expected to serve their lord on a full-time basis in the castle town. During the 18c and early 19c the goshi increasingly saw themselves as a rural elite (wealthy village-heads were often awarded goshi rank), and were hostile to the status, pretensions and privileges of the urban samurai. Many goshi participated in the anti-Tokugawa movement of the 1860s. ▷ **Tokugawa Shogunate**

Gosplan The State Planning Commission in the former USSR. Established in 1921, it had overall responsibility for state and regional planning, translating general economic objectives into specific blueprints. Its responsibilities varied over the years, but in the end it proved to be a liability as its bureaucratic functions prevented the Soviet economy from responding to new needs.

Gotha, Congress of (22–7 May 1875) This conference saw the union of the General German Workers' Association and the Social Democratic Workers' Party to form the Socialist Workers' Party, which was the direct forerunner of the **SPD**. The new party adopted a programme which demanded a democratic political order in Germany and a socialist society to be achieved 'by all legal means'. In Oct 1891 the Gotha Programme was replaced by the **Erfurt Programme**.

Goths A Germanic people who, by the end of 1c AD, had moved south from the Baltic area (Gotland) to the lower Vistula valley. By the 3c they had expanded into the Black Sea region and divided into two confederations, **Ostrogoths** and **Visigoths**. Displaced by the **Huns**, they created two kingdoms in the 5c out of the ruins of the Roman Empire in the West. ▷ **Claudius II Gothicus; Gallienus; Valens**

Goto Shojiro (1838–97) Japanese politician. He came from Tosa, one of the domains in the forefront of the **Meiji Restoration**. After 1868 Goto became a government minister, but resigned in 1873 after the government's refusal to sanction a military expedition to Korea. With another ex-**samurai** from Tosa, **Itagaki** Taisuke, Goto began to petition for a representative assembly, charging that the government was monopolized by leaders from **Satsuma** and **Choshu**. In 1881 he helped form Japan's first political party, the *Jiyuto* (Liberal Party), but like many party politicians of the time succumbed to the temptations of government bribes. He eventually abandoned the Jiyuto and joined the government as Communications Minister and then Minister for Agriculture and Commerce.

Gottwald, Klement (1896–1953) Czechoslovak politician. In **World War I** he fought with the Austro-Hungarian army. A Marxist, he helped to establish the Communist Party in 1921 and became its Secretary-General in 1929. He opposed the Munich Agreement of 1938 and later went to Moscow, where he was prepared by the Party for eventual office. In 1945 he became Vice-Premier in the Czechoslovak provisional coalition government. Prime Minister following elections in 1946, he pursued a pro-Soviet line and in Feb 1948 took advantage of his opponents' divisions to stage a coup d'état which averted a defeat for the Party at the polls; in June 1948 he became President. Strong in his support for **Stalin**, whose line he followed closely, he established a complete dictatorship that eliminated many of his Communist colleagues. Ironically, he died of an illness contracted while he was attending Stalin's funeral.

Gouin, Sir (Jean) Lomer (1861–1929) Canadian politician. The Liberal Premier of Quebec from 1905 to 1920, many considered him to be dominated by the English-speaking business community who controlled the hydro-electric power, transport and manufacturing industries. He became federal Minister of Justice in the administration of Mackenzie **King**. ▷ **Liberal Party** (Canada)

Goulart, João (Belquior Marques) (1918–76) Brazilian politician. Born in Rio Grande do Sul, he became the wealthy landowning neighbour of Getúlio **Vargas**. He was linked with the PTB in the late 1940s and, as Vargas' protégé, became Minister of Labour in 1954. He became leader of the PTB in 1960 and, having been accused by the army of nurturing pro-communist sympathies, was elected Vice-President against military hostility; the army reluctantly agreed to allow him to become President of a parliamentary regime in 1961. A weak and vacillating leader in 1963–4, he alienated moderate opinion by flirting with nationalist and left-wing groups. Goulart was ejected by a coup (Mar 1964) engineered by the army and supported by powerful conservative politicians in the UDN. The coup was precipitated by his insistence on recruiting support among non-commissioned officers in the army and navy.

Gouled Aptidon, Hassan (1916–) Djiboutian politician. While serving as a representative of French Somaliland in France, he became increasingly active in the independence movement and in 1967 founded the African People's League for Independence (APLI). Djibouti achieved self-government in 1977 and he became the country's first President, later merging the APLI with other groups to form the country's only political party, the People's Progress Party. His policy of neutralism in a war-torn region of the continent ensured his continuing popularity and in 1987 he was re-elected for a final six-year term.

Gourlay, Robert Fleming (1778–1863) Canadian reformer. A Scottish immigrant, disappointed by his failure to secure a large land grant and incensed by the bitterness of settlers at the crown and **Clergy Reserves** of Upper **Canada**, the lack of an emigration policy and the exclusion of Americans from settlement, complaints of which he learnt through replies to a questionnaire he had circulated to gather material for an emigrant's guide. Calling a convention of town delegates and agitating for reform, he was arrested and imprisoned when he refused to obey an order of banishment.

Government of India Acts Measures passed by the British Parliament to regulate the government of India (1883–1935). They included the 1858 Act which transferred British **East India Company** powers to the British Crown, and the 1919 and 1935 Acts which introduced limited constitutional change. Motivated in part by the need for retrenchment and increased taxation in the wake of India's involvement in **World War I**, the 1919 Act attempted to seduce moderate Indian politicians into cooperating with the colonial regime by offering a say in local and provincial government to a small proportion of the population from among the wealthier and more influential sections of society. The 1935 Act went further, although it still fell well short of a universal franchise, and led to the establishment of elected Congress ministries in most of the Indian provinces. Although these provincial governments had no say in matters of security, and the British governors retained a right of veto over both candidates and legislation, they were nonetheless a successful experiment in self-government, persuading some colonial officials that they could perhaps live with democracy. Unfortunately, representatives of minority political parties were largely excluded from the Congress governments, fuelling communal divisions in the country, whilst many officials merely saw provincial government as an undesirable concession, forced upon them by M K Gandhi's civil disobedience movement of 1930–2. The ministries resigned en masse in 1939, following the Viceroy, Linlithgow's, declaration of war with Germany without prior consultation with Indian politicians. ▷ **Communalism; India Acts; Montagu–Chelmsford Reforms; Scheduled Castes and Tribes**

Gowon, Yakubu (1934–) Nigerian soldier and politician. A Christian in a Muslim area, he was educated at a CMS missionary school and then Government College Zaria. His military training began in Ghana and continued in the UK where he attended the Royal Military Academy, Sandhurst, among other institutions. He was commissioned into the Nigerian army in 1956, serving with the **UN** force in the Congo (Zaire) in 1960–1. He became Adjutant-General in 1963 and Chief of Staff in 1966. The ethnic conflicts in the country precipitated a coup on 15 Jan 1966, led by Ibo officers, and Gowon headed a counter-coup (July 1966). He then became head of the Federal Military Government and Commander-in-Chief. Unable to prevent a civil war, he fought to retain **Biafra** (the Eastern Region) within a single Nigeria, while acceding to ethnic concerns by increasing the number of states; with the assistance of both the USA and the USSR, he prevailed. However, his retarded return to democracy encouraged another military coup; he was deposed in 1975 and went into exile.

Graaf, Sir de Villiers, Bt (1913–79) South African politician. Educated in South Africa, the UK and Netherlands, he saw military service in **World War II**. Elected a United Party MP in 1948, he became party leader in 1956, remaining so until 1977, when he transferred his allegiance to the New Republic Party. The political heir to Jan Smuts, his opposition to the **National Party** was too gentlemanly to challenge its hegemony and too conservative to build a new coalition across the race divide. He epitomized the failure of well-meaning liberalism in these years.

Gracchi (The Brothers), in full **Tiberius Sempronius Gracchus** (c.168–133BC) and **Gaius Sempronius Gracchus** (c.159–121BC) Roman politicians of aristocratic lineage. They attempted to solve the major social and economic problems of their day—the growing landlessness of the Roman peasantry and the consequent decline in army recruitment—by forcing through sweeping reforms while Tribunes of the Plebs (133BC and 123–122BC). The ruthlessness of their methods provoked such a backlash that on each occasion rioting broke out on the streets of Rome. Tiberius was lynched, and a decade later Gaius was forced to commit suicide. ▷ **Scipio Aemilianus**

Graeco-Turkish War (1921–2) This war was ostensibly provoked by Greek fears for the safety of the Greeks in the Izmir region of Anatolia in the face of growing Turkish nationalism. By the Treaty of Sèvres (1920), Greece had received the right to administer Izmir and its hinterlands for five years. When, in Dec 1920, **Constantine I** returned to Greece, he determined to bolster his position by championing the cause of the Anatolian Greeks. In July 1921 the government ordered 100 000 troops into Anatolia to attack Kemal **Atatürk**'s men. The Turks withdrew and the Greeks foolishly advanced with the intention of taking Ankara, but became bogged down in Sep 1921. No attempt was made to evacuate the Greek troops and, in Aug 1922, they were defeated by the Turks, who entered Izmir and destroyed the town. By the Treaty of **Lausanne**, Greece lost the major gains made after **World War I** and some 1.3 million Greeks were forced to leave Anatolia, while 380 000 Turks were expelled from Greece. Utterly discredited, Constantine I abdicated and was succeeded by **George II**.

Grafton, Augustus Henry Fitzroy, 3rd Duke of (1735–1811) British politician. He became MP in 1756, succeeding to his peerage in the following year. He was a prominent opponent of **Bute** in 1762–3 and became Secretary of State for the Northern Department (1765–6) under **Rockingham**. He accepted office under the Earl of **Chatham** as First Lord of the Treasury (1766–70) and took over leadership of the administration on his resignation (1768–70). His administration was weak and divided. He wished to pursue a more liberal policy towards the American colonies than his colleagues would allow and he handled **Wilkes**'s expulsion from the Commons ineptly. Soon after his resignation, he resumed office under Lord North as Lord Privy Seal (1771–5) but resigned when war broke out with the colonies. He served in the same office under Rockingham (1782–3) before retirement from politics when he became increasingly sympathetic to evangelicalism. ▷ **George III** of Great Britain

Gramsci, Antonio (1891–1937) Italian journalist, politician and political thinker. Born in Sardinia of a humble family, he was educated at Turin University, where he was drawn into political activity in the Socialist Party. A founder member of the **PCI** (Italian Communist Party) in 1921, he was Italian delegate at the Third International in Moscow (1922). In 1924 he became leader of the communists in parliament. He was one of a number of outspoken communist critics of the fascist regime to be arrested in 1928 and was sentenced to 20 years' imprisonment; he died a prisoner. His reputation rests primarily on his *Prison Notebooks*, a collection of thoughts and reflections written while in confinement and published posthumously.

Granada, Conquest of (2 Jan 1492) The conquest was achieved by **Ferdinand II, 'the Catholic'** and **Isabella I, 'the Catholic'** after 10 years of campaigning. Splits among the Muslim leadership helped the Christians; a key role was played by **Boabdil**, last King of Granada, who overthrew his father but refused to surrender the city, which underwent a nine-month siege and then capitulated on terms which assured respect for Muslim property and the Islamic faith. The campaigns helped to strengthen the Spanish monarchy by stimulating the emergence of regular military forces, and encouraged religious zeal under the form of a 'crusade'. The Pope in 1494 rewarded Ferdinand and Isabella with the title 'the Catholic Monarchs'. The Kingdom of Granada, however, suffered through the death or emigration of about half of its Muslim population.

Granby, John Manners, Marquis of (1721–70) British army officer. He was the eldest son of the Duke of Rutland. His reputation was made in the **Seven Years War**, when he led the British cavalry in a major victory over the French at Warburg (1760). He became a popular hero, and in 1763 was appointed Master-General of the Ordnance.

Gran Chaco The lowland plain covering part of northern Argentina, western Paraguay and southern Bolivia. Historically Bolivian, its ownership was disputed in the 1932–5 **Chaco War** between Paraguay and Bolivia. Paraguay wished to vindicate its losses in the war with Brazil, Uruguay and Argentina, which had led to the loss of lands in the Chaco; Bolivia sought to regain access to the sea, which had been lost in the War of the **Pacific** (1879–84). Bolivia eventually ceded 20 000 square miles in Paraguay in 1938. ▷ **Triple Alliance, War of the**

Gran Colombia Literally 'Greater Colombia', this is the name given by historians to the union of Venezuela, New Granada, and

Quito (Ecuador) formed in 1819 by Simón **Bolívar** and known by him as Colombia. The union dissolved in 1830, and the name Colombia was later adopted by New Granada.

Grand Alliance, War of the (1805–7) A phase in the **Napoleonic Wars**. A third coalition of states (Britain, Austria, Russia, Sweden, and Prussia) was formed to attack France by land and sea. Despite Britain's success at the Battle of **Trafalgar** (1805), the coalition was undermined by spectacular French victories at Ulm, **Austerlitz** (1805), and **Jena and Auerstädt** (1806). The Treaties of **Pressburg** (1805) and **Tilsit** (1807) ended hostilities.

Grand Army of the Republic (GAR) US veterans organization. Established in 1866 by ex-Union soldiers, the GAR became an important force in post-**American Civil War** politics.

Grand Council (*Junjichu*) A ruling institution in **Qing Dynasty** China whose origins date from 1726 when the Yongzheng Emperor (1722/35) was preparing for a military expedition against the **Dzungars**. As a compact, secret and informal group of trusted confidants that transcended the formal bureaucracy, the Grand Council greatly facilitated the consolidation of imperial autocracy. Grand Councillors transmitted important imperial edicts directly to provincial officials, while the latter were able to send secret memorials on local affairs to the Grand Council.

Grande Brigantaggio The term commonly used to describe the civil war in the south of Italy after unification. The 'Great Brigandage' was a euphemism, adopted by the military and political authorities of the newly united Kingdom of Italy, to conceal the political and social origins of discontent in the **Mezzogiorno**. There, large sections of the gentry and perhaps the majority of the peasantry showed little liking for the policies of **piemontizzazione** adopted by the government in Turin. The use of martial law and violent repression, legalized by the so-called **Pica Law** of 1863, enabled order to be effectively restored by 1865.

grandfather clause US political manoeuvre. It was a device used by Southern US states between 1895 and 1910 to prevent blacks from voting. It exempted from literacy requirements persons who were eligible to vote on 1 Jan 1867 or their descendants, thus excluding former slaves, who had not been given the right to vote by that date. It was ruled unconstitutional by the Supreme Court in 1915. ▷ **civil rights**

Grandi, Dino, Count (1895–1988) Italian politician. A powerful **ras** who in 1921, disillusioned with **Mussolini**, unsuccessfully offered the leadership of the fascist movement to Gabriele **D'Annunzio**. He was a quadrumvir in the **March on Rome**. Foreign Minister (1929–32) and Ambassador to London (1932–9), he became extremely anglophile and warned Mussolini about the likely hostile reaction of the British to his proposed Conquest of **Ethiopia**. Minister of Justice and President of the 'Chamber of Fasces and Corporations' (1939–43), he grew increasingly worried about the **Duce**'s enslavement to **Hitler**'s policies and moved the motion in the **Fascist Grand Council** (25 July 1943) that full constitutional powers be restored to **Victor Emmanuel III**. In 1944 he was sentenced to death in absentia by the Republic of **Salò**. After liberation, he retired from politics and spent most of the rest of his life in Brazil.

Grand Pensionary (*Raadspensionaris*) The leader of the provincial sovereign assemblies or states in the Dutch Republic. Each province had its own Pensionary, sometimes under another title (eg Secretary, Syndic), whose official job was to provide legal advice to the government. By far the most important was the Pensionary of Holland, who chaired the meetings of the states and executed its decisions, acting as Prime Minister and Foreign Minister. He led the Holland deputation to the States General, and the dominance of the province of Holland in the republic meant that the Holland Grand Pensionary was often effectively the leader of republic: naturally this caused periodic conflict with the holder of the other great Dutch office, the **Stadholder**. Famous pensionaries were J van Oldenbarnevelt, J **Cats**, J de **Witt**, G **Fagel**, A **Heinsius**, and S van **Slingelandt**. The title was also given to R J **Schimmelpenninck** as leader of the **Batavian Republic** in 1805–6.

Grand Remonstrance The statement of **Charles I** of England's abuses, and of reforms made by the **Long Parliament** in 1640–1; passed by 11 votes in the House of Commons (22 Nov 1641), and thereafter published as an appeal for support. The close vote reflected the formation of roughly equal parties of 'royalists' and 'parliamentarians'.

Granger Movement A US organization of farmers, officially known as the **Patrons of Husbandry**, founded in 1867, which adopted a radical stance towards farmers' problems and big business. The name stems from the title *grange* (or farm) adopted by local units. The organization still exists. ▷ **Populist Party**

Grant, Ulysses S(impson) (1822–85) US general and 18th President. After graduating from the US Military Academy at West Point in 1843, he fought in the **Mexican War** (1846–8), and later settled as a farmer in Missouri. On the outbreak of the **American Civil War** (1861), he rejoined the army and by 1862 was promoted to the rank of major general, leading Union forces to victory, first in the Mississippi Valley, then in the final campaigns in Virginia. He accepted Confederate general Robert E **Lee**'s surrender at **Appomattox Court House** (1865), and was made a full general in 1866. President from 1869 to 1877, he presided over the **Reconstruction** of the South, but his administration was marred by scandal.

Granvelle, Antoine Perrenot (1517–86) French-born Spanish prelate and diplomat. The son of the jurist and diplomat, Nicholas Granvelle, in 1540 he was appointed Bishop of Arras and Secretary of State to Emperor **Charles V**. On the latter's abdication in 1535, he transferred his services to **Philip II** of Spain. In 1559 he became Prime Minister to **Margaret of Parma** in the Netherlands, in 1560 Archbishop of Malines, and the following year cardinal. His policy provoked such hostility in the Low Countries, however, that at the King's advice he retired in 1564 to Franche-Comté. In 1570 he represented Spain in Rome at the drawing-up of a treaty of alliance with Venice and the papal see against the Turks. From 1570 to 1575 he was Viceroy of Naples and from 1579 to 1586 was Chief Minister of Spain.

Gratian (c.358–83) Roman Emperor (375/83). Appointed ruler of Gaul when only nine by his father, Emperor **Valentinian I**, Gratian became the virtual ruler of the entire West on his father's death (375), since his Co-Emperor, his half-brother, **Valentinian II**, was only four. Finding himself also Emperor of the East with the death of **Valens** in the Battle of **Adrianople** (378), he appointed the able **Theodosius** to be his Co-Emperor there. A feeble ruler himself,

much under the influence of Christian clerics and court favourites, Gratian lost control of his troops and was overthrown in a putsch led by the Roman army commander in Britain, **Magnus Maximus**.

Grattan, Henry (1746–1820) Irish politician. In 1775 entered the Irish parliament, where his oratory made him the leading spokesman for the patriotic party. He secured Irish free trade in 1779, and legislative independence in 1782. He was returned for Dublin in 1790, and in 1805 was elected to the House of Commons, where he fought for **Catholic Emancipation**.

Gravelotte, Battle of (1870) A critical engagement of the **Franco-Prussian War**. The French Army of the Rhine under Marshal Bazaine, though inflicting heavy casualties on the Germans, failed to break von **Moltke**'s troops, and retreated to nearby Metz; the decision led to **MacMahon**'s attempt to relieve Metz, and the French disaster at **Sedan**.

Graziani, Rodolfo, Marquis of Neghelli (1882–1955) Italian soldier. He served in Libya in 1913 and on the Italian front during **World War I**. In 1930 he became Vice-Governor of Cyrenaica and in 1936 was given command of the Italian forces on the Somalian front during the Conquest of **Abyssinia**. He succeeded **Badoglio** as Viceroy of Ethiopia. In July 1940 he was placed in charge of the Italian forces in North Africa but was replaced (Mar 1941) after a series of defeats. In Sep 1943 he accepted **Mussolini**'s invitation to become Defence Minister of the Republic of **Salò**. He was captured at the end of the war and put on trial for war crimes (Oct 1948). In 1950 he was sentenced to 25 years, but was released the same year. He was active in the **Italian Social Movement** until his death.

Great Depression The worldwide slump in output and prices, and the greatly increased levels of unemployment, which developed between 1929 and 1934. It was precipitated by the collapse of the US stock market (the Wall Street crash) in Oct 1929. This ended US loans to Europe and greatly reduced business confidence worldwide. A major Austrian bank also collapsed, producing destabilization in much of Central and Eastern Europe.

Greater East Asia Co-Prosperity Sphere The term applied to Japan's empire in East and South-East Asia after 1942. It implied the creation of a politically and economically integrated Asia under Japanese leadership and free of Western colonial domination. The concept had originated in 1938 with Japan's proclamation of a New Order in East Asia following her invasion of China in 1937. The New Order was designed to create an autarchic bloc comprising Japan, China and Manchuria that would be free of Anglo-Saxon liberalism and Soviet **communism**. Japan's rapid conquest of South-East Asia in 1942 meant that no detailed preparation had been carried out on the future of the Greater East Asia Co-Prosperity Sphere. Even its geographical boundaries remained vague (with some Japanese leaders including India and/or Australia). Although a Greater East Asia Ministry was created in 1943, it had little centralized control over the separate Japanese military administrations in South-East Asia. Long-term policy was sacrificed to the immediate needs of Japan's war economy, ultimately alienating Asian opinion which had initially welcomed the Japanese as liberators. Despite the granting, or promise, of independence to some South-East Asian countries (Burma, Philippines, Indonesia), the Sphere ended in ignominy with Japan's defeat in 1945.

Great Leap Forward A movement in China, initiated in 1958, which aimed at accelerating both industrial and agricultural progress, 'walking on two legs'. Abandoning Russian models, it planned the creation of 'communes' in a true collective system. It failed miserably.

Great Northern War (1700–21) A war in which Sweden under King **Charles XII** fought against a coalition of its neighbours, who were seeking to deprive it of the territories in the Baltic and northern Germany, which it had won during the previous century. Denmark was forced to withdraw early in the struggle, and the army of **Peter I, 'the Great'** of Russia was defeated by a far smaller Swedish force at Narva in 1700. But Charles failed to pursue his advantage and became involved in an attempt to dethrone Augustus of Saxony, King of Poland, who had also attacked him. After forcing Augustus to renounce the throne, Charles turned once more against Peter, but was defeated by him at the Battle of **Poltava** in the Ukraine (1709). This led to the re-formation of the anti-Swedish coalition, joined also by Brandenburg-Prussia and Hanover. By Charles' death (1718) Sweden had lost most of its Baltic possessions, and a series of treaties in

1720 and 1721 left Russia as the leading Baltic power, with Sweden reduced to one of second rank.

Great Patriotic War (1941–5) The name given by **Stalin** to the war against **Hitler**. His communist ideology had allowed him to make the 1939 **German–Soviet Pact**, but what he faced after 1941 was Hitler's determination to destroy the USSR and its Slav peoples. What he also discovered was that these peoples made incredible efforts to defend their country, not the system that **communism** had impressed on it. He therefore encouraged all forms of patriotic feelings: even the **Patriarchate of Moscow** was reinstated. However, after 1945 it was more or less back to Soviet communism. ▷ **World War II**

Great Schism (1378–1417) The 14c was a period of deep crisis for the papal monarchy. Seven successive popes resided at Avignon between 1309 and 1377. In 1378 the Church divided between supporters of Pope Urban VI in Rome and those of Pope Clement VII in Avignon, and the European monarchies took sides according to their own rivalries. The rival popes hurled anathemas at each other, and the crisis deepened in 1409 when the Council of Pisa, which had met to heal the schism, elected the scandalous **condottiere** Baldassare Cossa as **John XXIII** as a third pope. Only in 1417, with the election of Martin V at the Council of Constance, did the schism come to an end.

Great Society The name given to a legislative programme called for by US President Lyndon B **Johnson** ('LBJ') on 19 Jan 1965, which committed his administration to vigorous action on health insurance, education, housing and urban renewal. The opportunity and mandate for federal initiatives in what had previously been local responsibilities came from the extraordinary 1964 election results, which returned LBJ as President in his own right with a larger percentage of the popular vote (61 per cent) than ever before achieved, together with a two-thirds Democratic majority in both houses of Congress.

Great Trek The movement of parties of Boers (*Voortrekkers*) which made them the masters of large tracts of the interior of southern Africa. Objecting to British suzerainty, they began to leave Cape Colony in 1836 in separate trekking groups. Two parties were wiped out by black African resistance and malaria, when they headed for

Delagoa Bay in Mozambique. Some settled in the Transvaal, where they were threatened by the Ndebele. One party in Natal was massacred by the **Zulu**, an event avenged by the Battle of **Blood River** in 1838. When the British annexed Natal in 1843, the majority of the Boers returned to the interior. The British made several unsuccessful attempts to resolve the divisions in the area, but when the region was reunited it was largely under Boer control. ▷ **Afrikaners; Boer Wars**

Great Wall of China The defensive and symbolic frontier stretching 2 150 miles across northern China from the Yellow Sea to the central Asian desert. Under Qin Shihuangdi, using 300 000 troops, the earliest connected wall was built from 221BC to repel attacks from the Jung and Ti nomads to the north. It was improved during later dynasties, notably during the Han (202BC–AD220), by extension to Yumen in the west and the addition of 25 000 turrets. Considerably later is the conserved stretch of stone-faced wall now seen by visitors at Badeling Pass, north of Beijing, which dates to the **Ming Dynasty** (1368–1644). The wall is about eight metres high and four metres broad, made of earth and stone with a facing of bricks.

Grechko, Andrei Antonovich (1903–76) Soviet marshal and politician. He fought in the cavalry during the **Russian Civil War** and held several cavalry commands in the first half of **World War II**. As Commander-in-Chief in East Germany in 1953 he helped put down the Berlin rising, and he was Commander-in-Chief of the **Warsaw Pact** when the **Berlin Wall** was erected in 1961. He became Minister of Defence in 1967 and a **Politburo** member in 1973. In the debate about East–West détente he was regarded as a hardliner.

Greek Civil War (1944–9) Rooted in the struggle between communist and monarchist partisans for control of Greece, the conflict erupted as the Axis forces retreated at the end of **World War II**. Britain sent troops to back the monarchist forces, while the USSR supported the communists. With US financial aid, the British were able to remain in Greece after 1945, and helped to re-establish the monarchy. The rupture between Yugoslavia and Russia in 1948 also helped to weaken communist resistance and an end to hostilities was declared in Oct 1949.

Greek Colonels (1967–74) The name given to the right-wing military regime established in Greece after the coup led by Colonel

George Papadopoulos, Colonel Nikolaos Makarezos and Brigadier Stylianos Pattakos (21 Apr 1967). Militantly anti-communist, the regime imprisoned its political opponents, frequently on island camps, where torture was widely used. Strikes were forbidden during this period, and there was strict censorship of the arts and media. In 1973, Papadopoulos declared the monarchy abolished and had himself elected President for eight years. He was ousted in a counter-coup (Nov 1973) but the new regime under General Dimitrios Ioannidis was yet more conservative, and no attempt was made to restore constitutional rule. In July 1974 the regime backed an attempt to depose Archbishop **Makarios** in Cyprus and to declare **enosis**; Greece was on the brink of war with Turkey. Another military coup followed, in which Ioannidis was ousted and **Karamanlis** was brought back from exile. Leading members of the 'Colonels' regime were put on trial and imprisoned for life.

Greeks In the 8c–6c BC the Greeks settled throughout the eastern Mediterranean, establishing colonies along the shores of Asia Minor and the adjoining islands. In the southern part of the Balkan Peninsula, a distinctive Greek culture has persisted unbroken since antiquity; the Slav and Avar invaders who arrived in waves in the 6c and later settled in the southern part of the Balkan Peninsula were hellenized and assimilated into the original population. During the Byzantine Age (330–1204), the Greeks again enjoyed a period of political and cultural hegemony in the Balkans and eastern Mediterranean. After the sack of Constantinople (1204), the Balkan Greeks fell prey to the ambitions of the Franks and Venetians and finally to the Turks who occupied Greece from 1460 to 1830. The Greek national revival began in the late 18c, the Greeks drawing inspiration from the French revolutionaries as well as from the philosophers of the Enlightenment. After a long war against the Turks which wrecked much of Greece (1821–8), the Greeks gained formal recognition of their independence from the Ottoman Porte in 1832. Greek society has, however, remained riddled with divisions. The 19c saw continuous arguments over the constitution and form of government. In the 20c the Greeks were at war from 1912 to 1922: first the **Balkan Wars**, then **World War I**, both of which brought substantial territorial gains, and then the disastrous war against the Turks in Anatolia (1919–22) during which c.30 000 Christians were killed in Izmir (Smyrna) in Sep 1922, and over a million Greeks were forced to leave Asia Minor where their ancestors had lived for centuries. The Greeks were again at war continuously between 1940 and 1949; during **World War II**, they organized resistance against the occupying Axis forces but rivalries between resistance groups had played upon existing divisions in Greek society and erupted in a brutal and bloody civil war (1944–9). After a tentative period of democracy, the Greeks were subject to the right-wing dictatorship of the Colonels (1967–74). Only since 1974 have the Greeks enjoyed a period of relative peace and stability. ▷ **Constantinople, Patriarchate of; EAM; EDES; EKKA; ELAS; enosis; EOKA; Epirus; Filiki Etairia; Greek Civil War; Greek War of Independence; Klephts; Lausanne, Treaty of; Megale Idea; Navarino Bay, Battle of; PASOK; Tsintsars; Vlachs**

Greek War of Independence (1821–8) The struggle of the Greeks to gain independence from the **Ottoman Empire**. The revolt against the Ottoman Turks broke out in the Peloponnese and on several islands in 1821. At first the Turks were unable to retake the areas controlled by the rebels but, with the aid of Egyptian forces, in 1825 they invaded the Peloponnese, capturing Missolonghi (1826), and advanced to take Athens. Britain, Russia and eventually France came to the aid of the Greek rebels, destroying the Egyptian fleet at **Navarino Bay** (1827). By the Treaty of **Adrianople** (1829), the allies guaranteed Greek independence. The Ottoman Porte formally recognized Greek independence by the Treaty of Constantinople (1832). ▷ **Ali Pasha**

Greeley, Horace (1811–72) US journalist and politician. The founder of the *New York Tribune*, he was the most influential Republican journalist of his day, combining support for economic development ('Go West, Young Man') with vigorous anti-slavery attitudes. It was in response to his 1862 plea for emancipation, the 'Prayer of Twenty Million', that **Lincoln** emphasized that the aim of the **American Civil War** was to preserve the union, not to destroy slavery. In 1864 he undertook an unofficial and unsuccessful effort at peacemaking. By 1872 he was advocating a general amnesty for ex-Confederates and this won him an unexpected presidential nomination in that year by the splinter Liberal Republican Party and the **Democratic Party**.

greenback A popular term for paper currency in the USA, particularly in the **American Civil War** and **Reconstruction** eras, which saw strong debate about the place of currency in the monetary system. The Greenback Party was a minor party which sought a reflationary paper currency to solve the problems of farmers and working people. It ran presidential candidates in 1876 and (as the Greenback Labor Party) in 1880 and 1884. In 1892 it supported the **Populist Party**.

Green Gang (*Qingbang*) A Chinese underworld organization active in Shanghai during the 1920s, with its headquarters in the French Concession area. Green Gang leaders were often businessmen or had links with financial circles and were involved in prostitution, gambling and opium rackets. The Nationalist leader, **Chiang Kai-shek**, also formed close ties with the Green Gang, and after he gained control of Shanghai (Mar 1927) during the **Northern Expedition**, he used it to attack communist-led labour unions in the city, often with the connivance of foreign concession authorities and the National Revolutionary Army. Ironically, following the brutal suppression of the labour unions, Chiang then turned against the very bourgeoisie who had supported the suppression: Green Gang members launched a campaign of terror against wealthy businessmen, forcing them to buy government bonds and extend loans to Chiang's regime.

Green Mountain Boys The movement of landowners and speculators who created the state of Vermont from territory disputed between New York and New Hampshire. They defied the authority of New York's government and harassed New York settlers. Of many rural insurrections in early America, the Green Mountain Boys was the only one that succeeded. During the **American Revolution**, they redirected their energies and helped capture for the colonists the British fort at Ticonderoga, on Lake Champlain (1775). The cannon taken were important in the successful American siege of occupied Boston. ▷ **Allen, Ethan**

Greens, The (*Die Grünen*) German political party. This coalition of ecologist, pacifist, anti-nuclear and other special interest groups was established as a federal party in 1980 and dominates environmental politics in Germany. It has held seats in various **Land** (state) parliaments and has been represented in the **Bundestag** since 1983 and in the European parliament since 1984. Internally it is divided between *Realos* ('Realists') prepared to work with conventional parties (especially the **SPD**) and *Fundis* ('Fundamentalists') who are not.

Greenville, Treaty of (1795) The treaty concluded between the USA and the Delaware, Shawnee and Miami Confederacy **Native Americans** after the victory of General Anthony Wayne at the Battle of Fallen Timbers (Ohio). The Native Americans ceded their lands east of the Wabash River (which Britain had hoped to use as a buffer zone between the USA and Canada), thus allowing safe white settlement throughout most of Ohio and south-east Indiana and encouraging immigration into the North West Territories.

Grégoire, Henri (1750–1831) French prelate and revolutionary. His *Essai sur la régénération des juifs* (1789) became widely popular. He was sent to the **Estates General** of 1789 as a Deputy of the clergy. He was the first of his order to take the oaths of loyalty to the new constitution, and was elected 'Constitutional Bishop' of Loir-et-Cher. The **Concordat** (1801) forced him to resign his bishopric. He died unreconciled with the Church. Among his works are *Histoire des sectes religieuses* (1814) and *L'Eglise gallicane* (1818). ▷ **French Revolution**

Gregory I, 'the Great', St (c.540–604) Italian Pope (590/604). Appointed Praetor of Rome, he left this office (c.575), distributed his wealth among the poor, and withdrew into a monastery at Rome. It was here that he saw some Anglo-Saxon youths in the slave market, and was seized with a longing to convert their country to Christianity. As Pope, he was a great administrator, reforming all public services and ritual, and systematizing the sacred chants. In his writings the whole dogmatic system of the modern Church is fully developed.

Gregory II, St (669–731) Pope (715). He was by birth a Roman. The authority of the Eastern Emperors had shrunk in the West into little more than a name and the tyrannical measures of the Emperor Leo the Isaurian against image-worship weakened the tie even more. Gregory protested strongly against the imperial policy, the result being a notable aggrandizement of the political authority and influence of the popes in Italy. Under Gregory's auspices, Boniface began his missionary work in Germany.

Gregory VII, St (c.1020–85) Italian Pope (1073/85). He became a cardinal in 1049. As Pope, he worked to change the secularized condition of the Church, which led to conflict with the German Emperor **Henry IV**, who declared Gregory deposed in a diet at Worms (1076), but then yielded to him after excommunication. In 1080 Henry resumed hostilities, appointing an anti-pope (Clement III), and after a siege took possession of Rome (1084). Gregory was freed by Norman troops, but was forced to withdraw to Salerno, where he died. ▷ **anti-pope; pope**

Gregory IX (Ugo or Ugolino) (1155–1241) Pope (1227/41). A powerful advocate of papal supremacy, he was a strong supporter of the **Franciscans** and the Dominicans. After an initial phase of uneasy collaboration with the Emperor **Frederick II** in which the Pope supported the Emperor in his relations with the Lombard cities, while the Emperor supported the Pope against opposition in Rome, a ferocious conflict broke out over Frederick's Constitutions of Melfi which subjected Sicily to his will. Rome itself was under siege when the aged pope died.

Gregory XIII (Ugo Buoncompagni) (1502–85) Italian Pope (1572/85). A professor of law from Bologna, he became one of the theologians at the Council of **Trent**, then in 1565 a cardinal and legate to Spain. He displayed extraordinary zeal for the promotion of education and endowed many of the colleges in Rome. His pontificate is notable for the correction of the calendar and the introduction of the Gregorian Computation in 1582, but his reputation was sullied by his ordering a *Te Deum* for the slaughter of French protestants in the **St Bartholomew's Day Massacre** in 1572.

Gregory XVI (1765–1846) Pope (1831–46). Elected when the **Papal States** were in the midst of liberal revolt, he quickly demonstrated himself to be a reactionary with marked sympathy for the Jesuits. Under pressure from the powers, he and his Secretary of State, Cardinal Tommaso Bernetti, did initiate some reforms on paper, but in practice they often remained a dead letter or simply masked conservative intentions. ▷ **Centurioni**

Grenville, George (1712–70) British politician. He practised as a lawyer and was first MP in 1741, becoming Lord of the Admiralty (1744–7), Lord of the Treasury (1747–54) and Treasurer of the Navy (1754–5 and 1756–62).

He was briefly Secretary of State for the Northern Department (1762–3) and then became Prime Minister (1763–5). During his period in office, Wilkes was arrested for seditious libel under a general warrant for his attack on the King's speech (1763). The closer supervision of revenue collection (1764–5) and **Stamp Act** (1765) began the process of alienating the American colonies from British rule. His lack of tact and maladroit handling of arrangements to cover a possible regency during **George III**'s first serious illness (1765) led to his dismissal by the King and he remained in opposition for the rest of his life. ▷ **Bute, John; Pelham, Henry; Pelham, Thomas Pelham-Holles, 1st Duke of Newcastle**

Grenville, Sir Richard (1542–91) British naval commander. A cousin of Sir Walter **Raleigh**, he fought in Hungary and Ireland (1566–9) and was knighted c.1577. He commanded, in 1585, the seven ships carrying Raleigh's first colony to Virginia. In 1591, as commander of the *Revenge*, he fought alone against a large Spanish fleet off the Azores, dying of wounds on board a Spanish ship.

Grenville, William Wyndham, 1st Baron (1759–1834) British politician. The son of George **Grenville**, he studied at Eton and Oxford and entered parliament in 1782. He became Paymaster-General in 1783, Home Secretary in 1790, and Foreign Secretary in 1791. He resigned with **Pitt, 'the Younger'**, in 1801 on the refusal of **George III** to agree to **Catholic Emancipation**. In 1806–7 he formed the coalition government of 'All the Talents', which abolished the **slave trade**.

Grévy, François Paul Jules (1807–91) French politician. Vice-President of the Constituent Assembly of 1848, he opposed Louis Napoleon (**Napoleon III**), and after the coup d'état retired from politics. In Feb 1871 he was elected President of the National Assembly and in 1879 he became President of the Republic. Re-elected in 1885, he resigned in Dec 1887 after a financial scandal involving his son-in-law.

Grey, Charles Grey, 2nd Earl (1764–1845) British politician. He became a Whig MP in 1786, and was a leading supporter of parliamentary reform in the 1790s. In 1806 he became First Lord of the Admiralty, Foreign Secretary, and Leader of the House of Commons. In 1807 he succeeded his father as the 2nd Earl Grey. In 1830 he formed a government promising peace, retrenchment and reform, and after considerable difficulties secured the passage of the 1832 Reform Bill. In the new parliament he carried the Act for the abolition of slavery in the colonies, but was forced to resign in 1834 following disagreement over the Irish question. ▷ **Reform Acts; Whigs**

Grey, Sir George (1812–98) British colonial governor and Premier of New Zealand. He explored in Western Australia (1837–9), and became successively Governor of South Australia (1841), New Zealand (1845), and Cape Colony (1854). Again Governor of New Zealand (1861–8), he brought the **Maori Wars** to a close. As Premier of New Zealand (1877–9), he had much influence with the **Maoris**, and wrote on Polynesian culture. He returned to Britain in 1894.

Grey, Lady Jane (1537–54) Queen of England for nine days in 1553. She was the eldest daughter of Henry Grey, Marquis of Dorset, and great-granddaughter of **Henry VII**. In 1553 the Duke of Northumberland, foreseeing the death of **Edward VI**, aimed to secure the succession by marrying Jane (against her wish) to his fourth son, Lord Guildford Dudley. Three days after Edward's death (9 July), she was named as his successor, but was forced to abdicate in favour of **Mary I**, who had popular support. She was imprisoned in the Tower of London, and beheaded.

Gribeauval, Jean-Baptiste Vaquette de (1715–89) French military officer. As Inspector-General of artillery from 1776 onwards, he reformed French artillery equipment and operational practice, to make it the most effective in the world for a century. One of his early officer pupils was Napoleon Bonaparte. ▷ **Napoleon I**

Griboyedov, Alexander Sergeevich (1795–1829) Russian writer and diplomat. He wrote *Gore ot Uma* (1822–4; The Mischief of Being Clever), a comedy in rhymed iambics, which satirized the contemporary Moscow society so aptly that it has provided household phrases for the Russian people. Though sympathizing with the Decembrist Revolution, he was cleared, and in 1828 became Russian ambassador to Persia, where he had previously served in a lesser capacity. He was killed in an anti-Russian demonstration at the Embassy in Tehran.

Griffith, Arthur (1872–1922) Irish nationalist politician. He worked as a compositor, then as a miner and journalist in South Africa (1896–8), before editing *The United Irishman* (1899). In 1905 he founded the newspaper, *Sinn Féin*, editing it until 1914, was twice imprisoned (1916–17 and 1920–1), and became an MP (1918–22). He headed the delegation which signed the Anglo-Irish Treaty (Dec 1921) and was President of **Dáil Eireann** (1922). ▷ **Sinn Féin**

Griffith, Samuel Walker (1845–1920) Welsh-born Australian judge. Emigrating to Australia in 1854, he studied at Sydney University. From 1867 he practised law in Queensland, entered the state legislature in 1872 and was state Premier (1883–8 and 1890–3). He was an active proponent of **federation** and as chairman of the Constitutional Committee of the National Australasian Convention in 1891 had a major role in drafting what became, in amended form, in 1900 the Australian Commonwealth Constitution. Chief Justice of Queensland from 1893, he was first Chief Justice of the High Court of Australia (1900–19).

Grimaldi A noble Genoese house; from 1419, lords of the Principality of Monaco.

Grimké, Sarah Moore (1792–1873) and **Angelina Emily** (1805–79) US abolitionists and feminists. Born into a major slaveholding family, the sisters rejected their family's way of life and joined the Quakers, who were officially anti-slavery. They moved to Philadelphia and lived quietly until, in 1836, Angelina published a letter in the anti-slavery newspaper, *The Liberator*. They became public figures, and Angelina undertook an unprecedented speaking tour. She resisted efforts to silence her, but gave up public life after her marriage to the abolitionist, Theodore Weld (1803–95). Sarah lived with the couple thereafter, and the two remained committed to social change. ▷ **abolitionism**

Griqua People of mixed race who spoke Dutch and established stock-raising, hunting, and trading communities under patriarchal leadership on the frontier of Cape Colony in the late 18c and early 19c. Their peoples are now integrated into the **Cape Coloured** community.

Grishin, Viktor Vasilevich (1914–92) Soviet politician. He was a supporter of Leonid **Brezhnev**, whom he expected to succeed. A genuine railwayman, he only took up party work during **World War II**. From 1956 to 1967 he was head of the Soviet trade

unions and managed to keep them firmly in line. In 1967 he became First Secretary of the Moscow party and succeeded in making it toe the line for 18 years. In 1985 Mikhail **Gorbachev** replaced him almost immediately and put Boris **Yeltsin** in his place, an obvious sign of reform.

Grivas, Georgeios (Theodoros) (1898–1974) Greek-Cypriot nationalist leader. He commanded a Greek army division in the Albanian campaign of 1940–1, and led a secret ultra right-wing organization called 'X' (Khi) during the German occupation of Greece. An ardent nationalist, in 1955 he became head of the underground campaign against British rule in Cyprus; as founder and leader of **EOKA**, he began to call himself 'Digenis Akritas' after a legendary Greek hero. In 1959, after the Cyprus settlement, he left Cyprus and was promoted general in the Greek army. In 1971 he returned secretly to Cyprus and, as leader of EOKA-B, directed a terrorist campaign for **enosis** (union with Greece) until his death, at Limassol. He was accorded a hero's funeral.

Groener, Wilhelm (1867–1939) German military commander and politician. A prominent member of the German General Staff during **World War I**, General Groener led army negotiations with the Social Democratic government in Nov 1918 to guarantee the old army's survival in the republic. Successful in this, he later held various ministerial posts in Weimar governments, serving as Army Minister and as Interior Minister under **Brüning**. His failure to sustain a ban on the SA of the **Nazi Party** coupled with the fall of Brüning's government ended his political career in May 1932. ▷ **Weimar Republic**

Groen van Prinsterer, Guillaume (1801–76) Dutch historian and politician. After studying law and classics at Leiden University, he became Secretary to the King's cabinet and archivist to the Dutch royal family. Having converted to orthodox Calvinism c.1828, he advocated a Christian approach to political affairs, rejecting both reactionary conservatism and secular liberalism. In 1847 he published a seminal critique of the **French Revolution**, *Ongeloof en Revolutie* (Unbelief and Revolution), which became the classic statement of a renascent Calvinist political movement in the Netherlands. This gave rise to the **Anti-Revolutionary Party**, in defence of constitutional monarchy and parliamentary rights, which later joined with the Christian Historical

Union to form the Dutch **Christian Democratic Appeal** (CDA). He was a member of the Second Chamber of parliament (1849–57 and 1862–6). His spiritual and political heir was Abraham **Kuyper**.

Gromyko, Andrei Andreevich (1909–89) Soviet politician and diplomat. He studied agriculture and economics, and became a research economist at the Soviet Academy of Sciences. In 1939 he joined the staff of the Russian Embassy in Washington, becoming Ambassador in 1943; after **World War II** he was permanent delegate to the **UN** Security Council (1946–8) and then Deputy Foreign Minister for most of the period 1949–57. As longest-serving Foreign Minister (1957–85), he was responsible for conducting Soviet relations with the West during the **Cold War**, presenting an austere and humourless public demeanour for which he became notorious in diplomatic circles. Mikhail **Gorbachev** promoted him to the largely honorific and mainly domestic post of President in 1985, but he retired from office following the 19th Party Conference in 1988, when he was replaced in a much stronger presidency by Gorbachev himself.

Gronchi, Giovanni (1888–1978) Italian politician and President. One of the founders of the **Popolari**, he entered **Mussolini**'s first government as Under-Secretary of State for Industry and Commerce, but in 1923 he moved into the opposition and led his party in the **Aventine Secession**. He took part in the resistance and was elected to the post-war Constituent Assembly as a Christian Democrat. He was President of Italy from 1955 to 1962. ▷ **Christian Democrat Party**

Grósz, Károly (1930–) Hungarian politician. The son of a steel worker, he began his career in 1946 as a printer and rose to be a newspaper editor in 1958–61. Having joined the ruling Hungarian Socialist Workers' Party in 1945, he moved to Budapest in 1961 to work in the agitprop department, becoming its deputy head in 1968 and its head in 1974. Grósz served as Budapest Party chief (1984–7) and was inducted into the Politburo in 1985. He became Prime Minister in 1987 and succeeded János **Kádár** as Party leader in 1988, giving up his position as Prime Minister six months later. He moved pragmatically with the times and, following the lead given by Mikhail **Gorbachev** in Moscow, became an apparently committed and frank-speaking reformer in both the economic and political spheres, seeking to establish in Hungary a new system of 'socialist pluralism'. However, when, in Oct 1989, the Party reconstituted itself as the new Hungarian Socialist Party, he was replaced as leader by Rezsö Nyers, a more radical ex-Communist.

Grotius, Hugo (Huig de Groot) (1583–1645) Dutch jurist, politician, diplomat, poet and theologian. He studied at Leiden, practised in The Hague, and in 1613 was appointed Pensionary of Rotterdam. He was a politial champion of the **Remonstrants**, and in 1618 religious and political conflicts led to his imprisonment. In 1621 he escaped in a trunk from Loevestein Castle to Paris, where **Louis XIII** for a time gave him a pension. In 1625 he published his great work on international law, *De Jura Belli et Pacis* (On the Law of War and Peace). He also led diplomatic missions for Sweden, where he died. He is honoured as one of the founders of international law.

Grouchy, Emmanuel, Marquis of (1766–1847) French Napoleonic soldier. He greatly distinguished himself in Italy (1798), and fought at Hohenlinden, Eylau, **Friedland** (1807), **Wagram**, and in the Russian campaign of 1812. On **Napoleon I**'s escape from Elba, he destroyed the Bourbon opposition in the south of France, and helped to rout **Blücher** at Ligny, but failed to play an effective part at the Battle of **Waterloo** due to misleading orders (1815). He retired to the USA, returning in 1819, and was reinstated as marshal in 1831.

Groulx, Abbé Lionel (1878–1967) French-Canadian nationalist historian and novelist. In reaction to the more moderate interpretations of the early 20c, he depicted French-Canadian history as an unremitting struggle against English domination, and in such works as *Notre maître le passé* (1944) he celebrated the clerical and agrarian elements of that past, although he never explicitly advocated separatism.

Groza, Petru (1884–1958) Romanian politician. During the 1930s he led the Ploughmen's Front which drew its support from the Transylvanian peasantry. When Romania entered **World War II** in 1944, he joined the communist front organization, the National Democratic Front (FND). In Nov 1944 together with his fellow 'home Communist' **Gheorgiu-Dej** he represented the FND in the government of Sănătescu. In Feb 1945 **Stalin** approved his appointment as presiding minister in the FND government, a post he held until 1952 when he became President of the Presidium of the Romanian Communist Party.

Grundherrschaft A system of landlordship which developed in medieval Germany. It necessarily included public authority and aristocratic rule as opposed to simple estate ownership (*Gutsherrschaft*). At the centre of the system was the lord's hall or court (*Hof*), from which the lord exercised his economic and political powers in his estates.

Grundtvig, Nicolaj Frederik Severin (1783–1872) Danish theologian, historian, poet and educator. He dedicated his life to the spiritual regeneration of Denmark during the years following the **Napoleonic Wars**. Strongly influenced by his visits to England in 1829–31, Grundtvig worked for political and religious freedom, but above all for the enlightenment of the common people. He was the inspiration behind the folk high school movement, begun in 1844, which provided adults with education in both practical subjects and the humanities, and which contributed to the transformation of rural life in Denmark in the aftermath of the **German–Danish War** of 1864.

Grunwald (Tannenberg), Battle of (1410) A crushing defeat inflicted on the Teutonic Order under Grand Master Ulrich von Jungingen by King Ladislav of Poland and his cousin, Witold of Lithuania. The Grand Master of the Order, all but one of its commanders and 205 of its knights died in the battle and the conquest of the Order's lands was only prevented by Henry of Plauen's vigorous defence of them. The battle marked the end of the Order's military dominance in north-east Europe and the decline of its political and financial authority quickly followed. ▷ **Hermann of Salza; Teutonic Knights; Winrich of Kniprode**

Gruppi d'Azione Patriottica Anti-German and anti-fascist urban guerrillas during **World War II**. Usually attached to the communists, the so-called *Gappisti* were especially active in the closing stages of the war, where their daring and ruthless actions often elicited brutal German reprisals.

Guadalcanal, Battle of (1942) A battle in the South Pacific in **World War II**. Following the attacks on **Pearl Harbor** and Singapore (7–8 Dec 1941), Japan advanced into the South Pacific, reaching Guadalcanal in the Solomon Islands in May 1942. US forces

reinvaded and after six months of bitter fighting, in one of the crucial actions of the war, they halted the Japanese advance.

Guadalupe, Sentence of (1486) The judgement decreed by **Ferdinand II, 'the Catholic'** as arbiter in the long-running dispute between the Catalan *remensa* ('redemption') peasants and their lords. The remensa peasants in Catalonia were so called because of the custom obliging them to buy their freedom if they wished to move from their lord's land; their position was one of serfdom. By his judgement, Ferdinand abolished this custom, confirmed their right to liberty, and ended other feudal customs known as the *malos usos* ('evil usages'), in exchange for a payment to be made to the lords. The sentence brought freedom to the Catalan peasantry but did not improve their condition.

Guadalupe Hidalgo, Treaty of (2 Feb 1848) The agreement that settled the **Mexican War**, with Mexico yielding all of Texas, Arizona, Nevada, California and Utah, and parts of New Mexico, Colorado and Wyoming. The USA paid US$15 000 000, and assumed US$3 250 000 worth of Mexican debts.

Guandong (Kwantung) Army The Japanese military force that protected the leasehold territory on the Liaodong Peninsula (southern Manchuria) and the South Manchuria Railway, acquired by Japan in 1905 as a result of the **Russo-Japanese War**. During the 1920s, at a time when China was in turmoil, the Guandong Army began to act independently of the civilian government in Tokyo in pursuit of Japanese interests in the region, a situation helped by the fact that the Army's commander reported directly to the General Staff rather than to the Prime Minister. In 1931 the Guandong Army exploited a sabotage incident on the South Manchuria railway to justify a full-scale offensive in Manchuria, and by 1932 had created the puppet state of **Manzhuguo**. The Guandong Army henceforth exercised dominant political control in Manchuria, calling for a mobilization of all resources to counter the USSR, which it perceived as Japan's main threat. Tokyo's decision in 1941 to advance towards South-East Asia, however, precluded any decision to go to war with the USSR. Six days after the USSR itself declared war on Japan (9 Aug 1945), the Guandong Army had to surrender to Soviet forces. Thousands were sent to labour camps in the USSR, and the survivors were not repatriated until the mid-1950s.

Guangxu **(Kuang-hsu)** (1871–1908) Emperor (1875/1908) of the Manchu **Qing Dynasty**. The nephew of the Empress-Dowager **Cixi**, he ascended the throne as a minor in 1875. Cixi acted as regent until his majority in 1889 but continued to exercise influence thereafter. In 1898 Guangxu seized the opportunity to assert himself by supporting a programme of reform (the One **Hundred Days of Reform**). Hoping to emulate the Meiji Emperor of Japan, Guangxu issued edicts calling for the abolition of all sinecures, the creation of modern schools, and the establishment of an advisory council to discuss institutional change. Cixi, with the support of conservatives at court, terminated the reforms and placed the hapless Guangxu under virtual house arrest for the duration of his reign.

Guan Yu **(Kuan Yu)** (d.219) Chinese general of the Three Kingdoms Period. He was noted for his military exploits and unswerving loyalty to Liu Bei (Liu Pei) (d.223), ruler of the Shu Han (based in western China), one of the three successor dynasties following the break-up of the Han Empire. Guan Yu's daring exploits to foil the hegemonic ambitions of **Cao Cao**, the military strongman in north China, served as an inspiration for later fiction and drama. He was also canonized as the God of War.

Guan Zhong **(Kuan Chung)** (d.645BC) Chinese thinker. Traditionally regarded as one of the founders of **Legalism**, a school of thought in China that sought to strengthen the state (although his authorship of the *Guanzi*, a collection of disparate writings on administration, is now doubted). As Chief Minister to Duke Huan of Qi, one of a number of states that emerged during the Spring and Autumn period (722/481BC), Guan Zhong stressed the virtues of administrative efficiency, a sound economy, and a strong military. During the 7c BC Qi became the dominant Chinese state, exercising leadership over its neighbours.

Guchkov, Alexander I (1862–1936) Russian politician. From a business family he believed in gradual constitutional change and helped to found the Octobrist Party, which based itself on the representation promised in **Nicholas II**'s 1905 **October Manifesto**. But he became disillusioned with a powerless **Duma** and eventually with Nicholas, who would not prosecute the 1914 war seriously. In 1917, although he regretted the passing of the **Romanov Dynasty** with Nicholas's abdication, he became Minister of War in the **Russian Provisional Government** in the hope of promoting moderate change. But his advocacy of continuing the war and his opposition to far-reaching land-reform undermined his position and he was forced out of office in May, even before the main assault by the **Bolsheviks** in Oct 1917.

Guderian, Heinz (Wilhelm) (1888–1953) German general and creator of the German Panzer (armoured) forces. He was a career soldier from his first commission in 1908. After serving in **World War I**, he stayed in the small army allowed to Germany by the Treaty of **Versailles**, and was an ardent pioneer of mechanized warfare. Created general of Panzer troops in 1938, he advocated the idea of fast-moving 'Blitzkrieg' warfare which he later put into brilliant effect, commanding forces in France and the USSR. He had a stormy relationship with **Hitler**, being dismissed and reinstated several times. ▷ **World War II**

Guelfs The pro-papal, anti-imperial party in Italian cities in the 13–14c, opposed to the power of the Holy Roman Emperors, and successful in resisting the authority of the **Hohenstaufen Dynasty**, whose power was eclipsed after 1266. Allied with the papacy, the Guelfs resisted the claims of potential successors, and dominated Florentine politics. ▷ **Ghibellines; Holy Roman Empire; Welfs**

Guernica Historic Basque town. As a traditional meeting place for the **Basques**, Guernica is a symbol of Basque sovereignty. After the Autonomy Statute was approved in Oct 1936, the Basques' first President (or *Lendakari*) was chosen in Guernica. On 26 Apr 1937, a market day, the town was decimated by the German Condor Legion (*Luftwaffe*) on the orders of the Spanish High Command. Guernica's destruction became synonymous with the atrocities committed by the Nationalists and their fascist allies during the **Spanish Civil War**. The bombing was immortalized in Picasso's painting, 'Guernica'.

Guerra, Alfonso (1940–) Spanish politician. A close friend of Felipe **González** from the early 1960s, Guerra was largely responsible for the transformation of the **PSOE** in the 1970s into a major political organization. He has complemented the charismatic appeal of González well through his outstanding administrative abilities, though his control of the party machine has been heavily personalized and intolerant of dissent. A deputy in every election since 1977, he was Deputy Prime Minister from 1982 until his major split with González in 1991. A ruthless, sarcastic and demagogic politician, who specializes in inflammatory attacks on opponents, he has made many enemies both inside and outside the Socialist Party.

Guesclin, Bertrand du (c.1320–80) French knight. A military leader during the **Hundred Years War**, he entered royal service on the eve of **Charles V**'s accession. After becoming Constable of France in 1370, he assumed command of the French armies, reconquering Brittany and most of south-western France. He died while besieging Châteauneuf-de-Randon in the Auvergne.

Guesde, Jules (Bazile) (1845–1922) French politician. A supporter of the **Paris Commune**, he was sentenced in absentia, and fled abroad, where he was converted to Marxism. On his return to France (1876) he was a leading figure in the first attempts to create a workers' movement. In 1882 he founded his own party, the POF (*Parti ouvrier français*, 'French Workers' Party'), which he led until it was incorporated in the United Socialist Party (SFIO) in 1905. The united party accepted Guesde's rigid Marxism in theory, but in practice **Jaurès**'s parliamentary tactics had greater influence. Guesde was a Deputy (1893–8 and 1906–22), and accepted office during **World War I**. He did not join the **Communist Party** in 1920. ▷ **Socialist Party**

Guevara, Che (Ernesto Guevara (de la Serna)) (1928–67) Argentine revolutionary leader. He trained as a doctor (1953), and played an important part in the Cuban revolution (1956–9), after which he held government posts under Fidel **Castro**. He left Cuba in 1965 to become a guerrilla leader in South America, and was captured and executed in Bolivia. His career was important as an inspiration to a variety of left-wing groups throughout the continent, and his failure to stimulate peasant revolt in Bolivia indicated that the Cuban experience of revolution could not be repeated elsewhere.

Guicciardini, Francesco (1483–1540) Italian historian and diplomat. He was Professor of Law at Florence and also practised as an advocate. As a diplomat he served as Florentine ambassador to the court of **Ferdinand II 'the Catholic'** of Aragon (1512–14), then travelled widely in papal service, acting as Governor of Modena (1516) and Reggio (1517) before retiring in 1534. He secured the election of Cosimo I de' **Medici** as Duke of Florence, then withdrew to Arcetri, where he produced the phenomenal contemporary history, *Storia d'Italia* (History of Italy), an account of events in Italy in the period 1494–1534.

Guillaume de la Mark ('Wild Boar of the Ardennes') (d.1485) Liège politician. He opposed those Prince-Bishops of Liège supported by the House of **Burgundy** in its attempts to unite the Low Countries; in this he was aided by the French King **Louis XI**. In 1483 he ruled Liège as regent, and had his son elected bishop, but was defeated by the forces of neighbouring **Brabant** at the Battle of Hollogne in 1483; in the same year the Pope appointed Jean de Hornes as bishop instead. Hostilities were ended, but Jean de Hornes's brother, the Count of Montigny, captured Guillaume and took him to Maastricht, where he was condemned and beheaded.

Guillotin, Joseph Ignace (1738–1814) French physician and revolutionary. He proposed that the Constituent Assembly, of which he was a Deputy, should use a decapitating instrument as a means of execution. This was adopted in 1791 and named after him, though a similar apparatus had been used earlier in Scotland, Germany, and Italy.

Guiscard, Robert (c.1015–85) Norman adventurer. The son of Tancred de Hauteville, he campaigned with his brothers against the Byzantine Greeks, and created a duchy comprising southern Italy and Sicily. In 1059 the papacy recognized him as Duke of Apulia, Calabria, and Sicily. He ousted the Byzantines from Calabria by 1060, then conquered Bari (1071) and captured Salerno (1076). In 1081 he crossed the Adriatic, seized Corfu, and defeated the Byzantine Emperor, Alexius Comnenus, at Durazzo. He died while advancing on Constantinople. ▷ **Normans**

Guise, House of The French ducal house of Lorraine, named after the town of Guise. Members of the house were prominent as staunch leaders of the Catholic Party during the 16c civil wars, through their relationship with the royal houses of **Stuart** and Valois. The first duke was Claude of Lorraine, 1st

Duke of Guise (1496–1550), who served under **Francis I** of France in Italy and was given the ducal title in 1528. Henry, 3rd Duke of Guise, instigated the murder of **Coligny** in the **St Bartholomew's Day Massacre** (1572). On the death of the seventh duke, Francis Joseph (1675), the estates reverted to Mary of Lorraine, on whose death the line became extinct. ▷ **Religion, Wars of; Valois Dynasty**

Guise, Charles of (1525–74) French prelate and Archbishop of Reims, created Cardinal of Guise in 1547. He was the son of Claude of Lorraine, 1st Duke of **Guise** and brother of Mary of Lorraine Guise and Francis, 2nd Duke of **Guise**, with whom he became all-powerful in the reign of **Francis II** (of France). He introduced the **Inquisition** into France and exerted a great influence at the Council of Trent. ▷ **Guise, House of**

Guise, Claude of Lorraine, 1st Duke of (1496–1550) French nobleman and soldier. He fought under **Francis I** (of France) at Marignano in Italy in 1515, defeated the Imperial army at Neufchâteau. He was Regent during the captivity of Francis by **Charles V** (1525–7). For suppressing the peasant revolt in Lorraine (1527), Francis I created him Duke of Guise. He was the father of Mary of Lorraine Guise, who married **James V** of Scotland and became mother of **Mary, Queen of Scots**. ▷ **Guise, House of**

Guise, Francis, 2nd Duke of, 'the Scarred' (1519–63) French soldier and politician, son of Claude of Lorraine, 1st Duke of **Guise**. In 1556 he commanded the expedition against Naples, and took Calais (1558), bringing about the Treaty of Château Cambrésis (1559). He and his brother, Cardinal Charles of **Guise**, shared the chief power in the state during the reign of **Francis II** (of France). Heading the Roman Catholic Party, they sternly repressed Protestantism. Guise and **Montmorency** won a victory over the **Huguenots** at Dreux (1562), and Guise was besieging Orléans when he was assassinated by a Huguenot. ▷ **Guise, House of**

Guise, Henry, 3rd Duke of (1550–88) French soldier and politician, also known as 'the Scarred', son of Francis, 2nd Duke of Guise. He was one of the contrivers of the **St Bartholomew's Day Massacre** (1572), and was the head of the **Holy League** against the Bourbons (1576). ▷ **Bourbon, House of; Guise, House of**

Guise, Henry, 5th Duke of (1614–64) French prelate and soldier, grand-nephew of Henry, 3rd Duke of **Guise**. Having opposed **Richelieu**, he was condemned to death, but fled to Flanders. He put himself at the head of **Masaniello**'s revolt in Naples, but was taken by the Spanish (1647) and carried to Madrid. After another attempt to win Naples (1654) he settled in Paris. He published his *Mémoires* in 1669. ▷ **Guise, House of**

Guizot, François (Pierre Guillaume) (1787–1874) French historian and politician. He studied law in Paris, but in 1812 he became Professor of Modern History at the Sorbonne. A member of the *Doctrinaires* (a group of moderate constitutional liberals who elevated their policy of the *juste milieu*, or 'middle road', to a complete political philosophy), he was elected to the Chamber (1830), became Minister of the Interior (1830), and then of Public Instruction (1832). As **Louis-Philippe**'s chief adviser (1840), he relapsed into reactionary methods of government, and was forced to escape with him to London in 1848. After 1851 he gave himself up entirely to his historical publications.

Gulag The acronym of *Glavnoye Upravleniye Ispravitelno-Trudovykh Lagerey* ('Main Administration of Corrective Labour Camps'). From 1930 this was the Soviet secret police department that administered the system of forced labour camps for those found guilty of what were known as crimes against the state (and which were very broadly defined). Many Soviet dissidents were 'punished' in this way and many innocent victims died. The system was exposed by Alexander Solzhenitsyn in his *Gulag Archipelago*, which was finally published in 1973.

Gulf Co-Operation Council (GCC) An organization which provides for co-operation between the states surrounding the Persian Gulf. It was established in 1981 by Bahrain, Kuwait, Oman, Qatar, Saudi Arabia, and the United Arab Emirates.

Gulf of Tonkin Resolution (1964) The US constitutional authorization to escalate the **Vietnam War**, passed at the request of President Lyndon **Johnson** by an overwhelming majority in Congress, after two US destroyers had reportedly been attacked by North Vietnamese torpedo boats. Its repeal in 1970, the result of mounting opposition to the war and doubts as to the wisdom of giving such discretion to the President, was unopposed by President Richard **Nixon**, who believed that he had the necessary authority to achieve US aims in the war by virtue of his powers as Commander-in-Chief.

Gulf War (1980–8) ▷ **Iran–Iraq War**

Gulf War (16 Jan–27 Feb 1991) A war which followed the invasion of Kuwait by Iraq in Aug 1990. A rapid air and land campaign, codenamed 'Desert Storm', was mounted by a US-led international coalition based in Saudi Arabia on the authority of George **Bush** after Iraq failed to withdraw from Kuwait by the **UN** deadline. The Bush administration gained its highest popular approval ratings during the crisis, largely due to the president's impassioned attacks on the Iraqi leader, Saddam Hussein. Iraqi forces were expelled from Kuwait and a large part of Iraq's military resources was destroyed. US casualties were set at 79 killed, 213 wounded, 45 missing and 9 captured. Casualty figures for Iraq are unavailable, although they have been estimated at 35000 killed, 175000 captured.

Gulistan, Treaty of (Oct 1813) The peace treaty between Russia and Persia signed at Gulistan in the Caucasus. The actual date of the signing of the treaty is the subject of some dispute, but is given somewhere between 12 Oct and 24 Oct 1813. In any event, the treaty, achieved through the mediation of Britain as represented by Sir Gore Ouseley, resulted in the cession of several formerly Persian regions to Russia, in the recognition of Russia's sole rights to navigation in the Caspian Sea, and in the granting to Russia of the right to intervention in the support of nominated heirs to the throne of the Qajars. The treaty, which was the result of Persia's having to sue for peace after defeats at the hands of the Russians in 1812, presaged increased Russian (and British) intervention in Persia later in the 19c.

Gundibald ▷ **Gundobad**

Gundicarius, Gunther or **Gunnar** (c.385–437) First recorded King of the Burgundians. He was an ally of the Romans, but was killed when his army was annihilated by the Huns. In later Germanic and Norse heroic legend he was cast as the brother-in-law of **Attila** the Hun, who had not, in fact, taken part in the war against the Burgundians.

Gundobad (c.474–516) Barbarian general at the close of the Roman Empire and King of

the **Burgundians**. He was briefly supreme military commander under the Romans. After becoming joint ruler of **Burgundy** (with his brothers), he murdered his brother Chilperic and fought off Frankish attacks instigated by his niece, Clotilda, wife of the Frankish King **Clovis I**, and by another brother, Godesigel, whom he also murdered. He is known for the law code which bears his name, the Lex Gundobada. ▷ **Franks**

Gunpowder Plot A conspiracy by Catholic gentry, led by Robert Catesby, to blow up the English parliament. It failed when Guy **Fawkes**, who placed the explosives, was arrested (5 Nov 1605). The plot failed because one conspirator, Francis Tresham, warned his brother-in-law, Lord Monteagle, not to attend; and Monteagle reported the matter to the government. The scheme reflected Catholic desperation after the failure of previous plots to remove **James VI and I** in 1603; peace with Spain in 1604, which ended the prospect of foreign support; and new sanctions against recusant Catholics, resulting in 5000 convictions in the spring of 1605.

Guomindang (Kuomintang, KMT) The Chinese Nationalist Party, founded by **Sun Yat-sen** in 1919 and later led by **Chiang Kai-shek**. It ruled China from Nanjing (Nanking) 1927–37 and 1945–9, and from Chonqing during the war with Japan (1937–45). It retreated to Taiwan in 1949.

Guo Songdao (Kuo Sung-tao) (1818–91) Chinese official and diplomat. He took an active part in the resistance against the **Taiping Rebellion** and was an enthusiastic advocate of the use of a steamship fleet on the Yangzi River. In 1863 he was Provincial Governor of Guangdong and in 1875 a provincial judicial commissioner in Fujian. In 1876 Guo was appointed Minister to England, becoming China's first diplomatic representative abroad. In 1878 he was also appointed Minister to France. His positive appraisal of Western political institutions and his promotion of railways and telegraphs incurred the wrath of conservatives back home and he was recalled at the end of 1878. Thereafter, he withdrew from official life.

Gupta Empire (320–540) A decentralized state system covering most of northern India, with provinces (*desa*) and districts (*pradesa*). It was materially prosperous, especially in urban areas, and is known as India's 'Classical' or 'Golden' Age, when norms of

Indian literature, art, architecture, and philosophy were established, and Hinduism underwent revival.

Gurkhas An elite infantry unit of the British army recruited from the hill tribes of Nepal. Their characteristic weapon, the Kukri fighting knife with its curved blade, has contributed to their fame, in battles from the North West Frontier of India in the 19c, via the Western Front in **World War I**, to the Burma and Italian campaigns of **World War II**. Gurkha infantry also took part in the **Falklands War** of 1982.

Gursel, Cemal (1895–1966) Turkish general. He emerged as leader of the rebel grouping, the 1960 revolution, against the Menderes government, ending the period of control by the Democratic Party by arresting Menderes himself (who was later executed) and other members of his cabinet. Gursel and a group of officers formed a National Unity Committee and assumed control of the country. A new constitution was drawn up by a national constituent assembly and this was ratifed by popular vote in 1961. Gursel was President of the Turkish Republic from 1961 until his death.

Gush Emmunim An Israeli pressure group set up after the 1973 elections, dedicated to an active settlement policy in territories such as the West Bank, occupied by the Israelis after the 1967 war. The name is Hebrew, meaning 'Bloc of the faithful'. ▷ **Arab-Israeli Wars**

Gustav I Vasa (1496–1560) King of Sweden (1523/60). The founder of the **Vasa Dynasty**, he was born into a gentry family at Lindholmen in Uppland. In 1518 he was taken to Denmark as a hostage, on the orders of King **Christian II**, but managed to escape. After the death of his father in the **Stockholm Bloodbath**, he led an uprising against Christian. He captured Stockholm in 1523 and was elected King by the Diet, effectively ending the **Kalmar Union**. Despite several rebellions against him, Gustav strengthened monarchical power, and his long reign was a peaceful one.

Gustav II Adolf (1594–1632) King of Sweden (1611/32). He was the son of **Charles IX** of Sweden. After ascending the throne, he brought to an end the wars which he had inherited, with Denmark (1613) and Russia (1617), and set out to drive Poland from the eastern Baltic. Having carried the war to Poland itself (1626), he concluded in 1629 the six-year Truce of Altmark with that power, in order to have his hands free to enter the **Thirty Years War** in Germany in 1630. After establishing a bridgehead in Pomerania and winning a decisive victory over the opposing Catholic forces at Breitenfeld in Saxony (1631), he began a triumphal march through central and southern Germany, which carried him almost to the gates of Vienna. He was, however, drawn back to Saxony by the Imperial commander, **Wallenstein**, and was killed during the Swedish victory at **Lützen**. Working closely with his Chancellor, Axel **Oxenstierna**, Gustav reformed Sweden's central and local administration, and made Stockholm the administrative capital for the first time. He was himself a brilliant military commander and made the Swedish army one of the most formidable in Europe.

Gustav III (1746–92) King of Sweden (1771/92). He was the son and successor of King **Adolf Frederick** and **Lovisa Ulrika**. Reared by his mother in the spirit of the Enlightenment, he was at home with the most celebrated thinkers and artists of his day. On ascending the throne, he set about ending the party squabbles and noble oligarchy of the **Age of Liberty**, and in 1772 arrested the Council in a coup d'état and introduced a new constitution which restored a degree of royal power. He then set about a series of reforms which purged the bureaucracy, improved the state's finances, reformed the penal code and introduced a measure of religious toleration. His court became a northern Versailles, with the foundation of the Royal Opera House (1782), the Swedish Academy (1786) on the French model, and the Royal Dramatic Theatre (1788). But his reforming zeal ran out of steam after 1780, and his increasingly autocratic style of government alienated many nobles. When, in 1788, he launched an attack on Russia from Finland, he found himself faced with a mutiny of noble officers. This, however, brought an anti-noble reaction and enabled him to assume well-nigh absolute powers. Peace was made with Russia in 1790, and Gustav became involved with plans for the restoration of royal power in France, whose culture he much admired. He encouraged Count Hans Axel von **Fersen** to attempt the rescue of the French royal family in the abortive 'Flight to Varennes' (June 1792) and planned to land a Russo-Swedish army in Normandy for a march on Paris. But in Mar 1792 he was shot by a former army officer, Johan Jakob **Anckarström** during a masked ball in the Royal

Opera House, dying a lingering death. Married to Sofia Magdalena of Denmark, he was succeeded by his young son, **Gustav IV Adolf**.

Gustav IV Adolf (1778–1837) King of Sweden (1792/1809). He was the son and successor of **Gustav III**. During his minority, the regent was his uncle Karl, Duke of Södermanland. In the first years of his reign as an absolute monarch, he did much to improve Swedish agriculture with a General Enclosure Act (1803). But his aversion to **Napoleon I** induced him to abandon Swedish neutrality and declare war on France in 1805. When Russia changed sides as a result of the Treaty of **Tilsit** (1807) and became an ally of Napoleon, the Swedes were driven from Pomerania, their last German possession. In 1808 Sweden was attacked by France's ally, Denmark, and Finland was invaded by the Russia of **Alexander I**. Tactless and autocratic by nature, Gustav spurned an offer of help from a British force under Sir John Moore which was anchored off Gothenburg, and Finland was occupied by Russia in 1809. He was arrested by noble bureaucrats in Stockholm before he could escape to the south, and was forced to abdicate. He was exiled with his wife, Queen Frederika of Baden, and their children. After divorcing his wife (1812), he spent 25 years wandering in Europe before his death in St Gallen in Switzerland, as 'Colonel Gustafsson'. He was succeeded on the throne by his uncle as King **Charles XIII** under a new constitution which limited the power of the monarch.

Gustav V (1858–1950) King of Sweden (1907/50). The son and successor of **Oscar II**, he was the longest-reigning king in Swedish history. Shy and reserved by nature, he disliked pomp and spectacle and refused a coronation ceremony, thus becoming the first 'uncrowned king' on the Swedish throne. Nevertheless, he sought to assert the personal power of the monarchy and, in 1914, in his famous 'Courtyard Speech' to a farmers' rally, challenged the Liberal government with a call for greater spending on defence. The government resigned in protest, but demands for his abdication were stilled by the outbreak of **World War I**, when Sweden mobilized but remained neutral. Thereafter he reigned as a popular constitutional monarch, and in **World War II** came to symbolize the unity of the nation. He continued, however, to exercise political influence, and his threat to abdicate in 1941 was a factor in persuading the Swedish government to give

way to German demands. He married Princess Viktoria, daughter of the Grand Duke of Baden and great-granddaughter of **Gustav IV Adolf**, thus uniting the reigning house of Bernadotte with the former royal house of Vasa. His nephew was Count Folke **Bernadotte**. He was succeeded by his son, **Gustav VI Adolf**. ▷ **Vasa Dynasty**

Gustav VI Adolf (1882–1973) King of Sweden (1950/73). The son and successor of **Gustav V**, he was a respected scholar and archaeologist, and an authority on Chinese art. In 1905 he married Princess Margaret (the grand-daughter of Queen **Victoria**), by whom he had four sons and a daughter. In 1923 he married Lady Louise Mountbatten, the sister of Earl **Mountbatten** of Burma. His eldest son, Gustav Adolf, having been killed in an air-crash (1947), he was succeeded by his grandson, **Charles XVI Gustav**.

Gustavus II Adolphus ▷ **Gustav II Adolf**

Gustavus III ▷ **Gustav III**

Guthorm ▷ **Guthrum**

Guthrum (d.890) Danish King of East Anglia (880/90). The opponent of King **Alfred, 'the Great'**, he led a major Viking invasion of Anglo-Saxon England in 871 (the 'Great Summer Army'), seized East Anglia and conquered Northumbria and Mercia. He attacked Wessex early in 878 and drove Alfred into hiding in Somerset. By May of that year Alfred had recovered sufficiently to defeat the Danes at the crucial Battle of **Edington** in Wiltshire; in the ensuing treaty, Guthrum agreed to leave Wessex and accept baptism as a Christian, and he and his army settled down peacefully in East Anglia.

Gu Weijun (Ku Wei-chun) (1887–) Chinese diplomat, also known as Wellington Koo. He studied in the USA and joined the Ministry of Foreign Affairs in 1912. As a member of the Chinese delegation to the Paris Peace Conference (1919), he refused to sign the ensuing treaty in protest against the powers' decision to allow Japan to retain control of the Qingdao (Tsingtao) Peninsula, Germany's former leasehold territory in China. Gu was China's chief delegate at the first meeting of the **League of Nations** assembly (1920), helping to draft the League Covenant. He gained renown in 1932 when, as China's delegate to the League of Nations, he forcefully condemned Japanese aggression in Manchuria. In June 1945 Gu represented China at the signing of the **UN** Charter, of which China was the first signatory.

Gu Yanwu (Ku Yen-wu) (1613–82) Chinese scholar and official. He is celebrated for his loyalty to the **Ming Dynasty** and his refusal to serve the succeeding Manchu **Qing Dynasty**. He participated in the Ming resistance movement against the Manchus in the late 1640s and later led the life of an independent scholar, rejecting all offers by the Qing authorities to enter officialdom. Gu was to serve as an inspiration for early 20c anti-Manchu revolutionaries.

Guyenne (Guienne) A medieval duchy, including Gascony, in south-western France, bounded west by the Bay of Biscay. The rump of Aquitaine, it remained a possession of the English crown after **Normandy** and other French territories were lost in 1204–5. The claim of the kings of England to be independent rulers of Guyenne was one of the causes of the **Hundred Years War**. It was finally conquered by the French in 1453. The area is now occupied by the departments of Gironde, Dordogne, Lot, Aveyron, Tarn-et-Garonne, and Lot-et-Garonne. ▷ **Angevins**

Guy of Dampierre (c.1226–1305) Count of Flanders and Namur. The second son of William of Dampierre, the death of his elder brother (1251) brought Guy the County of Flanders in 1278; his second marriage, in 1265, to Isabella of Luxembourg having brought him Namur. In Flanders he strove to restore the Count's power, some of which had been lost to the rich and powerful industrial-commercial towns. In foreign policy, Guy allied himself with the English against King **Philip IV** of France, who was trying to extend his influence over Flanders. In 1300 France occupied the County, and Guy was forced to surrender; a general revolt broke out, leading to the Matins of **Bruges** and the Battle of the **Golden Spurs**, but Guy died in French captivity.

Guy of Lusignan (d.1194) French Crusader. He became King of Jerusalem in 1186 as consort of Sibylla, daughter of Amalric I, but was defeated and captured at the Battle of **Hittin** (1187) by **Saladin**, who overran most of the kingdom. On the death of his wife in 1190, the throne passed to **Conrad of Montferrat**, but as compensation Guy received **Cyprus**, where his family ruled until 1474.

Guzmán Blanco, Antonio (1829–99) Venezuelan dictator. Educated in Europe, he was violently anticlerical, and a bitter opponent of José Antonio **Páez**. He was Vice-President from 1863 to 1868, when he was driven from office. He then headed a revolution which restored him to power in 1870, and became dictator, holding the presidency on three occasions (1873–7, 1879–84 and 1886–8). He was prevented from returning from a visit to Paris by a rising in Caracas and died in exile.

H

Haakon I ▷ **Haakon the Good**

Haakon IV ▷ **Haakon the Old**

Haakon VII (1872–1957) King of Norway (1905/57). Born Prince Carl of Denmark, the second son of King **Frederick VIII**, he was elected King of Norway when the country voted for independence from Sweden. In 1896 he married Princess Maud, youngest daughter of King **Edward VII** of Britain. Known as the 'people's king', he dispensed with much of the pomp of royalty. When Germany invaded Norway in 1940 he refused to abdicate, and when further armed resistance was impossible, carried on the resistance from England, returning in triumph in 1945. He was succeeded by his son, **Olav V**. ▷ **Norway, German Invasion of**

Haakon the Good (?914–61) King of Norway (c.945/61). The youngest son of **Harald Fairhair**, he was reared in England at the Christian court of King **Athelstan** and became known as 'Haakon Athelstan's-fosterling'. When news came that his father had died in 945, he returned to Norway to dispute the right to the crown with his half-brother, **Erik Bloodaxe**, and seized the throne himself. He proved to be an able legislator and administrator. He brought missionaries from England and built some churches, but his attempts to convert Norway to Christianity met stubborn resistance. He had to fight off several attempts on the throne by the sons of Erik Bloodaxe, led by **Harald Greycloak**, and eventually died in battle against them.

Haakon the Old (1204–63) King of Norway (1217/63). The illegitimate grandson of the 'usurper' **Sverrir Sigurdsson**, he was placed on the throne as a boy of 13 by his powerful and ambitious uncle, Duke Skúli, who acted as regent. Eventually Skúli tried to rebel against his nephew, but was defeated and killed in 1240. Haakon strengthened relationships with the church, and was ceremoniously crowned in 1247. A great empire-builder, he annexed Iceland and Greenland to the Norwegian crown (1262), but in the following year, on an expedition to the Western Isles of Scotland to reassert Norwegian power there, he suffered a setback at

the Battle of Largs against **Alexander III** of Scotland and died at Kirkwall in the Orkneys on his way back to Norway.

Habash, George (192?–) Palestinian guerrilla leader. A radical, it was his Damascus-based Popular Front for the Liberation of Palestine (PFLP), created in 1967, which carried out the first Middle East airliner hijackings. Attacks carried out by the PFLP have included the May 1972 incident at Lod Airport (Tel Aviv), when 27 civilians were killed by Japanese Red Army gunmen who opened fire in the terminal building, and the June 1976 hijacking of an Air France airliner to Entebbe Airport in Uganda (which resulted in a successful Israeli commando rescue raid during which four civilians died). A brief furore was caused in early 1992 when Habash was flown from Tunis to Paris for emergency brain surgery following a stroke. He is now presumed back in Tunisia.

habitants The peasant settlers of **New France** (Canada). Since the feudal customs transplanted from France were not suited to pioneering conditions, the *habitants* gained certain advantages such as the reduction of the *corvée* (the forced labour duty) to six days or a commutation. Another benefit they gained (though only after government pressure) was the use of the *seigneur's* mill. Whilst the *seigneurs* still retained a certain status, their economic distinctions became increasingly less marked.

Habre, Hissene (c.1930–) Chadian nationalist and politician. The son of a desert shepherd, he worked as a clerk for the French army before becoming an administrator. He joined the FAN guerrillas in the early 1970s but, having made his peace with President Malloum in 1978, he was appointed Prime Minister. When Goukouni seized power in 1979, he became Defence Minister. However, supported by the CIA, he fought against Goukouni and took power himself in 1982. With French military assistance and support from African Heads of State, he forced Libya to withdraw from northern Chad and, although uneasily, retained power.

Habsburg Dynasty A major European dynasty whose origins lie in the Upper Rhine region. The name is derived from the Habichtsburg ('Hawk's Castle') in what is today Switzerland, built c.1020 by Bishop Werner of Strassburg. The title Count of Habsburg does not occur until 1090 but, by the time **Rudolf I** gained the German crown in 1273, the Habsburgs had accumulated a considerable mass of Swiss, Swabian and Alsatian possessions. The acquisition, in 1278, of Austria initiated the crucial shift of their power from the south-west to the south-east of the **Holy Roman Empire**, whose crown they were to hold with few interruptions (1292–8, 1308–1437 and 1742–5) until its fall. The international expansion of the House of Habsburg started in the late 15c when **Maximilian I** married the heiress of Burgundy and the Netherlands, with Spain added one generation later in the same way and followed by the conquest of Bohemia and Hungary in 1526. Including the Spanish colonies overseas, **Charles V** could thus truly claim to be the ruler of 'an empire on which the sun never sets'. After his abdication (1556), the Habsburg dominions were divided between the Spanish line which died out in 1700 and the German line whose members continued to rule over a varying collection of territories until 1918, having adopted the title of Emperor of Austria in 1804. In 1867 the venture of Archduke Maximilian (the title of all Habsburg princes since 1359) to establish himself as Emperor of Mexico ended with his execution. ▷ **Pragmatic Sanction**

Habsburg Serfs, Emancipation of the (1781 and 1849) A revolutionary social and economic transformation with political consequences for the Habsburg Empire. The practice of serfdom came under increasing criticism during the spread of the European Enlightenment. Peasant risings became more frequent and bitter; and serfs proved to be poor labourers and worse soldiers. In 1781 **Joseph II** abolished serfdom, although most peasants were still obliged to provide labour service or to make payments in lieu. It was not until 1849 that **Francis Joseph** abolished the remaining obligations as a means of ensuring that the peasants in his dominions would not join the other rebels in the **Revolutions of 1848–9**. Emancipation accelerated the **Industrial Revolution** by freeing peasant labour, but as they crowded into the cities and factories they became the backbone of national and socialist movements.

HABSBURG DYNASTY

Regnal Dates	Name
1273/91	Rudolf I
1298/1308	Albert I
1314/22	Frederick I
1438/9	Albert II
1440/93	Frederick III
1493/1519	Maximilian I
1519/58	Charles V
1558/64	Ferdinand I
1564/76	Maximilian II
1576/1612	Rudolf II
1612/19	Matthias
1619/37	Ferdinand II
1637/57	Ferdinand III
1658/1705	Leopold I
1705/11	Joseph I
1711/40	Charles VI
1740/2	Interregnum
1742/5	Charles VII
1745/65	Francis I
1765/90	Joseph II
1790/2	Leopold II
1792/1835	Francis II
1835/48	Ferdinand I
1848/1916	Francis Joseph
1916/18	Charles I

Habyarimana, Juvenal (1937–) Rwandan soldier and politician. He was educated at a military school, joined the National Guard and rose rapidly to the rank of major-general, and head of the Guard, by 1973. In the same year, as fighting between the Hutu and Tutsi tribes restarted, he led a bloodless coup against President Gregoire Kayibanda and established a military regime. He founded the National Revolutionary Development Movement (MRND) as the only legal party and promised an eventual return to constitutional government.

Hácha, Emil (1872–1945) Czechoslovak lawyer and politician. He became President of Czechoslovakia in Oct 1938 on **Beneš**'s resignation following the German annexation of Sudetenland; under duress, he made over the state to **Hitler** in Mar 1939. He was puppet president of the subsequent German protectorate of Bohemia and Moravia. Arrested after liberation in 1945, he died in prison.

hacienda The standard Spanish-American term for a large landed estate, usually worked by a resident population of tenant-labourers cultivating small plots of land and subject to labour obligations of various kinds. Haciendas emerged in the late 17c and early 18c due to the growth of local markets for their produce. By the mid-18c they had become clusters of buildings, including housing plus *estancias*, often held piecemeal. By the late 18c prominent families in Mexico and Peru owned strings of haciendas, organized as one substantial enterprise. These supplied an entire range of goods for domestic consumption and export. They were complemented by smaller ranchos, held by mestizo peasant farmers. A century later their position was strengthened with the growth of wage labour. ▷ **estancia**

Hadrian (Publius Aelius Hadrianus) (AD76–138) Roman Emperor (117/38). The ward, protégé and successor of the Emperor **Trajan**, he was a fellow Spaniard and relation by marriage. Coming to power in ambiguous circumstances, Hadrian was always unpopular at Rome, and even the object of a serious conspiracy there (118). He spent little of his reign at Rome, but tirelessly toured the empire, consolidating the frontiers, visiting the provinces and promoting urban life (as in Britain, where he initiated the building of **Hadrian's Wall**). ▷ **Britain, Roman**

Hadrian's Wall The principal northern frontier of the Roman province of Britain. Built AD122–8 on the orders of the Emperor **Hadrian** and possibly inspired by travellers' accounts of the **Great Wall of China**, it runs 117km/73ml from the Solway Firth to the River Tyne, the wall itself is 4.5m/15ft high (probably with a 2m/6ft timber parapet), its forward defensive ditch c.8.5m/28ft wide and 3m/10ft deep. Sixteen forts (the best preserved at Housesteads and Chester) were supplemented by 80 milecastles and numerous signal turrets. Overrun by **Picts** and northern tribes in AD139 and again in 367, the wall was finally abandoned c.400–10. It is now a world heritage site. ▷ **Antonine Wall; Britain, Roman**

Hafstein, Hannes Pétursson (1861–1922) Icelandic politician. He studied law in Copenhagen and returned to Iceland in 1887 to head the Independence Party in the campaign to secure home rule from Denmark. As Prime Minister (the first after the granting of home rule by the Danish crown) in 1904–7 and 1912–14, he was responsible for reforms in education and health and inaugurated a telegraph and telephone system. He was also a distinguished lyric poet.

Haganah The Jewish underground militia in Palestine, founded in the 1920s during the period of the British Mandate in response to nationalist Arab attacks on Jewish settlements. Banned by the British authorities, the *Haganah* ('self-defence') maintained a policy of restraint, opposing the terrorism of the **Irgun** and others. However, this changed when the British sought to limit Jewish immigration after **World War II**. The Haganah comprised a part-time membership, but 1941 saw the creation of a full-time striking force, the *Palmach*. After the War of Independence in 1948, in which it played a central role, the Haganah became the Israel Defence Force, the official Israeli army. ▷ **Jewish Agency; Israel, State of; Likud; Stern Gang**

Hague Peace Conferences Two conferences at The Hague, Netherlands, in 1899 and 1907. The first met on the initiative of Count Muravyov, the Russian Foreign Minister, to discuss the limitation of armaments, but the 26 countries represented made little progress. A permanent court of arbitration was set up for states in dispute wishing to use its services. The second met on the initiative of President Theodore **Roosevelt**, sat under the chairmanship of Tsar **Nicholas II** and, with 44 countries represented, produced a series of conventions to try to limit the horrors of war.

Haidar Ali (1722–82) Indian Muslim ruler of Mysore (1766/82). Having conquered Calicut and fought the Marathas, he waged two wars against the British, in the first of which (1767–9) he won several gains. In 1779 he and his son, Tippoo Sahib, again attacked the British, initially with great success; but in 1781–2 he was defeated. He died at Chittoor.

Haig, Alexander Meigs (1924–) US general and administrator. Educated at the US Military Academy at West Point and at Georgetown, he held a number of staff and field positions, serving in the **Vietnam War**. A full general by 1973, he then retired from the army to become White House Chief-of-Staff during the last days of Richard **Nixon**'s presidency. Returning to active duty, he became supreme **NATO** commander before returning again to civilian life. He served President Ronald **Reagan** as Secretary of State in 1981–2, and sought the Republican nomination for the presidency in 1988.

Haig, Douglas, 1st Earl Haig of Bemersyde (1861–1928) British field marshal. He obtained a commission in the 7th Hussars, and served in Egypt, South Africa and India. In 1914 he led the 1st Army Corps in France, and in 1915 became commander of the **British**

Expeditionary Force. He waged a costly and exhausting war of attrition, for which he was much criticized, but led the final successful offensive in front of Amiens (Aug 1918). In post-war years he devoted himself to the care of ex-servicemen, organizing the Royal British Legion. His earldom was awarded in 1919. ▷ **World War I**

Haile Selassie I (Prince Ras Tafari Makonnen) (1892–1975) Emperor of Ethiopia (1930/6 and 1941/74). He led the revolution in 1916 against Lij Eyasu and became regent and heir to the throne, becoming Emperor in 1930. He set about westernizing the institutions of his country, but was driven out when the Italians occupied Ethiopia in 1935 and settled in England. Restored in 1941 by the British, he became a father-figure of African nationalism and was central to the establishment of the **Organization of African Unity**, whose headquarters were established in Addis Ababa. His authoritarian rule, however, built up centres of opposition, both among the elite and among non-Amharic peoples. He survived an attempted coup in 1971, but the famine of 1973 led to economic crisis, industrial strikes and ultimately a mutiny in the army and he was deposed (12 Sep 1974). He died a year later at army headquarters.

Hailsham, Quintin (McGarel) Hogg, 2nd Viscount (1907–) British politician. He became a Conservative MP in 1938 and succeeded to his title in 1950. He was First Lord of the Admiralty (1956–7), Minister of Education (1957), Lord President of the Council (1957–9 and 1960–4), Chairman of the **Conservative Party** (1957–9), Minister for Science and Technology (1959–64), and Secretary of State for Education and Science (1964). In 1963 he renounced his peerage and re-entered the House of Commons in an unsuccessful bid to become Leader of the Conservative Party. In 1970 he was created a life peer (Baron Hailsham of Saint Marylebone) and was Lord Chancellor (1970–4), a post he held again from 1979 until his retirement in 1987.

Haitian Revolution (1791–1804) The only successful slave revolution in the New World, which led to the independence of Haiti in 1804. Started by the *grand blancs*' resistance to the French National Assembly's grant of representation to the *affranchis* of St Domingue, the white–coloured confrontation was superseded in Aug 1791 by a slave revolt which broke out on the Northern Plain. This uprising was taken over by **Toussaint L'Ouverture**, who expelled Maitland's British expeditionary force (1798), overcame the white and coloured armies by 1800 and, in 1801, sent an independence constitution to Paris. By then, France was under Bonaparte's control and he despatched a 20 000-strong military force under General Victor Le Clerc to crush the black **Jacobins**. Toussaint was captured by trickery but the French forces were decimated by yellow fever and withdrew (Nòv 1803), leaving the African-born slave, **Dessalines**, to proclaim himself Emperor of an independent Haiti (1804). ▷ **Napoleon I**

Hajduks South Slav bandits who resisted the Ottoman Turks, made a distinctive contribution to the Serbs' struggle for independence from the **Ottoman Empire** and, like the Greek **Klephts**, were celebrated in folklore.

Hajek, Jiri (1913–) Czechoslovak academic, diplomat, politician and dissident. A political scientist and social democrat, he was imprisoned in a **concentration camp** for much of **World War II**. On the left wing of his party, he joined with the communists in 1948 and soon began to rise: ambassador in London (1955–8); Deputy Foreign Minister (1958–62); Ambassador to the **UN** (1962–5); and Minister of Education (1965–8). In 1968 Alexander **Dubček** appointed him Foreign Minister, in which post he tried to act as broker between the USSR and the West and, after the Soviet invasion in Aug, tried to condemn the Soviet action by flying to the UN in New York. But he was summoned home and soon deprived of all his positions and privileges. In 1977 he was one of the founders of **Charter 77** and was frequently harassed thereafter. Thoroughly disillusioned by the communist subversion of socialism, he had the satisfaction of witnessing the so-called **Velvet Revolution** in 1989.

Hakim, al- (985–1021) Fatimid Caliph of Egypt (996/1021). He succeeded his father, al-'Aziz, at the age of 11 and the early part of his reign was characterized by the persecution of the Christian and Jewish minorities and the destruction of thousands of churches, including the Holy Sepulchre in Jerusalem. His extreme **Shiite** policies in Muslim affairs aroused the antagonism of the predominantly **Sunni** population. From 1017, he became convinced of his own divinity, which was publicly preached by his followers, Hamza and al-Darazi, and in the midst of a growing crisis the caliph disappeared in mysterious circumstances. His cult became the basis of the Druze religion which took root in the Lebanon, Syria and Galilee.

Hakka A people from north China who settled in southern China in the 12–13c and remained unassimilated. During the 18–19c they were involved in feuds over land, and many eventually migrated to other areas, including Taiwan, Hong Kong, Indonesia, Malaysia and Singapore.

Haldane, Richard Burdon, 1st Viscount (1856–1928) British politician, philosopher and lawyer. He entered parliament in 1879 as a Liberal. As Secretary of State for War (1905–12), he remodelled the army and founded the Territorials; British mobilization took place in 1914 on the basis of his plans. He was Lord Chancellor (1912–15) and again in 1924 following his move to the **Labour Party**. He also wrote on the philosophical aspects of relativity, and helped to found the London School of Economics (1895). ▷ **Liberal Party** (UK)

Hale, Nathan (1755–76) American Revolutionary War hero. Born in Coventry, Connecticut, he joined the Continental Army in 1775 and a year later volunteered for a dangerous information-gathering mission behind British lines on Long Island. He was captured and before being hanged as a spy reportedly stated, 'I regret that I have but one life to lose for my country.'

Halidon Hill, Battle of (19 July 1333) A battle between England and Scotland during the Scottish Wars of Independence. **Edward III** of England turned from besieging Berwick-upon-Tweed, and inflicted a massive defeat on the Scottish relief army. ▷ **David II; Scottish War of Independence**

Halifax, Charles Montagu, 1st Earl of (1661–1715) English politician. A Whig, he became MP for Maldon (1688) and a Lord of the Treasury (1692), establishing the National Debt and the Bank of England (1694). As Chancellor of the Exchequer (1694–5), he introduced a new coinage. In 1697 he was First Lord of the Treasury and Leader of the House of Commons, but resigned when the **Tories** came to power in 1699, and became Baron Halifax. On Queen **Anne**'s death he was made a member of the Council of Regency, and on **George I**'s arrival (1714) became an earl and Prime Minister. He was also a patron of letters, and a poet. ▷ **Whigs**

Halifax, Edward Frederick Lindley Wood, 1st Earl of (2nd creation) (1881–1959) British politician. He became a Conservative MP (1910–25), and held a range of political posts before becoming (as Baron Irwin, 1925) Viceroy of India (1926–31). He was Foreign Secretary (1938–40) under Neville **Chamberlain**, whose 'appeasement' policy he implemented, and Ambassador to the USA (1941–6). He was created an earl in 1944. ▷ **Conservative Party** (UK)

Halifax, George Savile, 1st Marquis of (1633–95) English statesman. He was created viscount (1668) for his share in the **Restoration**, and in 1672 was made a marquis and Lord Privy Seal. On the accession of **James II** of England (1685), he became President of the Council, but was dismissed soon after. He was one of the three Commissioners appointed to treat with William of Orange (later **William III**), after he landed in England (1688). He gave allegiance to William and resumed the office of Lord Privy Seal; however, joining the opposition, he resigned his post in 1689.

Hall, Ben (Benjamin) (1837–65) Australian bushranger. The son of an English convict, in 1862 he was arrested for armed robbery but was acquitted. Rearrested on suspicion of involvement in the Eugowra gold robbery with Frank Gardiner, he was again released, but returned home to find his farm burnt down by the police. The most glamorous of the Australian bushrangers, between 1863 and 1865 he led a series of audacious raids, most notably on Bathurst and the Sydney–Melbourne road. After the shooting of two policemen, Hall went into hiding, but was betrayed and killed in a police ambush (May 1865).

Hallstein Doctrine Federal German foreign policy stance, named after the State Secretary for Foreign Affairs, Dr Walter Hallstein. Following **Adenauer**'s visit to Moscow in 1955, which saw the opening of diplomatic relations between the USSR and the Federal Republic of Germany, the West German government declared that it would not maintain diplomatic relations with any state (other than the USSR) which maintained relations with East Germany. Relations were accordingly severed with Yugoslavia in 1957, but the Hallstein Doctrine fell into abeyance during the late 1960s and more particularly in the early 1970s with the inception of **Ostpolitik**. ▷ **Germany, East; Germany, West**

Hamaguchi Osachi (1870–1931) Japanese politician. He began his career as a Finance Minister bureaucrat and was elected to the lower house of the Diet in 1915. In 1927 he assumed the presidency of the Minseito, one of the two main political parties of the time, and became Prime Minister of a Minseito government in 1929. Renowned for his incorruptibility and dogged determination, he adopted a policy of domestic financial austerity and better relations with the USA and UK. He aroused the bitter hostility of the navy when, in 1930, he pushed through the Diet ratification of the London Naval Treaty, which placed restrictions on Japan's naval development. In assuming sole responsibility for the ratification of the treaty and ignoring the opinions of the navy, Hamaguchi was accused by both the military and ultra-nationalists of infringing the Emperor's prerogative of supreme command. In Nov 1930 he was shot by a right-wing fanatic and died the following year.

Hamburg The history of Germany's largest port began in 825 with the construction of the Mammaburg, a small moated castle between the Alster and Elbe rivers. After Lübeck, Hamburg was the premier Hanseatic town. Hamburg profited from the emigration of prosperous Dutch merchants to the Lower Elbe during the Dutch Wars of Independence. Its fortifications spared it from the ravages of the **Thirty Years War**. The Treaty of Gottorp (1768) created it an Imperial town freeing Hamburg from the titular rule of Denmark which had existed since 1459. It was annexed by Napoleon's French Empire in 1810 but became a free city again in 1815.

Hamdanids The Arab dynasty which, with its capital in Mosul, controlled northern Mesopotamia from 929 until 991. The Hamdanids also expanded westwards and took Aleppo, which they controlled from 944 until 1001. The most notable of the Hamdanids was Sayf al-Dawla of Aleppo (945/67), renowned for his defence of the northern marches against the Byzantines; this was no light task as the late 10c was a period of particular effectiveness for Byzantine arms.

Hamilton, Alexander (1755–1804) US politician. Educated at King's (now Columbia) College, New York, he fought in the **American Revolution**, becoming George **Washington**'s aide-de-camp (1777–81). After the war, he studied law, and in 1782 was returned to Congress. He was instrumental in the movement to establish the USA in its present political form. As Secretary of the Treasury (1789–95), his policy of funding a national debt and assuming the state debts restored the country's finances to a firm footing. He was the real founder and a leader of the **Federalist Party** until his death. His successful effort to thwart the ambition of his rival, Aaron **Burr**, led to a duel in Weekauken, New Jersey, in which Hamilton was killed.

Hamilton, James, 1st Duke of (1606–49) Scottish royalist commander during the **English Civil Wars**. He fought during the **Thirty Years War**, leading an army in support of **Gustav II Adolf** (1631–2), and later played a conspicuous part in the contest between **Charles I** and the **Covenanters**. Created duke in 1643, he led a Scottish army into England (1643), but was defeated by **Cromwell** at the Battle of **Preston**, and beheaded.

Hammarskjöld, Dag Hjalmar Agne Carl (1905–61) Swedish politician. He was the son of Hjalmar Hammarskjöld, Conservative Prime Minister of Sweden during the early years of **World War I**. He became in 1933 an assistant professor at the University of Stockholm, in 1935 State Secretary of Finance and from 1941 to 1948 was Chairman of the Bank of Sweden. He was a cabinet minister from 1951 to 1953, when he became Secretary-General of the **UN**. Hammarskjöld, who once described himself as 'the curator of the secrets of 82 nations', played a leading part in the setting up of the UN Emergency Force in Sinai and Gaza in 1956, in conciliatory moves aimed at securing peace and stability in the Middle East in 1957–8 and in sending observers to Lebanon in 1958. He was awarded the Nobel Peace Prize in 1961, after his death in an air crash near Ndola in Zambia while he was attempting to resolve the Congo crisis.

Hammer, Armand (1898–1991) US financier and philanthropist. Using his Russian origins and business contacts, he became an intermediary between five Soviet general-secretaries and US presidents from Franklin **Roosevelt** to Richard **Nixon**. With **Stalin**'s accession to power, Hammer left Russia, taking with him many Russian paintings which he used to found the Hammer Galleries in New York City. Retiring to Los Angeles after building a second fortune, in 1961 he bought Occidental Petroleum, a company near bankruptcy and by 1965 had made it a major force in the oil industry. Convicted of making illegal contributions to

Nixon's re-election fund, he was put on a year's probation and fined US$3 000. President **Bush** pardoned him in 1989.

Hammurabi (18c BC) Amorite King of Babylon (c.1792/1750BC). Best-known for his Code of Laws, he is also famous for his military conquests that made Babylon the greatest power in Mesopotamia. ▷ **Amorites; Babylonia**

Hampden, John (1594–1643) English parliamentarian and patriot. He became a lawyer, and in 1621 an MP. His opposition to **Charles I**'s financial measures led to his imprisonment (1627–8), and in 1634 he became famous for refusing to pay Charles's imposed levy for outfitting the navy ('ship money'). A member of both the **Short Parliament** and the **Long Parliament**, he was one of the five members whose attempted seizure by Charles (1642) precipitated the **English Civil Wars**. He fought for the parliamentary army at Edgehill and Reading, but was killed at Thame.

Hampi The site of the former Hindu capital of Vijayanagar, near the south-western Indian village of Hampi. The city was founded in the 14c, and remained the centre of a vast and powerful Hindu empire until 1565, when it was sacked. It remains an important religious and tourist centre, and is a world heritage site.

Han Dynasties The name of several early Chinese dynasties, now used to distinguish those of native Chinese stock from the national minorities. The Western (or 'Former') Han (206BC–AD24), founded by Liu Bang, a leader of the rebellion that overthrew the **Qin Dynasty**, was characterized by expansion of the Chinese empire into Korea and Central Asia, incessant campaigns against the Huns, the triumph of Confucianism as state orthodoxy, and great achievements in literature and learning. Its capital was at Changan (present-day Xi'an). After an interregnum (AD8–23), during which the reformist Wang Mang usurped the throne, the Eastern Han ruled China from Luoyang (AD25–220). During this period Buddhism was introduced to China, and trade links developed with Europe via the Middle East.

Han Fei (d.233BC) Chinese philosopher. He was noted for his espousal of **Legalism**, a school of thought that emphasized the effective use of state power. A nobleman

from the state of Han during the Warring States period (403–221BC), Han Fei later served the ruler of Qin, the state that would ultimately forge the first Chinese empire. He was critical of Confucian morality and insisted on the importance of institutions and the impartial imposition of laws as the basis of sound government. He also believed in the effectiveness of a strict system of rewards and punishments and argued that state policy should not be hampered by custom or precedent. Han Fei was forced to commit suicide by his arch-rival, **Li Si**.

Han Gaozu (Han Kao-tsu) (256–195BC) The founder of the Western (or 'Former') Han Dynasty, whose personal name was Liu Bang (Liu Pang). From a peasant family, he led an armed uprising against the ruling **Qin Dynasty** and captured its capital of Xianyang (near present-day Xi'an) in 206BC. He then defeated his main rival, Xiang Yu (Hsiang Yu), an aristocrat from the state of Chu, in 202BC and formally established the Han Dynasty, becoming the first commoner-ruler in China. As Emperor, he abolished the Draconian laws of the preceding dynasty and lowered tax rates. In heeding the advice of his ministers and assuming that government exists to serve the people's needs, Han Gaozu set an important precedent for future rulers. ▷ **Han Dynasties**

Hanlin Academy A central government institution in imperial China whose members lectured to the emperor on the **Confucian Classics**, prepared imperial edicts and officiated at ritual ceremonies. Originating in the 8c as a loosely organized group of litterateurs, it acquired status as a regular central government agency during the **Yuan Dynasty** (1264–1368). Only the top metropolitan degree-holders were appointed, and so membership of the Hanlin Academy often brought with it important official posts. A State Historiographer's Office within the Academy prepared a chronicle of each reign, made public after the reigning emperor's death.

Hannes Pétursson Hafstein ▷ **Hafstein, Hannes Pétursson**

Hannibal (247–182BC) Carthaginian general and statesman, the son of Hamilcar Barca. As a child, his father made him swear eternal enmity to Rome. He served in Spain under Hamilcar and Hasdrubal, and as general reduced most of southern Spain (221–219BC). In the Second Punic War, he left New

Carthage on his famous journey (218BC), defeated the Gauls, and crossed the Alps in 15 days, in the face of almost insuperable obstacles. He marched on Rome, and defeated the Romans at Lake Trasimene (217BC) and at **Cannae** (216BC). Denied support by his countrymen, he fought on for several years, until recalled to Africa in 203BC. He was defeated by **Scipio Africanus Major** at Zama (202BC), leaving Carthage at the mercy of Rome. After making peace, Hannibal turned to political reform, but raised such opposition that he voluntarily exiled himself, first to Syria, then Crete and finally Bithynia, where he committed suicide to avoid Roman capture. ▷ **Fabius Maximus, Quintus; Punic Wars**

Hanover, House of A branch of the Guelf Dynasty, more specifically the Brunswick–Lüneburg line which, in 1692, acquired the Electoral dignity for Hanover. On the death of Queen **Anne** in 1714, the Elector Georg Ludwig, who was descended through the female line from Princess Elizabeth, the sister of **Charles I**, became King of Great Britain and Ireland, as **George I**, thus securing the Protestant succession. Monarchs from the House of Hanover ruled their British and German dominions in personal union until the death of **William IV** in 1837. Thereupon, the British crown went to Queen **Victoria** who was, however, disqualified under the **Salic Law** from succession in Germany. In consequence, her uncle, the Duke of Cumberland, became King of Hanover under the name of Ernest Augustus. While the family name of the British dynasty changed to Saxe–Coburg and Gotha when Victoria married Prince **Albert** in 1840, the Hanoverians continued to rule their native country until 1866 when it was annexed by **Prussia** for siding with Austria in the preceding war. A descendant of the last King of Hanover succeeded to the Duchy of Brunswick in 1913 after the Brunswick–Wolfenbüttel line had become extinct, but was toppled by the revolution of 1918.

HOUSE OF HANOVER

Regnal Dates	Name
1714/27	George I
1727/60	George II
1760/1820	George III
1820/30	George IV
1830/7	William IV
1837/1901	Victoria

Hanover, State of Originally the principality of Brunswick-Calenberg-Göttingen, created in 1638, the state took its name from its largest city, Hanover. In 1692 Duke Ernest Augustus was made an elector by Emperor Leopold I. It was merged with the Duchy of Lüneberg in 1705. Ernest Augustus married Sophia of the Palatinate, granddaughter of **James VI and I** of Britain. In 1714, Sophia's son, George Louis, became **George I** of Britain after which the electorate was ruled by a minister of the British monarch. Britain lost claim to the electorate, which recognized only male rulers, when **Victoria** came to the British throne (1837).

Hanseatic League A late medieval association of 150 north German towns, including Bremen, Hamburg, and Lübeck. It had its origins in the practice of early medieval merchants from individual towns of travelling together for safety. The development of the Hansa, as it was also known, was given a great impetus by German colonization of Eastern Europe. It facilitated the exchange of raw materials from the east and manufactured goods from the West, dominated trade from the Atlantic to the Baltic, and fought successful wars against neighbours between 1350 and 1450. It declined because of internal divisions, English and Dutch competition, and the growth of princely power.

Hansson, Per Albin (1885–1946) Swedish politician. He rose to prominence in the Social Democratic youth movement and was elected to parliament in 1918. He served as Minister of Defence in Social Democrat administrations in 1918–25 under Hjalmar **Branting**, whom he succeeded as leader of the party (1925). Hansson became Prime Minister of a minority Social Democrat government in 1932, but secured the support of the Agrarians in the so-called 'cow deal' the following year and, apart for a brief period in 1936, was in office from then until his death. He presided over the foundation of the modern welfare state in Sweden and guided his country's successful policy of neutrality during **World War II**.

Han Wudi (Han Wu-ti) (141/87BC) Emperor of the Han Dynasty. He ruled longer than any other Chinese emperor until the 18c. Han Wudi enhanced imperial authority and centralized control by abolishing the semi-independent fiefdoms originally granted by **Han Gaozu** to his relatives and supporters and by expanding

the state's role in the economy with the institution of state monopolies over the production and distribution of iron, salt and liquor. During his reign, Confucianism was adopted as the official state orthodoxy. Han Wudi also pursued an aggressively expansionist policy, incorporating Mongolia, southern Manchuria, Korea and what is now southern and western China into the Han Empire. From 133BC, he launched a number of campaigns against the Xiongnu, frontier nomads on China's northern and western frontiers. Han armies penetrated as far as central Asia, where Chinese military governors were stationed to supervise native rulers.
▷ **Han Dynasties**

Han Yu (786–824) Chinese moralist. He condemned the pervasive influence of Buddhism and promoted a revival of Confucian thought during the **Tang Dynasty**. Han Yu considered Buddhism an invidious foreign superstition whose other-worldly philosophy and monastic way of life threatened the family system and eroded the Confucian tradition of public service. He was also concerned about the growing wealth of Buddhist institutions and their tax-exempt estates. A systematic persecution of Buddhism was to be carried out 20 years after Han Yu's death.

Hara Kei (1856–1921) Japanese politician. From a **samurai** family, he worked as a newspaper editor before joining the Ministry of Foreign Affairs (1882). He resigned from government service to join the **Seiyukai**, a political party formed in 1900, and shortly afterwards gained a seat in the lower Diet. As Home Minister in various non-party cabinets (1906–8, 1911–12 and 1913–14) and Leader of the *Seiyukai*, Hara was able to advance the party's interests by appointing pro-Seiyukai provincial governors and promoting regional economic development. As the head of the majority party in the Diet, he became Prime Minister in 1918 and presided over the first party cabinet since the establishment of the **Meiji Constitution**. He proved to be a conservative premier, however, moving cautiously on political and social reform. Although he expanded the electorate by lowering tax qualifications, he did not endorse the principle of universal manhood suffrage. He was assassinated by an ultra-nationalist fanatic.

Harald I Halfdanarson ▷ **Harald Fairhair**

Harald II Eriksson ▷ **Harald Greycloak**

Harald III Sigurdsson ▷ **Harald Hardrada**

Harald Bluetooth (c.910–85) King of Denmark (c.950/85). The son of Gorm the Old and father of **Svein I Haraldsson, 'Fork-Beard'**, he was the first king to unify all the provinces of Denmark under a single crown. He was converted to Christianity by a German missionary, Poppo (c.960) and made Christianity the state religion of Denmark. He erected the massive Jelling Stone at Jelling to proclaim his conversion of Denmark ('and made the Danes Christian'), and exhumed for proper Christian burial the bodies of his father and his mother, Thyri, from the great burial mounds at Jelling. He is also now thought to have built the fortified military barracks at Trelleborg and elsewhere in Denmark; he strengthened the unity and central administration of the country, and repelled attacks from Norway and Germany. Harald Bluetooth was eventually deposed by Svein Fork-Beard in 985, and died in exile soon afterwards.

Harald Fairhair (c.865–945) King of Norway (c.890/942). He was the first ruler to claim sovereignty over all Norway. The son of Halfdan the Black (King of Vestfold), he fought his way to power with a crushing defeat of his opponents at the naval Battle of Hafursfjord, off Stavanger, in c.890. His authoritarian rule caused many of the old aristocratic families to emigrate west to the Orkneys, Hebrides and Ireland, and to newly-settled Iceland. Harald made several punitive expeditions across the North Sea to subdue his former subjects and impose Norwegian rule over the Northern and Western Isles of Scotland. When he was nearly 80 years old, in 942, he abdicated in favour of his eldest son, **Erik Bloodaxe**.

Harald Gormsson ▷ **Harald Bluetooth**

Harald Greycloak (d.970) King of Norway (c.965/70). The eldest son of **Erik Bloodaxe**, after his father's death in England (954) he took refuge at the Danish court with his mother, Gunnhild, the sister of King **Harald Bluetooth**. With Danish support he and his four brothers made several assaults on Norway from 960 onwards against their uncle, King **Haakon the Good**, and eventually killed him in battle off Hardangerfjord. Harald Greycloak's reign was unpopular, especially when he tried to impose Christianity on his subjects. When he tried to break free of his alliance with Denmark one of his enemies, Earl Haakon of Lade, enlisted

Harald Bluetooth's help for another invasion, and Greycloak was caught and killed at Limfjord in 970.

Harald Hardrada (1015–66) King of Norway (1045/66). The half-brother of **Olaf II** (St Olaf), he was present at the Battle of Stiklestad in 1030 where St Olaf was killed, and sought refuge in Kiev at the court of his kinsman, Prince Yaroslav the Wise, together with his nephew, **Magnus I, 'the Good'**. He had a lurid career as a Viking mercenary with the Varangian Guard in Constantinople, and returned to Norway in 1045 to demand, and receive, a half-share in the kingdom from his nephew. He became sole king on his nephew's death in 1047, and earned the nickname Hardrada ('Hard-Ruler'). After long and unrelenting wars against King **Svein II Ulfsson** of Denmark, he invaded England in 1066 to claim the throne after the death of **Edward the Confessor**, but was defeated and killed by **Harold II** at Stamford Bridge.

Hardaknut (1018–42) King of Denmark (1035/42) and of England (1040/2). He was the son of **Canute** and Emma (the widow of King **Ethelred the Unready**), and was Canute's only legitimate heir. He inherited Denmark on his father's death in 1035, but was unable to come to England immediately to claim the throne there. The English elected his half-brother, **Harold I, 'Harefoot'** regent in his stead, and then confirmed Harold as King in 1037. Hardaknut mounted an expedition to invade England to claim the crown, but Harold died in Mar 1040, before he arrived. Hardaknut was thereupon elected King, and promptly punished the English by imposing a savage fleet-tax to pay for his expedition. His reign was universally disliked; he died (June 1042) of convulsions at a drinking party.

Hardenberg, Karl August, Prince von (1750–1822) Prussian politician. After holding appointments in Hanover, Brunswick, Ansbach, and Bayreuth, he became a Prussian minister in 1791, and Chief Minister in 1803. In 1806, under **Napoleon I**'s influence, he was dismissed, but later appointed Chancellor and Chief Minister (1810–22). In the war of liberation he played a prominent part, and after the Treaty of Paris (1814) was made a prince. He reorganized the Council of State (1817), of which he was appointed President, and continued the work of von **Stein**, carrying out many reforms in the army, social structure, culture, and education. ▷ **Prussia**

Hardie, (James) Keir (1856–1915) British politician. He worked in the mines between the ages of seven and 24, and was victimized as the miners' champion. He became a journalist and the first Labour MP, entering parliament for East Ham in 1892. He founded and edited *The Labour Leader*, and was Chairman of the **Independent Labour Party** (founded 1893). Instrumental in the establishment of the Labour Representation Committee, Hardie served as Chairman of the **Labour Party** (1906–8). His strong pacifism led to his becoming isolated within the party, particularly once **World War I** had broken out.

Hardinge (of Lahore), Henry Hardinge, 1st Viscount (1785–1856) British soldier and colonial administrator. After service in the **Peninsular War**, he became an MP (1820–44) and Secretary of War (1828–30 and 1841–4). In 1844 he was appointed Governor-General of India, and after the first Sikh War was created a viscount (1845). Returning in 1848, he succeeded **Wellington** as Commander-in-Chief of the British Army (1852), but was demoted following the disasters early in the **Crimean War** (1854–6). ▷ **Sikh Wars**

Harding, Warren G(amaliel) (1865–1923) US politician and 29th President. He became a successful journalist, gained a seat in the Ohio State Senate (1899) and the lieutenant-governorship (1902), after which he returned to journalism until 1914, when he was elected to the US Senate. Emerging as a power in the **Republican Party**, he won its nomination. As President (1921–3), he campaigned against US membership of the **League of Nations**. ▷ **Prohibition; Teapot Dome Scandal**

harijan The name (Hindi, 'children of God'), proposed by M K **Gandhi** for the untouchables. ▷ **caste**

Harley, Robert, 1st Earl of Oxford (1661–1724) British politician. He became a lawyer, and a Whig MP in 1689. In 1701 he was elected Speaker, and in 1704 became Secretary of State. Shortly after, he became sympathetic to the **Tories**, and from 1708 worked to undermine the power of the **Whigs**. In 1710 **Godolphin** was dismissed, and Harley made Chancellor of the Exchequer, head of the government, and (1711) Earl of Oxford and Lord High Treasurer. The principal Act of his administration was the Treaty of Utrecht (1713). In 1714 he was dismissed, and after the Hanoverian succession spent two years in prison. He then retired from politics. ▷ **Hanover, House of**

Harold I, 'Harefoot' (d.1040) King of England (1037/40). He was the younger son of **Canute** and his English mistress, Ælfgifu of Northampton. On Canute's death, the English elected Harold regent for his half-brother, **Hardaknut**, King of Denmark, the legitimate heir to the throne, who could not leave Denmark to claim the crown. In 1037 Harold was elected King; he died (Mar 1040) just as Hardaknut was poised to invade England to claim back the throne.

Harold II (c.1022–66) Last Anglo-Saxon King of England (1066). The second son of Earl Godwin, by 1045 Harold was Earl of East Anglia, and in 1053 succeeded to his father's earldom of **Wessex**, becoming the right hand of **Edward the Confessor**. After Edward's death (Jan 1066), Harold, his nominee, was crowned as King. He defeated his brother **Tostig** and **Harald III Sigurdsson**, King of Norway, at Stamford Bridge, Yorkshire (Sep 1066), but Duke William of Normandy (**William I, 'the Conqueror'**) then invaded England, and defeated him at the Battle of **Hastings** (14 Oct 1066), where he died, shot through the eye with an arrow.

Harpers Ferry Raid (1859) An attack on the federal arsenal in Virginia, led by abolitionist John **Brown**, intending to launch a slave insurrection. The raiders were captured, and Brown was executed amidst great publicity. ▷ **abolitionism**

Harriman, William Averell (1891–1986) US politician and diplomat. Educated at Yale, he became Ambassador to the USSR (1943) and to Britain (1946), Secretary of Commerce (1946–8), and special assistant to President **Truman** (1950–1), helping to organize **NATO**. He was Director of the Mutual Security Agency (1951–3), Governor of New York (1955–9), ambassador-at-large (1961 and 1965–8) and US representative at the Vietnam peace talks in Paris (1968). He negotiated the partial Nuclear Test Ban Treaty between the USA and USSR in 1963, and continued to visit the USSR on behalf of the government, making his last visit there at the age of 91. ▷ **Vietnam War**

Harrison, Benjamin (1833–1901) US politician and 23rd President. In 1854 he became a lawyer in Indianapolis, and during the **American Civil War** fought in **Sherman**'s Atlanta campaign. He was elected US Senator from Indiana in 1881. In 1888 he defeated Grover **Cleveland** on the free-trade issue, and was President from 1889 to 1893. Failing to gain re-election, he returned to his law practice in Indianapolis, Indiana, where he died.

Harrison, William Henry (1773–1841) US general and 9th President. He fought against the Native Americans, and when Indiana Territory was formed (1800) he was appointed Governor, serving for 12 years. He tried to avoid further **Indian Wars**, but was compelled to quell **Tecumseh**'s uprising, which ended in the Battle of Tippecanoe (1811). In the **War of 1812** he defeated the British in the Battle of the Thames (1813). In 1816 he was elected to the US House of Representatives, and in 1824 he became a Senator. With the slogan 'Tippecanoe and Tylertoo', he was elected to the presidency in 1840, but died in Washington a month after his inauguration. His grandson was Benjamin **Harrison**.

Harsha (Harshavardhana) (c.590–c.647) Ruler of a large empire (606/47) in north India. He was the second son of the King of Thanesar in Punjab and was crowned after the assassination of his elder brother. He became a Buddhist convert and his influence extended from Gujarat to Assam. Known chiefly through the works of Bana and Hsuan-tsang, a Chinese pilgrim, Harsha is said to have been a model ruler who established benevolent institutions for travellers, the sick and the poor. A patron of learning, Harsha initiated diplomatic relations between India and China.

Harshavardhana ▷ **Harsha**

Hartford Convention (1814–15) A gathering at Hartford, Connecticut, of delegates from the New England states to oppose the **War of 1812** and to propose changes in the **US Constitution**. The Treaty of Ghent, ending the war, and US victory at New Orleans discredited both the Convention and the **Federalist Party**, with which the Convention was associated.

Hartling, Poul (1914–) Danish politician. He represented the Liberal Party (*Venstre*) and was Danish Foreign Minister (1968–71) and Prime Minister (1973–5). From 1978 to 1985 he was the **UN** High Commissioner for Refugees.

Harun al-Rashid (766–809) 'Abbasid caliph (786/809). He came to the throne on the death of his brother, al-Hadi, with the help of the influential Barmakid family which he

'Abbasid Empire, 8–9c

Legend:

— Extent of 'Abbasid Empire at the time of Harun al-Rashid

IRAQ etc Province ruled by Harun al-Rashid (786/809)

● Baghdad, capital of the 'Abbasid Empire

◉ Samarra, capital from 836 to 892

Situation c.840:

Area under direct 'Abbasid control

Vassal states:

Tahirids (820-73), then Saffarids

Aghlabids (from 800)

★ Revolts

Qarmatians (end 9c)

→ Muslim naval attacks (9c)

permitted to dominate his early reign, but gradually removed from power. He was a great patron of the arts and enthusiastic in waging war against the Byzantines. He was, however, less interested in the detail of central government, and weakened the empire through his attempts to divide it among his three sons. ▷ **Barmakids**

Harvester Judgement (1907) A landmark decision of the Australian Conciliation and Arbitration Court made by Justice H B **Higgins** under the Excise Tariff Act (1906) which allowed firms paying fair wages to claim exemption from excise duty. Giving judgement on the claim of the harvester manufacturer, H V Mackay, Higgins calculated the fair wage for an unskilled labourer on the basis of need, establishing the principle of the minimum or family wage tied to the cost of living. It remained a central feature of the Australian industrial system until the end of the 1960s.

Haryana The northern Indian state carved out of the erstwhile state of Punjab in 1966. Haryana's population is largely Hindi-speaking. There remain disputes between Punjab and Haryana over the transfer of Chandigarh, their joint capital, to Punjab, and the transfer, in return, of Hindi-speaking areas to Haryana. Haryana, like Punjab, is a predominantly agricultural state, though industries have come up in the last few years. It has sites like Kurukshetra and **Panipat** where historic battles have been fought. Politics in Haryana is dominated dualistically by the Congress Party and the opposition **Lok Dal** which, under various guises, allies from time to time with the BJP and Congress fragments.

Haselrig (Heselrige), Sir Arthur (d.1661) English parliamentarian. In 1640 he sat in the **Long Parliament** and **Short Parliament** for his native county, Leicestershire, and he was one of the five members whose attempted seizure by **Charles I** in 1642 precipitated the **English**

405

Civil Wars. He commanded a parliamentary regiment, and in 1647 became Governor of Newcastle. After the **Restoration**, he was imprisoned and died in the Tower of London.

Hasluck, Sir Paul Meernaa Caedwalla (1905–93) Australian politician and historian. A journalist on the *West Australian* (1922–38), he was lecturer in history at the University of Western Australia (1939–40). Seconded during **World War II** to the Australian Department of External Affairs, he became head of the Australian mission to the United Nations, returning to the university in 1948. He entered federal politics in 1949, and was successively Minister for Territories (1951–63), for Defence (1963–4), and for External Affairs (1964–9). He was Governor-General of Australia (1969–74).

Hassan II (1929–) King of Morocco (1961–). Educated in France, Crown Prince Hassan served his father as head of the army and, on his accession as King in 1961, also became Prime Minister. He suspended parliament and established a royal dictatorship in 1965 after riots in Casablanca. Despite constitutional reforms in 1970 and 1972, he retained supreme religious and political authority. His forces occupied Spanish (Western) Sahara in 1957. He mobilized a large army to check the incursion of **Polisario** guerrillas across his western Saharan frontier from 1976 to 1988. Unrest in the larger towns led Hassan to appoint a coalition 'government of national unity' under a civilian prime minister in 1984.

Hastings, Battle of (14 Oct 1066) The most decisive battle fought on English soil, which led to the successful **Norman Conquest** of England. Norman cavalry overcame the resolute defence of the Anglo-Saxon army fighting on foot, and **Harold II**'s death in battle cleared the way for Duke William of **Normandy**'s coronation. Not until 1092 (the capture of Carlisle) were the **Normans** masters of all England. ▷ **Anglo-Saxons; William I, 'the Conqueror'**

Hastings, Warren (1732–1818) British colonial administrator. Educated at Westminster, he joined the British **East India Company** in 1750, and by 1774 was Governor-General of Bengal. Carrying out several reforms, he made the Company's power paramount in many parts of India. However, wars (1778–84) interfered with trade, and damaged his reputation, and on his return to England in 1784 he was charged with

corruption. After a seven-year trial, he was acquitted. The Company made provision for his declining years, which he spent as a country gentleman in Worcestershire, England.

Hatoyama Ichiro (1883–1959) Japanese politician. He was first elected to the Diet in 1915 and became a prominent leader of the **Seiyukai** in the 1930s. As Education Minister (1931–4), he clamped down hard on liberal university teachers who questioned the nature of the Japanese state. In 1946 he organized the conservative Japan Liberal Party (*Nihon Jiyuto*), which gained a victory in the elections of that year. On the verge of becoming Prime Minister, he was purged from official life by the US occupation authorities for his role in supporting the military cabinets of the 1930s. Although he was rehabilitated in 1951, he found that leadership of the Liberal Party was now firmly in the hands of **Yoshida** Shigeru. He formed a new conservative party, the Japan Democratic Party (*Nihon Minshuto*), which successfully ousted Yoshida from power (Dec 1954), when Hatoyama became Premier. During Hatoyama's premiership (1954–6), relations with the USSR were normalized, thus paving the way for Japan's entry into the UN in 1956, and the two conservative parties were merged to form the **Liberal Democratic Party** (LDP).

Hat Party (Sweden) ▷ **Age of Liberty**

Hatshepsut (Maatkare) (c.1489/1469BC) Queen of Egypt. A ruler in the 18th Dynasty, she was the daughter of **Thutmose I** and consort of Thutmose II. On the latter's death, **Thutmose III**, his son by a minor wife, succeded to the throne, with Hatshepsut, his step-mother, as regent. Supported by a group of officials, Hatshepsut soon had herself crowned king with full powers, regalia and titles. She was represented in male attire, including an artificial beard. The young Thutmose was kept in the background. During her 20-year reign, she built her mortuary temple at Deir el Bahri, erected obelisks at Karnak and despatched a trading expedition to Punt (modern Eritrea/Somalia).

Hatt-i Humayun (1 Feb 1856) The second edict of reform decreed in Istanbul as a result of pressure from the Western powers (Britain, France and Austria). The object of the edict was essentially to insist on internal reforms in Turkey to protect Christian subjects of the Ottomans and hence to bolster the effect of the peace treaty after the **Crimean War** by depriving Russia of pretexts for interfering in the internal affairs of the **Ottoman Empire**.

Haughey, Charles (James) (1925–) Irish politician. He became a **Fianna Fáil** MP in 1957. From 1961 he held posts in the Ministries of Justice, Agriculture, and Finance, but he was dismissed in 1970 after a quarrel with the Prime Minister, Jack **Lynch**. He was subsequently tried and acquitted on a charge of conspiracy to import arms illegally. After two years as Minister of Health and Social Welfare, he succeeded Lynch as Premier (1979–81), was in power again for a nine-month period in 1982, and again from 1987 to 1992, after defeating Garrett **Fitzgerald** in the 1987 elections. He resigned after allegations of illegal telephone-tapping led his Progressive Democrat coalition allies to withdraw their support.

Hausa ▷ **Fulani Emirates**

Haussmann, Georges Eugène, Baron (1809–91) French financier and town planner. He entered public service, and under **Napoleon III** became prefect of the Seine (1853), improving Paris by widening streets, laying out boulevards and parks, and building bridges. He was made a baron and Senator, and was elected to the Chamber of Deputies in 1881.

Havel, Václav (1936–) Czechoslovak dramatist and reluctant but distinguished politician. Educated at the Academy of Dramatic Art in his native Prague, he began work in the theatre as a stagehand and became resident writer for the Prague 'Theatre on the Balustrade' (1960–9). Having been chairman of the Writers' Union during the **Prague Spring**, his work was then judged subversive. He was one of the founders of Charter 77 in 1977 and was subsequently imprisoned several times, his plays only being performed abroad. During the so-called **Velvet Revolution** in Dec 1989, which ended **communism** in Czechoslovakia, he was elected President by direct popular vote. Although he subsequently opposed the division of Czechoslovakia into two separate states, he nevertheless agreed to stand for the presidency of the Czech Republic.

Havelock, Sir Henry (1795–1857) British soldier. A lawyer by training, he entered the army a month after the Battle of **Waterloo**, and went out to India in 1823. He distin-guished himself in the Afghan and Sikh Wars, and in 1856 commanded a division in Persia. On the outbreak of the **Indian Uprising** (1857–8), he organized a column of a 1 000 Higlanders and others at Allahabad with which to relieve Cawnpore and **Lucknow**, engaged and broke the rebels at Fatehpur, and, driving them before him, entered Cawnpore. Next crossing the Ganges, he fought eight victorious battles, but through sickness in his little army had to retire to Cawnpore. In Sep **Outram** arrived with reinforcements, and Havelock again advanced, Outram waiving his superior rank, and serving under Havelock as a volunteer. The relieving force fought their way to the Residency, where they in turn were besieged by the determined rebel forces until Nov, when Sir Colin Campbell forced his way to their rescue. A week after the relief, Havelock died of dysentery. ▷ **Afghan Wars**

Havlicek, Karel (1821–56) Czech political journalist. In the early days of the 1848 revolt in Prague he established *National News*, a newspaper devoted to the nationalist cause. It was closed down by the Habsburg authorities in 1849 but he started another, *The Slav*, in 1850. Late in 1851 he was arrested and exiled to Austria where he could not undertake political journalism. Released in 1855, he returned home to find his wife dead; and he died himself a year later. His contemporary impact was slight, but he served as a model to others who came after him.

Hawke, 'Bob' (Robert James Lee) (1929–) Australian politician. He worked for the **Australian Council of Trade Unions** for over 20 years, before becoming an MP in 1980. His **Australian Labor Party** defeated the **Liberal Party of Australia** in the 1983 election, only one month after adopting him as leader. The most successful Labor Prime Minister in Australian history, he won his fourth general election in 1990.

Hawke (of Towton), Edward Hawke, 1st Baron (1705–81) British admiral. As a young commander, he fought against the French and Spanish, for which he was knighted (1747). His major victory was against the French at Quiberon Bay (1759), which caused the collapse of their invasion plans. He also became an MP (1747), First Lord of the Admiralty (1766–71), and a baron (1776).

Hawkyns, Sir John (1532–95) British sailor. He was the first Englishman to traffic in slaves (1562) between West Africa and the

West Indies, but on his third expedition his fleet was destroyed by the Spanish (1567). He became navy treasurer (1573), and was knighted for his services against the Spanish **Armada** in 1588. In 1595, with his kinsman **Drake**, he commanded an expedition to the Spanish Main, but died at Puerto Rico.

Hay, John Milton (1838–1905) US politician and writer. Educated at Brown University, he became a lawyer, and private secretary to President **Lincoln**. After Lincoln's death (1865), he served as a diplomat in Paris, Vienna and Madrid. He returned to the USA and to journalism in 1870, and went on to write poetry, fiction, and a multivolume biography of Lincoln. He became Assistant Secretary of State (1879), Ambassador to Britain (1897), and Secretary of State (1898), serving under Presidents **McKinley** and **Roosevelt**. ▷ **Open Door Policy**

Haya de la Torre, Víctor Raúl (1895–1979) Peruvian politician and political thinker. Educated in Lima, he was the founder (1924) of APRA (*Alianza Popular Revolucionaria Americana*), known as the Aprista Party, the voice of radical dissent in Peru. Imprisoned (1931–3) after standing against Colonel Luis Sánchez Cerro, he was released on the latter's assassination (1933), and went into hiding (1934–45). The Aprista Party changed its name to the *Partido del Pueblo* (People's Party) in 1945, and supported the successful candidate, José Luis Bustamante; control of the government, however, lay in Haya's hands. On Bustamante's overthrow (1948), Haya sought refuge in the Colombian embassy in Lima and later (1954) left for Mexico. He returned to Peru when constitutional government was restored (1957) and fought the bitter 1962 election campaign which, after army intervention, he lost to Terry Fernando **Belaúnde**. Haya was instrumental in drafting the constitution of 1979 restoring parliamentary democracy, but died before the People's Party finally gained power in 1985 under Perez Alan **Garciá**.

Hayashi Razan (1583–1657) Japanese Confucian scholar and ideologist. He served as adviser to the **Tokugawa Shogunate**. As the promoter of Neo-Confucianism, with its emphasis on loyalty and its assumption that a hierarchical and harmonious polity reflected the natural order, Hayashi provided ideological support for the shogunate and the political ascendancy of the warrior class.

Hay–Bunau-Varilla Treaty (1903) An agreement between the USA and Panama creating the Panama Canal Zone under US sovereignty, and giving the USA the right to build and operate the Canal, in return for a US$10 000 000 fee and US$250 000 annual rent. The chief parties involved were US Secretary of State John Hay, and Philippe Bunau-Varilla, representing Panama.

Hayden, Bill (William George) (1933–) Australian politician. He entered the federal parliament in 1961, serving under Gough **Whitlam** whom he replaced as **Australian Labor Party** leader in 1977. In 1983 he surrendered the leadership to the more charismatic Bob **Hawke** and was Foreign Minister in his government (1983–8). In 1989 he became Governor-General of Australia.

Hayes, Rutherford B(irchard) (1822–93) US politician and 19th President. He practised law in Cincinnati (1849–61), served in the **American Civil War**, entered Congress (1865–7) as a Republican, and was elected Governor of Ohio three times (1867, 1869, 1875). The contested 1876 presidential election between Hayes and Samuel J Tilden was finally resolved in Hayes's favour, with concessions made to the Southern states in the Compromise of 1877. Hayes supported civil service reform but was unsuccessful in his efforts to prevent freer coinage of silver. ▷ **Republican Party**

Hay–Herrán Treaty (1903) An agreement between the USA and Colombia giving the USA the right to build a canal across the isthmus of Panama, then part of Colombia. Its rejection by the Colombian Senate led to the Panamanian revolt for independence, with US sponsorship. The parties involved were US Secretary of State John Hay, and Tomás Herrán, Colombian chargé d'affaires based in Washington. ▷ **Hay–Bunau-Varilla Treaty**

Haykal, Muhammad Hasanayn (1924–) Egyptian journalist and author. Early in his career he covered the 1948 War and the **Korean War**. He had contacts with the **Free Officers** before the 1952 coup, and his subsequent career has spanned the period from Gamal Abd al-**Nasser**'s presidency to the period in office of Hosni **Mubarak**. The most influential journalist of his generation, Haykal became editor of the respected Cairo newspaper *al-Ahram* in 1957, writing, on subjects such as Nasser's relations with world leaders such as Nikita **Khrushchev** and

Lyndon B **Johnson**, in addition to other Arab heads of state. He also had contacts with guerrilla leaders, including Che **Guevara**. Removed from the editorship of *al-Ahram* in 1974 following his criticism of Anwar **Sadat**'s conduct of the **October War**, Haykal was briefly held under arrest in 1981 when Sadat, ostensibly to deal with the religious extremism of the **Muslim Brotherhood**, extended his purge to include journalists and opposition party leaders.

Haymarket Square Riot (4 May 1886) A clash between police and demonstrators at a labour union rally in Chicago at which a bomb exploded, killing seven police and injuring some 70 others. Four persons were executed by the state of Illinois for their involvement. Violent labour disputes, fuelled by anarchist elements within the movement and culminating in the riot, led to a loss of public support for the union movement.

Haywood, William Dudley ('Big Bill') (1869–1928) US labour leader. After working as a miner, homesteader, and cowboy, he joined the Western Federation of Miners in 1896, and quickly achieved prominence. In 1905 he helped to found the Industrial Workers of the World (**IWW**), which was committed to revolutionary labour politics and to the organization of all workers in one big union. An active socialist, he was convicted of sedition in 1917 for his opposition to **World War I**. He fled from the USA in 1921, and took refuge in the USSR, dying in Moscow.

Heath, Edward (Richard George), 'Ted' (1916–) British politician. He served in **World War II**, and became a Conservative MP in 1950. Following a career in the Whips' office (1951–9), he was Minister of Labour (1959–60), then Lord Privy Seal (1960–3) and the chief negotiator for Britain's entry into the European Common Market (**EEC**). He became the **Conservative Party**'s first elected leader in 1965, and remained Leader of the Opposition until the 1970 election, when he became Prime Minister (1970–4). After a confrontation with the miners' union in 1973, he narrowly lost the two elections of 1974, and in 1975 was replaced as leader by Margaret **Thatcher**. He has continued to play an active part in politics, being particularly critical of his successor's policies.

Heaven and Earth Society A Chinese secret society, also known as the Triads (*tiandihui*), that originated in the 1670s

during the early years of the **Qing Dynasty** as a group pledging loyalty to the previous **Ming Dynasty**. The Triads first emerged in Taiwan, then spread to the southern provinces of Fujian, Guangdong and Guangxi, initially drawing recruits from seamen and poor urban-dwellers. Spawning a wide variety of local branches with different names, the Triads engaged in smuggling, racketeering and robbery in addition to organizing armed uprisings, particularly during the 19c. With its blood oath rituals and appeal to brotherhood, the society provided an attractive refuge for the homeless and destitute, but its conservative ideology harking back to a restoration of the Ming Dynasty made it increasingly irrelevant amidst the far-reaching political changes of the 20c. The Triads remain active today in Hong Kong and overseas Chinese communities.

Hébert, Jacques René (1757–94) French revolutionary. An extremist, he represented the aspirations of the **sans-culottes**. He became a popular political journalist, assumed the pseudonym 'Le père Duchesne' after launching a satirical newspaper of that name (1790), and joined both the Cordelier and Jacobin clubs. He had a major part in the September Massacres and the overthrow of the monarchy. After denouncing the Committee of **Public Safety** for its failure to help the poor, he tried to incite a popular uprising, but having incurred the suspicion of **Danton** and **Robespierre**, he and 17 of his followers ('Hébertists') were guillotined. ▷ **Cordeliers' Club; French Revolution; Girondins; Jacobins**

Hegel, Georg Wilhelm Friedrich ▷ **Marx, Karl**

Heian Era (794–1185) The period in Japanese history which began with the removal of the imperial capital from Nara to Heian (present-day Kyoto) and ended with the ascendancy of the warrior class and the establishment of the **Kamakura Shogunate**. The Heian period is seen as the apogee of the aristocratic age in Japan, when the imperial capital was the political, social and cultural centre. During this period an attempt was made to implement an emperor-dominated political system based on the Chinese model. After the mid-10c, however, a rising warrior class and the emergence of private landed estates (*shoen*), which became the principal form of landholding, vitiated such efforts.

Heimwehren Austrian volunteer defence leagues. These were organized after **World**

War I to protect Austria's southern (Yugoslav) frontier. By the late 1920s the *Heimwehren* were explicitly anti-socialist and anti-republican, receiving financial aid and encouragement from right-wing Austrian governments and from fascist Italy. Involved both in the crushing of the Austrian socialists (Feb 1934) and of the Austrian Nazis (July 1934), the Heimwehren were subsequently disbanded by the **Schuschnigg** government in 1936. ▷ **Austria, Republic of; Nazi Party**

Hein (Heyn), Piet (1577–1629) Dutch naval commander. After an adventurous career as a galley-slave of the Spanish and a merchant captain, in 1623 he became a vice-admiral under the Dutch. In 1624 he defeated the Spaniards near San Salvador in Brazil, and again in 1626 off Bahia, returning with an immense booty. In 1626 near Cuba he captured the Spanish silver flotilla, valued at 12 000 000 guilders; in 1629 was made Lieutenant-Admiral. He died in a sea battle against the **privateers** of Dunkirk.

Heinemann, Gustav (1899–1976) West German politician. He practised as an advocate from 1926 and lectured on law at Cologne (1933–9). After the war he was a founder of the Christian Democratic Union (**CDU**), and was Minister of the Interior in **Adenauer**'s government (1949–50), resigning over a fundamental difference over defence policy; being a pacifist, he opposed Germany's rearmament. He formed his own neutralist party, but later joined the Social Democratic Party (**SPD**), was elected to the **Bundestag** (1957) and was Minister of Justice in **Kiesinger**'s 'Grand Coalition' government from 1966. In 1969 he was elected President but resigned in 1974.

Heinsius, Anthony (1641–1720) Dutch politician. He was appointed Pensionary of Delft in 1672, and became an increasingly important friend and agent of the **Stadholder** William III. When William left for England in 1688 (to become King **William III**), Heinsius was left in charge as **Grand Pensionary** of Holland in 1689.

Hekmatyar, Gulbuddin (1949–) Afghan guerrilla leader. Formerly an engineer, in the 1970s he opposed the republican government of General Mohammad Daud Khan, and rose to prominence during the 1980s in the fight to oust the Soviet-installed communist regime in Afghanistan. As leader of one of the two factions of the Hizb-i Islami (Islamic Party), he was seen as the most intransigently

fundamentalist, refusing to join an interim 'national unity' government with Afghan communists as the USSR began to wind down its military commitment. He was injured in a car bomb attack on his group's headquarters in Peshawar in 1987, and in 1988 briefly served as President of the seven-party mujahadin alliance.

Hellenistic Age The period from the death of **Alexander III, 'the Great'** (323BC) to the death of **Cleopatra VII** (30BC), during which a number of Greek or Hellenized dynasties, many descended from Alexander's generals (such as the Ptolemies and **Seleucids**), ruled the entire area from Greece to the north of India. ▷ **Attalids; Bithynia; Hellenization; Ptolemy I Soter; Seleucids**

Hellenization The process by which the ancient Greek language, culture, and institutions were disseminated throughout the Mediterranean, Black Sea and parts of the Near East. This primarily resulted from the foundation of new *poleis* (city-states) in three major phases of 'colonization': c.1000BC along the west coast of Asia Minor; in the 8c–6c BC mainly in the west Mediterranean (primarily Sicily and southern Italy) and the Black Sea; and following the conquests of **Alexander III, 'the Great'**, throughout the Near East as far as Afghanistan. Greek culture was also commonly adopted voluntarily by neighbouring non-Greeks, particularly in the kingdoms of the **Hellenistic Age**. ▷ **polis**

He Long (Ho Lung) (1896–1977) Chinese Red Army general. The son of a lowly army officer and with little formal education, he was active as a bandit during the 1910s in his home province of Hunan, before enrolling in the provincial army. He Long joined the **Guomindang** in 1926 and became a commander in the National Revolutionary Army. He was a participant in the Nanchang army uprising against the Guomindang on 1 Aug 1927, a date that is now considered by the Chinese Communist Party to mark the birth of the Red Army. During the **Sino-Japanese War** (1937–45) he became a divisional commander in the communist **Eighth Route Army** and was elected a member of the party's Central Committee in 1945. Always a firm believer in party control of the army, he was made Marshal of the People's Republic of China (1955) and elected to the Politburo in 1956.

helots In ancient Greece, the descendants of the peoples conquered and reduced to a kind of serfdom by the Spartans. Mainly Messenians, they belonged to the Lacedaemonian state, not to individual Spartans, and had no political rights at all. ▷ **Cimon; Messenian Wars; Sparta**

Helsinki Conference (1975) A conference on security and co-operation in Europe, attended by the heads of 35 states, including the USA and USSR, with the objective of forwarding the process of détente through agreements on economic and technological co-operation, security, disarmament and human rights. These were set out in the Final Act within the principles of sovereignty and self-determination and existing frontiers. There have been several follow-up conferences, and there is now a permanent organization called the Conference on Security and Co-operation in Europe (CSCE). ▷ **détente**

Helvetii Celtic people forced south by Germanic tribesmen in the 2c BC into modern Switzerland. In 58BC, when renewed Germanic pressure prompted Helvetian migration into **Gaul**, Julius **Caesar** drove them back to their Swiss lands. They became allies then subjects of Rome, until c.400. The official names for Switzerland derive from this source: *Helvetia* and *Confederatio Helvetica*.

Henderson, Arthur (1863–1935) British politician. Several times Chairman of the **Labour Party** (1908–10, 1914–17 and 1931–2), he was elected an MP in 1903, served in the coalition cabinets (1915–17), and became Home Secretary (1924) and Foreign Secretary (1929–31) in the first Labour governments. He was President of the World Disarmament Conference in 1932, won the Nobel Peace Prize in 1934, and also helped to establish the **League of Nations**. ▷ **MacDonald, Ramsay**

Heng Samrin (1934–) Cambodian (Kampuchean) politician. He served as a political commissar and commander in **Pol Pot**'s **Khmer Rouge** (1976–8) but, alienated by his brutal policies, led an abortive coup against him, then fled to Vietnam. Here he established the Kampuchean People's Revolutionary Party (KPRP) and became head of the new Vietnamese-installed government in Cambodia in 1979. He has since remained in de facto control of Cambodia but, following Vietnam's withdrawal of its troops in 1989, his influence began to wane.

Henlein, Konrad (1898–1945) Sudeten German politician. A bank clerk and then gym teacher, he was the leader from 1935 onwards in the agitation and conspiracy that led, in 1938, to Germany's seizure of Sudetenland from Czechoslovakia, and in 1939 to the institution of its Protectorate of Bohemia and Moravia and the dissolution of Czechoslovakia. Gauleiter of Sudetenland in 1938–9 and Civil Commissioner for the Protectorate from 1939 to 1945, he committed suicide when in US hands.

Henry I (c.1008–60) King of France (1031/60). He was the son of Robert II. He was involved in struggles with **Normandy** and with **Burgundy**, which he had unwisely granted to his rival brother, Robert. Several of his conflicts were with William of Normandy (later **William I, 'the Conqueror'**).

Henry I (1068–1135) King of England (1100/35) and Duke of Normandy (1106/35). He was the youngest son of **William I, 'the Conqueror'**. Under Henry, the Norman empire attained the height of its power. He conquered Normandy from his brother, Robert Curthose, at the Battle of Tinchebrai (1106), maintained his position on the Continent, and exercised varying degrees of authority over the King of Scots, the Welsh princes, the Duke of Brittany, and also the Counts of Flanders, Boulogne, and Ponthieu. His government of England and **Normandy** became increasingly centralized and interventionist, with the overriding aim of financing warfare and alliances, and consolidating the unity of the two countries as a single cross-Channel state. His only legitimate son, William Adelin, was drowned in 1120, and in 1127 he nominated his daughter Empress Matilda, widow of Emperor **Henry V** of Germany, as his heir for both England and Normandy. But Matilda and her second husband, Geoffrey of Anjou, proved unacceptable to the King's leading subjects. After Henry's death, the crown was seized by **Stephen**, son of his sister, Adela. ▷ **Angevins**

Henry I, 'the Fowler' (c.876–936) King of Germany as Henry I (919/36). The founder of the Saxon Dynasty, he was Duke of Saxony from 912. He brought Swabia and Bavaria into the German confederation, regained Lotharingia (925), defeated the Wends in 928 and the Hungarians in 933 and seized Schleswig from Denmark in 934. He was about to claim the imperial crown as Holy Roman Emperor in 936 when he died. He was succeeded by his son, **Otto I, 'the Great'**. Another son was St Bruno (925–65).

Henry II (1133–89) King of England (1154/89). He was the son of Empress Matilda, **Henry I**'s daughter and acknowledged heir, by her second husband, Geoffrey of Anjou. Already established as Duke of Normandy (1150) and Count of Anjou (1151), and as Duke of Aquitaine by marriage to **Eleanor of Aquitaine** (1152), Henry invaded England in 1153, and was recognized (Treaty of Wellingford) as the lawful successor of **Stephen**. He founded the Angevin or Plantagenet Dynasty of English kings, and ruled England as part of a wider Angevin empire. Henry restored and transformed English governance after the disorders of Stephen's reign. His efforts to restrict clerical independence caused conflict with his former Chancellor, Thomas **Becket**, Archbishop of Canterbury, which was ended only with Becket's murder (1170). Henry led a major expedition to Ireland (1171), which resulted in its annexation. The most serious challenge to his power came in 1173–4 when his son, the young Henry, encouraged by Queen Eleanor, rebelled in alliance with **Louis VII** of France, **William I** of Scotland, and Count Philip of Flanders. All parts of the King's dominions were threatened, but his enemies were defeated. In 1189 he faced further disloyalty from his family when his sons, **John** and **Richard I**, allied with **Philip II** of France, who overran Maine and Touraine. Henry agreed a peace which recognized Richard as his sole heir for the Angevin empire, and he died shortly afterwards at Chinon. ▷ **Angevins; Clarendon, Constitutions of; Plantagenet Dynasty**

Henry II (1519–59) King of France (1547/59). The second son of **Francis I**, he became heir to the throne in 1536. In 1533 he married **Catherine de' Medici**; although he had 10 children by her, his mistress, **Diane de Poitiers**, was treated virtually as his consort. She was an ardent Catholic, favouring the Guise family, and her influence at court contributed to the oppression of his Protestant subjects. Through the influence of the Guises he formed an alliance with Scotland, and declared war against England, which ended in 1558 with the taking of Calais. He continued the long-standing war against Emperor **Charles V**, gaining Toul, Metz, and Verdun, but suffered reverses in Italy and the Low Countries, which led to the Treaty of Cateau-Cambrésis (1559). He was killed accidentally while taking part in a tournament to celebrate the signing of the treaty. ▷ **Guise, House of**

Henry II, 'the Holy' (973–1024) German King and Emperor of the West. Although originally intended for a life in holy orders, he was elected Duke of Bavaria on the death of his father, **Henry the Wrangler**, in 995 and crowned King of Germany in 1002. He waged several campaigns against the Christian Polish king, Bolesław I, in alliance with the heathen Liutitians and against Arduin of Ivrea, who claimed the Italian throne. He was crowned Emperor in 1014 and fought Greeks and Lombards in southern Italy at the request of the Pope. His main achievement was the elaboration of the so-called Ottonian system of government in Germany, ruthlessly using the church as a tool of imperial authority. He was canonized in 1146. ▷ **Ottonians**

Henry II Jasomirgott (1114–77) Duke of Austria. The second son of Leopold III, he was originally Count Palatine of the Rhine, and succeeded his younger brother, Leopold IV, as Margrave of Austria and Duke of Bavaria (1141). He married Theodora, the niece of the Byzantine Emperor Manuel Comnenas in 1149. Unable to hold Bavaria, he surrendered it to the **Welfs** in 1156; as compensation, Austria was made into a dukedom and the rights he received, the Privilegium minus, made it a semi-independent principality. He was a loyal supporter of **Frederick I**.

Henry III (1017–56) Holy Roman Emperor (1039–46). The son of Conrad II, he became Duke of Bavaria (1027), Duke of Swabia (1038), sole King of the Germans (1039), and Holy Roman Emperor (1046). He resolutely maintained the imperial prerogatives of power and made great use of Ministeriales to secure his authority. In 1046 he put an end to the intrigues of three rival popes by deposing them all and appointing Clement II in their stead. He promoted learning and the arts, founded monastic schools, and built many great churches. ▷ **Holy Roman Empire**

Henry III (1207–72) King of England (1216/72). He was the elder son and successor, at the age of nine, of **John**. He declared an end to his minority in 1227, and in 1232 stripped the justiciar, Hubert de **Burgh**, of power. His arbitrary assertion of royal rights conflicted with the principles of **Magna Carta**, and antagonized many nobles. Although he failed to recover Poitou (northern Aquitaine) in 1242, he accepted the Kingdom of Sicily (1254). This forced him to seek the support of the barons, who under the leadership of the King's brother-in-law, Simon de **Montfort**, imposed far-reaching reforms by the Provisions of **Oxford** (1258), which gave them a definite role in government. When Henry sought to restore royal power, the barons rebelled and captured him at Lewes (1264), but were defeated at Evesham (1265). The Dictum of Kenilworth (1266), though favourable to Henry, urged him to observe Magna Carta. Organized resistance ended in 1267, and the rest of the reign was stable. Henry was succeeded by his elder son, **Edward I**. ▷ **Barons Wars**

Henry III (1551–89) King of France (1574/89). The third son of **Henry II**, in 1569 he gained victories over the **Huguenots**, and took an active part in the **St Bartholomew's Day Massacre** (1572). In 1573 he was elected to the crown of Poland, but two years later succeeded his brother, **Charles IX**, on the French throne. His reign was a period of almost incessant civil war between Huguenots and Catholics. In 1588 he engineered the assassination of Henry, 3rd Duke of Guise, enraging the Catholic League. He joined forces with the Huguenot Henry of Navarre (**Henry IV**), and while marching on Paris was assassinated by a fanatical priest. The last of the Valois line, he named Henry of Navarre as his successor. ▷ **Guise, House of; Holy League** (1576); **Religion, Wars of; Valois Dynasty**

Henry IV (1050–1106) King of the Germans (1056/1106). He succeeded his father, **Henry III**, with his mother acting as Regent. He tried to break the power of the nobles; but his measures provoked a rising of the **Saxons**. After defeating them at Hohenburg (1075), he repressed both secular and ecclesiastical princes. This brought the intervention of Pope **Gregory VII**, and several years of conflict with the papacy, during which he appointed an anti-pope, Clement III, who crowned him Emperor in 1084. In his later years, he faced a further rebellion, in which his sons Conrad and Henry took part. He was compelled to abdicate, escaped, and found safety at Liège, where he died. ▷ **Canossa,; Tribur, Princes' Meeting at**

Henry IV (1366–1413) King of England (1399/1413). The first king of the House of **Lancaster**, he was the son of **John of Gaunt** (who was the fourth son of **Edward III**). In 1397 he supported **Richard II** against the Duke of **Gloucester**, and was created Duke of Hereford, but was banished in 1398. After landing at Ravenspur, Yorkshire, Henry

induced Richard, now deserted, to abdicate in his favour. During his reign, rebellion and lawlessness were rife, and he was constantly hampered by lack of money. Under Owen **Glendower** the Welsh maintained their independence, and Henry's attack on Scotland in 1400 ended in his retreat with no victories won. The Scots were, however, defeated by a force led by the Percies at Homildon Hill (1402), and it was partly annoyance at the King's apparent ingratitude which led the Percies to support the Scots and Welsh against Henry, which in turn led to the King's victory against them at Shrewsbury (1403). Henry was a chronic invalid in later years, and only rarely asserted himself in power struggles between the Prince of Wales and Archbishop Arundel, who was supported by Henry's second son, Thomas. ▷ **Percy**

Henry IV (Henry of Navarre) (1553–1610) First Bourbon King of France (1589/1610). The third son of Antoine de Bourbon, he was brought up a Calvinist. He led the Huguenot army at the Battle of Jarnac (1569) and became leader of the Protestant Party. Henry married Margaret of Valois in 1572, but this marriage was annulled in 1599, and in 1600 he married Marie de' Medici. After the **St Bartholomew's Day Massacre** (1572), he was spared by professing himself a Catholic, and spent three years virtually a prisoner at the French court. In 1576 he escaped, revoked his conversion, and resumed command of the army in continuing opposition to the Guises and the Catholic **Holy League** (1576). After the murder of **Henry III**, he succeeded to the throne. In 1593 he became a Catholic, thereby unifying the country, and by the Edict of **Nantes** (1598) Protestants were granted liberty of conscience. His economic policies, implemented by his minister, **Sully**, gradually brought new wealth to the country. He was assassinated in Paris by a religious fanatic. ▷ **Bourbon, House of; Guise, House of; Huguenots; Religion, Wars of; Valois Dynasty**

Henry V (1081–1125) German King and Emperor. In 1106 he allied himself with the nobility and dethroned his father, **Henry IV**. His reign was dominated by the issues involved in the **Investiture Controversy** and his power struggle with the princes, whose support he alienated by favouring the **Ministeriales** and the towns. In 1111 he agreed with Pope Paschal II to give up his rights to invest bishops in return for coronation as Emperor and the return of the royal insignia. This agreement was rejected by the German bishops and princes, whereupon Henry took the Pope prisoner and forced him to concede both coronation and rights of investiture: (1111). This concession was later withdrawn and Henry excommunicated. Finally negotiations with Pope Calixtus II led to the end of the Investiture Controversy in the Concordat of Worms, in which the princes, rather than the Emperor, took the initiative. ▷ **Worms, Concordat of**

Henry V (1387–1422) King of England (1413/22). The eldest son of **Henry IV**, he fought against **Glendower** and the Welsh rebels (1402–8), and became Constable of Dover (1409) and Captain of Calais (1410). To this time belong the exaggerated stories of his wild youth. The main effort of his reign was his claim, through his great-grandfather, **Edward III**, to the French crown. In 1415 he invaded France, and won the Battle of **Agincourt** against great odds. By 1419 Normandy was again under English control, and in 1420 was concluded the 'perpetual peace' of Troyes, under which Henry was recognized as heir to the French throne and Regent of France, and married **Charles VI**'s daughter, Catherine of Valois. ▷ **Hundred Years War**

Henry VI (1165–97) Holy Roman Emperor (1190/7). The son of **Frederick I, 'Barbarossa'**, he married Constance, the aunt and heiress of William II of Sicily (1186) and succeeded his father in 1190. He was opposed by the papacy, the **Guelfs**, **Richard I** of England and Constance's illegitimate brother **Tancred** who had been elected King by the Sicilian barons on the death of William. This hostile coalition collapsed when Richard fell into the hands of **Leopold V** of Austria, who turned his captive over to Henry. On the death of Tancred (1194) he overran Sicily, where Constance bore him a son, **Frederick II**. Emperor since 1191 and now king of Sicily, he was regarded by contemporaries as the most powerful man on earth, although he was unsuccessful in his plans to make the empire hereditary. Still a young man, he died at Messina, probably of malaria, while engaged in preparations for a crusade.

Henry VI (1421–71) King of England (1422/61 and 1470/1). He was the only child of **Henry V** and Catherine of Valois. During Henry's minority, his uncle John, Duke of **Bedford**, was Regent in France, and another uncle, Humphrey, Duke of **Gloucester**, was Lord Protector of England. Henry was crowned King of France at Paris in 1431, two years after his coronation in England. But once the Burgundians had made a separate peace with **Charles VII** (1435), Henry V's French conquests were progressively eroded, and by 1453 the English retained only Calais. Henry had few kingly qualities, and from 1453 suffered from periodic bouts of insanity. Richard, Duke of York, seized power as Lord Protector in 1454, and defeated the King's army at St Albans (1455), the first battle of the Wars of the **Roses**. Fighting resumed in 1459, and although York himself was killed at Wakefield (1460), his heir was proclaimed King as **Edward IV** after Henry's deposition (1461). In 1464 Henry returned from exile in Scotland to lead the Lancastrian cause, but was captured and imprisoned (1465–70). Richard Neville, Earl of **Warwick**, restored him to the throne (Oct 1470), his nominal rule ending when Edward IV returned to London (Apr 1471). After the Yorkist victory at the Battle of **Tewkesbury** (May 1471), where his only son was killed, Henry was murdered in the Tower. ▷ **Hundred Years War**

Henry VII (1274–1313) Holy Roman Emperor (1308/13) and King of Germany. Originally Count of Luxembourg, a French-speaking minor prince from the extreme west of the empire, he was elected Emperor in 1308 as an alternative candidate to **Charles of Valois**, mainly due to the skilful diplomacy of his brother, Baldwin, Archbishop of Trier. His family soon rose to great power with the marriage of his son John to Elizabeth, heiress of Bohemia (1311). In 1310 Henry led an army to Italy where he remained with the aim of restoring imperial authority, but made little progress against the opposition of King Robert of Naples and the Guelf cities, and the imperialist cause collapsed when he died near Siena, probably of malaria.

Henry VII (1457–1509) King of England (1485/1509). The founder of the Tudor Dynasty, he was the grandson of Owen Tudor, who married Queen Catherine of Valois, the widow of **Henry V**. After the Lancastrian defeat at the Battle of **Tewkesbury** (1471), Henry was taken to Brittany, where several Yorkist attempts on his life and liberty were frustrated. In 1485 he landed unopposed at Milford Haven, and defeated **Richard III** at the Battle of **Bosworth Field**. As King, he restored peace and prosperity to the country, which was helped by his marriage of reconciliation with Elizabeth of York. He was also noted for the efficiency of his financial and administrative policies. He dealt efficiently with Yorkist plots, such as those surrounding Lambert Simmel and Perkin Warbeck, who impersonated the Yorkist 'Princes in the Tower', Edward of Warwick and Richard of York respectively. Peace was concluded with France (1492), and the marriage of his heir Arthur to **Catherine of Aragon** cemented an alliance with Spain. He was succeeded by his son, as **Henry VIII**. ▷ **Tudor, House of**

Henry VIII (1491–1547) King of England (1509/47). The second son of **Henry VII**, soon after his accession he married **Catherine of Aragon**, his brother Arthur's widow. As a member of the **Holy League**, he invaded France (1512), winning the Battle of the **Spurs** (1513); and while abroad, the Scots were defeated at the Battle of **Flodden**. In 1521 he published a book defending the Catholic Sacraments in reply to **Luther**, receiving from the Pope the title 'Defender of the Faith'. From 1527 he determined to divorce Catherine, whose children, except for Mary (later **Mary I**), had died in infancy. This policy directly precipitated the Reformation in England. He tried to put pressure on the Pope by humbling the clergy, and in defiance of Rome was privately married to Anne **Boleyn** (1533). Using parliamentary statute to strengthen his actions against the Catholic Church, it was enacted in 1534 that his marriage to Catherine was invalid, and that the King was the sole head of the Church of England. The policy of suppressing the monasteries followed (1536–9). In 1536 Catherine died, and Anne Boleyn was executed for infidelity. Henry then married Jane **Seymour** (c.1509–37), who died leaving a son, afterwards **Edward VI**. In 1540 **Anne of Cleves** became his fourth wife, in the hope of attaching the Protestant interest of Germany; but dislike of her appearance caused him to divorce her speedily. He then married Catherine **Howard** (1540), who two years later was executed on grounds of infidelity (1542). In 1543 his last marriage was to Catherine **Parr**, who survived him. His later years saw further war with France and Scotland, before peace was concluded with France in 1546. He was succeeded by his son, Edward VI. ▷ **Cromwell, Thomas; More, Thomas; Reformation (England); Wolsey, Thomas**

Henry of Navarre ▷ **Henry IV** of France

Henry Raspe (c.1204–47) Landgrave of Thuringia and German anti-king. He was the last of the Ludovinger to rule Thuringia,

which he received from the Emperor c.1231. Although he was excommunicated (1240) for his support of the Emperor against the papacy, he went over to the papal side in 1245 and was elected King in 1246 by the clerical princes and supporters in Thuringia. He defeated **Conrad IV** (to whom he had been appointed as Regent (1246)) near Frankfurt in 1246 and died, without heir, the following year, having never been crowned.

Henry the Lion (1129–95) Duke of Saxony (1142/80) and Bavaria (1156/80). The head of the **Guelfs**, he pursued a vigorous policy of expansion in the north-east, conducted a crusade against the Wends and promoted trade by refounding Lübeck and setting up a series of trade agreements. In 1158 he founded Munich. His ambitious designs roused against him a league of princes in 1166, but he retained power through an alliance with Emperor **Frederick I, 'Barbarossa'**. After breaking with Frederick in 1176, he was deprived of most of his lands, and exiled. Ultimately he was reconciled to Frederick's successor, **Henry VI**.

Henry the Navigator (1394–1460) Portuguese prince. He was the third son of John I, King of Portugal, and Philippa, daughter of John of Gaunt, Duke of Lancaster. He set up court at Sagres, Algarve, and erected an observatory and school of scientific navigation. He sponsored many exploratory expeditions along the West African coast, and the way was prepared for the discovery of the sea route to India.

Henry the Wrangler (951–95) Duke of Bavaria. He ruled Bavaria under the regency of his mother, Judith, until he came of age c.970. In 974 he took part in a conspiracy against **Otto II** and was imprisoned, but escaped and fled to Bohemia in 976. After the death of Otto II he attempted, unsuccessfully, to become Regent to **Otto III**. He regained control of Bavaria in 985 and devoted himself to its internal development.

Henry, Patrick (1736–99) US politician. After training as a lawyer, he entered the colonial Virginia House of Burgesses, where his oratorical skills won him fame and before whom he delivered his famous lines 'Give me liberty or give me death'. He was outspoken in his opposition to British policy towards the colonies, particularly on the subject of the **Stamp Act** (1765), and he made the first speech in the **Continental Congress** (1774). In 1776 he became Governor of Virginia, and was four times re-elected. ▷ **American Revolution**

Hepburn, Mitchell Frederick (1896–1953) Canadian politician. A farmer who came to power as the Liberal Premier of Ontario (1934–42) with the promise of a 'swing to the left' and a fight in favour of the 'dispossesed and oppressed', he soon began to fight the CIO, which was asked in to help organize the General Motors plant at Oshawa in 1937, branding them as 'foreign agitators' and communists. After Mackenzie **King** refused to send in the **Mounties**, Hepburn organized his own anti-labour force, nicknamed 'Hepburn's Hussars' or the 'Sons of Mitch's' and attacked the federal government for its 'cowardice'. Although the strikers won company recognition, Hepburn gained increased electoral support, winning 75 per cent of the seats in the subsequent election. Hepburn continued his feud with the federal administration of Mackenzie King over both provincial rights (wrecking the 1941 conference on the recommendations of the **Rowell–Sirois Commission**) and its war policies, but this fight ruined his party and destroyed his health. Resigning from office in 1942, he lost his seat in the election of 1945 in which the **Liberal Party** was decimated. ▷ **AFL–CIO**

Heraclius (c.575–641) Byzantine Emperor (610/41). In 610 he headed a revolt against Emperor Phocas of Constantinople, killed him, and mounted his throne. He concluded a treaty with the Avars (620), who were threatening the north-west of the empire, and took the field against the Persians, who had captured Jerusalem (614), and all of Syria, Egypt, and Asia Minor. He routed them in a series of campaigns, won back the lost provinces, and restored the Cross to Jerusalem. After 634, however, his armies were defeated by the Arabs, and most of his achievements were lost. He died in Constantinople.

Herero Revolt (1907) A resistance movement by Bantu-speaking peoples in Namibia, crushed by the Germans with great brutality. They participated in the struggle for Namibian independence against South African rule.

Hereward, 'the Wake' (d.c.1080) Anglo-Saxon thegn. He returned from exile to lead in East Anglia the last organized English resistance against the Norman invaders. He held the Isle of Ely against **William I, 'the Conqueror'** for nearly a year (1070–1), then

disappeared from history, and entered medieval outlaw legend as a celebrated opponent of the forces of injustice. ▷ **Anglo-Saxons; Norman Conquest**

hermandad Literally 'brotherhood', this Spanish term refers to a popular 'vigilante' peacekeeping organization in medieval Castilian towns; it was adapted by the Castilian crown in the late 15c to act as local police and judiciary. These organizations lost much of their power and prestige during the 16c, and now the term is used only of ceremonial religious brotherhoods.

Hermann, Count of Salm (d.1088) German anti-king. Elected as the successor to the anti-king **Rudolf of Rheinfelden** (1080), he defeated **Frederick I** of Swabia and was formally crowned in Goslar in 1081. However his support evaporated and he fled from the Emperor's army to Denmark. With the support of Welf IV, he was able to undertake renewed campaigns in Germany but died storming a castle in 1088. No new anti-king was elected after his death.

Hermann of Salza (1170–1239) Grand Master of the Teutonic Order. Born into a family of **Ministeriales**, he became Grand Master in 1209. Under his leadership, the Order responded to Conrad of Masowia's appeal for help against the Prussians and he laid the basis of the Order's later power there. He was one of **Frederick II**'s closest advisers, acting as a diplomat in his service. His good relations with the Pope allowed him to mediate in the dispute between the empire and the papacy and he was able to use his position to gain many important concessions for the Teutonic Order. ▷ **Teutonic Knights**

Hermansson, Steingrímur (1928–) Icelandic politician. He trained as an electrical engineer in the USA, returning to pursue an industrial career. He became Director of Iceland's National Research Council (1957–78) and then made the transition into politics, becoming Chairman of the Progressive Party (PP) in 1979. He became a minister in 1978 and then Prime Minister, heading a PP–Independence Party (IP) coalition (1983–7) after which he accepted the Foreign Affairs portfolio in the government of Thorsteinn Pálsson. He became Prime Minister again in 1988.

Herod Antipas (d.39AD) The son of Herod the Great and Ruler (Tetrarch) of Galilee and Peraea (AD4/39), after Herod's death.

An able client of the Romans, he enjoyed an especially good relationship with the Emperor Tiberias, but fell foul of his successor, **Caligula**, largely through the machinations of his nephew, Herod Agrippa. In the Christian tradition, he looms large as the capricious murderer of John the Baptist.

Herod the Great (c.73–31/4BC) King of Judea. The younger son of the Idumaean chieftain, Antipater, he owed his initial appointment as Governor of Galilee (47BC) to Julius **Caesar**, his elevation to the kingship of Judea (40BC) to Mark **Antony**, and his retention in that post after **Actium** (31BC) to Octavian (later **Augustus**). Besides being a loyal and efficient Roman client king, who ruthlessly kept all his subjects in check, he was also an able and far-sighted administrator who did much to develop the economic potential of his kingdom, founding cities, and promoting agricultural projects. Life at court was marked by constant and often bloody infighting between his sister, his various wives, and their many offspring. Undoubtedly he was cruel, and this is reflected in the Gospel account of the Massacre of the Innocents.

Herriot, Edouard (1872–1957) French politician. Mayor of Lyons from 1905 until his death, he became Minister of Transport during **World War I**. A radical, he was three times Premier (1924–5, 1926 (for two days) and 1932), and was on several occasions President of the Chamber of Deputies. In 1942 he became a prisoner of the Nazis. After the war he was President of the National Assembly (1947–53). ▷ **Nazi Party; World War II**

Herstigte Nasionale Party ▷ **HNP**

Hertzog, J(ames) B(arry) M(unnik) (1866–1942) South African politician. He was a Boer general (1899–1902), and in 1910 became Minister of Justice in the first Union government. In 1913 he founded the Nationalist Party, advocating complete South African independence. As Premier, in coalition with Labour (1924–9), and with **Smuts** in a United Party (1933–9), he pursued a legislative programme which destroyed the African franchise, created job reservation for Whites, and also tightened land segregation. He renounced his earlier secessionism, but at the outbreak of **World War II** declared for neutrality, was defeated, and in 1940 retired.

Herules A Germanic tribe which originated in southern Sweden, they were subjected by the **Ostrogoths** and the **Huns**. The important kingdom they established in what is now western Slovakia was destroyed by the Langobards (505) and they disappeared in the 6c.

Herzen, Alexander Ivanovich (1812–70) Russian nobleman, political thinker and active propagandist. A brilliant student, he was arrested and exiled in 1834 and again in 1841 for his revolutionary ideas. In 1847 he left Russia for Paris but settled in London in 1851, becoming a powerful liberal socialist propagandist by his novels and treatises, and by the smuggling into Russia of his influential journal, *Kolokol* (The Bell). He died in Paris.

Herzl, Theodor (1869–1904) Hungarian Zionist leader. He moved to Vienna at the age of 18, where he trained as a lawyer and pursued a career as a journalist and author. In Paris as a newspaper correspondent (1891–5), he covered the **Dreyfus** trial in 1894 and was deeply affected by its anti-Semitism. He became convinced that the only adequate Jewish response was a political one. In 1895 he published *Der Judenstaat* (The Jewish State), in which he argued that the Jews should have their own state, which would receive Jews from those parts of the world where they experienced rejection or persecution. In 1897, in Basel, he convened the First Zionist Congress, which declared its goal to be the founding of a national Jewish home in Palestine and established the **World Zionist Organization** to that end. Herzl spent his remaining years strengthening this organization and seeking support for its aims from influential European leaders, and succeeded in moulding it into an efficient institution. While not original in his ideals, Herzl's efforts have rendered his name inseparable from the emergence of political **Zionism** in the modern period. ▷ **Ben-Gurion, David**

Heseltine, Michael (Ray Dibdin) (1933–) British politician. He built up a publishing business before becoming a Conservative MP in 1966. After holding junior posts in Transport (1970), Environment (1970–2), and Aerospace and Shipping (1972–4), he was appointed Secretary of State for the Environment (1979–83), and then Defence Secretary (1983–6). He resigned from the government in dramatic fashion by walking out of a cabinet meeting over the issue of the takeover of Westland helicopters. His challenge to Margaret **Thatcher**'s leadership of the **Conservative**

Party directly led to her resignation (Nov 1990) but he was defeated by John **Major** in the election to succeed her.

He Shen (Ho Shen) (1750–99) The son of a minor Manchu nobleman in China, he became the personal favourite of Emperor **Qianlong**. He attracted the interest of the Emperor in 1775 while serving as a member of the Imperial Bodyguard. Thereafter he was given important government posts and by 1778 was in charge of the Beijing gendarmerie and superintendent of customs. He used his influence with the Emperor to intervene in official appointments and amass a huge personal fortune, thus contributing to the depletion of the treasury and the spread of the corruption throughout the bureaucracy. Shortly after Qianlong's death, He Shen was arrested and forced to commit suicide.

Hess, (Walter Richard) Rudolf (1894–1987) German Nazi politician, **Hitler**'s deputy as party leader. Educated at Godesberg, he fought in **World War I**, then studied at Munich. He joined the **Nazi Party** in 1920, and became Hitler's close friend and (in 1934) deputy. In 1941, on the eve of Germany's attack on the USSR, he flew alone to Scotland to plead the cause of a negotiated Anglo-German peace. He was temporarily imprisoned in the Tower of London, then placed under psychiatric care near Aldershot. At the **Nuremberg Trials** (1946) he was sentenced to life imprisonment, and remained in Spandau prison, **Berlin** (after 1966, as the only prisoner), until his death. ▷ **World War II**

Hesse Established as an independent landgravate in the late 13c, the area experienced many problems until reunited by the Landgrave (1509–67), Philip the Magnanimous, who introduced Lutheranism in 1526 and founded the first Protestant University at Marburg (1527). The various subdivisions between subsequent heirs produced Hesse-Kassel and Hesse-Darmstadt. The former was allied with Sweden in the **Thirty Years War**. Frederick, son of Landgrave Charles (1654–1730) became Frederick I, King of Sweden in 1720. Hesse-Kassel became an electorate in 1803.

Heuss, Theodor (1884–1963) West German politician and President. Educated at Munich and **Berlin**, he became editor of the political magazine *Hilfe* (1905–12), professor at the Berlin College of Political Science (1920–33), and an MP (1924–8 and 1930–2). A prolific author and journalist, he wrote two books denouncing **Hitler**, and when the latter came to power in 1933, he was dismissed from his chair and his books publicly burnt. In 1946 he became a founder member of the Free Democratic Party (**FDP**), and helped to draft the new federal constitution. He was the first President of the Federal Republic of Gemany (1949–59).

He Xiangning (Ho Hsiang-ning) (1880–1972) Chinese revolutionary and feminist. Educated in Hong Kong and Japan, she married fellow revolutionary **Liao Zhongkai** in 1905 and was an active advocate of links with the communists and Russia. Her husband was assassinated in 1925, and when two years later **Chiang Kai-shek** broke with the communists, she returned to Hong Kong and was an outspoken critic of his leadership. She returned to Beijing in 1949 as head of the overseas commission. Ho Hsiang-ning was one of the first Chinese women to cut her hair short and publicly to advocate nationalism, revolution and female emancipation.

Hexi (Gansu) Corridor A natural corridor from central China through Gansu province to Xinjiang autonomous region. Some 750 miles long, it was a major part of the ancient Silk Road and the scene of numerous battles, from the 3c BC.

Heydrich, Reinhard (1904–42) Prominent Nazi functionary and Deputy-Chief of the **Gestapo**. As a youth, he joined the **Freikorps** ('Volunteer Corps'), and was later a naval sub-lieutenant; in 1931 he had to quit the navy and entered the **SS**, rising to be second-in-command of the secret police, and charged with pacifying occupied territories. In 1941 he was made protector of Bohemia and Moravia, but the following year was killed by Czech assassins parachuted in from the UK. In the murderous reprisals, Lidice village was razed and every man put to death.

Hidalgo (y Costilla), Miguel (1753–1811) Mexican revolutionary. The son of a poor farmer, he became a curate in several parishes. He was known to the Inquisition as an avid reader of Rousseau, and was banished to Dolores outside Mexico City. He led a rising against the Spanish authorities (16 Sep 1810), with the cry of 'Long live our Lady of Guadelupe, death to bad government and the Spaniards'. His following, a 'horde' some 60 000 strong, sacked Guanajuato, but his 'war of revenge' terrified wealthy Creoles into support for the colonial authorities.

Executed at Chihuahua, he remains a symbol of nationalism, and is often known as 'the Father of Mexican independence'.

Hiero I (d.467 or 466 BC) King of Syracuse, won a great naval victory over the Etruscans in 474. Though reputedly violent and rapacious, in contrast with his idealized brother and predecessor Gelon, he had a keen interest in poetry, and was the patron of Simonides of Ceos, Aeschylus, Bacchylides, and Pindar.

Hiero II (308–215 BC) King of Syracuse. The son of a noble Syracusan, he came to the fore during the troubles in Sicily after the retreat of **Pyrrhus** (275 BC), and in 269 was hailed as king. He joined the Carthaginians in besieging Messana, which had surrendered to the Romans; but was beaten by **Appius Claudius**. In 263 he concluded a 15-year peace with Rome, and in 258 a permanent one. In the second Punic war Hiero supported the Romans with money and troops. He was a patron of the arts, and was a relative and friend of Archimedes.

Higgins, Henry Bournes (1851–1929) Irish-born Australian politician and judge. His family emigrated to Melbourne in 1870 and he went on to become a successful lawyer, entering the Victorian assembly in 1894. He was a state representative at the Federal Convention (1897–8), where he criticized the powers reserved to the states and the rigidity of the federal constitution. As a supporter of Irish **Home Rule**, and opposing both the terms of **federation** and Australian participation in the **Boer Wars**, he lost his seat in the Victorian elections of 1900, although he remained popular with the Labor movement. In 1901 he entered Commonwealth politics as a Liberal, but became Attorney-General in the brief Labor administration of 1904. In 1906 he was appointed to the High Court, and in 1907 became President of the Commonwealth Conciliation and Arbitration Court. A firm believer in state intervention in industrial relations, he had, with **Kingston**, been responsible for the conciliation and arbitration provisions of the constitution. As President of the Arbitration Court he made the **Harvester Judgement** which established the principle of the minimum wage. He fought for the Commonwealth's right to arbitrate in the High Court, and resigned in protest against the interference of Prime Minister **Hughes** in 1921. By then arbitration had become an integral part of the Australian industrial system.

Hijaz Railway The railway, running between Damascus and Medina, which was built between 1901 and 1908, when the area was under Ottoman domination. The construction and subsequent operation of the railway was the province of a subdepartment of government later to become the Hijaz Railway Ministry. Financed by popular subscription and grants from the central treasury, the railway was constructed with German technical assistance. Its strategic importance to the Turkish military effort in the Hijaz during **World War I** made it an immediate target after the proclamation of the **Arab Revolt** by Sharif **Husayn ibn 'Ali** of Mecca in 1916. The Amir, Faysal, and British officers (among whom was T E **Lawrence**) successfully destroyed the railway as an effective transport system and were thus able to wrest control of Mecca and Jedda from the Ottomans, at the same time as isolating those Ottomans then in the Yemen. ▷ **Faysal I**

hijra (hegira) The migration of the Prophet **Muhammad** from Mecca to Medina in 622. The departure marks the beginning of the Muslim era.

Hillery, Patrick (John) (1923–) Irish politician. Following his election as an MP (1951), he held ministerial posts in Education (1959–65), then Industry and Commerce (1965–6), and Labour (1966–9), then became Foreign Minister (1969–72). Before becoming President of the Irish Republic (1976–90), he served as the **EEC** Commissioner for Social Affairs (1973–6).

Himiko (c.3c AD) Female ruler of a Japanese tribe known as the Yamato, which extended its control over other tribal groups in the area around Nara (Kyushu) at the eastern end of the Inland Sea. Chinese chronicles of the 3c describe her as a shamaness-ruler whose younger brother served as the non-spiritual ruler. She may have been killed by chieftains disillusioned with her waning religious powers in war. Evidence of female rule at this time and the claim of Yamato rulers that they were descended from the Sun Goddess (Amaterasu) have led some historians to suggest that early Japan may originally have been a matriarchal society that was only gradually transformed into the strongly male-dominated family system of later times.

Himmler, Heinrich (1900–45) German Nazi politician and Chief of Police. He joined the **Nazi Party** in 1925, and in 1929 was made head of the **SS**, which he developed from

Hitler's personal bodyguard into a powerful party weapon. In 1933 he commanded the Bavarian political police and in 1934 took over the secret police (**Gestapo**) in **Prussia**. Chief of Police from 1936, he later initiated the systematic liquidation of Jews. In 1943 he became Minister of the Interior, and in 1944 Commander-in-Chief of the home forces. He was captured by the Allies, and committed suicide at Lüneburg. ▷ **Holocaust; World War II**

Hincks, Sir Francis (1807–85) Canadian politician. Editor of the *Examiner*, the **Canada West** reform party newspaper founded in 1837, he united with Louis H **Lafontaine** in the campaign for **Responsible Government** which Lord Sydenham sought to evade. He became Prime Minister in 1851, and was primarily responsible for initiating **reciprocity** negotiations with the USA. He was also a sponsor of the Grand Trunk Railway, but some dubious financial dealings forced him out of office in 1854.

Hindenburg, Paul (Ludwig Hans Anton von Beneckendorff und) von (1847–1934) German general and President (1925–34). Educated at Wahlstatt and Berlin, he fought in the **Franco-Prussian War** (1870–1), rose to the rank of general (1903), and retired in 1911. Recalled at the outbreak of **World War I**, he won victories over the Russians (1914–15), and later directed the creation of strategic fortifications on the Western Front (the Hindenburg Line). A national hero, he became the second President of the German Republic in 1925 despite his known anti-republican views. He was re-elected in 1932 to block **Hitler**'s candidacy, but in 1933 appointed Hitler as Chancellor.

Hindu Mahasabha An Indian socio-political organization concerned with advancing Hindu nationalism. It started in Punjab in 1907 and claimed that the Congress and its concern for Hindu-Muslim unity would endanger Hindus. Within the Mahasabha, there was a divide between those who sought social reforms and those who were orthodox. The organization expanded under the leadership of **Lajpat Rai** and **Malaviya** who kept it linked with the **Congress**. Under Savarkar, it broke completely with the Congress in 1937 and strengthened links with the **RSS**. Its members included Nathuram Godse, M K **Gandhi**'s assassin. Mahasabha electoral support declined after 1952 as its Hindu nationalist themes were pre-empted by the Jan Sangh.

Hirata Atsutane (1776–1843) Japanese scholar and theologian. As an extreme chauvinist, he condemned Buddhist and Confucian influences in Japanese culture and insisted that the Japanese were superior to all other peoples. By elevating those Shinto beliefs in the divine character of the imperial institution, Hirata's teachings helped to undermine the legitimacy of the shogunate, influencing the imperial loyalist movement that was ultimately to overthrow the **Tokugawa Shogunate**.

Hirohito (1901–89) Emperor of Japan (1926/89). The 124th emperor in direct descent, his reign was marked by rapid militarization and the aggressive wars against China (1931–2 and 1937–45) and Britain and the USA (1941–5). The latter ended with the dropping of atomic bombs on **Hiroshima** and Nagasaki. Under US occupation, Hirohito in 1946 renounced his mythical divinity and most of his powers, and became a democratic constitutional monarch. ▷ **Akihito; World War II**

Hiroshima, Atomic Bombing of (6 Aug 1945) Hiroshima, the capital of Hiroshima prefecture, South Honshu Island, Japan, was chosen as the target for Little Boy, the first atomic bomb ever dropped, because of its importance as a centre of military and supply bases, shipyards and industrial plants. Approximately 150 000 people were killed or wounded as a result, and 75 per cent of the city's buildings were destroyed or severely damaged.

Hirota Koki (1878–1948) Japanese diplomat and politician. He had close links with the ultra-nationalist **Genyosha** and served in diplomatic posts in China, Britain, the USA and the USSR before becoming Foreign Minister in various non-party cabinets (1933–4 and 1934–6). He championed an assertive foreign policy to protect Japan's interests in China, and in 1935 laid down principles to guide Sino-Japanese relations: the formation of a Japan-China-Manchuria economic bloc, suppression of all anti-Japanese activities in China, and the creation of a Sino-Japanese front against **communism**. As Prime Minister (1936–7), he increased the military budget and signed the Anti-Comintern Pact with Germany and Italy, thus alienating Japan even further from the Anglo-Saxon powers. Appointed Foreign Minister again (1937–9), Hirota supported Japan's full-scale invasion of China in 1937. After the war, he was tried as a Class A war criminal and executed in 1948, the only civilian to be so sentenced.

Hiss, Alger (1904–) US civil servant. He reached high office as a State Department official, then stood trial twice (1949, 1950) on a charge of perjury, having denied before a Congressional Un-American Activities Committee that in 1938 he had passed secret state documents to Whittaker Chambers, an agent for an international communist spy ring. The case roused great controversy, but he was convicted at his second trial, and sentenced to five years' imprisonment. He did not return to public life after his release. The justice of his conviction continues to be disputed. ▷ **HUAC; McCarthy, Joseph**

Histadrut Israeli Zionist labour organization, formed in 1920, incorporated into the International Confederation of Free Trade Unions. Comprising both industrial and agricultural workers, its remit nonetheless includes activities beyond those normally associated with trade unions. *Histadrut* is involved in marketing and distribution, banking, building programmes, irrigation, healthcare, education and entertainment, as well as in traditional negotiations on working conditions and wages. Of considerable economic importance, Histadrut is run by an elected executive whose leaders have had strong ties with the **Mapai Party**. ▷ **Jewish Labour Movement in Palestine; World Zionist Organization**

Hitler, Adolf (1889–1945) German dictator and leader of the **Nazi Party**. The son of a minor customs official, he was educated at Linz and Steyr, attended art school in Munich, but failed to pass into the Vienna Academy. He lived on his family subventions in Vienna (1904–13), yet inhabited hostels and did a variety of menial jobs. In 1913 he emigrated to Munich, where he found employment as a draughtsman. In 1914 he served in a Bavarian regiment, became a corporal, was decorated, and was wounded in the last stages of **World War I**. In 1919 he joined a small political party which in 1920 he renamed as the National Socialist German Workers' Party. In 1923, with other extreme right-wing factions, he attempted to overthrow the Bavarian government as a prelude to a 'March on Berlin' in imitation of **Mussolini**'s 'March on Rome', but was imprisoned for nine months in Landsberg jail, during which time he dictated to Rudolf **Hess** his political testament, *Mein Kampf* (1925, My Struggle). He expanded his party

greatly in the late 1920s, won important parliamentary election victories in 1930 and 1932 and though he was unsuccessful in the presidential elections of 1932 against **Hindenburg**, he was made Chancellor in 1933. He then suspended the constitution, silenced all opposition, exploited successfully the burning of the **Reichstag** building, and brought the **Nazi Party** to power, having dozens of his opponents within his own party and the **SA** murdered by his bodyguard, the **SS**, in the **Night of the Long Knives** (1934). He openly rearmed the country (1935), established the Rome–Berlin 'axis' with Mussolini (1936) and pursued an aggressive foreign policy which culminated in **World War II** (3 Sep 1939). His domestic policy traded off social and economic improvements for political dictatorship enforced by the Secret State Police (**Gestapo**). His government established concentration camps for political opponents and Jews, over 6 million of whom were murdered in the course of World War II. With his early war successes, he increasingly ignored the advice of military experts and wantonly extended the war with his long-desired invasion of the USSR in 1941. The tide turned in 1942 after the defeats at **El Alamein** and **Stalingrad**. He miraculously survived the explosion of the bomb placed at his feet by Colonel **Stauffenberg** (July 1944), and purged the army of all suspects. When Germany was invaded, he retired to his *Bunker*, an air-raid shelter under the Chancellory building in Berlin. All available evidence suggests that Hitler and his wife committed suicide and had their bodies cremated (30 Apr 1945).

Hitler–Stalin Pact ▷ **German–Soviet Pact**

Hitler Youth (*Hitler-Jugend*) The organization, set up by Adolf **Hitler** in 1933, designed to inculcate Nazi principles in German youths. By 1935, membership accounted for almost 60 per cent of German boys. It became (1 July 1936) a state agency that all young 'Aryan' Germans were expected to join. On his tenth birthday, after various investigations (especially for 'racial purity'), a German boy would enter the *Deutsches Jungvolk* ('German Young People'). At 13, he was eligible to join the Hitler Youth, in which he remained until the age of 18, living an austere life, dominated by Nazi theory, generally with minimun parental guidance. When he was 18, he became a member of the Nazi Party, serving in the state labour service and the armed forces until at least the age of 21. A parallel organization, the *Bund Deutscher Mädel* ('League of German Girls'), trained girls for domestic duties and motherhood.

Hittin, Battle of (4 July 1187) This battle saw the destruction by the Sultan **Saladin** of the field army of the Latin Kingdom of Jerusalem and led directly to his capture of Jerusalem (2 Oct 1187). An ill-advised march from Sepphoris, with Tiberias as its objective, led to **Guy of Lusignan**'s Crusaders being caught at a disadvantage on hostile terrain by Saladin's combined muster, including as it did forces deriving from Egypt and the entire Fertile Crescent. The defeat of the Crusaders at Hittin, the capture of their nobility, and the destruction of the Latin field army, coupled with the subsequent loss of Jerusalem, constituted the proximate cause of the Third Crusade. ▷ **Crusade, Third**

Hittites A people of uncertain origin who became prominent in central Asia Minor in the first part of the second millennium BC; they spoke an Indo-European language, known as Hittite. At their zenith (1450–1200BC), their Empire covered most of Anatolia and parts of northern Syria (eg Carchemish). It was destroyed by marauding invaders, known as the Sea Peoples, around 1200BC.

Hizbullah (Hizbollah) The umbrella organization in south Beirut of militant Shiite Muslims with Iranian links; the name means 'Party of God'. They came to world attention after the TWA hijacking in Cairo in 1985, and the subsequent taking of hostages. ▷ **Shiites**

Hlinka, Andrei (1864–1938) Slovak priest and politician. As a young man he was attracted by the political stance of the Slovak National Party and by the concern for the peasants of the Magyar Populist Party. In 1905 he established the Slovak Populists Party as a compromise, but he was soon being harassed by the Hungarian authorities. In 1918 he supported the creation of Czechoslovakia but he was subsequently disappointed with centralist rule from Prague and his own non-involvement in governing his countrymen. In the 1920s and 1930s he built up his party and secured some political concessions from Prague. But in the middle of 1938 he used the opportunity of **Beneš**'s discomfiture to demand autonomy for Slovakia. However, he died in Aug and left **Tiso** to develop a treasonable relationship with Germany.

HNP (*Herstigte Nasionale Party*, 'Reconstituted National Party') Founded in 1969 by dissidents from the **National Party**, the HNP seeks to preserve **apartheid** undiluted, the Afrikaans language, and a public policy based upon Calvinist principles. It allied with the Conservative Party in the late 1980s to embarrass the Nationalist Party in individual constituencies, which it occasionally defeats.

Hoare–Laval Pact An agreement concluded in 1935 by the British Foreign Secretary Samuel Hoare and the French Prime Minister Pierre **Laval** aimed at the settlement of a dispute between Italy and Abyssinia. By this pact, large parts of Abyssinia were ceded to Italy. A public outcry against the pact led to its repudiation by Britain and to Hoare's resignation.

Hoche, Lazare (1768–97) French revolutionary soldier. Promoted from corporal to general, he defended Dunkirk against Frederick Augustus, Duke of York, and drove the Austrians out of Alsace (1793), ended the civil war in La Vendée (1795), commanded the attempted invasion of Ireland (1796), and defeated the Austrians at Neuwied (1797). ▷ **Vendée, Wars of the**

Ho Chi Minh (1892–1969) Vietnamese politician, born Nguyen That Thanh. From 1912 he visited London and the USA, and lived in France from 1918, where he was a founder member of the Communist Party. From 1922 he was often in China and then Moscow. He led the **Viet Minh** independence movement from 1941, and directed the successful military operation against the French (1946–54). Prime Minister (1954–5) and President (1954–69) of North Vietnam, he was the leading force in the war between North and South Vietnam during the 1960s. ▷ **Vietnam War**

Höchstädt, Battle of (1703) The battle won by the Elector of Bavaria over the Imperial general Styrum in the War of the **Spanish Succession**. The Battle of Blenheim (1704) is sometimes referred to as the Second Battle of Höchstädt as the latter is the nearest large town to the village of Blenheim.

Hodza, Milau (1878–1944) Slovak politician. A Lutheran, he worked with Catholics such as **Hlinka** before **World War I** in order to secure some kind of autonomy for Slovakia. He hoped for improvement within Austria-Hungary but failing that, he favoured a Czech-Slovak solution, which is what came in 1918. He never abandoned his Slovak sentiments, though he became mostly a convinced Czechoslovak and was appointed Czechoslovak Premier in 1935. The strain of dealing with **Hitler** and **Henlein** from 1937 through 1938 put his loyalties to test, and there is evidence that he was talking out of turn both to the Germans and to disloyal Slovaks at the height of the pre-Munich crisis. In the final days before the **Munich Agreement** he has dropped from the premiership, and even abroad during **World War II** his political contribution was slight.

Høegh-Guldberg, Ove (1731–1808) Danish politician. Of humble Jutland origin, he studied theology at the University of Copenhagen and was in 1761 appointed Professor at the Noble Academy in Sorø. In the same year, he also became the tutor of Prince Frederick, son of the late King Frederick V and his second wife, the powerful Queen Dowager, Juliane Marie. On 16 Jan 1772 Juliane Marie was the leader of a palace revolution that overthrew the self-appointed, progressive-minded dictator, Johann Friedrich **Struensee**, who since the summer of 1770 had filled the power gap created by the mental illness of King **Christian VII**. After the palace revolution, Høegh-Guldberg became Denmark's most influential politician, for 12 years pursuing his cautious policies from his power base, the King's 'court cabinet', of which he was the Secretary. Høegh-Guldberg's court rule culminated in the years 1780 to 1784. In 1784 his regime was overturned by another coup d'état led by Crown Prince Frederick, son of King Christian VII, and by Høegh-Guldberg's principal political adversary, Andreas Peter **Bernstorff**. After this, Høegh-Guldberg became a civil servant in the provincial town of Aarhus, where he loyally implemented the progressive policies of the new regime.

Hofer, Andreas (1767–1810) Tyrolese patriot leader and innkeeper. In 1808 he called the Tyrolese to arms to expel the French and Bavarians, and defeated the Bavarians at the Battle of Isel Berg (1809). The Treaty of **Vienna** between **Austria** and France after the Battle of **Wagram** (July 1809) left Tyrol unsupported. The French again invaded them; but in eight days Hofer routed them and retook Innsbruck, and for the next two months was ruler of his native land. By the Peace of Vienna (Oct) Austria again left Tyrol at the mercy of her enemies. Hofer once more took up arms, but this time the French and Bavarians were too strong for him; Hofer had to disband his followers and take refuge in the mountains. Two months later he was betrayed, captured and taken to Mantua, where he was tried by court martial and shot.

Hofkapelle As early as the Carolingian period all written work in the royal chancellory was undertaken by clerics. These clerics were referred to as the *Kapelle* ('chapel') and were under the direction of a head chaplain. From c.854, the chaplain was entrusted with the leadership of the chancellory and from 975 the office of chancellor was always held by the Archbishop of Mainz. The clerics in the *Hofkapelle* (literally 'court chapel') also undertook political and diplomatic missions and many, particularly in the Ottonian period, attained important feudal positions. Its importance declined from the 11c onwards, although the chancellor was a cleric until the 15c. ▷ **Ottonians**

Hofmeyr, Jan Hendrik (1845–1909) South African politician. He took to journalism, as 'Onze Jan', rose to be political leader of the Cape Dutch and dominated the **Afrikaner Bond**. He represented the Cape at the Colonial Conferences of 1887 and 1894. After the **Jameson Raid** (1895) he parted from **Rhodes**, and thereafter worked outside parliament. His nephew, Jan Hendrik (1894–1948), was Deputy Premier to **Smuts** and advocated a liberal policy towards the Africans.

Hogendorp, Gijsbert Karel (1762–1834) Dutch politician. A member of a patrician family, he studied law and became active in politics as a champion of the House of Orange during the revolutionary **Patriot Movement** in the 1780s. He became Pensionary of Rotterdam, but was out of office during the period of French domination of the Netherlands (1795–1813). As the French were withdrawing in 1812, he was instrumental in arranging the return of William of Orange (who became King **William I**), and chaired the committee which drew up the new Dutch constitutions in the post-Napoleonic period. He was Foreign Minister (1813–14), and Vice-President of the Council of State (1814–16), but disagreed with King William and spent the years 1816–25 as an MP highly critical of the government. His writings on political economy had considerable impact in the Netherlands, promoting both political and economic liberalism.

Hohenlinden, Battle of (1800) A confused but crucial battle in the closing stage of the

HOHENSTAUFEN DYNASTY

Regnal Dates (as Holy Roman Emperor)	Name
1138/52	Conrad III
1152/90	Frederick I, 'Barbarossa'
1190/7	Henry VI
1198/1208	Philip of Swabia
1198/1214	Otto IV
1215/50	Frederick II
1250/4	Conrad IV

French Revolutionary War, causing the Austrians to abandon the Second Coalition by the Armistice of Steyr. It was fought near Munich between the French, commanded by General Moreau, and Archduke John's Austrian forces, the latter suffering heavy casualties. ▷ **French Revolutionary Wars**

Hohenlohe-Schillingsfürst, Chlodwig Karl Victor, Prince von (1819–1901) Prussian politician and Chancellor. A supporter of **Bismarck**'s unification policies and a noted conservative, he served as a diplomat in Paris and Alsace-Lorraine, before becoming Chancellor (1894–1900) and Prime Minister of **Prussia**.

Hohenstaufen Dynasty The German royal dynasty named after the castle of Staufen in north-eastern Swabia. From 1138 to 1254 its members wore the crown of the **Holy Roman Empire**, starting with **Conrad III** and ending with Conrad IV, the dynasty reaching its zenith under **Frederick I, 'Barbarossa'** and **Frederick II**. They were also kings of Germany and of Sicily. The Hohenstaufen period is associated with a flowering of German courtly culture.

Hohenzollern Dynasty The German ruling dynasty of Brandenburg-Prussia (1415–1918) and Imperial Germany (1871–1918). Originating in Swabia in the 9c, one branch of the family became Burgraves of Nuremberg; a descendant, Frederick VIII, was rewarded by the Emperor with the title of Elector of Brandenburg (1415). After the **Thirty Years War**, the Hohenzollerns pursued a consistent policy of state expansion and consolidation, generating a long-standing rivalry with the **Habsburg Dynasty** (1740–1871), from which **Bismarck** ensured that the Hohenzollerns emerged successfully with the imperial title (1871). **World War I** ruined Hohenzollern militarism, and forced the abdication of the last Emperor, **William II** (1918). ▷ **Frederick**

I of Prussia; **Frederick II, 'the Great'**; **Frederick III** of Germany; **Frederick William ('The Great Elector')**; **Frederick William III**; **William I** (Emperor)

Ho Hsiang-ning ▷ **He Xiangning**

Hojo Family A Japanese warrior family during the **Kamakura Shogunate** whose members became hereditary regents virtually ruling Japan for more than a century. The patriarch of the family, Hojo Tokimasa (1138–1215), was the father-in-law of the first Kamakura shogun, Minamoto no Yoritomo (1147/99). After his death, Hojo exercised control over the shogunate, becoming regent in 1203; thereafter, the post became hereditary. Under the fifth Hojo regent, Hojo Tokimune (1268/84), the Mongol invasions of 1274 and 1281 were successfully repelled. The last effective Hojo regent, Hojo Takatoki (1316/26), frustrated Emperor Daigo II's two attempts to overthrow the shogunate and restore direct imperial rule. With the overthrow of the Kamakura Shogunate in 1333 by **Ashikaga Takauji**, the Hojo regency was abolished and the family ordered to commit suicide. ▷ **Minamoto Family**

HOHENZOLLERN DYNASTY

Regnal Dates	Name
Electors of Brandenburg	
1417/40	Frederick I
1440/70	Frederick II
1470/86	Albert Achilles
1486/99	John Cicero
1499/1535	Joachim I
1535/71	Joachim II
1571/98	John George
1598/1608	Joachim Frederick
1608/19	John Sigismund
1619/40	George William
1640/88	Frederick William ('The Great Elector')
Kings of Prussia	
1701/13	Frederick I (Frederick III as Elector of Brandenburg, 1688/1713)
1713/40	Frederick William I
1740/86	Frederick II, 'the Great'
1786/97	Frederick William II
1797/1840	Frederick William III
1840/61	Frederick William IV
Emperors of Germany	
1871/88	William I (King of Prussia, 1861/88)
1888	Frederick III
1888/1918	William II

Holkeri, Harri (1937–) Finnish politician. A political activist in his teens, he joined the youth league of the centrist National Coalition Party in 1959 and was its Information, Research and National Secretary between 1962 and 1971. Holkeri was elected to Helsinki City Council in 1969, entered Parliament the following year and became Prime Minister in 1987.

Holmes, Oliver Wendell (1841–1935) US judge. Known as the 'Great Dissenter', he was the son of the writer, Oliver Wendell Holmes (1809–94). Educated at Harvard, he became a lawyer, and served in the Union army in the **American Civil War**. From 1867 he practised law in Boston, became coeditor of the *American Law Review*, and Professor of Law at Harvard (1882). He became Chief Justice (1899–1902) of the Supreme Court of Massachusetts, and Associate Justice of the US Supreme Court (1902–32). He earned his nickname because he frequently dissented from the conservative court's majority opinions, especially as the court moved to dismantle social legislation, particularly relating to regulation of the economy.

Holocaust The attempt by Nazi Germany to destroy systematically European Jews. From the inception of the Nazi regime in 1933 Jews were deprived of civil rights, persecuted, physically attacked, imprisoned, pressurized to emigrate, and murdered. With the gradual conquest of Europe by Germany, the death toll increased, and a meeting at Wannsee (Jan 1942) made plans for the so-called 'final solution'. Jews were herded into concentration camps, slave labour camps, and extermination camps. By the end of **World War II** in 1945, more than 6 million Jews had been murdered out of a total Jewish population of 8 million in those countries occupied by the Nazis. Of these the largest number, 3 million, were from Poland. Other minorities (gypsies, various religious sects, homosexuals) and millions of Soviet prisoners were also subject to Nazi atrocities, but the major genocide was against the Jewish people. ▷ **Babi Yar; concentration camp; Nazi Party**

Holstein A county, then (1474) a duchy of the **Holy Roman Empire**. After the Peace of Prague (1866) it was incorporated into **Prussia** with Schleswig as the province of Schleswig-Holstein both of which had large Danish minorities.

Holt, Harold Edward (1908–67) Australian politician. He entered the House of Repre-

sentatives in 1935, becoming Deputy Leader of the **Liberal Party of Australia** (1956), and Leader and Prime Minister, when Robert **Menzies** retired (1966). During the **Vietnam War** he strongly supported the USA with the slogan 'all the way with LBJ'. He died in office while swimming at Portsea, near Melbourne.

Holy Alliance (20 Nov 1815) The alliance concluded on this day after the final defeat of **Napoleon I** between Austria, Britain, **Prussia** and Russia, which was designed to ensure the exclusion of the House of Bonaparte from power in France and to guarantee the monarchist order in Europe. Each power made specific military commitments in the event of war with France; however royalist France itself joined the alliance at the Congress of Aachen (Aix-la-Chapelle) in 1818.

Holy League (1510) An alliance of the papacy under **Julius II** with Venice, Aragon and England against France. ▷ **Italian Wars**

Holy League (1571) An alliance of the three Catholic powers, Venice, Spain, and the Papacy, after protracted negotiations by Pope **Pius V** (1570–1) to counter Turkish supremacy in the eastern Mediterranean. The league's fleet commanded by Don **John of Austria** smashed the Turks at the Battle of **Lepanto** (1571), before disagreements divided the allies; by 1573 Spain continued the struggle alone.

Holy League (1576) An association of militant French Catholics, led by Henry, 3rd Duke of **Guise**, until his death in 1588; one of its members, a monk, assassinated **Henry III** (of France), after which the League proclaimed the Cardinal de Bourbon king as 'Charles X'; however, **Henry IV** managed to impose himself as king by renouncing Protestantism ('Paris is worth a mass'). ▷ **Bourbon, House of; Guise, House of**

Holy League (1684) The union of the empire, Poland, Venice, and the Papacy against Turkey, following the imperial repossession of Vienna (1683). Pope **Innocent XI** planned further crusades in Hungary, Greece, and Moldavia; the latter failed (1686), but after several years' fighting (1683–99) the league recovered most of Hungary for the Habsburgs, and began the reconquest of Greece (1685–7). ▷ **Habsburg Dynasty**

HOLY ROMAN EMPERORS

Regnal Dates	Name	Regnal Dates	Name	Regnal Dates	Name
800/14	Charlemagne (Charles I)	1081/93	Hermann[2][4]	1346/78	Charles IV
814/40	Louis I, 'the Pious'	1093/1101	Conrad[2][4]	1378/1400	Wenceslas[4]
840/3	Civil War	1106/25	Henry V	1400/10	Rupert I[4]
843/55	Lothair I	1125/37	Lothair II	1410/37	Sigismund
855/75	Louis II	1138/52	Conrad III[4]	1438/9	Albert II[4]
875/7	Charles II, 'the Bald'	1152/90	Frederick I, 'Barbarossa'	1440/93	Frederick III
877/81	Interregnum	1190/7	Henry VI	1493/1519	Maximilian I[4]
881/7	Charles III, 'the Fat'	1198/1208	Philip of Swabia[2][4]	1519/56	Charles V[4]
887/91	Interregnum	1198/1214	Otto IV	1556/64	Ferdinand I[4]
891/4	Guido of Spoleto	1215/50	Frederick II	1564/76	Maximilian II[4]
892/8	Lambert of Spoleto[1]	1246/7	Henry Raspe[2][4]	1576/1612	Rudolf II[4]
896/9	Arnulf[2]	1247/56	William, Count of	1612/19	Matthias[4]
901/5	Louis III		Holland[2][4]	1619/37	Ferdinand II[4]
911/18	Conrad I[2][4]	1250/4	Conrad IV[4]	1637/57	Ferdinand III[4]
905/24	Berengar I	1254/73	Great Interregnum	1658/1705	Leopold I[4]
919/36	Henry I, 'the Fowler'[4]	1257/72	Richard[2][4]	1705/11	Joseph I[4]
936/73	Otto I, 'the Great'	1257/75	Alfonso (Alfonso X	1711/40	Charles VI[4]
973/83	Otto II		of Castile)[2][4]	1740/2	Interregnum
983/1002	Otto III	1273/91	Rudolf I[4]	1742/5	Charles VII[4]
1002/24	Henry II	1292/8	Adolf[4]	1745/65	Francis I[4]
1024/39	Conrad II	1298/1308	Albert I[4]	1765/90	Joseph II[4]
1039/56	Henry III	1308/13	Henry VII	1790/2	Leopold II[4]
1056/1106	Henry IV	1314/26	Frederick (III)[3][4]	1792/1806	Francis II[4]
1077/80	Rudolf of Rheinfelden[2][4]	1314/46	Louis IV, 'the Bavarian'		

[1] Co-Emperor   [2] Rival   [3] Co-Regent
[4] Ruler not crowned at Rome; therefore, strictly speaking, only King of Germany

Holyoake, Sir Keith Jacka (1904–83) New Zealand politician. A successful farmer who represented New Zealand's agricultural industry overseas, he sat in the House of Representatives as its youngest member (1932–8). Re-elected in 1943, he became Deputy Leader of the National Party in 1947, Deputy Prime Minister in 1949 and, briefly, Party Leader and Prime Minister in 1957. He was Prime Minister (1960–72) and Governor-General of New Zealand (1977–80).

Holy Roman Empire The revived medieval title of the Roman Empire, dating from the 9c, when the papacy granted the title to **Charlemagne**, King of the **Franks**. It was later bestowed upon German princely families, including the **Hohenstaufen Dynasty**, the House of **Luxemburg**, and the **Habsburg Dynasty**. After Charlemagne, imperial power was greatest under the Hohenstaufens in the 12–13c: the full title 'Holy Roman Empire' (*sacrum Romanum imperium*) was used from the reign of **Frederick I, 'Barbarossa'**; and **Frederick II** came close to uniting diverse imperial territories that covered much of central Europe and Italy. From the 14c, the empire's power declined with the rise of princely power and city-states; the title was dropped in 1806. ▷ **Electors; Swabian League**

Home Guard A home defence militia, raised during the summer of 1940, when the German armies seemed poised to complete the conquest of Western Europe by invading Great Britain. At first called the Local Defence Volunteers, the name was changed at Prime Minister Winston **Churchill**'s urging to the more evocative title of 'Home Guard'. The force was finally stood down in 1945. ▷ **World War II**

Homelands ▷ **apartheid**

Home of the Hirsel, Baron (formerly, **Sir Alec Douglas-Home**) (1903–) British politician. He became a Conservative MP in 1931 and was Neville **Chamberlain**'s Secretary during the negotiations with **Hitler** and beyond (1937–40). He became Minister of State at the Scottish Office (1951–5), succeeded to the peerage as 14th Earl of Home (1951), was Commonwealth Relations Secretary (1955–60), and Foreign Secretary (1960–3). After **Macmillan**'s resignation, he surprisingly emerged from the process of consultation as Leader of the **Conservative Party** and, thus, Premier (1963–4). He made history by renouncing his peerage and fighting a by-election, during which, although Premier, he was technically a member of neither House. After the 1964 defeat by the **Labour Party**, he was Leader of the Opposition until replaced in 1965 by Edward **Heath**, in whose 1970–4 government he was Foreign Secretary. In 1974 he was made a life peer.

Home Rule The handing down of certain legislative powers and administrative functions, previously exercised by a higher authority, to an elected body within a geographically defined area; usually put forward as an alternative to separatism. In British history, it has usually been applied to policies for Ireland, as with **Gladstone** in the 1880s and 1890s. It was also illustrated by the government of Northern Ireland (1922–72) when **Stormont**, the Northern Ireland parliament, was abolished. Since the early 1970s in the UK, for political movements such as the **Scottish National Party** and Irish republicans, home rule has tended to become synonymous with separatism. ▷ **IRA; Plaid Cymru**

Homestead Act (1862) A US law aimed at increasing the agricultural development of the West. It granted 160 acres of public land to settlers, who agreed to stay five years, and to cultivate their land. Homesteaders had to be US citizens or to have filed for citizenship, and either heads of families or over 21 years of age.

Homestead Steel Strike (1892) A five-month strike, one of the bitterest industrial disputes in US labour history, which seriously weakened organized labour in the steel industry at the Carnegie Steel Company, near Pittsburgh, USA. When the union would not agree to a wage-cut, the manager, Henry Frick, refused to negotiate except with individual employees. He then recruited strike-breakers and hired 300 **Pinkerton** detectives to protect them. The union seized the works, and an armed battle broke out when the Pinkertons attempted to break in, in which several men were killed or injured. Control of the factory was regained only when the National Guard was sent in at Frick's request by the governor of Pennsylvania.

Honda Toshiaki (1744–1821) Japanese political economist and navigator. He learnt Dutch in order to acquire knowledge of the West and, after surveying Japan's northern island of Hokkaido in 1801, he advocated a programme to bring about wealth and power focusing on the manufacture of gunpowder and metals, the encouragement of shipping, and the colonization of Hokkaido. Honda's programme envisaged an end to the traditional policy of isolation and the promotion of state-sponsored foreign trade, thus anticipating developments after the **Meiji Restoration** (1868).

Honecker, Erich (1912–) East German politician. Active in the communist youth movement from an early age, he was involved in underground resistance to **Hitler**, and was imprisoned for 10 years. Released by Soviet forces, he became the first Chairman of the Free German Youth in the German Democratic Republic (1946–55). He first entered the Politburo in 1958, oversaw the building of the **Berlin Wall** in 1961 and was elected party chief in 1971, becoming Head of State from 1976 to 1989. Although prepared to deal with the West, he maintained a tight grip on East Germany. He was dismissed as a consequence of the anti-communist revolution. Manslaughter charges, instigated against him for the deaths of those fleeing East Germany, who fell victim to his regime's 'shoot-to-kill' policy at her borders, were dropped in Jan 1993, after it was revealed that he was suffering from terminal illness. ▷ **Germany, East; Revolution of 1989**

Hong Kong, Cession of (1842) One of the terms of the Treaty of **Nanjing** signed by Britain and China following the end of the first of the **Opium Wars**. In addition to paying an indemnity, opening five **treaty ports** to foreign trade and abolishing the **Cohong**, China was compelled to cede the island of Hong Kong 'in perpetuity' to Britain. Under British rule, Hong Kong became a free-trade entrepot, attracting migrants from the nearby province of Guangdong. The Kowloon Peninsula on the adjoining mainland was added to Britain's colony of Hong Kong in 1860, following the second of the Opium Wars (1856–60).

Hong Rengan (Hung Jen-kan) (1822–64) Distant cousin and close associate of **Hong Xiuquan**, leader of the **Taiping Rebellion**. Left at home to look after family affairs when Xiuquan launched the rebellion (1850), he later went to Hong Kong, became a Christian, and studied Western culture. In 1859 he succeeded in reaching the rebel capital at Nanjing (Nanking), where he tried to introduce a programme of political, religious and military reforms. His aims were frustrated by the increasing madness of Xiuquan, the opposition of the rebellion's leaders, and the hostility of the British minister to China.

After the recapture of Nanjing by the Imperial forces (1864), he was caught and executed.

Hong Xiuquan (Hung Hsiu-ch'üan) (1813–64) Chinese revolutionary. Leader of the **Taiping Rebellion** in China, and self-styled Divine Sovereign of the Heavenly Kingdom of Transcendent Peace. The son of a poor Guangdong farmer of Hakka stock, during an illness he had religious visions which led him to preach a new Christian revelation in China. In 1843 he and two cousins began to preach and to destroy idols, arousing the opposition of Imperial forces. In 1851 he proclaimed a theocratic kingdom, and by 1853 his movement, half a million-strong, had taken Nanjing (Nanking). By 1855 the war against the Manchus had reached stalemate, and there were internal dissensions within his movement. In 1864 the troops of Zeng Guofan broke into Nanking and massacred the Taipings within. Hong was already dead, either by his own hand or as a result of the siege. ▷ **Hong Rengan**

Honorius (384–423) Roman Emperor of the West (395/423). He was the younger son of **Theodosius I**. A young and feeble ruler, he abandoned Britain to the barbarians, and cowered in Ravenna while **Alaric I** and the **Goths** besieged and sacked Rome (408–410). From 395 to 408, power was effectively in the hands of **Stilicho**.

Honorius III (Cencio Savelli) (d.1227) Pope (1216/27). Unanimously elected as successor to **Innocent III**, his pontificate was at first dominated by the need to involve **Frederick II** in crusade. Concessions to achieve this aim were exploited by the Emperor for his own ends. Honorius then devoted his energies to the suppression of heresy within the boundaries of Christendom and the extension of those boundaries in the Baltic and Spain.

Hood (of Whitley), Samuel, 1st Viscount (1724–1816) British admiral. He joined the navy in 1741, and fought during the **American Revolution**, when he defeated the French in the West Indies (1782), for which he was made a baron in the Irish peerage. In 1784 he became an MP, and in 1788 a Lord of the Admiralty. In 1793, he directed the occupation of Toulon and the operations in the Gulf of Lyons. He was made viscount in 1796. ▷ **American Revolution**

Hooks, Benjamin Lawson (1925–   ) US civil rights leader. A minister and lawyer, he

was appointed by President **Nixon** to the Federal Communications Commission (FCC) in 1972 and became the first black American to serve there. After leaving the FCC in 1977, he took over the leadership of the **NAACP**.

Hoover, Herbert C(lark) (1874–1964) US politician and 31st President. During **World War I** he was associated with food and relief efforts in Europe. In 1921 he became Secretary of Commerce. As President (1929–33), his belief in spontaneous economic recovery made him reluctant to provide massive federal assistance for the unemployed after the stock market crash of 1929. This unpopular position led to his defeat by Franklin D Roosevelt in 1932. Following **World War II**, he assisted **Truman** with the various US European economic-relief programs. ▷ **Great Depression; Republican Party**

Hoover, J Edgar (1895–1972) US public official. Director of the FBI, his length of service, from 1924 until his death (because President Lyndon B **Johnson** exempted him from civil-service retirement regulations) has been interpreted both as a tribute to his national importance in the fight against crime and as a recognition that he had learnt too much about the politicians. In the early days, his force was at a disadvantage in dealing with the gangsters of **Prohibition**, but with the **Lindbergh** kidnapping case the FBI's powers were considerably strengthened. His selection and training of the 'G-Men' created an effective and efficient organization. The application of modern scientific techniques enabled him to develop counter-espionage methods of value not only during **World War II** and the **Cold War**, but also in operations against the Mafia and the **Ku Klux Klan**. Very sensitive to criticisms of the FBI, Hoover responded angrily to the strictures contained in the Warren Commission's report on the assassination of President **Kennedy**, but he then used the urban riots of the 1960s with great political skill to increase the Bureau's powers and funding. A fanatical anti-communist, he saw much **civil rights** protest in this light and flagrantly abused his powers in some investigations of the civil rights and anti-**Vietnam War** movements (notably that of Martin Luther **King**).

Hopkins, Harry Lloyd (1890–1946) US administrator. He was federal emergency relief administrator in the 1933 **Great Depression**, became Secretary of Commerce (1938–40), and supervised the Lend-Lease programme in 1941. A close friend of Franklin D **Roosevelt**, he undertook several important missions to Russia, Britain, and other countries during **World War II**. ▷ **Lend-Lease Agreement; New Deal**

Horatii and Curiatii An early Roman legend used to justify appeals. Under Tullus **Hostilius** there was war between Rome and Alba. Two groups of three brothers were selected from Rome (the Horatii) and Alba (the Curiatii) to fight, the winners to decide the battle. All were killed except one Horatius. When his sister, who was betrothed to a Curiatius, abused him, he murdered her, but was acquitted after appealing to the Roman people.

Horatius Cocles (late 6c BC) Legendary Roman hero of early Republican times. He saved the newly-established **Roman Republic** (509 BC) from a return to the tyrannical rule of King **Tarquinius Superbus** by single-handedly holding the Pons Sublicius—at that time the only bridge across the Tiber—against the invading Etruscan army of Lars Porsenna, Tarquinius's would-be restorer. After the bridge had been cut down behind him, Horatius jumped into the river. According to one version of the legend, he swam safely back to Rome; in another, he perished.

Hore-Belisha (of Devonport), (Isaac) Leslie Hore-Belisha, 1st Baron (1893–1957) British barrister and politician. He became a London journalist, and a Liberal MP (1923). In 1934, as Minister of Transport, he gave his name to the 'Belisha' beacons, drafted a new highway code, and inaugurated driving tests for motorists. As Secretary of State for War (1937–40) he carried out several army reforms, and introduced conscription in 1939. He received a peerage in 1954. ▷ **Liberal Party** (UK)

Horemheb (Djeserkheprure) (c.1339/1304 BC) King of Egypt. A soldier, he was the commander-in-chief of **Tutankhamun's** forces, who prepared a tomb at Sakkara, the sculptured reliefs of which feature campaigns in Syria/Palestine and Nubia. There were attempts to revive Egyptian power in territories which had revolted in the reign of Akhenaten. The royal line became extinct on the death of Tutankhamun; he was succeeded by Ay, an army officer, who in turn died without an heir, leaving Horemheb to become king. Horemheb was buried in the Valley of the Kings at Thebes, rather than at Sakkara. His main achievement was to

prepare the way for the Ramesside rulers of the following dynasty, issuing an edict suppressing corruption and fraud, re-organizing district councils and reforming the army.

Horn, Arvid Bernhard (1664–1742) Swedish politician. Born in Finland, he began his career in the army and on the outbreak of the **Great Northern War** (1700) was a major-general. He won the favour of King **Charles XII** of Sweden, who in 1705 appointed him to the Royal Council and five years later made him Chancellor. Apart for a brief period under Queen **Ulrika Eleonora**, he held this office until the victory of his opponents, the Hat Party, in 1738. He dominated Swedish political life during the first two decades of the **Age of Liberty**, conducting a policy of peaceful reconstruction after the strains of the Great Northern War.

Horrocks, Sir Brian (Gwynne) (1895–1985) British general. He joined the army in 1914, and served in France and Russia. In 1942 he commanded the 9th Armoured Division and then the 13th and 10th Corps in North Africa, where he helped to defeat **Rommel**. Wounded at Tunis, he headed the 30th Corps during the Allied invasion (1944). Horrocks was well known as a military journalist and broadcaster. ▷ **North African Campaign; World War II**

Hortense Eugénie de Beauharnais (1783–1837) Queen of the Kingdom of Holland (1806/10). The daughter of General de **Beauharnais** and the future French Empress **Josephine**, she married **Napoleon I**'s brother **Louis Napoleon** in 1802, and so became Queen of Holland (present-day Netherlands). She took many lovers and had several children of uncertain fatherhood, including the future Emperor **Napoleon III**, who was said to be the child of a Dutch admiral. In 1810 she divorced her husband and went to Paris as the Duchess of Saint-Leu.

Horthy, Miklós Nagybányai (1868–1957) Hungarian sailor, politician and regent (1920/44). He became commander of the Austro-Hungarian fleet in 1918, and was then Minister of War in the counter-revolutionary 'white' government in 1919, opposing and suppressing Béla **Kun**'s communist regime in 1920. He became regent and presided over a resolutely conservative, authoritarian system. In 1937 he became politically more active and in **World War II** he supported the Axis Powers until Hungary was overrun by the Germans in 1944. He was imprisoned by the Germans, but released by the Allies in 1945. He lived thereafter in Portugal, where he died.

Horton, James Africanus (1835–83) Sierra Leonean doctor and surgeon-major. He served in the British army and was the author of *West African Countries and Peoples* (1868). He acted as an adviser to traditional chiefs in the Gold Coast, and is regarded as one of the intellectual founders of modern West African nationalism.

Horváth, Mihály (1809–78) Hungarian historian, prelate and revolutionary. Professor at the University of Vienna (1844) and Bishop of Csanád (1848), he took an active part in the revolution of 1848 and then became Minister of Education in **Kossuth**'s government. After the revolution was crushed in 1849, he lived in exile, but returned under the amnesty of 1867.

Hospitallers Members (priests or brother knights subject to monastic vows) of the Order of the Hospital of St John of Jerusalem, originally a purely charitable organization to care for sick pilgrims to the Holy Land. The warrior element developed and became predominant, and from the 12c they played a prominent role in the **Crusades** as an international religious-military order. After the loss of Acre in 1291, they transferred their headquarters to Limassol, Cyprus (1292), then Rhodes (1309), but were expelled by the Ottoman Turks in 1523. They moved to Malta (1530), which they held until dislodged by Napoleon I in 1798. The Sovereign Order is now based in Rome. It is known also as the Order of the Hospital of St John of Jerusalem, the Knights of Rhodes, Knights of Malta, or Knights of St John of Jerusalem.

hospodar The title given to the governors of the **Danubian Principalities** under Ottoman rule. The office was at first filled by native princes but after 1709 it was monopolized by the **Phanariots** who grew rich on the taxes raised from the Provinces. The Treaty of **Adrianople** (1829) decreed that hospodars were to be elected for life and this was confirmed by the **Organic Statutes**. In 1849 Russia and the Porte agreed to cooperate in the appointment, rather than the election, of the hospodars. The separate offices of Hospodar of Moldavia and Hospodar of Wallachia were first united in the person of Alexander **Cuza** and through him evolved into the office of Prince, and finally King, of Romania.

Hostilius, Tullus (7c BC) Third of the legendary Kings of Rome (673/642BC). He may well have destroyed Alba Longa and transferred its inhabitants to Rome but the other wars accredited to him are probably unhistorical, mere inventions to explain his warlike name (*hostilius* meaning 'hostile').

Hot Autumn of 1969 The term (in Italian, *Autunno caldo*) applied to the period of workers' sit-ins and strikes in Italy that represented the climax of student and worker demonstrations and agitation, begun in 1967.

Hotta Masayoshi (1810–64) Japanese feudal lord (**daimyo**). He became Senior Chief Councillor of the **Tokugawa Shogunate** in 1855 at a time when the Western powers, particularly the USA, were pressing for new treaties that would open more of Japan's ports to foreign trade. He negotiated a full commercial treaty with the USA (Feb 1858), allowing a US minister to reside at the shogunal capital and open four more ports to foreign trade (in addition to the two opened in an 1854 treaty). In an attempt to silence critics of the treaty, Hotta took the unprecedented step of personally seeking imperial approval of the treaty. The Emperor and his advisers, however, continued to favour seclusion and an imperial decree, while recognizing that foreign policy was the responsibility of the shogunate, did not specifically approve the treaty, thus damaging the shogunate's credibility. Hotta was shortly thereafter replaced as the regime's senior official by **Ii Naosuke**. ▷ **treaty ports**

Hottentots ▷ **Khoisan**

Houphouet-Boigny, Felix (1905–93) Ivorien politician. The son of a chief, he was educated in Cote d'Ivoire and at Dakar, and was a medical assistant and planter before turning to politics. He was President of the Syndicat Agricole Africain in 1944 and a founder of the Parti Democratique de la Cote d'Ivoire (PDCI). Elected to the French Constituent Assembly (1945–6) and then National Assembly (1946–58), he held a series of ministerial posts. He became Prime Minister of Cote d'Ivoire in 1959 and President, at independence, in 1960. His paternalistic rule, which also combined close relations with France and support for capitalist enterprises, saw Cote d'Ivoire initially develop more successfully than most other West African countries, but economic decline and profligacy, especially the building of a palace and cathedral at Yamoussoukro, reduced his popularity.

House of Representatives In the USA, one of the two chambers of Congress, in which, under the Constitution, legislative power is vested. The 435 members of the House are elected from Congressional districts according to population, although each state has at least one representative. Many state legislatures also have a House of Representatives. Although many bills are acted on by both the Senate and the House, all revenue bills must originate in the House. ▷ **Congress; Senate**

Houston, Sam (1793–1863) US politician. A former Governor of Tennessee, he moved to Texas in 1833 and led the force which overwhelmed the Mexican Army under **Santa Anna** at San Jacinto and won Texan independence in 1836. After Texas was admitted to the Union in 1845, he served as US Senator and later became its Governor (1859). A consistent unionist, he refused in 1861 to convene the legislature to vote on secession. Texas was therefore the last state to secede and Houston was deposed for refusing to swear allegiance to the Confederacy.

Howard, Catherine (c.1520–42) Queen of England. She was the fifth wife of **Henry VIII**, and was a granddaughter of the 2nd Duke of Norfolk. She became Queen in the same month as **Anne of Cleves** was divorced (July 1540). A year later she was charged by **Cranmer** with intercourse before her marriage with a musician and a kinsman, and was beheaded for treason.

Howard, Charles, 1st Earl of Nottingham (1536–1624) English admiral. A cousin of Queen **Elizabeth I**, he commanded the English fleet against the Spanish **Armada** (1588). He succeeded to his father's title in 1573, and became Lord High Admiral in 1585. For his role in the Cadiz expedition (1596) he was created an earl, and in 1601 he quelled **Essex**'s rising.

Howard, Thomas, 3rd Duke of Norfolk (1473–1554) English statesman. The brother-in-law of **Henry VII**, he held several high offices under **Henry VIII**. He was the uncle of Anne **Boleyn** and Catherine **Howard**, after whose execution (1542) he lost power. The father of the Earl of Surrey, who was executed for treason by Henry VIII, he would himself have been executed as an accessory, but for Henry's own death. He

remained in prison during the reign of **Edward VI**, but was released by the Catholic **Mary I**.

Howe, Clarence Decatur (1886–1960) Canadian businessman and politician. In 1936 he was appointed Minister of Transport in the Liberal government of Mackenzie **King** and played a major role in establishing Trans-Canada Airlines (later Air Canada). He proved to be a superb administrator during **World War II** as director of the Wartime Prices and Trade Board and Minister for Munitions and Supply. Faced with the refusal by private companies to produce synthetic rubber, he set up the Polymer Corporation as a crown company. Its success, both financial and in research and development, enabled the government to refuse its competitors' demands to close it down. Although he always had little patience for politics and politicians, Howe became Minister of Reconstruction in **Saint Laurent**'s administration in 1951, when the Defence Production Act gave him such wide economic powers that he became known as the 'Minister of Everything'. However, his management of the Trans-Canada Pipeline project, which he rammed through parliament in 1956 over outspoken opposition and charges that he had sold out the public interest to private American companies, marked the beginning of the end of more than 20 years of Liberal federal government and allowed the Conservatives a platform of reform on which they won the 1957 election. ▷ **Liberal Party** (Canada)

Howe, Joseph (1804–73) Canadian politician. In 1836 he entered Nova Scotia's assembly where he mobilized the reform party. His open letters to Lord John **Russell**, making the case for **Responsible Government**, were instrumental in winning it for Nova Scotia in 1848. As fishery commissioner Howe was out of politics during the **Confederation Movement** (which he opposed). He was Premier of Nova Scotia in 1860–3 and, after federation, entered the first Canadian government at Ottawa. In 1869 John A **Macdonald** persuaded him to join the Dominion cabinet (and increased the province's subsidy). His public opposition to administration policy caused some embarrassment and he resigned in 1873.

Howe, Julia Ward (1819–1910) US abolitionist and reformer, author of the 'Battle Hymn of the Republic', adopted as a rally song by the Union side in the **American Civil**

War. A respected writer, poet and lecturer, she was an early leader in the American women's suffrage movement. ▷ **abolitionism**

Howe, Richard, 1st Earl (1726–99) British admiral. The brother of William, 5th Viscount **Howe**, he entered the navy at 13, and distinguished himself in the **Seven Years War**. He became a Lord of the Admiralty (1763), Treasurer of the Navy (1765), First Lord of the Admiralty (1783), and earl (1788). In 1776 he was appointed commander of the British fleet during the American War of Independence and, in 1778, defended the American coast against a superior French force. On the outbreak of war with France (1793), he took command of the Channel Fleet, defeating the French off Ushant at the Battle of the **Glorious First of June** (1794). ▷ **French Revolutionary Wars**

Howe, Sir (Richard Edward) Geoffrey (1926–) British politician. He became a Conservative MP in 1964. Knighted in 1970, he became Solicitor-General (1970–2), Minister for Trade and Consumer Affairs (1972–4), Chancellor of the Exchequer (1979–83), and then Foreign Secretary (1983–9). A loyal supporter of Margaret **Thatcher**, in 1989 he was made Deputy Prime Minister, Lord President of the Council, and Leader of the House of Commons, but resigned from the government (Nov 1990) because of Thatcher's hostility towards European Monetary Union. His resignation speech set in train the events which led to the Premier's resignation. ▷ **Conservative Party (UK)**

Howe, William, 5th Viscount Howe (1729–1814) British soldier. The brother of Richard, 1st Earl **Howe**, he joined the army in 1746 and served under General James **Wolfe** at Louisbourg (1758) and **Quebec** (1759), where he led the famous advance to the Heights of **Abraham** (1759). He became an MP in 1758. He was a commander in North America during the **American Revolution**, and in the American War of Independence his victories included Bunker Hill (1775), the capture of New York City (1776, with naval support provided by his brother) and Brandywine Creek (1777). After his failure at **Valley Forge** (1778), he was superseded by Sir Henry Clinton. He returned to England and was made a viscount in 1799.

Hoxha, Enver (1908–85) Albanian politician. Born into a middle-class Muslim family, he joined the French Communist Party while

he was living in France (1930–6). Returning home during **World War II**, he joined the Albanian Labour Party (Puna), becoming provisional Secretary-General in 1941. With Mehmet **Shehu**, he was a leader of the Albanian National Liberation Movement which began in 1942 under the direction of the Yugoslav partisans of **Tito**, and he became Chief Political Commissar of the National Liberation Army. In 1946, after Albania was declared a People's Republic, Hoxha held office as Prime Minister, Foreign Minister and Minister of Defence until 1954 when, as First Secretary of the Albanian Communist Party, he preferred to rule through the party. He presided over the most doctrinaire and rigid of post-war communist governments. A Stalinist, he broke with Yugoslavia (1948), then the USSR (1960) and finally China (1978), denouncing them as revisionists and imperialists. With each turn in foreign policy, he eliminated his rivals and opponents but the late purge (1981–2) and the mysterious suicide of Shehu (1981) show he never succeeded in entirely destroying his critics. ▷ **Alia, Ramiz; Xoxe, Koci**

Hoysala A family of petty hill chiefs of the Western Ghats who carved out of the dismembered Chalukya state a southern Indian state (11–14c) in present-day Mysore. The most important Hoysala rulers were Vira Ballala II (1173/1220), Vira Someswara, their greatest ruler (1233/64), and Vira Ballala III. The Hoysalas started declining after c.1335. At the fall of the Hoysala state, some Hoysala officers founded the Vijayanagar kingdom. The Hoysalas made important contributions to South Indian art and architecture.

Hoyte, (Hugh) Desmond (1929–) Guyanese politician. After studies at London University and the Middle Temple, he taught in a boys' school in Grenada (1955–7) and then practised as a lawyer in Guyana. He joined the socialist People's National Congress (PNC) Party and in 1968, two years after Guyana achieved full independence, was elected to the National Assembly. He held a number of ministerial posts before becoming Prime Minister under Forbes **Burnham**. On Burnham's death, in 1985, he succeeded him as President.

Hrolf ▷ **Rollo**

Hrushevsky, Mikhail S (1866–1934) Ukrainian writer and political thinker. Russian-born and trained as a historian, he was appointed Professor of Ukrainian History in the University of Lvov, Galicia, in 1894, at a time of intensifying Russian nationalism. Since Galicia was then ruled by Austria, he was in a position to take up the Ukrainian case. He founded the Ukrainian National Democratic Party in exile, and he wrote extensively in Ukrainian which he helped to transform from a language of the peasantry to a medium for culture and for politics. He was able to return to Kiev in the **Duma** period, without however having much impact, but in 1917–18 he was among the founders of the short-lived Ukrainian Republic.

Hsuan Tsang ▷ **Xuan Zang**

HUAC (House Committee on Un-American Activities) A committee of the House of Representatives, it became a permanent committee in 1938 under the chairmanship of Democrat Martin Dies, with the purpose of investigating subversive activities. After the Republicans took control of the House of Representatives in 1946, the committee's focus became largely anti-communist. In the 1950s, when it became associated with Republican Senator Joseph **McCarthy**, it targeted alleged communists in the theatre, the movie industry, government and the trades. HUAC was notorious for basing its charges on loose gossip and for bullying witnesses. The committee was dissolved in 1975.

Hua Guofeng (Hua Kuo-feng) (c.1920–) Chinese politician. He was Vice-Governor of Hunan (1958–67), but came under attack during the **Cultural Revolution**. A member of the Central Committee of the Party from 1969 and of the Politburo from 1973, he became Deputy Prime Minister and Minister of Public Security (1975–6), and was made Prime Minister (1976–80) and Chairman of the Central Committee. Under him, China adopted a more pragmatic domestic and foreign policy, with emphasis on industrial and educational expansion, and closer relations with Western and Third World countries. He resigned as Chairman in 1981. ▷ **Mao Zedong**

Huai-hai, Battle of (1958–9) A crucial battle of the **Chinese Civil War** (1946–9) between the Communists and Nationalists. By the summer of 1948, communist armies already controlled Manchuria and much of the north China countryside. In order to open the way to the Yangzi River in central China, **Mao Zedong** launched a mass offensive (Oct 1948) against the Nationalist-held railway junction of Xuzhou (Hsuchow), which fell in Dec 1948. By the time the Battle of Huai-hai ended (Jan 1949), the Nationalists had lost 200 000 men; thereafter they were unable to prevent rapid communist advances throughout central and southern China.

Hua Kuo-feng ▷ **Hua Guofeng**

Huang Chao (Ch'ao) Rebellion (875–84) The large-scale peasant rebellion that devastated most of China during the last years of the **Tang Dynasty** and hastened China's political fragmentation. Under the leadership of a salt merchant, Huang Chao, the rebellion began in east and central China. By 879 the rebels had captured the southern city of Canton, and many of its inhabitants (including large numbers of Muslims, Jews, and Christians involved in overseas trade) were slaughtered. In 880 Huang Chao occupied the Tang capital of Chang'an, forcing the emperor to flee for his life. Huang Chao proclaimed a new dynasty (Great Qi) but his excessive cruelty lost him support and Tang loyalist forces dislodged him from the capital (883). He fled to eastern China, where he committed suicide. The Tang Dynasty never recovered, however, and in the early 10c was brushed aside by powerful militarists who established independent kingdoms.

Huang Hsing ▷ **Huang Xing**

Huang Tsung-hsi ▷ **Huang Zongxi**

Huang Xing (Huang Hsing) (1871–1916) Chinese revolutionary leader. He helped to overthrow the **Qing Dynasty** and bring the Chinese Empire to an end. In 1905 he fled to Japan, where he organized a revolutionary group which joined **Sun Yat-sen** as the Alliance Society. When the Republic was founded in 1912, he devoted himself to turning the society into a parliamentary party, a policy frustrated by President **Yuan Shikai**. Huang joined Sun Yat-sen in armed opposition to the President, but was defeated and fled to Japan. He returned to China in 1916 after the death of Yuan Shikai, but died later the same year in Shanghai.

Huang Zongxi (Huang Tsung-hsi) (1610–95) Chinese scholar. He was celebrated for his opposition to the Manchu **Qing Dynasty** and in 1644 joined the resistance movement in the south loyal to the previous **Ming Dynasty**. However, he retired to a life of scholarship after 1649, refusing to accept an official position from the new dynasty. His critique of imperial absolutism, written in 1662, exerted a considerable influence on early 20c Chinese reformers and revolutionaries.

Hudson's Bay Company A London-based corporation which was granted a Royal Charter to trade (principally in furs) in most of north and west Canada (Rupert's Land) in 1670. It annexed its main competitors, the **North West Company**, in 1821, and developed extensive sea-based trade in otter pelts along the coast of British Columbia. Rupert's Land was purchased by the Canadian Government in 1870.

Huggins, Godfrey Martin, 1st Viscount Malvern of Rhodesia and Bexley (1893–1971) Rhodesian politician. Born in England, he emigrated to Southern Rhodesia in 1911 as a doctor but was soon drawn into politics, being elected at the first election after internal self-government. He was catapulted into the premiership of Southern Rhodesia in 1933, a post he held until his elevation to the premiership of the Central African Federation, of which he was one of the chief architects. He retired in 1956. Although the Central African Federation proved short-lived and Huggins' readiness to respond to nationalist pressures was too limited, he established a liberal base in Southern Rhodesia where class was deemed more significant than race. The combined forces of African nationalism and white reaction squeezed such liberals into positions of no power in the 1960s, but the development of the state which Zimbabwe's politicians inherited owes a great deal to Huggins' leadership in difficult economic conditions in the 1930s, 1940s and 1950s.

Hughes, Charles Evans (1862–1948) US politician and jurist. Elected Governor of New York State (1907) after exposing huge frauds in the insurance industry, he served as an Associate Justice of the Supreme Court (1910–16). He resigned to run as the Republican candidate in the presidential election of 1916, when he narrowly lost to Woodrow **Wilson**. He was appointed Secretary of State in 1921 by President Warren **Harding**, and served until 1925.

Hughes, William M(orris) (1864–1952) British-born Australian politician and Prime Minister (1915–23). Hughes emigrated to Australia in 1884. He entered the New South Wales Legislature in 1894 and federal politics in 1901. He was Attorney-General (1908–9,

1910–13 and 1914–15), succeeding Fisher as Labor Leader and Prime Minister in 1915. A long-standing supporter of compulsory military service, he returned from a visit to Britain in 1916 to campaign for conscription. The referendum was lost, but Hughes and his followers were expelled from the **Australian Labor Party**. He formed the Nationalist Party in 1917, retained office and represented Australia at the **Paris Peace Conference** of 1919. After the election of 1922, the Country Party held the balance of power and forced his retirement in favour of S M Bruce (1923). He engineered the overthrow of the Bruce–Page government in 1929 for which he was expelled from the Nationalist Party. Involved in the foundation of the United Australia Party, he held various offices during the 1930s and was briefly party leader in 1941. He remained in parliament until his death in 1952. ▷ **National Party of Australia**

Huguenots French Calvinist Protestants whose political rivalry with Catholics (eg the House of **Guise**) led to the French Wars of **Religion** (1562–98). Their leader, Henry of Navarre (**Henry IV**), succeeded to the throne (1589), granting them important concessions on his conversion to Catholicism (Edict of **Nantes**, 1598); these were later revoked by **Louis XIV** (1685), resulting in persecution and emigration. ▷ **St Bartholomew's Day Massacre**

Hu Hanmin (Hu Han-min) (1879–1936) Chinese politician. An early leader of the Chinese Nationalist Party, he was a founder-member of the Alliance Society created (1905) in Tokyo by **Sun Yat-sen**, from which the Party later developed. After Sun's death (1925) he lost influence, and broke with **Chiang Kai-shek** in 1931. He was imprisoned briefly for his opposition, and thereafter played little part in politics until his death. ▷ **Guomindang**

Hukbalahap (Huk) Filipino peasant movement, concentrated in central Luzon. The term in fact refers to two related organizations: the People's Anti-Japanese Army, which was the most prominent of the indigenous resistance groups during the Japanese occupation of the Philippines; and the People's Liberation Army, which mounted a rising (the Huk Rebellion) against the newly-independent Filipino Republic from late 1946. The origins of the rebellion lay in the severe deterioration of agrarian relations in central Luzon from the 1930s, arising from the increasingly harsh treatment of tenant farmers by the big landowners, many of whom had collaborated with the Japanese during the war years. The Communist Party of the Philippines was sometimes aligned with, and occasionally provided leadership within, the Huks. However, the rebellion remained essentially a rural one. By 1953 it had been broken, by a combination of effective military operations and changes in government policy which appeared to offer an alleviation of rural grievances.

Hull, Cordell (1871–1955) US politician. He became Secretary of State under **Roosevelt** in 1933, and served for the longest term in that office until he retired in 1944, having attended most of the great war conferences. He was a strong advocate of maximum aid to the Allies. He helped to organize the **UN**, for which he received the Nobel Peace Prize in 1945.

Humanism The philosophy espoused by Kenneth **Kaunda** and based upon Julius **Nyerere**'s philosophy of **ujamaa**, it aimed to find a specifically African conception of man's place in society and the economy, in which human dignity and equality were the central principles. It was never taken as seriously as Nyerere's writings as a blueprint for public policy.

Humanists Those scholars who, from the 14c onwards, worked to recover the pure language of the classical past, removing the glosses and errors generated in the centuries which separated the new era from the ancient world ('the *medium aevum*' and hence 'Middle Ages'). The early humanists tended to find their ideal in the works of Cicero, but by the mid-15c there was a new interest in Greek learning, especially in the works of Plato. The application of humanist techniques to the text of the Bible by scholars such as Lorenzo Valla prepared the way for 'Christian humanists', most significantly Erasmus, who urged reform of the Church according to the principles of the Scriptures, an approach which links the Renaissance to the **Reformation**. In sum, the Italian Renaissance gave people who were not clerics a new sense of their creative powers. Moreover, the specific developments in the visual arts and humanism identified above all with perspective and with a more refined sense of history gave Europeans a new sense of space and time at precisely the moment when Europe was beginning to make its impact on the rest of the globe in the age of the great oceanic discoveries.

Humayun (1508–56) Mughal Emperor of India (1530/42 and 1554/6). He became the second Mughal Emperor of India upon the death of his father, **Babur**. The early part of his reign was spent fighting Sher Khan, an Afghan, by whom he was defeated in 1542. Sher Khan became Emperor Sher Shah and founded the Sur Dynasty. From 1539 to 1554, Humayun was in exile when his son, **Akbar the Great**, was born. In 1544, Humayun captured and ruled southern Afghanistan for some time. Sher Shah having died in 1545, in 1554 Humayun marched from Kabul to Lahore and defeated Sikandar Shah at Sirhind (1555), eventually recapturing the Delhi throne. He died the following year, after a fall from his library stairs.

Hume, Allan Octavian (1829–1912) British colonialist and naturalist. After studying medicine, Hume joined the Bengal Civil Service in 1849. He became Commissioner of Customs for the North West Provinces, and Director-General of Agriculture. Having served in the **Indian Uprising** of 1857–8, he carried with him a morbid fear of the repetition of these events. In order to provide an outlet for educated opinion, therefore, he organized the first National Congress in India, in Bombay in 1885, remaining the Secretary of this organization until 1908.

Hume, Joseph (1777–1855) British radical politician. He studied medicine at Edinburgh, and then in 1797 became assistant surgeon under the East India Company. After returning to England (1808), he sat in parliament (1812 and 1819–55), where his reform campaigns included the legalizing of trade unions, freedom of trade with India, and the abolition of army flogging, naval impressment, and imprisonment for debt. ▷ **East India Company, British**

Humphrey, Hubert Horatio (1911–78) US politician. He became Mayor of Minneapolis in 1945, and was elected Senator in 1948. He built up a strong reputation as a liberal, particularly on the **civil rights** issue, but, as Vice-President from 1965 under Lyndon B **Johnson**, alienated many of his supporters by defending the policy of continuing the **Vietnam War**. Although he won the Democratic presidential nomination in 1968, a substantial minority of Democrats opposed him, and he narrowly lost the election to Richard **Nixon**. He then returned to the Senate. ▷ **Democratic Party**

Hundred Associates The French colonization company organized by Cardinal

Richelieu in 1627. Its aim was to settle 4000 colonists in **New France** within 15 years and to support them for three years after their arrival. In return the Associates were given a monopoly of the **fur trade** and a claim to the North American continent from the Arctic circle down to Florida. Their first two fleets were both captured by privateers and Quebec was lost in 1629. The profitable fur trade had to be sublet to another company and only 2500 settlers had been sent out when the Associates' charter was revoked in 1663.

Hundred Days (Mar–June 1815) An interlude between **Napoleon I**'s escape from Elba and his defeat at the Battle of **Waterloo**, during which he returned to Paris and tried to reconstitute the First Empire. He was finally exiled to St Helena. ▷ **Empire, First** (France)

Hundred Days of Reform (1898) A reform movement in China, which lasted for just over a hundred days. During this period **Kang Youwei** and his supporters succeeded in securing Emperor **Guangxu**'s approval of radical reforms affecting the constitution, administration, army and education. All were rescinded on the intervention of Empress-Dowager **Cixi**. Six leading reformers were executed, and Kang fled abroad. ▷ **Qing Dynasty**

Hundred Flowers Campaign (1956–7) A campaign in China which encouraged freedom of expression, under the slogan 'Let a hundred flowers bloom and a hundred schools of thought contend', in art and literature as well as political debate. By June 1957 a clampdown was imposed on the violent criticism of the Communist Party, and an anti-rightist campaign was launched.

Hundred Years War A series of wars between England and France dated by convention 1337–1453. They formed part of a longer contest which began when England was linked with **Normandy** (1066), then with Anjou and Aquitaine (1154). In the 13c, the Capetians redoubled their efforts to rule all France. But when **Edward III** claimed the French throne, from 1340 styling himself 'King of England and France', traditional rivalries exploded into a dynastic struggle. Under **Henry V** (1415/22) the English turned from raiding to territorial conquest, a task ultimately beyond their resources. Eviction from Guyenne (1453) reduced England's French territories to Calais (lost in 1558) and the Channel Islands, but the title of King of

France was abandoned only in 1801. ▷ **Agincourt, Battle of; Angevins; Capetian Dynasty**

Hungarian Millennium (1869) The 1000th anniversary of the year in which the Magyars probably settled the Hungarian plain was used by the Hungarian government within Austria-Hungary to celebrate undoubted political and economic achievements in the course of the previous half century. It was also used as an anti-Habsburg demonstration and marked an intensification of the attempt to Magyarize Hungary's subject nationalities. Protests were made by Magyar poor as well as by Slavs and Romanians.

Hungarian Uprising (Oct–Nov 1956) National insurrection centred on Budapest following the denunciation of **Stalin** at the 20th Congress of the Soviet Communist Party for his oppressive rule. Rioting students and workers pulled down statues of Stalin and demanded radical reform. When the new Prime Minister, Imre **Nagy**, announced plans for Hungary's withdrawal from the **Warsaw Pact**, among other things, Soviet troops and tanks crushed the uprising. Many were killed, thousands fled abroad, and Nagy was executed. Reform was set back for more than a decade.

Hung Hsiu-ch'üan ▷ **Hong Xiuquan**

Hung Jen-kan ▷ **Hong Rengan**

Huns An Asiatic people who in 375 overran the Gothic tribes of southern Russia, and precipitated the great Germanic migration into the **Roman Empire**. They were feared for their brutality throughout the empire. United under **Attila**, they laid waste parts of **Gaul** and Italy (451–2), but were then forced to retreat, and Hunnic dominance was soon eclipsed. ▷ **Goths; Vandals**

Hunt, Henry ('Orator Hunt') (1773–1835) British radical agitator. He was a well-to-do farmer who in 1800 became a staunch radical, and spent the rest of his life advocating the repeal of the **Corn Laws**, democracy, and parliamentary reform. In 1819, on the occasion of the **Peterloo Massacre**, he delivered a speech which cost him three years' imprisonment. He became an MP in 1831.

Hunyadi, János (c.1407–56) Hungarian statesman and warrior. Apparently a Wallach by birth, he was knighted and in 1409 presented by Emperor **Sigismund** with the

Castle of Hunyad in Transylvania. His life was one unbroken crusade against the Turks, whom he defeated in several campaigns, notably in the storming of Belgrade (1456). During the minority of Ladislas V he acted as Governor of the Kingdom (1446–53). He died in Belgrade, of plague, shortly after his victory there. One of his sons, **Matthias I, 'Corvinus'**, became King of Hungary in 1458.

Hurd, Douglas (Richard) (1930–) British politician. He followed a career in the Diplomatic Corps (1952–66) before moving to work in the Conservative Research Department (1966–70). A Conservative MP from 1974, he was Northern Ireland Secretary (1984–5), Home Secretary (1985–9), and Foreign Secretary from 1989. He was an unsuccessful candidate for the **Conservative Party** leadership (Nov 1990). ▷ **Thatcher, Margaret**

Huron Iroquoian-speaking Native North Americans, who settled in large towns and farming villages in Quebec and Ontario in the 16–17c. They supplied furs to French traders, competing with tribes of the **Iroquois Confederacy**. Defeated by the Iroquois in 1649, many were driven to the west, and eventually settled on land in Ohio and Michigan, where they were known by the British as the Wyandots. In 1867 they were moved to the **Indian Territory** in Oklahoma, where many still live.

Hurrians An ancient, non-Semitic, non-Indo-European people first detected in the Caucasus area in the latter part of the third millennium. From there they migrated in great numbers to northern Mesopotamia, Syria, and eastern Anatolia, where in the next millennium they greatly influenced the Hittites.

Hurtado de Mendoza, Diego (1503–75) Spanish politician of Basque origin. The great-grandson of Iñigo López de **Mendoza**, he was entrusted by **Charles V** with the conduct of his Italian policy and the representation of his views at the Council of Trent. He inherited his ancestor's gifts as a statesman and man of letters. His *War of Granada* is a masterpiece of prose. ▷ **Basques**

Hus, Jan (c.1372–1415) Bohemian religious reformer. He was born at Husinec, from which his name derives. At the relatively new and intellectually lively University of Prague he became a bachelor of arts in 1393, master of arts in 1396 and was elected dean of the

faculty in 1401. He was influenced by the writings of Wycliffe among others. His preaching won him both royal and popular Czech support but in 1410 he was excommunicated by the Archbishop of Prague. He continued to preach even when, in 1412, the Pope issued a papal bull against him and put Prague under an interdict. He was, therefore, called before a General Council at Constance and, despite a guarantee of safe conduct from Emperor **Sigismund**, he was burned after refusing to recant. The anger of his followers in the Czech lands led to the **Hussite Wars**, which lasted almost until the mid-15c and for a time guaranteed Czech independence. Hus's ideas exerted an important influence on the Protestant reformers in the 16c. ▷ **Hussites; Reformation**

Husák, Gustáv (1913–) Czechoslovak politician. He trained as a lawyer, joined the Communist Party in 1939 and became a member of the resistance movement during **World War II**. After the war he was a parliamentary deputy and Party official and became Minister of Agriculture in 1948–9 before being imprisoned, as an alleged Slovak bourgeois nationalist, in 1951. Rehabilitated in 1960, he worked at the Academy of Sciences (1963–8) until he became First Secretary of the Slovak Communist Party and Deputy Premier during the **Prague Spring**. After the 1968 Soviet invasion, of which he approved, he replaced Alexander **Dubček** as General-Secretary of the entire Czechoslovak Communist Party in 1969. His task was to restore public order, 'cleanse' the Party and introduce a new federal constitution. He became state President in 1975 and, pursuing a policy of minimal economic reform, remained the dominant figure in Czechoslovakia until his retirement from the general-secretaryship, under pressure, in 1987. He was finally replaced as state President by Václav **Havel** in Dec 1989 in the course of the so-called **Velvet Revolution**.

Husayni, Amin al- (1897–74) Arab nationalist leader. Educated in Jerusalem, Cairo and Istanbul, he went on to serve in the Turkish artillery. In 1921 the British, under their Mandate for Palestine, appointed him Mufti of Jerusalem and Permanent President of the Supreme Muslim Council, the most important Palestinian Muslim body. In 1930, in an attempt to attract outside support for the Arab cause in Palestine, he told the German representative in Jerusalem that the Palestinians were in sympathy with the new Germany. This search for support had been prompted by the **Peel Commission**'s report, which recommended the partition of Palestine and was rejected by the Palestinian Arabs. A thorn in the side of the British, al-Husayni spent his life in an unsuccessful attempt to avert the partition of Palestine. His collaboration with Nazi Germany, his call for Egyptian aid for German and Italian troops and his support of Japan after **Pearl Harbor**, were more than enough to cast him in the darkest light in the eyes of the Allies. In 1945 he was captured by the French and kept under house arrest near Paris. By mid-1946, however, he had escaped to Damascus and was cordially greeted later the same year in Egypt by the Prime Minister, Isma'il Sidqi. He continued to work for the Palestinian cause from Gaza as leader of the 'All Palestine Government', recruiting guerrillas for raids into Israel. After 1956, however, with the growing influence of al-Fatah, his own power declined. ▷ **PLO**

Husayn ibn 'Ali (1856–1931) Sharif of Mecca (1908/16) and King of the Hijaz (1916/24). The founder of the modern Arab Hashimite Dynasty, when **World War I** began and the British tried to persuade him to rise up against the Turks, he negotiated with Sir Henry McMahon, British High Commissioner in Egypt, and proposed that Britain should accept as independent an area that included the present states of Syria, Lebanon, Iraq, Jordan and the Arabian Peninsula, except for Aden. McMahon accepted most of his demands but the British were making other agreements which conflicted with the promises made to Husayn, such as the **Sykes–Picot Agreement** with France (May 1916). Husayn began his revolt in June 1916, soon captured Mecca and in 1917 moved out of the Hijaz and supported Allenby as he advanced into Palestine. At the end of the war, he was frustrated and bitter, as the Allies recognized him only as King of the Hijaz and he was driven from there after a conflict (1919–24) with 'Abd al-'Aziz ibn Sa'ud. His sons, Faysal and Abdullah, became respectively King of Iraq and of Transjordan, but Husayn felt betrayed by Britain and France, who had left only Arabia as a truly independent Arab area. ▷ **Abdullah ibn Husayn; Arab Revolt; Faysal I; Husayn–McMahon Correspondence**

Husayn–McMahon Correspondence The notorious correspondence between Sharif **Husayn ibn 'Ali** of Mecca and Sir Henry McMahon, the British High Commissioner in

Egypt, initiated in 1915. It resulted in Husayn's becoming convinced that Britain supported the emancipation of the Arabs from Ottoman rule and the establishment of a Greater Arab Kingdom in the Arabian Peninsula and parts of the Fertile Crescent. This conviction derived from an assurance dispatched by McMahon in Oct 1915 that Britain was 'prepared to recognize and support the independence of the Arabs' in accordance with Husayn's demands, subject to three reservations. Despite these reservations (which concerned those parts of the Levant 'west of the districts of Damascus, Homs, Hama and Aleppo' as not being wholly Arab, an exclusion with regard to British interests in lower Iraq, and an allusion to the 'interests of her (Britain's) ally France'), this correspondence was (and remains) a major source of irritation amongst the Arabs where their relations with Britain are concerned. It undoubtedly played a decisive part in encouraging the 1916 **Arab Revolt**, and the conflict between the tenor of the correspondence with the **Sykes–Picot Agreement**, coupled with the absence of any specific mention in the correspondence of the status of Palestine (despite McMahon's much later avowal that he had always thought of Palestine as being excluded from the territories promised to the Arabs), has done nothing to promote cordial relations between Britain and the Arabs.

Huss, John ▷ Hus, Jan

Hussein (ibn Talal) (1935–) King of Jordan (1952/). Educated in Alexandria, and at Harrow and Sandhurst in England, he steered a middle course in the face of the political upheavals inside and outside his country, favouring the Western powers, particularly Britain, and pacifying Arab nationalism. After the 1967 war with Israel, the **PLO** (Palestine Liberation Organization) made increasingly frequent raids into Israel from Jordan; their power developed to such an extent that he ordered the Jordanian army to move against them and, after a short civil war (1970), the PLO leadership fled abroad. His decision to cut links with the West Bank (1988) prompted the PLO to establish a government in exile. He has been married four times; his second wife was an Englishwoman, by whom he had an heir, Abdullah, in 1962.

Hussein, Saddam (1937–) Iraqi soldier and President. He joined the Arab Baath Socialist Party in 1957, and was sentenced to death in 1959 for the attempted execution of General Abd al-Krim **Qassim**, but escaped to Egypt. He played a prominent part in the 1968 revolution, and became Vice-President of the Revolutionary Command Council in 1969. On the retirement of his colleague President al-**Bakr**, he became sole President (1979–   ). His attack on Iran in 1980, to gain control of the Strait of Hormuz, led to a war of attrition which ended in 1988. His invasion of Kuwait in Aug 1990 led to the 1991 **Gulf War**, but by Feb that year he had been defeated by an Allied Force backed by the **UN**. However, he defied UN ceasefire resolutions imposed on Iraq and made further raids on Iran in 1993. ▷ **Iran–Iraq War**

Hussites Followers of Jan **Hus**, who in early 15c Bohemia initiated a movement for the reform of the universal Church. They failed in their main purpose but, together and in various sects, they anticipated the 16c **Reformation** by demanding the moral reform of the clergy, free preaching of the Word of God, and the availability of the Eucharist for all believers in two species or kinds (ie bread and wine).

Hussite Wars (1419–36) The burning at the stake of Jan **Hus** aroused enormous religious and national unrest in Bohemia and led to the formation of a Hussite League. The movement spread rapidly under King Wenceslas IV and open war broke out under **Sigismund**, whom the Bohemians held responsible for Hus's death. In 1420 the pope called for a crusade against the **Hussites**. The Emperor suffered serious defeats, and raids into Silesia, Austria and as far as Danzig spread fear of the Hussites. For the first time, an imperial tax was levied to fund the war against them. Continued Hussite successes led to a diplomatic solution being reached in the pacts of Prague (1433) and Iglau (1436).

Hu Yaobang (Hu Yao-pang) (1915–89) Chinese politician. Born into a poor peasant family in Hunan province, he joined the Red Army in 1929 and took part in the **Long March**. He held a number of posts under **Deng Xiaoping** before becoming Head of the Communist Youth League (1952–67). During the **Cultural Revolution** he was purged as a 'capitalist roader' and 'rusticated'; briefly rehabilitated (1975–6), he did not return to high office until 1978, when, through his patron Deng, he joined the Communist Party's Politburo. From Head of

the Secretariat, he was promoted to Party Leader in 1981, but dismissed in 1987 for his relaxed handling of a wave of student unrest. Popularly revered as a liberal reformer, his death triggered an unprecedented wave of pro-democracy demonstrations.

Hu Yao-pang ▷ **Hu Yaobang**

Huysmans, Camille (1871–1968) Belgian politician. After studying at Liège University, he became a teacher (1893–7). He subsequently worked as a journalist and trade unionist, and was a socialist MP from 1910 to 1965. Active in the Second International, and also in the **Flemish Movement**, Huysmans was especially concerned that Dutch be made the language of instruction at Ghent University. He was involved in municipal politics in Antwerp (of which he was Mayor, 1933–40 and 1944–6) and in Brussels; he held several national cabinet posts and from 1946 to 1947 was Prime Minister. His party dropped him in 1965 (when he was in his nineties); he set up his own socialist group but was not elected.

Hyksos A term used by the Ptolemaic historian Manetho for a ruling class, known to the Egyptians as the 'rulers of foreign countries'. By c.1720BC they had gained control of the many groups of people who for generations had infiltrated into the northeastern Delta of Egypt from Western Asia. About 1675BC they set up the 15th Dynasty which ruled for over a century until the rise of the **New Kingdom**.

Hyrcanus I, John (2c BC) High priest of Israel and perhaps also a king subject to Syrian control (c.134/104BC). The son of the high priest Simon, and in the line of Hasmonean priestly rulers, Hyrcanus consolidated his own hold over Israel, destroyed the Samaritan temple on Mount Gerizim, and forced the **Edomites** (the inhabitants of southern Judea) to adopt Judaism. Eventually he supported the Sadduceans against the Pharisees, who opposed his combination of political and religious leadership. ▷ **Maccabees; Sadducees**

Hyrcanus II (d.30BC) Jewish high priest. He was the grandson of John **Hyrcanus** and son of Alexander. On his father's death (76BC) he was appointed high priest by his mother Alexandra, who ruled Judaea until her death (67BC). He warred for power with his younger brother Aristobulus, having varying fortune until Aristobulus was poisoned (49BC). In

47BC **Caesar** made **Antipater** of Idumaea Procurator of Judaea with supreme power; and a son of Aristobulus, with Parthian help, captured Hyrcanus, and carried him off to Seleucia. But when **Herod the Great**, son of Antipater, came to power, the aged Hyrcanus was invited home to Jerusalem, where he lived in peace till, suspected of intriguing against Herod, he was put to death in 30BC.

I

Iaşi, Treaty of (1792) ▷ **Jassy, Treaty of**

Ibárruri (Gómez), Dolores ('La Pasionaria') (1895–1989) Spanish communist orator and politician. Born into a Catholic mining family in the Basque country, she became a member of the Central Committee of the Spanish Communist Party (1930), served as Spanish delegate to the Third International (1933 and 1935), and was elected Deputy to the Spanish **Cortes** (1936). With the outbreak of the **Spanish Civil War** (1936), she became the Republic's most emotional and effective propagandist. After the war she took refuge in the USSR, becoming Secretary-General (1942–60) and then (1960) President of the Spanish Communist Party in exile. In 1977 she returned to Spain as Communist Deputy for Asturias.

Ibbetson, Denzil (1847–1948) British Lieutenant-Governor of Punjab. Educated at Cambridge, Ibbetson entered the Indian Civil Service in 1870 and was posted to Punjab. During his career, he held various posts among which were the posts of the Superintendent of Census, Financial Commissioner, and Secretary to the Government of India in the Department of Revenue and Agriculture. He was also a retired member of the Viceroy's Executive Council, India. Ibbetson published the census Report of Punjab in 1883 and the Gazetteer of Punjab in 1883–5.

Iberians A group of Iron Age peoples inhabiting the southern and eastern periphery of present-day Spain (Andalusia, Valencia, Aragon, and Catalonia), and extending north into present-day France as far as the Rhône Valley.

Ibn Khaldun (1332–1406) Arab philosopher, historian, and politician, born in Tunis. He was widely involved in political intrigues before he turned to history, eventually becoming a college president and judge in Cairo. He wrote a monumental history of the Arabs, best known by its *Muqaddima*, or introduction, in which he explains the rise and fall of states by the waxing and waning of the spirit of *asabiya* ('solidarity'). He died in Cairo.

Ibn Saud (Ibn Abd al-Rahman al-Saud) (1880–1953) First King of Saudi Arabia (1932/53). Seeking exile with his family in 1890, he was brought up in Kuwait. In 1901 he succeeded his father, and set out to reconquer the family domains from the Rashidi rulers, an aim which he achieved with British recognition in 1927. He changed his title from Sultan of Nejd to King of Hijaz and Najd in 1927, and in 1932 to King of Saudi Arabia. After the discovery of oil (1938), he granted substantial concessions to US oil companies. He died in Ta'if, Saudi Arabia. His son, Saud (1902–69) had been Prime Minister for three months when he succeeded his father in 1953. In 1964 he was peacefully deposed by the Council of Ministers, and his brother, Faysal (1904–75), became king, as well as remaining Prime Minister and Minister of Foreign Affairs.

Ibo ▷ **Igbo**

Ibrahim Pasha (1789–1848) Viceroy of Egypt. Born at Kavalla, Rumelia, he was the son (or adopted son) of **Muhammad 'Ali**. In Egypt from 1805, he became Governor of Cairo, and later commanded the army. In 1833 he invaded Syria, but European intervention forced his withdrawal in 1840. He succeeded his father as Viceroy when the latter became senile, but predeceased him, dying in Cairo after only 40 days in office.

Iceni An ancient British tribe occupying what is now Norfolk and north-west Suffolk. They rebelled in AD47 and again in 60, when their queen, **Boudicca**, led them and other tribes in a major revolt that briefly threatened the collapse of the Roman administration in Britain.

Ichikawa Fusaye (1893–1981) Japanese politician and feminist. Starting her working life as a teacher, she then became involved in politics and feminism, helping to found the New Women's Association (c.1920) which successfully fought for women's right to attend political meetings. During her time in the USA (1921–4) she was impressed by the US suffrage movement, and in 1924 formed the Women's Suffrage League in Japan. Following **World War II** she became head of the New Japan Women's League, which secured the vote for women in 1945, and went on to fight for their wider rights. She campaigned against legalized prostitution and served in the Japanese Diet (1952–71), where she continued to press for an end to bureaucratic corruption. After defeat in 1971 she was triumphantly returned to parliament in 1975 and 1980.

iconoclasm Literally 'image breaking', this Greek terms refers to the extreme rejection of the veneration of images. The practice was justified as an interpretation of the second of the Ten Commandments, and was supported by the Byzantine (or eastern Roman) emperor in the 8c, and again by certain reformers in the 16c.

Iconoclastic Riots ▷ Image-breaking Riots

Idris Aloma (d.c.1600) Ruler of Bornu (c.1569/c.1600). He was a warrior-king and the dominant figure in the central Sudan. During his reign, and those of his sons, the Karini peoples of Bornu became a distinct, unified nation.

Igbo or **Ibo** A people of eastern Nigeria, living in many small and traditionally autonomous communities, with a common culture (present-day population c.13 million). They dominated agricultural trade in Nigeria, and produced the earliest bronze art in the region. They established the short-lived state of Biafra (1960–70), during which time the genocide of Igbo living in other parts of Nigeria occurred.

Iglesias, Pablo (1850–1925) Spanish politician and trade union leader. He was the founder and father figure of both the Spanish Socialist Party and its trade union movement, the **UGT**. The Socialist movement was dominated by him until his later years when he was incapacitated by ill health. He was a highly moralistic, austere and cautious character who preached revolutionary ideas, while practising a pragmatic reformism. His twin obsessions were building up the Socialists' organizations and educating the working class. He became the Socialists' first Deputy to the Cortes through the alliance with the Republicans in 1910, though the **PSOE** never surpassed seven seats before his death in 1925.

Ignatiev, Nikolai Pavlovich, Count (1832–1908) Russian diplomat. He entered the diplomatic service in 1856 and, arriving as

Ambassador in Beijing in 1859, he used guile and foreign military pressure to induce the Chinese to accept the Treaty of Beijing, which gave Russia most of the Amur province that it wanted, including the site for Vladivostok. In 1864 he became Ambassador at Constantinople where, as an enthusiast for the Slav cause as well as for Russia's imperial interests, he encouraged the Balkan Slavs, and took a principal part in the diplomacy before and after the Russo-Turkish War of 1878. He was primarily responsible for the Treaty of San Stefano, which was then largely undone at the Congress of Berlin. He was appointed Minister of the Interior in 1881, but was dismissed the following year for expressing excessively liberal, if somewhat impractical, ideas. ▷ **Russo-Turkish Wars**

Ii Naosuke (1815–60) Japanese feudal lord. He was Chief Counsellor, or Elder (*tairo*), of the **Tokugawa Shogunate** in 1858–60. Ii took the initiative in signing a commercial treaty with the USA (July 1858) despite strong pro-seclusionist feelings both at the imperial court and amongst many feudal lords and **samurai**. He instituted repressive measures against his critics and was eventually assassinated by the retainers of one domain (Mito) that had borne the brunt of his repression.

Ikeda Hayato (1900–65) Japanese politician and economic expert. Educated in Kyoto, he became Finance Minister (1949) of the Liberal-Democratic (Conservative) Party, and introduced an 'income doubling policy' of economic growth and higher living standards. As Prime Minister (1960–4), he was a supporter of the US-Japan Security Treaty (1960), and developed a low-key style in international relations during the post-war recovery period.

Ikhshidid Dynasty A minor dynasty of Turkish origin which controlled Egypt from 935 until 969, when it fell to the Fatimid general, Jawhar. The first Ikhshidid ruler, Muhammad ibn Tughj, received from the 'Abbasid caliph in Baghdad, the title *al-Ikhshid* (Persian, 'Prince'), from which the dynasty derived its name. Muhammad expanded the area over which he held sway by adding much of greater Syria and Mecca and Medina to the territory which owed him allegiance. His two sons were little more than titular rulers: during their reigns effective control was exercised by Abu'l-Misk Kafur, an Abyssinian eunuch, who came into conflict with the Hamdanids of Aleppo. ▷ **'Abbasid Dynasty**

Ilbert Bill The bill, introduced in 1883 by Courtney Ilbert, according to which the privilege enjoyed by every British subject in India to be tried only by a magistrate of his own race was to be withdrawn. However in deference to strong expressions of European public opinion, this privilege was withdrawn merely to the extent of conferring jurisdiction in such cases on all magistrates of whatever race as well as on justices of the peace, who were European British subjects and also the highest magistrates. This stirred up resentment amongst Indians, including early nationalist politicians, who felt that a racial privilege was being perpetuated, and that a slur was being cast upon Indian magistrates.

ILGWU (International Ladies Garment Workers Union) US labour organization. Founded in 1900, it saw conflict in its early years as different ethnic and political groups and skilled and unskilled workers vied for control. Massive strikes in 1909–11 in New York led to a settlement with dress manufacturers that included the 'Protocol of Peace'. Negotiated under the aegis of Louis D **Brandeis**, the protocol offered improved wages and working conditions in exchange for a ban on strikes and lock-outs and imposed impartial arbitration as a means of ending disputes. By the 1920s, the presence of a strong communist faction had caused the union's fortunes to decline, but David Dubinsky's election as President in 1932, coupled with **New Deal** legislation favourable to labour, helped it regain strength. Membership continued to grow at a rapid pace until the 1960s, but later fell with the gradual decline of the labour unions. The ILGWU's advanced social welfare programs, which included such benefits as medical and disability insurance and unemployment compensation, provided a model for other unions.

Ili Crisis (1879–81) This term refers to the tense situation between Russia and China following the Russian occupation of the Chinese prefecture of Ili in northern Xinjiang (Chinese Turkestan) near the border of Russian Turkestan. Xinjiang had been conquered as a military colony by the **Qing Dynasty** in 1759 but the region's Turkic-speaking Muslims (Uighurs) remained hostile. A Muslim rebellion in 1864 was quickly exploited by an adventurer from neighbouring Khokand, Yakub Beg, who by 1870 had imposed his control over all of Xinjiang. The Russians then occupied the strategically important and mineral-rich Ili region to protect trading provileges obtained there in

1851. A promise to evacuate the region once the Qing had restored its authority was not fulfilled after Qing armies had defeated Yakub Beg and retaken Xinjiang (1877). Relations between China and Russia became extremely tense in 1879 when the Treaty of Livadia, signed by a Chinese diplomatic mission to Russia, allowed the latter to remain in effective control of Ili: in Beijing, officials denounced the treaty and called for war. A second mission was sent (1881), resulting in the Treaty of St Petersburg (24 Feb 1881), by which Russia finally agreed to hand back Ili to Chinese control. The resolution of the crisis gave a moral boost to hardline Chinese officials who advocated greater resistance to foreign encroachment.

Iliescu, Ion (1930–) Romanian politician. He joined the Communist Youth Union in 1944 and the Communist Party in 1953, and from 1949 to 1960 served on its Central Committee. In 1965 he began a three-year term as Head of Party Propaganda, and as a member of the Central Committee again from 1968 held office as First Secretary and Youth Minister (1967–71), and First Secretary of Jassy County (1974–9). In 1984 he withdrew from office but, in the wake of the 1989 revolution and the execution of Nicolae **Ceauşescu**, he returned to politics, becoming President of the National Salvation Front (Dec 1989) and, two months later, of its successor, the Provisional Council for National Unity. In May 1990 he was elected President and resigned his party posts. Discontent with the economic situation resulted in protests against his government in late 1990 and early 1991.

Ilinden Uprising (St Elijah's Day Revolt) (2 Aug 1903) **VMRO**, hoping to provoke the Great Powers to intervene, organized a rebellion among the peoples of **Macedonia** against Ottoman rule. The uprising was badly planned, its leader, Gotse Delchev, was captured and executed before it began and the Great Powers avoided involvement. The Ottoman authorities' brutal suppression of the revolt did, however, prompt Emperor **Francis Joseph** and Tsar **Nicholas II** to force the Ottoman government to pay compensation and to allow foreign advisers into Macedonia. ▷ **Macedonians**

Ilkhanid Dynasty A Mongol dynasty, the Ilkhans ruled in Iran and the central Islamic lands after the capture of Baghdad by Hulagu in 1258. Hulagu adopted Maragha as his capital, while his son, Abaqa, preferred

Tabriz. However, it was generally from what is now north-western Iran (or Iranian Azerbaijan) that the Ilkhans conducted their affairs. There was considerable internecine strife between the various Mongol groupings and with the Turks. Despite this, by the time of Ghazan, who took control after the execution of Baidu (4 Oct 1295), the economic position of the lands under Ilkhanid dispensation was healthy. This was particularly true of agriculture, which had benefited from Ghazan's reforms. Learning and scholarship also flourished. While Ghazan's predecessor, Baidu, had been a Christian, Ghazan, who was a Buddhist, ultimately converted to Islam. He then overthrew Baidu and brought to a close a curious interlude when the foremost ruler in the central Islamic lands was not a Muslim. Decay and collapse, however, soon followed; while details surrounding the fall of the Ilkhans is obscure, it seems that with the death of Togha-Temur in 1353, the Ilkhanid state ceased to exist.

Illyrian Movement The cultural and political movement among the Croats which, after 1830, aspired to Croatian independence and the unification of the **South Slavs** who inhabited the region known in antiquity as Illyria. Under the leadership of Ljudevit **Gaj** and Count Janko Drašković, it drew its support from the Croatian bourgeoisie. Identified with Croatian romanticism and the first phase of Croatian nationalism, after the revolutions of 1848–9, the Illyrian Movement faded away but its programme re-emerged in the **Yugoslavism** of **Strossmayer**.

Illyrian Provinces (1809–13) The name given by **Napoleon I** to the province which he formed from Dalmatia, Croatia, Carniola and Carinthia. Marshall Auguste Frédéric Marmont was appointed Governor of the Provinces and Ljubljana, now in modern Slovenia, was chosen as the administrative capital. ▷ **Croats; Istria**

Ilorin A state lying to the north of Yorubaland in central Nigeria which resisted European missionary and trading encroachment in the 19c, but was conquered by the Royal Niger Company and acted as a further springboard for the conquest of the northern emirates. Muslim Ilorin was an outlier of the Sokoto caliphate. It was annexed to British rule in 1896 when Sir George Goldie undertook a campaign against it and its neighbour Nupe.

Iltutmish (d.1236) Delhi Sultan of the Mamluk ('Slave') Dynasty (1211/36). The son-in-law and foremost slave of **Qutb-ud-Din Aibak**, he held fiefs under Aibak, whom he succeeded in 1211 after defeating Aram Shah, the latter's son. Iltutmish recovered Punjab, captured Sind and Bihar, and established his authority in Bengal. In Feb 1229, Iltutmish became Sultan of India as per the patent of the 'Abbasid Caliph of Baghdad. He also recaptured Gwalior and invaded Malwa and Ujjain successfully. The greatest of the Slave kings, on his death he named his daughter, **Raziya**, as his successor. ▷ **'Abbasid Dynasty; Mamluks**

Ilyushin, Sergei Vladimirovich (1894–1977) Soviet aircraft designer. Born of a peasant family in the Vologda region, he found his way to the military Aviation Academy in Moscow and by about 1930 was already working on new aeroplane designs. These were used to equip the wartime and post-war Soviet air force and increasingly to provide aircraft for Aeroflot, the Soviet civilian airline.

Image-breaking Riots (1566) Generally, the violent destruction of high-church statues and valuables, such as that carried out in England by the soldiers of Oliver **Cromwell**; however, the most famous outburst was in the Low Countries almost a century before. The riots of 1566 began in Aug in Steenvoorde in Flanders, where a mob smashed the decorations of a Catholic convent church; within a month the destruction had spread right through the Netherlands northwards to Groningen. The leadership was unidentified and much of the popular support was spontaneous; however Calvinist preachers were usually the immediate instigators. Besides the obvious anti-Catholicism, the movement was motivated by economic crisis and frustration that the Dutch Revolt against Spain seemed to be achieving little. The result of the riots was a hardening of Spanish attitudes: **Philip II** decided to send the Duke of **Alva** to restore order, and his harsh conduct signalled the start of the **Eighty Years War** (1568).

imam (1) A religious leader and teacher of a Sunni Muslim community, who leads worship in the Mosque. (2) A charismatic leader among Shiite Muslims, who believe that in every generation there is an imam who is an infallible source of spiritual and secular guidance. The line of imams ended in the 9c, and since then the ayatollahs serve as the collective caretakers of the office until the return of the expected imam. ▷ **Shiites; Sunnis**

Imam Ahmad (d.1962) Imam Ahmad of the Yemen succeeded his father the Imam Yahya who was assassinated in 1948, and ruled the country until his death in 1962, when with the backing particularly of Egypt, the Yemen Arab Republic (YAR) was proclaimed. A protracted civil war ensued with Egyptian troops being sucked into what was for them a particularly undesirable conflict, insofar as the so-called 'royalists', who supported Ahmad's son, the Imam Muhammad al-Badr and were backed by the Sa'udis (who naturally had no wish to see a left of centre republican regime on their back doorstep), were familiar with the mountainous terrain of the country, a terrain which was totally alien to the Egyptian forces sent to support the Republican cause.

impeachment A legal process for removing public officials from office. Originating in medieval England, the process was revived in that country in the 17c, when the Rump Parliament voted to bring Charles I to trial, resulting in his conviction and beheading. In the USA, the Constitution provides that the House of Representatives may move to impeach for 'high crimes and misdemeanors'. The case is then tried by the Senate, where a two-thirds majority is required for conviction. It is generally agreed that impeachment is a cumbersome method because of the problem of defining unacceptable behaviour and crimes. The move to impeach President Richard **Nixon** in 1974 did, however, have the effect of forcing his resignation. Earlier, the impeachment proceedings against President Andrew **Johnson** in 1867, which were politically inspired, resulted in his acquittal by the Senate.

Imperial Aulic Court (*Reichshofrat*) The Aulic Court was designed by **Maximilian I** in 1498 to be the Empire's highest executive and judicial body. The court was reorganized by **Ferdinand I** in 1559. Thereafter, it balanced the Imperial Cameral Tribunal, dealing with judicial matters and litigation, providing the Emperor with advice on foreign and domestic affairs. The court accompanied the Emperor's person and eventually made its permanent residence with him in Vienna.

Imperial British East Africa Company A British company founded and chartered to rule a large area of East Africa in 1888. It was designed to ward off the German and French threats to the area and maintain British access to Lake Victoria, Uganda, and the upper Nile. However, it was seriously undercapitalized, and could not find the resources to develop the region, create an infrastructure, or withstand African resistance. It was wound up in 1894, and its territories became the protectorates (later Crown Colonies) of Kenya and Uganda.

Imperial Cameral Tribunal (*Reichskammergericht*) Between 1495 and the Empire's end in 1806, the Cameral Tribunal was the highest court in the Empire. After reforms in 1555 it was composed of men trained in law and it was instrumental in introducing Roman law throughout the Empire. The court sat at Speyer until 1693 and thereafter at Wetzler. It dealt with civil cases; criminal cases were usually referred to the Aulic Court.

Imperial Conferences The consultative arrangements devised in 1907 by which the British and Dominion governments met on a regular basis. A permanent secretariat was established and meetings at four-year intervals were organized. The Canadian Prime Minister, Sir Wilfred **Laurier**, was suspicious of both the title and its implications, but he wished to challenge the London government's right to decide the foreign policy of the empire as a whole and thereby commit Canada without proper consultation. The 1911 conference provided the first occasion for at least some briefing by the imperial government when Sir Edward Grey gave the Prime Ministers a cagey description of the European situation. By 1926 the conference at last accepted the principle that the dominions were independent nations. The **Balfour Declaration** recommended a new constitutional framework for the Empire in which the dominions became 'autonomous communities within the **British Empire**, equal in status' but still 'united by a common allegiance to the crown', and this was embodied in the Statute of **Westminster**. However, there were limits to the British government's readiness to see the dominions as equal partners. At the 1930 conference it refused to consider the Canadian Prime Minister R B **Bennett**'s plea for imperial preferential tariffs. By 1944, however, the Imperial Conference had become a genuine means by which the Prime Ministers discussed problems and suggested mutually acceptable solutions.

Imperial Diet (*Reichstag*) The Diet was the assembly of the Holy Roman Empire (c.1100–1806). After 1489, the Diet was divided into three chambers or colleges. Seven lay and ecclesiastical princes (electors) formed the electoral college and were charged with electing a new emperor. The second college, also of princes, was composed of the other noble rulers, lay and ecclesiastical. The third college represented delegates from the Imperial towns. With the collapse of central authority during the **Thirty Years War** the Diet lost its legislative powers and became a largely ceremonial body.

Imperial Federation League (1884–94) A British pressure group, with branches in Canada, working towards federation for the British Empire. Its members saw this as answer to the challenge of industrial powers such as Germany and the USA, to Britain's isolation within Europe, and to the rivalry with other imperial powers that emerged after 1880. The British league split over the tariff in 1893 and was succeeded by the British Empire League; but this, with its Canadian counterpart, dwindled away in the early 1900s.

imperialism The extension of the power of the state through the acquisition, normally by force, of other territories, which are then subject to rule by the imperial power. Many suggest that the motivation behind imperialism is economic, through the exploitation of cheap labour and resources, and the opening up of new markets. Others suggest that non-economic factors are involved, including nationalism, racism and the pursuit of international power. The main era of imperialism was the 1880s to 1914, when many European powers sought to gain territories in Africa and Asia. Imperialism of the form associated with the establishment of European empires has in large measure disappeared, but the term is now often applied to any attempts by developed countries to interfere in underdeveloped countries. There is also increasing interest in the idea of *neo-colonialism*, where certain countries are subjugated by the economic power of developed countries, rather than through direct rule. ▷ **indirect rule**

Imperial Knights (*Reichsritter*) The Knights comprised a class of small landholders. Their holdings were usually poor and notoriously poorly managed. The Knights faced a constant threat of encroachment from the greater princes. To protect themselves they allied closely to the Emperor and the ecclesiastical states. They were some of the strongest supporters of the Imperial constitutional order and status quo.

Imperial Maritime Customs A Chinese government institution under foreign management during the late 19c and early 20c in charge of collecting customs duties accruing from foreign trade. In 1854 the Chinese Superintendent of Trade at Shanghai fled the city following its occupation by secret society rebels (Small Sword Society). UK and US consuls then assumed responsibility for collecting the maritime customs and remitting them to the Chinese governments, and this arrangement was extended to other **treaty ports**. In 1861 the Chinese government formally appointed Horatio Lay, a British subject, Inspector-General of Imperial Maritime Customs and the institution remained under foreign direction until its abolition in 1945. The most celebrated Inspector-General was Robert Hart, who served in the post from 1863 to 1908. Chinese nationalists cite the institution as an example of Western imperialism in China, while some Western historians underline its contribution to China's modernization.

Imperial Rescript on Education (30 Oct 1890) The rescript issued in the name of the Japanese **Meiji Emperor** that sought to provide the basic aims of education, emphasizing the importance of inculcating traditional values of loyalty to the Emperor, filial piety and concern for the common welfare. It represented a conservative reaction to the westernizing reforms of the 1870s and 1880s, which were thought to have encouraged individualism and materialism. The close relationship between the Emperor and his subjects, described as existing since time immemorial, was the central focus of the rescript. Copies were displayed in every school, where children had to recite the rescript every day. After **World War II**, US occupation authorities condemned the rescript for having contributed to the emergence of fanatical emperor-worship, ultra-nationalism and militarism during the late 1930s, and ordered its replacement by new educational aims to encourage a democratic spirit in Japan.

Imperial Rescript to Soldiers and Sailors (4 Jan 1882) The rescript issued in the name of the Japanese **Meiji Emperor** to provide a code of ethics for the military services. It was issued at a time when a national conscript army had only recently been formed (1873) and against a background of **samurai** discontent with modernizing reforms, which had led to several uprisings in the late 1870s. The support of the military services were therefore essential for the new Meiji government. The rescript described service to the state in terms of absolute loyalty to the Emperor and called for a spirit of patriotism, discipline and simplicity amongst the military (harkening back to traditional ethics of the samurai class). At the same time, all servicemen were to eschew politics, an injunction that was to be broken in the 1930s when ultra-nationalist army officers attempted a military takeover of government. Like the **Imperial Rescript on Education**, this rescript has been regarded since 1945 as providing the moral underpinning for the pre-war ideology of fanatical emperor-worship and extreme nationalism.

Imperial Rule Assistance Association (IRAA) An umbrella organization created in Japan (Oct 1940) to promote a New Order whereby all interests in society would be united behind mobilization for war and the national interest. Launched by the Prime Minister Fumimaro **Konoe** in the summer of 1940, the IRAA was originally intended to be the nucleus of a mass-based reformist party that would absorb all existing political parties and occupational groups, thereby challenging the political, bureaucratic and economic elites. It was supported by army officers who wanted to see a controlled economy as well as intellectuals attracted to models of European Fascism. In practice, however, the IRAA soon came under the control of the bureaucracy (in particular the Home Ministry) and became merely an instrument of government control. Although political parties were formally abolished, former party elites continued to exercise leadership in the Diet, while business elites were able to obstruct all attempts to impose total state control of the economy.

Imperial Towns (*Resichsstädte*) Cities in the **Holy Roman Empire** directly ruled by the Emperor. The term is often confused with Free Imperial City (*freie Reichstadt*), though the latter is correctly applied only to the seven cities which had won freedom from ecclesiastical control: Basle, Strasbourg, Speyer, Worms, Mainz, Cologne and Regensburg. Most of the Imperial towns were in South Germany. The largest grouping of them was the Hanseatic League. After the Peace of Westphalia (1648) their representatives made up the third college of the Imperial Diet. Many smaller towns lost their

Imperial privileges; the number declined from over 80 in 1521 to 51 in 1789. Most were governed by oligarchies through a town council (*Rat*).

Imperial Way Faction (*Kodo-ha*) Japanese army faction in the 1930s which stressed the importance of the **samurai** spirit and mystic devotion to the emperor. The faction comprised ultra-nationalist junior officers who denounced corruption amongst political and business elites (who were seen as insensitive to the economic hardships of the people as a result of the Great Depression) and advocated direct action to sweep away the civilian establishment and achieve national renovation in preparation for what they saw as an inevitable war with the USSR. In Feb 1936 the faction attempted a coup in Tokyo but it was suppressed by the army senior command.

Imrédy, Béla (1891–1946) Hungarian financier and politician. He was Director of the national bank from 1932 to 1935 and thereafter its President. Between 1932 and 1935 he was also Minister of Finance, and from May 1938 to Feb 1939 Prime Minister. Internally he supported authoritarian rule and externally he supported **Hitler**'s policies, particularly after the **Munich Agreement** in Sep 1938. During the Nazi occupation 1944–5 he acted as Minister of Economic Affairs. After the war he was executed as a war criminal.

IMRO ▷ **VMRO**

Incas Originally a small group of Quechua-speaking Indians living in the Cuzco Basin of the central Andean highlands. In the 11c, they established their capital at Cuzco, the Sacred City of the Sun, where they built huge stone temples and fortresses, and covered their buildings in sheets of gold. During the 15c, they brought together much of the Andean area, stretching along the entire western length of South America, from near the present Ecuador-Columbia border to south central Chile, and occupied much of the Andean regions of Bolivia as well. The Incas succeeded in creating an organizational structure that could hold a vast area together, and were able to extract from it the resources necessary to support armies of conquest and a sizable state apparatus. They used former rulers as regional administrators (provided they were loyal) but these were denied any independence, and Inca culture, language (Quechua), and the cult of the Sun were forcibly imposed. The Inca emperor was a despotic ruler of a highly stratified society, a quasi-religious figure, who was a direct descendant of the Sun-god, Inti. The population of the empire has been variously estimated between 5 and 10 million in 1500. The Incas were not innovative; they merely expanded and intensified existing practices, such as in agriculture. They had a system of more than 15 000 km of roads, and hundreds of way stations and administrative centres that provided an essential infrastructure for communication, conquest, and control. They also had impressive storage facilities, such as the food warehouses at the administrative city of Huanuco Pampa in central Peru. In 1523, Spanish invaders under Pizarro encountered the Incas. They captured the emperor, **Atahualpa**, whom they later murdered, and seized control of the empire, and by the 1570s Indian power was totally destroyed.

Indentured Labour, Indian Workers from India, imported in the period 1838 to 1917 into those British West Indies colonies which lost their labour force after Emancipation. After 1834, British West Indies governments set up emigration offices in Bombay, Calcutta and Madras and offered a five-year indenture, rations, housing and a free passage home. The latter condition was dropped after 1854 and when their term of indenture was completed many immigrants chose to stay, buying up cheap crown land and putting down roots. It is calculated that some 370 000 Indian labourers came to Jamaica, Trinidad and Guyana prior to 1917; their descendants make up half the population in Trinidad and Guyana today.

indentured servants The name given to Europeans who were contracted to serve as field labourers mainly in St Kitts and Barbados prior to the **Sugar Revolution.** In those colonies the native population was hostile or non-existent and a source of labour was found in the 'rejects' of England and France: common criminals, beggars and rebels, although some penurious gentlemen also served. The contract provided passage, board and lodging and the promise of land or a passage home after the 3–7 year period of indenture was completed. The civil unrest in England and Ireland between 1640 and 1660 resulted in many deportations and Barbados alone received 23 000 servants in the period 1645–60. As conditions were very harsh and mortality high, many indentured servants took to buccaneering, the most notable being Henry **Morgan**. ▷ **buccaneers**

indentured servitude A system of contract labour, developed to attract immigrants to the early American colonies, offering poor Englishmen Atlantic passage in exchange for a term of service. After serving their terms (generally four years, during which, in contrast to slaves, they retained legal rights), most indentured servants became wage-labourers on plantations or farms, although a few did succeed in becoming landowners. Through most of the 17c, some 1 500 indentured servants were brought to the Chesapeake Bay colonies every year. In the late 17c, however, the numbers declined significantly as large numbers of slaves were imported.

Independent Labour Party (ILP) British political party formed in 1893 with the objective of sending working men to parliament. It was socialist in aim, but wished to gain the support of working people whether they were socialist or not. One of its leading figures was Keir **Hardie**. Many of its leaders played a major part in founding the Labour Representation Committee (1900), which became the **Labour Party** in 1906. It was affiliated to the Labour Party but put up its own candidates, and was disaffiliated in 1932. It continued to have a few members of parliament up to 1950. ▷ **socialism**

Independent Republican Party French political party. Those members of the CNI (*Centre national des independants*, 'National Centre of Independents') who continued to support de **Gaulle** after 1962 and who formed a new party in 1966, led by **Giscard d'Estaing**. At first little more than a weak adjunct to the Gaullist Party, it emerged as an equal partner with its leader's election as President in 1973, and became one of the two main right-wing parties. In 1978 it was incorporated in the UDF (*Union pour la démocratie française* ('Union for French Democracy'), an electoral coalition, with various small centre groups. Often referred to as Giscardiens, after their leading figure. ▷ **Gaullists; Independents** (France)

Independents (England) The name given to those Puritans in favour of religious toleration who rejected a Presbyterian establishment in England during the 1640s and who founded their own independent congregations. From these developed Congregationalism. The term is also used to distinguish those parliamentarians who favoured an all-out war against **Charles I** involving, if necessary, his deposition from 'Presby-

Partition of India (1947)

terians' who wanted a defensive war and accommodation with the King. The leadership of the **New Model Army** from 1645 reflected 'independent' objectives. ▷ **Cromwell, Oliver; English Civil Wars; Puritanism**

Independents (France) French political party, officially known as the CNI (*Centre national des indépendants*, 'National Centre of Independents' or 'Independents'). The party was organized in 1948, and was the successor to the pre-**World War II** parties known collectively by the name *Modérés* ('**Moderates**'). In 1951 it incorporated the *Parti paysan* ('Peasant Party'), and in 1952 many former **Gaullists**. It was led by Antoine Pinay and supported de **Gaulle** in 1958, but its opposition to his Algerian policy led to its collapse in 1962. A small faction, led by **Giscard d'Estaing**, remained loyal to de

Gaulle's government, and resurrected the party as the **Independent Republican Party** in 1966.

India, Partition of (1947) Under the Indian Independence Act of July 1947, the formerly British-ruled Indian sub-continent was partitioned on 14–15 Aug into two independent countries, a predominantly Hindu India and a predominantly Muslim Pakistan. There was a lot of communal violence at this time which had started in the spring of 1947. Many Muslims migrated from India to Pakistan and many Hindus from Pakistan to India, resulting in a refugee population of some 6 000 000 Muslims (in Pakistan) and 4 500 000 Sikhs and Hindus (on the Indian side of the border). In places there was a total collapse of law and order, before, during and after the partition. The violence which accompanied the migration resulted in what is believed to have been near to a million deaths—although the official total was 180000. All princely states in the Indian subcontinent were left to choose their own fate but were advised to integrate with either India or Pakistan according to the religious affiliations of their peoples and their geographical positions. The state of Kashmir, however, remains in dispute. See map p449.

India Acts Passed by the British parliament, the Regulating Act of 1773 and India Act of 1784 attempted to reform the corrupt and inefficient administration of the British **East India Company** over the developing Indian empire, whilst avoiding the necessity for Parliament to have to take direct responsibility for governing the newly-acquired territories. The 1773 Act set up the post of Governor-General and a Governing Council in India and that of 1784 established a Board of Control in London, made up of members of the cabinet, to decide on strategic questions concerning the government of India. The Acts were intended to meet criticism amongst the English establishment of the all too evident speculation of Company funds, seen in the growing number of 'Nabobs' (merchants and Company employees returning from India with vast fortunes who then bribed their way into positions of influence), as well as the maladministration of Bengal (which resulted in the death of one third of the population in the famine of 1770) and the warmongering of Warren **Hastings** (Governor-General, 1773–85). Subsequent Acts in 1813 and 1830 deprived the East India Company of its monopoly of the East Indies trade and then of its trading functions altogether, allowing it to concentrate entirely on the business of administration. During this later period, the so-called 'era of reform', zealous attempts were made to improve the Company's administration along utilitarian lines, as well as to impress the mark of British rule on the Indian population. The result was the **Indian Uprising** of 1857 and the abolition of the Company the following year. ▷ **Government of India Acts**

Indian Civil Service (ICS) Formerly known as the Covenanted Civil Service because its nominated members entered into covenants originally with the British **East India Company**, and afterwards with the Secretary of State in council, ICS members filled the higher posts in the government secretariats in various departments. Under a decree dating 1853, the ICS was opened to all natural-born British subjects, regardless of race, who would be appointed as civil servants subject to their performance in a competitive examination held in England. The first Indian, the poet Tagore's brother, Satyendranath Tagore, entered the ICS in 1864. At Independence, the ICS was renamed as the Indian Administrative Service (IAS).

Indian National Congress A broad-based political organization, it was founded in 1885 and became a nationwide political party in 1920. It spearheaded the nationalist movement for independence from Britain under the leadership of charismatic figures such as M K **Gandhi** and Jawaharlal **Nehru**. An uneasy alliance of left and right, business and rural interests, it has been the dominant political party in India since 1947. Exceptions to its rule occurred in the periods 1977–80, when the Janata Party ruled, and 1989–91, when India was ruled by the Janata Dal and Janata Dal (S). ▷ **Non-Cooperation Movement; Quit India Movement**

Indian Uprising (1857–8) A serious rebellion against British rule, triggered off partly by the belief among Indian troops in British service that new cartridges had been greased with animal fat — something which would have been abhorrent to both Hindus and Muslims. At the same time, there was resentment among the old governing class over the reduction in their power, and Western innovations. The uprising at Meerut (10 May 1857) spread throughout northern India, with both urban and rural populations rising in revolt. Delhi quickly fell, and Kanpur and Lucknow garrisons were besieged. The British finally regained full control in mid-1858. The immediate result was the transfer of government from the British **East India Company** to the British Crown (1858), but the long-term result was a legacy of bitterness on both sides. The element of national consciousness present made the episode a source of inspiration for later Indian nationalists. The uprising is also known as the Indian Mutiny or the 1st National War of Independence.

Indian Territory The land designated by the US government as a 'permanent' homeland for Native Americans who were forced to give up their land in the southeast, which had been guaranteed by federal treaties, and relocate in the west in compliance with the Indian Removal Act of 1830. The boundaries of what was to be inviolable territory based on new treaties signed in the 1830s were redefined several times, beginning in 1834. The original area included most of Oklahoma and parts of Kansas and Nebraska. The passage of homestead and land allotment acts opened up parts of the area to white homesteaders and developers. The northern section was lost in 1854 when Kansas and Nebraska became territories, and by the end of the century most of the remaining Indian Territory had been absorbed into what is now Oklahoma. ▷ **Five Civilized Tribes**

Indian Wars (1622–1890) In American history, the process of invasion and conquest by which white people settled the present USA. The Europeans set out to remake the New World in the image of the Old, if possible by persuasion, if necessary by force. The result was the destruction of the indigenous population, cultures and economies. Through European diseases to which the Native Americans had no natural resistance, the imposition of white culture, and warfare, the native population of North America was reduced from roughly 1 million at first contact to about 250 000 by the end of the 18c. The list of specific Indian wars is very long, most of them actually being skirmishes between a local tribe and the white settlers usurping their land. They are generally accepted to have begun with the revolt of the **Powhatan Confederacy** against settlers at **Jamestown**, Virginia in 1622, and to have ended with the massacre at **Wounded Knee** in 1890. Specific early conflicts include the **Pequot War** (1637) and **King Philip's War** (1676) in New England and the Pueblo Revolt (1680–92) led by Popé against Spanish settlements in what is now New Mexico and Arizona. From 1689 to 1763 Native American warfare was bound up with the struggle between France and Britain for control of the continent, the **French and Indian War**. The **Algonquin** tribes sided with the French. The English, eventually victorious, enjoyed the support of the **Iroquois Confederacy** of western New York, important both for their internal strength and for their control of the Mohawk Valley and Lake Ontario plain, which formed the only natural break in the Appalachian Mountains. Further west, the Ottawa chief, Pontiac, seized almost all the British fur trading posts from upper Michigan to New York state before the French cut off their supplies. By 1830 the US government had formalized a policy of denying Indian rights and removing tribes from the lands east of the Mississippi to unsettled lands in the west. Despite resistance, the **Five Civilized Tribes** of the southeast and others were forced to move west and settle in **Indian Territory**. The **Seminole** people of Florida, whose number included escaped black slaves, fought for over 30 years, accepting defeat in 1842 when nearly all were lost. Some finally moved west, but a small group survived by living in the Everglades. The Indian wars generally followed the progress of white settlers as they moved their frontier westward. On the plains, the US Cavalry fought the **Sioux** and the **Cheyenne**, under such leaders as **Sitting Bull** and **Crazy Horse**. These 'Sioux Wars' lasted over 30 years until finally ended by the incident at **Wounded Knee** (1890). The massacre of warriors, women and children by the Cavalry at Sand Creek, Colorado (1864) inflamed Arapaho, **Comanche**, Kiowa and Cheyenne already fighting to avoid being placed on reservations. In the southwest, the **Navajo** conflict ended with their mass imprisonment (1864–8) at Fort Sumpter, while the **Apache** under such leaders as **Cochise** and **Geronimo**, fought on until 1900. At the same time Nez Percé under Chief **Joseph** and the Modoc fought for their lands in the northwest until their eventual defeat. Throughout the wars, the Native Americans fought at material and numerical disadvantage. They were disadvantaged as well by their own concept of warfare, for they understood it in wholly different terms from their foes. Finally they were handicapped by their own lack of unity. Specific tribes approached each war in terms of their own friendships and enmities. This gave some, such as the Iroquois, more power to shape their own futures. But only on a few occasions did such confederacies surmount tribal boundaries. ▷ **Little Bighorn, Battle of the; Native Americans; Pontiac's Conspiracy**

indirect rule A form of colonial rule especially characteristic of British rule in Africa during the inter-war years. In general terms it involved the use of existing political structures, leaders, and local organs of authority. Thus local political elites enjoyed considerable autonomy, although they still had to keep in accord with the interests of the colonial power. It was adopted on grounds of its cheapness and to allow for independent cultural development, but was increasingly criticized for its failure to introduce a modernizing role into colonial administration, and was gradually given up after 1945. ▷ **Fulani Emirates; Lozi**

Indochina The term, as currently used, refers to the present-day states of Vietnam, Laos and Cambodia. French Indochina, the Indochinese Union, was established in 1887, and comprised the protectorates of Cambodia, Laos, Tonkin and Annam, together with the colony of Cochinchina. French Indochina as a political unit ceased to exist in 1954, following the conclusion of the Geneva Agreements and the withdrawal of the French.

Indo-Pakistan Wars (1947–9, 1965 and 1971) The conflict between Hindus and Muslims that first led to partition at Independence in 1947 and the creation of India and Pakistan, has been kept alive since for a number of reasons, including, most obviously, resentment at the bloodshed which accompanied partition and the ineptitude with which the boundary between the two countries was delineated by the British in the months before their departure. Roughly drawn, the boundary often divided families, villages and communities and has been a cause of dispute ever since. The fate of various nominally still independent Princely states had also not been decided at the time of partition. Owing to their loyalty to the British, there had been a reluctance to force them into joining either of the new nations and in Kashmir, on the border between India and Pakistan, the Raja, Hari Singh, was in a dilemma since, although himself a Hindu, the majority of his population were Muslim. An uprising in the west of the country decided the matter for him, forcing him to turn to India for help, which was afforded only on the condition that Kashmir joined the Indian union. This decision, made without consulting the population, was contested by Pakistan, which supported the insurgents against the Indian army, the fighting in Kashmir only being brought to an end in 1949 after the **UN** arranged a ceasefire, pending a plebiscite to decide the fate of the territory. This plebiscite was never held, and fighting broke out between India and Pakistan again in 1965, a ceasefire being brokered by the Soviet Premier, Alexei Kosygin, after an arms embargo was imposed by the USA and USSR. In 1971 a third war was occasioned by the uprising in East Pakistan that led to the foundation of the independent state of Bangladesh. This time it was India that intervened in support of Sheikh Mujibur Rahman and the Awami League; fighting also occurred on the western frontier between India and Pakistan, and in Kashmir. On this occasion the superior size of the Indian army outmatched the Pakistanis and an uneasy peace has persisted ever since. In the 1980s the rearming of Pakistan by the USA following the Soviet invasion of Afghanistan, accelerated the arms race between the two countries, both sides acquiring the capacity to manufacture nuclear weapons (the first test explosion of an Indian bomb occurring in 1974). The foundation of the South Asian Association for Regional Cooperation in 1986 (comprising India, Pakistan, Bangladesh, Bhutan, Nepal and Sri Lanka) has helped to relieve tension in subsequent years. ▷ **India, Partition of; Princely States, Indian**

Indo-Sri Lankan Peace Accord (1987) The agreement signed by Rajiv **Gandhi**, then Prime Minister of India, and J R **Jayawardene**, the President of Sri Lanka. The Accord was Gandhi's attempt to impose a solution to Sri Lanka's Tamil secessionist problem, but collapsed due to a lack of support from all sections of Sri Lankan society. Troops from the Indian Peacekeeping Force (IPKF) were quickly embroiled in conflict with the militants of the **LTTE**, while Jayawardene's government was threatened by violent protests led by the **JVP**.

Industrial Revolution A term usually associated with the accelerated pace of economic change, the associated technical and mechanical innovations, and the emergence of mass markets for manufactured goods, beginning in Britain in the last quarter of the 18c with the mechanization of the cotton and woollen industries of Lancashire, Central Scotland, and the West Riding of Yorkshire. After the harnessing of steam power, cotton and woollen factories were increasingly concentrated in towns, and there were hugely increased rates of urbanization. A rapid population increase, stimulated by greater economic opportunities for early marriage, is also associated with this type of economic growth. The mechanization of heavier industries (iron and steel) was slower, but sustained the Industrial Revolution in its second phase from c.1830.

Industrial Workers of the World (IWW) US radical labour organization movement, whose members were known as Wobblies. An offshoot of the Western Federation of Miners, it was founded in 1905 by a group who opposed the craft unionism of the AFL and proposed instead a union of both skilled and unskilled workers. The movement was soon splintered because of the radical ideology of its leader, 'Big Bill' **Haywood**, who called for the destruction of capitalism and the formation of a new society and maintained that employers' violence must be met in kind. He was less interested in negotiation than in striking and sabotage. Lack of organization and funds meant that the IWW had few successes in industrial conflicts although its membership reached a peak of at least 60 000. It declined rapidly after the Red Scare of 1919. ▷ **AFL–CIO**

Indus Valley Civilization The earliest known South Asian civilization, flourishing c.2300–1750BC across half a million square miles around the River Indus in Pakistan. Over 100 sites have been identified with important urban centres at Mohenjo-daro and Harappa (Pakistan), and Kalibangan and Lothal (western India). There were uniform principles of urban planning, with streets set out in a grid pattern and public drainage systems. Weights and measures were standardized, and there was widespread trade with western Asia. A common writing system was used, which remains undeciphered. Great granaries on citadel mounts suggest the existence of priest-kings or a priestly oligarchy. There is no firm explanation for the decline of the civilization.

INF (Intermediate Nuclear Force) Treaty A treaty signed (Dec 1987) in Washington by US President Ronald **Reagan**, and Soviet General-Secretary Mikhail **Gorbachev**, involving the elimination of 1 286 missiles from Europe and Asia, and over 2 000 warheads. It was noted for its inclusion of the most comprehensive, stringent and intrusive verification procedures ever seen in an arms control treaty, including short notice on-site verification, and was a major break in the arms race and a step forward in arms control generally, leading to later agreements in both the nuclear and conventional fields.

Inkatha Freedom Party A loose political organization based in Zululand and answerable to Chief Gatsha **Buthelezi** which in the 1970s and 1980s offered an opposition voice to **apartheid** but then became the vehicle for Zulu nationalism and a sometimes violent antagonist to the **ANC** (African National Congress). It received clandestine support from the police and probably government sources as well.

INLA ▷ **Irish National Liberation Army**

Innocent I, St (360–417) Italian Pope (402/17). A native of Albano, his pontificate,

next to that of **Leo I, 'the Great'**, is the most important for the relations of Rome to the other Churches. He enforced the celibacy of the clergy; he maintained the right of the bishop of Rome to judge appeals from other churches, and his letters abound with assertions of universal jurisdiction. During his pontificate, Rome was sacked in 410 by **Alaric I**.

Innocent III (Lotario de' Conti di Segni) (1160–1216) Italian Pope (1198/1216). His pontificate is regarded as the high point of the temporal and spiritual supremacy of the Roman see. He judged between rival emperors in Germany, and had Otto IV deposed. He laid England under an interdict and excommunicated King **John** for refusing to recognize Stephen **Langton** as Archbishop of Canterbury. Under him the fourth Lateran Council was held in 1215. ▷ **Lateran Councils**

Innocent IV (Sinibaldo Fieschi) (d.1254) Italian Pope (1243/54). Genoese by birth and trained in the canon law at Bologna, Innocent IV took a view of papal supremacy very similar to that of **Innocent III**. He was unscrupulous in the construction of his own power network through the exercise of patronage, and his pontificate brought the struggle between the papacy and Emperor **Frederick II** to its climax. At Frederick's death (1250), he sought to establish papal overlordship in Sicily. This was acknowledged by Frederick's illegitimate son **Manfred** who nevertheless led a revolt in 1254. Innocent also put the **Inquisition** on a permanent basis in Italy.

Innocent X (Giambattista Pamfili) (1574–1655) Italian Pope (1644/55). An unscrupulous man, he was notorious for his nepotism. Scarcely had he been elected than he began systematic attacks on the Barbarini, relatives of his predecessor, Urban VIII. He was quickly forced to desist from this persecution when his victims fled to France and successfully appealed to Cardinal **Mazarin** for protection. When the latter threatened to annex the papal enclave of Avignon, Innocent backed down. In international affairs, Innocent's condemnation of the Peace of **Westphalia** served only to demonstrate the growing impotence of the papacy, while his support for Spanish claims to Portugal (which had regained its independence again in 1640) proved equally fruitless. Even the Bull *Cum Occasione* (1653) condemning Jansenist views on grace, rather than restoring unity to the Church, merely sparked over a century of internal religious controversy.

Innocent XI (Benedetto Odescalchi) (1611–89) Italian Pope (1676/89). Elected Pope despite the opposition of **Louis XIV** of France, he took over an empty treasury and an inefficient administration. To counter these, he embarked on a policy of retrenchment (including the abolition of many sinecures and a campaign against luxury) and tried, with some success, to end the practice of nepotism; he also sought financial aid from Catholic princes. The consequence of these reforms was that he was able to put papal finances on a sufficiently sound footing to aid **John III Sobieski** of Poland and the Holy Roman Emperor, **Leopold I**, to break the Turkish siege of Vienna (1683). However, in other areas he was less successful, most notably in his dealings with **Louis XIV**. Poor from the start, his relations with the French King further deteriorated because of his reluctance (like **Clement X**) to see the implementation of Louis's edict of 1673 which empowered him to seize the revenue of vacant sees. Matters came to a head when Louis summoned a French synod, which under royal pressure published the so-called Four or Gallican Articles (*Déclaration du clergé de France*), which fiercely affirmed the limitations of papal authority within France. In retaliation, Innocent refused to confirm the promotion of any French clergy involved in the synod. In 1685 he further angered the French monarch by condemning his treatment of the **Huguenots** and, in 1688, by opposing his candidate for the archbishopric of Cologne; Louis's response was to occupy the papal enclave of Avignon. In theological matters, Innocent was far from unsympathetic to Jansenist views, but he drew the line at the Quietist doctrines of his friend, the Spaniard Miguel de Molinos, whom he had tried and imprisoned.

Innocent XII (Antonio Pignatelli) (1615–1700) Italian Pope (1691/1700). Jesuit-educated, he was papal ambassador to Tuscany, Poland and Austria before becoming a Cardinal in 1681. It was Innocent who brought an end to the poor relations between **Louis XIV** of France and the papacy by persuading the latter to withdraw the Gallican Articles of 1682 and to relinquish the occupied papal enclave of Avignon. In return for this, Innocent championed the candidacy of Philippe of Anjou (Louis XIV's grandson)

as the heir to the Spanish throne and acknowledged the French monarch's right to administer vacant sees. In theological matters, he condemned both Jansenism (1696) and Quietism (1699), while in ecclesiastical and domestic affairs he carried on the struggle against nepotism which he condemned in the Bull *Romanum decet pontificem* (1692). ▷ **Innocent XI**

Innocent XIII (Michelangelo dei Conti) (1655–1724) Italian Pope (1721/4). A former papal ambassador to Switzerland and Portugal and a Cardinal from 1706, it was Innocent XIII who in 1721 invested the Holy Roman Emperor **Charles VI** with sovereignty over Naples. He recognized James Francis Edward **Stuart** (the Old Pretender) as King of England and promised him subsidies if he returned England to Roman Catholicism. Although he was hostile towards the Jansenists — he confirmed the Bull *Unigenitus* in 1722 — he was also distrustful of the Jesuits, taking particular issue with the modified 'Chinese rites' which they employed with some success to attract converts in Asia.

Inönü, Ismet (1884–1973) Turkish soldier and politician. He fought in **World War I**, then became **Atatürk**'s Chief-of-Staff in the war against the **Greeks** (1919–22), defeating them twice at Inönü. As the first Premier of the new republic (1923–37), he introduced many political reforms, and was elected President in 1938 on Atatürk's death. From 1950 he was Leader of the Opposition, and held office as Premier again from 1960 to 1965, when he resigned.

Inoue Kaoru (1836–1915) Japanese politician and elder statesman (**genro**). From a **samurai** family in **Choshu**, he took an active part in the overthrow of the **Tokugawa Shogunate**, purchasing arms from England and playing a key role in arranging the Chosu-**Satsuma** alliance (1866) against the Tokugawa regime. In the new Meiji government (1868–87) he served as Minister of Public Works, Minister of Agriculture and Commerce, Minister of Finance and Minister of Foreign Affairs. He was a keen advocate of economic modernization and developed close ties with business interests. As Foreign Minister (1879–87) he negotiated with the Western powers over treaty revision, but was unable to obtain their agreement to end the foreign privilege of extraterritoriality in Japan.

inquilino This Spanish term refers to tenants attached to the land by unilateral agreements, a practice which evolved during the colonial period in Chile. The *inquilino* provided some 240 days of labour, received nominal wages, a plot, a small house and the right to pasture stock on unused land. The growth of agro-industrial businesses and the cities has partially eroded *inquilinaje*, which was strongest during the late 19c and proved the bedrock of the family groups ruling Chilean society.

Inquisition A tribunal for prosecuting heresy, first created on a local and temporary basis in 13c France and Germany. In Spain, this medieval Inquisition existed in the realm of **Aragon**, with its chief seat in Tarragona. It was, however, superseded in the late 15c by the new Castilian or Spanish Inquisition, founded by papal bull in 1478 and set up in 1480: this was devoted primarily to investigating the orthodoxy of the cultural minorities that since 1492 (Jews) and 1502 (Muslims of **Castile**) had been forced to accept the Catholic faith. Of the 16 permanent tribunals of peninsular Spain, 11 were founded by 1500, three between 1505 and 1526, and one (Santiago) in 1574; the last, established in 1640, was that of Madrid. A contemporary estimated that in its first 10 years it burnt 2000 people and punished 15000 others. Portugal, like Castile, had no medieval Inquisition, and attempts by the authorities to introduce one on the Castilian model foundered until a tribunal was created temporarily in 1539; it was not until a papal bull was promulgated (July 1547) that the Inquisition was fully introduced. The Inquisition of Portugal was introduced into Goa in 1560, and into Brazil later that century; in the metropolis it held its last **auto-de-fe** in 1765 and was eventually abolished by decree in 1821. The Spanish Inquisition was established in Peru in 1570 and in Mexico the following year; in Spain it survived until the early 19c, until its abolition in 1834.

Institución Libre de Ensenañza ('Free Educational Institute') Spanish secular educational association. Beginning in 1875 as a small private school renowned for its excellence and defiance of catholic norms, the Institución greatly influenced liberal culture in Spain. The college it established at Madrid University became an important focus of liberal intellectual life, and it was also instrumental in the creation of various leading state research bodies.

integralismo A Brazilian fascist movement of the 1930s. Its supporters were noted for their green shirts and aggressive street actions. The Brazilian Integralists Party, led by Plinio Salgado, was suppressed after a vain attack on the presidential Catete Palace in Rio de Janeiro (10 May 1938). The party had been used as a tool by Getúlio **Vargas** against liberals and the communist-led *Aliança Nacional Libertadora* (ANL) headed by Luís Carlos Prestes, a leading *tenente* in the struggle against the old republic.

Intelligentsia (19c) A peculiarly Russian phenomenon, a small educated class, interested in ideas, but separated both from its social peers and those lower down the scale. In a population of millions they numbered only thousands. In a tsarist autocracy, ideas drove them to read and write about opposition, even revolution, and this split them from the nobility and the new class of businessmen. Although towards the end of the century some groups participated in movements to the people, they had few genuine contacts with ordinary peasants. However, they developed a debate that helped to produce the political parties of the period 1894–1917.

intendentes This Spanish term (literally, 'intendants') refers to well-salaried colonial officials with significant staff, responding directly to the Spanish Crown. The intendant system, instituted by the House of Bourbon in Spain, was transplanted from Spain to Cuba in 1764, the Viceroyalty of La Plata in 1782, Peru in 1784, Mexico in 1786, and in other regions in 1790. Military officers appointed for more than 10 years, in Hispanic America they were in charge of administration, finance, the military and justice: they were effectively a response to the growth and maturity of colonial society and larger changes in the international economy, principally the growth of English economic weight. Nevertheless, the system achieved centralization and rationalization, financing the growth of full-scale military forces in the Americas.

Intensive Development (post-1953) The term used by Soviet-style economists to describe the second stage of growth following initial industrialization, itself entitled **Extensive Development**. After **Stalin**'s death Nikita **Khrushchev** and later Leonid **Brezhnev** tried to diversify the economy of the USSR by expounding the production of consumer durables and introducing new materials and technologies. Other communist countries followed suit. Largely because of too much central planning, the communist world lagged behind the West, a fact which sapped confidence in the regimes and contributed to their downfall in the period 1989–91.

Intermediate Period, First (c.2181–2040BC) In Ancient Egyptian history, the period covering the 7th to 11th Dynasty of the Egyptian chronicler Manetho. Following the collapse of the **Old Kingdom**, the country suffered civil wars, infiltration of the Nile Delta by Bedawin, plundering, a breakdown of central government, poverty and the ephemeral rule of many kings. The 7th and 8th Dynasties in Memphis had limited authority; the rest of Egypt was ruled by the nomarchs who became independent princes. By c.2160BC the princes of Heracleopolis imposed their will over neighbouring nomes (governorates) and set up the 9th and 10th Heracleopolitan Dynasties in Middle Egypt. The warlike princes of Thebes later founded the 11th Dynasty in the south, overcame the Heracleopolitans and achieved the unification of the country c.2040BC, leading to the **Middle Kingdom**. ▷ **Mentuhotpe II**

Intermediate Period, Second (c.1786–1560BC) This term covers the two centuries of Egyptian history between the Middle Kingdom and **New Kingdom**. It comprises the 13th to 17th Dynasties inclusive. For the 13th Dynasty, with its numerous kings of ever decreasing power, the breakdown of authority was cushioned through the efforts of government officials. Possibly simultaneously, the 14th Dynasty, of which little is known, exercised some control at Xois in the Delta. The weakened state of the country allowed Asiatics to move in to the Delta where, under the leadership of the **Hyksos**, the 15th and 16th Dynasties came to power. The 15th or Great Hyksos had their capital at Avaris in the Delta by c.1675BC, while the minor kings of the 16th Lesser Hyksos seem to have reigned concurrently, although no details are preserved. To the south at Thebes, the local princes formed the 17th Dynasty c.1650BC. The early members of the family were confined to the Theban area, but later rulers challenged the Hyksos and, in a series of armed clashes, began the liberation of Egypt which was finally accomplished by **Ahmose I** of the succeeding 18th Dynasty.

Intermediate Period, Third (c.1085–656BC) This term refers to post-imperial Egypt, when the country was divided and sometimes under foreign domination. The 21st Dynasty ruled from Tanis in the Delta, while at Thebes the High Priests of Amun controlled the south. The kings at Tanis were buried there with rich grave goods. The Amun priests were responsible for rescuing the plundered royal burials of earlier kings and re-interring the remains. The 22nd Dynasty, of Libyan origin, assumed the throne c.945BC and ruled from Tanis (and possibly also Bubastis). In spite of a successful campaign into Palestine and ending the hereditary position of the High Priests of Amun by appointing royal nominees such as **Shoshenq I**, conditions in Egypt were greatly disturbed. About 818BC another line of kings, the 23rd Dynasty, was established in the Delta and ruled concurrently with the 22nd Dynasty, causing the country to fragment into smaller units. Following the Nubian invasion of Egypt (c.728BC), order was restored, the short-lived 24th Dynasty ended with **Tefnakhte**, and thereafter the 25th Dynasty ruled until 656BC. ▷ **Tantamani**

International An abbreviation originally of International Working Men's Association, the name given to successive organizations attempting to establish international co-operative mechanisms for socialist, communist, and revolutionary groups. The First International was created in London in 1864 and its leadership was initially assumed by **Marx**, but it slowly disintegrated not least because of differences between him and Bakunin. The Second International was formed in Paris in 1889, but it largely collapsed in 1914 as socialist parties took sides in **World War I**. The Third International (**Comintern**) was founded by **Lenin** in Moscow in 1919 and represented mainly communist parties. It became in effect a tool of **Stalin**'s foreign policy until he abolished it in 1943 during **World War II**. There was a brief attempt in the 1930s by **Trotsky** to launch a Fourth International, which came into existence in Périgny in France in 1938 but remained merely an umbrella for miscellaneous left-wing groups of no particular importance. ▷ **communism**

International Brigades In the **Spanish Civil War**, foreign volunteer forces recruited by the **Comintern** and by individual communist parties to assist the Spanish Republic. Almost 60000 volunteers, mostly workers, fought in Spain between Oct 1936 and the brigades' withdrawal in Oct 1938, playing a particularly important role in the defence of Madrid.

Interprovincial Conferences (Canada) A governmental consultative process. The first, in 1887, was convened by Honoré **Mercier**, and was essentially a convention of provincial Liberals. It passed resolutions against the federal government's disallowing power and for increases in provincial subsidies. In the short term Ottawa reacted to the resolutions in a limited way, refraining from disallowing a contentious Quebec law and introducing subsidies for Nova Scotia's iron and steel industry. With the growing complexity and interdependence of the Canadian government and economy dating from the late 19c onwards, inter-governmental conferences (both federal-provincial and interprovincial) have become an increasingly important aspect of policy making and administration. The some 158 federal-provincial and 30 interprovincial bodies now in existence focus mainly on economic and constitutional matters, headed by a First Ministers' Conference, with various ministerial conferences and Continuing Committees feeding up to them. Since 1960 there has also been an annual meeting of provincial premiers.

interregnum A period between rulers; normally, in British history, the period between **Charles I**'s execution (30 Jan 1649) and the **Restoration** of **Charles II** (5 May 1660); also, the period between the departure of **James VII and II** (22 Dec 1688) and the accession of **William III** and Mary II (23 Feb 1689; in Scotland until 20 Apr 1689).

Interregnum (1254–73) The term used to describe the period when the German throne was held by puppet kings appointed by the princes, which marks the end of the **Hohenstaufen Dynasty** and the beginning of the rise of the **Habsburg Dynasty**. After the deaths of **Conrad IV** (1254) and the anti-King **William of Holland** (1256), the princes elected two foreigners as kings of Germany: Richard of Cornwall and **Alfonso, 'the Astronomer'** of Castile. Neither spent much time in Germany, leaving the princes and towns free to pursue their own ends. The Interregnum was the culmination of a long period of decline in the power of the monarchy in Germany.

Intolerable Acts (1774) The American name for laws passed by parliament in London to punish Massachusetts for the **Boston Tea Party** (1773). They were called the Boston Port Act, the Massachusetts Government Act, the Administration of Justice Act, and a Quartering Act. The **Quebec Act**, though addressing a different problem, was also taken by colonists to add insult to the injury of the Intolerable Acts.

Inuit The indigenous peoples of the Canadian arctic; formerly also known as the eskimos. Traditionally their eight tribes live in regional groupings of bands (about 100 strong). They have been nomadic hunters and gatherers and some maintain this way of life, though increasing numbers live in established settlements with schools, medical stations, and airstrips. Their first sustained contact with Europeans came in the late 18c by way of Moravian missionaries in Labrador. Sporadic trading contacts were made during the 19c, but only after the end of commercial whaling at the time of **World War I** were permanent trading posts established. Politically they were never included under the Indian Act, but became a federal responsibility in 1939. During the 1950s exploitation of the arctic gas and oil reserves began to destabilize their communities and in 1972 the Inuit Tapirisat of Canada (ITC) was established to preserve their culture through voluntary separation from white communities. The result of its pressure has been more government consultation and increased subsidies.

Inukai Tsuyoshi (1855–1932) Japanese politician. He was a newspaper reporter before helping to form a political party, the *Kaishinto* (Progressives), in 1882. Inukai was elected to the first Diet in 1890 and was re-elected a further 18 times. He became known for his strong opposition to clique-government and his championing of constitutionalism. During the 1920s he was associated with the largest political party in the Diet, the **Seiyukai**, becoming its President in 1929. He became Prime Minister in 1931 at a time of economic hardship at home and independent Japanese military action in Manchuria to sever the region from China. He aroused the anger of ultra-nationalists when he attempted to reassert civilian control of the army in Manchuria and reach a compromise settlement with China. In May 1932 he was assassinated in an abortive army coup. Inukai's death marked the end of party cabinets in Japan until after **World War II**.

Investiture Controversy (1075–1122) A conflict between reforming popes and lay rulers, notably the German emperor, over the leadership of Christian society. It was named after the royal practice of investing a newly appointed bishop or abbot with a ring or pastoral staff, the symbols of his spiritual office. This was condemned in 1075 by Pope **Gregory VII** as epitomizing secular domination of the Church, and the ensuing power struggle between the emperors and the papacy led to the permanent weakening of the German monarchy in favour of the princes. ▷ **Canossa; Henry IV**

Ionescu, Take (1858–1922) Romanian politician. First a liberal, then a conservative, he was a founder and leader of the Conservative–Democratic Party in 1907. As Foreign Minister during **World War I**, he agreed (1916) to the entry of Romania on the side of the Entente. He was delegate to the Peace Conference at **Versailles** (1919) and worked for the creation of the **Little Entente**. He was, briefly, President of State from 1921 to 1922.

Ionian Revolt (499–494BC) The revolt of the Greeks of Asia Minor against the **Persian Empire**, to which they had been subject since 545BC, this was recounted by Herodotus as a prelude to the **Persian Wars** against Greece. After initial success, including the burning of Sardis, the seat of the Persian satrap (or governor), the Greeks were defeated at Lade; and **Miletus**, the greatest city of Ionia, was destroyed (494BC).

Iorga, Nicolae (1871–1940/1) Romanian politician and historian. As editor (1903–6) of 'The Sower' (*Sămănătorul*), he advocated conservative and patriotic values. Active in political life, he was elected to the Romanian parliament (1907) and founded the National Democrat Party. As Prime Minister and Minister of Education (1931–2), he supported **Charles II** of Romania. With the establishment of the **Antonescu** regime, he was one of several leading figures in Romanian political and cultural life who were murdered in the years 1940–1.

IPLA (Irish People's Liberation Army) An offshoot of the Irish National Liberation Army (itself an **IRA** breakaway group) that once had left-wing pretensions, but which in the 1980s became identified once more with drug-dealing — an activity forbidden to IRA supporters and punishable by execution.

Iqbal, Sir Mohammed (1875–1938) Indian poet and philosopher. He was educated at Lahore, Cambridge (where he read law and philosophy) and Munich. On his return to India, he achieved fame through his poetry, whose compelling mysticism and nationalism caused him to be regarded almost as a prophet by Muslims. His efforts to establish a separate Muslim state eventually led to the formation of Pakistan. He was knighted in 1923, and died at Lahore, Punjab.

iqta Land granted to army officials in the Islamic empire of the Caliphs for limited periods instead of a regular salary. The *iqta* system was established in the 9c. Land subject to the iqta was originally owned by non-Muslims and thus subject to a special property tax, the *kharaj*. While the land remained legally the property of its owner, the iqta was a grant of appropriation to a Muslim officer entitling him to collect the kharaj from the owner. Out of this, the officer was to pay a small tax, but could keep the rest as his salary.

IRA (Irish Republican Army) An anti-British paramilitary guerrilla force established in 1919 by Irish nationalists to combat British forces in Ireland. It opposed the Anglo-Irish Treaty of 1921 because Ireland was a dominion and the six counties of the North of Ireland were part of the UK, but it was suppressed by the Irish government in the 1922 rising, banned by Eamon **De Valera** in 1936 and remained largely inactive until the late 1960s. In 1969, a major split in its ranks led to the formation of the Provisional IRA alongside the Official IRA, and a serious schism between the two sides in the early 1970s. The Official IRA has been virtually inactive since 1972, and generally supports political action to achieve Irish unity. The Provisionals have become the dominant republican force, responsible for shootings and bombings in Northern Ireland, Britain, and Western Europe. Targets have mainly been security and military personnel and establishments, although there have been many sectarian killings and attempts to disrupt civilian life. ▷ **Sinn Féin**

Iran, Anglo-Soviet Invasion of (Aug 1941) Suspicions that Reza Shah was sympathetic to the Germans in **World War II** resulted in the Anglo-Soviet invasion of Iran in Aug 1941, although it is possible that a desire to protect oil supplies among other things was as much of a motive for the invasion on the British side as any inklings of pro-German leanings in the Shah. The invasion and subsequent occupation forced the abdication of Reza Shah in favour of his son, Muhammad Reza, and the presence of the Soviets allowed a brief reappearance of the Tudeh Party. The country was subjected to Anglo-Soviet military occupation until 1946.

Iran–Contra Affair (1986) A major US political scandal. It grew out of the **Reagan** administration's efforts to obtain the release of US hostages held in Lebanon by groups friendly to Iran by secretly supplying arms to Iran's strongly anti-American government. **National Security Council** officials (notably, Colonel Oliver North) had been involved in the diversion of the proceeds of the arms sales to Iran to Nicaragua, to support the anti-government Contra rebels, even though Congress had banned the supplying of arms to the Contras. Congressional hearings in 1987 centred on the legality of the arms-for-hostages deal and on whether Colonel North had acted on his own as the Administration claimed, or whether top government officials, including President Reagan himself, were involved. The issues have not been satisfactorily resolved.

Iran Hostage Crisis (1979–81) On 4 Nov 1979 the US Embassy in Tehran, Iran, was seized by a mob and its staff of 52 were taken hostage. The action was approved by the Ayatollah Khomeini who, like many Iranians, hated Americans for the role of the **CIA** in the overthrow of the Mossadegh government (1953) and for their training of Shah Muhammad Reza Pahlavi's secret police. The price demanded for the release of the hostages was the return of the Shah and all his wealth. Neither **UN** appeals nor President Jimmy **Carter**'s move to freeze all Iranian assets induced Iran to release the hostages. In 1980, an attempted helicopter rescue operation using US marines, failed, causing the Carter administration great political embarrassment. The crisis preoccupied Carter during his last months in office and may well have been the single most important factor in his defeat by Ronald **Reagan** in the 1980 election. After 444 days of captivity, the hostages were released on the day President Reagan was inaugurated, and Iranian assets were unfrozen.

Iranian Revolution The 1979 revolution in Iran which deposed the Shah (15 Jan) and led to the triumphant return (1 Feb) from his French exile of the Ayatollah **Khomeini**. Khomeini appointed Dr Mehdi Bazargan as Prime Minister (1979–80), although real power was to remain with Khomeini's 15-man Islamic Revolutionary Council. Revolutionary forces took control of the country, and Khomeini announced the establishment of the Islamic Republic.

Iran–Iraq War (1980–8) Although the 1975 peace agreement with Iran ended Iraq's Kurdish revolt, Iraq still wanted a readjustment of its borders with Iran. After the Islamic Revolution in Iran, the Iranians accused Baghdad of fomenting demands for autonomy by the Arabs of Iran's Khuzestan province. In addition, Iraq feared Iranian provocation of its own 60 per cent Shiite population. After some border fighting in 1980, Iraqi forces advanced into Iran (22 Sep). By the time a peace was agreed (1988), the war had cost about half a million lives on both sides, and represented a serious threat to shipping in the Gulf. Iraq accepted Iran's terms in Aug 1990. ▷ **Kurds; Shiites**

Irene (752–803) Byzantine Empress. She was a poor orphan of Athens whose beauty and talents led Emperor Leo IV to marry her in 769. After 780 she ruled as regent for her son, Constantine VI. She imprisoned and blinded him and her husband's five brothers, and ruled in her own right from 797, but in 802 she was banished to Lesbos. For her part in the restoration of the veneration of icons she was recognized as a saint by the Greek Church.

Ireton, Henry (1611–51) English soldier. At the outbreak of the **English Civil Wars** he fought for parliament, and served at Edgehill, Naseby, and the Siege of Bristol. **Cromwell**'s son-in-law from 1646, he was one of the most implacable enemies of the King (**Charles I**), and signed the warrant for his execution. He accompanied Cromwell to Ireland, and in 1650 became Lord Deputy. He died of the plague during the Siege of Limerick.

Irgun (Zvai Leumi) The terrorist organization operating in Palestine during the British Mandate and seeking the establishment of a Jewish state. Formed in 1931 after disagreement with the **Haganah** and reconstituted in 1937, it accepted **Jabotinsky**'s ideology and engaged in armed conflict with Arabs and the British. Led by Menachem **Begin** from 1943, Irgun bombed Jerusalem's **King David Hotel** in 1946, hanged two British sergeants in 1947 in response to the execution of its members, and attacked the Arab village of Deir Yassin in 1948. Condemned for this by the **Jewish Agency**, the Irgun became the nucleus of the right-wing Herut Party in Israel after 1948.

Irish Famine The widespread starvation of Irish peasantry which followed the potato blight in 1845–7, and the consequent destruction of the crop. Because of starvation and emigration (to Britain and the USA), the population of Ireland fell by almost 25 per cent between 1845 and 1851. The British government was widely blamed by the emigrants for the scale of the disaster. ▷ **Peel, Robert**

Irish Free State A form of **Home Rule**, established by the Anglo-Irish Treaty (Dec 1921). Accordingly, 26 counties (excluding the six of Northern Ireland) became a Dominion under the British crown. The treaty was ratified by a small majority in the **Dáil Eireann** and power was transferred from Westminster (Mar 1922). Republicans, led by **De Valera**, refused to accept the authority of the crown and civil war (1922–3) ensued. The name 'Irish Free State' was retained until Dominion status was dismantled with the new constitution of 1937. ▷ **Collins, Michael; Eire; Griffith, Arthur**

Irish National Liberation Army (INLA) The military wing of the **Irish Republican Socialist Party**, a small paramilitary group which commits few terrorist attacks, but is noted for the ruthless nature of those it does carry out. Probably created by former members of the Official **IRA** disenchanted with the 1972 ceasefire, it was responsible for the killing of the Conservative MP Airey Neave (Mar 1979). Its impact lessened with internal feuds in the 1980s.

Irish Republic The name given to the republic declared in Dec 1948 which came into effect in 1949 (Republic of Ireland Act). It changed the relationship between Ireland and Britain. The republic retained special citizenship arrangements and trade preference with Britain, but left the **Commonwealth of Nations**. The Westminster parliament passed the Ireland Act (1949) which confirmed a special relationship of Irish citizens in the UK, but declared that Northern Ireland would remain part of the UK until its citizens declared otherwise. ▷ **Eire; Irish Free State**

Irish Republican Socialist Party A political party formed in 1974 largely as a breakaway group from the official **Sinn Féin**, which disagreed with its political strategy and the ceasefire. Its most prominent member was Bernadette McAliskey. It was involved in a feud with the Official **IRA** in the 1970s, and subsequently moved closer to the Provisional Sinn Féin. ▷ **Irish National Liberation Army**

Iron Curtain A term formerly used to describe the separation of certain East European countries from the rest of Europe by the **Cold War** and in particular the political

and military domination of the USSR. It was first used by Nazi Propaganda Minister **Goebbels** in 1943, and became widely known after Winston **Churchill** used it in a speech in 1946.

Iron Guard The name commonly applied to the Legion of the Archangel Michael, a movement with a fascist ideology which in the 1930s, under the leadership of Corneliu Zelea **Codreanu**, established a mass following in Romania. Founded in 1927, the Legion was at first a quasi-religious organization encouraging moral regeneration. Chauvinist and anti-Semitic, it founded its military section, the Iron Guard, to combat the communists. First dissolved by the Romanian government in 1933, it operated under a front, 'All for the Fatherland'. In 1938 the Guard was again disbanded and Codreanu shot. Ion **Antonescu** established links with the Guard and its new leader, Horia Sima, but in 1941 the movement was crushed with German support. ▷ **Charles II** of Romania

Ironsi ▷ **Aguiyi-Ironsi**

Ironside, William Edmund, 1st Baron (1880–1959) British field marshal. He served as a secret agent disguised as a railwayman in the **Boer Wars**, held several staff appointments in **World War I**, and commanded the Archangel expedition against the **Bolsheviks** (1918). He was Chief of the Imperial General Staff at the outbreak of **World War II**, and placed in command of the Home Defence Forces (1940). The 'Ironsides', fast light-armoured vehicles, were named after him. He was made a peer in 1941.

Iroquois Confederacy A confederation of Iroquois tribes during the 17–18c in northern New York State consisting of the Mohawk, Oneida, Onondaga, Cayuga, and Seneca, later joined by the Tuscarora. Also known as the Iroquois League or the 'Six Nations', they were united largely for control of the **fur trade** and for war. Numbering close to 16000, they defeated most of their Native American rivals and dominated the area. The league broke up during the **American Revolution** when the tribes took sides: the four groups siding with the British were defeated in 1779. Today most of the Iroquois live in upstate New York, although some live on reservations elsewhere in the USA and Canada.

irredentism In the new nations of 19–20c Europe, the acquisition, by negotiation or more usually conquest, of 'unredeemed' territory. The term is most commonly applied to the Italians. The term *Italia irredenta* ('unredeemed Italy'), was used from the late 19c of those lands, such as Trieste, Istria, Gradisca and Trentino, which had Italian populations but remained under Austrian rule. The 'irredentists' were those who sought to regain these regions either by negotiation or war. By extension, the term came to be applied to similar cases of new nations claiming lands inhabited by compatriots but under foreign rule. Greek irredentists, for example, sought to incorporate Greek-speaking, Turkish-controlled areas into the new Greek kingdom. ▷ **enosis; Megale Idea; Risorgimento**

Isaac I, Comnenus (d.1061) Eastern Roman Emperor in Constantinople (1057/9). He established the finances of the empire on a sounder footing, laid the clergy under contribution at the tax collections, and repelled the Hungarians attacking his northern frontier; and then, resigning the crown (1059), retired to a monastery, where he died.

Isaacs, Sir Isaac Alfred (1855–1948) Australian jurist and politician, the son of a Jewish tailor. He became a barrister and, as Attorney-General for Victoria, helped prepare the federal constitution (1897–9). He sat in the federal parliament (1901–6), was a justice of the High Court (1906–30), and Chief Justice (1930–1). From 1931 to 1936 he was Governor-General, the first Australian to hold that office.

Isabella I, 'the Catholic' (1451–1504) Queen of **Castile** (1474/1504). The daughter of John II, King of Castile and Leon, in 1469 she married Ferdinand V of Aragon (**Ferdinand II, 'the Catholic'**), with whom she ruled jointly from 1479. During her reign, the **Inquisition** was introduced (1478), the Conquest of Granada completed (1482–92), and the Jews expelled (1492). She sponsored the voyage of Christopher Columbus to the New World. ▷ **Granada, Conquest of; Jews, Expulsion of the; Reconquest**

Isabella II (1830–1904) Queen of Spain (1833/68). The elder daughter of **Ferdinand VII** and **María Cristina** of Naples, she succeeded to the throne as an infant, with her mother and later (1840–3) General **Espartero**, as Regent. Her succession was disputed by her uncle, Don **Carlos**, and not until the Carlists' defeat in the First Carlist War (1833–40) was she secure. Her reign was characterized by acute political instability and repeated military intervention. Her own meddling in politics, together with her scandalous private life following an unsatisfactory marriage (1846) to Prince Francisco de Asís, weakened the crown, and led to her overthrow in the 1868 Revolution. Although her son, **Alfonso XII**, was restored to the throne in 1874, she spent the rest of her life in exile.

Isabella of France (1292–1358) Queen consort of **Edward II** of England. The daughter of **Philip IV** of France, in 1308 at Boulogne she married Edward. She became the mistress of Roger Mortimer, with whom she overthrew and murdered the King (1327). Her son, **Edward III**, had Mortimer executed in 1330, and Isabella was sent into retirement, eventually to join an order of nuns.

Isa ibn Sulman (1932–) Ruler of Bahrain (1971/). Despite encouragement from Britain to maintain a federal connection with Arab Emirates further down the Persian Gulf, he declared his island's full independence in 1971; in this he adopted much the same attitude as the ruler of Qatar, Khalifa ibn Ahmad al-Thani. He has also made a show of attempting a democratic approach to government, but after little more than a year dissolved the elected assembly and full powers reverted to the Shaykh and his family.

Isandlhwana, Battle of (1879) A notorious reverse for the British in the Zulu War of 1879. Through mismanagement, an entire British regiment, its ammunition in boxes which could not be opened, was virtually destroyed by the Zulu using their traditional tactics. It caused considerable public alarm in Britain, allayed only by the victory at Ulundi later in the same year. ▷ **Zulu Wars**

Ishibashi Tanzan (1884–1973) Japanese politician. In the 1930s he was an economic journalist and vociferous critic of the militarists. He joined the Liberal Party (*Nihon Jiyuto*) after the war and served as Finance Minister in 1946. In 1951 Ishibashi became head of **MITI**, a powerful government ministry created in 1949 to promote economic development. He served briefly as Prime Minister for two months in 1956 before illness forced him to retire. Ishibashi was a keen supporter of the **normalization** of relations between Japan and communist China during the 1950s and 1960s.

Ishiwara Kanji (1889–1949) Japanese army officer. He graduated from the prestigious

Army War College in 1918 and lectured there 1925–8. Influenced by the apocalyptic doctrines of the Japanese medieval Buddhist monk, Nichiren, Ishiwara believed in the inevitability of a final conflict between East and West, as represented by Japan and the USA. To prepare for this conflict, he maintained that Japan needed to harness resources in East Asia (especially Manchuria). After 1929, as an operations officer attached to the Japanese army (**Guandong Army**) that protected Japan's interests in south Manchuria and along the South Manchuria railway, Ishiwara helped plan the campaign in 1931 (without reference to the civilian government in Tokyo) that resulted in the transformation of Manchuria into the Japanese puppet-state of **Manzhuguo**. On his return to Japan (1932), his abrasiveness and independent way of thinking brought him into conflict with his military superiors. In 1937, especially, he criticized Japan's invasion of China, fearing that a long drawn-out war of attrition would sabotage Japan's efforts in building a national defence state. He was forced out of the army in 1941.

Ismail (1645–1727) Sultan of Maghrib (Morocco) (1672/1727). He consolidated the authority of the state and took firm control of piracy which he turned into a state enterprise. He also established an elite corps of black slaves (*abid al-Bukhari*), who owed personal devotion to the sultan.

Ismail I (1487–1524) Safavid Shah of Iran (1501/24). He was the founder of the Safavid Dynasty in Persia. Despite not having been accorded the renown of his illustrious successor, Shah **'Abbas I, 'the Great'**, his achievement was nonetheless considerable. Ismail, a Turkish-speaker from Tabriz, was astute enough to realize that the original quietist, Sunni Sufi Safavid order would not impart sufficient ideological impact to motivate Iranians against the Ottoman Turks. He therefore made a point of establishing Twelver Shiism as his state religion, thus converting his lands from the Sunni to the Shiite sect of Islam, to lend credibility to his confrontation with the Ottoman Turks, who were Sunnis. Furthermore, despite Ismail's Turkic origins and the fact that he chose Tabriz for his capital, the language of his administration was Persian.

Ismailis Adherents of a secret Islamic sect, one of the main branches of the Shiites; also known as the 'Seveners'. It developed from an underground movement (c.9c), reaching

political power in Egypt and North Africa in the 10–12c. It distinguished between inner and outer aspects of religion, was critical of Islamic law, and believed that in the eventual new age of the seventh imam, a kind of universal religion would emerge that was independent of the laws of all organized religions. Thus it welcomed followers of other religions, but retained its own secret traditions and rites.

Ismail Pasha (1830–95) Khedive of Egypt. The second son of Ibrahim Pasha, he was educated at St Cyr, France. In 1863 he became deputy of the Ottoman Sultan, and was granted the title of Khedive in 1866. His massive development programme included the building of the Suez Canal, which was opened in splendour in 1869. The accumulation of a large foreign debt led to European intervention; he was deposed by the Ottoman Sultan, and replaced by his eldest son, **Tewfik Pasha**. He died in exile in Istanbul.

isolationism A foreign policy strategy of withdrawing from international affairs as long as the country's interests are not affected. It is a means of avoiding involvement in international conflicts, and implies neutrality in most cases. It was practised most notably by the USA, which kept out of the League of Nations and **World War II** until attacked by the Japanese.

Israel, State of Democratic republic in the Middle East, with Jerusalem as its capital, bordered by Lebanon, Syria, Jordan, Egypt and the Mediterranean Sea. Since the 1967 **Six-Day War**, Israel has controlled the so-called 'occupied territories': the Golan Heights, West Bank, East Jerusalem and **Gaza Strip**. Excluding these, the population, mostly Jewish but with a sizable Arab minority, exceeds 4 500 000. Ultimate authority lay with the Knesset (parliament), consisting of 120 members elected for a four-year term. Zionists settled in Palestine in the 1880s under Ottoman rule, while the British declared support for a Jewish state there in 1917. However, this never materialized under the British Mandate (1918–47), although Jewish immigration in the 1930s and 1940s increased greatly due to Nazi persecution. Resultant tension between Arabs and Jews led the **UN** in 1947 to support the formation of two states in Palestine, one Jewish and the other Arab. When the Arab side rejected this, David **Ben-Gurion** announced the creation of the state of Israel on 14 May 1948. Military conflict with

Creation of the State of Israel

surrounding countries ensued in which Israeli forces were victorious. Further wars took place in 1958, 1967, 1973 and 1982. In contrast, a peace agreement between Israel and Egypt's President, Anwar **Sadat**, was reached in 1979. ▷ **Balfour Declaration; Irgun; Mapai Party**

Istria The peninsula at the north end of the Adriatic, divided between the republics of **Slovenia** and **Croatia**. Under Byzantine rule (538–787) and with Venice part of the Ravenna exarchate, it was settled by Slavs in the 7c. By the 15c, Istria was divided between the Austrian Habsburgs and the Republic of Venice, with the latter holding about three-quarters of the area. After **Napoleon I** took Venice in 1797, the French included the whole peninsula in the **Illyrian Provinces** (1809–13). Austrian forces took Istria in 1813 and Habsburg possession was confirmed at the Congress of **Vienna** (1814–15). In 1921 it was annexed by **Mussolini**'s Italy and the fascist government tried to suppress all expression of Slovene and Croatian national identity. After **World War II**, in 1947, it was formally ceded to the Socialist Federal Republic of Yugoslavia and was divided between the Republics of Croatia and Slovenia. ▷ **Habsburg Dynasty**

Itagaki Seishiro (1885–1948) Japanese army officer. Along with **Ishiwara Kanji**, he was a key player in the Japanese military conquest of Manchuria. He became Army Minister in 1937 and then Chief of General Staff of the China Expeditionary Army in 1939. After **World War II** he was tried as a war criminal and executed.

Itagaki Taisuke (1837–1919) Japanese politician. The leader of the **Freedom and People's Rights Movement** in the 1870s, he came from an upper **samurai** family in Tosa domain and was a participant in the **Meiji Restoration**. Although he entered the government in 1869, he resigned in 1873 when proposals for a military expedition to Korea were rejected. Condemning the monopoly of power held by those from the former domains of **Choshu** and **Satsuma**, from 1874 he began calling for a national representative assembly, drawing on ideas from Western liberalism. In 1881 he formed Japan's first political party, the *Jiyuto* (Liberals), which attracted the support of former samurai and wealthy landowners. Owing to government harrassment and internal rivalries, the party was disbanded in 1884, but was revived in time to contest the country's first elections for a national diet in 1890. In

463

The beginnings of Italian unity

1898 Itagaki, in alliance with the *Shimpoto* (Progressives) of **Okuma** Shigenobu, formed Japan's first party cabinet but it only lasted four months before internal bickering brought an end to the experiment. Thereafter Itagaki retired from active politics.

Italian National Society (*Società Nazionale Italiana*) Nationalist organization established by Giorgio Pallavicino

(1796–1878), Daniele **Manin** and Giuseppe **La Farina** in July 1857. It channelled the backing of many former republicans and Mazzinians, including **Garibaldi**, into the moderate, monarchist camp that sought unification through Piedmontese expansion. It also played an important role in preparing the ground in northern and central Italy for annexation by **Victor Emmanuel II**. ▷ **Risorgimento**

Legend:

- Kingdom of Italy in 1861
- Territory ceded to France in 1860
- ⊚ Capitulation of Francis II of the Two Sicilies (13 Feb 1861)

Acquisitions:
- in 1866
- in 1870
- ➡ Garibaldi's 1867 expedition

Italy, 1860–70

Italian Social Movement (*Movimento Sociale Italiano*) The post-war Italian neo-fascist movement that stands on the extreme right of Italian parliamentary politics. It is a fringe party which has never received more than 10 per cent of the national vote. However, it remains strong in some regions such as the Alto-Adige, where it is seen as defending the interests of the Italian-speaking population against the privileged German population and their *Südtiroler Volkspartei*. Its most able leader was Giorgio Almirante (1915–88).

Italian Wars (1494–1559) A long series of conflicts often described in terms of the rivalry between the French **Valois Dynasty** and the **Habsburg Dynasty**, but which in many ways form a continuity between the struggles of popes and emperors in the

Middle Ages and the religious wars of the **Reformation** era. The first war was prompted by **Charles VIII**'s decision in 1494 to activate the Angevin claim to Naples, dormant since the **Sicilian Vespers** of 1282. His invasion was triumphant, but on their return northward the French had to face a powerful Italian alliance at Fornovo on the Taro and performed wonders to cut their way through it. In 1499 **Louis XII** pressed the claims of his house (Orléans) to Milan, but was drawn south by the apparent disregard of **Ferdinand II, 'the Catholic'** of partition arrangements made at the Treaty of Granada (1500). In 1503 the great captain, Gonzalo **Fernández de Córdoba**, won decisive victories over the French at Cerignola and on the Garigliano. Franco-Spanish rivalry in Italy was effectively institutionalized and reached new heights during the long conflict between **Francis I** of France and Emperor **Charles V**. ▷ **Cambrai, League of; Cambrai, Treaty of; Cateau-Cambrésis, Treaty of; Créspy, Peace of; Madrid, Treaty of; Orléans, House of**

Italy A republic in southern Europe, comprising the boot-shaped peninsula extending south into the Mediterranean Sea, as well as Sicily, Sardinia, and some smaller islands. In pre-Roman times, Italy was inhabited by Etruscans in the north, Latins in the centre of the country, and Greeks in the south. Most regions were part of the Roman Empire by the 3c BC; barbarian tribes invaded in the 4c, and the last Roman emperor was deposed in AD476. Italy was later ruled by the **Lombards** and by the **Franks** under **Charlemagne**, who was crowned Emperor of the Romans in 800. It became part of the **Holy Roman Empire** under **Otto I, 'the Great'** in 962, and conflict between popes and emperors continued throughout the **Middle Ages**. There were disputes between **Guelfs** and **Ghibellines** in the 12c. Italy was divided amongst five powers during the 14c–15c (Kingdom of Naples, Duchy of Milan, republics of Florence and Venice, and the papacy). The country made a major contribution to European culture through the **Renaissance**. Numerous republics were set up after the **French Revolution**, and **Napoleon I** was crowned King of Italy in 1805. The 19c saw the upsurge of liberalism and nationalism (the **Risorgimento**); unification was achieved by 1870 under **Victor Emmanuel II** of Sardinia, aided by **Cavour** and **Garibaldi**; colonies were established in Eritrea (1870–89) and Somaliland (1889), but the attempt to secure a protectorate over Abyssinia was defeated at the Battle of **Adowa**

(1896). During **World War I**, Italy fought alongside the Allies. The Fascist movement brought **Mussolini** to power in 1922, and he led the Conquest of **Abyssinia** (1935–6) and Albania (1939). The alliance with **Hitler** in **World War II** led to the end of the Italian Empire. Political instability has resulted in over 45 governments in power since the formation of the democratic republic in 1946. Following corruption scandals in the early 1990s, a right-wing government was elected in 1994. See maps p464 and p465. ▷ **fascism**

Ito Hirobumi (1838–1909) Japanese politician. He was Premier (1885–8, 1892–6, 1898 and 1900–1). Ito visited Europe and the USA on several occasions, drafted the **Meiji Constitution** (1889), and played a major role in abolishing Japanese feudalism and building up the modern state. He was assassinated at Harbin by a supporter of Korean independence.

Iturbide, Agustín de (1783–1824) Mexican general and politician. Born in Valladolid of a Spanish father and Creole mother, he fought as part of Calleja's forces against **Hidalgo (y Costilla)** and **Morelos (y Pavón)**, defeating the latter. He seized the moment in 1821, when Mexican conservatives were caught off balance by the radical liberal regime in Spain, to group together the military, aristocracy and clergy in support of Mexican independence. His manifesto, the *Plan de Iguala*, attracted support from conservatives and rebels alike: it guaranteed the status of Catholicism, independence under a Bourbon monarch, and equality between Creoles and Spanish-born. He proclaimed himself Emperor as Agustín I (1822/3), after the Bourbons failed to provide the prince required by *Iguala*. However, beset with political and financial problems, he was forced to abdicate by a revolt of which one of the leaders was **Santa Anna**. He then travelled in Europe and, on his return to Mexico, was executed, having been sentenced in absentia.

Ituzaingó, Battle of (1827) The only significant land battle of the Argentine–Brazilian War of 1825–8. The battle, in the Argentine province of Corrientes, was a tactical stalemate, the organization of the Argentine forces being offset by the skill of the Brazilians.

Ivan I, 'Moneybag' (d.1341) Grand Prince of Moscow (1328 or 1332/41). A skilful diplomat and careful administrator, he expanded Moscow's territory and developed its economy. He also made Moscow the capital of Russia by transferring the metropolitan cathedral from Kiev in 1326. His two sons, Simeon the Proud (1341/53) and Ivan II, 'the Meek' (1353/9), reigned after him, continuing the tradition he had started.

Ivan III, 'the Great' (1440–1505) Grand Prince of Moscow (1462/1505). Building on his predecessors' work, he succeeded in ending his principality's subjection to the Mongols, and gained control over several important Russian principalities, notably Novgorod and Tver. In 1493 he assumed the title of 'Sovereign of all Russia' (including Kiev) and, upon marrying the Byzantine Princess Sofia, he acquired the emblem of the two-headed eagle of the Byzantine Empire. In many respects he was the real founder of Russia and won it international acceptance.
▷ **Golden Horde**

Ivan IV, 'the Terrible' (1530–84) Grand Prince of Moscow (1533/84). He was the first prince to assume the title of 'tsar' (from Latin, *Caesar*), indicating the power of Russia and asserting his own authority. He subdued Kazan and Astrakhan, made the first inroads into Siberia, and established commercial links with England. The first half of his reign was one of autocratic benevolence as he took account of the needs of his people. However, after the death, in 1560 of his first wife, Anastasia, he lost his sense of balance and saw treachery everywhere. He embarked on a ghastly reign of terror, directed principally at the feudal aristocracy (**boyars**), and killed his eldest son and heir, Ivan, in 1581. He nonetheless did much for Russian culture and commerce, not least in his moments of guilt and remorse.

Ivanov, Nikolai Veniaminovich (1952–) Russian lawyer. He was the junior partner of **Gdlyan** in proving corruption in high places during the last years of Leonid **Brezhnev**'s dictatorial rule. He helped Gdlyan in the 'Uzbek affair' and then in attacking senior Muscovite communists. With Gdlyan, he attracted both official disapproval and popular encouragement.

Ivashko, Vladimir Antonovich (1932–) Ukrainian politician. He became First Secretary of the Ukrainian Communist Party in 1989 and Deputy General-Secretary of the Soviet Communist Party in 1990, only to see the party as a whole dissolved a year later. He was engineer, lecturer and, more particu-

larly, party official who rose to the top quickly when the hardline and aging **Shcherbitsky** died and Mikhail **Gorbachev** seized the reform opportunity. He certainly outpointed Yegor **Ligachev**, but he was not particularly liberal and in any case did not have long to make an impact on a conservative USSR.

Iwakura Tomomi (1825–83) Japanese court noble. He supported the anti-Tokugawa movement and helped restore direct imperial rule in 1868. He helped formulate the **Charter Oath**, the manifesto of the new government's modernization drive. Between 1871 and 1873 he led a mission to the USA and Europe with the original aim of negotiating a revision of the treaties signed in the 1850s and 1860s, in particular the abolition of the foreign privilege of extraterritoriality in Japan. The Western powers were reluctant to countenance any change and Iwakura returned to Japan convinced more than ever of the need for internal modernization. Tokugawa Shogunate

Iwasaki Yataro (1835–85) Japanese entrepreneur. The son of a farmer who claimed **samurai** descent, Iwasaki became the financial agent for his domain (Tosa), taking over its interests in shipping and coal-mining. In 1873 he founded the Mitsubishi Trading Company and developed close personal links with the new Meiji government, receiving government subsidies and contracts. By 1877 Iwasaki owned over 80 per cent of all ships in Japan and monopolized the coastal trade, having successfully defeated his US and UK rivals. Mitsubishi became one of the largest *zaibatsu* (financial combines), with interests in banking, insurance and mining.

IWW ▷ **Industrial Workers of the World**

Iyasu I, 'the Great' (d.1706) Emperor of Ethiopia (1682/1706). He succeeded to the throne in 1682 and proved to be a brave and far-sighted ruler. A modernizer and patron of the arts, he made a determined effort to reunify the kingdom following the wholesale migration of Galla tribesmen into the empire, and to reform its institutions after a period of decline during the 17c. He was assassinated by a kinsman of his wife.

Izvolski, Alexander Petrovich (1856–1919) Russian diplomat and politician. He served as an envoy in Europe and Japan before becoming Foreign Minister in 1906. He negotiated the **Anglo-Russian Entente** in 1907 and also tried to improve relations with

Austria and simultaneously strengthen the Russian hold on Turkey. However, in 1908 Austria did not honour the understanding that he believed he had with it, unilaterally annexed Bosnia-Hercegovina and left him inadequately prepared diplomatically to get the Straits opened for Russian warships. From 1910 to 1917 he acted as ambassador in Paris, where he helped to strengthen the **Franco-Russian Alliance** of 1894.

J

Jabotinsky, Vladimir (1880–1940) Jewish writer and Zionist, born in Odessa. Realizing that **World War I** would spell the end of the **Ottoman Empire**, Jabotinsky and others persuaded the British government to allow Jewish involvement in the fight for Palestine. The result was a Jewish transport unit which fought in the **Gallipoli Campaign** but was disbanded in 1916. However, Jabotinsky was instrumental in convincing the British to sanction the more substantial Jewish Legion which took recruits from Britain, North America and, towards the end of the war, Jews from Palestine. Thereafter, the Legion became the basis for the **Haganah**. Unlike that of others, Jabotinsky's **Zionism** was right-wing and hostile to socialism. This led him to found in 1925 the Zionist Revisionist Movement, later renamed the New Zionist Organization. With growing resistance to Jewish immigration to Palestine under the British Mandate, Jabotinsky supported terrorist activities by the **Irgun**.

Jackson, Andrew ('Old Hickory') (1767–1845) US politician and 7th President. He trained as a lawyer, and became a member of the US House of Representatives for Tennessee (1796), its Senator (1797), and a judge of its Superior Court (1798–1804). In the **War of 1812**, he was given command of the South, and became famous for his defence of New Orleans (1814–15). Regarded as a folk hero, he won the presidency in 1828 in a campaign that gave him a large majority in the popular vote. His emphasis on the importance of the popular vote came to be known as 'Jacksonian democracy'. His presidency (1829–1837) was significant for its use of executive power, most notable in the **nullification** issue and in the **Bank War**.

Jackson, Jesse (1941–) US **civil rights** leader and minister. As Martin Luther **King**'s lieutenant, he established a strong branch of the **SCLC** in Chicago. In 1967 he initiated Operation Breadbasket, which aimed to create jobs by attracting business investment in black enterprises in the cities. In 1971 he became the executive director of Operation PUSH (People United To Serve Humanity), these two projects helped get him national attention, and in 1983 he became a candidate for the Democratic presidential nomination. His 'Rainbow Coalition' attracted a good deal of media attention, but without an organized political base, he had little chance of success. He was the first black American to mount a serious campaign for the office. He was a candidate again in 1987, but was again unsuccessful in gaining the nomination.

Jackson, Thomas Jonathan, 'Stonewall' (1824–63) US Confederate general. In 1851 he became a professor at the Virginia Military Institute. During the **American Civil War**, he became a Confederate general. He commanded a brigade at **Bull Run**, where his firm stand gained him his nickname. He showed tactical superiority in the campaign of the Shenandoah valley (1862), and won several victories, notably at Cedar Run, Manassas, and Harpers Ferry. He was accidentally killed by his own troops at Chancellorsville.

Jacoba of Bavaria ▷ **Jacqueline of Holland**

Jacobins A radical political group in the **French Revolution**, originally the Club Breton in Versailles, but renamed after transferring to the premises of the Dominican or 'Jacobin' fathers in Paris (1789). After successive purges, the club became the instrument of the Terror under **Robespierre**'s dictatorship (1793–4), the name being associated thereafter with left-wing extremism. ▷ **Terror, Reign of**

Jacobites Those who supported the claim of the Catholic **James VII and II** of England, and his successors, to the British throne. The Jacobites launched two major rebellions, in 1715 (the **Fifteen Rebellion**) and 1745 (the **Forty-Five Rebellion**), against the Protestant Hanoverian succession, and in the period 1714–60 some British Tory politicians had Jacobite sympathies. ▷ **Tories**

Jacqueline of Holland (1401–36) Dutch noblewoman. The only child of Count William VI of Holland and Zeeland and Duke of Bavaria and of Margaret of Burgundy, she made a series of marriages which caused her much trouble. She married, first (1415), Prince John of Touraine, Dauphin of France, who died in 1417, the year in which Jacqueline succeeded her father. She waged war against John of Bavaria for the right to succeed to her father's title there, then in 1418 married her cousin, Duke John IV of **Brabant**, who mortgaged Holland and Zeeland to John of Bavaria. Repudiating the marriage, she went to England, where she married (with debatable legality) Humphrey, Duke of Gloucester, in 1422. Deserted by him during an invasion to regain her lands in Hainaut, she surrendered to **Philip the Good** of Burgundy in 1428, and in 1433 relinquished to him her claims to sovereignty. In 1432 she married once more, this time to Frans van Borsele, a Zeeland nobleman.

Jacquerie (1358) Originally, a serious peasant rebellion in north-eastern France, noted for its savagery. Started by mercenaries following the English victory at Poitiers (1356), it degenerated (May 1358) into bitter violence between the oppressed peasantry, aggrieved Parisians, and their noble overlords; the latter massacred the insurgents indiscriminately at Meaux and Clermont-en-Beauvaisis (June 1358). The term then came to be used for any peasant rising.

Jagan, Cheddi (1918–) Guyanese socialist politician and writer. With **Burnham**, he led the nationalist People's Progressive Party (PPP) in demanding self-government in the early 1950s. The Jagan–Burnham alliance won the 1953 election but the Governor, accusing Jagan of 'communist' policies, suspended the constitution, dismissed Jagan and his cabinet and called in British troops. He came to power with the PPP again in 1957, but an austerity budget and Jagan's desire to hasten the end of imperial rule led to racial rioting and a long general strike in Georgetown only ended by further British military intervention (1961–4). In the 1964 election, based on a British-devised proportional representation constitution, when Burnham's **People's National Congress** was victorious, and Jagan became the leader of the official opposition.

Jagat Seths The title of the heads of the Hindu banking house of the Seths, awarded to them by Nawab Alivardi Khan of Bengal in the mid-18c. The Seths financed the large transit and foreign trade of Bengal in the early 18c. As lenders, they became politically influential and conspired with the British to remove the Nawab, **Siraj ud-Daula**, who had insulted them. In the 1760s, the Seths were removed by Mir Kasim from Murshidabad to

the new capital, Monghyr. In 1763, Mir Kasim put to death the two leading members of the house, suspecting them of complicity with the British **East India Company**.

Jagiełłon Dynasty The ruling dynasty of Poland-Lithuania, Bohemia, and Hungary, which dominated east central Europe from the Baltic to the Danube in the 15–16c. It was founded when Jagiełło, Grand-Duke of Lithuania, married Queen Jadwiga of Poland and so became King of Poland from 1386 to 1434, as Władysław II. The dynasty flourished under his acquisitive successors until Sigismund II Augustus (1548/72) died without heirs. In between times, Władysław III was also King of Hungary (1440/4), and a later Władysław ruled both Bohemia (1471/1516) and Hungary (1490/1516).

Jahangir (1569–1627) Mughal Emperor (1605/27). The son of **Akbar the Great**, he was named Salim and took the title of Jahangir on his accession. The earlier part of his reign was a period of peace and great prosperity for the empire, with a steady growth of trade and commerce and a great flowering of the arts. The latter part of the reign was characterized by continual rebellions against his rule, principally on behalf of his various sons, and he was only able to survive as ruler by dint of the courage and vigour of the empress, **Nur Jahan**. He was, however, a just and tolerant man and a consistent patron of the arts.

Jahn, Frederick Ludwig (1778–1852) Prussian physical educationist, known as the 'Father of gymnastics' (*Turnvater*). In 1811 he started the first gymnasium (*Turnplatz*) in **Berlin** and his methods soon became very popular. An ardent nationalist, he commanded a volunteer corps in the **Napoleonic Wars** (1813–15); after the peace of 1815, he resumed his teaching and published *Die deutsche Turnkunst* (1816). The gymnasia began to witness political gatherings which attracted students and intellectuals; these meetings were too liberal to please the Prussian government, and they were closed in 1818. Jahn, who had taken a prominent part in the movement, was arrested in 1819, and suffered five years' imprisonment. He was elected to the Frankfurt National Assembly in 1848.

Jaime I, 'the Conqueror' (1208–76) Count of Barcelona and King of Aragon, Valencia and Mallorca (1213/76). Possibly the greatest of the rulers of the Catalan lands, he spent his infancy in France with Simon de **Montfort**. Soon after, he succeeded to the throne of Aragon and committed himself to a campaign of military expansion against the Muslim powers in the Iberian Peninsula. His capture of Mallorca in 1229 was followed by the subjugation of the remaining Balearic Islands. From 1232 he commenced the campaigns that culminated in 1238 with the capture of Valencia. Catalan expansion threatened the already expanding Kingdom of **Castile**, and a treaty to define their respective limits was signed in 1244. In 1266 he conquered Murcia but handed it over to Castile. The marriage of his son, Peter, to the Princess of Sicily began Catalan expansion further into the Mediterranean. Under him, the first Catalan code of maritime law, the *Llibre del consolat de Mar*, was drawn up, and the key figures of early Catalan culture, Ramon Penyafort and Ramon Llull, were active.

Jainism An indigenous religion of India which regards Vardhamana Mahavira (599–527BC), said to be the last Tirthankara, as its founder. Jains believe that salvation consists in conquering material existence through adherence to a strict ascetic discipline, thus freeing the soul from the working of karma for eternal all-knowing bliss. Liberation requires detachment from worldly existence, an essential part of which is the practice of Ahimsa, non-injury to living beings, an ideal also used by M K **Gandhi** in his campaigns against British rule in India.

Jai Singh, Mirza Raja (d.1743) King of Amber, in present-day Rajasthan (1699/1743). He was a vassal and prominent general of the Mughal Emperor, **Aurangzeb**, on whose behalf he brought the troublesome Shivaji to heel after the latter's raid on the town of Surat. In 1708 Jai Singh rebelled against Bahadur Shah, Aurangzeb's son and successor. He was subsequently pardoned by him and, in 1722, was made Viceroy of Agra, where he succeeded in subduing the Jats. He was later made Viceroy of Malwa by the Mughal Emperor, Farrukh-siyar. However, in later years, he could not restrain the Marathas. It was Jai Singh who founded Jaipur, and built still extant astronomical observatories at Delhi and Jaipur.

Ja Ja of Opobo (1821–91) West African merchant prince. An ex-slave, he established a highly successful trading operation in the Niger Delta before the partition of Africa. He founded his kingdom in 1869, when he led many of the constituent houses of the Kingdom of Bonny to his new capital to command the palm oil trade. He shipped oil directly to Britain and resisted European encroachments upon his trade. However, he aroused the enmity of other traders, of missionaries and of British consuls. In 1885, without any authorization from London, Consul Sir Harry Johnston deposed him, a significant move in the development of total British command of the Niger Delta. ▷ **Africa, Partition of**

Jakeš, Miloš (1922–) Czechoslovak politician. Originally an electrical engineer, he joined the Communist Party of Czechoslovakia in 1945 and studied at the Higher Party School in Moscow (1955–8). He supported the Soviet invasion of Czechoslovakia in 1968 and later, as head of the Party's Central Control Commission, oversaw the purge of reformist personnel. He became a member of the Central Committee in 1977 and of the Politburo in 1981, and in Dec 1987 replaced Gustav **Husak** as Party leader. Although enjoying close personal relations with the Soviet leader, Mikhail **Gorbachev**, he emerged as a cautious reformer who made it clear that restructuring (*prestavba*) in Czechoslovakia would be a slow and limited process. He was forced to step down as CCP leader in Nov 1989, following a series of pro-democracy rallies.

Jallianwalla Bagh Massacre ▷ **Amritsar Massacre**

Jamaat-i Islami The party founded in 1941 by Maulana Abu'l Ala Maududi, to voice his opposition to the **Muslim League's demands** for Pakistan, which he regarded as not properly Islamic and liable to encourage Hindu nationalism. Following the Partition of India in 1947, Maududi moved to Pakistan and the party became a persistent critic of the government. Banned in 1953 for fomenting trouble over the Ahmadiyyas, it later staged a comeback. An Indian successor party, established in 1948, was banned by the Indian government in 1992 following the Ayodhya disturbances. ▷ **India, Partition of**

Jamaica Labour Party (JLP) One of the two major political parties which have shared power in Jamaica since independence in 1962. **Bustamante**'s JLP, founded in 1943, grew out of his Industrial Trade Union while its rival, the People's National Party (PNP), was the creation of Norman **Manley** in 1938. The PNP dominated politics from 1957 to

1962, but Bustamante won the election of that year and the JLP retained power until 1972 under Bustamante, Sangster and Shearer. The PNP returned to power in 1972 under Michael **Manley** but Manley's socialist policies, his troubles with the IMF and his inability to stimulate the economy saw the return of the JLP under Edward Seaga in 1980. However, the JLP's reliance on capitalism fared no better in creating economic stability and Manley and the PNP were returned in the 1989 election.

James I (1394–1437) King of Scots (1406/37). His father, Robert III, sent him for safety to France, but he was captured at sea (1406), held prisoner in England for 18 years, and did not begin to rule until his release in 1424. An accomplished poet, he wrote *The Kingis Quair* to celebrate his romance with Joan Beaufort, a cousin of **Henry V** of England, whom he married in 1424. He was acquisitive and vindictive, and his ruthlessness towards the House of **Stuart** led to his murder at Perth.

James I of England ▷ **James VI and I**

James II (1430–60) King of Scots (1437/60). The son of **James I** of Scotland, he came to the throne at the age of six, and took control of the government in 1449. The early years of his personal rule were dominated by his efforts to curb the power of the mighty Black Douglases, whom he eventually defeated in 1455. He later attempted to recover Roxburgh Castle from the English, and was killed during the siege. ▷ **Douglas**

James II of England ▷ **James VII and II**

James III (1452–88) King of Scots (1460/88). The eldest son of **James II** of Scotland, he came to the throne at the age of eight, and took control of the government in 1469. His marriage in that year to Margaret of Denmark led to the incorporation of Orkney and Shetland within the Scottish realm (1472). He was defeated and killed by rebel nobles at the Battle of Sauchieburn, near Stirling.

James IV (1473–1513) King of Scots (1488/ 1513). The eldest son of **James III** of Scotland, he became active in government at his accession, at the age of 15, and gradually exerted his authority over the nobility. In 1503 he married **Margaret Tudor**, the eldest daughter of **Henry VII**: an alliance which led ultimately to the union of the crowns. However, he adhered to the French alliance

when **Henry VIII** joined the **Holy League** against France, and was induced to invade England by the French. He was defeated and killed, along with the flower of his nobility, at the Battle of **Flodden**.

James V (1512–42) King of Scots (1513/42). The son of **James IV** of Scotland, and an infant at his father's death, he grew up amid the struggle between the pro-French and pro-English factions in his country. In 1536 he visited France, marrying Magdeleine, the daughter of **Francis I** (1537), and after her death, Mary of Guise (1538). War with England followed from the French alliance (1542), and after an attempt to invade England, he was routed at Solway Moss. He retired to Falkland Palace, Fife, where he died soon after the birth of his daughter, Mary (later, **Mary, Queen of Scots**).

James VI and I (1566–1625) King of Scotland (1567/1625) as James VI and, as James I, the first Stuart King of England and Ireland (1603/25). He was the son of **Mary, Queen of Scots**, and Henry, Lord **Darnley**. On his mother's forced abdication, he was proclaimed King, and brought up by several regents. When he began to govern for himself, he ruled through his favourites, which caused a rebellion, and a period of imprisonment. In 1589 he married Princess Anne from Kristiania. Hating Puritanism, he managed in 1600 to establish bishops in Scotland. On **Elizabeth I**'s death, he ascended the English throne as great-grandson of **James IV** of Scotland's English wife, **Margaret Tudor**. At first well received, his favouritism again brought him unpopularity. ▷ **Addled Parliament**

James VII and II (1633–1701) King of Scotland, as James VII, and of England and Ireland, as James II (1685/8). The second son of **Charles I** of England, he escaped to Holland nine months before his father's execution. At the Restoration (1660) he was made Lord High Admiral of England, and commanded the fleet in the Dutch Wars; but after converting to Catholicism he was forced to resign his post. The national ferment caused by the **Popish Plot** (1678) became so formidable that he had to retire to the Continent, and several unsuccessful attempts were made to exclude him from the succession. During his reign his actions in favour of Catholicism raised general indignation, and William, Prince of Orange, his son-in-law and nephew, was finally asked by leading clerics and landowners to invade. Deserted by ministers and troops, James escaped to France, where he was warmly received by **Louis XIV**. He made an ineffectual attempt to regain his throne in Ireland, which ended in the Battle of the **Boyne** (1690), and remained at St Germain until his death. ▷ **Anglo-Dutch Wars**

James, C(yril) L(ionel) R(obert) (1901–89) Trinidadian writer, lecturer, political activist and cricket enthusiast. James's aim was the freedom of the black race through **Marxism** and revolution. For his Trotskyite writings he was deported from the USA, while in Trinidad his former pupil, Eric **Williams**, the Prime Minister, put him under house arrest. His most influential book was *The Black Jacobins: Toussaint L'Ouverture and the San Domingo Revolution* (1938). ▷ **Toussaint L'Ouverture**

Jameson, Sir Leander Starr, 1st Baronet (1853–1917) South African politician. After studying medicine, he set up in practice in Kimberley (1878). Through Cecil **Rhodes**, 'Dr Jim' engaged in pioneer work, was in 1891 made administrator for the South Africa Company at Fort Salisbury, and won popularity among the whites for his lack of administrative scruple. In 1895 he withdrew the British South African Police from Mashonaland to Bechuanaland (Botswana) to support a supposed uprising of Uitlanders in Johannesburg. He invaded the Transvaal (the **Jameson Raid**) on 29 Dec 1895, but the expected rising failed to materialize. At Krugersdorp Jameson and his men were overpowered by a force of Boers, and after a sharp fight were compelled to surrender (2 Jan 1896). Handed over to the British authorities (July), Jameson was condemned in London to 15 months' imprisonment, but was released in Dec. In 1900 he was elected to the Cape Legislative Assembly, and in 1904–8 was (Progressive) Premier of Cape Colony. Made a baronet in 1911, he retired from politics the following year.

Jameson Raid (Dec 1895–Jan 1896) An expedition against the South African Republic, which was supposed to link up with a revolt by White workers on the Rand and topple the government of President **Kruger**. Leander Starr **Jameson**, administrator for the South Africa Company at Fort Salisbury, led a detachment of British South Africa Police into the Transvaal, but they were easily defeated and arrested. The German Emperor, **William II**, sent a telegram of congratulation to Kruger, and the incident caused a major government crisis in Britain as well as contributing to the tensions that led to the Boer War. ▷ **Boer Wars**

Jamestown (USA) A deserted town, 15 miles (24 km) inland from Chesapeke Bay, Virginia, USA, the site of the first successful British settlement in America. Excavated archaeologically (1934–56), it was founded in 1607 by 105 settlers as James Fort, but after 1699 was superseded as the capital of Virginia by Williamsburg, and abandoned.

Janata Dal A minority Indian political party, led by Prime Minister V P Singh, which governed India with the support of the BJP and CPIM during the period Dec 1989–Oct 1990. A faction of the Janata Dal, the Janata Dal (S), then held power, with Chandra Shekhar as Prime Minister, with the support of the much larger Congress (I) Party.

Janata Vimukti Peramuna (People's Liberation Front) ▷ **JVP**

Janissaries An elite force of soldiers in the Turkish Army established by **Murad I** during the 14c. Originally recruited from among prisoners of war, they were later raised by **devşirme** (levy) from among the Christian subjects of the **Ottoman Empire**. The recruits, who constituted a 'New Force' (*Yeni Ceri*, whence Janissary) of infantry, were converted to Islam, educated and given a military training. Always potentially mutinous and involved in power struggles at the Porte, they were finally disbanded after a revolt in Constantinople in 1826. ▷ **Janissaries, Massacre of the**

Janissaries, Massacre of the (June 1826) Also known as the 'Auspicious Incident', the massacre was the result of a revolt of the Janissaries against the formation of the elite Eskinciyan corps, which they perceived as the usurper of their own privileged position. The Ottoman Sultan, **Mahmud II**, had been paving the way for the dissolution of the Janissaries: over time, the corps had acquired a power out of all proportion to its original status and was riddled with corruption. By appointing personnel loyal to himself within the Janissary corps, winning over the religious hierarchy and establishing a popular perception of himself as a moderate reformer, Mahmud was able to muster sufficient force against the Janissaries to force them to retreat to their barracks. In the ensuing siege, the gates of the barracks were destroyed and troops moved in; those Janissaries in the open were slaughtered and the buildings of the depot were set ablaze, the Janissaries within perishing. Janissaries elsewhere in the empire were hunted down and the corps was abolished. ▷ **Ottoman Empire**

Jan Sangh 'The Hindu People's Party' was the Major Hindu Nationalist political party until the rise of the BJP (Bharatiya Janata Party). It was formed in 1951 by Syama Prassad Mookerjee and leaders of the **RSS** (*Rashtriya Swayamsevak Sangh*), a militant Hindu cultural organization, in order to promote and represent Hindu political interests more effectively in government. It was most specifically designed to offer a national alternative to the secularist Congress Party of Jawaharlal **Nehru**, from which Mookerjee himself had resigned in 1947. The Jan Sangh's support came primarily from the merchant and middle classes of the north Indian states. It is considered by its detractors to be a communal anti-Muslim political party with fascistic inclinations. This charge its members have always denied, although it has consistently demanded the maintenance of traditional Hindu institutions, replacement of English by Hindi as the sole official language of India, and. has opposed concessions to Muslims. These, it has argued, are legitimate and appropriate policies in a predominantly Hindu society. On economic issues, it supported liberalization. The Jan Sangh merged into the Janata Party which ruled India under the leadership of Morarji **Desai** in 1977–9, but broke away in the early 1980s to emerge as the BJP, the main opposition party since 1991. ▷ **Hindu Mahasabha**

Jansenism A heretical movement in the Roman Catholic Church in France and Holland in the 17c and 18c. It followed the teaching of Cornelius Jansen, who adopted the theology of St **Augustine**, particularly on predestination, and promulgated a rigorous and ascetic way of life. Condemned by the Papal Bull *Unigenitus* (1713), which was accepted in France in 1720, Jansenism was nevertheless defended by a party in the French Church and protected by the *Parlements*, who had their revenge on the Jesuits, seen as the chief agents of the papal campaign against Jansenism, in 1764, with the expulsion of the Jesuits from France. It has also survived in the Netherlands in the **Old Catholic Church**. ▷ **Parlement**

Japan An island state off the east coast of Asia. It comprises the four large islands of Hokkaido, Honshu, Kyushu and Shikoku,

and many small islands. Originally occupied by the Ainu, in the 4c the country developed from individual communities into small states; by the 5c, the Yamato dynasty was the most dominant. Its culture was strongly influenced by China (8c–12c). It was ruled by feudal shoguns for many centuries, and little contact was made with the West until the **Meiji Restoration** in 1868. Successful wars were waged with China in 1894–5, and Russia in 1904–5. Japan annexed Korea in 1910, occupied **Manchuria** in 1931–2 and entered **World War II** with a surprise attack on the US fleet at **Pearl Harbor**, Hawaii, in 1941. It occupied British and Dutch possessions in SE Asia (1941–2), and was pushed back during 1943–5. Atomic bombs were dropped on **Hiroshima** and **Nagasaki** in 1945. There was strong economic growth in the 1960s, which was affected severely by the international oil crisis in the 1970s. Investment in other countries led to increased economic success and a trade surplus with most trading partners. A new coalition government was formed in 1993 to replace that of the **Liberal Democratic Party**. See map p475 and panel p476.

Japan Communist Party (JCP; *Nihon Kyosanto)* Formed in July 1922 as a branch of the **Comintern**, it was to remain a small and illegal organization until 1945. Severe government repression in the late 1920s and in the 1930s resulted in many members being imprisoned. With Japan's defeat in 1945 and the ensuing US occupation, the JCP was legalized and played a leading role in the workers' movement of the late 1940s. In the 1946 elections the party garnered 2.1 million votes, obtaining five seats in the lower house. The suppression of the left-wing movement that coincided with the outbreak of the **Korean War** in 1950 forced the JCP underground and some of its members resorted to terrorist tactics. After the mid-1950s, under the leadership of Miyamoto Kenji, the JCP adopted a gradualist approach and regained parliamentary ground. In 1980 the party won 29 lower house seats with nearly 10 per cent of the popular vote. Communist-backed candidates were also elected mayors of several cities. The JCP remains one of Japan's largest political parties in terms of active membership and has increasingly adopted a nationalist orientation.

Japan Socialist Party (JSP; *Nihon Shakaito)* Japan's largest opposition party. Socialism was introduced to Japan at the end of the 19c and the country's first socialist party was formed in 1901, but was banned by

Japan, 1868–1939

the government two days later. Although several anti-communist 'proletarian' parties did emerge during the 1920s and contested Diet elections, they were all banned in the 1930s, except for the Socialist Masses Party (*Shakai Taishuto*), which supported the aggressive nationalism of the Japanese militarists. The present-day JSP was formed in Nov 1945, winning a plurality of seats in the 1947 elections for the lower house. The party then led a coalition government (1947–8) under **Katayama** Tetsu, the only time the JSP had been in power before economic crisis and

internal rivalries led to its downfall. The party has been plagued by a left-right division; in 1951–5 it split over the 1951 Security Treaty with the USA, while in 1959 a right-wing faction bolted to form the Democratic Socialist Party. Despite losing public support in the 1960s and 1970s, the JSP remained the largest opposition party, and championed neutralism and a non-nuclear defence policy. After 1986, under the leadership of Takako **Doi**, the JSP gained additional public support, making important gains in the 1989 and 1990 elections. The party suffered a

JAPANESE EMPERORS

The first 14 emperors (to Chuai are regarded as legendary, and the regnal dates for the 15th to the 28th emperor (Senka), taken from the early Japanese chronicle, *Nihon shoki* are not considered to be authentic.

Regnal Dates	Name	Regnal Dates	Name	Regnal Dates	Name
660/585BC	Jimmu	724/49	Shomu	1246/59	Go-Fukakusa
581/549BC	Suizei	749/58	Koken	1259/74	Kameyama
549/511BC	Annei	758/64	Junnin	1274/87	Go-Uda
510/477BC	Itoku	764/70	Shotoku	1287/98	Fushimi
475/393BC	Kosho	770/81	Konin	1298/1301	Go-Fushimi
392/291BC	Koan	781/806	Kammu	1301/8	Go-Nijo
290/215BC	Korei	806/9	Heizei	1308/18	Hanazono
214/158BC	Kogen	809/23	Saga	1318/39	Daigo II (Go-Daigo)
158/98BC	Kaika	823/33	Junna	1339/68	Go-Murakami
97/30BC	Sujin	833/50	Nimmyo	1368/83	Chokei
29BC/AD70	Suinin	850/8	Montoku	1383/92	Go-Kameyama
71/130	Keiko	858/76	Seiwa		Northern Court
131/190	Selmu	876/84	Yozei	1331/3	Kogon
192/200	Chuai	884/7	Koko	1336/48	Komyo
270/310	Ojin	887/97	Uda	1348/51	Suko
313/99	Nintoku	897/930	Daigo	1352/71	Go-Kogon
400/5	Richu	930/46	Suzaku	1371/82	Go-Enyu
406/10	Hanzel	946/67	Murakami	1382/1412	Go-Komatsu
412/53	Ingyo	967/9	Reizei	1412/28	Shoko
453/6	Anko	969/84	En'yu	1428/64	Go-Hanazono
456/79	Yuryaku	984/6	Kazan	1464/1500	Go-Tsuchimikado
480/4	Seinei	986/1011	Ichijo	1500/26	Go-Kashiwabara
485/7	Kenzo	1011/16	Sanjo	1526/57	Go-Nara
488/98	Ninken	1016/36	Go-Ichijo	1557/86	Ogimachi
498/506	Buretsu	1036/45	Go-Suzako	1586/1611	Go-Yozei
507/31	Keitai	1045/68	Go-Reizei	1611/29	Go-Mizunoo
531/5	Ankan	1068/72	Go-Sanyo	1629/43	Meisho
535/9	Senka	1072/86	Shirakawa	1643/54	Go-Komyo
539/71	Kimmei	1086/1107	Horikawa	1654/63	Go-Sai
572/85	Bidatsu	1107/23	Toba	1663/87	Reigen
585/7	Yomei	1123/41	Sutoku	1687/1709	Higashiyama
587/92	Sushun	1141/55	Konoe	1709/35	Nakamikado
592/628	Suiko	1155/8	Goshirakawa	1735/47	Sakuramachi
629/41	Jomei	1158/65	Nijo	1747/62	Momozono
642/5	Kogyoku	1165/8	Rokujo	1762/70	Go-Sakuramachi
645/54	Kotuko	1168/80	Takakura	1770/9	Go-Momozono
655/61	Saimei	1180/3	Antoku	1779/1817	Kokaku
662/71	Tenji	1183/98	Go-Toba	1817/46	Ninko
671/2	Kobun	1198/1210	Tsuchimikado	1846/66	Komei
673/86	Temmu	1210/21	Juntoku	1867/1912	Meiji
686/97	Jito	1221	Chukyo	1912/26	Taisho
697/707	Mommu	1221/32	Goshirakawa	1926/89	Hirohito
707/15	Gemmei	1232/42	Shijo	1989/	Akihito
715/24	Gensho	1242/6	Go-Saga		

set-back in 1991 local elections, however, and Doi was replaced by Masashi Ishibashi. The party is now known as the Social Democratic Party of Japan.

Jarring, Gunnar (1907–) Swedish diplomat. He was appointed a special representative to the **UN**, with responsibilities for the Middle East, in late 1965. However, despite many visits to the Middle East in the period 1967–9, he was unable to generate any real enthusiasm amongst either Israelis or Arabs in his attempts to gain acceptance of UN

Resolution 242, aimed at a Middle Eastern settlement, with the Israeli return of territories occupied in the wake of the June War of 1967. After the civil war in Jordan in late 1970, he was again involved in trying to broker a peace settlement in the area.

Jarrow March (Oct 1936) A march to London by unemployed workers in the Durham shipbuilding and mining town, to put the unemployed case. Jarrow was among the towns worst affected by the Depression, and the march took place at a time when the economy was recovering in much of the rest of the country. It alerted the more prosperous South and Midlands to the intractable problems of depressed areas.

Jaruzelski, Wojciech Witold (1923–) Polish general and President. He took part in the Soviet liberation of Poland from German occupation in 1944–5. Afterwards he rose to become Chief of the General Staff in 1965, Minister of Defence in 1968, a full member of the Politburo in 1971, and First Secretary of the Communist Party and Prime Minister in 1981. In Dec of that year, in order to end the power of the mass free trade union, **Solidarity**; to prevent the break-up of **communism** in Poland and to obviate Soviet intervention; and, at the same time, to promote moderate economic reform, he introduced martial law, which he only partially lifted a year later. His many attempts to find a middle way proved unsuccessful and in 1988 he had to negotiate a reform package with Solidarity. The communists lost power in the consequent elections that year, and Jaruzelski became a token president until Lech Wałesa was ready to run for election himself in 1990. Although a sad figure at the end, he did not entirely fail. It was probably largely due to him that the USSR did not invade Poland in 1981 and that the eventual transfer of power was essentially peaceful.

Jason of Pherae ▷ **Thessaly**

Jassy, Treaty of (1792) This treaty confirmed the terms of the 1774 Treaty of **Kuchuk Kainarji** and ended the Russo-Turkish War of 1787–92. The war had begun as a combined Russo-Austrian assault on the **Ottoman Empire** intended to partition it. Austria, however, quickly withdrew, and **Catherine II, 'the Great'** had to abandon her 'Grand Plan'. Nevertheless, under General **Suvorov**'s command, Catherine's armies conquered the entire northern shores of the Black Sea. Under the treaty, Russia extended her lands to the Dniester River, but returned Bessarabia and Moldavia and Wallachia to Ottoman rule.

Jaszi, Oszkar (1875–1957) Hungarian politician and scholar. Before **World War I** he held an appointment at the Ministry of Agriculture, but he was too radical in his views to progress far in administration or in politics. He was close to the Social Democrats in opposing vestiges of feudalism and in supporting minority rights against the prevailing policy of Magyarization; but in 1914 he founded his own Radical Party. After the war he tried to woo the minority peoples, but in the wake of the peace settlement this proved unpopular with the Magyars. In 1919 he left for the USA where he wrote extensively on Central Europe.

Jaurès, (Auguste Marie Joseph) Jean (1859–1914) French political leader, writer and orator. He lectured on philosophy at Toulouse, then became a moderate republican deputy in 1885. Defeated in 1889, he returned to parliament as a socialist; defeated again in 1898, he campaigned on behalf on **Dreyfus**, and founded the *Parti socialiste français* ('French Socialist Party'), which, unlike its rival the *Parti socialiste de France* ('Socialist Party of France'), led by Jules **Guesde**, supported Dreyfus and ministerial participation. Jaurès was persuaded to drop the latter policy as the price to pay for unification of the two factions in the United Socialist Party, known officially as the SFIO (*Section française de l'Internationale ouvrière*, 'French Section of the Workers' International') in 1905, but he retained much influence in parliament until his assassination in 1914. He helped to found the socialist newspaper *l'Humanité* (1904), and wrote in it frequently; the need to avert a war between the Great Powers was a major theme. ▷ **Socialist Party** (France)

Jawara, Alhaji Sir Dawda Kairabi (1924–) Gambian politician. Educated at a Muslim primary school, Methodist Boys' GS Bathurst and Achimota College (Ghana), he continued his veterinary studies at Glasgow and Edinburgh Universities. He returned to the Gambia as a veterinary officer (1954–60), before entering politics as leader of the People's Progressive Party, becoming Minister of Education (1960–2) and Prime Minister at independence in 1963. On Gambia becoming a republic in 1970 he became President. He was re-elected in 1972, 1977, 1983 and 1987, despite an abortive coup against him in 1981, which was put down by Senegalese troups and paved the way for the creation of the short-lived confederation of **Senegambia**.

Jay, John (1745–1829) US politician and jurist. Educated at King's (now Columbia) College, New York, he was admitted to the Bar in 1768. He was elected to the **Continental Congress** (1774–5), becoming its President in 1778. He helped negotiate (1781–3) peace with Great Britain under the Treaty of Paris, and he served as Secretary for Foreign

Affairs (1784–9). Jay contributed to the **Federalist Papers** in an effort to secure ratification of the Constitution. He became the first Chief Justice of the Supreme Court (1789–95), and in that capacity negotiated **Jay's Treaty**. From 1795 to 1801 he was governor of New York. ▷ **American Revolution**

Jayatilaka, Sir Baron (1868–1944) Ceylonese lawyer and government official. Representative of the Ceylon government in India. Educated in Colombo and Oxford, Jayatilaka became an advocate at the Supreme Court of Ceylon in 1913. He was a member of the Legislative Council of Ceylon from 1924 to 1931. He held during his career the posts of the Vice-Chairman of the Board of Ministers, the Leader of the State Council, and the Minister of Home Affairs, Ceylon. Jayatilaka also revised and edited a number of old Sinhalese works.

Jayavarman VII (1181/c.1218) Ruler of the Cambodian kingdom of Angkor. His reign was marked by vigorous building construction, notably of the city of Angkor Thom and of its central shrine, the Bayon. These are among the most remarkable constructions in the ancient world, although the demands which their erection placed upon the resources of Angkor may well have exhausted the state. Certainly, his successors did not undertake any further monumental constructions. Jayavarman VII also extended the authority of Angkor, making claims over parts of Burma and the Malay Peninsula.

Jayawardene, J(unius) R(ichard) (1906–) Sri Lankan politician. After studying law in Colombo, he became a member of the State Council (1943) and the House of Representatives (1947). Honorary Secretary of the Ceylon National Congress (1940–7), he went on to hold office as Minister of Finance (1947–53), Vice-President of the **UNP** (United National Party) and Deputy Leader of the Opposition (1960–5). As Leader of the Opposition after the 1970 election defeat, he rebuilt the UNP's organization and led it to a landslide victory in 1977, when he became Prime Minister. The following year he became the country's first Executive President under a new constitution and he won a second term of office in 1982. In 1988 he retired and was succeeded by his Prime Minister, Ranasinghe **Premadasa**. His period as head of state was marked by his pro-Western 'open economy' policies and by deteriorating relations between the **Sinhala**

and **Tamil** communities, culminating in the 1987 **Indo-Sri Lankan Peace Accord** and the second **JVP** (People's Liberation Front) insurrection of 1987–9.

Jay's Treaty (1794) An agreement between the USA and Britain to end the British occupation of military posts in the north-western parts of US territory, and for altering the terms of US commerce with Britain and its colonies. Negotiated by John **Jay**, it was very unpopular with the US public, largely because of the restrictions it imposed on US trade with the West Indies.

Jaziyah The 'poll tax' levied upon non-Muslims In India by Islamic rulers who tolerated idolatry on payment of tribute. According to strict Islamic law, this poll-tax was payable only by Jews and Christians, but these rulers claimed it from their Hindu subjects as commutation money for not embracing Islam. The *jaziyah* was abolished in Kashmir by Zain-ul-Abidin in the early 15c, and **Akbar the Great** abolished it in 1579. However, **Aurangzeb** reimposed the jaziyah in 1679, forcing many poor Hindus to convert to Islam in order to escape payment. Muhammad Shah proclaimed but abandoned the poll-tax in 1720, and declined later to levy it.

Jebtsundamba Khutuktu Literally 'living Buddha', this was the title given to head of the Tibetan Buddhist (Lamaist) church in outer Mongolia between the 17c and the early decades of the 20c. The installation of the *Jebtsundamba Khutuktu* took place at a time when the **Qing Dynasty** was extending its control throughout Mongolia and promoting the Yellow Sect of the Tibetan Lamaist church there. The eighth, and last, Jebtsundamba Khutuktu (1870–1924) was a Tibetan who was enthroned as head of state (*bogdo-khan*) in 1912 when a republican revolution in China overthrowing the Qing Dynasty enabled Outer Mongolia to break free from Chinese control. The Mongolian People's Party, founded in 1921 with the support of the USSR, declared a republic in 1924 and on the Jebtsundamba Khutuktu's death the same year no successor was chosen.

Jefferson, Thomas (1743–1826) US politician and 3rd President. He became a lawyer (1767) and a member of the Virginia House of Burgesses. A delegate to the Second Continental Congress (1775), he drafted the **Declaration of Independence**. Jefferson was Governor of Virginia (1779–81), Minister to

France (1785) and Secretary of State (1790). He served as Vice-President under John **Adams** (1797–1801), and as President (1801–9). Important events of his administration include the **Louisiana Purchase** (1803), and the Embargo Act of 1807. After he retired to Monticello, he founded the University of Virginia.

Jeffreys (of Wem), George, 1st Baron (1648–89) English judge. Called to the Bar in 1668, he rose rapidly, was knighted (1677), and became Recorder of London (1678). He was active in the **Popish Plot** prosecutions, became Chief Justice of Chester (1680), baronet (1681), and Chief Justice of the King's Bench (1683). In every state trial he proved a willing tool of the crown, and was raised to the peerage by **James II** (1685). His journey to the West country to try the followers of **Monmouth** earned the name of the 'bloody assizes' for its severity. He was Lord Chancellor (1685–8), but on James's flight was imprisoned in the Tower of London, where he died.

Jelačić, Josip (1801–59) Croatian politician and soldier. The Croatian national hero in the struggle against the Magyars, he was appointed Ban (Viceroy) of Croatia in 1848 by the Vienna government, which hoped he would secure Croatian support for Austria in the impending clash with the Magyar nationalists. He led the Croatian *sabor* (parliament) in its declaration of independence from Hungary, a move which temporarily lost him his office (June 1848). He was reinstated later the same year and, at Scwechat, defeated the Hungarian troops of Artúr **Görgey** which were marching on Vienna. Within Croatia, he oversaw the liberation of the serfs. He was made a count in 1855.

Jellicoe, John Rushworth, 1st Earl (1859–1935) British admiral. He became Third Sea Lord (1908), and was Commander-in-Chief, Grand Fleet at the outbreak of **World War I**. His main engagement was the inconclusive Battle of **Jutland** (1916), for which at the time he was much criticized. Promoted First Sea Lord, he organized the defences against German submarines, and was made Admiral of the Fleet (1919). He later became Governor of New Zealand (1920–4). He was created an earl in 1925.

Jemappes, Battle of (6 Nov 1792) Fought between the Austrians and the French in present-day Belgium during the **French Revolutionary Wars**, the battle was decisively won by the French General **Dumouriez**. For the Austrian southern Netherlands (now Belgium) the French victory was crucial, for in 1793 they were annexed as part of revolutionary France.

Jena and Auerstädt, Battles of (1806) French military victories of the **Napoleonic Wars**, both fought in Saxony on 14 Oct 1806 between two French armies under **Napoleon I** and **Davout** and combined Prussian-Saxon forces. The French smashed the obsolete Prussian Army inherited from **Frederick II, 'the Great'**, enforcing the reduction of **Prussia** to half its former size. ▷ **Grand Alliance, War of the; Tilsit, Treaties of**

Jenkins, Roy (Harris), Baron (1920–) British politician. He became a Labour MP in 1948, and was Minister of Aviation (1964–5), Home Secretary (1965–7), Chancellor of the Exchequer (1967–70), Deputy Leader of the **Labour Party** in opposition (1970–2) and again Home Secretary (1974–6). He resigned as an MP in 1976 to take up the presidency of the European Commission (1977–81). Upon his return to Britain, he co-founded the **Social Democratic Party** (1981), and became its first leader, standing down after the 1983 election in favour of David **Owen**. Defeated in the 1987 election, he was given a life peerage and also became Chancellor of Oxford University. ▷ **Liberal Party** (UK)

Jenkins' Ear, War of A war between Britain and Spain starting in 1739, and soon merging into the wider War of the **Austrian Succession** (1740–8). Some of the violent anti-Spanish indignation in Britain that provoked the war was due to Captain Robert Jenkins, who claimed to have had an ear cut off by Spanish coastguards in the Caribbean.

Jesuits' Estates Act (1888) A Quebec statute by which Honoré **Mercier**'s administration disposed of the compensation for Jesuit property sequestrated by the crown when the order was suppressed in the late 18c. After its re-establishment in Quebec (1842), successive governments had been unable to solve the question of how to allot the compensation, which had to be spent on education. The property was valued at C$400 000 and the Act granted C$70 000 to the province's Protestant schools while the rest was to be divided within Catholic community at the Pope's discretion. In Quebec this seemed a sensible solution, but in Ontario the **Orange Order** was enraged, and charged Mercier with inviting the Pope to intervene in Canadian affairs. John A **Macdonald**, however, refused to disallow the Act as it fell clearly within provincial powers over education.

Jewish Agency The executive body of the **World Zionist Organization**, established in 1922 as the Jewish Agency for Palestine. The shorter title was adopted in 1929 and, until 1948, the Jewish Agency regulated the **Yishuv**'s relations with world Jewry and the British authorities. The latter recognized its oversight of Jewish affairs in Palestine and its role as negotiator for the Zionist position. Although many of its functions passed to the Israeli government after 1948, the Agency continued to be involved in immigration and agricultural settlement, as well as in education abroad. With headquarters in Jerusalem and New York, the Agency was reconstituted in 1971 to take account of relations with non-Zionists. ▷ **Balfour Declaration**

Jewish Labour Movement in Palestine Labour was an issue which preoccupied many Jewish settlers in Palestine in the late 19c and early 20c, including David **Ben-Gurion**. This stemmed from Zionist-socialist critiques of the situation of Russian and European Jewry, who were experiencing both emancipation and anti-Semitism. Their aim was to create a Jewish homeland to whose economy Jews themselves would contribute through a complete range of occupations. Numerous trade unions and political parties resulted in the early 1900s. Most of the unions combined in 1920 to form the **Histadrut**, while **Mapai** became the main socialist party of the **Yishuv** and, after 1948, the State of Israel. ▷ **Aliyah; Zionism**

Jewish National Fund The fund established (Dec 1901) by the **World Zionist Organization**, with the aim of buying land in Palestine. Although initially based in Vienna, its headquarters were in Jerusalem by 1922. The fund spent most of its first 45 years acquiring land in Palestine for Jewish settlement, so that by 1947 it possessed 234 000 acres. It operated leases of 49 years to its lessees, based on Leviticus 25:10, 23–4. Since Israeli independence in 1948, the Fund has concentrated on land improvement, irrigation and afforestation. Supported by worldwide Jewish contributions, it is headed by a board of directors. ▷ **Jewish Agency**

Jews, Expulsion of the (31 Mar 1492) This decree, expelling Jews from Spain, was

issued by King **Ferdinand II, 'the Catholic'** and Queen **Isabella I, 'the Catholic'**. It was influenced in part by the Spanish **Inquisition**, which believed that the presence of Jews encouraged **Conversos** to practise Judaism. Jews were given four months to accept baptism or leave the country; the edict was in fact one of conversion and not of expulsion. A high proportion converted, including important community leaders, and others returned even after leaving, so that the final number of expulsions was probably less than 50 000. Those who left went mainly to Portugal (where a forced conversion was decreed in 1497), North Africa and Italy; there is no evidence of emigration to Turkey until much later. The expulsions had no significant impact on the economy of Spain, since Jews had been a small and persecuted minority with no access to commerce or the major professions. Some Spanish leaders criticized the decree, and in the early 17c there were proposals, considered seriously by the Count Duke of **Olivares**, to allow the émigrés back to Spain.

Jiang Jieshi ▷ **Chiang Kai-shek**

Jiang Jing'guo (Chiang Ching-kuo) (1910–88) Taiwanese politician. The son of **Chiang Kai-shek**, he studied in the USSR during the early 1930s, returning to China with a Russian wife in 1937 at the time of the Japanese invasion. After the defeat of Japan in 1945 he held a number of government posts before fleeing with his father and the defeated **Guomindang** forces to Taiwan in 1949. He became Defence Minister (1965–72), and was Prime Minister from 1972 to 1978. He succeeded to the post of Guomindang leader on his father's death (1975) and became state President in 1978. Under his stewardship, Taiwan's post-war 'economic miracle' continued, but in the political sphere there was repression. During the closing years of his life, with his health failing, he instituted a progressive programme of political liberalization and democratization, which was continued by his successor, **Lee Teng-hui**.

Jiang Qing (Chiang Ch'ing) (1914–91) Chinese politician. She trained in drama and literature, and then became an actress in Shanghai. In 1936 she went to Yenan to study Marxist-Leninist theory, met **Mao Zedong** and became his third wife in 1939. She was attached to the Ministry of Culture (1950–4), and in the 1960s began her attacks on bourgeois influences in the arts and literature. One of the leaders of the **Cultural Revolution**, she was elected to the Politburo (1969), but after Mao's death (1976) was arrested with three others — the **Gang of Four** — imprisoned, expelled from the Communist Party and tried in 1980. She was sentenced to death, but the sentence was later suspended.

Jiangxi (Kiangsi) Soviet The most important rural base area under the control of the Chinese Communist Party (CCP) between 1930 and 1934. It had its origins in **Mao Zedong**'s decision to abandon the cities and create a peasant-based Red Army controlling the countryside. Emphasis henceforth was on 'protracted revolution' in which liberated rural base areas would eventually surround the cities. Mao began (Feb 1930) organizing a rural soviet in the southern province of Jiangxi, which was to become the most important of several such soviets established in this region with control over an estimated 3 million inhabitants. In Nov 1931 the First National Congress of the Chinese Soviet Republic formally established a soviet government under Mao. After 1932, however, when the Moscow-trained urban party leadership came to Jiangxi, Mao lost influence. His flexible attitude towards rich peasants was condemned, while his guerrilla tactics were replaced by a strategy of conventional warfare to confront the series of encirclement campaigns launched against the soviet by **Chiang Kai-shek**'s Nationalist armies. By the end of 1933, the Jiangxi soviet had to be abandoned and the communists embarked on the **Long March** that would take them to the far north-west of China.

Jiang Zemin (Chiang Tse-min) (1926–) Chinese politician. The son-in-law of former President **Li Xian'nian**, after university he began a career as an electrical engineer and trained in the USSR. He was Commercial Counsellor at the Chinese Embassy in Moscow (1950–6) and during the 1960s and 1970s held a number of posts in the heavy and power industry ministries. Elected to the Chinese Communist Party (CCP)'s Central Committee in 1982, he was appointed Mayor of Shanghai in 1985. Here he gained a reputation as a cautious reformer, loyal to the party line. He was inducted into the CCP's Politburo in 1987 and in June 1989, following the **Tiananmen Square** massacre and the dismissal of **Zhao Ziyang**, was elected Party Leader. Fluent in English and Russian, Jiang has, as a compromise figure, pledged to maintain China's 'open door' economic strategy.

jihad Literally meaning 'striving' in Arabic, the term is often used with the specific sense of struggling against enemies of Islam in 'holy war'. According to the Quran, Muslims have a duty to oppose those who reject Islam, by armed struggle if necessary, and *jihad* has been invoked to justify both the expansion and defence of Islam.

Jim Crow Laws A term used to characterize US state laws passed from the 1890s onwards, to segregate blacks from whites in the south in schools, public transport, housing, and other areas. They were gradually abolished from the mid-20c, largely because of the **civil rights** movement, which led to Supreme Court decisions and changes in Federal policies. ▷ **Plessy v Ferguson**

Jin (Jurched) The Tartar tribe that founded the Jin Dynasty in northern China (1122–1234), captured (1126) Kaifeng, the capital of the **Song Dynasty**, and established a frontier with the southern Song along the River Huai. It was finally destroyed by the **Mongols** in 1234.

Jin (Chin/Tsin) Dynasty (266–317) Also known as the Western Jin, this was the last native Chinese dynasty to rule over a unified China before a period of division lasting until the 6c, in which independent Chinese kingdoms confronted non-Chinese dynasties of conquest in the north. The Jin Dynasty was founded by the Sima family when it usurped power from the reigning Cao family and overthrew the Wei state. By 280, the Jin had completed the reunification of China, thus ending the Three Kingdoms period, but came under increasing pressure from non-Chinese tribes in the north, who succeeded in capturing the Jin capital of Chang'an in 316. A member of the Sima family then established a separate dynasty (Eastern Jin, 318–420) in the south at Nanjing, the first of a series of independent kingdoms that engaged in constant warfare with the northern foreign dynasties.

Jinggangshan (Ching-Kang shan) The mountain stronghold on the border between the central Chinese provinces of Hunan and Jiangxi where **Mao Zedong** took the survivors of his armed force that had participated in one of the abortive **Autumn Harvest Uprisings** in 1927. During the ensuing year, Mao began the task of building a Red Army recruiting from amongst vagrants and bandits, as well as agricultural labourers and poor peasants. Mao also carried out a radical land redistribution policy, although he later adopted a more flexible policy towards rich peasants. He was forced to abandon Jinggangshan in 1928, following repeated Nationalist attacks and moved to south-east Jiangxi where he was to create the first rural soviet.

Jinnah, Muhammad Ali (1876–1948) Indian Muslim politician and founder of Pakistan. Educated in Bombay and London, he was called to the Bar in 1897, and practised in Bombay. He became a member of the **Indian National Congress** (1906) and the **Muslim League** (1913), and supported Hindu–Muslim unity until 1930, when he resigned from the Congress following disagreement over the demands attached to M K **Gandhi**'s programme of **civil disobedience**. His advocacy of a separate state for Muslims led to the creation of Pakistan in 1947, and he became its first Governor-General.

Joan of Arc, St (The Maid of Orléans) (c.1412–31) French patriot and martyr. She halted the English ascendancy in France during the **Hundred Years War**. Born into a peasant family, at the age of 13 she heard the voices of Saints Michael, Catherine, and Margaret bidding her rescue France from English domination. She was taken to the **Dauphin**, and eventually allowed to lead the army assembled for the relief of Orléans. Clad in a suit of white armour and flying her own standard, she entered Orléans (1429), forced the English to retire, and took the Dauphin to be crowned **Charles VII** at Rheims. She then set out to relieve Compiègne, but was captured and sold to the English by John of Luxembourg. Put on trial (1431) for heresy and sorcery, she was found guilty by an English-dominated court, and burnt. She was canonized in 1920.

Jodl, Alfred (1890–1946) German general and Nazi collaborator. An artillery subaltern in **World War I**, he became **Hitler**'s close associate. General of Artillery in 1940, he was the planning genius of the German High Command and Hitler's chief adviser. He was found guilty of war crimes at the **Nuremberg Trials** (1946), and executed. ▷ **World War II**

Joffre, Joseph Jacques Césaire (1852–1931) French general. He joined the army in 1870, and rose to be French Chief-of-Staff (1914) and Commander-in-Chief (1915), carrying out a policy of attrition against the German invaders of France. He retired as Commander-in-Chief and was made Marshal of France (1916). ▷ **World War I**

Johan III of Sweden ▷ **John III**

John ('John Lackland') (1167–1216) King of England (1199/1216). The youngest son of **Henry II** of England, he was one of the least popular monarchs in English history. He tried to seize the crown during **Richard I**'s captivity in Germany (1193–4), but was forgiven and nominated successor by Richard, who thus set aside the rights of Prince **Arthur**, the son of John's elder brother Geoffrey. Arthur's claims were supported by **Philip II** of France, and after Arthur was murdered on John's orders (1203), Philip marched against him with superior forces, and conquered all but a portion of Aquitaine (1204–5). In 1206 John refused to receive Stephen **Langton** as Archbishop of Canterbury, and in 1208 his kingdom was placed under papal interdict. He was then excommunicated (1209), and finally conceded (1213). His oppressive government, and failure to recover **Normandy**, provoked baronial opposition, which led to demands for constitutional reform. The barons met the King at Runnymede, and forced him to seal the Great Charter (**Magna Carta**) (June 1215), the basis of the English constitution. His repudiation of the Charter precipitated the first **Barons War** (1215–17).

John I (c.1255–94) Duke of Brabant. As the second son of Henry III, he succeeded to the Duchy on the death of his older brother, Henry VI, in 1267. In 1270 he married Margaret of France (the daughter of **Louis IX**), and in 1271 Margaret, daughter of **Guy of Dampierre**. He increased the power of the Duchy of **Brabant**, and obtained the Duchy of Limburg for his family as well.

John I Tzimisces (c.924–76) Byzantine Emperor (969/76). He was a successful general who intrigued with Empress Theodora to murder her husband, Nicephorus II Phocas, in 956. However, after seizing the throne, he was forced by the Church to repudiate her. He won a major victory over the Bulgars (971) and went on to reconquer much of Syria and Palestine from the Muslims.

John II, 'the Good' (1319–64) King of France (1350/64). The son of **Philip VI**, in 1356 he was taken prisoner by **Edward the Black Prince** at the Battle of Poitiers (1356), and carried to England. After the Treaty of Brétigny (1360) he returned home, leaving his second son, the Duke of Anjou, as a hostage. When the duke broke his parole and escaped (1363), John chivalrously returned to London, and died there.

John II Casimir Vasa (1609–72) King of Poland (1648/68). The son of King **Sigismund III Vasa** of Sweden, he was elected king to succeed his brother, Władysław IV, in 1648. Throughout his reign he was faced with external and internal threats, sometimes combined, a sign of Poland's growing weakness. A successful Swedish invasion in 1655 forced him to take refuge in Silesia while moves were made to elect **Charles X Gustav** of Sweden in his place. John Casimir returned to Poland in 1656 with widespread support but hostilities continued until the Peace of Oliwa (1660). On his return, he had solemnly promised to alleviate the plight of the Polish serfs and he made a strenuous effort to introduce constitutional reform (1660–1). However, all reformist legislation was opposed by conservative opponents and, when he persisted, they raised a bloody rebellion under their leader, Jerzy Lubomirski (1665–6). Although Lubomirski admitted defeat, John Casimir finally abdicated in 1668 and ended his life as a pensioner of **Louis XIV** in Paris. Poland's decline continued.

John II Comnenus (1088–1143) Byzantine Emperor (1118/43). He succeeded his father, **Alexius I Comnenus**. In government he relied on trusted servants rather than his immediate family, some of whom, such as his sister, Anna, and brother, Isaac, intrigued against him and were deprived of their positions. Apart from an abortive attempt to curtail the trading privileges of the Venetians, his energetic rule was distinguished by military and diplomatic success. In the Balkans his victory over the Patzinaks (1122) effectively ended a long-standing threat to the empire and was thereafter commemorated by a public holiday; in the east he recovered territory in Cilicia and asserted Byzantine overlordship over the Normans of Antioch (1137). He was killed in a hunting accident while on campaign.

John III (1300–55) Duke of Brabant and of Limburg. He was the son of John II and Margaret of York, the daughter of King **Edward I** of England. At the start of the **Hundred Years War** John tried to walk a tightrope between France and England; in 1338 he decided to secure the English wool staple at Antwerp by supporting England. When the staple was moved to Bruges in 1340, he switched to France.

John III (1537–92) King of Sweden (1569/92). He was the second son of King **Gustav I Vasa** by his second wife, Margareta Leijonhufvud, and the half-brother and successor to **Erik XIV**. Having been made Duke of Finland by his father, he married the Polish princess, Katarina Jagełłonica, and then embarked on his own pro-Polish foreign policy, which led to his imprisonment by King Erik. On his release, apparently reconciled to Erik, he joined his younger brother, Charles (later, King **Charles IX**), in a rebellion which ended in Erik's deposition and John's accession to the throne. He brought the Seven Years War with Denmark and Lübeck to an end with the Treaty of Stettin (1570) and thereafter fought against Russia in Livonia, side by side with his brother-in-law, King **Sigismund II** Augustus of Poland, driving Tsar **Ivan IV, 'the Terrible'** from the Baltic. An avid student of theology, he negotiated with the Pope for the return of Sweden to the Catholic fold and introduced (1577) a Catholic liturgy (the 'Red Book'). His son, who was raised as a Catholic, was elected King of Poland in 1587 as Sigismund III Vasa, and succeeded his father on the Swedish throne.

John III Sobieski (1629–96) King of Poland (1674/96). A military commander, or hetman, he defeated the Turks at Choczim in 1673, and was elected King the following year. He had ambitions in Germany but he was constantly plagued by Turkish incursions. In 1683 he raised the Turkish siege of Vienna in a famous victory but, although he won European fame, he got little thanks from Austria. His later campaigns against the Turks were not equally successful. Domestic unrest and especially financial and religious difficulties clouded the last years of his reign.

John (João) IV (1604–56) King of Portugal (1640/56). As Duke of Braganza, he was the leading aristocrat and greatest landowner in Portugal. When the country freed itself from Spanish rule in 1640, he became King of the newly independent Portugal. Despite alliances with France, Sweden and the Dutch and with Portugal's ancient ally, England, he was unable to secure Spanish recognition of independent Portugal during his lifetime.

John IV (1831–89) Emperor of Ethiopia (1868/89). He succeeded Emperor Theodore, who committed suicide after the Napier invasion of Ethiopia in 1867–8. Although John wielded even greater power in Ethiopia than his predecessor, his authority was threatened in the 1880s by the Italians in Eritrea, the Mahdist forces in the Sudan and King Menelik of Shoa to the South. In 1882 John came to terms with Menelik, accepting him as his successor. He was killed in battle with the Mahdists in 1889.

John VI (1535–1606) Count of Nassau-Dillenburg. The direct ancestor of the royal house of the Netherlands (Orange-Nassau), he was the eldest of the younger brothers of **William I, 'the Silent'**, Prince of Orange. He supported his brother during the **Eighty Years War** against Spain, and became **Stadholder** of Gelderland in 1578, which he proceeded forcibly to convert to Calvinism. He did not always see eye to eye with his brother, William, and returned to Germany in 1580. He was married three times and had 24 children.

John XII (Octavian) (c.937–64) Pope (955/64). Elected to the papacy when only 18, the Emperor **Otto I** had him deposed in 963 in a synod of the clergy because of his scandalous life, and caused Leo VIII to be elected in his stead. In the following year John drove Leo from Rome but then died suddenly.

John XXII (c.1249–1334) French Pope (1316/34). One of the most celebrated of the popes of Avignon, he intervened in the contest for the Imperial Crown between Louis of Bavaria and Frederick of Austria, supporting the latter. A long contest ensued both in Germany and Italy between the Guelf (papal) party and the Ghibelline (imperial) party. In 1327 Louis entered Italy, was crowned Emperor at Rome, and deposed the Pope, setting up an anti-pope (1328). Although Guelf predominance at Rome was later restored, John died at Avignon. ▷ **Ghibellines; Guelfs**

John XXIII (Baldassare Cossa) (d.1419) Anti-pope (1410/15). A scandalous and corrupt figure, he came to the papacy because of the conviction that his military skills were essential if Rome were to be won back from the dominion of Naples. He was one of three claimants to the papal throne, a rivalry which brought the **Great Schism** to its point of crisis. The Council of Constance eventually forced him to abdicate on grounds of simony, perjury and sodomy and swear not to renege on the decision.

John Frederick, 'the Magnanimous' (1503–54) Elector of Saxony (1532/54). A Lutheran, he was involved in Imperial politics and the **Schmalkaldic League** before he became Elector. He vacillated between support for Philip of Hesse and Emperor **Charles V**. He came near to war with his relative, **Maurice**, Duke of Saxony, in 1541. Shortly after war broke out between Charles V and the Schmalkaldic League, John Frederick was placed under the Imperial ban. He was captured at the Battle of **Mühlberg** (24 Apr 1547) and held until May 1552. He was stripped of the electorate, a loss he accepted in the Treaty of Naumburg (Feb 1554).

John George I (1585–1656) Elector of Saxony. He succeeded his elder brother, Christian II, in 1611. A leading Lutheran prince, his native conservatism and his strong distaste for Calvinism made him an unsteady defender of Protestantism. During the **Thirty Years War** he at first supported the Catholic emperor, **Ferdinand II**, before agreeing in 1631 to head a defensive Protestant alliance. His support for the cause remained lukewarm and in 1635 he signed the separate Peace of Prague with the emperor.

John Lackland ▷ John ('John Lackland')

John of Austria, Don (1547–78) Spanish soldier. The illegitimate son of Emperor **Charles V**, he defeated the **Moors** in Granada (1570) and the Turks at the Battle of **Lepanto** (1571). In 1573 he took Tunis, and was then sent to Milan and (1576) to the Netherlands as Viceroy. He planned to marry **Mary, Queen of Scots**, but died of typhoid at Namur.

John of Gaunt (1340–99) Duke of Lancaster. He was the fourth son of King **Edward III** of England, and ancestor of Kings **Henry IV**, V, and **VI** of England. In 1359 he married his cousin, Blanche of Lancaster, and through her succeeded to the dukedom in 1362. After her death (1369), he married Constance, daughter of **Pedro, the Cruel** of Castile, and assumed the title of King of Castile, though he failed by his expeditions to oust his rival, Henry of Trestamare. In England he became highly influential as a peacemaker during the troubled reign of **Richard II**. He was made Duke of Aquitaine by Richard (1390), and sent on several embassies to France. On his second wife's death (1394) he married his mistress, Catherine Swynford, by whom he had three sons; from the eldest descended **Henry VII**.

John of Nepomuk (c.1345–93) Catholic patron saint of Bohemia. He studied at the University of Prague, and became Vicar-General to the Archbishop of Prague. For crossing King Wenceslas IV, who wished to create a new bishopric, he was tortured and drowned in the Vltava. He was canonized in 1729 as part of the Habsburg and Jesuit campaign to ensure that there was an appropriate Catholic martyr to set against popular veneration for the reformist martyr, Jan **Hus**.

John Paul II (Karol Jozef Wojtyła) (1920–) Polish Pope (1978/). The first non-Italian pope in 456 years, he was educated and ordained in Kraków in 1946, received further education in Rome and Lublin, and became Professor of Moral Theology at Lublin and Kraków. Archbishop and Metropolitan of Kraków (1964–78), he was created cardinal in 1967. Noted for his energy and analytical ability, his pontificate has seen many foreign visits, in which he has preached to huge audiences. In 1981 he survived an assassination attempt, when he was shot and wounded in St Peter's Square by a Turkish national, Mehmet Ali Agca, possibly at Bulgarian instigation. A champion of economic justice and an outspoken defender of the Church in communist countries, he has been uncompromising on moral issues. In the 1980s his visits to Poland and his meetings with Mikhail **Gorbachev** were of great assistance to **Solidarity** in promoting Polish independence, achieved in 1989. ▷ **pope**

John the Fearless (1371–1419) Duke of Burgundy, the eldest son of **Philip the Bold**. His father's death in 1404 left him in possession of **Burgundy**, Flanders and Artois. He opposed Louis, Duke of **Orléans**, brother of the periodically insane **Charles VI**, 'the Foolish', whose assassination (1407) led to civil war between the Burgundian party and Orléans's supporters, the Armagnacs. John gained, lost and regained control of Paris, the King, and the government, but was murdered during a conference at Montereau-Faut-Yonne, probably at the instigation of the **Dauphin**, the future **Charles VII**. ▷ **Orléans, House of**

John Zapolya ▷ **Zapolya, John**

John, Patrick (1937–) Dominican politician. In the period before full independence he served in the government of Chief Minister Edward LeBlanc, and succeeded him in 1974. On independence in 1978 he became the country's first Prime Minister. His increasingly authoritarian style of government led to the loss of his assembly seat in 1980 and his replacement as Prime Minister by Eugenia **Charles**. The following year he was arrested for alleged complicity in a plot to overthrow Charles but was acquitted of the charge. A subsequent trial, in 1985, found him guilty and he was given a 12-year prison sentence.

Johnson, Andrew (1808–75) US politician and 17th President. With little formal schooling, he became alderman and Mayor in Greeneville, Tennessee, and a member of the Legislature (1835), state Senate (1841) and Congress (1843). He was Governor of Tennessee (1853–7), and a US Senator (1857–62). During the **American Civil War** he was made Military Governor of Tennessee (1862), and became Vice-President when Abraham **Lincoln** was re-elected in 1864. On Lincoln's assassination (1865), he became President (1865–9). A Democrat, his **Reconstruction** policies were opposed by the Republican Congress, who wished to make reconstruction of the Southern states dependent on a measure of protection for black civil rights. After he vetoed the **Civil Rights Acts** of 1866, his popularity declined rapidly. Politically motivated impeachment proceedings were brought against him, but fell short of conviction by one vote. ▷ **Democratic Party**

Johnson, Lyndon B(aines) ('LBJ') (1908–73) US politician and 36th President. Educated at Southwest Texas State Teachers College, he was a teacher and congressman's secretary before becoming a Democratic member of the House of Representatives in 1937. He became a Senator in 1949, and later an effective Democratic majority leader (1954). Vice-President under John F **Kennedy** in 1961, he assumed the presidency after Kennedy's assassination, and was elected to the office in 1964 with the biggest majority ever obtained in a presidential election up until that time. His administration (1963–9) passed the Civil Rights Act of 1964 and the **Voting Rights Act** of 1965, and his **Great Society** programme to reduce poverty, eliminate racial discrimination, provide medical care, and improve education. However, the escalation of the **Vietnam War** led to large-scale marches and protests and to his growing unpopularity, and he decided not to seek re-election in 1968. ▷ **Civil Rights Acts; Democratic Party**

Johnston, Sir Harry H (1858–1927) British administrator, explorer and artist. He played a significant part in the Partition of Africa. Trained as an artist, he also developed scientific and linguistic interests and in 1879 he went to Tunis to paint and explore. Later he travelled in Angola, the Congo and (in 1884) the Kilimanjaro region of East Africa, where he collected treaties with local chiefs. He subsequently served the Foreign Office in West Africa (1885–9), Lisbon in 1889, Mozambique (1889–91), British Central Africa (Malawi, 1891–6), Tunis (1897–9) and Uganda (1899–1901). He is generally credited with inventing the phrase 'Cape to Cairo'. ▷ **Africa, Partition of**

Joinville, Jean, Sire de (c.1224–1317) French historian. He took part in the unfortunate 7th Crusade of **Louis IX** (1248–54) and was imprisoned at Acre, and ransomed. He returned with Louis to France, and lived partly at court and partly on his estates. Throughout the crusade he kept notes on the events, which he later wrote up in his *Histoire de Saint Louis* (completed by 1309). ▷ **Crusades, Later**

Jonathan, Chief (Joseph) Lebua (1914–) Lesotho chief and politician. Educated in mission schools before working in South African mines and then in local government in Basutoland, he entered politics in 1952. He joined the Basutoland National Council in 1956 and in 1959 founded the Basutoland National Party, which favoured a free enterprise economy and cordial relations with South Africa. He was elected to the Legco in 1960 and became Prime Minister in 1965 but he suspended the Constitution in 1970. Parliamentary government was restored in 1973 and elections held regularly until 1985, when they were cancelled. Chief Jonathan was overthrown in a military coup (Jan 1986).

Jones, (John) Paul (1747–92) Scottish-born American naval commander. Originally named John Paul, he was apprenticed as a cabin boy, made several voyages to America, and in 1773 inherited property in Virginia. He joined the navy at the outbreak of the **American Revolution**, and performed a number of daring exploits off the British coast, capturing and sinking several ships. Outmanned and outgunned in the famous battle against the Serapis, he refused to surrender, declaring 'I have not yet begun to fight' and through sheer grit emerged victorious.

Jones, J Raymond (1900–91) US politician. The first black 'boss' of **Tammany Hall**. From his base in the Carver Democratic Club, Jones had run Harlem since the 1920s and formed an alliance with Adam Clayton **Powell**. When Tammany's image became tarnished by scandal in the 1950s, Jones split with Powell and backed Robert **Wagner** Jnr for Mayor of New York in 1957. In return, Wagner placed him charge of patronage, and he took over Tammany in 1964. This was a significant gain for the black community, and Jones became one of the major power brokers within the **Democratic Party**, until the machine all but collapsed under the pressure of black protest and Jones was challenged by Robert **Kennedy**. In 1967 the 'Harlem Fox' (as Jones was known) retired to the West Indies, leaving among his protégés the first black to become Mayor of New York, David Dinkins. ▷ **political machine**

Jones, Mary Harris ('Mother Jones') (1830–1930) Irish-born US labour activist. She migrated to the USA via Canada, lost her family in an epidemic in 1867, and thereafter devoted herself to the cause of labour. An effective speaker, she travelled to the scenes of major strikes, especially in the coal industry, and continued to work as a labour agitator almost until her death.

Jon Sigurdsson ▷ **Sigurdsson, Jón**

Jordan, Vernon E, Jr (1935–) US civil rights leader. After earning a law degree from Harvard University (1960), he became a field secretary for the **NAACP**, and in 1970 director of the United Negro College Fund. He was President of the **National Urban League** (1972–81), and became an influential voice in politics for black concerns.

Joørgensen, Anker (1922–) Danish politician. He worked his way up through the organizations of the Danish labour movement and has been a member of the Danish parliament (**Folketinget**) since 1964. From 1973 to 1987 he was leader of Denmark's **Social Democratic Party** and was Prime Minister in 1972–3 and again in 1975–82. Since 1982 he has been chairman of the Danish delegation in the Nordic Council.

Josel von Rosheim (c.1478–1554) Leader of the German Jewish community under Emperors **Maximilian I** and **Charles V**. He used his political skills and contacts at court to protect the Jews from persecution through his efforts as a *shtadlan* (advocate).

Joseph II (1741–90) Holy Roman Emperor (1765/90). The son of Emperor **Francis I** and **Maria Theresa**, until his mother's death (1780) he was co-regent, and his power was limited to the command of the army and the direction of foreign affairs. A sincere enlightened despot, he was known as 'the revolutionary emperor' for his programme of modernization. He was determined to assert Habsburg leadership, but some of his ambitious plans were thwarted variously by the diplomatic obstruction of France, Prussia, the United Provinces, and Britain, by war (with Prussia in 1778–9 and Turkey in 1788) and by insurrection (in the Netherlands in 1787, Hungary 1789, and the Tyrol 1790). ▷ **Habsburg Dynasty**

Joseph, Chief (c.1840–1904) Leader of the Nez Percé Native Americans, born in the Wallowa Valley of Oregon. The Nez Percé had agreed to settlement on a reservation, but when whites overran their territory and the government wanted to claim even more land, they resisted. Chief Joseph opposed any conflict, but helped lead his people on a gruelling fighting retreat from US troops through approximately 1 500 miles of wilderness. They were finally overwhelmed and forced to surrender close to the Canadian border. Chief Joseph died on a reservation in Washington State.

Joseph, Père (François Joseph le Clerc du Tremblay) (1577–1638) French diplomat and mystic. He became a Capuchin in 1599, and Cardinal **Richelieu**'s secretary in 1611. His byname, *L'Eminence Grise* (or 'Grey Eminence') derives from his contact with Richelieu (the 'Red Eminence'), for whom he went on several important diplomatic missions, especially during the **Thirty Years War**.

Josephine (*née*) **Marie Josèphe Rose Tascher de la Pagerie**) (1763–1814) First wife of Napoleon Bonaparte, and French Empress. In 1779 she married Alexandre, Viscount of **Beauharnais**, who was executed during the **French Revolution** (1794). She married Napoleon in 1796, and accompanied him on his Italian campaign, but soon returned to Paris. At Malmaison, and afterwards at the Luxembourg and the Tuileries, she attracted round her the most brilliant society of France. The marriage, being childless, was dissolved in 1809. She retained the title of Empress. ▷ **Napoleon I**

Josephinism The series of policies and reforms which Emperor Joseph II tried to introduce after the death of his mother, **Maria Theresa**, in 1780. He attempted to reform the Imperial structure, control the clergy (by severing all effective ties with Rome), introduce conscription and remove burdens on the peasants. Revolts in Tyrol and the Netherlands and a threatened uprising in Hungary forced him to reverse the entire reform programme.

Joubert, Petrus Jacobus (Piet) (1834–1900) Boer soldier and politician. Born in Cango, Cape Colony, he fought against the British in the Transvaal (1880–1), and became Vice-President under **Kruger** (1883). He organized the first Boer successes of Boer War (1899–1902), but died in Pretoria after a short illness. ▷ **Boer Wars**

Jouhaux, Léon (1879–1954) French trade-union leader. He became General-Secretary of the CGT (*Confédération générale du travail*, 'General Confederation of Labour') in 1909, remaining until 1947. Originally an advocate of revolutionary syndicalism, he soon adopted a more moderate position, supporting the French government during **World War I**, and rejecting **communism** in 1920. Nevertheless, he supported the reunification of the trade union movement in 1936, which rapidly led to commmunist domination of the CGT under his ineffective presidency. In Dec 1947 this led to his resignation from the CGT, and to his becoming President of the anti-communist trade-union federation (CGT-FO).

Jovellanos, Gaspar Melchor de (1744–1811) Asturian politician, historian and writer. One of the leading figures of the Spanish Enlightenment, he trained as a lawyer and entered the bureaucracy. In 1797 he was appointed Secretary of Justice, but was subsequently sacked by Manuel de **Godoy**. He is best known for his writings on the themes of justice, the rights of the crown against the Church and the **Inquisition**, reform of the universities, and economic liberalism. His most famous report, on the *Agrarian Law* (1795), proposed reforms in agriculture. He was imprisoned in 1801 by Godoy, but freed in 1808. After his release he withdrew to **Asturias** but refused to join the reforming **afrancesados** who supported José Bonaparte.

Jovian (c.331–364) Roman Emperor (363/4). He was appointed by the army in Mesopotamia on **Julian**'s death in battle. Jovian was immediately forced to make a humiliating peace with Shapur II, ceding great tracts of Roman territory to Sassanian Persia, and agreeing to pay her a subsidy.

Joyce, William ('Lord Haw-Haw') (1906–46) British traitor. As a child, he lived in Ireland and in 1922 his family emigrated to England. In 1937, he founded the fanatical British National Socialist Party, and fled to Germany before war broke out. Throughout **World War II**, he broadcast from Radio Hamburg propaganda against Britain, gaining his byname from his upper-class drawl. He was captured by the British at Flensburg, and was tried and executed in London.

Joyeuse Entrée (*Blijde Inkomst*) A processional entry into a town in the later Middle Ages to celebrate the accession or marriage of a ruler, especially in the Low Countries. Reminiscent of the Roman triumphal entries, they involved ceremonial arches, plays, and decorated floats. One *Joyeuse Entrée* in particular is remembered as the quasi-constitution of the Duchy of **Brabant**. It was granted on 3 Jan 1356 by Johanna of Brabant and Wenzel of Luxembourg and allowed the Brabantines some say in their own government. The document was used in the protests and revolts against the Spanish King **Philip II** (the **Eighty Years War**) and the Austrian Emperor **Joseph II** (**Brabant Revolution**), and also in drawing up the Belgian constitution of 1831.

Juana the Mad (1479–1555) Countess of Flanders and Queen of Castile (1505/55) and Aragon (1516/55). The daughter of **Ferdinand II**, 'the Catholic' and **Isabella I**, 'the Catholic', she became the wife of **Philip I**, 'the Handsome', of Flanders in 1495. The couple settled in Ghent and had several children, of whom the eldest was the future Emperor **Charles V**. On her mother's death (1505), she became Queen of Castile and she and Philip moved to Spain in 1506. Philip died the same year and Juana, who suffered from severe melancholia, was declared unfit to govern and was shut away under close watch in Tordesillas, while her father assumed the government of Castile (1510). Although Ferdinand died in 1516, her son, Charles, now King of Spain, did not release her and Juana remained incarcerated, along with her youngest daughter, Catalina, until her death.

Juan Carlos I (1938–) King of Spain (1975/). The son of Don Juan de Borbón y Battenberg, Count of Barcelona, and the grandson of Spain's last ruling monarch, **Alfonso XIII**, he was educated in Switzerland, and from 1948, by agreement between his father and General **Franco**, in Spain. He earned commissions in the army, navy, and air force, and studied at the University of Madrid before marrying (1962) Princess Sophia of Greece. In 1969 Franco named him as his eventual successor, and he was proclaimed King on Franco's death in 1975. Instead of upholding the Franco dictatorship (as had been intended), he decisively presided over Spain's democratization, helping to defeat a military coup (1981) and assuming the role of a constitutional monarch.

Juan José of Austria (1629–79) Spanish politician and soldier. The natural son of **Philip IV** of Spain and the actress Maria Calderón, he served as Viceroy of Naples from 1648 to 1651. After suppressing the revolt there, in 1650 he commanded the armies in Catalonia and received the surrender of Barcelona (1652). He was Viceroy of Catalonia (1652–6), of the Netherlands (1656–9) and commander of forces fighting Portugal (1661–4). On the accession of **Charles II** of Spain, he was involved in power struggles to control the government, against the King's mother, the Regent Mariana, and her confessor, Father Nithard. He eventually succeeded in obtaining power in 1676, as Chief Minister, but died suddenly three years later. A man of culture and vision, he patronized new trends in scientific thought.

Juárez, Benito (Pablo) (1806–72) Mexican national hero and politician. A Zapotec Indian, he was a clerk and lawyer and then Governor of Oaxaca (1847–52). Exiled by conservatives under **Santa Anna** (1853–5), he then returned to join the new Liberal government. Proposing fundamental change, he abolished the fueros, seized control of Church lands, and passed the anticlerical and liberal constitution of 1857. During the civil war of 1857–60, he assumed the presidency, upholding a free Church in a free state. He was elected President on the Liberal victory (1861), a post he held until his death. The French invasion under **Maximilian** forced him to the far north, from where he directed resistance until Maximilian's defeat in 1867. He then restored republican rule, creating the basis for the regime of Porfírio **Díaz**.

Jubogha, Jubo ▷ Ja Ja of Opobo

Judah, Kingdom of An ancient Jewish state which incorporated the tribal areas of Judah and Benjamin, established when the united monarchy split into the Kingdoms of Judah (in the south) and Israel (in the north) in the late 10c BC after the reign of Solomon. Each kingdom had separate kings, with Jerusalem being in the Kingdom of Judah. Both Judah and Jerusalem fell to the Babylonians in 587BC.

Jugnauth, Sir Aneerood (1930–) Mauritian politician. After qualifying as a barrister in London (1954), he returned to Mauritius and was elected to the Legco in 1963. In 1970 he helped found the socialist Mauritius Militant Movement, but broke from it to form his own Mauritius Socialist Party. He became Prime Minister (June 1982) in a coalition government, altered the name of his party to Mauritius Socialist Movement and retained leadership of the coalition after elections in 1983 and 1984.

Jugurtha (c.160–104BC) King of Numidia (118/105BC), after whom the Jugurthine War (112–104BC) is named. Rome's difficulty in defeating him provided Gaius **Marius** with a launching pad for his career, and led to important reforms in the Roman Army. Jugurtha's surrender to Marius' deputy, **Sulla**, ended the war, but was the starting point of the deadly feud between Marius and Sulla, which plunged Rome into civil war 20 years later.

Juin, Alphonse Pierre (1888–1967) French soldier. He passed out top of his class, which included Charles de **Gaulle**, at the Saint-Cyr military academy, fought in **World War I**; as divisional commander in the 1st French Army he was captured by the Germans in 1940, but was later released (June 1941). He became Military Governor of Morocco. After the Allied invasion of Tunisia, he changed sides, helped to defeat von Arnim's Afrika Corps remnants and distinguished himself in the subsequent Italian campaign. He was resident-general in Morocco (1947–51) and served in senior **NATO** commands. He broke with de Gaulle in 1960 over his Algerian policy, and retired. ▷ **World War II**

Julian (Flavius Claudius Julianus) (332–63) Roman Emperor (361/3). The son of a half-brother of **Constantine I, 'the Great'**, he was appointed Deputy Emperor (Caesar) in the West by his cousin, Constantius II, in 355. He served with great distinction on the Rhine, and was proclaimed emperor (Augustus) by his adoring troops in 360. As emperor, he publicly proclaimed himself a pagan (hence his nickname) and initiated a vigorous policy of reviving the old pagan cults, though without persecuting Christians. He was killed in battle against the Sassanid Persians.

Juliana (Louise Emma Marie Wilhelmina) (1909–) Queen of the Netherlands (1948/80). The daughter of Queen **Wilhelmina** and Prince Hendrik, she was educated at Leiden University and became a lawyer. In 1937 she married Prince **Bernhard Leopold**; they have four daughters. On the German invasion of Holland (1940), Juliana escaped to Britain and later resided in Canada. She returned to Holland in 1945, and became Queen on the abdication of her mother in 1948. In 1980 she herself abdicated in favour of her eldest daughter, **Beatrix**, and once more took the title of Princess.

Jülich–Cleves Succession Conflict A dispute over rival claims to the duchy upon the death, without issue, of Duke John William in 1609. The duchy was claimed by Philip Louis, Count Palatine of Neuburg, John Sigismund, Elector of Brandenburg, and the Elector of Saxony, among others. The assassination of **Henry IV** of France and the death of the leader of the Evangelical Union, Frederick IV, prevented a war. France and the Union supported Philip and John, while the Holy Roman Emperor **Rudolf II** and the **Catholic League** supported the Saxon Duke. The Treaty of Xanten (1614) averted another war by awarding Jülich and Berg to John, while Philip's successor, Wolfgang William, a convert to Catholicism, received the rest. Later (late 18c) another crisis arose when the extinction of the Neuburg line allowed **Frederick William I** of Prussia to claim (after agreeing to the **Pragmatic Sanction**) the duchy. Prussia abandoned its claim in 1742 and the duchy passed to Sulzbach, thence to Bavaria (1799).

Julio-Claudian Dynasty (c.27BC–AD68) The first dynasty to rule the **Roman Empire** after the collapse of the Republic. The name is a modern, not a Roman, one and reflects the fact that the first five emperors (**Augustus**, **Tiberius**, **Caligula**, **Claudius** and **Nero**) each belonged either to the Julian *gens* (the family of Julius **Caesar**) or to the Claudian, the two families having been brought together in 38BC by the marriage of Augustus (a Julian) to **Livia**, the recently divorced wife of a member of the Claudian family (Tiberius Claudius Nero). The subsequent members of the dynasty were either children of these two by their previous marriages or descendants of those children, Augustus and Livia's own long union being without issue. ▷ **Roman Republic**

Julius II (1443–1513) Italian Pope (1503/13). His public career was mainly devoted to re-establishing papal sovereignty in its ancient territory, and removing foreign domination in Italy. His participation in the League of Cambrai (1509) restored the **Papal States**, but the **Holy League** (1510) with Spain and England against **Louis XII** of France was less successful. A liberal patron of the arts, he employed Bramante for the design of St Peter's, begun in 1506, and commissioned works from Raphael and Michelangelo.

Julius III (1487–1555) Italian Pope (1550/5). He was one of the three delegates to the Council of **Trent**, which he reopened after his election. He sent Cardinal Reginald **Pole** to organize with **Mary I** the reunion of England with the Church of Rome.

July Days (16–20 July 1917) Largely spontaneous anti-government demonstrations in Petrograd in Russia, marking growing popular dissatisfaction with the Provisional Government's record since the beginning of the Revolution. Demonstrators demanded that Russia withdraw from **World War I**, the actual overthrow of the Provisional Government, and the transfer of 'All power to the soviets'. **Lenin** initially opposed the demonstrations, judging the time for a proletarian–socialist revolution to be premature, but he eventually gave half-hearted support. Despite several hundred deaths, nothing was achieved except a slight swing to the Right within the Provisional Government. Lenin was more convinced than ever of the need for a highly-organized revolutionary party and carefully-directed revolution of the kind he had advocated since first establishing the **Bolsheviks**. ▷ **April Theses; February Revolution** (Russia); **October Revolution**

July Revolution (1830) A three-day revolt in Paris which ended the Bourbon Restoration, forcing the abdication of the reactionary **Charles X**. It resulted in the establishment of a more liberal regime dominated by the wealthy bourgeoisie, the so-called 'July Monarchy', under the Orléanist, **Louis-Philippe**, 'King of the French'. ▷ **Bourbon, House of**

Jumblatt, Kemal (1919–77) Lebanese politician and hereditary Druze chieftain. He founded the Progressive Socialist Party in 1949, held several Cabinet posts (1961–4) and was Minister of the Interior (1969–70). The Syrian intervention on the side of the Christians in 1976 was a response to the increasing power of his authority in partnership with the Palestinians. He was assassinated in an ambush outside the village of Baaklu in the Chouf Mountains. His son Walid became leader of the Druze after his death.

June Days (1848) A violent episode in the French **February Revolution** (1848), when working-class radicals resisted the dissolution of the **National Workshops** in Paris. They were crushed by the **National Guard** and troops of the republican government under the direction of General Louis Eugène **Cavaignac**, thus exacerbating class divisions in France for generations.

Jung Bahadur (1816–77) Nepali politician. He was Prime Minister and virtual ruler of Nepal from 1846 to 1877. He visited Britain in 1850–1 and his closeness to that country was exemplified by his assistance in providing the British with a body of Gurkhas during the **Indian Uprising** of 1857–8; this led to the tradition of Gurkha military service in the British army. Jung Bahadur was the founder of the Rana Dynasty, which provided a line of prime ministers for the country until 1951, when the last hereditary prime minister, Mohun, retired.

Junín, Battle of (1824) A major cavalry battle of the **Spanish-American Wars of Independence**, fought at nearly 4300 metres in the Peruvian Andes. It was the last major victory of Simón **Bolívar**.

Junker Prussian aristocrats whose power rested on their large estates, situated predominantly to the east of the River Elbe, and on their traditional role as army officers and civil servants. Their position came increasingly under threat in late 19c Germany as a result of industrialization, but they jealously safeguarded their privileges and power. The loss of lands east of the Rivers Oder and Neisse in 1945 and the confiscation of their estates in East Germany destroyed their basis. ▷ **Germany, East; Prussia**

junta An administrative council, especially in Italy and Spain. The term is now commonly applied to a military leadership who have taken control of a country, particularly in Latin America.

juros In Spain, annuities paid out of state income for loans to the crown. The practice was begun systematically by **Ferdinand II, 'the Catholic'** and **Isabella I, 'the Catholic'** as a means of raising funds for the wars against Granada, and assumed overwhelming importance in the 16c and 17c, when the crown had to borrow to cover its commitments. The loans yielded interest of about seven per cent in the 16c, which made them attractive to all investors as a form of national debt. Repayment consumed in 1556 some 68 per cent of normal state revenue, and in 1565 some 84 per cent; by the 17c, their repayments exceeded available revenue. The system continued until the mid-19c.

justicialismo This was the populist doctrine, lying midway between capitalism and **communism**, espoused by the followers of Juan Domingo **Perón** between 1946 and 1970. It was a combination of creole nationalism, support for the *descamisados* ('shirtless masses'), and the massive extension of state power into every aspect of Argentine social and economic life. It also entailed government controls over employment and social security provision. Industrial and trading corporations were designed to maintain the descamisados as passive support to Perón, while destroying opposition groups, whether the Church, British investors or trade unions. After he was ousted in 1955, *justicialismo* became the official doctrine of the Peronists. ▷ **Peronism**

Justinian I, 'the Great' (c.482–565) Roman Emperor (527/65). He was the protégé of his uncle, the Byzantine Emperor Justin (518/27), and was at first Co-Emperor with him. On Justin's death, he became sole ruler. Along with his wife, Theodora, Justinian presided over the most brilliant period in the history of the late Roman Empire. Through his generals, **Belisarius** and **Narses**, he recovered North Africa, Spain, and Italy, and carried out a major codification of the Roman law. ▷ **Byzantine Empire; Justinian Code**

Justinian Code The emperor Justinian's codification of Roman law, carried out under the direction of Tribonian and published in four sections between 529 and 565. Also known as the *Corpus Juris Civilis*, it is regarded as the pinnacle of Roman law.

Jutes A Germanic people whose original homeland was the northern part of the Danish peninsula (Jutland). The tradition preserved by Bede, that Jutes participated in the 5c Germanic invasions of Britain and settled in Kent and the Isle of Wight, is confirmed by archaeological evidence. ▷ **Anglo-Saxons**

Jutland, Battle of (31 May–1 June 1916) A sea battle of **World War I** (and the first major challenge to British naval supremacy since the Battle of **Trafalgar** in 1805), in which Admiral **Jellicoe** led the British Grand Fleet from Scapa Flow and intercepted the German High Seas Fleet of the west coast of Jutland, Denmark. Though the battle itself was inconclusive, German naval chiefs withdrew their fleet to port, and turned to unrestricted submarine warfare as a means of challenging British command of the sea.

JVP (*Janata Vimukti Peramuna*, 'People's Liberation Front') Left-wing Sri Lankan political group, founded in the late 1960s by Rohan Wijeweera and other left-wing activists from the small group of Sri Lankan Maoists. In 1971 Wijeweera was detained just before the JVP launched an insurrection against the government of Sirimavo **Bandaranaike**. After a brief period of legality in the late 1970s, the party was again proscribed after the 1983 anti-Tamil riots, but it re-emerged to lead the opposition to the 1987 **Indo-Sri Lankan Peace Accord**. Between 1987 and 1989 a huge number of people died in the JVP's clash with the government's security forces, which eventually ended with the capture and killing of Wijeweera.

K

Kabaka Yekka Literally 'the King Alone', this was a neo-traditionalist movement in Buganda organized round allegiance to, and support of, the *Kabaka* (or 'King') of Buganda in the 1960s. It disintegrated when the Kabaka was forced into exile in 1966.

Kabir (1440–1518) Indian mystic and poet. He tried to unite Hindu and Muslim thought and preached the essential unity of all religions and was a forerunner of Sikhism, which was established by his disciple, Nanak. Kabir was brought up by a Muslim weaver and later influenced by a Hindu ascetic, Ramananda. He took the best tenets of both Hinduism and Islam and preached his own religion called *sahaja-yoga* ('simple union'): from Hinduism, he took the ideas of transmigration and the law of karma, but rejected idolatry, asceticism and **caste**; from Islam, he accepted the idea of one God and the equality of all men before God.

Kabra Bassa A major dam and hydroelectric plant in Mozambique. Kabra Bassa was a set of cataracts on the Zambezi just above the town of Tete which were seen by David Livingstone on his second African journey between 1858 and 1863. In the late 1960s, the Portuguese rulers of Mozambique embarked upon the building of a dam, funded by foreign investment, which would supply electricity to South Africa and create a vast lake which would provide irrigation for new areas of white settlement in the Zambezi Valley. **Frelimo** saw it as a symbol of continuing white domination and from 1968 began a campaign to sabotage it. They failed, but pinned down Portuguese troops in its defence. South African military and air forces were also involved.

Kabyle A Berber people of Algeria. Organized into different castes with serfs, they speak Kabyle, a Hamito-Semitic language, and are predominantly Muslims. They live in villages, grow grains and olives, and herd goats. Population c.2 million.

Kadalie, Clements (c.1895–1951) Nyasaland (Malawian) trade union leader. A migrant, he founded in 1919 the Industrial and Commercial Workers' Union of South Africa, the first large-scale trade union for black people. Kadalie started the union in the Cape, where he led a series of dock strikes. By 1923, it had become a mass movement reaching a peak of membership of 86 000 in 1928. However, it declined rapidly from 1929 onwards and was defunct by 1933, failing because Kadalie led it into political action, split it into moderate and radical factions, expelled the Communists and forced the creation of a separate organization in Natal. It never secured a large membership among the workforce of the Rand gold mines and failed to gain international recognition.

Kádár, János (1912–89) Hungarian politician. He joined the illegal Communist Party in 1931, and was arrested several times. He became a member of its Central Committee (1942) and of the Politburo (1945). As Minister of the Interior from 1948 to 1951, he organized the trial of László **Rajk**, but he was arrested and imprisoned for his anti-Stalinist views (1951–4). When the anti-Soviet **Hungarian Uprising** broke out in 1956, he was a member of the 'national' government of Imre **Nagy**, but he then formed a puppet government which invited measured Soviet intervention and helped to suppress the uprising. He resigned in 1958, becoming Prime Minister again in 1961. His long reign as Party Secretary ended in 1988, and during that time he did manage to introduce elements of reform into the Hungarian economy. However, by the mid-1980s he had become comparatively conservative, and reform petered out, to the immediate advantage of Hungarian **communism**. ▷ **Stalin, Joseph**

Kadets (1905–18) The short name for the Russian Constitutional Democratic Party that was established in the Russian **Revolution of 1905** to represent liberal non-Marxist interests. The main plank in their programme was their demand for a constituent assembly completely to reform Russia's political structure. This was unacceptable to **Nicholas II**; and even though they were the largest group in the first **Duma**, their numbers dropped in the succeeding three, which were in any case powerless assemblies. Eventually in 1917 they participated in the **Russian Provisional**

Government, with Pavel **Miliukov** as Foreign Minister, but they were already falling behind popular cries for change. When the **Russian Constituent Assembly** was finally elected in Nov, they had a mere 15 out of 703 representatives. When it was disbanded in Jan 1918, they were declared illegal.

Kaganovich, Lazar Moiseyevich (1893–1991) Soviet politician. He joined the Communist Party in 1911 and, after participating actively in the 1917 **Russian Revolution**, became First Secretary of the Ukrainian Party in 1925. In 1928 he moved to the secretariat of the All-Union Party and in 1930 became a full member of the **Politburo**, as well as serving for five years as First Secretary of the Moscow Party. He played a prominent role in the brutal, forced collectivization programme in the early 1930s, and in the great purges of 1936–8. He also served as Commissar for Railways and was responsible for building the Moscow metro. A close ally of **Stalin**, he survived the latter's death in 1953 but, having fallen foul of Nikita **Khrushchev** and participated in the **Anti-Party Plot**, was dismissed in 1957, being posted to a managerial position in a Siberian cement works. He retired into obscurity in Moscow, to die just as the USSR was about to collapse.

Kagawa Toyohiko (1888–1960) Japanese social reformer and evangelist. A convert to Christianity, he was educated at the Presbyterian College in Tokyo, and Princeton Theological Seminary in the USA. Returning to Japan, he became an evangelist and social worker in the slums of Kobe. He became a leader in the Japanese labour movement, helping to found the Federation of Labour (1918), Farmers' Union (1921), as well as establish agricultural collectives. In 1928 he founded the Anti-War League and after **World War II** was a leader in the women's suffrage movement, and helped with the process of democratization.

Kaiser The title assumed (Dec 1870) by the Prussian King, **William I**, following the unification of Germany and the creation of the German Empire. He was succeeded on his death in 1888 by his son **Frederick III**, who survived him by only three months, and then by his grandson **William II**, who ruled until his enforced abdication in 1918.

Kalashnikov, Mikhail Timofeevich (1919–) Soviet military designer. He invented the famous Soviet rifle also used extensively by foreign armies and international

terrorists. Born of peasant stock in the Altai area, he joined the army in 1938. Seriously wounded in 1941, he began experimenting with what was to be the AK 7.62 assault rifle taken into Soviet service in 1949. Other versions were produced later.

Kalimantan (Borneo) A huge island straddling the equator, directly east of Singapore. Historically, Kalimantan has had a very low population density. The interior is home to an extremely large number of diverse ethnic groups, including the Dayak and the Iban. During the colonial period, a major part of the island (the southern portion) came under Dutch rule. When the Netherlands Indies achieved independence (1949–50) that part was integrated into the unitary state of Indonesia. During the colonial period, the northern portion of the island came under British protection: it comprised Sarawak (under the Brooke family), Sabah (formerly British North Borneo) and Brunei. Sarawak and Sabah became independent in 1963, and entered the Malaysian federation, while Brunei remained a British protectorate until 1984, when it became an independent state.

Kalinga Ancient Indian kingdom in the modern eastern Indian state of Orissa. It was the sole conquest of **Ashoka**, the third Mauryan emperor c.261BC, but it regained its independence some time after his death (c.232BC). Ashoka, by now a Buddhist, declared that he was so appalled by the suffering caused by the Kalinga War that he resolved to give up warfare in favour of 'conquest by righteousness'. The greatest early ruler of Kalinga was Kharavela (probably mid- to late 1cBC) of the Chedi Dynasty, known to us from his mutilated Hathigumpha ('Elephant Cave') inscription in the Udayagiri Hill near Bhubaneswar (close to the site of the Ashokan inscription at Dhauli).

Kalinin, Mikhail Ivanovich (1875–1946) Soviet politician. He was the formal head of state after the 1917 Revolution and during the years of **Stalin**'s dictatorship (1919–46). A peasant and metal-worker, he entered politics as a champion of the peasant class, and won great popularity. He became President of the Soviet Central Executive Committee (1919–38), and of the Presidium of the Supreme Soviet (1938–46). A member of the **Politburo** from 1926 onwards, he was an influential figure; but he was sufficiently pliable to survive the purges in the late 1930s and to die a natural death.

Kallay, Miklos (1887–1976) Hungarian politician. A big landowner, he became lord lieutenant of Szabolcs county. To the right in politics, he was Minister of Agriculture from 1932 to 1935. During **World War II** he served as Prime Minister (Mar 1942–Mar 1944). Initially he cooperated with Germany but after the Battle of **Stalingrad** he tried to make a separate settlement with the Allies, only to be imprisoned in Nov 1944 in Mauxhaussen concentration camp. He subsequently settled in the USA.

Kalmar Union The dynastic union of Denmark, Norway and Sweden achieved at Kalmar in Sweden in 1397, when **Erik of Pomerania** was crowned king of all three kingdoms. It came about partly as a result of previous dynastic marriages, partly to satisfy the interests of nobles with landed property in more than one country, but principally to present a more united front against the threat of dominance by the German Hanseatic League. Many Swedish nobles came to resent what they saw as infringements on their rights by a king residing in Copenhagen and, on several occasions in the course of the 15c, broke away from the Union under their own head of state, until finally under **Gustav I Vasa** Sweden withdrew from the Union altogether (1523). Norway, however, with a much weaker nobility, remained united with Denmark until 1814. ▷ **Karl Knutsson; Sture, Sten, 'the Elder'**

Kalmuks Western Mongols (also known as Eleuthes or **Dzungars**) who were conquered by the Manchu **Qing Dynasty** in the 1750s. Their homeland (Chinese Turkestan) was incorporated into the Qing Empire in 1759 with its modern name of Xinjiang (Sinkiang), now a Chinese province.

Kalonga (mid-17–18c) The dynastic title of the paramount chiefs of the Maravi kingdoms of central southern Africa. *Kalonga* Muzura in the mid-17c allied himself with the Portuguese. A formidable warrior, he was able to subjugate the lesser kingdoms of the area but, by the beginning of the 18c, the empire was collapsing from fragmentation amongst the ruling group and from competition from the subject-peoples, particularly the Chewa kingdom whose rulers, the Undi replaced the *Kalonga* as the dominant political authority in the area during the 18c.

Kamakura Shogunate (1192–1333) Japan's first warrior government, established by Minamoto no Yoritomo (1147/99). In 1192

KAMAKURA SHOGUNATE

Regnal Dates	Name
1192/9	Minamoto Yoritomo
1202/3	Minamoto Yoriie
1203/19	Minamoto Sanetomo
1226/44	Fujiwara Yoritsune
1244/52	Fujiwara Yoritsugu
1252/66	Munetaka Shinno
1266/89	Koreyasu Shinno
1289/1308	Hisaaki Shinno
1308/33	Morikuni Shinno

the Emperor, recognizing his paramount position, bestowed on Minamoto the title of **shogun** (military generalissimo), although Minamoto had already in 1180 established a military government (*bakufu*) in Kamakura (south of Tokyo). Minamoto used his power to appoint military governors and estate stewards, principally in the eastern part of the country. There were altogether nine Kamakura shoguns, although from the 13c onwards effective power was in the hands of members of the **Hojo Family**, who occupied the hereditary post of regent. The Kamakura shogunate was overthrown in 1333 by **Ashikaga Takauji**. ▷ **Ashikaga Shogunate**

Kambujiya ▷ **Cambyses II**

Kamenev, Lev Borisovich (1883–1936) Soviet politician. He was an active revolutionary throughout Russia and abroad from 1901 onwards, associating with **Lenin**, **Trotsky** and **Stalin**, and was exiled to Siberia in 1915. Liberated after the **February Revolution**, he was active as a Bolshevik throughout 1917, became the first Chairman of the Central Executive Committee of the All Russian Congress of Soviets and subsequently held various Party, government and diplomatic appointments. Expelled from the Party as a Trotskyist in 1927, he was readmitted the next year but again expelled in 1932. The same happened in 1933–4. He was finally executed for allegedly conspiring against **Stalin**. Like many others falsely accused, he was rehabilitated in 1988 during the **Gorbachev** years.

kamikaze A Japanese term (literally, 'divine wind') identifying the volunteer suicide pilots of the Japanese Imperial Navy, who guided their explosive-packed aircraft onto enemy ships in **World War II**. They emerged in the last year of the Pacific War, when Allied forces were closing on the Japanese homeland.

Kanaris, Constantine (1790–1877) Greek admiral and politician. He was one of several merchant-captains who provided their own ships for service in the struggle for Greek independence. He used fireships to blow up the Turkish flagship in the Strait of Chios (1822), repeated the feat in the harbour of Tenedos, and in 1824 burnt a Turkish frigate and some transport ships. He held high commands, and was made a senator in 1847. He was Prime Minister of Greece on three occasions between 1848 and 1877, and took part in the revolution that put **George I** on the throne in 1863.

Kanauj An ancient city in the state of Uttar Pradesh in India, Kanauj rose after the Gupta period during **Harsha**'s time and was the capital of the kingdom of the Gurjara **Pratiharas** c.AD1000 in north India. It was taken by Mahmud of Ghazni c.1018. A later Gahrwal ruler, Jayachandra, is initially said to have been allied to **Muhammad Ghuri** whose forces, led by **Qutb-ud-Din Aibak**, later destroyed Kanauj in 1193. Kanauj became part of the kingdom of Jaunpur and later became part of the Lodi kingdom. In 1540, Sher Shah defeated **Humayun** at Kanauj, and built a fort there. After his death, Kanauj was taken by the Mughals.

Kandyan Kingdom The last independent kingdom in Sri Lanka. It was based in the city of Kandy in the mountainous interior of the country and was founded in the late 15c/early 16c, after the demise of the great classical kingdoms of **Anuradhapura** and Polonnaruwa, and as their successors in the southwest of the country were threatened by the Portuguese. For most of its existence, the kingdom had to deal with a hostile European presence in the lowlands, first the Portuguese, then the Dutch, and finally the British, who captured the kingdom in 1815 with the assistance of a conspiracy against the king by the leading aristocratic famililes.

Kanem West African kingdom situated to the north-east of Lake Chad under the Sefuwa Dynasty, which survived from the 10c to the 19c. The strength of Kanem was based on its position between the forest and the desert and its ability to trade salt and copper from the north with forest goods and cottons from the south. Kanem's power was replaced by that of Bornu in the 15c.

K'ang-hsi ▷ **Kangxi**

Kanghwa, Treaty of (27 Feb 1876) Korea's first treaty with a foreign power (Japan), signed after considerable pressure from the new Meiji government in Tokyo. Following the **Meiji Restoration** (1868), the Japanese government sent envoys to the Korean court to seek diplomatic relations and bilateral trade. With the Korean court dominated (until 1873) by the xenophobic regent, **Taewon'gun**, Japan's requests were rejected. When three Japanese gunboats were fired upon off the coast of Kanghwa island (near the Korean capital of Seoul) in 1875, Japan used this as a pretext to demand a commercial treaty, a demand backed up by the sending of an armed naval force to Korea. The resulting treaty established formal diplomatic relations between the two countries and opened three ports for trade in which Japanese consuls were stationed. The treaty was to encourage the Western powers to seek similar concessions, beginning a process of ending Korea's traditional isolation and its long-established dependence on China as its vassal state.

Kang Sheng (1899–1975) Chinese politician. He studied Soviet security and intelligence techniques in Moscow during the early 1930s. He was a prominent member of the Chinese Communist Party during the 1960s, and exercised considerable behind-the-scenes influence in his capacity as Head of Party Security. During the **Cultural Revolution** he was associated with the radical left group led by **Mao Zedong**'s wife, **Jiang Qing**. Since Mao's death in 1976, Kang's role in the persecution of party members and intellectuals during the Cultural Revolution has been condemned.

KaNgwane A national state or nonindependent Black homeland in Natal province, South Africa, it gained self-governing status in 1971. It ceased to exist in May 1994 after the first all-race elections in South Africa.

Kangxi (K'ang-hsi) (1661/1722) Emperor of China. The third son of the first Manchu Qing Emperor, he presided over the consolidation of Manchu rule in China. He suppressed the Rebellion of the **Three Feudatories** in the south and captured Taiwan from Ming loyalist forces in 1682. He patronized Confucian learning and promoted himself as the ideal Confucian monarch, touring the country extensively. His secret palace memorial system, allowing certain provincial officials to report directly to him on confidential matters without going through official nels at the capital, allowed Kangxi to exercise personal supervision over the bureaucracy. The last years of his reign were marked by factional struggles over the succession. His fourth son, Yongzheng (1722/36), eventually succeeded. ▷ **Qing Dynasty**

Kang Youwei (K'ang Yu-wei) (1858–1927) Chinese reformer. Leader of the **Hundred Days of Reform** in China (1898). In 1895 he organized thousands of young scholars to demand drastic national reforms. The young Emperor **Zai Tian** summoned him to implement reforms as the first step to creating a constitutional monarchy, but the movement was ended when **Cixi** seized the Emperor, executed six of the young reformers, and punished all who had supported them. Kang and his disciple, **Liang Qichao**, escaped to Japan with foreign help. He returned to China in 1914, and died at Tsingtao, Shandong.

K'ang Yu-wei ▷ **Kang Youwei**

Kanishka (c.78/c.101) Third and most important of the Kushana rulers of northwest India and Afghanistan. During his reign control of the Silk Route between China and the Roman Empire brought great prosperity to the kingdom (manifested in Kushana patronage of the Gandhara and Mathura schools of art). Traditionally he is regarded as a great patron of Buddhism and is linked with the rise of Mahayana Buddhism (which did indeed spread along the trade routes into Central Asia and China).

Kanpur, Massacre of (1857) The native cavalry of the garrison of Kanpur (Cawnpore), based in Uttar Pradesh in northern India, rebelled against their British masters on 4 June 1857 and the garrison, led by Sir Hugh Wheeler, was besieged for three weeks. On 27 June, members of the garrison were offered a safe passage to Allahabad on thatched barges. However, as they were leaving, the barges came under gunfire and were set ablaze. The survivors, including women and children, were later transferred to a small house called the Bibighar where they were killed on 15 July by the Nana Sahib's men.

Kansas–Nebraska Act (1854) A bill passed by the US Congress in 1854 to establish the territories of Kansas and Nebraska. Because it opened up the possibility of extending slavery into western territories, by allowing popular sovereignty, it led to bitter debates.

The ensuing protests contributed to the formation of the **Republican Party**, which was hostile to the expansion of slavery.

KANU (Kenyan African National Union) The party which led Kenya to independence in 1963. It was founded in 1960 as a successor to the Kikuyu Central Association of 1929 and the Kenya African Union of 1947. The Kenya African Democratic Union (KADU) was a rival body which represented mainly non-Kikuyu groups. KANU won the first Kenyan election, with President Kenyatta becoming the leader of independent Kenya, although he tried to bring KADU into a coalition.

Kao Kang ▷ **Gao Gang**

Kapodistrias, Ioannis (1776–1831) Greek national leader. An Ionian nobleman born on Corfu, he entered the service of Tsar **Alexander I** and from 1816 was joint Foreign Minister of Russia. In 1828 he became President of the new Greek state. Authoritarian and paternalistic, he attempted to create a national army, administrative bureaucracy and education system. He tried to revive the economy, which had been wrecked by the **Greek War of Independence**, but his plan to create a stable landowning peasantry was frustrated by powerful clan leaders. In 1831, in the course of a feud, he was assassinated at Nafplion by members of a local clan seeking revenge.

Kapp Putsch (Mar 1920) An unsuccessful coup by some **Freikorps** units against the **SPD**-dominated German government led by extreme right-wing politicians and a small number of army commanders. Scheduled reductions in the size of Germany's armed forces under the terms of the Treaty of **Versailles** led one of the affected commanders, von Lüttwitz, to order forces loyal to him to seize **Berlin** and force a change in policy. The government fled rather than comply, leading to the creation of a rebel government under Wolfgang Kapp, a civil servant, which lasted three days. He was toppled by a general strike organized by the **ADGB** and by passive resistance from the Civil Service and the national bank. Significant was the failure of the army to oppose the coup, even if it did not actively support it.

Kapwepwe, Simon (1922–89) Zambian nationalist leader and politician. Educated in mission schools before becoming a teacher, he helped found the Northern Rhodesian

African National Congress in 1946. After a period of study in India, he returned to be Treasurer and then helped form the breakaway United National Independence Party (**UNIP**) of which he became Treasurer 1960–7. After holding several ministerial posts in the early days of independence, including the vice-presidency, he resigned from UNIP to form his own party, the United Progress Party, in 1971 in order to oppose Kenneth **Kaunda**. The party was banned in 1972, when Zambia became a one-party state and Kapwepwe was detained. He rejoined UNIP in 1977.

Karadžić, Vuk Stefanović (1787–1864) Leader of the Serb national revival. Born in a remote village in western Serbia, he is said to have been taught to write with ink made from gunpowder and water. During the first Serbian Uprising (1804), he was secretary to a leader of the **hajduks**. The next year he studied briefly at Sremski Karlovci, then in southern Hungary. He returned to teach in Belgrade, but fled to Vienna when the Turks reoccupied the city and crushed the uprising of 1813. Influenced by the ideas of Herder and Kopitar, he was persuaded by Goethe to collect Serbian folk poetry and folklore. Among his many literary and scholarly achievements, he tried to create a standard Serbian orthography, grammar and dictionary based on the dialect used in Herzegovina, compiled a Serbian-German dictionary (1818) and translated the New Testament into Serbian (published 1869). ▷ **Kosovo, Battle of; Obradović, Dositej**

Karageorge (George Petrović) (c.1768–1817) Serbian national leader. The leader of the Serbian uprising in 1804, he was elected Governor of Serbia in 1808. After the Turks regained control of Serbia in 1813, he fled to Austria but was murdered on his return in 1817 with the connivance of his rival, Prince Miloš **Obrenović**. He was founder of the Karageorgević Dynasty. ▷ **Serbian Uprisings**

Karakhan Manifesto (25 July 1919) A declaration issued by the Soviet Assistant Foreign Commissar, Leo Karakhan, that renounced all former Tsarist rights and privileges in China. A similar declaration had been issued the year before by the Foreign Commissar, G V Chicherin. Although the Soviet government in 1920 insisted that such a declaration had not implied handing over the **Chinese Eastern Railway** without compensation (it remained, in fact, under Soviet control until 1935, when it was sold to Japan), the Karakhan Manifesto had a profound effect on young Chinese radicals, convincing them that the new Soviet state was the only foreign country willing to treat China as an equal.

Karamanlis, Constantine (1907–) Greek politician. A lawyer, he was elected to parliament in 1935, became Minister of Public Works (1952), then in 1955 succeeded Alexander **Papagos** as Prime Minister and reconstituted the right-wing Greek Rally as the National Radical Union. Confronting the Cyprus dispute and sensitive to US and **NATO** anxiety over the activities of **EOKA**, in 1959 he signed a treaty with the Greek and Turkish Cypriot communities whereby Cyprus would become an independent republic in the British **Commonwealth of Nations**. After his party's election defeat in 1963, he left politics and lived abroad. He returned to become Prime Minister again in 1974, when he supervised the restoration of civilian rule after the collapse of the Colonels' dictatorship (1967–74) led by Georgios **Papadopoulos**. He served as President from 1980 to 1985, and was re-elected in 1990.

Karami, Rashid (d.1987) Lebanese politician. The son of Abd al-Hamid Karami, he succeeded to the leadership, albeit disputed, of the Muslims in the Tripoli area of Lebanon while still a young man. In the 1950s Karami established himself, along with Sa'ib Salam, as a politician with pro-**Nasser** sympathies, and became a member of the newly-formed National Front, which constituted a concentration of all Camille **Chamoun**'s opponents. After Chamoun's departure following the disturbances of 1958, and Chehab's assumption of the presidency, Karami formed a predominantly National Front cabinet. A subsequent Christian strike drove home the fact that some Phalange and pro-Christian elements would have to be included and, accordingly, a new and more representative cabinet was formed. During the civil war in the 1970s, Karami was himself called upon to become Prime Minister. He was confronted with the problem of trying to ensure stability while, on the one hand, negotiating with the President to bring an end to the fighting and, on the other hand, having to recognize that, in the environs of Tripoli, Tony Franjiyeh's ultra-Right Zghorta Liberation Army was at daggers drawn with his own supporters. Much later Karami, who must be regarded as amongst those Lebanese politicians who strove to save the country, headed the coalition government formed by President Amin **Gemayel** in 1984. Karami was assassinated in 1987.

Kara Mustafa (d.1683) Turkish grand vizier. He was brought up in the family of Grand Vizier Mehmet **Köprülü**, whose daughter he married. On the death of Fazil Ahmed **Köprülü** in 1676, Kara Mustafa became Grand Vizier and in 1682 he conquered the whole of upper Hungary while gathering a huge army for an assault upon Vienna. The Austrians, reinforced by the Polish King **John III Sobieski**, forced the Ottomans to retreat, and Kara Mustafa was dismissed and executed in Belgrade.

Karamzin, Nikolai Mikhailovich (1766–1826) Russian historian. In 1790–2 he wrote the *Moscow Journal*; in 1802 he began publishing the *Messengers of Europe*; and in 1804 he started compiling his *History of Russia*, which appeared in 12 volumes. In the years of the war against **Napoleon I** he helped to shape Russian patriotism. He also argued in favour of modernizing the language as a means of linking Russia with European ideas. Yet in his *Memorandum on Ancient and Modern Russia* in 1811, while attacking ministries, he still supported aristocracy. In short, he defended tsarism while enabling its critics to have access to the ideas that would destroy it.

Karavelov, Ljuben (1834/5–79) Bulgarian revolutionary and writer. Influenced by the Russian Slavophiles and radical socialists he met while studying in Odessa, he joined the Bulgarian revolutionary organizations active in Serbia (1867) and founded the Bulgarian Revolutionary Committee with Khristo **Botev** and Vasil Levski in Bucharest (1871). He published the two journals *Freedom* (1869–72) and *Independence* (1873–4), and in his novels and memoirs attacked both the Greeks and the Turks as the Bulgarians' oppressors.

Kardelj, Edvard (1910–79) Yugoslav (Slovene) politician. A schoolteacher, he joined the Communist Party and was among the many imprisoned during the dictatorship of **Alexander I**. He lived in the USSR and joined **Tito** as a partisan during **World War II**, becoming Vice-President of **AVNOJ** and in 1946 Foreign, and Deputy Prime Minister. With **Djilas** he went to Moscow in 1948 to face **Stalin**'s criticism of Yugoslavia's independent foreign policy and stood firm with Tito in demonstrating that Yugoslavia would not become merely a Soviet satellite. He was the prominent theoretician of Tito's post-war regime, drawing up the federal constitution and leading the search for a **Marxism** purified of all Stalinist accretions.

Karen Heterogeneous peoples, found in parts of Lower Burma, along the Thai-Burmese border and in north-west Thailand. At the present time, over 90 per cent of the estimated 3 million Karen live in Burma. It is generally accepted that the Karen first appeared in the territory of present-day Burma c.500AD, thus preceding Burman, Thai and Mon. From the 1820s, US Baptist missionaries found large numbers of converts among the Karen, thus encouraging further a distinct Karen identity, and the National Karen Association was founded in 1881. In granting Burma independence in 1948, the British refused Karen appeals for the creation of a separate Karen state and the following year the Karen National Union declared a rebellion against Rangoon. Although the Karen forces were driven back, their demands for autonomy continue.

Karl VIII of Sweden ▷ **Karl Knutsson**

Karl XVI Gustav ▷ **Charles XVI Gustav**

Karl Knutsson (1408–70) King of Sweden (1448/57, 1464/5 and 1467/70) and of Norway (1449/50). A powerful Swedish magnate, he was appointed guardian of the realm after the rebellion of **Engelbrekt Engelbrektsson** and during the reign of Christopher III (Christopher of Bavaria) he was given large fiefs in Finland. On Christopher's death in 1448, he was elected King of Sweden by his fellow nobles. In 1457 he was driven from Sweden by an insurrection in favour of **Christian I** of Denmark, but was twice recalled by factions opposed to the **Kalmar Union**.

Karlowitz, Treaty of (1699) The peace settlement which was concluded at the end of the so-called Vienna War (1684–99) between the Ottoman sultan, Mustafa II, and Emperor **Leopold I** with his allies in the Holy League (Poland, Venice and Russia). The Emperor gained all the liberated Croatian and Hungarian lands (except the Banat of Temesvár) and Transylvania. The Republic of Venice gained the Peloponnese and regained the Dalmatian coast. Poland regained Podolia and a part of the Ukraine but surrendered its conquests in Moldavia. The treaty marked the beginning of the Ottoman retreat from Europe.

Karmal, Babrak (1929–) Afghan politician. The son of an army officer. Educated at Kabul University, where he studied law and political science, he was imprisoned for anti-government activity during the early 1950s. In 1965 he formed the Khalq ('Masses') Party and, in 1967, the breakaway Parcham ('Banner') Party. These two groups merged in 1977 to form the banned People's Democratic Party of Afghanistan (PDPA), with Karmal as deputy leader. After briefly holding office as President and Prime Minister in 1978, he was forced into exile in Eastern Europe, returning in 1979, after the Soviet military invasion, to become head of state. Karmal's rule was fiercely opposed by the Mujahidin guerrillas and in 1986 he was replaced as president and PDPA leader by Najibullah Ahmadzai.

Karolyi, Mihalyi, Count (1875–1955) Hungarian politician. In 1901 he classified himself a liberal, but from 1906 an independent. Despite his aristocratic background he struggled for democratic reforms, and during **World War I** he opposed the alliance with Germany. In 1918 he was briefly Prime Minister, and President from Jan to July 1919. His well-known willingness to accommodate the subject nationalities won him the wrath of most of his fellow Magyars and he was forced into exile. Before and during **World War II** he won an international reputation as a champion of democratic Hungary, and he served as Ambassador in Paris (1947–9). With the triumph of **communism**, he was once more compelled to flee abroad.

Karolyi, Sandor, Baron (1668–1743) Hungarian landowner, soldier and politician. Lord-Lieutenant of Szatmár county, he became a leading general in Ferenc **Rákóczi**'s army revolting against Austrian rule in the period 1703–11. Without Rákóczi's consent he concluded the compromise peace of Szatmár. He was subsequently successful in institutionalizing this compromise so that the Hungarian diet enjoyed privileges not granted to others in the Habsburg Empire. He also began textile manufacturing on his estates, assisting his country's recovery from its long wars. ▷ **Habsburg Dynasty**

Kartini, Raden Adjeng (1879–1904) Javanese aristocrat, one of the first to advocate equal opportunities for Indonesian women. Her ideas and aspirations, as expressed in letters to a Dutch pen-friend, were published as *Door duisternis tot licht* (1911). She set up a school in her house in 1903, with the blessing of the Education Minister. She later started another school with her husband, the Regent of Renbang, but died soon after giving birth to her first child.

Karume, Sheikh Abeid (1905–72) Zanzibari politician. A sailor, he became active in local politics in the 1940s, was elected a town councillor in 1954 and helped found the Afro-Shirazi Party in 1957. Following the 1964 coup which deposed the Sultan of Zanzibar, he became President of the Revolutionary Council. When Zanzibar united with Tanganyika in 1964 to form Tanzania, he became Vice-President, but his expressed opposition to democratic changes made him enemies and he was assassinated in 1972.

Kasavubu, Joseph (1910–69) Zairean politician. Educated locally in a seminary, he worked as a teacher and civil servant in the Belgian colonial administration before entering politics. He was Mayor of Leopoldville in 1957 and, supported by the **UN** in his struggle for power against Patrice **Lumumba**, became President of the Republic of the Congo in 1960. In the ensuing civil war he first defeated **Mobutu**'s challenge and recaptured the presidency, but was later deposed by Mobutu, whom he had appointed as Commander-in-Chief.

Kashmir Problem In 1947, at the time of the partition of India, Kashmir was a largely Muslim-populated state with a Hindu king. In Oct 1947 there was an uprising of Muslims in western Kashmir, supported from across the border in Pakistan. Kashmir appealed to India, which sent troops in exchange for the accession of the kingdom to the Indian Union. After fighting had continued for several months, the **UN** intervened in 1949, establishing along the cease-fire line a provisional demarcation line, which left most of Kashmir with India. India and Pakistan fought a second war over Kashmir in 1965, with a truce being agreed at Tashkent the following year. After the 1971 **Bangladesh War**, both countries accepted, under the terms of the 1972 Simla Agreement, that the Kashmir problem ought to be settled bilaterally. Subsequent years have witnessed further turmoil in Kashmir, with some Kashmiris demanding an independent nation.

Kassites A people, possibly of Iranian origin, who were the dominant power in Babylonia and Lower Mesopotamia after the

Hittite destruction of Babylon in 1595BC. They were conquered by the Assyrians and Elamites around 1150BC. ▷ **Assyria; Elam; Hittites**

Katanga The southernmost province of Zaire, rich in minerals. In 1960, when the Congo (Zaire) achieved independence from Belgium, Katanga (now Shaba) attempted to secede under the leadership of Moïse **Tshombe**. In the ensuing chaos the government of Patrice **Lumumba** was overthrown. Lumumba was assassinated in 1961, and the unitary state was later re-created under the military leadership of President **Mobutu**.

Katayama Tetsu Japanese politician. A Christian socialist, he helped form the Socialist People's Party (*Shakai Minshuto*) in 1926, one of a number of 'proletarian parties' founded during the 1920s. In 1945 Katayama emerged as the leader of the newly-created **Japan Socialist Party**, which achieved a plurality of votes in the first elections held under the 1947 Peace Constitution. He headed a coalition government in 1947–8, the country's first and, to date, only socialist Prime Minister. Katayama's government created a new Ministry of Labour, enacted the Anti-Monopoly Law, and presided over the dissolution of the *zaibatsu,* the pre-war financial combines. The government became increasingly unpopular, however, when economic crisis forced it to impose price and wage controls. After his resignation in 1948, Katayama became identified with the party's right wing. In 1960 he joined a breakaway group that formed the moderate Democratic Socialist Party, which, unlike the larger Socialist Party, supported the 1951 Security Treaty with the USA.

Katholieke Volkspartij ▷ **Catholic People's Party (Netherlands)**

Katkov, Mikhail Nikiforovich (1818–87) Russian journalist. He was Professor of Philosophy at Moscow from 1845 to 1850, when the teaching of his subject was stopped, and after 1861 he was editor of the *Moscow Gazette*. He was at first an advocate of reform, a vaguely Panslav liberal, but he was converted by the Polish rising of 1863 into a crudely chauvinist Russian, increasingly supportive of reactionary Tsarist government. Because of his success as a publicist, he accordingly did great damage to the cause of moderate reform in 19c Russia.

Kato Takaaki (Komei) (1860–1926) Japanese politician. He initially worked for the firm of Mitsubishi, marrying the daughter of its founder, Yataro **Iwasaki**. He studied in England (1883–5) and was to remain an enthusiastic Anglophile throughout his life. As Minister to Britain (1894–1900), he supported the idea of an **Anglo-Japanese Alliance**. Elected to the Diet in 1902 he joined a political party, the *Doshikai* (Constitutional Association of Friends) in 1913, soon becoming its leader. While Foreign Minister (1914–16) Kato attempted to follow a policy free from the interference of the **genro**. He engineered Japan's entrance into **World War I** on the side of the Allies in 1914 as a means of expanding Japan's influence in China. As leader of the moderately progressive **Kenseikai**, which became the largest single party in the 1924 elections, Kato became Prime Minister (1924–6). During his premiership, universal manhood suffrage was enacted (1925), but attempts to reform the upper house (House of Peers) failed. In order to placate conservative critics, Kato's government also enacted the Peace Preservation Law (1925) to restrict left-wing thought. He died in office. ▷ **Peace Preservation Laws**

Katsura Taro (1847–1913) Japanese army general and politician. A member of the **Choshu** clique, he was a general in the **Sino-Japanese War** (1894–5), Governor-General of Japan's colony of Taiwan (1896–8) and Army Minister, before serving as Prime Minister on three occasions (1901–6, 1908–11 and 1912–13). He helped reorganize the army on the German model, and during his terms as Prime Minister Japan became a major imperialist power, forging an alliance with Britain (1902), defeating Russia (1905) and annexing Korea (1910). In 1912 he came under increasing attack in and outside the Diet for his increased military expenditures and his attempts to stay in power by creating his own party (*Doshikai*) to rival the majority party, the **Seiyukai**. He resigned in Feb 1913 and died shortly afterwards.

Katyn Massacre (May 1940) A massacre of more than 10 000 Polish army officers in the Katyn forest near Smolensk, Belorussia. The officers were shot and buried, and their mass graves were discovered by German occupying forces in 1943. Soviet authorities persistently denied responsibility for the massacre, blaming it on the Germans. In 1989 the Soviet–Polish Historical Commission (set up in 1987 to establish the truth) reported that the crime was most probably committed by the Soviet security service (NKVD). This was later confirmed by the Soviet authorities. ▷ **World War II**

Kaufmann, Konstantin Petrovich (1818–82) Russian general and administrator. He distinguished himself at the successful siege of Kars (1855) which was during the **Crimean War**, and from 1867 to 1882 was Governor of Turkestan. In 1868 he occupied Samarkand, and in 1873 conducted the campaign against Khiva. He effectively brought the three khanates of Bukhara, Khiva and Kokand under the control of the Russian Empire.

Kaunda, Kenneth (David) (1924–) Zambian nationalist leader and politician. Educated in mission schools and Munali Secondary School, he became a teacher and welfare officer before entering politics and becoming the Secretary-General of the (Northern Rhodesian) **African National Congress** in 1953, breaking away from it to form the Zambian African National Congress in 1958. After a spell in prison as a result of his nationalist activities, he replaced Mainza Chona as leader of the United National Independence Party (**UNIP**) in 1960 and, after UNIP won elections in 1961, he was made Minister of Local Government and Social Welfare (1962–3) in the first black African government and then, on independence in 1964, he became President. A close friend of Julius **Nyerere**, he espoused a version of African socialism called **humanism**, made UNIP the sole legitimate party and oversaw a steady decline in the country's economic position and political liberalism. Forced by the democratic movement elsewhere in the world and internal pressures, he called an election in 1991 and was defeated.

Kaunitz-Rietberg, Wenzel Anton, Prince von (1711–94) Austrian statesman. He distinguished himself in 1748 at the congress of Aix-la-Chapelle, and as Austrian ambassador at the French court from 1750 to 1752 converted old enmity into friendship. In 1753 he was appointed chancellor, and for almost 40 years directed Austrian politics. Active in the ecclesiastical reforms of **Joseph II**, he was a liberal patron of arts and sciences.

Kautilya (fl.300BC) Hindu statesman and author. He was the supposed writer of the **Arthashastra** ('Textbook of Politics'), the most important extant Sanskrit work on political theory, which was edited, in part from older texts, into its present form (perhaps by Vishnugupta) c.AD2c. At a later date, the Indian tradition identified Kautilya as the outstanding political theorist with Chanakya; according to legend, he was the minister and real power behind the rise of **Chandragupta** Maurya. As the prime practitioner of statecraft, he has been dubbed the 'Indian Machiavelli'.

Kautsky, Karl Johann (1854–1938) German socialist leader. In 1883 he founded and edited *Die Neue Zeit*. A disciple of **Marx**, he wrote a study of Marxist economic theory (1887), and of Sir Thomas More and his *Utopia* (1888). He also wrote against Bolshevism in *Die Diktatur des Proleteriats* (1918, trans 1931). ▷ **Marxism**

Kawakami Hajime (1879–1946) Japanese economist. He played a significant role in popularizing Marxism in Japan after 1918. As Professor of Economics at Kyoto University (1908–28), Kawakami placed most emphasis on the moral aspects of Marxism, and drew the public's attention to the poverty-stricken conditions of Japanese workers and tenant farmers. He was forced to resign his university post in 1928 as part of the government's campaign against left-wing thought. After an unsuccessful attempt to run for the Diet in 1930, he joined the **Japan Communist Party** (1933). He was arrested shortly afterwards and imprisoned until 1937.

Kawawa, Rashidi Mfaume (1929–) Tanzanian trade unionist, nationalist leader and politician. From an early age he was involved in labour politics, becoming President of the Tanganyika African Civil Servants' Association. He joined the Tanganyika African Association (1951–6) and was a founder member, and later Secretary-General and President, of the Tanganyika Federation of Labour. From 1957 he was a member of the Tanganyika Legislative Council and, when Julius **Nyerere** resigned as Prime Minister (1962), Kawawa briefly replaced him. He became first Vice-President (1962–4) and was re-elected after the amalgamation of Tanganyika and Zanzibar until 1972, when he was once again appointed Prime Minister. As a result of his overly zealous commitment to the **Tanganyika African National Union** Guidelines set forth in the **Arusha Declaration**, he was demoted to Minister of Defence and National Service in 1977, but returned to the office of President in 1980. He lost status in government when **Mwinyi** replaced Nyerere, but he was re-elected almost unanimously as Secretary-General of **Chama Cha Mapinduzi** (CCM) in the 1987 Congress.

Kazembe, Kingdom of Central African kingdom founded in the mid-18c by one of the dynasties that were offshoots of the Lunda empire, situated in the Luapula Valley between Lake Mweru and Katanga. It occupied a strategic position rich in resources of salt, iron and copper and attracted the interest of the Portuguese. However it was divided in the late 19c between King Leopold of the Belgians and Cecil **Rhodes**' British South Africa Company.

Keita, Modibo (1915–77) Mali politician. Educated at William Ponty School, Dakar, he helped to found the **Rassemblement Democratique Africaine** in 1946 and was elected to the territorial assembly in 1948. He was a deputy in the French Assembly (1956–9) before becoming President of the Mali Federation (1959–60) and President of Mali (1960–8). A radical who looked to **Nkrumah** for leadership, he was overthrown by the military in 1968 and was imprisoned until his death.

Keitel, Wilhelm (1882–1946) German field marshal and Nazi collaborator. He joined the army in 1901, and became an artillery staff officer in **World War I**. An ardent Nazi and close associate of **Hitler**, he was made Chief of the Supreme Command of the Armed Forces (1938). In 1940 he signed the Compiègne armistice with France, and in 1945 was one of the German signatories of surrender in Berlin. He was convicted of war crimes at the **Nuremberg Trials**, and executed. ▷ **Nazi Party; World War II**

Kekkonen, Urho Kaleva (1900–86) Finnish politician. After studying law at Helsinki University and fighting against the **Bolsheviks** in 1918, he entered the Finnish parliament as an Agrarian Party deputy, and held ministerial office in 1936–9 and 1944. He was Prime Minister on four occasions in the early 1950s before being elected President (1956), in succession to Juo **Paasikivi**. Although Kekkonen had always been hostile to Stalinist Russia, as President he encouraged a policy of cautious friendship with the USSR. At the same time his strict neutrality ensured that he retained the confidence of his Scandinavian neighbours. He supported Finland's membership of the European Free Trade Association (1961) and in 1975 was host to the 35-nation European Security Conference in Helsinki. Five years later he accepted a Lenin peace prize. His popularity in Finland led to the passage of special legislation enabling him to remain in office until 1984, but his health gave way and he resigned in 1981. ▷ **Stalinism**

Kellogg–Briand Pact (27 Aug 1928) A proposal made by French Foreign Minister Aristide **Briand** to US Secretary of State Frank B Kellogg that the two countries should sign a pact renouncing war as an instrument of national policy. At Kellogg's suggestion, a Paris conference in 1928 formally condemned recourse to war, and the pact was subsequently signed by 65 states (the Pact of Paris). However, no provision was made for the punishment of aggressors. ▷ **Paris, Pact of**

Kelly, Ned (1855–80) Australian bushranger, the son of an Irish convict. Brought up in an environment of lawlessness, stock theft and conflicts with the police, Kelly was arrested four times between 1869 and 1871, served three years in prison for horse-stealing (1871–4), and began horse-stealing again in 1876. In 1878 the attempt to arrest his brother, Dan, also for horse-stealing, led to allegations that Ned, Dan, Mrs Kelly and two others had tried to murder a trooper named Fitzpatrick. Mrs Kelly was sentenced to three years' imprisonment, and Ned and Dan went into hiding where they were joined by Steve Hart and Joe Byrne. At Stringybark Creek three of the four policemen in pursuit were killed by the gang, which then robbed banks at Euroa and Jerilderee. Kelly's plan to lure the police into a trap and derail their train at Glenrowan backfired when the police were warned. Trapped in the Glenrowan hotel, three of the gang were killed and Kelly, despite his body armour and headgear, was shot and captured. He was hanged in Melbourne in 1880. By far the most famous of the bushrangers, his feats and defiance of authority made him a legendary figure.

Kennan, George Frost (1904–) US diplomat and historian. After graduating from Princeton in 1925 he joined the US foreign service. During **World War II** he served in diplomatic posts in Berlin, Lisbon and Moscow, and in 1947 was appointed director of policy planning by Secretary of State George C **Marshall**. He advocated the policy of 'containment' of the USSR by political, economic and diplomatic means, which was adopted by Secretaries of State Dean **Acheson**, and John Foster **Dulles**. Kennan subsequently served as US Ambassador in

Moscow (1952–3) and Yugoslavia (1961–3). From 1956 to 1974, as Professor of History at the Institute for Advanced Study at Princeton, he revised his strategic views and called for US 'disengagement' from Europe.

Kennedy, Edward Moore (1932–) US politician. The younger brother of John F **Kennedy** and Robert F **Kennedy**, he was educated at Harvard and the University of Virginia, he was called to the Bar in 1959, and elected a Democratic Senator in 1962. In 1969 he became the youngest ever majority whip in the US Senate, where he has established a notable record on advancing liberal issues. But his involvement the same year in a car accident at Chappaquidick, in which a companion (Mary Jo Kopechne) was drowned, dogged his subsequent political career. In 1979, he was an unsuccessful candidate for the presidency; the nomination went to Jimmy **Carter**, who became President in 1980.

Kennedy, John F(itzgerald) (1917–63) US politician and 35th President. Educated at Harvard, he joined the US navy in 1941 and became a torpedo boat commander in the Pacific. Elected to the House of Representatives as a Democrat in 1947, he became Senator from Massachusetts in 1952 and President in 1960. He was the first Catholic, and the youngest person, to be elected President. His domestic policies called for a 'new frontier' in social legislation, involving a federal desegregation policy in education, and **civil rights** reform. Although criticized for his handling of the **Bay of Pigs**, he later displayed firmness and moderation in foreign policy. In 1962 he induced the USSR to withdraw its missiles from Cuba, and he achieved a partial nuclear test ban treaty with the Soviets the following year. On 22 Nov 1963, he was assassinated by rifle fire while being driven in an open car through Dallas, Texas. The alleged assassin, Lee Harvey Oswald, was himself shot and killed two days later, during a jail transfer. ▷ **Cuban Missile Crisis; Democratic Party; Kennedy, Robert F**

Kennedy, Joseph Patrick (1888–1969) US businessman and diplomat. The grandson of an Irish Catholic immigrant, he was educated at Harvard. During the 1930s, as a strong supporter of **Roosevelt** and the '**New Deal**', he was rewarded with minor administrative posts, and the ambassadorship to Great Britain (1937–40). He had political ambitions for his sons, and placed his large fortune at their disposal for that purpose.The eldest,

Joseph Patrick (1915–44), was killed in a flying accident while on naval service in **World War II**. The others achieved international political fame. ▷ **Kennedy, Edward M; Kennedy, John F; Kennedy, Robert F**

Kennedy, Robert Francis (1925–68) US politician. Educated at Harvard and the University of Virginia, he served in the US navy during **World War II**, was admitted to the Bar (1951), and became a member of the staff of the Senate Select Committee on Improper Activities (1957–60). He managed the presidential campaign of his brother, John F **Kennedy**, and as his Attorney-General (1961–4) and closest advisor, actively sought to enforce laws that guaranteed blacks **civil rights**. In 1964 he was elected Senator for New York. On 5 June 1968, he was shot after winning the Californian primary election, and died the following day. His assassin, Sirhan Sirhan, was later convicted of murder.

Kenseikai The Japanese political party (literally, 'Constitutional Association') formed in 1916 by **Kato Takaaki**, calling for moderate reform and constitutional government. In 1924 the *Kenseikai* became the majority party in the Diet and joined with other parties to bring down a **genro**-chosen non-party cabinet. Kato then became Prime Minister of a Kenseikai-dominated coalition government (1924–6). This government promoted international cooperation, normalized relations with the USSR, reduced the number of army divisions and enacted universal manhood suffrage. In 1927 the Kenseikai fell from power and shortly thereafter became the *Rikken Minseito* ('Constitutional Democratic Party').

Kentucky and Virginia Resolutions (1798 and 1799) Declarations by two state legislatures that the **Alien and Sedition Acts** violated the **US Constitution**. This laid the foundation for the future development of the doctrine of 'state sovereignty' and the state's right to nullify Federal law. The resolutions were written by Thomas **Jefferson** (Kentucky) and James **Madison** (Virginia).

Kenyatta, Jomo (Kamau Ngengi) (1891–1978) Kenyan nationalist and politician. Educated by Scots missionaries, he joined the Young Kikuyu Association in 1922 and politics thereafter dominated his life. He edited the Kikuyu Central Association's news-sheet, *Mwigwithania*, and played a major role in representing progressive black

Kenyan opinion in the 1930s, visiting London on more than one occasion to lobby government. He visited the USSR several times and got to know most of the anti-colonial lobby in the UK, where he worked throughout **World War II**. He attended the famous Fifth Pan-Africanist Conference at Manchester (1945) and, on his return, to Kenya in 1946, he was elected President of the Kenyan African Union, becoming the country's major spokesman for the anticolonial movement. On the outbreak of the **Mau Mau** uprising and the subsequent emergency, he was tried, found guilty on what later proved to be perjured evidence and was detained until 1961. Chosen in absentia to be President of the Kenyan African National Union in 1960, he was elected in 1962 to the Legco and then, after the independence elections, became Prime Minister in 1963 and President when Kenya became a republic in 1964. A remarkable mixture of Kikuyu nationalist, pragmatic politician and father-figure (he was known as *Mzee* or 'old man'), he surprised observers by leading Kenya into a period of economic growth and unexpected tribal harmony.

Kerekou, Mathieu Ahmed (1933–) Benin soldier and politician. The son of a soldier, he joined the colonial army, being trained in France whose army he served. He joined the Dahomey army at independence in 1961, rising to command it in 1966. He took part in the 1967 coup which overthrew President Soglo but returned to the army, while remaining Vice-President of the Military Revolutionary Council (CNR). In 1972 he led a further coup, establishing a National Council of Revolution and espousing 'scientific socialism'. He renamed Dahomey Benin and began to return the country to democracy, being first elected to the presidency in 1980 and re-elected in 1984 and 1989. He dissolved the CNR and finally resigned from the army in 1987 as a gesture of his commitment to democracy.

Kerensky, Alexander Fyodorovich (1881–1970) Russian socialist. He studied law in St Petersburg and made a name for himself as counsel for the defence in Tsarist times in several leading political trials. He was a critical but reasonable member of the Third and Fourth Dumas. In the 1917 **Russian Revolution** he became Minister of Justice in Mar, Minister of War in May, and Prime Minister in July in the Provisional Government. Though crushing **Kornilov's** military revolt in Aug, he found it increas-

ingly difficult to put through moderate reforms in a deteriorating political situation, and in Oct was swept away by the **Bolsheviks**, and fled to France. In 1940 he went to Australia and in 1946 to the USA, writing several books on the Revolution. He died in New York City. He was a talented, well-meaning politician, possibly too superficial and flamboyant to deal with a turbulent society and dedicated revolutionaries. ▷ **Mensheviks; October Revolution**

Kesselring, Albert (1885–1960) German air commander and field marshal in **World War II**. He led the **Luftwaffe** attacks on France and (unsuccessfully) on Britain. In 1943 he was made Commander-in-Chief in Italy, and in 1945 in the West. Condemned to death as a war criminal in 1947, he had his sentence commuted to life imprisonment, but was released in 1952. ▷ **Nazi Party**

KGB (*Komitet Gosudarstvennoy Bezopasnosti*, 'Committee for State Security') From 1953 to 1991 one of the Soviet Union's two secret police organizations with joint responsibility for internal and external order and security and espionage. Its tasks included the surveillance of key members of the Communist Party, the administration, and the military; the monitoring and regulation of dissidents and the population at large; and espionage and subversion abroad.

Khafre (Chephren) (c.2558/2532BC) King of Egypt. He was the fourth king of the 4th Dynasty in the **Old Kingdom**, who constructed the second largest of the pyramids at Giza (towering to a height of 4474 feet). The mortuary temple at the eastern base of the pyramid was connected by a causeway with a valley temple near the edge of the cultivated land. The valley temple is a massive building of limestone faced inside and out with slabs of Aswan granite. In this temple there was found a magnificent diorite seated statue of Khafre, now in the Cairo Museum. One of over 20 similar sculptures in various stones which originally stood in the temple, it conveys the calm dignity of an absolute monarch. Another outstanding monument of the King's reign is the great Sphinx.

Khaironeia, Battle of ▷ **Chaeronea, Battle of**

Khalid, ibn Abdul Aziz (1913–82) King of Saudi Arabia (1975/82). The fourth son of the founder of the Saudi Dynasty, he ascended the throne after the assassination of his brother, Faysal. His caution and moderation served as a stabilizing factor in the Middle East: Khalid's personal influence was seen in the halting of the Lebanese Civil War (1975–6), and in his country's disagreement with the other members of OPEC over oil price increases. He died at Ta'if, Saudi Arabia.

Khaljis A Turkish tribe, long-settled in Afghanistan, which ruled the kingdom of Delhi for 30 years from 1290, when Firuz Khalji, a Balban noble, ascended the throne. Firuz's nephew, Alauddin, treacherously slew Firuz and proclaimed himself King in 1296. In 1304 and 1306, invading Mughal armies were defeated by Alauddin's forces. Further expeditions in 1310 plundered the Hoysalas and the Pandyas. Alauddin died in 1316 and his son, Mubarak, seized the throne. Mubarak quelled rebellions in Gujarat and Deogir, but was treacherously killed in 1320 by his chief minister, Khusrav Khan, who proclaimed himself King and wiped out the Khaljis.

Khalkas The collective name for tribes in eastern Mongolia who allied with the Manchu **Qing Dynasty** during the 18c, helping the dynasty to extend its control over western Mongolia.

Khama (c.1837–1923) King of the Ngwato, one of the Tswana peoples occupying the north of modern Botswana (1875/1923). He was a successful modernizing ruler, who avoided the direct conquest of his kingdom by seeking an accommodation with Europeans. In the late 19c Khama tried to protect his state from the Ndebele to the north and the Boers to the east by securing the protection of missionaries and of British imperial rule. He first sought the protection of Queen **Victoria** in 1876, but a protectorate was not granted until 1885 and imperial rule not fully established until 1891. He succeeded in avoiding control by the British South Africa Company which had secured a charter to rule in Rhodesia. Khama had already become a Christian, insisting on the conversion of his entire people when he did so. He issued laws to reform African traditional customs such as bride-price and initiation ceremonies and banned the brewing of strong liquor in his kingdom. He visited London in 1895 on the occasion of the centenary of the founding of the London Missionary Society.

Khama, Sir Seretse (1921–80) Botswana Chief and politician. Educated Fort Hare College and London, where he trained as a lawyer. The heir to the chieftainship of the Ngwato, he only inherited the title in 1963. He was banned by the colonial authorities from returning to Bechuanaland because of his marriage to a white woman. When he was permitted to return as a private citizen in 1956, he founded the Bechuanaland Democratic Party, won a seat to Legco in 1965 and became President of the Republic of Botswana from its independence in 1966 to his death in 1980. Plagued by health problems, he nevertheless managed to steer Botswana with great skill along a democratic path in the shadow of South Africa.

Khan, Sir Sayyid Ahmad (1817–1898) Indian Muslim educationist, jurist, and author. After a traditional Muslim education, he was employed by the British in 1837, becoming a subordinate judge in Bijnor in 1850, and receiving a special pension for his loyal services during the **Indian Uprising** of 1857–8. In 1875, to encourage Western education among Indian Muslims, he set up the Mohammedan Anglo-Oriental School in Aligarh. Opposed to the **Indian National Congress**, he then formed the All-India Muhammadan Educational Conference in 1886. Through his educational and religious reforms, he became the principle motivating force behind the revival of Indian Islam in the late 19c.

Kharijites This sect is regarded as the first in Islam, having its origin in 657–8 at the Battle of **Siffin**. The Kharijites objected strongly to the decision of the fourth of the Rashidun, or 'Rightly-guided' Caliphs, **'Ali**, to go to arbitration to settle his dispute with **Mu'awiya**, the de facto Governor of Syria, and, saying 'Arbitration belongs to God alone', they left (*kharaja* = 'he went out') the battlefield of Siffin, maintaining thereafter not only that they were the only true Muslims but, since all others were not, conflict with them was not only permissible but a duty. They thus remained a problem for caliphs down the years and it was one of their number, a certain Ibn Muljam, who was responsible for the death of 'Ali, striking him down at the mosque in Kufa. A subgrouping of the Kharijites, called Ibadis after their founder, Ibn Ibad (7–8c), has survived to the present day.

khedive An ancient Persian title acquired from the Ottoman Sultan by the effectively independent Viceroy of Egypt, **Ismail Pasha**, in 1867. It was used until Egypt became a British protectorate (1914).

Khilafat Movement A protest campaign by Indian Muslims (1919–24) against British policy towards the Sultan of Turkey, who was also Caliph of Islam. It joined forces with the **Non-Cooperation Movement** for Indian independence. However, it was weakened by the Turks' own deposition of the Sultan (1923) and the abolition of the Caliphate (1924).

Khitan (Ch'i-tan) A federation of proto-Mongolian nomadic tribes who dominated north China in the 10–12c. Their ruler, Yelu Abauji (Yeh-lu A-pao-chi) (872–926) proclaimed himself Emperor of the Liao Dynasty (916–1125), which held sway over inner Mongolia and north China. Attempts by the Chinese **Song Dynasty** to dislodge them failed and from the 11c the Song was forced to pay annual tribute to pacify the Khitan. Unlike many non-Chinese conquest dynasties, the Khitan Liao resisted sinicization, preserving its nomadic and shamanist practices and treating the Chinese under its rule as an inferior caste. The Khitan were conquered by a forest-hunting tribe from eastern Manchuria, the Jurchen, who established their own dynasty the Jin (Chin) (1127–1234), in northern China. ▷ **Jin Dynasty**

Khmer Empire An empire in mainland South-East Asia, founded in the 7c, with its capital at **Angkor Thom** from 802 onwards. In the 11–12c it extended to South Laos and a large part of Thailand. It was eventually overthrown by the Thais in the 15c.

Khmer Rouge A Cambodian communist guerrilla force which opposed the right-wing government that deposed Prince **Sihanouk** in 1970 and the subsequent US invasion of eastern Cambodia. After gaining control of the country in 1975, its government, led by **Pol Pot**, set about a drastic transformation of 'Democratic Kampuchea', involving the mass forced evacuation from the towns to the countryside, the creation of agricultural cooperatives, and the execution of thousands of 'bourgeois elements'. In late 1978, Vietnam invaded Cambodia, and the Khmer Rouge were ousted, retiring to the Thai-Cambodian border region. Following the Vietnamese withdrawal from Cambodia in 1989, they have mounted a major offensive, especially in the western and southern provinces. Western intelligence estimates suggest that the force consists of 20–35000 armed men, with 50–100000 refugees in Khmer Rouge-controlled camps along the border and in Thailand. Pol Pot is still

regarded as the overall leader; other senior personnel include the deputy leader Ieng Sary (1930–), guerrilla commander Son Sen (1930–), and the leader of Khmer Rouge delegations at international conferences seeking a settlement of Cambodia's political future, Khieu Samphan (1931–).

Khoisan Groups of peoples inhabiting the Cape of Good Hope and encountered by the Dutch when landing at the Cape to trade and after their settlement of 1652. They are made up of the Khoikhoi or Hottentot and San or Bushman people. The Khoikhoi were pastoralists, while the San were hunter-gatherers. However, there was a great deal of marital and economic interaction between them and they are generally grouped together. They spoke a language with distinctive click sounds which survives among the Bushmen and has lent its clicks to the Bantu language of the **Nguni** people. The Dutch at first traded amicably with the Khoisan, but relations soon became bitter and violent. The Khoi, whose decentralized political system made it difficult for them to combine for military success, were devastated by war, the loss of their cattle through drought and raids, and outbreaks of smallpox. The Khoi are now one element in the Cape coloured community while the San are marginalized in the Kalahari desert. In 18c Europe, the word 'Hottentot' was used to mean any uncivilized person.

Khomeini, Ayatollah Ruhollah (1900–89) Iranian religious and political leader. A Shiite Muslim who was bitterly opposed to the pro-Western regime of Shah Mohammad Reza Pahlavi, he was exiled to Turkey and Iraq in 1964, and from Iraq to France in 1978. He returned to Iran amid great popular acclaim in 1979 after the collapse of the Shah's government and became virtual head of state. Under his leadership, Iran underwent a turbulent 'Islamic Revolution' in which a return was made to the strict observance of Muslim principles and traditions. In 1979, a new Islamic constitution was sanctioned, into which was incorporated his leadership concept of the *Vilayet-i faqih* (Trusteeship of the Jurisconsult). This supreme religious and political position was recognized as belonging to Khomeini, as was the title *Rabhar* (Leader). In 1989 he provoked international controversy by publicly commanding, through the issue of a fatwa, the killing of Salman **Rushdie**, author of the novel *The Satanic Verses*.

Khosrow I, II ▷ Chosroes I, II

Khrushchev, Nikita Sergeevich (1894–1971) Soviet politician. Coming from a poor background and with little education but a sharp intellect, he joined the Communist Party in 1918, fought in the **Russian Civil War** and rose rapidly in the Party organization through working with **Kaganovich** and **Stalin**. In 1939 he was made a full member of the **Politburo** and of the Presidium of the Supreme Soviet. During **World War II** he served as a senior political officer on the Ukrainian front. In 1953, on the death of Stalin, he became First Secretary of the **Communist Party of the Soviet Union**, though his position was not secure until 1955. In 1956, at the 20th Party Congress, he denounced **Stalinism** and the 'personality cult' in a well-known secret speech that fundamentally altered the course of Soviet history. Among the events of his administration were the 1956 Poznan Riots that he quietened down, and the **Hungarian Uprising** that he crushed, and the failed attempt to install missiles in Cuba (1962). The latter and his inability fundamentally to improve the Soviet economy led to his being deposed in 1964 and replaced by Leonid **Brezhnev** and Alexei **Kosygin**. He died in retirement in Moscow. ▷ **Cuban Missile Crisis**

Khuen-Héderváry, Károly (1849–1918) Ban (Governor) of Croatia (1883–1903). A Hungarian landowner, he was supported by the Unionist Party which sought closer ties between Zagreb and Budapest. As ban, he established a Hungarian-dominated regime which ignored the historical rights of the Kingdom of Croatia and exploited antagonism between the Serbs, whom he conspicuously favoured, and the **Croats** over **Bosnia and Herzegovina**. In 1903 he left Croatia to become Prime Minister of Hungary (1903 and 1910–12). ▷ **Nagodba; Starčević, Ante**

Khufu (Cheops) (c.2589/2566BC) Builder of the Great Pyramid at Giza and second king of the 4th Dynasty. The pyramid rose to a height of 481 feet, covered 13.1 acres in area and was composed of 2 300 000 blocks of limestone, each averaging two and a half tons in weight. Surrounding the pyramid were rows of tombs for the royal family and the king's officials. Near by were a number of pits designed to hold boats connected to the solar cult or the transportation of the dead king in the after-life. Two held dismantled wooden boats, one of which is now re-assembled and displayed in a museum on the south side of the pyramid.

Kiakhta, Treaty of (1728) A treaty signed by Tsarist Russia and **Qing Dynasty** China, which attempted to solve border disputes and provide more trading opportunities between the two countries. The earlier Treaty of **Nerchinsk** (1689) had provided for Qing control of the Amur River region (in north Manchuria); the Treaty of Kiakhta drew a line between Kiakhta (south of Lake Baikal in Siberia) and the Argun River (flowing south from the Amur). The treaty also allowed Russia to trade at Kiakhta and other border settlements. The Russians were also permitted to maintain an Orthodox Church and hostel in Beijing for the benefit of visiting Russian merchants, the first time foreigners were allowed a permanent official presence in the Chinese capital.

Kido Koin (Takayoshi) (1833–77) Japanese **samurai** politician. He played a prominent part in the **Meiji Restoration** (1868) and helped cement the anti-Tokugawa alliance between his own domain of **Choshu** and that of **Satsuma** in 1866. After 1868, Kido became one of the architects of the new centralized state. He was a member of **Iwakura Tomomi**'s mission to the West (1871–3) and, on his return, was the first Japanese leader to propose a constitution for Japan, based on the German model. ▷ **Tokugawa Shogunate**

Kiesinger, Kurt Georg (1904–) West German politician. Educated at **Berlin** and Tübingen, he then practised as a lawyer (1935–40), and served during **World War II** at the Foreign Office on radio propaganda. Interned after the war until 1947, he was exonerated of Nazi crimes. In 1949 he became a member of the **Bundestag**, and succeeded **Erhard** as Chancellor (1966). A Christian Democrat and long a convinced supporter of **Adenauer**'s plans for European unity, he formed with Willy **Brandt** a government combining the Christian Democratic Union (**CDU**) and the Social Democrats (**SPD**). He was Chancellor from 1966 to 1969, when, following election defeat, he was succeeded by Brandt.

Kiev Rus (c.882–1240) The first settled Russian state, famed for princes such as Oleg, Igor, Sviatoslav, Vladimir, Jaroslav and Vladimir Monomakh, but also for periods of civil war. At times it extended towards the Baltic and Black Seas, but it was frequently threatened by other tribes on the move; in the end it succumbed to the Mongols. It arose around Kiev on the strength of trade routes and declined as the routes shifted to the Mediterranean. Possibly its most important contribution to history was its conversion to Christianity in 988 or thereabouts. This guaranteed that Russia would be neither Muslim nor Judaic and would become part of Europe. Kiev Rus, of course, has also been one of the bases for Ukrainian nationalism, requited in 1991.

Kiheitai A volunteer militia unit (literally, 'irregular militia') organized by the Japanese domain of **Choshu** in 1863 at a time when the Western powers were threatening to take military action in response to attacks on foreigners in the **treaty ports**. Significantly, it recruited from amongst all social classes, including peasants, thus breaking with the tradition whereby military functions were monopolized by the **samurai** class. The unit was equipped with modern rifles and its leaders were chosen on the basis of ability rather than hereditary status. It played a part in the overthrow of the **Tokugawa Shogunate**. Although the *Kiheitai* was disbanded in 1869, it served as a model for the 1873 Conscription Law, which provided for a national army drawing on all ranks in society.

Kikuyu Central Association (KCA) A society founded in Kenya in 1922 under the leadership of Harry Thuku. Jomo **Kenyatta**, the future nationalist leader and President of Kenya, became Secretary-General of the KCA, which became the basis of African politics in the British colony. It took up African grievances such as the European occupation of Kikuyu lands in the 'White Highlands' and the missionary campaign to abolish female circumcision. It established the Kikuyu leadership of nationalism in Kenya, but was banned during **World War II**. The Kenya African Union emerged as its successor in 1944.

Kilwa A great trading town on the coast of southern Tanzania, which acted as the major entrepot of the trade of the interior of East-Central Africa with the Middle East and the Indian Ocean. Kilwa owed its rise to the migration of Shirazi merchants from the Persian Gulf in the 12c. By the early 14c it had supplanted Mogadishu as the greatest port on the coast, the southern limit of the Arab traders who used the annual monsoons to connect Africa to Asia. It flourished for the succeeding two centuries until sacked by the Portuguese. Its remaining ruins are testimony to its magnificence in its heyday with palaces, mosques and warehouses built of coral. It became a slaving port in the 18c.

Kimberley, Siege of (1899–1900) One of the three sieges of the second Boer War, in which Boer forces attempted to pen up their British opponents and secure control of vital lines of communication. The siege lasted from the middle of Oct 1899 until Feb 1900, when the town was relieved by General **French**. ▷ **Boer Wars**

Kim Chong-il (1942–) North Korean politician. The eldest son of the North Korean communist leader **Kim Il Sung**, he was born in the USSR where his mother had retreated from the Korean anti-Japanese guerrilla base in Manchuria. Kim Chong-il played a leading part in ideological and propaganda work, helping to create the cult that surrounded his father. In 1980 he became First Secretary of the Party's Central Committee. From 1982, frequently referred to as the 'dear leader', he was regarded as heir-apparent, and he succeeded his father in 1994.

Kim Dae Jung (1924–) South Korean politician. A Roman Catholic, he was imprisoned by communist troops during the **Korean War**. He challenged General **Park** for the presidency in 1971 and was later imprisoned (1976–8 and 1980–2) for alleged 'anti-government activities'. He lived in exile in the USA (1982–5) and on his return successfully spearheaded an opposition campaign for democratization. Although popular among blue-collar workers and fellow Chollans, Kim is distrusted by the business and military elite and in the 1987 presidential election was defeated by the government nominee, **Roh Tae Woo**.

Kim Il Sung (Kim Song-ju) (1912–94) North Korean soldier and politician. He founded the Korean People's Revolutionary Army in 1932, and led a long struggle against the Japanese. He proclaimed the Republic in 1948, and remained effective head of state until his death. He was re-elected President in 1982, having named his son, **Kim Chong-il**, as his eventual political successor. His death in 1994 was greeted by scenes of massive public grief.

Kim Ok-kyun (1851–94) Korean revolutionary. From a prominent family, he served in the government of King Kojong (1864/1907) and, after visiting Japan in 1882, promoted modernization on the Japanese model and an end to Korea's traditional tributary relationship with China. His reform proposals, however, were blocked by the family of the King's consort (the Min), who dominated the court. In 1885, with the connivance of the Japanese Minister and the assistance of Japanese troops stationed in the Korean capital, Kim staged a palace coup. A new cabinet was formed with Kim as Finance Minister, but two days later Chinese troops intervened and he fled to Japan. He was assassinated by a Korean government agent in Shanghai.

Kimon ▷ **Cimon**

Kim Yong-sam (1927–) South Korean politician. After election to the National Assembly in 1954, he was a founder member of the opposition New Democratic Party (NDP), becoming its President in 1974. His opposition to the **Park** regime resulted in his being banned from all political activity. In 1983 he staged a 23-day pro-democracy hunger strike and in 1985 his political ban was formally lifted. In that year he helped form the New Korea Democratic Party (NKDP) and in 1987 the centrist Reunification Democratic Party (RDP). In his 1987 bid for the presidency he came second, behind the governing party's candidate, **Roh Tae Woo**. In 1990 he merged the RDP with the ruling party to form the new Democratic Liberal Party (DLP).

King, Martin Luther (1929–68) US civil rights leader. The son of a Baptist minister, he studied at Morehouse College and Boston University, set up his first ministry in Montgomery, Alabama. In 1957 he helped found the **SCLC** (Southern Christian Leadership Conference) as a base for coordinating efforts in the struggle for racial equality. Embracing M K **Gandhi**'s message of achieving change through non-violent resistance, he mobilized the black community to challenge segregation laws in the South through non-violent marches and demonstrations, boycotts and freedom rides, and broadened support for the 1964 Civil Rights Act. His voter registration drive in Alabama, culminating in the Selma march, led to the passage of the Voting Rights Act in 1965. In 1968, he was assassinated in Memphis, Tennessee, by James Earl Ray. ▷ **civil rights movement**

King, (William Lyon) Mackenzie (1874–1950) Canadian politician. He studied law at Toronto, and became an MP (1908), Minister of Labour (1909–11), **Liberal Party** leader (1919), and Prime Minister (1921–6, 1926–30 and 1935–48). His great ability to find common ground among differing political views made a major contribution to the Liberal domination of national politics for a whole generation, and his view that the dominions should be autonomous communities within the **British Empire** resulted in the Statute of **Westminster** (1931). He resigned from office in 1948. ▷ **Compulsory Service Act; Rowell–Sirois Commission**

King–Crane Commission The commission, composed of two US members, Henry King and Charles Crane, which carried out its work in June, July and Aug 1919. Its remit — to ascertain local reactions to the proposed Middle Eastern mandatory arrangements — resulted in their reporting opposition to separation from Palestine and to the proposal for a French mandate in Syria. The commission also found that the Zionist programme for Palestine could not, at least in its extreme form, be reconciled with the **Balfour Declaration** in which the rights of the non-Jewish population of Palestine were enshrined. The Commission's report was published in 1922 and its findings were all but disregarded.

King David Hotel, Bombing of the (22 July 1946) The attack by the **Irgun** on a wing of the King David Hotel in Jerusalem, the headquarters of British rule in Palestine. It took place as part of a wider campaign by the Irgun and others in response to opposition from the British Labour government to Jewish immigration into Palestine. ▷ **Jewish Agency; Zionism**

King George's War ▷ **Austrian Succession, War of the**

King Philip's War (1675–6) US colonial war. An attempt by the Native Americans of central New England to stop further white expansion. It was led by Metacom, King Philip, or chief of the Wampanoags, who tried to build an inter-tribal coalition. The Native Americans lost, and were killed or enslaved, but not before killing hundreds of colonists. ▷ **Indian Wars**

Kingston, Charles Cameron (1850–1908) Australian politician. A lawyer, he entered South Australian politics in 1881, and was state Attorney-General (1884–5 and 1887–9), Chief Secretary (1892) and Premier (1893–9). His ministry was the first in Australia to give votes to women (1894), and to introduce state conciliation and arbitration (1894). A leading figure in the **federation** movement, he attended the National Australasian Convention in 1891 and the Federal Convention of

1897–8, at which, with H B **Higgins**, he included conciliation and arbitration powers in the federal constitution. He entered federal politics in 1901, and was Minister of Trade and Customs in **Barton**'s government. Disputes with his colleagues over the scope of his conciliation and arbitration Bill led to his resignation in 1903, and although an arbitration Act was passed in 1904, ill health prevented any return to office.

King William's War (1689–97) The first of the great wars between France and England for the control of North America. Known in Europe as the War of the League of **Augsburg**, it was settled by the Treaty of Rijswijk (1697). ▷ **William III**

Kinnock, Neil (Gordon) (1942–) British politician. He became a Labour MP in 1970, joined the **Labour Party**'s National Executive Committee (1978), and was chief opposition spokesman on education (1979–83). He was elected Party Leader in 1983, following Michael **Foot**. During the 1980s he reorganized the party and led successsful attacks on its left-wing influence and on **Militant Tendency**. He resigned the Labour Party leadership in 1992, following his defeat by John **Major** in the general election of Apr 1992.

Kirk, Norman Eric (1923–74) New Zealand politician. While working as an engine-driver, he joined the Labour Party and became involved in local, then national politics, becoming President of the party in 1964. He entered parliament in 1957, was Leader of the Opposition (1965–72) and became Prime Minister in 1972, at a time when his country's economy was in difficulties. Forced by Britain's entry into the **EEC** and the USA's disengagement in Asia, he sought a more independent regional role for New Zealand, opposed French nuclear testing in the Pacific and sent ships into the test area. He died in office.

Kirov, Sergey Mironovich (1886–1934) Russian revolutionary and politician. In and out of prison from 1905 onwards, he played an active part in the **October Revolution** and **Russian Civil War**, and during the 1920s held a number of leading provincial Party posts. He had been elected a full member of the Central Committee by 1923, and in 1934 he became a full member of the **Politburo** at the 17th Party Congress and was elected as a secretary of the Central Committee. Later that year he was assassinated at his Leningrad

headquarters, possibly at the instigation of **Stalin**, who then used his death as the pretext for a widespread campaign of reprisals. ▷ **Bolsheviks; Bukharin, Nikolai Ivanovich; communism; Trotsky, Leon**

Kisan Sabhas 'Peasant associations' in India. The first All-India Kisan Congress of Apr 1936 brought together regional groups which had developed during the **civil disobedience** movement of 1930–4. After the second congress (Dec 1936), relations between the Congress and the Kisan Sabha movement were strained; after the Sabha's demands for radical agrarian reform became very insistent, Congress forbade (1938) its members from joining any Sabhas. During **World War II**, the Sabha came increasingly under communist control and went underground soon after independence. It reemerged as part of the Communist Party of India in 1952, but its strength varied regionally.

Kiselev, Pavel Dmitriyevich, Count (1788–1872) Russian general and politician. An efficient and not inhumane soldier, he was Governor of the Danubian Principalities following the Treaty of **Adrianople** of 1829, until in 1836 he was put in charge of a new Fifth Department to look after the state peasantry, who comprised about a third of the Russian population. Over the next 20 years he introduced several reforms affecting everything from landholding to health and education; these were some of the better aspects of **Nicholas I**'s autocratic reign. However, Kiselev's concentration was on administration, and his reforms were often ignored or simply spoiled by malpractices at local level.

Kishi Nobusuke (1896–1991) Japanese politician. The brother of Eisaku **Sato**, he took the name of Kishi when he was adopted into his uncle's family. He entered the Ministry of Agriculture and Commerce (1920) and during the interwar years was identified as one of the 'new bureaucrats' (*shinkanryo*), who championed more extensive economic planning. While he served in the Japanese puppet-state of **Manzhuguo** (1936–9), Kishi worked closely with the military in developing heavy industry. On returning to Japan, he became a vice-minister of Commerce and Industry, helping to place the economy on a war footing. He then served in the wartime cabinet of Hideki **Tojo**. After the war, he was imprisoned by the US occupation authorities but was released in 1948. Kishi was one of the architects, in 1955, of the Liberal Democratic Party (LDP), formed when the two major conservative parties merged. A controversial Prime Minister (1957–60), he ensured ratification of the renewed Security Treaty with the USA (1960) in the face of an opposition boycott in the Diet and massive public demonstrations. He resigned shortly afterwards, but remained influential within the LDP.

Kissinger, Henry Alfred (1923–) US political scientist and politician. His family emigrated from Germany to the USA in 1938, to escape the Nazi persecution of Jews. He was educated at Harvard, served in **World War II**, and subsequently joined the Harvard faculty. He became President Richard **Nixon**'s adviser on national security affairs in 1969, was the main US figure in the negotiations to end the **Vietnam War**, and became Secretary of State in 1973, serving under Nixon and **Ford**. His 'shuttle diplomacy' during the Arab–Israeli War of 1973 helped bring about a cease-fire, and resulted in a notable improvement in Israeli–Egyptian relations. He left public office in 1977.

Kita Ikki (1883–1937) Japanese national socialist. A promoter of a Japanese-led Pan-Asianism, in 1919 he wrote *An Outline Plan for the Reorganization of Japan* in which he argued that a radical reordering of Japanese society was required in order for Japan to take her rightful place as leader of Asia. He called for a military coup that would sweep away the constitution and civilian political establishment and establish direct rule under the Emperor. Kita also advocated nationalization of industry, confiscation of all excess wealth and land reform. His ideas influenced the radical army officers of the **Imperial Way Faction**. When they staged an abortive coup in 1936, Kita was arrested as an accomplice and executed.

Kitchen Cabinet Term used in US politics to describe an informal group of advisers surrounding a US president. It originated in the mid-19c in the administration of President Andrew **Jackson**.

Kitchener (of Khartoum and of Broome), (Horatio) Herbert, 1st Earl (1850–1916) British field marshal and statesman. He joined the Royal Engineers in 1871, and served in Palestine (1874), Cyprus (1878), and the Sudan (1883). By the final rout of the Khalifa at **Omdurman** (1898), he won back the Sudan for Egypt, and was made a peer. Successively Chief-of-Staff and Commander-

in-Chief in South Africa (1900–2), he brought the Boer War to an end, and was made viscount. He then became Commander-in-Chief in India (1902–9), Consul-General in Egypt (1911), and Secretary for War (1914), for which he organized manpower on a vast scale ('Kitchener armies'). He was lost with HMS *Hampshire*, mined off the Orkney Islands. ▷ **Boer Wars; World War I**

KKE (*Kommunistikon Komma Ellados*, 'Communist Party of Greece') Founded in 1918 as the Socialist Workers' Party of Greece by Greek socialists, the character of the KKE changed after 1924 as Moscow-trained communists started to 'bolshevize' and take control of the party. The most 'westernized' of Greek political parties, at least a quarter of its support came from the urban middle classes as well as industrial workers and peasants, but particularly among refugees from Anatolia after the **Graeco-Turkish War**. In the 1926 election, the KKE gained 10 seats in parliament, although total party membership did not exceed 2000. In 1936, the KKE's plans for a general strike on 5 Aug were foiled when the **Metaxas** regime arrested all leading members on the preceding day — a black day, still not forgotten, in the history of Greek communism. Until 1939 the KKE was incapable of action, with its members in prison or having been released after signing 'declarations' denouncing the party. The government infiltrated and manipulated the party so that, in 1940, there were no less than three central committees. During **World War II** the KKE was the dominant force behind the **EAM** (National Liberation Front); it tried to seize power during the German occupation, and again in Dec 1944 after the German withdrawal and during the **Greek Civil War**.

Klapka, György (1820–92) Hungarian soldier and patriot. He became a lieutenant general in the Austrian army, but in the Hungarian Uprising of 1848–9 fought he valiantly against the Austrians, holding Komárom for eight weeks after the rest of Hungary had submitted. Although he later conducted anti-Austrian activities abroad, he was permitted under the amnesty of 1867 to return from exile, and he died in Budapest.

Klaras, Athanasios (Aris Veloukhiotis) (1905–45) Greek resistance leader. He was the leader of **ELAS** resistance bands in Greece during **World War II**. He took part in the settlement of Greek refugees from Asia Minor (1922) and joined the Greek

Communist Party (1924). Under the dictatorship of Ioannis **Metaxas** he was interned (1936–9), but was released after retracting his communist convictions. After the German occupation of Greece (Apr 1941), he was impatient to organize resistance but it was not until Mar 1942 that he received orders from **EAM**, the communist-led National Liberation Front, to form guerrilla bands and to take to the mountains. Committed to the establishment of a communist regime, he organized communist-led self-administration in the liberated regions, oversaw the brutal coercion of the often recalcitrant local population and waged war against the other resistance organizations. He attacked **EKKA** (May 1943) and, with the agreement of EAM, launched a campaign against **EDES**, led by his cousin, Napoleon **Zervas** (Oct 1943). Opposed to any compromise, however expedient, he condemned the EAM leaders for their compliance with the Allies and the Greek government-in-exile at the Lebanon Conference (May 1944) and at Varkiza (Feb 1945). For the sake of party unity, he formally agreed to the demobilization of ELAS, but withdrew with sections of his followers to the mountains. At its Apr 1945 plenum, the Greek Communist Party, now led by Nikos **Zachariadis**, condemned Veloukhiotis who, hounded from village to village by the communists and Greek government officials, committed suicide.

Kléber, Jean Baptiste (1753–1800) French general. He served in the Austrian army (1776–82), became an architect, and then joined the National Guard (1792). He commanded in the Vendean War, but was recalled for leniency. He later won victories at Fleurus (1794) and Altenkirchen (1796), and he accompanied Bonaparte to Egypt, was wounded at Alexandria, and won the Battle of Mount Tabor (1799). When **Napoleon** Bonaparte left Egypt, Kléber was left in command. He attempted to reconquer Egypt, but was assassinated by a Turkish fanatic at Cairo.

Kleist, Ewald von (1881–1954) German military commander. He joined the army in 1900 and served as a cavalry officer during **World War I**. During **World War II** he commanded an armoured group in the French campaign (1940) and from 1942 to Mar 1944 commanded an army group on the Russian front. Promoted field marshal in 1943, he was later dismissed by **Hitler** and was subsequently taken prisoner by the Allies. He died in captivity in the USSR.

Kleisthenes ▷ **Cleisthenes**

Klephts Greek folklore celebrated the Klephts as bandits who robbed the rich to give to the poor, and for their ability to worst the Ottoman Turks. While the heroic image presented in folk-songs was grounded in fact, it should not be forgotten that many klephts were simply brigands and opportunists.

Klondike Gold Rush A flood of prospectors (largely US) when gold was discovered in Canada Yukon Territory in 1896. The rush lasted for five years, generated an estimated US$50 million in gold, established the town of Dawson, and invigorated the economies of British Columbia, Alberta, Alaska and Washington State.

Knights of Labor (1878–93) An early US labour organization. It tried to organize all workers in support of a large-scale political and social programme, regardless of their age, race or colour. Its membership peaked at around 700 000 in 1886, but then declined.

Knossos A centre of habitation from Neolithic times, it became from c.2200BC the location of a large and increasingly elaborate complex of buildings. The so-called 'Palace of Minos', excavated by Arthur Evans, is thought to be the main centre of **Minoan Civilization**. After the destruction of this civilization (c.1450BC), Knossos continued to be inhabited as a town throughout antiquity.

Knut Sveinsson ▷ **Canute**

Know-Nothings (1856) US political party. A popular name for the short-lived anti-immigrant American Party. It was so called because of the response members were instructed to give to questions from outsiders: 'I know nothing'. ▷ **nativism**

Knox, John (c.1513–72) Scottish Protestant reformer, born near Haddington, Lothian. A Catholic priest, he acted as notary in Haddington (1540–3), and in 1544 was influenced by George Wishart to work for the Lutheran reformation. After Wishart was burned (1546), Knox joined the reformers defending the castle of St Andrews, and became a minister. After the castle fell to the French, he was kept a prisoner until 1549, then became a chaplain to Edward VI, and was consulted over the Second Book of Common Prayer. On Mary's accession (1553), he fled to Dieppe, and then to Geneva, where he was much influenced by **Calvin**. He returned to

Scotland in 1555 to preach, and then again in 1559, where he won a strong party in favour of reform, and founded the Church of Scotland (1560). He played a lasting part in the composition of *The Scots Confession*, *The First Book of Discipline*, and *The Book of Common Order*. He died in Edinburgh. ▷ **Mary, Queen of Scots; Reformation** (Scotland)

Kobayashi Takaji (1903–33) Japanese revolutionary. A literary activist and prominent leader of the proletarian literature movement in the late 1920s, he participated in strikes while his short stories and novellas (all censored or banned outright until after 1945) championed the heroic struggle of the working class against oppression and exploitation. Forced to go underground after 1929, Kobayashi was eventually arrested, tortured, and executed in 1933.

Kogălniceanu, Michael (1817–91) Romanian politician and historian. With Ion **Brătianu** he led the Liberal Party and was appointed Prime Minister by Alexander **Cuza** (1862). He presided over a period of economic and social reform, sequestering the lands of the Dedicated Monasteries which were controlled by the **Phanariots**, introducing a civil code based on the **Code Napoléon**, reorganizing local government and establishing more schools. He lost the support of Cuza, however, and was dismissed in 1865. He later served in the Liberal government (1876) and strongly supported Prince Charles (later King **Charles I** of Romania).

Koguryo, Kingdom of A Korean state whose influence stretched from southern Manchuria to central Korea. First mentioned in Chinese records of the 1c BC, Koguryo tribes were used by the Han Dynasty as a buffer on its north-eastern frontier against more hostile tribes. After AD 12, a Koguryo warrior aristocracy increasingly asserted its independence from China and assumed leadership over other tribes in northern Korea. At the height of its power, Koguryo was one of the three kingdoms that dominated the Korean Peninsula (the other two being **Silla** and **Paekche**). From 427, its capital was located in Pyongyang (the present-day capital of North Korea). Repeated Chinese attacks, first during the **Sui Dynasty** and then during the **Tang Dynasty** finally led to Koguryo's collapse in 668. ▷ **Han Dynasties**

Kohl, Helmut (1930–   ) German politician. Educated in Frankfurt and Heidelberg, he became a lawyer, and joined the **Christian Democrats**. In 1976 he moved to **Bonn** as a member of the Federal Parliament, became leader of the opposition, and his party's candidate for the chancellorship. After the collapse of the **Schmidt** coalition in 1982, Kohl was installed as interim Chancellor (1982–   ), and in the elections of 1983 he formed a government which has since adopted a central course between political extremes. Following the **Revolution of 1989** in East **Germany**, Kohl played a decisive part in ensuring the integration of the former communist state within the Federal Republic of Germany.

Koht, Halvdan (1873–1965) Norwegian politician and historian. He was a professor of history at Oslo University from 1910 to 1935, when he became Foreign Minister under the Labour government (1935–40). A prolific writer on Norwegian history and literature, he was also a highly controversial figure in Norwegian political life. Koht was strongly criticized for his failure to anticipate the German invasion of Norway (Apr 1940) and was replaced as Foreign Minister in the government-in-exile by Trygve **Lie**. ▷ **Norway, German Invasion of**

Koivisto, Mauno (1925–   ) Finnish politician. A Social Democrat, he served as Minister of Finance in 1966–7 and Prime Minister in 1968–70 and 1979–81. As Governor of the Bank of Finland after 1968 (retaining office while serving as Prime Minister, with another politician serving as acting governor), he presided over a period of tight monetary policy which helped to consolidate the country's economic growth. President from 1982, he had a more relaxed political style than his predecessor, Urho **Kekkonen**, although maintained the latter's policy of close cooperation with the USSR until its demise in 1991.

Kojiki Japan's oldest extant chronicle ('The Record of Ancient Matters'), compiled in the early 8c, recording events from a mythical past to the time of Empress Suiko (593/628). Purporting to be an official history, the chronicle sought to emphasize Japan's uniqueness as the land of the gods: Jimmu, the great-grandson of the Sun Goddess, Amaterasu, was said to have founded the Japanese empire in 660 BC. During the 1930s, the *Kojiki* became the bible of fanatical ultra-nationalists, who accepted the myths as fact confirming Japan's superiority.

Kokovstov, Vladimir N (1853–1943) Russian politician. He had two spells as Finance Minister before becoming Prime Minister following **Stolypin**'s assassination in 1911. He was good at reducing budget expenditure and resisting right-wing corruption, at raising French loans and giving sound advice to **Nicholas II**. However, he exercised little power and was replaced in 1914 by someone more conservative and compliant.

Kokutai A Japanese term, meaning 'national essence', used to denote the country's unique polity, in particular the role of an unbroken imperial line descended from the gods. The term was first used during the **Tokugawa Shogunate** (1603–1867) as a reaction against Chinese influence on Japanese culture. From the 1890s onwards, the idea of Japan as a family-state in which the close relationship between the Emperor and his subjects was likened to that of a father and his children increasingly took hold. During the 1920s and 1930s, protection of the *kokutai* was used as justification for the suppression of dissident thought. With the dismantling of the Emperor-centred state after **World War II**, the term was no longer used and it has little meaning in today's Japan.

Kolchak, Alexander Vasilievich (1874–1920) Russian naval commander. In **World War I** he was in command of the Black Sea fleet. After the **Russian Revolution** of 1917, he went to Omsk as War Minister in an anti-Bolshevik government. He cleared Siberia in co-operation with **Denikin** and other leaders of the White Army, styling himself latterly 'supreme ruler of Russia'. In 1919 Omsk fell to the **Bolsheviks**; Kolchak was betrayed, and shot.

Kolettis, Ioannis (1774–1847) Greek politician. A Vlach doctor from **Epirus**, he served at the court of **Ali Pasha**. He joined the civilian government of George Kountouriotes at Kranidi before becoming, with Agostino Kapodistrias and Theodoros **Kolokotronis**, joint-head of the administration established after the assassination of Ioannis **Kapodistrias** (1831). While serving as Greek representative in Paris, he was influenced by French political thought and became leader of the 'French Party' in Greece during the 1840s. He played an important role in drawing up the 1844 Greek constitution which was inspired by the French July Monarchy and which established Greece as a constitutional monarchy. From 1845 until his death, he led the government and

won wide support for King **Othon**, formulating the programme of Greek territorial expansion known as the **Megale Idea**. ▷ **Mavrokordatos, Alexander**

Kollar, Jan (1793–1852) Slovak writer. He was one of the early formative group of Czech and Slovak intellectuals who helped to give their peoples a sense of being and purpose. He wrote about the Slavs in general and was anxious to promote unity among them. Though a Slovak, he worked in the Czech Lands and also wrote in Czech, determined to bring the two groups together. After the failure of the 1848–9 rebellions, he was seduced into working with the authorities in Vienna in the hope of influencing them to defend Slovakia against Hungarian pressure. He gained nothing and lost respect. The Slovak national movement lost its unity and impetus for some years to come.

Kollontai, Alexandra Mikhailovna (1872–1952) Russian feminist and revolutionary. The world's first female ambassador, she was born in St Petersburg into an upper-class family, but rejected her privileged upbringing and became interested in socialism. Married to an army officer, she nevertheless joined the Russian Social Democratic Party and, for her revolutionary behaviour and the radical views she expressed at the First All-Russian Congress of Women, was exiled to Germany in 1908. In 1915 she travelled widely in the USA, begging the nation not to join **World War I**, and urging the acceptance of socialism. In 1917, following the **Russian Revolution**, she returned to Russia, becoming Commissar for Social Welfare. In this post she agitated for reforms, including collective childcare and easier divorce proceedings. Partly because her private liaisons and aggressive feminist advocacy shocked the Party, she was appointed Minister to Norway, Mexico and Sweden, becoming ambassador in 1943. She played a vital part in negotiating the termination of the **Continuation War** (1944).

Kolokotronis, Theodoros (1770–1843) Greek military leader. The captain of a band of **Klephts** in the Morea, he played an important role in the **Greek War of Independence**. Inspired by the ideals of the **French Revolution**, he was recruited to the **Filiki Etairia** and supported Alexander **Ypsilanti** in his bid to head the revolutionary government (1821). He refused to support Kountouriotes' government at Kranidi and organized raids against it from his base at Nauplion. In 1824 he was bribed into surrender and lent his support to Ioannis **Kapodistrias**, whom he succeeded in 1831, heading an administration with Agostino Kapodistrias and Ioannis **Kolettis**. Conservative and Orthodox in outlook, he led the 'Russian Party'.

Komeito The 'Clean Government' Party of Japan, which achieved the power of veto over the traditional ruling Social Democratic Party by winning 20 seats in the Upper House in the 1989 elections, following revelations about government corruption. *Komeito* is an offshoot of *Soka Gakkai*, a born-again Buddhist cult founded in 1930 but based on the teachings of a 13c holy man. In **World War II**, Soka Gakkai's leader was jailed by Japan's thought police and starved to death. The organization was unbanned in 1964 and formed Komeito as its political wing, but six years later the party broke its secular links to broaden its appeal.

Komenský, Jan Ámos ▷ **Comenius, John Amos**

Komorowski, Tadeusz Bór (1895–1966) Polish soldier. As 'General Bór' he led the heroic but unsuccessful Warsaw rising against the occupying Germans in 1944, and settled in England after **World War II**.

Komsomol The All-Union Leninist Communist League of Youth, founded in 1918, incorporating the majority of persons between the ages of 14 and 28. Its purpose being the socialization of youth in the thought and ways of the **Communist Party of the Soviet Union**, it served as a recruiting ground for Party membership until 1991.

Kongo, Kingdom of An African kingdom situated to the south of the River Congo which by the 15c had a coastline of 150 miles and reached inland for 250 miles. It was already involved in trade in ivory, copper, and slaves when the Portuguese arrived in the area in 1482. Some of its kings accepted Christianity, but it was disrupted by the stepping up of the **slave trade**, and declined during the 18c when the Portuguese turned their attention southwards to Angola.

Kong Xiangxi (K'ung Hsiang-hsi) ▷ **Kung, H H**

Koniev, Ivan Stepanovich (1897–1973) Soviet military commander. Born into a peasant family, he was drafted into the Tsarist army in 1916, and joined the **Red Army** and the Communist Party in 1918. For some time he was a political commissar, but after graduating from the Frunze Military Academy in 1934 he held various commands, including in the Far East, before the USSR was drawn into **World War II**. In the years 1941–5 he served with great distinction on several sections of the Western front. Made Marshal of the USSR in 1944, he was Commander-in-Chief, Ground Forces in 1946–50, First Deputy Minister of Defence, and, in 1956–60, Commander-in-Chief of the **Warsaw Pact** forces, which he built into an effective fighting force. ▷ **Russian Civil War**

Königgrätz-Sadowa, Battle of (3 July 1866) The decisive Prussian victory in the 1866 war against **Austria**. The battle itself was hard-fought and close-run, but by the next day it was apparent that the Austrians (who suffered much higher casualties) were in full retreat and the Prussian pursuit began. Diplomatic intervention by the French Emperor **Napoleon III** led to the Peace of **Nikolsburg**. ▷ **Austro-Prussian War; Prussia**

Königsberg A city in East Prussia (now Russia) which arose around a Teutonic castle built in 1255. In 1340 it became a Hansa town. From 1547 it was the seat of the Grand Master of the **Teutonic Knights** and then (1525–1618) the Dukes of Prussia. Albert I created a Lutheran university in Königsberg in 1544. It was viewed as the royal city of the Prussian dukes and kings.

Konoe Fumimaro (1891–1945) Japanese politician. From an aristocratic family, he inherited the title of prince from his father. Konoe was a prominent member of the Upper House (House of Peers), before becoming Prime Minister for the first time in 1937. He favoured the growth of Japanese influence in Asia, criticizing what he felt was an Anglo-American attempt to preserve the status quo. During his first term as Premier (1937–9) he led Japan into full-scale war with China in an attempt to create a New Order in East Asia. During his second term (1940–1), Japan's relations with the USA worsened, especially after his government signed a military alliance with the Axis powers (Tripartite Pact) in Sep 1940. He resigned when his offer of a summit meeting with President **Roosevelt** was rebuffed. Although Konoe was a member of the first post-war government (1945), he was indicted as a war criminal by the US occupation authorities. He committed suicide on the day he was to turn himself in for confinement and trial.

Koo, Wellington ▷ Gu Weijun

Köprülü (late 17c) The name of three Turkish grand viziers who effectively controlled the Ottoman government for most of the late 17c. Mehmet Köprülü (d.1661) was an Albanian by birth who rose from working in the imperial kitchen to become Grand Vizier in 1656 when he was in his seventies. He ruthlessly consolidated his power and rebuilt the Ottoman fleet for service against the Venetians. He retired shortly before his death in 1661 in favour of his son, Fazil Ahmed Köprülü (c.1676), who, during his 15 years as Grand Vizier, built upon the foundation laid down by his father. He personally led the army against Austria, securing advantageous terms at the Peace of Vasvar (Eisenberg) in 1664, and against Crete which was taken in 1669. He died of dropsy and his place was taken by his foster-brother Kara Mustafa, who brought the Ottomans to the gates of Venice. Fazil Ahmed's younger brother, Fazil Mustafa Köprülü (d.1691), became Grand Vizier in 1689. Like his predecessors, he reformed the administration and reorganized the army. He showed particular concern for non-Muslim subjects in the Balkans. He was killed in battle near Karlowitz.

Korean War (1950–3) A war between communist and non-communist forces in Korea, which had been partitioned along the 38th parallel in 1945 after Japan's defeat in **World War II**. The communist North invaded the South in 1950 after a series of border clashes, and a **UN** force intervened, driving the invaders back to the Chinese frontier. China then entered the war and, together with the North Koreans, occupied Seoul. The UN forces counter-attacked, and by 1953, when an armistice was signed, had retaken all territory south of the 38th parallel. ▷ **MacArthur, Douglas**

Kornilov, Lavr Georgevich (1870–1918) Russian general. With previous intelligence and diplomatic experience, he was a divisional commander in **World War I**, tried to turn the tide against the Germans by an offensive in June 1917 and, in Aug 1917, marched on St Petersburg, in an attempt to set up a military directorate. He was forced to surrender by **Kerensky**, but subsequently escaped. Kornilov then organized a Cossack force against the **Bolsheviks**, but fell in battle. ▷ **Kornilov Affair**

Kornilov Affair (1917) A military attempt to prevent the **Bolsheviks** coming to power.

The failure of the **Brusilov offensive** in July 1917 greatly weakened the **Russian Provisional Government**. **Kerensky** appointed the adventurous General **Kornilov** as Commander-in-Chief, but he apparently succumbed to right-wing influence and in Aug attempted a military coup by sending cavalry to Petrograd. He failed and simply increased support for the Bolsheviks.

Korošec, Anton (1872–1940) Slovene politician. He studied theology at Maribor and was ordained priest, taking a leading role in the Slovene People's Party before **World War I**. An advocate of **trialism**, he became President of the coalition of **South Slav** members in the Austrian parliament (1917) and President of the National Council of Slovenes, Croats and Serbs in Zagreb (Oct 1918). After the creation of the Kingdom of Serbs, Croats and Slovenes (later Yugoslavia), he served as Vice-Premier (1919). Conservative and opportunistic, he continued to represent the interests of the Slovenes and was the only non-Serb inter-war Prime Minister and Minister of the Interior (July 1928–Jan 1929). During the dictatorship of **Alexander I**, he was interned on the island of Hvar (1933) but was released during the regency to serve again as Minister of the Interior (1935–8).

Koryo, Kingdom of The name given to Korea (of which it is the original form) by Wang Kon, founder of the Koryo Dynasty (918–1392) which had its capital at Kaesong (Songdo). It was an abbreviation of the ancient name Koguryo.

Kościuszko, Tadeusz Andrzej Bonawentura (1746–1817) Polish soldier and patriot. He was trained in the military acaedmies in Warsaw and Paris. In 1776 he went to North America, where he fought for the colonists in the American War of Independence and was eventually promoted to brigadier-general and became a US citizen. He returned to Poland in 1784; and when Russia attacked his country in 1792, he held Dubienka for five days, with 4000 men against 18000. In 1794, after initial hesitation, he took charge of a national uprising in Kraków, being appointed dictator and Commander-in-Chief. In spite of his defeat of a greatly superior force of Russians at Racławice, he had to withdraw to Warsaw, winning popular support by suspending serfdom. He conducted a difficult but brilliant defence of the city but, overpowered by superior numbers in the Battle of Maciejowice (10 Oct 1794) and wounded, he was taken prisoner. Two years later Emperor

Paul of Russia had him freed. He went first to England, then to America, and in 1798 to France. In 1806 he refused to support **Napoleon I**'s plan for the restoration of Poland, the Grand Duchy, because it would not secure genuine independence; similarly, in 1815 he refused to support Alexander I's so-called Congress Poland. He settled in Switzerland in 1816, and died when his horse fell over a precipice.

Kosice Programme (Apr 1945) The political programme on which post-1945 Czechoslovakia was based. It consisted of a compromise between 'Westernizers' and communists, the pre-war ministries who had accompanied **Beneš** to exile in London and Klement **Gottwald** and his colleagues coming home from Moscow. It was based on the hope that good East–West relations would continue after the war; and while it excluded some parties and concentrated on socializing the economy, it stipulated free elections and did not contemplate collectivizing agriculture. However, Kosice in Slovakia was liberated by the **Red Army** and when the **Cold War** got under way, the compromise was abandoned in 1948 to fit the objectives of **communism**.

Kosovo The region of southern Serbia, bounded by Montenegro, Albania and Macedonia. The heart of medieval Serbia, it encompasses many sites of religious significance for the Serbs as well as the scene of their defeat by the Ottoman Turks (1389). Settled by **Albanians** as well as Serbs, it has long been the cause of friction between the two nations. In the 19c it was the centre of the Albanian national revival, but was granted to Serbia when the first Albanian state was established (1913). During **World War II** it was included within Albania by the Italian fascists and its future was a contentious issue between Albanian resistance movements (79 per cent of the population is Albanian). Returned to Yugoslavia in 1945, it became an autonomous province within the Socialist Federal Republic of Serbia, with Albanian and Serbian as its official languages. In 1981 Albanian students led demands for the establishment of Kosovo as the seventh Yugoslav republic and the ensuing riots led to the declaration of a state of emergency. Since then, there has been constant unrest culminating in the removal of the province's autonomous status in 1989. ▷ **Balli Kombëtar; Kosovo, Battle of; LNC; Milošević, Slobodan; Prizren, League of**

Kosovo, Battle of (28 June 1389) The Ottoman Turks' victory over the Serbs on the Kosovo plain marked the end of the medieval Kingdom of **Serbia**. The battle was the subject of Serbian ballads in the oral tradition including the celebrated *Maiden of Kosovo*. ▷ **Kraljević, Marko; Lazar, Hrebeljanović**

Kossuth, Lajos (1802–94) Hungarian revolutionary. Part Slovak, part local German, he was born into a poor but noble family near Zemplén. He practised law for a time and in 1832 was a deputy at the Diet of Pressburg. He edited a journal which, owing to the law, could not be printed, but only transcribed and widely circulated. The issue of a lithographed paper led, in 1837, to imprisonment. Freed in 1840, he became editor of the twice-weekly *Pesti Hirlap*, advocating extreme Liberal, and somewhat chauvinistic, views. In 1847, sent by the county of Pest to the diet, he became leader of the radical opposition; and in Mar 1848 after the French Revolution he demanded an independent government for Hungary. In Sep 1848, pushing aside the more conservative nobility and heading the Committee of National Defence, he prosecuted the war with extraordinary energy and in Apr 1849 induced the National Assembly at Debrecen to declare that the Habsburg Dynasty had forfeited the throne. Appointed Provisional Governor of Hungary, he sought in vain to secure the intervention of the Western Powers; and finding that the dissensions between himself and his generals were damaging the national cause, he resigned his dictatorship in favour of Artúr **Görgey**. After the defeat at Temesvár (9 Aug 1849), he fled to Turkey, where he was made a prisoner, but not extradited. In Sep 1851, liberated by British and US influence, he came to England, where, as subsequently in the USA, he was received with respect and sympathy, but no more. From 1852 he lived mainly in England till, on the Franco-Italian War with Austria in 1859, he proposed to **Napoleon III** to arrange a Hungarian rising against Austria. The Peace of Villafranca bitterly disappointed Kossuth; and in 1861 and in 1866 he again tried in vain to bring about a rising against Austria. When in 1867 **Deák** effected the reconciliation of Hungary with the dynasty, Kossuth retired from active political life, and afterwards lived mostly in Turin. In 1867 he refused to avail himself of the general amnesty. ▷ **Villafranca Armistice**

Kostov, Traicho (?1897–1949) Bulgarian politician. He studied law and joined the

Bulgarian Communist Party (BCP) in 1920. Tortured and imprisoned under the regime of **Boris III**, he was left a cripple. During **World War II**, a 'home' rather than a 'Moscow' communist, he served in the post-war **Fatherland Front** government as Secretary of the Central Committee of the BCP (1944–8), Deputy Prime Minister (1946–9) and Minister for Electrification (1947–9). After criticizing the terms of economic deals with the USSR, he was summoned with the Yugoslavs **Kardelj** and **Djilas** to justify himself before **Stalin** (1948). In 1949 he was tried on charges of wartime collaboration with the police and the British and plotting to assassinate Georgi **Dimitrov**. He was executed in Dec 1949, a victim of Stalin's purges of 'home communists' and 'Titoists'. However, he was posthumously rehabilitated and decorated (1956). ▷ **Tito; Velchev, Damian**

Kosygin, Alexei Nikolaievich (1904–80) Soviet politician. A textile-worker by training, he owed his advancement in the 1930s to the vacancies resulting from **Stalin**'s purges. Elected to the Supreme Soviet (1938), he held a variety of political industrial posts, and became a member of the Central Committee in 1939 and of the **Politburo** in 1948. He had a chequered career in the post-**World War II** period, falling in and out with both Stalin and Nikita **Khrushchev**. It was only really when, in 1964, he succeeded the latter as Chairman of the Council of Ministers (or Prime Minister) that he could attempt serious, if decentralizing, reforms. However, he was blocked in the late 1960s by the Party machine and the caution of Leonid **Brezhnev**. He soldiered on until 1980, when he resigned because of ill health, and he died soon after, having failed to rescue the economy from over-centralization and -planning.

Kotoku Shusui (1871–1911) Japanese socialist and anarchist. In 1898 he joined the newly-founded Society for the Study of Socialism (*Shakai shugi Kenkyukai*) and in 1901 helped to form Japan's first social democratic party, which was quickly outlawed by the government. Kotoku became a fierce critic of Japanese imperialism, opposing the **Russo-Japanese War** (1904–5). His paper, *Heimin shimbun* ('Common People's Newspaper') published the first Japanese translation of the *Communist Manifesto* in 1904. By 1906, Kotoku had abandoned parliamentary tactics and adopted an anarcho-syndicalist position, calling for direct action and a general strike. He was arrested for supposed involvement in a plot to

assassinate the **Meiji Emperor** in 1910 and executed the following year.

Kountche, Seyni (1931–87) Niger soldier and politician. Trained in France, he served with the French army in Indochina and Algeria. He joined the Niger army at independence in 1961, undertaking further military training in France before becoming Chief of Staff in 1973. He led the military coup against Hamani **Diori** in 1974 and established a military government. However, he set about restoring the country's economy and a return to civilian rule, but died in Paris while undergoing surgery.

Koxinga (**Zheng Chenggong/Cheng Ch'eng-kung**) (1624–62) Chinese warrior general. Born of a Japanese mother, his father was a pirate and trader along China's east coast during the last years of the **Ming Dynasty**, before being made an official. The young Zheng was given the imperial surname, and was thus known as *Kuo-hsing yeh* ('Lord of the Imperial Surname'), from whence came the Dutch derivation of Koxinga. Although his father submitted to the Manchu **Qing Dynasty** in 1646, Zheng himself resisted Manchu rule, continuing to support a Ming loyalist movement, controlling much of the south-eastern coast around Amoy. After an abortive attack on Nanjing in 1659, he retreated to Taiwan where he expelled the Dutch from their fortress of Zeelandia. Although he died later in the same year (1662), his sons continued to monopolize trade between Taiwan and the mainland until Qing forces captured the island in 1683.

Kozlov, Frol Romanovich (1908–65) Soviet politician. Graduating in 1936 from what later became the Leningrad Polytechnic, he held Communist Party functions in various parts of the country before returning to Leningrad in 1949 to work his way up to be First Secretary there. In 1957 he became a member of the **Politburo** in the wake of the **Anti-Party Plot**. Thereafter he held two brief ministerial posts before becoming Second Secretary to Nikita **Khrushchev** in the Soviet party as a whole. As such he tried to restrain Khrushchev's reforms in the interests of conservative forces and was reputed to be behind an unsuccessful coup in 1963, but that year he suffered a stroke and had to leave the field to Leonid **Brezhnev**.

KPD (*Kommunistische Partei Deutschlands*, 'Communist Party of Germany') German

political party. Founded at New Year 1919, the KPD was, initially, a coalition of left-wing Social Democrats within the Spartacus League (Spartakus Bund) and various anarcho-syndicalist groupings which opposed the **Weimar Republic**. At first an independent-minded party led by Rosa **Luxemburg** and Karl **Liebknecht**, the KPD later came increasingly under Russian control and became virulently hostile to the **SPD** by the mid-1920s. Cooperation with the SPD, which it branded 'Social Fascist', or with other republican parties to defend the Weimar Republic during the early 1930s was therefore out of the question. Its relationship with the **Nazi Party**, however, although highly violent, became more and more equivocal. When the organization was banned by the Nazis (Mar 1933), many members left politics or even switched to the Nazi Party or **SA**, but a minority put up sustained if low-level passive resistance to the end of the Third **Reich**. After **World War II**, the revived KPD in eastern Germany forced the SPD there into a merger to form the **SED**, the ruling party of the German Democratic Republic. Soon afterwards it was banned in the Federal Republic. During Weimar, the KPD failed to gain a significant foothold in the trade-union and working-class cultural movement and towards the end of Weimar relied on the unemployed and marginalized working-class groups for its growing, if minority, support.
▷ **communism; Spartacists**

Krag, Jens Otto (1914–78) Danish politician. He was Minister of Foreign Affairs (1958–62), when he became Leader of Denmark's **Social Democratic Party**, which he led until 1972. During this time he had two periods as Prime Minister (1962–8 and 1971–2). In 1972 he led Denmark into the Common Market, but after the EEC referendum (Oct 1972), which showed 63.3 per cent of the votes in favour of membership and 36.7 per cent against, he surprisingly decided to resign and was succeeded by Anker **Jørgensen**.

Kraljević, Marko (1335–94/5) Serbian Prince. The ruler of a small principality within **Serbia**, he fought with Prince **Lazar** at the Battle of **Kosovo** (1389). Later he became a vassal of the Turks and died fighting for Sultan **Bayezid I** against the Wallachians led by **Mircea the Old** at the Battle of Rovine. He is celebrated in Serbian epic poetry for his prodigious strength and supernatural powers and, like many folk heroes, is said not to have died but to be asleep, ready to rescue his country in its hour of need.

Kramar, Karel (1860–1937) Czechoslovak politician. He almost became a professor, but took up politics in the 1890s as a member of the Young Czech Party that wished to improve the lot of all Slavs within Austria-Hungary. He was also pro-Russian, and at the beginning of **World War I** he tried to float a scheme that would make Bohemia and Moravia a kingdom with a Russian prince. He was accordingly imprisoned by the Austrian authorities for much of the war but emerged at the end as provisional Prime Minister in **Masaryk**'s government. He was then very active, pressing the Czechoslovak case during the **Versailles** peace conference. However, in the middle of 1919, he lost his place in the government as too conservative for the majority. Although he remained in parliament, his influence waned; he had been overtaken by history.

Krasin, Leonid Borisovich (1870–1926) Soviet politician, diplomat and engineer. Expelled from St Petersburg Technological Institute in 1888 for radical political activity, he graduated from Kharkov Technological Institute in 1900 and continued thereafter to be both practising engineer and occasional revolutionary activist. He took part in the negotiations leading up to the Treaty of **Brest-Litovsk** in 1918; and as Commissar for Foreign Trade (1920–6), he was deeply involved in most of the negotiations leading to the **normalization** of Soviet relations with other European states. Increasingly pragmatic in his approach, he died shortly after being appointed Ambassador to Britain.

Krausism Spanish cultural movement. Based on the ideas of Karl Krause, the German idealist, Krausism had a major impact on educational, religious, political and ethical thought in Spain. As interpreted in Spain, Krausism contributed to liberalism by stressing harmonious social development through reason. Its advocates became a secular priesthood for ethical progress.

Kreisau Circle (*Kreisauer Kreis*) A German anti-Nazi resistance group founded by Count Helmuth von Moltke in 1940, which met on his estate at Kreisau. The Circle drafted a Christian–conservative political programme for post-war Germany. Von **Moltke** was arrested in Jan 1944 after which most of his colleagues attached themselves to von **Stauffenberg**'s group which tried, unsuccessfully, to kill **Hitler** in July 1944.

Kreisky, Bruno (1911–90) Austrian politician. Educated at Vienna University, he joined the Social Democratic Party of **Austria** (**SPÖ**) as a young man and was imprisoned for his political activities from 1935 until he escaped to Sweden in 1938. He returned to Austria and served in the Foreign Service (1946–51) and the Prime Minister's office (1951–3). He was increasingly active in party politics and in 1970 became Chancellor in a minority SPÖ government. He steadily increased his majority in subsequent elections but in 1983, when that majority disappeared, he refused to serve in a coalition and resigned.

Kremlinology The once essential art of deducing by 'reading between the lines' from various, often indirect, sources what was happening in Soviet politics. The need arose from the 'monolithic unity' presented by Soviet leaders to their own people and the outside world, hiding their conflicts and divisions through strict control of the media. Under Mikhail **Gorbachev**, **glasnost** lessened the need for Kremlinology to the point where the supply of information became as abundant as elsewhere.

Kriegel, Frantisek (1908–79) Czechoslovak politician. Active in the Communist Party from the 1930s, a doctor by training, he practised his profession in both the **Spanish Civil War** and **Chinese Civil War** from 1936 through to 1945. He subsequently held a series of party and government appointments and acted as health adviser in Cuba in the years 1960–3. In 1968 he played an important role as chairman of the National Front and he was abducted to Moscow along with Alexander **Dubček** and others after the invasion. The Soviet authorities initially refused to release him, and he never signed the protocol that was extracted in Moscow; that and his subsequent outspokenness lost him all his positions and privileges.

Krishnadevaraya (1509/29) Ruler of the Hindu empire of Vijayanagar. A warrior king, he spent much of his reign at war with the Sultan of Bijapur, inflicting a severe defeat upon the Muslims at the Battle of Raichur in 1520. A poet himself, he was a liberal patron of writers in the Telugu language of the region.

Krishna Menon, Vengalil Krishnan (1896–1974) Indian politician. He was educated at the Presidency College, Madras, and at London University. He came to

Britain in 1924 and became a history teacher and a London barrister. In 1929 he became Secretary of the India League and the mouthpiece of Indian nationalism in Britain. When India became a Dominion in 1947 he became India's High Commissioner in London. In 1952 he became leader of the Indian delegation to the **UN**, bringing Jawaharlal **Nehru**'s influence to bear on international problems as leader of the Asian 'uncommitted' and 'neutralist' bloc. During the first 1956 **Suez Crisis** on the nationalization of the Canal he formulated a plan to deal with it. As Defence Minister (1957–62) he came into conflict at the UN with Britain over Kashmir. He was Minister of Defence Production for a short time in 1962.

Kristallnacht (*Reichskristallnacht*) (9–10 Nov 1938) A **pogrom** against the Jews in National Socialist Germany unleashed by the **SA** and **Nazi Party** members following a provocative speech by Joseph **Goebbels**. The ostensible reason was the murder in Paris of a German official by a Polish Jew. The result was the massive destruction of Jewish property in Germany, the death of 91 Jews, and subsequently heightened pressure on Jews to emigrate from the country combined with the further isolation and persecution of those remaining.

Kritias ▷ **Critias**

Krofta, Kamil (1876–1945) Czechoslovak historian and diplomat. A professor at Charles University in Prague, he entered diplomatic service as Ambassador to the Vatican (1920–2), and then held postings in Vienna and Berlin. He became Deputy Foreign Minister in 1927 and Foreign Minister in 1936. It was not easy to follow **Beneš** or even to serve him when he was elected President, but Krofta proved both able and loyal in the pre-Munich struggle to preserve Czechoslovakia. He was imprisoned in a **concentration camp** during **World War II** and died just after he was set free.

Kronstadt Rebellion (Mar 1921) An uprising of sailors from the Baltic fleet stationed at Kronstadt in the Gulf of Finland. Protesting against the dictatorial Bolshevik policy of 'war communism', the mutineers demanded political and economic reforms under the slogan of 'free soviets', and established a revolutionary commune on the orders of **Lenin**. The rising was crushed by **Red Army** units after fierce fighting and heavy losses on both sides. But at the 10th Communist Party

Congress in the same month, Lenin was sensitive enough to introduce his 'New Economic Policy', which at least improved the material conditions of the Soviet people. ▷ **Bolsheviks**

Kropotkin, Prince Peter (1842–1921) Russian geographer, savant, radical and anarchist. In 1857 he entered the corps of pages. After five years' service and exploration in Siberia, he returned to Moscow to study mathematics, while acting as Secretary to the Geographical Society. In 1871 he explored the glacial deposits of Finland and Sweden; but in 1872, critical of the limited nature of reform in Russia, he associated himself with the extremist section of the International Workingmen's Association. Arrested in 1874 and imprisoned in Russia, he escaped to England in 1876. At Lyons he was condemned in 1883 to five years' imprisonment for anarchism; but, released in 1886, he settled in England until the **Russian Revolution** of 1917 took him back to Russia. Well-known for his *Memoirs of a Revolutionist* (1900), he wrote widely and contributed both to the revolutionary ferment in his own country and to criticism abroad of its political backwardness.

Kruchina, Nikolai Yefimovich (1928–91) Soviet politician. Graduating as an agronomist in 1952, he was a **Komsomol** official from then until 1962 when he was transferred to the Communist Party proper. From 1978 to 1983 he was second-in-command of the agricultural section of the Central Committee and came into close contact with Mikhail **Gorbachev**. He was then made chief administrator of party affairs, a post that gave considerable financial responsibility. Suddenly in 1991, as the **August Coup** crumbled, he committed suicide, suggesting corruption as well as disloyalty among Gorbachev's former lieutenants.

Kruger, Stephanus Johannes Paulus (Paul) (Oom ('Uncle') Paul) (1825–1904) Afrikaner politician. He took part in the Great Trek of the 1830s, becoming leader of the independence movement when Britain annexed Transvaal (1877). In the first Boer War (1881), he was head of the Provisional Government, and subsequently became President of the South African Republic (1883–1902). During the second Boer War (1899–1902), he came to Europe to seek (in vain) alliances against Britain, making his headquarters at Utrecht. He died at Clarens, Switzerland. ▷ **Boer Wars; Great Trek**

Krupskaya, Nadezhda Konstantinova (1869–1939) Russian revolutionary, and wife and widow of **Lenin**. A Marxist activist before she met Lenin in 1894, she was sentenced to exile about the same time as he was and allowed to join him in Siberia in 1898 on condition that they got married. Thereafter they were inseparable, and Krupskaya acted as his agent, organizer and fellow-thinker in both Europe and Russia. She disliked the political limelight and, following the Bolshevik **Russian Revolution**, she was mainly active in promoting education and the status of women. As Lenin's widow she at first opposed **Stalin** but subsequently supported some of his policies, and was accordingly exploited. She left a rather brief *Reminiscences of Lenin*. ▷ **Bolsheviks**

Kryuchkov, Vladimir Alexandrovich (1924–) Soviet lawyer, diplomat and secret policeman. Born and educated in Volgagrad (Stalingrad), he immediately threw himself into local Communist Party work. However, in 1954 he was recruited into the diplomatic service and became Third Secretary in Budapest, where Yuri **Andropov** was serving as ambassador. Thereafter he went everywhere with Andropov, to the Central Committee as a sector head in 1957 and to the **KGB** in a similar posting in 1967. From 1974 to 1988 he was deputy chairman, mainly responsible for foreign intelligence; but in 1988, under Mikhail **Gorbachev**, he became Chairman. Obviously expected to support reform, he was brought into the **Politburo** in 1989 and transferred to the presidential council in 1990. But in 1991, disenchanted or ambitious, he helped organize the attempted **August Coup** that led to his own imprisonment and Boris **Yeltsin**'s advancement.

Kuan Chung ▷ **Guan Zhong**

Kuang-hsu ▷ **Guangxu**

Kuan Yu ▷ **Guan Yu**

Kubitschek (de Oliveira), Juscelino (1902–76) Brazilian politician. The grandson of a Czech immigrant, he studied medicine in Belo Horizonte, Minas Gerais, and went on to become Mayor of the city (1940–5). He was elected to Congress by the PSD (*Partido Social Democrático*) in 1945 and was Governor of Minas Gerais in 1951–5. As President (1956–61), his ambitious *Programa de Metas* ('Programme of Goals') emphasized transportation, energy, manufacturing and the building of Brasília, rather than social measures, and was the blueprint for subsequent programmes during military rule. The political necessity for high GDP growth-rates hampered effective counter-inflationary policies and the achievement of a modus vivendi with international creditors, bequeathing massive problems to subsequent **Quadros/Goulart** and **Castelo Branco** administrations. He was a candidate for the presidency in 1965 when he was exiled by Castelo Branco.

Kublai Khan (1214–94) Mongol Emperor of China (1279/94). He was the grandson of **Genghis Khan**. An energetic prince, he suppressed his rivals, adopted the Chinese mode of civilization, encouraged men of letters and made Buddhism the state religion. He established himself at Cambaluc (modern Beijing), the first foreigner ever to rule in China, and ruled an empire which extended as far as the River Danube. The splendour of his court was legendary.

Kučan, Milan (1941–) Slovenian politician. During the late 1980s, Kučan as the communist President of Slovenia, resisted pressure from Belgrade to stifle the emergence of opposition parties in his republic, long the most liberal in the Yugoslav federation. In 1990, after the Slovenes held the first free elections anywhere in Yugoslavia since **World War II**, he was re-elected as non-Party President of Slovenia. He declared Slovenia's secession from the Yugoslav Federation on 25 July 1991. With the backing of Serbia's President, Slobodan **Milošević**, Yugoslav Federal army units attacked Slovenia, but Milošević was obliged to withdraw and to accept Slovenia's independence.

Kuchuk Kainarji, Treaty of (21 July 1774) The treaty signed at the end of the Russo-Turkish War of 1768–74, **Catherine II, 'the Great'**'s first war against the **Ottoman Empire**. The war had begun when Sultan Mustafa III, egged on by his French and Austrian allies, made a pre-emptive attack on Russian forces. Following several notable victories, Russia greatly improved its strategic position on the Black Sea by gaining control of the estuaries of the Don, Dnieper and Bug Rivers. The treaty gave the Russians the right to represent the Sultan's Orthodox subjects in Moldavia and Wallachia and the Aegean Islands, and marked the first stage in the establishment of Russian interests in the **Danubian Principalities**. Russia was also granted trading privileges throughout the Ottoman Empire, free passage through the Straits and the right to set up consulates throughout the empire. Among the other terms, Greek merchants gained the right to sail under the Russian flag. The treaty marked a turning-point for Russia: henceforward, Tsarist policy moved from domestic consolidation to foreign conquest. ▷ **Russo-Turkish Wars**

Ku Klux Klan US white supremacist organization. The first klan was founded after the **American Civil War** to oppose **Reconstruction** and the new rights being granted to blacks. The members, disguised in white robes and hoods, engaged in whippings, lynchings, and cross burnings to terrorize blacks and their sympathizers in the rural areas of the South. The Klan declined in influence after federal laws were passed against it, but was re-established after **World War I**. This time its influence was felt far beyond the South, and its targets were enlarged to include Catholics, foreigners, and Jews as well as blacks. It declined during the 1930s, but was revived by the fear of **communism** in the 1950s. In the 1960s, its violent opposition to the **civil rights movement** led to a federal government crackdown, and the prosecution of key members. Subsequently the Klan moved toward working through traditional political channels in order to further its agenda.

kulaks The most progressive stratum of the late 19c and early 20c Russian peasantry. The kulaks became significant after the final emancipation of the serfs in 1905, building up successful medium-sized farms with encouragement from the Tsarist government, which was anxious to broaden its very narrow support. During the collectivization of agriculture in the 1930s, **Stalin** 'liquidated' the kulaks as a class, asserting that they were enemies of the revolution. In fact he eliminated an important source of agricultural wealth that his successors tragically lacked. ▷ **Russian Serfs, Emancipation of the**

Kulikov, Viktor Georgevich (1921–) Soviet commander. He rose to be Chief of Staff of a tank brigade during **World War II**, then worked his way up until in 1969 he became the commander of Soviet forces in Germany. His subsequent promotion was even quicker: Chief of the General Staff and first Deputy Defence Minister in 1971; and Commander-in-Chief of the **Warsaw Pact** and Marshal of the USSR in 1977. He was therefore deeply involved in Leonid **Brezhnev**'s military build-up and opposed

Mikhail **Gorbachev**'s cutbacks. He was relieved of his appointment in 1989 not long before the disbandment of the Warsaw Pact, the two events obviously being connected.

Kulturkampf In the German Empire, a 'cultural conflict' between the Prussian state and the Roman Catholic Church. It was inspired by liberal suspicion of Catholics' extra-German loyalties, and involved discriminatory legislation against the Church's position within **Prussia**. Exploited by **Bismarck** to consolidate his position, it was most intense during the period 1870–8, but gradually subsided following the election of Pope Leo XIII (1878), and effectively ended by 1886.

Kumazawa Banzan (1619–91) Japanese **samurai** administrator and Confucian scholar. The son of a masterless samurai (*ronin*), Kumazawa entered the service of the **daimyo** (feudal lord) of Bizen, where he was instrumental in promoting administrative reforms. His writings stressed the importance of empirical knowledge of the external world and of the need to adopt practical solutions to changing circumstances. Kumazawa's thought influenced later samurai activists of the early 19c dissatisfied with the rigidities of the status quo.

Kun, Béla (1886–1939) Hungarian political leader and revolutionary. He was a journalist and social democrat, who was conscripted into the Austro-Hungarian army and became a prisoner of war in Russia in 1916. In 1917 he sympathized with the **Bolsheviks**, and in 1918 founded the Hungarian Communist Party. In Mar 1919 he organized a communist revolution in Budapest and set up a Soviet republic which succeeded **Károlyi**'s post-**World War I** government. His policy of nationalization and other socialist measures failed, however, to gain popular support, and he was forced to flee for his life in Aug of that year. After escaping to Vienna, he returned to Russia where, in 1921, he became a member of the Executive Committee of the **Comintern**. He then fell victim to the Stalinist purges of the late 1930s. ▷ **Stalin, Joseph**

Kunaev, Dimmukhamed Akhmedovich (1912–) Kazakh politician. A metallurgist by occupation and communist by inclination, he worked his way up the Kazakh party ladder in the 1940s and 1950s, coming into close contact with Leonid **Brezhnev** and being made First Secretary in 1960. He was demoted by Nikita **Khrushchev** in 1962, but reappointed in 1964 by Brezhnev who also brought him into full membership of the **Politburo**. This gave Brezhnev support and the Politburo a nationality following; inevitably it meant his dismissal by Mikhail **Gorbachev** in 1986. His ousting led to riots in Alma Ata but these were countered by charges of extensive corruption.

Kunersdorf, Battle of (12 Aug 1759) A battle, during the **Seven Years War**, in which **Frederick II, 'the Great'** suffered a tremendous defeat at the hands of an Austro-Russian force commanded by Loudon and Soltykov. The engagement resulted in immense loss of life and the near-ruin of Frederick's army.

Kung, H H (Kong Xiangxi/K'ung Hsiang-hsi) (1881–1967) Chinese politician and banker. He came from a family of traditional bankers and received a missionary education in China before studying in the USA (1901–7). Through marriage, Kung developed close ties with **Sun Yat-sen** and **Chiang Kai-shek** (their wives were sisters), joining the **Guomindang** in 1924 and becoming Minister of Industry and Commerce of the new Nationalist government in 1928. As Governor of the Bank of China and Minister of Finance (1933–44), Kung attempted to increase the government's financial control of the modern sector. Through control of the four major banks, the government floated more bond issues to finance its military projects. Kung's abandonment of the silver standard in favour of a managed paper currency in 1935 was to lead ultimately to hyperinflation in the 1940s. During the war against Japan, Kung was instrumental in obtaining US loans and was China's representative at the **UN** Bretton Woods Conference (1944). He moved to the USA permanently in 1948.

Kuomintang (KMT) ▷ **Guomindang**

Kuo Sung-tao ▷ **Guo Songdao**

Kurds A nationalistic West Iranian-speaking ethnic group settled in neighbouring mountainous areas of Anatolia, Iraq, Iran and Turkey (including some in Syria and Armenia), an area which they themselves call Kurdistan, and numbering 9–10 million. They were originally pastoral nomads with some agriculture, but the creation of national boundaries after **World War I** restricted their seasonal migrations, and most are now urbanized. They have been Sunni Muslims since the 7cAD. They are politically oppressed in Turkey, and have suffered religious presecution in Iran, especially after the Iranian Revolution of 1979. In Iraq, the Kurds' failure to achieve autonomous status for Kurdistan during the 1970s, despite promises by the Ba'athist government, resulted in hostilities between Kurds and government forces.

Kuril Islands, Dispute over the A territorial dispute between the USSR and Japan over ownership of the southern group of Kuril Islands. During the 18c Russia began settling the northern and central Kurils, while the **Tokugawa Shogunate** laid claim to the southern islands, an arrangement that was formalized by the Treaty of Shimoda (7 Feb 1855). With the Treaty of St Petersburg (7 May 1875), Russia surrendered its claim to the northern and central Kurils (in return for which, Japan gave up her claims to Sakhalin Island), and the islands were then administered by Japan as part of Hokkaido (1875–1945). The Kurils were occupied by Soviet forces shortly after the USSR declared war on Japan (9 Aug 1945) and were formally declared Soviet territory. Since Japan insisted on the return of the southern Kurils (Kunashiri, Etorofu, Shikotan, Habomai islands), which it regards as inalienable Japanese territory (and are referred to as the Northern Territories), a Soviet–Japanese peace treaty was never signed, although relations were normalized in 1955. Even with the dismantling of the USSR in 1991, the dispute remains unresolved.

Kuropatkin, Alexei Nikolaievich (1848–1925) Russian general. He was Russian Chief-of-Staff under **Skobeleff** in the Turkish War (1877–8), and Commander-in-Chief in Caucasia (1897); as Minister of War (1898–1904) and Commander-in-Chief in Manchuria (1904–5), his record against the victorious Japanese was at best mediocre. He commanded the Russian armies on the northern front Feb–Aug 1916, and then was Governor of Turkestan until the **Russian Revolution** in 1917. ▷ **Russo-Turkish Wars**

Kush An independent kingdom on the Nile which emerged from the Egyptian province of Nubia in the 11cBC. In the 8cBC Kush conquered Egypt, and established the 25th Dynasty which ruled until the Assyrian conquest in 671–666BC. The Kush kings became Egyptianized, but after their withdrawal from Egypt in the 7cBC they moved to the more southerly capital of Meroe, where

there were good supplies of iron ore and timber. It became an important centre of iron smelting, and large slag heaps can still be seen there. ▷ **Axum; Napata**

Kushana Dynasty The chief tribe of the Yueh-chi people of China, the Kushanas ruled over much of north Indian, Afghanistan and Central Asia in 1–3cAD; their empire extended southwards as far as Sanchi, and to the east as far as Benares, with Mathura having the status of almost a second capital. The Kushana were Buddhist and also patronized some Hindu sects. The history of northern India under the Kushanas was closely associated with events in Central Asia. Kujula Khadhises and his son, Vima, were the first Kushanas; they came from Central Asia and gained control of northwest India in the 1cAD. Vima Kadphises was succeeded by **Kanishka**. It was under the latter that the Kushana Dynasty flourished, and this period ranks as one of the significant phases in the cultural development of northern India. Although Kanishka's successors ruled for 150 years, Kushana power gradually diminished after his reign.

Kusunoki Masashige (d.1336) Japanese warrior chieftain. Celebrated for his loyalty to Emperor **Daigo II**, Kusunoki supported Daigo's abortive attempt to restore direct imperial rule (1333–6), but was defeated in battle by the forces of **Ashikaga Takauji**, who supported a rival claimant to the throne. Kusunoki committed suicide shortly afterwards. He became a folk hero in later centuries and in school textbooks of the 1930s was eulogized for his faithful devotion to the throne and his spirit of self-sacrifice. ▷ **Ashikaga Shogunate**

Kut al-Amara, Battles of (28 Sep 1915 and 29 Apr 1916) **and Siege of** (1915–16) Kut al-Amara, on the west bank of the Tigris, some 100 miles from Baghdad, was taken first by the British under Major-General Charles Townshend in Sep 1915. Townshend later over-reached himself and was forced to fall back on Kut al-Amara, having suffered a reverse near the site of the ancient Ctesiphon. The Turks laid siege to Kut in Dec 1915 and, despite attempts to relieve Kut by British forces in Iraq, Townshend was forced to ask for terms. Townshend's proposals for terms were refused by the Turks and he surrendered, having first obtained a guarantee for his troops, in 1916.

Kutuzov, Mikhail Ilarionovich, Prince of Smolensk (1745–1813) Russian field marshal. He distinguished himself in Poland and in the **Russo-Turkish Wars**, and from 1805 to 1812 he commanded against the French. In 1812, as Commander-in-Chief, he fought **Napoleon I** obstinately at the Battle of **Borodino**, and later obtained a great victory over **Davout** and **Ney** at Smolensk. His army pursued the retreating French out of Russia into Prussia, where he died.

Kuusinen, Otto Vilgelmovich (1881–1964) Finnish-born Soviet politician. An active Bolshevik in both the 1905 and 1917 Russian Revolutions, he founded the Finnish Communist Party in 1918, but emigrated to Moscow when it was outlawed in 1930. He had already been working there as Secretary of the **Comintern** Executive Committee, a function he performed until 1939. He was then briefly Chairman of the Presidium of the so-called Karelo-Finnish Republic, which won him membership of the Soviet Party's Central Committee. A survivor, he was selected by Nikita **Khrushchev** in 1957 to be a member of the **Politburo** in the aftermath of the **Anti-Party Plot**. However, he died before it could be known how he would fare with Leonid **Brezhnev**.

Ku Wei-chun ▷ **Gu Weijun**

Ku Yen-wu ▷ **Gu Yanwu**

Kuyper, Abraham (1837–1920) Dutch theologian and politician. As a clergyman, founder of the Free University of Amsterdam (1880), member of the Dutch parliament and Prime Minister (1900–5), Kuyper sought to develop a Christian world-view of society. He founded and edited two newspapers and wrote numerous books, few of which have been translated into English, apart from *Lectures on Calvinism* (1898), *Principles of Sacred Theology* (1898), and *The Work of the Holy Spirit* (1900). His theology of common grace, the kingdom of God, and the 'sphere-sovereignty' of the Church and other social institutions, offer a Calvinistic version of Social Christianity. In the Netherlands he is remembered as the emancipator of the orthodox Calvinists and as the founder of the **Anti-Revolutionary Party**.

Kuznetsov, Vasili Vasilevich (1901–90) Soviet politician. He joined the Communist Party in 1927, and so managed to steer clear of trouble that in 1952 he became a member of the **Politburo**. Although he held various second-level political posts, he achieved little. Mikhail **Gorbachev** took the first opportunity to get rid of him in 1986 in order to free the system and make room for new blood.

Kwantung Army ▷ **Guandong Army**

KwaZulu A former national state or non-independent Black homeland in Natal province, eastern South Africa. Situated close to the Indian Ocean between the Transkei and Durban, it was granted self-governing status in 1971. It ceased to exist in May 1994 following the first all-race elections in South Africa. ▷ **apartheid**

L

Labadie, Jean de (1610–74) French ex-Jesuit Protestant reformer. A former member of the Jesuits, he became a Calvinist convert in 1650 and was minister at Middelburg in the Netherlands from 1666. He became increasingly pietistic, and preached a return to primitive Christianity. He was suspended by the Dutch Church in 1669, whereupon he moved his Labadist colony to Germany, where he died.

Labourers' Statute (1351) A law passed in an endeavour to stabilize the English economy in the wake of the Black Death, it represented the first ever attempt to control wages and prices by freezing wages and the prices of manufactured articles, and by restricting the movement of labour. Like most subsequent attempts, it failed abysmally to achieve its aims and contributed largely to the 1381 **Peasants Revolt**.

Labour Party (Norway) Despite the pioneering activities of Marcus **Thrane**, working-class political organization did not develop on a large scale in Norway until the beginnings of rapid industrialization at the end of the 19c. The Norwegian Labour Party was founded in 1884. Following the enactment of manhood suffrage (1898), four Labour candidates were elected to the Storting (parliament) in 1904, and by 1915 the party had won the support of 32 per cent of the electorate. Initially a moderate, reformist party, Labour moved sharply to the left during **World War I**. Its youth movement was represented at the Zimmerwald Conference in 1915 and established links with **Bukharin**. Led by Martin Tranmæl, the Left gained control at the 1918 Party Congress. In 1919 the Norwegian Labour Party became the second foreign party (after the Bulgarian) to join the **Comintern**. The right wing of the party split away in 1920 to form the Social Democratic Party. In 1923 the party broke with the Comintern: the Left then broke away to form the Norwegian Communist Party. The Social Democrats rejoined the party in 1927; in the elections of that year it became the largest single party in the country and in Jan–Feb 1928 formed a short-lived minority government under Christopher Hornsrud. Committed to parliamentarism

and measures to combat the depression, Labour obtained 40 per cent of the vote in 1933 and a deal with the Agrarian Party enabled it to form a government under Johan Nygaardsvold in 1935. Despite its achievements in social reform, the Labour government had neglected defence and was forced into exile in London (June 1940) following the German invasion of Norway. Labour won an absolute majority in the first post-war elections with a programme of extensive economic reconstruction and nationalization. Einar **Gerhardsen** was Prime Minister from 1945 to 1951 and again from 1955 to 1965. The defection of part of its left wing to form the Socialist People's Party deprived Labour of its majority in 1961, and from 1965 to 1971 Norway was ruled by a coalition of non-socialist parties. Labour returned to office under Trygve Bratteli, but his government resigned when the Norwegian electorate rejected EEC membership in the referendum of Oct 1972. In the election of 1973 the party's vote fell to 35 per cent but it remained in office through the support of the Socialist Electoral Alliance (anti-EEC socialists). In 1976 the leadership passed from Bratteli to Odvar Nordli, who was in turn succeeded briefly as Prime Minister by Gro Harlem **Brundtland** in 1981. After a period of minority Conservative and centre-right coalition government, Brundtland returned to power in 1986. ▷ **Koht, Halvdan; Lie, Trygve; Norway, German Invasion of**

Labour Party (UK) A British socialist/social democratic political party, originally formed in 1900 as the Labour Representation Committee to represent trade unions and socialist societies as a distinct group in parliament. In 1906, 26 MPs were elected, and the name changed to the **Labour Party**. In 1922 it overtook the Liberals as the main opposition party, and the first minority Labour government was elected in 1924, lasting 11 months. The first majority Labour government under Clement **Attlee** (1945–51) established the welfare state and carried out a significant nationalization programme. Since then Labour have been in office 1964–70 and 1974–9. The breakaway **Social Democratic Party** of the 1980s hurt the party's electoral chances throughout that decade. Outside parliament, the annual conference and the National Executive Committee share policy-making, though their influence is greater in opposition. The leader and deputy leader are elected annually when in opposition by an electoral college composed of trade unions, constituency parties, and the parliamentary Labour Party. The British Labour Party has been little influenced by **Marxism**, unlike the corresponding parties in Europe. ▷ **socialism**

Lacoste, Robert (1898–1989) French social-ist politician. He began his career as a civil servant, becoming a trade-union official. In **World War II** he began the first trade-union Resistance group. In 1944 he was Minister of Industrial Production, and was Minister for Industry and Commerce in 1946–7 and again in 1948. From 1956 to 1958 he was resident minister in Algeria, and was accused of allowing the military authorities to use torture and other ruthless measures against the rebels. He was Senator for the Dordogne (1971–80). ▷ **Resistance Movement** (France)

Ladislas IV of Poland ▷ **Władysław IV Vasa**

Ladysmith, Siege of (1899–1900) One of the three sieges of the second Boer War in which Boer forces attempted to pen up their British opponents, and around which many of the actions of the war took place. An attempt to relieve the town was frustrated at the Battle of **Spion Kop** (Jan 1900), but General Sir Redvers Buller (1839–1908) succeeded in raising the siege on 28 Feb 1900. ▷ **Boer Wars; Kimberley, Siege of; Mafeking, Siege of**

La Farina, Giuseppe (1815–63) Italian revolutionary and writer. In 1837 La Farina was forced to leave his native Sicily and settled in Florence; he returned when revolu-tion broke out in 1848 and joined the Provisional Government. After the failure of the **Revolutions of 1848–9**, he went to live first in Paris and then in Turin. By 1853 he had come to believe in the idea of Italian unification under the King of Sardinia-Pied-mont and in 1856 he founded the **Italian National Society**. In 1859 he helped to instigate and orchestrate a number of liberal/nationalist revolutions in central Italy which were used by **Cavour** as a pretext for subsequent annexation by Piedmont. The following year he was sent by **Cavour** to Sicily to try to prevent **Garibaldi** exerting too much influence over the course of events on the island, but poor relations with the great military hero led to La Farina's withdrawal.

Lafayette, Marie Joseph (Paul Yves Roch Gilbert du Motier), Marquis of (1757–1834) French soldier and revolutionary. After a period at court, he fought in the USA against the British during the War of Independence (1777–9 and 1780–2), and became a hero and a friend of George **Washington**. A liberal aristocrat, in the National Assembly of 1789 he presented a draft of a Declaration of the Rights of Man, based on the US Declaration of Indepen-dence. Hated by the **Jacobins** for his mod-eration, he defected to Austria, returning to France during the **Consulate**. During the Restoration he sat in the Chamber of Depu-ties (1818–24), became a radical Leader of the Opposition (1825–30), and commanded the **National Guard** in the 1830 **July Revolu-tion**. ▷ **American Revolution; Declaration of the Rights of Man and Citizen**

Laffitte, Jacques (1767–1844) French finan-cier and politician. He acquired great wealth as a Paris banker, and in 1814 became Governor of the Bank of France. He was elected to the Chamber of Deputies in 1817. In 1830 his house was the headquarters of the July Revolution, and he supplied a great part of the funds needed. In Nov 1830 he formed a cabinet, but he only held power until Mar 1831. From the ruins of his fortune he founded a Discount Bank in 1837. In 1843 he was elected President of the Chamber of Deputies.

La Follette, Robert Marion, Snr (1855–1925) US politician. Three times Progressive Governor of Wisconsin, he began his political career by winning election as a district attorney after exposing corruption in the local Republican Party **machine**. From 1885 to 1891, he served in the US House of Representatives. As Governor of Wisconsin, he reformed the primary election process and the civil service, strengthened the railroad commission and introduced measures for workers' compensation and the conservation of natural resources. His widely publicized and imitated reforms became knowns as the 'Wisconsin Idea'. He would have been the **Progressive Party** presidential candidate in 1912 but for the re-entry into politics of ex-President Theodore **Roosevelt**; in 1924 he became the nominee; although he failed in his presidential bid, he received nearly 5 million votes.

Lafontaine, Louis Hippolyte (1807–64) Canadian lawyer and politician. He recog-nized that French-Canadian culture would best be served by full French-Canadian participation in politics and by achieving **Responsible Government**. Although a follower of **Papineau**, he opposed the rebellion of 1837, and went to London to request constitutional reform. As the leader of the French-Canadians of **Canada East**, he joined in a coalition with **Canada West**'s reform leaders, Robert **Baldwin** and **Hincks**. The British government had sought to assimilate the French-Canadians by insisting on equal representation in the provincial legislature and on the use of English as the language of debate. The French-Canadians, however, became more politically cohesive and were able to unite with the English-speaking reformers to form an alliance which became the majority party. With the arrival of the realist Sir Charles **Bagot** in 1841, Lafontaine and Baldwin were eventually accepted as the leaders of a ministry. They therefore not only introduced a semblance of a responsible government, but demonstrated the potential of bi-cultural cooperation. There was a short interruption to reform when Sir Charles **Metcalfe** replaced Bagot, but with the introduction of free elections in 1848, the Baldwin–Lafontaine coalition came into office and served until 1851.

Lafontaine, Oskar (1943–) West German politician. Educated at Bonn University, he became leader of the Saar regional branch of the Social Democratic Party (**SPD**) in 1977 and served as Mayor of Saarbrücken (1976–85). He gained a reputation for radicalism and was variously dubbed 'Red Oskar' and the 'Ayatollah of the **Saarland**'. He began to mellow, however, after his election as Minister-President of the **Saarland** state parliament in 1985. In 1987 he was appointed a deputy chairman of the SPD's federal organization and served as the SPD's unsuccessful chancellor-candidate in the 1990 **Bundestag** elections after surviving an assassination attempt.

La Guardia, Fiorello Henry (1882–1947) US politician. He became Deputy Attorney-General (1915–17) and served seven terms in the House of Representatives as a Republican (1917–21 and 1923–33). Three times mayor of New York City (1934–46), he was a popular and effective leader who initiated broad reforms in public services, fought corruption, and undertook a major rebuilding program. New York's La Guardia Airport is named after him. ▷ **Republican Party**

La Hogue, Battle of (13–17 May 1692) A naval victory in the Channel, won by an Anglo-Dutch force after a five-day running battle over a numerically inferior French fleet. The defeat seriously reduced **Colbert**'s navy, ended French hopes of invading England, and gave the Allies control of the seas for the duration of the Nine Years War (1689–97).

laissez-faire An economic doctrine (in French literally 'leave alone') advocating that commerce and trade should be permitted to operate free of government controls. It was a popular view in the mid-19c and is still part of modern-day conservative political thinking. The phrase originated with the French 18c free trade economists.

Lajpat Rai, Lala (1865–1928) Indian politician and writer. He was a follower of the **Arya Samaj** and when, in 1893, it split, he and Hans Raj led the moderate 'college faction' which concentrated on building up a chain of 'Dayanand Anglo-Vedic colleges'. At the same time, Lajpat Rai developed a somewhat sporadic interest in Congress politics, as well as a more sustained involvement in **Swadeshi** enterprises. In the two articles published (1901) in the *Kayastha Samachar*, Lajpat Rai advocated technical education and industrial self-help and criticized the Congress as being a gathering of English-educated elites. He also argued that Congress should openly and boldly base itself on the Hindus alone. He led the wave of so-called extremist nationalism in Punjab between 1904 and 1907. The Congress split in the Surat session in 1907 and Lala Lajpat Rai formed the famous 'extremist' trio of Lal, Pal and Bal, with Tilak and Bipin Chandra Pal. Deported on charges of instigating the peasants, he led the **Non-Cooperation Movement** in Punjab in 1921.

Lakshmibai (d.1858) Maratha Rani (Queen) of Jhansi. The state of Jhansi was absorbed in 1853 by the British under the annexation policy made by Lord **Dalhousie**. According to this policy, all 'dependent' Indian states without direct heirs were to lapse to the British. In 1857, Jhansi was besieged and taken by the British despite desperate resistance from the Rani. The Rani then went first to Kalpi, and then to Gwalior with Tantia Tope where after proclaiming the Nana as Peshwa, she died fighting in 1858. She is regarded by some as the best and bravest military leader of the Indian forces during the war of 1857.

La Marmora, Alfonso Ferrero (1804–78) Piedmontese soldier and politician. He fought in the campaign against Austria in 1848 and was involved in the suppression of the Genoese revolt of 1849. During the 1850s he was instrumental in reforming the Piedmontese army, which formed the basis of the Italian army after 1860. In 1855 he commanded the Italian contingent in the **Crimean War**, and in 1860 he became Prime Minister on the resignation of **Cavour**. In 1860 he was made Governor of recently annexed Milan and the following year took the same job in Naples. He was Prime Minister again in 1864 and, as Foreign Minister, concluded the 1866 alliance with Prussia which was to lead to the Italian acquisition of Venetia. In 1870 he was once again made a royal governor, this time of Rome, just seized from the papacy. He subsequently retired from public life.

Lamartine, Alphonse (Marie Louis) de (1790–1869) French poet, politician, and historian. His best-known work was his first volume of lyrical poems, *Méditations poétiques* (1820). He became a member of the Provisional Government after the 1848 **July Revolution**, and acted as Minister of Foreign Affairs. He then devoted himself to literature, publishing several historical and other works.

Lambert, John (1619–84) English general. He studied law, then joined the parliamentary army in the **English Civil Wars**, commanding the cavalry at the Battle of **Marston Moor** (1644), and participating in several victories. He headed the army group which overthrew Richard Cromwell (1659), and virtually governed the country with his officers as the 'Committee of Safety'. After the **Restoration** (1661) he was tried, and imprisoned on Drake's Island, Plymouth, until his death.

Lambing Flat Riots (1860–1) In Australian history, a series of anti-Chinese riots on the Burrangong goldfields (Young, New South Wales) which expelled the Chinese and destroyed their camps. Police intervention led to further rioting in which one miner was killed. The riots reflected the racial and economic hostility to the Chinese which was general on Australian goldfields, leading to immigration restrictions and ultimately the **White Australia Policy**.

Lamennais, Félicité Robert de (1782–1854) French priest and writer. He began in 1816 his famous *Essai sur l'indifférence en matière de religion* (1818–24), a denunciation of private judgement and toleration, which was favourably received in Rome. However, notions of popular liberty began to change his outlook, and *L'Avenir*, a journal founded by him in 1830 with **Montalembert** and others, was condemned by the Pope in 1832. The *Paroles d'un croyant* (1834) brought about complete rupture with the Church, and revolutionary doctrines in his later work got him a year's imprisonment. Active in the 1848 **February Revolution**, he sat in the Assembly until the coup d'état. At his death he refused to make peace with the Church.

Lampião (Virgulino Ferreira da Silva) (d.1938) Brazilian bandit. Dubbed the 'King of the Cangaçeiros', he began his career in 1921. His fame rested on the size of his band, some 40–50 men on routine raids, who attacked large properties and even interior cities within the states of north-eastern Brazil. His brother's savage attack on Sousa (Paraíba) in 1924 and his equivocal role in combatting the Prestes Column (a group of young soldiers, led by Luís Carlos Prestes, which were in conflict with the federal government under President Washington Luís from 1926 to 1928) stimulated the growth of federal rule in the interior, limiting the control previously exercised by *coroneis*. Nevertheless, he was regarded as a popular hero in the country at large, and was the subject of a vast popular literature. ▷ **cangaço; coronelismo**

Lancaster, House of The younger branch of the Plantagenet Dynasty, founded by Edmund 'Crouchback', the younger son of **Henry III** and 1st Earl of Lancaster (1267–96), whence came three kings of England: **Henry IV**; **Henry V**; and **Henry VI**. ▷ **Edward IV; Roses, Wars of the; York, House of**

HOUSES OF LANCASTER AND YORK

Regnal Dates	Name
1399/1413	Henry IV
1413/22	Henry V
1422/61	Henry VI
1461/70	Edward IV
1470/1	Henry VI
1471/83	Edward IV
1483	Edward V
1483/5	Richard III

Lancaster House The London venue for various conferences preparing the way for independence in several parts of the British empire. It is most noted for the 1961 conference, which paved the way to Kenyan independence and the 1989 conference in which the British Foreign Secretary, Lord Carrington, managed to forge agreement for an independence constitution for Zimbabwe and procedures to end the civil war in that country.

Land A constituent 'state' in the German (and also the Austrian) federation. The majority of the Federal (West) German *Länder* (the plural form of the word) were set up by the Allied occupation authorities before the Federation (**Bund**) was created. Most *Land* constitutions are strongly plebiscitary in nature and envisage the democratization of broad aspects of society. The Länder enjoy sovereign rights in defined fields and are further strengthened in German constitutional life by the fact that the upper house of the Federal Parliament (the **Bundesrat**) consists of nominees of the Land governments. However, in practice the *Bund* has considerable influence over the shape of legislation at Land level. ▷ **Basic Law; Germany, West**

Land Acts, Irish A succession of British Acts passed in 1870, 1881, 1903, and 1909 with the objective first of giving tenants greater security and compensation for improvements, and later of enabling tenants to buy the estates they farmed. The Acts also aimed at reducing nationalist grievances and agitation. ▷ **Land League**

Landdrost Full-time officials and magistrates of the Dutch East India Company in South Africa who administered the interior regions of the colony. They were normally strangers to their areas, and were assisted by a secretary, a messenger and a number of soldiers. They managed all legal matters, border conflicts and wars and frequently came into conflict with the Boer citizens of their districts.

Länder ▷ **Land**

Landfriede An imperial measure (literally, 'country-wide peace') to restrict private warfare. This institution is linked to the **Treuga Dei**, which originated in France, but it was not limited to specific feast days or times. The first imperial *Landfriede* was promulgated by **Henry IV** in Mainz, with the aim of regulating feuds between princes. Breach of the peace was punishable by imperial sanctions and the policy was vigorously pursued by **Frederick I**, reaching a high-point in the Mainz imperial Landfriede of 1235. It made a significant contribution to securing law and order in the empire. There were also parallel local Landfrieden, the first of which was enacted for Bavaria in 1094.

Land League An association formed in Ireland in 1879 by Michael **Davitt** to agitate for greater tenant rights, in particular the '3 Fs': *fair rents*, to be fixed by arbitration if necessary; *fixity of tenure* while rents were paid; and *freedom* for tenants to sell rights of occupancy. **Gladstone** conceded the essence of these demands in the 1881 Land Act. ▷ **Land Acts, Irish**

Landsknechte German mercenary troops of the 16c first raised by Maximilian I. The term originally differentiated them from the more numerous Swiss mercenaries, whose reputation declined after the Battles of Marignano and Padua. The *Landsknechte* were the mainstay of the Imperial and German armies and fought on both sides of the **Thirty Years War**. Their organizational structure formed the pattern of the later regimental system, which is still in use at the present time.

Landtag Literally 'state diet' or 'parliament', this term describes the parliament of German (and Austrian) states (*Länder*). ▷ **Basic Law; Bund; Germany, West; Land**

Lange, David Russell (1942–) New Zealand politician. After studying law at Auckland University and qualifying as a solicitor and barrister, he worked as a crusading lawyer for the underprivileged in Auckland. Elected to the House of Representatives in 1977, he became Deputy Leader of the Labour Party in 1979 and Leader in 1983. He won a decisive victory in the 1984 general election on a non-nuclear defence policy, which he immediately put into effect, despite criticism from other Western countries, particularly the USA. Re-elected in 1987, he resigned the premiership in 1989, following bouts of ill health and disagreements within his party.

Langevin, Sir Hector-Louis (1826–1906) Canadian lawyer, journalist and politician. Mayor of Quebec in 1856, and Solicitor-General in the coalition ministry that achieved confederation, he replaced George Étienne **Cartier** as the French-Canadian representative in the cabinet of John A **Macdonald**. However, he was an extremist Catholic, gaining much of his support from the intolerant ultramontane wing of the Church, and Macdonald found it necessary to balance his power by inviting into the cabinet the Grand Master of the **Orange Order**, Mackenzie **Bowell** and later Joseph Adolphe **Chapleau**. Langevin was forced to resign in the railway scandal of 1891. ▷ **Confederation Movement**

Langton, Stephen (c.1150–1228) English prelate and Archbishop of Canterbury. Pope Innocent III made him a cardinal (1206) and Archbishop (1207), but King John refused to accept his appointment, and Langton was kept out of the see until 1213. He took sides with the barons against John, and his name is the first of the subscribing witnesses of Magna Carta. ▷ **John ('John Lackland')**

Lansbury, George (1859–1940) British politician. Active as a radical since boyhood, he became a convinced socialist in 1890 and a Labour MP in 1910, resigning in 1912 to stand in support of women's suffrage. He was defeated and not re-elected until 1922. He founded and edited the *Daily Herald* (1912–22), and became Commissioner of Works (1929) and Leader of the **Labour Party** (1931–5). ▷ **MacDonald, Ramsay; socialism**

Lansing–Ishii Agreement (2 Nov 1917) The name given to the exchange of diplomatic notes between the Japanese ambassador to the USA, Ishii Kikujiro, and US Secretary of State, Robert Lansing, which agreed on a set of principles concerning policy towards China. The agreement helped soothe tensions between the two countries at a time when the USA was becoming increasingly critical of Japan's attempts to enhance its influence in China. Respect for China's territorial integrity and commitment to the Open Door policy (ie that all powers should have equal economic opportunities in China) were confirmed; at the same time, the USA recognized that Japan had special interests in China because of 'territorial propinquity'. The agreement was superseded by the Washington Treaties of 1921–2, which committed all the powers to respect China's independence.

Lao-tzu ▷ **Lao Zi**

Lao Zi (Lao-tzu) (6c BC) Chinese philosopher and sage, literally 'the old master'. Little

is known of his life, but he is regarded as the inspiration for Taoism and for one of its principal works, the *Tao-te-Ching* (The Way of Power), compiled some 300 years after his death, which teaches self-sufficiency, simplicity and detachment. Taoism venerates the 'feminine' qualities which promote longevity, equanimity and an instinctive unity with nature.

La Pérouse, Jean François de Galaup, Count of (1741–88) French navigator. In 1785, in command of an expedition of discovery, he visited the north-west coast of America, explored the north-east coasts of Asia, and sailed through La Pérouse Strait between Sakhalin and Yezo. In 1788 he sailed from Botany Bay, and his two ships were wrecked north of the New Hebrides.

Lapointe, Ernest (1876–1941) Canadian politician. As a Liberal with **Rouge** tendencies, he was very critical of the **Borden–Meighen** stand against the **Winnipeg General Strike**. In 1921 he was appointed to a minor position in the Mackenzie **King** administration, but it was as an adviser on French-Canadian affairs and attitudes that the Prime Minister valued him. In 1924 he became Minister of Justice. Like King, he believed the unity of the country was the foremost issue and therefore put his concern for social reform to one side (accepting, for instance, the notorious anti-communist **Padlock Act** in Quebec). Although he opposed conscription, he played an important role in generating support within Quebec for Canada's participation in **World War II**, and when Maurice **Duplessis** challenged the **War Measures Act**, Lapointe's threat to resign was an effective contribution to the return of a more amenable provincial administration. ▷ **Liberal Party** (Canada)

Lapua Movement A semi-fascist political movement which originated in the Finnish town of Lapua in 1929. Composed mainly of small farmers who were influenced by Lutheran pietism and who were fiercely both nationalist and also anti-communist, the movement agitated for the suppression of the Finnish Communist Party (which had been formally illegal in Finland since 1919). Its pressure on parliament and acts of violence led to the banning of the Communist Party's front organizations in Oct 1930. The Lapua Movement was itself declared illegal in 1932 following an abortive armed uprising against the government. However, during its short period of existence Lapua was one of the most significant manifestations of right-wing extremism in inter-war Europe. ▷ **Communist Party** (Finland)

Largo Caballero, Francisco (1869–1946) Spanish trade union and socialist leader. Secretary-General of the **UGT** from 1918 to 1936, his corporativist aspirations led him to collaborate with the dictatorship of **Primo de Rivera** of 1923–30. As Minister of Labour (1931–3) under the Second Republic, he altered the exploitative economic and social relations of rural Spain. From 1934 to 1935 he was the leader of the socialists' increasingly revolutionary left wing as the Right reversed the reforms of 1931–3. His revolutionary stance contributed significantly to the polarization of the Republic in 1936. Appointed Prime Minister (Sep 1936) after the **Spanish Civil War** broke out, he proved a conservative and rigid war leader, curtailing the social revolution and re-establishing state authority. He was nonetheless ousted by the communists in May 1937 for opposing the suppression of the **CNT** and **POUM**. First detained in exile by the **Vichy** French and then, in Feb 1943, by the **Gestapo**, he was liberated from a **concentration camp** in Apr 1945. ▷ **Republic, Second** (Spain)

Lari Massacre (26 Mar 1953) A notorious incident during the 'Mau Mau' emergency in Kenya in which over 100 Kikuyu of the loyal chief Luka were killed by insurgents of the secret society. As with the assassination of the senior chief, Waruhiu, in the previous year, the massacre revealed the extent to which the emergency was in one of its aspects a Kikuyu civil war.

La Rochefoucauld, François, 6th Duke of (1613–80) French writer. An active member of the opposition to Cardinal **Richelieu**, he was forced to live abroad (1639–42). He then joined in the revolts known as the **Fronde** (1648–53), and was wounded at the Siege of Paris. He retired to the country in 1652, returning to the court on **Mazarin**'s death in 1661. His major works were written while in retirement: *Mémoires* (1664) and the epigrammatic collection, *Réflexions*, which is commonly known as the *Maximes* (1665). ▷ **Paris, Siege of**

La Rocque, François, Colonel, Count of (1886–1946) French regular army officer. He resigned from the army in 1928 to enter business; in 1931 he became leader of the Ligue des **Croix de Feu** which expanded its membership very rapidly under him. In 1936

he became leader of the *Parti social français* ('French Social Party') which replaced the *Croix de Feu*. During **World War II** he supported the **Resistance Movement**.

Las Casas, Bartolomé de (1474–1566) Spanish missionary priest. Dubbed the 'Apostle of the Indians', he sailed in the third voyage of Columbus (1502) to Hispaniola, was ordained (1512), and travelled to Cuba (1513). His desire to protect the natives from slavery led him to visit the Spanish court on several occasions. Appointed Bishop of Chiapa, he was received (1544) with hostility by the colonists, returned to Spain, and resigned his see (1547). ▷ **slave trade**

Lassalle, Ferdinand (1825–64) German socialist. He studied philosophy at Breslau, **Berlin**, and Paris, and in 1846 engaged in eight years of divorce litigation on behalf of the Countess Hatzfeld, for which he received a pension. He took part in the **Revolution of 1848**, and was imprisoned for six months for an inflammatory speech. He lived in the **Rhineland** until 1857, developing his theories of **socialism**, much influenced by **Marx**. He then returned to Berlin, and at Leipzig in 1863 he founded the Universal German Workers' Association to agitate for universal suffrage. He was killed in a duel over a love affair, at Geneva. ▷ **Marxism**

Late Period In Ancient Egyptian history this term refers to the period of the 25th to 30th Dynasties. The 25th Dynasty (Nubian) kings were devoted to the worship of Amun and stressed the importance of the position of the Divine Adoratrice of the god at Thebes. Royal princesses held the office, being appointed by adoption. New buildings were erected and others restored, both in Egypt and Nubia. The dynasty ended with the invasions of the Assyrians in 671BC and 663BC. Princesses loyal to Ashurbanipal were installed in the Delta, with Thebes under the control of the Divine Adoratrice. The prince of Sais was strong enough to unite the country and set up the 26th Dynasty. There was an upsurge in artistic and cultural expression inspired by the best works of the **Old Kingdom** particularly. Babylon had overwhelmed Assyria and inevitably there was a clash with Egypt. The Persians invaded Egypt in 525BC and under the 27th Dynasty the country became a satrapy of the Persian Empire. From this time onwards, frequent revolts to gain independence are recorded in Greek sources. Following the ephemeral 28th and 29th Dynasties, the last native kings formed the 30th Dynasty, but by 343BC, Egypt was once more subject to Persia until the conquest of **Alexander III, 'the Great'**. ▷ **Necho II; Nectanebo II; Psamtik I**

Lateran Councils A series of councils of the Church held at the Lateran Palace, Rome, between the 7c and the 18c. Those held in 1123, 1139, 1179, and especially 1215 are the most significant. The Fourth or Great Council defined the doctrine of the Eucharist ('transubstantiation'), and represents the culmination of medieval papal legislation.

Lateran Pacts (Feb 1929) The name given to agreements, between the Italian fascist state and the papacy, reached after negotiations between **Mussolini** and Pius XI's Secretary of State, Cardinal Gaspari. The pacts brought an end to the Church–state conflict which had been raging in Italy since the **Risorgimento**. By them, Italy recognized the sovereignty of the Vatican city, gave substantial compensation to the papacy for the loss of its territories during the **Risorgimento**, and guaranteed religious education at all levels of state schooling. In return, the Church recognized the Italian state for the first time. The pacts were confirmed in the constitution of 1948.

Latimer, Hugh (c.1485–1555) English Protestant reformer and martyr. He was appointed a university preacher in 1522. Converted to Protestantism, he was one of the divines who examined the lawfulness of **Henry VIII**'s marriage, and declared on the King's side. In 1535 he was made Bishop of Worcester, but opposed the Six Articles of Henry VIII, for which he was imprisoned in 1536, 1546, and 1553. He became known as a preacher under **Edward VI**, but under **Mary I** was tried for heresy and was burnt. ▷ **Reformation** (England)

Latium In antiquity, the area south-east of Rome between the Apennine Mountains and the sea. It was the territory of the Latini, Latin-speaking peoples of whom the Romans are the most famous. Densely populated in early Roman times, by the imperial period it had become the recreation area of the Roman rich who filled it with luxurious villas.

Lattre de Tassigny, Jean de (1889–1952) French soldier. He commanded an infantry battalion during **World War I**, and in 1940 he commanded the 14th Division; he was then sent by the **Vichy** government to command in Tunisia. He was recalled for sympathy with

the Allies and arrested in 1942. He escaped from Riom prison via North Africa to London in 1943. As commander of the French 1st Army he took a brilliant part in the Allied liberation of France (1944–5), signing the German surrender. He was responsible for the reorganization of the French Army and was appointed Commander-in-Chief of Western Union Land Forces under **Montgomery** in 1948. In 1950 as Commander-in-Chief in French Indo-China, for a time he turned the tide against the Vietminh rebels. He was posthumously made a Marshal of France in 1952. ▷ **Riom Trial**

Laud, William (1573–1645) Archbishop of Canterbury. He was ordained in 1601. His learning and industry brought him many patrons, and he rapidly received preferment, becoming King's Chaplain (1611), Bishop of St David's (1621), Bishop of Bath and Wells and a Privy Councillor (1626), Bishop of London (1628), and Archbishop of Canterbury (1633). With **Strafford** and **Charles I**, he worked for absolutism in Church and state. In Scotland, his attempt (1635–7) to Anglicize the Church led to the **Bishops Wars**. In 1640 the **Long Parliament** impeached him. He was found guilty, and executed on Tower Hill.

Lauderdale, John Maitland, Duke of (1616–82) Scottish statesman. He was an ardent supporter of the **Covenanters** (1638), and in 1643 became a Scottish Commissioner at Westminster. Made earl in 1645, he was taken prisoner at Worcester (1651), and imprisoned. At the **Restoration** (1660) he became Scottish Secretary of State. A Privy Councillor, he was a member of the **Cabal** advisers to **Charles II**, and was created duke in 1672. ▷ **English Civil Wars**

Lauenburg A duchy associated with Holstein and Denmark. Duke Magnus I (d.1543) introduced the Reformation to the Duchy. The extinction of the ruling house in 1689 resulted in claims by John George III, Elector of Saxony, and George William, Duke of Brunswick, among others. George William prevailed and, after an indemnity, was recognized as Duke by the Saxon Elector. His nephew, George Louis, Elector of Hanover, later George I of Britain, became Duke in 1692. It was occupied (1803) by France, reverted to Hanover (1813) and was eventually ceded to Prussia (1816).

Laurier, Sir Wilfrid (1841–1919) Canadian politician. He became a lawyer, a journalist, and a member of the Quebec Legislative Assembly. He entered federal politics in 1874, and became Minister of Inland Revenue (1877), leader of the **Liberal Party** (1887–1919), and the first French-Canadian and Roman Catholic to be Prime Minister of Canada (1896–1911). A firm supporter of self-government for Canada, in his home policy he was an advocate of compromise and free trade with the USA. ▷ '**Commercial Union**'; **Imperial Conferences**

Lausanne, Treaty of (1923) After the Graeco-Turkish war, it replaced the Treaty of Sèvres and granted considerable concessions to the Turks, freeing them from paying the reparations imposed on them as a defeated power at the end of **World War I**. The Turks retained their lands in Anatolia and Thrace, while Greece lost most of its major war gains: Eastern Thrace, the Smyrna region and the Imvros and Tenedos islands. The Turkish minister **Inönü** and the Greek Eleuthérios **Venizélos** agreed to the exchange of populations which led to the uprooting of 380 000 Turks from Greece and 1.3 million **Greeks** from Anatolia. The treaty also confirmed the British annexation of Cyprus.

Lausanne Conference (1932) The conference held between the Allied powers and Germany to discuss the question of German reparation payments, which had been suspended by the moratorium imposed by the unilateral decision of US President Herbert **Hoover** in 1931, after the onset of the Great Depression. A final reparation payment by Germany was agreed, but the Lausanne convention was never ratified, and no more payments were actually made.

Laval, Pierre (1883–1945) French politician. He became a lawyer, Deputy (1914), and Senator (1926), before serving as Premier (1931–2, 1935–6). From a position on the extreme left of the **Socialist Party**, he moved rightwards during the 1920s and 1930s, and in the **Vichy** government was **Pétain**'s deputy (1940). He was removed from office in Dec 1940 but restored with much greater power in Apr 1942. Again Prime Minister in 1942–4, he openly collaborated with the Germans. Fleeing after the liberation to Germany and Spain, he was brought back, charged with treason, and executed in Paris. ▷ **World War II**

La Vallière, Louise Françoise de la Baume le Blanc, Duchess of (1644–1710) Mistress of **Louis XIV** of France. She was

maid of honour to Henrietta Anne of England, Duchess of Orléans, before becoming the royal mistress (1661–7). She bore the King four children, and remained at court reluctantly after Mme de **Montespan** superseded her (1667). Eventually she was allowed to retire to a Carmelite nunnery in Paris (1674), where she died.

Lavigerie, Charles Martial Allemand (1825–92) French prelate. As Primate of Africa and Archbishop of Algiers (1884) he became well known for his missionary work, and founded the order of the White Fathers (1868). In 1888 he founded the Anti-Slavery Society. In 1890 his 'toast of Algiers' launched Pope Leo XIII's campaign to persuade French Catholics to rally to the republic.

Lavrentev, Mikhail Alexevich (1900–80) Soviet mathematician. He held several influential academic appointments in both Moscow and Kiev, and during and after **World War II** came into close contact with Nikita **Khrushchev**. He was a full member of the Soviet Academy of Sciences from 1946, a deputy in the Supreme Soviet from 1958, and a candidate member of the Central Committee from 1961. This enabled him to build Akademgorodok, or Academic City, in Novosibirsk, designed to educate generations of superbrains and promote outstanding research. His creation partly achieved its purpose but it also helped to expand the intellectual frustration that built up under Leonid **Brezhnev**.

Law, (Andrew) Bonar (1858–1923) British politician. He was an iron merchant in Glasgow, became a Unionist MP in 1900, and in 1911 succeeded **Balfour** as Unionist leader. He acted as Colonial Secretary (1915–16), a member of the war cabinet, Chancellor of the Exchequer (1916–18), Lord Privy Seal (1919), and from 1916 Leader of the House of Commons. He retired in 1921 through ill health, but returned to serve as Premier for several months in 1922–3.

Lawrence, Sir Henry Montgomery (1806–57) British soldier and colonial administrator. In 1823 he joined the Bengal Artillery and took part in the first Burmese War (1828), the first of the **Afghan Wars** (1838), and the Sikh Wars (1845 and 1848). In 1856 he pointed out the danger of reducing the British army, and the latent germs of rebellion. The following year he was appointed to Lucknow, and did all he could to restore contentment there, but the **Indian Uprising** broke out in May. It was owing to his foresight that it was made possible for 1 000 Europeans and 800 Indians to defend the Residency for nearly four months against 7 000 rebels. He was mortally injured during this defence.

Lawrence, T(homas) E(dward) ('Lawrence of Arabia') (1888–1935) British soldier and author. Before **World War I** he travelled in the Middle East, studying Crusader castles and participating in the excavation of Carchemish. In 1914 he joined military intelligence and was sent to Cairo, where he became a member of the Arab Bureau. In 1916 he was appointed the British liaison officer to the **Arab Revolt**, led by **Faysal**, the son of Sharif **Husayn ibn 'Ali** of Mecca, and was present at the taking of Aqaba (1917) and of Damascus (1918). He was an adviser to Faysal at the **Paris Peace Conference** and a member of the Middle East Department at the Colonial Office (1921). His account of the Arab Revolt, *Seven Pillars of Wisdom*, abridged by himself as *Revolt in the Desert*, became one of the classics of war literature. His exploits received so much publicity that he became a legendary figure, and so he attempted to escape his fame by enlisting in the ranks of the RAF (1922) as J H Ross, in the Royal Tank Corps (1923) as T E Shaw, and again in the RAF in 1925. He retired in 1935 and was killed in a motorcycling accident the same year.

Lawrence (of the Punjab and of Grately), John Laird Mair, 1st Baron (1811–79) British colonial administrator. He joined the Indian Civil Service in Delhi, and became Commissioner, then Lieutenant-Governor, of the Punjab. He carried out many economic and social reforms, for which he was nicknamed 'the Saviour of the Punjab'. After helping to put down the **Indian Uprising** of 1857–8, he was made a baronet, and in 1863 became Governor-General of India. He returned to England in 1869, was made a baron, and died in London.

Lawson, Nigel (1932–) British politician. He spent some time working for various newspapers and also for television (1956–72), and during this time edited the *Spectator* (1966–70). Elected to parliament in 1974, when the Conservatives returned to office he became Financial Secretary to the Treasury (1979–81), Energy Secretary (1981–3), and Chancellor of the Exchequer (1983–9). During his time at the Exchequer, Britain saw lower direct taxes, but high interest rates and record trade deficits. ▷ **Conservative Party** (UK)

Lazar, Hrebeljanović (1329–89) Prince of Serbia (1371/89) and Serbian national hero. He led his people into battle against the Ottoman Turks, repulsing Sultan Murad I at Pločnik (1386) but was captured and executed by the Turks at the Battle of **Kosovo** which marked the end of the medieval Kingdom of Serbia (1389). He was buried in the monastery at Ravenica but was later reburied at Vrdnik (1683) and finally at Belgrade, in the Orthodox cathedral built by Miloš **Obrenović** (1845). ▷ **Kraljević, Marko**

League of Nations A former international organization whose constitution was drafted at the **Paris Peace Conference** in 1919 and incorporated into the Treaty of **Versailles**. The main aims were to preserve international peace and security by the prevention or speedy settlement of disputes and the promotion of disarmament. With its headquarters in Geneva, the League operated through a Council, which met several times a year, and an annual Assembly. Its original members included the victorious Allies of **World War I**, except for the USA, which refused to join, and most of the neutral nations. Germany joined in 1926, and the USSR in 1934, but Germany and Japan withdrew in 1933, and Italy in 1936. Although the League succeeded in settling some minor disputes, it became increasingly ineffective in the later 1930s, when it failed to stop major acts of aggression by Japan, Italy, and Germany. In 1946 it transferred its functions to the **UN**. ▷ **Wilson, Thomas Woodrow**

leagues (*ligues*) The name given to French political movements, which, while being in some ways akin to political parties, also had an extra-parliamentary dimension, which made them appear proto-fascist. The most important were the *Ligue des patriotes* ('League of Patriots', 1882), and *Ligue de la patrie française* ('League of the French Fatherland', 1899), the *Ligue de l'action française* ('League of French Action', 1899) and the Ligue des **Croix de Feu** (1927).

Learn from the PLA Campaign (1963–4) A political campaign in China which began within the **People's Liberation Army** (PLA), aiming to stress the importance of service to the Communist Party and commitment to socialist ideals. A key aspect of the campaign was to elevate the position of **Mao Zedong**

and his thought at a time when his influence within the party had waned following the disasters of the **Great Leap Forward**. With the active support of **Lin Biao**, appointed by Mao in 1959 as Defence Minister and head of the PLA, a compilation of Mao's sayings (*Quotations from Chairman Mao*, known as the 'Little Red Book') was studied and memorized throughout the PLA, thereby initiating the cult of Mao that was to attain grotesque proportions during the **Cultural Revolution**. By the end of 1963, Mao was calling upon the entire country to 'learn from the PLA', implying that it was the army rather than the party that incarnated the spirit of self-sacrifice and dedication to collective values. The campaign marked the beginning of the PLA's increasing involvement in politics (army personnel were assigned to work in various government organizations) and Mao's attack on the party hierarchy.

Lease, Mary Elizabeth (1853–1933) US reformer. She spoke out in favour of women's suffrage, **prohibition** of alcohol and other causes. Nicknamed the 'Kansas Pythoness' for the strength of her populist rhetoric, her command to 'raise less corn and more hell' became the Populist Party's slogan.

Lebeau, Joseph Jean Louis (1794–1865) Belgian politician. Trained as a lawyer and active as a journalist in liberal opposition to the government of King **William I**, after the **Belgian Revolution** of 1830 Lebeau helped draw up the constitution of the new state of Belgium, and became an MP and (briefly) Foreign Minister in 1831. He was Minister for Justice (1832–4), and Governor of Namur (1834–40); he formed the first purely liberal Belgian government (without the Catholics) in 1840, in which he was himself Foreign Minister (1840–1).

Lebensraum An expansionist concept (literally, 'living space') developed by the Nazis (especially **Hitler**) from the early 1920s onwards, which planned to extend German control far into the USSR to provide land for colonization. Hitler argued that Germany was over-populated, and needed more agriculturally productive land to guarantee future food supplies for an expanded German population. The alleged inferiority of East European peoples was used to justify this, parallels being made with European/British colonialism in America and Australia. ▷ **Nazi Party; World War II**

Lebowa A former national state or non-independent Black homeland in northern Transvaal province, north-east South Africa. Situated north-east of Pretoria, it was granted self-governing status in 1972. It ceased to exist in May 1994 following the first all-race elections in South Africa. ▷ **apartheid**

Lebrun, Albert (1871–1950) French politician and President (1932–40). He became a Deputy in 1900, was Minister for the Colonies (1911–14), for Blockade and Liberated Regions (1917–19), Senator (1920), and President of the Senate (1931). The last President of the **Third Republic,** he surrendered his powers to **Pétain** in 1940.

Leburton, Edmond (1915–) Belgian politician. He studied at Liège University and in 1946 became a MP for the **Belgian Socialist Party**. From 1954 to 1971 he held numerous cabinet posts with economic and social portfolios; in 1973–4 he was Prime Minister.

Le Chapelier, Isaac René Guy (1754–94) French revolutionary politician. He is best known for the law he introduced in June 1791, and known by his name, forbidding associations of members of the same trade, and thus banning trade unions and strikes, as well as employers' associations. It was the keystone of economic liberalism. He was executed in 1794.

Lechfeld, Battle of the (955) After the invading Hungarians had besieged Augsburg and attacked the rearguard of the King's army, they were defeated to the west of Augsburg by the **Franks** under **Conrad the Red**, who died in battle, and the Saxons, led by **Otto I, 'the Great'**, and thereafter driven out of their camp beyond the River Lech. The following day Otto surrounded them and won a historic victory. After this battle, Hungarian raids ceased and the Hungarians became settled and part of Western civilization. The victory marked an important step in Otto's progress towards becoming emperor.

Le Clerc (de Hauteclocque), Jacques Philippe (1902–47) French soldier. After fighting in 1940, he joined the **Free French** forces under de **Gaulle** in England. He became military commander in French Equatorial Africa, and led a force across the desert to join the British 8th Army, in 1942. He commanded the French 2nd Armoured Division in **Normandy**, and received the surrender of Paris in 1944. ▷ **Normandy Campaign; World War II**

Ledru-Rollin, Alexandre Auguste (1807–74) French republican politician. In 1841 he was elected Deputy for Le Mans. At the **February Revolution** (1848) he became Minister of the Interior in the Provisional Government. As candidate for the presidency against Louis Napoleon (**Napoleon III**) he was beaten, and an unsuccessful attempt to provoke an insurrection in June 1849 drove him to England. He was amnestied in 1870, and after his return was elected to the National Assembly (1871).

Le Duc Tho (Phan Dinh Khai) (1911–93) Vietnamese politician. He joined the Indo-Chinese Communist Party in 1929 and was exiled to the penal island of Con Dia by the French in 1930. Released in 1937, he became head of the Nam Dinh revolutionary movement, but was re-arrested and imprisoned (1939–44). After **World War II**, he worked for the Communist Party of Vietnam (CPV), entering its Politburo in 1955. As leader of the Vietnamese delegation to the Paris Conference on Indo-China (1968–73), he was awarded the 1973 Nobel Peace Prize, jointly with Henry **Kissinger**, but he declined to accept it. He retired from the Politburo in 1986.

Lee (of Asheridge), Jennie, Baroness (1904–88) British politician. The daughter of a Scottish miner, she made her own way in socialist politics, becoming the youngest elected woman MP (1929–31). She married Aneurin **Bevan** in 1934. Re-elected to parliament in 1945, she became Minister for the Arts (1967–70), and was given the task of establishing the Open University. She retired from the House of Commons in 1970 to be made a life peer. ▷ **Labour Party** (UK); **socialism**

Lee, Robert E(dward) (1807–70) US general. Educated at the US Military Academy at West Point, he received a commission in the Engineer Corps. He fought in the Mexican War and later became Superintendent of West Point. He commanded the US troops that captured John Brown at Harpers Ferry. When the southern states seceded from the Union, he resigned from the US Army so he would be free to serve his native state of Virginia. In 1861 he accepted the position of Commander-in-Chief of the Confederate Army of Virginia. His achievements are central to the history of the **American Civil War**. He was in charge of the defences at Richmond, and halted federal forces in the **Seven Days Battles** (1862). His forces were victorious in the second battle of **Bull Run**. His first northern invasion was stopped at the Battle of **Antietam**. His troops repulsed the Union side in the Battle of **Fredericksburg** and were victorious at the Battle of Chancellorsville. His second northern invasion ended in defeat at the Battle of **Gettysburg** (1863). In the **Wilderness** campaign (1864) Lee's forces were badly battered. In Feb 1865 Lee became Commander-in-Chief of all of the sourthern armies, but the confederate cause was hopeless at that point and two months later he surrendered his army to General Grant at **Appomattox Court House**, Virginia. After the war, Lee became President of Washington College at Lexington.

Leeds, Thomas Osborne, 1st Duke of (1631–1712) English politician. He became MP for York in 1665. After opposition to **Clarendon**, he was appointed Treasurer of the Navy (1668) and Privy Councillor (1673). He became Lord Treasurer in 1673, succeeding Clifford as King **Charles II**'s Chief Minister until his fall during the **Exclusion Crisis** (1679). He was successively Viscount Osborne of Dunblane, Baron Osborne of Kiveton and Viscount Latimer (1673), Earl of Danby (1674), Marquis of Carmarthen (1689) and Duke of Leeds (1694). Under Charles, he increased the yield from taxes and thus the King's financial independence. He also worked for the marriage of Mary, daughter of James, Duke of York, to **William III** (1677). He was impeached on charges of secret financial dealings with **Louis XIV** of France on Charles's behalf, and imprisoned in the Tower (1684). During **James VII and II**'s reign, he opposed the King's Catholic policies. His negotiations with the Dutch were part of a process which culminated in William of Orange's arrival in England (1688) and assumption of the crown. He was rewarded with the Presidency of the Council (1689–99) but further impeachment proceedings, for taking a bribe to secure a charter for the new East India Company (1695), ended his career as Chief Minister. In semi-retirement during Queen **Anne**'s reign, he supported the **Tories**, especially defending the Church of England. ▷ **East India Company, British; Popish Plot**

Lee Kuan Yew (1923–) Singaporean politician, born into a wealthy Chinese family. He studied law at Cambridge and qualified as a barrister in London before returning to Singapore in 1951 to practise. He founded the moderate, anti-communist

People's Action Party (PAP) in 1954, and entered the Singapore Legislative Assembly in 1955. He became the country's first Prime Minister in 1959, a position he held until 1990. He acquired a formidable reputation for probity and industry, and oversaw the implementation of a successful programme of economic development. His son, Brigadier-General Lee Hsien Loong (1952–), is viewed as a possible successor in the longer term.

Lee Teng-hui (1923–) Taiwanese politician. Educated at universities in the USA and Japan, he taught economics at the National Taiwan University before becoming Mayor of Taipei in 1979. A member of the ruling **Guomindang** and a protégé of **Jiang Jing'guo**, he became Vice-President of Taiwan in 1984 and state President and Guomindang leader on Jiang's death in 1988. The country's first island-born leader, he is a reforming technocrat who has significantly accelerated the pace of liberalization and 'Taiwanization'.

Left-Republicans Spanish political parties. In the 1920s two new Republican parties emerged in reaction against the old-style populism and patronage politics of Alejandro **Lerroux**'s **Radical Republican Party**: Republican Action in 1925 and the Radical–Socialist Party in 1929. They aimed to provide the Republican movement with a more progressive and modern content, their most coherent and articulate representative being Manuel **Azaña**. Under the Second Republic, the Left-Republicans dominated the liberal reformist administrations of 1931–3, but were devastated in the general election of Nov 1933. They were nonetheless central to the creation of the Popular Front coalition which won the election of Feb 1936. However, the Left-Republicans' vacillatory leadership during the spring and summer of 1936 not only contributed to the polarization of the political climate, but also was critical in the conversion of the military rising of July 1936 into a civil war. ▷ **Republic, Second** (Spain); **Spanish Civil War**

Legalism An important school of Chinese thought during the Warring States Period (403–222BC). Legalist thinkers such as Shang Yang and **Han Fei** were concerned above all else with the power and authority of the state, rather than the well-being of the population. They rejected the Confucian emphasis on the innate moral goodness of man and insisted that people be ruled by a strict and uniform system of rewards and punishments

impartially imposed. Legalist measures were adopted by the Qin state, which eventually conquered its neighbours to establish China's first empire. The brutal policies adopted by the short-lived **Qin Dynasty** gave legalism a bad name in subsequent centuries, although many legalist precepts (eg an emphasis on the penal nature of law codes) were incorporated into official orthodoxy.

Lega Lombarda The main party of the *Lega Nord*, a coalition of north Italian political parties seeking autonomy from Rome, which has become an increasingly potent political force in the early 1990s. Its appeal is based on traditional **campanilismo** and north–south hostility (which have been exacerbated by anxieties over immigration, both from the **Mezzogiorno** and from outside Italy) and on the premise that politicians in Rome are too ready to tax the prosperous north to provide for the backward and endemically criminal south. Under the leadership of Umberto Bossi, the Lega Nord won over 50 seats in the 1992 general election.

Legien, Carl (1861–1920) German trade-union leader. Active in the trade-union movement from 1886, he became Convener of the General Trade Union Commission in 1890 and Convener of the **ADGB** in 1919. He was also an active member of the **SPD** from 1885, sitting in the **Reichstag** in 1893–8 and 1903–20. His aim was to shape the pro-SPD unions into a powerful bargaining force for German labour and his efforts were crowned by the Stinnes–Legien Agreement (Nov 1918) under which German employers recognized the trade unions as sole legitimate bargaining partners. Months before his death, Legien organized the general strike which toppled the **Kapp Putsch**. Many of his achievements were overturned by the employers after his death.

Legislative Assembly (1791–2) In France, the first assembly elected under the constitution drawn up by the revolutionary Contituent Assembly. It was dispersed after the rising of 10 Aug 1792, and was replaced by the National Convention. ▷ **Convention, National**

Legitimists In France, the supporters of **Charles X** and of his heir, as opposed to the **Orléanists**, supporters of the Orléans branch of the French royal house. The division between the two factions was an important cause of the eclipse of royalism in late 19c France, especially in the National Assembly

(1871–5), where the two royalist groups together had a majority, but which nevertheless established the Third Republic. ▷ **Orléans, House of; Republic, Third** (France)

Legnano, Battle of (1176) This was the decisive victory of the Italian communes of the **Lombard League** over the armies of the Holy Roman Emperor, **Frederick I, 'Barbarossa'**. As a result, Frederick was forced to acknowledge the liberty of the Italian cities and to come to terms with Pope **Alexander III** in the Treaty of Venice (1177).

Leicester, Robert Dudley, Earl of (c.1532–88) English nobleman. The favourite of **Elizabeth I**, he became Master of the Horse, Knight of the Garter, a privy councillor, baron, and finally Earl of Leicester (1564). He continued to receive favour in spite of his unpopularity at court and a secret marriage in 1573 to the Dowager Lady Sheffield. In 1578 he bigamously married the widow of Walter, Earl of Essex; yet Elizabeth was only temporarily offended. In 1585 he commanded the expedition to the Low Countries, but was recalled for incompetence in 1587. He was nonetheless appointed in 1588 to command the forces against the Spanish **Armada**, and died later that year.

Leipzig, Battle of (1813) The overwhelming defeat of **Napoleon I**'s forces by the armies of the Fourth Coalition, also called the Battle of the Nations. Heavily outnumbered by the Allied force of Austrians, Prussians, Russians and Swedes, Napoleon tried to withdraw, but his troops were badly mauled; he effectively surrendered French control east of the Rhine. ▷ **Napoleonic Wars**

Leipzig Manifesto (1631) This manifesto was designed to establish a neutral, third force in Germany during the **Thirty Years War**. Protestant Saxony and Brandenburg wanted some means of driving all foreign armies (eg the Swedes) from the Empire while working to relax the Edicts of Restitution which was aimed at reintroducing Catholicism. The manifesto doomed Swedish hopes for a rising by the Protestant princes against the Emperor in support of the invading Swedish troops.

Lena Goldfields Strike (1912) A landmark on the road to the unrest that led to the **Russian Revolution** (1917). In the British-owned goldfields about 5000 workers protested against poor living conditions in the difficult climate of Eastern Siberia; their complaints were ignored. When they went on strike, troops opened fire and killed over 200. The **Duma**, the public and foreign observers were equally distressed. Improvements were promised but did not materialize. The number of strikes then increased year by year down to the outbreak of **World War I**.

Lenart, Jozef (1923–) Slovak politician. He fought in the **Slovak uprising**, then gained industrial experience in the Bata shoe concern. He rose quite suddenly to the premiership in 1963 while Czechoslovakia experienced industrial stagnation; and as a pragmatic reformer he achieved important results in the next few years. However, discontent increased with the **Novotny** regime and Lenart found himself turning away from reform. When the **Prague Spring** eventually broke through in 1968 he lost the premiership.

Lend-Lease Agreement (1941) The arrangement by which the USA lent or leased war supplies and arms to Britain and other Allies during **World War II**. It was a measure in which President **Roosevelt** took a close personal interest. The Lend–Lease Act was passed by Congress in Mar 1941, when British reserves were almost exhausted. By the time the agreement terminated in 1945, the allies had received about £5000 million worth of materials.

Lenin, Vladimir Ilyich (V I Ulyanov) (1870–1924) Russian Marxist revolutionary and political leader. He was educated at the Universities of Kazan and St Petersburg, where he graduated in law. From 1895 to 1897 he was in prison and from 1897 to 1900 he was exiled to Siberia for participating in underground revolutionary activities; there he used his time to study and write extensively about **Marxism**. At the Second Congress of the Russian Social Democratic Labour Party (1903) he caused the split between what came to be called the Bolshevik and Menshevik factions. Apart from the frustrating period of the Russian **Revolution of 1905**, he spent the entire period until 1917 abroad, developing and publicizing his political views. Following the **February Revolution** in 1917, he returned to Petrograd from Zurich, and urged the early seizure of power by the proletariat under the slogan 'All Power to the Soviets'. In Oct 1917 he initiated the Bolshevik revolution and became head of the first Soviet government. He made peace with Germany at **Brest-Litovsk** in order to concentrate on defeating the Whites in the ensuing **Russian Civil War** (1918–21) and then changed tactics again by switching from a ruthless centralized policy of 'war communism' to the **New Economic Policy**, which his critics in the Party saw as a 'compromise with capitalism' and a retreat from strictly socialist planning. On his death, his body was embalmed and placed in a mausoleum in Red Square until Jan 1994 when it was removed and buried in St Petersburg. In 1924 Petrograd (formerly St Petersburg) was renamed Leningrad in his honour. Much was subsequently done in his name by **Stalin** and others, some of which he would not have approved of. But the nature of the USSR and the reasons for its final collapse in 1991 owed much to him; and it was not altogether surprising that the citizens of Leningrad voted for their city to resume the name of St Petersburg. ▷ **April Theses; Bolsheviks; Mensheviks; October Revolution; Russian Revolution**

Leningrad, Siege of (1941–4) One of the more heroic incidents in Soviet and world history. The Soviet Union's second city, formerly Tsarist Russia's capital, **St Petersburg**, was besieged for 28 months and lost over a third of its population from the fighting or from starvation. It received less help than it might have from **Stalin** though it played a large part in the defeat of **Hitler**; it survived largely on the will of its people. Memories of the siege influenced many Leningraders to object to the reversion to the former name, St Petersburg, in 1991.

Leninism ▷ Marxism–Leninism

Lenshina, Alice The leader of a millenarian movement, the Lumpa Church, which from 1964 led opposition to the newly independent regime in Zambia. The church and its followers represented the split between urban politics and rural aspirations, between modernizers and traditionalists. Lenshina's church became a major focus of opposition to the regime of Kenneth **Kaunda**.

Leo I, 'the Great', St (c.390–461) Pope (440/61). One of only two popes (the other being **Gregory I**) to take the title 'the Great', Gregory was one of the most eminent of the Latin Fathers. He summoned the Council of Chalcedon (451), which accepted his doctrine of the Incarnation as defined in his 'Dogmatical Letter'. He made treaties with **Attila** the Hun and with the **Vandals** in defence of Rome.

Leo III (c.680–741) Byzantine Emperor (717/41). He reorganized the army and

financial system, and in 718 repelled a formidable attack by the Arabs on Constantinople. In 726 he prohibited the use of images in public worship, which led to more than a century of controversy. In 740 he defeated the Arabs at Amorium, thus halting their incursions into Asia Minor. He died in Constantinople. ▷ **iconoclasm**

Leo III, St (c.750–816) Italian Pope (795/816). In 799, opposition to his election forced him to flee from Rome to the protection of **Charlemagne**. After returning safely, he crowned Charlemagne Emperor of the West (800), thus initiating the **Holy Roman Empire**.

Leo X (Giovanni de' Medici) (1475–1521) Italian Pope (1513/21). 'Let us enjoy the papacy!' he is said to have remarked on his elevation, and he set about so doing, with consequences which he could scarcely have imagined. His vast project for the rebuilding of St Peter's made it necessary to preach an indulgence in order to raise funds to do so and this provoked Martin **Luther**'s 95 theses. Leo's failure to respond either promptly or effectively helped to increase the **Reformation**'s early momentum.

Leo XIII (1810–1903) Pope (1878/1903). Elected on the death of **Pius IX**, he was less reactionary than his predecessor and his more conciliatory stance was instrumental in ending the so-called **Kulturkampf** in Germany and getting the French clergy to accept the republic. However, nominally at least, he continued Pius IX's policy of refusing to recognize the Italian state. ▷ **Lateran Treaties**

Leonidas (d.480BC) King of **Sparta** (c.491/480BC) and hero of the **Persian Wars**. He perished at the Battle of **Thermopylae**, along with his entire bodyguard of 300, fighting vainly to check the advance of the Persian king, **Xerxes**, into central Greece.

Leopold I (1640–1705) Holy Roman Emperor (1658/1705). The second son of Ferdinand III and the Infanta Maria Anna, he was elected to the crowns of Hungary (1655) and Bohemia (1657), and succeeded to the Imperial title in 1658. In 1666 he married his niece, Margaret Theresa, second daughter of **Philip IV** of Spain. Following her early death (1673), he took a second Habsburg bride, Claudia Felicitas, before his third marriage (1676) to Eleonore of Palatinate-Neuburg, by whom he had two sons, the future Emperors Joseph I and Charles VI. Committed throughout his long reign to the defence of the power and unity of the House of Habsburg, he faced constant external threats from the Ottoman Turks and the King of France, in addition to the hostility of the Hungarian nobility. Treaties of neutrality (1667, 1671) between Leopold and **Louis XIV** of France gave way to military conflict over the Rhine frontier (1674–9 and 1686–97), as the issue of the Spanish inheritance loomed closer. To substantiate the rights of his son, Charles, against the French claimant, Leopold took the Empire into the Grand Alliance (1701). He died in Vienna while his armies were still deeply involved in the War of the **Spanish Succession** and the Hungarian revolt of Rákóczi (1703–11). ▷ **Habsburg Dynasty**

Leopold I (1790–1865) First King of the Belgians (1831/65). The son of Francis, Duke of Francis Saxe-Coburg, he was the uncle of Queen **Victoria**. He distinguished himself in the wars against **Napoleon I,** and in 1816 he married Charlotte, daughter of the future **George IV** of England; he lived in England after her death in 1817. He declined the crown of Greece (1830), but the following year became King of the Belgians. His second marriage in 1832 to Marie Louise of Orléans, daughter of **Louis-Philippe**, ensured French support for his new kingdom against the Dutch. An influential force in European diplomacy prior to **Bismarck**'s ascendancy. ▷ **Belgian Revolution**

Leopold II (1747–92) Holy Roman Emperor (1790/2). The third son of Emperor **Francis I** and **Maria Theresa**, he succeeded his father as Grand-Duke of Tuscany in 1765, and his brother, **Joseph II**, as Emperor in 1790. He succeeded in pacifying the Netherlands and Hungary, and was led by the downfall of his sister, **Marie Antoinette**, to form an alliance with Prussia against France. He died, however, before the war broke out.

Leopold II (1835–1909) King of the Belgians (1865/1909). The son of **Leopold I**, in 1853 he married Maria of Habsburg. His chief interest was the expansion of Belgium abroad. In 1879 he founded a company to develop the Congo, in 1885 became King of the Congo Free State, and presided over the infamous 'Red Rubber Regime' there; the Belgian state was forced to annex the colony in 1908.

Leopold III (1901–83) King of the Belgians (1934/51). The son of **Albert I**, in 1926 he married **Astrid** of Sweden, and after her death Liliane Baels in 1941. On his own authority he ordered the capitulation of the Belgian Army to the Germans (1940), thus opening the way to Dunkirk. He then remained a prisoner in his own palace at Laeken until 1944, and afterwards in Austria. After returning to Belgium in 1945, he was forced to abdicate in 1951 in favour of his son, **Baudouin I**. ▷ **World War II**

Leopoldovna, Anna (1718–46) Regent of Russia. Born Elisabeth Katharine Christinem, she was the daughter of Charles Leopold, Duke of Mecklenburg Schwerin, and the niece of the Empress **Anna Ivanovna**. In 1739 she married Prince Anton Ulrich, Duke of Brunswick. Their son, Ivan, was declared Emperor of Russia at the age of eight weeks on the death of Anna Ivanovna, and Anna Carlovna was appointed regent. A year later, however, Ivan was deposed by the Empress **Elizabeth Petrovna**, and Anna Carlovna was thrown into prison, where she died.

Leovigild (d.586) Leader of the **Visigoths** and ruler of Spain. He became sole ruler of Spain (572) on the death of his brother and waged constant wars against the **Suebi** in the north and the Greeks in the south. He did much to restore the extent and power of the Visigothic kingdom. ▷ **Germanic Invasions**

Lepanto, Battle of (7 Oct 1571) The naval battle fought by the forces of the Christian Holy League against those of the **Ottoman Empire**, off the coast of Greece. The Christian forces were raised by the papacy, Venice, the Italian states and Spain, and commanded by Don **John of Austria**, with 208 warships. The Turks mustered 230 warships. At stake was the security of Western Europe, threatened by successful Ottoman expansion. The battle was a clear victory for the Christians, who lost 10 galleys and 8000 men. On the Turkish side, the commander, Ali Pasha, was killed; all but 30 of the galleys were destroyed or captured; 30000 casualties were sustained and 3000 men taken prisoner. Although a decisive watershed in the Christian–Muslim conflict in the Mediterranean, the victory did not stop the Ottomans from putting to sea with a further fleet the following year.

Le Pen, Jean-Marie (1928–) French politician. The son of a Breton fisherman, he served in the 1950s as a paratrooper in Indochina and Algeria. In 1956 he was elected as a right-wing Poujadist Deputy. During the 1960s he had connections with the extremist **OAS** (*Organisation Armée Secrète*), before forming the National Front in 1972. This party, with its extreme right-wing policies, emerged as a new 'fifth force' in French politics, winning 10 per cent of the national vote in the 1986 Assembly elections. A controversial figure and noted demagogue, he unsuccessfully contested the presidency in 1988.

Lepidus, Marcus Aemilius (d.c.13BC) Aristocratic Roman politician of the civil war era (49–31BC), who first rose to prominence under **Caesar**, becoming his deputy at Rome. He reached the high point of his career in 43BC, when he formed the second triumvirate with Mark **Antony** and Octavian (Emperor **Augustus**). Outmanoeuvred by Octavian in the power struggle of the 30s BC, he retired from active politics, but remained head of state religion (Pontifex Maximus) until his death.

Lerma, Don Francisco Gómez de Sandoval y Rojas, Duke of (1553–1625) Spanish politician. The minister and confidant of **Philip III** of Spain, during the period 1598–1618 he played an important role in government policy. A peaceful foreign policy was being pursued at this time: various treaties were signed with the French (1598), English (1604), and Dutch (1609, the **Twelve Years' Truce**); and there was a rapprochement with France (the marriage, in 1615, of Philip to Elizabeth of France). In domestic affairs, he was notable in having influenced the transfer of the court from Madrid to Valladolid (1601–6), and the decree expelling the **Moriscos** (1609). Created cardinal in 1618, he was dislodged by a palace coup the same year, and was forced to give up some of his accumulated wealth.

Lerroux, Alejandro (1864–1949) Spanish politician and journalist. During the first decade of the 20c he was the highly innovative and audacious populist leader of Barcelona. In forging a new basis for collaboration between the working class and republicanism, he formed the first modern party in Spain. Mythologized by his fiery anticlerical demagogy, the charismatic Lerroux was known as the 'Emperor of the Parallel' (a working-class thoroughfare). After he founded the **Radical Republican Party** in 1908, he became increasingly conservative, even offering in 1923 to become the civilian figurehead of **Primo de Rivera**'s

dictatorship. Although he also dedicated more and more time to his own varied business interests, Lerroux retained an extraordinary hold over his party. During the Second Republic, he led the Radicals as the principal source of opposition to the progressive Republican–Socialist coalition of 1931–3, having left the government in Dec 1931. He was crucial to the formation of the alliance with the non-Republican Right, which ruled Spain from Nov 1933 to Oct 1935 and which polarized the regime to an unprecedented degree. During this period he headed five administrations before falling from power through a bribery scandal. Despite backing the Nationalists during the **Spanish Civil War**, he was prevented from returning to Spain from his exile in Portugal until 1947, because of his earlier involvement with freemasonry. ▷ **Republic, Second** (Spain)

Lesage, Jean (1912–80) Canadian politician. He became the Liberal Premier of Quebec in 1960, carried into power on a wave of nationalist fervour, although the Liberals won only 50 out of the 95 seats. He then introduced the **Quiet Revolution** against corruption, the Catholic Church's involvement in lay issues such as education, welfare and health, and against the economic domination of the USA and of anglophone Canadians in Quebec. His demands for a more active governmental role in the province, because of its special situation within the Confederation, began to cause unease among other Canadian provinces, especially when he asked for an increased share of tax revenue. In 1966 his government was defeated by the **Union Nationale**. He remained leader of the Provincial Party until his retirement in 1970. ▷ **Liberal Party** (Canada)

Lesseps, Ferdinand (Marie), Viscount of (1805–94) French engineer. After holding several diplomatic posts in Europe, in 1854 he began to plan the Suez Canal, finally built 1860–9. He was knighted, and received several other honours. In 1881 work began on his scheme for a Panama Canal; but in 1892–3 the management was charged with breach of trust, and Lesseps and his son, Charles, were found guilty.

Le Tellier, Michel (1603–85) French politician. A lawyer, and government official, specializing in military supply, he was loyal to **Mazarin** during the **Fronde**, and became one of the principal advisers of **Louis XIV**.

Together with his son, **Louvois**, he was the creator of Louis XIV's army; he was a great rival of **Colbert**; his last act was to draw up the revocation of the Edict of Nantes.

Lettow-Vorbeck, General Paul Emil von (1870–1964) Prussian officer. He commanded the German forces in East Africa in **World War I**. These forces, largely composed of black troops recruited from warlike peoples in Tanganyika, were expanded and reorganized by him and raided the Uganda railway early in the war. He failed to hold the Kilimanjaro area, where most German settlers were located, and fell back to the Tanganyika Central Railway. In 1916 the railway was captured by forces led by General Smuts and he moved south to the Rufiji. He subsequently invaded Portuguese East Africa and Northern Rhodesia and surrendered after the Armistice at Abercorn (now Mbala, Zambia) on 25 Nov 1918.

lettres de cachet A royal order of the French kings, sealed with the monarch's private seal, issued for the arrest and imprisonment of individuals during the **ancien régime**. The practice was abolished in the **French Revolution** (1790).

Leuctra, Battle of (371BC) The occasion of the crushing defeat of the Spartans by the Thebans under **Epaminondas**, which ended **Sparta**'s hegemony in Greece for good. ▷ **Thebes**

Levant, The A general name formerly given to the eastern shores of the Mediterranean Sea, from western Greece to Egypt. The Levant States were Syria and Lebanon, during the period of their French mandate (1920–41). ▷ **mandates**

Levellers A radical political movement during the **English Civil Wars** and the **Commonwealth**. It called for the extension of manhood franchise to all but the poorest, religious toleration, and the abolition of the monarchy and the House of Lords. Led by John Lilburne (c.1614–57), Richard Overton (c.1631–64), and William Walwyn (1600–80), it was supported by 'agitators' in the parliamentary army 1647–9, and was defeated at Burford (May 1649).

Leven, Alexander Leslie, 1st Earl of (c.1580–1661) Scottish general. He became Field Marshal of Sweden under **Gustav II Adolf**. Recalled to Scotland in 1639, he took command of the Covenanting army in the

Bishops Wars against **Charles I**, who made him an earl in 1641 in the hope of winning his allegiance. He fought for the parliamentary army in the **English Civil Wars**, and received Charles's surrender at Newark. After the execution of the King, he supported **Charles II**, was captured in 1651, and imprisoned until 1654. ▷ **Dunbar, Battle of** (1650)

Lévesque, René (1922–87) Canadian politician. He founded the **Parti Québecois** in 1968 after **Lesage**'s defeat and the refusal of the **Liberal Party** to become more nationalist. By uniting the majority of francophones who wished greater autonomy for Quebec and those who wanted complete political independence for the province, he won a stunning victory in 1976, with 41 per cent of the vote. He then introduced electoral and labour reforms, pressed hard for the completion of the huge Quebec Hydro scheme and initiated legislation to place foreign-owned and other corporations under public ownership. More controversial were Bill 101, which legislated for a unilingual province, and a referendum law on the question of Quebec's future. With the other provinces refusing to commit themselves to economic relationships with Quebec, and with Prime Minister Pierre **Trudeau**'s full involvement in the campaign, the Quebeckers voted against secession. Lévesque then began to demand enhanced provincial powers, along with Alberta's Premier Peter Lougheed. In 1981 Quebec became increasingly isolated, with Lévesque refusing to endorse Trudeau's constitutional reforms which challenged not only Bill 101 but also Lévesque's demand for compensation from Ottawa if the province opted out of federal socio-economic programmes. The party became deeply divided over the secession issue, but Lévesque maintained his leadership in 1985 with a 75 per cent vote.

Lewis, John L (1880–1969) US labour leader. Born the son of a Welsh coalminer, he grew up to hold the presidency of the Union of United Mineworkers from 1920 to 1960. When its membership was reduced by the **Great Depression** to 150 000 in 1933, fearing a communist takeover, Lewis led a vigorous recruitment drive which increased the membership to 500 000. When, in 1935, he was unsuccessful in his attempts to change the AFL's traditional exclusion of industrial workers, he reacted by founding the Committee for Industrial Organizations, which became the CIO after its expulsion from the AFL in 1938. He took the coal miners out on several strikes during **World War II**, and his fiery personality and stubborn drive led to clashes with Presidents Franklin D **Roosevelt** and Harry S **Truman**. Although he swung the vote of organized labour behind Roosevelt in 1936, he reverted to his original Republicanism in 1940, and was a member of the isolationist **America First Committee**. ▷ **AFL–CIO**

Lexington and Concord, Battles of (19 Apr 1775) The first battles of the **American Revolution**, fought in Massachusetts after British troops tried to seize supplies stored at the village of Concord, and were confronted by colonial militia.

Leyte Gulf, Battle of (1944) A battle during **World War II**, when the Japanese fleet converged on the US 3rd and 7th Fleets protecting Allied landings on Leyte in the central Philippines. The Japanese suffered irreplaceable losses of 300 000 tonnes of combat ships, compared to US losses of 37 000 tonnes. The way was opened for further US gains in the Philippines and on islands nearer Japan.

L'Hôpital, Michel de (1507–73) French politician. In 1554 he became Superintendent of Finances, in 1560 Chancellor of France. He strove to pacify the religious quarrel by staying the hand of the Catholic persecutors, but resigned in 1568 and retired to his estate near Etampes.

Liang Ch'i-ch'ao ▷ **Liang Qichao**

Liang Qichao (Liang Ch'i-ch'ao) (1873–1929) Chinese reformer and intellectual. He was a student and follower of **Kang Youwei**, with whom he served during the **Hundred Days of Reform** (1898). He escaped to Japan, thereafter devoting himself to journalism, through which he became the most influential political writer of his generation. Liang returned to China in 1912, and was influential in creating the Progressive Party, which supported **Yuan Shikai** in the hope of maintaining national unity. However, the violence and corruption prevalent under Yuan led him to despair of the possibility of democracy in China, and he retired from politics to study Buddhism.

Liang Shuming (Liang Shu-ming) (1893–1981) Chinese rural reformer. While teaching at Beijing University (1917–24), he argued that Confucianism, with its stress on harmony and adaptation to nature, was relevant to the modern world as an antidote to the materialism and aggressive individualism associated with Western culture. During the 1930s Liang was involved in the rural reconstruction movement, an attempt to create model villages based on economic cooperation and the harmonization of social relations. In 1945–6 he was Secretary-General of the **China Democratic League**, formed in 1944 to represent a 'third force' in Chinese politics independent of both the communists and nationalists. Liang stayed on in China after the communist victory in 1949, and during the early 1950s was an outspoken critic of party politics towards the peasants.

Liao Chung-k'ai ▷ **Liao Zhongkai**

Liao Zhongkai (Liao Chung-k'ai) (1878–1925) Chinese politician. Born into an overseas Chinese family in the USA, he studied in Japan before becoming the **Guomindang**'s leading financial expert after 1912. Associated with its left wing, he supported the United Front with the communists in 1923, advocating a planned economy along socialist lines. In 1924 he played an important role in setting up both the workers and peasant departments under Guomindang auspices as part of its new strategy of mass mobilization. As the leading Guomindang representative at the Whampoa Military Academy, Liao also laid the basis for the political commissar system that was to be used throughout the National Revolutionary Army. He aroused opposition from right-wing members of the Guomindang who opposed the United Front, and who may have been involved in his assassination.

Liaquat Ali Khan (1895–1951) Pakistani politician. After leaving Oxford he became a member of the Inner Temple. He joined the **Muslim League** in 1923, and became Prime Minister of Pakistan in 1947. He was assassinated in 1951.

Liberal Democratic Party (LDP; *Jiyu minshuto*) The conservative party that ruled continuously in Japan from its formation in Nov 1955 until its defeat in Aug 1993. It was created by the merger of the two principal conservative parties established after 1945. The party gained the support of business groups because of its commitment to economic growth, the free enterprise system and traditional values, while its policy of subsidizing domestic rice production proved popular with the farmers. Until the late 1960s, the party won every Diet election with substantial margins (although never achieving the ⅔ majority required for any revision of the 1947 **Peace Constitution** which some LDP members desired). From the 1970s, however, its popularity dipped and its share of the popular vote never exceeded 50 per cent. The fragmentation of the opposition, though, ensured the LDP's position as the majority party until 1993. Bribery scandals and the increasing importance of money politics, whereby factions expended huge sums of money to get their candidates elected, tarnished the LDP's reputation. In 1992 a group of rebel LDP MPs formed the Japan New Party (JNP) and brought down the government in a vote of no confidence (June 1993). Two further groups of rebel MPs formed the Japan Renewal Party (JRP) and the Sakigate (Harbinger) Party, and the LDP lost its majority in the general election which followed. These three new parties then formed a coalition with several other existing parties, and the new government came into power in Aug 1993.

Liberal Party of Australia Australia's largest conservative party, formed by R G **Menzies** in 1944–5 from existing conservative groups. It built up a mass following in the late 1940s, and was victorious in 1949. It governed from 1949 to 1972 and again from 1975 to 1983, sometimes in coalition with the Country/National Party. As the major anti-Labor grouping in Australian politics, the party is the descendant of **Deakin**'s Liberal Party in the early years of **federation**, W M **Hughes**'s Nationalist Party (1917) and the United Australia Party (1931). Organized through branches in federal and state electorates, the party stands for individual liberty, private enterprise and economic competition, law and order, the family, and state rights. Out of office since 1983, the party lost its fourth successive general election in 1990. ▷ **National Party of Australia**

Liberal Party (Belgium) After playing an important role in events during the French revolutionary period and in the **Belgian Revolution**, Belgian liberals first formed a party in June 1846. Besides embracing the general liberal principles of personal, constitutional and economic liberty, the Belgian liberals were particularly anti-clerical. There were liberal governments in Belgium in 1847–55, 1857–70 and 1878–84; they dominated politics in the third quarter of the 19c. Two factors caused their decline: internal splits between progressive radicals and 'doctrinaire' conservatives, and universal male suffrage (1893 in Belgium). However, on a smaller scale, liberalism has continued to be a force in Belgian politics. It has now dropped its anti-clericalism, and tends to represent employers' viewpoints. In 1961 the Liberal Party split into two wings, the French-speaking *Parti pour la Liberté et le Progrès*, and the Flemish *Partij voor Vrijheid en Vooruitgang*. In 1971 these two wings separated and decided to act independently with their own programmes. The Francophone wing joined part of the **Rassemblement Wallon** in 1976 to form the *Parti des Reformées et des Libertés Wallones*.

Liberal Party (Canada) This party evolved from the reform groups of **Canada East** and **Canada West** in the late 1840s and early 1850s, joined by the **Clear Grits** in 1855 and the **Rouges** after confederation. The party's early lack of cohesion and its failure to organize at a federal level meant that it was easily distracted by provincial issues and without the Conservatives' ability to distribute patronage it could not attract new members or erode Conservative support. After the 1871 Treaty of **Washington**, however, Liberals had the necessary issues to unite their provincial groups and were ready, under the leadership of Alexander **Mackenzie**, to take advantage of the railway scandal of 1873 to win power. Their failure to negotiate a reciprocity agreement with the USA in 1874 and refusal to adopt a higher tariff policy, combined with the effects of depression and the accusation of atheism levelled by Quebec's Catholic Church, lost them the 1878 election and they remained in opposition under the leadership of Edward **Blake** in the 1880s. It was not until the end of the century that the party developed a formula for success, which essentially followed the example of the Conservatives. This was an anglo-francophone coalition, tempering reform with pragmatism, and cemented by a new emphasis on patronage. Sir Wilfrid **Laurier** led the party to success in 1896, and by recruiting provincial premiers to his cabinet he increased the government's appeal to the provinces. The party was severely damaged by the defection of Clifford **Sifton** (over reciprocity in 1911) and Henri **Bourassa** (over naval policy), and joined the union government of R L **Borden** to bring in conscription during **World War I**. After Laurier's death, W L Mackenzie **King** led the party back into office in 1921, adding to the old formula a unique ability to blur political issues which enabled distinctly antagonistic groups to remain within the Liberal fold, and which kept them in power (with Progressive Party allies) until 1930, and from 1935 until his retirement in 1948. His successor, Louis **Saint Laurent** was not able to maintain this unity and the party began to alienate itself from Western Canada, resulting in the defeat of 1957. Although Lester **Pearson** led the party back into minority government in 1963, it was not until Pierre **Trudeau** took the leadership that the party was successful in re-establishing itself nationally.

Liberal Party (Netherlands) Liberalism was first found in the Netherlands at the end of the 18c in the **Patriot Movement**, but became politicially mature as an opposition group to the government of King **William I**. The most prominent liberal was J R **Thorbecke**, who was responsible for the new constitution of 1848, and formed several governments in the third quarter of the 19c. Despite their domination and the usual splits between left and right, there was no formal parliamentary party until 1885 when the Liberal Union (*Liberale Unie*) was formed as a loose association. There were several splinter-actions in the 1890s, caused by dissent over the issue of universal suffrage; in 1901 the less conservative liberals formed the Progressive Democratic League (*Vrijzinnig Democratische Bond*), which in 1938 became the National Liberal Party (*Liberale Staatspartij*). This became the Party of Freedom (*Partij van de Vrijheid*) in 1946, which after another merger in 1948 became the present liberal party, the People's Party for Freedom and Democracy (*Volkspartij voor Vrijheid en Democratie*, VVD). The Dutch liberals are now the party of the employers; they were in government with the Christian Democrats in the 1980s, when they commanded nearly a fifth of the vote.

Liberal Party (Sweden) Formed in 1900 to fight for parliamentary government and an extension of the franchise, it is the oldest of Sweden's modern political parties. It formed an administration for the first time in 1905 under Karl Staaff. Divided in 1924 over the question of prohibition, it was reunited in 1934. Under its leader Ola Ullsten, it participated in the non-socialist government formed in 1976 and, when this collapsed in 1978, Ullsten was briefly Prime Minister at the head of a minority administration.

Liberal Party (UK) One of the two major political parties in the UK in the 19c and early 20c. It developed from the aristocratic Whig Party in the middle years of the 19c when,

especially under **Gladstone**'s leadership, it appealed to the rapidly growing urban middle classes, to skilled working men and to religious nonconformists. Many of its land-owning supporters and also radical imperialists were alienated by Gladstone's Irish **Home Rule** policy from the mid-1880s. Based on values of economic freedom and, from the late 19c, social justice, the last Liberal government enacted in the decade before **World War I** many important social reforms which anticipated the Welfare State. Internal splits and the challenge of a reorganized **Labour Party** weakened it from 1918 onwards and by the end of the 1920s the Liberals were clearly a minority third party on the centre-left of British politics, a position they have not been able to escape despite revivals in the 1970s and alliance with the **Social Democratic Party** in the 1980s. The party became known as the Liberal Democrats after the decision to merge with the Social Democrats in 1987. ▷ **Conservative Party** (UK); **Tories**; **Whigs**

liberation theology A style of theology originating in Latin America in the 1960s, and later becoming popular in many developing countries. Accepting a Marxist analysis of society, it stresses the role and mission of the Church to the poor and oppressed in society, of which Christ is understood as liberator. Its sympathy for revolutionary movements led to clashes with established secular and religious authorities.

Liberation Tigers of Tamil Eelam ▷ **LTTE**

Liberman, Yevsesi Grigorevich (1897–1983) Soviet economist. Born and educated in Kharkov, he spent all his working life practising there as an academic economist. In 1962 he published an article in *Pravda* entitled 'Plan, Profit, Bonuses', which in a mild way advocated something of a market mechanism. Though far short of Mikhail **Gorbachev**'s ideas, this was the basis for the reforms introduced by **Kosygin** in 1965 but undermined by the **Brezhnev** hardliners after the **Prague Spring** in 1968.

'Liberty, Equality, Fraternity' The motto of the French Republic; adopted in June 1793, it remained the official slogan of the state until the Bourbon Restoration (1814). It was re-adopted during the Second Republic (1848–51), and has remained the national slogan from 1875 to the present day, except during the German Occupation (1940–4). ▷ **French Revolution; Republic, Second** (France)

Li-chia System ▷ Lijia System

Li Chih ▷ Li Zhi

Licinius (Valerius Licinianus Licinius) (d.AD325) Roman Emperor (308/24). A protégé of Emperor **Galerius**, who appointed him Emperor of the West, he ruled in fact only over the Balkan area. In 313, with his defeat of **Maximin Daia**, he became sole Emperor of the East, a position he held until his defeat by **Constantine I, 'the Great'**, the Emperor of the West, at the Battle of Adrianople (324). His fame rests primarily on his promulgation, jointly with Constantine, of the Edict of Milan (313), the first imperial enactment ever to guarantee Christians freedom of worship throughout the whole Roman empire. ▷ **Milan, Edict of**

Li Dazhao (Li Ta-chao) (1888–1927) Chinese revolutionary. One of the founders of the Chinese Communist Party, whose interpretation of Marxism as applied to China had a profound influence on **Mao Zedong**. Appointed Head Librarian of Beijing University and Professor of History (1918), he had the young Mao as a library assistant, and founded one of the first of the communist study circles which in 1921 were to form the Communist Party. In 1927, when the Manchurian military leader, Zhang Zuolin (Chang Tso-lin), then occupying Beijing, raided the Soviet Embassy, Li was captured and executed.

Lidice, Destruction of (1942) A Nazi-German act of savage revenge on innocent Czech villagers. In late May resistance fighters fatally wounded Reinhard **Heydrich**, the **Gestapo** officer who was in charge of the **Bohemian Protectorate**. Heydrich had a nasty reputation, but that was quickly overshadowed by actions to avenge his death. The worst of these was in June when, as an example, the village of Lidice was destroyed, its almost 200 males shot, its 200 females sent off to Ravensbruck **concentration camp**, and its 100 children dispersed, many to their deaths. However, the tragedy was to stiffen the Czech resistance and convince the Allies of the need to expel the Germans from Czechoslovakia after the war.

Lie, Trygve Haldvan (1896–1968) Norwegian lawyer. After becoming an MP, he

was appointed Minister of Justice and of Shipping before fleeing to Britain with other members of the Norwegian Government in 1940, where he acted as Foreign Minister until the end of **World War II**. In 1946 he was elected **UN** Secretary-General, but resigned in 1952. He served as Minister for Industry (1963–4) and for Commerce and Shipping until his death.

Liebknecht, Karl (1871–1919) German barrister and politician. The son of Wilhelm **Liebknecht**, he was a member of the **Reichstag** (1912–16). During **World War I** he was imprisoned as an independent, anti-militarist, social democrat. He was a founder member with Rosa **Luxemburg** of the German Communist Party (**KPD**) in 1918–19 and led an unsuccessful revolt in **Berlin**, the 'Spartacus Rising', in Jan 1919, during which he and Rosa Luxemburg were killed by army officers. ▷ **Spartacists**

Liebknecht, Wilhelm (1826–1900) German politician. He studied at Giessen, Marburg and Berlin, became a lawyer (1847), and developed an interest in **socialism**. For his part in the Baden insurrection (1848–9), he had to take refuge in Switzerland and in England, where he worked closely with **Marx**. He returned to Germany in 1862 and during a two-years' imprisonment was elected to the **Reichstag** (1874). A co-founder of the German Social Democratic Party (**SPD**) (1875), he became one of its leading spokesmen. ▷ **Marxism**

Liechtenstein, Principality of Originally the medieval counties of Vaduz and Schellenberg, this small territory lying between **Austria** and Switzerland came into the hands of the princes of Liechtenstein between 1699 and 1712. A principality of the **Holy Roman Empire** from 1719, Liechtenstein became a member of the Confederation of the Rhine in 1806 and of the **German Confederation** from 1815 to 1866. In 1862 it became a constitutional state and from 1866 was fully independent. Close economic and political ties have existed at different times with Austria and Switzerland.

Ligachev, Yegor Kuzmich (1920–) Soviet politician. After graduating as an engineer in 1943, he worked in the Urals region before joining the Communist Party in 1944. From then until 1961 he worked in his native Novosibirsk as an official first of **Komsomol** and then of the local Party. As Party Chief of the new 'science city' of

Akademgorodok, he gained a reputation as an austere opponent of corruption. He was brought to Moscow by Nikita **Khrushchev** in 1961 but, after the latter was ousted in 1964, he was sent to Tomsk, where he was regional party boss for 18 years. However, he became a full member of the Central Committee in 1976, and in 1983 he was promoted to the Secretariat by Yuri **Andropov**, becoming Ideology Secretary in 1984. With the accession to power of Mikhail **Gorbachev** in 1985, he was brought into the **Politburo**. He initially served as Gorbachev's deputy, but they became estranged over the issue of reform and, in 1988, he was demoted to the position of Agriculture Secretary. As Gorbachev became more radical, he became more conservative, and in 1990 he was expelled from the Central Committee as well as the Politburo. He remained an anti-reform critic even after the USSR collapsed.

Li Hongzhang (Li Hung-chang) (1823–1901) Chinese scholar and soldier. He rose to prominence in the resistance to the **Taiping Rebellion**, and became the most influential Chinese statesman of the late 19c. A protégé of **Zeng Guofan**, he was the chief representative of China in its relations with foreign powers, and supported limited industrialization at home.

Li Hsien-nien ▷ **Li Xian'nian**

Li Hung-chang ▷ **Li Hongzhang**

Lijia (Li-chia) System This term refers to a sub-bureaucratic level of government in imperial China inaugurated by the founder of the **Ming Dynasty**, **Ming Hongwu**. It represented an attempt to extend the government's reach below the district (*xian*), the lowest level of the formal bureaucracy. A community (*li*), comprising 110 households, was subdivided into units (*jia*) of 10 households. The heads of the 10 wealthiest households were to be responsible for population registration and the levying and collection of taxes, each head serving a one-year term. The system continued to be used during the succeeding **Qing Dynasty**, although its functions were increasingly blurred with those of the **Baojia System**.

Likud The coalition of right-wing political parties in Israel, named *Likud Liberalim Leumi* in full ('National Union of Liberals'). Formed in 1973 in opposition to the Israel Labour Party, it governed Israel from 1977 to 1990 under Menachem **Begin** and Yitzhak

Shamir. The coalition was composed mainly of the Herut Party and Liberal Party. The former was constructed in 1948 out of the **Irgun** and **Haganah**, while the latter was created in 1961. To maintain a working majority, Likud has sometimes negotiated the support of small parties, which have been influential beyond their size as a result. ▷ **Mapai Party**

Lilburne, John (c.1614–57) English revolutionary. Imprisoned by the **Star Chamber** in 1638 for importing Puritan literature, he rose in the parliamentary army, but resigned from it in 1645 over the Covenant. He became an indefatigable agitator for the **Levellers** during the **English Civil Wars**, thought Cromwell's republic too aristocratic, and demanded greater liberty of conscience and numerous reforms. He was repeatedly imprisoned for his treasonable pamphlets.

Li Lisan (Li Li-san) (1900–67) Chinese politician. Chinese Communist Party leader and effective head of the Party (1928–30), he enforced what has since become known as the 'Li Lisan line', in which the Party's weak and undeveloped military forces were used in futile attempts to capture cities. His authoritarian methods alienated his fellow leaders. He was demoted in 1930, and lived in the USSR until 1945. Thereafter, he was employed by the Chinese Communist Party in various minor roles.

Limann, Hilla (1934–) Ghanaian diplomat and politician. He was educated in Ghana and then at the LSE and the Sorbonne, where he earned a doctorate. He was a teacher before joining the Ghanaian diplomatic service as Head of Chancery at Lome (1968–71). Limann then served his country at many international gatherings while being his country's counsellor at its permanent mission to the UN in Geneva (1971–5) and senior officer Ministry of Foreign Affairs (1975–9). In 1979 he was chosen to lead the People's National Party and was its successful presidential candidate in the 1979 elections, becoming President until his removal from office (31 Dec 1981) as a result of a military coup led by Flt-Lt Jerry **Rawlings**.

Limes A Latin word (plural, *limites*) originally meaning track or pathway (especially for troops marching through enemy territory), which came ultimately to denote the fixed frontiers of the Roman empire. These might take the form either of a solid wall, as in northern Britain, or of a palisade, earth bank and ditch complex, as in Upper Germany, or of a line of connected forts along a river (eg the Rhine) or across a stretch of desert, as in the area between the Red Sea and the Euphrates. ▷ **Hadrian's Wall**

limpieza de sangre 'Blood purity' (signifying purity from Jewish origins) was a requirement of some institutions in Spain from the late 15c onwards. Apparently first introduced by the University College of St Bartolomé in Salamanca in 1482, the requirement was a symptom of anti-Semitism in Spanish society, and discriminated against **Conversos**. Several bodies subsequently adopted statutes of *limpieza*, among them the Jeronimite Order (1486) and the Cathedral of Seville (1515). The tendency gained force when in 1547 Siliceo, Archbishop of Toledo, forced through a statute in his cathedral. However, by the late 16c there was widespread criticism of the social implications of *limpieza*, and prominent figures including the Spanish **Inquisition** began attempts to abolish the practice. Despite this, statutes of *limpieza* remained in force in many parts of Spain until the 19c.

Lin Biao (Lin Piao) (1907–71) Chinese military leader. He was one of the leaders of the Chinese Communist Party and a Marshal of the Red Army. Lin became Minister of Defence in 1959, and in 1968 replaced the disgraced **Liu Shaoqi** as heir-apparent to **Mao Zedong**. He was one of the promoters of the **Cultural Revolution**, and appears to have been a patron of extreme left-wing factions. In 1971, after a political struggle, he was killed in a plane crash in Mongolia, apparently in the course of an attempt to seek refuge in the USSR.

Lincoln, Abraham (1809–65) US politician and 16th President. Elected to the Illinois legislature in 1834, he became a lawyer in 1836. A decade later, he was elected to a single term in Congress, where he spoke against the extension of slavery, and in 1860 was elected President as the **Republican Party**'s candidate on a platform of hostility to slavery's expansion. When the **American Civil War** began (1861), he defined the issue in terms of national integrity, not anti-slavery, a theme he restated in the **Gettysburg Address** (1863). Nonetheless, in his Emancipation Proclamation that same year, he announced his intention of freeing all slaves in areas of rebellion. He was re-elected in 1864; after the final Northern victory he proposed to reunite the nation on the most generous terms, but on 14 Apr 1865 he was shot at Ford's Theater, in Washington DC, by an actor, John Wilkes **Booth**, and died next morning. He immediately became a national hero, and is regarded as one of the finest symbols of American democracy.

Lindbergh, Charles Augustus (1902–74) US aeronaut. His 1927 flight from New York to Paris, taking 334 hours in his monoplane, *Spirit of St Louis*, won him a prize of US$25 000 for the first solo transatlantic flight and instant fame. To this was added national sympathy when his son was abducted and murdered in 1932. In 1940 he became a member of the isolationist America First Committee, and his popularity was seriously damaged in 1941 because of his suggestion to negotiate a settlement with **Hitler**'s Germany.

Linlithgow, Victor Alexander John Hope, 2nd Marquess of (1887–1952) British politician. He served during **World War I** on the Western Front. He was Chairman of the Royal Commission on Agriculture in India (1926–8) and was also a member of the Select Committee on Indian Constitutional Reform. In 1936 he became Viceroy of India, in succession to Lord Willingdon, and held the post until 1943, thus becoming the longest holder of that office. In 1939, he declared war against Germany before consulting the Indian political parties; the Congress Party was offended by this step, and provincial Congress ministries resigned in protest. Although he suppressed opposition to British rule in India during **World War II**, under him provincial autonomy functioned smoothly. He was responsible for jailing the Congress leaders of the **Quit India Movement** in 1942–3.

Lin Piao ▷ **Lin Biao**

Lin Tse-hsü ▷ **Lin Zexu**

Lin Zexu (Lin Tse-hsü) (1785–1850) Chinese politician. He was regarded in China as the first great patriot to resist the incursions of foreign powers into China. Lin was appointed Imperial Commissioner to deal with the problem of the increase in illegal imports of opium. At Guangzhou (Canton) he held members of the British community hostage in their warehouses until they surrendered their stocks of opium, thus precipitating a British punitive expedition. When China suffered defeat, he was exiled to Chinese Turkestan, but later recalled. ▷ **Opium Wars; Taiping Rebellion**

Lion of Janina ▷ **Ali Pasha**

Li Peng (1928–) Chinese politician. He was the son of the radical communist writer, Li Shouxun, who was executed by the **Guomindang** in 1930. Adopted by **Zhou Enlai** on his mother's death (1939), he trained as a hydro-electric engineer and was appointed Minister of the Electric Power Industry in 1981. He became a vice-premier in 1983, was elevated to the Politburo in 1985 and made Prime Minister in 1987. As a cautious, orthodox reformer, he sought to retain firm control of the economy and favoured improved relations with the USSR. In 1989 he took a strong line in facing down the student-led, pro-democracy movement, and became in the process a popularly reviled figure.

Li Shih-tseng ▷ **Li Shizeng**

Li Shizeng (Li Shih-tseng) (1881–1973) Chinese anarchist, educator and prominent member of the **Guomindang**. From an influential official family, Li went to France in 1902 to study. While there he became attracted to anarchism and founded a journal, *Xin Shiji* ('New Century'). This not only called for the overthrow of the **Qing Dynasty** but also condemned Confucian social institutions, such as the family, for stifling the individual and entrenching sexual inequality. As an enthusiastic Francophile, Li organized a work-study programme for Chinese students in France (1919–21). He championed work-study as part of his vision to create a harmonious and cooperative society, in which class divisions would be dissolved through education and the integration of intellectual and manual labour. Ironically, many work-study students later became prominent members of the Chinese **Communist Party**. Li's hostility to **communism** and his close personal ties with **Sun Yat-sen** and **Chiang Kai-shek** drew him into the Guomindang and he became a member of the party's supervisory committee in 1924. In the 1950s he was a policy adviser to Chiang Kai-shek's regime in Taiwan.

Li Si (Li Ssu) (c.280–208BC) Chinese adviser to the state of Qin, which unified China by force in 221BC. As chief counsellor to the first emperor, **Qin Shi Huangdi** (221/210BC), Li Si was the principal architect of the harsh system of centralized control imposed throughout the empire. Laws, weights and measures, and the written script were all standardized. Li Si was also associated with

the notorious 'burning of the books and burial of the scholars' in 213BC, when Confucian texts were destroyed and many scholars were executed. As a result of factional rivalries at court, Li Si himself was executed two years after the death of Qin Shi Huangdi.

Lissa, Battle of (20 July 1866) The clash between the Italian and Austrian navies, in which, despite possessing a marked superiority in numbers and quality of vessels, the Italian admiral, Count Carlo di Persano, contrived through his own incompetence to turn probable victory into defeat.

Li Ssu ▷ **Li Si**

List, (Georg) Friedrich German political economist. A disciple of Adam Smith, he was charged with sedition in 1824, went to the USA, and became a naturalized citizen. He was US consul at Baden, Leipzig and Stuttgart successively. A strong advocate of protection for new industries, he did much by his writings to form German economic practice.

Lister, Enrique (1907–) Spanish Communist leader and general. During the **Spanish Civil War** he became commander of the Republic's famous Fifth Regiment. Exiled in the USSR, he fought with the Soviet army in **World War II**, reaching the rank of general. A member of the Spanish Politburo from 1946, he was expelled in 1970. In 1973 he founded the stalinist Spanish Workers' Communist Party (PCOE), and returned to Spain in 1977, where his party made little impact.

Listone The Italian word (literally, 'big list') used to describe the fascist-approved candidates put forward by **Mussolini** when contesting the Apr 1924 Italian elections. It included not only members of the **Fascist Party** but also nationalists, right-wing liberals (including **Orlando**, **Salandra** and De Nicola) and even a few **Popolari**. Indeed, of the 374 victorious candidates on the *Listone* under two-thirds were genuine fascists. The Listone was remarkably successful, bringing Mussolini a comfortable parliamentary majority.

Li Ta-chao ▷ **Li Dazhao**

Little Bighorn, Battle of the (25–6 June 1876) The famous battle, popularly called 'Custer's Last Stand', between US cavalry, under General Custer, and the **Sioux** and **Cheyenne**, under **Sitting Bull** and **Crazy**

Horse. The Native Americans destroyed Custer's force. Issues behind the battle included Custer's bloody dawn attack on a Cheyenne village at the Washita in 1868, and the white invasion of the Black Hills, sacred to the Sioux. ▷ **Indian Wars**

Little Entente A system of alliances between Czechoslovakia and Yugoslavia (1920), Czechoslovakia and Romania (1921), and Yugoslavia and Romania (1921), consolidated into a single treaty signed in Belgrade in 1929. The alliances aimed to maintain post-1919 boundaries in central Europe, and prevent a Habsburg restoration. ▷ **Habsburg Dynasty**

Litvinov, Maxim Maximovich (1876–1951) Soviet revolutionary and diplomat. He was an early critic of Tsarist rule and joined the Social Democratic Party in 1898. He was soon exiled abroad and joined the Bolshevik faction after 1903. Having lived in Britain for over a decade, he was appointed Bolshevik Ambassador in London (1917–18), and held various roving commissions before becoming Deputy Commissar (1921), then Commissar (1930) for Foreign Affairs. Until **Stalin** dismissed him in the spring of 1939, he was the chief architect of improved relations between the USSR and the West in the face of **Hitler**. He did not return to favour until after Hitler's attack in 1941, when he became Ambassador to the USA (1941), and Vice-Minister of Foreign Affairs (1942–6). A strong advocate of co-operation between the USSR and the West even at the onset of the Cold War, he died in Moscow. ▷ **Bolsheviks; Litvinov Protocol**

Litvinov Protocol (1929) The term used to describe Soviet attempts to improve security by working with Western proposals. Maxim **Litvinov**, Soviet Deputy Foreign Commissar, had been attempting to normalize relations with neighbouring states and to secure guarantees against Germany. When the US Secretary of State, Frank B Kellogg, proposed the renunciation of war as the core of a new international treaty (**Kellogg–Briand Pact**), Litvinov managed to persuade the USSR's Western neighbours to adhere to his protocol, also renouncing war, as a kind of Eastern alliance against Germany.

Li Tzu-ch'eng ▷ **Li Zicheng**

Liu Shao-ch'i ▷ **Liu Shaoqi**

Liu Shaoqi (Liu Shao-ch'i) (1898–1969) Chinese politician. A leading figure in the Chinese communist revolution, he was educated in the USSR, returned to China in 1922 and became a communist trade-union organizer. In 1939 he joined **Mao Zedong** at Yan'an, where he emerged as the chief party theorist on questions of organization. In 1943 he became Party Secretary, and succeeded Mao in 1959. After the **Cultural Revolution**, the extreme left made Liu their principal target, and in 1968 he was stripped of all his posts and dismissed from the party. ▷ **Great Leap Forward**

Liutprand (Luitprand) (c.922–72) Italian prelate and historian. Emperor **Otto I** made him Bishop of Cremona, and sent him on an embassy to Constantinople. He wrote important chronicles covering events from 886 to 950 and from 960 to 964.

Liverpool, Robert Banks Jenkinson, 2nd Earl of (1770–1828) British politician. He entered parliament in 1790, and was a member of the India Board (1793–6), Master of the Royal Mint (1799–1801), Foreign Secretary (1801–4), Home Secretary (1804–6 and 1807–9), and Secretary for War and the Colonies (1809–12). He succeeded his father as Earl of Liverpool in 1807. As Tory Premier (1812–27), he oversaw the final years of the **Napoleonic Wars**, the war of 1812–14 with the USA, and a difficult and lengthy process of readjustment to peace. His administrations adopted trade liberalization policies in the 1820s. He resigned after suffering a stroke early in 1827. ▷ **Tories**

Livia (58BC–AD29) **Augustus**'s wife (39BC–14AD) and key backroom figure in the early days of the Roman Empire. The mother of **Tiberius** by her first husband, Tiberius Claudius Nero, she plotted strenuously to ensure his succession, thus gaining from her great-grandson, the future Emperor **Caligula**, the nickname 'Ulysses in Petticoats'.

Livonian Knights Brothers of the Knighthood of Christ in Livonia, commonly known as the Sword-Brothers, their order was founded c.1202 to support the Bishop of Riga in his missionary work among pagan Latvians. They achieved significant successes against the Estonians (1211 and 1217) but were unable to establish a secure power base. After a crushing defeat in battle against the Lithuanians (Saule, 1236), the remnants of the order formed part of the Livonian branch of the **Teutonic Knights**. By the 14c they controlled the eastern Baltic lands of Courland, Estonia, and Livonia. However, in 1561 they disbanded in the face of threats from Russia.

Li Xian'nian (Li Hsien-nien) (1909–92) Chinese politician. Born into a poor peasant family in Hubei province, he worked as a carpenter before serving with the **Guomindang** forces (1926–7). After joining the Chinese Communist Party (CCP) in 1927 he established the Oyuwan Soviet (People's Republic) in Hubei, participated in the **Long March** and was a military commander in the war against Japan and in the Chinese Civil War. He was inducted into the CCP Politburo and secretariat in 1956 and 1958, but fell out of favour during the **Cultural Revolution**. He was rehabilitated, as Finance Minister, by **Zhou Enlai** in 1973, and later served as state President in the 'administration' of **Deng Xiaoping** (1983–8).

Li Yuanhong (Li Yuan-hung) (1864–1928) Chinese militarist. As the commander of the army division in central China whose mutiny (Oct 1911) against the **Qing Dynasty** signalled the collapse of the monarchy and creation of a republic, Li served briefly and reluctantly as the overall leader of the revolutionary army. He failed to curb the growing influence of the northern (Beiyang) militarists during his two terms as President of the Chinese Republic (1916–17 and 1922–3) and was a virtual figurehead.

Li Yuan-hung ▷ **Li Yuanhong**

Li Zhi (Li Chih) (1527–1602) Chinese iconoclast during the **Ming Dynasty**. After serving as a minor government official (1555–81), Li led the life of a Buddhist recluse. He aroused the ire of officials and scholars with his radical critique of traditional Confucian morality and condemnation of enforced conformity. He considered selfishness and profit to be respectable motivations, advocated free choice in marriage, and insisted that Confucianism, Buddhism and Daoism all had equal truth and value. Li was arrested in 1602 and committed suicide in jail. His unorthodox views form part of a significant dissident tradition in imperial China.

Li Zicheng (Li Tzu-ch'eng) (1605–45) Chinese bandit. The leader of a peasant rebellion that overthrew the **Ming Dynasty**, he came from a peasant family in north-west China (Shaanxi province) and was a soldier before resorting to banditry in the 1620s. By the spring of 1644, he had amassed a huge peasant army with his promotion of tax relief

and distribution of goods and controlled much of north and north-west China. He captured Beijing in Apr 1644 and the last Ming Emperor committed suicide. Although Li proclaimed a new dynasty (Shun), he was forced to evacuate Beijing (June 1644) by invading Manchu forces from the north-east, who gained the support of Chinese military commanders appalled by the disorder and cruelty of Li's regime. He was killed one year later. ▷ **Qing Dynasty**

Ljotić, Dimitrije (1891–1945) Serbian lawyer. He held a number of minor offices under King **Alexander I** then, during **World War II**, working for the collaborationist government of General Milan **Nedić**, he led the Serbian fascist movement, Zbor, and its youth movement, the White Eagle. Serbnationalist in ideology, Zbor aspired to the creation of a corporate regime on the model of **Mussolini**'s Italy. Ljotić was killed while trying to escape from Yugoslavia at the end of the war.

Lliga Catalan regionalist party. Originally founded in 1901 as the *Lliga Regionalista*, it became the principal representative of the Catalan bourgeoisie. It was instrumental in the creation of the Mancomunitat, a limited form of autonomous government, in 1913. However, the *Lliga*'s principal aim was to establish the Catalan bourgeoisie as the ruling class within Spain. The general strike of 1917 led the Lliga to withdraw into an alliance with the central government, thereby gravely undermining the opposition to the monarchy. The party split in 1922. Rebuilt by Francesc **Cambó** under the Second Republic as the *Lliga Catalana*, it was overshadowed throughout the regime by the *Esquerra* (Catalan Left). ▷ **Republic, Second** (Spain)

Lloyd-George (of Dwyfor), David, 1st Earl (1863–1945) British politician. Born of Welsh parentage, he became a solicitor, and in 1890, as a strong supporter of **Home Rule**, a Liberal MP for Caernarvon Boroughs (a seat he was to hold for 55 years). He was President of the Board of Trade (1905–8), and Chancellor of the Exchequer (1905–15). His 'people's budget' of 1909–10 was rejected by the House of Lords, and led to a constitutional crisis and the Parliament Act of 1911, which removed the Lords' power of veto. He became Minister of Munitions (1915), Secretary for War (1916), and superseded **Asquith** as coalition Prime Minister (1916–22), carrying on a forceful war policy. After **World War I**, he continued as head of a coalition government dominated by Conservatives. He negotiated with **Sinn Féin**, and conceded the **Irish Free State** (1921) — a measure which precipitated his downfall. His energies could not sufficiently revive the fortunes of a divided **Liberal Party** and, following the 1931 general election, he led a 'family' group of Independent Liberal MPs. He was made an earl in 1945. ▷ **Boer Wars; New Deal**

Llywelyn The name of two Welsh princes. **Llywelyn ap Iorwerth** or **Llywelyn the Great** (d.1240) successfully maintained his independence against King **John** and **Henry III**, and gained recognition of Welsh rights in the **Magna Carta** (1215). **Llywelyn ap Gruffydd** (d.1282) helped the English barons against Henry III, and opposed **Edward I**, who forced his submission. He was slain near Builth, at which point Wales lost her political independence.

LNC (*Lufta Nacional Çlirimtare*, 'National Liberation War') Dominated from its inception by the communists, this Albanian movement also included members from other political parties. Closely supervised by the Yugoslav resistance, it was forced by **Tito** to abandon any hope of acquiring **Kosovo**, and reached an agreement with the other Albanian resistance group, **Balli Kombëtar**. In May 1944, following the Yugoslav example of **AVNOJ**, the LNC met at Permët and founded an Anti-Fascist Council of National Liberation with Enver **Hoxha** as leader. When the regime in Tirana collapsed, following the withdrawal of German forces (Nov 1944), the LNC quickly established its authority, trying and executing members of the former government and eliminating all opposition to the establishment of a communist regime. Renamed the Democratic Front, in Dec 1945 it alone fielded candidates in the elections and in Jan 1946 it declared Albania a people's republic.

Lobengula (1870/93) King of the Ndebele or Matabele people of Zimbabwe. After a two-year succession crisis, he succeeded his father, **Mzilikazi**, to rule directly over Matabeleland. He frequently raided and established authority over many of the chieftaincies of the Shona people in Mashonaland. During his reign many Europeans, prospectors, hunters, missionaries, traders and concession-seekers, reached his kingdom from the south. He became embroiled in complex diplomatic negotiations and set out to protect his kingdom with great astuteness. However, Cecil Rhodes succeeded in securing key concessions for mining and land alienation in Mashonaland which enabled him to secure a charter for his British South Africa Company and invade Mashonaland (1890). Lobengula attempted to maintain a peaceful co-existence with the white settlers, but was forced into war in 1893. The Ndebele were defeated and Lobengula died, possibly of smallpox, while fleeing north to the Zambezi. He left a number of sons who were claimants to the throne of Matabeleland, but the region was incorporated into Southern Rhodesia. The Ndebele rose in revolt in 1896 and made Nyamanda king, but they sued for peace later the same year. Their chieftaincies survive and they now constitute 20 per cent of the population of Zimbabwe.

Locarno Pact (Oct 1925) The international agreement, held at Locarno, Italy, which guaranteed the post-1919 frontiers between France, Belgium and Germany, and the demilitarization of the Rhineland. The treaty was guaranteed by Italy and Britain as well as signed by the three states directly concerned, France, Germany and Belgium. At the same time, Germany agreed to arbitration conventions with France, Belgium, Poland and Czechoslovakia, and France signed treaties of mutual guarantee with Poland and Czechoslovakia.

Lockheed Scandal A political scandal in Japan that revealed the close links between the **Liberal Democratic Party** (LDP) and business interests. It broke in 1976, when Kakuei **Tanaka** (who had resigned as Prime Minister in 1974 amidst allegations of shady financial dealings) was named during US Senate hearings into the bribery of foreign officials by US multinationals. The American Lockheed Aircraft Corporation was alleged to have paid Tanaka, as Prime Minister, 500 million yen to ensure the purchase of its planes by a Japanese civil airline. Subsequent investigations in Japan highlighted the extent of bribes and kickbacks involved, and several businessmen and politicians, including Tanaka, were prosecuted. In 1983 Tanaka was sentenced to four years in prison but was released on bail pending appeal; the case has dragged on since then. Significantly, however, Tanaka remained a Diet member and his faction continued to be influential within the LDP during the 1980s.

Lodge, Henry Cabot (1850–1924) US politician, historian and biographer. He became a Republican Senator from Massachusetts in 1893, and after **World War I** led the opposition to the Treaty of **Versailles** (1919). The treaty was not ratified, preventing the USA from joining the **League of Nations** in 1920.

Lodi, Peace of (1454) The Fall of Constantinople in 1453 inspired the Pope to act as peacemaker between the warring states of Italy, and the league formed at Lodi was to defend Italy against the Turkish threat. Its principal result was to define the spheres of influence of the dominant Italian powers: Venice, Milan, Florence, Naples and, more indirectly, the papacy. Although there remained overlaps and sources of friction, the treaty was more or less effective until the outbreak of the **Italian Wars**.

Lodi Dynasty After the Timurid invasion in 1398, a new dynasty, the Sayyid, arose in Delhi. A number of Afghan generals established themselves in Punjab, the most

Italy after the Peace of Lodi (1454)

1 Montferrat
2 Asti
3 Mantua
4 Lucca
5 Modena
6 Ferrara
7 Piombino
8 Saluzzo

Possessions of Aragon

Patrimony of St Peter

Dependencies of Patrimony of St Peter

◆ Peace of Lodi (1454)

important of whom was Bahlul Lodi. He checked the growing power of the Khokhars, a fierce tribe which lived in Salt Ranges, and soon dominated the entire Punjab. Called in to help the ruler of Delhi against an impending attack by the ruler of Malwa, Bahlul Lodi stayed on. Before long, his men took over the control of Delhi. Bahlul formally crowned himself in 1451 when the ruler of Delhi died in exile. The Lodis dominated the upper Ganges valley and Punjab from the mid-15c. As distinct from early Delhi rulers who were Turks, the Lodis were Afghans. The most important of the Lodi Sultans was Sikandar Lodi (1489/1517), an efficient administrator who laid great emphasis on justice. During his reign all the highways of the empire were made safe from robbers and bandits. It was he who selected the site for the city of Agra in 1506, which in the course of time became the second capital of the Lodis. The Lodi Dynasty came to an end with the defeat of Ibrahim Lodi by **Babur** at the Battle of **Panipat** (1526).

Lok Dal The Lok Dal, an agrarian-based political party, started as the Bharatiya Lok Dal (BLD) in 1969 under the leadership of Charan **Singh**. Its supporters belonged mainly to the so-called backward or middle-status peasant castes. The BLD merged into the Janata Party towards the end of the Emergency. The Janata government collapsed in 1979 when the BLD reemerged as the **Lok Dal**, ruling India briefly with Charan Singh as Prime Minister. Upon Charan Singh's death in 1987, the party split into two and his son, Ajit Singh, presided over one faction. The two factions merged into the Janata Dal, which ruled briefly from 1989, but soon parted company in 1990 when the Janata Dal government fell.

Lollards A derisive term applied to the followers of the English theologian John **Wycliffe**. The movement, responsible for the translation of the Bible into the vernacular, was suppressed; however, it continued among the enthusiastic but less literate of society, generally anticlerical in attitude, and in some ways anticipated the **Reformation** in England.

Lombard League A coalition of northern Italian cities, established in 1167 to assert their independence as communes (city-republics) confronting the German Emperor **Frederick I, 'Barbarossa'**. The league, of which new versions were later formed, set a model for inter-city alliances, and underlined the rising political importance of urban communities in the medieval West.

Lombards A Germanic people settled in Hungary (their name deriving from the long beards (*langobardi*) they traditionally wore) who invaded northern Italy in AD568 under their King, **Alboin**. They founded a new capital at Milan, and in time controlled most of the peninsula except for the south and the area around Ravenna. Their kingdom was annexed by **Charlemagne** in 774, but the Lombard duchies (Benevento, Spoleto) survived as autonomous entities until the 11c.

Lombardy-Venetia, Kingdom of The title given to the Habsburg Kingdom in northern Italy established by the Vienna Settlement and administered as part of the Austrian Empire. Although ruled with a fair degree of efficiency, there were major anti-Austrian insurrections in the kingdom in 1848–9. Lombardy was lost by the Austrians to **Victor Emmanuel II** of Piedmont after the war of 1859 and Venetia was acquired by the newly united Kingdom of Italy in 1866. ▷ **Plombières, Agreement of; Revolutions of 1848–9**

Lomé Convention A series of agreements, named after the capital of Togo where the first Convention was signed, between the European Communities and a number of developing nations in Africa, the Caribbean and the Pacific (ACP). It came into force on 1 Apr 1976 and was intended to provide preferential trading arrangements for the ACP countries within the Common Market. The fourth agreement, intended to last 10 years, began in Mar 1990.

London, Treaties of (1827, 1830, 1913 and 1915) By the 1827 treaty, France, Britain and Russia agreed to work for Greek autonomy and to mediate between the rebels and the Ottoman Porte. By the 1830 treaty, the Great Powers agreed to Greek independence and established the boundaries of the new Greek kingdom. By the 1913 treaty at the end of the **Balkan Wars**, it reduced Ottoman possessions in Europe to the area around Constantinople, while Crete was ceded to Greece and Bulgaria gained Adrianople. The 1915 treaty secured Italian entry into **World War I** on the side of the Allies and promised the Italians the South Tyrol, Trentino, Gorizia, Gradisca, **Trieste**, **Istria**, part of **Dalmatia**, Saseno and Vlorë in Albania, as well as continued possession of the Dodecanese Islands and a share in the Turkish and German colonies.

London Convention (1884) A convention agreed between President Paul Kruger and the British Government which revised the Pretoria Convention of 1881. The British secured the definition of the western border of the Transvaal which laid the way open to their annexation of Bechuanaland and the maintenance of the 'road to the north', while in exchange Kruger persuaded the British to reduce the republic's debt, remove the British resident from Pretoria, recognize the name 'South African Republic' and abolish the Queen's suzerainty except in respect of specific powers.

Long, Huey Pierce (1893–1935) US politician. Flamboyant, astute and ambitious, he used the grievances of poor whites and his record as Public Service Commissioner to win the governorship of Louisiana, and then (1928–31) proceeded to build one of the most effective political machines in the history of US politics. His programme of extensive public spending on roads, educational institutions and hospitals not only reformed and developed Louisiana's public services, but also mitigated the impact of the Depression upon the state. Although a ruthless manipulator of the state legislature and judiciary, Long refused to use race as a political issue. Aiming at a national audience, he developed the 'Share Our Wealth' plan for income redistribution. A Democratic US Senator from 1931, by 1935 he claimed to have a following of 7.5 million for the plan. Initially supportive of the **New Deal** and President Franklin D **Roosevelt**, he became a vehement critic of the president and planned to run against him as a third-party candidate in 1936. However, he was widely feared and reviled as a potential dictator, and was assassinated in Sep 1935.

Long March (1934–5) The long trek in China, covering over 5000 miles, made by approximately 100000 communists under **Mao Zedong** to reach their base in Shaanxi from the **Jiangxi Soviet**, which had been encircled by nationalist government troops. See map p557.

Long Parliament An English parliament called (Nov 1640) by **Charles I** after his defeat by the Scots in the second of the **Bishops Wars**. It was legally in being 1640–60, but did not meet continuously. It attacked prerogative rights and alleged abuses of power by the King and his ministers, and abolished the Court of **Star Chamber**, the Councils of the North and for Wales, and the Ecclesiastical Court of High Commission (1641), the bishops and the Court of Wards (1646), and the monarchy and the House of Lords (1649). Moderates were eliminated in **Pride**'s Purge (Dec 1648), and the remaining **Rump Parliament** was dismissed by **Cromwell** in 1653. The Rump was recalled in the death-throes of the **Protectorate** (May 1659), and all members in Dec 1659.

Longueville, Anne, Duchess of (1619–79) French noblewoman. Known as the 'soul of the **Fronde**', she exerted a considerable influence on politics, in which she first began to interest herself as the mistress of the Duke de **La Rochefoucauld**. In the first war of the Fronde (1648) she sought in vain to win over her brother, 'the Great Condé'. In the second she won over both him and **Turenne**. After the death of her husband and her desertion by La Rochefoucauld, she entered a convent but continued to have influence at court. ▷ **Condé, Louis II of Bourbon, Prince of**

Lopes, Francisco Higino Craveiro (1894–1964) Portuguese politician. Born into a distinguished military family, Lopes was educated at the Military School in Lisbon and then fought in the expeditionary force in Mozambique in **World War I**. As a full colonel, in 1942 he entered negotiations for cooperation with the Allies and was responsible for the modernization of the Portuguese air force. In 1944 he entered parliament, in 1949 was promoted to general, and was President of Portugal from 1951 to 1958.

López, Francisco Solano (1826–70) Paraguayan dictator. He was the son of Carlos Antonio López, the dictator of Paraguay from 1844 to 1862. On his father's death, he succeeded him in power, leading his country into internecine war with Brazil, Argentina and Uruguay. He himself died in action at Cerro Corá, Paraguay, in the last battle of the War of the **Triple Alliance**.

Lopéz Rodó, Laureano (1920–) Spanish politician, academic and lawyer. He was the most influential **Opus Dei** technocrat to serve in a **Franco** government. As Secretary-General of the Presidency and Commissar of the Plan of Development, he formed part of the Opus Dei group which undertook the economic modernization of Spain from the late 1950s onwards. An intimate ally of Admiral **Carrero Blanco**, he became one of Franco's closest associates, being the dominant minister in the cabinet from 1965 to 1973. He was also Minister of Foreign Affairs

Long March (Oct 1934–Oct 1935)

(1973–4) and Ambassador to Austria (1974–7). He played an important role in persuading Franco to accept the candidacy of **Juan Carlos I** as heir to the throne. After Franco's death, he joined the *Alianza Popular* on its foundation in 1976, being elected as a deputy for Barcelona in 1977. He left the party in 1979.

Lords, House of The non-elected house of the UK legislature. Its membership, currently c.1200, includes hereditary peers and life peers (including judicial members — the *Lords of Appeal in Ordinary*); also the two archbishops and certain bishops of the Church of England. The House can no longer veto, though it can delay, bills passed by the House of Commons, with the exception of a bill to prolong the duration of a parliament. Its functions are mainly deliberative, its authority based on the expertise of its membership. The House of Lords also constitutes the most senior court in the UK. Appeals heard by the House are confined to matters of law.

Loris-Melikov, Mikhail Tariyelovich (1825–88) Russian general and political reformer. Having made a name for himself during the Russo-Turkish War of 1877–8, he was appointed in 1880 to head a supreme commission to suppress revolution and advise on its causes. He came up with a proposal for limited representative participation in government. **Alexander II** was examining this favourably when he was assassinated in 1881. On the conservative intervention of Konstantin **Pobedonostsev**, **Alexander III** rejected the idea (which did not surface again until 1905), and so Loris-Melikov resigned. ▷ **Russo-Turkish Wars**

Lothair I (795–855) King of the **Franks** and Emperor of the West. The eldest son of **Louis I, 'the Pious'**, at his father's accession he became ruler of Bavaria and later (822) of Italy. After his father's death, he became involved in a war with his brothers for the succession. He became Emperor in 840 but after the Battle of Fontenoy (841) he had to relinquish the supremacy he claimed over his brothers and agree to the partition of the empire under the terms of the Treaty of **Verdun** (843). He was allocated the Middle Kingdom. On his death, it was divided between his sons, **Lothair II** and Charles.

Lothair II (825–69) King of Lotharingia. Lothair inherited Francia, later called Lotharingia, from his father, **Lothair I**. His kingdom extended from the North Sea to the Alps and was bounded to the west by the rivers Maas, Schelde and Saone and to the east by the Rhine, with its capital at Aachen (Aix-la-Chapelle); on the death of his brother, Charles (863), he added part of Burgundy. In order to secure the realm for his descendants, in 862 he married the mother of his illegitimate son, the Frankish concubine Waldrada, but this aroused opposition and she was excommunicated (863). Attempts to reconcile the popes to his plan were unsuccessful and on his death his lands were divided by the Treaty of **Mersen**.

Lothair III, 'of Supplinburg' (c.1075–1137) German King and Emperor. He succeeded to extensive lands in Saxony and was involved in an uprising against **Henry IV** in 1088. His marriage to the heiress Richenza (1110) made him the most powerful noble in Germany. As a reward for supporting **Henry V** against Henry IV, he was made Duke of Saxony (1106) but he was soon involved in revolts against the King (1112–15). He was elected King on Henry's death (1125) and his reign was dominated by a long struggle against Frederick and Conrad Hohenstaufen, which was finally resolved at the Diet of Bamberg (1135). ▷ **Conrad III**

Lotharingia Originally, the kingdom of Lothar II (855–69), great-grandson of **Charlemagne**; subsequently, though disputed with France, two duchies of the Kingdom of Germany. Only one, Upper Lotharingia (modern Lorraine), survived the 12c, and it was eventually incorporated into France (1766).

Louis I, 'the Great' (1326–82) King of Hungary (1342/82) and Poland (1370/82). He succeeded his father, **Charles Robert**, as King of Poland in 1342 and until 1356 his reign was mostly devoted to campaigns against Queen Johanna of Naples, who was implicated in the murder (1344) of her husband, Andrew, Louis's younger brother. Louis's ultimate lack of success in Italy was compensated for by the conquest of Dalmatia (including the port of Dubrovnik) from Venice, recognized in the Peace of Zara (1358); and in 1370 he became King of Poland on the death of his uncle, Casimir III. A notable patron of the arts, Louis founded the first Hungarian university at Pécs in 1367.

Louis I, 'the Pious' (778–840) King of Aquitaine (781/814) and, as sole surviving son of **Charlemagne**, Emperor of the Western or Carolingian Empire (814/40). In 817 he attempted to secure his succession by dividing his territories between his three sons, **Lothair I** (d.855), **Pepin II** (d.838) and **Louis the German** (d.876), with Lothair to be the Emperor. In 829, a further share was given to a fourth son, **Charles II, 'the Bald'**. Louis's reign was marked by his reforms of the church in which he collaborated with the monk St Benedict of Aniane. It was also significant for the raids of the Norsemen in the north-west of the empire, especially the Seine and Scheldt basins. It is greatly debated how far the proliferation of hereditary countships and of the institutions of vassalage, often thought to result from these raids, caused a general decline in imperial authority. After his death, the empire disintegrated as his sons fought for supremacy.

Louis II (c.822–75) German King and Emperor. The eldest son of **Lothair I**, he took over the administration of Italy and was crowned King in 844, becoming Emperor in 850. After his father's death (855), he became sole Emperor and later acquired territory from his brothers, **Lothair II** of Lotharingia and Charles of Provence. In 866 he began an extensive campaign against the Arabs who had invaded southern Italy, and with the help of the Byzantine fleet he conquered their headquarters at Bari (871). However, he was unable to enforce his rule and withdrew to northern Italy where he died without a male heir.

Louis II, 'the Stammerer' (846–79) King of France (877/9). The second son of **Charles II, 'the Bald'**, he was King of Maine (856) and Aquitaine (867). He was often in revolt against his father, whom he succeeded with great difficulty as King of 'Francia' from 877 to 879.

Louis III (c.863–882) King of France, eldest son of **Louis II**, on whose death (879) he was proclaimed joint king with his brother Carloman. He took Francia and Neustria as his territories. After his short reign, he was succeeded by Carloman.

Louis IV, 'd'Outremer' (d.954) King of France (936/54). He was the son of **Charles III, 'the Simple'**, himself the posthumous son of **Louis II, 'the Stammerer'**. His early life was spent in exile but he was recalled from England on the death of King Raoul, by Hugh the Great (father of Hugh **Capet**) from whose political domination he sought successfully to escape. Nevertheless, during his reign (936–54) many territorial princes in France consolidated their power to the detriment of royal authority. He was succeeded by his son, Lothair IV, and his grandson **Louis V**.

Louis IV, 'the Bavarian' (c.1283–1347) Holy Roman Emperor, a younger son of Louis, Duke of Upper Bavaria. He was elected King of Germany in 1314, opposed by a rival candidate, Frederick II, Duke of Austria, whom he eventually defeated in battle at Mühldorf (1322). Pope John XXII however refused to recognize his title, referring to him only as 'Louis the Bavarian', a name which stuck. In 1328 he received the imperial crown from the people of Rome, but was forced to leave Italy the next year. Thereafter Louis remained mostly in Germany, maintaining his position against internal opposition with the financial support of the cities. He waged a war of propaganda against the papacy with the help of Marsilius of Padua, William of Ockham, and the Spiritual Franciscans; he invaded Italy (1327–30), captured Rome and set up an anti-pope, Nicholas V (1328/30), in opposition to Pope John. In 1338, at the Diet of Rense, the electoral princes precipitated a Church/state division by declaring that the Emperor did not require papal confirmation of his election. His energetic policy of family aggrandizement, however, cost him his alliance with the House of Luxembourg, who raised up a rival emperor, **Charles IV**, a year before Louis met his death while hunting.

Louis V, 'the Do-Nothing' (c.967–987) King of France (986/7), son of Lothair IV, with whose kingship he was associated in 978. He died heirless and was thus the last Carolingian ruler of France. The throne passed to Hugh **Capet**, the first of the Capetian line. ▷ **Capetian Dynasty**

Louis VI, 'the Fat' (1081–1137) King of France. He succeeded his father **Philip I** in 1108. Despite an inclination to gluttony and a corpulence which left him unable to mount a horse after the age of 46, he was one of the most active of the House of Capet, and greatly increased the power and prestige of the monarchy. ▷ **Capetian Dynasty**

Louis VII (c.1120–1180) King of France (1137/80). The second son of **Louis VI, 'the Fat'**, in 1137 he became King, married Eleanor, heiress of Aquitaine, and continued the consolidation of royal authority begun by his father. The marriage was annulled in 1152, whereupon Eleanor married Henry Plantagenet, Count of Anjou, who became King of England in 1154 as **Henry II**. Faced with a vast agglomeration of power on both sides of the Channel, Louis succeeded in staving off the Angevin threat, enlisting the aid of the papacy and fomenting discord within Henry's family. ▷ **Angevins; Eleanor of Aquitaine**

Louis VIII, 'the Lion' (1187–1226) King of France (1223/6). The son of **Philip II** and Isabella of Hainault, his short reign was marked chiefly by his acquisition of the Montfort claim to the County of Toulouse (1224) and the resumption of the Albigensian Crusade in the south in 1226. This led to the submission of Count Raymond VII to his widow, Blanche of Castile (1229), and the eventual absorption of all Languedoc into the royal domain. ▷ **Albigenses; Crusades, Later**

Louis IX, St (1214–70) King of France (1226/70). He was the son of **Louis VIII, 'the Lion'**. By his victories he compelled **Henry III** of England to acknowledge French suzerainty in **Guyenne** (1259). He led the Seventh Crusade (1248), but was defeated in Egypt, taken prisoner, and ransomed. He embarked on a new, eighth, crusade in 1270, but died of plague at Tunis. He was canonized in 1297.

Louis X, 'the Quarrelsome' (1289–1316) King of Navarre (1305/16) and of France (1314/16). The son of **Philip IV, 'the Fair'**, during his brief reign, which was marked by unrest among his barons, he was guided in his policy by **Charles of Valois**.

Louis XI (1423–83) King of France (1461/83). The eldest son of **Charles VII**, he made several unsuccessful attempts against his father's throne, and had to flee to Dauphiné. His severe measures as king led to a coalition against him (1465), which he survived. During his reign he added to his lands, defeated **Charles the Bold**, Duke of Burgundy (1477), and actively encouraged trade and industry.

Louis XII (1462–1515) King of France (1498/1515). He was the son of Charles, Duke of Orléans, to whose title he succeeded in 1465. He commanded the French troops at Asti during **Charles VIII**'s invasion of Italy (1494–5) before succeeding him to the French throne (1498) and marrying the King's widow, **Anne of Brittany**. His forces were driven from Italy (1512) and then defeated by an Anglo-Imperial alliance at the Battle of Guinegate (1513). To guarantee peace, Louis married Mary Tudor, sister of **Henry VIII** (1514), but died shortly afterwards. ▷ **Tudor, House of**

Louis XIII (1601–43) King of France (1610/43). The eldest son of **Henry IV** and **Marie de Médicis**, he succeeded to the throne on the assassination of his father (1610). He was, however, excluded from power, even after he came of age (1614), by the Queen Regent. In 1617 Louis took over the reins of government, and exiled Marie de Médicis to Blois (1619–20). By 1624 he was entirely dependent upon the political acumen of **Richelieu**, who became his Chief Minister. Louis's later years were enhanced by French military victories in the **Thirty Years War** against the Habsburgs. ▷ **Habsburg Dynasty; Huguenots**

Louis XIV (Louis the Great or The Sun King) (1638–1715) King of France (1643/1715). He was the son of **Louis XIII**, whom he succeeded. During his minority (1643–51) France was ruled by his mother, **Anne of Austria**, and her Chief Minister, Cardinal **Mazarin**. In 1660 Louis married the Infanta **Maria Theresa**, elder daughter of **Philip IV** of Spain, through whom he was later to claim the Spanish succession for his second grandson. In 1661 he assumed sole responsibility for government, advised by various royal councils. His obsession with France's greatness led him into aggressive foreign and commercial policies, particularly against the Dutch. His patronage of the Catholic Stuarts also led to the hostility of England after 1689; but his major political rivals were the Austrian Habsburgs, particularly **Leopold I**. From 1665 Louis tried to take possession of the Spanish Netherlands, but later became obsessed with the acquisition of the whole Spanish inheritance. His attempt

to create a Franco-Spanish Bourbon bloc led to the formation of the Grand Alliance of England, the United Provinces, and the Habsburg Empire, and resulted in the War of the **Spanish Succession**. In his later years Louis was beset by other problems. His determination to preserve the unity of the French state and the independence of the French Church led him into conflict with the Jansenists, the **Huguenots** and the papacy, with damaging repercussions. His old age was overshadowed by military disaster and the financial ravages of prolonged warfare. Yet Louis was the greatest monarch of his age, who established the parameters of successful absolutism. In addition, his long reign marked the cultural ascendancy of France within Europe, symbolized by the Palace of Versailles, where he died, to be succeeded by his great-grandson as **Louis XV**. ▷ **Bourbon, House of; Colbert, Jean Baptiste; Fouquet, Nicolas; Fronde, The; Grand Alliance, War of the; Habsburg Dynasty; Jansenism; Stuart, House of**

Louis XV, 'the Well-Beloved' (1710–74) King of France (1715/74). He was the son of **Louis**, Duc de Bourgogne and Marie-Adelaide of Savoy, and the great-grandson of **Louis XIV**, whom he succeeded. Until he came of age (1723), he was guided by the Regent, Philippe d'Orléans, and then by the Duc de Bourbon, who negotiated a marriage alliance with Maria Leczczynska, daughter of the deposed King Stanislas I of Poland. In 1726 Bourbon was replaced by the King's former tutor, the elderly **Fleury**, who skilfully steered the French state (*Etat français*) until his death (1744). Thereafter Louis vowed to rule without a First Minister, but allowed the government to drift into the hands of ministerial factions, while indulging in secret diplomatic activity, distinct from official policy, through his own network of agents. This system (*le secret du roi*) brought confusion to French foreign policy in the years that preceded the Diplomatic Revolution (1748–56), and obscured the country's interests overseas. Instead, France was drawn into a trio of continental wars during Louis's reign, which culminated in the loss of the French colonies in America and India (1763). Among innumerable mistresses, the two who were most famous and influential were the Countess du **Barry** and Madame de Pompadour. In 1771 Louis tried to introduce reforms, but these came too late to staunch the decline in royal authority. He was succeeded by his grandson, **Louis XVI**. ▷ **Austrian Succession, War of the; Fleury,**

Cardinal; Poland, Partitions of; Savoy, House of; Seven Years War

Louis XVI (1754–93) King of France (1774/93). He was the third son of the **Dauphin** Louis and Maria Josepha of Saxony, and the grandson of **Louis XV**, whom he succeeded in 1774. He was married in 1770 to the Archduchess **Marie Antoinette**, daughter of the Habsburg empress, **Maria Theresa**, to strengthen the Franco-Austrian alliance. He failed to give consistent support to ministers who tried to reform the outmoded financial and social structures of the country, such as **Turgot** (1774–6) and **Necker** (1776–81). He allowed France to become involved in the War of American Independence (1778–83), which exacerbated the national debt. To avert the deepening social and economic crisis, he agreed in 1789 to summon the **Estates General**. However, encouraged by the Queen, he resisted demands from the National Assembly for sweeping reforms, and in Oct was brought with his family from Versailles to Paris as hostages to the revolutionary movement. Their attempted flight to Varennes (June 1791) branded the royal pair as traitors. Louis reluctantly approved the new constitution (Sep 1791), but his moral authority had collapsed. In Aug an insurrection suspended Louis's constitutional position, and in Sep the monarchy was abolished. He was tried before the National Convention for conspiracy with foreign powers, and was guillotined in Paris. ▷ **American Revolution; Convention, National; French Revolution**

Louis (Charles) XVII (1785–95) Titular King of France (1793/5). He was the second son of **Louis XVI** and heir to the throne from June 1789. After the execution of his father (Jan 1793), he remained in the Temple prison in Paris. His death there dealt a blow to the hopes of royalists and constitutional monarchists. The secrecy surrounding his last months led to rumours of his escape, and produced several claimants to his title. ▷ **French Revolution**

Louis XVIII (Louis Stanislas Xavier, Count of Provence) (1755–1824) King of France, in name (1795/1824) and in fact (1814/24). The younger brother of **Louis XVI**, he fled from Paris (June 1791), finally taking refuge in England, and becoming the focal point for the royalist cause. On **Napoleon I**'s downfall (1814) he re-entered Paris, and made promise of a Constitutional Charter. His restoration was interrupted by

Napoleon's return from Elba, but after the Battle of **Waterloo** (1815) he again regained his throne. His reign was marked by the introduction of parliamentary government with a limited franchise. The system of constitutional monarchy practised in France under the Restoration, a system in which the King was more than a mere figurehead ('the King governs as well as reigns'), was defended by François **Guizot** and the *Doctrinaires*. ▷ **French Revolution**

Louisiana Purchase (1803) The sale by France to the USA of an area between the Mississippi River and the Rocky Mountains for US$15 000 000. The purchase gave the USA full control of the Mississippi Valley.

Louis Napoleon (1778–1846) King of Holland (1806/10). He was the younger brother of the French Emperor, **Napoleon I**. A marriage was arranged in 1802 between him and **Hortense** de Beauharnais, and in 1808 the future Emperor **Napoleon III** was born, although there is some doubt about his father's identity. In 1806 Napoleon I put his brother on the throne of the Kingdom of Holland (present-day Netherlands), intending to make it a satellite state of France. Louis Napoleon, however, took his kingship seriously, learned the Dutch language, and was generally well liked by his new subjects, often defending them against the demands of the French; for this he was dethroned by his brother in 1810, who annexed the Netherlands to France. Louis left for England, where he wrote an apology for his reign in Holland.

Louis Napoleon (1808–73) ▷ **Napoleon III**

Louis of Male (1330–84) Count of Flanders, Nevers and Rethel. The son of **Louis of Nevers**, he became Count of Flanders in 1346. In 1357 he also became Duke of **Brabant** through his wife Margaret's family. He expanded his County with Walloon Flanders (1369), and also inherited Artois and Franche-Comté through his mother. Internationally he tried to remain neutral, and to keep the trading connection open with England; in Flanders he tried to limit the growing power of the industrial towns, which brought him into conflict with Philip van **Artevelde**, who defeated him at Beverhoutsveld in 1382.

Louis of Nassau (1538–74) German nobleman. A younger brother of **William I**, Prince of Orange (and of **John VI, Count of**

Nassau), he played a significant role in the early years of the **Eighty Years War** in support of his brother, William, and the Dutch against Spain. He led a military expedition from Germany into Groningen in 1568, and was active in the Huguenot struggles against France, where he abandoned Lutheranism for Calvinism. In 1572 he captured Mons from the Spanish (though it was lost again the same year), and died in the Battle of Mokerheide.

Louis of Nevers (c.1304–46) Count of Flanders, Nevers and Rethel. He was brought up at the French court, married Margaret, daughter of the French King **Philip V**, and supported France heavily when he became Count in 1322. This meant cutting off Flanders from England (and English wool) in the **Hundred Years War**, which, together with heavy taxation, caused a general revolt in Flanders led by Jacob van **Artevelde**. Louis left his County to fight for the French against England, and died in the Battle of **Crécy**. His successor was his son, **Louis of Male**.

Louis-Philippe (1773–1850) King of the French (1830/48). Known as the 'Citizen King', he was the eldest son of Louis Philippe Joseph, Duke of **Orléans** (Philippe Egalité). At the **French Revolution** he entered the **National Guard**, and with his father he renounced his titles to demonstrate his progressive sympathies. He joined the Jacobin Club (1790), and fought in the Army of the North before deserting to the Austrians (1793). He lived in exile and married Marie Amélie, daughter of **Ferdinand I** of the two Sicilies. He returned to France (1814), but fled to England again in the **Hundred Days**. On the eve of **Charles X**'s abdication (1830) he ruled with the title of King of the French. He strengthened his power by steering a middle course with the help of the upper bourgeoisie; but political corruption and industrial and agrarian depression (1846) caused discontent, and united the radicals in a cry for electoral reform. The dominant figure in his governments from 1840 to 1848 was François **Guizot**. When the Paris mob rose (1848), he abdicated, and escaped to England with Guizot. ▷ **Bourbon, House of; February Revolution** (France)**; July Revolution (1830); Jacobins**

Louis the German (c.804–76) Frankish King. The third son of **Louis I, 'the Pious'**, he was granted Bavaria by his father in 817. The conflicting ambitions of his father and his two brothers, **Charles II, 'the Bald'** and **Lothair I**, led to a series of disputes which were finally settled by the Treaty of **Verdun** (843). Louis received the area east of the Rhine and Aare, along with Speyer, Worms and Mainz on the left of the Rhine. He extended his realm as far as the Maas and the Mosel by the Treaty of **Mersen** (870). On his death, his realm was divided among his sons **Carloman**, Louis III and **Charles III, 'the Fat'**.

Louvois, François Michel le Tellier, Marquis of (1641–91) French politician. The son of Michel **Le Tellier**, he was Secretary of State for War under **Louis XIV**. He reformed and strengthened the army, and was recognized as a brilliant administrator and the King's most influential minister in the years 1683–91. ▷ **Nantes, Edict of**

Lovisa Ulrika (1720–82) Queen of Sweden. Born in Berlin, she was the daughter of King Frederick William I of Brandenburg-Prussia and the sister of **Frederick II, 'the Great'**. In 1744 she married **Adolf Frederick**, heir to the Swedish throne. After her husband came to the throne in 1751, she worked tirelessly to increase royal power and formed a Court Party in the Diet to struggle for this. She saw her dreams realized with the accession of her son, **Gustav III**, in 1771; however relations between them cooled and they were reconciled only just before her death.

Loyalists Colonial Americans who remained loyal to Britain during the **American Revolution**. Britain defined the term carefully, since loyalists were eligible for compensation. It was not enough to have been born or been living in the American colonies at the onset of revolution; it was necessary to have served the British cause in some substantial manner and to have left the USA before or soon after the termination of hostilities. During the revolution special corps were established for over 19000 loyalist troops. Half of the 80000–100000 refugees went to Canada, especially to the Maritime Provinces, and their presence contributed to the creation of **Upper Canada** in 1791. Their influence was not insubstantial in the establishment of governmental, social, educational and religious institutions. In 1789 Lord Dorchester ordained that both they and their children were entitled to add the letters 'UE' after their names, indicating their belief in the Unity of Empire. They then became known as the United Empire Loyalists. ▷ **Carleton, Sir Guy**

Loyola, Ignatius de (Iñigo López de Recalde) (1491 or 1495–1556) Spanish theologian and founder of the Jesuits. He became a soldier, was wounded, and while convalescing read the lives of Christ and the saints. In 1522 he went on a pilgrimage to Jerusalem, studied in Alcalá, Salamanca, and Paris, and in 1534 founded with six associates the Society of Jesus. Ordained in 1537, he went to Rome in 1539, where the new order was approved by the Pope. The author of the influential *Spiritual Exercises*, he was canonized in 1622.

Lozi (Barotse) State A state formed by a cluster of Bantu-speaking agricultural and cattle-herding people of western Zambia, living in the floodplain of the upper Zambezi. It was penetrated by hunters, traders and missionaries in the late 19c and, under King Lewanika, peacefully accepted colonial rule. During the colonial period, the state was known as Barotseland and was controlled by **indirect rule**, so that their kingship and distinctive institutions survived.

LTTE (Liberation Tigers of Tamil Eelam) Also known simply as the 'Tigers', the Sri Lankan secessionist group which has been fighting to establish a separate Tamil state (**Eelam**) in the north and east of the country. The group was founded in Jaffna in the mid-1970s and gradually grew in size and effectiveness, particularly after the anti-Tamil violence of the early 1980s. A reluctant partner to the **Indo-Sri Lankan Peace Accord** overseen by Rajiv **Gandhi**, it soon found itself fighting the Indian Peacekeeping Force (IPKF) and it was widely believed to have been responsible for Gandhi's assassination in Tamil Nadu in 1991.

Lu (d.180BC) Empress of China. A formidable ruler, she was virtual regent for 15 years following the death of her husband, **Han Gaozu** (256/195BC), the founder of the Han Dynasty. By the time of her death, she had firmly established the authority of the ruling Liu family, although Chinese historiography condemns her for her resort to nepotism and employment of **eunuchs** at court. ▷ **Han Dynasties**

Luba-Lunda Kingdoms A succession of African states occupying territory in what is now Zaire. They were powerful by the 17c, involved in slave and ivory trading with the Portuguese and later with Zanzibar. The Luba states were relatively unstable, but the Lunda Empire seems to have consolidated its power through trade. The central Lunda state did not survive the ending of the Angolan **slave trade** in the 1840s, and the others fell to European imperialism.

Lubbers, Rudolf Franz Marie (1939–) Dutch politician. After graduating from Erasmus University, Rotterdam, he joined the family engineering business of Lubbers Hollandia. He made rapid progress after entering politics, becoming Minister of Economic Affairs in 1973 and, in 1982, at the age of 43, Prime Minister, leading a **Christian Democratic Appeal** (CDA) coalition.

Lublin, Union of (1569) An Act uniting Poland and the Grand Duchy of Lithuania. The Union, separately confirmed by the Polish and Lithuanian assemblies (*sejms*), completed the formal unification of the two states begun in the 14c. It established a common political system and currency, and a Commonwealth headed by a king jointly elected by the Polish and Lithuanian aristocracy. This greatly enlarged Poland and brought it increasingly into conflict with an expanding Russia.

Lu Buwei (Lu Pu-wei) (d.235BC) Chinese official. He served as Chief Minister (250–237BC) in the state of Qin. Originally from an émigré merchant family, Lu supported the imposition of Draconian laws and centralized control that was to make Qin a formidable power in the region. A court intrigue led to his suicide and he was succeeded by **Li Si**, one of his protégés.

Lucknow, Siege of (1857–8) The siege of the Lucknow garrison began on 1 July 1857. On 25 Sep, Henry Havelock's forces broke through the siege and reinforced the garrison. Additional British forces under Sir Colin Campbell broke through on 18 Nov and women, children, the sick and the wounded were removed to safety. Two days later Havelock died and Campbell left for Kanpur. During Campbell's absence, Tantia Tope attacked the garrison forcing Campbell to return to Lucknow. Campbell defeated Tantia on 6 Dec and went to Kanpur from where he returned with a large army on 28 Feb 1858 and succeeded in repossessing Lucknow for the British on 21 Mar.

Lucretia (Lucrece) According to Roman legend, the wife of Collatinus. She was raped by Sextus, son of **Tarquinius Superbus**; after telling her story, she committed suicide. The incident led to the expulsion of the Tarquins from Rome.

Lucullus, Lucius Licinius (c.110–57BC) Roman politician and general. He is famous for his victories over Mithridates VI Eupator, and also for his enormous wealth, luxurious lifestyle, and patronage of the arts. He is believed to have introduced the cherry to Italy from Asia Minor, the scene of his greatest military triumphs and administrative reforms. ▷ **Pompey the Great**

Luddites The name given to the group of workers who destroyed newly-introduced textile machinery in Nottingham, Yorkshire, and Lancashire (1811–12). Their fear was that the output of the equipment was so much faster than the output of a hand-loom operator that many jobs would be lost. Known as 'the Luds', after their leader, Ned Ludd, when the movement ended with a mass trial in York in 1813 many were hanged or transported to Australia. The term has since been used to describe any resistance to technological innovation.

Ludendorff, Erich von (1865–1937) German general. He and **Hindenburg** defeated the Russians at the Battle of Tannenberg (1914). In 1916 he became Chief of Staff under Hindenburg and conducted the 1918 spring offensives on the Western Front. In 1923 he was a leader in the unsuccessful **Hitler** putsch at Munich, but was acquitted of treason. He became involved with the **Nazi Party**, but from 1925 led a minority party of his own. ▷ **World War I**

Ludwig I (1786–1868) King of Bavaria (1825/48). His lavish expenditure on pictures, public buildings and favourites, and by taxes and reactionary policy, provoked active discontent in 1830, and again in 1848, when he abdicated in favour of his son, Maximilian II.

Ludwig II (1845–86) King of Bavaria (1864/86). The son of Maximilian II, on his accession he devoted himself to patronage of Wagner and his music. In the 1870 Franco-Prussian War he threw Bavaria on the side of **Prussia**, and offered the imperial crown to **William I**, though he took no part in the war, and lived the life of a recluse. He was almost constantly at feud with his ministers and family, mainly on account of his insensate outlays on superfluous palaces, and was declared insane in 1886. A few days later he was found drowned, with his physician, in the Starnberger Lake near his castle of Berg. It is not known whether his death was suicide, murder, or simply accidental.

Ludwig Wilhelm I (d.1709) Margrave of Baden. The Imperial general at the Battle of Heilbronn (1693), he commanded Imperial troops against the French in the War of the **Spanish Succession**.

Luftwaffe The correct name for the German Air Force, re-established in 1935 under **Goering**, in contravention of the Treaty of **Versailles**. Dominant in the early years of German victory in **World War II**, the *Luftwaffe* suffered production shortfalls and poor central leadership which led to defeat in the Battle of Britain. It had all but ceased to exist by 1945, having lost around 100 000 aircraft. The Federal Republic of Germany's air force, also known as the *Luftwaffe*, was re-established in 1956, and today is a critical element in **NATO**. It operates over 600 combat aircraft. ▷ **Britain, Battle of**

Lugard, Frederick John Dealtry, Baron Lugard (1858–1945) British soldier and colonial administrator. In 1878 he was commissioned as an army officer, serving in the Sudan against **Mohammed Ahmed**, the Mahdi (1885), and in Burma after the fall of King Thibaw (1886), and commanded an expedition against slavers in Nyasaland (1888). His activities in rough-and-ready Uganda peacekeeping led to its being made a British protectorate in 1894. Appointed Commissioner in the Nigerian hinterland by Joseph **Chamberlain** (1897), he kept a French challenge at bay and kept the peace. Britain having declared a protectorate over Northern and Southern Nigeria, Lugard was high commissioner for the North (1900–7), and established administrative paternalistic control with minimal force. He was Governor of Hong Kong from 1907, helping to establish its University in 1911. He returned to Nigeria as Governor of the two protectorates, becoming Governor-General (1914–19) on their amalgamation. His principle was one of use of existing tribal institutions as the infrastructure for British rule.

Lukács, György (1885–1971) Hungarian Marxist philosopher, critic and politician. From a wealthy Jewish family, he studied in Budapest, Berlin and Heidelberg. He published two important early works on literary criticism, *Soul and Form* (1910) and *The Theory of the Novel* (1916). In 1918 he joined the Hungarian Communist Party, but after the defeat of the uprising in 1919 he lived abroad in Vienna (1919–29) and Moscow (1930–44). He returned to Hungary after **World War II** as Professor at Budapest;

he came in for political criticism in the early 1950s and, more or less inevitably, joined **Nagy**'s short-lived revolutionary government in 1956 as Minister of Culture. After the Russian suppression he was briefly deported and interned but returned to Budapest in 1957. His major book on Marxism, *History and Class Consciousness* (1923), was repudiated as heretical by the Russian Communist Party and in the 1950s, in abject public confession, by Lukács himself. His situation and influence grew in the 1960s as his works were published.

Lukyanov, Anatoli Ivanovich (1930–) Soviet lawyer, bureaucrat and political conspirator. Born in Smolensk and educated in Moscow, he held a series of legal positions within the Soviet and the party. A moderate reformer, he began to rise very quickly first with Yuri **Andropov** and then with Mikhail **Gorbachev**. In 1989 he was elected deputy chairman under Gorbachev's chairmanship of the new Supreme Soviet, and in 1990, when Gorbachev was elevated to the presidency, then Luykanov in turn became chairman. In 1991 it was to save his vision of the USSR that he participated in the **August Coup** to oust Gorbachev; but he achieved quite the opposite of what he wanted and landed in prison.

Lula (Luis Inácio Lula da Silva) (1944–) Brazilian labour leader. He came to national prominence as leader of the Metalworker's Union of São Bernardo, a São Paulo industrial zone housing key industries, especially in motor vehicles. Forced by the military regime's labour legislation to concentrate on local issues, Lula led strikes in the Saab–Scania plant in May 1978 and 1979 involving 500 000 workers and making the employers concede higher wages through direct negotiations rather than via government-led labour courts. In Oct 1979 he founded the PT (*Partido dos Trabalhadores*), to achieve representation for workers in Congress; it has drawn support from a range of traditional radical movements and the left wing of the Church. Elected to Congress in 1986, he narrowly defeated Leonel **Brizola** as the candidate for the Left against Fernando **Collor de Mello** in the 1989 presidential race.

Lumey, William of (c.1542–78) Nobleman from the southern Netherlands and a leader of the Dutch Revolt against Spain. A great-grandson of **Guillaume de la Mark**, he was active in opposition to the town authorities at an early age. In the **Eighty Years War** he

joined the revolt against Spain, and became admiral of the Sea-**Beggars**, leading the attack on the port of Brielle in Apr 1572. However, **William I**, Prince of Orange, considered his violent persecution of Catholics a liability and had him imprisoned in 1573; in 1574 he left for Germany.

Lumumba, Patrice (Hemery) (1925–61) Congolese (Zairois) politician. Educated at mission schools, both Catholic and Protestant, he was a post office clerk and then director of a brewery. He helped form the *Mouvement National Congolais* in 1958 to challenge Belgian rule and, when the Congo was granted independence, he was made its first Prime Minister (1960). A major symbolic figure in the African history of the period, he sought a unified Congo and opposed the secession of Katanga under Moise **Tshombe**. He was arrested by his own army in Sep 1960, handed over to the Katangese and murdered. His name, however, remains significant as the embodiment of African nationalism and the opponent of balkanization manipulated by ex-colonial countries and their allies.

Lunacharsky, Anatoli Vasilevich (1875–1933) Russian philosopher and revolutionary. As a student and writer he dabbled in Marxism. He was imprisoned several times for his political activities and spent much time associating with émigrés in Western Europe. In 1917 he offered his services to **Lenin** who made him in effect the Minister of Education, a function he performed none too well down to 1929 when he took up a somewhat similar party port. He died on his way to becoming ambassador to Spain, a cultural adornment who was perhaps fortunate not to have to face the purges of the 1930s.

Lundy's Lane, Battle of (1814) The only Canadian engagement in the **War of 1812** which was not simply a skirmish. Casualties were high on both sides, with the Americans suffering more fatalities. The Americans retreated and were unable to continue their campaign in the Niagara district.

Luns, Joseph Marie Antoine Hubert (1911–) Dutch politician. After studying law, he joined the Dutch diplomatic service (1940–52). In 1952 he became Minister without Portfolio for the Dutch **Catholic People's Party**, and from then on was inextricably bound up with Dutch foreign affairs. For the whole of the period 1957–71 he was Foreign Minister, and from 1971 to 1984 he was Secretary-General of **NATO**. He was integrally involved in the formation and consolidation of the European Communities, and was a central figure in international relations during the days of the **Cold War**.

Lupescu Magda (1902–) Mistress and second wife of King **Charles II** of Romania. Her Jewish descent as much as her dissolute behaviour earned her the disapproval of Romanian society, itself notorious for its profligacy. Because of the scandal surrounding their affair, Charles renounced his claim to the throne and when he returned to Romania in 1930 it was on condition that she remained abroad. When she also returned and took up residence in the palace, the Prime Minister, Iuliu **Maniu**, resigned. Upon her marriage in 1947 to Charles, she took the name Princess Elena and lived in exile with the former king.

Lusitania, Sinking of the (May 1915) A Cunard passenger liner torpedoed by a German submarine off the Irish Coast while in transit from New York to Liverpool, when 128 Americans were among those lost. The German government had announced (Feb 1915) that any passenger ship caught within a designated war zone around the British Isles would be sunk without warning. President Woodrow **Wilson** declared he would hold Germany accountable for such deaths in the future. Although the German authorities argued that the *Lusitania* was carrying war munitions for the Allies, they did eventually make **reparations**. However, any US sympathy toward Germany up to this point disappeared, and many called for a declaration of war.

Luther, Hans (1879–1962) German politician. Following his early career in local government, Luther entered the national government in 1922. He served in various cabinets and, as Finance Minister, succeeded in re-establishing a stable German currency (the *Rentenmark*) after the Great Inflation of 1923. He became Chancellor in Jan 1925 at the head of the centre-right coalition which concluded the **Locarno Pact** with the Allies. He resigned in 1926, but served as President of the National Bank between 1930 and Mar 1933 and then as Ambassador to Washington until 1937. He held various public and academic offices in the Federal Republic and published a number of books.

Luther, Martin (1483–1546) German religious reformer. He spent three years in an Augustinian monastery, obtained his degree at Erfurt, and was ordained in 1507. His career as a reformer began after a visit to Rome in 1510–11 and the preaching and selling of indulgences, to raise money (for St Peter's Basilica and the Elector/Archbishop of Mainz), by the monk, Tetzel, in lands around Saxony. In 1517 he drew up 95 theses on indulgences, which he nailed on the church door at Wittenberg. Violent controversy followed, and he was summoned to Rome to defend his theses, but did not go. He then began to attack the papal system more boldly, and publicly burned the papal bull issued against him. An order was issued for the destruction of his books; he was summoned to appear before the Diet at Worms, and was put under the ban of the Empire. In 1525 he married a former nun, Katharina von Bora. The drawing up of the Augsburg Confession, where he was represented by Melanchthon, marks the culmination of the German Reformation (1530). His translation of the Bible became a landmark of German literature.

Luthuli, Albert (John Mvumbi) (1898–1967) South African nationalist. He qualified as a teacher and taught for 15 years before succeeding to the chieftainship of Groutville, the community in Natal in which he had been raised, in 1935. He joined the **ANC** (African National Congress) in 1946, became President of the Natal branch and led a campaign of passive resistance against **apartheid**, for which he was deposed from his chieftainship by the South African government. He became President of the ANC in 1952, reflecting the 'colour-blind' traditions of the party, but was repeatedly 'banned', and was imprisoned (1956–7). He was awarded the Nobel Peace Prize in 1960.

Lützen, Battle of (1632) A battle during the **Thirty Years War**, fought near Leipzig in Saxony between forces led by King **Gustav II Adolf** of Sweden and an Imperial army commanded by Albrecht von **Wallenstein**. Wallenstein withdrew into Bohemia after the battle, during which Gustav was slain.

Lützen, Battle of (1813) A battle of the **Napoleonic Wars** between **Napoleon I**'s advance guard and Russo-Prussian armies. It resulted in heavy casualties, but was inconclusive.

Luwum, Janani (1922–77) Ugandan bishop. The son of a Christian, he became a teacher and was converted in 1948. He was ordained into the Anglican Church and, despite his evangelicanism which disturbed more conventional Christians in Uganda, he became a theological college principal, Bishop of Northern Uganda and was then elected Archbishop of Uganda in 1974. He spoke out fearlessly against the atrocities committed during Idi **Amin**'s period of rule, as a result of which he was murdered. So concerned was the Amin government that a memorial service for him was forbidden.

Luxemburg, House of Taking their name from the Castle of Lützelburg, this family, which owned lands in the area between the Maas and the Mosel from the 13c, came to prominence when **Henry VII** was elected to the throne in 1308. Although they lost the throne after his death, his son John gained control of Bohemia and the Luxemburgers' power base was now comparable with that of the Habsburgs. Their most important representative was **Charles IV**, the greatest of the late medieval German rulers, who elevated Luxemburg to a duchy. From 1346 until 1437 (when the dynasty died out in the male line with the death of **Sigismund**), all but one of the German kings came from the House of Luxemburg. ▷ **Habsburg Dynasty**

Luxemburg, Rosa (1871–1919) German social democrat. She emigrated to Zurich in 1889, where she studied law and political economy, and subsequently became a German citizen in 1895. A radical, she and the German politician, Karl **Liebknecht**, formed the Spartacus League (1916), which later became the German Communist Party (**KPD**, 1919). She was arrested and murdered during the 'Spartacus Rising' in **Berlin**. ▷ **Marxism; Spartacists**

Lvov, Giorgiy Yevgenievich, Prince (1861–1925) Russian liberal politician. Educated in Moscow, he joined the imperial civil service, then entered local government and became a member of the **Duma**. He was in effect prime minister in the first and second provisional governments after the **February Revolution** of 1917, but his moderate policies and his determination to continue the war against Germany and Austria led to the collapse of his government. He was succeeded by **Kerensky**, and subsequently arrested by the **Bolsheviks**, but he escaped to Paris, where he died. ▷ **Russian Revolution**

Lyautey, Louis Hubert Gonzalve (1854–1934) French marshal and colonial administrator. He held administrative posts in Algeria, Tonkin and Madagascar, and

became resident Commissary-General in Morocco (1912–16 and 1917–25), and also War Minister (1916–17). He was made a Marshal in 1921.

Lydia In antiquity, the area of western Asia Minor lying inland of Ionia. Its capital was Sardis. At the height of its power in the 7c and 6c BC, it was the centre of an empire which stretched from the Aegean to central Turkey. Conquered by the Persians in 546BC, it lost its political independence for ever, and was ruled in succession by Persians, Seleucids, Attalids, and Romans. ▷ **Persian Empire**

Lynch, Jack (John) (1917–) Irish politician. Following a career in the Department of Justice (1936), he was called to the Bar (1945). Elected an MP in 1948, he held ministerial posts in Lands (1951), the Gaeltacht (1957), Education (1957–9), Industry and Commerce (1959–65) and Finance (1965–6), before becoming Prime Minister (1966–73 and 1977–9). Perceived as a strong supporter of the Catholic minority in Ulster, he drew criticism from both Ulster and mainland Britain. In 1979 he resigned both as Prime Minister and from the leadership of **Fianna Fáil**. He retired from politics in 1981. ▷ **Haughey, Charles**

Lyons, Joseph Aloysius (1879–1939) Australian politician. He became a teacher, entering politics in 1909 as Labor member in the Tasmanian House of Assembly. He held the posts of Treasurer, Minister of Education and Railways (1914–16), and was Premier (1923–8). Then in the federal parliament (1929–39), he was in turn Postmaster-General and acting Treasurer. Lyons favoured balanced budgets and reduced public expenditure to meet the Depression and when these were rejected, left the **Australian Labor Party** to found the **United Australia Party**; he became Prime Minister (1932/9) after the election of Dec 1931.

Lyons, Treaty of (1601) In 1599 in an attempt to define and defend the frontiers of France, **Henry IV** laid claim to the Marquisate of Saluzzo, which brought him into conflict with Savoy and its Spanish allies. Through the mediation of Pope Clement VIII, agreement was reached at Lyons in 1601. France ceded Saluzzo in return for Bresse, Bugey, Gex, Valromey, and financial compensation. For an additional sum, the Duke of Savoy was allowed to use routes connecting Savoy with the Franche-Comté. France, however, was not well placed to sustain any of its allies who might be threatened from the Spanish power base in Lombardy.

Lysander (d.395BC) Spartan naval commander. He commanded the fleet which defeated the Athenians at the Battle of **Aegospotami** (405BC), and in 404BC took Athens, thus ending the **Peloponnesian War**. He died while unsuccessfully besieging Haliartus in **Boeotia** in 395BC.

Lysenko, Trofim Denisovich (1898–1976) Soviet agronomist. He first became famous in 1929 for 'vernalization', making possible the spring sowing of winter wheat, a technique of beating nature which appealed to **Stalin** and,

later, to Nikita **Khrushchev**. He began to produce attractive theories to transform agricultural production, he discredited genetics and had geneticists imprisoned or shot, and he dominated the scene as President of the Soviet Academy of Agricultural Sciences (1938–56 and 1961–2). Although an investigation in 1965 proved his innovations useless, he continued to exert some influence until his death.

Lysimachus (d.281BC) Macedonian general of **Alexander III, 'the Great'**. He later became King in Thrace, to which he subsequently added north-west Asia Minor and **Macedonia**. He was defeated and killed at Koroupedion by Seleucus I.

M

Macanaz, Melchor Rafael de (1670–1760) Spanish legist and politician. A leading protagonist of Bourbon absolutism in Spain, he came to prominence during the War of the **Spanish Succession**, when he was appointed Intendant in Valencia and then in **Aragon**, where he helped to abolish the *fueros* of these realms and to establish the new Bourbon authority. In 1714 he was appointed *fiscal* (Attorney-General) of the Council of **Castile**, and drew up several reform plans, including one for the reform of the **Inquisition**. Conflict with the latter, and the coming of Elizabeth Farnese as queen, led to his exile in France. While in exile, he carried out several diplomatic missions for the Spanish government, and on the accession of a new king he was in 1748 allowed to return to Spain. He was, however, arrested on his arrival, and kept in prison until shortly before his death. ▷ **Bourbon, House of; Farnese Family**

Macao, Portuguese Settlement of The settlement in the Pearl River Delta on the southern coast of China acquired by Portugal in 1557. It was used as a base for Catholic missionaries in the 17c and 18c as well as being a port of call for British traders on their way to Canton in the early 19c. Until the 19c, Macao was a flourishing trade centre, but the silting of its harbour and increasing competition from Hong Kong led to its decline. With the overthrow of the **Salazar** dictatorship in Portugal in 1975 and the new government's commitment to decolonization, China exercised further influence in the colony. In 1987 it was agreed that Macao be formally returned to Chinese control in 1999 under the same arrangements applying to the British return of Hong Kong to China in 1997 (ie that the capitalist system should remain in place).

MacArthur, Douglas (1880–1964) US general. Educated at the US Military Academy at West Point, he joined the US army, and in **World War I** served with distinction in France. In 1941 he became commanding general of the US armed forces in the Far East, and, after losing the Philippines, from Australia directed the recapture of the south-west Pacific (1942–5). He formally accepted the Japanese surrender, and commanded the occupation of Japan (1945–51). In 1950 he led the UN forces in the **Korean War**, defeating the North Korean Army, but was relieved of command when he tried to continue the war against China.

Macartney, George, 1st Earl (1737–1806) Irish diplomat. In 1764 he was sent as an envoy to Russia, from 1769 to 1772 was Chief Secretary of Ireland, and in 1775 was Governor of Grenada. There (an Irish baron from 1776) he was taken prisoner by the French in 1779. Governor of Madras (1781–5), in 1792 he was made an earl and headed the first diplomatic mission to China. After a mission to **Louis XVIII** at Verona (1795–96), he went out as Governor to the Cape (1796), but returned in ill health in 1798.

Macbeth (c.1005–57) King of the Scots (1040/57). He was probably a grandson of Kenneth II (971/95), son of Findleach, Mormaer of Moray, and nephew of Malcolm II. Macbeth overthrew and killed **Duncan I** in 1040 and defeated a challenge to his kingship from Crinan, father of Duncan I, in 1045. Despite his malign Shakespearean image, he seems to have ruled wisely, avoiding expensive and debilitating raids on England; he was a benefactor of the Church and went on pilgrimage to Rome (1050). He was defeated and killed by **Malcolm III, 'Canmore'**, son of Duncan I, at Lumphanan on 15 Aug 1057 after an invasion from England aided by Earl Siward of Northumbria.

Maccabees An important Jewish family, and those of its party (also known as the Hasmoneans) who initially resisted the influences of Greek culture on Israel and its religion during Syrian rule over Palestine. Judas Maccabeus (or ben Mattathias) led a revolt in 168BC by attacking a Jewish apostate, and it was continued by his sons through a kind of guerrilla warfare. It resulted eventually in semi-independence from Syrian control, with Jonathan and Simon beginning a Hasmonean dynasty of high priestly rulers which lasted until the rise of Herod the Great under Roman patronage (c.37BC).

Macdonald, Flora (1722–90) Scottish heroine. Following the **Forty-five Rebellion**, she conducted the Young Pretender, Charles

Edward Stuart, disguised as 'Betty Burke', to safety in Skye. For this she was imprisoned in the Tower of London, but released in 1747. She married in 1750, and in 1774 emigrated to North Carolina, where her husband fought in the **American Revolution**. When he was captured (1779), Flora returned to Scotland, to be rejoined there in 1781 by her husband. They settled at Kingsburgh, Skye.

Macdonald, John Alexander (1815–91) Scottish-born Canadian politician. His family emigrated to Canada in 1820, and he was educated in law at Kingston. Entering politics in 1843, he became leader of the Conservative Party and joint Premier in 1856. Prime Minister in 1857–8 and 1864, he played an important role in bringing about the confederation of Canada, and in 1867 formed the first government of the new dominion. The Pacific Scandal brought down his government in 1873, but he regained the premiership in 1878, retaining it until his death in office. ▷ **Jesuits' Estate Act; Tariff Policy (Canada)**

Macdonald, John Sandfield (1812–72) Canadian politician. From an Irish background, he became Solicitor-General in Robert **Baldwin**'s ministry (1849–51), but Francis **Hincks** passed him over and he, like George **Brown**, became a bitter critic of the government. When George Étienne **Cartier** was defeated in 1862, Macdonald was asked to form a ministry. As a reformer and a Catholic, he believed in the 'double-majority' principle, requiring a government to hold majorities within each half of the province, in order to contain both Protestants and Catholics within the party. However as Reform Premier in 1862–4 he forgot his principles and voted for a Separate School bill against the wishes of his Protestant supporters. He was Premier of Ontario (1867–71).

MacDonald, (James) Ramsay (1866–1937) British politician. He had little formal education, worked as a clerk, then joined the **Independent Labour Party** in 1894, eventually becoming its leader (1911–14 and 1922–31). He became an MP in 1906, and was Prime Minister and Foreign Secretary of the first British Labour government (1924). Prime Minister again (1929–31 and 1931–5), he met the financial crisis of 1931 by forming a largely Conservative 'National' government, most of his party opposing, and reconstructed it the same year after a general election. Defeated by Shinwell in the 1935 general election, he returned to parliament in

1936, and became Lord President. He died on his way to South America. ▷ **Labour Party** (UK)

MacDougall, William (1822–1905) Canadian politician. He was the first Governor of the North West Territories in 1869. A Clear Grit before confederation, he became a Minister of Public Works in the **MacDonald** cabinet of 1867. Exploration of the North West Territories had established the agricultural potential of the 64 000 square mile belt beyond the Red River along North Sasketchewan to the mountains. MacDougall was one of the negotiators for the purchase of these **Hudson's Bay Company** lands, but the **métis** of the Red River colony were not informed either of this fact or of his appointment as Governor. Thus his entry was blocked, and the rebellion began. ▷ **Clear Grits; Red River Rebellion**

Macedonia The region between the Balkans and the Greek Peninsula; in antiquity the centre of a kingdom whose royal family, the Argeadae, claimed Greek descent. Militarily weak until **Philip II** (382–336BC) consolidated his rule over the mountainous districts of Upper Macedonia and annexed the Strymon valley and Chalcidice Peninsula, it thereafter dominated peninsular Greece under Philip and his son, **Alexander III, 'the Great'**. The Argead Dynasty ended with the death of Alexander's young son (Alexander IV) in 310BC; later the Antigonid Dynasty established power there. Divided into four republics after Rome's defeat of its last king, **Perseus** (167BC), it became a Roman province in 146BC. ▷ **Antigonus; Antigonus Gonatas; Archelaus; Demetrius Poliorcetes**

Macedonians The nation inhabiting the area of ancient Macedonia and speaking a Slav language closer to Bulgarian than Serbo-Croat. Through the centuries many tribes and nations have settled in Macedonia and its ethnic composition is accordingly complex; the French *macédoine* is a synonym for 'medley' or 'mixture'. Slav tribes arrived in the 7c and mixed with the Greek and romanized Illyrians and Thracians, while the Byzantine rulers established settlements of Scythians and Christianized Turks. In the 9c the **Bulgars** conquered Macedonia but the region returned to Byzantine rule until the Ottoman conquest (1355). Under the Turks, Sasi, Tartars, Čerkezi, Gypsies and Jews all settled and mixed with the local population. At the end of the 19c, a Macedonian nationalist movement emerged, its members insisting that the Macedonians were neither Bulgars nor Serbs, but a distinct Slav nation with its own language; this was a claim which the neighbouring Serbs, Bulgars and **Greeks**, nations all bent on territorial expansion, were determined to discount. ▷ **Ilinden Uprising; Samuel** (Emperor of Macedonia); **South Slavs; VMRO**

Maček, Vladko (1879–1964) Croatian politician. A doctor of law, he served in the Austrian Army during **World War I**. As a member of the Croatian Peasant Party, he was imprisoned in 1924 with its leader, Stephen **Radić**, becoming party leader himself in 1928. Again imprisoned in 1933, on charges of treason, he was released the following year under the regency of Prince Paul Karageorgević. In 1939 he signed the **Sporazum** with **Cvetković**, thus securing Croatian participation in government, and became Vice-President of Yugoslavia, continuing in this position under General Dušan Simović who seized power in a coup (27 Mar 1941). He refused **Ribbentrop**'s offer of assistance in creating an independent **Croatia** and at first urged the **Croats** to support the **Ustaša** regime of **Pavelić**. He retired from political life shortly afterwards and was interned on his farm until the end of **World War II** when he went into exile in France and the USA.

Machel, Samora Moises (1933–86) Mozambique nationalist leader and politician. He trained as a medial assistant before he joined **Frelimo** in 1963, soon becoming active in the guerrilla war against the Portuguese colonial power. Commander-in-Chief in 1966, he succeded **Mondlane** on the latter's assassination in 1969 and was President of Mozambique from its independence in 1975 until his death in an air crash. Avowedly a Marxist, his success at politicizing the peasantry in northern Mozambique during the liberation war led him to believe in the dominant role of the party but, after the flight of white Portuguese in 1974 and the economic failure of his policies, he became more pragmatic, turning to the West for assistance, advising **Mugabe** to temper principle with prudence, and began establishing more harmonious relations with South Africa.

Machiavelli, Niccolò (di Bernardo dei) (1469–1527) Italian statesman and political theorist. He travelled on several missions in Europe for the republic (1498–1512). On the restoration of the **Medici**, he was arrested on a charge of conspiracy (1513) and, although pardoned, was obliged to withdraw from public life. He devoted himself to literature, writing historical treatises, poetry, short stories, and comedies. His masterpiece is *Il Principe* (1532, The Prince), whose main theme is that all means may be used in order to maintain authority, and that the worst acts of the ruler are justified by the treachery of the governed. It was condemned by the Pope, and its viewpoint gave rise to the adjective 'machiavellian'.

machine ▷ **political machine**

Macía, Francisco (1859–1933) Catalan leader. The leader and founder, in 1922, of *Estat Català*, the Catalan nationalist party, he was a central figure in the Catalan struggle to achieve autonomy. After **Primo de Rivera**'s dictatorship collapsed, Macía forged a coalition of the Catalan Republican Party and his own *Estat Català*, creating the Republican Left of Catalonia. He was the first President of Catalonia under the autonomy statute of 1932 granted by the Second Republic. His Republican Left was defeated in the elections of 1933 and Macía died a few weeks later. ▷ **Catalan Autonomy Statutes; Republic, Second** (Spain)

Mackenzie, Alexander (1822–92) Canadian politician, a Clear Grit before confederation and leader of the **Liberal Party** afterwards. He came to the fore when George **Brown** retired from public life and Oliver Mowat restricted his political ambitions to Ontario. Mackenzie lacked sufficient support in parliament when he tried to form a government after the railway scandal of 1873 and he opted for a general election. A good majority established him as Prime Minister, but his tenure was cautious and inept. His go-slow public construction of the Canadian Pacific Railway (for which he took personal responsibility as Minister of Public Works), nearly lost British Columbia to the USA, while his inability to deal with the severe depression and his refusal to raise the tariff lost him the election of 1878. In 1880 the party threatened to rebel and he was succeeded by Edward **Blake**. ▷ **Clear Grits**

Mackenzie, William Lyon (1795–1861) Canadian politician. He emigrated to Canada in 1820, established the *Colonial Advocate* in 1824, and entered politics in 1828. In 1837 he published in his paper the 'Declaration of the Toronto Reformers' (modelled on the US Declaration of Independence), headed a band of reform-minded insurgents, and after a skirmish with a superior force fled to the USA, where he was imprisoned. He returned to Canada in 1849, becoming a journalist and MP (1851–8). ▷ **Canada, Upper; Rebellions of 1837**

Mackinnon, William (1823–93) Scottish merchant and shipowner. A significant late 19c imperialist figure, he went to India in 1847 and founded a prosperous general mercantile company in Calcutta with his partner, Robert Mackenzie. In 1856 he formed the Calcutta and Rangoon Steam Navigation Company (later renamed the British India Steam Navigation Company), which became one of the largest shipping companies in the world. Mackinnon developed an interest in East Africa and secured (1877) a concession from Barghash, Sultan of Zanzibar, to develop the mainland territories of Zanzibar. The British government refused to support Mackinnon, but once German competition had become a real threat in the area a charter was granted to Mackinnon's Imperial British East Africa Company (1888). The chartered company ruled Kenya and Uganda for only a few years but failed through lack of capital and the costs of suppressing African resistance. The territories were taken over by the British government in 1893.

Maclean, Donald (Duart) (1913–83) British double agent. He studied at Cambridge at the same time as **Burgess** and **Philby**, and was similarly influenced by **communism**. He joined the diplomatic service in 1935, serving in Paris, Washington (1944–8), and Cairo (1948–50), and from 1944 acted as a Soviet agent. He became head of the American Department of the Foreign Office, but by 1951 was a suspected traitor, and in May of that year, after Philby's warning, disappeared with Burgess to the USSR. He died in Moscow.

MacMahon, Marie Edme Patrice Maurice de, Duke of Magenta (1808–93) French marshal and President of the Third Republic. He was descended from an Irish Jacobite family. In the **Franco-Prussian War** (1870–1) he was defeated at Wörth and surrendered at **Sedan** (1870). After the war he suppressed the **Paris Commune** (1871), and succeeded **Thiers** as Head of State (1873). Failing to assume dictatorial powers, he resigned in 1879, thus ensuring the supremacy of parliament. ▷ **Republic, Third** (France)

Macmillan, (Maurice) Harold, 1st Earl of Stockton (1894–1986) British politician. He became a Conservative MP in 1924. He was Minister of Housing (1951–4) and Defence (1954–5), Foreign Secretary (1955), Chancellor of the Exchequer (1955–7), and succeeded **Eden** as Premier (1957–63). He became popular and respected during a period of economic boom, earning the sobriquet 'Supermac'. He was re-elected in 1959. After several political setbacks, and a major scandal (the **Profumo** Affair), he resigned through ill health in 1963, and left the House of Commons in 1964. He became Chancellor of Oxford University in 1960, an earl in 1984. ▷ **Conservative Party** (UK)

Macquarie, Lachlan (1761–1824) British soldier and colonial administrator. He became Governor of New South Wales in 1810 after the deposition of **Bligh**. He raised the colony to a state of lawfulness and prosperity, but his liberal policies towards ex-convicts united his opponents, and caused his resignation. He returned to Britain in 1822.

Madariaga y Rojo, Salvador de (1886–1978) Spanish diplomat and writer. Educated in Madrid and Paris, he became a journalist in London (1916–21), a member of the **League of Nations** secretariat (1922–7), Professor of Spanish Studies at Oxford (1928–31), and Spanish Ambassador to the USA (1931) and France (1932–4). During 1934 he was briefly Minister of Education and Justice under the Spanish Second Republic. An opponent of the **Franco** regime, he was in exile from 1936 to 1976. The author of many historical works, especially on Spain and Spanish-America, he died at Locarno, Switzerland. ▷ **Republic, Second** (Spain)

Madero, Francisco Indalécio (1873–1913) Mexican revolutionary and politician. The son of a wealthy landowner, groomed in Paris and educated in the USA, he was no social revolutionary, although he greatly improved the *peons'* condition on his own estates. He unsuccessfully opposed Porfirio **Díaz**'s local candidates in 1904, and in 1908, when Díaz was quoted as saying that he would not seek another term, Madero took the dictator at his word and launched his own presidential campaign. A spiritualist, vegetarian, and practitioner of homoeopathic medicine, he was an unlikely challenger, and at first was not taken seriously. But his popularity grew rapidly and Díaz turned to repression, imprisoning Madero and many of his supporters. He escaped to the USA, from where he directed a military campaign. His supporters, including **Villa**, captured Ciudad Juárez, where he established his capital (May 1911), and the dictatorship crumbled. Once elected President (Oct 1911), Madero's moderate political reform programme pleased no one and he faced a succession of revolts by Emiliano **Zapata** and others demanding land reform, as well as by supporters of the old dictatorship. On the night of 23 Feb 1913, he and his Vice-President were murdered following a military coup led by General Victoriano Huerta, planned with the assistance of US ambassador Henry L Wilson. ▷ **peon**

Madison, James (1751–1836) US politician and 4th President. He entered Virginia politics in 1776, played a major role in the **Constitutional Convention** of 1787, which framed the federal **US Constitution**, and collaborated in the writing of the **Federalist Papers**. He served as a Congressman from Virginia (1789–97) in the first federal Congress, and was a strong advocate of the Bill of Rights. He was Secretary of State under **Jefferson**, and President himself for two terms (1809–17). His period in office was dominated by the **War of 1812** with Britain. ▷ **US Constitution**

Madiun Rebellion (Sep–Oct 1948) A rebellion by major elements in the Indonesian Communist Party (**Partai Komunis Indonesia**, PKI) against the Indonesian government, at a time when the peoples of Indonesia were still engaged in their violent post-war struggle to prevent the restoration of Dutch colonial rule. The rebellion was primarily driven by deep disagreements with other forces in Indonesia over the ways in which the struggle with the Dutch should be pursued and over the aims of the revolution. It was fiercely crushed by government forces, with much loss of life. In launching the rebellion against the government, the PKI provoked the charge, long-sustained, of treachery against the revolution. The defeat of the communists, however, opened the way for stronger US support for the Indonesian government, which was crucial in effecting the final Dutch withdrawal in 1949–50.

Madrasas Islamic schools which concentrate on theology and linguistics, in addition to teaching Islamic science, history, poetry and literature. They originated in the Middle East in the medieval period and then spread throughout the Islamic world, including India. The schools were attached to mosques and, as with similar institutions linked to Hindu temples, an emphasis was placed on religious training. The madrasas were state-financed, and it is estimated that during the Tughlaq period in India there were as many as a thousand madrasas in Delhi alone. To this day, madrasas remain an important part of Indian life, as elsewhere in the Islamic world.

Madrid, Treaty of (Jan 1526) The treaty signed by King **Francis I** of France while a prisoner of **Charles V** in Madrid, after the former had been captured by the Imperial forces at the Battle of Pavia (Feb 1525). By the treaty, Francis was to surrender **Burgundy** to Charles, but on his release he refused to honour his promise. At the time a small town, Madrid was in 1561 adopted by **Philip II** as capital of Spain.

Madvig, Johan Nicolai (1804–86) Danish politician and classical scholar. He was Professor of Latin at Copenhagen (1829–70), and Inspector of Higher Schools (from 1848). He was one of the chief speakers of the national Liberal Party, was Minister of Religion and Education (1848–51), and was repeatedly President of the Danish parliament.

Maecenas, Gaius (Cilnius) (d.8BC) Roman politician of ancient Etruscan lineage, who together with **Agrippa** played a key role in the rise to power of Octavian (**Augustus**), and his establishment of the empire after 31BC. Besides being a trusted counsellor and diplomatic agent, he also helped the new regime by his judicious patronage of the arts, encouraging such poets as Horace, Virgil and Propertius.

Mafeking, Siege of (Oct 1899–May 1900) The most celebrated siege of the second Boer War, during which Colonel Robert **Baden-Powell** and a detachment of British troops were besieged by the Boers. The news of their relief aroused public hysteria in Britain, the celebrations being known as 'mafficking'. The truth about the siege was rather different from the heroic action depicted by the British press. It is now known that the White garrison survived in reasonable comfort as the result of appropriating the rations of the Blacks, who were faced either with starvation or with running the gauntlet of the Boers by escaping from the town. ▷ **Boer Wars; Kimberley, Siege of; Ladysmith, Siege of**

Magadha One of the greatest empires of ancient India. The capital was originally Rajagriha and was later shifted to the River Ganges at **Pataliputra**. The geographical position of Magadha gave it control over the lower Ganges plain, including the river, supplying it with revenue from river trade. The first important king of Magadha was Bimbisara, a man of determination and political foresight, who reigned in the second half of the 6c BC. He was murdered by his son, Ajatashatru, who was impatient to rule, c.493BC. After Ajatashatru's death (461BC), Magadha was ruled by a succession of weak kings until 413BC, when the Shishunaga Dynasty assumed the throne and ruled for half a century. The **Nandas** followed as the rulers of Magadha until 321BC, when Chandragupta Maurya usurped the throne and built the great Mauryan empire, which ruled India until 185BC. This last period is considered as one of the most glorious phases of Indian history.

Magenta, Battle of (4 June 1859) French victory in the Franco-Piedmontese campaign against Austria. The battle was marked by extremely high casualties on both sides.

Magersfontein, Battle of (1899) An engagement of the second Boer War in which British forces were defeated by the Boers. It followed on the defeat of the British at **Modder River** several days previously, both actions taking place a few miles from Kimberley as part of the British attempts to relieve that town. ▷ **Boer Wars; Kimberley, Siege of**

Maghrib (Maghreb) An area of northwest Africa including the countries of Morocco, Algeria, and Tunisia; largely occupied by sedentary and nomadic Berbers of the Kabyle, Shluh, and Tuareg groups. In Arabic, the word refers to Morocco only.

Maginot Line French defensive fortifications stretching from Longwy to the Swiss border, named after André Maginot (1877–1932), who was the French Minister of Defence (1924–31). The line was constructed (1929–34) to act as protection against German invasion, but Belgium refused to extend it along her frontier with Germany. The German attack of 1940 through the Low Countries largely by-passed the Maginot Line, whose name became synonymous with passive defence and defeatism. ▷ **World War II**

Magna Carta The 'Great Charter', imposed (June 1215) by rebellious barons on King **John** of England, it was designed to prohibit arbitrary royal acts by declaring a body of defined law and custom which the King must respect in dealing with all his free subjects. The principle that kings should rule justly was of long standing, but in Magna Carta the first systematic attempt was made to distinguish between kingship and tyranny. While failing to resolve all the problems raised by the nature of the English crown's relations with the community, it endured as a symbol of the sovereignty of the rule of law, and was of fundamental importance to the constitutional development of England and other countries whose legal and governmental systems were modelled on English conventions. ▷ **Barons Wars**

Magnus I, 'the Good' (1024–47) King of Norway (1035/47) and of Denmark (1042/7). The illegitimate son of King **Olaf II** (St Olaf), he was named after Emperor **Charlemagne** (Carolus Magnus). After St Olaf's death at the Battle of Stiklestad in 1030, the boy was given refuge at the court of Prince Jaroslav the Wise in Kiev, and was brought back by popular acclaim in 1035 to assume the Norwegian throne. In 1042 he inherited the Danish throne, and in the following year won a notable victory over the Wends at Lürschau Heath in southern Jutland. In 1045 he agreed to share the throne of Norway with his uncle **Harald Hardrada**, and died two years later during a campaign in Denmark.

Magnus III, 'Barelegs' (c.1074–1103) King of Norway (1093/1103). The son of King **Olaf III, 'the Peaceful'**, he was one of the last of the Norse Viking sea-kings bent on strengthening Norway's hold over her North Sea territories. He harried the Orkneys and Shetland (1098–9), and in 1102–3 led another punitive naval expedition west to Scotland and Ireland; he took Dublin, and built new fortifications in the Isle of Man, but was killed in an ambush in Ulster. He earned his nickname because he abandoned Norse trousers in favour of the Scottish kilt.

Magnus V Erlingsson (1156–84) King of Norway (1162/84). The son of Earl Erling the Crooked, he was raised to the throne as a child under his father's regency; in 1164 he was crowned by Archbishop Eystein at a church ceremony in Bergen, the first religious coronation in Denmark. After his father's death in 1179 he was engaged in a long war against a rival claimant to the throne, the Faroese-born 'usurper', **Sverrir Sigurdsson**; he was forced to flee to Denmark for safety, and lost his life in a naval battle in an attempt to regain his kingdom.

Magnus VI, 'the Law-Mender' (1238–80) King of Norway (1263/80). The son of King **Haakon the Old**, he succeeded to the throne when his father died in the Orkneys on his return to Norway after the Battle of Largs (1263). He made peace with King **Alexander III** of Scotland and ceded the Western Isles and the Isle of Man. He revised and standardized the laws of the land in a series of legal codes, from which he earned his nickname, and which were based on the 'four sisters' of Mercy, Truth, Fairness and Peace.

Magnus Eriksson (1316–74) King of Sweden (1319/65) and, as Magnus VII, of Norway (1319/55). He was the son of Duke Erik Magnusson of Sweden and Ingeborg, the daughter of King Haakon V of Norway. He inherited the throne of Norway from his grandfather and was elected to the Swedish throne in the same year on the deposition of his uncle, Birger Magnusson. In 1335 he married Blanche of Namur, by whom he had two sons. In 1355 he handed over the crown of Norway, his younger son, Haakon VI, and in the following year was deposed in Sweden by his elder son, Erik. Magnus regained the throne in 1359, but lost the island of Gotland to Valdemar IV 'Atterdag' of Denmark and was again deposed in 1365 in favour of his nephew, Albrekt of Mecklenburg. He died in a shipwreck. He is associated with a code of law which covered the whole of Sweden and which remained in force until the 18c.

Magnus Maximus Roman Emperor (383/8). He was a Roman army commander in Britain who, after being proclaimed Emperor by his troops, crossed to Gaul and overthrew the emperor of the West, **Gratian**. Recognized as Emperor by the Emperor of the East, **Theodosius I, 'the Great'**, who was then preoccupied with problems nearer home, Maximus proceeded to rule over Gaul, Spain and Britain. His attempts to add Italy to his empire backfired: Theodosius marched against him, decisively defeated him in battle and had him executed.

Magnússon, Skúli (1711–94) Icelandic reformer. He was the first Icelander to hold the important post of treasurer (*landfógeti*) on the island (in 1749). He worked hard to develop industry and fought against the abuses committed by the Danish merchants who enjoyed a monopoly of trade with Iceland.

Magnús Stephensen ▷ Stephensen, Magnús

Mahajanapadas Sixteen important states ('great lands') in northern India (600–321BC), containing both republics (eg Vrijji) and monarchies (eg **Magadha**). They displayed the growth of a stable agrarian economy and urbanization. The expansion of trade necessitated the use of coins and the Brahmi script. During this time there emerged new reformist schools of thought, principally Buddhism and Jainism.

Mahathir bin Mohamad (1925–) Malaysian politician. He practised as a doctor (1957–64) before being elected to the House of Representatives as a United Malays' National Organization (UMNO) candidate. He won the support of UMNO's radical youth wing through his advocacy of 'affirmative action' in favour of *bumiputras* (ethnic Malays). Following sharp attacks on the then Prime Minister, Tunku **Abdul Rahman**, in the wake of the 1969 race riots, he was expelled from UMNO. He was, however, subsequently readmitted and, after holding several ministerial posts, he was appointed UMNO Leader and also Prime Minister in 1981. He immediately launched a 'look east' economic policy, which sought to emulate East Asian industrialization. Despite severe divisions within UMNO, he has seen off all challengers and led the ruling alliance to successive electoral victories.

Mahdi The name (literally, 'divinely guided one') given by Sunni Muslims to those who periodically revitalize the Muslim community. **Sunnis** look forward to a time before the Last Day when a Mahdi will appear and establish a reign of justice on Earth. **Shiites** identify the Mahdi with the expected reappearance of the hidden Imam. Many Muslim leaders have claimed the title, such as **Mohammed Ahmed**, who established a theocratic state in the Sudan in 1882. His great-grandson, Sadiq al-Mahdi, became Prime Minister of the Sudan in 1986.

Mahdi's Revolt Mohammed Ahmad, the Mahdi of the Sudan, joined the Samaniyya dervish order, but c.1872 he proclaimed privately that he was *al-Mahdi al-Muntazar* ('the awaited or expected Mahdi'), who promised believers that a new order was imminent. He made a tour of the Sudan from

Dongola to Sennar, from the Blue Nile to Kordofan, and convinced himself of the people's disaffection and discontent with the established order. In 1881 he made his first public appearance as Mahdi and Mahdism spread from Kordofan and Bahr al-Ghazal to the eastern Sudan, despite the dispatch of several fruitless and occasionally disastrous (as in the case of Hicks Pasha) expeditions against him. In 1884 he laid siege to Khartoum and in 1885 the Governor-General Charles George (Chinese) **Gordon** was killed. Muhammad Ahmad died later in 1885 but the Sudan was to remain under Mahdist control until Kitchener reduced the Sudan in the following decade finally defeating the Mahdists at **Omdurman**.

Mahmud II (1785–1839) Ottoman Sultan (1808/39). His reign was marked by the cession of Bessarabia to Russia (1812), Greece's successful struggle for independence (1820–8), a disastrous war with Russia (1828–9), and the triumphs of **Muhammad 'Ali**. He shattered the power of the **Janissaries** by a massacre in 1826, introduced many domestic reforms, and did much to westernize Turkey. He died in Constantinople.

Mahmud of Ghazni (971–1030) Muslim Afghan conqueror of India. The son of Sebuktigin, a Turkish slave who became ruler of Ghazni (modern Afghanistan), he succeeded to the throne in 997. He invaded India 17 times between 1001 and 1026, and created an empire that included Punjab and much of Persia. A great patron of the arts, he made Ghazni a remarkable cultural centre.

Maichew (Mai Ceu), Battle of (31 Mar 1936) The decisive battle of the Italian invasion of Abyssinia, in which the Emperor **Haile Selassie** was defeated and the Italian commander, Marshal Badoglio, prepared for the final advance on Addis Ababa. The Emperor decided that, instead of withdrawal, he would attack the Italian camp at Maichew with forces which consisted of the Imperial Guard and large numbers of Galla under feudal chiefs. The Italians had forewarning of the attack, harried the Ethiopians with air power, and were able to repulse the Ethiopian forces with superior artillery. It became Selassie's last despairing gesture before he fled into exile and the Italians were able to complete their conquest. Ethiopian resistance passed from the traditional leaders to the guerrilla Patriots.

Maintenon, Madame de (Françoise d'Aubigné, Marchioness of Maintenon) (1635–1719) Second wife of **Louis XIV** of France. In 1652 she married the crippled poet, Paul Scarron, and on his death was reduced to poverty. In 1669 she took charge of the King's two sons by Madame de **Montespan**, and moved with them to the court in 1673. By 1674 the King's generosity enabled her to purchase the estate of Maintenon, near Paris, which was converted to a marquisate. After the Queen's death (1683) Louis married her secretly. On the King's death (1715) she retired to the educational institution for poor girls which she had founded at Saint-Cyr (1686).

Mainz Republic The government established (1793) in Mainz by the occupying armies of Revolutionary France which had ousted the Elector. The vote to ratify the changes and the new relationship with France was almost totally boycotted by the citizens of Mainz.

Maipú (Maipó), Battle of (1818) A decisive battle of the **Spanish–American Wars of Independence**, fought near Santiago. A notable victory for the Argentine general, José de **San Martín**, it secured the final liberation of Chile from Spanish rule.

Maitraka Dynasty The Indian dynasty which ruled Gujarat and Saurashtra from the 5c to the 8c. Its founder, Bhatarka, was a Gupta general, who took advantage of the decline of the Gupta Empire to establish Valabhi (present-day Vala) as his capital. Under Shiladitya I (c.6c), the kingdom extended into Malwa and Rajasthan, but later suffered at the hands of **Harsha** and the **Chalukyas**. After Harsha's death (c.647), the dynasty revived until c.780, when the last Maitraka king, Shiladitya VI, was killed, and his capital razed, by the Arabs. The Maitraka Empire played a significant role in the history of Jainism and Buddhism.

Majapahit A Javanese state of the 14c and 15c. Majapahit was a Hindu–Buddhist kingdom, and by far the most important of the pre-Islamic states of Indonesia. It was both a land-based and a trading empire, and an important naval power. Majapahit's authority was said to extend to Sumatra, the Malay Peninsula, Kalimantan and the islands of the eastern Indonesian archipelago, although given difficulties of communication over that vast area, it would rarely have been effectively exercised. Majapahit also maintained relations with Cambodia, Siam, Burma and Vietnam and sent missions to China. The capital was witness to great annual religious festivals.

Maji Maji (1905) A rising against German rule which took place in southern Tanganyika. People from a variety of ethnic backgrounds rose against harsh tax exactions and compulsory cotton growing. Priests and messengers moved from village to village urging people to rise and claiming that they had a medicine which would turn bullets into water or *maji*. German administration broke down for several months, but the rising was put down with great brutality causing a famine, in which a million people died, and a major ecological disaster in the region.

Major, John (1943–   ) British politician. He had a career in banking before becoming a Conservative MP in 1976. He rose to become Chief Secretary to the Treasury, was unexpectedly made Foreign Secretary in Margaret **Thatcher**'s cabinet reshuffle in 1989, and soon after replaced Nigel **Lawson** as Chancellor of the Exchequer. He won the leadership contest following Thatcher's resignation, and became Prime Minister (1990–   ). ▷ **Conservative Party** (UK)

Majuba Hill, Battle of (1881) An engagement which ended the first Boer War. In 1877 the British had attempted to federate the British and Boer territories of South Africa by invading and annexing the Transvaal. The latter was successfully accomplished, but the plan was destroyed by the British victory at Ulundi in the Zulu War of 1879. With the **Zulu** threat removed, the Boers resolved to re-establish their independence. The British suffered several small reverses, culminating in their defeat at Majuba Hill. **Gladstone**'s government then restored a limited independence to the Orange Free State and the Transvaal under the Pretoria Convention, subsequently modified by the London Convention of 1884. Disagreements about the interpretation of these Conventions were to increase tensions later in the 19c. ▷ **Boer Wars; Jameson Raid**

Makarios III (Mihail Khristodoulou Mouskos) (1913–77) Cypriot political and religious leader. He was ordained priest in 1946, elected Bishop of Kition in 1948, and Archbishop and Primate of the Orthodox Church of Cyprus in 1950. He reorganized the **enosis** (union) movement, was arrested and detained in 1956, but returned to a tumultuous welcome in 1959 to become chief Greek–Cypriot minister in the new Graeco-Turkish provisional government. Later that year he was elected President (1960–74 and 1974–7).

Malacca/Melaka A small state on the west coast of the Malay Peninsula. The Malacca/Melaka sultanate, founded in c.1400, was a great trading port, a major centre of Malay statecraft and culture and a central point for the dissemination of Islam in the Malay world. Malacca/Melaka was captured by the Portuguese in 1511, the Dutch in 1641 and was taken by the British, finally, in 1824. Together with Singapore and Penang, it formed the Straits Settlements from 1826, although as a trading and administrative centre it was easily dwarfed by its two partners.

Malan, Daniel F(rançois) (1874–1959) South African politician. Educated at Stellenbosch and Utrecht Universities, in 1905 he joined the ministry of the Dutch Reformed Church but in 1915 left to become editor of *Die Burger*, the Nationalist newspaper. Elected an MP in 1918, he held the portfolios of Interior, Education and Public Health by 1924. He helped reform the **National Party** with Hertzog and became leader of the Opposition to Smuts's United Party. He led the National Party to its decisive electoral victory in 1948 and oversaw the initial implementation of the policy of **apartheid**. He retired in 1954.

Malatesta Lords of the state of Rimini in north-east Italy from the 13c to the 16c; among the most durable of several families of *signori* who dominated political life in the Italian **Renaissance**. Originally the political 'vicars' of the papacy, the Malatesta state was overthrown in 1500 by a coalition of the papacy and the French. ▷ **Papal States**

Malaviya, Madan Mohan (1861–1946) Indian politician and journalist. A nationalist, he joined the Congress in 1886 and was a prominent member of the Uttar Pradesh Legislative Council and the Central Legislature. Mainly concerned with the furtherance of Hindu interests, Malaviya campaigned for the use of Hindi and was the dominant force in the creation of the Benares Hindu University in 1916. He was an important member of the **Hindu Mahasabha**, from which he broke away in 1928, although he remained the chief Hindu spokesman within Congress. He opposed the Communal Award of 1932, which created separate electorates representing different religious and social groups, and left the Congress to form a new party to fight the award, which he regarded as 'communal'. ▷ **Communalism**

Malawi Congress Party (MCP) Founded in 1959, this party grew out of the Nyasaland African National Congress. It is the only legal party in Malawi and has, as its Life President, Hastings Kamuzu **Banda**.

Malayan Emergency (1948) The name given to the insurrection led by the Malayan Communist Party (MCP) against British rule, and the campaign to crush that insurrection, in post-war Malaya. Following growing MCP violence, including the murder of European estate managers, on 18 June 1948 the British administration declared a state of emergency throughout Malaya. In the early years of the insurrection, the MCP achieved a number of notable successes, including the assassination of the High Commissioner, Sir Henry Gurney, in Oct 1951. However, by the mid-1950s, through a combination of fierce military measures, substantial resettlement of the Chinese rural population (which had provided much of the MCP's support) and the introduction of political initiatives that clearly would soon take Malaya to independence, the insurrection was broken, although, officially, it did not end until 31 July 1960.

Malcolm III, 'Canmore' ('large-headed') (c.1031–93) King of Scots (1058/93). He was the son of **Duncan I**, who was slain by **Macbeth** in 1040. He returned from exile in 1054, and conquered southern Scotland; but he did not become king until he had defeated and killed Macbeth (1057), and disposed of Macbeth's stepson, Lulach (1058). He first married Ingibjorg, daughter of the Earl of Orkney, by whom he had a son, **Duncan II**, briefly King of Scots (1094). His second marriage was to the English Princess Margaret (later St **Margaret**), sister of Edgar the Atheling. He launched five invasions of England between 1061 and died in a skirmish near Alnwick, Northumberland. ▷ **Northumbria**

Malcolm IV, 'the Maiden' (c.1141–65) King of Scots (1153/65). He was the grandson and successor of **David I**. Compelled to restore the northern English counties to **Henry II** in return for the earldom and honour of Huntingdon (1157), he served on Henry's expedition to Toulouse (1159), and

was then knighted. Malcolm continued to implement David I's Normanizing policies, despite native opposition. He defeated Fergus, Lord of Galloway, in 1161, and in 1164 Somerled, Lord of Argyll, was vanquished and slain at Renfrew. His byname was coined in the 15c, in recognition of his well-attested reputation for chastity.

Malcolm X (1925–65) US militant black activist, who became the most effective spokesman for **Black Power**. Born Malcolm Little, he took the name 'X' to symbolize the stolen identities of the generations of black slaves. After an adolescence of violence, narcotics and petty crime, he came under the influence of Elijah **Muhammad** while in prison for burglary and after his release in 1952 became Muhammad's chief disciple within the **Black Muslims**, greatly expanding the organization's following. In 1963 Malcolm was suspended from the Nation of Islam after disagreements with Muhammad and gained the deep hatred of the leader's loyal followers. Malcolm founded the Organization for Afro-American unity, dedicated to the alliance of American blacks and other non-white peoples. In the last year of his life, following a pilgrimage to Mecca, Malcolm announced his conversion to orthodox Islam and put forward the belief in the possible brotherhood between blacks and whites. Malcolm's extreme stance and the inflammatory nature of his oratory had scared many whites, appealed to many northern blacks in the urban ghettos, and had been met with criticism by moderate civil rights leaders who deplored his violent message. In 1965 Malcolm was the victim of Black Muslim assassins who retaliated against the man they viewed as a traitor.

Malenkov, Giorgiy Maximilianovich (1902–88) Soviet politician. He joined the **Red Army** in 1919 and the Communist Party in 1920, and by 1925 he was a Central Committee official. He was very closely involved in the collectivization of agriculture and the purges of the 1930s under **Stalin**. Malenkov became a member of the Central Committee in 1939 and of the **Politburo** in 1946; he became Deputy Premier in the same year, succeeding Stalin as Party General-Secretary and Premier in 1953. However, he was very quickly forced out of his Party post and, under pressure from Nikita **Khrushchev**, in 1955 he resigned as Premier, admitting responsibility for the failure of Soviet agricultural policy. Having participated in the so-called **Anti-Party Plot** in 1957, he was sent by Khrushchev to Kazakhstan as manager of a hydroelectric plant. He died an obscure pensioner in Moscow. ▷ **communism**

Malesherbes, Chrétien (Guillaume de Lamoignon) de (1721–94) French politician. In 1744 he became a counsellor of the **Parlement** of Paris, and in 1750 was made chief censor of the press. At **Louis XVI**'s accession (1774) he was made Secretary of State for the royal household, instituting prison and legal reforms in tandem with **Turgot**'s economic improvements. He resigned in 1776 on the eve of Turgot's dismissal. Despite his reforming zeal, he was mistrusted as an aristocrat during the **French Revolution**. Arrested as a royalist (1794), he was guillotined in Paris.

Mali, Kingdom of Major medieval kingdom of the Western Sudan which flourished between the 13c and 15c and dominated the trade routes of the Sahara with North Africa. It had a quasi-Islamic ruling group but was dominated by Muslim merchants. It was visited in 1352–3 by the great Arab traveller and geographer, Ibn Battuta, who commented on its prosperity and freedom from violence. It declined in the late 15c.

Malik, Jakub Alexandrovich (1906–80) Soviet politician. Having been educated and having practised as an economist in the Ukraine until 1935, he studied at the Diplomatic Institute in Moscow from then until 1937, when he entered the Foreign Service. Said to be one of **Stalin**'s favourite 'juniors', he was ambassador to Japan from 1943 to 1945 and Deputy Foreign Minister with particular responsibility for Far Eastern affairs in 1946–53. From 1948 to 1952 he was also Soviet spokesman at the **UN**, succeeding Andrei **Gromyko**. Ambassador to Britain in 1953–60, from 1960 he was again Deputy Foreign Minister, serving a second term as Ambassador to the UN in 1968 to 1976.

Malinovsky, Rodion Yakovlevich (1898–1967) Soviet general. He was a corporal in **World War I**, when, after the Russian collapse, he escaped via Siberia and Singapore to fight in a Russian brigade in France. He joined the **Red Army** in 1919 after the **Russian Revolution**, built up experience as a military adviser and instructor, and was major-general at the time of the Nazi invasion in 1941. He commanded the forces which liberated Rostov, Kharkov and the Dnieper basin and led the Russian advance on Budapest and into Austria (1943–5). When Russia declared war on Japan, he took a leading part in the Manchurian campaign and after **World War II** he held important commands in the Far East. In Oct 1957 he succeeded **Zhukov** as Nikita **Khrushchev**'s Minister of Defence and remained in that post under Brezhnev until his death. He therefore bore considerable responsibility for the great Soviet build-up of the 1960s.

Malou, Jules (1810–86) Belgian politician. He was MP for Ypres (1841–86), Minister for Finance (1847–8), and Prime Minister and Finance Minister (1871–8 and 1884). A leader of the Catholics in their struggle for state-sponsored Catholic education, he is remembered for his work with Belgium's finances and its railways. ▷ **Schools Question (Belgium)**

Malplaquet, Battle of (1709) A bitter military engagement of the War of the **Spanish Succession** between the French army led by Marshals Villars (1653–1734) and Boufflers (1644–1711) and the Grand Alliance army commanded by **Marlborough** and Prince **Eugene of Savoy**. Malplaquet, a very costly victory for the Allies, stiffened French resistance and swung English opinion behind the **Tories**' peace policy. ▷ **Grand Alliance, War of the**

Malraux, André (Georges) (1901–76) French politician and novelist. He studied oriental languages and spent much time in China, where he worked for the **Guomindang** and was active in the 1927 revolution. He also fought in the **Spanish Civil War**, and in **World War II** escaped from a prison camp to join the French Resistance. He was Minister of Information in de **Gaulle**'s government (1945–6) and Minister of Cultural Affairs (1960–9). He is known for his novels, notably *La Condition humaine* (1933), winner of the Prix Goncourt, and *L'Espoir* (1937). ▷ **Resistance Movement (France)**

Malwa Situated on the high plateau between Narmada and Tapti rivers in central India. The earliest mention of Malwa in history is made in context of the 6c BC empire of Avanti (modern Ujjain). Another great ancient Indian dynasty to rule Malwa was the **Shaka** who remained in this region until AD 5c. By the second half of the 10c, the Pawars had established their control over Malwa with their capital in Dhar near Indore. During the period 1400–1525 Malwa commanded the trunk routes between Gujarat and northern

MAMLUKS

Regnal Dates	Name	Regnal Dates	Name	Regnal Dates	Name
Bahri Line		1345/6	Sha'ban I	1405/12	Faraj (2nd reign)
1250	Shajar al-Durr	1346/7	Hajji I	1412	al-'Adil al-Musta'in
1250/7	Aybak	1347/51	al-Nasir al-Hasan	1412/21	al-Mu'ayyad Shaykh
1257/9	'Ali		(1st reign)	1421	al-Muzaffar Ahmad
1259/60	Qutuz	1351/4	Salih	1421	Tatar
1260/77	Baybars I	1354/61	al-Nasir al-Hasan	1421/2	al-Salih Muhammad
1277/80	Baraka Khan		(2nd reign)	1422/37	Barsbay
1280	Salamish	1361/3	al-Mansur Muhammad	1437/8	Yusuf
1280/90	Qala'un	1363/76	Sha'ban II	1438/53	al-Zahir Jaqmaq
1290/4	Khalil	1376/82	al-Mansur 'Ali	1453	'Uthman
1294/5	al-Nasir Muhammad	1382/9	al-Salih Hajji II	1453/61	Inal
	(1st reign)		(1st reign)	1461	al-Mu'ayyad Ahmad
1295/7	Kitbugha	(1382	Barquq)	1461/7	Khushqadam
1297/9	Lajin	1389	al-Salih Hajji II	1467/8	Bilbay
1299/1309	al-Nasir Muhammad		(2nd reign)	1468	Timurbugha
	(2nd reign)			1468/96	al-Ashraf Qa'it Bay
1309	Baybars II	**Burji (Circassian) Line**		1496/8	al-Nasir Muhammad
1309/40	al-Nasir Muhammad	1382/9	Barquq (1st reign)	1498/1500	Qansuh
	(3rd reign)	(1389/90	al-Salih Hajji II)	1500/1	Janbalat
1340/1	Abu Bakr	1390/9	Barquq (2nd reign)	1501	al-'Adil Tuman Bay
1341/2	Kujuk	1399/1405	Faraj (1st reign)	1501/17	Qansuh al-Ghawri
1342	Ahmad	1405	al-Mansur 'Abd al-'Aziz	1517	al-Ashraf Tuman Bay
1342/5	Isma'il				

India, as also between north and south India. During the 15c, the kingdom of Malwa reached the height of its glory. The capital was shifted from Dhar to Mandu. Here the rulers of Malwa constructed a large number of buildings, the ruins of which are still impressive. One of the early rulers of Malwa, Hushang Shah, adopted a broad policy of religious tolerance. Mahmud Khalji (1436/69), who is considered as the most powerful of Malwa rulers, fought nonetheless with almost all of his neighbours. This feuding with neighbouring territories continued after his death until Malwa was taken over by Rana Sanga of Mewar in 1517.

Mamaev Kurgan (Mamai Hill) An area in the heart of Volgograd, USSR, and the scene of the most severe conflict during the Battle of **Stalingrad** (1942–3).

Mamelukes ▷ Mamluks

Mamluks Slave soldiers who constituted the army of the Ayyubid sultanate established in Egypt by **Saladin** in the 1170s. Their commanders (*amirs*) created a professional army of high quality. In 1250 they overthrew the Ayyubids, and established Muslim dynasties until conquered by the Turks in 1516–17. They continued to rule in Egypt with Ottoman blessing until their massacre by **Muhammad 'Ali** in 1811. ▷ **Ottoman Empire**

580

Ma'mun, al- (813/33) 'Abbasid Caliph. The son of **Harun al-Rashid**, he was the victor in a succession struggle with his brother, al-Amin, after their father's death. Criticized for running the caliphate from Khurasan (where the bulk of his support lay) and for nominating al-Rida, the eighth Imam, as his successor, al-Ma'mun was persuaded to move to Baghdad and to repudiate his support for al-Rida, who died in suspicious circumstances in Nishapur. Al-Ma'mun is further noted for his espousal of Mutazili doctrine, of which the principal dogma, that the Quran was created in time, formed the basis of his *mihna* or inquisition, and for his support in Baghdad for scholarly activity centring on the so-called *Bayt al-Hikma* (House of Wisdom).

Man, Hendrik de (1885–1953) Belgian politician. He took a doctorate at Leipzig University in economic history, and was appointed to a Chair at Frankfurt University in 1929. In 1933 he was forced to leave Germany, and entered active politics in his native Belgium. He rejected Marxism, and developed his own socialist theory, laid out in his Labour Plan (*Plan du Travail*) of 1934. This non-revolutionary socialism, working with the bourgeoisie and using the democratic state as the instrument of socialism, was highly influential in Europe in the 1930s. De Man served as a cabinet minister (1935–8), and was chairman of the **Belgian Socialist Party** from 1939. When the Germans invaded, he entered into collaboration with the New Order, and dissolved his Socialist Party. He escaped to Switzerland in 1942, where he died in a traffic accident; in Belgium he was convicted in absentia in 1945.

Manchu Originally a people of Tartar stock from Manchuria (an area that included present-day Liaoning, Jilin, and Heilongjiang), they ruled all China from 1644 to 1911 under the **Qing Dynasty**. (Both *Qing* and *Man* mean 'pure'.)

Manchuria A former region of north-east China. A mountainous area, sparsely populated by nomadic tribes, this was the home of the Manchus, who overthrew the **Ming Dynasty** to become the last Chinese emperors as the **Qing Dynasty**. Rich in natural resources (timber, coal, iron, magnesite, oil, uranium and gold), Manchuria came under Russian military control in 1900. Captured by Japan in 1932, it became part of the puppet-state of **Manzhuguo**, until Russian control was reasserted in 1945. Chinese sovereignty was recognized in 1950, but the border area with USSR remains a continuing focus of political tension. ▷ **Puyi**

Mandalay The last capital of the last dynasty of Burma. Situated in the dry central plains, Mandalay was founded by King Mindon in 1857. Like most Burmese capitals, it was designed to represent the ordered structures of the Buddhist universe. During the brief Third Anglo-Burmese War in late 1885, much of Mandalay was destroyed; its records and treasures were looted and the last king of the dynasty, Thibaw, was deposed and exiled. ▷ **Anglo-Burmese Wars**

Mandal Commissions The name commonly given to the Backward Classes Commission, appointed by India's Janata government in 1978 (under President Morarji **Desai**) to examine the position of the former 'untouchable' castes and other low status groups within Indian society. The Commission, under Janata Party member Bindeshwari Prasad Mandal, was asked to report on the effectiveness of the measures taken since independence (1947) to end discrimination against the so-called 'backward classes' and to recommend means by which anti-discriminatory policies could be improved. Following a national survey, the report was published in Dec 1980, but later the same year the Congress Party, under Indira

Gandhi, was returned to power, and its proposals were never implemented. Viewed by some, particularly on the political right, as a divisive political initiative, Mandal himself resigned from the Janata Party soon after publication of the report. However, after the defeat of the Congress Party in Dec 1989, the Commission's proposals were revived by the new Prime Minister, V P Singh, in an attempt to boost the popularity of his minority government. Subsequent attempts to increase the reservation of student places in higher education and make appointments in the government service for members of the backward classes proved highly controversial, provoking widespread rioting and unrest in the towns and cities of northern India. The agitation was led mostly by students and younger members of high-caste groups, who adopted the self-immolation as a means of protest. The widespread outrage this provoked, together with the controversy over attempts by Hindu fundamentalist groups, backed by the Janata Party, to demolish a Muslim shrine at Ayodhya in northern India to make way for the construction of a Hindu temple on the site, led ultimately to the collapse of V P Singh's government, following a motion of no-confidence in the Indian parliament (Nov 1990). In practice, the Commission's proposals would have proved of little benefit to the untouchables; nor did they pose much of a threat to the upper castes. However, the implementation of the recommendations caused widespread opposition amongst the increasingly desperate, unemployed, educated youth of north India, a discontent that persists. After the restoration of the Congress Party to power (May 1991), new proposals were discussed for the modification of positive discrimination, placing more emphasis on economic rather than social disadvantage and thus avoiding the issue of **caste**

Mandarins (Scholar-Official Class) A 19c Western term used to refer to the class of officials in imperial China who obtained their appointment through success in the **Civil Service Examination System** based on the **Confucian Classics**. Since the number of government posts was always less than the total number of degree-holders, officials were part of a much larger scholarly elite (sometimes referred to in English as 'the gentry') that derived its status from being representatives of the Confucian moral order.

Mandate of Heaven (*Tianming*/*T'ien-ming*) An important doctrine in imperial China first introduced by the **Zhou Dynasty** to justify its overthrow of the preceding **Shang Dynasty**. Early Zhou leaders claimed that rulers were entrusted to rule by Heaven (*tian*), an impersonal but all-powerful presence that dominated the cosmos; since the last Shang ruler had been corrupt, Heaven had commanded the Zhou to remove the Shang. To symbolize the mandate to rule granted by heaven, the first Zhou king (and all subsequent rulers) came to be known as the Son of Heaven. The Confucian philosopher Mencius provided a further moral imperative to the doctrine, implying that any ruler who failed to attend to the needs of the people could justifiably be overthrown. Throughout subsequent Chinese history, a popular insurrection or even a natural calamity might be interpreted as a sign of Heaven's displeasure with the ruler, while the leader of a rebellion who succeeded in establishing a new dynasty would legitimize his rule by claiming that the Mandate of Heaven had been withdrawn from the previous dynasty.

mandates A system under which former territories of the German and Ottoman empires were to be administered by the victorious powers of **World War I** under international supervision. The mandates were granted by the **League of Nations**, and annual reports had to be submitted to its Permanent Mandates Commission. Britain and France acquired mandates in the Middle East (Palestine, Iraq, Transjordan, Syria, Lebanon) and Africa (Tanganyika, Togo, Cameroon); Belgium acquired Rwanda-Urundi; South Africa acquired South-West Africa; Australia and New Zealand acquired New Guinea and Western Samoa. The functions of the Commission were later assumed by the Trusteeship Council of the **UN**.

Mandela, Nelson Rohlihlahla (1918–) South African nationalist leader. Educated at Fort Hare College (1938–40), he practised law in Johannesburg before joining the **ANC** (African National Congress) in 1944 and founding the Congress Youth League. For the next 20 years he was at the forefront of black opposition to **apartheid**, being 'banned' (1956–61) and sentenced to life imprisonment in 1964 for his leadership of the ANC. He spent most of the next 25 years in prison on Robben Island before being released, on President F W **De Klerk**'s orders, on 11 Feb 1990. He was elected Deputy President of the ANC by the party in exile (Apr 1990) and in July 1991 he was elected President. In 1993

he was jointly awarded the Nobel Peace Prize with F W De Klerk, and in 1994 he became South Africa's first black President.

Mandelstam, Osip (1891–1938) Russian poet. Born of Jewish parents in Warsaw, he was brought up in St Petersburg. His early success with *Kamen* (1913, Stone), *Tristia* (1922, Sad Things), and *Stikhotvorenia 1921–25* (1928, Poems) was followed by suspicion and arrest (1934) by the Soviet authorities. His death was reported from Siberia in 1938. His *Sobranie sochineny* (Collected Works) were published in three volumes (1964–71). His wife, Nadezhda, wrote their story in *Hope Against Hope* (1970).

Manfred (1232–66) King of Sicily (1258/66). The illegitimate son of Emperor **Frederick II**, he was made Prince of Tarentum. He bravely defended the interests of the empire for his nephew **Conradin of Swabia** against the aggression of Pope **Innocent IV**. However, the Pope compelled Manfred to flee to the **Saracens** for shelter. With their aid he defeated the papal army, and in 1257 he became master of the kingdom of Naples and Sicily. On the false rumour of Conradin's death (1258) he was crowned King at Palermo, but was killed in the Battle of **Benevento**.

Mangu Khan (1251/9) Great Khan of the Mongol Empire. He was the grandson of **Genghis Khan**. During his rule the Mongols began their offensive against **Song Dynasty** China. He died while campaigning, and the conquest of China was completed by his brother, **Kublai Khan**.

Manhattan Project The codename for the most secret scientific operation of **World War II**, the development of the atomic bomb, undertaken successfully in the USA from 1942 onwards. The project culminated in the detonation of the first atomic weapon near Alamogordo, New Mexico (16 July 1945).

Manifest Destiny A term for US expansion throughout North America in the mid-19c, used particularly to rationalize the conquest of Native American and Mexican lands and southern and western settlements. The phrase was coined by the editor of the *United States Magazine and Democratic Review*, John O'Sullivan, who, in 1845, stated that it was the country's 'manifest destiny to overspread the continent allotted by Providence for the free development of our yearly multiplying millions'.

Manila Galleon A collective term applied to the Spanish vessels which sailed across the Pacific between Manila and Acapulco from 1565 to 1815. Carrying rich cargoes of silver from Mexico and Peru, and goods from China, the vessels were an attraction for pirates, particularly English.

Manin, Daniele (1804–57) Venetian lawyer and politician. Arrested with Niccolò Tommaseo (1802–74) in Jan 1848 because of his demands that the Austrian government of the Kingdom of **Lombardy-Venetia** undertake extensive reforms and concede greater autonomy to the Italian population, he was freed (Mar 1848) after anti-Habsburg insurrection broke out in Venetia. He rapidly emerged as the leader of the revolution, proclaiming the restoration of the Republic of Saint Mark and being elected its President. The pressing need to resist Austria obliged him to cooperate with the revolutionary government in Milan and **Charles Albert** of Sardinia-Piedmont: in July 1848, following widespread support for fusion with Lombardy and Piedmont among the population of the Venetian *Terraferma*, he allowed the Venetian assembly to vote on whether the republic should become part of a greater north Italian kingdom. He resigned over the assembly's pro-fusion stance, but by Aug had returned to power and continued to resist the Austrians, despite growing tension with more radical elements led by Giuseppe Sirtori. After the defeat of King Charles Albert by the Austrians at Novara, Manin continued the heroic defence of Venice, assuming virtually dictatorial powers (Aug 1849) until typhus, bombardment and food shortages forced the city's eventual surrender later that month. He fled Venice and settled in Paris, where he gradually shifted from his republican and essentially Venetian stance, towards a position as a monarchist and Italian patriot. In 1856 he supported **La Farina** in his creation of the **Italian National Society**. His ashes were returned to Venice in a public ceremony in 1868.

Manin, Ludovico (1726–1802) Last Doge of Venice. Elected in Mar 1789, during his rule the Venetian Republic ill-advisedly antagonized the French revolutionary regime by allowing émigrés sanctuary, but declined to join the league of Italian states advocated by **Victor Amadeus III** to counter the growing French threat. The republic was forced to capitulate in 1797 in the face of overwhelming French military superiority. ▷ **Campo Formio, Treaty of**

Manitoba Schools Act (1890) Canadian educational legislation. Passed by the Manitoba provincial assembly under pressure from the campaign of D'Alton **McCarthy**, it established a non-sectarian educational system and reversed the act under which Manitoba had been admitted to the Confederation with denominational schools specified. Popular outrage among Catholics, especially in Quebec, challenged the act in the courts, but the privy council found in favour of the law. After the Supreme Court had declared remedial legislation to be within federal jurisdiction, the Conservative administration reluctantly introduced it, but not in time to be carried before the election of 1896. When the Liberals won the election, **Laurier** ensured that the matter was settled by negotiation rather than coercion. While separate schools were not re-established, denominational religious instruction was accepted, as was bilingual teaching where there were more than 10 pupils with a native language other than English. This solution satisfied all except the Catholic Church, which eventually relented after Vatican approval had been sought by the Liberals.

Maniu, Iuliu (1873–1953) Romanian politician. The leader of the National Party, he directed the provisional government in Transylvania which proclaimed union with Romania (Dec 1918). Later, as leader of the National Peasant Party, he served as Prime Minister and tried to carry out agrarian reform (1928–30) but resigned from office when King **Charles II** of Romania introduced his mistress, Magda **Lupescu**, into the Romanian court. He was again Prime Minister (1932–3) and his electoral alliance with the **Iron Guard** was an expediency aimed at curbing the King's power (1937). He played a major role in the coup (Aug 1944) and was a minister without portfolio in General Sănătescu's national government which declared war on Germany. The postwar communist regime, in a move intended to destroy the Peasant Party, had him arrested, accused of conspiring with US intelligence agents. He received a life sentence (1947) and died in prison.

Manley, Michael Norman (1923–) Jamaican politician. The son of Norman **Manley**, he was educated in Jamaica, served in the Royal Canadian Air Force in **World War II**, and then studied at the London School of Economics (1945–9). He worked as a journalist in Britain before returning to Jamaica, where he became a leader of the National

Workers' Union in the 1950s, sat in the Senate (1962–7) and was then elected to the House of Representatives. In 1969 he became Leader of the People's National Party (PNP) and, in 1972, Prime Minister. He embarked on a radical, socialist programme, cooling relations with the USA and forming links with Cuba, and despite rising unemployment was re-elected in 1976. He was decisively defeated in 1980 and 1983, but returned to power in 1989 with a much more moderate policy stance.

Manley, Norman Washington (1893–1969) Jamaican politician. A Rhodes scholar at Oxford, he was called to the Bar and then became a respected QC. In 1938 he won fame by successfully defending his cousin, and political opponent, Alexander **Busta-mante**, who was then an active trade unionist, on a charge of sedition. In the same year Manley founded the People's National Party (PNP) and in 1955, seven years before Jamaica achieved full independence, he became Chief Minister. He handed over leadership of the PNP to his son, Michael **Manley**, in 1969.

Mannerheim, Carl Gustav Emil, Baron (1867–1951) Finnish soldier and politician. When Finland declared her independence (1918), he became Supreme Commander and Regent. Defeated in the presidential election of 1919, he retired into private life, but returned as Commander-in-Chief against the Russians in the **Russo-Finnish War** of 1939–40. He continued to command the Finnish forces until 1944, when he became President of the Finnish Republic until 1946. He died at Lausanne, Switzerland. ▷ **World War II**

Mannix, Daniel (1864–1963) Irish-born Australian Catholic archbishop. He was appointed Coadjutor-Archbishop of Melbourne in 1912 and Archbishop in 1917, and campaigned strongly for the rights of Catholics in Australian society, especially state aid for church schools. After the **Easter Rising** in Ireland (1916) he became an outspoken supporter of Irish **Home Rule**, and opposed **Hughes** demands for conscription in 1916–17. His position verged on a populist identification with the working classes, with whom he enjoyed an immense prestige which he never lost; the social establishment demanded his deportation. In 1920, returning to Europe, he was fêted in the USA, but refused entry to Ireland by the British government. His social views involved a hostility to capitalism that

for many years made him close to the **Australian Labor Party**, but increasingly he came to regard **communism** as the greater threat, and he supported the **Democratic Labor Party** after the Labor Party split of the mid-1950s. His involvement with the Catholic laity and combative nature made him a powerful force in Australian society and politics for half a century.

Mansabdar The name (literally, 'holder of an office') given to a member of the military/civil hierarchy created by the Mughal emperor, **Akbar the Great**. All *mansabdars* owed direct allegiance to the emperor and were liable to contribute a contingent to the Mughal army, thus augmenting the size of the army at the emperor's disposal. Akbar drew his mansabdars from all ethnic groups — Irani and Turani, native Muslim, Rajput and other Hindus — which served to weaken the parochialism and factional interests then rife. Every office was graded and assigned one of 33 ranks, from the lowest rank (*mansab*) of 10 to the highest of 7000. Each officer was assigned a pair of numbers: the zat, a personal rank which determined the person's status and thus salary, was in Akbar's time usually the same as or higher than the *sawar* rank, which indicated the number of cavalrymen — and an appropriate number of infantry and so on — that the mansabdar was required to maintain. Mansabdars were paid handsomely (although they were of course expected to maintain their contingent out of their revenue) by *jagirs*, assignments of land revenue in lieu of salary (the territory assigned for this purpose being regularly changed: the 'rotation of jagirs').

Mansfeld, Count Ernst (1580–1626) German soldier of fortune in the **Thirty Years War**. The illegitimate son of Peter Ernst Mansfeld, he refused his father's possessions, the promised reward for his brilliant services in Hungary and elsewhere, and went over to the Protestant princes. After he had defended the Count-Palatine Frederick for a time (1618–20), he was driven by the disaster of the Weissenberg to retreat to the Palatinate, from which he carried on for two years a predatory war on the imperialists, defeating **Tilly** in 1622. Thereafter he served the United Netherlands, beating the Spaniards at Fleurus (1622). At **Richelieu**'s solicitation he raised an army of 12000 men (mostly in England), but in 1626 he was crushed by **Wallenstein** at Dessau. He died near Sarajevo in Bosnia, when marching to join Gabriel **Bethlen** of Transylvania.

Mansfield (of Caen Wood), William Murray, 1st Earl (1705–93) British judge. He became Solicitor-General (1742), an MP, Attorney-General (1754), Chief Justice of the King's Bench (1756), a member of the cabinet, and baron. He was impartial as a judge, but his opinions were unpopular, and during the **Gordon Riots** of 1780 his house was burnt. Made earl in 1776, he resigned office in 1788.

Mansfield Judgement (1772) The name given to the ruling by Lord Justice **Mansfield** in a case involving a runaway black slave that slavery was neither allowed nor approved under English law, and which effectively abolished slavery in England and Wales. ▷ **slave trade**

Manstein, Fritz Erich von (1887–1973) German soldier. At the outset of **World War II** he became Chief of Staff to **Rundstedt** in the Polish campaign and later in France, where he was the architect of **Hitler's Blitzkrieg** invasion plan. In 1941 he was given command of an army corps on the Eastern Front and though not trained in armoured warfare handled his panzers with great resource in the Crimea. After the disaster of **Stalingrad**, he contrived to extricate the right wing in sufficient strength to stage a successful counter-attack at Kharkov, though he failed to relieve **Paulus's** 6th Army. After being captured in 1945 he was imprisoned as a war criminal but released in 1953. A strong advocate of fluid defence for preventing the enemy from exploiting an advantage, he embodied his theories and an account of his military career in his *Lost victories* (trans 1959).

Mansur, al- (c.710–75) 'Abbasid Caliph (754/75). This was the name (literally, 'the Victorious') adopted by Abu Jafar Abd Allah ibn Muhammad as Caliph. He held important military commands during the struggle against the Umayyads under his brother, al-Saffah, whom he succeeded. An astute politician, he defeated several revolts, establishing a firm government dominated by the 'Abbasid family, and founded a new capital for the empire, Baghdad (762). He overcame considerable opposition to ensure the succession of his own son, al-Mahdi, and died while leading his fifth pilgrimage to Mecca. ▷ **'Abbasid Dynasty; Umayyad Dynasty**

Mansur, al- (Ibn Abi Amir) (940–1002) Ruler of Cordoba (978/1002). He rose from humble origins to become one of the greatest political and military figures of medieval Spain. From 981 he was effective ruler of the Caliphate of Cordoba and won a series of impressive victories which earned him the sobriquet *al-Mansur bi-llah* ('Victorious through Allah'). In some 20 years he undertook 50 successful expeditions against the Christians, the most famous being the sacking in 997 of Santiago de Compostela, the key Christian shrine.

Mantua, Duchy of ▷ **Cherasco, Peace of; Gonzaga**

Manuel I Comnenus (c.1122–1180) Byzantine Emperor (1143/80). He was the youngest son of John II. His initial successes against the Turks and the Normans were halted by the massive defeat of his army at the hands of the Seljuks at Myriokephalon (1176), which marked the beginning of the downfall of the empire.

Manuel II (1889–1932) King of Portugal (1908/10). On the assassination of his father, King Charles (Carlos) I, and Crown Prince Luis, on 1 Feb 1908, he became king, but was forced to abdicate at the revolution of 3 Oct 1910. He subsequently settled in England.

Manuel II Palaeologus (1350–1425) Byzantine Emperor (1391/1425). He was the son of John V Palaeologus (1341/91). For much of his reign, Manuel was besieged in Constantinople by the Turks. At one point he was relieved by the advance of **Timur** into Asia Minor, but he failed to profit from this diversion and was overwhelmed.

Manzhuguo (Manchukuo) A Japanese puppet-state established in 1932 in Manchuria, which Japanese forces had invaded in 1931. Henry **Puyi**, the last Qing Emperor, was its nominal head. The regime ended with the defeat of Japan in 1945. ▷ **Qing Dynasty; Sino-Japanese War**

Manzikert, Battle of (1071) The Byzantine Emperor, Romanus IV Diogenes (1068/71), tried to extend his empire into Armenia but was defeated at Manzikert near Lake Van by the Seljuk Turks under **Alp Arslan** (1063/72), who then launched a full-scale invasion of Anatolia.

Mao Dun (1896–1981) Chinese writer. Born Shen Yanbing, he was educated at Beijing University, and became one of the foremost left-wing intellectuals and writers in China, adopting the pseudonym Mao Dun. In 1926 he joined the Northern Expedition as a propagandist, but had to go underground in Shanghai as a communist activist. In 1930 he helped to organize the influential League of Left-Wing Writers. After the communists came to power in 1949, he was China's first Minister of Culture (1949–65), and was also founder-editor of the literary journal, *People's Literature* (1949–53). During the **Cultural Revolution** he was kept under house arrest in Beijing (1966–78).

Maoism Specifically, the thought of **Mao Zedong**, and more broadly a revolutionary ideology based on Marxism–Leninism and adapted to Chinese conditions. Maoism shifted the focus of revolutionary struggle from the urban workers or proletariat to the countryside and the peasantry. There were three main elements: strict Leninist principles of organization; Chinese tradition; and armed struggle as a form of revolutionary activity. Mao gained political power in 1949 through a peasant army, his slogan being 'Political power grows through the barrel of a gun'. While there were attempts to take account of the views of the masses, the Chinese Communist Party was organized along strict centralist, hierarchical lines, and increasingly became a vehicle for a personal dictatorship. In domestic terms, Mao pursued a radical and far-reaching attempt to transform traditional Chinese society and its economy, using thought reform, indoctrination and the psychological transformation of the masses. Maoism was regarded in the 1960s at the height of the **Cultural Revolution** as a highly radical form of Marxism–Leninism that was distinct from the bureaucratic repression of the USSR, and had a strong appeal among the New Left. Since his death, his use of the masses for political purposes, his economic reforms and his conception of political power have been increasingly criticized inside and outside China as seriously misguided and too rigid.

Maoris Polynesian people who were the original inhabitants of New Zealand. The first of them arrived, probably from the Marquesas, about AD800, bringing with them dogs and rats, and some cultivated plants, including the kumara (sweet potato). They also ate fern roots, fish and birds, including the large flightless moa, which they hunted to extinction. By 1200 they had explored the whole country, and by 1800 numbered over 100000. They were skilful carvers of wood and greenstone (jade). Politically they were divided into loose tribes linked by trade and

sporadic warfare, and ruled by hereditary chiefs. In the 19c they came to be outnumbered and dominated by European (*pakeha*) settlers. Their culture declined; they lost most of their land; and by 1896 their population had shrunk to 42200. There has been some improvement in the 20c. Numbers have risen (279000 in 1981), and since the 1970s they have become politically more assertive. The Maori language has been officially encouraged, and they have obtained the return of some of their land. ▷ **Maori Wars**

Maori Wars A succession of conflicts (1843–7 and 1860–72) in which the Maori people attempted, unsuccessfully, to resist the occupation of New Zealand by British settlers. The wars, both in the 1840s and the 1860s, concerned the settlers' demands for land and the growing opposition of a section of Maori opinion to land sales, with the colonial government caught between them, but in practice favouring the settlers. The fighting involved the contrasting slow, methodical sieges of efficiently defended Maori strongholds and widespread guerrilla conflict as Maori resistance was often localized and tribal. Nevertheless, time and numbers were on the side of the Europeans; Maori resistance was worn down, and they were forced to surrender or retreat to the wilder central North Island where pursuit was both difficult and unnecessary. An uneasy stand-off was reached by the early 1870s but peace was not formalized until 1881.

Mao Tse-tung ▷ **Mao Zedong**

Mao Zedong (Mao Tse-tung) (1893–1976) Chinese political leader. He was the leading theorist of the Chinese communist revolution which won national power in China in 1949. The son of a farmer, at the age of 12 he sought an education in Changsha, where he was introduced to Western ideas. After graduating from a teachers' training college there, he went to Beijing, where he came under the influence of **Li Dazhao**. He took a leading part in the **May Fourth Movement**, then became a Marxist and a founding member of the Chinese Communist Party (CCP) (1921). During the first United Front with the Nationalist Party, he concentrated on political work among the peasants of his native province, and advocated a rural revolution, creating the **Jiangxi Soviet**. After the break with the Nationalists in 1927, the communists were driven from the cities, and with the assistance of **Zhu De**, he evolved the guerrilla tactics of the 'people's war'. In 1934 the nationalist government was at last able to destroy the Jiangxi Soviet, and in the subsequent **Long March** the communist forces retreated to Shaanxi to set up a new base. When in 1936, under the increasing threat of Japanese invasion, the nationalists renewed their alliance with the communists, Mao restored and vastly increased the political and military power of his party. His claim to share in the government led to civil war; the regime of **Chiang Kai-shek** was ousted from the Chinese mainland; and the new People's Republic of China was proclaimed (1 Oct 1949) with Mao as both Chairman of the CCP and President of the Republic. He followed the Soviet model of economic development and social change until 1958, then launched his **Great Leap Forward**, which encouraged the establishment of rural industry and the use of surplus rural labour to create a new infrastructure for agriculture. The failure of the Great Leap lost him most of his influence, but by 1965, with China's armed forces securely in the hands of his ally, **Lin Biao**, he launched a **Cultural Revolution**, and the Great Leap strategy was revived (though with new caution) when the left wing was victorious in the ensuing political struggles (1965–71). He died in Beijing after a prolonged illness, which may well have weakened his judgement during his last years. A strong reaction set in against the excessive collectivism and egalitarianism which had emerged, but his anti-Stalinist emphasis on rural industry and on local initiative was retained and strengthened by his successors. ▷ communism; Maoism

Mapai Party Acronym for the Hebrew *mifleget poalei eretz yisrael* ('Party of the Workers of the Land of Israel'). A political party created in 1930 from two already existing parties by David **Ben-Gurion** among others, Mapai aimed to establish a national Jewish homeland in Palestine built on socialist principles and became the main party in the **Yishuv**. During **World War II**, Mapai opposed British policy in Palestine but supported the war against the Nazis; after 1948 it maintained a dominant position within Israeli politics. Mapai combined with two other socialist parties in 1968 to form the Israel Labour Party (Hebrew *mifleget ha-avodah ha-yisraelit*), which remained in power until 1977. ▷ Jewish Agency; Likud

Mapillas Descendants of early Arab settlers in many of the coastal towns of peninsular India. Arabs visited India long before the

days of **Muhammad**, and there is evidence of small Muslim communities from the 8c. Unlike the Roman traders, the Arabs settled permanently in the coastal regions of south India, where they were welcomed as traders and given land for their trading stations; they were free to practise their religion. The Malabar Muslims, being mainly traders, were not concerned with converting others to Islam, and therefore coexisted peacefully with local society. However, social and economic changes under British rule and the poverty which resulted, as well as instances of favouritism by police and the local administration, provoked a succession of uprisings in the 19c and early 20c, which often took on a 'communal' or sectarian character. The most serious outbreak was that of 1921, which was marked not only by murder and mayhem, but attempts at the forcible conversion of Hindus. The price for this was paid during the pacification campaigns of the British and the famine that stalked the country in this part of India for many years afterwards. A wider significance of these events lay in the way in which they helped to undermine the cooperation between Muslims and Hindus which had characterized the early years of the Indian independence movement.

Maquiladoras A Spanish term used in Mexico (literally, 'assembly') that signifies foreign-owned industrial assembly plants built on the US border, in order to take advantage of lower wage rates and less onerous labour legislation in Mexico. The growth of *maquiladora* industries was most rapid in the 1960s as both the US and Mexican authorities sought to limit the flight of the *braceros* to California and Texas, while major multinational manufacturing firms sought to take advantage of tax-breaks conceded under Mexican legislation designed to stimulate industrial growth and exports. Their effective contribution to Mexican growth is hotly debated, while their existence is also unpopular with US labour unions.

Maquis The local name given to the dense scrub in Corsica; adopted in German-occupied France by groups of young men who hid in the hills and forests to escape forced labour in Germany. Organized into Resistance groups, they led the national rising against the Germans on and after **D-Day**. ▷ Resistance Movement (France); World War II

Marat, Jean Paul (1743–93) French revolutionary politician. He studied medicine at

Bordeaux, and lived in Paris, the Netherlands, and London. At the Revolution he became a member of the Cordelier Club and established the radical paper *L'Ami du peuple* ('The Friend of the People'). His virulence provoked hatred, and he was several times forced into hiding. Elected to the National Convention, he became a leader of the **Mountain**, and advocated radical reforms. After **Louis XVI**'s death he was locked in a struggle with the **Girondins**, and was fatally stabbed in his bath by a Girondin supporter, Charlotte **Corday**; thereafter he was hailed as a martyr. ▷ **Convention, National; Cordeliers' Club; Girondins; French Revolution**

Maratha Kingdom A west Indian regional power, founded by Maratha warrior-leader Shivaji (1627–80), which filled the vacuum left by Mughal decline. It later became a confederacy of leading families (Bhonsle, Gaekwad, Holkar, Sindhia) under hereditary chief ministers (Peshwas). The kingdom was defeated by the Afghans at the Battle of **Panipat** (1761). Internal disputes caused the Peshwa to seek British protection at one stage, but the kingdom was finally destroyed by the British in the last of three wars, fought in 1775–82, 1803–5 and in 1818.

Marathon, Battle of (490BC) The decisive Athenian victory over the Persians on the eastern coast of Attica, which brought the first of the **Persian Wars** to an end.

Maravi, Kingdom of An African kingdom situated north of the Zambesi and south of Lake Malawi, which has given its name to the modern Malawi. It was a rather loose confederation of chiefdoms under a titular head which occupied territory spanning land in Malawi, Zambia, and Mozambique. Its peoples were involved in long-distance trade, and in the 17c its power reached the eastern African coast; but it was disrupted by the migrations of the Ngoni in the early 19c.

Marbury v Madison (1803) The first US Supreme Court decision declaring a federal law unconstitutional. William Marbury had received a minor judicial appointment as one of the last acts of President John **Adams**'s administration. James **Madison**, the new Secretary of State, refused to deliver the commission and Marbury took legal action. Chief Justice John **Marshall** admonished Madison but found that the clause of the Federal Judiciary Act (1789) under which Marbury brought his case was contrary to the US Constitution. In a classic assertion of the doctrine of judicial review he argued that 'it is emphatically the province and duty of the judicial department to say what the law is'.

Marcellus, Marcus Claudius (c.268–208BC) Roman general of the time of the second of the **Punic Wars**. Nicknamed the 'Sword of Rome', his main exploits were the defeat of the Insubrian Gauls (222BC) and the capture of Syracuse (212BC). His namesake, who lived from 42 to 23BC, was a nephew of the Emperor **Augustus** by his sister, **Octavia**. As Augustus's first intended successor, his early death was widely regarded as a national calamity.

March, Juan (1884–1962) Spanish business magnate. If Barcelona was the nexus of his financial empire, Mallorca (where he was born) became his own personal fiefdom. Imprisoned for fraud by the Second Republic, he retaliated by aiding the military rebellions of 1932 and July 1936. During the **Spanish Civil War** he was a key backer of the Nationalists. He died the richest person in modern Spain, allegedly the seventh in the world. Republic, Second (Spain)

March Through Georgia (1864) A campaign in the American Civil War by the Northern army under General Sherman, resulting in devastation of the area between Atlanta and the ocean. In military terms it completed the task of splitting the Confederacy on an E–W line. ▷ **American Civil War Sherman**

Marchais, Georges (1920–) French communist politician, the son of a miner. A former metalworker, he joined the French **Communist Party** (PCF) in 1947, becoming its General-Secretary in 1972. Under his leadership the PCF pledged its commitment to the 'transition to socialism' by democratic means, and joined the **Socialist Party** (PS) in a new 'Union of the Left'. This union was, however, severed by Marchais in 1977 and the party returned to an orthodox 'Moscow line', although PCF ministers participated in the **Mitterrand** government (1981–4). He unsuccessfully contested the 1981 presidential election.

Marchand, Jean Baptiste (1863–1934) French soldier and explorer. He explored the White Nile, and caused a Franco-British crisis by hoisting the tricolour at Fashoda in 1898. As a general he distinguished himself in **World War I**. ▷ **Fashoda Incident**

Marchenko, Anatoli Tikhonovich (1938–86) Soviet dissident. One of the small group of prominent Soviet dissidents whose continuing courage did much to bring down the communist system. A young worker and writer, he was first imprisoned in 1960 for attempting to travel abroad and spent 18 of his remaining 26 years in jails or camps for championing his rights. He wrote the first detailed account of Buzhnev labour camp in *My Testimony* in 1968, and died in prison on hunger strike but in suspicious circumstances.

March First Movement (1919) A non-violent protest in Korea led by religious groups (both Buddhist and Christian) in response to the failure of the Paris Peace Conference to grant Korean independence from Japan (Korea had been a colony since 1910). The timing of the demonstration coincided with funeral ceremonies for the former Korean king, Kojong (1864/1907). Mourners signed a declaration of independence amidst rumours that Kojong had been poisoned for having refused to sign a statement supporting permanent unity with Japan. Japanese troops responded with violence and hundreds of Koreans were killed (553 according to Japanese figures at the time; 7189 according to later Korean figures). Colonial control was relaxed for a time during the 1920s by party governments in Japan anxious to atone for the incident, but with the emergence of military-led cabinets in the 1930s Japanese policy in Korea once more became oppressive.

March on Rome (Oct 1922) The largely symbolic march on the Italian capital by several thousand fascists. Although **Mussolini** subsequently liked to portray the event as a glorious seizure of power, he had already successfully negotiated and bullied his way into office before his supporters actually arrived in the capital. He did not reach Rome himself until he was already certain of success in his bid for power and had been invited to form a government by **Victor Emmanuel III**.

March to the Sea ▷ **Sherman, William Tecumseh**

Marcomanni A Germanic tribe. Members of the Suebi group, they originated in the area between the rivers Main and Danube. At the end of the 1c AD they settled in southern Moravia and Lower Austria and, under their leader, Marbod, became the core of a significant league of Germanic peoples.

They then became clients of the Roman Empire until a series of wars with **Marcus Aurelius** (c.167–80) ended their relationship with Rome. At the end of the 4c, they settled in the area around Vienna and are sometimes regarded as the original Bavarians. ▷ **Germanic Invasions**

Marco Polo Bridge Incident (7 July 1937) A clash between Chinese and Japanese troops near the Marco Polo Bridge, southwest of Beijing, that was to lead to full-scale war between China and Japan (1937–45). Exercising their right under the Boxer Protocol (1901), which allowed foreign troops to be stationed in the vicinity of Beijing, Japanese soldiers were engaged in manoeuvres when skirmishes with local Chinese forces took place. Although a local ceasefire was arranged (11 July 1937), the Japanese Prime Minister, **Konoe**, announced plans to mobilize five divisions for north China. The head of the Chinese Nationalist government, **Chiang Kai-shek**, reversing the appeasement policy he had followed regarding persistent Japanese attempts to remove north China from Chinese central government control, responded by reinforcing the Chinese forces. Chiang's unyielding stand was prompted by the anti-Japanese united front agreement he had been compelled to sign in 1936 with the communists. On 29 July 1937 Japanese troops attacked and occupied Beijing, signalling the start of the war between the two countries.

Marcos, Ferdinand (Edralin) (1917–89) Filipino politician and President (1965–86). He trained as a lawyer, and as a politician obtained considerable US support as an anti-communist. His regime as President was marked by increasing repression, misuse of foreign financial aid, and political violence (in particular, the assassination of Benigno **Aquino** in 1983). He declared martial law in 1972. Overthrown in 1986 by a popular revolt led by Corazon **Aquino**, he went into exile in Hawaii, where he and his wife, Imelda, fought against demands from US courts investigating charges of financial mismanagement and massive corruption. He died in Honolulu.

Marcus Aurelius (121–180) Roman Emperor (161/80). The adopted son of **Antoninus Pius**, he ruled as his junior partner from 146, discharging his duties with the utmost fidelity, despite his continuing study of law and philosophy, especially Stoicism. On his succession to the throne, he voluntarily divided the government with his adopted brother, Lucius Verus. His reign saw constant warfare. Trouble in Britain, the East, and Germany was handled by his generals, but he himself, for almost a decade, personally directed operations along the Danube frontier, where he died of sheer exhaustion. His Meditations, devotional jottings written while on campaign, make him among the best known of Roman emperors. ▷ **Antonine Emperors**

Marengo, Battle of (14 June 1800) The important, but narrow, French victory over the Austrians, fought in northern Italy during the War of the Second Coalition. It enabled **Napoleon I** to ensure his restored hegemony in northern Italy, to guarantee the re-establishment of the **Cisalpine Republic** and to assert his political authority in France. ▷ **Napoleonic Wars**

Margai, Albert Michael (1910–80) Sierra Leone politician. The son of a trader and the brother of Sir Milton **Margai**, he was educated in Roman Catholic schools before becoming a nurse and pharmacist. He studied law in London (1944–7) and was elected a member of Legco in 1951, when he was appointed Minister of Education, Welfare and Local Government. A member of the Sierra Leone People's Party from 1951–8, he helped found the People's National Party and became Minister of Finance at independence. When his brother died, he succeeded him as party leader and Prime Minister (1964–7). Following the military coup led by Siaka **Stevens** in 1967, he went into exile in London.

Margai, Milton A S (1895–1964) Sierra Leone nationalist leader and politician. The elder brother of Sir Albert **Margai**, he was educated in Roman Catholic mission schools, Fourah Bay College and in the UK, where he qualified as a doctor. Appointed a member of the Protectorate Assembly in 1940, he was elected to Legco in 1951, when he helped found the Sierra Leone People's Party and played a major role in pressing for independence. He was Chief Minister (1954–8) and, on independence, Prime Minister until his death in 1964.

Margaret ('Maid of Norway') (1283–90) Infant Queen of Scotland (1286/90). The grand-daughter of **Alexander III** of Scotland, she was the only child of Alexander's daughter, Margaret (who died in childbirth) and King Erik II of Norway. When Alexander III

died in 1286, Margaret was the only direct survivor of the Scottish royal line. In 1289 she was betrothed to the infant Prince Edward (the future **Edward II** of England), son of **Edward I**; but she died at sea the following year on her way from Norway to the Orkneys.

Margaret, St (c.1045–93) Scottish Queen. Born in Hungary, she came to England, but after the **Norman Conquest** fled to Scotland with her boy brother, **Edgar the Atheling**. She married the Scottish king, **Malcolm III**, **'Canmore'**, and did much to civilize the realm, and to assimilate the old Celtic Church into the rest of Christendom. She was canonized in 1250.

Margaret I and II of Denmark ▷ **Margrethe I and II**

Margaret of Angoulême ▷ **Margaret of Navarre**

Margaret of Anjou (1429–82) Queen Consort of **Henry VI** of England (1445/82). She was the daughter of René of Anjou. Because of Henry's madness, she became deeply involved in political life, and during the Wars of the **Roses**, was a leading Lancastrian. Defeated at the Battle of **Tewkesbury** (1471), she was imprisoned in the Tower for four years, until ransomed by **Louis XI** of France. She then retired to France, where she died. ▷ **Lancaster, House of**

Margaret of Austria (1480–1530) Duchess of Savoy and Regent of the Netherlands. The daughter of the Emperor **Maximilian I** and **Mary of Burgundy**, in 1497 she married, first, the Infante Juan of Spain, who died within a few months, and then in 1501, Philibert II, Duke of Savoy. In 1507 her father appointed her Regent of the Netherlands and guardian of her nephew, the future Emperor **Charles V**. In 1519 she was appointed regent again, by Charles V, and proved herself an effective and capable stateswoman. She was convinced of the importance of the Low Countries to Habsburg interests, and was a great patron of the arts. ▷ **Habsburg Dynasty**

Margaret of Navarre (1492–1549) Queen of Navarre. The sister of Francis I of France, in her youth she was known as Marguerite d'Angoulême. In 1509 she was married to the Duke of Alençon, who died in 1525; and in 1527 to Henri d'Albret, titular King of Navarre. Their daughter, Jeanne d'Albret, was the mother of **Henry IV** of France. A patroness of humanism and literature in the Renaissance tradition, she sheltered religious reformers at her court in Angoulême.

Margaret of Parma (1522–86) Regent of the Netherlands. The illegitimate daughter of the Emperor **Charles V**, she married first Alessandro **de' Medici** (1536) and second Ottavio Farnese, Duke of Parma (1538), to whom she bore Alessandro **Farnese** (later Duke of Parma) in 1546. From 1559 to 1567 she was Regent of the Netherlands, masterful, able, and a staunch Catholic. She rapidly restored peace after the **Image-breaking Riots** (1566), but was replaced by the Duke of **Alva**. While her son Alessandro was governor of the Netherlands (1578–86), later ruling as regent for **Philip II** of Spain, Margaret was made head of the civil administration for a time.

Margaret Tudor (1489–1541) Queen of Scotland. The eldest daughter of **Henry VII** of England, she became the wife of **James IV** of Scotland (1503) and the mother of **James V**, for whom she acted as Regent. After James IV's death in 1513 she married twice again, to the Earl of Angus (1514) and Lord Methven (1527). She was much involved in the political intrigues between the pro-French and pro-English factions in Scotland, but lacking Tudor shrewdness, she was discredited (1534). Her great-grandson was **James VI and I**. ▷ **Tudor, House of**

Margrethe I (1353–1412) Queen of Denmark (1375/1412), Norway (1380/1412), and Sweden (1388/1412). She became Queen of Denmark in 1375, on the death of her father, Valdemar IV, without male heirs; by the death of her husband, Haakon VI, in 1380, she became ruler of Norway; and in 1388 she aided a rising of Swedish nobles against their King, Albert of Mecklenburg, and became Queen of Sweden. She had her infant cousin, **Erik of Pomerania**, crowned King of the three kingdoms at Kalmar in 1397, but remained the real ruler of Scandinavia until her death at Flensburg. ▷ **Kalmar Union**

Margrethe II (1940–) Queen of Denmark (1972/). The daughter of **Frederick IX**, whom she succeeded, she is an archaeologist, and was educated at the universities of Copenhagen, Aarhus and Cambridge, the Sorbonne, Paris, and the London School of Economics. In 1967 she married a French diplomat, Count Henri de Laborde de Monpezat, now Prince Henrik of Denmark. Their children are the heir-apparent, Prince

Frederik André Henrik Christian, and Prince Joachim Holger Valdemar Christian.

Maria Carolina (1725–1814) Queen of Naples. The daughter of Maria Theresa of Austria, she married Ferdinand IV of Naples (**Ferdinand I**) in 1768 and rapidly came to dominate him. She appointed her English lover, John Acton, Prime Minister and brought Naples into the Austro-British coalition against revolutionary France. She fled to Sicily with her husband during the uprising that led to the establishment of the **Parthenopean Republic** and again in 1806 when the French invaded Naples. However, the British forces defending Sicily thought her a danger and had her exiled to Austria where she spent the remainder of her life.

María Cristina (1806–78) Queen Consort and Regent (1833/40) of Spain. She was the daughter of **Francis I**, King of the Two Sicilies, and fourth wife of Ferdinand VII of Spain. On his death (1833), she became regent for their daughter, **Isabella II**. A Carlist war broke out, and in 1836 she was forced to grant a constitution; in 1840 she resigned the regency and fled to France, but returned in 1843. Her share in the schemes of **Louis-Philippe** over the marriage of her daughter in 1846, and her reactionary policy, made her unpopular. In 1854 a revolution drove her again to France, where, except for a time in Spain (1864–8), she lived thereafter.

Maria II da Gloria (1819–53) Queen of Portugal (1826/8 and 1834/53). Proclaimed Queen under a regency following the death of her grandfather, **John IV**, in 1826, Maria was overthrown by her uncle, Miguel, in 1828. A civil war between Liberals and Absolutists ensued (1832–4), returning Maria to the throne. In Nov 1836 she tried to engineer a coup d'etat against a leftist government. Similarly, the civil war of 1846–7 was caused by Maria's imposition of the conservative Saldanha as Prime Minister. Although Maria was forced to abdicate, the English and Spanish enforced the Peace of Gramido (June 1847), which restored her to power until her death in childbirth. Through both her interference and her favouritism, she undoubtedly exacerbated the political instability of the years 1836–51, being personally responsible for several crises.

Maria Theresa (1717–80) Archduchess of Austria and Queen of Hungary and Bohemia (1740/80). The daughter of Emperor Charles VI, in 1736 she married Francis, Duke of

Lorraine, and in 1740 succeeded her father in the hereditary Habsburg lands. Her claim, however, led to the War of the **Austrian Succession**, during which she lost Silesia to Prussia. In 1741 she received the Hungarian crown, and in 1745 her husband was elected Holy Roman Emperor. Although her Foreign Minister, Kaunitz, tried to isolate Prussia by diplomatic means, military conflict was renewed in the **Seven Years War**, and by 1763 she was finally forced to recognize the status quo of 1756. In her later years she strove to maintain international peace, and reluctantly accepted the partition of Poland (1772). Of her 10 surviving children, the eldest son, Joseph II, succeeded her. ▷ **Frederick II, 'the Great'; Habsburg Dynasty; Poland, Partitions of**

Marie Antoinette (Josèphe Jeanne) (1755–93) Queen Consort of France (1774/93). She was the daughter of Maria Theresa and Emperor **Francis II** of Austria, and sister of Leopold II. Married in 1770 to the **Dauphin** (later **Louis XVI**), in order to strengthen the Franco-Austrian alliance, she exerted a growing influence over him. Capricious and frivolous, she aroused criticism by her extravagance, disregard for conventions, devotion to the interests of Austria, and opposition to reform. From the outbreak of the **French Revolution**, she resisted the advice of constitutional monarchists such as **Mirabeau**, and helped to alienate the monarchy from the people. In June 1791 she and Louis tried to escape from the Tuileries to her native Austria, but were apprehended at Varennes and imprisoned in Paris. After the King's execution, she was arraigned before the Revolutionary Tribunal and guillotined.

Marie de' Medici (1573–1642) Queen Consort of **Henry IV** of France. The daughter of Francesco de' Medici, Grand Duke of Tuscany, she married Henry in 1600, following his divorce from his first wife, Margaret of Valois. She gave birth to a son (later **Louis XIII**) in 1601 and, after her husband's death (1610), she acted as regent. Confined in Blois when Louis assumed royal power (1617), she continued to intrigue him and her former protégé, **Richelieu**, who had become the King's adviser. She escaped to Brussels (1631) and her last years were spent in poverty.

Marie-Louise (1791–1847) Empress of France (1811/14). The daughter of Emperor **Francis II** of Austria, she married **Napoleon I** in 1810, after his divorce from **Josephine**. In 1811 she bore him a son, who was created King of Rome and who became **Napoleon II**. On Napoleon's abdication, she returned to Austria. By the Treaty of Fontainebleau (1814), she was awarded the Duchies of Parma, Piacenza, and Guastalla in Italy.

Marignano, Battle of ▷ **Italian Wars**

Marinheiro The pejorative name (literally, 'sailor') often used to describe a Portuguese in 19c Brazil. The Portuguese frequently dominated the retail trades in the major cities and were often accused of cartelizing trade. *Mata Marinheiro* ('Death to the Portuguese') was a popular slogan of the 1830s, and was used by the revolutionaries of 1848 in Recife. Anti-Portuguese sentiment fomented riots in the 1870s and 1890s, particularly in Rio de Janeiro, and Pará, where they were led by the Jacobins.

Maritsa River, Battle of (1371) At this battle, the Ottoman Turks defeated the Serbs and overran Macedonia and southern Serbia, forcing the Serbian Prince, Marko **Kraljević** to become a vassal of Sultan **Murad I**.

Marius, Gaius (157–186BC) Roman general and politician from Arpinum. Of comparatively humble extraction, Marius's military talents and ruthless ambition enabled him to rise to the very top at Rome, where he held an unprecedented number of consulships (seven) and married into the heart of the aristocracy—the Julian *gens*. Famous in his lifetime for his victories over **Jugurtha** (105BC), the Teutones (102BC), and the Cimbri (101BC), it was by his army reforms that he made his greatest impact on the state. His final years were dominated by his rivalry with **Sulla**. The violence with which he recaptured Rome for **Cinna** from the forces backing Sulla (87BC) permanently damaged his reputation.

Marj Dabiq, Battle of (1516) This battle, between the Ottoman Turks of Sultan **Selim I, 'the Grim'** and the **Mamluks** of Qansawh, resulted in a crushing defeat for the Mamluks and the death of Qansawh himself. It was during the reign of **Bayezid II** (1481/1512) that the Ottomans began to pose a serious threat to Mamluk influence in northern Syria. After various provocations, the promise of support for Shah Ismail the Safavid on the part of Qansawh proved too much for the Ottomans and despite Qansawh's attempts while on a visit to Aleppo to appear to be acting merely as an intermediary between Ismail and Selim, Selim's intelligence had told him of Qansawh's inclination towards Ismail. By murdering the attendants of Qansawh's envoy Selim left Qansawh in no doubt as to his intentions. The Battle of Marj Dabiq ensued; after his victory, Selim was popularly acclaimed in Aleppo as a liberator from the harshness of Mamluk rule. The battle also opened up Syria to Sultan Selim and the Ottoman Turks.

Marj Rahit, Battle of (684) This battle was fought between al-Dahhak ibn Qays al-Fihri, in support of Abdullah ibn al-Zubayr, the so-called 'anti-caliph', and forces supporting the Umayyad Marwan ibn al-Hakam. A further factor was the antagonism between Qaysite and Kalbite which surfaced at this time, with al-Dahhak leading the Qaysites or North Arabian party against the Kalbites (Yemenites or South Arabians) who supported Marwan. Al-Dahhak's defeat in the battle gave Syria to Marwan and opened the way for Marwan's son and successor, '**Abd al-Malik**, finally to crush Zubayrid aspirations (691). ▷ **Umayyad Dynasty**

market economy An economic system where prices, wages, and what is made and sold are determined primarily by market forces of supply and demand, with no state interference. The contrast is with a command economy, where the state takes most, if not all, economic decisions. Most Western economies these days are mixed, with varying degrees of state control or intervention.

Markievicz, Constance (Georgine), Countess (1868–1927) Irish nationalist. The daughter of Sir Henry Gore-Booth of County Sligo, she married the Polish count, Casimir Markievicz. She fought in the **Easter Rising** (1916), and was sentenced to death but reprieved. Elected the first British woman MP in 1918, she did not take her seat, but was a member of the **Dáil Eireann** from 1923.

Marković, Ante (1924–) Yugoslav politician. He joined the Communist Youth Movement in Yugoslavia in 1940 and fought in **Tito**'s partisans, becoming a member of the Communist League of Yugoslavia in 1943. He was a member of the Central Committee of the League of Communists of Croatia (1982–6) and, as Prime Minister of the Socialist Federal Republic of Croatia, introduced a programme of economic reform. A member of the Central Committee of the League of Communists of Yugoslavia since 1986, he succeeded Branko Mikulić as Prime

Minister of Yugoslavia (Mar 1989). A liberal and pro-Western, he was hailed as 'man of the year' by the popular Croatian magazine *Danas* (1990). After six months of civil war between the Serbs and Croats, he announced his resignation as Prime Minister of Yugoslavia (Dec 1991).

Marlborough, John Churchill, 1st Duke of (1650–1722) English general. Commissioned as an ensign in the Guards (1667), he fought in the Low Countries. In 1678 he married Sarah Jennings, a close friend and attendant of Princess Anne, and was further promoted. On **James VII and II**'s accession (1685), he was elevated to an English barony and given the rank of general. He took a leading part in quelling **Monmouth**'s rebellion at Sedgemoor but, concerned for the integrity of the Anglican Church under James, in 1688 he deserted to the Prince of Orange (later **William III**), and served the Protestant cause in campaigns in Ireland and Flanders. Under Queen **Anne**, he was appointed Supreme Commander of the British forces in the War of the **Spanish Succession**, and he became Captain-General of the Allied armies. His military flair and organization skills resulted in several great victories — Donauwörth and Blenheim (1704), Ramillies (1706), Oudenarde and the capture of Lille (1708) — for which he was richly rewarded with Blenheim Palace and a dukedom. Forced by political interests to align himself with the Whig war party (1708), his influence waned with theirs after 1710. When his wife fell from royal favour, the **Tories** pressed for his downfall. Dismissed on charges of embezzling, he left England for continental Europe (1712), returning after **George I**'s accession (1714), when he was restored to his former offices. ▷ **Whigs**

Marmont, Auguste Frédéric Louis Viesse de (1774–1852) French soldier. He went with **Napoleon I** to Italy, and fought at Lodi, in Egypt, and at **Marengo** (1800). He was sent to Dalmatia in 1805, defeated the Russians there, and was made Duke of Ragusa. He was next Governor of the **Illyrian Provinces**, and in 1811 succeeded Masséna in Portugal. In 1813 he fought at **Lützen**, Bautzen and Dresden. In 1814 he deserted to the Allies, compelling Napoleon to abdicate, and earned Marmont from the Bonapartists the title of traitor. At the **July Revolution** (1830) he endeavoured to reduce Paris to submission, and finally retreating with a few faithful battalions, conducted **Charles X** across the frontier, living thereafter in exile.

Marne, Battle of the (1914) A battle early in **World War I**, in which General **Joffre**'s French armies and the **British Expeditionary Force** halted German forces which had crossed the Marne and were approaching Paris, thus ending German hopes of a swift victory. The German line withdrew across the River Aisne, dug in, and occupied much the same positions until 1918.

Marnix, Philippe de, Lord of St Aldegonde (c.1540–98) Netherlands politician and writer. He studied under **Calvin** and Beza at Geneva, and was active in the Reformation in the Netherlands, and in 1566 in the revolt against Spain. An intimate friend of **William I** of Orange, he represented him at the first meeting of the Estates of the United Provinces, held at Dordrecht in 1572, and was sent on special missions to the courts of France and England. As burgomaster of Antwerp, he defended the city for 13 months against the Spaniards; but having then capitulated, he incurred so much ill-will that he retired from public life. He is said to have written the patriotic 'Wilhelmus' song; the prose satire, *The Roman Beehive* (1569); a metrical translation of the Psalms (1580); and part of a prose translation of the Bible.

Maronites Under the influence of Monotheletism, the 'Syrian' Christians of Lebanon became the separate Maronite Church in the 8c. They united with Rome towards the end of the 12c, and as a result of the influence of Rome from the late 15c, the Maronite Christians of Lebanon became distinctly westward-leaning. In modern Lebanon, the constitution has stipulated that the President should be a Christian (which, in Lebanese terms, means a Maronite Christian) and the Prime Minister a Muslim. The privileged position accorded to the Maronites (largely as a result of the French occupation) was built on the fiction of there being a Christian majority in the country or, at least, equal numbers of Christians and Muslims. The **Ta'if Accord** of 1989 addressed the constitutional majority enjoyed by the Christians (Maronites) in Lebanon.

Maroons Name derived from the Spanish *cimarrones* for runaway slaves who fled the estates for the refuge of the mountains (*cima* meaning 'summit'). Maroon communities existed in Hispaniola, Dominica, St Vincent and St Lucia but the best known and documented are the Maroons of Jamaica. Living in the rugged interior of the island in a number of separate settlements, they were a constant threat to British rule and the plantations which they occasionally raided. In the 18c there were two Maroon Wars. The first (1734–8) was concluded by a peace treaty in which the Maroon chief of Trelawny Town, Cudjoe, agreed to assist in the defence of the island and hand over runaway slaves in return for sovereignty over 1500 acres of land. The Second Maroon War (1795–6) led to the deportation of 556 Maroons to Nova Scotia and then to Sierra Leone.

Marprelate Tracts Seven pamphlets covertly published in London in 1587–9. The pseudonymous author, 'Martin Marprelate', satirized the Elizabethan Church and bishops, and favoured a Presbyterian system. One alleged author, John Penry, was executed; another, John Udall, died in prison; a third, Job Throckmorton, successfully refuted the accusations. The Tracts led to statutes against dissenting sects and sedition (1593).

Marranos A derogatory word used since at least the 15c in Spain and Portugal to describe Jews or, more specifically, those **Conversos** who secretly continued to practise their Jewish faith. The word was, and is, commonly used as a synonym for 'pig', although its etymological origins are obscure.

Marryshow, Albert (1885–1958) Grenadian champion of a federation of the British West Indies. In 1913 he founded a newspaper, *The West Indian*, which campaigned for greater West Indian unity and for an extension of the franchise, based on his belief that the 'People's Parliament' should be founded on universal adult suffrage. Marryshow lived long enough to sit in the Federation of the **West Indies**, for which he had so long struggled, but not long enough to see it dissolved four years later.

Marshall, George Catlett (1880–1959) US general and politician. Educated at the Virginia Military Institute, he became Chief-of-Staff (1939–45), and directed the US Army throughout **World War II**. After two years in China as special representative of President **Truman**, he became Secretary of State (1947–9), originating the **Marshall Plan** for the post-war reconstruction of Europe, and Secretary of Defense (1950–1). He retired (Sep 1951) after nearly 50 years of military and civilian service, and was awarded the Nobel Peace Prize in 1953.

Marshall, John (1755–1835) US jurist. The foremost Chief Justice in the history of the

US Supreme Court, in the 1790s he became a supporter of the Federalist measures of George **Washington** and Alexander **Hamilton**, and was named Chief Justice by the outgoing President John **Adams** in 1801. From then until his death he dominated the Supreme Court, establishing the US doctrine of Supreme Court judicial review of federal and state legislation. ▷ **American Revolution; Marbury v Madison; McCulloch v Maryland**

Marshall, Thurgood (1908–93) US jurist. Associate justice of the US Supreme Court and civil rights advocate. Educated at Lincoln and Howard universities, he joined the legal staff of the National Association for the Advancement of Colored People, and argued many important civil rights cases. He served as a judge of the US Court of Appeals (1961–5), and as Solicitor-General of the United States (1965–7), before becoming the first black Associate Justice of the US Supreme Court, a post he held until his retirement in 1991. ▷ **civil rights**

Marshall Plan The popular name for the European Recovery Program, a scheme for large-scale, medium-term US aid to war-ravaged Europe, announced in 1947 by the US Secretary of State, George Marshall. 'Marshall Aid' was rejected by the USSR and the Eastern bloc, but during the period 1948–50 it materially assisted Western Europe's economic revival.

Marsilius of Padua (c.1275–c.1342) Italian political theorist and philosopher. He was rector of the University of Paris from 1313, where he lectured on natural philosophy, engaged in medical research, and involved himself actively in Italian politics. In 1324 he completed *Defensor Pacis*, a political treatise much influenced by Aristotle's *Politics*, which argued against the temporal power of clergy and the pope and developed a thoroughgoing, secular theory of the state based on popular consultation and consent and on natural rights. When the authorship of the work became known he was forced to flee Paris (1326). Excommunicated by Pope **John XXII**, he took refuge at the court of **Louis IV, 'the Bavarian'** in Munich, and remained under his protection till his death.

Marston Moor, Battle of (2 July 1644) A major conflict in the first of the **English Civil Wars**, in which a force of 27 000 parliamentary and Scottish troops defeated 18 000 royalists near York. The royalist cavalry was led by Prince **Rupert**; the parliamentary horse by Oliver **Cromwell**. The defeat led to the fall of the royalist stronghold of York, and the virtual collapse of **Charles I**'s cause in the north.

Martens, Wilfried (1936–) Belgian politician. Educated at Louvain University, he was adviser to two governments, in 1965 and 1966, before becoming Minister for Community Problems in 1968. He was President of the Dutch-speaking Social Christian Party (CVP) from 1972 to 1979, when be became Prime Minister at the head of a coalition. He continued in office, apart from a brief break in 1981, heading no fewer than six coalition governments.

Martí, José (Julián) (1853–95) Cuban national hero. Educated in Havana, Madrid and Saragossa, he devoted his life to the liberation of Cuba from Spain. Much of his adult life was spent in exile, and he became famous for his journalism, plays and poems. In 1892 he helped to found the Cuban Revolutionary Party (*Partido Revolucionario Cubano*), which in 1895 mounted an armed rebellion in the island, during which he was killed near Dos Ríos. The independence of Cuba was achieved seven years after his death. ▷ **Cuban Revolution**

Martin I, St (d.655) Pope (649/55). A Tuscan, he held the first Lateran Council (against the Monothelites) in 649, and was banished by Constans II in 654 to the Crimea, where he died. ▷ **Lateran Councils**

Martin V (Oddone Colonna) (1368–1431) Italian Pope (1417/31). Through his election, during the Council of Constance, the **Great Schism**, which had begun in 1378, was finally extinguished. He died in Rome, just after calling the Council of Basle.

Martínez Barrio, Diego (1883–1962) Spanish politician. Under the Second Republic he was Minister of Communications (Apr–Dec 1931) and caretaker Prime Minister (Oct–Dec 1933). A leading freemason, he was national Grand Master from 1931 to 1934. His opposition to the alliance with the non-Republican Right led him to split with the **Radical Republican Party** in May 1934, taking up to a quarter of the party with him. After the Popular Front victory of Feb 1936, he was elected President of the **Cortes** and, on the outbreak of the military rising of July 1936, tried to form a government of conciliation. A man of immense integrity and reserve, he was President of the republic in exile until his death. Republic, Second ▷ (Spain)

Marwan I (623–85) Umayyad Caliph (684/5). He defeated the forces of Dahhak ibn Qays, a supporter of the rival and so-called anti-caliph Abdullah ibn al-Zubayr, at the Battle of **Marj Rahit** (684). The significance of Marwan's accession, his rights to which he was initially tempted to waive, is that it marked the end of the Sufyanid line of Umayyad caliphs, paving the way for the establishment of the Marwanids and by extension the Umayyad caliphate as undisputed master of the then Islamic world by Marwan's son, **'Abd al-Malik**, who succeeded his father in 685, Marwan having died of the plague. ▷ **Umayyad Dynasty**

Marwaris One of the largest trading communities in India. The Marwaris, originally from Marwar in Rajasthan, started to establish their reputation as merchants in medieval India. In this period some communities specialized in wholesale trade and others in retail trade; the former being called *seth* or *bohra* and the latter *beoraris* or *bania*. The wealthy merchants lived in an ostentatious manner and adopted the manners of the nobles.

Marx, Karl (Heinrich) (1818–83) German founder of modern international **communism**, the son of a Jewish lawyer. He studied law at **Bonn** and **Berlin** but took up history, Hegelian philosophy and Feuerbach's materialism. He edited a radical newspaper in the **Rhineland**, and after it was suppressed, moved to Paris (1843) and Brussels (1845). There, with **Engels** as his closest collaborator and disciple, he reorganized the Communist League, which met in London in 1847. In 1848 he finalized the *Communist Manifesto* (1848), which attacked the state as the instrument of oppression, and religion and culture as ideologies of the capitalist class. He was expelled from Brussels, and in 1849 settled in London, where he studied economics, and wrote the first volume of his major work, *Das Kapital* (1867). He died with this work unfinished. ▷ **Marxism; Marxism–Leninism; socialism**

Marx, Wilhelm (1863–1946) German politician. A member of the **Centre Party**, Marx pursued a varied legal and political career before serving in the National (constituent) Assembly (1919–20) and then as Chairman of the Centre Party (1922–8). He served as

Chancellor between Nov 1923 and Jan 1925 at the head of a centre-right coalition which renegotiated Germany's **reparations** obligations with the Allies (**Dawes Plan**). In Mar 1925 he was, as the republican candidate, narrowly defeated by **Hindenburg** in the presidential elections. After this he held further ministerial posts, including that of Chancellor (Jan 1927–May 1928). He withdrew from public life in 1932.

Marxism The body of social and political thought informed by the writings of Karl **Marx**. It is essentially a critical analysis of capitalist society contending that such societies are subject to crises which create the conditions for proletarian revolutions and the transformation to socialism. Much of Marx's writing, especially *Das Kapital*, was concerned with the economic dynamics of capitalist societies, seeing the state as an instrument of class rule supporting private capital and suppressing the masses. Because of private capital's need to earn profits or extract surplus value, wages have to be kept to a subsistence minimum. This results in economic contradictions, because it restricts the purchasing power of workers to consume the goods produced. Capitalism is, therefore, inherently unstable, being subect to crises of booms and slumps. Marx's view was that these crises would become increasingly worse, and eventually lead to revolution, whereby the working class would seize the state and establish a dictatorship of the proletariat, productive power would be in public hands, and class differences would disappear (socialism). This classless society would eventually lead to the withering away of the state, producing a communist society. Marxism has sought to popularize and extend this method of analysis to contemporary conditions. In particular, Western Marxism has examined the impact of state intervention in smoothing out the crises of capitalism and establishing a legitimacy for the existing capitalist order through its control over education and the media. In non-industrialized societies Marxism has been adapted to account for revolution in countries where there is no extensive development of capitalism, in contrast to Marx's view of history. It is generally recognized that his writings regarding the transformation to, and the nature of, socialism lacked detail. Consequently, Marxism has adopted a wide range of interpretations. ▷ **Marx, Karl; Marxism–Leninism**

Marxism–Leninism A distinct variant of Marxism formulated by **Lenin** who, prior to the Bolshevik Revolution, argued for direct rule by the proletariat, defined as workers and poor peasants, and in the circumstances of Russia after 1905 advocated direct democracy through the soviets (councils). In practice, the Bolshevik Revolution did not produce a democratic republic, but gave a 'leading and directing' role to the Communist Party, seen as the vanguard of a working class which had insufficient political consciousness to forge a revolution; such a well-organized and disciplined party, operating according to the principles of democratic centralism, would be able to exploit the revolutionary situation and create a new socialist society. Leninist principles of a revolutionary vanguard became the central tenet of nearly all communist parties. They were organized according to the idea of democratic centralism that afforded the leadership, on the grounds of its revolutionary insight, the right to dictate party policy, to select party officials from above, and to discipline dissenting party members. In addition, Lenin modified Marx's theory of historical materialism, contending that revolutionary opportunities should be seized when they arose, without waiting for the social and economic crisis of bourgeois capitalism leading to proletarian revolution. He also developed a theory of imperialism which held that it was the last stage of a decaying capitalism. This was used to justify revolution in feudal Russia, because it was an imperial power, and subsequently to justify communist intervention in underdeveloped countries as part of the struggle between socialism and imperialism. Serious doubts were cast upon Lenin's views by the many failures of the socialism they led to and eventually the collapse of the USSR in 1991. ▷ **Maoism; Russian Revolution**

Mary I (1516–58) Queen of England and Ireland (1553/8). She was the daughter of **Henry VIII** of England by his first wife, **Catherine of Aragon**. A devout Catholic, during the reign of her half-brother, **Edward VI**, she lived in retirement, refusing to conform to the new religion. Despite Northumberland's conspiracy to prevent her succession on Edward's death (1553), she relied on the support of the country, entered London and ousted Lady Jane **Grey**. Thereafter she proceeded cautiously, repealing anti-Catholic legislation and reviving Catholic practices, but her intention was to restore papal supremacy with the assistance of Cardinal **Pole**, and to cement a Catholic union with **Philip II** of Spain. These aspirations provoked a rebellion led by the Protestant Sir Thomas Wyatt (1554), followed by the execution of Lady Jane **Grey** and the imprisonment of Mary's half-sister, Elizabeth (later **Elizabeth I**), on suspicion of complicity. Mary's unpopular marriage to Philip (1554) was followed by the persecution of some 300 Protestants, which earned her the name of 'Bloody Mary' in Protestant hagiography, though her direct responsibility is unproven. Broken by childlessness, sickness, grief at her husband's departure from England, and the loss of Calais to the French, she died in London. ▷ **Cranmer, Thomas; Latimer, Hugh; Reformation** (England); **Ridley, Nicholas**

Mary of Burgundy (1457–82) Daughter of Duke **Charles the Bold** of **Burgundy** and Isabella of Bourbon, she inherited all the Burgundian possessions in France and the Netherlands, as Duchess, in 1477. France repossessed Burgundy and Picardy while the Netherlands rose up against her; Mary married Emperor **Maximilian I** of Austria who restored order in Mary's dominions. By this means the Burgundian possessions came into Habsburg hands; Mary's son **Philip I**, 'the Fair', succeeded her in 1482 when she fell from her horse during hunting and died.

Mary of Hungary (1505–58) Queen of Hungary and Bohemia. The daughter of **Philip the Fair** and Johanna of Aragon, she married Louis II of Hungary, thus becoming Queen of Hungary and Bohemia. In 1531 her brother, Emperor **Charles V**, confident of her administrative capabilities, asked her to act as regent in his Low Countries possessions, which she did from 1531 to 1555. Despite her patronage of the arts and her efficient government, Mary's rule subjugated the interests of the Netherlands provinces to those of Spain and the empire, which, along with the persecution of Protestant heretics, helped lay the ground for the **Eighty Years War**.

Mary of Modena (1658–1718) Queen of Great Britain and Ireland (1685/8). The only daughter of Alfonso IV, Duke of Modena, she married the future James VII of Scotland and II of England, as his second wife, in 1673 when he was Duke of York. They lost five daughters and a son in infancy, but in 1688 she gave birth to James Francis Edward **Stuart** (the future 'Old Pretender'). When William of Orange (the future **William III**) landed in England later that year at the start of the **'Glorious Revolution'**, she escaped to France with her infant son, to be joined there later by her deposed husband. She later gave birth to a daughter and spent the rest of her life at St Germain. ▷ **James VII and II**

Mary, Queen of Scots (1542–87) Queen Consort of France (1559/60). She was the daughter of **James V** of Scotland by his second wife, Mary of Guise. Queen of Scotland at a week old, her betrothal to Prince Edward (later **Edward VI**) of England was annulled by the Scottish parliament, precipitating war with England. After the Scots' defeat at **Pinkie** (1547), she was sent to the French court and married (1558) the Dauphin (later **Francis II**), but was widowed at 18 (1560) and returned to Scotland (1561). A Catholic with a clear dynastic claim, she was ambitious for the English throne, and in 1565 she married her cousin, Henry Stuart, Lord **Darnley**, a grandson of **Margaret Tudor**, but disgusted by his debauchery, was soon alienated from him. The vicious murder of Rizzio, her Italian secretary, by Darnley and a group of Protestant nobles in her presence (1566) confirmed her insecurity. The birth of a son (the future **James VI and I**) failed to bring a reconciliation. When Darnley was found, strangled, after an explosion at his residence (1567), the chief suspect was the Earl of **Bothwell**, who underwent a mock trial and was acquitted. Mary's involvement is unclear, but she consented to marry Bothwell, a divorcee with whom she had become infatuated. The Protestant nobles under Morton rose against her; she surrendered at Carberry Hill, was imprisoned at Loch Leven, and compelled to abdicate. After escaping, she raised an army, but was defeated again by the confederate lords at Langside (1568). Placing herself under the protection of Queen **Elizabeth I**, she found herself instead a prisoner for life. Her presence in England stimulated numerous plots to depose Elizabeth. Finally, after the **Babington** conspiracy (1586) she was brought to trial for treason, and executed in Fotheringay Castle, Northamptonshire. ▷ **Moray, James; Morton, James**

Masaniello (Tommaso Aniello) (1623–47) Neapolitan patriot. A fisherman of Amalfi, he led the successful revolt of the Neapolitans against Spanish rule in July 1647. However, the revolt degenerated into murder and massacre, and Masaniello was assassinated by agents of the Spanish viceroy.

Masaryk, Jan (1886–1948) Czechoslovak diplomat and politician. The son of Tómaš **Masaryk**, after a youth of travelling and developing a variety of skills, he entered the diplomatic service in 1918, and from 1925 to 1938 was Czechoslovak envoy in London. There, his fluent English and personal charm won him many friends, but proved inadequate to prevent Chamberlain imposing the Munich Agreement on his country. He became a popular broadcaster during the war. In July 1941 he was appointed Foreign Minister of the Czechoslovak government in exile, returning with President **Beneš** to Prague in 1945 and remaining in office in the hope of bridging the growing gap between East and West in the developing **Cold War**. On 10 Mar 1948, following the Communist takeover of power in Czechoslovakia, his body was found beneath the open window of the Foreign Ministry in Prague, and it is generally believed that he killed himself in protest at the Stalinization of his homeland. ▷ **Stalin, Joseph**

Masaryk, Tomáš (Garrigue) (1850–1937) Philosopher, politician and first President of the Czechoslovak Republic. Half Czech and half Slovak, he received his university education in Vienna and Leipzig, read and travelled widely, and married an American before becoming Professor of Philosophy at the newly authorized Czech University of Prague in 1882. Entering politics in the nationalistic atmosphere of the 1880s and 1890s, he made his name as an independent of courage and common sense through his many writings and his intervention in several fraught disputes. A deputy in the Czech and Austrian Imperial parliaments off and on after 1891, he was variously a 'realist' and a 'progressive'; but his main political contribution came after 1914 when he travelled abroad to France, Britain, Russia and the USA to win support and recognition for an independent state, first Czech, then Czechoslovak. He became its first President in 1918 and was regularly re-elected until he retired in 1935. His character and authority were crucial in developing a prosperous, democratic republic which, tragically, Britain and France helped Germany to destroy in 1938–9 after his death.

Masinissa (c.240–148BC) Numidian prince. Brought up at Carthage, it was his switch of allegiance to the Romans towards the end of the Second Punic War and help at the Battle of Zama (202BC), which earned him Roman recognition as King of Numidia. A faithful ally of the Romans from then on, he exploited his good relations with them over the next 40 years to encroach upon the territory of the defeated Carthaginians and to carve out for himself a huge kingdom in north Africa. The greatest of the kings of Numidia, his ambitions ultimately came to be feared by Rome and so, on his death, his territory was split up between his sons.

Masire, Quett Ketumile Joni (1925–) Botswanan journalist and politician. A journalist, he was Director of African Echo in 1958 before, with Sir Seretse **Khama**, founding the Botswana Democratic Party in 1962, whose Secretary-General he became. Deputy Prime Minister in 1965, he became Minister of Finance in 1966 and Vice-President 1966–80, taking over the presidency on Sir Seretse Khama's death in 1980.

Mason–Dixon Line The border between Maryland and Pennsylvania, drawn in 1763–7 by the British astronomer Charles Mason (1730–87) and his colleague Jeremiah Dixon (of whom little is known). It is regarded as the boundary of 'the South'.

Massachusetts Bay Company A joint stock company established in 1629 by royal charter to promote trade and colonization along the Merrimack and Charles rivers in New England. Its Puritan stockholders won the right to acquire all of the company's stocks. The company became self-governing, and it elected John Winthrop its first governor. Puritan settlers began what would become the Great Puritan Migration. The first group arrived in Salem in 1630, and later established a settlement in Boston. The company and the Massachusetts Bay Colony were one in the same, but in 1684 the company lost its charter, two years later the colony became part of the Dominion of New England.

Massey, Charles Vincent (1887–1967) Canadian politician and diplomat. In 1952 he became the first native-born Governor-General. In 1925 Mackenzie **King** invited him to join his cabinet but he failed to win a seat in 1926 and he was appointed instead as Canada's first minister to the USA. He was chairman of the 1949 Royal Commission on National Development in the Arts, Letters and the Sciences which inquired into the federal cultural agencies, such as the Canadian Broadcasting Corporation, the National Film Board, the National Gallery and the National Research Council. Its report, submitted in 1951, suggested that a Canadian Council for the 'Encouragement of the Arts, Letters, Humanities and Social Sciences be established' and that Canada's cultural institutions be supported in order to limit US influence.

Massey, William Ferguson (1856–1925) Irish-born New Zealand politician. He emigrated to New Zealand (1870), where he became a farmer. Elected to the House of Representatives (1894), he became Leader of the Opposition (1903) and, in 1912, Prime Minister. The creator of the Reform Party, Massey represented small property owners' fears of **socialism** and crushed the industrial unrest of 1912–13. During **World War I**, he formed a coalition government (1915–19) with Sir Joseph Ward, but remained Prime Minister until his death.

Matabeleland The name given to the region of western and southern Zimbabwe, between the Zambezi and Limpopo Rivers. It was named after the Matabele or Ndebele, a **Nguni** tribe (related to the Zulu) originally located in Natal and the Transvaal. Acquired by the British South Africa Company in 1893, it became part of Southern Rhodesia in 1923.

Mata Hari (Margaretha Gertruida Zelle) (1876–1917) Alleged Dutch spy. She became a dancer in France (1903), had many lovers, several in high military and governmental positions (on both sides during and before **World War I**) and, found guilty of espionage for the Germans, was shot in Paris.

Mataram A major Javanese kingdom, in south-central Java, which rose to prominence towards the end of the 16c. Mataram reached the height of its power under Sultan Agung (1613–46), in a series of strikingly successful military campaigns. However, its domination was short-lived, partly because its expansion soon brought it into conflict with the Dutch East India Company but also because internal rebellion within its territories could not be long suppressed. Under Sultan Agung's incompetent son, Amangkurat I (1646/77), Mataram came close to complete collapse. In the late 17c and the first half of the 18c, the Mataram court was torn apart by internal rivalries, while the Dutch became increasingly influential in the Javanese interior. Finally, under the Giyanti settlement of 1755, Mataram was divided. ▷ **East India Company, Dutch**

Mather, Cotton (1662–1728) US colonial minister. Educated at Harvard, he became the foremost Puritan minister in New England during his time. A polymath, he reported on American botany, and was one of the earliest New England historians. But his reputation suffered lasting disfigurement because of his involvement in the Salem Witch Trials of 1692.

Mathura Situated in the state of Uttar Pradesh and popularly known as the birthplace of Lord Krishna, Mathura is a famous centre of pilgrimage for Hindus. It features prominently in the history of the Indo-Greeks, and the Central Asian empires of India. Menander, the Indo-Greek king (155/ 130BC), the Shakas (88BC) and the Kushanas (AD78) all visited Mathura. Possessing the status of a second capital during **Kanishka**'s reign, in **Harsha**'s time Mathura became renowned for its temples and was also a centre for the textile trade. The Mathura school of art probably began at the end of 1cBC; from it evolved the style of art known as Gupta, which produced some of the greatest Indian religious sculptures.

Matica Slovenska (1861) Slovak cultural-nationalist organization. Modelled on the **Matice Ceska**, this was equally meant to raise funds to publish Slovak works of an essentially political character. It quickly became the centre of the nationalist movement, so much so that the Hungarian authorities closed it down in 1875 and refused to open it despite repeated requests. Other secret bodies took its place from time to time, and it remained a symbol of frustrated nationalism.

Matice Ceska (1831) Czech cultural-nationalist organization. The Czech Foundation was established by František **Palacký** and other writers to publish books in Czech about the Czech people. By 1848 its membership had risen from essentially a handful to over 2 000. However, in due course other organizations took over its leading nationalist role.

Matilda of Tuscany (c.1046–1115) The 'Great Countess' of Tuscany. She was a devoted supporter of the papacy and, in particular, **Gregory VII**, even taking the field at the head of her troops to aid him in his struggle against the **Holy Roman Empire**. In 1077 it was at her stronghold of Canossa that the Emperor **Henry IV** did barefoot penance to the Pope. After Gregory's death in 1085 her lands were ravaged by the Emperor's allies, but she refused to make peace or recognize the anti-pope Clement III. Instead she steadfastly supported Pope **Urban II** until his death in 1099.

Matsudaira Sadanobu (1758–1829) Japanese feudal lord (**daimyo**). He was Chief Senior Councillor of the **Tokugawa Shogunate** from 1787 to 1793, at a time of growing financial crisis for the regime and **samurai** indebtedness to an emerging merchant class. Matsudaira imposed Draconian sumptuary laws to curb merchant extravagance and cancelled the debts of shogunal retainers. His attempt to reinforce the traditional hierarchy (which placed samurai at the top and merchants at the bottom) ultimately failed to stem the tide of social and economic change.

Matsukata Masayoshi (1835–1924) Japanese **genro** (senior statesman). He was a member of the **Satsuma** clique of former samurai (which included **Saigo Takamori** and **Okubo Toshimichi**) who had all played an important role in the **Meiji Restoration** and rose to prominence in the new government after 1868. As Finance Minister in the 1880s and 1890s, Matsukata tackled the serious problem of inflation by pursuing a deflationary policy: withdrawing inconvertible paper notes, increasing indirect taxes and cutting administrative expenditures. He also established the Bank of Japan in 1882 with the monopoly right of convertible note issue and sold off government enterprises to private entrepreneurs to build up the government's specie reserves. Although Matsukata's policies are credited with putting the Japanese economy on a sound footing (Japan adopted the gold standard in 1897), they also contributed to hardship in the countryside, where many small landowners were forced into tenancy as a result of falling prices and increased taxes. Matsukata served twice as Prime Minister (1891–2 and 1896–8).

Matsuoka Yosuke (1880–1946) Japanese diplomat and politician. After studying in the USA, Matsuoka joined the diplomatic service (1904) and attended the Paris Peace Conference (1919) as a member of the Japanese delegation. As Vice-President, and later President, of the South Manchuria Railway, he supported the expansion of Japan's interests in Manchuria. Matsuoka led the withdrawal of the Japanese delegation from the **League of Nations** in 1933 in response to the league's adoption of the Lytton Commission report, which had criticized the actions of the Japanese military in Manchuria. As Foreign Minister (1940–1), Matsuoka sought to strengthen Japan's position in the Far East and counter US hostility to its war in China by concluding the

Tripartite Pact with Germany and Italy (27 Sep 1940) and signing a neutrality pact with the USSR (13 Apr 1941). Matsuoka's grand scheme ultimately failed; **Hitler**'s invasion of the USSR brought the latter into the allied camp, while US hostility to Japan's war in China (1937–45) merely intensified. In 1946 he was indicted as a class-A war criminal, but died before the trial was concluded.

Matteotti, Giacomo (1885–1924) Italian politician. As a talented young deputy, belonging to Filippo **Turati**'s moderate Socialist Unity Party, Matteotti bravely and openly denounced the corruption and intimidation practised by the **Fascist Party** in the 1924 elections, only to be murdered by thugs acting on the orders of **Mussolini**. The murder resulted in widespread hostility and disgust towards Mussolini and a wave of anti-fascist feeling, which briefly threatened to bring an end to his rule.

Matthias (1557–1619) Holy Roman Emperor (1612/19). He was the third son of the Emperor **Maximilian II**. A tolerant man in religious matters, he favoured a policy of moderation towards German Protestants although, as Governor of Austria, he was responsible for suppressing risings of Protestant peasants (1594–7). Elected Emperor on his brother **Rudolf II**'s death, he continued to pursue a conciliatory policy which aroused the antagonism of other Catholic princes, including his nephew and heir, Ferdinand (later **Ferdinand II**), whose more rigid policy was instrumental in provoking the **Thirty Years War** in 1618.

Matthias I, 'Corvinus' (c.1440–90) King of Hungary (1458/90). He was the second son of János **Hunyadi**. He drove back the Turks, and made himself master of Bosnia (1462), Moldavia and Wallachia (1467), Moravia, Silesia, and Lusatia (1478), Vienna, and a large part of Austria proper (1485). He greatly encouraged the arts and letters, founded the Corvina Library and the Pozsony Academy, promoted industry, and reformed finances and the system of justice. However, his rule was arbitrary and his taxes heavy and in the end he had to compromise with the nobility who feared for the loss of their privileges.

Maududi, Maulana Abu'l Ala (1903–79) Muslim revivalist thinker and founder of the **Jamaat-i Islami Party**. Beginning as a journalist, he became known as an opponent of both Pakistani and Indian nationalism. After India gained its independence, he was several times imprisoned by the Pakistan government.

Mau Mau The phrase used by the colonial authorities for the uprising in Kenya, largely among the Kikuyu, which caused a state of emergency in the early 1950s. Its aims were anti-colonial and anti-settler (especially in the formerly Kikuyu 'White Highlands', rather than self-consciously nationalist, and much of its violence was directed against fellow Kikuyu who were thought to be collaborating with the colonial authorities. But the disruption it caused hastened the transition to independence. However, very few of those who fought for Mau Mau benefited materially from the transfer of power.

Maura, Antonio (1853–1925) Spanish politician. As the leader of a regenerationist movement within the Conservative Party, he sought a revolution from above. Autocratic and clerical, he was, however, unable to implement his nebulous ideas because of opposition from both Right and Left. In 1903 he tried, as Prime Minister, to replace *caciquismo* with an indirect, corporate franchise, but was dismissed the following year by King **Alfonso XIII**. His second period in office was from 1907 to 1909; he fell from power after the **Tragic Week**, a popular revolt in Barcelona against conscription. Four years later, he organized a proto-fascist party. Appointed Premier again in 1913, he hoped to become the 'iron surgeon' of the national government, but the Cabinet fell that same year. He headed a further two governments in 1919 and 1921–2.

Maurice (1521–53) Duke (1541/53) and Elector (1547/53) of Saxony. A Protestant, he sided with Emperor **Charles V** and refused to join the Schmalkaldic League when promised the electorship then held by his relative, John Frederick I, the Magnanimous. Made Elector in 1547, Maurice was wary of Charles's Catholic goals; he changed sides and forced the Emperor to accept the Lutheran position in the Treaty of Passau (1552). He then returned to the Imperial camp and was killed, at the Battle of Sievershausen (1553), fighting against Albert II Alcibiades of Brandenburg, who had refused to accept the Passau accord.

Maurice (1567–1625) Stadholder of the United Provinces (1585/1625). The son of **William I, 'the Silent'**, he was elected **Stadholder** of Holland and Zeeland in 1585 and later (1589 onwards) of Utrecht, Overijssel, and Gelderland, also becoming in 1587 Captain-General of the armies of the United Provinces during their War of Independence from Spain. During this period he was probably the leading soldier in Europe. He checked the Spanish advance, and by his steady offensive (1590–1606) liberated the northern provinces of the Netherlands from Spain. During the **Twelve Years' Truce** he entered into domestic political conflict with Oldenbarnevelt, and won the day at the Synod of **Dodrecht** in 1618–19. In the renewed conflict with the Habsburgs in 1621, he commanded the republic, with help from England and France, this time with rather less military success. ▷ **Habsburg Dynasty; United Provinces of the Netherlands**

Maurice (1696–1750) Marshal of Saxony. He was the illegitimate son of Elector Frederick Augustus I of Saxony. In 1711 he was created Count of Saxony. He served with the French against his half-brother, King Augustus III of Poland, in the War of the **Polish Succession**. In 1744 he was put in charge of Louis IV's force set to invade Britain in support to Charles Edward **Stuart**, the Young Pretender. The wreck of the fleet in a storm forced the plan to be abandoned. He was then promoted to field marshal. He won France's last great military victory before the Revolution at **Fontenoy** when he defeated the Duke of Cumberland (11 May 1745) during the War of the **Austrian Succession**.

Mauroy, Pierre (1928–) French politician. He was a teacher before becoming involved with trade unionism and socialist politics, and was prominent in the creation of a new French **Socialist Party** in 1971. He became Mayor of Lille in 1973, and was elected to the National Assembly the same year. A close ally of **Mitterrand**, Mauroy acted as his spokesman during the socialists' successful election campaign. He was Prime Minister from 1981 to 1984.

Maurras, Charles (1868–1952) French royalist journalist and political theorist. He was early influenced by the ideas of Auguste Comte. By 1894 he was established as an avant-garde journalist and a proponent of monarchism. From 1908, in the newspaper *Action française*, his articles wielded a powerful influence on the youth of the country. In 1936 he was imprisoned for violent attacks on the government. At the fall of France (1940), he supported the **Vichy** government, and in 1945 was sentenced to life imprisonment, but released on medical grounds in 1952. ▷ **collaboration** (France); **World War II**

Mauryan Empire A powerful north Indian kingdom (321–185BC) stretching from Afghanistan to southern India, the earliest example in the subcontinent of a state system. Its third ruler, Ashoka, was famous for his Buddhist beliefs and policy of dharma (a code of conduct based on social responsibility).

Mausolus (377/353BC) Dynast of Caria under Persian overlordship. He pursued a policy of expansionism and artistic patronage and **Hellenization**. Mausolus transferred his capital to Halicarnassus on the coast, and encouraged the secession of Chios, Cos, **Rhodes** and Byzantium from their alliance with Athens (357BC); Rhodes and Cos both came under his control. His monumental tomb, the Mausoleum, was regarded as one of the seven wonders of the world. ▷ **Confederacy, Second Athenian**

Mavrokordatos, Alexander (1791–1865) Greek politician. From one of the 11 Phanariot families, during the **Greek War of Independence** he headed the Senate which governed the newly liberated areas of western Greece. In 1822 he helped to draft the provisional constitution known as the Epidaurus Constitution. Under King **Othon**, he led the 'English Party' which favoured constitutional rule. He was briefly the Greek representative in London but was recalled to become, briefly, Foreign Minister and alternate President of the Council (1841). He again held office in 1844 but was replaced by **Kolettis**. During the Russo-Turkish War (1854–7) when the Piraeus was occupied by British and French troops, he was appointed to form a new administration which would maintain Greek neutrality. ▷ **Kolokotronis, Theodoros; Phanariots; Russo-Turkish Wars**

Mavrokordatos, Constantine (1711–69) Alternately Hospodar (Governor) of Wallachia and Moldavia (1730–69). From a Greek Phanariot family, in 1730 he was chosen by the clergy and boyars to succeed his father as Hospodar of Wallachia; in 1733 he was chosen as Hospodar of Moldavia. He cooperated with the Ottoman Porte in resisting the spread of Habsburg and Russian influence into the **Danubian Principalities**. Mavrokordatos introduced a wide-ranging programme of reform, easing the tax burden on the peasantry and abolishing serfdom in Wallachia (1746) and Moldavia (1749). He built schools throughout the provinces and founded the academies at Bucharest and Jassy. In his foreign policy he achieved the reintegration of **Oltenia** into Wallachia (1739). During the Russo-Turkish War (1768–74), he was seized by the Russians and died in captivity. ▷ **Moldavia and Wallachia; Phanariots; Russo-Turkish Wars**

Max, Adolphe (1869–1939) Belgian politician and patriot. First a journalist, then an accountant, he became the Burgomaster of Brussels in 1909. When the German troops approached Brussels in Aug 1914, he boldly drove to meet them and opened negotiations. He defended the rights of the Belgian population against the invaders, and in Sep was imprisoned by the Germans, later refusing an offer of freedom on condition that he went to Switzerland and desisted from anti-German agitation. In Nov 1918 he returned to Belgium, was elected to the House of Representatives, and became a minister of state.

Maxentius (Marcus Aurelius Valerius Maxentius) (d.AD312) Roman Emperor (306/12). Passed over for the succession by Emperor **Diocletian** (305), Maxentius, with the help of his father, the ex-emperor **Maximian**, successfully bid for the throne the following year. Restricted mainly to Italy by his rivals for power, he ruled there from Rome until his defeat by **Constantine I, 'the Great'** in the battle of the Milvian Bridge (312).

Maximian (Marcus Aurelius Valerius Maximianus) (d.AD310) Emperor of Rome (286/305). Roman army officer and friend of **Diocletian**, who made him co-emperor in 286, entrusting him with the government of the western half of the Roman empire and the suppression of the breakaway empire of **Carausius** in Britain and northern Gaul. Forced by Diocletian to abdicate on the same day as himself in 305, Maximian did so only reluctantly and was soon back in active politics again supporting the bid of his son **Maxentius** for the throne (306). Forced to abdicate again in 308, he could not settle down, revolted against **Constantine I, 'the Great'**, now effective Emperor of the West, and ended up committing suicide.

Maximilian (Ferdinand Maximilian Joseph) (1832–67) Emperor of Mexico (1864/7). Born in Vienna, he was the younger brother of Emperor Francis Joseph I, and was an archduke of Austria. In 1863, supported by the French, he accepted the offer of the crown of Mexico, falsely believing that he had the general support of the people of Mexico. This offer was in fact the result of conniving between those conservative Mexicans who sought the overthrow of the government of Benito **Juárez** and the French Emperor, Napoleon III, who wished to further his own interests in Mexico. When the French troops were forced, under US pressure, to withdraw from Mexico, Maximilian refused to abdicate, seeing this as the desertion of his people. He made a brave defence at Querétaro, but his forces were starved into surrender. He was captured and executed, despite petitions for clemency by many European monarchs.

Maximilian I (1459–1519) Holy Roman Emperor (1493/1519). Born Archduke of Austria at Weiner Neustadt, he was the eldest son of Emperor Frederick III and Eleanor of Portugal. Elected King of the Romans (1486), he inherited the Habsburg territories and assumed the imperial title in 1493. He pursued an ambitious foreign policy, based on dynastic alliances, with far-reaching results for Habsburg power. His marriage to **Mary of Burgundy** in 1477 gave his family the Burgundian inheritance, including the Netherlands, of which he was twice regent (1482/93 and 1506/7). This was followed by union with the Spanish kingdoms of Castile and Aragon, when the Spanish crown passed to his grandson, Charles (1516). A double marriage treaty between the Habsburgs and the **Jagiełlon Dynasty** (1506) eventually brought the union of Austria-Bohemia-Hungary (1526). He was involved in conflict with the Flemish, the Swiss, the German princes, and especially with the Valois kings of France. Financial difficulties weakened his campaigns, and he was later forced to cede Milan (1504) to **Louis XII**. He incurred the hostility of the Venetians, and despite the League of Cambrai (1508), suffered defeat. He died, leaving his extended empire to his grandson, as **Charles V**. ▷ **Habsburg Dynasty; Holy Roman Empire; Valois Dynasty**

Maximilian I (1573–1651) Duke (1598/1651) and Elector of Bavaria (1623/51). Educated at the Jesuit college at Ingolstadt, on his succession to the dukedom 1598 he instituted energetic reforms of the country's inefficient bureaucracy and disordered finances. He placed himself at the head of the

Catholic League in 1609 and pledged his support to Emperor **Ferdinand II** in the **Thirty Years War**, obtaining as a reward the confiscated lands of **Frederick V** of the Palatinate. By the Peace of **Westphalia** (1648), the Palatinate was returned to Frederick's heir, Charles Louis, but Maximilian retained the electoral title. The foremost Catholic prince in Germany after the Emperor, Maximilian was a keen defender of German liberties and resisted imperial attempts to turn the empire into a centralized Habsburg monarchy.

Maximilian I Joseph (1756–1825) King of Bavaria. An eventful early political and military career culminated in his accession to the Bavarian throne in Dec 1805. Advised by his minister, Montgelas, Maximilian succeeded in consolidating Bavaria's territory and, in 1818, established a constitutional monarchy.

Maximilian II (1527–76) Holy Roman Emperor (1564/76). The eldest son of Emperor **Ferdinand I** and Anna of Bohemia and Hungary, he became King of Bohemia in 1548 and Emperor in 1564. An intelligent, tolerant and cultivated man who considered himself 'neither Catholic nor Protestant but a Christian', he embarrassed his family by his Protestant leanings and was obliged in 1562 to swear to live and die within the Catholic Church. As Emperor he secured substantial religious freedom for Austrian Lutherans and deplored the intolerance of the Catholic reaction in Spain and France. A patron of the arts and sciences, he set out to make Vienna a centre of European intellectual life.

Maximilian II Emmanuel (1662–1726) Elector of Bavaria (1679/1726). A military leader, he distinguished himself at the capture of Belgrade (1688). He was Governor of the Spanish Netherlands (1692) while fighting for the Habsburgs against **Louis XIV** of France. He supported the French in the War of the **Spanish Succession** and lost his lands as a result (after Blenheim). He was restored to his former possessions after the Peace of Utrecht (1713). ▷ **Habsburg Dynasty**

Maximilian III Joseph (1727–77) Elector of Bavaria. The son of Charles VII, he renounced all claim to the Imperial throne and made peace with **Maria Theresa**. In return, he was able to recover his state which the Austrians had occupied. His capitulation to Maria complicated the plans of **Frederick II, 'the Great'** for checking Austrian power.

Maximilian IV Joseph (1756–1825) Elector of Bavaria and, as Maximilian I, first Wittelsbach King of Bavaria (1806/25). In 1795 he succeeded his brother as Duke of Zweibrücken after having served in a French regiment in Alsace from 1777 to 1789. Austria forced him to attack France in 1799 but he signed a separate peace in 1801. He supported **Napoleon I** but switched to Austria after Napoleon's defeat in Russia and was thereby able to retain his kingdom. He created a liberal state, granting a constitution in 1808 and establishing a bicameral parliament in 1818. ▷ **Napoleonic Wars**

Maximin (d.238) Roman Emperor (235/8). A Roman army officer of Thracian peasant extraction, he spearheaded the mutiny at Mainz in 235 which resulted in the overthrow and murder of the last emperor of the **Severan Dynasty**, **Alexander Severus**. With his elevation to the throne by his troops, the Roman Empire entered upon half a century of internal confusion and civil war.

Maximin Daia (Gaius Galerius Valerius Maximinus) (d.313) Roman Emperor (310/13). He was the favourite of his uncle, the Emperor **Galerius**, and was his loyal deputy in the East (305–10). A noted persecutor of the Christians, Maximin Daia was overthrown by **Licinius** in 313.

Mayakovsky, Vladimir Vladimirovich (1893–1930) Russian poet. He began writing at an early age, and was regarded as the leader of the Futurist school. Involved in underground activity before the **Russian Revolution** (1917) and deeply committed to its success, he emerged as the propaganda mouthpiece of the Communist Party but also wrote satirical plays. Travelling abroad frequently in the 1920s, he became critical of the regime and eventually committed suicide in Moscow.

Mayas The best-known civilization of the classic period of Mesoamerica (250–900). The Maya rose to prominence c.300 in present-day southern Mexico, Guatemala, northern Belize, and western Honduras. Inheriting the inventions and ideas of earlier civilizations, such as the Olmec and Teotihuacan, they developed astronomy, calendrical systems, hieroglyphic writing, and ceremonial architecture, including pyramid temples. The tropical rainforest area was cleared for agriculture, and rain water was stored in numerous reservoirs. They also traded with other distant people, clearing routes through jungles and swamps. Most people farmed, while centres such as Tikal and Bonampak were largely ceremonial and political, with an elite of priests and nobles ruling over the countryside. Maya civilization started to decline, for reasons unknown, c.900, although some peripheral centres still thrived, under the influence of Mexico.

Mayflower Compact (1620) An agreement to establish a 'civil body politic', signed aboard the ship *Mayflower* by members of the Pilgrim party about to settle in the Cape Cod region.

May Fourth Movement (1919) A student demonstration in Beijing which crystallized the political and cultural aspirations of those who struggled for a new China. Originally a protest against the Japanese takeover of Germany's rights in Shandong (agreed by the Western powers at the Versailles Peace Conference), the movement spread nationwide, rallying students and intellectuals across a broad political spectrum. ▷ **Versailles, Treaty of**

May Thirtieth Movement (1925) The large-scale anti-imperialist demonstrations in China which resulted in increased membership for both the Chinese **Communist Party** and the **Guomindang**. On this day, a crowd of workers and students in Shanghai protesting against the earlier killing of a Chinese worker in a Japanese textile mill was fired upon by the British-led International settlement police force. The incident, during which 13 died and many more were injured, led to nationwide strikes and boycotts. The most significant of these was the 15-month boycott against the British colony of Hong Kong following the killing of 52 demonstrators by British and French troops in Canton (23 June 1925). The movement clearly revealed the strength of opposition to foreign privilege in China. The powers, adapting to the new situation, began discussions in 1925 on the return to China of tariff autonomy.

Mazarin, Jules, Cardinal (Giulio Mazarini) (1602–61) Neapolitan cleric, diplomat and politician. He became Papal Nuncio to the French court (1634–6) and entered the service of **Louis XIII** in 1639. Through the influence of **Richelieu** he was elevated to cardinal, succeeding his mentor as First Minister in 1642. After Louis's death (1643), he retained his authority under the Queen Regent, **Anne of Austria**. Blamed by many for the civil disturbances of the **Fronde**,

he twice fled the kingdom, and returned to Paris in 1653 after the nobles' revolt had been suppressed. His foreign policy was more fruitful: he concluded the Peace of **Westphalia** (1648), whose terms increased French prestige, and negotiated the Treaty of Pyrenees (1659), ending the prolonged Franco-Spanish conflict. ▷ **Bourbon, House of**

Mazeppa, Ivan Stepanovich (c.1644–1709) Russian nobleman, and hetman of the Cossacks. Having become a page at the court of Poland, he was involved in an intrigue with a nobleman's wife, and was sent home bound naked upon his horse. Mazeppa now joined the Cossacks, and in 1687 was elected hetman of the Ukraine. He won the confidence of **Peter I, 'the Great'**, who made him Prince of the Ukraine; but when Peter curtailed the freedom of the Cossacks and seemed in any case likely to be defeated by his Swedish enemy, **Charles XII** of Sweden, Mazeppa entered into treasonable negotiations. However, his hopes of an independent crown for the Ukraine perished in the disaster of **Poltava** (1709), and he fled with Charles to Bender, where he died.

Mazzini, Giuseppe (1805–72) Italian patriot. Initiated into the **Carbonari** as a young man, he was arrested by the Piedmontese police and exiled to France, where in 1833 he founded his own movement, **Young Italy**. Expelled from France, he travelled widely in Europe, calling for republican insurrection. During the **Revolutions of 1848–9** he took part first in the Lombard revolt against Austrian rule and, subsequently, in the governing triumvirate of the Roman Republic established after **Pius IX** fled the city. A number of abortive Mazzinian insurrections during the 1850s (notably that of Pisacane) and a growing support for the moderate views embodied by the **Italian National Society** largely discredited Mazzini. In the final decade of his life he continued to preach republicanism and women's emancipation and played a small part in the establishment of the First International, but never managed to reconcile his ideas to those of socialism.

M'ba, Leon (1902–67) Gabon politician. Educated in Catholic schools, he was in turn accountant, journalist and administrator. He was elected for the **Rassemblement Democratique Africaine** to the Gabon Assembly in 1952 and, in the French tradition, used the mayoral position (of Libreville) to enhance his political ambitions. He was Head of Government (1957–60) and President from Gabon's independence until his death in 1967.

Mboya, Tom (Thomas Joseph) (1930–69) Kenyan trade unionist and politician. Educated at Catholic mission schools and Ruskin College, Oxford, he was an employee of the Nairobi City Council when he became Treasurer of the Kenyan African Union in 1953. He was elected Secretary-General of the Kenyan Federation of Labour in 1955 and a member of Legco in 1957. Mboya was a founder member, and Secretary-General (1960–9) of the Kenyan African National Union (**KANU**). His reformist instincts brought him into conflict with his fellow Luo, Oginga **Odinga**, but he eventually won out, forcing Odinga out of KANU after the party's conference at Limuru (1966), thus binding himself closer to Jomo **Kenyatta**. He was Minister of Labour (1962–3), Minister of Justice and Constitutional Affairs (1963–4), Minister for Economic Planning and Development (1964–9) when his essentially Fabian philosophy established the 'free enterprise with state regulation' economic system which Kenya epitomizes. He was assassinated in 1969.

McCarthy, D'Alton (1836–98) Canadian politician. From an Ulster Protestant background, he rose to be one of John A Macdonald's lieutenants, but when Macdonald refused to disallow Quebec's **Jesuits' Estates Act**, he established the Equal Rights Association. The association's title was curiously inappropriate since it sought to limit the use of French in Ontario's schools and to annul Ottawa's acceptance of French as an official language in the North West Territories. The McCarthyites' assertion that they were ready to use force to maintain Anglo-Saxon Protestantism destabilized the Conservative Party, in which moderates argued that confederation required tolerance of French rights. French-Canadians also began to question the old alliance between the **Bleus** and the Ontario Tories. One of the results of his campaign was the enactment of the Manitoba Schools Act.

McCarthy, Joseph Raymond (1909–57) US politician. Educated at Marquette University, Milwaukee, he became a circuit judge in 1939, and after war service was elected Senator in 1946. He achieved fame for his unsubstantiated accusations in the early 1950s that communists had infiltrated

the State Department, and in 1953 became chairman of the Senate permanent subcommittee on investigations. By hectoring cross-examination and damaging innuendo he arraigned many innocent citizens and officials, overreaching himself when he came into direct conflict with the army. This kind of anti-communist witchhunt became known as 'McCarthyism'. His power diminished after he was formally condemned by the Senate in 1954. ▷ **Fifth Amendment; HUAC**

McClellan, George B(rinton) (1826–85) US general. Educated at the US Military Academy at West Point, when the **American Civil War** began, he drove Confederate forces out of West Virginia, and was called to Washington to reorganize the Federal Army of the Potomac. His Virginian campaign ended disastrously at Richmond (1862). He forced **Lee** to retreat at the Battle of **Antietam**, but failed to follow up his advantage, and was recalled. In 1864 he opposed **Lincoln** for the presidency, and in 1877 was elected Governor of New Jersey.

McCulloch v Maryland (1819) US Supreme Court decision which prevented a state interfering with the exercise of a legitimate federal power. McCulloch was a clerk in the Baltimore branch of the Bank of the United States who appealed against an indictment for his failure to affix a state tax stamp on US banknotes. The court sustained his appeal with Chief Justice John **Marshall** declaring that although sovereignty was divided between the national government and the states, the former was supreme 'within its sphere of action'.

McKinley, William (1843–1901) US politician and 25th President. He served in the **American Civil War**, then became a lawyer. As a Republican, he was elected to the US House of Representatives in 1877, and in 1892 was elected Governor of Ohio, despite his name being identified with the unpopular high protective tariff carried in the McKinley Tariff Act of 1890. During the presidential election of 1896 he secured a large majority as an advocate of the gold standard. During his term as President (1897–1901), the **Spanish–American War** (1898) broke out, culminating in the acquisition of Cuba and the Philippines. He was re-elected in 1900, but his second term ended when he was shot by an anarchist in Buffalo, New York. ▷ **Republican Party**

McNamara, Robert Strange (1916–) US politician and businessman. After service in the air force (1943–6), he worked his way up in the Ford Motor Company to the office of President by 1960. A Democrat, in 1960 he joined the J F **Kennedy** administration as Secretary of Defence, being particularly involved in the **Vietnam War**. He resigned in 1967 to become President of the World Bank (a post he held until 1981). In the 1980s he emerged as a critic of the nuclear arms race. ▷ **Democratic Party**

Mecca and Medina, Capture of (1803–4) The holy city of Mecca was vacated in 1803 by Ghalib, the Sharif; thereupon, Saud ibn Abd al-Aziz with his Wahhabis entered and destroyed everything which, in the Wahhabi view, smacked of idolatrous practices, executing all those suspected of being involved in them. Unsuccessful in his attempts to take Medina and Jedda, Saud withdrew and his garrison in Mecca was massacred by the native Meccans. An unsuccessful attempt to mount an attack on the Wahhabis from Baghdad gave Saud the opportunity to return to campaigning in the Hijaz, where he took Medina in 1804, Mecca in 1806, and subsequently Jedda.

Mecklenburg A region which first came under German control in 1160. It converted to Lutheranism during the Reformation. Mecklenburg sided with Denmark and Sweden in the **Thirty Years War** and ceded part of its territory, Wismar, to Sweden in the Peace of Westphalia (1648), which was not returned until 1803. The area, divided into two duchies, joined Napoleon's Rhine Confederation (1808). The Congress of **Vienna** (1814–15) recognized the two as Grand Duchies. The University of Rostock was founded in Mecklenburg in 1419.

Medes An ancient people living to the south-west of the Caspian Sea, often wrongly identified with the Persians. At their peak in the 7c and 6c BC, they conquered Urartu and Assyria, and extended their power as far west as central Turkey. In the east they ruled most of Iran. Their Empire passed to the Persians c.550BC. ▷ **Persian Empire**

Medici A family which made its wealth through banking and which ruled Florence from 1434 to 1494, though without holding formal office. They were overthrown at the start of the **Italian Wars** in 1494, but they returned to power in 1512. They became hereditary Dukes of Florence in 1537 and Grand Dukes of Tuscany from 1569. By that stage, however, their dynastic power base

had shifted away from Florence, first to Rome when Giovanni (1475–1521) became Pope **Leo X** in 1513 and then when Catherine, the niece of another Medici Pope, **Clement VII**, was married to the heir to the throne of France who became **Henry II**. ▷ **Catherine de' Medici**

Medici, Cosimo de', 'the Elder' (1389–1464) Florentine financier, statesman and philanthropist. His father, Giovanni de Bicci de' Medici, appears to have created the Medici wealth, and Cosimo was to use it to fuel the machine of his own power in Florence. He was exiled by the ascendant Albizzi faction in 1433, having opposed the imposition of taxes for what proved a disastrous war. He returned in 1434 and stifled family faction while maintaining the facade of republican government with an attractive mixture of ruthlessness and urbanity. He employed some of his wealth in patronage of the arts, including Europe's first public library, though his encouragement of the platonic revival among humanists may have been designed to make them espouse the contemplative life and stay out of politics. He was posthumously commemorated as 'Pater Patriae'.

Medici, Cosimo I de', 'the Great' (1519–74) Duke of Florence (1537/74) and Grand Duke of Tuscany (1569/74). A skilled soldier, he annexed the republic of Siena in 1555, and doubled the territory of Tuscany during his rule. He devoted his considerable energies to developing the trade and agriculture of Tuscany and to the expansion of its military. He was a notable patron of the arts and a great collector of Etruscan antiquities.

Médici, Emílio Garrastazú (1905–90) Brazilian military dictator. A career military officer, he was Chief-of-Staff to Artur da Costa e Silva in the late 1950s, Military Academy Commander in 1964 and Head of the SNI (National Information Service, the military intelligence operation attached to the presidency) during Costa's government. Nominated President by the military junta in 1969, he governed until 1974, using a military-technocratic team to balance repression and rapid economic growth. He manipulated elections and liquidated guerrillas in major cities as well as Araguaía in Goiás and Pará, at the cost of creating an almost autonomous security apparatus, and stimulated settlement of Amazonia.

Medici, Lorenzo de', 'the Magnificent' (1449–92) Florentine ruler, son of Piero de'

Medici and grandson of Cosimo de' **Medici**. He succeeded as head of the family upon the death of his father, Pietro, in 1469, and was an able, if autocratic, ruler who made Florence the leading state in Italy. In 1478 he showed courage and judgement in thwarting an attempt by malcontents, with the encouragement of Pope **Sixtus IV**, to overthrow the Medici, although the rising led to the assassination of Lorenzo's brother, Giuliano (1453–78). Lorenzo was a distinguished lyric poet as well as being, in the words of **Machiavelli** 'the greatest patron of literature and art that any prince has ever been'.

Medici, Piero de', 'the Gouty' (1416–69) Ruler of Florence (1464/8). The son of Cosimo de' **Medici** and father of Lorenzo de' **Medici**, he revealed his abilities as prince in surmounting a notable constitutional crisis by the judicious use of force. The illness which killed him so young was also to claim Lorenzo.

Medici, Piero de', 'the Unfortunate' (1471–1503) Florentine ruler. The eldest son of Lorenzo de' **Medici**, he succeeded his father in 1492, but his disregard of republican forms made him unpopular. With the invasion of Italy by **Charles VIII** of France in 1494, Piero was obliged to surrender key Florentine forces to the aggressor, a step strongly resented by the civic authorities, who banished the Medici from the state. Piero died fighting against the French in the **Italian Wars**.

Medina Sidonia, Alonso Pérez de Guzmán el Bueno, 7th Duke of (1550–1619) Spanish naval commander and Captain General of Andalusia. He was a distinguished administrator with a good record in conquest of Portugal. Appointed to command the Great **Armada** in the Enterprise of England on the death of the Marquis of Santa Cruz (1588), he led the Armada successfully up the English Channel to rendezvous with Parma off the Dutch coast. He was, however, thwarted by the latter's failure to break out, action by the English fleet and adverse weather. He returned to Spain north-about round Britain, and continued in royal service. He was one of the wealthiest and most influential men in Spain.

Medvedev, Roy Alexandrovich (1925–) Soviet historian, dissident and politician. Although remaining a Marxist, he was highly critical of **Stalin** and other communist leaders. In 1968 he was expelled from the

608

Communist Party and denied employment in academic bodies. However, he continued writing as a private individual; for example he published his best book *Let History Judge* in 1971. In this way he helped to sustain ideological criticism of Leonid **Brezhnev**'s dictatorship. Under Mikhail **Gorbachev** he was able to enter politics. He was readmitted to the party and elected to the Congress and the Supreme Soviet in 1989. His twin brother, Zhores **Medvedev**, also suffered as a critic of Brezhnev.

Medvedev, Zhores Alexandrovich (1925–) Soviet geneticist and dissident. Like his twin brother, Roy **Medvedev**, he became an opponent of the communist system through his scientific studies. As a reputable geneticist, he was particularly critical of the damage **Lysenko** had done with political support. In 1970 he was confined to a psychiatric hospital but was released as a result of protests from abroad. On visiting Britain in 1973, he was deprived of his Soviet citizenship and he stayed on working as a genontological researcher. His publications include *The Rise and Fall of Lysenko*, helping to set the Soviet scientific record straight.

Meech Lake Accord (1987) Canadian constitutional amendment, which recognized French-speaking Quebec as a 'distinct society', in response to the province's demands for special status within the confederation. The agreement was concluded in 1987 but did not receive enough support from the English-speaking provinces to be ratified. The failure of the Accord intensified Quebec separatism and also fuelled resentment among the native Inuit and Indians at their own lack of representation. The Charlottetown Agreement, which balanced concessions for greater autonomy for Quebec and the Inuit and Indian populations with other consitutional reforms aimed at the Western provinces, was put to a referendum on 26 Oct 1992. This was defeated by 54.4 per cent to 44.6 per cent.

Megale Idea Literally, 'the Great Idea', this describes the programme of Greek expansion which was first formulated in the 1840s by Ioannis **Kolettis** and which aspired to the revival of the Byzantine Empire. With Constantinople as its capital, this new Greek empire was to embrace **Epirus**, **Thessaly**, **Macedonia**, **Thrace**, the Aegean islands, Crete, **Cyprus**, the west coast of Asia Minor and **Eastern Rumelia** and all other areas which were Hellenized. This programme of

irredentism was to dictate the course of Greek foreign policy well into the 20c and had a staunch advocate in Eleuthérios **Venizélos**. At the end of **World War I**, the Treaty of Sèvres (1920) brought Greece closer to realizing the Megale Idea but after the Anatolian debacle it forfeited its territorial gains by the Treaty of **Lausanne** (1923). ▷ **Deligiannis, Theodoros; enosis; Rigas, Velestinlis Pheraios**

Megiddo In antiquity, an important town in northern Palestine controlling the main route from Egypt to Syria. Under Israelite control from around 1000BC, it was rebuilt by Solomon (c.970–933BC) as a military and administrative centre. Among its most impressive remains are the 9c stables of the Israelite kings.

Mehemed-Pasha Sokollu, Sokolović (c.1505–79) Grand Vizir of the **Ottoman Empire**. Born to a Serb family and recruited by devşirme, he was trained as a janissary and entered the service of the Sultan. Enjoying the trust of **Suleyman I, 'the Magnificent'**, he was appointed dragoman of the Ottoman fleet (1546) and *beglerbeg* (Governor) of **Rumelia** (1549). After a series of military victories, he rose from Third to Grand Vizir (1555–65). He accompanied Süleyman on his Hungarian campaign and directed operations at the siege of Sigetvár, keeping secret the death of the Sultan lest it demoralize the troops. Under **Selim II** (1566/74) he enjoyed great authority, overseeing the rebuilding of the fleet after the Battle of **Lepanto** (1571). Under Murad III (1574/96) opposition to him mounted and he was murdered. ▷ **Janissaries**

Mehmed I (c.1387–1421) Ottoman Sultan (1413/21). His reign marks the beginning of the recovery from the devastating effects of the conquests of **Timur**. He was the father of Sultan **Murad II**.

Mehmed II, 'the Conqueror' (1432–81) Ottoman Sultan (1451/81). The founder of the **Ottoman Empire**, he was born in Adrianople. He succeeded his father, **Murad II**, in 1451, and took Constantinople in 1453, renaming it Istanbul, thus extinguishing the **Byzantine Empire** and giving the Turks their commanding position on the Bosphorus. Checked by János **Hunyadi** at Belgrade in 1456, he nevertheless annexed most of Serbia, all Greece, and most of the Aegean Islands. He threatened Venetian territory, was repelled from Rhodes by the Knights of St John (1479), took Otranto in 1480 and died in a campaign against Persia.

Mehmed III (1566–1603) Ottoman Sultan (1595/1603). He was the son of **Murad III**, whom he succeeded. On his accession to the throne, he invoked the Law of **Fratricide** by which the sultan could have his brothers put to death. All 19, of whom the eldest was only 11, were accordingly executed by strangulation.

Mehmed IV (1642–93) Ottoman Sultan (1648/87). He succeeded his deposed father, Ibrahim I, as a child, in the middle of a long war with Venice (1645–64). Anarchy in the country was quelled by the appointment of able viziers, Mohammed Köprülü (1656) and his son, Ahmed (1661). In 1664 the Turks were defeated by the Austrians under Montecucculi at the battle of St Gotthard; in a war with Poland (1672–6) the Turks were twice defeated by King **John III Sobieski**, but gained Polish Ukraine, which they lost to Russia in 1681. In 1683 the Turks, under a new Grand Vizier, Kara Mustafa, laid siege to Vienna, which was relieved by John Sobieski. After defeat at the second Battle of Mohács (1687), Mehmed was deposed, and replaced by **Suleyman II**.

Mehmed V (1844–1918) Ottoman Sultan (1909/18). He was Turkey's first 'constitutional monarch', having gained his elevation through the victory of the Young Turks and their deposition of **Abd ul-Hamid II**. A pious and mild man, Mehmed reigned under the control of the Unionist Party, whose power became total in 1913. He was constrained to proclaim a holy war (*jihad*) against the Entente Powers in 1914, but this did not greatly influence his Muslim subjects. As a constitutional monarch, he was unable to wield effective power and as a result it was not he, but initially his Grand Vizier and subsequently Unionist leaders such as Enver and Talat, who controlled affairs. Significantly, it was Enver's German sympathies which turned Turkey's initially neutral stance into a German alignment at the outbreak of **World War I** in 1914.

Mehmed VI (1861–1926) Last Ottoman Sultan (1918/22). He was the brother of **Mehmed V**. Unsuccessful in suppressing the nationalists led by Mustafa Kemal, he died in exile.

Mehta, Pherozeshah (1845–1915) Indian political leader and lawyer. A Parsi from

Bombay, he came under the influence of Dadabhai Naoroji, a successful businessman and nationalist politician, in the late 1860s and early 1870s. Along with Tilak and Gokhale, he was one of the founder-members of the **Indian National Congress**. Mehta started taking a more active interest in the Congress from 1889 and was a prominent leader of the 'moderate' or right-wing faction of the Congress movement, playing an important role in the so-called 'split' in the Congress at a famous session in Surat in 1907. A pioneering journalist and a member of the Bombay Legislative Council since 1886, Mehta was also a member of the Imperial Legislative Council after 1898, until ill health forced him to retire in 1902. He devoted himself in later years not only to Congress politics (of which he became increasingly suspicious), but also to business education and municipal reform, for which he was knighted in 1904.

Meighen, Arthur (1874–1960) Canadian lawyer and politician. A Conservative, in 1913 he became Solicitor-General in Robert **Borden**'s Union government and was the architect of much of its strategy during **World War I**: railway nationalization, conscription and the deeply-resented Wartime Elections Act. It was Meighen who also orchestrated the government's draconian response to the **Winnipeg General Strike** (1919), insisting that organized labour was revolutionary. Both the Immigration Act and the criminal code were amended so that strike leaders would face either deportation or long prison sentences. In 1920 Meighen succeeded Borden as Prime Minister and his high tariff policy was a major factor in the defeat of the Conservative Party in 1921. He became Prime Minister again in 1925 but when the Progressives deserted him, the Governor-General allowed him to dissolve parliament, a mechanism which had not been afforded to Mackenzie **King** in a similar situation. King won the election by promising to prevent such imperial intervention. Meighen then resigned as Conservative leader a few months later, and was replaced by R B **Bennett**. In 1940 the Conservatives invited him to lead the party again but he failed to win a seat and retired from politics.

Meiji Constitution (1889) Promulgated by the Japanese **Meiji Emperor** on 11 Feb 1889, this constitution was to remain in effect until 1947. It was the result of a long debate that had begun with the **Meiji Restoration** (1868), when the new government promised greater

public participation in the political process. By the 1870s, some government leaders like **Kido Koin** were advocating a written constitution on the Western model as a means of unifying the country and to enhance Japan's credentials as a modern state (and thereby persuade the Western powers to revise their unequal treaties with Japan). There was disagreement, however, over the timing and scope of such a constitution. In order to deflect the more radical demands of the **Freedom and People's Rights Movement**, an imperial rescript (12 Oct 1881) promised a parliament by 1890. **Ito Hirobumi**, who had led an investigative mission to Europe in 1882, was charged with drafting a constitution. Influenced by the ideas of German constitutional theorists (whom Ito had met while in Europe) the constitution, presented as a gift by the Emperor to the people, was an authoritarian, if ambivalent, document. Article One stated that sovereignty lay with the Emperor; at the same time, he was to be above the political fray and rule only through his ministers. In line with the notion of 'transcendental' cabinets, such ministers were responsible solely to the Emperor and not to the Diet, which comprised two houses: an appointed upper house and a lower house to be elected on a limited franchise. The Diet could not initiate legislation, although it could veto the government's budget. Basic rights were guaranteed, but could be modified by law. Like cabinet ministers, the military, Imperial Household Ministry, and Privy Council were not subject to Diet control and were directly responsible to the Emperor. The Meiji constitutional system was therefore inherently unstable since each of these institutions could claim to represent the imperial will, while in time political parties in the Diet would demand more power and influence.

Meiji Emperor (Mutsuhito) (1852–1912) Emperor of Japan (1867/1912). He became the symbol of Japan's modernization. He is commemorated by the Meiji Shrine and the Meiji Memorial Picture Gallery, Tokyo, and a large mausoleum at Momoyama, near Kyoto. ▷ **Meiji Restoration; Tokugawa Shogunate**

Meiji Restoration (1868) An important point in Japanese history, when the last **Shogun** was overthrown in a short civil war, and the position of the **Meiji Emperor** was restored to symbolic importance. Powerful new leaders set about making Japan into an industrial state; the four hereditary classes of

Tokugawa Japan were abolished; and new technology and technical experts were acquired from the West. ▷ **daimyo; samurai; Tokugawa Shogunate**

Meir, Golda (1898–1978) Israeli politician. Born in Kiev, she emigrated with her family to Milwaukee, USA, when she was eight. She married in 1917 and settled in Palestine in 1921. She was Israeli Ambassador to the USSR (1948–9), Minister of Labour (1949–56), and Foreign Minister (1956–66). As Prime Minister (1969–74), her efforts for peace in the Middle East were halted by the fourth Arab–Israeli War (1973). ▷ **Arab-Israeli Wars; Mapai Party**

Melanchthon, Philipp (Philipp Schwarzerd) (1497–1560) German religious reformer, whose name is a Greek translation of his German surname, 'black earth'. Educated at Heidelberg and Tübingen, he became Professor of Greek at Wittenberg in 1516 and Luther's fellow worker. His *Loci Communes* (1521) is the first great Protestant work on dogmatic theology, and he composed the Augsburg Confession (1530).

Melbourne, William Lamb, 2nd Viscount (1779–1848) British politician. He became a Whig MP in 1805, and Chief Secretary for Ireland (1827–8). Succeeding as second viscount (1828), he became Home Secretary (1830–4) under **Grey**. Prime Minister in 1834 and 1835–41, he formed a close, almost avuncular, relationship with the young Queen **Victoria**. Defeated in the election of 1841, he resigned and thereafter took little part in public affairs. His wife (1785–1828) wrote novels as Lady Caroline Lamb, and was notorious for her nine months' devotion (1812–13) to Lord Byron. ▷ **Chartists; Whigs**

Méline, (Félix) Jules (1838–1925) French politician. He was a Deputy (1872–1903) and Senator (1903–25), and famous as the champion of the peasantry. He was several times Minister of Agriculture (1883–5, 1896–8 and 1915–16) and campaigned for increases in tariffs on both agricultural and industrial products, which he imposed by the law of 1892 (the Méline tariff). He was Prime Minister (1896–8) of a moderate republican ministry, supported by the *Ralliés*, Catholics who had accepted the republic; in this position he refused to allow the reopening of the **Dreyfus** case.

Menderes, Adnan (1899–1961) Turkish politician. Though educated for the law, he became a farmer, and entered politics in 1932, at first in opposition, then with the party in power under Kemal **Atatürk**. In 1945 he was one of the leaders of the new Democratic Party and became Prime Minister when it came to power (1950). He was deposed (1960) in an army coup, put on trial, and hanged at Imrali.

Mendès-France, Pierre (1907–82) French politician. He entered parliament in 1932 as a member of the **Radical Party**, in 1941 escaping to join the **Free French** forces in England. He was Minister for National Economy under de **Gaulle** in 1945. As Prime Minister (1954–5), he ended the war in Indo-China, but his government was defeated on its North African policy. A firm critic of de Gaulle, he lost his seat in the 1958 election.

Mendoza, Iñigo López de (fl.1450) Spanish statesman and poet. The father of Pedro Gonzalez de **Mendoza** and great-grandfather of Diego Hurtado de Mendoza, he was created Marquis of Santillana by John II of **Castile** in 1445 for his services on the field. Mendoza was a wise statesman, a sturdy patriot, and an admired poet of Petrachan sonnets, lyrics, allegories and didactic poems. He left an excellent account of the Provençal, Catalan and Valencian poets, and was an early folklorist and collector of popular proverbs.

Mendoza, Pedro Gonzalez de (1428–95) Spanish prelate and statesman. The son of Iñigo López de **Mendoza**, he was created a cardinal in 1473 and was later made Chancellor of Castile. As Archbishop of Castile, in 1474 he helped Isabella of Castile gain the throne (as **Isabella I, 'the Catholic'**). He became the Archbishop of Toledo and Primate of Spain in 1482, and was a trusted minister of Isabella and her husband, **Ferdinand II, 'the Catholic'**.

Menelik (1845–1913) Emperor of Ethiopia. The King of Shoa, he succeeded John IV when the latter was killed (1889) in battle with the Mahdists in the Sudan. Menelik had conquered the Galla and Somali people, adding the Ogaden to the Ethiopian state, and had cultivated Europeans, particularly the Italians. He was probably the most powerful indigenous ruler in Africa, but he faced threats from a number of quarters: Egyptian imperialism from the North, the Mahdists in the Sudan, and the Italians in Eritrea and Somalia. He concluded the

Treaty of Wichale or Ucciali with the Italians, interpreting this as a sign of diplomatic friendship. The Italians considered that it gave them a protectorate over Ethiopia and advanced into the interior to make good their claims. However, Menelik had supplied himself with modern arms and the Italians were defeated at the Battle of **Adowa** in 1896, perhaps the greatest success of Africans against Europeans in the Partition of Africa. Mussolini's invasion of Ethiopia in 1936 was a conscious act of revenge. ▷ **Africa, Partition of**

Menem, Carlos Saul (1935–) Argentine politician. While training for the legal profession, he became politically active in the Peronist (Justice Party) movement, founding the Youth Group in 1955. In 1963 he was elected President of the party in La Rioja and in the same year unsuccessfully contested the governorship of the province, eventually being elected in 1983 and re-elected in 1987. In 1989 he defeated the Radical Union Party (UCR) candidate and became President of Argentina. A highly pragmatic ruler, he rapidly jettisoned inflammatory rhetoric to move towards discussion of the Falklands/Malvinas issue, and to begin an ambitious privatization policy.

Menendez y Pelayo, Marcelino (1856–1912) Spanish Catholic thinker. Spanish conservatism owed him a great debt as an ardent and prolific defender of Spanish orthodoxy and tradition. He attacked the ideas of the Enlightenment and even praised the work of the **Inquisition**. He represented the Conservative Party in both the Cortes and the Senate.

Menes ▷ **Narmer**

Mengistu, Haile Mariam (1941–) Ethiopian soldier and politician. He trained at Guenet Military Academy and took part in the attempted coup against Emperor Haile Selassie in 1960, but was not put on trial. He was a member of the Armed Forces Co-ordinating Committee (**Dergue**) which helped overthrow **Haile Selassie** in 1974. He manipulated himself into the chairmanship of the Dergue and became undisputed leader and Head of State in 1977. Allying himself with the USSR and modelling himself upon Cuba's **Castro**, he sought a socialist transformation for Ethiopia, while retaining its territorial borders intact. Mismanagement, drought and internal war weakened his hold on the country and he fled from Addis Ababa

on 21 May 1991, travelling to Zimbabwe where he was offered political asylum.

Menkaure (Mycerinus) (c.2532–2504BC) King of Egypt. The fifth king of the 4th Dynasty, he was the builder of the third pyramid at Giza, forming with those of **Khufu** and **Khafre** the only surviving monuments of the Seven Wonders of the World. At an original height of 218 feet, a much smaller building than either of its predecessors, it was partly cased in granite from Aswan. This material was brought down river from the southern quarries in contrast to the more easily obtained and worked local limestone. A series of finely sculpted slate statues of the king accompanied by his queen or various goddesses was recovered by the Harvard University–Boston Museum of Fine Arts excavations. These were conducted between 1905 and 1927 at the Giza site and included the valley building and mortuary temple connected with the pyramid, where the statues were found.

Mennonites The Dutch and Swiss Anabaptists who later called themselves Mennonites after one of their Dutch leaders, Menno Simons (1496–1559). They adhere to the Confession of Dordrecht (1632), baptize on confession of faith, are pacifists, refuse to hold civic office, and follow the teachings of the New Testament. Most of their one million adherents live in the USA. ▷ **Anabaptists**

Menotti, Ciro (1798–1831) Italian revolutionary. He was involved, with Enrico **Misley**, in an attempt to create a united Italian state. However, his attempt to launch an insurrection in the Duchy of Modena resulted in his arrest and summary execution by **Francesco IV d'Este**.

Mensheviks In Russian literally 'minority-ites', the members of the moderate faction of the Marxist Russian Social Democratic Labour Party, led by J Martov, which split with **Lenin**, who engineered a false majority for his supporters (hence called **Bolsheviks** or 'majority-ites') at the Party's Second Congress in 1903. The Mensheviks particularly opposed Lenin's policy of organizing a small disciplined party dedicated to promoting and provoking revolution. In 1917 some Mensheviks joined the Provisional Government; but from 1918 onwards they were subject to increasing persecution, their leaders forced abroad in 1921 and many one-time members put on trial in 1930–1. ▷ **Russian Revolution**

Menshikov, Alexander Danilovich (1673–1729) Russian field marshal and politician. Born of poor parents in Moscow, he entered the army, distinguished himself at the siege of Azov, and afterwards accompanied **Peter I**, **'the Great'** in his travels to Holland and England. During the war with Sweden (1702–13) he played an important part at **Poltava**, — Peter made him a field marshal on the spot — Riga, Stettin and elsewhere. At the capture of Marienburg the girl who became **Catherine I** fell into Menshikov's hands, and was through him introduced to the Tsar. Towards the end of Peter's reign, Menshikov lost favour owing to extortions and suspected duplicities. But, when Peter died, he secured the succession of Catherine, and during her reign and that of her young successor, **Peter II**, he governed Russia with almost absolute authority. He was about to marry his daughter to the young tsar when the jealousy of the old nobility led to his banishment to Siberia and the confiscation of his estates.

Menshikov, Alexander Sergeevich (1789–1869) Russian soldier. The great-grandson of Alexander Danilovich **Menshikov**, he rose to the rank of general in the Napoleonic campaigns of 1812–15. Seriously wounded at Varna in the Turkish campaign of 1828, he was made head of the Russian navy. His overbearing behaviour and incompetent diplomacy as ambassador at Constantinople contributed greatly to the outbreak of the **Crimean War**. He commanded at Alma and Inkerman with no great skill, and defended **Sevastopol**, but in 1855 was recalled because of illness. ▷ **Napoleonic Wars**

Mentana, Battle of (3 Nov 1867) The defeat of **Garibaldi** at the hands of French troops rushed to Italy by **Napoleon III** to defend Rome. Garibaldi's ill-organized and diplomatically ill-considered attempt to march on the papal capital resulted in the return of the French garrison, which had been withdrawn (Dec 1866) under the terms of the so-called September Convention.

Mentuhotpe II (Nebhepetre) (c.2060/2010BC) King of Egypt. A king of the 11th Dynasty from Thebes, he reunified Egypt c.2040BC, following a period of instability, and inaugurated the Middle Kingdom. He fostered a period of peace and prosperity, winning the loyalty and support of local princes in the provinces. There was a gradual return to fine craftmanship in place of the careless, ungainly work of the preceding Intermediate Period. Mentuhotpe's ruined mortuary temple at Deir al Bahri in western Thebes had a raised terrace approached by a ramp, supporting a square building, either pyramidal or flat-topped, fronted by porticos on two levels.

Menzies, Robert Gordon (1894–1978) Australian politician. He practised as a barrister, entering the Victoria parliament in 1928. In 1934, he moved to federal politics as member for Kooyang. He was Attorney-General (1935–9), Prime Minister (1939–41), and Leader of the Opposition (1943–9), during which time he rebuilt the conservative elements in Australian politics from the disintegrating **United Australia Party** into the formidable **Liberal Party of Australia**. Successful in the 1949 election, he became Prime Minister, an office he held for 16 years, until his retirement in 1966. Old-fashioned in his regard for British traditions, Menzies was also strongly anti-communist and supported US involvement in the Pacific. He led Australia into SEATO, the **ANZUS** pact and actively supported the USA in the **Vietnam War**. He shrewdly exploited the **Australian Labor Party**'s divisions over **communism** in the 1950s, but failed in his attempt to ban the Australian Communist Party. The 'Menzies Era' was one of economic growth and prosperity which made Australia briefly 'the lucky country'. In 1956 he headed the Five Nations Committee which sought to come to a settlement with Gamal Abd al-**Nasser** on the question of the **Suez Crisis**.

Mercia A kingdom of the Anglo-Saxon heptarchy, with its main centres at Tamworth, Lichfield and Repton. Mercian supremacy over the other Anglo-Saxon kingdoms reached its height under **Offa**, whom **Charlemagne** treated as an equal, but by the early 10c Mercia had been brought under the direct rule of **Wessex**. ▷ **Anglo-Saxons**

Mercier, Désiré Joseph (1851–1926) Belgian Roman Catholic primate and theologian. He took holy orders in 1874 and was appointed to a chair at Leuven (Louvain) University in 1882. In 1906 he was appointed Archbishop of Mechelen (Malines) and primate of Belgium; he received a cardinal's hat in 1906. In Flanders (northern Belgium) he was often disliked for his opposition to the **Flemish Movement**, and to the use of the Flemish language in Catholic schools in particular; his social Catholicism also won him much support.

Mercier, Honoré (1840–94) Canadian politician. Leader of the Quebec liberals, he revived the **Parti National** in response to the execution of **Riel** in 1885, bringing both **Rouges** and conservatives into a 'united front' to preserve French Canadian rights. In 1887 he became Premier of Quebec, and sought the support of the Catholic Church with the passage of the **Jesuits' Estates Act**. Realizing that a majority of the English-speaking provinces also sought a greater measure of autonomy, he called an **Interprovincial Conference** in 1887 which supported **Compact Theory of Confederation**. His popular premiership was curtailed by charges of corruption in 1891, when the lieutenant-governor removed him from office. The charges were unproven but the party was badly beaten in the following year and he only just retained his seat.

Merenptah (Baenre) (c.1224/c.1213BC) King of Egypt. He was the thirteenth son of **Ramesses II**. In the fifth year of his reign, the Egyptian army repelled an invasion by Libyans and their allies, the 'people of the sea' somewhere in the Delta. From his reign there exists the only Egyptian written record of the name 'Israel', implying its recognition as an entity possibly some two generations following the Exodus from Egypt (c.1275BC). ▷ **Sea Peoples**

Meroe ▷ **Kush**

Merovingians The original Frankish royal family, formerly chiefs of the Salians, named after the half-legendary Merovech or Meroveus (the 'sea-fighter'). **Clovis I** was the first Merovingian king to control large parts of Gaul; the last to hold significant power was **Dagobert I** (died 638), though the royal dynasty survived until Childeric III's deposition in 751. ▷ **Carolingians; Franks; Huns**

Merriman, John Xavier (1841–1926) English-born South African politician. He went early to South Africa, where his father was Bishop of Grahamstown. He was a member of various Cape ministries from 1875, and Premier (South African Party) from 1908 to 1910.

Merritt, William H (1793–1862) Canadian entrepreneur. He built the Welland Canal, bypassing the Niagara cataract, to provide a major route for exports and imports into American-Canadian interior. The canal was completed by 1829 but essential improvements were not completed until 1848, when the US railways provided a satisfactory alternative which Canadians were ready to use. Merritt was also one of the foremost proponents of **reciprocity**.

Mersen, Treaty of (9 Aug 870) After the death of **Lothair II**, **Charles II, 'the Bald'** annexed all of Lotharingia. The threat of war from his brother, **Louis the German**, led to negotiations in 870 by which Lothair's kingdom was divided between the two, with the land to the east of a line running along the Maas, Ourthe, Mosel and Saone going to Louis and the lands to the west going to Charles. The border followed the language line but took no account of political or religious considerations and was revised in 879 by the Treaty of Ribemont.

Mesopotamia Literally, 'the land between the rivers'; the name in antiquity for the area between the Tigris and Euphrates. It was conventionally divided into two: Lower Mesopotamia, the home of the Sumerian and Babylonian civilizations, stretched from the alluvial plain at the head of the Persian Gulf to Baghdad (central Iraq); Upper Mesopotamia, the home of the Assyrians, extended from Baghdad to the foothills of eastern Turkey. Historically, the former is more important: here the world's first urban civilization emerged during the fourth millennium BC. ▷ **Assyria; Babylonia; Sumer**

Mesopotamia Campaign This campaign in **World War I** represented an effort by the British to safeguard both the route to India and the newly discovered oilfields of Persia. The Ottomans had declared for the German interest in the war and it was thus essential, for the realization of the above two aims, that British arms prevail in Iraq. After the catastrophe of **Kut al-Amara** earlier in the war, a regrouped British offensive under General Maude took Kut early in 1917 and entered Baghdad in Mar of the same year. Further operations on the River Euphrates and the River Tigris as far as Mosul resulted in a complete British occupation of Mesopotamia.

Messalina, Valeria (c.25–c.48) Great grand-daughter of Octavia (sister of the Roman Emperor **Augustus**) and third wife of the Emperor **Claudius**, whom she married at the age of 14. She bore Claudius two children, Octavia (wife of **Nero**) and Britannicus. Messalina's name has became a byword for avarice, lust and cruelty. In the Emperor's absence she publicly married one of her favourites, the consul-designate Silius; eventually Claudius had her executed.

Messenian Wars The three wars by which **Sparta** subjugated and kept control over the neighbouring Messenians in the south-west Peloponnese. The initial conquest (the First Messenian War, late 8c BC) allegedly lasted 20 years, after which the Messenians were made **helots** (serfs). The Second Messenian War (c.650BC) resulted from a revolt and led to the development of Spartan militarism. In 464BC, the Messenians revolted again (the Third Messenian War); after their defeat some were settled by the Athenians at Naupactus (c.456BC). The Messenians were finally liberated after the Battle of **Leuctra** (371BC), and the city of Messene was founded in 369BC. ▷ **Cimon**

Mesta The Spanish guild of sheepowners, instituted in 1273 by **Alfonso X, 'the Wise'**, the *Mesta* was given extensive privileges to protect the country's biggest industry, wool. It was granted rights to pasture its more than 2 million sheep across lengthy tracts (*cañadas*) of countryside, and the right to have its own officials and judges to protect it in the courts; in return, it paid substantial taxes to the Castilian crown. Flourishing in the early 16c, the Mesta decayed later when the country's trade and industry declined. It was fiercely attacked by reforming ministers in the 18c, notably **Campomanes**, to whom its bad reputation is chiefly due, and was eventually abolished in 1836.

Metaxas, Ioannis (1870–1941) Greek general and dictator. He fought against the Turks in 1897, studied military science in Germany, and in 1913 became Chief of the General Staff. On the fall of King **Constantine I** in 1917 he fled to Italy, but returned with him in 1921. In 1935 he became Deputy Prime Minister, and as Premier in 1936 established a fascist dictatorship. He led the resistance to the Italian invasion of Greece in 1940. He remained in office until his death, which, it was rumoured, was brought about by posion administered by agents of **Hitler**.

Metcalfe, Charles Theophilus Metcalfe, Baron (1785–1846) British colonial official. He went in 1808 as an envoy of Lord Minto to the Sikh ruler Ranjit Singh of Lahore, in order to cement the cracks in the East India Company's north-western front. After heading the Delhi Residency (1811–18), he was Resident in Hyderabad (1820–5), where he exposed irregularities in the Nizam's financial relations with the House of Palmer and Co, in whose Hyderabad branch Lord **Hastings**, the then Governor-General, was personally interested. Serving continously in India from 1800, he was Lord Bentinck's right-hand man during most of his government and, following his retirement (1835), acted as Governor-General until the arrival of his permanent successor. He resigned from the service in 1837 and became Governor-General of Jamaica (1839) and Governor-General of Canada (1843). Having succeeded Sir Charles **Bagot** in 1843, he attempted to reverse the trend towards responsible government and reassert his independence of ministers. On his pressing the crown's right to make all appointments, the ministry, including Robert **Baldwin** and **Lafontaine**, resigned, and the assembly showed their support for them in a vote of no confidence. Metcalfe then dismissed the government and, in the following bitterly-fought election campaign, appealed to the country for support; he won, but with a dangerously narrow margin. His ministers were weak and unpopular, although they managed to remain in power for two years. With the end of the mercantile system and repeal of the **Corn Laws**, the need to maintain the colonies in political dependence was diminished and in 1845 Metcalfe resigned, to allow for the introduction of responsible government.

Metellus Numidicus, Quintus Caecilius (2c–1c BC) Roman commander. He achieved great success, though not outright victory, in the war against the Numidian King, **Jugurtha** (109–107BC) (hence the title Numidicus, belatedly awarded him in 106BC). His attempts to thwart the political career of his able and ambitious officer in Numidia, **Marius**, were not only unsuccessful in the short term but they led to a bitter and protracted feud from which Metellus's own career never recovered. He never regained prominence after his return from exile c.99BC.

métis Canadians of Indian and white stock (both French and Scottish, but especially the former). They thought of themselves as a separate people, with a culture which blended their French heritage with Aboriginal skills. Living a semi-nomadic life and dependent on buffalo-hunting, the semi-military structure of their society enabled them to resist the pressures of new settlements. However, the failures of the rebellions in Red River (1869–70) and

Saskatchewan (1885) meant that the *métis* either sank further into poverty or were absorbed into the city, for they did not benefit even from the slender privileges which treaties bestowed on the Indians. ▷ **Red River Rebellion**

Metternich, Klemens (Wenzel Nepomuk Lothar), Prince of (1773–1859) Austrian politician. He studied at Strasbourg and Mainz, was attached to the Austrian embassy at The Hague, and became Austrian Minister at Dresden, **Berlin** and Paris. In 1809 he was appointed Foreign Minister, and negotiated the marriage between **Napoleon I** and **Marie Louise**. He took a prominent part in the Congress of **Vienna** (1814–15), and between 1815 and 1848 was the most powerful influence for conservatism in Europe. His suppression of liberal and nationalist movements contributed much to the tension that produced the upheaval of 1848. After the fall of the Imperial government in that year, he fled to England, and in 1851 retired to his castle of Johannesburg on the Rhine. ▷ **Revolution of 1848**

Mexican War (1846–8) A war between Mexico and the USA, declared by US Congress after it received a message from President **Polk** calling for war. The culmination of a decade of friction resulting from the secession of Texas from the republic in 1835, the war began with General Zachary Taylor's advance into the area between the River Neuces and the Rio Grande. US troops assaulted Mexico City in Sep 1847 and Mexico was subsequently forced to cede most of the present-day south-west USA. This 'national catastrophe' provided the basis for the subsequent struggle between conservatives under **Santa Anna** and liberals under Juárez. ▷ **Guadalupe Hidalgo, Treaty of; Wilmot Proviso**

Mexican War (1862–7) The Mexican government having suspended interest payments on its foreign debt to France, Spain and Britain, **Napoleon III** tried to use this default as a pretext for intervention designed to turn Mexico into a client state of France. A joint expedition of the three European powers in 1862 was followed by a larger French force in 1863, and the proclamation of the Austrian Archduke Maximilian as Emperor of Mexico. The end of the **American Civil War** forced the French to withdraw their troops; Maximilian was captured and executed. The war had always been unpopular in France, and the outcome was seen as a humiliation.

Mezzogiorno The Italian word (literally, 'midday') used to describe Italy to the south of Rome, usually in contrast to the more developed north and centre of the country.

Michael, King of Portugal ▷ **Miguel**

Michael (1921–) King of Romania (1927/30 and 1940/7). The son of **Charles II** of Romania, he first succeeded to the throne on the death of his grandfather, **Ferdinand**, his father having renounced his own claims in 1925. In 1930 he was supplanted by Charles, but was again made king in 1940 when the Germans gained control of Romania. In 1944 he played a considerable part in the overthrow of the dictatorship of Ion **Antonescu**. He announced the acceptance of the Allied peace terms, and declared war on Germany. His attempts after the war to establish a broader system of government were foiled by the progressive communization of Romania. In 1947 he was forced to abdicate and has since lived in exile.

Michael VIII Palaeologus (c.1225–82) Eastern Roman Emperor (1259/82) and founder of the last dynasty to rule in the Byzantine Empire. He distinguished himself as a soldier, and was made regent for the heir to the throne, John Lascaris, whom he ultimately deposed and blinded. His army took Constantinople in 1261, thus re-establishing the Byzantine Empire. He was responsible for the abortive reunion of the Church of Constantinople with that of Rome (Council of Lyons, 1274).

Michael Romanov (1596–1645) Tsar of Russia (1613/45). The great-nephew of **Ivan IV, 'the Terrible'**, he was the founder of the **Romanov Dynasty** that ruled Russia until the revolution of 1917. He was elected by a remarkably widely representative **Zemski Sobor** after a successful revolt against the Poles, when Russia was also threatened with invasion from Sweden. Michael brought to an end the **Time of Troubles** that had plagued Russia since the death of **Boris Godunov** in 1605. He concluded peace with Sweden (1617) and Poland (1618), but he left the business of government largely in the hands of his father, the extremely able Patriarch Filaret (Fedor Nikitch Romanov). The latter reorganized the army and industry with the help of experts from abroad and consolidated the system of serfdom, although raising enough money to fund the state remained a serious problem.

Michael the Brave (1558–1601) Hospodar (Governor) of Wallachia. Threatened by the Ottoman Turks, he submitted to the suzerainty of Sigismund Báthory, Prince of **Transylvania**, and achieved two victories over the Turkish forces (1595). He then pledged his loyalty to the Habsburg Emperor **Rudolf II** and made peace with the Turks (1598), before turning against his erstwhile protector, Báthory, in 1599. He proclaimed himself Prince of Transylvania and went on to conquer Moldavia (1600) taking the title 'Prince of Ungro-Wallachia, Transylvania and Moldavia' but was forced into retreat by the Emperor, whom he then helped to crush a Hungarian rebellion at Goràslàu (1601). His swift changes of allegiance in the past made his loyalty suspect again and he was put to death on the orders of one of Rudolf's generals. Having briefly united the Romanian lands of Transylvania, **Moldavia and Wallachia**, in the 19c he was hailed by the Romanian nationalists as the father of their nation. ▷ **Romanians**

Michurin, Ivan Vladimirovich (1855–1935) Soviet agronomist. In 1875 he started improving fruit varieties by stock-scion grafting on his plot in Kozlov. It was **Lenin** who drew attention to him in 1920, and **Stalin** then exploited him as an example of what could be done through collectivization. He never developed any theories, but after his death **Lysenko** claimed to be his scientific heir and managed in this way to raise his own respectability. In 1932 Kozlov, in the Soviet manner, was renamed Michurinsk.

Mickiewicz, Adam Bernard (1798–1855) National poet of Poland. Born in Lithuania, he was educated in Vilna and published his first poems in 1822. He was arrested and exiled to Siberia for a while for his revolutionary activities, and after the failure of the Polish revolt of 1830–1 he had to flee to the West. After travelling in Germany, France and Italy he wrote his masterpiece, the epic *Pan Tadeusz* (1834). He taught at Lausanne and Paris. Generally he tried to keep the Polish spirit alive through his writings, and in 1853 he went to Italy to organize a Polish legion. He died in Constantinople, his country still not free, but eternally in his debt. ▷ **Napoleon III**

Middle Ages The period of European history between the collapse of the **Roman Empire** in the West and the Renaissance (c.500–c.1500); sometimes, however, the term is restricted in its use to the four or five centuries after the year 1000. By the early 16c, humanists regarded the civilization that followed the fall of Rome as distinctly different from the classical culture that preceded it and the classical revival of their own day. The notion of a separate but inferior medieval civilization has since been transformed into a more positive appreciation of the age and its achievements, notably the emergence of national states, the vigour of cultural life, and the spiritual attainments of the Church in what was above all an age of faith. Though quite a well-defined period between ancient and modern times, it has no obvious beginning, still less an obvious end.

Middle Kingdom In Ancient Egyptian history, the period c.2040–1786BC covering the last 50 years of the 11th Dynasty to the end of the 12th Dynasty. The founders were the princes of Thebes who extended their authority throughout Upper and Lower Egypt, reunifying the country with a central government control, in place of the disruption of the First **Intermediate Period**. Mines and quarries were again worked and trade renewed. Architecture and art regained their former high standard of design and crisp execution. In the 12th Dynasty, by strong government, the adoption of a co-regency to ensure the smooth transition from one ruler to another and the establishment of an almost feudal system to obtain the support of the provincial governors, the kings put the country into a stable, prosperous condition. The conquest of Lower Nubia was undertaken with the boundary set at the 2nd cataract on the Nile. Contacts were maintained with Western Asia, particularly the port of Byblos. The craftsmanship of the Middle Kingdom jewellers and goldsmiths was unsurpassed in taste, beauty of design and technical skill. The strength of the Middle Kingdom administration is demonstrated by its being continued for over a century by officials in the succeeding 13th Dynasty in spite of the short and ever weaker rule of a number of petty kings.

Midway, Battle of (1942) US naval victory. Admiral Chester **Nimitz**, forewarned of Japanese intentions by the breaking of their naval codes, reinforced Midway Island and forced the Japanese to withdraw with the loss of four aircraft carriers. This was the first battle in which the use of aircraft enabled engagement beyond visual range, and together with the Battle of the Coral Sea, saved Australia and Hawaii and stemmed the Japanese push into the Central Pacific.

Miguel (1802–66) King of Portugal (1828/34). The third son of King John VI, he plotted (1824) to overthrow the constitutional form of government granted by his father, but was banished with his mother, his chief abettor. On John's death in 1826, the throne devolved upon Miguel's elder brother, **Pedro I**, Emperor of Brazil; he, however, resigned it in favour of his daughter, **Maria II da Gloria**, making Miguel regent. Miguel then summoned a **Cortes**, which proclaimed him King in 1828. In 1832 Pedro captured Oporto and Lisbon, and Charles Napier destroyed Miguel's fleet off Cape St Vincent (1833). The following year Maria was restored, and Miguel withdrew to Italy.

Mihailović, Draža (1893–1946) Serbian soldier. He rose to the rank of colonel in the Yugoslav Army, and in 1941 remained in Yugoslavia after the German occupation, forming groups (**Chetniks**) to wage guerrilla warfare. He later allied himself with the Germans and then with the Italians to fight the communists. He was executed in Belgrade by the **Tito** government for collaboration. ▷ **World War II**

Mikołajczyk, Stanisław (1901–67) Polish politician. He was born the son of an émigré miner in Westphalia and, returning to independent Poland at the end of **World War I**, he soon entered politics and became leader of the Peasant Party (1931–9). From 1940 to 1943 he held office in the exiled Polish government in London and, following General **Sikorski**'s death, became Prime Minister (1943–4). After the German defeat, he became Deputy Premier in the new coalition government in Warsaw, promoted by the USSR and accepted by the Western Allies. With a large peasant following, he hoped to resist a total takeover by the pro-Soviet communists. However, following rigged elections in 1947 he had no alternative but to flee to the West, where he settled in the USA.

Mikoyan, Anastas Ivanovich (1895–1970) Soviet politician. Educated in a seminary, he became a Bolshevik in 1915 and was active in the Caucasusu. A candidate member of the Central Committee from 1922 and of the **Politburo** from 1926, he supported **Stalin** against **Trotsky** in the 1920s and survived the former's purges in the 1930s. He held various ministerial posts connected with trade, doing much to improve Soviet standards of living and introducing several ideas from the West. Mikoyan survived Stalin and allied with Nikita **Khrushchev**. He was Vice-Chairman of the Council of Ministers (1955–64) and President of the Presidium of the Supreme Soviet (1964–5). An extremely versatile politician, he helped Khrushchev survive the **Anti-Party Plot** in 1957, and in 1962 persuaded Fidel **Castro** to accept the withdrawal of Soviet missiles from Cuba.

Milan, Edict of (313) The edict, issued jointly by the Roman emperors **Constantine I, 'the Great'** and **Licinius** at Milan, which guaranteed Christians freedom of worship throughout the entire empire for the first time. The impetus for the measure came from Constantine's victory over the rival emperor, **Maxentius**, at the Milvian Bridge in Rome (312), which he believed was due to the support of the Christian god.

Miletus The southernmost of the 12 Ionian Greek cities on the western coast of Asia Minor, prosperous and commercially oriented, which founded more than 60 cities in the Hellespont and Black Sea. The birthplace of Thales (c.635–c.545BC), it is commonly regarded as the cradle of Western philosophy. It led the **Ionian Revolt** against Persia in 499BC, and was sacked in 494BC. In the 5c BC, it belonged to the **Delian League**, revolting from Athens in 412BC. In the 4c BC it became subject to the dynasts of Caria. ▷ **Athenian Empire; Hellenization; Mausolus**

Militant Tendency A British political group which came to prominence in the 1980s. Ostensibly, *Militant* is a newspaper published by **Labour Party** members espousing Marxist positions. In practice, critics have argued, the newspaper is a front for a 'party within a party', a separate organization of revolutionary Trotskyists who have entered the Labour Party (*entryism*) to use its organizational base for its own political ends. To all intents and purposes Militant is a cover for the Revolutionary Socialist League, the original British section of the Fourth International. In the 1980s, its supporters infiltrated a number of local Labour parties and the Young Socialists (its youth wing). Fearing the adverse electoral publicity resulting from Militant activities, the Labour Party moved to expel members of Militant on the grounds that they were members of a separate political party, which is against the party's constitution. Many of those expelled took the party to court, but their cases were not upheld. Since then, Militant's influence has declined.

Military Frontier (*Militärgrenze*; *Vojna Krajina*) The broad stretch of borderland which the Habsburgs maintained from the 16c as a militarized buffer zone between their lands and the **Ottoman Empire**. First established along the Croatian-Ottoman border, it was later extended through the Banat of Temesvár and **Transylvania**. It was directly under the control of the War Council in Vienna until 1881 when it was dissolved. ▷ **Croatia, Kingdom of; Habsburg Dynasty; Slavonia**

Military Service Act (1917) Canadian conscription legislation. It was introduced because Canada's voluntary militia had been unable to fulfil the commitment to provide four full divisions on the Western Front. Robert Laird **Borden**'s Minister for Militia, Sir Sam Hughes, had deterred many French-Canadians from volunteering by his Ulster Protestant prejudices. The Act was particularly unpopular in Quebec, where many believed they were being asked to fight for the empire, while being denied equal rights at home. With **World War II** the government tried to maintain a policy of 'no conscription' to ensure national unity, despite continuous pressure coming from the English-speaking provinces, especially after the fall of France. In response **King** held a referendum which showed that although 80 per cent of the English-speaking population wished to free the government from its pledge, 72 per cent of French-Canadians were against doing so. King therefore retained the policy and sacked his Defence Minister when he was advised that there were not enough volunteers to maintain the Canadian commitment after the Normandy landings in 1944. But with the failure of the policy to enlist home defence draftees, King was forced to reintroduce conscription. Protestation from French-Canadians, both among civilians and in the forces, was fierce, while one French-Canadian minister resigned from the government and 34 Quebec Liberals voted against it in a vote of confidence. Even so, King managed to survive the election of 1945, albeit with a reduced majority.

Militia Bill (1862) Canadian legislation to provide better protection against incursions from the USA during their **American Civil War**, and from **Fenian Raids**. The first bill proposed a force of 50000 at a cost of C$1 million per year. Its rejection in favour of a cheaper alternative was seen by the British government as Canadian reluctance to assume their defensive responsibilities, but it was countered by the insistence that Canadians had the right to determine their own defence and how much they would allocate to it. This argument indicated the colony's progress towards autonomy.

Miliukov, Pavel Nikolaevich (1849–1943) Russian historian and politician. As a professor of history in Moscow he wrote extensively on the condition of the people and was almost inevitably drawn into criticizing the Tsarist regime. During the Russian **Revolution of 1905** he campaigned for the establishment of a constituent assembly. In the dumas that followed he led the Constitutional Democrats or **Kadets**, whose aim remained the eventual establishment of a constituent assembly. That became the official policy of the **Russian Provisional Government** in 1917 in which Miliukov was Minister of Foreign Affairs. Unfortunately his wish that Russia should continue the war cost him his job in May and helped to undermine the government that might have made his assembly a reality. It was easy for **Lenin** to dismiss the one and only **Russian Constituent Assembly** in Jan 1918. ▷ **Duma**

Millerand, Alexandre (1859–1943) French politician. He entered parliament (1885) and was Minister of Commerce (1899–1902), the first socialist to hold ministerial office. However, in 1905 he refused to join the SFIO and moved towards the Right, holding office as Minister of Works (1909–10) and of War (1912–13 and 1914–15), when he resigned on complaints of deficiency of supplies. His chief critic, **Clemenceau**, later appointed him *commissaire général* in Alsace–Lorraine (1919). As Prime Minister (1920), he formed a right-wing coalition (**Bloc national**) and gave support to the Poles during the Russian invasion of 1920. He became President in 1920 and resigned in 1924 in face of opposition from the **Cartel des gauches** under **Herriot**. He later entered the Senate. ▷ **Socialist Party** (France)

millet An administrative unit within the **Ottoman Empire**. The subjects of the Ottoman Sultan were divided into millets, according to religious affiliation. There were five major millets or divisions, each under its own religious leaders: Muslim; Orthodox; Jewish; Roman Catholic; and Gregorian Armenian. Tax collection, education and legal matters were organized within each millet.

Milner (of St James's and Cape Town), Alfred, 1st Viscount (1854–1925) British politician and colonial administrator. He established his reputation in Egypt and was appointed Governor of the Cape and High Commissioner in South Africa (1897). There he became convinced that the British position was endangered by the South African Republic (Transvaal), and set about the political rationalization of the region through the **Boer Wars**. He hoped to encourage sufficient English-speaking immigration to outnumber the Boers in a South African dominion. He additionally became Governor of the Transvaal and Orange River Colony in 1901, but was forced to resign in 1905 as a result of irregularities over Chinese labour he had introduced for the Rand gold mines. He was Secretary for War (1916–19) and Colonial Secretary (1919–21), and died in Kent, England.

Milorg Abbreviated form of *Militær Organisasjonen*, the secret resistance force formed in Norway following the German invasion of the country in Apr 1940. ▷ **Norway, German Invasion of**

Milošević, Slobodan (1941–) Serbian politician. He joined the Communist League in 1959 while a student. In 1966 he entered government service as an economic adviser to the Mayor of Belgrade and later held senior posts in the Yugoslav federal banks and gas industry (1969–83). Appointed President of the Serbian League of Communists in 1984, he became President of Serbia in 1988. Both a Serbian nationalist and a hardline Communist Party leader in the pre-**perestroika** mould, he withdrew the status of Kosovo and Vojvodina as autonomous provinces within the Republic of Serbia. He remained in power after the multi-party elections held in Serbia in 1990. The crisis in Yugoslavia gathered pace in 1991, when Milošević at first refused to accept a Croat, Stipe Mesić, as President of Yugoslavia, and when it was revealed that he had appropriated £875-worth of Yugoslav federal reserves to buttress the Serbian economy. Bitterly opposed to the break-up of Yugoslavia, after Slovenia and Croatia declared their independence in June 1991, he agitated for the Yugoslav federal army to be sent into Slovenia and Croatia and later, in Apr 1992, into Bosnia Herzegovina. An unrepentant champion of a 'Greater Serbia', he has done nothing to prevent the fighting in Bosnia led by avowedly 'independent' Serbian militias bent on joining the greater part of the newly-independent Republic of Bosnia to the Republic of Serbia and eliminating all non-Serb residents

through '**ethnic cleansing**'. ▷ **Kučan, Milan; Tudjman, Franjo**

Miltiades (c.550–489BC) Athenian aristocratic general and politician. He was the chief architect of the Greek victory at the Battle of **Marathon**. He was also the father of **Cimon** by the Thracian princess, Hegesipyle. ▷ **Persian Wars**

Milyutin, Vladimir Petrovich (1884–1937) Russian economist. Menshevik, turned Bolshevik, turned practical economist, he joined the Russian Social Democratic Party in 1903 when only 19; but by 1917 he was as well schooled in prisons as in splits in the party. He tended to waver in his politics which may have turned him to economics, a discipline in which the communists were short of specialists. He held various posts, including both Commissar for Agriculture (1919–22) and vice-chairman of Gosplan (1929–37). ▷ **Bolsheviks; Mensheviks**

Min (1851–95) Consort of the Korean king, Kojong (1864/1907). She was the leader of a powerful faction at court, mainly comprising members of her own family, which was strongly opposed to increased Japanese influence in Korea. Min was assassinated in a palace coup instigated by the Japanese Minister to Korea, Miura Goro, in an attempt to secure control over the Korean King. The plot misfired, however; Miura was cashiered by his own government while King Kojong increasingly looked to China for protection.

Minamoto Family An important Japanese family that dominated politics for most of the **Heian Era** (794–1185). The family was an offshoot of the imperial line when Emperor Saga (809/23) gave the surname Minamoto to 33 of his 50 children. They were treated as ordinary nobles and in time comprised individual lineages that were only loosely unified. Most members of the Minamoto clan remained in the capital as high civil officials. Others distinguished themselves in the eastern provinces as warrior chieftains, of whom the most notable was Minamoto no Yoritomo (1147/99). After defeating his rivals in 1185, Minamoto no Yoritomo established a military government in eastern Japan, which became the basis of the **Kamakura Shogunate** — the first of Japan's warrior governments which dominated the country until the 19c.

Mindon (1814–78) Burmese king of the Konbaung Dynasty. Mindon came to the throne in Feb 1853, having launched a revolt against his half-brother, King Pagan Min, in the final stages of the Second Anglo-Burmese War. Quickly bringing that war to an end, Mindon sought throughout his long reign to prevent a further extension of British power at his kingdom's expense. He established comparatively cordial relations with the British (important commercial treaties were concluded); Burmese diplomatic missions were sent to a number of the other European powers, in an attempt to secure arms and alliances; and domestic reforms were undertaken, notably the improvement of internal communications. In 1857 he established a new capital at Mandalay. Mindon gave Burma 25 years of comparative peace, but the fundamental internal and external problems facing Burma could not be solved. His death led to a bloody succession struggle at the court: Burma entered a new period of extreme instability, leading to the Third Anglo-Burmese War (1885) and the final collapse of Burmese independence.

Mindszenty, József (1892–1975) Roman Catholic Primate of Hungary. He became a priest in 1915, Archbishop of Esztergom and Primate in 1945, and Cardinal in 1946. He then acquired international fame in 1948 when he was charged with treason by the communist government in Budapest. He was sentenced to life imprisonment the following year, but in 1955 was released on condition that he did not leave Hungary. At the end of the **Hungarian Uprising** in 1956 he was granted asylum in the US legation, where he remained as a voluntary prisoner until 1971, when conditions in Hungary eased and he was allowed to go abroad. He spent his last years in a **Hungarian** religious community in Vienna.

Ming Dynasty (1368–1644) The last indigenous Chinese dynasty, founded by **Ming Hongwu**, and finally replaced by the Manchu **Qing Dynasty** after peasant rebels had sacked Beijing and driven the last emperor to commit suicide. Its capital was shifted from Nanjing (Nanking) to Beijing in 1420 by the Yongle Emperor, who was responsible for building such monuments as the Forbidden City and the Temple of Heaven.

Ming Hongwu (Ming Hung-wu) (1328–98) Emperor of China (1368/98). This was the reign title of Zhu Yuanzhang (Chu Yuanchang), founder of the Chinese **Ming Dynasty**. The son of a peasant, he became a leader of the Red Turbans, one of a number

of Buddhist and Daoist-inspired millenarian sects that rose in revolt against the Mongol **Yuan Dynasty** during the 1340s. In 1356 he captured Nanjing and during the next few years disposed of his rivals to establish his own dynasty, the Ming. His reign was marked by the consolidation of imperial power (the post of Senior Chancellor was abolished and all central government organs were placed directly under the Emperor), agrarian reconstruction (low land taxes, reforestation, and resettlement of abandoned land) and intimidation of the landed and scholarly elites, a reflection of Zhu Yuanzhang's commoner origins.

Ming Yongle (Ming Yung-lo) (1360–1424) Emperor of China (1402/24). The reign title of Zhu Di (Chu Ti), the third Emperor of the Chinese **Ming Dynasty**. The fourth son of **Ming Hongwu**, he had been enfeoffed as the Prince of Yan (Yen), present-day Beijing. When he was passed over in the succession by his nephew, Ming Jianwen (1398/1402), he rose in revolt, eventually seizing the throne for himself. In 1421 Ming Yongle transferred the capital from Nanjing to Beijing, where it has remained ever since, and began the construction of the Imperial Forbidden City. Ming Yongle's reign also witnessed the expansion of China's land frontiers and an attempt to assert China's influence in South-East Asia, with the maritime expeditions organized by the court eunuch, **Zheng He** (Cheng Ho).

Ministeriales A group of court officials who were originally unfree retainers. In the 9–10c German kings looked increasingly to this group for their warriors and officials in order to curb the power of the nobility. They came to be of great political importance, particularly in the 12c when they became the chief instruments in the attempts of the **Hohenstaufen Dynasty** to rebuild the power of the monarchy after the **Investiture Controversy**.

Minoan Civilization The Bronze Age culture, named after Minos, the legendary King of Crete, which flourished in the Aegean area in the third and second millennia BC, reaching its zenith around the middle of the second millennium (1700–1450BC). Its most impressive remains come from Crete: the large palace-like structures at **Knossos**, Phaestus, Mallia and Zakron reveal a sophisticated society, with a complex centrally-controlled economy, a highly developed bureaucracy, and evidence of trading contacts far beyond the Aegean itself (eg the Levant and Egypt).

Minoan civilization came abruptly to an end c.1450BC. The cause is unknown: earthquakes, tidal waves and invading Mycenaeans are all possible reasons for its demise. ▷ **Mycenaean Civilization**

Minobe Tatsukichi (1873–1948) Japanese constitutional scholar. A member of the House of Peers (Upper House of the Diet), he was accused by the military in 1935 of *lèse-majesté* for his views on the Emperor. A supporter of party cabinets and democratic constitutionalism, Minobe asserted that the Emperor was an 'organ' of the state, a notion that was seen as an attack on the sacred nature of the imperial institution. Amidst growing calls during the 1930s by both the military and civilian ultra-nationalists for the elimination of 'dangerous thoughts', Minobe was forced to resign from the House of Peers and many of his works were banned.

Minto, Gilbert John Elliot-Murray-Kynynmound, 4th Earl of (1845–1914) British colonial administrator. After serving in the Scots Guards (1867–70) and working as a journalist in Spain and Turkey (1874–7), he fought in the second Afghan War (1879) before going to Canada. As Governor-General (1898–1905) he was an intermediary between the Prime Minister, Wilfrid **Laurier**, and Joseph Chamberlain, the British Colonial Secretary. As Viceroy of India (1905–10), in succession to Lord Curzon, he found an associate in John Morley, the radical Secretary of State. Both were convinced that something must be done to associate articulate Indian opinion more closely with the government. The two men, though different in their origins and natures, made an effective team. Among the problems tackled by Minto and Morley were the securing of better representation of important Indian interests and the enlargement of the powers of the existing legislative councils. The Indian Councils Act, the core of what is generally known as the **Morley–Minto Reforms**, became law in 1909. As a result of a campaign by a Muslim delegation for representation of Muslim interests through special constituencies this law introduced the principle of communal representation. Six special Muslim constituencies of land-holders were created for the Imperial Legislative Council, and others in some other provinces. This measure is considered as the official germ of Pakistan.

Minutemen Militiamen, particularly in New England, who were prepared to take up arms at very short notice. They were important in the first months of the US War of Independence, before the creation of a regular continental army under George **Washington**. ▷ **Bunker Hill, Battle of; Lexington and Concord, Battles of**

mir A peasant commune in pre-revolutionary Russia (also known as *obshchina*). Its origins and functions were disputed, but after the emancipation of the serfs in 1861 it exercised collective authority of an economic and quasi-judicial nature over the peasants. Among its most important functions were the periodic redistribution of land-allotments among its members and the collection and payment of taxes and redemption dues. ▷ **Russian Serfs, Emancipation of the**

Mirabeau, Honoré Gabriel Riqueti, Count of (1749–91) French revolutionary politician and orator. Elected to the **Estates General** by the Third Estate of Marseilles (1789), his political acumen made him a force in the National Assembly. He advocated a constitutional monarchy on the English model, but failed to convince **Louis XVI**. As the popular movement progressed, his views were also rejected by the revolutionaries. He died in Paris before the climax of the Revolution. ▷ **French Revolution**

Mirambo (c.1840–84) King of the Nyamwezi. He was the most important of the warrior kings of the Nyamwezi people of Tanzania, who became traders connecting the East African coast to the interior in the 19c. Mirambo created military bands of followers called ruga-ruga who were influenced by the age-regiment system of the Ngoni people, and by the 1870s was able to control the Swahili traders conveying ivory and slaves to the coastal ports.

Miranda, Francisco de ('the Precursor') (1750–1816) Venezuelan revolutionary. After serving in the Spanish army, he fled in 1783 to the USA, and travelled widely in Europe. Actively plotting for Spanish-American independence, he organized (from New York) a disastrous expedition to Venezuela (1806). In 1810, he returned to Venezuela to take part in the struggle for independence then under way. Two years later, having been given dictatorial powers, he was captured by royalists and sent to Spain, where he died in prison in Cádiz. ▷ **Spanish–American Wars of Independence**

Mircea the Old (1386/1418) Prince of Wallachia. Threatened by the Ottoman

Turks in the south and by the Hungarians in the north, he preserved the independence of his principality through a mixture of diplomacy and warfare. His alliance with Władysław II Jagiełłon of Poland deterred the Hungarians from further advance (1389) so that, as the Ottomans approached yet closer, he was able to conclude a defensive alliance with the Hungarian King Sigismund (1395). He extended his territory to rule over Muntenia, **Oltenia**, Banatul, Severinuliu, **Dobrudja** and Moldavia as far as the River Prut. His fortunes changed after the accession of Sultan Mehmed I (1413/21) and after 1415 he was obliged to pay tribute to the Porte and to surrender Dobrudja. ▷ **Moldavia and Wallachia; Romanians**

Mishima Yukio (Hiraoka Kimitake) (1925–70) Japanese writer. He passionately believed in the chivalrous traditions of Imperial Japan, became expert in the martial arts, and in 1968 founded the Shield Society, a group of a hundred youths dedicated to a revival of **bushido**, the **samurai** knightly code of honour. The most extreme expression of his elitist right-wing views was in an essay *Sun and Steel* (1970); in the same year he committed suicide by performing hara-kiri after a carefully-staged token attempt to rouse the nation to a return to pre-war nationalist ideals.

Misley, Enrico (1801–63) Italian revolutionary. Having been introduced to Italian nationalist ideas as a young man, he conceived the bizarre plan of persuading one of the most reactionary rulers in Italy, **Francesco IV d'Este**, to put himself at the head of a liberal, nationalist movement. Francesco seems initially to have been flattered by the plans but he had no love for liberalism and in 1829 Misley (who it has been suggested may have been a paid agent provocateur) left Italy for France. In 1832 he published a shrill and mendacious attack on Austrian hegemony in Italy. He spent most of the rest of his life in Spain, where he pursued a successful career as a financier and industrialist.

Missouri Compromise (1820) An agreement to admit Missouri, with slavery, and Maine (formerly part of Massachusetts), without it, to statehood simultaneously, in order to preserve a sectional balance in the US Senate. The compromise also forbade slavery in the rest of the **Louisiana Purchase** lands, north of 36°30. It was in effect until 1854, when it was repealed by the **Kansas–Nebraska Act**.

Mita A Spanish word (originally meaning 'turn') which refers to a forced labour system, instigated by the Spanish crown in 1574, which provided a regular trained workforce for its great colonial mining complexes in the Andes. First used in Inca times for rotary labour, the term was then applied to labour recruitment under the **encomienda** and, later, to *repartimiento* labour. Under Spanish rule, each year one seventh of all adult males in Indian communities were sent to work in the mines and refining mills; these *mitayos* worked one week in three at fixed wages, hiring themselves out as free labourers (*mingados*) for the other two weeks. Mitayos provided a subsidy for the vast Spanish mining operation in the 17c, but were displaced by free labour by 1812, when labour tributes were abolished.

Mitakshara A commentary on the lawbook of Yajnavalkya, written by Vijnaneshvara, a medieval jurist, who was at the court of the great Chalukya emperor, Vikramaditya VI (1075–1127). There are two great schools of family law, Mitakshara, and Dayabhaga. Most families of Bengal and Assam followed the rules of Dayabhaga, while the rest of India generally followed Mitakshara. These two schools became the basis of civil law and were to remain so until very recently. They deal with property rights in a Hindu joint-family system. Both systems refer among other things to property held jointly by the male members of the family. According to the Dayabhaga school it is only on the death of the father that the sons can claim rights to the property, whereas in the Mitakshara school the sons can claim this right during the lifetime of the father. In either case the father does not have absolute rights over property.

Mitbestimmung As early as 1848, German working-class organizations had demanded their rights of *Mitbestimmung*, or co-determination, in the workplace. However, effective employee rights of co-determination (as against mere consultation) have only come into existence with the establishment of the Federal Republic. The 1952 Factory Constitution Law (or *Betriebsverfassungsgesetz*) allowed co-determination in social matters, but similar rights across a broad range of company affairs was introduced in the iron, steel and coal industries at that time and universally in larger firms in 1976. Elected workers' and staff representatives sit on the upper board (*Aufsichtsrat*) of German companies where they enjoy equal rights with shareholders' representatives in defined key areas. Co-determination is not unrestricted in Germany, but the contemporary system is regarded by the trade unions and the **SPD** as an important element of the democratic order.

Mitchell, James Fitzallen (1931–) St Vincent and the Grenadines politician. He trained and worked as an agronomist (1958–65) and then bought and managed a hotel in Bequia, St Vincent. He entered politics through the St Vincent Labour Party (SVLP) and in the pre-independence period served as Minister of Trade (1967–72). He was then Premier (1972–4), heading the People's Political Party (PPP). In 1975 he founded the New Democratic Party (NDP) and, as its leader, became Prime Minister in 1984, achieving re-election in 1989.

Mithridates VI Eupator (d.63BC) King of Pontus (c.115/63BC). He was a Hellenized ruler of Iranian extraction in the Black Sea area, whose attempts to expand his empire over Cappadocia and Bithynia led to a series of wars (the Mithridatic Wars) with Rome (88–66BC). Though worsted by Sulla (c.86BC) and Lucullus (72–71BC), he was not finally defeated until Pompey took over the eastern command (66BC). Mithridates avoided capture, but later took his own life.

MITI (Ministry of International Trade and Industry) The powerful Japanese government ministry created in 1949 to formulate and implement trade and industrial policy. The initial aim was to provide unified control over industrial recovery and export growth so as to end dependence on US aid. Until the mid-1960s MITI exercised total control over imports and exports, and allocated imported technology, investment funds and resources to those sectors (coal, steel, shipbuilding) deemed crucial for industrial growth. After the mid-1960s, in response to foreign accusations of protectionism, MITI relaxed its controls and began to liberalize foreign trade, although it continued to exercise influence over the economy through informal 'administrative guidance', encouraging rationalization of industry (such as mergers) and recommending loans for chosen institutions. As a key component of the 'economic bureaucracy', MITI has played a crucial role in Japan's post-war recovery and its attainment of economic superpower status. On retirement, many of its officials become executives of leading private corporations, illustrating the close ties that exist between government and business.

Mitre, Bartolomé (1821–1906) Argentine politician. Exiled by General Juan Manuel de **Rosas**, he returned to the country as a follower of General Justo José de Urquiza after the Battle of Monte Caseros, which brought about Rosas's downfall. He became Governor of Buenos Aires in 1860. As President (1862–8), he created a national administrative structure in Buenos Aires, set about the construction of railroads and encouraged immigration, while eliminating *caudillos*. He was defeated by Domingo **Sarmiento** in the 1868 presidential elections. In 1870 he founded the newspaper *La Nación*, and in 1874 attempted a coup against Sarmiento's choice for President, Nicolas Avellanada. Mitre failed, however, to rally support among the *estancieros*, and was jailed. He made another bid for the presidency in 1891 as the candidate for the *Union Civica*, but withdrew in favour of the Conservative candidate.

Mitsotakis, Costas (Constantine) (1918–) Greek politician. Leader of the New Liberals, a party on the centre-right founded in 1977 which claims to be the successor to the Liberal Party of his uncle, Eleuthérios **Venizélos**. Since 1990 he has served as Prime Minister and Minister for the Aegean in the government of Constantine **Karamanlis**.

Mitterrand, François (Maurice Marie) (1916–) French politician. Having served in the French Army (1939–40) and been taken prisoner, he escaped from capture and was active in the **Resistance Movement**. Elected a Deputy in 1946, and at once appointed a cabinet minister, he continued to hold office frequently for the rest of the Fourth Republic; he belonged to none of the major parties, but was a member of a tiny faction, the UDSR (*Union démocratique et socialiste de la Résistance*, 'Democratic and Socialist Union of the Resistance'). In 1958 he was a stubborn opponent of de **Gaulle**, and of the new constitution, which he characterized as being semi-fascist, in a book entitled *Le Coup d'Etat permanent* (1964). He worked assiduously to unify the left, standing unsuccessfully as the left-wing candidate in the 1965 presidential elections. After the collapse of the Left in 1968, and its very poor showing in the 1969 presidential elections, in which he was not a candidate, he achieved this aim in 1971 when the SFIO (**Socialist Party**) merged with various left-wing groups, including Mitterrand's own, to form the new Socialist Party of which he was at once elected leader. This was followed by agreement with the French Communist Party on a common programme (1972). Although this was later denounced by the communists, the two parties remained close allies. After he was elected President in 1981, a coalition government that included communists was formed (1981–4), which embarked on a major programme of nationalization and job creation; in 1983 this produced economic crisis, and had to be abandoned. The right won the parliamentary elections of 1986, opening a period of 'cohabitation', in which his powers as President were restricted, but Mitterrand won the presidential elections of 1988, and managed to achieve in the parliamentary elections of the same year an assembly with no overall majority, but in which it was possible to form left-wing cabinets, thus restoring his political authority. ▷ **Republic, Fourth** (France)

Mlada Bosna The revolutionary organization (literally, 'Young Bosnia') opposed to **trialism** and to the Austrian annexation of Bosnia (1908). Its members were drawn from the Bosnian–Serb intelligentsia.

Mlynar, Zdenek (1930–) Czechoslovak politician. Coming of age in communist Czechoslovakia, educated in law in Moscow in the last years of **Stalin** and the first years of **Khrushchev**, and then observing the slow stagnation of the **Novotný** years in Czechoslovakia, he became a reformer through disillusionment. However, during the period of the **Prague Spring**, when he became a secretary of the purged Communist Party Central Committee, he made a major contribution to Alexander **Dubček**'s action programme and was one of the leaders abducted to Moscow following the Soviet invasion. Released with the others, he quickly lost his party function and eventually, when he signed **Charter 77**, he lost his employment and went abroad.

MNR ▷ **Renamo**

Moabites An ancient Semitic people who in Old Testament times inhabited the area to the south-east of the Dead Sea. Like the Ammonites, they were believed to be descended from Lot.

Mobutu, Sese Seko Kuku Ngbendu Wa Za Banga (Joseph Desire) (1930–) Zairean soldier and politician. After army training and a period of study in Brussels, he joined the Belgian Force Publique in 1949. By 1956 he was a colonel. He joined Patrice

Lumumba's Mouvement National Congolais in 1958 and was Chief of Staff in 1960 at the time of independence. The indecisiveness of government in Leopoldville led him to take over the government to deal with the problem of Katanga's secession but he handed power back to civilians within five months. After the 1963–5 civil war, he intervened again, this time permanently. He renamed the country Zaire in place of the Belgian Congo and imposed a degree of stability on to the country which had hitherto been unknown. Backed by US money and the power of the army, his regime has become increasingly corrupt and unpopular.

Modder River, Battle of (1899) One of the engagements of the second Boer War through which the British hoped to relieve the Siege of **Kimberley**. The Boers had command of a hilltop, a traditional Boer tactic; but as this made them vulnerable to modern artillery, they gave up the hilltop and dug trenches by the river. The British failed to take the positions, and were defeated two weeks later at Magersfontein, putting back the relief of Kimberley by three months. ▷ **Boer Wars**

Moderate Party (*Partido Moderado*) The party which dominated Spanish party politics from 1834 to 1868, together with the **Progressive Party**. The Moderate Party was more conservative than its chief rival, though their differences were more of degree than principle. The representative of the large landowners and aristocrats, loosely organized and venal, the Moderate Party dominated the period 1843–50 under General **Narváez**, supported the rule of the Liberal Union 1858–63, and returned to power under Narváez again in 1863–8. The Constitution of 1845 best embodied its principles. The Moderates' oligarchical style of rule was revived under the **Restoration System** of 1875–1923.

Moderates (*Modérés*) French political grouping. The name applied for most of the Third Republic to the more conservative part of the republicans, as opposed to the radicals and socialists. Originally known as the **Opportunists**, and then as the Progressists, between 1900 and 1940 they were usually known as the Moderate Republicans, or simply as the Moderates. They were organized in two factions: the *Alliance démocratique* ('Democratic Alliance'), more to the Left, and the *Fédération républicaine* ('Republican Federation'), more to the

Right. The heirs to this tradition were the **Independents** (1948–62) and then (since 1966) the **Independent Republican Party**. ▷ **Republic, Third** (France)

Moderate Unity Party (Sweden) The name adopted in 1969 by the party of Swedish Conservatives, previously called 'The Right', whose origins can be traced back to 1904. It last formed an administration in 1928–30 under Arvid Lindman, but has participated in non-socialist coalitions since **World War II**. In the person of Carl Bildt it provided a prime minister for the administration formed in 1991.

Moeller van den Bruck, Arthur (1876–1925) German writer. A radical right-winger, he was strongly opposed to Weimar's parliamentary order and toyed with Bolshevik as well as right-wing and racist ideas. In 1923 he published *The Third Reich* whose title was subsequently adopted by the National Socialists to describe the successor state to the **Weimar Republic**. ▷ **Bolsheviks; Nazi Party; Reich**

Mohács, Battle of (1526) A significant Turkish victory in Europe, when the army of the Ottoman sultan, **Suleyman I, 'the Magnificent'** annihilated a Hungarian force one fifth its size under King Louis II outside Buda. Louis was killed, Hungary was plunged into civil war, and the way was opened for a long period of Turkish and particularly Habsburg domination of the old Hungarian kingdom. Since Louis was simultaneously King of Bohemia/Moravia, the Czech throne was also made vacant and was likewise occupied by the Habsburg Archduke Ferdinand, marking the beginning of an Austrian rule that lasted until 1918. ▷ **Habsburg Dynasty**

Mohamed, Murtala Ramal (1937–76) Nigerian soldier. A Muslim Hausa from Northern Nigeria, he trained at Sandhurst and the Royal School of Signals before returning to Nigeria and then serving in the **UN** Congo operations in 1960. He commanded the Nigerian 2nd Battalion at the start of the Biafran War and was made federal Commissioner of Communications in 1974. When General **Gowon** was deposed in 1975, he became Head of State, but he was himself assassinated in an unsuccessful uprising on 13 Feb 1976.

Mohammadan Educational Association The body founded by Sayyid Ahmed Khan

to disseminate elements of European knowledge to Indian Muslims. In 1872 Khan was instrumental in the establishment of a Select Committee which discussed the educational needs of the various classes within Muslim society. The Committee's report led to the concept of a school that was intended to serve all Muslims and cut across sectarian differences. A number of Hindus donated to his cause, and after 1873 Hindus were expected to participate in the student body. In June 1875 the Mohammadan Anglo-Oriental College of Aligarh was opened. The institution enrolled students at the elementary level and adopted the standard government curriculum under an English headmaster within a carefully constructed Islamic environment. Between 1882 and 1902 Aligarh had sent up 220 Muslim graduates. Aligarh elites formed a very important section of the Muslim intelligentsia and played a crucial role in the formation of the **Muslim League**.

Mohammed Ahmed (1844–85) The **Mahdi**. Born in Dongola, he was for a time in the Egyptian civil service, then a slave trader, and finally a relentless and successful rebel against Egyptian rule in the eastern Sudan. He made El Obeid his capital in 1883, and defeated Hicks Pasha and an Egyptian army. In 1885 Khartoum was taken, and General **Gordon** killed. He died later that year, at **Omdurman**.

Mohammed Nadir Shah (c.1880–1933) King of Afghanistan (1929/33). The brother of **Dost Muhammad**, as Commander-in-Chief to **Amanullah Khan** (ruler and later King of Afghanistan from 1926) he played a prominent role in the third of the **Afghan Wars** against Britain (1919), which secured the country's full independence in 1922. He subsequently fell into disfavour and was forced to live in exile in France. In 1929, with British diplomatic support, he returned to Kabul and seized the throne, immediately embarking on a programme of economic and social modernization. These reforms, however, alienated the Muslim clergy and in 1933 he was assassinated. He was succeeded by his son, Mohammed **Zahir Shah**.

Moi, Daniel T arap (1924–) Kenyan politician. Educated in local schools he was a primary school, and unqualified, teacher (1946–56). He entered Legco in 1957 and then was elected for the Baringo constituency which he represented 1963–78. Chairman of the Kenyan African Democratic Union

(KADU) 1960–1, he was Minister of Education in the coalition pre-independence government 1960–1 and, after KADU had merged with the Kenyan African National Union (**KANU**), he was made Minister of Home Affairs (1964–7). He became Vice-President of Kenya in 1967 and succeded Jomo **Kenyatta** on the latter's death in 1978. He has shifted the ethnic balance of central politics away from the Kikuyu towards the Kalenjin peoples of the Rift Valley and has cracked down hard on dissidents and opponents, reducing the already limited opportunities for meaningful political participation available to Kenyans. Despite an attempted coup in Aug 1982 he has remained in power.

Moldavia and Wallachia Two independent Balkan principalities formed in the 14c: Moldavia lies in north-eastern Romania, south-west of the River Prut; Wallachia lies in southern Romania, south of the Transylvanian Alps. In the 16c they were incorporated into the **Ottoman Empire**, but the **Russo-Turkish Wars** during the 18–19c weakened Turkish control of the Balkans, and the two states gained autonomy under a Russian protectorate by the Treaty of **Adrianople** (1829). In 1862 Moldavia and Wallachia merged to form the unitary Principality of Romania; Russian Moldavia became a Soviet Socialist Republic in 1940.

Molé, Louis Matthieu, Count (1781–1855) French politician and writer. His father was guillotined during the Terror. In his *Essai de morale et de politique* (1806) he vindicated **Napoleon I**'s government on the ground of necessity, and was made a count. **Louis XVIII** made him a peer and minister for the navy. **Louis-Philippe** made him Foreign Minister and, in 1836, Prime Minister, but his regime was unpopular. He left politics after the coup d'état of 1851. ▷ **Terror, Reign of**

Molinos, Miguel de (1640–97) Spanish divine. Ordained in 1652, in 1675 he published his *Spiritual Guide*. He was arrested for his views, which embodied an exaggerated form of Quietism, and after a public retraction, was condemned to life imprisonment.

Mollet, Guy Alcide (1905–75) French socialist politician. A schoolteacher and member of the **Socialist Party**. In 1946 he became Mayor of Arras, a Deputy in the National Assembly, Secretary-General of the Socialist Party and a cabinet minister in the Léon **Blum** government. He survived the

international crisis over the Anglo-French intervention in Suez (Nov), but fell from office in May 1957. In 1959 he was elected a Senator, remaining leader of the SFIO until its absorption into the new Socialist Party in 1971, which ended his political influence.

Molly Maguires A secret organization of (primarily) Irish miners, involved in industrial disputes in Pennsylvania, USA, during the 1870s. The prosecution of their leaders led to hangings and imprisonments, which crushed their group.

Molotov (Skriabin), Vyacheslav Mikhailovich (1890–1986) Soviet politician. Of middle-class origin and a student at Kazan University, he became a Bolshevik in 1906 and was close to **Lenin** and **Stalin** during the **Russian Revolution** in 1917. He subsequently acted as Stalin's right-hand man, first in domestic politics and, from 1939 onwards, as Foreign Minister, in foreign affairs. Holding office until 1949, he negotiated the Nazi–Soviet Pact with Ribbentrop and was then Stalin's chief adviser at the **Tehran Conference** and **Yalta Conference**, and was present at the founding of the **UN** (1945). After **World War II**, he emerged as the uncompromising champion of Soviet ambition; his *nyet* ('no') at meetings of the UN became a byword, and helped to foster the **Cold War**. He was less in favour in Stalin's last years, but became Foreign Minister again in 1953 until he was forced out by Nikita **Khrushchev** in 1956. He was then a leading figure in the failed **Anti-Party Plot** in 1957, but was gracefully allowed to occupy two further official posts before retiring in 1962. ▷ **Bolsheviks; communism; German–Soviet Pact**

Molotov Cocktail (1939–40) A bottle filled with petrol, kerosene and tar used by Finnish soldiers as an anti-tank weapon during the Russo–Finnish War with the USSR. Originally the fuse was a rag ignited with a match, but eventually ampules of sulphuric acid were used. With little armour themselves the Finns used their Molotov Cocktails with devastating effect. The name 'Molotov' was that of the Soviet Foreign Minister. ▷ **Molotov (Skriabin), Vyacheslav Mikhailovich**

Moltke, Helmuth (Karl Bernhard), Count von (1800–91) Prussian field marshal. He entered Prussian service in 1822, and became Chief of the General Staff in **Berlin** (1858–88). His reorganization of the Prussian Army led to the successful wars with

627

Denmark (1863–4), **Austria** (1866) and France (1870–1). ▷ **Austro-Prussian War; Franco-Prussian War; Prussia**

Moluccans, South The name given to the inhabitants of a group of islands in the Indonesian archipelago, also known as the Spice Islands, of which the largest is Ambon; many South Moluccans now live in the Netherlands. Since the 14c, the islands have been heavily integrated into the European colonial empires, and under the Dutch East Indies regime the South Moluccans often assisted the Dutch in running the colony, especially as soldiers in the colonial army. With the independence of Indonesia in 1949, the South Moluccans were denied their own republic (*Republik Maluku Selatan*, RMS), and many soldiers and their families were transported to the Netherlands as a temporary measure in 1949–50. At that time both the South Moluccans and the Dutch government expected the soldiers and their families to return to South-East Asia; they were therefore put in temporary camps and were kept largely isolated from Dutch society. After 20 years the situation had become impossible: in the 1970s a younger generation of South Moluccan militants in the Netherlands tried to attract attention to their problems in the Netherlands and Indonesia by a series of terrorist actions, including hostage-taking and the hijacking of two trains. No progress has been made towards a Moluccan republic, but the South Moluccans in the Netherlands have now been rather better integrated into Dutch society as a whole.

Moluccas (Maluku) Islands in the eastern Indonesian archipelago, commonly known as the Spice Islands. The most important islands include Ternate, Tidore, Ambon, Ceram and the Banda group. From the beginning of the 16c, the islands became the focus of fierce rivalry between the Portuguese and the Spanish, and then between the Dutch and the English, for control over their valuable clove, nutmeg and mace production. By the mid-17c, the Dutch had achieved pre-eminence, and used their domination to restrict production in order to secure monopoly profits. Dutch intervention and control of the local population and economy was intense, and was reflected, in part, in the emergence of a substantial Christian population, particularly on Ambon. The islands were brought within the Indonesian Republic in 1950, although local resistance and resentment has never been fully stilled.

Momoh, Joseph Saidu (1937–   ) Sierra Leone soldier and politician. Educated in secondary school in Freetown and military academies in Ghana, Britain and Nigeria, he was commissioned into the Sierra Leone army in 1963. He was a battalion commander by 1968 and was appointed a minister of state in 1975. When Siaka **Stevens** announced his retirement in 1985, Momoh, who had been hand-picked to be Stevens's successor, was endorsed by the country's only political party, the All People's Congress, as the sole presidential candidate. Having won the election, he has sought to distance himself from his predecessor's policies in an attempt to restrain corruption and reform the economy.

Mon An agricultural people of Burma and Thailand, thought to have come originally from western China, establishing a kingdom in Burma in about the 9c. They introduced Buddhism and Pali writing into Burma, and were subjugated by the Burmans by the 18c. They speak an Austro-Asiatic language, also known as Tailang. Population now c.670 000.

Mon, Alejandro (1801–82) Spanish politician and administrative reformer. As Minister of Finance in 1844–5, he created the tax system that was the basis of government finance for the rest of the 19c. Accordingly, he has been dubbed 'The Peel of Spain'.

Monash, Sir John (1865–1931) Australian soldier. He practised as a civil engineer and also held a commission in the Australian Citizen Force (1887), rising to command the 13th Infantry Brigade by 1913. He commanded the 4th Australian Infantry Brigade at Gallipoli (1914–15), the 3rd Australian Division in France (1916), and the Australian Corps as Lieutenant-General (1918). Recognized as one of the outstanding generals of **World War I**, he was noted for the meticulous preparation and planning of his operations. After the war, he was chairman of the Victorian State Electricity Commission. ▷ **Gallipoli Campaign**

Monck, George (1608–70) English general. He fought in the Low Countries, and with the royalists in Scotland, then joined the **Commonwealth** cause and served successfully in Ireland, Scotland, and (1652–4) in the first of the **Anglo-Dutch Wars**. He feared a return to civil war during and after Richard Cromwell's regime (1658–9), and was instrumental (as commander of the army in Scotland) in bringing about the **Restoration** of **Charles II**, for which he was created Duke of Albermarle. ▷ **English Civil Wars**

Mondlane, Eduardo (1920–69) Mozambiquan nationalist leader. Educated in mission schools, he furthered his training at Fort Hare College and Lisbon University and developed into a respected sociologist with research posts in the USA and with the UN. He returned to Mozambique in 1961 to form **Frelimo** and launched the guerrilla war against Portuguese colonialism in 1964. He was murdered by a parcel bomb in Dar es Salaam.

Mongkut (1804–68) The 4th King of the **Chakri Dynasty** of Thailand. Passed over for the throne on the death of his father in 1824, Mongkut entered the monkhood. By the late 1830s he had emerged as, in effect, the leader of a reformist order, the *Thammayutika*. Mongkut ascended the throne in 1851. His reign, which lasted until his death in 1868, is perhaps most noted for the opening of the kingdom to political and commercial intercourse with the Western powers, a process marked by the signing of the Bowring Treaty between Thailand and Britain in 1855. Mongkut also undertook a limited measure of internal reform, and he paid close attention to the education and training of his son, Chulalongkorn, who was to succeed him in 1868.

Mongolia Originally the homeland of nomadic tribes, which united under **Genghis Khan** in the 13c to become part of the great Mongol Empire, Mongolia was assimilated into China, and divided into Inner and Outer Mongolia. Outer Mongolia declared itself an independent monarchy in 1911; the Mongolian People's Republic was formed in 1924, but was not recognized by China until 1946.

Mongols The general name applied to the linguistically related tribes of Central Asia and southern Siberia who effected the violent collapse of the 'Abbasid Empire before converting to Islam. United under **Genghis Khan** in 1206, they spread into what are now Iran and Russia and then conquered China under his grandson, **Kublai Khan**, who ruled as first emperor of the **Yuan Dynasty**. After Kublai's death they began splitting up, and over the next two or three centuries they were gradually pushed back to the territories they now inhabit. About 3 million now live in the Chinese autonomous region of Inner Mongolia, and about 2 million in the People's Republic of Mongolia. ▷ **'Abbasid Dynasty; Golden Horde**

Monkey Trial ▷ **Darrow, Clarence**

Monmouth, Battle of (1778) An engagement in New Jersey between British and American troops during the US War of Independence. It was notable for Washington's suspension of General Charles Lee (1731–82) from command, and for the discipline of American troops under fire. ▷ **American Revolution; Washington, George**

Monmouth, James, Duke of (1649–85) Illegitimate son of **Charles II** of England. He was created Duke of Monmouth in 1663, and became Captain-General in 1670. He had substantial popular support, and as a Protestant became a focus of opposition to Charles II. After the discovery of the **Rye House Plot** (1683), he fled to the Low Countries. In 1685 he landed at Lyme Regis, and asserted his right to the crown. He was defeated at the Battle of **Sedgemoor**, captured, and beheaded. ▷ **James VII and II**

Monnet, Jean (1888–1979) French political economist and diplomat. He introduced in 1947 the Monnet Plan for the modernization of French industry. He was President of the European Coal and Steel High Authority (1952–5), and of the Action Committee for the United States of Europe (1956–75). ▷ **EEC**

Monroe, James (1758–1831) US politician and 5th President. After serving in the War of Independence, he entered politics, becoming a member of the Senate (1790–4), Minister to France (1794–6), Governor of Virginia (1799–1802), Minister to England and Spain (1803–7), and Secretary of State (1811–17). During his 'era of good feeling' he signed the **Missouri Compromise**, acquired Florida, and set forth the principles of the **Monroe Doctrine**. He won an easy re-election in 1820. ▷ **American Revolution**

Monroe Doctrine A major statement of US foreign policy, proclaimed in 1823, attributed to President James **Monroe**, but written by Secretary of State John Quincy **Adams**. The doctrine was issued after renewed interest in the Americas by European powers, especially Britain and Russia, following the Spanish-American revolutions for independence. It announced (1) the existence of a separate political system in the Western Hemisphere, (2) US hostility to further European colonization or attempts to extend European influence, and (3) non-interference with existing European colonies and dependencies or in European affairs.

Monseny, Federica (1905–) Spanish anarchist writer and leader. She fought for women's rights within both the **CNT** and the **FAI**. Monseny strongly supported anarchist participation in the Popular Front elections of Feb 1936. She became Minister of Public Health in the Republican government of Sep 1936–May 1937 — the first woman in Spain to achieve a ministerial portfolio. Exiled to France in 1939, she remained active in anarchist circles, returning to Spain in 1975.

Mons Graupius, Battle of (AD83) The battle fought at an unidentified site (possibly near Mount Bennachie, Aberdeenshire) between Roman forces under Gnaeus Julius **Agricola** and Caledonians under Galgacus. The Roman victory enabled them to establish extensive, though temporary, settlement in north-eastern Scotland. Agricola's ambition to conquer the whole of Britain was not realized; fortifications were abandoned and legions withdrawn from northern Scotland later in the same decade. ▷ **Britain, Roman**

Montagu–Chelmsford Reforms After a report (Apr 1918) by the Secretary of State for India, E S Montagu, and the Viceroy, Lord Chelmsford, the British agreed the 1919 Government of India Act. Promising progressive moves towards Indian self-government within the British Empire, it provided as a first step enlarged electorates, and partial provincial autonomy whereby responsibility for certain aspects of government was transferred to elected Indian ministers; at the centre a bicameral legislature comprising a Council of State and a Legislative Assembly with increased powers. The number of Indians on the central executive council was also enlarged; the Indian government gained a larger degree of independence from the control of Whitehall. It was rejected by many Indians, and its promise of future progress was resisted by some British Conservatives, but a further step was taken, with full provincial autonomy under Indian control, in 1935. ▷ **Government of India Acts**

Montalembert, Charles René Forbes de, Count of (1810–70) French historian and politician, the eldest son of a noble French *émigré* and his English wife. In 1830 he eagerly joined the Abbé **Lamennais** and Henri Lacordaire in *L'Avenir*, a Catholic liberal newspaper. Montalembert, who had succeeded to his father's peerage, pleaded with great eloquence the cause of religious liberty, in spite of the papal condemnation of

L'Avenir. A famous protest against tyranny was his great speech (Jan 1848) upon Switzerland. After the **February Revolution** (1848) he was elected a member of the National Assembly; and he supported Louis Napoleon (**Napoleon III**) until the confiscation of the Orléans property, when he became a determined opponent of the imperial regime. He visited England in 1855, and wrote *De l'Avenir politique de l'Angleterre*, and many other works on medieval Church history, and on contemporary political topics; he sought, in vain, to reconcile Catholicism and liberalism.

Montcalm (de Saint Véran), Louis Joseph de Montcalm-Grozon, Marquis of (1712–59) French general. During the **Seven Years War**, he took command of the French troops in Canada (1756), and captured the British post of Oswego and Fort William Henry. In 1758 he defended Ticonderoga, and proceeded to the defence of **Quebec**, where he died in the battle against General James **Wolfe** on the Plains of Abraham.

Montefeltro Lords of Urbino in north-east Italy in the **Renaissance**. Federigo (d.1484) was the ideal prince: a successful **condottiere**, politician, and patron of the arts. The most famous Renaissance handbook for courtiers, by Castiglione, was based on the author's experience of the Montrefeltro court of Federigo's son, Guidobaldo, c.1504. ▷ **Papal States**

Montenegro A constituent republic of the Federal Republic of Yugoslavia, a mountainous region bounded south-west by the Adriatic Sea and south-east by Albania. The area was part of the Roman province of Illyria, settled by Slavs in the 7c and established as the independent province of Zeta. In the late 12c it was incorporated into the Serbian empire. Montenegrin independence was recognized at the Congress of **Berlin** (1878), although border disputes with Albania continued. The country retained its independent monarchy until 1918, when King Nicholas was deposed and Montenegro absorbed into Serbia. Of the six republics that made up Yugoslavia as established in 1945 (Croatia, Slovenia, Bosnia-Herzegovina, Macedonia, Montenegro and Serbia), only Serbia and Montenegro remained as the Federal Republic of Yugoslavia declared on 27 Apr 1992. In the elections of 1993, Momir Bulatovic was appointed President and Radoje Kontic as Prime Minister-designate. There were demonstrations in 1993 by elements of the Montenegrin population who favoured independence from Serbia.

Montesa, Order of A military order founded in the crown of **Aragon** by King Jaime II, to replace the Order of Templars, abolished by the Pope in 1312. It derived its name from the Castle of Montesa in Valencia, formerly a Templar stronghold. Granted approval by the Pope in 1317, it came to possess extensive estates (*encomiendas*). Members were in theory subject to semi-monastic discipline. ▷ **encomienda**

Montespan, Françoise Athenäs de Rochechouart, Marchioness of (1641–1707) Mistress of **Louis XIV**. She replaced Mlle de La Vallière as the king's mistress c.1667, and after her marriage was annulled (1674) received official recognition of her position. She bore the king seven children who were legitimized (1673). Supplanted first by Mlle de Fontanges and later by Mme de **Maintenon**, she left court in 1687 and retired to the Convent of Saint-Joseph, Paris, eventually becoming the Superior.

Montesquieu, Charles-Louis de Secondat, Baron of la Brède and of (1689–1755) French philosopher and jurist. Educated at Bordeaux, he became an advocate, but turned to scientific research and literary work. He settled in Paris (1726), then spent some years travelling and studying political and social institutions. His best-known work is the comparative study of legal and political issues, *De l'esprit des lois* (1748), which was a major influence on 18c Europe.

Montezuma I (c.1390–1464) Aztec Emperor of Mexico (c.1437/64). His reign is notable for the annexation of Chalco and the crushing of the Tlascalans.

Montezuma II (1466–1520) The last Aztec Emperor of Mexico (1502/20). A distinguished warrior and legislator, he died at Tenochtitlán during the Spanish conquest. One of his descendants was Viceroy of Mexico from 1697 to 1701. ▷ **Cortés, Hernan**

Montfort, Simon de, Earl of Leicester (c.1208–65) English politician and soldier. In 1238 he married **Henry III** of England's youngest sister, Eleanor, and as the king's deputy in Gascony (1248) put down disaffection with a heavy hand. He returned to England in 1253, became the leader of the barons in their opposition to the king, and defeated him at Lewes (1264). He then became virtual ruler of England, calling a parliament in 1265; but the barons soon grew dissatisfied with his rule, and the ing's army defeated him at Evesham, where he was killed. ▷ **Barons Wars**

Montgomery (of Alamein), Bernard Law, 1st Viscount (1887–1976) British field marshal. Commissioned into the Royal Warwickshire Regiment (1908), in **World War II** he gained renown as arguably the best British field commander since **Wellington**. A controversial and outspoken figure, he was nevertheless a 'soldier's general', able to establish a remarkable rapport with his troops. He commanded the 8th Army in North Africa, and defeated **Rommel** at the Battle of **El Alamein** (1942). He played a key role in the invasion of Sicily and Italy (1943), and was appointed Commander-in-Chief, Ground Forces, for the Allied **Normandy Campaign** (1944). On his insistence, the invasion frontage was widened, and more troops were committed to the initial assault. Criticized for slow progress after **D-Day**, he uncharacteristically agreed to the badly-planned airborne landings at Arnhem (Sep 1944), which resulted in the only defeat of his military career. In 1945, German forces in north-western Germany, Holland, and Denmark surrendered to him on Lüneberg Heath. Appointed field marshal (1944) and viscount (1946), he served successively as Chief of the Imperial General Staff (1946–8) and Deputy Supreme Commander of **NATO** forces in Europe (1951–8). ▷ **North African Campaign**

Montluc, Blaise de (1502–77) French soldier. He fought in Italy, and as governor of **Guyenne** treated the **Huguenots** with great severity. His *Mémoires* were called 'la bible du soldat' by **Henry IV** (of France).

Montmorency, Anne, 1st Duke of (1493–1567) Marshal and Constable of France. He distinguished himself under his childhood friend, **Francis I** of France, at Marignano (1515) and became Constable (1538); suspected by the king of siding with the **Dauphin**, he was banished from court in 1541. He was restored to his dignities by **Henry II** (1547), commanded at the disaster of St Quentin (1557), and was taken prisoner by the Spaniards. He opposed the influence of **Catherine de' Medici** and commanded against the **Huguenots** at Dreux (1562). In 1563 he drove the English out of Le Havre. He again engaged the Huguenot leader,

Louis I of Bourbon, Prince of **Condé** at St Denis (1567), where he received his death-wound.

Montoire sur Loir A village in central France, where **Laval**, and two days later **Pétain**, met **Hitler** (22–4 Oct 1940) to define the policy of Franco-German **collaboration**.

Montoneros Argentine urban guerrillas claiming allegiance to **Peronism** and (from 1970) staging terrorist actions against the military regime then in power. Repudiated by Juan Domingo **Perón** himself (1974), the Montoneros renewed their attacks on the regime installed in 1976, meeting with severe repression. Their activities encouraged the Argentine military to embark on the 'Dirty War' against the urban guerrillas, culminating in the Malvinas (Falklands) imbroglio.

Montreux Convention (1936) This agreement revised the terms of the Treaty of **Lausanne** (1923) and allowed Turkey to remilitarize the Straits. Turkey was given absolute control of the waterway and could regulate the passage of warships through it in times of conflict, and in peacetime if it felt threatened. These generous concessions are explained by Britain's desire to prevent Turkey allying itself with **Hitler**.

Montrose, James Graham, 1st Marquis of (1612–50) Scottish general. He helped to draw up the Covenant in support of Presbyterianism. He served in the Covenanter army in 1640, but transferred his allegiance to **Charles I**, and led the royalist army to victory at Tippermuir (1644). After the royalist defeat at the Battle of **Naseby** (1645), his army became disaffected, and his remaining force was defeated at Philiphaugh. He fled to Europe, returning to Scotland after Charles's execution to avenge his death; but his army was largely lost by shipwreck, and the remnant defeated at Invercharron (1650). He was taken prisoner, and hanged in Edinburgh. ▷ **Covenanters; English Civil Wars**

Moonje, Balakrishna Shivaram (1872–1948) Indian nationalist. A reputed eye surgeon who joined the Indian freedom struggle. He studied at Hislop College, Nagpur and at Grant Medical College, Bombay. He attended the Bombay Congress session and adopted **Tilak** as his guru. He subsequently gave up his medical practice to enter politics. He worked for the **Swadeshi** boycott and took a prominent part in the Home Rule Movement. He was elected President of the Central Legislature in 1926, but resigned the post at the call of Congress. He represented **Hindu Mahasabha** on the joint parliamentary committee and in 1937 formed a Hindu Military Education Society and started the Bhonsle Military School. He wrote a new Manusmriti which was never published. He received the popular title Dharmavira for his religious activities and was nicknamed Field Marshal Moonje for his military qualities.

Moore, John (1761–1809) British general. From 1794 he served in many countries in Europe, and in the West Indies, but is remembered for his command of the English Army in Spain (1808–9), where he was forced to retreat to Corună. There he defeated a French attack, but was mortally wounded. ▷ **Peninsular War**

Moors The name applied in Spanish to Muslims from North Africa who conquered the Iberian Peninsula in the 8c. The Hispanic Christian kingdoms (**Castile**, above all) fought wars of **Reconquest**, which by the mid-13c eliminated the Moors from all but the small southern Kingdom of Granada. Granada was conquered in 1492, and in 1502 all professed Muslims were expelled by order of **Isabella I, 'the Catholic'**. ▷ **Granada, Conquest of**

Moplahs ▷ **Mapillas**

Moral Majority A US pressure group founded in 1979 which campaigns for the election of morally conservative politicians and for changes in public policy in such areas as abortion, homosexuality, and school prayers. It is associated with Christian fundamentalists who in the 1980s played a prominent role in US politics.

Morant Bay Rebellion (1865) Black uprising against the colonial government in Morant Bay, St Thomas, Jamaica. Infuriated by the violence of the local militia's response to a peaceful demonstration, a group of black smallholders led by Paul Bogle, a charismatic Baptist preacher, fired the Court House and in the ensuing riot 30 people of both sides were killed. The Governor, Edward John Eyre, blamed the discontent on George William Gordon, a coloured landowner and ex-magistrate. Gordon was tried, convicted and hanged for high treason in Kingston, Bogle and 400 other 'rebels' were executed, and 600 people were flogged in St Thomas. Embarrassed by Eyre's savage reaction to this 'African uprising', London recalled the Governor (although many in Britain continued to regard him as the saviour of the island). Gordon and Bogle are now revered as nationalist heroes in Jamaica.

Morat, Battle of (22 June 1476) A decisive battle in the war between the Burgundians under **Charles the Bold** and the Swiss Confederation (1474–6). A crushing defeat was inflicted on the Burgundians who lost c.11 000 men, against Swiss losses of only c.410.

Moravian Brethren (Unitas Fratrum) A Protestant movement descended from the so-called Unity of Czech Brethren formed in Bohemia in 1457 by Petr Chelčický among others and subsequently at the centre of the Czech reformation in its struggle with the Austrian Counter-Reformation. Most were driven out of Bohemia and Moravia by Ferdinand II after his victory at the Battle of the **White Mountain** in 1620, but some survived until 1725, when Charles VI completed their expulsion. The survivors found refuge in Saxony where they became known as Moravians. Some spread across Europe and on to North America where, in 1734, they established the Moravian Church.

Moray, James Stuart, 1st Earl of (1531–70) Regent of Scotland (1567/70). He was the illegitimate son of **James V** of Scotland, and half-brother of **Mary, Queen of Scots**. He acted as Mary's chief adviser (1560), but supported John **Knox** and opposed Mary's marriage to **Darnley**. After an attempted coup, he was outlawed and took refuge in England (1565). Pardoned the following year, he became regent for Mary's baby son when she abdicated (1567), and defeated her army at Langside (1568). His Protestant and pro-English policies alienated some Scots nobles, and he was killed at Linlithgow by one of Mary's supporters.

More, Sir Thomas (St Thomas More) (1478–1535) English statesman. He became a lawyer, then spent four years in a Carthusian monastery to test his vocation for the priesthood. He did not take holy orders, and under **Henry VIII** of England became Master of Requests (1514), Treasurer of the Exchequer (1521), and Chancellor of the Duchy of Lancaster (1525). On the fall of **Wolsey** (1529), he was appointed Lord Chancellor, but resigned in 1532 following his opposition

to Henry's break with Rome. On refusing to recognize Henry as head of the English Church, he was imprisoned and beheaded. A leading humanist scholar, as revealed in his Latin *Utopia* (1516) and many other works, he was canonized in 1935. ▷ **Reformation** (England)

Morelos (y Pavón), José María (1765–1815) Mexican revolutionary. Born in Michoacán, New Spain a mestizo, his early life was spent as a muleteer before he entered the priesthood. He then joined **Hidalgo (y Costilla)** in the struggle for Mexican independence as the leader in the south and reorganized the insurgents in the period 1810–13. A brilliant guerrilla leader, he regrouped opposition to Spanish rule in 1811 under a supreme junta. In opposition to the Spanish Constitution of Cádiz, he convened a 'sovereign congress' at Chilpancingo which, though beleaguered, declared independence at Apatzingán (22 Oct 1814). This first Mexican constitution was republican, and abolished the fuero and slavery. Isolated and trapped by the royalist forces under Viceroy Felix Calleja, he was captured, defrocked and executed in Mexico City. He was one of the founders, with Vicente Guerrero, Guadalupe Victoria and Juan Álvarez, of the radical liberal tradition of Mexican politics.

Morgan, Henry (c.1635–88) British buccaneer. Morgan's 'Brethren of the Cross' terrorized Spanish settlements in the Caribbean between 1655 and 1671. Welsh-born, Morgan went to Barbados as an indentured servant but later joined the cosmopolitan **buccaneers** in St Domingue. In 1655 he took part in the capture of Jamaica and Mansfield's raid on Cuba. Provided with letters of marque by the Governor of Jamaica, Thomas Modyford, Morgan made daring, brutal and profitable attacks on Puerto Bello (1668), Maracaibo (1669) and Rio de la Hacha and Panama (1670–1). When buccaneering was outlawed by the Treaty of Madrid (1670), Morgan returned to Port Royal and was twice made Deputy Governor of Jamaica. ▷ **indentured servants**

Morgarten, Battle at the Pass of (1315) The decisive battle between Duke Leopold of Austria and the Swiss Cantons. Leopold suffered a crushing defeat while attempting to impose the imperial ban on the Cantons and reassert Habsburg rights there. As a result of their victory, the Cantons renewed the Confederacy and had their rights recognized by **Louis IV, 'the Bavarian'**, while

Habsburg lands in the area were confiscated by the empire. ▷ **Habsburg Dynasty**

Mori Arinori (1847–89) Japanese politician. From a **Satsuma** samurai family, Mori studied in Britain and the USA (1865–8) and on his return became a vigorous proponent of westernization, advocating the abolition of traditional customs and even the replacement of the Japanese language by English. He was Japan's first envoy to the USA (1871–3) and Vice-Foreign Minister (1878–9) before heading the newly-established Education Ministry in 1885. He created a centralized and secular education system with emphasis on practical instruction and service to the state. A series of higher schools, culminating in the prestigious Tokyo Imperial University, were also founded to train a governing elite. Mori was assassinated by a religious fanatic on the same day the **Meiji Constitution** was promulgated (11 Feb 1889).

Moriscos The name given to Spanish Muslims and their descendants who accepted Christian baptism. They came into existence on a large scale when the Castilian government in 1502 ordered Muslims in Granada and **Castile** to choose between baptism and expulsion. The Muslims of the crown of **Aragon** were not forced to convert until 1526. *Moriscos* formed a high proportion of the Mediterranean population of Spain, and most resisted all attempts to convert them effectively. In Granada they were responsible for a major uprising in the Alpujarra region (1569). They were eventually expelled en masse in 1609–14, to a total of some 300000. The economic effects of their departure were serious in certain areas. ▷ **Alpujarras, Revolts of**

Morlaks Originally the Venetian term for non-urban Slavs and Vlachs living along the Dalmatian coast, the name came to be used erroneously as a synonym for **hajduks**.

Morley–Minto Reforms The popular name given to the 1909 Indian Councils Act. They broadened the basis of Indian Government, allowed Indians to sit on the Imperial Legislative Council, introduced direct elections for non-official seats in provincial legislative councils, and granted separate or communal electorates to minorities. They were not intended to progress to full parliaments, and were soon criticized for holding up administration, dividing Muslims and Hindus, and failing to appease Indian opinion.

Mornay, Philippe de, Lord of Plessay-Marly (1549–1623) French Huguenot leader and polemicist. Converted to Protestantism in 1560, he was nicknamed the 'Pope of the **Huguenots**' for his role in the Wars of Religion (1562–98). A trusted counsellor of Henry of Navarre (**Henry IV**), he undertook many embassies for the Protestant cause; however, he lost the King's favour after Henry's conversion to Catholicism (1593) and played no further part in national affairs. ▷ **Religion, Wars of**

Morny, Charles Auguste Louis Joseph, Duke of (1811–65) French nobleman, believed to be the son of Queen Hortense and the Count of Flahaut, and so half-brother of **Napoleon I**. In 1838 he became a manufacturer of beet sugar and was mixed up in all sorts of speculations. Chosen a Deputy in 1842, he quickly became prominent in financial questions. After 1848 he supported Napoleon, took a leading part in the coup d'état, and became Minister of the Interior. From 1854 to 1865 he was President of the *corps législatif*, and was Ambassador to Russia in 1856–7. He is the 'Duc de Mora' in Alphonse Daudet's *Le Nabab* (1877).

Moro, Aldo (1916–78) Italian politician. A leading figure in the **Christian Democrats**, he served twice as Prime Minister (1963–8 and 1974–6) and was Foreign Minister (1970–2). During the 1970s he was one of the DC moderates who sought to cooperate with **Berlinguer**. He was one of several important figures to die at the hands of the **Red Brigades**.

Morrill Land Grant Act (1862) US educational legislation. The act (sponsored by Representative Justin Morrill of Vermont) provided for the sale of public lands to establish 'land-grant' colleges in every state. The majority of these were agricultural and technical colleges, many of which have grown into the state universities. The act was a major precedent for the provision of federal aid for education in the 20c.

Morrison (of Lambeth), Herbert Stanley, 1st Baron (1888–1965) British politician. Largely self-educated, he helped to found the London **Labour Party** of which he became Secretary (1915). First elected an MP in 1923, he was Minister of Transport (1929–31), Minister of Supply (1940), and Home Secretary (1940–5). He served in the war cabinet from 1942, and became a powerful post-war figure, acting as Deputy Prime Minister

(1945–51), but was defeated by **Gaitskell** for the leadership of the Labour Party in 1955. He was made a life peer in 1959.

Morton, James Douglas, 4th Earl of (c.1525–81) Regent of Scotland (1572/8). Although a Protestant, he was made Lord High Chancellor by **Mary, Queen of Scots** (1563); yet he was involved in the murders of Rizzio (1566) and **Darnley** (1567), and played an important part in the overthrow of the Queen. He joined the hostile noble confederacy, leading its forces at Carberry Hill and Langside, and succeeded **Moray** as regent for **James VI and I**. However, his high-handed treatment of the nobles and Presbyterian clergy caused his downfall (1581). He was arraigned for his part in Darnley's murder, and executed at Edinburgh.

Morton, John (c.1420–1500) English statesman and cardinal. He practised as a lawyer, and adhered with great fidelity to **Henry VI**, but after the Battle of **Tewkesbury** made his peace with **Edward IV**, and became Master of the Rolls (1473) and Bishop of Ely (1479). **Richard III** imprisoned him (1483), but he escaped, and after the accession of **Henry VII** was made Archbishop of Canterbury (1486), Chancellor (1487), and cardinal (1493). ▷ **Roses, Wars of the**

Mosaddeq, Mohammad (1880–1967) Iranian politician. He held office in Iran in the 1920s, returned to politics in 1944, and directed his attack on the Anglo-Iranian Oil Co, which, by his Oil Nationalization Act of 1951 (in which year he became prime minister), he claimed to have expropriated. His government was overthrown by a royalist uprising in 1953, and he was imprisoned. He was released in 1956.

Mosaic Theory of Ethnicity Canadian social theory. The concept emerged in the 1920s to describe the pluralism of Canadian society. The analogy facilitated the description of each racial group, its status and influence within the whole society as well as its cultural and institutional contributions to the nation. In 1965 John Porter suggested the refinement of a vertical mosaic, with status and prestige indicated by layers, so that some ethnic groups were heavily represented in the upper strata whilst others, without power, remained in the lower strata. He believed the idea of the mosaic (as opposd to that of the melting pot) impeded social mobility, and thus encouraged the persistence of conservative traits within Canadian society.

Mościcki, Ignacy (1867–1946) Polish politician and scientist. Opposed to Tsarist rule as a young man, he spent many years in Switzerland, where he became a chemist. He later returned to Poland, where he was Professor of Chemistry at Lvov (1912–26). In 1926, as part of his coup d'état, Józef **Piłsudski** made him President of Poland, a respectable figure hiding a virtual dictatorship. In 1939 he fled to Romania and then retired to Switzerland, where he died.

Moshesh (c.1786–1870) King of the southern Sotho people. He was the founder of the state which has survived as the independent Lesotho, surrounded by South Africa. Moshesh was the son of a small chieftain who succeeded in creating a congeries of people to protect themselves from the marauding **Nguni** flooding out of northern Natal in the diaspora known as the *Mfecane*. From his stronghold at Thaba Bosiu he was able to build his power and play off the rivalries of Boer and Briton in the 1840s and 50s. He invited French Protestant missionaries to his kingdom and, although he himself was never baptized, he adapted some traditional customs to missionary demands. In turn he used the missionaries as his protectors and go-betweens. In 1868 he persuaded the British to annex his kingdom to avoid further encroachments and attacks from the Boers. After a brief period when Basutoland, as Lesotho was then known, was administered from the Cape, Moshesh's state was transferred directly to the British in 1880.

Moshoeshoe II (Constantine Bereng Seciso) (1938–) King of Lesotho (1960/). Educated at Roma College, Ampleforth and Corpus Christi College, Oxford, he was installed as Paramount Chief of the Basotho in 1960 and then proclaimed King when Lesotho became independent in 1966. His political involvement resulted in his being twice placed under house arrest and in 1970 he spent eight months of exile in Holland. He returned on the understanding that he would behave as a constitutional monarch. He remained King after the military coup in Jan 1986, but was exiled (Mar 1990) to England and did not take up Major-General Lekhanya's invitation to return to Lesotho. In Nov 1990 his eldest son succeeded to the throne as King Letsie II.

Mosley, Sir Oswald (Ernald), 6th Baronet (1896–1980) British politician. He was successively a Conservative, Independent and Labour MP, and a member of the

635

1929 Labour government. He resigned from the **Labour Party**, and founded, first, the New Party (1931), and then, following a visit to Italy, the British Union of Fascists, of which he became leader, and which is remembered for its anti-Semitic violence in the East End of London and its support for **Hitler**. Detained under the Defence Regulations during **World War II**, he founded another racialist party, the **Union Movement**, in 1948. He died in Orsay, near Paris, where he mainly lived after the war. ▷ **Blackshirts**

Mosquera, Tomás Cipriano de (1798–1878) Colombian politician. Born into a prominent colonial family, he served under **Bolívar** as a boy. A brigadier at 30, he was 'an unreliable friend and an implacable enemy'. Well-travelled and pragmatic, he was instrumental in repressing a revolt led by religious interests against constitutionalist measures in 1839–42. By the time of his presidency of New Granada (1845–9), he had begun to move to the conservative camp, favouring centralist rule, supported by his brother, the Archbishop of Bogotá, and the army. A beneficiary of increasing prosperity and international trade, he switched towards a conservative liberal view, becoming President of Colombia for a second time (July 1861). Architect of the anticlerical, liberal and ultra-federalist constitution of 1863, he manipulated a shifting alliance of Radicals, Liberals and Independents against the ever-present Conservatives. Elected to a further term in 1865, he assumed dictatorial powers, and was toppled and exiled in 1867.

Motlana, Nthato (1925–   ) South African doctor and politician. Educated at Kilnerton High School and Fort Hare College where he came into contact with the **ANC** (African National Congress) Youth league, he qualified as a doctor at the University of the Witwatersrand. Involved in establishing a network of ANC branches on the Witwatersrand, he was banned in 1953 for five years. By the mid-1970s he had became a leading figure in Soweto and played a major role in the 1976 uprising, helping to establish the Soweto Committee of Ten, which developed into the Soweto Civil Association, of which he is Chairman. One of the few figures to have lived in the townships and retained the respect of ordinary citizens, he became an articulate spokesman for black interests in the 1980s while the ANC was still banned.

Motodo Eifu (1818–91) Japanese Confucian scholar. As tutor to the **Meiji Emperor**, his call for a return to traditional values during the 1880s represented a conservative backlash against the westernizing trends of the 1870s. Appointed Court Adviser in 1886 and a member of the Privy Council in 1888, Motoda helped draft the **Imperial Rescript on Education** (30 Oct 1890), which emphasized the inculcation of patriotism and reverence for the emperor.

Motoori Norinaga (1730–1801) Japanese scholar. He championed the superiority of Japan's ancient culture and beliefs as a reaction against the influence of rational Chinese thought. Condemning Japanese deference to Chinese civilization, Motoori reaffirmed Shinto myths portraying Japan as the 'Land of the Gods' and highlighted the uniqueness of Japan's sacred imperial institution (an unbroken line of emperors descended from the gods) in contrast to the succession of dynasties that prevailed in China. Known as *Kokugaku* ('National Learning'), Motoori's ideas were to influence the imperial loyalist movement of the 19c that overthrew the **Tokugawa Shogunate** and to provide the basis of ultra-nationalist ideology in the 1930s.

Mott, Lucretia (1793–1880) US abolitionist and feminist. A Quaker, she became deeply involved in anti-slavery agitation in the 1830s, helping to organize the Philadelphia Female Anti-Slavery Society (1833). She was one of the driving forces at the world's first women's rights convention, held at Seneca Falls, New York, in 1848. ▷ **abolitionism**

Mountain, The A group of Jacobin extremist Deputies in the French Convention, led by **Robespierre**, so-called because they sat on the highest tiers of seats in the chamber, where they overlooked their political opponents, the **Girondins**, and the uncommitted majority who were known collectively as 'the Plain'. ▷ **Convention, National; French Revolution; Jacobins**

Mountbatten (of Burma), Louis (Francis Albert Victor Nicholas), 1st Earl (1900–79) British Admiral of the Fleet and statesman. He was the younger son of Prince Louis of Battenberg (later Louis Mountbatten, Marquess of Milford Haven) and Princess Victoria of Hesse, the granddaughter of Queen **Victoria**. Having joined the Royal Navy in 1916, in **World War II** he became chief of **Combined Operations Command** (1942), and played a key role in preparations for **D-Day**. In 1943 he was appointed Supreme Commander, South-East Asia, where he defeated the Japanese offensive into India (1944), and worked closely with **Slim** to reconquer Burma (1945). He received the Japanese surrender at Singapore, and in 1947 was sworn in as last Viceroy of India prior to independence. Created an earl in 1947, he returned to the Admiralty, and became First Sea Lord (1954) and Chief of the Defence Staff (1959). Retiring in 1965, he remained in the public eye, and was assassinated by Irish terrorists while fishing near his summer home in the Irish Republic.

Mounties (The Royal Canadian Mounted Police) The force was founded as the Royal North-West Mounted Police in 1873 by Lt Col George Arthur French who was the first commissioner, recruited mainly from the British Army and retaining its red jackets and pillbox hats. Organized on strictly military lines, the Mounties established tight control over the new territories as compared with law enforcement in the American West. Policing was only one of their many roles in the North West until 1953, when the Department of Northern Affairs took over most of their civic duties. In the other provinces the Mounties were amalgamated with the federal Dominion Police in 1920 and became the Royal Canadian Mounted Police. In 1928 Saskatchewan became the first province to contract the RCMP to provide a police force, followed by Alberta and other provinces in the later decades. Ontario and Quebec have not followed their example.

Moyne Commission (1940) A royal commission of the British government set up after the **Disturbances** to investigate the social and economic conditions prevailing in the British West Indies. Headed by the Lord Moyne, its members toured the British Caribbean colonies (1938–9) and its recommendations were made public in 1940, although because of its critical nature, the full report was not published until 1945. It attributed social discontent to the current appalling socioeconomic conditions and recommended the creation of an imperially-financed Colonial Development and Welfare Fund to encourage spending on health, education and housing projects. The Commission also supported the growth of trade unions, but was ambivalent towards constitutional progress.

Moynihan, Daniel Patrick (1927–) US politician. Educated at the City College of New York and Tufts University, he taught at Syracuse, Harvard, and the Massachusetts Institute of Technology. He served in the administrations of Presidents **Johnson** and **Nixon**, acquiring notoriety as the author of *The Negro Family: The Case for National Action* (1965). He became Ambassador to India (1973–4), and won a seat in the US Senate as a Democrat from New York in 1976. ▷ **Democratic Party**

Mozarabs The term, derived from Arabic, designating Christians who lived under Muslim rule in Spain. Mozarabs were given their own administration and their religion was tolerated, but they had to live in separate areas. Under later Muslim rulers in Spain, such as the **Almoravids** and especially the **Almohads**, they were frequently persecuted. Toledo was regarded as their chief city. The term *mozarab* is also used of their culture, in particular their traditional church liturgy.

Mozi (Mo-tzu) (c.270–391BC) Chinese thinker. Living at the time of the Warring States Period, he broke away from the Confucian school to found his own system of thought. Rejecting the Confucian emphasis on family relationships and filial piety, he adopted a rigorous utilitarian approach in advocating universal love — equal concern for the benefit of all. At the same time, he argued that people had to be regimented into total obedience to their rulers, although the latter in turn had to submit to the will of an anthropomorphic god who had the power to reward good and punish evil. Mozi condemned aggressive war, but trained his followers in the techniques of defensive warfare, creating a well-organized private army that assisted any state threatened with aggression. Although the influence of Mozi's thought waned after the 3cBC, the tradition of professional knight-errantry spawned by his military organization survived well into the Han Dynasty. ▷ **Han Dynasties**

MPLA (*Movimento Popular de Libertação de Angola*) Formed in 1975, under the leadership of Agostinho **Neto**, by the merger of several nationalist groups, the organization faced opposition from **UNITA** and **FNLA** which could not be defused through negotiation. After the ensuing civil war, the MPLA with its Cuban and Soviet allies formed the government in Angola, but was faced with a continuing insurrection from UNITA with its South African and US allies. With neither side being able to prevail, negotiations took place and a cease fire was agreed in Estoril, Portugal, in May 1991.

MRP (*Mouvement républicain populaire*, 'Popular Republican Movement') French political party, founded in 1944 by a group of Catholics, led by **Bidault**, who were active in the **Resistance Movement**. It was heir to the tradition of Christian democracy that had found expression before **World War II** in the *Parti démocrate populaire* ('Popular Democratic Party'), founded in 1924. It won nearly a quarter of the vote in 1945–6, and was one of the three pillars of the coalition government (Tripartism) in 1945–7. However, its support declined rapidly, being halved in the 1951 elections. It supported Charles de **Gaulle** in 1958, but was divided by his Algerian policy, as some of its leaders, notably Bidault, opposed Algerian independence. Other members of the MRP objected to de Gaulle's opposition to European integration, and it withdrew from the government in 1962. Its electoral support continued to decline, and it merged in a new political formation, the *Centre démocrate* ('Democratic Centre') in 1963.

Mu'awiya (c.602–80) First Umayyad Caliph (661/80). He opposed the prophet **Muhammad** until the conquest of Mecca in 630, then he became his secretary. Under the second caliph, **'Umar**, he took part in the conquest of Syria and was made Governor in 640. He rebelled against the fourth caliph, **'Ali**, for the murder of his kinsman, the caliph **'Uthman**, and fought him at the indecisive Battle of **Siffin** (657). With the help of **Amr ibn al-As** he gained control of Egypt, and after the assassination of 'Ali in 661 took over the caliphate, thus founding the **Umayyad Dynasty**, and moved the capital to Damascus. He centralized control of the caliphate and extended it through conquests in North Africa and Afghanistan. He was succeeded by his son, Yazid.

Mubarak, Hosni (c.1928–) Egyptian politician. A former pilot and flying instructor who rose to become Commander of the Egyptian Air Force, he was Vice-President under Anwar **Sadat** from 1975 until the latter's assassination in 1981. The only candidate for the presidency, Mubarak pledged to continue Sadat's domestic and international policies, including firm treatment of Muslim extremists and the peace process with Israel.

muckrakers A derogatory term coined in 1906 by President Theodore **Roosevelt** for crusading journalists, authors, and critics whose accounts of social evils were attracting widespread attention. Among the most

important were Ida M Tarbell (1857–1944), Lincoln Steffens (1866–1936), Ray Stannard Baker (1870–1946) and Upton Sinclair (1878–1968).

Mudejars The **Moors** remaining, mostly as peasants or craftsmen, in regions of medieval Spain reconquered for Christianity. Many were expelled during the final stages of **Reconquest** in the 15c.

Mudros Armistice (30 Oct 1918) The armistice which took the Ottomans out of **World War I**, signed at Mudros, a harbour on the Aegean island of Lemnos. The principal participants were Huseyn Rauf Bey, the Ottoman Navy Minister, and Vice-Admiral Calthorpe, commander of the British forces in the Aegean, representing the Entente. The armistice provided for an immediate end to hostilities, demobilization of the Ottoman land forces, surrender of the Ottoman fleet, the withdrawal of Ottoman troops from certain specified territories, and the breaking of all contact with the Austro-Hungarian and German empires. This break in relations was to be accompanied by the expulsion of all nationals of the two Powers' name. The agreement also covered the opening of the Dardanelles and Bosphorus, the stationing of appropriate personnel in strategic positions and access to all Ottoman naval and military facilities. Despite the theoretically provisional nature of the armistice, the British handling of it left suspicions of British intent in the minds of both the French and the Turks. Calthorpe had been ordered by the British government to exclude the French from the talks, and the British approach to enforcing the terms of the armistice, particularly regarding demobilization and the surrender of important positions, led the Turks to suspect that the British intention was no less than a piecemeal dismemberment of what remained of the **Ottoman Empire** in Thrace and Anatolia. Although the Nationalists were able successfully to oppose some of the armistice provisions, the British handling of the matter did little for future relations between the two countries.

Mugabe, Robert (Gabriel) (1924–) Zimbabwean nationalist leader and politician. Educated in Catholic missions schools and Fort Hare College, he was a teacher successively in Southern Rhodesia, Northern Rhodesia and Ghana before returning to Southern Rhodesia in 1960 as Publicity Secretary to the National Democratic Party. He was Deputy Secretary-General of **ZAPU**

in 1961 before being detained and then imprisoned, but co-founded **ZANU** in 1963. He was detained again (1964–74) during which period he replaced Ndabaningi **Sithole** as President of ZANU and qualified as a lawyer. Released in 1974, he went to Mozambique to oversee the guerrilla war against the white regime. United uncomfortably with Joshua **Nkomo**'s ZAPU in the **Patriotic Front**, Mugabe essentially retained his independence and, to the surprise of many, led ZANU (PF) as his party was called to a decisive victory in 1980 and hence became Prime Minister in the first Zimbabwe independence government. In Dec 1987 he became executive President but his radical views, both on the virtues of socialism and the one-party state, have not prevailed.

Mughal Empire An important Indian Muslim state (1526–1857), founded by **Babur**. It temporarily declined under **Humayun** (1530–40), who lost control to the Afghan chieftain, Sher Shah (1540–5). His son, **Akbar the Great**, defeated the Afghan challenge at **Panipat** (1556) and extended the empire to include territory between Afghanistan and Deccan. This was a period of religious freedom, in which a policy of conciliation was pursued with the Rajput states. Akbar was succeeded by Jahangir (1605–27) and **Shah Jahan** (1627–58). Its last great emperor was **Aurangzeb** (1658–1707), who extended the limits of the empire further south; however, religious bigotry alienated

MUGHAL DYNASTY

Regnal Dates	Name
1526/30	Babur
1530/56	Humayun
1556/1605	Akbar the Great
1605/27	Jahangir
1627/58	Shah Jahan
1658/1707	Aurangzeb (Alamgir)
1707/12	Bahadur Shah I (Shah Alam I)
1712/13	Jahandar Shah
1713/19	Farrukh-siyar
1719	Rafi-ud-Darajat
1719	Rafi-ud-Daulat
1719	Neku-siyar
1719	Ibrahim
1719/48	Muhammad Shah
1748/54	Ahmad Shah
1754/9	Alamgir II
1759/1806	Shah Alam II
1806/37	Akbar II
1837/57	Bahadur Shah II

non-Muslim supporters and undermined the empire's unity. The empire disintegrated under Maratha and British pressure. By the mid-18c it ruled only a small area around Delhi, but its administrative forms and culture continued to have great influence. Its last emperor, Bahadur Shah II (1837–57) was exiled by the British to Rangoon after the 1857–8 **Indian Uprising**. See map p640. ▷ **Maratha Kingdom**

mugwump US political epithet used to describe an Independent Republican in the US election of 1884 who, preferring reform to party discipline (particularly on the question of ending the **spoils system**), supported the Democrat Grover **Cleveland**, rather than the Republican James Blaine. The name is said to derive from an Algonquian word meaning 'chief'. ▷ **Republican Party**

Muhammad (c.570–632) Founder of the Islamic religion. Born in Mecca, the son of a poor merchant, he was orphaned at six and earned his living by tending sheep. At 25 he led the caravans of a rich widow, Khadija, whom he later married. He continued as a merchant, but spent much of his time in solitary contemplation, and was moved to teach a new faith, which would dispense with idolatry, narrow Judaism, and corrupt Christianity. When he was 40, Gabriel appeared to him on Mount Hira, near Mecca, and commanded him in the name of God to preach the true religion. Four years later he was told to come forward publicly as a preacher. The basis of his teaching was the Quran, which had been revealed to him by God. He attacked superstition, and exhorted people to a pious, moral life, and belief in an all-powerful, all-just, and merciful God, who had chosen him as his prophet. God's mercy was principally to be obtained by prayer, fasting, and almsgiving. At first dismissing him as a poet, the Meccans finally rose against him and his followers. He sought refuge at Medina in 622 (the date of the **Hijra**), and assumed the position of highest judge and ruler of the city. He then engaged in war against the enemies of Islam. In 630 he took Mecca, where he was recognized as chief and prophet, and thus secured the new religion in Arabia. In 632 he undertook his last pilgrimage to Mecca, and there on Mount Arafat fixed the ceremonies of the pilgrimage (*Hajj*). He fell ill after his return, and when too weak to visit the houses of his nine wives, chose as his last sojourn that of Aisha, his best beloved, the daughter of **Abu Bakr**. See map p641.

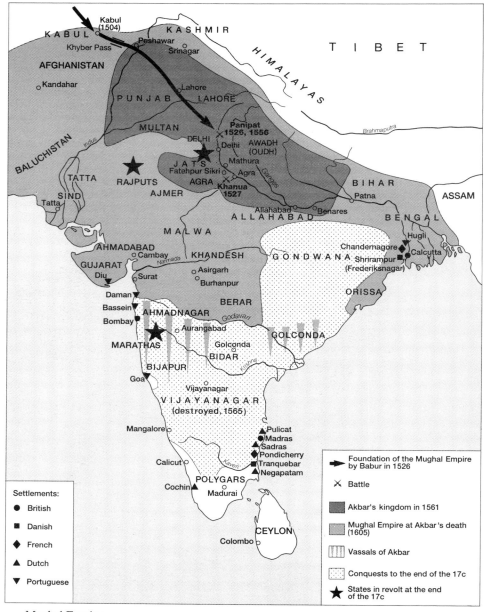

Mughal Empire

Muhammad 'Ali (c.1769–1849) Viceroy of Egypt (1805/48). An Albanian military officer, he was sent to Egypt with a Turkish–Albanian force on the French invasion in 1798. After the French left, he supported the Egyptian rulers in their struggles with the **Mamluks**, and became the chief power in Egypt (1805). He formed a regular army, improved irrigation, and also introduced elements of European civilization. He

640

extended Egyptian territory, routing the Ottoman army at Koniya (1832), but the Quadruple Alliance of 1840 compelled him to limit his ambition to Egypt. In 1848 he became insane, and was succeeded by his adopted son, Ibrahim.

Muhammad bin Tughlaq Sultan of Delhi (1325/51). The son of Ghiyasuddin Tughlaq, he is best remembered as a ruler who

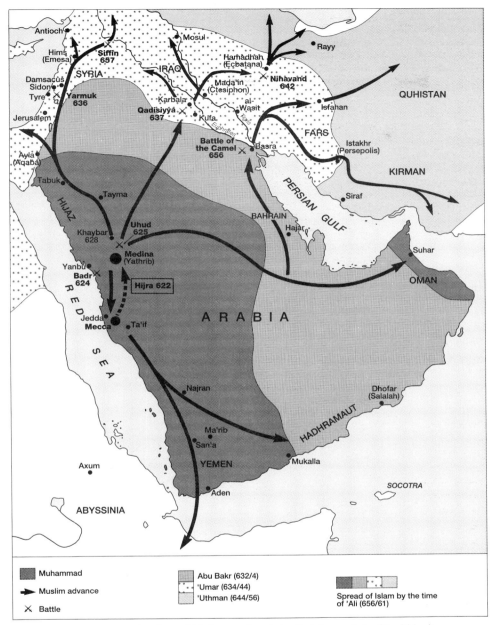

Islamic conquests at the time of Muhammad and the first four caliphs (Rashidun)

undertook a number of bold experiments. He was a scholar in his own right and spent a lot of time in theological and philosophical debates. He was a secular ruler and was accused by many orthodox theologians for being a 'rationalist', ie someone unwilling to accept religious beliefs as a matter of faith. Tughlaq had a reputation of being hasty and impatient and many of his experiments

failed. The best-known of his misadventures was the transfer of the capital from Delhi to Deogiri which he undertook. Deogiri had been a base for the expansion of the Muslim rule in south India. He wanted to make Deogiri a second capital so that he might be able to control south India better. For this purpose, he ordered many of the officers and leading men, including many Sufi saints, to shift to Deogiri which he renamed Daulatabad. The transfer of capital however proved traumatic for many involved and in the end the effort failed. Another failed experiment was the introduction of token currency.

Muhammad Ghuri (d.1206) Conqueror of north India. Assigned Ghazni by his elder brother, Ghiyas ud-Din, after its capture in 1173, Muhammad used it as a base for expansion into India, starting with a successful attack on Multan in 1175–6 and establishing himself in the Punjab in 1186. Conflicts with various Rajput dynasties culminated in his victory at the second Battle of Tarain in 1192, giving him control of all north India as far as Delhi; after the battle, Muhammad returned to Khurasan, leaving the conduct of the campaign to **Qutb ud-Din Aibak**, who secured all north India, except Gujarat and Rajasthan, by 1203.

Muhammad Shah (1702–48) Mughal ruler (1719/48). During his ineffectual rule, the Mughal Empire continued to decline (with the Marathas making large gains) and Delhi was sacked by Nadir Shah in 1739, although **Ahmad Shah Durrani** was repelled in 1748.

Muhammad, Elijah (1897–1975) US black leader. Born Elijah Poole, he moved to Detroit from Georgia in 1923, where eight years later he came into contact with Wali Farad, the founder of the **Black Muslims**. In 1934, Muhammad became the leader of the movement as 'Messenger of Allah'. During **World War II** he was arrested and imprisoned for discouraging his followers from registering for the draft. After his release he initiated a period of fast expansion for the Black Muslims. ▷ **Malcolm X**

Mühlberg, Battle of (1547) The battle at which the Duke of Alba defeated the forces of the **Schmalkaldic League**. The victory was the highwater mark of the power of Emperor **Charles V**.

Mujahidin Muslim guerrillas (literally, 'holy warriors') who resisted the Soviet occupation of Afghanistan after the invasion (Dec 1979). Based in Iran and Pakistan, they formed various armed bands united by their common aim of defeating the invaders, and the conflict was proclaimed a **jihad** ('holy war'). The Russians withdrew from Afghanistan in 1989, and the Mujahidin subsequently experienced much internal dissent over their role in the country's future.

Mujibur Rahman (Sheikh Mujib) (1920–75) Bangladesh politician. Born in Tungipana, into a landowning family, he was educated in Calcutta and Dacca University, from which he was expelled for political activities. In 1949 he co-founded the **Awami League**, campaigning for autonomy for East Pakistan (Bangladesh), became its leader in 1953, and led it to electoral victory in 1970. In 1972, after the civil war between East and West Pakistan, he became Prime Minister of newly independent Bangladesh. He introduced a socialist economic programme but became increasingly intolerant of opposition, establishing a one-party state. In Aug 1975 he and his wife were assassinated in a military coup.

Mukhitdinov, Nuritdin Akramovich (1917–) Soldier and apparatchik, the first central Asian to achieve prominence in Soviet politics. Having fought during **World War II**, he rose to be First Secretary of the Communist Party in Uzbekistan in 1955. Nikita **Khrushchev** then made him a candidate member of the **Politburo** in 1956 and a full member in 1957, essentially to boost his own support, but also to secure backing from beyond the Slav states. But he failed to measure up and was dismissed in 1961.

Mukhopadhyay, Ashutosh (1864–1924) Indian legal figure. After a brilliant academic career, he obtained his doctorate in law in 1894. Made a judge in the Calcutta High Court in 1904, he was a member of the Legislative Council and the Vice-chancellor of Calcutta University for 10 years. He was the President of the Asiatic Society of Bengal, and a chairman and trustee of the Indian Museum and the Council of Imperial (now National) Library.

Muldoon, Robert David (1921–92) New Zealand politician. He served as an infantryman in **World War II** before becoming an accountant. He was elected to parliament in 1960 as an MP for the New Zealand National Party, was Minister of Finance (1967–72) and briefly Prime Minister (1972) when the government was defeated. He became Party Leader and Leader of the Opposition (1974) and was Prime Minister (1975–84). He resigned the party leadership in 1984, and became shadow Foreign Affairs Spokesman (1986–92).

Mulroney, (Martin) Brian (1939–) Canadian politician. The son of an Irish immigrant, he studied law and then practised as a labour lawyer in Montreal, while becoming increasingly active in the Progressive Conservative Party. In 1976 he failed to wrest the party leadership from Joe **Clark** and returned to business as President of a US-owned iron-ore company. In 1983 he replaced Clark and in 1984 became Prime Minister, with a landslide victory over the Liberals. He initiated a number of radical measures, including the **Meech Lake Accord**, settling disputes between the provinces and the centre, and negotiating a free-trade agreement with the USA. Decisively re-elected in 1988, he resigned abruptly from office in 1993. ▷ **Constitution Act of 1982**

Munich Agreement (29 Sep 1938) One of the more infamous acts in history that has come to stand for a betrayal for the worst of reasons and with the worst of consequences. After a long period of pressurizing Czechoslovakia to make whatever concessions its Sudeten German subjects demanded, the Prime Ministers of Britain and France, **Chamberlain** and **Daladier**, sat down with the two fascist dictators of Italy and Germany, **Mussolini** and **Hitler**, and, in the absence of **Beneš**, they agreed to its virtual dismemberment, allegedly in the interest of European peace. But the peace Chamberlain and Daladier bought at the price of Czechoslovakia only encouraged Hitler and Mussolini and, a year later, they had to go to war in worse circumstances for the sake of Poland.

Munich Putsch (1923) The abortive attempt by **Hitler** to overthrow the state government of Bavaria, as a prelude to the March on Berlin and the establishment of the Nazi regime in Germany. It was supported by General **Ludendorff**, but badly planned, and it disintegrated in the face of firm Bavarian police action. Hitler was tried for treason, and sentenced to five years' imprisonment. ▷ **Nazi Party**

Muñoz Marín, Luis (1898–1989) Puerto Rican politician and architect of the modern state. Son of the nationalist, Muñoz Rivera, and educated in the USA, he took up the cause of the peasant in 1938 and founded the Popular Democratic Party which took power in that year. Muñoz, with the aid of the last US Governor, Guy Rexford Tugwell, introduced social reforms and industrialization and was the creator of 'Operation Bootstrap'. He was elected Governor himself in 1948 and held the post until his retirement (1960). Previously a supporter of Puerto Rican independence, in 1950 he devised the status of commonwealth (associated free statehood) for the island in its relationship with the USA.

Munro, Sir Thomas (1761–1827) British colonial administrator. A British **East India Company** official, of humble Scottish origins, he contributed significantly to early British knowledge of, and authority over, its subject population in India. He was associated with the introduction, in the early 19c, of the Ryotwari system of land revenue collection, which advocated settlement direct with the cultivator. As with many of his other innovations, Ryotwari grew out of Munro's understanding of Indian traditions and problems acquired through many years of service both as a soldier and administrator. During his governorship of Madras, the Ryotwari system became a rule, although it only acquired its modern methodical form after 1885.

Münster, Capture of (1535) A city in north-western Germany originally called Mimigernaford. The name was changed to Münster in 1068. It was chartered in 1137 and later joined the Hanseatic League. It was seized by Anabaptist radicals in 1534 who began a programme of change meant to make the city the 'New Jerusalem'. When it was obvious that a combined Catholic Protestant army was to move against Münster, many Anabaptists rallied to the city. The city was taken in 1535 and three of its leaders (including Jan Bokelson) were executed (1536). The city was later the site of the negotiations which produced the Peace of **Westphalia** (1645–8).

Münster, Treaty of (30 Jan 1648) The peace treaty which brought to an end the **Eighty Years War** between the Dutch Republic and Spain, and part of the Peace of Westphalia. In the treaty Spain recognized the sovereign independence of the Dutch Republic of the **United Provinces of the Netherlands**; both sides recognized each other's current possessions in Europe and the colonies, the Dutch were permitted to close the Scheldt River to trade, and both countries granted freedom of conscience to each other's citizens. It represented the victory of the Dutch Republic, and the final split between the northern and southern Netherlands.

Müntzer, Thomas (c.1489–1525) German preacher and Anabaptist. He studied theology, and in 1520 began to preach at Zwickau, but his socialism and mystical doctrines soon brought him into conflict with the authorities. In 1525 he was elected pastor of the Anabaptists of Mülhausen, where his communistic ideas soon aroused the whole country. A leader of the Peasants' War (1524–5), he was captured at the Battle of Frankenhausen, and executed at Mülhausen.

muqti A governor under the **Delhi Sultanate** (1200–1526). The sultanate was divided into provinces, each under a *muqti*, who was responsible for the administration of the province and the collection of revenue from those peasants who paid their tax directly to the state. From the share which he received, the muqti was required to maintain a quota of horses and foot soldiers which were at the sultan's disposal. The muqti's appointment was not permanent, and he could be transferred at any time to another part of the kingdom.

Murad I (c.1326–89) Ottoman Sultan (1360/89). The son of **Orhan**, his main achievement lay in his being the first of the Ottomans to carry Ottoman arms into Europe. Details of his campaigns are difficult to disentangle reliably from the sources, but in broad outline western Thrace was conquered and raids were mounted into western Bulgaria. Murad established Adrianople (Edirne) as the European capital of the Ottomans (1366) and the Byzantine Emperor John V Palaeologus submitted to him as a vassal. There is little doubt that the Ottomans derived advantage from the Byzantine–Bulgar animosities at this time. Later (c.1371) the Turks checked a Serbian advance and were able, as a result, to establish themselves in Macedonia. Further conquests followed, with Murad's troops taking Sofya and Niš in the mid-1380s, thereby securing a firm foothold for the Ottomans in the Balkans. Murad also campaigned in Anatolia, and his leniency there provoked friction amongst the Serbs in his army. It is suggested that this in some way contributed to the general growth in feeling against the Turks among the Serbs as a whole, which led to the defeat (1388) of a Turkish force at Plocnik by a combined force of Serbs and Bosnians. This defeat caused Murad himself to move against the Serbs, and the Battle of **Kosovo** in 1389 cost Murad his life, although the Ottoman forces in the event emerged victorious under the leadership of **Bayezid I**, Murad's successor. Murad's reign represents the transition in the role of the Ottoman ruler from being one of a group of warring princelings in Asia Minor to being the ruler of a state of a size and consequence requiring complexities of government and administration not hitherto associated with the minor Turkish dynasties of Anatolia.

Murad II (c.1401–51) Ottoman Sultan (1421/44 and 1446/51). The son of **Mehmed I**, he was faced initially with two pretenders supported by the Byzantine Emperor, Manuel II Palaeologus. Having dealt with both, he began a siege of Constantinople in 1422. He was, however, again beset by the problem of rivals, who caused him to raise the siege, and it was not until 1425 that Murad II was safely ensconced upon his throne. The death of Manuel (1424) and the accession of John VIII Palaeologus enabled Murad to negotiate a peace and the Ottomans were able once again to turn their attention to problems on their frontiers. They captured Thessalonica (1430) and took fortresses in Epirus and Albania, and mounted raids into Serbia and, in 1438, into Hungary. In 1440 they unsuccessfully laid siege to Belgrade. A reaction, represented by a crusading army under János **Hunyadi**, resulted in defeat for the Turks, but Murad was able to conclude a peace in 1444 which effectively represented a recognition of the *status quo ante* as far as the geographical extent of Ottoman political influence was concerned. The brief period (1444–6) following Murad's abdication in favour of his son, **Mehmed II, 'the Conqueror'**, ended with Hungarian aggression in contravention of the peace treaty. The remaining years of Murad's reign were spent largely in campaigns in the Balkans. Despite the necessity of warlike dispositions to consolidate and maintain his rule, his policies were essentially of a peaceful nature, and he is the first of the Ottoman rulers to have maintained a court where letters, the arts, poetry and science flourished.

Murad III (1546–95) Ottoman Sultan (1574/95). He appears to have had no great taste for politics and the affairs of state, preferring to trust his viziers and only becoming involved when rivalries between groups threatened to get out of hand. Factions in the palace were responsible for war with Safavid Persia (1578–90) and the start of the 'Long War' (1593–1606) between the Ottomans and the Habsburgs. Foreign policy was also under the control of viziers and, at times, a harem clique; there were contacts with Venice, France, and even Queen **Elizabeth I** of England. Murad is remembered as a generous sultan, who was particularly fond of his harem. A cultivated ruler, he both patronized and involved himself in letters and the arts, and under his rule architecture flourished, notable among his architects being the great Sinan.

Murad IV (c.1611–40) Ottoman Sultan (1623/40). Until 1632, he was under the influence of those who had engineered his preferment and the Ottoman state itself was perceived (correctly) as weak by its enemies, who included the Safavid Shah **Abbas I, 'the Great'** (d.1629), who took Baghdad and Iraq, except for Mosul and Basra. It was, however, uprisings among the soldiery and divisions among the rebellious troops that gave Murad the chance to assert his authority. This he did ruthlessly by hunting down all rebels and having them executed. Discipline was restored by 1635, corruption (which had been rife) eradicated, and Murad's rule was enforced by a network of informers who served to alert the Sultan to any impending problems. His major achievement in foreign affairs was to bring to a close the hostilities with Safavid Persia, which had lasted for well over a century, by creating the conditions for the signature of a peace treaty between the two countries (1639). Iraq was thenceforward to be in the Ottoman sphere of influence, with Erevan and parts of the Caucasus remaining under Safavid control. By the time of his death, Murad had, in eight years, successfully returned the **Ottoman Empire** from a state of enfeebling anarchy to some semblance of stability and its former glory.

Murat, Joachim (1767–1815) French soldier and King of Naples (1808/15). Having enlisted in the cavalry on the eve of the Revolution, he was promoted to general during **Napoleon I**'s Egyptian campaign of 1799. He helped the latter become First Consul and subsequently married his sister, Caroline. In 1808 he replaced Napoleon's brother, Joseph, as King of Naples, where he introduced a number of reforms. He commanded Napoleon's cavalry during the 1812 invasion of Russia but resigned his commission in 1812 and returned to Naples. After Napoleon's defeat at **Leipzig** (1813), Murat sought to keep his throne by a treaty with the Austrians, but when Napoleon escaped from Elba, Murat rallied to his cause, hoping to conquer the whole of Italy. Defeated by the Austrians at Tolentino (3 May 1815), he fled to France and then Corsica; in Sep 1815 he sailed for Calabria, intending to reclaim his old kingdom, but was captured and executed by the troops of **Ferdinand I**.

Muraviev-Amursky, Nikolai N, Count (1809–81) Russian politician. Appointed Governor-General of Siberia in 1847 by **Nicholas I**, he was strongly supported by him and latterly by **Alexander II** in his determined efforts to explore and then control the Amur River, formally under Chinese rule. By 1859 he was in an unassailable position, and it was left to the diplomats to secure the territory from China by the Treaty of **Beijing** in 1860. Vladivostok became Russia's open declaration of Pacific ambition.

Murray, General Sir James (1721–94) British soldier and administrator. Military commander after the death of General James **Wolfe**, he was responsible for the application of the 1763 Proclamation which excluded Catholics from holding public office. It was impossible for the very few Protestants to supply an Assembly, and it was also dangerous to retain the judiciary within the control of such a small number. Murray, therefore, had to make adjustments in order to establish a stable government. Already on bad terms with the English-speaking merchants (he thought them subversive, while they disliked military rule), Murray modified the proclamation to allow Catholics to sit on juries and to practise law, and introduced French legal customs into the judicial system. These concessions, as well as the lack of habeas corpus, angered the English-speaking merchants, who petitioned London for his replacement. In 1766 he was recalled, although the **Quebec Act** later adopted many of his administrative arrangements, and was one of the factors which prevented the colony from joining the **American Revolution**.

Musa Ibn Nusair (640–717) Arab soldier. He conquered northern Africa from 699 to 709 and Spain in 712. However, he fell under the displeasure of the caliph of Damascus, and died in poverty in the Hijaz.

Muscovy Company An English trading company granted a charter in 1554 allowing it to monopolize trade between England and Russia. In 1568 Tsar **Ivan IV, 'the Terrible'** allowed the company to conduct trade with the Orient via the River Volga. Political intrigues led to the expulsion of the company's agents from Russia in 1649, after which it ceased to exist.

Museveni, Yoweri Kaguta (1944–) Ugandan revolutionary leader and politician. A graduate of Dar es Salaam University, he was Assistant Secretary for Research in

645

President Obote's office until Idi **Amin**'s coup of 1971. He returned to Dar es Salaam as an exile and headed the Front for National Salvation against Amin while teaching at the Cooperative College, Moshi. He led the attack on Mbarar, with Tanzanian troops, and participated at the forefront of the fighting which drove Amin from power. Museveni became Minister of Defence in the governments of Yusof Lulu and Godfrey Binaisa (1979–80) but he fell out with Obote on the latter's return to power. When the Tanzanian troops left in 1982 a virtual civil war ensued until 1986, when Museveni's forces prevailed and Obote once again fled the country. Museveni has since attempted to follow a policy of national reconciliation.

Muslim Brotherhood An Islamic movement, founded in Egypt in 1928 by an Egyptian schoolteacher, Hasan al-**Banna**. Its original goal was the reform of Islamic society by elimination of Western influences and other decadent accretions. Subsequently, it became more radical, and its goal of a theocratic Islamic state found support in many other Sunni countries. ▷ **Sunnis**

Muslim League Founded in 1906 by politicized Muslims, many of whom were active in the Muhammadan Educational Conference established by Sayyid Ahmed Khan, the league saw itself as the spokesman for all Muslims in British India. By the 1930s, it had begun to articulate a Muslim nationalism expressed through the concept of Pakistan, a separate Muslim state. In 1927 the league split over the question of the Simon Commission. Muslim fear of a Hindu self government led to the reorganization of the league under Muhammad Ali **Jinnah** in 1934. The search for a positive programme led the league in two directions. The first was that of safeguards: Muslims welcomed federation as it gave provinces greater freedom and thus tended to safeguard Muslims in their majority areas. They sought to reduce the scope of the centre as much as possible. The second direction was towards autonomy in the Muslim majority areas. In 1930 Iqbal suggested the union of the Frontier Province, Baluchistan, Sind, and Kashmir as a Muslim state within a federation. Choudhari Rahmat Ali Khan developed the concept of a separate Muslim state at Cambridge and invented the term Pakistan in 1933. The ideology of Iqbal and the vision of Rahmat ali Khan were turned into a practical programme by Jinnah, the future President of Pakistan, and the

Muslim League was the dominant party in Pakistan after 1947. ▷ **India, Partition of**

Mussert, Antoon Adriaan (1894–1946) Dutch politician. He made his early career as a hydraulic engineer in Dutch government service, but under the influence of fascism and Nazism he founded the **National Socialist Movement** (*Nationaal Socialistische Beweging*, NSB), the main Dutch fascist party. During the German occupation of the Netherlands he collaborated fully, and was given the title of 'Leader of the Dutch People'; however he had little real power. After the war he was captured, sentenced to death and executed by firing squad.

Mussolini, Benito (1883–1945) Italian politician. The son of a blacksmith and a schoolteacher, he fled Italy in 1902 to avoid military service. In 1904 he returned to Italy as editor of the socialist newspaper *Avanti!*, but resigned in 1914 because of his refusal to support Italian neutrality. He was wounded while serving on the front and began to edit his own nationalist paper, *Il Popolo d'Italia*. In Mar 1919 Mussolini established the fascist movement, borrowing ideas from Gabriele **D'Annunzio** and the 'futurists'; in Oct 1921 he converted this into the **Fascist Party**. Profiting from the economic and political instability of post-war Italy and the support of para-military **squadristi** and local **ras**, as well as a readiness to ally with politicians of differing ideologies, he was able first to take control of a number of provincial cities and then present himself as the only man capable of restoring order to a country that seemed to be slipping ever more rapidly into political chaos. In Oct 1922 he was asked by **Victor Emmanuel III** to form a government and the following month assumed dictatorial powers. His rule came under serious threat only once after the ill-judged murder of **Matteotti** (1924) and during the course of the mid-1920s he was able to consolidate power. Using a mixture of intimidation, patronage and propaganda, he was able to turn Italy into a totalitarian state by 1929. Despite his early aggression over **Corfu** and his fierce nationalism, his foreign policy was not marked by overt expansionism or aggression until the mid-1930s. However, in 1935 he launched the Conquest of **Abyssinia** which was followed by large-scale intervention in the **Spanish Civil War** on the side of **Franco**. During this period he moved increasingly towards cooperation with **Hitler**, which culminated in the Pact of Steel and eventually in the invasion of France in 1940. In 1939 Mussolini annexed Albania but (Oct 1940) failed to seize Greece. The arrival of German troops to assist in the conquest of Greece signalled the beginning of his dependence on Hitler, and henceforth his actions were dictated largely by the needs of Berlin. Dissatisfaction with this policy and a realization of the likely victory of the Allies persuaded many of his **gerarchi** to oppose him, and at a meeting of the **Fascist Grand Council** (25 July 1943) it became clear that he had lost the support of most of his closest associates. The following day he was arrested after being summoned by **Victor Emmanuel III**, but was subsequently rescued by German paratroopers. In Sep 1943 he was established at the head of the puppet Republic of **Salò** in German-occupied northern Italy but was no more than an impotent quisling. On 28 Apr 1945 he was captured by partisans and shot while trying to flee Italy. ▷ **Duce**

Mu'tazilites An Islamic religious group, said to have its origin in the departure of one Wasil ibn Ata from a mosque in which Hasan of Basra was speaking, as a result of which he provoked the comment *itazala anna* 'he has dissociated himself from us'. The point at issue was the apportionment of blame or sinfulness in the conflict between **'Ali** on the one side and Talha, al-Zubayr and **'Aisha** on the other, which resulted in the Battle of the **Camel**. Wasil, and Amr ibn Ubayd, maintained that they were all true believers, but that in the war itself both sides could not be in the right and that human agencies could not decide between them. The Mutazila, who were very strictly monotheistic, developed their own *Usul* or 'Principles' and they were in general devoted, in the early period at least, to the cause of the 'Abbasid caliphs. They are best known in a political context for the espousal of their doctrines by the caliph al-**Ma'mun** and his establishment of an inquisition (*Mihna*) to root out the unregenerate. The doctrine used as a test was that of the 'creation' of the Quran, the Mu'tazila maintaining that the Quran was created in time, the Orthodox that the Quran was uncreated and eternal. There was an orthodox reaction in the reign of the caliph al-Mutawakkil (847/61) but the major challenge on a doctrinal level was mounted by al-Ashari, the founder in Islam of *kalam* or scholastic theology.

Mutesa I (c.1837–84) Long-reigning Kabaka (King) of Buganda (1856/84). Under his rule the power of the monarch and the extent of the kingdom on the northern shore of Lake Victoria were greatly increased. Mutesa was

fascinated by the Muslim Zanzibari traders who visited his court and was eager to supply himself with modern firearms. His court developed Islamic practices, but Mutesa was also beset with Christian Europeans. In 1876 a religious persecution created Muslim martyrs. He invited both Catholic and Protestant missionaries to Buganda to try to balance them against each other and also encouraged the restoration of indigenous religion. His successor, Mwanga, inherited a religious powder keg.

Mutesa II ('King Freddie') (1924–69) Kabaka or King of Buganda (1939/53 and 1955/66). Mutesa was educated in England and was an honorary captain in the Grenadier Guards. He succeeded as Kabaka during **World War II** and set about safeguarding the position of his kingdom within Uganda, even attempting to lead it to separate independence. At the centre of several controversies relating to the independence and post-colonial politics of Uganda, Mutesa was exiled (1953–5) by the Governor, Sir Andrew Cohen, for opposing British plans for unitary decolonization. On independence, he was briefly President of Uganda with Milton Obote as his Prime Minister, but in 1966 Obote overthrew him in a coup. Mutesa escaped to London, where he died.

mutilated victory The term (in Italian, *vittoria mutilata*) coined originally by Gabriele **D'Annunzio** to describe the consequences of Italy's treatment by its allies after **World War I**. Italy, having been brought into war by promises of extensive territorial and colonial gains, suffered among the greatest human and material losses of any of the Western states. However, the Italian delegates at the Paris Peace Conference were virtually ignored by those of Britain, France and the USA. While most of the territory promised by the Treaty of **London** (1915) was handed over, Italian claims for colonies and mandates were disregarded (doubly offensive given the readiness to allow Australia and South Africa control of mandated territory) and the Dalmatian littoral was given to Yugoslavia. This not entirely unfounded sense of being cheated played a large part in stimulating aggressive nationalist sentiment which helped contribute to the growth of **fascism**.

Muzorewa, Abel (Tendekayi) (1925–) Zimbabwean cleric and politician. Educated in Methodist schools in Southern Rhodesia and at theological college in the USA, he was ordained in 1963 and became a bishop of the United Methodist Church in Southern Rhodesia in 1968. Founder President of the African National Council in 1971, he failed to hold together the differing elements of the nationalist movement and chose the path of an 'internal settlement' rather than guerrilla war. After the ANC won the first universal suffrage election in 1979, he was Prime Minister of 'Zimbabwe–Rhodesia' for a few months before the 1980 election swept Robert **Mugabe** into power.

MVSN (*Milizia Volontaria per la Sicurezza Nazionale*) The fascist militia set up in Jan 1923 by **Mussolini**. Recruited mainly from ex-**squadristi**, paid out of state funds and answerable only to Mussolini himself, the militia was established primarily to keep the fascist movement under the **Duce**'s own control. By organizing the members of the fascist squads, Mussolini was able to prevent powerful **ras** from mustering their own private armies and to prevent also the worst excesses of *squadrismo*, so fostering his image as the one man able to keep order. However, the MVSN served little real military or policing purpose.

Mwata Yamvo (1600–mid-19c) The dynastic title of the paramount chiefs of the Lunda empire of central Africa. The empire expanded steadily from its inception c.1600 so that by the mid-19c as many as 36 great chiefs of the region were reputed to pay tribute to the *mwata yamvo*.

Mwene Mutapa The dynastic title of the kings of northern Zimbabwe with whom Portuguese traders established close relations in the 16c. Gatsi Rusere (d.1622) appealed to the Portuguese for aid in suppressing a rebellion, ceding in return the mineral wealth of the kingdom to his 'brother-in-arms', the king of Portugal. Towards the end of his reign relations with the Europeans deteriorated although the king received Christian baptism on his deathbed. His son Nyambo Kapararidze broke openly with the Portuguese and placed himself at the head of an uprising in 1631. He was defeated in battle in 1633 and then replaced by the puppet-king Mavura (d.1652), after which the dynasty survived only in subordination to the Portuguese.

Mwinyi, (Ndugu) Ali Hassan (1925–) Tanzanian politician. Having trained as a teacher, he taught in Zanzibar (1954–61) before going to the UK to study for two years.

On his return, he joined the Zanzibari Ministry of Education and then the Zanzibar State Trading Corporation. In 1969 he became a Minister of State in the Office of President Julius **Nyerere** and thereafter Minister of Health and Home Affairs, Minister of Natural Resources and Tourism, and Minister of State in the Vice-President's Office. In Apr 1984 he was elected President of Zanzibar and in Oct 1985 he succeeded Nyerere as President of Tanzania. Since then, he has attempted to loosen the state's control over the country's economy while retaining a faith in the single party, the **Chama Cha Mapinduzi** (CCM).

Myall Creek Massacre (1838) In Australian history, the massacre of 28 **Aboriginals** in north-east New South Wales by a party of assigned convicts for an alleged attack on cattle. Seven of the men charged with the massacre were found guilty and hanged, the first whites executed for murdering Aboriginals. The accused attracted considerable support from other colonists, who regarded Aboriginals as less than human; thereafter the murder of Aboriginals was carefully concealed.

Mycale, Battle of (479BC) A decisive Greek action in coastal Ionia against the Persians, which brought the Second Persian War to an end. ▷ **Persian Wars**

Mycenaean (Mycenean) Civilization The Bronze Age culture which flourished in Greece and the Aegean during the second millennium, reaching its high point in Greece in the 13c BC. Important sites are Mycenae, Pylos, and Tiryns. These show the existence in Greece of the palace system of government with its complex redistributive economy, found earlier in Minoan Crete. An important difference, however, is the existence in Mycenaean society of a distinct warrior class. The chief Mycenaean palace sites were destroyed or abandoned towards the end of the 13c BC. Inter-state strife may have been the cause; invading **Dorians** are no longer considered responsible. ▷ **Minoan Civilization**

Mycerinus ▷ **Menkaure**

Mylae, Battle of (260BC) A famous sea battle off Sicily in the first of the **Punic Wars**. It was the first victory Rome achieved with her newly-built navy.

My Lai incident (Mar 1968) The massacre of several hundred unarmed inhabitants of the South Vietnamese village of My Lai by US troops, an incident exposed by *Life* magazine photos in 1969. The officer responsible, Lieutenant Calley, was court-martialled in 1970–1. ▷ **Vietnam War**

Mzilikazi (c.1790–1868) Chief of the Ndebele (c.1820/68). The Ndebele were one of the **Nguni** groups which clashed with Shaka, King of the Zulu. During the early 1820s, Mzilikazi led his people over the Drakensberg on to the high veld, where he attacked a number of peoples and finally settled in what is now the western Transvaal. The missionary, Robert Moffat, made contact with him and they established a close relationship. Mzilikazi came into conflict with the Boer **Voortrekkers** and was defeated by a Boer commando under Hendrik Potgieter in 1837 near the modern Pretoria. He and his people then moved northwards, settling in what is now southwestern Zimbabwe. There he established his power over many of the Shona peoples and succeeded in keeping whites at bay until his death.

N

NAACP (National Association for the Advancement of Colored People) US civil rights organization established in 1910. This biracial association developed from the National Negro Committee Conference, held in 1909 in the aftermath of riots in Springfield, Illinois, in which eight people had died. Though Booker T **Washington** refused to join the association, its founding members included Jane **Addams**, William Monroe Trotter and W E B **Du Bois**, who became editor of its magazine, *Crisis*. The NAACP's aim was to 'make 11 000 000 Americans physically free from peonage, mentally free from ignorance, politically free from disenfranchisement and socially free from insult', through educating public opinion, lobbying for legislative reform and sponsoring court action. Its first major success came in 1915 when the Supreme Court ruled the **grandfather clause** to be unconstitutional, and a series of victories over aspects of segregation culminated in **Brown v Board of Education of Topeka, Kansas** (1954). The membership of the movement grew from 6 000 in 1914 to 500 000 in the early 1990s.

Nabuco (de Araújo), Joaquim Aurélio (1849–1912) Brazilian politician and abolitionist. Born into a major Liberal political dynasty, he was a diplomat, then became a deputy (1878–80, 1885 and 1887–9). He founded the Brazilian Society for the Abolition of Slavery and led the campaign to abolish slavery through the legislature and the courts, rather than by extrajudicial means. He triumphed, largely as a result of the slave insurrections in São Paulo in 1887–8, the refusal of the Cabinet to face possible civil war, and the acceptance of abolition as a fait accompli by the Chamber of Deputies in May 1888. An admirer of **Pedro II**, he left public life after the former's deposition (Nov 1889), returning as a special envoy and ambassador to the USA.

Nacertanije (1844) Literally 'outline', the term describes the Serbian national programme presented by Ilija **Garašanin** to Alexander Karageorgević. It advocated the creation of Great Serbia which was to include **Serbia**, **Montenegro**, Bosnia and Herzegovina and, for the sake of a corridor to the

sea, north Albania. Serbian foreign policy continued to be informed by the *Nacertanije* throughout the 19c. After the creation of the Kingdom of Serbs, **Croats** and Slovenes (later Yugoslavia) at the end of **World War I**, the continued desire of many Serbs for the Great Serbia of the Nacertanije bedevilled their relations with the other nations within Yugoslavia.

Nadir Shah (1688–1747) King of Persia (1736/47). Born in Khurasan, he expelled the Afghan rulers of Persia, defeated the Turks (1731), conquered Afghanistan, and ravaged the north-west of India, taking Delhi. His domestic policy led to revolts, especially on religious matters, and he was assassinated at Fathabad.

Nagano Osami (1880–1947) Japanese naval officer. Educated at the Naval Academy, Etajima, he studied law at Harvard and served as naval attaché in Washington (1920–3). Promoted rear-admiral in 1928, he was superintendent of the Naval Academy (1928–9). As head of the Japanese delegation to the 2nd London Naval Conference (1935–6), he advocated the expansion of Japanese naval power. He was Navy Minister (1936–7), Commander-in-Chief Combined Fleet (1937), and Chief of Naval General Staff (1941–4). He planned and ordered the Japanese attack on **Pearl Harbor** (Dec 1941) and died while on trial for war crimes.

Nagasaki The capital of Nagasaki prefecture, western Kyushu, Japan, it was the target for the second atomic bomb of **World War II** (9 Aug 1945) which killed or injured c. 75 000 people and destroyed over one-third of the city.

Nagodba (1868) Literally 'compromise', this term describes the agreement which regulated Croatia's status within the Dual Monarchy of **Austria-Hungary**. After the **Ausgleich** (1867), **Dalmatia** and **Istria** came under the Austrian half of the Dual Monarchy, while **Croatia** and **Slavonia** were joined and placed under Hungarian jurisdiction. The *Nagodba* recognized Croatia as a distinct political unit within Hungary and allowed the **Croats** to elect their own *sabor* (parliament) and to have a measure of control over their internal affairs; however, in matters concerning external affairs, finance, defence and trade, they were subject to the joint parliament at Pest. The overall effect of the Nagodba was to effect Croatia's subordination to Hungary: the Croats were then left without direct access to the central government of the empire and their ban was chosen by the Hungarian Prime Minister and the Emperor, a provision which shortly led to the appointment of the much-reviled **Khuen-Hédervány**. In Sep 1668 the sabor, which had fallen prey to Hungarian gerrymandering, accepted the Nagodba which remained in force until the collapse of the Habsburg Empire (1918).

Nagy, Imre (1896–1958) Hungarian politician. Born into a poor peasant family, he came into contact with Bolshevism as a prisoner in Russia in **World War I** and, after returning to Hungary, he held a minor post in the Béla **Kun** revolutionary government in 1919. He fled to the USSR for two years, but returned to participate in the illegal Hungarian communist movement until 1929, when he again had to flee. Returning with the **Red Army** in 1944, he held various ministerial posts in a chequered career until he became Prime Minister. As a moderate he was ousted in 1955 and brought back during the **Hungarian Uprising** the following year. His decision to declare Hungary neutral and to appeal to the **UN** for help provoked Soviet suppression of the uprising. He was displaced by János **Kádár** and executed in 1958. What was regarded as his martyrdom was avenged with the overthrow of the communists in 1989. ▷ **Russian Revolution**

Nahayan, Sheikh Zayed bin Sultan al- (1918–) Amir of Abu Dhabi. He was governor of the eastern province of Abu Dhabi, one of seven Trucial States on the southern shores of the Persian Gulf and the Gulf of Oman, which were under British protection, until in 1969 he deposed his brother, Sheikh Shakhbut, and became Amir. When the States decided to federate as the United Arab Emirates in 1971 he became President of its Supreme Council. He was unanimously re-elected in 1986.

Nahhas, Mustafa al- (1879–1965) Egyptian politician. He was the leader of the Wafd Party in Egypt in 1923 and Premier in 1928, 1930 and 1950. In addition, al-Nahhas acted as regent for King Farouk in his early years and, despite their being dismissed by Farouq

in 1938, the Wafd were brought back in 1941 at Britain's behest. The damage done to the reputation of the Wafd by their cooperation with the British was irreparable. Although al-Nahhas became Premier again in 1950 after the Wafd's victory in the elections, and despite his endeavours to regain credibility for the Wafd by giving the party an anti-British bias, they were again dismissed by Farouk in 1952. Al-Nahhas then left the political stage, charged with but not tried for corruption and in the same year (1952) King Farouk was deposed by General Neguib on behalf of the **Free Officers**. The Wafd Party was dissolved in 1953.

Naicker, E V Ramaswami (1879–1973) Indian social reformer. A fiery anti-Brahmin crusader, he was responsible for reorganizing the Justice Party, a rival of the **Indian National Congress**, into the *Dravid Munnetra Kazagam* (DMK), an exclusively Tamil party. He began his public career as an exponent of social equality and became a crusader against 'untouchability' — the synonym for the range of prejudices (particularly acute in the south of India) which were directed against low-caste members of Indian society. He was elected Chairman of Erode Municipal Council and joined the Congress in the 1910s. Naicker participated in the **Non-Cooperation Movement** and courted arrest in 1922. In 1925 he launched the Self Respect Movement and, in 1933, led his first anti-Hindu march. He was elected President of the Justice Party in 1938 and reorganized it into the DMK in 1944. He denounced Hinduism, the **caste** system and child marriage, and opposed the imposition of Hindi, the northern language, on the population of southern India, the 'Dravidians'. ▷ **Untouchables**

Naidu, Sarojini (1879–1949) Indian feminist, politician and poet. Educated at Madras, London and Cambridge, she became known as 'the Nightingale of India' as the author of three volumes of lyric verse between 1905 and 1915. She lectured widely on feminism and campaigned for the abolition of purdah, and in 1925 became the first President of M K **Gandhi**'s **Indian National Congress**. She was imprisoned several times for **civil disobedience**, and took a leading part in the negotiations that led to her country's independence in 1947, when she was appointed Governor of the United Provinces, now Uttar Pradesh.

Najibullah, Major General (1947–) Afghan politician. He became active in the

Moscow-inspired People's Democratic Party of Afghanistan (PDPA) in the mid-1960s, and was twice imprisoned for his political activities. After King Mohammed **Zahir Shah** was deposed in a military coup and abdicated (1973), he rose rapidly in the party hierarchy, and as a member of the PDPA's Central Committee, played a key role in the negotiations that led to the 1978 Treaty of Friendship with the USSR that served as a pretext for the Russian invasion the following year, when he was made Information Minister. He was admitted to the Afghan Politburo in 1981, and became President in 1987. Strong guerrilla resistance by the members of the National Islamic Front continued, and insistence by the Russian army, in the wake of continued attacks by Pakistani **Mujahidin** guerrillas on the Kabul-Soviet border, that Najibullah's regime should continue to be funded despite the USSR's own economic difficulties was a factor in the resignation in Dec 1990 of Foreign Minister Eduard **Shevardnadze**. In 1991, the **UN** renewed its call for elections in mujaheddin-controlled territories with a view to replacing Najibullah's regime with a democratically-elected Government. Najibullah finally resigned, handing over power to a coalition of Mujahidin leaders in May 1992.

Nakasone Yasuhiro (1918–) Japanese politician. Educated at Tokyo University, he was a junior naval officer in **World War II**, and entered the Ministry of Home Affairs in 1945. Elected to the Diet at the age of 29 for the Liberal-Democratic (Conservative) Party, he held a range of ministerial posts from 1959 to 1982. As Prime Minister (1982–8), he supported the renewal of the US–Japan Security Treaty, and maintained close relations with US President Ronald **Reagan**.

Nakaz (1767) Literally the 'instruction' from **Catherine II, 'the Great'** to the Legislative Commission she summoned to discuss and reshape the laws of Russia that had last been codified in 1649. It took her 18 months to prepare and she drew heavily on the works of Montesquieu and other writers of the European Enlightenment. However, she modified their ideas to suit her own autocratic purposes. The commission excluded the largest segment of the population, the serfs, and in the course of a year and a half of discussion it became divided along interest group lines. Catherine dismissed it without its achieving other than the accumulation of

papers useful to administrators and historians. Yet it did help to establish her prestige in Russia and abroad.

Nalanda A Buddhist monastery in Bihar founded in the Gupta period (320–500), Nalanda became one of the most famous teaching centres of medieval Buddhism. The Chinese traveller, Hsuan Tsang, described Nalanda in the 7c as being a monastery which was full of intellectual activities. Under its aged and saintly abbot, Silabhadra, Nalanda became the foremost educational centre in the north and attracted students and scholars from places as distant as China and south-east Asia. It grew from being a monastery which trained Buddhist novices to an institute where Vedas, Hindu philosophy, logic, grammar, medicine and various other subjects were taught. The students were predominantly Buddhist but candidates from other orders who passed an examination were admitted. Nalanda was supported by the revenues of an enormous estate of one hundred villages, and by many wealthy patrons including the great king, Harsha. It continued to be a centre for learning until its destruction by the Turkish invaders.

Namboodripad, E M S (1909–) Indian politician. Hailing from Kerala, he was educated in Victoria College, Palghat, and St Thomas College, Trichur. He was Chief Minister of Kerala in 1957–9 and again in 1967–9. Acting General-Secretary of the Communist Party in 1962–3, he became its Secretary-General in 1978 and went on to hold the post of Secretary-General of the Communist (Marxist) Party of India (CPM). He has also written on various Indian political and economic issues. ▷ **Communist Parties of India**

Nana Sahib (Brahmin Dundhu Panth) (c.1820–c.1859) Indian rebel. The adopted son of the ex-peshwa of the Marathas, he became known as the leader of the 1857–8 **Indian Uprising**. On its outbreak, he was proclaimed peshwa, and was held responsible for the massacres at Cawnpore (Kanpur). After the collapse of the uprising he escaped into Nepal.

Nandas A dynasty described as the first empire-builders of India. Mahapadma Nanda founded the dynasty in the mid-4c BC. He was Emperor of Magadha and succeeded in gaining control of **Kalinga** and of other parts of Deccan. The Nandas were the first of a number of non-kshatriya dynasties. The

Nandas built up a vast army anticipating the Greek invasion but never had the opportunity to use the army against them since the campaign of **Alexander III, 'the Great'** campaign terminated in Punjab. The Nandas made a methodical collection of taxes and land revenue became a substantial source of income. The Nandas also built canals and carried out irrigation projects. The possibility of an imperial structure based on an essentially agrarian economy began to germinate in the Indian mind. The further development of the Nandas was however cut short by Chandragupta Maurya, who usurped the Nanda throne in 321BC.

Nanjing, Treaty of (29 Aug 1842) Signed at the conclusion of the **Opium War** between China and Britain, it was to be the first of a series of unequal treaties that gave extensive privileges to the foreign powers in China. Five **treaty ports** were opened for British residence and trade; British consuls were to be stationed permanently in these ports; the **Cohong** monopoly system was abolished; a huge indemnity was imposed on the Chinese government to compensate for the opium confiscated in 1839 and to cover the expenses of the British military expedition; and the island of Hong Kong was ceded to Britain 'in perpetuity'. A supplementary treaty (1843) fixed tariff rates, thus infringing on China's tariff autonomy, and stipulated a 'most-favoured nation' clause: any privileges or immunities granted to the nationals of other foreign countries were to be automatically extended to those of Britain. The USA and France concluded similar treaties with China in 1844; additional privileges granted included the enjoyment of extraterritoriality (foreigners in the treaty ports to be subject to the jurisdiction of their own consuls) and the right of missionaries to build churches and proselytize in the treaty ports. While the **Qing Dynasty** regarded such concessions as minor irritants, by the turn of the century Chinese nationalists were to view the Nanjing Treaty as the opening move in a full-scale imperialist onslaught on China.

Nansen, Fridtjof (1861–1930) Norwegian explorer, scientist and statesman. Educated at Oslo and Naples, in 1882 he travelled into the Arctic regions, and in 1888 made an east–west journey across Greenland. His greatest scheme was to reach the North Pole by letting his specially built ship, the *Fram*, get frozen into the ice north of Siberia and drift with a current setting towards Greenland. During the union crisis with Sweden

(1905) he was one of the leading spokesmen for Norwegian independence and Norway's unofficial representative in Britain. In 1906–8 he was the first ambassador of independent Norway in London and played an active part in the negotiations leading to the Norwegian integrity treaty of 1907. During **World War I** he headed a trade delegation to the USA which led to a war trade agreement in Apr 1918. As Norway's first delegate to the **League of Nations** (1920), Nansen became deeply engaged in post-war relief work. He was appointed League Commissioner for Refugees, and thousands of displaced persons were issued with special 'Nansen passports'. In 1921 he organized relief for the victims of famine in Russia, saving 1.5–2 million people from death by starvation. In 1922 he was awarded the Nobel Peace Prize in recognition of his relief efforts.

Nantes, Edict of (1598) A law promulgated by **Henry IV** of France granting religious and civil liberties to his Huguenot subjects at the end of the Wars of **Religion**. **Richelieu** annulled its political clauses (1629) as a threat to the integrity of the state; and the same motive led **Louis XIV** to order the revocation of the edict (1685). ▷ **Huguenots**

Naoroji, Dadabhai (1825–1917) Indian politician. He became Professor of Mathematics at Elphinstone College, Bombay, and was later a member of the Legislative Council. From 1892 to 1895 Naoroji represented the London constituency of Finsbury in the House of Commons — the first Indian MP — and was also President of the **Indian National Congress**. He was particularly renowned for his economic critiques of British rule in India, despite his admiration for the British system of education and the country's tradition of liberal political philosophy.

Napata An ancient city, situated on the western bank of the Nile in what is now the Sudan. It was the capital of the kingdom of **Kush** c.750–590BC. Although political dominance passed to Meroe in that year, Napata remained the kingdom's religious capital.

Napier, Sir Charles James (1782–1853) British general and colonial administrator. He fought in the **Peninsular War** from 1808 to 1811, against the USA (1812), and in 1842 was sent to India to take command of the war in Sind. He defeated the amirs at Miani (1843), and was made Governor of the province. In 1847 he returned to England, but went back to India before the end of the second of the **Sikh Wars** to command the army. He left India in 1851.

Napier (of Magdala), Robert (Cornelis), 1st Baron (1810–90) British field marshal. Born in Ceylon, he joined the army in 1826 and distinguished himself at the Siege of **Lucknow** (1857–8). He carried out successful expeditions during the Chinese War (1860) and in Abyssinia (1868), and became Commander-in-Chief in India (1870), Governor of Gibraltar (1876–82), and Constable of the Tower of London (1887). Created a baron in 1868, he died in London. ▷ **Indian Uprising**

Napoleon I (Napoleon Bonaparte) (1769–1821) French general and Emperor (1804/15). He entered the military schools at Brienne (1779) and Paris (1784), commanded the artillery at the Siege of Toulon (1793), and was promoted Brigadier-General. In 1796 he married **Josephine**, widow of the Viscount of **Beauharnais**, and soon after left for Italy, where he skilfully defeated the Piedmontese and Austrians, and made several gains through the Treaty of Campo Formio (1797). Intending to break British trade by conquering Egypt, he captured Malta (1798), and entered Cairo, defeating the Turks; but after the French fleet was destroyed by Nelson at the Battle of the Nile, he returned to France (1799), having learnt of French reverses in Europe. The coup d'état of 18th Brumaire followed (9 Nov 1799) in which Napoleon assumed power as First Consul, instituting a military dictatorship. He then routed the Austrians at **Marengo** (1800), made further gains at the Treaty of Luneville (1801), and consolidated French domination by the **Concordat** (1801) with Rome and the Peace of Amiens with England (1802). Elected consul for life, he crowned himself Emperor in 1804. His administrative, military, educational, and legal reforms (notably the **Code Napoléon**) made a lasting impact on French society. War with England was renewed, and extended to Russia and Austria. Forced by England's naval victory at **Trafalgar** (1805) to abandon the notion of invasion, he attacked the Austrians and Russians, gaining victories at Ulm and **Austerlitz** (1805). Prussia was defeated at **Jena and Auerstädt** (1806), and Russia at **Friedland** (1807). After the Peace of Tilsit, he became the arbiter of Europe. He then tried to cripple England with the Continental System, ordering the European states under his control to boycott British goods. He sent armies into Portugal and Spain, which resulted in the bitter and ultimately unsuccessful Peninsular War (1808–14). In 1809, wanting an heir, he divorced Josephine, who was childless, and married the Archduchess **Marie Louise** of Austria, a son being born in 1811. Believing that Russia was planning an alliance with England, he invaded, defeating the Russians at **Borodino**, before entering Moscow, but he was forced to retreat, his army broken by hunger and the Russian winter. In 1813 his victories over the allied armies continued at **Lützen**, Bautzen and Dresden, but he was routed at the Battle of **Leipzig**, and France was invaded. Forced to abdicate, he was given the sovereignty of Elba (1814). The unpopularity which followed the return of the Bourbons motivated him to return to France in 1815. He regained power for a period known as the **Hundred Days**, but was defeated by the combination of **Wellington**'s and **Blücher**'s forces at **Waterloo**. He fled to Paris, abdicated, surrendered to the British, and was banished to St Helena, where he died. ▷ **Amiens, Treaty of; Bourbon, House of; Brumaire Coup; Campo Formio, Treaty of; French Revolution; Napoleonic Wars; Nelson, Horatio; Peninsular War; Tilsit, Treaties of**

Napoleon II (François Charles Joseph Bonaparte) (1811–32) King of Rome. He was the son of **Napoleon I** by the Empress **Marie Louise**. Styled King of Rome at his birth, after his father's abdication he was brought up in Austria and in 1818 given the title of the Duke of Reichstadt, though allowed no active political role.

Napoleon III (Louis Napoleon) (1808–73) President of the Second French Republic and Emperor of the French (1852/70). Born in Paris, the third son of Louis Bonaparte, King of Holland (the brother of **Napoleon I**) and Hortense Beauharnais, he was brought up in Switzerland. On the death of the Duke of Reichstadt (1832), he became head of the Napoleonic dynasty. He made two abortive attempts on the French throne (1836 and 1840), for which he was imprisoned at Ham, near Amiens. He escaped to England (1846), but when the Bonapartist tide swept France after the **February Revolution** (1848) he was elected first to the Assembly and then to the Presidency (1848–52). He carried out a coup d'état in 1851 and assumed the title of Emperor (1852); in 1853 he married Eugénie de Montijo de Guzman (1826–1920), a Spanish countess, who bore him a son, the Prince Imperial (1856). He actively

Napoleonic Europe, c.1812

encouraged economic expansion and the modernization of Paris. His search for prestige in foreign affairs was at first successful in the **Crimean War** (1854–6) and in the war against Austria (1859), which brought France Nice and Savoy (1860); it also led, not in accordance with his plans, to the unification of Italy. Outside Europe, he joined with Britain in expeditions to open China to commerce (1857–60), and acquired colonies in Senegal and Indo-China, but his ill-starred intervention in Mexico (1862–5) ended in disaster. Encouraged by the Empress Eugénie, he unwisely declared war on Prussia in 1870 and suffered humiliating defeat, culminating in the Battle of **Sedan**. Confined at Wilhelmshohe until 1871, he went into exile in England, where he lived until his death. ▷ **Empire, Second** (France)**; Franco-Prussian War; Haussmann, Georges Eugène, Baron; Mexican War; Napoleon II**

Napoleon Bonaparte ▷ **Napoleon I**

Napoleonic Wars (1800–15) The continuation of the **French Revolutionary Wars**, fought to preserve French hegemony in Europe. They increasingly became a manifestation of **Napoleon I**'s personal ambitions. The wars began with Napoleon's destruction of the Second Coalition (1800); after a peaceful interlude (1802–3) Britain resumed hostilities, prompting Napoleon to prepare for invasion, and encouraging the formation of a Third Coalition (1805–7). While Britain retained naval superiority (1805), Napoleon established territorial domination, sustained by economic warfare, resulting in the invasions of Spain (1808) and Russia (1812). Gradually the French were overwhelmed by the Fourth Coalition (1813–14); the **Hundred Days**' epilogue ended with the Battle of **Waterloo** (1815). ▷ **Austerlitz/Copenhagen/ Leipzig/Marengo/Trafalgar/Wagram, Battles of; Confederation of the Rhine; Grand Alliance, War of the; Paris, Treaties of; Peninsular Wars; Tilsit, Treaties of; Vienna, Congress of**

Nara Period (710–94) The period in Japanese history when the imperial capital was located in Nara near present-day Kyoto. It represented the height of Chinese political and cultural influence on Japan. The city

655

itself was patterned on the Chinese **Tang Dynasty** capital of **Chang'an** and a short-lived attempt was made to introduce a Chinese-style centralized bureaucracy in order to buttress the power of the imperial institution. After the removal of the capital to Heian (Kyoto) in 784, the political influence of Japanese emperors waned until they became virtually symbolic figureheads.

Narayan, Jaiprakash ('JP') (1902–79) Indian freedom fighter and politician. He was educated in a village primary school and abandoned his studies in 1921 to join the **Non-Cooperation Movement**. He went to the USA on a scholarship and obtained a masters degree from the University of Ohio. Influenced by Marxist ideas, he joined the communist movement. He however accepted **Nehru**'s offer to take charge of the Labour Department in Congress, joined the **civil disobedience** movement after the failure of the M K **Gandhi**–Irwin talks and was jailed. One of the founders of the Congress Socialist Party in 1934, he advocated the abolition of the zamindari system and the nationalization of heavy industries. The author of a number of books and booklets on social, political and economic problems, he took an active part in the **Quit India Movement** of 1942, but gave up politics after India gained independence and joined the **Bhoodan** movement of Vinoba **Bhave**. Later, he was closely involved in the protest movement against the Chinese policy on Tibet and also toured the tribal areas of Nagaland in an attempt to bring about a rapprochement between the rebel Nagas and the government of India. He organized famine relief for the affected people of Bihar in 1967 and persuaded several dacoits of Madhya Pradesh to surrender their arms in 1972. He led the movement for restoration of democracy and liberties after the imposition of the 'emergency' by Indira **Gandhi** in 1975, for which he was arrested. Released in 1977, he led the Janata Party to victory in the general election of that year.

Narmer (Menes) (c.3100BC) King of Egypt. The founder of the 1st Dynasty, he is considered by some scholars to be the king who accomplished the unification of Egypt c.3100BC. Strong evidence for this exists in a ceremonial slate palette now in the Cairo Museum, which shows the king wearing the crowns of Upper and Lower Egypt, symbolizing his claim to be ruler of both lands. The palette is also important in recording the development at this early period of a method of writing, the hieroglyphic script. Memphis,

the capital of Egypt, was traditionally established by Narmer at the apex of the Nile Delta. Some authorities hold that the 'Menes' of Manetho, an Egyptian priest who wrote a history of Egypt during the **Ptolemaic Period**, combines in a single character both Narmer and his successor, Aha.

Narodna Obrana Literally 'National Defence', this term refers to the Serbian nationalist society which was founded after the annexation of Bosnia-Herzegovina by Austria (1908).

Narodniki Russian populists, revolutionaries who turned their backs on intellectual arguments and looked to an awakened peasantry as the hope for political and social change. The movement really got under way in the early 1870s as young people, mostly the privileged and educated from the towns, went into the countryside to harangue the frequently baffled peasants. Many were arrested, and following mass trials in 1877–8 many were exiled to Siberia. Thereafter the movement became more conspiratorial and turned to terrorism and assassination. The first group to emerge was 'Land and Liberty'; and it was an offshoot of this, 'The People's Will', that organized **Alexander II**'s assassination in 1881. Populism and terrorism in various forms continued down to 1917.

Narses (c.478–573) Byzantine general. The famous general of Emperor **Justinian I, 'the Great'**, and rival of **Belisarius**, he reasserted Byzantine control over Rome and Italy by his victories over the Ostrogoths (550–4).

Narváez, Ramón María (1800–68) Spanish soldier and politician. A supporter of **Isabella II**, he defeated the Carlists in 1836, and then took part in an unsuccessful insurrection against **Espartero** in 1840 and fled to France, where he was joined by **María Cristina**. In 1843 he led a Republican insurrection in Madrid that drove Espartero from power, and became virtual dictator. He lost power temporarily in 1851, and was briefly exiled as special ambassador to France, but from 1856 he was Premier again several times.

Naseby, Battle of (14 June 1645) A major conflict of the **English Civil Wars** in Northamptonshire. The royalist forces of **Charles I**, outnumbered by two to one, were defeated by parliament's **New Model Army** led by **Fairfax**, with **Cromwell** commanding the cavalry. Royalist cavalry, led by Prince **Rupert**, left the main battle, fatally weakening Charles's forces.

Nash, Sir Walter (1882–1968) British-born New Zealand politician. Nash went to New Zealand in 1909. From 1919 to 1960 he served on the national executive of the New Zealand Labour Party, encouraging the adoption of a moderate reform programme in the Christian socialist tradition. A member of parliament from 1929, he held numerous ministerial appointments from 1935 onwards and in **World War II** was Deputy Prime Minister to Peter **Fraser**, although from 1942 to 1944 he headed a special mission to the USA. He was Prime Minister (1957–60), retiring from the party leadership in 1963.

Nasir al-Din Shah (1831–96) Qajar Shah of Persia (1848/96). He visited England in 1873 and 1889, introduced some European ideas into Persia, granted trade concessions to Britain and Russia, and was shot near Tehran by an assassin. He was succeeded by his second son, Muzzaffar al-Din.

Nasriddimova, Yadgar Sadykovna (1920–) Soviet bureaucrat and politician. Born in Uzbekistan and educated in the Tashkent Institute of Railway Engineering, she rose through various party and government offices eventually to become chairman of the Soviet of Nationalities in Moscow (1970–4). Her corruption was such, however, that she had to be demoted to a ministry in 1974; it was not until 1988 that she could be removed from the party itself.

Nassau A Burgundian noble family, who rose as servants of the Habsburgs, then rebelled against their authority in the Low Countries. They were made *stadtholders* of Holland, Zeeland, and Friesland, Counts of Nassau, and Princes of Orange by Emperor **Charles V**. The heirs to the titles, William of Orange (1533–84), and his brother Louis (1538–74), Count of Nassau, supported and led the Dutch Revolt (1566–1648) against their former masters. ▷ **Habsburg Dynasty**

Nasser, Gamal Abd al- (1918–70) Egyptian politician. An army officer, he became dissatisfied with the corruption of the regime of King **Farouk**, and was involved in the military coup of 1952. He became Prime Minister (1954–6) and then President (1956–70), deposing his fellow officer, General Mohammed **Neguib**. During his term of office, he nationalized the Suez Canal, which led to Israel's invasion of Sinai, and the intervention of Anglo-French forces. He aimed to build a North African Arab empire, and in 1958 created a federation with Syria,

the **United Arab Republic**, from which Syria withdrew in 1961. After the Arab–Israeli **Six-Day War** (1967), heavy losses on the Arab side led to his resignation, but he was persuaded to stay on, and died while still in office in Cairo.

Nation, Carry Amelia (1846–1911) US temperance advocate, born in Kentucky. After the death of her first husband from alcoholism, she moved to Kansas, where she took up the temperance cause. She gained notoriety as a prohibitionist following her numerous saloon-smashing expeditions, for which she was frequently arrested for disturbance of the peace, and during which this large and powerful woman wielded a hatchet to destroy bars and the alcohol they contained.

National American Woman Suffrage Association (NAWSA) A US feminist organization. Founded in 1890, it united the National Woman Suffrage Association (for which the suffrage was only one cause amongst others) with the American Woman Suffrage Association (for which the suffrage was the only cause). Elizabeth Cady **Stanton** was President of the new organization for the first two years, followed by Susan B **Anthony** until 1900. By 1912, under the leadership of Carrie Chapman **Catt**, the movement had become increasingly staid in contrast to the more militant National Women's Party organized by Alice **Paul**. Nevertheless its policy of intense lobbying was instrumental in achieving passage of the 19th Amendment, giving women the vote, which was finally ratified in June 1919, and went into effect in Aug 1920.

National Defence, Government of (1870–1) In France, the government that replaced the Second Empire on 4 Sep 1870. As its name indicates, its primary task was seen as continuing the war against **Prussia**; it consisted of republicans, and continued in office until replaced by a government under **Thiers**, appointed by the National Assembly elected in Feb 1871. ▷ **Empire, Second** (France)

National Front (NF) A strongly nationalist political party in Britain which centres its political programme on opposition to immigration, and calls for the repatriation of ethnic minorities even if they were born in the UK. The party was created in 1960 by the merger of the White Defence League and the National Labour Party, and in its early years was a small neo-Nazi grouping. In the mid- and late 1970s it had some minor impact in elections and its membership grew. It tried to develop a more respectable face and recruited some members from the right of the **Conservative Party** to widen its base beyond hardline neo-fascists. Its political appeal declined with the election of a Conservative government in 1979.

National Guard The body created (13 July 1789) in France to replace the royal troops that the National Assembly refused to allow to enter Paris. Other towns followed the example, and soon most towns had their own guard under the control of the municipal council. It consisted of active (richer) citizens, and played a prominent part in the revolutionary events of 1792–3. Having shown royalist sympathies in 1795, it was suppressed; revived in a different form under the First Empire, and reorganized again in 1815, it became a bastion of the 'bourgeois' monarchy of **Louis-Philippe**. The refusal of some elements of the Paris National Guard to defend the regime in Feb 1848 was the signal for the **February Revolution**. It was virtually suspended during the Second Empire, but the Paris National Guard was enormously expanded and transformed in 1870 in a vain attempt to defeat the Prussian invader. Its revolt (Mar 1871) was the catalyst of the **Paris Commune**, in which many of its rank and file perished. It was finally suppressed after the defeat of the Commune. ▷ **Empire, Second** (France)

National Labor Relations Act (Wagner Act) (1935) US labour legislation. Instigated and steered through Congress by Senator Robert Wagner, the act sought to find an effective means of guaranteeing the right of collective bargaining. It established a National Labor Relations Board with legal powers to ensure compliance by employers, especially in allowing employees to elect their own bargaining agent without fear of discrimination. It also prohibited company unions and opened the way for a huge expansion in union membership. ▷ **Lewis, John L; Taft–Hartley Act; United Automobile Workers**

National Party (NP) A party formed in South Africa, in 1912, to reflect the Boer (Afrikaner) interest. Over the years it absorbed smaller parties like the Afrikaner Party and developed an explicit programme of Afrikaner advancement and separation of the races. It gained power in 1948 and has retained power since then. Originally an almost exclusively Afrikaner party, it has recently begun to lose some Afrikaners to more specifically nationalist organizations while gaining the support of conservative English-speaking white South Africans. Under the leadership of F W **De Klerk**, the party has begun to orchestrate the transfer of power from whites to a more democratic political base.

National Party of Australia The third largest party in Australia, it grew out of the Australian Country Party formed in 1920. Renamed the National Country Party in 1975, it took its present title in 1982, but except in Queensland it remains sectional in both its support and its policies. Socially conservative, favouring low tariffs and support for agriculture, it has generally acted in coalition with the major anti-Labor grouping of the time, most notably the **Liberal Party of Australia** (1949–72). Only in Queensland, where the National Party title was adopted in 1974, has the party been able to rule in its own right.

National Republican Party US political party. It emerged in the winter of 1824–5 from remnants of the US Democratic-Republican Party. Opposed to Andrew Jackson and centred on John Quincy **Adams** (President, 1825–9) and Henry **Clay**, his Secretary of State, the National Republicans espoused active intervention in the economy. By 1836 they were absorbed into the **Whig Party**. ▷ **Republican Party**

National Revolution (1940) In France, the name given by the supporters of **Pétain** and the **Vichy** regime to the abolition of the Third Republic; it symbolized their political programme, also epitomized in the national motto, *Travail, Famille, Patrie* ('Work, Family, Fatherland'), that was imposed in place of the republican **'Liberty, Equality, Fraternity'**. ▷ **collaboration** (France); **Republic, Third** (France); **World War II**

National Road A road built in the early 19c from Cumberland, Maryland, to Vandalia, Illinois, and eventually to St Louis, Missouri. Its construction and repair were financed initially by government sales of land, but in the 1830s this became the responsibility of the states through which it passed. The National Road played an important role in the expansion of the West.

National Security Council (NSC) A body created by Congress in 1947 to advise the US

President on the integration of domestic, foreign, and military policies relating to national security. It was designed to achieve effective coordination between the military services and other government agencies and departments, and is composed of the President, Vice-President, Secretary of State, and Secretary of Defence. The Chairman of the Joint Chiefs of Staff and the Director of Central Intelligence are advisers.

National Socialist Movement (*Nationaal Socialistische Beweging*, NSB) Dutch fascist party. Founded in 1931 by A A **Mussert** and C van Geelkerken (1901–76), the party attracted some support in the Netherlands in the 1930s, achieving 8 per cent of the votes in the local elections of 1935. During the German occupation of **World War II** there were 87000 members, but the German authorities gave the leaders of the NSB very little real power. After the war the NSB members were widely persecuted, interned, tried and imprisoned; several of the leaders, such as Mussert, were executed.

National Urban League US civil rights organization. Founded in 1911 by professional blacks and progressive whites, it aimed to provide for rural blacks arriving in Northern cities the same services as those provided to white arrivals by settlement houses and charities. The definition of its aims demonstrates the influence of Booker T **Washington**: 'to promote, encourage, assist and engage in any and all kinds of work for improving the industrial, economic, social and spiritual condition among Negroes'.

National Workshops (1848) Set up in France after the **February Revolution** of 1848, the name suggested an attempt to create a state-supported cooperative system of production, advocated by Louis **Blanc** in his book *L'Organisation du travail* (1839). In reality, they amounted to little more than a scheme of unemployment pay, and were soon seen as impossible to continue because of the huge cost. Restriction of entitlement to the payments led to the rising of the Parisian workers known as the **June Days**.

Nation of Islam ▷ **Black Muslims**

Native Americans (American Indians) The original inhabitants of the Western Hemisphere who arrived during the last Ice Age, estimated at 20000 to 40000 years ago. They came in several migrations over a land bridge connecting Alaska with Siberia, and

Native Americans: Location of tribes at the time of the discovery

659

spread gradually throughout the Americas. In what is now the USA, the Native Americans developed ways of life that suited the area in which they lived. Those of the Northwest Coast lived off the sea; those living on the buffalo-rich Great Plains were hunters and gatherers; those in the warm and abundant southeast were skilled farmers and fishermen. Columbus, mistakenly believing he had reached India, called the indigenous people he encountered 'Indians'. Friendships with the Native Americans were indispensable to the survival of the early European settlers, who were shown how to grow native crops and where to hunt and fish, saving them from almost certain starvation. The Europeans unwittingly brought diseases to which the native people had no immunity, wiping out thousands and nearly destroying whole tribes. In addition, as more Europeans came and spread further west, Native American resistance to the encroachment of white settlers increased and the long conflict known as the **Indian Wars** began. The numerous tribes with their diverse languages lacked the cohesion to repel the influx of well-supplied, determined settlers. Since Native American land was increasingly in demand, most of the tribes east of the Mississippi River were pushed west. But as western land was opened to settlers, the Native Americans were forced onto reservations in hostile terrain and far from their original lands, sometimes close to traditional tribal enemies. With their affairs administered by the federal government, they lost control over their lives and were not granted US citizenship until 1924. In the USA today the Native American population is growing quickly (38% growth according to the 1990 census). Of the current population of almost 2 million, more than half live off reservations in metropolitan areas. Over 50 languages are now spoken among the more than 500 tribes. As a group, Native Americans are among the poorest in the nation and continue to contend with both the prejudice and romanticized images of the past. Throughout the second half of the 20c they have been pressing for increasing self-determination, striving to balance their economic and political survival against the preservation of their cultural and spiritual identities.

nativism US anti-immigrant attitude, generally expressed by native-born white Protestants. From the early 19c, a major focus of anti-immigrant feeling was directed toward Irish Catholics who were accused by nativists of bringing the papacy into US politics. Nativist antagonism was also extended to other immigrant groups. Between 1854 and 1858, the nativist movement made significant political gains with the American Party, popularly known as the **Know-Nothings**. Nativism began to diminish in importance as the slavery issue became a dominant American concern. With the renewal of immigration in the late 19c and early 20c, nativist sentiment resurfaced and contributed largely to the passage of the Immigration Act of 1924, which eventually brought a sharp curtailment to immigration by establishing immigration quotas.

NATO (North Atlantic Treaty Organization) An organization established by a treaty signed in 1949 by Belgium, Canada, Denmark, France, Iceland, Italy, Luxembourg, the Netherlands, Norway, Portugal, the UK, and the USA; Greece and Turkey acceded in 1952, West Germany in 1955, and Spain in 1982. NATO is a permanent military alliance established to defend Western Europe against Soviet aggression. The treaty commits the members to treat an armed attack on one of them as an attack on all of them, and for all to assist the country attacked by such actions as are deemed necessary. The alliance forces are based on contributions from the member countries' armed services and operate under a multinational command. The remit includes the deployment of nuclear, as well as conventional, weapons. Its institutions include a Council, an International Secretariat, the Supreme Headquarters Allied Powers, Europe (SHAPE), and various committees to formulate common policies. In the 1970s and 1980s, NATO policy of a first-strike nuclear attack to fend off a Soviet conventional attack became controversial in Western Europe, where many thought it increased the possibility of nuclear war. In 1966 France under Charles de **Gaulle** withdrew all its forces from NATO command, but it remains a member. After the 1989 changes in E Europe, a NATO summit in London (July 1990) began the process of redefining NATO's military and political goals. ▷ **nuclear weapons**

Navajo (Navaho) Athabascan-speaking Native North Americans. They are thought to have migrated to the Southwest some time around 1000AD. With a population numbering c200000, they are one of the largest Native American groups in the USA. In the 18c they carried out raids on Spanish settlers and Pueblo in the area, but were themselves eventually defeated by US troops led by Kit **Carson** in 1863–4. They settled in 1868 on a reservation covering much of Arizona and some of New Mexico and Utah, measuring c16 million acres. Tribal income is derived from the raising of sheep and horses, metalworking, weaving, and some mining of gas, uranium, and oil resources found on their reservation. The Navajo remain among the poorest of Native Americans.

Navarino Bay, Battle of (1827) A battle fought when the British and French (with the agreement of the Russians) destroyed the Turkish and Egyptian fleets off south-west Greece. The outcome was an important factor in the achievement of Greek independence from the **Ottoman Empire**, which was formally recognized in 1828.

Navarre, Kingdom of A former kingdom of northern Spain, co-extensive with the modern province of Navarre. It was an early centre of resistance to the **Moors** and united with **Castile** in 1515.

Navas de Tolosa, Battle of Las (1212) The key battle of the medieval Spanish **Reconquest**, won by Alfonso VIII of Castile at the head of a joint army from Castile, France, Aragon, Navarre and Portugal, which routed the Almohad rulers, checked the Muslim advance permanently and prepared the way for the further extension of Christian territory.

Navigation Acts (1650–96) Protective legislation in Britain, designed to increase England's share of overseas carrying trade. The laws stated that all imports to England had to be in English ships or in those of the country of origin. The laws were frequently contentious in the 18c, adding to the 13 American colonies' sense of grievance against the mother country. These Acts were not repealed until 1849. ▷ **American Revolution**

Naxalites An extremist group which broke away from the Communist Party of India in 1969, with the aim of forming a truly revolutionary Marxist-Leninist party; their name derived from the 1967 Naxalbari revolts in west Bengal. Influenced and approved by the Chinese Communist Party, their intention was to seize power by violent means, rather than through parliamentary channels. In the early 1970s the group was involved in political violence, including murder, in a number of Indian states. Most members were subsequently arrested, and

what had been a serious threat to law and order removed.

Nayaks Telugu chieftains of the **Vijayanagara** empire, often at odds with their overlords; some of them founded small kingdoms of their own at Ikkeri, Jinji (Gingee), Thanjavur (Tanjore) and Madurai, which became more prominent after the sack of Vijayanagara in 1565. These Nayak dynasties were in conflict not only with one other but with the **Deccani Sultanates**, the Mughals and the European powers of the British and the French. The greatest of the Madurai Nayaks was Tirumala Nayak (1623/59), known both for his military campaigns and for his rebuilding of the great Minakshi temple at Madurai.

Nazarbaev,   Nursultan   Abishevich (1940–) Kazakhstan politician. He was elected President of his state in 1991. Originally a metal worker, he turned to party duties in 1969 and rose steadily in the 1970s and dramatically in the 1980s. By 1984 he was Chairman of the Kazakhstan Council of Ministers, and by 1989 he had been selected as First Secretary of the Kazakh Communist Party. In 1990 he was chosen for the Soviet **Politburo** and became President of the Kazakh Supreme Soviet. As elected President of Kazakhstan in 1991 he took his republic out of the USSR but kept it in the new Commonwealth of Independent States (CIS).

Nazi–Soviet Pact ▷ **German–Soviet Pact**

Nazi Party (NSDAP) A German political party which originated as the German Worker's Party (DAP), founded in 1919 as a patriotic working-man's party to protest against the German surrender of 1918 and the Treaty of **Versailles**, and renamed the *Nationalsozialistische Deutsche Arbeiterpartei* ('National Socialist German Worker's Party', NSDAP or Nazi Party) in 1920. Adolf **Hitler** became the party's leader the following year. Its ideology was a blend of imperialist nationalism, racism, **socialism** and more traditional ideas. Nazi ideology maintained that the world was divided into a hierarchy of races: Aryans, of whom Germans were the purest example, were the supreme culture-bearing race, while the Jews were the lowest. It was also contended that the Jews were intent on world conquest through infesting the Aryan race. This set of ideas was set out by Hitler in *Mein Kampf* (1925), although public opinion forced the NSDAP to play down this theme until after 1933. It was not until the 1930s, with the onset of economic crisis, that the Nazi Party gained a position of significant support: in 1932 with 37.3 per cent of the vote it became the largest party in the **Reichstag**. Support came from people of all backgrounds, although its electorate was strongly Protestant and its membership young. In 1933 Hitler was appointed Chancellor in a coalition government, a position from which he was able to build up a personal dictatorship, through legal measures, terror, and propaganda. Once in power, the Nazis ruthlessly crushed opposition, initiated a vigorous job-creation programme, from 1935 engaged in extensive rearmament, and in the late 1930s invaded **Austria** and the **Sudetenland** (1938), and Bohemia-Moravia and Memel (1939) as a strategic and economic prerequisite for the conquest of Eastern Europe to obtain land (**Lebensraum**) for the 'master race'. During **World War II**, Nazi policies included slave labour, plunder, and mass extermination, leading to the **Nuremberg Trials** of 1946. Nazism as a political ideology is now viewed as a terrifying combination of populism and technocracy with inhumanity, Social-Darwinistic imperialism, and almost nihilistic amorality. ▷ **Anschluss; Holocaust**

Ndebele (Matabele) A Bantu-speaking people of south-western Zimbabwe and northern South Africa. They originated in the 19c as an offshoot of **Nguni** groups who moved north, conquering some of the indigenous Shona peoples, and established a highly stratified state. In the 1890s they resisted White pioneers' encroachment on their land, but were ruthlessly suppressed. Today they constitute 20 per cent of the population of Zimbabwe. ▷ **Zulu Kingdom**

Ndongo A kingdom to the south of the Congo mouth which the Portuguese first encountered in the late 15c. Its ruler was known as the Ngolo and gave his name to Angola. The Portuguese attempted to turn Ndongo into a major slaving partner and also embroiled it in wars with the kingdom of Kongo. A new kingdom known as Matamba emerged from it in the 16c, but like its neighbours it was eventually subsumed within the Portuguese colony.

Nearchus (4c BC) Macedonian general. Born in Crete, he settled in Amphipolis during the reign of **Philip II** of Macedon, and became the companion of the young **Alexander III, 'the Great'**. In 330BC he was Governor of

Lycia; in 329BC he joined Alexander in **Bactria** with a body of Greek mercenaries, and took part in the Indian campaigns. Having built a fleet on the Hydaspes (Jhelum), Alexander gave Nearchus the command. He left the Indus in Nov 325BC, and, skirting the coast, reached Susa in Feb 324BC.

Nebuchadnezzar (Nebuchadrezzar) (c.630–562BC) King of Babylon (605/562BC). The son of Nabopolassar, founder of the New Babylonian Empire, and the most famous king of Babylon. Under him, Babylonian civilization reached its height, and its empire extended as far as the Mediterranean. In the West, he is remembered chiefly for his deportation of the Jews to Babylonia (586BC). ▷ **Babylonian Exile; Chaldaeans**

Nechaev, Sergei Gennadievich (1847–82) Russian revolutionary. The schoolteacher son of a workman, he left St Petersburg for Geneva in 1869 at the age of 21 and teamed up with **Bakunin** to write a book called *Revolutionary Cathechism* on how to be a professional revolutionary. He returned home before the end of the year to found a small organization, the 'People's Reckoning', which achieved notoriety for killing one of its members, allegedly a police spy. He immediately escaped to Zurich, but in 1872 he was extradited and imprisoned in St Petersburg. From the Peter and Paul Fortress he kept in touch with his fellow revolutionaries until his death 10 years later.

Necho II (Wehemibre) (610/595BC) King of Egypt. For information on the reign of this king of the 26th Dynasty, the chief source is the historian Herodotus. Necho attempted to link the Nile with the Red Sea by means of a canal, but the undertaking had to be abandoned. In commissioning Phoenician ships to circumnavigate Africa, however, the king had more success. After the fall of Nineveh to the Medes and Babylonians (612BC) and the end of the Assyrian Empire, Necho was the chief opponent of Nabopolassar of Babylon. Referred to in the Old Testament as 'Pharaoh-necho', the killing of Josiah of Judah at the Battle of Megiddo by the Egyptian King is mentioned in 2 Kings XXIII 29–30. Necho, with a fleet, was able to control the coast of Phoenicia and in 606–605BC mounted attacks on the Babylonians on the Euphrates. In 605BC the tide turned and the Egyptians were defeated at Carchemish by Nebuchadnezzar, son of

Nabopolassar. In 601BC the Babylonians marched against Egypt once more but were driven off and retreated to Babylon.

Necker, Jacques (1732–1804) French politician and financier. Initially a banker's clerk, he moved to Paris (1762), founded a bank, and became a wealthy speculator. By 1776–7 he became Director of the French Treasury and Director-General of Finances. He attempted some administrative reforms, but tried to finance French involvement in the War of American Independence by heavy borrowing, while concealing the large state deficit. He was dismissed in 1781, but recalled in 1788 to deal with the impending financial crisis. He summoned the **Estates General**, but his proposals for social and constitutional change aroused royal opposition. He was dismissed and hastily recalled (1789), but finally resigned in 1790. He retired to his estate near Geneva, where he died. ▷ **American Revolution; Louis XVI**

Nectanebo II (360/343BC) King of Egypt. He came to the throne as the result of a disastrous expedition, led by Teos of the 30th Dynasty with the help of Greek allies, against the Persians in Phoenicia. The Greeks supported Nectanebo and following the defeat of Teos, who fled to Persia and exile, he returned to Egypt as the last native king. A considerable number of buildings, particularly in the Memphite area, owed their construction to him. In Persia, meanwhile, Artaxerxes III Ochus was bringing order to his shaky empire. Dealing first with revolts in Phoenicia and Palestine, by 343BC he had attacked Egypt at Pelusium and two other points in the Delta; Nectanebo retreated to Memphis and prepared for a siege. Pelusium surrendered, the garrison having been promised fair treatment. Soon other Delta towns surrendered and Nectanebo, realizing that further resistance was hopeless, set off for Nubia and vanished from history.

Nedić, Milan (1877–1946) Serbian politician and soldier. Chief of Staff and Minister of War during the 1930s, he collaborated with the German occupation during **World War II** and was President of the puppet government in Belgrade from 1941 to 1944. At the end of the war, he was imprisoned and committed suicide. ▷ **Ljotić, Dimitrije**

Nefertiti (Neferneferuaten) (14c BC) Queen of Egypt. She was the consort of **Amenhotpe IV (Akhenaten)** and the mother of his six daughters. Nefertiti was closely associated with the king as is evident from the painted reliefs in the Aten temple at Karnak, where she figures prominently, and at El Amarna in tomb scenes. The new realism in art is nowhere better shown than in the portrait head of the queen now held in the Berlin museum.

Negrín (López), Juan (1892–1956) Spanish politician. He studied medicine in Germany, and became Professor of Physiology at the University of Madrid (1923–31). As a moderate Socialist, he was a parliamentary deputy throughout the Second Republic (1931–6). During the **Spanish Civil War** he served as Finance Minister (1936–7) and Prime Minister (1937–9), and for a time was also Defence Minister. As Premier he adopted a pro-Soviet, pro-communist but anti-revolutionary position, aimed at winning the Western democracies' support for the Republic, but his 'Thirteen Points' (1938) failed to impress Britain and France. In 1939, shortly before the end of the war, he was overthrown by an anti-communist coup. He died in exile in France. ▷ **Republic, Second** (Spain)

Negritude Associated above all with francophone writers, such as Aime Cesaire and Leopold **Senghor**, negritude was an orientation which valued the contribution of black people and held that black people had a special intellectual approach which was less rational than the Graeco-Roman tradition and more instinctual.

Neguib, Mohammed (1901–84) Egyptian leader. As general of an army division in 1952 he carried out a coup d'état in Cairo which banished King **Farouk I** and initiated the 'Egyptian Revolution'. Taking first the offices of Commander-in-Chief and Prime Minister, he abolished the monarchy in 1953 and became President of the republic. He was deposed in 1954 and succeeded by Colonel Gamal Abd al-**Nasser**.

Nehru, Jawaharlal ('Pandit') (1889–1964) Indian politician. Educated at Harrow and Cambridge, he became a lawyer, and served in the Allahabad High Court. He joined the Indian Congress Committee (1918), became an admirer and follower, if sometimes a critic, of M K **Gandhi**, and was imprisoned several times by the British. In 1929 he was elected President of the **Indian National Congress**. From 1947 to 1964 he was India's first Prime Minister and Minister of External Affairs, following a policy of neutrality during the **Cold War**. He introduced a policy of industrialization, reorganized the states on a linguistic basis, and brought the dispute with Pakistan over Kashmir to a peaceful, though not final, solution.

Nehru, Motilal (1861–1931) Indian nationalist leader, lawyer and journalist. The father of Jawaharlal **Nehru**, he became a follower of M K **Gandhi** in 1919, founded the *Independent* of Allahabad and became the first President of the reconstructed **Indian National Congress**. In the 1920s he co-headed the **Swaraj** Party (with Chittaranjan **Das**) in which members of the Congress entered the legislatures, and wrote a report as a basis for Indian constitutional development and to solve the political differences between Hindus and Muslims. The report was not, however, acceptable to members of the All-India **Muslim League**, led by Muhammad Ali **Jinnah**.

Nejedly, Zdenek (1878–1962) Czechoslovak communist ideologue. A professor of music in the Charles University, Prague, from before **World War I**, he joined the Communist Party during the depression in 1929 and emigrated to Moscow with other leaders during **World War II**. In subsequent National Front governments down to 1953 he held ministerial posts, usually education; and in 1952 he became chairman of the Academy of Sciences. A man of many words but simple thoughts, he restricted the education of a whole generation of Czechoslovaks to narrow Marxist ideas; however, he was very popular with sympathizers abroad.

Nelken, Margarita (1896–1968) Spanish politician and feminist. The daughter of German Jews, she was born in Madrid but did not achieve Spanish nationality until 1931. During her early years she was a painter, exhibiting her works in Paris and Vienna as well as Spain, but following a severe eye-illness dedicated herself to literary criticism. She was also active on behalf of women's rights, publishing *The Social Condition of Women* (1922), as well as being involved in land reform movements in Estremadura and Andalucia. Under the Second Republic (1931–6) Nelken was successful in all three general elections as a deputy for the Socialist Party (**PSOE**). She agitated for land reform, was active in the national arbitration boards, and formed part of the National Committee of Women against War and Fascism. Her impatience with the parliamentary process led her to become one of the most radical Socialist deputies. During the **Spanish Civil War** (1936–9) she led various campaigns for the mobilization of women. In 1937 Margarita Nelken entered the Communist Party (**PCE**). After the war, she was exiled in Paris, Moscow and finally Mexico, where she died. ▷ **Republic, Second** (Spain)

Nelson, Horatio, Viscount (1758–1805) British admiral. He joined the navy in 1770, and was sent to the West Indies (1784) to enforce the Navigation Act against the newly independent USA. There he married Frances Nisbet, and in 1787 retired with her to Burnham Thorpe. In 1794 he commanded the naval brigade at the reduction of Bastia and Calvi where he lost the sight of his right eye, and in an action at Santa Cruz had his right arm amputated. In 1798 he followed the French fleet to Egypt, destroying it at the Battle of **Aboukir Bay**. On his return to Naples, he fell in love with Emma, Lady Hamilton, and began a liaison with her which lasted until his death. In 1801 he was made rear-admiral, and led the attack on Copenhagen. Previously created a baron, he then became a viscount, and Commander-in-Chief. In 1805 he gained his greatest victory, against the combined French and Spanish fleet at the Battle of **Trafalgar**. During the battle he was mortally wounded on his flagship, HMS *Victory*. His body was brought home and buried in St Paul's Cathedral, London. ▷ **Hood, Samuel; Napoleonic Wars**

Nemanja (Nemanjić) Dynasty (1168–1372) The Serbian ruling family which rose to prominence in **Raška**. In 1168 the Byzantine emperor, Manuel Comnenus, granted **Stephen I Nemanja** and his brothers great tracts of land which they held as vassals. These estates were part of the core of the medieval state of **Serbia**. In 1372, with the death of Uroš V, son of **Stephen Dushan**, the dynasty died out.

Nenni, Pietro (1891–1980) Italian politician. As editor of the socialist paper *Avanti!* he was exiled by the fascists in 1926, and served as a political commissar for the International Brigades during the **Spanish Civil War**. He became Secretary-General of the Italian Socialist Party (PSI) in 1944, Vice-Premier in the **De Gasperi** coalition (1945–6) and Foreign Minister (1946–7). In 1963–8 he once again served as Vice-Premier in the four-party left-centre coalition headed by Aldo **Moro**. In Dec 1968 he accepted the post of Foreign Minister but resigned in July 1969.

Neo-Confucianism A reassertion of Confucian political and moral values in China during the **Song Dynasty** in reaction against the otherworldly concerns of Buddhism, which had been influential in China since the 6c. Neo-Confucian scholars refocused attention on the traditional **Confucian Classics** and promoted the virtues of public service and social welfare activism. Only through active engagement in society, they argued, could one bring one's own self-cultivation to fruition. In order to rival Buddhist metaphysics, Neo-Confucian scholars also constructed a metaphysical system of their own, claiming that correct relationships prescribed by Confucian thought (eg within the family, or between ruler and ruled) were manifestations of abstract principles (*li*) immanent in the cosmos. The commentaries on the classics written by Zhu Xi (1130–1200), the most important Neo-Confucian thinker, became accepted orthodoxy from the 14c and were designated as the only correct interpretations to be used in education and the **Civil Service Examination System**.

Nerchinsk, Treaty of (7 Sep 1689) China's first treaty with a foreign country (Russia) which was regarded as an independent state rather than a vassal. It settled, for the time being, border disputes between tsarist Russia and **Qing Dynasty** China in the wake of Russian expansion eastwards across Siberia. By the 1640s, Russian traders were moving south into the Amur River region (northern Manchuria) demanding tribute from tribes that owed allegiance to the Qing. Following a siege of the Russian stockade at Albazin (on the Amur River) by Qing forces in 1686 both countries decided on a peace settlement since each was fearful that the other would ally with neighbouring Mongol tribes to the west. Envoys met at Nerchinsk (founded by the Russians in 1658) and the resulting treaty provided for Qing control of the Amur River region in exchange for which Russia was allowed to send trading caravans to the Chinese capital at Beijing. The treaty held good until the mid-19c when further Russian expansion in the Amur region led to territorial concessions being wrung from an enfeebled Qing Dynasty. ▷ **Beijing, Treaty of**

Nero (Nero Claudius Caesar) (AD37–68) Roman Emperor (AD54/68). Born Lucius Domitius Ahenobarbus, the son of Gnaeus Domitius Ahenobarbus and **Agrippina the Younger** (daughter of **Germanicus**), he owed his name and position to the driving ambition of his mother, who engineered his adoption by the Emperor **Claudius**, her fourth husband. Initially his reign was good, thanks to his three main advisers: his mother, the philosopher **Seneca**, and the Praetorian Prefect, Burrus. However, after Agrippina's murder (AD59), and their fall from favour, Nero, more interested in sex, singing, acting and chariot-racing than government, neglected affairs of state, and corruption set in. He was blamed for the Great Fire of Rome (AD64), despite assiduous attempts to make scapegoats of the Christians. A major plot to overthrow him (the Conspiracy of Piso) was formed (AD65) but detected, and Rome had to endure three more years of tyranny before he was toppled from power by the army, and forced to commit suicide. ▷ **Poppaea Sabina**

Nerva, Marcus Cocceius (c.32–98) Roman Emperor (96/8). Elected by the Senate after the assassination of **Domitian**, he introduced liberal reforms but lacked military support, and had to adopt **Trajan** as his successor.

Nesselrode, Karl Robert Vasilevich, Count (1780–1861) Russian politician. He was born in Lisbon, the son of a diplomat. After experience in the army, the navy and the foreign service, he represented Russia at the Congress of **Vienna** (1814–15), and was one of the most active diplomats in the subsequent Holy Alliance. He became Foreign Minister in 1822, and dominated Russian foreign policy on behalf of **Alexander I** and **Nicholas I** for 30 years. His Balkan policy of trying to extend Russia's influence over the **Ottoman Empire** at the expense of Britain and France contributed to the outbreak of the **Crimean War** in 1854.

Nestorians Followers of Nestorius, Bishop of Constantinople (d.c.451), who is alleged to have taught the doctrine, later declared heretical, of two persons (one human, one divine) as well as two natures in the incarnate Christ. They formed a separate Church which survived in parts of Persia.

Neto, Antonio Agostinho (1922–79) Angolan nationalist and politician. The son of a methodist missionary, he was educated in a methodist school in Luanda before studying medicine in Portuguese universities. He returned to Angola to work in the colonial medical service and joined the **MPLA**. He was imprisoned several times (1952–62) but escaped from the Cape Verde Islands to Zaire where he soon became President of the

MPLA and its leader in the guerrilla war against Portuguese colonialism. His close ties with **Castro** gave him both Cuban and Soviet backing and this assistance enabled him to prevail in the civil war which followed the Portuguese retreat from Angola. He became the first President of Angola in 1974, holding the post until his death.

Neuilly, Treaty of (27 Nov 1919) This agreement dictated the terms to be paid by Bulgaria as a defeated power at the end of **World War I**. Bulgaria surrendered to Greece the gains it had made in Western Thrace after the **Balkan Wars** and ceded to Serbia four regions of strategic significance. The Bulgarians were also to pay an indemnity of US \$450 million, about a quarter of the national wealth, and a great quantity of their livestock. The size of the Bulgarian Army, police force and border guard was greatly reduced. ▷ **Boris III; Stamboliski, Alexander; Thrace**

Neustria The western part of the Frankish kingdom in the Merovingian period. It had been conquered by the **Franks** in the 5c and in the 7c became a kingdom with its capital in Paris. Its rivalry with the other Frankish kingdom, **Austrasia**, came to an end in 607 when Austrasia became predominant in Frankish affairs. ▷ **Merovingians**

Neutrality Acts A series of US acts passed in the 1930s which aimed to prevent the USA becoming involved in the escalating European conflict. The 1935 Act authorized a temporary embargo on arms shipments to all belligerents; the 1936 Act outlawed loans or credits to belligerents; and the 1937 Act forbade munitions shipments to either side in the **Spanish Civil War**. By the time of the attack on **Pearl Harbor**, the bans had been lifted and the neutral course had been abandoned.

Neva, Battle of the (1240) A battle between Russian and Swedish forces on the River Neva, where Russian troops led by Prince Alexander of Novgorod (subsequently referred to as **Alexander Nevsky**) attacked and defeated Swedish forces under cover of fog. The victory thwarted Sweden's attempts to control the northern end of the trade route from the Baltic to the Black Sea. Two years later Alexander won a famous victory over the **Teutonic Knights** at Lake Peipus, proving that in the end the emerging Russian society could resist German as well as Swedish incursions.

Neves, Tancredo de Almeida (1910–85) Brazilian politician. He was a local politician in the 1930s and became a federal deputy for the **PSD** in the 1950s. Justice Minister under Getúlio **Vargas** in 1953–4, he was Head of the Banco do Brasil under **Kubitschek (de Oliveira)** (1956–8) and first Prime Minister and Justice Minister under João **Goulart**. Neves was a master of **conciliação**, both as architect of the 1961 compromise, which allowed President Goulart to assume office under a 'parliamentary regime', and the referendum of Jan 1963, which restored traditional powers to the President. His inability to cobble together cross-party support for moderate policies was a leading factor in the coup of 1964. A man of moderate centrist views, he managed to gain the confidence of conservative groups in the 1970s for the transition to civilian rule. As **PMDB** Governor of Minas Gerais (1982–4), he articulated the 'Democratic Alliance' which won the presidential nomination in 1985, with José **Sarney (Costa)** as running-mate. Overtaken by illness a few hours before he was to take office, he remained the 'President who never was'.

Newcastle, Duke of ▷ **Pelham, Thomas Pelham-Holles, 1st Duke of Newcastle**

New Deal (Canada) The name given to the legislation influenced by US President **Roosevelt**'s New Deal, passed in 1935 by the Conservative administration of R B **Bennett**, after the failure of more orthodox measures to solve the problems of the Depression. It established a social insurance plan, maximum hours and minimum wages, a marketing board for natural products, and farm credit provisions. This programme and the fears of several Conservative supporters that the government would involve itself in economic planning and price-fixing led to a split in the party and the formation of the Reconstruction Party, which let in the Liberals under Mackenzie **King** with a landslide victory in the 1935 elections. Bennett's New Deal measures were declared unconstitutional in 1937, but they served as a basis for the **Liberal Party** programme after constitutional amendment. ▷ **New Deal (USA); Price Spreads Commission; Stevens, Harry H**

New Deal (USA) The administration and policies of US President Franklin D **Roosevelt**, who pledged a 'new deal' for the country during the campaign of 1932. He embarked on active state economic involvement to combat the **Great Depression**, setting the tone in a hectic 'first hundred days'. Although some early legislation was invalidated by the Supreme Court, the New Deal left a lasting impact on US government, economy and society, not least by the effective creation of the modern institution of the presidency. Major specific initiatives included the National Recovery Act (1933), the Tennessee Valley Authority (1933), the Agricultural Adjustment Act (1933), the National Youth Administration (1935), the **National Labor Relations Act** or Wagner Act (1935) and the Social Security Act (1935). The 'first New Deal' (1933–4), concerned primarily with restarting and stabilizing the economy, is sometimes distinguished from the 'second New Deal' (1935), aimed at social reform. Although Roosevelt was triumphantly re-elected in 1936 (losing only two states), his reform programme slowed considerably after his failure to reorganize the Supreme Court (1937), growing opposition to government spending and taxes, and the worsening situation in Europe, which increasingly directed Roosevelt's attention to foreign affairs.

New Democratic Party (NDP) Canadian political party. It was established in 1961 by the merger of the **CCF** and the **CLC**. Whilst it did not attract much support in the Atlantic provinces, it presented a much wider appeal to the urban electorate of British Columbia, Saskatchewan, Ontario and Manitoba. Under the leadership of T C (Tommy) Douglas the party won 19 seats in the federal elections of 1962, while in 1969 it was elected into government in Manitoba. In the early 1970s a group of Trotskyites, the 'Waffle' group, seized power until they were expelled from the party in 1972. Later that year the NDP managed to win 30 seats in the federal elections and was able to keep the Liberals in power, giving its support in return for policies of economic nationalism. By the 1980s the NDP had become more centrist because the Liberals had taken over its characteristic policies. In 1984, however, under the leadership of Ed Broadbent the party was still able to muster 19 per cent of the vote and 30 seats in the legislature. The greatest contribution of the NDP to Canadian political life has been to present the country with an alternative to the major parties and exert a constant pressure from the left, which has ensured that social issues retained political importance.

New Economic Policy (NEP) A partly experimental economic system introduced by **Lenin** in the USSR in 1921. Its main objective was to help the country recover from the ravages of the **Russian Civil War** and the diseconomies of the policy of 'war communism'; but it also emerged from a dispute about the best way to organize economic development in the new society. The system privatized some small-scale business, decentralized major parts of industry and encouraged foreign investment. **Stalin** abandoned it in 1928 after Lenin's death and as part of his battle with **Trotsky**. He forged ahead instead with the collectivization of agriculture and forced industrialization.

New England Confederation (1643–84) An agreement of the American colonies of Massachusetts, Plymouth, Connecticut, and New Haven aiming to establish a common government for the purposes of war and Native American relations. The confederation declined in importance after 1664.

New Fourth Army Incident (4 Jan 1941) The military clash in central China between the communist New Fourth Army and Nationalist forces that effectively ended the second of the **United Fronts** forged in 1937 to counter Japanese aggression. The New Fourth Army had been created (1937) from communist remnants in south China and had been allowed to operate south of the Yangzi River against the Japanese. Tension grew, however, as the army expanded its operations north of the Yangzi, leading to frequent clashes with Nationalist troops. **Chiang Kai-shek**, fearing an expansion of communist influence, ordered an attack on the headquarters force of the New Fourth Army at Maolin (Anhui province) in Jan 1941 as it was evacuating the region in accordance with an agreement reached the previous year. Most of the force was annihilated and the New Fourth Army was dissolved. This, together with Chiang's economic blockade of the communists' principal base in the north-west, signified the end of any cooperation between the communists and nationalists for the remainder of the Russo–Japanese War.

New France Technically this name was given to all the North American territories claimed by France between 1524 and 1803. Generally, however, it is used for the north-eastern colonies. In 1534 a cross was planted on the shores of the Gaspée by Jacques Cartier, who thus claimed the territory for the King of France. However, it was Quebec, founded in 1608 by **Champlain** as a base for exploration and fur-trading, which became the centre of the French colony. By

1663 the colony had become a royal province with a governor responsible for foreign relations and defence, an intendant to administer justice, and a bishop to impose spiritual discipline. It was therefore not given the opportunity to develop the early expressions of political responsibility and the sense of community which characterized the English colonies. It was, however, one of the early intendants, Jean Talon, who encouraged fishing, farming, lumbering, ship-building and the production of tar and potash, to ensure the colonies' economic development.

New Freedom The political programme on which US President Woodrow **Wilson** was elected in 1912. It was directed against the acceptance of large-scale enterprise by his opponent, Theodore **Roosevelt**, and was intended to return the spirit of free enterprise to the market-place, restoring an open society which would benefit individual entrepreneurs, immigrant minorities and women. The chief architect of Wilson's central argument that trusts and monopolies should be broken up by the federal government was Louis **Brandeis**, but the domestic record of Wilson's administration showed a very partial adherence to these principles. ▷ **New Nationalism**

New Frontier The administration and policies of US President John F **Kennedy** (1961–3). The programme was characterized by a high international profile and a liberal domestic stance. ▷ **Peace Corps**

New Granada (Nueva Granada) The official name in the Spanish-American Empire for the area now covered by the Republic of Colombia. It was also the name (1739–1810) of a Spanish viceroyalty embracing Venezuela and Quito in addition to New Granada.

New Guard In Australian history, an extreme right-wing organization formed in New South Wales in 1932 by Eric Campbell, which claimed 100 000 members by 1933. Its principal achievement was the disruption of the official opening of Sydney Harbour Bridge (1932). In some respects a fascist organization, the Guard was defunct by 1935.

Ne Win (1911–) Burmese politician. He was an active anti-British nationalist in the 1930s. In **World War II** he became Chief of Staff in the collaborationist army after the Japanese invasion of Burma, but joined the Allied forces later in the war. He held senior

military and cabinet posts after Burma's independence (1948), before becoming caretaker Prime Minister (1958–60). In 1962, following a military coup, he ruled the country as chairman of the revolutionary council and became state President in 1974. After leaving this office in 1981, he continued to dominate political affairs as chairman of the ruling Burma Socialist Programme Party (BSPP). He followed an isolationist foreign policy and a unique domestic 'Burmese Way to Socialism' programme, a blend of **Marxism**, Buddhism and Burmese nationalism. In 1988, with economic conditions rapidly deteriorating and riots in Rangoon, he was forced to step down as BSPP leader although he remained a formidably powerful political figure.

New Kingdom In Ancient Egyptian history, the great era which began with the expulsion of the **Hyksos** (c.1567BC). This was when Egypt became an imperial power, with a sphere of influence extending, at its height, from the 4th Cataract of the Nile in the south, to the Amanus mountains of Anatolia in the north. The commitment of the early kings of the 18th Dynasty to a policy of expansion, with political control over Palestine and Syria, the exploitation of Nubia and the dedication of the spoils of war to Amun Re at Thebes as thanks offerings for their victories, was continued by succeeding ruling families. In the reign of **Amenhotpe III**, the country reached the peak of its achievements culturally, economically and politically. Following the religious and artistic revolution of the Amarna period under Akhenaten (**Amenhotpe IV**), the Ramesside kings attempted to reimpose Egypt's hold in western Asia. However, the balance among the neighbouring nations began to shift away from economies based on bronze to those using iron. This, combined with ethnic movements in the Mediterranean after 1200BC and the ever-increasing power of the priesthood of Amun, led to a steady decline in Egypt's prestige and the end of the empire in the early 11c BC.

New Left A neo-Marxist movement which espoused a more libertarian form of socialism compared to orthodox Marxism. In part, it was inspired by the earlier writings of Marx, which were essentially humanistic, and the ideas of Italian politician Antonio Gramsci (1891–1937) regarding the importance of ideological hegemony. It also drew on dialectical sociology and radical forms of existentialism. It is, however, difficult to pinpoint any central ideas specific to the New Left.

The movement had some influence in the 1960s, particularly in student politics and in opposition to the **Vietnam War**, but it never became an effectively organized political force. Its importance in the 1980s declined, and it gave way in part to the **New Right**.

New Liberal Club (*Shin Jiyu Kurabu*) The Japanese political party formed in 1976 when six members of the ruling **Liberal Democratic Party** (LDP) broke away to form their own party in protest against government corruption. Although only ever gaining a handful of parliamentary seats, the New Liberal Club formally entered into a coalition with the LDP following the 1983 elections in which the LDP had fallen short of a majority (the only time the LDP has entered a coalition with another party). The LDP's renewed parliamentary strength after 1983, plus the fact that New Liberal Club members always tended to support government policy, made the party's existence increasingly redundant. It was quietly disbanded in 1985 and its members rejoined the ranks of the LDP.

New Model Army An English army established by Parliament (15 Feb 1645) to strengthen its forces in the first civil war against royalists. The county and regional armies of Essex, Manchester, and Waller were merged into a successful national force. The cavalry and artillery were augmented; the battle tactics of **Gustav II Adolf** adopted; discipline and pay improved; and religious toleration introduced. ▷ **English Civil Wars; Naseby, Battle of**

New Nationalism The US political programme outlined by ex-President Theodore **Roosevelt** in a speech at Osawatomie, Kansas in Aug 1910, and on which he campaigned as the **Progressive Party**'s candidate in the election of 1912. Roosevelt advocated such policies as graduated income and inheritance taxes, compensation for employee accident, closer supervision of female and child labour, and more effective corporate regulation. Greatly influenced by Herbert Croly's *The Promise of American Life*, the programme was essentially a call for government intervention to achieve social justice, and it later influenced such **New Deal** brain trusters as Raymond Moley. ▷ **New Freedom**

New Netherland A Dutch colony in the Hudson River valley. The first settlement was Fort Orange (Albany), founded in 1617; Nieuw Amsterdam (New York City) followed in 1624. Conquered by the English and named New York in 1664, it was restored by treaty to the English in 1674 after a second brief period of Dutch rule. Initially established on feudal social lines, the colony prospered on the basis of the **fur trade**.

New Right A wide-ranging ideological movement associated with the revival of conservatism in the 1970s and 1980s, particularly in the UK and USA. Its ideas are most prominently connected with classical liberal economic theory from the 19c. It is strongly in favour of state withdrawal from ownership, and intervention in the economy in favour of a free-enterprise system. There is also a strong moral conservatism — an emphasis on respect for authority, combined with a strong expression of patriotism and support for the idea of the family. Politically, the New Right adopts an aggressive style which places weight on pursuing convictions rather than on generating a consensus. In the USA in the 1980s it has been associated with the emergence of Christian fundamentalism (eg the **Moral Majority**).

New Spain (Nueva España) The formal title of the Spanish viceroyalty covering the area of modern Mexico.

Ney, Michel, Duke of Elchingen (1769–1815) French marshal. He fought in the **French Revolutionary Wars**, became a General of Division in 1799, and a Marshal of the Empire. He commanded the 3rd Corps of the Grand Army in the Russian campaign (1813), for which he received the title of Prince of Moskowa. After **Napoleon I**'s abdication in 1814 he accepted the Bourbon restoration, but instead of obeying orders to retake Bonaparte (1815), Ney deserted to his side and led the centre at the Battle of **Waterloo**. On **Louis XVIII**'s second restoration, he was condemned for high treason, and shot in Paris. ▷ **Bourbon, House of; Napoleonic Wars**

Nghe-An/Ha-Tinh Uprisings (1930–1) A fierce revolt against French colonial rule, which took place in the northern **Annam** provinces of Nghe-An and Ha-Tinh. The precise causes of the revolt are a matter of considerable scholarly dispute but important elements would include the markedly harsh agricultural conditions of that region, the burden of colonial taxation, social disintegration and the organizational skills of the **Indochina** Communist Party. For a short period the rebels were able to seize power. However, French repression, including the bombing of demonstrations from the air, broke the revolt. Approximately 2 000 Vietnamese were killed.

Ngo Dinh Diem (1901–63) Vietnamese political leader. He became Prime Minister of the State of Vietnam in June 1954. This was the territory south of the 'temporary' demarcation line, established at the 1954 Geneva Conference. Ngo Dinh Diem quickly consolidated his position, securing the abdication of **Bao Dai** and suppressing the political-religious sects. He allied himself strongly with the USA, which saw in him an instrument by which the reunification of Vietnam, under the communists, might be prevented. However, by the beginning of the 1960s, Ngo Dinh Diem's internal position was weakening, largely because his encouragement of Catholic interests greatly angered the Buddhist majority. His violent treatment of Buddhist protest lost him US support. Ngo Dinh Diem was assassinated on 2 Nov 1963, in the course of a military coup that had, at the very least, tacit US approval.

Nguni A group of Bantu-speaking peoples of southern Africa. They originally occupied present-day Natal and Transkei and in the 19c they carried out a series of migrations. The main groups today include the Zulu, Swazi and Xhosa of South Africa and Swaziland, the Ndebele of Zimbabwe, and the Ngoni of Zambia, Malawi and Tanzania.

Nguyen Van Thieu (1923–) Vietnamese army officer and political leader. His military career began in the late 1940s and by 1963 he was Chief of Staff of the Armed Forces of the Republic of Vietnam (South Vietnam), becoming Minister of Defence and Deputy Premier in the following year. In 1965 he became Head of State. Under a new, American-style presidential constitution, he was President from 1967 until the collapse of the Saigon regime in 1975. During those years, his relationship with the USA, and with American public opinion, was central to his survival. He was roundly condemned in the West for his authoritarian, commonly corrupt, methods; he, in turn, felt betrayed by the US withdrawal from Vietnam, agreed with his northern enemies in Paris in early 1973. With the communist victory in 1975, he went into exile, first in Taiwan and then in the UK.

Niagara Movement US civil rights movement. Founded in 1905 by W E B **Du Bois** and others to resist the public acceptance of segregation advocated by Booker T **Washington**, and to agitate for 'every single right that belongs to a freeborn American, political and social'. The movement was superseded by the establishment of the **NAACP**.

Nian Rebellion (1852–68) A peasant insurrection in north-central China. Armed bandit gangs, known as *Nian* (literally 'twist', this may either be a reference to the twisted paper torches they used or a description of them as tightly-knit outlaw bands), had been active in the region since the 1790s. Amidst the worsening economic situation in the 1850s and the turmoil caused by the **Taiping Rebellion**, the Nian rebels gained control over entire villages, from where they conducted seasonal plundering expeditions. Unlike the Taipings, the Nian had no systematic ideology and no organization, although one leader, Zhang Luoxing (Chang Lo-hsing) declared himself leader of a Nian confederacy in 1852. After 1864, when they were dislodged from their fortified bases, the Nian resorted to mobile cavalry warfare until they were finally suppressed in 1868 by Qing forces carrying out a strategy of blockade. ▷ **Qing Dynasty**

Nicaea, Conquest of (1331) One of the Byzantine towns of Asia Minor, Nicaea (Iznik) came under threat from the nascent Ottoman state in the early 14c. A Byzantine relief army was defeated at Philocrene in 1330 and Nicaea fell to the Ottomans under **Orhan** on 2 Mar 1331.

Nicaea, Council of (325) The first ecumenical Council of the Church, called by Emperor Constantine to settle the doctrinal dispute between the Arians and the Orthodox on the person of Christ.

Nicaea, Council of (787) A Council of the Church called to deal with the question of the veneration of images. ▷ **iconoclasm**

Nicaea, Empire of The successor state of the **Byzantine Empire**, established after the Latins had conquered Constantinople (1204). It was founded by Theodore Lascaris, whose court at Nicaea (modern Iznik, Turkey) maintained the traditions of Byzantine administration and culture. **Michael VIII Palaeologus**, co-emperor with John Lascaris at Nicaea, recovered Constantinople (1261) and restored the Byzantine Empire.

Nichiren (1222–82) Japanese Buddhist priest. He founded his own sect in 1253, condemning all other sects as evil. The fanatical zeal of his sect often led to violent clashes between his followers and the members of other sects. The nationalist tone of Nichiren's teachings, emphasizing that Japanese Buddhism was the one true Buddhism, made him a hero to some ultra-nationalist ideologies of the 1930s and 1940s.

Nicholas I, St (c.820–67) Italian Pope (858/67). He asserted the supremacy of the Church over the actions of several secular rulers and local bishops. He supported the appeal of the deposed Bishop of Soissons against his Archbishop, Hincmar of Reims (862), and forbade the divorce of **Lothair II**, King of Lorraine (863). In the East, he deposed Photius as Patriarch of Constantinople (863). ▷ **pope**

Nicholas I (1796–1855) Emperor of Russia (1825/55). The third son of **Paul I**, he was an absolute despot, whose first action was ruthlessly to suppress the December Revolution and whose subsequent domestic policy was scrupulously devoted to preventing subversion. In 1830–1 he crushed the rising in Congress Poland and abolished its constitution, and then attempted to Russianize all the inhabitants of the empire. He helped to quell the 1848–9 Hungarian insurrection on Austria's behalf, and drew closer the alliance with Prussia. The re-establishment of the French Empire confirmed these alliances, and led him to intensify his policy of southwards expansion aimed particularly at dominating Turkey; but the opposition of Britain and France brought on the **Crimean War**, during which he died. Ironically, Russia's defeat in 1856 strengthened the pressure for social and political change and precipitated the emancipation of the serfs under **Alexander II** in 1861. ▷ **Napoleon III; Nesselrode, Karl; Russian Serfs, Emancipation of the**

Nicholas I (1841–1921) Prince and King of Montenegro (1860/1918). As the autocratic ruler of a backward state, he introduced a measure of reform calculated not to diminish his authority. He reorganized the state in 1879, issued a new law code (1888), reformed the army, issued a constitution (1905) and declared Montenegro a kingdom (1910). His foreign policy was determined by his dependence on subsidies from Russia and Austro-Hungary and he made a series of marriage alliances with Russia, **Serbia** and Italy. During **World War I**, when the Habsburg Army overran Montenegro, he fled to Italy

(1916). He was declared deposed by the Montenegrin National Assembly (Nov 1918) and Montenegro then became part of the Kingdom of Serbs, Croats and Slovenes (later Yugoslavia). ▷ **Petrović-Njegoš Dynasty**

Nicholas II (1868–1918) Last Emperor of Russia (1895/1917). He was the son of **Alexander III**. In foreign affairs his reign was marked by a switch from co-operation with Austria and Germany to an alliance with France, an *entente* with Britain, the disastrous **Russo-Japanese War** (1904–5) and, eventually, involvement in **World War I**. Inadequate industrialization and insufficient social change helped precipitate the Russian **Revolution of 1905**. His failure to concede any real power to the assembly or **Duma** instituted in 1906 and also his incompetence as commander of the army against the Central Powers in turn helped to precipitate the 1917 **Russian Revolution** that led to his immediate abdication and to the murder of himself and his family by Red Guards at Ekaterinburg in 1918.

Nicholas V (Tommaso Parentucelli) (1397–1455) Italian Pope (1447/55). He prevailed on the anti-pope, Felix V (**Amadeus VIII, 'the Peaceful'**) to abdicate in 1449, and thus restored the peace of the Church. A liberal patron of scholars, he rebuilt the Vatican and restored St Peter's and the Vatican Library. He vainly endeavoured to arouse Europe to the duty of succouring the Greek empire.

Nicias (c.470–413BC) Wealthy Athenian politician and general, prominent during the **Peloponnesian War**. A political moderate, he was opposed to the strident warmongering of Cleon and **Alcibiades**, and in 421BC arranged the short-lived peace named after him. Appointed commander in Sicily in 415BC, his lack of sympathy with his mission, along with bad luck, ill health, and sheer incompetence, led to the total destruction of the Athenian forces and his own death at the hands of the Syracusans.

Nicomedia, Conquest of (1337) Nicomedia (Izmit) was taken by the Ottoman **Orhan** after a siege lasting six years in 1337. (It was at Nicomedia that Orhan set up the first Ottoman madrasa to establish a name for himself as a credible Muslim prince by demonstrating his care for learning.)

Nicopolis, Battle of (1396) A disastrous attack by Christians against the Turks, conquerors of much of Eastern Europe since the early 14c. The battle centred on the major fortress on the River Danube. The Christian forces were led by King Sigismund of Hungary (later Holy Roman Emperor) and John the Fearless (1371–1419), Duke of Burgundy. John was captured by the Turks, and ransomed for a huge sum.

Niemöller, Martin (1892–1984) German theologian and resistance figure. After serving as a **U-boat** commander in **World War I**, Niemöller entered the Lutheran Church and held various positions, most notably as Pastor in Berlin-Dahlem from 1931. He was a prominent member of the anti-Nazi **Confessing Church** for which he was arrested in 1937 and sent to Sachsenhausen and **Dachau** concentration camps. Freed in 1945, he resumed his church career and adopted outspoken views on current affairs, most notably on German reunification and nuclear disarmament. ▷ **concentration camp**

Nien Rebellion ▷ **Nian Rebellion**

Night of the Long Knives (30 June–1 July 1934) The event which took place in Germany when the **SS**, on **Hitler**'s orders, murdered **Röhm** and other leaders of the **SA** (Stormtroopers). The aim was to crush the political power of the SA, reassure the German establishment which was worried by SA excesses and settle old political scores. It has been estimated that up to 150 of Hitler's political opponents and rivals were killed, including von **Schleicher**, the former Chancellor.

nihilism A term made popular by Ivan Turgenev's *Fathers and Sons* (1861), referring to any outlook that denies the possibility of justifying moral values. It was a caricature but it came to characterize several members of the Russian radical intelligentsia, including Nikolai **Chernyshevsky** and particularly Dmitri Pisarev (1840–68), who advocated the total rejection of all existing institutions as well as moral values in the name of an unrestricted individual freedom intended to improve the lot of the Russian people.

Nihon Shoki The first Japanese official court history (literally, 'Chronicles of Japan'), completed in 720. Like the earlier *Kojiki* ('Record of Ancient Matters'), it sought to glorify the Japanese imperial family, tracing its descent from the gods. In the 1930s both works were lifted out of relative obscurity by ultra-nationalists anxious to prove Japan's superiority over other nations.

Nijmegen, Treaties of (1678–9) A peace settlement ending the Dutch War (1672–8) between the Netherlands and France and their allies, effectively recognizing French supremacy in Western Europe. Negotiations began in 1676, but fluctuated with the fortunes of war. The Dutch and Spanish governments acceded to **Louis XIV** of France's territorial demands, Spain being the principal loser (1678). After further military defeats, the Emperor **Leopold I** concluded a separate treaty (1679). ▷ **Anglo-Dutch Wars**

Nikolaevna, Klavdiya Ivanovna (1893–1944) Russian and Soviet women's rights activist. Born in St Petersburg, a bookbinder by trade, she was early involved in revolutionary activities and frequently arrested from 1908 onwards. After 1917 she organized women's groups in St Petersburg and in 1924 she was appointed head of *zhenotdel*, the Communist Party's women's section. In 1926 she was dismissed for supporting **Zinoviev** but survived to hold various lower rank appointments until her death.

Nikola Petrović ▷ **Nicholas I** of Montenegro

Nikolai Nikolaevich, Grand-Duke (1859–1929) Russian general. The nephew of **Alexander II**, in **World War I** he was the not particularly successful Russian commander-in-chief until he was displaced in 1915 by Tsar **Nicholas II** himself, who was particularly unsuccessful. Transferred to be commander in the Caucasus (1915–17), he fared rather better. He was inclined to favour some concessions in politics but after 1915 he had no influence. At least he was able to die peacefully in France.

Nikolsburg, Peace of (26 July 1866) The provisional peace settlement after the Battle of **Königgrätz-Sadowa** between **Prussia** and Austria and, days later, Prussia and the north German states, which ended the **Austro-Prussian War** and secured Prussian dominance in Germany. The Prussian Minister-President, **Bismarck**, succeeded in creating a **North German Confederation** in which Prussia was pre-eminent, in excluding Austria from German affairs, and in gaining French acceptance of this major shift in the European balance of power. The south German states remained independent until after the **Franco-Prussian War** (1870–1).

Nikon (1606–81) Russian religious leader and reformer. Having made a name for himself as Metropolitan of Novgorod, he achieved the highest office in the Russian Church (that of Patriarch) in 1652, and immediately began to rectify mistakes that had crept into texts and rituals. Although he was attacked by many priests, he won the backing of a series of Church Councils. Those who would not agree split off to become the **Old Believers**. But Nikon then exceeded his powers by asserting that the Church stood above the state, just as the sun was greater than the moon. Tsar **Alexei** quarrelled with him in 1658 and a church council deposed him in 1667.

Nile, Battle of the ▷ **Aboukir Bay, Battle of** (Aug 1798)

Nimeri, Gaafar Mohamed al- (1930–) Sudanese soldier and politician. Educated at Sudan Military College in Khartoum, he joined the army, and continued his training in Egypt, where he became a disciple of Gamal Abd al-**Nasser**. In 1969, with the rank of colonel, he led the military coup which removed the civilian government and established a Revolutionary Command Council (RCC). In 1971, under a new constitution, he became President. Although twice re-elected, by the 1980s his regional policies and his attempts to impose strict Islamic law had made his regime unpopular and in 1985, while visiting the USA, he himself was deposed by an army colleague, General Swar al-Dahab.

Nimitz, Chester William (1885–1966) US admiral. He trained at the US Naval Academy, served mainly in submarines, and by 1938 had become rear-admiral. Chief of the Bureau of Navigation during 1939–41, he then commanded the US Pacific Fleet, his conduct of naval operations contributing significantly to the defeat of Japan. He was made Fleet Admiral (1944) and Chief of Naval Operations (1945–7). ▷ **World War II**

Ninety-Two Resolutions (1834) Canadian political reform demands. The list of complaints against the government of Upper **Canada** was drawn up by a committee of reformers led by William Lyon **Mackenzie**. The system of patronage, the dispensation of the **Clergy Reserves** and various economic policies were all attacked and coupled with the demand for an elective legislature.

Ninomiya Sontoku (1787–1856) Japanese rural moralist. His conservative teachings (emphasizing frugality, obedience, harmony and self-help) were used by the state in the late 19c and early 20c to reinforce social order in the countryside. Statues of Ninomiya were erected in every elementary school and national ethics textbooks of the 1930s portrayed him as a model of virtue.

Nisei The term used to describe US citizens of Japanese descent. Technically the term should be restricted to the second generation, the first being called *Issei*, and the third *Sansei*. The first generation, mainly market-gardeners and farmers who had settled in Hawaii and California, were legally prohibited from applying for US citizenship. They numbered less than 25 000 at the beginning of the 20c, but their rapid increase led to President Theodore **Roosevelt** concluding a 'gentleman's agreement' with the Japanese government in 1907 to discourage further immigration. California and other states passed laws preventing them from owning or leasing real estate. After **Pearl Harbor**, President Franklin D **Roosevelt** ordered the *Issei* and the *Nisei*, even though the latter had been born with US citizenship, to be removed to concentration camps, and there was little protest from the rest of US society. In 1983 it was recognized by the federal government that these *Nisei* internees had been subjected to racial injustice and those still alive were awarded compensation of US$20 000 each.

Nishihara Loans The secret loans (totalling 145 million yen) made by the Japanese government to the Chinese Premier, **Duan Qirui**, between 1917 and 1918. Named after Nishihara Kamezo (1873–1954), who personally represented the Japanese Prime Minister, Terauchi Masatake, in Beijing, the loans were ostensibly granted for China's economic development. In reality they were used to keep Duan Qirui in power, in exchange for which Duan recognized Japan's retention of the former German leasehold territory in China it had occupied in 1914. The loan agreements were signed without the knowledge of the Chinese parliament; when details became known in 1919 they helped ignite the **May Fourth Movement** student demonstrations. The loans were not recognized by subsequent Chinese governments and were never repaid.

Nishio Suehiro (1891–1981) Japanese labour leader and politician. A moderate trade union leader in the 1920s, Nishio was first elected to the Diet in 1928 as a member of the *Shakai Minshuto* (Social Masses Party), a proletarian party founded in 1926 that subsequently supported the military cabinets of the 1930s. He joined the **Japan Socialist Party** (JSP) in 1945 and was a member of Tetsu **Katayama**'s socialist cabinet in 1947. Condemning the party's left-wing bias, in particular its opposition to Japan's security treaty with the USA, Nishio left the JSP in 1959 to form the Democratic Socialist Party, of which he remained Chairman until 1967.

Nithsdale, William Maxwell, 5th Earl of (1676–1744) Scottish Jacobite. In 1699 he married Lady Winifred Herbert, the youngest daughter of the Marquis of Powis. A Catholic in 1715, he joined the English **Jacobites** and was taken prisoner at Preston, tried for treason, and sentenced to death. The night before his execution he escaped from the Tower in woman's clothes, through the heroism of his countess. They settled at Rome, where he died.

Nitti, Francesco Saverio (1868–1953) Italian politician and professor. A deputy of radical and socialist sympathies from 1904, he grew closer to **Giolitti** in whose 1911–14 government he served as Minister of Agriculture and Industry. After **Caporetto**, he became **Orlando**'s Finance Minister, before replacing him as Prime Minister (1919). A victim of fascist attacks on account of his consistent and outspoken attacks on **Mussolini**, he went into self-imposed exile but returned to Italy after the war and remained active in politics until his death.

Nivelle, Robert (1857–1924) French soldier. He was an artillery colonel in Aug 1914, and made his name when in command of the army of Verdun by recapturing Douaumont and other forts (Oct–Dec 1916). He was Commander-in-Chief from Dec 1916 to May 1917, when his Aisne offensive failed and he was superseded by **Pétain**. ▷ **Verdun, Battle of; World War I**

Nixon, Richard M(ilhous) (1913–94) US politician and 37th President. He became a lawyer, then served in the US Navy. A Republican, he was elected to the House of Representatives in 1946, where he played a prominent role in **HUAC**. He became Senator in 1950 and Vice-President under **Eisenhower** for two terms (1952–9). He lost the 1960 presidential election to John F **Kennedy** but won in 1968. As president he sought to bring an end to the **Vietnam War**, but did so only after the US invasion of Cambodia and Laos and the heaviest US bombing of North Vietnam of the entire conflict. He had diplomatic successes with China and the USSR. In his domestic policy he reversed many of the social programmes that had come out of the previous Democratic administrations. He resigned under the threat of impeachment after several leading members of his staff had been found guilty of involvement in the **Watergate** affair, and because he was personally implicated in the cover-up. He was given a full pardon by President Gerald **Ford**.

Nkomati Accord Essentially this was a non-aggression treaty, signed between Mozambique and South Africa in 1984, in which the former agreed not to support the **ANC** (African National Congress) militarily and the latter agreed not to support **RENAMO** militarily. In practice, the superior power of South Africa meant that the agreement was implemented unilaterally.

Nkomo, Joshua (Mqabuko Nyongolo) (1917–) Zimbabwean nationalist and politician. Educated in Natal and at Fort Hare College, where he joined the **ANC** (African National Congress), he returned to Bulawayo as a social worker and became General-Secretary of the Rhodesian Railway African Employees Association in 1951. Elected Chairman of the (Southern Rhodesian) African National Congress in 1951, he became its President in 1957, leaving the country for exile in 1959. When the ANC was banned, he became President of its successor, the National Democratic Party, but that, too, was banned. He then helped form the Zimbabwe African People's Union (**ZAPU**) of which he became President. His non-confrontationist tactics and tendency to spend time outside Rhodesia led to a more radical group breaking away to form the Zimbabwe African National Union (**ZANU**). ZANU and ZAPU, with different international patrons and separate military wings, competed for the representation of African opinion but were persuaded to unite to form the **Patriotic Front** in 1976. ZAPU, however, was increasingly an Ndebele party and in the 1980 elections won only 20 seats. Nkomo, who still saw himself as the father of Zimbabwean nationalism, was disappointed to be offered only the post of Minister of Home Affairs, from which he was dismissed in 1981. Violence in Matabeleland encouraged him into a period of further exile, but he returned and agreed to integrate his party into ZANU, a union ratified in Apr 1988. He became Vice-President of the new party and was one of three senior members in the President's office forming in effect a 'super cabinet'.

Nkrumah, Kwame (1909–71) Ghanaian politician. Educated in a Catholic primary school and Achimota College, he then went to Lincoln and Pennsylvania Universities in the USA. He studied law in London (1945–7) and was Co-Chairman of the famous Fifth Pan-African Congress held in Manchester in 1945. He returned to the Gold Coast as Secretary-General of the **United Gold Coast Convention**, but broke with it to form the **Convention People's Party (CPP)** in 1949. Imprisoned briefly (he was elected to Legco while in prison), he became leader of government business (1951), Prime Minister (1952–7) and continued in that post on independence until Ghana became a republic in 1960, when he became President. A radical Pan-Africanist, for which he was widely admired throughout much of the continent, he created considerable opposition within Ghana, most of which was repressed; ultimately, however, the military intervened while he was abroad, symbolically on a visit to Beijing. He spent his years of exile in Guinea, where Sekou **Toure** gave him the status of co-head of state. He died in Bucharest.

Nkumbula, Harry M (1916–83) Zambian nationalist. Educated in local schools, he became a teacher before studying at Makerere College and the London School of Economics (1946–50). He was elected President of the Northern Rhodesian African National Congress (1951) and he was imprisoned briefly for his political activities. His support for a moderate independence constitution cost him the support of **Kaunda**, who left the **ANC** to form **UNIP**. He was a member of the pre-independence coalition government but was leader of the opposition during the first Republic, being restricted for a while in 1970. With the one-party state Second Republic, he joined UNIP in 1973 but remained outside politics in his last years.

Nobel Peace Prize A prize awarded annually (providing a suitable candidate is identified) since 1901 from the income of a trust fund established by the will of Swedish chemist and industrialist, Alfred Nobel (1833–96). The prize, which is given to an individual or to an institution for important contributions to peace, consists of a gold medal and a sum of money, and is presented in Oslo on 10 Dec, the anniversary of Nobel's death. See panel p676.

Noli, Fan S (1882–1965) Albanian bishop and politician. Born into an Orthodox family in Thrace, he was educated in Greece and taught at a Greek school in Egypt, where he first encountered the Albanian national movement. After studying law at Harvard, he was ordained a priest and became a bishop in the Albanian Orthodox Church (1908). In 1920 he returned to Albania to represent the American Albanians at the National Assembly held in Lushnjë. Left-wing and known as the 'Red Bishop', he was Foreign Minister in the 1921 Popular Party regime, but he criticized the conservative policies of King **Zog** and went on to form his own opposition party. After Zog fled (1924), Noli formed a government and tried to establish constitutional rule. He introduced agrarian reforms, tried to minimize Italian influence in Albania and made steps towards recognizing the Soviet regime. However, his government collapsed after only seven months, when Zog invaded the country. In 1930 he retired from political life and resumed his religious duties in the USA. ▷ **William of Wied**

Nomenklatura (post-1930) A list of official positions in the Communist Party of the USSR, and in Soviet government at most levels, and of people suited to fill them, predominantly communist. It was originally intended to identify good candidates in a developing society, but it was gradually abused first to support dictatorship and then to create and perpetuate an elite. By 1985 a corrupt system had paradoxically made reform essential in party and state and at the same time difficult to implement, as Mikhail **Gorbachev** found to his cost.

Nomonhan Incident (May–Sep 1939) A military clash between Japanese and Soviet troops on the border between north-west Manchuria and Outer Mongolia. When the Japanese **Guandong Army** engaged in hostilities with Mongolian troops on the border at Nomonhan, Soviet troops intervened under the terms of a mutual defence treaty with Outer Mongolia. A full-scale border war ensued involving the use of aircraft and armoured divisions. Soviet mechanized units under Georgii **Zhukov** inflicted a heavy defeat on the Japanese forces (17 450 dead or missing). Japan's humiliation at Nomonhan convinced Tokyo that war with the USSR (which the Guandong Army had consistently advocated) was to be avoided, and led to the signing of the Japan–USSR Neutrality Pact in 1941.

NOBEL PEACE PRIZE WINNERS

Year	Name	Year	Name	Year	Name
1901	(Jean) Henri Dunant	1931	Jane Addams	1964	Martin Luther King Jr
	Frédéric Passy		Nicholas Murray Butler	1965	United Nations Children's
1902	Élie Ducommun	1932	no award		Fund (UNICEF)
	Charles Albert Gobat	1933	Sir Norman Angell	1966	no award
1903	Sir William Cremer	1934	Arthur Henderson	1967	no award
1904	Institute of International	1935	Carl von Ossietzky	1968	René Cassin
	Law	1936	Carlos Saavedra Lamas	1969	International Labour
1905	Bertha von Suttner	1937	Viscount Cecil of Chelwood		Organisation
1906	Theodore Roosevelt	1938	Nansen International Office	1970	Norman Borlaug
1907	Ernesto Teodoro Moneta		for Refugees	1971	Willy Brandt
	Louis Renault	1939	no award	1972	no award
1908	Klas Pontus Arnoldson	1943	no award	1973	Henry Kissinger
	Fredrik Bajer	1944	International Red Cross		Le Duc Tho (declined)
1909	Baron d'Estournelles		Committee	1974	Sean MacBride
	de Constant	1945	Cordell Hull		Sato Eisaku
	Auguste Beernaert	1946	Emily Green Balch	1975	Andrei Sakharov
1910	International Peace Bureau		John R Mott	1976	Mairead Corrigan
1911	Tobias Asser	1947	American Friends Service		Betty Williams
	Alfred Fried		Committee (USA)	1977	Amnesty International
1912	Elihu Root		Friends Service Council	1978	Menachem Begin
1913	Henri Lafontaine		(UK)		Anwar al-Sadat
1914	no award	1948	no award	1979	Mother Teresa
1915	no award	1949	Lord Boyd-Orr	1980	Adolfo Pérez Esquivel
1916	no award	1950	Ralph Bunche	1981	Office of the United Nations
1917	International Red Cross	1951	Léon Jouhaux		High Commissioner for
	Committee	1952	Albert Schweitzer		Refugees
1918	no award	1953	George Catlett Marshall	1982	Alfonso García Robles
1919	Woodrow Wilson	1954	Office of the United Nations		Alva Myrdal
1920	Léon Bourgeois		High Commissioner for	1983	Lech Walesa
1921	Karl Branting		Refugees	1984	Desmond Tutu
	Christian Lous Lange	1955	no award	1985	International Physicians for
1922	Fridtjof Nansen	1956	no award		the Prevention of Nuclear
1923	no award	1957	Lester Bowles Pearson		War
1924	no award	1958	Dominique Georges Pire	1986	Elie Wiesel
1925	Sir Austen Chamberlain	1959	Philip Noel-Baker	1987	Oscar Arias Sánchez
	Charles G Dawes	1960	Albert Luthuli	1988	United Nations
1926	Aristide Briand	1961	Dag Hammarskjöld		Peacekeeping Forces
	Gustav Stresemann	1962	Linus Pauling	1989	HH the Dalai Lama of
1927	Ferdinand Buisson	1963	International Red Cross		Tibet
	Ludwig Quidde		Committee	1990	Mikhail Gorbachev
1928	no award		League of Red Cross	1991	Aung San Suu Kyi
1929	Frank B Kellogg		Societies	1992	Rigoberta Menchu
1930	Nathan Söderblom				

Non-Aligned Movement A movement of states in the early years of the **Cold War** which positively espoused the cause of not taking sides in the major division within world politics between the USA and the USSR. Non-alignment was different from neutralism in that it was associated with moves to mediate between the **superpowers**, and aimed to make a direct contribution to the achievement of peace. It was particularly associated with countries like India and statesmen like **Nehru**. Attempts by Mediterranean, African and Asian countries in the 1960s to give renewed impetus to the movement were badly shaken by continuing superpower hostility. However, conferences were still being held in the 1980s.

Non-Cooperation Movement A nationalist campaign (1919–22) led by M K **Gandhi** and Congress in protest against the **Amritsar Massacre** and the **Montagu-Chelmsford Reforms**, and to force the British to grant Indian independence. Locally, it took up many issues, and was linked, especially by Gandhi, with the **Khilafat Movement**. The movement marked M K **Gandhi**'s rise to pre-eminence in the Congress. It involved the boycott of Government institutions and for-

RULERS OF ENGLAND TO THE NORMAN CONQUEST

Regnal Dates	Name
West Saxon Kings	
802/39	Egbert
839/58	Ethelwulf
858/60	Ethelbald
860/5	Ethelbert
865/71	Ethelred I
871/99	Alfred the Great
899/924	Edward the Elder
924/39	Athelstan
939/46	Edmund I
946/55	Edred
955/9	Edwy
959/75	Edgar
975/8	Edward the Martyr
978/1016	Ethelred the Unready
1016	Edmund II, 'Ironside'
Danish Kings	
1016/35	Canute
1035/7	Harold I, 'Harefoot' (Regent)
1037/40	Harold I, 'Harefoot'
1040/2	Hardaknut
1042/66	Edward the Confessor
1066	Harold II

eign goods, and was abandoned when the protest became violent.

non-violent resistance The use of non-violent means to resist occupation by a foreign power or other political purposes. It can involve an appeal to wider world opinion, as well as various forms of peaceful political reistance, such as general strikes and **civil disobedience**. Damage to property is not necessarily ruled out. Non-violent resistance is most famously associated with M K **Gandhi**'s resistance to British rule in India, and was popular with the civil rights movements of the 1960s.

Noriega, Manuel (Antonio) (1939–) Panamanian military leader. The ruling force behind the presidents of Panama in the period 1983–9, he had been recruited by the CIA in the late 1960s and supported by the US government until 1987. Alleging his involvement in drug trafficking, the US authorities ordered his arrest in 1989: 13 000 US troops invaded Panama to support the 12 000 already there. He surrendered in Jan 1990 after taking refuge for 10 days in the Vatican nunciature, and was taken to the USA for trial.

normalization A term used to describe the restoration of previously ostensibly friendly

relations between states or other political organizations after a period of tension or conflict. It was more specifically applied to what was frankly the reimposition of Soviet-style **communism** on those East European socialist states, such as Czechoslovakia in 1968, that had attempted to modify Soviet forms to suit their own conditions. ▷ **detente**

Norman Conquest A fundamental watershed in English political and social history, though some of its consequences are much debated. It not only began the rule of a dynasty of Norman kings (1066–1154), but entailed the virtual replacement of the Anglo-Saxon nobility by **Normans**, Bretons, and Flemings, many of whom retained lands in northern France. Moreover, between 1066 and 1144 England and **Normandy** were normally united under one king-duke, and the result was the formation of a single cross-Channel state. The Angevin conquest of Normandy (1144–5) and takeover of England (1154) ensured that England's fortunes would continue to be linked with France, even after the French annexation of Normandy in 1204. ▷ **Angevins; Domesday Book; Hastings, Battle of; Henry I** of England; **Hundred Years War; William I, 'the Conqueror'; William II, 'Rufus'**

Normandy Former duchy and province in north-western France, along the littoral of the English Channel between Brittany and French Flanders; now occupying the regions of Haute-Normandie and Basse-Normandie. A leading state in the **Middle Ages**, **William I, 'the Conqueror'**, as Duke of Normandy, conquered England in 1066. Captured by France in 1204, the ownership of Normandy was disputed between France and England in the **Hundred Years War** until it became part of France in 1449. In 1944 it was the scene of the Allied invasion of occupied France. ▷ **Normandy Campaign**

Normandy Campaign (1944) A **World War II** campaign which began on **D-Day** (6 June 1944). Allied forces under the command of General **Eisenhower** began the liberation of

NORMAN DYNASTY

Regnal Dates	Name
1066/87	William I, 'the Conqueror'
1087/1100	William II, 'Rufus'
1100/35	Henry I
1135/54	Stephen

Western Europe from Germany by landing on the **Normandy** coast between the Orne River and St Marcouf. Artificial harbours were constructed along a strip of beach so that armoured vehicles and heavy guns could be unloaded. Heavy fighting ensued for three weeks, before Allied troops captured Cherbourg (27 June). Tanks broke through the German defences, and Paris was liberated (25 Aug), followed by the liberation of Brussels (2 Sep), and the crossing of the German frontier (12 Sep).

Normans By the early 11c, a label (derived from 'Northmen', ie **Vikings**) applied to all the people inhabiting **Normandy**, a duchy (and later province) in northern France, though probably only a small element was actually of Scandinavian descent. During the second half of the 11c and the first decade of the 12c, their achievements, especially as conquerors, were remarkable. They completed the conquest and aristocratic colonization of England and a large part of Wales, established a kingdom in southern Italy and Sicily, and founded the Norman principality of Antioch. They also fought against the Muslims in Spain and settled peacefully in Scotland. ▷ **Guiscard, Robert**

Norodom I (1838–1904) King of Cambodia (1860/1904). When Norodom succeeded his father as king in 1860, Cambodia fell into civil war. Norodom fled to Bangkok, having spent much of his childhood at the Siamese court. On his return to Cambodia in 1863, Norodom was approached by the French, recently established in **Cochin-China**, who offered him protection in exchange for commercial rights. Eager to escape from the influence of Siam, Norodom accepted. However, this action simply secured French domination. Cambodia became a French protectorate. Until the 1880s, Norodom retained considerable freedom but from the middle of that decade the French greatly tightened their control.

North, Frederick, 8th Lord North (1732–92) British politician. He became a Lord of the Treasury (1759) and Chancellor of the Exchequer (1767), and as Prime Minister (1770–82) brought **George III** a period of political stability. He was widely criticized both for failing to avert the **Declaration of Independence** by the North American colonies (1776) and for failing to defeat them in the subsequent war (1776–83). He annoyed the King by resigning in 1782, then formed a coalition with his former Whig

opponent, 'Fox (1783), but it did not survive royal hostility. After this coalition was dismissed (1783), he remained an opposition politician until his death. ▷ **American Revolution**

North African Campaign (1940–3) A campaign fought during **World War II** between Allied and Axis troops. After an initial Italian invasion of Egypt, Italian forces were driven back deep into Libya, and **Rommel** was sent to North Africa with the specially trained Afrika Corps to stem a further Italian retreat. The British were driven back to the Egyptian border, though they defended Tobruk. They counter-attacked late in 1941, and fighting continued the following year, with Rommel once more gaining the initiative. In Oct, British troops under **Montgomery** defeated Rommel at the Battle of **El Alamein**, and drove the German troops W once more. In Feb 1943, the Germans attacked US troops in Tunisia, were driven back, and finally 250 000 Axis troops, half of them German, were caught in a pincer movement by Allied forces advancing from the east and west. ▷ **Axis Powers**

North Atlantic Treaty Organization ▷ **NATO**

Northern Expedition (1926–8) The military expedition undertaken by the Chinese Nationalists (**Guomindang**) and their communist allies to defeat provincial warlords and reunify the country. Under the command of **Chiang Kai-shek**, the National Revolutionary Army marched northwards from south China (July 1926) and had reached the Yangzi River (central China) by early 1927. At this point the left wing of the Guomindang, with the support of the communists, established its own government at Wuhan, while the right wing under Chiang Kai-shek, after taking Shanghai (Apr 1927), embarked on a campaign of terror against communists and their labour supporters. By June 1927 the left-wing Guomindang government had collapsed, effectively ending the United Front between Nationalists and communists. Chiang then proceeded northwards, capturing Beijing (1928). Although a Nationalist government was formally proclaimed (with the capital at Nanjing), Chiang's control over the country was tenuous. Most warlords had simply enrolled under the Nationalist banner and continued to exercise control of their own armies. Furthermore, although the communists' urban base had been destroyed during the

Northern Expedition they developed rural bases after 1928 that were ultimately to engulf the entire country.

North German Confederation The state system and constitutional arrangement created in 1866 by **Bismarck**, Minister-President of **Prussia**, following the Prussian defeat of Austria and the dissolution of the **German Confederation**. Utterly dominated by Prussia, the new confederation was itself dissolved with the creation of the German Empire in 1871. ▷ **Austro-Prussian War**

Northumbria The largest kingdom of the Anglo-Saxon heptarchy. In the 7c it established a broad dominance in Britain both north and south of the Humber, while in the 8c the Northumbrian monasteries gained a European-wide reputation for sanctity and learning. The kingdom came to an end in 876, and by the 12c Northumbria was equivalent to the earldom or county of Northumberland. ▷ **Anglo-Saxons**

North West Company Canadian fur-trading association. Established in 1779, it set up a string of trading partnerships and achieved a remarkable record of exploration. The Montreal partners managed finance and marketing, meeting the 'wintering' partners once a year in Fort William to collect the furs and make policy decisions. The 'wintering' partners in turn organized the trappers and canoeists. In 1821, however, the company was absorbed into the **Hudson's Bay Company** with which it had been conducting a bitter and often violent competition. ▷ **Fraser, Simon**

Northwest Ordinance of 1787 An Act of the American Continental Congress establishing procedures by which newly settled Western territories could become states on the basis of full political equality with the original states. It was one of several Northwest Ordinances passed in 1784–7.

North-West Rebellion (1885) Canadian revolt. The **métis** of the Saskatchewan, like those of Red River, had suffered from the encroachments of English-speaking settlers without any governmental assurances or safeguards. Although they had an effective leader in Gabriel Dumont, they appealed to Louis **Riel**, who returned from the USA to lead them. When two Indian tribes also gave their support it began to look as if the North West was about to explode, but a large body of militia crushed the revolt. Dumont

escaped but Riel was captured and later executed. The speed with which the militia were able to get from Ottawa to Winnipeg (six days instead of the two months taken in 1870 by the Wolseley expedition) showed the value of the Canadian Pacific Railway, encouraging the government to lend it the money essential for its completion. ▷ **Red River Rebellion**

Norway, German Invasion of (8–9 Apr 1940) A daring seaborne operation, undertaken in defiance of British naval superiority, which was carried out as a preliminary to the German invasion of France and in order to protect Germany's supply of iron ore from northern Sweden. It brought all major Norwegian cities, including Oslo, Bergen, Trondheim and Narvik under German control within a single night. Refusing to capitulate or to hand over authority to **Quisling**, the Norwegian government and King **Haakon VII** maintained a resistance to the Germans which lasted, with British and French support, until June 1940. ▷ **World War II**

Notables, Assemblies of the (1787–8) In France, the name originated with consultative assemblies called by the monarchy in 15–17c. They fell into disuse until **Calonne** convoked such a meeting in 1787, hoping that these representatives of the privileged orders would agree to the ending of their exemption from certain taxes. They refused, and the first assembly was dissolved, leading to Calonne's fall. In 1788 **Necker**, who replaced him, called a second assembly to advise on the method of calling the **Estates General**.

Nothomb, Jean Baptiste (1805–81) Belgian politician. Trained as a lawyer, he was active as a journalist-editor, and in political opposition to the union between the northern and southern Netherlands (present-day Netherlands and Belgium, 1815–30). After the **Belgian Revolution** he became a member of the National Congress and helped draft the constitution. He served as an MP (1831–48), Minister for Public Works (1837–40) and Minister for Home Affairs (1841–5), when he also led the government. He then became Belgian ambassador to Berlin.

Notting Hill Riots (1958) A series of violent demonstrations in north-west London. Directed at non-white immigrants living there, they brought immigration into the British political arena for the first time.

Novara, Battle of (23 Mar 1849) The defeat by **Radetzky** of the Piedmontese forces under the command of the Polish General, Chrzanowsky, which led to the abdication of **Charles Albert**.

Novatian (fl.3c) Hard-line Christian cleric. Formerly a Stoic, in the aftermath of the persecution of **Decius** (251), he challenged the papal policy of readmitting lapsed Christians to communion and formed instead his own sect (the Novatiani) with rigorous views on Christian purity. The first theologian at Rome to write in Latin, Novatian is believed to have perished in the persecution of **Valerian**. His sect survived until the 6c.

Novikov, Nikolai I (1744–1818) Russian Freemason. Like other phenomena of the Enlightenment, Freemasonry spread to the imitative Russia of **Catherine II, 'the Great'**; and from 1779 to 1791 Novikov was active as publisher and journalist in Moscow. His main interests were education and philanthropy, and initially he had widespread support from fellow nobles and from Catherine. But particularly following the **French Revolution**, she began to object to the criticism inherent in Novikov's activities. In 1791 she suspended his publications and in 1792 imprisoned him without trial. The idea of secret societies working for reform (one aspect of Freemasonry) revived in the 1820s and helped shape the activity of the **Decembrists**.

Novi Pazar ▷ **Sandžak of Novi Pazar**

Novosiltsev, Nikolai Nikolaeva, Count (1761–1836) Russian bureaucrat. He was one of the 'unofficial committee' of four friends and advisers of Tsar **Alexander I**, who helped him to make a liberal start to his reign in the years 1801–3. In 1805 he headed a special mission to Britain, and the resulting treaty brought Alexander into the alliance against **Napoleon I**. In 1815 he became imperial commissioner in Warsaw, generally supervising the so-called **Congress Kingdom of Poland**. In 1820 he presented the Tsar with the definitive form of his Constitutional Charter of the Russian Empire, which advocated something approaching a federation of 12 provinces. Alexander favoured it but implemented it only marginally. With **Nicholas I**'s accession, however, Novosiltsev lost influence.

Novotný, Antonín (1904–75) Czechoslovak politician. He became a communist at the age of 17 and held various party jobs in the years before **World War II**. Arrested in 1941, he survived four years in a Nazi concentration

camp. After his release, he rose rapidly in the Czechoslovak Communist Party, becoming Regional Secretary in Prague in 1945 and a member of the Central Committee in 1946. He played a leading part in the communist takeover of the Czechoslovak government in 1948. Novotný became all-powerful First Secretary of the Party in 1953 and from 1958 to 1968 he was also President of the republic. He was essentially a Soviet-style communist so much committed to central planning and the needs of heavy industry that by 1961 there was an economic recession. His unpopularity forced him to make token concessions from 1962 onwards, especially in the hope of placating the Slovaks, but these empty gestures failed to satisfy his critics within the Party. He was therefore forced out, and succeeded as First Secretary by, the reformist Slovak, Alexander **Dubček**, in Jan 1968, and was also forced to resign the presidency two months later. However, his negative and protracted tenure of office lost the Czechoslovak reform movement more time than it could make up in the course of the **Prague Spring**. ▷ **Stalinism**

NPD (*Nationaldemokratische Partei Deutschlands*, 'National Democratic Party of Germany') German political party. Founded in 1964 through the amalgamation of extreme right-wing splinter parties, notably the German Reich Party (DRP) and German Party (DP), the NPD became increasingly radical, especially under von Thadden's leadership from 1967. In its internal structure, politics and membership the NPD showed some disturbing parallels with the **Nazi Party**, but although it gained seats temporarily in various **Land** (state) parliaments, it failed to enter the **Bundestag** and by the mid-1970s had, to all intents and purposes, collapsed.

NSDAP ▷ **Nazi Party**

Nu, U (1907–) Burmese politician and Prime Minister (1948–56, 1957–8 and 1960–2). He became a teacher, and in 1934 came to prominence through the student political movement. Imprisoned by the British for sedition (1940), he was released by the Japanese and served in Ba Maw's puppet administration. In 1946 he became President of the Burmese Constituent Assembly, and the first Prime Minister of the independent Union of Burma (1948). He was overthrown by a military coup in 1962, and imprisoned, but released in 1966. He then lived abroad, organizing resistance to the military regime, but returned to Burma in 1980 to become a Buddhist monk.

Nuclear Non-Proliferation Treaty (NPT) A treaty signed in 1968 by the USA, the USSR, the UK and an open-ended list of over 100 other countries. It sought to limit the spread of nuclear weapons, those possessing them agreeing not to transfer the capability to produce them, and those not possessing them agreeing not to acquire the capability. Recent reductions in US and Russian nuclear stockpiles appear to have reinforced the Treaty, but a number of other states are thought to be close to producing their own nuclear arms.

nuclear weapons Bomb, missile or other weapon of mass destruction deriving its destructive force from the energy released during nuclear fission or nuclear fusion. According to their size and the means of delivery, they may be classified as tactical short-range weapons (for use on the battlefield), theatre medium-range weapons (for use against deep military targets), or strategic long-range weapons (for use against enemy cities and command centres). ▷ **CND; Nuclear Non-Proliferation Treaty**

Nujoma, Sam Daniel (1929–) Namibian nationalist. Educated at a Finnish missionary school in Windhoek, he was a railway worker and clerk until entering politics as the co-founder of the South West Africa People's Organization (**SWAPO**). He was exiled in 1960, set up a provisional headquarters in Dar es Salaam and led SWAPO's armed struggle from 1966 until 1989 when he returned to Namibia for the pre-independence elections, which his party won. He became the first President of Namibia in Mar 1990.

nullification A US political doctrine that a state has the power to render laws of the federal government void within its borders. It was tested by South Carolina during the 'Nullification Crisis' in 1832, over the issue of enforcing a federal tariff. That immediate issue was resolved by the **Jackson** administration's Force Bill, authorizing the president to use armed forces to enforce the laws of Congress. However, in larger terms the problem was not resolved until the **American Civil War**, and in some ways continued through the **civil rights** movement.

Numantia, Siege of (133BC) The scene of the last struggle between the Celtiberians and the Romans in the Iberian Peninsula. The Celtiberian city was besieged by the Romans in 153BC and 140BC, but each time the Romans suffered a spectacular defeat. Eventually **Scipio Aemilianus**, the conqueror of Carthage, reorganized the Roman forces and laid siege to the city in 133BC: after eight months, the starving Celtiberians surrendered and the city was reduced to ashes. ▷ **Celtiberia**

Numa Pompilius (8c–7c BC) The second of Rome's early kings. According to tradition he ruled from 715 to 673BC. He is described as a peaceful ruler, and was credited with organizing the religious life of the community.

Numidia The Roman name for the region in North Africa to the west and south of **Carthage** which roughly corresponds to modern Algeria.

Núñez, Rafael (1825–94) Colombian politician. Trained as a lawyer, he rose to prominence as a Liberal leader in the 1870s but, influenced by radical Spencerian ideas, such as the 'survival of the fittest', turned to Conservatism. Governor of Bolivar, he was elected President (1880–2) with the support of moderate Liberals and Conservatives. Returned to office 1884–94, he fought the Liberals, assuring centralized government in the constitution of 1886, which lasted until 1936. He restored the power of the Church, and the Jesuits returned to dominate the education system. His governments were also marked by attempts at modernization. The secession of Panama in 1903 partially resulted from Núñez's centralization of administration in Bogota, and his concern for the interests of his birthplace, Cartagena, the historic rival to Panama.

Nupe An Islamic state in central Nigeria which resisted the encroachments of Europeans in the 19c. It was conquered in 1896 by Sir George Goldie and forces of the Royal Niger Company. The southern half of the emirate was ceded to the British and a new emir was installed likely to be sympathetic to the company. It was subsequently incorporated into the colony of Nigeria.

Nur al-Din (1118–74) Sultan of Egypt and Syria (1146/74). Also known as al-Malik al-Adil ('the Just Ruler'), he was the son of the Turkish Atabeg Zangi, whom he succeeded as ruler of Aleppo in 1146. He devoted himself to the **jihad**, the holy war against the Christian Franks of the crusader states, defeating and killing Prince Raymond of Antioch (1149) and completely extinguishing the most exposed Frankish state, the county of Edessa (1146–51). He saw the unification of the Muslim Middle East as the key to his aim, and worked to bring about the conquest of Damascus (1154) and Mosul (1170), while through his generals Shirkuh and **Saladin** he took control of Egypt and abolished the Fatimid caliphate. Nur al-Din's empire began to fall apart soon after his death, and it was left to Saladin, who by this time had made himself independent, to carry on his mission.

Nuremberg Laws (1935) Two racial laws promulgated in Nuremberg at a **Reichstag** meeting held during the **Nazi Party** Congress of that year. The first deprived of German citizenship those not of 'German or related blood'; the second made marriage or extramarital relations illegal between Germans and Jews. Following on earlier arbitrary terror, the laws were the first formal steps in the process of separating off Jews and other 'non-Aryans' in Nazi Germany.

Nuremberg Trials Proceedings held by the Allies at Nuremberg after **World War II** to try Nazi war criminals, following a decision made in 1943. An International Military Tribunal was set up in Aug 1945, and sat from Nov 1945 until Oct 1946. Twenty-one Nazis were tried in person, including **Goering** and **Ribbentrop** (who were sentenced to death), and **Hess** (who was given life imprisonment). ▷ **Nazi Party**

Nurhaci (1559–1626) Manchu (Jurchen) leader. He unified the tribes on China's north-eastern frontier, laying the foundations for the eventual Manchu conquest of China in 1644. Nurhaci belonged to a clan whose forebears had owed allegiance to the Chinese **Ming Dynasty**, but his policy of unifying the tribes through warfare and marriage ties, and his assumption of the title of Khan (ruler) in 1616 symbolized open defiance of the Ming. The creator of the **Banner System**, he developed a sophisticated military and bureaucratic organization, employing Chinese advisers and devising a Manchu written script. After his death, following an unexpected setback to his offensive on China, his sons and grandsons completed the task of conquest to establish the **Qing Dynasty**.

Nur Jahan (fl.1611–27) Wife of Jahangir, the eldest son of Emperor **Akbar the Great**. In 1611 her first husband, Sher Afghan, died in a clash with the Mughal Governor of Bengal. Nur Jahan's father, Itimaduddaula, was made joint Diwan by Jahangir in the first year of his reign and, after Jahangir's marriage to Nur Jahan, he was raised to the office of Chief Diwan; furthermore Nur Jahan's brother, Asaf Khan, who appointed Khan-i-saman, a post reserved for nobles in whom the emperor had full confidence. Along with her father and brother, and in alliance with Khurram (Shah Jahan), Nur Jahan formed a group or *junta* which 'managed' Jahangir and his political activities. This led to the division of court into two factions. Although her precise political role in this period is not clear, Nur Jahan was a dominant figure in the royal household and set new fashions based on Persian traditions.

Nyamwezi A people of the highlands of north-central Tanzania, south of Lake Victoria. In the 18c they created a trading network between the East African coast and some of the states of Uganda. Later they extended their commercial influence to the Kazembe kingdom in Zambia. Coastal Swahili and Europeans were in touch with them in the 19c, particularly during the reign of their chief, Mirambo. ▷ **Buganda; Luba-Lunda Kingdoms; Swahili**

Nyerere, Julius (Kambarage) (1922–) Tanzanian nationalist leader and politician. While working as a schoolteacher, he became President of the Tanganyika African Association (1953). He left the profession to co-found (1954) the Tanganyika African National Union, of which he became President, and led the movement to independence. After a brief spell as a nominated member of Legco (from which he resigned), Nyerere was elected (1958) in his own right, becoming Chief Minister (1960–1) and, on independence, Prime Minister. He resigned from the post to reorganize the party and returned to central politics as President, negotiating the union of Tanganyika and Zanzibar in 1964. His idealism, reflected in the **Arusha Declaration**, dominated Tanzania's public policy and the country's reputation abroad. He resigned the presidency in 1985, but retained the presidency of the party until 1987.

Nyoro A Bantu-speaking agricultural people of western Uganda. The original feudal kingdom of Bunyoro-Kitara was founded in the 14–15c with a pastoralist ruling class (Hima) and farming peasants (Iru). It was the most powerful kingdom in the area during the 19c, but was destroyed by the British in the

1890s. The kingship was abolished by the Ugandan government in 1966.

Nystadt, Treaty of (1721) The Russo-Swedish treaty, signed at Nystadt, Finland, ending the Great Northern War and recognizing Russia's total victory. The cost of the war to Russia in terms of money and manpower was immense. However, so was the profit from the treaty: the area now occupied by Estonia, Latvia and Lithuania; and the south-east corner of post-**World War I** Finland, above all the fortress of Vyborg. In this way, Russia was ensured permanent access to the Baltic Sea. The treaty marked the emergence of Russia as a major European power. ▷ **Peter I, 'the Great'**

Nzinga (d.1663) Queen of Matamba. A royal princess of the Ndongo (a small kingdom adjoining the Portuguese colony of Angola), she fought to establish a kingdom independent of the Portuguese, free from war and the depredations of the **slave trade**. In 1623 she went personally to Angola to negotiate with the governor and was baptized a Christian as Dona Aña de Souza. Driven out of Ndongo by Portuguese troops the following year, she created the new kingdom of Matamba. Here she trained up military élites to resist the Portuguese and allied herself with the Dutch following their capture of Luanda, the Angolan capital, in 1641. Although she had abandoned Christianity, she reconverted towards the end of her life, by which time Matamba had become a successful commercial kingdom (largely through acting as a broker in the Portuguese slave trade).

O

OAPEC (Organization of Arab Petroleum Exporting Countries) An organization formed under the umbrella of the Organization of Petroleum Exporting Countries (OPEC) in 1968 by Saudi Arabia, Kuwait, and Libya, with its headquarters in Kuwait. By 1972 all the Arab oil producers had joined. ▷ **OPEC**

OAS (*Organisation Armée Secrète*, 'Secret Army Organization') The clandestine organization of French Algerians, led by rebel army generals Jouhaud and Raoul **Salan**, active (1960–2) in resisting Algerian independence. It caused considerable violence in Algeria and metropolitan France until thrown into rapid decline by the Franco-Algerian cease-fire (Mar 1962), Salan's capture (Apr 1962) and Algerian independence (July 1962). ▷ **Algerian War of Independence; FLN**

Oastler, Richard (1789–1861) British social reformer. A Tory humanitarian, he attacked the employment of children in factories and advocated a shorter working day, in campaigns resulting in the Factory Act (1833) and Ten Hours Act (1847). He was a strong opponent of **laissez-faire** political economy, and campaigned against the implementation of the Poor Law Amendment Act (1834), which he believed reduced paupers to the status of slaves. His *Fleet Papers*, attacking the Poor Law and criticizing the government, were edited from prison, where he had been placed for debts owing to his former employer. ▷ **Poor Laws; Tories**

Oba ▷ **Benin, Kingdom of**

Obasanjo, Olusegun (1937–) Nigerian soldier and politician. Educated at Abeokuta Baptist High School and Mons Officers' School, he joined the Nigerian army in 1958, training in both the UK and India, specializing in engineering. He served with the Nigerian unit in the **UN** Congo (Zaire) operations and was military commander of the federal forces during the **Biafran War** (1967–70). He was made Federal Commissioner of Works and Housing (1975) as well as Chief of Staff. After the short interim military rule led by Murtala Mohammed, he became Head of State (1976–9) overseeing the transfer back to civilian rule. Since then, he has played an important role on the international stage, especially within the Commonwealth, and as founder and leader of the African Leadership Forum.

Obote, (Apollo) Milton (1924–) Ugandan politician. Educated in mission schools and Makerere College, he worked in Kenya (1950–5), being a founder member of the Kenyan African Union. He kept his political links with his home country and was a member of the Uganda National Congress (1952–60), being elected to Legco in 1957. He helped form the Uganda People's Congress in 1960, became its leader and then leader of the opposition during the Kiwanuka government of 1961–2. The 1962 elections resulted in a coalition between Obote's UPC and the neo-traditionalist **Kabaka Yekka** and he became Prime Minister. When fundamental differences between himself and the Kabaka could not be mediated, he staged a coup in 1966, deposing the Kabaka and establishing himself as Executive President. In 1971, however, his government was overthrown in a military coup, led by Idi **Amin**. He went into exile in Tanzania and returned to Uganda with the Tanzanian army in 1979, regaining the presidency after elections in 1980. But he was once more overthrown by the military (July 1985) and went into exile again, this time in Zambia.

Obradović, Dositej (1743–1811) Leading figure in the Serbian national revival. Born into a Serbian family in the Banat of Temesvár, as an Orthodox monk he travelled widely in the Near East, England, France and Germany. On his travels he absorbed the ideas of the Enlightenment and became fiercely anticlerical. During the **Serbian Uprisings**, he was responsible for education in the administration of George **Karageorge**. ▷ **Karadžić, Vuk Stefanović**

Obrenović, Alexander (1876–1903) King of Serbia (1889/1903). The son of Milan **Obrenović**, he became King after his father's abdication (1889), the last of the Obrenović Dynasty. Governing at first through a regency, he used the army to take control of the country in 1893 and introduced some limited reform, reinstating the 1869 constitution which allowed more power to the executive (1894). He lacked popular support and his marriage in 1897 to a widow of ill-repute undermined yet further his authority. In June 1903 a group of Serbian army officers staged a coup and brutally murdered the King and Queen with the Prime Minister, War Minister and the Queen's brothers. ▷ **Pašić, Nikola**

Obrenović, Michael (1822–1868) Prince of Serbia (1839/42 and 1860/8). The second son of Miloš **Obrenović**, he succeeded his father and governed through a regency until 1842, when he was overthrown and replaced by **Alexander Karageorgević**. He succeeded his father as Prince once again in 1860. Well-educated and a clever politician, he looked to expand the Serbian state on the lines of Ilija **Garašanin**'s **Nacertanije**. He increased and improved the army, created a War Ministry and built up a system of alliances with the other Balkan states against the **Ottoman Empire**. While maintaining the form of the constitution, he controlled the assemblies and concentrated supreme power in his own hands. He was assassinated in June 1868.

Obrenović, Milan (1854–1901) Prince (1868/82) and King (1882/9) of Serbia. In 1868 he succeeded his cousin, Michael **Obrenović**, and governed through a regency. In 1869 he issued a new constitution which gave the assembly a stronger role, but his rule was both authoritarian and ineffectual. In 1889 he abdicated in favour of his son, Alexander **Obrenović**. ▷ **Ristić, Jovan**

Obrenović, Miloš (1780–1860) Prince of Serbia (1858/60). The founder of the Obrenović Dynasty, in 1815 he led the second stage of the **Serbian Uprisings** and was ruler of the semi-independent Serbian state, before finally becoming the first Prince of autonomous Serbia (1830). Eliminating his rivals, including George **Karageorge**, he ruled autocratically and amassed a great fortune. He considered that the so-called Turkish Constitution (1838) placed too many limitations on his authority and he left Serbia. After the fall of the constitutionalist regime of **Alexander Karageorgević**, he returned to Serbia and ruled as an absolute prince.

O'Brien, William (1852–1928) Irish journalist and nationalist. He became editor of the weekly *United Ireland*, and sat in parliament as a Nationalist (1883–95). Several times prosecuted, and imprisoned for two years, he later returned to parliament (1900–18), and founded the United Irish League (1898) and the All-for-Ireland League (1910).

O'Brien, William Smith (1803–64) Irish nationalist. He entered parliament in 1826, joining Daniel **O'Connell**'s Repeal Association (1843), but withdrew in 1846 after disputes over the use of force. Leader of the **Young Ireland** movement, he organized an unsuccessful rebellion in 1848, and was given a death sentence, commuted to transportation for life. In 1854 he was released, on condition of his not returning to Ireland, and in 1856 he received a free pardon.

O'Connell, Daniel (1775–1847) Irish political leader. He became a lawyer, and in 1823 formed the Catholic Association, which successfully fought elections against the landlords. His election as MP for County Clare precipitated a crisis in **Wellington**'s government, which eventually granted **Catholic Emancipation** in 1829, enabling him to take his seat in the Commons. In 1840 he founded the Repeal Association, and agitation to end the union with Britain increased. In 1844 he was imprisoned for 14 weeks on a charge of sedition. In conflict with the **Young Ireland** movement (1846), and failing in health, 'the Liberator' left Ireland in 1847, and died in Genoa.

O'Connor, Feargus Edward (1794–1855) Irish Chartist leader. He studied at Dublin, became a lawyer, and entered parliament in 1832. Estranged from **O'Connell**, he devoted himself to the cause of the working classes in England. His Leeds *Northern Star* (1837) became the most influential Chartist newspaper. He attempted, without great success, to unify the Chartist movement via the National Charter Association (1840), and presented himself as leader of the Chartist cause. Elected MP for Nottingham in 1847, in 1852 he became insane. ▷ **Chartists**

O'Connor, Sandra Day (1930–) US lawyer and jurist. She studied at Stanford, and after practising law she entered Arizona politics as a Republican, becoming majority leader in the state Senate before moving to the state bench. In 1981 President **Reagan** named her to the US Supreme Court. She was confirmed, becoming the first woman in that position. ▷ **Republican Party**

Octavia (d.11BC) Roman matron. The sister of Emperor **Augustus**, distinguished by her beauty and 'womanly' virtues. On the death of her first husband, Marcellus, in 40BC she consented to marry Mark **Antony**, to reconcile him and her brother; but in 32BC Antony divorced and forsook her in favour of **Cleopatra VII**.

October Crisis (1970) Terrorist crisis in Quebec. After the arrest of Pierre Vallière and Charles Gagnon, the **Front de Libération de Québec (FLQ)** changed its tactics from bombing to kidnapping. One plan was foiled, but on 5 Oct the group kidnapped the British Trade Commissioner in Quebec, James Cross. A ransom of C$500 000 was demanded, along with the release of a number of 'political prisoners'. There was to be no police pursuit, transport out of the country was to be provided for the gang and the FLQ manifesto was to be broadcast on radio and television. The last two demands were accepted, and the Attorney-General of Quebec promised to support parole for a number of 'political prisoners'. Cross was not released, however, and on 10 Oct the Minister of Labour and Immigration, Pierre Laporte, was also kidnapped. Three days later students began a campaign of rallies and sit-ins, and the **Parti Québecois** began to put pressure on Premier Robert **Bourassa** to form an emergency coalition government. Instead, he brought in the army to back up the police and the **War Measures Act** was implemented to round up FLQ sympathizers. Although over 450 were arrested, only 20 were convicted in the 62 cases brought. Protest against the Act died down after Laporte's murder on 17 Oct. Cross was discovered and his release obtained after safe passage to Cuba was guaranteed to the kidnappers. Later that month the murderers of Laporte were apprehended and imprisoned.

October Manifesto (17 Oct 1905) The proclamation issued by **Nicholas II** at the height of the Russian **Revolution of 1905**, promising the Russians freedom of speech and assembly and the election of a legislative body. This took the steam out of the opposition. But gradually the freedoms were ignored, while the dumas that were elected were increasingly unrepresentative and powerless. This breach of promise was one of many factors decreasing Tsarism's chances of survival. ▷ **Duma**

October Revolution (1917) The overthrow of the Russian Provisional Government by Bolshevik-led armed workers (Red Guards), soldiers and sailors (25–6 Oct 1917 old style;

7–8 Nov new style). The revolution was organized by the Military Revolutionary Committee of the Petrograd Soviet, but was based on **Lenin**'s tactical exploitation of the Provisional Government's failure to provide effective leadership in a rapidly escalating crisis. The members of the government were arrested and it was replaced by the Soviet of People's Commissars (*Sovnarkom*), chaired by Lenin. This first Soviet government then proceeded to totally reorganize the economy and polity of Russia on lines that lasted for over 70 years. ▷ **April Theses; Bolsheviks; February Revolution; July Days**

October War (1973) This war, which followed the launching of a surprise attack by Egypt and Syria on Israel on the Jewish Day of Atonement (*Yom Kippur*), gave the Arabs an important lift in morale as a result of some initial success. The Israeli counter-attack could not, however be contained by the Egyptian and Syrian forces, and the USA was persuaded by the Saudis to get Israel to cease her military activities pending mediation by the **UN**. The importance of the war from the Egyptian point of view was that it went some way to salving the national pride which had taken a severe pounding in the **Six Day War** (June 1967).

Octobrists (1905–18) The short name for the Union of 17 Oct, those Russian liberals who, in contrast with the **Kadets**, accepted the Tsar's **October Manifesto** in 1905 as a basis on which to achieve moderate reform. Their numbers were greatest in the third and fourth dumas for which the franchise was most biased, but they still achieved little. In 1911 their leader, Alexander **Guchkov**, was elected **Duma** President but could not even exercise influence upon **Nicholas II**. Although Guchkov was Minister of War in the **Russian Provisional Government** of 1917, they were even more out of touch than the Kadets with the changing public mood and had virtually no representation in the **Russian Constituent Assembly** in 1918.

Oda Nobunaga (1534–82) Japanese warrior. The first of the three great historical unifiers of Japan, followed by **Toyotomi Hideyoshi** and **Tokugawa Ieyasu**, born into a noble family near Nagoya. He became a general, and occupied the old capital, Kyoto, in 1568, destroying the power of the Buddhist Church, and favouring Christianity as a counterbalance. He built Azuchi Castle, near Kyoto, as his headquarters. He was assassinated by one of his own generals, in Kyoto.

Oder–Neisse Line The new Polish–German border, drawn by the **World War II** Allies in a series of conferences and negotiations in 1944–5, and involving the transfer to Poland of a sizeable area of the Third Reich. The decision was partly based on historical arguments but also facilitated the transfer of territory in the east of Poland claimed by the USSR. A source of contention between the Federal Republic of Germany on the one hand and the German Democratic Republic and Poland on the other, the border was finally recognized by the Federal Republic in 1970 and by the reunited Germany in 1990.

Odinga, (Zaramogi) Oginga (Ajuma) (1911–94) Kenyan nationalist and politician. Educated at Alliance High School and Makerere College, he was a schoolteacher when he became active in local Luo politics. He was elected to Legco in 1957 and was Vice-President of **KANU** (1960–6), during which period he pressed unflinchingly for independence, his apparent extremism being contrasted with the moderation of **Mboya**. He was Minister of Home Affairs (1963–4) and then Vice-President (1964–6). At the Limuru Party Conference in 1966, Mboya managed to remove Odinga from positions of authority and he soon resigned to form the Kenya People's Union. He was re-elected on the KPU ticket in the Little General Election of 1966 and provided a charismatic figure round which dissidents might congregate. Consequently, the party was soon banned and Odinga spent some of the next 25 years in and out of detention.

Odoacer (d.493) Germanic warrior who destroyed the western Roman Empire, and became the first barbarian King of Italy (476–493). An able ruler, he was challenged and overthrown by the Ostrogothic King Theoderic (489/93) at the instigation of the Eastern Roman emperor, Zeno.

O'Donnell, Leopoldo (1809–67) Spanish soldier and politician. Descended from an Irish family, he was born in Tenerife. He supported the infant queen **Isabella II** against her uncle Don **Carlos** and later supported her mother, the regent **María Cristina**, but was forced into exile with her in 1840. In 1843 his intrigues against **Espartero** were successful, and as Governor-General of Cuba he amassed a fortune. He returned to Spain in 1846, was made War Minister by Espartero in 1854, but in 1856 supplanted him as Prime Minister by a coup d'état. After only three months in office, he was succeeded by **Narváez**, but in 1858 returned to power; in 1859 he led a successful campaign against the Moors in Morocco and was made Duke of Tetuan. He was Prime Minister again in 1863 and 1865, but in 1866 his government was upset by Narváez.

Offa (d.796) King of Mercia (757/96). He was the greatest Anglo-Saxon ruler in the 8c, treated as an equal by **Charlemagne**. Styling himself 'King of the English', he asserted his authority over all the kingdoms south of the Humber, and treated their rulers as subordinate provincial governors. He was responsible for constructing Offa's Dyke, and established a new currency based on the silver penny which, with numerous changes of design, remained the standard coin of England for many centuries. His reign represents an important but flawed attempt to unify England, with the Mercian supremacy collapsing soon after his death. ▷ **Anglo-Saxons; Mercia**

Official Nationality (1833) A crude analysis of the domestic policy of Tsar **Nicholas I** that gradually became his government's doctrine. It was originally propounded in 1833 by Count Sergei Uvarov, then Minister of Education, who held that the three fundamental elements were the following: Orthodoxy (the attitudes and practices of the Russian Orthodox Church), Autocracy (maintaining the absolute authority of the Tsars), and Nationality (maintaining the singular loyalty of the Russian people to their Church, their Tsars and their heroic past). Nicholas was by nature dictatorial and fundamentally opposed to change. The new doctrine helped him to resist it until his death and therefore made his successor's task all the more difficult.

Ogaden The disputed region of south-eastern Ethiopia which became part of Abyssinia in 1890 and part of Italian East Africa from 1936 to 1941. It is largely inhabited by Somali-speaking nomads and was claimed by Somalia in the 1960s. The Somalis invaded in 1977, but were repulsed by Ethiopian forces. Fighting continued throughout the 1980s.

Ogarkov, Nikolai Vasilevich (1917–94) Soviet military adviser and politician. Son of a peasant, he joined the **Red Army** in 1938 and rose through wartime experience and subsequent commands to become First Deputy Chief of the General Staff in 1968 and full member of the Communist Party Central

Committee in 1971. From 1977 to 1984 he was Chief of Staff and Deputy Defence Minister. For over a decade he helped to strengthen and expand the Soviet forces. But his advocacy of further improving conventional forces met opposition even from Leonid **Brezhnev** and certainly from Yuri **Andropov**. His removal in 1984 got rid of an obstacle to East-West arms control talks.

Ogedei (1186–1241) Mongol ruler. Third son of the Mongol conqueror **Genghis Khan**. He was elected by the Mongol nobility in 1229 to succeed his father. Ogedei continued with his father's expansionist policy, seizing north China in 1234 and initiating a western campaign that took the Mongols to the borders of Hungary and Poland. His construction of a new, permanent capital at Karakorum (Outer Mongolia) and his use of Chinese-educated advisers to establish a civilian administration signified a growing concern with settled government rather than periodic plunder.

O'Higgins, Bernardo (1778–1842) Chilean revolutionary. The son of Ambrosio O'Higgins, an Irish-born Governor of Chile and Viceroy of Peru, he was educated in Peru and England. He played the major role in the Chilean struggle for independence, having been influenced by others involved in the struggle for Latin American independence, especially Francisco **Miranda**. He became the first leader ('supreme director') of the new Chilean state in 1817. However, his reforms aroused antagonism, particularly in the Church and among the aristocracy and business community, and he was deposed in 1823, thereafter living in exile in Peru, where he died.

Ohira Masayoshi (1910–80) Japanese politician. A Finance Ministry bureaucrat, Ohira was first elected to the Diet in 1952 and later went on to serve as Foreign Minister and Finance Minister in **Liberal Democratic Party (LDP)** cabinets of the 1970s. He became LDP President (and Prime Minister) in 1978 under new party election rules that aimed to give a greater role to the party rank and file in the constituencies. During his premiership, Ohira hosted the 1979 Tokyo economic summit of developed countries. Following a no-confidence vote against him in 1980, when rival LDP factions joined the opposition, Ohira dissolved the Diet. He died 10 days before new elections, but the LDP won handsome majorities in both houses.

Ojukwu, Chukwenmeka Odumegwu (1933–) Nigerian soldier and politician. Educated in church schools in Lagos, Epsom College and Lincoln College, Oxford, he joined the Nigerian Army in 1957. After attending military college in England, he served with the Nigerian force in the **UN** Congo (Zaire) operations and was named Military Governor of the mainly Ibo-speaking Eastern Region of Nigeria after the military coup of Jan 1966. He proclaimed the Eastern Region the independent Republic of Biafra in May 1967, thus precipitating the **Biafran War**, and for three years acted as Head of Government and Supreme Commander. When his forces were finally defeated in 1970, he fled to the Ivory Coast.

Okawa Shumei (1886–1957) Japanese ultra-nationalist. He was involved in several right-wing plots against the civilian government. A fierce critic of Western colonialism in Asia, Okawa founded societies to protect the **Kokutai** ('national essence') and promote renovation of the state. Unlike Ikki **Kita**, Okawa was willing to work with military and bureaucratic elites, and lectured to the Army Academy on the need for Asian unity and struggle against the West. He was imprisoned in 1932 for his participation in an abortive military coup but was released in 1934. Okawa was indicted by allied authorities as a class-A war criminal in 1945 (the only person to be so indicted who was not a military or government figure). Judged to be insane, however, Okawa was never brought to trial.

Okhranka (1881–1917) The secret police in the last decades of Tsarist rule. With the assassination of **Alexander II** in 1881, following the abolition of the Third Section, **Alexander III** felt it essential to find an alternative. From a law on state protection, all sorts of far-reaching powers were conferred on government agents, to send people into exile without a trial, for example. In this way much opposition was controlled, but some went underground and became, like the **Bolsheviks**, more dangerous. Eventually the Okhranka brought Tsarism into widespread disrepute.

Okubo Toshimichi (1830–78) Japanese **samurai** official. He participated in the overthrow of the **Tokugawa Shogunate** and became one of the most powerful members of the new Meiji government after 1868. His commitment to modernization was reinforced after his visit to the West with the

Iwakura Tomomi mission (1871–3). As Head of the newly-created Home Ministry, Okubo laid the foundations for a national police force. In 1877 he commanded the new imperial conscript army which defeated the samurai rebellion led by **Saigo Takamori**. Considered a traitor by many disgruntled samurai, he was assassinated in 1878.

Okuma Shigenobu (1838–1922) Japanese politician. He came from a **samurai** family in Saga domain, one of the four domains (along with Choshu, Satsuma and Tosa) that took the lead in the overthrow of the **Tokugawa Shogunate** (1868). He became a councillor in the new Meiji government and was a keen advocate of industrial development. He aroused the ire of his government colleagues in 1881 when he proposed the immediate establishment of constitutional government based on the British parliamentary system. He was purged from government and, in the following year, he created Japan's second political party, the *Rikken Kaishinto* (Constitutional Reform Party), which gained support amongst the urban educated and mercantile classes. In 1898 Okuma joined with Taisuke **Itagaki**, Leader of the *Jiyuto* (Liberal Party) to form Japan's first party cabinet, but it collapsed within four months due to internal rivalries. In 1914 Okuma was chosen by the **genro** to head a non-party cabinet but his aggressive attempt to enhance Japan's influence in China brought him into conflict with the more cautious *genro* and he was forced to resign.

Olaf I Trygveson (c.964–c.999) King of Norway (995/9). The great-grandson of **Harald Fairhair**, he took part in Viking expeditions against England, and came to the throne of Norway after overthrowing King Haakon. Having turned Christian, he attempted the conversion of Norway and Iceland, with limited success. He was killed in a naval battle against the Danes and Swedes. ▷ **Vikings**

Olaf II (St Olaf) (c.995–1030) King of Norway (1015/30). He fought in England (1009–11), became a Christian, and completed the work of conversion begun by **Olaf I Trygveson**. His reforms provoked dissension, and he was killed by a rebel army at Stiklestad. He later became the patron saint of Norway.

Olaf III, 'the Peaceful' (d.1093) King of Norway (1067/93). He was at the Battle of Stamford Bridge in Yorkshire (1066) when his father, **Harald Hardrada**, was defeated and killed by King **Harold II** of England. He was, however, allowed to return to Norway with the survivors of the Norwegian invasion force, and assumed the throne of Norway the following year. His long reign was marked by unbroken peace and prosperity in Norway. He was succeeded by his illegitimate son, **Magnus III, 'Barelegs'**.

Olav V (1903–91) King of Norway (1957/91). A keen sportsman and Olympic gold medallist, Crown Prince Olav escaped from Oslo with his father, King **Haakon VII**, following the German invasion in Apr 1940, accompanying him into exile in Britain (June 1940). He participated actively in the war effort and from 1944 to 1945 served as chief of the Norwegian armed forces. He succeeded his father as king in 1957, but performed a mainly ceremonial role as monarch. ▷ **Norway, German Invasion of**

Old Believers (1653) Those who split from the Russian Orthodox Church because of the reforms introduced by Patriarch **Nikon** in 1652. Among the first and most famous to protest was the Archpriest Avvakum, who in 1653 accused Nikon of heresy. However, when a series of Church Councils supported Nikon it was Avvakum and his like who were persecuted as heretics. Avvakum was burned at the stake in 1682. But the Old Believers survived, generating many sects in the 18c and 19c, varying in their beliefs from being upholders of ancient Russian practices to being social and political rebels.

Oldcastle, Sir John (c.1378–1417) English Lollard leader and knight. After serving in the Scottish and Welsh wars, and becoming an intimate of **Henry V** when Prince of Wales, he was tried and convicted on charges of heresy in 1413. He escaped from the Tower, and conspired with other **Lollards** to capture Henry V at Eltham Palace, Kent, and take control of London. The rising was abortive. Oldcastle remained free until caught near Welshpool in 1417, and was hanged and burnt. Shakespeare's character Falstaff is based partly on him.

Old Catholic Church An independent religious denomination in the Netherlands (and parts of Germany and Switzerland), founded in 1723 as a result of a dispute with the Roman Catholic Church. The Old Catholics maintained that the **Reformation** and **Eighty Years War** had not destroyed the Catholic Church in the Netherlands; the

Jesuits denied this, and accused the Old Catholics of **Jansenism**. In 1725 the Old Catholics founded their own seminary at Amersfoort; the Church still thrives in the Netherlands today in small numbers, rejecting many Roman Catholic dogmas such as the Immaculate Conception, papal infallibility, celibacy for priests, and the use of Latin in church services.

Oldenburg A city and duchy in north-western Germany, lying near the North Sea district of East Frisia (Ostfriesland). The city received its charter in 1345 and was the capital of the Duchy of Oldenburg. The Duchy was neutral in the **Thirty Years War**. In 1667 it passed to the Danish crown, thence to Emperor **Paul I** of Russia in 1773. He ceded it to Frederick Augustus who also controlled the neighbouring bishopric of Lübeck. It became a grand duchy in the 19c.

Old Kingdom In Ancient Egyptian history, the kingdom founded on the basis of the Archaic or **Early Dynastic Period**. The Old Kingdom was the period of pyramid-building, with a central government under the absolute power of a god-king. Through the king, authority was delegated to officials (often members of his family). He controlled their training, granted them land and made provision for their burials and funerary endowments. The administrative structure included the treasury, the granaries, the public works department, the royal household and temple estates. Alongside the massive pyramids, there is in contrast simple, elegant design of furniture, jewellery and burial equipment. During this period expeditions were sent to Sinai and Nubia, while trading for timber with western Asia was conducted by sea. Economic factors and the growing independence of local governors led to the breakdown of central control and the resulting confusion of the First **Intermediate Period**.

Old Pretender ▷ **Stuart, James Francis Edward**

Olga, St (c.890–968) Russian Princess and Regent of Kiev (945/64). The wife of Prince Igor of Kiev, she ruled Kiev firmly during the minority of her son, Svyatoslav. She was baptized at Constantinople (c.957) and, returning to Russia, laboured for the new creed. She had little success in her lifetime but, subsequently sanctified, she played an important part in the development of Kievan Christianity. Her grandson was **Vladimir I, 'the Great'**.

Olivares, Guzmán y Pimentel, Count-Duke of (1587–1645) Spanish statesman. The favourite and Chief Minister of **Philip IV** of Spain from 1623 to 1643, he cultivated the arts, and tried to modernize Spain's anachronistic administration and to build up military resources. However, his introduction of the Union of Arms brought revolts in Portugal and Catalonia (1640–3). He took Spain into renewed conflict with the United Provinces, challenged France over the Mantuan Succession (1628–31) and was **Richelieu**'s great opponent in the **Thirty Years War**. After the Spanish fleet was destroyed at the Battle of the Downs (1639) and Roussillon was overrun by the French, he was dismissed (1643), and died mad in exile at Toro. ▷ **Habsburg Dynasty**

Ollivier, Emile (1825–1913) French politician. One of the five republican opposition deputies elected to parliament in 1857, from 1864 he came closer to the regime, as one of the members of the 'third party'. **Napoleon III** charged him to form a constitutional ministry (Jan 1870), but 'with a light heart' he rushed his country into war with Prussia. He was overthrown on 9 Aug 1871.

Olmecs Members of a highly elaborate Mesoamerican Indian culture on the Mexican Gulf Coast, at its height 1200–600 BC. The Olmecs influenced the rise and development of the other great civilizations of Mesoamerica. They probably had the first large planned religious and ceremonial centres, at San Lorenzo, La Venta, and Tres Zapotecs, where the resident elite and their families lived, served by much larger populations dispersed throughout the lowland area. The centres had temple mounds, monumental sculptures, massive altars, and sophisticated systems of drains and lagoons. They were probably also the first people in the area to devise glyph writing and the 260-day Mesoamerican calendar.

Oltenia Part of western Wallachia, sometimes known as the County of Severin, it was subject to the Habsburg Emperor after the Treaty of **Passarowitz** (1718) but was returned to Wallachia by the Peace of Belgrade (1739). Its chief town is Craïova. ▷ **Danubian Principalities; Romanians**

Olympio, Sylvanus (1902–63) Togolese politician. Educated at the London School of Economics, he returned to Africa as District Manager of the United Africa Company. He was President of the Togolese Assembly in

1946 and then led the country's government from 1958 to 1960 when, on independence, he became President. He was killed on 13 Jan 1963 in a military coup.

Omar Pasha (Michael Latas) (1806–71) Croatian-born Ottoman general. He served in the Austrian Army but in 1828 he deserted, fled to Bosnia, and became a Muslim. He was appointed writing-master to **Ab dul-Majid I**, on whose accession to the Ottoman throne (1839) Omar Pasha was made colonel, and, in 1842, Governor of Lebanon. From 1843 to 1847 he suppressed insurrections in Albania, Bosnia and Kurdistan. On the invasion of the Danubian Principalities by the Russians in 1853, he defeated the Russians in two battles. In the **Crimean War** he repulsed the Russians at Eupatoria (Feb 1855) but was sent too late to relieve Kars. He was Governor of Baghdad (1857–9); in 1861 he again pacified Bosnia and Herzegovina, and overran **Montenegro** in 1862.

Omdurman, Battle of (1898) An engagement outside Khartoum, across the Nile, which confirmed the British reconquest of the Sudan. The British campaign under **Kitchener** had been authorized in 1895, and instituted with powerful Anglo-Egyptian forces in 1896. The overwhelming defeat of the massed forces of the Khalifa (the successor of the **Mahdi**), with many casualties, illustrated the power of modern weapons. ▷ **Fashoda Incident; Mohammed Ahmed**

O'Neill (of the Maine), Terence (Marne), Baron (1914–90) Ulster politician. He served in the Irish Guards during **World War II**. A member of the Northern Ireland parliament (1946–70), he held junior posts before becoming Minister for Home Affairs (1956), Finance (1956–63), and then Prime Minister (1963–9). A supporter of closer cross-border links with the Irish Republic, he angered many Unionists. Following a general election in 1969, dissension in the Unionist Party increased, and he resigned the premiership soon after. Made a life peer in 1970, he continued to speak out on Northern Ireland issues. ▷ **Democratic Unionist Party**

Onin War (1467–77) The long drawn-out struggle in Japan between rival **daimyo** (feudal lords), named after the Onin Era (1467–9) in which it began. The *daimyo* had been granted territorial powers by the **Ashikaga Shogunate** and by the end of the 14c had considerable autonomy. The political situation became increasingly unstable from the mid-1460s when rival daimyo took sides in a shogunal succession dispute. Full-scale war broke out in the Kyoto region, lasting for 10 years. The Ashikaga Shogunate was permanently weakened, continuing in name only to 1573, and there ensued a period of disunity and periodic warfare that was essentially to last until the end of the 16c, when a new military hegemony under the **Tokugawa Shogunate** began to take shape.

OPEC (Organization of Petroleum Exporting Countries) An international economic organization set up in 1960 with its headquarters in Vienna; the longest-surviving major cartel. It consists of 13 oil-producing countries: the founder members were Iran, Iraq, Kuwait, Saudi Arabia, and Venezuela; and they have since been joined by Algeria, Ecuador, Gabon, Indonesia, Libya, Nigeria, Qatar, and the United Arab Emirates (formerly Abu Dhabi). Its purpose is to co-ordinate the petroleum policy of members to protect their interests, especially in relation to the fixing of prices for crude oil and the quantities to be produced.

Open Door Policy US foreign policy towards China, formulated in response to the weakness of the later **Qing Dynasty**. Announced in Mar 1900 by Secretary of State John **Hay**, the Open Door policy sought to preserve Chinese integrity and US trade rights by opposing the development of spheres of influence dominated by Britain, Germany, Russia, France, Italy and Japan.

Opium Wars Two wars (1839–42 and 1856–60) between Britain and China, fought over the question of commercial rights in China, specifically relating to the opium trade. The British were victorious on each occasion, and gained increased access to China through the Treaties of **Nanjing** (Nanking) (1842) and **Tianjin** (Tientsin) (1858). ▷ **Arrow War; treaty ports**

Oppenheimer, John Süss (1698/99–1738) A prominent financier in the Palatinate and Hesse. He was also Chief Minister under Charles Alexander (Duke, 1733–7). He established various monopolies and was involved in the programme of the Duke, a Catholic, to break his subjects' Lutheranism by a system of harsh taxation. He was so disliked that he was executed soon after the Duke's death.

Opportunists French political tendency. The more conservative tendency among the republicans. The name was coined in 1874, and was applied to the supporters of **Gambetta**, and **Ferry**, who ruled for most of the period 1879–95; after that time the term went out of use, being replaced first by Progressists, and then by **Moderates**.

Opus Dei Established in Spain in 1928 by an Aragonese priest, José María Escrivá, Opus Dei (literally, 'the Work of God') is a lay order within the Catholic Church which has sought secular power through the recruitment of leading professionals. With its ultra-conservative theology and its severe subjugation of women, the sodality has moved in the opposite direction to most other orders within the church. Under the **Franco** regime Opus Dei, dubbed 'the Holy Mafia', rose rapidly to a position of considerable power. It orchestrated Spain's economic modernization from the late 1950s on and remained the major force within the government until 1973. The three ministers involved in the most notorious scandal of the Franco regime, the Matesa affair of 1969, were all Opus Dei members. Elsewhere, Opus has been linked to numerous dictatorial regimes in Latin America, often in collaboration with the **CIA**. Under Pope John Paul II, Opus Dei has become the most powerful order in the Roman Catholic Church. Its extreme secretiveness, its unique semi-autonomous status, and its colossal wealth have combined to produce what is, in effect, a church within the church.

Orán, Conquest of (1509) The most spectacular of the several conquests by Christians of Muslim forts on the North African coast. After the easy capture in 1508 of the fort of Peñon de Vélez de Gomera, attempts were made to seize other forts. In May 1509 Cardinal Cisneros personally financed and led an expedition which sailed from Cartagena with 90 ships, and captured Orán on 18 May. The fort was unsuccessfully besieged several times in later years by Muslim forces.

Orange Order An association that developed from the Orange Society, which had been formed in 1795 to counteract growing Catholic influence in Ireland and 'to maintain the laws and peace of the country and the Protestant constitution'. The name was taken from the Protestant Dutch dynasty represented by **William III**. Organized in 'Lodges', it provided the backbone of resistance to **Home Rule** proposals from the mid-1880s, and has operated as organized Protestantism in Northern Ireland since partition.

Orange Order (Canada) The First Grand Lodge was established in Canada in 1830, and the order had grown to 2 000 lodges with 100 000 members by the 1980s. Its growth and activities have made it one of the most powerful pressure groups in Canadian politics. Not only did Orangemen reinforce the pro-British and Tory sentiments of the loyalists; they introduced the rigid hostilities nurtured in the old country, transferring their antagonism from Irish Catholics to the French-Canadian 'Papists'. In 1848 **Lafontaine** introduced a Secret Societies Bill to counteract their activities, but this only incited the Orangemen of Upper **Canada** to further demonstrations. During a visit by the Prince of Wales in 1860 they attempted, by various ruses, to force him to acknowledge a relationship between the order and the monarchy. This he managed to refuse, but John A **Macdonald** apologized to the order for him. The murder of the Orangeman Thomas **Scott** during the **Red River Rebellion** led indirectly to the campaign of D'Alton **McCarthy** and the **Manitoba Schools Act**. The murder of another Orangeman which occurred in Montreal during a provocative 12 July parade in 1877 also incensed the order, and Macdonald was able to use this anger to swing it behind the Conservatives to win the next election. In 1878 he included the Grand Master, Mackenzie **Bowell** in his cabinet.

Ordinance of 1787 ▷ Northwest Ordinance

Ordzhonikidze, Gregori Konstantinovich (1886–1937) Georgian politician. The son of a small landowner, he had already joined the **Bolsheviks** before graduating as a director at Tiflis in 1905. Between then and 1917 he was in and out of prison and in and out of Russia for his revolutionary activities. In 1920–1 he helped establish Soviet rule in Georgia and Armenia; and by 1930 he was a **Politburo** member and chairman of the council for Soviet economy. However, as friends and relatives were shot in **Stalin**'s purges, he lost heart and took his own life.

Oregon Boundary Dispute A disagreement between the British and US governments over the frontier between respective possessions on the west coast of North America. Britain claimed the northwest basin of the Columbia River to its mouth at Fort Vancouver, while the USA sought a boundary farther north. The Oregon Treaty (1846) settled the US–Canadian boundary on the 49th parallel, dipping south at Juan de Fuca Strait to maintain British claims to

Vancouver Island. Residual disputes over the disposition of the Gulf/San Juan Islands in the strait were settled by arbitration in 1872.

Oregon Trail The main route for emigration to the far west of the USA during the 1840s. The trail began at Independence, Missouri, crossed the Rockies at South Pass in Wyoming, and terminated at the mouth of the Columbia River. Extending some 2 000 miles in length, it took approximately six months to travel it by wagon train.

Organic Acts Statutes of the US Congress which laid down the relationship of Puerto Rico to the USA between 1900 and 1950. The First Organic Act of 1900 (the Foraker Act) effectively made Puerto Rico a US dependency in that supreme power was vested in the US governor and a nominated executive council. The Second Organic Act of 1916 (the Jones Act) conferred universal male suffrage and made Puerto Ricans citizens of the USA. The Public Law Act of 1950 allowed the new Commonwealth (a status devised by **Muñoz Marín**) to draft its own constitution.

Organic Statutes (1831–2) These statutes regulated the government in the **Danubian Principalities**, introducing similar highly centralized administrations into Moldavia and Wallachia. Political power rested in the hands of the high boyars who sat in the legislative assembly and from whose ranks the hospodars were to be elected for life. The statutes acknowledged the boyars as the owners of their land, strengthened their hold over the peasantry and confirmed their exemption from taxation. Drawn up under Russian supervision, the Organic Statutes gave Russia a large measure of influence over internal affairs in the Principalities. ▷ **Akkerman, Convention of; Sturdza, Mihail**

Organization of African Unity (OAU) An organization founded in 1963 by representatives of 32 African governments meeting in Addis Ababa, which reflected the views of the moderate leaders, such as **Nyerere**, rather than radicals such as **Nkrumah**. By protecting territorial integrity, the organization accepted the artificial boundaries bequeathed by the colonial powers and preserved individual self-interest over continental political and economic unity. It remained, however, the main forum for the African continent to express its political views and, through its Liberation Committee in Dar es Salaam, assisted the decolonization of southern Africa. It has had some success at mediation,

but its lack of sanctions has resulted in its inability to solve problems where major African powers disagree.

Organization of American States (OAS) A regional agency established in 1948 to coordinate the work of a variety of inter-American departments recognized within the terms of the United Nations Charter. The organization was formed to promote more peace, economic cooperation, and social advancement in the Western hemisphere. Its central organ, the General Secretariat, is housed in Washington DC, and consists of one representative from each member country. Thirty-one countries within the Americas are members. ▷ **Pan-American Union; UN**

Organization of Central American States An agency established in 1951 by Costa Rica, El Salvador, Guatemala, Honduras, and Nicaragua (Panama refused to join) to promote economic, social, and cultural cooperation. In 1965 this was extended to include political and educational cooperation. The Organization has also been involved in legal reform.

Orhan (1288–1360) Ottoman Sultan (1324/60). The son of **Osman I**, he took Bursa in his father's time, and afterwards reduced Nicaea and Mysia. He organized the state and established the Ottoman bridgehead in Europe. ▷ **Ottoman Empire**

Orlando, Vittorio Emanuele (1860–1952) Italian politician. Professor of Law at Palermo University, he was elected to parliament in 1897. He served as Minister of Education, before becoming Minister of Justice in 1916. At the height of the **Caporetto** crisis he became Prime Minister, remaining in office until June 1919. His inability to force Woodrow **Wilson** and **Clemenceau** to honour the terms of the Treaty of **London** (1915) at the Paris peace talks, coupled with post-war economic dislocation and growing political violence, brought about his downfall. He made little attempt to resist **Mussolini** and appeared on the fascist **Listone** in the Apr 1924 election. He belatedly adopted a more openly anti-fascist stance in 1925. After **World War II** he became a Senator.

Orléanists Supporters of the Orléans branch of the French royal house, which reigned in the person of **Louis-Philippe** (1830–48). Rivalry between them and the **Legitimists**, supporters of **Charles X**, and of his heir, the

Count of **Chambord** was an important factor in the eclipse of the royalist cause, especially in the National Assembly (1871–5), in which the two royalist factions together had a majority, but which nevertheless established the Third Republic. The death of the legitimist claimant in 1883 reunited the monarchists. ▷ **Orléans, House of; Republic, Third** (France)

Orléans, House of The junior branch of the **Valois** and Bourbon dynasties in France, the title of which fell to four individual lines: Philippe de Valois, created Duke in 1344 but died without issue; Louis I de Valois (1372–1407), whose descendants held the title until 1544; Gaston (1608–60), the Bourbon third son of **Henry IV**, made Duke in 1626; and **Louis XIV**'s younger brother Philippe (1640–1701), from whom descended the Regent Orléans (1674–1723), Louis Philippe Joseph, Duke of **Orléans**, 'Philippe Egalité' (1747–93), who died in the **French Revolution**, and **Louis-Philippe** (1773–1850), 'King of the French'. The latter's son was the last to hold the ducal title. ▷ **Bourbon, House of**

Orléans, Louis Philippe Joseph, Duke of (Philippe Egalité) (1747–93) French Bourbon prince. The cousin of King **Louis XVI** and father of **Louis-Philippe**, he inherited his father's title in 1785. At the **French Revolution** he proved a strong supporter of the Third Estate against the privileged orders, and in 1792 renounced his title of nobility for his popular name. At the National Convention he voted for the King's death but was himself arrested after the defection of his eldest son to the Austrians (1793), and guillotined. ▷ **Convention, National; Estates General; Marie Antoinette**

Orléans, Philippe, Duke of (1674–1723) Regent of France during the minority of **Louis XV**, son of the first duke Philippe, and grandson of **Louis XIII**. He had been appointed Regent by **Louis XIV**'s will, but with limited powers as President of a **Regency** Council. He persuaded the **Parlement** to override the will, thus acquiring full powers, but at the expense of restoring the authority of the *Parlement*, which he later tried to restrict. He entrusted the conduct of foreign affairs to the Abbé **Dubois**, who formed the Quadruple Alliance with the Netherlands, Britain and Austria (1718), defeating Spain and producing the fall of Alberroni (1719). His adoption of John Law's scheme led to financial disaster. In 1720 he accepted the

Papal Bull *Unigenitus*, condemning **Jansenism**. His power ended when Louis XV came of age in 1723.

Orléans, Siege of (Oct 1428–May 1429) The English blockade of the main stronghold still loyal to **Charles VII** of France, during the **Hundred Years War**. Orléans was relieved by troops inspired by **Joan of Arc**. Anglo-Burgundian forces, who already controlled most of northern France, were prevented from pressing south; but the event was less of a turning point in the war than the Franco-Burgundian rapprochement of 1435. ▷ **Philip the Good**

Orlov A Russian family that rose to eminence when one of its members, Gregory (1734–1783), an officer in the Imperial Guards, succeeded King Stanislas Augustus **Poniatowski** of Poland as the favourite of **Catherine II, 'the Great'**. It was he who planned the murder of **Peter III**, and his brother Alexis (1737–1808) who committed the deed (1762). The legitimate line of Orlov became extinct; but Feodor, a brother of Gregory and Alexis, left four illegitimate sons, one of whom, Alexis (1787–1862), distinguished himself in the French and Turkish wars. He negotiated the Treaty of Unkiar-Skelessi with the **Ottoman Empire** in 1833, in 1844 became head of **Nicholas I**'s secret police, the Third Department, and he frequently acted in the role of senior diplomat as, for example, at the Congress of Paris in 1856. His last appointment was under **Alexander II** as chairman of a committee to consider the abolition of serfdom.

Ormonde, James Butler, 1st Duke of (1610–88) Anglo-Irish general. In the **English Civil Wars** he commanded the royalist army in Ireland (1641–50), and was compelled to retire to France. At the **Restoration** he was rewarded by the ducal title of Ormonde, and twice became Lord-Lieutenant of Ireland.

Orsini A powerful Roman noble family which periodically dominated papal politics and appointments (including the election of family members to the papacy itself) from the 11c. In the 1400s, 'by custom', one Orsini, along with a French and a Venetian cardinal, was entitled to sit in the College of Cardinals. The family inter-married with the **Medici** of Florence in the same period. ▷ **pope**

Orsini, Felice (1819–58) Italian patriot, revolutionary and follower of **Mazzini**. Elected to the Roman Constituent Assembly in 1848, he took part in the defence of the city under the command of **Garibaldi**. In Jan 1858, after a decade of agitation and exile, he went to Paris to try to assassinate **Napoleon III** whom he considered to have betrayed the Italian cause: in the attempt, 10 people were killed but the Emperor survived unharmed. Orsini was sentenced to death, but before his execution he wrote a personal appeal to Napoleon begging him to assist the Italian struggle. It is possible that fear of further attempts on his life or the passion of Orsini's plea contributed to Napoleon's readiness to meet with **Cavour** at **Plombières** and to declare war on Austria in 1859.

Ortega (Saavedra), Daniel (1945–) Nicaraguan military leader. Educated in Managua, he became active in his teens in the resistance movement against the **Somoza** regime, and in 1963 joined the Sandinista National Liberation Front (FSLN), which had been founded in 1960. He became National Director of the FSLN in 1966, was imprisoned for seven years for urban guerrilla bank raids, and then, in 1979, played a major part in the overthrow of Anastasio Somoza. A junta led by Ortega established a provisional government, and in 1985 he became President, but US-backed counter-revolutionary forces, the 'Contras', threatened his government's stability. By 1989, however, there were encouraging signs of peace being achieved. He surprisingly lost the 1990 general election to Violeta Chamorro, and supervised the peaceful handover of power.

Ortega y Gasset, José (1883–1956) Spanish politician, philosopher and journalist. From a well-to-do family of newspaper proprietors, he studied philosophy in Germany before becoming a professor at the Central University of Madrid. He promoted the cultural regeneration of Spain through his voluminous journalistic and other writings, his extensive speech-making, and the foundation of cultural institutions and numerous publications, such as the League of Political Education of Spain (1914), the leading liberal newspaper *El Sol* (1917), and the cultural journal *Revista de Occidente* (1923). In the process, he became one of the most influential makers of public opinion. With the advent of the Second Republic in 1931, he founded the Group at the Service of the Republic, was elected as one of its deputies, but soon became disillusioned, dissolving the group in 1932 and abandoning politics altogether in 1933. He spent the **Spanish Civil War** in France, estranged from either side. After the war, he continued to publish a great deal and lectured widely, both in Europe (including Spain) and America. He returned to Spain in 1955 to die. ▷ **Republic, Second** (Spain)

Oscar I (1799–1859) King of Norway and Sweden (1844/59). He was the only son and successor of **Charles XIV John**. Born in Paris, he accompanied his father to Sweden when the latter was elected heir to the Swedish throne in 1810. A liberal by temperament, he sought to conciliate nationalist feelings in Norway, encouraged social and economic development, but opposed any attempts to limit his political power. He took a particular interest in foreign policy. He favoured the political union of the Scandinavian monarchies and nearly involved Sweden in the **Crimean War** in the hope of regaining Finland. He married Josephine of Leuchtenberg, the daughter of Empress **Joséphine**'s son, Eugène de Beauharnais. Oscar suffered from a brain tumour during the last two years of his reign, during which his eldest son acted as regent, succeeding him as **Charles XV**.

Oscar II (1829–1907) King of Sweden (1872/1907) and of Norway (1872/1905). He was the younger son of **Oscar I** and brother of **Charles XV**, whom he succeeded. A vigorous, intelligent and highly cultured man, his foreign policy was marked by admiration of the new German Empire of Otto von **Bismarck**. His reign saw growing tension between his Norwegian and Swedish subjects until in 1905 he was compelled to surrender the crown of Norway to Prince Carl of Denmark, elected King of Norway as **Haakon VII**. The sacrifice saddened the last years of Oscar's life. He was married to Sofia of Nassau, by whom he had four sons, of whom **Gustav V** succeeded him as King.

Osceola (c.1804–38) American Seminole Native American leader. He refused to accede to US government demands in 1835 that the Seminoles give up their lands in the Florida Everglades and move to the West. He fought for many months in the Everglades, but in 1837 he was tricked by a false peace overture to come out and have talks with General Thomas S Jesup. He was captured and died in prison in South Carolina.

Osman I (1259–1326) Founder of the **Ottoman Empire**. Born in Bithynia, the son of a border chief, he founded a small Turkish state in Asia Minor called Osmanli (or

Ottoman). On the overthrow of the Seljuk sultanate of Iconium in 1299 by the Mongols, he gradually subdued a great part of Asia Minor.

Osman Nuri Pasha (1832–1900) Turkish general. He fought in the **Crimean War** (1853–56) and numerous other campaigns, and became a national hero for his defence of Plevna against the Russians, in 1877.

Ossory An ancient Irish kingdom, co-extensive with the diocese of Ossory (seat, Kilkenny), conquered by Anglo-Norman invaders in the late 12c. The most powerful families in the area were the Marshals, Earls of Pembroke, Wales, and Lords of Leinster (1199–1245), and the Butlers, created Earls of Ormond (1328) and Ossory (1528).

Ostend Manifesto (1854) A statement presented by the US ministers to Great Britain, France and Spain, effectively asserting US claims over the then Spanish colony of Cuba. It stated that if Spain refused to sell Cuba, then the USA was justified in taking it by force. Although repudiated by the US government, the manifesto gave notice of future US interest in Cuba and in the Caribbean.

Ostpolitik The policy initiated in West Germany in the 1960s as part of the process of detente to normalize relations with communist countries which recognized the German Democratic Republic (GDR) and with the GDR itself. It led to treaties with Poland and the USSR, the recognition of the Polish border (the **Oder–Neisse Line**) and, most significantly, the recognition of the GDR. Largely masterminded by Willy **Brandt**, the policy sought to prevent, and even reverse, the deepening schism between the Federal Republic and GDR and had the broader aim of generally improving relations between West and East. It culminated in German reunification in 1990. ▷ **Germany, East; Germany, West**

ostracism In ancient Athens, the means whereby unpopular citizens could be banished for up to 10 years without loss of property or citizenship. Votes were cast by writing on *ostraka* (potsherds) the names of the citizens to be banished.

Ostrogoths Germanic tribe. By the beginning of the 4c they had migrated from the Baltic to southern Russia but were conquered by the **Huns** in 375. After **Attila**'s death, they freed themselves and under their leader, **Theodoric the Great** (471–526), they conquered Italy and established a powerful and highly civilized kingdom. After Theodoric's death, the kingdom disintegrated under pressure from the Eastern Empire. ▷ **Germanic Invasions**

Otho, Marcus Salvius (AD32–69) Second Roman Emperor in the Year of the **Four Emperors** (69). Ex-drinking companion of the emperor **Nero** and ex-husband of Nero's consort, the empress **Poppaea Sabina**, from 58 until Nero's downfall (68), Otho governed in Spain virtually as an exile from court. A supporter briefly of **Galba**, in Jan 69 he organized a coup against him and with the backing of the **Praetorian Guard** became emperor in his place, only to find his own position immediately challenged by the governor of Lower Germany, **Vitellius**. In the brief civil war that followed, Otho was comprehensively defeated and committed suicide (Apr 69).

Othon (Frederick Otto of Wittelsbach) (1815–67) King of Greece (1832/62). The son of King **Ludwig I** of Bavaria, in 1832 he was chosen by the Great Powers to rule the newly independent Greek kingdom. At first he governed through a regency appointed by his father but, after assuming full control, he showed himself increasingly inclined to rule as an absolute monarch, surrounding himself with Bavarian advisers. The growing frustration of many Greek politicians at the domination of their country by a German oligarchy culminated in a coup (1843), after which Othon was forced to form a new government and to accept a new constitution (1844). He was driven from Greece after another coup in 1862 and retired to Bavaria. ▷ **Kolettis, Ioannis; Mavrokordatos, Alexander**

Otis, James (1725–83) US politician. A leading Boston attorney, Otis was advocate general in 1760, when royal revenue officers demanded his assistance in obtaining from the Massachusetts superior court general search warrants allowing them to enter any man's house in quest of goods that violated the Sugar Act of 1733. Otis refused and argued powerfully before the court against taxation without representation and violation of the rights of colonists. In 1761, elected to the Massachusetts assembly, he became a radical opponent of British rule. In 1769 he was beaten in an altercation with revenue officers and received a head injury from which he never fully recovered.

Ottawa Conferences (1894, 1932) British **Imperial Conferences**. The main topic in 1894 was the development of communications between the individual units of the **British Empire**. Underlying the conference was a realization that the nature of imperial relationships had altered and that a new way of dealing with them had to be found. A major evolution was evident by 1932 in the agreements at the Ottawa economic conference held between Britain and its dominions at the height of the world depression. The conference negotiated a limited amount of imperial preference following the adoption of a new protective tariff by the British government earlier that year.

Otto I, 'the Great' (912–73) German King and Holy Roman Emperor (936/73). The son of **Henry I, 'the Fowler'**, he brought the great tribal duchies under the control of the monarchy and made the Church the main instrument of royal government. He was married in 930 to Edith, daughter of **Edward the Elder** and sister of **Athelstan** of England; and later, in 951, to St Adelaide. He preserved Germany from the Hungarian invasions by his great victory on the **Lechfeld** near Augsburg (955), and re-established imperial rule in Italy in a revival of the Carolingian tradition.

Otto II (955–83) German King (961/83) and Holy Roman Emperor (973/83). The son of **Otto I, 'the Great'**, he became Emperor in 973, successfully fought the Danes and Bohemians, and subdued insurgent Bavaria which he reduced in size by splitting it up. In 972 he married **Theophano**, daughter of the Byzantine Emperor, Romanus II. He invaded France, but overreached himself in attempts on the Eastern Empire, suffering a crushing defeat at Cotrone in southern Italy (982). During his absence, the Slavs and Danes rebelled (983) and destroyed settlements and missions in north-east Germany. He died of malaria while preparing another Italian campaign and is the only German emperor to be buried in Rome.

Otto III (980–1002) German King and Holy Roman Emperor (983/1002). The son of **Otto II**, he came to the throne at the age of three. His mother, Empress **Theophano**, ruled as regent until her death in 991; thereafter his grandmother, Adelaide, widow of **Otto I, 'the Great'**, was regent until his accession in 996. Under the influence of Adalbert of Prague, he undertook a campaign against the heathen Slavs on the Elbe (997) and promoted the cult of **Charlemagne** in an attempt to enhance the standing of the Western Empire. In his brief reign he managed to engineer into the papacy first his cousin, Gregory V, and then his tutor, Sylvester II. He lived most of his short life in Rome and tried to make it the capital of the empire, but was driven out by the hostility of the people in 1002.

Otto IV (c.1174–1218) German King and Holy Roman Emperor (1198/1214). The son

OTTOMAN DYNASTY

Regnal Dates	Name	Regnal Dates	Name
1281/1324	Osman I	1623/40	Murad IV
1324/60	Orhan	1640/8	Ibrahim
1360/89	Murad I	1648/87	Mehmed IV
1389/1402	Bayezid I	1687/91	Suleyman II
1403/13	Interregnum	1691/5	Ahmed II
1413/21	Mehmed I	1695/1703	Mustafa II
1421/44	Murad II (1st reign)	1703/30	Ahmed III
1444/6	Mehmed II, 'the Conqueror'	1730/54	Mahmud I
	(1st reign)	1754/7	Osman III
1446/51	Murad II (2nd reign)	1757/74	Mustafa III
1451/81	Mehmed II, 'the Conqueror'	1774/89	Abd ul-Hamid I
	(2nd reign)	1789/1807	Selim III
1481/1512	Bayezid II	1807/8	Mustafa IV
1512/20	Selim I, 'the Grim'	1808/39	Mahmud II
1520/66	Suleyman I, 'the Magnificent'	1839/61	Abd ul-Majid I
1566/74	Selim II	1861/76	Abd ul-Aziz
1574/95	Murad III	1876	Murad V
1595/1603	Mehmed III	1876/1909	Abd ul-Hamid II
1603/17	Ahmed I	1909/18	Mehmed V
1617/18	Mustafa I (1st reign)	1918/22	Mehmed VI
1618/22	Osman II	1922/4	Abd ul-Majid II (Caliph only)
1622/3	Mustafa I (2nd reign)		

Formation of the Ottoman Empire

of **Henry the Lion** and Matilda, the daughter of **Henry II** of England, he grew up at the court of his uncle **Richard I** of England, who created him Count of Poitou. He was elected King in 1198 in opposition to **Philip of Swabia**, against whom he struggled for supremacy for 10 years. Philip's murder in 1208 left the way free for his coronation as Emperor (1209), but his subsequent invasion of Sicily lost him the support of Pope **Innocent III** who raised up Philip's nephew **Frederick II** as a rival, and Otto's cause finally collapsed after his defeat by **Philip II** of France at **Bouvines** in 1214.

Ottoman Empire A Muslim empire founded c.1300 by Sultan **Osman I**, and originating in Asia Minor. Ottoman forces entered Europe in 1345, conquered Constantinople in 1453, and by 1520 controlled most of south-eastern Europe, including part of Hungary, the Middle East, and North

Africa. Following the 'golden age' of **Suleyman I, 'the Magnificent'**, the empire began a protracted decline. During the 19c and early 20c, Ottoman power was eroded by the ambitions of Russia and Austria in south-east Europe, the ambitions of France, Britain, and Italy in North Africa, the emergence of the Balkan nations, and internal loss of authority. It joined the Central Powers in 1914, and collapsed with their defeat in 1918. See panel p697 and map p699.

Ottonians German royal dynasty. Also known by their family name, the Liudolfinger, the family was founded in the 9c. They ruled Germany from 919 until 1024 under the kings Henry I, **Otto I, 'the Great'**, Otto II, **Otto III** (hence the name Ottonians) and **Henry II, 'the Holy'**, and completed the transformation of the eastern Frankish kingdom into the German kingdom. They supported church reform and pursued a

Break-up of the Ottoman Empire

policy of elevating churchmen as a counter-balance to the ambitions of the nobility. They reannexed **Lotharingia** and established the principle that the country could not be divided by inheritance. Their support of the church led to the so-called Ottonian Renaissance, with notable achievements in architecture, literature and the arts.

Oudenarde, Battle of (1708) A Grand Alliance victory in Flanders during the War of the **Spanish Succession**. While laying siege to Oudenarde, the French under the Duke of Vendôme and Burgundy were surprised by Allied troops commanded by Prince Eugene of Savoy and the Duke of Marlborough. A bitter contest followed, and later (1709) the French withdrew to their frontier.

Oudinot Expedition The French military expedition under the command of General Nicolas-Charles Oudinot sent, with the backing of Louis Napoleon Bonaparte (later **Napoleon III**), to crush the Roman Republic and to restore Pope **Pius IX**. Having finally overcome the republic's forces commanded by **Garibaldi**, a French garrison was left in Rome to protect the Pope. ▷ **Roman Question**

Outram, James (1803–63) British general and political officer. He joined the Bombay native infantry in 1819, and became political agent in Gujarat (1835–8). He fought in the first of the **Afghan Wars** (1838–42), and took part in the relief of Lucknow (1857–8). Known as 'the Bayard of India' because of his reputation for chivalry, he was made a baronet in 1858. ▷ **Indian Uprising**

ÖVP (*Österreichische Volkspartei*, 'Austrian People's Party') Austrian political party. Founded in 1945, the ÖVP represented the key Christian (Catholic) political groupings of inter-war **Austria** and identifies with contemporary European Christian Democracy. It has played a major role in Austrian government (1945–70, 1986–) sometimes in coalition with the **SPÖ**, but in 1986–7 became embroiled in the controversy surrounding Kurt **Waldheim**'s candidacy for the Austrian presidency.

OVRA In Italy, the name given to **Mussolini**'s secret police force. Never really an integral part of the **Fascist Party** machinery, the OVRA was little more than a slightly expanded version of the old secret branch of the Ministry of the Interior police.

Owen, David (Anthony Llewellyn) (1938–) British politician. He trained in medicine, then became an MP (1966) and Under-Secretary to the Navy (1968). He was Secretary for Health (1974–6), and Foreign Secretary (1977–9). One of the so-called 'Gang of Four' who formed the **Social Democratic Party** (SDP) in 1981, he succeeded Roy **Jenkins** as its leader in 1983. Following the Alliance's disappointing result in the 1987 general election, he opposed Liberal leader David **Steel** over the question of the merger of the two parties. In 1988, after the SDP voted to accept merger, Owen led the smaller section of the party to a brief independent existence. He retired from parliament in 1992 and went on to become, along with Cyrus Vance, a peace-broker in the troubles that erupted after the disintegration of Yugoslavia.

Oxenstierna, Count Axel Gustafsson (1583–1654) Swedish statesman. He was born in Uppland into one of Sweden's leading noble families. Trained abroad for the Church, he entered royal service in 1605 and was instrumental in achieving the smooth accession of **Gustav II Adolf** in 1611. From then on, he was Gustav's chancellor, responsible for administrative reform and Sweden's relations with foreign powers. He implemented a thorough reform of central and local administration, setting up new 'colleges' headed by the great officers of state. The Diet of four estates was also given a defined membership and procedure. After the King's death in 1632, Oxenstierna became regent for his young daughter, **Christina**, and directed Sweden's war effort in Germany. He set up the Heilbronn league of German princes in 1633 and after control of southern Germany was lost in 1635, he returned to Sweden to presuade his fellow councillors to fight on until the country's war aims had been

achieved. He continued as chancellor after Christina came of age in 1644, but thereafter lost influence to the Queen's own favourites.

Oxford, Provisions of (1258) A baronial programme imposing constitutional limitations on the English crown. **Henry III** of England had to share power with a permanent council of barons, parliaments meeting three times a year, and independent executive officers (chancellor, justiciar, treasurer). In 1261 the Pope absolved Henry from his oath to observe the Provisions. ▷ **Barons Wars**

Oyama Iwao (1842–1916) Japanese soldier and prince. In the **Sino-Japanese War** of 1894–5 he took Port Arthur and Wei-hei-Wei from China, and in the **Russo-Japanese War** of 1904–5 defeated General Alexei **Kuropatkin** in several encounters.

Oyo, Kingdom of The dominant Yoruba (Nigeria) state of the 17c and 18c. Both the Oyo Dynasty and those of the other kingdoms of the Yoruba were said to have been founded by descendants of a King of Ife, and their peoples were notably town dwellers. The success of Oyo was based on its cavalry, which extended the kingdom southwestwards and also jostled for power with its neighbouring savanna states Borgu and Nupe. Its expansion was based on securing the salt trade and trading routes to the coast associated with European slaving. In the 18c it came into conflict with Dahomey and won the war of 1726–30. In the early 19c, Oyo became a victim of the **jihads** or holy wars of the period. Its northern territory became the Fulani emirate of Ilorin, and the state broke up into a series of small states competing with each other in incessant rivalries and warfare.

Ozaki Yukio (1859–1954) Japanese politician. A journalist before he turned to politics, Ozaki participated in the formation of the *Rikken Kaishinto* (Constitutional Reform Party) in 1882 and was elected to the first Diet in 1890 (he was to be elected a further 24 times). Ozaki remained a consistent advocate of party government and expansion of the suffrage. Outspoken, he maintained an independent stance even during **World War II**, criticizing the dictatorial style of Prime Minister Hideki **Tojo**. He retired from politics in 1953.

Özal, Turgut (1927–93) Turkish politician. Educated at Istanbul Technical University, he entered government service and in 1967 became Under-Secretary for State Planning. From 1971 he worked for the World Bank, in 1979 joined the office of Prime Minister Bülent **Ecevit**, and in 1980 was Deputy to Prime Minister Bülent Ulusu, within the military regime of Kenan Evren. When political pluralism returned in 1983, Ozal founded the Islamic, right-of-centre Motherland Party (ANAP, *Anavatan Partisi*) and led it to a narrow, but clear victory in the elections of that year. In the 1987 general election he retained his majority, and in 1989 became Turkey's first civilian President for 30 years.

P

Paardeberg, Battle of (1900) The first major British victory of the second Boer War, following the relief of the Siege of **Kimberley**. The Boers abandoned the position they had held at **Magersfontein**, and moved east to defend Bloemfontein. Their defeat at Paardeberg opened the way for the full-scale attack on the Orange Free State and the Transvaal, and the taking of the Boer cities. ▷ **Boer Wars**

Paasikivi, Juo Kusti (1870–1956) Finnish politician. He became Conservative Prime Minister after the civil war in 1918. He recognized the need for friendly relations with Russia, and took part in all Finnish–Soviet negotiations. He sought to avoid war in Sep 1939, conducted the armistice negotiations and became Prime Minister again in 1944. He succeeded Carl Gustav **Mannerheim** as President (1946–56). ▷ **Continuation War; Russo-Finnish War**

Pacific, War of the (1879–83) A war fought between Chile on the one hand and Peru and Bolivia (in alliance since 1873) on the other, arising out of Chilean grievances in the Atacama Desert, then Bolivian-held. Chile won command of the sea in the early months of the war, and sent large expeditions to Peru, occupying the capital, Lima (Jan 1881). Peace treaties gave Chile large territorial gains.

Paderewski, Ignacy (Jan) (1860–1941) Polish pianist, composer, and patriot. He studied in Warsaw, becoming a professor in the Conservatoire (1878), and a virtuoso pianist, appearing throughout Europe and the USA. During **World War I** he used his popularity abroad to argue the case, particularly in the USA, for Poland regaining its independence, and in 1919 he became for a time Prime Minister of Poland in order to establish a sense of political unity. But he soon retired from politics, lived in Switzerland, and resumed concert work. He was elected President of Poland's provisional parliament abroad in 1940, though poor health prevented him pursuing an active role. He died in New York City.

Padilla, Juan de (1490–1521) Leading noble of Toledo. He emerged as one of the principal leaders of the Revolt of the **Comuneros** in 1520, but his forces were eventually defeated at the Battle of **Villalar** (1521) and he and his companions were beheaded. His wife, Maria (d.1531), held Toledo against the royal forces from 1521 to 1522, and then fled to Portugal.

Padlock Act (1937) Canadian anti-communist legislation. Enacted by the **Duplessis Union Nationale** administration of Quebec, it authorized the closure of any premises which were suspected of producing communist propaganda. Since the term 'communist' was not properly defined, the government was able to hinder the growth of the **CCF** and also to use it against trade unions. The law was declared unconstitutional by the Supreme Court in 1957.

Padmore, George (1902–59) Trinidadian international revolutionary and Pan-Africanist. He spent most of his life campaigning against colonialism in Africa and preaching African **socialism** and unity; his memory is revered in West Africa.

Paekche State One of the three kingdoms of early Korean history (along with **Koguryo** and **Silla**) that held sway over the south-west of the peninsula between 350 and 663. Paekche's rulers and aristocracy were originally sinicized migrants from eastern Manchuria. It was through Paekche that Buddhism was first introduced to Japan in the 6c, while Paekche scholars and artisans played a crucial role in Japan's attempts to emulate Chinese civilization. In 660 **Tang Dynasty** China, determined to restore a Chinese presence in the peninsula lost during the 3c, intervened in a war between Paekche and Silla on the latter's behalf. By 663, despite Japanese assistance (involving the first known clash between Chinese and Japanese forces), Paekche had been defeated. It was temporarily occupied by Chinese troops, before being swallowed up by Silla in 673.

Páez, José Antonio (1790–1873) Venezuelan general and politician. He commanded forces of *llaneros* ('cowboys') in the **Spanish–American Wars of Independence** as principal lieutenant of Simón **Bolívar**. On the break-up of Gran Colombia, he became President of Venezuela (1831) and ruled the country until the late 1840s, again assuming power in 1861–3. He died in exile in New York City.

Pagan The capital of the first Burman state, located in the dry plains of central Burma, at the point where the great Irrawaddy River turns towards the East. The state of Pagan emerged in the middle of the 9c. In the 11c, under Anawrahta, it extended its authority both to the north and to the south, the latter securing important access to the port cities on the Gulf of Martaban and the Kra Isthmus, and thus to their commercial and cultural connections. The most important physical legacy of Pagan was its astounding pro-gramme of temple construction. The ruins of over 2 000 temples, within an area of 26 square miles, still stand. Pagan began to weaken in the 13c, initially probably as a result of the heavy and continuous religious donations of the state in the form of skilled labour and irrigated rice fields. A Mongol invasion and Shan incursions at the end of the century brought about its final collapse.

Page, Sir Earle Christmas Grafton (1880–1961) Australian politician. He practised medicine and sat in the federal parliament from 1919 until his death. He became Leader of the Country Party in 1921 and Deputy Prime Minister and Treasurer in the Bruce–Page coalition government of 1923–9. He was Deputy Prime Minister (1934–9) and briefly Prime Minister in 1939. In 1941 he became Australian minister in London, representing Australia on war cabinet committees. Minister of Health in 1949, he retired to the backbenches in 1956. ▷ **National Party of Australia**

Pahlavi, Mohammad Reza (1919–80) Shah of Persia (1941/79). He succeeded on the abdication of his father, Reza Shah, in 1941. His reign was for many years marked by social reforms and a movement away from the old-fashioned despotic concept of the monarchy, but during the later 1970s the economic situation deteriorated, social inequalities worsened, and protest at West-ern-style 'decadence' grew among the relig-ious fundamentalists. After several attempts at parliamentary reform the Shah, having lost control of the situation, left the country, and a revolutionary government was formed under Ayatollah **Khomeini**. The ex-Shah having been admitted to the USA for medical treatment, the Iranian government seized the US embassy in Tehran and held many of its staff hostage for over a year, demanding his return to Iran. He made his final residence in Egypt at the invitation of President Anwar **Sadat** and died there.

Paine, Thomas (1737–1809) British-Ameri-can political writer. In 1774 he sailed for Philadelphia, where his pamphlet *Common Sense* (1776) argued for complete independ-ence from Britain. He served with the American Army, and was made Secretary to the Committee of Foreign Affairs. In 1787 he returned to England, where he wrote *The Rights of Man* (1791–2) in support of the **French Revolution**. Indicted for treason, he fled to Paris in 1792, where he was elected a Deputy to the National **Convention**, but imprisoned for his proposal to offer the King asylum in the USA. At this time 1794–5 he wrote *The Age of Reason*, in favour of deism. Released in 1796, he returned to the USA in 1802.

Paisley, Rev Ian (Richard Kyle) (1926–) Northern Ireland militant Protestant clergy-man and politician. An ordained minister since 1946, he formed his own Church (the Free Presbyterian Church of Ulster) in 1951, and from the 1960s became deeply involved in Ulster politics. He founded the Protestant **Democratic Unionist Party** and stood as its MP for four years until 1974, since when he has been the Democratic Unionist MP for North Antrim. He has been a member of the European Parliament since 1979. A rousing orator, he is strongly in favour of maintaining the Union with Britain, and fiercely opposed to the **IRA**, Roman Catholicism, and the unification of Ireland.

Pal, Bipin Chandra (1858–1932) Indian nationalist and freedom fighter. Though born into an orthodox Zamindar family in Sylhet (in present-day Bangladesh), he opposed traditional orthodoxy and religious practices. He entered politics in 1877 and his associa-tion with the great reformist **Brahmo Samaj** leader, Keshab Chandra Sen, drew him into this movement in 1880. He was also greatly influenced by B G **Tilak**, **Lala Lajpat Rai** and Aurobindo **Ghosh**. In 1898 he went to England on a scholarship for theological studies and, on his return, launched a weekly journal, *Young India* (1902), through which he championed the complete freedom of India. He campaigned for the boycott of British goods and also advocated a policy of passive resistance and non-cooperation. A member of the famous Congress trio 'Lal, Pal and Bal', he spent the years 1908–11 in England, where he worked for India's freedom and published *Swaraj*. In the later stages of the freedom movement, he withdrew from political life, although he continued to write on national matters. ▷ **Lajpat Rai, Lala; Non-Cooperation Movement; Swaraj**

Palach, Jan (1948–69) Czech philosophy student. As a protest against the invasion of Czechoslovakia by **Warsaw Pact** forces (Aug 1968) and its subsequent '**normalization**', he burnt himself to death in Wenceslas Square in Prague in Jan 1969. He became a hero and symbol of hope, and was mourned by thousands. Huge popular demonstrations marking the 20th anniversary of his death were held in Prague in 1989.

Palacký, František (1798–1876) Czech historian and a leading light in the Czech national revival. Politically he argued the case before and during the 1848–9 revolutionary outburst in the Habsburg Empire for the restoration of Czech autonomy. Subsequently, and particularly after the **Ausgleich** of 1867 recognized the equality of Hungary alongside Austria, he became more radical in looking towards eventual independence. However, his greatest contribution was his mammoth *History of Bohemia* (1836–67), which established the historical case for the burgeoning national movement.

Palafox y Melzi, José de (1780–1847) Spanish patriot. Nominally head of the heroic defence of Saragossa (July 1808–Feb 1809), he was carried prisoner to France, and not released until 1813. He was made Duke of Saragossa (1836) and Grandee of Spain (1837).

Palas One of the three dynasties vying with one other for supremacy in north India in the 8–10c. Established by Gopala (supposedly elected by the people) in the mid-8c in Bengal, the dynasty soon came into conflict with the **Pratiharas** over control of **Kanauj**. In decline in the mid-10c, the kingdom recovered under Mahipala I (c.975/1027); Rampala (1072/1126) successfully put down the Kaivarta rebellion (recorded in Sandhyakaranandin's *Ramacarita*). Buddhists by persuasion, the Palas encouraged the development of great Buddhist monasteries as educational centres but never themselves had a permanent seat of government.

Palatinate, The A German Rhenish principality, with Heidelberg as its capital.

Acquired by the Wittelsbach family (1214), it was elevated to an imperial electorate by the Golden Bull of 1356, and became increasingly wealthy and important in the 13–15c. After the introduction of Calvinism by Frederick III (1559/76), it was the leading Protestant German state and head of the Protestant Union (1608), before its division and systematic devastation in the **Thirty Years War** (1618–48) and later by France (1685). In the 18c it lost significance, being successively reunified as a single state (1706), linked dynastically with Bavaria (1777), and occupied by the French (1793–4). Shared between Baden and Bavaria (1815), it was finally absorbed into the German Reich (1871).

Pale (Ireland) The 'land of peace' where English rule prevailed in late medieval Ireland. It shrank during this period because of aggrandizement by Anglo-Irish nobles (the Earls of Desmond, Kildare, and Ormond), and continued to diminish until its reconquest under **Henry VIII** of England. It was defined as the four counties of Dublin, Kildare, Louth, and Meath in 1464, but the Act of 1495 under **Poynings' Law** showed a smaller area.

Pale, The (Russia) In the 19c and early 20c, the area within which the bulk of the Jewish population of imperial Russia was forced to live. This was fairly broadly defined in **Alexander I**'s time, but following the assassination of **Alexander II** in 1881 it was restricted to the narrow confines of what had been eastern Poland plus part of south-west Russia. In typical anti-Semitic fashion it was alleged by Konstantin **Pobedonostsev**, Procurator of the Holy Synod, and others that Jews had been involved in the assassination and were enemies of the state. There were frequent **pogroms** within the Pale; and Jews were officially discriminated against throughout Russia. The result was that more Jews did become involved in opposition activities and that some contributed to the emergence of the Zionist movement; most Jews were forced to follow those occupations they were accused of monopolizing.

Palestine A region bordering the east Mediterranean, historically settled by Philistines then Israelites. During the 20c it has been disputed by Jewish and Arab interests. Palestine was viewed by the Jews as the 'Promised Land', but it also contains Islamic holy sites associated with Muhammed. After **World War II** a mandate was granted to the

UK by the **UN** to administer the territory (1920–48). The **Balfour Declaration** supported the establishment of a Jewish homeland. After World War II the UN recommended that there should be separate Jewish and Arab states in Palestine. The State of Israel came into being in 1948 and was immediately invaded by its Arab neighbours. The Israelis were victorious, and gained more land than had been allotted by the UN. Over 700 000 Arab refugees left the Israeli-occupied areas. The **PLO** was recognized by the Arab League in 1974 as the official voice of Palestinian Arabs.

Pallava Dynasty South Indian dynasty. The Pallavas ruled from the 4c to the end of the 9c, when their territories were annexed by the Chola kings of Thanjavur (Tanjore). The Pallava period in south India saw the growth of the Aryan institutions in the south. Amongst the later group of Pallava rulers, Mahendra-Varman I (600/30) was responsible for the growing political strength of the Pallavas and during his reign some of the finest cut rock temples, including the famous one sited at Mahabalipuram, were built. Another famous Pallava king, who ruled for 40 years, was Narsimha-Varman II. The Pallavas developed a navy, built dockyards at Mahabalipuram and Nagapattinam and conducted extensive maritime trade with South-East Asia. ▷ **Chola Dynasty**

Palme, (Sven) Olof (1927–86) Swedish politician. He graduated in law from the University of Stockholm in 1951 and became private secretary to the Social Democratic Prime Minister, Tage **Erlander** in 1954. He was elected to parliament four years later and was appointed minister without portfolio in 1963. He succeeded Erlander as Prime Minister on the latter's resignation in 1969. Palme lost power in 1976, but returned at the head of a minority government in 1982. He was shot dead by an unknown assailant in the centre of Stockholm after a visit to the cinema with his wife. His leadership of the Social Democratic Labour Party saw a leftward swing in its policies, and he was an outspoken critic of US policy in the **Vietnam War**.

Palmerston (of Palmerston), Henry John Temple, 3rd Viscount (1784–1865) British politician. He became a Tory MP in 1807, served as Secretary of War (1809–28), joined the **Whigs** (1830), and was three times Foreign Secretary (1830–4, 1835–41 and 1846–51). His brusque speech, assertive manner, and robust defences of what he considered to be British interests abroad made him a controversial figure and secured him the name of 'Firebrand Palmerston'. He was unpopular with Queen **Victoria** and many of his political colleagues but cultivated public opinion. Home Secretary in **Aberdeen**'s coalition (1852), he became Premier in 1855, when he vigorously prosecuted the **Crimean War** with Russia. He remained in office until 1858, and was Prime Minister again in 1859–65. ▷ **Liberal Party** (UK); **Tories; Wellington, Duke of**

Pan-Africanism An ideal and a movement, drawing its ideas from black American and West Indian writers and activists. In part, it reflects a pride in the African continent and Africanness (and thus has some similarities with **negritude**) and, in part, a commitment to self-rule. Although the pull towards continental unity is strong in rhetoric and emotion, Pan-Africanism has failed ultimately to provide a strong enough ideology to transcend local self-interest and rivalries, nor has its political manifestation, the **Organization of African Unity**, managed to provide the institutional framework for continental unity.

Pan-Africanist Congress (PAC) A South African political party and offshoot of the **ANC** (African National Congress), the PAC was formed in 1959 as a movement rejecting the multi-racial assumptions of the ANC as well as its communist and Soviet links. It was banned in 1960 and its leaders went into exile, organizing opposition to the **apartheid** regime in South Africa from Zambia. The ban was lifted in 1990, and it remains a smaller, but perhaps more closely knit, party than the ANC, despite its leadership problems in the years of exile.

Panama A republic occupying the southeast end of the isthmus of Central America. It was visited by Columbus in 1502 and quickly gained strategic importance as a centre of Spanish trade movement, a vital link between the Caribbean and Pacific. It remained under Spanish colonial rule until 1821, when it joined the Republic of Greater Columbia. The US-inspired revolution of 1903 led to a break from Columbia. Panama assumed sovereignty of the **Panama Canal**, previously administered by the USA, in 1979. Although Panama has an elected president and Legislative Assembly, the military have been the ruling force, led by Manuel Noriega until 1989. In Dec 1989 US forces invaded Panama City after allegations of corruption and drugs trafficking against Noriega had led to strict US sanctions and heightened tensions in the area, and Noriega was tried and convicted for drugs offences in the USA.

Panama Canal A canal bisecting the Isthmus of Panama and linking the Atlantic and Pacific Oceans. It is 82 km/51 ml long, and 150 m/490 ft wide in most places; built by the US Corps of Engineers (1904–14). In 1979, US control of the Panama Canal Zone (8 km/5 ml of land flanking the canal on either side passed to the Republic of Panama, which has guaranteed the neutrality of the waterway itself when control of the canal is passed to it in 2000. ▷ **Bunau-Varilla, Philippe Jean; Hay-Bunau-Varilla Treaty; Hay-Herran Treaty; Panama**

Panama Congress (1826) Attended by delegates from Mexico, Peru, Gran Colombia and the Central American Federation at the invitation of Simón **Bolívar** (who did not himself attend). The treaty of Spanish-American confederation agreed at the meeting had no practical effect, but the Congress remains a symbol of the quest for Latin American unity.

Pan-American Union An organization founded in 1890 (and first called the International Bureau for American Republics) to foster political and economic cooperation among American states, and to draw North and South America closer together. Until **World War II** the Union concluded many agreements covering trade, migration, and neutrality zones around their coasts, despite fears among many members of domination by the USA. In 1948 it became part of the wider Organization of American States (OAS), and now forms its permanent administrative and advisory machinery. It has four departments: economic and social affairs; international law; cultural affairs; and administrative services.

Pan-Arabism The belief that Arabs should unite to form one nation had its origins in the Arab nationalist movement before **World War I**. With the collapse of the **Ottoman Empire** in that war and the foundation of separate Arab states after it, the belief in a single Arab nation declined. It was revived in the late 1930s when the Palestinian Arabs, revolting against Jewish colonization and British rule, appealed to Arabs everywhere for support. Egypt took up pan-Arabism as a means of asserting Egyptian leadership in the Middle East. In 1945 the Arab League was formed with its headquarters in Cairo, but it foundered in 1948 as it was unable to prevent the formation of the state of Israel. In the 1950s the cause of Arab unity was taken up by Gamal Abd al-**Nasser** in Egypt and by the Ba'ath Party in Syria, in order to oppose Israel and domination by foreign powers. There was a short-lived union of Syria and Egypt (1958–61) but the rivalries of Egypt, Syria and Iraq prevented Arab unification. With the defeat of Arab states by Israel in the 1967 war, Nasser's leadership was discredited and the idea of pan-Arabism lost its appeal.

Pan Chao ▷ **Ban Zhao**

Pan Ch'ao ▷ **Ban Chao**

Panchayati Raj A form of local self government in rural India initially advocated by M K **Gandhi** which advocated rule by village councils and other rural local bodies. It was promoted by the central government as a matter of national policy from 1957 to 1963, when the state governments were pressured to adopt some form of democratic decentralization and to involve the people down to the village level directly in the planning process. By the mid-1960s, however, support for Panchayati Raj had declined, even in its stronghold of Maharashtra and Gujarat. In 1977, the Janata government began to reopen the question of the importance and relevance of Panchayati Raj institutions, an issue which has since become important in the national political debate.

Pandhya Dynasty South Indian dynasty which, along with the **Chola Dynasty**, began to dominate the east coast after the turn of the 1c BC and was associated with the emergence of **Tamil** culture. The Cheras, Cholas and Pandyas were continually at war with one other. From the mid-6c, south India was ruled by the Pallavas of Kanchi, Chalukyas of Badami, and the Pandyas with their capital at Madurai. The Pandyas had established their position in the area of the south of Tamil-nad, and were to remain in control of this region for many centuries. The conflict between these warring states persisted for several centuries, and in the 9c the Pallavas succumbed to a combined attack from the Pandyas and the Cholas. By the 13c, the Pandyas had superseded the Cholas as the dominant power in the Tamil country and might well have maintained this position in the subsequent century had it not been for the attacks from Turkish rulers from the north and the threat of interference from the northern

Deccan, which was virtually in the hands of the **Delhi Sultanate**. ▷ **Pallava Dynasty**

Pandit, Vijaya Lakshmi (1900–) Indian politician and diplomat. The sister of Jawaharlal **Nehru**, she was the leader of the Indian **UN** delegation (1946–8 and 1952–3), and also held several ambassadorial posts (1947–51). In 1953 she became the first woman president of the UN General Assembly and from 1954 to 1961 she was Indian High Commissioner in London.

Panipat, Battles of (1526, 1556 and 1761) Three battles which took place 50 miles north of Delhi, India. The first (1526), between **Babur** and the Sultan of Delhi, represented the beginning of the **Mughal Empire**. The second (1556) marked the restoration of Mughal power when **Akbar the Great** defeated the Afghan challenge. The third (1761) saw the defeat of Maratha forces by the Afghan **Ahmad Shah Durrani**, which paved the way for British supremacy.

Pan-Islamism A movement to unite all Muslims against the threat from Christian states. It was born in the 1860s and 1870s among the Young Ottomans, who criticized the Ottoman government for failing to help the Central Asian Khans, who had been overrun by the Russians. A militant supporter of pan-Islamism was al-**Afghani**, who criticized reformers such as Sir Sayyid Ahmad Khan for weakening loyalty to Islam by making concessions to infidel imperialists in India. Muhammad **Abduh** was another leading figure in the intellectual revival of Islam, regarding nationalism with suspicion as it weakened the religious ties which bound Muslims together. 'He who professes the Muslim faith…ceases to concern himself with his race or nation', he wrote. Yet liberalism and nationalism overshadowed religion among the radical elites who identified Islam with social conservatism and political backwardness. In Turkey the success of **Atatürk** in obtaining a negotiated peace on his own terms at Lausanne (1923) gave a great boost to secular nationalism among young army officers in Arab lands in the 1920s and 1930s. After **World War II**, there was a great revival of Islamic beliefs and movements, which responded to the feelings of the suppressed lower classes, opposed to their westernized rulers. The **Muslim Brotherhood** in Egypt was the most successful of these movements until the revolution which brought the Ayatollah **Khomeini** to power in Iran in 1979. In the 1980s military, secular regimes were

struggling to hold on to power by resisting the tide of Islamic fundamentalism, which won elections in Algeria in 1991.

Pankhurst, Emmeline (1858–1928) British suffragette. In 1905 she organized the Women's Social and Political Union, and fought for women's suffrage by violent means, on several occasions being arrested and going on hunger strike. After the outbreak of **World War I**, she worked instead for the industrial mobilization of women. Of her daughters and fellow workers, Dame Christabel turned later to preaching Christ's Second Coming; and Sylvia diverged to pacificism, internationalism, and Labour politics. ▷ **suffragettes**

Pan Ku ▷ **Ban Gu**

Pan-Turkism A movement which sought to unite all Turks. In the late 19c it was strongest among the Turkish peoples of the Russian Empire. The Ottoman Turks at first rejected pan-Turkism, as it would disrupt their multinational empire but, as the **Ottoman Empire** lost its provinces in Europe, many sought a new unity in joining all Turks together. Sultan **Abd ul-Hamid II** suppressed these ideas but, after the Young Turk revolution of 1908, the desire to unite the Turkish peoples of Central Asia with those of Anatolia spread. This seemed possible with Russia's defeat in **World War I**, but **Atatürk** rejected Pan-Turkism to concentrate on ruling the new Turkish Republic which arose after the collapse of the Ottoman Empire. ▷ **Young Turks**

Pao-chia System ▷ **Baojia System**

Paoli, Pasquale de (1725–1807) Corsican patriot. He returned from exile in 1755 to take part in the struggle against the island's Genoese overlords. After Corsica's purchase by the French in 1768, he led a renewed rebellion but was defeated and fled to England. With the **French Revolution** he was made Governor of his native island. However, he again grew dissatisfied with French rule and launched an insurrection against the Convention. This too failed and in 1796 he returned to live in exile in England.

Papacy ▷ **Pope**

Papadopoulos, George (1919–) Greek soldier and politician. He underwent army training in the Middle East and fought in Albania against the Italians before the

German occupation of Greece in **World War II**. A member of the resistance during the occupation, he then rejoined the army, reaching the rank of colonel. In 1967 he led a coup against the government of King **Constantine II** and established a virtual military dictatorship. In 1973, following the abolition of the monarchy, he became President under a new republican constitution, but before the year was out he was himself ousted in another military coup. In 1974 he was arrested, tried for high treason and convicted, but his death sentence was commuted.

Papagos, Alexandros (1883–1956) Greek soldier and politician. After a brilliant military career involving service in the **Balkan Wars** (1912–13) and the Greek invasion of Turkey (1919–22), he was made Minister of War in 1935 and Chief of Staff the following year. In 1940, as Commander-in-Chief, he repelled the Italian attack on Greece, pushing the enemy forces back into Albania. Less successful against a German attack in Apr 1941, he was captured and taken as a hostage to Germany. After his release at the end of **World War II**, he led the campaign in Greece against the communist guerrillas. He was made field marshal in 1949, but resigned as Commander-in-Chief two years later in order to concentrate on a political role. He formed a new political party, the Greek Rally, and was Prime Minister of an exclusively Greek Rally government from 1952 until his death in 1955.

Papal Allocution (Apr 1848) The formal message delivered by **Pius IX** in which he made it clear that he would not back war against Austria. It marked the point where Pius IX ceased to be the darling of Italian patriots and showed his true reactionary colours.

Papal States The 'States of the Church', straddling rural, mountainous areas of central Italy, comprised of territories received by treaties and donations in the Middle Ages. The papal government was often ineffective, and relied upon local lords (Malatesta of Rimini, Montefeltro of Urbino) who were appointed as 'vicars in temporal matters'. Annexed in 1870, the papacy refused to recognize their loss until the **Lateran Pacts** (1929), which established the Vatican papal state.

Papandreou, Andreas George (1919–) Greek politician. The son of George **Papandreou**, before entering active politics

he had an impressive academic career, holding professorial posts at universities in the USA and Canada. He became a US citizen in 1944, but returned to Greece as Director of the Centre for Economic Research in Athens (1961–4) and Economic Adviser to the Bank of Greece, and resumed his Greek citizenship. His political activities led to imprisonment and exile after the military coup led by **Papadopoulos** in 1967. He returned to Greece in 1974 and threw himself wholeheartedly into national politics, founding the Pan-Hellenic Liberation Movement, which later became **PASOK** (the Pan-Hellenic Socialist Movement). He was leader of the opposition from 1977 and in 1981 became Greece's first socialist Prime Minister. Re-elected in 1985, in 1988 a heart operation and news of his impending divorce, following his association with a young former air stewardess, created speculation about his future. The 1989 general election produced no clear result and, after unsuccessful attempts to form a new government, he resigned and was succeeded by Tzannis Tzannetakis.

Papandreou, George (1888–1968) Greek politician. A lawyer by training, he moved into politics in the early 1920s. The monarchy had been temporarily removed in 1923 and reinstated by the army in 1925 but Papandreou, a left-of-centre republican, held office in several administrations including the brief period when the monarchy was temporarily removed (1923–5) and in the following decade. In 1942 he escaped from Greece during the German occupation and returned in 1944 to head a coalition government, but, suspected by the army because of his socialist credentials, remained in office for only a few weeks. He remained an important political figure, founding the Centre Union Party (1961), and returning as Prime Minister (1963 and 1964–5). A disagreement with the young King **Constantine II** in 1965 led to his resignation, and in 1967, when a coup established a military regime, he was placed under house arrest. His son, Andreas **Papandreou**, was to carry forward his political beliefs.

Papen, Franz von (1879–1969) German politician and Nazi collaborator. He was military attaché in Mexico and Washington, Chief of Staff with a Turkish army, and in 1921 joined the **Centre Party**. He was Chancellor (1932), playing a major part in undermining the **Weimar Republic**, **Hitler**'s Vice-Chancellor (1933–4), and Ambassador to **Austria** (1936–8) and Turkey (1939–44). Taken prisoner in 1945, he was acquitted at the **Nuremberg Trials**.

Papineau, Louis-Joseph (1786–1871) French-Canadian politician. The speaker of Lower Canada's House of Assembly (1815–37), he opposed union with Upper Canada, and agitated for a greater degree of governmental independence from Britain. His leadership of the *Patriotes* during the **Rebellions of 1837** led to charges of treason. He escaped to Paris, but returned to Canada after a general amnesty was granted in 1844.

Paraguayan War ▷ **Triple Alliance, War of the**

parcería The system of 'sharecropping' unsuccessfully attempted by major coffee producers in São Paulo in the 1850s. Immigrants would be contracted to work on *fazendas* against a '*parcería* contract'. These contracts were of two types: those where payment was dependent on the coffee-market and those where it was independent of it. In the first case, the profits from the crop were divided; in the second, a price was fixed in advance. The system failed, mainly because *fazendeiros* saw the effective working of a labour market as a threat to their overall control of their fazendas, many of which were not only undivided but also largely worked by slave-labour until 1887–8. The mistreatment of *parceiros* led European governments to discourage, if not prohibit, emigration to Brazil until the 1890s. ▷ **fazenda; fazendeiro**

parentela A term used in Brazil meaning 'extended family', including all relatives (*parentes*) by blood, marriage and ritual, generally living in a number of households. Colloquially, the term is understood as a plethora of obedient kin, and elite *parentelas* have crucial national significance. The practice of endogamous marriage conserved patrimony (especially on *fazendas*) within the family group by preventing the dividing-up of property among legitimate heirs entailed by inheritance laws. *Patria potestas* — the authority of the head of the household — denied wives the right to alienate landed property without their husband's consent. By no means limited to the elite, parentelas explain the preponderance of **coronelismo** throughout Brazil, especially in the northeast. ▷ **fazenda**

Paris, Congress of (1856) The peace conference which ended the **Crimean War**. Russia

gave up southern Bessarabia (acquired in 1813), which cut her off from the mouth of the River Danube, to Moldavia and Kars to Turkey. The Straits Convention of 1841, which did not allow any warships to pass through the Bosphorus, was re-affirmed. The most serious clause for Russia was that neutralizing the Black Sea: neither Russia nor Turkey was allowed warships or naval bases there. Russia regarded this as a serious threat to her security in the south, as in wartime British and French warships could rapidly enter an undefended Black Sea. She took advantage of France's defeat in the **Franco-Prussian** War (1870–1) to repudiate this clause. Russia also gave up her claim to act as protector of the Orthodox Christians in the **Ottoman Empire**.

Paris, Louis Philippe, Count of (1834–94) French nobleman, grandson of King **Louis-Phillippe**, and pretender to the French throne. He returned to France in 1871 and renounced his claim to the throne in favour of the Count of **Chambord; the latter's death in 1883 made him head of the House of Bourbon.** ▷ **Bourbon, House of**

Paris, Pact of (27 Aug 1928) ▷ **Kellogg–Briand Pact**

Paris, Siege of (1870–1) The siege of Paris carried out by the Prussian Army. Attempts by the **National Guard** from inside the city, and by the new armies raised by **Gambetta** south of the River Loire failed to lift the siege. Food shortages forced the Government of National Defence to ask for an armistice. The hysterical atmosphere of the siege, and the existence of the National Guard, which was not disarmed by the terms of the armistice, were important causes of the insurrection of 18 Mar, leading to the **Paris Commune**. ▷ **National Defence, Government of**

Paris, Treaties of (1814–15) Successive peace settlements involving France and the victorious coalition of Britain, Austria, Prussia, Russia, Sweden, and Portugal, restoring the Bourbon monarchy to France in place of the Napoleonic Empire, before and after the **Hundred Days** (1815). In 1815 a large indemnity and army of occupation replaced the generous terms of 1814. ▷ **Bourbon, House of; Napoleonic Wars**

Paris, Treaty of (1763) The peace settlement ending the **Seven Years War** (1756–63), signed by Britain, France, and

Spain. Spain surrendered Florida to the British, but received the Louisiana Territory and New Orleans from France, and Havana and Manila from Britain. In exchange for minor concessions, France ceded Canada, America east of the Mississippi, Cape Breton and the St Lawrence islands, Dominica, Tobago, the Grenadines, and Senegal to Britain. In the short term, Britain was isolated by the French determination for revenge, but the final consequence was British colonial supremacy.

Paris, Treaty of (30 Mar 1856) The treaty bringing to an end the **Crimean War** and enshrining the defeat of Russia by Britain and France. Russia had to cede southern **Bessarabia** to **Moldavia**, had to give up its virtual protectorate over Moldavia and Wallachia, and had to accept the neutrality of the Black Sea, including the dismantling of its own coastal fortresses. The **Ottoman Empire** was admitted to the so-called Concert of European Powers, but did not keep its promise to respect the rights of its subjects. Russia was driven back in on itself and under **Alexander II** embarked upon its first serious programme of domestic reform.

Paris, Treaty of (10 Feb 1947) This treaty exacted indemnities from nations allied with Germany during **World War II**. Italy was obliged to surrender the Dodecanese Islands to Greece.

Paris Commune An uprising that followed France's humiliating defeat in the **Franco-Prussian War** (18 Mar–28 May 1871). A bungled attempt to disarm the **National Guard** produced an uprising and the election of a municipal council, which took the name of Commune, with its revolutionary associations. The government, headed by the veteran Orléanist, **Thiers**, retreated to Versailles, where the monarchist National Assembly refused all compromise, as did the Commune. When a sufficient military force had been assembled, Paris was recaptured with huge loss of life. Members of the National Guard fighting for the Commune were massacred in thousands, and others were sentenced to long terms of imprisonment, leaving an unprecedented legacy of bitterness. ▷ **Orléanists**

Paris Pacts (1954) A series of amendments and protocols to the Treaty of Brussels and the Brussels Treaty Organization. Italy and the Federal Republic of Germany became members of what became known as the

Western European Union. Germany agreed not to manufacture atomic, bacteriological, or chemical weapons, thus clearing the way for its rearmament and membership of **NATO**.

Paris Peace Conference (1919–20) A meeting of 32 'allied and associated powers' who met in Paris to draw up a peace settlement after **World War I**. Five treaties were concluded: with Germany (Treaty of **Versailles**, 1919), Austria (Treaty of **St Germain**, 1919), Hungary (Treaty of **Trianon**, 1920), Bulgaria (Treaty of **Neuilly**, 1919) and Turkey (Treaties of **Sèvres**, 1920, and Lausanne, 1923).

Paris Peace Conference (1946–7) Meetings of the five members of the Council of Foreign Ministers, representing the main **World War II** Allies (USA, Russia, UK, France and China), and delegates from 16 other nations involved against the **Axis Powers**. It drew up peace treaties with Bulgaria, Finland, Hungary, Romania and Italy. Despite repeated divisions, agreement was finally reached and the treaties signed in the spring of 1947.

Park Chung-hee (1917–79) South Korean soldier and politician. Educated at a Japanese military academy, he fought with the Japanese forces during **World War II**. Park joined the South Korean army in 1946, becoming a major general by 1961, when he ousted the civilian government of Chang Myon in a bloodless coup. He formed the Democratic Republican Party (DRP) and was elected State President in Dec 1963. He embarked on an ambitious, and remarkably successful, programme of export-led industrial development, based on strategic government planning and financial support, which attained 'miracle' annual growth rates of 10–20 per cent during the 1960s and 1970s. However, he ruled in an austere and authoritarian manner, imposing martial law (Oct 1972) and introducing restrictive 'emergency measures' (May 1975). In Oct 1979, during a brief economic downturn, he was assassinated by the head of the Korean Central Intelligence Service.

Parkes, Sir Henry (1815–96) Australian politician. He emigrated to New South Wales in 1839, and became a well-known journalist in Sydney. A member of the colonial parliament in 1854, his early career was interrupted by the financial difficulties that troubled him for most of his life. He was five times Premier of New South Wales between 1872 and 1891. During his last ministry, he displayed a new interest in **federation**, his speech at Tenterfield (Oct 1889) reviving the question and leading to the Australasian Federation Conference (1890) and the National Australasian Convention in 1891 in which he played a leading role. He was knighted in 1877.

Parks, Rosa Lee (1913–) US civil rights protester. Her action as a black woman who refused to give up her seat to a white man on a bus in Montgomery, Alabama, led in 1955 to the Montgomery bus boycott by the black community. The boycott led to the Supreme Court decision in 1956 that declared bus segregation unconstitutional. Parks became an inspiration to other blacks and a symbol of the nonviolent protest advocated by the **civil rights movement**.

parlamentarismo A political term used in Brazil, which denotes a belief that presidential power should be checked by an executive directly responsible to the lower house of Congress. Since such an executive functioned under the imperial constitution and opponents of Floriano **Peixoto** espoused this ideal, it has largely been seen as conservative. Certainly, politicians from Rio Grande do Sul and Minas Gerais, such as Raul Pilla and Afonso Arinos de Melo Franco, have repeatedly this sort of viewpoint, especially during the constitutional crisis of the 1960s and the redemocratization of the late 1980s. On the other hand, pragmatists like Tancredo **Neves** have called for a parliamentary regime as a way of checking chief executives (such as **Goulart** or **Sarney (Costa)**) and bringing about a **conciliação** between the army and civilian politicians. The chaotic experience of 1961–3 indicated to many that political parties lacked the discipline to implement such a system and Sarney managed to prevent the **PMDB** leadership and the more conservative PSD from imposing it in 1987–8.

Parlement The French court of law in **ancien régime** France, originally a single institution, the *Parlement* of Paris, which developed from the medieval king's Court or *curia regis*, and subsequently assumed both political and judicial functions. Between the 14c and 17c a network of provincial Parlements emerged, but all were abolished in 1790. In the 18c (especially 1763–89) the Parlements assumed the role of opposition to the monarchy, and as a result were abolished by Maupeou in 1771. Their restoration on the accession of

Louis XVI in 1774 is often seen as a fatal mistake on the part of the monarchy.

Parnell, Charles Stewart (1846–91) Irish politician. He studied at Cambridge, and in 1875 became an MP, supporting **Home Rule**, and gaining great popularity in Ireland by his audacity in the use of obstructive parliamentary tactics. In 1878 he was elected President of the Irish National Land League, and in 1886 allied with the Liberals in support of **Gladstone**'s **Home Rule** Bill. He remained an influential figure until 1890, when he was cited as co-respondent in a divorce case, and was forced to retire as leader of the Irish nationalists. ▷ **Liberal Party** (UK)

Parr, Catherine (1512–48) Queen of England (1543/7). The daughter of Sir Thomas Parr of Kendal, she married first Edward Borough, then Lord Latimer, before becoming Queen of England (1543), as the sixth wife of **Henry VIII**. A learned, tolerant and tactful woman, she persuaded Henry to restore the succession to his daughters, and showed her stepchildren much kindness. Very soon after Henry's death (1547), she married a former suitor, Lord Thomas Seymour of Sudeley, and died in childbirth the following year.

Parri, Ferruccio (1890–1982) Italian politician. Imprisoned for helping Fillipo **Turati** to escape from fascist Italy, he was one of the founders of the **Party of Action**. Briefly Prime Minister in 1945, he remained a constant champion of left-wing cooperation and solidarity throughout the 1950s and 1960s.

Partai Komunis Indonesia (PKI) The Indonesian Communist Party. The mid-1910s saw the establishment of a small social-democratic movement in the Netherlands East Indies, entirely Dutch in its membership. By the beginning of the 1920s, the movement had evolved into a communist organization and the membership had become predominantly Indonesian. It took the name 'Partai Komunis Indonesia' in 1924. In 1926–7 the PKI launched an ill-planned rebellion against the Dutch, and was fiercely crushed, re-emerging as a major political force in 1945, as the Indonesian rebellion against the post-war return of the Dutch got underway. In 1948 elements within the PKI launched a rebellion at Madiun against the republican government. This rebellion was also quelled, leaving the PKI open to the charge that it had threatened the revolution. The PKI rose again in the late 1950s and early

1960s, developing as a very powerful political force in **Sukarno**'s 'Guided Democracy'. But its power was broken in 1965–6 when, in the aftermath of an attempted coup, hundreds of thousands of PKI members and sympathizers were slaughtered.

Parthenopean Republic The short-lived satellite republic established in Naples by an uprising assisted by the French revolutionary armies under the control of General Championnet. The republic was brought down by the **Sanfedisti** of Cardinal **Ruffo**. ▷ **Ferdinand I; Maria Carolina**

Parthians The inheritors of the eastern territories of the **Seleucids**, from the 3c BC ruling an empire that stretched from the Euphrates to the Indus. Rome's main rivals for power in the east, they resisted conquest by her in the decaded 60–50BC, but failed in their turn to take over her eastern provinces. In the end, both had to settle for uneasy co-existence.

Parti National Canadian political party. Originally formed in 1871 by young liberals in Quebec who wished to assert their devotion to the Church, it was revived as an alliance of Liberals and rebel Conservatives who deeply resented the execution of Louis **Riel**. Under Honoré **Mercier**'s leadership, the party managed to oust Quebec's Conservative government in 1886, but scandal brought an early end to its administration in 1891.

Parti Québecois Canadian political party. Formed by **Lévesque** after the **Liberal Party** under **Lesage** was defeated in 1966, essentially for refusing to be more nationalistic. The party members (or *Péquistes*) gained support from all classes and from organized labour as well as from the business community. The major aim of the party has been to attain sovereignty-association for Quebec, that is parity of status with the federal government. The pressure for this, however, has had to be balanced against the wish of the majority of Québecois to remain within Canada. As a result, the parliamentary party lost the support of its more radical *indépendentistes* in 1984.

Party Cadres (post-1920) Highly trained, dedicated communist or communist-model party functionaries whose task was to win and maintain support for policies decided from above and to ensure absolute party loyalty. **Stalin** developed the idea during his rise to power in the 1920s and was fond of saying

712

that 'cadres decide everything'. They became somewhat less important in the more sophisticated society of the 1970s and 1980s.

Party Congress (post-1898) The supreme policy-making body of Soviet and other communist-model parties. The first to meet was that of the All-Russian Social Democratic Party in Minsk in 1898. The second was in Brussels and London in 1903 and witnessed the split between the **Bolsheviks** and the **Mensheviks**. At the seventh in 1918 the party changed its name to Communist Party. From then until the 16th in 1930 Soviet Party Congresses saw genuine and often fierce debates. **Stalin** summoned only three between 1934 and 1952, using them to rubber-stamp his policies. Nikita **Khrushchev** used the 20th in 1956 to attack the dead Stalin and begin a very slow process of reform; but Leonid **Brezhnev** again made them dull adulatory performances. Mikhail **Gorbachev** used the 27th in 1986 to launch his more rapid reform programme. The 29th, scheduled for the autumn of 1991 and intended to radicalize the Soviet party, never met. The party had already been abolished following the failed **August Coup**. The experience of most East European communist-model parties was similar.

Party of Action (*Partito d'Azione*) The underground Italian anti-fascist movement founded in July 1942, formed of a broad coalition of left-wing liberals, republicans and radicals, most of whom came from the educated and professional classes. The *Azionisti* remained outside both the 'United Freedom Front' established by **Bonomi** and its successor, the **Committee of National Liberation**. They were, however, actively involved in the creation of local CLNs and fiercely supported the **Committee for the Liberation of Upper Italy**: in Nov 1944 they published an open letter to other anti-fascist parties urging the strengthening of both as instruments of popular democracy. The Action Party played a key role in the anti-German risings in the north of Italy in Apr 1944, but was too radical and idealistic to win substantial electoral support after the end of the war. Among the most prominent Azionisti was Ferruccio **Parri**.

Party of Labour (*Partij van de Arbeid*, PvdA) Dutch political party, founded in 1946 to replace the Social Democratic Workers Party (*Sociaal-Democratische Arbeiders Partij*, SDAP), founded in 1894 in Amsterdam. The SDAP was originally a Marxist socialist party, although there were always debates between Marxists and revisionists. In 1918 the Marxists, led by P J **Troelstra**, launched an abortive coup attempt. Thereafter, the labour unions gained a greater role in the party; in the 1930s the Dutch socialists fully embraced the Plan Socialism of Hendrik de **Man**. In 1939 the socialists first joined the government. After **World War II**, in 1946, in an attempt to create a broad left party, the PvdA was formed to replace the SDAP, and indeed a number of liberals and confessionals joined for a short time; however in the long run there was little change. The PvdA, as the second most popular party, joined the Catholics (the largest) in a long spell of coalitions after the war (1945–58); after another stint of government (1965–6), the party underwent considerable radicalization, with the emergence of a New Left movement. In 1973 the socialists again formed a government with the confessionals, but it fell because of internal strife in 1977; in the ensuing election Labour increased its vote, but was unable to find any coalition partners. It spent the 1980s out of office, but returned to power in 1989 (again with the confessionals), by then reformed along social-democratic lines.

pasdaran A name applied since 1979 to the revolutionary guards of the Islamic Republic of Iran. ▷ **Iranian Revolution**

Pašić, Nikola (c.1846–1926) Serbian politician. Condemned to death in 1883 for his part in the plot against King Milan, he survived on the accession of King Peter to be Prime Minister of Serbia (five times, from 1891) and later of Yugoslavia (1921–4 and 1924–6), which he helped to found.

Paskevich, Ivan Feodorovich (1782–1856) Russian general. He served against the French in 1805, and against the Turks, and took a prominent part in the campaign of 1812. In 1827, conquering Persian Armenia and taking Yerevan, he was made Count of Yerevan; in 1828–9 he made two campaigns against the Turks in Asia, taking Kars and Erzerum. In 1831 he suppressed the rising in Poland, and was made Prince of Warsaw. Under his governorship, Poland was incorporated with Russia (1832). In 1848, sent to the support of Austria, he defeated the insurgent Hungarians. In 1854 he commanded the Russian army on the Danube, was wounded at Silistria and retired to Warsaw, where he later died. A loyal imperial servant and trusted by **Nicholas I**, he was typical of those who helped to expand Russia territorially and to suppress it politically.

PASOK (*Panellinion Socialistikou Kinema*, 'Panhellenic Socialist Movement') Established in 1974 under the leadership of Andreas **Papandreou**, its original programme was based on socialization, decentralization and worker self-management. In foreign policy it advocates neutrality: it opposed Greece's entry into the EEC (1979); it remains hostile to **NATO**; and is opposed to the establishment of US military bases in Greece.

Passarowitz, Treaty of (1718) The treaty signed at Požarevac in modern Serbia which established peace after the Austro-Turkish and Venetian-Turkish wars (1716–18). Venice surrendered the Morea to the Ottomans, while the Habsburg Emperor gained Belgrade and parts of liberated Serbia, Oltenia and the Banat of **Temesvár**. The subjects of the Emperor also gained favourable terms for trade within the **Ottoman Empire**.

Passau, Treaty of (1552) The treaty forced upon Emperor **Charles V** by the rebellion of **Maurice**, Elector of Saxony. Charles V had to acknowledge the position of Lutheranism in the Holy Roman Empire. It marked the effective failure of his plan to reintroduce Catholicism to the empire by force of arms.

Passchendaele, Battle of (31 July–10 Nov 1917) The third battle of Ypres during **World War I**; a British offensive which was continued despite no hope of a breakthrough to the Belgian ports, the original objective. It was notable for appallingly muddy conditions, minimal gains, and British casualties of at least 300 000. In the final action, Canadians captured the village of Passchendaele, six miles north-east of Ypres.

Pasternak, Boris Leonidovich (1890–1960) Russian poet, translator and novelist. Before and after the 1917 **Russian Revolution** he established his reputation as a poet. It was because of political pressure during the **Stalin** years that he became the official translator into Russian of several major authors, such as Shakespeare, Verlaine, and Goethe. His major work, *Dr Zhivago* (completed in 1956), caused a political furore and was banned in the USSR, but was an international success after its publication in Italy in 1957. Expelled by the Soviet Writers' Union, he was compelled to refuse the Nobel Prize for Literature in 1958. *Dr Zhivago* was finally published in the USSR in 1988, a clear indication of how Mikhail **Gorbachev** had changed official attitudes.

Pasvanoglu, Osman Pasha (1758–1807) Balkan rebel leader. He was one of the most important rebel bandit leaders in the Balkans during the late 18c. In 1795 he declared himself and his lands independent from the Sultan. From his base at Vidin on the Danube he waged a constant rebellion against the Ottoman Porte and gained control of extensive territories in the area of modern Bulgaria and Romania.

Pataliputra On the site of modern-day Patna, the grand **Mauryan** capital of Pataliputra was the capital of most north Indian dynasties until the time of **Harsha** in the 7c. It was founded as a river port early in the 5c BC by Ajatashatru, whose successor transferred his seat of government there from the earlier capital of Rajagriha in the hills. It became a major metropolis under the first Mauryan emperor, Chandragupta. During **Ashoka**'s reign the meeting of the Third Buddhist Council took place at Pataliputra (250BC). The Mauryans built a Royal highway from Taxila to Pataliputra, a road which was rebuilt throughout the centuries and which today survives as the Grand Trunk road. Pataliputra was connected by road with Tamluk in the Ganges delta, the chief port for Burma, the east coast of India, and Ceylon. For centuries, Pataliputra remained a centre of art and culture.

Patel, Vallabhbhai Jhaverbhai ('Sardar') (1875–1950) Indian politician and lawyer. A Gujarati peasant leader, described as M K **Gandhi**'s right-hand man, he was Deputy Prime Minister and the first Minister of Home Affairs in independent India. By background a staunch Hindu, conservative and broadly identified with the interests of the business community, he was a lawyer by training and began his political career after being elected as a municipal councillor in Ahmadabad (1917). Soon after, he joined the Gujarat Sabha, a political body of great assistance to M K **Gandhi** during his political campaigns. Patel distinguished himself during India's independence struggle by his leading role in the Kheda peasants' **Satyagraha** (1918) and the Bardoli Satyagraha (1928), both launched in opposition to the colonial government's attempts to raise the land tax on peasant farmers. Following the successful conclusion of these campaigns, he

was given the honorific title, Sardar ('Leader') by Gandhi. He joined the Salt Satyagraha of 1930, the individual **civil disobedience** movement of 1940–1 and the **Quit India Movement** of 1942, following each of which he spent long periods in prison. A great party organizer, he was also, along with Jawaharlal **Nehru**, a key negotiator on behalf of the **Indian National Congress** during the talks leading to the transfer of power from the British in 1947. As Deputy Prime Minister of Independent India, Patel assumed responsibility for the Indian States as well as Home Affairs and Information and Broadcasting, and was responsible for persuading, or coercing, the nominally independent Indian Princely States into joining the Indian Union soon after independence. In tackling these and many other problems of post-Partition India, he acted with a thoroughness and ruthless efficiency that has caused him to be greatly admired, both as a statesman and politician, by subsequent generations.

Pathet Lao Laotian nationalist movement (literally, 'Land of Lao') founded in 1950. In alliance with the **Viet Minh** of North Vietnam, it employed armed resistance to French rule in Indochina. After the country's civil war, the movement (officially renamed the Lao People's Liberation Army in Oct 1965), took part in the coalition government set up in 1974; early the following year it assumed effective control of the country. In Dec 1975 it abolished the monarchy in Vientiane and made its leader, Prince **Souphanouvong**, President of the newly proclaimed Lao People's Democratic Republic.

Patiño, José (1667–1736) Spanish politician. Chief Minister of Spain in 1726–36, he rose to prominence during the War of the **Spanish Succession**. In 1726 he was Minister of the Navy and Finance, and subsequently took charge of War (1730) and Foreign Affairs (1733), an area he had in practice controlled for some time. The first notable minister of the Bourbon monarchy in Spain, Patiño's efforts were centred on three fields: the armed forces, the economy and foreign policy. His lasting achievement was the creation of the Spanish navy. He pursued the interests of the royal family in Italy, particularly the rights of Elizabeth Farnese's son, Don Carlos, to the Duchy of Parma (1731). Thanks to the first Family Pact (1733), which ensured agreement between the Bourbon states of France and Spain against Austria, Spanish forces ensured the succession (1734) of Carlos to the Kingdom of Naples. Spain was obliged, however, to cede Parma to Austria, a failure which was severely criticized in Madrid, where a pamphlet war was unleashed against the minister and embittered his last years. ▷ **Bourbon, House of**

Patriarchate of Moscow, Establishment of (1589)

The establishment of the Patriarchate was one of the most significant achievements of **Boris Godunov**, acting as regent for the young Tsar Theodore. He obtained the consent of Jeremiah the Patriarch of Constantinople, and all the Eastern Patriarchs in effect to upgrade the Russian Orthodox Church and to make it the symbol and support of Moscow and tsarism. This not only contributed in due course to ending the **Time of Troubles**; it was the base upon which the **Romanov Dynasty** duly built.

Patriotic Front (PF)

A Zimbabwean movement formed by the merging of the Zimbabwe African National Union (**ZANU**), led by Robert Mugabe, and the Zimbabwe African People's Union (**ZAPU**), led by Joshua Nkomo, in 1976. It was intended to unite the major exiled nationalist movements in a concerted opposition, both political and military, to Ian **Smith**'s white minority regime. In the elections held under the Lancaster House Agreement in 1980 the PF won an overwhelming victory. In the post-independence period, however, the Front broke up when Nkomo, whose principal power base was among the Ndebele people in Matabeleland, and Mugabe, who represented the majority Shona people, became estranged. Later they were reconciled as moves were made to create a one-party state.

Patriot Movement

A late 18c Dutch political movement, which called for a role for the wealthy middle classes in politics, until then dominated by patricians and aristocrats. Reliant on rationalism and other Enlightenment ideologies, the Patriots can be seen as the Dutch version of the French revolutionaries, and as the precursors of Dutch liberals. They took the name 'Patriot' from their insistence that policy should benefit the entire nation (*patria*), rather than just the élite classes. Their efforts were directed against the government of the **Stadholder**; one of the main activists was J D van der **Capellen tot den Poll**. In the confusion after the fourth of the **Anglo-Dutch Wars** (1780–4), the Patriots gained a measure of political power in certain regions; in 1787 **William V** was restored to power with Prussian military help. The Patriots fled to France, returned

with the French revolutionary troops in 1795, and played a significant role in several of the governments of the French period (1795–1814), notably the **Batavian Republic**.

Patrons of Husbandry ▷ Granger Movement

Patton, George (Smith) (1885–1945)

US general. Known as 'Old Blood and Guts', Patton trained at the US Military Academy at West Point and became one of the most daring and flamboyant US combat commanders in **World War II**. An excellent strategist and proponent of mobile tank warfare, he played a key role in the Allied invasion of North Africa (1942–3), led the US 7th Army in its assault on Sicily (1943), commanded the 3rd Army in the invasion of France, and contained the German counter-offensive in the Ardennes (1944). He was fatally injured in a motor accident near Mannheim, and died at Heidelberg. ▷ **Bulge, Battle of the; Normandy Campaign**

Pauker, Ana (1893–1960)

Romanian politician. The daughter of a Moldavian rabbi, she joined the Social Democrat Party in 1915 and took part in revolutionary movements in Romania (1917–18). She married Marcel Pauker (1920) and with him joined the Communist Party, becoming a member of the Central Committee in 1922. She was arrested in 1925, but escaped to the USSR where she worked for **Comintern**. She returned to Romania in 1934 and was again arrested. A 'Moscow communist' who spent **World War II** in the USSR, she returned home after the overthrow of Ion **Antonescu** (Sep 1944). Summoned to Moscow with **Gheorgiu-Dej** (Jan 1945), she was instructed by **Stalin** to establish a government under the control of the National Democratic Front, the communist front in Romania. She entered the Foreign Ministry in 1947 and took part in organizing the collectivization of all land. With Stalin's consent, she was relieved of her offices in 1952.

Paul I (1754–1801)

Emperor of Russia (1796/1801). He was the second son of **Peter III** and **Catherine II, 'the Great'**. A man of highly unstable temperament, he reversed many of his mother's policies (and, in time, many of his own), thereby arousing hostility from the nobility and army. His foreign policy, first attacking and then supporting France, won him considerable military successes but led to Russia's isolation. His officers conspired against him, and he was assassinated in St Petersburg, being succeeded by his son, **Alexander I**.

Paul I (1901–64) King of Greece (1947/64). In 1922 he served with the Greek Navy against the Turks; but in 1924, when a republic was proclaimed, went into exile. In 1935 he returned to Greece as Crown Prince. In **World War II** he served with the Greek general staff in the Albanian campaign, and was in exile in London (1941–6). His reign covered the latter half of the **Greek Civil War** and its difficult aftermath; during the early 1960s his personal role, and that of his wife Queen Frederika, became sources of bitter political controversy.

Paul III (Alessandro Farnese) (1468–1549) Italian Pope (1534/49). The first of the popes of the Counter-Reformation, in 1538 he issued the bull of excommunication and deposition against **Henry VIII** of England, and also the bull instituting the Order of the Jesuits in 1540. He also summoned the Council of **Trent** (1545).

Paul IV (Giampietro Carafa) (1476–1559) Italian Pope (1555/9). As a bishop, he showed rigorous opposition to heresy and was instrumental in the re-establishment of the **Inquisition** in Rome and Italy. As Pope, he sought to enforce discipline among the clergy, established censorship and a full *Index* of forbidden books. His Neapolitan origins helped to make him ferocious in his hatred of things Spanish. He was an opponent of the Jesuits, and declared war on Emperor **Charles V** in 1555 on the grounds that the Emperor could not abdicate his title without papal permission. Defensive of papal authority, he was also opposed to a reconvening of the Council of **Trent**.

Paul V (Camillo Borghese) (1552–1621) Italian Pope (1605/21). He became nuncio in Spain and cardinal prior to his election as pope. In 1606 he issued a decree of excommunication against the Doge and Senate of Venice, and placed the republic under Interdict. The crisis, and the fierce anti-papal propaganda of the Venetian Paolo Sarpi, prompted the English ambassador to suggest that Venice might become a Protestant state, but it ended in a messy compromise.

Paul Karageorgević (1893–1976) Prince Regent of Yugoslavia (1934/41). The son of Arsen and brother of King **Peter I Karageorgević**, he became regent for King **Peter II** of

Yugoslavia after the assassination of the latter's father, King **Alexander I**. Although he upheld the constitution of the previous dictatorial regime, his regency marked the beginning of a more relaxed period in the government of Yugoslavia. He worked closely with **Stojadinović** and his right-wing party, the Yugoslav Radical Union (1935–9), and with **Cvetković** and **Maček** played a leading role in bringing about the **Sporazum** (1939). In foreign affairs he developed relations with Germany and Italy so that at the outbreak of **World War II** Yugoslavia, although officially neutral, was in the Axis camp. After signing the Tripartite Pact with **Hitler** and Benito **Mussolini**, the regency was overthrown in a coup led by General Dušan Simović (Mar 1941). He left Yugoslavia for Kenya and later settled in Paris.

Paul, Alice (1885–1977) US feminist. Involved with the British suffragette movement while living in England, on her return to the USA (1912) she became the leader of the **National American Woman Suffrage Association** (NAWSA) congressional committee and organized a march of several thousand women in Washington (1913). Although her tactics generated much publicity, they proved too militant for most members of NAWSA and she left the organization to found the National Women's Party. After the Nineteenth Amendment (1920) gave women the right to vote, she turned her efforts to working for other women's rights. ▷ **Pankhurst, Emmeline; suffragettes**

Paullus, Lucius Aemilius (d.216BC) Roman general and politician. The father of Lucius Aemilius **Paullus Macedonicus**, he is chiefly remembered for his disastrous generalship at the Battle of **Cannae** (216BC), where the Roman army, though numerically superior, was heavily defeated by **Hannibal** and the Carthaginians, and suffered one of its worst defeats ever. Paullus himself, consul at the time, died on the field of battle.

Paullus Macedonicus, Lucius Aemilius (d.160BC) Roman general and politician. The son of Lucius Aemilius **Paullus**, he was famous primarily for his defeat of Perseus, King of Macedon, at the Battle of Pydna (168BC) and his suppression of the Macedonian monarchy, whence his title 'Macedonicus'. With Perseus' book collection, which fell to him as booty, he created the first private library at Rome. His second son, whom he gave in adoption to P Scipio, was the notorious destroyer of Carthage and Numantia, **Scipio Aemilianus**.

Paulus, Friedrich (1890–1957) German field marshal and tank specialist. He capitulated to the Soviets with the remnants of his army at the siege of Stalingrad in 1943. Released from captivity in 1953, he became a lecturer on military affairs under the East German government. ▷ **Stalingrad, Battle of; World War II**

Pausanias (d.c.470BC) Spartan soldier and Regent, nephew of **Leonidas**. He commanded the Greek forces at Plataea (479BC), where the Persians were routed. Capturing the Cyprian cities and Byzantium (478BC), he negotiated with **Xerxes** in the hope of becoming ruler under him of all Greece, and was twice recalled for treachery. He tried to stir up the **helots**, was betrayed, and fled to a temple of Athena on the Spartan acropolis, where he was walled up and only taken out when dying of hunger (c.470BC).

Pavel, Josef (1908–73) Czechoslovak soldier, politician and reformer. Joining the Communist Party in the depression in 1929, he studied with the **Comintern** in Moscow in 1935–7, fought in the **Spanish Civil War** in 1937–8 and in the West in 1939–45. He then rose to be commander of the people's militia that gave their backing to the **February Revolution** (1948) and acted as deputy to the Minister of the Interior until his arrest (1950). Because of his service in the West he was viewed as suspect by the puppets who did **Stalin**'s dirty work in Prague and was sentenced to 25 years in prison. Released in 1955, he did little until he became Minister of the Interior during the **Prague Spring**. His attempt to make the political police reponsible won him enemies and soon after the Soviet invasion he was dismissed. Experiences such as his were one of the ingredients that made for the revulsion against **communism** expressed in Europe in 1989.

Pavelić, Ante (1889–1959) Croatian fascist leader. A member of the extreme nationalist wing of the Croatian Party of (State) Right established by **Starčević**, he left Yugoslavia for Italy where, with Benito **Mussolini**'s support, he organized the **Ustaša**, the Croatian fascist movement. Chosen by Mussolini to run the puppet government of the Independent State of **Croatia** (1941–5), he instituted a reign of terror. At the end of the war, he escaped with the retreating German Army and settled in Argentina.

Pavia, Battle of (1525) A Habsburg victory over French forces laying siege to Pavia during the **Italian Wars**. The assailants were commanded by **Francis I** of France, taken prisoner after an abortive French cavalry attack on the garrison. The defeat temporarily checked the French threat in Italy, which had seen them take Milan in 1524. ▷ **Habsburg Dynasty**

Paz Estenssoro, Víctor (1907–) Bolivian revolutionary and politician. He was the founder of the left-wing *Movimiento Nacionalista Revolucionario* (MNR, National Revolutionary Movement) in 1941, going on to become its principal leader. Following the 1952 revolution, he served as President (1952–6) and held office again from 1960 to 1964, when he was ousted by a military coup. He went into exile in Peru, returning to Bolivia in 1971 as an adviser to the government of President Hugo Banzer Suárez. He failed to win election in 1979, but in 1985, after no candidate managed to achieve a majority, Congress elected him President. His main achievement in office (1985–9) was to reduce the raging inflation which had crippled Bolivia's economy.

Pazmany, Peter, Cardinal Archbishop (1570–1637) Hungarian religious leader. Born into a Protestant family, he became a Jesuit and was elevated to the archbishopric of Esztergom in 1616. He helped convert many of his fellow nobles, and during the **Thirty Years War** he steadily supported the Austrian Habsburg cause in Europe. His religious writings were very influential, as was the university he founded at Nagyszombal, north-west of Estergom, in 1635. ▷ **Habsburg Dynasty**

PCE (*Partido Comunista Español*, 'Spanish Communist Party') Established in 1920, the PCE was of little significance in the 1920s. Under the Second Republic of 1931–6 it played a minor role in the Asturias rising of Oct 1934 and, as part of the Popular Front coalition, won a total of 16 parliamentary seats in the Feb 1936 general election. However, once the **Spanish Civil War** broke out, the PCE soon became the dominant force in the Republic. This was because the USSR, in the absence of support from Britain and France, was the Republic's principal backer. The Communists opposed all other tendencies within the Republican camp, partly in order to meet the needs of **Stalin**'s foreign policy, and partly because of its authoritarian nature. This policy culminated in the May Days of 1937 when the **CNT** and **POUM** were defeated by the Communists. Under the **Franco** dictatorship (1939–75) the PCE emerged as the leading opposition force, due in great measure to the **CCOO** (*Comisiones Obreras*). After Franco, the party failed to capitalize on its widespread support during the last years of the regime, despite having evolved from neo-Stalinism to, in 1978, Eurocommunism. Having won 23 seats in the 1979 election, it was reduced to a mere four in 1982. The PCE subsequently split into various factions, the official party forming the backbone of the *Izquierda Unida* (United Left) coalition. In the general election of 1986 the PCE won seven seats. ▷ **Republic, Second** (Spain)

PCI (*Partito Communista Italiano*, 'Italian Community Party') Established in 1921 after the split in socialist ranks which followed the decision of the majority to join the Third International, the party was driven underground during the fascist regime. However, at the end of **World War II** it emerged as the most active force in the resistance, dominating the partisan struggle against the Germans and the Republic of **Salò**. Under the leadership of **Togliatti**, it initially sought to work together with the other anti-fascist parties but found itself increasingly at loggerheads with the **Christian Democrat Party**. It remained, however, consistently the second-biggest party in parliament, reaching its pinnacle under the leadership of **Berlinguer** during the 1970s. In the course of the 1980s it declined, losing direction completely with the collapse of Eastern European **communism** after 1989. It has since changed its name to *Partito Democratico della Sinistra*, with a more militant splinter group calling itself *Rifondazione Communista*. Both performed poorly in the Apr 1992 elections.

PDS (*Partido Democrático Social*) The heir to a long tradition of Brazilian conservatism, the immediate progenitor of this party was the UDN (*União Democrático Nacional*) formed in 1945 to challenge the power of Getúlio **Vargas**, and it is arguably the descendant of the Spanish Empire's Liberal Party (1831–89). The UDN had conspired with the army to break the natural majority achieved by the PDS and PTB (*Partido Trabalhista Brasileiro*), which were both Vargas's creations, in the 1950s; it supported **Castelo Branco** in 1964 and in 1965 united with a conservative PDS faction to form the ARENA (*Aliança Renovadora Nacional*) Party. The Figueiredo government's attempt

(1979–85) to reshuffle political groupings to divide the opposition created the PDS, in turn, as the successor to ARENA. The PDS became notorious as the personal vehicle for wealthy beneficiaries of the military regime, such as Paulo Salim Maluf, whose bid for the presidency divided the party in 1985, forcing a major faction to form the PFL (*Partido do Frente Liberal*). Ostracized during the mid-1980s, the PDS forms part of the coalition upon which President Collor has based his government.

Peace Constitution (1947) The name given to the post-**World War II** Japanese constitution that replaced the authoritarian **Meiji Constitution** (1889). Based on the draft imposed (Feb 1946) on the Japanese cabinet by US occupation authorities, the constitution attributed sovereignty to the people rather than the Emperor, who was now to be considered merely as a symbol of state. (In Jan 1946 **Hirohito** had renounced his divinity.) In contrast to the 1889 Constitution, an elected bicameral Diet, to which cabinets were collectively responsible, was to be the sole law-making organ of the state; furthermore, the lower house (House of Representatives) clearly had precedence over the upper house (House of Councillors) since it could override any veto by the upper house by repassing a disputed bill by a two-thirds majority. Prime ministers were to be chosen by the Diet (and hence the majority party), thus enshrining the principle of party government so fiercely opposed by governing elites in the pre-war period, while most cabinet ministers had to be both civilian and members of the Diet. The constitution also provided for an extensive guarantee of civil rights and freedoms (including women's suffrage), which could not be limited by law. The most controversial aspect of the constitution was Article 9 (Peace Clause), which renounced war as a sovereign right of the nation and provided for permanent disarmament. Subsequent interpretations of this article, however, led to the creation of the Self-Defence Forces, an army in all but name to be used solely for defence of the homeland. The constitution could be amended by a two-thirds majority of both houses followed by approval from a majority of voters. It was formally promulgated by Emperor Hirohito on 3 Nov 1946 and came into effect on 3 May 1947. The constitution has never been amended.

Peace Corps A corp of volunteers created during the Kennedy Administration in 1961

to assist and educate people in developing countries. By 1966, volunteers numbered more than 10 000 in 52 countries. The programme concentrates on education, health, agriculture, and public works and emphasizes self-sufficiency. ▷ **Kennedy, John F**

Peace Preservation Laws The repressive legislation in pre-**World War II** Japan that sought to clamp down on all strands of dissident thought. The first Peace Preservation Law was passed in 1887 to restrict the activities of the **Freedom and People's Rights Movement**, and led to the arrest and internal exile of many activists calling for the election of a national assembly. The Peace Preservation Law of 1925 outlawed any association calling for an alteration of the **Kokutai** ('national essence') or denying the system of private property. Although the law was applied to both rightists and leftists, it was primarily used to detain suspected communists, of whom 66 000 were arrested between 1928 and 1941. The law was repealed in Oct 1945.

Pearl Harbor US naval base on the island of Oahu, Hawaii. On 7 Dec 1941, the bombing of the base by the Japanese, before any declaration of war, brought the USA into **World War II**. Nineteen US ships were sunk or disabled in the surprise attack, and over 2 000 lives were lost.

Pearse, Patrick (Pádraic) Henry (1879–1916) Irish writer, educationist, and nationalist. A barrister, he was a leader of the Gaelic League, and editor of its journal. Having commanded the insurgents in the **Easter Rising** (1916), he was proclaimed President of the Provisional Government. After the revolt had been quelled, he was court-martialled and shot, along with his brother, William.

Pearson, Lester Bowles (1897–1972) Canadian politician. Educated in Toronto and at Oxford, he was leader of the Canadian delegation to the **UN**, becoming President of the General Assembly in 1952–3. Secretary of State for External Affairs (1948–57), his efforts to resolve the Suez Crisis were rewarded with the Nobel peace prize in 1957. As prime minister (1963–8), he introduced a comprehensive pension plan, socialized medicine and sought solutions to the growing separatist feeling in Quebec. ▷ **Bilingualism and Biculturalism, Royal Commission on**

Peasants Land Bank (1883) The Russian government bank intended to help free peasants or communes to buy land in order to produce a peasantry loyal to the existing order. It was established by the Minister of Finance, Nikolai **Bunge** and was, comparatively speaking, so successful during its first two years that a Nobles Land Bank also had to be instituted, with a lower rate of interest, to prevent impoverished aristocrats losing too much of their land. The Peasants Bank was even more successful after the Russian **Revolution of 1905**, once the peasants were wholly free. It loaned almost five times as much in the following decade as in the previous.

Peasants Revolt (June 1381) An English popular rising, among townsmen as well as peasants, based in Essex, Kent, and London, with associated insurrections elsewhere. It was precipitated by the three oppressive poll taxes of 1377–81, the underlying causes being misgovernment, the desire for personal freedom, and an assortment of local grievances. It was quickly suppressed.

Peasants War (1524–5) Probably the largest peasant uprising in European history, raging through Germany, from the Rhineland to Pomerania. It sought to defend traditional agrarian rights against lords and princes, and appealed to notions of divine law fostered by the Lutheran Reformation. It was denounced by Luther, and brutally suppressed by the princes.

Peć, Patriarchate of The seat of the Serbian Orthodox Church was moved c.1345 from Žiča to Peć in modern **Kosovo**. It remained there after the Ottoman conquest of **Serbia** (1389) until Sultan Mustafa III abolished the Serbian Patriarchate (1766), at which point the Serbian Church fell under the control of the Greek **Phanariots**. The Sultan restored the autonomy of the Serbian Orthodox Church in 1830 when Serbia was established as an autonomous state. ▷ **Bulgarian Exarchate; Constantinople, Patriarchate of; Sava, St**

Pedro I (1798–1834) First Emperor of Brazil (1822/31). Born in Lisbon, he was the second son of John VI of Portugal. He fled to Brazil with his parents on Napoleon's invasion, and became Prince Regent there when his father returned to Portugal (1821). Liberal in outlook, he declared for Brazilian independence in 1822, and was crowned as Pedro I. His failure to hold Montevideo, Brazilian fears for his involvement in Portugal after the death of his father, and the army's defeat in the **Argentine-Brazilian War** (1825–8) all contributed to his abdication in favour of his son, **Pedro II**, on 7 Apr 1831. He withdrew to Portugal, having become Pedro IV of Portugal on the death of his father. He abdicated the Portuguese throne in favour of his daughter, **Maria II da Gloria**, and died in Lisbon.

Pedro II (1825–91) Emperor of Brazil (1831/89). The son of **Pedro I**, he came to the throne as a minor following his father's abdication, and assumed full power in 1840. His reign is generally divided into a period of both consolidation (1831–49), **conciliação** (1850–68) and decline (1868–89). By supporting, in turn, Liberal and Conservative governments (he presided over almost 40 cabinets during his reign), he exercised a moderating influence. Gradualist in the extreme, he manipulated the system of patronage to achieve the consolidation of the empire and to implement strategic reforms, including the emancipation of slaves. The two regencies of his daughter, Izabel, in 1871–2 and 1887–8 witnessed the passage of the first emancipation law and the abolition of slavery through parliament. In Nov 1889 he was toppled by a military coup against the reform cabinet of Ouro Preto, and went into exile, dying in Paris.

Pedro the Cruel (1334–69) King of Castile and Leon (1349/69). The attempts of both Pedro and his father, Alfonso XI, to assert strong monarchic government aroused resentment among the nobility, who found a leader in Pedro's illegitimate brother, Henry of Trastámara. A revolt in 1354 was suppressed and Henry fled to France, but returned in 1366 with French and Aragonese support. With the help of **Edward, the Black Prince**, Pedro defeated his rival at Najera (1367) but, after Edward's departure from Spain, Pedro was finally routed and killed by Henry at Montiel (1369).

Peel, Sir Robert (1788–1850) British politician. He became a Tory MP in 1809. He was made Secretary for Ireland (1812–18), where he displayed a strong anti-Catholic spirit, and was fiercely attacked by **O'Connell**, earning the nickname 'Orange Peel'. As Home Secretary (1822–7 and 1828–30), he carried through the **Catholic Emancipation** Act (1829) and reorganized the London police force ('Peelers' or 'Bobbies'). As Prime Minister (1834–5 and 1841–6), his second

ministry concentrated upon economic reforms, but his decision to phase out agricultural protection by repealing the **Corn Laws** (1846) split his party and precipitated his resignation. He remained in parliament as leader of the 'Peelites' (1846–50). ▷ **Tories; Whigs**

Peel Commission The report of this commission (issued 7 July 1937) is famous (or notorious) for being the first formal recommendation of the partition of Palestine into separate states, Arab and Jewish, with the retention by the British of a corridor to the Mediterranean. Serious rioting by the Arabs, directed against the Jews, had led Stanley **Baldwin**, the British Prime Minister, to appoint a royal commission to enquire into the working of the British mandate under the leadership of Earl Peel. Despite the commission's evident recognition that there was an intractable problem in Palestine (a situation which had been foreseen by Henry King and Charles Crane nearly two decades before) and their earnest endeavour to find a solution of some sort, the commission's recommendations found favour with only some Arabs and Zionists, and was rejected by the British House of Lords. ▷ **King–Crane Commission**

Peisistratos ▷ **Pisistratus**

Peixoto, Floriano Vieira (1839–95) Brazilian military leader. He was educated in the Escola Militar in Rio and fought in the War of the **Triple Alliance** (or Paraguayan War). As Adjutant-General, he refused to order troops against forces under **Deodoro da Fonseca** on 15 Nov 1889. A Liberal in politics, Peixoto was virtual Minister of War under the Republic, and promoted young radical officers (Jacobins) to power. As Vice-President (1891–3), he defeated both the federalist and naval revolts. Haunted by fears of the restoration of the monarchy and European intervention, his government was both antiforeign and highly arbitrary. He cultivated a sphinx-like cult among young military officers and urban society, which inspired attacks on subsequent regimes and still prevails.

Pei-yang Army ▷ **Beiyang Army**

Pelham, Henry (c.1695–1754) British politician. He became a Whig MP in 1717 and regularly supported **Walpole** and **Townshend**, his relatives by marriage. His political advance was steady; he became Lord of the Treasury (1721–4), Secretary for War (1724–30) and Paymaster-General (1730–42). After Walpole's fall, he refused to serve under Wilmington, but replaced him as First Lord of Treasury in Aug 1743, a post he held until his death, acting also as Chancellor of the Exchequer. He admitted several **Tories** to his ministry (1744), which became colloquially known as the 'Broad Bottom', and defeated a challenge to his leadership by Carteret and the Prince of Wales (1746). His ministry presided over the peace negotiations ending the War of the **Austrian Succession** (1748). Buttressed by a comfortable parliamentary majority largely achieved through deployment of patronage considered by his opponents as corrupt, Pelham provided **George II** with secure, if unimaginative, government until his death in London while still in office. ▷ **Seven Years War**

Pelham, Thomas Pelham-Holles, 1st Duke of Newcastle (1693–1768) English politician. He became Earl of Clare in 1714 and Duke of Newcastle in 1715. A Whig and a supporter of **Walpole**, in 1724 he became Secretary of State, and held the office for 30 years. He succeeded his brother, Henry **Pelham** as Premier (1754–6), and was extremely influential during the reigns of **George I** and **II**. In 1757 he was in coalition with **Pitt** 'the Elder' during the **Seven Years War**, but resigned in 1762 after hostility from the new King, **George III**. ▷ **Whigs**

Pelikan, Jiri (1923–) Czechoslovak student politician and media reformer. An underground member of the Communist Party in **World War II**, he was President of the Czechoslovak Students Union in 1948 and became President of the International Union of Students for the period 1953–63. He then switched to another political appointment as Director of Czechoslovak state television. In the course of the **Prague Spring** this brought him into the forefront of the reform movement, for the opening of television had an important impact within Czechoslovakia and abroad. But after the events of Aug 1968, he had to leave the country, much to the detriment of Czech broadcasting for some 20 years.

Pelloux, Luigi Girolamo (1839–1924) Italian general and politician. A patriot who took part in all the major wars for Italian unification, he was a deputy from 1880 and twice served as Minister of War (1891–3 and 1896–7); in 1898 he briefly became Prime Minister and Interior Minister following the

fall of **di Rudini**. He pursued a policy of harsh repression against the parties of the left, but a poor showing in the general elections of 1900 forced him to resign.

Pelopidas (c.410–364BC) Theban general and politician. Together with his friend, **Epaminondas**, he established the short-lived Theban hegemony over Greece in the decade 360–350BC. After playing a prominent part in the Theban victory over **Sparta** at the Battle of **Leuctra** (371BC), he subsequently operated mainly to the north of Greece in **Thessaly** and **Macedonia**. ▷ **Thebes**

Peloponnesian League The alliance formed in the late 6c BC under Spartan leadership consisting of most Peloponnesian states (except **Argos**), and others, notably **Corinth**. Although largely a vehicle for Spartan dominance abroad, it never fully developed into an empire as did the **Delian League** under Athenian leadership. It fought the **Peloponnesian War** against Athens and her allies (431–404BC). It was dissolved in 366BC following the collapse of Spartan power after the Battle of **Leuctra** (371BC). ▷ **Sparta**

Peloponnesian War (431–404BC) The war waged throughout the Greek world on land and sea between the Spartans and the Athenians and their respective allies. According to its historian, **Thucydides**, the underlying cause was Athenian imperialism and the fear this produced among the Spartans and their allies, especially **Corinth**. The initial Spartan strategy of annual invasions of Attica produced a stalemate; peace was concluded in 421BC. However, when Athens became embroiled in the expedition against Sicily (415–413BC), **Sparta** renewed the war, occupying Decelea in Attic territory and, with Persian money, built a fleet to challenge Athens' maritime supremacy. After the final defeat of the Athenian fleet at the Battle of **Aegospotami** (405BC) Athens was besieged and soon capitulated, and a Spartan-backed puppet regime, the '**Thirty Tyrants**', was installed. ▷ **Alcibiades; Lysander; Nicias; Pericles; Thucydides**

Peloponnesus The southern Balkan Peninsula joined to mainland Greece by a narrow isthmus at **Corinth**. Dominated in antiquity by **Sparta**, in 146BC it became the Roman senatorial province of Achaea. Invaded by the **Goths** (267), by Alaric I (395) and the Ostrogoths (549), it was settled by the Slavs and Avars in the 6c. Known as the Morea, it became a theme in Byzantium in 805. After the fall of Constantinople (1203) it was subject to barons from France, Flanders and Burgundy and to the Neapolitan House of Angevin (1318–83). It was held continuously by the Ottoman Turks from 1460 to 1828 except for an interlude of Venetian government (1699–1718), the Venetians having had trading interests there since the 11c. A centre of insurgence in the **Greek War of Independence**, in 1828 it became part of the Kingdom of Greece. Apart from Corinth, the main city was Nauplia, the capital of Ottoman Morea after 1540 and of the newly independent Kingdom of Greece until 1834. ▷ **Karlowitz, Treaty of; Othon; Passarowitz, Treaty of**

Pelshe, Arvid Yanovich (1899–1983) Latvian politician. He joined the **Bolsheviks** in 1915, participated in the Petrograd Soviet in 1917, and failed with others to establish **communism** in Latvia in 1919. He then drifted through various jobs until the USSR seized Latvia in 1941. From then on he rose within the Latvian Communist Party. By 1959 he was its First Secretary; in 1966 he was called to the **Politburo** in Moscow of which he was still a member when he died at the age of 84. He acquired a reputation as illiberal but corrupt, which did little to endear his fellow Latvians to communism.

PEMEX (*Petróleos Mexicanos*) One of the largest state-owned corporations in Latin America, and a virtual state within a state in Mexico, the oil company was created in 1938 by President Lázaro **Cárdenas**. He seized the assets of foreign (mainly British) multinationals as a result of the failure to implement the wage rates decreed by the 1917 Constitution's *junta de arbitraje y conciliación*, invoked by Cárdenas to rule on labour practices; the companies received compensation in Mexican bonds. PEMEX was charged with the management, regulation and production of oil found on Mexican soil. A logical outcome of the Criollo nationalism enshrined in the constitution, PEMEX was free from other ministries; only after the 1982 debt crisis was its autonomy curtailed.

Penal Laws Collectively, statutes passed in the 16–17c against the practice of Roman Catholicism in Britain and Ireland, when Catholic nations were perceived as a threat. They prevented Catholics from voting and holding public office. Fines and imprisonment were prescribed for participation in Catholic services, while officiating priests could be executed. The laws were repealed in

stages, from the late 18c, the last not until 1926. ▷ **Catholic Emancipation**

penal settlements Places of secondary punishment in Australia where convicts found guilty of serious offences were sent; also used for colonial criminals sentenced to **transportation**, and (after 1842) for British convicts transported for life. About 10 per cent of the 162 000 convicts transported to Australia spent some time in these settlements, which were mainly at Newcastle (1801–24), Port Macquarie (1821–30), Moreton Bay (1824–39), Macquarie Harbour (1822–33), Port Arthur (after 1830) and Norfolk Island (after 1825). Life in these settlements varied from hard to savage, with hard labour and frequent and severe floggings; the last three named had deservedly fearsome reputations.

Penda (c.575–655) King of Mercia (c.632/55). He established mastery over the English Midlands, and was frequently at war with the kings of **Northumbria**. His forces defeated and killed Edwin, King of Northumbria, at Hatfield, Yorkshire (633), and also Edwin's successor, Oswald, when he invaded Penda's territories (642). Penda was himself slain in battle near Leeds while campaigning against Oswald's successor, Oswiu. ▷ **Anglo-Saxons**

P'eng Chen ▷ **Peng Zhen**

Peng Dehuai (Peng Te-huai) (1898–1974) Chinese communist general. He fought in the **Sino-Japanese War** (1937–45), became second-in-command to **Zhu De**, and led the Chinese 'volunteer' forces in the **Korean War**.

P'eng P'ai ▷ **Peng Pai**

Peng Pai (P'eng P'ai) (1896–1929) Chinese rural revolutionary. From a landlord family, Peng studied in Japan before joining the Chinese **Communist Party** and organizing rural tenants in his home district of Haifeng in the southern province of Guangdong. In 1923 he succeeded in establishing a peasants' association, which campaigned for lower rents, led anti-landlord boycotts, and organized welfare activities. When the association was crushed by a local warlord in 1924 Peng fled to the **Guomindang** base at Canton, where he became Secretary of the Peasants' Bureau and Director of the Peasant Movement Training Institute. By 1925 Peng had helped form the Guangdong Provincial Peasant Association, which claimed 200 000 members. During the **Northern Expedition** (1926–8) Peng returned again to his home district and organized China's first rural soviet. In the wake of **Chiang Kai-shek's** counter-revolution against the communists, however, Peng's soviet was crushed in 1928. Peng was captured and executed by the Guomindang the following year.

Peng Te-huai ▷ **Peng Dehuai**

Peng Zhen (P'eng Chen) (1902–) Chinese politician. A leading member of the Chinese **Communist Party** and Mayor of Beijing (1951–66), he was the first high-ranking party member to be purged during the **Cultural Revolution**. Accused by **Mao Zedong** of protecting party intellectuals who had been critical of the policies of his **Great Leap Forward**, he disappeared from public view in 1966 and was not rehabilitated until 1979, three years after Mao's death. He was reappointed to the party's Central Committee and became known as a hardliner opposed to **Deng Xiaoping's** free market reforms. Peng retired in 1987.

Peniakoff, Vladimir ('Popski') (1897–1951) Belgian soldier and author. Born in Belgium of Russian parentage, he was educated in England. He joined the British army and from 1940 to 1942 served with the Long Range Desert Group and the Libyan Arab Force. In Oct 1942, with the sanction of the army, he formed his own force, Popski's Private Army, which carried out spectacular raids behind the German lines. He rose to the rank of lieutenant-colonel and was decorated for bravery by Britain, France and Belgium.

Peninsular Campaign (1862) In the **American Civil War**, an extended attempt by the Union army under General McClellan to take Richmond, Virginia (the Confederate capital), by moving up the peninsula between the James and York Rivers. Although Union troops won most of the battles, McClellan acted overcautiously, failed to take the offensive, and instead slowly moved his troops away from the capital. ▷ **Seven Days Battles**

Peninsular War (1808–14) The prolonged struggle for the Iberian Peninsula between the occupying French and a British army under **Wellington** (formerly Wellesley), supported by Portuguese and Spanish forces. Known in Spain as the 'War of Independence' and to Napoleonic France as 'the Spanish ulcer', it started as a Spanish revolt against the imposition of **Napoleon I's** brother Joseph **Bonaparte** as King of Spain, but developed into a bitter conflict, as British troops repulsed Masséna's Lisbon offensive (1810–11) and advanced from their base behind the Torres Vedras to liberate Spain. Following Napoleon's Moscow campaign (1812), French resources were overextended, enabling Wellington's army to invade south-west France (1813–14). ▷ **Napoleonic Wars**

Penn, William (1644–1718) English Quaker leader and founder of Pennsylvania. Expelled from Oxford for his Puritan leanings, he joined the Quakers in 1666, was imprisoned for his writings (1668), and while in the Tower of London wrote the most popular of his books, *No Cross, No Crown*. In 1681 he obtained a grant of land in North America, which was called Pennsylvania in honour of his father. In 1682 he was granted land that later became Delaware. He referred to Pennsylvania as a 'Holy Experiment', where religious and political freedom could flourish.

Pensionary ▷ **Grand Pensionary**

peon A day-labourer (originally a footsoldier), the lot of the *peon* has long been the subject of travellers' accounts, novels and histories. *Peonaje* (peonage or debt servitude) emerged between 1870 and 1930 in many regions, especially in Mesoamerica and the Amazon, where massive capital investment and technological change combined with the absence, or resistance, of local sources of labour to make debt-peonage a viable form of operation. In general, major property owners used labour contractors (*enganchadores*), paternalistic measures, wage increases and advances to attract the labour needed on *haciendas*, *fincas*, *fazendas*, *usinas* or *estancias*. The 'golden age' of peonage came to an end in the 1940s, with the advent of significant population growth in many agricultural regions of Latin America. ▷ **estancia; fazenda; hacienda**

People's Democracy A term applied by the former communist regimes (other than the USSR) to themselves. It correctly indicated that in theory they had some form of machinery enabling mass participation in government. However, since there was only one political party or so-called popular front and no secret ballot, there were no democratic elections, and the description was therefore a misnomer. ▷ **communism**

People's Liberation Army (PLA) The Chinese army, numbering over 3 million troops. It is a significant political as well as military force, although in recent years its political role has been somewhat reduced. ▷ **Cultural Revolution**

People's Liberation Front (Sri Lanka) ▷ **JVP**

People's National Congress (PNC) The major political party in Guyana, which has provided the government since 1964. Founded in 1955 by **Burnham** as a breakaway African party after a split in **Jagan**'s People's Progressive Party, it took Guyana to independence in 1966 and has generally implemented socialist policies. Since Burnham's death in 1985, the PNC has retained power under the leadership of Desmond Hoyte.

People's National Movement The major political party in Trinidad, which provided the government of that state from its inception in 1956 until 1986. The personal party of Eric **Williams**, its founder, until his death in 1981, its rivals, the People's Democratic Party of Bhadase Maraj and the Democratic Labour Party of Dr Rudranath Capildeo, never mounted an effective challenge to its monopoly of power. In 1986 it was ousted by the National Alliance for Reconstruction led by Arthur Robinson, but returned to power in the election of 1991.

People's Party ▷ **Populist Party**

Pepe, Florestano (1778–1851) Italian patriot and general. He was the brother of Guglielmo **Pepe** and served the **Parthenopean Republic**, Joseph **Bonaparte** and Joachim **Murat**. In 1811 he was made a general and in 1815 became Governor of Naples. He was an important member of the revolutionary government established by the liberal insurrection of 1820, but fiercely opposed the Sicilian rebels who sought independence and the restoration of the **Bentinck** constitution.

Pepe, Guglielmo (1783–1855) Italian patriot and general. The brother of Florestano **Pepe**, he saw service with the Italian legion attached to French forces in 1800 and tried to seize Naples in 1802. Like his brother, he served both Joseph Bonaparte and Joachim **Murat**. In 1810 he was made a baron by Murat and, in 1815, a lieutenant-general. He led the Neapolitan insurrection of July 1820 but was defeated at the Battle of

Rieti (7 Mar 1821) by Austrian troops sent to restore the full powers of **Ferdinand I**. Condemned to death, he managed to flee abroad, returning to Naples in 1848 when the city was once again in the hands of liberal revolutionaries. He was sent by the new constitutional government to assist **Charles Albert** of Sardinia-Piedmont in his efforts to drive the Austrians from the north of Italy. When, after a conservative monarchist coup d'état, the Neapolitan forces were recalled, Pepe decided to carry on the patriotic struggle and went to assist the Venetian Republic of Daniele **Manin**. After the collapse of the **Revolutions of 1848–9**, he settled in Piedmont. ▷ **Napoleon I**

Pepi II (Phiops) (c.2278/2184BC) King of Egypt. According to the chronicle of Egyptian kings drawn up by Manetho, an Egyptian priest of the **Ptolemaic Period**, Pepi came to the throne when six years of age and lived to be a hundred. Some support for this is found in a papyrus known as the Turin Canon of Kings from the reign of **Ramesses II**, which gives Pepi a reign of over 90 years. The very human reactions of the boy king are recounted in a letter sent to Harkhuf, the Governor of Elephantine, on the latter's return from an expedition into Nubia, bringing a dancing dwarf as a gift to his royal master. Under Pepi's rule, foreign trade was carried on, together with expeditions to the turquoise mines in Sinai and quarrying operations in the eastern desert.

Pepin I (d.639) Frankish Mayor of the Palace. Leader of the Austrasian nobility under **Chlotar II**, in 613 he helped him to victory over **Brunhilde**. He was mayor of the palace under **Dagobert I**, although his political influence decreased in this period. After Dagobert's death, he assumed the reins of government once again and on his death the government passed to his son, Grimoald I.

Pepin II (c.823–64) King of Aquitaine. He succeeded his father as King of Aquitaine in 838 and, after the death of **Louis I** (840), fought on the side of **Lothair I** in the Battle of Fontenoy (841). He was, however, passed over in favour of **Charles II, 'the Bald'** in the Treaty of **Verdun**. Charles was able to enforce his hold on Aquitaine because of the support of the local nobility and Pepin was forced to enter a monastery (852–6 and 864).

Pepin II, 'of Heristal' (d.714) King of the Franks (687/714). He was Mayor of the Palace in Austrasia, to which he added after

687 the similar vice-royalties of Neustria and Burgundy, and called himself 'Duke and Prince of the Franks'. Although he held no actual office, he strengthened and extended the Frankish kingdom by promoting missions among the heathen and by undertaking campaigns against the Frisians and the Alemanni. He was succeeded by his son, **Charles Martel**. ▷ **Franks**

Pepin III, 'the Short' (c.715–768) King of the Franks (751/68). The illegitimate son of **Charles Martel** and father of **Charlemagne**, he was the founder of the Frankish dynasty of the **Carolingians**. Pepin was chosen king in place of Childeric III, the last of the **Merovingians**, in 751. When Pope Stephen III was hard pressed by the Longobards, Pepin led an army into Italy (754), compelled the Longobard Aistulf to become his vassal, and laid the foundation of the temporal sovereignty of the popes (756). The rest of his life was spent in wars against **Saxons** and **Saracens**.

Péquistes Members of the **Parti Québecois**.

Pequot War (1637) Colonial North American War between English settlers and the Pequot tribe of Connecticut. After the Pequots murdered an English trader, the settlers retaliated with the aid of their allies, the Mohegans and the Narrangansetts. They attacked the main Pequot town on the Mystic River and slaughtered hundreds of men, women and children, effectively destroying the tribe.

Perceval, Spencer (1762–1812) British politician. He became an MP in 1796 and went on to become Solicitor-General (1801), Attorney-General (1802) and Chancellor of the Exchequer (1807). He was Premier from 1809 until 1812, when he was shot dead while entering the lobby of the House of Commons by a bankrupt Liverpool broker, John Bellingham. An efficient administrator, he had succeeded in establishing a firm Tory government. ▷ **Tories**

Percy A noble family from the north of England, whose founder, William de Percy (c.1030–96), went to England with **William I, 'the Conqueror'**. The best-known member of the family was Henry (1364–1403), the famous 'Hotspur', who fell fighting against **Henry IV** at Shrewsbury. His father, who had helped Henry of Lancaster to the throne, was dissatisfied with the King's gratitude, and plotted the insurrection with his son.

Peres, Shimon (1923–) Israeli politician. He emigrated with his family from Poland to Palestine as a child in 1934, and was raised on a kibbutz, but received most of his education in the USA. In 1948 he became Head of Naval Services in the new state of Israel, and later Director-General of the Defence Ministry (1953–9). In 1959 he was elected to the Knesset. He was Minister of Defence (1974–7), and in 1977 became Chairman of the Labour Party and leader of the opposition until 1984, when he entered into a unique power-sharing agreement with the leader of the **Likud** Party, Yitzhak **Shamir**. Under this agreement, Peres was Prime Minister from 1984 to 1986, when Shamir took over. After the inconclusive 1988 general election, Peres rejoined Shamir in a new coalition. In 1992 Peres was defeated as Labour leader by Itzhak **Rabin**. ▷ **Mapai Party**

perestroika The process of 'reconstructing' the Soviet economy and society through a programme of reforms gradually introduced after 1985 by General-Secretary Mikhail **Gorbachev**. These reforms, meant to be consistent with the ideals of the Bolshevik Revolution, were directed at relaxing control over the economy, reducing the power of the bureaucracy and eliminating its corruption, and in due course democratizing the **Communist Party of the Soviet Union** itself. Unfortunately from Gorbachev's point of view, they exposed the failings of the previous regime without removing enough of them, and actually worsened the state of the Soviet economy. Challenged first by the conservatives and then by the radicals, Gorbachev was swept from power in Dec 1991, his reconstruction still incomplete. ▷ **Bolsheviks; glasnost**

Pérez, Antonio (1540–1611) Spanish statesman. Secretary to **Philip II** of Spain, he was a close confidant of the King during the period 1566–79. Pérez became even more powerful when in 1573 his patron, Ruy Gómez, Prince of **Eboli**, died and he assumed influence at court over the Eboli faction, headed by Ruy Gómez's widow, the Princess of Eboli. In 1578 he arranged the murder of a political rival, Juan de Escobedo, and obtained the King's complicity in it. When Philip learnt the full story, however, he ordered (1579) the arrest and imprisonment of Pérez and the Princess. In 1590 Pérez escaped from prison and went to Aragon, where he was a key figure in the troubles of Saragossa (1591). He then fled to France and to England, where he was befriended by the Earl of Essex and inspired several plots against Philip. His writings, notably his *Relations*, served to inflame public opinion against the person and policies of Philip II.

Pérez de Cuellar, Javier (1920–) Peruvian diplomat. After graduating from Lima University, he embarked on a career in the Peruvian diplomatic service and represented his country at the first **UN** assembly in 1946. He succeeded the openly ambitious Kurt **Waldheim** as UN Secretary-General in 1982, his quiet, modest approach contrasting sharply with that of his predecessor. His patient diplomacy secured notable achievements, particularly in his second term, including a ceasefire in the **Iran–Iraq War** and the achievement of independence for Namibia. His work enhanced not only his own reputation but that of the UN as well. He was succeeded as Secretary-General in 1992 by Boutros Boutros-Ghali.

Pergamum (Pergamon) An ancient city in north-western Asia Minor, which in Hellenistic times was the capital of the Attalids. Under their patronage it became a major centre of art and learning; its school of sculpture was internationally renowned, and its library came second only to that of Alexandria. ▷ **Hellenistic Age**

Pericles (Perikles) (c.495–429BC) Athenian politician and general. He was from the aristocratic Alcmaeonid family, whose political predominance at Athens coincided with the period of her greatest political and cultural supremacy. Pericles fostered the full development of Athenian democracy, eg proposing the introduction of pay for jurymen. Associated with the leading philosophers and artists of the time, he was responsible for the construction of the Parthenon and other great buildings on the Athenian acropolis. A staunch opponent of **Sparta**, it was his unremitting hostility to her and her allies that brought about the **Peloponnesian War**. He died of the plague which afflicted Athens in the early years of that war. ▷ **Alcmaeonids; Athenian Empire**

Perkins, Frances (1882–1965) US politician. She was the first woman to hold cabinet rank, as Secretary of Labor (1933–45) in President Franklin D **Roosevelt**'s cabinet. This appointment recognized her reputation as a social reformer, especially concerned with child labour and factory legislation. In 1945 she resigned from President Harry S

Truman's cabinet, became a member of the Civil Service Commission (1946–52). Her memoir, *The Roosevelt I Knew* (1946), was the first, and in many ways remains one of the best, recollections of the **New Deal**.

Permanent Revolution (post-1918) Trotsky's adaptation of Marxism and Bolshevism in Russia in the wake of **World War I**. When communist revolutions did not materialize in Germany and other advanced countries, Trotsky pronounced that Marxist revolution was a continuous process and ought to be supported everywhere in the world, including in backward countries. This contrasted with **Lenin**'s and **Stalin**'s adoption of **Socialism in One Country**, Russia, and exacerbated the quarrel that led to his exile and death. ▷ **Bolsheviks**

Perón, Evita (Maria Eva Duarte) (1919–52) Argentine political figure. The second wife of Juan **Perón**, she was a radio and screen actress before her marriage in 1945. She became a powerful political influence and a mainstay of the Perón government. Idolized by the poor, after her death in Buenos Aires, support for her husband waned. Her body was stolen, taken to Europe, and kept in secret until 1976.

Perón, Isabelita (María Estrela Martínez Cartas) (1931–) Argentine political figure. A dancer, she became the third wife of Juan **Perón** in 1961. She lived with him in Spain until his return to Argentina as President in 1973, when she was made Vice-President. She took over the presidency on his death in 1974, but her inadequacy in office led to a military coup in 1976. She was imprisoned for five years, and on her release settled in Madrid.

Perón, Juan (Domingo) (1895–1974) Argentine soldier and President. He took a leading part in the army coup of 1943, gained widespread support through his social reforms, and became President (1946–55). He derived immense popularity by cultivating the support of the urban working and middle classes of Buenos Aires, expanding government expenditure in the wake of an export boom. He was deposed and exiled in 1955 when the boom burst, having antagonized the Church, the armed forces and many of his former Labour supporters. He resumed the presidency in triumph in 1973, and won an overwhelming electoral victory, but died the following year. ▷ **Perón, Evita; Perón, Isabelita; Peronism**

Peronism A heterogeneous Argentine political movement formed in 1945–6 to support the successful presidential candidacy of Juan **Perón** and his government thereafter. The movement later underwent division, some left-wing Peronists forming the **Montoneros** guerrilla group, but it survived Perón's death (1974). Despite continued internal disputes, the party made a good showing in the congressional elections of 1986. The ideology of Peronism (formally labelled Justicialism (**justicialismo**) in 1949) has proved difficult to describe, and can perhaps best be viewed as a unique amalgam of nationalism and social democracy, strongly coloured by loyalty to the memory of Perón.

Perry, Matthew Galbraith (1794–1858) US naval officer. The brother of Oliver Hazard Perry (who defeated the British at the Battle of Lake Erie in the War of 1812), in 1837 he was appointed commander of the *Fulton*, one of the first naval steamships. He was active in suppression of the slave trade on the African coast in 1843, and in the **Mexican War** (1846–8) he captured several towns and took part in the siege of Veracruz. From 1852 to 1854 he led the naval expedition to Japan that forced it to open diplomatic negotiations with the USA and grant the first trading rights with Western powers.

Persepolis An ancient Persian city in Fars province, south-west Iran. Its construction was begun by **Darius I, 'the Great'** and further developed by his successors **Xerxes I** and **Artaxerxes I, Longimanus** until it was sacked by **Alexander III, 'the Great'** in 330 BC. The palaces and graves of the Achaemenid rulers of Persia are located here, and it is a World Heritage site.

Perseus (c.212–c.165BC) Last King of **Macedonia** in the Antigonid Dynasty (179/ 168BC). He succeeded his father, **Philip V** of Macedon, and pursued Philip's policy of consolidating his kingdom after the defeat by Rome. However, his success provoked the jealousy of Rome and her supporters in the Greek world, who accused him of hostile designs. This brought about the Third Macedonian War (171–168BC), in which Perseus was defeated at the Battle of Pydna (168BC) and taken to Italy, where he died in captivity. The Macedonian monarchy was then abolished.

Pershing, John Joseph ('Black Jack') (1860–1948) US general. He trained at the US Military Academy at West Point, and served in several **Indian Wars** (1886–91), in the Spanish–American War (1898), in the Philippines (1899–1903), in the **Russo-Japanese War** (1904–5), and in Mexico (1916). In 1917 he commanded the American Expeditionary Forces in Europe, and after the war became Chief of Staff (1921–4). His book *My Experiences in the World War* (1931) won a Pulitzer Prize. ▷ **World War I**

Persian Empire An empire created by the Achaemenids in the second half of the 6c BC through their conquests of the Medes, Babylonians, Lydians and Egyptians, extending from north-western India to the eastern Mediterranean. Although it was overthrown by **Alexander III, 'the Great'** in the decade 330–320BC, its administrative structure, the satrapal system, survived. ▷ **Babylonia; Bactria; Lydia; Persian Wars; satrapy**

Persian Wars The name given to the two punitive expeditions launched by the Persian kings, **Darius I, 'the Great'** and **Xerxes**, against Greece in 490 and 480–479BC. The first was in retaliation for Greek intervention in the **Ionian Revolt** (499–494BC), and was directed only at Eretria and Athens; it ended in catastrophe for the Persians at the Battle of **Marathon**. The second was to wipe out the disgrace of Marathon; it ended in the twin defeats for the Persians at Plataea and Mycale. ▷ **Leonidas; Pausanias; Salamis, Battle of; Themistocles; Thermopylae, Battle of**

Persigny, Jean Gilbert Victor Fialin, Duke of (1808–72) French politician. He secured the favour of Louis Napoleon (**Napoleon III**), and had the chief hand in the affairs of Strasbourg (1836) and Boulogne (1840), where he was captured and condemned to 20 years' imprisonment. Released in 1848, he strongly supported his patron then and in 1851, in 1852–5 and 1860–3 he was Minister of the Interior, 1855–60 Ambassador to England, and a Senator until the fall of the Second Empire.

Peruzzi ▷ **Bardi and Peruzzi**

Pétain, (Henri) Philippe (1856–1951) French soldier and politician. During **World War I** he became a national hero for his defence of **Verdun** (1916), and was made Commander-in-Chief (1917) and Marshal of France (1918). When France collapsed in 1940, the National Assembly voted him full powers to negotiate the armistice with

Germany and Italy, and made him Chief of State, with his government at **Vichy**. His aim to unite France under the slogan 'Work, Family and Country', and keep it out of the war, involved active **collaboration** with Germany. After the liberation, he was tried in the French courts, his death sentence for treason being commuted to life imprisonment on the Ile d'Yeu, where he died. His role remains controversial, and some still regard him as a patriot rather than a traitor. ▷ **French State; World War II**

Peter I, 'the Great' (1672–1725) Tsar (1682/1721) and Emperor (1721/5) of Russia. The son of Tsar **Alexei Mikhailovich** and his second wife, Natalia Naryshkina, he was joint tsar with his mentally retarded half-brother, Ivan, under the regency of their sister, Sophia (1682/9). On Ivan's death (1696), he became sole tsar, and embarked on a series of sweeping military, fiscal, administrative, educational, cultural and ecclesiastical reforms. Many of these were based on Western European models, pulled Russia into the mainstream of European history, and provided the economic and political basis on which Peter and his successors could defend and expand their dominions. However, all classes of society felt the impact of the changes and the frequent brutality of their implementation; his own son, Alexei, died under torture (1718), suspected of leading a conspiracy against his father. Peter encouraged expansion eastwards towards China, fought major wars with the **Ottoman Empire**, Persia, and in particular Sweden, which he defeated in the **Great Northern War**. All this established Russia as a major power, and specifically gained it a maritime exit on the Baltic coast, where Peter founded his new capital, St Petersburg. Whether what Peter achieved was worth the cost then and later is a subject still much debated by historians. The fact that he died without naming his successor contributed to the loss of direction which followed his reign. ▷ **Romanov Dynasty**

Peter I Karageorgević (1844–1921) King of Serbia (1903/18) and King of the Serbs, Croats and Slovenes (1918/21). The son of Prince **Alexander Karageorgević**, he fought in the French Army in the **Franco-Prussian War** (1870–1), and was elected King of Serbia by the Serbian parliament in 1903. In **World War I** he accompanied his army into exile in Greece in 1916. He returned to Belgrade in 1918 and was proclaimed titular King of the Serbs, Croats and Slovenes until his death,

although his second son, Alexander (later **Alexander I Karageorgević**), was regent.

Peter II (1715–30) Tsar of Russia (1727/30). The grandson of **Peter I, 'the Great'** and son of the tsarevich Alexis (1690–1718), he succeeded to the throne on the death of his step-grandmother, **Catherine I**. He died of smallpox on the day designated for his wedding and was succeeded by Empress **Anna Ivanova**, daughter of Peter the Great's half-brother and co-tsar, Ivan V. Peter II was too young and his reign was too short for him to do other than allow faction-fighting around the tsar to become more or less an established tradition.

Peter II (1923–70) King of Yugoslavia (1934/45). The son of **Alexander I Karageorgević**, he was at school in England when his father was assassinated in 1934. His uncle, Prince **Paul Karageorgević** was regent until 1941 when he was ousted by pro-Allied army officers, who declared King Peter of age and the latter assumed sovereignty. The subsequent German attack on Yugoslavia forced the King to go into exile within three weeks. He set up a government in exile in London, but lost his throne when Yugoslavia became a republic in 1945. From then on the ex-king lived mainly in California.

Peter II Petrović (1812–51) Prince-Bishop of Montenegro. He succeeded his uncle, Peter I, in 1830 and tried to introduce a measure of modernization into his backward, isolated country. A cultured man with a knowledge of German, French, Latin and Russian, he wrote poetry which is still highly acclaimed, his most famous work being *The Mountain Wreath* (1847).

Peter III (1728–62) Tsar of Russia (1762). He was the grandson of **Peter I, 'the Great'**, the son of Peter's youngest daughter, Anna, and Charles Frederick, Duke of Holstein Gottorp. In 1742 he was declared heir-presumptive to his aunt, Empress **Elizabeth Petrovna** (the daughter of Peter the Great and **Catherine I**), and in 1745 he married Sophia-Augusta von Anhalt-Zerbst (the future empress **Catherine II, 'the Great'**). An unstable and violent man, and a great admirer of **Frederick II, 'the Great'**, he withdrew Russia's forces from the Seven Years War as soon as he succeeded to the throne (Jan 1762), and restored East Prussia to Frederick. This enraged the army and aristocracy, and in June of that year Peter was deposed by a group of nobles inspired by his ambitious wife, Catherine, and led by her lover, Count **Orlov**. He was strangled in captivity a few days later, and Catherine was proclaimed Empress. His main domestic act had longlasting unfortunate consequences: he freed the gentry from their obligation to serve the state, while in no way diminishing the obligation of the serfs to serve the gentry.

Peterloo Massacre (1819) The name given to the forcible breakup of a mass meeting about parliamentary reform held at St Peter's Fields, Manchester. The Manchester Yeomanry charged into the crowd, killing 11 people. The incident strengthened the campaign for reform. 'Peterloo' was a sardonic pun on the **Waterloo** victory of 1815. ▷ **Reform Acts**

Peter the Hermit (Peter of Amiens) (c.1050–c.1115) French monk and a preacher of the First Crusade. When **Urban II** launched the First Crusade at a council in Clermont (France) in 1096, Peter traversed Europe, producing extraordinary enthusiasm. He rallied an army of 20 000 peasants, and led one section of the crusading army to Asia Minor, where it was utterly defeated by the Turks at Nicaea. ▷ **Crusade, First**

Pétion de Villeneuve, Jérôme (c.1756–1794) French revolutionary. In 1789 he was elected Deputy to the Third Estate. He was a prominent member of the Jacobin Club, and became a great ally of **Robespierre**. He was one of those who brought back the royal family from Varennes (1791) and advocated the deposition of King **Louis XVI**. He was elected Mayor of Paris and was the first President of the National Convention. He voted at the King's trial for death, but headed an unsuccessful attack on Robespierre. Proscribed on 2 June 1793, he escaped to Caen, and thence, on the failure of the attempt to make armed opposition against the Convention, to the Gironde, where his body was later found, partly devoured by wolves. ▷ **Convention, National; Estates General; Jacobins**

Petkov, Nikola (1893–1947) Bulgarian politician. The son of Prime Minister Dimitŭr Petkov, he studied law in Paris and was later attached to the embassy there. He remained in exile in France after the military coup which overthrew **Stamboliski** (June 1923) until 1931, when he returned to Bulgaria and led the left-wing Pladne group of the Bulgarian Agrarian National Union. During **World War II** he worked with the **Fatherland Front** and was interned (1942–4). He was a minister

without portfolio in the Provisional Government (Sep 1944–July 1945) and then edited the *National Agrarian Banner* (1945–7), leading the pro-Western opposition to full communist rule. After the 1946 elections, he attacked Georgi **Dimitrov** as a Soviet puppet. Dimitrov waited until the USA had ratified the Bulgarian peace agreement (June 1947) before executing Petkov after a farcical show trial.

Petöfi, Sándor (1823–49) Hungarian poet. He was successively actor, soldier, and literary hack, but by 1844 had secured his fame as a genuine poet, his most popular work being *János vitéz* (1845, Janos the Hero). An admirer of France and its successive revolutions, he threw himself into the revolutionary cause in 1848, somewhat to the discomfiture of the gentry leader, Lajos **Kossuth**. He wrote numerous war songs, and fell in battle at Segesvár, possibly to a Russian bullet. He was ever after regarded as a martyr in the cause of popular nationalism; in the **Hungarian Uprising** in 1956, for example, one of the revolutionary centres was the Petöfi Circle. ▷ **Revolutions of 1848–9**

Petri, Olaus (c.1493–1552) Swedish reformer and statesman. After his return in 1519 from Wittenberg, where he had become a follower of Martin Luther, he gained the ear of King **Gustav I Vasa**, who made him Chancellor in 1531. His directness, however, brought him into disfavour and in 1539 he was charged with high treason and condemned to death. He was pardoned and in 1543 made First Pastor of Stockholm.

Petrokov, Nikolai Yakovlevich (1937–   ) Soviet reform economist. A brilliant graduate of Moscow University in 1959, he joined the party and became the Deputy Director of the Institute of Mathematical Economics in 1965. He joined Mikhail **Gorbachev**'s team of advisers in 1985 and was appointed personal assistant in 1990. But in the autumn of that year he failed to persuade him to adopt serious economic reforms, which proved to be part of Gorbachev's undoing.

Petrov Affair The defection by Soviet Embassy Third Secretary, Vladimir M Petrov, in Canberra (Apr 1954); he was granted political asylum by the Australian government. The Soviet government tried to fly Petrov's wife back to Moscow, but the aircraft was intercepted at Darwin, and she too was granted asylum. Later the Petrovs revealed they had been spying in Australia, and in one of their documents they implicated two members of the staff of Dr H V **Evatt**, the federal leader of the **Australian Labor Party** opposition. Evatt defended his staff before a Royal Commission (1954–5), but it refused to clear them. The affair exacerbated the split in the Labor Party over **communism** during the 1950s. ▷ **Democratic Labor Party**

Petrović-Njegoš Dynasty The ruling house of Montenegro (1696–1918), founded by Prince-Bishop Danilo (1670–1735). Its principal members were the prince-bishops Peter I (1784–1830), Peter II Petrović-Njegoš (1813–51), Prince Danilo (1826–60) and **Nicholas I** (Nikola Petrović), Prince and King of Montenegro.

Phalange Party The *Phalanges Libanaises* (Arabic, *kata'ib*) were founded in Lebanon in 1936 by Pierre **Gemayel**, a young Maronite Christian, to counteract the provocative activities of Muslim elements seeking union with Syria. Originally a Christian youth movement, the Phalanges Libanaises then crystallized into a political party under the leadership of Gemayel, adding yet another factor to the Lebanese political equation. This factor was to have a destabilizing influence some four decades later when the Phalange aimed at the eradication of the **PLO** (Palestine Liberation Organization) in Lebanon. Gemayel himself played a leading part in the Lebanese politics of the 1960s and led the Phalange militia in the 1975–6 civil war. Gemayel's son, Amin, subsequently became leader of the Maronite Christians and was able to gain support also from the Sunni Muslims. President of Lebanon from 1982 to 1988, Amin **Gemayel** was no friend of extremists as his relations with Shiite factions and the more headstrong elements of the Phalanges bear witness.

Phanariots A small Greek elite of 11 families which in the 18c rose to prominence in the administration of the **Ottoman Empire**, first as interpreters, then in the 19c as hospodars of the **Danubian Principalities**, Dragoman (or Interpreter) of the Fleet and Grand Dragoman (a post equivalent to Minister of Foreign Affairs). Their name was derived from the Phanar district of Constantinople where they lived. ▷ **hospodar; Mavrokordatos, Constantine; Peć, Patriarchate of**

Phan Boi Chau (1867–1940) Vietnamese nationalist. Together with **Phan Chau Trinh**, he dominated the anti-colonial movement in

Vietnam in the early 20c. Born into a Confucian scholar family, he was in essence a Confucian revolutionary. In 1905 he went to Japan where, working under the supervision of the exiled Liang Ch'i-ch'ao, he wrote a history of Vietnam's loss of independence to the French, copies of which were then smuggled back to Vietnam. In 1912, now in China, he was involved with other Vietnamese in the establishment of the 'Revival Society' (*Quang Phuc Hoi*) which sought to bring about a democratic republic in Vietnam. Forces were raised which launched, from South China, poorly-organized attacks on French units (1915). In 1925, Phan Boi Chau was arrested by French agents in Shanghai and returned to Vietnam. Brought before the Criminal Commission (Nov 1925), he was sentenced to life imprisonment. The ensuing widespread public outcry led to his release and he spent the rest of his life, in gently guarded retirement, at Hue.

Phan Chau Trinh (1871–1926) Vietnamese nationalist. Along with **Phan Boi Chau**, he was a leading figure in the anti-colonial movement in Vietnam in the early 20c. In contrast to Phan Boi Chau's commitment to a revolutionary monarchism, Phan Chau Trinh advocated Western-style republicanism. Between 1911 and 1925 he was in France, spending some of that time in prison. From France he launched strong attacks on the Vietnamese monarchy. Phan Chau Trinh's funeral in 1926 was held in Saigon, provoking unprecedented mass demonstrations and student strikes. This heralded a new phase in the anti-colonial struggle in Vietnam, one that would involve greater popular participation.

Pharsalus, Battle of (48BC) Julius **Caesar's** decisive defeat in Thessaly, northern Greece, of his main rival, **Pompey**.

Phibunsongkhram (1897–1964) Thai military and political leader. Of humble origin, Phibun was educated at the Thai Military Academy and then, on a government scholarship, at the French Artillery School. In France he came into contact with a group of Thai students who were disaffected with the absolute monarchy in Bangkok and became involved in the coup which brought down the absolute regime (24 June 1932). Phibun gathered increasing authority in the first constitutional governments, becoming Prime Minister in 1938. During that premiership, he cultivated a close relationship with Japan, in late 1941 agreeing to allow Japanese forces to pass through his country in order to attack the British in Burma and Malaya. However, when the war turned against Japan, Phibun fell from office (July 1944). He returned as Prime Minister in 1947, this time aligning Thailand closely with the USA. Phibun remained in office until Sep 1957, when he was overthrown in a Sarit Thanarat coup. He died in exile in Japan.

Philby, Kim (Harold Adrian Russell) (1912–88) British double agent. He was educated at Cambridge, where, like **Burgess**, **Maclean** and **Blunt**, he became a communist. Already recruited as a Soviet agent, he was employed by the British Secret Intelligence Service (MI6), from 1944 to 1946 as head of anti-communist counter-espionage. He was First Secretary of the British Embassy in Washington, working in liaison with the **CIA** (1949–51), and from 1956 worked in Beirut as a journalist. In 1963 he disappeared to the USSR, where he was granted citizenship.

Philip I (1052–1108) King of France (1067/ 1108). The son of **Henry I**, his reign marked a low point in the prestige of the Capetian monarchy, largely due to his elopement with Bertrada, wife of Fulk of Anjou, a scandal which led to his excommunication. ▷ **Capetian Dynasty**

Philip I, 'the Handsome' (1478–1506) King of Castile (1506). He was the son of Emperor **Maximilian I** and **Mary of Burgundy**. As Archduke of Austria and Duke of Burgundy, he married (1496) the Infanta of Spain, **Juana the Mad**, daughter of **Ferdinand II, 'the Catholic'** of **Aragon** and **Isabella I, 'the Catholic'**. Isabella's death in 1504 made Juana the legal heiress to Castile, but Ferdinand promptly declared himself her regent. In 1506 Philip went to claim the throne, but died in the same year; Juana lost her reason and was put into confinement. Their children were Emperor **Charles V** and his successor, **Ferdinand I**.

Philip II (382–336BC) King of Macedon (359/336BC). He used his military and diplomatic skills first to create a powerful unified state at home (359–353BC), then to make himself the master of the whole of independent Greece. His decisive victory at the Battle of **Chaeronea** (338BC) established Macedonian hegemony there for good. The planned Macedonian conquest of Persia, aborted by his assassination in 336BC, was eventually carried out by his son, **Alexander III, 'the Great'**. ▷ **Aeschines; Demosthenes; Macedonia**

Philip II (1165–1223) King of France (1179/ 1223). The son of **Louis VII**, his reign formed a key period in the development of the medieval kingdom of France. He embarked on the Third Crusade in 1190, but returned the following year to concentrate on attacking the continental lands of the Angevin kings of England. When he died, Capetian power was firmly established over most of France. ▷ **Angevins; Capetian Dynasty; Crusade, Third**

Philip II (1527–98) King of Spain (1556/98) and (as Philip I) King of Portugal (1580/98). He was the only son of Emperor **Charles V** and Isabella of Portugal. Following the death of his first wife, Maria of Portugal, in childbirth (1545), he married **Mary I** (1554), becoming joint sovereign of England. Before Mary's death (1558) he had inherited the Habsburg possessions in Italy, the Netherlands, Spain, and the New World. To seal the end of Valois–Habsburg conflict, he married Elizabeth of France (1559), who bore him two daughters. His brief fourth marriage to his cousin, Anna of Austria (1570), produced another son, the future **Philip III** of Spain. As the champion of the Counter-Reformation, he tried to destroy infidels and heretics alike. He sought to crush Protestantism, first in the Low Countries (from 1568), then in England and France. The destruction of the **Armada** (1588) and the continuing revolt of the Netherlands, along with domestic economic problems and internal unrest, suggest a reign marked by failure. However, among his political achievements were the curbing of Ottoman seapower after the Battle of Lepanto (1571) and the conquest of Portugal (1580). ▷ **Alba, Fernando Álvarez de Toledo, 3rd Duke of; Eighty Years War; Habsburg Dynasty; Valois Dynasty**

Philip III (1578–1621) King of Spain (1598/ 1621). The son and successor of **Philip II** of Spain, he reacted against his dominating father by choosing his own advisers, notably the Duke of Lerma. A pious Catholic, he was actively concerned to restore the military fortunes of Spain. He was, however, uninterested in politics, and delegated administration to his advisers, Juan de Idiáquez and Lerma, preferring to travel elsewhere in the country. His reign was thus distinguished by a renewed role for administrative bodies such as the councils and the Cortes. After Lerma's fall in 1618, Philip played an increased role in government, but died shortly thereafter. It was during his reign that the **Moriscos** were expelled.

Philip III, 'the Bold' (1245–85) King of France from 1270. He was with his father **Louis IX** (St Louis) at his death in Tunis (1270), and fought several unlucky campaigns in Spain, the last of which, the attack on Aragon, caused his death.

Philip IV (1605–65) King of Spain (1621/65). The son and successor of **Philip III**, he was an active scholar and patron of the arts. He took a close interest in politics, supporting the government of his mentor, the Count-Duke of **Olivares**, but turned against him when the latter's policies collapsed. His reign experienced serious reverses which confirmed Spain's decline as a European power. In 1640 both Catalonia and Portugal rebelled, and in 1647 Naples followed suit. The Dutch Netherlands won their independence at the Peace of Westphalia (1648), and the war with France (1635) ended with the cession of northern Catalonia in the Treaty of the Pyrenees (1659). He was succeeded by his only surviving child, the sickly **Charles II**.

Philip IV, 'the Fair' (1268–1314) King of France. He succeeded his father, **Philip III**, in 1285. By his marriage with Queen Joanna of Navarre he acquired Navarre, Champagne and Brie. He overran Flanders, but was defeated by the Flemings at Courtrai (1302). His struggle with Pope **Boniface VIII** arose from his attempts to tax the French clergy. The King's reply to the Papal Bull *Unam Sanctam* was to send his minister William de Nogaret to seize Boniface, who escaped but died soon afterwards (1303). After the short pontificate of Benedict XI, Philip procured the elevation of the pliant Frenchman, **Clement V** (1305), who came to reside at Avignon, thus beginning the 70 years' 'Babylonish captivity' of the papacy. Coveting the wealth of the Templars, Philip forced the Pope to condemn and dissolve the order, whose property he appropriated (1314).

Philip V (238–179BC) King of Macedonia in the Antigonid Dynasty (221/179BC). Ambitious and active, he inherited a strong kingdom from his predecessor, Antigonus Doson, in 221BC, but came into conflict with the growing power of Rome. He made an alliance with **Hannibal** in 215BC during the second of the **Punic Wars**, which resulted in a first (indecisive) conflict with Rome (214–205BC). Conflict broke out again with Rome, in the Second Macedonian War of 200–196BC. Decisively defeated at Cynoscephalae in 197BC, he had to give up all control of

Greece and follow Rome's dictates. He was succeeded by his son, **Perseus**.

Philip V (1683–1746) First Bourbon King of Spain (1700/46). He occupied the throne twice, abdicating briefly in 1724 in favour of his son, Luis I, who died within a few months. King at the age of 17, Philip was never given the opportunity to assert himself as a ruler. At the beginning of his reign, dominated by the War of the **Spanish Succession**, policy was determined by his grandfather, **Louis XIV** of France. On the death of his first wife, Marie Louise of Savoy (1714), Philip married Isabel Farnese of Parma. She was an imperious woman, who completely changed the political complexion of the court, placing in charge of affairs her confidant, the priest Giulio **Alberoni**. For the rest of the reign, Farnese effectively imposed on ministers her obsession with securing the dynastic interests of her family in her native Italy and specifically in Parma. Philip's reign marked an important phase of readjustment to Spain's new role in Europe, and the importation of foreign tastes showed itself in the construction of new royal palaces in Madrid and Aranjuez.

Philip V, 'the Tall' (1293–1322) King of France (1316/22). The second son of **Philip IV**, he succeeded his brother, **Louis X**, in 1316. The main achievements of his reign were the ending of the war with Flanders (1320), and his attempt to unify the coinage.

Philip VI (1293–1350) First Valois King of France (1328/50). The nephew of **Philip IV**, he became king on the death of **Charles IV**. His right was denied by **Edward III** of England, son of the daughter of Philip IV, who declared that females, though excluded by the **Salic Law**, could transmit their rights to their children. The **Hundred Years War** with England thus began (1337), and in 1346 Edward III landed in **Normandy**, defeating Philip at the Battle of **Crécy**, just as the Black Death was about to spread through France. ▷ **Valois Dynasty**

Philip of Swabia (c.1177–1208) German King (1198/1208). The youngest son of **Frederick I, 'Barbarossa'**, he succeeded his brother Conrad as Duke of Swabia in 1196. After the death of **Henry VI**, he became embroiled in a struggle for the throne with **Otto IV**, who had been elected King with English support in 1198. Despite being temporarily excommunicated (1201) by Pope **Innocent III**, who wanted to weaken the Hohenstaufen position in Italy, he came to a settlement with Otto IV and was formally recognized in 1207. He was assassinated in 1208. ▷ **Bouvines, Battle of; Hohenstaufen Dynasty**

Philippi, Battle of (42BC) The decisive battle in northern Greece in which Antony and Octavian (later Emperor Augustus) defeated Brutus and Cassius, and thus avenged the murder of Julius **Caesar**. ▷ **Antony, Mark**

Philip the Bold (1342–1404) Duke of Burgundy (1364/1404). The youngest son of John the Good, King of France, he fought at Poitiers (1356), and shared his father's captivity in England. He married Margaret, heiress of Flanders in 1369, subdued a Flemish rebellion at Roosebeke (1382), and gained that country in 1384–5. Following the insanity of his nephew, the French king, **Charles VI**, he became virtual ruler of France.

Philip the Good (1396–1467) Duke of Burgundy (1419/67). The grandson of **Philip the Bold**, he at first recognized **Henry V** of England as heir to the French crown, but concluded a separate peace with the French in 1435. Philip created one of the most powerful states in later medieval Europe. A committed crusader, he maintained a fleet for operations against the Ottoman Turks. ▷ **Ottoman Empire**

Philip the Magnanimous (1504–67) Landgrave of Hesse. He was converted to Lutheranism in 1524 and was a major driving force in the Protestant **Schmalkaldic League** of 1531. He established Hesse as a sovereign state where the Protestant church was prominent in the provision of state schools and hospitals. Despite pressure from radical Anabaptists, Hesse maintained a tolerant religious regime that accommodated pastors of different Protestant persuasions and where no one was executed for religious reasons. In 1539 Philip developed syphilis and in 1540 contracted a bigamous marriage with Margaret van der Saale. This moral ambiguity, and his long imprisonment after the Schmalkaldic War (1547–52), lessened his influence in European affairs.

Philistines The ancient warlike inhabitants of the coastal area of the south-eastern Mediterranean between present-day Jaffa and Egypt. They were constantly at odds with the Israelites of the hinterland — a struggle epitomized by the stories of Samson and of **David** and Goliath.

Phillips, Wendell (1811–84) US abolitionist. He graduated from Harvard in 1831, and was called to the bar in 1834. By 1837 he was the chief orator of the anti-slavery party, closely associated with William Lloyd Garrison. He also championed the causes of prohibition, women's suffrage, organization of labour, and currency reform. ▷ **abolitionism**

Philopoemen (c.253–182BC) Greek soldier and politician. As Commander-in-Chief of the **Achaean League**, he crushed the Spartans at Mantinea (208BC), and sought to unite Greece against the Romans. In his old age he took part in an expedition against Messene, but was captured and poisoned by the Messenians.

Philosophes The leaders of the French Enlightenment (often political commentators, writers, and propagandists) who were critical of the **ancien régime** and advocates of rational criteria. Their great collective work was the *Encyclopédie* (1751–72). ▷ **Encyclopedists**

Phiops ▷ **Pepi II**

Phocion (c.397–318BC) Athenian soldier and politician. Elected general 45 times, in 341BC he crushed the Macedonian party in **Euboea**, and in 340BC forced **Philip II** of Macedon to evacuate the Chersonesus, but advised Athens to make friends with him. The advice was not taken, but the disastrous Battle of **Chaeronea** (338BC) proved its soundness. Subsequently, he consistently opposed resistance to **Macedonia**; on the death of **Alexander III, 'the Great'** in 323BC, he vainly endeavoured to prevent the Athenians from going to war with **Antipater**, Regent in Macedonia. During a brief return to democracy in Athens, he was put to death on a charge of treason.

Phoenicia A narrow strip in the east Mediterranean between the mountains of Lebanon and the sea, where the ancient cities of Arad, Byblos, Sidon and Tyre were located. It derived its name from the Phoenicians (descendants of the Canaanites) who were the dominant people of the area from the end of the second millennium BC, and was their base for trading all over the Mediterranean. From the 8cBC, they established trading posts and colonies in the western Mediterranean (eg Leptis Magna and Carthage in North Africa). The Phoenician alphabet is the ancestor of modern western alphabets.

Phoenix Park Murders (6 May 1882) The murder in Dublin of the recently appointed Chief Secretary for Ireland, Lord Frederick Cavendish, brother of Spencer Compton **Cavendish**, 8th Duke of Devonshire, and his Under-Secretary, Thomas Henry Burke, by a terrorist nationalist group called 'The Invincibles'. More murders followed during the summer. The British government responded with a fierce Coercion Act, which permitted trials for treason and murder to take place before a judicial tribunal and without a jury, and gave police extensive additional search powers. Five of the Phoenix Park murderers were arrested and hanged.

Photius (c.820–91) Patriarch of Constantinople (858–67 and 877–86). On the deposition of Ignatius from the patriarchate, he was hurried through all the stages of holy orders, and installed in his stead. In 862, Pope Nicholas I called a Council at Rome, which declared Photius's election invalid, and reinstated Ignatius. Supported by the Emperor, Photius assembled a Council at Constantinople (867), which withdrew from communion with Rome. He was then deposed and reinstated on several occasions, and excluded the *Filioque* clause from the Creed (879). In 886 he was finally exiled to Armenia, where he died.

Phrygia The name of the kingdom in antiquity with whom the legendary Midas is associated. At its widest extent around the beginning of the first millennium, it consisted of the central plateau of Asia Minor and its western flank. After its conquest by Lydia in the 6c BC, it never regained its political independence.

Phule, Jyotirao (1827–90) Indian social reformer. He led the anti-brahmin campaign in Maharashtra in the late 1800s and wrote *Ghulam Giri* (1872), which exposed the evils of a caste-based society. His organization, *Satyashodhak Samaj* (1873), proclaimed the need to save the lower castes from the hypocritical Brahmanas and their opportunistic scriptures. The Satyashodhak movement contained both an elite-based conservative trend and a more genuine mass-based radicalism, and struck some roots among the Maratha peasantry. ▷ **caste**

Physiocrats A group of French economic and political thinkers of the later 18c, led by François Quesnay, and committed to *a priori* principles of reason and natural law. Their theories made them critics of internal trade barriers and controls, and advocates of reform, to produce a system of economic liberalism.

Piast Dynasty The first rulers of Poland, a line of princes descended from a legendary Polish ploughman named Piast (fl.c.870), whose name was only applied to the dynasty 800 years later. Piast's son, Siemowit, was first of the new line of princes of Gniezno (Gnesen), commencing the loose consolidation of Great Poland which was to culminate in the great-great-grandson of Piast, Bolesław I, 'the Brave', being crowned king shortly before his death in 1025. Bolesław's great-grandson, Bolesław II, 'the Bold', briefly won back the title of king after it had fallen into abeyance, but after his death (1079) his successors lost it once more, Bolesław III, 'the Wry-Mouthed' restoring lost lands to include the territories of Pomerania, Silesia and Little Poland (first held under Mieszko I, Christianizer of Poland and father of Bolesław I). Bolesław III divided the lands among his descendants, resulting in constant struggles among the cousins and attempts at unification. Bolesław III's great-great-grandson, Przemysł II of Great Poland, was crowned king in 1295, but died in 1296. But the kingship then passed to his Bohemian son-in-law, Wenceslas (or Wacław) II (1300/5). It then passed to the Mazovian Piast line from Władysław I, 'the Short' who became king in 1320, and consolidated his situation by marriage alliances with Hungary and Lithuania. His son, Casimir III, 'the Great', reigned from Władysław's death in 1333 until his own in 1370, during which time he finally relinquished Silesia and Pomerania but annexed Galicia, modernized its state and army administration, strengthened its economy and founded the university at Kraków (1364), also codifying the Polish laws. His death marked the end of the Piast Dynasty as he was succeeded by his nephew, Louis I (d'Anjou) of Hungary, from whom eventually descended the **Jagiełłon Dynasty**.

Pica Law The title, derived from the name of moderate Deputy Giuseppe Pica, given to emergency measures adopted in Italy in Aug 1863 to deal with the **Grande Brigantaggio**. Effectively, it did no more than legalize the existing policy of reprisals and martial law which had already been adopted by the military authorities in the **Mezzogiorno**.

Piccolomini, Ottavio, Duke of Amalfi (c.1600–56) Italian soldier. He entered the

Spanish service and, sent to aid the Emperor Ferdinand II, fought against the Bohemians (1620), in the Netherlands, and against Wallenstein's army at **Lützen** (1632), and contributed to the fall of Wallenstein. He won great distinction at Nördingen (1634) and next year was sent to aid the Spaniards in the Netherlands to drive out the French. In 1640 he stopped the advance of the Swedes for a time, but he was worsted by them in Silesia. In 1643 he commanded the Spanish armies in the Netherlands, and after the Peace of **Westphalia** (1648) was created field marshal.

Pichegru, Charles (1761–1804) French soldier, a labourer's son. He enlisted in 1783, and by 1793 was a General of Division. With **Hoche**, he drove back the Austrians and overran the Palatinate; then defeating the Austrians at Fleurus in 1794, he entered Amsterdam in 1795. Recalled by the Thermidorians, he crushed an insurrection in Paris. In 1797 he became President of the Council of Five Hundred, but as a result of his Bourbon intrigues, he was deported to Cayenne. Escaping next year, he made his way to London, and thereafter lived in Germany and England until the Bourbon conspiracy of **Cadoudal** for the assassination of **Napoleon I**. The pair reached Paris but were betrayed; Pichegru was imprisoned and later found strangled in bed. ▷ **Bourbon, House of; Thermidor**

Pichincha, Battle of (1822) A decisive battle of the **Spanish–American Wars of Independence**, fought on the slopes of Mount Pichincha overlooking the city of Quito. It secured the liberation of Quito (now Ecuador) from Spanish rule.

Pichon, Stéphen Jean Marie (1857–1933) French politician and journalist. He served on **Clemenceau**'s newspaper *La Justice* before entering the Chamber of Deputies in 1885. Becoming a diplomat, he served in Port-au-Prince, San Domingo, Rio de Janeiro, Beijing and Tunis; he represented the powers in negotiations with China during the Boxer Rebellion. He was Minister of Foreign Affairs twice (1906–11 , 1917–20), after which he joined *Le Petit Journal* as its political editor. He was always seen as Clemenceau's protégé, and abandoned control of foreign policy to him in 1917–20.

Picts A general term coined by the Romans in the 3c for their barbarian enemies in Britain north of the **Antonine Wall**, and then used to describe the subjects of kings ruling north and south of the East Grampians. The name derives from the local custom of body tattooing. They disappear from history soon after being united with the Scots under Kenneth I. Traces of their language and art (notably the enigmatic Pictish symbol stones) survive.

PIDE (*Policia Internacional de Defensa do Estado,* 'International Police for State Defence') Portuguese secret police. With the establishment in 1933 of the PVDE ('Police of Vigilance and State Defence'), the secret police in Portugal became the most feared institution of the **Estado Novo** under **Salazar**. The Salazar dictatorship, in common with other authoritarian regimes, created an unscrupulous secret police force to safeguard its interests. In the 1930s the PVDE drew on the police state techniques of Nazi Germany and Fascist Italy. The creation of a nationwide network of spies and informers effectively banned the discussion of politics in public for almost half a century. In 1945 the secret police was renamed the International Police for State Defence (PIDE). With even greater powers than those of its predecessor, the PIDE lasted until the end of the Salazar era, reaching the height of its influence during the 1960s. Not only did it have a leading role in the colonial war being fought in Portuguese Africa (launching vicious dirty tricks campaigns), but it also dealt a devastating blow to the opposition through the murder of General **Delgado** in 1965. The PIDE was undoubtedly the most loathed of all the state institutions of the Salazar dictatorship. In 1969 it was rechristened the General Directorate of Security (DGS) and its powers were curtailed.

Pieck, Wilhelm (1876–1960) East German politician. The son of a labourer, he initially worked as a carpenter and was active from an early age in socialist politics. In 1915 he helped found the Spartacus League and in 1918–19 the German Communist Party (**KPD**), leading the unsuccessful 'Spartacus Uprising' in **Berlin** in 1919. During the **Weimar Republic**, Pieck was elected as a communist to the **Reichstag** in 1928, but was forced into exile in 1933 when **Hitler** came to power. He fled to Moscow where he became, in 1935, Secretary of the **Comintern**. In 1945 he returned to Berlin in the wake of the **Red Army** and created, in 1946, the dominant Socialist Unity Party (**SED**) out of the former KPD and Social Democratic Party (**SPD**). From 1949 he served as President of the

German Democratic Republic, the post being abolished on his death.

piemontizzazione The Italian term used to describe the policy adopted by the government in Turin after 1859 to extend Piedmontese laws, institutions and often personnel to the territories newly annexed by **Victor Emmanuel II**. The practice was extended to all of the peninsula with the exception of Tuscany, which briefly enjoyed considerable autonomy. In the **Mezzogiorno** it caused much ill-will and was an important contributory factor in the outbreak of the **Grande Brigantaggio**.

Pierce, Franklin (1804–69) US politician and 14th President. He studied law and was admitted to the Bar in 1827. From 1829 to 1833 he was a Democratic member of the state legislature, was elected to the House of Representatives, and in 1837 to the US Senate. Returning to his private law practice in 1842, he volunteered for the **Mexican War** (1846–8), where he was made brigadier general. In 1852 he was nominated as a compromise candidate for the presidency against Winfield Scott, the Whig nominee, and elected. As President (1853–7), he favoured an expansionist policy succeeding in the purchase from Spain of a significant strip of land in the Southwest. On the issue of slavery, he had supported the **Compromise of 1850**, but then signed the **Kansas–Nebraska Act**, which kindled a flame that ultimately led to the **American Civil War**. Because of the unpopularity of this act, he was not renominated, and he retired from politics in 1857.

Pierlot, Hubert (1883–1963) Belgian politician. After training and practising as a lawyer, he became a senator in 1926. He served as Minister for Internal Affairs (1934–5) and Agriculture (1936–8), and formed a government in Apr 1939. After the surrender of the Belgian forces in June 1940, he led the government in exile in London, leaving King **Leopold III**, who had decided to stay with the army. His negative attitude to the King continued during his post-war government (1944–5), but his **Christian People's Party** in general supported the King, so he retired from public life in 1945.

Pietism Originally, a movement within Lutheranism in the 17c and 18c stressing good works, Bible study, and holiness in Christian life. It was a reaction against rigid Protestant dogmatism, and influenced other groups, such as Moravians, Methodists, and Evangelicals.

Pig War (1906–11) The name given to the period of 'economic warfare' between the Habsburg government and Serbia. In 1905 Serbia and Bulgaria had agreed to closer economic ties which would lead to eventual economic union. To force Serbia to break this agreement, the government in Vienna banned the import of all Serbian livestock (chiefly pigs) into the Habsburg Empire. The embargo, combined with the annexation of Bosnia and Herzegovina (1908), caused Austro-Serb relations to deteriorate yet further and drove Serbia closer to France and Russia.

Pi i Margall, Francesc (1824–1901) Spanish politician and thinker. Emerging as a leading political activist in the revolution of 1854, he was an anti-absolutist and anti-Catholic radical democrat. In 1868 he was elected to the constituent Cortes before becoming head of the Federal Republican Party. After he became President of the First Republic in Apr 1873, the Cortes voted for a federal regime. He resigned in July 1873, unable to solve the clash between the cantonalists and the antifederal democrats. He not only became the chief theoretician of federalism but was also widely regarded as a secular saint for his doctrinal purity and incorruptibility. ▷ **Cantonalist Risings; Republic, First** (Spain)

Pilate, Pontius (Pontius Pilatus) (1c AD) The best known of all the Roman governors of Judaea because of his role in the trial and condemnation of Jesus of Nazareth, he held the office under **Tiberius** from 26–36. Though to the Jews his behaviour often seemed provocative — his appropriation of Temple funds to build an aqueduct and his smuggling of imperial portrait busts into Jerusalem by night both provoked near-riots — to the strict Tiberius, who kept him in post for a decade, he must have seemed a reasonably capable administrator. Deposed by the Governor of Syria for mishandling a public demonstration in Samaria, he was sent back to Rome in disgrace. Disappearing then from history, he reappears much later in Christian apocryphal literature as the subject of innumerable colourful legends and was actually canonized by the Coptic church in Egypt.

Pilgrimage of Grace (Oct 1536–Jan 1537) A major Tudor rebellion in England, a series of armed demonstrations in six northern counties. It was directed against the policies and ministers of **Henry VIII**, and combined upper-class and popular discontent over religious and secular issues, especially the Dissolution of the Monasteries. It was led by Lord Thomas Darcy, Robert Aske, and 'pilgrims' carrying banners of the Five Wounds of Christ. Darcy and Aske were subsequently executed for treason.

Pilgrim Fathers The English religious dissenters who established Plymouth Colony in America in 1620, after crossing the Atlantic on the *Mayflower*. The men, women and children included Puritan separatists and non-separatists. Before disembarking the adult males aboard signed the **Mayflower Compact**. ▷ **Plymouth Colony**

Piłsudski, Józef (1867–1935) Polish marshal and politician. Born near Vilna in Russian Poland, he was educated at the University of Kharkov. Imprisoned several times by the tsarist authorities for his activities in the cause of Polish independence, he was the founder and leader of the Polish Socialist Party (1892). He formed a band of troops which fought on the side of Austria against Russia for part of **World War I** but in 1917 he was imprisoned in Germany. Freed the following year, he was in a good position to declare Poland's independence and to become head of state and commander-in-chief. Still anti-Russian, he was not unhappy to lead his country in the Polish-Soviet War in 1920–1 and to emerge with considerable territorial gains. In 1922 he was pushed out of power by more moderate politicians, but in 1926 he organized a coup d'état to become Prime Minister, Minister of War and leader of an authoritarian, right-wing nationalist regime until his death.

Pimen, Patriarch (1910–90) Russian Orthodox patriarch. Ordained a priest in 1932, he spent the later **Stalin** years in jail. However, in Nikita **Khrushchev**'s time, in 1957, he was consecrated a bishop and in Leonid **Brezhnev**'s time, in 1971, became the Patriarch. He supported Soviet peace initiatives and was a member of the World Peace Committee. Finally, in 1988, he met Mikhail **Gorbachev** and secured his permission to celebrate the millennium of Christianity in Russia.

Pinckney, Charles Cotesworth (1746–1825) US statesman. Educated at Oxford, he became a lawyer. He was Washington's aide-de-camp at Brandywine and Germantown, but was taken prisoner at the surrender of **Charleston** (1780). He was a member of the convention that framed the US consti-

tution (1787). His refusal to pay bribes extorted by French agents brought the **XYZ Affair** into the open. He was twice Federalist candidate for the presidency (1804 and 1808). ▷ **American Revolution**

Pindling, Sir Lynden Oscar (1930–) Bahamanian politician. Educated in the Bahamas and at London University, he practised as a lawyer before becoming centrally involved in politics, eventually as Leader of the Progressive Liberal Party (PLP). He became Prime Minister in 1969 and led his country to full independence, within the **Commonwealth of Nations**, in 1973. The PLP, under Pindling, was re-elected in 1977, 1982 and 1987.

Pinkerton, Allan (1819–84) Scottish-born US detective. He was a Chartist who in 1842 settled at Dundee, Illinois, became a detective and deputy-sheriff, and in 1850 founded the Pinkerton National Detective Agency. He headed a federal intelligence network for General McClellan during the **American Civil War**, and his agency later took a leading part in breaking up the **Molly Maguires** and in policing other labour disputes.

Pinkie, Battle of (10 Sep 1547) A battle fought between the English and the Scots at Musselburgh, east of Edinburgh. The English forces under Protector Somerset were victorious, but the aim of the war, of 'rough wooing' (to secure **Mary, Queen of Scots** as a bride for **Edward VI**) was frustrated. Mary and Scotland formed an alliance with the French; and England was forced to evacuate by the Treaty of Boulogne (1550).

Pinochet (Ugarte), Augusto (1915–) Chilean dictator. A career army officer, he led the military coup overthrowing the government of Salvador **Allende** (1973), establishing himself at the head of the ensuing military regime. In 1980 he enacted a constitution giving himself an eight-year presidential term (1981–9). A plebiscite held in 1988 rejected his continuation as president beyond 1990. Free elections were held in 1990 and the Christian Democrat Patricio Aylwin was installed as President.

Pintasilgo, Maria de Lurdes (1930–) Portuguese politician. From 1970 to 1974 she was the Chairwoman of the National Committee on the status of women. After the 1974 revolution she was made Minister for Social Affairs, legislating above all on women's rights. In 1976–9 she was Ambassador to

UNESCO, and from 1979 to 1980 acted as caretaker Prime Minister. She has also written widely on international affairs and women's issues.

Pinzón, Vicente Yáñez (c.1460–c.1524) Spanish discoverer of Brazil, from a wealthy Andalusian family. He commanded the *Nina* in the first expedition of Christopher Columbus (1492), and his brother, Martin, commanded the *Pinta*. In 1499 he sailed on his own account, and in 1500 landed near Pernambuco on the Brazil coast, which he followed north to the Orinoco. He was made Governor of Brazil by **Ferdinand II, 'the Catholic'** and **Isabella I, 'the Catholic'**.

Pirogov, Nikolai I (1810–81) Russian surgeon. He was in charge of the medical service during the Siege of **Sevastopol** and performed virtual miracles in improving appalling hospital conditions. He had the assistance of a sister-in-law of the Tsar, the Grand Duchess Elena Pavlovna, who organized 250 nurses into the Community of the Elevation of the Cross. Subsequently he played an important part in developing medical education. He also contributed more widely to higher education and took steps, for example, that eventually led to the establishment of the University of Odessa. His liberal ideas led to the loss of his last public appointment in 1866.

Pisacane, Carlo (1818–57) Italian revolutionary. An ex-officer in the Bourbon army, he served in the French Foreign Legion and took part in the defence of the Roman Republic in 1849. In 1857 he tried to launch an insurrection in the Kingdom of the **Two Sicilies**, but was captured and killed by peasants.

Pisistratus (c.600–527BC) Tyrant of Athens (561/c.556BC and 546/527BC). A moderate and far-sighted ruler, he did much to improve the lot of the small farmer in Attica, and to boost Athenian trade abroad, especially in the Black Sea area. He invited the leading Greek poets of the day to settle in Athens, where he set about fostering a sense of national unity by instituting or expanding great religious and cultural festivals. He was succeeded by his sons Hippias and Hipparchus, the so-called *Pisistratidae*, but the dynasty was overthrown in 510BC.

Pitt, William, 1st Earl of Chatham, 'the Elder' (1708–78) British politician and orator. He joined the army (1731) and then entered parliament for the family borough,

Old Sarum (1735). He led the young 'Patriot' **Whigs**, and in 1756 became nominally Secretary of State, but virtually Premier. The enmity of **George II** led him to resign in 1757, but public demand caused his recall. Again compelled to resign when his cabinet refused to declare war with Spain (1761), he vigorously attacked the peace terms of the Treaty of Paris (1763) as too generous to France. He formed a new ministry in 1766, but ill health contributed to his resignation in 1768. He died in the House of Lords. His eldest son, John, 2nd Earl of Chatham (1756–1835), commanded the luckless Walcheren Expedition (1809). ▷ **Pitt, William, 'the Younger'**; **Seven Years War**

Pitt, William, 'the Younger' (1759–1806) British politician. The second son of William Pitt, 'the Elder', he studied law, but then became an MP (1781), his first post being Chancellor of the Exchequer under **Shelburne** (1782). He became First Lord of the Treasury (1783), and was confirmed as Prime Minister at the election of 1784. During his long first ministry (1783–1801), he carried through important administrative and financial reforms, his policy being influenced by the political economy of Adam Smith. He negotiated coalitions against France (1793 and 1798), but these had little success. After the Irish rebellion of 1798, he proposed a legislative union which would be followed by Catholic emancipation. The union was effected in 1800, but Pitt resigned office in 1801 rather than contest **George III**'s hostility to emancipation. He resumed office in 1804. He drank very heavily, and this contributed to his early death while still in office. ▷ **Napoleonic Wars**

Pittsburgh Agreement (1918) The agreement between **Masaryk**, the future President of Czechoslovakia, and Czech and Slovak immigrants to the USA, setting out the possible lines of a Czechoslovak constitution. As leader of the exiles struggling to win support from the Allied Powers in **World War I**, Masaryk wanted the immigrants' backing and promised the Slovaks that, to ensure the autonomy of Slovakia, it might be possible to create a federal state. When a unitary state emerged, the Slovaks in the USA felt betrayed and, particularly in the 1930s, worked hard to secure the separation of Slovakia that transpired in 1939 when **Hitler** occupied the Czech Lands and set up a puppet Slovakia.

Pius II (*Eneo Silvio de Piccolomini*) (1405–64) Italian Pope (1458/64). He was employed on diplomatic missions before taking orders and becoming Bishop of Trieste (1447) and a cardinal (1456). As Pope, he attempted to organize an armed confederation of Christian princes to resist the Turks, following their victory at Constantinople (1453). One of the most eminent humanist scholars of his age, his works are chiefly historical.

Pius IV (Giovanni Angelo de' Medici) (1499–1565) Italian Pope (1559/65). He brought to a close the deliberations of the Concil of **Trent**. In many ways, this signalled an end to the conflict between the principles of papal monarchy and conciliarism: the council endorsed its declaration of faith as the Creed of Pius IV, even though it is still known as the Tridentine Creed, which connects it to the council.

Pius V, St (Michele Ghislieri) (1504–72) Italian Pope (1566/72). As Pope, he implemented the decrees of the Council of **Trent** (1545–63), excommunicated Queen **Elizabeth I** (1570), and inspired the **Holy League** (1571) against the Turks. The league's campaign culminated in the great victory of the Christian fleet under Don **John of Austria** at the Battle of **Lepanto** in the Gulf of Corinth.

Pius VI (Giovanni Angelo Braschi) (1717–99) Italian Pope (1775/99). His long pontificate saw the papacy confronted with repeated threats and crises: the growth of anticlerical Enlightenment thought; the increasing tendency of monarchs to ignore the papacy and view the Church only in terms of their own interests and from a national context; and, above all, the devastating changes brought by the **French Revolution** and subsequent European wars. Pius VI was ill-suited to cope with so stormy a period and, from the outset, was beset with problems. Under Bourbon pressure to continue the anti-Jesuit policies of his predecessor, **Clement XIV**, he sought vainly to dissuade **Catherine II, 'the Great'** of Russia and **Frederick II, 'the Great'** of Prussia from offering the Jesuits refuge, while simultaneously having to cope with rumours among ultra-conservative **Zelanti** that he was secretly sympathetic towards the outlawed society. In 1781 he faced another blow to papal authority when Joseph II of Austria published his Edict of Toleration, which not only allowed greater rights to non-Catholics but also constituted a broad assault on the privileges, property and status of the Church within the Habsburg Empire. Although

Joseph's death in 1790 meant an effective end to the Josephist anticlerical experiment, it was by this stage a trifling worry for Pius compared with the problems posed by events in France. The French Civil Constitution of 1790 struck a crippling blow to the Church, forcing Pius to denounce the revolution openly the following year. In 1796, however, Napoleon invaded the Papal States at the head of a revolutionary army and, two years later, the Holy City was occupied and Pius expelled. In 1799 Rome was formally seized by France; Pius died the same year, a defeated and dejected prisoner.

Pius VII (Luigi Barnaba Chiaramonti) (1742–1823) Italian Pope (1800/23). He was responsible for the **Concordat** (1801) with **Napoleon I**, and was forced in 1804 to consecrate him as Emperor. When the French occupied the **Papal States** in 1809, Pius was taken to France and made to sign a new Concordat sanctioning their annexation. The fall of Napoleon in 1814 allowed his return to Rome and the restoration of the Papal States. ▷ **Consalvi, Ercole**

Pius IX (Giovanni Maria Mastai Ferretti) (1792–1878) Italian Pope (1846/78). Originally hailed as the patriot Pope longed for by **Gioberti**, his early reforms and apparently anti-Austrian stance evaporated in the face of the growing radicalism of the **Revolutions of 1848–9**. After the **Papal Allocution** of Apr 1848 it became clear that he was embarking on an increasingly conservative course. On the assassination of Pellegrino **Rossi** he fled Rome, returning only after the **Oudinot Expedition** had enabled the restoration of his full temporal powers. He was violently opposed to the unification of Italy which was accomplished through the annexation by **Victor Emmanuel II** of the **Papal States** (1860–70) and refused to recognize the new united Kingdom of Italy. His ever more reactionary stance was manifest in the **Syllabus of Errors** (1864) and the decree of Papal Infallibility of the first **Vatican Council** (1870). He spent the last years of his life in self-imposed 'imprisonment' in the Vatican city.

Pizarro, Francisco (c.1478–1541) Spanish conquistador. He served in Italy, and with the expedition which discovered the Pacific (1513). In 1526 he and **Almagro** sailed for Peru, and in 1531 began the conquest of the **Incas**. He killed King **Atahualpa**, then worked to consolidate the new empire, founding Lima (1535) and other cities.

Dissension between Pizarro and Almagro led to the latter's execution; in revenge, Almagro's followers assassinated Pizarro at Lima.

Pizarro, Gonzalo (c.1506–48) Spanish conquistador. The half-brother of Francisco **Pizarro**, he accompanied him in the conquest of Peru, and did good service when the Indians besieged Cuzco (1535–6), and in the conquest of Charcas. In 1539 he undertook an arduous expedition to the east of Quito. One of his lieutenants, Francisco de Orellana, sent ahead for supplies, deserted his starving comrades, discovered the whole course of the Amazon, and returned to Spain. Only 90 out of 350 Spaniards returned with Pizarro in June 1542. On his brother's assassination (1541), he retired to Charcas. In 1544 the new viceroy, Vela, arrived in Peru to enforce the 'New Laws'. The Spaniards, dismayed, entreated Pizarro to protect their interests. He mustered 400 men, entered Lima (Oct 1544), and was declared Governor of Peru; Vela was defeated and killed in battle (1546). When news of this revolt reached Spain, Pedro de la Gasca, an able ecclesiastic, was sent to Peru as President to restore order, and landed at Tumbes in June 1547. Pizarro defeated a force sent against him, and met Gasca near Cuzco (Apr 1548). However, his forces deserted him, he gave himself up and was beheaded.

PKI ▷ **Partai Komunis Indonesia**

Plaatje, Sol T (1876–1932) South African journalist, politician and literary figure. One of the founders of black nationalism, he first worked as a Post Office messenger and later a magistrates' court interpreter in Kimberley. He was in the town throughout the siege during the Boer War and kept a lively diary of those events. After the war he founded and edited newspapers, wrote books (including *Native Life in South Africa*), translated Shakespeare into his native tongue, Tswana, and was one of the founders of the South African Native National Congress, later the ANC (African National Congress).

Placidia, Galla (c.390–450) Daughter of **Theodosius I** and mother of **Valentinian III**, for whom she acted as regent, with the title Augusta, during the early part of his reign. She died at Ravenna, where her tomb is still to be seen.

Plaid Cymru The Welsh National Party, founded in 1925, with the aim of achieving independence for Wales. It stands for election throughout Wales, but finds support mainly in the north of the country. It had one MP following the 1987 general election, and has never had more than three.

Plain, The Known in French as the *Marais*, the term refers to the majority of deputies in the French revolutionary National Convention, politically uncommitted to a particular faction although broadly aligned with the **Girondins**. They were ultimately outmanoeuvred by extremists, the **Jacobins** of the **Mountain**. ▷ **Convention, National; French Revolution**

Plantagenet Dynasty The name given by historians to the royal dynasty in England from **Henry II** to **Richard II** (1154–1399), then continued by two rival houses of younger lines, Lancaster and York, until 1485. The dynasty was so called because, allegedly, Henry II's father Geoffrey of Anjou, sported a sprig of broom (Old French, *plante genêt*) in his cap. ▷ **Angevins; Edward I; Edward II; Edward III; Henry III; John ('John Lackland'); Lancaster, House of; Richard I, 'the Lionheart'; York, House of**

Plantation of Ireland The colonization and conquest of Ireland, begun in 1556 and continued to 1660; at first mainly English, but Scottish settlers came to Ulster (1608–11). The policy led to rebellions by the native Irish and Anglo-Irish aristocracy (1563–9, 1580–3, 1598–1603 and 1641) and the eventual conquest of Ireland under **Cromwell**, in which possibly two-thirds of the Irish died.

Plassey, Battle of (1757) The decisive victory of Robert **Clive of Plassey** over **Siraj ud-Daula**, Nawab of Bengal, India. Clive's success was aided by the treachery of the Nawab's general, Mir Jafar, whom the British subsequently placed on the throne. The victory was an important step in the British acquisition of Bengal. ▷ **East India Company, British**

PLANTAGENET DYNASTY

Regnal Dates	Name
1154/89	Henry II
1189/99	Richard I, 'the Lionheart'
1199/1216	John ('Lackland')
1216/72	Henry III
1272/1307	Edward I
1307/27	Edward II
1327/77	Edward III
1377/99	Richard II

Plastiras, Nikolaos (1883–1953) Greek politician. A Republican close to **Venizélos**, he organized the 1922 coup d'état following the humiliation of the Greek army by Kemal **Atatürk** in Asia Minor. Determined to be seen to punish those responsible for the debacle, he contrived the execution of six politicians and military commanders, charging them with treason. After the Republicans' election defeat (1933), he organized another coup which failed and fled with Venizélos to France. Remaining in exile during **World War II**, he was recognized as nominal leader of **EDES**. In 1945, during the regency of **Damaskinos**, he replaced George **Papandreou** as Prime Minister. After the **Greek Civil War**, he led the National Progressive Union (EPEK) and was again Prime Minister in one of the many coalition governments during 1951.

Platov, Matvei Ivanovich, Count (1757–1818) Russian soldier. He served in the Turkish campaign of 1770–1, and in 1801 was named by **Alexander I** 'Hetman of the Cossacks of the Don'. He took part in the campaigns against the French (1805–7), and hung on their retreat from Moscow with pitiless pertinacity (1813), defeating Lefebvre at Altenburg, gaining a victory at Laon, and making his name memorable by the depredations of his fierce horsemen.

Platt Amendment (1902) Appendage to the Cuban independence constitution after the **Spanish–American War** (1898) which gave the USA the right to 'intervene for the preservation of Cuban independence'. Such interventions took place in 1906, 1912 and 1920 and, while the Platt Amendment was annulled in 1934, the USA's lease of the naval base at Guantanamo Bay was retained. The Reciprocal Trade Treaty of 1903 continued to allow the USA to dominate the Cuban economy, particularly under the **Batista** administration. The **Castro** revolution of 1959 can be seen as a response to that alien control while the US response (the **Bay of Pigs** invasion of 1961) was another manifestation of the rights claimed under the Platt Amendment.

Plekhanov, Georgei Valentinovich (1856–1918) Russian Marxist philosopher, historian and journalist. Dubbed 'the Father of Russian Marxism', he left Russia in 1880, having already been involved in revolutionary action, and in 1883 founded the first Russian Marxist organization, the Liberation of Labour Group, in Geneva, where he remained until 1917. Arguing against the traditional idea of a peasants' revolt, and propounding the case for a bourgeois, followed by a proletarian, revolution, he was a major intellectual influence on the young **Lenin**. However, in 1903 he sided with the **Mensheviks** against Lenin's **Bolsheviks**, and in 1917 he denounced the **October Revolution**. He then moved to Finland, where he died. ▷ **Russian Revolution**

Plessy v Ferguson (1896) US Supreme Court decision that opened the way to racial segregation under the **US Constitution** by upholding the concept of 'separate but equal'. Homer Plessy was appealing against his conviction for refusing to leave a railroad car reserved for whites. The court ruled that if the facilities offered blacks were equal to those for whites, there was no infringement of the **Fourteenth Amendment**. Justice John M Harlan dissented with the prescient warning that the ruling was 'inconsistent with civil freedom' and would support prejudice. The decision came to underpin the whole structure of segregation in the Southern states during the first half of the 20c, eventually being overturned by **Brown v Board of Education of Topeka, Kansas** (1954).

Pleve, Vyacheslav Konstantinovich (1846–1904) Russian police chief and politician. A lawyer by training, he was director of state police by the age of 35. He attacked the relatively conservative **zemstvos**, confiscated Armenian Church lands, and regularly persecuted Jews, Finns and Poles. He became Minister of the Interior after the assassination of the incumbent in 1902 by a socialist revolutionary, and was himself murdered the same way in 1904. He acquired notoriety for urging **Nicholas II** to fight Japan since what Russia needed was 'a small victorious war', which of course it lost. His repressive activities gave Tsarism an evil press in Russia and abroad.

PLO (Palestine Liberation Organization) An organization that consists of several of the Palestinian groups opposed to Israel, led by Yasser Arafat. Founded in 1964, its charter denied the right of Israel to exist and called for Palestine to be liberated by armed conflict. In 1974 the Arab Summit in Rabat, Morocco, recognized the PLO as the sole legitimate representative of the Palestinian people. In 1982 its forces in Lebanon were attacked and expelled by Israel, with the support of the US Reagan administration; many US servicemen and diplomats in

Lebanon were killed as a result. Secret talks in Norway (1991–3) between the Israeli Prime Minister Itzhak Rabin and the PLO led to the agreement signed in Washington, DC (13 Sep 1993) by Rabin and Arafat on mutual recognition and limited self-rule in the Gaza Strip and West Bank town of Jericho.

Plojhar, Josef (1902–81) Czechoslovak politician. A member of the People's Party and an active Catholic priest, he agreed to support the communists in their takeover of power in 1948 and be a member of the new National Front government. He became Minister of Health and remained such until 1968 when the reformers removed him. Archbishop **Beran** banned him from preaching, but his clerical collar gave his government some degree of respectability in foreign parts.

Plombières, Agreement of (July 1858) A secret accord negotiated by **Cavour** with **Napoleon III**, in which the latter promised extensive military and financial assistance to Sardinia-Piedmont to drive the Austrians from the Kingdom of **Lombardy-Venetia**. In return, France was to receive Savoy and probably Nice, while Clotilde, daughter of **Victor Emmanuel II** was to marry Jerome Napoleon. The agreement provided the basis for a defensive-offensive alliance concluded on 18 Jan 1859, war eventually breaking out in Apr of the same year.

Plunkitt, George Washington (1842–1924) US politician. Tammany leader of the New York Fifteenth Assembly District, Sachem of the Tammany Society and chairman of the Election Committee of **Tammany Hall**, he was at various times an Assemblyman, State Senator, Police Magistrate, County Supervisor and Alderman. At one time he held four public offices and drew salaries from three of them simultaneously, a fact of which he was inordinately proud. He was immortalized in a series of 'Very Plain Talks on Very Practical Politics', recorded by the journalist William L Riordon, and published under the title *Plunkitt of Tammany Hall* in 1905. It was a cheerfully ingenuous defence of machine politics, and has become a minor classic of US political science. ▷ **political machine**

Pluralism Both a description of and prescription for circumstances where political power is widely dispersed, so that no one interest group or class predominates. The principal conditions for pluralism are free elections, many and overlapping interests,

low barriers to ways of organizing pressure on government, and a state that is responsive to popular demands. The term is commonly applied to liberal democracies, where it is argued that the large number of pressure groups complement electoral politics in allowing citizens to get their preferences reflected in government decisions. However, the argument that pluralism is democratic is criticized by some on the grounds that social and economic inequalities make political competition unequal.

Plutarch (AD c.46–c.120) Greek historian, biographer, and philosopher. Educated in Athens, he paid several visits to Rome, where he gave public lectures in philosophy. His extant writings comprise *Opera Moralia*, a series of essays on ethical, political, religious, and other topics, and several historical works, notably *Bioi paralleloi* (Parallel Lives), a gallery of 46 portraits of the great characters of preceding ages, each book consisting of a Greek and a Roman figure, sharing some resemblance. Thomas North's translation of this work into English (1579) was the source of Shakespeare's Roman plays.

Plymouth Colony The American colony established by the *Mayflower* Pilgrims in 1620, comprising the south-east corner of modern Massachusetts. It existed as a separate entity until 1686, when it was absorbed into the Dominion of New England. In 1691 it became part of Massachusetts Bay. ▷ **Pilgrim Fathers**

PMDB (*Partido do Movimento Democrático Brasileiro*, 'Brazilian Democratic Movement Party') The political party created in Brazil (1979) by opposition groups in response to the military government's attempts to dissolve the two-party system created in the aftermath of the 1964 military coup. This system pitted ARENA (*Aliança da Renovação Nacional*), heir to the conservative and golpista UDN (*União Democrática Nacional*) and conservative **PSD**, against the MDB (*Movimento Democrático Brasileiro*), itself the successor to **Vargas'** PSD (pro-**Kubitschek (de Oliveira)**) and the pro-**Goulart** PTB (*Partido Trabalhista Brasileiro*). By 1979, the strength of the PMDB in the cities and industrial zones of Brazil meant that it could outflank the Figueiredo government. Although the regime did succeed in dividing the PMDB between adherents to **Brizola's** PDT, a rump PTB, **Lula's** PT (*Partido dos Trabalhadores*) and Tancredo **Neves'** *Partido*

Popular, the PMDB gained decisive victories in 1982. It provided the platform for Neves' presidential campaign in 1984–5, and was an uneasy supporter of **Sarney (Costa)** in the gubernatorial contest of 1986. Its identification with Sarney, and the 'old politics' lost it the presidential campaign of 1989 to Fernando **Collor de Mello**.

PNC ▷ **People's National Congress** (Guyana)

PNV (*Partido Nacionalista Vasco*, 'Basque Nationalist Party') Founded in 1895, the PNV (or *Eusko Alderdi Jeltzalea* in Basque), was the first political party to defend Basque nationalism. Under the Second Republic of 1931–6 it was the leading party in Basque politics, though it never had a majority. With the outbreak of the **Spanish Civil War** (July 1936), the PNV backed the Republic in exchange for an autonomy statute, which was passed in Oct 1936. Under the dynamic leadership of José Antonio **Aguirre**, the PNV gained control of the autonomous government. During the Basque government's exile of 1939–75 the PNV provided most of its leadership. From 1977 to 1984 the PNV was again the leading force in the Basque country, but splits in the 1980s reduced its share of the Basque vote to 22 per cent in 1987. ▷ **Basque Autonomy Statutes; Republic, Second** (Spain)

Pobedonostsev, Konstantin Petrovich (1827–1907) Russian jurist and politician. Tutor, and later adviser, to **Alexander III** and **Nicholas II**, he became Professor of Civil Law at Moscow in 1858 and, as a member of a judicial commission in 1863, favoured liberal reforms in the law. However, after becoming Procurator of the Holy Synod in 1866, he reacted against this, becoming strongly opposed to any westernizing changes in Russia and the most influential as well as the most uncompromising champion of the autocracy and of the supremacy of the Russian Orthodox Church. He was eventually forced to resign in 1905 in the midst of the revolution of that year, but he had by then done immeasurable damage to the progress of normal constitutional change. ▷ **Revolution of 1905**

Pocahontas (1595–1617) Native American princess, the daughter of a chief, Powhatan, who is said to have saved the life of Captain John Smith, leader of a group of colonists who settled in Chesapeake Bay in 1607. She was captured and taken to Jamestown in 1612, where she embraced Christianity, was baptized Rebecca, married an Englishman, John Rolfe (1585–1622), and went to England with him in 1616. She embarked for Virginia the following year, but died of smallpox off Gravesend in England, leaving one son. ▷ **Powhatan Confederacy**

Podgorny, Nikolai Viktorovich (1903–83) Soviet politician. Born in the Ukraine, the son of a foundry worker, he worked in the sugar industry and in due course held managerial, educational and ministerial posts connected with food. In 1930 he joined the Communist Party, and after **World War II** took a leading role in the economic reconstruction of the liberated Ukraine. He held various senior posts (1950–65), becoming a full member of the **Politburo** in 1960. Following the dismissal of Nikita **Khrushchev** (1964), he became Chairman of the Presidium and therefore titular head of state in 1965. He was relieved of this office in 1977 and replaced by Leonid **Brezhnev**, partly because his performance was lacklustre, but mainly because Brezhnev wanted to be head of state as well as General-Secretary of the Party. ▷ **communism**

pogrom A violent racialist assault on a minority ethnic or religious group, especially Jews. The first great outbreak of pogroms was in Russia in 1881–2 following the assassination of Tsar **Alexander II**, for which Jews were falsely blamed. Despite the findings of a commission in 1883–8 that Russian Jews were sinned against rather than sinning, pogroms and anti-Semitism in general grew more widespread and in fact provoked many Jewish intellectuals into revolutionary activities.

Poincaré, Raymond (Nicolas Landry) (1860–1934) French politician. He studied law, becoming a Deputy (1887) and Senator (1903), holding office as Minister of Public Instruction (1893 and 1895), of Finance (1894–5 and 1906), and of Foreign Affairs (1912–3 and 1922–3). Elected Prime Minister (1912–13) and President (1913–20), he sought to play a more directive role than previous incumbents. He had some success at first, especially in foreign affairs, but when **Clemenceau** became Prime Minister in 1917, he found himself sidelined, and was unable to influence decisions at the post-war peace conference. As Prime Minister once again (1922–4) he sought to enforce the terms of the Treaty of **Versailles** (notably the payment of reparations) against a recalcitrant Germany by occupying the Ruhr (1923–4). Although Germany was thus forced to negotiate, Poincaré had by then been defeated in the 1924 elections, and his successor as Prime Minister, **Herriot**, bowing to British and US pressure, conceded much of what Poincaré had hoped to achieve. He was brought back to power (1926–9), as Prime Minister and Finance Minister, to deal with a financial crisis; he stabilized the franc, inaugurating a brief period of prosperity before France succumbed to the **Great Depression**.

Poissy, Synod of (1561) A meeting of theologians called by the French Regent, **Catherine de' Medici**, and her adviser, Michel de **l'Hôpital**, in an attempt to reconcile Catholics and Protestants. It failed, due to the intransigence of both sides on the question of transubstantiation.

Poitiers, Battle of (732) The battle at which **Charles Martel** defeated the Arab invaders, coming from Spain, turning them back definitively from Europe, north of the Pyrenees.

Poitiers, Battle of (19 Sep 1356) A battle between England and France during the **Hundred Years War**. The English forces, under **Edward the Black Prince** (son of **Edward III**), were victorious and King **John II** of France was captured. The battle had important consequences, the French King agreeing to return all possessions in France which had been held by **Henry II** of England. When the French nobility resisted these terms, Edward III invaded France and laid siege to Paris. The Treaty of Bretigny (1360), which ceded much territory in France to Edward III together with a large ransom for King John, represented one of the high-water marks of English success during the war.

Poland, Partitions of Agreements between Russia, Austria and Prussia to partition a weakening Poland in the late 18c. The first, second and third partitions (1772, 1793 and 1795) deprived Poland of its independent statehood and gave Russia the lion's share of its territories. Throughout the 19c and early 20c, the Poles constantly struggled for national liberation which they eventually won at the end of **World War I** in 1918.

Pole, Reginald (1500–58) English Roman Catholic churchman and Archbishop of Canterbury. He received several Church posts, and was at first high in **Henry VIII**'s favour; but after opposing the King on divorce, he left for Italy, and lost all his preferments. In 1536 the Pope made him a cardinal, and in 1554, in the reign of the Catholic Queen **Mary I**, he returned to England as papal legate. He became one of her most powerful advisers, returned the country to Rome, and became Archbishop of Canterbury. ▷ **Reformation** (England)

Polignac, Auguste Jules Armand Marie, Prince of (1780–1847) French politician. An exponent of papal and royal authority, he received the title of prince from the Pope in 1820 and became in 1829 head of the last Bourbon ministry. He promulgated the St Cloud Ordinances that cost **Charles X** of France his throne (1830). He was imprisoned until 1836, then lived in exile in England, returning in 1845 to Paris. ▷ **Bourbon, House of; July Revolution (1830)**

polis Conventionally translated 'city-state', the principal political, social and economic unit of classical Greece. There were differences of political colouring between one *polis* and another. Some (eg Athens) were democracies, while others (eg **Corinth**, **Thebes**, **Sparta**) were more oligarchical in character. But all possessed the same basic organs of government: an assembly of male citizens, an advisory council, and elected executive officers. The ideals of autonomy and economic self-sufficiency were in practice not attained by many *poleis*.

Polisario Properly, the Popular Front for the Liberation of Saguia el-Hamra and Rio de Oro, this is a movement of tribesmen from what is now called Western Sahara, which aims at resisting the attempts of King Hasan II of Morocco to absorb these areas into Morocco itself. This move on the part of Hasan followed Spain's granting of independence to the region (its former colony), and the division of the region between Morocco and Mauretania. Hostilities in 1975 and Polisario's establishment (1976) of a 'government-in-exile' of the so-called Sahrawi Arab Democratic Republic (SADR) was the prelude to Mauritania's renouncing the portion of the former Spanish Sahara it had shared with Morocco. Polisario guerrillas put up armed resistance from bases in Algeria, where they were supplied with arms by both Algeria and Libya, thereby provoking a Moroccan response which included the building of defensive works on the 'borders'. In 1988 the **UN** proposed a referendum to enable the indigenous population to choose between the area becoming an independent state under Polisario or becoming part of Morocco.

Polish Corridor An area of formerly Polish territory, acquired by Prussia at the time of the Partitions and transferred from Germany to Poland by the Treaty of **Versailles** (1919). It linked the Polish heartland with the free city of Danzig (or Gdansk) and the Baltic Sea, but divided East Prussia from the rest of Germany. Its recovery was one of **Hitler**'s aspirations during the late 1930s, providing him with a pretext for his aggression against Poland.

Polish Succession, War of the (1733–8) Upon the death of the Polish King, Augustus I (1 Feb 1733), France and Spain opposed the Austrian- and Russian-backed claimant to the throne, Frederick Augustus I of Saxony. The ensuing war engulfed much of Europe and was ended by the Treaties of Vienna (1635 and 1738) which recognized the claim of Frederick Augustus. The principal results of the war though were a redistribution of Italian territories and an increase in Russian power in Poland. France also agreed conditionally to accept the **Pragmatic Sanction** of Emperor **Charles VI**.

Politburo The Political Bureau of the Central Committee of the **Communist Party of the Soviet Union**; at various times, known as the Presidium. It was the highest organ of the Party, and, therefore, of the entire Soviet political system. Formally elected by the Central Committee, there were latterly about 15 members plus about seven candidate members who had no votes; in practice, though, membership was decided by the Politburo itself under the General-Secretary, who presided over it. Its functions might be compared to those of a cabinet, though its authority varied over the years. It was seldom questioned by the Party Congress or even by the Central Committee; in turn, it could only question the General-Secretary at times of crisis. Most other communist parties adopted the Soviet model.

political machine A term used to describe the US urban political organization developed in the late 19c in response to the constitutional decentralization of local politics intersecting with the flood of immigration into Northern cities such as New York, Philadelphia and Boston at a time of very rapid physical growth. Hierarchically structured from the city level, down through the ward to the precinct, the machine depended on the ability of the 'boss' to respond to the individual needs of constituents who voted at his direction in return, thus allowing him to control nominations and to discipline office holders. Developed by both parties and sizable ethnic groups, political machines have been characterized by endemic corruption and inefficiency, and many contemporary observers regard them as a degradation of democratic politics.

Polk, James K(nox) (1795–1849) US politician and 11th President. He was admitted to the Bar in 1820, served in the House of Representatives as a Democrat (1825–39), and was Governor of Tennessee (1839–41). Polk ran for President in 1844 as a 'dark horse' candidate who favoured the annexation of Texas. He became an activist President (1845–9) and a strong leader who set himself major objectives and achieved them. They included reducing the tariff, restoring the independent treasury system, settling the Oregon boundary dispute with Great Britain, and bringing Texas and California (which was under Mexican rule) into the Union. Texas was admitted to the Union in 1945. Unable to acquire California by peaceful negotiations, Polk ordered US troops to advance to the Rio Grande, precipitating war with Mexico. After the **Mexican War** (1846–8) the USA acquired California, New Mexico, and most of the Southwest. ▷ **'Fifty-Four Forty or Fight'**

Pollock, Sir George (1786–1872) British soldier. Entering the British **East India Company**'s army in 1803, he was engaged at the siege of Bhartpur (1805) and in other operations. Pollock saw service in the Nepal (Gurkha) campaigns of 1814–16, and was promoted colonel in the first Burmese War (1824–6). In 1838 he was made major-general. After the massacre of General **Elphinstone** in Afghanistan, the Indian government sent him to the relief of Sir Robert Sale in Jelalabad. In Apr 1842 he forced his way through the Khyber Pass and reached Sale, pushed on to Kabul, defeated the Afghan army, and recovered 135 British prisoners. He conducted the united armies back to India, and was rewarded with a political appointment at Lucknow. He returned to England in 1846, was Director of the East India Company from 1854 to 1856 and was created a field marshal in 1870.

Polonnaruwa A city in northern Sri Lanka and the centre of the island's second great Buddhist kingdom after the demise of

Anuradhapura. The city was established by members of the invading South Indian Chola Dynasty, but was retained as the centre of government by the Sri lankan kings who successfully fought them off during the 12c and 13c. The kingdom reached its zenith during the reigns of King Parakramabahu I (1153/86) and Nissanka Malli (1187/96), but rapidly declined after further attacks from South India and, possibly, the effects of malaria in the surrounding area.

Pol Pot (Saloth Sar) (1926–) Kampuchean (Cambodian) politician. After working on a rubber plantation in his early teens, he joined the anti-French resistance movement during the early 1940s, becoming a member of the Indo-Chinese Communist Party and Cambodian Communist Party in 1946. During the 1960s and early 1970s he led the communist **Khmer Rouge** in guerrilla warfare against the governments of Prince **Sihanouk** and then Lieutenant General Lon Nol. After the destruction of the Lon Nol regime in 1975, he became Prime Minister. He proceeded brutally to introduce an extreme regime which resulted in the loss of perhaps more than 2 500 000 lives. The regime was overthrown by Vietnamese troops in Jan 1979 and Pol Pot took to the resistance struggle once more. Despite announcing his retirement as the Khmer Rouge military leader in Aug 1985, he remained an influential and feared figure within the movement.

Poltava, Battle of (1709) The famous Russian victory in the **Great Northern War**. The Russians outnumbered the Swedes by two to one in soldiers and artillery (although at the Battle of Narva, in 1700, they had enjoyed better odds, yet had been beaten). The difference now was the quality of **Peter I, 'the Great'**'s army and of his own generalship. The war dragged on for another 12 years, but its outcome had in fact already been decided.

Polyansky, Dmitri Stepanovich (1917–) Ukrainian politician. Of peasant stock, he graduated in agriculture in Kharkov in 1939 and immediately became a Communist Party functionary. However, in 1958 his career blossomed when Nikita **Khrushchev** made him chairman of the Russian Council of Ministers. In 1960 he became a member of the **Politburo**. Even under Leonid **Brezhnev** he held several other ministerial posts, but in 1976 he was dropped from all but ambassadorial appointments as he was no longer in favour.

Polybius (c.200–after 118BC) Greek politician, diplomat and historian. From Megalopolis in the Peloponnese, he wrote of the rise of Rome to domination of the Mediterranean (264–146BC), however only five of his 40 books survive complete. The 18 years he spent in Rome as a political hostage (168–150BC) gave him a unique insight into Roman affairs, and led to lasting friendships with some of the great figures of the day, notably **Scipio Aemilianus**.

polycentrism A political term, first used by the Italian Communist Party (**PCI**) leader, Palmiro **Togliatti** after the 20th Congress of the Soviet Communist Party in Feb 1956 to describe and support the growing independence of other communist parties from the Soviet party after the **Stalin** era. The trend was forced on Yugoslavia when it was expelled from the **Cominform** in 1948; it became more difficult to believe in after the Soviet suppression of the **Hungarian Uprising** in Oct 1956; but it reasserted itself in the late 1950s and early 1960s. It was no longer used after the Soviet invasion of Czechoslovakia in 1968. ▷ **Marxism–Leninism; Stalinism**

Polycrates (536/522BC) **Tyrant** of Samos. One of the most conspicuous and powerful Greek tyrants of his time, he turned Samos into a major naval power, as well as the cultural centre of the Eastern Aegean. He made an alliance with **Ahmose II**, King of Egypt, but later broke it by giving support to the Persian King, **Cambyses II**, in his invasion of Egypt. He successfully resisted an attack from Spartans, Corinthians and disaffected Samians, but was later lured to the mainland by a Persian satrap (or governor), seized, and crucified.

Pomaks Bulgarian Muslims who converted to Islam during the Ottoman occupation. In 1970 there were c.170000 Pomaks still in Bulgaria, predominantly in the Meglen district of Macedonia. They use the Bulgarian language, but with many Turkish words. During the 1970s and 1980s they were subject to a programme of forced assimilation, which included changing their Islamic surnames for Slav ones.

Pombal, Sebastião (José) de Carvalho (e Mello), Marquis of (1699–1782) Portuguese statesman. He became Ambassador to London (1739) and Vienna (1745), and Secretary for Foreign Affairs (1750). He showed great resourcefulness in replanning the city of Lisbon, following the disastrous earthquake of 1755, and was made Prime Minister in 1756. He opposed church influence, reorganized the army, and improved agriculture, commerce, and finance. He was made count (1758) and marquis (1770), but fell from office on the accession of Maria I (1777).

Pomerania A region of north-central Europe along the Baltic Sea from Stralsund to the River Vistula in Poland. It was a disputed territory in the 17–18c, and was divided among Germany, Poland and the free city of Danzig in 1919–39. It was divided again, between East Germany and Poland, in 1945.

Pompadour, Madame de (Jeanne Antoinette Poisson, Marchioness of Pompadour) (1721–64) Mistress of **Louis XV**. A woman of remarkable grace, beauty, and wit, she attracted the eye of the King at a ball. Installed at Versailles (1745), and ennobled as Marquise de Pompadour, she assumed the entire control of public affairs, and for 20 years swayed state policy, appointing her own favourites. She was a lavish patroness of architecture, the arts and literature. ▷ **Seven Years War**

Pompey the Great (Gnaeus Pompeius Magnus) (106–48BC) Roman politician and general of the late republic. His outstanding military talents, displayed in his victories over the Marians (83–82BC), Sertorius (77BC), **Spartacus** (71BC), the pirates (67BC) and Mithridates VI Eupator (66BC), put him at the forefront of Roman politics from an early age. He was also an organizer of genius, and his settlement of the East after the Mithridatic Wars (63BC) established the pattern of Roman administration there for well over a century. Consistently outmanoeuvred in the 50s BC by Julius **Caesar**, he was finally defeated by him in the Battle of **Pharsalus** (48BC), and was assassinated in Egypt shortly after. ▷ **Crassus, Marcus Licinius; Roman Republic**

Pompidou, Georges (Jean Raymond) (1911–74) French politician. He trained as an administrator, joined Charles de **Gaulle**'s staff in 1944, and held various government posts from 1946. He helped to draft the constitution for the Fifth Republic (1959) and negotiate a settlement in Algeria (1961) and in the student-worker revolt of 1968. Prime Minister from 1962 to 1968, he was elected President, as the socialist candidate, after de Gaulle's resignation in 1969, and died in office. ▷ **Republic, Fifth** (France)

Poniatowski, Józef Antoni (1763–1813) Polish patriot and French marshal. The nephew of King **Stanisław II August Poniatowski**, he trained in the Austrian army, then commanded Polish armies against the Russians in the wars of the Second and Third Partitions of Poland. In 1807–9 he commanded Polish troops in Napoleon's Duchy of Warsaw, invading Galicia in 1809, hoping on both occasions to liberate his country. However, he was drowned while covering the French retreat at the Battle of **Leipzig**, thus losing his life as well as his cause. ▷ **Napoleonic Wars; Poland, Partitions of**

Poniatowski, Stanisław (1676–1762) Polish soldier and official. He was the father of **Stanisław II August Poniatowski**, the last King of Poland. He joined **Charles XII** of Sweden in supporting **Stanislaus Leszczynski** for the vacant Polish throne in the 1700s but later under Augustus II and III he was appointed to several administrative posts in Lithuania and Poland. He conspired deeply with Russia in securing his son's eventual election in 1764. Interested in promoting the future of a reformed Poland, he found little alternative but to work within the national and international system.

Poniatowski, Stanisław II August, King of Poland ▷ **Stanisław II August Poniatowski**

Ponomarev, Boris Nikolaevich (1905–) Soviet ideologue. He joined the Communist Party at 14, and at 21 became an official propagandist. His subsequent appointments included spells at the **Comintern** and at the Institute of Marxisim-Leninism. In 1955 he became director of the international department of the Central Committee and was only moved when Mikhail **Gorbachev** came to power in 1985. Throughout 30 years he was a conservative influence, asserting the ideological aspects of foreign policy.

Pontiac's Conspiracy (1763) An attempt by Native Americans of the Ohio and Great Lakes country to drive whites out of the area, led by Pontiac (c.1720–69), Chief of the Ottawa tribe, in retaliation against the English treatment of the Native Americans and the threat of expanding white settlements. The movement reached its peak with an unsuccessful siege of Detroit, and a final peace was signed in 1766. ▷ **Indian Wars**

Pontius Pilate ▷ **Pilate, Pontius**

Pontus In antiquity, the territory in north-eastern Asia Minor lying east of Bithynia and south of the Black Sea. In the early 1c BC, it was the centre of the empire of Mithridates VI, and with his defeat the area became a Roman province.

Poona Sarvajanik Sabha An Indian association, run by intellectuals and the middle class, which played an important role in the country's early freedom struggle. It came to prominence in 1896–7, when famine conditions in Deccan Maharashtra led to a demand for revenue remissions under the famine code — a demand which the government rejected. The *Poona Sarvajanik Sabha* sent agents into the countryside between Oct 1896 and Apr 1897 to popularize the legal rights of Raiyats in a famine situation. Along with the Indian Association, it also took up other issues, including the first all-India agitations on the Civil Service and the Press Act (1877–8).

Poor Laws Legislation in Britain originally formulated in 1598 and 1601, whereby relief of poverty was the responsibility of individual parishes under the supervision of Justices of the Peace and the administration of Overseers. Funds were provided by local property rates. As the population grew and rates rose at the end of the 18c, the Poor Laws were increasingly criticized. The Poor Law Amendment Act of 1834 radically changed the system, aiming to make application for poor relief less attractive and instituting a centralized poor law commission. The laws continued to operate in the 20c.

pope The title of the Bishop of Rome as head or Supreme Pontiff of the Roman Catholic Church; also, the title given to the head of the Coptic Church. The Bishop of Rome is elected by a conclave of the College of Cardinals, his authority deriving from the belief that he represents Christ in direct descendancy from the Apostle Peter, said to be the first Bishop of Rome. After the decline of the ancient churches of the Eastern Roman Empire, resulting from the spread of Islam, the Pope in Rome became the undisputed centre of the Christian Church, and enjoyed considerable political power as the temporal sovereign of extensive **Papal States** in Europe (now restricted to the Vatican City in Rome). The claim to infallibility was formalized at the First Vatican Council in 1870. See panel pp749–50.

Popiełuszko, Jerzy (Alfons) (1947–84) Polish priest. Serving in several Warsaw parishes after ordination, and inspired by the faith of his compatriot, St Maximilian Kolbe, he became an outspoken supporter of the **Solidarity** trade union, especially when it was banned in 1981 with the introduction of martial law. His sermons at 'Masses for the Country' regularly held in St Stanisław Kostka church were widely acclaimed. He ignored harassment and resisted official moves to have him silenced, but was kidnapped and murdered by the secret police in Oct 1984 more than a year after the lifting of martial law. It was probably this tragedy more than any other event that, in a profoundly Catholic country, spelt the eventual demise of the Communist Party. His grave and his church became a place of national pilgrimage.

Popish Plot An apocryphal Jesuit conspiracy in 1678 to assassinate **Charles II** of England, burn London, slaughter Protestants, and place James, Duke of York (later James VII of Scotland and II of England), on the throne. Created by opportunist rogues, Titus Oates and Israel Tonge, it resulted in 35 executions, bills in three parliaments for the exclusion of James from the succession, and the fall of the Danby government. ▷ **James VII and II**

Popolari Members of the Italian Popular Party (*Partito Popolare Italiano*) which briefly emerged as a major force in Italian politics in the period between **World War I** and the fascist seizure of power. It appealed basically to the Catholic voter and helped undermine the traditional liberal parties which could no longer guarantee Catholic support simply by promising not to introduce anticlerical measures. It ceased to exist under **fascism**, but many of its leaders subsequently played a part in the formation of the **Christian Democrat Party**.

Popov, Gavril Kharitonovich (1936–) Soviet economist and politician. Of Greek ethnic background, he graduated in economics in Moscow and joined the Communist Party in 1959. He was appointed Dean of the Faculty of Economics in 1971 and, with official backing, proceeded to introduce management studies. He blossomed on Mikhail **Gorbachev**'s accession to power. In 1989 he was elected to the Congress of Deputies and in 1990 became Mayor of Moscow. A fierce critic of the slow pace of change, he left the party in 1990 to survive Gorbachev's downfall in 1991.

POPES

Antipopes (who claimed to be pope in opposition to those canonically chosen) are given in parentheses.

Dates of Pontificate	Name	Dates of Pontificate	Name	Dates of Pontificate	Name
until c.64	Peter	483/92	Felix III (or II)	757/67	Paul I
c.64/c.76	Linus	492/6	Gelasius I	[767/9	Constantine II]
c.76/c.90	Anacletus	496/8	Anastasius II	[768	Philip]
c.90/c.99	Clement I	498/514	Symmachus	768/72	Stephen III (or IV)
c.99/c.105	Evaristus	[498 and 501/5	Laurentius]	772/95	Adrian I
c.105/c.117	Alexander I	514/23	Hormisdas	795/816	Leo III
c.117/c.127	Sixtus I	523/6	John I	816/17	Stephen IV (or V)
c.127/c.137	Telesphorus	526/30	Felix IV (or III)	817/24	Paschal I
c.137/c.140	Hyginus	530/2	Boniface II	824/7	Eugenius II
c.140/c.154	Pius I	[530	Dioscorus]	827	Valentine
c.154/c.166	Anicetus	533/5	John II	827/44	Gregory IV
c.166/c.175	Soter	535/6	Agapetus I	[844	John]
175/89	Eleutherius	536/7	Silverius	844/7	Sergius II
189/98	Victor I	537/55	Vigilius	847/55	Leo IV
198/217	Zephyrinus	556/61	Pelagius I	855/8	Benedict III
217/22	Calixtus I	561/74	John III	[855	Anastasius (III)]
[217/c.235	Hippolytus]	575/9	Benedict I	858/67	Nicholas I
222/30	Urban I	579/90	Pelagius II	867/72	Adrian II
230/5	Pontian	590/604	Gregory I	872/82	John VIII
235/6	Anterus	604/6	Sabinian	882/4	Marinus I
236/50	Fabian	607	Boniface III	884/5	Adrian III
251/3	Cornelius	608/15	Boniface IV	885/91	Stephen V (or VI)
[251/c.258	Novatian]	615/18	Deusdedit (or	891/6	Formosus
253/4	Lucius I		Adeodatus I)	896	Boniface VI
254/7	Stephen I	619/25	Boniface V	896/7	Stephen VI (or VII)
257/8	Sixtus II	625/38	Honorius I	897	Romanus
259/68	Dionysius	640	Severinus	897	Theodore II
269/74	Felix I	640/2	John IV	898/900	John IX
275/83	Eutychian	642/9	Theodore I	900/3	Benedict IV
283/96	Caius	649/55	Martin I	903	Leo V
296/304	Marcellinus	654/7	Eugenius I[1]	[903/4	Christopher]
308/9	Marcellus I	657/72	Vitalian	904/11	Sergius III
310	Eusebius	672/6	Adeodatus II	911/13	Anastasius III
311/14	Miltiades	676/8	Donus	913/14	Lando
314/35	Sylvester I	678/81	Agatho	914/28	John X
336	Mark	682/3	Leo II	928	John X
337/52	Julius I	684/5	Benedict II	928	Leo VI
352/66	Liberius	685/6	John V	928/31	Stephen VII (or VIII)
[355/65	Felix (II)]	686/7	Conon	931/5	John XI
366/84	Damasus I	[687	Theodore]	936/9	Leo VII
[366/7	Ursinus]	[687/92	Paschal]	939/42	Stephen VIII (or IX)
384/99	Siricius	687/701	Sergius I	942/6	Marinus II
399/401	Anastasius I	701/5	John VI	946/55	Agapetus II
402/17	Innocent I	705/7	John VII	955/64	John XII
417/18	Zosimus	708	Sisinnius	963/5	Leo VIII
418/22	Boniface I	708/15	Constantine	964/6	Benedict V
[418/19	Eulalius]	715/31	Gregory II	965/72	John XIII
422/32	Celestine I	731/41	Gregory III	973/4	Benedict VI
432/40	Sixtus III	741/52	Zacharias	[974	Boniface VII (1st
440/61	Leo I, 'the Great'	752	Stephen II[2]		pontificate)]
461/8	Hilarius	752/7	Stephen II (or III)	974/83	Benedict VII
468/83	Simplicius				

[1] Elected during the banishment of Martin I
[2] Although not actually consecrated, he is variously regarded and disregarded as pope: the numbering of subsequent popes named Stephen has, accordingly, been somewhat confused

POPES continued

Antipopes (who claimed to be pope in opposition to those canonically chosen) are given in parentheses.

Dates of Pontificate	Name	Dates of Pontificate	Name	Dates of Pontificate	Name
983/4	John XIV	[1159/64	Victor (IV)][1]	1471/84	Sixtus IV
[984/5	Boniface VII (2nd pontificate)]	1164/8	Paschal (III)]	1484/92	Innocent VIII
		[1168/78	Calixtus (III)]	1492/1503	Alexander VI
985/96	John XV (or XVI)	[1179/80	Innocent (III)]	1503	Pius III
996/9	Gregory V	1181/5	Lucius III	1503/13	Julius II
[997/8	John XVI (or XVII)]	1185/7	Urban III	1513/21	Leo X
999/1003	Sylvester II	1187	Gregory VIII	1522/3	Adrian VI
1003	John XVII (or XVIII)	1187/91	Clement III	1523/34	Clement VII
1004/9	John XVIII (or XIX)	1191/8	Celestine III	1534/49	Paul III
1009/12	Sergius IV	1198/1216	Innocent III	1550/5	Julius III
[1012	Gregory (VI)]	1216/27	Honorius III	1555	Marcellus II
1012/24	Benedict VIII	1227/41	Gregory IX	1555/9	Paul IV
1024/32	John XIX (or XX)	1241	Celestine IV	1559/65	Pius IV
1032/44	Benedict IX (1st pontificate)	1243/54	Innocent IV	1566/72	Pius V
		1254/61	Alexander IV	1572/85	Gregory XIII
1045	Sylvester III	1261/4	Urban IV	1585/90	Sixtus V
1045	Benedict IX (2nd pontificate)	1265/8	Clement IV	1590	Urban VII
		1271/6	Gregory X	1590/1	Gregory XIV
1045/6	Gregory VI	1276	Innocent V	1591	Innocent IX
1046/7	Clement II	1276	Adrian V	1592/1605	Clement VIII
1047/8	Benedict IX (3rd pontificate)	1276/7	John XXI[2]	1605	Leo XI
		1277/80	Nicholas III	1605/21	Paul V
1048	Damasus II	1281/5	Martin IV	1621/3	Gregory XV
1049/54	Leo IX	1285/7	Honorius IV	1623/44	Urban VIII
1055/7	Victor II	1288/92	Nicholas IV	1644/55	Innocent X
1057/8	Stephen IX (or X)	1294	Celestine V	1655/67	Alexander VII
[1058/9	Benedict X]	1294/1303	Boniface VIII	1667/9	Clement IX
1059/61	Nicholas II	1303/4	Benedict XI	1670/6	Clement X
1061/73	Alexander II	1305/14	Clement V	1676/89	Innocent XI
[1061/72	Honorius (II)]	1316/34	John XXII	1689/91	Alexander VIII
1073/85	Gregory VII	[1328/30	Nicholas (V)]	1691/1700	Innocent XII
[1080 and 1084/1100	Clement (III)]	1334/42	Benedict XII	1700/21	Clement XI
		1342/52	Clement VI	1721/4	Innocent XIII
1086/7	Victor III	1352/62	Innocent VI	1724/30	Benedict XIII
1088/99	Urban II	1362/70	Urban V	1730/40	Clement XII
1099/1118	Paschal II	1370/8	Gregory XI	1740/58	Benedict XIV
[1100/2	Theodoric]	1378/89	Urban VI	1758/69	Clement XIII
[1102	Albert]	[1378/94	Clement (VII)]	1769/74	Clement XIV
[1105/11	Sylvester (IV)]	1389/1404	Boniface IX	1775/99	Pius VI
1118/19	Gelasius II	[1394/1423	Benedict (XIII)]	1800/23	Pius VII
[1118/21	Gregory (VIII)]	1404/6	Innocent VII	1823/9	Leo XII
1119/24	Calixtus II	1406/15	Gregory XII	1829/30	Pius VIII
1124/30	Honorius II	[1409/10	Alexander (V)]	1831/46	Gregory XVI
[1124	Celestine (II)]	[1410/15	John (XXIII)]	1846/78	Pius IX
1130/43	Innocent II	1417/31	Martin V	1878/1903	Leo XIII
[1130/8	Anacletus (II)]	[1423/9	Clement (VIII)]	1903/14	Pius X
[1138	Victor (IV)][1]	[1425/30	Benedict (XIV)]	1914/22	Benedict XV
1143/4	Celestine II	1431/47	Eugenius IV	1922/39	Pius XI
1144/5	Lucius II	[1439/49	Felix (V)]	1939/58	Pius XII
1145/53	Eugenius III	1447/55	Nicholas V	1958/63	John XXIII
1153/4	Anastasius IV	1455/8	Calixtus III	1963/78	Paul VI
1154/9	Adrian IV	1458/64	Pius II	1978/	John Paul I
1159/81	Alexander III	1464/71	Paul II	1978/	John Paul II

[1] Different individuals
[2] There was no John XX

Poppaea Sabina (d.AD65) Roman society beauty and voluptuary. Before her marriage to the Emperor **Nero** (AD62), she had been the wife of his playboy friend, the future Emperor **Otho**. She shared the then fashionable interest in Judaism, and has been thought by many to have encouraged Nero in his vicious attack on the Christians in the aftermath of the Fire of Rome (AD64).

Popular Front A strategy of the communist movement begun in the 1930s as a means of fostering collaboration among left and centre parties to oppose the rise of right-wing movements and regimes, most obviously fascist ones. There were Popular Front governments in France, Spain, and Chile. The strategy virtually died with the signing of the **German–Soviet Pact** (1939), but re-emerged after **Hitler** had invaded the USSR.

populism Essentially a political outlook or mentality rather than an ideology, identified by a popular reaction to dramatic change, such as rapid industrialization. People feel that events are beyond their control, which is blamed on some conspiracy of foreigners, ethnic groups, economic interests, or intellectuals. The populist reaction is to 'regain' control from the suggested centres of power, usually through some form of participation, and to seek revenge and redemption. Beyond that, populism is an obscure and variable outlook, and has failed to establish political parties successfully. It is often found in underdeveloped countries as a reaction against more developed countries.

Populist Party US political party. It was founded in 1892 by farmers and labourers in the West who had become disenchanted with the economic and commercial policies imposed by the East. Running on a programme of economic and political reform, its first presidential candidate, James B Weaver, took more than 1 million votes in 1892, but at the next election (1896), the populists endorsed the Democratic nominee, William Jennings Bryan, and by the end of the century the party had disappeared as a political entity.

Portales, Diego (1793–1837) Chilean politician. A major trader in Valparaiso, he acquired a major interest in national affairs in 1824 when he was awarded the government monopoly on the sale of tobacco, tea and alcoholic beverages in return for servicing a British loan. A pragmatist, he was principally concerned with power, discipline, stability

and directed order and, as Chief Minister (1830–2 and 1835–7), he was the key figure in creating a new and stable political system. He imposed the conservative constitution of 1833, which lasted until 1925, and created a centralized state, dominated by the Church and the landed classes. By 1835, he was effectively a dictator, having evolved a government of merchants and powerful landowners, whose *inquilinos* served as an effective military force. He was murdered near Valparaiso by a group of soldiers during the war against General Andrés Santa Cruz's Peru-Bolivian Confederation, which was seen as a direct threat to the country. ▷ **inquilino**

Porte, The Sublime Originally the ministerial department of the Grand Vizier of the **Ottoman Empire**, it was finally established under the name *Bab-i Ali* ('Sublime Porte') in 1718 during the sultanate of **Ahmed III**. The Porte (or Gate) was used to refer to the buildings housing the central offices of government in Istanbul including the Ministries of the Interior and Foreign Affairs and the Council of State. By extension, the term then came to be used of the government itself.

porteño This Spanish term describes an inhabitant of the city of Buenos Aires. The early history of Argentina can be seen as a struggle between *unitarios*, who saw Buenos Aires as the dominant force in the Platine Basin, and federalists, who viewed the interests of upriver states such as Entre Rios, the province of Buenos Aires or Santa Fé as more important. The high profile assumed by Buenos Aires after 1810 stimulated cities of the interior to struggle against *porteños*, such as liberal-centralist Bernardino **Rivadavia**, intent on the rapid creation of a modern state. The tyranny of Rosas epitomized the pre-eminence of provincial caudillo and **gaucho** over the civilized urban liberal; the porteños finally regained influence under **Mitre** and **Sarmiento** in the 1860s. By 1880, their economic supremacy was secure and the city of Buenos Aires was brought under congressional rule.

Portland, William Henry Cavendish Bentinck, 3rd Duke of (1738–1809) British politician. He became an MP in 1761, succeeding to the dukedom in 1762. His first cabinet post was as Lord Chamberlain of the Household under **Rockingham** (1765–6). Along with other aristocratic **Whigs**, he maintained connection with Rockingham which kept him in opposition until 1782, when he was Lord Lieutenant of Ireland. Portland was nominal head of the ministry (Apr–Dec 1783) usually known as the **Fox–North** coalition which **George III** hated and rapidly dismissed. He led the Whigs in opposition to **Pitt, 'the Younger'** until 1794 when he agreed to join him in a coalition government to provide order and stability and to meet the challenge of the **French Revolutionary Wars**. Some have seen the Pitt–Portland coalition as the foundation of the modern Tory (later Conservative) Party. He served as Home Secretary (1794–1801) during a period of considerable radical disturbance in England and rebellion in Ireland (1798) and as Lord President of the Council under Addington (1801–3). In Pitt's last ministry he was successively Lord President (1804–5) and Minister without Portfolio (1805–6). He was summoned by **George III** in 1807 to head an administration of Pittites after the fall of the 'Ministry of all the Talents'; by now old, frail and gouty, he was little more than titular leader until his death in office. ▷ **Tories**

Port Royal A French religious and intellectual community occupying the former convent of Port-Royal-des-Champs, near Paris. It was associated with the Jansenist movement, and founded by the Abbé de Saint-Cyran (1637), a friend and admirer of the theologian, Cornelius Jansen, himself a devotee of Augustinian philosophy. The community was dispersed in 1665, and the convent destroyed (1710–11). ▷ **Jansenism**

Portsmouth, Treaty of (5 Sep 1905) The treaty, signed in Portsmouth, New Hampshire (USA), which concluded the **Russo-Japanese War**. Japan acquired south Sakhalin from Russia as well as the Russian leasehold in south Manchuria (Liaodong Peninsula) and the Russian-built South Manchuria Railway. Japan's predominant position in Korea was also confirmed, enabling Tokyo to declare a protectorate over Korea and then to annex it as a formal colony (1910). The Japanese demand for an indemnity, however, was abandoned when Russia adamantly refused, a compromise that provoked angry public demonstrations in Tokyo. This treaty marked the beginning of Japanese expansion on the Chinese mainland, which was increasingly to arouse the suspicion of the USA.

Portugal, Revolt of (1640–68) The union of the crowns of Spain and Portugal in 1580 led to increasing dissatisfaction in Portugal, principally because of the failure of Spain to protect the vulnerable Portuguese overseas empire. In 1640 the troubles in Catalonia encouraged a group of Portuguese to rally round the Duke of Braganza, proclaimed by them as King João IV. An uprising in Lisbon (1 Dec 1640) ended with the murder of the viceroy, Miguel de Vasconcellos, a confidant of the Spanish minister, **Olivares**. Spain's commitments, especially in Catalonia, made it difficult to deal with the national rising, which soon gained the support of France, which sent naval and military help. In 1660 the marriage of Princess **Catherine of Braganza** to **Charles II** of England ensured English help. Repeated failures by Spanish troops to subdue the rebellion ended with the Treaty of Lisbon (Feb 1668), which recognized Portugal's independence. ▷ **Braganza, House of**

Porvoo, Diet of (1809) The meeting of the Finnish estates convened by Tsar **Alexander I** at Porvoo (Borgå) following the Russian conquest of Finland (hitherto part of the Swedish kingdom) in 1808–9. On this occasion the Tsar guaranteed the rights enjoyed by the Finns under Swedish rule, thus allowing Finland considerable autonomy within the Russian Empire. The Diet has generally been regarded as marking the emergence of Finland as a modern state.

Postumus, Marcus Cassianus Latinius (d.268) Roman Emperor (260/8). Proclaimed emperor by his troops on the Rhine in 260, Postumus went on to establish a breakaway state in the western half of the Roman empire which at its height (268) embraced Gaul, Spain, Britain and, briefly, northern Italy. Its capital was Treves (Augusta Treverorum). Tacitly recognised by the Emperor **Gallienus** who could make no headway against him, Probus only fell from power when his troops mutinied against him and killed him.

Potemkin (1905) The Russian warship immortalized in Sergei Eisenstein's 1926 film for mutinying in the course of the Russian **Revolution of 1905**. The crew put to sea and resisted the attempts of loyal ships to capture them but eventually surrendered to the Romanian authorities. There were subsequent mutinies in the naval bases of Kronstadt and Sevastopol. Tsar **Nicholas II** rode out the revolution, but disaffection in his forces was an ominous sign of what was to unseat him in 1917.

Potemkin, Grigori Alexandrovich (1739–91) Russian field marshal and statesman. He entered the Russian army, attracted the attention of **Catherine II, 'the Great'** and became her intimate and most enduring favourite, heavily influencing Russian foreign policy in particular. There is some reason to believe they were secretly married. He distinguished himself in the **Russo-Turkish Wars** (1768–74 and 1787–92), during which Russia gained the Crimea and the northern coast of the Black Sea. He also helped to develop Catherine's unsuccessful Greek project which would have replaced the Ottoman Empire with a new Greek Empire based on Constantinople. Within Russia he became famous for the Potemkin villages, apparently prosperous artificial centres quickly built ahead of Catherine's carriage-routes and subsequently dismantled.

Potsdam Conference (17 July–2 Aug 1945) The last of the great **World War II** strategic conferences, following the **Tehran Conference** and **Yalta Conference**. During this period Winston **Churchill** (and later Clement **Attlee**), **Stalin** and **Truman** met to discuss the post-war settlement in Europe. Soviet power in Eastern Europe was recognized *de facto*, and it was agreed that Poland's western frontier should run along the **Oder–Neisse Line**. The decision was also made to divide Germany into four occupation zones. The political differences which began to emerge between the USA and the USSR could be said to have marked the start of the **Cold War**.

Poujade, Pierre (1920–) French right-wing political leader. A small shopkeeper in a tiny town, in 1951 he was elected a member of the Saint Cére municipal council, and in 1954 he organized his Poujadist movement (union for the defence of tradesmen and artisans) as a protest against the French tax system. His party had successes in the 1956 elections to the National Assembly, but disappeared in 1958. Jean-Marie **Le Pen**, leader of the National Front, was first elected as a Poujadist Deputy in 1956.

POUM (*Partido Obrero de Unificación Marxista*, 'Workers' Marxist Unification Party') Independent Spanish Marxist party. The POUM, founded in Sep 1935, never had a mass following, but its outstanding thinkers led it to exert considerable influence. Its leading figures were the Marxist theoreticians Joaquín Maurín, the originator of the *Alianza Obrera* ('United Workers' Front'), and Andreu Nin. The POUM's defence of a revolutionary war effort and general independence during the **Spanish Civil War** resulted in its persecution by the Communist Party (**PCE**) in the May Days of 1937. It was vigorously repressed thereafter until the end of the war.

Powell, Adam Clayton (1908–72) US clergyman and politician. Pastor of the Abyssinian Baptist Church in Harlem, he was a charismatic community leader. In 1941 he was elected as a Democrat to the City Council of New York and the following year he founded the People's Voice. Elected to the US House of Representatives in 1945, he was chairman of the House Committee on Education and Labor from 1951, though persistent absenteeism did inhibit his effectiveness. It was Powell who first used the phrase '**Black Power**' (at Howard University in 1966), and who acted as convenor of the first National Conference on Black Power. In 1967 he was expelled from the US House of Representatives for misusing public funds and for unbecoming conduct. Re-elected in 1968, he had the satisfaction of a Supreme Court ruling in favour of his appeal against expulsion, but he lost his seat in 1970. ▷ **Jones, J Raymond**

Powell, (John) Enoch (1912–) British politician. He was Professor of Greek at Sydney (1937–9), and became a Conservative MP in 1950. He held several junior posts before he became Minister of Health (1960–3). His outspoken attitude on the issues of non-white immigration and racial integration came to national attention in 1968, and as a consequence of this he was dismissed from the shadow cabinet. He was elected as an Ulster Unionist MP in Oct 1974, losing his seat in 1987. ▷ **Conservative Party (UK)**

Powhatan Confederacy A group of Algonquian-speaking Native North American tribes inhabiting the Tidewater region of Virginia at the time of the first white settlements. Named after Chief Powhatan, the group was initially receptive to the settlers, but grew suspicious of the newcomers, and in 1622 and 1644 launched massive attacks on them. They were defeated on both occasions. Scattered descendants of these tribes are still found in Virginia. ▷ **Indian Wars; Pocahontas**

Poynings' Law (1495) Statutes enacted by the Irish parliament at the direction of Sir

Edward Poynings, English Lord Deputy, in 1494, removing its right to meet without the English government's agreement and to pass laws without prior approval. The immediate object was to crush Yorkist support, but over the long term it bolstered English claims to sovereignty and conquest. It was effectively repealed in 1782. ▷ **Roses, Wars of the**

Pozzo di Borgo, Carlo Andrea, Count (1764–1842) Corsican-born Russian diplomat. He practised as an advocate in Ajaccio, in 1790 joined the party of Paoli, who made him President of the Corsican Council and Secretary of State, but in 1796 was obliged to seek safety from the Bonapartes in London. In 1798 he went to Vienna and effected an alliance of Austria and Russia against France. In 1803 he entered the Russian diplomatic service. Though he resigned again over the Treaty of Tilsit in 1807, he returned in 1812 and laboured strenuously to unite **Napoleon**'s enemies against him, seduced **Bernadotte** from the Napoleonic cause, and urged the allies to march on Paris. He represented Russia in Paris, at the Congress of **Vienna** (1814–15) and the Congress of Verona, and was ambassador to London from 1834 to 1839, when he settled in Paris, where he died.

PP (*Partido Popular*) Spanish conservative party. Founded in 1976 as *Alianza Popular* (AP, 'Popular Alliance') and headed by 'the magnificent seven', all former Francoists under the leadership of Manuel **Fraga Iribarne**. The party defended laissez-faire capitalism alongside more traditional Spanish conservative values. In the 1977 election AP won only 16 seats, but in 1982 it came second to the Socialist Party with a quarter of the vote cast. In 1989 the party was renamed *Partido Popular*, with Manuel Fraga stepping down as leader the following year.

Praetorian Guard An elite military corps in early imperial Rome which was effectively the Emperor's bodyguard. Their real influence dates from the decade 20–30AD, when they were concentrated in a single barracks in Rome by **Sejanus**, and put under the control of a single commander (initially Sejanus himself). From then on they often intervened in imperial politics as, for example, when they nominated **Claudius** as Emperor (41), deserted **Nero** (68), murdered **Galba** (69), forced **Nerva** to nominate **Trajan** as his successor (97) and murdered Pertinax (193) and **Elagabalus** (222). The Praetorians were

replaced by **Constantine I, 'the Great'** (312) with a new corps of guards called the Scholae.

Pragmatic Sanction A Habsburg family law devised in 1713 by Emperor **Charles VI** to alter an earlier pact in favour of the undivided succession of his heirs, male or female, to the Habsburg lands (1713). Later, much effort was deployed in achieving internal and international guarantees for his daughter **Maria Theresa**'s claims, though these were repudiated by **Frederick II, 'the Great'** of Prussia (1740). ▷ **Habsburg Dynasty**

Prague Spring (1968) The name given to the events associated with the attempt made to reform **communism** in Czechoslovakia and to create instead what Alexander **Dubček** called '**Socialism with a Human Face**'. The action programme anticipated many of Mikhail **Gorbachev**'s subsequent reforms in the USSR and attracted widespread popular support. But the thought that Czechoslovakia might develop a political system with several parties in which the communists could be defeated at the polls and themselves divided on Czech/Slovak ethnic grounds did not occur to Leonid **Brezhnev**, who saw his control over Eastern Europe and within the USSR itself threatened. Hence the Soviet invasion in Aug, the Dubček Doctrine, and the removal of Dubček and his colleagues who had not had quite enough time to dispose of conservative opposition. The whole area lost a great opportunity.

Prajadhipok (1893–1941) The 7th King of the **Chakri Dynasty** of Thailand, and the last absolute monarch in that line. He was educated in England, at Eton and the Woolwich Military Academy. Prajadhipok ascended the throne in 1925. His apparent instincts for political reform were smothered by an older generation of ministers and advisers. In June 1932 the absolute monarchy was overthrown in a bloodless coup. Prajadhipok remained as a constitutional monarch until Mar 1935, when he abdicated. He then lived in England until his death.

Prasad, Rajendra (1884–1963) Indian politician. Having been active in Bihari politics, he left legal practice to become a supporter of M K Gandhi, helped found the *Searchlight* newspaper, and was President of the **Indian National Congress** on several occasions between 1934 and 1948. In 1946 he was made Minister for Food and Agriculture, and was India's first President (1950–62). He died at Patna.

Prat de la Riba, Enric (1870–1917) Catalan nationalist and conservative theorist of the Catalan bourgeoisie. A founder in 1901 of the *Lliga Regionalista* (which sought autonomy within the Spanish state), he was Secretary of the party. His ideas on autonomy contributed to the creation of a regional government, the Mancomunitat, in 1914. He served as President of the Mancomunitat until his death, undertaking numerous projects to strengthen Catalan culture. ▷ **Lliga**

Pratiharas The most important of the Gurjara kingdoms which sprang up in the 7c in western India. The first major ruler, Nagabhata I, made his mark by repelling the Arabs of Sind when they attempted to overrun Rajasthan and Malwa c.725. The next ruler, Vatsaraja (c.778/92), campaigned successfully against the **Palas** but was himself invaded and defeated by the Rashtrakuta ruler; these were the opening moves in a triangular contest for dominance in north India which lasted for more than a century. Employing a markedly decentralized administration, the greatest of their rulers was Mihira Bhoja (c.835/c.888), who had successes against both the Palas and Rashtrakutas.

Prazos Estates granted by the Portuguese crown on the basis of African concessions to estate-holders (*prazeros*) in the Zambezi Valley of South-Central Africa in the 17c and 18c. These were designed to promote settlement and develop Portuguese trade with the region. Regulations to prohibit absenteeism and pluralism and to encourage Portuguese women to emigrate were generally ignored and the estates became progressively Africanized, by the 19c becoming African chieftaincies with only vestiges of Portuguese culture.

Prchlik, Václav (1922–) Czechoslovak general and politician. He joined the forces and the Communist Party at the end of **World War II**, rose through various official appointments to be political administrator of the army from 1955 to 1968, and in Jan 1968 apparently foiled an attempt by some of his colleagues to suppress the reform movement before it began. During 1968 he began a purge of the top security services and prepared to transfer the political responsibility for them from the party to parliament. After the Soviet invasion in Aug, which he was prepared to resist, he was dismissed, and fear of the secret police returned to Czechoslovakia.

Predynastic Period Human occupation of the Nile Valley is evidenced by Palaeolithic flint implements found in Upper Egypt before 1200BC. In the Neolithic period, the cultivation of crops and domestication of animals began. Certain localities have given their name to Predynastic cultures such as Badarian in Middle Egypt, where by c.4500BC the transition from stone technology to the gradual introduction of copper termed 'Chalcolithic' can be observed. By c.4000BC, a community at el Amra (hence Amratian or Naqada I culture), produced pottery of red ware, burnished, often with a black rim or white painted incised decoration. The later Gerzean or Naqada II culture (from el-Gerza) was characterized by buff-coloured pottery decorated with scenes in purplish paint and began c.3500BC. In the late Predynastic period there appear to have been two confederations consisting of local communities corresponding roughly to the later provinces of Egypt. The leaders of the two were 'kings' of Upper and Lower Egypt. In the century prior to c.3100BC Upper and Lower Egypt vied for supremacy until the conquest of the north by the south led to the unification under **Narmer** and the start of the historic Dynastic period in Egypt.

Premadasa, Ranasinghe (1924–93) Sri Lankan politician. The first Sri Lankan head of government to have emerged from the urban working classes rather than the traditional elite families, he began his political career attached to the Ceylon Labour Party. He formed a temperance group dedicated to moral uplift, then joined the **UNP** (United National Party) in 1950 and became Deputy Mayor of the Colombo municipal council (1955). Elected to Sri Lanka's parliament in 1960, he served, successively, as UNP Chief Whip (1965–8 and 1970–7), the Minister of Local Government (1968–70) and Leader of the House (1977–8), before becoming Prime Minister, under President **Jayawardene**, in 1978. During 10 years as Prime Minister, Premadasa implemented a popular house-building and poverty alleviation programme, which provided the basis for his election as President (Dec 1988).

Prempeh (d.1931) Last King of the **Ashanti** (1888/96). He was deposed by the British, imprisoned at Elmina, and exiled to the Seychelles. He was allowed to return in 1924, with chief's rank from 1926.

Prem Tinsulanonda, General (1920–) Thai soldier. Educated at the Chulachomklao

Royal Military Academy, Bangkok, he entered the army as a sub-lieutenant in 1941 and rose to become Commander-General of the 2nd Army Area in 1974, and assistant Commander-in-Chief of the Royal Thai Army in 1977. During the administration of General Kriangsak Chomanam (1977–80) he served as deputy Minister of the Interior and, from 1979, as Defence Minister. He was appointed Prime Minister (Mar 1980). Prem then formally relinquished his army office and established a series of civilian coalition governments. He withstood coup attempts in Apr 1981 and Sep 1985, and ruled in a cautious manner, retaining the confidence of key business and military leaders. Under his stewardship, 'newly industrializing' Thailand achieved annual growth rates in excess of 9 per cent. He retired, on 'personal grounds', in July 1988.

Premyslids (8c–early 14c) The native dynasty ruling more or less the area of the present Czech lands in their formative period. Its origin is attributed to the marriage between a princess Libuse and a peasant Premysl. It came to an end with the death of Vaclav III in 1306. However, in the meantime, the dynasty presided over a highly successful development. This did not simply embrace the foundation of the bishopric of Prague in 973 or the acquisition of a permanent royal title by Otakar I (1197–1230), but also the growth of a prosperous agricultural community interspersed with highly successful trading towns. In addition, the Premyslids left a legacy of involvement in Germany, and vice versa, which made subsequent Czech history both glorious and disastrous, as in the period of Jan **Hus** and the **Hussite Wars**.

Preobrazhensky, Yevgeni Alexandrovich (1886–1937) Soviet economist. The son of a priest in the Urals, he developed revolutionary tendencies quite early in life. After the 1917 **Russian Revolution** he spent some time in his home territory, but mainly he was active in Moscow, drafting, amongst other things, the 1919 party programmes. He associated with **Trotsky** and **Bukharin** and joined with the latter in publishing the *ABC of Communism*, thereby incurring **Stalin**'s anger. He died in prison in 1937. His writings have now attracted renewed interest.

Pressburg, Treaty of (1491) An agreement concluded by the Habsburgs, securing their rights to the Hungarian succession on King Vladislav II's death without heirs. ▷ **Habsburg Dynasty**

Pressburg, Treaty of (1805) A treaty following **Napoleon I**'s victories at Ulm and **Austerlitz**, which imposed harsh terms on Austria, effectively ending the **Holy Roman Empire** and establishing a ring of French client states. ▷ **Napoleonic Wars**

Prester John Mythical Christian priest-king of a vast empire in Central Asia. Reports of his existence, wealth and military might, substantiated by a famous letter purporting to have come from him in 1165, raised the morale of Christian Europe as it faced the Muslim threat. The story almost certainly related to the Christian kingdom of Ethiopia, which had been cut off by the Islamic conquest of Egypt. 'Prester' comes from Old French *prestre*, 'priest'.

Preston, Battle of (17–19 Aug 1648) A series of engagements between the English Parliamentary Army under **Cromwell** and **Lambert** and a numerically superior Scottish force in support of **Charles I** under the Duke of **Hamilton**. Hamilton's inability to concentrate his forces enabled them to be picked off piecemeal. The defeat ended the Second Civil War. Hamilton was captured and executed (1649). ▷ **English Civil Wars**

Pretoria Convention (1881) The agreement which brought to an end the first Boer War, establishing limited independence for the Boers in the Transvaal. In 1877 the Secretary of State for the Colonies, Lord Carnarvon, and the High Commissioner in South Africa, Sir Bartle Frere, resolved to attempt to reunite the two British colonies and two Boer states in southern Africa. The Transvaal was invaded and annexed by Sir Theophilus Shepstone in an attempt to place its bankrupt finances on a sound footing, but after the British suffered reverses in the Zulu war in 1879, the Boers set about re-establishing their independence. The British were defeated at a number of small engagements in the eastern Transvaal, notably **Majuba Hill** where the British commander, General Sir George Colley, was killed. **Gladstone**'s Cabinet resolved to abandon imperial responsibilities in return for a vague declaration of suzerainty, under which the British would control Boer foreign policy. The interpretation of the extent of such 'suzerainty' beggared relations between British and Boer up to the Boer War of 1899–1902. ▷ **Boer Wars**

Pretorius, Andries (Wilhelmus Jacobus) (1799–1853) Afrikaner leader. Born at Graaff-Reinet, Cape Colony, he was a prosperous farmer, who joined the **Great Trek** of 1835 into Natal, where he was chosen Commandant-General. He later accepted British rule, but after differences with the Governor he trekked again, this time across the Vaal. Eventually the British recognized the Transvaal Republic, later the South African Republic, whose new capital was named Pretoria after him.

Pretorius, Marthinus (Wessel) (1819–1901) Afrikaner soldier and politician. The son of Andries **Pretorius**, he succeeded his father as Commandant-General in 1853, and was elected President of the South African Republic (1857–71), and of the Orange Free State (1859–63). He fought against the British again in 1877, until the independence of the Republic was recognized (1881), then retired, and died at Potchefstroom. ▷ **Boer Wars**

PRI (*Partido Revolucionario Institucional*) Mexican political party, previously known as the PRN (*Partido Revolucionario Nacional*, National Revolutionary Party) and the PRM (*Partido de la Revolución Mexicana*, Mexican Revolutionary Party). Founded by Plutarco **Calles** in 1929, in the wake of the Mexican Revolution (1910–20), as an instrument for change through the achievement of unified and dictatorial centralism, the party has dominated Mexican political life ever since. The PRN was a coalition of local military chiefs, officeholders and CROM, the largest labour organization, and owed its strength to Calles' steady erosion of the autonomy of the states. **Cárdenas**, Calles' successor, created the succeeding PRM by replacing regional chiefs with military, labour, peasant and popular groups: labour and peasant organizations were seen as an effective counterpoise to the military, while the resolution of conflict lay in the hands of the President. By the time the PRM became the PRI (in 1945, under Avila Camacho), the military sector had been disbanded, other interest groups had been included and the state organization strengthened. The party's political monopoly remained unchallenged until the late 1970s when opposition parties began to win congressional seats; the 1988 elections saw the PRI's first-ever loss of Senate seats, and in 1989 the PRI state governorship monopoly was broken for the first time.

Pribičević, Svetozar (1875–1936) Serbian politician. Head of the Serbian Independent Party, which represented the Serbs within the Habsburg Empire, during **World War I** he advocated union with Serbia to form a South Slav state. Soon disillusioned with the organization of the Kingdom of Serbs, Croats and Slovenes (later Yugoslavia) under the arch-Serbian nationalists, Nikola **Pašić** and King **Alexander I**, in 1919 he led the Democratic Party, a breakaway group from the Serbian Radical Party. He was Minister of Education (1921–2). After 1927 he advocated the reorganization of the Kingdom of Yugoslavia as a federation. He was imprisoned during the royal dictatorship but was released to seek medical treatment in Czechoslovakia, where he died. ▷ **Korošec, Anton; Maček, Vladko; Radić, Stjepan**

Price, George (1919–) Belize politician. Educated in Belize City and the USA, he was elected to the Belize City Council in 1947 and in 1950 founded the People's United Party (PUP), a left-of-centre grouping which grew out of the People's Committee, a smaller group calling for the independence of Belize. Partial self-government was achieved in 1954 and Price became Prime Minister, continuing to lead his country until it achieved full independence in 1981. In 1984 PUP's 30 years of uninterrupted rule ended when the general election was won by the United Democratic Party (UDP), led by Manuel Esquivel, but Price unexpectedly returned to power in 1989.

Price Spreads Commission (1934) Canadian governmental inquiry. Instituted by the Ministry of Trade and Commerce to investigate the retail trade, the Commission found that retailers, especially the large department and chain stores, made their employees work very long hours for very low wages. Premier R B **Bennett** went public with its findings, condemning employers for their exploitation. His radio addresses on 'the state of the times' upset many of his conservative adherents, but Bennett insisted on the reforms, such as the Wages and Hours Bill and Unemployment Insurance, which had been suggested by the commission. Employers who broke the new laws were to be punished as criminals, not civil offenders. It was the controversy over the commission that led Harry H **Stevens** to resign from the cabinet to lead the Reconstruction Party of disaffected conservatives in the 1935 election. ▷ **New Deal** (Canada)

Pride, Sir Thomas (d.1658) English army officer during the **English Civil Wars**. Little is known of his early life. He commanded a regiment at the Battle of **Naseby** (1645), and served in Scotland. When the House of Commons betrayed a disposition to effect a settlement with **Charles I**, he was appointed by the army (1648) to expel its Presbyterian royalist members ('Pride's Purge'). He sat among the King's judges, and signed the death warrant. He was knighted by **Cromwell** in 1656. ▷ **Long Parliament**

Pridi Phanomyong (1900–83) Thai politician. Trained as a lawyer, notably in France in the 1920s, Pridi was a leading civilian figure in the coup group which overthrew the absolute monarchy in June 1932. He was then a prominent, but also highly controversial, government minister for much of the rest of the 1930s. In 1933 he drafted a National Economic Plan. This radical initiative, widely seen as communist, created a storm in Bangkok and forced Pridi into a brief exile in France. During the Japanese occupation (1941–5) Pridi acted as Regent for the absent King Ananda but also, towards the end of that period, as a clandestine leader of the anti-Japanese 'Seri Thai' movement, codename 'Ruth'. He was briefly Prime Minister in 1946. However, he remained a highly controversial figure in Thai politics. He left Thailand for exile in 1949, never to return, but living first in China and then, from 1970, in France.

Prieto, Indalecio (1883–1962) Spanish socialist leader. He served under the Second Republic first as Minister of Finance in 1931 and then as an innovative Minister of Public Works from 1931–3. The outstanding parliamentary orator of the Socialist Party, Prieto was also the leader of its moderate wing. He was unable to take up the premiership in May 1936 because of the opposition of **Largo Caballero**, the leader of the party's left wing. Such a move may have thwarted the military rising of July 1936 which led to civil war. During the **Spanish Civil War**, he proved a defeatist Minister of the Navy and Air Force (Sep 1936–May 1937) and Minister of Defence (May 1937–Apr 1938). He was forced to resign because of his opposition to the Communist Party. After the war, he tried to unite the socialists with the Republicans and even the monarchists in an effort to overthrow the **Franco** regime. ▷ **Republic, Second** (Spain)

Prim (y Prats), Juan (1814–70) Spanish soldier. As a Progressive he opposed the dictatorship of **Espartero**, and was exiled (1839), but came back and defeated him in 1843. He was Captain General of Puerto Rico

from 1847 to 1848, and deputy in the **Cortes** (1850–6). Failing in an insurrectional attempt in 1866, he fled to England and Brussels, and from there guided the revolution that in 1868 overthrew **Isabella II**. He was War Minister under **Serrano**, but soon became a virtual dictator. Prim secured the election of Amadeus as King in 1870, but was later shot by an assassin.

primary In US politics, a preliminary election to determine which candidates for public office are to appear on the ballot for a general election. There are various forms of primary, the most common being the closed primary, in which any voter who has registered with a particular party can vote for that party's respective candidate.

Primo de Rivera, José Antonio (1903–36) Spanish fascist leader. The son of the dictator, General Miguel **Primo de Rivera**, he was an aristocratic playboy turned charismatic political leader. He founded the **Falange Española**, a totalitarian and nationalistic movement, in Oct 1933. After the Falange fused with the *Juntas de Ofensiva Nacional Sindicalista* (JONS) in Feb 1934, he was elected leader. Detained in Mar 1936 by the Popular Front, he supported the rising of July 1936 against the Republic. He was shot on 20 Nov 1936 in Alicante jail. The cult of 'the absent one' became a central myth of the **Franco** regime.

Primo de Rivera (y Orbaneja), Miguel (1870–1930) Spanish dictator. He served in Cuba, the Philippines, and Morocco, and in 1923 led a military coup, inaugurating a dictatorship which lasted until 1930. During 1928–9 he lost the support of the army, the ruling class, and the King, **Alfonso XIII**, and in 1930 gave up power. He died in Paris. His son, José Antonio **Primo de Rivera** founded the Spanish Fascist Party, **Falange Española**, in 1933, and was executed by the Republicans in 1936. ▷ **fascism; Spanish Civil War**

Princely States, Indian Before the colonial period, India was composed of various independent kingdoms, with only the north of the country being dominated by the Mughal Empire. With the slow collapse of this empire, many of its constituent parts broke off to become effectively independent states (such as Hyderabad). With the rise of British colonial rule, many of these newly emergent successor states, as well as others with much longer histories, succeeded in maintaining their independence by entering into treaties with the British. Those which resisted, such as Mysore, were often crushed, but even those which were defeated, such as Gwalior and Holkar, having been deprived of much of their territory, continued as nominally independent rulers. This meant that, although the British dominated the subcontinent by the 19c, they never directly administered more than two-thirds of the country. Under Lord **Dalhousie**'s notorious policy of lapse, some independent states (such as Jhansi) were taken over in the 1850s; others, such as Awadh (Oudh), were too wealthy a prize to be resisted and were annexed without a pretext. Such high-handedness, however, caused resentment which was a factor in the **Indian Uprising** of 1857–8. Subsequently, the British propped up the Indian aristocracy wherever possible, provided they were willing to serve as loyal collaborators. The rewards for this loyalty were sumptuous, giving many rulers fabulous wealth which, combined with a lack of real power, earned them a reputation for decadence. On independence in 1947, the government of Independent India and Pakistan saw the Indian princes as a relic of colonial rule and had little use for them. Some, such as Hyderabad, Kashmir and Junagadh, made a bid for independence, but all were sooner or later annexed. Some ex-rulers went on to enjoy successful political careers but, following the abolition of aristocracy and all its privileges by Indira **Gandhi** in 1971, the majority sank into obscurity. ▷ **Communalism; India, Partition of**

Princip, Gavrilo (1895–1918) Serbian nationalist and revolutionary. He was a member of the secret Serbian terrorist organization known as the **Black Hand**, dedicated to the achievement of independence for the South Slav peoples from the Austro-Hungarian Empire. He and a group of young zealots assassinated **Francis Ferdinand**, Archduke of Austria, and his wife Sophie on a visit to Sarajevo (28 June 1914). The murder precipitated **World War I**, after Austria declared war on Serbia (28 July 1914). Princip died in an Austrian prison.

Priscillian (c.340–385) Bishop of Ávila. He was excommunicated by a synod at Saragossa in 380, then tolerated, but ultimately executed (the first case of capital punishment for heresy in the history of the Church). His doctrine, said to have been brought to Spain from Egypt, contained Gnostic and Manichean elements, and was based on dualism. The Priscillianists were ascetics, eschewed

marriage and animal food, and were said to hold strict truth obligatory only between themselves.

privateers Quasi-legal European freebooters who attacked Spanish shipping and settlements in the Caribbean in the period 1520–1650. Some were simply pirates; others were issued with letters of marque by their home governments which gave their captains the right to raid Spanish treasure ships and towns as instruments of war in periods of conflict with Spain. The most infamous were the French corsairs Jean Ango, François Le Clerc and Jacques de Sore operating in the period 1530–55, the Englishmen Hawkins and **Drake** in the period 1562–96, and the Dutchman Piet Heyn in the 1620s.

Privilegium Maius (1358–9) The most important of the documents forged by **Rudolf IV of Habsburg** to secure a position for Austria in the Electoral College. Rudolf was not one of the **Electors** named in the Golden Bull (1356) and to remedy this he forged several documents, which he claimed dated as far back as Julius **Caesar** and had been ratified by **Henry IV**. These were rejected by **Charles IV**, on the advice of Petrarch, but ratified by **Frederick III**. They were not exposed as forgeries until 1852.

Prizren, League of (Albanian League) Its founding in 1878 at Prizren in southern Kosovo marked the first stage in the creation of an Albanian state. The original aim of its members was to defend the Albanian national lands from expansionist foreign powers; at the Congress of **Berlin** they advocated the maintenance of the **Ottoman Empire** and autonomy and unification for the districts of Janina, Monastir, Üskub and Shkodër. Organized by the leading Albanian nationalist, Abdul Frashëri, its members were mainly Gheg landlords and notables, with a few southern **Tosks**. By 1880 the autonomists had control of the League and in Apr 1881 the movement was crushed by Sultan Abdul Hamit II. ▷ **Albanians; Ghegs**

Probus, Marcus Aurelius (d.282) Roman Emperor (276/82). Nominated emperor by the armies of Syria and Egypt, he was a man of outstanding military and administrative ability, who carried on the work of **Aurelian** in restoring order to the provinces, notably Gaul, Pisidia and Egypt, and re-establishing discipline among the unruly soldiery of the Empire. The latter was much resented and cost him his life.

Profumo, John (Dennis) (1915–) British politician. He became a Conservative MP in 1940, and held several government posts before becoming Secretary of State for War in 1960. He resigned in 1963 after admitting that he had been guilty of a grave misdemeanour in deceiving the House of Commons about the nature of his relationship with Christine Keeler, who was at the time also involved with a Soviet diplomat. He later sought anonymity in social and charitable services. ▷ **Conservative Party** (UK)

Progressive Party (Canada) The political party established in 1920 with the support of the farming community, it fought the 1921 federal election on a platform of lower tariffs and a reciprocity agreement with the USA. When it won 65 seats it became the second largest group in the Commons, to the surprise of the country. Its leader, T A **Crerar**, chose not to make the party the official opposition and over the next few years Mackenzie **King** was able to cut away the farmers' support, so that by 1926 the party had all but disappeared.

Progressive Party (Spain; *Partido Progresivo*) The Spanish political party which dominated the period 1834–68 along with the **Moderate Party**. The more liberal of the two parties, the Progressive Party supported the legitimacy of revolution and national rather than monarchical sovereignty. The Constitution of 1837 was its classic statement. The party ruled 1835–40, drawing on the authoritarian General **Espartero** to remain in power from 1840 to 1843 and in 1854–6. The party declined thereafter until its collapse in 1868.

Progressive Party (USA) (1912–16, 1924, and 1948) US political parties. The name was used by three separate third-party political initiatives. The first, essentially a breakaway from the Republican Party, centred on former President Theodore **Roosevelt**, who was its presidential candidate in 1912. The second developed in 1924 from midwestern farmer and labour discontent. Its presidential candidate, Senator Robert **La Follette** of Wisconsin, won 4 million votes. In the 1948 election, Democrats opposed to President Harry S **Truman**'s cold war policy ran Henry A Wallace, who received only 1 million popular votes. ▷ **New Nationalism; Republican Party**

Prohibition (1920–33) An attempt to forbid the manufacture, transportation and sale of all alcoholic drinks in the USA, authorized by the 18th Amendment to the **US Constitution** (1919). Building on 19c temperance movements and the powerful lobbying of the Anti-Saloon League, Congress passed the national legislation as a wartime emergency measure. Its enforcement, through the Volstead Act, gave rise to one of the great political controversies of the 1920s, and led to various 'bootlegging' operations that created new opportunities for organized crime. It also gained celebrity for J Edgar **Hoover** and his 'G-Men'. It was repealed in 1933 by the 21st Amendment. ▷ **Capone, Al**

Prokopovich, Feofan (1681–1736) Russian prelate and politician. He was educated at Kiev Orthodox Academy (where in 1711 he was appointed rector), and Rome. In St Petersburg in 1716 his sermons and theories for church reforms brought him to the notice of **Peter I, 'the Great'**, who made him his adviser and Bishop of Pskov, and in 1724 Archbishop of Novgorod. He was responsible for a new Spiritual Regulation which included setting up a Holy Synod instead of the existing patriarchate (which Peter had kept vacant since 1700). This consisted of 10, and later 12, clerics presided over by a lay procurator, and by and large ensured tsarist control of the Orthodox Church.

pronunciamiento Spanish army rising. The 'pronouncement' of the army (or a section thereof) for a particular regime amounted to an attempted coup d'état. Its origins lay in the role of the army in the administration of the 18c and the clashes of the War of Independence between soldiers and politicians. In the 19c, when there were · numerous *pronunciamientos*, it became the instrument of liberal revolution. Although there were far fewer in the 20c, those of 1923, 1936 and 1981 had far-reaching consequences.

Proprietary Church (*Eigentumskirche*) In the Middle Ages, the term used to describe a church standing on the land of a secular lord. As a result of his authority over the land, the lord also had the right to appoint clerics and to the Church's financial revenue. This arrangement was extensively regulated during the Carolingian period and also underlay the Emperor's relationship to the imperial churches. The **Investiture Controversy** represented the attempt of the Church to abolish this practice and it was effectively outlawed in the Concordat of Worms (1122). ▷ **Worms, Concordat of**

Protectorate A regime established by the Instrument of Government (1653), the work of army conservatives, England's only written constitution. The Lord Protectors, Oliver Cromwell (1653/8) and his son Richard (ruled 1658/9), issued ordinances and controlled the armed forces, subject to the advice of a Council of State and with parliament as legislative partner. It failed to maintain support, and its collapse led to the **Restoration**. ▷ **Commonwealth**

Protocols of the Elders of Zion A fraudulent document, originally printed in Russia (1903) and much translated, ostensibly reporting discussions among Jewish elders of plans to subvert Christian civilization and erect a world Zionist state. Exposed as forgeries in *The Times* (1921), the 'Protocols' have nevertheless been, and remain, a staple of right-wing, anti-Semitic propaganda. ▷ **Zionism**

Proudhon, Pierre Joseph (1809–65) French socialist and political theorist. In his first important book, *Qu'est-ce que la propriété?* (1840), he affirmed the bold paradox 'property is theft', because it involves the exploitation of the labour of others. He then published his greatest work, the *Système des contradictions économiques* (1846). During the **February Revolution** (1848), the violence of his utterances brought him three years' imprisonment, and after further arrest (1858) he retired to Belgium. Amnestied in 1860, he was seen by Karl **Marx** as his chief rival in the international socialist movement.

Prussia A North European state, originally centred in the East Baltic region as a duchy created by the Teutonic Knights, but later owing suzerainty to Poland. Inherited by the German House of Brandenburg in the early 17c, Brandenburg-Prussia was consolidated and expanded, and Polish sovereignty thrown off, by **Frederick William, the 'Great Elector'**. The Kingdom of Prussia was founded in 1701; under **Frederick William I** and **Frederick II, 'the Great'**, it acquired western Prussia and **Silesia**, and gained considerable territory in western Germany at the Congress of **Vienna** (1814–15). During the 19c it emerged as the most powerful German state, and was ultimately the focus of German unification. Within the federated German Empire (1871–1918) it was dominant, and within the **Weimar Republic** (1919–33) it retained considerable autonomy and influence. As a legal entity, Prussia ceased to exist with the post-1945 division of Germany and the establishment of a revised East German–Polish frontier. ▷ **Austro-**

Prussian War; Franco-Prussian War; Frederick William III; German Confederation; North German Confederation; Zollverein

Prussian Law Code (*Allgemeines Preussisches Landrecht*) (1794) The code was drawn up by Johann H C Carmer (1721–1801). It was Germany's first legal code and it combined traditional German laws with Roman Law and elements of natural law.

Prynne, William (1600–69) English Puritan pamphleteer. In 1633 his *Histrio-Mastix: the Players Scourge* appeared, which contained an apparent attack on Queen Henrietta Maria, wife of **Charles I**; for this he was tortured, fined and imprisoned. Released in 1640 by the **Long Parliament**, he prosecuted **Laud** (1644), and became an MP (1648). Purged from the House in 1650, he was again imprisoned (1650–2). After **Cromwell's** death he returned to parliament as a royalist, for which he was made Keeper of the Tower Records. ▷ **Protectorate; Puritanism**

Psammetichus ▷ **Psamtik**

Psamtik I (Wahibre) (664/610BC) King of Egypt. A prince of Sais in the Delta, Psamtik was installed there by the Assyrians following their overthrow of the 25th Dynasty (Nubian). Relying on Ionian and Carian mercenaries, Psamtik reunited Egypt by the ninth year of his reign through skilful use of manpower and the resources of his kingdom. He had his daughter, Nitocris, adopted as God's Wife of Amun at Thebes, an important religious and administrative post which helped unite the country. His long reign saw a renaissance of Egyptian culture, with a revival of **Old Kingdom** art styles. Many foreigners entered Egypt — Greeks, Syrians and Jews — the latter forming a community at Elephantine.

Psamtik II (595/589BC) King of Egypt. A member of the 26th Dynasty, it is known from several sources (including graffiti inscribed by the King's foreign mercenaries on the colossi of **Ramesses II** at Abu Simbel) that in 593BC Psamtik sent an expedition south into Nubia in response to a threat posed by a Nubian ruler. It appears that Psamtik remained at Aswan while the army was taken south by Potasimto, the leader of the Greek and Carian soldiers and Amasis, leader of the Egyptians. Their subsequent victory, which was the origin of a common tradition of rivalry between Egypt and Nubia, was celebrated in grand style. Elsewhere, Psamtik II maintained relations with Phoenecia, visiting Byblos and fostering the long-standing trading connections (dating from the early **Old Kingdom**) between the two countries.

PSD (*Partido Social Democrático*) The Brazilian party, formed in 1945, as a coalition of rural *coroneis* and urban leaders, including industrialists who had benefited substantially from the rule of **Vargas**, yet could not readily support his own PTB (*Partido Trabalhista Brasileiro*, Brazilian Labour Party). The PSD effectively retained control of Vargas' political machine in 1945, electing Eurico Gaspar Dutra as President, and receiving nearly 43 per cent of the vote. The party's 'natural alliance' with the PTB came to the fore during the 1950 presidential election, when the bulk of its leaders supported Vargas rather than its 'own' candidate. The blend of populist politics espoused by the PTB and the **coronelismo** of the countryside provided a powerful base for **Kubitschek (de Oliveira)**'s *Programa de Metas*, but foundered under the weak leadership of João **Goulart**. Much of the PSD merged with the ARENA party after 1965, inexorably delivering the rural vote to the military government.

PSOE (*Partido Socialista Obrero Español, 'Spanish Socialist Workers' Party'*) Spanish political party, founded in 1879, which established itself slowly, limited both by organizational rigidity and theoretical shortcomings. Although the party proclaimed a revolutionary rhetoric, it remained wedded to reformist practices, even to the extent of collaborating with the dictatorship of Miguel **Primo de Rivera** (1923–30). Under the Second Republic of 1931–6 the PSOE was the leading political force on the Left, forming the backbone of the reformist Republican–Socialist administrations of 1931–3. However, the reversal of reform after the electoral victory of the Right in Nov 1933 rapidly radicalized the PSOE, culminating in the Asturian rising of Oct 1934. The insurrection's defeat divided the party between the 'revolutionary' stance of **Largo Caballero** and the moderate Indalecio **Prieto**. After the **Spanish Civil War** broke out, Largo Caballero was made Premier in Sep 1936, but in May 1937 he was ousted by the Communists to be replaced by Juan **Negrín**, a socialist who supported communist policies. In Apr 1938, Negrín removed Indalecio Prieto, the last obstacle to communist domination. As the Republic plunged to defeat, the PSOE

collapsed and during **Franco**'s dictatorship PSOE opposition was negligible. However, it played an important role during the transition to democracy. Moreover, in 1982 the PSOE won an overall majority in the general election, repeating its success in 1986. The PSOE in power has done much to modernize Spain and raise its international profile, though it has proved intolerant of dissent, lost the support of the trade unions, and been discredited by corruption scandals. ▷ **Republic, Second** (Spain)

Psusennes I (Akheperre Setepenamun) (c.1040/992BC) King of Egypt. A member of the 21st Dynasty, he was closely attached to Amun of Thebes, something clearly signalled in his adoption of the title 'High Priest of Amun' in addition to his royal titulary. At Tanis, the capital established in this dynasty, the importance of the Theban triad of Amun, Mut and Khonsu was underlined by the building of a temple to the three deities.

Ptolemaic Period (332–30BC) This is the name applied to the time when Ancient Egypt was ruled by the Macedonian descendants of **Alexander III, 'the Great'**. Egypt became part of the Hellenistic world: Greek methods of administration were introduced and the Greek language was employed officially. The Egyptian army was reorganized on the Macedonian model. It was only in matters of religion that the old traditions were maintained, and some of the best preserved temples belong to this period. The new dynasty adopted pharaonic titles and dress, while writing their names in hieroglyphics within cartouches. Commercial activities were developed and learning was encouraged. Internal dynastic upheavals and intervention by Rome brought this period to an end.

Ptolemy I Soter (d.283BC) Macedonian general and ruler of Egypt. He was one of the greatest of the generals of **Alexander III, 'the Great'**, upon whose death he obtained Egypt (323BC). Nominally subject to the Macedonian kings, Ptolemy occupied the first half of his reign in repelling outside attacks and consolidating his government. In 306BC he was defeated by **Demetrius Poliorcetes** in a sea-fight off Salamis in Cyprus. He was nevertheless able to assume the royal title (305BC), and defended his territories against Antigonus and Cyclops and Demetrius. In 305BC he defended the Rhodians against Demetrius, and received from them his title *Soter* ('Saviour'). Alexandria, his capital, became the centre of commerce and Greek culture, where he founded the Museum and Library. ▷ **Ptolemaic Period**

Ptolemy II Philadelphus (283/246BC) King of Egypt (283–246BC), son and successor of **Ptolemy I Soter**, it was under him that the power of Egypt attained its greatest height. He was generally successful in his external wars, enlarged the Museum and Library, purchased many valuable manuscripts of Greek literature, and attracted leading Greek intellectuals to his court. The Egyptian history of Manetho was dedicated to him, but the story that he commissioned the Greek translation of the Hebrew scriptures (the Septuagint) is open to doubt. ▷ **Ptolemaic Period**

Ptolemy III Euergetes I (246/222BC) King of Egypt. He was the son and successor of **Ptolemy II Philadelphus**. As king, he conquered Syria and Cilicia and returned with immense booty which benefited the temples of Egypt. He was an ally of the Spartans against the Achaean League. ▷ **Ptolemaic Period**

Ptolemy IV Philopator (222/204BC) King of Egypt. The son and successor of **Ptolemy III Euergetes I**, he began his reign by murdering his mother, Berenice. A hostile tradition portrays him as indolent and ascribes to him the decline of Ptolemaic power at home and abroad. ▷ **Ptolemaic Period**

Ptolemy V Epiphanes (c.210/180BC) King of Egypt. He succeeded his father, **Ptolemy IV Philopator**, while still a boy. It was during his reign that the court intrigues and internal conflicts began which were to affect the dynasty increasingly for the remainder of the **Ptolemaic Period**. The ceremonies connected to his coronation, together with steps to secure the allegiance of the priesthood, are recorded on the Rosetta Stone in Greek, demotic and hieroglyphic, issued in 196BC. This trilingual inscription provided the key to understanding the ancient scripts of Egypt.

Ptolemy VI Philometor (180/145BC) King of Egypt. He came to the throne at a time when court intrigues and the clash of rival factions were on the increase. Acceding to the throne as a child, his mother, Cleopatra, governed the country during his minority. On her death, power devolved on courtiers, who were rash enough to go to war with the Seleucid King, Antiochus IV of Syria. The result was an invasion of Egypt in 170BC;

Memphis was attacked and the young Ptolemy was captured. He was well treated by Antiochus and reinstalled as king. Meanwhile, his brother (later, **Ptolemy VIII Euergetes II**) in Alexandria had assumed the title of King. In 168BC the **Seleucids** attacked a second time, to be met by a Roman embassy, which ordered the withdrawal of Antiochus from Egypt. In 164BC Euergetes expelled Philometor, who went to Rome and was restored by the Romans to his kingdom, while Euergetes obtained Cyrene as a separate realm; from this time onward, Egypt was under the protection of Rome. ▷ **Ptolemaic Period**

Ptolemy VIII Euergetes II (170/163 and 145/116BC) King of Egypt. One of the most unsavoury of the kings of the Ptolemaic Dynasty, he was nicknamed *Physcon* ('Potbelly') on account of his corpulence, and his cruelty and luxurious habits were notorious. He clashed with his brother, **Ptolemy VI Philometor**, and in 164BC drove him from Egypt. The intervention of Rome restored Ptolemy VI, and Euergetes II was established as ruler of Cyrene. Intrigue and ruthless elimination of rivals characterized his rule as Ptolemy VIII. He married his sister, Cleopatra II, the widow of Ptolemy VI, and executed his nephew, Ptolemy (Eupator), to have sole right to the throne. Following a revolt in Alexandria, he was forced to flee to Cyprus and his sister, Cleopatra, was declared queen in Egypt (130BC). This so enraged Ptolemy that he put to death Memphitis, his son by Cleopatra, sending the boy's head and hands to Cleopatra — some versions assert parts of the dismembered body were served to Cleopatra at a meal. ▷ **Ptolemaic Period**

Ptolemy XII Neos Dionysos (Auletes) (80/51BC) King of Egypt. Proclaimed King by the Alexandrians, he earned the name *Auletes* ('flute-player') because he performed in public on the instrument. Eager for the Roman senate's support for his title to the throne of Egypt, it was only on the appointment of Julius **Caesar** to the consulship that he was able to purchase this by bribery. His over-taxed subjects forced him into exile (58–55BC) in Rome, where he endeavoured to get the senate to restore him to his kingdom. Members of a delegation from Alexandria were sent to Rome to plead their cause, but Ptolemy arranged for them to be intercepted and the majority put to death. By further bribes, Ptolemy was again placed on the throne through the agency of the pro-consul of Syria. On his return, he executed his eldest daughter, Berenice IV, who had ruled Egypt during her father's exile. In his will, Ptolemy bequeathed the kingdom jointly to **Cleopatra VII** and her elder son, Ptolemy XIII, asking Rome to ensure the succession. ▷ **Ptolemaic Period**

Public Against Violence (1989) The Slovak offshoot and equivalent of Czech **Civic Forum** that united most of the anti-communist groups in Slovakia in Nov 1989 to help bring down the Czechoslovak communist government. There was no bloodshed and the 'party' won more seats than any other in the June 1990 election. But it subsequently split on the issue of relations with the Czech Lands. Even Jan Carnogursky, Slovak Prime Minister and leader of the rump 'party', had inevitably to talk in nationalist terms.

Public Safety, Committee of French revolutionary political body, set up in the war crisis (Apr 1793) to organize defence against internal and external enemies. Its members, elected by the National Convention, came to exercise dictatorial powers during the Reign of **Terror**, particularly under **Robespierre**'s leadership. After his downfall (July 1794), its powers were strictly limited. ▷ **Convention, National; French Revolution**

pueblo Means both 'the village' and 'the village dwellers' or 'the people'. Underlines the enormous importance attached to local ties in Spanish life. National unity came late to Spain, the persistence of the 'pueblo' providing the most significant yardstick.

Pugachev, Emelyan (c.1742–75) Russian Don Cossack. He fled to the Urals, from where he launched a mass rebellion against **Catherine II, 'the Great'**. This was neither the first nor the last such insurrection based on the simmering discontent of an exploited peasantry and led by a largely free Cossack. Pugachev carried his revolt to the Volga, proclaimed himself to be Peter III, Catherine's murdered husband, and promised to restore ancient freedoms. The rebellion was marked by great ferocity on both sides, and Pugachev's name later became a byword for the spirit of peasant revolution in Russia. He was captured in 1774 and taken to Moscow, where he was tortured and executed. Catherine's handling of the episode was in stark contrast to her allegedly enlightened social philosophy and only contributed in the long run to the downfall of tsarism. ▷ **Cossacks; Razin, Stenka**

Pułaski, Kazimierz (1747–79) Polish nobleman and soldier. One of the few who fought successfully against Russia, he was outlawed at the First Partition of Poland (1772). In 1777 he went to America, and for his conduct at Brandywine was given command of a brigade of cavalry. In 1778 he organized 'Pułaski's legion', in May 1779 entered Charleston, and held it until it was relieved. He was mortally wounded at the siege of Savannah. ▷ **American Revolution; Poland, Partitions of**

Pullman Strike (1894) A US labour conflict. During the depression of 1894 the Pullman Palace Car Company in Chicago cut workers' wages by 25–40 per cent, but maintained their high rents in the residential town founded by the company. The workers were members of the newly-formed American Railway Union, which retaliated by refusing to handle Pullman cars, and thereby interfering with the mail service. Despite pleas from Governor John Altgeld, President Grover **Cleveland** ordered federal troops to the site and after much violence, the strike was broken. The Attorney-General's court injunction, which forbade interference with the mail and interstate commerce, established the principle that a strike could violate the Sherman Anti-Trust Act. ▷ **Anti-Trust Acts; Debs, Eugene**

Pulszky, Ferenc Aurelius (1814–97) Hungarian politician and author. He studied law, travelled, and published (1837) a successful book on England. In 1848 he became **Esterházy**'s factotum, but, having joined the revolution, went to London in 1849 to plead for help, which was never given. He stayed on to become a journalist. When Lajos **Kossuth** came to England, Pulszky became his companion and went with him to America. He was condemned to death in 1852, but after living in Italy (1852–66) and being imprisoned in Naples as a Garibaldian, he was pardoned in 1867 at the time of the **Ausgleich**. He returned to Hungary, sat in parliament and was Director of Museums.

Punic Wars The three wars fought and won in the 3c and 2c BC by Rome against her only remaining rival for supreme power in the western Mediterranean, the Phoenician (Punic) city, Carthage. The first (264–241BC) resulted in Rome's acquisition of her first overseas province, Sicily, hitherto a Carthaginian territory. The second war (218–201BC) saw Carthage surrender to Rome all her remaining overseas possessions, and become a dependent, tribute-paying ally. The third (149–146BC) ended in the capture and total destruction of Carthage itself.

Puritanism The belief that further reformation was required in the Church of England under **Elizabeth I** and the Stuarts. It arose in the 1560s out of dissatisfaction with the 'popish elements', such as surplices, which had been retained by the Elizabethan religious settlement. It was not always a coherent, organized movement; rather, a diverse body of opinions and personalities, which occasionally came together. It included the anti-episcopal Presbyterian movement of John Field and Thomas Cartwright in the 1570s and 1580s; the separatist churches that left England for Holland and America from 1590 to 1640; the 'presbyterian', 'independent', and more radical groups which emerged during the **English Civil Wars** and **interregnum**; and the nonconformist sects persecuted by the **Cavalier Parliament**'s 'Clarendon Code' under **Charles II**. ▷ **Restoration; Stuart, House of**

Puyi (P'u-yi) (1906–67) Last Emperor of China (1908/12) and the first of Manzhuguo (1934/5). This was the personal name of **Hsuan T'ung**. Emperor at the age of two, after the **Chinese Revolution** (1911) he was given a pension and a summer palace. Known in the West as Henry Puyi, in 1932 he was called from private life by the Japanese to be provincial dictator of Manzhuguo, under the name of Kang Teh. Taken prisoner by the Russians in 1945, he was tried in China as a war criminal (1950), pardoned (1959) and became a private citizen. The story of his life was made into a film, The Last Emperor, in 1988.

Pyat, Félix (1810–89) French journalist and revolutionary. He signed **Ledru-Rollin**'s appeal to the masses to arm in 1849, escaped to London, and became a member of the 'European revolutionary committee'. Returning to Paris on amnesty in 1870, he was a leader of the communards, and again escaped to London. He was condemned to death, in absence, in 1873, but pardoned in 1880.

Pym, John (1584–1643) English politician. He left Oxford without taking a degree, studied law, and entered parliament (1614). In 1641 he took a leading part in the impeachment of **Strafford**, helped to draw up the **Grand Remonstrance**, and in 1642 was one of the five members whom **Charles I** singled out by name. He stayed in London during the **English Civil Wars**, and died soon after, being appointed Lieutenant of the Ordnance.

Pyramids, Battle of the (1798) A battle fought between French forces under **Napoleon I** and the Mamluk rulers of Egypt. The battle enabled Napoleon to take Cairo and establish control of Egypt. The Egyptian campaign aimed at strangling British lines of communication with India. ▷ **Mamluks**

Pyrenees, Treaty of the (7 Nov 1659) The peace treaty between France and Spain ending the hostilities of the **Thirty Years War**. It followed a series of Spanish Habsburg defeats since 1643 (the Austrian Habsburgs made a separate peace in the Treaty of **Westphalia**, 1648). The French King, **Louis XIV**, had ambitions in the Low Countries, and this treaty gave him part of the Spanish Netherlands: nearly all Artois, Grevelingen, and several other parts. The French, for their part, withdrew from most of Italy. The treaty also arranged Louis's marriage to **Philip IV** of Spain's daughter, **Maria Theresa**. The treaty brought to an end the war in the southern Netherlands (now Belgium) and marked the end of Spanish military and political dominance in Western Europe. ▷ **Habsburg Dynasty**

Pyrrhus (c.319–272BC) King of Epirus (307/303BC and 297/272BC). An ambitious ruler, his aim was to revive the empire of his second cousin, **Alexander III, 'the Great'**. Unsuccessful in this goal (283BC), Pyrrhus turned to the West, where he became embroiled in Italian affairs and hence conflict with Rome. Though he won two battles against her (280–279BC), his losses, particularly at Asculum (279BC), were so great that they gave rise to the phrase 'Pyrrhic victory'.

Q

Qaboos bin Said (1940–) Sultan of Oman (1970/). The son of Sa'id bin Taimur, he is the 14th descendant of the ruling dynasty of the Albusaid family. Educated in England, where he was trained at Sandhurst, the Royal Military Academy, he disagreed with the conservative views of his father and in 1970 overthrew him in a bloodless coup and assumed the sultanship. He proceeded to pursue more liberal and expansionist policies, while maintaining an international position of strict non-alignment.

Qadhdhafi, Mu'ammar ▷ **Gaddafi, Mu'ammar**

Qajar Dynasty A Turcoman tribe which furnished Persia with a dynasty which ruled from 795 to 1924. Qajar authority over Persia was established by Aqa Muhammad Khan at the expense of the Zand Khans whom he ousted. Murdered in 1797, Aqa Muhammad Khan was succeeded by his nephew, Fath Ali Khan, then Governor of Fars, who reigned with the title of Fath Ali Shah. The period of Qajar rule saw a great increase in the influence in Persia of both the British and the Russians, interference by which latter in the internal affairs of Persia was established in the Treaty of **Gulistan** which gave the Tsar the right, not only to recognize the Prince nominated as heir to the Qajar throne, but also to intervene on his behalf should there be dissension over his accession. The absolute nature of Qajar rule, coupled with the affectation of ostentatious luxury on the part of some Qajar Shahs, led to many disturbances, and this coupled with foreign interference led to difficulties with the religious hierarchy. A coup d'état in the early 1920s at the instigation of Reza Khan led in due course to the deposition of the last Qajar ruler, Ahmad Shah, and the coronation of Reza as Reza Shah Pahlavi.

Qarakhanid Dynasty A Turkish dynasty which ruled in Central Asia from the 10c to the early 13c. Initially a tribal confederation which, in the 10c, was instrumental in bringing down the Samanid Dynasty in Transoxiana, the Qarakhanids after an initial period of cordiality had hostile relations with **Mahmud of Ghazni**. In the early 11c the Qarakhanids accepted Sunni Islam and the

spiritual suzerainty of the 'Abbasid caliph. In the mid-11c the khanate split into an eastern and a western branch, the eastern branch being situated in Semirechye and adjoining territories, the western situated in Transoxiana until the early 13c when, caught between the Khwarazm-Shahs and the Qara-Khitay, the last Qarakhanid, 'Uthman Khan, succumbed to the Kharazm-Shah, Ala al-Din Muhammad, who captured Samarkand and had 'Uthman executed. Adopting Persian and Islamic values, both cultural and religious, the Qarakhanids patronized architecture, the arts and scholarship, while at the same time not losing sight of their own Turkish identity. ▷ 'Abbasid Dynasty

Qara-Qoyunlu The so-called 'Black Sheep' Turcomans ruled over portions of Eastern Anatolia, Iraq and much of Iran in the second half of the 14c and for much of the 15c. The first Qara-Qoyunlu leader to achieve prominence was Bayram Khoja, who, by the time of his death (1380), had brought the territories from Mosul to Erzerum under the sway of his tribe. His successors, Qara-Mehmet and Qara-Yusuf, both had to contend with **Timur**, but it was Qara-Yusuf who established the reputation of the Qara-Qoyunlu, bequeathing territories stretching from Erzinjan (Erzincan) to Qazvin and from Shirvan to Basra. Amongst those whose hostility he faced was Shah-Rukh the Timurid. However, after Qara-Yusuf's death, Shah-Rukh, realizing that he would not be able completely to reduce the Qara-Qoyunlu, supported individual members of the ruling family; his declaration in 1434 of Jihan-Shah as leader of the Qara-Qoyunlu led subsequently to the development of Qara-Qoyunlu lands into an empire. After Shah-Rukh's death, Jihan-Shah was able to take Rayy and Isfahan, and extend his rule to Kerman and Fars. However, a disastrous expedition against Uzun Hasan Beg of the Aq-Qoyunlu (or 'White Sheep' Turcomans) resulted in Jihan-Shah's death in 1467; by 1469, the authority of the Qara-Qoyunlu was almost completely in the hands of the Aq-Qoyunlu.

Qashqais A Turkish people living in Iran in the province of Fars. A relatively recent community (the earliest mention of them dates from the 18c), the nomadic Qashqais have a history of clashes with central authority in Iran. They were, for instance, disarmed by Reza Shah in 1930, and in **World War II** they refused to surrender German agents who had sought asylum amongst them. In 1963 land reforms were imposed on the territories of the Qashqais and their attempts to resist were forcibly put down; their tribesmen were disarmed and the ruling family of khans forced into exile.

Qassim, Abd al-Krim (1914–63) Iraqi soldier and revolutionary. The son of a carpenter, he joined the army and by 1955 had risen to the rank of brigadier. In 1958 he led the coup which resulted in the overthrow of the monarchy and the deaths of King **Faysal II**, his uncle Prince Abdul Ilah, and the pro-Western Prime Minister, General Nuri al-**Said**. Qassim suspended the constitution and established a left-wing military regime with himself as prime minister and head of state, but soon found himself increasingly isolated in the Arab world. He survived one assassination attempt, but failed to crush a Kurdish rebellion (1961–3) and was killed in a coup led by Colonel Salem Aref, who reinstated constitutional government.

Qianlong   (Ch'ien-lung)   (1736/96) Emperor of the Manchu **Qing Dynasty**. During his reign the Chinese empire attained its zenith of power and prosperity. Tibet and Mongolia were incorporated into the empire and neighbouring states (eg Korea, Burma, Annam) regularly sent tribute missions to Qianlong's court. The supreme confidence in China's superiority and self-sufficiency as the Middle Kingdom was dramatically illustrated by Qianlong's rejection of requests made by the Macartney mission (1793) for increased Sino-British trade. Peace and stability at home, however, led to a huge increase in population that outstripped the availability of land, while Qianlong's final years were marked by bureaucratic complacency and widespread corruption. When he abdicated in 1796 (so as not to reign longer than his grandfather, **Kangxi**) government financial resources were depleted, official morale was low, and the efficiency of Manchu military forces much impaired, all of which boded ill for the dynasty's ability to meet internal and external threats from the early 19c onwards.

Qin Dynasty (221–206BC) The first dynasty to rule over a united China. Its founder, **Qin**

Shi Huangdi, led the state of Qin (in present-day Shaanxi) to victory over the other 'warring states', and installed a regime of strict authoritarian **Legalism**. Its achievements included abolition of the ancient feudal order in favour of a prefectural system, the standardization of the Chinese script, weights, and measures, and the construction of roads, canals, and the Great Wall.

Qing Dynasty (1644–1911) The last dynasty of imperial China, it was founded by the Manchus following their conquest of China in 1644. **Kangxi** (1661/1722) made concerted attempts to suppress corruption and reduce taxation and was also a great patron of the arts and sciences. During his reign, Jesuit missionaries from France were allowed to settle in China and, with his permission, they were responsible for the first geographical survey of the empire in 1718. Much of the reign was taken up with military matters, the Rebellion of the **Three Feudatories** and wars with the Mongols and with Russia. The early years of **Qianlong**'s long reign (1736/96) were peaceful and prosperous, but the latter half was marred by corruption at court. Military conquests and the suppression of internal rebellions, especially the White Lotus Rebellion (1796–1807), were a considerable drain on the treasury. He formally abdicated in 1796, although he continued to 'instruct' his son on the conduct of national affairs until his death. The dynasty entered a period of decline in the 19c as China fell more and more under the domination of the European powers but did not finally collapse until the **Chinese Revolution** in 1911, when China became a republic. See map p768.

Qin Shi Huangdi (259–210BC) Chinese Emperor (221/210BC). He was the founder of the **Qin Dynasty** and was the creator of the first unified Chinese empire. His extension and consolidation of the empire involved the establishment of a centralized administration, with the abolition of territorial feudal power, and far-reaching measures for standardization (embracing all aspects of life, from the written language and the law to weights and measures) throughout the empire. He ordered the construction of a system of roads and built the Great Wall, completed in 214BC, to keep out barbarians. He had all historical documents, except those relating to the Qin and those in the imperial library, burnt in 212BC to maintain himself and his successors in power. Traditionally viewed as a despotic ruler, who handed out Draconian

China under the Qing Dynasty

punishments, his behaviour should perhaps be seen in the light of his belief in **Legalism**. Certainly, his establishment of an administrative and bureaucratic system which endured in subsequent dynasties, is of at least equal importance. When Shi Huangdi died, the recently-excavated 'Terracotta Army' of several thousand life-size soldiers and horses was buried with him.

Qishan (Ch'i-shan) (d.1854) Manchu official of the Chinese government. He was appointed Imperial Commissioner at Canton in 1840 to negotiate with the British expeditionary force during the **Opium War**. Qishan's attempt to compromise with the British led to the signing of the Chuenpi Convention (Jan 1841), which proposed the cession of Hong Kong to Britain and the reopening of the port of Canton to foreign trade. The convention was disowned by both the Qing Emperor (for having ceded too much) and by the British government (which felt it had not granted enough). Qishan was dismissed and the war dragged on until 1842.

Qiu Jin (Ch'iu Chin) (1875–1907) Chinese feminist and revolutionary. In 1904 Qiu Jin abandoned her family to study in Japan, where she became actively involved in radical Chinese student associations calling for the overthrow of the Manchu **Qing Dynasty**. On her return to China in 1906, she founded a women's journal in which she argued that the liberation of women was an essential prerequisite for a strong China. In 1907 Qiu Jin was implicated in an abortive anti-Manchu uprising and was executed by the Qing authorities.

Qiying (Ch'i-ying) (d.1858) Chinese official. A member of the Imperial clan, he held a succession of senior posts in central government (1823–36), and in 1842 was sent to Nanjing (Nanking) to defend the city against the British. He negotiated the Treaty of **Nanjing**, followed by similar treaties with the USA, France, and other countries, and pursued a policy of conciliation until recalled in 1848. In 1858, when the Chinese had again been defeated by the British, he was sent to join in the negotiations for the Treaty of **Tianjin**, but the British representatives confronted him with evidence of the insincerity of his former protestations of friendship. He left his post in despair and against orders, and was commanded by the Emperor to commit suicide.

Quadrilateral The defensive position on the borders of Lombardy and Venetia formed by the four fortified cities of Verona, Mantua, Peschiera and Legnano. Following the **Cinque Giornate**, the Austrian commander, **Radetzky**, retreated to the Quadrilateral and used it as the basis for his eventual recapture of the rebellious Italian provinces of the Habsburg Empire. During the war of 1859, the difficulty in dislodging the Austrians from the Quadrilateral seems to have played a large part in persuading **Napoleon III** to seek peace after the Battles of **Solferino** and **Magenta** (1859); it fell into Italian hands only in 1866. ▷ **Habsburg Dynasty**

Quadros, Jânio da Silva (1917–92) Brazilian politician. Trained as a teacher, he was elected to the municipal council of São Paulo in 1947. He was a masterful campaigner and orator, with a unique personal style: as the 'man of destiny', he won election to the São Paulo State Assembly, Prefecture and Governorship between 1951 and 1955. He began preparing for the presidential race in 1960, as the only hope of the UDN (*União Democrático Nacional*), mobilizing popular support in the process. He defeated his **PSD** opponents and assumed the presidency in 1961, determined to overcome the economic crisis bequeathed by **Kubitschek (de Oliveira)**. This he did by exercising near-dictatorial prerogatives to temper crisis economic measures with a strongly nationalist foreign policy. He incurred the wrath of Congress and the far right, led by Carlos Lacerda, and resigned (25 Aug 1961), pitching the country into crisis. Banned from political life in 1965, he returned to politics in 1985 as Prefect of São Paulo, failing in another bid for the presidency in 1989.

Quadruple Alliance (1718) A treaty signed by Britain, France, and the Habsburg Emperor, Charles VI, to which the Dutch were expected to accede, to ensure the principle of collective security in Western Europe. It provided for mutual guarantees of titles, possessions, and rights of succession, despite Spain's hostility to Italian territorial provisions, and secured peace for a generation (1718–33).

Quakers ▷ **Society of Friends**

Quayle, (J) Dan(forth) (1947–) US politician. Born in Indianapolis, Indiana, he was educated at DePauw and Indiana Universities, then served as a captain in the Indiana National Guard (1970–76). He worked as a lawyer, journalist, and public official, becoming a member of the House of Representatives (1977–81) and Senate (1981–8) representing the state of Indiana. He was elected Vice-President under George **Bush** in 1988. As Vice President he was a proponent of political conservatism and of a business community unhindered by federal regulation.

Quebec, Battle of (13 Sep 1759) A battle fought during the **Seven Years War** between British forces under General James **Wolfe** and French forces defending Quebec under the Marquis of **Montcalm**. It followed an audacious plan by Wolfe to transport British troops from the St Lawrence River up steep, wooded cliffs. British victory led to speedy capture of Quebec and the subsequent collapse of French power in Canada. Both Wolfe and Montcalm were killed in the battle.

Quebec Act (1774) British statute enacted to remedy the anomalous situation of Quebec within the empire. In 1769 the Board of Trade advised the extension of British institutions to the new colony and suggested that the French should participate in the government of the colony. Sir Guy **Carleton** took a different view of the problem, believing that the French seigniorial system should be maintained and that Responsible Government should be withheld. The Board of Trade report was suppressed and the Quebec Act, which reversed the established principle of colonial rule through British institutions, was passed. The governor was to rule with the assistance of a council which included the French seigniors; the seigniorial system of tenure continued and the position of the Catholic Church was maintained. The Act showed generosity to a conquered people but omitted to consider the expectations of either the **habitants** or the English-speaking settlers who were unhappy at the retention of the civil law embodied in the Custom of Paris and the absence of *habeas corpus*. The Act was superseded by the Constitutional Act of 1791.

Queen Anne's War (1702–13) The second of the four intercolonial wars waged by Britain and France for control of colonial North America, known in Europe as the War of the **Spanish Succession**. Both sides made considerable use of Native American allies. Settled by the Treaty of **Utrecht** (1713), the war resulted in British control of Newfoundland, **Acadia**, and Hudson's Bay. Britain also gained the Asiento, allowing trade with Spanish America.

Queenston Heights, Battle of (1812) Military engagement in the **War of 1812**. A victory for the British regular army, it reassured Canadians who doubted Britain's commitment to their defence, while pro-Americans were forced to reconsider their loyalties. A monument was erected as a memorial to Isaac Brock, the commanding officer who charged somewhat injudiciously up the face of the Heights.

Queipo de Llano, Gonzalo, Marquis of Queipo de Llano y Sevilla (1875–1951) Spanish soldier. After military service in Cuba and Morocco, he was promoted to the rank of major-general in the Republican army, but went over to the rebel side at the beginning of the **Spanish Civil War**. In July 1936 he led the forces which captured Seville, and became Commander-in-Chief of the Southern army. In his many propaganda broadcasts from Seville, he drew on General Emilio Mola's phrase '**fifth column**', as used to describe the rebel supporters inside Madrid, who were expected to add their strength to that of the four columns attacking from outside. In Apr 1950 he was given the title of marquis.

Quezon, Manuel Luis (1878–1944) President of the Commonwealth of the Philippines. He studied in Manila, served with **Aguinaldo** during the insurrection of 1899 and in 1905 became Governor of Tayabas under the US regime. In 1909 he went to Washington as one of the resident Filipino commissioners. President of the Filipino Senate (1916–35), he played a major role in the negotiation of Filipino independence in the early 1930s, and was elected first President of the Filipino Commonwealth (1935). Here he established a highly centralized government verging on 'one-man' rule. Quezon displayed great courage during the Japanese onslaught from Dec 1941, refusing to evacuate to the USA until President **Roosevelt** intervened.

Quiet Revolution (1960–6) Quebec reform programme. Pursued by Jean **Lesage**'s Liberal government of Quebec with the slogan, *Il faut que ça change* ('Things must change'), it sought to counteract the influence of the Catholic Church in civic spheres such as education and promoted state activism to 'decolonize' Quebec's economy from the influence of American and English-speaking institutions. It also began to participate in the federal/provincial shared-cost programmes, though previously shunned by **Duplessis** and the **Union Nationale**, to provide the range of social services available elsewhere in Canada. However, the resulting huge increases in the size of the provincial civil service and the tax burden gave the **Union Nationale** a platform for their return to power under Daniel Johnson. ▷ **Liberal Party** (Canada)

Quinet, Edgar (1803–75) French writer and politician. Appointed Professor of Literature in 1839, he began the lectures which formed his brilliant *Du génie des religions* (1842); then he joined Michelet in attacking the Jesuits. His lectures caused so much excitement that the government suppressed them in 1846. After the **February Revolution** (1848) he was elected to the National Assembly and voted with the extreme left. After the coup d'état he was exiled to

Brussels and Switzerland. After the downfall of **Napoleon III**, he returned to Paris and was elected to the National Assembly (1871).

Quisling, Vidkun (Abraham Lauritz Jonsson) (1887-1945) Norwegian fascist leader. He embarked on a military career, graduating from military academy with high honours in 1911, and went on to serve as a military attaché in Russia and Finland (1918–21) and to work with Fridtjof **Nansen** as a relief administrator in the USSR (1922–6). Quisling entered politics in 1929 and was Minister of Defence in 1931–2. In May 1933 he founded a new party, *Nasjonal Samling* ('National Union') in imitation of the German National Socialist Party. However, the party met with little electoral success and disintegrated after 1936. He then turned to Germany and in Dec 1939 made contact with the Nazi leader, Alfred Rosenberg, and the head of the German navy, Admiral **Raeder**, as well as with **Hitler** himself. Following the German invasion of Norway (Apr 1940), Quisling declared himself head of a government but won no support and was forced to step down six days later. It was from this point onward that his name became synonymous with 'traitor'. The German occupation authorities reluctantly allowed Quisling to head a puppet government from May 1942 onwards. At the end of **World War II** he was arrested and put on trial, and executed by firing squad on 24 Oct 1945. ▷ **fascism; Norway, German Invasion of**

Quit India Movement A campaign launched (Aug 1942) by the **Indian National Congress** calling for immediate independence from Britain, and threatening mass non-violent struggle if its demands were not met. M K **Gandhi** and other Congress leaders were arrested, and the movement was suppressed, though not without difficulty. It was described by the Viceroy, Lord Linlithgow, as 'by far the most serious rebellion since that

of 1857': 57 army battalions had to be used to help restore order and there were more than 1 000 deaths. It contributed significantly to the eventual decision by Britain to withdraw from India soon after the end of **World War II**. ▷ **Indian Uprising**

Qutb-ud-Din Aibak (d.1210) Founder of the Delhi Sultanate. A former slave become general, he was entrusted by **Muhammad Ghuri** with the continuation of his conquest of north India after 1192. Following Muhammad's death in 1206, Qutb-ud-Din declared himself Sultan of Muhammad's Indian possessions (1206/10), throwing off subordination to the Ghurids and establishing the so-called 'Slave' or Mamluk Dynasty of the Delhi Sultanate. He was succeeded, briefly, by his son, Aram Singh, and then by his son-in-law, **Iltutmish**.

Quwwatli, Shukri al- (1891–1967) He was early a member of the Young Arab Association, which was founded in Paris but later moved to Syria. This group aimed originally to free Arabs from Turkish rule, while at the same time discouraging the Western powers from interfering in Arab affairs. Al-Quwwatli went on to become a leader of the National Bloc in Syria, which distinguished itself by winning the first elections permitted by the French (1943). However, despite a declaration of independence in 1944, full independence was not achieved until 1946. Al-Quwwatli had a resurgence of political influence when he returned to power after the election of 1955, but this only lasted until the following year, when the government fell. He was President in 1958 and, with Gamal Abd al-**Nasser**, proclaimed the short-lived **United Arab Republic** (effectively the creation of Salah al-Din **Bitar** of the Syrian Ba'th party).

QwaQwa National state or non-independent Black homeland in South Africa; self-governing status, 1974. ▷ **apartheid**

R

Rabin, Itzhak (1922–) Israeli soldier and politician. He fought in the 'War of Independence' (1948–9) and represented the Israeli Defence Forces (IDF) at the armistice in Rhodes. In the IDF he rose to become Chief-of-Staff in 1964, heading the armed forces during the successful **Six-Day War** of 1967. After serving as Ambassador to the USA (1968–73), he became Labour Party leader and Prime Minister (1974–7) and Defence Minister from 1984. He became Labour leader and Prime Minister again (1992–), and signed the Israel–PLO peace accord with Yasser **Arafat**. ▷ **Arab-Israeli Wars; Gaza Strip; Mapai Party; West Bank**

Rabuka, Sitiveni (1948–) Fijian soldier and politician. He completed his army training at Sandhurst Military College in England, and then served with a **UN** peacekeeping force in the Lebanon, before returning to Fiji with the rank of colonel. When the 1987 elections produced an Indian-dominated coalition government, he engineered a coup that deposed the Prime Minister, Kamisese Mara, and established his own provisional administration. In Dec 1987, he declared the country a republic and reinstated Mara as Premier, while retaining control of the security forces and of internal affairs.

Radbod (d.719) King of the Frisians. Under his rule the Frisian kingdom (in the north of the Netherlands) reached its greatest extent at the expense of the Frankish kingdom. In 689 **Pepin II** of the **Franks** defeated Radbod's forces at Dorestad (near present-day Wijk-bij-Duurstede in the Netherlands), which meant that Christian evangelists were free to work among the Frisians. Radbod rose up in 714, but was finally defeated by the Frank **Charles Martel** in 717.

Radek, Karl Berngardovich (1885–1939) Russian revolutionary and politician. Educated in Kraków and Bern and left-wing in his views, he became a journalist in Germany and Switzerland. He was active in Petrograd following the Bolshevik Revolution and participated obliquely in the unsuccessful German revolution. Returning to the USSR, he became a leading member of the Communist International, but lost standing with his growing distrust of extremist tactics. He was charged as a supporter of **Trotsky**, and expelled from the Party (1927–9). He was readmitted after recanting, but in 1937 he was a victim of one of **Stalin**'s show trials, being sentenced to 10 years in prison, where he is believed to have been murdered by fellow-prisoners two years later. ▷ **Bolsheviks; communism; Russian Revolution**

Radetzky von Radetz, Joseph, Count (1766–1858) Austrian general. He saw action against the Turks (1788–9) and French (1792–1815). In 1831 he became Commander-in-Chief of the Austrian forces in Italy. Forced from Milan after the famous **Cinque Giornate** of street fighting in 1848, he took refuge in the **Quadrilateral**, before rallying his forces and defeating the Piedmontese army at **Custozza** (25 July 1848). When **Charles Albert** once again invaded Lombardy in 1849, Radetzky's forces routed them at the Battle of **Novara** (23 Mar 1849), resulting in the Piedmontese King's abdication. It was Radetzky who negotiated with the new King, **Victor Emmanuel II,** at Vignale the following day; contrary to popular tradition, he did not demand the abolition of the **Statuto**. Following the collapse of the **Revolutions of 1848–9**, Radetzky became Governor-General and military commander of the Kingdom of **Lombardy-Venetia** until he retired in 1857.

Radhakrishnan, Sarvepalli (1888–1975) Indian philosopher and politician. Educated in Madras, he taught at Mysore and Calcutta Universities, and became Professor of Eastern Religions and Ethics at Oxford (1936–52). In 1946 he was chief Indian delegate to UNESCO, becoming its Chairman in 1949. A member of the Indian Assembly in 1947, he was Indian Ambassador to the USSR (1949), Vice-President of India (1952–62) and President (1962–7). He was knighted in 1931.

Radić, Stjepan (1871–1928) Croatian politician. An admirer of the Czech leader, Thomas **Masaryk**, he and his brother, Antun, founded the Croat People's Peasant Party (HPSS, *Hrvatska Pučka Seljačka Stranka*) in 1904. A member of the National Council which represented the South Slavs of the

Habsburg monarchy in the months before the creation of the Kingdom of Serbs, Croats and Slovenes (Dec 1918), he was deeply suspicious of the motives of Nikola **Pašić** and of the Serbs in general. After unification, he and the HPSS maintained their vehement opposition to the new Belgrade-based government. Imprisoned in Mar 1919, on his release (Dec 1920) he sought foreign support for an autonomous Croatian republic. He visited Moscow (1924) and affiliated the HPSS with the Communist Peasant International. The Belgrade government charged him with cooperation with **Comintern** and imprisoned him and the other HPSS leaders until 1925 when, in an apparent volte-face, he accepted the constitution and agreed to cooperate with the Serbian Radical Party. He alternately sat and withdrew from the Belgrade parliament until 1928, when he and his nephew, Pavle Radić, were shot by a Montenegrin deputy during a parliamentary sitting. His death shortly afterwards brought an end to any semblance of Croat-Serb cooperation and precipitated the establishment of the royal dictatorship. ▷ **Alexander I; Korošec, Anton; Maček, Vladko; Pribičević, Svetozar**

radicalism Any set of ideas, normally of the left but not exclusively so, which argues for more substantial social and political change than is supported in the political mainstream. What is radical is a matter of judgement, and so the term is very widely applied. In a number of countries there are radical parties which are left of centre.

Radical Party (Argentina) Formed as the Radical Civic Union (*Unión Cívica Radical*) in 1891, it commanded wide support in the early 20c, remaining a leading Argentine party thereafter, though at times divided into two separate branches. The party gained its great strength from the support of the lower middle classes in Buenos Aires, and from the ability of the first **Yrigoyen** administration (1916–22) to secure their loyalty against lower classes. Radicals won the Argentine presidency in 1916, 1922, 1928, 1958, 1963 and 1983.

Radical Party (France) Political party founded in 1901. Radicalism as a political tendency came into existence around 1840, and after 1870 the term designated the left-wing faction of the republicans, as opposed to the **Opportunists**, or **Moderates**. However, an organized political party only appeared in 1901, with the title *Parti républicain radical et radical-socialiste* ('Republican

Radical and Radical-Socialist Party'). It at once became the largest political party in France, and had representatives in office throughout the remaining years of the Third Republic. Its most important leaders were **Caillaux**, **Herriot**, and **Daladier**. Paradoxically **Clemenceau**, the most important representative of the radical tendency before 1901, was never close to the organized party. It was always loosely organized and undisciplined, and was discredited by the collapse of the Third Republic. It was revived after **World War II**, but was much reduced in strength; its most important leader in that period was **Mendès-France**, Prime Minister in 1954. After 1958 it faded even more, and was eventually absorbed in other political formations. ▷ **Republic, Third** (France)

Radical Republican Party (*Partido Republicano Radical*) Spanish political party. Founded in 1908, the Radical Party soon moved away from its revolutionary working class origins in Barcelona to become a federation of largely middle class regional parties centred on the charismatic figure of the populist leader Alejandro **Lerroux**. By the advent of the Second Republic, the Radical Party was not only the most historic Republican party, but also by far the largest. It had also become staunchly conservative. From 1931 to 1933 it was the most formidable source of opposition to the reforms of the progressive Republican-Socialist administrations under Manuel **Azaña**. From 1933 to 1935, the Radical Party was the principal element in a succession of right-wing coalition governments formed in alliance with the non-Republican Right (resulting in a major internal party split in May 1934), which overturned the reforms of the first two years and thereby polarized the Republic to an unprecedented degree. The resulting breakdown of the regime culminated in the **Spanish Civil War** of 1936–9. Republic, Second (Spain)

Radishchev, Alexander Nikolaevich (1749–1802) Russian noble, official and writer. He exposed the hollowness of **Catherine II, 'the Great'**'s profession of enlightened views. Influenced by his studies at Leipzig, he was critical of much that he then observed in Russia. In 1790 he published *A Journey from St Petersburg to Moscow*, an account of the evils of serfdom and the iniquities of the bureaucracy told in the form of a genuine traveller's tale. What might have been acceptable to Catherine when she issued her **Nakaz** in 1767, was anathema in the wake of the **French Revolution**. She had Radishchev arrested and sentenced to death; in the end, he was exiled to Siberia. The *Journal* remains a testament to the true state of Catherine's Russia.

Radowitz, Joseph von (1797–1853) Prussian soldier. In 1813 he entered the Westphalian Army, in 1823 the Prussian, and in 1830 became Chief of the Artillery Staff. Connected by marriage with the Prussian aristocracy, he headed the anti-revolutionary party during and after 1848, and was **Frederick William IV**'s adviser. After 1848 the abortive Prussian scheme of a German constitution by means of the alliance of the three kings was largely his work. He wrote political treatises. ▷ **Prussia**

Raeder, Erich (1876–1960) German grand admiral. He joined the navy in 1894, and became a Chief of Staff during **World War I**. In 1928 he was made Commander-in-Chief of the navy, a Grand Admiral in 1939, and in 1943 head of an anti-invasion force. At the **Nuremberg Trials** (1946), he was sentenced to life imprisonment, but released in 1955. ▷ **World War II**

Raffles, Sir (Thomas) Stamford (1781–1826) British colonial administrator. He became the Lieutenant-Governor of Java (1811–16), where he reformed the administration during that British **interregnum**. In 1816 ill health brought him home to England, where he was knighted. As Lieutenant-Governor of Benkoelen (1818–23), he established a British settlement at Singapore, which rapidly grew into one of the more important trading centres in the East. He was closely involved in the establishment of the Zoological Society of London in the early 1820s. ▷ **East India Company, British**

Rafsanjani, Ali Akbar (1934–) Iranian cleric and political leader. He trained as a mullah under Ayatollah Ruholla **Khomeini** at the holy city of Qom, from 1950. His friendship with Khomeini led him into opposition against Shah Mohammed Reza **Pahlavi** and brief imprisonment in 1963. During the 1970s he became wealthy through the construction business in Tehran, but continued to keep in close touch with the exiled Khomeini. Following the 'Islamic Revolution' of 1979–80 he became Speaker of the Iranian parliament (Majlis), emerging as an influential and pragmatic power-broker between fundamentalist and technocrat factions within the ruling Islamic Republican

Party (which he helped to found), playing a key role in securing an end to the Gulf War (1980–8). In Aug 1989, soon after the death of Ayatollah Khomeini, Rafsanjani became State President and 'de facto' national leader.

Raglan (of Raglan), Fitzroy James Henry Somerset, 1st Baron (1788–1855) British general. He joined the army in 1804, fought at the Battle of **Waterloo** (1815), became an MP, and was made a baron in 1852. In 1854 he led an ill-prepared force against the Russians in the **Crimean War**, but though victorious at Alma he did not follow up his advantage. His ambiguous order led to the **Charge of the Light Brigade** (1854) at Balaclava. He died at **Sevastopol**. His name was given to the raglan sleeve, which came into use in the 1850s.

Railroad, Transcontinental The first transcontinental system in the USA, formed when the Central Pacific and Union Pacific railroads were connected in 1869. The route surveys undertaken during the 1850s all had serious sectional implications and not until after the Republican victory in 1860 was the central route chosen. This had the advantage of being straight and using the lowest mountain passes; however, building was still delayed by Native American attacks and high costs. The two railroads joined at Promontory Point near Ogden, Utah, in 1869. Both had received huge land-grants in order to finance the project, but Leland Stanford and his associates of the Central Pacific used their economic power as much for their own private financial gain as for national economic objectives. Their evasion of taxes and their discriminatory freight charges were largely responsible for the establishment of the Interstate Commerce Commission (1887) and the move toward regulation by the Populist and Progressive reformers of the late 19c and early 20c.

Rainald of Dassel (c.1120–67) Archbishop of Cologne. He became State Chancellor in 1156 and was one of **Frederick I**'s most influential advisers, staunchly asserting imperial rights against those of the papacy. He was responsible for the canonization of **Charlemagne** in Cologne in 1165, the model for Frederick's administration during Rainald's chancellorship. His death marked the end of Frederick's policy of military aggression.

Rajagopalachari, Chakravarti (1878–1972) Indian political leader. The first

Governor-General of free India, he was educated at Central College, Bangalore, and Presidency and Law Colleges, Madras. He joined the Bar in 1900 and practised until 1919 at Salem. Rajagopalachari joined the non-cooperation and **Satyagraha** movements and was elected Congress General-Secretary in 1921–2. He was a member of the Congress Working Committee in 1922–42, 1946–7 and 1951–4. Prime Minister of Madras from 1937 to 1939, he was a member of the interim government in 1946–7, Governor of West Bengal in 1947–8, acting Governor-General of India (Nov 1947), and then Governor-General from June 1948 to Jan 1950. He was Chief Minister of Madras between 1952 and 1954 and founded the **Swatantra Party** in 1959. ▷ **Non-Cooperation Movement**

Rajk, László (1908–49) Hungarian politician. An early convert to **communism**, he was expelled from Budapest University for his political activities and became a building worker. Leader of the left-wing faction of his union, he organized an important building workers' strike in 1935 but then deemed it wise to go abroad. He was Party Secretary to the Hungarian battalion of the **International Brigades** during the **Spanish Civil War** but was eventually imprisoned in France. He returned to Hungary in 1941 to become a secretary to the Communist Party Central Committee, but he was first interned by the Hungarians and then imprisoned by the Germans. He rose rapidly after 1945, becoming a full member of the Central Committee, Minister of the Interior, then Foreign Minister. In 1949 he was arrested and tried on trumped-up charges during the Stalinist purges and, like many others who had first-hand experience of the West, was executed. In 1955 he was rehabilitated, but his fate had much to do with undermining **communism** in Hungary. ▷ **Stalinism**

Rajputs Descended either from the Huns settled in northern and western India or from those tribes and peoples who had entered India along with the Hun invaders, the Rajputs rose to political importance in the 9c and 10c, when they were divided into a number of clans, of which four claimed a special status. These four — the **Pratiharas**, the **Chauhans**, the Chaulukyas (or Solankis) and the Parmaras (or Pawars) — claimed descent from a mythical figure which arose out of a vast sacrificial fire pit near Mount Abu in Rajasthan. These clans, which came to be known as the Agnikula or Fire Family, dominated early Rajput activities; other Rajput clans, claiming descent from the solar and lunar races, established themselves as local kings in various parts of western and central India.

Rákóczi, Ferenc, II (1676–1735) Hungarian Prince of Transylvania (1704/11). An energetic and cultured member of a famous family, in 1703 he led a revolt of Hungarian nobles against Austrian Habsburg rule and in 1704 was officially elected Prince of Transylvania. He struggled hard but was defeated by the Austrians at Trencsén in 1708 and had to leave the country after the Hungarian–Austrian Treaty of Szatmár in 1711. Although he sought help in Poland until 1712, in France until 1717, and finally in Turkey, he could not reactivate the struggle against Austria. All that he left was inspiration for later generations.

Rakosi, Matyas (1892–1971) Hungarian politician. He was already active in the labour movement before **World War I**. Conscripted in 1914, he spent most of the war years as a prisoner in Russia and moved further to the Left, joining the Hungarian Communist Party on his return home. He was commander of the Red Guard in Béla **Kun**'s Soviet Republic in 1919 and then fled to the USSR where he became Secretary of the Communist International. Returning to Hungary in 1924, he spent the years 1925–40 in prison until he was released to return to Moscow. He led the Hungarian communist émigrés there and came back to Budapest in 1945 as their General-Secretary. Rakosi was then responsible for many of the changes introduced and was deeply implicated in the Stalinist purges. He was much criticized after **Stalin**'s death, but in 1955 he attempted to reinstate Stalinist practices, thus helping to provoke the 1956 **Hungarian Uprising**. He was then removed from office and, in 1962, expelled from the party. ▷ **Stalinism**

Raleigh (Ralegh), Sir Walter (1552–1618) English courtier, navigator and author. He became prime favourite of Queen **Elizabeth I**. He was knighted in 1584, and that year sent the first of three expeditions to America. After the arrival of the Earl of **Essex** at court, he lost influence, and spent some years in Ireland. On his return, Elizabeth discovered his intrigue with Bessy Throckmorton, one of her maids-of-honour, and he was committed to the Tower of London. On his release, he married Bessy, and lived at Sherborne. He took little part in the intrigues at the close of Elizabeth's reign, but his enemies turned

James VI and I against him, and he was imprisoned (1603), his death sentence being commuted to life imprisonment. While in the Tower, he wrote his *History of the World* (1614), and several other works. Released in 1616, he made an expedition to the Orinoco in search of a goldmine, which was a failure. His death sentence was invoked, and he was executed.

Ralliement French political movement, launched on behalf of Pope Leo XIII by Cardinal **Lavigerie** in 1890, and confirmed by the *Encyclical Inter innumeras sollicitudines* (1892), appealing to Catholics to accept the Third Republic, and to stop supporting the monarchist right. It was hoped that it would be met by a new attitude on the part of the moderate republicans, who would abandon their anti-clericalism, thus allowing some realignment in French politics. It had some success, although it was rejected by many Catholic politicians, and produced the conservative **Méline** government (1896–8). However, any chance it might have had of leading at that time to a reconciliation between the Catholic Church and the republic was destroyed by the **Dreyfus** Affair. ▷ **Republic, Third** (France)

Rama V ▷ **Chulalongkorn**

Ramananda (fl.14c) Indian religious reformer. He was a Vaishnava and was associated with the Bhakti movement. He tried to abolish the **caste** system among his followers and like other Bhakti movement saints, he introduced a more personal element into Hindu religious activities.

Ramaphosa, Matamela Cyril (1952–) South African trade unionist. He became Chairman of the all-black South African Students' Organization in 1974. After 11 months of detention in 1974–5, he became an articled clerk in Johannesburg and was active in the BPC (Black People's Convention). He was detained again in 1976 but, after graduating from the University of South Africa with a law degree in 1981, he joined CUSA as an adviser in its legal department. He became General-Secretary of the National Union of Mineworkers in 1982 and led (Sep 1984) the first legal strike by black mineworkers. He brought the NUM into COSATU (Congress of South African Trade Unions) and was elected Secretary-General of the **ANC** in July 1991 at the party's congress held in Durban.

Ramesses II (Usermaatre) (c.1290/1224BC) King of Egypt. He enjoyed a long and prosperous reign. Following a drawn battle with the **Hittites** at Kadesh in northern Syria (1286BC), a series of campaigns was concluded by a peace treaty in 1270BC and a marriage alliance with a Hittite princess contracted in 1257BC. Ramesses II built on an enormous scale and often usurped the works of earlier kings. Among his outstanding monuments were the hypostyle hall of the Temple of Amun at Karnak and the rock-cut temples at Abu Simbel.

Ramesses III (Usermaatre-meryamun) (c.1186/1154BC) Ruler of the 20th Dynasty and the last great warrior king of Egypt. He repelled three invasions, as recorded in reliefs and inscriptions on his funerary temple at Medinet Habu in Western Thebes. In the fifth year of his reign he defeated the Libyans and in the eighth year the advance by land and sea of the northern sea peoples was halted; Ramesses's the eleventh year saw repulsion of yet another Libyan attack. The King made generous donations to the temples of Egypt. A conspiracy to assassinate Ramesses and place the son of a secondary wife on the throne was thwarted and the plotters put on trial.

Ramgoolam, Sir Seewoosagur (1906–86) Mauritian doctor and politician. Educated in Mauritius and London University, he practised as a doctor before becoming a member of Legco (1940–48) and then the Executive Council (1948–58). He was Ministerial Secretary to the Treasury (1958–60), then Minister of Finance (1961–5), and also Prime Minister (1965–80). After retirement, he was Governor-General of Mauritius from 1984 until his death.

Ramillies, Battle of (1706) A spectacular victory in the War of the **Spanish Succession** won by **Marlborough** over **Louis XIV** of France's army commanded by Marshal Villeroi. The French suffered heavy casualties. The forces of the Grand Alliance overran large areas of the northern and eastern Spanish Netherlands, but were unable to exploit their success to force France to make peace. ▷ **Grand Alliance, War of the**

Ram Mohan Roy, Raja (1774–1833) Indian religious reformer. He did much to awaken the Hindu social conscience and, indirectly, the birth of nationalism. Of high Brahman status, he came early to question his ancestral faith, and studied Buddhism in Tibet. He published various works, with the aim of uprooting idolatry, and supported the British wish to outlaw suttee. In 1828 he began the **Brahmo Samaj** association, and in 1830 was given the title of Raja.

Ramon Berenguer III, 'the Great' (1082–1131) Count of Barcelona (1096/1131). He was born only a few days after the murder of his father, Ramon Berenguer II. As ruler, he was actively at war with the **Almoravids** to the south of his lands, and distinguished himself in his expedition (1114–5) to the islands of Ibiza and Mallorca, which he captured and held for a while. In 1112 he married, as his third wife, Douce of Provence, who brought him as a dowry the county of Provence. In 1117 he also inherited the county of Cerdaña, and in 1118 restored the metropolitan see of Tarragona as the central see of the Catalan lands.

Ramphal,   Shridath   Surrendranath ('Sonny') (1928–) Guyanan and Commonwealth lawyer and diplomat. After studying law in London, he was called to the bar in 1951. He returned to the West Indies, and from 1952 held increasingly responsible posts in Guyana and the West Indies before becoming Guyana's Foreign Minister and Attorney-General in 1972, and Justice Minister in 1973. During much of this time he sat in the Guyanan National Assembly. From 1975 to 1989 he was Secretary-General of the Commonwealth.

Ramses ▷ **Ramesses**

Ranade, Mahadev Govind (1842–1901) Indian lawyer and reformer. He is popularly known for his association with the *Prarthana Samaj* ('Prayer Society') in the Marathi-speaking western part of India. This society, founded in Pune in 1869, initially had a vague, undeveloped set of ideas. Ranade actively participated in its activities and helped to reshape it into a patriotic association espousing a reinterpretation of Hindu tradition. His position as a subordinate judge in Pune prevented him from joining the **Indian National Congress** when it was formed in 1885. However, as an active sympathizer, he encouraged many others, including Gopal Krishna Gokhale, to join and to take a leading role in the early Indian independence movement.

Randolph, A Philip (1889–1979) US labour organizer, socialist and civil rights activist. Initially a supporter of Marcus **Garvey**, he opposed the idea of economic separatism in his journal, *The Messenger*. In 1925 he organized the Brotherhood of Sleeping Car Porters, the first black union to gain major successes, such as recognition by the Pullman Company. In 1941 he organized a march on Washington to demand equal employment opportunities for blacks in the defence industries, and racial desegregation in the armed forces. The march was called off after President Franklin D **Roosevelt** established the **Fair Employment Practices Committee**, but the tactic was revived during the civil rights movement of the 1960s, when he became the director of the March on Washington for Jobs and Freedom (Aug 28, 1963).

Ranjit   Singh (1780–1839)   Sikh   ruler (1801/39). Known as the 'Lion of the Punjab', he succeeded his father as ruler of Lahore. He fought to unite all the Sikh provinces and, with the help of a modernized army trained by Western soldiers, became the most powerful ruler in India. In 1813 he procured the Koh-i-noor diamond from an Afghan prince, as the price of assistance in war. He died in Lahore.

Rankin, Jeannette (1880–1973) US feminist and pacifist, the first female member of Congress. Educated at Montana University and the New York School of Philanthropy, she went on to work as a social worker in Seattle (1909), where she became involved in the fight for women's rights. In 1914 she was appointed Legislative Secretary of the **National American Woman Suffrage Association**, and in 1916 entered the House of Representatives as a Republican, the first woman to do so. During her two terms there (1917–19 and 1941–3) she consistently voted against US participation in both world wars, promoted women's welfare and rights, and was instrumental in the adoption of the first bill granting married women independent citizenship. Continuing to campaign for women's issues throughout her career, she worked for the National Council for the Prevention of War from 1928 to 1939, and led the Jeannette Rankin March (1968) in which 5000 women gathered on Capitol Hill, Washington, to protest against the **Vietnam War**.

Rankovié, Aleksander (1909–) Yugoslav politician. He joined the Communist Party in 1928 and was imprisoned during the dictatorship of King **Alexander I Karageorgevié**. During **World War II** he fought with **Tito** and the partisans and in 1945 became Director of the secret police, overseeing the ruthless elimination of all opposition to communist rule. He was also Minister of the Interior (1946–53) and Vice-President of Yugoslavia (1963). After 'bugging' Tito's home, he was accused of abusing his authority and was forced to resign (July 1966).

Rapallo, Treaty of (12 Nov 1920) The treaty of friendship and neutrality bringing together a defeated Germany and an ostracized Russia. It recognized Istria as Italian and **Fiume** (Rijeka) as a free city; it also made provision for future economic accords and stressed a mutual obligation to uphold the Treaties of Trianon and St Germain. The countries both gained diplomatically and economically. Their military cooperation was of particular benefit to the USSR, whose communist revolution was never seriously challenged thereafter: Allied intervention in Russia finally ended the same year. It was a triumph for the conciliatory policy of **Chicherin**, then Foreign Minister, and was echoed in the **German–Soviet Pact** of 1939.

Rapallo, Treaty of (16 Apr 1922) The treaty signed by Germany and the Russian Federation during the World Economic Conference in Genoa. German fears of an agreement between the Western Allies and the USSR on German **reparations** payments and a Russian desire to escape economic and diplomatic isolation led to this agreement which, first, saw both parties renounce all claims arising from **World War I** and, second, saw economic and trade links established on a 'most favoured nation' basis. The treaty was extended to the whole of the USSR and was a significant blow against the post-**World War I** settlement. German–Soviet military and diplomatic cooperation subsequently became more extensive.

ras Derived from the Arabic word for 'head', used in Abyssinia to denote a feudal warlord, this term was adopted and used in Italy to describe local fascist bosses in the 1920s. Amongst the *ras* numbered many figures who were to play a key role in the development of the **Fascist Party**, such as **Farinacci**, Italo **Balbo** and Dino **Grandi**. After attaining power in 1922, however, **Mussolini** felt it essential to check the power of the ras and to control the excesses of the **squadristi**, both because his position was threatened by other charismatic fascist leaders and because he needed to prove that he could restore order to an Italy scarred by political violence. Some ras consequently fell victim to purges, while

others were brought within the establishment and given important jobs in the party and government.

Rashtrakutas An Indian dynasty which produced a long line of warriors and successful administrators. It was founded by Dantidurga who overthrew the **Chalukyas** in 750 and established his capital at Malkhed near modern Sholapur. The Rashtrakutas soon dominated the entire area of northern Maharashtra. They also contested with the **Pratiharas** for the control of Gujarat and Malwa. The Rashtrakutas constantly fought the eastern Chalukyas of Vengi, the Pallavas of Kanchi and the Pandyas of Madurai. The greatest Rashtrakuta rulers were Indra III (915/27) and Krishna III (939/65). The Rashtrakuta rule in Deccan lasted for almost 200 years until the end of the 10c. The Rashtrakuta rulers were tolerant in their religious views and patronized not only Shaivism and Vaishnavism but Jainism as well. The famous rock cut temple of Shiva at Ellora was built by one of the Rashtrakuta kings, Krishna I in the 9c. The Rashtrakuta kings were great patrons of arts and letters. In their courts, we find not only Sanskrit poets but scholars who wrote in Prakrit and Kannada.

Rasin, Alois (1867–1923) Czechoslovak politician. He took part in a famous student riot in 1893 and became involved in serious radical politics in the later 1890s. Rasin was imprisoned during **World War I** and was then the first Finance Minister of the new Czechoslovak Republic. His tight monetary policies were, however, unpopular with particular groups and he was assassinated in 1923. Despite his unpopularity, it was Rasin who had set the new state on its feet economically, both domestically and internationally.

Raška The medieval name for the Serbian state derived from Rasa, the seat of the bishopric founded by Christianized Serbs and first mentioned in 1020. ▷ **Serbia, Kingdom of**

Rasputin, Grigoriy (1871–1916) Russian peasant and self-styled religious 'elder' (*starets*). A member of the schismatic sect of *Khlysty* (flagellants), he was introduced into the royal household, where he quickly gained the confidence of Tsar Nicholas II and the Empress, Alexandra, by his apparent ability to control through hypnosis the bleeding of the haemophiliac heir to the throne, Tsarevich Alexei. He was also a notorious lecher and drunkard, and created a public scandal through the combination of his sexual and alcoholic excesses, and his political influence in securing the appointment and dismissal of government ministers. His influence was particularly baneful during **World War I**, especially when the Tsar was away from St Petersburg commanding his army; it helped destroy cooperation between the Tsar and the **Duma** that might have won the war and prevented the 1917 **Russian Revolution**. He was murdered by a clique of aristocrats, led by Prince Felix Yusupov, a distant relative of the Tsar.

Rassemblement Démocratique Africaine (RDA)

Established in 1944, the RDA was a cross-national political party with branches in most parts of the French African empire, which sent members to the National Assembly in Paris. Its major figure was Felix **Houphouet-Boigny**.

Rassemblement Wallon (RW)

Belgian political party of Walloon (French-speaking southern Belgian) nationalist/separatists. Formed in 1968 from a number of small Walloon groupings in reaction to increasing **Flemish Movement** activity, it elected 14 MPs in 1971, and took part in the government coalition in 1974–7. The Francophone wing of the liberals joined the RW in 1976 to form the *Parti des Reformées et des Libertés Wallones*, which gained only four seats in the 1978 election.

Rastafarianism

A religious movement from Jamaica, followed by c.1 million people. It largely derives from the Old Testament and the thought of Jamaican political activist Marcus **Garvey**, who advocated a return to Africa as a means of solving the problems of black oppression. When **Haile Selassie I** was crowned Emperor of Ethiopia in 1930, he came to be viewed as the Messiah, with Ethiopia seen as the promised land. Rastafarians follow strict taboos governing what they may eat (eg no pork, milk, coffee); ganja (marijuana) is held to be a sacrament; they usually wear their hair in long dreadlocks; and they cultivate a distinctive form of speech.

Rastatt, Congress of

(1797–9) This congress was convened under the articles of the Treaty of **Campo Formio** to conclude a peace between the German states and France. The process failed when France refused to compensate the Germans for territories which they were expected to cede in an attached secret protocol.

Rastatt, Treaty of

(6 Mar 1714) Emperor Charles VI signed this personal treaty ending hostilities which had lingered after the Peace of **Utrecht** (1713) which had closed the War of the **Spanish Succession**. The Emperor renounced his claim to Spain but did not recognize the Bourbon claimant, **Philip V**, until 1720. The Treaty of **Baden** (Sep 1714) concluded an official peace between the entire Empire and France.

Rathenau, Walther

(1867–1922) German industrialist and politician. He organized German war industries during **World War I**, and in 1921, as Minister of Reconstruction, and after Feb 1922 as Foreign Minister, dealt with **reparations**. His attempts to negotiate a reparations agreement with the victorious Allies, and the fact that he was Jewish, made him extremely unpopular in nationalist circles, and he was murdered by extremists in the summer of 1922.

Ratsiraka, Didier

(1936–) Malagasy naval officer and politician. Educated in Madagascar and then at naval college in France, he served in the Navy (1963–70) before becoming military attaché in Paris (1970–2). A coup brought him to the centre of power in 1972, when he became Minister of Foreign Affairs and then, in 1975, President of the Supreme Revolutionary Council. He established a political party, the Advanced Guard of the Malagasy Revolution, and won elections in 1983 and 1989, although dissent remained high.

Rattazzi, Urbano, Count

(1808–73) Italian politician. Elected deputy in the Piedmontese parliament in 1848, he led the centre-left anticlericals. Minister first of Education and then of Justice, he opposed the armistice with Austria in Mar 1849. In 1852 he brought the centre-left into an alliance with **Cavour**, the so-called **Connubio**. Restored to government, he was first given his old position as Justice Minister (1853) and then became Interior Minister, a post he held from 1855 to 1858. The *Connubio* was based on an anticlerical policy (typified by the 1855 project to suppress all contemplative orders), which was in the end its undoing: as Cavour recognized the need to enlist the support of Napoleon III to drive the Austrians from northern Italy, he also realized that he would have to moderate his anticlerical stance to calm the French Emperor's fears about domestic Catholic opinion. The sweeping successes of clerical candidates in the elections of Nov 1857 gave Cavour the opportunity he needed to relocate the basis of his support and in the new year Rattazzi was made to resign. Rattazzi returned to office in **La Marmora**'s 1859 government, and was himself Prime Minister twice (Mar–Dec 1862 and Apr–Oct 1867).

Rau, Johannes (1931–) West German politician. He began his career as a salesman for a church publishing company before being attracted to politics as a follower of Gustav **Heinemann**. He joined the Social Democratic Party (**SPD**) and was elected to the parliament of his home state, North Rhine-Westphalia, the country's most populous, in 1958. He served as chairman of the SPD's parliamentary group (1967–70), and as Minister of Science and Research in the state parliament (1970–8) before becoming its Minister-President in 1978. His successful record as state leader, his moderate policy outlook, and his optimistic and youthful personality persuaded the SPD to elect him federal party deputy chairman in 1982 and chancellor-candidate for the 1987 **Bundestag** election. However, the party was heavily defeated, and since this setback he has concentrated on his work as state Premier.

Rawlings, Jerry (John) (1947–) Ghanaian soldier and politician. Educated at Achimota College and the University of Ghana, he joined the air force. He led an unsuccessful coup in 1979, was imprisoned and then escaped to mount a successful one later the same year. He headed the Armed Forces Revolutionary Council, returning power to an elected government, led by Hilla **Limann**, in that year, when he retired from the air force. However, he re-entered the political scene in Dec 1982 when he led another successful coup and has remained head of government since then, despite attempts to overthrow him in 1983 (twice) and 1987.

Razin, Stenka (Stepan Timofeevich) (c.1630–71) Russian Don Cossack, freebooter and rebel leader. He was the leader of a Cossack and peasant revolt in 1670–1 directed against the boyars and landowning nobility, at a time when the tsars were extending their authority. At one point he had as many as 200000 rebels under his command. However, they were no match for the Tsar's well-trained troops. In Apr 1671 he was captured, taken to Moscow and publicly executed. He became a folk-hero celebrated in later legend and song as the embodiment of popular rebellion against authority. ▷ **boyars; Cossacks; Pugachev, Emelyan**

Raziya (1236/40) First woman ruler of the Delhi Sultanate. She was named by her father, **Iltutmish**, as his successor, none of her brothers being considered worthy of the throne. The nomination of a woman in preference to a man was a novel step and, in order to assert her claim, Raziya had to contend with the hostility of her brothers as well as that of powerful Turkish nobles. In the event, she retained the throne for only four years. However, though brief, her rule had a number of interesting features. It marked the beginning of a power-struggle between the monarchy and the Turkish chiefs, sometimes called 'the forty' or the *chahalgani*. She put up a brave defence against these hostile forces, discarding female apparel and holding court with her face unveiled, hunting and leading the army. This behaviour, coupled with her attempt to create her own party and to raise non-Turks to high positions was, however, found unacceptable: a powerful group of provincial nobles banded against her and, despite a spirited defence, she was defeated and killed.

Reagan, Ronald (Wilson) (1911–) US politician and 40th President. He began his career as a radio sports announcer, then went to Hollywood in 1937, where he acted in more than 50 films, and served as President of the Screen Actors Guild (1947–52 and 1959). Originally a Democrat and supporter of liberal causes, he became actively involved in politics as a union leader and increasingly anti-communist. He registered as a Republican in 1962. Governor of California for two terms (1967–75), he campaigned unsuccessfully for the Republican presidential nomination in 1968 and 1976. He was elected President in 1980, defeating Jimmy **Carter**, and, with George **Bush** as his running mate, won a second term in 1984. Reagan's popularity enabled him to make sweeping changes in social and economic policy, including cuts in social services, the deregulation of many industries, and a tax cut that mainly benefited the wealthy. His foreign policy was dominated by a strong anti-communist stand, which led to a massive increase in defence spending and the introduction of the Strategic Defence Initiative (**SDI**), or 'Star Wars'. During his second term, when his attitude toward the USSR became less confrontational, largely as a result of President Mikhail **Gorbachev**'s policy of **perestroika**, he reached a major accord on nuclear arms reduction. The

Iran–Contra Affair (Irangate) tarnished the reputation of his administration in its last two years. Instead of the balanced budget Reagan had sought, 'Reaganomics' left behind a huge federal deficit.

Reaya In the **Ottoman Empire** the term was first applied to both Muslim and non-Muslim subjects, usually tradesmen and peasants; according to the model of the ideal Islamic society propounded by Nasireddin Tusi, they were the 'men of negotiation' and the 'men of husbandry'. From the 16c onwards, the term was customarily applied only to the non-Muslim subjects of the Sultan who were all liable to pay the capitation tax.

Rebellions of 1837 (1) A rebellion in Quebec in Lower Canada generated by a stalemate between the legislative council and the appointed executive council over control of provincial revenues. Led by **Papineau** and his *Parti Patriote*, it sought to dissolve the unsatisfactory imperial tie with Britain. It was crushed by British government troops after several brief confrontations. (2) Later in 1837, a rebellion in Ontario in Upper Canada, which opposed the oligarchical control exercised by the **Family Compact**, and the position of preferment enjoyed by the Church of England. Armed radicals led by **Mackenzie** marched on Toronto to seize the government, but were repulsed by pro-government troops and volunteers. Mackenzie and Papineau both fled to the USA. ▷ **Canada, Lower; Canada, Upper**

reciprocity A movement begun in British North America during the 1840s for the bilateral reduction of tariffs between the British colonies and the USA; it resulted in the Reciprocity Treaty of 1854. The treaty negotiations represented an important step in the growth of Canadian political autonomy. Arrangements became a source of discord in Washington, however, and the treaty was dissolved by the USA in 1866. Attempts to renew reciprocity failed up to 1911, when the idea was finally shelved. ▷ **Blake, Edward; Canada, Dominion of; 'Commercial Union'; Merritt, William H**

Reconquest The term (in Spanish, *Reconquista*) applied to the campaigns by Christian forces in medieval Spain to recover territory from the Muslims, who had begun to overrun the peninsula in 711. The Reconquest is normally said to have begun with the victory of the Christian chieftain, Pelayo, from his base in the cave of Covadonga (718) in the

Asturias. By the 10c, the successful advance of the Christian frontier led to the creation of the Kingdom of Leon. Occupation of the valley of the Duero led to the creation at the end of the 10c of the county of **Castile**, and a decisive step forward was then made with the capture of Toledo (1085). The last great victory of the Reconquest was Las **Navas de Tolosa** (1212), which opened the way to Andalusia and the occupation in less than 40 years of the whole valley of the Guadalquivir (Cordoba in 1236 and Seville in 1248). On the Mediterranean side of the peninsula, the Aragonese and Catalan forces moved south into Valencia. By the end of the 13c the main drive of the Reconquest was at an end, leaving only the Kingdom of Granada under Muslim rule. Two centuries passed before that finally fell, in 1492. The Reconquest had important social consequences, since it cultivated a warrior ethic among Spaniards, and emphasized the notion of religious crusade. ▷ **Granada, Conquest of.** See map p782.

Reconstruction The period following the **American Civil War** when the South, reeling from the physical and economic devastation it had sustained, was moving toward recovery and the status of the former Confederate states and the process of integration of the freed slaves was yet to be determined. President Andrew Johnson favoured a conciliatory approach toward the region, but radical Republicans took a hard line against what they viewed as recalcitrant Southern legislators dedicated to maintaining the power of the old order and determined to limit blacks' rights by evading the spirit of the Thirteenth Amendment by passing restrictive **Black Codes**. The Republican-controlled Congress responded by passing four Reconstruction Acts, two Civil Rights Acts, and the Fourteenth and Fifteenth Amendments. Military law was established throughout the South. Eventually, however, Republican control of the area was weakened due in large part to corruption in the federal government, and Southern states were slowly readmitted to the Union. The **Ku Klux Klan**, founded in 1866, gained in power, and the era ended with the Compromise of 1877, when a bargain among politicians gave a disputed presidential election to the Republican candidate Rutherford B Hayes in return for 'home' (ie white) rule in the South. Once white rule was fully restored, a policy of racial segregation evolved to keep black people firmly subordinate.

Reconquest of Spain, 11c

Recopilación de las leyes de los reinos de las Indias Published in four volumes in Madrid in 1681, the 'Compilation of the Laws of the Kings of the Indies' was the most famous of all attempts to compile all the laws and orders pertaining to each section of the Spanish royal government which dealt with its overseas dominions. This and similar colonial compilations became the bases for law in the successor states (eg *Ordenações Filipinas* for the dominions of the Portuguese crown). Iberian laws did not shape events, rather they approximated historical events, or commented upon them. Law and regulations were better developed in some parts of the continent than others; they also varied in their substance and timing.

Red Army The Red Army of Workers and Peasants (RKKA, *Raboche Krest'yanskaya Krasnaya Armiya*), the official name of the army of the USSR from 1918 to 1945. It was built around the original Bolshevik Red Guards from 1917, but was the most important land force engaged in the defeat of Nazi Germany in the period 1941–5. The epithet 'Red' gave it a political connotation which it never lost, even when 'Red' was changed to 'Soviet' in 1946. ▷ **Bolsheviks**

Red Brigades (*Brigate Rosse*, **BR**) An Italian left-wing terrorist organization founded in 1970 by Alberto Franceschini, Renato Curcio and Margherita Cagol. Its early years were marked by little real violence, but by 1974 the organization had hardened. The BR was at its most active in the period 1976–80, its energies directed at the killing and kidnapping of judges, politicians, businessmen and journalists. Lack of public sympathy and a more efficiently coordinated anti-terrorist campaign (based on using former BR members as informers) led to widespread arrests and a virtual end to its activities by the early 1980s. ▷ **Moro, Aldo**

Red Crescent ▷ Red Cross

Red Cross An international agency founded by the **Geneva Convention** (1864) to assist those wounded or captured in war. There are national branches; the British Red Cross performs relief duties throughout the world; the US Red Cross also runs a blood supply service. All branches use the symbol of the red cross on a white ground, except Muslim branches, which use the red crescent, and Iran, which uses a red lion and sun.

Red Front (*Roter Frontkampferbund*, **RFB**) German paramilitary league. This organization was founded by the Communist Party (**KPD**) in July 1924 as a counter-weight to the monarchist **Stahlhelm** and the republican **Reichsbanner Schwarz-Rot-Gold**. Its membership grew to 100000, but it was banned by the authorities in May 1929 after bloody disturbances between it and the police in **Berlin**. It nonetheless continued to operate and was involved in violent confrontations with the Nazi **SA** in the early 1930s. After **Hitler**'s takeover it ceased to function effectively and some of its members deserted to the SA.

Red Guards Young radical Maoist activists (mostly students) who spread the **Cultural Revolution** across China, destroying whatever was 'old', and rebelling against all 'reactionary' authority. The first Red Guards were a group formed in Qinghua University in Beijing on whom **Mao Zedong** bestowed his blessing (18 Aug 1966) at a mass rally in the capital. ▷ **Maoism**

Redmond, John Edward (1856–1918) Irish politician. He entered parliament in 1881. A champion of **Home Rule**, he was Chairman of the Nationalist Party in 1900. He declined a seat in **Asquith**'s coalition ministry (1915), but supported **World War II**, deplored the Irish rebellion, and opposed **Sinn Féin**.

Redondo, Nicolás (c.1927–   ) Spanish trade union leader. He helped revive the Spanish Socialist Party (the **PSOE**) in the late 1960s and early 1970s. Redondo was arrested 13 times during the period 1951–73, but in 1971 he became the leader of the **UGT**. In 1974 he was effectively offered the leadership of the PSOE, but turned it down. From 1984, he was increasingly critical of the socialist government, breaking with it in 1988. In the same year he organized Spain's first general strike since 1934.

Red River Rebellion (1869–70) An uprising among the **métis**, caused by the failure of the Canadian government to treat their problems seriously after it had assumed sovereignty from the **Hudson's Bay Company**. Bitter resentment was generated by the government's square survey system, which brought into doubt the land titles of the *métis* whose boundaries were based on river-front lots. The settlement of Manitoba by waves of Anglo-Protestant immigrants from Canada and the USA also brought huge problems, including the destruction of the buffalo on which the métis depended. The métis organized a 'National Committee' with Louis **Riel** as its Secretary, prevented Lieutenant-Governor **MacDougall** from entering the settlement, seized Upper Fort Garry and invited both English- and French-speaking inhabitants to discuss a 'List of Rights'. Some Canadians organized themselves to resist the committee, but Riel, now head of the Provisional Government, ordered their imprisonment. The committee issued the 'Declaration of the People of Rupert's Land and the North West'. Meanwhile the government decided to delay the transfer of sovereignty from the Hudson's Bay Company and sent a delegation to meet with the committee and negotiate the territory's entrance into the confederation. When some of the imprisoned Canadians escaped and attempted to raise support among the Scots of the area, the métis captured them and also court-martialled Thomas Scott, an obstreperous Orangeman, whom they executed. News of an amnesty for all rebels arrived four days later. Riel freed the other prisoners and sent representatives to Ottawa. They reached agreement with the Canadian government and as a result the Manitoba Act was passed, granting the métis 1400000 acres and bilingual rights. However only verbal assurances of amnesty were given. When Ontario's Orangemen maintained pressure to punish Scott's executioners, the government sent in a military force and Riel fled to the USA.

Red Shirts The name given to the volunteer forces which served under **Garibaldi** and which adopted their leader's distinctive red smock as a uniform. Red Shirts played a key part in the events of 1848–9, 1859–60 and 1866, as well as in a number of other minor campaigns.

Reeves, William Pember (1857–1932) New Zealand politician and writer. Trained in law and journalism, he became an MP (1887–96), and as a cabinet minister under Ballance and **Seddon**'s government (1891–6) introduced important reforms in industrial legislation, especially the innovative Conciliation and Arbitration Act of 1894 (the first in the world to be compulsory), which he hoped would stimulate trade unionism. He moved to England in 1896 as Agent-General, and was Director of the London School of Economics (1908–19).

Reforma, La The name given to the period of Liberal rule in Mexico from 1855 to 1860 and its major reforming measures, which were generally associated with the governments of Benito **Juárez** and Sebastián Lerdo de Tejada. The reforms included the abolition of military and ecclesiastical *fueros*, the secularization of education and the constitution of 1857. These changes not only sparked off the War of the Reforma (1857–60) but legitimized gradual changes taking place in the Mexican countryside as *haciendas* encroached on collective lands and wage labourers emerged in more prosperous zones of the country. It created the legal basis for the dramatic transformations achieved during the presidency of Porfirio **Díaz** (the period known as the Porfiriato). ▷ **fuero; hacienda**

Reform Acts Legislation in Britain which altered parliamentary constituencies and increased the size of the electorate. The main Acts were: 1832, which gave the vote to almost all members of the middle classes, and introduced a uniform £10 franchise in the boroughs; 1867, which gave the vote to all settled tenants in the boroughs, thus creating a substantial working-class franchise for the first time; 1884, which extended a similar franchise to rural and mining areas; 1885, which aimed to create parliamentary constituencies of broadly equal size; 1918, which created a universal male suffrage and gave the vote to women of 30 years and over; 1928, which gave the vote to all adult women; and 1969, which lowered the minimum voting age from 21 years to 18. The 1832 Reform Act

was the subject of furious controversy, and was preceded by widespread agitation.

Reformation The Protestant reform movements in the Christian Church, inspired by and derived from Martin Luther, John Calvin, and others in 16c Europe. A complex phenomenon, various factors are common to all reforms: a Biblical revival and translation of the Word of God into the vernacular; an improvement in the intellectual and moral standards of the clergy; emphasis on the sovereignty of God; and insistence that faith and scriptures are at the centre of the Christian message. Non-religious factors aiding the spread of the Reformation included the invention of the printing press; the political, social and economic uncertainties of the age; and a general feeling of revival caused by the Renaissance. In Germany, Luther's 'ninety-five theses' (1517) questioned the authority of the Church and led to his excommunication. The Lutheran Church then spread rapidly, in Switzerland under Zwingli and later under Calvin, neither of whom allowed any form of worship or devotion not explicitly warranted by scripture. The authority of scripture, the cornerstone of the Reformation, required a degree of ecclesiastical authority (and power) to justify and maintain it. The doctrine of the priesthood of all believers and the importance placed on preaching the Word of God led to an educated clergy, and decentralized church communities were better able to prevent abuse of ecclesiastical privilege. ▷ **Reformation** (England); **Reformation** (Scotland)

Reformation (England) The process by which the English Church rejected the authority of the Roman Catholic Church and established its own doctrine and liturgy. The English Reformation, unlike that of most European countries, was not predominantly doctrinal in origin. It was precipitated by **Henry VIII** after the Church refused to permit his divorce from **Catherine of Aragon** in order to marry Anne **Boleyn** with the intention of producing a male heir. Henry's response was to use parliament to pass statutes distancing the English Church from Rome. The English clergy were permitted to recognize Henry, rather than the Pope, as Supreme Head of the Church in 1531 and the Act of Supremacy (1534) ended the Pope's formal authority in England. Monasteries were dissolved during the later 1530s and their treasures forfeit to the Crown. Catholic doctrine was upheld by the 'Six Articles'

(1539) but, during the reign of **Edward VI**, Protestant usages were promoted in two Acts of Uniformity (1549 and 1552). During the reign of **Mary I**, England was formally reunited with Rome but the succession of **Elizabeth I** (1558) confirmed England as a non-Catholic country. The Act of Uniformity (1559) and the 39 Articles of Religion (1563) were recognizably Protestant although Elizabeth's Church Settlement rejected extreme Protestantism. Elizabeth's control over the Church as 'Supreme Governor' was established by the Act of Supremacy (1559). ▷ **Cranmer, Thomas; Cromwell, Thomas; Pilgrimage of Grace; Reformation** (Scotland)

Reformation (Scotland) The term used to describe the religious changes whereby the authority of the Pope was repudiated and Protestant forms of doctrine and worship established. Following a period of toleration for Protestants under the Regent, Mary of Guise, in the 1550s, 'Lords of the Congregation' asserted their intention to overthrow Catholicism (1557). The Regent's attempts to suppress Protestantism (1558–9) failed but **Elizabeth I**'s intervention in Scotland was decisive. The Protestant party, aided by John Knox, gained control. Catholicism was repudiated at a meeting of the Estates in 1560 ('Reformation Parliament') and celebration of Mass proscribed. One third of ecclesiastical revenues were appropriated to pay Ministers of the Reformed Church and to augment royal finances (1562). **Mary, Queen of Scots**, did not ratify the religious changes which were finally confirmed by **Moray**, Regent for James VI, in 1567. Controversy between Presbyterians (led by Andrew Melville), who insisted on equality of ministers, and Episcopalians, who upheld the hierarchy of bishops, continued within the Church in the late 16c and 17c. ▷ **James VI and I; Reformation** (England)

Reformatio Sigismundi An anonymous pamphlet, probably written in 1439 during the Council of Basle. It was drawn up in the name of Emperor **Sigismund** and shows the influence of Hussite ideas. It demanded the reform of both ecclesiastical and lay society, including the abolition of slavery, tithes and taxes. The pamphlet was widely disseminated and its demands echoed during the **Peasants Wars**.

reformism Any doctrine or movement that advocates gradual social and political change rather than revolutionary change; most commonly applied to socialism. The underlying premise is that democratic procedures provide the most suitable means through which to build social change.

Reform League (1863) An organization of middle-class radicals and skilled trade unionists by working-class radicals to extend male suffrage, whose 1866 demonstrations against the fall of the Liberal Reform Bill was a factor in persuading the subsequent Conservative administrations of Lord **Derby** and Benjamin **Disraeli** to introduce their own reform proposals. It won the support of the Liberals in their 1868 election campaign, but was dissolved soon afterwards. ▷ **Reform Acts**

Regalia In German history, the privileges reserved, in the first instance, for the king, especially taxation, coinage, the right to establish markets and to forests, fishing, hunting and mining. In the Middle Ages the regalia formed the core of royal finances. Later, they were devolved into the hands of landowners. In a narrower sense, regalia also refers to the secular rights of bishops, and the rights of the king to appoint bishops and endow with these rights were at the centre of the **Investiture Controversy**.

Regat The name given to **Moldavia and Wallachia**, the core of the pre-**World War I** Kingdom of Romania. ▷ **Danubian Principalities; Romanians**

Regency The period of **Louis XV** of France's minority (1715–23) during which the country was ruled by a Regency Council presided over by Philippe, Duke of **Orléans**. The main events of this period were the financial disaster of John Law's scheme (1719–20) and the acceptance in France of the Papal Bull *Unigenitus*, condemning **Jansenism** (1720). The Regent entrusted foreign affairs to the Abbé **Dubois**, who formed the Quadruple Alliance with the Netherlands, Britain and Austria, and went to war with Spain. The Regency was notorious for the extravagance and debauchery of its ruling group.

Regulus, Marcus Atilius (3c BC) Roman general and statesman of the first of the **Punic Wars**. After capture by the Carthaginians, he was sent to Rome on parole to sue for peace. Having dissuaded the Senate from agreeing to their terms, he voluntarily returned to **Carthage**, where he was tortured to death. His heroic death at the hands of the Carthaginians earned him legendary status.

rehabilitation The (usually posthumous) restoration to Party favour, and even membership, of communists who had been purged under a previous leadership. It was most prominently applied to Soviet communist leaders executed under **Stalin**, but was also a common practice in Eastern Europe. It was noticeable, however, that it usually remained selective; not all the innocents were rehabilitated. ▷ **communism**

Rehnquist, William H(ubbs) (1924–) US jurist. Educated at the Universities of Stanford and Harvard, he became a law clerk to Justice Robert H Jackson on the US Supreme Court before entering private practice. He served as Assistant Attorney-General from 1968 to 1971, became head of the Office of Legal Counsel of the Justice Department, and challenged many laws protecting the rights of defendants, such as Miranda v Arizona, giving him the reputation of a protector of law enforcement. In 1971, he was named Associate Justice of the Supreme Court by President Richard **Nixon**. He was chosen by President Ronald **Reagan** in 1986 to succeed Warren E **Burger** as Chief Justice of the Supreme Court, a controversial nomination due to his history of extremely conservative opinions. As Chief Justice, he has presided over a Supreme Court that has followed a conservative trend away from the more liberal Warren Court.

Reich The term used to describe the German Empire and the German national state between 1918 and 1945. The **Holy Roman Empire** was regarded as the First Reich, and unified Germany after 1870 was referred to as the Second Reich (*Kaiserreich*). After 1933, the enlarged Germany envisaged in **Hitler**'s plans was known as the Third Reich. The term is no longer used. ▷ **Kaiser**

Reichsbanner   Schwarz-Rot-Gold German paramilitary league (literally, 'National Flag Black-Red-Gold'). Founded in Feb 1924, the republican *Reichsbanner* sought to provide a counter-attraction to the monarchist leagues for Weimar military veterans and youth. Organized by the **DDP**, **Centre Party** and **SPD**, but dominated by the last, its membership exceeded 3.5 million by 1932, although with just 400000 activists. It fought the Nazi **SA** and, occasionally, the communist **Red Front** and monarchist **Stahlhelm** on the streets during the early 1930s, but was ineffective against the dismantling of republican democracy and **Hitler**'s eventual takeover. It dissolved itself in Mar 1933.

Reichsdeputationshauptschluss (24 Mar 1803) Following the loss of German territories west of the Rhine to France (1795, 1797–9 and 1801), the remaining secular states sought compensation through the secularization of the extensive church lands (in return for financial compensation) and the absorption of most self-governing imperial cities. This was achieved, ending papal involvement in and Catholic predominance in German affairs, but further wars with France delayed the full implementation of these agreements until 1815.

Reichstag Literally 'imperial diet', the term refers to three German political institutions: (1) The lower, elected house of the German parliament (1871–1918). Seen by **Bismarck** as a symbolic concession to national and liberal sentiment, the *Reichstag*, although elected by universal male suffrage, possessed very limited functions in Imperial Germany where power rested primarily with the crown and the Emperor's ministers. However, it could block legislation and budgets and, as parties seeking an extension of parliamentary power gained a majority in the Reichstag, in 1912 a constitutional crisis, delayed by **World War I**, developed. (2) The lower, elected house of the German parliament (1920–33). In this period (the **Weimar Republic**), governments were formed by dominant coalitions in the Reichstag, but political polarization and the growing strength of anti-republican parties (**Nazi Party**, **KPD**) necessitated the conduct of government under Article 48 of the constitution (presidential emergency powers) from 1930 to 1933. (3) An assembly dominated by the Nazi Party in the Third **Reich**, 1933–45. **Hitler** periodically addressed the Reichstag, but real power had passed to Hitler, his ministers and to party officials.

Reichstag Fire (27 Feb 1933) The deliberate burning down of Germany's parliament building, shortly after the Nazi accession to power. A deranged Dutch ex-communist, van der Lubbe, was accused of arson and executed. The new Nazi government, insisting that the act was evidence of a wider communist conspiracy, used the situation to ban and suppress the German Communist Party (**KPD**). Communist conspiracy was certainly not behind the fire; nor were the Nazis themselves, though it was long believed to be so. It is now agreed that, however convenient the fire may have been to the regime, van der Lubbe acted alone. ▷ **Nazi Party**

Reichswehr Literally 'national defence', this is the term used to describe the armed forces of Germany in the period 1919–35. Consisting of 100000 soldiers and 15000 sailors, the Reichswehr was a professional force with junior ranks serving 12 years and officers 25 years. Relations between the Reichswehr and the republic were equivocal. The officers were opposed to any open, violent challenge to the state, but secretly supported anti-republican paramilitary leagues in Germany and undertook secret rearmament in collaboration with the USSR. Allegedly 'above politics', senior *Reichswehr* officers such as **Groener** and **Schleicher** were active in late Weimar government affairs and did much indirectly to pave the way for **Hitler**'s takeover. In 1935, with rearmament, the Reichswehr, by now bound by oath of personal loyalty to Hitler, was reorganized as the **Wehrmacht**.

Reid, Sir George Houstoun (1845–1918) British-born Australian politician. He arrived in Melbourne with his parents in 1852, and in 1858 moved to Sydney, where he obtained a post with the Colonial Treasury. He studied law, and in 1878 became Secretary to the Attorney-General of New South Wales. A strong supporter of free trade, in 1880 he was elected to the Legislative Assembly of New South Wales, and in 1891 succeeded Sir Henry **Parkes** as Leader of the Opposition, becoming Premier of the state from 1894 to 1899. A cautious supporter of **federation**, he moved to the first federal parliament in 1901, still representing his old constituency, and became Leader of the Opposition in the House of Representatives. He was Prime Minister of Australia (1904–5) and retired from politics in 1908. In 1909 he was appointed Australia's first High Commissioner to London, a post he held with distinction until 1916. He then took up the seat for Hanover Square in the British House of Commons, which he held until his death.

Reign of Terror ▷ **Terror, Reign of**

Religion, Wars of (1562–98) A series of religious and political conflicts in France, caused by the growth of Calvinism, noble factionalism, and weak royal government. After 1559 there were a number of weak and/or young Valois kings whose mother, **Catherine de' Medici**, attempted abortive compromises. Calvinist or 'Huguenot' numbers increased from the 1550s, fostered by the missionary activities of Geneva. The noble factions of Bourbon, Guise, and Montmorency were split by religion as well as by family interests. Civil wars were encouraged by **Philip II** of Spain's support of the Catholic Guise faction and by **Elizabeth I** of England's aid to the **Huguenots**. They ended when the Huguenot Henry of Navarre (**Henry IV**), returned to Catholicism and crushed the Guise Catholic League (1589–98). ▷ **Bourbon, House of; Guise, House of; Valois Dynasty**

Remonstrants Christians adhering to the Calvinistic doctrine of Jacobus **Arminius** (17c Netherlands), whose followers were also known as Arminians. They were named after the 'Remonstrance', a statement of Arminian teaching dating from 1610, and lost their theological and political case against the Counter-Remonstrants at the Synod of **Dordrecht** (1618–19). Small in number, they have been influential among Baptists, and in Methodism and Calvinism.

Rémusat, Charles François Marie, Count of (1797–1875) French aristocrat. He early developed liberal ideas, and took to journalism. He signed the journalists' protest which brought about the **July Revolution** (1830), was elected Deputy for Toulouse, in 1836 became Under-Secretary of State for the Interior and in 1840 Minister of the Interior. Exiled after the coup d'état of 1848, he devoted himself to literary and philosophical studies, until, in 1871, **Thiers** called him to the Portfolio of Foreign Affairs, which he retained until 1873.

Renaissance From the French for 're-birth', the term is applied to several significant revivals of interest in the classical past which punctuate European history. One such revival is identified with the age of the Emperor **Charlemagne** (hence 'Carolingian Renaissance'), another with the Emperor **Otto I, 'the Great'** in the 10c ('Ottonian Renaissance') while the '12c Renaissance' was marked by the fusion of Christian learning with the rediscovered works of Aristotle in the great intellectual synthesis known as scholasticism. Most famously, however, the term is applied to the cultural achievements of the Italians in the 14c and 15c. In turn, the absorption of Italian values in a general European context in the 16c then paved the way for the Scientific Revolution of the 17c and the Enlightenment of the 18c. The idea was first formulated by the Florentine Vasari in his *Lives of the Artists* (c.1550). He identified three great eras of creativity: the first, c.1300, identified above all with Giotto, the second, around 1400 with the architect Brunelleschi, the sculptor Donatello and the painter Masaccio, while the climax, he thought, was reached in his own time in the work of Michelangelo. Vasari's vision was confined to achievements in the visual arts and within them he laid particular stress on the unique achievements of the Florentines. Subsequently, particularly since the work of Michelet and Burckhardt in the 19c, the application of the term has broadened to take in intellectual and social developments and other centres of creativity, notably Rome and Venice.

Renamo (*Resistencia Nacional Mozambicana*) An armed movement set up in 1976, first with Rhodesian and later with South African support, to oppose the **Frelimo** government of Mozambique. Although lacking a clear political aim, it has managed to disrupt Mozambique's economy and transport system and was responsible for pressurizing the government into signing the **Nkomati Accord**.

René I, 'the Good' (1409–80) Duke of Anjou, Count of Provence and Piedmont. He was known as the 'Last of the Troubadours'. Having failed in his efforts (1438–42) to make good his claim to the crown of Naples, he married his daughter, **Margaret of Anjou**, to **Henry VI** of England (1445). In his last years, he devoted himself to Provençal poetry and agriculture at Aix.

René, France-Albert (1935–   ) Seychelles politician. Educated locally, and in Switzerland and at King's College, London, he was called to the bar in 1957. He returned to the Seychelles and entered politics, founding the socialist Seychelles People's United Party in 1964, which he led. A member of the National Assembly since 1965, he formed a coalition at independence in 1976 with his opponent James Mancham (who became President) while Rene became Prime Minister. When Mancham was abroad in 1977, René staged a coup, created a one-party state and made himself Executive President.

Rennenkampf, Pavel Karlovich von (1853–1918) Russian cavalry officer. Of Baltic German origins, he commanded a force in the **Russo-Japanese War** (1904–5) and earned a reputation as a tough soldier, restoring order westwards from Harbin along the Trans-Siberian Railway. In **World War I**, in command of the 1st Army, he defeated the German 8th Army at Insterburg and Gumbinnen (Aug 1914), but was decisively defeated by **Hindenberg** in the wake of the Battle of Tannenberg a few days later. He was appointed Governor of Petrograd in 1915, and commander-in-chief of the northern front in 1916. After the **October Revolution** he was shot by the **Bolsheviks**.

Renner, Karl (1870–1950) Austrian politician. He trained as a lawyer, joined the Austrian Social Democratic Party (**SPÖ**), and became the first Chancellor of the Austrian Republic (1918–20). Imprisoned as a socialist leader, following the brief civil war (Feb 1934), he was Chancellor again (1945) after **World War II**, and first President of the new republic (1945–50).

reparations Payments imposed on the powers defeated in war to cover the costs incurred by the victors. For example, they were levied by the Allies on Germany at the end of **World War I**, though the final sum of £6000 million plus interest was not fixed until Apr 1921. The Dawes (1924) and Young (1929) Plans revised the payment schedule and reduced the scale of the payments, which were finally abandoned after 1932, because of the Depression.

Republic, First (France) The regime that was established in France in Sep 1792, and which lasted officially until **Napoleon I** proclaimed himself Emperor in 1804 (although the period 1795–9 is usually referred to as the **Directory**, and the period 1799–1804 as the **Consulate**).

Republic, First (Portugal) (1910–26) The transition from the oligarchical rule of the monarchy to the pluralistic democracy of the new regime produced acute political instability because of a weak party system enhanced by the 1911 Constitution. The reforms of the Republic largely benefited the urban lower middle classes, its main constituency, spurning the aspirations of the urban working class, women, and the rural peasants and labourers. For example, the labourers' strike in Alentejo of 1911–12 was brutally suppressed. Political uncertainty, a lack of resources, and the exclusivity of the Republicans all combined to prevent change. Military discontent and Republican divisions resulted in a conservative dictatorship, Jan–May 1915. Back in power, the Republican politicians entered **World War I** in 1916 on the side of the Allies. Rocketing prices, food shortages, and heavy losses in France led to the coup under Bernardino Sidonio Pais (5 Dec 1917); this young charismatic man became the first Republican dictator of the 20c. The so-called New Republic was a forerunner of the authoritarian and corporatist state created by **Salazar** in the 1930s. Unable to secure his power-based and thrown into crisis by the Allied victory of Nov 1918, Sidónio Pais was assassinated in Lisbon on 14 Dec 1918. From 1918 to 1926 the Republic was more unstable than ever. In 1919 there were four governments and in 1920, nine. Civil war broke out in northern Portugal, the economy collapsed and violence mounted. Several Republican politicians were murdered, including Antonio Machado Santos, the leading figure of the 1910 revolution. The failure to maintain public order and protect living standards, and the political stranghold of the PRP (preventing the emergence of other parties), alienated many of the Republic's own supporters. Though the internecine party warfare seemed remote, it reflected wider economic conflicts. The progressive governments of Dec 1923–July 1925 further consolidated the rapidly growing forces of counter-revolution. A marked swing to the Right took place in the 1920s. Following the abortive coups of Apr and July 1925, the Republic was finally overthrown by the military rising of 28 May 1926.

Republic, First (Spain) (1873–4) The First Spanish Republic may be divided into four periods. The **Figueras** government sought a unitary regime based on a presidential system. Its failure led to a rising of the provinces when scores of city-states, or cantons, declared their independence and pursued primitive **communism**. Under **Castelar** the cantonalists were crushed by the army and a unitary republic was partially restored. Political infighting led to a coup in Jan 1873 and the rule of the aristocratic General **Serrano** until a further coup in Dec 1874 brought the republic to an end. ▷ **Cantonalist Risings**

Republic, Second (France) The regime established in France after the **February Revolution** (1848), which lasted until the proclamation of the Second **Empire** in 1852.

Republic, Second (Spain) (1931–6) Spain's first democratic regime in nearly 60 years was established (14 Apr 1931) amidst great popular expectation following the disastrous policies of the monarchy. The Left-Republican–Socialist administrations of 1931–3 under Manuel **Azaña** made the most

determined effort yet to transform Spain from a reactionary and backward society into a modern and progressive 'European' state. The failure of reform was partly due to the lack of unity and expertise within the governmental coalition, but more so to a scarcity of resources and the world depression. Above all, reform proceeded slowly because of the hostility of the traditional ruling classes to meaningful change, especially the landowners. The course of the Republic was fundamentally altered by the general election of Nov–Dec 1933. A parliamentary alliance was formed between the **Radical Republican Party** and the Catholic **CEDA**. The Centre-Right administrations of Dec 1933 to Oct 1935 moved steadily to the Right while demolishing the reforms of the first two years. This led to a major Radical schism (May 1934) and to mounting socio-economic conflict. The entry of three members of the proto-fascist CEDA into the government (4 Oct 1934) resulted in a Socialist general strike, a declaration of Catalan independence, and an armed rising in Asturias. The brutal repression of the Oct protest polarized the Republic to an unprecedented extent. As the CEDA gained more and more power at the expense of the Radicals throughout 1935, so the previously divided Left rallied to the banner of the Popular Front. In the general election of Feb 1936 the Popular Front won a narrow victory. The political climate became increasingly volatile as the weak Left-Republican governments, now bereft of Socialist support, proved unable to impose themselves. The military rising of 17–18 July 1936 resulted in a civil war that lasted until Apr 1939. The origins of the **Spanish Civil War** were overwhelmingly domestic in nature, embracing not one but several conflicts, ranging from social and political tensions to religious and regional ones.

Republic, Third (France) The regime established in France on 4 Sep 1870, which lasted until the National Assembly voted full powers to **Pétain** on 10 July 1940; it remains by far the longest French regime since 1789.

Republic, Fourth (France) The regime established unofficially in France in 1944 on the country's liberation; it was, however, only legally confirmed by the referendum of 13 Oct 1946, which approved the new constitution by a small majority. The republic was brought down by the Algerian crisis of 13 May 1958, which led, first, to de **Gaulle** being voted into office as the last Prime Minister of the Fourth Republic and, second, to its replacement by the Fifth Republic on 5 Oct 1958. ▷ **Republic, Fifth** (France)

Republic, Fifth (France) The regime established in France by the referendum of 28 Sep 1958, approving the new constitution embodying the political ideas of de **Gaulle**.

Republican Party US political party. It was formed in 1854 by Northern anti-slavery factions of the existing Whig and Democratic Parties who opposed the Fugitive Slave Act (1850) and the **Kansas–Nebraska Act** (1854). The party's presidential candidate, Abraham **Lincoln**, won the 1860 election, precipitating Secession and the **American Civil War**. With the exception of four terms, the Republicans continued to hold the presidency until the **Great Depression**, which set the stage for the election of Franklin Delano **Roosevelt** in 1932 and 20 years of Democratic Presidents. Although the Republicans had espoused isolationism before **World War II**, they won the 1952 presidential election with the popular war hero Dwight D **Eisenhower**. The next 40 years saw a series of split governments on the national level, with the Republicans often winning the presidency while the Democrats held majorities in Congress. The **Watergate** scandal, which led to the first resignation of an American president, Richard M **Nixon**, was a black mark for the party, but it regained the presidency with the election of Ronald **Reagan** in 1980 and held it for the next 12 years through George **Bush**'s one-term administration. The party has traditionally been identified with big business rather than with labour, and favoured states' rights, limited government regulation, free market economic policies, and (in the **Cold War** period that followed World War II) a strong military and firm anticommunistic stance. It has generally had the support of voters of high socioeconomic status and of white Anglo-Saxons rather than of ethnic minorities; however, Ronald Reagan managed to broaden the party's historical base, drawing in many so-called Reagan Democrats, who were disillusioned with the policies of Democratic President Jimmy **Carter**, and including right-wing conservatives and religious fundamentalist groups as well. ▷ **mugwump; National Republican Party; Progressive Party** (USA)

Resistance Movement (Belgium, *Weerstand*) Clandestine opposition to the German occupation of Belgium during **World War II**, which took on serious proportions after the severe winter of 1940–1. Aid was provided to escaped prisoners of war and to Allied airmen, and there was also a lively underground press. Alongside there were sabotage and guerrilla groups, ranging from right-wing nationalist to communist; the largest was the Independence Front, with its own armed units (Patriotic Militias). The government in exile in London provided financial help; the Belgian resistance made an important contribution to the country's liberation in 1944.

Resistance Movement (France) There was very little active resistance for the first two years of the German occupation during **World War II**, but it developed rapidly from the summer of 1942. A great number of different organizations existed, covering the whole range of political opinion from Left to Right, although after the German invasion of the USSR communist recruitment was especially high. De **Gaulle** sought to coordinate the different groups from London and then, after the Allied invasion of North Africa, from Algiers; his delegate, Jean Moulin, was able to bring them all together in the *Conseil national de la résistance* ('National Council of the Resistance') before being murdered by the Germans. As well as guerrilla warfare against the occupying forces, there was a large political dimension to the Resistance, and elaborate and idealistic programmmes were drawn up; only some of these found any embodiment after 1944. ▷ **World War II**

Resistance Movement (Netherlands, *Het Verzet*) Also known as the 'Illegality' and the 'Underground', most Dutch resistance to the German occupation during **World War II** was clandestine. Only a few strikes, notably on the railways from Sep 1944, and limited actions by individual students, doctors and churchmen in particular, were public displays of resistance. The underground resistance was active, however, especially in producing and distributing newspapers, and looking after the several hundred thousand people, many of them Jewish, trying to evade the German authorities. Help was also provided for Allied airmen, and espionage work was carried out, though not always with success. Finance was provided by the National Support Fund (*Nationaal Steunfonds*). ▷ **Englandspiel; Frank, Anne; Resistance Movement** (Belgium); **Resistance Movement** (France)

Responsible Government A Canadian adaptation of British parliamentary practice.

Developed by Robert **Baldwin**, the doctrine held that the government of the Province of Canada should be exercised by a ministry chosen from the elected representatives of the people, and that it should be replaced if defeated in the elective legislature. Recommended in the Durham Report, it was several years before its practical implications were fully understood, and not until 1848 with the Baldwin–Lafontaine ministry in Canada and the Uniacke ministry in Nova Scotia did it come into operation.

Resquesens y Zúñiga, Luis de (1528–76) Spanish soldier and political figure, and Regent of the Spanish Netherlands (1573/6). He was already a sick man when he succeeded the Duke of **Alva** as regent; his military achievements in the Low Countries were few and the country's finances remained chaotic. He tried to follow a more conciliatory line than his precedessor, announcing a general pardon in 1574 (excluding heretics), and abolishing the Council of **Blood** and the hated **Tenth Penny** tax. He died in Brussels; the lack of an immediate successor led to a general uprising against Spanish authority in the **Eighty Years War**.

Restitution, Edict of (29 Mar 1629) The imperial edict promulgated by Emperor **Ferdinand II** during the **Thirty Years War**, which decreed that all ecclesiastical property confiscated since the Treaty of Passau in 1552 (including archbishoprics, bishoprics and monasteries) should be restored to those people who owned it in 1555. In this way, Ferdinand hoped to recover all the lands which had been lost to Protestantism in the intervening years. The edict also stipulated that only adherents of the **Augsburg Confession** were to have free exercise of religion and that all other 'sects' were to be broken up. Habsburg and Wittelsbach nominees were imposed on many bishoprics, and the edict was enforced by **Wallenstein**'s 100 000-strong army. After Wallenstein's dismissal, the edict was enforced less strenuously and was superseded, in 1635, by the Peace of Prague. ▷ **Habsburg Dynasty**

Restitution Agreement (Sep 1952) The settlement reached between representatives of the State of Israel and Chancellor **Adenauer** of the Federal Republic of Germany. Signed in Luxembourg, the agreement committed Germany to make material reparations to Israel, deemed to represent the Jewish people, and to another Jewish body representing the **Diaspora**, for persecutions suffered by the Jews under the Third Reich. As a result, and despite some opposition in both Israel and Germany, large sums of money were paid out to Israel and to individual survivors of **World War II** in subsequent years. ▷ **Holocaust; Israel, State of**

Restoration The return of **Charles II** to England (May 1660) at the request of the Convention Parliament, following the collapse of the **Protectorate** regime; but many royal prerogative powers and institutions were not restored. The bishops and the Church of England returned, but parliament took the lead in passing the **Clarendon Code** (1661–5) outlawing dissent from the Book of Common Prayer (1662).

Restoration System (1875–1923) Spanish political system. The rotation in power of the two dynastic parties — the Liberal-Conservatives and the Liberals — through an institutionalized form of electoral corruption. Election results were fixed by the Minister of the Interior through the local party bosses (or *caciques*). This was known as the *turno pacifico* ('peaceful rotation'). Although it quelled the interventionism of the army and brought a measure of political stability, it effectively excluded the non-monarchical opposition from the political process. The system was dismantled by the dictatorship of **Primo de Rivera** in 1923, though the caciques continued to exercise considerable influence under the Second Republic. ▷ **Republic, Second** (Spain)

Retief, Piet (1780–1838) One of the leaders of the Boer Trek which left the Cape in the 1830s to escape British rule. in 1837 Retief, originally from Stellenbosch but later resident in Grahamstown, published an explanatory manifesto and left the colony with about one hundred followers. His manifesto indicated that the British had disrupted proper white-black, master-servant relations and offended the law of God. He entered the Transvaal, crossed the Drakensberg into Natal and was killed by Dingane, King of the Zulu, in 1838 when attempting to negotiate a land concession.

Retz (Rais, Raiz), Gilles de Laval, Baron (1404–40) Breton nobleman. He fought by the side of **Joan of Arc** at Orléans, but soon retired to his estates, where for over 10 years he is alleged to have indulged in satanism and the most infamous orgies. He was hanged and burnt at Nantes, after being tried and condemned for heresy.

Retz, (Jean François Paul de Gondi), Cardinal (1614–79) French prelate. He plotted against **Mazarin**, and exploited the **Fronde** (1648) to further his own interests and the power of the Church. After transferring his allegiance between the rebel factions and the crown, he received a cardinal's hat, though in 1652 he was imprisoned on **Louis XIV**'s personal orders. After making peace with Louis in 1662, he received the abbacy of St Denis. ▷ **Richelieu, Cardinal**

Réveil A revival movement in early 19c northern European Protestantism, especially in the Netherlands, but also in Switzerland and France, with strong literary connections and political influence. It was a reaction to the rationalizing effects of the Enlightenment on religion, and as a deeply romantic movement it looked back in nostalgia to before the French revolutionary upheavals, and in the Dutch case to the Golden Age of the 17c. The theology was orthodox Calvinist, but with an emphasis on personal piety; much practical work was also achieved in education and social work. Leading figures in the Netherlands included Willem Bilderdijk (1756–1831); the Réveil's orthodox Calvinist political legacy was enacted by **Groen van Prinsterer** (who became a member in 1830) and the **Anti-Revolutionary Party**.

Revels, Hiram Rhodes (1822–1901) US politician and educator. Born in North Carolina, he was chaplain of a Union black regiment in the **American Civil War**, and later settled in Mississippi and served in the State Senate. Elected to the US Senate in 1869, he was the first black American to serve in that body. He founded a school for former slaves, and became President of Alcorn College, a newly formed state college for blacks.

Reventlow, Christian Ditlev (1748–1827) Danish civil servant. He was the driving force behind a number of agricultural reforms carried out by the Danish government during the last 13 years of the 18c. The aims of the reforms were to increase agricultural productivity and dampen a growing dissatisfaction among Danish peasants with the feudal conditions under which they lived, particularly with the considerable amount of day-labour they were obliged to provide for their feudal lord. In 1786 Reventlow influenced Denmark's de facto ruler, Crown Prince Frederick (later King **Frederick VI**), to set up the Great Agricultural Commission whose work (June 1788) led to the abolition of serfdom which had hitherto bound the peasant to the land of the lord. This reform, however, caused the break-up of the government, resulting in a more cautious, landowner-friendly reform policy during the 1790s.

Revere, Paul (1735–1818) US patriot. He served as a lieutenant of artillery in the French and Indian War, then followed the trade of silversmith and copperplate printer. He was one of the party that destroyed the tea in Boston harbour, and was at the head of a secret society formed to watch the British. On 18 Apr 1775, the night before **Lexington and Concord**, Revere rode from Charleston to Lexington and Lincoln, rousing the **Minutemen** as he went. His ride was immortalized in a poem by Longfellow. ▷ **American Revolution; Boston Tea Party**

Revolutionary Party of Tanzania ▷ **Chama Cha Mapinduzi**

Revolution of 1830 (Germany) The overthrow of the Bourbon monarchy in France led to liberal and populist revolts in many parts of Germany. In a number of German states constitutions were renewed or granted, but the monarchies of the key German powers, **Prussia** and **Austria**, were not challenged effectively and in 1834 the Vienna Conference of Ministers restored monarchist rule in most of Germany. ▷ **Bourbon, House of; July Revolution (1830)**

Revolution of 1848 (Germany) Following the overthrow of the Orléanist monarchy in France, revolution broke out in most German states. By the end of Mar 1849, the monarchs, including those of **Prussia** and **Austria**, had agreed to the formation of liberal-dominated constituent assemblies, while in Frankfurt-am-Main a German parliament sought to draft a national and liberal constitution for all Germany. By the end of 1849 the revolution had failed, however. The Austrian monarchy retained control of its army which, area by area, suppressed the revolution in the Habsburg lands. Non-German minorities and German radicals refused to accept Frankfurt's writ and, since the new parliament had insufficient military forces, it relied heavily on the monarchist Prussian Army. A successful counter-revolution in Prussia and the refusal of the Prussian King, **Frederick William IV**, to accept the German crown offered by Frankfurt therefore finished the revolution. The political self-confidence of the German middle classes was dealt a severe blow, but limited constitutional concessions by the German monarchs paved the way for the Prussian constitutional crisis of 1861 and, subsequently, German unification under **Bismarck**. ▷ **February Revolution** (France); **Habsburg Dynasty; Orléans, House of**

Revolution of 1905 A series of nationwide strikes, demonstrations, and mutinies in Russia, given added stimulus by the massacre by soldiers of workers demonstrating peacefully in St Petersburg on what came to be called 'Bloody Sunday' (9 Jan 1905 new style). Faced with continuing popular unrest, Tsar **Nicholas II** was forced to make some marginal concessions, including the legalization of most political parties, and qualified elections to a form of national assembly — the **Duma**. ▷ **Russian Revolution**

Revolution of 1918 (Germany) In the hour of Germany's defeat in **World War I**, attempts to preserve the monarchy failed in the face of growing civil disorder. On 9 Nov a republic was declared by the **SPD** leader **Scheidemann** and a provisional government of majority and independent socialists formed. Although the Workers' and Soldiers' Councils, which were established spontaneously at this time, bore a superficial resemblance to the Russian soviets, the former supported the principle of parliamentary government in Dec 1918 and a National Assembly met in Weimar on 19 Jan 1919 to draft a constitution. Controversy has raged over how far the Social Democrats were wise to restrict major socio-economic change and changes in non-parliamentary institutions (army, Civil Service, judiciary) at this point, as well as relying on monarchist and right-radical military forces to restrain the radical left. The survival of many monarchist institutions and grandees was subsequently to weaken the **Weimar Republic**.

Revolution of 1989 (Germany) Once the Soviet government under Mikhail **Gorbachev** had declared it would not intervene in the affairs of its Eastern European allies, the future of East **Germany** (German Democratic Republic) was in doubt. Militarily dependent on the USSR and economically dependent on the Federal Republic of Germany and the USSR, East Germany's economy and society were wracked by increasing difficulties. During the summer of 1989, East German tourists in Hungary spilled across the recently demilitarized border into Austria and also invaded Federal German embassies in Prague and Warsaw.

As East Germany's population haemorrhaged, widespread civil unrest broke out within the country and culminated in the storming of the **Berlin Wall** on 9 Nov. The communist regime collapsed and unification with the Federal Republic of **Germany** followed in 1990.

Revolutions of 1848–9 A succession of popular uprisings in various West and Central European countries during 1848–9, some fuelled by political and economic grievances against established governments, often inspired by liberal and socialist ideas, others by demands for national independence from foreign rule, as in the Italian states, Bohemia and Hungary. In Italy particularly a growing distaste for Austrian rule in the Kingdom of Lombardy-Venetia and for Habsburg hegemony elsewhere in the peninsula combined with incipient liberalism and nationalism, and separatist and economic grievances to stimulate protest and revolt. The granting of concessions by many rulers simply served to encourage greater demands from the populace and briefly most Italian states fell under some form of constitutional or republican control. However, regional and ideological differences, the fear of the propertied classes of radical social change and the re-establishment of conservative governments in Paris and Vienna led to the suppression of revolt and the restoration of the old order in almost every state: only in the Kingdom of **Sardinia** was there any significant change, the **Statuto** granted by **Charles Albert** being retained as the basis for constitutional government. In France the abdication of Louis Philippe was followed by the Second Republic and the socialist experiment of National Workshops; liberal constitutions were granted in Austria and in many German states; Britain experienced Chartism. The revolutions collapsed from internal weakness or military suppression, and aroused reaction; but they presaged the ultimate triumph of nationalism, if not liberalism.

Rexism Belgian fascist political movement, founded by Léon **Degrelle**, and named after his publishing firm. Rexism grew out of right-wing Roman Catholic circles in Walloon (French-speaking) Belgium in the 1930s. In 1936 the Rex Party contested the national elections, and gained several seats in both chambers. During the late 1930s the party became increasing fascist and authoritarian, and during **World War II** collaborated fully with the Nazi occupation forces. By 1944 it had lost all its support.

Reynaud, Paul (1878–1966) French politician. Elected a Deputy in 1919, he sat as an independent on the centre right, frequently holding office, notably as Finance Minister (1930 and 1938–40) and Colonial Minister (1931–2). During his second term as Finance Minister he instigated a remarkable recovery from the economic crisis in which France found herself after the **Popular Front** experiment. He was influenced by de **Gaulle**'s advocacy of armoured warfare, and opposed appeasement. His appointment as Prime Minister (Mar 1940) was seen as a move towards a more vigorous prosecution of the war, but he had achieved little before the German onslaught led to his fall, and replacement by **Pétain**, who asked for an armistice, which Reynaud had refused to do. He was imprisoned by the Germans during the war, re-entering politics after 1944, but without regaining his former influence. ▷ **Independents** (France); **World War II**

Reynolds, Albert (1932–   ) Irish politician. His early career was as an entrepreneur in the entertainment and food-manufacturing industries. He became **Fianna Fáil** MP for Longford-West Meath (1977) and was Minister for Industry and Commerce (1987–9) and Finance (1989–91). Dismissed after an unsuccessful challenge to Charles **Haughey** (1991), he nevertheless won the party leadership by a large majority after Haughey's resignation (Feb 1992), becoming Prime Minister the same year.

Rhee, Syngman (1875–1965) Korean politician. Imprisoned (1897–1904) for his part in an independence campaign, he later went to the USA, returning to Japanese-annexed Korea in 1910. After the unsuccessful rising of 1919, he became President of the exiled Korean Provisional Government. On Japan's surrender (1945) he returned to become the first elected President of South Korea (1948). Re-elected for a fourth term (1960), he was obliged to resign after only one month, following major riots and the resignation of his cabinet. He died, in exile, in Honolulu.

Rhenish Federation (*Rheinbund*) The federation was established (1658) to preserve the Peace of Westphalia (1648). Headed by Johann Philip von Schönborn, Elector of Mainz, the federation was generally supportive of France and included both Catholic and Protestant princes.

Rhenish League (1254–7) A league of Rhineland towns which began in Mainz and Worms. After two years it included over 70 cities from Lübeck in the north to Zurich in the south. Many lay and ecclesiastical princes also joined. Its founder and administrator was Wolpode Arnold (d.1268). The purpose of the league was to secure law and order in the face of the breakdown of central power and to protect property, commerce, trade and the rights of the estates. It was recognized by **William of Holland** in 1255 but foundered on differences between its members caused by the disputed elections of 1257. ▷ **Interregnum**

Rhense, Electoral Assembly at (1338) A meeting of the Electors to discuss Emperor **Louis IV**'s conflict with the papacy. They formed an alliance for the defence of the empire, the first instance of the **Electors** acting together politically other than when electing the king. At the same time, they declared it was a traditional right that whoever was elected by the Electors was entitled to call himself King and to rule the empire, and that papal approval was not necessary.

Rhineland German territory largely to the west of the River Rhine demilitarized and occupied by the victorious Allies from 10 Jan 1920. Governed by an Inter-Allied High Commission based in Koblenz, a customs frontier was established between the Rhineland and the rest of Germany. French attempts to establish a separate Rhine Republic failed and the occupation forces withdrew between 1926 and 1930. In Mar 1936 **Hitler** violated the area's demilitarized status (Treaty of **Versailles**, **Locarno Pact**) when troops were ordered back into the territory.

Rhodes, Cecil (John) (1853–1902) South African politician. After studying in Oxford, he entered the Cape House of Assembly, securing Bechuanaland as a protectorate (1885) and the charter for the British South Africa Company (1889), whose territory was later to be named after him, as Rhodesia. In 1890 he became Prime Minister of Cape Colony, but was forced to resign in 1896 because of complications arising from the **Jameson Raid**. He was a conspicuous figure during the Boer War of 1899–1902, when he organized the defences during the Siege of **Kimberley**. He died at Muizenberg, Cape Colony, and in his will founded scholarships at Oxford for Americans, Germans, and colonials ('Rhodes scholars'). ▷ **Boer Wars**

Rhodesia Crisis The series of events that began with the declaration by Prime Minister

Ian **Smith** of a Unilateral Declaration of Independence (11 Nov 1965), following the Rhodesian Government's failure to agree with successive British Administrations on a constitutional independence settlement that ensured the continuance of white supremacy. The British Government was successful in gaining **UN** support for sanctions while ruling out the use of force and, in 1966 and 1968, Smith engaged with Prime Minister Harold **Wilson** in (ultimately unsuccessful) attempts to resolve the crisis. An agreement was reached with Edward **Heath**'s Conservative Government in 1971, but was ruled out after an independent fact-finding mission determined that it would be unacceptable to the black majority. The growing influence of the **ANC** (African National Congress), and the withdrawal of the Portuguese from Angola and Mozambique, served to remind Smith of his isolationism, and in 1977 he announced that he was willing to enter into new talks on a one-man, one-vote basis, and released nationalist leaders Ndabaningi **Sithole** and Joshua **Nkomo** as a sign of good faith. However, they initially refused to participate in negotiations, and the escalation of terrorist activities continued unabated despite Smith having attained in 1978 an internal settlement, thus providing for multiracial government, with the moderate Sithole and Bishop Abel **Muzorewa**. The return of a Conservative Government in 1979 provided the springboard for fresh talks and a new settlement, leading to elections in 1980 that were won by the former Marxist guerrilla leader, Robert **Mugabe**.

Rhodesian Front (RF) The Rhodesian political party formed in 1962 to oppose the relatively liberal United Federal Party, with Winston Field as its leader. Ian **Smith** replaced him in a putsch in 1964 and led Rhodesia to its **UDI** (Unilateral Declaration of Independence). The RF, which gained a majority of seats in the 1962 general election, made a clean sweep of all contested seats thereafter and sought to preserve white political and economic dominance in the country. In 1977, however, under pressure of civil war and outside influence, it accepted the principle of universal adult suffrage and attempted to devise an 'internal settlement'. At independence in 1980, it changed its name to Republican Front and soon afterwards to Conservative Alliance of Zimbabwe.

Riade, Battle near (933) The victory of **Henry I, 'the Fowler'** over the Hungarians. Having secured the western, northern and

frontiers, Henry then turned his attention to the empire's most dangerous enemies, the Hungarians. Leading an army assembled from all over the empire, he defeated them resoundingly at Riade in Thuringia, the battle contributing materially to securing Henry's authority.

Ribbentrop, Joachim von (1893–1946) German Nazi politician. He became a member of the **Nazi Party** in 1932, and as **Hitler**'s adviser in foreign affairs, was responsible in 1935 for the Anglo-German naval pact. He became Ambassador to Britain (1936) and Foreign Minister (1938–45). Captured by the British in 1945, he was condemned and executed at the **Nuremberg Trials**. ▷ **World War II**

Ribot, Alexandre (1842–1923) French politician. A member of parliament from 1878 to 1923, he was a quintessential moderate republican, opposed to excesses of either right or left. In a very long political career, he occupied high office on several crucial occasions, notably as Prime Minister (1892–3, 1895, 1914 and 1917), Minister of Foreign Affairs (1890–3, when he was largely responsible for the Franco-Russian alliance, and 1917, at a very difficult period of **World War I**), and as Minister of Finance (1895 and 1914–17).

Ricasoli, Bettino, Baron (1809–80) Italian politician. A Tuscan aristocrat who participated in the national movement of 1848, he became the leader of the Tuscan moderates. He accepted **Cavour**'s vision of Italian unity and played a large part in smoothing the process of Tuscan annexation by **Victor Emmanuel II**. He was elected a deputy in the new Italian parliament and became Prime Minister on Cavour's death (1861–2), holding the office again five years later (1866–7). As Prime Minister for the second time, he wanted to continue the war against Austria but was forced to consent to peace.

Ricci, Matteo (1552–1610) Italian founder of the Jesuit missions in China. He studied in Rome, then travelled to India, where he was ordained (1580), and went on to China in 1582. He so mastered Chinese as to write works which received much commendation from the Chinese literati, and met with great success as a missionary. He died in China.

Richard I, 'the Lionheart' (1157–99) King of England (1189/99). Known also as Richard, Cœur de Lion, he was the third son of

Henry II of England and **Eleanor of Aquitaine**. Of his 10-year reign, he spent only five months in England, devoting himself to crusading, and defending the Angevin lands in France. Already recognized as an outstanding soldier, he took Messina (1190), Cyprus, and Acre (1191) during the Third Crusade, and advanced to within sight of Jerusalem. On the return journey, he was arrested at Vienna (1192), and remained a prisoner of the German Emperor **Henry VI** until he agreed to be ransomed (1194). The rest of his reign was occupied in warfare against **Philip II** of France, while the government of England was conducted by the justiciar, Hubert **Walter**. Richard was mortally wounded while besieging the castle of Châlus, Aquitaine. ▷ **Angevins; Crusades**

Richard II (1367–1400) King of England (1377/99). He was the younger son of **Edward the Black Prince**, and succeeded his grandfather, **Edward III** of England, at the age of 10. He displayed great bravery in confronting the rebels in London during the **Peasants Revolt** (1381); but already parliament was concerned about his favourites, and the reign was dominated by the struggle between Richard's desire to act independently, and the magnates' concern to curb his power. He quarrelled with his uncle, **John of Gaunt**, and his main supporters were found guilty of treason in the 'Merciless Parliament' of 1388. After Richard had declared an end to his minority in 1389, he built up a stronger following, and in 1397–8 took his revenge by having the Earl of Arundel executed, the Duke of Gloucester murdered, and several lords banished, the exiles including Gaunt's son, Henry Bolingbroke (later **Henry IV** of England). His final act of oppression was to confiscate the Lancastrian estates after Gaunt's death (1399). Having failed to restrain the King by constitutional means, the magnates resolved to unseat him from the throne. Bolingbroke invaded England unopposed, and Richard was deposed in his favour (Sep 1399). He died in Pontefract Castle, Yorkshire, possibly of starvation. ▷ **Lancaster, House of**

Richard III (1452–85) King of England (1483/5). He was the youngest son of Richard, Duke of York. Created Duke of Gloucester by his brother, **Edward IV**, in 1461, he accompanied him into exile (1470), and played a key role in his restoration (1471). Rewarded with part of the Neville inheritance, he exercised viceregal powers in northern England, and in 1482 recaptured

Berwick-upon-Tweed from the Scots. When Edward died (1483) and was succeeded by his under-age son, **Edward V**, Richard acted first as protector; but within three months, he had overthrown the Woodvilles (relations of Edward IV's Queen, Elizabeth Woodville), seen to the execution of Lord Hastings, and had himself proclaimed and crowned as the rightful King. Young Edward and his brother Richard were probably murdered in the Tower on Richard's orders. He tried to stabilize his position, but failed to win broad-based support. His rival, Henry Tudor (later **Henry VII**), confronted him in battle at **Bosworth Field**, and Richard died fighting bravely against heavy odds. Though ruthless, he was not the absolute monster Tudor historians portrayed him to be. Nor is there proof he was a hunchback.

Richard, Cœur de Lion ▷ **Richard I, 'the Lionheart'**

Richelieu, Armand Jean du Plessis, Cardinal and Duke of (1585–1642) French politician. A protégé of the Queen Mother, **Marie de Médicis**, he became Minister of State in 1624 and, as Chief Minister, was the effective ruler of France from then until 1642. His chief adviser and agent between 1624 and 1630 was a Capuchin friar, François Joseph de Tremblay, known as Père **Joseph** and nicknamed *L'Eminence Grise*. Richelieu's twin aims — to secure obedience to the Bourbon monarchy within France and enhance French prestige abroad — were achieved at the expense of recalcitrant groups in French society. His principal achievement was to check Habsburg power, ultimately by sending armies into the Spanish Netherlands, Alsace, Lorraine, and Roussillon. ▷ **Bourbon, House of; Habsburg Dynasty; Louis XIII**

Ridgway, Matthew B(unker) (1895–1993) US general. Educated at the US Military Academy at West Point, he commanded the 82nd Airborne Division in Sicily (1943), and Normandy (1944). He commanded the 18th Airborne Corps in the North-West Europe campaign (1944–5) and the US 8th Army in **UN** operations in Korea (1950). He succeeded Douglas **MacArthur** in command of US and UN forces (1951), and was supreme allied commander Europe in succession to **Eisenhower** (1952–3), and Army Chief of Staff (1953). He received the Presidential Medal of Freedom in 1986.

Ridley, Nicholas (c.1500–55) English Protestant martyr. He was ordained c.1524, and studied in Paris and Louvain (1527–30). He then held a variety of posts, including chaplain to Thomas **Cranmer** and **Henry VIII**, and Bishop of Rochester (1547). An ardent reformer, he became Bishop of London (1550), and helped Cranmer prepare the Thirty-Nine Articles. On the death of **Edward VI** he espoused the cause of Lady Jane **Grey**, was imprisoned, and executed at Oxford. ▷ **Reformation** (England)

Rieger, František Ladislav (1818–1903) Czech politician. A lawyer by training and son-in-law of František **Palacký**, he took part in the unsuccessful constituent assembly in 1848–9 and had to lie low in the 1850s. But he re-emerged in 1861 in alliance with the provincial nobility to demand the restoration of the old Czech state. The Emperor **Francis Joseph** would not yield and Rieger led his so-called Old Czech Party into a policy of abstention which was also unsuccessful except as a backdrop to the first great popular outburst of national feeling. By the late 1870s abstention was clearly discredited and Rieger joined the return to the Czech estates and the imperial parliament. Among concessions won in 1881 was the division of the Charles University, Prague, into two, a small German and a much larger Czech. Thereafter Rieger's influence declined and a Young Czech and other new parties took over.

Riel, Louis (1844–85) Canadian politician. The leader of the **métis** during both the **Red River Rebellion** and **North-West Rebellion**, he fled to the USA when the federal government sent a military force into the Red River settlement in 1870, but he returned to live there quietly, although Ontario orangemen had offered a reward for his capture as the murderer of Thomas Scott. He was still regarded by French-speaking Canadians as a hero. When the USA threatened Manitoba with a **Fenian Raid** in 1871, he mustered a métis cavalry force in defence and received public (though anonymous) thanks from the governor. John A **Macdonald** provided him with funds in the hope that he might return to exile, but in 1873 he was elected to the House of Commons in Ottawa. After his re-election in 1874, a motion was introduced by Mackenzie **Bowell** demanding his expulsion from the House. He was finally granted amnesty in 1875 on condition of a further five years' exile. By this time he had suffered a nervous breakdown and was detained in a mental asylum in Quebec. In 1878 he had recovered sufficiently to leave for the USA where he became a school-

teacher. In 1884 Riel responded to the pleas of the métis in Saskatchewan and so became involved in his second rebellion. However, he provoked opposition by his religious manias, while his claims against the government for $35 000 also gave his motivation a mercenary cast. When he surrendered he was charged with treason, but he refused to let his defence counsel enter a plea of insanity. With a verdict of guilty the jury also recommended clemency, but after several reprieves and an assessment of his sanity, he was hanged. His body was interred in front of St Boniface Cathedral. French-Canadian outrage at his execution helped Honoré **Mercier** to gain power in 1886 and has continued to agitate their nationalist feelings ever since.

Rienzi (Rienzo), Cola di (1313–54) Italian patriot. In 1347 he incited the citizens to rise against the rule of the nobles. The senators were driven out, and he was made tribune. Papal authority then turned against him, and he fled from Rome. He returned in 1354, and tried to re-establish his position, but was killed in a rising against him. Wagner's opera on his story was completed in 1840.

Rif (Riff) A cluster of Berber agricultural and herding groups of north-east Morocco. Famed as warriors, in the 1920s they defeated the Spanish, but were eventually conquered by combined French and Spanish forces in 1926. They later served in the French and Spanish regiments in Morocco. Population c.700 000. ▷ **Abd al-Krim, Muhammad**

Rigas, Velestinlis Pheraios (1757–98) Greek national hero, writer and revolutionary. Well-educated, he worked for the **Phanariots** in Constantinople and the **Danubian Principalities**. Inspired by the ideals of the Enlightenment and the **French Revolution**, he translated various French works into vernacular Greek and wrote many revolutionary pamphlets. In Vienna in 1796 he began publishing revolutionary literature including the *Declaration of the Rights of Man* and he issued a map of the Balkan Peninsula and Asia Minor which anticipated the Greater Greece of the **Megale Idea**. He drew up proposals for a Greek constitution and composed the *War Hymn* for which he is now best remembered. Involved in many conspiracies, he was arrested by the Austrian government, handed over to the Ottoman authorities and executed.

Rijswijk, Treaty of (1697) A settlement ending the Nine Years War or the War of the

League of **Augsburg** (1688–97), mediated by Sweden, between plenipotentiaries of **Louis XIV** of France on the one hand, and on the other **Charles II** of Spain, **William III** of Britain (also representing the Netherlands), and the Emperor **Leopold I**. Although the treaty ostensibly checked French expansionism, peace was short-lived; it freed Louis XIV to concentrate on the War of the **Spanish Succession**.

Rio de Janeiro Treaty (1947) The Inter-American Treaty of Reciprocal Assistance, signed in Rio, which enshrines principles of hemispheric defence laid down during **World War II**, especially a US-Brazilian alliance. It provides for certain types of mutual assistance in the case of an armed attack on any American state from outside the region and for mutual consultation in the event of any aggression between them or warlike action affecting territories situated outside them. It was the first permanent collective defence treaty signed by the USA and has remained the cornerstone of its military commitment to Latin America and the institutional basis for its hegemony. It has been applied on 16 occasions since 1948, in all cases to long-standing inter-American disputes, and to incidents within the Caribbean and Central American regions. It was not, however, invoked during the Falklands/Malvinas conflict. Directed mainly against Cuba, Latin American diplomats have argued that it has disguised, but not modified, the extent of US hegemony in Latin America. Since the breakup of the USSR, its purpose has become more questionable. ▷ **Falklands War**

Riom Trial (1942) The trial by the **Vichy** regime of General **Gamelin** and the leading figures of France's pre-war governments, notably **Blum** and **Daladier**, held responsible for the defeat of 1940; it was abandoned when it proved embarrassing for the military and for many who were in positions of authority under Vichy, but the defendants remained imprisoned, and were later handed over to the Germans. ▷ **World War II**

Riot Act Legislation in Britain concerned to preserve public order, first passed at the beginning of the Hanoverian era in 1714. When 12 or more people were unlawfully assembled and refused to disperse, they were, after the reading of a section of this Act by a person in authority, immediately considered felons having committed a serious crime.

Ripka, Hubert (1895–1958) Czechoslovak journalist and politician. Prominent in the National Socialist Party (totally different from **Hitler**'s of the same name), he was given a place in **Beneš**'s government in exile during **World War II**. Returning to Czechoslovakia in 1945, he became Minister of Foreign Trade until Feb 1948 when he joined the group of democratic politicians who tried to force an election by resigning. Since they constituted a minority, the **February Revolution** went the other way. Ripka found himself, like others, forced once again to flee abroad.

Rishon Massacre (Mar 1991) The murder, at a labour market in Rishon le Zion, of seven Arab workmen from the **Gaza Strip** by a 22-year-old Israeli, Ami Popper, served to refocus political attention on the conditions of Palestinians under Israeli occupation after the distraction of the 1991 Gulf War.

Rising in the North (1569–70) A rebellion (sometimes known as 'The Rebellion of the Northern Earls') against **Elizabeth I** by the Earls of Northumberland and Westmoreland. It was motivated by strong support for Catholicism in the north of England and precipitated by the arrival of **Mary, Queen of Scots**, in England (1568). A general rising was aborted when the Duke of Norfolk refused to lead it and the northern rising, beginning in Nov 1569 and centering on Durham, was confused and aimless, collapsing by Feb 1570. Westmoreland fled to the Netherlands but Northumberland was captured in Scotland and executed (1572). Despite its outcome, the rising demonstrated the limited impact of the Reformation in northern England. ▷ **Reformation** (England)

Risorgimento The Italian term (literally, 'resurgence') applied to the 19c movement by which Italy achieved unity. Although its origins lay in the administrative reforms and enlightenment ideas of the 18c and the Napoleonic period, it is usually held to have started properly in the decades after the Congress of **Vienna** (1814–15). In its early stages it is associated with the insurrections of 1820–1 and the early 1830s, and **Revolutions of 1848–9**, as well as with the growing nationalist and anti-Austrian feelings expressed by thinkers such as **Mazzini** and the more moderate **Gioberti**. After the failure of the popular revolts of the 1848–9 period, the *Risorgimento* came to fruition with the wars of unification (1859–70) and the creation of a single state under **Victor Emmanuel II**. Since the 19c many historians have mythologized the Risorgimento, stressing the wide support for unification and ignoring both the excesses perpetrated in the name of the new Italian state and the complete absence of nationalist feeling among much of the population. ▷ **Charles Albert; Cavour, Camillo; Garibaldi, Giuseppe; Grande Brigantaggio; Mazzini, Giuseppe; Thousand, Expedition of the; Young Italy**

Ristić, Jovan (1831–99) Serbian politician. In charge of Serbia's foreign policy at the outbreak of the Bosnian revolt (1875–8), he was briefly out of office but returned in 1876 to lead the government, which took Serbia into war against the Ottoman Porte in support of the Bosnians. The Serb Army was all but destroyed and the Treaty of **San Stefano** (1878), which established Bulgaria, shocked the Serbs, marking as it did the end of Russian support for Serbia. Still head of the Liberal government, Ristić set about the reconstruction of Serbia's diplomatic relations. He turned to the Habsburg government and later in 1878 concluded an agreement which secured Vienna's support in return for favourable trading arrangements. When Vienna tried to dictate terms for the extension of Serbia's railways, Ristić became disillusioned with the Serb-Habsburg concord and resigned (Oct 1880). ▷ **Obrenović, Milan**

Rites Controversy The dispute between the Vatican and the **Qing Dynasty** between 1693 and 1705 over interpretation of Chinese rites to honour **Confucius** and family ancestors. The Jesuits, who had begun to enter China at the end of the 16c and who were anxious to gain the support of the Chinese **Mandarins**, adopted a tolerant approach to indigenous elements of Chinese culture, insisting that the rites were social ceremonies of respect rather than acts of idolatrous worship. Their approach was criticized as too lax by Jesuit leaders in Europe and other Catholic missionaries (Dominicans, Franciscans) in China. In 1704 the Papacy decided in favour of the Jesuits' opponents, insisting that the rites had to be condemned. The papacy's attempt to enforce this decision in China was viewed as unwarranted interference by the Qing Emperor **Kangxi**, who reversed his previous policy of toleration towards missionaries. Under his successor, Yongzheng (1722/35), Christianity was formally proscribed.

Rivadavia, Bernardino (1780–1845) Argentine politician. A well-read **porteño**, he fought in the patriot militia which evicted the British in 1807. He supported the independence movement from Spain in 1810 and dominated the first revolutionary triumvirate in 1811. Rivadavia was greatly influenced by the reforms of **Charles III** of Spain (which created the **intendentes**) and by the French radicals, and was a convinced Benthamite. Once in power, a torrent of legislation decreed the end of the **audiencia** and the slave trade, liberalized commerce and standardized the currency. When he returned to Argentina in 1821, after several years in Europe, he became a minister and propounded schemes to encourage immigration, abolished ecclesiastical privileges (fueros) and founded the University of Buenos Aires. His land law of 1824 established the system of landholding which has prevailed to the present, and encouraged large amounts of public land to fall into the hands of the few able to rent them; by 1827 over 6 500 000 acres had been rented to 112 corporations. Elected President in 1826, he was forced to resign in the wake of the inconclusive conflict with Brazil and provincial reaction to his centralist constitution. He was exiled to Paris, where he died. ▷ **Argentine-Brazilian War; fuero**

Rivas, Angel de Saavedra, Duke of (1791–1865) Spanish politician and writer. Educated in Madrid, he served in the Civil War. He lived in exile (1823–34), became Minister of the Interior in 1835, and was soon exiled again. In 1837 he returned, became Prime Minister, and later was ambassador in Naples, Paris (1856) and Florence (1860).

Rizal, José (1861–96) Filipino patriot and writer. He studied medicine in Madrid. He went on to publish political novels, *Noli me tangere* (1886) and *El Filibusterismo* (1891), which had a strong anti-Spanish tone. On his return to the Philippines, he was exiled to Mindanao. He returned to Manila just as an anti-Spanish revolt was erupting; he was accused of instigating it, and was publicly shot.

Rizzio, David (c.1533–66) Italian courtier and musician. He entered the service of **Mary, Queen of Scots** in 1561, and rapidly becoming her favourite, was appointed Private Foreign Secretary in 1564. He negotiated Mary's marriage (1565) with **Darnley**, with whom he was at first on friendliest terms, but the Queen's husband soon became jealous of his influence over Mary and of his strong political power, and entered with other nobles into a plot to kill him. Rizzio was dragged from the Queen's presence and brutally murdered at the palace of Holyrood.

Roanoke (North Carolina) The site of Sir Walter **Raleigh**'s two attempts to found an English colony in North America. The first, in 1585, ended after trouble with the island's native inhabitants and the threat of an attack from Spanish forces. The second, an expedition of 117 men, women, and children in 1587, had disappeared without trace by 1591 when a relief force found the town of 'Ralegh' deserted. The failures demonstrated that colonization was too expensive an enterprise for one individual to support, even with the monarch's blessing; and that settlements had to be defensible, Roanoke being an exposed island without a good harbour.

'Robber Barons' US political epithet. First applied to railroad magnates like Jay Gould and Jim Fisk who exploited both national and local government, shareholders and the public in their ruthless operations, it was later extended to those like Cornelius Vanderbilt, Andrew Carnegie and John D Rockefeller who developed large-scale enterprises by coercive horizontal and vertical integration.

Robert II (1316–90) King of Scots (1371/90). He was the son of Walter, hereditary Steward of Scotland. Robert acted as sole regent during the exile and captivity of **David II**; on the latter's death, he became King in right of his descent from his maternal grandfather, Robert **Bruce**, and founded the Stuart royal dynasty. ▷ **Stuart, House of**

Robert of Anjou, 'the Wise' (1278–1343) King of Naples. The grandson of **Charles of Anjou**, he succeeded his father, Charles II, to the throne in 1309. A leader of the Guelf papal party, he nonetheless broke with Pope **John XXII** in 1330. A notable patron of learning and the arts, he was a friend of Boccaccio and Petrarch. ▷ **Guelfs**

Roberts (of Kandahar, Pretoria, and Waterford), Frederick Sleigh Roberts, 1st Earl (1832–1914) British field marshal. He took an active part in the **Indian Uprising** of 1857–8, for which he was decorated with the Victoria Cross in 1858. He became Commander-in-Chief in India (1885–93), and served as Supreme Commander in South Africa during the Boer War, relieving the Siege of **Kimberley** (1900). He was created earl in 1901, and died while visiting troops in the field in France. ▷ **Afghan Wars; Boer Wars**

Robespierre, (Maximilien François Marie Isidore de) (1758–94) French revolutionary leader. He became a lawyer, was elected to the **Estates General** (1789), became a prominent member of the Jacobin Club, and emerged in the National Assembly as a popular radical, known as 'the Incorruptible'. In 1791 he was public accuser, and in 1792 presented a petition to the **Legislative Assembly** for a Revolutionary Tribunal. Elected for Paris to the National Convention, he emerged as leader of the **Mountain**, strenuously opposed to the **Girondins**, whom he helped to destroy. In 1793 he became a member of the Committee of **Public Safety** and for three months dominated the country, introducing the Reign of **Terror** and the cult of the Supreme Being. However, as his ruthless exercise of power increased, his popularity waned. He was attacked in the National Convention, arrested, and guillotined on the orders of the Revolutionary Tribunal. ▷ **Convention, National; French Revolution; Jacobins**

Robinson, Arthur Napoleon (Ray) (1926–) Trinidad and Tobago politician. Educated in Trinidad and at Oxford, he qualified as a barrister. On his return to the West Indies, he became politically active and in 1967, on independence, was Deputy Leader of the moderate-centrist People's National Movement (PNM). In 1984, with other colleagues, he broke away to form a left-of-centre coalition which became the National Alliance for Reconstruction (NAR), and which in the 1986 general election swept the PNM from power, making Robinson Prime Minister. Wounded in the Aug 1990 attempted coup, he fought another election in Dec 1991, but he and the NAR were ousted by a rejuvenated PNM under Patrick Manning.

Robinson, Sir John Beverley (1791–1863) Canadian politician. A prominent member of the **Family Compact**, he became Attorney-General in 1818 and later Chief Justice (1829). In his determination to protect the imperial connection and the elite status of the Compact, he insisted on classifying American settlers as aliens and depriving them of both their property and their political rights. In 1830 he became President of the Executive Council and during the rebellion of 1837 he was responsible for the execution of two rebels and the banishment of 25.

Robinson, Mary (1944–) Irish politician. She trained as a lawyer and was Professor of

Law at Trinity College, Dublin, from 1969. She was a member of the Irish Senate (1969–89) and participated in numerous legal associations in the European Community (**EC**). She became an activist on many social issues, including women's and single-parents' rights and the decriminalization of homosexuality. Nominated by the Labour Party, from which she had resigned in 1985 over the **Anglo-Irish Agreement**, she unexpectedly defeated the **Fianna Fáil** candidate Brian Lenihan in the presidential elections of Nov 1990.

Rob Roy (properly, **Robert MacGregor**) (1671–1734) Scottish outlaw. After his lands were seized by the Duke of Montrose, he gathered his clansmen and became a brigand. His career gave rise to many stories, often unsubstantiated, about his brave exploits, and of his generosity to the poor. Captured and imprisoned in London, he was sentenced to transportation, but pardoned in 1727. He is later thought to have become a Catholic.

Rocard, Michel (1930–) French politician. He trained at the Ecole National d'Administration, where he was a classmate of Jacques **Chirac**, and in 1967 became leader of the Unified Socialist Party (PSU). He joined the Socialist Party (PS) in 1973, emerging as leader of its moderate social democratic wing, and unsuccessfully challenged François **Mitterrand** for the party's presidential nomination in 1981. After serving as Minister of Planning and Regional Development (1981–3) and Agriculture (1983–5) in the ensuing Mitterrand administration, he resigned in Apr 1985 in opposition to the government's expedient introduction of proportional representation. In May 1988, however, as part of a strategy termed the 'opening to the centre', he was appointed Prime Minister by President Mitterrand. He was replaced as Prime Minister by Mme Edith Cresson in 1991. ▷ **Socialist Party**

Roca–Runciman Pact (May 1933) A commercial treaty between Britain and Argentina, referred to by the names of the chief negotiators, Vice-President Julio Argentino Roca (Argentina) and Walter Runciman (Britain). The pact guaranteed Argentina a share of the British meat market in return for various economic concessions. Nevertheless, the debates over the pact weakened the *Concordancia* or 'coalition' government of General Augustín Justo, which was faced with a vigorous nationalist campaign.

Rochefort, Victor Henri, Marquis of Rochefort-Luçay (1832–1913) French journalist and politician. In 1868 he founded the satirical paper *La Lanterne*, which was quickly suppressed, but in 1869 on his election to the *Corps législatif* he started the *Marseillaise*, in which he continued his attacks on the imperial regime. He was elected to the National Assembly (1871), but having sided with the **Paris Commune**, he was excluded, and sentenced to transportation to New Caledonia, in the south Pacific. He escaped in 1874, returning to France after the amnesty of 1880. He continued his journalistic career with the popular and profitable newspaper *L'Intransigeant*, and became involved in the Boulangist movement. This producd a further period of exile in London (1889–95), after which he returned to French political journalism, moving to the extreme right, as a virulent anti-Semite, and anti-Dreyfusard. He wrote his autobiography, *Adventures of My Life* (trans 1896). ▷ **Boulanger, Georges; Dreyfus, Alfred**

Rockingham, Charles Watson Wentworth, 2nd Marquess of (1730–82) British politician. He was created Earl of Malton in 1750 and served as gentleman of the bedchamber to **George II** and **George III**. As leader of a prominent Whig opposition group, he was called upon to form a ministry in 1765. He repealed the **Stamp Act**, affecting the American colonies, then court intrigues caused his resignation (1766). He opposed Britain's war against the colonists. His was the most consistent opposition Whig group to George III's government in the 1760s and 1770s, and leading spokesmen, such as **Fox** and **Burke**, were adherents. He became Prime Minister again in 1782, the year he died. ▷ **American Revolution**

Rodney (of Stoke-Rodney), George Brydges Rodney, 1st Baron (1719–92) British admiral. He joined the navy in 1732, became Governor of Newfoundland (1748–52), and won several victories during the **Seven Years War** and after the **American Revolution**, when he defeated French fleets in the West Indies, notably off Dominica in 1782. He was made a baron after his return to England.

Rodney, Walter (1942–80) Guyanese historian and politician. Formerly Professor of African History at the University of Dar es Salaam, Rodney provoked a riot when he was deported from Jamaica in 1968 for his supposed connections with **Black Power**.

Although debarred from holding the history chair at the University of Guyana, he returned to his homeland and founded the Working People's Alliance which was antipathetic to the policies of **Burnham**'s ruling **People's National Congress**. The author of *How Europe Underdeveloped Africa* (1972), he was killed by a bomb in mysterious circumstances in Guyana.

Rodzianko, Mikhail V (1859–1924) Russian politician. An **Octobrist**, he was President of the third and fourth dumas and, after the outbreak of **World War I**, he became the chairman of a special **Duma** committee working to assist the war effort. The committee was, however, frustrated at every turn. In the wake of events of Feb 1917, Rodzianko appealed to **Nicholas II** to appoint a government that would enjoy public confidence; Nicholas simply refused to respond, and it fell to Rodzianko to ask him to abdicate, which he did. Thereafter, Rodzianko played little role in events.

Roe v Wade (1973) US Supreme Court decision legalizing abortion. It struck down state laws which prohibited abortion within the first three months of pregnancy on the grounds that the right to privacy, which included the right to have an abortion, was protected by due process.

Roger I (1031–1101) Norman ruler in Sicily. He joined his brother, Robert **Guiscard**, in South Italy, and helped him to conquer Calabria. In 1060 he was invited to Sicily to fight against the **Saracens**, and took Messina. Everywhere the Normans were welcomed as deliverers from the Muslim yoke; in 1071 the Saracen capital, Palermo, was captured, and Robert made Roger Count of Sicily. After Robert's death (1085), Roger succeeded to his Italian possessions, and held the reins of Norman power in southern Europe.

Roger II (1095–1154) First Norman King of Sicily. The second son of **Roger I**, he succeeded his older brother as Count of Sicily in 1105 and became Duke of Apulia in 1127, thus welding Sicily to the lands of Robert **Guiscard**, his grandfather's brother, and creating a strong Norman kingdom. He added Capua (1136), Naples and the Abruzzi (1140). He forced recognition of his royal titles from the Pope and after the Byzantine Emperor had insulted Roger's ambassador, his fleet ravaged the coasts of Dalmatia and Epirus, took Corfu and plundered both Corinth and Athens (1146). In 1147 he took

Tripoli, Tunis and Algeria. His court at Palermo was one of the most magnificent in Europe, and formed a critical point of contact for Christian and Arab scholars.

Rogers, John (c.1500–55) English Protestant reformer and martyr. He was a London rector who converted to Protestantism at Antwerp, and helped to prepare the new translation called 'Matthew's Bible' in 1537. He returned to England in 1548, preached an anti-Catholic sermon at St Paul's Cross in 1553, just after the accession of **Mary I**, and was burnt. ▷ **Reformation** (England)

Rogier, Charles Latour (1800–85) Belgian politician. He trained and practised as a lawyer in Liège, worked in journalism, and was active in politics during the **Belgian Revolution**, joining both the Provisional Government and the National Congress. During the 1830s he was Governor of Antwerp, and became a cabinet minister (for Internal Affairs) for the first time in 1832–4. From the late 1840s onward he was the leading liberal politician of his day, forming and participating in governments (1847–52, 1857–61 and 1861–8). The **Liberal Party** dominated the middle of the 19c, and so Rogier presided over their achievements: the industrial revolution, the 1848 Constitution, free trade, and the battle with the Catholics over the **Schools Question**. As a 'doctrinaire' liberal, he came into conflict with the radicals at the end of his career.

Rohan-Gié, Henri, Duke of (1579–1638) French Duke of Léon, and Huguenot leader. On the surrender of La Rochelle (1628) a price was set on his head, and he made his way to Venice, but soon after was summoned by **Richelieu** to serve his king in the Valtellina, out of which he drove Imperialists and Spaniards. ▷ **Huguenots**

Rohan-Guéménée, Louis René Edouard, Prince of (1734–1803) French prelate. In 1778 he became a cardinal, and in 1779 became Bishop of Strasbourg. He fell prey to Cagliostro and the Comtesse de La Motte, who tricked him into believing that Queen **Marie Antoinette**, who knew nothing of the affair, wished him to stand security for her purchase by instalments of a priceless diamond necklace. The adventurers collected the necklace from the jewellers supposedly to give it to the Queen, but left Paris in order to sell the diamonds for their own gain. When the plot was discovered, Rohan-Guéménée was arrested, but was acquitted by the

Parlement of Paris (1786). He was elected to the **Estates General** in 1789, but refused to take the oath to the constitution in 1791, retiring to the German part of his diocese.

Röhm, Ernst (1887–1934) German soldier, Nazi politician and paramilitary leader. He became an early supporter of **Hitler** and played a vital role in fostering good relations between the **Nazi Party** and the Bavarian authorities up until Nov 1923. The organizer and commander of the **SA** or stormtroopers ('Brownshirts') during the mid-1920s and from 1931 to 1934, his plans to pursue policies independently of the NSDAP and his wish to supplant the traditional army, led to his execution on Hitler's orders, in Munich. ▷ **Night of the Long Knives**

Roh Tae Woo (1932–) South Korean politician. He was educated at the Korean Military Academy (1951–5), where he was a classmate of a future president, **Chun Doohwan**. He fought briefly in the **Korean War** and was a battalion commander during the **Vietnam War**. He became commanding general of the Capital Security Command (1979), from which position he helped General Chun seize power in the coup of 1979–80. He retired from the army in 1981 and successively served, under President Chun, as Minister for National Security and Foreign Affairs (1981–2) and for Home Affairs (from 1982). He was elected Chairman of the ruling Democratic Justice Party in 1985 and in 1987, following serious popular disturbances, drew up a political reform package which restored democracy to the country. He was elected President in 1987.

Rojo, Vicente (1894–1966) Spanish soldier. The most brilliant strategist on the Republican side during the **Spanish Civil War**. He organized the remarkable defence of Madrid in Nov 1936 as well as the Jarama and Guadalajara campaigns of 1937. Having been made Chief of the General Staff in May 1937, he not only reorganized the Popular Army, but planned the offensives of Brunete, Teruel, and the Ebro. He returned to Spain from exile in 1957 and lived under virtual house arrest until his death in 1966.

Rokossovsky, Konstantin Konstantinovich (1896–1968) Russian soldier. Born in Warsaw of a Polish father and a Russian mother, he served in **World War I** in the tsarist army and joined the Red Guards in 1917. He served in the Red Army cavalry during the **Russian Civil War** and after, but

was lucky to survive imprisonment during the **Stalin** purges. In **World War II** he was one of the defenders of Moscow, played a leading part in the Battle of **Stalingrad** (1942–3), recaptured Orel and Warsaw, and led the Russian race for Berlin. In 1944 he was promoted Marshal of the USSR and then served as Commander-in-Chief of Soviet forces in Poland (1945–9). In 1949 he was appointed Polish Minister of Defence as Stalin's man in Warsaw, a post he was made to resign in 1956 during the anti-Soviet unrest in Poland, as part of the bargain under which **Gomułka** became Premier, with greater control over Polish domestic affairs in return for supporting Soviet foreign policy. Rokossovsky then became a Deputy Minister of Defence of the USSR from 1956 to 1962, apart from a brief period in a military command in Transcaucasia.

Roland, Manon ▷ **Roland de la Platière, Jean Mari**

Roland de la Platière, Jean Mari (1734–93) French politician. He married Marie Jeanne Phlipon (1754–93) in 1780. In 1791 Roland was sent to Paris by Lyons to watch the interests of the municipality; and Madame Roland established a salon patronized by the leading **Girondins**. In Mar 1792 Roland became Minister of the Interior, but made himself hateful to the **Jacobins** by his protests against the September Massacres (1792), in which demagogues had incited the Paris mob to invade the prisons, murdering innocent victims. He took part in the last struggle of the Girondins. On 31 May 1793, he was arrested, but escaped and fled to Rouen, hoping to organize insurrection, but in vain; the next day, Madame Roland was arrested. During her five months in prison she wrote her unfinished Memoirs, in which we have a serene and delightful revelation of her youth. On 8 Nov 1793 she was guillotined. Two days later her husband committed suicide.

Rollo (c.860–c.932) Viking founder of the duchy of Normandy. The son of a Norse earl of Orkney (Rognvald of Möre), he was the leader of a band of mercenary **Vikings** foraging in France in 911. He laid siege unsuccessfully to Chartres, but in peace talks with King **Charles III, 'the Simple'** he was offered a large tract of land on the lower Seine in return for becoming Charles' vassal. This territory was the nucleus of the future duchy of Normandy ('Northmandy'). One of his descendants was **William I, 'the**

ROMAN EMPERORS

Dates overlap where there are periods of joint rule (eg Marcus Aurelius and Lucius Verus (161–9), and where the government of the empire divides between East and West.

Regnal Dates	Name	Regnal Dates	Name	Regnal Dates	Name
27BC/AD14	Augustus (Caesar Augustus)	238	Maximus	337/50	Constans
14/37	Tiberius	238	Balbinus	337/61	Constantius II
37/41	Caligula (Gaius Caesar)	238/44	Gordian III	350/3	Magnentius
41/54	Claudius	244/9	Philip	361/3	Julian
54/68	Nero	249/51	Decius	363/4	Jovian
68/9	Galba	251	Hostilian	364/75	Valentinian I–(West)
69	Otho	251/3	Gallus	364/78	Valens–(East)
69	Vitellius	253	Aemilian	365/6	Procopius–(East)
69/79	Vespasian	253/60	Valerian	375/83	Gratian–(West)
79/81	Titus	253/68	Gallienus	375/92	Valentinian II–(West)
81/96	Domitian	268/70	Claudius II Gothicus	379/95	Theodosius I, 'the Great'
96/8	Nerva	269/70	Quintillus	395/408	Arcadius–(East)
98/117	Trajan	270/5	Aurelian	395/423	Honorius–(West)
117/38	Hadrian	275/6	Tacitus	408/50	Theodosius II–(East)
138/61	Antoninus Pius	276	Florian	421/3	Constantius III–(West)
161/80	Marcus Aurelius	276/82	Probus	425/55	Valentinian III–(West)
161/9	Lucius Verus	282/3	Carus	450/7	Marcian–(East)
180/92	Commodus	283/5	Carinus	455	Petronius Maximus–(West)
193	Pertinax	283/4	Numerian	455/6	Avitus–(West)
193	Didius Julianus	284/305	Diocletian–(East)	457/74	Leo I–(East)
193/211	Septimius Severus	286/305	Maximian–(West)	457/61	Majorian–(West)
211/17	Caracalla	305/11	Galerius–(East)	461/7	Libius Severus–(West)
211/12	Geta	305/6	Constantius I, 'Chlorus'– (West)	467/72	Anthemius–(West)
217/18	Macrinus			472/3	Olybrius–(West)
218/22	Elagabalus	306/7	Severus–(West)	474/5	Julius Nepos–(West)
222/35	Alexander Severus	306/12	Maxentius–(West)	474	Leo II–(East)
235/8	Maximin	306/37	Constantine I, 'the Great'	474/91	Zeno–(East)
238	Gordian I	308/24	Licinius–(East)	475/6	Romulus Augustulus– (West)
238	Gordian II	337/40	Constantine II		

Conqueror'. Rollo was such a huge man that no horse could carry him, hence his nickname of Hrolf 'the Ganger' (walker).

Roman Empire (31BC–AD476 in the West (1453 in the East)) Cobbled together out of the wreckage of the **Roman Republic**, the Roman Empire was the creation of one man, **Augustus**. Pretending that he had restored the Republic, he studiously avoided titles that smacked of absolute power, calling himself *princeps* or first citizen, a Republican term, from which the name for the early Empire 'the Principate', also derived. In reality, he and his successors were absolute monarchs; later titles make this clear — the Emperor being called *dominus* ('master'), and the name for the later Empire 'the Dominate'. Abroad, too, Augustus' arrangements affected the nature of the Empire permanently — the unbridled expansionism of Republican days was abandoned, and territorial limits were set — the Rhine and Danube in Europe, the Euphrates in Asia. Subsequent modifications were few; Britain

(43), Dacia, and Arabia (both annexed by Trajan in 106) were the only significant later additions. From the outset, the Rhine–Danube frontier was the hardest to hold, with the tribes across the rivers exerting a relentless pressure upon the Roman defences. Rome managed to contain this pressure for several centuries, but only at an increasing cost to herself. The area saw a steady military build-up and ultimately constant fighting. The foundation in the 3c of a new imperial capital (Nicomedia) nearer this frontier shows how the Empire's centre of gravity had shifted from Rome and Italy to the north and east. This was the point where the very integrity of the Empire was threatened; and it was here that Rome's defences in the end were breached. In the 5c, hordes of transriverine tribesmen (eg Huns, Vandals, Visigoths, Ostrogoths) poured into the west provinces carrying all before them. In 476 with their deposition of the last Emperor, Romulus Augustulus, they marked symbolically their destruction of the western half of the Empire. The eastern provinces, however, proved more resilient; here the barbarian challenge was contained for another thousand years, until the eastern capital Constantinople fell to the Ottoman Turks in 1453.

Romanians The descendants of the Dacians, the Romans, Vlachs, Slavs and the other settlers in **Moldavia and Wallachia** (modern Romania) who speak Romanian. While the culture of the Slav settlers came to dominate elsewhere in the north Balkans, the Romanians' ancestors assimilated to the Latin culture of the earlier Romanized inhabitants. Under the Ottomans (15–19c), the Romanians began their movement for national independence in the 1820s, aspiring to the unification of Moldavia, Wallachia and **Transylvania**. The Romanians of Moldavia and Wallachia were united under one **hospodar** (governor) in 1859 and received full independence from the **Ottoman Empire** in 1881. Not until 1920, however, were the Romanians in Transylvania joined to the Kingdom of Romania by the Treaty of Trianon (1920). ▷ **Bessarabia; Bukovina; Dacia; Dobrudja; Oltenia; Regat; Supplex Libellus Valachorum**

Roman Monarchy (753–509BC) Founded, according to tradition, in 753BC, Rome was initially ruled by kings, of whom Romulus was the first and **Tarquinius Superbus** the seventh and last. Expelled in 509BC because of his tyrannical ways, the latter left the Romans with a long-abiding hatred of monarchy. ▷ **Romulus and Remus**

Romanov, Grigori Vasilevich (1923–) Soviet politician. The son of a Novgorod peasant, he educated himself as a shipbuilding engineer at night classes and by correspondence. It was 1955 before he agreed to be a party functionary, but by 1970 he was in charge of the Leningrad party as First Secretary and by 1976 in the **Politburo**. Yuri **Andropov** made him a secretary of the Central Committee in 1983, a jumping-off platform for the general secretaryship, but he lacked Mikhail **Gorbachev**'s skill and commitment to change and was simply brushed aside for the party succession in 1985.

Romanov Dynasty The second (and last) Russian royal dynasty (1613–1917). The first Romanov tsar, Mikhail, was elected in 1613 after the **Time of Troubles**. The Romanovs soon ruled as virtually absolute autocrats, allowing no constitutional or legal checks on their political power. Even when **Nicholas II** conceded the establishment of a national assembly or **Duma** in 1905, he allowed it little

power in practice. The dynasty ended with Nicholas II's abdication in Feb 1917, and his execution by Bolshevik guards in July 1918. ▷ **Alexander I; Catherine II, 'the Great'; February Revolution** (Russia); **Nicholas I** (of Russia); **Peter I, 'the Great'; Revolution of 1905; Russian Revolution**

Roman Question After the creation of a united Italian state in 1861, two substantial areas remained outside the kingdom: Venetia (which was acquired by war in 1866) and those areas of the **Papal States** not seized in 1860. The question of the acquisition of the latter came to be known as the 'Roman Question'. Two factors complicated the situation. The first was the loyalty felt by many Italians to the Catholic Church and their consequent reluctance to use force to wrest the Eternal City from papal rule. The second was the presence since 1849 of a French garrison defending the Pope, meaning any attack would result in a clash with France. Initial attempts to acquire Rome in 1860–1 hinged on negotiation and offers of purchase, but eventually it was taken by force (1870), when the French troops were withdrawn for use in the **Franco-Prussian War**. Even after Rome's annexation, the problem was not resolved since **Pius IX**, already hostile to the Italian state which had first annexed much of his territory in 1860, became even more intransigent in his position that good Catholics should not recognize the Italian state or take any part in its politics. Tensions were to remain between Church and state until the **Lateran Pacts** of 1929. ▷ **Aspromonte, Battle of; Mentana, Battle of**

Roman Republic (509–31BC) Brought into being with the overthrow of the **Roman Monarchy**, the Republican system of government was designed to prevent a tyrant ever ruling Rome again. Executive power was entrusted to two annually elected officials (consuls); their advisory council, the Senate, an ex-officio body of magistrates, provided the necessary elements of experience and continuity. The system brought stability, and Rome grew rapidly from a small city-state into an empire. The **Punic Wars** brought the western Mediterranean under her control, while the campaigns against the rulers of the Hellenistic world added Macedon, Greece, Asia Minor, and the Levant. But the system which had served the city-state so well could not cope with the government of this Empire. The Republic perished at the Battle of **Actium** (31BC) after decades of civil war in which great warlords

1	Spoletium
2	Sora
3	Fregellae
4	Interamna
5	Beneventum
6	Signia
7	Norba
8	Narnia
9	Nepete
10	Sutrium
11	Sinuessa
12	Luceria

Roman territory in 298BC at the beginning of the Third Samnite War

Area under Roman control in 264BC at the beginning of the First Punic War

Extent of Roman power in 201BC after the Second Punic War

✕ Battle

Principal colonies, mid-2c BC :

◆ Roman colonies

■ Latin colonies

● Rome in 509BC

★ Capture of Veii (396 BC)

Roman conquest of Italy

such as Julius **Caesar**, **Pompey the Great**, Mark **Antony**, and Octavian fought for supreme power.

Romanus I Lecapenus (c.872–948) Byzantine Emperor (920/44). The son of an Armenian peasant, he was to prove one of the most astute and effective Byzantine emperors. He contrived to outmanoeuvre Emperor **Simeon** of Bulgaria, whose aim was nothing less than the establishment of an empire which would take the place of that of Byzantium; a man of some perspicacity, Romanus, while pursuing a course largely characterized by compromise, never lost sight of his own aims. This resulted in the acceptance, almost imperceptibly, of Byzantine influence in Bulgaria, the establishment of Romanus as 'senior' emperor and the setting up of his own dynasty, all by non-

violent methods, especially notable being his alliance of the legitimate dynasty to himself by ties of kinship. He also demonstrated considerable acumen as a legislator particularly in his measure for the protection of smallholders, the erosion of whose landed rights through purchase by the rich constituted a major danger for the Byzantine state. Threatened late in life by his sons, Stephen and Constantine, Romanus was forced into exile as a monk. This miscalculation by the younger Lecapeni rebounded on them by opening the way for a legitimist reaction in Byzantium and the resultant preferment of **Constantine VII Porphyrogenitus**.

Rome, Sack of (1527) The storming of the papal capital by the unpaid imperial mercenaries used by Emperor **Charles V** in the **Italian Wars**. Pope **Clement VII** had deserted

806

the Habsburg cause and joined the League of Cognac after the Battle of Pavia (1525), and the full wrath of his erstwhile allies was unleashed in the massacre of an estimated 8000 civilians and widespread plunder. Clement escaped from the city and, after signing a treaty with Charles, fled to Orvieto. This was an event so shattering that in many ways it can be said to have brought the Italian **Renaissance** to an end.

Rommel, Erwin (Johannes Eugen) (1891–1944) German field marshal and Nazi sympathizer. Educated at Tübingen, he fought in **World War I** and taught at Dresden Military Academy. He commanded **Hitler**'s headquarters guard during the early occupations, and led a Panzer division during the 1940 invasion of France. He then commanded the **Afrika Corps**, where he achieved major successes. Eventually driven into retreat by a strongly reinforced 8th Army, the 'Desert Fox' was withdrawn, a sick man, from North Africa, and appointed to an Army Corps command in France. Returning home wounded in 1944, he condoned the plot against Hitler's life. After its failure and his implication in it, he committed suicide at Herrlingen. ▷ **El Alamein, Battle of; World War II**

Romulus and Remus In Roman legend, the twin sons of Mars and the Vestal Virgin Rhea Silvia; an example of an invented myth, to explain the name of the city. They were thrown into the River Tiber, which carried them to the Palatine, where they were suckled by a she-wolf. In building the wall of Rome, Remus made fun of the work and was killed by Romulus or one of his followers. Having founded Rome, Romulus was later carried off in a thunderstorm.

Romulus Augustulus (5c) Roman Emperor (475/6). Elevated to the throne by his father, the army commander Orestes, Romulus is remembered solely because he happened to be the last Roman emperor of the West. Deposed by the German leader, **Odoacer**, his life was spared because of his extreme youth and he was pensioned off to southern Italy.

Roncesvalles, Battle of (778) An incident of the **Reconquest**, when part of the rearguard of the Emperor **Charlemagne** was wiped out in the Pass of Roncesvalles by Pyrenean forces aided by Muslim troops. Various versions of the story later took the form of the *Song of Roland*, a key narrative in the literature of chivalry which became popular in the Iberian Peninsula.

Roon, Albrecht (Theodor Emil), Graf von ('Count of') (1803–79) Prussian Army officer. He became War Minister (1859–73), and with **Bismarck**'s support effectively reorganized the army, which helped make possible Prussian victories in the Danish, Austrian, and Franco-Prussian Wars of the 1860s and 1870s. ▷ **Austro-Prussian War; Danish-German War; Franco-Prussian War; Prussia**

Roose, Pieter (1586–1673) Southern Netherlands politician. He trained as a lawyer and was appointed to the Secret Council (*Geheime Raad*) of the Spanish Netherlands in 1622. From 1627 to 1631 he was a member of the High Council for Flanders and Burgundy in Madrid, and had the ear of King **Philip IV** of Spain. In 1632 he was President of the Secret Council, and after restoring Spanish power in the southern Netherlands, exercised it there in the later 1630s. He was relieved of his office in 1653.

Roosevelt, (Anna) Eleanor (1884–1962) US humanitarian and diplomat. The niece of Theodore **Roosevelt** and wife of Franklin D **Roosevelt**, she became active in politics during her husband's illness from polio and proved herself invaluable to him as an adviser on social issues when he became President. In 1941 she became Assistant Director of the Office of Civilian Defence and after her husband's death in 1945 extended the scope of her activities, becoming a US delegate to the UN Assembly (1945–53, 1961), chairman of the UN Human Rights Commission (1946–51), and US representative to the General Assembly (1946–52).

Roosevelt, Franklin D(elano) ('FDR') (1882–1945) US politician and 32nd President, the fifth cousin of Theodore **Roosevelt**. He became a lawyer (1907), a New York State Senator (1910–13), and Assistant Secretary of the Navy (1913–20), and was Democratic candidate for the vice-presidency in 1920. Stricken with polio in 1921, he recovered partial use of his legs and went on to become Governor of New York (1929–33). During his first 'hundred days' as President (1933–45), he bombarded the economic crises with his **New Deal** for national recovery (1933), and became the only President to be re-elected three times. At the outbreak of **World War II** he strove to avoid US involvement and instead provided economic resources to the Allies in the form of a 'lend-lease' agreement, but Japan's attack on **Pearl Harbor** (1941) left him no choice and the US entered the war. He met with **Churchill** and **Stalin** at the **Tehran Conference** (1943) and **Yalta Conference** (1945) to formulate post-war plans, including the **UN**, but died three weeks before the German surrender. Throughout his presidency, his wife, Eleanor **Roosevelt**, was active in human rights and after his death became the US delegate to the **UN**.

Roosevelt, Theodore ('Teddy') (1858–1919) US politician and 26th President. Educated at Harvard, he became a member of the New York legislature (1881–84). In 1898 he raised a volunteer cavalry of cowboys and college athletes known as the **Rough Riders** in the **Spanish–American War**. Upon his return he was elected Governor of New York State (1898–1900). A Republican, he was elected Vice-President in 1900, became President on **McKinley**'s assassination (15 Sep 1901), and was re-elected in 1904. During his presidency (1901–9), he strengthened the navy, initiated the construction of the Panama Canal, and introduced a '**Square Deal**' policy for enforcing anti-trust laws. He received the Nobel Peace Prize in 1906 for his mediation during the **Russo-Japanese War** (1904–5). As organizer of the **Progressive Party** as well as its candidate for the presidency in 1912, he was defeated by **Wilson**. ▷ **New Nationalism; Republican Party**

Roosevelt Corollary (1904) Amendment to the **Monroe Doctrine** enunciated by Theodore **Roosevelt** which stated that the USA had a duty to prevent political instability and financial mismanagement in the countries of its Caribbean 'backyard'. In its crudest form it was a justification for Roosevelt's 'big stick' and **Taft**'s 'dollar diplomacy' policies, and sanctioned US military intervention in Haiti (1915–34) and the Dominican Republic (1916–24). Such interference was theoretically reversed by F D **Roosevelt**'s 'good neighbour' policy of 1934 but this has not precluded further overt and covert interventions in Guatemala (1954), Cuba (1961), Dominican Republic (1965), Nicaragua (1979–87), Grenada (1983) and Panama (1989).

Root, Elihu (1845–1937) US politician and international lawyer. Educated in New York, he became a lawyer, US Secretary of War (1899–1904), and Secretary of State (1905–9). He helped to establish civilian government in Puerto Rico, as well as governing policies for Cuba and the Philippines. A supporter of the League of Nations and the development of the World Court, he was awarded a Nobel Peace Prize in 1912 for his promotion of international arbitration.

Rosas, Juan Manuel de (1793–1877) Argentine dictator. The son of an *estanciero*, he himself became an enterprising rancher and exporter of salted beef, with a loyal following among the *gauchos* on his lands. Rising to prominence as a federalist leader, he acted as Governor of Buenos Aires and *de facto* ruler of Argentina from 1829 until 1852, except for a brief interval in 1832–3. His regime was a form of personal terrorism, and witnessed a dramatic concentration of estanciero landholdings among major merchant families in Buenos Aires. Anti-foreign sentiment was encouraged, and Rosas' actions against local nationals and their interests resulted in an Anglo-French naval blockade in 1845–50. By 1850, opposition to his rule had coalesced around Urquiza, Governor of Entre Rios, while a generation of exiles, including **Mitre**, **Sarmiento** and **Alberdi** demanded modernization. Defeated by a force drawn from Brazil and the interior provinces at Monte Caseros in Feb 1852, he died in exile in England. ▷ **estancia; gaucho**

Rosebery, Archibald Philip Primrose, 5th Earl of (1847–1929) British politician. He succeeded to the earldom in 1868, and after holding various educational and political posts, became Foreign Secretary (1886 and 1892–4) under **Gladstone**, whom he briefly (1894–5) succeeded as Premier before the Liberals lost the election of 1895. He was noted for his racehorse stables, and in his later years as a biographer of British statesmen. ▷ **Liberal Party** (UK)

Rose-Innes, Sir James (1855–1942) South African judge. Educated at the University of the Cape of Good Hope, he became Attorney-General (1890–93 and 1900–02), and then Judge President (later Chief Justice) of the Supreme Court of the Transvaal (1902–10), Judge of Appeal (1910–14), and Chief Justice of the Union of South Africa (1914–27). He advocated a liberal policy towards the Africans and, as head of a strong bench, was probably the greatest of all South African judges. His opinions are notable for their clarity and their willingness to rely on both the English and Roman-Dutch traditions in South African law.

Rosenberg, Alfred (1893–1946) German Nazi ideologue. A fervent advocate of national socialism, he joined the **Nazi Party** in 1920, edited Nazi journals, for a time (1933) directed the party's foreign policy, and in 1934 was given control of its cultural and political education policy. In his *The Myth of the 20th Century* (1930) he expounded the extreme Nazi doctrines which he later put into practice in eastern Europe, for which crime he was hanged at Nuremberg in 1946. ▷ **Nuremberg Trials**

Rosenberg Affair (1953) US treason trial. Julius and Ethel Rosenberg were found guilty, like Klaus Fuchs in Britain, of passing atomic bomb secrets to the USSR. The worth of the information they had passed to the Russians was dubious and the sentence of death passed by Judge Irving Kaufman was more a measure of US fears of **communism** and the anger felt at betrayal than a judicial decision. The Rosenbergs' prison letters aroused great sympathy in Europe, and their execution compounded the fears aroused by McCarthyism. ▷ **McCarthy, Joseph**

Roses, Wars of the (1455–85) A series of civil wars in England, which started during the weak monarchy of King **Henry VI**; named from the emblems of the two rival branches of the House of Plantagenet, York (white rose) and Lancaster (red rose) — a symbolism which was propagated by the Tudor Dynasty (1485–1603), which united the two roses. The wars began when Richard, Duke of York, claimed the protectorship of the crown after the King's mental breakdown (1453–4), and effectively ended with Henry Tudor's defeat of **Richard III** at Bosworth (1485). The armies were small, and the warfare intermittent, although marked by brutal executions. The wars were not purely dynastic in origin, and were exacerbated by the gentry and by aristocratic feuds, notably between the Neville and the **Percy** Family, and by the unstable 'bastard feudal' system, in which relations among landed élites were increasingly based upon self-interest — a system that the Tudors sought to control. ▷ **Henry VII; Lancaster, House of; Plantagenet Dynasty; Tudor, House of; York, House of**

Rosetti, Constantin A (1816–85) Romanian politician, nationalist leader and journalist. In 1848, he led the radical Liberals during the period of political agitation and was General-Secretary of the Provisional Government (June 1848). He fled to Paris where he was active in Romanian revolutionary organizations and founded two Romanian newspapers (1850–1). He returned home in 1857 and took part in the *divan ad hoc*. He attacked Alexander **Cuza** for being too autocratic and made an alliance with Ion **Brătianu** for the purpose of ousting the former. During the **interregnum** he was Minister of Education and, under Brătianu, Minister of the Interior (1878 and 1881–2). ▷ **Moldavia and Wallachia; Romanians**

'Rosie the Riveter' US epithet. The generic name given to US women employed in defence production during **World War II**. By 1944, over 50 per cent of workers in aircraft manufacture and shipbuilding were women and the number of married women in work had increased from around 15 per cent to almost 25 per cent. Their level of performance, in jobs for which they had previously been considered unsuitable, was so high that attitudes towards women in work were permanently altered.

Rossbach and Leuthen, Battles of (5 Nov and 6 Dec 1757) The battles took place in the **Seven Years War**. At Rossbach, Prussia defeated Austrian and French forces. A month later, at Leuthen (Lutynia), Prussian forces routed a much larger Austrian army.

Rossi, Pellegrino, Count (1787–1848) Economist and politician. Forced to leave Italy in 1815 because of his sympathies for Joachim **Murat**, he settled first in Geneva and then in France, where he was elected to the Upper House of the French Chamber (1839). In 1845 Guizot sent him as ambassador to Rome where he arrived just after the death of Gregory XVI. He encouraged the new Pope, **Pius IX**, to undertake liberal reforms and (Sep 1848) became his Prime Minister at the head of a constitutional government but was assassinated by Roman radicals in Nov of the same year.

Rostopchin, Feodor Vassilievich, Count (1763–1826) Russian soldier, statesman and writer. He won great influence over the unbalanced Tsar **Paul I** and was for two years his Foreign Minister. As a conservative, he was out of favour in **Alexander I**'s early years, but as a patriot he regained favour in the war against Napoleon as Governor of Moscow. It was he who may have planned, or at least had a share in, the burning of Moscow against **Napoleon I** in 1812. He wrote historical memoirs and two comedies and other plays, in Russian and French.

Rothschild, Meyer Amschel (1743–1812) German financier. Named after the 'Red

Shield' signboard of his father's house, he began as a moneylender, and became the financial adviser of the Landgrave of Hesse. The house transmitted money from the English government to Wellington in Spain, paid the British subsidies to Continental princes, and negotiated loans for Denmark (1804–12). His five sons continued the firm, establishing branches in other countries, and negotiated many of the great government loans of the 19c. ▷ **Napoleonic Wars**

Rouges French-Canadian political party. The reform party of **Canada East** which began to emerge from the late 1840s as the Institut Canadien acquired branches in the major towns of the province, and as the newspaper, *L'avenir*, spread ideas derived from American republicanism and French radicalism. Under **Papineau**, and after his retirement, A A Dorion, the party grew to be the major opposition to the conservative bloc, seeking repeal of the 1840 Act of Union, universal education for all and a democratic suffrage. Although the rouges opposed confederation, they joined with the **Clear Grits** and cooperated thereafter with the **Liberal Party** in federal politics. Within Quebec their liberalism earned the opposition of the Catholic Church and the ultra-montane **Castors**.

Rouget de Lisle, Claude Joseph (1760–1836) French army officer. He composed the words and music of a battle hymn for the French Army of the Rhine at Strasbourg in 1792. This became the 'Marseillaise', the revolutionary and, eventually, the French National Anthem.

Rough Riders The nickname created by the press for the First US Volunteer Cavalry Regiment, commanded during the **Spanish–American War** (1898) by Colonel Leonard Wood (1860–1927) and Lieutenant-Colonel Theodore **Roosevelt**. The fabled Rough Riders' 'charge' up San Juan Hill in Cuba (1 July 1898) was actually carried out on foot. Roosevelt emerged from the conflict a war hero.

Rouher, Eugène (1814–84) French politician. In 1848 he was returned to the Constituent Assembly, and until 1869 held various offices in the government. He negotiated the treaty of commerce with England in 1860 and with Italy in 1863. In 1870 he was appointed President of the Senate. A staunch Napoleonist, after the fall of the French Second **Empire** he fled abroad. Later he represented Corsica in the National Assembly.

Roundheads ▷ **Cavaliers**

Round Table Conferences (1930–2) A series of meetings in London between British government and Indian representatives to discuss the future constitution of India. It was prompted by the Simon Commission Report (1930) on the working of the 1919 Government of India Act. It helped in the formulation of the 1935 Government of India Act. ▷ **Government of India Acts; Montagu–Chelmsford Reforms**

Rousseau, Jean Jacques (1712–78) French political philosopher, educationist, and essayist. Largely self-taught, he carried on a variety of menial occupations, until after he moved to Paris in 1741, where he came to know Diderot and the **Encyclopedists**. In 1754 he wrote *Discourse on the Origin of Inequality* (1755), emphasizing the natural goodness of human beings, and the corrupting influences of institutionalized life. He later moved to Luxembourg (1757), where he wrote his masterpiece, *The Social Contract* (1762), a great influence on French revolutionary thought, introducing the slogan **'Liberty, Equality, Fraternity'**. The same year he published his major work on education, *Emile*, in novel form, but its views on monarchy and governmental institutions forced him to flee to Switzerland, and then England, at the invitation of David Hume. There he wrote most of his *Confessions* (published posthumously in 1782). He returned to Paris in 1767, where he continued to write, but gradually became insane. ▷ **philosophes**

Rowell–Sirois Commission (1940) Canadian Royal Commission on national economic problems. Appointed by Mackenzie **King** in 1937, the commission was chaired by N W Rowell and, after his resignation in 1938, by J N Sirois. Its remit was to find a way by which the Dominion government, after R B **Bennett**'s New Deal had been declared unconstitutional, could administer federal aid without infringing provincial rights. The commission's report analysed regional economic inequalities in depth and recommended a fundamental revision in the balance of federal and provincial powers. In particular it suggested that the Dominion should take over responsibility for social services (the major area of provincial expenditure), while in return the provinces should cease to levy income taxes and succession duties. A federal-provincial conference called to discuss the report in 1941 was torpedoed by the hostility of Ontario, Quebec and British Columbia (while Alberta had already boycotted the Commission itself), but in 1946 new revenue sharing proposals were accepted by all the provinces except Ontario, which acceded in 1950, and Quebec, which made its own agreement in 1954.

Rowlatt Act (1919) Passed by the British colonial government, the Anarchical and Revolutionary Crimes Act, popularly known by the name of its author, Sir Sidney Rowlatt, made the suspension of civil liberties during wartime by the Defence of India Act of 1915 a permanent feature of India's peacetime constitution. The Act aroused opposition amongst Indian nationalist politicians and caused M K **Gandhi** to organize the first all-India **Satyagraha**, an initially peaceful protest involving strikes, demonstrations and the deliberate courting of arrest, in opposition to the measure. Popular support was widespread, partly because of economic distress but also due to anger amongst the Muslim community at the proposed post-war division of the empire of the Ottoman Sultan, Khalifa, the protector of Islam's holy places in the Middle East and the organization and involvement of India's Sikh community as part of a general movement of religious revivalism in India at this time. Unfortunately, the Satyagraha was accompanied by violent incidents, some of them committed by Ghadrites, which led to the imposition of martial law in the Punjab and the infamous Amritsar Massacre. Shocked at this outcome, Gandhi called the Satyagraha a 'Himalayan blunder', but the real blunder was committed by the British, as clumsy attempts to cover up the massacre and to absolve those involved from responsibility convinced many moderate and reformist Indian politicians (including Gandhi himself) of the impossibility of Indians ever securing justice under colonial rule.

Royal Niger Company A company founded to secure the Niger regions for the British against French competition. British traders on the River Niger had been amalgamated into the National African Company, which in 1886 obtained a royal charter to rule a large part of what later became Nigeria. They secured the navigable portions of the Niger, frustrated the French, and destroyed the power of African middlemen. The charter was wound up in 1898, and the various parts of Nigeria were later amalgamated as a British colony, which achieved independence in 1960.

Roy Manabendra Nath (Narendranath Bhattacharya) (1887–1954) Indian political leader. Involved with terrorist groups against British rule, he was sent in 1915 to request aid from the Germans in Batavia. His mission having failed, he arrived in San Francisco in 1916, where he changed his name. He then went to Mexico, where he helped to found the Mexican Communist Party, and to Moscow, where he became a member of the Executive Committee of the **Comintern**, and founded the Communist Party of India in Tashkent (1920). He broke with the Comintern in 1929 but was arrested and imprisoned on his return to India. After independence, he abandoned **communism**.

RPF; **RPR**; **UDR**; **UNR** ▷ **Gaullists**

RSS (*Rashtriya Swayamsevak Sangh*, 'National Self-Service Society') A militant Hindu cultural organization, founded in Nagpur in the 1930s by K B Hedgewar with help from B S **Moonje**, organized into cells, whose members practise martial arts, and which promotes an exclusively Hindu definition of the Indian nation. By 1940 its membership numbered 100000 under the leadership of Golwalkar. The **Jan Sangh**, a political party which was originally an offshoot of the RSS, is now an independent political party but the RSS provides the Jan Sangh with the most vigorous canvassers at election time. ▷ **Hindu Mahasabha**

Rudolf I (1218–91) King of Germany (1273/91) and uncrowned Holy Roman Emperor. The founder of the **Habsburg Dynasty**, he was the most powerful prince in Swabia when he was elected King of Germany in 1273. He attempted to restore the power of the monarchy by the resumption of lands and rights usurped by the princes since 1245. His victory at **Durnkrüt** on the Marchfeld in 1278 over Ottokar II of Bohemia, who had occupied Austria and Styria, brought him control of these two duchies, which passed to his son, **Albert I**, and became the seat of Habsburg power.

Rudolf II (d.937) King of Burgundy (912/37). He was the son of Rudolf I, whom he succeeded, and father of the Empress St Adelaide. He became King of Italy in 922, but resigned the throne in 926 in return for Provence.

Rudolf II (1552–1612) Holy Roman Emperor (1576/1612). The eldest son of Maximilian II, he became King of Hungary in

1572, and King of Bohemia and King of the Romans (or German King) in 1575. A mentally unstable and incompetent ruler, he was soon faced with revolts, and Hungary, Bohemia, Austria and Moravia were taken from him by his brother, Matthias.

Rudolf IV of Habsburg (1339–65) Duke of Austria. He assumed power at the age of 19 and, excluded from the Electoral College by the Golden Bull, tried to establish Austria's independence by a series of forgeries, the most important of which was the **Privilegium Maius**; these were, however, rejected by the emperor. He built up a number of dynastic links to strengthen Austria's position, founded Vienna University and rebuilt St Stephen's Cathedral in the city.

Rudolf of Rheinfelden (1030–80) Duke of Swabia and German anti-king. He was enfeoffed with Swabia in 1037 by the Empress Agnes, entrusted with the administration of Burgundy and given her daughter Matilda in marriage. After Matilda's death, he married **Henry IV**'s sister-in-law, Adelaide (1066). From 1076 he went over to the papal side and had himself elected King when Henry IV was deposed (1077). He enjoyed little support, though, and was not recognized by Pope **Gregory VII** until 1080. Deposed as Duke of Swabia in favour of Frederick of Hohenstaufen, Rudolf was killed in battle in the same year.

Ruffo, Fabrizio, Cardinal (1744–1827) Cardinal and leader of the army of **Sanfedisti** that overthrew the **Parthenopean Republic** and restored the Bourbon Monarchy in Naples. ▷ **Ferdinand I**

Ruiz Zorrilla, Manuel (1833–95) Spanish politician. As Prime Minister (July–Oct 1871 and Aug 1872–Feb 1873), he reformed the Church, abolished slavery in Puerto Rico, and, on 11 Feb 1873, received the abdication of King Amadeus I. That same day, the First Republic was proclaimed. After the restoration of the monarchy in 1875, he went into exile in France. He continued to defend the Republican cause through military conspiracies, becoming a symbol of Republican idealism in the process. He returned to Spain in 1895, to die. ▷ **Republic, First** (Spain)

Rumelia Literally 'the land of the Romans', this was the name given by the Ottoman Turks to the province which included **Thessaly**, **Epirus**, **Macedonia** and **Thrace**. Divided into timars and later *vilayets*, it was lost to the

Ottoman Turks in stages, beginning with the annexation of **Eastern Rumelia** by Bulgaria (1885). After the Treaty of Bucharest (1913), by which Greece gained Salonica and Serbia Monastir, the Ottoman Porte was left with only Edirne. ▷ **timar**

Rump Parliament The members of the English **Long Parliament** who were left after **Pride**'s Purge of conservative and moderate 'presbyterian' elements (Dec 1648). It numbered about 60, but by-elections brought it up to 125 by 1652. It abolished the monarchy and the House of Lords. When it fell out with the army, **Cromwell** dismissed it (Apr 1653). It was recalled in 1659 with the fall of the **Protectorate**, and dissolved itself in 1660.

Rum Rebellion (1808) An uprising in Sydney which deposed the Governor of New South Wales, Captain William **Bligh**. Led by John Macarthur, a former army officer turned pastoralist, Major George Johnston and officers of the New South Wales Corps, the rebellion occurred because of personal antagonisms, and Bligh's attempt to end the use of rum as a currency. Bligh returned to England but was not reinstated as governor; Johnston was court-martialled and dismissed from the army; and Macarthur, on going to Britain, was forbidden to return to Australia until 1817.

Rundstedt, (Karl Rudolf) Gerd von (1875–1953) German field marshal. He served in **World War I**, and in the early 1930s became Military Commander of Berlin. In 1939 he directed the attacks on Poland and France. Checked in the Ukraine in 1941, he was relieved of his command, but in 1942 was given a new command in France. He was recalled after the success of the 1944 Allied invasion, but returned to direct the Ardennes offensive. War crimes proceedings against him were dropped on the grounds of his ill health. ▷ **World War II**

Rupert (1619–82) Prince and royalist commander in the **English Civil Wars**. He was the third son of the Elector Palatine Frederick V and Elizabeth, daughter of **James VI and I**. A notable cavalry leader, he won several victories in the major battles of the war, but was defeated at **Marston Moor** (1644), and after his surrender of Bristol, was dismissed by **Charles I**. Banished by parliament, he led the small royalist fleet until it was routed by Robert **Blake** (1650). He escaped to the West Indies, returning to Europe in 1653, and living in Germany until the **Restoration**.

Rupert I (1352–1410) King of Germany. Elected King the day after the deposition of King **Wenceslas** by the **Electors** of Mainz, Trier and Cologne, he was crowned in Cologne in 1400. After an unsuccessful Italian campaign (1401–2), he was accepted by the Pope in 1403. Rupert continued to support the Pope in Rome during the **Great Schism**, unlike the majority of the German princes, who supported Alexander IV. His active efforts to strengthen the crown led to opposition from the princes and only his premature death prevented war with the Archbishop of Mainz.

Rush, Benjamin (1746–1813) American physician and political figure. A member of the Continental Congress, he was a signatory of the **Declaration of Independence**. In 1786 he set up the first free dispensary in the US. His method of treatment of yellow fever was controversial, but he did pioneering work with the mentally ill and was the author of *Medical Inquiries and Observations upon the Diseases of the Mind* (1812).

Rush–Bagot Convention (1817) An agreement between the USA and Britain to demilitarize the Great Lakes by limiting the number, tonnage, and armament of ships on each side. The convention ended the threat of a Great Lakes arms race, but complete disarmament on the US/Canada border did not follow until decades later. The parties involved were acting US Secretary of State Richard Rush, and British Minister to the USA, Charles **Bagot**.

Rushdie, (Ahmad) Salman (1947–) British writer. Born in Bombay in India of Muslim parents, he was educated there and in England, at Rugby and Cambridge. He became widely known after the publication of his second novel, *Midnight's Children* (1981). *The Satanic Verses* (1988) caused worldwide controversy because of its treatment of Islam from a secular point of view, and in Feb 1989 he was forced to go into hiding because of a sentence of death passed on him by Ayatollah **Khomeini** of Iran.

Russell (of Kingston Russell), John, 1st Earl (1792–1878) British politician. He became an MP in 1813. He was Home Secretary (1835–9) and Secretary for War (1839–41), and became Whig–Liberal Prime Minister (1846–52) after the **Conservative Party** split over the repeal of the **Corn Laws**. In **Aberdeen**'s coalition of 1852 he was Foreign Secretary and leader in the Commons. He lost popularity over alleged incompetent management of the **Crimean War**, and in 1855 he retired; but he became Foreign Secretary again in the second **Palmerston** administration (1859), and was made an earl in 1861. On Palmerston's death (1865), he again became Premier, but resigned the following year. ▷ **Liberal Party** (UK); **Whigs**

Russell, Lord William (1639–83) English politician. He travelled in Europe, and at the **Restoration** became an MP. A supporter of the 1st Earl of **Shaftesbury**, he was a leading member of the movement to exclude James VII of Scotland and II of England from the succession. He was arrested with others for participation in the **Rye House Plot** (1683), found guilty by a packed jury, and beheaded in London. ▷ **James VII and II; Whigs**

Russia A republic occupying much of eastern Europe and northern Asia. Russia has been settled by many ethnic groups, initially

RULERS OF RUSSIA

Regnal Dates	Name
1283/1303	Daniel
1303/c.1328	Yuri
c.1328/41	Ivan I, 'Moneybag'
1341/53	Simeon the Proud
1353/9	Ivan II
1359/89	Dmitri Donskoi
1389/1425	Vasili I
1425/62	Vasili II
1462/1505	Ivan III, 'the Great'
1505/33	Vasili III
1533/84	Ivan IV, 'the Terrible'
1584/98	Fyodor I
1598/1605	Boris Godunov
1605	Fyodor II
1605/6	'False Dimitri'
1606/10	Vasili IV
1613/45	Michael Romanov
1645/76	Alexei Mikhailovich
1676/82	Fyodor III
1682/96	Ivan V[1]
1682/1725	Peter I, 'the Great'[1]
1725/7	Catherine I
1727/30	Peter II
1730/40	Anna Ivanovna
1740/1	Ivan VI
1741/62	Elizabeth Petrovna
1762	Peter III
1762/96	Catherine II, 'the Great'
1796/1801	Paul
1801/25	Alexander I
1825/55	Nicholas I
1855/81	Alexander II
1881/94	Alexander III
1894/1917	Nicholas II

[1] Co-Tsar

the nomadic **Slavs**, Turks and **Bulgars** (3c–7cAD). The Byzantine Christian Church had been established by the end of the 10c. Moscow was established as a centre of political power in the north during the 14c. The **Tatar** people were expelled under Russia's first tsar, **Ivan IV, 'the terrible'**. Internal disorder amongst a feudal nobility and constant warfare with border countries (eg Poland and Sweden) prevented Russian development until Tsar **Peter I, 'the Great'**. Under **Catherine II, 'the Great'** Russia became a great power, extending its territory into southern and eastern Asia. Defeat in the **Russo-Japanese War** (1904–5) precipitated a revolution which, although unsuccesful, brought Russia's first constitution and parliament. The **Russian Revolution** in 1917 ended the monarchy, and within the communist Union of Soviet Socialist Republics (formed in 1920), Russia was the dominant political force, covering 75% of the Soviet area with 50% of its population. With the disbandment of the Union in 1991, Russia became an independent republic and assumed the Soviet Union's permanent seat on the **UN** Security Council. Relations with some former Soviet republics deteriorated in the early 1990s, and the process of transition to a market economy caused a severe economic crisis in 1993, followed by a referendum and increased presidential powers. ▷ **CIS; USSR**

Russian Civil War A war which took place in Russia following the 1917 **October Revolution**. Anti-Bolshevik forces (Whites) led mostly by tsarist generals mounted a series of military and political campaigns against the new Soviet regime, supported by the intervention of Allied troops with the support of the governments of Britain, France, the USA, and Japan. They were opposed by the Soviet **Red Army**, created by **Trotsky**, which successfully fought back against them between 1918 and 1922. There were five main theatres of war: the Caucasus and southern Russia; the Ukraine; the Baltic provinces; the Far North; and Siberia. After the end of **World War I**, the military justification for intervention disappeared and the Allied governments eventually lost heart. The Red Army, which increasingly enjoyed more popular support than the Whites, gradually defeated the counter-revolutionary forces on all fronts, and established Soviet military and political power throughout the whole of Russia and its borderlands, with the exception of Poland, Finland, and the Baltic states, which received their independence. Among the legacies of the war was continuing

Soviet–Western mutual suspicion, and the inclusion within the USSR of peoples such as the Ukrainians, Armenians and Georgians, who had tried to regain their independence, which had been lost to Tsarist Russia. ▷ **Bolsheviks; Czechoslovak Legion; Russian Revolution; White Russians**

Russian Constituent Assembly (1918) Russia's first-ever, genuinely representative, constitution-making body. One reason behind the **February Revolution** (1917) was Tsar **Nicholas II**'s autocratic government. What emerged was the **Russian Provisional Government**, which was to hold power until a more democratic system could be decided upon by a representative constituent assembly. This was elected (Nov 1917) on the basis of proportional representation. The **Socialist Revolutionary Party** gained over half of the seats (380 out of 703); the **Bolsheviks** less than a quarter (168). **Lenin** still let the Assembly meet in Jan 1918 in the half-hearted hope that it would legitimize his new government. When it refused on the first day, he dissolved it on the second, thus ending all democratic experimentation for the next 70 years.

Russian Imperial Academy of Science (1725) The summit of the intellectual achievements of **Peter I, 'the Great'**, finally established just after his death. To bring Russia into mainstream Europe, Peter had already set up a School of Mathematics and Navigation, a Medical School and a Naval Academy. The new academy covered four main areas, mathematics, physics, history and art and was the basis for the reputation that scientists built up during the 18c and 19c in sharp contrast to the backward state of politics. The same might be said of its direct successor, the Soviet Academy of Sciences, though that is now the Russian Academy.

Russian Orthodox Church A Church originating in missionary activity on the part of the see of Constantinople and in political interest on the part of Kiev Rus in the 10c. In 988 Prince Vladimir declared Christianity the official faith; in the 14c Moscow became the see of the metropolitan; and in the 15c the Church effectively declared itself autonomous. In 1589 **Boris Godunov** secured a patriarchate for Moscow, thus elevating the Russian Orthodox Church internationally. In 1667 Patriarch **Nikon** managed to reform the church but was himself removed from office. And in 1721 **Peter I, 'the Great'** engineered a Spiritual Regulation that virtually brought the Patriarch and the church under the tsar's control right until 1917. Subsequently the church was separated from the state and suffered considerable persecution. Gaining some recognition as a result of its support for **Stalin** during the Great Patriotic War (1941–5), it was still largely controlled by government agencies. In the mid-20c there was some revival of interest in the church on the part of the intelligentsia, conscious of the role it formerly played in Russian art and culture. The contemporary Russian Church retains its former doctrine and liturgy, but since **Gorbachev**'s time and the collapse of **communism** it has become more popular, not least among young people.

Russian Provisional Government (1917) The government that was supposed to rule Russia until the **Russian Constituent Assembly** could produce a legitimate alternative, although its interim approach to revolutionary events flawed it from the start. It discussed minor issues, rather than making the big decisions that were required. It also lacked military power, was constantly opposed by the **Soviets**, and was too slow to move from modest liberal to reasonable centrist. In the end, it was swept away by **Lenin** and his **Bolsheviks**.

Russian Revolution (1917) The revolution which overthrew the Russian imperial regime and brought to power the first communist government. Mass demonstrations of discontented and revolutionary workers and soldiers in Petrograd led to the abdication of **Nicholas II** in Feb 1917. There followed a period of power-sharing between a liberal-minded provisional government and the more socialist Petrograd Soviet, known as 'dual power'. **Lenin**'s **Bolsheviks** soon refused to collaborate, and in Oct led an insurgency of armed workers, soldiers and sailors, removing the provisional government, seizing political power and establishing the first Soviet government. This very quickly shaped the revolution to its own Leninist/Stalinist prescription. ▷ **April Theses; February Revolution; July Days; Mensheviks; October Revolution**

Russian Serfs, Emancipation of (1861) The abolition by Tsar **Alexander II** of the legal possibility of anyone owning serfs. A crucial, but belated, reform in Russia, this emancipated about 20 million serfs (half the population) from their landlords, thus signalling the beginning of Russia's transition from a feudal to a capitalist economy.

Frequently ill-treated, the serfs formed an increasingly uneconomic labour force and they fought badly in the **Crimean War**. The new tsar had little alternative but to free them, and in any case he was afraid of a massive peasant rising. However, although the emancipation manifesto freed the serfs from their human bondage, the liberated peasants were organized into communes (**mir**) and obliged to find so-called redemption payments for the little land they received. This meant that economic bondage continued and, with it, economic backwardness and social discontent. It was not until the Russian **Revolution of 1905** that the payments were cancelled.

Russo-Finnish War (Winter War) (1939–40) The war between the USSR and Finland during the winter of 1939–40. Soviet forces invaded Finland in order to secure Finnish territory from which to defend Leningrad against a possible German attack. In spite of courageous and damaging Finnish resistance and early Russian bungling and because of lack of support from Britain and France, Finland capitulated (Mar 1940) and was forced to cede valuable territory to the USSR. ▷ **Continuation War; World War II**

Russo-Japanese War (1904–5) The war between an expanding Russian Empire and a modernizing Japan over rival territorial claims and imperial ambitions in northern China. Tsar **Nicholas II** and most of his ministers were keen on a war that they expected to win and that they hoped would divert attention from internal unrest, but it turned out to be a series of military and naval disasters for Russia; it had little popular support, and was marked by ineffectual command and political confusion. The war ended in Japanese victory with the Treaty of **Portsmouth** (1905). It also precipitated the Russian **Revolution of 1905**.

Russo-Turkish Wars A series of wars between an expanding Russian and a decaying Ottoman empire from the 17c to the 19c, principally for domination of the Black Sea and access to the Mediterranean. From the mid-18c they also involved national liberation struggles of the non-Turkish, Orthodox Christian peoples of the Balkans from Turkish, Islamic rule. As a result of the wars (the last in 1877–8), much of the northern Black Sea coast and the Caucasus was incorporated into the Russian Empire and the greater part of the Balkans gained its independence or was set firmly on the road to independence. ▷ **Ottoman Empire**

Ruthenia, Emergence and Disappearance of (1918–45) An ethnically mixed area of about half a million people, moved through four countries' control in a quarter of a century. In 1918 Ruthenia was part of Austria-Hungary but was summarily transferred to the new Czechoslovakia. Between Sep 1938 and Mar 1939 it hovered uncertainly on the brink of independence, which it enjoyed for a few days, before it passed to Hungary. In 1945 it was transferred to the Ukraine, part of the USSR. Its population was 60 per cent Ruthenian, related to Ukrainians, but it had Slovak and Hungarian minorities (and Polish). It was neither Catholic nor Orthodox, but Greek Catholic (Uniate). Small and divided, its fate was decided by crude power politics. Post-1991, it provided some of the internal drive towards the separation of the Ukraine from Russia.

Ruusbroec, Jan van (1293–1381) Southern Netherlands mystic. He worked as a priest in Brussels from 1317, but in 1344 left to live in the woods south of the city in the Groenendaal valley. In 1350 he became Prior of an order of Augustinians there, the Congregation of Groenendaal, which was a formative influence on the Modern Devotion. Van Ruusbroec's writings were well known even in his lifetime, and were characterized by his allegorical symbolism and his distinction between the holy and the profane life.

Ruyter, Michiel Adriaanzoon de (1607–76) Dutch admiral. He gave distinguished service in the **Anglo-Dutch Wars** of 1652–4, 1665–7 and 1672–8, winning notable victories in the Four Days' battle off Dunkirk (1666) and a daring raid up the Rivers Medway and Thames (Dutch descent on Chatham, 1667), in which much of the English fleet was destroyed. In the third war, his victories prevented a seaborne invasion of the United Provinces, but he was mortally wounded in a battle against the French off Sicily. ▷ **Chatham, Dutch Descent on**

Ryan, Claude (1925–) Canadian politician. Replacing Robert **Bourassa** as the Quebec **Liberal Party** leader after the defeat of 1976, he was largely responsible, with Jean **Chrêtien**, for the successful campaign against secession in **Lévesque**'s referendum of 1980. However, his own suggestions for a decentralized federation with a Federal Council

serving as a provincially-based watchdog were not favourably received by anglophones and he resigned the Liberal leadership after defeat by the **Parti Québecois** in the elections of 1981. He has remained a Minister of the National Assembly, and following the Liberal victory in 1985, he was named minister of education in the Bourassa government.

Rye House Plot (Apr 1683) An alleged plot by **Whigs** to murder **Charles II** of England and James, Duke of York, at Rye House near Hoddesdon, Hertfordshire. A counterpart to the alleged **Popish Plot** of 1678, it was foiled by the early departure of the royal pair from Newmarket. The conspirators were betrayed and captured; two of them, Algernon **Sidney** and William, Lord **Russell**, were executed. ▷ **James VII and II**

Ryerson, Adolphus Egerton (1803–82) Canadian educationalist and politician. A Methodist minister and editor of the widely read *Christian Guardian*, Ryerson wielded tremendous influence. He constantly attacked the privileges of the Anglican church, pressing for the secularization and sale of the **Clergy Reserves**, and for the proceeds to be used to support a compulsory school system. A reformer until a visit to England in 1833, he was absent during the rebellion of 1837, and condemned William Lyon **Mackenzie**'s radicalism and readiness to use force. He opposed **Responsible Government**, supporting Sir Charles **Metcalfe** in the struggle with Robert **Baldwin** and **Lafontaine**, who suspected that he had joined the **Tories**. In 1844 he was appointed chief superintendent of education in Canada West, a post he held until 1876 and in which he established the educational system of Ontario.

Rykov, Alexei Ivanovich (1881–1938) Russian revolutionary and Communist Party and government official. Born in Saratov into a poor peasant family, he was educated at Kazan University and soon became involved in social democratic politics, being arrested, imprisoned and exiled several times. In mid-1917 he was elected to the Moscow Soviet and helped to organize the Bolshevik Revolution there, becoming People's Commissar for Internal Affairs in the first Soviet government. He held a number of senior government posts (1919–36), and was also a member of the **Politburo** (1919–29). But in 1928, together with **Bukharin** and Tomsky, he led the 'right opposition' to **Stalin**'s economic policies and had to give up his Party positions. In 1937 he was arrested for alleged anti-Party activities, and was shot the following year. He was among other prominent victims of Stalin's purges rehabilitated during the **Gorbachev** era. ▷ **Bolsheviks; February Revolution** (Russia)

Ryzhkov, Nikolai Ivanovich (1929–) Soviet politician. A Russian born in the Donetsk region in the Ukraine, he worked as a miner before studying engineering in Sverdlovsk. He then worked his way up from welding foreman in a heavy machine building plant to head of the giant Uralmash engineering conglomerate, the largest industrial enterprise in the USSR. A member of the Communist Party since 1956, he was brought to Moscow in 1975 to work as First Deputy Minister for Heavy Transport and Machine Building. Four years later, he became First Deputy Chairman of Gosplan, and in 1982 was inducted into the Party Secretariat by Yuri **Andropov**, as Head of Economic Affairs. He was made a member of the **Politburo** by Mikhail **Gorbachev** in Apr 1985 and became Prime Minister in Sep 1985, with the task of restructuring the Soviet planning process on the quasi-autonomous Uralmash model. He was not particularly successful in introducing economic change, and living standards declined. In the reform debate that followed in the autumn of 1990, Ryzhkov produced a very modest scheme compared with Stanislav **Shatalin**'s radical plan. Gorbachev opted for a middle course and Ryzhkov was relieved of his post.

S

SA (*Sturmabteilung*, 'Storm Division') German paramilitary league. Founded in 1921, the SA (sometimes dubbed the Brownshirts by virtue of its uniform) served as the paramilitary arm of the **Nazi Party**. In its early years it vied with the Nazi Party for supremacy within the movement and its leader, Ernst **Röhm**, envisaged a military rising against the **Weimar Republic**. However, the failure of **Hitler's Munich Putsch** in Nov 1923 persuaded the latter to seek power through electoral means. The SA was subordinated to the Nazi Party in which role it gave excellent service as a proselytizer, propaganda vehicle, defence league and terrorist organization. Following Hitler's takeover, its 400 000, largely working-class, members were joined by over 2 million recruits, often blue-collar unemployed. Their impatience with Hitler's relative caution in political matters resulted in mounting lawlessness, which their leaders, still resenting their subordination to the party, did too little to control. Furthermore, Röhm openly aspired to replace the **Reichswehr** by the SA and carry the revolution further. All these factors combined to trigger the purging of the SA in mid-1934. After this it played a minor role in the Third **Reich**.

Saarland Territory in south-west Germany, now a **Land** of the Federal Republic. A heavily industrialized region on the north-eastern border of France, the Treaty of **Versailles** placed the Saarland under a **League of Nations** administration and economically at France's disposal. The referendum scheduled for Jan 1935 to decide on the territory's ultimate future witnessed an overwhelming vote for, and a return to Germany. After **World War II** the region was again detached from Germany, being constituted as an autonomous territory under French occupation, but the referendum of Jan 1957 saw the Saarland return to Germany.

Sabah Family The ruling family of the oil-rich Gulf shaykhdom of Kuwait. Founded in the 18c, the current Amir (or Shaykh) of Kuwait is Jabir III bin Ahmad al-Sabah. A protectorate of Britain until 1971, Kuwait has been ruled by the Shaykh through his Prime

Minister, Saad al-Abdullah al-Sabah, the Crown Prince. Most senior posts in Kuwait have been held by members of the ruling family, a matter which has given rise to much discontent not least in the aftermath of the recent Gulf War when members of the ruling family, who had amassed enormous wealth as a result of oil revenues, fled the country on the Iraqi invasion (1990), only to return after the coalition forces had duly expelled the occupying Iraqis and, it would appear, to make few concessions to the political aspirations of the remainder of the population.

Sabines A people of ancient Italy, inhabiting the mountainous country north-east of Rome. Often at war with the Romans, they were ultimately conquered and absorbed by them.

Sabra Palestinian refugee camp on the outskirts of Beirut, Lebanon, created following the evacuation of Palestinians from the city after the June 1982 Israeli attack. It was the scene of a massacre of Palestinians by Christian Phalangists in Sep 1983.

Sacajawea (c.1786–1812) Shoshone Native American, also known as Bird Woman. She was sold into slavery to a French-Canadian trader, who took her with him in 1804 when he joined the US transcontinental expedition of Lewis and Clark. Her participation was vital to the success of the expedition, which established an American presence in the Pacific Northwest.

Sacco and Vanzetti Affair (1921–7) US political *cause célèbre*. Nicola Sacco and Bartolomeo Vanzetti were arrested in 1920, during the Red Scare, for a post office robbery and murder in South Braintree, Massachusetts. During the trial, the prosecutor was allowed to deliver inflammatory anti-communist speeches by the judge, who privately called the two defendants 'those anarchist bastards'. Their conviction and sentence to death therefore caused an uproar throughout the world. In response Governor Fuller of Massachusetts appointed a committee to examine the case. It found that, although the trial judge had been in grave breach of official decorum, justice had been done. The two men died in the electric chair in 1927. Debate on the case continues.

Sachsenspiegel Literally 'Saxon Mirror', the term refers to the most important of the medieval compilations of Saxon law, which was used by many towns as a basis for their constitutions. It was compiled by a knight, Eike von Repgow between 1220 and 1225. Originally in Latin, it was later translated into the vernacular. It is divided into two sections, the first dealing with constitutional, criminal and civil law, and the second with feudal law.

Sacred Wars In ancient Greece, the name for wars involving the oracular shrine of **Delphi**. The First Sacred War occurred c.590BC over the rights of the neighbouring city of Cirrha to levy dues on visitors to the shrine: Cirrha was destroyed and Delphi declared independent. In the Second Sacred War, **Sparta** liberated Delphi from the control of the Phocians; however, Phocian control was immediately restored by the Athenians under **Pericles** (448BC). The Third Sacred War (355–346BC) was also precipitated by the Phocians' seizure of Delphi: their use of Delphic treasures to pay mercenaries prolonged the war but incurred the charge of sacrilege. **Philip II** of Macedon was invited by **Thessaly** and **Thebes** to intervene against Phocis; although initially defeated (353BC), and prevented from penetrating central Greece (352BC), the war resulted in Philip's acquisition of influence in central Greece.

Sadat, Anwar el- (1918–81) Egyptian politician. He trained for the army in Cairo, and in 1952 was a member of the coup which deposed King **Farouk**. After becoming President in 1970, he temporarily assumed the post of Prime Minister (1973–4), after which he sought settlement of the conflict with Israel. He met Menachem **Begin**, the Israeli Premier, in Jerusalem (1977) and at Camp David, USA (1978), in which year he and Begin were jointly awarded the Nobel Peace Prize. Following criticism by other Arab statesmen and hard-line Muslims, he was assassinated while still in office in Cairo by extremists. ▷ **Arab–Israeli Wars**

Sadducees A major party within Judaism (c.2c BC–AD70), the name probably deriving from the priest Zadok, whose descendants held priestly office from Solomon's times. They were mainly aristocrats, associated with the Jerusalem priesthood (with the high priest from among their number), and

influential in Israel's political and economic life. Josephus suggests that they differed from the Pharisees by their denials of the legal force of oral traditions, of bodily resurrection, and of divine determinism.

Sadowa, Battle of ▷ **Königgrätz-Sadowa, Battle of**

Safavid Dynasty The dynasty, possibly of Kurdish origin, which provided the shahs of Persia from 1501 to 1722. Its eponymous founder, Safi al-Din, an Azerbaijani, married the daughter of leader of a Muslim Sufi order. After becoming the order's head in 1301, he gradually developed it into a revolutionary religious movement, the *Safaviyya*, under the hereditary leadership of his descendants, and was based at Ardabil near the Caspian Sea. Its military strength was provided by many of the Turkmen tribesmen of Azerbaijan and eastern Anatolia, who came to be known as Qizilbash ('redheads') from their distinctive headwear. By the end of the 15c the *Safaviyya* had grown strong enough to challenge for political power in Persia, and at Sharur in 1501 Isma'il I (1487–1524) defeated the leading Turkmen confederation, the Ak-Koyunlu ('White Sheep'), and proclaimed himself shah. He proceeded to impose a variety of Islam called Twelver Shiism which has remained the predominant religion of Iran up to the present. Although Isma'il took over a Persian bureaucracy, military power remained with the Qizilbash leaders whose internecine struggles led to civil war in the reign of his son Tahmasp I (1514–76). Their supremacy was not ended until the reign of **Abbas I, 'the Great'**, whose military and administrative reforms constituted a lasting achievement which enabled the Safavid state to survive a series of mediocre successors and pressure from Ottomans and Uzbeks until its overthrow by the Afghans in 1722.

Sagasta, Práxedes Mateo (1827–1903) Spanish politician. He was a member of the **Cortes** from 1855 and took part in insurrections in 1856 and 1866, having twice to flee to France. Seven times Prime Minister (1871–2, 1874, 1881–3, 1885–90, 1892–5, 1897–9 and 1901–2), he introduced a number of reforms including universal male suffrage and trial by jury.

Saguna, Andreiu (1809–73) Romanian political and religious leader. He studied philosophy, law and theology before being ordained priest (1833). During 1848, the year of revolutions, he took a leading role among the Transylvanian Romanian nationalists, becoming their chief spokesman at the Viennese court and presenting their case against the Hungarians. Loyalty to the Habsburg emperor remained his guiding principle and in 1849 he presented a petition for the political and religious autonomy of the Romanians within the Habsburg Empire. He worked for the recognition of the equality of the Romanian people and their two churches and was appointed the first Metropolitan of the ecclesiastical province of Transylvania (1864). His popularity among his own people later declined when he pledged loyalty to Emperor **Francis Joseph** and supported the Austro-Hungarian settlement of 1867.

Sa'id, Nuri al- (1888–1958) Iraqi politician. After military training at the Istanbul Staff College for the Turkish army, he fled to Egypt when his Pan-Arab activities became suspect, taking an active part in the **Arab Revolt** in which he served under T E **Lawrence** and the Amir, **Faysal**. He followed Faysal to Iraq, where he was active in the establishment of the Iraqi army. In 1921 he became Iraq's first Chief of the General Staff and a year later Defence Minister. From 1930 onwards he held office as Prime Minister several times. Strongly pro-British and anti-communist in his sympathies, he fell foul of the Left and, in particular, those with pro-**Nasser** leanings. He was captured at the time of Abd al-Krim **Qassim**'s coup d'état in 1958, and killed.

Sa'id Pasha (1822–63) Ottoman Viceroy of Egypt (1854/63). He granted the concession for making the Suez Canal.

Saigo Takamori (1827–77) Japanese **samurai** leader. He commanded the pro-imperial forces that overthrew the **Tokugawa Shogunate**. One of the most important leaders of the new Meiji government, Saigo resigned (1873) when his proposal for a punitive expedition to Korea to enforce the opening of diplomatic relations was turned down by his more cautious colleagues. He retired to Satsuma, his native domain, and there he became increasingly critical of the government's reforms to create a centralized state and abolish the samurai class. His disaffected samurai followers resorted to open rebellion in 1877 which Saigo, initially reluctantly, agreed to lead. The rebellion, the last significant samurai uprising against the new Meiji government, was suppressed by the new (non-samurai) conscript army

created in 1873, and Saigo committed suicide shortly afterwards. He has remained a popular hero in Japan, the symbol of traditional virtues and resistance against arbitrary government.

Saint Arnaud, Jacques Leroy de (1796–1854) French soldier. Louis Napoleon (**Napoleon III**) made him War Minister (1851–4) and he took an active part in the coup d'état of 2 Dec 1851 that gave Napoleon the crown. He was rewarded with the marshal's baton. In the **Crimean War** he commanded the French forces, and cooperated with Lord **Raglan** at Alma, but nine days later died on his way home to France.

Saintes, Battle of the (12 Apr 1782) A major Caribbean Anglo-French naval action during the **American Revolution**. In that war, France and Spain sided with Britain's rebellious North American colonists and used the British preoccupation with the Americans to obtain naval supremacy and capture British colonies in the Caribbean. In 1782 the British admiral George **Rodney** (who had taken St Lucia in 1778) returned from Europe to shadow the French commander, the Count de Grasse, who was planning to attack Jamaica with 35 warships. Battle was joined off the Saintes (the small rocky islets between Dominica and Guadeloupe) on 12 Apr and, after a day of heavy fighting, de Grasse, his flagship, the *Ville de Paris*, and six other ships were captured by the British. Rodney was hailed as the saviour of Jamaica.

Saint-Just, Louis (Antoine Léon Florelle) de (1767–94) French revolutionary. He wrote poetry and essays, notably *L'Esprit de la révolution* (1791). He was elected to the National Convention (1792), attracted notice by his fierce tirades against **Louis XVI**, and as a devoted follower of **Robespierre** was sent on diplomatic and military missions. He joined the Committee of **Public Safety** (1793), contributing to the destruction of **Danton** and **Hébert**. He became President of the National Convention (1794), and sponsored the radical Ventôse Laws, redistributing property to the poor. He was guillotined with Robespierre in the Thermidorian Reaction. ▷ **Convention, National; French Revolution; Thermidor**

Saint Laurent, Louis Stephen (1882–1973) Canadian lawyer and politician. In 1914 he became Law Professor at Laval University and was appointed counsel to the **Rowell–Sirois Commission** between 1937 and 1940. In

1941 Mackenzie **King** appointed him Minister of Justice and, unlike other Quebec Liberals, he supported King on conscription in 1944, for which he was made Secretary of State for External Affairs in 1946. King's own choice as his successor, Saint Laurent became Prime Minister in 1948, and enacted such social programmes as the extension of the old-age pension scheme and hospital insurance. Under his leadership, the Liberals were re-elected in 1949 and again, with a huge majority, in 1953; but he was defeated by the Conservatives under **Diefenbaker** in 1958 after a campaign that focused on the Liberals' arrogance in power.

Saint-Simon, Claude Henri de Rouvroy, Count of (1760–1825) French social reformer and founder of French socialism. He served in the American War of Independence, and during the **French Revolution** was imprisoned as an aristocrat. His writing was a reaction against the great savagery of the revolutionary period, and proclaimed a brotherhood of man in which science and technology would become a new spiritual authority. ▷ **American Revolution**

Saionji Kimmochi (1849–1940) Japanese politician. The son of a court noble, Saionji studied law in France (1871–80) before becoming a member of the Privy Council and House of Peers. In 1903 he became Leader of the largest party in the Diet, the **Seiyukai**, and served two terms as Prime Minister (1906–8 and 1911–12). After 1924, as the sole surviving **genro** (the only one not to have come from Choshu or Satsuma), Saionji unsuccessfully attempted to restrain the military's increasing influence over politics.

Sakharov, Andrei (1921–89) Russian physicist and dissident. In 1948 he joined the nuclear weapons research group, and played a critical role in developing the Soviet hydrogen bomb. He received many honours and was elected a full member of the Academy of Sciences in 1953 at a very early age. While still supporting the USSR's possession of nuclear arms, he began opposing nuclear testing in the late 1950s because of the harmful effects of fall-out, thereafter supporting East–West co-operation and human rights, and in 1975 he was awarded the Nobel Peace Prize. All of this brought him criticism and harassment at home and, exiled to Gorky in 1980 as a leading dissident, he lived under poor conditions until he was restored to favour, somewhat reluctantly, by Mikhail **Gorbachev** in 1987. He was elected to the Congress of People's Deputies in 1989 as a representative of the Academy and was active within it until the day he died of a heart attack. His contribution to the promotion of political tolerance in the USSR and the relaxation of East–West tension was almost unmatched. ▷ **civil rights**

Sakoku The Japanese expression (literally, 'national seclusion') first coined in the early 19c, to refer to the seclusion policy adopted by the **Tokugawa Shogunate** and formalized in five directives issued between 1633 and 1639. The Tokugawa, fearing the subversive political impact of Christianity, excluded Spanish and Portuguese missionaries, persecuted Japanese Christians, and prohibited all Japanese from engaging in foreign trade or travelling abroad. The policy was also designed to strengthen Tokugawa control by preventing the **daimyo** from becoming too economically powerful through the profits of foreign trade. Not all foreign trade was banned, however. Carefully-regulated trade under Tokugawa control was permitted at Nagasaki (for the Dutch and Chinese) and at Tsushima (for the Koreans). It was through contact with the Dutch that Japan acquired a substantial body of Western knowledge during the 18c and early 19c. The seclusion policy was formally ended in 1854, when the Shimoda Treaty with the USA opened two ports to US ships. ▷ **treaty ports**

Saladin (Salah al-Din Yusuf ibn Ayyub) (1137–93) Sultan of Egypt and Syria and leader of the Muslims against the Crusaders in Palestine. Born in Mesopotamia, he entered the service of **Nur al-Din**, Amir of Syria, and on his death (1174) proclaimed himself Sultan, reduced Mesopotamia, and received the homage of the Seljuk princes of Asia Minor. His remaining years were occupied in wars with the Christians, whom he defeated near Tiberias in 1187, recapturing almost all their fortified places in Syria. A further crusade, headed by the kings of France and England, captured Acre in 1191, and he was defeated. He died soon after at Damascus. ▷ **Ayyubid Dynasty; Crusade, Third**

Salamis, Battle of (480BC) Island off the west coast of Attica, site of the naval victory by the Greek, mainly Athenian, fleet over the Persian forces of **Xerxes**. Consequently Xerxes retreated from Greece with part of his army; however, the bulk of the Persian infantry remained in Greece until defeated at Plataea the following year. ▷ **Persian Wars**

Salan, Raoul (1899–1984) French general. From 1956 he was Commander-in-Chief of the French army in Algeria. In 1958 he played an important part in the crisis that brought Charles de **Gaulle** back to power, and was appointed by him as delegate of the government in Algeria, with full powers. An opponent of Algerian independence, he was brought back to France in 1959, and retired in 1960. In 1961 he joined in an attempted putsch led by General Challe. When this failed, he went underground in Algeria, and launched the **OAS** (*Organisation Armée Secrète*), using terrorist methods in its struggle against de Gaulle's Algerian policy. He was arrested in 1962, condemned to life imprisonment, but later amnestied.

Salandra, Antonio (1853–1931) Italian politician and university professor. Elected a deputy in 1886, Salandra was a right-wing liberal who held various ministerial posts in the Pelloux and **Sonnino** governments. After 1910, he tried to become the focus for moderate and conservative forces, becoming Prime Minister in 1914. Together with Sidney Sonnino he was responsible for Italy's entry into **World War I**, deciding to back France and Britain against Italy's former allies, Austria and Germany, feeling such a policy would bring greater territorial gains. He was replaced as Prime Minister in 1916, but formed part of the delegation to the Paris Peace Conference. He refused to form a government in Oct 1922 and made little effort to oppose **Mussolini**, actually being on the fascist **Listone** in the Apr 1924 elections. After the murder of **Matteotti**, Salandra withdrew his support from the fascists.

Salasco Armistice (9 Aug 1848) The armistice which brought fighting between the Piedmontese army of **Charles Albert** and the Austrian forces under **Radetzky von Radetz** to an end after the Battle of **Custozza**. The peace was not long-standing, Charles Albert declaring war again in 1849.

Salazar, António de Oliveira (1889–1970) Portuguese dictator. From the conservative, devout smallholding peasantry of the north, Salazar's seminary education allowed this reserved and studious individual to become a lecturer in economics at Coimbra, the university of the elite. He was active in a Catholic lay group and stood as a parliamentary candidate under the First Republic on three occasions. His economic expertise led to his ascendancy under the military dictatorship of General **Carmona** (1926–32). During the early 1930s he laid the foundations of the **Estado Novo** which he would dominate as dictator for over 35 years. The authoritarian and supposedly corporatist Salazarist state was underpinned by the army and the feared security police, the **PIDE**. Salazar's retrogressive economic policies made Portugal the poorest country in Europe (in 1960 per capita income was lower than that of Turkey), while greatly enhancing the wealth of its opulent oligarchy. Indeed, Salazar's economic failure made Portugal determined not to give up its African colonies. Yet it was the revolt of the army against the war in Africa against the independence movements (1961–74) that led to the downfall of the regime after his death. Although he fell from power in 1968 through ill health, he died in 1970 still thinking that he was dictator. ▷ **Republic, First** (Portugal)

Saldanha, João Carlos, Duke of (1790–1876) Portuguese politician and soldier. He fought at Busaco (1810), helped Brazil against Montevideo (1817–22) and sided with Dom Pedro against Dom Miguel as a moderate constitutionalist. From 1846 to 1856, he was alternately head of government and in armed opposition. Created a duke in 1846, he was twice ambassador in Rome, Prime Minister in 1870, and ambassador in London from 1871.

Saleh, Ali Abdullah (1942–) North Yemeni soldier and politician. A colonel in the army of the Yemen Arab Republic, he took part in the 1974 coup when Colonel Ibrahim al-Hamadi seized power, with rumours that the monarchy was to be restored. Hamadi was assassinated in 1977 and Colonel Hussein al-Ghashmi took over, only to be killed by a South Yemen terrorist bomb in 1978. Against this background of death and violence Saleh became President. Under his leadership, the war with South Yemen was ended and the two countries agreed to eventual reunion. He was re-elected in 1983 and 1988.

Salem Witch Trials (1692) An outbreak of hysteria in colonial Massachusetts in which accusations were made that witchcraft was being practised. The situation quickly outran the control of the town authorities. Arrests were made on the unsupported testimony of young girls and 19 people were executed. Judge Samuel Sewall later publicly confessed that the trials had been in error and that he believed no witchcraft had been practised. The ramifications of the episode have been attributed to the breakdown of Puritan control, the tensions of economic and social change focused on conflict between Salem Village and Salem Town, and wider provincial fears (awakened by the recall of the charter) as to its future after the Glorious Revolution.

Salians (1) A Frankish tribe, first heard of in the 4c, which took over the leadership of the Frankish kingdom under the **Merovingians**. They are best known for the codification of Frankish law bearing their name, the *Lex Salica*. (2) The royal dynasty which came to power with **Conrad II** and encompassed the reigns of **Henry III**, **Henry IV** and **Henry V**, who was the last in the line. It is not clear whether the name of the dynasty refers to the Frankish tribe, to whom they were undoubtedly related, or whether it derives from the Old High German term *sal*, meaning 'lordship'. ▷ **Franks**

Salic Law In normal usage, a rule of succession to the throne barring women, and men whose royal descent is only through females. The principle was established in France from 1316, partly by ingeniously invoking the law-code of the Salian **Franks**, which was issued c.511 and given definitive form c.798 — Salic Law (Latin *Lex Salica*) in its original sense.

Salisbury, Marquis of ▷ **Cecil, Robert**

Saljuks A family of Turkish mercenary soldiers that rose to prominence and conquered much of Asia Minor in the 11–12c. They were converted to the Muslim faith, and became established as sultans in the area of present-day Syria and eastern Turkey. Their decline in the 13c was brought on by Mongol pressure from the east and their defeat at Kösedagh (1243). ▷ **Mongols**

Salò, Republic of The fascist 'Italian Social Republic' established in the north of Italy under German protection in autumn 1943, with **Mussolini** as its puppet ruler. The republic had no single administrative centre, different ministries being located in different towns eg Public Works in Venice, Finance in Brescia, Propaganda at Salò. It is from the last that it derived its usual name, a reflection of the fact that it was little more than a propaganda exercise, real power being located not in Italy but in Germany.

SALT (Strategic Arms Limitation Talks) The name given to two rounds of talks held between the USA and USSR to limit their nuclear weapons arsenals and slow down the arms race. The first began in Helsinki in 1969, designed to place a numerical limit on intercontinental nuclear weapons. An agreement (SALT I) was reached in 1972. SALT II talks began that same year, and agreement was reached in 1979. There developed, however, a hardening of attitudes in the West towards the USSR, brought on in large part by the Soviet refusal to allow on-site verification. Once the USSR invaded Afghanistan, US Senate ratification of SALT II was doomed. Both countries, nevertheless, initially kept to the limitations established in the agreement. The arms situation was ultimately transformed by the **Reagan–Gorbachev** arms reduction accord, the revolutions of 1989 and the break-up of the USSR in 1991.

Samaria The site in central Palestine of the ancient capital of the northern kingdom of the Hebrews, Israel. Destroyed by the Assyrians c.722BC, Herod the Great rebuilt and enlarged it in the decade 30–20BC. It remained a flourishing Greek-style city throughout the Roman period. It is now in the Israeli-occupied West Bank. ▷ **Assyria; West Bank**

Samaritans A sect of Jewish origin, living in Samaria, the northern territory of Israel, who apparently were not deported in the Assyrian conquest of c.721BC and who were in tension with the Jews of Judea during the rebuilding of Jerusalem after the return from exile and well into New Testament times. Jews criticized them for their mixed ancestry, their building of a rival temple on Mount Gerizim, and their schism from true Judaism. A small remnant survives today.

Samarkand, Capture of (1497) The capture of the old Timurid capital of Samarkand by **Babur**, who was to be the first of the Great Mughal rulers in India, represents the successful assertion of his authority over his kinsmen. Babur had earlier succeeded to his father's position as Mirza of Ferghana, which position his uncles, Sultan Ahmad Mirza of Samarkand and Sultan Mahmud of Tashkent, were attempting to usurp. Although he only held Samarkand for a few months, Babur's success in wresting control of the city from his paternal uncle served notice of his promise for the future.

samizdat From the Russian *sam*, 'self' and *izdatelstvo*, 'publishing', the term refers to privately-circulated editions of books and pamphlets not authorized for publication by the state censorship in the former USSR, and usually reproduced laboriously in typescript. The habit caught on in Poland and other communist countries, and helped to mould critical public opinion.

Samnites A warlike, Oscan-speaking, people of the southern Apennines against whom the Romans fought a protracted series of wars during the late fourth and early third centuries BC. Though defeated in 290 BC, the Samnites continued to oppose the Romans right down to the 1c, their resistance only being ended for good after their crushing defeat by **Sulla** at the Battle of the Colline Gate in 82BC. They then virtually disappear from history.

Samori (c.1830–1900) West African Islamic leader. Possessed of great military talent, he established in the 1870s an empire in the upper Niger region from Sierra Leone to Bamako and south into the modern Ivory Coast. After an initial confrontation in 1883, the French co-existed with Samori for a number of years, but between 1891 and 1894 conquered Samori's empire. Samori re-established himself further east between the Ivory Coast and northern Ghana, but he was captured by the French in 1898 and exiled to Gabon.

Samsonov, Alexander (1859–1914) Russian general. He was in charge of a force in the **Russo-Japanese War** (1904–5). In **World War I** he commanded the army which, in order to take pressure off Russia's French ally, was given the task of invading East Prussia in Aug 1914, but was decisively defeated by **Hindenburg** at the Battle of **Tannenberg** (26–31 Aug). His shame and losses were so great — 100000 prisoners — and his awareness that the last Battle of Tannenberg (Grunwald) in 1410 had been a huge Russian victory over the **Teutonic Knights** so strong, that he committed suicide.

Samudragupta (d.c.375) Northern Indian Emperor (c.335/c.375). With a reputation as a warrior, poet, and musician, he epitomized the ideal king of the golden age of Hindu history.

Samuel (d.1014) Emperor of Macedonia (c.976/1014). It appears that c.976 he became ruler of the small Slav state of Macedonia which had been under the nominal authority of Byzantium since 971. While the Byzantine Emperor, Basil II, was distracted by rebel-

lions in Asia Minor, Samuel set out to increase his territory by conquest. He marched into Thessaly, central Greece and the Peloponnese and into the Bulgarian lands between the Danube and the Balkan Mountains. He took Larissa in Greece (985) but was unable to seize Salonica. By the end of the 10c, he had subdued Dioclea (modern Montenegro) and had marched as far as Zadar. He established his capital at Ohrid and proclaimed himself Emperor. Samuel's progress was halted when the armies of Basil II fell on Macedonia, crushing his forces at Strumica. According to legend, Samuel died from shock when he beheld the sorry spectacle of his returning men who, on the orders of the Emperor, had been blinded, except for one in every hundred who had been left with one eye so that he might lead the others home. ▷ **Macedonians**

Samuel, Herbert (Louis), 1st Viscount (1870–1963) British politician and philosopher. Educated at Oxford, he became an MP in 1902, and held various offices, including Postmaster-General (1910–14 and 1915–16), Home Secretary (1916 and 1931–2), and High Commissioner for Palestine (1920–5), where he pursued a policy of trying to establish a multi-national commonwealth to include the Jews. He was Leader of the **Liberal Party** in the Commons (1931–5), and later Liberal Leader in the Lords (1944–55). He was created a viscount in 1937.

samurai Japanese warrior. Tokugawa Japan (1603–1868) had four hereditary classes: samurai, farmers, craftsmen and merchants (outcasts, or **burakumin**, were not part of this system). Only samurai were allowed to bear weapons, and they carried two swords. They had to serve their **daimyo** masters loyally and follow the warrior's code, **bushido**; in return they received lodging and income. ▷ **Meiji Restoration; Tokugawa Shogunate**

Sandinistas ▷ Sandino, Augusto César

Sandino, Augusto César (1895–1934) Nicaraguan revolutionary. From the mountains of northern Nicaragua, he led guerrilla resistance to US occupation forces after 1926. His success in evading the US forces and the Nicaraguan National Guard generated sympathy for his cause, as well as a significant degree of anti-American feeling. After the withdrawal of the US Marines (Jan 1933), Anastasio **Somoza**, Chief of the National Guard, arranged a meeting with him, apparently to discuss peace. It transpired, however, that this was a ruse: Sandino was murdered, on Somoza's orders, near Managua. The Nicaraguan revolutionary government of 1979–90 (later known as the *Sandinistas*) took him as their principal hero.

Sand River Convention (1852) An agreement whereby the British acknowledged the independence of the Boers beyond the Vaal River. After the Great Trek, the Boers had established a number of communities in the interior of southern Africa north of the Orange and the Vaal Rivers. In 1848 Governor Sir Harry Smith of the Cape proclaimed the authority of Queen Victoria over these territories. Further frontier problems and Boer resistance under Andries Pretorius caused the British to reconsider their responsibilities beyond the borders of the Cape colony. The Sand River Convention was followed within two years by the Bloemfontein Convention, under which the British relinquished authority over the Orange River Sovereignty. The British re-established imperial power over these territories between 1877 and 1881, and 1902 and 1906–7.

Sandžak of Novi Pazar Under the **Ottoman Empire**, the administrative region (*sandžak* or *sanjak*) based around the town of Novi Pazar, now in modern Serbia. After gaining autonomy in 1830, the young state of Serbia soon aspired to the acquisition of the sandžak, but at the Congress of **Berlin** (1878) it was awarded to Austria-Hungary (although it still remained under Ottoman suzerainty). By the Treaty of **Bucharest** (1913), it was divided between the Kingdoms of Serbia and Montenegro and in 1918 it became part of the Kingdom of Serbs, Croats and Slovenes (later Yugoslavia). With the redrawing of the internal boundaries of Yugoslavia at the end of **World War II**, it became part of the Republic of Serbia within the Socialist Federal Republic of Yugoslavia.

Sanjak of Novi Pazar ▷ **Sandžak of Novi Pazar**

Sanfedisti The name, applied in 1799, to the so-called 'Army of the Holy Faith' (*Santafede*) organized by the reactionary Cardinal Fabrizio **Ruffo** to overturn the **Parthenopean Republic** and to restore the Bourbon monarchy. Composed largely of peasants and Neapolitan poor, the irregular bands which made up the Santafede were often motivated by the chance to loot and settle vendettas rather than by genuine loyalty to the Bourbon throne.

San Francisco, Treaty of (8 Sep 1951) The treaty which brought to an end the war between Japan and the 48 other signatory nations. Those other signatories were the nations which had declared war on Japan (with the exceptions of the USSR, the Republic of China (Taiwan) and the People's Republic of China) and those nations which had been created since the Japanese surrender in 1945 in territories which had been occupied by Japan. The San Francisco Treaty brought to an end the post-war occupation of Japan, and marked the restoration of Japan to the community of nations.

Sanga of Mewar (1509/28) Medieval Indian ruler. He was associated with the rise of Mewar during the 16c, which played an important part in the political history of north India. Rana ('King') Sanga, a grandson of Rana Kumbha ascended to the throne of Mewar in 1508, and the following year began to defy the power of Delhi. The Lodi kings were, however, too involved with their own internal problems to bother much about Mewar, and Sanga contemplated an attack on Delhi. He allied himself with **Babur** against Ibrahim Lodi, and agreed to attack Delhi from the south and west, whilst Babur attacked from the north. Trouble from Gujarat, however, prevented Sanga from keeping his part of the agreement and the Battle of **Panipat** ended in victory for Babur. Sanga did not expect Babur to stay in India and rule from Delhi. The alliance broke on this and in 1527 Sanga fought a war with Babur in which he was defeated. After his death, Mewar's power gradually declined to that of a minor state.

Sanger, Margaret Louise (1883–1966) US social reformer and founder of the birth control movement. Educated at Claverack College, she became a trained nurse, and married William Sanger in 1902. Appalled by the tragedies she encountered as a nurse, in 1914 she published a radical feminist magazine, *The Woman Rebel*, with advice on contraception, and two years later founded the first American birth-control clinic, in Brooklyn, New York, for which she was imprisoned. After later completing a world tour, she founded the American Birth Control League in 1921. Divorced in 1920, she married J Noah H Slee in 1922.

Sanguinetti, Julio María (1936–) Uruguayan politician. A member of the long-established, progressive Colorado Party (PC), which had its origins in the civil war of

1836, he was elected to the assembly in 1962, and then headed the Ministry of Labour and Industry, and then Education and Culture (1969–73). The oppressive regime of Juan Maria Bordaberry (1972–6) was forcibly removed, and military rule imposed before democratic government was restored in 1985. The 1966 constitution was, with some modifications, restored, and Sanguinetti was elected President. He took office in 1986, leading a government of National Accord. Sanguinetti's major achievement was the restoration of democracy and human and civil rights. However, the means by which he brought this about — a general amnesty to the military, rather than criminal trials — weakened his popular support. He lost the presidency, in 1989, to Luis Alberto Lacalle of the Blanco Party.

Sanjurjo, José (1872–1936) Spanish soldier. As director of the **Civil Guard** he played an important role in the establishment of the Second Republic in 1931 by refusing to place his forces at the service of the King, **Alfonso XIII**. Nevertheless, he led an abortive monarchist rising against the new regime in 1932. Sentenced to life imprisonment, he was amnestied by the right-wing government of **Lerroux** in 1934. Popular in the army for his down-to-earth style, he accepted the leadership of the Nationalist rising of 17–18 July 1936 against the Republic, only to die on 20 July 1936 in an air crash. ▷ **Republic, Second** (Spain)

Sankara, Thomas (1950–87) Burkina Faso soldier and politician. He joined the army in Ouagadougou in 1969 and attended the French Parachute Training Centre (1971–4) where he began to acquire radical political ideas. As a minister in Saye Zerbo's government, he increasingly came to believe in the need for a genuinely popular revolution to expunge the consequences of French colonialism. Leading a coup in 1983, he became Prime Minister and Head of State and introduced a wide range of progressive policies which made him enemies. Despite his great symbolic popularity among young radicals (outside Burkina Faso as much as inside the country), he was shot during a coup led by his close associate, Blaise **Compaore**, on 15 Oct 1987.

San Martín, José de (1778–1850) Argentine soldier and politician. After military training, he served the Spanish crown against the Moors in Oran (1791), the British (1798), the Portuguese (1801) and the French during their occupation of Spain (1808–13). Rewarded for his distinguished service with high command, he travelled instead to Buenos Aires. In a dramatic change of allegiance, thereafter he played a major role in winning independence from Spain for Argentina, Chile, and Peru. In 1817 he led an army across the Andes into Chile, defeating the Spanish at Chacubuco (1817) and **Maipú** (1818). He then captured Lima, and became Protector of Peru (1821), but resigned the following year after failing to reach an agreement with **Bolívar** over the future of Peru, and died in exile in France. ▷ **Spanish–American Wars of Independence**

San Remo, Conference of (Apr 1920) This conference, attended by representatives of Britain, France and Italy, reached agreement on the Middle East settlement after **World War I**. The agreement covered the peace treaty with Turkey (eventually signed in Sèvres, Aug 1920), and the eventual independence of the Middle Eastern states. However, it also granted interim mandates to Britain over Iraq and Palestine, and to France over Syria and Lebanon (as had earlier been formulated in principle by the **Sykes–Picot Agreement**). Japan, Greece and Belgium were also party to the Conference, but not the USA or USSR.

sans-culottes The French name (literally, 'without trousers') for the mass of the working populace in French towns at the time of the Revolution; it was, however, more specifically applied to small-time Parisian shopkeepers, craftsmen, wage-earners, and unemployed who were politically active. Their demands for food controls and democratic government made them temporary allies of the **Jacobins**. ▷ **French Revolution**

San Stefano, Treaty of (1878) A pre-emptive treaty concluding the Russo-Turkish War of 1877–8. Under its terms Russia gained considerable diplomatic advantages against the other European powers and weakened Ottoman power in the Balkans, particularly through the creation of a large Bulgarian state, ostensibly independent but arguably under Russian influence. Under pressure from Britain and Austro-Hungary, it was superseded by a multilateral treaty at the Congress of **Berlin** (1878), the terms of which were less favourable to Russia, although they guaranteed the independence of a much smaller Bulgaria. Tsar **Alexander II** was particularly upset at **Bismarck**'s false claim to have acted as 'honest broker' in mounting the

Congress in Germany. ▷ **Ottoman Empire; Russo-Turkish Wars**

Santa Anna, Antonio López de (1797–1876) Mexican soldier and dictator. The son of a colonial official, he served in the Spanish army and supported **Iturbide** in the struggle for Mexican independence, although he was one of those who deposed him in 1823. Dubbed the 'Hero of Tampico' because of his role in defending his country against Spanish attempts at reconquest, he was President from 1833 to 1836. Following a revolt in Texas by US settlers and the state's declaration of independence from Mexico (1836), Santa Anna defeated Texan forces at the **Alamo**, but was routed at San Jacinto River, and imprisoned. Dictator in 1839 and 1841–5, he returned to power on two occasions (1846 and 1853) at the head of Conservative groups, from Mexico and Puebla, anxious to preserve their *fueros* from Liberal attack and to preserve central control over the republic. An exile for many years, he was permitted to return to Mexico in 1872, and died in Mexico City. ▷ **fuero; Mexican War**

Santa Fe Trail A trading route from west Missouri through Kansas and Colorado to Santa Fe in New Mexico. The trail was pioneered by William Becknell in 1821, the year of Mexico's independence from Spanish rule. It remained a commercially important route for over 50 years, but declined after the Santa Fe railway was opened in 1880.

Santander, Francisco de Paula (1792–1840) Colombian politician. He took part in the **Spanish–American Wars of Independence**, acted as Vice-President of Gran Colombia (1821–7) during **Bolívar**'s campaigns, and was President of New Granada (modern Colombia) in 1832–7. An opponent of Bolívar, especially regarding the latter's decision to retain Venezuela in Colombia, Santander was the effective founder of Colombia, constructing a unitary regime in which the *fueros* of Church and army were set aside. ▷ **fuero**

Santarosa, Annibale de' Rossi di Pomarolo, Count Santorre di (1783–1825) Piedmontese general and politician. One of the key figures in the Piedmontese conspiracy of 1821 which forced the abdication of **Victor Emmanuel I**, he became the *de facto* head of the Provisional Government established under the regency of **Charles Albert**. After the defeat of the revolution, he emigrated to France and then England. In 1824 he went to

Greece to fight against Turkish rule and died in battle at Spakteria.

Santerre, Antoine Joseph (1752–1809) French revolutionary and soldier. A wealthy brewer, he received a command in the **National Guard** in 1789, took part in the storming of the **Bastille** and was in charge at King **Louis XVI**'s execution. Appointed general of division (1793), he marched against the Vendéan royalists, but, miserably beaten, was recalled and imprisoned. ▷ **Vendée, Wars of the**

Santiago, Order of One of the military orders founded in **Castile** during the **Reconquest**. It was founded in 1170, with a red cross in the shape of a sword as its symbol, and came to possess extensive estates (*encomiendas*), numbering 94 in 1616. Members were in theory subject to semi-monastic discipline. From 1523 the crown of Spain became, with papal permission, head of the order. The order was named after St James, one of the apostles of Jesus, who was said to have ended his days in Spain. From the 9c the alleged discovery of his tomb at Compostela made him the inspiration for the Reconquest, and he was known as Santiago Matamoros ('St James the Moor-Slayer').

Sapru, Tej Bahadur (1875–1949) Indian political leader and lawyer. He studied law and practised as a lawyer in Allahabad. Entered politics in 1907 as a moderate, joined Annie Besant's Home Rule League Movement (1917) and became a member of Lord Reading's Executive Council in 1921. As a member of the government of India, Sapru took the initiative to remove restrictions on the press following the Press Act 1910, and to withdraw the Criminal Law Amendment Act, 1910. He represented India at the Imperial Conference London in 1923 and after M K **Gandhi**'s conviction and imprisonment, resigned from the Executive Council in 1923. At the Round Table Conference in London in 1930, he reiterated the demand for provincial autonomy with responsibility to the legislature at the centre. He was member of the Privy Council in 1934 and was in favour of a new constitution under the Government of India Act in 1935. As a leader of the Non-Parties Conference at Allahabad in 1942, Sapru demanded that Winston **Churchill** declare India's position equal to that of dominions. He was the first President of the Indian Council of World Affairs (1943), a position which he held until his death. He was a Persian and Urdu scholar, with a keen judicial mind free of religious and communal prejudices — one of the greatest statesmen of the Indian freedom movement. ▷ **communalism**

Saracens General term for Muslim forces, particularly during the Middle Ages. The name, which usually referred to Arab or Turkish groups, was used by Christians for all followers of Islam or Islamic subjects of the caliph.

Saratoga, Battle of (Oct 1777) One of the most important engagements of the American Revolution. Actually fought near modern Schuylerville, New York, the battle brought the defeat of a large British army under John Burgoyne by American continental troops and militia under Horatio Gates. The outcome ended British plans to cut New England off from the rest of the states, and encouraged French intervention on the American side.

Sardinia, Kingdom of The Italian kingdom created (1718–20) through the Duchy of Savoy's acquisition of Sardinia in exchange for Sicily. Despite its name, the kingdom's heart remained Savoy and Piedmont: to avoid confusion, it is generally called the Kingdom of Sardinia-Piedmont. During the course of the **Risorgimento**, the kingdom became the driving force behind unification and in 1861 **Victor Emmanuel II** of Sardinia became Italy's first king.

Sarekat Islam The first mass political movement in the Netherlands East Indies (Indonesia), indeed the only mass movement in the colony prior to 1945. Sarekat Islam (Islamic Union) was founded in 1912 by a prominent batik merchant from Surakarta, Hadji Samanhudi, to protect the economic interests of batik traders at a time of increasing organization within the Chinese commmercial community. However, the movement soon moved beyond this narrow aim, attracting a wide range of frequently disparate elements. Indeed, at one time or another during its brief history, virtually every persuasion within the Indies population had come within it, and the membership had grown to more than 2 million in 1919. That figure may mean little. Only a few tens of thousands were in any sense formal members while far more than 2 million were swept along by the movement. At the close of the 1910s, socialist elements achieved a growing influence within Sarekat Islam, provoking a major split with the

Muslim wing. In 1921 the Indies Communist Party (PKI) was forced out of the central organization. However, by the late 1920s Sarekat Islam had largely faded into inactivity. ▷ **Partai Komunis Indonesia**

Sargon II (d.705BC) King of Assyria (721/705BC). He was probably a son of **Tiglath-pileser III**, and was possibly named partly after **Sargon of Akkad**. One of the most powerful of Assyrian kings, he consolidated the empire he had inherited in a long series of campaigns to the north, east, and west of Assyria. He was succeeded by his son, **Sennacherib**.

Sargon of Akkad (fl.c.2370BC) Mesopotamian ruler. He extended his power over the Sumerian cities in Mesopotamia, and established the first large empire of the ancient Near East. He was long remembered as a conquering ruler and a model for later Near Eastern empire-builders.

Sarit Thanarat (1908–63) Thai military and political leader. Educated at the Royal Thai Military Academy, Sarit first saw combat during the suppression of the 1933 royalist Boworadet rebellion. Following distinguished service during the Pacific War, in the post-war years Sarit played an increasingly important role in military politics. He became Commander-in-Chief of the army in 1954, supreme commander of the armed forces in 1957. In Sep the same year, he staged a coup against Phibun. He became Prime Minister in 1958. Sarit ruled in a highly authoritarian manner, dealing harshly with all dissent. He was fiercely anti-communist. However, during his premiership, considerable attention was also given to improvement in the country's infrastructure and the development of the economy. He died in office, leaving behind a great fortune; most of it was confiscated by the government which succeeded him.

Sarmiento, Domingo Faustino (1811–88) Argentine writer and politician. An outspoken critic of the dictator Juan Manuel de **Rosas** and the *caudillo* Juan Facundo Quiroga, he spent much of the first part of his life in exile in Chile (1831–6, 1840–5 and 1848–51), also travelling to Europe and the USA. He later served as Governor of San Juan (1862–4) before becoming, at a time of dramatic change, his country's first civilian President (1868–74). An especially vigorous promoter of education and immigration, he was also a prolific and forceful writer. With

Alberdi and **Mitre**, he was one of the most important architects of modern Argentina.

Sarney (Costa), José (1930–) Brazilian politician. A follower of the UDN Bossa Nova (nationalist) group in the early 1950s, he became ARENA (National Renewal Alliance) Governor of Maranhão in 1965 under **Castelo Branco**. A prominent Senator during the 1970s, he led the Social Democratic Party (PDS) under Figueiredo. Running-mate to Tancredo **Neves** in 1985 on a breakaway ticket, he became President on Neves' sudden death. Saddled with the latter's commitments, but without either the backing or skill to carry them through himself, he drifted from crisis to crisis. His attempt to retain the executive during the 1987–8 Constituent Congress succeeded, but at enormous political and economic cost. He was succeeded in 1990 by Fernando **Collor de Mello**.

Sarrail, Maurice Paul Emmanuel (1856–1929) French soldier. In **World War I** he led the 3rd Army at the Battle of the **Marne** (1914), commanded the Allied forces in the East (Salonica) from 1915 to 1917, where he deposed **Constantine I** of Greece. He was High Commissioner in Syria (1924–5), but was recalled after the bombardment of Damascus during a rising.

Sassanid Dynasty The aggressive Persian dynasty that overthrew the Parthian Empire in AD224 and became Rome's fiercest challenger in the east. They were driven from Mesopotamia by the Arabs in 636. ▷ **Parthians**

Sassou-Nguesso, Denis (1943–) Congolese soldier and politician. After completing his secondary education in the Congo Republic, he joined the army and trained in Algeria and France. An active member of the radical Parti Congolais du Travail (PCT), he was appointed Minister of Defence in 1975 and survived the military coup of 18 Mar 1977 in which President N'Gouabi was assassinated. In 1979, under popular pressure, power was transferred to the PCT and Sassou-Nguesso became President later in the year. Since then, he has moved politically towards the centre, rebuilding links with France and establishing more harmonious relations with the USA.

Sastri, V S Srinivasa (1869–1946) Indian politician. Greatly influenced by Annie Besant, C P Ramaswami Aiyar and Gokhale,

he was the Secretary of the Madras session of Congress (1908). He took an active part in drawing up the Lucknow Pact between the Congress and **Muslim League**, which demanded 'responsive government for India', and was opposed to M K **Gandhi**'s policy of non-violence and non-cooperation. Elected to the Madras Council in 1913, he became a member of the Imperial Legislative Council in 1915 and of the Council of State in 1921. Sastri was a member of the delegation to South Africa which led to the Cape Town agreement, committing the South African government to shelve its Class Area Bill to segregate Indians. He also struggled for the cause of Indians living in Kenya and British East Africa and was President of the Servants of India Society for some years. In 1945, he strongly opposed Muhammad Ali **Jinnah**'s two-nation theory. ▷ **Non-Cooperation Movement**

Satavahana Dynasty An early Hindu dynasty which ruled over the North Deccan (1c BC to 3c AD) prior to the rise of the Gupta Dynasty. The area of origin of the Satavahanas is a matter of some dispute, but while in power they were centred on the Krishna Valley. The Satavahanas had a loose confederation of chiefdoms rather than a centralized empire. Ties were based on kinship and socio-religious connections; the Satavahana rulers were Brahma-Kshatriyas. Their main sources of revenue were products of the land and both regional and international trade. While not a naval power, the Satavahana appear to have taken over much of the coastal and high-seas trading after the decline of Rome's Far Eastern merchant navy. The Satavahana Dynasty saw the rise of urbanism in South India. Although Hindu, the Satavahana were tolerant of both Jainism and Buddhism in order not to prejudice trade with societies of those faiths.

Sato Eisaku (1901–75) Japanese politician. The younger brother of Nobusuke **Kishi**, he was an official in the Ministry of Railways before **World War II**, and was first elected to the Diet in 1949. Indicted for corruption in 1954, he was released in 1956 before completion of his trial as part of a general amnesty celebrating Japan's entry into the UN. During Sato's premiership (1964–72), relations with South Korea were normalized (1965) and US-held Okinawa was returned to Japan (1972). Although the 1960 security treaty with the USA was automatically extended in 1970, a dispute over Japanese textile exports and President Richard **Nixon**'s **normalization**

of relations with China without consulting Japan soured US-Japan relations during the last years of Sato's premiership. It is widely believed that Sato's three non-nuclear principles (non-manufacture, non-possession and non-introduction into Japan of nuclear weapons) earned him the Nobel Peace Prize in 1974.

satrapy The chief territorial sub-division of the Achaemenid Empire, administered by a satrap (literally, 'a protector of the kingdom'). About 20 in number, the most westerly was Ionia and the most easterly Gandhara.

Satsuma A feudal domain in south-west Japan created in the 7c. Designated an 'outside' (*tozama*) domain by the **Tokugawa Shogunate** (ie one which had originally opposed the imposition of Tokugawa rule in 1601), its territory was much reduced in the 17c. **Samurai** activists from Satsuma played a leading role in the overthrow of the Tokugawa shogunate in 1867 and then went on to dominate the new Meiji government along with former samurai from **Choshu**. The Satsuma–Choshu monopoly of power lasted virtually throughout the Meiji period (1868–1912).

Satyagraha Literally 'truth-force', the term refers to M K **Gandhi**'s philosophy of non-violent resistance to evil. It was conceived in South Africa in response to laws discriminating against Asians (1906), and used in campaigns against British rule in India. The approach involved fasting, economic boycotts, hand-spinning, and hand-weaving.

Sava (Sabas), St (c.1174–1235/6) Monk, founder of the Serbian Orthodox Church and member of the **Nemanja Dynasty**. Born Rastko Nemanja, the son of **Stephen I Nemanja**, King of **Serbia**, he took the name Sava upon entering monastic life at Mount **Athos**. There, with the help of his father, he founded the Monastery of Hilandar which became a centre for Serbian culture and religious life. Returning to Serbia c.1208, he became head of the Studenica Monastery and founded a monastery at Žiča. Endeavouring to counter the influence of the **Bogomils** and of the Roman Church, he organized the Serbian Orthodox Church and, with the sanction of the Patriarch of **Constantinople**, he became its first Archbishop in 1219. He made a pilgrimage to the Holy Land and died at Trnovo in north Bulgaria. ▷ Peć, **Patriarchate of; Stephen II**

Savage, Michael Joseph (1872–1940) Australian-born New Zealand politician. In 1907 he emigrated to New Zealand, where he became a moderate trade unionist. He later moved into politics, and helped to found the Labour Party in 1916. He was elected to parliament in 1919 and in 1933 became leader of the New Zealand Labour Party. By cultivating the support of rural interests he secured a win for his party in the Nov 1935 general election, thus becoming the country's first Labour Prime Minister. His popularity grew and he was re-elected in 1938 but died in office two years later, to be succeeded by Peter **Fraser**.

Savimbi, Jonas Malheiro (1934–) Angolan soldier and nationalist. Educated in Angola and at Lausanne University, he returned to Zambia and became a leader of the Popular Union of Angola, being Foreign Minister of the Angolan government-in-exile (1962–4). After a period with the **FNLA**, he broke away to form **UNITA** and fought against the Portuguese until independence. Unable to agree with the leaders of the **MPLA** and the FNLA, he continued the struggle against the MPLA from bases in the south of Angola, supported by South Africa and the USA. A man of considerable charisma, he stood for a democratic and capitalist Angola, but his associations with South Africa and the USA made him a pariah in third world circles. However, the strength of his position and diplomatic bargaining by the USA led to a series of meetings designed to end the civil war and remove the Cubans from Angola. Agreement for a cease-fire and democratic elections was finally achieved in Estoril in 1991.

Savonarola, Girolamo (1452–98) Florentine religious and political reformer. He became a Dominican at Bologna in 1474, and came to be recognized as an inspiring preacher. He became Vicar-General of the Dominicans in Tuscany in 1493, and his preaching began to point towards a political revolution as the means of restoring religion and morality. When a republic was established in Florence (1494), he became its guiding spirit, fostering a Christian commonwealth, with stringent laws governing the repression of vice and frivolity. In 1495 he was called to Rome to answer a charge of heresy. He disregarded the order, was excommunicated in 1497, and burnt in Florence.

Savornin Lohman, Alexander Frederik de (1837–1924) Dutch Protestant politician.

From 1879 to 1921 he sat in the Second Chamber, initially as a member of the Calvinist **Anti-Revolutionary Party** (ARP). In 1884–95 he was also Professor of Law at the Calvinist Free University in Amsterdam. He was the leader of the more conservative tendency within the ARP, and as such objected to A **Kuyper**'s schism from the Dutch Reformed Church in 1886, and his democratic politics; Savornin Lohman therefore led a splinter group away from the ARP in 1894, calling itself the Free Anti-Revolutionary Party, which in 1908 became the **Christian Historical Union**. In 1890–1 he was Minister for Internal Affairs in a confessional government.

Savoy, House of Rulers of the duchy of Savoy, a transalpine area in present-day Switzerland and France, from the 11c to the 19c. Its heyday was from the mid-14c to the mid-15c; thereafter it was hemmed in by French and Spanish monarchies. In the 16c it suffered in the **Italian Wars** and thereafter was often locked in conflict with Calvinist Geneva. The damage of the **Thirty Years War** and the **Napoleonic Wars** added momentum to the process of decline.

'Saw-off' Canadian political manoeuvre. It was used by the Conservative Party during the late 19c in order to deplete the already impoverished Liberal Party's funds. After a particularly close election result, they would file a petition alleging irregularities under the Controverted Elections Act. Given the number of numerically small constituencies, there were many opportunities to use the device. Whether or not the petition was successful, the Liberal Party had to pay. If it was upheld then the election was void, and the expense of another election incurred. If the Liberals won, they still had to bear the legal costs.

Saxe, (Hermann) Maurice, Count of ('Marshal de Saxe') (1696–1750) Marshal of France. He was the illegitimate son of **Augustus II**, King of Poland (formerly Elector of Saxony). He served in the French Army in the War of the Polish Succession (1733–8), and in the War of the Austrian Succession (1740–8) invaded Bohemia, taking Prague by storm. In 1744 **Louis XV** appointed him commander in Flanders, where he won victories at **Fontenoy** (1745), Raucoux (1746), and Lauffeld (1747), and was promoted to Marshal of France.

Saxe-Coburg-Gotha The name of the British royal family, 1901–17. King **Edward VII** inherited it from his father, Prince **Albert**, the second son of the Duke of Saxe-Coburg-Gotha. The obviously Germanic name was abandoned during **World War I** as a means of asserting the 'Englishness' of royalty and playing down the extent of its German blood. ▷ **Windsor, House of**

Saxons A Germanic people from the north German plain. With the Angles, they formed the bulk of the invaders who in the two centuries following the Roman withdrawal from Britain (409) conquered and colonized most of what became England. They were especially prominent in Essex, Sussex, and **Wessex**. ▷ **Anglo-Saxons; Britain, Roman**

Saxony A German ducal and electoral state which experienced many changes of fortune. Prominent from the 9c to the 11c, it was reduced by Emperor Frederick I to two small areas on the River Elbe (1180–1422). Dynastic alliances enlarged the Saxon state on the Middle Elbe in the 15c. Frederick the Wise adopted Lutheranism (1524), establishing Saxony's Protestant leadership, and despite family divisions, it grew prosperous in the 16c. The reign of John George I (1611/56) marked its steady eclipse by Brandenburg, and new duchies (eg Hanover) were formed out of Lower Saxony. Under the Catholic elector Frederick Augustus (1694/1733), Saxony's prestige improved with the acquisition of the Polish crown, but his namesake became a client of Napoleon, only to lose two-fifths of his territory at the Congress of **Vienna** (1814–15). Saxony was merged in the North German Confederation (1866) and the German Reich (1871).

HOUSE OF SAVOY

Regnal Dates	Name
1553/80	Emmanuel Philibert
1580/1630	Charles Emmanuel I
1630/7	Victor Amadeus I
1637/8	Francis Hyacinth
1638/75	Charles Emmanuel II
1675/1730	Victor Amadeus II
1730/73	Charles Emmanuel III
1773/96	Victor Amadeus III
1796/1802	Charles Emmanuel IV
1802/21	Victor Emmanuel I
1821/31	Charles Felix
1831/49	Charles Albert
1849/78	Victor Emmanuel II
1878/1900	Umberto I
1900/46	Victor Emmanuel III
1946	Umberto II

Saya San Rebellion (1930–1) A major anti-colonial uprising in Burma, named after its leader, Saya San. In inspiring rebellion, Saya San utilized both modern political organization at the local level and the millenarian expectations of folk belief, casting himself as the *Setkya-min*, the avenging king in Burman legend. However, the rebellion also took its strength from harsh economic conditions in the rural areas, as the world depression struck Burma, and the burden of colonial taxation borne by the peasantry. In the course of the rebellion, some 3 000 were killed or wounded. A further 350 were executed for their part in the rebellion, including Saya San himself.

Sayyid Dynasty An Indian dynasty that arose in Delhi after the Taimurid invasion in the earlier half of the 15c. The first Sayyid sultan was a nominee of Taimur. The Sayyids kept the **Delhi Sultanate** going until the Lodis took over.

Sazonov, Sergei Dmitriyevich (1861–1927) Russian diplomat and politician. He served in several diplomatic posts in Western Europe before becoming Foreign Minister in 1910. His role was somewhat ambivalent, helping to impose Russian control on Mongolia in 1911–13, encouraging the Balkan powers to turn against Turkey in 1912, and indicating his readiness to go to war with Germany in 1914, while at the same time attempting to restrain the Russian Army and looking for peaceful settlements with both Austria and Germany. In this he simply reflected the Russian dilemma. Although he did everything possible after war broke out in 1914 to secure a Russian victory, he was dismissed by **Nicholas II** in 1916 on the issue of self-government for Poland.

SBZ (*Sowjetische Besatzungs zone*, 'Soviet Zone of Occupation') The territories in central Germany, between the western and Polish-occupied zones, which, in 1949, became the German Democratic Republic (East **Germany**, GDR). For many years thereafter the territory continued to be described by official and other sources in Federal (West) **Germany** as the SBZ so as to question the GDR's legitimacy.

Scalawags US political epithet. A derogatory term for white Southerners who cooperated with occupying forces during the era of **Reconstruction** following the **American Civil War**. Many Scalawags had never favoured secession, and some were principled opponents of slavery.

Schacht, (Horace Greely) Hjalmar (1877–1970) German financier. In 1923 he became President of the Reichsbank, and founded a new currency which ended the inflation of the mark. He was Minister of Economics (1934–7), but in 1939 was dismissed from his bank office for disagreeing with **Hitler** over rearmament expenditure. Involvement with the resistance led to his internment. He was acquitted of war crimes at the **Nuremberg Trials**. In 1953 he set up his own bank in Düsseldorf. ▷ **Nazi Party**

Schaepman, Hermanus Johannes Aloysius Maria (1844–1903) Dutch Roman Catholic priest and politician, journalist and poet. He took holy orders in 1867, and taught church history at the Roman Catholic seminary in Rijsenburg from 1870. As a journalist and editor his work was prodigious: he was editor-in-chief of *De Tijd* ('Time') and later of *Het Centrum* ('The Centre'), as well as being closely involved with several other publications. In 1880 he became the first Roman Catholic priest to enter the Dutch Second Chamber as an MP; he remained one until 1903, and effectively achieved the political emancipation of Dutch Roman Catholics. In 1883 he published a programme which called for Catholics to drop their alliance with the liberals, and to work with the Calvinist **Anti-Revolutionary Party** to achieve their similar aims in the **Schools Question** and in expanding the electorate. This position meant that very few of the Catholic élite, least of all the bishops, supported him. Nonetheless in 1896 he managed to unite all the Dutch Catholic political groups around a single programme based on the 1891 papal encyclical *Rerum Novarum*.

Scharnhorst, Gerhard Johann David von (1755–1813) Prussian general and military reformer. He worked with **Gneisenau** to reform the Prussian Army after its defeat by **Napoleon I**, served as Chief of Staff to **Blücher**, and was fatally wounded fighting the French at **Lützen**. ▷ **Prussia**

Scheduled Castes and Tribes Initially defined by the Government of India Act of 1919 and later by that of 1935, the schedule included all the castes and tribes in India considered by the British to be either of too inferior a social standing in the Indian caste system or too economically backward to be capable of exercising a vote and having a say in local government. Ostensibly, the scheduling of these groups was intended to protect them from exploitation and discrimination, but by insisting that the so-called 'untouchable' castes and those living in India's tribal areas should be represented by officials, the schedule also provided a convenient pretext for packing provincial councils with British nominees. On Independence, the Indian government adopted a universal adult franchise and the scheduled castes and tribes were temporarily forgotten. Soon, however, the government realized that, to carry out its commitment to abolish all social discrimination, it would need to adopt measures of positive discrimination and would have need of a convenient definition of those so disadvantaged. A proportion of all government posts and university and college places was therefore reserved for those from the tribal communities and 'backward' castes, and the 'schedule' of the 1930s was revived. The list of scheduled castes has expanded in accordance with political expediency. In 1991 the attempts to implement further increases in reservation, in line with the recommendations of the controversial 1980 Mandal Commission, led to widespread rioting in northern India and helped to bring down the minority Janata Dal government under V P Singh. ▷ **communalism; Government of India Acts; Janata Dal**

Scheel, Walter (1919–) West German politician. After serving in the **Luftwaffe** in **World War II** he went into business, joined the Free Democratic Party (**FDP**), and was elected to the **Bundestag** in 1953. He was Minister for Economic Cooperation (1961–6) and Foreign Minister (1969–74), and in 1970, as part of the **Ostpolitik**, negotiated treaties with the USSR and Poland. Scheel was President of West Germany from 1974 to 1979. ▷ **Germany, West**

Scheidemann, Philipp (1865–1939) German political leader. A leading member of the Social Democratic Party (**SPD**), he proclaimed the German Republic in Nov 1918. He was Minister of Finance and Colonies in the Provisional Government of 1918, and first Chancellor of the republic in 1919. He resigned rather than sign the Treaty of **Versailles**.

Scheldt Question The dispute over the status of the Scheldt River, which connects the port of Antwerp with the sea, and which services a large and densely populated hinterland in Belgium and northern France. During the **Eighty Years War**, the Sea-**Beggars** closed the river after the fall of Antwerp

to the Spanish in 1585; the Treaty of **Münster** in 1648 confirmed their right to do this, until the French opened it again in the 1790s. A new chapter of the Scheldt Question began after the **Belgian Revolution**: in the settlement the Dutch were awarded Zeeland Flanders on the left bank of the river, which gave them control of its mouth; indeed they imposed a toll on all shipping until 1863 (when the Belgians bought it off). Belgium tried without success to gain Zeeland Flanders after **World War I**; there have been long negotiations concerning Belgium's access to the sea through Dutch territory. In 1963 there was a treaty agreeing the construction of a canal joining the Scheldt and the Rhine rivers, which was completed in 1965.

Schiller, Karl (1911–) German economist and politician. A distinguished academic career, latterly at the University of Hamburg, was complemented from 1949 by a growing involvement as an **SPD** member in municipal and national politics. In 1966 he became Economics Minister in the **CDU/SPD** coalition, retained the post in the SPD/**FDP** coalition (1969–72) and also served as Finance Minister (1971–2) before resigning from the government. He is credited with Germany's economic recovery from the 1966 recession and with introducing a Keynesian style of economic management to Germany.

Schimmelpenninck, Rutger Jan (1761–1825) Dutch politician. He practised law in Amsterdam, and in the 1780s joined the **Patriot Movement** as a supporter of change from the *ancien régime*. In 1796 he became a member of the National Congress in the French-sponsored **Batavian Republic**, and was appointed its representative in Paris in 1798, in London in 1802, and then in Paris again. In 1804 **Napoleon I** charged him with drawing up a constitution for the Netherlands, which came into effect in 1805 and which created Schimmelpenninck **Grand Pensionary** at the head of the Republic. In 1806 Napoleon installed his own brother **Louis Napoleon** as King of Holland, and Schimmelpenninck retired to his estate near Deventer. He joined the First Chamber after the restoration in 1815; his achievement had been to introduce the Napoleonic administrative reforms to the Netherlands, for example in taxation and education.

Schleicher, Kurt von (1882–1934) German soldier and politician. He was on the general staff during **World War I**. Politically active behind the scenes during **Brüning**'s chancellorship, he became Minister of War in von **Papen**'s government of 1932, then succeeding him as Chancellor. However, his failure to obtain either a parliamentary majority or emergency powers provided the preconditions for **Hitler**'s appointment as Chancellor in 1933. Schleicher and his wife were murdered by the Nazis in mid-1934 on a trumped-up charge of treason. ▷ **Night of the Long Knives**

Schleswig-Holstein Problem The southern part of the Jutland Peninsula, linking Denmark and Prussia, whose ownership has been hotly contested throughout the 19c and 20c. Since the Middle Ages, the two duchies had been ruled by the King of Denmark, despite their markedly different populations: Schleswig comprised a mixed population, while Holstein (which had joined the German Confederation in 1815) was almost completely German. Denmark sought, in 1848, to annex Schleswig, and war broke out between the Confederation and Denmark. A compromise was reached in 1852, although the Danes' demands remained unresolved. War broke out again in 1863, prompted by a dispute over the right of **Christian IX**, **Frederick VII** of Denmark's successor, to rule. At stake was the principle of the Salic Law, which did not recognize a female line of succession. The German population argued that the duchies should be ruled by the Duke of Augustenberg, and Prussia and Austria added their weight. A brief war followed, in which the Danes were defeated and, under the Treaty of Prague (1866), Schleswig-Holstein passed, as a province, under Prussian rule. Plebiscites following the Treaty of **Versailles** (1919) led to the awarding of northern Schleswig to Denmark (July 1920); after a referendum, the remainder of Schleswig-Holstein was absorbed (1946) into West Germany as a state. **Palmerston** allegedly said of the problem: 'There are only three men who have ever understood it: one was Prince Albert, who is dead; the second was a German professor, who became mad. I am the third — and I have forgotten all about it.'

Schlieffen, Alfred, Count von (1833–1913) Prussian field marshal. He advocated the plan which bears his name (1895), on which German tactics were unsuccessfully based in **World War I**. He envisaged a German breakthrough in Belgium and the defeat of France within six weeks by a major right-wheel flanking movement, cutting off Paris

from the sea, holding off the Russians meanwhile with secondary forces.

Schlüter, Poul Holmskov (1929–) Danish politician. After studying at Aarhus and Copenhagen Universities, he qualified as a barrister and Supreme Court attorney but was politically active at an early age, becoming leader of the youth movement of the Conservative People's Party (KF) in 1944. He became its national leader in 1951 and in 1952 a member of the Executive Committee of the KF. He was elected to parliament (**Folketinget**) in 1964 and 10 years later became Chairman of the KF (Conservative People's Party), and in 1982 Prime Minister, heading a centre-right coalition which survived the 1987 election but was reconstituted, with support from one of the minor centre parties, *Det Radikale Venstre*, in 1988. Since the election in Dec 1990 the coalition has consisted of only two parties: Schlüter's Conservative Party and the Danish Liberal Party, *Venstre*, led by the Foreign Minister, Uffe Elleman-Jensen.

Schmalkaldic League (1531) The league was created by the Protestant German princes who desired to defend their Protestantism against the attempts of Emperor **Charles V** to reintroduce Catholicism. It was led by **Philip the Magnanimous** of Hesse and **John Frederick**, Elector of Saxony. Charles was forced to grant it a form of recognition in 1544 but was able to destroy it militarily a few years later (1547) at the Battle of **Mühlberg**.

Schmerling, Anton von (1805–93) Austrian politician. After a training in law and an early career in the Civil Service, Schmerling served between July and Dec 1848 as a liberal minister in the Frankfurt Parliament. He then served in various Austrian offices between 1849 and 1851 before resigning in protest at the neo-absolutist policies of the Habsburg monarchy. However, in Feb 1861 he was the author of the February Patent which failed to settle the monarchy's nationality problems, but marked the beginning of constitutional government. Schmerling thereafter resumed his legal career as President of the Supreme Court and, from 1867, served as a member of the Upper House of the Austrian parliament. ▷ **Habsburg Dynasty**

Schmidt, Helmut (Heinrich Waldemar) (1918–) West German politician. After service in **World War II**, he studied at Hamburg, joined the Social Democratic

Party in 1946, and became a member of the **Bundestag** in 1953. He was Minister of Defence (1969–72) and of Finance (1972–4), in which role he created a firm basis for Germany's continued economic growth. He succeeded Willy **Brandt** as Chancellor in 1974, describing his aim as the 'political unification of Europe in partnership with the United States'. In 1982 his **SPD/FDP** coalition collapsed, to be replaced by a **CDU/FDP** administration. ▷ **Germany, West; Kohl, Helmut**

Schnaebele Affair (20–30 Apr 1887) A war scare between France and Germany. Following the arrest of the French (Alsatian-born) commissioner for the Franco-German border, Schnaebele, on German soil on suspicion of espionage, French public opinion and even the Prime Minister, **Boulanger**, called for war. However, the French President merely made a formal protest and since Schnaebele had been promised safe conduct while in Germany on official business, **Bismarck** agreed to his release thereby defusing the crisis.

Schoelcher, Victor (1804–93) French politician. A republican, he was an advocate of the emancipation of the slaves of French colonies, which he accomplished as a member of the Provisional Government of 1848. He opposed the 1851 coup d'état, and remained in exile throughout the French Second **Empire**. He returned to France in 1870, was elected to the National Assembly in 1871, as Deputy for Martinique, and became a life Senator in 1875.

Schools Question (Belgium) The extended political conflict between the supporters of neutral state education and of Roman Catholic schools, dominating the third quarter of the 19c, and also the 1950s. The French revolutionary period had removed the traditional monopoly held by the Catholic Church over education; during the union with the northern Netherlands (1815–30) King **William I** insisted that education be regulated by the state, which became one of the contributory causes of the **Belgian Revolution**. The liberals held sway in Belgian politics around the middle of the 19c, and much of their anti-clericalism was manifested in Education Acts which progressively reduced the influence of the Church in primary education. During the years 1878–84 more anti-Catholic provisions in education brought the Schools Question to a head; at the elections of 1884 the liberals were soundly beaten and the

Catholics, embarking on 30 years of uninterrupted power, reversed the legislation. After **World War II** the battleground switched to secondary education, and in 1954–8 education dominated Belgian politics once more. In 1958 the Schools Pact was signed, by which the three major parties (Catholics, socialists and liberals) agreed to a free choice of education at secondary level, with largely equivalent state funding.

Schools Question (Netherlands) The extended political conflict surrounding Calvinist and Roman Catholic attempts to gain equal status for confessional education, especially in terms of state funding. In Napoleonic times primary education had been made a state monopoly; from the 1820s both Catholics and Calvinists began to raise objections to this, for example by means of petitions. The issue dominated Dutch domestic politics from 1850 to 1917: the confessionals objected to the 'neutral' religious content of state education, and so set up their own schools, demanding state funds to run them. The liberals refused; the Schools Question became a battleground in the emancipation of the Catholics and orthodox Calvinists. Further Education Acts in 1857 and 1878 only served to sharpen the conflict, and in 1889, during the first confessional government in the Netherlands, an Act was introduced giving partial subsidy to 'free' or non-state schools. During the government of 1901–5 led by A **Kuyper** there were more laws increasing subsidies to religious schools; in 1917 a great compromise was struck, granting universal male suffrage, and financial equality to 'free' and state education: the constitution was amended accordingly. Since the pacification of 1917 the heat has left the debate, but education continued to be a highly divisive issue in the Netherlands in the interbellum and after **World War II**.

Schumacher, Kurt Ernst Karl (1895–1952) German politician. He studied law and political science at the universities of Leipzig and **Berlin**, and from 1930 to 1933 was a member of the **Reichstag** and of the executive of the Social Democratic parliamentary group. An outspoken opponent of National Socialism, he spent 10 years from 1933 in Nazi concentration camps, where he showed outstanding courage. He became in 1946 Chairman of the Social Democratic Party (**SPD**) and of the parliamentary group of the **Bundestag, Bonn**. He strongly opposed **Adenauer**'s policy of integration with Western Europe at the expense of reunification.

Schuman, Robert (1886–1963) French politician. He was a popular Christian Democrat Deputy (1919–40) and then (1945–62) one of the leaders of the **MRP** ('Popular Republican Movement'). After holding office as Prime Minister (1947–8), he remained Foreign Minister (1948–53), during which time he carried through the Schuman Plan (1950) for pooling the coal and steel resources of Western Europe, the predecessor of the European Economic Community. He was Minister of Justice (1955–6) after which he concentrated on the European movement, becoming President of the **EEC** assembly (1958–60). ▷ **EC**

Schuschnigg, Kurt von (1897–1977) Austrian politician. He served in **World War I**, practised law, was elected a Christian Socialist Deputy (1927), and became Minister of Justice (1932) and of Education (1933). He was Chancellor of Austria from 1934 to 1938. His attempt to prevent **Hitler** occupying **Austria** led to his imprisonment until 1945. He then lived in the USA, where he became Professor of Political Science at St Louis (1948–67).

Schwabenspiegel A south German reworking of the law code known as the **Sachsenspiegel**, it originated in Augsburg in the second half of the 13c. Originally called the *Deutschspiegel*, the document was later revised (c.1287) and the name *Schwabenspiegel* became established for the revised version in the 17c. It is not as coherent as the *Sachsenspiegel*, but it served as a basis of law in southern Germany and as far north as Hessen until the 17c–18c.

Schwarzenberg, Felix (Ludwig Johann Friedrich) (1800–52) Austrian politician. During the **Revolution of 1848**, he was made Prime Minister, and created a centralized, absolutist, imperial state. He then sought Russian military aid to suppress the Hungarian rebellion (1849), and demonstrated Austrian superiority over **Prussia** at the Olmütz Convention (1850). His bold initiatives temporarily restored Habsburg domination of European affairs. ▷ **Habsburg Dynasty**

Schwarzenberg, Karl Philipp, Prince of (1771–1820) Austrian soldier and diplomat. He entered the army in 1787 and took part in the War of the Second Coalition (1792–1802). He was Ambassador to Russia in 1808, and when **Austria** declared war on France in 1809 he participated in the unsuccessful campaign. After the peace treaty, he pursued a diplomatic career until **Napoleon I** demanded him as general of the Austrian contingent in the invasion of Russia in 1812. When Austria turned on Napoleon, he became generalissimo of the allied armies which won the Battles of Dresden and **Leipzig** in 1813. In 1814 he helped to occupy Paris.

Schwimmer, Rosika (1877–1948) Hungarian feminist and pacifist. As a journalist she was active in the Hungarian women's movement, and was a co-founder of a feminist-pacifist group. She became Vice-President of the Women's International League for Peace and Freedom, and in 1918–19 was Hungarian minister to Switzerland. In 1920, fleeing from the country's anti-Semitic leadership, she emigrated to the USA, but was refused citizenship since, as a pacifist, she could not promise to fight should war break out. For the rest of her life she continued to campaign for pacifism and before the outbreak of **World War II** was outspoken in her criticism of growing European Fascism.

Scipio Aemilianus (Scipio Africanus Minor) (185–129BC) Roman statesman, general and orator. He is famous primarily for the sack of Carthage in the third of the **Punic Wars** (146BC), the destruction of Numantia (133BC), and his patronage of the arts. Members of the so-called 'Scipionic Circle' included the historian Polybius, the Stoic Panaetius, the poet Lucilius, and the playwright Terence. His opposition to the reforms of the **Gracchi** may have been the cause of his sudden death, possibly by poison.

Scipio Africanus Major, Publius Cornelius (236–c.183BC) Roman general. An innovative military commander, in the second of the **Punic Wars** his victory at Ilipa (206BC) forced the Carthaginians out of Spain; his subsequent defeat of **Hannibal** at Zama (202BC) broke the power of Carthage altogether. Honoured for this with the title 'Africanus', he remained in the forefront of affairs until forced into retirement by his political enemies in the 180s.

SCLC (Southern Christian Leadership Conference) US **civil rights** organization. Formed in 1957 by Martin Luther **King** and other ministers to pursue racial integration, primarily in the South, through non-violent protest. As ministers they were natural leaders in their communities, able to explain their aims in terms of the Christian creed, and in a rhetoric which their people understood. An unsuccessful campaign in Albany, Georgia, in 1961, demonstrated the need for careful planning and preparation. In later campaigns the movement sought to develop a 'creative tension', inciting whites to over-react, attracting the media, and forcing the federal government to intervene. The success of this strategy was seen in Birmingham and Selma. However it did not succeed in Chicago where blacks lacked unity, the issues were far more complicated and white opposition was far more skilful. After the death of Martin Luther King, the organization lost much of its moral authority, though it still remained an important platform for leaders such as Ralph Abernathy and, later, Jesse **Jackson**.

Scott, Thomas (c.1842–70) Canadian Orangeman. He became an Protestant martyr when he was executed in 1870 during the **Red River Rebellion**. This disastrous incident was the root of later troubles which split the country, such as the execution of Louis **Riel**, the campaign of D'Alton **McCarthy**, and the **Manitoba Schools Act**.

Scotland The northern constituent part of the **United Kingdom**, comprising all the mainland north of the border that runs from the Solway Firth to Berwick-upon-Tweed, and the island groups of the Outer and Inner Hebrides, Orkney and Shetland. Roman attempts to limit incursions of northern tribes were marked by the building of both the **Antonine Wall** and **Hadrian's Wall**. There were the beginnings of unification in the 9c, and wars between England and Scotland during the **Middle Ages**. Scottish independence was declared by Robert **Bruce**, and recognized in 1328. The Stuarts succeeded to the throne in the 14c and united the crowns of Scotland and England in 1603; parliaments were united under the Act of **Union** in 1707. There were unsuccessful Jacobite rebellions in 1715 and 1745. A proposal for devolution failed in a referendum in 1979. Scotland retains a separate legal and educational system and other institutions which are distinct from those of England or Wales. ▷
Fifteen Rebellion; Forty-Five Rebellion; Stuart, House of

Scottish National Party (SNP) A political party formed in 1928 as the National Party of Scotland, which merged with the Scottish Party in 1933. It first won a seat at a by-election in 1945. Its greatest success was in

RULERS OF SCOTLAND

Regnal Dates	Name
1005/34	Malcolm II
1034/40	Duncan I
1040/57	Macbeth
1057/8	Lulach
1058/93	Malcolm III, 'Canmore'
1093/4	Donald III (Donald Bane)
1094	Duncan II
1094/7	Donald III (Donald Bane)
1097/1107	Edgar
1107/24	Alexander I
1124/53	David I
1153/65	Malcolm IV, 'the Maiden'
1165/1214	William I, 'the Lion'
1214/49	Alexander II
1249/86	Alexander III
1286/90	Margaret ('Maid of Norway')
1290/2	Interregnum
1292/6	John Balliol
1296/1306	Interregnum
1306/29	Robert I, 'the Bruce'
1329/71	David II
1371/90	Robert II
1390/1406	Robert III
1406/37	James I
1437/60	James II
1460/88	James III
1488/1513	James IV
1513/42	James V
1542/67	Mary, Queen of Scots
1567/1625	James VI

the 1974 general election, when it took nearly a third of Scottish votes and won 11 seats. Since then its support has declined, although in 1988 it achieved a surprise victory in the Govan by-election. Its principal policy aim is independence for Scotland from the UK. ▷
Home Rule

Scottish War of Independence The conflict between the Scots and English in the late 13c and early 14c. After heavy defeats by **Edward I** at the Battle of **Dunbar** (1296) and Falkirk (1298), the Scots regrouped first under William **Wallace** and then Robert **Bruce**. The fall of Stirling Castle (1304) led to the capture and execution of Wallace but Bruce was crowned (1306) and, after Edward I's death (1307), increasingly asserted his authority. His victory at the Battle of **Bannockburn** (1314) secured Scotland from English rule and the Scottish barons declared their allegiance to Bruce in the face of papal opposition to his kingship (Declaration of **Arbroath**, 1320). A truce between England and Scotland (1323) was broken when the Scots crossed into Northumberland and ravaged it (1327–8). Queen **Isabella of France** and her lover Roger Mortimer sued for peace. The English renounced all claims to feudal superiority over Scotland (1328) and recognized Bruce as its king. In 1329 Pope **John XXII** issued a Bull authorizing Robert to be crowned and anointed. ▷ **Edward II**

SDI (Strategic Defense Initiative) The proposal first made by President **Reagan** in 1983 (dubbed by the press 'Star Wars') that the USA should develop the technologies for a defensive layered 'shield' of weapons based primarily in space, able to shoot down incoming ballistic missiles. SDI has remained controversial because it seemed to overthrow the principle of 'mutual assured destruction' on which the idea of deterrence rested. Also the technologies it would need to perfect, such as directed energy, as well as being extremely difficult to achieve, might ultimately be used for offensive as well as defensive purposes.

Seaga, Edward Philip George (1930–) US-born Jamaican politician. He went to school in Kingston, Jamaica and then studied at Harvard University. On the staff of the University of West Indies before moving into politics, he joined the Jamaica Labour Party (JLP) and became its leader in 1974. Seaga entered the House of Representatives in 1962 and served in the administration of Hugh Shearer (1967–72) before becoming leader of the opposition. In 1980 he and the JLP had a resounding, and surprising, win over Michael **Manley**'s People's National Party (PNP), and Seaga became Prime Minister. He called a snap election in 1983 and won all the assembly seats, but in 1989 Manley and the PNP returned to power with a landslide victory.

Sea Peoples An assortment of marauders, probably from the Mycenaean world, who destroyed the Hittite empire in Anatolia (c.1200BC), and penetrated as far south as Egypt before being checked and dispersed. The Achaeans (pre-Dorian Greeks) may have been among the invaders. ▷ **Hittites; Mycenaean Civilization**

Sebastian (1554–78) King of Portugal (1557/78). The grandson of Emperor **Charles V** and nephew of **Philip II** of Spain, he succeeded his grandfather, John III. Following the regencies of his grandmother, Catalina (1557/62) and great-uncle, Cardinal Henry (1562/8), he took control of the government at the age of 14. Lost in dreams of conquest and crusading zeal, he launched a futile and costly war against the **Moors** of North Africa, and fell in the Battle of

Alcazarquivir in Algeria. His death without an heir opened the way for the union of Portugal with Spain under his uncle, but continuing rumours that he was still alive fuelled Portuguese nationalism and gave rise to a series of impostors. The popular belief that he would return revived as late as 1807–8 when Portugal was occupied by the French.

Securities and Exchange Commission (SEC) A body set up in 1934 in the USA during the **Great Depression** to regulate and control the issue of shares by corporations. It ensures that statements about the stocks being sold are accurate, and generally regulates the way US stock markets operate.

SED (*Sozialistische Einheitspartei Deutschlands*, 'Socialist Unity Party of Germany') East German political party. Formed in East **Germany** in 1946 out of the **KPD** and a somewhat unwilling **SPD**, the SED became the Marxist-Leninist party of government in East Germany. Led initially by Wilhelm **Pieck** and Otto Grotewohl, it then saw Walter **Ulbricht** become General-Secretary in 1950 (1963 renamed First Secretary) and Erich **Honecker** replace him in 1971 (1976 renamed General-Secretary). The SED claimed its moral authority as the German proponent of Soviet-style socialism, but despite a membership of over 2 million in 1987, its style of government was never popular. Following the **Revolution of 1989**, the SED reconstituted itself as the PDS (Party of Democratic Socialism), but only enjoys limited support. ▷ **Marxism**

Sedan, Battle of (1870) The crucial French defeat of the **Franco-Prussian War**, bringing the end of the Second Empire in France. **MacMahon**'s plan to relieve the French Rhine Army, besieged in Metz, was foiled when German forces under **Moltke** encircled Sedan. **Napoleon III** surrendered the town with 83 000 men; the Germans then advanced on Paris. ▷ **Empire, Second** (France)

Seddon, Richard John (1845–1906) British-born New Zealand politician. He emigrated to Australia in 1863, arriving in New Zealand in 1866. He entered national politics in 1879 and in 1890 became a minister in Ballance's reforming Liberal government, succeeding Ballance as Prime Minister in 1893. Under Ballance and Seddon, New Zealand gained its reputation as a pioneer of state experiments in social reform. Their governments facilitated the extension of small farming by graduated land and income taxes, the repurchase of alienated crown lands, the purchase of further Maori lands, reform of land law and cheap credit; introduced the enfranchisement of women (1893); compulsory conciliation and arbitration (1894), old-age pensions (1898) and free secondary education (1903). These last two were Seddon's personal concerns, but his main contribution was political, disciplining the party and overcoming opposition in the Legislative Council. An imperialist, he sent troops to South Africa during the **Boer Wars** (1899–1902), but his aim of annexing Fiji and Samoa to New Zealand was frustrated by the British government. As 'King Dick' he dominated New Zealand politics from 1893 until his death in office. ▷ **Reeves, William Pember**

Sedgemoor, Battle of (5 July 1685) A battle near Bridgwater, Somerset, which ended the Duke of **Monmouth**'s rebellion against James VII of Scotland and II of England. The rebel army received popular support and outnumbered the royal army by 4000 to 2500, but desertions provoked an abortive night attack. Monmouth was executed, and his supporters suffered under Judge **Jeffreys**' 'Bloody Assizes'. ▷ **James VII and II**

Seeckt, Hans von (1866–1936) German army officer. After serving with merit as a staff officer in **World War I**, Seeckt acted as military expert to the German delegation at the Treaty of **Versailles** before becoming Army Chief of Staff in 1920. His equivocal attitude to the republic saw him uphold order with emergency powers during the troubles of late 1923 and early 1924, but also saw him fail to act decisively against far-right conspirators (**Kapp Putsch**, 1920). Eventually this equivocation forced his resignation in 1926. As Chief of Staff he had been a strong advocate of military cooperation with the USSR, not least to undermine Poland. He sat in the **Reichstag** (1930–2), and functioned briefly thereafter as a military adviser in China.

segregation The cultural, political, and typically geographical separation imposed by one racial or ethnic group over another. The term is most often applied to the subjugation of blacks by a politically dominant white elite, particularly through **apartheid** (literally 'separateness') in South Africa, and in the southern states of the USA c.1900–60. Segregation of blacks has been most apparent in housing, public facilities and transportation, and education. ▷ **civil rights; Jim Crow Laws**

Segu A West African state, founded (c.1650) by the Bambara, a Mande-speaking agricultural people. They also formed the state of Kaarta (now in Mali) c.1753–4.

Seguí, Salvador (1887–1923) Spanish anarcho-syndicalist. He took part in the **Tragic Week** of 1909 and had to flee the repression afterwards. Having participated in the foundation of the **CNT** in 1910, he became President of the Federation of Construction Workers of Barcelona in 1914. Seguí was the architect of the Pact of Saragossa (1916) with the Socialist trade union movement, the **UGT**, which led the two movements to pressure the government jointly in the fight against inflation and unemployment. Indeed, he believed that common action against capitalism not only required cooperation with the Socialists, but even with groups beyond the organized working class. Consequently, in 1917 he participated in the general strike committee, even though the CNT was not officially part of the Republican-Socialist coalition. After **World War I**, the down-to-earth Seguí was the most prominent figure in the CNT, and in 1919 almost single-handedly persuaded it to accept the agreement reached in the La Canadiense strike, only to be undermined by the revolutionary anarchists. On 10 Mar 1923 Seguí, despite his moderation, was assassinated in Barcelona by the employers. His 'libertarian possibilism' maintained that the working class should not renounce politics in order to achieve its ends, and his untimely death robbed the Spanish anarcho-syndicalists not just of an outstanding organizer, but of their most gifted figure.

Seipel, Ignaz (1876–1932) Austrian politician. After an early career as a theologian, Seipel played a leading role in Austrian politics from 1918 until his death. A member of the Christian Social Party, he served on the Constituent Assembly (1919–20) and as the Federal Chancellor (1922–4, 1926–9). Throughout the period he was a determined opponent of Social Democracy and gradually came to question the efficacy of democracy as such. His foreign policy achievements included the Geneva Protocol (1922) which obtained foreign credit and stabilized the Austrian economy, but at the cost of economic deflation and social suffering.

Seiyukai Literally, 'Association of Political Friends', the leading political party in Japan between 1900 and 1940. Created by **Ito Hirobumi** in 1900 as a pro-government party in the Diet, the *Seiyukai* attracted the support of bureaucrats and landowners. Under the leadership of **Hara Kei** after 1914, the Seiyukai became the largest single party in the Diet. In 1918 Hara became Prime Minister of a Seiyukai-dominated cabinet, the first time a government had been formed from the majority party in the Diet. Despite high hopes, his government (1918–21) proved to be conservative on issues of political and social reform. The Seiyukai supported the military cabinets of the 1930s and advocated a hardline policy in China. The party was dissolved in 1940 as part of a government attempt to bring all political parties under the umbrella of the **Imperial Rule Assistance Association**.

Sejanus, Lucius Aelius (d.AD31) Prefect of the **Praetorian Guard** (AD14–31), and all-powerful at Rome after the Emperor **Tiberius**'s retirement to Capri (AD26). He systematically eliminated possible successors to **Tiberius**, such as Agrippina's sons, so that he himself might wield supreme power after Tiberius's death as regent for his young grandson Gemellus. His plans, however, were made known to Tiberius, and his fall from grace was sudden and spectacular. ▷ **Agrippina the Elder**

Sekigahara, Battle of (Oct 1600) A decisive battle in Japan in which the forces of **Tokugawa Ieyasu** (mainly from the eastern part of the country) defeated their rivals in the west. One year later, Tokugawa Ieyasu was awarded the title of **Shogun** by the emperor, allowing him to impose a military hegemony over the country that was to last until 1867.

selectors Men or women who selected land made available on credit terms by the Australian states in land Acts (1859–72) to encourage small farming. Selectors had to live on and work the farms. Many came from the goldfields, and too often inexperience, squatter opposition, limited acreage or unsuitable land resulted in a depressed rural proletariat rather than yeoman farmers. They provided the social environment of the **bushrangers** (1860–80). ▷ **closer settlement; Squatters**

Seleucids The Greek dynasty descended from Selecus, the general of **Alexander III, 'the Great'**. As the main beneficiaries of Alexander's Persian conquests, initially the Seleucids ruled a vast empire stretching from Asia Minor to north-west India. However, by the time Rome suppressed them in 63BC, all

that was left was their Syrian heartland. ▷ **Hellenistic Age; Persian Empire**

self-determination A doctrine dating back to the 18c that cultural communities and national groupings have the right to determine their own destiny, including political independence and the right to self-rule. The principle that each nation has the right to fashion its own state is incorporated in the **UN** Charter, and is a major plank in anti-colonialism.

Self-Strengthening Movement The ultimately abortive attempt by the **Qing Dynasty** between the 1860s and 1890s to strengthen China militarily and economically against foreign encroachment, through the selective importation of Western military technology and the establishment of modern economic enterprises. First rationalized by the Chinese scholar-official **Feng Guifen** as a means to 'learn the techniques of the barbarians in order to control them', self-strengthening was supported by Prince **Gong** at court and carried out by several high-ranking provincials, many of whom had participated in the suppression of the **Taiping Rebellion**. Military projects included the construction of a shipyard at Fuzhou (1866) and arsenals at Shanghai (1865) and Nanjing (1867). Economic projects included the founding of the China Merchants Steam Navigation Company (1872) to compete with foreign shipping, and the opening of modern coal mines at Kaiping (1877) near Beijing. The period also witnessed the beginnings of institutional change. In 1861 a proto-Foreign Office (*Zongli Yamen*) was created, to which was attached a foreign language school for the training of interpreters. At no time, however, was a fundamental overhaul of China's institutions or education system envisaged. This, together with the piecemeal and uncoordinated nature of the projects themselves, bureaucratic corruption, and persistent conservative opposition both at court and in most of the provinces to any modernizing change, contributed to the movement's failure, which was dramatically illustrated by China's military defeats at the hands of France (1885) and Japan (1895).

Selim I, 'the Grim' (1467–1520) Ottoman Sultan (1512/20). Having dethroned his father, **Bayezid II**, and caused him, his own brothers, and nephews to be put to death, in 1514 Selim declared war against Persia, and took Diyarbakir and Kurdistan. In 1517 he conquered Egypt, Syria and the Hijaz, including the holy cities of Medina and Mecca, receiving the keys of the latter from the Sharif, and thus winning from the nominal 'Abbasid caliph at Cairo, al-Muta-wakkil III, the headship of the Muslim world. Selim chastised the insolence of the **Janissaries**, sought to improve the condition of the peoples he had conquered, and cultivated the poetic art. He was succeeded by his son, **Suleyman I, 'the Magnificent'**. ▷ **Marj Dabiq, Battle of**

Selim II (1524–74) Ottoman Sultan (1566/74). The son of **Suleyman I, 'the Magnificent'**, he proved to be an indolent drunkard, who delegated the handling of state affairs to his able Grand Vizier, Mehmed Sokollu. During Selim's reign Cyprus was sacked by Turkish troops and 30000 inhabitants of Nicosia were massacred. A naval force mustered by the pope, Italian states and Spain, under Don **John of Austria**, succeeded in defeating the Turkish fleet at the Battle of **Lepanto** in 1571. However, the victors did not follow up their success: Venice was forced to recognize Ottoman supremacy in the Mediterranean in 1573 and, the following year, Ottoman forces recaptured Tunisia from the Spanish (who had taken it in 1574).

Selim III (1761–1808) Ottoman Sultan (1789/1807). Having succeeded his uncle, Abd ul-Hamid I, he prosecuted the war with Russia. However, the Austrians joined the Russians, and Belgrade surrendered to them, while the Russians took Bucharest, Bender, Akkerman and Ismail. Inspired by the reformist zeal of his father, Mustafa III (1757/74), and the changes brought about by the **French Revolution**, Selim embarked on a plan of westernization for his country. Having established a committee for reform in 1792–3, he set about implementing a series of changes, known as the New Order (*Nizam-i Cedid*). These reforms affected the organization of the army, and the system of tax and land tenure. To promote contact with the West, he also opened Ottoman embassies in the major European capitals. However, these attempts at change engendered the hostility of conservative elements, such as the Janissaries and ulama, and Selim was forced, in 1807 after a series of mutinies, to abandon his programme of reorganization. His dream of a New Order was ultimately to cost him both his throne and his life (by strangulation, on the orders of his successor, Mustafa IV).

Seminole A Muskogean-speaking Native North American group of south-east USA,

descended from Creeks who settled in Florida in the late 18c, many intermarrying with runaway Negro slaves. One of the **Five Civilized Tribes**, they were drawn into war after aiding their fellow Creeks and fought against troops led by Andrew Jackson. They eventually surrendered to US forces in the 1820s and 1830s, and were moved to reservations in Oklahoma. Population c.3500. ▷ **Native Americans**

Semites A group of peoples found in south-west Asia. In antiquity they included the Ammonites, Amorites, Assyrians, Babylonians, Canaanites, and Phoenicians; today the most prominent Semitic peoples are the Jews and the Arabs. ▷ **Assyria; Babylonia; Phoenicia**

Sempach, Battle of (1386) This battle was the culmination of a dispute between the city of Lucerne and the Duke of Austria, Leopold III. In it, Lucerne and the Swiss Cantons inflicted a crushing defeat on the Austrians, losing only 200 of their 1600 men, while Austrian losses amounted to around 1800.

Senanayake, Don Stephen (1884–1952) Sri Lankan politician. Born in Colombo, he was educated there and then worked on his father's rubber estate. Entering the Legislative Council in 1922, he founded the cooperative society movement in 1923, and was elected to the State Council in 1931 where he was Minister of Agriculture for 15 years. Following independence, he was Sri Lanka's first Prime Minister (1947–52), and also held the posts of Minister of Defence and External Affairs. He died after falling from his horse in Colombo.

Senate One of the two chambers of the US Congress in which legislative power is vested. It consists of two Senators from each state (100 in all) chosen by the people to serve for six years; the terms of a third of the members expire every two years. It has powers of 'advice and consent' on presidential treaties and appointments. It is presided over by the US Vice-President, who has no part in its deliberations, but can cast the deciding vote if there is a tie. Legislation must pass both the House and the Senate before being signed by the President and becoming law. ▷ **Congress; House of Representatives**

Sendero Luminoso Literally 'Shining Path', the name refers to a Maoist rural guerrilla movement of uncompromisingly revolutionary character, operating in the Peruvian central Andes (though capable, also, of mounting terrorist actions in cities) during the 1980s and 1990s. Its leader, Abimael Guzman, was captured in Sep 1992 and sentenced to life imprisonment.

Seneca, Lucius Annaeus, 'the Younger' (c.5BC–AD65) Roman philosopher, statesman, and author; and the son of Seneca (the Elder). Banished to Corsica (41–49) by **Claudius**, on a charge of adultery, he was recalled by **Agrippina the Younger**, who entrusted him with the education of her son **Nero**. Made consul by Nero in AD57, his high moral aims gradually incurred the Emperor's displeasure, and he withdrew from public life. Drawn into conspiracy, he was condemned, and committed suicide in Rome.

Seneca Falls Women's Rights Convention (1848) US feminist conference. It was organized by Elizabeth Cady **Stanton** and Lucretia **Mott**, who met after they had been denied seats at the World Anti-Slavery Conference in London. Stanton and Mott protested against the contradiction of fighting for the rights of blacks when they themselves did not have the right to vote. The Convention adopted a Declaration of Sentiments modelled on the **Declaration of Independence**, maintaining that 'all men and women are created equal'. It not only claimed the vote for women but demanded equality in property, marriage and education. ▷ **slavery**

Senegambia, Confederation of An association between The Gambia and Senegal, begun in 1982, designed to integrate military, economic, communications, and foreign policies, and to establish joint institutions, while preserving independence and sovereignty. It proved to be of limited value and was ended by mutual agreement in 1989.

Senghor, Leopold Sedar (1906–) Senegalese poet and politician. Educated in Roman Catholic schools in Dakar, he went to the University of Paris and, after graduation, taught in France itself (1935–9). He joined the French army at the outbreak of war and was a prisoner (1940–2). A member of the Resistance (1942–4), he was a member of the French Constituent Assembly in 1945 and was Deputy for Senegal in the French Assembly (1948–58), during which period he was a university lecturer. He was one of the founders of *Presence Africaine* in 1947 and wrote widely in that, and other intellectual magazines, establishing himself as a major

poet and an exponent of the philosophy of **negritude**. He formed the *Union Progressiste Senegalaise* in 1958 and, as its leader, became President of Senegal on the country's independence in 1960. He retained cordial links with France and, although nominally a socialist, espoused a mixed economy. In 1981 he retired from politics.

senhores de engenho In colonial Brazil (1500–1822), these mill-owners were men of significant political power. Of varied origins, their investment in capital stock, including slaves, made them risk-taking entrepreneurs. They rented their lands to *lavradores de cana*, who owned slaves and equipment to cultivate cane; this ensured a large supply of sugar to the *engenho* (mill) throughout the long harvest period. Free labour was contracted for specialized and occasional tasks. Mill-owners also controlled cattle ranches (*fazendas*) in the interior, so that their activities dominated the economy and society of major regions of Brazil. By the mid-18c many had evolved into strong *parentelas*. ▷ **fazenda; parentela**

Sennacherib (8–7c BC) King of Assyria (704/681BC). The son of **Sargon II** and grandfather of Assurbanipal, he was an able ruler, whose fame rests mainly on his conquest of Babylon (689BC), and his rebuilding of Nineveh. He figures prominently in the Bible, because of his attack on Jerusalem.

Senusret I (Kheperkare) (c.1971/1928BC) King of Egypt. The second king of the 12th Dynasty, he was a man of great energy and ability. He was active in Nubia, where expeditions penetrated beyond the Second Cataract, and was responsible for extensive building works throughout Egypt.

Senusret II (Khakheperre) (c.1897/1878BC) King of Egypt. One of the most vigorous rulers of the 12th Dynasty, he was the fourth king of that family. There are no records of his having tried to extend Egypt's foreign conquests. Instead, he was concerned with the exploitation of mines and quarries and economic and agricultural improvements in Egypt. It was apparently Senusret II who began a scheme of land reclamation and flood control of the Nile waters in the Fayum.

Senusret III (Khakaure) (c.1878/1843BC) King of Egypt. The fifth king of the 12th Dynasty, he was a key figure in the Middle Kingdom. His reign was significant in two important respects. Firstly, he intervened during the second half of his reign to deprive the nomarchs or provincial governors of their status and privileges. The manner in which he did this is unknown, but the construction of nomarchs' tombs was brought to an end and there is no further mention of their activities. A new administrative system was introduced: Lower, Middle and Upper Egypt became departments (*waret*) of the central government, staffed by officials responsible to a vizier. The king's other achievement was the strengthening of Egypt's hold on Nubia: campaigns were mounted in the eighth, tenth, sixteenth and nineteenth years of his reign to enforce Egyptian authority. An armed foray was also made into Palestine as far as the biblical Shechem. The southern boundary was settled at Semna at the head of the Second Cataract, protected by a line of forts situated at strategic points.

Senussi A Sufi order found in North Africa, particularly the Sahara. Founded by Muhammad al-Sanusi (1791–1855), the Senussi is to be regarded as one of the reforming modern movements in Islam, preaching as it does a simple and purified form of the religion. Its political importance lies in its opposition to the Italians in Libya and the fact that after **World War II** the then leader of the Sanusiyya, Muhammad Idris al-Sanusi became King of Libya as Idris I. He ruled Libya until 1969, when he was deposed by a military coup and Muammar al-**Gaddafi** came to power.

Separation of Church and State (France) (1905) The conflict between the Church and the French Republic had been renewed as a result of the **Dreyfus** Affair (1898–9) and the Law on Associations (1901), which was used to dissolve the religious orders. **Combes's** government (1902–4) opened a conflict with the papacy which led to the law of 1905 abrogating the **Concordat** (1801), ending the position of the Catholic Church as an established Church, financially supported and to some extent controlled by the state. The separation was at first fought bitterly by the Church, but the mollifying policies of **Briand**, Minister of Religious Worship in the **Clemenceau** government (1906–9), reduced the confrontation, and in a short time the new regime proved acceptable to both sides. ▷ **Republic, Third** (France)

separation of powers A political doctrine, associated with the 18c philosopher Montesquieu, which argues that, to avoid tyranny, the three branches of government (legislature, executive, and judiciary) should be separated as far as possible, their relationships governed by checks and balances. The **US Constitution** is a practical example of an attempt at separation of powers. Parliamentary systems such as that of the UK do not have a complete separation, as the heads of the executive (ie government ministers) sit as members of the legislature. Nonetheless, most systems claim independence of the judiciary.

Séparatisme French-Canadian independence movement. It has played a significant role in Canadian politics since the 1960s. Some groups such as the **Front de Libération de Québec (FLQ)** were prepared to resort to the sort of violence which resulted in the **October Crisis**. One of the largest groups was the *Rassemblement Démocratique pour l'Indépendence* which was important in the defeat of **Lesage**, and became even stronger after the defeat of the **Parti Québecois** by the Liberals in 1985. Initially the federal government responded by attempting to remedy French-Canadian dissatisfactions through such initiatives as the Royal Commission on **Bilingualism and Biculturalism**. As Prime Minister, Pierre **Trudeau** reasserted the tradition of tolerant Canadianism for which **Laurier** had stood, in the hope that the province might be prevented from becoming racist and introverted. As a Québecois Liberal, his own success controverted the image of disadvantage that the separatist groups attempted to convey.

Sephardim The name (from Hebrew *Sepharad*, 'Spain') given to the Jews of Spain and Portugal, and hence applied to all Jews who trace their descent from the Iberian Peninsula, more particularly to those descended from the Jews expelled in 1492. Their language and culture were Spanish (*Ladino*), distinguishing them sharply from the Jews of Eastern European origin. ▷ **Jews, Expulsion of the**

Septennial Act (1716) Legislation repealing the Triennial Act (1694) which extended the maximum life of parliament from three years to seven. Remaining in force until the Parliament Act (1911) restricted parliaments to five years, it was important in easing the transition to political stability and to Whig supremacy in the early years of the Hanoverian monarchy. ▷ **Hanover, House of; Triennial Acts; Whigs**

Septimius Severus (c.146–211) Roman Emperor (193/211). The founder of the

Severan Dynasty), he was the first Roman emperor to be born in Africa (at Leptis Magna, of Romanized Punic stock). Declared Emperor by the army in 193, he spent the early years of his reign securing his position against his rivals. Once established, he proved to be an able administrator, effecting many reforms, and showing a particularly close interest in the army and the law. His final years were spent in Britain, trying unsuccessfully to restore order in the north of the province. ▷ **Britain, Roman**

Septinsular Republic The name given to the separate state formed from the Ionian Islands in 1800 on the basis of a treaty between the Russian Tsar and the Ottoman Sultan. First a protectorate of the Porte, then of Russia, the history of the short-lived republic was bloody and brutal. By the Treaty of **Tilsit** (1807) the islands were returned to France and became part of the **Illyrian Provinces**.

Sequoia (Sequoyah) (c.1770–1843) Cherokee leader. He was a major figure behind the decision of the Cherokee to adopt as much as possible of white culture, while retaining their own identity, and personally invented an alphabet for their language. ▷ **Indian Wars**

Serbia, Kingdom of The medieval Kingdom of Serbia was part of Byzantium until the 12c, when the Nemanja Dynasty established its authority over the emerging Serbian state. After the fall of **Stephen Dushan**, the state disintegrated and fell to the Turks (1389). In the 19c, after the Serbs' long struggle for independence from the Ottoman Turks, the Kingdom of Serbia was reestablished at the Congress of **Berlin**, with its capital at Belgrade. After **World War I** it became part of the Kingdom of Serbs, Croats and Slovenes (later Yugoslavia).

Serbian Uprisings (1804 and 1815) When the Serbs of the *pašaluk* of Belgrade rose in protest against the abuses of the local Ottoman administration, they were brutally suppressed by the **Janissaries**. This led to the first Serbian uprising of 1804 under the leadership of **Karageorge**. What began as little more than a peasant revolt, attracted in time the support of Russia and of educated Romanians, Greeks and Serbs under Habsburg rule. By 1806, the insurgents had seized Belgrade and in 1807 the first Serbian constitution declared Karageorge the hereditary leader of **Serbia**. The Turks retook

Belgrade in 1813 and the first uprising collapsed. The second uprising took place in 1815 under Miloš **Obrenović** and ended with his recognition as the 'supreme prince of Serbia'. ▷ **Karadžić, Vuk Stefanović; Obradović, Dositej; Šumadija**

Sergei (1876–1944) Russian Orthodox religious leader. Already a bishop in 1901, he managed to survive the **Russian Revolution** (1917) and the subsequent campaigns against religion. In 1925 he became Patriarch by default when Patriarch **Tikhon** died, and in 1927 made a declaration of loyalty to the state which allowed something of Orthodoxy to continue. During **World War II**, **Stalin** sought his support in defence of the country and allowed him to call a council in 1943 at which he was finally properly elected.

Serrano, Francisco, Duke de la Torre (1810–85) Spanish politician. He fought against the Carlists and, nominally a liberal, was favoured by **Isabella II** and played a conspicuous part in various ministries. Banished in 1866, in 1868 he drove out Isabella and was regent until the accession of Amadeus I of Savoy (1870). He waged successful war against the Carlists in 1872 and 1874; again regent in 1874, he resigned power into the hands of **Alfonso XIII**. ▷ **Carlism**

Sertorius, Quintus (123–72BC) Roman soldier. He fought with **Marius** in **Gaul** (102BC) and supported him against **Sulla**. In AD83, as praetor, he was given Spain as his province: in AD80 he headed a successful rising of natives and Roman exiles against Rome, holding out against Sulla's commanders (including **Pompey the Great**) for eight years until he was assassinated by his chief lieutenant.

Servile Wars The collective name for the official attempts to suppress the slave uprisings of the late 2c and early 1c BC in Sicily and southern Italy. The most serious was the revolt led by Spartacus, in which tens of thousands of slaves were involved. It took the Romans two years to suppress it (73–71BC).

Servius Tullius (578–535BC) Semi-legendary 6th King of Rome. He allegedly distributed all freeholders (for military purposes primarily) into tribes, classes and centuries, making property, not birth, the standard of citizenship.

Sesostris I, II, III ▷ **Senusret I, II, III**

Sethos ▷ **Seti I**

Seti I (Men-maat-Re) (c.1303/1290BC) King of Egypt. The second king of the 19th Dynasty, Seti succeeded his elderly father, Ramesses I, who ruled for only a very short period. Following the disruptive effects of the Amarna episode, Seti restored Egypt's standing as a great power in western Asia. Scenes carved on the walls of the temple of Amun at Karnak show campaigns waged to re-establish Egyptian influence in Palestine/Syria. The fourth of these operations was against the Libyans, and provided a foretaste of the trouble experienced by later Ramesside kings. In Egypt itself the effectiveness of the administration is shown by the amount of building undertaken by Seti.

Settlement, Act of An important statute of 1701 which determined the succession of the English throne after the death of Queen **Anne** and her heirs, if any. It excluded the Catholic Stuarts from the succession, which was to pass to the Electress Sophia of Hanover, descendant through the female line of James VI of Scotland and I of England. Future monarchs were to be communicant members of the Church of England, and were not permitted to leave the country without the consent of parliament. ▷ **James VI and I; Stuart, House of**

Sevastopol, Siege of (1854–5) The centre-piece of the **Crimean War**. Britain, France and Turkey chose to attack Russia's main naval base in the Black Sea in order to reduce its alleged threat to the status quo in the **Ottoman Empire** and the Mediterranean. Time was lost through opting to surround it, and initial successes were not followed up. The result was that General Totleben was able to build formidable defences which Admiral Nakhimov used to good effect. In the event it took 12 months and many casualties to capture Sevastopol. Although Russia therefore lost the war, the battle honours were shared. The Russian surgeon, Nikolai **Pirogov**, played a similar role inside the fortifications to Florence Nightingale outside.

Seven Days Battles (25 June–1 July 1862) The final conflict in the Peninsular Campaign during the **American Civil War**, in which the Union drive to capture Richmond was halted.

Seven Years War (1756–63) A major European conflict rooted in the rivalry between Austria and Prussia and the imminent colonial struggle between Britain and France in the New World and the Far East. Hostilities in North America (1754) pre-dated the Diplomatic Revolution in Europe (1756), which created two opposing power blocs: Austria, France, Russia, Sweden and Saxony against Prussia, Britain and Portugal. British maritime superiority countered Franco-Spanish naval power, and prevented a French invasion. The European war, precipitated by Prussia's seizure of Saxony, was marked by many notable pitched land battles. Saved from total defeat when Russia switched sides, **Frederick II, 'the Great'** of Prussia retained Silesia in 1763. ▷ **Elizabeth Petrovna; George II** of Great Britain; **Granby; Louis XV** of France; **Maria Theresa; Montcalm, Marquis of; Paris, Treaty of; Vendôme, Duke of; Villars, Duke of**

Severan Dynasty (193–235) The **Roman Empire**'s fourth and last stable dynasty before the military and economic chaos of the 3c erupted. Founded by **Septimius Severus** from Leptis Magna in north Africa (193), the dynasty lasted for another two generations, the other rulers being Septimius's sons **Caracalla** (211/17) and Geta (211/12) and his wife's great–nephews, **Elagabalus** (218/22) and **Alexander Severus** (222/35). The most remarkable feature of the dynasty was the dominant role in politics played by its women, especially Julia Maesa, the grandmother of the last two Severan emperors and her daughter, the formidable Julia Mamaea.

Seward, William Henry (1801–72) US politician. He won the governorship of New York State in 1838 and during the 1850s became a major spokesman for the anti-slavery movement and a leader of the **Republican Party**. His 'irrepressible conflict' speech was thought by many Democrats to be responsible for John **Brown**'s violence at **Harpers Ferry Raid**. He served as a very effective Secretary of State under Abraham **Lincoln**, taking an uncompromising attitude towards French support for Archduke **Maximilian** as Emperor of Mexico, which he saw as a breach of the **Monroe Doctrine**. Severely injured during the assassination of Lincoln, he recovered to remain Secretary of State in President Andrew **Johnson**'s cabinet. In 1867 he secured the purchase of Alaska from Russia, known as 'Seward's folly' by persuading a reluctant Congress of its vast mineral wealth.

Seymour, Jane (c.1509–37) Queen of England. She was the third wife of **Henry VIII**, the mother of **Edward VI**, and the sister of Protector Somerset. She was a lady-in-waiting to Henry's first two wives, and married him 11 days after the execution of Anne **Boleyn**. She died soon after the birth of her son.

Seyss-Inquart, Artur von (1892–1946) Austrian politician. He practised as a lawyer in Vienna and saw much of **Schuschnigg**. When the latter became Chancellor in 1938, he took office under him, informing **Hitler** of every detail of Schuschnigg's life, in the hope of becoming Nazi leader in **Austria** after the **Anschluss**. Instead, he was appointed Commissioner for the Netherlands in 1940. In 1945 he was captured by the Canadians, tried at the **Nuremberg Trials** and executed for war crimes.

Seyyid Said (1791–1856) Sultan of Oman and Zanzibar (1806/56). The greatest of the sultans of the al-Busaid Dynasty, he was a merchant prince who ruled in both the Arabian Peninsula and East Africa between 1806 and his death. He visited the East African coast, over which Oman had a vague suzerainty dating from the late 17c, in 1827–8. He recognized the potential of the islands of Zanzibar and Pemba and encouraged members of his Omani aristocracy to found clove plantations there. By 1840, he had moved his capital to Zanzibar. Under his rule, Indian merchants and capitalists moved into his dominions and Zanzibar became the major strategic and commercial port of the East African coast. The USA opened trading relations and the British established a powerful consulate. On Said's death, the British arbitrated the succession dispute. Under the Canning 'Award' of 1862, the combined sultanate of Oman and Zanzibar was divided between two of his sons.

SFIO ▷ **Socialist Party** (France)

Sforza, Carlo (1872–1952) Italian diplomat and politician. As Foreign Minister (1920–1), he negotiated the **Rapallo** Treaty. In 1922 he was made Ambassador to Paris, but resigned on **Mussolini**'s seizure of power and chose to live in exile. After the fall of Mussolini, he returned to Italy and was a member of the first democratic governments. As Foreign Minister (1947–51), he backed European unity and Italian membership of **NATO**.

Sforza, Francesco (1401–66) Duke of Milan from 1450. The illegitimate son of Muzio Attendolo Sforza, he was the father of Galeazzo Maria and Ludovico **Sforza**. He

sold his sword to the highest bidder, fighting for or against the Pope, Milan, Venice and Florence. From the Duke of Milan he obtained his daughter's hand and the succession to the duchy; and before his death had extended his power over Ancona, Pesaro, all Lombardy and Genoa.

Sforza, Galeazzo Maria (1444–76) Italian nobleman, son of Francesco **Sforza** and Duke of Milan from 1466. A competent ruler, he was nonetheless notorious for debauchery and prodigality, and was assassinated.

Sforza, Ludovico, 'the Moor' (1451–1508) Ruler of Milan. The son of Francesco **Sforza**, he acted as regent for his nephew Gian Galeazzo (1469–94) from 1476, but expelled him in 1481 and usurped the Dukedom for himself. He made alliance with Lorenzo de' **Medici** of Florence; under his rule, Milan became the most glittering court in Europe. He helped to defeat the attempts of **Charles VIII** of France to secure Naples, but in 1499 was expelled by **Louis XII** and imprisoned in France, where he died.

Shaftesbury, Anthony Ashley Cooper, 1st Earl of (1621–83) English statesman. He became a member of the **Short Parliament** (1640) and of the **Barebone's Parliament** (1653), and was made one of **Cromwell**'s Council of State, but from 1655 was in opposition. At the **Restoration** he became a baron and Chancellor of the Exchequer (1661–72), a member of the **Cabal** (1667), an earl (1672), and Lord Chancellor (1672–3). He was dismissed in 1673, and led the opposition to the succession of James, Duke of York (later **James II**). Charged with treason in 1681, he was acquitted, but fled to Holland in 1682, and died soon after in Amsterdam. ▷ **English Civil Wars**

Shaftesbury, Anthony Ashley Cooper, 7th Earl of (1801–85) British factory reformer and philanthropist. He entered parliament in 1826, and become the main spokesman of the factory reform movement. He piloted successive **Factory Acts** (1847 and 1859) through parliament, regulated conditions in the coalmines (1842), and provided lodging houses for the poor (1851). A leader of the evangelical movement within the Church of England, he succeeded to his earldom in 1851.

Shagari, Alhaji Shehu Usman Aliyu (1925–) Nigerian politician. Educated in Northern Nigeria, he became a schoolmaster before being elected as a member of the Federal Parliament (1954–8). He was Minister of Economic Development (1959–60), Minister of Establishments (1960–2), Minister of Internal Affairs (1962–5) and Minister of Works (1965–6). After the 1966 coup, he was both State Commissioner for Education in Sokoto province and Federal Commissioner for Economic Development and Reconstruction (1968–70) and then Commissioner for Finance (1971–5). He was a member of the Constituent Assembly which drew up the Constitution for the Second Republic and was the successful presidential candidate for the National Party of Nigeria in 1979. He was President of Nigeria from 1979 until 1983, when he was overthrown in a military coup.

Shah Jahan (1592–1666) Mughal Emperor of India (1627/58). His reign saw two wars in the Deccan (1636 and 1655), the subjugation of Bijapur and Golconda (1636), and attacks on the Uzbegs and Persians. A ruthless but able ruler, the magnificence of his court was unequalled. His buildings included the Taj Mahal, the tomb of his beloved third wife, Mumtaz Mahal. In 1658 he was held prisoner by his son, **Aurangzeb**, until his death, at Agra. ▷ **Mughal Empire**

Shah Wali Ullah (1703–62) Muslim theologian. He took refuge in the concept of the community of the faithful looking only to God. He sought to meet the Hindu intellectual challenge by maintaining that the mystical experience of the divine union did not imply or involve absorption in the deity. Thus Sufi practice, the Islamic religion of the heart, could be reconciled with the orthodox doctrine of God's sovereignty over his creation. He called for a return to the religion of the Quran, which he translated into Persian. Historians trace the seed of Pakistan to the work of Shah Wali Ullah and his school of theologians.

Shaka (1727–1828) King of the Zulu (1817/28). The most famous of the Zulu kings, he built on the military achievements of his predecessor, **Dingiswayo**, extended the Zulu state, and contributed to the great dispersal of **Nguni** peoples in southern Africa known as the *Mfecane*. Shaka was the illegitimate son of Senzangakona, the chief of the small clan known as the Zulu which was conquered by Dingiswayo's Mthethwa. When Dingiswayo was killed in battle with the rival Ndwandwe, Shaka's military genius enabled him to take over the Mthethwa

army. In 1819 his troops, using the short stabbing assegai and the encircling attacking formation which he introduced, defeated the Ndwandwe and welded together a considerable state in northern Natal. His rule became a by-word for ruthlessness although he maintained reasonably good relations with the European traders settled at Port Natal. His victories sent shock waves of Nguni people into southern Natal, the Transvaal and areas of Central and East Africa as far north as Lake Victoria.

Shalaev, Stepan Alexevich (1929–) Soviet trade union leader. He spent his early years working in the timber industry, became a manager and then, in 1963, changed occupations to become a trade union official. Yet his function remained that of running the workforce. So in 1980 he could become Minister of the Timber Industry and two years later was chairman of the whole trade union movement. This kind of dual role could not survive the reform period, and in 1990 he was pushed out.

Shamil (Imam Samuel) (c.1797–1871) Caucasian chief. He led Avar and Chechen tribesmen in the Caucasus in their 30-year-long struggle against Russia. Having become a Sufi mullah or priest, he strove to end the tribal feuds. A passionate believer and brilliant soldier, he was prominent in the defence of Gimry against the Russians in 1831; in 1834 he was chosen head of the Lesghians and, by abandoning open warfare for guerrilla tactics, secured numerous successes for the mountaineers. In 1839, and again in 1849, he escaped from the stronghold of Ahulgo after the Russians had made themselves masters of it, to continue preaching a **jihad** against the infidels. The Russians were completely baffled, their armies sometimes disastrously beaten, though Shamil began to lose ground. During the **Crimean War** the Allies supplied him with money and arms, but after peace was signed the Russians compelled the submission of the Caucasus. In 1859, Shamil's chief stronghold, Vedeno, was taken. He was hunted for several months and, after a desperate resistance, was captured and exiled to Kaluga, south of Moscow. In 1870 he was finally allowed to go to Mecca, where he died. He and his like provide some of the inspiration for current Caucasian feelings against Russia.

Shamir, Yitzhak (1915–) Israeli politician. Born in Poland, he studied law at Warsaw University and, after emigrating to

Palestine, at the Hebrew University of Jerusalem. In his twenties he became a founder member of the **Stern Gang**, the Zionist terrorist group which carried out anti-British attacks on strategic targets and personnel in Palestine. He was arrested by the British (1941) and exiled to Eritrea in 1946, but given asylum in France. He returned to the new State of Israel in 1948 but spent the next 20 years on the fringe of politics, immersing himself in business interests. He entered the Knesset in 1973, becoming its Speaker (1977–80). He was Foreign Minister (1980–3), before taking over the leadership of the right-wing **Likud** Party from Menachem **Begin**, and becoming Prime Minister (1983). From 1984 to 1992 he shared power in an uneasy coalition with the Israel Labour Party and its then leader, Shimon **Peres**. Peres was replaced as Labour leader by Itzhak **Rabin** in Feb 1992, and in June 1992 Likud was defeated in the general election by the Labour Party. ▷ **Mapai Party**

Shan A Tai-speaking people, the second largest minority group in Burma. Buddhists, with a strong cultural identity, they are mainly concentrated in the Shan state, constituting half of its population of 3.1 million. Most are rice farmers.

Shang Dynasty (1766–1122BC) The first Chinese dynasty for which there are historical records, although archaeological evidence suggests that the Shang monarchy emerged from an earlier neolithic culture. Shang civilization stretched from the western edge of the Yellow River plain to Shandong in the east, with its core area in present-day northern Henan province (north China). There may have been several capitals although only the last one, Yin (near present-day Anyang), has been firmly identified. The inscriptions on the oracle bones excavated from the royal tombs around Anyang are the oldest known form of Chinese writing. Shang civilization, which clearly distinguished itself from non-Chinese 'barbarians' to the north, was characterized by sophisticated use of bronze, ancestor worship, large cities, and a chariot-riding warrior aristocracy ruling over a dependent peasantry and specialized craftsmen. The Shang state was overthrown by a Chinese-speaking people known as Zhou (Chou) from the west in the Wei River valley (present-day Shanxi province), who established the **Zhou Dynasty** (1122–256BC).

Shaposhnikov, Boris Mikhailovich (1882–1945) Russian officer and Soviet marshal.

Once he went over to the **Bolsheviks** after 1917, he rose rapidly through the ranks until in 1928 he became Chief of Staff. He was commandant of the Frunze Military Academy (1932–7) and was promoted to be Chief of the General Staff (1937–40 and 1941–2). His role was particularly important in the wake of **Stalin**'s army purge. During **World War II** his subservience to Stalin made him less valuable than several other commanders.

Shapur II, 'the Great' (309–79) King of Persia (309/79). Declared King at his birth by the Persian nobility, he ruled with the help of regents until the age of 16. Under him the Sassanian Empire reached its zenith. He successfully challenged Roman control of the Middle East, forcing Jovian to cede five provinces to him (363), and establishing Persian control over Armenia. ▷ **Artaxerxes I; Sassanid Dynasty**

sharecropping A post-slavery system of tenant farming in the USA in which short-term tenants (usually black) worked land for landlords (usually white) for a percentage of the crop raised. As much a means of labour and racial control as of economic production, sharecropping provided the economic basis of post-slavery white supremacy, although it also provided a limited economic autonomy for tenants.

Sharett, Moshe (1894–1965) Israeli politician. Born in the Ukraine, he settled in Palestine in 1906. Sharett served in the Turkish Army during **World War I**, after which he studied at the London School of Economics. Returning to Palestine, he was prominent in the **Jewish Agency** in the 1930s and 1940s, and was arrested by the British authorities along with other Jewish leaders in 1946. Sharett was Israel's first Foreign Minister, and was then Prime Minister (1954–5). From 1960 he headed the executive of the **World Zionist Organization** and the Jewish Agency, spending his remaining years engaged in Zionist work. ▷ **Ben-Gurion, David; Zionism**

Sharm al-Shaykh This area, which commands the western side of the Straits of Tiran, was occupied by the Egyptians in May 1967 by order of President Gamal Abd al-**Nasser**. Because of the threat posed to the rights of passage through the Straits of Tiran and hence the effect on shipping passing from the Gulf of Aqaba to the Red Sea particularly from the Israeli port of Eilat, the Israelis regarded this as a provocative act. The June War of 1967 can be seen as having in some measure the Egyptian occupation of Sharm al-Shaykh and the implied threat to Israeli shipping as its pretext.

Sharon, Ariel (1928–) Israeli general and politician. Prominent in the War of Independence (1948) and Sinai Campaign (1956), he became a major general shortly before the **Six-Day War** of 1967, during which he recaptured the Milta Pass in the Sinai Peninsula. Leaving the army (July 1973), he was recalled to fight in the **Yom Kippur War**. That year he helped to form **Likud** and was voted into the Knesset. As Defence Minister (1981–3) under Menachem **Begin**, Sharon planned Israel's invasion of Lebanon in 1982.

Sharpeville An African township outside Johannesburg in South Africa. It was here, on 21 Mar 1960, that the police opened fire on a crowd demonstrating against laws restricting non-white movements and requiring non-Whites to carry indentification cards (the so-called pass laws), killing 69 people and wounding 180 others. It led to the banning of both the **ANC** and the **Pan-Africanist Congress** (PAC) and remains a symbolic day for all Black nationalists in South Africa as a mark of their determination for self-rule and white intransigence.

Sharpsburg, Battle of ▷ **Antietam, Battle of**

Shastri, Lal (Bahadur) (1904–66) Indian politician. He joined the independence movement at the age of 16, and was often imprisoned by the British. He excelled as a Congress Party official, and in **Nehru**'s Cabinet became Minister of Transport (1957), Commerce (1958), and Home Affairs (1960). He succeeded Nehru as Prime Minister (1964–6), but died of a heart attack in Tashkent, USSR, the day after signing a 'no war' agreement with Pakistan. ▷ **Indian National Congress**

Shatalin, Stanislav Sergeievich (1934–) Soviet economist. In 1989 he was appointed Secretary of the Economics Division of the Academy of Sciences and in 1990 he was made a member of Mikhail **Gorbachev**'s new presidential council. He acquired particular fame in the autumn of 1990 when he proposed a very radical economic reform, the '500-days plan', as an alternative to **Ryzhkov**'s more conservative one. Gorbachev promised to amalgamate the two but

retreated before his right-wingers, in this way undermining both the cause of **perestroika** and his own position.

Shatt al-Arab Tidal river formed by the union of the Tigris, Euphrates and Karun Rivers, in south-east Iraq; part of the Iraq–Iran border in its lower course; international commission in 1935 gave control to Iraq, but disputes over navigational rights continued, and were one of the issues that led to the outbreak of the **Gulf War** (1980–8).

Shays, Daniel (c.1747–1825) American revolutionary soldier. A farmer, who became a captain in the American army, after the War of Independence he returned to farming in Pelham, Massachusetts. However, like many of his fellows, he found himself subject to impossible economic demands. In 1786–7 he led a short-lived rural insurrection, known as Shays' Rebellion, against his state's policies on taxes and debt repayment. The rebellion was crushed by state troops, but it provided a major impetus to the drafting of the Federal Constitution at the **Constitutional Convention** of 1787.

Shcharansky, Natan (Anatoli Borisovich) (1948–) Soviet dissident. A brilliant mathematician who was disillusioned with Soviet society, in 1973 he applied for a visa to emigrate to Israel. This was repeatedly refused, prompting him to become increasingly active in the Soviet dissident movement. In 1976 he joined Yuri Orlov's Helsinki Watch Group, a body formed to monitor Soviet human rights violations, and in 1977 was sentenced to 13 years in a labour colony for allegedly spying on behalf of the **CIA**. He was freed from confinement in Feb 1986 as part of an East–West 'spy' exchange and joined his wife, Avital, in Israel, where he assumed the name Natan. In 1989 he was nominated as Israeli Ambassador to the UN.

Shchelokov, Nikolai Anisimovich (1910–84) Soviet politician. A Ukrainian metallurgist, he had close associations with Leonid **Brezhnev** in party work based in Dnepropetrovsk, as political officers in the army during **World War II**, and subsequently in party work in Moldavia. In 1966 Brezhnev brought him to Moscow to become Minister of Internal Affairs (and Central Committee member from 1968). He utilized his position to help himself and his friends to have an easy life: his corruption became notorious. In 1983 Yuri **Andropov** dismissed him immediately on entering office; a year later he killed himself before charges could be brought against him.

Shcherbitsky, Vladimir Vasilevich
(1918–90) Ukrainian politician. A chemical engineer and wartime soldier, after 1945 he climbed up the Communist Party bureaucratic ladder until, by 1971, he was a member of the **Politburo** and, by 1972, First Secretary for the Ukraine. He silenced both dissidence and nationalism, and in dealing with the latter he was also of help to Mikhail **Gorbachev**. He was typical of the obstacles facing **perestroika**, paying it lip-service, but resisting it by all possible means. He was the last of the old guard, and Gorbachev was only able to get rid of him a few months before his death.

Sheffield Disturbances (1866–7) The name given to an outbreak of violence against non-unionized labour in the cutlery trade which prompted the British government to establish the first ever Royal Commission on trade unionism.

Shehu, Mehmet (1913–81) Albanian politician. Born into a prosperous Muslim family, he studied at the American school in Tirana and later at an Italian military college, from which he was expelled for communist activities. He fought with the communists in the **Spanish Civil War** and returned to Albania to fight in the resistance during **World War II**. After the war, he studied at the military academy in Moscow (1945–6) and returned to Albania to become Chief of Staff in the Albanian army. With the ascendancy of the pro-Yugoslav faction within the Albanian Communist Party, he was expelled from party meetings but after the purges which followed Yugoslavia's expulsion from Cominform (June 1948), Shehu was readmitted and replaced **Xoxe** as Minister of the Interior. He resumed his position as Chief of Staff and in 1954 became Prime Minister. He survived successive purges but it is a matter of speculation whether his suicide in 1981 was entirely voluntary. ▷ **Hoxha, Enver**

Shelburne, William Petty Fitzmaurice, 2nd Earl of (1737–1805) British politician and Prime Minister. He entered parliament, succeeded to his earldom in 1761, became President of the Board of Trade (1763) and Secretary of State (1766). Made Premier on the death of **Rockingham** (1782), he resigned in 1783 when outvoted by the coalition between **Fox** and **North**. In 1784 he was made Marquis of Lansdowne.

Shelest, Petr Yefimovich (1908–)
Ukrainian politician. A poor peasant, he became a Communist Party official and won Nikita **Khrushchev**'s patronage. By 1957 he was First Secretary in Kiev, by 1963 First Secretary in the Ukraine, and by 1964 a Central Committee member. In 1968, under Leonid **Brezhnev**, he took an interventionist approach in the Czechoslovak crisis. However, he tended to be soft on Ukrainian nationalism and lost Brezhnev's backing in 1972. In any case Brezhnev had his own more subservient candidate, **Shcherbitsky**.

Shepilov, Dmitri Trofimovich (1905–)
Soviet politician. Educated at Moscow University, from 1926 to 1931 he was a public prosecutor in Siberia and later became a lecturer in political economy. During **World War I** he was a political commissar in the Ukraine, where he came into contact with Nikita **Khrushchev**, and in 1945 he joined the Central Committee Secretariat. In 1952 he became chief editor of *Pravda*; in 1954 a member of the Supreme Soviet; and in 1956 Foreign Minister. But, disillusioned with Khrushchev, he participated in the **Anti-Party Plot** in 1957, was 'purged' by the Party leadership and banished to a distant teaching post.

Sherbrooke, Sir John Coape (1764–1830)
British general and Lieutenant-Governor of Nova Scotia (1811–16). His reputation was made during the Peninsular War and in the **War of 1812** he conducted a vigorous defence, which included the capture of Castine (Maine). He served as Governor-in-Chief at Quebec from 1816 until he suffered a stroke in 1818.

Shere Ali (1825–79) Amir of Afghanistan (1863/79). He was the younger son of **Dost Muhammad**, whom he succeeded as amir. Disagreements with his half-brothers soon arose, which kept Afghanistan in anarchy; Shere Ali fled to Kandahar; but in 1868 regained possession of Kabul, with assistance from the viceroy of India, Sir John Lawrence. In 1879 his eldest son, Yakub Khan, rebelled but was captured and imprisoned. Shere Ali's refusal to receive a British mission (1878) led to war; and, after severe fighting, he fled to Turkestan, where he died. He was succeeded by Yakub Khan.

Sheridan, Philip Henry (1831–88) US general. Educated at the US Military Academy at West Point, he commanded a Federal division at the beginning of the

American Civil War, and took part in many of the campaigns. In 1864 he was given command of the Army of the Shenandoah, turning the valley into a barren waste, and defeating General Robert E **Lee**. He had a further victory at Five Forks in 1865, and was active in the final battles which led to Lee's surrender. He died at Nonquitt, Massachusetts, never having lost a battle.

Sherman, William Tecumseh (1820–91) US general. Trained at the US Military Academy at West Point, he became a general in the Union Army during the **American Civil War**. His most famous campaign was in 1864, when he captured and burned Atlanta. He then commenced his famous 'March to the Sea', in which his 60000 men totally destroyed everything in their path en route to the coastal town of Savannah. His forces then moved north through the Carolinas causing even more devastation and gaining further victories which helped to bring forward the Confederate surrender. ▷ **Indian Wars; March through Georgia**

Sher Shah (c.1486–1545) Emperor of north India (1540/5). From the power base he had established in eastern North India, he contested the supremacy of the Mughals, defeating Emperor **Humayun** at Chausa on the Ganges in 1539 and forcing him into exile. A formidable warrior and able administrator, he also built a new city at Delhi and a fine mausoleum at Sahasram in Bihar. Only his death in battle and the inefficiency of his successors allowed the Mughals to emerge triumphant.

Shevardnadze, Eduard Amvrosievich (1928–) Soviet politician. Having studied history at the Kutaisi Institute of Education, he joined the Communist Party in 1948, and rose rapidly through the Komsomol youth league to the party apparatus during the 1950s and to the Georgian Ministry of the Interior in 1964 as minister. There from 1965 to 1972, he gained a reputation as a stern opponent of corruption, including that on the part of Mahavanadze, the Georgian Party Secretary. For his courage, he became Georgian Party Secretary himself in 1972 and introduced imaginative agricultural experiments. In 1978 he was brought into the **Politburo** as a candidate member and, having enjoyed longstanding connections with Mikhail **Gorbachev**, was promoted to full Politburo status and appointed Foreign Minister in 1985, contrasting starkly with his dour predecessor, Andrei **Gromyko**. He rapidly overhauled the Soviet foreign policy machine and, alongside Gorbachev, was responsible for the Soviet contribution to the ending of the **Cold War**. He was also a powerful influence for political reform inside the USSR and over the winter of 1990–1 constantly warned Gorbachev against the danger of a coup. In 1992 he returned to Georgia in the midst of a virtual civil war and, eventually becoming President of the newly independent state, took on himself the task of making it stable.

Shidehara Kijuro (1872–1951) Japanese politician. From a wealthy landlord family who had close links (through marriage) with the Mitsubishi financial combine, Shidehara was ambassador to the USA and a delegate to the Washington Conference (1921–2) before becoming Foreign Minister in the reforming **Kenseikai** government of 1924–6, and again in 1929–31. He adopted a policy of cooperation with the Western powers in China and aroused the ire of ultra-nationalists when he supported the 1930 London Naval Treaty, which placed restrictions on Japan's naval build-up. He served as the second post-war Prime Minister in 1945–6 (because of his pro-Western reputation), seeing as his main task the preservation of the emperor system. This may have been behind Shidehara's suggestion that a disarmament clause (the eventual Article 9) be included in the 1947 **Peace Constitution**. Shidehara was defeated in Japan's first post-war election in Apr 1946.

Shigemitsu Mamoru (1887–1957) Japanese diplomat and politician. During the 1930s, as vice-Foreign Minister, Shigemitsu was associated with the Asia faction of diplomats, who favoured an aggressive and independent foreign policy in China rather than working with the West. As Ambassador to the USSR (1936) and Britain (1938), however, he also cautioned against war with the USA and opposed the alliance with **Hitler**'s Germany in 1940. He served as Foreign Minister in 1943–5, trying unsuccessfully during the last year of **World War II** to involve the USSR as a mediator to bring about an early peace. Convicted as a war criminal in 1946, Shigemitsu served four years of a seven-year sentence before being released in 1950. He was Foreign Minister again in the cabinet of **Hatoyama Ichiro** (1954–6), helping to normalize relations with the USSR in 1956.

Shiites Members of an Islamic religious movement prominent in Iran and Iraq. After the murder of 'Ali, the son-in-law and

851

nephew of the Prophet **Muhammad**, his followers continued to support his claim to the Muslim caliphate and became known as *Shi'*at 'Ali ('partisans of 'Ali'), usually anglicized as Shiites. They believe that 'Ali and his followers were both temporal rulers and imams. Today about 99 per cent of Iranians and 60 per cent of Iraqis are Shiites. The most important group is the 'Twelver' Shiites, who believe that there were twelve imams — 'Ali and his descendants — after the Prophet Muhammad, and that the twelfth did not die, but disappeared, and one day will return to bring justice to the world. Since the 16c, Twelver Shiism has been Iran's state religion.

Shiloh, Battle of (6–7 Apr 1862) An engagement in the **American Civil War** in Tennessee, near Corinth, Mississippi, between Union forces under General Ulysses S **Grant** and Confederate forces under Albert Sidney Johnston (1803–62). Losses were heavy on both sides, with 13 000 Union and 11 000 Confederate casualties.

Shimabara Rebellion (1637–8) A peasant uprising in Japan that broke out on the Shimabara Peninsula (in present-day Nagasaki prefecture). Its leader, Amakusa Shiro, was an impoverished **samurai** whose millenarian teachings drew huge support from amongst the inhabitants of a region suffering from famine, overtaxation and religious persecution. Forces of the **Tokugawa Shogunate** finally took the rebel stronghold of Hara castle in Apr 1638, sparing no-one; 37 000 rebels perished. Since the Shimabara region had been Christianized before official persecution began in 1614, the Tokugawa viewed the uprising as a Christian-inspired rebellion, reinforcing its decision to sever all contacts with the West.

Shimonoseki, Treaty of (17 Apr 1895) The treaty which concluded the **Sino-Japanese War** (1894–5), fought over which country would exercise dominant influence in Korea. Japan's victory in the war brought it considerable gains. The treaty formally ended Korea's tributary relationship with China; henceforth Japan was to be the dominant power in Korea. China also had to pay an indemnity and to cede to Japan the island of Taiwan and the Liaodong Peninsula (southern Manchuria). More significantly, Japan gained the same treaty rights as the Western powers in China's **treaty ports**. Although Japan was forced to return the Liaodong Peninsula to China in 1896 as a result of pressure from Russia, France and

Germany (known as the Triple Intervention), this treaty was a significant turning-point in the emergence of Japan as an imperialist power in China.

Shining Path ▷ **Sendero Luminoso**

Shipov, Dimitri N (1851–1920) Russian political philanthropist. Chairman of the board of the **zemstvo** in St Petersburg, he organized a meeting of his fellow chairmen in the summer of 1896 to exchange views and present them to the Tsar. They encountered many official obstacles but held to their view that consultation was essential. Some became more radical and formed the Union of Liberation in 1903 to seek full representative government. In 1905 they went on to form the **Kadets**. But Shipov split to join **Guchkov** in establishing the **Octobrists** who were altogether less radical.

Shivaji (1627–80) Indian King and founder of the Maratha Kingdom (1674/80). He was the son of Shahaji Bhosle, a Maratha nobleman who had defied the power of the Mughals in Bijapur. Shivaji was able to gather a considerable following among the Mawali hill-dwellers of the region, and, when the Bijapur authorities sent a large army against him in 1659, he succeeded in killing their general and ambushing the leaderless army. During the 1660s Maratha power continued to increase and he had himself crowned as Raja in 1674. He profited from the conflict between the Mughal emperor, **Aurangzeb**, and the Afghans to make extensive conquests in the South before his death. Although his empire remained essentially a 'robber-state', exacting 'protection-money' from areas under its control, he was also intensely devoted to the cause of Hinduism, and the Maratha Empire that he created maintained its independence until 1818.

Shmelev, Nikolai Petrovich (1936–) Soviet academic reformer and politician. An economist graduate of Moscow University, he had a short period in the 1960s in the propaganda section of the Central Committee. But he spent most of his career from the time of Nikita **Khrushchev** to that of Mikhail **Gorbachev** between three of the major institutes of the Soviet Academy, latterly having the opportunity to influence people in high places with his liberal ideas. From 1989 to 1991 he was a member of the Soviet Congress of Deputies.

Shogun A Japanese general; the head of a system of government which dates from 1192, when a military leader received the title *seii-tai-shogun* ('Barbarian-Quelling Generalissimo') from the Emperor. Most important were members of the **Tokugawa Shogunate** (1603–1868), who ruled as military dictators, the Emperor remaining a figurehead, without power. The shoguns' rule strictly regulated and controlled life down to the smallest detail. The system ended in 1868. ▷ **Meiji Restoration**

Short Parliament (Apr–May 1640) The brief parliament summoned by **Charles I** of England to vote supplies for his campaigns against the Scots. It refused to do so, however, whereupon the King dissolved it after only three weeks, adding to parliament's sense of grievance.

Shoshenq I (Hedjkheperre) (c.945/924BC) King of Egypt. The founder of the 22nd Dynasty (Libyan or Bubastite), he was descended from a line of Libyan chiefs. Linked indirectly to the preceding dynasty, the new king made his capital at their city of Tanis. Shoshenq appointed members of the royal family to key positions in the Theban priesthood and strengthened the bond between Upper and Lower Egypt by marriage alliance, thus breaking the hereditary succession of the Amun high priests, which had formed a state within a state during the previous dynasty. In Shoshenq's reign, there was Egyptian activity in Syria, Nubia and Palestine. The latter is commemorated at Karnak in a scene of the king smiting his enemies and a list of places captured during the campaign in 925BC against Rehoboam of Judah. Confirmation is found in the Bible (I Kings 14: 25–6), 'in the fifth year of King Rehoboam...Shishak [Shoshenq] king of Egypt came up against Jerusalem...'

show trials Originally a series of political trials held in Moscow in the late 1930s under **Stalin**'s direct control. Because of what happened, the term came to refer to any political trial where the accused under pressure made public confessions of their alleged crimes, although their guilt would not have been established in any normal court. The process was an attempt to obscure personal vendettas and to justify political repression by demonstrating the use of apparently proper and just judicial procedures in dealing with so-called enemies of the state. ▷ **Stalinism**

Shuvalov, Count Pyotr Andreevich (1827–89) Russian officer, politician and diplomat. He served in the **Crimean War**, became head of the Third Department or secret police in 1866 and proved himself a dangerous opponent of reform. In 1873, sent on a secret mission to London, he was able to do less damage and arranged the marriage between the Duke of **Edinburgh** and the only daughter of **Alexander II**. In general he proved a sound diplomat; in 1878 he was one of the Russian representatives at the Congress of **Berlin**.

Sicilian Vespers (1282) The wholesale massacre of the French in Sicily which began the Sicilian revolt against **Charles of Anjou**, King of Naples-Sicily, and a war ending in 1302. It was so called because the first killings occurred during a riot in a church outside Palermo at vespers (evensong) on Easter Monday, 1282. ▷ **Angevins**

Sidi Muhammad (1757–90) Sultan of Maghrib (Morocco). He restored peace and prosperity after a period of political chaos. He developed Mogador as the principal port for trade with Europe, strengthened central authority and limited the intervention of Europeans in Moroccan affairs.

Sidi Muhammad ben Yusuf (1911–61) Sultan of Morocco (1927/61). A member of the Alouite Dynasty, he exercised both spiritual and temporal power; privately supporting the nationalist Istaqlal Party, he constantly obstructed French hegemony. Tribal hostility to him gave the French the chance to depose him in 1953, but he was restored in 1955, and when Morocco attained independence in 1957 he became King Mohammed V. He died suddenly after a minor operation and was succeeded by his eldest son, Prince Moulay Hassan, who had already emerged as the spokesman of chauvinistic Moroccan youth. His eldest daughter, Princess Lalla Ayesha, repudiated the yashmak and became a leader of the women's emancipation movement.

Sidmouth (of Sidmouth), Henry Addington, 1st Viscount (1757–1844) British politician. He left law for politics, and became an MP in 1783. He was Speaker of the House (1789–1801) when, upon the resignation of **Pitt, 'the Younger'**, he was invited to form a ministry. His Tory administration negotiated the Treaty of Amiens (1802), which held for barely a year. His government ended in 1804, when he was created a viscount. He later became Home Secretary under **Liverpool** (1812–21), unpopular for coercive measures such as the Six Acts (1819), which restricted newspaper publication and the holding of political meetings. It was during his period of office that the **Peterloo Massacre** took place in Manchester. ▷ **Napoleonic Wars**

Sidney, Algernon (1622–83) English politician. He became a cavalry officer in the **English Civil Wars** on the parliamentary side, and was wounded at the Battle of **Marston Moor** (1644). In 1645 he entered parliament, and served as governor in several cities. An extreme republican, he resented **Cromwell's** usurpation of power, and retired from public life (1653–9). After the **Restoration** he lived on the Continent, but in 1677 was pardoned and returned to England. However, in 1683, he was implicated on very little evidence in the **Rye House Plot**, and beheaded in London. ▷ **Whigs**

Siegfried Line A fortified defensive line on Germany's western border with Belgium and France, known in German as the *Westwall* or 'Western Wall'. Built from 1936, to a large degree with conscripted labour, the Westwall turned out to be of limited military significance upon the Allied invasion of Germany (1944–5). ▷ **World War II**

Sieyès, Emmanuel Joseph, Count of (**'Abbé Sieyès'**) (1748–1836) French cleric and political theorist. His pamphlet, *Qu'est-ce que le tiers-état?* (1789, What is the Third Estate?), stimulated bourgeois awareness and won him great popularity. He was elected to the **Estates General**, and suggested the name National Assembly when it united into one body. He was a prominent figure in the early years of the **French Revolution**, being one of the founders of the Jacobin club. However, as the Revolution became more extreme, he withdrew from centre stage, being famous for his reply to the question of what he had done during the Revolution, 'I survived'. He became one of the Directors, and in 1799 was a leading figure in the **Brumaire coup** that brought **Napoleon I** to power. He withdrew from public life under the First Empire, but was exiled at the Restoration (1815) and lived in Brussels until 1830, when the **July Revolution** allowed him to return to Paris. ▷ **Empire, First** (France); **Jacobins**

Siffin, Battle of (658) This battle, fought in the aftermath of the murder of the third Orthodox caliph, **'Uthman**, was essentially a conflict between the Umayyad family (the family of 'Uthman), represented by **Mu'awiya**, and the Hashimites (the family of **Muhammad**), represented by 'Ali ibn Abi Talib. On another level, it was a conflict between Syria and Iraq; and on yet another it may be seen as a clash between the old Meccan aristocracy and the bedouin soldiery, together with newly converted Muslims. The battle itself was inconclusive and the subsequent so-called arbitration worse than unsatisfactory. The decision, the result of a ruse suggested by Mua'wiya's henchman, **Amr ibn al-As**, to go to arbitration gave rise to one of the more implacable sects of Islam, the Kharijites, and sowed the seeds of an enmity between certain elements of the Muslim and Middle Eastern communities which, in one form or another, has lasted to the present day. ▷ **Umayyad Dynasty**

Sifton, Sir Clifford (1861–1929) Canadian politician. As Manitoba's provincial Attorney-General (1891–6) he vigorously defended the province's educational policy during the **Manitoba Schools Act**. After the problem was resolved, **Laurier** appointed him Minister of the Interior, and he established a very effective immigration policy which drew large numbers of Ukrainians and Doukhobors to the north-west. He broke with the Liberal government first in 1905, when he resigned over the restoration of separate schools in the north-west; and again when his defection over **reciprocity** helped the Conservatives to win the election of 1911. ▷ **Liberal Party** (Canada)

Sigibert I (535–75) Frankish King of the Merovingian Dynasty. The son of **Chlotar I**, he inherited **Austrasia** on his father's death and defended it successfully against the attacks of the Avars. His marriage to **Brunhilde**, daughter of the Visigothic king Athanagild, led to a feud with his brother, Chilperic, who had married and then murdered Brunhilde's sister. After a long and bitter war, Chilperic was defeated, but Sigibert was assassinated at the moment of victory. ▷ **Franks; Merovingians**

Sigismund (1368–1437) Holy Roman Emperor (1410/37). The son of **Charles IV**, he became King of Hungary in 1387, German King in 1410 and King of Bohemia in 1419. In 1396 he was defeated by the Ottoman Turks at Nicopolis, but later conquered Bosnia, Herzegovina, and Serbia. As German King, he induced the Pope to call the Council of Constance to end the Hussite schism (1414), but in the end made no effort to uphold the safe conduct he had granted to Jan **Hus**, and permitted him to be burnt at the stake in 1415. As a result, his succession in Bohemia was opposed by the Hussites in 1420 and he was only accepted in 1436 a year before his death.

Sigismund I, 'the Old' (1467–1548) King of Poland (1506/48). His court was filled with factions stirred up by his second wife, the daughter of the Duke of Milan, and the Reformation raised new troubles. In a war with Russia he lost Smolensk, but gained eastern Prussia (1525) and Moldavia (1531). A great patron of the Renaissance, he died at Kraków.

Sigismund II Augustus (1520–72) King of Poland (1548/72). During his reign Lithuania was joined to Poland, and Poland acquired Livonia, thus greatly expanding the kingdom. He died at Knyszyn.

Sigismund III Vasa (1566–1632) King of Poland (1587/1632). Born in Sweden, from 1592 he was also King of Sweden, but was deposed by his uncle in 1599. This led to wars between the two countries until 1629, during which he lost Livonia (1621), and gave up his right to the Swedish crown. He died in Warsaw.

Sigurd I, 'the Crusader' (c.1090–1130) King of Norway (1103/30). The youngest of the three sons of **Magnus III, 'Barelegs'**, he ruled jointly with his brothers until their deaths (1115 and 1122). Between 1107 and 1111 he made an expedition with 60 ships to the Holy Land, the first Scandinavian king to take part in the Crusades (hence his nickname, *Jorsalafari*, 'Jerusalem-farer'). At home he did much to strengthen the church, building cathedrals and imposing tithes for the first time.

Sigurdsson, Jón (1811–79) Icelandic politician and scholar. Born in the west of Iceland, he was educated in Copenhagen, where he spent the rest of his life. As a politician, he led the struggle for autonomy under the Danish crown, earning himself the title 'the Father of Icelandic Independence'. He persuaded King **Christian VIII** to restore the **Althing** as a consultative assembly in 1843, and King **Christian IX** to give it legislative powers in internal affairs in 1874, on the thousandth anniversary of the traditional date of the founding of Iceland's first settlement. His birthday — 17 June — is Iceland's National Day.

Sihanouk, Prince Norodom (1922–) Cambodian (Kampuchean) politician. Educated in Vietnam and Paris, he became King of Cambodia in 1941. He negotiated the country's independence from France (1949–53), before abdicating in 1955 in favour of his father, so as to become an elected leader under the new constitution. As Prime Minister and then, from 1960 after his father's death, also as head of state, he steered a neutralist course during the **Vietnam War**. In 1970 he was deposed in a right-wing military coup led by the US-backed Lieutenant-General Lon Nol. Fleeing to Peking (Beijing), he formed a joint resistance front with **Pol Pot**, which overthrew Lon Nol in Apr 1975. Prince Sihanouk was reappointed head of state, but a year later was ousted by the **Khmer Rouge** leadership. In 1982, while living in North Korea, he became head of a broad-based Democratic Kampuchea (Cambodia) government-in-exile, which aimed to overthrow the Vietnamese-installed regime in Cambodia. Following the Vietnamese troop withdrawal in 1989, he has been involved in the attempts to negotiate a settlement of the country's civil war.

Sikandar Hayat Khan (1892–1942) Indian politician. He came from a rich, landed family and after matriculating from school in Aligarh, entered University College, London to study medicine, but returned after two years. In **World War I** he offered his services to the British government. He was appointed an honorary recruiting officer and was granted a commission. During the third of the **Afghan Wars** he acted as a company commander (1919). He was elected to the Punjab legislative council in 1921, and was appointed chairman of Punjab Reforms Committee to work with the Simon Commission. He was knighted in 1933 and was appointed Governor of Reserve Bank in 1935. He was elected Chief Minister of Punjab at the start of **World War II** and held this office until 1942. During this time he launched rural reconstruction programmes, extended irrigation facilities, laid new roads, and established and strengthened panchayats. In his lifetime, the **Muslim League** could not get hold on the Punjab province. After his death Punjab plunged into political turmoil.

Sik, Ota (1919–) Czechoslovak economist and politician. Imprisoned in a concentration camp during **World War II**, he joined the Communist Party in 1945. His main claim to fame was then as an economist, becoming

Director of the Institute of Economics of the Academy of Sciences in 1962. This put him at the heart of the minor economic reform in the early 1960s and of the major political reform in 1968. He became a member of the Central Committee and a deputy premier. Not all of his ideas would necessarily have prospered, but he and they were swept away by the Soviet invasion in Aug; he then found it wiser to go abroad.

Sikh Wars (1845–6 and 1848–9) Two campaigns between the British and the Sikhs which led to the British conquest and annexation of the Punjab, north-west India (Mar 1849).

Sikorski, Władysław (Eugeniusz) (1881–1943) Polish general and politician. Educated at Kraków and Lvov, he fought in the Russian-Polish War (1920-1), became Commander-in-Chief (1921), and Premier (1922–3). After **Piłsudski**'s coup (1926) he retired and wrote military history in Paris. He returned to Poland in 1938, but on being refused a command, fled to France, becoming Commander of the Free Polish forces and from 1940 Premier of the Polish government in exile in London. He was killed in an air crash at Gibraltar.

Silesia Region of east-central Europe on both banks of the River Oder in south-west Poland and north-central Czechoslovakia, bounded on the south by the Sudetes Mountains. It was a disputed area between Austria and **Prussia** in the 17–18c, passing largely to the latter. In 1921 Poland received part of industrial, Upper Silesia and in 1945 the greater part was granted to Poland, with the removal or flight of the German population. ▷ **Silesian Wars**

Silesian Wars (1740–2 and 1744–5) These wars represent two campaigns in the War of the Austrian Succession and the Seven Years War. In both, Austria and Prussia fought to control Silesia, an area rich in minerals and ores. In the first war, Prussia conquered the area by 1741. In the Treaties of Berlin (1742) and Dresden (1745), Austria recognized Prussia's control of Silesia. In the second war, Austrian troops failed to retake Silesia and, once again, Austria was forced to acknowledge, by the Treaty of Hubertusberg (1763), Prussian sovereignty in the province.

Silk Road The ancient trade route from East China to Central Asia and Europe; from the 2c AD, the best-known route ran from Xi'an

through the Hexi Corridor to the Eastern Mediterranean coast. During the **Sui Dynasty** (581–618), a route further north ended at Istanbul. In exchange for silk, China received grapes, cotton, chestnuts, lucerne and pomegranates. Chinese techniques for silkworm breeding, iron-smelting, paper-making and irrigation spread westwards, and the route also brought Buddhism to China.

Silla, Kingdom of One of the three early Korean kingdoms (along with **Koguryo** and **Paekche**) that emerged in the late 4c following the collapse of China's presence in the peninsula a century previously and which lasted until the 9c. Originally occupying the south-west of the peninsula, Silla expanded in the late 7c to take over its neighbour, Paekche, in the wake of China's invasion of Koguryo in the north. During the height of its prosperity (late 7c–late 8c) Silla became a vital trading link between China and Japan. Block-printing was introduced in the mid-8c and the Chinese examination system was adopted. Students from Silla also studied in China and some became bureaucrats there. Succession disputes and the growing independence of provincial landed families led to the disappearance of the Silla monarchy in the late 9c. The Chinese-style administrative structures and education system that Silla had adopted, however, were inherited by later Korean dynasties.

Sillon A French Catholic review, founded in 1894. In 1899 it was taken up by Marc Sangnier (1873–1950) to express his ideas of democratic Catholicism, and developed into a movement of clubs with a membership of students and workers; condemned by Pope Pius X in 1910, it is seen as one of the roots of later Christian democracy.

Sima Qian (Ssu-ma Ch'ien) (c.145–87BC) Chinese historian. He succeeded his father, Sima Tan (Ssuma T'an), in 110BC as Grand Astrologer, but incurred Emperor Han Wudi's wrath for taking the part of a friend who, in command of a military expedition, had surrendered to the enemy. Sima Qian was imprisoned for three years and castrated, but was gradually restored to favour. He is chiefly remembered for the *Shih Chi*, the first history of China compiled as dynastic histories in which annals of the principal events are supplemented by princely and other biographies and notes on economic and institutional history. It had been begun by his father.

Simcoe, Sir John Graves (1752–1806) British colonial administrator. As Lieutenant-Governor of Upper Canada (1792–94), his intention was to re-create British social and political patterns in the colony, but his disagreements with both London and Canadian administrators caused his recall in 1796. His most positive accomplishment was the use of the army in a huge road-building programme.

Simeon (c.864/5–927) Emperor of Bulgaria (893/927). The son of Boris Mihajl, he was the most powerful ruler in the first Bulgarian Empire. Waging war against Byzantium, he achieved victories at Bulgarophygon in **Thrace** (896) and Arnchialos (917), captured Adrianople twice (914 and 923) and forced the Byzantine emperor, Romanus I Lecapenus, to pay him tribute. He extended the boundaries of his empire to include Thrace, Macedonia, Albania and Raška, which he took in 924 in the course of a dispute with the Croatian King, **Tomislav**. ▷ **Bulgars**

Simeon (1937–) King of Bulgaria (1943/6). The son of **Boris III** and Tsaritsa Giovanna, he was proclaimed King on 28 Aug 1943 but was never crowned. Since he was too young to rule, Prince Kiril, together with the former Prime Minister, Bogdan Filov, and the former War Minister, General Nikola Mikhov, formed a council of regents. In Dec 1944 the **Fatherland Front** regime put the regents on trial and secured their execution. After the plebiscite (Sep 1946), Bulgaria was declared a People's Republic and Simeon went with his mother to Spain, where he still lives as a businessman.

Simmonds, Kennedy Alphonse (1936–) St Christopher-Nevis politician and physician. He practised medicine in the USA and Caribbean before entering politics and founding (1965) the People's Action Movement (PAM) as a centre-right alternative to the Labour Party. After a series of unsuccessful elections, in 1980 Simmonds and PAM won enough seats in the Assembly to form a coalition government with the Nevis Reformation Party (NRP) and he became Prime Minister. Full independence was achieved in 1983 and Simmonds' coalition was re-elected in 1984. In the 1989 election, Simmonds and his party were again victorious.

Simon (of Stackpole Elidor), John (Allsebrook), 1st Viscount (1873–1954) British politician and lawyer. A Liberal, he entered parliament in 1906, and was knighted in 1910. He was Attorney-General (1913–15) and Home Secretary (1915–16), before resigning from the cabinet for his opposition to conscription. Deserting the Liberals to form the Liberal National Party, he supported Ramsay **MacDonald**'s coalition governments and became Foreign Secretary (1931–5), Home Secretary in the Conservative government (1935–7), Chancellor of the Exchequer (1937–40), and Lord Chancellor in Winston **Churchill**'s war-time coalition (1940–5). Created viscount in 1940. ▷ **Liberal Party** (UK)

Simon, Jules François (1814–96) French politician and philosopher. A lecturer at the Sorbonne in 1839, he became a Republican Deputy in 1848, and later one of the opposition Deputies in the *Corps Législatif* of the Second Empire. He was a member of the Government of **National Defence** (1870–1), and was elected to the National Assembly (1871). He was Minister of Public Instruction (1871–3), and Prime Minister (1876–7). Describing himself as 'profoundly republican and profoundly conservative', he was nevertheless dismissed by President **MacMahon** on 16 May 1877, opening a major constitutional crisis. ▷ **Empire, Second** (France)

Sinai Campaign (1956) This campaign, which can be seen as forming a prelude to the Suez Crisis, took Israeli armour to the Suez Canal. Terrorist raids from Gaza in 1955 were put forward as the reason for Israel's move into the Gaza Strip, which caused the Egyptians to close the Gulf of Aqaba. Egypt consulted on a joint military response with Syria and Jordan, but secret talks between Britain, France and Israel (so effectively secret that it appears that not even the British Ambassador in Cairo knew of them) resulted in an Israeli attack on the Sinai Peninsula on 29 Oct 1956. By 5 Nov, when the UN imposed a ceasefire, the Israelis under the leadership of Moshe **Dayan** had occupied Sinai and reached the Suez Canal.

Sindia The title of the Maratha princes of Gwalior. Their founder was Ranaji Sindia, who rose to high rank in the bodyguard of the Peshwa, and had a grant of half the province of Mala. ▷ **Sindia, Baji Rao; Sindia, Madhava Rao; Sindia, Mahadaji**

Sindia, Baji Rao (d.1886) Maratha Prince of Gwalior. During the **Indian Uprising** of 1857–8 he took the field against the rebels; but most of his troops deserted him, and he fled to Agra. He was reinstated, and was succeeded by his adopted son.

857

Sindia, Daulat Rao (1779–1827) Maratha Prince of Gwalior. The grandnephew of Ranaji Sindia, he ravaged Indore and Pune, but was routed by Holkar (1802), and next year brought upon himself the vengeance of the British **East India Company**. The Marathas were routed at Assaye and Argaum by Sir Arthur Wellesley (**Wellington**), and were scattered at Laswari by Lord Lake. Thereupon Sindia ceded all his possessions in the Doab and along the right bank of the River Jumna to the British. Gwalior was restored in 1805.

Sindia, Madhava Rao (d.1794) Maratha Prince of Gwalior. The illegitimate son of Ranaji Sindia, he joined the Maratha confederation, and was crippled for life at the Battle of **Panipat** (1761). In 1770, along with the Peshwa and Holkar (the chief general), he helped the Mughal to expel the Sikhs and became virtually supreme in Hindustan. He came into conflict with the British in 1779, and was defeated by Warren **Hastings**, but by the Treaty of Salbai (1783) was confirmed in all his possessions. In 1784 he captured Gwalior, in 1785 marched on Delhi, and subsequently seized Agra, Alighar and nearly the whole of the Doab. He raised and drilled an army in European fashion and crushed Jodhpur, Udaipur and Jaipur (all Rajput states), while Holkar remained his ally. He died (possibly murdered) at Pune.

Sindia, Mahadaji (1727–94) Maratha Ruler of Gwalior (1761/94). He succeeded Madu Rao in 1772 as Peshwa ('commander') of the combined Maratha forces. In addition to Maratha lieutenants, he used mercenary troops, hired adventurers and obtained assistance from the battalions of the French officer, de Boigne. He used his trained troops in the decisive encounters that made him dominant in the Delhi kingdom and secured his supremacy in Rajputana. His dominion soon stretched from the River Sutluj to the Narmada and he became the recognized Mughal agent as Deputy Regent of the empire. However, his ambition was to control Pune and in 1792 he marched there to assert his claims against Holkar and Fadnavis in the Pune court. His death left his lands in the far less capable hands of Daulat Rao, and his disciplined troops passed to the correspondingly weak Perron.

Singh, Charan (1902–87) Indian politician. Born into a poor peasant family in Meerut District, Uttar Pradesh, he obtained a law degree in 1925. He started practising law in Ghaziabad, and soon became involved in the freedom movement. He courted arrest in the Salt **Satyagraha** in 1932. In 1929 he joined the Congress, and was elected to the Uttar Pradesh Legislative Assembly in 1937, going on to represent his constituency for 40 years until 1977, when he was elected for the Lok Sabha. He joined both the **Non-Cooperation Movement** and **Quit India Movement** in 1940. He was Chief Minister of Uttar Pradesh twice, and in 1969 formed the ministry of *Bharatiya Kranti Dal* (BKD). Charan Singh's *Bharatiya Lok Dal* revolted against Morarji **Desai**'s 28-month-old Janata government and he was sworn in as the fifth prime minister of India in July 1979. He served in this capacity until Congress won the general elections in 1980.

Singh, V(ishwanath) P(ratap) (1931–) Indian politician. The son of an influential Raja in Uttar Pradesh, he was educated at Pune and Allahabad Universities and was elected (1971) to the Lok Sabha (federal parliament) as a representative of the Congress (I) Party. During the administrations of Indira **Gandhi** and Rajiv **Gandhi**, he served as Minister of Commerce (1976–7 and 1983), Chief Minister of Uttar Pradesh (1980–2), Minister of Finance (1984–6) and Minister of Defence (1986–7), instigating a zealous anticorruption drive in the finance and defence posts. In 1987 he was ousted from the government and Congress (I) when he unearthed the 'Bofors Scandal', which involved the payment of alleged arms deal 'kickbacks' to senior officials closely connected to Rajiv Gandhi. Respected for his probity and sense of principle, as head of the broad-based Janata Dal coalition he emerged as the most popular opposition politician in India. He was elected Prime Minister in 1990.

Sinhala A language of North Indian origin. The speakers of the language, the Sinhala or Sinhalese, form the largest group in the population of Sri Lanka and have dominated the country's politics since independence in 1948. Most Sinhala people are Buddhists and modern Buddhist nationalists believe that the Buddha himself entrusted the care of the island to the Sinhala people as custodians of his teaching. The election of S W R D **Bandaranaike** in 1956, with a promise to make Sinhala the sole language of used in government led to opposition from the country's predominantly Hindu Tamil minority, which has continued ever since.

Sinn Féin Irish political party (literally, 'Ourselves Alone') which developed during the period 1905–8 under the direction of Arthur **Griffith** in support of Irish independence from Britain. By the end of **World War I** it had become the main Irish nationalist party. It formed a separate assembly from the UK parliament, and succeeded in creating the **Irish Free State** (1922). Following the Anglo-Irish Treaty (1921), it split to form the two main Irish parties, and in 1970 it split again into official and provisional wings. It has remained active in Northern Ireland, and has close contacts with the **IRA**. ▷ **Fianna Fáil; Fine Gael**

Sino-Japanese War (1894–5) A long-standing conflict between Chinese and Japanese interests in Korea, which resulted in war during the Ming period. China suffered a humiliating defeat, and by the Treaty of **Shimonoseki** (1895) recognized Korean independence and ceded Taiwan, the Liaodong Peninsula, and the Pescadores to Japan.

Sino-Japanese War (1937–45) The war proper broke out in 1937 with the Japanese invasion of Tianjin (Tientsin) and Beijing, but this was only the ultimate phase of Japan's territorial designs on China. Manchuria had already been occupied (1931) and the puppet-state of **Manzhuguo** created in 1932. Nanjing was invaded in Dec 1937, and most of northern China was soon under Japanese control. From Dec 1941, US intervention became the major factor in the Pacific War, which ended with Japan's surrender in 1945. ▷ **United Fronts; World War II**

Sino-Soviet Dispute (1960–89) The period of extreme tension between the USSR and China, even leading to border war in 1969. **Stalin** had been a half-hearted supporter of the Chinese Communist Party down to 1953; Nikita **Khrushchev** had subsequently been more generous; but both had been patronizing. **Mao Zedong** objected to being treated as inferior, and he had developed his own somewhat different brand of **communism**. Ideological sparring led to Khrushchev withdrawing all Soviet assistance and advisers in 1960. Behind the border dispute also lay serious territorial differences. The situation only improved after **Deng Xiaoping** launched China on an outward-looking reform programme in 1978 and Mikhail **Gorbachev** started his revolutionary upheaval in 1985. Their meeting in Beijing in 1989 signalled the end of the dispute, though internal developments in both countries have since renewed the strain.

Sioux (Dakota) A cluster of Siouan-speaking Native North American groups belonging to the Plains culture. Having moved from further north into present-day north and south Dakota, they acquired horses, fought wars against other native groups, and hunted buffalo. They were later involved in clashes with advancing white settlers and prospectors, and were finally defeated at **Wounded Knee** (1890).

Sipahi (Spahi) Ottoman cavalryman. In return for service in the army, Sipahis drew their income from a grant of land, a **timar**, which they held on a non-hereditary basis.

Siraj ud-Daula (Mirza Muhammad) (c.1732–57) Nawab (Ruler) of Bengal under the nominal suzerainty of the **Mughal Empire** (1756/7). He came into conflict with the British over their fortification of Calcutta, and marched on the city in 1756. The British surrender led to the infamous **Black Hole of Calcutta**, for which he was held responsible. Following the recapture of Calcutta, the British under **Clive of Plassey** joined forces with Siraj ud-Daula's general, Mir Jafar, and defeated him at the Battle of **Plassey** in 1757. He fled to Murshidabad, but was captured and executed.

Siroky, Viliam (1902–71) Czechoslovak politician. As a young Slovak railway worker, he helped create the Communist Party in Bratislava in 1921 and by 1935 he was both a secretary of the Central Committee and a communist member of parliament. His experiences in **World War II** included imprisonment in Slovakia and service in Moscow. Siroky's subsequent rise made him Deputy Prime Minister (1945–53), Foreign Minister (1950–3), following the executed **Clementis**, and Prime Minister (1953–63), in succession to **Zapotocky**. He survived the purges, but his bureaucratic credentials were inadequate to cope with the transitional needs of the late 1950s/early 1960s and he was dropped in favour of another Slovak, **Lenart**, whose supposed reform credentials achieved little more.

Sistova, Peace of (1791) The peace established between the Habsburg and the Ottoman Empires at Sistova on the borders of modern Bulgaria and Romania. Emperor **Leopold II**, eager to end the war begun by his brother, Joseph II, agreed to return Belgrade to the Turks in exchange for modest gains in Bosnia. ▷ **Habsburg Dynasty; Ottoman Empire**

Sisulu, Walter Max Ulyate (1912–) South African nationalist. After working as a labourer in Johannesburg and then running his own real estate agency, he joined the **ANC** in 1940, becoming Treasurer of the Youth League in 1944. A leader of the Programme of Action in 1949, he was elected Secretary-General of the ANC in the same year. He resigned his post in 1954 because of banning orders, but continued to work underground. Sisulu was captured in 1963 and found guilty of treason, being sentenced in 1964 to life imprisonment. He was released in 1989 and took responsibility for the party's internal organization after its legalization in 1990.

Sithole, Ndabaningi (1920–) Zimbabwean cleric and politician. He worked as a teacher (1941–53) before going to the USA to study theology (1953–6) and was ordained a congregational minister in 1958. He wrote *African Nationalism* in 1959, when he was also President of the African Teachers' Union. Sithole was Treasurer of the National Democratic Party in 1960 and, after it was banned, formed with Joshua **Nkomo** the Zimbabwe African People's Union (**ZAPU**), from which he split in 1963 and formed the Zimbabwe African National Union (**ZANU**). Imprisoned by the RF government from 1964 to 1975, during which time the leadership of ZANU was wrested from him by Robert **Mugabe**, he went into exile in Zambia in 1975, forming his own faction of the **African National Council**. He negotiated with Ian **Smith** and was a member of the Executive Council of the transitional government in Rhodesia-Zimbabwe (1978–80). Although he was elected to the first post-independence parliament, he ceased thereafter to play a major role in politics.

sitiante The Spanish term used to describe a South American small-scale livestock or mixed farm. In the interior of north-eastern Brazil, it denotes an estate usually devoted to stockraising as its primary economic activity. *Sitiantes* in the southern states commonly cultivated cash crops, but historically employed a few slaves and engaged in subsistence agriculture, such as planting beans, manioc or maize. Sitiantes normally made up the following of local *coroneis* or *fazendeiros*, who often controlled credit and communications. In the Planalto and south, small-scale proprietors were known as *lavradores* or *camponeses* (peasants). By the mid 1960s, such lands had been subdivided to such an extent that they could not support the families of their owners. ▷ **fazendeiro**

Sitting Bull (c.1834–90) Native American warrior. The chief of the Dakota Sioux, he was a leader in the Sioux War of 1876–7. He is remembered especially for his role in the Battle of the **Little Bighorn**, following which he escaped to Canada, but surrendered in 1881. After touring with Buffalo Bill's Wild West Show, he returned to his people, and was present in 1890 when the army suppressed the 'ghost dance' messianic religious movement inspired by the Paiute Wovakq. Sitting Bull was killed during the army's action. ▷ **Cody, William F; Indian Wars; Native Americans**

Six-Day War (5–10 June 1967) Arab-Israeli war. In May 1967 President Gamal Abd al-**Nasser** of Egypt blocked the Tiran Straits to Israeli shipping and massed troops in the Sinai Peninsula, while King Hussein allowed Iraqi forces into Jordan. Taking preemptive action, Israel paralysed the Egyptian air force and then, responding to Jordanian and Syrian attacks, captured East Jerusalem, the West bank, Golan Heights and Sinai. Israel's unexpected victory was achieved in six days. Afterwards, Arab states refused to negotiate peace with Israel which has therefore held on to the so-called 'occupied territories', except Sinai which was returned to Egypt after the peace agreement of 1979. ▷ **Arab-Israeli Wars; Israel, State of; Sharon, Ariel; West Bank**

Sixtus IV (Francesco della Rovere) (1414–84) Italian Pope (1471/84). A Genoese, he became a renowned Franciscan preacher, and was made a cardinal in 1467. His was a worldly pontificate. He fostered learning and built the Sistine Chapel, but his nepotism led to many abuses. He lowered the moral authority of the papacy, especially through his involvement in the Pazzi conspiracy against the **Medici** in Florence in 1478, and his sale of indulgences. ▷ **Franciscans**

Sixtus V (Felice Peretti) (1521–90) Italian Pope (1585/90). Elected for his apparent feebleness, his rule proved vigorously reformist. He repressed licence and disorder, reformed the law and the disposal of patronage, and secured a surplus for the treasury. A fierce opponent of Protestantism, he extended a measure of liberty to the Jews. He also instigated the building of the Vatican Library at the Lateran Palace.

Skanderbeg (George Kastrioti) (1405–68) Albanian patriot, of Serb descent. Carried away by Ottoman Turks at the age of seven, he was brought up a Muslim, and became a favourite commander of Sultan Murad II, who gave him his byname, a combination of *Iskander* ('Alexander') and the rank of bey. In 1443 he changed sides, renounced Islam, and drove the Turks from Albania. For 20 years he maintained Albanian independence, but after his death, opposition to the Turks collapsed.

Skobeleff, Mikhail Dmitrievich (1843–82) Russian soldier. He fought against the Polish insurgents (1863), and from 1871 to 1875 was at the conquest of Khiva and Khokland. In the Russo-Turkish War of 1877–78 he played a conspicuous part at Plevna, in the Shipka pass, and at Adrianople; in 1881 he stormed the Turkoman stronghold of Göktepe. He was an ardent Panslavist. ▷ **Russo-Turkish Wars**

Skobtsova, Maria (1891–1945) Russian Orthodox nun. She early identified herself with the Social Revolutionaries when a student in St Petersburg, where she was the first woman to enrol at the Ecclesiastical Academy. Bolshevik excesses having disillusioned her, she was among those who escaped to France. She began work with the Russian Orthodox Student Christian Movement which administered also to refugees, and in 1932, despite having had two divorces, became a nun. Unconventional and radical, she worked among society's cast-offs whom she fed and housed. Nazi measures against the Jews in wartime Paris provided a new challenge. She was arrested and sent to Ravensbrück concentration camp in 1943, where she brought Christian light and hope despite appalling conditions. She was gassed on the eve of Easter, 1945, reportedly going voluntarily 'in order to help her companions to die'.

Skúli Magnússon ▷ **Magnússon, Skúli**

Slankamen, Battle of (20 Aug 1691) This battle, fought between the Ottoman army under Mustafa Koprulu and Habsburg forces under Louis of Baden, resulted in the ambush and defeat of the Ottomans and the death of Mustafa. His expedition had been aimed at reversing the Ottoman failures of the previous decade in Hungary and the Balkans by carrying Ottoman arms into Hungary, and the defeat was significant in that, since the Habsburgs were preoccupied by affairs in the west and since the Ottoman advance had been halted by the battle, the Danube became established as the boundary between the Ottoman and Habsburg Empires. ▷ **Habsburg Dynasty; Ottoman Empire**

Slánský, Rudolf (1901–52) Czechoslovak politician. Born in Moravia, an intellectual, he joined the Communist Party when it was founded in 1921 and, in 1929, became one of Klement **Gottwald**'s chief aides in revolutionizing or 'bolshevizing' it. He spent much of **World War II** in Moscow but in 1944 was flown in to assist the Slovak uprising. From 1945 to 1951 he held the most important party post as Secretary-General, masterminding much of what produced and followed the **February Revolution** in 1948. However, he was arrested, then executed during the purges, a victim of **Stalin**'s dislike of independent-minded communists, especially Jewish intellectuals. It was little comfort to the majority of his countrymen that he suffered the self-same fate he had imposed on others.

Slave Rebellions The normal slave response to bondage was indirect resistance through sham illness, non-cooperation, vandalism and maroonage but when driven to extremes by white brutality or unfulfilled expectations, such as the **Amelioration** proposals of 1823 in the British West Indies, outright rebellion erupted. There were major slave uprisings in Cuba virtually every 10 years from 1792 to 1844, and in Jamaica from 1655 to 1831; indeed, these were commonplace in almost every Caribbean colony. The only successful revolt was the **Haitian Revolution** of 1791, but the rebellion of Cuffy in Berbice (1763) came near to triumph and the revolt of Sam Sharpe in Jamaica (1831) seriously frightened the Jamaican plantocracy.

slavery A system of social inequality in which some people are treated as items of property belonging to other individuals or social groups. There have been different types and conditions of slavery throughout human history, and slavery has been present in societies that have otherwise been considered advanced. Slaves have often been captured peoples, considered part of the spoils of war. At one extreme, slaves have been worked to death, as in the Greek mining camps of the 5c and 4c BC. At the other, slaves have been used less as chattels and more as servants, working in households, and to an extent even administering them and acting as tutors to young children. The institution of slavery was one of the major issues over which the **American Civil War** was fought.

slave trade A trade in Africa which started in ancient times. Slaves were sent across the

Sahara and were traded in the Mediterranean by Phoenicians; Graeco-Roman traders in the Red Sea and beyond traded slaves from East Africa to Egypt and the Middle East. These trades continued in medieval times, but the scale of the trade built up with the arrival of the Portuguese in Africa and the development of the labour-intensive plantation system in the West African islands of São Tomé and Principe, Brazil, the Caribbean, the southern American colonies, and later the Indian Ocean islands, and South and East Africa. The Portuguese dominated the trade in the 16c, the Dutch in the early 17c, while the late 17c was a period of intense competition with the French, British, Danes, and Swedes joining the early practitioners. The trade reached its peak in the second half of the 18c, and from this period the East African **slave trade** became more significant, particularly during the period of Omani power up to the 1860s. The British abolished the slave trade in 1807, and the institution of slavery in 1833. They then instituted Royal Naval anti-slavery squadrons on the coasts of western and eastern Africa. There have been various estimates of the number of slaves removed from Africa, the most reliable figure being c.12.5 million between 1650 and 1850. Many other people must have lost their lives in the wars stimulated by the trade, and the total drain meant that at the very least the African population remained static for over two centuries.

Slave Trade, Abolition of the Effected in the **British Empire** by an Act of parliament of 1807. The Society for Effecting the Abolition of the Slave Trade was founded in 1787 and was spearheaded by the 'Clapham Sect' or 'Saints', whose membership included Ramsay, Clarkson, Stephen and Fowell Buxton and which found a political voice in William **Wilberforce**, the MP for Yorkshire. Although Wilberforce's abolition bill had lacked government support during the **Pitt** administration, in 1806 the **Tories** were replaced by the **Whigs** of Charles James **Fox**, the bill became law a year later and the last British slave trader, the *Kitty Amelia* left Liverpool in May 1808. Denmark had abolished its trade in 1804, the USA in 1808, France in 1818 and Spain in 1820.

Slavonia The region of **Croatia** lying between Bosnia and Hungary. The first recorded reference to Slavonia as a kingdom dates from 1240. The Hungarian King Béla IV administered it as a *banovina* with its own *ban* (viceroy) within the Kingdom of Croatia

(1260). In the 13–14c, it was ruled by members of the ruling dynasty in Hungary, but was returned to the Croatian ban in 1476. The Slavonian *sabor* (parliament) was joined to that of Croatia in the mid-16c but Slavonia was then occupied by the Ottomans until the Treaty of **Karlowitz** (1699), when it passed to the Habsburg Emperor and was absorbed into the **Military Frontier**. ▷ **Triune Kingdom**

Slavonic Congresses (1848, 1868 and 1908) The series of meetings of Slav delegates in Prague, aimed at showing the unity of the Slav peoples in their struggles against other ethnic ruling groups. The Czechs were probably the least self-centred of the Slav peoples, but they also had local anti-Austrian and anti-German reasons for calling the congresses. The first congress was organized by František **Palacký**, the second was addressed by him, and the third was summoned by **Kramar**. All of them drummed up general sentiments of solidarity, but showed evidence of international divisions. In Czech terms, the first two were the more succcessful in strengthening national feeling; the third, however, was too much dedicated to Kramar's personal political views.

Slavophils and Westerners Opposing schools of thought in Russia during the 1840s. The Westerners argued that backward Russia should emulate the political, legal, scientific, and rational traditions of Western Europe. The Slavophils believed in the superior quality of traditional Russian religious and social values, including Orthodox worship, a benevolent autocracy, and social and spiritual community (*sobornost*).

Slavs The largest group of European peoples sharing a common ethnic and linguistic origin, consisting of Russians, Ukrainians, Belorussians, Poles, Czechs, Slovaks, Bulgarians, Serbs, Croats, Montenegrins, and Macedonians. The ancient Slavs, inhabiting central and Eastern Europe, were first mentioned in 2c AD sources. Since **World War II**, most of the Slav nations have been ruled by socialist governments.

SLFP (Sri Lanka Freedom Party) Left-of-centre Sri Lankan political party formed by S W R D **Bandaranaike** after his departure from the **UNP** in 1951. The SLFP formed the largest party in government in 1956–9, 1960–5 and 1970–7. Each time, the party achieved power as leader of a coalition formed with smaller left-wing parties, and each time the coalition was undermined by internal friction and gradual defections to the opposition. The leadership of the party has been dominated by Bandaranaike, his widow, Sirimavo **Bandaranaike**, and their children and close relatives.

Slim (of Yarralumia and of Bishopston), William (Joseph), 1st Viscount (1891–1970) British field marshal. He served during **World War I** in the **Gallipoli Campaign** and in Mesopotamia. In **World War II**, his greatest achievement was to lead his reorganized forces, the famous 14th 'forgotten' army, to victory over the Japanese in Burma. He was Chief of the Imperial General Staff (1948–52) and a highly successful Governor-General of Australia (1953–60). Knighted in 1944, he became a viscount in 1960.

Slingelandt, Simon van (1664–1736) Dutch politician and political thinker. From 1690 to 1725 he was Secretary to the Council of State, then became Thesaurier-General to the republic, and in 1757 **Grand Pensionary** of the Province of Holland. He believed firmly that the Dutch Republic should have a much stronger central authority, which he suggested could be vested in the Council of State; his best chance of achieving this programme was at the Great Meeting held in 1716 on the structure of the republic; however, the particularism of the provinces carried the day. His works were admired in the 1780s by members of the **Patriot Movement**.

Slovak National Movement (19c and 20c) A movement somewhat similar to, although much slower and less certain than, the **Czech National Movement**. The Slovaks were poorer than the Czechs, were more effectively oppressed by their Hungarian rulers, and had a less remarkable history to look back on. But they, too, had a cultural revival and gained strength from demographic movement. However, nationalism at home was much more dependent on support from abroad: from the US Slovaks through the **Pittsburgh Agreement**, and from **Masaryk** and **Stefanik** in the West in **World War I**. The creation of a united Czechoslovak state in 1918 did not entirely satisfy all the Slovaks, as witnessed the **Slovak Republic** during **World War II**.

Slovak Republic (1939–45) The supposedly independent republic carved out of Czechoslovakia by Slovak nationalists on **Hitler's** instructions. Many Slovaks had genuine

complaints: the Czechs had established a centralized state in 1918, were less devoutly Catholic and economically better off. However, those who led the new republic (such as **Tiso** and **Tuka**) soon lost popularity as the Germans exploited the Slovak economy and expected Slovaks to fight in the hated Russian front. Resistance produced the **Slovak Uprising** in 1944. Although it was put down by the Germans, their presence and brutality simply recruited more volunteers to fight against them and Tiso. Little was done after 1945 to meet legitimate Slovak aspirations, but in Jan 1993 Slovakia finally gained its independence.

Slovak Uprising (Sep–Oct 1944) A rising against **Tiso**, President of the **Slovak Republic**, and his German masters. The rebels comprised partisans, civilians, Allied helpers and insurgent regiments from the Slovak army. Their aim was to free eastern Slovakia as the **Red Army** advanced and to block German reinforcements. For two months they held a large area around Banska Bystrice. But the Germans moved quickly, the Russians slowly, and there were divided counsels. Despite great heroism, the rising was put down. Many fighters escaped to the mountains; inevitably the civilians suffered. The Slovaks gained little except an important historical memory.

Slovenia, Republic of Like the Republics of Croatia and Bosnia, one of the new independent successor states to the old Socialist Federal Republic of Yugoslavia. In June 1991, Milan Kučan declared the Republic's independence from the Yugoslav Federation. The Yugoslav National Army invaded but, after the so-called 'Ten-Day War', Serbia's President, Slobodan **Milošević**, acknowledged Slovenia's independence in the vain hope that he could arrest the secession of the Republics of Croatia and Bosnia.

Slovo, Joe (1926–) South African nationalist. Born in Lithuania, he emigrated to South Africa in 1935, where he worked as a clerk before volunteering for service in **World War II**. After joining the South African Communist Party (SACP), he qualified as a lawyer and defended many figures in political trials. He married Ruth First, daughter of the SACP Treasurer, and was a founding member of the Congress of Democrats in 1953. Charged in the treason trial of 1961, he nevertheless escaped the country in 1963 working for the **ANC** and SACP abroad.

In 1985 he became Chief of Staff of **Umkhonto we Sizwe** but resigned to become Chairman of the SACP. He returned to South Africa after the legalization of the SACP and has been a major figure in the negotiations between the nationalist parties and the government.

Sluys, Battle of (1340) A naval battle fought in the Zwyn estuary in Flanders, the first major English victory in the **Hundred Years War**. **Edward III**, King of England, personally commanded the English fleet, which wiped out or captured all but 24 of 200 French ships. However, he failed to follow up his victory, either on land or sea.

Smalls, Robert (1839–1915) US sailor and politician. A slave in Charleston, South Carolina, who with his brother shanghaied a Confederate paddle steamer, the *Planter*, and sailed it through Confederate guns to the Union fleet blockading the port. Later he enlisted as a pilot in the Union navy. Smalls was one of the 200 000 blacks who crossed to the Union lines and served as spies and guides in unfamiliar territory, as well as working as labourers. After the war his military service provided a springboard for a local political career in South Carolina, in the course of which he served in the US House of Representatives.

Smeral, Bohumir (1880–1941) Czechoslovak politician. A lawyer, he joined the Social Democratic Party in 1897 and was editing its paper by 1906. During **World War I** he was slow to join the struggle for Czechoslovak independence, and following the 1917 **Russian Revolution** his loyalty swung increasingly towards the left. In 1921 he helped found the Communist Party and became very active in Czechoslovak politics in the 1920s. In the 1930s he was also very active in the **Comintern**, which involved much travelling. Although he fled to Moscow in 1938 and died there, he was never a Stalinist, preserving some traces of his social democratic moderation. ▷ **Stalinism**

Smirnov, Georgi Lukich (1922–) Soviet communist ideologue. Of Cossack stock with a long career in the Communist Party bureaucracy, he became adviser to Mikhail **Gorbachev** in 1985 and Director of the Institute of Marxism–Leninism in 1987. In both positions he attempted to modify Brezhnevite orthodoxy; he was still trying, with only moderate success, when the party was closed down in 1991.

Smith, Alfred Emanuel (1873–1944) US politician. He rose from newsboy to be Governor of New York State (1919–20 and 1923–8) with an impressive record of liberal reform. 'Al' Smith was beaten as Democratic candidate for the US presidency in 1928, and later became an opponent of President Franklin D **Roosevelt**'s **New Deal**.

Smith, Goldwin (1823–1910) Canadian publicist. Regius Professor of Modern History at Oxford (1858–66), he settled permanently in Canada in 1871, and founded a chair of history at Toronto. He became one of the major figures in **Canada First**, and in *Canada and the Canadian Question* (1891) he argued for the union of Canada with the USA.

Smith, Ian (Douglas) (1919–) Rhodesian politician and farmer. Educated at Chaplin High School and Rhodes University, he served with the Royal Airforce in **World War II** before returning to his farm. He was elected a member of the Southern Rhodesian Legislative Assembly in 1948 for the United Party and then, for the United Federal Party (UFP), to the Federal Parliament in 1953, becoming Chief Whip. He broke with the UFP, ostensibly on the question of Britain's failure to grant independence to the white minority-ruled states of central Africa, and helped found the **Rhodesian Front** in 1962. He replaced Winston Field as leader after a putsch and was Prime Minister from 1964 to 1978, when he became a member of the Executive Council of the transitional government in Zimbabwe-Rhodesia. A cautious and secretive man, he declared **UDI** (Unilateral Declaration of Independence) in 1965, negotiated without success with successive British governments and was immensely popular with his white voters. He was elected to the post-independence parliament and remained a vigorous opponent of Robert **Mugabe** and his government.

Smith, John (1580–1631) English colonist and explorer. He fought in Transylvania and Hungary, where he was captured by the Turks, and sold as a slave. After escaping to Russia, he joined an expedition to colonize Virginia (1607), and helped found **Jamestown**. He was saved from death by **Pocahontas**. His energy and tact in dealing with the Indians led to his being elected president of the colony (1608–9). He wrote valuable accounts of his travels, and died in London.

Smrkovsky, Josef (1911–74) Czechoslovak politician. A baker's assistant, he joined the

Communist Party in 1933 and was active in the resistance during **World War II**. He was one of the leaders of the Prague rising in 1945 and held a series of party and government posts until, in 1951, he was imprisoned during the Stalinist purges. It was 1963 before he was rehabilitated and 1966 before he was readmitted to the party. In 1967–8 he was a prime mover in the reforms and became a popular chairman of parliament. His very moderation made him a Soviet target; and like Alexander **Dubček** himself he was taken to Moscow in Aug 1968 and then removed from power at the first opportunity the following year.

Smuts, Jan (Christian) (1870–1950) South African general and politician. Educated at the University of Cambridge, England, he became a lawyer, fought in the second Boer War (1899–1902), and entered the House of Assembly in 1907. He held several Cabinet posts, led campaigns against the Germans in south-west Africa and Tanganyika, was a member of the Imperial War Cabinet in **World War I**, and succeeded Louis **Botha** as Prime Minister (1919–24). He was a significant figure at Versailles, and was instrumental in the founding of the **League of Nations**. As Minister of Justice under **Hertzog**, his coalition with the Nationalists in 1934 produced the United Party; he was Premier again from 1939 to 1948. ▷ **Boer Wars**

Snamek, Jan (1870–1956) Czechoslovak politician. Born and educated in Moravia, he was variously a priest, professor of theology and papal negotiator, and helped found Christian democracy in the late 1890s. A deputy from 1907, he supported **Masaryk** during **World War I** and, as leader of the Populist Party in the interwar period, held several ministerial appointments. During **World War II** he was Prime Minister in **Beneš**'s government-in-exile in London, and Deputy Prime Minister (1945–8) in the National Front government. Usually a moderate, he nevertheless joined those resigning in 1948 and precipitating the **February Revolution**. The middle road had not been easy and it became impossible under **communism**.

Sneferu (Neb-maat) (c.2613/2589BC) King of Egypt. He was the founder of the 4th Dynasty. The highlights of his reign are recounted in his annals, partly preserved on the Palermo Stone. Named from the city where it is now housed, the stone contains inscriptions of the names of rulers, lengths of reigns and outstanding events for the early

Egyptian period. From it we know that Sneferu campaigned against Nubians and Libyans while trading expeditions were sent by sea to the coast of Syria for timber (no fewer than 40 ships laden with cedar returned to Egypt). A number of building constructions were undertaken — temples, fortresses and palaces. In Sinai rock carvings show that the copper mines were worked and the Bedawin kept in check. The king built two pyramids at Dahshur near Sakkara. The southern one is known as the Bent or Rhomboidal Pyramid because of the lower angle of its upper part, while the north pyramid is of normal shape. From reliefs, recovered from the valley temple connected to the Bent Pyramid and tombs in its vicinity, a picture of the centralized administration, official religion and daily life of the early **Old Kingdom** is obtained.

Snorri Sturluson ▷ **Sturluson, Snorri**

Soares, Mario Alberto Nobre Lopez (1924–) Portuguese politician. Educated at Lisbon University and in the Faculty of Law at the Sorbonne, Paris, he was politically active in the democratic socialist movement from his early twenties and was imprisoned for his activities on 12 occasions. In 1968 he was deported by **Salazar** to São Tomé, returning to Europe in 1970 and living in exile in Paris until 1974 when he returned to co-found the Social Democratic Party (PSD). In the same year he was elected to the Assembly and was soon brought into the government. He was Prime Minister (1976–8 and 1983–5), and then in 1986 was elected Portugal's first civilian President for 60 years.

Sobbuza II (1899–1982) King of Swaziland. Educated at Lovedale College, he was installed as Paramount Chief or Ngwenyama of the Swazi people in 1921. He was Head of State when Swaziland became independent in 1968, but in 1973 he assumed full executive and legislative powers and introduced a new Constitution in 1978 which re-established traditional authorities, rather than universal suffrage, as the basis of legitimate authority.

Sobchak, Anatoli Alexandrovich (1937–) Russian politician. A talented law graduate who became Dean of the Faculty of Law in Leningrad (now St Petersburg), long before turning to politics. In the **Gorbachev** period he became critical of many past communist practices and was chosen in 1989 as a member of both the Congress of Deputies and the Supreme Soviet, where he demonstrated his investigative and debating skills. In May 1990 he was elected Mayor of St Petersburg and in July abandoned the Communist Party to become both locally and nationally one of the driving forces for serious reform.

Sobukwe, Robert (1924–77) South African nationalist leader. Educated at mission schools and Fort Hare College, he was President of the Students' Representative Council in 1949 and a member of the **ANC** Youth League. He was dismissed from his teacher's post in 1952 because of his participation in the Defiance Campaign, but taught for the next seven years at Fort Hare College. He helped found the **Pan-Africanist Congress** (PAC) in 1959 and was elected its President. He was banned in 1960 and then imprisoned until 1969 when he was released, but restricted to Kimberley where he died in 1977.

Social and Liberal Democratic Party (SLDP) ▷ **Liberal Party** (UK)

Social Credit Party Canadian political party. The monetary theory known as social credit (regarded as nonsense by most economists) was developed by a British engineer, Major Clifford H Douglas, during the early 1930s. It held that government should issue payments (social credits) to everyone, in order to balance consumers' buying power with agricultural and manufacturing productivity. It attracted the attention of an Albertan radio-evangelist, William Aberhardt, who spread the doctrine to the depression-hit prairie farmers. In the provincial election of 1935, the Social Credit Party came to power. The federal government, however, disallowed its attempts to implement its policies, and in a short time the party became just another free enterprise neo-conservative political party. As such, it retained power and had cleared the province's debts by the mid-1950s. In 1952 it also defeated the Liberal–Conservative coalition in British Columbia, and throughout the 1950s it grew in federal strength. By 1962 **Diefenbaker** required its support to maintain his fragile hold on power, but in 1979 it contributed to a Conservative defeat when Joe **Clark** refused to bargain for its support in a vote of confidence. By the 1980s, however, the party had all but disappeared. ▷ **Créditistes**

Social Darwinism A school of thought which developed within 19c sociology based on the belief that social evolution depended on society adapting most efficiently to its environment. The associated 'eugenics movement' argued that Western society had developed because of the superior abilities of Whites compared with other 'racial' groups.

Social Democratic Party (Denmark) Founded in 1871 as a section of the socialist First International, in 1878 it was divided into a trade union wing and a political party wing, which in 1884 for the first time became represented in the Danish parliament, **Folketinget**. After the general election in 1924, the Social Democrats became the largest party in parliament and formed their first government, with Thorvald **Stauning** as Premier. The party has remained Denmark's largest. During the interwar period the party, under Stauning's leadership, moved away from the socialist idea of a class struggle. Instead, it became the party's ambition to create a welfare state for all social groups through democratic, parliamentary reforms. This ambition was fulfilled during the post-war period under the party leaders Hedtoft, Hansen, Kampmann and **Krag**, all of whom were also prime ministers. After 1973, when the Danish economy was hit by recession, the party, led by Joørgensen (1972–87) and Auken (1987–92), became the chief defender of the welfare system, since 1982 as the main opposition party. In 1992 Poul Nyrup Rasmussen was elected the new party leader.

Social Democratic Party (Finland) Founded in 1899, the party adopted a revolutionary, Marxist programme. It collaborated with Russian socialists against the Tsarist regime but was also committed to achieving Finland's independence from the Russian Empire. By 1916 it had won an absolute majority in the Finnish parliament, but was taken by surprise by the 1917 **Russian Revolution**. Despite its collaboration with the bourgeois parties, the SDP's radicalism alarmed its partners in government, who achieved a parliamentary majority in the elections of Oct 1917. At this point, the SDP was urged by the new Bolshevik regime in Russia and by its own working-class supporters to seize power in its own right. The workers took control of the country through a revolutionary general strike, but the party leadership hesitated. When the bourgeois parties gave in to their demands for reform, the SDP called off the strike and a bourgeois government was formed. In Jan 1918 the Social Democrats declared this government deposed and set up a provisional workers' government. Civil war followed, in which the Reds were supported by the **Bolsheviks** and the Whites by the Germans. The Reds were defeated (Apr 1918) and much of the leadership went into exile in Russia; in Aug 1918 they formed the Finnish Communist Party. The SDP in Finland was suppressed after the civil war but was revived, largely through the efforts of Väinö **Tanner**, in late 1918. From this point dates the deep division between the two wings of the Finnish workers' movement and the hostility of the communists towards Tanner's revisionism. Although the SDP retained the loyalties of the majority of the working class, an important minority was attracted to the communist-influenced Finnish Socialist Workers' Party, formed in 1920. Tanner formed a minority government, with the support of the Swedish People's Party, in 1926–7, but lost the leadership of the SDP for four years. SDP support grew steadily in the 1930s despite the attempt by the **Lapua Movement** to repeat against the SDP the success of its anti-communist agitation. Excluded from office in 1936 by the opposition of President Svinhufvud, the Social Democrats formed a stable, broad-based coalition with the Agrarians and the Progressives following Svinhufvud's defeat in the presidential election of 1937, and were in government throughout Finland's two disastrous wars with the USSR in 1939–40 and 1941–4. A minority of the party opposed the war and linked up with the Communist Party when the latter was legalized after Finland's defeat, forming part of the communists' parliamentary organization, the Finnish People's Democratic League (SKDL). Tanner regained control of the SDP in Nov 1944 but was imprisoned as a war criminal (1946–9). Throughout the 1950s the party was weakened by internal struggles and was under the shadow of Soviet suspicion, heightened by the re-election of Tanner as Party Chairman in 1957. A major realignment of Finnish politics occurred in 1966; from this point onwards, the majority of Finnish governments were coalitions of Social Democrats, SKDL and the Centre Party, usually with a Social Democrat as Prime Minister. The 1980s saw a strong revival of the Finnish Conservative Party (which had also been the object of Soviet mistrust), but the SDP remained the largest party. In 1982 a Social Democrat, Mauno **Koivisto**, was elected President. ▷ **Communist Party** (Finland)

Social Democratic Party (Sweden) The party was founded in Stockholm in 1889. Under the leadership of Hjalmar **Branting**, who became its first parliamentary representative in 1896, it came to adopt a reformist programme and was the largest party in the directly-elected chamber of the parliament by 1915. Social Democratic ministers sat in a coalition government with the Liberals in 1917, and Branting headed purely Social Democrat administrations in 1920–5. Under Per Albin **Hansson**, Tage **Erlander** and Sven Olof **Palme** the Social Democrats enjoyed continuous power from 1932 to 1976 (except for a brief break in 1936) either alone or in coalition with the Agrarians, but only rarely have they enjoyed an overall majority.

Social Democratic Party (SDP) UK political party formed in 1981 by a 'gang of four', comprising David **Owen**, Shirley **Williams**, Roy **Jenkins**, and Bill Rogers. They broke away from the **Labour Party** primarily over disagreements on policy and the degree of influence exerted on party policy by the trade unions. Although espousing socialist principles, the party was a moderate centrist one. The SDP formed an electoral pact with the Liberals in 1981, but despite some early electoral successes failed to break the two-party 'mould' of British politics. It merged with the **Liberal Party** in 1988 becoming the **Social and Liberal Democratic Party**, although a rump, led by David Owen, continued in existence as the SDP until 1990.

Social Gospel An early 20c movement in the USA concerned with the application of Christian principles to the social and political order in the service of the Kingdom of God. Among its most prominent leaders were Washington Gladden (1836–1918), Walter Rauschenbusch (1861–1918), and Shailer Matthews (1863–1941).

socialism A wide-ranging political doctrine which first emerged in Europe during industrialization in the 18c. Most socialists would agree that social and economic relationships play a major part in determining human possibilities, and that the unequal ownership of property under capitalism creates an unequal and conflictive society. The removal of private property or some means of counterbalancing its power, it is held, will produce a more equal society where individuals enjoy greater freedom and are able to realize their potential more fully. A socialist society will thus be more co-operative and fraternal. Possibly the major division within socialism is between those who believe that to bring it about revolution is necessary, and those who believe change can be achieved through reforms within the confines of democratic politics. There are also differences as to how far capitalist production needs to be eradicated to bring about a socialist society.

Socialism in One Country (post-1918) The slogan epitomizing Soviet policy after the **Russian Revolution**. **Lenin** forced the events of late 1917 on the basis that a few workers and a mass of poor peasants constituted a genuine 'working class'. However, he still expected communist revolutions in more advanced industrial countries. When these did not materialize, he and **Stalin** opted for a policy of building socialism within formerly Tsarist Russia, using their 'working class' to build the industry that the country needed to have a genuine proletariat. What resulted was not socialism, but a personal dictatorship within a forcibly industrialized country. The USSR also developed a very defensive foreign policy.

Socialism with a Human Face (1968) The description applied to the reform **communism** proposed by Alexander **Dubček** in Czechoslovakia in 1968. It included genuine elections, an end to censorship, and freedom of assembly and travel. The threat this seemed to pose to communist parties everywhere provoked the Soviet invasion in Aug of the same year and the end of reform. Ironically, Mikhail **Gorbachev** adopted a somewhat similar but more radical approach which helped to destroy his party.

Socialist Party (France) Officially known (1905–71) as the SFIO (*Section française de l'Internationale ouvrière*, 'French Section of the Workers' International'). Organized socialist parties emerged from 1879, but were for 20 years only tiny sects, divided among themselves, usually known by the name of their leaders, as Guesdists, Broussists, Allemanistes, etc, with very little representation in parliament. By 1901, two main parties had emerged, the *Parti socialiste de France* ('Socialist Party of France') under **Guesde**, more dogmatically Marxist, and the *Parti socialiste français* ('French Socialist Party') under **Jaurès**, more prepared to work within the existing system, and supporting the entry of a socialist, **Millerand**, into the cabinet. Under pressure from the Second International (the umbrella organization, created in 1889, in which all recognized Socialist parties of the world are represented) they united in 1905, accepting in theory the intransigent Marxism of Guesde, but in reality more influenced by Jaurès. Nevertheless the policy

of refusing to accept office in 'bourgeois' cabinets was accepted, and maintained until 1936, except for **World War I**, leading to defection from the party of many of its Deputies who had ministerial ambitions. The majority of the party agreed to support the government in 1914 *Union Sacrée* ('Sacred Union'), but as the war continued, a growing minority turned to opposition. This split foreshadowed the division of 1920 between socialists and communists. The majority of party members voted to join the Third International, and founded a new party. The leading figures in the Socialist Party after 1920 were Léon **Blum**, the leader of the parliamentary group, and Paul Faure, the General-Secretary of the party. In opposition for most of the inter-war period, the socialists overtook the radicals as the largest party of the left in 1936, allowing Blum to form a coalition government, the **Popular Front** (1936–7, 1938). The party was divided over support for **Pétain** in 1940, but emerged in 1945 as one of the three large parties that ruled France (1946–7) in a coalition (Tripartism). In 1947 the communists were excluded from that coalition, and the division of the left between socialists and communists reduced the political influence of both parties for over 30 years. By 1971 the SFIO, which had been led by Guy **Mollet** since 1946, appeared almost moribund; it combined in that year with other small parties and was renamed the *Parti socialiste* ('Socialist Party') with François **Mitterrand** as leader. In 1981 it achieved the feat of winning a majority of seats in parliament, something very rarely achieved in France by a single party, although the majority was lost in 1986. ▷ **socialism**

Socialist Revolutionary (SR) Party A neo-populist revolutionary party in Russia, founded in 1902 and led by Victor Chernov (1873–1952). The SR's radical agrarian programme envisaged the uncompensated redistribution and 'socialization' of the land among a communally organized peasantry. Their 'fighting detachments' carried out a number of spectacular political assassinations between 1902 and 1918. In 1917 Chernov was Minister of Agriculture in the Provisional Government. ▷ **Russian Revolution**

social market economy (*soziale Marktwirtschaft*) Otherwise known as neo-liberalism, the social market economy was adopted first in the western zones of Germany (1948) and then by the Federal Republic (1949). Its guiding principle is that economic stability should be achieved through market forces, although the state is accorded a role in ensuring the smooth operation of a competitive market and in providing social security and welfare benefits in as far as they did not flout market principles. In the 1950s the **CDU** government and its Economics Minister, **Erhard**, were staunch proponents of the social market economy and credited it with Federal Germany's 'economic miracle' (**Wirtschaftswunder**) and by the end of the 1950s all major German parties accepted the principle of a market economy. In practice, however, there had always been and there continue to be deviations from this principle in areas such as competition policy, social policy and labour policy.

Sokolov, Sergei Leonidovich (1911–) Soviet military commander. He rose rapidly during **World War II** and was subsequently given a series of staff posts. In 1965 he became Commander of the Leningrad district and in 1967 Deputy Defence Minister. He was long retired when he was chosen to succeed **Ustinov** as Defence Minister in 1984. This represented a downgrading of the army, a process that was completed when dismissal came in 1987 because of the forces' failure to intercept a German light plane that landed provocatively in Red Square.

Sokolovski, Vasili Danilovich (1897–1968) Soviet marshal. He was already a staff officer by 1921 and led several assaults against Germany in **World War II**, aiding the capture of Berlin. From 1945 to 1949 he was head of the Soviet military administration in Germany and was held responsible for the failure of the **Berlin Blockade**. Yet he became a deputy defence minister for the years 1949–60 and Chief of the General Staff for the period 1952–60. He wrote standard studies of Soviet military strategy.

Solemn League and Covenant (Sep 1643) An alliance between the English parliament and the Scottish rebels against King **Charles I**. Parliament promised £30 000 a month to the Scots and the introduction of full Presbyterianism in England; the Scots agreed to provide an army to the hard-pressed parliamentarians to fight Charles. The pact facilitated parliamentary victory in the first of the **English Civil Wars**, but Presbyterianism was never fully implemented. ▷ **Covenanters**

Solferino, Battle of (20 June 1859) An indecisive engagement between Austrians and invading Franco-Piedmontese forces in Lombardy. Extremely heavy casualties on both sides so revolted **Napoleon III** that he was encouraged to offer the Austrians an armistice without even consulting his Piedmontese allies. ▷ **Villafranca Armistice**

Solidarity An organization established in Poland (Sep 1980) as the National Committee of Solidarity (*Solidarność*) to co-ordinate the activities of the emerging independent trade union following protracted industrial unrest, notably in the Lenin shipyard in Gdańsk. Its first President was Lech **Walesa** (later to become President of Poland). It organized a number of strikes in early 1981 for improved wages and conditions, and became a force for major political reform. It attempted to seek reconciliation with the Polish government through proposing a council for national consensus, but suffered continuous harassment and was rendered largely ineffective by the declaration of martial law (Dec 1981) and by being made illegal. It remained underground, but came back into the political arena in mid-1988. Following its successes in the 1989 elections, Solidarity entered into a coalition government with the communists, with one of its members (Tadeusz Mazowiecki) eventually becoming Prime Minister.

Solon (fl. early 6c BC) Athenian politician, lawgiver, and poet. As eponymous **archon** (594BC), he enacted many economic, constitutional, and legal reforms, and paved the way for the development of democracy at Athens, and her emergence as a great trading state. Enslavement for debt was abolished and citizenship granted to foreign craftsmen settling in Athens. Wealth rather than birth was made the criterion for participation in political life, and **Draco**'s inhumane legal code was largely repealed.

Solzhenitsyn, Alexander Isayevich (1918–) Russian writer. Educated at Rostov in mathematics and physics, he fought in **World War II**, and was imprisoned (1945–53) for unfavourable comment on **Stalin**'s conduct of the war. On his release, he became a teacher, and started to write. His first novel, *Odin den iz zhizni Ivana Denisovicha* (1962, One Day in the Life of Ivan Denisovich), set in a prison camp, was acclaimed both in the USSR and the West; but his subsequent denunciation of Soviet censorship led to the banning of his later, semi-autobiographical novels, *Rakovy korpus* (1968, Cancer Ward) and *V kruge pervom* (1968, The First Circle). He was expelled from the Soviet Writers' Union in

1969, and awarded the Nobel Prize for Literature in 1970 (received in 1974). His later books include *Arkhipelag Gulag* (1973–8, The Gulag Archipelago), a factual account of the Stalinist terror, for which he was arrested and exiled (1974). He now lives in the USA.

Somers (of Evesham), John, 1st Baron (1651–1716) English politician. A Whig, he became a lawyer (1676) and an MP (1689). He helped to draft the **Declaration of Rights** (1689), and after the **Glorious Revolution** (1688) held several posts under **William III**, culminating as Lord Chancellor (1697). William's most trusted minister, he was the object of frequent attacks, which led to his impeachment (and acquittal) in 1701. He was President of the Privy Council under Queen **Anne** (1708–14). ▷ **Whigs**

Somme, Battle of the (1 July–19 Nov 1916) A major **World War I** British offensive against German troops in north-western France which developed into the bloodiest battle in world history, with more than a million casualties. It was launched by British Commander-in-Chief, Douglas **Haig**. When the attack was abandoned, the Allies had advanced 10 miles from previous positions. The battle formed part of the war of attrition on the Western Front.

Somoza (García), Anastasio (1896–1956) Nicaraguan dictator. The son of a wealthy coffee planter, he was educated in Nicaragua and the USA. As Chief of the National Guard (Nicaragua's army), he established himself in supreme power in the early 1930s. With army backing, he deposed President Juan Bautista Sacasa, replacing him at the beginning of 1937. Exiling most of his political opponents and amassing a huge personal fortune, he retained power until his assassination. His sons, Luis Somoza Debayle (1923–67) and Anastasio Somoza Debayle (1925–80), continued dynastic control of Nicaragua until the 1979 revolution.

Sonderbund A political and military league of seven Swiss Catholic cantons (Uri, Schwyz, Unterwalden, Zug, Fribourg, Lucerne, Valais), formed in 1845 to resist liberal plans for centralization. The 25-day Sonderbund War (1847) ended with the government's defeat of the Sonderbund, and the creation of a Federal State (1848).

Song (Sung) Dynasty (960–1279) The Chinese dynasty founded by Zhao Kuangying, with its capital at Kaifeng. From the beginning, it was threatened by the **Khitan**, who in 1125 conquered all northern China, which they then ruled from Beijing. The Song court was re-established at Hangzhou (then called Linan), but the 'Southern Song Dynasty' was destroyed by the Mongols, who had earlier overcome the Khitan.

Songhai A West African state which rose to power in the region formerly dominated by Mali in the second half of the 15c, commanding the trade routes of the Sahara, the great market at Timbuktu, and the area westwards to Senegal. It declined as a result of the Portuguese re-orientation of trade routes, and was attacked by Moroccan forces in the 1590s. Songhai peoples still control much of the Saharan caravan trade. ▷ **Berber**

Song Jiaoren (Sung Chiao-jen) (1882–1913) Chinese revolutionary and champion of parliamentary government. He was a leading member of **Sun Yat-sen**'s revolutionary anti-Manchu organization, the *Tongmenghui* ('Alliance League'), before 1911, helping to set up a branch in central China. Following the establishment of the republic in 1912, the Tongmenghui was transformed into a political party, the **Guomindang** (Nationalist Party). Song became its principal spokesman in the elections of Dec 1912, carrying out a vigorous Western-style electioneering campaign calling for a figurehead presidency, a responsible cabinet system and local autonomy. The Guomindang won the elections and Song was widely tipped to become Prime Minister. Song's programme, however, was a direct challenge to the hegemonic ambitions of the president, **Yuan Shikai**. On his way to Beijing, in Mar 1913, Song was assassinated at Shanghai railway station by Yuan's henchmen.

Song Qingling (Soong Ch'ing-ling) (1892–1981) Chinese politician. The wife of the Chinese revolutionary leader, **Sun Yat-sen**, she played an increasingly active political role after his death (1925) and became associated with the left wing of the **Guomindang**. After a Christian education in the USA, she became Sun Yat-sen's English-language secretary (1913) and married him in 1914. She was elected to the Central Executive Committee of the Guomindang (1926) and was a member of the left-wing Guomindang government established at Wuhan in 1927 in opposition to **Chiang Kai-shek**. (Ironically her younger sister, Meiling, married Chiang Kai-shek in

1927.) After the collapse of the Wuhan government, Song Qingling spent two years in the USSR (1927–9). During the 1930s she was a prominent member of the China League for Civil Rights, which was constantly harrassed by Chiang Kai-shek's government. She stayed on in China following the victory of the Chinese communists (1949), becoming one of three non-communist vice-chairpersons of the People's Republic. As the widow of Sun Yat-sen, of whom the communists claimed to be the legitimate heirs, she was accorded much respect by the Chinese Communist Party, although her presence in the new government remained an honorary one.

Song Ziwen (Sung Tzu-wen/Soong, T V) (1894–1971) Chinese financier and politician. His sister, **Song Qingling**, married **Sun Yat-sen**, and through this Song became closely associated with the **Guomindang**. He provided the financial stability which made possible the 1926 **Northern Expedition** that reunited China under the Nationalists. A second sister, Meiling, married **Chiang Kai-shek** in 1927. Song served as Finance Minister of the new government until 1931, and was Foreign Minister from 1942 to 1945. When the Nationalist government was overthrown in 1949, he moved to the USA, where he died.

Sonnino, Giorgio Sidney (1847–1922) Italian diplomat and politician. He entered parliament in 1880 and occupied various ministerial posts, including Treasury Minister (1894–6). He was twice Prime Minister (1906 and 1909–10), and as Foreign Minister was responsible with **Salandra** for bringing Italy into **World War I** on the side of the Allies. He remained Foreign Minister throughout the war and was part of the Italian delegation to the post-war conference in Paris.

Sons of Liberty An organization in the **American Revolution** that provided popular leadership in the resistance movement against Britain. Composed mainly of merchants, lawyers, artisans, and small traders, it operated as an organized inter-colonial group in 1765–6, opposing the Stamp Act. Thereafter, the men who had taken part continued to provide popular leadership, helping to organize the First Continental Congress in 1774. The term was also used to describe all Americans involved in the revolutionary movement.

Sophia Alexeevna (1657–1704) Regent of Russia (1682/9). She was the daughter of Tsar **Alexei Mikhailovich** and his first wife, Maria Miloslavskaya. On the death of her brother, Tsar Fyodor Alexeyevich (1682), Sophia opposed the accession of her half-brother, Peter (the future **Peter I, 'the Great'**), and took advantage of a popular uprising in Moscow to press the candidature of her mentally deficient brother, Ivan. A compromise was reached whereby both Ivan (V) and Peter were proclaimed joint Tsars, with Sophia as Regent. Supported by leading boyars she became the *de facto* ruler of Russia. A faction of the nobility succeeded in removing her from power in 1689, and (apart from a failed attempt to regain power in 1698) she spent the rest of her life in a convent in Moscow.

Sophie Frederica Mathilda (1818–77) Queen of the Netherlands (1849/77). The daughter of King William of Württemberg and Catherine Pavlovna of Russia, she married the future Dutch King **William III** on 18 June 1839. They succeeded to the Dutch throne in 1849. Sophie bore her husband three sons, none of whom outlived their father. Their marriage was not a success, and she lived estranged from her husband until her death in The Hague.

Sorbs (Wends) A slavic minority concentrated near Dresden in Lusatia who were never forced out or assimilated by German immigration in the Middles Ages. They maintain their own linguistic and cultural identity to this day.

Sorsa, (Taisto) Kalevi (1930–) Finnish politician. After graduating from Tampere University, he worked in publishing and with the **UN** in the Ministry of Education. In 1969 he became Secretary-General of the Social Democratic Party and went on to become its President in 1975. He was elected to the Eduskunta in 1970, and served two terms as Foreign Minister between 1977 and 1987. When the SPP formed a government with the conservative National Coalition Party in 1987, he became Deputy Prime Minister.

Soult, Nicolas Jean de Dieu (1769–1851) French marshal. Created Marshal of France by **Napoleon I** (1804), he led the French armies in the Peninsular War (1808–14) until defeated at Toulouse (1814). A skilled opportunist, Soult turned royalist after Napoleon's abdication, but joined him in the **Hundred Days**, acting as his Chief-of-Staff at

871

the Battle of **Waterloo**. Exiled until 1819, he was gradually restored to all his honours, and presided over three ministries of **Louis-Philippe** (1832–4, 1839–40 and 1840–7).

Souphanouvong, Prince (1902–) Lao prince and politician. On graduating as a civil engineer in 1937, he worked under the French administration in Vietnam. Following the capitulation of the Japanese in Aug 1945, he was returned to Laos, with the assistance of **Ho Chi Minh**, to assist in the liberation of his country from the French. He was badly wounded when his forces were routed by the French in Mar 1946. In the early 1950s he became head of a Vietnamese front organization (later known as the **Pathet Lao**), accompanying the Vietnamese invasion of Laos in 1953–4. Souphanouvong entered the government in 1957, but his strongly pro-Vietnamese, communist ties inevitably caused great tensions and he was imprisoned in 1959–60. In the 1960s it proved impossible to secure an integrated government in Laos, which consequently was driven apart by civil war, and Souphanouvong and the Pathet Lao left for the hills. The communist victory in Vietnam in 1975 brought the Pathet Lao to power in Laos and Souphanouvong became President of the Lao People's Democratic Republic, in effect a Vietnamese colony; a position he held until 1986. ▷ **Vietnam War**

South Africa Act (1909) The act of the British parliament which created the Union of South Africa, with dominion status, in 1910. After the Boer War, the Liberal government which came to power in 1905 moved rapidly to restore responsible self-government to the Transvaal (1906) and the Orange Free State (1907). A series of constitutional conventions then set about federating the two Boer territories with the British colonies of the Cape and Natal. In the event, a union constitution was agreed upon, with the parliamentary capital in Cape Town, the administrative capital in Pretoria and the major law courts in Bloemfontein. The Union constitution ensured that the **Afrikaners** would remain the dominant political force in South Africa. It was hailed as a colonial triumph for **Asquith**'s government in keeping South Africa within the British Empire and ultimately ensuring its participation in two world wars. However, the British failed to establish black political rights or protect the franchise enjoyed by limited numbers of Africans at the Cape. It led not to a liberalizing of the South African system, as the British had hoped, but to white supremacist rule and **apartheid**. ▷ **Boer Wars**

South-East Asia Treaty Organization (SEATO) An organization founded in 1954 to secure South-East Asia against communist 'aggression'. The eight signatories to the treaty were Australia, France, New Zealand, Pakistan, the Philippines, Thailand, UK, and USA. SEATO's headquarters was in Bangkok. It was phased out in the mid-1970s.

Southern African Development Coordination Conference (SADCC) An association of 10 states (Angola, Botswana, Lesotho, Malawi, Mozambique, Namibia, Swaziland, Tanzania, Zambia and Zimbabwe) with its headquarters in Gaberone. Its first meeting was held in Arusha in 1979 and its Lusaka Declaration (Apr 1980) set forth a commitment to a peaceful transition to majority rule in Zimbabwe and opposition to **apartheid** in South Africa. Intended to help limit members' dependence on South Africa, it is based upon sectoral coordination and acts as a conduit for international aid to the region.

South Sea Bubble A financial crisis in Britain (1720) arising out of speculation mania generated by parliament's approval of the South Sea Company proposal to take over three-fifths of the National Debt. Many investors were ruined in the aftermath, but Robert **Walpole**'s plan for stock transfer retrieved the situation and made his reputation.

South Slavs The Slavs began to establish themselves as farmers in the Balkans in the first decades of the 6c and eventually covered the entire peninsula. In the 7c a second wave of invaders, including the Croats and Serbs, who were Slavs, and the Turkic **Bulgars**, who assimilated to the earlier Slav settlers, entered the Balkans and established the first South Slavic states, Bulgaria, Croatia and Serbia. During the 15–17c, Croat, Slovene and Serb scholars became conscious of their common Slav ancestry and referred to themselves as Illyrians or simply Slavs, in addition to their more specific national name. In the 19c, under the influence of romantic nationalism, this Slav consciousness grew and gave rise to various movements for South Slav unification which led to the establishment of the Kingdom of Serbs, Croats and Slovenes (later Yugoslavia) at the end of **World War I**. ▷ **Bosnia and Herzegovina; Carinthia;**

Carniola; Dalmatia; Istria; Macedonians; Montenegro; Serbian Uprisings; Slovenia, Republic of; Yugoslavism; Yugoslavs

South Tirol That part of the Tirol south of the Brenner Pass and currently in Italy. Although overwhelmingly German-speaking, the region passed to Italy after **World War I** (Treaty of **St Germain**). Under **Mussolini**, a ruthless policy of Italianization, later condoned by **Hitler**, was pursued but ultimately failed. Since 1945 considerable tension in the area has been largely defused by various agreements between Austria and Italy which accord the region far-reaching cultural autonomy.

soviet Originally, a workers' council established in Russia after the 1905 revolution. They re-appeared as workers' and soldiers' councils, important instruments of the 1917 revolution. Members of soviets are now elected by popular vote, and lower soviets cannot control higher ones. The highest is the Supreme Soviet, the legislative body of the USSR.

Soviet–Chinese Friendship Treaty (1950) The treaty bringing together the longest-established communist power and the most important new one, and settling some of their differences. **Stalin** had been less helpful to **Mao Zedong** than most had expected, but he now promised him protection against Japan and gave him $300 million in aid. However, he did not offer protection against the USA, and kept him waiting for 10 weeks in the middle of a Moscow winter to give him in fact less aid than Poland. On the other hand he did agree to abandon Soviet positions within China. Relations prospered for a few years but gradually deteriorated into the **Sino-Soviet dispute**.

Soviet–Finnish War ▷ **Continuation War**

Soviet Union ▷ **USSR**

Soweto Riots (Apr 1976) The student disturbances which took place in the Transvaal African township of Soweto, when several hundred people were killed resisting the teaching of Afrikaans in schools. The township (whose name derives from *South West Township*) has remained a source of tension and violence in South Africa. ▷ **apartheid**

Spaak, Paul Henri (1899–1972) Belgian politician. He became Belgium's first socialist Premier (1938–9) and was Foreign Minister with the government-in-exile during **World War II**. In 1945 he was chairman of the first General Assembly of the **UN**. After his later periods as Premier (1946 and 1947–9), he was again Foreign Minister (1954–7 and 1961–8), in which role he became one of the founding fathers of the **EEC**. Secretary-General of **NATO** in 1957–61, he was sometimes known as 'Mr Europe'.

Spanish–American War (1898) In 1898 Spain lost the final remnants — Cuba, Puerto Rico, and the Philippines — of its empire to the USA. If the war signalled the emergence of the USA as an imperial power, it marked the eclipse of Spain as one. Although the material loss to Spain was substantial, the psychological blow was devastating. The end of the once vast empire confronted Spaniards not just with their declining power and status, but also their sheer backwardness. There emerged a generalized, if unfocused, demand for the 'regeneration' of a 'decadent' nation. The 'Disaster of 1898' thereby triggered off a protracted internal crisis which culminated in the fall of the monarchy in 1931.

Spanish–American Wars of Independence (1810–26) The wars fought in South America, following **Napoleon**'s invasion of Spain (1808). Reformers in the major South American colonies set up semi-independent governments (1810), which were rejected both by royalists in the colonies and by the Spanish King Ferdinand VII, when restored in 1814. The ensuing wars were fought in two main theatres: Venezuela, New Granada and Quito, where Simón **Bolívar** was the leading patriot general, and Argentina and Chile, from where General José de **San Martín** mounted an invasion of the Viceroyalty of Peru, still held by Spain (1820–1). The final liberation of Peru was effected in 1824 by Bolívar. The last Spanish garrisons in South America, at Callao (Peru) and on the island of Chiloé (Chile), surrendered to the patriots in 1826.

Spanish Civil War (1936–9) The conflict between supporters and opponents of the Spanish Second Republic (1931–6). The 'Republicans' included moderates, socialists, communists, and Catalan and Basque regionalists and anarchists. The 'Nationalist' insurgents included monarchists, Carlists, conservative Catholics, and fascist Falangists. The armed forces were divided. Both sides attracted foreign assistance: the Republic from the USSR and the **International Brigades**; the Nationalists from fascist

Italy and Nazi Germany. The Nationalist victory was due to the balance of foreign aid; to 'non-intervention' on the part of the Western democracies; and to greater internal unity, achieved under the leadership of General **Franco**. The war took the course of a slow Nationalist advance. The Nationalists initially (July 1936) seized much of north-west Spain and part of the south-west, then (autumn 1936) advanced upon but failed to capture Madrid. They captured Malaga (Mar 1937) and the north coast (Mar–Oct 1937); advanced to the Mediterranean, cutting Republican Spain in two (Apr 1938); overran Catalonia (Dec 1938–Feb 1939); and finally occupied Madrid and south-east Spain (Mar 1939). ▷ **Basques; Carlism; Falange Española; fascism; Republic, Second** (Spain)

Spanish Succession, War of the (1702–13) The war fought nominally over the throne of Spain, but which involved worldwide interests in trade and the colonies. The succession, in dispute for a generation because of the lack of an heir to **Charles II**, the last Habsburg ruler of Spain, had initially been resolved by partition treaties between the major European powers. Charles II's will aimed to avoid any carve-up of the monarchy by settling the throne on **Louis XIV** of France's grandson, Philip, Duke of Anjou; in 1700, the latter became King of Spain, thereby provoking a declaration of war by the other disappointed powers. The Grand Alliance of the Hague (1701) united England, the **Holy Roman Empire** and the **United Provinces of the Netherlands** against France and Spain. The main centre of land operations was in the Netherlands, where the Duke of Marlborough inflicted major defeats on the French at Blenheim (1704) and Ramillies (1706), but there were also crucial spheres of conflict in Italy and the Iberian Peninsula. In Italy the successful Imperial forces, commanded by Eugene of Savoy, defeated the French at Turin (1706) and subsequently drove the Spanish out of the greater part of Italy. In the Iberian Peninsula, the Allies were supported by the Portuguese and the Catalans, enabling their armies to capture all the major cities of the peninsula by 1706. Gibraltar fell into Allied hands in 1704. Strong Franco-Spanish forces under the Marshal Duke of **Berwick**, however, won a decisive victory at **Almansa** (1707), and the Bourbon forces laid siege to Barcelona, which fell in 1714. The general European war was settled by the Peace of Utrecht (1713), which confirmed the Bourbon succession in Spain, and by the Peace of Rastatt (1714). ▷ **Bourbon, House of**

Sparta (Lakedaimon) One of the leading city-states of ancient Greece, situated in the south Peloponnese. She initially expanded her power by subjugating the neighbouring Lakonians and Messenians as **helots** (serfs); the revolt of Messenia (c.650BC) led to a series of military and social reforms, traditionally associated with the lawgiver Lycurgus, designed to deter further uprisings. By the later 6cBC, Sparta was the foremost military power in Greece, and, through leadership of the **Peloponnesian League**, dominated Peloponnese and exercised wider influence. Her victory over Athens in the **Peloponnesian War** (431–404BC) led to a brief and unpopular naval empire. However, culturally and economically, Sparta became increasingly inward-looking and backward; by the early 4cBC, her citizen manpower had declined drastically. Thus, when defeated at the Battle of **Leuctra** (371BC) by the Thebans under **Epaminondas** (who reinforced his victory with the liberation of Messenia), Spartan power collapsed and never revived. Spartan government was basically oligarchic, with the addition of two hereditary kings who ruled simultaneously (the Agiad and Eurypontid houses); their duties were primarily military and religious. ▷ **Agesilaus; Cleomenes I; Corinthian War; Leonidas; Lysander; Pausanias**

Spartacists A left-wing revolutionary faction (the *Spartakusbund*), formed by Rosa **Luxemburg** and Karl **Liebknecht** in 1917, which advocated ending **World War I** and worked for a German socialist revolution. Initially part of the Independent **SPD**, it formed the core of the German Communist Party (**KPD**) when the latter was founded in 1919. Luxemburg and Liebknecht were murdered in disturbances during the German revolution in early 1919. ▷ **Revolution of 1918** (Germany)

Spartacus (d.71BC) Thracian-born slave and gladiator, who led the most serious slave uprising in the history of Rome (73–71BC). With a huge army of slaves and dispossessed, he inflicted numerous defeats on the Roman armies sent against him, until defeated and killed by **Crassus**. His supporters were crucified wholesale, their bodies left hanging along the Appian Way to act as a deterrent to other would-be rebels. ▷ **Pompey the Great; Servile Wars**

SPD (*Sozialdemokratische Partei Deutschlands*, 'Social Democratic Party of Germany') German political party. In 1875 the two main workers' parties in Germany (Association of German Workers, Social Democratic Workers' Party) merged to form the SAP (Socialist Workers' Party). Despite severe persecution by the Bismarckian state, the party steadily gained support and because of this persecution its politics became increasingly Marxist and revolutionary in tone. In 1890 the SAP was renamed the SPD and in 1891 formally adopted a Marxist ideology (the **Erfurt Programme**). However, the more pragmatic stance of the trade unions and the increasing involvement of south German Social Democrats in public affairs encouraged the growth of 'revisionism' within the party, as advocated by Eduard **Bernstein**. By 1914 the SPD had over 1 million members and the support of 34.8 per cent of voters and although it split in 1917 on whether to tolerate the war effort, the majority SPD played the pre-eminent role in the founding of the **Weimar Republic** (1918–19). During the Weimar Republic the SPD pursued a reformist policy which found little favour either among political conservatives or the radicals of other parties. Banned by **Hitler** in 1933, the SPD was refounded in 1945 and in 1959, at Bad Godesberg, formally abandoned its Marxist ideology and committed itself to achieving reforms in the existing social order. In 1966 it entered government in coalition with the **CDU/CSU** and from 1969 to 1982 governed in coalition with the **FDP** when it achieved noteworthy successes in foreign policy (**Ostpolitik**) and domestic policy (**Mitbestimmung**). Current membership is around 900 000. ▷ **Bismarck, Otto von; Marxism**

Special Operations Executive (SOE) An

organization set up with British war cabinet approval in July 1940 in response to Winston **Churchill**'s directive to 'set Europe ablaze'; it later also operated in the Far East. It promoted and coordinated resistance activity in enemy-occupied territory until the end of World War II. ▷ **FFI; Free French; Maquis; Resistance Movement** (France)

Speenhamland system The most famous of

many local expedients in Britain to improve the operation of the old **Poor Laws** at a time of crisis. The name was taken from the Berkshire parish whose magistrates in 1795 introduced scales of relief for labourers dependent both on the prevailing price of bread and the size of labourers' families. The principles spread to many southern and eastern parishes in the early 19c. It was much criticized by political economists for encouraging the poor to breed!

Speer, Albert (1905–81) German Nazi official. An architect by training, he joined the **Nazi Party** in 1931 and became **Hitler**'s chief architect (1934) and Minister of Armaments (1942). Always more concerned with technology and administration than ideology, he openly opposed Hitler in the final months of **World War II**, and was the only Nazi leader at the **Nuremberg Trials** to admit responsibility for the regime's actions. He was imprisoned for 20 years in Spandau, **Berlin**, and after his release in 1966 became a writer.

Spence, William Guthrie (1846–1926) British-born Australian trade unionist and politician. His family emigrated to Australia in 1852. Without formal education and working by the age of 13, his beliefs stemmed from his experiences, eclectic reading and Nonconformist background. Secretary of the Amalgamated Miners Association (1882–91), and foundation President of the Amalgamated Shearers Union (1886–93), his activities contributed to the maritime strike of 1890 and the shearers' strike of 1891, both of which ended in defeat for the workers. In 1894 he founded the **Australian Workers Union**, becoming Secretary (1894–8) and President (1898–1917). A member of the New South Wales assembly (1898–1901), he entered federal politics in 1901, but although he became Postmaster-General (1914–15), his major contribution to the Australian labour movement lay in his leadership and organization of rural unionism. Forced out of the union and the **Australian Labor Party** for supporting conscription in 1916–17, he sat as a Nationalist until defeated in 1919.

Speransky, Mikhail Mikhailovich (1772–1839) Russian politician. He entered government service in 1797, and was soon to achieve distinction, in 1807 becoming Secretary of State to **Alexander I**, who commissioned him to draft a plan for governmental reform. However, the plan was shelved, and in 1812 a conservative conspiracy brought about his banishment. In 1819 he was appointed Governor-General of Siberia, where he initiated a programme of far-reaching administrative reforms. In 1821 he was recalled to St Petersburg where he was restored to Imperial favour. Now a firm supporter of absolute autocracy, he continued to serve both Alexander and **Nicholas I** in a number of senior posts. His greatest achievement at this time was the publication of a 30-volume collection of the laws of the Russian Empire (1830). ▷ **Decembrists; Nicholas II; Romanov Dynasty**

Spiegel Affair (Oct–Nov 1962) A political scandal in the Federal Republic of **Germany**. Following the publication of an article in the periodical *Der Spiegel* on 10 Oct 1962, which questioned the efficacy of West German defence policy, the authorities reacted by arresting its publisher (Rudolf Augstein) and several journalists. Augstein was charged with treason and *Der Spiegel* in effect subjected to censorship. However, a vigorous public reaction and opposition from **SPD** and **FDP** members of parliament revealed government complicity in the affair, in particular by Franz-Josef **Strauss**, the Minister of Defence. The government backed down, delivering a setback to Strauss's wider political ambitions, undermining the authority of the Chancellor, **Adenauer**, but consolidating individual and press freedoms and wider democratic values in post-war Germany.

Spinola, Ambrogio, Marquis of Los Balbases (1539–1630) Genoese soldier in Spanish service. In 1602 he raised and maintained at his own cost 9000 troops and fought against **Maurice**, Count of Nassau in the Spanish Netherlands. He was one of the plenipotentiaries at the Hague Conference which made the 12-year truce in 1609. In the early stages of the **Thirty Years War** he served the Habsburg cause by subduing the Lower Palatinate. He was recalled to the Netherlands to fight once more against Maurice of Nassau, who, however, died of a fever while attempting to relieve Breda, which fell to Spinola in 1625, an event commemorated in Velazquez's famous painting. ▷ **Habsburg Dynasty**

Spínola, António de (1910–   ) Portuguese general and politician. From a well-to-do landed family which was a pillar of the Establishment, he fought on the side of **Franco** during the **Spanish Civil War** and was sent to Nazi Germany for training. A teetotaller and non-smoker, Spínola's trade-marks were his monocle, riding crop and African cane. As Governor-General of Guinea-Bissau (1968–73) he endeavoured to halt the independence movement through a combination of welfare and community projects (designed to win over the local population) and the latest counter-insurgency methods. Though he believed the war was militarily unwinnable, he returned to Portugal a war hero. After the bloodless coup of 25 Apr 1974 toppled the remnants of the **Salazar** regime, the conservative Spínola became President as a compromise candidate. He proved a limited

and naive politician. Moreover, he clashed gravely with the Armed Forces Movement (MFA) over the granting of independence (July 1974) to Angola, Mozambique and Guinea. The ensuing power struggle led to his resignation (30 Sep 1974). After staging an unsuccessful coup attempt (Mar 1975), he fled into exile. He returned the following year, but played no further part in events.

Spinoza, Benedict de (1632–77) Dutch-Jewish philosopher and theologian. His deep interest in the new natural sciences (including astronomy and optics) and Cartesian rationalist philosophy made him unpopular in traditional religious circles, and he was expelled from the Jewish community in 1656 and persecuted by Calvinists. His major works include the *Tractatus Theologico-Politicus* (1670), which despite its anonymity made him famous, and his *Ethica* (published posthumously, 1677). In 1673 he refused the chair of philosophy at Heidelberg University in order to keep his independence.

Spion Kop, Battle of (1900) A battle of the second Boer War which was part of the British attempt to relieve the Siege of **Ladysmith**, a town in Natal besieged by the Boers since Oct 1899. British forces attempted to take a hill a few miles from the town, and although they were close to success at one stage, the Boers succeeded in beating them off. There were 1500 British casualties, and together with the reverse at Vaal Krantz in the same week, it continued the succession of defeats which the British suffered during the early months of the war. ▷ **Boer Wars**

Spiritualia The staff and ring, symbols of a bishop's spiritual authority. The practice of laymen investing bishops with these symbols was at the centre of the **Investiture Controversy**.

Spiritual Regulation (1721) The reform by **Peter I, 'the Great'** of the Russian Orthodox Church, which greatly reduced its former power. In the previous century Patriarch **Nikon** had tried and failed to make the Church superior to the state but he had nevertheless made it extremely powerful and rich. Peter extracted much of its wealth to pay for his wars; but in 1721 he also abolished the independent patriarchate and replaced it with a body of 10 clerics, the Holy Synod, with a state official, the Procurator, to ensure that it obeyed the Tsar's will. Thereafter the Church was more or less automatically a loyal organ of state, though the patriarchate was reinstated in 1943 when a beleaguered **Stalin** was looking for patriotic support.

SPÖ (*Sozialistische Partei Österreichs*, 'Socialist Party of Austria') Austrian political party. Founded in 1889, the SPÖ functioned as a democratic Marxist party which attracted substantial support before 1914 and held power between 1919 and 1920 at the birth of the Austrian Republic. In opposition there-after, it was opposed by the right with increasing stridency and crushed in 1934 when it tried to resist by force the institution of crypto-fascist constitutional measures. Refounded in 1945, the SPÖ has held office in **Austria** for much of the inter-war period, either alone or in coalition. In 1978 it eschewed **Marxism**, instead supporting the democratization of society at all levels and the furtherance of workers' co-determination in the private sector.

spoils system The practice in US politics of filling public offices on the basis of loyalty to the party in power. Such appointments were made beginning with the early presidencies but became widespread in Andrew Jackson's administration. The term itself derives from Senator William Marcy's defence of the system: 'to the victors belong the spoils'. The corruption and scandals in Ulysses S **Grant's** administration led to the passage of civil service reforms and examination requirements, resulting in the establishment of a career structure in government bureau-cracies. ▷ **Albany Regency; mugwump**

Sporazum (1939) The agreement reached on the eve of **World War II** between the Yugoslav government led by Dragiša **Cvetko-vić** and the Croatian Peasant Party (HSS) led by Vladko **Maček**. The **Croats** agreed to cooperate with the Belgrade government in return for a large measure of self-government. The internal administration of Yugoslavia was reorganized to include Dal-matia, Slavonia and parts of Bosnia Herze-govina within Croatia, and a Croatian assembly met at Zagreb to regulate Croatian domestic affairs. ▷ **Subašić, Ivan**

Spurs, Battle of the (16 Aug 1513) A battle between France and England, who had joined the **Holy League** of the Pope, Spain, and Venice against the French. **Henry VIII** laid siege to Thérouanne, near St Omer (Pas-de-Calais), and beat off the French relieving force in this battle, which was so called because of the precipitate French retreat. Thérouanne and Tournai were taken, but these successes had no lasting significance.

Spurs, Battle of the Golden ▷ **Golden Spurs, Battle of the**

squadristi The term applied to members of the fascist para-military movement that developed in Italy in the period after 1919. *Squadrismo* was often no more than a manifestation of political thuggery and inti-midation, often directed against members of left-wing groups, strikers and ethnic minori-ties. However, in some cases, particularly in rural areas, it represented an understandable reaction to intimidation by similar left-wing groups. Local 'squad' leaders came to be known as **ras**. After **Mussolini's** seizure of power, he tried to reduce the threat to order posed by these militant supporters of **fascism**, channelling them with considerable success into the **MVSN**.

Square Deal The popular name for the domestic policies of US President Theodore **Roosevelt**, especially the enforcement of the **Anti-Trust Acts**. The term was coined by Roosevelt during a speaking tour in the summer of 1902.

Squatters In Australian history, pastoralists who occupied unallocated land initially beyond the limits of crown land grants; their position was formalized by the late 1840s. The term was subsequently used to denote large-scale landholders in general. Squatters formed a social and economic élite and used their power to impede government efforts to settle small farmers. ▷ **closer settlement; selectors**

Sri Lanka Freedom Party ▷ **SLFP**

Srivijaya An early state in South-East Asia, which dominated the maritime trade passing through that region between the close of the 7c and the early 11c. The task of locating the precise site of the capital of Srivijaya conti-nues to tax students of early South-East Asian history: but it was in the region of Palembang, in south-east Sumatra. Srivi-jaya's power was built on well-developed political and trading relationships with China, its ability to dominate local trade (that involved a capacity to suppress sea piracy) and its wide reputation as a centre of culture, learning and civilization. It was also an important centre of Buddhist observance and study, sustained and sponsored by part of the great wealth created by trade. When I Ching visited Srivijaya in 671, he found a very substantial community of Buddhist monks.

Srobar, Vavro (1867–1950) Slovak politician. As a medical student in Prague he was greatly influenced by **Masaryk**, and in 1898 he established a journal for Slovak youth that developed the idea of collaboration with the **Czech National Movement**. During and just after **World War I** he was able to give effect to the idea in the establishment of the Czechoslovak state. He did the same during and just after **World War II** to get Czechoslovakia re-established. On both occasions, other Slovak attitudes were pushed aside.

SS (*Schutz staffel*, 'protective squad') A Nazi organization founded in 1925 as **Hitler**'s personal bodyguard. From 1929 it was transformed and expanded by **Himmler** into an élite force. Within the Third **Reich** it became an independent organization, controlling the police forces, and responsible for concentration camps and racial policy. It formed its own armed detachments, which after 1939 became the *Waffen* ('armed') SS. During **World War II** it became an alternative army, an autonomous power within the Third Reich, and the principal agent of racial extermination policy. ▷ **Nazi Party**

Ssu-ma Ch'ien ▷ **Sima Qian**

Stabilization Plan (1959) The economic autarky sought since 1939 by the **Franco** regime by means of a heavily protected command economy had failed so signally by the late 1950s that the country was on the verge of bankruptcy. The Stabilization Plan of 1959 was the cornerstone of the regime's programme of capitalist modernization. This dramatic change in policy was engineered above all by Mariano Navarro Rubio (Minister of Finance, 1957–65) and Alberto Ullastres (Minister of Commerce, 1957–65), both prominent members of **Opus Dei**. Although the regime's switch to laissez-faire capitalism proved economically successful, the short-term social cost was extremely high. However, the economic modernization of Spain did more than anything else to undermine the political foundations of the Franco dictatorship.

Stack, Lee (d.1924) British soldier. He was Sirdar (British Commander-in-Chief of the Egyptian Army) in 1924, at a time when a combination of the first Wafdist government in Egypt and the first Labour government in Britain was resulting in a certain amount of British sympathy being shown for Egyptian nationalist aspirations. Unfortunately for both sides, when Sa'd **Zaghlul** came to London for negotiations his demands were well beyond what the British government was prepared to concede. The upshot was increased hostility to the British in Egypt and particularly to the rank and status of the Sirdar. Stack was murdered in Cairo in late 1924 to some extent as a result of this. The subsequent ultimatum presented to Egypt by the British, although certainly not strong enough for the British expatriates in Egypt, was sufficient to jolt the Egyptian government. This, coupled with the complicity in a number of political murders with which certain Wafdists were charged, was enough to bring down the Wafdist government.

Stadholder (*Stadhouder*) The office of the chief executive of the Dutch Republic. Originally the Stadholder had been the King's representative and military commander in a given district; when the northern Netherlands broke formally with their Spanish monarch in 1581 the provincial assemblies (states) took it on themselves to appoint the Stadholder. This meant that his position was highly ambivalent: he was appointed by the states, but had the right to appoint officials, often including the members of the states themselves. Each province could appoint its own Stadholder, but in practice the offices always went to a prominent member of the House of Orange-Nassau (the northern provinces often chose a different member). The Stadholder was not a monarch, but successful ones like **Frederick Henry**, **William II** and **William III** had many of the trappings of kings; conversely, power-

HOUSE OF ORANGE-NASSAU

Regnal Dates	Name
1572/84	William I, 'the Silent'
1585/1625	Maurice
1625/47	Frederick Henry
1647/50	William II
1672/1702	William III
1747/51	William IV
1751/95	William V
1815/40	William I
1840/9	William II
1849/90	William III
1890/1948	Wilhelmina
1948/80	Juliana
1980/	Beatrix

ful leaders of the states party like Johan de **Witt** tried to reduce the centralizing power of the Stadholders. There were two periods when no Stadholder ruled in most of the provinces: 1650–72 and 1702–47. Under William III the office became hereditary; in 1815 the son of the last Stadholder, **William V**, became King **William I**.

Stefanik, Milan Rastislav (1880–1919) Hero of the **Slovak National Movement**. Born in Slovakia and educated in Prague, he migrated to Paris in 1904 and became a French citizen in 1910. An astronomer, then civil servant, he volunteered for the French air force in 1914 and was appointed general in 1918. He also worked with **Masaryk** and **Beneš** as a representative of the Slovaks. A spokesman at the **Versailles** peace conference in 1919, his words carried great weight with the French and with his own Slovaks. In 1919 he was killed in an air crash while travelling back to Slovakia.

Stahlberg, Kaarlo Juho (1865–1952) Finnish politician. Having established his reputation as Professor of Law at Helsinki University, as well as a judge and a member of the Finnish Diet, in 1919 he drafted Finland's constitution and served as the republic's first president until 1925. Kidnapped by members of a pro-Fascist movement in 1930, he was narrowly defeated in the elections of 1931 and 1937.

Stahlhelm Bund der Frontsoldaten German paramilitary league (literally, 'Steel Helmet League of Front-line Soldiers'). This monarchist paramilitary veterans' association was founded in Nov 1918 to resist radical left-wing unrest. It then quickly became the main focus of anti-republican paramilitary activity in the **Weimar Republic**, propagating extreme nationalist and racist views, and did much thereby to undermine the democratic parliamentary order. Its political links to the **DNVP**, which formed a coalition with the **Nazi Party** in Jan 1933, allowed the *Stahlhelm* a minor role in **Hitler**'s consolidation of power after which its members were either absorbed into the **SA** (1933) or eventually saw their units disbanded (1935).

Stakhanov, Alexei Grigorievich (1906–77) Russian coalminer. He started an incentive scheme (1935) for exceptional output and efficiency by individual steel workers, coalminers, etc. Such prize workers were called Stakhanovites.

Stakhanovism An economic system in the USSR designed to raise productivity through incentives. It was named after the first worker to receive an award, coalminer Alexei Grigorievich **Stakhanov**, who in 1935 reorganized his team's workload to achieve major gains in production. The movement lasted only until 1939.

St Alban's Raid (1865) A Confederate attack made from Canada, on the town of St Albans, Vermont, during the **American Civil War**. Such raids heightened tension between Great Britain and the USA during the Civil War, and fears of retaliation were one of the factors leading Canadians to Confederation.

Stalin, Joseph (Iosif Vissarionovich Dzhugashvili) (1879–1953) Georgian Marxist revolutionary and virtual dictator of the USSR. The son of a cobbler and ex-serf, he was educated at Tiflis Orthodox Theological Seminary, from which he was expelled in 1899. After joining a Georgian Social Democratic organization (1898), he became active in the revolutionary underground, and was twice exiled to Siberia (1902 and 1913). As a leading Bolshevik he played an active role in the **October Revolution**, and became People's Commissar for Nationalities in the first Soviet government and a member of the Communist Party **Politburo**. In 1922 he became General-Secretary of the Party Central Committee, a post he held until his death, and also occupied other key positions which enabled him to build up enormous personal power in the party and government apparatus. After **Lenin**'s death (1924) he pursued a policy of building 'socialism in one country', and gradually isolated and disgraced his political rivals, notably Leon **Trotsky**. In 1928 he launched the campaign for the collectivization of agriculture during which millions of peasants perished, and the first five-year plan for the forced industrialization of the economy. Between 1934 and 1938 he inaugurated a massive purge of the party, government, armed forces, and intelligentsia in which millions of so-called 'enemies of the people' were imprisoned, exiled, or shot. In 1939 he signed the Non-Aggression Pact with **Hitler** which bought the USSR two years respite from involvement in **World War II**. After the German invasion (1941), the USSR became a member of the Grand Alliance, and Stalin, as war leader, assumed the title of Generalissimus. He took part in the **Tehran Conference**, **Yalta Conference** and **Potsdam Conference** which with other factors resulted in Soviet military and political control over the liberated countries of postwar Eastern and central Europe. From 1945 until his death he resumed his repressive measures at home, and conducted foreign policies which contributed to the **Cold War** between the USSR and the West. He was posthumously denounced by Nikita **Khrushchev** at the 20th Party Congress (1956) for crimes against the party and for building a 'cult of personality'. Under Mikhail **Gorbachev** many of Stalin's victims were rehabilitated, and the whole phenomenon of '**Stalinism**' officially condemned by the Soviet authorities. ▷ **Bolsheviks; Russian Revolution**

Stalingrad, Battle of (1942–3) One of the great battles of **World War II**, fought between Nazi German and Soviet troops in and around Stalingrad (now Volgograd) on the River Volga during the winter of 1942–3. After savage fighting, which cost 70 000 German lives, the German 6th army surrendered (Feb 1943), yielding 91 000 prisoners of war to the Russians. The battle is regarded as a major turning-point in the Allied victory over Germany.

Stalinism A label used pejoratively outside (and ultimately inside) the USSR to refer to the nature of the Soviet regime during the period 1929–53. It referred to a monolithic system, tightly disciplined and bureaucratic, with the party hierarchy having a monopoly of political and economic power. It also encompassed the total subservience of society and culture to political ends, the suppression of political opponents and total disregard of human rights, and especially the promotion of an individual above the party. ▷ **communism; Stalin, Joseph**

Stamboliski, Alexander (1879–1923) Bulgarian politician. A staunch republican, in 1906 he took over the leading role in the Bulgarian Agrarian National Union (BANU). During **World War I**, he was imprisoned by the pro-German King **Ferdinand I** for his outspoken support of the Allies. In 1918 he led a march on Sofia and forced the King to abdicate, briefly declaring a republic. After the 1919 elections, he became Prime Minister and represented defeated Bulgaria at the **Paris Peace Conference**. He established an authoritarian regime, organizing the anti-communist Orange Guard, undermining the position of the urban middle class and introducing a programme of radical reform designed to turn Bulgaria into a model agricultural state. Abroad, he tried to improve Bulgaria's

international position, joining the **League of Nations** and attempting to mend relations with Yugoslavia. The military and the parties of the centre and right united against him while the Communist Party and **VMRO** agitated against his policies. In 1923 he was overthrown in a military coup and was tortured and decapitated by members of VMRO. ▷ **Tsankov, Alexander**

Stambolov, Stephan Nikolov (1854–95) Bulgarian politician. He took part in the rising of 1875–6 and became the leading member of the Russophobe regency (1886). As Premier (1887–94), he ruled with a strong hand. Forced to retire, he was assassinated.

Stamp Act (1765) A British Act passed by the administration of George **Grenville**, which levied a direct tax on all papers required in discharging official business in the American colonies. It was the first direct tax levied without the consent of the colonial assemblies, and it caused much discontent in the colonies, six of which petitioned against it. (The measure provoked the colonists' famous slogan, 'No taxation without representation'.) The Act was withdrawn by the **Rockingham** government in 1766. ▷ **American Revolution**

Stanfield, Robert Lorne (1914–   ) Canadian politician. In 1967 he took over the leadership of the Conservative Party from John **Diefenbaker** after a bitter fight. He sought French-Canadian support by proposing to accept bilingualism and special conditions for Quebec, but in doing so, he lost the support of many anglophone Conservatives. A successful Premier of Nova Scotia, he failed to project himself in national politics and in 1976 was replaced by Joe **Clark**.

Stanhope, Charles, 3rd Earl (1753–1816) British scientist and politician. He became an MP and married the daughter of **Pitt**, 'the Elder'. A strong enthusiast for the **French Revolution**, he advocated peace with **Napoleon I** (1800). As a scientist, he invented a new microscope lens, two types of calculating machine, the first iron hand-printing press, and several other devices.

Stanhope, James, 1st Earl (1675–1721) British soldier and politician. He entered parliament as a Whig in 1701, and commanded in Spain during the War of the **Spanish Succession** (1702–13). He was Secretary of State for Foreign Affairs under **George I**, and became his Chief Minister in 1717. ▷ **Whigs**

Stanislaus Leszczynski (1677–1766) King of Poland (1704/9 and 1733/5). After his election in 1704, under the influence of Charles XII of Sweden, he was driven out by **Peter I, 'the Great'**. Re-elected in 1733, he lost the War of the Polish Succession, and formally abdicated in 1736, receiving the Duchies of Lorraine and Bar.

Stanisław II August Poniatowski (1732–98) Last King of Poland (1764/95). He was the son of Stanisław **Poniatowski**. In St Petersburg in 1755, while in the suite of the British ambassador, he became much favoured by Empress **Catherine II, 'the Great'**. Largely through her influence and that of his father, he was elected king in 1764. A cultured and enlightened individual with reforming ideas and an independent streak, he was not necessarily the person most suited to countering the intrigues of his neighbours and the unruliness of the *sejm* or diet. **Frederick II, 'the Great'**, who had gained the consent of Austria to a partition of Poland, soon made a similar proposal to Russia, and despite Stanisław the first partition was effected in 1772. The sejm then agreed to try, too late, to introduce reforms. The intrigues of discontented nobles were used to facilitate Russian and Prussian intervention, and a second fruitless resistance was followed in 1793 by the second partition. The Poles now became desperate; under **Kościuszko's** leadership a much more widespread rising took place in 1794, the Prussians were driven out, and the Russians were several times routed. But Austria again intervened, Kościuszko was defeated, Warsaw was taken, and the independent Polish state and with it the Polish monarchy were at an end. Stanisław abdicated in 1795 and died in St Petersburg. ▷ **Poland, Partitions of**

Stanton, Elizabeth Cady (1815–1902) US feminist. Educated at Troy (New York) Female Seminary, she involved herself in the anti-slavery and temperance movements, and in 1840 married the abolitionist Henry B Stanton. In 1848 she and Lucretia Mott organized the first women's rights convention in Seneca Falls, NY. She was personally responsible for the emergence of women's suffrage as a public issue, but she regarded women's rights as a much larger problem. ▷ **National American Woman Suffrage Association**

Starace, Achille (1889–1945) Italian politician. An interventionist in 1914 and a **Bersaglieri** officer in **World War I**, Starace was one of the most energetic of the **Fascist Party** (PNF) bosses in the immediate post-war era, dominating the PNF in both the Veneto and Venezia-Tridentina. Party Vice-Secretary (1921–2 and 1926–31), and Secretary (1931–9), he was most renowned for his profound stupidity and was a constant butt of popular jokes. In May 1941 he was made head of the **MVSN**, but was imprisoned under the Republic of **Salò** for insufficient attachment to the regime. He was captured and executed by partisans in Milan.

Starčević, Ante (1823–96) Croatian nationalist. At first a follower of Ljudevit **Gaj** and the **Illyrian Movement**, in 1861 with Eugen Kvaternik he founded the Croatian Party of Right (ie state-right). An extreme nationalist, he advocated the creation of an independent Croatia which would include not only all the **Croats** but also all the Slovenes and Serbs, whom he considered to be of Croatian nationality. During the anti-Croat regime of Ban **Khuen-Héderváry**, membership of his party grew to dominate Croatian political life in the 1880s.

Star Chamber, Court of The royal prerogative court in Britain for hearing subjects' petitions and grievances, of uncertain date but increasingly prominent under the Tudors and early Stuarts. It consisted of privy councillors and two chief justices, who dealt swiftly and efficiently with cases, particularly those involving public order. **Charles I** used it against government opponents. It was abolished by the **Long Parliament** in 1641. ▷ **Stuart, House of; Tudor, House of**

Starhemberg Family A prominent Austrian family. Ernest Rüdiger (1638–1701) is the most notable member. He was the field marshal who defended Vienna when it was attacked by the Turks (during the Turkish Wars), for the last time, in 1683.

START (Strategic Arms Reduction Talks) Discussions held between the USA and the USSR, beginning in 1982–3 after President Ronald **Reagan** came to power and resuming after Mikhail **Gorbachev** became General-Secretary in 1985. They were concerned with a reduction in the number of long-range missiles and their nuclear warheads and were complicated partly by issues of mutual distrust and partly by the need to deal also with other types of weapons. Agreements were reached on the abolition of intermediate-range nuclear missiles in 1987 (the INF Treaty) and on conventional forces in Europe in 1990 (the CFE Treaty). The way was then open for President George **Bush** to agree the START I Treaty with President Gorbachev in July 1991 and the START II Treaty with President Boris **Yeltsin** in Jan 1993. Roughly speaking, the two powers agreed to cut their long-range nuclear capability by two-thirds within 10 years.

Star Wars ▷ **SDI**

States General ▷ **Estates General**

States Reorganization Act (1956) The process of linguistic reorganization of states in India was a prolonged and divisive one and raised fundamental questions of centre–state relations. The first step occurred in the aftermath of a major movement in the Andhra region of the former province of Madras. This led to the appointment of the States Reorganization Commission which published its report in 1955. Following the States Reorganization Act, the boundaries of the southern states were reorganized in closer conformity with traditional linguistic regions. The bifurcation of Bombay province into the present states of Gujarat and Maharashtra followed in 1960. In 1966, Punjab was reorganized and its several parts distributed among three units: Punjab, the new state of Haryana, and Himachal Pradesh. Several new states have also been carved out in response to tribal demands in the north-eastern region of the country from time to time. Presently India has 25 states and seven union territories.

states' rights A US constitutional doctrine based on the Tenth Amendment that the separate states enjoy areas of self-control which cannot be breached by the federal government. Debate has surrounded the interpretation of this Doctrine. At issue are the concepts of the implied power of the federal government and the extent or limitations of that power. The doctrine has been applied inconsistently and to support opposing points of view. It was adopted by white Southerners between **Reconstruction** and the **civil rights** movement, and amounted to a code term for white supremacy.

Statists A late 18c Southern Netherlands conservative political faction, also known as Nootists after their leader Hendrik van der Noot (1731–1837). In reaction to the rationalist reforms of Emperor **Joseph II**, two groups rose up in the **Brabant Revolution** of 1789; the **Vonckists** and the Statists. The latter wanted

a return to the old situation where effective power had been in the hands of the provincial assemblies or states, hence their name.

Statuto In Italy, the name given to the constitution granted by Charles Emmanuel in Mar 1848. It remained more or less unaltered as the constitution of united Italy after 1860. Extensive powers were vested in the king and the right to vote was limited by a very high property qualification.

Statutum in favorem principum (1231–2) A document enacted by **Frederick II**, at the instigation of lay and clerical princes, on whom the Emperor depended for his Italian policy. The statute places limits on the role and influence of the towns and the extent to which they can intervene in what the princes regarded as their prerogatives.

Stauffenberg, Claus, Count von (1907–44) German soldier. Initially welcoming the advent to power of **Hitler**, he quickly became alienated by Nazi brutality. He was a colonel on the German general staff in 1944, and placed the bomb in the unsuccessful attempt to assassinate Hitler at Rastenburg (20 July 1944). He was shot the following day. ▷ **Nazi Party; World War II**

Stauning, Thorvald (1873–1942) Danish politician. He became a member of the Danish parliament, the **Folketinget** (1906), leader of the Danish Social Democratic Party (1910) and Scandinavia's very first Social Democratic minister in 1916. After the general election of 1924, he became Premier of Denmark's first Social Democratic government. The longest-serving Danish Premier of the 20c (1924–6 and 1929–42), one of the achievements of the parliamentary reform policies of the Stauning administration was the social reform bill of May 1933 based upon the principle of the needy citizen's *right* to public support. In the general election of 1935, fought by the Social Democrats under the slogan 'Stauning or Chaos', the party's popularity reached its peak when 46 per cent of the electorate voted for it. Stauning's reform policy was interrupted (Apr 1940) with the German occupation of Denmark, but he continued as Premier of a national coalition government. He died on 3 May 1942 and his funeral became a manifestation of popular and national solidarity. ▷ **Denmark, German Invasion of**

St Bartholomew's Day Massacre (24 Aug 1572) The slaughter of French **Huguenots** in

Paris, ordered by King **Charles IX** and connived at by the Queen Mother, **Catherine de' Medici**, to coincide with celebrations for the marriage of Margaret of Valois and **Henry IV** (18 Aug). An attempted assassination of the Huguenot leader, Admiral **Coligny**, failed (22 Aug), but mass butchery of Huguenots followed. ▷ **Valois Dynasty**

Steel, Sir David (Martin Scott) (1938–) British politician. He became an MP in 1965, sponsored a controversial Bill to reform the laws on abortion (1966–7), and was active in the anti-**apartheid** movement. He became Liberal Chief Whip (1970–5), before succeeding Jeremy Thorpe as Liberal Party leader (1976–88). In 1981 he led the party into an alliance with the **Social Democratic Party**. Following successful merger negotiations between the two parties (1987–8), he was the last leader of the Liberal Party. He remains active in politics both as an MP and party spokesman.

Steel, Pact of (28 May 1939) An offensive alliance concluded between fascist Italy and Nazi Germany and based on the earlier Rome–Berlin Axis. It committed either power to join the other should it become involved in hostilities.

Stein, (Heinrich Friedrich) Karl, Baron von (1757–1831) Prussian politician. He studied law at Göttingen, and entered the service of **Prussia** in 1780, becoming Secretary for Trade (1804–7) and Chief Minister (1807–8), when he carried out important reforms in the army, economy, and both national and local government. In 1812 he went to St Petersburg, and built up the coalition against **Napoleon I**. He was later adviser to **Alexander I** (1812–15), then retired to Kappenberg in Westphalia, where he died. ▷ **Napoleonic Wars**

Steinem, Gloria (1934–) US feminist and writer. A journalist and activist in the 1960s, she emerged as a leading figure in the women's movement. She co-founded *New York* magazine in 1968, was a co-founder of Women's Action Alliance in 1971, and was a founder of the feminist *Ms Magazine*.

Stephen (c.1090–1154) Last Norman King of England (1135/54). He was the son of Stephen, Count of Blois, and Adela, the daughter of **William I, 'the Conqueror'**. He had sworn to accept **Henry I**'s daughter, Empress Matilda, as Queen, but seized the English crown and was recognized as Duke of Normandy on Henry's death in 1135. Though defeated and captured at the Battle of Lincoln (Feb 1141), he was released nine months later, after Matilda's supporters had been routed at Winchester. However, Matilda strengthened her grip on the West Country; **David I** of Scotland annexed the northern English counties by 1141; and Matilda's husband, Count Geoffrey of Anjou, conquered Normandy by 1144–5. Stephen was also repeatedly challenged by baronial rebellions, and after 18 years of virtually continuous warfare, he was forced in 1153 to accept Matilda's son, the future **Henry II**, as his lawful successor. His reputation as the classic incompetent king of English medieval history is nevertheless undeserved. He was remarkably tenacious in seeking to uphold royal rights, and his war strategy was basically sound. His inability to defend the Norman Empire was due largely to the sheer weight of his military burdens, especially the major offensives of the Scots in the north and the **Angevins** in the south.

Stephen I (997/1038) First King of Hungary. He formed Pannonia and Dacia into a regular kingdom, organized Christianity, and introduced many social and economic reforms. He received from the pope the title of 'Apostolic King' and, according to tradition, St Stephen's Crown, now a Hungarian national treasure. He died at Esztergom, and was canonized in 1083.

Stephen I Nemanja (d.1200) King of Serbia (1169/96). He was the founder of the Kingdom of Serbia and of the **Nemanja Dynasty**. After receiving a grant of land from the Byzantine Emperor, Manuel I Comnenus, with his brothers he drew together the Serbian *župani* (chieftains) in the **Raška** region and established himself as their king in 1169. He abdicated in favour of his second son (1196) and, taking the name Simeon, became a monk on Mount Athos. ▷ **Sava, St**

Stephen II (or **III**) (d.757) Pope (752/7). When Rome was threatened by the **Lombards**, he turned to **Pepin III, 'the Short'**, King of the **Franks**, who forced the Lombards to withdraw, and gave the Pope the exarchate of Ravenna, the real foundation of the temporal power.

Stephen IV, 'the Great' (1435–1501) Prince of Moldavia (1457/1504). He defended Moldavia against invasions by Hungary in 1467 and 1471 and by the Ottoman Turks, defeating the latter at Vaslui

(1475) and Valca Alba (1476). He won a reputation as the 'Athlete of Christ' because of his determination to drive back the Turks from Christendom. ▷ **Moldavia and Wallachia; Romanians**

Stephen Báthory (1533–86) Hungarian King of Poland (1575/86). Elected Prince of Transylvania in 1571, he succeeded to the Polish throne four years later. An able administrator and fine soldier, he easily suppressed a revolt of dissident burghers in Danzig and went on to defeat an attempted Russian invasion of Livonia under **Ivan IV, 'the Terrible'** and retake Polotsk. He was responsible for many administrative reforms and was notably successful in achieving a tolerant resolution of the religious divisions brought about by the Reformation in Poland.

Stephen Dushan (c.1308–55) King (1331/46) and Emperor (1346/55) of Serbia. He was the last of the Nemanjić family, who extended Serbian rule into **Macedonia**, Bulgaria and Albania, and instituted a legal code.

Stephensen, Magnús (1762–1833) Icelandic administrator. The first Icelandic governor of the island, he was the leading representative on Iceland of the European Enlightenment. After studying in Copenhagen, he was sent by the Danish government to report on the effects of the great volcanic eruption of 1783. In 1789 he was appointed Justice for the southern and western areas of the island and in 1800 was made President of the new Supreme Court, which replaced the **Althing**. He encouraged reform in a number of fields and published Iceland's first monthly journal. He was, however, an arrogant man, who was somewhat insensitive to the traditions dear to his countrymen.

Stepinac, Aloysius (1898–1960) Yugoslav prelate and cardinal, and Primate of Croatia. He was imprisoned by **Tito** (1946–51) for alleged wartime collaboration and, with failing health, was released but lived the remainder of his life under house arrest.

Stepnyak ('Son of the Steppe') (1852–95) Russian revolutionary. An artillery officer, born Sergius Mikhailovich, he adopted this nom de guerre. Having become obnoxious to government as an apostle of freedom, he was arrested, and subsequently kept under such surveillance that he left Russia and settled (1876) in Geneva, and then (1885) in London. He was, however, held to be the

assassin of General Mesentzieff, head of the St Petersburg police (1878). He was run over by a train in a London suburb. Among his works were *La Russia Sotteranea* (1881, trans *Underground Russia*, 1883), studies of the Nihilist movement; *Russia under the Tsars* (trans 1885); and the novel *The Career of a Nihilist* (1889).

Stern Gang Palestinian covert organization formed under Avraham Stern in 1940 after disagreement with the **Irgun** over a cease-fire with the British during **World War II**. Conflict between the Stern Gang and the British climaxed in 1942, when British forces sought and killed members of the group, including Stern himself. Thereafter, his followers adopted the name *Lohamei Herut Yisrael* ('Fighters for Israel's Freedom'), but others dubbed them the Stern Gang/Group. Their aim was to attack British installations and personnel in Palestine in the struggle for a Jewish state. Although collaborating with the **Haganah** and Irgun during 1945, many found the Stern Gang unnecessarily brutal. After 1948 the group was disbanded.

Stevens, Harry H (1878–1973) Canadian politician. A member of **Meighen's** Conservative administrations in 1921 and 1926, he was Minister of Trade and Commerce in **Bennett's** government from 1930. In 1934 he became chairman of the **Price Spreads Commission**, and after the controversy surrounding its recommendations, he resigned to found the Reconstruction Party. He was its only successful candidate in the 1935 election, and returned to the Conservative Party in 1939.

Stevens, Siaka Probyn (1905–88) Sierra Leone politician. Educated in Freetown, he was a railwayman and miner, founding the Mineworkers Union in 1943. Appointed a representative in the Protectorate Assembly, he then went to study at Ruskin College, Oxford in 1945. On his return, he helped found the Sierra Leone People's Party (APC) in 1951. The APC won the 1967 general election but the result was disputed by the army and Stevens withdrew from the premiership. In 1968 an army revolt brought him back and in 1971 he became President. He established a one-party state and remained in power until his retirement at the age of 80.

Stevens, Thaddeus (1792–1868) US politician. After graduating from Dartmouth College, he began a law practice at Gettysburg, Pennsylvania. He was an outspoken opponent of slavery throughout his years in Congress (1849–53 and 1859–68). A radical Republican leader during reconstruction, he actively pressed for the impeachment of President Andrew **Jackson** (1868).

Stevenson, Adlai Ewing (1900–65) US politician. Educated at Princeton, he became a lawyer, took part in several European missions for the State Department (1943–5), and was elected Governor of Illinois (1948) as a Democrat. He helped to found the **UN** (1946), ran twice against **Eisenhower** as a notably liberal presidential candidate (1952 and 1956), and was the US ambassador to the UN in 1961–5.

Stewart, Charles Edward, 'the Young Pretender' ▷ Stuart, Charles Edward

Stewart, House of ▷ Stuart, House of

Stewart, James Francis Edward, 'the Old Pretender' ▷ Stuart, James Francis Edward

Steyn, Martinus Theunis (1857–1916) South African politician. Born in Winburg, Orange Free State, he was state president (from 1896), joining with the Transvaal in the war (1889–1902). He promoted the Union of 1910, but later encouraged Boer extremists and their rebellion of 1914. His son, Colin Fraser (1887–1959), mediated between Generals **Botha** and **de Wet**, and was Minister of Justice in the **Smuts** government (1939–45) and of Labour (1945–8).

St Germain, Treaty of (10 Sep 1919) The treaty between the Allied victor powers and **Austria**, signed unwillingly by the latter, which defined the limits of the rump Austrian state, confirmed its separation from Hungary, and in effect blocked the desired union of German Austria with Germany. ▷ **World War I**

Stilicho, Flavius (d.408) Half-Roman, half-Vandal Roman general. He was virtual ruler of the Western Roman Empire (395–408) under the feeble Emperor **Honorius**. His greatest achievements were his victories over **Alaric I** and the **Visigoths** in northern Italy at Pollentia (402) and Verona (403).

Stimson, Henry L (1867–1950) US politician. Appointed a US District Attorney in New York by President Theodore **Roosevelt**, he made his reputation in anti-trust actions.

In 1911 he became Secretary of War in President **Taft**'s administration and modernized the army in which, as an artillery colonel, he fought in France in 1917. President Calvin **Coolidge** sent him to Nicaragua to negotiate an end to the civil war, and then to the Philippines as Governor-General. He became Secretary of State in President Herbert **Hoover**'s cabinet, and was the chief negotiator for the USA at the London Naval Conference (1930). At the 1932 Geneva Conference on arms limitation, he issued the 'Stimson Doctrine', condemning the Japanese occupation of Manchuria. Recalled as Secretary of War (1940) by President Franklin D **Roosevelt**, his experience made him a formidable influence on wartime policy, and (fearing that an invasion would be too costly in Allied lives) his advice was crucial in President Harry S **Truman**'s decision to use the atom bomb against Japan.

Stirling, William Alexander, 1st Earl of (1567–1640) Scottish statesman, poet and scholar. Having gained the patronage of King **James VI and I** through his poetry and his kinship to the Earl of Argyll, he gained the King's support for his aim of acquiring a colony for Scotland, along the lines of **New France** and New England. He was granted (1621) the proprietorship of Nova Scotia ('New Scotland'), the three Atlantic provinces and the Gaspé Peninsula. The last was also claimed by the French, and the renewal of their claim eventually led to the failure of his ambitions. Alexander's major problem was to find Scots willing to settle in the colony, and James sought to help him by the promise of hereditary baronetcies and territory in the colony to Scots who would support a number of settlers. However, this measure failed under both James and his son, **Charles I**. In 1631 Alexander was commanded to yield Port-Royal to the French, after a challenge from **Richelieu**'s Company of One **Hundred Associates**. He died with his dream unfulfilled, surrounded by creditors.

Stockholm Bloodbath (1520) After the fall of Stockholm to King **Christian II** at the beginning of 1520 and his coronation in Nov, he allowed the trial and execution of 82 leading Swedes, including two bishops. The main charge against them was one of heresy and the main instigator was probably Archbishop Gustav Trolle, but the King also in this way disposed of many of his opponents. The event led on to the successful rebellion by **Gustav I Vasa**, whose father had been a victim.

Stojadinović, Milan (1888–1961) Serbian politician and economist. After studying law at Belgrade University, he began his career in finance, becoming a minister in the Serbian Treasury (1914), Director of the English bank in Belgrade (1919) and Finance Minister in successive Yugoslav governments (1922–35). As head of the Yugoslav Radical Union, he was Prime Minister and Foreign Minister (1935–9). He led Yugoslavia away from the **Little Entente** and **Balkan Entente** towards the Axis camp, but his consent to Italian domination in Albania lost him the support of the regent, Prince **Paul Karageorgević**, and he was dismissed. Interned by the **Cvetković–Maček** government (1939), he made his way to the British at Athens, who deported him to Mauritius and held him there until 1948. He then went to Argentina, where he worked as an economist and journalist. ▷ **Ljotić, Dimitrije**

Stolypin, Peter Arkadevich (1862–1911) Russian politician. After service in the Ministry of the Interior (from 1884) he became Governor of Saratov province (1903–6), where he ruthlessly put down local peasant uprisings and helped to suppress the revolutionary upheavals of 1905. As Premier (1906–11), he introduced a series of agrarian reforms, which had only limited success. In 1907 he suspended the second **Duma**, and arbitrarily limited the franchise. He was assassinated in Kiev. ▷ **Nicholas II; Revolution of 1905**

Stormberg, Battle of (1899) One of the battles of the 'black week' when the British suffered several reverses during the Boer War. They were defeated while attempting to take an important railway junction to the south of the Orange River, one of the keys to Bloemfontein. ▷ **Boer Wars**

Stormont A suburb of east Belfast and site of a castle which housed the seat of government in Northern Ireland from 1921 to 1972. The Northern Ireland parliament, created by the Government of Ireland Act 1920, comprised a Senate and a House of Commons, both dominated by Protestants. It had jurisdiction over domestic affairs in the province until suspended by the Northern Ireland (Temporary Provisions) Act, 1972 which established direct rule from Westminster. ▷ **Bloody Sunday (1972); Ulster 'Troubles'**

St Petersburg, Foundation of (1703) This city was the symbol of the advance of **Peter I,** 'the Great' into Europe and formed the basis of Russian naval power in the Baltic and beyond. He started building it near the mouth of the Neva River in a strategic position, but on swampy ground that cost thousands of lives. It was not until 1721, the year of the Treaty of **Nystadt**, that the city was secure, and it took a century of construction, from Bartolomeo Rastrelli's **Winter Palace** through to Andrei Voronikhin's Kazan Cathedral, before it could claim to be one of the great cities of Europe. However, by that time, Tsar **Alexander I**'s Russia was one of the great European powers.

St Quentin, Battle of (1557) The battle fought near the town of that name in Picardy, resulting in a victory for the troops of **Philip II** of Spain, commanded by the Count of Egmont and the Duke of Savoy, over the French troops commanded by the Dukes of Montmorency and Nevers. Philip II built his palace-monastery of El Escorial in part as a memorial of the battle, fought on the Feast of St Lawrence, to whom the building was dedicated.

Strachan, John (1778–1867) Canadian bishop. Prominent in the **Family Compact**, he sought to maintain the ascendancy of the Anglican Church against the challenge of the Methodists (whom he accused of being American in origin and loyalty). As President of the Board of Education, his policy of keeping education under the clergy's control caused resentment throughout Upper **Canada**. In 1839 he became first Bishop of Toronto and opposed the Reformers over such issues as the secularization of King's College in 1849 and the **Clergy Reserves** in 1854.

Strafford, Thomas Wentworth, 1st Earl of (1593–1641) English statesman. He was knighted in 1611, and in 1614 succeeded to his baronetcy, and entered parliament. He acted with the Opposition (1625–8), but after being appointed President of the North and Baron Wentworth (1628), he supported **Charles I**. In 1632 he became Lord Deputy of Ireland, where he imposed firm rule. In 1639 he became the King's principal adviser, and Earl of Strafford. His suppression of the rebellion in Scotland failed, and he was impeached by the **Long Parliament**. Despite a famous defence at Westminster, he was executed on Tower Hill. ▷ **Bishops Wars**

Straits Convention (1841) By this treaty, the Straits, the passage from the Bosphorus to the Dardanelles which links the Black Sea to the Mediterranean, was placed under international control. The treaty between the Great Powers closed the Straits to foreign warships during peacetime, a provision intended to reconcile Russian and British shipping interests since neither country would be able to menace the other's fleet on the Black Sea or the Mediterranean.

Straits of Tiran, Closure of the (22 May 1967) The Straits of Tiran, which control entry to the Red Sea from the Gulf of Aqaba, were closed in May 1967 by the Egyptian President Gamal 'Abd al-**Nasser** operating from the vantage point of Sharm al-Shaykh which commands the western side of the straits. The closure of the straits, whereby the Israeli port of Eilat was effectively cut off from the sea, was seen by Israel as direct provocation and may be regarded as in part at least as the casus belli of the June War of 1967 between Israel and the Arabs which resulted in the Israeli occupation of Golan, the West Bank, the Old City of Jerusalem, the Gaza Strip, and Sinai as far as the Suez Canal.

Straits Settlements The name given to the former British crown colony which consisted of Singapore, Malacca, the Dindings, Penang, and Province Wellesley. Singapore became a separate city state in 1965; the remaining components are now part of Malaysia.

Strauss, Franz-Josef (1915–88) West German politician. He served in the German Army during **World War II** and in 1945 joined the **CDU**'s Bavarian-based sister party, the Christian Social Union (**CSU**), being elected to the **Bundestag** (federal parliament) in 1949. He became leader of the CSU in 1961 and held a succession of ministerial posts. His career was seriously blighted when, for security purposes, he authorized a raid on the offices of the journal *Der Spiegel*, leading to his sacking as Minister of Defence in 1962. Throughout the 1970s he vigorously opposed the **Ostpolitik** initiative of the Willy **Brandt** and Helmut **Schmidt** administrations. In 1980 he sought election as Federal Chancellor for the CDU and CSU alliance, but was heavily defeated. Nevertheless, from 1978 he had success as State Premier of Bavaria, using this base to wield significant influence within the **Bundesrat** (federal upper house) and, from 1982, in the coalition government headed by Chancellor **Kohl**. ▷ **Spiegel Affair**

Streicher, Julius (1885–1946) German Nazi journalist and politician. He was associated with **Hitler** in the early days of Nazism, taking part in the 1923 putsch. A ruthless persecutor of the Jews, he incited anti-Semitism through the newspaper *Der Stürmer*, which he founded and edited and also served as Nazi *Gauleiter* (Party Regional Leader) for Nuremberg–Franconia. He was hanged at Nuremberg as a war criminal. ▷ **Gau; Nazi Party; Nuremberg Trials**

Streltsy (1550–1698) The first regular regiment of Russian soldiers who gradually took upon themselves a political role. Musketeers, they were recruited by **Ivan IV, 'the Terrible'** and initially helped the expansion and the consolidation of the Russian state. During the minority of **Peter I, 'the Great'** they became involved in attempting to keep Sophia, his half-sister, on the Russian throne; and in 1698, when Peter was abroad, they tried in effect to prevent him coming back. Peter extracted a terrible revenge and disbanded what was left of them. However, he proceeded to build up the guards as his own elite military unit.

Stresa, Conference of (11–14 Apr 1935) Following **Hitler**'s declaration of German rearmament (16 Mar 1935), the Italian, French and British governments condemned the move at a meeting in Stresa. They guaranteed Austria's independence and agreed on future cooperation (Stresa Front). The Front was quickly undermined by the Anglo-German Naval Treaty (18 June 1935) and Italy's invasion of Abyssinia and intervention in the **Spanish Civil War**.

Stresemann, Gustav (1878–1929) German politician. Entering the **Reichstag** in 1907 as a National Liberal, he became leader of the party, and later founded and led its successor, the German People's Party. He was Chancellor of the new German Republic in 1923, then Minister of Foreign Affairs (1923–9). He pursued a revisionist policy through the medium of diplomacy, helped to negotiate the **Locarno Pact** (1925), and secured the entry of Germany into the **League of Nations** (1926). He shared the Nobel Peace Prize for 1926. ▷ **Weimar Republic**

Strijdom, Johannes Gerhardus (1893–1958) South African politician. Educated at Stellenbosch and Pretoria Universities, he was first a farmer and then a lawyer. Elected to parliament in 1929, he became the major spokesman for the least flexible members of the **National Party** (NP) but was nonetheless made Minister of Lands and Irrigation when the NP came to power in 1948. He was chosen to succeed **Malan** as leader and so became Prime Minister in 1954. He saw one of his cherished objectives achieved, namely **apartheid**, but died before South Africa became a republic.

Stroessner, Alfredo (1912–) Paraguayan dictator. The son of a German immigrant, he took up a military career, fighting in the **Chaco War** (1932–5). He became President in 1954 after leading an army coup which deposed Federico Chávez. He was re-elected at regular intervals (having had the constitution modified to allow this) but was forced to stand down after a military coup in 1989, led by Andres Rodríguez.

Stroganov, Pavel, Count (1772–1817) Russian landowner and political adviser. With extensive property in the Urals and Siberia, he acted as adviser to **Alexander I** both before and after his accession in 1801. A believer in autocratic government retraining the privileged and benefiting the downtrodden, he advocated the 'unofficial committee' of four that established the Tsar's liberal reputation in the years 1801–3. He soon became disillusioned because of the lack of fundamental change, and sought alternative outlets in military and diplomatic service.

Strossmayer, Josip Juraj (1815–1905) Croatian politician, prelate and man of letters. As Leader of the Croatian National Party, he defended Croatian interests by pursuing a course of compromise and tactical opportunism towards Vienna. A passionate believer in South Slav unity, he developed the Illyrism of Ljudevit **Gaj** and is considered the intellectual founder of Croatian **Yugoslavism**; the strength of his commitment is manifest in his efforts to reconcile the Catholic and Orthodox **South Slavs**. ▷ **Illyrian Movement**

Strougal, Lubomir (1924–) Czechoslovak politician. A lawyer who entered the Communist Party bureaucracy in 1955 and government office in 1959. In 1961 he took over the Ministry of the Interior at a sensitive time, managing to correct some of its worst excesses before reverting to a Central Committee function in 1965. His reputation was sufficient to make him a deputy prime minister in 1968, but he was a half-hearted supporter of the **Prague Spring**. In Aug he took the **Husak** line of ostensibly trying to

save something through working with the Soviet authorities. He was Prime Minister (1970–87) and was regarded as the man who might yet reinvigorate the reform movement; he never did.

Strozzi, Filippo, 'the Younger', properly **Giovanni Battista** (1489–1538) Florentine nobleman. He was prominent in the revolt which overthrew the **Medici** in 1527, but the republic then established lasted only three years. The restored Medici, Alessandro, having been assassinated in 1537, Filippo judged the time opportune to launch an attack on his successor, **Cosimo I, the Great**, but was captured and executed.

Strozzi, Piero (1510–58) Italian soldier. The son of Filippo the Younger, he fought the **Medici** and escaped to France. There he was made a marshal of France by **Henry II** in 1556 after campaigns in Italy. Strozzi found out the weaknesses of the defences of Calais before its capture by Francis, 2nd Duke of **Guise** in 1558, and was killed at the siege of Thionville. ▷ **Strozzi, Filippo**

Struensee, Johann Friedrich, Count (1737–72) German-born Danish politician. The son of a Halle pastor, in 1768 he became physician to **Christian VII** of Denmark. He soon gained the confidence of the young king and queen and, with their backing, sought to free Denmark from Russian influence and win Sweden as an ally. Court intrigue, however, thwarted his ambitions and he was found guilty of treason and beheaded.

Struve, Peter Bergardovich (1870–1944) Russian political economist. The grandson of Friedrich Struve, he was a leading Marxist and wrote *Critical Observations on the Problem of Russia's Economic Development* (1894), which **Lenin** attacked for its 'revisionism'. He edited several political magazines with Liberal tendencies, was professor at the St Petersburg Polytechnic (1907–17) and was closely connected with the 'White' movement in South Russia after the **Russian Revolution**. After 1925 he lived in exile in Belgrade and Paris, where he died during the Nazi occupation. His principal work is *Economy and Price* (1913–16).

St Stephen, Crown of (1000) The name given to the Hungarian royal title. Stephen (or Istvan in Magyar) was the baptismal name of Vajk, the son of Geza, who drew the Hungarian tribes together to form a feudal state. His baptism, like his marriage to a

Bavarian princess, Giselle, was part of the process of raising the state's international standing. In 1000 he succeeded in obtaining the Emperor's permission to raise Hungary to the status of a kingdom, the crown allegedly being donated by the Pope. This rare double achievement gave the new creation some security at the time and, since Stephen was canonized in 1083 after his death, considerable pretensions thereafter.

Stuart, Charles Edward (Louis Philip Casimir), 'the Young Pretender' (1720–88) Claimant to the British crown. The son of James Francis Edward **Stuart**, he became the focus of Jacobite hopes. In 1744 he went to France to head the planned invasion of England, but after the defeat of the French fleet he was unable to leave for over a year. He landed with seven followers at Eriskay in the Hebrides (July 1745) and in Aug raised his father's standard at Glenfinnan. The clansmen flocked to him, Edinburgh surrendered, and he kept court at Holyrood. Victorious at Prestonpans, he invaded England, but turned back at Derby for lack of evident English support, and was routed by the Duke of **Cumberland** at the Battle of **Culloden** (1746). The rising was ruthlessly suppressed, and he was hunted for five months. With the help of Flora **Macdonald** he crossed from Benbecula to Portree, disguised as her maid. He landed in Brittany, then lived in France and Italy, where (after his father's death in 1766) he assumed the title of Charles III of Great Britain. ▷ **Forty-Five Rebellion; Jacobites; Stuart, House of**

Stuart, House of The Scottish royal family, commencing with **Robert II** (1371/90), which succeeded to the English throne in 1603 with the accession of **James VI and I**, the cousin of **Elizabeth I**, and the great-grandson of **Henry VIII**'s sister, Margaret. As English monarchs the family's fortunes were mixed. James VI and I and **Charles II** were both successful politicians (although the second spent his first 11 years as king in exile). But **Charles I** and **James VII and II** were not, and both lost their thrones. The Stuart monarchy ended in 1714 with the death of Queen **Anne**, although pretenders laid claim to the throne and invaded Britain in support of their claims as late as 1745. ▷ **Stuart, Charles Edward; Stuart, James Francis Edward**

Stuart, James Francis Edward, 'the Old Pretender' (1688–1766) Claimant to the

HOUSE OF STUART

Regnal Dates	Name
1371/90	Robert II
1390/1406	Robert III
1406/37	James I
1437/60	James II
1460/88	James III
1488/1513	James IV
1513/42	James V
1542/67	Mary, Queen of Scots
1567/1625	James VI of Scotland (as James I of England, 1603/25)
1625/49	Charles I
1649/59	Commonwealth and Protectorate
1660/85	Charles II
1685/8	James VII and II
1689/1702	William III (joint ruler, with Mary, 1689/94)
1702/14	Anne

British throne. He was the only son of James VII of Scotland and II of England and his second wife, Mary of Modena. As a baby he was conveyed to St Germain, and proclaimed successor on his father's death (1701). After failing to land in Scotland in 1708, he served with the French in the Low Countries. In 1715 he landed at Peterhead during the Jacobite rising, but left Scotland some weeks later. Thereafter he lived mainly in Rome, where he died. ▷ **Fifteen Rebellion; Jacobites; James VII and II; Stuart, Charles Edward; Stuart, House of**

Stur, Ludovit (1815–56) Slovak writer and politician. One of a small group of educated Slovaks who resisted the growing policy of Magyarization in Hungary in the 1840s. He started publishing the Slovak *National News* in 1845 and chose the central Slovak dialect as the basis on which to found a proper literary language. In 1848 he helped to formulate demands for Slovak autonomy and appealed to Vienna for help. He also made contact with his Czech opposite members and helped found the Czechoslovak idea. Despite Slovak help for the Habsburg Emperor there was no concession after the defeat of the Magyars in 1849.

Sturdza, Mihail (1795–1884) Ruler of Moldavia (1834/49). He was chosen as **hospodar** (governor) of Wallachia by Russia and the Ottoman Porte at the Convention of St Petersburg (1834). During his rule, the **Danubian Principalities** were a Russian protectorate and Sturdza showed himself adept at working with the Russians to his own benefit and to that of his subjects. Following

889

the guidelines of the **Organic Statutes**, he attempted internal reforms and achieved genuine improvements in the standard of education, roads and postal service. In 1848 he quelled by force the petitioners led by Alexander **Cuza** who had called for moderate social and political reform. ▷ **Moldavia and Wallachia**

Sture, Sten, 'the Elder' (c.1440–1503) Regent of Sweden (1471/97 and 1501/3). On the death of his uncle, King **Karl Knutsson**, in 1470, Sten claimed the regency and defeated his opponents (who wished to restore the **Kalmar Union** under the Danish king, **Christian I**) at the Battle of Brunkeberg north of Stockholm (1471). In 1497 King Hans of Denmark and Norway successfully reasserted his claim to Sweden and forced Sten to step down. In 1503 the Swedish nobility again revolted and Sten was again chosen to be regent. Traditionally pictured as a selfless patriot fighting for Sweden's independence, recent research has revealed a ruthless opportunist with a driving personal ambition.

Sture, Sten Svantesson, 'the Younger' (c.1492–1520) Regent of Sweden (1512/20). He was the son of Svante Nilsson, Swedish regent (1504–12). An able but ambitious and ruthless man, he forced the nobles of the Council to accept him as regent on his father's death. He attempted to turn the regency into a hereditary monarchy and, while he enjoyed support among the commons and the lower nobility, he encountered growing opposition from the great nobles and Archbishop Gustav Trolle, whom he imprisoned in 1518. King **Christian II**, who sought to restore the **Kalmar Union**, took up the Archbishop's cause. After several unsuccessful attacks, he invaded Sweden in 1520 and defeated the Regent at the Battle of Åsunden (1520). Sten was mortally wounded in the encounter and died on the journey back to Stockholm. His wife, Christina Gyllenstierna, bravely defended the city against Christian for eight months.

Sturluson, Snorri (1179–1241) Icelandic chieftain and historian. He was born in western Iceland and fostered at Oddi in the south by the powerful Jón Loptsson. He acquired the estates of Borg and Reykholt, where he lived much of his life. He was Lawspeaker of the **Althing** for 15 years and became deeply involved in the turbulent politics of Iceland in the period which led to its loss of independence, first as an ally of the King of Norway and then as his opponent. He was finally slain at Reykholt by one of the King's followers. He is the author of two of the most important works of Icelandic literature, the *Prose Edda*, from which much of our knowledge of the Old Norse religion derives, and *Heimskringla*, a history of the early kings of Norway.

Stuyvesant, Peter (c.1610–1672) Dutch administrator. He became Governor of Curaçao, Arubq, and Bonaire (1643) and from 1646 directed the New Netherland colony. He proved a vigorous but arbitrary ruler, a rigid sabbatarian, and an opponent of political and religious freedom, but did much for the commercial prosperity of New Amsterdam until his reluctant surrender to the English in 1664.

Suárez, Adolfo (1932–) Spanish politician. He was a high-ranking Francoist bureaucrat who owed much to his good looks, great charm and single-minded ambition. Appointed Prime Minister in Mar 1976, Suárez carried out a swift transition from the **Franco** dictatorship to democracy, the elections of June 1977 proving a personal triumph. Backed by the newly established centrist party, the **UCD**, he undertook the creation of the new democratic state. Having embodied consensual change in the Constitution of 1978, Suárez triumphed again in the general election of 1979. However, economic and regional problems, divisions within both the government and UCD, as well as his own secretiveness and authoritarian style, led to his resignation in Jan 1981. The following year he founded the CDS ('Democratic and Social Centre Party'), which has won little support. The most important politician of the transition, Suárez helped establish democracy in Spain through pragmatism and conciliation.

Subašić, Ivan (1882–1955) Croatian politician. A leading member of the Croatian Peasant Party (HSS) between the two World Wars, he became *ban* (governor) of **Croatia** after the 1939 **Sporazum** between **Cvetković** and **Maček**. During **World War II**, he served in the Yugoslav government-in-exile in London and, as its Prime Minister, met **Tito** on the British-occupied island of Vis where he agreed to recognize **AVNOJ** as the only political authority within Yugoslavia (June 1944). In accordance with the provisions of the Vis agreement, in Mar 1945 he and two colleagues from the London-based regime joined Tito's Provisional Government, but he resigned as Foreign Minister six months later and was under house arrest until after the communist victory in the Nov 1945 elections. Obliged to retire from public life, he settled in Croatia.

Sucre, Antonio José de (1793–1830) South American soldier-patriot, born in Venezuela. He was **Bolívar**'s lieutenant, defeated the Spaniards at Ayacucho (1824), and became the first President (1826) of Bolivia. He tried to establish stability in the country, but was beset by warring political factions, as well as an incursion by Peruvian troops, and resigned in 1828. He took service with Colombia, and won the Battle of Tarqui (1829) against Peru. He was assassinated at Berruecos, near Pasló, possibly on the orders of José María Obando, a Colombian soldier. ▷ **Spanish–American Wars of Independence**

Sudan People's Liberation Movement The proclamation of an Islamic state in the Sudan by Numayri in 1977, led to unrest in the south which found its expression in the emergence of the Sudan People's Liberation Movement. This movement initially represented a political refusal to accept the dictates of the government in Khartum but subsequently moved to armed rebellion under Colonel John **Garang**.

Sudetenland Mountainous territory on Polish–Czech border. After **World War I**, the name also applied to the parts of Bohemia and Moravia occupied by German-speaking people; occupied by Germany after the **Munich Agreement** in 1938, and restored to Czechoslovakia in 1945 when the German-speaking population was expelled. ▷ **World War II**

Suebi A Germanic tribe, which included the **Marcomanni**, Quadi, Semnones and the Langobardi (Lombards). They originated around the Havel and the Spree and spread westwards towards the rivers Elbe and Neckar, south Germany, Bohemia and Moravia. Some crossed the Rhine and entered Spain in 409. The kingdom they set up there survived until c.585 when it was annexed by the Visigothic state. The leading Suebi tribe, the Semnones, settled in southern Germany and their name was transferred to the Alemanni, hence modern Swabia. ▷ **Germanic Invasions; Visigoths**

Suez Crisis (1956) A political crisis focused on the Suez Canal. Intensive rearmament by Egypt, the Egyptian nationalization of the Suez Canal, and the establishment of a unified command with Jordan and Syria aimed at surrounding and eliminating Israel, led in Oct to a pre-emptive strike by Israel in Sinai. Following this attack, the UK and France asked both sides to withdraw from the Canal Zone and agree to temporary occupation. When this was rejected by Egypt, the British and French invaded, but had to withdraw following diplomatic action by the USA and USSR. Israel was also forced to relinquish the Sinai Peninsula. There have been many allegations of collusion between Israel, France, and the UK. ▷ **Arab-Israeli Wars; Eden, Anthony; Nasser, Gamal Abd al-**

suffragettes Those women who identified with and were members of the late 19c movement to secure voting rights for women. The vote was 'won' after the end of **World War I** (1918), though it was limited to those women of 30 years of age or over. There were many men and women opponents of female suffrage, and in England it was not until 1928 that women over 21 achieved the right to vote. ▷ **Pankhurst, Emmeline**

Suffren de Saint Tropez, Pierre André de (1729–88) French naval commander. He served six years in Malta amongst the Knights Hospitallers; he was captured in Admiral Boscawen's destruction of the Toulon fleet (1759), took part in the bombardment of Sallee (1765), was again four years in Malta, and returned to France as captain in 1772. In 1781 he was placed in command of a French squadron for service in the Indian Ocean, and captured Trincomalee. Returning to Paris in 1784, he was received with great honour as one of France's greatest admirals.

Sugar Act (1764) British statute that attempted for the first time to raise colonial revenue without reference to the colonial assemblies. Its main aim was to impose and collect customs duties and to prevent illegal trade. The colonials responded with protest, but not outright resistance, and the Act was sporadically enforced until the complete breakdown of British–American relations. ▷ **American Revolution; Boston Tea Party; Stamp Act; Townshend Acts**

Sugar Revolution The term used to denote the change from diversified, smallholding, family agriculture to large-scale, plantation/estate sugar monoculture which took place throughout the Caribbean c.1650. Prior to this date, European colonists had grown maize and ground food as subsistence crops and tobacco and cotton as cash crops on small farms of a few acres using their own and indentured labour. However, the demand for sugar in Europe, its profitability and the suitability of the Caribbean coastal plains for its cultivation led to a widespread switch to the crop once its technology had been mastered. The change replaced the small-holder with the capitalist planter, the small-holding with the estate or plantation of several hundred acres and the indentured white labourer with the black African slave. The cultivation of 'King Sugar' was responsible for the slave trade, **slavery**, a dependent monoculture export economy and a hier-archical, racist and class-ridden society.

Suger (c.1081–1151) French prelate and politician. As Abbot of St Denis from 1122, he reformed the abbey and rebuilt its church in the first example of the Gothic style. **Louis VI** and **Louis VII** both employed him on diplomatic missions, and during Louis VII's absence on the Second Crusade, Suger served as Regent, displaying particular skills in financial administration. ▷ **Crusades**

Suharto, Thojib N J (1921–) Indonesian soldier and statesman. Educated for service in the Dutch colonial army, in 1943 he was given a command in the Japanese-sponsored Indonesian army and played an important role in the revolutionary struggle against the Dutch. He became a major political figure during the crises of 1965 and 1966, and assumed full executive power in 1967, order-ing the mass arrest and internment of alleged communists. He became President in 1968, thereafter being re-elected every five years. Suharto's virtual dictatorship uner the 'New Order' saw an improvement in Indonesia's relations with her neighbours in South-East Asia, the republic's return to membership of the **UN**, and considerable economic advance, sustained in large part by buoyant oil revenues.

Suhrawardy, Husein Shaheed (1893–1963) Pakistani politician. Born in East Bengal, he was educated at Oxford Univer-sity in England. In 1921 he became a member of the Bengal Assembly. He was Pakistan's Minister of Law (1954–5) and Prime Minister (1956–7).

Sui Dynasty (581–618) The short-lived Chinese dynasty which unified the country after three centuries of division. The founder of the dynasty, Yang Jian, came to power through a palace coup which toppled the Northern Zhou (557–81), the last of a series

of 'barbarian' conquest dynasties that had held sway in north China since the 4c. Under the reign title of Sui Wendi (581/604), Yang Jian had united China by 589 and imposed centralized control through the promotion of the **Civil Service Examination System** to end entrenched aristocratic privilege. His son, Sui Yangdi (605/17), embarked on costly military adventures in Korea and Vietnam. This, together with the implementation of large-scale public works such as the Grand Canal (built between 605 and 607) and the construction of a second capital using con-scripted labour, exhausted government rev-enues and made the dynasty increasingly unpopular. Sui Yangdi, whose extravagance and cruelty confirmed Confucian stereotypes of the 'last bad ruler', was murdered by one of his officials in 617 amidst large-scale popular revolts. One of the rebels, a frontier general called Li Yuan (566–635), then inaugurated the **Tang Dynasty**.

Sukarno, Ahmed (1902–70) Indonesian statesman and first President of Indonesia (1945–66). He formed the Indonesia National Party (PNI) in 1927, was imprisoned by the Dutch in Bandung (1929–31), and lived in forced exile until 1942, when he emerged as a major nationalist leader during the Japanese occupation. He became Presi-dent when Indonesia was declared indepen-dent in 1945 and was a crucial unifying figure during the subsequent struggle against the Dutch. His popularity waned as the country suffered increasing internal chaos and poverty in the late 1950s and 1960s, while his governments laid themselves open to charges of corruption and extremism. An abortive coup (1965) led to massive violence and a takeover by the army, Sukarno's powers gradually devolving to General Suharto. Sukarno finally retired in 1968.

Sukhothai An ancient state and ruined city of Thailand, 273 miles north of Bangkok. Founded in the mid-13c, Sukhothai's power waned with the emergence of the southern state of Ayudhya in the mid-15c.

Sulaiman (1838–92) Turkish soldier. He entered the army in 1854, fought in Mon-tenegro, Crete and Yemen, and in peace taught at the military academy in Constanti-nople, of which he became director. He distinguished himself against the Serbians in 1876. When the Russians declared war (1877) Sulaiman checked them at Eski Zagra, but destroyed his army in heroic attempts to force them from the Shipka Pass. In Oct 1877 he became commander-in-chief of the army of the Danube, but suffered defeat near Philippopolis (Jan 1878). Court-martialled, he was condemned to 15 years' imprisonment, but the Sultan pardoned him.

Suleyman I, 'the Magnificent' (1494–1566) Ottoman Sultan (1520/66). He added to his dominions, by conquest, Belgrade, Budapest, Rhodes, Tabriz, Baghdad, Aden and Algiers. His fleets dominated the Mediterranean, although he failed to capture Malta. His system of laws regulating land tenure earned him the name *Kanuni* ('lawgiver'), and he was a great patron of arts and architecture. He died during the siege of Szigeth in his war with Austria. ▷ **Ottoman Empire**

Suleyman II (1641–91) Ottoman Emperor (1687/91). The son of Ibrahim I, he succeeded his brother, Muhammad IV, when he was deposed in 1687. He was defeated by the Austrians in 1688, but from 1689 his grand vizier, Mustafa Köprülü, drove the Austrians out of Bulgaria, Serbia and Transylvania and retook Belgrade; Köprülü also introduced numerous liberal reforms, but was killed in battle in 1691.

Sulh, Taqi al-Din al- (1909–88) Lebanese Sunni politician. He was a fervent campaigner on behalf of the Arab peoples against any form of foreign interference in their affairs. Initially focusing on the way in which the Ottoman Turks had kept the Arab peoples in subjection, when the problems of Ottoman dominion had receded, he turned his attentions to the French and British. A moderate who aimed at reconciliation between Christians and Muslims in Lebanon, Taqi al-Din, together with his brother Kazim, maintained that, although the Lebanese people were part of the great Arab nation, the regional peculiarities of Lebanon made the country's independence an essential concomitant of its peaceful development. Politically active throughout his life, he played a prominent role in the late 1960s and early 1970s, and was Prime Minister in 1973–4.

Sulla, Lucius Cornelius, 'Felix' ('Lucky') (138–78BC) Roman politician. Ruthless and enigmatic, his bitter feud with **Marius**, begun in Africa in 107BC during the Jugurthine War, twice plunged Rome into civil war in the decade 90–80sBC. In 88BC he chose to lead his army against the state rather than surrender to Marius his command of the war against

Mithridates VI Euphator; on returning to Rome (83BC), he used his forces to defeat the Marians and secure his own (illegal) position. Appointed 'Dictator' in 82BC, he set about reforming the state, and enacted a number of measures to boost the authority of the Senate. These did not long survive his sudden retirement in 79BC, but his reform of criminal jurisdiction lasted into the empire. ▷ **Jugurtha; Roman Republic**

Sully, Maximilien de Béthune, Duke of (1560–1641) French Huguenot soldier, financier and politician. He fought in the later stages of the Wars of **Religion** (1574–98) and was wounded at Ivry (1590). Instrumental in arranging **Henry IV**'s marriage to Marie de' Medici (1600), he became the King's Chief Minister and trusted counsellor. His major achievement was the restoration of the economy after the civil wars. In 1606 he was created duke, but after Henry's assassination (1610) was forced to retire to his estates. ▷ **Huguenots**

Sultan-Galiev, Mivza Said (1892–1939) Tatar intellectual and politician. He attempted to synthesize Islam and **communism**. He joined the **Bolsheviks** in 1917 in his native Kazan and soon had an official post. **Stalin** welcomed him on to the commissariat of nationalities in 1920 as one of the few non-Russians and then had him arrested in 1923 for his dissident Islamic views. Freed, he continued to preach communism as a means of liberating his fellow non-Russian Muslims. However, he was rearrested in 1929 and disappeared. His name has been much revered among Muslims ever since.

Šumadija Literally 'the forested land', this term describes the region of Central Serbia which lies to the south of Belgrade. After the fall of Serbia to the Ottoman Turks (1389), it was ruled from the 15c to 1697 by the Crnojević Dynasty of Montenegro. In 1804 the first of the **Serbian Uprisings** began in Šumadija and its chief town, Kragujevac, was the capital of Prince Miloš **Obrenović**.

Sumatra A large island, straddling the equator, at the western extremity of the Indonesian archipelago. Historically, the island has been only very lightly populated and, even today, large areas of the mountainous interior are covered by dense, unpopulated jungle. The south-east part of the island, in the region of Palembang, was the site of the great empire of **Srivijaya**, dominating the maritime trade of the archipelago from the close of the 7c. As the Dutch colonial state extended its control outside Java from the middle of the 19c, it encountered in Sumatra a large number of small states. Most were brought under Dutch administration by treaty, but the north Sumatran state of **Aceh** put up fierce armed resistance and was not subdued until 1902. In 1958 West Sumatra was the site of a major rebellion against the central government in Jakarta.

Sumer The name given to the part of Lower Mesopotamia between Babylon and the Persian Gulf. It is the place where the world's first urban civilization evolved; among the greatest of Sumerian city-states were Eridu, Ur, and Uruk. Surviving art forms date from c.2500BC, and include the stone statues of Gudea and many coloured bas-reliefs.

Sunderland, Robert Spencer, 2nd Earl of (1641–1702) English statesman. He became an influential adviser, successively, of **Charles II**, **James VII and II** and **William III**. He was dismissed as Secretary of State in 1681 for voting to exclude James from the succession, but reinstated in 1683, becoming Chief Minister under James in 1685, and a Catholic (1688). On William's accession, he fled to Europe, but after renouncing his Catholicism was allowed to return in 1691. He was Lord Chancellor for a while in 1697.

Sung Dynasty ▷ **Song Dynasty**

Sunnis Members of an Islamic religious movement representing 'orthodoxy' in Islam, comprising about 80 per cent of all Muslims. They recognize the first four caliphs as 'rightly-guided' (*rashidun*), and base their *sunnah* (the 'path' of the Prophet **Muhammad**) upon the Quran and the *hadith* or 'traditions' of the Prophet. They are organized into four legal schools which all enjoy equal standing. The other major Islamic group is made up of **Shiites**.

Sun Tzu ▷ **Sun Zi**

Sun Yat-sen (Sun Zhongshan/Sun Yixian) (1866–1925) Chinese politician. The founder and early leader of China's Nationalist Party, the **Guomindang**, he first trained as a doctor in Hawaii and Hong Kong. Alarmed by the weakness and decay of China, he founded the Society for the Revival of China, and sprang to fame when, on a visit to London, he was kidnapped by the Chinese legation, and released through the interven-

tion of the Foreign Office. He then helped to organize risings in southern China. He returned to China after the 1911 Wuhan rising, realized that he would not be widely acceptable as President, and voluntarily handed over the office to **Yuan Shikai**. After the assassination of his follower, **Song Jiaoren**, civil war ensued (1913), and he set up a separate government at Guangzhou (Canton). He died in Beijing, widely accepted as the true leader of the nation. ▷ **Lenin**

Sun Zi (Sun Tzu) (4c BC) Chinese general and military philosopher. A native of the state of Qi (Ch'i, modern Shantung), he was the author of *Ping-fa* (The Art of War), the first known military treatise, containing profound and still-relevant insights into the philosophy of human conflict. He moved to Wu, whose armies he led to great victories over the rival principalities of Qu (Ch'u), Qi (Ch'i) and Qin (Ch'in).

superpowers The description applied during the **Cold War** period to the USA and the USSR, the two nations with economic and military resources far exceeding those of other powers. With the collapse of the USSR in 1991, it is sometimes argued that there is only one superpower left. But arguments concerning gross national product and real or potential military strength suggest that China, Japan and the European Community might merit the description if still in use.

Supilo, Frano (1870–1917) Croatian politician. A Croat from **Dalmatia**, during **World War I** he worked closely with Ante **Trumbić**, co-founding with him the Social Democrat Party. Supilo helped to found the **Yugoslav Committee** which, from its base in London, tried to win Allied support for South Slav unification. ▷ **South Slavs; Yugoslavs**

Suppiluliumas (14c BC) King of the Hittites (c.1380/1346BC). Under Suppiluliumas, Hittite power reached its zenith. He rebuilt the capital Hattusas, and re-established Hittite control over northern Syria, installing his sons as rulers of Carchemish and Aleppo. ▷ **Hittites**

Supplex Libellus Valachorum (1791) The petition addressed from the **Romanians** in Transylvania to Emperor **Leopold II**, in which they demanded the same rights as those enjoyed by the privileged nations of the province, the Magyars, **Saxons** and **Szeklers**. This was an attempt by the Romanians to seek representation in Transylvania's political institutions, which were then dominated by Magyar nobles.

Supreme Court In the USA, the highest federal court established under the constitution, members of which are appointed by the President with the advice and consent of the Senate. In addition to its jurisdiction relating to appeals, the court exercises oversight of the Constitution through the power of judicial review of the acts of state and federal legislatures, and the executive. It was created in 1789 and has comprised nine members since 1869. ▷ **US Constitution**

Surat A coastal town in present-day Gujarat, which was subordinated by the British in 1709. Surat was a big trading and export centre under the Mughals and its value as a fort and as a strategic point between the Deccan and Gujarat was very high. In its heyday, ships from Surat traded with East Africa, the Middle East and throughout the Indian Ocean, and fortunes were made from the sale of textiles, precious metals and spices. In 1664 Surat was sacked by the Maratha leader, Shivaji. Although it subsequently recovered from this, in the declining years of the **Mughal Empire** the port became increasingly vulnerable. After the death of Muhammad Ali, the last great merchant of Surat, at the hands of the Mughal governor in 1733, a British blockade in 1734 and an attack on the merchant fleet in 1735, the majority of merchants fled to the relative safety of the British-controlled port of Bombay. After the establishment of British paramountcy in western India in 1803, the fortunes of the port then slowly recovered. Surat became important to the Indian national movement when a famous session of the **Indian National Congress** was held there in 1907. This session witnessed a clash between so-called 'moderates' and 'extremists'. The meeting broke up in disorder because of extremist attempts at coercion, but the episode ended with the assertion of the supremacy of the 'moderate' faction under Gokhale Banerjee, Sinha and Mehta.

Susa (Greek *Shusan*) An ancient city of Elam and the capital of the Achaemenid Empire under **Darius I, 'the Great'** and his succesors. It is the site of the the world's best-preserved ziggurat.

Suslov, Mikhail Andreevich (1902–82) Soviet politician. He joined the Communist Party in 1921, and was a member of the

Central Committee from 1941 until his death. An ideologist of the Stalinist school, he became a ruthless and strongly doctrinaire administrator. Very different from Nikita **Khrushchev** in temperament and political outlook, he opposed Khrushchev's 'de-Stalinization' measures, economic reforms, and foreign policy, and was instrumental in unseating him in 1964. ▷ **Stalinism**

Suspects, Law of (17 Sep 1793) This French law, drafted in sweeping terms, allowing the arrest of all who supported tyranny or federalism, former nobles or emigrés or their relatives, was the basis of the Reign of **Terror**; it was repealed in 1795.

Suvorov, Alexander Vasilyevich, Count (1729–1800) Russian general. He fought in the **Seven Years War**, and in Poland and Turkey, then aided the Austrians against the French in Italy (1799), where he won several victories. Directed to join other Russian forces in Switzerland, he found them already defeated, and was forced into a winter retreat across the mountains to Austria, which he completed with great success. ▷ **French Revolutionary Wars**

Suzman, Helen (1917–) South African politician. Educated at Parktown Convent and Witwatersrand University, she lectured part-time at the University (1944–52) but became deeply concerned by the rightward shift of the **National Party** (NP); she joined the opposition United Party and was elected to parliament in 1953. Closely involved with the South African Institute of Race Relations in the 1970s, she was often a solitary voice against the NP's policy of **apartheid** in parliament. A formidable debater, Suzman earned the respect of opponents of apartheid and received the UN Human Rights Award in 1978. She retired from parliament in 1989 after 36 uninterrupted years of service.

Suzuki Zenko (1911–) Japanese politician. He was elected in 1947 to the lower house of the Diet as a Socialist party deputy, but moved to the Liberal Party in 1949 and then, on its formation in 1955, to the conservative **Liberal Democratic Party (LDP)**. During the 1960s and 1970s he held a succession of ministerial and party posts, including Post and Telecommunications (1960–4), Chief Cabinet Secretary (1964–5), Health and Welfare (1965–8) and Agriculture, Forestry and Fisheries (1976–80). Following the death of his patron, Masayoshi **Ohira**, he succeeded to the dual positions of

LDP President and Prime Minister in 1980. His premiership was marred by factional strife within the LDP, deteriorating relations with the USA and opposition to his defence policy. He stepped down in 1982, but remained an influential LDP faction leader.

Svehla, Antonin (1873–1933) Czechoslovak politician. Born near Prague, he was active in the Agrarian Party from its foundation in 1899, establishing its newspaper in 1906 and chairing its executive committee from 1909 until his death in 1933. Half-way through **World War I** he threw his weight behind **Masaryk**'s drive for complete independence. As Minister of the Interior (1918–20), he protected the new state against threats from the revolutionary left. As Prime Minister for most of the period 1922–9, he gave it economic prosperity and social stability, based on a combination of middle-of-the-road agrarian and socialist interests.

Svein I Haraldsson, 'Fork-Beard' (d.1014) King of Denmark (985/1014) and, for five winter weeks, of England (1014). He was the son of **Harald Bluetooth**, but rebelled against his father and deposed him in 985. His reign was notable for a series of military campaigns against England from 994 onwards. On each occasion, King **Ethelred the Unready** paid escalating amounts of *Danegeld* to buy off the Danish invaders but each time they returned for more. In 1013 Svein Fork-Beard launched another expedition with imperial intent, taking with him his son, **Canute**. By the end of the year, King Ethelred had fled to safety in Normandy, leaving Svein to take up the crown; but five weeks later, on 3 Feb 1014, Svein died, and Canute returned for a time to Denmark.

Svein II Ulfsson (Estridsson) (d.1074) King of Denmark (1047/74). The son of a regent of Denmark, Earl Ulf, and nephew of **Canute** (his mother was Canute's sister, Estrid), he was appointed Regent of Denmark in 1045 by King **Magnus I, 'the Good'** of Norway (and Denmark), and was himself acclaimed King when Magnus died in 1047. **Harald Hardrada**, who became sole King of Norway, laid claim to Denmark as well, and now began a long and unrelenting war of attrition against Svein. Svein lost every battle, but never lost the war, and in 1064 peace was made and Harald accepted Svein's right to the throne of Denmark. In 1069, after the conquest of England by **William I, 'the Conqueror'**, Svein's army descended on the north of England and captured York, but

Svein made peace with William the following year and withdrew. He was succeeded by five of his sons in turn.

Sveinn Björnsson ▷ Björnsson, Sveinn

Sverdlov, Yakov Mikhailovich (1885–1919) Bolshevik politician. Born and brought up in Nizhni Novgorod, he embraced socialism early and was arrested for the first time when he was 17 years old. Between 1902 and 1907 he was often in prison or in exile. In 1917 he rose rapidly to become Chairman of the Central Executive Committee, running both the party and the country while others fought their military and political battles. However, in 1919 he died suddenly, leaving a serious gap at the top which was never really filled.

Sverdrup, Johan (1816-92) Norwegian politician. A combative and charismatic figure, Sverdrup was elected to parliament (the *Storting*) in 1850. His prolonged fight to establish parliamentary sovereignty in Norway was rewarded with success in 1884. Since Norway was ruled by the King of Sweden, this entailed challenging both the prerogatives of the crown and the union with Sweden. In 1869 Sverdrup became leader of Norway's first organized political party, the Left (*Venstre*). Following repeated challenges by Sverdrup and his supporters, King Oscar II was finally obliged, in 1884, to turn to Sverdrup as the only leader who commanded the support of a majority in the Storting. Sverdrup was Prime Minister of Norway from 1884 to 1889.

Sverrir Sigurdsson ('the Usurper') (c.1150–1202) King of Norway (1184/1202). Brought up in the Faroes, he claimed to be the illegitimate son of Sigurd Haraldsson, 'the Mouth' (d.1155), King of Norway. He emerged from obscurity in 1179 to lay claim to the throne from **Magnus V Erlingsson**, whom he finally defeated and killed in 1184. He turned out to be one of Norway's greatest kings, strengthening the crown against both Church and nobles with the support of the freeholding farmers. He commissioned one of the first Icelandic Sagas — a biography of himself, *Sverris saga*, written during his lifetime by his contemporary and friend, Karl Jónsson, Abbot of the Monastery of Thingeyrar in Iceland.

Svestka, Oldrich (1922–) Czechoslovak editor and politician. A journalist, he joined the Communist Party in 1945 and became one of the editors of its daily *Rudé Právo*. In 1958

he became editor-in-chief, and in 1962 he became a member of the Central Committee, and so held an influential political position. In 1968 he was admitted to the presidium of the party, but his allegiance to the **Prague Spring** was only formal. With **Bil'ak** and others he welcomed the Soviet invasion, and by 1975 he was once more editor-in-chief of *Rudé Právo*, but it disappeared with the party in 1990.

Svoboda, Ludwik (1895–1979) Czechoslovak soldier and politician. He fought with the Czechoslovak Legion in Russia in 1917 before becoming a professional soldier. After escaping from Czechoslovakia in 1939 he became commanding general of the Czechoslovak army corps attached to the **Red Army** in 1943, and helped to liberate Kosiče, Brno and Prague in 1944 to 1945. In 1948 he joined the Communist Party and was Minister of Defence until 1950. From 1952 to 1963 he lived in obscurity, mistrusted by the Stalinists; but, with Nikita **Khrushchev**'s backing, he was subsequently brought forward as a 'safe' patriotic father-figure and, in 1968, he succeeded the discredited Antonín **Novotný** as President. He gave loyal support to the abortive reforms of Alexander **Dubček** and, after the hostile Soviet intervention in 1968, he travelled to Moscow to seek relaxation of the repressive measures imposed on the Czechoslovaks. He remained in office until 1975, when failing health forced his retirement.

Swabia A south-western medieval German duchy, extending from the River Rhine in the west to the Alps in the south, Bavaria in the east, and Franconia in the north, containing the cities of Strasbourg, Constance, and Augsburg. The **Peasants War** of 1524–5 began here, because landlords and peasants were at odds, imperial authority was increasing, and Lutheran doctrines were spreading.

Swabian League (1488) Various leagues existed throughout the Middle Ages but in 1488, at Esslingen, 22 Imperial towns joined with the Imperial Knights' League of St George, some ecclesiastical princes (eg Mainz, Bavaria, Baden) to create a new league. This body, governed by three colleges of knights, princes and towns, possessed its own army. It was actively involved in the suppression of the Peasants Revolt (1524–5). The league was disbanded in 1534 as a result of tensions produced internally by the Reformation and the introduction of Lutheranism into some of the member states.

Swadeshi A Hindi term meaning 'of one's own country', this was a slogan used as part of an Indian campaign of boycotting foreign-made goods, initiated in protest against the partition of Bengal into two separate administrative divisions by the British in 1905, in defiance of Indian public opinion. The policy was viewed as an attempt to perpetuate British rule by dividing the Indian population, particularly the Muslims of East Bengal from the Hindus of West Bengal. Advocates of *Swadeshi* urged the Indian people to wear *khadi* or home-made country-cloth, amongst other things. The first example of mass opposition to British rule, the campaign led eventually to the abandonment of the partition of Bengal in 1911. ▷ **Bengal, Partition of**

Swahili A language spoken in East Africa, especially in Tanzania. A hybrid of Arabic and local languages, it has provided a bridge across tribal divides and has been seen by many East Africans as a national, or even regional, language which is indigenous rather than imported from the colonial power.

Swatantra Party The only authentic Indian political party of the traditional Right, as the term would be understood in Europe. It was a coalition of big urban business and rural aristocratic and landlord elements in which the later were dominant. The Swatantra Party was formed on an all-India basis in 1959 and was of consequence nationally only in three general elections: 1962, 1967 and 1972. In 1967, it succeeded in winning 44 seats in the Lok Sabha (the lower house of Parliament), emerging as the second largest party in the House after Congress. During its heyday, the Swatantra Party was the leading party of the Right offering a full scale critique of the Congress policies of centralized planning, nationalization of industries, agrarian reform, and nonalignment.

SWAPO (South West Africa People's Organization) Founded in 1958 as the Ovambo People's Organization, SWAPO became the main nationalist movement for South-West Africa (Namibia) and organized the guerrilla war against the South African administration of the country. Based initially in Tanzania and then Zambia, the guerrilla movement established bases in Angola in the 1970s and became embroiled in the general conflict involving South Africa, **UNITA**, and the **MPLA** government in Luanda with its Cuban and Soviet support. Recognized by the **Organization of African Unity** (OAU), and later by the world community, as the authentic voice of Namibian aspirations, an international agreement was reached in Geneva in 1988 which linked Namibia's independence with Cuban withdrawal from Angola and the cessation of South African support for UNITA. In the ensuing 1989 election, SWAPO won over half the votes and a majority of seats and formed the first independent government.

Swaraj A Hindi term meaning 'self-government' or 'home rule'. It was used by Indian nationalists to describe independence from British rule.

Swing Riots (1830–1) A movement of agricultural workers, especially in the south and east of England, consisting of a series of arson attacks and the destruction of threshing machines. The uprising was put down by the Whig government, resulting in 19 executions and nearly 500 transportations, but the labourers won some wage concessions and delayed the introduction of mechanization.
▷ **Luddites**

Swiss Guards The papal police corps, originally instituted by Pope **Julius II** and recruited from the mercenaries of the cantons of the Swiss confederacy, whose reputation as infantrymen was established after their victories over the Burgundian calvary in 1476. Their dark blue, yellow, and red uniforms were designed by Michelangelo.

Sykes–Picot Agreement (1916) A secret agreement concluded in this year by diplomat Sir Mark Sykes (for Britain) and Georges Picot (for France) partitioning the **Ottoman Empire** after the war. France was to be the dominant power in Syria and Lebanon, and Britain in Transjordan, Iraq, and northern Palestine. The rest of Palestine was to be under international control, and an Arab state was to be established.

Syllabus of Errors Appended to the papal encyclical *Quanta cura* of 1864 was a 'Catalogue of the Principal Errors of Our Time' in which Pope **Pius IX** not only condemned **socialism** and nationalism, but also rejected any notion that the Catholic Church could tolerate 'progress, liberalism and modern civilization'. Rather than halting the forces that Pius feared, the Syllabus served to foster greater anti-clericalism both within Italy and the rest of Europe.

Sylvester II (Gerbert Aurillac) (c.940–1003) French Pope (999/1003). Renowned for his achievements in chemistry, mathematics, and philosophy, he is said to have introduced Arabic numerals and to have invented a species of clock. As Pope, he upheld the primacy of Rome against the separatist tendencies of the French Church.

Symmachus, Coelius (d.514) Pope (498/514). Strongly orthodox, he expelled the Manicheans from Rome.

syndicalism A revolutionary socialist doctrine that emphasized workers taking power by seizing the factories in which they worked; developed in the 1890s, and common in France, Italy, and Spain in the early 20c. The state was to be replaced by worker-controlled units of production. Often a general strike was advocated as part of the strategy. By 1914 it had lost its political force. The name, deriving from *syndicat* (French, 'trade union'), has also been applied to various non-revolutionary doctrines supporting worker control.

Syracuse Greek city in eastern Sicily founded by **Corinth** c.734BC, in antiquity noted for its prosperity from agriculture and trade. Periods of democratic government alternated with periods of tyranny: 485–467BC under Gelon, Hieron I and Thrasybulus; from 405BC under **Dionysius the Elder** and his son Dionysius II (who ruled 367/344BC until expelled by Timoleon of Corinth); Agathocles (317/289BC) took the title of King (304BC). Thereafter Syracuse declined in the face of Carthaginian, and later Roman, power. ▷ **Peloponnesian War**

Syrian National Bloc Formed in 1931, the National Bloc (*al-kutla al-wataniyya*) was a heterogeneous assortment of regional factions bound together by the common cause of the independence to which Syrian nationalists opposed to the French mandate aspired. After the national strike of 1936, which was not of the Bloc's making, the French invited delegates from the Bloc to negotiations in Paris. Despite the preparation of a draft treaty, granting Syria a form of independence (while providing guarantees for the special position of France), by the outbreak of **World War II**, the Syrian nationalist aim of freedom from France had been frustrated. After the invasion of the Free French and British in 1940, the Bloc continued to press for independence, despite opposition from the Free French. The British, however, began to lend their support to the Bloc, which was led from 1940 by

Shukri **Quwwatli**, who was later to become President of the Syrian Republic. Independence was achieved in 1946, but the failure of the old elite, who came to power in 1946, to recognize the need for reform in the face of pressing social and economic difficulties, led to military coups in 1949. As a result of the third of these, Colonel Adib Shishakli was to hold power until 1954. Despite the re-emergence of Quwwatli in 1955 and the reforming efforts of Khalid al-Azm, the Ba'th Party in Syria, by dint of proposing a **United Arab Republic** of Egypt and Syria in 1958, managed in due course to supplant the existing party structure.

Syrian Wars (274–168BC) The series of six wars in which the Seleucid and Ptolemaic Dynasties vied for control of 'Hollow Syria' ie Palestine and southern Syria. Initially under Ptolemaic control, the area was definitively transferred to Seleucid control at the Battle of Panion (200BC), in the Fifth Syrian War (202–200BC). Later, the Ptolemies renewed their claim to the area, saying that it constituted the dowry of Ptolemy V's wife, Cleopatra, daughter of the Seleucid King, Antiochus III; but in the Sixth Syrian War (170–168BC) the Seleucid King, Antiochus IV, retaliated with two invasions of Egypt, and might have secured permanent control of Egypt had not the Roman envoy, Gaius Popillius Laenas, compelled him to withdraw.

Szabo, Ervin (1877–1918) Hungarian intellectual. A lawyer by training and a librarian by occupation, he was very active in shaping socialist ideas from 1899 onwards. After a few years he switched from support for the Social Democratic Party to syndicalism. He translated **Marx** and **Engels** and wrote extensively about Marxism. He left behind a circle of young critics of bureaucracy, opportunism and militarism.

Szalasi, Ferenc (1897–1946) Hungarian soldier and politician. A major on the general staff, he joined a secret racist group in 1930, and in 1933 published his *Plan for the Building of the Hungarian State*, which became the ideological handbook for Hungarian pacifism. Retired from military service in 1935, he formed the first of a series of fascist parties culminating in the **Arrow Cross** in 1940. Under Nazi pressure he became Prime Minister in 1944 and instituted a racist reign of terror. In 1946 he was executed as a war criminal.

Szechenyi, Istvan, Count (1791–1860) Hungarian landowner, soldier, innovator and reformer. He was responsible for establishing the Hungarian Academy of Sciences, which from 1825 onwards contributed a cultural core and a broadening social base to aristocratic protests against Habsburg rule. He was also behind the building of Adam Clark's famous Chain Bridge across the Danube joining the political weight of Buda to the commercial weight of Pest to form a new capital. He eventually despaired both of the aristocracy and of the new nationalists and committed suicide. ▷ **Habsburg Dynasty**

Szeklers A tribe in **Transylvania** which served as frontiersmen in medieval Hungary, then assimilated to the Magyars and came to speak the Hungarian language. The medieval kings of Hungary granted them the right of self-government in their districts: they elected their own count, who was responsible to the King, and their land was administered by the Transylvanian diet. During the **Reformation**, many became members of the Lutheran and Unitarian Churches. Today many Szeklers remain in Transylvania and form a Hungarian-speaking majority in the counties between Tîrgu Mureş and Braşov. ▷ **Supplex Libellus Valachorum**

T

Taaffe, Eduard Franz Josef, Count von (1833–95) Austrian politician. Born 11th Viscount Taaffe and Baron of Ballymote in the Irish peerage, he became Austria's Minister of the Interior (1867) and Chief Minister (1869–70 and 1879–93). He showed great tact in an attempt to unite the various nationalities of the empire into a consolidated whole.

Table of Ranks (1722) The grading by **Peter I, 'the Great'** of the Russian nobility into 14 different ranks for military and civil service. Peter was intent on exploiting all the resources of his state. In accordance with the Table, the nobility had to carry out service from a very young age; new men who did not happen to be nobles could also get on to the ladder; and promotion was dependent on performance. The fifth rank brought ennoblement, the ninth rank made it hereditary. Two-thirds served in the army or navy, the rest in the bureaucracy. Peter's successors were less able to dominate and exploit the nobility in this way; and **Catherine II, 'the Great'** produced a **Charter of the Nobility** mainly to keep them out of power.

Tacna-Arica Question A prolonged diplomatic dispute between Peru and Chile concerning sovereignty over Tacna and Arica provinces, occupied by Chile in the War of the **Pacific**. It was finally resolved in 1929 by the award of Tacna to Peru and Arica to Chile.

Taewon'gun (Yi Ha-ung) (1820–98) Korean courtier. The father of the Korean king, Kojong (1864/1907), he became the dominant figure at court in his capacity as Grand Prince (*Taewon'gun*). He favoured an exclusionist foreign policy, rejecting requests from Japan and the Western powers for the opening of diplomatic and commercial relations and preferring to maintain Korea's tributary relationship with China. His formal retirement in 1873 paved the way for the Treaty of **Kanghwa** (1876) with Japan, which signalled the end of Korean seclusion.

Taft, Robert Alphonso (1889–1953) US politician. The son of President William **Taft**, he studied law at Yale and Harvard and in 1917 became counsellor to the American Food Administration in Europe under **Hoover**. A conservative Republican, he was elected to the Senate from Ohio in 1938, and co-sponsored the **Taft–Hartley Act** (1947) directed against the power of the trade unions and the 'closed shop'. A prominent isolationist, he was Republican leader from 1939 to 1953, failing three times (1940, 1948 and 1952) to secure the Republican nomination for the presidency.

Taft, William Howard (1857–1930) US politician and 27th President. Educated at Yale, he became a lawyer, solicitor general (1890), the first civil Governor of the Philippines (1901), and then Secretary of War (1904–8) under President Theodore **Roosevelt**. As President (1909–13), he continued both Roosevelt's aggressive foreign policy and his policies favouring conservation and regulation of big business, and achieved an excellent record of legislation. But he was handicapped by having followed the flamboyant and popular Roosevelt. While he was in fact a fairly progressive president, the public, in favour of reform as a result of Roosevelt's politics, perceived him as conservative, and he was not re-elected. From 1913 he was Professor of Law at Yale, and from 1921 Chief Justice of the US Supreme Court, where he made administrative improvements. He was the father of Robert Alphonso **Taft**, the US Senator and Republican leader.
▷ **Republican Party**

Taft–Hartley Act (1947) US labour legislation. It outlawed 'unfair' labour practices such as the closed shop, and demanded that unions supply financial reports and curtail their political activities. It also gave the US government the power to postpone major strikes endangering national health or safety for a cooling-off period of 80 days. The National Management Relations Act, its official name, was passed over President Truman's veto by the first Republican-controlled Congress in almost 20 years to limit the power of the **National Labor Relations Act** (the 'Wagner Act') of 1935, which the Republicans believed had shifted the balance between employers and workers far too much in favour of the unions.

Tagliacozzo, Battle of (1268) The victory of **Charles of Anjou** over the armies of **Conradin of Swabia** secured for him the crown of Sicily and Naples, and marked the ruin of the empire in Italy. Conradin, the last legitimate Staufen heir, was taken. He appealed to the Pope to intervene with his captors, but Clement IV did not respond and the 16-year-old and his entourage were publicly hanged in Naples. The papal triumph over the Staufen was complete, but short-lived, for Charles of Anjou cared even less for ecclesiastical rights and privileges than the heirs of **Frederick II**.

Tahirid Dynasty The first of the so-called Independent Dynasties in the eastern Islamic lands. It was founded by Tahir ibn al-Husayn, one of the 'Abbasid Sultan al-**Ma'mun**'s generals in the conflict with the former's brother, al-Amin. Granted the governorship of the territories east of Baghdad by al-Ma'mun in 820, Tahir established himself in Khurasan with his capital at Merv. It was Tahir's omission of the caliph's name from the *khutba* (a prayer or sermon) in the mosque rather than any overtly aggressive action that proclaimed his assertion of independence. Tahir's successors expanded the Tahirid domains and they moved their capital westwards to Nishapur. The Tahirids fell with the rise of the Saffarids in 872. ▷ 'Abbasid Dynasty

Ta'if Accord (1898) When Amin **Gemayel** left office as President of Lebanon in Sep 1988, the country found itself without a government. Michel Awn, then Commander-in-Chief of the Lebanese army and a Maronite Christian, took over the presidential palace and went on to attack Syrian forces in Beirut. In response to the crisis, the **Arab League**, represented by King Fahd of Saudi Arabia and King Hasan of Morocco, together with President Chadli of Algeria, proposed a peace plan (Oct 1989) and the Lebanese members of parliament gathered in Ta'if in Saudi Arabia. The Ta'if Accord was the result of their talks on the need to reduce Maronite Christian domination in government. The essence of the agreement was that the cabinet and the National Assembly, to whom the President would be subject, would be equally divided between Christian and Muslim members. Not surprisingly, this proposal was criticized by both Druze and Shi'a, and rejected by Awn.

Taifa Kings The name (literally, 'party' or 'faction' kings) given to the rulers of the petty kingdoms that were formed in Muslim Spain after the fall of the Caliphate of Cordoba in 1031. There was a total of 23 Taifa realms, many of which were conquered by the invading **Almoravids** under Yusuf ibn Tashfin in the late 11c.

Taiping Rebellion (1850–64) A rebellion that spread all over southern China, led by **Hong Xiuquan**. Its programme, which aimed at ushering in a 'Heavenly Kingdom of Great Peace' (*Taiping tianguo*) was a mixture of religion and political reform. The rebels took Nanjing (Nanking) in 1853 and made it their capital, but internal strife, foreign intervention, and the Qing forces under **Zeng Guofan** eventually brought the downfall of the movement. ▷ **Qing Dynasty**

Taisho Emperor (Yoshihito) (1879–1926) Emperor of Japan (1912/26). The only son of the **Meiji Emperor (Mutsuhito)**, he was proclaimed Crown Prince in 1889 and succeeded his father on the imperial throne in 1912. His 14-year reign saw the emergence of Japan as a world great power. Unlike his father, however, he took little part in active politics, for his mental health gave way in 1921. In the last five years of his life, Crown Prince **Hirohito** was regent.

Takeshita Noboru (1924–) Japanese politician, The son of an affluent sake brewer, he trained as a kamikaze pilot during World War II. After university and a brief career as a schoolteacher, he was elected to the House of Representatives as a **Liberal Democratic Party (LDP)** deputy in 1958, rising to become Chief Cabinet Secretary (1971–2) to Prime Minister **Sato** and Minister of Finance (1982–6) under Prime Minister **Nakasone**. Formerly a member of the powerful 'Tanaka faction', he founded his own faction, the largest within the party, in 1987, and three months later was elected LDP President and Prime Minister. Although regarded as a cautious, consensual politician, he pushed through important tax reforms. His administration was undermined by the uncovering of the Recruit-Cosmos insider share dealing scandal, which, though dating back to 1986, forced the resignation of senior government ministers, including, eventually, Takeshita himself (June 1989).

Talat Pasha, Mahmud (1872–1921) Initially a civil servant, he was a supporter of the liberal Young Turks movement along with Enver Pasha who had been a military attaché in Berlin. An associate of Enver, who as Minister of War was regarded as having been largely responsible for bringing Turkey into the Great War on the German side, Talat was excluded from the peace negotiations after the conclusion of the Mudros Armistice in Oct 1918 and fled to Germany. He was assassinated by an Armenian in Berlin.

Talleyrand (-Périgord), Charles Maurice de (1754–1838) French politician. Educated for the Church, he was ordained (1779), appointed Bishop of Autun (1788), elected to the **Estates General**, and made President of the National Assembly (1790). He lived in exile in England and the USA until after the fall of **Robespierre**. As Foreign Minister under the **Directory** (1797–1807), he helped to consolidate **Napoleon I**'s position as Consul (1802) and Emperor (1804); but alarmed by Napoleon's ambitions, he resigned in 1807, becoming leader of the anti-Napoleonic faction. He became Foreign Minister under **Louis XVIII**, representing France with great skill at the Congress of **Vienna** (1814–15). He then lived largely in retirement, but was **Louis-Philippe**'s chief adviser at the **July Revolution** (1830), and was appointed French Ambassador to England (1830–4). ▷ **French Revolution**

Tallien, Jean Lambert (1767–1820) French revolutionary politician. As President of the National Convention (1794), he was denounced by **Robespierre**, but conspired with **Barras** and **Fouché** to bring about the former's downfall. He became a member of the Council of Five Hundred under the **Directory** (1795–9), and accompanied **Napoleon I** to Egypt (1798). ▷ **Convention, National; French Revolution**

Talukdars A class of landholders in eastern India which grew in the first half of the 18c. Zamindars (literally, 'lords of the land') were at the apex of a pyramid of revenue collecting agents. Below them were hundreds of small tenure holders, usually called Talukdars. Sometimes Talukdars paid directly to the government, although they more often did so through the Zamindars. Some 18c Taluks originated from older revenue rights which had been incorporated into a new Zamindari, but most appear to have been recent creations, granted to those who had settled new lands, or sold by existing Zamindars who wished to raise money. Even in the great Zamindaris in the last years of the Nawabs, men who wished to invest in revenue rights seem to have been able to purchase taluks.

Tamberlaine ▷ **Timur**

Tambo, Oliver (1917–93) South African politician. The son of a peasant farmer, he went to Johannesburg to attend a school set up by the Community of the Resurrection, where he came under the influence of Trevor Huddleston. Having graduated from Fort Hare College, he embarked upon a teaching diploma but was expelled for political activity. He joined the **ANC** Youth League in 1944, rising to be a member of the ANC executive (1949), Secretary-General (1955), and Deputy President (1959). He then went into exile and was President of ANC in exile from 1977. He returned to South Africa in 1989 as titular leader of the party, but gave up this position at the meeting of the party in exile in 1990.

Tamerlane ▷ **Timur**

Tamil A Dravidian language originally found in South India and Sri Lanka. The term 'Tamil' also refers to the speakers of the language, most of whom live in the South Indian state of Tamil Nadu, although there are substantial Tamil populations in Sri Lanka, where some have been agitating for secession from the state dominated by the Sinhala majority, and Malaysia. Nationalist political aspirations have been promoted by Tamil parties like the DMK in India as well as the militant LTTE in Sri Lanka.

Tammany Hall US **political machine** of the Democratic Party in New York City and State. It was originally a club (the Society of Tammany) founded in 1789, and in the late 19c and early 20c became notorious for its political corruption. Its power declined in the 1932 election, and although revived for a short time, it has ceased to exist as a political power in New York politics.

Tanaka Giichi (1864–1929) Japanese militarist and politician. A member of the **Choshu** clique, Tanaka served in both the **Sino-Japanese War** (1894–5) and the **Russo-Japanese War** (1904–5) and became a vigorous supporter of army expansion. He became leader of the **Seiyukai** in 1925 (signalling that party's close association with the military) and Prime Minister in 1927. During his premiership (1927–9) thousands of suspected communists were arrested under the **Peace Preservation Laws**. Tanaka also initiated the policy of direct Japanese military intervention in China when he sanctioned three expeditions (1927–8) to east China (Shandong province), ostensibly to protect Japanese residents in the wake of **Chiang Kai-shek**'s **Northern Expedition**.

Tanaka Kakuei (1918–) Japanese politician. After training as a civil engineer and establishing a successful building contracting business, he was elected to Japan's House of Representatives in 1947. He rose swiftly within the dominant **Liberal Democratic Party (LDP)**, becoming Minister of Finance (1962–5), Party Secretary-General (1965–7) and Minister of International Trade and Industry (1971–2), before serving as LDP President and Prime Minister (1972–4). He was arrested in 1976, while he was Prime Minister, on charges of accepting bribes as part of the **Lockheed Scandal**, and eventually in 1983 was found guilty and sentenced to four years' imprisonment. He had resigned from the LDP in 1976, becoming an independent deputy, but remained an influential, behind-the-scenes, faction leader. His appeal against the 1983 verdict was rejected by the High Court in 1987, but a further appeal was lodged.

Tancred (c.1076–1112) Norman crusader. The grandson of Robert **Guiscard**, he went on the First Crusade. He distinguished himself in the sieges of Nicaea, Tarsus, Antioch, Jerusalem, and Ascalon, and was given the principality of Tiberias (1099). He also ruled at Edessa and Antioch, where he died. ▷ **Crusade, First; Normans**

Taney, Roger Brooke (1777–1864) US jurist. He was admitted to the bar in 1799 and Andrew **Jackson** made him Attorney-General in 1831, and Secretary of the Treasury in 1833. The Senate, after rejecting his appointment as Chief Justice in 1835, confirmed it in 1836. His most famous decision was in the **Dred Scott** case, when he ruled that the Missouri Compromise was unconstitutional and that slaves and their descendants had no rights as citizens. This precipitated the Civil War, and injured the reputation of the Court for years thereafter.

Tanganyika African National Union (TANU) This party, founded in 1954, grew out of the Tanganyika African Association and was the dominant party in Tanganyika during the period leading to independence. Under the leadership of Julius **Nyerere**, it became first *de facto* the only party in the country and then, in 1966, *de jure* the only party. Noted for the internal competition it provided at election time and for its unique brand of socialist ideology, laid out in the **Arusha Declaration**, the party merged in 1977 with the Afro-Shirazi Party of Zanzibar to form **Chama Cha Mapinduzi (CCM)**.

Tang Dynasty (618–907) The Chinese dynasty founded by Li Yuan, with its capital at Chang'an (present-day Xi'an). In 690 Wu Zetian, a former concubine of the second Emperor and the Empress of the third, became herself Emperor of China — the only woman ever to do so. In 755 the Rebellion of **An Lu-shan**, though crushed, left the dynasty unable to control all its provinces as before, and there resulted a period of political disunity known as the Period of the **Five Dynasties and Ten Kingdoms**. The Tang Dynasty is generally regarded as the golden age of Chinese poetry.

T'ang Hsuan-tsung ▷ **Tang Xuanzong**

T'ang T'ai-tsung ▷ **Tang Taizong**

Tang Taizong (T'ang T'ai-tsung) (600–49) Chinese Emperor (626/49). The second emperor of the **Tang Dynasty**, this is the posthumous title of Li Shimin (Li Shih-min). Considered the real founder of the dynasty and one of the most heroic emperors in Chinese history, Li Shimin persuaded his father, Li Yuan, to rebel against the **Sui Dynasty** and then commanded the forces that defeated rival rebel armies and unified the country in 624. As Emperor (his father abdicated in his favour), Li Shimin expanded the frontiers of the Chinese empire to cover the northern steppes, Central Asia and Tibet. At home, he gained a reputation for benevolent rule, delegating authority and practising toleration of Daoism, Buddhism and Nestorian Christianity.

Tang Xuanzong (T'ang Hsuan-tsung) (685–762) Chinese Emperor (712/56). The sixth emperor of the **Tang Dynasty**, he presided over a golden age of cultural achievement in China. He continued with the enlightened domestic policies of **Tang Taizong** and established the **Hanlin Academy** to foster talented scholars and litterateurs. Towards the end of his reign, however, he became dependent on palace **eunuchs**, while on the frontiers non-Chinese mercenary generals asserted increasing independence. Corruption at court intensified once Tang Xuanzong became besotted with one of his son's concubines, Yang Guifei (Yang Kuei-fei), whose relatives monopolized all ministerial posts. The neglect of administration and the decline of the military establishment led to the gradual disintegration of the Tang Empire. The 755 Rebellion of **An Lu-shan**, a frontier general, forced Tang Xuanzong to flee his capital. En route, his palace guard, blaming the troubles on Yang Guifei, insisted on her death, an incident immortalized in Chinese poetry and painting. Tang Xuangzong abdicated shortly afterwards. Although the dynasty was restored in 763, its power and influence were much diminished.

Thanjavur (Tanjore) Capital of the **Chola Dynasty**, situated by the River Kaveri. The Cholas built a number of Shiva and Vishnu temples, the most famous of which is the Brihadiswara temple at Thanjavur which was completed in 1010. Probably the largest temple built in India up to that time, it contains elaborate pillared halls and beautiful decorations. This was possibly the richest temple during this period, had an income of 500 lb troy of gold, 250 lb troy of precious stones, and 600 lb troy of silver, which was acquired through donations and contributions in addition to the revenue from hundreds of villages. Thanjavur became an important centre of art and culture in south India during the Chola reign.

Tannenberg, Battle of (26–30 Aug 1914) A **World War I** battle between Russian and German forces. The Russian army under General Alexander **Samsonov** was completely routed; 100 000 prisoners of war were taken, and Samsonov himself committed suicide. German nationalists claimed the victory as revenge for the defeat of the **Teutonic Knights** by Russian, Polish and Lithuanian forces at the first Battle of Tannenberg (Grunwald) in 1410.

Tanner, Väinö (1881–1966) Finnish politician. A controversial figure in Finnish politics, Tanner emerged as leader of the **Social Democratic Party** after the end of the civil war in 1918. Tanner distanced the party from the radical Left in order to cooperate with the Centre, a policy which enabled the Social Democrats to participate in a majority government in 1937. He was identified by the USSR as one of those who had blocked a peaceful outcome to the negotiations which resulted in the **Russo-Finnish War** (1939–40). Tanner earned further Soviet hostility through his role in government, first as Foreign Minister and later, during the **Continuation War** of 1941–4, as Minister of Finance. In 1946 he was one of eight Finnish war leaders who were tried and convicted as war criminals. Following his release from prison in 1949 Tanner returned to parliament and in 1957 was re-elected Leader of the Social Democratic Party.

Tantamani (Tanuatamun) (Bakare) (664/ 656BC) King of Egypt. The last king of the 25th Dynasty (Nubian), for a brief time he reconquered Egypt, which had been occupied by the Assyrians under Assurbanipal, with delta princes appointed as vassals. On the return of the Assyrians (664–663BC), Tantamani lost Memphis and fled south to Thebes. This city also fell, a disaster which resulted in the looting of centuries of accumulated treasures. The king made his way to Napata in Nubia, where he continued to rule; the Nubian domination of Egypt had come to an end.

Tantia Topee (Ramchandra Pandurangez) (d.1859) Indian Brahman soldier and rebel. Hailing from Gwalior, he was **Nana Sahib**'s lieutenant in the **Indian Uprising** (1857–8). He took part in the massacre of the British at Cawnpore (July 1857). With the Rani of Jhansi he occupied Gwalior and then held the field after his chief had fled. After a skilful campaign and march through central India and Khandesh, in an attempt to raise up the Marathas in revolt, he was betrayed, captured and executed in Apr 1859.

Tanuatamun ▷ **Tantamani**

Tanucci, Bernardo (1698–1783) Neapolitan politician and administrator. From 1754, he was the principal minister of Charles VII (1716–88; King of Spain as Charles III, 1759/98), under whom he pursued a lively anticlerical policy. After Charles's departure for Spain, he remained the main adviser of **Ferdinand I** (IV of Naples), and continued to pursue anticlerical and enlightened policies, including the expulsion of the Jesuits and the introduction of civil marriage. In 1776 he fell from favour and was forced to resign; henceforth affairs were increasingly dominated by the Queen, **Maria Carolina**, and her lover, Acton.

Tanzimat The term (literally, 'reorganization') used to describe the reforms in the **Ottoman Empire** during the period 1839–78. Sultan **Abd ul-Majid I** (1839/61) showed that he was determined to carry on the reforms of his father, Mahmud II, when he issued the Noble Rescript (*Hatt-i Sherif*) in 1839. This marked a radical break with Islamic tradition, which had always regarded non-Muslims as separate and inferior. The Rescript recognized the equality of all religious groups before the law. Equal treatment for Muslims and non-Muslims was again promised in the Imperial Rescript (**Hatt-i**

Humayun) of 1856 and in 1867 Christians began to be appointed to state councils. The aim was to integrate them (40 per cent of the Sultan's subjects were Christians early in the century) in the Ottoman Empire and this meant replacing the traditional educational and legal systems, dominated by the *ulama* (religious leaders), by secular organizations. From 1840, Western-type courts and codes were introduced and administration was centralized on the French model, with prefects and departments. A new educational system, with elementary and secondary schools to prepare students for higher technical education, grew slowly and painfully to create a new elite committed to reform. The economy was also improved, as land was reclaimed, new factories set up, postal (1834) and telegraph (1855) systems established and railways begun (1866). All these reforms were revolutionary, as they seemed to secure the triumph of the Christian enemy over Islam by imposing, often with the help of European advisers, European practices and institutions. Most Turks were unaffected by the Tanzimat — their lives, beliefs and loyalties were still dominated by Islam — but power had nevertheless passed to secular bureaucrats.

Tardieu, André (1876–1945) French politician. A well-known journalist before 1914, he was a Deputy (1914–24 and 1926–36), High Commissioner in the USA (1917–18), and one of **Clemenceau**'s chief advisers during the negotiation of the peace treaties. His political position was right of centre; he was Minister of Public Works (1926–8), Prime Minister (1929–30), Minister of the Interior (1928–30), of Agriculture (1931–2), and of Foreign Affairs during his own second term as Prime Minister (1932), thus clearly being the dominant figure throughout the 1928–32 parliament. During that time, he practised what he called a 'prosperity policy', providing government assistance for the modernization of agriculture and industry, the electrification of rural areas, etc, and put through measures to abolish fees in state secondary schools and to improve social insurance. The victory of the left in the 1932 elections put him in opposition, but after the crisis of Feb 1934 he was brought back to office in the **Doumergue** cabinet with the task of producing proposals for constitutional reform. When it became evident that they were not going to be adopted, he left active politics to defend his plans for a stronger executive power in books and articles.

Tariff Policy (Canada) After 1846 Britain's policy of free trade allowed the colonial governments to cease imposing duties on foreign imports. Canada, however, needing revenue for development, decided to raise tariffs from a general level of 10 per cent in 1846 to 20 per cent or 25 per cent by 1859. British manufacturers protested through the Duke of Newcastle to the Finance Minister, A T **Galt**, but he asserted Canada's economic independence. In the early years of confederation tariffs produced three-quarters of all federal government revenue, and by 1879 they had been raised to an average of 25 per cent through the **Macdonald** government's National Policy, despite the complaints of fishermen and farmers. In 1897 **Fielding** sought to solve their problems by introducing a two-tier system, which he also tried to embody in an agreement with the USA in 1911. Later tariff agreements within the **Commonwealth of Nations** were negotiated through **Imperial Conferences**, and since **World War II** within the framework of the General Agreement on Tariffs and Trade (GATT). The Tokyo round, completed in 1979, envisaged an average of 9 per cent on dutiable goods (comprising 35 per cent of Canadian imports) by 1987. These tariff reductions, however, have been coupled with Canadian import restrictions on textiles, clothing and agricultural products.

tarimbeiro Brazilian army slang for an officer who had risen through active service, rather than through formal qualifications gained at the military schools in Rio de Janeiro, Fortaleza or Rio Grande do Sul. *Tarimbeiros*, men who had seen service in the War of the **Triple Alliance** (or Paraguayan War) (1864–70), became sceptical of the ability of the Spanish Empire to sustain a modern army and formed an alliance with the *doutores* (those who had studied under the guidance of well-known but bookish teachers) to overthrow the regime in 1889. Both groups became convinced that the army, rather than political elites, had become the defender of national interests. Their influence was broken in 1897–8, with the **Canudos Campaign** and the advent of **Campos Salles**.

Tarquinius Priscus Traditionally the fifth King of Rome, whose dates are conventionally given as 616–579BC. The first of two Etruscans with the name Tarquinius who ruled Rome, he was nicknamed Priscus ('the Elder') to distinguish him from the other monarch of that name, the tyrannical **Tarquinius Superbus** ('the Proud'). Among the many things accredited to him, the most important is probably the introduction of Etruscan cults to Rome, among them the worship of the Capitoline Triad of Jupiter, Juno and Minerva.

Tarquinius, Superbus (Lucius Tarquinius) Traditionally, the seventh and last King of Rome (534/510BC). According to Roman tradition, his cruelty and the rape of **Lucretia** by his son, Sextus, provoked an uprising of the Roman people under Lucius Junius Brutus, his expulsion from Rome, and the establishment of the republic. Tarquinius is then said to have tried to re-establish himself in Rome with the help of Lars Porsena of Clusium, but this attempt failed and he died in exile. ▷ **Roman Republic**

Tatar (Tartar) A Turkic-speaking people living in the USSR. Sunni Muslims since the 14c, they were a highly stratified medieval society. Traditionally farmers and pastoralists, in the 18–19c, they became important as political agents, traders, teachers, and administrators in the Russian Empire.

Taylor, Zachary (1784–1850) US general, politician and 12th President. He joined the army in 1808 and fought in several campaigns against the Native Americans. In the **Mexican War** (1846–8) he captured Matamoros, and won a major victory at Buena Vista, though heavily outnumbered. He emerged from the war as a hero, and was given the Whig presidential nomination. The main issues of his presidency (1849–50) were the status of the new territories and the extension of slavery there, but he died only 16 months after taking office. He was succeeded by Millard **Fillmore**. ▷ **Whig Party**

Teamsters' Union (International Brotherhood of Teamsters, Chauffeurs, Warehousemen and Helpers of America) The largest US labour union, with over 1.5 million members. Founded in 1903, it was expelled from the **AFL–CIO** in 1957 for corruption, but was reaffiliated in 1987.

Teapot Dome Scandal (1923) US political scandal. One of several in the administration of President Warren G **Harding**, it involved the lease of naval oil reserves at Teapot Dome (Wyoming) and Elk Hills (California) by the Secretary of the Interior, Albert B Fall. He allowed no competition to the bids of Harry F Sinclair (Mammoth Oil) and Edward Doheny (Pan-American Petroleum), who had both lent him considerable sums of money. A Senate investigation uncovered the scandal and Fall was eventually sentenced to prison for one year and fined US$100 000. Sinclair and Doheny were cleared of bribery charges, although Sinclair did serve nine months in jail for contempt of the Senate. In 1927 the Supreme Court found that neither of the leases was valid and the oilfields were returned to the government.

Tecumseh (1768–1813) Native American chief of the Shawnee and a gifted orator. He joined his brother, 'The Prophet', in a rising against the whites, which was suppressed at the Battle of Tippecanoe in 1811. He then passed into British service, commanding the Native American allies in the **War of 1812** and fell fighting at the Thames in Canada. ▷ **Indian Wars; Native Americans**

Tefnakhte (Shepsesre) (c.727/720BC) King of Egypt. He was a prince of Sais in the Delta and a great chief of the Ma, who made himself master of the Princedom of the West towards the end of the 23rd Dynasty. He formed a confederacy of minor rulers and was the main opponent of the Nubian king, Piankhy. The latter advanced (c.728BC) into Egypt, paving the way for the establishment of the 25th Nubian Dynasty. Tefnakhte moved southward and laid siege to Heracleopolis, but the Nubians steadily overcame the opposition from the north. One by one, Tefnakhte's allies were defeated. Finally he retreated to Memphis, which he garrisoned with 8 000 troops and tried to rally the Delta princes to his side. Memphis was, however, captured and Tefnakhte submitted. Shortly afterwards, Piankhy retired to Napata, while Tefnakhte presented himself as king in the shortlived 24th Dynasty, when he assumed royal titles.

Tehran Conference (28 Nov–1 Dec 1943) The first inter-allied conference of **World War II**, attended by **Stalin**, **Roosevelt** and Winston **Churchill**. The subjects discussed were the coordination of Allied landings in France with the Soviet offensive against Germany, Russian entry in the war against Japan, and the establishment of a post-war international organization. Failure to agree on the future government of Poland foreshadowed the start of the **Cold War**.

Teleki, Count Paul (1879–1941) Hungarian politician. He became Professor of Geography at Budapest University in 1919 and, combining politics with an academic career, was in the same year appointed Foreign

Minister and, from 1920 to 1921, Premier. The founder of the Christian National League and chief of Hungary's boy scouts, he was Minister of Education in 1938 and again Premier in 1939. He was fully aware of the German threat to his country, but all measures to avert it, including a pact with Yugoslavia, were unavailing through lack of support. When Germany marched against Yugoslavia through Hungary, he took his own life.

Tel el-Kebir, Battle of (1882) An engagement between British and Egyptian forces which resulted in the British becoming the effective rulers of Egypt. It followed a period of increasing Egyptian ambition to extend her power, which had led to a financial crisis. In 1875 the Egyptian Khedive Ismail sold his Suez Canal shares to the British government, and in 1880 an international debt commission was established. These inroads on Egyptian independence stirred the nationalism of young army officers. In 1881 an army faction under Colonel 'Urabi Pasha forced the Khedive to appoint a new ministry with 'Urabi as Minister for War. The British regarded this as a dangerous destabilization of the country; the Royal Navy bombarded Alexandria and landed a British army under Sir Garnet **Wolseley**, who defeated 'Urabi at Tel el-Kebir. ▷ 'Urabi Revolt

Telengana Disturbances Telengana, in northern Hyderabad, India, was the scene of the most widespread, violent and long-lived peasant insurrection in South Asia in the 20c. (It was also possibly one of the largest communist-led insurrections seen in all Asia (outside China and Vietnam) in modern times.) Beginning in 1946, at its height, the movement against the Nizam, the pro-British ruler of the independent princely state of Hyderabad, covered 3000 villages spread over 16000 square miles. A peasant army was established, and communes set up in the villages under communist control which, among other things, raised agricultural wages and redistributed waste lands to the poor. Unwilling to come to terms even after the granting of independence from Britain and the formal incorporation of Hyderabad into the Union of India, central government troops were sent to the area in Sep 1948, although the movement was not finally suppressed until 1951. Nonetheless, a guerrilla movement is still active in the hills and communist MPs are regularly elected to the Lok Sabha (or Parliament) in Delhi. Since

the **States Reorganization Act** of 1956, Hyderabad has been part of the modern Telugu-speaking state of Andhra Pradesh, and Telengana has seen continuing protest movements against immigration to the region and the alleged control of the Andhra state by what are said to be politicians and business interests originating in the north.

Temesvár (Timişoara), Banat of Within the Habsburg Empire, this was the province between Transylvania, Wallachia and the Danube, Tisza and Mures Rivers. Settled by the **Goths**, Slavs and **Huns**, from the 9c it was tied to Hungary, becoming in 1233 the Banat of Severin. From the mid-16c it was subject to the Ottomans, but by the Treaty of **Passarowitz** (1718) it passed to Austria and was administered as the Banat of Temesvár. After 1779, it was attached to Hungary. By the Treaty of **Trianon** (1920), Hungary retained the region around Szeged while Romania acquired the eastern portion, with the remainder going to Yugoslavia. The population is a mixture of nationalities: as well as Hungarians, Romanians, Vlachs, Tsintsars and Serbs, there remain the descendants of those Germans sent by the Habsburg emperors to repopulate the devastated Banat during the 18c.

temperance movement An organized response to the social disruption caused by the alcoholism so widespread in the 18c and 19c. Temperance societies were started first in the USA, then in Britain and Scandinavia. The original aim was to moderate drinking, but prohibition became the goal. Federal prohibition became a reality in the USA in 1919, but was impossible to enforce and was repealed in 1933.

Templars The Poor Knights of Christ and of the Temple of Solomon; an international religious-military order, whose members were subject to monastic vows. The order was founded c.1120 chiefly to protect pilgrims to the Holy Land; its name derives from the location of its headquarters near the site of the Jewish Temple in Jerusalem. It developed into a widespread institution, acquiring wealth and property all over Europe, and was suppressed by Pope **Clement V** in 1312.

Ten Days Campaign (2–12 Aug 1831) The militarily successful Dutch expedition against the Belgians during the **Belgian Revolution**, but one which failed to suppress the revolt. The Great Powers had recognized Belgium, but King **William I** of the Netherlands refused to accept their terms and ordered the campaign, led by his son, the future King **William II**. Two Belgian armies were defeated at Hasselt and Leuven (Louvain); a French army arrived to help the Belgians, but the Dutch pressed their attack anyway. After 13 Aug the Dutch largely withdrew; the campaign gained them some concessions in the eventual settlement.

tenentismo Deriving from the Portuguese *tenente* ('lieutenant'), this term originally referred to the generation of young Brazilian army officers who graduated from the military school in Realengo after 1919. Trained by the 'indigenous mission' of officers who had been seconded to the Imperial German Army before **World War I**, they emerged to general service highly critical of both superior officers and the regime they served. As a result, they took leading roles in the 1922 Copacabana Revolt, the Revolt of São Paulo, the Prestes Column and Revolution of 1930. Many continued in politics until the 1960s. Such men included Luís Carlos Prestes (leader of the Communists), Eduardo Gomes (éminence grise of the UDN), Cordeiro de Farias (the major support for **Castelo Branco**), Jauréz Távora and Jurac de Maghalâes, and were the progenitors of the military regime of 1964–85.

Teng Hsiao-p'ing ▷ **Deng Xiaoping**

Tennis Court Oath (1789) An oath taken in a tennis court at the Palace of Versailles by representatives of the Third Estate locked out of their assembly place. Declaring themselves to be the National Assembly, the Deputies swore never to separate until a constitution was established for France. ▷ **Estates General; French Revolution**

Tenth Penny The most famous of a series of taxes which were an important cause of the **Eighty Years War**. In 1559 the Duke of **Alba** introduced a new tax system in the Netherlands designed to centralize and standardize all the anomalous local ones which existed in the various provinces. The largest was the Tenth Penny, a 10 per cent tax put on all commercial transactions except in real estate. In the first two years it brought in 2 million gilders; in 1571 there were widespread revolts against it. The Spanish gave up trying to collect it in 1574.

Ten Years War (1868–78) Nationalist Cuban uprising against Spanish illiberal rule provoked by the Special Laws of 1867. Led by

Carlos Manuel de **Céspedes**, 'The Father of the Country', Maximo Gomes, Antonio Maceo and Tomás **Estrada Palma**, the 10 000-strong rebel force conducted an intermittent, desultory campaign against the Spanish Army for 10 years but, holding no port, having no seat of government and unable to enlist international support, it could not prevail. Hostilities were brought to an end when a new Spanish commander, Martinez Campos, promised reform and representation. The Peace of Zanjón (Feb 1878) reiterated these promises but they proved a dead letter and the only positive outcome of the conflict was the abolition of **slavery**.

tercios The name given to the elite regiments formed in the Spanish army in the 1560s, consisting of 12–15 companies, each of 250–300 men. Recruited exclusively from Castilians, they were used mainly in the battlefields of northern Europe, where they were feared and respected. In the early 18c they were superseded by regiments based on the French model.

Territorial Princes Rulers of various secular principalities in the **Holy Roman Empire**. These princes had strong dynastic lines and answered directly to the Emperor, such as those of Saxony, were Electors. With the Ecclesiastical Princes, the Imperial Knights, the free cities and the Imperial towns, they constituted the level of overlordship beneath the Emperor.

territory In US history, the political status of an area prior to the attainment of statehood. It was held in two stages: in the first, an 'unorganized territory' was ruled by a judge; in the second, an 'organized' territory could elect its own legislature and non-voting delegate to Congress. ▷ **Ordinance of 1787**

Terror, Reign of (1793–4) The extreme phase of the **French Revolution**, characterized by the systematic execution of political opponents of the **Jacobins** and supposed sympathizers of the Counter-Revolution, who were brought before the Revolutionary Tribunal and guillotined. Around 40 000 people are thought to have been killed in Paris and the provinces.

Terror, White In French history, a term first used in 1795, when the **Jacobins** were pursued by those they had persecuted in the revolutionary Reign of **Terror** of 1793–4. It revived on a larger scale (1815–16), against those who had supported **Napoleon I** during the **Hundred Days**, especially in the south of France.

Tessin, Carl-Gustaf (1695–1770) Swedish politician. He was the son of the architect, Nicodemus Tessin, 'the Younger'. As a young man he travelled extensively in France, Germany and Italy, and on his return to Sweden assumed a leading position in the pro-French and anti-Russian Hat Party, which hoped to regain territory lost to Russia at the end of the **Great Northern War**. He was elected chairman of the Estate of Nobles when the Hats gained a majority in 1738. As envoy in Paris, he secured French support for the war launched against Russia in 1741. He gained the favour of King **Adolf Frederick** and Queen **Lovisa Ulrika** and in 1746 was appointed governor to the future King **Gustav III**, a post he held until 1755. By then, his relations with the court had cooled, and he spent much of the rest of his life on his estate at Åkerö. He had immense influence on the Swedish culture of the period: his interior decoration of the Royal Palace in Stockholm introduced the rococo style into the country and the collections he sold to the royal family formed the basis of the National Museum and Royal Library in Stockholm.

Test Act (1673) A British Act passed by a parliament anxious to curb Catholic influence at **Charles II**'s court. Every office holder had to take Oaths of Supremacy and Allegiance, and to take communion according to the rites of the Church of England. A declaration against transubstantiation also had to be made. The passage of the Act necessitated the resignation of the King's brother, James, Duke of York, as Lord High Admiral. The Act remained in force until 1828. ▷ **Catholic Emancipation**

Tet Offensive (Jan–Feb 1968) A campaign in the **Vietnam War**. On 30 Jan 1968, the Buddhist 'Tet' holiday, the Viet Cong launched an attack against US bases and more than 100 South Vietnamese towns (which had been considered safe from guerrilla attack), the targets including the US Embassy in Saigon and the city of Hue. There were heavy casualties, including large numbers of civilians. US public opinion was shocked by the scale of death and destruction, and support for the war declined rapidly. The offensive proved to be a turning-point in the war: on 31 Mar 1968, President Lyndon B **Johnson** announced an end to escalation and a new readiness to negotiate.

Teutoburg Forest, Battle of (AD9) A defeat inflicted on the Romans by Germanic tribes. After repeated Roman campaigns east of the Rhine, the Cherusci became Roman clients in AD4. Five years later, the troops of the Roman Governor, P Quinctilius Varus, marching from their summer quarters in the lands of the Cherusci on the rivers Weser and Elbe to their winter quarters on the Rhine, were attacked by the Cherusci and other tribes under the leadership of Arminius and almost completely annihilated. As a result, the Romans lost their forts between the Weser and the Rhine but were able to hold the Rhine. The defeat caused great concern in Rome and influenced the decision not to undertake the conquest of the Germanic tribes. ▷ **Germanic Invasions**

Teutonic Knights The Order of St Mary of the Germans, a religious-military order founded in Acre in 1190. The Order grew quickly in Germany and the Mediterranean and, as a result of Conrad of Mazovia's appeal for help in 1226, also gained a foothold in northern Europe. The Golden Bull of Rimini (1226) confirmed its position there and granted the Order all lands conquered from the heathen Prussians outside the borders of the Empire. With the loss of the Holy Land in 1291 all the Order's efforts were concentrated there and by the end of the 14c they controlled the Baltic lands of the **Livonian Knights**, Prussia and East Pomerania. The Order's power declined after the battle of Grunwald (1410) and the secularization of the Order in Prussia in 1525 led to Prussia becoming part of the **Holy Roman Empire**. The Order was dissolved in Germany in 1809 but re-established in Austria in 1834. ▷ **Grunwald, Battle of; Winrich of Kniprode**

Teutons A Germanic tribe whose homeland was in modern Schleswig-Holstein. In about 200BC they left their homeland with the neighbouring **Cimbri** tribe and migrated south and west, finally entering **Gaul** and defeating several Roman armies. They failed to take advantage of their victories, however, and were annihilated by the Roman general Marius (156–86BC) at Aquae Sextiae (102BC). Their invasions were the prelude to the more important Germanic invasions which were to follow.

Tewfik Pasha, Mohammed (1852–92) Khedive of Egypt (1879/92). The eldest son of **Ismail Pasha**, he succeeded his father on the latter's abdication in 1879. The chief events of his reign were 'Urabi's insurrection (1882), the British intervention, the war with the Mahdi **Mohammed Ahmed** (1884–5), the pacification of the Sudan frontiers, and the improvement of Egypt under British administration. He was succeeded by his son, Abbas Hilmi. ▷ 'Urabi Revolt

Tewkesbury, Battle of (4 May 1471) A decisive battle in the Wars of the **Roses** at which **Edward IV** defeated Lancastrian forces hastily assembled by Queen Margaret, wife of **Henry VI**. Their son, Prince Edward, was killed as were many other leading Lancastrian supporters. Soon afterwards, Edward IV was able to re-enter London, order the death of Henry VI in the Tower of London and resume his reign, which was not thereafter seriously challenged.

Thakurdas, Purshottamdas (1879–1961) Indian industrialist and social reformer. He joined the family cotton business and started rooting out evil practices in the cotton industry. At the age of 28, the 'Cotton King of Bombay' was elected Vice-President of the Indian Merchants Chamber, Bombay. A founding member of the Federation of Indian Chambers of Commerce and Industry (FICCI), he went on to become its President. He was a member of the Retrenchment Committee (1922) and served on the Royal Commission on Indian Finance, Currency and Practice (1925), where he fought for a better exchange-rate for the Indian rupee. He was appointed Sheriff of Bombay in 1920. Secretary of the Gujarat Famine Relief Fund in 1911, he also made generous contributions to schemes involving education and self-help. It was thanks to his initiative that the Indenture Act was abolished.

Thalmann, Ernst (1886–1944) German politician. After joining the **SPD** in 1903, Thalmann switched to the **KPD** in 1920, joining its Central Committee in 1921. Convener of the KPD from 1925, he was heavily reliant on the **Comintern** in Moscow for his authority and steered the party increasingly along lines acceptable to the USSR. Arrested by the National Socialists in 1933, he was shot in **Buchenwald** concentration camp in 1944. ▷ **Nazi Party**

Thani, Khalifa ibn Hamad al- (1932–) Shaykh and Prime Minister of Qatar. The oil-rich Persian Gulf state of Qatar entered into treaty relations with Britain in 1916, having earlier been under Ottoman control. As with the Trucial States (now the United

Arab Emirates), it was arranged that the foreign affairs of Qatar would be conducted by the British in return for naval protection, while internal affairs should be regulated by the state itself (and thus by extension the Al-Thani family). The discovery of oil made Qatar extremely wealthy and the state became fully independent in 1971.

Thant, U (1909–74) Burmese diplomat. He was a teacher who became a civil servant when Burma became independent in 1948; he became Burma's **UN** representative in 1957. As Secretary-General of the UN (1962–71), he played a major diplomatic role during the **Cuban Missile Crisis**. He also formulated a plan to end the Congolese Civil War (1962) and mobilized a UN peace-keeping force in Cyprus (1964). He died in New York City. The return of his body to Burma provoked major anti-government demonstrations.

Thapsus, Battle of (46BC) A decisive victory in North Africa for the forces of Julius **Caesar** over those of **Pompey the Great**. It paved the way for the Caesar's dictatorship. ▷ **Pharsalus, Battle of**

Thatcher, Margaret (Hilda) (1925–) British politician. Elected to parliament in 1959, and after holding junior office, she became Minister of Education (1970–4). In 1975 she replaced Edward **Heath** as Leader of the **Conservative Party** to become the first woman party leader in British politics. Under her leadership, the Conservative Party moved towards a more 'right-wing' position, and British politics and society became more polarized than at any other time since **World War II**. Her government (1979–90) privatized several nationalized industries and utilities, made professional services, such as healthcare and education, more responsive to market forces, and reduced the role of local government as a provider of services. Her election for a third term of office in 1987 was aided, as in 1983, by divisions in the **Labour Party** and a more equal division of votes between the opposition parties than had hitherto been usual. She became the longest serving 20c Prime Minister in 1988 but her popularity waned and her anti-European statements caused damaging division within the Conservative Party. She resigned soon after failing to win a sufficiently large majority in the Conservative leadership contest of Nov 1990, and retired from her parliamentary seat of Finchley in 1992.

Thebaw (1858–1916) Last King of Burma. He reigned from 1878 to 1885, when he was deposed by the British, and sent into exile.

Thebes In ancient Greece, the most powerful city-state in **Boeotia**. Although prominent in Greek legend (the Oedipus cycle is based there), in historical times it was rarely able to rival Athens and **Sparta**. Only under the brilliant **Epaminondas** in the decade 380–370BC did it succeed briefly in being the leading power in Greece. ▷ **Leuctra, Battle of; Pelopidas**

Themistocles (c.525–c.462BC) Athenian general and politician. By persuading the Athenians to develop Piraeus as a port (493BC), and to use their rich silver deposits to build a fleet (483BC), he not only made possible their great naval victory at the Battle of **Salamis** (480BC), but also laid the foundations of their maritime empire. He fell from favour c.470BC, and was ostracized. After many adventures, he served the Persian King in Asia Minor as the Governor of Magnesia and two other cities. ▷ **Delian League; ostracism; Persian Wars**

Theodora (c.500–47) Byzantine Empress (527/47). An actress, dancer, and prostitute, she became mistress, then wife, of Emperor **Justinian I, 'the Great'** (522). A woman of great intelligence and courage, she played a major backstage role throughout his long and distinguished reign, and probably saved his throne during the Nika riots by her intervention (532).

Theodore, Kassai (1816–68) King of Abyssinia, as Theodore II (1855/68). In 1853 he crushed the vice-regent, Ras Ali, and, overthrowing the Prince of Tigré in 1855, had himself crowned Negus of Abyssinia as Theodore II. At first he was guided by two Englishmen, Plowden and Bell; but after they were killed in a rebellion (1860) he became more hostile to Europeans. He had made several vain attempts to procure the alliance of England and France against his Muslim neighbours, but without success. A letter sent to Queeen **Victoria** in 1862 went somehow unnoticed, and a fancied slight was also received from **Napoleon III**. Theodore imprisoned the consuls along with other Europeans. Negotiations failed, and a British military expedition under General **Napier** landed in Abyssinia in the spring of 1867, and reached Magdala in Apr. An Abyssinian attack was repulsed. Theodore sued for peace and released the prisoners, but, as he declined to surrender, the fort was stormed and Theodore shot himself.

Theodoric I (d.451) King of the Visigoths (418/51). The son of Alaric I, he was elected King in 418. Alternately an ally and an enemy of Rome, in 421 (or 422) he treacherously joined the Vandals and attacked the Roman troops from behind. In 435 he attacked the Romans in Gaul and besieged Narbonne. Forced to retreat to Toulouse, he there defeated a Roman army (439). On the invasion of **Attila** in 451, he joined the Romans, under **Aëtius**, and at Troyes commanded the right wing. He drove back the **Huns** under Attila but was killed. ▷ **Visigoths**

Theodoric (Thierry) III (673/91) Puppet King of **Neustria** and Burgundy. He became King in 673 at the instigation of **Ebroin**, the Mayor of the Palace, as successor to his brother, Chlotar III. Deposed by another brother, Childeric II, he was restored to the throne in 676. He was King of **Austrasia** from 679 until **Pepin II,' of Heristal'** and the Austrasians defeated the Neustrians at the Battle of Tertry (687).

Theodoric the Great (d.526) King of the **Ostrogoths** (471/526). He invaded Italy in 489, defeating the barbarian ruler, Odoacer. His long reign secured for Italy tranquillity and prosperity, the Goths and the Romans continuing as distinct nations, each with its own tribunals and laws. He established his capital at Ravenna, where he died.

Theodosius I, 'the Great' (c.346–95) Roman Emperor of the East (379/95). Made Emperor because of his military abilities, he solved the long-standing problem of the **Goths** by allowing them to settle south of the River Danube as allies of Rome. His title comes from his vigorous championship of orthodox Christianity. ▷ **Theodosius II**

Theodosius II (401–50) Roman Emperor (408/50). The grandson of **Theodosius I, 'the Great'** and, like him, a staunch champion of orthodox Christianity, he is chiefly remembered for his codification of the Roman law.

Theophano (c.955–91) German Empress. Niece of the Byzantine Emperor, she married King **Otto II** in Rome as a symbol of the union of the Eastern and Western Empires. She had six children, including Emperor **Otto III**. Theophano took an active role in politics and with her mother-in-law, Adelaide, secured the throne for Otto III on his father's death.

She dealt successfully with enemies at home and abroad during the king's minority, including **Henry the Wrangler** and Boleslav II of Bohemia. She secured Lotharingia for the empire and ruled Italy as her son's regent. Her influence is visible in many of Otto III's policies, especially his ambitions for the Empire.

Thermidor (16–17 July 1794/8–9 Thermidor Year II) The coup d'état when **Robespierre** and his Jacobin supporters were overthrown, ending the most radical phase of the **French Revolution**. Among the instigators of Thermidor were such former **Jacobins** as Joseph **Fouché** and Paul **Barras** who, with members of the National Convention, set about dismantling the machinery of the Reign of **Terror**. ▷ **French Republican Calendar; Convention, National**

Thermopylae, Battle of (480BC) A pass between mountains and sea in central Greece. The failure of the Greeks to hold the pass enabled the Persians to invade Attica, capture Athens, and sack the Acropolis. ▷ **Leonidas; Persian Wars**

Thessaly In antiquity, an area of northern Greece noted for its cavalry, its chief cities being Larissa and Pherae. The aristocratic Aleuadae family actively supported the Persian invasion of Greece in 480BC. A tyranny established at Pherae in the late 5c challenged the power of the Aleuadae: Jason of Pherae (**tyrant** c.380/370BC) briefly united Thessaly into a powerful state, but was assassinated before this power could be consolidated. From c.353BC, Thessaly came under the influence of neighbouring **Macedonia**; the Thessalian cavalry accompanied **Alexander II, 'the Great'** on his conquest of Persia. In 196BC the Romans liberated Thessaly from Macedonian control; in 146BC it became part of the Roman province of Macedonia. In the 7–13c it was invaded by the Slavs, Saracens and Bulgars, and then the **Vlachs** who took control of the region and made it part of Great Wallachia. In the 14c it was invaded by the Catalans and Serbs and fell to the Ottoman Turks after the collapse of the Kingdom of **Serbia** (1389). After the Congress of **Berlin** (1878), the Ottoman Porte ceded Thessaly to Greece in stages: the greater part in 1881 and the remainder north of the Vale of Tempe in accordance with the Treaty of **London** (1913). ▷ **Sacred Wars**

Theux de Meylandt, Barthélemy Théodore, Count (1798–1874) Belgian politician.

In 1828 he and other liberal Catholics in the southern Netherlands formed a union with the liberals and so assisted the **Belgian Revolution**. From 1830 to 1850 he led the Belgian right in politics, and was a cabinet minister (usually of Internal Affairs) in 1831–2, 1834–40 and 1846–7. He formed his final government in 1871.

Thiers, (Louis) Adolphe (1797–1877) French politician and historian. He held several posts in the government of **Louis-Philippe**, and was twice Prime Minister (1836 and 1839). He supported **Napoleon III**'s candidacy as President of the republic in 1848, but was arrested and banished at the coup d'état of 1851, only to re-enter the Chamber in 1863 as a critic of Napoleon's policies. After the collapse of the Second Empire and the demise of the Government of **National Defence**, he was elected Chief of the Executive Power by the National Assembly, suppressed the **Paris Commune**, and was elected first President of the Third Republic (1871–3). ▷ **Charles X** (of France); **Empire, Second** (France); **Republic, Second** (France); **Republic, Third** (France)

Third Department (1826–81) The department of Russian government, established by **Nicholas I**, with responsibility for state security. It was part of his reaction against **Alexander I**'s attempts at reform and, although it professed to be concerned with welfare and collected information for this purpose, it became in effect the secret police. Even under **Alexander II** it had a very nasty reputation. He abolished it before his own assassination in 1881, but it was quickly replaced by the **Okhranka**.

Third Rome (1510) The concept of Moscow as the successor to Rome and Constantinople. In 1510 Philotheus, an abbot from Pskov, wrote passionately to Basil III, Grand Prince of Moscow, about Rome falling to heresy and Constantinople to Islam, which left his dominion as the sole survivor and the heart of Christendom. Basil's father, Ivan III, had married a Byzantine princess and adopted the title Tsar from Caesar. So Basil was prepared to harness the Third Rome myth and give it political significance. It was a view of Russia's role in the world that survived down to the 20c.

thirty-eighth parallel The boundary line proposed for the partition of Korea at the Potsdam Conference in 1945, after the defeat of Japan (who had annexed Korea in 1910).

In 1948 the Democratic People's Republic of North Korea was proclaimed (but not recognized by the Western powers). Since the **Korean War**, the 38th parallel again forms the line of division between North and South Korea.

Thirty Tyrants The Spartan-backed clique which seized power in Athens at the end of the **Peloponnesian War** (404BC), overthrew the democracy, and instituted a reign of terror. They were overthrown in 403BC and the democracy restored. ▷ **Critias; Lysander; Sparta; tyrant**

Thirty Years War (1618–48) A complex phase, specifically German in origin, of a long and intermittent power struggle between the kings of France and the Habsburg rulers of the **Holy Roman Empire** and Spain (1491–1715). The background was complicated by the developing confrontation between militant Calvinism and reinvigorated, post-Tridentine Catholicism; also by the underlying constitutional conflict between the Holy Roman Emperor and the German princes, illustrated in the Bohemian Revolt (1618). With the Elector Frederick V's defeat (1620) and intervention by other powers (eg Sweden, Transylvania, Denmark and France), the conflict intensified, spreading to other theatres. Isolated as Spain collapsed, the Emperor opened negotiations (1643–8) which ended the German war, at the Peace of **Westphalia**. ▷ **Habsburg Dynasty; Trent, Council of**

Thokoly, Imre, Count (1657–1705) Hungarian landowner. He was typical of those who used Turkish support to try to diminish Habsburg dominance. Basing himself in Transylvania, he managed to establish control over northern Hungary for much of the period 1677–83. Although he even became Prince of Transylvania for a short time in 1690, he was soon forced into powerless exile in Turkey. ▷ **Habsburg Dynasty**

Thorbecke, Johan Rudolf (1798–1872) Dutch politician. He studied at Amsterdam, Leiden and several German universities, and in 1825 was appointed Professor of History at Ghent University (then part of the United Kingdom of the Netherlands). In 1831 he moved to Leiden University. In the 1830s he became a liberal, and from 1840 sat in parliament. In 1844 he (with eight others) produced a proposal for a new constitution; in 1848 King **William II** panicked at riots in other European capitals and made Thor-

becke chairman of a constitutional committee; the resulting constitution was a classic liberal document and the foundation of modern democratic politics in the Netherlands. Thorbecke, who is often referred to as the founder of the modern Dutch state, led three governments (1849–53, 1862–6 and 1871–2). During his periods of office most of the crucial bills were passed concerning free trade, the abolition of **slavery**, centralized government, the separation of church and state, and the construction of the transport infrastructure. Towards the end of his career, despite great respect from all parts of the House, he came into conflict with the more radical wing of the liberals.

Thorez, Maurice (1900–64) French politician. Having worked briefly as a coalminer, he joined the **Communist Party** in 1920; he was made General-Secretary in 1930, when the earlier generation of leaders fell foul of **Stalin**, and remained in undisputed command of a highly disciplined party until his death. He was one of the creators of the **Popular Front**, thus bringing the party out of the political wilderness, although communists tended not to join in the Popular Front governments. He survived the difficult period of the **German–Soviet Pact** (1939–41) by deserting from the French Army into which he had been conscripted and fleeing to the USSR. He was amnestied, and returned to France in 1944, becoming Deputy Prime Minister in the cabinet of the socialist Ramadier (Nov 1946–May 1947). After the exclusion of the party from office he led it through its most Stalinist period, adopting a position of unwavering support for the USSR on all questions until 1956, when he refused to accept Nikita **Khrushchev**'s denunciation of Stalin.

Thousand, Expedition of the (1860) In Italian history, the expedition of volunteer **Red Shirts** led by **Garibaldi** to assist Sicilian rebels against Bourbon rule.

Thrace The region which lies between the Maritsa and Nestos Rivers, the Aegean and the Stara Planina range, now divided between Greece, Bulgaria and Turkey. Annexed by the Roman Emperor **Claudius** (AD46), Thrace was settled by the **Visigoths** and Slavs and in the 7c became part of Bulgaria. It fell to the Turks (1453) and parts of it remained under Ottoman rule until the 20c. An integral part of Greece according to the **Megale Idea**, it was also the object of Russian and Bulgarian territorial ambitions throughout the 19c. By the Treaty of **Bucharest** (1913), Thrace was awarded to Bulgaria but was then ceded to Greece at the end of **World War I** by the Treaty of **Neuilly** (1919); at the end of the **Graeco-Turkish War**, however, the eastern part went to Turkey (1922).

Thrane, Marcus (1817–90) Norwegian labour reformer. An outstanding figure in the history of pre-Marxist socialism, he was a pioneer of the labour movement in Norway. Between 1848 and 1850 he organized 'workers' unions' to campaign for manhood suffrage and improved working and living conditions for labourers and poor farmers. Despite Thrane's advocacy of non-violent methods, he alarmed the authorities and was imprisoned without trial (1850–4). He was then sentenced to a further four years in prison. Thrane emigrated to the USA in 1862 and became politically active in the Norwegian-American community. He returned only once to Norway (1882–3), to find himself a largely forgotten figure.

Three Emperors' League (*Dreikaiserbund*) An entente (1873, renewed 1881 and 1884) between Emperors **William I** of Germany, Francis Joseph of Austria-Hungary, and **Alexander II** of Russia. It was designed by **Bismarck** to protect Germany by isolating France and stabilizing South-East Europe. Largely superseded by the **Dual Alliance** (1879) of Germany and Austria-Hungary, it lapsed in 1887.

Three Feudatories, Rebellion of the (1673–81) A rebellion in China that threatened the newly-established Manchu **Qing Dynasty**. As a reward for helping them to consolidate their rule in south China, the Manchus awarded three Chinese generals (Wu Sangui, Shang Zhixin and Geng Jingzhong) control of the entire region. Known as 'the Three Feudatories', these generals resorted to open rebellion in 1673 when Emperor **Kangxi** made it known that their bailiwicks were to be brought under central control. Wu Sangui (Wu San-Kuei), the northern frontier general who had originally allowed the Manchus to pass through the Great Wall in 1644 on their way to capture Beijing, declared himself emperor of a new dynasty in 1678. For a while it seemed the Manchus might be driven from China but poor coordination amongst the rebel armies and Kangxi's vigorous counter-attack led to the rebellion's collapse in 1683. The Qing Dynasty was henceforth firmly entrenched in

China and was not to be seriously threatened again until the mid-19c with the outbreak of the **Taiping Rebellion**.

Throckmorton, Sir Nicholas (1515–71) English diplomat. He fought at the Battle of **Pinkie** (1547), was knighted in 1547, and became Ambassador to France and Scotland. In 1569 he was imprisoned for promoting the scheme to marry **Mary, Queen of Scots**, to the Duke of Norfolk, but soon released. His daughter, Elizabeth, married Sir Walter **Raleigh**; his nephew, Francis (1554–84) was executed for planning a conspiracy to overthrow **Elizabeth I**.

Thucydides (c.460–c.400BC) Athenian general and historian of the **Peloponnesian War**. Though scrupulously accurate in his narrative of events, he is not altogether unprejudiced. Exiled for 20 years by the democracy for military incompetence in the northern Aegean (424BC), he is consistently critical of the Athens' imperialism, her democratic system and most political leaders in the war years.

Thuggee A form of banditry in rural central India, said to be a cult which combined robbery and ritual murder (usually by strangling) in the name of Kali (the Hindu goddess of destruction). Under British Governor-General Lord Bentinck (1833–5), and his agent Captain William Sleeman, vigorous steps were taken to eradicate the problem.

Thuringia A historic area of Germany, including the Harz Mountains and Thuringian Forest, a march or frontier region against the Slavs. Controlled by various dynasties, from the 10c Dukes of Saxony to the House of Wettin (1265), it was divided between Saxony, Hesse-Kassel, and others from 1485–1920, and was subsequently a part of East Germany. ▷ **Germany, East**

Thutmose I (Akheperkare) (c.1526/1508BC) King of Egypt. It appears that he came to the throne through marriage to Ahmose, the sister of King Amenhotpe I. Thutmose may have belonged to a collateral branch of the royal family, but his mother, Seniseneb, was neither a king's wife nor daughter. Thutmose waged war in Nubia, where he extended Egyptian control into **Kush** beyond the Third Cataract and in Syria, where he campaigned as far as the Euphrates against Naharin (Mitanni). At Karnak the king enlarged the temple of Amun, where he constructed the present 4th and 5th pylons (monumental gateways) and erected a pair of granite obelisks, one of which still stands. For his burial, the king selected the site of the Valley of the Kings and established a pattern for royal internments which was followed for the next 400 years.

Thutmose III (Menkheperre) (c.1490/1436BC) King of Egypt. One of the greatest of Egypt's rulers, he was the son of Thutmose II, born to a minor wife, Isis. Following the joint rule with his stepmother, Hatshepsut, in which she took the dominant part, Thutmose restored Egyptian influence in Palestine and Syria, leading 17 campaigns in the course of his reign. Under this soldier, statesman and administrator, Egypt was established as a leading power, with her empire extending from the Euphrates to the 4th Cataract on the Nile in the Sudan. Thutmose built a festival hall and the 7th pylon at Karnak. He put up obelisks both there (one now in Istanbul) and at Heliopolis (now in London, 'Cleopatra's Needle') and rebuilt temples elsewhere in Egypt.

Tiananmen Square The largest public square in the world, covering 40 hectares and lying before the gate to the Imperial Palace in central Beijing. It was here that the People's Republic was proclaimed in Oct 1949. In June 1989, it was the scene of mass protests by students and others against the Chinese government. The demonstrations were crushed by troops of the Chinese Army, leaving an undisclosed number of people dead.

Tianjin, Treaty of (1858) The second unequal treaty imposed on China by the Western powers following the invasion of an Anglo-French expeditionary force in 1856 to enforce revision of the Treaty of **Nanjing** (1842) to allow for an expansion of foreign trade. Under the terms of the treaty, China was compelled to open 10 new **treaty ports** and to allow permanent foreign legations in the capital. Furthermore, foreigners could travel in the interior (where they would continue to enjoy the privilege of extraterritoriality), while the Yangzi River was opened to foreign navigation. When the Qing court refused to ratify the treaty, a second Anglo-French offensive was launched, which led to the occupation of the Chinese capital in 1860. The Beijing Convention (1860) confirmed the terms of this treaty, although additional concessions were wrung from the Qing: Britain acquired the Kowloon peninsula (which became part of the colony of Hong Kong), while missionaries gained the right to travel and own property in the interior. ▷ **Qing Dynasty**

Tianjin Massacre (1870) A major anti-foreign and anti-Christian incident in China, one of a number of 'missionary cases' during the second half of the 19c in which the arrogance of Western missionaries aroused the hostility of the local population already whipped up by grotesque rumours spread by conservative gentry elites. In 1869 a French Catholic cathedral with an attached orphanage had been built in Tianjin on the site of a razed Buddhist temple. When it became known that missionaries were offering payment to receive orphans, rumours abounded that Christians were maiming and torturing Chinese children. As Tianjin had already been occupied twice by Anglo-French forces in 1858 and 1860 during the **Arrow War** (1856–60), anti-foreign feeling was already rife. In an altercation with the local magistrate, the French consul (Henri Fontanier) accidentally shot and killed a bystander. An angry mob then killed the consul and several French traders, before destroying the cathedral and orphanage, in the process also killing 10 nuns. The Chinese government was compelled to pay an indemnity and send a mission of apology to France.

Tiberius (Tiberius Julius Caesar Augustus) (42BC–AD37) Roman Emperor (AD14/37). He was the son of **Livia**, and stepson and successor of Emperor **Augustus**. Deeply conservative by nature, he was content to continue Augustus' policies and simply consolidate his achievements. Despite the soundness of his administration and foreign policy, politically his reign was a disaster. While the suspicious death of his heir, **Germanicus** (AD19), followed by the excesses of his chief henchman, **Sejanus** (Prefect of the **Praetorian Guard**), made him unpopular, the reign of terror that followed Sejanus' downfall (AD31) made him an object of universal loathing. Few mourned when he died on Capri, the island retreat that had been his home since AD26. ▷ **Agrippina the Elder**

ticket of leave A pass issued to convicts in Australia as a reward for good behaviour; it was a form of parole which could be issued after 4, 6, or 8 years depending on whether the sentence was for 7, 14 years, or life, respectively. About 30 per cent of convicts received tickets of leave by 1840. ▷ **transportation**

Tientsin, Treaty of; Tientsin Massacre ▷
Tianjin, Treaty of; Tianjin Massacre

Tiglathpileser I (1115/1077BC) King of
Assyria. He extended his dominions to the
upper Euphrates, and defeated the King of
Babylonia.

Tiglathpileser III (745/727BC) King of Assyria. A great empire-builder, he was the
driving-force behind the greatest phase of
Assyrian expansion. He defeated Sarduri II
of **Urartu** (743BC) and conquered the cities of
northern Syria and Phoenicia, including
Damascus and Babylon, ruling the latter as
King Pulu. Under his rule, Assyria was
strengthened by military and administrative
reforms: a standing army was created,
replacing the traditional annual conscription
of peasants; large provinces were subdivided
in order to curb moves towards independence; a policy of mass resettlement of
peoples from conquered territories was
implemented; and Assyrian officials were
appointed by Tiglathpileser in territories not
immediately within the empire.

Tikhon (1865–1925) Patriarch of the Russian
Orthodox Church. He was the first to have to
face up to the new communist regime. A
bishop by 1898, he had few crises to face until
he became patriarch in 1918. His first
approach was to condemn the new Soviet
state; but before his death he called on the
faithful to show it political loyalty. Neither
policy was to prove successful, and his *de
facto* successor, **Sergei**, faced the same
problem.

Tikhonov, Nikolai Alexandrovich
(1905–) Soviet politician. He began his
career as an assistant locomotive driver,
before training in the late 1920s at the
Dnepropetrovsk Metallurgical Institute,
where he met Leonid **Brezhnev**, then a
Communist Party (CPSU) organizer. Tikhonov worked for two decades in the ferrous
metallurgy industry, before being appointed
Deputy Minister for the Iron and Steel
Industry (1955–7), Deputy Chairman of
Gosplan (1963–5) and Deputy Chairman of
the Council of Ministers (1965–80). He was
inducted into the CPSU **Politburo** as a full
member by party leader Brezhnev in 1979
and appointed Prime Minister in 1980, a post
which he held until 1985. A cautious, centralist Brezhnevite, his period as state Premier
was characterized by progressive economic
stagnation.

Tilak, Bal Gangadhar (1856–1920)
Militant Indian nationalist, scholar, and
philosopher. After teaching mathematics, he
became owner and editor of two weekly
newspapers. A member of the so-called
'extremist' wing within the **Indian National
Congress**, he was twice imprisoned by the
British for his nationalist activities. He
helped found the Home Rule League in 1914,
and died in Bombay.

Tilley, Sir Samuel Leonard (1818–96)
Canadian politician. He was one of the few
who supported confederation in New Brunswick and this lost him the 1865 election. John
A **Macdonald** ensured that he was given
massive aid, including direct grants to help
him win the 1866 election and he joined the
federal government in 1867. When Macdonald fell in 1873, he became Lieutenant-
Governor of New Brunswick, but on Macdonald's return to power he again entered
government as Minister of Finance, bringing
in the National Policy tariff. Ill health forced
his retirement in 1885, although he remained
as Lieutenant-Governor until 1893. ▷ **Tariff
Policy (Canada)**

Tilly, Johann Tserclaes, Count von
(1559–1632) Bavarian general. Tilly was the
chief commander of the **Catholic League's**
army in the **Thirty Years War**. He campaigned in 1594 with Emperor **Rudolf II**
against the Turks. He reorganized the
Bavarian army in 1610 into a disciplined,
efficient fighting force. He became Imperial
commander in 1630 after **Wallenstein's** fall.
His string of victories ended when he was
decisively beaten by the Swedes at Breitenfeld (1631). He was subsequently fatally
wounded in battle at the Lech River.

Tilsit, Treaties of (1807) Agreements of
France with Russia and Prussia, following the
breakup of the Third Coalition. After spectacular victories at **Jena and Auerstädt** and the
Battle of **Friedland**, **Napoleon I** imposed a
blockade on Continental trade with Britain,
and established the Grand Duchy of Warsaw
and the Kingdom of Westphalia. The treaties
contained secret clauses intended to mollify
Russia. ▷ **Grand Alliance, War of the;
Napoleonic Wars**

timar In the **Ottoman Empire**, the right to a
share in the income drawn from taxation
upon an area of land acquired by conquest.
The holder of a *timar* (a *timariot*) was usually
obliged to serve in the Ottoman cavalry. A
zaim was a timariot granted a *zeamet*, a timar

yielding an annual income of more than 20 000 *akchas*. After the introduction of gunpowder, the military importance of the timariots was eclipsed by the **Janissaries**. ▷ **Ayans; Sipahi**

Time of Troubles (1598–1613) A period of intense social and political turmoil in Russia, involving a series of successive crises, civil war, famines, Cossack and peasant revolts, foreign invasions, and widespread material destruction. The period ended with a national uprising against the invading Poles, and the election of the first Romanov tsar. ▷ **Cossacks; Romanov Dynasty**

Timor An island in the eastern Indonesian archipelago. In the colonial period, the island was divided between the Dutch in the west and the Portuguese in the east, the border between the two being laid down at the beginning of the 20c. Neither territory was of great economic importance to its colonial masters, although there was a modest cattle industry in the west and some coffee plantations in the east. West Timor was incorporated into the Republic of Indonesia in May 1950; colonial rule was maintained in East Timor until 1975 when, following the fall of the **Salazar** regime in Portugal, the colonial administration withdrew. In East Timor, Fretilin, which had sought immediate independence, emerged as the major domestic political force, but in Oct 1975, Indonesian forces invaded, alleging that Fretilin was a communist movement. The capital, Dili, was taken and Timor was declared a province of Indonesia (July 1976). A guerrilla struggle between Indonesian forces and Fretilin continues.

Timoshenko, Semyon Konstantinovich (1895–1970) Russian general. He joined the Tsarist army in 1915, and in the **Russian Revolution** took part in the defence of Tsaritsyn. In 1940 he smashed Finnish resistance during the **Russo-Finnish War**, then commanded in the Ukraine, but failed to stop the German advance (1942). He also served as People's Commissar of Defence, improving the system of army training. He retired in 1960. ▷ **World War II**

Timur ('Timur the Lame', Timur Lenk) (1336–1405) Tatar conqueror. Born near **Samarkand**, in 1369 he ascended the throne of Samarkand, and in a series of devastating wars (in which he sustained the wounds which gave him his nickname) subdued nearly all Persia (1392–6), Georgia, and the **Tatar**

Empire, and conquered all the states between the Indus and the lower Ganges (1398). He won Damascus and Syria from the Mamluk sovereigns of Egypt, then defeated the Turks at **Ankara** (1402), taking Sultan **Bayezid I** prisoner. He died while marching to conquer China. ▷ **Mamluks; Timurids**

Timurids The dynastic group descended from **Timur**, which ruled in Persia and in Central Asia following his death. The major achievement of the Timurids, of whom Shah-Rukh (1404/47) was arguably the greatest, lay in the realms of learning, architecture and the arts; despite the steady erosion of the empire as a result of rivalries between individual Timurids, these were cultivated at a high level until the end of the sultanate of Husayn Bayqara. The latter's son, Badi al-Zaman (who died in 1517 in Constantinople, a prisoner of **Selim I, 'the Grim'**), was the last of the Timurids to rule in Persia. Although a descendant of Timur, **Babur** was to found the Mughal Dynasty in India.

Tindemans, Leo (1922–) Belgian politician. He studied economics and social sciences at Antwerp, Ghent and Leuven universities; in 1958 became Secretary to the **Christian People's Party** (CVP). In 1961 he entered parliament for Antwerp. From 1968 he regularly held cabinet posts, and led the government from 1974 to 1978. In 1979 he became chairman of the CVP, and is particularly known for his role in the European Community.

Ting Ling ▷ **Ding Ling**

Tippoo Sahib (Tipu Sultan) (1749–99) Sultan of Mysore (1782/99). The son of Haidar Ali, he continued his father's policy of opposing British rule, and in 1789 invaded the British-protected state of Travancore. In the ensuing war (1790–2) he was defeated by **Cornwallis** and had to cede half his kingdom. After recommencing hostilities in 1799, he was killed during the siege of Seringapatam.

Tippu Tib (1837–1905) One of the most powerful of the traders and plantation owners of Zanzibar in the 19c. He created a personal empire in the eastern Congo region (Zaire) in the years before the Scramble for Africa. Tippu began to lead large and powerful trading caravans, financed by Indian capitalists, into the interior of East Africa from the 1850s. Together with other Zanzibari traders, he helped to establish networks of trade in ivory and slaves throughout eastern central Africa. In 1869 he settled in the rich ivory grounds of eastern Zaire, became powerful in the markets there, and virtually ruled a large area for some 12 years. By the 1890s, he was back in Zanzibar and owned seven plantations and some 10 000 slaves.

Tirpitz, Alfred (Friedrich) von (1849–1930) German admiral. He joined the Prussian Navy in 1865, was ennobled in 1900, and rose to be Lord High Admiral (1911). As Secretary of State for the Imperial Navy (1897–1916), he raised a fleet to challenge British supremacy of the seas, and acted as its commander (1914–16). He advocated unrestricted submarine warfare, and resigned when this policy was, initially, opposed in government circles (to be implemented later, on 1 Feb 1917); he later sat in the **Reichstag**. ▷ **World War I**

Tiso, Jozef (1887–1947) Slovak priest and politician. Like many other Slovak priests he was attracted to politics by Catholic and ethnic feelings against the Czechs in the united state established in 1918. In 1938 he succeeded **Hlinka** as leader of the Populist Party and began talks with **Henlein**, the Sudeten leader, whose objective was to enable **Hitler** to destroy Czechoslovakia. Following the **Munich Agreement**, ably assisted by **Durcansky**, he conspired with Hitler and in Mar 1939 obeyed the order to declare Slovakia independent, leaving Czechs to Hitler's mercy in the **Bohemian Protectorate**. As President of the new Slovakia he eventually, in 1944, invited the Germans in to suppress the patriotic **Slovak uprising**. In 1947 he was tried and executed in Bratislava. The Slovak-Czech relationship had been little improved by his efforts.

Tissaphernes (d.395BC) Persian satrap. A satrap in Asia Minor from 413BC, he was notorious for his duplicity in the conflicts between Athens and Sparta. Deprived of a province in favour of **Cyrus the Younger**, brother of **Artaxerxes II**, he denounced him to Artaxerxes, for whom he fought and won the Battle of Cunaxa (401BC). He then murdered the leaders of the Greeks, including Cyrus, and harassed **Xenophon** and the ten thousand Greek mercenaries who had fought in the battle. But he was himself defeated by **Agesilaus** in the war with Sparta, and murdered for the murder of Cyrus on the orders of Artaxerxes.

Tisza, Kalman (1830–1902) Hungarian politician. The father of Stephen **Tisza**, he was Premier and virtual dictator of Hungary from 1875 to 1890.

Tisza, Stephen (1861–1918) Hungarian politician. He was the son of Kalman **Tisza**. A patriotic Magyar, he was Premier of Hungary in the periods 1903–5 and 1913–17. He supported Germany and was assassinated on 31 Oct 1918, the first day of the Hungarian Revolution.

Tito (Josip Broz) (1892–1980) Yugoslav politician. In **World War I** he served with the Austro-Hungarian Army, was taken prisoner by the Russians, and became a communist. He was imprisoned for conspiring against the regime in Yugoslavia (1928–9), and became Secretary of the Communist Party in 1937. In 1941 he organized partisan forces against the Axis conquerors, and after the war became the country's first communist Prime Minister (1945), consolidating his position with the presidency (1953–80). He broke with **Stalin** and the Cominform in 1948, developing Yugoslavia's independent style of **communism** ('Titoism'), and played a leading role in the association of nonaligned countries. ▷ **Axis Powers; Chetniks**

Titulescu, Nicolae (1883–1941) Romanian politician. At the end of **World War I**, he was one of the Romanian representatives at the peace negotiations in Paris and later signed the Treaty of **Trianon** (1920). He worked at the Romanian embassy in London (1922–6 and 1928–32), returning to Romania to serve as Foreign Minister (1927 and 1932–6). He negotiated Romania's membership of the **Little Entente** and the **Balkan Entente** and courted the support of France and the USSR. He was dismissed by **Charles II** of Romania in 1936.

Titus (Titus Flavius Vespasianus) (AD39–81) Roman Emperor (AD79/81). He was the elder son and successor of **Vespasian**. Popular with the Romans for his generosity, charm, and military prowess, he is execrated in Jewish tradition for his destruction of Jerusalem (AD70) and suppression of the Jewish Revolt. His brief reign was marred by many natural calamities, notably the eruption of Vesuvius (AD79). He completed the Colosseum, begun by his father.

Tobruk, Battles of (1941–2) A key city in Libya, Tobruk was taken from the Italians in Jan 1941 by Wavell, then in command of the

Eighth Army. The arrival, however, in Libya of **Rommel** with his Afrika Corps in Mar of the same year saw the British withdrawing eastward. The subsequent siege of Tobruk, which was garrisoned largely by Australian troops, lasted for some eight months until the garrison was able to break out. Auchinleck, who was now in command of the Eighth Army and whom they managed to join, mounted a major offensive which was to extend British control over Cyrenaica as far as Benghazi bringing back Tobruk with it. However, Rommel's counter-offensive towards Egypt meant that Tobruk was again placed under siege, this time falling in June 1942. In the event, Auchinleck was able to check Rommel's advance at the first Battle of **El Alamein** and it was the successful western drive of Montgomery which finally recaptured Tobruk in Nov 1942.

Tocqueville, Alexis (Charles Henri Maurice Clérel) de, (1805–59) French historian and political scientist. In 1831 went to the USA to report on the prison system. On his return, he published a penetrating political study, *Democracy in America* (1835), which gave him a European reputation. He became a member of the Chamber of Deputies in 1839, and in 1849 was Vice-President of the Assembly and briefly Minister of Foreign Affairs. After Louis Napoleon's coup, he retired to his estate, where he wrote the first volume of *L'Ancien Régime et la Révolution* (1856). ▷ **Napoleon III**

Todarmal (d.1589) Indian administrator. A brilliant revenue officer, he first served under **Sher Shah** and then joined the court of **Akbar the Great**. He was instrumental in devising the 'Zabti System' or 'Todarmal's Bandobast', a system of revenue assessment and collection introduced during Akbar's reign. According to this system, the peasant was required to pay taxes on the basis of local produce as well as local prices. There were a number of advantages of this system. As soon as the area sown by the peasant had been measured, both the peasant and the state knew what the dues were. The peasant was, furthermore, given remission in the land revenue if crops failed on account of drought, floods etc. Akbar successfully introduced this system in the area from Lahore to Allahabad, and in Malwa and Gujarat. A very efficient system of revenue administration thus evolved under his guidance.

Todd, Sir (Reginald Stephen) Garfield (1908–92) Rhodesian politician. Born in New Zealand, he was educated there and in South Africa. Having come to Southern Rhodesia in 1934 as a missionary, he was elected to the Legislative Assembly (1946) and then to the leadership of the United Rhodesia Party (1953) which made him Prime Minister of Southern Rhodesia. He was removed from the leadership by an internal putsch because of his liberalism and he helped form the overtly liberal Central African Party in 1959. After the party's failure in 1962, he returned to farming but remained the spokesman for white liberalism in the country, as a result of which he was restricted by the **Rhodesian Front** government under Ian **Smith** (1965–6 and 1972–6). A close friend and ally of Joshua **Nkomo**, he supported the latter in the 1980 elections.

Todleben, Eduard Ivanovitch (1818–84) Russian soldier and military engineer. Born of German descent in Mitau in Courland, he served in the Caucasus, and in the Danubian principalities in 1853. He conducted with skill and energy the defence of **Sevastopol** until he was severely wounded (June 1855); thereafter he completed the fortification of Nikolaieff and Cronstadt. During the Turkish War of 1877–8 he was called to besiege Plevna, which he took after a brilliant defence.

Togliatti, Palmiro (1893–1964) Italian politician. A member of the Italian Socialist Party in 1914, he was one of the founders of the Italian Communist Party (**PCI**) in 1921. Forced to flee Italy by the fascists in 1926, he organized the activities of the party from abroad and was part of the **Comintern** secretariat in charge of communists fighting in the **Spanish Civil War**. In Mar 1944 he returned to Italy, played a key part in the coalition governments that controlled Italy until 1947 and was instrumental in stressing the need to avoid insurrectionary attempts. Until his death (while visiting Nikita **Khrushchev** in Yalta), he was Party Secretary, presiding over the PCI's development from a relatively small group of militants into the largest communist organization in the West. ▷ **Berlinguer, Enrico**

Togo Heihachiro (1848–1934) Japanese admiral. After training at the Royal Naval College at Greenwich, London, he served against China (1894). As commander during the **Russo-Japanese War** (1904–5), he bombarded Port Arthur. Togo defeated the Russian fleet at the Battle of Tsushima (1905), the first victory of an Asian power over a European nation in modern times.

Tojo Hideki (1885–1948) Japanese general and politician. He attended military college, became military attaché in Germany (1919), served in **Manchuria** as Chief of Staff (1937–40), and during **World War II** was Minister of War (1940–1) and Prime Minister (1941–4). Arrested in 1945, he attempted to commit suicide, but was hanged as a war criminal in Tokyo.

Tokugawa Ieyasu (1542–1616) Japanese warrior leader. The third of the three great historical unifiers of Japan, after **Oda Nobunaga** and **Toyotomi Hideyoshi**, he was a noble from eastern Japan. He took power after the Battle of **Sekigahara** (1600), and founded the **Tokugawa Shogunate**. He completed Edo Castle (the present Tokyo Imperial Palace) as his headquarters, and instituted an all-pervading centralized control of Japanese life, whose effects are still felt.

Tokugawa Shogunate (1603–1867) Japan's third warrior government, established by **Tokugawa Ieyasu** when he was awarded the hereditary title of **shogun** in 1603 by the Emperor, following his military victory over rival warrior families at the Battle of **Sekigahara** (1601). The Tokugawa Shogunate (or *bakufu*, 'tent government') was located in Edo (present-day Tokyo) and proved to be the most durable of the three shogunates (the other two being the **Kamakura Shogunate** and the **Ashikaga Shogunate**), providing peace and stability until the mid-19c, when domestic social and economic change together with external pressure from Western powers combined to bring about its collapse. Tokugawa Japan has been described by historians as a centralized feudalism: although the **daimyo** (feudal lords) were allowed considerable autonomy, they were subject to restrictions on the size of their castle towns and the number of retainers they could have. The Tokugawa also retained the right to reduce or confiscate their domains. Furthermore, Daimyo were forbidden to engage in foreign trade and were obliged to reside in Edo six months every year (**Alternate Attendance System**). From the mid-18c, however, Tokugawa control gradually loosened as its financial situation worsened and attempts to impose a rigidly hierarchical social order foundered on the rocks of social and economic change, while the **samurai** elite became indebted to an emerging merchant class. Dissatisfaction with the status quo led to an imperial loyalist movement in the early 19c which was to culminate in the overthrow of the Tokugawa and the **Meiji Restoration** (1868).

Tolbert, William Richard (1913–80) Liberian politician. Educated at Liberia College in Monrovia, he was a civil servant (1935–43) before becoming a member of the House of Representatives for the True Whig Party (1943–51). Vice-President from 1951 to 1971, he became President in 1971 and remained in this post until he was assassinated in a military coup on 12 Apr 1980.

Tolpuddle Martyrs Agricultural labourers at Tolpuddle, Dorset, in England, who were organized in 1833 into a trade union by a Methodist local preacher, George Loveless (1796–1874), convicted of taking illegal oaths, and transported. The action provoked substantial protests, and the labourers were eventually pardoned.

Tolstoy (Tolstoi) A family of Russian nobles. Count Peter (1645–1729) was a trusted agent of **Peter I, 'the Great'**. Count Peter Alexandrovich (1761–1844) was one of **Suvorov**'s generals and, under **Nicholas I**, head of a government department. Count Dmitri Andreevich (1823–89) was a reactionary Minister of Education, champion of Russian orthodoxy and a 'russifier' of the Poles.

Toltecs A people (or peoples) who controlled most of central Mexico between c.900 and 1150, and were the last such dominant culture prior to the **Aztecs**. Their capital was at Tula, 80 km north of Mexico City. The most impressive Toltec ruins are at Chichen

TOKUGAWA SHOGUNATE

Regnal Dates	Name
1603/5	Tokugawa Ieyasu
1605/23	Tokugawa Hidetada
1623/51	Tokugawa Iemitsu
1651/80	Tokugawa Ietsuna
1680/1709	Tokugawa Tsunayoshi
1709/12	Tokugawa Ienobu
1713/16	Tokugawa Ietsugu
1716/45	Tokugawa Yoshimune
1745/60	Tokugawa Ieshige
1760/86	Tokugawa Ieharu
1787/1837	Tokugawa Ienari
1837/53	Tokugawa Ieyoshi
1853/8	Tokugawa Iesada
1858/66	Tokugawa Iemochi
1866/7	Tokugawa Yoshinobu

Itzá in Yucatán, where a branch of the culture survived beyond the fall of its central Mexican hegemony.

Tombalbaye, N'Garta (François) (1918–75) Chadian politician. Educated locally, he was a teacher before becoming a trades union organizer. He then helped organize the **Rassemblement Démocratique Africaine** (RDA) in Chad in 1947 and was elected to the territorial assembly (1953). He rose to be Prime Minister in 1959 and then President on Chad's independence in 1962. He remained in this position until the military coup of 13 Apr 1975, during which he was killed.

Tomislav (c.925/8) First King of Croatia. A member of the Croatian Trpimirović Dynasty, he is thought to have been the son of Prince Muncimir who acceded c.892. At first bearing only the title 'Prince', c.925 he was granted the title 'King' by Pope John X. He increased the territory of Croatia and built up its military strength, successfully repulsing the Magyar incursions into Pannonia. ▷ **Croats**

Tomsky, Mikhail Pavlovich (1880–1937) Soviet trade unionist. Born into a poor working-class family in St Petersburg, he organized factory strikes from his mid-teens. From 1909 to 1917 he was either in prison or in exile. He returned to trade union activity in Moscow in 1917, and by 1919 was Chairman of the Central Council of Trade Unions and by 1922 a full-blown member of the **Politburo**. In these capacities he destroyed the unions in the Western sense and made them vehicles for party and government control. In the period 1928–30 he changed his stance and defended workers' rights. He was thereupon dismissed and committed suicide in protest against **Stalin**'s purges.

Tone, (Theobald) Wolfe (1763–98) Irish nationalist. He acted as Secretary of the Catholic Committee, helped to organize the Society of **United Irishmen** (1791), and had to flee to the USA and to France (1795). He induced France to invade Ireland on two occasions, and was captured during the second expedition. He was condemned to be hanged, but committed suicide in Dublin.

Tooke, John Horne (1736–1812) British politician. Born John Horne, he became a lawyer, and in 1760 a vicar. A radical, in 1771 he formed the Constitutional Society, supporting the American colonists and parliamentary reform. His spirited opposition to an enclosure bill procured him the favour of the rich Mr Tooke of Purley in Surrey, which led to his new surname and *The Diversions of Purley* (1786), written while in prison for supporting the American cause. He was tried for high treason in 1794, acquitted, and became an MP in 1801. ▷ **American Revolution; Wilkes, John**

Tories (UK) The British political party which emerged in 1679–80 as the group opposed to the exclusion of James, Duke of York, from succession to the throne. The name was taken from 17c Irish outlaws who plundered and killed English settlers. The party developed after the **Glorious Revolution** (1688) as the supporters of the divine right of monarchy, and had particular support from the country squirearchy and most sections of the Anglican Church. It opposed religious toleration for Catholics and Dissenters. The Tories enjoyed periods of power in the reign of Queen **Anne**, but the party went into decline after the Hanoverian succession, when some of its supporters became **Jacobites**. It is generally agreed to have revived under **Pitt, 'the Younger'** as the leading opposition to French revolutionary ideology in the 1790s, and Lord **Liverpool** became the first Prime Minister to acknowledge the title 'Tory' in the early 19c. Toryism developed into Conservatism under **Peel**, but survived as a nickname for the Conservatives. ▷ **Conservative Party** (UK); **James VII and II; Whigs**

Tories (USA) Also known as Loyalists, those who remained loyal to the crown during the **American Revolution**. After the **Declaration of Independence**, loyalty to the crown became treason, punishable by imprisonment and confiscation of property. It was estimated that one third of the colonial population were loyalists. Many chose to leave the country during or after the revolution and sufficient numbers enlisted in the British Army to make up several regiments.

Torquemada, Tomás de (1420–98) The first Inquisitor-General of Spain. He entered the Dominican Order in Valladolid, was later appointed Prior of the Convent of Santa Cruz in Segovia, and at about the same time was chosen to be a confessor of **Isabella I, 'the Catholic'** and **Ferdinand II, 'the Catholic'**. In 1482 he was appointed as one of the seven new inquisitors to continue the work of the recently founded (1480) **Inquisition**. In 1483 he was chosen to head it as Inquisitor-General, and played a key role in forcing through the introduction of the new Inquisition in the realms of the crown of **Aragon**. No evidence exists for attributing to Torquemada the anti-Semitic philosophy evident in the early Inquisition, or responsibility for its excesses, but it is unquestionable that he was a major force behind the Expulsion of the **Jews** in 1492.

Tosks Part of the Albanian nation from southern Albania, during the years of Ottoman rule they mainly lived as peasants working on large estates. Both Sunni and Bektashi Muslims, they were loyal to the Sultan and less open to political reform. Their dialect was the basis for the Albanian literary language. ▷ **Albanians; Ghegs**

Tostig (d.1066) Earl of Northumbria. He was the son of Godwin and brother of **Harold II**. After return from banishment in 1052, **Edward the Confessor** created him Earl of Northumbria (1055) over which he ruled both violently and as a frequent absentee. He was supplanted by Morcar, whose title was confirmed by Edward and Harold. Tostig was banished and, upon Harold's succession (1066), plotted to overthrow him. He aided **Harald Hardrada**'s invasion from Norway in Sep and was killed at the Battle of Stamford Bridge (25 Sep 1066).

totalitarianism In its modern form, a political concept first used to describe the USSR's communist regime and Italy and Germany's fascist regimes during the period between the two World Wars. It is difficult to distinguish empirically from related concepts such as authoritarianism and dictatorship, but certain common features can be identified. These relate to the use of power and the means of government employed by the leadership, which claims exclusive rights to govern, usually on behalf of the party and its ideology. Furthermore, all aspects of social, political, industrial, military, and economic life are controlled or permeated by the state apparatus. Political opposition is suppressed, and decision-making is highly centralized. ▷ **authoritarianism; communism; fascism**

Touré, Ahmed Sékou (1922–84) Guinean politician. Educated in Quran schools and at Conakry (1936–40), he turned to trade union activity and attended the *Conféderation Générale des Travailleurs* (CGT) Congress in Paris in 1947, after which he was imprisoned for a brief period. He was a founder member of the **Rassemblement Démocratique Africaine** (RDA) in 1946 and became its Secretary-General in 1952, as well as Secretary-General of the local CGT branch. He was a member of the Territorial Assembly from 1953, Mayor of Conakry in 1955 and then Deputy in the French National Assembly in 1956. In 1958 he organized an overwhelming 'non' vote to de **Gaulle**'s referendum on self-government within a French Community. Guinea was granted its independence at once, the French removing as much of their possessions as possible. He was President from 1958 to 1984, and retained his uncompromisingly radical views of domestic and foreign politics. He survived several attempts, supported by outside powers, to overthrow him. Soon after his death, the military did take control.

Tours, Congress of (25–30 Dec 1920) The Congress of the **Socialist Party** (SFIO) at which the majority of members decided to join the Third International, and thus to create a new party, the **Communist Party** (SFIC). His impassioned oratory against this decision made Léon **Blum** the most influential figure among those who decided to stay with the 'old firm', the Socialist Party. The subsequent general election (1924) revealed that the majority of socialist voters agreed, and the Communist Party had little support until the **Popular Front** period (1934–6).

Toussaint L'Ouverture (François Dominique Toussaint) (1746–1803) Haitian black revolutionary leader. He was born of African slave parents but was freed in 1777. In 1791 he joined the black insurgents, and by 1797 was effective ruler of the former colony. He drove out British and Spanish expeditions, restored order, and aimed at independence. **Napoleon I** sent a new expedition to St Domingue, and proclaimed the re-establishment of slavery. Toussaint was eventually arrested, and died in a French prison. His surname comes from his bravery in once making a breach (*ouverture*) in the ranks of the enemy.

Townshend (of Rainham), Charles, 2nd Viscount (1674–1738) English politician. He succeeded his father as viscount (1687), was made Secretary of State by **George I** (1714–16 and 1721–30), and became a leading figure in the Whig ministry with his brother-in-law, Robert **Walpole**. After a resignation engineered by Walpole, he became known as 'turnip Townshend' for his interest in agricultural improvement, and his proposal to use turnips in crop rotation. ▷ **Whigs**

Townshend Acts (1767) British statutes imposing taxes on five categories of goods imported into the American colonies, after successful colonial resistance to the **Stamp Act** (1765). The Townshend Taxes likewise met resistance from the colonists, and four categories were repealed in 1770. The fifth, on tea, remained in effect until the **Boston Tea Party**. The Acts are named after British Chancellor of the Exchequer, Charles Townshend (1725–67), who sponsored them. ▷ **American Revolution**

Toyotomi Hideyoshi (1536–98) Japanese warrior leader. The second of the three great historical unifiers of Japan, between **Oda Nobunaga** and **Tokugawa Ieyasu**, sometimes called 'the Napoleon of Japan'. Unusually, he was an ordinary soldier who rose to become Oda's foremost general. His law forbade all except **samurai** to carry swords (1588), and he banned Christianity for political reasons (1597). His armies invaded Korea (1592–8), but withdrew after his death at Fushimi Castle, Kyoto.

Trade Unions (Belgium) As one of the first industrialized nations, with strong mining and heavy industrial sectors in Wallonia and Ghent, Belgian socialism developed early, having a radical syndicalist trade-union movement as one of the moving forces. In 1898 the various socialist organizations joined a Syndical Committee, which in 1938 became the Belgian Labour League, and after **World War II** the General Belgian Labour League (*Algemeen Belgisch Vakverbond*; *Fédération Générale du Travail de Belgique*). The Catholics were much slower to adopt organizations exclusively for workers, but after the papal encyclical *Rerum Novarum* in 1891 work started, and in 1904 the General Secretariat for Christian Professional Organizations was set up, which, after several changes, in 1923 became the General Christian Labour League (*Algemeen Christelijk Vakverbond*; *Confédération des Syndicats Chrétiens*). The importance of heavy industry to the Belgian economy has always meant that the more radical socialist Belgian trade unions have had a strong political influence, albeit sometimes rather negative, eg in the strikes of the 1880s; in the 20c both branches have been integrated into Belgian political culture and the power-sharing mechanism of Belgian society.

Trade Unions (Netherlands) Due to late industrialization, the trade union movement was slow to achieve strength in the Netherlands; it has always been characterized by ideological fragmentation (**Verzuiling**) into socialist, Calvinist, Catholic and liberal/ neutral organizations. The first unions were found in the skilled trades in Amsterdam in the 1860s; in 1871 the General Netherlands Workers' League (*Algemeen Nederlandsch Werkliedenverbond*, ANWV) was set up as the first nationwide organization. Mainly out of fear for socialism, in 1877 the Calvinists set up Patrimonium as their national umbrella for workers, which in 1909 gave way to the Christian National Labour League (*Christelijk Nationaal Vakverbond*, CNV); the Roman Catholics were much slower and did not achieve a proper workers' national organization until the 1920s, which in 1963 became the Netherlands Catholic Labour League (*Nederlands Katholieke Vakverbond*, NKV). The socialists set up a National Labour Secretariat in 1893, which in 1905 led into the Netherlands League of Trade Unions (*Nederlandse Verbond van Vakverenigingen*, NVV). There was also a neutral league, the 'General' (*Algmemeen Nederlands Vakverbond*, NVC, 1919), but it had limited influence. In 1975 the socialists and Catholics merged into the Federative Netherlands Labour Movement (*Federatie Nederlands Vakbeweging*, FNV). Dutch trade unionists have, in the 20c, had close relations with their political parties and have often sent their leaders into parliament; by means of the consultative system within *Verzuiling* they are very well represented in policy-making, for example in the Social and Economic Council (SER).

Trafalgar, Battle of (21 Oct 1805) The most famous naval engagement of the **Napoleonic Wars**, which destroyed **Napoleon I**'s hopes of invading England and established British naval supremacy for a century. Fought off Cape Trafalgar, Spain, between the British and Franco-Spanish fleets, the British triumph was marred by the death of **Nelson** at the moment of victory.

Tragic Week, The (July 1909) Spanish popular protest. The Tragic Week (*La Semana Tragica*) took place when a public demonstration in Barcelona against the conscription of soldiers for the war in Morocco developed into a violent popular protest with the widespread burning of churches and convents. This was largely a spontaneous backlash against the oppressive and anti-regionalist policies of the monarchy (with the church being seized on as the most visible manifestation of the ancien regime), though the inflammatory anticlerical propaganda of the **Radical Republican Party** had done much to create the volatile climate of opinion. The Tragic Week was a turning-point in the history of modern Spain because it brought the Republican and Socialist movements together, which eventually culminated in the establishment of the Second Republic in 1931. ▷ **Republic, Second** (Spain)

Trajan (Marcus Ulpius Trajanus) (c.53–117AD) Roman Emperor (AD98/117). Selected as successor by the aged **Nerva** for his military skills, he was the first emperor after **Augustus** to expand the Roman Empire significantly. The wealth from **Dacia**'s goldmines enabled him to launch an ambitious building programme, especially in Rome, where he constructed a new forum, library, and aqueduct. A sensitive but firm ruler, he was one of Rome's most popular emperors. ▷ **Hadrian**

transportation Sentence of banishment from England for those convicted of certain offences, introduced in 1597. Increasingly large numbers of English convicts were shipped to North America in the 17c and 18c, but the practice was ended by the **American Revolution**. As a result, the British government turned their attention to Australia. 162 000 convicts (137 000 males and 25 000 females) were transported to Australia from 1788 to 1868, mainly to New South Wales (1788–1840), Van Diemen's Land (1803–52) and Western Australia (1850–68). Most of the convicts were young, poorly-educated urban-dwellers convicted of some form of theft. In the early years of settlement, convict labour was used on public works; later the typical fate of most convicts was assignment to private service. ▷ **penal settlements; ticket of leave**

Transylvania A former province of northern and central Romania, separated from **Moldavia and Wallachia** by the Carpathian Mountains. Transylvania was a principality that became part of the Austro-Hungarian Empire and was incorporated into Romania in 1918. It was part of the region ceded to Hungary by **Hitler** in **World War II**.

trasformismo The term applied to the Italian political practice of forming parliamentary alliances, almost regardless of political ideology, in order to guarantee a government majority. The origins of *trasformismo* can be traced back to the **Connubio** and to some extent it continues even today;

however, it reached its pinnacle in the late 19c governments of Agostino **Depretis**. Because coalitions were not based on ideological considerations, *trasformismo* usually demanded extensive use of patronage and even blatant corruption to function effectively; it discredited the parliamentary system and led to a blurring of ideological distinctions.

treaty ports The ports opened by China during the 19c as a result of unequal treaties with the West. The first five (Canton, Amoy (Xiamen), Fuzhou, Ningbo and Shanghai) were opened by the Treaty of **Nanjing** (1842) and by the end of the 19c there were over 50 treaty ports. Situated along China's coast and inland on major rivers, the treaty ports were places in which foreigners could reside, trade, and (after 1895) establish manufacturing enterprises whose goods were not subject to Chinese taxation. Foreigners enjoyed the privilege of extraterritoriality. In a number of treaty ports (eg Shanghai) foreign powers also leased land (known as concession areas) where they exercised legal jurisdiction and collected taxes. Condemned as bastions of foreign privilege by a growing Chinese anti-imperialist movement from the 1920s on, the treaty ports came to an end when the unequal treaties were formally abolished in 1943.

Trenchard (of Wolfeton), Hugh Montague, 1st Viscount (1873–1956) British marshal of the RAF. He joined the army in 1893, served in India, South Africa, and West Africa, and developed an interest in aviation. He commanded the Royal Flying Corps in **World War I**, helped to establish the RAF (1918), and became the first Chief of Air Staff (1918–29). As Commissioner of the London Metropolitan Police (1931–5), he founded the police college at Hendon. He became a peer in 1930.

Trent, Council of (1545–63) A series of councils of the Catholic Church, held at Trent, Italy. The Emperor **Charles V** had long advocated the convocation of such a council as a means of restoring the unity of the Church which the **Reformation** had broken. The Popes tended to prevaricate because of the potential threat which a council posed to papal supremacy. After some efforts at compromise with Protestant doctrine, Jesuit influence helped to secure a powerful restatement of traditional dogma which included an emphatic reassertion of papal authority. The clarification on doctrinal matters was to form the ideological spearhead of the Counter-Reformation.

Trent Affair (1861) An incident between the USA and Britain during the **American Civil War**, in which the USS *San Jacinto* forcibly removed two officials of the Confederate States from the British ship *Trent* while in international waters. The issue provoked considerable British anger until the Confederate officials were released by the American Secretary of State.

Treuga Dei During the early Middle Ages private wars and feuds were almost unrestricted. The reforming church in France at the end of the 10c introduced the *pax dei*, which compelled warriors to respect the rights and persons of non-combatants. The *Treuga Dei* (or 'truce of God') was a development of this, forbidding private warfare from Wednesday evening until the following Monday and during Lent. This was later extended to cover other seasons. The Salian emperors were instrumental in trying to implement it in Germany. ▷ **Landfriede; Salians**

Treurnicht, Andries Petrus (1921–) South African politician. He studied at the Universities of Cape Town and Stellenbosch and was a minister in the Dutch Reformed Church from 1946 until his election as a **National Party** representative in 1971. Elected Transvaal provincial leader in 1978, he held several cabinet posts under P W **Botha**, gaining a reputation as an unreconstructed supporter of **apartheid**. He opposed even Botha's partial liberalization of the regime and was forced to leave the party with 15 colleagues in 1982. He formed a new party, the **Conservative Party of South Africa**, which pressed for a return to traditional apartheid values and effective partitioning of the country. The party gained seats and votes, especially from among the less well-off Afrikaners, over the next decade and took over from the moderate Progressive Federal Party as the official opposition within parliament.

Triads ▷ **Heaven and Earth Society**

trialism First formulated in 1894 by Josip Frank's Pure Party of Right, a breakaway group from **Starčević**'s Party of Right, the proponents of trialism sought the creation within the Habsburg Empire of a Croatian state which would embrace all the Habsburg South Slavic possessions and would possess all the prerogatives that the Hungarians enjoyed under dualism. Frank and his followers hoped that Vienna would accept a trialist solution in order to secure the **Croats** as allies against the Hungarians. ▷ **Khuen-Héderváry, Károly; Nagodba**

Trianon, Treaty of (1920) The treaty agreed between the new state of Hungary and the Allies of **World War I**, which reduced the territory of Hungary to about a third of its pre-war size. Romania received almost all that it had hoped to gain by entering the war, acquiring Transylvania with its mixed Romanian and Magyar population, Bessarabia, Crişana and **Bukovina** with part of the Banat, the rest of which was ceded to the Kingdom of Serbs, Croats and Slovenes (later Yugoslavia). Czechoslovakia also benefited from the treaty, gaining areas of mixed Czech and Magyar population.

Tribur, Princes' Meeting at (1076) In the face of the intensifying power-struggle between **Henry IV** and the German princes and the papacy, the king entered into negotiations with the princes, who had assembled with the papal legates at Tribur, in an attempt to stem his own increasing loss of support and in the hope of splitting the alliance between princes and papacy, thus preventing the election of an anti-king. After Henry had made concessions, including a promise to obey the pope, the princes agreed to recognize him as king, but only if his ban of excommunication was lifted within a year. The king responded with a submission to the pope at **Canossa** (1077), where he was absolved and his authority over the princes theoretically restored.

Triennial Acts (1641, 1664 and 1694) The collective name given to legislation passed requiring Parliament to assemble at least once every three years, as a reaction to the personal rule of **Charles I**. The 1694 Act also limited the life of each parliament to three years. ▷ **Septennial Act**

Trieste, Free Territory of This Adriatic port, at the north-west junction of the Istrian Peninsula, was promised to Italy in the Treaty of **London** (1915). In the inter-war years it was the subject of dispute between Italy and Yugoslavia and, following **World War II**, it was established as the 'Free Territory of Trieste', with the northern zone administered by the USA and Britain and the southern zone under Yugoslav control (1946). In 1954 the status of Trieste was revised and the northern zone was returned to Italy.

Trikoupis, Spyridon (1788–1873) Greek politician and writer. He was private secretary to Lord Guilford in the Ionian Islands, studied in Rome, Paris and London, and joined the patriots on the outbreak of the **Greek War of Independence** (1821). He was thrice envoy-extraordinary to London, was Minister of Foreign Affairs and of Public Instruction (1843), Vice-President of the Senate (1844–9), and Envoy-Extraordinary to Paris (1850). His son, Kharilaos (1832–96), was Foreign Minister (1866) and Premier repeatedly from 1875 to 1895.

Tripartite Declaration (May 1950) This represented an attempt by Britain, France and the USA to limit arms supplies to Israel and the Arab states in the wake of the emergence of the state of Israel, in the hope that this would ensure some stability for the area. Arms supplies were to be conditional on non-aggression, and the signatories to the Declaration undertook to take action both within and outside the framework of the **UN** in cases of frontier violation. Closer French relations with Israel subjected the Declaration to some strain, and with the Soviet arms deal with Gamal Abd al-**Nasser**'s Egypt in 1955 it became a dead letter.

Triple Alliance (1882) Following France's annexation of Tunisia, Italy joined the German-Austro-Hungarian Dual Alliance in order to protect her Mediterranean interests against France. The complex provisions of the resulting Triple Alliance protected Germany and Italy from French attack and all partners from unprovoked attack from a fourth party. Austro-Italian rivalries repeatedly threatened to destroy the Alliance and, with the coming of war in 1914, Italy's initial neutrality was followed by a declaration of war on Germany and Austria in 1915. ▷ **World War I**

Triple Alliance, War of the (Paraguayan War) (1864–70) A devastating war, fought by Paraguay against the combined forces of Brazil, Argentina and Uruguay (the Triple Alliance), which was provoked by the ambitions of the Paraguayan dictator, Francisco Solano **López**. The eventual victory of the Allies (most of the troops were provided by Brazil) was achieved at the cost of reducing the male population of Paraguay by nine-tenths.

Triple Entente A series of agreements between Britain and France (1904) and Britain and Russia (1907) initially to resolve outstanding colonial differences. It aligned Britain to France and Russia, who had concluded a military alliance in 1893–4. In 1914, the Triple Entente became a military alliance.

Tripolitania Region of North Africa, lying between Tunis and Cyrenaica; former province of western Libya; under Turkish control from the 16c until 1911; under Italian control until 1943; British control until 1952.

Tripolitanian War (1911–12) The war between Italy and Turkey, in which Italian forces invaded and occupied the Turkish province of Tripolitania (present-day Libya) to gain useful ports and to prevent an extension of French influence in North Africa. After the declaration of war (Sep 1911), the initial invasion went smoothly but the Italians were surprised to discover that the local Arab population did not welcome them as liberators from Turkish rule. The Italians therefore found themselves fighting not only the Turkish Army, but also Arab tribesmen. **Giolitti**'s response was to try to put pressure on the Turks elsewhere, and, in May 1912, 13 Turkish Aegean islands were seized. The outbreak of the Balkan war (Oct 1912) obliged Turkey to concentrate on resisting the threat from Bulgaria, Serbia, Montenegro and Greece, and so peace negotiations were begun with Italy, leading to the surrender of both Tripolitania and neighbouring Cyrenaica. Although the Italians were able to claim a considerable victory, the war brought them little real advantage: the colony was of little economic value and until the early 1930s required a constant and expensive military presence to combat a hostile native population.

Triune Kingdom During the 19c, the name given by Croatian nationalists to the kingdom which they hoped to create within the Habsburg Empire and which would consist of the three parts of the medieval Croat kingdom (Croatia, Slavonia and Dalmatia) with, according to some, Bosnia and Herzegovina. ▷ **trialism**

Trochu, Louis Jules (1815–96) French soldier. After a distinguished military career in the Crimea and elsewhere, he entered the Ministry of War. However, the unpalatable truths contained in his *L'Armée française en 1867* set the court against him. On 17 Aug

1870 he was made Governor of Paris, and became President of the Government of **National Defence** (Sep 1870). Regarded as overcautious and timid, he resigned as Military Governor of Paris in Jan 1871; his functions as President of the Government of National Defence were ended by the election of the National Assembly (Feb 1871). ▷ **Crimean War**

Troelstra, Pieter Jelles (1860–1930) Dutch politician. Trained as a lawyer, he disagreed with the anarchist tendencies of F **Domela Nieuwenhuis**, and helped set up the Social Democratic Workers' Party (SDAP) in 1894. From 1897 onwards he sat in parliament, and led the socialist group there. Often caught between the extreme left and the moderates, he never held a government post, but managed to keep the Dutch socialists together in their most turbulent period. In 1918 he tried to stage a coup, announcing the revolution in parliament, but support was insufficient and the effort collapsed; he remained an MP until 1925. ▷ **Party of Labour**

Trojan War In Greek legend, the 10-year conflict between the Greeks and Trojans, which began when Paris carried off Helen, the wife of Menelaus, and ended in the sacking of Troy. The story was the subject of Homer's *Iliad*, and is tentatively dated on the basis of archaeology to c.1260BC.

Tromp, Cornelis (Maartenszoon) (1629–91) Dutch naval commander. The son of Maarten **Tromp**, he shared the glory of Michiel de **Ruyter**'s Four Days' battle (1666) off Dunkirk, and won fame in the battles against the combined English and French fleets, 7 and 14 June 1673. On a visit to England in 1675 he was created baron by **Charles II** and was appointed lieutenant-governor of the United Provinces (1676).

Tromp, Maarten (Harpertszoon) (1598–1653) Dutch admiral. In 1639 he defeated a superior Spanish fleet off Gravelines, and won the Battle of the Downs later that year. Knighted by **Louis XIII** of France (1640) and by **Charles I** of England (1642), he then fought the French pirates based on Dunkirk, while his encounter with Robert **Blake** in 1652 started the first of the **Anglo-Dutch Wars**. Victorious off Dover, he was defeated by a superior English fleet off Portland, and finally off Terheijde, near Scheveningen, where he was killed. His son, Cornelis (Maartenzoon) **Tromp**, was a Lieutenant-Admiral in the later Anglo-Dutch Wars.

Tron, Andrea (1712–85) Venetian nobleman, diplomat and politician. He was perhaps the outstanding political figure of the 18c Venetian Republic. Known as 'el paron' for the way he dominated the Republic's councils, he was at various times ambassador to Vienna, Paris and Rome and was one of that minority of far-sighted patricians who recognized the need for wide-ranging reform of the Venetian state.

Trotsky, Leon (Lev Davidovich Bronstein) (1879–1940) Russian revolutionary. Educated in Odessa, in 1898 he was arrested as a Marxist and exiled to Siberia. He escaped in 1902, joined **Lenin** in London, and in the abortive **Revolution of 1905** was President of the St Petersburg Soviet. He then worked as a revolutionary journalist in the West, returning to Russia in 1917, when he joined the **Bolsheviks** and played a major role in the **October Revolution**. In the **Russian Civil War** he was Commissar for War, and created the **Red Army**. After Lenin's death (1924) his influence began to decline; he was ousted from the Party by **Stalin**, who opposed his theory of 'permanent revolution', exiled to Central Asia (1927), and expelled from the USSR (1929). He continued to agitate as an exile, and was sentenced to death *in absentia* by a Soviet court in 1937. He finally found asylum in Mexico, where he was assassinated by one of Stalin's agents. ▷ **Russian Revolution; Trotskyism**

Trotskyism A development of Marxist thought by Leon **Trotsky**. Essentially a theory of permanent revolution, Trotskyism stressed the internationalism of socialism, avoided coexistence, and encouraged revolutionary movements abroad; this conflicted with **Stalin**'s ideas of 'socialism in one country'. Trotskyism has since inspired other extreme left-wing revolutionary movements but they are factionally divided, and have little support outside some Western capitalist states. ▷ **communism; Marxism–Leninism; Stalinism**

Trucial States The former name of the United Arab Emirates of Abu Dhabi, Ajman, Dubai, Fujairah, Ras al Khaimah, Sharjah and Umm al Qaiwain on the Persian Gulf and Gulf of Oman. The name derives from a truce signed between the ruling sheiks and Great Britain in 1820; in 1892 the states accepted British protection.

Trudeau, Pierre (Elliott) (1919–) Canadian politician. Educated at Montreal,

Harvard, and London, he became a lawyer, helped to found the political magazine, *Cité Libre* (1950), and was Professor of Law at the University of Montreal (1961–5). Elected a Liberal MP in 1965, he became Minister of Justice (1967) and an outspoken critic of Québecois **séparatisme**. His term of office as Prime Minister (1968–79 and 1980–4) saw the **October Crisis** (1970) in Quebec, the introduction of the Official Languages Act, federalist victory during the Quebec Referendum (1980), and the introduction of the **Constitution Act of 1982**. He resigned as leader of the **Liberal Party** and from public life in 1984.

Trujillo (Molina), Rafael Leonidas (1891–1961) Dominican Republic dictator. He was dictator of the Dominican Republic from 1930 until his assassination in Santo Domingo, a city he had renamed Ciudad Trujillo. Born in San Cristóbal, Dominican Republic, he rose to prominence as commander of the police. His regime was both highly repressive and highly corrupt.

Truman, Harry S (1884–1972) US politician and 33rd President. He fought in **World War I**, was a presiding judge in the Jackson County Court in Missouri (1926–34), was elected to the US Senate as a Democrat in 1934 and became chairman of a senate committee investigating defence spending. He became Vice-President (1944) and, on Franklin D **Roosevelt**'s death (Apr 1945), President. He was re-elected in 1948 in a surprise victory over Thomas E Dewey. As president (1945–53) he ordered the dropping of the first atomic bomb on Japan in Aug 1945, which led to Japan's surrender. Following **World War II**, he established a 'containment' policy against the USSR, developed the **Marshall Plan** to rebuild Europe and created **NATO** (1949). He authorized the sending of US troops to South Korea in 1950, and promoted the Four-Point Programme that gave military and economic aid to countries threatened by communist interference. He established the CIA (1947) and ordered the **Berlin Airlift** (1948–9). At home, he introduced his '**Fair Deal**' programme of economic reform. ▷ **Democratic Party**

Trumbić, Ante (1864–1938) Croatian politician. A proponent of **trialism**, with Frano **Supilo** he founded the Croatian Social Democrat Party in 1895. During **World War I** he was a founder and President of the **Yugoslav Committee**, helping to formulate the Declaration of Corfu in which the Committee

and the Serbian government agreed to cooperate in establishing a South Slav state (July 1917). He was Minister for Foreign Affairs in the post-1918 Provisional Government but became disillusioned with the Serb nationalist programme of Nikola **Pašić** and **Alexander I** and retired from political life in 1921.

Trusteeship A system developed by the **UN** after 1945 for the international supervision of colonial territories that had been removed from the German and Ottoman empires at the end of **World War I**. These territories had been supervised originally under the mandates commission of the **League of Nations** and mandates in the Middle East, Africa and the South Pacific were held by Britain, France, South Africa, Australia and New Zealand. Only South Africa refused to hand over South-West Africa (now Namibia) to the UN, leading to the long-running dispute over the independence of that territory. The British Palestine mandate became the setting for Arab/Jewish conflict and the British were forced to hand it over to the UN in 1948. The trusteeship system, in internationalizing key areas of colonial rule, has been seen as pressing forward decolonization.

Truth, Sojourner (c.1797–1883) US abolitionist. Born into slavery in New York State, she escaped from her master in 1827 and settled in New York City, where she involved herself in the religious enthusiasms of the day until 1843, when she became a travelling preacher. She joined the abolitionist movement and became an effective antislavery speaker. She eventually settled in Battle Creek, Michigan but remained active after the Civil War in the causes of freed slaves and also of women's rights. ▷ **abolitionism**

Ts'ai Ch'ang ▷ **Cai Chang**

Tsai T'ien ▷ **Zai Tian**

Tsankov, Alexander (1879–1959) Bulgarian politician. He became Prime Minister in 1923 after the military coup which overthrew **Stamboliski**. Drawing his support from a coalition of parties called the Democratic Concord, his government tried to eliminate **VMRO** and the Bulgarian Communist Party. In Jan 1926 he was replaced by Andrei Liapchev.

Ts'ao Ts'ao ▷ **Cao Cao**

Tseng Kuo-fan ▷ **Zeng Guofan**

Tshombe, Moise Kapenda (1919–69) Congolese politician. Educated in mission schools, he was a businessman who helped to found the Confederation des Associations du Katanga in 1957. When Belgium granted the Congo independence in 1960, he declared the copper-rich province of Katanga independent and became its President. On the request of **Lumumba**, **UN** troops were called in to reintegrate the province and Tshombe was forced into exile in 1963; he returned again in 1964, supported by some of the mining interests and white settlers of Katanga. Forced into exile again after **Mobutu**'s 1966 coup, Tshombe was kidnapped in 1967 and taken to Algeria, where he died. A talented conservative, he became the representation of neo-colonialism's ugly face in the mythology of African nationalism throughout the continent.

Tsintsars Hellenized, multilingual, city-dwelling Vlach merchants in Greece, **Macedonia** and **Serbia**. ▷ **Vlachs**

Tsiranana, Philibert (1912–) Madagascar politician. Educated on the island and in France, he organized the Social Democratic Party, on whose ticket he was elected a member of the Representative Assembly in 1956, as well as the French National Assembly in 1957. He was Deputy President of Madagascar in 1958 and President in the following year. He remained in the post until being overthrown in a military coup in 1972.

Tsouderos, Emmanuel (1882–1956) Greek politician. A banker from Crete, he was a republican and follower of Eleuthérios **Venizélos**. In Apr 1940, after the suicide of Alexander Koryzis, he became Prime Minister and fled with King **George II** after Greece's surrender to Germany. He continued as Prime Minister in the Greek government-in-exile but, following the mutinies in the Greek Army and Navy in Egypt (Apr 1944), he was succeeded briefly by Sofoklis **Venizélos** and then by George **Papandreou**.

Tsushima, Battle of (27 May 1905) Admiral Togo's crushing victory over the Russian Baltic fleet, in the Tsushima Straits, during the **Russo-Japanese War**. It is remarkable for being the only instance in world history of a decisive engagement between all-gun iron-clad ships. The battle gave the Japanese naval supremacy and dashed Russian hopes of achieving a land victory.

Tuan Ch'i-jui ▷ **Duan Qirui**

Tubman, Harriet (c.1820–1913) US abolitionist. She escaped from slavery in Maryland (1849), and from then until the **American Civil War** she was active on the slave escape route (the **Underground Railroad**), making a number of dangerous trips into the South. She acquired fame among abolitionists, and counselled John **Brown** before his attempt to launch a slave insurrection in 1859. During the Civil War she was a Northern spy and scout, but was denied a federal pension until 1897. ▷ **abolitionism**

Tubman, William V S (1895–1971) Liberian politician. Educated in a methodist seminary, he was a teacher, lawyer and Methodist preacher. Tubman was elected for the True Whig Party, which protected the interests of the Americo-Liberian elite, and became a member of the Liberian Senate in 1922. In 1937 he was appointed Deputy President of the Supreme Court and, in 1944, was chosen as President of Liberia, a post he retained until his death.

Tudeh The Communist Party of Iran, founded in 1920. It had the varying fortunes to be expected of a communist party in a primarily Islamic state and despite its temporary demise in 1930, it had its heyday with the Soviet intervention in Northern Iran during **World War II**. It helped, with the USSR, in the founding of the Kurdish Republic of Mahabad which lasted about a year, but was itself again outlawed in 1946. Surfacing yet again to support the left wing leader Mosaddeq in the early fifties, the Tudah Party was once more banned, this time by Shah Muhammad Reza.

Tudjman, Franjo (1922–) Croatian politician and historian. He served in the partisan army led by **Tito** and in 1945 became the youngest general in the Yugoslav Federal Army. In 1972 he was imprisoned during the purge of the Croatian nationalist movement and in 1981 was again sentenced to three years' imprisonment in the first major political trial since Tito's death. A professor of modern history at the Faculty of Political Science at Zagreb, he became Chairman of the History of the Workers' Movement of Croatia. Following the elections in Apr 1990, as leader of the right-wing Croatian Democratic Union, he became President of Croatia. He declared the Republic of Croatia's independence from the Yugoslav federation (25 June 1992), but the republic soon found itself engaged in a brutal war against the Yugoslav Federal Army, which occupied eastern Slavonia, besieged and destroyed Vukovar and shelled cities and towns, including Dubrovnik, on the Dalmatian coast. While international recognition of the independence of the Republic of Croatia followed in Dec 1991 and spring 1992, over a third of the republic still remained beyond the reach of Tudjman's government in Zagreb. He was re-elected as President of Croatia in Sep 1992.

Tudor, House of A North Wales gentry family, one of whose scions married a Plantagenet in the early 15c. Elevated to the peerage in the mid-15c, they ruled England from 1485 to 1603. The dynasty began when Henry (later **Henry VII**), 2nd Earl of Richmond and son of Margaret Beaufort (a Lancastrian claimant to the crown), overthrew **Richard III** in 1485. It ended with **Elizabeth I**'s death in 1603. ▷ **Edward VI; Henry VIII; Mary I; Plantagenet Dynasty**

Tu Duc (1829–83) Emperor of Vietnam (1847/83). His reign saw the establishment of French rule over the whole of Vietnam. These years were marked by frequent outbreaks of internal rebellion and by a series of severe natural disasters. Allied with his own profoundly pessimistic and diffident nature, these circumstances fatally handicapped the Vietnamese court as it sought to come to terms with French commercial, religious and territorial ambitions from the late 1850s. By treaties concluded in 1862 and 1874 against a background of severe internal unrest, Tu Duc was forced into major concessions to France. His death provoked a major succession crisis, during which the French finally achieved complete domination over Vietnam.

Tughlaq Dynasty Indian dynasty, which came to power in Delhi in 1320, when Ghiyasuddin Tughlaq raised the banner of revolt against the much-weakened **Khaljis** and defeated Khusrau. Ghiyasuddin Tughlaq established a new dynasty which ruled until 1412. The Tughlaqs provided three competent rulers: Ghiyasuddin, his son, **Muhammad bin Tughlaq** (1324/51), and his nephew, Firuz Shah Tughlaq (1351–87). The first two of these rulers ruled over an empire which comprised almost the entire subcontinent; the empire of Firuz was smaller but still almost as large as that of Allauddin Khalji. After Firuz's death, the **Delhi Sultanate** disintegrated and north India was divided into a series of small states. Although the

Tughlaqs continued to rule until 1412, the invasion of Delhi by **Timur** in 1398 may be said to mark the end of their empire.

Tughrul Beg, Muhammad (c.990–1063) He was the grandson of Seljuk, a leader of Ghuzz tribesmen in central Asia from whom the Great Seljuks derive their name. Tughrul (or Toghril) moved westwards through Khurasan and Persia and in 1055 was welcomed by the 'Abbasid caliph, al-Qa'im, particularly because his arrival put an end to Buyid control of Baghdad and the central Islamic lands (a matter of some embarrassment to the (Sunni) Caliph since the Buyids were Shiite). There was a hiccup in that during a temporary absence of Tughrul, the general al-Basasiri, previously in the Buyid camp, but now a Fatimid supporter, re-emerged in Baghdad and forced him to recognize the suzerainty of the Fatimid al-Mustansir in Cairo. This was however short-lived for with the return of Tughrul Sunni control of Baghdad was restored. Tughrul died in 1063 to be succeeded by his nephew, Alp Arslan.

Tuka, Vojtech (1880–1946) Slovak politician. Of Magyar parentage and pro-Hungarian orientation, he was a member of **Hlinka**'s Slovak Populist Party during the 1920s and encouraged it to be more assertive in demanding Slovak autonomy. But in 1929 he was proved to be a Hungarian agent and was imprisoned, to the serious embarrassment of Hlinka and the whole party. In 1939 he reappeared as Deputy Prime Minister and then as Prime and Foreign Minister in the puppet government of **Tiso**. In 1946 he was condemned to death.

Tukhachevsky, Mikhail Nikolaevich (1893–1937) Soviet military leader. From 1926 he was Chief-of-Staff of the **Red Army**, which he was influential in transforming from a peasant army into a modern, mechanized force. His vigour and independence made him suspect to **Stalin**, and in 1937 he was executed, an early victim of the great purge which decimated the Red Army's officer corps.

Tulip Mania (1634–7) A speculation bubble on the markets of the Dutch Republic; highly advanced financial institutions and an excess of capital led to spiralling prices for tulip bulbs, for which sometimes gigantic sums of money changed hands, based on the estimated resale price rather than on any intrinsic value. The bubble burst in 1637, ruining many throughout Dutch society.

Tulsidas (1532–1623) Indian poet. His most famous work is the *Ramcharitmanas*, which is the *Ramayana* retold in a simple and popular form. Pleading for a modified **caste** system based not on birth but on individual qualities, Tulsidas was essentially a humanistic poet, who upheld family ideals and complete devotion to the Hindu god, Rama, as a way of salvation open to all, irrespective of caste. He is considered a very prominent poet from the Bhakti Movement, whose religious ideas have had a profound, and egalitarian, effect on Indian social development.

Tulunid Dynasty The dynasty, founded and named after a Turk, Ahmad ibn Tulun, which ruled from 868 until 905 in Egypt and Syria, with its capital at Fustat. It was under Ahmad that Egypt first emerged as an independent state during the Islamic era, the effective declaration of which was the refusal by Ahmad to assist the 'Abbasid caliph, al-Mu'tamid, financially when the latter was faced with the Zanj revolt. Ahmad made a considerable contribution to the development of Egyptian agriculture with his irrigation schemes, he beautified the capital architecturally, and underpinned his authority by his strict control of army organization. Under his more extravagant and personally weaker progeny, Tulunid power declined, with the country returning to 'Abbasid rule under his son, Shayban (904/5). ▷ 'Abbasid Dynasty; Fatimid Dynasty

Tung Chung-shu ▷ **Dong Zhongshu**

Tunglin Movement ▷ **Donglin Movement**

Tupamaros Uruguayan urban guerrillas belonging to the *Movimiento de Liberación Nacional* (National Liberation Movement). The movement was founded by Raúl Sendic, a labour organizer, in 1963 and was named after the 18c Peruvian Indian rebel, Tupac Amaru. The organization was suppressed by the military-controlled government of 1972–85, and since then has been re-created as a legitimate political party.

Tupolev, Andrei Nikolaevich (1888–1972) Soviet military and civilian aircraft designer. The son of a lawyer and product of Moscow Higher Technical School, he was already working in a Moscow aircraft factory in the pre-revolutionary period. In the 1920s and 1930s he designed several bombers of world class, and even when imprisoned on false accusations of treason in 1937 he combined designing and was therefore released in 1943.

Subsequently he worked on everything down to the supersonic passenger plane, becoming the best-known international name in the business and keeping the Soviet air force at least on a par with the American.

Tupper, Charles (1821–1915) Canadian politician and diplomat. As Nova Scotia's Premier (1864–7), his was the primary responsibility for persuading it to join the confederation; but Joseph **Howe**'s opposition had been so effective that he delayed until John A **Macdonald** persuaded the imperial government to apply direct pressure, and terms more favourable to Nova Scotia had been included. He entered Macdonald's administration in 1870 and again in 1878. In 1884 he became High Commissioner in London and in 1896 Secretary of State in Mackenzie Bowell's short-lived government. In the same year he himself became Premier for 10 weeks and committed the havering Conservative Party to remedial legislation in the controversy over the **Manitoba Schools Act**. The bill was talked out, however, and after the Liberals won the election of 1896, he led the Conservative opposition until 1900.

Turati, Filippo (1857–1932) Italian politician. In 1892 he helped to found the party that three years later was to become the Italian Socialist Party (PSI). He was elected deputy in 1896 and remained one until he fled the country in 1926. In 1898 he was condemned to 12 years' imprisonment for his part in protests in Milan, but was released the following year. He refused to participate in **Giolitti**'s governments, but was always on the moderate wing of the socialist movement. He opposed the **Tripolitanian War** and Italian intervention in 1915. In the aftermath of **World War I** and the Bolshevik Revolution, Turati found it hard to check the increasing radicalism of the PSI; he left the party when it joined the Third International (1919) and founded the Socialist Unity Party. With the assertion of fascist power, he fled Italy for France, where he died.

Turenne, Henri de la Tour d'Auvergne, Viscount of (1611–75) French marshal. The grandson of William the Silent, in the **Thirty Years War** he fought with distinction for the armies of the Protestant alliance. He captured Breisach (1638) and Turin (1640), and for the conquest of Roussillon from the Spaniards (1642) was made Marshal of France (1643). In the civil wars of the **Fronde**, he joined the *frondeurs* at first, but then switched sides; his campaigning (1652–3)

931

saved the young King **Louis XIV** and **Mazarin**'s government. In the Franco-Spanish war he conquered much of the Spanish Netherlands after defeating Louis II de Bourbon, Prince of **Condé** at the Battle of the Dunes (1658). He won lasting fame for his campaigns in the United Provinces during the Dutch War (1672–5), but advancing along the Rhine he was killed at Sasbach.

Turgot, Anne Robert Jacques (1727–81) French economist and politician. He became a magistrate in the **Parlement** of Paris and was then promoted to Intendant at Limoges (1761–74), where he carried out reforms. Here he published his best-known work, *Réflexions sur la formation et la distribution des richesses* (1766). Appointed Controller-General of Finance by **Louis XVI** (1774), he embarked on a comprehensive scheme of national economic reform, but the opposition of the privileged classes to his Six Edicts led to his overthrow (1776), and he died forgotten, his reforms abandoned.

Turkish Wars (1662–4 and 1683–9) The campaigns undertaken by Emperor Leopold I (1657–1705) to drive the Turks from Hungary. The first ended with an Austrian victory at St Gothard and the Peace of Vasvár (1644). In the second, persecution of Hungarian Protestants by the Emperor led them to ally with the Turks who marched, for the last time, on Vienna itself (1683). The Turks were defeated by John Sobieski on 12 Sep 1683. A string of Turkish defeats followed: Párkány (1683), Esztergom (1685), the fall of Budapest (1686), Mohács and the fall of Belgrade (1688), **Slankamen** (1691), and Zenta (1697). The Treaty of **Karlowitz** (1699) ended the wars with substantial Turkish concessions.

Turkmanchai, Treaty of (Feb 1828) The treaty under which Russia acquired eastern Armenia from the Persian Empire. Russian expansion southwards continued from **Alexander I**'s reign into **Nicholas I**'s, and following almost three years of fighting the foundations were laid for control of the Caucasus. This kind of warfare also became almost standard training for the Russian army.

Turner, Nat (1800–31) US slave insurrectionary. He learned to read, and in 1831 planned a slave uprising. He succeeded in killing his master's family and some 50 other whites, but as many as 100 slaves were killed and the revolt quickly collapsed. Captured after six weeks in hiding, he was brought to trial and hanged at Jerusalem, Virginia.

Tutankhamun (Nebkheperure) (c.1352/1343BC) King of Egypt. Made famous through the discovery in 1922 by Lord Carnarvon and Howard Carter of his virtually intact tomb with its treasures in the Valley of the Kings in Upper Egypt, he was nine years old when he came to the throne. As Tutankhaten, he succeeded Smenkhkare, who had been co-regent with Akhenaten and duly married the priestess Ankhesenpaaten. In his nine-year reign the king reconciled the priesthood of Amun after the Amarna interlude. The 'Restoration Stela' from Karnak discloses the confused state of Egypt and the measures taken to regain confidence, repair shrines and revive offerings and services in the temples. The worship of Amun was restored and the king and queen changed their names to Tutankhamun and Ankhesenamun respectively. Tutankhamun died in his 19th year. He left no children, and was the last male of the 18th Dynasty royal family. The application of modern medical techniques to the mummified remains of the Tutankhamun and Smenkhkare have proved them to be brothers, but uncertainty still surrounds the identity of their father.

Tuthmosis I, III ▷ **Thutmose I, III**

Tutu, Desmond Mpilo (1931–) South African cleric. Educated in mission schools and at Pretoria Bantu Normal College, he studied at St Peter's Theological College and King's College, London. He was ordained a deacon in the Anglican Church in 1960 and held a variety of church positions in England, South Africa and Lesotho, including lecturing at the Federal Theological Seminary in Cape Province (1967–9), the University of Botswana, Lesotho and Swaziland (1970–2). He returned from England to South Africa in 1975 as Dean of Johannesburg, from where he went to be Bishop of Lesotho. As Secretary-General of the South African Council of Churches from 1978 to 1985, he spoke out strongly from the relative safety of his church position against the extremes of **apartheid** and was awarded the Nobel Peace Prize in 1984. He was elected Bishop of Johannesburg in 1985 and Archbishop of Cape Town in 1986. A critic of the apartheid system, he has nonetheless also criticized violence in the townships.

Tvardovsky, Alexander Trifonovich (1910–71) Soviet poet, editor and **samizdat** publisher. Writing during and after **World War I**, he was editor of *Novy Mir* in the years 1958–70 when he exposed the excesses of

Stalinism; for example, he secured the publication of Alexander **Solzhenitsyn**'s *One Day in the Life of Ivan Denisovich*. His task became increasingly difficult following Leonid **Brezhnev**'s rise to power in 1964, hence his resort to underground publication. However, he had laid the foundations for the **Gorbachev** years of open debate.

Tver Manifesto (1894) An appeal made by the Tver **zemstvo** to the new tsar, **Nicholas II**, that institutions such as theirs should have the opportunity and the right to express their opinions to him. It was composed by a talented lawyer, Fedor Rodichev, but it evoked the reply in 1895 that the **zemstvo** had been 'carried away by senseless dreams', and that Nicholas would 'uphold the principle of autocracy', which he did until he was forced to abdicate in 1917.

Tvrtko I (1353/91) King of Bosnia. The greatest of all the Bosnian rulers, he assumed the royal title and laid claim to the thrones of **Serbia**, **Dalmatia** and **Croatia**. During his reign, Bosnia included all the Dalmatian towns except Zadar and Dubrovnik and became a stronghold of the heretical **Bogomils**.

Twelve Tables Drawn up by a commission of 10 men in 451–450BC, this was the first attempt by the Romans to codify their laws. Produced under pressure from the plebeians, their publication (on 12 tablets) was intended to curb the power of the patricians. Although the original tablets themselves do not survive, quotations from them in ancient authors indicate that they contained rulings from all branches of the law as it existed at that time.

Twelve Years' Truce (1609–21) Extended cease-fire in the **Eighty Years War** between Spain and the Netherlands, thus giving a welcome rest to the war-exhausted parties and especially to the southern Netherlands after 41 years of being a theatre of war. The truce was against the wishes of the Dutch Stadholder **Maurice** of Nassau, but forced by the states party which needed peace to restore its trade. During the truce, conflict flared up in the Dutch Republic between Maurice and the states party (led by Oldenbarnevelt), much of it manifested in the struggle between the **Remonstrants** and the **Counter-Remonstrants**. The Orange Party won the struggle, removed the states leaders from power, and renewed the war with Spain in 1621. ▷ **Stadholder**

Twenty-Four Parganas Revenue districts ceded to the British **East India Company** by Mir Jafar, Nawab of Bengal, in 1757.

Twenty-One Demands A series of demands presented by Japan to China in 1915, which included: the recognition of Japanese control of **Manchuria**, Shandong, Inner Mongolia, south-eastern China and the Yangzi Valley; the imposition of Japanese advisers in the Chinese administration; and the compulsory purchase of 50 per cent of its munitions from Japan. President **Yuan Shikai** accepted them as the basis of a treaty, but the resulting popular patriotic protest movement gave impetus to the rise of Chinese nationalism.

Two Sicilies, Kingdom of the The Bourbon kingdom in the south of Italy, restored in 1815 after the collapse of Joachim **Murat**'s Kingdom of Naples, and comprising the Island of Sicily and that part of the peninsula lying to the south of the **Papal States**. It ceased to exist in 1860 after it was successfully overrun by **Garibaldi** and annexed by **Victor Emmanuel II**.

Tyler, John (1790–1862) US politician and 10th President. He became a lawyer, member of the Virginia state legislature (1811–16), a US Congressman (1817–21), Governor of Virginia (1825–7), and then a US Senator (1827–36). Elected Vice-President in 1840, he became President on the death of William Henry **Harrison** in 1841, only a month after his inauguration. He remained in office from 1841–5. His most important accomplishments were the annexation of Texas and the **Webster–Ashburton Treaty**. He later remained active in politics, adhering to the Confederate cause until his death.

Tyler, Wat (d.1381) English leader of the **Peasants Revolt** (1381). The rebels of Kent, after taking Rochester Castle, chose him as captain, and marched to Canterbury and London. At the Smithfield conference with **Richard II** blows were exchanged, and Tyler was wounded by the Mayor of London, William Walworth. He was taken to St Bartholomew's Hospital, where Walworth had him dragged out and beheaded.

tyrant In Greek city-states of the 7c and 6c BC, a neutral term, possibly of Lydian origin, simply describing an absolute ruler who had seized power illegally. Only later (5c BC) did it acquire its present meaning: a cruel and oppressive ruler. ▷ **Lydia**

Tzimisces, John I ▷ **John I Tzimisces**

U

U-2 Incident (1960) On 1 May 1960 a US U-2 spy plane was brought down over Sverdlovsk in the USSR. After US denials, Premier Nikita **Khrushchev** produced the pilot, Francis Gary Powers, and his photographs of military installations. President **Eisenhower** justified the flights as essential for US national security. Khrushchev took advantage of the situation at the scheduled Paris Summit Meeting a few days later, when he withdrew Eisenhower's invitation to visit the USSR and demanded that he condemn the flights. The President's refusal allowed Khrushchev to walk out of the summit and to blame the USA for its failure.

U-boat An abbreviation of the German *Unterseeboot* ('submarine'). The German Navy launched large-scale submarine offensives in both world wars, and each time the U-boats came close to victory.

UCD (*Unión Central Democrática*, 'Central Democratic Union') (1977–82) A coalition of liberal, regional, Christian and social democratic groups under the leadership of Adolfo **Suárez** which formed a political party after its success in the 1977 Spanish general election. Having formed the minority governments of 1977–82, numerous schisms and defections, caused by struggles over the party apparatus and ideological differences, led to the Union's rout in the 1982 election and its disbandment shortly thereafter. However, although it had failed as a party, the UCD had succeeded in transforming Spain from a dictatorship into a democracy.

UDI (Unilateral Declaration of Independence) (11 Nov 1965) The declaration by Ian **Smith**'s Rhodesia Front government which attempted to maintain white supremacy in Southern Rhodesia (Zimbabwe). After the dissolution of the Central African Federation at the end of 1963, Nyasaland and Northern Rhodesia achieved independence as Malawi and Zambia. The British government then expected that Southern Rhodesia would also pursue unimpeded progress to black majority rule, but the white settlers attempted to maintain their dominance of the economy and politics of the territory. Harold **Wilson**'s British Labour government declined to use force against them, but imposed sanctions. Because of South Africa's initial support of Rhodesia, these took some time to take effect, but the Smith regime was ultimately defeated by guerrilla incursions from Zambia and Mozambique and by economic collapse. Zimbabwe achieved its independence in 1980.

Uganda Martyrs A group of 22 African youths, converted to Roman Catholicism, who were killed for their faith in Uganda between 1885 and 1887. Canonized in 1964, they were among a number of Christians put to death in the reign of King Mutesa II of Buganda.

Ugolino della Gherardesca, Count (d.1289) Ghibelline Count of Donoratico. By intriguing with Pisa's enemies and treachery in the city itself, Ugolino came to power in 1284. The tyrant was overthrown in 1289, and he and his relations starved to death in the tower to which they were confined. The grisly episode is recalled in Dante's *Inferno*. ▷ **Ghibellines**

UGT (Unión General de Trabajadores, 'General Union of Workers') Spanish socialist trade union movement. The UGT grew extremely slowly after its foundation in 1888, not achieving a national presence until the Second Republic of 1931–6. Throughout this period it was distinguished by its rigid centralism, ideological confusion, and practical moderation. The pragmatism of the UGT was shown above all by its collaboration with the dictatorship of Miguel **Primo de Rivera** (1923–30) in an effort to reshape the trade unions along corporatist lines. Under the Second Republic the UGT grew spectacularly, especially among the landless day labourers. The failure of reform led to demands for action from an increasingly militant rank and file, culminating in the agricultural strike of June 1934 and the general strike and rising of Oct 1934. The defeat of these protests and their savage repression led the UGT to adopt a revolutionary line in 1935, though it still backed the Popular Front in the general election of Feb 1936. Once the Popular Front came to power, the UGT's rural section, frustrated by the lack of reform, encouraged landless labourers to take the law into their own hands, thereby polarizing the political climate further. During the **Spanish Civil War** the UGT lost more and more influence to the **PCE** and b y the end of the war it had been torn apart by internal divisions. Like the **PSOE**, it played an extremely limited role in the opposition to the **Franco** regime. With the restoration of democracy in Spain in 1977, the UGT was re-established. By 1982 it had become the largest trade union body in Spain, but it fell out with the socialist government in 1988 over its modernization programme. ▷ **Republic, Second** (Spain)

Uighurs One of China's national minorities, now numbering over 6 million and for the most part settled in Xinjiang. They are a people of Turkic origin who emerged as an independent force as early as the 7c. They developed their own script, and practised a religion which was a form of Manicheism.

Uitlanders The name given to Europeans of a variety of national origins who flocked to the Transvaal after the discovery of gold there in 1886. They soon came to outnumber the Boers who feared that they would be politically and culturally swamped. Their grievances, particularly relating to the franchise and citizenship rights, were used by Sir Alfred Milner and the British as a pretext for the escalation of tension which led to the **Boer Wars**.

Ujamaa A Swahili word, usually translated as 'familyhood', which is applied to the special brand of African Socialism espoused by Julius **Nyerere** in Tanzania. It emphasizes cooperation and equality, and it is based upon his conception of traditional African society.

UK (United Kingdom of Great Britain and Northern Ireland) A kingdom in western Europe, comprising England, Scotland, Wales and Northern Ireland. Wales was effectively joined to England in 1301, then Scotland was joined under one crown in 1603 (and by legislative union in 1707) and Ireland in 1801 (the United Kingdom of Great Britain and Ireland). The present name dates from 1922, following the establishment of the **Irish Free State**. The UK has a population of 57.2m (1989e). It is a kingdom with a monarch as head of state, governed by a bicameral parliament comprising an elected 650-member House of Commons and a House of Lords with hereditary peers, life

peers, Anglican bishops, and law lords. A Cabinet is appointed by the Prime Minister. See table p936. ▷ **Union, Acts of**

Ulbricht, Walter (1893–1973) East German politician. At first a cabinetmaker, he entered politics in 1912, and in 1928 became communist Deputy for Potsdam. He left Germany on **Hitler**'s rise in 1933, spending most of his exile in the USSR. In 1945 he returned as head of the German Communist Party (**KPD**), and became Deputy Premier of the German Democratic Republic and General-Secretary of the Socialist Unity Party (**SED**) in 1950. He was largely responsible for the 'sovietization' of East **Germany**, and had the **Berlin Wall** built in 1961. ▷ **communism**

Ulrich (890–973) Bishop of Augsburg. Educated in St Gallen, he became Bishop of Augsburg in 923 and made it an important centre for church reforms. He was a loyal servant of **Otto I, 'the Great'**, supporting him during the uprising of his son Liudolf (952/4) and finally mediating between the two. In 955 he successfully defended Augsburg, which he had newly fortified, against the Hungarians, and took part in the final defeat of the Hungarians at the Battle of the Lechfeld. He was canonized in 993.

Ulrich of Württemberg (1487–1550) Duke of Württemberg, his excessive taxes sparked a peasant rebellion in 1514. He was expelled from his possessions in 1519 by the Swabian League and did not recover them until 1534. He was a Lutheran and a member of the Schmalkaldic League.

Ulrika Eleonora (1688–1741) Queen of Sweden (1719/20). The younger sister of, and successor to, **Charles XII**, she married Prince Frederick of Hesse in 1714, and declared herself Queen after her brother's death. She was, however, compelled by the Estates to renounce her hereditary right to the throne. She was subsequently elected to the throne on condition that she accepted a new constitution which severely limited royal power. She found these limitations difficult to accept and in 1720 agreed to abdicate in favour of her husband, who ascended the throne as Frederick I.

Ulster 'Troubles' The name conventionally given to violence in Northern Ireland from 1968. They originated in conflict between Catholics and Protestants over civil rights and perceived discrimination against the Catholic minority in the Province. The promise of

UNITED KINGDOM: PRIME MINISTERS

Dates	Name	Party	Dates	Name	Party
1721–42	Robert Walpole	Whig	1855–8	Viscount Palmerston (Henry	
1742–3	Earl of Wilmington (Spencer			John Temple)	Lib
	Compton)	Whig	1858–9	Earl of Derby	Con
1743–54	Henry Pelham	Whig	1859–65	Viscount Palmerston	Lib
1754–6	Duke of Newcastle (Thomas		1865–6	Lord John Russell	Lib
	Pelham-Holles)	Whig	1866–8	Earl of Derby	Con
1756–7	Duke of Devonshire (William		1868	Benjamin Disraeli	Con
	Cavendish)	Whig	1868–74	William Ewart Gladstone	Lib
1757–62	Duke of Newcastle	Whig	1874–80	Benjamin Disraeli	Con
1762–3	Earl of Bute (John Stuart)	Tory	1880–5	William Ewart Gladstone	Lib
1763–5	George Grenville	Whig	1885–6	Marquess of Salisbury (Robert	
1765–6	Marquess of Rockingham			Gascoyne-Cecil)	Con
	(Charles Watson Wentworth)	Whig	1886	William Ewart Gladstone	Lib
1766–70	Duke of Grafton (Augustus		1886–92	Marquess of Salisbury	Con
	Henry Fitzroy)	Whig	1892–4	William Ewart Gladstone	Lib
1770–82	Lord North (Frederick North)	Tory	1894–5	Earl of Rosebery (Archibald	
1782	Marquess of Rockingham	Whig		Philip Primrose)	Lib
1782–3	Earl of Shelburne (William		1895–1902	Marquess of Salisbury	Con
	Petty-Fitzmaurice)	Whig	1902–5	Arthur James Balfour	Con
1783	Duke of Portland (William		1905–8	Henry Campbell-Bannerman	Lib
	Henry Cavendish)	Coal	1908–15	Herbert Henry Asquith	Lib
1783–1801	William Pitt	Tory	1915–16	Herbert Henry Asquith	Coal
1801–4	Henry Addington	Tory	1916–22	David Lloyd George	Coal
1804–6	William Pitt	Tory	1922–3	Andrew Bonar Law	Con
1806–7	Lord Grenville (William		1923–4	Stanley Baldwin	Con
	Wyndham)	Whig	1924	James Ramsay MacDonald	Lab
1807–9	Duke of Portland	Tory	1924–9	Stanley Baldwin	Con
1809–12	Spencer Perceval	Tory	1929–31	James Ramsay MacDonald	Lab
1812–27	Earl of Liverpool (Robert		1931–5	James Ramsay MacDonald	Nat
	Banks Jenkinson)	Tory	1935–7	Stanley Baldwin	Nat
1827	George Canning	Tory	1937–40	Arthur Neville Chamberlain	Nat
1827–8	Viscount Goderich (Frederick		1940–5	Winston Churchill	Coal
	John Robinson)	Tory	1945–51	Clement Attlee	Lab
1828–30	Duke of Wellington (Arthur		1951–5	Winston Churchill	Con
	Wellesley)	Tory	1955–7	Anthony Eden	Con
1830–4	Earl Grey (Charles Grey)	Whig	1957–63	Harold Macmillan	Con
1834	Viscount Melbourne (William		1963–4	Alex Douglas-Home	Con
	Lamb)	Whig	1964–70	Harold Wilson	Lab
1834–5	Robert Peel	Con	1970–4	Edward Heath	Con
1835–41	Viscount Melbourne	Whig	1974–6	Harold Wilson	Lab
1841–6	Robert Peel	Con	1976–9	James Callaghan	Lab
1846–52	Lord John Russell	Lib	1979–90	Margaret Thatcher	Con
1852	Earl of Derby (Edward		1990–	John Major	Con
	George Stanley)	Con			
1852–5	Lord Aberdeen (George				
	Hamilton-Gordon)	Peelite			

Coal Coalition
Con Conservative
Lab Labour
Lib Liberal
Nat Nationalist

reforms by the Ulster Premier Terence O'Neill lost him the confidence of loyalists in his Unionist Party and he resigned in 1969. Reforms implemented by his successor, James Chichester-Clark, provoked rioting between Protestants and Catholics and an increase in the specific acts of sectarian violence. The British Army was sent to maintain peace in 1969 but continuing violence resulted in the imposition of internment without trial for Catholics only under Brian Faulkner's administration. Anti-British Army feeling among the Catholics and mainland **IRA** attacks increased markedly after the **Bloody Sunday** demonstrations (30 Jan 1972) and direct rule was imposed in Mar.

In Dec 1973, the British, Ulster and Irish governments signed the power-sharing Sunningdale Agreement, providing for representation in the Province's government of both the Catholic and Protestant populations, but continued Protestant Unionist resistance to the agreement led to the collapse of the **Stormont** executive in May 1974. Since then Ulster has been ruled directly from Westminster and sectarian killings have continued. The IRA has from time to time concentrated its attention on England with bombings and assassinations of prominent Conservative politicians, such as Airey Neave in 1979 and Ian Gow in 1990. Political initiatives to find a solution to an apparently intractable problem have been frustrated.

Ultramontanism Literally, 'beyond the mountains'; a movement, deriving from France, asserting the centralization of the authority and power of the Roman Catholic Church in Rome and the Pope. It gained impetus after the **French Revolution** (1789), and reached its high point with the First Vatican Council (1870) and the declaration of papal infallibility.

Ultras The name given to the extreme right in French politics (1815–30), because they were more royalist than the King, while **Louis XVIII** reigned; **Charles X** adopted Ultra policies and lost his throne in 1830; the leading Ultras were Villèle and **Polignac**.

'Umar (c.581–64) Second of the Rashidun, or 'Rightly-Guided' Caliphs (634/44). The father of one of the Prophet **Muhammad**'s wives, he succeeded **Abu Bakr**. He built up an empire comprising Persia, Syria, and all North Africa. He was assassinated at Medina by a slave.

Umar ibn Tal, al Hajj (c.1795–1864) A Tukulor from Futa Toro who made the pilgrimage to Mecca, he was a member of the highly disciplined Tijaniyya order, and led one of the important jihads in the western Sudan. He conquered Bambara, Segu and the territories formerly welded together by **Ahmadu ibn Hammada**. His conquests brought him into conflict with the French, but he recognized that he was not strong enough to dislodge them.

Umayyad Dynasty A Damascus-based dynasty, founded by the Muslim general **Mu'awiya**, which ruled from 661 until 750. It replaced the era of the four Medina-based Rashidun or 'Rightly-Guided' Caliphs, of whom the last, **'Ali**, was murdered in 661. See map p938. ▷ 'Abbasid Dynasty

Umberto I (1844–1900) King of Italy (1878/1900). The son and successor of **Victor Emmanuel II**, he distinguished himself at the Battle of **Custozza**. He is often portrayed as a model constitutional monarch, who despite his conservative sympathies and considerable pressure from reactionary politicians, rarely interfered in parliamentary affairs. In reality, he was perfectly content to block ministerial appointments and to use the royal prerogative, especially in matters concerning the army or foreign affairs. Despite a genuine concern for his subjects (manifest particularly at times of natural disaster: earthquakes, floods and epidemics), there were attempts on his life in 1878 and 1897, before he was finally assassinated by an anarchist.

Umberto II (1904–83) King of Italy (May/June 1946). Made *de facto* Regent ('Lieutenant-General of the Realm') by his father, **Victor Emmanuel III**, in June 1944, he ascended the throne on the latter's abdication in 1946, at a time when the monarchy had become widely unpopular. In a referendum later the same year 12718641 Italians voted in favour of a republic and 10718502 for the retention of the monarchy, most support for the latter stance being located in the **Mezzogiorno**. Victor Emmanuel was forced to leave Italy, setting up residence in Portugal as the self-styled Count Di Sarre.

Umkhonto we Sizwe The military wing (literally, 'Spear of the Nation') of the **ANC** (African National Congress), which was established when the party was banned. Its main bases were in Angola and its Chief of Staff in the 1980s was Joe **Slovo**. It has provided a number of the new generation of leaders in the ANC.

UMW ▷ United Mine Workers of America

UN (United Nations Organization) An organization formed to maintain world peace and foster international cooperation, formally established on 24 Oct 1945 with 51 founder countries. The UN Charter, which was drafted during the war by the USA, UK and USSR, remains virtually unaltered despite the growth in membership and activities. There are six 'principal organs'. The General Assembly is the plenary body which controls much of the UN's work, supervises the subsidiary organs, sets priorities, and debates major issues of international affairs. The

Islamic conquests in the Umayyad period (661–750)

Legend:

Umayyad lands in 661

Umayyad conquests

↑ Muslim advance to the East

↑ Muslim advance to the West

--- Arab attacks and invasions

✕ Battle

⇡ Arab naval and military attacks against Byzantine Empire

◎ Arab sieges of Constantinople (674–8 and 717–18)

Areas contested by Byzantines and Muslims

Byzantine Empire in the second half of the 7c

Byzantine Empire in 750

Chinese protectorate under the Tang Dynasty (618–907)

UNITED NATIONS MEMBERSHIP

Grouped according to year of entry

Date	
1945	Argentina, Australia, Belgium, Belorussian SSR, Bolivia, Brazil, Canada, Chile, China (Taiwan) (to 1971), Colombia, Costa Rica, Cuba, Czechoslovakia, Denmark, Dominican Republic, Ecuador, Egypt, El Salvador, Ethiopia, France, Greece, Guatemala, Haiti, Honduras, India, Iran, Iraq, Lebanon, Liberia, Luxembourg, Mexico, Netherlands, New Zealand, Nicaragua, Norway, Panama, Paraguay, Peru, Philippines, Poland, Saudi Arabia, South Africa, Syria, Turkey, Ukrainian SSR, USSR, UK, USA, Uruguay, Venezuela, Yugoslavia
1946	Afghanistan, Iceland, Sweden, Thailand
1947	Pakistan, Yemen
1948	Burma
1949	Israel
1950	Indonesia
1955	Albania, Austria, Bulgaria, Kampuchea (formerly Cambodia), Sri Lanka (formerly Ceylon), Finland, Hungary, Ireland, Italy, Jordan, Laos, Libya, Nepal, Portugal, Romania, Spain
1956	Japan, Morocco, Sudan, Tunisia
1957	Ghana, Malaya (Malaysia, 1963)
1958	Guinea
1960	Benin (formerly Dahomey), Burkina Faso (formerly Upper Volta), Cameroon, Central African Republic, Chad, Congo, Ivory Coast (Côte d'Ivoire), Cyprus, Gabon, Madagascar, Mali, Niger, Nigeria, Senegal, Somalia, Togo, Zaire
1961	Mauritania, Mongolia, Sierra Leone, Tanganyika (within Tanzania, 1964)

Date	
1962	Algeria, Burundi, Jamaica, Rwanda, Trinidad and Tobago, Uganda
1963	Kenya, Kuwait, Zanzibar (within Tanzania, 1964)
1964	Malawi, Malta, Zambia, Tanzania
1965	Gambia, Maldives, Singapore
1966	Barbados, Botswana, Guyana, Lesotho
1968	Equatorial Guinea, Mauritius, Swaziland
1970	Fiji
1971	Bahrain, Bhutan, China (People's Republic of), Oman, Qatar, United Arab Emirates
1973	Bahamas, German Democratic Republic, German Federal Republic
1974	Bangladesh, Grenada, Guinea-Bissau
1975	Cape Verde, Comoros, Mozambique, Papua New Guinea, São Tomé and Príncipe, Surinam
1976	Angola, Seychelles, Western Samoa
1977	Djibouti, Vietnam
1978	Dominica, Solomon Islands
1979	St Lucia
1980	St Vincent and the Grenadines, Zimbabwe
1981	Antigua and Barbuda, Belize, Vanuatu
1983	St Christopher and Nevis
1984	Brunei
1990	Namibia, Yemen (formerly North Yemen and South Yemen) (Germany replaced GDR and GFR)
1991	Estonia, Latvia, Lithuania, Marshall Islands, Micronesia, North Korea, Russia, South Korea
1992	Armenia, Azerbaijan, Kazakhstan, Kirgizia, Moldavia, San Marino, Tadzhikistan, Turkmenistan, Uzbekistan

15-member Security Council is dominated by the five permanent members (China, France, UK, USSR and USA) who each have the power of veto over any resolutions; the remaining 10 are elected for two-year periods. The primary role of the Council is to maintain international peace and security; its decisions, unlike those of the General Assembly, are binding on all other members. It is empowered to order mandatory sanctions, call for ceasefires, and establish peacekeeping forces (these forces were awarded the Nobel Peace Prize in 1988). The use of the veto has prevented it from intervening in a number of disputes, such as Vietnam. The Secretariat, under the Secretary-General, employs some 16000 at the UN's headquarters in New York City and 50000 worldwide. The staff are answerable only to the UN, not national governments, and are engaged in considerable diplomatic work. The Secretary-General is often a significant person in international diplomacy and is able to take independent initiatives. The International Court of Justice consists of 15 judges appointed by the Council and the Assembly. As only states can bring issues before it, its jurisdiction depends on the consent of the states who are a party to a dispute. It also offers advisory opinions to various organs of the UN. The Economic and Social Council is elected by the General Assembly; it supervises the work of various committees, commissions, and expert bodies in the economic and social area, and co-ordinates the work of UN specialized agencies. The Trusteeship Council oversees the transition of Trust territories to self-government. In addition to the organs established under the Charter, there is a range of subsidiary agencies, many with their own constitutions and membership, and some pre-dating the UN. The main such agencies are the Food and Agriculture Organization, the Inter-

UNITED NATIONS: SECRETARY-GENERAL

Dates	Name
1946–53	Trygve Lie
1953–61	Dag Hammarskjöld
1962–71	U Thant
1971–81	Kurt Waldheim
1982–91	Javier Pérez de Cuéllar
1991–	Boutros Boutros-Ghali

governmental Maritime Consultative Organization, the International Atomic Energy Authority, the International Bank for Reconstruction and Development ('World Bank'), the International Civil Aviation Organization, the International Development Association, the International Finance Corporation, the International Fund for Agricultural Development, the International Labour Organization, the International Monetary Fund, the United Nations Educational, Scientific and Cultural Organization, the Universal Postal Union, the International Telecommunication Union, the World Meteorological Organization, and the World Health Organization. The UN has presently 160 members. It is generally seen as a forum where states pursue their national interest, rather than as an institution of world government, but it is not without considerable impact.

Underground Railroad In US history, a loose network of safe houses, hiding places, and routes to aid fugitive American slaves to reach freedom in the North or Canada. Never formally organized, it was active as early as 1786, but was most widespread and active between 1830 and 1860. Estimates suggest that it may have assisted some 50000 runaways.

Unidad Popular Literally 'Popular Unity', this was a coalition of six left-wing political parties in Chile (Communists, Socialists, Radicals, and three minor groups) formed to support the presidential candidacy and government (1970–3) of Salvador **Allende**.

Uniformity, Acts of (1549, 1552, 1559 and 1662) A series of acts passed by English parliaments which sought to impose religious uniformity by requiring the use of the Church of England liturgy as contained in the Book of Common Prayer (various editions, 1549–1662). The act of 1552 penalized Catholic recusants; that of 1662 excluded dissenting Protestant clergy.

Unilateral Declaration of Independence (11 Nov 1965; Rhodesia) ▷ **UDI**

Union, Acts of (1707 and 1800) The Acts which joined England in legislative union with Scotland (1707) and Ireland (1800). The 1707 Act brought 45 Scottish MPs to join the new House of Commons of Great Britain, and 16 peers became members of the House of Lords; the Scottish legal system, however, remained separate. The 1800 Act created the United Kingdom of Great Britain and Ireland, which came into effect in 1801, and lasted until 1922. Union was brought about after the collapse of the Irish rebellion (1798) in order to increase British security during the French wars. The Irish parliament was abolished; 100 Irish MPs were added to the UK House of Commons, and 32 Peers to the Lords. The Churches of England and Ireland were united.

Union Movement A party formed by Sir Oswald **Mosley** in 1948 as a successor to his New Party (1931) and the British Union of Fascists (1932). It put up a handful of candidates during the period 1959–66, but failed to secure a significant number of votes. The party's main platform was opposition to immigration, but it also included a call to unite Europe into a vast market to buy from and sell to Africa. Mosley gave up the leadership in 1966, and the movement went into decline, dying out by the end of the 1960s. ▷ **Blackshirts**

Union Nationale French-Canadian political party. It was formed by a coalition of the Conservatives and *Action Libérale Nationale* to fight the 1935 provincial elections in Quebec. Its failure to win led to an amalgamation under Maurice **Duplessis**. With the support of the rural and small-business sector, it won an easy victory in 1936 on a platform of political, social and economic reform. In practice, this turned out to be anti-radicalism and pro-corporatism. In 1939 it was defeated after the intervention of Quebec Liberals in the federal government, but it returned to power in 1944 after accusing them of betraying nationalist rights, and it was to emphasize nationalist leanings thereafter. Duplessis maintained a very personal control of the party until his death in 1959, following which the party lost the 1960 election. In 1966 it regained power under Daniel Johnson, but he died in 1968 and very soon the **Parti Québecois** had seized the nationalist mantle. The *Union Nationale* lost the 1970 election and its support declined precipitously.

Union of Arms (July 1624) The proposal drawn up by the Count-Duke of **Olivares** for a force of 140000 men to be raised and maintained by each component state of the Spanish monarchy, in proportion to its resources. The plan was intended to solve the serious financial difficulties of the crown of **Castile**, which shouldered most of the defence burden. The plan was partially put into effect in America, Flanders and Italy. The strongest opposition came from the crown of **Aragon**, notably from Catalonia. The proposal was one of the major grievances leading to the Revolt of Catalonia in 1640. ▷ **Catalonia, Revolt of**

Union of Liberation (1903) A loose alliance of Russian liberals coming together to advocate some form of representative government. The members included the former Marxist, Peter **Struve**; but predominantly they were well-to-do **zemstvo** activists annoyed at **Nicholas II**'s incompetence and continued refusal to meet them. As the Russian **Revolution of 1905** developed, they split: **Shipov** and **Guchkov** to form the moderate **Octobrists**, and **Miliukov** and Muromtsev the more far-seeking **Kadets**. The Union represented an important transitory stage in Russian politics.

Union of Soviet Socialist Republics ▷ **USSR**

UNIP (United National Independence Party) Formed in 1959 with Kenneth **Kaunda** as its leader, UNIP was the strongest party in the last years of Northern Rhodesian colonial rule and provided the first independence government of Zambia. It became the only legal party in 1972, but in 1991, after pressure from the international community and widespread signs of dissatisfaction within the country, multiparty elections were held and UNIP was convincingly defeated.

UNITA (*União Naçional para a Independência Total de Angola*, 'National Union for the Total Independence of Angola') An Angolan nationalist party, founded in 1966 by Jonas Savimbi. Its support was based in south-eastern Angola and, even after Angola gained independence from Portugal in 1975, it waged a guerrilla war against the **MPLA** government, receiving backing from the

USA and South Africa. When the civil war seemed to have reached an inconclusive position of stalemate, after long and difficult negotiations, UNITA and the MPLA agreed upon a ceasefire in Estoril in early 1991.

United Arab Republic (UAR) The short-lived union between Egypt and Syria proclaimed in 1958. Gamal Abd al-**Nasser** was elected as head of state and the union generated considerable euphoria in both countries. Syria seceded however in late 1961, although Egypt retained the name until 1971 when it adopted the name Arab Republic of Egypt (ARE).

United Australia Party Australian political party formed in 1931 from the Nationalist Party and dissident Australian Labor Party members under the former Labor minister, Joseph **Lyons**. Although the party governed through the 1930s (in coalition with the Country Party after 1934), it was never stable, and merged into the **Liberal Party of Australia** (1944–5).

United Automobile Workers (UAW) US labour union. Originally formed by the AFL under the aegis of the NRA, an attempt to impose a president on the UAW led to a revolt in the spring of 1936, when the members elected their own leader, Homer Martin, and enrolled in the CIO. The UAW had to operate in an industry dominated by three aggressively anti-union companies, General Motors, Chrysler and Ford. However, by Dec 1936 the union had become strong enough to demand official recognition from General Motors. This was refused, despite the Wagner Act, so an official strike began in Jan 1937, the workers sitting in rather than walking out. The employers brought in the police, who used tear gas, but ineffectually. Michigan Governor Frank Murphy refused to use the state militia to remove the strikers and demanded negotiations between the employers and John L Lewis, President of the CIO. Backed also by President Franklin D **Roosevelt**, these discussions led to the UAW being recognized by General Motors, who also promised not to discriminate against union workers. Later that year, the same tactic was used to gain recognition from Chrysler. ▷ **AFL–CIO**

United Fronts Two political movements in China, which promoted cooperation between the Chinese **Communist Party (CCP)** and **Guomindang**. In the first, begun in 1924, to promote the defeat of regional militarists and reunify the country, **Sun Yat-sen** agreed to members of the Communist Party joining the Guomindang as individuals, while still retaining CCP membership, in exchange for Soviet military and organizational aid. The alliance relied heavily on Sun's personal prestige, however, and after his death (1925) friction developed between the right wing of the Guomindang and the communists, culminating in Mar 1926 when **Chiang Kai-shek**, the commander of the Guomindang army, expelled communists from senior positions within the organization. After the success of Chiang's Northern Expedition, he initiated (Apr 1927) a purge of all communists in areas under his control; the alliance was subsequently officially dissolved (July 1927). In Dec 1936, the **Xi'an Incident** ended with an anti-Japanese alliance between the two parties and, after the outbreak of the **Sino-Japanese War** in 1937, the Communist Party initiated the second United Front. Clashes between Guomindang and Communist forces made it an uneasy alliance from the start, and by 1941 it had virtually disintegrated, although efforts were made to revive it in 1943.

United Fruit Company The company organized in 1899, by the legendary Minor Cooper Keith, to cultivate and ship bananas from eastern Costa Rica. Keith extended his ventures into Honduras and Salvador, against competition from the USA, using refrigerated ships to transport the crop to the US market. The combination of buccaneering tactics and chicanery practised by the company during its early years earned it the sobriquet *el pulpo* ('the octopus'). At the height of its activities, United Fruit held extensive terrain and feeder railroads in many parts of Central American countries; Minor Keith was known as 'the uncrowned King of Central America', and the company remained a powerful force in the region and the Caribbean through the 1950s. It played a significant role in the US intervention of 1954 against Guatemala's President Jácobo Arbenz Guzmán.

United Gold Coast Convention (UGCC) The political party founded in 1947, which was led originally by Dr J B Danquah. It was the first organization to seek self-government within a short time frame. For a while its General-Secretary was Kwame **Nkrumah**, but he broke away to form the more radical **CPP** (Convention People's Party) and defeated the UGCC in the 1951 elections, after which the latter was dissolved.

United Irishmen, Society of A society formed in Belfast in 1791 by Protestant lawyer Wolfe **Tone**, which supported the **French Revolution** and espoused both religious equality and parliamentary reform. Its early support was primarily located in Ulster. As agitation increased, so United Irishmen became increasingly associated with support for Catholicism. The society was instrumental in organizing French support for the unsuccessful Irish rebellion of 1798, and afterwards went into decline.

United Kingdom ▷ **UK**

United Mine Workers of America (UMW) US labour union. Formed in 1890 by an amalgamation of mining unions within the AFL and the Knights of Labor. After unexpectedly successful strikes in 1897 and 1900, and the election in 1898 of a vigorous young president, John Mitchell, the union consolidated its position in 1902 with a strike in the anthracite fields. When it demanded recognition, an increase in wages and shorter hours, the coalfield operators responded aggressively and lost public sympathy when violence broke out. President Theodore **Roosevelt** saw the conflict as of national economic importance, and the intransigence of the operators led him to force arbitration. This established an important precedent for government intervention in the future. Under the leadership of John L **Lewis** (1920–60) the union became part of the CIO, which merged with the AFL in 1957. Its membership, which was as high as 500 000 in the 1930s, declined steeply in the latter half of the 20c, along with the decline of the labour movement itself. ▷ **AFL–CIO**

United National Party (Sri Lanka) ▷ **UNP**

United Nations Organization ▷ **UN**

United Provinces of the Netherlands Seven sovereign states of the Dutch Republic (Holland, Zeeland, Gelderland, Utrecht, Friesland, Groningen and Overijssel), roughly comprising the present kingdom of the Netherlands, but originally part of the Burgundian lands until they achieved independence from the Spanish crown in the **Eighty Years War**. Also known as the Dutch Republic, it declined in the 18c, collapsing during the **French Revolutionary Wars** (1795).

United States of America ▷ **USA**

Unkiar-Skelessi, Treaty of (1833) The treaty of alliance concluded between Tsar **Nicholas I** and Sultan **Mahmud II** at a time when the **Ottoman Empire** was under serious threat from **Muhammad** 'Ali's Egyptian revolt. To the chagrin of the other European powers, Russia gained not only the closure of the straits of the Dardanelles against them but also a virtual protectorate over what was left of the Ottoman Empire. This helped to produce the Russophobia, particularly in Britain, that led to the **Crimean War**.

UNP (United National Party) Sri Lankan political party. A right-of-centre alliance, it was originally formed out of the disbanded Ceylon National Congress at independence in 1948. The UNP held power from then until 1956, when it was defeated by a coalition headed by S W R D **Bandaranaike**'s **SLFP**. It only enjoyed one sustained period of government in the next 20 years, under the leadership of Dudley Senanayake from 1965 to 1970, but after J R **Jayawardene**'s landslide victory of 1977 it won all subsequent elections, not least because of weakness and division among the opposition parties.

untouchables ▷ **caste**

Ur The early home of the Jewish patriarch, Abraham, Ur was an ancient Sumerian city-state lying to the south-east of Babylon. It was at its zenith in the third millennium BC, when twice it became the capital of **Sumer**. Destroyed by Elam c.2000BC, the city recovered but never attained its former greatness. It was finally abandoned in the 4c BC.

'Urabi Pasha (1839–1911) Egyptian soldier and nationalist leader. An officer in the Egyptian army, he fought in the Egyptian–Ethiopian War of 1875–9 and took part in the officers' revolt that deposed the Khedive, **Ismail Pasha**, in 1879. He was the leader of a rebellion against the new Khedive, **Tewfik Pasha**, in 1881 (the **'Urabi Revolt**); this led to the setting up of a nationalist government, in which he was War Minister. The British intervened to protect their interests in the Suez Canal, and he was defeated at **Tel el-Kebir** in 1882. Sentenced to death, he was exiled to Ceylon instead and was pardoned in 1901.

'Urabi Revolt (1881–2) A demonstration in Egypt, led by Colonel Ahmad **'Urabi Pasha**, an officer of Egyptian peasant origin, which forced the Khedive to accept a nationalist government. 'Urabi was initially as Under-

Secretary and subsequently became Minister for War. The revolt was in essence a reaction of junior officers of native Egyptian origin against the Turko-Circassians who tended to monopolize the senior ranks of the army. Unfortunately for 'Urabi, these developments occasioned disquiet among the British and French, who demanded that the Khedive dismiss the nationalist government. This dismissal provoked xenophobic disorder and 'Urabi prepared to face the possibility of direct British and French intervention. The British eventually moved against 'Urabi, destroying the defences of Alexandria he had prepared and defeating the Egyptian army at Tel el-Kebir.

Urartu A state which flourished from the 9c to the 7c BC in the mountains of eastern Turkey around Lake Van. Abutting onto the territory of the Assyrians, then at the height of their power, Urartu was often engaged in hostilities with them. ▷ **Assyria**

Urban II (Odo of Lagery) (1042–99) French Pope (1088/99). He became a monk at Cluny, and was made Cardinal Bishop of Ostia in 1078. As Pope, he introduced ecclesiastical reforms, drove foreign armies from Italy, and launched the First Crusade.

Urban VIII (Maffeo Barberini) (1580–1644) Italian Pope (1623/44). As Pope, he supported **Richelieu**'s policy against the Habsburgs in the **Thirty Years War**, and took no action against the French alliance with Protestant Sweden in 1631. He carried out much ecclesiastical reform, revising the breviary and rewriting some of the hymns himself, and offered firm support to missionary activity. His condemnations of heresy included the works of **Galileo** (despite a long-standing personal friendship) and those of Jansen. ▷ **Habsburg Dynasty; Jansenism**

Uruk One of the greatest city-states of Sumer, lying to the north-west of Ur. The home of the legendary Gilgamesh, it is also the site of the earliest writing ever found. Although it came under the domination of Ur c.2100BC, it outlasted its powerful neighbour, surviving well into the Parthian period (3c AD).

USA (United States of America) A federal republic in North America and the fourth-largest country in the world. The country was first settled by migrant groups from Asia over 25 000 years ago. These **Native Americans**

943

UNITED STATES OF AMERICA: PRESIDENTS
Vice-Presidents in parentheses

Dates	Name	Party	Dates	Name	Party
1789–97	George Washington (1st) (John Adams)		1889–93	Benjamin Harrison (23rd) (Levi P Morton)	*Rep*
1797–1801	John Adams (2nd) (Thomas Jefferson)	*Fed*	1893–7	Grover Cleveland (24th) (Adlai E Stevenson)	*Dem*
1801–9	Thomas Jefferson (3rd) (Aaron Burr, 1801–5) (George Clinton, 1805–9)	*Dem-Rep*	1897–1901	William McKinley (25th) (Garret A Hobart, 1897–9) no Vice-President 1899–1901 (Theodore Roosevelt, 1901)	*Rep*
1809–17	James Madison (4th) (George Clinton, 1809–12) no Vice-President 1812–13 (Elbridge Gerry, 1813–14) no Vice-President 1814–17	*Dem-Rep*	1901–9	Theodore Roosevelt (26th) no Vice-President 1901–5 (Charles W Fairbanks, 1905–9)	*Rep*
1817–25	James Monroe (5th) (Daniel D Tompkins)	*Dem-Rep*	1909–13	William Howard Taft (27th) (James S Sherman, 1909–12) no Vice-President 1912–13	*Rep*
1825–9	John Quincy Adams (6th) (John C Calhoun)	*Dem-Rep*	1913–21	Woodrow Wilson (28th) (Thomas R Marshall)	*Dem*
1829–37	Andrew Jackson (7th) (John C Calhoun, 1829–32) no Vice-President 1832–3 (Martin Van Buren, 1833–7)	*Dem*	1921–3	Warren G Harding (29th) (Calvin Coolidge)	*Rep*
1837–41	Martin Van Buren (8th) (Richard M Johnson)	*Dem*	1923–9	Calvin Coolidge (30th) no Vice-President 1923–5 (Charles G Dawes, 1925–9)	*Rep*
1841	William Henry Harrison (9th) (John Tyler)	*Whig*	1929–33	Herbert Hoover (31st) (Charles Curtis)	*Rep*
1841–5	John Tyler (10th) no Vice-President	*Whig*	1933–45	Franklin D Roosevelt (32nd) (John Nance Garner, 1933–41) (Henry A Wallace, 1941–5) (Harry S Truman, 1945)	*Dem*
1845–9	James K Polk (11th) (George M Dallas)	*Dem*	1945–53	Harry S Truman (33rd) no Vice-President 1945–9 (Alben W Barkley, 1949–53)	*Dem*
1849–50	Zachary Taylor (12th) (Millard Fillmore)	*Whig*	1953–61	Dwight D Eisenhower (34th) (Richard M Nixon)	*Rep*
1850–3	Millard Fillmore (13th) no Vice-President	*Whig*	1961–3	John F Kennedy (35th) (Lyndon B Johnson)	*Dem*
1853–7	Franklin Pierce (14th) (William R King, 1853) no Vice-President 1853–7	*Dem*	1963–9	Lyndon B Johnson (36th) no Vice-President 1963–5 (Hubert H Humphrey, 1965–9)	*Dem*
1857–61	James Buchanan (15th) (John C Breckinridge)	*Dem*	1969–74	Richard M Nixon (37th) (Spiro T Agnew, 1969–73) no Vice-President Oct–Dec 1973 (Gerald Ford, 1973–4)	*Rep*
1861–5	Abraham Lincoln (16th) (Hannibal Hamlin, 1861–5) (Andrew Johnson, 1865)	*Rep*	1974–7	Gerald Ford (38th) no Vice-President Aug– Dec 1974 (Nelson A Rockefeller, 1974–7)	*Rep*
1865–9	Andrew Johnson (17th) no Vice-President	*Dem-Nat*	1977–81	Jimmy Carter (39th) (Walter F Mondale)	*Dem*
1869–77	Ulysses S Grant (18th) (Schuyler Colfax, 1869–73) (Henry Wilson, 1873–5) no Vice-President 1875–7	*Rep*	1981–9	Ronald Reagan (40th) (George Bush)	*Rep*
1877–81	Rutherford B Hayes (19th) (William A Wheeler)	*Rep*	1989–93	George Bush (41st) (J Danforth Quayle)	*Rep*
1881	James A Garfield (20th) (Chester A Arthur)	*Rep*	1993–	Bill Clinton (42nd) (Al Gore)	*Dem*
1881–5	Chester A Arthur (21st) no Vice-President	*Rep*			
1885–9	Grover Cleveland (22nd) (Thomas A Hendricks, 1885) no Vice-President 1885–9	*Dem*			

Dem Democrat
Fed Federalist
Nat National Union
Rep Republican

remained undisturbed until the country was explored by the Norse (9c) and the Spanish (16c), who settled in Florida and Mexico. In the 17c, there were settlements by the British, French, Dutch, Germans, and Swedish. Many Black Africans were introduced as slaves to work on the plantations. In the following century, British control grew throughout the area. A revolt of the English-speaking colonies in the **War of Independence** (1775–83) led to the creation of the United States of America, which then lay between the Great Lakes, the Mississippi, and Florida; the **Declaration of Independence** was made on 4 July 1776. Louisiana was sold to the USA by France in 1803 (the **Louisiana Purchase**) and the westward movement of settlers began. Florida was ceded by Spain in 1819, and further Spanish states joined the Union between 1821 and 1853. In 1860–1, 11 Southern states left the Union over the slavery issue, and formed the Confederacy; the Civil War (1861–5) ended in victory for the North, and the Southern states later rejoined the Union. As a result of the North's victory, **slavery** was abolished in 1865. In 1867 Alaska was purchased from Russia, and the Hawaiian Islands were annexed in 1898 (both admitted as states in 1959). The USA entered **World War I** on the side of the Allies in 1917. Native Americans were given the right to become US citizens in 1924. In 1929 the stockmarket on Wall Street crashed, resulting in the **Great Depression**. After the Japanese attack on **Pearl Harbor** in 1941 the USA entered **World War II**. The campaign for black civil rights developed in the 1960s, accompanied by much civil disturbance. From 1964 to 1975 the USA intervened in the **Vietnam War**, supporting non-communist South Vietnam. The USA led the space exploration programme of the 1960s and 1970s (in 1969 US astronaut Neil Armstrong was the first person on the moon). The **Watergate** scandal (1972–4) forced President **Nixon** to resign; there was further scandal in 1986 over arms sales to Iran to fund Contra rebels in Nicaragua. The **Cold War** between the USA and the **USSR** came to an end in 1990. In the 1991 **Gulf War**, US troops led the assault against **Saddam Hussein** following Iraq's invasion of Kuwait. In 1992 there was rioting in Los Angeles and other cities over racial issues. ▷ **civil rights movement; Indian Wars; Iran–Contra Affair**

US Constitution The US Constitution embodies the concepts on which the US system of government is based. The law of the land since 1789, it establishes a federal republic, balancing the power of the states and that of the federal government. In the federal government, power is divided among three independent branches: legislative, executive and judicial. The constitutional document comprises a short preamble followed by seven articles which include: the organization, powers and procedures of the legislative branch (Congress); the powers of the President and executive; the powers of the judiciary, including the Supreme Court; the rights of the states; and procedures for amending the Constitution. The articles are followed by 26 amendments, the first 10 of which are known as the **Bill of Rights** (although later amendments also deal with civil rights issues). The others cover such matters as the election, death or removal of the President, and eligibility to stand for election to Congress. Drafted at the **Constitutional Convention** of 1787 held in Philadelphia, the Constitution was adopted after it had been ratified by nine of the states. ▷ **Articles of Confederation**

Usman dan Fodio (1754–1817) Ruler of Hausaland. He was the leader of a **jihad** or holy war in northern Nigeria, which resulted in the creation of a large Islamic empire extending over some 180000 square miles and 10 million people. A member of an Islamic brotherhood in the small state of Gobir, Usman began to preach about 1775. His repeated calls for reform in line with strict Islamic doctrine were resisted by successive Hausa rulers. In 1804 he launched a jihad against the ruling Hausa aristocracy and founded his capital at Sokoto. Many similar jihads followed and Usman, as *Shehu* (or Chief) of Sokoto, was able to establish client Muslim rulers over a vast area. This was an important part of the late 18c and early 19c movements to create African Islamic states, which were to prove resistant to the advance of European rule.

USSR (Union of Soviet Socialist Republics), Russian **Soyuz Sovyetskikh Sotsialisticheskikh Republik**, also called **Soviet Union** A former federation of 15 Union Republics which, until its dissolution in 1991, jointly formed the world's largest sovereign state. Under Empress **Catherine II, 'the Great'**, Russia had become a great power, its territory extending into southern and eastern Asia. The 1917 **Russian Revolution** ended the monarchy, initiating a five-year struggle between the **Mensheviks** and the **Bolsheviks**. The first Soviet government was headed by **Lenin**, then in the 1920s **Stalin**

USSR (UNION OF SOVIET SOCIALIST REPUBLICS)

President

1917	Lev Borisovich Kamenev
1917–19	Yakov Mikhailovich Sverdlov
1919–46	Mikhail Ivanovich Kalinin
1946–53	Nikolai Shvernik
1953–60	Kliment Yefremovich Voroshilov
1960–4	Leonid Ilich Brezhnev
1964–5	Anastas Ivanovich Mikoyan
1965–77	Nikolai Viktorovich Podgorny
1977–82	Leonid Ilich Brezhnev
1982–3	Vasili Vasilevich Kuznetsov *Acting President*
1983–4	Yuri Andropov
1984	Vasili Vasilevich Kuznetsov *Acting President*
1984–5	Konstantin Ustinovich Chernenko
1985	Vasili Vasilevich Kuznetsov *Acting President*
1985–8	Andrei Andreevich Gromyko
1988–90	Mikhail Sergeevich Gorbachev

Executive President

1990–1	Mikhail Sergeevich Gorbachev
1991	Gennadi Ivanovich Yanaev *Acting President*
1991	Mikhail Sergeevich Gorbachev

Chairman (Prime Minister)

Council of Ministers

1917	Giorgiy Yevgenievich Lvov
1917	Alexandr Fyodorovich Kerensky

Council of People's Commissars

1917–24	Vladimir Ilich Lenin
1924–30	Alexei Ivanovich Rykov
1930–41	Vyacheslav Mikhailovich Molotov
1941–53	Joseph Stalin

Council of Ministers

1953–5	Giorgiy Maximilianovich Malenkov
1955–8	Nikolai Alexandrovich Bulganin
1958–64	Nikita Khrushchev
1964–80	Alexei Nikolaevich Kosygin
1980–5	Nikolai Alexandrovich Tikhonov
1985–91	Nikolai Ivanovich Ryzhkov
1991	Valentin Pavlov
1991	Ivan Silaev *Acting Chairman*

General-Secretary

1922–53	Joseph Stalin
1953	Giorgiy Maximilianovich Malenkov
1953–64	Nikita Khrushchev
1964–82	Leonid Ilich Brezhnev
1982–4	Yuri Andropov
1984–5	Konstantin Ustinovich Chernenko
1985–91	Mikhail Sergeevich Gorbachev

began vigorous socialist reforms, including the **Collectivization** of agriculture and rapid industrialization. Soviet territories were extended to the west after **World War II**, creating a corridor of Communist-dominated countries between the USSR and western

Europe and heralding the start of the **Cold War**. The Soviets intervened to suppress the 1956 Hungarian uprising and the 1968 Czech programme of liberalization. Afghanistan was invaded between 1979 and 1988. In the 1980s there was a series of disarmament agreements with a new approach to international relations (**glasnost**). Constitutional reforms were implemented in 1989, Communist power weakened and local independence movements emerged. Lithuania, Estonia, and Latvia became independent sovereign states in 1991; Georgia also became independent in 1991; Russia, Belorussia and the Ukraine then formed the Commonwealth of Independent States (**CIS**); they were soon joined by Armenia, Azerbaijan, Moldavia, Kazakhstan, Kirghizia, Tajikistan, Turkmenistan and Uzbekistan. In Dec 1991 the Soviet Union was formally dissolved.

Ustaša The name (meaning 'uprising') of the Croatian fascist movement which was organized in the 1930s by Ante **Pavelić** and supported by **Mussolini**'s Italy, and Hungary. Its right-wing nationalist ideology was an extension of the politics of Ante **Starčević**'s Croatian Party of (State) Right. A terrorist organization, it carried out the assassination of the Yugoslav King, **Alexander I**. During **World War II** it upheld the regime of Pavelić in **Croatia** and brutally massacred many thousands of Serbs, Jews, gypsies, communists and non-Ustaša **Croats**.

Ustinov, Dmitri Fedorovich (1908–84) Russian politician and Soviet marshal. Born into a working-class family, he acquired a technical eduation in his twenties, and by 1938 he was manager of an arms factory in Leningrad. In 1941 he was appointed as People's Commissar for Armaments; from then until 1976, when he became Minister of Defence, his primary function was to develop the arms industry. He gave it a civilian element and secured it an unfair share of the Soviet budget. He also helped find it an outlet by supporting the invasion of Afghanistan in 1979. His death removed from the ministry and the **Politburo** a fierce opponent of Mikhail **Gorbachev**'s campaign to reduce expenditure on the military.

US War of Independence ▷ **American Revolution**

'Uthman (d.656) Third of the Rashidun, or 'Rightly-Guided' Caliphs (644/56). Elected in succession to **'Umar**, and in preference to

'**Ali**, he established a commission of scholars who collected the Revelations of **Muhammad** to produce the definitive version of the Quran. However, 'Uthman's administration was badly organized, and disagreements concerning the division of the gains made in the Muslim conquests gave rise to increasing social tensions, culminating in a revolt in which he was killed.

Utrecht, Peace of (11 Apr 1713) The treaty which ended the War of the **Spanish Succession**, signed between England, the Dutch Republic, Spain and France, with the other powers agreeing in due course. By its terms Philip of Anjou became King **Philip V** of Spain, but the southern Netherlands went to the Austrian Habsburgs, along with Spanish parts of Italy. England obtained Gibraltar, and parts of Canada (from France). The Dutch contained France, obtained some possessions in Gelderland, and gained English support for the **Barrier Treaties**. ▷ **Habsburg Dynasty**

Utrecht, Union of (1579) The defensive alliance of the northern Dutch provinces against Spain in the **Eighty Years War**, provoked by the Union of **Arras** which threatened to take the southern Netherlands back into the Spanish fold. The union was signed by the provinces of Holland, Zeeland, Utrecht, Groningen and Gelderland, and later by Ghent, some Frisian towns, Antwerp, Breda, Bruges, Lier, Drenthe, and eventually Prince **William I**, Prince of Orange. The union arranged taxes for defence purposes, and stipulated freedom of religion. Later the union gained the status of a sort of constitution for the northern Dutch Republic.

V

Vaal Kraantz Reverse (5–8 Feb 1900) An incident in the Boer War in which the British general Sir Redvers Buller attacked Boers on a ridge of kopjes a few miles east of Spion Kop in an attempt to relieve Ladysmith. He was forced to withdraw and the British commander-in-chief, Roberts, was given authority to dismiss Sir 'Reverses' Buller.

Vafiadis, Markos (1906–92) Greek politician. Like many other Greeks driven from Anatolia in 1923, he found work in the Greek tobacco industry. He joined the **KKE** (Communist Party of Greece) in 1928 and was frequently imprisoned during the 1930s for his communist activities. In 1941 he escaped from the island where he was being held and went to Macedonia where he became Captain of the **ELAS** 10th Division operating there. During the **Greek Civil War** (1944–9), he led the Democratic Army of Greece which was founded by the KKE (Oct 1946). He organized communist bases in the villages and was one of those responsible for the abduction and forced enrolment in the army of many Greek youths and girls. Often at variance with the KKE leadership, he fled to Albania in 1949 after the KKE made a clumsy attempt on his life. He was expelled from the KKE the following year and was condemned for never having been 'a real communist'. ▷ **Lausanne, Treaty of; Zachariadis, Nikos**

Vakatakas An Indian dynasty which rose to power in the second half of the 3c, emerging after the collapse of the Satavahana kingdom, which was spread over present-day Madhya Pradesh, Maharashtra and northwest Andhra Pradesh. Pravarsena I, ruling in the early 4c, conquered large parts of the western Deccan and central India. The Vakataka kingdom was divided into four parts under the successor of Pravarsena I. This weakened the state but at the same time prevented the complete take over of the kingdom by Samudragupta, since he was content to obtain the homage of the Vakataka feudatories in central India and did not harass the main line of the Vakataka kings. Their survival after the **Gupta** campaigns gave them the opportunity to rearrange their territory which dominated the Deccan. A marriage alliance with the Gupta made the Vakataka kingdom virtually a part of the Gupta Empire.

Valckenier, Johan (1759–1821) Dutch politician. He made his career in academic law, holding chairs at the Universities of Franeker (1782–7), Utrecht (1787), and Leiden (1795–6). Politically he was a fervent supporter of the **Patriot Movement**, following the ideals of the **French Revolution** in the Netherlands, and working for a new unitary Dutch state. During the period of French domination of the Netherlands (1795–1813) he held political office: he was a member of the National Assembly in 1796, ambassador to Spain in 1796 and 1799–1801, and was a close adviser to King **Louis Napoleon** in 1806–10.

Valdemar I, 'the Great' (1131–82) King of Denmark (1157/82). The son of King Knut Lavard, he emerged victorious from 30 years of civil strife to give Denmark an unparalleled period of prosperity and expansion. In 1169 he destroyed the power of the Wends by capturing the island of Rügen. He strengthened the defences of the Danevirke and increased the size and effectiveness of the Danish army. He was succeeded by his eldest son, Knud VI.

Valdemar II, 'the Victorious' (1170–1241) King of Denmark (1202/41). The son of **Valdemar I, 'the Great'** and the brother of King Knud VI, he continued the expansionist policies of his predecessors, culminating in the conquest of Estonia (1219). He created a Danish Baltic empire which at its climax (c.1220) stretched from Holstein in the west to Estonia in the east. This empire, however, crumbled rapidly after the kidnapping of King Valdemar by a German vassal in 1223. In 1225 a huge ransom and the relinquishing of the bulk of the conquered territories secured the King's release. Only Estonia remained under Danish rule until 1346. At the domestic level, however, Valdemar was was not weakened, keeping a firm hold on power. He was succeeded by his brother, Erik (1216–50).

Valdivia, Pedro de (c.1510–1559) Spanish soldier. He went to Venezuela (c.1534) and

948

then to Peru, where he became **Pizarro**'s lieutenant. He won renown at Las Salinas (1538), and was in real command of the expedition to Chile. He founded Santiago (1541) and other cities, including Concepción (1550) and Valdivia (1552). In 1559, attempting, with a small force, to relieve Tucapel, which was besieged by the Araucanians, he was captured and killed by the Indians.

Valencia, Conquest of (1233–53) The campaigns to conquer the Muslim Kingdom of Valencia were begun by **Jaime I, 'the Conqueror'**, and continued until the siege of Valencia city (Apr 1238). The city capitulated on 28 Sep and Jaime I entered in triumph on 9 Oct. Campaigns continued in later years until the whole of the kingdom was reduced by 1253.

Valens (c.328–78) Roman Emperor (364/78). Appointed Emperor of the East by his brother, **Valentinian I**, Valens' entire reign was taken up with fighting either the Sassanids in the east or the marauding **Visigoths** in the north, who became a major threat to the security of the provinces south of the Danube once again in his reign. It was in battle against the Visigoths at **Adrianople** in Moesia that Valens's army was routed and he himself killed. ▷ **Sassanid Dynasty**

Valentinian I (321–75) Roman Emperor (364/75). A Roman army officer of Pannonian extraction, he was proclaimed emperor by his troops on the death of **Jovian**. Realizing that the task of governing the empire was too much for one man, he appointed his brother, **Valens**, as Co-Emperor, entrusting him with the difficult eastern half of the empire, while he himself took the even more problematic west. An energetic and capable ruler, Valentinian's greatest achievement was the complete refurbishment of the defences of Rome's northern frontiers along the Danube and Rhine.

Valentinian II (371–92) Roman Emperor (375–92). The second son of **Valentinian I**, he ruled as Co-Emperor with his half-brother, **Gratian**. He received from Gratian the provinces of Italy, Illyricum and Africa. During his minority the Empress, Justina, administered the government; about three years after her death, Valentinian was murdered, probably by Arbogastes, Commander-in-Chief of his army.

Valentinian III (c.419–455) Roman Emperor (425/55). The grand-nephew of

Valentinian II and the son of Constantius III, he was given the Western Empire by **Theodosius II**, Emperor of the East, in 425. A weak prince, he never really ruled during his 30 years' reign. At first his mother Placidia was the dominant influence, then after 433 the Commander-in-Chief, **Aëtius**. He lost control of Africa to the Vandal **Gaiseric** in 442. Valentinian stabbed Aëtius to death in 454, but the next year was himself slain by two of Aëtius's bodyguards.

Valerian (d.260) Roman Emperor (253/60). Proclaimed Emperor jointly with his son, **Gallienus**, by the Roman army in Raetia (Switzerland), Valerian's reign is notable for two things: the renewal of the persecution of the Christians, abandoned on **Decius**'s death (251), and the virtual collapse of the Roman frontier system of defence—in the North through pressure from Germanic tribes like the **Goths** and in the East through Sassanid (Persian) aggression. It was in combat with the latter that Valerian was captured (260). His subsequent fate is unknown.

Valerius Poplicola, Publius (6c BC) According to Roman tradition, a popular lawgiver. He was one of Rome's first two consuls after the overthrow of the monarchy and the establishment of the **Roman Republic** (509BC), his partner being Lucius Junius **Brutus**. A figure of doubtful historicity, most of the achievements popularly accredited him were later inventions, designed to explain his name Poplicola ('cultivator of the people').

Valley Forge An area in Chester County, Pennsylvania, USA, which was the winter headquarters of George **Washington** in 1777–8. His troops are renowned for the endurance and loyalty they showed while stationed there during the severe winter. ▷ **American Revolution**

Valois Dynasty The ruling dynasty of France from the accession of **Philip VI**, Count of Valois (1328), to the death of **Henry III** (1589). The succession was maintained in the direct male line from the 14c until **Louis XII** of the Orléans branch assumed the crown (1498). The last three Valois kings — **Francis II** (1559–60), **Charles IX** (1560–74) and **Henry III** (1574–89) — were all childless. See table p950. ▷ **Orléans, House of**

Van Buren, Martin (1782–1862) US politician and 8th President. He became a lawyer, state Attorney-General (1816–19), Senator (1821), Governor of New York (1828),

VALOIS DYNASTY

Regnal Dates	Name
1328/50	Philip VI
1350/64	John II, 'the Good'
1364/80	Charles V, 'the Wise'
1380/1422	Charles VI, 'the Foolish'
1422/61	Charles VII, 'the Victorious'
1461/83	Louis XI
1483/98	Charles VIII
1498/1515	Louis XII
1515/47	Francis I
1547/59	Henry II
1559/60	Francis II
1560/74	Charles IX
1574/89	Henry III

Secretary of State (1829–31) and Vice-President (1833–7). He was a supporter of Andrew **Jackson** and a member of the group which evolved into the **Democratic Party**. His presidency (1837–41) began during the financial panic of 1837 and in response to this, he introduced the Independent Treasury system. This crisis overshadowed his term in office and he was overwhelmingly defeated for re-election by the **Whig Party** in 1840. In 1848 he ran unsuccessfully for President as the candidate of the **Free-Soil Party**, which opposed the spread of slavery.

Vandals A Germanic people, originally perhaps from the Baltic area, who settled in the Danube valley in the 4c. Pushed west by the **Huns**, they invaded **Gaul** (406), crossed into Spain, conquered Roman Africa (429–439), and sacked Rome (455). The Byzantine general **Belisarius** reconquered North Africa in 533–534.

Vandervelde, Emile (1866–1938) Belgian politician. Having studied law, he joined parliament as a socialist in 1894 and became the leader of the **Belgian Socialist Party**. He repeatedly held cabinet posts from 1916 to 1937, and was also a noted theorist in revisionist Marxism. He published widely and was chairman of the Second International from 1900.

Vane, Sir Henry (1613–62) English statesman. He travelled in Europe, became a Puritan, and sailed for New England in 1635, where he was Governor of Massachusetts; but his advocacy of religious toleration lost him popularity, and he returned in 1637. He entered parliament, became joint Treasurer of the Navy, and was knighted (1640). He helped to impeach **Strafford**, promoted the

Solemn League and Covenant (1643), and was a strong supporter of the parliamentary cause in the **English Civil Wars**. During the **Commonwealth** he was appointed one of the Council of State (1649–53), but he opposed **Cromwell**'s becoming Lord Protector in 1653, and retired from politics. On Cromwell's death he returned to public life (1659), opposed the **Restoration**, and was imprisoned and executed. ▷ **Protectorate**

Vanunu, Mordechai (1948–) Israeli nuclear technician. A relatively junior member of the technical staff developing Israel's nuclear arsenal, Vanunu's disillusionment with the duplicity of his country's government, which had always claimed that it would not be the first Middle East country to acquire atomic weapons, led him to resign his post in 1986, and later that year the *Sunday Times* published an interview with Vanunu in which he revealed that Israel had already stockpiled up to 200 atomic bombs at an underground factory in the Negev Desert. In Sep of that year, he was abducted at Rome airport by agents of Mossad, the Israeli secret service, and returned to Jerusalem. After a secret trial, Vanunu was found guilty of treason and sentenced to life imprisonment in solitary confinement. ▷ **Israel, State of**

Vargas, Getúlio (Dornelles) (1883–1954) Brazilian politician. After serving in the army and training as a lawyer, he was elected a Federal deputy in 1923. He was Minister of Finance under Washington Luís Pereira de Souza and headed the Liberal Alliance ticket for the presidency in 1930. Defeated in the polls, he won the support of significant military force to govern with the army from 1930–45. A man who stood aloof from party politics, he sought a **conciliação** based upon support from the army, major industrial groups in Sao Paulo and Minas Gerais to achieve a more centralized state. Ousted in 1945 by the army, he returned as constitutional President in 1951. Four years later, in the face of mounting opposition from the right wing, he committed suicide. He created two political parties, the **PSD** and PTB, but his political heirs were Leonel **Brizola** and João **Goulart**.

Varna, Battle of (1828) A three-month siege and battle between Russian and Turkish troops during the Russo-Turkish War, which took place at Varna, a fortress on the Black Sea coast of Bulgaria. The Turkish garrison fell in Oct 1828, and was occupied by Russian forces. ▷ **Russo-Turkish Wars**

Varotnikov, Vitali Ivanovich (1926–) Soviet politician. He began work as a fitter in 1942, joined the Communist Party in 1947, and started to climb the bureaucratic and political ladder in his native Voronezh and Kubyshev. In 1975 he was brought to Moscow to become Deputy Chairman of the Russian Ministerial Council, but quickly clashed with Leonid **Brezhnev** and was sent to Cuba as ambassador in 1979. Yuri **Andropov** brought him back as full Chairman in 1938, and Mikhail **Gorbachev** then made him Chairman of the Presidium of the Supreme Soviet in 1988. Not quite able, however, to accept full-blooded reform, he was dropped in 1990.

Varus, Publius Quinctilius (d. AD9) High-ranking Roman official from the reign of **Augustus**. He is principally remembered as the army commander responsible for the Varian Disaster — the catastrophe in which three Roman legions were ambushed and annihilated by the Germans under **Arminius** (AD9). Prior to this, he had been, among other things, Governor of Syria with overall responsibility for Judaea. The revolt which he had put down there after Herod's death (4BC) is known in Jewish sources as the War of Varus.

Vasa Dynasty A royal dynasty which provided Sweden's monarchs, with two exceptions, from 1523 to 1818. Originally a minor noble family, it gained the throne for the first time in the person of **Gustav I Vasa**, who finally broke the Danish-dominated **Kalmar Union** and carried through the Reformation. He was succeeded by three of his sons: **Erik XIV**, **John III** and (after the deposition of John's son, **Sigismund**) **Charles IX**. The latter's son, **Gustav II Adolf**, was a great statesman and soldier, whose daughter, **Christina**, abdicated in 1654 in favour of her cousin, **Karl X**. His son, **Karl XI**, introduced absolute monarchy, but this was again abolished after the death of his childless son, **Karl XII**. The abdication of the latter's sister, **Ulrika Eleonora**, in 1720 brought a breach in the line with the accession of her husband, **Frederick I**. His successor, **Adolf Frederick**, was descended from Karl IX's sister, and his son, **Gustav III**, had even less of the blood in his veins. The line ended with his brother, **Karl XIII**, who died without heirs.

Vasilevski, Alexander Mikhailovich (1895–1977) Soviet marshal. An ensign in the Tsarist army in 1915, he joined the **Red Army** in 1919 and served in the war with Poland. He

VASA DYNASTY

Regnal Dates	Name
1523/60	Gustav I Vasa
1560/9	Eric XIV
1569/92	John III
1592/1604	Sigismund
1604/11	Charles IX
1611/32	Gustav II Adolf
1632/54	Christina
1654/60	Charles X
1660/97	Charles XI
1697/1718	Charles XII
1718/20	Ulrika Eleonora
1720/51	Frederick
1751/71	Adolf Frederick
1771/92	Gustav III
1792/1809	Gustav IV Adolf
1809/18	Charles XIII

subsequently demonstrated great skill in staff work. By 1940 he was Deputy Chief of the General Staff, and in 1942 he was confirmed as Chief. Along with **Zhukov** he planned the **Stalingrad** counter-offensive; he went on to liberate White Russia and take Konigsberg. In 1945 he directed the rapid defeat of the Japanese in the Far East. After **World War II** he supervised the reorganization of the Soviet forces, eventually serving as Deputy Defence Minister in 1953–6. In 1959 he retired from active service, disenchanted with Nikita **Khrushchev**'s military doctrine.

Vatican Councils Two councils of the Roman Catholic Church. The first, called by **Pius IX** in 1869 to deal with a wide range of ecclesiastical and doctrinal issues, produced the decree of Papal Infallibility. The second (1962–5), called by John XXIII, was aimed at renewing religious life and bringing the belief, structure and the discipline of the Church up to date.

Vauban, Sebastien le Prestre de (1633–1707) French soldier and military engineer. After serving in the **Fronde** (1651), he joined the government forces in 1653, and by 1658 was chief engineer under Turenne, serving with him at the siege of Lille (1667). He brought about a revolution in siege warfare and fortification; he directed siege operations throughout **Louis XIV**'s campaigns, and surrounded the kingdom with a cordon of fortresses (1667–88). He was created Marshal of France in 1703.

Vaudreuil, Philippe de Rigaud, Marquis of (c.1643–1725) French soldier and colonist.

Vaudreuil resented the French government's aim of controlling the colony of Canada, while failing to support it adequately. The failure to resolve the differences between the French forces under the Marquis of **Montcalm** and the *Canadiennes* under Vaudreuil did much to weaken their defences against British invasion. After the defeat, he attained the best possible terms for the **habitants**, securing both their religious and their property rights.

Vedic Age A period (1500–600BC) in the history of India, which began with the migration of Indo-European tribes (Indo-Aryans) to northern India. It was a period of transition from nomadic pastoralism to settled village communities, with cattle representing the major form of wealth. There was religious worship of personified forces of nature and abstract divinities, centred on a ritual of sacrifice.

Veii The Etruscan city, situated nine miles north of ancient Rome, which became Rome's arch rival for the control of **Latium** in the late 5c BC. Sacked by the Romans under the command of the dictator **Camillus** in 396BC after a ten year siege, its territory was annexed and it effectively ceased to exist.

Velchev, Damian (1883–1954) Bulgarian politician. A member of the Military League, in 1934 he led the military coup supported by **Zveno**. In the 1944 government of the **Fatherland Front**, he became Minister of War but lost his position in 1946 during the communist purge and was sent to Switzerland as the Bulgarian representative. ▷ **Dimitrov, Georgi; Kostov, Traicho; Petkov, Nikola**

Veldkornet A Boer functionary during the period of Dutch East India Company rule at the Cape. It was a powerful, though part-time position, generally filled by a farmer, important in matters relating to legal affairs and black labour.

Vellore Uprising (1806) The rebellion at Vellore, a small town in the state of Tamil Nadu in India, was fostered by changes in regulations which were thought to reflect upon religion and encouraged by the proximity of the exiled Mysore princes. It was not comparable to the later **Indian Uprising** of 1857–8 because the discontent was wholly military, however it cost Lord Bentinck his governorship of Madras.

Velvet Revolution (1989) The sudden, almost bloodless, process by which the communist regime in Czechoslovakia collapsed. Ever since the **Prague Spring** was blighted in 1968 by the Soviet invasion, **communism** had been tolerated but lacked popularity. Its mainstay remained the USSR with local military and police assistance. As Mikhail **Gorbachev** tolerated change elsewhere in Eastern Europe, the public in Czechoslovakia saw their opportunity. On 17 Nov a crowd of 50000 in Wenceslas Square was attacked by the police, but for the last time. The crowds grew, Miloš **Jakeš** resigned on 24 Nov, and Václav **Havel** became the new President on 30 Dec.

Vendée, Wars of the French counter-revolutionary insurrections in the western provinces against the central government in Paris. The brutal rising in La Vendée (1793), when priests and nobles encouraged the conservative peasantry to rebel against the National Convention's conscription and anti-clerical policies, was a precedent for other provincial revolts in 1795, 1799, 1815 and 1832. ▷ **Convention, National; French Revolution;**

Vendémiaire, 12th and 13th (4–5 Oct 1795) In France, a royalist rising in protest against a decree of the National Convention, stating that in the elections for a new assembly at least two-thirds of the seats should be reserved for the out-going members of the Convention. It was crushed by **Barras**, who brought in Napoleon Bonaparte to quell the uprising; he used cannon to disperse the insurgents gathered in front of the church of St Roch, Paris. ▷ **Convention, National; Napoleon I**

Vendôme, Louis Joseph, Duke of (1654–1712) French general. The great-grandson of **Henry IV** (of France). He commanded in Italy and Flanders during the War of the **Spanish Succession** (1701–14) and was defeated at Oudenarde by **Marlborough** (1708). Sent to Spain in 1710 to aid **Philip V**, he recaptured Madrid, defeated the English at Brihuega and the Austrians at Villaviciosa, but died soon after.

vendus A derogatory term for those French-Canadians who, like Sir George Étienne **Cartier**, were alleged to have 'sold out' to anglophone Canada.

Venezia Giulia The name given by Italy to **Istria** and Gorizia, two regions which the Italians gained from Austria at the end of **World War I**. With Venezia Tridentina and

Venezia Euganea, it was part of the so-called *Le Tre Venezie* (the Three Venices). At the end of **World War II**, Italy ceded Istria to Yugoslavia and reorganized the remaining parts of Venezia Giulia as Friuli-Venezia Giulia.

Venezuelan Boundary Dispute A dispute between Britain and Venezuela over the boundary of British Guiana (now Guyana). In 1895 this provoked a brief but acute crisis in Anglo-American relations, the USA forcing Britain to accept arbitration. The dispute was settled in 1899.

Venizélos, Eleuthérios (Kyriakos) (1864–1936) Greek politician. He became a lawyer and journalist, joined the Cretan Chamber of Deputies and took a prominent part in the rising against the Turks in 1896. As Prime Minister (1910–15) after the 1909 military coup, he restored law and order, promoted the Balkan League against Turkey and Bulgaria (1912–13), extended Greek territory and enacted land reform. His sympathies with France and Britain in **World War I** clashed with those of King **Constantine I** and led him to establish a rival government (1917–20), forcing the King's abdication. During the 1920s and early 1930s, he was leader of the anti-royalist political faction. In 1935 he came out of retirement to support a military revolt staged by his sympathizers, but after its failure he fled to Paris, where he died.

Venizélos, Sofoklis (1894–1964) Greek politician. The son of Eleuthérios **Venizélos**, in 1944 he was briefly Prime Minister of the Greek government-in-exile, resigning in favour of George **Papandreou**. In the elections of Mar 1946 he led the National Political Union with Papandreou and Panayiotis Kanellopoulos. After the **Greek Civil War** (1944–9), in the elections of Mar 1950, as leader of the Liberal Party he joined the coalition government with the National Progressive Centre Union and Papandreou's Democratic Socialist Party, becoming Prime Minister later that year.

Vercingetorix (d.46BC) Chieftain of the Arverni, a Gallic tribe. A charismatic leader, he masterminded and led a general revolt of the Gauls against Julius **Caesar** in 52BC. After a number of notable successes such as that at Gergovia, he was badly defeated and forced to take refuge inside the hill-fort at Alesia. Forced to surrender (52BC), he was taken to Rome, kept in captivity and executed after Caesar's triumph (46BC). ▷ **Alesia, Siege of**

Vercors A mountain plateau near Grenoble in the Alps which became a stronghold of the French **World War II** resistance movement. It was captured by the German Army after heroic struggle with great loss of life (13 June–5 Aug 1944).

Verdinaso Belgian fascist political party, founded in 1931 by Joris Van Severen (1894–1940). The name is a shortened form of the League of Low Countries National Solidarists (*Verbond van Dietsch-Nationaal Solidaristen*). The party was influenced by French and Italian right-wing politics, and opposed parliamentary processes and all forms of liberalism and socialism; it never achieved a large membership. Originally heavily supportive of the **Flemish Movement**, Van Severen later championed a neo-Burgundian nationalist ideal; at the outbreak of **World War II** he was executed by French forces (20 May 1940), and Verdinaso rapidly disappeared.

Verdun, Battle of (1916) A battle in **World War I**. The German army chose to attack a salient in the French line at this point because it was thought that its symbolic value would force the French to defend it to the bitter end. This did happen but, in spite of huge losses on both sides, Verdun did not fall. General **Pétain**, the French commander for most of the battle, earned his reputation at Verdun.

Verdun, Treaty of (Aug 843) After his defeat at the Battle of Fontenoy (841), **Lothair I** was forced to negotiate with his brothers, **Charles II, 'the Bald'** and **Louis the German**, about the division of the Frankish empire. The apportioning was decided on the basis of an inventory of all bishoprics, monasteries and imperial lands, and based around the central areas of Bavaria, Italy and Aquitaine. Lothair received the middle kingdom, containing Italy, Provence and the lands north as far as Frisia, bordered on the West by the Rhone, Saone, Maas and Schelde rivers and on the east by the Alps and the Rhine. Charles received the lands to the west of this area and Louis those to the east. The treaty paved the way for the decline of the empire into an eastern and western Frankish kingdom. See map p954.

Vereeniging, Peace of (1902) The peace treaty which ended the Boer War, signed at Pretoria. The Boers won three important concessions: an amnesty for those who had risen in revolt within the Cape Colony; a promise that the British would deny the

Division of the Carolingian Empire under the Treaty of Verdun (843)

franchise to Africans until after the Boer republics were returned to representative government; and additional financial support for reconstruction. The Peace ensured that there would be no significant change in the political relationship of Whites and Blacks in South Africa. ▷ **Boer Wars**

Vergennes, Charles Gravier (1717–87) French politician. As **Louis XVI**'s Foreign Minister, he sought to humble Britain by promoting the independence of the USA. He negotiated the Peace of Paris (1783) and also **Pitt**'s commercial treaty (1786). ▷ **American Revolution**

Vergniaud, Pierre Victurnien (1753–93) French politician. He settled as an advocate at Bordeaux in 1781, and was sent to the National Assembly in 1791. His eloquence made him the leader of the **Girondins**. In the National Convention he voted for King **Louis XVI**'s death, and as President announced the result. When the Girondins clashed with the rival revolutionary faction, known as the **Mountain**, who wanted to retain power by dictatorial means, Vergniaud and his party were arrested and guillotined (31 Oct 1793).

▷ **Convention, National; French Revolution; Jacobins**

Vernon, Edward (1684–1757) British admiral. He joined the navy in 1700, and also became an MP (1727–41). In 1739, during the War of **Jenkins' Ear**, he was sent to harry the Spaniards in the Antilles, and his capture of Portobello made him a national hero. During the Jacobite **Forty-Five Rebellion** Vernon's effective dispositions in the Channel successfully kept the standby Gallic reinforcements in their ports. He was nicknamed 'Old Grog', from his grogram coat, and in 1740 ordered the dilution of navy rum with water, the mixture being thereafter known as 'grog'.

Verres, Gaius (d.43BC) Roman politician. He was notorious for his cruel and corrupt governorship of Sicily (73–71BC), for which he was successfully prosecuted by the rising young barrister **Cicero** (70BC). To escape conviction, he fled to Massilia (Marseilles), taking enough of his ill-gotten gains with him to live in comfort for the rest of his life. His riches made him an obvious target for the Triumvirs and he died in their proscriptions in 43BC.

Versailles, Treaty of (1919) A peace treaty drawn up between Germany and the Allied powers at Paris. Of the 434 articles, the most controversial was article 231 assigning to Germany and her allies responsibility for causing **World War I**, and establishing liability for reparation payments. Germany lost all overseas colonies, and considerable territory to Poland in the East. The **Rhineland** was demilitarized and to be occupied by Allied troops for up to 15 years, and German armed forces were strictly limited. ▷ **Paris Peace Conference**

Verwoerd, Hendrik Freusch (1901–66) South African politician, born in Amsterdam, the Netherlands. He was educated at Stellenbosch, where he became Professor of Applied Psychology (1927) and Sociology (1933), and edited the nationalist *Die Transvaler* (1938–48). Elected Senator in 1948, he became Minister of Native Affairs (1950) and Prime Minister (1958–66). His administration was marked by the highly controversial policy of apartheid, an attempt on his life (1960), the establishment of South Arica as a republic (1962) and his assassination in Cape Town.

Verzet, Het ▷ **Resistance Movement** (Netherlands)

Verzuiling Literally 'pillarization', this is the Dutch term which describes the division of society into vertical ideological groups, rather than into horizontal socio-economic ones, particularly used of the Netherlands. Also known as vertical pluralism and consociationalism. Dutch *verzuiling* consists of two things: the division of society into four camps characterized by an ideology such as Roman Catholicism, Calvinism, socialism, or humanism; and a complex of rules, regulations, committees and consultative processes allowing the efficient running of the country despite the vertical differences, and with proportional input from each group. Historically, the system arose out of demands made in the course of the 19c by the Roman Catholics, the Calvinists and the socialists for a share in the power held by the ruling liberals; in the 20c the institutions in the 'pillars' continued to expand until c.1960, since when there has been a process of de-pillarization (*ontzuiling*). The term *verzuiling* is also used of Belgian politics, but refers more to the development of the pillars than to the mechanism of consultation for running the country.

Vespasian (Titus Flavius Vespasianus) (AD9–79) Roman Emperor (AD69/79). The founder of the **Flavian Dynasty** (AD69–96), he was declared emperor by the troops in the East, where he was engaged in putting down the Jewish Revolt. He ended the civil wars that had been raging since **Nero**'s overthrow, put the state on a sound financial footing, and restored discipline to the army. Among his many lavish building projects was the Colosseum. He was succeeded by his son, **Titus**. ▷ **Domitian**

Vichy The informal name of the French political regime between 1940 and 1945; officially the **French State** (*Etat français*). Established at the spa town of Vichy following Germany's defeat of France (1940), its head of state was Marshal Philippe **Pétain** and its other dominant political figure Pierre **Laval**, Prime Minister from 1942. Although a client regime of Germany, Vichy at first succeeded in maintaining a degree of autonomy. ▷ **collaboration** (France); **Riom Trial; World War II**

Vicksburg, Battle of (1863) A major success for Union forces during the **American Civil War**, in which General Ulysses S **Grant** captured Vicksburg and thus the Mississippi River, splitting the Confederate forces in two. Pressured by an impatient President

Lincoln, Grant circumvented the impregnable cliffs protecting the city, captured the nearby city of Jackson and only then laid seige to Vicksburg. With bombardment from Unionist gunboats on the Mississippi River that lasted for six weeks, he forced the Confederate General, Pemberton, to surrender. The victory proved Grant's abilities as a general and Lincoln placed him in command of all the Union's western forces. The cause of emancipation was also helped by the use of black units in the campaign.

Victor Amadeus II (1666–1732) Duke of Savoy (1675/1730), King of Sicily (1713/20) and King of Sardinia (1720/30). He reigned under influence of his mother, Jeanne de Nemours, until 1684. After taking power in his own right, he pursued a domestic policy of administrative rationalization, fiscal reform and economic development. For most of his reign, his foreign policy was based on switching allegiance between **Louis XIV** of France and the Habsburgs, according to the demands of the moment. Despite defeats at the hands of both imperial and French armies, he managed to extend his territories considerably, becoming King of Sicily by the Treaty of **Utrecht** in 1713. Feeling Sicily too distant from Savoy, he swapped it for Sardinia in 1720, but retained his royal title. From 1720 he avoided involvement in international conflict and concentrated on domestic reform, establishing a new legal code (1723–9) and a land register (1730). In 1730 he abdicated in favour of his son, **Charles Emmanuel III**, on condition that the latter kept him well informed of his actions. When Charles Emmanuel failed to do so, Victor Amadeus tried to restore his own rule, but was captured by his son and imprisoned at the fortress of Rivoli, where he died. ▷ **Habsburg Dynasty**

Victor Amadeus III (1726–96) King of Sardinia (1773/96). The son and successor of **Charles Emmanuel III**, from the outset of the **French Revolution** he offered sanctuary to aristocratic émigrés, including **Louis XVI**'s brother, the Count of Artois, who wished to use Savoy as a base from which to launch a counter-revolutionary invasion. Attacked by the revolutionary regime in 1792, Victor Amadeus was driven into the arms of the Habsburgs, but defeat by Napoleon Bonaparte forced him to leave the anti-French coalition in 1796. By the Treaty of Paris of May that year he was forced to cede Nice and Savoy and to accept the presence of a French garrison. ▷ **Habsburg Dynasty**

Victor Emmanuel I (1759–1824) King of Sardinia (1802/21). The son of **Victor Amadeus III**, he took part in wars against the French from 1793 to 1796. He became King on the abdication of his brother, **Charles Emmanuel IV**, and until 1814 lived at Cagliari in Sardinia, as his mainland possessions were in the hands of the French. After the Vienna Settlement (which awarded Genoa and the Ligurian littoral to the Kingdom of Sardinia), he returned to Turin, where he pursued a policy of extreme reaction, rejecting any legacy of French rule and appointing to high office almost only conservative aristocrats who had followed him to Sardinia. In this climate of reaction, discontent grew, especially among those of his subjects who had served the Napoleonic regime; it found expression in the liberal insurrection led by **Santarosa** in 1821. Faced with an army mutiny and demands for a liberal constitution, Victor Emmanuel abdicated in favour of his brother, **Charles Felix**, appointing the young **Charles Albert** as Regent until the latter's return from Modena.

Victor Emmanuel II (1820–78) King of Sardinia (1849/61) and King of Italy (1861/78). He came to the throne on his father's abdication, after the defeat of the Battle of **Novara**. He did not, as was once commonly held, have to defend the retention of the **Statuto** against Austrian pressure to abolish it, but rather saw eye-to-eye with **Radetzky** on the need to repress democracy and revolution. The early years of his rule did, however, witness a series of more or less liberal ministries under **D'Azeglio** and **Cavour**, although he was often unhappy about the anticlerical nature of much of their legislation. It was largely on his own initiative that Piedmont sent troops to fight alongside the British and French in the Crimea in 1855. In 1859 he went to war in alliance with France to drive out the Austrians from the north of Italy, securing Lombardy but failing to take Venetia. In return for French assistance, he ceded Nice and Savoy to **Napoleon III**. During the spring of 1860 he also acquired Parma, Modena and Tuscany, their transfer to his rule being engineered largely by the **Italian National Society**. Later that year, Umbria, the Papal Marches and the Kingdom of the **Two Sicilies** were annexed and in Mar 1861, he was crowned King of Italy. He did not, however, change his title to Victor Emmanuel I. Nor did he control the entire peninsula, having to wait until 1866 before acquiring Venetia, and 1870 until he gained Rome. ▷ **Roman Question**

Victor Emmanuel III (1869–1947) King of Italy (1900/46). He came to the throne after the assassination of his father, **Umberto I**. After Italy's entrance into **World War I**, he took an active part in the campaign, appointing his uncle, the Duke of Aosta, as Regent. With the arrival of peace, he took little active part in politics. In 1922, however, faced with **Mussolini**'s bid to seize power he refused to declare a state of emergency, which would have enabled the army to crush the fascist movement. Instead, when **Salandra** declined to form a government, he asked Mussolini to do so, opening the way for the creation of the fascist regime. Among suggested motives for Victor Emmanuel's ready capitulation to the fascists are his fear that the alternative to Mussolini might have been a socialist revolution, anxieties about the loyalty of the army and rumours that the Duke of Aosta was planning to depose him. Mussolini's regime effectively deprived the monarchy of its powers, but it did make Victor Emmanuel Emperor of Ethiopia (1936) and King of Albania (1939). Eventually, however, the King was to play a part in toppling the **Duce**: on 24 July 1943, the **Fascist Grand Council**, disillusioned by the progress of the war and dissatisfied with Mussolini's gutless readiness to accept orders from **Hitler**, begged Victor Emmanuel to assume power. On 25 July, Mussolini was summoned by the King and dismissed; shortly afterwards, with Mussolini under arrest, Victor Emmanuel invited General **Badoglio** to form a government. However, he was irredeemably tarnished by his association with **fascism** and did little in the final stages of the war to improve his or his dynasty's popularity. In May 1946, in a last effort to save the monarchy, he abdicated in favour of his son, **Umberto II**. He died in exile in Egypt.

Victoria (1819–1901) Queen of Great Britain (1837/1901) and Empress of India (1876/1901). She was the only child of **George III**'s fourth son, Edward, and Victoria Maria Louisa of Saxe-Coburg, sister of **Leopold I**, King of Belgium. Taught by Lord **Melbourne**, her first Prime Minister, she had a clear grasp of constitutional principles and the scope of her own prerogative, which she resolutely exercised in 1839 by setting aside the precedent which decreed dismissal of the current ladies of the bedchamber, thus causing **Peel** not to take up office as Prime Minister. In 1840 she married Prince **Albert** of **Saxe-Coburg-Gotha**, and had four sons and five daughters. Strongly influenced by her husband, with whom she worked in closest harmony, after his death (1861) she went into lengthy seclusion, neglecting many duties, which brought her unpopularity and motivated a republican movement. However, with her recognition as Empress of India, and the celebratory golden (1887) and diamond (1897) jubilees, she rose high in her subjects' favour, and increased the prestige of the monarchy. She had strong preferences for certain prime ministers (notably **Melbourne** and **Disraeli**) over others (notably Peel and **Gladstone**), but did not press these beyond the bounds of constitutional propriety. At various points in her long reign she exercised some influence over foreign affairs, and the marriages of her children had important diplomatic, as well as dynastic, implications in Europe. She and was succeeded by her son, **Edward VII**.

Vieira, Antonio de (1608–97) Portuguese Jesuit missionary. Born in Lisbon, he grew up in Bahia in Brazil, where he attended the Jesuit College and became a missionary. He returned to Portugal after the restoration of independence (1640), was appointed court preacher (1641–52) to King João IV and became influential. In 1653 he returned to Brazil as Superior of Jesuit missions, but in defending the local Indians fell foul of the colonists. Eventually, after years of conflict, Vieira and his fellow Jesuits were expelled from the Amazon and sent back to Lisbon in 1661. There he was put under house arrest and imprisoned by the **Inquisition** (1663–8). He subsequently went to Rome where he was well received, and in 1681 was able to return with the Jesuits to Brazil, where he remained until his death.

Vieira, Joao Bernardo (1939–) Guinea-Bissau politician. He joined the Party for the Independence of Portuguese Guinea and Cape Verde (PAIGC) in 1960, and in 1964 became a member of the political bureau during the war for independence from Portugal. After independence in 1974, he served in the government of Luiz **Cabral**, but in 1980 led the coup which deposed him. In 1984 constitutional changes combined the roles of head of state and head of government, making Vieira Executive President.

Vienna, Congress of (1814–15) A European assembly convened at the instigation of the four victorious Powers to redefine the territorial map of Europe after the defeat of **Napoleon I**. The negotiators were concerned to create a balance of power and to avoid alienating any major state.

Metternich in particular was concerned to contain the forces of nationalism and liberalism and to preserve the prerogatives of the monarchies of Europe. ▷ **Napoleonic Wars**

Vienna, Siege of (1529) The first Ottoman siege of Vienna, undertaken by **Suleyman I, 'the Magnificent'**, was indirectly the result of an agreement made by Zapolya, King of Hungary, with the Ottomans, whereby Zapolya was prepared to recognize Suleyman's suzerainty in return for the latter's help against the Habsburgs. Suleyman was, for his part, content that Hungary should be autonomous under Zapolya and act as a buffer state against the Habsburgs. An expedition against Hungary ensued, with the object of expelling Ferdinand; Buda was occupied (Sep 1529) and Suleyman went on to lay siege to Vienna. The main reason behind the failure of the siege was climatic in that the season was too well advanced. Despite early success in the suburbs of Vienna, Suleyman, who was having difficulties with his own troops, particularly the **Janissaries**, decided to return to Istanbul for the winter. ▷ **Habsburg Dynasty; Ottoman Empire**

Vienna, Siege of (1683) The second Ottoman siege of Vienna, undertaken by the Grand Vizier Qara Mustafa in the reign of Muhammad IV, was the culmination of a campaign provoked by the emergence of a Hungarian nationalist movement against the Habsburgs. As with the first siege of Vienna in 1529, Ottoman help was sought on the condition that Ottoman suzerainty would be recognized. After a campaign in Hungary in late 1682, a great army was mustered in Edirne (Adrianople) and the Ottomans eventually advanced on Vienna in June 1683. Faced by a European coalition (Pope Innocent XI had managed to get men and money from Poland, Portugal and Spain to aid the beleaguered Habsburgs) and a vigorous defence of the city, the Ottomans were forced to retire. Polish assistance, led by Jan Sobieski, had been instrumental in saving Vienna and also played a major part in the subsequent defeat of the Ottomans at Gran. Qara Mustafa was made the scapegoat for the whole debacle, being dismissed and then executed in Belgrade in 1683. ▷ **Habsburg Dynasty; Ottoman Empire**

Vienna, Treaties of (1735 and 1738) These two treaties began and ended the negotiations which concluded the War of the **Polish Succession**. They recognized the claim of Frederick Augustus I of Saxony to the Polish throne.

Vienna, Treaty of (Peace of Schönbrunn)
(14 Oct 1809) A peace treaty between **Austria**
and France following the French victory at
the Battle of **Wagram**. Austria lost most of
her remaining Alpine and Adriatic lands as
well as some northern border territories. She
accepted French hegemony in Europe and
adjusted her foreign policy to French
requirements, as well as paying **reparations**.
On 12 Aug 1813 Austria renounced the
treaty.

Vienna Award (1st) (2 Nov 1938) The
alteration of the Czechoslovak-Hungarian
frontier following the **Munich Agreement**.
Hitler's success against Czechoslovakia
encouraged other predators, and Hungary
laid claim to **Ruthenia** and part of Slovakia.
Ribbentrop and **Ciano** acted as arbitrators,
although Hitler was still not sure what he
wanted to happen to Ruthenia. But the
Vienna Award gave Hungary a fertile slice of
Slovakia with almost a million inhabitants,
just over half of whom were, admittedly,
Hungarian. Most of the area was restored to
Czechoslovakia in 1945.

Vienna Award (2nd) (29 Aug 1940) The
alteration of the Hungarian–Romanian frontier following the **German–Soviet Pact**. When
Stalin moved his forces into **Bessarabia** (July
1940) in accordance with the terms of his pact
with **Hitler**, Hungary saw its opportunity to
reclaim Transylvania, which had been lost to
Romania at the end of **World War I**. Hitler
was anxious to weaken Romania to his own
advantage but not to encourage Hungary (or
Mussolini) excessively. Eventually **Ribbentrop** and **Ciano** again acted as arbitrators.
This 2nd Vienna Award gave Hungary
two-thirds of Transylvania. Most of this area,
too, was restored to Romania in 1945.

Viet Cong or **Vietcong** ('Vietnamese communists') The name commonly given in the
1960s to the communist forces that fought the
South Vietnamese government during the
Vietnam War.

Viet Minh or **Vietminh** The abbreviation of
Vietnam Doc Lap Dong Minh ('League for
the Independence of Vietnam'), a politico-
military organization formed by **Ho Chi Minh**
in 1941. It included nationalists and communists, and aimed at liberating Vietnam from
the Japanese and then gaining independence
from France. In 1945, on the Japanese
surrender, it formed a government following
the dropping of the bombs on Hiroshima and
Nagasaki, in Hanoi. Its army defeated the

French at Dien Bien Phu in 1954. ▷ **Vietnam
War**

Vietnam War (1964–75) A war between
communist North Vietnam and non-communist South Vietnam which broadened to
include the USA. It was preceded by the
Indo-China War (1946–54) between France
and the Viet Minh, which ended with the
defeat of the French at Dien Bien Phu. The
Geneva Conference left North Vietnam
under the rule of Ho Chi Minh, while the
South was ruled first by the Emperor Bao Dai
and then by Ngo Dinh Diem. Elections were
planned to choose a single government for all
of Vietnam, but when they failed to take
place, fighting was renewed. From 1961, in
an attempt to stop the spread of **communism**,
the USA increased its aid to South Vietnam
and the number of its 'military advisors'. In
1964 following a North Vietnamese attack on
US ships, President Lyndon **Johnson** ordered
retaliatory bombing of North Vietnam.
Although the US Congress never declared
war officially, it passed the **Gulf of Tonkin
Resolution** which authorized US forces in
South-East Asia to repel any armed attack
and to prevent further aggression. US bombing of North Vietnam was continued, and in
1965 the USA stepped up its troop commitment substantially. By 1968 over 500 000 US
soldiers were involved in the war. As the
conflict dragged on, victory against the
elusive communist guerrilla forces seemed
unattainable. Opposition to the war within
the USA badly divided the country, and
pressure mounted to bring the conflict to an
end. In 1968 peace negotiations were begun
in Paris, and in 1973 a ceasefire agreement
was signed. Hostilities did not end until two
years later when North Vietnam's victory was
completed with the capture of Saigon
(renamed Ho Chi Minh City).

Vígdis Finnbogadóttir ▷ Finnbogadóttir,
Vígdis

Vijayanagar Empire The last great medieval Hindu state, located in southern India
(1336–c.1614). It served as a barrier against
invasion by north Indian Muslim sultanates,
and created the conditions for creative
productivity in which Sanskrit and regional
literatures thrived.

Vikings Raiders, traders, and settlers from
Norway, Sweden and Denmark, who
between the late 8c and the mid-11c conquered and colonized large parts of Britain,
Normandy and Russia; attacked Spain,

Vietnam War (approximate situations, Dec 1967)

Morocco and Italy; traded with Byzantium, Persia and India; discovered and occupied Iceland and Greenland; and reached the coast of North America. As sea-borne raiders they gained a deserved reputation for brutality and destructiveness, but as merchants and settlers they played an influential and positive role in the development of medieval Europe. Their earliest overseas settlements were in the Orkney and Shetland Islands, which remained united to the Norwegian crown until 1472. ▷ **Canute; Danelaw; Normans; Rollo**

Villafranca Armistice (11 July 1859) The armistice between **Napoleon III** and Francis Joseph of Austria after the Battle of **Solferino** that brought to an end the 1859 campaign to seize Lombardy and Venetia. By seeking peace with the Austrians, Napoleon III broke the promises he made in the **Plombières Agreement** to secure the whole of the Kingdom of **Lombardy-Venetia** for the Kingdom of **Sardinia**: indeed, his actions led to the resignation of a furious **Cavour**. However, the armistice did provide the basis for Piedmontese acquisition of most of Lombardy by the Treaty of Zurich (Nov 1859).

Villalar, Battle of (23 Apr 1521) A relatively small engagement fought between the forces representing Emperor **Charles V** (Charles I of Spain) and the rebel **Comuneros**, commanded by Juan **Padilla**. In bad weather conditions, the dispirited Comunero force was routed by the royal cavalry, suffering about 500 losses to about 20 on the royalist side. Padilla, with his principal colleagues, Juan Bravo and Francisco Maldonado, was summarily executed the next day in Villalar.

Villa, Pancho (Francisco) (1877–1923) Mexican revolutionary. The son of a field labourer, he followed a variety of modest occupations until he joined **Madero**'s uprising against **Díaz** (1911) and the Mexican Revolution made him famous as a military commander. In a fierce struggle for control of the revolution, he and **Zapata** were defeated (1915) by Venustiano **Carranza**, with whom Villa had earlier allied himself against the dictatorship of General Victoriano Huerta. Both Villa and Zapata withdrew to strongholds in north and central Mexico, from where they continued to direct guerrilla warfare. In 1916 Villa was responsible for the shooting of a number of US citizens in the town of Santa Isabel, as well as an attack on the city of Columbus, New Mexico, which precipitated the sending of a US punitive force by President Woodrow **Wilson**. The troops failed to capture Villa and he continued to oppose Carranza's regime until the latter's death (1920), when he laid down his arms and was pardoned. He was murdered at his hacienda in Chihuahua.

Villars, Claude Louis Hector, Duke of (1653–1734) French soldier. He fought with distinction in the third Dutch War (1672–8) and in the War of the **Spanish Succession** (1701–14). In 1711 he headed the last army France could raise, and with it fell upon the British and Dutch at Denain (July 1712). He became principal adviser on military affairs and foreign policy, and fought again in his 80s at the outbreak of the War of the Polish Succession (1733–8). He died at Turin. ▷ **Marlborough, Duke of; Spanish Succession, War of the**

Villeneuve, Pierre (Charles Jean Baptiste Sylvestre) de (1763–1806) French admiral. He commanded the rear division of the French Navy at the Battle of the Nile, and in 1805 was in charge of the French fleet at the Battle of **Trafalgar**, where he was taken prisoner. Released in 1806, during his return journey to Paris to face **Napoleon I**, he committed suicide at Rennes. ▷ **Napoleonic Wars**

Vimy Ridge An escarpment five miles north-east of Arras (Pas-de-Calais), and a strongly held part of the German defence line on the Western Front in **World War I**. It was successfully stormed during the Battle of Arras by the Canadian Corps of the British 1st Army (1917). This feat of arms had great symbolic significance in establishing Canada's identity as an independent nation.

Violencia, La The name given in Colombia to the undeclared civil war between Conservatives and Liberals, at its most intense between 1948 and 1955. The period was marked by numerous atrocities, especially in the countryside. Deaths attributable to the conflict probably exceeded 200 000.

Visconti Lords of Milan and Lombardy from 1277, and the most powerful family in northern Italy. The foundations were laid by Ottone, Archbishop of Milan (d.1295). Giovanni (1290–1354), who was archbishop, brought Genoa and Bologna under his jurisdiction. From 1395, the Visconti were hereditary Dukes of Milan (then probably

the largest city in Italy) and Gian Galeazzo Visconti threatened for a time to conquer the whole of the peninsula. The male line died out in 1447, and after a brief republican interlude the succession passed to the Sforza.
▷ Visconti, Gian Galeazzo

Visconti, Gian Galeazzo (1351–1402) Milanese statesman. He succeeded his father, Galeazzo II, as joint ruler (1378/85) with his uncle Bernabo, whom he put to death (1385). As Duke (1385) he made himself master of the northern half of Italy, bringing many independent cities into one state, arranging marriage alliances with England, France, Austria and Bavaria, and acting as a great patron of the arts.

Visigoths A Germanic people who fled from the **Huns** in 376 into the Roman Empire and founded several Visigothic kingdoms extending through Portugal, most of Spain and southern Gaul. At their peak in the 6c in the Iberian Peninsula, the Visigoths absorbed elements of Roman culture and, despite their official Arian Christianity, allowed Catholic Christianity to coexist. Toledo was adopted as their capital under King Leovigildo, whose son, Recared, embraced Catholicism. The Council of Toledo of 589 initiated Catholic supremacy and the extension of Roman culture. Visigothic civilization has left many impressive artefacts and treasures, but decayed after the Arab conquests that began in 711.

Vitellius, Aulus (AD 15–69) The third of the four emperors who ruled at Rome during the so-called Year of the **Four Emperors** (AD 69). Appointed by **Galba** as Governor of Lower Germany in 68, he was proclaimed emperor by his troops there in Jan 69 but did not actually come to power until his victory over Galba's short-lived successor **Otho** in Apr of that year. As Emperor, Vitellius achieved nothing, except a reputation for gluttony. With his overthrow and brutal murder in Dec by troops loyal to Vespasian, Rome's year of civil war was brought to an end.

Vittorio Veneto, Battle of (Oct 1918) The major victory for the Italians and their allies under General **Diaz** over Austrian forces at the end of **World War I**.

Viviani, René (1862–1925) French politician. As Prime Minister at the outbreak of **World War I**, in order to demonstrate France's peaceful intentions he withdrew French forces from the German frontier. He was Minister of Justice in 1915 and French representative at the **League of Nations** in 1920.

Vlachs A Balkan people whose name is derived from *Walh*, the Germanic word for all peoples of Roman and Celtic ancestry. In the early Middle Ages most Vlachs lived in Great Wallachia in **Thessaly**, **Thrace** and in the Carpathian region. The Vlachs in the region of modern Romania romanized the Slavs between the Carpathians and the Danube and created the principalities of Vlaška or Wallachia, and Moldavia. Elsewhere, they generally became assimilated to the Slavs although some authentically Vlach communities still remain: the Aromuns of **Macedonia** and eastern **Serbia**; the Ćići in **Istria**. Typically nomadic or semi-nomadic, they worked as shepherds and cowherds but some settled in towns and became wealthy hellenized merchants known as **Tsintsars** (or Cincars). ▷ **Moldavia and Wallachia**

Vladimir (Svyatoslavich) I, 'the Great' (d.1015) Grand Prince of Kiev (c.978/1015). One of ancient Russia's most illustrious rulers, he consolidated the state, and led victorious campaigns against the Viatichi, Lithuanians, and Bulgars. Under his rule the economy and culture of Kievan Russia generally flourished. In 988 he was converted to Christianity, and adopted the Greek Orthodox rite from Byzantium as the official religion of Russia. After his death, Kievan Russia was torn apart by dynastic rivalries among his 12 sons. He was later canonized.

Vladimir II, 'Monomachus' (1053–1125) Grand Prince of Kiev (1113/25). The great-grandson of **Vladimir I, 'the Great'**, he became by popular demand Grand Prince of Kiev in 1113 instead of the prior claimants of the Syiatoslav and Izyaslav families, thus founding the Monomakhovichi Dynasty. A popular, powerful, enlightened and peaceful ruler, he colonized, built new towns, dethroned unruly princes and introduced laws against usury. He left careful instructions to his son and cousin in the manuals *Puchenie* and *Poslanie*.

Vladimirescu, Todor (1780–1821) Romanian national leader. Born into a family of free peasants in Wallachia, he led the ill-fated 1821 revolt in **Moldavia and Wallachia**. Drawing on the support of the peasants and small landowners and cooperating with Greek leaders of the **Filiki Etairia**, he raised an insurrection against Ottoman rule which was the prelude to the **Greek War of Independence**. When Russia did not lend its support, he realized that the revolt would fail and so he opened negotiations with the Ottoman Porte. When the Greek leader, Alexander **Ypsilanti** (1783–1828), learnt of this, he had Vladimirescu kidnapped and murdered.

Vlasov, Andrei Andreevich (1900–46) Soviet general. During **World War II** he distinguished himself defending his country until he was captured during 1942 when he emerged as the leader of a Russian group intending to overthrow **Stalin**. It was only subsequently in 1944 that he was allowed to raise two divisions to serve on the Russian front. In 1945 he surrendered to the Americans who handed him over to the Soviet authorities, who tried and hanged him in 1946. He was seen as a traitor to his country, but later revelations concerning Stalin and the more recent collapse of **communism** have caused some observers to question that judgement.

VMRO (*Vnutrašnja Makedonska Revolucionarska Organizacija*, 'Internal Macedonian Revolutionary Organization') Founded in Salonica in 1893, the organization's goal was 'Macedonia for the Macedonians'. The failure of the **Ilinden Uprising** of 1903, however, divided its membership: the federalists wanted autonomy within a Balkan federation; the centralists wanted annexation to Bulgaria. After the **Balkan Wars** and **World War I**, when Macedonia was divided, VMRO, with Italian and Hungarian backing, waged a terrorist campaign from Bulgaria against the Yugoslav government. It kidnapped, tortured and murdered **Stamboliski** after he signed the Treaty of Niš (1923) and was involved in the assassination of King **Alexander I** of Yugoslavia (1934). ▷ **Macedonians; Tsankov, Alexander**

Vogel, Hans-Jochen (1926–) West German politician, successor to Helmut **Schmidt** as leader of the Social Democratic Party (**SPD**). A former Minister of Housing and Town Planning (1972–4) and Minister of Justice (1974–81), he also served briefly as governing Mayor of West Berlin (1981). ▷ **Germany, West**

Vogel, Sir Julius (1835–99) British-born New Zealand politician. He emigrated to Australia in 1852 and on to New Zealand in 1861. He edited and founded newspapers in both countries, entered the New Zealand

parliament in 1863 and became Colonial Treasurer in 1869. He embarked on an extensive but inadequately regulated programme of public works funded by overseas borrowing, successfully stimulating rapid economic development on uncertain foundations. Conflicts with the provinces led to the abolition of provincial governments in 1875. He became Prime Minister in 1873, but retired in 1876 to become Agent-General in London. He returned to New Zealand politics and office in 1884 but renewed borrowing failed to stem the recession. The ministry fell in 1887 and Vogel retired from politics in 1889.

Vogt In German history, an official appointed by the king or the emperor to administer imperial lands or a royal abbey. The most extensive of the lands administered in this way was the so-called *Vogtland*, which during the Hohenstaufen period was centred on the river Elster and had its administrative centre in Plauen. ▷ **Hohenstaufen Dynasty**

Vojvodina Literally 'duchy', the name refers to the region bounded by Hungary, Croatian **Slavonia** and the River Danube, with its chief town at Novi Sad. Settled by the Slavs (6–7c) and by the Magyars (9–10c), it fell to the Turks in 1526. By the Treaties of **Karlowitz** (1699) and **Passarowitz** (1718), it came under the rule of Vienna. Under the Habsburgs, its fertile plains were settled by Germans, Slovaks, Hungarians, Ruthenians and Romanians. In Nov 1918, at the end of **World War I**, the National Assembly of the Vojvodina voted to join the Kingdom of Serbs, **Croats** and Slovenes (later Yugoslavia). Occupied by the Germans (Apr 1941), it was divided between the Nazi-collaborating governments of Hungary and the Independent State of **Croatia**. In 1945 it became an autonomous unit within the Republic of **Serbia** in the Socialist Federal Republic of Yugoslavia. ▷ **Habsburg Dynasty**

Volkspartij voor Vrijheid en Democratie ▷ **Liberal Party** (Netherlands)

Volksraad The ruling council of the Boer republics in South Africa. Volksraads were established by the various Boer communities in the interior of southern Africa after the **Great Trek** which commenced in 1835. They became the legislative bodies of the Transvaal and the Orange Free State up to the Boer War of 1899–1902. Volksraads were also created by the Griqua or half-caste republics established on the frontier of the Cape in the 19c. ▷ **Boer Wars**

Volstead, Andrew John (1860–1947) US politician. A lawyer, he entered Congress for the Republicans in 1903 and is best remembered as the author of the 1919 Volstead Act, which prohibited the manufacture, transportation and sale of alcoholic beverages. The purpose of the legislation, which remained in force until 1933, was to placate the influential temperance movement, and to divert grain to food production in the wake of **World War I**. In fact, prohibition proved impossible to enforce effectively, and did little other than to create enormous profits for bootleggers and speakeasies, and to provide Hollywood with the inspiration for countless gangster movies.

Vonckists A late 18c Southern Netherlands progressive political faction, named after their leader J F Vonck (1743–92). In reaction to the rationalist reforms of Emperor Joseph II, two groups rose up in the **Brabant Revolution**; the **Statists** and the Vonckists. The latter were mainly from the middle classes, and represented the forces of the **French Revolution** in the southern Netherlands. In 1790 many had to flee to France, but they returned with the revolutionary armies in 1792 and 1794.

Voortrekkers The Boer migrants who left the Cape Colony from 1835 onwards to escape British rule and create independent republics in the interior of southern Africa. The British took the Cape during the **Napoleonic Wars** and held it after the peace settlement at Vienna. New land-owning systems, legal and administrative concepts, the English language, British settlers and more missionary activity were all introduced under their rule. The Boers took particular exception to the new legal status of their black workers, the emancipation of slaves in 1833 and the inability of the British to introduce acceptable frontier policies. A number of columns of Voortrekkers left under a series of leaders, including Louis Tregardt, Piet **Retief**, Gerrit Maritz, and Hendrik Potgieter. About 6000 left the Colony and established a number of small republics in the region across the Orange and Vaal Rivers and Natal. Many withdrew from Natal when it was declared a British colony in 1843, and the republics coalesced into the Orange Free State and the South African Republic or Transvaal. For the rest of the 19c, the British made repeated and largely unavailing attempts to bring them back within their jurisdiction. The Voortrekkers

are commemorated by a powerful and romantic monument in Pretoria.

Voroshilov, Kliment Yefremovich (1881–1969) Soviet Marshal and politician. He joined the Russian Social Democratic Labour Party in 1903, but political agitation soon brought about his exile to Siberia, where he remained a fugitive until 1914. He played a military rather than a political role in the 1917 **Russian Revolution**, and as Commissar for Defence (1925–40) was responsible for the modernization of the **Red Army**. He was removed from office after the failure to prevent the German siege of Leningrad, but stayed active in the party, and after **Stalin**'s death became head of state (1953–60). ▷ **World War II**

Vorrink, Jacobus Jan (1891–1955) Dutch politician. Beginning as a schoolteacher, he joined the Socialist Party (SDAP) in 1918, and was highly active in the socialist youth movements, eventually becoming Party Chairman in 1934. He sat in the First Chamber of parliament from 1935 to 1946, and was a member of the Second Chamber (1946–54). Despite having spent the period 1943–5 in a **concentration camp**, after **World War II** a press campaign accused him of having harboured fascist sympathies; perhaps this was the reason that he never held a cabinet post. ▷ **Party of Labour**

Vorster, John (Balthazar Johannes Vorster) (1915–83) South African politician. Educated at Stellenbosch University, he later became a lawyer and was a leader of the extreme Afrikaner group, Ossewa Brandwag, in **World War II**, as a result of which he was interned for the duration of the war. He was elected to parliament for the **National Party** in 1953 and was Minister of Justice (1961–5) before becoming Prime Minister (1966–78) and, for a brief moment, President. He was largely responsible for the imposition of the repressive **apartheid** laws and did not hesitate to employ state power to protect white interests. However, he was implicated in the 'Muldergate' scandal in which government funds had been misappropriated and was forced to resign.

Vortigern (5c) Semi-legendary King of Britain. According to Bede, he recruited Germanic mercenaries led by Hengist and Horsa to help fight off the **Picts** after the final withdrawal of the Roman administration from Britain (AD409). Tradition has it that the revolt of these troops opened the way for the Germanic conquests and settlements in England. ▷ **Angles; Britain, Roman; Jutes; Saxons**

Voting Rights Act (1965) US suffrage legislation. The law prohibited all means by which the segregationist Southern states had been able to prevent blacks from registering to vote. The Attorney-General was empowered to dispatch federal registrars anywhere that local officials were obstructing registration of blacks; the act was so effective that 250 000 new black voters had been able to register before the end of the year.

Voznesenksy,   Nikolai   Alexeevich (1903–50) Soviet economist. Educated after the **Russian Revolution** (1917) in the Institute of Red Professors, he lectured there until in 1935 **Zhdanov** recruited him as a planning assistant. He then became Chairman of the State Planning Bureau (1938–49), with one short interval in 1941–2 when Giorgiy **Malenkov** was in the ascendant. He managed both the war-time economy and the post-war recovery, but **Stalin** had him arrested in 1949 and executed in 1950, seemingly because of the Zhdanov connection.

Vranitzky,   Franz (1937–) Austrian politician. Educated at what is now the University of Commerce, Vienna, he embarked on a career in banking and in 1970 became adviser on economic and financial policy to the Minister of Finance. After holding senior appointments in the banking world he became Minister of Finance himself in 1984 and two years later succeeded Fred Sinowatz as Federal Chancellor.

Vyshinsky, Andrei Yanuaryevich (1883–1954) Russian jurist and politician. He studied law at Moscow, joined the Communist Party in 1920, and became Professor of Criminal Law and then Attorney-General (1923–5). He was the public prosecutor at the state trials (1936–8) which removed **Stalin**'s rivals, and later became the Soviet delegate to the **UN** (1945–9 and 1953–4), and Foreign Minister (1949–53).

W

Wacha Dinshaw Edulji (1844–1936) Indian politician. A member of the Bombay Legislative Council and the Imperial Legislative Council, he worked in close association with Dadabhai Naoroji and Ferozshah Mehta for the peaceful development of his country through social reform, education and participation in politics. A founder-member of the Congress, he was its President in 1901. He criticized the British government's economic and financial policies and freely expressed his nation's viewpoint before the Welby Commission in London.

Wafd Party The name of the Egyptian nationalist party which sent a delegation under the nationalist leader Sa'd **Zaghlul** to the British High Commissioner in 1919; the word means 'delegation'. The 'New Wafd' became Egypt's official opposition party in 1984, but was replaced as such in 1987 by an alliance headed by the **Muslim Brotherhood**.

Wagner Act ▷ **National Labor Relations Act**

Wagram, Battle of (1809) A victory achieved by **Napoleon I** over the Austrians under Archduke Charles (1771–1847), fought north-east of Vienna, notable for the unparalleled concentration of artillery fire. Napoleon forced **Austria** to seek an armistice and negotiate the Treaty of **Vienna** (1809). ▷ **Napoleonic Wars**

Wahhab, Muhammad ibn Abd al- (1703–92) Eponymous founder of the strict Wahhabi sect in Islam. Born at Uyayna, he received his early education in Medina whereafter he travelled widely in Iraq and Persia, teaching and studying. He also became an advocate of the Hanbali school of jurisprudence and returned to Uyayna whence he was expelled for disruptive activities. Moving to Dar'iyya where the local chieftain, Muhammad ibn Saud, accepted his doctrine and undertook its defence and propagation, he aimed to get rid of *bid'a* (innovation) later than the 3cADand was vigorous in his opposition to the cult of saints. Abd al-Wahhab's religious views (which were of extreme simplicity) underpinned the aggressive and expansionist policies of Ibn

Saud, and by the time of Abd al-Wahhab's death, Ibn Saud's son, Abd al-Aziz, was master of the whole of Najd. ▷ **Wahhabis**

Wahhabis An Islamic movement which derives from Muhammad ibn Abd al-**Wahhab**, a religious reformer from Uyayna near Riyadh, and Muhammad ibn Saud, the ancestor of the present rulers of Saudi Arabia. The alliance was to lead to the unification in the 18c of most of the peninsula under the Saudi banner. The modern reunification of the kingdom was carried out 1902–32 by King Abd al-Aziz, otherwise known as 'Ibn Saud'. Arabs call the followers of Abd al-Wahhab *muwahhidun* or 'unitarians' rather than *Wahhabis*, which is an anglicism. The movement maintains that legal decisions must be based exclusively on the Quran and the *Sunna*. The original Wahhabis banned music, dancing, poetry, silk, gold, and jewellery, and in the 20c, the *ikhwan* ('brotherhood') have attacked the telephone, radio and television as innovations not sanctioned by God.

Waitangi, Treaty of (1840) The treaty that marked the formal assumption of sovereignty over New Zealand by a reluctant British government. Based on the fiction that Maori society resembled European in concepts of sovereignty and organization of government, it recognized Maori property rights in which they were promised undisturbed possession, gave the crown the sole right of purchase should they wish to sell, and bestowed upon them the rights and privileges of British subjects. The land question nevertheless remained a source of contention and warfare between settlers and **Maoris** for much of the 19c. ▷ **Maori Wars**

Wakefield, Edward Gibbon (1796–1862) English colonial politician. Sentenced for abduction in 1827, he wrote in prison *A Letter from Sydney* (1829), which outlined his theory (expanded in several other books) of systematic colonization by the sale of crown lands at a price sufficient to oblige intending purchasers to work for wages while amassing capital. The intention was to re-create English society as a basis for future self-government, attracting landowners by ensuring a supply of respectable labour, both male and female, and assisting labourers to emigrate from the proceeds of the land sales. He influenced the South Australian Association (which founded South Australia in 1836) and, as secretary (1838) to Lord Durham, the **Durham Report** on Canada. He formed (1837) the New Zealand Association and sent a shipload of colonists there (1839) to force the British government to recognize it as a colony. With George William, 4th Baron Lyttleton, he founded (1850) the Anglican colony of Canterbury, where he emigrated in 1853.

Waldeck-Rousseau, Pierre Marie René

(1846–1904) French politician. A successful lawyer, he was a Deputy (1879–89) and Senator (1894–1904), first holding office in **Gambetta**'s cabinet (1881–2) and then under **Ferry** (1883–5) as Minister of the Interior. In 1884 he was responsible for a law legalizing trade unions. He retired from politics in 1889 to concentrate on his legal practice, but was brought back as Prime Minister (1899–1904) at the high point of the crisis caused by the **Dreyfus** Affair. His ministry, known as the Ministry of Republican Defence, pardoned Dreyfus and survived the noisy attacks of the nationalist and anti-Semitic **leagues**. It was a coalition that included a wide spectrum of opinion from the conservative republicans of which he was himself one, through the radicals to the socialist **Millerand**, and was supported by the Bloc des gauches ('Left-wing Bloc'). It passed the law on associations, which Waldeck-Rousseau saw as a way of legalizing the position of Catholic religious orders in France. The law was used instead to begin a process that led to the dissolution of the great majority of the orders. Profoundly out of sympathy with the fervent anti-clericalism that had developed in his majority, he resigned after winning the 1902 elections.

Waldheim, Kurt (1918–) Austrian politician. He entered the Austrian foreign service (1945) and was Minister and subsequently Ambassador to Canada (1955–60), Director of Political Affairs at the Ministry (1960–4), Austrian representative at the **UN** (1964–8 and 1970–1), Foreign Minister (1968–70), and then UN Secretary-General (1972–81). His presidential candidature was controversial, because of claims that he had lied about his wartime activities, and had been involved in anti-Jewish and other atrocities in the Balkans. He denied the allegations and, despite international

pressure, continued with his campaign, winning the presidency in 1986. ▷ **Austria, Republic of**

Waldo, Peter (fl.1175) French religious leader. He became a preacher in Lyons (1170) and practised voluntary poverty. He was eventually excommunicated and banished from Lyons in 1184 with his followers, who because of their vow of poverty were known as 'The Holy Paupers'. They became known as the Waldenses.

Wałesa, Lech (1943–) Polish trade unionist. A former Gdansk shipyard worker, he became the leader of the independent trade union, **Solidarity**, which in 1980 openly challenged the Polish government's economic and social policies. He held negotiations with the leading figures in the Communist Party and had tacit but strong support from the Roman Catholic Church, but was detained by the authorities when martial law was declared in 1981. He was released in 1982, and was awarded the Nobel Peace Prize in 1983. Despite restrictions imposed on him, he continued to be a prominent figure in Polish politics, and was mainly responsible for the success of the negotiations which led to Solidarity effectively forming the first Polish non-Communist government in Sep 1989. This not only transformed the course of events in Poland but was an important contributory factor in the whole East European revolution in the winter of 1989–90. Wałesa became President in Dec 1990.

Wall Street Crash The collapse of the US stock market in Oct 1929. The Crash followed an artificial boom in the US economy (1927–9) fuelled by speculation. Panic-selling resulted in 13 million shares changing hands on 24 Oct, and 16 million on 29 Oct, causing widespread bankruptcy and a massive rise in unemployment. ▷ **Great Depression**

Wallace, William (c.1274–1305) Scottish knight and champion of the independence of Scotland. He routed the English Army at Stirling (1297), and took control of the government of Scotland as 'Guardian', but was defeated by **Edward I** at Falkirk (1298). He was eventually captured near Glasgow (1305), and was hanged, drawn, and quartered at Smithfield, London. Many legends collected around him due to his immense popular appeal as a national figure resisting foreign oppression.

Wallenberg, Raoul (1912–?47) Swedish diplomat. He was a member of a prominent Swedish business family. In 1944 he was sent to Hungary under the auspices of the American War Refugee Board to attempt to rescue the 700 000 Jews put at risk by the German occupation of the country. With the help of special passports and warnings to the occupying power of post-war retribution, he managed to save over 100 000 Hungarian Jews. He was arrested by the Russians when they marched into Budapest in 1945, and disappeared. In spite of Russian claims that he died in 1947 as their prisoner, rumours continued to circulate that he was alive even in the 1970s.

Wallenstein (Waldstein), Albrecht (Wenzel Eusebius), Herzog von (1583–1634) Bohemian general. During the **Thirty Years War** he became Commander of the Imperial armies and won a series of victories (1625–9), gaining the titles of the Duke of Mecklenburg and 'General of the Baltic and Oceanic Seas'. His ambition led to his dismissal in 1630, but he was reinstated to defend the Empire against Swedish attack. He recovered Bohemia, but was defeated by **Gustav II Adolf** at **Lützen** (1632), and was again dismissed. His intrigues led to an Imperial proclamation of treason, resulting in his assassination at Eger by Irish mercenaries.

Walloon Movement Belgian political movement, formed largely in reaction to the progress made by the **Flemish Movement**. Ever since Flemish rights were claimed in the early 19c, Walloon (southern Belgium, French-speaking) counter-claims have been lodged; since the early 20c there have been Walloon congresses each year in Liège. The movement has often been rather negative, perhaps because of the decline of Wallonia in economic and demographic terms in relation to Flanders in the 20c. After **World War II** a National Walloon Congress spoke out for such alternatives as federalism, Walloon independence, or even annexation of Wallonia by France. In 1961 the Popular Walloon Movement was founded, agitating for the federal solution. In 1968 all the various Walloon organizations came together in the **Rassemblement Wallon**; its power to win seats had declined by the late 1970s. The movement's contribution to Belgian politics has been to accelerate the country's federalization.

Walpole, Sir Robert (1676–1745) English politician. He became a Whig MP in 1701, and was made Secretary for War (1708) and Treasurer of the Navy (1710). Sent to the Tower for alleged corruption during the Tory government (1712), he was recalled by **George I**, and made a Privy Councillor and (1715) Chancellor of the Exchequer. After the collapse of the South Sea Scheme, he again became Chancellor (1721), and was widely recognized as 'Prime Minister', a title (unknown to the constitution) which he hotly repudiated. A shrewd manipulator of men, he took trouble to consult backbench MPs, and followed policies of low taxation designed to win their favour. He was regarded as indispensable by both George I and **George II**. His popularity began to wane in the 1730s over the Excise Scheme and also over his determination to avoid foreign wars. He did not fully recover from the outbreak of a war he had opposed in 1739, and resigned in 1742. His period in office is widely held to have increased the influence of the House of Commons in the constitution. He was created Earl of Orford. ▷ **South Sea Bubble**

Walsingham, Sir Francis (c.1530–90) English statesman. He studied at Cambridge, became a diplomat, and was made a Secretary of State to **Elizabeth I** (1573–90), a member of the Privy Council, and knighted. A Puritan sympathizer, and a strong opponent of the Catholics, he developed a complex system of espionage at home and abroad, enabling him to reveal the plots of **Throckmorton** and **Babington** against the Queen, and was one of the commissioners to try **Mary, Queen of Scots** at Fotheringay. ▷ **Puritanism**

Walter, Hubert (c.1140–1205) English churchman and statesman. He became Bishop of Salisbury (1189), and accompanied **Richard I, 'the Lionheart'** on the Third Crusade. Appointed Archbishop of Canterbury in 1193, he played key roles in raising the ransom to secure Richard's release from captivity, and in containing the rebellion of the King's brother, **John**. At the end of 1193, he became justiciar of England, and was responsible for all the business of government until his resignation in 1198. On John's accession (1199), he became Chancellor, and was consulted on important matters of state. ▷ **Crusades**

Wandervogel German and Austrian youth movement. Founded in Germany in 1901 and **Austria** in 1909, this movement asserted youthful values in society and an affinity with nature. Organized hikes, rural trysts and a search for adventure attracted a significant membership to the various *Wandervogel* associations. These continued to function during the **Weimar Republic**, but were closed by the **Nazi Party** in 1933, with members being transferred to the Hitler Youth.

Wang Ching-wei ▷ **Wang Jingwei**

Wang Jingwei (Wang Ching-wei) (1883–1944) Chinese politician. An associate of the revolutionary and Nationalist leader **Sun Yat-sen**, he studied in Japan, where he joined Sun's revolutionary party, and from 1917 became his personal assistant. In 1927 he was appointed head of the new **Guomindang** government at Wuhan, and in 1932 became the party's President, with his main rival for control of the Guomindang, **Chiang Kai-shek**, in charge of the military. In 1938, after the outbreak of war with Japan, Wang offered to cooperate with the Japanese, and in 1940 he became head of a puppet regime ruling the occupied areas.

war A military conflict between two states, or, in the case of civil war, between different groups within a state. International war is subject to international law, and wars can be either lawful or unlawful. There have been a series of treaties since the 18c covering the conduct of war, largely designed to prevent 'unnecessary suffering', or action that has no military advantage. The use of more overtly ideological wars and modern weapons have made it more difficult to regulate the conduct of war (eg greater difficulty in protecting civilians from aerial bombardment). Today the main source of international law on war or the use of force is the **UN** Charter, notably article 2(4). Distinctions are also now drawn between conventional warfare, which does not involve the use of nuclear weapons, nuclear warfare, chemical warfare, and biological warfare. A guerrilla war is conducted by non-regular forces, often avoiding direct engagement, designed to make a state ungovernable prior to a seizure of power.

warlords Chinese provincial military rulers who engaged in a bitter power struggle and civil war after the death of President **Yuan Shikai** in 1916. They were eventually subdued by the 1926–8 **Northern Expedition** of **Chiang Kai-shek**.

War Measures Act (1914) Canadian statute. Enacted in the first weeks of **World War I**, it gave the federal government extraordinary powers. It could bypass the

normal legislative process, suspend habeas corpus and deport without trial. It also included emergency economic regulations. Under the Act, immigrants from Germany and Austria-Hungary were forced to carry special identity cards and to register at regular intervals, while 8 300 aliens were interned in special camps. During **World War II** 6 414 orders were made under the War Measures Act; and it was still in force in 1945 when a defector from the USSR, Igor Gouzenko, informed on a Soviet spy ring in Canada. The findings of a Royal Commission led to the arrest, under the Act, of the single communist MP, a prominent scientist and members of the civil and military service. In 1970 the Act was again invoked to deal with the **October Crisis** in Quebec.

War of 1812 The name given to the hostilities between the UK and the United States between 1812 and 1814. Its deepest causes went back to some unfulfilled provisions of the Peace of 1783, which secured American independence. However, war was eventually provoked by the persistent refusal of Britain to recognize American neutral and maritime rights. After 1793, in the course of the Anglo-French war, American trade was incessantly disrupted and American ships continually subjected to boarding and their crews to impressment. The most notorious of these incidents, the surrender of the USS *Chesapeake* to HMS *Leopard* in 1807, provoked commercial retaliation with President Thomas **Jefferson**'s embargo policy. The failure of both this and the subsequent Non-Intercourse Act to alter British policies eventually left the USA no other option but to declare war, if independence was to mean anything at all. Ironically, war began as British policy was changed with the suspension of the Orders in Council, while the most decisive military engagement, the American victory at the Battle of New Orleans, occurred after peace had been made at the Treaty of **Ghent** (Dec 1814). Apart from this defeat, the British were militarily more effective, victorious with their Native American allies against American attempts to gain Canadian land, and even burning down the Capitol and the White House in Washington. The peace treaty marked a change in the attitude of Britain towards the USA, allowing a mutually beneficial commercial relationship to develop and for the USA marking the achievement of substantive, as well as formal, independence.

War of Independence, US ▷ **American Revolution**

War Powers Act (1973) US legislation requiring that Congress be consulted before the President dispatch US forces into battle, and that Congress approve any continuance of war beyond 60 days. Public confidence in the executive branch had been greatly diminished after the **Vietnam War** and **Watergate** and, like the Freedom of Information Act, this act aimed to limit its power.

Warren, Earl (1891–1974) US jurist. He attended the University of California law school and was admitted to the bar. An active Republican, he became Governor of California (1943–53) and made an unsuccessful run for the vice-presidency in 1948. He became Chief Justice of the US Supreme Court in 1953. The Warren Court (1953–69) was active and influential, notably in the areas of civil rights and individual liberties. It was responsible for the landmark decision in **Brown v Board of Education of Topeka, Kansas** (1954), which outlawed school segregation, and for Miranda v Arizona (1966), which ruled that criminal suspects be informed of their rights before being questioned by the police. Warren was chairman of the federal commission (the Warren Commission) that investigated the assassination of President John F **Kennedy**.

Warsaw Pact The shorthand name for the East European Mutual Assistance Treaty signed in Warsaw in 1955 by Albania, Bulgaria, Czechoslovakia, East Germany, Hungary, Poland, Romania and the USSR. Albania withdrew in 1968. The pact established a unified military command for the armed forces of all the signatories who were committed to giving immediate assistance to one another in the event of an attack in Europe. It was a Soviet bloc response, in part, to the formation of **NATO** by the West. But it also had a political purpose, as was demonstrated when it was used in Czechoslovakia to restore communism, allegedly endangered by the **Prague Spring** in 1968. In the wake of the East European revolution in the winter of 1989–90, the pact effectively disintegrated before it was officially terminated in 1991.

Wars of the Coalition A series of wars against Revolutionary France. The first coalition (1793) began to collapse as a result of **Napoleon I**'s victories in 1797. In 1799, a second coalition arose after **Nelson**'s victory over the French in Egypt (**Aboukir Bay**) but dissolved with the overthrow of the French First Republic by Napoleon. A third coalition

was created in 1805 to defeat Napoleon. ▷ **Republic, First** (France)

Wartburg A castle near Eisenach on a hill first fortified in 1080. After 1485 the castle belonged to the Dukes of Saxony. Martin Luther, after the Diet of Worms, hid at the Wartburg (May 1521–Mar 1522) to avoid Imperial persecution.

Warwick, Richard Neville, Earl of ('the Kingmaker') (1428–71) English soldier and politician. He exercised great power during the first phase of the Wars of the **Roses**. Created Earl of Warwick in 1450, he championed the Yorkist cause. In 1460 he defeated and captured **Henry VI** at Northampton, had his cousin, Edward of York, proclaimed King as **Edward IV** (1461), and then destroyed the Lancastrian army at Towton. When Edward tried to assert his independence, Warwick joined the Lancastrians, forced the King to flee to Holland, and restored Henry VI to the throne (1470). He was defeated and killed by Edward IV at the Battle of Barnet. ▷ **Lancaster, House of; York, House of**

Washington, Booker Taliaferro (1856–1915) US black leader and educationist. He was born a slave in Franklin County, Virginia. After emancipation (1865), he was educated at Hampton Institute, Virginia, and Washington DC, then became a teacher, writer, and speaker on black problems and the importance of education and vocational training. In 1881 he was appointed principal of the newly-opened Tuskegee Institute, Alabama, and built it into a major centre of black education. The foremost black leader in the late 19c, he encouraged blacks to focus on economic equality rather than fight for social or political equality. He was strongly criticized by W E B **Du Bois**, and his policies were repudiated by the 20c **civil rights** movement. He is the author of *Up From Slavery* (1901).

Washington, George (1732–99) US general and 1st President of the USA. He had an informal education, worked as a surveyor, and first fought in the campaigns of the French and Indian War (1754–8). He then managed the family estate at Mount Vernon, Virginia, becoming active in politics as a member of the Virginia House of Burgesses (1758–74). He then represented Virginia in the first (1774) and second (1775) Continental Congresses. In 1775 he was given command of the American forces, where he displayed great powers as a strategist and leader of men. Following reverses in the New York area, he retreated through New Jersey, inflicting notable defeats on the enemy at Trenton (1776) and Princeton (1777). He suffered defeats at Brandywine and Germantown, but held his army together through the severe winter of 1777–8 at **Valley Forge**. After the alliance with France (1778), he forced the surrender of **Cornwallis** at Yorktown in 1781, marking the end of the war. He then retired to Mount Vernon, and sought to secure a strong government by constitutional means. In 1787 he presided over the Constitutional Convention, and became the first President, an office he held from 1789 to 1797. He tried to remain neutral as political differences increased between the Federalists and Jeffersonians, and refused to continue for a third term in office. He retired to Mount Vernon and died two years later. ▷ **American Revolution**

Washington, Treaty of (1871) Treaty between the USA and Great Britain (whose delegation included the Canadian Prime Minister, John A **Macdonald**). The USA demanded compensation for the damage inflicted during the **American Civil War** by Confederate raiders using arms manufactured in Britain, together with arbitration of the boundary south of Vancouver Island and the possession of the strategic island of San Juan. Canada hoped to negotiate a trade agreement in return for the admission of US fishermen to her inshore waters. Macdonald was well aware that Britain, above all, wished to establish good relations with the USA and he was determined that Canadian interests should not suffer. While the USA secured compensation and a favourable settlement of the boundary question, Macdonald ensured that Canada gained free navigation of the rivers of Alaska (crucial for the **Hudson's Bay Company**) in exchange for free US use of the St Lawrence. Fishing and trade agreements were also negotiated between Canada and the USA which formed the basis for a consultative arrangement to resolve problems before they became international crises involving the British.

Watergate (1972–4) US political scandal. It led to the first resignation of a President in US history (Richard **Nixon**, in office 1968–74). The actual 'Watergate' is a hotel and office complex in Washington, DC, where the **Democratic Party** had its headquarters. During the presidential campaign of 1972, a team of burglars was caught inside Democratic headquarters, and their connec-

tions were traced to the White House and to the Committee to Re-elect the President. Investigations by the *Washington Post*, a grand jury and two special prosecutors revealed that high officials who were very close to Nixon were implicated, and that Nixon himself was aware of illegal measures to cover up that implication. A number of officials were eventually imprisoned. Nixon himself left office when it became clear that he was likely to be impeached and removed. ▷ **Iran–Contra Affair**

Waterloo, Battle of (18 June 1815) The final defeat of **Napoleon I**, ending the **Napoleonic Wars** and the Emperor's last bid for power in the **Hundred Days**. A hard-fought battle, in which **Blücher**'s Prussian force arrived at the climax to support **Wellington**'s mixed Allied force. A number of crucial blunders by the French contributed to their defeat.

Wavell, Archibald Percival, 1st Earl (1883–1950) British field marshal. He served in South Africa and India, became **Allenby**'s Chief-of-Staff in Palestine, and in 1939 he was given the Middle East Command. He defeated the Italians in North Africa, but failed against **Rommel**, and in 1941 was transferred to India, where he became Viceroy (1943). He was made field marshal and viscount (1943), earl (1947), Constable of the Tower (1948), and Lord-Lieutenant of London (1949). ▷ **World War II**

Webb, Sidney (James) (1859–1947) and **(Martha) Beatrice** (1858–1943) British social reformers, historians, and economists, married in 1892. Sidney became a lawyer, and joined the **Fabian Society**, where he wrote many powerful tracts. Beatrice interested herself in the social problems of the time. After their marriage they were committed to advancing the causes of **socialism** and trade unionism, publishing their classic *History of Trade Unionism* (1894), *English Local Government* (1906–29, 9 vols), and other works. They also started the *New Statesman* (1913). Sidney became an MP (1922), President of the Board of Trade (1924), Dominions and Colonial Secretary (1929–30), and Colonial Secretary (1930–1), and was created a baron in 1929.

Weber, Max (1864–1920) German sociologist. Educated at Heidelberg and **Berlin**, he held university posts at Berlin (1893), Freiburg (1894), Heidelberg (1897) and Munich (1919). His best-known works include *Die protestantische Ethik und der Geist des*

Kapitalismus (1904, The Protestant Ethic and the Spirit of Capitalism) and *Wirtschaft und Gesellschaft* (Economy and Society) which were major influences on sociological theory. He helped to draft the constitution for the **Weimar Republic** (1919).

Webster, Daniel (1782–1852) US lawyer and statesman. He was called to the Bar in 1805, and served in the US House of Representatives (1813–17). Settling in Boston as an advocate in 1816, he distinguished himself before the US Supreme Court in the Dartmouth College case (1818) and **McCulloch v Maryland** (1819), and as an orator became famous by his speech on the bicentenary of the landing of the **Pilgrim Fathers**. He returned to Congress (Dec 1823) as a Massachusetts Representative, and in 1827 he became a Senator. Having previously favoured free trade, in 1828 he defended the new protective tariff. His career was marked by a deep reverence for established institutions and for the principle of nationality. When the **Whig Party** triumphed in 1840, Webster was called into Benjamin **Harrison**'s cabinet as Secretary of State (1841–3). Under President **Tyler**, he negotiated the **Webster–Ashburton Treaty** (1842) with Britain, but resigned in May 1843. In 1844 he refused his party's nomination for President and supported Henry **Clay**. He opposed the **Mexican War**. In 1850 he voiced his abhorrence of slavery, and unwilling to break up the Union to abolish it, supported compromise measures. Under President **Fillmore**, he was recalled as Secretary of State (1850–2) to settle differences with England. He was one of the greatest of US orators.

Webster–Ashburton Treaty (1842) An agreement between Britain and the USA which established the boundary between north-east USA and Canada. Among specific issues were disputed territory between Maine and New Brunswick and at the north end of Lake Champlain, navigation rights on the St John's River, and control of the Mesabi iron deposits. The treaty also established provisions for later joint action between the USA and Britain.

Weerstand, Het ▷ **Resistance Movement** (Belgium)

Wehrmacht Literally 'defence force', this is the term used to describe the German armed forces during the period 1935–45. Recruited by conscription, the *Wehrmacht* constituted the military strength of the National Socialist state and conducted the victorious **Blitzkrieg** campaigns of the period 1939–41. However, from 1938 the *Waffen-SS* ('Armed' **SS**) was developed as a parallel, Nazi army which, in the closing months of the war, came to overshadow the Wehrmacht. The members of the Wehrmacht were bound to **Hitler** by a personal oath of loyalty and its commanders generally carried out Hitler's orders willingly, although individuals, such as those involved in the July 1944 plot against him, did offer resistance. ▷ **Nazi Party**

Wei Ching-sheng ▷ **Wei Jingsheng**

Wei Jingsheng (Wei Ching-sheng) (1949–) Chinese political prisoner. A Red Guard during the **Cultural Revolution**, Wei served in the **People's Liberation Army** during the early 1970s before becoming an electrician at Beijing Zoo. During the **Democracy Wall Movement** (1978–9) he called for greater democracy (what he called the 'fifth modernization') and became the editor of an outspoken unofficial journal. He was arrested in Mar 1979 and brought to trial six months later on charges of divulging state secrets to foreigners and spreading counter-revolutionary propaganda. He was sentenced to 15 years in prison.

Weil, Simone (1909–43) French philosophical writer and mystic. She taught philosophy in several schools, interspersing this with periods of manual labour to experience the working-class life. In 1936 she served in the republican forces in the **Spanish Civil War**. In 1941 she settled in Marseilles, where she developed a deep mystical feeling for the Catholic faith, yet a profound reluctance to join an organized religion. She escaped to the USA in 1942 and worked for the **Free French** in London, before her death at Ashford, Kent. Her posthumously published works include *La Pesanteur et la Grâce* ('Gravity and Grace') and *Attente de Dieu* ('Waiting for God').

Weimar Republic The name by which the German Federal Republic of 1918–33 is known. In 1919 a National Constituent Assembly met at Weimar, on the River Elbe, and drew up a constitution for the new republic. The government moved from Weimar to **Berlin** in 1920. In 1933, two months after becoming Chancellor, **Hitler** passed an Enabling Act suspending the Weimar constitution.

Weisse Rose The German anti-Nazi resistance group (literally, 'White Rose'), centred on Professor Kurt Huber and the students Hans and Sophie Scholl of Munich University. From autumn 1942 until their arrest on 18 Feb 1943 the group pursued a leafleting campaign in which they called for resistance against a morally-bankrupt National Socialism. Arrested by the **Gestapo**, the Scholls were executed on 22 Feb 1943 and Huber on 13 July 1943.

Weizmann, Chaim (Azriel) (1874–1952) Israeli politician. Born in Russia, he studied in Germany and Switzerland, then lectured on chemistry at Geneva and Manchester. He helped to secure the **Balfour Declaration** of 1917, and became President of the **World Zionist Organization** (1920–30 and 1935–46), and of the **Jewish Agency** (from 1929). He played a major role in the establishment of the state of Israel (1948), and was its first President (1949–52). ▷ **Zionism**

Weizsäcker, Richard Freiherr, Baron von (1920–) West German politician, the son of a baron-diplomat who was tried at Nuremberg. He was educated at **Berlin**, Oxford, Grenoble and Göttingen universities, studying history and law. During **World War II** he served in the **Wehrmacht**. After the war he worked as a professional lawyer and was active in the German Protestant Church, becoming President of its congress (1964–70). A member of the conservative Christian Democratic Union (**CDU**) since 1954, he served as a Deputy in the **Bundestag** from 1969, as CDU Deputy Chairman (1972–9) and, from 1981, as a successful Mayor of West Berlin, before being elected federal President in May 1984. He was re-elected in May 1989. ▷ **Germany, West**

Welensky, Roland (Roy) (1907–92) Rhodesian politician. Born in Bulawayo, he was educated in local schools and then started work on the railways at the age of 14. He became leader of the Railway Workers' Union in Northern Rhodesia in 1933, by which time he had also been heavyweight boxing champion (1926–8). Elected to the Northern Rhodesia Legco in 1938, he founded the Northern Rhodesia Labour Party in 1941 and was appointed Director of Manpower by the Governor. He became Chairman of the unofficial opposition in 1946. A strong supporter of the proposed Federation of Rhodesia and Nyasaland, he was elected to its first parliament. Welensky was appointed Minister of Transport and Development in 1953, to which he soon added the portfolios of Communications and

Posts. Promoted to Deputy Prime Minister in 1955, he succeeded Sir Godfrey **Huggins** (Lord Malvern) as Prime Minister in 1956, which post he held until the Federation's demise at the end of 1963. Although considered a doughty champion of white rule, he was strongly opposed to Southern Rhodesia's **UDI** and tried, unsuccessfully, to return to politics as an opponent of Ian **Smith**. He retired to a smallholding near Salisbury (Harare).

Welfs (Guelfs) A Frankish aristocratic family. They were the chief rivals of the **Hohenstaufen** dynasty in Germany and Italy, with extensive lands in Saxony and Bavaria. They were at their most powerful under **Henry the Lion**, whose son, **Otto IV**, became king and emperor. The Welfs and Hohenstaufen were reconciled when **Frederick II** enfeoffed Otto's grandson with the Duchy of Brunswick-Lüneberg, the shrunken remains of his ancestors' lands. The term **Guelf** came to be used in Italy for supporters of the papacy against the emperor.

Wellesley (of Norragh), Richard (Colley), 1st Marquis (1760–1842) British administrator. He became an MP (1784), a Lord of the Treasury (1786), a marquis (1799), and Governor-General of India (1797–1805). Under his administration British rule in India became supreme: the influence of France was extinguished, and the power of the princes reduced by the crushing of **Tippoo Sahib** (1799) and the Marathas (1803). After his return to England, he became Ambassador to Madrid (1805), Foreign Minister (1809), and Lord-Lieutenant of Ireland (1821 and 1833).

Wellington, Arthur Wellesley, 1st Duke of (1769–1852) British general and politician. He joined the army in 1787, was sent to India with his regiment, and there defeated **Tippoo Sahib**, became Governor of Mysore, and broke the power of the Marathas. Knighted in 1804, he became an MP (1806), and Irish Secretary (1807). He defeated the Danes during the Copenhagen expedition (1807), and in the **Peninsular War** drove the French out of Portugal and Spain, gaining victories at Talavera (1809), Salamanca (1812), and Toulouse (1814). For his role in this campaign he was given many honours, and created Duke of Wellington. After **Napoleon** I's escape from Elba, he defeated the French at the Battle of **Waterloo**. He supported **Liverpool**'s government, and joined it as Master-General of the Ordnance (1818). He also became Constable of the Tower (1826) and army Commander-in-Chief (1827). His period as Prime Minister (1828–30) significantly weakened the Tory Party, which split over the question of **Catholic Emancipation** (1829), and was further weakened by disagreements over trade and reform. Wellington's opposition to parliamentary reform brought down his government, which was succeeded by the **Whigs**. He was Foreign Secretary under **Peel** (1834–5), retired from public life in 1846. ▷ **Napoleonic Wars**

Welser Family A powerful banking family established in Augsburg in 1498 by Anton Welser. They were noted for their involvement in projects in the New World.

Weltpolitik A concept (literally, 'world policy') widely promoted in post-Bismarckian Imperial Germany and taken to mean the acquisition of new colonies, a greater German share in international trade and parity with the other major powers, especially Britain. The creation of a large, high-seas battle fleet by **Tirpitz** was seen as essential to the realization of these aims, but this attempt led in turn to a costly and ultimately futile arms race with Britain. *Weltpolitik* was further seen as a means of diverting public attention from the steadily growing constitutional tensions within Germany, but its limited success led to failure in this regard. The resulting crises in domestic and foreign policy led to calls for war from sections of the establishment from 1912 onwards. ▷ **Bismarck, Otto von**

Wenceslas IV (1361–1419) Holy Roman Emperor (1378/1400). The son of Emperor **Charles V** and elder brother of Emperor **Sigismund**, he was crowned King of Bohemia in 1378 and Emperor in the same year. In the papal schism he followed his father's policy of supporting the Pope in Rome, Urban VI, although he negotiated secretly with Clement VII in Avignon. He intervened ineffectually in the conflict between the princes and the towns by attempting to impose peace. Although capable, he was inactive and increasingly given to bouts of drunkenness. He allowed Germany to slide into anarchy and was deposed in 1400.

Wenceslaus (Wenceslas), St ('Good King Wenceslas') (c.903–35) Duke and patron of Bohemia. He received a Christian education, and after the death of his father (c.924) encouraged Christianity in Bohemia, against the wishes of his mother. Probably at her instigation, and because he had put his duchy under the protection of Germany, he was murdered by his brother, Boleslaw. He became the patron saint of Bohemia and Czechoslovakia.

Wentworth, William Charles (1793–1872) Australian politician, born at sea, his mother being a transported convict. He took part in 1813 in the first crossing of the Blue Mountains, and in 1816 returned to England where he had been educated, to study law. When called to the Bar in 1822, he had already published his classic *Statistical Historical and Political Description of the Colony of New South Wales* (1819). A staunch protagonist of self-government, which he made the policy of his newspaper, *The Australian* (established 1824), he demanded an elected legislature, taxation by consent and trial by jury. He entered the Legislative Council in 1843, and was chairman of the committee that drafted the New South Wales constitution. As a wealthy landowner and defender of squatter interests, he proposed a lower house elected on a property-owning franchise and an upper house of colonial peers, derisively called the 'bunyip aristocracy' by his opponents who deleted this provision. Wentworth accompanied the constitution to London where it was passed in the House of Commons in 1855, and retired to Dorset. A firm believer in education, he played a leading role in the foundation of Sydney University, and in establishing a state primary education system.

Wesley, John (1703–91) British evangelist and founder of Methodism. He was ordained deacon (1725) and priest (1728), and in 1726 became a fellow at Oxford and lecturer in Greek. Influenced by the spiritual writings of William Law, he became leader of a small group which had gathered round his brother Charles, nicknamed the Methodists, a name later adopted by John for the adherents of the great evangelical movement which was its outgrowth. On his father's death, the brothers went as missionaries to Georgia (1735–8), but the mission proved a failure. In 1738, at a meeting in London, during the reading of Luther's preface to the epistle to the Romans, he experienced an assurance of salvation which convinced him that he must bring the same assurance to others; but his zeal alarmed most of the parish clergy, who closed their pulpits against him. This drove him into the open air at Bristol (1739), where he founded the first Methodist chapel, and then the Foundry at Moorfields, London, which became his headquarters. His life was frequently in danger, but he outlived all persecution, and the itineraries of his old age were triumphal processions throughout the country. He was a prolific writer, producing grammars, histories, biographies, collections of hymns, his own sermons and journals, and a magazine.

Wessex A kingdom of the Anglo-Saxon heptarchy, with its main centres at Winchester and Hamwic (Southampton). Under **Alfred, 'the Great'**, Wessex (by then incorporating Kent and Sussex) was the only English kingdom to withstand the onslaughts of the **Vikings**. Alfred's successors reconquered the **Danelaw**, and had united all England under a single monarchy by 954. ▷ **Anglo-Saxons; Mercia**

West Bank The region of the Middle East west of the River Jordan and the Dead Sea. Administered by Jordan (1949–67), the area was seized by Israel in the **Six-Day War**. Because of Arab refusal to negotiate peace terms, Israel retained it, administered it as the district of Judea-Samaria and allowed Jewish settlement. The West Bank includes Old (East) Jerusalem, as well as Bethlehem, Jericho, Hebron and Nablus, and has been a focus of territorial aspirations by the **PLO** (Palestine Liberation Organization). It was the scene of the *intifada* ('uprising') against the Israelis between 1988 and 1993. Israel reached agreement with the PLO in 1993 on the implementation of limited Palestinian self-rule in the area. ▷ **Arab–Israeli Wars; Israel, State of; Zionism**

West India Regiment Founded in 1795 in response to the need for local defence in the war with France, the force had 12 regiments by 1799. However, after mutinies in Dominica (1802) and Jamaica (1808), parts of the force were disbanded (1815). Of the remaining units, the First Regiment mutinied in 1837 in Trinidad led by Daaga (Donald Stewart) and the Third Regiment was disbanded in 1870. In the Asante Wars (1873–4), the First and Second Regiments again saw action and in 1888 the two regiments were reconstituted to form the rank and file of two battalions led by white officers. That regiment served in both East and West Africa in **World War I** and was finally disbanded in 1927.

West Indies, Federation of the (1958–62) Ill-fated union of the British West Indies devised at the Montego Bay Conference (Sep 1947). Damaged from the outset by the

failure of Guyana, Belize, the Bahamas and the British Virgin Islands to join, the federation was further weakened by disputes. These ranged from the powers of the federal government, taxation and the constitutional backwardness of the union relative to constitutional progress in Jamaica, Trinidad and Barbados, to the under-representation in the federal parliament of these states, given their contribution in population and finance. As it was, the West Indian Federal Labour Party led by Grantley **Adams** relied on small island support to maintain its majority over the Democratic Labour Party of **Bustamante**; when the latter withdrew Jamaica from the federation (1961) and **Williams** took out Trinidad (1962), the union collapsed and was dissolved.

Westminster, Statute of (1931) Legislation which clarified that Dominions in the **British Empire** were autonomous communities and effectively independent, though owing common allegiance to the crown. The statute closely followed the formulation made by Arthur **Balfour** in the 1920s about the relationship of the Dominions to Britain and it also established a free association of members in the '**Commonwealth of Nations**'.

Westminster, Statutes of (1275, 1285 and 1290) Part of a comprehensive programme undertaken by **Edward I** to reform English law and administration. The first statute (1275) was concerned mainly with criminal matters, notably compulsory trial by jury; the second (1285) covered many fields of law, and facilitated the creation of entailed estates; the third (1290) protected lords' feudal incidents.

Westminster Assembly A body of clerics (120) and laymen (30) convened by the English **Long Parliament** in 1643 to arrange a religious settlement to replace the Church of England. Dominated by Presbyterians, it produced a directory of public worship to replace the Prayer Book, and the Westminster Confession of Faith. Its influence declined when the power of the army, which favoured toleration, increased after 1648.

Westphalia A north-west German principality, first settled by Saxons c.700, given to the Archbishop of Cologne (1180), and later forming part of the Lower Rhine-Westphalian Circle of the **Holy Roman Empire** (1512). In 1803–6 it was divided between Brandenburg-Prussia and neighbouring states. Although the name was coined for

Napoleon's satellite kingdom (1807), the princes regained possession (1814–15). ▷ **Napoleon I**

Westphalia, Peace of (1648) A series of treaties ending the **Thirty Years War** between France and the Empire, and the Eighty Years War between Spain and the Dutch, negotiated at the Westphalian towns of **Münster** and Osnabrück. The Peace marked the triumph of the French Bourbons over the Habsburgs, and enshrined the concept of *raison d'état* — the primacy of the interests of the sovereign state over other considerations, such as dynastic or religious factors. ▷ **Bourbon, House of; Habsburg Dynasty**

Wettin Dynasty The Wettin family gained the electorate of Saxony in 1423. Later, in 1485 the family divided into two branches, the Ernestines and the Albertines. The Ernestines lost the electorship in 1547 to the Albertines. The Albertines were to produce two Polish kings (1697–1763) and numerous Saxon kings (1806–1918). The Ernestines provided kings for Belgium, Portugal, Bulgaria, and Britain in the 19c and 20c.

Weygand, Maxime (1867–1965) French soldier. As Chief of Staff to **Foch** (1914–23), he rendered great services in **World War I**. Then he was High Commissioner in Syria (1923–4), and appointed Chief of Staff (1930), and then designated Commander-in-Chief in a future war (1931). Retired in 1935, he was recalled and sent to command in Syria in 1939. In May 1940, in the middle of the battle, he was recalled to replace **Gamelin** as Commander-in-Chief, but arrived too late to do much more than recommend an armistice. The **Vichy** government sent him as its delegate to North Africa, but he was recalled in response to German pressure and imprisoned in Germany until the end of **World War II**. In 1948 he was brought before the High Court for his role in 1940, but the case was dropped.

Whig Party (USA) One of two major US political parties during the decades prior to the **American Civil War**. The name was adopted in 1834 to signify opposition to President Andrew **Jackson** (1829–37). The Whigs stood for greater governmental intervention in the economy than did the Democrats, who followed Jackson, but both parties agreed on the necessity of keeping the slavery issue out of politics. The Whigs collapsed in 1854, precisely because the slavery issue

could no longer be contained. Daniel **Webster** and Henry **Clay** were prominent members of the party.

Whigs (UK) A British political party which emerged in 1679–80 as the group agitating for the exclusion of James, Duke of York (later **James VII and II**), on the grounds of his Catholicism. The name was probably a contraction of 'Whiggamores' — militant Scottish Presbyterians. The party benefited from the political changes of the **Glorious Revolution** of 1688 and, during its long period of dominance in British politics after 1714, drew much strength from defending 'the principles of 1688', which included limited monarchy and the importance of parliament. Whiggery is better seen as a general set of beliefs along these lines, rather than as a unified party. Most of its leaders were great landowners who used political patronage to create family-based groupings in parliament. The party was supported by many in the moneyed and commercial classes, and by Nonconformists who looked to the Whigs (usually mistakenly) to provide religious toleration. Whig fortunes waned in the late 18c, and Whigs became leading members of the new **Liberal Party** from the mid-19c. ▷ **Tories**

Whiskey Rebellion (1794) An insurrection of farmers in western Pennsylvania and Virginia, USA, against the excise tax imposed by the federal government on whiskey, which they made in large quantities from their crops of grain. The rebellion was suppressed by government forces led by Henry Lee and Alexander **Hamilton**.

Whiskey Ring (1875) A conspiracy of distillers and tax officials during the administration of President Ulysses S **Grant** to defraud the government of taxes due on liquor: 238 people were indicted, including Grant's private secretary.

Whitby, Synod of (664) A meeting in Britain before Oswiu, King of **Northumbria**, where the differences in organization between Roman and Celtic Christianity were debated. Roman concepts of church order prevailed, with the result that the two Christian traditions in Britain were eventually united in their acceptance of the authority and practices of Rome.

White Australia Policy The unofficial national policy of Australia from 1901 until the late 1960s, designed to exclude non-

European migrants; it was particularly aimed at Asians and Pacific Islanders. It also assumed the decline and ultimate extinction of the native **Aboriginals**. The policy enjoyed general support, including that of the trade-union movement to protect union wage rates. In the late 1960s, the policy was progressively dismantled, and race was replaced as a basis for admission by other, largely economic, criteria. ▷ **Dictation Test**

Whitehead, Edgar (1905–71) Southern Rhodesian politician. Born in England, he emigrated to Southern Rhodesia in 1928 and, after two years in the civil service, went into farming. He was elected to the legislative assembly in 1939 and, after war service, became the country's High Commissioner in London (1945–6) before being called back as Minister of Finance (1946–53). After a further period of farming, he was asked to be the Central African Federation's representative in the USA, from where he was recalled again, this time to be Prime Minister. His term of office introduced several liberalizing measures but, lacking charisma and facing a more avowedly racist opposition in the Rhodesian Front, he lost office in the 1962 elections and retired, yet again, to his farm.

White Mountain, Battle of the (1620) The battle in which Duke Maximilian of Bavaria, acting on behalf of the Habsburg Emperor, Ferdinand II, defeated the motley forces of Frederick V, Elector Palatine and recently elected King of Bohemia and Moravia, and put paid to what remained of Czech independence for three centuries. Frederick fled ignominiously and Ferdinand succeeded him as King, proceeding to execute or expel all those who had led the last-ditch fight for the right to pursue their own Czech Protestant faith. This was also an important first Habsburg victory in what was subsequently, and not altogether accurately, termed the **Thirty Years War**. ▷ **Habsburg Dynasty**

White Russians The name collectively given to counter-revolutionary forces led by ex-tsarist officers, which fought unsuccessfully against the Bolshevik **Red Army** during the **Russian Civil War** (1918–22). The Whites were supported by the military intervention of British, American, French, and Japanese troops; when these withdrew, White resistance to the Red Army collapsed. ▷ **Bolsheviks**

White Terror ▷ **Terror, White**

Whitlam, (Edward) Gough (1916–) Australian politician. A lawyer, he entered politics in 1952 and led the **Australian Labor Party** (1967–77), forming the first Labor government since 1949. His administration (1972–5) was notable for its radicalism, ending conscription and withdrawing Australian troops from the **Vietnam War**, recognizing communist China, relaxing the restrictions on non-white immigrants, abolishing university fees and creating Medibank (the state-funded healthcare system). He was controversially dismissed by the Governor-General in 1975, after the Senate had blocked his money bills, and lost the subsequent election. He retired from politics in 1977 and in 1983 became Australian Ambassador to Unesco in Paris.

Wichale, Treaty of (1889) The friendship treaty between Italy and Abyssinia, which, according to the Italians, established Abyssinia as an Italian protectorate. The treaty was used by subsequent Italian governments to legitimize further extension of influence in East Africa, although the Abyssinians claimed that the Amharic text had been falsely rendered in the Italian version.

Wilberforce, William (1759–1833) British politician, evangelist, and philanthropist. He became an MP (1780), and in 1788 began the movement which resulted in the abolition of the slave trade in the British West Indies in 1807. He next sought to secure the abolition of all slaves, but declining health compelled him in 1825 to retire from parliament. He died, one month before the Slavery Abolition Act was passed in parliament. A lifelong friend of **Pitt** 'the Younger', he was like him a strong opponent of reformers in the 1790s. His evangelical beliefs led him to urge the aristocracy to practise 'real Christianity', and to give a moral lead to the poor. ▷ **slave trade**

Wilderness, Battle of (1864) An indecisive conflict in the **American Civil War** between the Union army under General Ulysses S **Grant** and the Confederate army under General Robert E **Lee**, fought in the Wilderness area of Virginia. Both sides sustained heavy losses in a month of relentless fighting.

Wilhelm, Crown Prince of Germany and Prussia (1882–1951) After serving as an army field commander during **World War I**, he sought exile in the Netherlands on 13 Nov 1918 and renounced his claims to the German and Prussian thrones in Dec. He returned to Germany in 1923 and despite identifying with monarchist groups and, for a time, with the **Nazi Party**, he played a limited role in political life. ▷ **Prussia**

Wilhelmina (Helena Pauline Maria) (1880–1962) Queen of the Netherlands (1890/ 1948). She succeeded her father **William III** at the age of 10, her mother Emma acting as Regent until 1898. In 1901 she married Duke Henry of Mecklenburg-Schwerin. An upholder of constitutional monarchy, she especially won the admiration of her people during **World War II**. Though compelled to seek refuge in Britain, she steadfastly encouraged Dutch **resistance** to the German occupation. In 1948 she abdicated in favour of her daughter **Juliana**, and assumed the title of Princess of the Netherlands.

'Wilhelmus' The Dutch national anthem. It was originally a song of the **Beggars** (irregulars in the early part of the **Eighty Years War** of the Dutch against Spain), composed c.1570 by an admiring follower of **William I**, Prince of Orange. The melody is derived from a French army marching song. In 1932 it became the official Dutch anthem, emphasizing the bond between Dutch nationalistic feeling and the House of Orange-Nassau.

Wilkes, John (1727–97) British politician and journalist. He studied at Leiden, became an MP (1757), and attacked the ministry in his weekly journal, *North Briton* (1762–3). He was imprisoned, released, then expelled from the house for libel. Re-elected on several occasions, and repeatedly expelled, he came to be seen as a champion of liberty, and an upholder of press freedom. In 1774 he became Lord Mayor of London, and in the same year finally gained readmission to parliament, where he remained until his retirement in 1790.

Wilkins, Roy (1901–81) US civil rights leader. He began working for the NAACP in 1931, and became its executive director (1965–77). Throughout his career he fought to end segregation, rejecting the concept of separate development for blacks and opposing the black nationalism of both Marcus **Garvey** and the **Black Power** movement. Because of his insistence on using constitutional means to effect change, he fell out of favour in the 1960s with the more militant civil rights leaders.

William I (Willem Frederik) (1772–1843) King of the Netherlands (1806/40), Grand Duke of Luxembourg and Prince of Orange-Nassau. He was the son of the last **Stadholder**, **William V**, and Princess Wilhelmina of Prussia; the **French Revolution** and Napoleonic period obliged him to spend his youth in exile from the Netherlands. In 1793–4 he led the Dutch forces against the French, but had to flee to England in 1795. He then entered the Prussian Army as a general and moved to Berlin; in 1802 he became sovereign of the small German states of Fulda and Corvey, and chose the Prussian side against **Napoleon I**. He entered Austrian service in 1809, but then left for England again. In 1813 he was invited back to the Netherlands to lead the post-Napoleonic government as sovereign prince. When the Congress of **Vienna** (1814–15) decided to unite the southern and northern Netherlands (present-day Belgium and the Netherlands) as a buffer against France, William took the title of King of the United Kingdom of the Netherlands. In 1791 he had married his cousin Princess Wilhelmina of Prussia, who died in 1837; in 1841 he was married again, controversially, to the Roman Catholic Duchess Henriëtte d'Oultremont. He was an exceptionally able monarch, but wanted no interference from parliament, and ruled by decree as a self-styled enlightened despot. His economic politics were interventionist: he founded the Netherlands Bank, the Netherlands Trading Company, the **Culture System** in the Dutch East Indies, and was known as the King-Merchant. His policies were also of benefit to modern Belgium: he founded the *Société Générale* in 1822, and gave great support to the industrial revolution there. His relentless centralization (in finance, religion and administration) created discontent, especially in the southern provinces, which led to the **Belgian Revolution** in 1830. William became increasingly unpopular in the 1830s as he refused to relinquish Belgium and maintained an armed peace; finally he abdicated in 1840 in favour of his son **William II**, and moved to **Berlin**, where he died.

William I (1797–1888) King of Prussia (1861/88) and first German Emperor (1871/88). The second son of **Frederick William III**, his use of force during the **Revolution of 1848** made him unpopular, and he was forced to leave **Prussia** temporarily for London. As King, he consolidated the power of the monarchy following the relative failure of the 1848 Revolution, and strengthened the army: renewed constitutional tensions led to his appointing (1861) **Bismarck** as Prussian Minister-President, who initiated victorious wars against Denmark in 1864, **Austria** (1866), and France (1871), when William was proclaimed Emperor. A semi-absolute monarch, he entrusted his Chancellor, Bismarck, with the reins of government. He survived two attempts at assassination in 1878. ▷ **Austro-Prussian War; Franco-Prussian War**

William I, 'the Conqueror' (c.1028–87) Duke of Normandy and the first Norman King of England (1066/87). He was the illegitimate son of Duke Robert of Normandy. **Edward the Confessor**, who had been brought up in Normandy, most probably designated him as future King of England in 1051. When Harold Godwin, despite an apparent oath to uphold William's claims, took the throne as **Harold II**, William invaded with the support of the papacy, defeated and killed Harold at the Battle of **Hastings**, and was crowned King (25 Dec 1066). The key to effective control was military conquest backed up by aristocratic colonization, so that by the time of **Domesday Book** (1086), the leaders of Anglo-Saxon society south of the Tees had been almost entirely replaced by a new ruling class of **Normans**, Bretons, and Flemings, who were closely tied to William by feudal bonds. He died while defending Normandy's southern border. ▷ **Anglo-Saxons; Norman Conquest**

William I, 'the Lion' (c.1142–1214) King of Scots (1165/1214). He was the brother and successor of **Malcolm IV**. In 1173–4 he invaded Northumberland during the rebellion against **Henry II** of England, but was captured at Alnwick, and by the Treaty of Falaise (1174) recognized Henry as the feudal superior of Scotland. Despite his difficulties with England, he made Scotland a much stronger kingdom, and in 1192 Celestine III declared the Scottish Church free of all external authority save the Pope's. ▷ **David I**

William I, 'the Silent' (1533–84) Prince of Orange. First of the hereditary Stadholders of the United Provinces of the Netherlands (1572/84). He joined the aristocratic protest to the oppressive policies of **Philip II** of Spain, and in 1568 took up arms against the Spanish crown. After initial reverses, he began the recovery of the coastal towns with the help of the Sea-**Beggars**, and became the leader of the northern provinces, united in the Union of **Utrecht** (1579) in revolt against Spain in the **Eighty Years War**. He was assassinated at Delft by a Spanish agent. His byname comes from his ability to keep secret **Henry II** of France's scheme to massacre all

the Protestants of France and the Netherlands, confided to him when he was a French hostage in 1559. ▷ **United Provinces of the Netherlands**

William II (1626–50) Stadholder and Captain-General of the Netherlands. He was the son of the Stadholder Frederick Henry, who had succeeded his brother, **Maurice** of Nassau, in 1625. Anglo-Dutch diplomacy established what would prove a fateful marital linkage of the houses of Orange and Stuart by William's marriage in 1641 to Mary, daughter of **Charles I**, and William was elected to follow his father in office, which he duly did in 1647. Dutch independence was recognized at the end of the Thirty Years War in the Peace of **Westphalia** (1648), but William wished to support the French in their continued war with Spain, in the hope of conquering the remaining Spanish Netherlands. He arrested his leading opponents in Holland, laid siege to Amsterdam and won an advantageous compromise, but died of smallpox before he could make much use of its results. His posthumous son, the future **William III** of Britain and Ireland, would spend his life in opposition to France, for whose alliance William II had laboured in vain.

William II (Willem Frederik George Lodewijk) (1792–1849) King of the Netherlands (1840/9), Grand Duke of Luxembourg and Prince of Orange-Nassau. The son of King **William I** and Princess Wilhelmina of Prussia, he married the Russian Princess **Anna Pavlovna** in 1816. He had a distinguished early career as a soldier, fighting under **Wellington** in Spain (1811–13), present at Quatre-Bras and the Battle of **Waterloo**, and as leader of the **Ten Days Campaign** against the Belgians (1831). On 7 Oct 1840 he succeeded his father as King; his interests were not overtly political, and he generally maintained his father's autocratic line, although he was more tolerant in matters of religion. The European **Revolutions of 1848–9** seem to have panicked him into entrusting charge of the new Dutch constitution to the liberal J R **Thorbecke**, and thus William was responsible for allowing the liberal floodgates to open in the Netherlands. He was succeeded by his son, **William III**, in 1849.

William II (1859–1941) German Emperor and King of **Prussia** (1888/1918). He was the eldest son of Frederick (II) and Victoria (the daughter of Britain's Queen **Victoria**), and grandson of **William I**. He dismissed **Bismarck** (1890), and began a long period of personal rule, later displaying a bellicose attitude in international affairs. He and his government pledged full support to Austria-Hungary after the assassination of the Archduke **Francis Ferdinand** at Sarajevo (1914), thereby setting Europe on the road to war. During **World War I** he became a mere figurehead, and when the German armies collapsed, and US President Woodrow **Wilson** refused to negotiate while he remained in power, he abdicated and fled to the Netherlands, living as a country gentleman until his death. ▷ **Jameson Raid**

William II, 'Rufus' (c.1056–1100) King of England (1087/1100). He was the second surviving son of **William I, 'the Conqueror'**. His main goal was the recovery of Normandy from his elder brother, Robert Curthose, and from 1096, when Robert relinquished the struggle and departed on the First Crusade, William ruled the duchy as *de facto* duke. He also led expeditions to Wales (1095 and 1097); conquered Carlisle and the surrounding district (1092); and after the death of **Malcolm III, 'Canmore'**, exercised a controlling influence over Scottish affairs. Contemporaries condemned his government of England as arbitrary and ruthless. He exploited his rights over the Church and the nobility beyond the limits of custom, and quarrelled with Anselm, Archbishop of Canterbury. His personal conduct outraged many, for he was most likely a homosexual. He was killed by an arrow while hunting in the New Forest. It has been supposed that he was murdered on the orders of his younger brother, who succeeded him as **Henry I**, but his death was almost certainly accidental. ▷ **Crusades**

William III (1817–90) King of the Netherlands and Grand Duke of Luxembourg (1849/90). The son of King **William II** and **Anna Pavlovna**, he married his cousin, **Sophia Frederika Mathilde** of Württemberg, with whom his relations were not good; after her death (1877), he married Princess **Emma** of Waldeck-Pyrmont. Three sons from his first marriage failed to outlive him; from the second marriage a daughter, the future Queen **Wilhelmina**, was born in 1880. William was a difficult sovereign: he wanted to rule directly, but found it hard to adapt to the conditions of constitutional monarchy. He had furious rows with his ministers, and took a personal dislike to the leading liberal of the day, J R **Thorbecke**. His inability to operate with

parliament led to the end of royal ministries, which were replaced by parliamentary ones; after the Luxembourg question of 1866–8 (in which William's government was heavily criticized from all sides) Dutch governments had to be able to count on a parliamentary majority. William's health deteriorated; in the months before he died, Queen Emma was made regent during Wilhelmina's minority.

William III, 'of Orange' (1650–1702) Stadholder of the United Provinces (1672/1702) and King of Great Britain (1689/1702). Born in The Hague, he was the son of William II of Orange by Mary, the eldest daughter of **Charles I** of England. In 1677 he married his cousin, Mary (1662–94), the daughter of **James VII and II** by Anne Hyde. Invited to redress the grievances of the country, he landed at Torbay in 1688 with an English and Dutch army, and forced James VII and II to flee; William and Mary were proclaimed rulers early the following year. He was defeated by James's supporters at Killiecrankie (17 July 1689) but overcame James at the Battle of the **Boyne** (1 July 1690), then concentrated on the War of the **Grand Alliance** against France (1689–97), in which he was finally successful. In later years, he had to withstand much parliamentary opposition to his proposals. He died, childless, the crown passing to Mary's sister, **Anne**. ▷ **Glorious Revolution**

William IV (1711–51) Stadholder and Captain-General of the Netherlands. He was born Charles Henry Friso, of a cadet branch of the House of Orange (Nassau-Dietz). In 1711 he was named Friesland's Stadholder in succession to his father, John William Friso. He was chosen as Stadholder in the other provinces at various intervals, all these posts having been untenanted since the death of **William III, 'of Orange'** in 1702. His appointments were not completed until 1747 when Holland, Zeeland and Utrecht bowed to popular Orangist pressure in the riots after a French invasion. His offices were then declared hereditary in male and female lines, a tribute to the historical reputation of the House of Orange. Thus in possession of near-absolute power, he failed to arrest the general decline of the Dutch Republic.

William IV, 'the Sailor King' (1765–1837) King of Great Britain and Ireland, and King of Hanover (1830/7). The third son of **George III**, he entered the navy in 1779, saw service in the USA and the West Indies, became Admiral in 1811, and Lord High Admiral in

1827–8. His elder brother having died, he succeeded **George IV** in 1830. Widely believed to have Whig leanings to his accession, he developed Tory sympathies, and did much to obstruct the passing of the first Reform Act (1832). He was the last monarch to use prerogative powers to dismiss a ministry with a parliamentary majority when he sacked **Melbourne** in 1834 and invited the **Tories** to form a government. He was succeeded by his niece, **Victoria**. ▷ **Reform Acts; Whigs**

William V (1748–1806) Last hereditary **Stadholder** and Captain-General of the Netherlands. He succeeded his father, **William IV**, in 1751 but did not rule until 1766. He abandoned the old alliance of Orange and Britain, leaning instead towards alliance with Prussia, itself hostile to Britain after its loss of British support towards the end of the **Seven Years War**. During the **American Revolution**, Britain declared war on the Netherlands because of its financial and moral support for the American rebels, but it was the pro-French 'Patriots', pressing for domestic reforms, who led William to leave The Hague in order to live outside what was now the hostile Province of Holland. Prussian armed intervention restored him in 1787. French revolutionary armies invaded the Netherlands in 1794, and in 1795 William fled to England, whose occupation of the Dutch provinces he took part in, including the abortive Anglo-Russian invasion of 1799. After that he lost heart, and allowed his followers to accept office in the **Batavian Republic**, the French client state which had been formed in his absence.

William, Count of Holland (1228–56) German King. The son of Count Florence IV of Holland, he was elected King (1247) after the death of the anti-king **Henry Raspe**, and crowned in Aachen in 1248. He was unable to assert his claim until the death of **Frederick II** (1250) and was recognized by pope Innocent IV in 1251. He won the support of north Germany by his marriage to the daughter of the Duke of Brunswick, and that of the Hohenstaufen towns after the death of **Conrad IV** (1254). He died in 1256 on a campaign against the Frisians, sinking unnoticed with his horse into a frozen swamp.

William of Wied (1876–1945) Prince of Albania (7 Mar/3 Sep 1914). He arrived in newly-independent Albania in Mar 1914, as a 35-year-old captain in the German Army, with 75 million francs for financing the government. Seeing him as an Austrian protégé, the Italian government intrigued against him. He never gained control of the country which was split into factions and, after losing the support of the Emperor **Francis Joseph**, he left Albania in 1914. Fan **Noli**'s verdict upon him was that 'he can be criticized only for being unable to perform miracles'. ▷ **Albanians**

William of Wykeham (Wickham) (1324–1404) English churchman and statesman. Possibly the son of a serf, he rose to become the chief adviser of **Edward III** of England. He was appointed Keeper of the Privy Seal (1363), Bishop of Winchester (1367), and was twice Chancellor of England (1367–71 and 1389–91). He founded New College, Oxford, and Winchester College, both of which were fully established by the 1390s.

Williams, Eric (1911–81) Trinidadian politician and historian. Williams was Prime Minister of Trinidad and Tobago for 30 years. In 1956 he founded the PNM and, as Chief Minister, took Trinidad into the Federation of the **West Indies** (1958), insisting on a powerful centralized government. When that failed to materialize, Williams took Trinidad out of the union and obtained independence (1962) with the slogan 'Discipline, Production and Tolerance'. Thanks to a favourable economic situation and PNM expenditure on public works and social services, Williams's popularity soared until 1970, when an economic downturn and his increasing authoritarianism led to **Black Power** violence. Saddened by the materialism his own policies had helped to create, Williams committed suicide in 1981.

Williams, Roger (c.1604–83) English colonist, founder of Rhode Island. A member of the Anglican church, his espousal of Puritan beliefs led him to emigrate in 1630 to the Massachusetts Bay colony. He refused to participate in the church in Boston, believing it had not separated from the English church, and moved to Salem where, after challenging the authority of the Puritan magistrates over matters of personal conscience, he was persecuted and eventually banished. He took refuge with Native Americans, then purchased land from them on which he founded the city of Providence in 1636. His colony was a model of democracy and religious freedom; he went to England in 1643 and 1651 to procure a charter for it and served as its President (1654–7).

Williams, Shirley (Vivien Teresa) (1930–) British politician. A former journalist, and Secretary of the Fabian Society (1960–4), she became a Labour MP in 1964. After many junior positions, she was Secretary of State for Prices and Consumer Protection (1974–6), and for Education and Science (1976–9). She lost her seat in 1979, became a co-founder of the Social Democratic Party in 1981, and the Party's first elected MP later that year. She lost her seat in the 1983 general election, but remained as the SDP's President (1982–7). She supported the merger between the SDP and the Liberal Party. ▷ **Labour Party** (UK); **Liberal Party** (UK); **Social Democratic Party** (UK)

Williams Thesis Revolutionary argument postulated by Eric **Williams** in *Capitalism and Slavery* (1944) that British emancipation was more the consequence of 'laissez-faire' self-interest than imperial altruism. The idea that the abolition of the slave trade and **slavery** was simply the result of the high-minded idealism of the Abolitionists had been set in historical truth by books such as Reginald Coupland's *The British Anti-Slavery Movement* (1933), but Williams argued cogently that while slavery and the slave trade had provided the necessary capital to finance the **Industrial Revolution** in England, by the beginning of the 19c the British West Indies sugar plantocracy with its expensive production, captive, monopolistic market and inefficient labour force had become an obstacle to a booming industrial society and its metropolitan, free-trading entrepreneurs.

Willibrord (658–739) English monk. He was born in Northumbria and trained in Ripon Abbey; after working in Ireland, he and 11 others left for the Netherlands as missionaries in 690 and successfuly converted much of the Netherlands to Christianity. The Merovingian and Carolingian Frankish kings legitimized his work in Friesland, which they welcomed as a stabilizing political influence in their interests. Willibrord visited Rome c.692 and 695, and was made Archbishop of the Frisians, based in Utrecht, in 694.

Wilmot Proviso (1846) A motion introduced in US Congress by David Wilmot (Democrat, Pennsylvania) to forbid the expansion of slavery into territory acquired during the Mexican War. It passed the House of Representatives but not the Senate, where the South and the North had equal strength. The debate was a major step in the politicization of the slavery issue.

Wilson, Arnold (1884–1940) British administrator. Having carried out surveying work in southern Persia as a young Indian Army officer, he was appointed, by the British, to the commission charged with looking into the Ottoman–Persian Shatt al-Arab frontier dispute in 1913. He was a member of Cox's civil administration in 1915–16 and became (mid-1918) Acting Civil Commissioner, on Cox's departure to Tehran. Wilson's administration, although generally fair and efficient, was distinctly unsympathetic towards local, and particularly nationalist, aims. After **World War I**, he urged opposition both to the Anglo-French Declaration and to the notion of an Iraq run by a prince from the Sharifian family. His government appeared increasingly intolerant, giving rise to Iraqi fears that they had merely exchanged a Turkish master for a British, and that their political aspirations would be thwarted; this helped to bring about the insurrection of 1920. Later that year, Cox returned to Iraq, relieving Wilson of the task of carrying out the proposed constitutional programme for the country. He went on to become an MP, was arrested early in **World War II** because of alleged fascist sympathies and was killed in action, having volunteered as a rear-gunner in the RAF.

Wilson, Sir Henry Hughes (1864–1922) British field marshal. He joined the Rifle Brigade in 1884, and served in Burma (1884–7) and South Africa (1899–1901). As Director of Military Operations at the War Office (1910–14), he elaborated plans for the rapid support of France in the event of war with Germany. By the end of **World War I**, he was Chief of the Imperial General Staff. Promoted field marshal and created a baronet (1919), he resigned from the army in 1922, and became an MP. His implacable opposition to the leaders of **Sinn Féin** led to his assassination on the doorstep of his London home.

Wilson (of Libya and of Stowlangtoft), Henry Maitland, 1st Baron (1881–1964) British field marshal. He fought in South Africa and in **World War I**, and at the outbreak of **World War II** was appointed Commander of British troops in Egypt. Having led the initial British advance in Libya (1940–1) and the unsuccessful Greek campaign (1941), he became Commander-in-Chief Middle East (1943) and Supreme Allied Commander in the Mediterranean theatre (1944). Wilson headed the British Joint Staff Mission in Washington (1945–7) and was raised to the peerage in 1946.

Wilson (of Rievaulx), (James) Harold, Baron (1916–) British politician. He became a lecturer in economics at Oxford in 1937. An MP in 1945, he was President of the Board of Trade (1947–51), and the principal opposition spokesman on Economic Affairs. An able and hard-hitting debater, in 1963 he succeeded **Gaitskell** as Leader of the **Labour Party**, then he became Prime Minister (1964–70). His economic plans were badly affected by balance of payments crises, leading to severe restrictive measures and devaluation (1967). He was also faced with the problem of Rhodesian independence, opposition to Britain's proposed entry into the Common Market, and an increasing conflict between the two wings of the Labour Party. Following his third general election victory, he resigned suddenly as Prime Minister and Labour leader in 1976. Knighted in 1976, he became a life peer in 1983. ▷ **EC; EEC; Rhodesia Crisis**

Wilson, (Thomas) Woodrow (1856–1924) US politician and 28th President. He practised law in Atlanta, later became a university professor and, in 1902, President of Princeton University. He served as Democratic Governor of New Jersey (1911–13), and was elected President in 1912, running against Theodore **Roosevelt** and William H. Taft, and served two terms (1913–21). His 'New Freedom' program, establishing equality and opportunity for all men, created the Federal Reserve Board and the Clayton Anti-Trust Act (1914), which accorded many rights to labour unions. Wilson tried to keep the USA out of **World War I** but was compelled to enter the war in Apr 1917 to make the world 'safe for democracy'. He laid out his peace plan proposal in the **Fourteen Points**, and actively championed the idea of forming a **League of Nations**, which was part of the Treaty of **Versailles**. When the Senate rejected the treaty, his idealistic vision of world peace was shattered. In 1919 he was awarded the Nobel Peace Prize, but thereafter his health declined severely, and he never recovered.

Windischgrätz, Prince Alfred (1787–1862) Austrian soldier. As commander in Bohemia from 1840, he suppressed the **Revolution of 1848**–49 in Prague, and another in Vienna. In 1848 he helped to bring **Francis Joseph** to the throne. He defeated the Hungarians repeatedly, but was superseded after his defeat by them at Gödöllö.

Windsor, House of The name of the British royal family since 1917. This unequivocally

HOUSE OF WINDSOR

Regnal Dates	Name
1837/1901	Victoria
1901/10	Edward VII
1910/36	George V
1936	Edward VIII
1936/52	George VI
1952/	Elizabeth II

English name resulted from a declaration by **George V**, a member of the House of **Saxe-Coburg-Gotha**. It was felt that a Germanic surname for the British monarchy was inappropriate during a war against Germany.

Windthorst, Ludwig (1812–91) German Catholic politician. He became distinguished as an advocate and politician in Hanover. After the absorption of Hanover by **Prussia**, he became leader of the Ultramontanes in the German parliament and, as leader of the Catholic **Centre Party**, chief opponent of **Bismarck** during the **Kulturkampf**.

Wingate, Orde (Charles) (1903–44) British general. He was commissioned in 1922, and served in the Sudan (1928–33) and Palestine (1936–9), where he helped create a Jewish defence force. In the Burma theatre (1942) he organized the Chindits — specially trained jungle-fighters who were supplied by air, and thrust far behind the enemy lines. He was killed in a plane crash in Burma. ▷ **World War II**

Winnipeg General Strike (1919) One of the most significant Canadian strikes, it began when the employers in the building and metal trades refused to negotiate a collective bargaining procedure or to raise wages. After two weeks, the Winnipeg Trades and Labour Council voted to strike in sympathy. Fearing, like business leaders, that unionization would damage industrial profitability, the federal government immediately intervened. Despite the strikers' non-violence, specials were brought in to replace the city police force. A peaceful march was broken up, one spectator killed and 30 injured. The strike came to an end; its leaders jailed for sedition and the premier's promise of a Royal Commission. It did, however, politicize the issues, and in Manitoba's provincial elections of 1920 four of the jailed strike leaders were elected as socialists. The following year J S **Woodsworth** became the first socialist member of the federal House of Commons, as a representative from Winnipeg. ▷ **Meighen, Arthur**

Winrode of Kniprode (c.1310–82) Grand Master of the Teutonic Order. After a career in the Order as Commander in Danzig (Gdansk), Balga and Königsberg, he became Supreme Commander in Marienburg in 1346 and Grand Master in 1351. He presided over the period of the Order's great successes, when it became the centre for crusading chivalry from all over northern Europe. He was active as a diplomat and did much to enhance the prosperity of the German towns and the Order's trading links, especially with England and Flanders. He maintained peace with Poland and had many successes against the pagan Lithuanians. ▷ **Hermann of Salza; Teutonic Knights**

Winter, Jan Willem de (1750–1812) Dutch naval commander. He was defeated by Adam Duncan at the Battle of Camperdown (1797) and was ambassador to France from 1798 to 1802.

Winter Palace, Storming of (1917) A symbolic victory for the Bolshevik revolutionaries. The Tsar's residence had become the headquarters of the **Russian Provisional Government**. With the Neva River on one side, and an open square on the other, it could have been defended. However, before the attack began on the night of 7 Nov (25 Oct old style) **Kerensky**, the Prime Minister, had already fled, and those left to face the attacking soldiers, sailors and workers' red guards were mainly young cadets and a women's battalion. An easy triumph subsequently made good political theatre. The Winter Palace is now the Hermitage Museum, one of the richest storehouses of art and artefacts in the world. ▷ **Bolsheviks**

Winter War ▷ **Russo-Finnish War** (1939–40)

Winthrop, John (1588–1649) English colonist. Educated at Cambridge, England, he became a lawyer, and in 1629 the first Governor of the Bay Company. He crossed the Atlantic to settle what would become Massachusetts and Massachusetts colony, and was re-elected Governor 12 times. His political and religious conservatism greatly influenced the political institutions that were formed in the Northern states of America.

Wirth, Josef (1879–1956) German politician. After an early teaching career, Wirth entered politics in Baden as a member of the **Centre Party** (1913) and national politics as a member of the **Reichstag** (1914). National Finance Minister after **World War I**, he became Chancellor in May 1921. As such he headed a minority coalition of the republican parties (Centre, **SPD**, **DDP**) which tried to fulfil Allied **reparations** demands so as to demonstrate their excessiveness. He resigned in Nov 1922, held further ministerial posts between 1929 and 1931 and then sought exile in Switzerland (1933) when **Hitler** took power. He returned to Germany in 1948, where he advocated a policy of German neutrality.

Wirtschaftswunder Literally 'economic miracle', this is the term given to Federal Germany's rapid economic recovery from the devastation of **World War II**. Rapid growth from 1948 onward appeared to confirm the efficacy of the **social market economy** and also helped to legitimize the democratic-parliamentary order.

witan (witenagemot) The council (Old English, 'meeting of wise men') of the Anglo-Saxon kings, once regarded as the first English 'parliament'. It was not a popular assembly imposing constitutional restraints on kingship, but in essence an informal advisory body of great men. It nevertheless upheld the convention that kings should take into account the views of important subjects. ▷ **Anglo-Saxons**

Witt, Johan (Jan) de (1625–72) Dutch statesman and mathematician. The son of Jacob de Witt, he was made Pensionary of Dordrecht in 1650, and in 1653 **Grand Pensionary** of the Province of Holland. As such, he was the leader of the States (republican or oligarchic) Party from 1653 to 1672, a party which strove to reduce the influence of the House of Orange in the Dutch Republic, and to leave power in the hands of the merchant élite of the towns and provinces. De Witt was effectively the Foreign Minister of the Dutch Republic during its most powerful period, and his authority was largely unchallenged. In foreign policy he supported the economic interests of the republic, playing England and France off against each other. At the close of the first of the **Anglo-Dutch Wars**, at Oliver **Cromwell's** insistence, he put through an Act of Seclusion, which prevented members of the House of Orange from holding office in the republic; the Act was repealed after the end of Cromwell's reign in 1660. As the young

William III, 'of Orange' came of age and was supported strongly by his uncle, **Charles II** of England, the Orange Party gained influence in the Netherlands, and in 1672, as scapegoats for a situation in which a French army was threatening the southern borders, De Witt and his brother Cornelius were lynched by an Orangist mob in The Hague (20 Aug 1672). William III then became the uncontested leader of the republic.

Witte, Sergei Yulevich (1849–1915) Russian politician. He became a recognized authority on transport economics, and was appointed Minister of Transport and then of Finance (1892). He actively encouraged the development of capitalism in Russia, and presided over the industrialization boom of the late 1890s, attracting foreign investment, and launching the construction of the Trans-Siberian Railway. Under the 'Witte system', Russia became a leading industrial power. As Prime Minister (1905–6) during the **Revolution of 1905**, he combined repression of popular disturbances with a policy of urging political concessions to the middle classes. He also headed the Russian delegation which signed the Treaty of **Portsmouth** (1905) ending the **Russo-Japanese War**. He resigned in 1906, unable to satisfy either conservative or liberal opinion with his policies; but remained active in government circles until his death in Petrograd. ▷ **Duma; Nicholas II**

Wittelsbach The premier Bavarian family, the Wittelsbachs provided successive dukes and kings for Bavaria from medieval times until the early 20c. They still have a disputed claim to the Spanish throne.

Wittenberg A city southwest of Berlin chartered in 1293. It was the residence of the Dukes and Electors of Saxony (1212–1547). The university, founded in 1502, is famous for its associations with Luther and Melanchthon. Luther nailed his 95 Theses to the doors of Wittenberg's Church of All Saints on 31 Oct 1517.

Witwatersrand (The Rand) The region (literally, 'white water's reef') centred on a ridge of gold-bearing rock in southern Transvaal province, South Africa; Johannesburg located near its centre; the power house of the South African economy, with many Black townships nearby providing a reserve of labour; gold discovered in 1886 (produces over half the world's supply).

Władysław IV Vasa (1595–1648) King of Poland (1632/48). The son of **Sigismund III**

Vasa of Sweden, he was elected to the Polish throne in 1632. His reign was a peaceful one, since Poland, despite attempts to draw the country into the conflict, remained neutral during the **Thirty Years War**. At home, he suffered from the religious controversies between Catholics and Protestants, but he crushed the Cossack rebellions in 1637–8, initiating 10 years of 'golden peace' in the Ukraine. Although he harboured grandiose plans to gain the Swedish throne and to drive the Turks from the Balkans, he lacked sufficient support amongst the Polish gentry to achieve this aim.

Wojtyla, Karol Jozef ▷ **John Paul II**

Wolfe, James (1727–59) British general. Commissioned in 1741, he fought against the **Jacobites** in Scotland (1745–6) and was sent to Canada during the **Seven Years War** (1756–63). In 1758 he was prominent in the capture of Louisbourg in Nova Scotia; the following year he commanded at the famous capture of **Quebec**, where he was killed.

Wollstonecraft, Mary (1759–97) Pioneer advocate of women's rights. After working as a teacher and governess, she became a translator and literary adviser. In 1792 she published *Vindication of the Rights of Woman*, which advocated equality between the sexes, radical social change and economic independence for women. She also supported the **French Revolution** and her ideas were vilified by the authorities. After a failed first marriage, she married William Godwin in 1797 and died giving birth to a daughter, Mary (later Mary Shelley, author of *Frankenstein*).

Wolof A West Atlantic language-speaking agricultural people of Senegal and Gambia, traditionally grouped into a state with elaborate hierarchical distinctions. They developed a powerful empire (14–16c), were involved in the European slave trade, and later worked in factories and on European trading vessels.

Wolseley, Garnet Joseph, 1st Viscount (1833–1913) British field marshal. He joined the army in 1852, and served in the Burmese War (1852–3), the **Crimean War** (where he lost an eye), the **Indian Uprising** (1857–8), and the Chinese War (1860). He put down the **Red River Rebellion** (1870) in Canada, and commanded in the Ashanti War (1873). After other posts in India, Cyprus, South Africa and Egypt, he led the attempted rescue of General **Gordon** at Khartoum. He became a baron (1882) and, after the Sudan campaign (1884–5), a viscount. As army Commander-in-Chief (1895–1901), he carried out several reforms, and mobilized forces for the Boer War (1899–1902). ▷ **Boer Wars**

Wolsey, Thomas (c.1475–1530) English cardinal and statesman. He was ordained in 1498, appointed chaplain to **Henry VII** in 1507, and became Dean of Lincoln. Under **Henry VIII**, he became Bishop of Lincoln, Archbishop of York (1514), and a cardinal (1515). Made Lord Chancellor (1515–29), he pursued legal and administrative reforms. He was Henry VIII's leading adviser, in charge of the day-to-day running of government. He aimed to make England a major power in Europe, and also had ambitions to become Pope, but his policy of supporting first Emperor **Charles V** (1523) then **Francis I** of France (1528) in the Habsburg–Valois conflict was unsuccessful, and high taxation caused much resentment. When he failed to persuade the Pope to grant Henry's divorce, he was impeached and his property forfeited. Arrested on a charge of high treason, he died while travelling to London. ▷ **Habsburg Dynasty; Valois Dynasty**

Woodsworth, James Shaver (1874–1942) Canadian social worker, Methodist minister and politician. Having emerged as the country's conscience following the **Winnipeg General Strike** and the federal elections of 1921, his social work in the cities showed him that his church's complicity with capitalist society compromised any capacity for reform. He then turned to politics, but in 1917 lost his job in provincial government for criticizing conscription. He also resigned his ministry as a protest against the Church's support for the war. Arrested for sedition (as an editor of the Winnipeg strikers' bulletin), although not convicted, the resulting publicity helped to spread his reputation as a spokesman for the disadvantaged. Well-informed also on the problems of the prairie farmers, he was a founder and President of the **CCF**. In 1926 he and A A Heaps were able to take advantage of the government's tiny majority: while **Meighen** refused to negotiate with them, Mackenzie **King** promised to introduce an Old Age Pensions Act and rescind the 1919 amendments to the Immigration Act and the Criminal Code. Woodsworth argued that both parties were corrupt and that it was his duty to use his parliamentary position to promote the cause of socialism. Although it took 10 years to repeal the 1919 amendments, the Old Age Pensions Act was passed in 1927. Winning his last election in 1940, Woodsworth was the one MP who voted against Canada's involvement in **World War II**, and his speech of conscience was heard in respectful silence.

Worcester, Battle of (3 Sep 1651) The last battle of the **English Civil Wars**, fought between the English Army, supported by local militia, under Oliver **Cromwell** and an invading Scottish army led by **Charles I**, who had been crowned King of Scotland at Scone (1 Jan 1651). The English forces decisively overpowered their opponents and Charles was a fugitive for several weeks before escaping to Normandy to begin an exile in France, Germany and the Spanish Netherlands which lasted for almost nine years.

Works Projects Administration (WPA) (1935–43) A US federal agency established under President Franklin D **Roosevelt** to combat unemployment during the **Great Depression**. Originally called the **Works Progress Administration**, it built transportation facilities, parks and buildings. Some 8 500 000 people were employed during its history, including artists and writers as well as manual workers. ▷ **New Deal**

World War I (1914–18) A war whose origins lay in the increasingly aggressive foreign policies as pursued by Austria-Hungary, Russia and, most significantly, Germany. The assassination of the heir to the Habsburg throne, **Francis Ferdinand**, at Sarajevo in Bosnia (28 June 1914), triggered the war which soon involved most European states following Austria's declaration of war on Serbia (28 July). Russia mobilized in support of Serbia (29–30 July); and Germany declared war on Russia (1 Aug), and on France (3 Aug). The German invasion of neutral Belgium (4 Aug) brought the British into the war on the French side. Japan joined Britain, France and Russia under the terms of an agreement with Britain (1902, 1911), and Italy joined the Allies in May 1915. Turkey allied with Germany (Nov 1914), and they were joined by Bulgaria (Oct 1915). Military campaigning centred on France, Belgium and, later, Italy in Western Europe, and on Poland, western Russia and the Balkans in Eastern Europe. The French Army prevented the Germans from executing the **Schlieffen** Plan and then, with the **British Expeditionary Force**, at the first Battle of Ypres, from reaching the Channel ports. By the end of 1914, a static defence line had been

FRONTS

1917

Nov 1914

Dec 1915

1916

NETHERLANDS

GERMANY

Berlin

GERMAN OFFENSIVES
1915

Tannenberg
26 Aug 1914 X

Prague

POLAND

Lodz

Vienna

Brest-
Litovsk

Riga

RUSSIA

AUSTRIA -

FALKENHAYN
OFFENSIVE
Sep 1916

Budapest

Gorlice

GALICIA
Lvov

Pinsk

BRUSILOV OFFENSIVE
June–Aug 1916

HUNGARY

Belgrade

Czernowitz

MONTENEGRO

SERBIA

ROMANIA

Jassy (Iaşi)

DATE OF ENTRY INTO THE WAR:

BULGARIA   5 Oct 1915
ROMANIA   28 Aug 1916
GREECE   30 June 1917

ALBANIA

Sofia

Bucharest

BULGARIA

MACKENSEN

Salonica

GREECE

Mudros Armistice
(30 Oct 1918)

Constantinople

SALONICA
Oct 1915

DARDANELLES
Apr 1915–Jan 1916

OFFENSIVES

OTTOMAN

EMPIRE

Trebizond
(Apr 1916)

Erzurum
(Feb 1916)

Allies

1914

1915

1916

1917

1918

Cyprus
(GB)

Aleppo
(25 Oct 1918)

Beirut

Mosul
(4 Nov 1918)

EGYPT

German–Turkish raid
on Suez Canal
(Feb 1915)

Gaza

Damascus
(1 Oct 1918)

Jerusalem

Baghdad

ALLENBY OFFENSIVE
Oct–Dec 1917

Kut al-Amara

Central Powers

1915

1916

1917

986   World War I: Eastern Europe and the Middle East, 1914–18

established from the Belgian coast to Switzerland. The Allies attempted to break the stalemate by the **Gallipoli Campaign** aimed at re-supplying Russia and knocking out Turkey (Apr 1915–Jan 1916), but failed. On the eastern and south-eastern fronts, the **Central Powers** occupied Russian Poland and most of Lithuania, and Serbia was invaded. After staunch resistance, Serbia, Albania and, latterly, Romania were overrun. For three years, an Allied army was involved in a Macedonian campaign, and there was also fighting in Mesopotamia against Turkey. Naval competition had played a crucial role in heightening tension before 1914, but in the event, the great battle fleets of Germany and Britain did not play an important part in the war. The only significant naval encounter, at Jutland in 1916, proved indecisive. The Allies organized a large offensive for the Western Front in 1916, but were forestalled by the Germans, who attacked France at Verdun (Feb–July). To relieve the situation, the Battle of the Somme was launched, but proved indecisive. The Germans then unleashed unrestricted submarine warfare (Jan 1917) to cripple Britain economically before the USA could come to her aid. The USA declared war on Germany (2 Apr 1917) when British food stocks were perilously low, and the German submarine menace was finally overcome by the use of convoys. Tanks were used effectively by the Allies at the Battle of Cambrai (1916). By 1917, the Russian armies were broken and revolution broke out in St Petersburg and Moscow. In late 1917 **Lenin**'s Bolshevik government sued for peace and in Mar 1918 Germany and her allies imposed the punitive peace of Brest-Litovsk on the USSR (annulled after Germany's defeat). Following this, in the spring of 1918, the Germans launched a major attack in the west, but after several months of success were driven back, with the USA providing an increasing number of much-needed troops. By Sep, the German Army was in full retreat, and signified its intention to sue for peace on the basis of President **Wilson**'s **Fourteen Points**. By Nov, when the armistice was signed, the Allies had recaptured western Belgium and nearly all French territory. Military victories in Palestine and Mesopotamia resulted in a Turkish armistice (31 Oct 1918); Italian victories and a northward advance by Franco-British forces finished Austria-Hungary (and Bulgaria). Estimated combatant war losses were: British Empire, just under 1 million: France, nearly 1.4 million; Italy, nearly ½ million; Russia, 1.7 million; USA, 115 000; Germany 1.8 million; Austria-Hungary 1.2 million, and Turkey 325 000. About double these numbers were wounded. ▷ **ANZAC; Marne, Battle of the; Paris Peace Conference; Passchendaele, Battle of; reparations; Somme, Battle of the; Triple Entente; Verdun, Battle of; Versailles, Treaty of; Vimy Ridge, Battle of**

World War II (1939–45) A war whose origins lay in three different conflicts which merged after 1941: **Hitler**'s desire for European expansion and perhaps even world domination; Japan's struggle against China; and a resulting conflict between Japanese ambitions and US interests in the Pacific. The origins of the war in Europe lay in German unwillingness to accept the frontiers laid down in 1919 by the Treaty of **Versailles** and the National Socialists' hegemonial foreign policy. After the German invasion of rump Bohemia-Moravia (Mar 1939), Britain and France pledged support to Poland. Germany concluded an alliance with the USSR (Aug 1939), and then invaded Poland (1 Sep), with Soviet troops joining in the attack on 17 Sep. Britain and France declared war on Germany (3 Sep), but could not prevent Poland from being overrun in four weeks. For six months there was a period of 'phoney war', when little fighting took place, but the Germans then occupied Norway and Denmark (Apr 1940), and Belgium and Holland were invaded (10 May), followed immediately by the invasion of France. A combination of German tank warfare and air power brought about the surrender of Holland in four days, Belgium in three weeks, and France in seven weeks. Italy declared war on France and Britain in the final stages of this campaign. There followed the Battle of Britain, in which Germany tried to win air supremacy over Britain, but failed. As a result, German attempts to force Britain to come to terms came to nothing, not least because of Winston **Churchill**'s uncompromising stance. Germany launched submarine (**U-boat**) attacks against British supply routes, but then moved east and invaded Greece and Yugoslavia (Apr 1941) and, following an Italian military fiasco there, Greece. British military efforts were concentrated against Italy in the Mediterranean and North Africa. After early reverses for Italy, **Rommel** was sent to North Africa with the German **Afrika Corps** to reinforce Italian military strength, and here fiercely-contested campaigning continued for three years until Allied troops finally ejected German and Italian forces in mid-1943, invaded Sicily and then Italy itself,

Thrust of Axis troops in successive campaigns:

| Poland | Norway | France | Balkans | Russia |

Axis territory on 1 Sep 1939

Territory conquered or occupied by Wehrmacht

Allied territory

Territory contested throughout the war

FRONTS:
1 Dec 1941
Jan–Mar 1942
Sep 1942

SOVIET CAMPAIGN AGAINST FINLAND
Nov 1939–Mar 1940

NORWEGIAN CAMPAIGN
Apr–June 1940

BATTLE OF BRITAIN
Aug 1940–May 1941

POLISH CAMPAIGN
Sep 1939

BALKANS CAMPAIGN
Apr 1941

GREEK CAMPAIGN
28 Oct 1940

FRENCH CAMPAIGN
May–June 1940

FINLAND

SWEDEN

NORWAY

DENMARK

GREAT BRITAIN

IRELAND

GERMANY

FRANCE

SPAIN

SWITZER-LAND

ITALY

HUNGARY

ROMANIA
7 Oct 1940

BULGARIA
2 Mar 1941

GREECE

ALBANIA

TURKEY

IRAN

IRAQ
1941

SYRIA
1941

BLACK SEA

CAUCASUS

Stalingrad

Moscow

Leningrad

Tikhvin

Narvik

Namsos

Trondheim

Lillehammer

Andalsnes

Bergen

Oslo

Stavanger

Kristiansand

Stockholm

Copenhagen

Memel

DANZIG

EAST PRUSSIA

POLAND

Warsaw

Brest Litovsk

Lvov

Minsk

Smolensk

Vitebsk

Riga

Tallinn

Valkyie

Ufa

Rybinsk

Kalinin

Tula

Kaluga

Orel

Kursk

Bryansk

Gomel

Kiev

Zhitomir

Uman

Odessa

Dnepropetrovsk

Zaporozhye

Kharkov

Belgorod

Voronezh

Velets

Taganrog

Rostov

Kerch

Sebastopol

Novorossiysk

Maykop

Armavir

Vorochilovsk

Grozny

P. OF BOHEMIA AND MORAVIA

SLOVAKIA

Vienna

AUSTRIA

Zagreb

Belgrade

Sarajevo

Trieste

Nice

Toulon

Lyons

Vichy

Bordeaux

Saumur

Paris

Sedan

Dunkirk

London

Coventry

Rotterdam

NETHER-LANDS

BELGIUM

L. Onega

L. Ladoga

988

and forced Italy to make a separate peace (3 Sep 1943). In June 1941, in line with Hitler's longheld hostility to the USSR, and in his quest for **Lebensraum**, Germany invaded her ally Russia along a 2000 mile front, and German armies advanced in three formations: to the outskirts of Leningrad in the north, towards Moscow in the centre, and to the Volga River in the south. After spectacular early successes, the Germans were held up by bitter Soviet resistance, and by heavy winter snows and Arctic temperatures, for which they were completely unprepared. From Nov 1942 they were gradually driven back, suffering decisive reverses at **Stalingrad** (winter 1942–3) and Kursk (May 1943). Leningrad was under siege for nearly 2½ years (until Jan 1944), and about a third of its population died from starvation and disease. The Germans were finally driven out of the USSR (Aug 1944). A second front was launched against Germany by the Allies (June 1944), through the invasion of Normandy, and Paris was liberated (25 Aug). Despite German use of flying bombs and rockets against Allied bases, the Allies advanced into Germany (Feb 1945) and linked with the Russians on the River Elbe (28 Apr). The Germans surrendered unconditionally at Rheims (7 May 1945). In the Far East, Japan's desire for expansion, combined with a US threat of economic sanctions against her, led to her attack on **Pearl Harbor** and other British and US bases (7 Dec 1941), and the USA declared war against Japan the next day. In reply Japan's allies, Germany and Italy, declared war on the USA (11 Dec). Within four months, Japan controlled South-East Asia and Burma. Not until June 1942 did naval victories in the Pacific stem the advance, and Japanese troops defended their positions grimly. Bitter fighting continued until 1945, when, with Japan on the retreat, the USA dropped two atomic bombs on Hiroshima and Nagasaki (6 and 9 Aug). Japan then surrendered 14 Aug. Casualty figures are not easy to obtain accurately, but approximately 3 million Russians were killed in action, 3 million died as prisoners of war, 8 million people died in occupied Russia, and about 3 million in unoccupied Russia. Germany suffered 3¼ million military casualties, around 6 million total casualties, and lost a million prisoners of war. Japan suffered just over 2 million military casualties and just over ¼ million civilian deaths. France lost a total of ½ million dead, and Britain and her Commonwealth just over 600000. The USA suffered just over 300000 casualties. It is also estimated that in the course of the German

occupation of a large part of Europe, about 6 million Jews were murdered in extermination and labour camps, along with a million or more other victims. ▷ **Anschluss; appeasement; Atlantic, Battle of the; Atlantic Charter; Blitzkrieg; Britain, Battle of; Bulge, Battle of the; Casablanca Conference; D-Day; Desert Rats; El Alamein, Battle of; Free French; Gestapo; Holocaust; kamikaze; Lend-Lease Agreement; Maginot Line; Munich Agreement; Normandy Campaign; North African Campaign; Nuremberg Trials; Paris Peace Conference; Potsdam Conference; Special Operations Executive; SS; Yalta Conference**

World Zionist Organization The political institution established under the leadership of Theodor **Herzl**, its first President, at the First Zionist Congress, held in Basel (29–31 Aug 1897). The goal of the organization was the establishment of a national home for world Jewry in Palestine. For this purpose, the first Zionist bank and the **Jewish National Fund** were also formed. With time, the World Zionist Organization opened offices all around the world and, in the years before his death, Herzl shaped it into an efficient and effective political institution. ▷ **Zionism**

Worms, Concordat of (1122) This agreement, negotiated under **Henry V**, brought a temporary end to the **Investiture Controversy**. It was decided that bishops were to be invested with their fiefs, symbols of their secular office, by the emperor, but were to receive the ring and staff, the symbols of their spiritual authority, from the Pope. The emperor retained a limited control over ecclesiastical appointments, but his power in this sphere was considerably weakened.

Wörner, Manfred (1934–) West German politician. He studied law at the universities of Heidelberg, Paris and Munich, then joined the conservative Christian Democratic Union (**CDU**) and was elected to the **Bundestag** (federal parliament) in 1965. Establishing himself as a specialist in strategic issues, he was appointed Defence Minister in 1982 by Chancellor **Kohl** and then oversaw the controversial deployment of US Cruise and Pershing-II nuclear missiles in West Germany, an extension of military service from 15 to 18 months to compensate for a declining birthrate, and, in 1984, the dismissal of General Gunter Kiessling, for alleged, though subsequently disproven, homosexual contacts. Wörner succeeded Lord **Carrington** as Secretary-General of **NATO** in 1988.

Wounded Knee (29 Dec 1890) The site in South Dakota (USA) of the final defeat of the **Sioux**. The 'battle' was in fact a massacre of men, women, and children by US troops, finally suppressing the Ghost Dance cult inspired by the visions of the Paiute religious leader Wovoka. In 1973, members of the American Indian Movement occupied the site to protest at the conditions of **Native Americans**. Two people were killed in the ensuing seige by **FBI** agents and federal marshals. ▷ **Indian Wars**

Wrangel, Pyotr Nikolaievich, Baron (1878–1928) Russian army officer. He entered military service in 1904 and commanded a cavalry corps during **World War I**. In the **Russian Civil War**, he commanded cavalry divisions and the Volunteer Army in the Ukraine, and in 1920 became Commander-in-Chief of the White armies in the south. After the **Red Army** victory, he fled to Turkey with the remnants of his troops. He died in Brussels, and was buried in Belgrade.

Wu (625–705) Empress of China (690/705). The only woman in Chinese history who formally bore the title of Emperor, she was originally the concubine of the first Tang Emperor, **Tang Taizong** (626/49). She became Empress on marriage to Taizong's son, Tang Gaozong (649/83), and by 660 she was in virtual charge of government. After the death of her husband, Empress Wu placed first one and then a second son on the throne. In 690 she deposed her second son, Tang Ruizong (684/90 and 710/12), and proceeded to establish a dynasty of her own, the Zhou, ruling as Emperor until she was forced to abdicate at the age of 80. Her first son, Tang Zhongzong (683/4 and 705/10), then re-established the **Tang Dynasty**. Although condemned by Chinese historians as a despotic and corrupt usurper, her reign witnessed further refinement of the **Civil Service Examination System** and a resurgence of Chinese influence in the Korean Peninsula.

Wu P'ei-fu ▷ Wu Peifu

Wu Peifu (Wu P'ei-fu) (1874–1939) Chinese warlord. A major figure in the warlord struggles of China (1916–27). He joined the **Beiyang Army**, newly created by

Yuan Shikai, and rose rapidly in its ranks. After Yuan's death (1916), when **Duan Qirui** sought to reunite China by force and in dependence on Japan, Wu and other northern generals refused Duan's orders. In the civil war which followed, he was unable to sustain his government of national unity (1923). He died in Japanese-occupied Beijing.

Württemberg Originally part of Swabia, Württemberg became a Duchy in 1495. Duke Ulrich siezed church lands and introduced Lutheranism. Duke Christopher (1550/68) made substantial reforms while Duke Frederick (1593/1608) freed the Duchy from the titular overlordship of the Habsburgs. The dukedom was devastated in the **Thirty Years War** and by the French during the Wars of the Coalition (the War of the Grand Alliance). ▷ **Habsburg Dynasty**

Wycliffe, John (c.1330–84) English religious reformer. He taught philosophy at Oxford, then entered the Church, becoming Rector of Lutterworth, Leicestershire, in 1374. He was sent to Bruges to treat with ambassadors from the Pope about ecclesiastical abuses, but his views were found unacceptable, and he was prosecuted. He then attacked the Church hierarchy, priestly powers, and the doctrine of transubstantiation, wrote many popular tracts in English (as opposed to Latin), and issued the first English translation of the Bible. His opinions were condemned, and he was forced to retire to Lutterworth, where he wrote prolifically until his death. The characteristic of his teaching was its insistence on inward religion in opposition to the formalism of the time. His followers were known as '**Lollards**', and the influence of his teaching was widespread in England, in many respects anticipating the **Reformation**.

Wyszynski, Stepan (1901–81) Polish cardinal. Educated at Włocławek and Lublin, he was ordained in 1924, and became Bishop of Lublin (1946), Archbishop of Warsaw and Gniezno (1948), and a cardinal (1952). Following his indictment of the communist campaign against the Church, he was imprisoned (1953). Freed in 1956, he agreed to a reconciliation between Church and state under the **Gomułka** regime, but relations remained uneasy.

X

Xenophon (c.427–355BC) Athenian historian, essayist and soldier. A pupil of Socrates, in 401BC he joined the 10000 Greek mercenaries under the Persian Prince Cyrus, who was secretly preparing to supplant his brother as King of Persia. On the death of Cyrus, and the treacherous murder of the Greek officers of the 10000, Xenophon was elected their leader, and they successfully fought their way back over 900 miles from the River Tigris to the Black Sea. Exiled from Athens, he fought for the Spartans under his friend, King **Agesilaus**, and was rewarded with an estate in the Peloponnese, where he lived as a gentleman farmer and writer.

Xerxes I (c.519–465BC) Achaemenid King of Persia (485/465BC). The son of **Darius I, 'the Great'**, he is remembered in the West mainly for the failure of his forces against the Greeks in the Second Persian War at Salamis, Plataea, and Mycale. ▷ **Persian Wars**

Xi'an Incident (12–25 Dec 1936) The incident during which the **Guomindang** leader, **Chiang Kai-shek**, was kidnapped and held hostage in Xi'an by some of his own troops, under the 'Young Marshal', Zhang Xueliang (Chang Hsueh-liang). The hostage-taking was designed to force Chiang Kai-shek into acceding to demands for an alliance between the Guomindang and the Communists against the Japanese, who had occupied Manchuria in 1931. He was released, after 13 days, thanks to intervention by the Communist leader, **Zhou Enlai** (further to urging by **Stalin**). Chiang Kai-shek made a verbal agreement to review Guomindang policy, and the second of the **United Fronts** followed.

Xoxe, Koci (d.1949) Albanian politician. A member of the Communist Party, and a wartime protégé of the Yugoslav partisan leader, **Tito**, he was Minister of the Interior in the post-war government, presiding over the trials of 'war criminals' which consolidated the position of Enver **Hoxha**. As a supporter of Albania's ties with Yugoslavia, his position weakened after Yugoslavia was expelled from Cominform and Hoxha moved closer to **Stalin**. From being second only to Hoxha in importance, he was demoted, then tried for treason and executed in 1949, a victim of Stalin's purge of 'Titoists'.

Xuan Zang (c.600–664) Chinese Buddhist traveller, born in Honan. He became a Buddhist monk in 620 and made a long pilgrimage through China and India during which he travelled 40000 miles in 16 years. His books graphically describe the Buddhist world in the Middle Ages.

XYZ Affair (1797) A diplomatic incident between the USA and France. It arose when French agents, identified as 'X', 'Y', and 'Z', solicited a bribe from US agents sent to negotiate an end to maritime hostilities.

Y

Yaba Higher College A college founded in Lagos, Nigeria in 1934 by the British Governor General, Sir Donald Cameron, with the intention of training Africans for administrative work. By **World War II** it offered some degree courses.

Yadavas The name of a late Vedic tribe which settled in the Mathura area in northern India. Subsequently, the name was used of a dynasty which ruled in northern Deccan (Aurangabad region) from 900 to 1300, whose contribution to the final disintegration of the **Chola Dynasty** was significant. In 1296, Allauddin Khalji attacked the city of Deogiri, the Yadava capital. He defeated the Yadavas and the Yadava king was forced to pay a vast amount of gold to Allauddin as part of the ensuing peace treaty. Between 1327 and 1330 **Muhammad bin Tughlaq** moved his capital from Delhi to Deogiri and renamed it Daulatabad. Yadavas patronized the Marathi language and played an important part in establishing Marathi as the language of intellectual communication.

Yagoda, Genrikh Grigorevich (1891–1938) Soviet police chief. A shadowy figure of Jewish origin, he became number two in the OGPU (or secret police) in 1924 and head of its successor, the NKVD, in 1934. He was **Stalin**'s agent in the great purges that started in that year. Yagoda was dismissed as inefficient in 1936 and brought before a firing squad in 1937. His successor, **Yezhov**, was a much nastier figure.

Yahya Khan, Agha Muhammad (1917–80) Pakistani soldier. The son of a Pathan police superintendent, he was educated at Punjab University and the Indian Military Academy, Dehra Dun. He was commissioned in 1938, fought with the British Eighth Army during **World War II** and afterwards rose to become Chief of the Army General Staff (1957–62). He supported General **Ayub Khan**'s successful coup in 1958, became Army Commander-in-Chief in 1966 and, in 1969, with popular unrest mounting, replaced Ayub Khan as military ruler. In 1980 he sanctioned the nation's first national elections based on universal suffrage, but his mishandling of the Bangladesh separatist issue led to civil war and the dismemberment of the republic in 1971. After defeat by India in the **Bangladesh War**, Yahya Khan resigned and was sentenced to five years' house arrest.

Yakovlev, Alexander Nikolaevich (1923–) Soviet party official and intellectual. Born into a simple peasant family in the Yaroslavl area, he first became an apparatchik after being invalided out of the army and by 1953 had been called to Moscow where, with the exception of four years of academic leave, he spent the period down to 1973 servicing the Central Committee of the Communist Party. He was then exiled as Ambassador to Canada for a decade for offending communist hardliners. It was on Mikhail **Gorbachev**'s advice that he was brought back to the Central Committee to assist with ideological work and by 1987 he was a full member of the **Politburo**. Although previously anti-American he did much to give body to Gorbachev's new thinking on home and foreign affairs. He was eventually more reformist than Gorbachev but still did everything possible to rescue him politically after the attempted **August Coup** in 1991. ▷ **apparat**

yakuza Literally 'good-for-nothing', the Japanese word used to describe a gangster. Like the Mafia, its Western equivalent, Japanese organized crime has a long history. Gangsters belong to recognized groups of racketeers (*boryokudan*). Often tattooed, gangsters cultivate a **samurai**-like loyalty and are proud of their traditions. Like the Mafia, they are widely involved in such activities as gambling, extortion, racketeering, and the 'protection' of pachinko halls.

Yalta Conference (4–11 Feb 1945) A meeting at Yalta, in the Crimea, during **World War II**, between Winston **Churchill**, **Stalin** and **Roosevelt**. Among matters agreed were the disarmament and partition of Germany, the Russo-Polish frontier, the establishment of the **UN**, and the composition of the Polish government. In a secret protocol it was also agreed that Russia would declare war on Japan after the war with Germany ended. ▷ **Curzon Line**

Yamagata Aritomo (1838–1922) Japanese soldier and politician. Made commanding officer of the **Kiheitai** in 1863, he went on to become Vice-Minister of War (1871) and then Army Minister, issuing in 1878 the 'Admonition to the Military', which emphasized the traditional virtues of bravery and loyalty to the **Meiji Emperor**, in an attempt to counteract the trend of liberalization. As Chief of Staff, he was the driving force behind the promulgation of the 1882 **Imperial Rescript to Soldiers and Sailors** and 1890 **Imperial Rescript on Education**. He was Home Minister (1883–9) and was Japan's first Prime Minister (1889–91 and 1898–1900). His modernization of the military system led to Japanese victories in the **Sino-Japanese War** (1894–5) and **Russo-Japanese War** (1904–5), for which he was made Prince (*Koshaku*), and the emergence of Japan as a significant force in world politics. From 1903 he alternated with **Ito Hirobumi** as President of the Privy Council; after the latter's death (1909), he was the dominant senior statesman, with the backing of the military and bureaucracy. His downfall came about in 1921 when he interfered in the marriage of the Crown Prince; he was publicly censured and died in disgrace the following year.

Yamamoto Isoroku (1884–1943) Japanese naval officer. Educated at the Naval Academy, Etajima, he was wounded in the Battle of Tsushima in the **Russo-Japanese War** (1904–5). He studied at Harvard (1917–19), serving thereafter as a language officer (1919–21) and as naval attaché at the Japanese embassy in the USA (1926–2). He became Chief of the Aviation Department of the Japanese navy in 1935, and was vice-Navy Minister from 1936 to 1939. Opposed to the Japanese entry into **World War II**, Yamamoto was nevertheless made Admiral (1940) and Commander-in-Chief Combined Fleet (1939–43). A great strategist, it was he who planned and directed the attack on **Pearl Harbor** in Dec 1941. His forces were defeated at the Battle of **Midway** (June 1942), and he was killed when his plane was shot down over the Solomon Islands.

Yamani, Sheikh Ahmed Zaki (1930–) Saudi Arabian politician. Educated in Cairo, New York and Harvard, he worked as a lawyer before entering politics. Yamani has been Minister of Petroleum and Mineral Resources since 1962, and an important and 'moderate' member of **OPEC** (the Organization of Petroleum-Exporting Countries).

Yamashita Tomoyuki (1885–1946) Japanese soldier. After serving in the **Russo-Japanese War**, **World War I** and **Sino-Japanese War**, he commanded the Japanese 25th Army which overran Malaya and captured Singapore (15 Feb 1942). He then took over the Philippines campaign, capturing Bataan and Corregidor. Still in charge when General **MacArthur** turned the tables in 1944–5, he was captured and hanged in Manila for atrocities perpetrated by his troops.

Yameogo, Maurice (1921–) Burkina Faso politician. Educated in Upper Volta (now Burkina Faso), he was a civil servant and trade unionist before turning to politics and being elected to the Territorial Assembly in 1946. He was Vice-President of the Upper Volta section of the Confédération Français du Travailleurs Chrétiens and was active within the **Rassemblement Démocratique Africaine** (RDA). The founder of the Mouvement Démocratique Voltaique, he was Minister of Agriculture (1957–8), Minister of the Interior (1958) and President (1958–66), before being toppled by a military coup on 4 Jan 1966 led by Lt-Col Sangoule Lamizana. He was imprisoned until 1970, when he went into exile in the Ivory Coast.

Yanaconazco A Peruvian term, originally signifying the Indian servants of Spaniards. By the mid-17c, the term had come to mean city labourers and servants dependent upon Spanish artisans or traders; and by the late 19c, the term *yanacona* signified a dependent sharecropper, producing a cash crop. Yanaconas were lent money by the estate to buy seed and fertilizers and to hire day-labourers from the sierra. In return, they serviced the loan and paid their shares in cotton.

Yanaev, Gennadi Ivanovich (1937–) Soviet lawyer and politician. He made his career in the **Communist Party of the Soviet Union** as a **Komsomol** official and union apparatchik. That he had some genuine popularity was proved in 1989, when he was elected by the unions to the Congress of Deputies. In 1990 his promotion was remarkably fast: Chairman of the trade unions, a **Politburo** member, and Soviet Vice-President. In all these positions he attempted to steer a middle course between reform and reaction; but in 1991 he opted for reaction, whether of his own free will or under pressure. His leadership of the attempted coup was so disastrous as to suggest that

993

neither his heart nor his mind was in it. He was arrested with the others from the '**junta**'.
▷ **apparat**

Yang Shangkun (Yang Shang-k'un) (1907–) Chinese politician. The son of a wealthy Sichuan province landlord, he joined the Chinese Communist Party (CCP) in 1926 and studied in Moscow (1927–30). He took part in the **Long March** and the liberation war (1937–49), and became an alternate member of the CCP's secretariat in 1956, but during the **Cultural Revolution** was purged for alleged 'revisionism'. He was subsequently rehabilitated in 1978 and in 1982 inducted into the CCP's Politburo and Military Affairs Commission. A year later he became a vice-chairman of the state Central Military Commission and in 1988 was elected state President. Viewed as a trusted supporter of **Deng Xiaoping**, he has strong personal ties with senior military leaders and in June 1989 it was 27th Army troops, loyal to him, who carried out the brutal massacre of pro-democracy students in **Tiananmen Square**, Beijing.

Yankee The nickname for an inhabitant of New England, or Northerner in general (especially during and since the **American Civil War**). It is also a general term for people of the USA, especially among non-Americans. The source is obscure, but it may derive from the Dutch *Janke* (a derivation of *Jan*), used as a nickname by early settlers.

Yazdegerd III (d.651) Last Sassanid ruler of Persia (632/51). A young man when he came to the throne, he had the misfortune of having to face the vibrant forces of nascent Islam. His capital, Ctesiphon, was taken by Sa'd ibn Abi Waqqasin in 637, after his major victory over the Persians at the Battle of al-Qadisiyya (636). From the time of the capture of Ctesiphon, Yazdegerd, with his court, spent the remainder of his life in flight. The Battle of Nehavand (641–2) saw the final defeat of the Persians and the downfall of the Persian Empire. The major Persian cities of Isfahan and Istakhr (the ancient Persepolis) then fell to the advancing Arabs, and Yazdegerd fled north and east to Khurasan. In 651–2 Yazdegerd, who had with him his imperial crown and treasure, was murdered on the premises of a miller who had offered him refuge near Marv in north-eastern Khurasan.

Yazov, Dmitri Timofeevich (1923–) Soviet marshal. Of peasant stock from Omsk,

he fought in **World War II** as a young officer. He subsequently rose through various junior and senior commands, went through the General Staff Academy in 1967, and in 1984 became commander of the important Far East military district. In 1987 Mikhail **Gorbachev** appointed him Deputy Minister, then Minister of Defence to bring the army into line with his reforms. However, Yazov supported only limited changes and was particularly unpopular with radical deputies. In Aug 1991 he felt that reform had proceeded to the point of endangering the army, but in the event his men would not obey him and fire on the crown. When the attempted **August Coup** failed, he was arrested.

Yegarov, Alexander Ilich (1883–1939) Soviet marshal. Of relatively humble origins in Samova, he was a colonel in the Tsarist army by 1917. He then threw in his lot with the **Bolsheviks** and rose rapidly in the course of the **Russian Civil War** during which he came into close contact with **Stalin**. By 1935 he was Chief of the General Staff and in 1937 he succeeded the executed **Tukhachevsky** as Deputy Defence Minister, only to be shot himself two years later. The loss of his fighting experience and his organizational talent was sorely felt.

Yeltsin, Boris Nikolaevich (1931–) Soviet politician. He joined the **Communist Party of the Soviet Union** in 1961 and was appointed First Secretary of the Sverdlovsk region in 1976. He became a full member of the Central Committee in 1981 and was made its Secretary by Mikhail **Gorbachev** in 1985 for a few months, before being appointed Moscow Party Chief, replacing the disgraced Viktor Grishin. Yeltsin, a blunt-talking, hands-on reformer, rapidly set about renovating the corrupt 'Moscow machine' and was elected a candidate member of the **Politburo** in 1986, but in 1987–8, after he had bluntly criticized party conservatives at two meetings of the Central Committee for sabotaging political and economic reform, he was downgraded to a lowly administrative post. No longer in the Politburo, he returned to public attention in 1989 by being elected to the new Congress of People's Deputies and becoming an outspoken critic of Gorbachev's failings. In May 1990 he was elected President of the Russian Federation and achieved even greater fame. But his moment of triumph came in Aug 1991, when he took the open stand that foiled the anti-Gorbachev coup and in Dec effectively put an end to both Gorbachev and the USSR. ▷ **August Coup**

Yehenala ▷ Cixi

Yevtushenko, Yevgeny (Alexandrovich) (1933–) Soviet poet. His early poetry, such as *The Third Snow* (1955), made him a spokesman for the young post-**Stalin** generation. His long narrative poem *Stantsiya Zima* (1956, Zima Junction), considering issues raised by the death of Stalin, prompted criticism, as did his *Babi Yar* (1962) which attacked anti-Semitism. In 1960 he began to travel abroad to give readings of his poetry. ▷ **Babi Yar**

Yezhov, Nikolai Ivanovich (1894–1939) Soviet police chief. He first emerged in 1933 as a member of a small group charged by **Stalin** with the task of purging the Communist Party of undesirable elements, essentially those opposed to him. In 1936 he succeeded **Yagoda** as head of the NKVD (secret police) and turned the confined purges into mass terror. The bloodletting took on the title, the *Yezhovshchina*. Succeeded by **Beria** in 1938, he too disappeared for ever in 1939.

Yi Dynasty (1392–1910) The dynasty which ruled Korea under the official dynastic name of *Choson* ('morning serenity'). Founded by Yi Song-gye (1335–92), a prominent general under the preceding **Koryo** Dynasty (918–1392), the Yi Dynasty provided Korea with a long period of political and social stability until the incursions of Japan and the Western powers in the late 19c and its annexation as a Japanese colony in 1910. The Yi rulers were assisted by a centralized bureaucracy recruited through competitive civil service examinations on the Chinese pattern. Until the late 19c, the Yi maintained Korea's traditional tributary relationship with China.

Yishuv The Hebrew term (literally, 'settlement') used to describe the Jewish community living in Palestine before 1948. It was also used for the declaration of the State of Israel in that year. ▷ **Balfour Declaration; Israel, State of; Jewish Agency**

Yogyakarta (Jogjakarta) A court city and sultanate in Java, founded in the mid-18c following the partition of central Java at the Treaty of Giyanti (1755). In 1810 and again in 1812, Yogyakarta was invaded by European forces. On the second occasion, British troops took and looted the *kraton* (court) itself and Yogyakarta subsequently lost considerable territory. During the Java War (1825–30), many officials in Yogyakarta made common cause with Prince **Dipa-**nagara. Following the defeat of the rebel forces, Yogyakarta therefore lost all its remaining outlying territories as well as a great deal of its income. In the early 20c Yogyakarta became an important centre for emerging nationalist and religious reformist movements. During the war against the Dutch for independence, following the Japanese surrender in 1945, the Indonesian Republic government resided in Yogyakarta.

Yohannes IV ▷ **John IV** of Ethiopia

Yom Kippur War (1973) The hostilities that broke out towards the end of Golda **Meir**'s last term as Israeli Premier, when an attack on the State of Israel by Egypt and Syria coincided with Yom Kippur, the holiest day in the Jewish calendar. A cease-fire was reached after three weeks of fighting in which there were heavy losses on both sides. ▷ **Arab-Israeli Wars**

Yonai Mitsumasa (1880–1948) Japanese naval officer and politician. Born of **samurai** descent, he was educated at the Naval Academy, Etajima and served in Russia (1915–17). He was Commander of the Imperial Fleet (1936–7), Navy Minister (1937–9 and 1944–5), and was briefly Prime Minister in 1940.

York, House of The younger branch of the **Plantagenet Dynasty**, founded by Edmund of Langley, the fourth son of **Edward III** and first Duke of York, whence came three kings of England: **Edward IV**, who usurped the Lancastrian king **Henry VI**; **Edward V**; and **Richard III** killed at the Battle of **Bosworth Field**, and succeeded by **Henry VII**, first of the Tudors. ▷ **Lancaster, House of; Roses, Wars of the; Tudor, House of**

Yorktown Campaign (30 Aug–19 Oct 1781) The final campaign of the **American Revolution**, in which the British Army under General **Cornwallis** was trapped at Yorktown in Virginia, by troops under George **Washington** and a French fleet under Admiral de Grasse (1722–88). The defeat destroyed the political will on the English side to continue the war. It brought the fall of Lord **North**, Prime Minister since 1770, and opened the way for peace negotiations.

Yoruba City States A cluster of politically autonomous units in Nigeria and Benin, inhabited by Kwa-speaking peoples, and each ruled by a king who is both political and religious head. The dominant state in the

17–18c was the kingdom of Oyo, which broke up in the early 19c. Ibadan was the largest pre-colonial city in Black Africa, and the states are famed for their art. Missionaries were highly active in Yorubaland in the 19c, but Islam and traditional religions are also represented.

Yoshida Shigeru (1878–1967) Japanese politician. Educated at Tokyo Imperial University, he served as a diplomat in several capitals. Vice-Foreign Minister (1928–30), in 1930–2 he was Ambassador to Italy and in 1936–8, after the army had blocked his appointment as Foreign Minister, he was Ambassador in London. As a fervent advocate of Japanese surrender, he was imprisoned (June 1945) for this view in the closing stages of **World War II**. He was released (Sep 1945) under the US occupation and was appointed Foreign Minister. After **Hatoyama**'s removal by the US authorities from public office, he stepped into his shoes as leader of the Liberal Party. As Prime Minister (1946–7 and 1949–54), he was instrumental in the socio-economic development of post-war Japan and in fostering relations with the West. In 1954, Hatoyama (who had been rehabilitated in 1951) forced him out of office and, when the **Liberal Democratic Party** was formed (1955), with Hatoyama as its leader, Yoshida withdrew from politics.

Youlou, Abbe Fulbert (1917–72) Congo politician. Educated in Catholic seminaries and ordained a priest in 1946, he became Mayor of Brazzaville in 1957 and formed a moderate party to oppose the local socialists. He was elected to the territorial assembly in 1957 and was, in turn, Minister of Agriculture (1957–8), Prime Minister (1958–9) and President of the Congo Republic (1959–63), before being forced into exile in Spain as the result of popular opposition within the country.

Young, Whitney M, Jr (1921–71) US civil rights leader. Born in Kentucky, he was a graduate in social work from the University of Minnesota. Executive director of the **National Urban League** from 1961 until his death, some of his social welfare proposals were incorporated into President **Johnson**'s anti-poverty programmes.

Young Ireland An Irish protest movement, founded in 1840, which produced *The Nation* magazine, arguing for repeal of the Act of Union. It set up an Irish Confederation in 1847, which returned several nationalists to parliament, and an unsuccessful Young Ireland rising took place in Tipperary (1848). ▷ **O'Connell, Daniel; Union, Acts of**

Young Italy (*Giovine Italia*) The organization founded by the Italian patriot, Giuseppe **Mazzini**, in 1831 after he had grown dissatisfied with the poor organization and muddled programme of the **Carbonari**. Limited in all but exceptional circumstances to individuals under 40 years of age, the organization sought to develop Italian national feeling, aiming to generate a national, republican uprising. In reality, it merely inspired a handful of invariably abortive conspiracies, but it did play an important part in fostering patriotic sentiment among many future leaders of the **Risorgimento**, including **Garibaldi**. During the early 1830s, various sister organizations (Young Switzerland, Young Germany, Young Poland, Young Europe) were formed but they never achieved the same degree of support. Young Italy itself fell victim to the repressive measures of the Piedmontese government in the period 1833–5 and never again attained the widespread support of its earliest years.

Young Pretender ▷ **Stuart, Charles Edward (Louis Philip Casimir)**

Young Turks The modernizing and westernizing reformers in the early 20c **Ottoman Empire**. With the support of disaffected army elements under **Enver Pasha**, they rebelled against Sultan **Abd ul-Hamid II** in 1908, and deposed him (1909). The Young Turk revolution helped precipitate Austria-Hungary's occupation of Bosnia-Herzegovina (1908), the somewhat similar Greek officers' revolt of 1909, the Italian attack on Libya (1911), and the **Balkan Wars** (1912–13).

Ypres, Battle of (Oct–Nov 1914) In **World War I** the halting of a German offensive to outflank the **British Expeditionary Force**. It left Ypres (Belgium) and its salient dominated on three sides by German-occupied heights.

Ypres, Battle of (Apr–May 1915) A series of German attacks, using poison gas (chlorine) for the first time in warfare. It forced the British to shorten their defence line in the Ypres salient.

Ypres, Battle of ▷ **Passchendaele, Battle of**

Ypsilanti, Alexander (1725–1805) Greek administrator. He became Ottoman **hospodar** (governor) of Wallachia, but was put to death on suspicion of fostering Greek ambitions.

Ypsilanti, Alexander (1783–1828) Greek soldier. The eldest son of Constantine **Ypsilanti**, he served with distinction in the Russian Army (1812–13), and was chosen by the Greek 'Hetairists' as their chief in 1820. In 1821 he led a Romanian uprising in the Danubian Principalities, but was defeated by the Turks. He took refuge in Austria, where he died.

Ypsilanti, Constantine (d.1816) Greek administrator. The son of Alexander **Ypsilanti** (1725–1805), he became Ottoman **hospodar** (governor) of **Moldavia and Wallachia**. Deposed in 1805, he came back with some thousands of Russian soldiers and stirred the Serbs to rebellion; he made another plan for restoring Greece, but had to flee to Russia.

Ypsilanti, Demetrius (1793–1832) Greek soldier. The younger son of Constantine **Ypsilanti**, he served in the Russian Army, and aided the schemes of his brother, Alexander **Ypsilanti** (1783–1828), for emancipating the Christian population of Turkey. In Greece, he took part in the capture of Tripolita (Oct 1820). His gallant defence of Argos stopped the victorious march of the Turks, and from 1828 to 1830 he was commander-in-chief of the Greek army.

Yrigoyen, Hipólito (1852–1933) Argentine politician. A lawyer and teacher, he was the principal leader of the **Radical Party** (*Unión Cívica Radical*) from 1896. He mounted a successful attack on the dominant conservative governments of the time, ushering in a period of Radical dominance. Yrigoyen was President in 1916–22, during which term he maintained Argentine neutrality in **World War I**, and again in 1928–30. His second presidential term was ended by a military coup, precipitated by the country's prevailing economic depression and Yrigoyen's growing senility and weakening grasp on national affairs.

Yuan Dynasty (1279–1368) The Chinese dynasty founded by **Kublai Khan**, who completed the conquest of the Southern Song, and built a new capital (Marco Polo's 'Cambaluc') at Beijing. The Chinese never accepted their foreign rulers, however, and after Kublai's death (1294) Mongol power rapidly declined. Civil war between Mongol princes broke out in 1328, and the dynasty was eventually overthrown by a Chinese uprising led by Zhu Yuanzhang.

Yuan Shih-k'ai ▷ **Yuan Shikai**

Yuan Shikai (Yuan Shih-k'ai) (1859–1916) Chinese politician and soldier. He was careful to remain neutral during the **Boxer Rising**, from which he thus emerged with his army intact and with the gratitude of the foreign powers. On the death of his patron, the Empress Dowager **Cixi** (1908), he was removed from influence, but recalled after the successful **Chinese Revolution** of 1911. As the first President of the Republic (1912–16), he lost support by procuring the murder of the parliamentary leader of the **Guomindang** and making war on them, accepting Japan's **Twenty-One Demands**, and proclaiming himself Emperor (1915). Forced to abdicate, the humiliation may have hastened his death. ▷ **Hundred Days of Reform; Qing Dynasty**

Yugoslav Committee Established during **World War I** (Apr 1915) in Paris by, among others, Ivan Meštrović, Ante **Trumbić** and Frano **Supilo**, the Yugoslav Committee held that the **South Slavs** were entitled to their own state on the principles of national right and self-determination. Claiming to represent the interests of the South Slavs in the Habsburg Monarchy, it moved to London where it campaigned to win the support of the Allies for the political unification of the South Slavs. By the Declaration of Corfu, it agreed to cooperate with the Serbian government in establishing a South Slav state (July 1917). At the end of **World War I**, the National Council of Slovenes, **Croats** and Serbs in Zagreb authorized the Yugoslav Committee to act as its representative in international negotiations. After the Serbian regent, **Alexander I Karageorgević**, accepted the Council's proposals (1 Dec 1918), the South Slavs were united for the first time within the Kingdom of Serbs, Croats and Slovenes (later Yugoslavia). ▷ **Yugoslavs**

Yugoslavia A federal republic in the Balkan peninsula of south-east Europe, consisting of the republics of Serbia and Montenegro. Serbs, Croats and Slovenes united under one monarch in 1918, and the kingdom was renamed Yugoslavia in 1929. There followed civil war between Serbian royalists (**Chetniks**), Croatian nationalists and Communists in the early 1940s. Yugoslavia was occupied by Germany during **World War II**; in 1945

Territory freed from Turkish occupation:

- 1800–76
- in 1878
- in 1913
- Formerly, Sandžak of Novi Pazar
- •••• Frontier between Montenegro and Serbia, 1912–13

Territory freed in 1919 from:

- Austrian occupation
- Hungarian occupation
- Austro-Hungarian occupation
- Frontier of the Kingdom of Serbs, Croats and Slovenes in 1920; later (1929) Kingdom of Yugoslavia

Territory freed from Italian occupation

- after World War II (1945–54)

Formation of Yugoslavia

the Federal People's Republic was established under **Tito**. Following a break with the **USSR** in 1948, the country followed an independent form of communism and a general policy of non-alignment. At the end of the 1980s, political disagreement between the federal republics increased; in 1989 **Slovenia** declared its sovereignty and its strong opposition to the Communist Party. In an attempt to preserve Yugoslavian unity the government announced plans to allow a multiparty system with direct elections, but ethnic unrest in Serbia and Croatia placed further strains on the federal system. Croatia and Slovenia ceded from Yugoslavia in 1991, and Bosnia-Herzegovina in 1992. Macedonia

declared its independence in 1992. Since 1991 there has been prolonged civil war and atrocities between ethnic factions in Bosnia-Herzegovina, forcing economic sanctions by the **UN**. A new Federal Republic of Yugoslavia consisting of Serbia and Montenegro was declared in Apr 1992 but is unrecognized by the UN. In 1992 rigorous sanctions were imposed upon Yugoslavia, regarded as a supply route and ally for the Serbian forces in Bosnia-Herzegovina.

Yugoslavism During the 19c, the ideology of a primarily Croatian movement which sought to promote closer cultural and political ties among the **South Slavs**. An extension of the Illyrianism of Ljudevit **Gaj**, its chief proponents were Bishop Juraj **Strossmayer** and Canon Franjo Rački. Originally aimed at unifying the South Slavs through their common culture and literary language, Yugoslavism developed into a political movement for the unification of the South Slavs of the Habsburg Monarchy within a South Slav state which would remain part of a federalized monarchy. In time, its ultimate goal became a federal South Slav state including **Serbia** and **Montenegro**. ▷ **Yugoslavs**

Yugoslavs Literally the 'South Slavs', this is the collective name for the inhabitants of Yugoslavia who are members of several different nations; while the Serbs, **Croats**, Slovenes, Bosnian Muslims and Macedonians are all South Slavs, Yugoslavia has many non-Slav inhabitants including the Hungarians in the **Vojvodina** and the Albanians in Kosovo. At the end of **World War I**, the South Slavs of the former Habsburg Monarchy, the Croats, Slovenes and some Serbs were joined to the Serbs of the Kingdom of Serbia and Montenegro within a new independent state, the Kingdom of Serbs, Croats and Slovenes. The head of the new state was **Peter I**, the King of Serbia and head of the Karageorgević Dynasty, and formal unification was proclaimed by the **Regent Alexander I Karageorgević** (1 Dec 1918), who, later as King, renamed the kingdom the Kingdom of Yugoslavia (1929). During **World War II**, Yugoslavia capitulated to the Axis forces and puppet governments were established in Zagreb and Belgrade. The resentment which had built up during the inter-war years among different nations within Yugoslavia combined with longstanding national rivalries to erupt in a 'civil war' of brutal reprisals; the only semblance of 'Yugoslav' unity remained in the communist-led partisan army which

waged a brave and effective tactical campaign against the occupying Axis forces. After the war, **Tito**'s version of **communism** promised to neutralize old national rivalries and to unite the nations of Yugoslavia in pursuit of a common future. While Yugoslavia was reorganized as a federation of six republics and two autonomous provinces, each of which was based around a core nation, the different nationalisms were strictly repressed and the expression of national identities stifled. Uneven economic development among the republics, however, continued to fuel resentment among the nations. After Tito's death, nationalisms resurfaced and Yugoslavia fell into political and economic decline. In 1990 individual republics held democratic elections and in 1991 **Slovenia** and **Croatia** declared secession and achieved international recognition as independent republics in winter and spring 1991–2. When the President of Bosnia and Herzegovina, Alia Izetbegović, declared his republic's secession in Mar 1992, international recognition again followed, but the Yugoslav National Army and nationalist militia groups fought to divide the republic on ethnic lines, plunging the civilian population into a brutal war. While Tito's old Socialist Federal Republic of Yugoslavia has ceased to exist, the name Yugoslavia is still used by the Republics of Serbia, Montenegro and Macedonia. ▷ **AVNOJ; Bosnia and Herzegovina; Chetniks; Dalmatia; Istria; Macedonia; trialism; Ustaša; Yugoslavism**

Yusuf bin Hassan (Jeronimo Chingulia)

(1526/31) Last sheik of the Malindi Dynasty of Mombasa (Kenya). As a youth he studied under Portuguese tutelage in Goa and was baptized a Christian as Dom Jeronimo Chingulia. Following his succession in 1526 he took up arms in 1531 against Portuguese domination. He was driven out of Mombasa and direct Portuguese rule was established.

Z

Zab, Battle of the Greater (750) The major battle which compassed the eclipse of the **Umayyad Dynasty** (661–750). The Khurasani troops of Abu Muslim defeated the Umayyads under Marwan II on the banks of the Greater Zab, a tributary of the River Tigris. As a result of this, the **'Abbasid Dynasty** was proclaimed, with al-Saffah as its first caliph. This change of dynasty signalled a shift in the centre of power in the central Islamic lands from Syria (Damascus) to Iraq (eventually Baghdad). The subsequent persecution of the Umayyad House led to the flight of the surviving Umayyads westwards, where eventually the Umayyad Emirate was established in Spain (later the Umayyad Caliphate under Abd al-Rahman III).

Zachariadis, Nikos (1903–73) Greek political leader. The son of a tobacco worker, he was one of the many Greeks who were forced to leave Anatolia in 1923 after the **Graeco-Turkish War** and who became communists. He was Secretary-General of the **KKE** (Communist Party of Greece) from 1931 to 1941. Imprisoned during **World War II** in **Dachau** concentration camp, he lived to return home in 1945 to direct communist opposition to the British-backed Greek government and resumed his post as Secretary-General of the KKE. Believing that the communists would achieve their victory in the towns, he quickly came into conflict with Markos **Vafiadis**, who was based in the country, and succeeded Vafiadis as commander of the Democratic Army in 1949. ▷ **Lausanne, Treaty of**

Zaghlul, Sa'd (c.1857–1927) Egyptian politician and lawyer. Effectively the founder of the Egyptian **Wafd Party**, he headed a campaign to change the political position of Egypt, leading the delegation (*wafd*) of Egyptians who petitioned Britain for an end to the protectorate. This petition failed and, as a result, he was banished to Malta (1919). Anti-British riots followed and he was released, later achieving the desired recognition of independence for Egypt. After varying fortunes, during the course of which he was once more arrested and banished, Zaghlul eventually led his Wafd Party to success in Egypt's first election. By 1924

Zaghlul had become Egypt's first Prime Minister; a modern campaign conducted during the first Wafd government meant, however, that despite the success once more of the Wafdists in the 1926 election, the British refused to accept Zaghlul as Prime Minister. He was allowed, though, to become President of the Chamber, a cabinet containing six members of the Wafd, three Liberals and an independent, with the cabinet as a whole headed by the Liberal leader. Zaghlul, however, relinquished office shortly afterwards.

Zahir Shah, Mohammed (1914–) King of Afghanistan (1933/73). Educated in Kabul and Paris, he was Assistant Minister for National Defence and Education Minister before succeeding to the throne in 1933 after the assassination of his father, Nadir Shah. His reign was characterized by a concern to preserve neutrality and promote gradual modernization. He became a constitutional monarch in 1964, but, in 1973, while in Italy receiving medical treatment, was overthrown in a republican coup led by his cousin, General Daud Khan, in the wake of a three-year famine. Since then he has lived in exile in Rome and remains a popular symbol of national unity for moderate Afghan opposition groups.

Zahle, Carl Theodore (1866–1946) Danish politician. After studying law, he became a member of the Danish parliament, **Folketinget**. In Jan 1905, he and seven other members were expelled from the then leading Danish political party, *Venstrereformpartiet* ('Left Reform Party'), because they advocated a reduction in Denmark's defence expenditure. In response to the expulsion, Zahle in May 1905 became one of the founding members of a new centre party, *Det Radikale Venstre* ('The Radical Left'), which was to develop into a major middle-ground force of Danish pre-war and interwar politics. It was a socially committed, non-socialist party that wanted Denmark declared 'lastingly neutral' and the working-class party, *Socialdemokratiet*, drawn into the democratic process. The party's core electorate was made up of the unusual alliance of smallholders, schoolteachers and Copenhagen academics. As early as Oct 1909, Det Radikale Venstre formed its first, shortlived government, with Zahle as Premier. After the general election in 1913, he headed a much stronger government which, supported by the Social Democrats, secured the Danish policy of neutrality during **World War I**. After the war, there was in financial and nationalistic circles a growing dissatisfaction with Zahle's government which resulted in his being dismissed by the Danish King, **Christian X**, on 29 Mar 1920, causing the so-called Easter Crisis.

Zai Tian (Tsai T'ien) (1871–1908) Emperor of China (1875/1908). A ruler of the **Qing Dynasty**, he took the reign-title **Guangxu** (Kuang-hsu). He remained largely under the control of the Empress Dowager **Cixi** until 1898 when, after China's defeat in the **Sino-Japanese War** (1894–5), he was determined to reform and strengthen his country. He threatened to abdicate if not given full authority and issued a series of reforming edicts. However, his attempts to gain power precipitated a coup; thereafter, he was confined to his palace until his mysterious death one day before the death of the Empress Dowager. ▷ **Hundred Days of Reform; Kang Youwei**

Zalygin, Sergei Pavlovich (1913–) Soviet fiction writer. Born in the Bashkin autonomous region, he spent much of his life in Siberia. He came into his own under Mikhail **Gorbachev**, being one of the main campaigners against the project to reverse the Siberian rivers. In 1986 he became Chief Editor of *Novy Mir* and was responsible for securing the publication of Solzhenitsyn's previously banned works.

Zambezi Expedition An official British expedition (1858–64), led by David Livingstone, to investigate the potentiality of the Zambezi River for steamship communication with the interior of Africa, in order to promote the destruction of the **slave trade**, its replacement by 'legitimate' commerce, and the extension of missionary activity in the region. The expedition was a failure: the Zambezi was found to be non-navigable, Livingstone's relations with his associates were difficult and helped to thwart the scientific objectives, and the earliest missionary endeavours met with disaster.

zamindar A Persian term meaning 'holder/occupier of the land'. Its use in India ranged from hereditary tax collectors (Bengal) to large landowners with full proprietory rights (parts of northern India) to all local hereditary revenue officers (western and central India). The term was adopted by the British to mean 'landowner', notably in the permanent settlement of the land revenue in Bengal in 1793, designed to provide an aristocracy of improving landlords.

Zamyatin, Evgeny Ivanovich (1884–1937) Russian novelist and short-story writer. He was exiled in 1905 after joining the Bolshevik Party, and again in 1911, but on each occasion soon returned to Russia. In 1921 he was a founder member of the Modernist group, the Serapion Brothers, and was briefly imprisoned by the Soviets in 1922. In 1932 he travelled to Paris, where he remained until his death. He is best known for the novel *My* (1920, We). ▷ **Bolsheviks**

Zanardelli, Giuseppe (1826–1903) Italian politician. He took part in the anti-Austrian uprisings in his native Brescia during the **Revolutions of 1848–9** and supported the Piedmontese invasion of Lombardy in 1859. In 1860 he was elected to the new Italian parliament. Following the electoral victories of the left in 1876, he held a number of ministerial posts until finally becoming Prime Minister in 1901. A left-wing liberal, he was violently anticlerical and a supporter of divorce. He was also responsible for the reform of the penal code. As Prime Minister, he was particularly concerned with improving the economic conditions of the **Mezzogiorno**.

Zangid Dynasty Also known as the Atabeg Dynasty, it was established by Imad al-Din Zangi, who became Governor of Mosul in 1127 and took control of Aleppo in 1128. His power in the Fertile Crescent, resulting from his control of these two major cities, brought him into not always happy contact in the east with the great Seljuk sultanate, and in the west with the Crusaders and the Burid Dynasty which controlled Damascus. Chiefly remembered in the West for his capture of Edessa (1144), which feat precipitated the preaching of the unsuccessful Second Crusade, Zangi was murdered in 1146 and the dynasty's influence was then split between Syria and the Jazira. He had expended much effort in endeavouring to gain control of Damascus but this was only finally achieved by his son, Nur al-Din. Zangid influence waned after the latter's death, chiefly as a result of the rise in power of one of his junior lieutenants, **Saladin**, who subsequently gained control not only of Damascus, but also

Aleppo. This finally confined Zangid influence once more to Mosul and and the northern Jazira. The Zangids can, however, be credited with the first effective prosecution of holy war (**jihad**) against the crusading Franks. ▷ **Crusade, Second**

Zanj ▷ **Azania**

ZANU (Zimbabwe African National Union) The party which was formed in 1963, under the leadership of Ndabaningi **Sithole**, as a breakaway from **ZAPU** in opposition to ZAPU's strategy. The party split again, as a result of which Robert **Mugabe** became leader. Banned from Southern Rhodesia, the party relocated to Mozambique and became, through its military wing, the Zimbabwe African National Liberation Army (ZANLA), the most effective guerrilla movement. Associated with ZAPU in 1976 to form the Patriotic Front, it nevertheless fought the 1980 elections separately as ZANU (PF) and won 57 of the 80 seats available to black voters. It has been the dominant party since then, increasing its majorities at both subsequent general elections. In 1988, after long discussions, it absorbed **Nkomo**'s wing of the **Patriotic Front**.

Zapata, Emiliano (1879–1919) Mexican revolutionary. The son of a mestizo peasant, he became a sharecropper and local peasant leader. After the onset of the Mexican Revolution, he occupied estates by force and mounted a programme for the return of land in the areas he controlled to the native Indians. He initially supported Francisco **Madero** and, with a small force of men was largely responsible for toppling the dictatorship of Porfirio **Díaz**. Along with Pancho **Villa**, he subsequently fought the **Carranza** government. Meanwhile, he continued to implement agrarian reforms in the southern area under his control, creating impartial commissions responsible for land distribution and setting up the Rural Loan Bank. He was eventually lured to his death at the Chinameca hacienda in Morelos.

Zapolya, John (1487–1540) King of Hungary (1526/40). A prince of Transylvania, he was proclaimed king despite the superior Habsburg claim of Emperor **Ferdinand I**, who drove him out in 1527. John was, however, supported by **Suleyman I, 'the Magnificent'**, who reinstated him as a puppet ruler.

Zapolya, John Sigismund (1540–71) King of Hungary. The son of John **Zapolya**, he succeeded his father. However, as **Suleyman I, 'the Magnificent'** had made Hungary a Turkish province, he had to content himself with the voivodship of Transylvania.

Zapolya, Stephen (d.1499) Hungarian soldier. He gained renown as a military leader under **Matthias I, 'Corvinus'** by his defeat of the Turks and his conquest of Austria, of which he was made Governor (1485). He was the father of John **Zapolya**, King of Hungary.

Zapotecs A Precolumbian Mesoamerican Indian civilization of southern Mexico (300BC–AD300), influenced by Olmec culture. It was centred on Monte Alban, a ceremonial site located on a high ridge in the Valley of Oaxaca.

Zapotocky, Antonin (1884–1957) Czechoslovak trade unionist and politician. A stonemason from Kladno, he was active in the socialist youth movement from 1900 and in the Socialist Party from 1907. In 1920 he was a major organizer of an unsuccessful general strike, and in 1921 helped found the Communist Party. Imprisoned during **World War II**, he emerged in 1945 to become the President of the revolutionary trade-union organization that played a key role in seizing power in 1948. He was appointed Prime Minister and succeeded to the presidency when Klement **Gottwald** died unexpectedly in 1953. His responsibility for the purges was probably less than Gottwald's, but despite the moderation of old age, he lost much of the opportunity to make amends.

ZAPU (Zimbabwe African People's Union) Founded in 1961 with Joshua **Nkomo** as its leader, in the 1960s it was the most popular party in Southern Rhodesia, espousing the end to white minority rule. It was banned in 1964 and moved to Zambia where it organized, through its military wing, the Zimbabwe Independent People's Revolutionary Army (ZIPRA), guerrilla attacks within Southern Rhodesia. It reassociated itself with **ZANU** to form the **Patriotic Front** (PF) in 1976, but fought the independence elections in 1980 independently from its partner, although under the Patriotic Front label. It became effectively an Ndebele Party and finally fused with **ZANU** (PF) on 1988.

Zaslavskaya, Tatyana Ivanovna (1927–) Soviet economist, sociologist and political reformer. Born into an academic family in Kiev, she was educated in and researched economics in Moscow until in 1963 she joined **Aganbegyan** in Novosibirsk and turned her attention to sociology. In the early 1980s she came into contact with Mikhail **Gorbachev** through her writings on the countryside and at the same time earned herself a reputation for criticism of Soviet life. In 1988 she returned to Moscow to head a centre devoted to the study of public opinion and became in effect a most influential member of Gorbachev's reform team, including the Congress of Deputies.

Zaydis A moderate Shiite grouping who take their name from Zayd, son of the fourth Imam, 'Ali Zayn al-Abidin. 'Ali's son, Muhammad al-Baqir, is the traditionally accepted fifth Imam of both the Seveners (Isma'ilis) and the Twelvers (Ithna ashariyya). Of a more militant disposition than his elder brother, Muhammad, Zayd attracted his own following. In modern times most Zaydis are to be found in the Yemen. Under Turkish rule from 1517 to 1918, the Zaydi Imam Yahya was established as ruler of the Yemen as a kingdom, principally with support from the British in Aden. Assassinated in 1948, Yahya was succeeded by his son, Ahmad, who ruled until 1962. Despite the subsequent proclamation of Yemen as a republic, discontent having been principally fomented by Gamal Abd al-**Nasser**'s Egypt, the religious basis of the Yemen continues to be principally Zaydi, with pockets of Isma'ilism principally in the Jabal Haraz.

Zeeland, Paul van (1893–1973) Belgian politician. He studied law and political science at Leuven (Louvain) University, where he held a chair from 1928 to 1963. He first became cabinet minister (without portfolio) in 1934, and in 1935–7 was Prime Minister and Minister of Foreign Affairs. Having spent **World War II** in England, he became Minister of Foreign Affairs (1949–54), and was intensively involved in the moves towards European union during those years.

Zelanti The Italian term (literally, 'zealots') used to describe the ultra-reactionary cardinals who resisted the more reforming tendency typified by Cardinal **Consalvi** after the Congress of **Vienna** (1814–15).

Zemski Sobor (1550–1694) A Russian form of estates that helped to strengthen central government until it was itself discarded by a

forceful **Peter I, 'the Great'**. It can be traced back to 1471, but assumed importance only in 1550 when **Ivan IV, 'the Terrible'** summoned it to help him in his law-making. It frequently played this role, but in 1613 it elected the first of the **Romanov Dynasty** to be Tsar. In 1649 it assisted in codifying the laws, but it often met mainly to deal with disturbances. Although it was appointed, not elected, it nonetheless represented a cross-section of opinion, sometimes including peasants, and gave a flavour of popular participation in government, which was lost in Peter's time.

zemstvo An organ of rural local self-government established in Russia following the emancipation of the serfs (1861). The zemstvos consisted of elected councillors, paid officials, and professional employees responsible for such matters as local education, health care, sanitation, and public welfare. Their activities were, however, severely curtailed by the bureaucratic and financial constraints imposed by central government. ▷ **Duma; Russian Serfs, Emancipation of the**

Zeng Guofan (Tseng Kuo-fan) (1811–72) Chinese politician, soldier and philosopher. When ordered in 1852 to raise a militia with which to quell the **Taiping Rebellion**, he built a force as committed to Confucianism as the rebels were to their form of Christianity. His successes led to his appointment as Governor-General of the Nanjing (Nanking) area (1860); Nanjing was besieged, and recovered from the rebels in 1864.

Zenkl, Peter (1884–1975) Czechoslovak politician. Born in Tabor and educated in Prague, he was a relatiely late entrant to politics. He was elected to the city council in 1923 as a National Socialist (Czechoslovak-style, totally different from **Nazi Party**) and became Mayor in 1937. He became a government minister just before the **Munich Agreement** and remained one for a few more months. He was then imprisoned in **Buchenwald** concentration camp. In 1945 he resumed as Mayor but became a deputy prime minister in the National Front government in 1946. In 1948 he was one of those who resigned to provoke a fresh election and instead gave the communists an excuse for their **February Revolution**. He died in exile.

Zeno (c.440–491) Byzantine Emperor (474/91). An Isaurian noble, he married Ariadne, daughter of Leo I (466) and became sole ruler on the death of their son, Leo II. He tried to achieve a reconciliation between the orthodox church and the monophysite churches of the east, but his doctrinal compromise, the *Henoticon*, merely antagonized both parties and caused a schism with the Roman church.

Zenobia (3c) The widow and successor of Odaenathus, Roman client ruler of Palmyra (c.266). An ambitious and intelligent woman, she wrested control of Syria, Egypt, and most of Asia Minor from Rome, and ruled in the name of her infant son Vaballathus, whom she declared Emperor (271). Defeated by Aurelian (272), she was taken to Rome and exhibited in his victory parade. Palmyra itself was totally destroyed.

Zentrum ▷ **Centre Party** (Germany)

Zervas, Napoleon (1891–1957) Greek resistance leader. In 1926 with General Kondylis he led a coup against the military dictatorship of General Pangalos (1925–6). During **World War II** he was the leader in Greece of the non-communist resistance movement **EDES**, the National Republican Greek League. At the end of the war he bitterly opposed the communists in their attempts to seize power. ▷ **EAM; EKKA; ELAS; Greeks; Plastiras, Nikolaos**

Zeta The name of the medieval state ruled by the Crnojević family until the Ottoman incursions in the late 15c and which from the 1690s formed part of Montenegro. The last ruler of Zeta, Ivan Crnojević, retreating from the Turks, transferred his court to Cetinje which later became the capital of Montenegro and seat of the **Petrović-Njegoš Dynasty**.

Zhang Guotao (Chang Kuo-t'ao) (1897–1979) Chinese politician. As a student he played a part in the **May Fourth Movement** of 1919, and in 1921, as a founding member, joined the new Chinese Communist Party. He rose to prominence as a labour leader and played a leading role in the Nanchang Mutiny (1927). He opposed the elevation of **Mao Zedong** as Leader of the Party, but his army was destroyed by Muslim forces in the north-west. He defected to the **Guomindang** in 1938. When the Chinese Communist Party won national power in 1949, he moved to Hong Kong.

Zhang Zhidong (Chang Chih-tung) (1837–1909) Chinese scholar and provincial

official. A pioneer of industrialization in late 19c China, he was successively Governor of Shanxi (1882–4), Guangdong and Guangxi (1884–9), and Hunan and Hubei (1889–1907). An impassioned patriot, he led the 'Purist' party, opposed to French encroachments in Indo-China, with disastrous results. After China's defeat in 1885, he turned his attention to education and industrialization, building a steelworks, mills, and factories, but his efforts met with only limited success. ▷ **Kang Youwei; Li Hongzhang**

Zhao Ziyang (Chao Tzu-yang) (1918–) Chinese politician. He joined the Communist Youth League (1932) and worked underground as a Chinese Communist Party (CCP) official during the liberation war (1937–49). Zhao rose to prominence implementing land reform in Guangdong, becoming the province's CCP First Secretary in 1964. As a supporter of the reforms of **Liu Shaoqi**, was dismissed during the **Cultural Revolution**, paraded through Canton in a dunce's cap and sent to Nei Monggol. However, enjoying the support of **Zhou Enlai**, he was rehabilitated (1973) and appointed Party First Secretary of China's largest province, Sichuan (1975). Here he introduced radical and successful market-orientated rural reforms, which attracted the eye of **Deng Xiaoping**, leading to his induction into the CCP Politburo as a full member in 1979 and his appointment as Prime Minister a year later. As Premier, he oversaw the implementation of a radical new 'market socialist' and 'open door' economic programme, and in 1987 replaced the disgraced **Hu Yaobang** as CCP General-Secretary, relinquishing his position as Premier. However, in June 1989, like his predecessor, he was controversially dismissed for his allegedly overly liberal handling of the **Tiananmen Square** pro-democracy demonstrations.

Zhdanov, Andrei Alexandrovich (1896–1948) Soviet politician. A school inspector's son, he joined the **Bolsheviks** in 1915 and took part in the 1917 **Russian Revolution** and the **Russian Civil War**. He then rose through the Communist Party bureaucracy until in 1934 he became Secretary of the Central Committee and in 1939 was appointed to the **Politburo**. He performed a prominent role in the defence of **Leningrad** from 1941 to 1944, and subsequently assumed responsibility for ideological purity, bitterly attacking the West and its alleged imitators in the USSR.

Zheng Chenggong (Cheng Ch'eng-kung) ▷ **Koxinga**

Zheng He (Cheng Ho) (1371–1433) Chinese eunuch. He led a series of maritime expeditions to South-East Asia, India, and the east coast of Africa between 1405 and 1433 during the **Ming Dynasty**. He came from a Muslim family and became a close aide of Emperor **Ming Yongle** (1402/24). Ming Yongle promoted the maritime expeditions as a means both to assert the universality of the Chinese empire and expand trade. The expeditions were thought to be too extravagant by critics at court and were ended in the 1430s. China would never again have ambitions of being a seafaring power.

Zhivkov, Todor (1911–) Bulgarian politician. A Communist Party member since 1932, in **World War II** he fought in the resistance movement that in 1944 overthrew the pro-German Sofia regime. He was made Party Secretary in 1954 and Prime Minister in 1962 and, as Chairman of the Council of State from 1981, he was effectively the republic's President. In 1989 Zhivkov was replaced by Petur Mladenov as leader of the Bulgarian Communist Party, and in 1990 he was indicted on charges of 'especially gross embezzlement'. When his trial began in Feb 1991, he pleaded not guilty, complaining that the trial was 'a farce'.

Zhou (Chou) Dynasty A Chinese dynasty founded between 1122 and 1027BC; accounts of its origins are a mixture of history and legend. It is traditionally held to have been founded by King Wu, who overthrew the last tyrannical ruler of the Shang Dynasty, Zhouxin. Its capital was at Hao (near Xi'an) until 771BC, and at Luoyi (near Luoyang) until its occupation by the Win in 256BC. A form of feudal monarchy, the Zhou saw the first flowering of Chinese historical, philosophical, and literary writing, and the establishment of the culture that has endured to the present.

Zhou Enlai (Chou En-lai) (1898–1976) Chinese politician. One of the leaders of the Chinese Communist Party (CCP), he was Prime Minister of the Chinese People's Republic from its inception (1949) until his death. After pursuing his studies in Japan, he returned to China after the 1919 **May Fourth Movement**. Imprisoned in 1920 as an agitator, on his release he spent four years in Europe, where he dedicated himself to the communist cause. In 1927, under the first of the **United Fronts**) he organized the revolt in Shanghai for the **Guomindang**; he became a member of the CCP Politburo later the same

year. In 1932 he was appointed to succeed **Mao Zedong** as Political Commissar of the Red Army, but after 1935, following Mao's elevation, he served him faithfully, becoming the Party's chief negotiator and diplomat. As Prime Minister (1949–76) and Minister of Foreign Affairs (1949–58) he vastly increased China's international influence. Perhaps his greatest triumph of mediation was in the **Cultural Revolution** in China, when he worked to preserve national unity and the survival of government against the forces of anarchy. ▷ **Chiang Kai-shek; Comintern; communism; Xi'an Incident**

Zhu De (Chu Teh) (1886–1976) Chinese soldier. He was one of the founders of the Chinese Red Army and was closely associated throughout his later career with **Mao Zedong**. Zhu took part in the Nanchang Mutiny (1927) and his defeated troops joined with those of Mao to found the **Jiangxi Soviet**. There, he and Mao evolved the idea of 'people's war', beating off attacks by **Chiang Kai-shek**'s vastly superior **Guomindang** forces until finally driven out in 1934. The Red Army then undertook the **Long March**, in which Zhu De was the leading commander. During the **Sino-Japanese War** (1937–45), he was in charge of the **Eighth Route Army**. After the Japanese surrender and the renewal of civil war in China (1946), Zhu was Supreme Commander of the renamed **People's Liberation Army**, which expelled the Nationalists from mainland China. He was Chairman of the Standing Committee of the National People's Congress from 1959. 'Purged' at the beginning of the **Cultural Revolution**, he was rehabilitated in 1967.

Zhukov, Giorgiy Konstantinovich (1896–1974) Soviet marshal. He joined the **Red Army** in 1918, commanded Soviet tanks in Outer Mongolia (1939), and became army Chief-of-Staff (1941). He lifted the siege of Moscow, and in 1943 his counter-offensive was successful at the Battle of **Stalingrad**. In 1944–5 he captured Warsaw, conquered Berlin, and accepted the German surrender. After the war he was Commander of the Russian zone of Germany, and became Minister of Defence (1955), but was dismissed by Nikita **Khrushchev** in 1957. ▷ **World War II**

Zia, Begum Khaleda Bangladeshi politician. The widow of General **Ziaur Rahman** who was President of Bangladesh from 1977 until his assassination in 1981, she became leader of the Bangladesh Nationalist Party (BNP) in 1982. In 1990, when President Hussain Muhammad **Ershad** was forced to resign, elections were called. The BNP's main contestant was the **Awami League** led by Sheikh Hasina Wajed; in the event, the latter only gained 30 per cent of the seats and in 1991 Begum Zia became the first woman prime minister of Bangladesh.

Zia ul-Haq, Muhammad (1924–88) Pakistani general and President. He served in Burma, Malaya, and Indonesia in **World War II**, and in the wars with India (1965, 1971), rising rapidly to become general and Army Chief-of-Staff (1976). He led a bloodless coup in 1977, was President (1978–88), imposed martial law, banned political activity, and introduced an Islamic code of law. Despite international protest, he sanctioned the hanging of former President **Bhutto** in 1979. He was killed in an air crash near Bahawalpur.

Ziaur Rahman (1935–81) Bangladeshi soldier and President. He played an important part in the emergence of the state of Bangladesh. Appointed Chief of Army Staff after the assassination of Mujibur Rahman (1975), he became the dominant figure within the military. President from 1977 to 1981, his government was of a military character, even after the presidential election of 1978 which confirmed his position. He survived many attempted coups, but was finally assassinated in Dhaka.

Zimbabwe African National Union ▷ **ZANU**

Zimbabwe African People's Union ▷ **ZAPU**

Zimmermann, Arthur (1864–1940) German politician. After diplomatic service in China, he directed from 1904 the eastern division of the German Foreign Office and was Foreign Secretary (Nov 1916–Aug 1917). In Jan 1917 he sent the famous 'Zimmermann telegram' to the German minister in Mexico with the terms of an alliance between Mexico and Germany, by which Mexico was to attack the USA with German and Japanese assistance in return for the US states of New Mexico, Texas and Arizona. This telegram finally brought the hesitant US government into the war against Germany. ▷ **World War I**

Zinoviev, Grigoriy Yevseyevich (1883–1936) Russian revolutionary and politician.

Educated at Berne University, in 1924 he was made a member of the ruling **Politburo**, but because of opposition to **Stalin**'s policies was expelled from the **Communist Party of the Soviet Union** (1926). Reinstated in 1928, he was again expelled in 1932, and in 1935 was arrested after the assassination of Kirov. Charged with organizing terrorist activities, he was executed following the first of Stalin's Great Purge trials in Moscow. The so-called Zinoviev Letter urging British Communists to incite revolution in Britain contributed to the downfall of the Labour government in the 1924 general elections. ▷ **Bolsheviks; Lenin; October Revolution**

Zinzendorf, Nicolaus Ludwig, Count von (1700–60) German religious leader. Educated at Wittenberg, he later held a government post at Dresden. He invited the persecuted Moravians to his estates, and there founded the colony of *Herrnhut* ('the Lord's keeping') for them. His zeal led to conflict with the government, and he was exiled from Saxony in 1736. Ordained at Tübingen (1734), he became Bishop of the **Moravian Brethren**, wrote over 100 books, and died at Herrnhut.

Zionism The movement which sought to recover for the Jewish people its historic Palestinian homeland (the *Eretz Israel*) after centuries of dispersion. The modern movement arose in the late 19c with plans for Jewish colonization of Palestine, and under Theodor **Herzl** also developed a political programme to obtain sovereign state rights over the territory. Gaining support after **World War I**, its objectives were supported by the British **Balfour Declaration** in 1917, as long as rights for non-Jews in Palestine were not impaired. After **World War II**, the establishment of the Jewish state in 1948 received **UN** support. Zionism is still active, as a movement encouraging diaspora Jews to immigrate to and take an interest in the Jewish state. ▷ **Aliyah; Israel, State of**

Ziska (Žižka), John (c.1370–1424) Bohemian Hussite leader. He fought against the Poles, Turks, and French, and soon after the murder of Jan **Hus**, became Chamberlain to King **Wenceslas**. During the Civil War he was chosen leader of the popular party, captured Prague (1421), and erected the fortress of Tabor, his party coming to be called Taborites. Having lost both his eyes in battles, he continued to lead his troops in a series of victories, compelling Emperor

Sigismund to offer the Hussites religious liberty, but he died at Przibislav before the war was over.

Zoë (980–1050) Byzantine Empress (1028/50). The daughter of the Byzantine Emperor Constantine VIII, in 1028 she married Romanus III. She had him murdered in 1034 and made her paramour Emperor as Michael IV. When his successor, Michael V, was deposed in 1042 she became Empress jointly with her sister, Theodora, and married her third husband, Constantine IX.

Zog I (1895–1961) King of Albania (1928/39). Educated in Istanbul, he became leader of the Nationalist Party, and formed a republican government in 1922. Forced into exile in 1924, he returned with the assistance of Yugoslavia, and became President (1925–8), proclaiming himself King in 1928. After Albania was overrun by the Italians (1939), he fled to Britain, and later lived in Egypt and France. He formally abdicated in 1946, and died in France.

Zollverein A German customs union, based on the enlarged **Prussia** of 1814, and officially constituted in 1834. It comprised all of Germany save the Austrian Empire, Hanover, Brunswick, Oldenburg, and three northern maritime states: a total of 17 states embracing 26 million people. It represented an important stage in the German unification process.

Zouaves A body of troops in the French army, first raised from Algerian tribes in 1830, who dressed in flamboyant Moorish costume. During the **American Civil War**, several 'Zouave' style volunteer regiments were raised on the US side.

Zubatov, Sergei Vasilyevich (1863–1917) Russian colonel. He was in the **Okhranka**, which organized trade unions to try to direct revolution. As unrest increased at the turn of the century, he was authorized to set up a 'Society for Mutual Help of Workers in Mechanical Production' to organize loyalist demonstrations. But another 'union' became entangled in a strike in Odessa, and Zubatov was dismissed and his idea dropped in 1904. Ironically the net effect was to increase union activity during the Russian **Revolution of 1905**.

Zulu Kingdom The Zulu kingdom was formed in the early 19c, when **Shaka**, building on the military achievements of his predecessor, **Dingiswayo**, welded the northern **Nguni** into an expansive and highly militarized state. His troops became a formidable fighting force, dispersing many of the other peoples of southern Africa far afield; however, they were defeated by the Boers and British, and much of their territory annexed. They have retained a strong self-identity, and are organized politically into the modern **Inkatha Freedom Party** under their leader Chief Gatsha **Buthelezi**. Their territory, greatly contracted, became one of the 'Homelands' of modern South Africa: **KwaZulu**. ▷ **Afrikaners**

Zulu War (1879) A war between British forces and the Zulu kingdom characterized by initial reverses for the British but final defeat for the Zulu. From the time of the arrival of Boer settlers in northern Natal in 1836, there had been uneasy border relations between white and black. The boundary was set at different times on the Tugela, Black Umfolosi and Buffalo Rivers, but Boer farmers continued to penetrate Zululand in search of land. A boundary commission was appointed (1878), but the colonial authorities refused to accept its recommendations because the High Commissioner, Sir Bartle Frere, considered that they were too favourable to the Zulu. When a party of Zulu crossed the Natal border to kidnap two wives of a Zulu chief, war was declared. After initial reverses at Isandlhwana and Rorke's Drift, the British forces under Sir Garnet **Wolseley** defeated the Zulu at Ulundi. **Cetewayo**, King of the Zulu, was exiled and Zululand was divided into 13 chieftaincies. The removal of the Zulu military threat encouraged the Boers to throw off British power in the Transvaal, leading to the first Boer War and the British defeat at **Majuba Hill** (1881).

Zumalacárregui, Tomás de (1788–1835) Spanish soldier. He fought against **Napoleon**, and on the re-establishment of absolutism was made Governor of Ferrol, but in 1832, with other Carlists, was dismissed from the army. Head of the Carlist insurrection (1833), he kept his opponents at bay, and gained a series of victories over the Madrid generals. This turned the head of Don **Carlos**, and led him to interfere with the plans of his general, who was anxious to strike for Madrid; ordered to lay siege to Bilbao instead, Zumalacárregui died of a wound sustained as he observed enemy lines nearby.

Zurich, Peace of (10 Nov 1859) A treaty between Austria, Piedmont and France at the end of the north Italian war. Lombardy passed from Austrian, through French, into Piedmontese hands in return for compensation paid to Austria on Piedmont's behalf by France. This peace marked the first significant permanent reduction in Austrian power in northern Italy in the post-Napoleonic age and paved the way for Italian unification during the 1860s.

Zveno Literally 'the Link', this is the name given to the Bulgarian civilian organization, formed in 1927 under the leadership of Colonel Kimon Georgiev, which aimed at the modernization of Bulgaria through the development of technology and industry. The government of Colonel Damian **Velchev**, who had come to power in the 1934 military coup, implemented the Zveno programme and depended on the support of its members. During **World War II**, members of Zveno joined the communist-backed **Fatherland Front** and Georgiev became Prime Minister in the new Bulgarian government organized by the Front (Sep 1944). In 1946, when Zveno became the target of the communists, Georgiev was demoted in stages as the Soviet-backed Georgi **Dimitrov** established himself in power.

Zwangendaba (d.c.1845) General in the Ndwandwe army of northern Natal. After defeat at the hands of **Shaka** in 1819, he took his followers northwards and settled near Delagoa Bay in Portuguese Mozambique. In 1831 Zwangendaba moved on, attacked the Shona in Zimbabwe, crossed the Zambezi River in 1835 and established military states in both the modern Malawi and Tanzania. These states resisted the establishment of European rule in the Partition of Africa. ▷ **Africa, Partition of**

Zwide (d.1819) Chief of the Ndwandwe, one of the northern Nguni tribes of northern Natal. The Ndwandwe and the Mthethwa under **Dingiswayo** battled for power in the emerging **Nguni** state. Dingiswayo was killed when attacked by Zwide in 1817, thus enabling **Shaka** to take over the Mthethwa army and forge the Zulu state, which was one of the most celebrated of all African states in the 19c.